THE ACCESS BIBLE

New Revised
Standard Version

THE ACCESS BIBLE

New Revised
Standard Version

THE ACCESS
BIBLE®

NEW REVISED STANDARD VERSION

GAIL R. O'DAY   DAVID PETERSEN

General Editors

OXFORD

UNIVERSITY PRESS

OXFORD UNIVERSITY PRESS

Oxford   New York
Athens   Auckland   Bangkok   Bogotá   Buenos Aires   Calcutta
Cape Town   Chennai   Dar es Salaam   Delhi   Florence   Hong Kong   Istanbul
Karachi   Kuala Lumpur   Madrid   Melbourne   Mexico City   Mumbai   Nairobi
Paris   São Paulo   Singapore   Taipei   Tokyo   Toronto   Warsaw

and associated companies in
Berlin   Ibadan

CONTRIBUTORS

David L. Barr   Revelation

John Barton   "The Nature and Formation of the Canon"

Ronald E. Clements   Isaiah

Richard J. Clifford   Job, Proverbs

Theodore Hiebert   Hosea, Joel, Amos, Obadiah, Jonah, Micah, Nahum, Habakkuk,
Zephaniah, Haggai, Zechariah, Malachi

Kenneth G. Hoglund   1 and 2 Chronicles, Ezra, Nehemiah

Carl R. Holladay   Romans, 1 and 2 Corinthians, Galatians

Amy-Jill Levine   Matthew, Mark

J. Clinton McCann Jr.   Psalms,

Steven L. McKenzie   1 and 2 Samuel, 1 and 2 Kings

Richard D. Nelson   Deuteronomy, Joshua, Judges

Jerome H. Neyrey, s.j.   Hebrews, James, 1 and 2 Peter, Jude

Julia M. O'Brien   Ruth, Esther (Hebrew), Ecclesiastes, Song of Solomon,
Lamentations,

Kathleen M. O'Connor   Jeremiah

David L. Petersen   "A Guide to the Features and Uses of the Access Bible," "What Is
Bible Study?" "A Reader's Guide to the Books of the Bible"

Dennis T. Olson   Genesis, Exodus, Leviticus, Numbers

John Painter   John, 1, 2, and 3 John

Abraham Smith   Ephesians, Philippians, Colossians, 1 and 2 Thessalonians,
1 and 2 Timothy, Titus, Philemon

Marvin A. Sweeney   Ezekiel, Daniel,

David L. Tiede   Luke, Acts of the Apostles

TO THE READER

This preface is addressed to you by the Committee of translators, who wish to explain, as briefly as possible, the origin and character of our work. The publication of our revision is yet another step in the long, continual process of making the Bible available in the form of the English language that is most widely current in our day. To summarize in a single sentence: the New Revised Standard Version of the Bible is an authorized revision of the Revised Standard Version, published in 1952, which was a revision of the American Standard Version, published in 1901, which, in turn, embodied earlier revisions of the King James Version, published in 1611.

In the course of time, the King James Version came to be regarded as "the Authorized Version." With good reason it has been termed "the noblest monument of English prose," and it has entered, as no other book has, into the making of the personal character and the public institutions of the English-speaking peoples. We owe to it an incalculable debt.

Yet the King James Version has serious defects. By the middle of the nineteenth century, the development of biblical studies and the discovery of many biblical manuscripts more ancient than those on which the King James Version was based made it apparent that these defects were so many as to call for revision. The task was begun, by authority of the Church of England, in 1870. The (British) Revised Version of the Bible was published in 1881–1885; and the American Standard Version, its variant embodying the preferences of the American scholars associated with the work, was published, as was mentioned above, in 1901. In 1928 the copyright of the latter was acquired by the International Council of Religious Education and thus passed into the ownership of the churches of the United States and Canada that were associated in this Council through their boards of education and publication.

The Council appointed a committee of scholars to have charge of the text of the American Standard Version and to undertake inquiry concerning the need for further revision. After studying the questions whether or not revision should be undertaken, and if so, what its nature and extent should be, in 1937 the Council authorized a revision. The scholars who served as members of the Committee worked in two sections, one dealing with the Old Testament and one with the New Testament. In 1946 the Revised Standard Version of the New Testament was published. The publication of the Revised Standard Version of the Bible, containing the Old and New Testaments, took place on September 30, 1952. A translation of the Apocryphal/Deuterocanonical Books of the Old Testament followed in 1957. In 1977 this collection was issued in an expanded edition, containing three additional texts received by Eastern Orthodox communions (3 and 4 Maccabees and Psalm 151). Thereafter the Revised Standard Version gained the distinction of being officially authorized for use by all major Christian churches: Protestant, Anglican, Roman Catholic, and Eastern Orthodox.

The Revised Standard Version Bible Committee is a continuing body, comprising about thirty members, both men and women. Ecumenical in representation, it includes scholars affiliated with various Protestant denominations, as well as several Roman Catholic members, an Eastern Orthodox member, and a Jewish member who serves in the Old Testament section. For a period of time the Committee included several members from Canada and from England.

Because no translation of the Bible is perfect or is acceptable to all groups of readers, and because discoveries of older manuscripts and further investigation of linguistic features of the text continue to become available, renderings of the Bible have proliferated. During the years following the publication of the Revised Standard Version, twenty-six other English translations and revisions of the Bible were produced by committees and by individual scholars—not to mention twenty-five other translations and revisions of the New Testament alone. One of the latter was the second edition of the RSV New Testament, issued in 1971, twenty-five years after its initial publication.

Following the publication of the RSV Old Testament in 1952, significant advances were made in the discovery and interpretation of documents in Semitic languages related to Hebrew. In addition to the information that had become available in the late 1940s from the Dead Sea texts of Isaiah and Habakkuk, subsequent acquisitions from the same area brought to light many other early copies of all the books of the Hebrew Scriptures (except Esther), though most of these copies are fragmentary. During the same period early Greek manuscript copies of books of the New Testament also became available.

In order to take these discoveries into account, along with recent studies of documents in Semitic languages related to Hebrew, in 1974 the Policies Committee of the Revised Standard Version, which is a standing committee of the National Council of the Churches of Christ in the U.S.A., authorized the preparation of a revision of the entire RSV Bible.

For the Old Testament the Committee has made use of the *Biblia Hebraica Stuttgartensia* (1977; ed. sec. emendata, 1983). This is an edition of the Hebrew and Aramaic text as current early in the Christian era and fixed by Jewish scholars (the "Masoretes") of the sixth to the ninth centuries. The vowel signs, which were added by the Masoretes, are accepted in the main, but where a more probable and convincing reading can be obtained by assuming different vowels, this has been done. No notes are given in such cases, because the vowel points are less ancient and reliable than the consonants. When an alternative reading given by the Masoretes is translated in a footnote, this is identified by the words "Another reading is."

Departures from the consonantal text of the best manuscripts have been made only where it seems clear that errors in copying had been made before the text was standardized. Most of the corrections adopted are based on the ancient versions (translations into Greek, Aramaic, Syriac, and Latin), which were made prior to the time of the work of the Masoretes and which therefore may reflect earlier forms of the Hebrew text. In such instances a footnote specifies the version or versions from which the correction has been derived and also gives a translation of the Masoretic Text. Where it was deemed appropriate to do so, information is supplied in footnotes from subsidiary Jewish traditions concerning other textual readings (the *Tiqqune Sopherim*, "emendations of the scribes"). These are identified in the footnotes as "Ancient Heb tradition."

Occasionally it is evident that the text has suffered in transmission and that none of the versions provides a satisfactory restoration. Here we can only follow the best judgment of competent scholars as to the most probable reconstruction of the original text. Such reconstructions are indicated in footnotes by the abbreviation Cn ("Correction"), and a translation of the Masoretic Text is added.

For the New Testament the Committee has based its work on the most recent edition of *The Greek New Testament*, prepared by an interconfessional and international committee and published by the United Bible Societies (1966; 3rd ed. corrected, 1983; information concerning changes to be introduced into the critical apparatus of the forthcoming 4th edition was available to the Committee). As in that edition, double brackets are used to enclose a few passages that are generally regarded to be later additions to the text, but which we have retained because of their evident antiquity and their importance in the textual tradition. Only in very rare instances have we replaced the text or the punctuation of the Bible Societies' edition by an alternative that seemed to us to be superior. Here and there in the footnotes the phrase, "Other ancient authorities read," identifies alternative readings preserved by Greek manuscripts and early versions. In both Testaments, alternative renderings of the text are indicated by the word "Or."

As for the style of English adopted for the present revision, among the mandates given to the Committee in 1980 by the Division of Education and Ministry of the National Council of Churches of Christ (which now holds the copyright of the RSV Bible) was the directive to continue in the tradition of the King James Bible, but to introduce such changes as are warranted on the basis of accuracy, clarity, euphony, and current English usage. Within the constraints set by the original texts and by the mandates of the Division, the Committee has followed the maxim, "As literal as possible, as free as necessary." As a consequence, the New Revised Standard Version (NRSV) remains essentially a literal translation. Paraphrastic renderings have been adopted only sparingly, and then chiefly to compensate for a deficiency in the English language—the lack of a common gender third person singular pronoun.

During the almost half a century since the publication of the RSV, many in the churches have become sensitive to the danger of linguistic sexism arising from the inherent bias of the English language towards the masculine gender, a bias that in the case of the Bible has often restricted or obscured the meaning of the original text. The mandates from the Division specified that, in references to men and women, masculine-oriented language should be eliminated as far as this can be done without altering passages that reflect the historical situation of ancient patriarchal culture. As can be appreciated, more than once the Committee found that the several mandates stood in tension and even in conflict. The various concerns had to be balanced case by case in order to provide a faithful and acceptable rendering without using contrived English. Only very occasionally has the pronoun "he" or "him" been retained in passages where the reference may have been to a woman as well as to a man; for example, in several legal texts in Leviticus and Deuteronomy. In such instances of formal, legal language, the options of either putting the passage in the plural or of introducing additional nouns to avoid masculine pronouns in English seemed to the Committee to obscure the historic structure and literary character of the original. In the vast majority of cases, however, inclusiveness has been attained by simple rephrasing or by introducing plural forms when this does not distort the meaning of the passage. Of course, in narrative and in parable no attempt was made to generalize the sex of individual persons.

Another aspect of style will be detected by readers who compare the more stately English rendering of the Old Testament with the less formal rendering adopted for the New Testament. For example, the traditional distinction between *shall* and *will* in English has been retained in the Old Testament as appropriate in rendering a document that embodies what may be termed the classic form of Hebrew, while in the New Testament the abandonment of such distinctions in the usage of the future tense in English reflects the more colloquial nature of the koine Greek used by most New Testament authors except when they are quoting the Old Testament.

Careful readers will notice that here and there in the Old Testament the word LORD (or in certain cases GOD) is printed in capital letters. This represents the traditional manner in English versions of rendering the Divine Name, the "Tetragrammaton" (see the notes on Exodus 3.14, 15), following the precedent of the ancient Greek and Latin translators and the long established practice in the reading of the Hebrew Scriptures in the synagogue. While it is almost if not quite certain that the Name was originally pronounced "Yahweh," this pronunciation was not indicated when the Masoretes added vowel sounds to the consonantal Hebrew text. To the four consonants YHWH of the Name, which had come to be regarded as too sacred to be pronounced, they attached vowel signs indicating that in its place should be read the Hebrew word *Adonai* meaning "Lord" (or *Elohim* meaning "God"). Ancient Greek translators employed the word *Kyrios* ("Lord") for the Name. The Vulgate likewise used the Latin word *Dominus* ("Lord"). The form "Jehovah" is of late medieval origin; it is a combination of the consonants of the Divine Name and the vowels attached to it by the Masoretes but belonging to an entirely different word. Although the American Standard Version (1901) had used "Jehovah" to render the Tetragrammaton (the sound of Y being represented by J and the sound of W by V, as in Latin), for two reasons the Committees that produced the RSV and the NRSV returned to the more familiar usage of the King James Version. (1) The word "Jehovah" does not accurately represent any form of the Name ever used in Hebrew. (2) The use of any proper name for the one and only God, as though there were other gods from whom the true God had to be distinguished, began to be discontinued in Judaism before the Christian era and is inappropriate for the universal faith of the Christian Church.

It will be seen that in the Psalms and in other prayers addressed to God the archaic second person singular pronouns (*thee*, *thou*, *thine*) and verb forms (*art*, *hast*, *hadst*) are no longer used. Although some readers may regret this change, it should be pointed out that in the original languages neither the Old Testament nor the New makes any linguistic distinction between addressing a human being and addressing the Deity. Furthermore, in the tradition of the King James Version one will not expect to find the use of capital letters for pronouns that refer to the Deity—such capitalization is an unnecessary innovation that has only recently been introduced into a few English translations of the Bible. Finally, we have left to the discretion of the licensed publishers such matters as section headings, cross-references, and clues to the pronunciation of proper names.

This new version seeks to preserve all that is best in the English Bible as it has been known and used through the years. It is intended for use in public reading and congregational worship, as well as in private study, instruction, and meditation. We have resisted the temptation to introduce terms and phrases that merely reflect current moods, and have tried to put the message of the Scriptures in simple, enduring words and expressions that are worthy to stand in the great tradition of the King James Bible and its predecessors.

In traditional Judaism and Christianity, the Bible has been more than a historical document to be preserved or a classic of literature to be cherished and admired; it is recognized as the unique record of God's dealings with people over the ages. The Old Testament sets forth the call of a special people to enter into covenant relation with the God of justice and steadfast love and to bring God's law to the nations. The New Testament records the life and work of Jesus Christ, the one in whom "the Word became flesh," as well as describes the rise and spread of the early Christian Church. The Bible carries its full message, not to those who regard it simply as a noble literary heritage of the past or who wish to use it to enhance political purposes and advance otherwise desirable goals, but to all persons and communities who read it so that they may discern and understand what God is saying to them. That message must not be disguised in phrases that are no longer clear, or hidden under words that have changed or lost their meaning; it must be presented in language that is direct and plain and meaningful to people today. It is the hope and prayer of the translators that this version of the Bible may continue to hold a large place in congregational life and to speak to all readers, young and old alike, helping them to understand and believe and respond to its message.

For the Committee,
Bruce M. Metzger

NAMES AND ORDER OF THE BOOKS
of the Old and New Testaments

THE HEBREW SCRIPTURES

Genesis   1 OT
Exodus   69 OT
Leviticus   123 OT
Numbers   162 OT
Deuteronomy   219 OT
Joshua   265 OT
Judges   296 OT
Ruth   328 OT
1 Samuel   334 OT
   (1 Kingdoms in Greek)
2 Samuel   378 OT
   (2 Kingdoms in Greek)
1 Kings   414 OT
   (3 Kingdoms in Greek)
2 Kings   454 OT
   (4 Kingdoms in Greek)
1 Chronicles   495 OT
   (1 Paralipomenon in Greek)
2 Chronicles   534 OT
   (2 Paralipomenon in Greek)
Ezra   580 OT
   (2 Esdras in Greek)
Nehemiah   600 OT
   (2 Esdras in Greek)

Esther   624 OT
Job   634 OT
Psalms   679 OT
Proverbs   807 OT
Ecclesiastes   847 OT
Song of Solomon   859 OT
Isaiah   868 OT
Jeremiah   963 OT
Lamentations   1046 OT
Ezekiel   1058 OT
Daniel   1129 OT
Hosea   1151 OT
Joel   1168 OT
Amos   1175 OT
Obadiah   1189 OT
Jonah   1192 OT
Micah   1196 OT
Nahum   1207 OT
Habakkuk   1211 OT
Zephaniah   1216 OT
Haggai   1221 OT
Zechariah   1225 OT
Malachi   1240 OT

THE NEW TESTAMENT

Matthew   1 NT
Mark   48 NT
Luke   80 NT
John   129 NT
Acts of the Apostles   170 NT
Romans   222 NT
1 Corinthians   244 NT
2 Corinthians   266 NT
Galatians   280 NT
Ephesians   289 NT
Philippians   297 NT
Colossians   304 NT
1 Thessalonians   310 NT
2 Thessalonians   315 NT

1 Timothy   319 NT
2 Timothy   326 NT
Titus   331 NT
Philemon   335 NT
Hebrews   338 NT
James   355 NT
1 Peter   362 NT
2 Peter   369 NT
1 John   375 NT
2 John   382 NT
3 John   384 NT
Jude   386 NT
Revelation   389 NT

CONTENTS

Note: In accordance with traditional practice, the pages of the separate Testaments are numbered independently; thus, the Introductions to Genesis and to Matthew are respectively the first page of the Old Testament and the first page of the New Testament. As an aid to the reader the page numbers in the lists of contents are distinguished by the abbreviations OT and NT. The reference materials at the back of the book continue the numbering of the New Testament, but without the distinguishing letters.

SIDEBAR ESSAYS, MAPS, CHARTS

ALPHABETICAL LISTING OF THE BOOKS OF THE BIBLE

OT—Old Testament   NT—New Testament

Acts	170 NT	James	355 NT	Nehemiah	600 OT
Amos	1175 OT	Jeremiah	963 OT	Numbers	162 OT
1 Chronicles	495 OT	Job	634 OT	Obadiah	1189 OT
2 Chronicles	534 OT	Joel	1168 OT	1 Peter	362 NT
Colossians	304 NT	John	129 NT	2 Peter	369 NT
1 Corinthians	244 NT	1 John	375 NT	Philemon	335 NT
2 Corinthians	266 NT	2 John	382 NT	Philippians	297 NT
Daniel	1129 OT	3 John	384 NT	Proverbs	807 OT
Deuteronomy	219 OT	Jonah	1192 OT	Psalms	679 OT
Ecclesiastes	847 OT	Joshua	265 OT	Revelation	389 NT
Ephesians	289 NT	Jude	386 NT	Romans	222 NT
Esther	624 OT	Judges	296 OT	Ruth	328 OT
Exodus	69 OT	1 Kings	414 OT	1 Samuel	334 OT
Ezekiel	1058 OT	2 Kings	454 OT	2 Samuel	378 OT
Ezra	580 OT	Lamentations	1046 OT	Song of Solomon	859 OT
Galatians	280 NT	Leviticus	123 OT	1 Thessalonians	310 NT
Genesis	1 OT	Luke	80 NT	2 Thessalonians	315 NT
Habakkuk	1211 OT	Malachi	1240 OT	1 Timothy	319 NT
Haggai	1221 OT	Mark	48 NT	2 Timothy	326 NT
Hebrews	338 NT	Matthew	1 NT	Titus	331 NT
Hosea	1151 OT	Micah	1196 OT	Zechariah	1225 OT
Isaiah	868 OT	Nahum	1207 OT	Zephaniah	1216 OT

ABBREVIATIONS

The following abbreviations are used for the books of the Bible:

OLD TESTAMENT

Gen	Genesis	2 Chr	2 Chronicles	Dan	Daniel
Ex	Exodus	Ezra	Ezra	Hos	Hosea
Lev	Leviticus	Neh	Nehemiah	Joel	Joel
Num	Numbers	Esth	Esther	Am	Amos
Deut	Deuteronomy	Job	Job	Ob	Obadiah
Josh	Joshua	Ps	Psalms	Jon	Jonah
Judg	Judges	Prov	Proverbs	Mic	Micah
Ruth	Ruth	Eccl	Ecclesiastes	Nah	Nahum
1 Sam	1 Samuel	Song	Song of Solomon	Hab	Habakkuk
2 Sam	2 Samuel	Isa	Isaiah	Zeph	Zephaniah
1 Kings	1 Kings	Jer	Jeremiah	Hag	Haggai
2 Kings	2 Kings	Lam	Lamentations	Zech	Zechariah
1 Chr	1 Chronicles	Ezek	Ezekiel	Mal	Malachi

NEW TESTAMENT

Mt	Matthew	Eph	Ephesians	Heb	Hebrews
Mk	Mark	Phil	Philippians	Jas	James
Lk	Luke	Col	Colossians	1 Pet	1 Peter
Jn	John	1 Thess	1 Thessalonians	2 Pet	2 Peter
Acts	Acts of the Apostles	2 Thess	2 Thessalonians	1 Jn	1 John
Rom	Romans	1 Tim	1 Timothy	2 Jn	2 John
1 Cor	1 Corinthians	2 Tim	2 Timothy	3 Jn	3 John
2 Cor	2 Corinthians	Titus	Titus	Jude	Jude
Gal	Galatians	Philem	Philemon	Rev	Revelation

In the notes to the books of the Old Testament the following abbreviations are used:

Ant.	Josephus, *Antiquities of the Jews*
Aram	Aramaic
Ch, chs	Chapter, chapters
Cn	Correction; made where the text has suffered in transmission and the versions provide no satisfactory restoration but where the Standard Bible Committee agrees with the judgment of competent scholars as to the most probable reconstruction of the original text.
Gk	Septuagint, Greek version of the Old Testament
Heb	Hebrew of the consonantal Masoretic Text of the Old Testament
Josephus	Flavius Josephus (Jewish historian, about A.D. 37 to about 95)
Macc	The book(s) of the Maccabees
Ms(s)	Manuscript(s)
MT	The Hebrew of the pointed Masoretic Text of the Old Testament

OL	Old Latin
Q Ms(s)	Manuscript(s) found at Qumran by the Dead Sea
Sam	Samaritan Hebrew text of the Old Testament
Syr	Syriac Version of the Old Testament
Syr H	Syriac Version of Origen's Hexapla
Tg	Targum
Vg	Vulgate, Latin Version of the Old Testament

A GUIDE TO THE FEATURES AND USES OF THE ACCESS BIBLE

THE TRANSLATION

This Bible contains the full text of the New Revised Standard Version (NRSV) Bible translation. The NRSV is the most complete translation of the biblical text into English: it contains the Hebrew Scriptures, the Apocryphal/Deuterocanonical Books, and the New Testament. Some editions of the Access Bible are published without the Apocryphal/Deuterocanonical Books. In editions that do contain these books, the individual introductions contain information about the status of these works in the various Christian churches.

The NRSV Preface, "To the Reader," explains the nature of the NRSV translation, its history, and the scholarly research that lies behind it. The translation also includes footnotes, prepared by the scholars on the translation committee. These footnotes, an important tool for Bible study, explain places where the original language text is unclear, where there is a difference among the various manuscripts that the scholars have consulted (usually indicated in the notes by the phrase, "other ancient authorities read"), or where the original language allows for an alternate translation of the word or phrase (indicated by the word "or"). Some notes provide information about other ancient translations of the Bible that scholars consulted in their translation work. The glossary at the back of this Bible provides information about these different translations (see the entry **ancient translations**). See also "Language and Text" in the essay "What Is Bible Study?" on p. 4.

THE STUDY MATERIALS

The Access Bible is designed to provide study helps that enable the reader to engage the biblical text directly and not simply read about the Bible. That is, the study helps are designed to lead readers into their own careful and reflective reading of the biblical text. The study materials range from full length essays on topics of general interest to the Bible reader to short, dictionary-like entries on particular words or topics. All of the helps are intended to assist the reader in discovering the richness and diversity of the biblical texts.

The Introductory Essays   Three introductory essays provide an overview of the Bible as a whole and discuss the nature of Bible study today. "What Is Bible Study?" explains the various ways in which the Bible may be studied. "A Reader's Guide to the Books of the Bible" explains the different books within the Bible and the types of literature they represent. "The Nature and Formation of the Biblical Canon" describes how these many different books came to be gathered together as the Bible and why Jewish, as well as Protestant, Catholic, and Orthodox Christian communities, each hold to a slightly different definition of "canon."

The Book Introductions In this study Bible, each biblical book is preceded by a brief introduction. The first part enables the modern reader to imagine how the book's content may have been understood by its ancient readers. Information about historical setting, type of literature (e.g., letter, poetry, story), social issues or theological themes all assist in bridging the gap between the ancient world and today's world.

Each introduction also contains a section labeled "Reading Guide," that is primarily directed toward the reading concerns of the modern reader, rather than the questions and needs that probably guided the book's original readers. The included outline helps the reader see a picture of the general sweep of the book before attending to its details.

The Sectional Comments This Study Bible includes section by section comments on the biblical text. In most cases, the comments follow a segment of Scripture and explain unusual words, ancient religious and social customs, literary features, or the historical setting of that text. They orient the modern reader to the places, people, and events of the biblical world. They also identify key themes or ideas that may be relevant to the reader's own situation.

Within these comments, words in *italics* are those quoted directly from the NRSV text; words in **boldface** describe divisions or individual passages; numbers in boldface are chapter and verse numbers which the comments address.

To refer to a translators' footnote, the words "see note on . . ." are used. "See comment" refers to the running comment on the biblical text, and "see map, chart, or sidebar" refers to the respective study help at the location given.

Other Features within the Text In addition to section by section comments on the biblical text, this edition contains other helps—maps, charts, and sidebar essays. Each of these helps expands on information mentioned in the comments. The sidebar essays often point beyond the particular biblical text under consideration to broader biblical themes.

Helps at the Back of the Study Bible At the end of the Bible are three sets of materials that supplement the helps located at each individual book of the Bible. First is a glossary. This lists and defines specialized terms that are used in the running comments; these terms have been marked with a star symbol (⋆) to indicate that their definitions can be found in the glossary. The glossary also contains a discussion of other terms not explicitly mentioned in the running comments, but that are helpful for interpreting the biblical text and understanding the biblical world. In addition, many of the glossary entries refer to passages in the Bible that illustrate the entry. The glossary therefore moves in two directions: from the study materials to an explanation in the glossary, or from an explanation in the glossary to an illustration in the biblical text.

Second, the helps contain a brief concordance to the NRSV text. A concordance is a tool for Bible study that enables the reader to compare the use of a word in one biblical verse to its usage elsewhere—either in the same biblical book or another one. By using a concordance, the reader begins to achieve a sense of what individual words meant to the biblical writers and their original readers.

Finally, a full-color set of Oxford Bible Maps is included, along with an index to all of the place names found on the maps. These maps are an important tool for locating the places mentioned in the biblical text and becoming familiar with the geography of the ancient world. The maps also provide a glimpse of the history of the ancient Mediterranean world, since the different maps cover a period of 1,000 years.

Calendar Designation   This Study Bible employs the designations BCE ("before the common era") and CE ("common era") to refer to the time periods often marked by the designations BC ("before Christ") and AD ("in the year of the Lord," *anno domini* in Latin). The designations BCE and CE reflect the way that years are counted in the Western calendar without using terms that derive from the Christian faith tradition, since not all people who follow the Western calendar are members of a Christian community.

USING THIS STUDY BIBLE

The Access Bible is designed to be used in group Bible study settings, classrooms, and for individual Bible reading and study. The helps outlined above can be used in a variety of ways—to assist in verse by verse, chapter by chapter reading of the Bible or to provide information and insight about a particular text or topic.

The editors of the study Bible have designed it in such a way as to put the best resources of biblical scholarship in the hands of the general reader. We have tried to anticipate readers' questions about the ancient world and the complexities of many biblical texts, but in a way that respects both the reader and the Bible. That is, no matter how much Bible study one does, there are some texts in the Bible that are always going to be difficult to understand and that will seem challenging rather than comforting. Nonetheless, the editors hope that the Access Bible will make Bible study a rewarding experience and will make the Bible accessible to the reader—accessible in its contradictions and complexities as well as in its comfort and inspiration.

WHAT IS BIBLE STUDY?

People read the Bible in many settings, such as religious services, personal homes, libraries, hospitals and hotel rooms. Not all Bible reading constitutes Bible study, however. When you read the Bible in a hospital room, you may be seeking to understand your condition from the perspective of your particular religious tradition. You may thus reflect upon illness using the kind of metaphorical language in, for example, Psalm 22:

> I am poured out like water,
> and all my bones are out of joint;
> my heart is like wax;
> it is melted within my breast;
> my mouth is dried up like a potsherd,
> and my tongue sticks to my jaws;
> you lay me in the dust of death. (Ps 22.14–15)

Moreover, you may gain some comfort from the confidence in God expressed in psalms of lament, for example, Ps 55.17. In such a reading, the Bible will have played an important role in your life, but it would be inappropriate to designate that sort of activity as Bible study.

"Bible study" means different things to different people. To some it means sitting at home, reading, and underlining passages in red pencil. To some it means gathering with members of one's church to read and share perceptions about a biblical text or theme. To some it means taking a course devoted to an aspect of the Bible in a college or university classroom. The only real common denominator for these various approaches is attention to the biblical text.

For the purposes of these introductory essays, Bible study means "the disciplined and active reading of the Bible in order to gain new understandings about the biblical text or the reader's own situation." This way of thinking about Bible study includes learning about ancient Israel or early Christianity as well as coming to a new understanding of one's own condition.

We would add one other initial comment about Bible study. Since the Bible derives from ancient cultures, it is, in many ways, a foreign document that requires study in order to be understood properly. Put another way, for the person who takes the Bible seriously, Bible study is not an option but a requirement. The appropriateness of such Bible study is attested in biblical times. Acts 8.26–40 recounts an episode in which an Ethiopian eunuch is reading from the book of Isaiah. Philip approaches him and asks, "Do you understand what you are reading?" The Ethiopian responds, "How can I, unless someone guides me?" The need for guides, whether in the form of a teacher, a book, study materials or an internet site, is even more powerful today than it was in Philip's time.

PRIMARY FEATURES OF BIBLE STUDY

Language and Text   The ancient biblical manuscripts were written in three languages: Hebrew, Aramaic, and Greek. (Aramaic is, like Hebrew, a Semitic language, one that became particularly prominent during the Persian period.) As a result, all English Bibles are translations, scholarly attempts to convey the meaning of these texts into English.

Such a task is no easy enterprise since different theories of translation abound. Some focus on the meaning of individual words, whereas others think the sentence is of primary importance. The former perspective may be called "literal" or "word for word," whereas the latter has often been characterized as a "dynamic-equivalence" approach. Though no translation of the Bible belongs to one or the other approach all the time, the NRSV tends toward the "word for word" style. Such a translation can be useful for Bible study since it will usually translate a Greek or Hebrew word with the same English word, thereby allowing the reader of the English to study individual terms like *mishpat* (a Hebrew word for justice) or *agape* (a Greek word for love) in translation. Still, there are instances in which the original language offers no easy "word for word" option. John 8.15 provides a good example. The NRSV reads: "You judge by human standards" whereas a more literal rendition of the Greek is cited in the translators' note, "You judge according to the flesh."

Despite the best efforts of hundreds of scholars, certain biblical texts remain difficult to translate. As a result, those who created the NRSV have noted many instances in which they have encountered problems in moving from a Hebrew or Greek text to an English version. They also place notes where they have had to interpret the evidence attested in manuscripts written in other languages, such as Latin, Syriac or Coptic. For example, in Habakkuk 3.14, the translators' note on the word "warriors" reads "Vg Compare Gk Syr: Meaning of Heb uncertain." This shorthand statement conveys considerable information. Since the Hebrew term and the phrase in which it is embedded do not follow the normal rules of Hebrew grammar, the translators indicate that they have solved this problem by following the understanding conveyed in the Vulgate (Vg), an early Latin translation. In addition, ancient translations in two other languages—the Gk (Greek or Septuagint) and Syr (Syriac or Peshitta)—provide important information that has helped corroborate their judgments.

Most readers of this study Bible will not be able to consult the Hebrew or Greek texts, much less the Latin and Syriac versions. However, attention to notes of this sort, which are more common than one might suspect, helps the reader to be alert to places of uncertainty. In such a place, one needs to be careful about placing too much interpretive emphasis. In addition, these notes help us appreciate the remarkable complexity of the biblical manuscript traditions along with the various religious communities that produced and used them.

The work of translators is absolutely essential. Without their efforts, there would be no Bibles in modern languages. At the same time, we should recognize subjectivity at work in the creation of a translation, as well as the influence of newly available information for interpreting the ancient texts. Perhaps the best way to appreciate this issue is to compare the NRSV with its earlier counterpart, the Revised Standard Version (RSV).

We offer two such points of comparison. First, compare these two versions of the initial lines of Deut 33.27:

The eternal God is your dwelling place, and underneath are the everlasting arms. (RSV)

He subdues the ancient gods, shatters the forces of old; (NRSV)

"The everlasting arms" have become, as it were, "the forces of old." These two readings represent differing assessments of the rich idioms in ancient Hebrew poetry. The NRSV reflects knowledge about ancient Semitic languages that was unavailable to the translators of the RSV.

Those readers of the biblical text who do not know Hebrew or Greek may well feel at a disadvantage when confronted with such disparities. But there is a way to deal with this issue: It is always appropriate to compare several translations in order to see if there are major differences. At such points of difference, the reader should be careful of placing too much emphasis on a disputed element in the translation. So, in the just mentioned case, the reader of the RSV would do well to avoid offering broad statements concerning the arms of God until after having consulted other good translations, for example, the Revised English Bible, Tanakh or the New American Bible.

As another example, it is useful to compare the RSV and NRSV renditions of Ezek 7. In the RSV, the chapter is printed as prose whereas in the NRSV, most of the chapter is printed as poetry. The scholars responsible for the NRSV had benefitted from recent studies of Hebrew poetry, which enabled them to discern more texts as poetry than had earlier been the case. As we shall see later in this essay, approaching poetry requires different interpretive strategies than reading prose does. And the decision about whether or not a text is poetry can rest in the hands of the translator.

The issues we have just been addressing involve, primarily, questions of language (philology) and translation. However, there is another range of issues related to the texts preserving these ancient readings. None of the original compositions, called "autographs," has been preserved. Moreover, though there is remarkable fixity in the ancient manuscript traditions, they do, on occasion, diverge. The study of the significance of these differences among ancient biblical manuscripts is called textual criticism. Indeed, there are several kinds of text critical issues.

One type of text critical issue is that some manuscripts clearly have a faulty text, one in which a copyist's error or some other accident has occurred. The Cain and Abel story (Gen 4) offers a compelling example. In this well-known tale, God accepts the offering of Abel but not the offering of Cain, whereupon Cain is challenged to "do well." Then, according to the NRSV, "Cain said to his brother Abel, 'Let us go out to the field' " (Gen 4.8). As the translators' note makes clear, the words "Let us go out to the field" are not present in the Hebrew manuscripts, though they are present in the Samaritan Pentateuch, the Septuagint and the Peshitta (the Syriac Old Testament). The phrase has almost certainly fallen out of the Hebrew tradition by mistake, since the text certainly seems to suggest that Cain had engaged in premeditated murder. Scholars who are able to assess the various ancient manuscript evidence have in this case supplied what they deemed to be the more original reading, which has been preserved in manuscripts written in languages other than Hebrew.

Another text critical issue is that ancient texts may offer contrary readings, alternate forms of a story or saying. One of the most interesting examples occurs at the end of Mark's Gospel. Here the question is not one of a mistake but of varying texts. In the ancient manuscripts, the Gospel of Mark can end in three ways: with Mk 16.8, with Mk 16.8 plus what is referred to as "The Shorter Ending of Mark," and with Mk

16.9–20, "The Longer Ending of Mark." The layout of the NRSV, along with the translators' note at the first ending, makes these options very clear.

Option 1 concludes the Gospel on a note of fear. Three women, Mary Magdalene, Mary the mother of James, and Salome, had come to tend to the body of Jesus in the tomb. When they arrived, they were informed by "a young man" that Jesus "has been raised." Whereupon they fled; "and they said nothing to anyone, for they were afraid" (16.8). The note of fear is accompanied by an ironic tone, because they must have told someone, or the scene could not have been recounted in Mark's Gospel. Option 2 removes that ironic tone by reporting explicitly that the women did indeed recount what they had seen and heard "to those around Peter," moving the story beyond the empty tomb into the realm of the disciples. The final portion of the verse introduces the motif of a commission, similar to that found in Mt 28.19. Option 3 removes the note of incompleteness with which Mk 16.8 ends by adding a series of post-resurrection appearances of Jesus. With these verses, the ending of Mark more closely resembles the endings of the other Gospels, which all contain stories of post-resurrection appearances.

The NRSV prints all three options because it is impossible to know how the Gospel of Mark originally ended. The ending at Mk 16.8, while well attested by some very ancient manuscripts, nonetheless seems an abrupt way to end, and the alternatives proposed in many manuscript traditions show how the earliest Christians tried to work with and around this unexpected abruptness. Holy writ there is, but it is on occasion written in more than one way.

Careful study of the Bible, then, particularly for those who do not have access to the ancient languages, will involve comparison of several translations as well as attention to the notes provided by the translators. This form of active reading will alert readers to problem areas in the text as well as to differences among the early biblical witnesses.

Literary Form and Style   If a story begins with "Once upon a time," the reader expects that it will be a traditional tale. The focus will almost certainly be on people and places, not on economic or social history. Similarly, when hearing the phrase "This is the last will and testament of . . . ," the listener knows that the text is a legal document that will outline the disposition of someone's estate. Our initial perception of these texts depends in considerable measure on the sort of literature we think we are hearing.

Just as there are identifiable forms of literature in our own time, so too, both in the ancient Near East and in the Greco-Roman era, readers and listeners (there were far more listeners than readers) were accustomed to encountering discrete forms of literature, many of which are preserved in the Bible. Contemporary readers of the Bible, however, are not always attuned to those ancient forms of literature. Hence, part of Bible study involves becoming aware of and understanding some of these ancient styles of writing.

We have already referred to a primary distinction that occurs in Old Testament literature—prose versus poetry—and we have noted that translators of the Bible differ in their judgments about whether a text is prose or poetry. Some cases are ambiguous. Others are less so, particularly as we learn more about the nature of the Hebrew language and literature. In any case, the reader should discern which style is being used and whether it has significance to the message of the text.

The first two chapters of Genesis in the NRSV present a particularly interesting illustration. The reader can note immediately that Gen 1.27 and Gen 2.23 are written as poetry, surrounded by prose. Is this an accident, or is it important for the interpretation of this literature? Surely, the latter. Both chapters concern God's acts of creation. In the first chapter the entire universe is in view, whereas in the second only the earth and life on it are of concern to the writer. In both cases, these brief poetic pieces occur near the end of the text. In Gen 1 the poem relates to what is happening on the sixth day (vv. 24–31), and in Gen 2 the poem occurs in the final scene (vv. 18–23) of creative activity. These final elements of creation appear as the high point of the texts—creation of humanity in Gen 1 and of woman in Gen 2—and the poetic elements in the text underscore these important moments.

Poetry requires the reader to slow down and focus on the taut relationship between the lines. In Gen 1.27, one confronts the pregnant phrase "the image of God." Though the primary connotation offered by the phrase is something visual—an image, the poem itself offers another angle of vision, by comparing "the image of God" in the second line with "male and female" in the third line. Those relationships make the reader wonder what indeed is conveyed by the notion of God's image. Perhaps it has more to do with community as represented by the relation of the genders and less to do with something visible.

As for Gen 2.23, the writer for the first time gives explicit voice to a human being, and what that individual speaks is a poem. The man testifies to the inextricable connection between male and female, as attested by a wordplay in the Hebrew words for Man (*ish*) and Woman (*ishshah*). (See translators' notes.)

Gaining a better understanding of the categories of prose and poetry is important for readers of biblical literature. Within each of these two basic categories, one may discern a number of sub-types. For example, the following sorts of literature are composed in prose: list (Lev 11.29–30), genealogy (Gen 10), letter (Jer 29.24–28), report (Gen 6.1–2), and story (the book of Ruth). Similarly, another set of literature is written in poetry: e.g., song (Ex 15), prophetic oracle (Mic 1.2–7), and wisdom speech (Prov 6.20–35). To understand a prose text as a story or a poetic text as a song offers the reader special insight into the workings of such literature. Some basic questions can be asked of any story or poem to gain a deeper understanding of the type of literature in question.

Much of the Bible is written in prose. And much, though not all, of the prose conveys stories. Though not all readers are literary critics, everyone knows how to read a story—whether in the historical books of the Old Testament or the parables of the New Testament. We suggest that those engaged in Bible study ask at least three questions of each story that they read. First, what is the basic movement in the plot? Second, what sort of important characters act in the story? Third, what is the main idea or theme of the story?

Let us comment briefly on each of these categories. First, the plot of the story will often begin with a basic situation, from which a complication arises; for example, a husband and wife are unable to bear children. By the end of the story, some change has occurred so that the tension created by the complication has been resolved. Attention to this movement helps readers identify the plot of a story. Second, most stories in the Bible have only a few important characters, and it is always interesting to see if the characters change or develop. Daniel does not seem to change, Paul does. Moreover, some characters are complex: We observe people who struggle, who make mistakes and yet also sometimes do the right thing; they are round, full of depth. Other characters are depicted as totally perfect or sinful; they are flat, without depth. Finally, the reader should try to identify the primary idea with which an author is wrestling in a story. To create that statement of theme requires an active engagement with the art of the author. Individual readers will often write quite different statements of theme, in part because the story may be read in several ways, and in part because the readers understand the story differently. Discussing our statements of theme with others helps us understand the various ways readers respond to prose in biblical literature.

Another type of prose, as mentioned earlier, is the letter. Although there are some letters preserved in the Old Testament, twenty-one of the New Testament books are themselves letters. Hence, it helps to know something about letters in antiquity before encountering this remarkable corpus in the New Testament. Letters in the Greco-Roman world characteristically began by identifying the sender and the receiver or addressee, followed by a thanksgiving to the gods. They concluded with an exchange of greetings. When reading NT letters, it is interesting to look for these opening and closing sections, addressees, and thanksgivings; see, for example, the opening in 1 Cor 1.1–9 and the conclusion in Rom 16.

What special characteristics does poetry have? As we have had occasion to see, poetry challenges readers in a way that prose often does not. Readers of the New Testament will face those challenges less frequently than will readers of the Old Testament because poetry simply does not appear as often in the New Testament. Moreover, much of the poetry that does appear in the New Testament is a quotation of Old Testament texts (for example, Mt 13.14–15). Hence, in most cases, attending to poetry in the Bible involves the reading of Hebrew poetry.

We possess no guidebook in which the rules of ancient Hebrew poetry have been preserved. Rather, the workings of that poetry have been inferred, based on an assessment of poetic texts. For many years, it has been clear that the dominant element in Hebrew poetry is parallelism, typically the juxtaposition of two lines of comparable length. The relationship between the meaning of each line can vary significantly. Often, the lines bear similar meaning, though rarely are they absolutely identical. For example,

> For the bed is too short to stretch oneself on it,
> and the covering too narrow to wrap oneself in it. (Isa 28.20)

These lines offer two related examples of something that is too small, but the absence of a good fit is expressed in different ways: a cramped bed and a skimpy blanket.

So-called antithetic proverbs operate in a different way:

> A soft answer turns away wrath,
> but a harsh word stirs up anger. (Prov 15.1)

The two lines comment on differing forms of behavior, one positive, one negative. Together they work to admonish the reader or hearer toward one form of behavior, the positive one.

Finally, some lines that stand in parallel fashion operate more as a narrative: the thought simply flows from one line to the next.

> My beloved had a vineyard
> > on a very fertile hill.
> He dug it and cleared it of stones,
> > and planted it with choice vines; (Isa 5.1–2)

The person who reads Hebrew poetry will need to be alert to the various ways in which such parallel lines work.

If parallelism is a hallmark of Hebrew poetry, there are other elements that make it similar to that written in other languages: It is filled with rich images, similes (comparisons using "like" or "as") and metaphors (direct comparisons). For example, many psalms give voice to an individual who is suffering (these psalms are often called "individual laments"). These psalms, such as the one that follows, include remarkable descriptions of an individual's plight.

> . . . my bones burn like a furnace.
> My heart is stricken and withered like grass;
> > I am too wasted to eat my bread.
> Because of my loud groaning
> > my bones cling to my skin.
> I am like an owl of the wilderness,
> > like a little owl of the waste places. (Ps 102.3–6)

Four similes depict this person's distress, and because this figure of speech is so prominent, it would be unwise to try to guess precisely what the physical or psychological plight is. Rather than giving a clinical description, the psalm presents images, which could be applied by this person, another Israelite, or even a reader today to reflect on a current situation. To read this psalm as poetry helps us gain access to it as a resource and prevents it from remaining simply a historical artifact of an ancient Israelite's experience.

Formation of Biblical Literature   Many books of the Bible grew or developed over time. To be sure, some, like Ruth and 1 Corinthians, were written by a single author. However, many books possess a core of prose or poetry that has been arranged, rearranged and supplemented over time by an editor or reviser (known as a "redactor"). Scholars who study this process engage in "redaction criticism." There are numerous examples of this growth process in the Bible.

In the New Testament, the Synoptic Gospels include many of the same sayings of Jesus. However, their order and configuration is not uniform. For example, the parable of the sower occurs much earlier in Mark's Gospel (4.1–9) than it does in the Gospel of Matthew (13.1–9). Each of the Gospels narrates the account of Jesus and the money-changers in the Jerusalem temple ("the cleansing of the temple"), but whereas in

Matthew, Mark, and Luke that story is positioned in the last week of Jesus' life, in John it is one of the first acts of Jesus' ministry. What we see in such comparisons is the freedom with which ancient collectors and authors could assemble and cast their material.

The Old Testament is full of comparable examples. The book of Psalms is a collection of various songs. The process whereby that collection was made is far from clear. However, even the casual reader soon learns that one element in that organization involves the notion of "books." Just before Psalms 1, 42, 73, 90 and 107, the NRSV includes rubrics, "Book I, II, III, IV and V." Moreover, Ps 41.13; 72.18–19; 89.52; 106.48 and all of Psalm 150 comprise doxologies that conclude each of these "books." In each case, these doxologies stand outside the poetic flow of the psalms to which they have been attached. As a result, one has good reason to think that the psalms have been configured to make them appear in five books. Such a pattern of organization would, of course, make them appear similar to the five book collection—the Pentateuch or Torah—with which the Hebrew Bible begins.

These two examples, taken from the Gospels and Psalms, involve primarily the organization of existing traditions or texts. However, the formation of biblical literature can result from far more aggressive activity than simply the ordering of poems or sayings. The book of Isaiah offers a classic example. Isaiah ben Amoz was active as a prophet in the mid-late eighth and early seventh centuries BCE. During this period, he addressed the people of Judah as they lived through several crises. The sayings of this Isaiah are concentrated in early portions of the book, especially chs. 2–10 and 28–33. Elsewhere in the book, particularly chs. 40–66, the style of the literature changes and the historical context is different. For example, Isa 45.1–8 refers to Cyrus, emperor of the Persian empire (he ruled in the mid sixth century). Moreover, the poetry is more rhetorical and occurs in longer units than does that in the earlier chapters. As a result of such observations, scholars have argued that chs. 40–66 along with many others, for example, chs. 1, 34–35, reflect authors other than Isaiah ben Amoz. Hence, one may surmise that the book of Isaiah reflects a long process of growth, from c. 700 BCE to at least 500 BCE, during which the words of Isaiah were collected and supplemented. Later poets/prophets, particularly in the Persian period, contributed new sayings, which grew out of the theological and literary resources provided by the seminal figure, Isaiah ben Amoz. Understood in this way, the book of Isaiah is very much the product of organic growth. To understand this prophetic book is to understand the generative power of the core sayings along with the literatures that were stimulated by them.

The book of Jeremiah includes a story about how an early form of that book was created. God commands Jeremiah to "Take a scroll and write on it all the words that I have spoken to you. . . " (Jer 36.2). Soon after the scroll is written, it is destroyed, whereupon a new one is created. At the end of Jer 36, which describes this process, the narrator writes, "Then Jeremiah took another scroll and gave it to the secretary Baruch son of Neriah, who wrote on it at Jeremiah's dictation all the words of the scroll that King Jehoiakim of Judah had burned in the fire; and many similar words were added to them" (Jer 36.32). There can be no more graphic statement about one way in which a biblical book developed. Such formative processes hint at the appropriateness, even need, for biblical literature to readdress each new age of readers.

Historical and Cultural Context   One question that readers regularly pose to a biblical text is: When was it written? Knowing something about the people, places or political forces at the time the book was written will help readers gain a deeper understanding of that text. For example, the book of Hosea stems from the early part of the second half of the eighth century BCE (roughly 750–720 BCE). However, as one reads that book, few specific historical references to that period appear. Instead, Hosea uses many ornate figures of speech to depict the fate that awaits Israel: e.g., "they shall reap the whirlwind" (8.7) or "they shall be like the morning mist or like the dew that goes away early" (13.3). In addition, God speaks as if the deity would be an enemy arrayed against Israel: "I will destroy you, O Israel" (13.9) or "I will become like a lion to them" (13.7). This way of speaking does not enable the reader to speak about what, concretely, will happen to Israel.

When one places such language of destruction within the context of what we know about the ancient Near Eastern history of that period, we discover what it is that the prophet is probably anticipating. Other biblical texts are also helpful, in this regard, since the time that Hosea was active is also treated by the biblical historian whose work is preserved in the book of Kings. In addition, archaeologists have discovered texts from the royal archives of the Neo-Assyrian empire, the dominant political force of this era. These varied sources help us understand that the Neo-Assyrian empire was exerting considerable influence on Syria-Palestine during the last half of the eighth century. Their armies were campaigning in the Levant. Hence, when Hosea speaks about sounding an alarm (5.8) or "the tumult of war shall rise against your people" (10.14), we know that there is a very specific reference in Hosea's mind. He perceives that the Neo-Assyrians will destroy Israel. Moreover, he understands military activity from a theological perspective, namely, that such destruction is consistent with Israel's God's intent for Israel—that it be punished.

This is only one of many instances in which understanding the historical context helps the reader. Hence it is always appropriate to raise questions involving a text's historical background when one is studying the Bible. Still, there is a remarkable number of chapters, narratives, and poems about which we can say very little concerning a precise historical context. Such is the case for many psalms. For example, it would be interesting to know when Ps 113 was written or in what specific context it was used in ancient Israel. However, no word or idea in this psalm is specific to a particular moment in ancient Israelite history. The God who dwells above the heavens is a prominent motif in many periods, as is the deity's concern for the poor and the barren woman. Hence, the reader will be wise to avoid struggling to identify a historical setting for this psalm. Instead, a different range of questions—perhaps literary or theological analysis—would be more likely to yield results.

To attend to the context of biblical literature can involve more than simply asking about the historical point of origin. Both the Old and New Testaments are literatures that emerged within cultural contexts that influenced them in important ways. Jewish and Greco-Roman religious impulses fed into early Christian discourse at the very outset of its existence. Likewise, ancient Israelite society and culture was informed by the cultural heritage of the ancient Near East.

Let us take the example of two types of legal material in the Old Testament to demonstrate the importance of paying attention to cultural context. Many of the laws in the Israelite collections follow a standard form: If something happens, then such and such will be the penalty, often termed "case law." Exodus 21.33–34 offers a biblical example, and similar case laws were also prominent in collections from ancient Mesopotamian cultures. These laws surely grew out of actual cases adjudicated by Israelite or Mesopotamian courts. However, elsewhere in the Israelite collections, we find laws of a different sort: "you shall not do something." Exodus 22.18 is characteristic of this form, as are several of the ten commandments. When consulting the ancient Near Eastern collections, one learns that this form of law is much less frequent than it is in the Israelite material. This comparison suggests that these laws of prohibition directed to an individual, a "you," do not seem to derive from the ancient court system and may reflect some other tradition, which was particularly prominent in ancient Israel.

When undertaking Bible study, it is often useful to consult a commentary or the notes in a study Bible to discover if there is an important issue of cultural context that might be pursued. Many of the ancient texts with which biblical literature may be compared are now available in translations and are more readily available than they have been in the past: for example, texts from ancient Egypt or those written by Flavius Josephus. Attention to such literatures can help us understand the ways in which ancient Israelites, Jews, and early Christians shared important beliefs and values with those with whom they interacted. Moreover, such study can make clear instances in which those who wrote the Bible stood apart from others in their culture.

Finally, we should note the important resource that the work of archaeologists provides for biblical study. Though few would now speak of something called "biblical archaeology," the work of archaeologists has informed significantly the way in which we understand ancient Israel and early Christianity, not so much by attesting or verifying events or places mentioned in the Bible as by helping us understand how these ancient societies worked. Of course, the discovery of texts has a special significance, whether ancient flood stories from Babylon or the Dead Sea Scrolls from the Wadi Qumran, but even when excavations or surveys do not yield texts, we learn a great deal about the context out of which biblical literature emerged.

For example, there are numerous references to city gates in the Old Testament. North American readers of the Bible are probably more familiar with city gates in a European context than those of the ancient Near East. The typical city gate in ancient Israel was like a major corridor into which a number of open rooms were built. When one entered the city, one passed through several chambers, often lined with benches. The ancient city gate had several functions. It afforded the opportunity for assembly as well as entry and, of course, defense. Such knowledge about city gates helps us understand a text such as Ruth 4.1–2, which in this case refers to the city gate as a place of legal assembly. As did Boaz, one could go to the gate and collect a group of individuals—here they were elders of the city—who were those enfranchised to constitute the legal assembly. Were we to have only the European picture, we might imagine this group of elders clogging a small door to the village of Bethlehem.

Recently, archaeologists have been doing more than excavating monuments (for example, city walls) and finding texts—they have attempted to reconstruct the ways in which people lived. Hence, the nature of family life, for example, has become part of their scope. How many people lived in a household? What sort of food did they produce and eat? What relation did a family outside of a city have to the city? Such studies are having a major impact on the ways we understand the forms of social life depicted in biblical literature.

Social World Issues Attention to the world of family life is also consistent with another way of studying the Bible: namely, asking broader questions about social structure, economics, culture, and political order. These four labels are related directly to what some would call the social sciences. Earlier in this chapter, we were addressing literary, historical, and philological questions, topics that would normally be addressed in humanities courses. Now we move to another range of discourse, that represented especially by sociology, economics, anthropology, and political science.

Since ancient Israel was a society that existed in a particular period, it is amenable to all these forms of analysis, just as are early Christian communities. In both settings, it is useful to know something about the economies in which people lived. Such knowledge helps us either when we have questions about the economic "sins" that the prophets attack or when we want to ask what early Christians thought about the relation of their faith to possession of property. Similarly, Israel existed in quite different political modes over time—clans, monarchy, religious communities. Other nations and communities have existed in these forms as well. And it is useful to compare the various communities that have been ruled by priests (hierocracies) in order to understand the internal dynamics that were at work in those societies. In this regard, it is no accident that the role of the "high priest" apparently did not exist until after Israel and Judah ceased to exist as nations.

When addressing social world issues, it is very important to distinguish, at least initially, the social world in the text versus the social world behind the text. We may use the book of Genesis as a case in point. In order to study the social world that produced the text, one would need to determine the time it was produced. If, for example, one thought that Genesis had been written during the time of Solomon (tenth century BCE), one would attempt to discern the ways in which issues important to that time are addressed by the Genesis narratives. Similarly, if one thought that Genesis had been written during the time of Ezra (fifth century BCE), then one would seek ways in which Israel's existence as a district in the Persian empire is reflected in it. One would read the book of Genesis in quite different ways, based upon differing judgments about its point of origin.

Scholars currently disagree about when Genesis was written. Hence it would be risky indeed to postulate a social world that produced this important biblical book. It would be very difficult to speak about the social structure or economic system in which its author or authors were embedded. So, unlike the situation with Amos or Romans, it would be unwise to attempt to speak with precision about the social world behind or outside this particular text.

On the other hand, there is a social world conveyed in the book of Genesis. We read about the people planting crops, engaging in animal husbandry, buying and selling land. Hence, we can attempt to determine whether these reports make up an intelligible economic system. The same may be said of family life. People are born, undergo puberty rites, marry, have children, grow old and die. Some of the patterns of family behavior may seem strange to us—for example, Abraham marrying Sarah and then having a child with Sarah's servant Hagar, or Jacob's marrying two sisters, Rachel and Leah. However, scholars familiar with family life in many cultures recognize these practices as part of a well-attested family structure in which property is passed through a particular type of kinship structure. Similar things can be said about patterns of religious behavior. People build altars, engage in blood rituals, whether circumcision or animal sacrifice. Here too, these patterns of religious activity can be understood, based on cross-cultural analysis—without appeal to a specific historical context. This world in the text—whether that of social structure or religious behavior—can be studied and found to be intelligible, even though we may not know when the text was written.

Many readers of the Bible will be familiar with their own social worlds, but not with those of other cultures, including those that might be more similar to those in the Bible. In such situations, it will be important, at a minimum, to allow the biblical text to speak for itself. In the previous paragraph, we mentioned marriage patterns in Genesis that are quite different from those practiced in North America today. Whether or not readers know about other cultures in which such marriages are practiced, they should attempt to discern what cultural values are being addressed by such practices and whether or not these marriage patterns elicit censure by the biblical authors. We need to be careful not to impose our own culture's practices and values on texts that derive from a radically different context. Attention to the social world in the text will help us understand how different that world might be from that of our own.

The Worlds of Readers   All texts are the products of human authors, and readers have often assumed that their task is to figure out what the authors intended them to find in the text. The act of reading itself, however, is very important for the "creation of meaning." Reading involves far more than discovering "the meaning" of a text. Readers come from varied social, economic, and geographical contexts. Some are women, some are men. And, most important, each reader brings his or her own unique history to the text. All these factors regularly manifest themselves in diverse questions or sensitivities that readers bring to texts.

We offer two examples of the ways in which Bible study can be affected by different readers' worlds. First, women will often bring a different set of experiences and questions to biblical texts than will men. Such modes of interpretation, as exemplified by *The Women's Bible Commentary*, have significantly enriched our ability to study the Bible. One scholar has written an interpretation of the book of Judges based on a study of the female characters in it. Seen from this vantage point, Judges, particularly after the time of Deborah, is truly a violent world, one in which "all the people did what was right in their own eyes" (Judg 21.25). And not much was right. In the New Testament, scholars have noted the remarkable prominence of women among Jesus' early followers. Even more, the first resurrection reports are attributed to women: "Now it was Mary Magdalene, Joanna, Mary the mother of James, and the other women with them . . ." (Lk 24.10).

Second, people's own individual experiences affect their interpretations of biblical materials. Genesis 22 offers a useful example. This narrative, often called "the sacrifice of Isaac," has both perplexed and stimulated readers for centuries. It perplexed the Danish theologian Søren Kierkegaard, and it stimulated the Dutch artist Rembrandt. Reading and seeing the results of their work enriches our perception of this text. However, the reader who has suffered as a child at the hands of an abusive parent reads this text from a very different perspective. And that reader's perception, too, can enrich our study of this problematic tale.

There is, of course, a danger in emphasizing the role of the reader. Readers can import their own meanings into the text (often called "eisegesis" or "reading into") as opposed to drawing meaning out of the text (often called "exegesis" or "reading out of"). Each reader should be aware of critical elements in his or her identity. They are obviously important and will, inevitably, affect the way that an individual constructs meaning during the reading process. Such awareness will enable that individual to learn from other readers who might share certain elements of that identity, but that same awareness will make it possible for the individual to seek out others whose experience is different, creating the possibility for true dialogue in Bible study.

The text should, in principle, be able to challenge any reader's preconceptions about what it is saying. Hence, it is always appropriate for readers to be conscious of the questions and the perspectives with which they are approaching a text. Readers might well ask whether their question is literary, sociological, theological or historical.

SUMMARY

There are many ways to study the Bible. Obviously the materials provided in this study Bible do not offer an exhaustive guide. They hint at possible points of engagement and provide some of the basic information needed in order to begin to understand the text. Still, an important element of study are the questions that each reader brings to the text. Readers will serve themselves well if they routinely address a broad range of questions, ranging from literary, historical, and philological subjects to social world issues. In so doing, they will make fruitful biblical study possible for themselves and for others.

A READER'S GUIDE TO THE BOOKS OF THE BIBLE

The signs in a bookstore or the category headings in the card catalogue at the library inform us whether a book is history or science, fiction or non-fiction, poetry or drama, and so we are able to prepare ourselves for our reading in advance. We would read a biography with a different set of expectations, for example, from those with which we would read an autobiography; a collection of essays on contemporary social problems calls for a different approach to reading than does a novel that focuses on one of those problems. The more readily we as readers are able to recognize the type of literature that we are reading, the more deeply we will be able to engage what that literature has to offer.

For example, the knowledge that *Anne Frank: The Diary of a Young Girl* is the actual journal of a young Jewish girl who lived in hiding during the Nazi occupation of the Second World War raises a different set of reading expectations and responses than would a novel built around the same set of circumstances. Reading the journal of a real person's experiences is different from reading a fictional representation of what those experiences might have been like. Moreover, our reading can be diminished if we misunderstand what type of literature we are reading. If, for example, we read a book on military tactics and strategy with the expectation that it will focus on the emotional costs of battle and so enable us to experience the human face of war, we will inevitably be disappointed or confused. Likewise, if we read a war novel expecting to learn how the high command developed its specific strategies and deployed the troops, we most likely will be disappointed again.

Although it is common to refer to the Bible as a faith community's book (singular), in reality the Bible is a collection of many different books (plural). The very word "bible" signifies a collection of books, because the word's origins can be traced back (through the Latin *biblia*) to the Greek phrase *ta biblia*, which means "the little scrolls." In the Jewish community as well, the diversity of books is reflected in the word used to refer to its Scriptures; "Tanakh" is an acronym formed from the first letters of the Jewish threefold division of Scripture: Law ("torah"), Prophets ("nevi'im") and Writings ("kethubim").

Bound within one cover, then, are many different books, each of which demands something different from the reader. In the New Testament, for example, one can read Paul's own accounts of his ministry in his letters and someone else's account of Paul's ministry in the stories of the Acts of the Apostles. As with *The Diary of A Young Girl*, reading Paul's own words and reading what someone else presents as Paul's words are two very different reading experiences. And unlike the signs and classifications that guide the modern reader through the bookstore or the library, the markers that identify the various types of literature found in the Bible are not as obvious at a casual glance. The titles of the different books of the Bible, for example, do not automatically indicate what we will find there. A man's personal name is the title of many books of the Bible, but reading Amos and reading Philemon are completely different experiences. The rest of this essay suggests the categories in the card catalogue at the library under which the books of the Bible might be filed, if they were filed as individual books, and so equips all readers for a deeper and fuller engagement with the Bible.

NARRATIVE AND NON-NARRATIVE BOOKS

One of the first classifications would involve the broad distinction between narrative and non-narrative books. Narrative books are those that tell a story and that, by and large, follow the traditional forms of storytelling—plot, character, setting, dialogue, etc. The narrative books of the Bible are often the best-known and the most beloved because they tell stories that people remember and retell—Genesis, 1 and 2 Samuel, Ruth, Esther, the four Gospels—but in reality, narrative and non-narrative books are fairly evenly balanced in the full sweep of biblical literature. Non-narrative books are those that, in contrast, do not tell stories. Non-narrative books in the Bible range from the poetry of the Psalms to the community instructions in Paul's letters.

Again, a comparison between Paul's letters and the book of Acts may be the most helpful way to illustrate the difference between narrative and non-narrative books. In the Acts of the Apostles, one of the goals of the author, Luke, is to tell the story of the rise of the Christian church, as the good news of Christ spread to the Gentile world. The reader is positioned to see the story of early Christianity the way Luke sees it and to understand that this story forms the foundation of the future life of the Christian church in the world, right up to the present day. As such, the stories about the mission to individuals or communities stand as illustrations of this basic story line. Paul's letters, by contrast, are not stories about the spread of the gospel in the Gentile world, nor does Paul write them so that the reader can see how the church grew and developed. Rather, Paul's letters are the urgent writings of someone on the front lines, so to speak, written to communities who have only a beginning sense of what it means to embrace the gospel that Paul preaches. A story could be constructed about each of the communities to which Paul writes (which to some extent Luke does in Acts), but that is not Paul's goal in writing. Paul writes to help these newly formed communities resolve particular theological and pastoral issues or crises with which they struggle. He addresses his readers directly through the letter: He talks to them about their own situation, not about another situation, as is the case with the audience of the stories in Acts.

Acts and the letters of Paul, then, give the Bible reader very different exposures to the life of the early Christian church by virtue of the differences in their literary type. Acts, a narrative book, offers a story of the church that has a beginning, middle, and end (however open-ended that ending may be; see the commentary on Acts). It has a cast of characters and a clearly defined plot. Paul's letters, non-narrative books, have none of that. With the exception of Paul and a few of his co-workers, there is no clear cast of characters, only the largely anonymous members of the church to whom each letter is sent. There is no defined story line, because Paul's letters are written out of and to ongoing struggles and situations, so we as modern readers find ourselves in the middle of a situation to which we are outsiders.

Paul cannot provide what Acts does—an ordered story—and Acts cannot provide what Paul's letters do—the sense of urgency and intensity that comes from addressing a crisis. Reading a story and reading a letter are two very different things. Each of these two types of literature, one narrative, the other non-narrative, has something valuable to contribute to our engagement with the biblical writings, but in order to grasp this experience we must read, assess, and appreciate each one on its own terms.

DIFFERENT TYPES OF NARRATIVE BOOKS

The broad distinction between narrative and non-narrative books is a start in orienting us to the spectrum of books gathered together in the Bible. It needs further specification, however, because there are many variations among the books that constitute these two large categories. The category "narrative" is a good way to begin to look at the storytelling of the Bible, but narrative books of the Bible tell different types of stories and tell them in different ways. Some narrative books of the Bible tell one continuous story from beginning to end. The most notable examples of this *novelistic* type of narrative would be the books of Ruth and Esther in the Hebrew Scriptures, and Judith, Tobit, Susanna, and Bel and the Dragon in the Apocrypha. Jonah also fits into this category, because even though it is one of the books of the prophets, it is a narrative of the adventures of one prophet who is trying to avoid his call.

Some narrative books are formed from the combination of many smaller stories and are more like *epics* than novels. Genesis, for example, combines many different stories— the story of the genesis of human beings and their foibles and failings (Gen. 1–11), and the stories of Abraham and his descendants (Gen. 12–50) that tell the distinctive story of the ancestors of the Israelite people. The remaining books of the Pentateuch— Exodus, Leviticus, Numbers, and Deuteronomy—work together to tell the sweeping story of Israel's exodus from slavery in Egypt, journey in the wilderness, and arrival at the promised land, while at the same time telling the life story of one man, Moses.

Shorter story units are also brought together to construct the *historical narratives* that play such a major role in biblical literature. Historical narratives appear in the Hebrew Scriptures, the Apocrypha, and the New Testament. These narratives tell the stories of a particular period in biblical history, but do so not by providing a simple record or chronicle of the events, but by looking at the events through the authors' understanding of the role and place of God in those events. Joshua and Judges tell the story of the conquest and occupation of the promised land, and the books of Samuel, Kings, and Chronicles tell the rich and contentious story of the rise and fall of the Davidic monarchy and dynasty. The last chapters of 2 Chronicles take the story through the fall of Jerusalem at the hands of the Babylonians and the Babylonian exile to the rise of King Cyrus and the Persian Empire. The books of Ezra and Nehemiah pick up the historical narrative at that point, and tell the story of the restoration of Jerusalem under Persian rule.

A comparison of the books of Samuel and Kings with those of Chronicles clearly illustrates that biblical histories are not simply objective recordings of events. The same events are recounted with very different narrative and theological emphases, because the Samuel–Kings tradition and the Chronicles tradition interpreted the events through different lenses (see the commentaries on the respective books). Interestingly, despite their different perspectives, both traditions end their storytelling of the Babylonian exile on a note of hope rather than desolation, another indication that biblical historical narratives are about more than simply recording the "facts."

In the Apocrypha, historical narratives are represented by the books of 1 Esdras and 1 and 2 Maccabees. First Esdras, like the books of Chronicles before it, draws heavily on other biblical histories (2 Chron 35–36, Ezra, and parts of Nehemiah) to tell its story of the Persian period. First and Second Maccabees tell the story of Israel after the death of Alexander the Great, when the Jews, under Hasmonean leadership, rebelled against foreign domination. First Maccabees in particular is highly reminiscent in style and tone of the biblical histories of Samuel and Kings. Again, the fact that 1 Esdras retells so much of a history already available in other books provides an important clue about the nature of biblical histories. Their function is not simply to record the facts—if that were the case, one version of any event would suffice—but to use the telling and retelling of history to think through what it means to be a people who have these stories as part of its heritage.

The Acts of the Apostles is the New Testament's example of a biblical history. The focus and function of the history change dramatically from the historical narratives cited above to Acts. Acts is no longer concerned with telling Israel's national story, but the author of Acts uses the models of the biblical histories that were at his disposal to shape his telling of the story of the rise of the Christian church.

Two other types of biblical narrative need to be discussed—*gospel* and *apocalypse*. The predominant form of narrative literature in the New Testament is the *gospel*, which has many similarities to the narrative forms discussed above, but is also distinct from them. Like Genesis and the biblical historical narratives, each of the four New Testament Gospels, Matthew, Mark, Luke, and John, also combine many smaller stories into one narrative unity, but they do so not to tell the sweeping story of many generations of a family or to cover several centuries in Israel's history. Rather, like the more novelistic narratives of Ruth or Jonah, the Gospels tell one continuous story from beginning to end—the story of the life and death of one man, Jesus. Yet because the focus of this story is primarily on the words and works of Jesus' public ministry and not on the full scope of his life, it is not accurate to label the Gospels as biography either, because their shaping concern is not a portrait of the life of a great man. The Gospels tell the story of Jesus as a way of telling the story of God at work in the world, and are written by people who believe God to be at work in the story they tell. In this way, the Gospel writers are like the authors of the historical narratives of the Hebrew Scriptures, recounting not "facts" alone, but what those facts tell about God and the people who attempt to live in accordance with their faith in that God. The Gospels represent a unique narrative form in the Bible, but one that is closely linked to the various narrative types of the Jewish Scriptures.

The *apocalypse* is represented in the Bible by the books of Daniel and Revelation, and in the Apocrypha by 2 Esdras. To be more specific, Daniel contains two distinct narrative types: Daniel 1–6 belongs to the novelistic type of narrative and so is closely linked in form to the Additions to Daniel found in the Apocrypha (Susanna and Bel and the Dragon), while Daniel 7–12 is an apocalyptic narrative. Daniel 7–12, Revelation, and 2 Esdras do tell a story, but it is not a story that adheres to the conventional expectations of storytelling. Indeed, the "story" of these books is the most sweeping in scope of any narrative in the Bible, for it tells God's cosmic story of the present and future of the created order. Much of Daniel 7–12, Revelation, and 2 Esdras are presented as visions revealed to the author, so that these books, like other biblical narratives, combine shorter narrative units to form the whole. An apocalypse can be among the most difficult books of the Bible to read, because we are tempted to ignore the narrative world that it creates and force it to adhere to our storytelling expectations. More than any other narratives in the Bible, the apocalypses ask the reader to step completely into the imagistic world created by the storyteller and view the whole creation through that perspective. The challenge is to allow these cosmic stories to shape our reading, rather than the other way around.

NON-NARRATIVE BOOKS

As different as the types of narrative books are, they all share the common trait that they tell stories. There is no comparable common characteristic among the non-narrative books of the Bible, and one finds a vast array of such literature—from poetical books to prophetic books to wisdom books to letters. The non-narrative books of the Bible present the reader with a completely different reading challenge and experience than do the narrative books.

Prophetic Books   The prophetic books of the Old Testament may be the furthest removed from the biblical narratives. Stories draw the reader into someone else's life or history, but these books directly address a particular audience and focus on the diagnosis and resolution of a particular community problem. The prophetic books are not telling stories about foreign domination and economic injustice for anyone to read; they are engaging in political, economic, and theological analysis for a very specific community situation in what is for them the present moment.

The prophetic books give the reader access to many prophets whose words and actions have been preserved in writing: Isaiah, Jeremiah, Ezekiel, Hosea, Joel, Amos, Obadiah, Micah, Nahum, Habakkuk, Zephaniah, Haggai, Zechariah, Malachi. (Although Jonah appears in the group of the twelve minor prophets, between Obadiah and Micah, it is closer in form to the narrative books than the other prophets; see discussion of Jonah above.) But the narratives of the Hebrew Scriptures also describe many other prophets, most notably Elijah and Elisha in 1 and 2 Kings. We must therefore be careful not to view the nature and place of prophecy in Israel solely through the prophetic books. The prophetic books of the Bible contain a particular form of religious literature which forms part, but not all, of an important religious activity in the life of Israel.

The dominant literary characteristic of the prophetic books is the presence of preaching and prophetic oracles in poetic form. The prophetic oracle, usually a poem, is the prophet's announcement of the word and will of God, often prefaced by the phrase, "Thus says the LORD. . . . " The prophets used the poetry of their preaching and the prophetic oracle to analyze their current political and economic situations, often highlighting the failure of Israel's political and religious leadership, as well as the ordinary people, to live out the righteousness and justice of God.

It may seem odd to the modern reader, used to thinking of poetry primarily as fanciful and artistic language, that the prophets should use poetry to deliver their often harsh messages of social and economic injustice and impending judgment, instead of speaking in the nuts and bolts language common to newspaper editorials and other contemporary forms of social criticism. Perhaps it would help to think instead of the eloquent sermons of Martin Luther King, Jr., whose preaching combined poetry, social urgency, and theological conviction just as the prophets do.

The prophetic books also contain autobiographical and biographical material about the prophets' lives and work. This material may locate a prophet's ministry in a particular historical setting (for instance, Am 1.1) or show how the prophet's own life embodies the will of God that he speaks about in the oracles and sermons (for instance, Am 1.10–17; Jer 13.1–11). Just as biblical narratives are formed from a combination of shorter stories, the prophetic books are formed from a combination of different traditions. And interestingly, as is the case with the biblical histories of Samuel and Chronicles (and Acts in the New Testament), in most instances, the traditions have been gathered together in such a way as to end on a note of hope (for example, Am 9.9–15, Hab 3). The oracles of hope do not diminish the urgency of the judgment, but point toward the ongoing possibility of this faith community's future with God.

Wisdom Literature   At the other end of the spectrum from the prophets are the wisdom books. In the Hebrew Scriptures, Proverbs, Ecclesiastes and Job are classified as wisdom books, with Sirach and Wisdom of Solomon representing wisdom in the Apocrypha. Where the prophets are radically devoted to Yahweh, the God of Israel, constantly appeal to the possibilities for righteousness and faithfulness in Israel's history with this God, and call for reform of specific religious and political institutions, the wisdom books are almost completely silent on these topics (Sir 44–50 and Wis 10.1–21, 11–19 are exceptions). Where the prophetic books are a distinctly biblical literary form, without real parallels in the literature of the ancient Near East, the wisdom books are a universal literary form, one also found in Egypt, Mesopotamia, and other parts of the ancient Mediterranean world. The wisdom books are concerned with everyday experience and what it means to be human, and their subject matter runs from mundane instructions on proper behavior (Proverbs) to a skeptical consideration of the meaning of life (Ecclesiastes).

Wisdom books are poetic in form, with one of their central literary traits being the use of aphorisms or proverbs. The aphorisms usually have an instructional purpose—either to educate the younger generation about what it means to be a productive and moral member of society, or to inculcate traditional wisdom literature values more generally (teachings of wealth and poverty, appropriate speech, how to select one's friends). Proverbs 10–31 and Sirach both represent this traditional didactic wisdom book. Some wisdom teachings are less concerned with practical wisdom and more with an almost philosophical wisdom, reflecting on the nature of wisdom itself (for instance, Prov 1–9, Wis 6–9) and on the goodness and reliability of God's created order (for instance, Prov 8, Sir 16–18, Wis 19.18–21).

Yet biblical wisdom literature also contains two books, Job and Ecclesiastes, that present other important strands of the wisdom tradition, that which engages in skeptical wisdom and questions traditional religious assumptions about God and creation. Job is a complex poetic dialogue on the nature of divine justice and the problem of suffering, and the famous opening lines of Ecclesiastes, " . . . vanity of vanities, all is vanity," set the tone for this skeptical reflection on the meaning of human existence. It is as essential for all readers to struggle with the often jarring and disturbing reflections of Job and Ecclesiastes as it is to read the more traditionally affirmative aphorisms of Proverbs, because it is only when all the perspectives voiced in wisdom literature are taken together that one begins to get a sense of the complexity of biblical faith.

The New Testament book of James, even though its opening address gives it the external form of a letter (see below), is actually much closer to the wisdom teachings of Proverbs or Sirach. Like these books, its focus is instructional and it explicitly hails wisdom as a virtue and equates wisdom with righteousness (Jas 3.13–18).

Poetical Books   The discussions of prophetic and wisdom books noted their use of poetic forms, but there are some books of the Bible that consist entirely of poems. The poetical books of the Bible include songs, hymns, and prayers. The best-known of these poetical books is Psalms, a collection of Israel's hymns and prayers. Psalms is often referred to as Israel's hymnbook, and that term gives an accurate sense of the place of poetical books in the Bible. Lamentations also contains hymns for the faith community's worship, in this case laments over the destruction of Jerusalem. The poetical books in the Apocrypha (the Prayer of Manasseh, the Prayer of Azariah and Song of the Three Jews, and Psalm 151) are also in this hymnic and prayer tradition. One poetical book stands slightly apart from the hymns and prayers of the other poetical books: the Song of Solomon (Song of Songs). This book contains joyous love songs between a man and a woman, perhaps to be used at a wedding.

Although the techniques used in Hebrew poetry may seem complicated to modern readers (see discussions of Hebrew poetry in comments and glossary), the power of the poetical books to communicate deeply and immediately to almost everyone remains undiminished. This poetry is able to span chronological and cultural distance and speak as directly to us as it did to its first readers. Not only that, the biblical hymns and prayers have provided Jews and Christians across the centuries with the words needed to pray and sing their own laments and fears, hopes and thanksgivings.

Epistles   Like wisdom literature, epistles are a literary form common to the literature of the ancient Mediterranean world. Letter writing was the only way to communicate across long distances, and it therefore should not be surprising, given the missionary nature of the early Christian church, that epistles (letters) are the predominant literary form in the New Testament. Ancient letter writing followed certain conventions and these conventions are adhered to in the New Testament epistles. For example, ancient letters always began with a greeting, in which the letter's sender and recipient are both named. This opening greeting was followed by an expression of thanksgiving, often for a safe journey or rescue from danger, or a prayer on behalf of the recipient. Ancient letters also closed with greetings, in which the writers often passed along greetings from those with them to those at the letter's destination point. The letter of Paul to Philemon, the shortest of Paul's letters, gives the modern reader a good sense of what ancient letters were like.

Although New Testament readers tend to identify the letter form with Paul's writings, twenty-one of the New Testament's twenty-seven books have characteristics of the letter form. Some of these books, most notably James and Revelation, share important characteristics with other literary types (see the discussions of apocalyptic and wisdom books above), but nonetheless contain some stylistic conventions that link them with the letter form. There are no epistles as separate books in the Hebrew Scriptures, but the Apocrypha contains one, the Letter of Jeremiah.

Perhaps the most important thing to remember when reading the New Testament letters is that they are real letters, real communication between two parties, preserved through time, and when we read them we are quite literally eavesdropping on someone else's conversation. This puts modern readers at a certain disadvantage to the original recipients, who knew more about the circumstances that evoked and shaped those letters than we ever can. It is our task to find meaning for ourselves in these letters through the prior experience and struggles of the original readers, and we must be attentive to what those prior situations may have been before leaping to our own situation. Yet these letters also give modern readers a vivid portrait of ancient faith communities struggling with the meaning of their emerging Christianity for their own lives and their conduct in the world, and so provide an invaluable conversation partner for contemporary communities of faith. The reader of the New Testament epistles is never a solitary reader, but is always in the company of the letter's sender and original recipients.

CONCLUSION

This essay began by broadly categorizing the various books of the Bible under the headings "narrative" and "non-narrative." Those basic divisions hold true, but they also need some final clarification, because many of the books of the Bible combine these two categories to some degree. Many of the Bible's narratives contain non-narrative material, and many non-narrative books have strong narrative elements. Exodus and Numbers, for example, narrative books of the Pentateuch, contain important non-narrative sections, most notably the sections of legal codes (for instance, Ex 20–23). The Gospels, likewise, incorporate much non-narrative material into their stories (for instance, the Sermon on the Mount in Mt 5–7). As noted above, the prophetic books include biographical and autobiographical stories about the prophets. Job, a wisdom book, is set within a narrative frame. A letter is part of the narrative in Ezra (4.11–22).

As we have also seen, one biblical book can fit into more than one category. Revelation is the Bible's fullest example of an apocalypse, a narrative form, but it also can be categorized as one of the New Testament epistles. Jonah is a novelistic narrative, but it also is categorized canonically as one of the prophetic books. Daniel is both novelistic and apocalyptic narrative. Some Psalms, for instance Ps 37, can also be considered as wisdom literature, or at least as having been influenced by wisdom traditions. Also, many of the broad categories can be further refined. Hebrews and 1 Peter, for example, New Testament epistles, can also be categorized as sermons in letter form.

The categories suggested in this essay, then, are only a starting point. They provide the basic tools necessary to recognize the varieties of literary types that make up the books of the Bible, but each reader will discover ways to refine, expand, and deepen these categories through continued Bible reading and study. And while each of us will have our favorite biblical book or favorite literary type, it is only when the Bible is allowed to speak in all its variety that we can perceive the span and depth of biblical faith.

THE NATURE AND FORMATION
OF THE BIBLICAL CANON

DEFINITION

By the *biblical canon* is meant the official list of the books which make up the Scriptures of the Old and New Testaments. Books which appear on this list are called *canonical* and all other books *non-canonical*. There are also books accepted as Scripture by some Christians but not others, and these are called *deuterocanonical*, meaning "belonging to a second level of canonicity" (Greek *deuteros* means "second"). These categories do not express value judgments about the books in question: to call a book non-canonical is not to say that it is necessarily unimportant or worthless. It is simply to say that it does not belong to the Christian Bible.

CONTENTS

The New Testament contains twenty-seven books, and all Christians agree on which these are. They fall into three categories. First, there are the four Gospels and the Acts of the Apostles, which contain the story of Jesus and of the earliest days of the Christian Church. Secondly, there are a number of letters or "epistles," some written to churches and others to individuals. The bulk of the letters are, or claim to be, by Paul. One of these is to the church in Rome, two to Corinth, one to Galatia, one to Ephesus, one to Colossae, and two to Thessalonica, together with personal letters to Timothy (two), Titus, and Philemon. Other letters claim to be by James, Peter (two), and Jude. Tradition ascribes three letters to John, though the name does not appear in the text itself. In addition there is the Letter to the Hebrews, which does not tell us who wrote it, though some people since ancient times have thought it was by Paul. Thirdly, we have the book of Revelation, sometimes called the Apocalypse. This begins with letters to churches, but consists mostly of a series of visions of the end of the world and the creation of a "new heaven and new earth." All these books were written in Greek.

Things are more complicated where the Old Testament is concerned, because here Christians do not agree. We will begin by discussing the books about which there is no disagreement, which are also regarded as Holy Scripture by Jews. If we follow the order presented in the NRSV (and there are others), we can say that, as in the New Testament, there are basically three kinds of books.

First, there are books of *narrative* or history. Together these amount to about half of the Old Testament. Genesis, Exodus, Leviticus, Numbers, Deuteronomy, Joshua, Judges, Ruth, 1 & 2 Samuel, and 1 & 2 Kings tell the story of God and his people from the creation of the world down to the exile of the people of Israel from their own land to Babylon, after the Babylonians conquered Jerusalem. This story is then repeated, but with enormous differences, in the two books of Chronicles. Following Chronicles, Ezra and Nehemiah relate the return of some Israelites to their land and the establishment of the Jewish state once again during the time of the Persian empire. The Old Testament does not take the story any further than this. The book of Esther tells us of some events at the Persian court which affected the safety of the Jews.

Secondly, the Old Testament contains books of *poetry* and *wisdom*. Job presents the problem of innocent suffering through a story about a righteous man whom God allows to suffer severe trials. Psalms contains many of the hymns that may have been used in Israel's worship. Proverbs includes collections of wise sayings. Ecclesiastes (also known by its Hebrew name, Qoheleth) provides a sceptical reflection on the teachings of other wise men. The Song of Solomon (or Song of Songs) is a collection of love poetry. None of these books is connected to any particular event in the history of Israel, and it is difficult to date them precisely.

The third part of the Old Testament consists of the books of the *prophets*. Three of these (Isaiah, Jeremiah together with Lamentations, and Ezekiel) are very long, and along with a fourth, shorter book—Daniel—are known as the *major prophets*. Last come the twelve *minor prophets*, Hosea, Joel, Amos, Obadiah, Jonah, Micah, Nahum, Habakkuk, Zephaniah, Haggai, Zechariah, and Malachi. ("Major" and "minor" here refer to length, not to importance.) The prophetic books consist of the prophets' *oracles*, which offer comments on contemporary society and predictions of the future, together with some stories about the prophets' lives.

Thus there is a certain parallel between the shape of the Old and New Testaments as they have come down to us—though as we shall see it is partly accidental. Both start with history (Genesis–2 Kings, Gospels and Acts), continue with books of teaching (poetic and wisdom books, letters) and conclude with prophecy (prophetic books, Revelation):

OLD TESTAMENT	NEW TESTAMENT
1. Histories	1. Gospels and Acts
2. Poetry and Wisdom	2. Letters
3. Prophecy	3. Revelation

Remembering this (rough) parallel can be useful as an aid to remembering how the Old and New Testaments are arranged in our Bibles.

All the books of the Old Testament were written in Hebrew, with the exception of a few chapters in Ezra and Daniel which are in Aramaic, a related language spoken across wide areas of the ancient world.

The Old Testament canon thus contains a wide variety of books. In fact the variety is even greater than indicated so far. Among the narrative or "historical" books there are wide variations in content. For example, whereas Genesis consists almost entirely of stories about the beginnings of the world and the early Hebrew ancestors, Exodus contains both history and law. It starts with the story of the exodus from Egypt under the leadership of Moses, but once the escaping Israelites reach Mount Sinai, the narrative pauses while we hear of the laws that Moses received from God. These begin with the Ten Commandments (Ex 20) but go on to include detailed rules for social life and the right ordering of worship. The laws continue all the way through Leviticus and the first half of Numbers, and it is only at Num 20 that continuous narrative resumes. Deuteronomy also consists mostly of laws.

In the same way the books of the prophets are far more varied than people often expect. Alongside oracles about the future (both optimistic and pessimistic) there are also stories, poems, passages that read like sermons, and denunciations of the state of society. It is often difficult or impossible to understand how the prophetic books are organized, with the result that they present a muddled appearance to the reader.

As well as the Old and New Testaments, many Bibles contain a section headed *The Apocrypha* (NRSV: *The Apocryphal/Deuterocanonical Books*). This consists of books whose authority as Scripture is accepted by some Christians but not others. Some Christians regard them as authoritative, but on a lower level from the books of the Old Testament; no Jews regard them as scriptural. The ancient texts of these books are available only in Greek (or certain other languages) rather than Hebrew. Although we know that some of them were originally written in Hebrew, for the most part the original Hebrew text is lost. (A partial exception is the book called Ecclesiasticus. Large portions of this book in Hebrew were found in Egypt at the beginning of the twentieth century.)

There is a traditional way of listing these additional books, but the NRSV prefers to collect them in sections according to which Christian communities accept their authority.

1. There are some books found in all Greek, Latin, and Slavonic Bibles, and are consequently accepted by Catholics, and by Greek and Russian Orthodox Christians. Tobit and Judith, two stories about the adventures of pious Jews, are in some ways rather reminiscent of Esther. Esther itself exists in a short form in the Hebrew Bible, but in Greek, Latin, and Slavonic Bibles it appears in a longer form with additional incidents, speeches, and prayers. Protestant Apocryphas usually print simply the parts that are additional under the heading "Additions to Esther." But these make no sense on their own, so the NRSV has translated The Greek Esther in full. Then there are two wisdom books that stand in the tradition of Proverbs: the Wisdom of Solomon and Ecclesiasticus, also known as the Wisdom of Jesus Son of Sirach (sometimes Sirach or Ben Sira). The book of Baruch combines further wisdom with prophetic teaching about the future glory of Jerusalem. Its sixth and final chapter, known as the Letter of Jeremiah, is sometimes printed separately, as it is in the NRSV. Additions to the book of Daniel follow: the Prayer of Azariah and the Song of the Three Jews, which belongs in the story of the burning fiery furnace (Dan 3), and the stories called Susanna and Bel and the Dragon. Then there are two history books, 1 and 2 Maccabees, which tell the story of Israel in the second century BCE.

2. Christians in the Greek and Russian Orthodox churches recognize four other works beyond even those in the Latin Bible. One is 1 Esdras, a narrative book—the Slavonic Bible calls it 2 Esdras, and Latin Bibles sometimes print it as an appendix under the name 3 Esdras. The Prayer of Manasseh, a penitential text, is also found in an appendix in some Latin Bibles. Psalm 151 and 3 Maccabees are peculiar to the Greek and Slavonic Bibles and not found in Latin Bibles.

3. The Slavonic Bible alone recognizes a work which it calls 3 Esdras, but which in the Latin Bible appendix is called 4 Esdras. This was originally written in Latin, and may be dated to the early Christian era. It is basically a Jewish work, but contains some Christian insertions. So it is later than many books in the New Testament. In Protestant Apocryphas it is usually called 2 Esdras. The titles and numbers of the books said to be composed by Ezra (Esdras in Greek) seem designed to baffle the memories of most readers!

4. Finally, the Greek Bible too has an appendix, which contains a further narrative book called 4 Maccabees. This is found in no other Bibles.

Whereas in Protestant Bibles, and in the NRSV, the apocryphal/deuterocanonical books are thus kept in a special section, in Greek, Slavonic, and Latin Bibles they are mingled in among the other books of the Old Testament, usually placed next to those they are most like. Thus Tobit and Judith stand next to Esther, and Wisdom and Ecclesiasticus next to Proverbs.

This overview demonstrates that the Old Testament and Apocrypha is a much more complex body of material than the New Testament. All Christians agree on the contents of the New Testament, but the Old Testament—though it obviously has a fixed core, the books that exist in Hebrew and are regarded as Scripture in Judaism—is much fuzzier at the edges. If one asks a well-informed Christian in a Protestant, Catholic, Greek Orthodox, or Russian Orthodox church what the books of the Old Testament are, one will get four different answers, though they will all agree in including the books which Jews recognize as their Bible.

ARRANGEMENT

The arrangement of the New Testament, like its contents, is now standardized among Christians. But it is interesting to note that the current arrangement was not the usual one in the first few Christian centuries. Modern Bibles group together all the narratives—the four Gospels and Acts. But Christians in the early centuries linked Acts with the so-called catholic epistles. "Catholic" here means "addressed to all Christians," and in practice the catholic epistles are the letters which are neither by Paul nor attributed to him. His letters each had a specific Christian church in mind, whereas the letters of the other apostles (James, Peter, John, and Jude) seem to envisage a wider group, rather like later papal encyclicals. Early Christian Bibles put Acts, the story of what the apostles did, at the beginning of the section containing the letters they wrote. The Gospels form a section on their own, and so do the letters of Paul (usually taken to include Hebrews). Revelation is the only member of a fourth category. So an early Christian Bible does not have quite the pattern we traced above, and the parallel drawn above with the Old Testament breaks down.

The Old Testament once again offers a more complicated case. Christian Bibles of all sorts usually have the shape described above, with histories followed by poetic books followed by prophets. As we have seen, what is included in each section varies. Catholic Bibles include Wisdom and Ecclesiasticus along with Proverbs and Ecclesiastes, Protestant Bibles exclude them. But the big difference in the arrangement of the Old Testament lies between Christian and Jewish Bibles.

The Hebrew Bible, as we saw, contains only the books that Protestants now accept as Holy Scripture. This does not mean that Jews follow Protestants! It results from the fact that, at the Reformation, Protestants decided to follow the Jewish canon for the books of the Old Testament. But the internal arrangement of the Hebrew books is strikingly different from that of Christian Bibles. There are still three sections, but their logic is a completely different one. The arrangement can be seen by looking at modern Jewish translations of the Bible into English, such as that of the Jewish Publication Society.

The first section of the Hebrew Bible is called the Torah, sometimes translated into English as "the Law." However, Torah has a wider meaning than the English word "law" Though Torah includes the sense of law, it also means teaching, instruction, and guidance. By calling the first section of the Bible "Torah," Jews are signalling that for them it forms the heart of Scripture, the books which are the supreme authority in matters of faith and life. The Torah consists of the *Pentateuch* or five "books of Moses"— Genesis, Exodus, Leviticus, Numbers, and Deuteronomy. Christians often think of these simply as five "historical books," running on without a break into Joshua. But in Judaism they are see not primarily as history but as instruction. They do of course contain historical narratives, but the purpose of these is to guide the life of their Jewish readers, not simply to record information about the past.

The second section of the Hebrew Bible is called the Prophets. This contains all the books called prophets in Christian Bibles (except Daniel), but it also includes the books of Joshua, Judges, Samuel, and Kings. Since the Middle Ages these historical books have come to be known as the "Former Prophets," with the books that are prophetic in the ordinary sense (for example Isaiah, Jeremiah, Amos) described as the "Latter Prophets," but this is not seen as a very important distinction. Why the histories were included under the same heading as the prophecies no-one knows: perhaps they were thought to have prophets as their authors. (Jewish sources tend, for example, to regard Samuel as the author of the books of Samuel, and Jeremiah of the books of Kings.) The Prophets section is important in Jewish worship. After the weekly reading from the Torah, there is a second reading, and it always comes from the Prophets, whether Former or Latter. There is a tendency to think of the Prophets as a kind of second tier in Scripture, of slightly lower status than the Torah though still, of course, highly authoritative.

For the third section the rather bland name Writings is the official term—sometimes modern writers use the Greek form Hagiographa, meaning "sacred writings." This is the section to which everything in Scripture that is not Torah or Prophets is assigned. Such an organization of the texts causes some surprises to those used to the Christian Bible. Chronicles, Ezra, and Nehemiah, which Christian Bibles treat as histories and place after Kings, appear in Hebrew Bibles in the Writings section. What is more, they are usually arranged out of chronological order: Ezra, Nehemiah, Chronicles. Daniel is also reckoned among the Writings, not with the Prophets. Here appear also the five books that were read at Jewish festivals: Lamentations, Ruth, Esther, Song of Solomon, and Ecclesiastes. The order of books in the Writings is not regarded as very significant: ancient and medieval manuscripts sometimes have different orders. The Writings are sometimes thought of as somewhat lower in status than the Prophets, though for practical purposes it is the distinction between the Torah and the rest that is really important. Early rabbis sometimes lumped Prophets and Writings together as "Qabbalah," or tradition.

There has never been a Christian Bible that followed the Jewish arrangement, and this perhaps is puzzling. When Protestants decided to remove the deuterocanonical books from their canon, leaving only the same Hebrew books that were also accepted by Jews, they did not rearrange what remained to make it follow the Hebrew order. They simply extracted the deuterocanonical books, and left everything else as it was.

Consequently we could say that the Protestant "Old Testament" is the Hebrew Bible arranged in the Christian order—something of a hybrid Scripture.

FORMATION OF THE OLD TESTAMENT

The canon of the Old Testament was not fixed by a decision of some authoritative body. In the New Testament period, we do hear dimly from a few Jewish sources that some books were of doubtful status. The Song of Solomon, Ezekiel, Esther, Ecclesiastes, and Proverbs were all regarded by some as anomalous or of doubtful status, though it is far from clear that there was ever any suggestion that that they were not yet canonical, or that they should be removed from the canon. Only in the case of Ecclesiasticus is there record of a decision by rabbis to exclude it from the canon. This decision was taken on the grounds that, though edifying, the book was known to have been written (in 180 BCE) long after the time at which, according to Jewish belief, scriptural books ceased to be written (roughly sometime in the fifth or fourth century BCE). (Daniel, though also written in the second century BCE, did become part of the canon, probably because its attribution to a figure of the sixth century was believed to be correct.) The books that form the Hebrew Bible were never controversial. The canon simply grew, as books were gradually accepted as Holy Scripture and revered by successive generations.

The threefold division of the Hebrew Bible reflects, to some extent, the order in which the books came to be recognized as Scripture. The Pentateuch—the Torah—must have been completed at some time during the Persian period, which lasted from 540 BCE or so until 333 BCE, when Alexander the Great conquered the Persian empire. A date sometime in the fifth century BCE is likely. If so, then we have an explanation for the high prestige of this part of the canon: it is the oldest part of the Bible. There may be books, or parts of books, in the Prophets and Writings that are older, taken individually. For example, the books of Amos, Hosea, Isaiah, and Micah probably include genuine words of those prophets who lived in the eighth century BCE. But as a *collection* the Torah is older than the Prophets and the Writings.

Possibly the Prophets formed next, with the Writings put together last of all, some time not long before the period when the New Testament was written. This would help to explain why the last books to be written appear, on the whole, in the Writings: Daniel, for example, and probably also Ruth and Esther. By the time these books were written, the Torah already existed as a finished whole. Daniel, in fact, even refers to the book of Jeremiah (see Dan 9.1), which indicates that the book of Jeremiah already existed, and possibly that the collection of the Prophets did as well.

Still, there is one piece of evidence that makes it less certain that Prophets and Writings represent successive stages in the formation of the canon. We have already observed that some rabbinic sayings link the two collections together under the single term "Qabbalah." Moreover, the New Testament also tends to treat them as a single whole, when it speaks of "the law and the prophets," meaning by this not Torah and Prophets in the technical sense, but Torah and other scriptural books. In other words, for the New Testament writers the distinction between Prophets and Writings seems not to exist. At most there could be an allusion to it in Lk 24.44, which refers to Scripture as "the law of Moses, the prophets, and the psalms"—the psalms might stand for the Writings. There may also be a reference to the threefold division in the Prologue to Ecclesiasticus, which speaks of "the law and the prophets and the other writings"—though the third category here may mean "other writings in general," not necessarily "the Writings." It seems likely that many people, even as late as the New Testament writers (first century CE), were not yet familiar with the threefold division of the canon, and that it was not generally established until some time in the Common Era.

The situation of all the books other than the Torah forming a single, shapeless category as late as the first century CE might help to explain why the Jewish and Christian Bibles diverge in the way they are arranged, and also in which books they contain. Most of the early Christians whose writings are represented in the New Testament were Greek speakers; and many Jews by this time also spoke Greek as their first, or even their only language. For their benefit the Hebrew Bible had been translated into Greek, mostly in Egypt at Alexandria, during the last three centuries BCE. Moreover, most of the deuterocanonical books, as we have seen, were written in Greek or else existed in Greek translations. For a Greek-speaking Jew living in Egypt it would have been far from clear that (for example) Proverbs, which he or she would know in its Greek version, was Holy Scripture, whereas the (rather similar) Wisdom of Solomon, which was originally composed in Greek, was not. The Jews of Alexandria probably had, alongside the Torah, a rather larger category of second-order books than their fellow Jews in Palestine who knew only the Hebrew books. This "Alexandrian canon" was what the Christians inherited, for most of them lived outside Palestine and did not understand Hebrew: they naturally adopted the Greek version of the Jewish Bible as their own. In arranging the books other than the Torah in a different way from what would become the Hebrew canon, they may not, therefore, have been deliberately changing anything. No one had yet had the idea that there was a "correct" way of arranging them.

An important witness to the state of the canon in the first century CE is the Jewish writer Josephus. He lived in Palestine, but was familiar with the Bible in Greek (he wrote in Greek himself). In one of his writings he claims that the Jews recognize only twenty-two books as Scripture. Most scholars think he is referring to the books of the Hebrew Bible as Jews now have it, though this is usually said to contain twenty-*four* books—the exact number depends on whether, for example, 1 and 2 Samuel are counted as one book or two, whether Lamentations is thought of as part of Jeremiah, and so on. But what is interesting is that Josephus' description of what these twenty-two books contain actually sounds as though he knew them in an order different from any known to us, but having similarities to the Greek Bible—which was to become the Christian Bible. Thus he says that

> five are the books of Moses, comprising the laws and the traditional history down to the death of the lawgiver. . . . From the death of Moses until Artaxerxes, who succeeded Xerxes as king of Persia, the prophets subsequent to Moses wrote the history of the events of their own times in thirteen books. The remaining four books contain hymns to God and precepts for the conduct of human life (*Against Apion* 1.42).

Like the Hebrew Bible, this appears to lump together the Former and the Latter Prophets, treating their writers primarily as historians. But it also recognizes a category of poetic and wisdom books, which is more like the central, poetic section of the Greek Bible than it is like the Writings of the Hebrew one. Perhaps what Josephus shows us is that Jews had not yet agreed on any particular way of arranging the books outside the Torah, so that he was free to classify them in whatever way would be most helpful to his readers.

At some point all Jews came to the conclusion that only the books that are now in the Hebrew Bible were to be treated as Holy Scripture. Christians, on the other hand, tended to follow the longer selection which we find in the Greek Bible and its descendants, the Latin and Slavonic Bibles. We do not know why Jews opted for the shorter canon, nor why they divided it into the three sections described above. But the threefold division was definitely established by the end of the second century CE.

We also do not know why the Church decided to accept the longer Greek canon. But it is clear that many early Christian writers thought that many of the works only to be found there had great authority. Manuscripts of the Christian Old Testament also contain the additional Greek books. There were occasional disagreements. For example, toward the end of the second century CE Melito, bishop of Sardis (in what is now Turkey), went on a fact-finding tour to the Holy Land and discovered that the Jews there accepted only the Hebrew books. (This is one reason why we know that for Jews the Hebrew canon must have been in force by then.) He decided on the strength of this that Christian Old Testaments ought not to contain the extra books; but no one paid him much attention.

Two later Christian leaders also tried to limit the canon to the Hebrew books. Athanasius (c. 296–373 CE), bishop of Alexandria, maintained that the deuterocanonical books ought not to be part of the canon. He would have reduced the Old Testament to the Hebrew books and treated the other books as non-canonical. Strikingly, however, he himself continued to make just as much use of these books after he had pronounced on the subject as he had before—especially the Wisdom of Solomon, which for him as for many early Christian writers was a favorite text.

In the following century Jerome (c. 345–420) set himself the task of translating the whole Bible into Latin, producing the work known as the Vulgate, which is the official version still used by the Catholic Church. (Latin translations already existed, but they were less accurate than Jerome's.) In the process Jerome learned Hebrew from Jewish friends, and inevitably became aware that the Jews recognized only the Hebrew books. He proposed that the Church, too, should abandon the deuterocanonical works. He engaged in a fierce debate with Augustine (345–430), bishop of Hippo in North Africa. Augustine believed that the universal consensus among Christians that the deuterocanonical books were part of the Bible should overrule the fact that the Jews did not accept them. The matter was resolved in Augustine's favor, because the Church continued to use these additional books, and Jerome, indeed, translated them despite his misgivings about their status.

It is important to see that the point at issue was whether the deuterocanonical books should be thought of as Scripture. No one suggested that they were bad or worthless. There is no contradiction in thinking a book to be good but not regarding it as part of the Bible! The problem was that the Church always had regarded these books as Scripture. Although they are quoted little in the New Testament, Christian writers throughout the second century CE used them freely, and treated them exactly as if they were on a par with the "canonical" books. Hence writers like Augustine could argue that, whatever Jews thought about the canon, for Christians the matter was settled by a long tradition in the Church.

Augustine may have had the best of the argument. If we thought of the deuterocanonical books as books added to the Bible by Christians, it would be natural to say that the "original" Old Testament did not contain them. Then we might, with Jerome, think they should be removed. But as we have seen, this way of thinking is not likely to be the explanation of the longer canon in the Christian Bible. There are two more likely explanations. One is the "Alexandrian canon" theory, which says that some Jews already had a longer canon in the New Testament period. The shorter canon is the Bible of Palestinian Jews, the longer is that of the Jews of Alexandria. Everyone agrees that the majority of the Greek books in the longer canon, after all, are Jewish in origin—no one is suggesting that Christians *wrote* them, only that they accepted them. The other plausible explanation is that in New Testament times neither Jews nor Christians had yet decided on the exact selection of books they would regard as canonical. When they did eventually decide, Jews opted for the shorter, Hebrew canon, Christians for the longer, Greek one. In other words, Jerome's argument rested on what Jews *in his own day* thought about the limits of Scripture, but this is not necessarily what Jews had believed several centuries earlier.

After Augustine the matter was regarded as closed in the Christian Church, and throughout subsequent centuries Christian Bibles always included the deuterocanonical books, incorporated into the main body of the Old Testament in the way we have described. It was not until the Reformation in the sixteenth century that the matter was discussed fully again. The major Reformers, Luther and Calvin, both went back to Jerome and Athanasius, and argued strongly that only the Hebrew books should be accepted as Holy Scripture. However, even within Protestantism there were differences of opinion. Calvin and those who followed him in the Reformed tradition regarded the deuterocanonical books as no different in principle from any other ordinary books, and wanted them to have no special position in the Church at all. Sometimes they even argued—which was not strictly necessary to this point of view, as we have seen—that the deuterocanonical books were badly flawed. Luther, on the other hand, regarded these books as good and edifying, and wanted to see Christians continue to read them. But he placed them in an appendix to the Old Testament. In practice Lutherans do not make much use of these additional books, and most Lutheran Bibles do not contain them. Of the other churches of the Reformation, the Anglican (Episcopalian) churches have adopted a position like the Lutheran one, but have tended to use these books in worship and private reading to a greater extent. According to the Church of England's thirty-nine Articles of Religion (1571) "the other books [that is, the deuterocanonical books] the Church doth read for example of life and instruction of manners; but yet doth it not apply them to establish any doctrine." Even so, few Anglicans know these books at all well, and they are read in Church rather seldom, though the *Book of Common Prayer* includes the Song of the Three Jews in its service of Morning Prayer, and Anglican lectionaries have always drawn on the Apocrypha to provide readings for saints' days. Sirach 44.1ff. is familiar to many as a reading for All Saints' Day, is commonly used in Britain at memorial services, and will be familiar to many from the opening of the film "Chariots of Fire."

The Catholic church had to react to the Reformers' decisions about the deuterocanonical books, and did so at the Council of Trent in 1546. The traditional teaching that all the books of the Latin Bible were to be regarded as canonical was reaffirmed, and the special place of the Vulgate translation was emphasized. The Council expressed doubts only about the books usually called 1 and 2 Esdras (see above), which it placed in an appendix following the New Testament. The First Vatican Council in 1870 reaffirmed the position set out at Trent.

Because of the special status allowed for the deuterocanonical books in the thirty-nine Articles of Religion, the translators of the King James Version translated these books, which therefore form a third section to this Bible, between Old and New Testaments, called "The Apocrypha." Consequently their influence on English literature has been greater than might be expected on the basis of official pronouncements about their status.

In the twentieth century nothing has changed regarding the status of the deuterocanonical books. Catholics still regard them as part of the Bible, on an equal footing with the universally accepted books. In the Orthodox churches there have been no debates about them like those at the Reformation in the West, so they remain firmly in place within that religious tradition. The Protestant churches have continued to reject them or to be ambivalent about them. Consequently it is possible to buy Bibles either with or without the Apocrypha. The NRSV is the first western Bible to include the books which are not recognized even in the Catholic church, but only by the Orthodox churches. In this it recognizes an important fact about this vexed issue, namely, whatever status the churches officially claim for the deuterocanonical books, they are certainly important, and deserve to be read and studied. In practice all students of the Bible, whether they are Jewish, Catholic, Protestant, Orthodox, or of no religion need to know about these books. Discussion of the status of the Apocrypha does not seem to be on the agenda in any of the churches; in practice old feuds about them have become rather less important in the modern period.

FORMATION OF THE NEW TESTAMENT

Compared with the Old Testament, the books of the New Testament were all written in a very short space of time—probably not much more than fifty or sixty years, from the 40s CE till the beginning of the second century. As we saw above, by the time there were manuscripts of the whole New Testament the books clearly fell into groups, and presumably this is how they were first collected. One obvious group is the collection of Paul's letters, sometimes called the *Pauline corpus*. Paul's letters were all written to a very specific situation, dealing with problems and difficulties that had arisen in this or that Christian community. But he himself probably expected his letters to be read outside the church to which they were originally written—though the only explicit statement of such an intention is found in Col 4.16 ("when this letter has been read among you, have it read also in the church of the Laodiceans; and see that you read also the letter from Laodicea"), in a letter regarded by many modern scholars as not genuinely Pauline. The custom seems to have grown up of passing Paul's letters around, and it was a short step from this to making a collection of them.

The Pauline corpus seems to go back to the second or third generation after Paul himself. In almost all manuscripts, the letters are arranged in order of length, within two categories. The first category consists of letters to churches: Romans, 1 and 2 Corinthians, Galatians, Ephesians, Philippians, Colossians, 1 and 2 Thessalonians (Ephesians is in fact slightly longer than Galatians, but this is always the order). The second category comprises letters to individuals: 1 and 2 Timothy, Titus, and Philemon. Some people have speculated that Philemon holds the clue to the collection. Perhaps Onesimus, the runaway slave who is the subject of this letter, became a leader in one of the churches founded by Paul, and decided to collect all his letters together. This theory might explain why a letter so completely personal is included in a collection intended for the Church at large. However, such speculation is really the stuff of a biblical novel rather than a matter of hard evidence! Whatever the cause, copies of Paul's letter collection were circulating by the beginning of the second century CE.

The collection of the Four Gospels seems to be equally old. It had a greater effect on the way the Gospels came to be understood than the collection of Paul's letters had on the individual letters. Each Gospel seems originally to be intended to tell the definitive version of the life, death, and resurrection of Jesus. Luke, in fact, tells us explicitly that he wanted to correct existing accounts and to tell the story in its true form (see Lk 1.1). If everything in any one of the Gospels is true exactly as stated, then none of the other Gospels can be completely true, for they present divergent accounts of the same events. But once it came to be accepted that there were four Gospels, all with equal authority, people inevitably had to read them as complementing and completing, rather than contradicting each other. This perspective was fully established by the late second century, when Irenaeus of Lyons (c. 130–c. 200 CE) defended the existence of four Gospels, rather than a single authoritative one, as a positive blessing to the Church. His argument was that four witnesses to such crucial events provided a guarantee greater than would be given by only one, and that the discrepancies do not affect the overall reliability of all four accounts.

Before Irenaeus there had been two attempts to establish just one version of the Gospel as definitive. Marcion (died 160 CE), a native of Asia Minor who taught for a time in Rome, believed that there was only one correct Gospel, the Gospel according to Luke. But he thought that even that Gospel had been contaminated by wrong teaching, so he "corrected" it, and combined it with a selection of Paul's letters to form a kind of rudimentary New Testament. Marcion's attachment to Luke resulted from the fact that it is the least "Jewish" of the Gospels, in the sense that it stresses more than the others the central importance of non-Jews in God's plan, and does not quote the Old Testament as much as does (for instance) Matthew. Even so, Marcion had to delete a number of passages to remove references to the Old Testament. He wanted to do this because he believed that the God of Jesus was quite distinct from the Jewish God, and that Christianity had no kind of connection or continuity with Judaism. For this the Church condemned him as a heretic, because Christians believed that the God revealed in Jesus was, on the contrary, the God who had been known to the Jews for so long through the pages of the Old Testament. But in condemning Marcion, the Church also ruled out the possibility of allowing anyone to claim that only one of the Gospels was a true record, and endorsed the four-Gospel canon.

The second attempt to produce a single Gospel account was made by Tatian (who wrote about 160 CE), who came from Assyria but also studied in Rome. He worked differently from Marcion. Instead of taking one Gospel and expurgating it, he accepted all four Gospels but made a "harmony" of them. He followed different Gospels for different incidents and sayings in Jesus' life, blending the four accounts together to make a single, consistent one. His work, the Diatessaron, became widely popular in the Church, especially in Syria and the East, and was still in use there instead of the four Gospels two or more centuries later. Indeed, it was translated into many languages, and was still used by some people in Western Europe in the Middle Ages. It represents in many ways a common sense reaction to the problem of four inconsistent Gospels. That the Church eventually rejected it shows that the prestige of the four-Gospel canon was high in most areas of Christendom from an early period.

We do not know when the "catholic" letters (James, 1 and 2 Peter, 1, 2, and 3 John, and Jude) were collected together, but we do know that they usually circulated with the Acts of the Apostles. It is almost as if these works together were felt to add up to a kind of apostolic equivalent of the Gospels: just as in the Gospels we learn of Jesus' actions and his teaching, so in this collection we learn of the deeds of the apostles (in Acts) and their teachings (in the letters). From early times, this section of the New Testament was used conspicuously less by Christian writers than the Gospels and Paul. Quotations from Acts are far less common than those from its "first volume," Luke, and the catholic letters are rarely mentioned. Nevertheless, there is no record of any opposition to these books. They were accepted by all as authoritative, even if they were not much used.

Finally, there are the book of Revelation and the Letter to the Hebrews. Revelation had a checkered history. When Christian writers such as Eusebius of Caesarea (c. 260– c. 340 CE), the first Church historian, discuss which books are part of the New Testament, they often express doubts about the status of Revelation. It seems to have been especially unpopular in the Eastern Mediterranean world, and to have been more widely accepted in the West. Revelation's acceptance there may be connected with its predictions of the end of the world in the context of fierce denunciations of the Roman empire. By the fourth century, however, Revelation was firmly ensconced in the canon, perhaps partly because, like the Fourth Gospel and the three Letters of John, it was assumed to have been written by the Apostle John.

As the case of Revelation demonstrates, authorship was often an important factor in deciding which books would be accepted into the canon. We see this also in the case of Hebrews. This letter (if it really is a letter) had the opposite fate from Revelation, since doubts about it tended to be expressed chiefly in the West—possibly because of its very harsh attitude to sins committed after baptism (10.26–31). But doubts about its authority may have been related to doubts about who wrote it. Many Christians assumed it was by Paul, even though it nowhere says so. (Paul's authorship is stated in the *title* in the King James Version, "The Epistle of Paul the Apostle to the Hebrews," but there is nothing about it in the *text* of the letter.) When they did, they tended also to think it must be a valid part of the New Testament, and to quote it more often than those who thought it was by someone else. The question of authorship also affects where it appears in the Pauline corpus. For people who thought Hebrews was written by Paul, it was natural to include it between Romans and 1 Corinthians, because it is next to Romans in length. Where it was not thought to be Pauline, it tended to appear where we now have it, after all the Pauline letters.

The formation of the New Testament differs from that of the Old in two particularly important ways. First, the Old Testament began life as a series of scrolls. Each major book had its own scroll, which had the effect of determining how long a book could be. Although the Pentateuch is a continuous whole, it was divided up into five separate scrolls. Similarly, the "Former Prophets" tell a continuous story from the exodus to the exile, but they are divided up—not always in the most natural places—to make a set of scrolls of roughly equal length. On the other hand, several short books might be grouped together on a single scroll. This is the case with the twelve minor prophets, which in Judaism in ancient times tended to be regarded as a single book—the "Book of the Twelve"—and not seen as having much individual character, because they all appeared on the same scroll. But the New Testament did not start as a set of scrolls. For some reason which no-one has yet discovered, Christian texts from the very beginnings were written in what are technically known as "codices" (singular: "codex"), which are what we call "books"—many pages sewn together with covers, and opening flat. In the ancient world codices were normally used only for informal purposes, as notebooks, and it was a startling innovation for Christians to write their most treasured possessions, the Gospels, in this form.

The use of a codex form had a major effect on the emergence of the New Testament. For one thing, a codex can hold considerably more than a scroll without becoming unwieldy, and so it was possible to have a codex of all four Gospels, of all the Pauline letters, and in due course of the whole New Testament. Secondly, books arranged in a codex come in a certain order. Mark follows Matthew in the straightforward sense that you finish reading Matthew, turn the page, and there is Mark. Scrolls can never be in an "order" in quite this sense, and Jewish discussions of the order of biblical books in ancient times were always rather more theoretical than Christian ones, because scrolls can be moved around relative to each other whereas the order of books in a codex, once they have been written out, is fixed. Christians soon began transferring their methods of writing their own books in codices on to the Old Testament too, so that the Greek Old Testament has a definite order in a stronger sense than the Hebrew Bible ever had—at least until the time when Jews, too, began to use the codex.

Secondly, and possibly linked with their use of the codex form, Christians seem to have had a rather different attitude to their own books, or at least to the Gospels, than they had towards the Old Testament Scriptures. Whereas the Old Testament was seen as a fixed and sacred text, the Gospels were often perceived more as rather informal records of the life and teaching of Jesus, on the basis of which early Christian preachers could to some extent improvise. Although there was enormous reverence for what Jesus had said and done, this referent was not necessarily seen as identical with exactly the words of this or that Gospel, but more as a matter of tradition passed on by word of mouth, which the Gospels were an aid to remembering and recalling. People knew that Jesus had spoken in Aramaic, and that the Gospels contained only translations of his words, not the very words themselves. This is probably one reason why four partly inconsistent Gospels were not seen as a problem. Nothing hung on the *precise* details of this or that incident or saying.

There is something of a paradox here. Only the Old Testament was "Scripture" for the very earliest Christians: their own books were still seen as something less formal than a "Bible." Yet on the other hand those books were their own special possession in a way that the Old Testament was not; and the traditions about Jesus that they knew, whether they were recorded in books or not, were of literally earth-shaking significance in their minds. So they saw the New Testament as less "scriptural" than the Old Testament, yet in many ways as more important. This is a vital point to grasp if we are to understand the significance of what would become the New Testament in the minds of early Christians. Sometimes people say that only the Old Testament was Holy Scripture for the first Christians, and that the New Testament only gradually came to be accepted as of equal status. This is true in one sense; but at another level it fails to take account of how committed Christians were to their not-yet-scriptural writings, which contained the record of something which they thought had changed the world.

Whereas with the Old Testament we cannot point to a definite date when the collection was complete (either for the Hebrew or the Greek version), with the New Testament it is possible to identify a series of official decisions about what was to count as "Scripture." The matter was discussed and ruled on at the council of Laodicea 363 CE, and soon after this we can point to a final moment of "canonization" in the writings of Athanasius, bishop of Alexandria (296–373). Every year before Easter Athanasius wrote to the churches under his care a so-called "Festal Letter." In 367 CE he chose to include an account of the books of the New Testament, and there for the first time we find exactly the list which is now accepted in all the churches. The arrangement is still the old one, with Acts at the head of the catholic letters rather than between the Gospels and Paul, but the specific books are precisely those that are now in our New Testament. In the western Church, councils at Hippo (393) and Carthage (397 and 419) confirmed Athanasius' list as definitive.

THE EXCLUSIVE CANON

There is one further element that needs to be present before we can speak strictly of the biblical canon as fixed and complete. This is that the books in the list are seen as *exclusive*, in the sense that these *and only these* books form the Bible. It is theoretically possible to have an official list of all the books that have *so far* been recognized as authoritative. Perhaps this is what Josephus, for example, is doing in the passage quoted above from *Against Apion*: listing the books that Jews do in fact recognize, and saying that they could only recognize others if they were equally ancient. But when Athanasius lays down the limits of the New Testament canon, he is saying these books are *for all time* the Bible that Christians must accept.

The idea that some books are to be excluded from the Bible is much older than the fourth century CE. As we saw, Jewish authorities had already decided that the Wisdom of Jesus ben Sirach (Ecclesiasticus) did not qualify for the status of Holy Scripture. Tertullian (c. 160–c. 225) tells us that the Church of his day had a list of books that Christians were not supposed to read, the remote ancestor of the Vatican's *Index of*

Prohibited Books, which persisted down into our own time. But it seems to have been in roughly the fourth century that Christians started to abandon a rough-and-ready system in which some books were definitely in and others definitely out, but in which there was a grey area of books whose status was rather unclear. Instead they tried to formulate a definitive and exclusive list of canonical works. The creation of such a list does not mean the works on it were of doubtful authority until then. The great majority of books in the New Testament, like the great majority in the Old, did not become "scriptural" because some authority decided they should be, but established themselves over time in people's minds. All that someone like Athanasius did was to endorse the books that everyone accepted already, and to give a ruling on a few doubtful cases. No-one created the biblical canon: it grew.

THE HEBREW SCRIPTURES COMMONLY
CALLED THE OLD TESTAMENT

New Revised
Standard Version

GENESIS

Introduction

Genesis is made up of two large sections. The first part (chs. 1–11) begins with stories of God's creation of the heavens and the earth and the first generations of human beings on the earth. Other ancient cultures in biblical times also had their own stories of the beginnings of the world, worldwide floods, and interaction between multiple gods and humans. Some parallels exist between these other ancient accounts and chs. 1–11. However, the biblical writers reshaped these ancient traditions in distinctive ways that were true to their Israelite understanding of the one God who created all things. The second part (chs. 12–50) involves stories about one particular family line whom God selected from among all the families of the earth. This family eventually became the people of Israel, whose story continues throughout the rest of the Old Testament. Israel's family line begins with Abraham and Sarah and their son Isaac (chs. 12–25). These family stories continue with tales about Isaac's son Jacob (chs. 25–36). Genesis concludes with stories about Jacob's children, especially Joseph and Judah (chs. 37–50).

In the first part of Genesis (chs. 1–11), God works with all humanity to restore the broken relationships caused by human rebellion and disobedience. God's repeated attempts to respond to these rebellions through punishment and continued blessing do not succeed in restoring harmony between God and humans. Thus, in the second part (chs. 12–50), God embarks upon a new strategy. God concentrates on working with and through one particular family, the ancestors of the people of Israel. This one family is chosen so that through them "all the families of the earth shall be blessed" (12.3). In this way, the two major parts of Genesis depend upon one another. Most scholars believe that the present form of the book of Genesis is the result of various stages of oral storytelling, writing, and editing over hundreds of years. Certain texts in Genesis may have arisen quite early in ancient Israel's history. Other texts may have been written much later. They have, however, been combined into an artful and extended story about the beginning of the world and Israel's earliest ancestors.

The date and setting for the final form of Genesis is probably the time when the people of Judah were in exile in Babylon (sixth century BCE) or when the Babylonian exiles returned home to Judah under the Persian empire (fifth century BCE). The time of exile and the return home forced Israel to think hard about its identity as a people and its mission as the people of God among the nations of the world. Remembering the Genesis stories about the beginnings of the world and Israel's earliest ancestors was a way to return to their roots and think about who they were as an exiled people who were returning home to Judah. They could identify with the Genesis ancestors of Israel , who were also a family on the move. Just as the family of Abraham and Sarah migrated back and forth from Mesopotamia to Canaan, so the exiles would migrate from Babylon back to Judah. The key promise in the midst of this wandering and yearning to return home was the promise God made to Jacob: "Know that I am with you and will keep you wherever you go, and will bring you back to this land" (28.15).

READING GUIDE

Chapters 1–11, which describe the beginnings of the world and the human race, contain elements that are clearly not part of our everyday experience. These include a talking serpent (3.1), individuals who live to be nearly a thousand years old (5.5), divine beings called "sons of God" who came down to earth (6.1–4), a worldwide flood (7.17–24), and all people of the world talking one language (11.1). The world of these stories may seem strange to us and very distant. Nevertheless, the narratives✶ seek to teach profound truths about the nature of reality, the meaning of life, and the purpose of human existence. Two major themes weave in and out among these initial stories of all humankind. The first theme is the emergence of broken relationships among humans, God, and nature. Examples include the human disobedience in the Garden of Eden (ch. 3), the flood story of Noah and the ark (chs. 6–9), and the building of the tower of Babel (ch. 11). The second theme is God's good creation and his continued blessing of humans and creation in spite of human disobedience.

A similar two-part theme also moves in and out of the family stories of Israel's ancestors in chs. 12–50. God makes a major promise of blessing, land, and many descendants to the family of Abraham and Sarah (12.1–3). One theme repeated throughout these stories is the regular endangerment and threat to God's promise coming true. Sarah is unable to have children (11.30). God tells Abraham to kill his only son (22.1–2). Jacob's life is threatened by his brother Esau (27.41). Joseph's own brothers threaten to kill him and then sell him into slavery in Egypt (37.17–28). The second major theme in these ancestor stories is God's continuing commitment to the promise he first made to Abraham and Sarah. The family line continues in spite of all the struggles and obstacles. This sustained blessing of God is marked most clearly throughout Genesis by the birth of children, the gift of prosperity, and the recurring family trees or genealogical lists that form the literary backbone of the narrative.

1–11	The creation of the world and the beginning of humankind
12–25	The family stories of Abraham and Sarah and their son Isaac
25–36	The family stories of Isaac's son, Jacob
37–50	The family stories of Jacob's sons, especially Joseph and Judah

1 In the beginning when God created[a] the heavens and the earth, 2the earth was a formless void and darkness covered the face of the deep, while a wind from God[b] swept over the face of the waters. 3Then God said, "Let there be light"; and there was light. 4And God saw that the light was good; and God separated the light from the darkness. 5God called the light Day, and the darkness he called Night. And there was evening and there was morning, the first day.

6 And God said, "Let there be a dome in the midst of the waters, and let it separate the waters from the waters." 7So God made the dome and separated the waters that were under the dome from the waters that were above the dome. And it was so. 8God called the dome Sky. And there was evening and there was morning, the second day.

9 And God said, "Let the waters under the sky be gathered together into one place, and let the dry land appear." And it was so. 10God called the dry land Earth, and the waters that were gathered together he called Seas. And God saw that it was good. 11Then God said, "Let the earth put forth vegetation: plants yielding seed, and fruit trees of every kind on earth that bear fruit with the seed in it." And it was so. 12The earth brought forth vegetation: plants yielding seed of every kind, and trees of every kind bearing fruit with the seed in it. And God saw that it was good. 13And there was evening and there was morning, the third day.

14 And God said, "Let there be lights in the dome of the sky to separate the day from

a Or when God began to create or In the beginning God created   b Or while the spirit of God or while a mighty wind

the night; and let them be for signs and for seasons and for days and years, [15]and let them be lights in the dome of the sky to give light upon the earth." And it was so. [16]God made the two great lights—the greater light to rule the day and the lesser light to rule the night—and the stars. [17]God set them in the dome of the sky to give light upon the earth, [18]to rule over the day and over the night, and to separate the light from the darkness. And God saw that it was good. [19]And there was evening and there was morning, the fourth day.

20 And God said, "Let the waters bring forth swarms of living creatures, and let birds fly above the earth across the dome of the sky." [21]So God created the great sea monsters and every living creature that moves, of every kind, with which the waters swarm, and every winged bird of every kind. And God saw that it was good. [22]God blessed them, saying, "Be fruitful and multiply and fill the waters in the seas, and let birds multiply on the earth." [23]And there was evening and there was morning, the fifth day.

24 And God said, "Let the earth bring forth living creatures of every kind: cattle and creeping things and wild animals of the earth of every kind." And it was so. [25]God made the wild animals of the earth of every kind, and the cattle of every kind, and everything that creeps upon the ground of every kind. And God saw that it was good.

1.1–2.3: The creation of the heavens and the earth. 1.2: *The face of the deep* and *the face of the waters* are descriptions of a watery and disordered chaos. God's creation involves separating, setting boundaries, and ordering this watery chaos in order to create a space for life to flourish. **3:** God creates by simply speaking a verbal command. **6:** God's creation of *a dome in the midst of the waters* assumes a flat earth and a clear dome that pushes back the lower waters and the blue upper waters to form the space for the sky. **11:** *Let the earth put forth vegetation:* Parts of creation are invited to join with God in the process of creating and ruling (1.17, 24, 28). **14:** The first three days of creation form three regions: Day 1—the region of light and darkness (1.3–5); Day 2—the region of the sky (1.6–8); and Day 3—the region of the earth with its vegetation (1.9–13). Beginning in v. 14, the

next three days of creation provide the inhabitants for each of these regions: Day 4—the sun, moon, and stars occupy the region of light and darkness (1.14–19); Day 5—the birds fill the sky and the fish fill the lower waters (1.20–23); and Day 6—the animals and humans occupy the earth. **21:** *So God created the great sea monsters:* In other ancient stories of creation, the sea monsters are portrayed as independent gods of evil and chaos. Here the sea monsters are made by God and subject to God's control (Ps 148.7).

---

26 Then God said, "Let us make humankind[a] in our image, according to our likeness; and let them have dominion over the fish of the sea, and over the birds of the air, and over the cattle, and over all the wild animals of the earth,[b] and over every creeping thing that creeps upon the earth."
27 So God created humankind[a] in his image,
    in the image of God he created them;[c]
    male and female he created them.
[28]God blessed them, and God said to them, "Be fruitful and multiply, and fill the earth and subdue it; and have dominion over the fish of the sea and over the birds of the air and over every living thing that moves upon the earth." [29]God said, "See, I have given you every plant yielding seed that is upon the face of all the earth, and every tree with seed in its fruit; you shall have them for food. [30]And to every beast of the earth, and to every bird of the air, and to everything that creeps on the earth, everything that has the breath of life, I have given every green plant for food." And it was so. [31]God saw everything that he had made, and indeed, it was very good. And there was evening and there was morning, the sixth day.

1.26–31. 26: The plural *us* and *our image* is probably a reference to an ancient motif* of an assembly of divine beings, here God and God's divine advisers (compare 1 Kings 22; Job 1). They resolve to create humankind in their *image* or *likeness.* The divine image characterizes the human vocation of *dominion* or caring for the fish, birds, and animals. Human dominion

a Heb *adam*   *b* Syr: Heb *and over all the earth*
c Heb *him*

Two Different Creation Stories

The Bible begins with two different versions of the story of the beginning of the world. The two versions arose at different periods in Israel's history. Most scholars would date the creation story in Gen 2.4–25 earlier than 1.1–2.3. The former was probably written during the time Israel had kings reigning in Jerusalem and before the exile to Babylon in 587 BCE. The usual scholarly designation for this earlier tradition, which extends intermittently throughout the Pentateuch* (Genesis—Deuteronomy), is the Yahwist or J tradition. Most scholars would date the later creation story in Gen 1.1–2.3 to a time after 587 BCE and the exile to Babylon. It may have been written even later, after the return to Judah in 539 BCE during the Persian period. Scholars call this later tradition the Priestly or P tradition. The Priestly tradition also extends into other parts of Genesis as well as the Pentateuch, especially the books of Leviticus and Numbers. There are a number of differences between the Priestly (P) creation story and the Yahwist's (J) creation story: the divine names (P—"God"; J—"LORD God"); the condition of the world before creation (P—watery chaos–1.2; J—dry desert–2.5–6); the sequence of creation (P—six days with both man and woman created at the same time; J—man created first, then animals, then woman); the manner of creation (P—the word of God–1.3, 6, 9; J—God "formed," "planted," "made"); the depiction of the deity (P—more majestic and transcendent; J—more intimate and hands-on); and the recurring literary structure and refrains in P versus the absence of such repetitions in J. Allowing two different versions of the creation story to stand side by side suggests that the ancient writers were not interested in defining precisely how the world began in a scientific sense. Rather, they were interested in exploring larger questions of meaning and purpose through multiple perspectives on the same event of creation.

or rule is to be similar to the way God rules over and cares for all creation. **27:** The human *image of God* includes both *male and female*. **31:** God's final evaluation that the creation *was very good* concludes a series of refrains throughout Gen 1 about the goodness of creation (1.4, 12, 18, 21).

2 Thus the heavens and the earth were finished, and all their multitude. ²And on the seventh day God finished the work that he had done, and he rested on the seventh day from all the work that he had done. ³So God blessed the seventh day and hallowed it, because on it God rested from all the work that he had done in creation.

2.1–3: God's resting *on the seventh day* of creation became an explanation for one of the Ten Commandments, that the seventh day of every week be set apart as a sabbath, a day of rest and no work (Ex 20.8–11).

The word "sabbath" comes from the Hebrew word "shabat" meaning "to rest."

4 These are the generations of the heavens and the earth when they were created.

In the day that the LORD God made the earth and the heavens, ⁵when no plant of the field was yet in the earth and no herb of the field had yet sprung up—for the LORD God had not caused it to rain upon the earth, and there was no one to till the ground; ⁶but a stream would rise from the earth, and water the whole face of the ground— ⁷then the LORD God formed man from the dust of the ground,ᵃ and breathed into his nostrils the breath of life; and the man became a living being. ⁸And the LORD God planted a gar-

a Or *formed a man* (Heb *adam*) *of dust from the ground* (Heb *adamah*) den in Eden, in the east; and there he put the man whom he had formed. 9Out of the ground the LORD God made to grow every tree that is pleasant to the sight and good for food, the tree of life also in the midst of the garden, and the tree of the knowledge of good and evil.

10 A river flows out of Eden to water the garden, and from there it divides and becomes four branches. 11The name of the first is Pishon; it is the one that flows around the whole land of Havilah, where there is gold; 12and the gold of that land is good; bdellium and onyx stone are there. 13The name of the second river is Gihon; it is the one that flows around the whole land of Cush. 14The name of the third river is Tigris, which flows east of Assyria. And the fourth river is the Euphrates.

2.4–14: A second creation story—the garden of Eden. 4: The opening formula, *These are the generations of* (sometime alternately translated as "these are the descendants of" or "this is the story of"), marks the beginning of new sections throughout Genesis (6.9; 10.1; 11.27; 25.19; 37.2). *In the day that the LORD God made the earth and the heavens:* a heading for this second and different creation story. The creation story in Gen 2 uses a different divine name, *LORD God*, instead of simply "God" in Gen 1. Genesis 2 begins not with chaotic waters of the deep as in 1.1–2 but with a dry desert. Like the watery deep, the dry wilderness is a biblical image of evil and chaos (Isa 21.1–3; 43.15–21). **7:** The Hebrew word for *man* ("adam") is closely related to the word for *ground* ("adamah"). This Hebrew wordplay underscores the close relationship of humans and the soil (3.19). *The LORD God formed man from the dust* like a potter forming clay. This earth creature becomes a living human only when the LORD God breathes into it *the breath of life.* **8:** The *garden of Eden* means literally "garden of delight." **9:** Two trees, *the tree of life* and *the tree of the knowledge of good and evil*, stand in the middle of the garden. They will become important later in the story (2.17; 3.1–7, 22–24). Eating from the tree of life would give immortality, and eating from the tree of knowledge would provide wisdom, moral discernment, and the experience of pleasure and pain. **10–14:** The image is that of a lush garden at the center of the known world from which four major rivers flow to water the earth. We know the location of only two

of the rivers, the *Tigris* and the *Euphrates*. They are in Mesopotamia. *Havilah* (v. 11) may be in Arabia, and *Cush* (v. 13) may be associated with Africa.

15 The LORD God took the man and put him in the garden of Eden to till it and keep it. 16And the LORD God commanded the man, "You may freely eat of every tree of the garden; 17but of the tree of the knowledge of good and evil you shall not eat, for in the day that you eat of it you shall die."

18 Then the LORD God said, "It is not good that the man should be alone; I will make him a helper as his partner." 19So out of the ground the LORD God formed every animal of the field and every bird of the air, and brought them to the man to see what he would call them; and whatever the man called every living creature, that was its name. 20The man gave names to all cattle, and to the birds of the air, and to every animal of the field; but for the man*a* there was not found a helper as his partner. 21So the LORD God caused a deep sleep to fall upon the man, and he slept; then he took one of his ribs and closed up its place with flesh. 22And the rib that the LORD God had taken from the man he made into a woman and brought her to the man. 23Then the man said,

"This at last is bone of my bones
    and flesh of my flesh;
  this one shall be called Woman,*b*
    for out of Man*c* this one was taken."

24Therefore a man leaves his father and his mother and clings to his wife, and they become one flesh. 25And the man and his wife were both naked, and were not ashamed.

2.15–25. 15: The garden of Eden is not a paradise of luxury but a place for human work. Humans will *till* the garden *and keep it.* **16–17:** The command not to eat from the tree of the knowledge of good and evil carries a grave consequence, which in Hebrew reads literally: "you shall *surely* die." **18:** The term *helper* does not imply an inferior assistant but a genuine partner who comes to the aid of another. God is often

a Or *for Adam*   *b* Heb *ishshah*   *c* Heb *ish*

called a "helper" for those in need (Ps 10.14; 54.4). **19–20:** God's first attempt to satisfy the human's loneliness (animals) fails. God invites the human to participate in shaping the character of the animals by giving them names. **21–22:** God tries a second strategy to satisfy the human's loneliness. God fashions a woman from the rib of the sleeping man. **23:** Unlike the animals, the woman instantly evokes a joyous response from the man. The man's brief poetic response plays on the Hebrew words "ish" (*Man*) and "ishshah" (*Woman*). **24:** *They become one flesh* suggests not only sexual union but also a unity through a common household and the raising of children.

3 Now the serpent was more crafty than any other wild animal that the LORD God had made. He said to the woman, "Did God say, 'You shall not eat from any tree in the garden'?" 2The woman said to the serpent, "We may eat of the fruit of the trees in the garden; 3but God said, 'You shall not eat of the fruit of the tree that is in the middle of the garden, nor shall you touch it, or you shall die.' " 4But the serpent said to the woman, "You will not die; 5for God knows that when you eat of it your eyes will be opened, and you will be like God,*a* knowing good and evil." 6So when the woman saw that the tree was good for food, and that it was a delight to the eyes, and that the tree was to be desired to make one wise, she took of its fruit and ate; and she also gave some to her husband, who was with her, and he ate. 7Then the eyes of both were opened, and they knew that they were naked; and they sewed fig leaves together and made loincloths for themselves.

8 They heard the sound of the LORD God walking in the garden at the time of the evening breeze, and the man and his wife hid themselves from the presence of the LORD God among the trees of the garden. 9But the LORD God called to the man, and said to him, "Where are you?" 10He said, "I heard the sound of you in the garden, and I was afraid, because I was naked; and I hid myself." 11He said, "Who told you that you were naked? Have you eaten from the tree of which I commanded you not to eat?" 12The man said, "The woman whom you gave to be with me, she gave me fruit from the tree, and

I ate." 13Then the LORD God said to the woman, "What is this that you have done?" The woman said, "The serpent tricked me, and I ate." 14The LORD God said to the serpent,

"Because you have done this,
    cursed are you among all animals
    and among all wild creatures;
upon your belly you shall go,
    and dust you shall eat
    all the days of your life.
15 I will put enmity between you and the
        woman,
    and between your offspring and hers;
    he will strike your head,
    and you will strike his heel."
16To the woman he said,
    "I will greatly increase your pangs in
        childbearing;
    in pain you shall bring forth children,
yet your desire shall be for your
        husband,
    and he shall rule over you."
17And to the man*b* he said,
    "Because you have listened to the voice
        of your wife,
    and have eaten of the tree
about which I commanded you,
    'You shall not eat of it,'
cursed is the ground because of you;
    in toil you shall eat of it all the days
        of your life;
18 thorns and thistles it shall bring forth
        for you;
    and you shall eat the plants of the
        field.
19 By the sweat of your face
    you shall eat bread
until you return to the ground,
    for out of it you were taken;
you are dust,
    and to dust you shall return."

20 The man named his wife Eve,*c* because she was the mother of all living. 21And the LORD God made garments of skins for the man*d* and for his wife, and clothed them.

22 Then the LORD God said, "See, the man has become like one of us, knowing

a Or *gods*   *b* Or *to Adam*   *c* In Heb *Eve* resembles the word for *living*   *d* Or *for Adam*

good and evil; and now, he might reach out his hand and take also from the tree of life, and eat, and live forever"— 23 therefore the LORD God sent him forth from the garden of Eden, to till the ground from which he was taken. 24 He drove out the man; and at the east of the garden of Eden he placed the cherubim, and a sword flaming and turning to guard the way to the tree of life.

3.1–24: A serpent's temptation and human disobedience. 1: The *serpent* is not an alien being but simply one of the garden's more intelligent and *crafty* animals *that the LORD God had made*. 3: The woman repeats the command given by God in 2.17 but then attaches her own additional prohibition, *nor shall you touch it*. Once she disobeys her own prohibition (touching the fruit), it will be easier to take the next step and disobey God's prohibition (eating the fruit). 4–6: The serpent assures the woman that *you will not die*. In an odd way, the serpent will be correct. God will not cause the humans to die "in the day that you eat of it." However, the humans will come to *know good and evil* by experiencing new intensities of pain as a consequence of their rebellion. The man's quick willingness to eat the forbidden fruit along with the woman suggests equal responsibility for the disobedient act. 7: The humans now know *that they were naked*. They experience shame and the pain of an intimate human bond that has been broken. The innocence, trust, and openness of their former relationship must now be hidden behind clothes made of *fig leaves*. The prickly fig leaves would make for uncomfortable clothing. 8: The portrait of *the LORD God walking in the garden* in the cool of the evening implies God's close relationship and involvement with the creation. God's closeness contrasts with the humans' sudden desire for distance as they *hid themselves from the presence of the LORD God*. 14–15: The serpent is directly cursed by God. The curse provides an ancient explanation for why the snake has no legs and why humans often have a negative reaction to snakes. 16–17: Neither the woman nor the man are directly cursed as was the serpent. But negative consequences flow from the disobedient act. For the woman, the pain of childbirth will increase, and the man *shall rule over you*. This inequality contrasts with God's original will for mutuality and interdependence between the man and woman in 2.18–22. 17–19: Like the woman and unlike the serpent, the man is not directly cursed. However, God declares, *cursed is the ground because*

of you. The man will struggle in hard *toil* and *sweat* to produce food from the ground. The earlier story of human creation in 2.7 had already recounted the man's origin from the dust of the ground. Now, for the first time, human death is explicitly mentioned: *to dust you shall return* (3.19). However, the original prohibition in 2.17 had decreed death on the very day that the forbidden fruit would be eaten. God does not enforce this death sentence immediately. God mercifully allows the humans to continue to live for some time and produce children for future generations. 21: God graciously replaces the prickly fig leaf clothing (2.7) with softer *garments of skins*. 22–24: God seals the entrance to the garden to make sure the humans do not *take also from the tree of life, and eat, and live forever*. The *cherubim*✷ are winged creatures who are half human and half beast. They guard holy areas. For example, cherubim guard the holiest sections of the Temple✷ in Jerusalem (1 Kings 8.6–7).

4 Now the man knew his wife Eve, and she conceived and bore Cain, saying, "I have produced*a* a man with the help of the LORD." 2 Next she bore his brother Abel. Now Abel was a keeper of sheep, and Cain a tiller of the ground. 3 In the course of time Cain brought to the LORD an offering of the fruit of the ground, 4 and Abel for his part brought of the firstlings of his flock, their fat portions. And the LORD had regard for Abel and his offering, 5 but for Cain and his offering he had no regard. So Cain was very angry, and his countenance fell. 6 The LORD said to Cain, "Why are you angry, and why has your countenance fallen? 7 If you do well, will you not be accepted? And if you do not do well, sin is lurking at the door; its desire is for you, but you must master it."

8 Cain said to his brother Abel, "Let us go out to the field."*b* And when they were in the field, Cain rose up against his brother Abel, and killed him. 9 Then the LORD said to Cain, "Where is your brother Abel?" He said, "I do not know; am I my brother's keeper?" 10 And the LORD said, "What have you done? Listen; your brother's blood is crying out to me from the ground! 11 And now you are cursed from the ground, which has

a The verb in Heb resembles the word for *Cain*
b Sam Gk Syr Compare Vg: MT lacks *Let us go out to the field*

opened its mouth to receive your brother's blood from your hand. 12When you till the ground, it will no longer yield to you its strength; you will be a fugitive and a wanderer on the earth." 13Cain said to the LORD, "My punishment is greater than I can bear! 14Today you have driven me away from the soil, and I shall be hidden from your face; I shall be a fugitive and a wanderer on the earth, and anyone who meets me may kill me." 15Then the LORD said to him, "Not so!*a* Whoever kills Cain will suffer a sevenfold vengeance." And the LORD put a mark on Cain, so that no one who came upon him would kill him. 16Then Cain went away from the presence of the LORD, and settled in the land of Nod,*b* east of Eden.

17 Cain knew his wife, and she conceived and bore Enoch; and he built a city, and named it Enoch after his son Enoch. 18To Enoch was born Irad; and Irad was the father of Mehujael, and Mehujael the father of Methushael, and Methushael the father of Lamech. 19Lamech took two wives; the name of the one was Adah, and the name of the other Zillah. 20Adah bore Jabal; he was the ancestor of those who live in tents and have livestock. 21His brother's name was Jubal; he was the ancestor of all those who play the lyre and pipe. 22Zillah bore Tubal-cain, who made all kinds of bronze and iron tools. The sister of Tubal-cain was Naamah.

23 Lamech said to his wives:

"Adah and Zillah, hear my voice;
    you wives of Lamech, listen to what I
        say:
    I have killed a man for wounding me,
        a young man for striking me.
24 If Cain is avenged sevenfold,
        truly Lamech seventy-sevenfold."

25 Adam knew his wife again, and she bore a son and named him Seth, for she said, "God has appointed*c* for me another child instead of Abel, because Cain killed him." 26To Seth also a son was born, and he named him Enosh. At that time people began to invoke the name of the LORD.

Eve (3.20). Now Eve in turn names a man, her son *Cain*. In a wordplay on the name *Cain* ("qayin"), the woman creates or "produces" ("qnh") *a man with the help of the LORD*. **4–5**: The text gives no reason why God accepts Abel's animal offering but rejects Cain's grain offering. God reserves the divine right to accept or be merciful to whomever he wills (Ex 33.19). **7**: If Cain acts properly in response to his brother's acceptance and his own rejection, then Cain himself will be accepted. But if Cain does not *do well, sin is lurking at the door* like an animal eager to consume his life. This is the first occurrence of the word *sin* in the Bible. **9**: Cain's cynical question, *Am I my brother's keeper?*, may imply that God should be the one responsible for "keeping" or "guarding" his brother (Ps 121.5; Isa 27.3). **10–11**: The blood of any human or animal is considered sacred because it is believed to contain the essence of life. Thus, any spilling of blood is a matter for God's attention (Deut 12.23–24; Lev 17.10–14). **14**: As a *fugitive and wanderer* in foreign lands, Cain will have no rights or protection. He will be vulnerable to blood revenge for the murder of his brother. 2 Sam 24.1–24 provides an example of such a case. **17–22**: Cain is a fugitive from the settled rural life of farming. His descendants become the founders of cities (v. 17), wandering shepherds (v. 20), developers of culture (v. 21), and makers of tools (v. 22). **23–24**: Lamech takes revenge into his own hands in an increasing spiral of violence. He kills someone in revenge for a simple injury against himself. Earlier, the LORD had tried to limit revenge and violence (4.15). **25–26**: Adam and Eve have a third son, Seth. The family line of Adam and Eve, through their son Seth, will be traced over ten generations in Gen 5.

5 This is the list of the descendants of Adam. When God created humankind,*d* he made them*e* in the likeness of God. 2Male and female he created them, and he blessed them and named them "Humankind"*d* when they were created.

3 When Adam had lived one hundred thirty years, he became the father of a son in his likeness, according to his image, and named him Seth. 4The days of Adam after he became the father of Seth were eight hundred years; and he had other sons and

4.1–26: Cain and Abel—the first murder. 1: *The man knew his wife* implies intimate knowledge, in this case sexual intercourse. The man had earlier named his wife

---

a Gk Syr Vg: Heb *Therefore*   *b* That is *Wandering*
c The verb in Heb resembles the word for *Seth*
d Heb *adam*   *e* Heb *him*

daughters. [5]Thus all the days that Adam lived were nine hundred thirty years; and he died.

6 When Seth had lived one hundred five years, he became the father of Enosh. [7]Seth lived after the birth of Enosh eight hundred seven years, and had other sons and daughters. [8]Thus all the days of Seth were nine hundred twelve years; and he died.

9 When Enosh had lived ninety years, he became the father of Kenan. [10]Enosh lived after the birth of Kenan eight hundred fifteen years, and had other sons and daughters. [11]Thus all the days of Enosh were nine hundred five years; and he died.

12 When Kenan had lived seventy years, he became the father of Mahalalel. [13]Kenan lived after the birth of Mahalalel eight hundred and forty years, and had other sons and daughters. [14]Thus all the days of Kenan were nine hundred and ten years; and he died.

15 When Mahalalel had lived sixty-five years, he became the father of Jared. [16]Mahalalel lived after the birth of Jared eight hundred thirty years, and had other sons and daughters. [17]Thus all the days of Mahalalel were eight hundred ninety-five years; and he died.

18 When Jared had lived one hundred sixty-two years he became the father of Enoch. [19]Jared lived after the birth of Enoch eight hundred years, and had other sons and daughters. [20]Thus all the days of Jared were nine hundred sixty-two years; and he died.

21 When Enoch had lived sixty-five years, he became the father of Methuselah. [22]Enoch walked with God after the birth of Methuselah three hundred years, and had other sons and daughters. [23]Thus all the days of Enoch were three hundred sixty-five years. [24]Enoch walked with God; then he was no more, because God took him.

25 When Methuselah had lived one hundred eighty-seven years, he became the father of Lamech. [26]Methuselah lived after the birth of Lamech seven hundred eighty-two years, and had other sons and daughters. [27]Thus all the days of Methuselah were nine hundred sixty-nine years; and he died.

28 When Lamech had lived one hundred eighty-two years, he became the father of a son; [29]he named him Noah, saying, "Out of the ground that the LORD has cursed this one shall bring us relief from our work and from the toil of our hands." [30]Lamech lived after the birth of Noah five hundred ninety-five years, and had other sons and daughters. [31]Thus all the days of Lamech were seven hundred seventy-seven years; and he died.

32 After Noah was five hundred years old, Noah became the father of Shem, Ham, and Japheth.

5.1–32: Ten generations from Adam and Eve to Noah. This list of ten generations links the story of Adam and Eve (Gen 2–4) with the next major character and story, Noah and the flood (Gen 6–9). Such genealogies, or family trees, occur at important transition points throughout Genesis (from Adam and Eve to Noah—5.1–32; from Noah's son Shem to Abraham—11.10–26; the descendants of Abraham's grandson Jacob—46.8–27). **3:** Adam has a son Seth who is *in his likeness, according to his image*. These same words are used for the first humans before the disobedient act in the garden of Eden (1.26–27; 5.1). The humans' sin did not erase God's image from them as it passes on to the next generation (9.6). **24:** *Because God took him* suggests that Enoch* did not die a normal death. An analogy may be the way in which the prophet* Elijah was taken up into heaven by God (2 Kings 2.11–12). Enoch comes to have a place of honor in later Jewish tradition as one who *walked with God.* **27:** Methuselah's age of 969 years makes him the oldest human being. **29:** *The ground that the LORD has cursed* refers to Adam's punishment in 3.17 and Cain's punishment in 4.11. The verb "to bring relief" (Hebrew "nhm") is seen as a wordplay on the name Noah (Hebrew "nh").

---

6 When people began to multiply on the face of the ground, and daughters were born to them, [2]the sons of God saw that they were fair; and they took wives for themselves of all that they chose. [3]Then the LORD said, "My spirit shall not abide[a] in mortals forever, for they are flesh; their days shall be one hundred twenty years." [4]The Nephilim were on the earth in those days—and also

a Meaning of Heb uncertain

afterward—when the sons of God went in to the daughters of humans, who bore children to them. These were the heroes that were of old, warriors of renown.

6.1–4: The origins of a legendary★ line of giant warriors. 1–2: This brief story portrays the breaking of the created boundary between heaven and earth. Divine beings called *the sons of God* cross the boundary and have sexual intercourse with human daughters. **3:** God decides to place tighter limits on the length of human life. Before this, individuals had lived for over 900 years (5.5, 8). In this next stage, humans will live no more than 120 years. Later biblical tradition will declare the typical limit of human life to be 70–80 years which is closer to our normal experience (Ps 90.10). The advancing power of death accompanies the appearance of human sin. **4:** *The Nephilim* were remembered as a superhuman race of legendary warriors born of mixed human and divine parents. Later in Israel's history, Israelite spies will report seeing the giant Nephilim warriors in the land of Canaan (Num 13.32–33).

STARTING OVER—NOAH AND THE FLOOD

6.5–8.22: Many scholars believe that two parallel versions of this flood story were woven together into the present combined single story. For example, two separate introductions to the flood story stand side by side (compare one version in 6.5–8, 7.1–5 with the second version in 6.9–22). Scholars have also noted some striking parallels and differences between the biblical flood story and ancient flood stories from Babylon and Mesopotamia.

5 The LORD saw that the wickedness of humankind was great in the earth, and that every inclination of the thoughts of their hearts was only evil continually. 6And the LORD was sorry that he had made humankind on the earth, and it grieved him to his heart. 7So the LORD said, "I will blot out from the earth the human beings I have created—people together with animals and creeping things and birds of the air, for I am sorry that I have made them." 8But Noah found favor in the sight of the LORD.

9 These are the descendants of Noah. Noah was a righteous man, blameless in his generation; Noah walked with God. 10And

Noah had three sons, Shem, Ham, and Japheth.

11 Now the earth was corrupt in God's sight, and the earth was filled with violence. 12And God saw that the earth was corrupt; for all flesh had corrupted its ways upon the earth. 13And God said to Noah, "I have determined to make an end of all flesh, for the earth is filled with violence because of them; now I am going to destroy them along with the earth. 14Make yourself an ark of cypress*a* wood; make rooms in the ark, and cover it inside and out with pitch. 15This is how you are to make it: the length of the ark three hundred cubits, its width fifty cubits, and its height thirty cubits. 16Make a roof*b* for the ark, and finish it to a cubit above; and put the door of the ark in its side; make it with lower, second, and third decks. 17For my part, I am going to bring a flood of waters on the earth, to destroy from under heaven all flesh in which is the breath of life; everything that is on the earth shall die. 18But I will establish my covenant with you; and you shall come into the ark, you, your sons, your wife, and your sons' wives with you. 19And of every living thing, of all flesh, you shall bring two of every kind into the ark, to keep them alive with you; they shall be male and female. 20Of the birds according to their kinds, and of the animals according to their kinds, of every creeping thing of the ground according to its kind, two of every kind shall come in to you, to keep them alive. 21Also take with you every kind of food that is eaten, and store it up; and it shall serve as food for you and for them." 22Noah did this; he did all that God commanded him.

6.5–22. 5: The human *heart* is the point where the intellect (knowing what is right or wrong) and the will (wanting to do right or wrong) come together. **9:** To be *righteous* means to be in a trusting and loyal relationship with God. To *walk with God* means to obey and follow God's will (Judg 2.22; 2 Kings 21.22). **14:** An *ark* is a "chest," "box," or "basket." The baby Moses floated in the Nile River in a "basket" (same Hebrew word as *ark*). Like Noah's ark, the basket was sealed with pitch, and it saved Moses from death (Ex

a Meaning of Heb uncertain   *b* Or *window*

Clean and Unclean Animals

The difference between *clean animals* (7.2) and *animals that are not clean* (7.8) involves a whole system of dividing animals and other parts of life into two categories: clean and unclean. Thus, any animals that have two or more characteristics that usually go together are considered clean. For example, animals that live in the sea typically have fins and scales. Therefore, all fish are clean since they have the fins and scales that sea creatures usually have. However, other sea creatures such as clams or oysters are unclean, because they live in the sea but they do not have fins or scales. They cross created boundaries or mix characteristics that do not normally belong together. See Lev 11.1–47 and Deut 14.3–21. This system of dividing between clean and unclean underlies the Jewish dietary laws of kosher* eating.

2.1–10). **15:** A *cubit* is the length of a forearm, about 20 inches long. Thus, the size of the ark or large boat is about 450 feet long, 75 feet wide, and 45 feet high. **18:** A *covenant** is a formal agreement or promise made between two parties. One or both of the covenant partners commit themselves to fulfill certain promises or obligations. Here God makes a covenant with Noah and his family. The content of the covenant will be spelled out more fully later (9.8–17). God makes several important covenants with his people throughout the Old Testament.

7 Then the LORD said to Noah, "Go into the ark, you and all your household, for I have seen that you alone are righteous before me in this generation. ²Take with you seven pairs of all clean animals, the male and its mate; and a pair of the animals that are not clean, the male and its mate; ³and seven pairs of the birds of the air also, male and female, to keep their kind alive on the face of all the earth. ⁴For in seven days I will send rain on the earth for forty days and forty nights; and every living thing that I have made I will blot out from the face of the ground." ⁵And Noah did all that the LORD had commanded him.

6 Noah was six hundred years old when the flood of waters came on the earth. ⁷And Noah with his sons and his wife and his sons' wives went into the ark to escape the waters of the flood. ⁸Of clean animals, and of animals that are not clean, and of birds, and of everything that creeps on the ground, ⁹two and two, male and female, went into the ark with Noah, as God had commanded Noah. ¹⁰And after seven days the waters of the flood came on the earth.

11 In the six hundredth year of Noah's life, in the second month, on the seventeenth day of the month, on that day all the fountains of the great deep burst forth, and the windows of the heavens were opened. ¹²The rain fell on the earth forty days and forty nights. ¹³On the very same day Noah with his sons, Shem and Ham and Japheth, and Noah's wife and the three wives of his sons entered the ark, ¹⁴they and every wild animal of every kind, and all domestic animals of every kind, and every creeping thing that creeps on the earth, and every bird of every kind—every bird, every winged creature. ¹⁵They went into the ark with Noah, two and two of all flesh in which there was the breath of life. ¹⁶And those that entered, male and female of all flesh, went in as God had commanded him; and the LORD shut him in.

17 The flood continued forty days on the earth; and the waters increased, and bore up the ark, and it rose high above the earth. ¹⁸The waters swelled and increased greatly on the earth; and the ark floated on the face of the waters. ¹⁹The waters swelled so mightily on the earth that all the high mountains under the whole heaven were covered; ²⁰the waters swelled above the mountains, covering them fifteen cubits deep. ²¹And all flesh died that moved on the earth, birds, domestic animals, wild animals, all swarm-

ing creatures that swarm on the earth, and all human beings; 22everything on dry land in whose nostrils was the breath of life died. 23He blotted out every living thing that was on the face of the ground, human beings and animals and creeping things and birds of the air; they were blotted out from the earth. Only Noah was left, and those that were with him in the ark. 24And the waters swelled on the earth for one hundred fifty days.

7.11–24. 11: In this version, the flood results from the upper and lower waters of chaos pouring back into the earth. In essence, God reverses the creation of Gen 1. *All the fountains of the great deep burst forth* from below the earth. Above the earth, God opens *the windows of the heavens* in the dome of the sky (1.6–8) and allows the watery chaos to pour onto the earth. 17–24: The gradual flooding and disappearance of the dry land and the death of humans, animals, creeping things, and birds returns the world to its pre-creation state, undoing what God did in Gen 1.9–27.

8 But God remembered Noah and all the wild animals and all the domestic animals that were with him in the ark. And God made a wind blow over the earth, and the waters subsided; 2the fountains of the deep and the windows of the heavens were closed, the rain from the heavens was restrained, 3and the waters gradually receded from the earth. At the end of one hundred fifty days the waters had abated; 4and in the seventh month, on the seventeenth day of the month, the ark came to rest on the mountains of Ararat. 5The waters continued to abate until the tenth month; in the tenth month, on the first day of the month, the tops of the mountains appeared.

6 At the end of forty days Noah opened the window of the ark that he had made 7and sent out the raven; and it went to and fro until the waters were dried up from the earth. 8Then he sent out the dove from him, to see if the waters had subsided from the face of the ground; 9but the dove found no place to set its foot, and it returned to him to the ark, for the waters were still on the face of the whole earth. So he put out his hand and took it and brought it into the ark with him. 10He waited another seven days,

and again he sent out the dove from the ark; 11and the dove came back to him in the evening, and there in its beak was a freshly plucked olive leaf; so Noah knew that the waters had subsided from the earth. 12Then he waited another seven days, and sent out the dove; and it did not return to him any more.

13 In the six hundred first year, in the first month, on the first day of the month, the waters were dried up from the earth; and Noah removed the covering of the ark, and looked, and saw that the face of the ground was drying. 14In the second month, on the twenty-seventh day of the month, the earth was dry. 15Then God said to Noah, 16"Go out of the ark, you and your wife, and your sons and your sons' wives with you. 17Bring out with you every living thing that is with you of all flesh—birds and animals and every creeping thing that creeps on the earth—so that they may abound on the earth, and be fruitful and multiply on the earth." 18So Noah went out with his sons and his wife and his sons' wives. 19And every animal, every creeping thing, and every bird, everything that moves on the earth, went out of the ark by families.

20 Then Noah built an altar to the LORD, and took of every clean animal and of every clean bird, and offered burnt offerings on the altar. 21And when the LORD smelled the pleasing odor, the LORD said in his heart, "I will never again curse the ground because of humankind, for the inclination of the human heart is evil from youth; nor will I ever again destroy every living creature as I have done. 22 As long as the earth endures,

seedtime and harvest, cold and heat,
summer and winter, day and night,
shall not cease."

8.1–22. 1: The great turning point in the story is the phrase, *God remembered Noah* and all the animals that were with him in the ark. God remembered the covenant* promises made to Noah in 6.18 and shifted from destruction to reconstruction. God's remembering previous covenant promises is often the signal of a major positive change in the fortunes of his people (Ex 2.24). God begins a whole new creation. He makes *a wind blow* over the watery chaos, just as God's wind

Two Biblical Versions of the Flood Story

Two different versions of the flood story have been woven together to form the present unified story in Gen 6–9. The two versions correspond to two originally separate traditions in ancient Israel, the earlier Yahwist (J) tradition and the later Priestly (P) tradition (see sidebar, "Two Different Creation Stories," p. 4). The existence of two originally separate versions is evident from a number of consistent variations, doublets, and other tensions in the story. These include the following:

- Focus only on human corruption and the destruction of only living things in 6.5–7 (J) versus a broader focus on the corruption of "all flesh" (both humans and animals) and the destruction of "the earth" in 6.11–13 (P)
- The reason God chose Noah is that he "found favor" in God's eyes in 6.8 (J) versus "Noah was a righteous man" in 6.9 (P)
- The portrayal of the flood as a simple rainstorm in 7.4 (J) versus the flood as the return to the watery chaos before creation in Gen 1.2 in 6.17 (P)
- The number of animals as seven pairs of all clean animals and one pair of unclean animals in 7.2 (J) versus one pair of all animals of every kind in 6.19 (P)
- The duration of the flood as 40 days and nights in 7.12, 17; 8.6 (J) versus 150 days with the water standing for over a year in 7.11, 24; 8.3b–5, 13a, 15 (P)
- The divine name of "the Lord" in J versus "God" in P

The two biblical versions of the flood story may be divided in the following way:

	Yahwist version (J)	Priestly version (P)
The condition of the world and God's decision	6.5–8	6.9–13
Instructions concerning the ark and the animals	7.1–5	6.14–22
Boarding the ark as the flood begins	7.7–8, 10, 12, 16b	7.6, 9, 11, 13–16a
The flood	7.17, 22–23	7.18–21, 24
The end of the flood	8.2b–3a, 6–12, 13b	8.1–2a, 3b–5, 13a, 14–19
God's promise	8.20–22	9.1–7
The covenant* of the rainbow		9.8–17
The sons of Noah	9.18–27	
The age of Noah and his death		9.28–29

over the deep had begun the first creation (1.2). **2–12:** The destroying flood of 7.11–24 is gradually reversed. *The mountains of Ararat* are located in a region in modern-day southeast Turkey and northwest Iran. The *raven* and the *dove* are sent out to test whether they find dry land. The dove is sent out three times. The first time the dove returns with nothing, then returns with an *olive leaf* or branch (v. 11), and finally does not return at all (v. 12). The dove with an olive branch has become a symbol of peace, hope, and new life. In the story, the dove with the olive branch is a sign of hope that the waters have partially receded below the level of olive trees. **17:** The phrase *be fruitful and multiply* calls to mind the same words used in the first creation story in 1.28. **20–22:** Noah's first building project after leaving the ark is an altar. Noah offers ritually clean animals (7.2–3) upon the altar as burnt offerings to give thanks to God. God smells *the pleasing odor* of the burnt offerings as the smoke rises to the heavens (Lev 1.9). God resolves never again to *curse the ground* as he had done before (3.17; 4.11) and never again to *destroy every living creature* (v. 21). The flood is not successful in changing the basic problem: *the inclination of the human heart is evil from youth* (v. 21). From here on, God will have to live with that fact and work within its reality. In the meantime, God promises not to disrupt the basic created order of the seasons and the agricultural rhythms of life (v. 22).

9 God blessed Noah and his sons, and said to them, "Be fruitful and multiply, and fill the earth. ²The fear and dread of you shall rest on every animal of the earth, and on every bird of the air, on everything that creeps on the ground, and on all the fish of the sea; into your hand they are delivered. ³Every moving thing that lives shall be food for you; and just as I gave you the green plants, I give you everything. ⁴Only, you shall not eat flesh with its life, that is, its blood. ⁵For your own lifeblood I will surely require a reckoning: from every animal I will require it and from human beings, each one for the blood of another, I will require a reckoning for human life.

6 Whoever sheds the blood of a human,
  by a human shall that person's blood
    be shed;
  for in his own image
    God made humankind.

⁷And you, be fruitful and multiply, abound on the earth and multiply in it."

8 Then God said to Noah and to his sons with him, ⁹"As for me, I am establishing my covenant with you and your descendants after you, ¹⁰and with every living creature that is with you, the birds, the domestic animals, and every animal of the earth with you, as many as came out of the ark.ᵃ ¹¹I establish my covenant with you, that never again shall all flesh be cut off by the waters of a flood, and never again shall there be a flood to de-

stroy the earth." ¹²God said, "This is the sign of the covenant that I make between me and you and every living creature that is with you, for all future generations: ¹³I have set my bow in the clouds, and it shall be a sign of the covenant between me and the earth. ¹⁴When I bring clouds over the earth and the bow is seen in the clouds, ¹⁵I will remember my covenant that is between me and you and every living creature of all flesh; and the waters shall never again become a flood to destroy all flesh. ¹⁶When the bow is in the clouds, I will see it and remember the everlasting covenant between God and every living creature of all flesh that is on the earth." ¹⁷God said to Noah, "This is the sign of the covenant that I have established between me and all flesh that is on the earth."

18 The sons of Noah who went out of the ark were Shem, Ham, and Japheth. Ham was the father of Canaan. ¹⁹These three were the sons of Noah; and from these the whole earth was peopled.

20 Noah, a man of the soil, was the first to plant a vineyard. ²¹He drank some of the wine and became drunk, and he lay uncovered in his tent. ²²And Ham, the father of Canaan, saw the nakedness of his father, and told his two brothers outside. ²³Then Shem and Japheth took a garment, laid it on both their shoulders, and walked backward and covered the nakedness of their father; their faces were turned away, and they did not see their father's nakedness. ²⁴When Noah awoke from his wine and knew what his youngest son had done to him, ²⁵he said,
  "Cursed be Canaan;
    lowest of slaves shall he be to his
      brothers."
²⁶He also said,
  "Blessed by the LORD my God be Shem;
    and let Canaan be his slave.
27 May God make space forᵇ Japheth,
    and let him live in the tents of Shem;
    and let Canaan be his slave."

28 After the flood Noah lived three hundred fifty years. ²⁹All the days of Noah were nine hundred fifty years; and he died.

a Gk: Heb adds *every animal of the earth*   *b* Heb *yapht*, a play on *Japheth*

9.1–29: God's covenant* with creation and Noah's curse of Canaan. 3–4: God expands the original vegetarian diet for humans (1.29) to include the meat of animals, which *shall be food for you*. However, the blood of any animal is to be drained from it before its flesh is eaten (Deut 12.23–25). The blood represents life, and returning it to the ground acknowledges that life belongs to God. **5–6:** Every killing of a human being is a serious threat to the social and moral order of society since it crosses the created boundary between life and death. In addition, God requires *a reckoning* or severe consequence (a life for a life) because humans are created in God's *own image* (1.26–27). God requires a reckoning even from an animal that kills a human (v. 5; Ex 21.28–32). **8–17:** God establishes a covenant relationship with Noah and with all living creatures. God promises never again *shall there be a flood to destroy the earth* (v. 11). This promise fills out the contents of the earlier covenant mentioned in 6.18. The *sign of the covenant* is the rainbow in the sky. The bow will be a sign to jog the divine memory so that God will *remember the everlasting covenant between God and every living creature* (v. 16). In the ancient world, the rainbow was associated with the bow used by God to shoot arrows of lightning (Ps 7.12–13). To hang up the bow in the sky symbolized peace. Worldwide destruction would no longer be a strategy used by God. **18–19:** The three sons of Noah become the ancestors of all living human beings because all other humans had died in the flood (7.21–23). **20:** Noah becomes the world's first winemaker. The intoxicating effect of wine fulfills the words Noah's father spoke at his birth concerning Noah's role in producing something that would bring relief from work (5.29). **21–23:** Noah overindulges in the intoxicating fruits of his own labors and lies *uncovered in his tent*. Noah's son Ham, the father of Canaan, sees *the nakedness of his father*. This may suggest some form of incest or other improper sexual activity (Lev 18.6–8, 24–30). **24–27:** Although Ham is the one who acted improperly, it is Ham's son Canaan who is cursed to be a slave and Shem who is blessed. As the following genealogy, or family tree, in Gen 10 shows, these sons of Noah represent geographical nations and peoples in the known world of the ancient Near East. Ham represents the Hamitic peoples associated with Egypt and areas under Egyptian control, including at some time the land of Canaan. Shem represents the Semitic people, which will eventually include Israel and other related nations. Japheth included a number of groups from Asia Minor. The cursing of Canaan and the blessing of Shem provide a backdrop and justification for the eventual conquest of the Canaanites and the settlement of the Israelites into the land of Canaan in the book of Joshua.

~~~~~~~~~~~~~~~~~~~~

10 These are the descendants of Noah's sons, Shem, Ham, and Japheth; children were born to them after the flood.

2 The descendants of Japheth: Gomer, Magog, Madai, Javan, Tubal, Meshech, and Tiras. ³The descendants of Gomer: Ashkenaz, Riphath, and Togarmah. ⁴The descendants of Javan: Elishah, Tarshish, Kittim, and Rodanim.ᵃ ⁵From these the coastland peoples spread. These are the descendants of Japhethᵇ in their lands, with their own language, by their families, in their nations.

6 The descendants of Ham: Cush, Egypt, Put, and Canaan. ⁷The descendants of Cush: Seba, Havilah, Sabtah, Raamah, and Sabteca. The descendants of Raamah: Sheba and Dedan. ⁸Cush became the father of Nimrod; he was the first on earth to become a mighty warrior. ⁹He was a mighty hunter before the LORD; therefore it is said, "Like Nimrod a mighty hunter before the LORD." ¹⁰The beginning of his kingdom was Babel, Erech, and Accad, all of them in the land of Shinar. ¹¹From that land he went into Assyria, and built Nineveh, Rehoboth-ir, Calah, and ¹²Resen between Nineveh and Calah; that is the great city. ¹³Egypt became the father of Ludim, Anamim, Lehabim, Naphtuhim, ¹⁴Pathrusim, Casluhim, and Caphtorim, from which the Philistines come.ᶜ

15 Canaan became the father of Sidon his firstborn, and Heth, ¹⁶and the Jebusites, the Amorites, the Girgashites, ¹⁷the Hivites, the Arkites, the Sinites, ¹⁸the Arvadites, the Zemarites, and the Hamathites. Afterward the families of the Canaanites spread abroad. ¹⁹And the territory of the Canaanites extended from Sidon, in the direction of

a Heb Mss Sam Gk See 1 Chr 1.7: MT *Dodanim*
b Compare verses 20, 31. Heb lacks *These are the descendants of Japheth*   c Cn: Heb *Casluhim, from which the Philistines come, and Caphtorim*

The Gilgamesh Epic

Other cultures in the ancient Near East had their own versions of a story about a worldwide flood. A Mesopotamian version, the story of Atrahasis, tells of a flood, a boat sealed with bitumen (pitch or tar), and other details that parallel the Genesis story. The Babylonian version involves a scene from the "Epic of Gilgamesh"* and dates roughly to 3000 BCE. A comparison of the biblical flood story and its Babylonian counterpart displays a number of striking parallels. The hero's name in the Babylonian flood story is Utnapishtim. The god Ea tells Utnapishtim in a dream to build an ark or large boat shaped as an exact cube. Ea warns him that other gods are planning to send a flood to destroy the earth. Utnapishtim builds the wooden ark and seals it with pitch. He loads the ark with his family, possessions, animals, and skilled workers. A fierce storm blows in, and even the gods cower in terror before the storm. The rain covers the whole earth by the seventh day. The ark eventually comes to rest on a mountain. After six days, Utnapishtim sends out a dove and then later a swallow. Both birds return because they cannot find a resting place. Then he sends out a raven which does not return, indicating that the waters have receded and dry land has appeared.

Utnapishtim then leaves the ark and offers up a burnt animal sacrifice to delight the gods. The gods "smelled the sweet odor" and "hovered like flies" over the sacrifice. They are apparently hungry because no sacrifices have been offered to them during the flood. The gods vow that there will never be a flood like this again. The gods take Utnapishtim away from his human and earthly existence to live in the heavens as an immortal divine being.

Gerar, as far as Gaza, and in the direction of Sodom, Gomorrah, Admah, and Zeboiim, as far as Lasha. 20These are the descendants of Ham, by their families, their languages, their lands, and their nations.

21 To Shem also, the father of all the children of Eber, the elder brother of Japheth, children were born. 22The descendants of Shem: Elam, Asshur, Arpachshad, Lud, and Aram. 23The descendants of Aram: Uz, Hul, Gether, and Mash. 24Arpachshad became the father of Shelah; and Shelah became the father of Eber. 25To Eber were born two sons: the name of the one was Peleg,ᵃ for in his days the earth was divided, and his brother's name was Joktan. 26Joktan became the father of Almodad, Sheleph, Hazarmaveth, Jerah, 27Hadoram, Uzal, Diklah, 28Obal, Abimael, Sheba, 29Ophir, Havilah, and Jobab; all these were the descendants of Joktan. 30The territory in which they lived extended from Mesha in the direction of Sephar, the hill country of the east. 31These are the descendants of Shem, by their families, their languages, their lands, and their nations.

32 These are the families of Noah's sons, according to their genealogies, in their nations; and from these the nations spread abroad on the earth after the flood.

10.1–32: A list of nations descended from Noah's three sons. This genealogy* traces the family line of all the known peoples of the earth back to the three sons of Noah: Japheth, Ham, and Shem. Each of the peoples or groups listed have their own *families, their languages, their lands, and their nations:* This refrain is repeated three times (10.5, 20, 31). **2–5:** *The descendants of Japheth* include peoples to the north and west of Canaan in Greece and Asia Minor and the *coastland peoples* of the Mediterranean Sea such as the Philistines. **6–20:** *The descendants of Ham* represent the nations under Egypt's influence at the time in Africa and Mesopotamia, including the land in and

a That is *Division*

around Canaan itself (vv. 15–20). The list of nations contains an old legend* about a great warrior named Nimrod. Nimrod conquered *the land of Shinar* or Babylon (see *Babel* in v. 10) and the land of Assyria with its *great city* of *Nineveh* (vv. 11–12; see Mic 5.5–6). The story of the tower of Babel will be set in the land of Shinar (11.2). **21–31:** *Shem* is the ancestor of the Semitic peoples who lived in and around Assyria and the Arabian Peninsula. Shem is *the father of all the children of Eber* (v. 21). *Eber* may be related to the word "Hebrew," which describes a number of wandering peoples on the margins of society. One of these groups formed the core of the Hebrew or Israelite people (14.13; Ex 9.13).

human pride and presumption. **2:** *The land of Shinar* is Babylon (10.10). **4:** *A tower with its top in the heavens* probably alludes to a very high pyramid-like structure called a ziggurat. The tall structure functioned as a temple in which to worship the gods in ancient Babylon. In the story, however, the humans' root desire is not to worship the gods but to *make a name* for themselves. **7:** God says, *Let us go down.* He is speaking to a divine council of advisers as in 1.26. **9:** The name *Babel* in the language of Babylon means "Gate of God," which would be appropriate for a temple. However, the Hebrew storyteller links the name instead with the Hebrew word "balal" ("to confuse").

11 Now the whole earth had one language and the same words. 2And as they migrated from the east,*a* they came upon a plain in the land of Shinar and settled there. 3And they said to one another, "Come, let us make bricks, and burn them thoroughly." And they had brick for stone, and bitumen for mortar. 4Then they said, "Come, let us build ourselves a city, and a tower with its top in the heavens, and let us make a name for ourselves; otherwise we shall be scattered abroad upon the face of the whole earth." 5The LORD came down to see the city and the tower, which mortals had built. 6And the LORD said, "Look, they are one people, and they have all one language; and this is only the beginning of what they will do; nothing that they propose to do will now be impossible for them. 7Come, let us go down, and confuse their language there, so that they will not understand one another's speech." 8So the LORD scattered them abroad from there over the face of all the earth, and they left off building the city. 9Therefore it was called Babel, because there the LORD confused*b* the language of all the earth; and from there the LORD scattered them abroad over the face of all the earth.

10 These are the descendants of Shem. When Shem was one hundred years old, he became the father of Arpachshad two years after the flood; 11and Shem lived after the birth of Arpachshad five hundred years, and had other sons and daughters.

12 When Arpachshad had lived thirty-five years, he became the father of Shelah; 13and Arpachshad lived after the birth of Shelah four hundred three years, and had other sons and daughters.

14 When Shelah had lived thirty years, he became the father of Eber; 15and Shelah lived after the birth of Eber four hundred three years, and had other sons and daughters.

16 When Eber had lived thirty-four years, he became the father of Peleg; 17and Eber lived after the birth of Peleg four hundred thirty years, and had other sons and daughters.

18 When Peleg had lived thirty years, he became the father of Reu; 19and Peleg lived after the birth of Reu two hundred nine years, and had other sons and daughters.

20 When Reu had lived thirty-two years, he became the father of Serug; 21and Reu lived after the birth of Serug two hundred seven years, and had other sons and daughters.

22 When Serug had lived thirty years, he became the father of Nahor; 23and Serug lived after the birth of Nahor two hundred years, and had other sons and daughters.

11.1–9: The tower of Babel and the confusion of human language. This story of the tower of Babel explains the geographical scattering of humans and the division of human speech into many different languages (Gen 10). Like that of the garden of Eden, the story continues the theme of God's limits on excessive

a Or *migrated eastward*　　*b* Heb *balal,* meaning *to confuse*

24 When Nahor had lived twenty-nine years, he became the father of Terah; 25 and Nahor lived after the birth of Terah one hundred nineteen years, and had other sons and daughters.

26 When Terah had lived seventy years, he became the father of Abram, Nahor, and Haran.

27 Now these are the descendants of Terah. Terah was the father of Abram, Nahor, and Haran; and Haran was the father of Lot. 28 Haran died before his father Terah in the land of his birth, in Ur of the Chaldeans. 29 Abram and Nahor took wives; the name of Abram's wife was Sarai, and the name of Nahor's wife was Milcah. She was the daughter of Haran the father of Milcah and Iscah. 30 Now Sarai was barren; she had no child.

31 Terah took his son Abram and his grandson Lot son of Haran, and his daughter-in-law Sarai, his son Abram's wife, and they went out together from Ur of the Chaldeans to go into the land of Canaan; but when they came to Haran, they settled there. 32 The days of Terah were two hundred five years; and Terah died in Haran.

11.10–32: The family line from Shem to Abraham. The genealogy in Gen 10, before the tower of Babel story, had named all the siblings of a given generation. These siblings had represented the spread of God's blessing over all peoples of the earth. A major transition occurs with the genealogy in Gen 11. The family line of promises becomes more narrowly focused on one person in each generation. The family line begins with Noah's son Shem (v. 10) and extends for ten generations until we come to Abram (later called Abraham; 17.5) and Sarai (later called Sarah; 17.15). This genealogy builds the literary bridge from stories about all humanity in Gen 1–11 to the more narrowly focused stories on the one family of Abraham and Sarah, the ancestors of Israel, in Gen 12–50. **28:** The memory of this family includes the tragedy of a son *(Haran)* who died at a young age, while his father was still living. The theme of a son's premature death will continue to haunt this family line. The young sons of Abraham (22.2), Isaac (27.41), and Jacob (37.29–36) will all be endangered or presumed to be dead. **30:** Abram's wife, Sarai, *was barren* and unable to have children. This condition will become a major obstacle and cause for suspense when God promises Abram and Sarai that

they will have many descendants and become a great nation (12.2; 17.16). The theme of the barren mother unable to have children will also be repeated in succeeding generations with Rebekah (25.21) and Rachel (29.31). **31:** *Haran,* a city in northern Mesopotamia, is the place where Abraham grew up. Abraham will later see to it that his son Isaac obtains a wife from his hometown of Haran, also known as the city of Nahor (24.10). Abraham's grandson, Jacob, will likewise return to Haran to work for his uncle Laban and marry Laban's two daughters (29.4).

12 Now the LORD said to Abram, "Go from your country and your kindred and your father's house to the land that I will show you. 2 I will make of you a great nation, and I will bless you, and make your name great, so that you will be a blessing. 3 I will bless those who bless you, and the one who curses you I will curse; and in you all the families of the earth shall be blessed."[a]

4 So Abram went, as the LORD had told him; and Lot went with him. Abram was seventy-five years old when he departed from Haran. 5 Abram took his wife Sarai and his brother's son Lot, and all the possessions that they had gathered, and the persons whom they had acquired in Haran; and they set forth to go to the land of Canaan. When they had come to the land of Canaan, 6 Abram passed through the land to the place at Shechem, to the oak[b] of Moreh. At that time the Canaanites were in the land. 7 Then the LORD appeared to Abram, and said, "To your offspring[c] I will give this land." So he built there an altar to the LORD, who had appeared to him. 8 From there he moved on to the hill country on the east of Bethel, and pitched his tent, with Bethel on the west and Ai on the east; and there he built an altar to the LORD and invoked the name of the LORD. 9 And Abram journeyed on by stages toward the Negeb.

12.1–9: God calls Abram and promises great blessing. 1–3: This first promise to Abram of *land*, many descendants in the form of *a great nation*, and bless-

---

a Or *by you all the families of the earth shall bless themselves*   b Or *terebinth*   c Heb *seed*

ings that will extend to *all the families of the earth* is a foundation for all of God's future promises to Israel. The promise of land and descendants will run like a thread throughout Genesis (13.15–17; 15.5–7, 18–21; 17.1–8; 22.15–18; 26.2–4; 28.1–4, 13–15) and beyond (Ex 6.4, 8; Deut 34.4). God promises Abram to *make your name great* as one who will be a blessing to other nations (v. 2). This element stands in contrast to the tower builders of Babel, who sought to make a name for themselves by their own selfish efforts (11.4). **4:** Abram immediately obeys God's command to leave his homeland and go to a place where he will receive great blessing. Later God will call Abraham a second time to go and sacrifice his son and apparently give up his blessing (22.1–3).

〰〰〰〰〰〰〰

10 Now there was a famine in the land. So Abram went down to Egypt to reside there as an alien, for the famine was severe in the land. ¹¹When he was about to enter Egypt, he said to his wife Sarai, "I know well that you are a woman beautiful in appearance; ¹²and when the Egyptians see you, they will say, 'This is his wife'; then they will kill me, but they will let you live. ¹³Say you are my sister, so that it may go well with me because of you, and that my life may be spared on your account." ¹⁴When Abram entered Egypt the Egyptians saw that the woman was very beautiful. ¹⁵When the officials of Pharaoh saw her, they praised her to Pharaoh. And the woman was taken into Pharaoh's house. ¹⁶And for her sake he dealt well with Abram; and he had sheep, oxen, male donkeys, male and female slaves, female donkeys, and camels.

17 But the LORD afflicted Pharaoh and his house with great plagues because of Sarai, Abram's wife. ¹⁸So Pharaoh called Abram, and said, "What is this you have done to me? Why did you not tell me that she was your wife? ¹⁹Why did you say, 'She is my sister,' so that I took her for my wife? Now then, here is your wife, take her, and be gone." ²⁰And Pharaoh gave his men orders concerning him; and they set him on the way, with his wife and all that he had.

12.10–20: Abram pretends Sarai is his sister and not his wife. 10: *A famine in the land* of Canaan forces Abram and Sarai to travel to Egypt. The same situation

will occur later with Abraham's descendants when Jacob's sons come to Egypt looking for food (41.53–42.3). *An alien* is a traveler who lives for a time in a foreign land. Such a person has no rights as a citizen and thus is vulnerable to abuse. **11–16:** Sarai is so *beautiful in appearance* that Abram is convinced that the Egyptians will take Sarai and kill Abram if they find out they are husband and wife. Therefore, Abram instructs Sarai to lie and say that she is Abram's sister. Abram endangers Sarai's life in order to save his own. **17–20:** The LORD afflicts the Egyptian Pharaoh with plagues to force him to let go of Sarai. During the Israelite exodus out of Egypt, the LORD will again send plagues on Egypt and Pharaoh, which will cause him to set free the Israelite slaves (Ex 11.1). This wife-sister story will reappear with Abraham and Sarah in 20.1–17 and with Isaac and Rebekah in 26.6–11.

〰〰〰〰〰〰〰

13 So Abram went up from Egypt, he and his wife, and all that he had, and Lot with him, into the Negeb.

2 Now Abram was very rich in livestock, in silver, and in gold. ³He journeyed on by stages from the Negeb as far as Bethel, to the place where his tent had been at the beginning, between Bethel and Ai, ⁴to the place where he had made an altar at the first; and there Abram called on the name of the LORD. ⁵Now Lot, who went with Abram, also had flocks and herds and tents, ⁶so that the land could not support both of them living together; for their possessions were so great that they could not live together, ⁷and there was strife between the herders of Abram's livestock and the herders of Lot's livestock. At that time the Canaanites and the Perizzites lived in the land.

8 Then Abram said to Lot, "Let there be no strife between you and me, and between your herders and my herders; for we are kindred. ⁹Is not the whole land before you? Separate yourself from me. If you take the left hand, then I will go to the right; or if you take the right hand, then I will go to the left." ¹⁰Lot looked about him, and saw that the plain of the Jordan was well watered everywhere like the garden of the LORD, like the land of Egypt, in the direction of Zoar; this was before the LORD had destroyed Sodom and Gomorrah. ¹¹So Lot chose for himself all the plain of the Jordan, and Lot journeyed

eastward; thus they separated from each other. 12Abram settled in the land of Canaan, while Lot settled among the cities of the Plain and moved his tent as far as Sodom. 13Now the people of Sodom were wicked, great sinners against the LORD.

14 The LORD said to Abram, after Lot had separated from him, "Raise your eyes now, and look from the place where you are, northward and southward and eastward and westward; 15for all the land that you see I will give to you and to your offspring[a] forever. 16I will make your offspring like the dust of the earth; so that if one can count the dust of the earth, your offspring also can be counted. 17Rise up, walk through the length and the breadth of the land, for I will give it to you." 18So Abram moved his

tent, and came and settled by the oaks[b] of Mamre, which are at Hebron; and there he built an altar to the LORD.

_____

13.1–18: Abram and his nephew Lot separate into different territories. 3: After the famine is over, Abram and Sarai return to Canaan *where his tent had been at the beginning* (12.8). **8–9:** As the elder uncle, Abram could have chosen whatever land he wished. Instead, Abram graciously allows his young nephew Lot to select land first. **10:** The green and lush *plain of the Jordan* looked *like the garden of the LORD*, an allusion to the garden of Eden in Gen 2. *Like the land of Egypt* points forward to Israel's experience in Egypt where the Nile River provides fertile crops. But the lush

a Heb *seed*   b Or *terebinths*

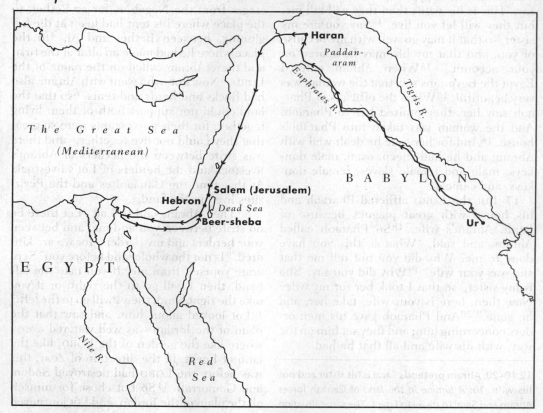

Map The journeys of Abram and Sarai

appearance of the area is deceptive: The people of the area are *wicked, great sinners* (v. 13). Genesis 19 will tell the story of the destruction of *Sodom and Gomorrah*. This destruction will dramatically change the lush land into a dry desert (19.24–25). **11:** Lot will become the ancestor of two nations that will border Canaan or Israel on its eastern boundary, Moab and Ammon (19.30–38). **14–18:** The first promise to Abram had not specified the exact land God would give him (12.2). But now God invites Abram to lay claim to a specific piece of real estate by making a full survey of it. God also reaffirms that Abram will have descendants as numerous as *the dust of the earth* (v. 16). God's promises of land and children become more visible and real to Abram.

14 In the days of King Amraphel of Shinar, King Arioch of Ellasar, King Chedorlaomer of Elam, and King Tidal of Goiim, 2these kings made war with King Bera of Sodom, King Birsha of Gomorrah, King Shinab of Admah, King Shemeber of Zeboiim, and the king of Bela (that is, Zoar). 3All these joined forces in the Valley of Siddim (that is, the Dead Sea).*a* 4Twelve years they had served Chedorlaomer, but in the thirteenth year they rebelled. 5In the fourteenth year Chedorlaomer and the kings who were with him came and subdued the Rephaim in Ashteroth-karnaim, the Zuzim in Ham, the Emim in Shaveh-kiriathaim, 6and the Horites in the hill country of Seir as far as El-paran on the edge of the wilderness; 7then they turned back and came to En-mishpat (that is, Kadesh), and subdued all the country of the Amalekites, and also the Amorites who lived in Hazazon-tamar. 8Then the king of Sodom, the king of Gomorrah, the king of Admah, the king of Zeboiim, and the king of Bela (that is, Zoar) went out, and they joined battle in the Valley of Siddim 9with King Chedorlaomer of Elam, King Tidal of Goiim, King Amraphel of Shinar, and King Arioch of Ellasar, four kings against five. 10Now the Valley of Siddim was full of bitumen pits; and as the kings of Sodom and Gomorrah fled, some fell into them, and the rest fled to the hill country. 11So the enemy took all the goods of Sodom and Gomorrah, and all their provisions, and went their way; 12they also took Lot, the son of Abram's brother, who lived in Sodom, and his goods, and departed.

13 Then one who had escaped came and told Abram the Hebrew, who was living by the oaks*b* of Mamre the Amorite, brother of Eshcol and of Aner; these were allies of Abram. 14When Abram heard that his nephew had been taken captive, he led forth his trained men, born in his house, three hundred eighteen of them, and went in pursuit as far as Dan. 15He divided his forces against them by night, he and his servants, and routed them and pursued them to Hobah, north of Damascus. 16Then he brought back all the goods, and also brought back his nephew Lot with his goods, and the women and the people.

17 After his return from the defeat of Chedorlaomer and the kings who were with him, the king of Sodom went out to meet him at the Valley of Shaveh (that is, the King's Valley). 18And King Melchizedek of Salem brought out bread and wine; he was priest of God Most High.*c* 19He blessed him and said,

"Blessed be Abram by God Most High,*c*
    maker of heaven and earth;
20 and blessed be God Most High,*c*
    who has delivered your enemies into
      your hand!"

And Abram gave him one-tenth of everything. 21Then the king of Sodom said to Abram, "Give me the persons, but take the goods for yourself." 22But Abram said to the king of Sodom, "I have sworn to the LORD, God Most High,*c* maker of heaven and earth, 23that I would not take a thread or a sandal-thong or anything that is yours, so that you might not say, 'I have made Abram rich.' 24I will take nothing but what the young men have eaten, and the share of the men who went with me—Aner, Eshcol, and Mamre. Let them take their share."

14.1–24: The rescue of Lot and the blessing of Abram. 1–11: A coalition of kings from the east attacks the area around Sodom and Gomorrah. *Shinar* (v. 1) is probably Babylon (10.10; 11.2). Most of these

a Heb *Salt Sea*   *b* Or *terebinths*   *c* Heb *El Elyon*

names of kings are not known historically from other ancient sources. **12:** The mention of *Lot, the son of Abram's brother,* gives the reason the story is included. The story suggests that Lot's choice of this initially attractive land may not have been so wise (13.10–11). **13–16:** Abram's small band of 318 fighters is able to defeat the coalition of forces from the east. Abram rescues Lot and his family. Abram's concern for Lot is an example of Abram as a blessing to other families of the earth (12.3). **17–18:** Two kings of Sodom and Salem come out to thank Abram for defeating the eastern kings who had attacked them. Salem is another name for the city of Jerusalem (Ps 76.2). The Canaanite king, *Melchizedek of Salem,* was also a Canaanite priest of a god named *God Most High* (v. 18). The title ''Most High'' or ''God Most High'' is an ancient divine title used also for the LORD in the Old Testament (Num 24.16; Deut 32.8) and especially in the Psalms (Ps 57.2). Abram himself links Melchizedek's *God Most High* with *the LORD* in 14.22. The king-priest Melchizedek is not known from other historical sources. He is mentioned only once elsewhere in the Old Testament, in a psalm or blessing addressed to one of Israel's later kings (Ps 110.4). **19–24:** Abram again shows great generosity to people of other nations. He is a blessing to other families of the earth (12.3).

15 After these things the word of the LORD came to Abram in a vision, "Do not be afraid, Abram, I am your shield; your reward shall be very great." [2]But Abram said, "O Lord GOD, what will you give me, for I continue childless, and the heir of my house is Eliezer of Damascus?"[a] [3]And Abram said, "You have given me no offspring, and so a slave born in my house is to be my heir." [4]But the word of the LORD came to him, "This man shall not be your heir; no one but your very own issue shall be your heir." [5]He brought him outside and said, "Look toward heaven and count the stars, if you are able to count them." Then he said to him, "So shall your descendants be." [6]And he believed the LORD; and the LORD [b] reckoned it to him as righteousness.

[7] Then he said to him, "I am the LORD who brought you from Ur of the Chaldeans, to give you this land to possess." [8]But he said, "O Lord GOD, how am I to know that I shall possess it?" [9]He said to him, "Bring me a heifer three years old, a female goat three years old, a ram three years old, a turtledove, and a young pigeon." [10]He brought him all these and cut them in two, laying each half over against the other; but he did not cut the birds in two. [11]And when birds of prey came down on the carcasses, Abram drove them away.

12 As the sun was going down, a deep sleep fell upon Abram, and a deep and terrifying darkness descended upon him. [13]Then the LORD [b] said to Abram, "Know this for certain, that your offspring shall be aliens in a land that is not theirs, and shall be slaves there, and they shall be oppressed for four hundred years; [14]but I will bring judgment on the nation that they serve, and afterward they shall come out with great possessions. [15]As for yourself, you shall go to your ancestors in peace; you shall be buried in a good old age. [16]And they shall come back here in the fourth generation; for the iniquity of the Amorites is not yet complete."

17 When the sun had gone down and it was dark, a smoking fire pot and a flaming torch passed between these pieces. [18]On that day the LORD made a covenant with Abram, saying, "To your descendants I give this land, from the river of Egypt to the great river, the river Euphrates, [19]the land of the Kenites, the Kenizzites, the Kadmonites, [20]the Hittites, the Perizzites, the Rephaim, [21]the Amorites, the Canaanites, the Girgashites, and the Jebusites."

15.1–21: God's covenant* with Abram. This story probably developed over a long period of time. It contains a very ancient covenant ceremony (vv. 7–10, 17) and later additions that point to future events in the exodus out of Egypt and the conquest of Canaan (vv. 12–16). **2–3:** Abram complains to God that the promise of many children and descendants shows no signs of being fulfilled. Abram's only apparent heir is his household slave, Eliezer, which reflects a custom that a chief servant could inherit the possessions of a couple who died without children. **6:** This key verse is the basis for Abram's reputation as a man of great trust in God (Gal 3.6–9). *He believed the LORD* means Abram trusted God to make good on the promise. *The LORD* in turn *reckoned* or evaluated Abram's trust in God as

a Meaning of Heb uncertain   *b* Heb *he*

righteousness. Righteousness denotes a relationship that is in good order. **7–8:** The topic turns from the promise of children to the promise of land. Again, Abram pleads for a sign of reassurance. **9–10:** God responds to Abram's request for a sign by setting up an ancient covenant ceremony. The bodies of animals are cut in two and laid out on two sides with a path between them. By walking down the path, the one making the covenant promise apparently pledges that he will be cut in two like the animals if he does not fulfill the promise made. Jeremiah 34.18 mentions a similar covenant ceremony. **11:** The hovering *birds of prey* symbolize future obstacles that will threaten the fulfillment of the promise. **12–16:** The general future threat symbolized in v. 11 is specified in Abram's dream. Abram's *offspring shall be aliens* and *slaves* in a *land that is not theirs* (v. 13), a reference to Israel's future slavery in Egypt (Ex 1–15). The LORD promises that Abram's family will eventually return and settle in the land of Canaan (v. 16). *Amorites* (v. 16) is an alternate name for Canaanites. **17–21:** The *smoking fire pot* and the *flaming torch* represent the LORD walking down the path between the animal carcasses. In effect, the LORD's action means, "I will be split in two like these animals if I do not fulfill the promise." Abram does not walk through the animals. This is a one-sided and unconditional promise from God to Abram.

16 Now Sarai, Abram's wife, bore him no children. She had an Egyptian slave-girl whose name was Hagar, ²and Sarai said to Abram, "You see that the LORD has prevented me from bearing children; go in to my slave-girl; it may be that I shall obtain children by her." And Abram listened to the voice of Sarai. ³So, after Abram had lived ten years in the land of Canaan, Sarai, Abram's wife, took Hagar the Egyptian, her slave-girl, and gave her to her husband Abram as a wife. ⁴He went in to Hagar, and she conceived; and when she saw that she had conceived, she looked with contempt on her mistress. ⁵Then Sarai said to Abram, "May the wrong done to me be on you! I gave my slave-girl to your embrace, and when she saw that she had conceived, she looked on me with contempt. May the LORD judge between you and me!" ⁶But Abram said to Sarai, "Your slave-girl is in your power; do to her as you please." Then Sarai dealt harshly with her, and she ran away from her.

7 The angel of the LORD found her by a spring of water in the wilderness, the spring on the way to Shur. ⁸And he said, "Hagar, slave-girl of Sarai, where have you come from and where are you going?" She said, "I am running away from my mistress Sarai." ⁹The angel of the LORD said to her, "Return to your mistress, and submit to her." ¹⁰The angel of the LORD also said to her, "I will so greatly multiply your offspring that they cannot be counted for multitude." ¹¹And the angel of the LORD said to her,

"Now you have conceived and shall bear
     a son;
   you shall call him Ishmael,ᵃ
   for the LORD has given heed to your
     affliction.
¹² He shall be a wild ass of a man,
   with his hand against everyone,
     and everyone's hand against him;
   and he shall live at odds with all his
     kin."

¹³So she named the LORD who spoke to her, "You are El-roi";ᵇ for she said, "Have I really seen God and remained alive after seeing him?"ᶜ ¹⁴Therefore the well was called Beer-lahai-roi;ᵈ it lies between Kadesh and Bered.

15 Hagar bore Abram a son; and Abram named his son, whom Hagar bore, Ishmael. ¹⁶Abram was eighty-six years old when Hagar bore himᵉ Ishmael.

16.1–16: Hagar, Sarai, and the birth of Ishmael. 2: Because Sarai could have no children on her own, ancient custom allowed her to have a child through one of her women servants (30.3, 9). **6:** Sarai *dealt harshly* with the Egyptian slave-girl, Hagar. The same Hebrew verb meaning "to deal harshly, oppress" is used to describe the Egyptians' treatment of the Israelite slaves in Ex 1.11. Israel was capable of the same oppression it would experience at the hands of the Egyptians. **10:** *The angel of the LORD* gives a promise to Hagar that is virtually identical to the promise the LORD made to Abram (15.5). **11:** The name of Hagar's son will be *Ishmael,* which means "God hears." The LORD *has given heed to* or heard Hagar's cry for help. God responds to the cry of the oppressed, including non-

---

a That is *God hears*   *b* Perhaps *God of seeing* or *God who sees*   *c* Meaning of Heb uncertain   *d* That is *the Well of the Living One who sees me*   *e* Heb *Abram*

Israelites like Hagar. **12:** Ishmael will be the ancestor of a people known for their defiance and conflict. **13:** Hagar *named the* LORD: *"You are El-roi,"* which means "You are a God who sees." This is the only example in the Old Testament of a human being giving a name to God. In all other cases, God is the one who reveals the divine name to humans. **14:** Place names in Genesis often recall important stories or events. Here *Beer-lahai-roi* means "the well of the living one who sees me."

17 When Abram was ninety-nine years old, the LORD appeared to Abram, and said to him, "I am God Almighty;*a* walk before me, and be blameless. ²And I will make my covenant between me and you, and will make you exceedingly numerous." ³Then Abram fell on his face; and God said to him, ⁴"As for me, this is my covenant with you: You shall be the ancestor of a multitude of nations. ⁵No longer shall your name be Abram,*b* but your name shall be Abraham;*c* for I have made you the ancestor of a multitude of nations. ⁶I will make you exceedingly fruitful; and I will make nations of you, and kings shall come from you. ⁷I will establish my covenant between me and you, and your offspring after you throughout their generations, for an everlasting covenant, to be God to you and to your offspring*d* after you. ⁸And I will give to you, and to your offspring after you, the land where you are now an alien, all the land of Canaan, for a perpetual holding; and I will be their God."

9 God said to Abraham, "As for you, you shall keep my covenant, you and your offspring after you throughout their generations. ¹⁰This is my covenant, which you shall keep, between me and you and your offspring after you: Every male among you shall be circumcised. ¹¹You shall circumcise the flesh of your foreskins, and it shall be a sign of the covenant between me and you. ¹²Throughout your generations every male among you shall be circumcised when he is eight days old, including the slave born in your house and the one bought with your money from any foreigner who is not of your offspring. ¹³Both the slave born in your house and the one bought with your money must be circumcised. So shall my covenant

be in your flesh an everlasting covenant. ¹⁴Any uncircumcised male who is not circumcised in the flesh of his foreskin shall be cut off from his people; he has broken my covenant."

15 God said to Abraham, "As for Sarai your wife, you shall not call her Sarai, but Sarah shall be her name. ¹⁶I will bless her, and moreover I will give you a son by her. I will bless her, and she shall give rise to nations; kings of peoples shall come from her." ¹⁷Then Abraham fell on his face and laughed, and said to himself, "Can a child be born to a man who is a hundred years old? Can Sarah, who is ninety years old, bear a child?" ¹⁸And Abraham said to God, "O that Ishmael might live in your sight!" ¹⁹God said, "No, but your wife Sarah shall bear you a son, and you shall name him Isaac.*e* I will establish my covenant with him as an everlasting covenant for his offspring after him. ²⁰As for Ishmael, I have heard you; I will bless him and make him fruitful and exceedingly numerous; he shall be the father of twelve princes, and I will make him a great nation. ²¹But my covenant I will establish with Isaac, whom Sarah shall bear to you at this season next year." ²²And when he had finished talking with him, God went up from Abraham.

23 Then Abraham took his son Ishmael and all the slaves born in his house or bought with his money, every male among the men of Abraham's house, and he circumcised the flesh of their foreskins that very day, as God had said to him. ²⁴Abraham was ninety-nine years old when he was circumcised in the flesh of his foreskin. ²⁵And his son Ishmael was thirteen years old when he was circumcised in the flesh of his foreskin. ²⁶That very day Abraham and his son Ishmael were circumcised; ²⁷and all the men of his house, slaves born in the house and those bought with money from a foreigner, were circumcised with him.

17.1–27: Another covenant* promise to Abraham and Sarah. God provides another version of the cov-

a Traditional rendering of Heb *El Shaddai*   *b* That is *exalted ancestor*   *c* Here taken to mean *ancestor of a multitude*   *d* Heb *seed*   *e* That is *he laughs*

enant promise, similar to the one made in Gen 15. For the first time, however, God clearly names both Abraham *and* Sarah as the parents of the promised child. The names of Abram and Sarai are changed to mark the importance of this new promise. God also introduces the ritual of circumcision⋆ as a physical sign of belonging to the covenant people of God. **1:** Abram is 99 years old, which makes his son Ishmael 13 years old (16.16). **5:** God changes the name *Abram* (meaning "exalted ancestor") to *Abraham* (meaning "ancestor of a multitude") as a further guarantee that God will keep the promise of many descendants. **7–8:** God introduces a new element of assurance involving time. The covenant is *everlasting*, and Abraham's family will possess the land of Canaan as a *perpetual holding*. God also promises a continuing relationship: *I will be their God.* **9–14:** The ritual of circumcision involves cutting off the foreskin of the male penis. The ritual was practiced by neighboring cultures around Israel as well as by Israel itself. It continues to be practiced by Jews and Muslims today. Circumcision is a physical sign for males that they are members of the covenant people of God. The story in Ex 4.24–26 apparently alludes to the rite of circumcision, although the story is somewhat unclear. **15–16:** God changes *Sarai's* name to *Sarah* to indicate that she is now clearly part of the promise. She will be the mother of the long expected child and of future kings. **17–22:** Abraham laughs at the thought that he and Sarah will have a child at their ages of 100 and 90 years old. Abraham pleads with God to keep Ishmael, who is now 13 years old, as the promised son rather than wait for yet another son (v. 18). But God insists that Sarah will have another son whose name will be *Isaac,* which means "he laughs." The theme of laughter and Isaac will come up again (18.12–15; 21.5–6). God also responds to Abraham's concern for Ishmael. God promises to *bless him,* make him *exceedingly numerous,* and *a great nation.* These are the same promises that Abraham originally received (12.1–3) and that now extend to Isaac as the child of promise.

18 The LORD appeared to Abraham*ᵃ* by the oaks*ᵇ* of Mamre, as he sat at the entrance of his tent in the heat of the day. ²He looked up and saw three men standing near him. When he saw them, he ran from the tent entrance to meet them, and bowed down to the ground. ³He said, "My lord, if I find favor with you, do not pass by your servant. ⁴Let a little water be brought, and wash your feet, and rest yourselves under the tree. ⁵Let me bring a little bread, that you may refresh yourselves, and after that you may pass on—since you have come to your servant." So they said, "Do as you have said." ⁶And Abraham hastened into the tent to Sarah, and said, "Make ready quickly three measures*ᶜ* of choice flour, knead it, and make cakes." ⁷Abraham ran to the herd, and took a calf, tender and good, and gave it to the servant, who hastened to prepare it. ⁸Then he took curds and milk and the calf that he had prepared, and set it before them; and he stood by them under the tree while they ate.

9 They said to him, "Where is your wife Sarah?" And he said, "There, in the tent." ¹⁰Then one said, "I will surely return to you in due season, and your wife Sarah shall have a son." And Sarah was listening at the tent entrance behind him. ¹¹Now Abraham and Sarah were old, advanced in age; it had ceased to be with Sarah after the manner of women. ¹²So Sarah laughed to herself, saying, "After I have grown old, and my husband is old, shall I have pleasure?" ¹³The LORD said to Abraham, "Why did Sarah laugh, and say, 'Shall I indeed bear a child, now that I am old?' ¹⁴Is anything too wonderful for the LORD? At the set time I will return to you, in due season, and Sarah shall have a son." ¹⁵But Sarah denied, saying, "I did not laugh"; for she was afraid. He said, "Oh yes, you did laugh."

18.1–15: The LORD visits Abraham and Sarah. This epiphany⋆ occurs at *the oaks of Mamre,* namely, "a tree shrine at Mamre," a holy place. The depiction of the deity is ambiguous. Is the LORD one among the *three men?* Or is the LORD symbolized by all three individuals? **4–5:** Abraham's description, *little water* and *little bread,* understates the lavish feast that Abraham and Sarah actually prepare for the guests (vv. 7–8). **9–15:** Sarah's laughter at the apparently impossible promise of a child appears to provoke the deity. *Laugh* ("tshq") puns on the name Isaac ("yitshaq").

16 Then the men set out from there, and they looked toward Sodom; and Abraham

a Heb *him*   *b* Or *terebinths*   *c* Heb *seahs*

went with them to set them on their way. ¹⁷The LORD said, "Shall I hide from Abraham what I am about to do, ¹⁸seeing that Abraham shall become a great and mighty nation, and all the nations of the earth shall be blessed in him?ᵃ ¹⁹No, for I have chosenᵇ him, that he may charge his children and his household after him to keep the way of the LORD by doing righteousness and justice; so that the LORD may bring about for Abraham what he has promised him." ²⁰Then the LORD said, "How great is the outcry against Sodom and Gomorrah and how very grave their sin! ²¹I must go down and see whether they have done altogether according to the outcry that has come to me; and if not, I will know."

22 So the men turned from there, and went toward Sodom, while Abraham remained standing before the LORD.ᶜ ²³Then Abraham came near and said, "Will you indeed sweep away the righteous with the wicked? ²⁴Suppose there are fifty righteous within the city; will you then sweep away the place and not forgive it for the fifty righteous who are in it? ²⁵Far be it from you to do such a thing, to slay the righteous with the wicked, so that the righteous fare as the wicked! Far be that from you! Shall not the Judge of all the earth do what is just?" ²⁶And the LORD said, "If I find at Sodom fifty righteous in the city, I will forgive the whole place for their sake." ²⁷Abraham answered, "Let me take it upon myself to speak to the Lord, I who am but dust and ashes. ²⁸Suppose five of the fifty righteous are lacking? Will you destroy the whole city for lack of five?" And he said, "I will not destroy it if I find forty-five there." ²⁹Again he spoke to him, "Suppose forty are found there." He answered, "For the sake of forty I will not do it." ³⁰Then he said, "Oh do not let the Lord be angry if I speak. Suppose thirty are found there." He answered, "I will not do it, if I find thirty there." ³¹He said, "Let me take it upon myself to speak to the Lord. Suppose twenty are found there." He answered, "For the sake of twenty I will not destroy it." ³²Then he said, "Oh do not let the Lord be angry if I speak just once more. Suppose ten are found there." He answered, "For the sake of ten I will not destroy

it." ³³And the LORD went his way, when he had finished speaking to Abraham; and Abraham returned to his place.

18.16–33: Dialogue about Sodom. 16–21: After reflecting on the promises already made to Abraham, the LORD tells Abraham why he is concerned about Sodom. **22–33:** Abraham addresses the LORD six times, pleading for the fate of the *righteous* people in a sinful city. God clarifies the status of Sodom, should some righteous people be found in it. There is talk of forgiveness (v. 26) but, more frequently, simply the absence of destruction is indicated. Abraham may be negotiating on behalf of his nephew, Lot, who lives in Sodom.

19 The two angels came to Sodom in the evening, and Lot was sitting in the gateway of Sodom. When Lot saw them, he rose to meet them, and bowed down with his face to the ground. ²He said, "Please, my lords, turn aside to your servant's house and spend the night, and wash your feet; then you can rise early and go on your way." They said, "No; we will spend the night in the square." ³But he urged them strongly; so they turned aside to him and entered his house; and he made them a feast, and baked unleavened bread, and they ate. ⁴But before they lay down, the men of the city, the men of Sodom, both young and old, all the people to the last man, surrounded the house; ⁵and they called to Lot, "Where are the men who came to you tonight? Bring them out to us, so that we may know them." ⁶Lot went out of the door to the men, shut the door after him, ⁷and said, "I beg you, my brothers, do not act so wickedly. ⁸Look, I have two daughters who have not known a man; let me bring them out to you, and do to them as you please; only do nothing to these men, for they have come under the shelter of my roof." ⁹But they replied, "Stand back!" And they said, "This fellow came here as an alien, and he would play the judge! Now we will deal worse with you than with them." Then they pressed hard against the man Lot, and came near the door to break it down. ¹⁰But

a Or *and all the nations of the earth shall bless themselves by him* *b* Heb *known* *c* Another ancient tradition reads *while the* LORD *remained standing before Abraham*

the men inside reached out their hands and brought Lot into the house with them, and shut the door. 11And they struck with blindness the men who were at the door of the house, both small and great, so that they were unable to find the door.

19.1–11: The wickedness of Sodom. The generous hospitality that the visitors received from Abraham and Sarah in 18.1–15 contrasts sharply with the incredible lack of hospitality shown by the inhabitants of Sodom. **1:** *Two angels* come to Sodom. The angels are divine messengers who look like ordinary human beings. They are apparently two of the same "men" who visited Abraham and Sarah (18.22). **5:** The men of Sodom desire to *know* the visitors sexually. They threaten homosexual rape.

12 Then the men said to Lot, "Have you anyone else here? Sons-in-law, sons, daughters, or anyone you have in the city—bring them out of the place. 13For we are about to destroy this place, because the outcry against its people has become great before the LORD, and the LORD has sent us to destroy it." 14So Lot went out and said to his sons-in-law, who were to marry his daughters, "Up, get out of this place; for the LORD is about to destroy the city." But he seemed to his sons-in-law to be jesting.

15 When morning dawned, the angels urged Lot, saying, "Get up, take your wife and your two daughters who are here, or else you will be consumed in the punishment of the city." 16But he lingered; so the men seized him and his wife and his two daughters by the hand, the LORD being merciful to him, and they brought him out and left him outside the city. 17When they had brought them outside, they*a* said, "Flee for your life; do not look back or stop anywhere in the Plain; flee to the hills, or else you will be consumed." 18And Lot said to them, "Oh, no, my lords; 19your servant has found favor with you, and you have shown me great kindness in saving my life; but I cannot flee to the hills, for fear the disaster will overtake me and I die. 20Look, that city is near enough to flee to, and it is a little one. Let me escape there—is it not a little one?—and my life will be saved!" 21He said to him,

"Very well, I grant you this favor too, and will not overthrow the city of which you have spoken. 22Hurry, escape there, for I can do nothing until you arrive there." Therefore the city was called Zoar.*b* 23The sun had risen on the earth when Lot came to Zoar.

24 Then the LORD rained on Sodom and Gomorrah sulfur and fire from the LORD out of heaven; 25and he overthrew those cities, and all the Plain, and all the inhabitants of the cities, and what grew on the ground. 26But Lot's wife, behind him, looked back, and she became a pillar of salt.

27 Abraham went early in the morning to the place where he had stood before the LORD; 28and he looked down toward Sodom and Gomorrah and toward all the land of the Plain and saw the smoke of the land going up like the smoke of a furnace.

29 So it was that, when God destroyed the cities of the Plain, God remembered Abraham, and sent Lot out of the midst of the overthrow, when he overthrew the cities in which Lot had settled.

19.12–29: The LORD destroys Sodom and Gomorrah. 24: This area southeast of the Dead Sea is an arid desert region with extensive sulfur and other mineral deposits. This story explains why the area is no longer the green "garden of the LORD" that Lot first saw (13.10). **26:** This comment probably explained a certain salt formation in the area. **29:** Abraham again plays a role in saving his nephew Lot and Lot's two daughters. Abraham continues to be a blessing to other families of the earth (12.3).

30 Now Lot went up out of Zoar and settled in the hills with his two daughters, for he was afraid to stay in Zoar; so he lived in a cave with his two daughters. 31And the firstborn said to the younger, "Our father is old, and there is not a man on earth to come in to us after the manner of all the world. 32Come, let us make our father drink wine, and we will lie with him, so that we may preserve offspring through our father." 33So they made their father drink wine that night; and the firstborn went in, and lay with her father; he did not know when she lay down

a Gk Syr Vg: Heb *he*   *b* That is *Little*

or when she rose. 34On the next day, the firstborn said to the younger, "Look, I lay last night with my father; let us make him drink wine tonight also; then you go in and lie with him, so that we may preserve offspring through our father." 35So they made their father drink wine that night also; and the younger rose, and lay with him; and he did not know when she lay down or when she rose. 36Thus both the daughters of Lot became pregnant by their father. 37The firstborn bore a son, and named him Moab; he is the ancestor of the Moabites to this day. 38The younger also bore a son and named him Ben-ammi; he is the ancestor of the Ammonites to this day.

19.30–38: Lot becomes the ancestor of Moab and Ammon. The unflattering story of drunkenness and incest explains the origins of two nations that border Canaan on the east, Moab and Ammon. **31–32:** *Come in to us* and *lie with him* describe sexual intercourse.

20 From there Abraham journeyed toward the region of the Negeb, and settled between Kadesh and Shur. While residing in Gerar as an alien, 2Abraham said of his wife Sarah, "She is my sister." And King Abimelech of Gerar sent and took Sarah. 3But God came to Abimelech in a dream by night, and said to him, "You are about to die because of the woman whom you have taken; for she is a married woman." 4Now Abimelech had not approached her; so he said, "Lord, will you destroy an innocent people? 5Did he not himself say to me, 'She is my sister'? And she herself said, 'He is my brother.' I did this in the integrity of my heart and the innocence of my hands." 6Then God said to him in the dream, "Yes, I know that you did this in the integrity of your heart; furthermore it was I who kept you from sinning against me. Therefore I did not let you touch her. 7Now then, return the man's wife; for he is a prophet, and he will pray for you and you shall live. But if you do not restore her, know that you shall surely die, you and all that are yours."

8 So Abimelech rose early in the morning, and called all his servants and told them all these things; and the men were very much afraid. 9Then Abimelech called Abraham, and said to him, "What have you done to us? How have I sinned against you, that you have brought such great guilt on me and my kingdom? You have done things to me that ought not to be done." 10And Abimelech said to Abraham, "What were you thinking of, that you did this thing?" 11Abraham said, "I did it because I thought, There is no fear of God at all in this place, and they will kill me because of my wife. 12Besides, she is indeed my sister, the daughter of my father but not the daughter of my mother; and she became my wife. 13And when God caused me to wander from my father's house, I said to her, 'This is the kindness you must do me: at every place to which we come, say of me, He is my brother.' " 14Then Abimelech took sheep and oxen, and male and female slaves, and gave them to Abraham, and restored his wife Sarah to him. 15Abimelech said, "My land is before you; settle where it pleases you." 16To Sarah he said, "Look, I have given your brother a thousand pieces of silver; it is your exoneration before all who are with you; you are completely vindicated." 17Then Abraham prayed to God; and God healed Abimelech, and also healed his wife and female slaves so that they bore children. 18For the LORD had closed fast all the wombs of the house of Abimelech because of Sarah, Abraham's wife.

20.1–18: Abraham again pretends Sarah is his sister and not his wife. Abraham had earlier lied about Sarah's being his wife in 12.10–20. It was not at that point clear that Sarah was supposed to be the mother of the child promised to Abraham. However, now Sarah will be the mother of the child (18.10). Thus, Abraham's willingness to endanger his wife Sarah and the promise of God in this case is a much more serious matter. In this story, Abraham appears much less righteous than his hosts. **3–7:** The narrator wants to make clear that there is absolutely no possibility that the child born to Sarah in the next chapter (ch. 21) is King Abimelech's child rather than Abraham's child. *He is a prophet:** the only time Abraham is called a prophet (v. 7). **11:** Abraham's concern that Abimelech and the people of Gerar would have *no fear of God* is directly contradicted by 20.8. **12:** Abraham tries, weakly, to justify his lie by indicating that technically Sarah is his half-sister. Later biblical laws prohibited such marriages (Lev 18.9–11). **16:** The payment of money is an *exoneration* designed to compensate Sarah's family for any injury to her family's honor.

21 The LORD dealt with Sarah as he had said, and the LORD did for Sarah as he had promised. ²Sarah conceived and bore Abraham a son in his old age, at the time of which God had spoken to him. ³Abraham gave the name Isaac to his son whom Sarah bore him. ⁴And Abraham circumcised his son Isaac when he was eight days old, as God had commanded him. ⁵Abraham was a hundred years old when his son Isaac was born to him. ⁶Now Sarah said, "God has brought laughter for me; everyone who hears will laugh with me." ⁷And she said, "Who would ever have said to Abraham that Sarah would nurse children? Yet I have borne him a son in his old age."

21.1–7: The birth of Isaac. At long last, the LORD begins to fulfill the promises of a great nation and many descendants (12.2; 15.5) through the birth of Isaac. **4:** Circumcision* is the ritual cutting off of the foreskin of the male penis. It is a physical sign of a male's belonging to God's covenant* people (17.9–14). **6:** The words *laughter* and *laugh* ("tshq") are puns on the child's name Isaac ("yitshaq") in v. 4.

8 The child grew, and was weaned; and Abraham made a great feast on the day that Isaac was weaned. ⁹But Sarah saw the son of Hagar the Egyptian, whom she had borne to Abraham, playing with her son Isaac.ᵃ ¹⁰So she said to Abraham, "Cast out this slave woman with her son; for the son of this slave woman shall not inherit along with my son Isaac." ¹¹The matter was very distressing to Abraham on account of his son. ¹²But God said to Abraham, "Do not be distressed because of the boy and because of your slave woman; whatever Sarah says to you, do as she tells you, for it is through Isaac that offspring shall be named for you. ¹³As for the son of the slave woman, I will make a nation of him also, because he is your offspring." ¹⁴So Abraham rose early in the morning, and took bread and a skin of water, and gave it to Hagar, putting it on her shoulder, along with the child, and sent her away. And she departed, and wandered about in the wilderness of Beer-sheba.

15 When the water in the skin was gone, she cast the child under one of the bushes. ¹⁶Then she went and sat down opposite him a good way off, about the distance of a bowshot; for she said, "Do not let me look on the death of the child." And as she sat opposite him, she lifted up her voice and wept. ¹⁷And God heard the voice of the boy; and the angel of God called to Hagar from heaven, and said to her, "What troubles you, Hagar? Do not be afraid; for God has heard the voice of the boy where he is. ¹⁸Come, lift up the boy and hold him fast with your hand, for I will make a great nation of him." ¹⁹Then God opened her eyes and she saw a well of water. She went, and filled the skin with water, and gave the boy a drink.

20 God was with the boy, and he grew up; he lived in the wilderness, and became an expert with the bow. ²¹He lived in the wilderness of Paran; and his mother got a wife for him from the land of Egypt.

21.8–21: Abraham and Sarah send Hagar and Ishmael away. This episode contains elements similar to the earlier story of Hagar and Ishmael in 16.1–16: conflict between Sarah and Hagar, journey into the desert, encounter with a divine angel, a well of water, promises concerning Ishmael, and a play on the word "hear" related to the name Ishmael. A key difference this time is that Hagar is forcibly expelled by Sarah, whereas before Hagar had left voluntarily. **10–13:** Sarah's demand to send Hagar and Ishmael away is *very distressing* to Abraham because it will mean giving up his son Ishmael. But God commands Abraham to send Ishmael away, and Abraham obeys. In 22.2, God will similarly command Abraham to give up his only remaining son Isaac. **16:** Hagar's words *Do not let me look* reflect the theme of seeing and not seeing in the story (21.9, 16, 19). **17:** That God *heard* and *has heard* ("shm") is a pun on the child's name, Ishmael, which means "God hears."

22 At that time Abimelech, with Phicol the commander of his army, said to Abraham, "God is with you in all that you do;

a Gk Vg: Heb lacks *with her son Isaac*

23 now therefore swear to me here by God that you will not deal falsely with me or with my offspring or with my posterity, but as I have dealt loyally with you, you will deal with me and with the land where you have resided as an alien." 24And Abraham said, "I swear it."

25 When Abraham complained to Abimelech about a well of water that Abimelech's servants had seized, 26Abimelech said, "I do not know who has done this; you did not tell me, and I have not heard of it until today." 27So Abraham took sheep and oxen and gave them to Abimelech, and the two men made a covenant. 28Abraham set apart seven ewe lambs of the flock. 29And Abimelech said to Abraham, "What is the meaning of these seven ewe lambs that you have set apart?" 30He said, "These seven ewe lambs you shall accept from my hand, in order that you may be a witness for me that I dug this well." 31Therefore that place was called Beer-sheba;*a* because there both of them swore an oath. 32When they had made a covenant at Beer-sheba, Abimelech, with Phicol the commander of his army, left and returned to the land of the Philistines. 33Abraham*b* planted a tamarisk tree in Beer-sheba, and called there on the name of the LORD, the Everlasting God.*c* 34And Abraham resided as an alien many days in the land of the Philistines.

21.22–34: Abraham reconciles with Abimelech. The Canaanite king *Abimelech,* who Abraham had earlier thought had no "fear of God" (20.11), shows a remarkable reverence toward Abraham's God and a willingness to reconcile a human conflict with Abraham. **31:** *Beer-sheba* can mean either "well of the oath" (referring to the loyalty oath between Abraham and Abimelech in vv. 22–24) or "well of seven" (referring to the *seven ewe lambs* Abraham gave to Abimelech in return for acknowledging that the well belonged to Abraham in vv. 28–30). **33:** The planting of the *tamarisk tree* establishes the site as a holy place of worship. *Everlasting God* ("El Olam") may have been the name of an earlier deity worshipped at the site that the story now appropriates as an additional title for the LORD.

And he said, "Here I am." 2He said, "Take your son, your only son Isaac, whom you love, and go to the land of Moriah, and offer him there as a burnt offering on one of the mountains that I shall show you." 3So Abraham rose early in the morning, saddled his donkey, and took two of his young men with him, and his son Isaac; he cut the wood for the burnt offering, and set out and went to the place in the distance that God had shown him. 4On the third day Abraham looked up and saw the place far away. 5Then Abraham said to his young men, "Stay here with the donkey; the boy and I will go over there; we will worship, and then we will come back to you." 6Abraham took the wood of the burnt offering and laid it on his son Isaac, and he himself carried the fire and the knife. So the two of them walked on together. 7Isaac said to his father Abraham, "Father!" And he said, "Here I am, my son." He said, "The fire and the wood are here, but where is the lamb for a burnt offering?" 8Abraham said, "God himself will provide the lamb for a burnt offering, my son." So the two of them walked on together.

9 When they came to the place that God had shown him, Abraham built an altar there and laid the wood in order. He bound his son Isaac, and laid him on the altar, on top of the wood. 10Then Abraham reached out his hand and took the knife to kill*d* his son. 11But the angel of the LORD called to him from heaven, and said, "Abraham, Abraham!" And he said, "Here I am." 12He said, "Do not lay your hand on the boy or do anything to him; for now I know that you fear God, since you have not withheld your son, your only son, from me." 13And Abraham looked up and saw a ram, caught in a thicket by its horns. Abraham went and took the ram and offered it up as a burnt offering instead of his son. 14So Abraham called that place "The LORD will provide";*e* as it is said to this day, "On the mount of the LORD it shall be provided."*f*

a That is *Well of seven* or *Well of the oath*   b Heb *He*
c Or *the LORD, El Olam*   d Or *to slaughter*
e Or *will see;* Heb traditionally transliterated *Jehovah Jireh*   f Or *he shall be seen*

22 After these things God tested Abraham. He said to him, "Abraham!"

15 The angel of the LORD called to Abraham a second time from heaven, 16and said, "By myself I have sworn, says the LORD: Because you have done this, and have not withheld your son, your only son, 17I will indeed bless you, and I will make your offspring as numerous as the stars of heaven and as the sand that is on the seashore. And your offspring shall possess the gate of their enemies, 18and by your offspring shall all the nations of the earth gain blessing for themselves, because you have obeyed my voice." 19So Abraham returned to his young men, and they arose and went together to Beersheba; and Abraham lived at Beer-sheba.

20 Now after these things it was told Abraham, "Milcah also has borne children, to your brother Nahor: 21Uz the firstborn, Buz his brother, Kemuel the father of Aram, 22Chesed, Hazo, Pildash, Jidlaph, and Bethuel." 23Bethuel became the father of Rebekah. These eight Milcah bore to Nahor, Abraham's brother. 24Moreover, his concubine, whose name was Reumah, bore Tebah, Gaham, Tahash, and Maacah.

22.1–24: God commands Abraham to sacrifice Isaac. God puts Abraham through a remarkable test of his obedience and trust in God. God commands Abraham to sacrifice his only remaining son, an act that seems to deny everything God had promised concerning a great nation and many descendants (12.2; 15.5). 2: The location of Mount Moriah is not known. A later tradition identified Moriah with the mountain on which the Temple* in the city of Jerusalem stood (2 Chr 3.1). 14: The phrase the LORD will provide plays on the verb "to see" and may be translated "the LORD will see to it" or "the LORD will be seen." 15–18: God reaffirms the earlier promises of many descendants because of Abraham's extraordinary obedience and trust in God. 20–24: The list of children born to Abraham's extended family includes Rebekah (v. 23), who will eventually become the wife of his son Isaac (24.1–67).

23 Sarah lived one hundred twenty-seven years; this was the length of Sarah's life. 2And Sarah died at Kiriath-arba (that is, Hebron) in the land of Canaan; and Abraham went in to mourn for Sarah and to weep for her. 3Abraham rose up from beside his dead, and said to the Hittites, 4"I am a stranger and an alien residing among you; give me property among you for a burying place, so that I may bury my dead out of my sight." 5The Hittites answered Abraham, 6"Hear us, my lord; you are a mighty prince among us. Bury your dead in the choicest of our burial places; none of us will withhold from you any burial ground for burying your dead." 7Abraham rose and bowed to the Hittites, the people of the land. 8He said to them, "If you are willing that I should bury my dead out of my sight, hear me, and entreat for me Ephron son of Zohar, 9so that he may give me the cave of Machpelah, which he owns; it is at the end of his field. For the full price let him give it to me in your presence as a possession for a burying place." 10Now Ephron was sitting among the Hittites; and Ephron the Hittite answered Abraham in the hearing of the Hittites, of all who went in at the gate of his city, 11"No, my lord, hear me; I give you the field, and I give you the cave that is in it; in the presence of my people I give it to you; bury your dead." 12Then Abraham bowed down before the people of the land. 13He said to Ephron in the hearing of the people of the land, "If you only will listen to me! I will give the price of the field; accept it from me, so that I may bury my dead there." 14Ephron answered Abraham, 15"My lord, listen to me; a piece of land worth four hundred shekels of silver—what is that between you and me? Bury your dead." 16Abraham agreed with Ephron; and Abraham weighed out for Ephron the silver that he had named in the hearing of the Hittites, four hundred shekels of silver, according to the weights current among the merchants.

17 So the field of Ephron in Machpelah, which was to the east of Mamre, the field with the cave that was in it and all the trees that were in the field, throughout its whole area, passed 18to Abraham as a possession in the presence of the Hittites, in the presence of all who went in at the gate of his city. 19After this, Abraham buried Sarah his wife in the cave of the field of Machpelah facing Mamre (that is, Hebron) in the land of Canaan. 20The field and the cave that is in it

passed from the Hittites into Abraham's possession as a burying place.

23.1–20: Abraham buys a piece of the promised land. Sarah dies and Abraham buys a cave and field in Canaan as a burial place for her. In the indirect style of Near Eastern bargaining, the Hittites' extravagant offers of generosity (vv. 6, 11, 15) mean that the price Abraham will have to pay for the land will be very high. But, in the end, Abraham does hold title to at least a small piece of the land God had promised (15.18–21). **15:** *Four hundred shekels** of silver is a very high price for the field. The prophet* Jeremiah bought a field for only seventeen shekels (Jer 32.9). **19:** The land becomes the burial place for Sarah. It will also be the burial place for Abraham (25.8–10), Isaac, Rebekah, Jacob, and Leah (49.29–31).

〰〰〰〰〰〰〰〰〰〰〰〰〰〰〰

24 Now Abraham was old, well advanced in years; and the LORD had blessed Abraham in all things. 2Abraham said to his servant, the oldest of his house, who had charge of all that he had, "Put your hand under my thigh 3and I will make you swear by the LORD, the God of heaven and earth, that you will not get a wife for my son from the daughters of the Canaanites, among whom I live, 4but will go to my country and to my kindred and get a wife for my son Isaac." 5The servant said to him, "Perhaps the woman may not be willing to follow me to this land; must I then take your son back to the land from which you came?" 6Abraham said to him, "See to it that you do not take my son back there. 7The LORD, the God of heaven, who took me from my father's house and from the land of my birth, and who spoke to me and swore to me, 'To your offspring I will give this land,' he will send his angel before you, and you shall take a wife for my son from there. 8But if the woman is not willing to follow you, then you will be free from this oath of mine; only you must not take my son back there." 9So the servant put his hand under the thigh of Abraham his master and swore to him concerning this matter.

10 Then the servant took ten of his master's camels and departed, taking all kinds of choice gifts from his master; and he set out and went to Aram-naharaim, to the city of Nahor. 11He made the camels kneel down outside the city by the well of water; it was toward evening, the time when women go out to draw water. 12And he said, "O LORD, God of my master Abraham, please grant me success today and show steadfast love to my master Abraham. 13I am standing here by the spring of water, and the daughters of the townspeople are coming out to draw water. 14Let the girl to whom I shall say, 'Please offer your jar that I may drink,' and who shall say, 'Drink, and I will water your camels'— let her be the one whom you have appointed for your servant Isaac. By this I shall know that you have shown steadfast love to my master."

15 Before he had finished speaking, there was Rebekah, who was born to Bethuel son of Milcah, the wife of Nahor, Abraham's brother, coming out with her water jar on her shoulder. 16The girl was very fair to look upon, a virgin, whom no man had known. She went down to the spring, filled her jar, and came up. 17Then the servant ran to meet her and said, "Please let me sip a little water from your jar." 18"Drink, my lord," she said, and quickly lowered her jar upon her hand and gave him a drink. 19When she had finished giving him a drink, she said, "I will draw for your camels also, until they have finished drinking." 20So she quickly emptied her jar into the trough and ran again to the well to draw, and she drew for all his camels. 21The man gazed at her in silence to learn whether or not the LORD had made his journey successful.

22 When the camels had finished drinking, the man took a gold nose-ring weighing a half shekel, and two bracelets for her arms weighing ten gold shekels, 23and said, "Tell me whose daughter you are. Is there room in your father's house for us to spend the night?" 24She said to him, "I am the daughter of Bethuel son of Milcah, whom she bore to Nahor." 25She added, "We have plenty of straw and fodder and a place to spend the night." 26The man bowed his head and worshiped the LORD 27and said, "Blessed be the LORD, the God of my master Abraham, who has not forsaken his steadfast love and his faithfulness toward my master. As for me,

the LORD has led me on the way to the house of my master's kin."

28 Then the girl ran and told her mother's household about these things. 29Rebekah had a brother whose name was Laban; and Laban ran out to the man, to the spring. 30As soon as he had seen the nose-ring, and the bracelets on his sister's arms, and when he heard the words of his sister Rebekah, "Thus the man spoke to me," he went to the man; and there he was, standing by the camels at the spring. 31He said, "Come in, O blessed of the LORD. Why do you stand outside when I have prepared the house and a place for the camels?" 32So the man came into the house; and Laban unloaded the camels, and gave him straw and fodder for the camels, and water to wash his feet and the feet of the men who were with him. 33Then food was set before him to eat; but he said, "I will not eat until I have told my errand." He said, "Speak on."

34 So he said, "I am Abraham's servant. 35The LORD has greatly blessed my master, and he has become wealthy; he has given him flocks and herds, silver and gold, male and female slaves, camels and donkeys. 36And Sarah my master's wife bore a son to my master when she was old; and he has given him all that he has. 37My master made me swear, saying, 'You shall not take a wife for my son from the daughters of the Canaanites, in whose land I live; 38but you shall go to my father's house, to my kindred, and get a wife for my son.' 39I said to my master, 'Perhaps the woman will not follow me.' 40But he said to me, 'The LORD, before whom I walk, will send his angel with you and make your way successful. You shall get a wife for my son from my kindred, from my father's house. 41Then you will be free from my oath, when you come to my kindred; even if they will not give her to you, you will be free from my oath.'

42 "I came today to the spring, and said, 'O LORD, the God of my master Abraham, if now you will only make successful the way I am going! 43I am standing here by the spring of water; let the young woman who comes out to draw, to whom I shall say, "Please give me a little water from your jar to drink,"

44and who will say to me, "Drink, and I will draw for your camels also"—let her be the woman whom the LORD has appointed for my master's son.'

45 "Before I had finished speaking in my heart, there was Rebekah coming out with her water jar on her shoulder; and she went down to the spring, and drew. I said to her, 'Please let me drink.' 46She quickly let down her jar from her shoulder, and said, 'Drink, and I will also water your camels.' So I drank, and she also watered the camels. 47Then I asked her, 'Whose daughter are you?' She said, 'The daughter of Bethuel, Nahor's son, whom Milcah bore to him.' So I put the ring on her nose, and the bracelets on her arms. 48Then I bowed my head and worshiped the LORD, and blessed the LORD, the God of my master Abraham, who had led me by the right way to obtain the daughter of my master's kinsman for his son. 49Now then, if you will deal loyally and truly with my master, tell me; and if not, tell me, so that I may turn either to the right hand or to the left."

50 Then Laban and Bethuel answered, "The thing comes from the LORD; we cannot speak to you anything bad or good. 51Look, Rebekah is before you, take her and go, and let her be the wife of your master's son, as the LORD has spoken."

52 When Abraham's servant heard their words, he bowed himself to the ground before the LORD. 53And the servant brought out jewelry of silver and of gold, and garments, and gave them to Rebekah; he also gave to her brother and to her mother costly ornaments. 54Then he and the men who were with him ate and drank, and they spent the night there. When they rose in the morning, he said, "Send me back to my master." 55Her brother and her mother said, "Let the girl remain with us a while, at least ten days; after that she may go." 56But he said to them, "Do not delay me, since the LORD has made my journey successful; let me go that I may go to my master." 57They said, "We will call the girl, and ask her." 58And they called Rebekah, and said to her, "Will you go with this man?" She said, "I will." 59So they sent away their sister Rebekah and her nurse

along with Abraham's servant and his men. 60And they blessed Rebekah and said to her,

"May you, our sister, become
thousands of myriads;
may your offspring gain possession
of the gates of their foes."

61Then Rebekah and her maids rose up, mounted the camels, and followed the man; thus the servant took Rebekah, and went his way.

62 Now Isaac had come from*a* Beer-lahai-roi, and was settled in the Negeb. 63Isaac went out in the evening to walk*b* in the field; and looking up, he saw camels coming. 64And Rebekah looked up, and when she saw Isaac, she slipped quickly from the camel, 65and said to the servant, "Who is the man over there, walking in the field to meet us?" The servant said, "It is my master." So she took her veil and covered herself. 66And the servant told Isaac all the things that he had done. 67Then Isaac brought her into his mother Sarah's tent. He took Rebekah, and she became his wife; and he loved her. So Isaac was comforted after his mother's death.

24.1–67: Isaac secures a wife, Rebekah. 2: Abraham's command to the servant to *put your hand under my thigh,* near his reproductive organs, was a customary way of taking an intimate and solemn oath. **10:** *Aram-naharaim* and *Nahor* are part of Abraham's original home territory in Mesopotamia where he and his family lived before migrating to Canaan (11.31). Most of his extended family apparently remained there. **12–14:** The servant asks the LORD to guide the selection process for Isaac's wife. Rebekah fulfills the conditions perfectly (vv. 15–21). **62:** Isaac comes from *Beer-lahai-roi,* the place where the LORD had guided and comforted Hagar (16.14).

25 Abraham took another wife, whose name was Keturah. 2She bore him Zimran, Jokshan, Medan, Midian, Ishbak, and Shuah. 3Jokshan was the father of Sheba and Dedan. The sons of Dedan were Asshurim, Letushim, and Leummim. 4The sons of Midian were Ephah, Epher, Hanoch, Abida, and Eldaah. All these were the children of Keturah. 5Abraham gave all he had to Isaac. 6But to the sons of his concubines Abraham gave gifts, while he was still living, and he sent them away from his son Isaac, eastward to the east country.

7 This is the length of Abraham's life, one hundred seventy-five years. 8Abraham breathed his last and died in a good old age, an old man and full of years, and was gathered to his people. 9His sons Isaac and Ishmael buried him in the cave of Machpelah, in the field of Ephron son of Zohar the Hittite, east of Mamre, 10the field that Abraham purchased from the Hittites. There Abraham was buried, with his wife Sarah. 11After the death of Abraham God blessed his son Isaac. And Isaac settled at Beer-lahai-roi.

12 These are the descendants of Ishmael, Abraham's son, whom Hagar the Egyptian, Sarah's slave-girl, bore to Abraham. 13These are the names of the sons of Ishmael, named in the order of their birth: Nebaioth, the firstborn of Ishmael; and Kedar, Adbeel, Mibsam, 14Mishma, Dumah, Massa, 15Hadad, Tema, Jetur, Naphish, and Kedemah. 16These are the sons of Ishmael and these are their names, by their villages and by their encampments, twelve princes according to their tribes. 17(This is the length of the life of Ishmael, one hundred thirty-seven years; he breathed his last and died, and was gathered to his people.) 18They settled from Havilah to Shur, which is opposite Egypt in the direction of Assyria; he settled down*c* alongside of*d* all his people.

25.1–18: Abraham's death and the family he leaves behind. 1–6: Abraham takes another wife, Keturah. She is a *concubine** (v. 6), a woman servant with whom he has additional children. However, Isaac remains the favored son (v. 5). The *sons of Midian* are associated with nomadic tribes called Midianites who live *eastward* from Canaan (vv. 4, 6). **10:** The story of the field *purchased from the Hittites* is told in 23.1–20. **16:** Ishmael's descendants form twelve tribes, a grouping similar to the twelve tribes of Israel. They dwell in Arabia (v. 18).

19 These are the descendants of Isaac, Abraham's son: Abraham was the father of

a Syr Tg: Heb *from coming to*   *b* Meaning of Heb word is uncertain   *c* Heb *he fell*   *d* Or *down in opposition to*

Isaac, 20and Isaac was forty years old when he married Rebekah, daughter of Bethuel the Aramean of Paddan-aram, sister of Laban the Aramean. 21Isaac prayed to the LORD for his wife, because she was barren; and the LORD granted his prayer, and his wife Rebekah conceived. 22The children struggled together within her; and she said, "If it is to be this way, why do I live?"*a* So she went to inquire of the LORD. 23And the LORD said to her,

"Two nations are in your womb,
    and two peoples born of you shall be
        divided;
the one shall be stronger than the other,
    the elder shall serve the younger."

24When her time to give birth was at hand, there were twins in her womb. 25The first came out red, all his body like a hairy mantle; so they named him Esau. 26Afterward his brother came out, with his hand gripping Esau's heel; so he was named Jacob.*b* Isaac was sixty years old when she bore them.

27 When the boys grew up, Esau was a skillful hunter, a man of the field, while Jacob was a quiet man, living in tents. 28Isaac loved Esau, because he was fond of game; but Rebekah loved Jacob.

29 Once when Jacob was cooking a stew, Esau came in from the field, and he was famished. 30Esau said to Jacob, "Let me eat some of that red stuff, for I am famished!" (Therefore he was called Edom.*c*) 31Jacob said, "First sell me your birthright." 32Esau said, "I am about to die; of what use is a birthright to me?" 33Jacob said, "Swear to me first."*d* So he swore to him, and sold his birthright to Jacob. 34Then Jacob gave Esau bread and lentil stew, and he ate and drank, and rose and went his way. Thus Esau despised his birthright.

25.19–34: The birth and rivalry of Jacob and Esau. 23: The twin boys in Rebekah's womb represent the *two nations* of Israel (Jacob; 32.28) and Edom (Esau; 36.1). Esau is the elder son. Thus, according to the LORD's prediction, the nation of Edom will be less powerful and serve Israel. **25:** The first baby born is *Esau,* whose body is *red* (Hebrew "admoni"). This is a wordplay on the name "Edom" (v. 30). **26:** The name *Jacob* may have two meanings, both of which describe Ja-

cob's character throughout his life. The name may mean "he takes by the heel" in line with Jacob's tendency to take advantage of others for his own self-interest. The other meaning is "he supplants"; Jacob the younger brother will supplant or take over the privileged position of his elder brother Esau by stealing his birthright and blessing. **30:** A famished Esau asks for Jacob's stew, *that red stuff* ("adom"), a pun on Esau's other name, *Edom.*

26 Now there was a famine in the land, besides the former famine that had occurred in the days of Abraham. And Isaac went to Gerar, to King Abimelech of the Philistines. 2The LORD appeared to Isaac*e* and said, "Do not go down to Egypt; settle in the land that I shall show you. 3Reside in this land as an alien, and I will be with you, and will bless you; for to you and to your descendants I will give all these lands, and I will fulfill the oath that I swore to your father Abraham. 4I will make your offspring as numerous as the stars of heaven, and will give to your offspring all these lands; and all the nations of the earth shall gain blessing for themselves through your offspring, 5because Abraham obeyed my voice and kept my charge, my commandments, my statutes, and my laws."

6 So Isaac settled in Gerar. 7When the men of the place asked him about his wife, he said, "She is my sister"; for he was afraid to say, "My wife," thinking, "or else the men of the place might kill me for the sake of Rebekah, because she is attractive in appearance." 8When Isaac had been there a long time, King Abimelech of the Philistines looked out of a window and saw him fondling his wife Rebekah. 9So Abimelech called for Isaac, and said, "So she is your wife! Why then did you say, 'She is my sister'?" Isaac said to him, "Because I thought I might die because of her." 10Abimelech said, "What is this you have done to us? One of the people might easily have lain with your wife, and you would have brought guilt upon us." 11So Abimelech warned all the people, saying,

a Syr: Meaning of Heb uncertain   *b* That is *He takes by the heel* or *He supplants*   *c* That is *Red*
d Heb *today*   *e* Heb *him*

"Whoever touches this man or his wife shall be put to death."

12 Isaac sowed seed in that land, and in the same year reaped a hundredfold. The LORD blessed him, 13and the man became rich; he prospered more and more until he became very wealthy. 14He had possessions of flocks and herds, and a great household, so that the Philistines envied him. 15(Now the Philistines had stopped up and filled with earth all the wells that his father's servants had dug in the days of his father Abraham.) 16And Abimelech said to Isaac, "Go away from us; you have become too powerful for us."

17 So Isaac departed from there and camped in the valley of Gerar and settled there. 18Isaac dug again the wells of water that had been dug in the days of his father Abraham; for the Philistines had stopped them up after the death of Abraham; and he gave them the names that his father had given them. 19But when Isaac's servants dug in the valley and found there a well of spring water, 20the herders of Gerar quarreled with Isaac's herders, saying, "The water is ours." So he called the well Esek,ᵃ because they contended with him. 21Then they dug another well, and they quarreled over that one also; so he called it Sitnah.ᵇ 22He moved from there and dug another well, and they did not quarrel over it; so he called it Rehoboth,ᶜ saying, "Now the LORD has made room for us, and we shall be fruitful in the land."

23 From there he went up to Beer-sheba. 24And that very night the LORD appeared to him and said, "I am the God of your father Abraham; do not be afraid, for I am with you and will bless you and make your offspring numerous for my servant Abraham's sake." 25So he built an altar there, called on the name of the LORD, and pitched his tent there. And there Isaac's servants dug a well.

26 Then Abimelech went to him from Gerar, with Ahuzzath his adviser and Phicol the commander of his army. 27Isaac said to them, "Why have you come to me, seeing that you hate me and have sent me away from you?" 28They said, "We see plainly that the LORD has been with you; so we say, let

there be an oath between you and us, and let us make a covenant with you 29so that you will do us no harm, just as we have not touched you and have done to you nothing but good and have sent you away in peace. You are now the blessed of the LORD." 30So he made them a feast, and they ate and drank. 31In the morning they rose early and exchanged oaths; and Isaac set them on their way, and they departed from him in peace. 32That same day Isaac's servants came and told him about the well that they had dug, and said to him, "We have found water!" 33He called it Shibah;ᵈ therefore the name of the city is Beer-shebaᵉ to this day.

26.1–33: Stories about Isaac and Abimelech. Several incidents in Isaac's life repeat similar events in the life of his father Abraham. Examples include divine promises of land and descendants (12.1–3; 26.1–5, 24), the building of altars (12.7–8; 13.18; 26.25), a wife-sister incident with Abimelech (20.1–18; 26.6–11), conflicts over the ownership of wells (21.25–34; 26.17–25), and a covenant* of peace with Abimelech (21.22–24; 26.26–31). **8:** The writer again puns on the name Isaac: The king saw *Isaac* ("yitshaq") *fondling* ("metsaheq") his wife. **33:** *Shibah* is a wordplay on the Hebrew verb "to exchange an oath" ("shb," v. 31). Shibah is an alternate place name for *Beer-sheba* ("Well of the oath," 21.31).

---

34 When Esau was forty years old, he married Judith daughter of Beeri the Hittite, and Basemath daughter of Elon the Hittite; 35and they made life bitter for Isaac and Rebekah.

27 When Isaac was old and his eyes were dim so that he could not see, he called his elder son Esau and said to him, "My son"; and he answered, "Here I am." 2He said, "See, I am old; I do not know the day of my death. 3Now then, take your weapons, your quiver and your bow, and go out to the field, and hunt game for me. 4Then prepare for me savory food, such as I like, and bring it to me to eat, so that I may bless you before I die."

ᵃ That is *Contention*   ᵇ That is *Enmity*   ᶜ That is *Broad places* or *Room*   ᵈ A word resembling the word for *oath*   ᵉ That is *Well of the oath* or *Well of seven*

5 Now Rebekah was listening when Isaac spoke to his son Esau. So when Esau went to the field to hunt for game and bring it, 6Rebekah said to her son Jacob, "I heard your father say to your brother Esau, 7'Bring me game, and prepare for me savory food to eat, that I may bless you before the LORD before I die.' 8Now therefore, my son, obey my word as I command you. 9Go to the flock, and get me two choice kids, so that I may prepare from them savory food for your father, such as he likes; 10and you shall take it to your father to eat, so that he may bless you before he dies." 11But Jacob said to his mother Rebekah, "Look, my brother Esau is a hairy man, and I am a man of smooth skin. 12Perhaps my father will feel me, and I shall seem to be mocking him, and bring a curse on myself and not a blessing." 13His mother said to him, "Let your curse be on me, my son; only obey my word, and go, get them for me." 14So he went and got them and brought them to his mother; and his mother prepared savory food, such as his father loved. 15Then Rebekah took the best garments of her elder son Esau, which were with her in the house, and put them on her younger son Jacob; 16and she put the skins of the kids on his hands and on the smooth part of his neck. 17Then she handed the savory food, and the bread that she had prepared, to her son Jacob.

18 So he went in to his father, and said, "My father"; and he said, "Here I am; who are you, my son?" 19Jacob said to his father, "I am Esau your firstborn. I have done as you told me; now sit up and eat of my game, so that you may bless me." 20But Isaac said to his son, "How is it that you have found it so quickly, my son?" He answered, "Because the LORD your God granted me success." 21Then Isaac said to Jacob, "Come near, that I may feel you, my son, to know whether you are really my son Esau or not." 22So Jacob went up to his father Isaac, who felt him and said, "The voice is Jacob's voice, but the hands are the hands of Esau." 23He did not recognize him, because his hands were hairy like his brother Esau's hands; so he blessed him. 24He said, "Are you really my son Esau?" He answered, "I am." 25Then he said,

"Bring it to me, that I may eat of my son's game and bless you." So he brought it to him, and he ate; and he brought him wine, and he drank. 26Then his father Isaac said to him, "Come near and kiss me, my son." 27So he came near and kissed him; and he smelled the smell of his garments, and blessed him, and said,

"Ah, the smell of my son
   is like the smell of a field that the
     LORD has blessed.
28 May God give you of the dew of heaven,
   and of the fatness of the earth,
     and plenty of grain and wine.
29 Let peoples serve you,
   and nations bow down to you.
Be lord over your brothers,
   and may your mother's sons bow
     down to you.
Cursed be everyone who curses you,
   and blessed be everyone who blesses
     you!"

30 As soon as Isaac had finished blessing Jacob, when Jacob had scarcely gone out from the presence of his father Isaac, his brother Esau came in from his hunting. 31He also prepared savory food, and brought it to his father. And he said to his father, "Let my father sit up and eat of his son's game, so that you may bless me." 32His father Isaac said to him, "Who are you?" He answered, "I am your firstborn son, Esau." 33Then Isaac trembled violently, and said, "Who was it then that hunted game and brought it to me, and I ate it all*a* before you came, and I have blessed him?—yes, and blessed he shall be!" 34When Esau heard his father's words, he cried out with an exceedingly great and bitter cry, and said to his father, "Bless me, me also, father!" 35But he said, "Your brother came deceitfully, and he has taken away your blessing." 36Esau said, "Is he not rightly named Jacob?*b* For he has supplanted me these two times. He took away my birthright; and look, now he has taken away my blessing." Then he said, "Have you not reserved a blessing for me?" 37Isaac answered Esau, "I have already made him your

a Cn: Heb *of all*   *b* That is *He supplants* or *He takes by the heel*

lord, and I have given him all his brothers as servants, and with grain and wine I have sustained him. What then can I do for you, my son?" 38 Esau said to his father, "Have you only one blessing, father? Bless me, me also, father!" And Esau lifted up his voice and wept.

39 Then his father Isaac answered him:
  "See, away from*a* the fatness of the
        earth shall your home be,
    and away from*b* the dew of heaven on
        high.
40 By your sword you shall live,
        and you shall serve your brother;
    but when you break loose,*c*
        you shall break his yoke from your
        neck."

41 Now Esau hated Jacob because of the blessing with which his father had blessed him, and Esau said to himself, "The days of mourning for my father are approaching; then I will kill my brother Jacob." 42 But the words of her elder son Esau were told to Rebekah; so she sent and called her younger son Jacob and said to him, "Your brother Esau is consoling himself by planning to kill you. 43 Now therefore, my son, obey my voice; flee at once to my brother Laban in Haran, 44 and stay with him a while, until your brother's fury turns away— 45 until your brother's anger against you turns away, and he forgets what you have done to him; then I will send, and bring you back from there. Why should I lose both of you in one day?"

46 Then Rebekah said to Isaac, "I am weary of my life because of the Hittite women. If Jacob marries one of the Hittite women such as these, one of the women of the land, what good will my life be to me?"

28 Then Isaac called Jacob and blessed him, and charged him, "You shall not marry one of the Canaanite women. 2 Go at once to Paddan-aram to the house of Bethuel, your mother's father; and take as wife from there one of the daughters of Laban, your mother's brother. 3 May God Almighty*d* bless you and make you fruitful and numerous, that you may become a company of peoples. 4 May he give to you the blessing of Abraham, to you and to your offspring with you, so that you may take possession of the

land where you now live as an alien—land that God gave to Abraham." 5 Thus Isaac sent Jacob away; and he went to Paddan-aram, to Laban son of Bethuel the Aramean, the brother of Rebekah, Jacob's and Esau's mother.

6 Now Esau saw that Isaac had blessed Jacob and sent him away to Paddan-aram to take a wife from there, and that as he blessed him he charged him, "You shall not marry one of the Canaanite women," 7 and that Jacob had obeyed his father and his mother and gone to Paddan-aram. 8 So when Esau saw that the Canaanite women did not please his father Isaac, 9 Esau went to Ishmael and took Mahalath daughter of Abraham's son Ishmael, and sister of Nebaioth, to be his wife in addition to the wives he had.

26.34–28.9: Jacob steals Esau's blessing. Jacob deceives his old and blind father Isaac. Jacob pretends to be his older brother Esau so that he can receive the blessing and inheritance that belong to the firstborn son. 26.34–35: Esau marries two Hittite or native Canaanite women who bring trouble to the family. This comment places Esau in a negative light. 27.34–38: The grief and anger of Isaac and Esau presuppose that the words and power of a blessing cannot be taken back once they have been spoken. 39: Esau can only receive the opposite of what Jacob already received. Jacob will receive *of* (the Hebrew preposition "min") *the fatness of the earth* (v. 28) while Esau will live *away from* (the same preposition "min") *the fatness of the earth.* The land of Edom was not an agriculturally rich area. 41: *I will kill my brother Jacob:* These are the last words we hear from Esau concerning Jacob until they meet many years later in ch. 33. 46: Rebekah's excuse to Isaac for sending Jacob away is to avoid Jacob's marrying one of the Hittite or Canaanite *women of the land* as Esau had done (26.34–35). Her real reason is to stop Esau from murdering his brother Jacob (vv. 42–45). 28.1–5: Isaac instructs Jacob to return to the original homeland of Abraham and of his mother Rebekah in Mesopotamia to obtain a wife as Isaac had done (ch. 24; 25.20).

10 Jacob left Beer-sheba and went toward Haran. 11 He came to a certain place and

---

a Or *See, of*   *b* Or *and of*   *c* Meaning of Heb uncertain   *d* Traditional rendering of Heb *El Shaddai* stayed there for the night, because the sun had set. Taking one of the stones of the place, he put it under his head and lay down in that place. [12]And he dreamed that there was a ladder[a] set up on the earth, the top of it reaching to heaven; and the angels of God were ascending and descending on it. [13]And the LORD stood beside him[b] and said, "I am the LORD, the God of Abraham your father and the God of Isaac; the land on which you lie I will give to you and to your offspring; [14]and your offspring shall be like the dust of the earth, and you shall spread abroad to the west and to the east and to the north and to the south; and all the families of the earth shall be blessed[c] in you and in your offspring. [15]Know that I am with you and will keep you wherever you go, and will bring you back to this land; for I will not leave you until I have done what I have promised you." [16]Then Jacob woke from his sleep and said, "Surely the LORD is in this place—and I did not know it!" [17]And he was afraid, and said, "How awesome is this place! This is none other than the house of God, and this is the gate of heaven."

18 So Jacob rose early in the morning, and he took the stone that he had put under his head and set it up for a pillar and poured oil on the top of it. [19]He called that place Bethel;[d] but the name of the city was Luz at the first. [20]Then Jacob made a vow, saying, "If God will be with me, and will keep me in this way that I go, and will give me bread to eat and clothing to wear, [21]so that I come again to my father's house in peace, then the LORD shall be my God, [22]and this stone, which I have set up for a pillar, shall be God's house; and of all that you give me I will surely give one-tenth to you."

28.10–22: This story of Jacob's encounter with God and God's blessing as he leaves Canaan is the first of two such encounters. When Jacob returns to Canaan twenty years later, he will encounter angels or divine messengers a second time (32.1–2). He will also wrestle with God and receive a blessing (32.22–32). **13–15:** God reaffirms the promises made to Abraham and Isaac as belonging also to Jacob (12.1–3; 26.2–5). **17:** *The house of God* ("beth'el") becomes the basis for the name of the place, Bethel (v. 19). **18:** Jacob's act

of *pouring oil on top of* the stone *pillar* marked the location as a holy place. **20–21:** Jacob is always a tough negotiator for his own self-interest (25.29–34). True to his nature, Jacob vows to let God *be my God* on the condition that God cares for all his needs.

29

Then Jacob went on his journey, and came to the land of the people of the east. [2]As he looked, he saw a well in the field and three flocks of sheep lying there beside it; for out of that well the flocks were watered. The stone on the well's mouth was large, [3]and when all the flocks were gathered there, the shepherds would roll the stone from the mouth of the well, and water the sheep, and put the stone back in its place on the mouth of the well.

4 Jacob said to them, "My brothers, where do you come from?" They said, "We are from Haran." [5]He said to them, "Do you know Laban son of Nahor?" They said, "We do." [6]He said to them, "Is it well with him?" "Yes," they replied, "and here is his daughter Rachel, coming with the sheep." [7]He said, "Look, it is still broad daylight; it is not time for the animals to be gathered together. Water the sheep, and go, pasture them." [8]But they said, "We cannot until all the flocks are gathered together, and the stone is rolled from the mouth of the well; then we water the sheep."

9 While he was still speaking with them, Rachel came with her father's sheep; for she kept them. [10]Now when Jacob saw Rachel, the daughter of his mother's brother Laban, and the sheep of his mother's brother Laban, Jacob went up and rolled the stone from the well's mouth, and watered the flock of his mother's brother Laban. [11]Then Jacob kissed Rachel, and wept aloud. [12]And Jacob told Rachel that he was her father's kinsman, and that he was Rebekah's son; and she ran and told her father.

13 When Laban heard the news about his sister's son Jacob, he ran to meet him; he embraced him and kissed him, and brought him to his house. Jacob[e] told Laban all these

a Or *stairway* or *ramp*   *b* Or *stood above it*
c Or *shall bless themselves*   *d* That is *House of God*
e Heb *He*

things, ¹⁴and Laban said to him, "Surely you are my bone and my flesh!" And he stayed with him a month.

15 Then Laban said to Jacob, "Because you are my kinsman, should you therefore serve me for nothing? Tell me, what shall your wages be?" ¹⁶Now Laban had two daughters; the name of the elder was Leah, and the name of the younger was Rachel. ¹⁷Leah's eyes were lovely,ᵃ and Rachel was graceful and beautiful. ¹⁸Jacob loved Rachel; so he said, "I will serve you seven years for your younger daughter Rachel." ¹⁹Laban said, "It is better that I give her to you than that I should give her to any other man; stay with me." ²⁰So Jacob served seven years for Rachel, and they seemed to him but a few days because of the love he had for her.

21 Then Jacob said to Laban, "Give me my wife that I may go in to her, for my time is completed." ²²So Laban gathered together all the people of the place, and made a feast. ²³But in the evening he took his daughter Leah and brought her to Jacob; and he went in to her. ²⁴(Laban gave his maid Zilpah to his daughter Leah to be her maid.) ²⁵When morning came, it was Leah! And Jacob said to Laban, "What is this you have done to me? Did I not serve with you for Rachel? Why then have you deceived me?" ²⁶Laban said, "This is not done in our country—giving the younger before the firstborn. ²⁷Complete the week of this one, and we will give you the other also in return for serving me another seven years." ²⁸Jacob did so, and completed her week; then Laban gave him his daughter Rachel as a wife. ²⁹(Laban gave his maid Bilhah to his daughter Rachel to be her maid.) ³⁰So Jacob went in to Rachel also, and he loved Rachel more than Leah. He served Labanᵇ for another seven years.

29.1–30: Jacob marries Leah and Rachel. Jacob the deceiver (ch. 27) meets his match in his uncle Laban, who deceives Jacob (v. 25). Jacob agrees to work seven years in order to marry Rachel. Laban tricks Jacob into working for him for twice as many years (14 years). Jacob also ends up marrying both of Laban's daughters instead of only Rachel, the wife he truly wanted. 17: The Hebrew word for *lovely* is unclear and may also mean weak or unattractive. This may

partly explain why Jacob preferred Rachel over Leah (v. 30).

31 When the LORD saw that Leah was unloved, he opened her womb; but Rachel was barren. ³²Leah conceived and bore a son, and she named him Reuben;ᶜ for she said, "Because the LORD has looked on my affliction; surely now my husband will love me." ³³She conceived again and bore a son, and said, "Because the LORD has heardᵈ that I am hated, he has given me this son also"; and she named him Simeon. ³⁴Again she conceived and bore a son, and said, "Now this time my husband will be joinedᵉ to me, because I have borne him three sons"; therefore he was named Levi. ³⁵She conceived again and bore a son, and said, "This time I will praiseᶠ the LORD"; therefore she named him Judah; then she ceased bearing.

30 When Rachel saw that she bore Jacob no children, she envied her sister; and she said to Jacob, "Give me children, or I shall die!" ²Jacob became very angry with Rachel and said, "Am I in the place of God, who has withheld from you the fruit of the womb?" ³Then she said, "Here is my maid Bilhah; go in to her, that she may bear upon my knees and that I too may have children through her." ⁴So she gave him her maid Bilhah as a wife; and Jacob went in to her. ⁵And Bilhah conceived and bore Jacob a son. ⁶Then Rachel said, "God has judged me, and has also heard my voice and given me a son"; therefore she named him Dan.ᵍ ⁷Rachel's maid Bilhah conceived again and bore Jacob a second son. ⁸Then Rachel said, "With mighty wrestlings I have wrestledʰ with my sister, and have prevailed"; so she named him Naphtali.

9 When Leah saw that she had ceased bearing children, she took her maid Zilpah and gave her to Jacob as a wife. ¹⁰Then Leah's maid Zilpah bore Jacob a son. ¹¹And Leah said, "Good fortune!" so she named him Gad.ⁱ ¹²Leah's maid Zilpah bore Jacob a second son. ¹³And Leah said, "Happy am

a Meaning of Heb uncertain   b Heb *him*   c That is *See, a son*   d Heb *shama*   e Heb *lawah*   f Heb *hodah*   g That is *He judged*   h Heb *niphtal*   i That is *Fortune*

I! For the women will call me happy"; so she named him Asher.[a]

14 In the days of wheat harvest Reuben went and found mandrakes in the field, and brought them to his mother Leah. Then Rachel said to Leah, "Please give me some of your son's mandrakes." [15]But she said to her, "Is it a small matter that you have taken away my husband? Would you take away my son's mandrakes also?" Rachel said, "Then he may lie with you tonight for your son's mandrakes." [16]When Jacob came from the field in the evening, Leah went out to meet him, and said, "You must come in to me; for I have hired you with my son's mandrakes." So he lay with her that night. [17]And God heeded Leah, and she conceived and bore Jacob a fifth son. [18]Leah said, "God has given me my hire[b] because I gave my maid to my husband"; so she named him Issachar. [19]And Leah conceived again, and she bore Jacob a sixth son. [20]Then Leah said, "God has endowed me with a good dowry; now my husband will honor[c] me, because I have borne him six sons"; so she named him Zebulun. [21]Afterwards she bore a daughter, and named her Dinah.

22 Then God remembered Rachel, and God heeded her and opened her womb. [23]She conceived and bore a son, and said, "God has taken away my reproach"; [24]and she named him Joseph,[d] saying, "May the LORD add to me another son!"

29.31–30.24: The birth of Jacob's eleven sons and one daughter. The sons born to Jacob will become the ancestors of the twelve tribes of Israel. The birth of the twelfth and last son, Benjamin, is described in ch. 35. The relative status of the mother of each of the sons reflected the relative status of the corresponding tribe at some point in Israel's history. For example, the Joseph tribe was once one of the most powerful tribes, a status reflected by his mother, the most favored wife (vv. 22–24; 29.30). Leah's children and the children of the maid would have been less favored or influential. Each child's name has some meaning attached to it. **30.14–16:** As the favored wife, Rachel has the first rights of sleeping with Jacob. However, she barters that right away to Leah for a night in exchange for some *mandrakes*. Mandrakes are herbs thought to aid in fertility. The childless Rachel is apparently anxious

to do what she can to have children with Jacob. Rachel eventually succeeds with God's help (30.22–24).

25 When Rachel had borne Joseph, Jacob said to Laban, "Send me away, that I may go to my own home and country. [26]Give me my wives and my children for whom I have served you, and let me go; for you know very well the service I have given you." [27]But Laban said to him, "If you will allow me to say so, I have learned by divination that the LORD has blessed me because of you; [28]name your wages, and I will give it." [29]Jacob said to him, "You yourself know how I have served you, and how your cattle have fared with me. [30]For you had little before I came, and it has increased abundantly; and the LORD has blessed you wherever I turned. But now when shall I provide for my own household also?" [31]He said, "What shall I give you?" Jacob said, "You shall not give me anything; if you will do this for me, I will again feed your flock and keep it: [32]let me pass through all your flock today, removing from it every speckled and spotted sheep and every black lamb, and the spotted and speckled among the goats; and such shall be my wages. [33]So my honesty will answer for me later, when you come to look into my wages with you. Every one that is not speckled and spotted among the goats and black among the lambs, if found with me, shall be counted stolen." [34]Laban said, "Good! Let it be as you have said." [35]But that day Laban removed the male goats that were striped and spotted, and all the female goats that were speckled and spotted, every one that had white on it, and every lamb that was black, and put them in charge of his sons; [36]and he set a distance of three days' journey between himself and Jacob, while Jacob was pasturing the rest of Laban's flock.

37 Then Jacob took fresh rods of poplar and almond and plane, and peeled white streaks in them, exposing the white of the rods. [38]He set the rods that he had peeled in front of the flocks in the troughs, that is, the watering places, where the flocks came to

a That is *Happy*   *b* Heb *sakar*   *c* Heb *zabal*
d That is *He adds*

drink. And since they bred when they came to drink, 39the flocks bred in front of the rods, and so the flocks produced young that were striped, speckled, and spotted. 40Jacob separated the lambs, and set the faces of the flocks toward the striped and the completely black animals in the flock of Laban; and he put his own droves apart, and did not put them with Laban's flock. 41Whenever the stronger of the flock were breeding, Jacob laid the rods in the troughs before the eyes of the flock, that they might breed among the rods, 42but for the feebler of the flock he did not lay them there; so the feebler were Laban's, and the stronger Jacob's. 43Thus the man grew exceedingly rich, and had large flocks, and male and female slaves, and camels and donkeys.

30.25–43: Jacob prospers and Laban loses. Laban promises to give Jacob all the sheep and goats that are spotted or black (vv. 32–34). But then Laban secretly removes all the spotted and black animals from the herd and sends them away so nothing is left for Jacob (vv. 35–36). Jacob places striped or spotted almond or poplar branches in front of the strong sheep and goats as they mate. The assumption was that whatever the animals saw while they mated would determine whether their offspring would be a solid or a spotted color. An underlying biological fact is that even though the parent animals were both all white, they could carry the recessive gene for black or a spotted color. As a result of his genetic engineering, Jacob *grew exceedingly rich* (v. 43).

31 Now Jacob heard that the sons of Laban were saying, "Jacob has taken all that was our father's; he has gained all this wealth from what belonged to our father." 2And Jacob saw that Laban did not regard him as favorably as he did before. 3Then the LORD said to Jacob, "Return to the land of your ancestors and to your kindred, and I will be with you." 4So Jacob sent and called Rachel and Leah into the field where his flock was, 5and said to them, "I see that your father does not regard me as favorably as he did before. But the God of my father has been with me. 6You know that I have served your father with all my strength; 7yet your father has cheated me and changed my

wages ten times, but God did not permit him to harm me. 8If he said, 'The speckled shall be your wages,' then all the flock bore speckled; and if he said, 'The striped shall be your wages,' then all the flock bore striped. 9Thus God has taken away the livestock of your father, and given them to me.

10 During the mating of the flock I once had a dream in which I looked up and saw that the male goats that leaped upon the flock were striped, speckled, and mottled. 11Then the angel of God said to me in the dream, 'Jacob,' and I said, 'Here I am!' 12And he said, 'Look up and see that all the goats that leap on the flock are striped, speckled, and mottled; for I have seen all that Laban is doing to you. 13I am the God of Bethel,^a where you anointed a pillar and made a vow to me. Now leave this land at once and return to the land of your birth.' " 14Then Rachel and Leah answered him, "Is there any portion or inheritance left to us in our father's house? 15Are we not regarded by him as foreigners? For he has sold us, and he has been using up the money given for us. 16All the property that God has taken away from our father belongs to us and to our children; now then, do whatever God has said to you."

17 So Jacob arose, and set his children and his wives on camels; 18and he drove away all his livestock, all the property that he had gained, the livestock in his possession that he had acquired in Paddan-aram, to go to his father Isaac in the land of Canaan.

19 Now Laban had gone to shear his sheep, and Rachel stole her father's household gods. 20And Jacob deceived Laban the Aramean, in that he did not tell him that he intended to flee. 21So he fled with all that he had; starting out he crossed the Euphrates,^b and set his face toward the hill country of Gilead.

22 On the third day Laban was told that Jacob had fled. 23So he took his kinsfolk with him and pursued him for seven days until he caught up with him in the hill country of Gilead. 24But God came to Laban the Aramean in a dream by night, and said to him,

a Cn: Meaning of Heb uncertain   b Heb *the river*

"Take heed that you say not a word to Jacob, either good or bad."

25 Laban overtook Jacob. Now Jacob had pitched his tent in the hill country, and Laban with his kinsfolk camped in the hill country of Gilead. 26Laban said to Jacob, "What have you done? You have deceived me, and carried away my daughters like captives of the sword. 27Why did you flee secretly and deceive me and not tell me? I would have sent you away with mirth and songs, with tambourine and lyre. 28And why did you not permit me to kiss my sons and my daughters farewell? What you have done is foolish. 29It is in my power to do you harm; but the God of your father spoke to me last night, saying, 'Take heed that you speak to Jacob neither good nor bad.' 30Even though you had to go because you longed greatly for your father's house, why did you steal my gods?" 31Jacob answered Laban, "Because I was afraid, for I thought that you would take your daughters from me by force. 32But anyone with whom you find your gods shall not live. In the presence of our kinsfolk, point out what I have that is yours, and take it." Now Jacob did not know that Rachel had stolen the gods.*a*

33 So Laban went into Jacob's tent, and into Leah's tent, and into the tent of the two maids, but he did not find them. And he went out of Leah's tent, and entered Rachel's. 34Now Rachel had taken the household gods and put them in the camel's saddle, and sat on them. Laban felt all about in the tent, but did not find them. 35And she said to her father, "Let not my lord be angry that I cannot rise before you, for the way of women is upon me." So he searched, but did not find the household gods.

36 Then Jacob became angry, and upbraided Laban. Jacob said to Laban, "What is my offense? What is my sin, that you have hotly pursued me? 37Although you have felt about through all my goods, what have you found of all your household goods? Set it here before my kinsfolk and your kinsfolk, so that they may decide between us two. 38These twenty years I have been with you; your ewes and your female goats have not miscarried, and I have not eaten the rams of your flocks. 39That which was torn by wild beasts I did not bring to you; I bore the loss of it myself; of my hand you required it, whether stolen by day or stolen by night. 40It was like this with me: by day the heat consumed me, and the cold by night, and my sleep fled from my eyes. 41These twenty years I have been in your house; I served you fourteen years for your two daughters, and six years for your flock, and you have changed my wages ten times. 42If the God of my father, the God of Abraham and the Fear*b* of Isaac, had not been on my side, surely now you would have sent me away empty-handed. God saw my affliction and the labor of my hands, and rebuked you last night."

43 Then Laban answered and said to Jacob, "The daughters are my daughters, the children are my children, the flocks are my flocks, and all that you see is mine. But what can I do today about these daughters of mine, or about their children whom they have borne? 44Come now, let us make a covenant, you and I; and let it be a witness between you and me." 45So Jacob took a stone, and set it up as a pillar. 46And Jacob said to his kinsfolk, "Gather stones," and they took stones, and made a heap; and they ate there by the heap. 47Laban called it Jegar-sahadutha:*c* but Jacob called it Galeed.*d* 48Laban said, "This heap is a witness between you and me today." Therefore he called it Galeed, 49and the pillar*e* Mizpah,*f* for he said, "The LORD watch between you and me, when we are absent one from the other. 50If you ill-treat my daughters, or if you take wives in addition to my daughters, though no one else is with us, remember that God is witness between you and me."

51 Then Laban said to Jacob, "See this heap and see the pillar, which I have set between you and me. 52This heap is a witness, and the pillar is a witness, that I will not pass beyond this heap to you, and you will not pass beyond this heap and this pillar to me, for harm. 53May the God of Abraham and

a Heb *them*   *b* Meaning of Heb uncertain
c In Aramaic *The heap of witness*   *d* In Hebrew *The heap of witness*   *e* Compare Sam: MT lacks *the pillar*
f That is *Watchpost*

the God of Nahor"—the God of their father—"judge between us." So Jacob swore by the Fear*a* of his father Isaac, 54and Jacob offered a sacrifice on the height and called his kinsfolk to eat bread; and they ate bread and tarried all night in the hill country.

55*b* Early in the morning Laban rose up, and kissed his grandchildren and his daughters and blessed them; then he departed and returned home.

31.1–55: Jacob flees from Laban with his family and flocks. 1–2: Envy and conflict within the extended families of Jacob and Laban increase as Jacob's wealth and flocks increase. **14–16:** After having experienced conflict between themselves (30.1, 15), Leah and Rachel are now united in their negative feelings toward their father Laban. **19:** The *household gods* were idols that were believed to carry with them power, prosperity, and the legal claim to the family's property. **32:** Jacob unknowingly predicts what will happen to Rachel. She will soon die prematurely in childbirth (35.16–20). **35:** *The way of women* refers to her menstrual period. **47–48:** The site for the boundary covenant* or agreement between Jacob and Laban has two names. One name, *Jegar-sahadutha*, means "the heap of witness" in the Aramaic* language spoken by Laban the Aramean (25.20). The other name for the same site, *Galeed*, also means "the heap of witness," but in the Hebrew language spoken by Jacob. The names refer to the heap of stones that mark the boundary between Laban's Arameans and Jacob's Israelites. **49:** Laban names the pillar *Mizpah*, meaning "watchpost."

32 Jacob went on his way and the angels of God met him; 2and when Jacob saw them he said, "This is God's camp!" So he called that place Mahanaim.*c*

3 Jacob sent messengers before him to his brother Esau in the land of Seir, the country of Edom, 4instructing them, "Thus you shall say to my lord Esau: Thus says your servant Jacob, 'I have lived with Laban as an alien, and stayed until now; 5and I have oxen, donkeys, flocks, male and female slaves; and I have sent to tell my lord, in order that I may find favor in your sight.' "

6 The messengers returned to Jacob, saying, "We came to your brother Esau, and he is coming to meet you, and four hundred men are with him." 7Then Jacob was greatly afraid and distressed; and he divided the people that were with him, and the flocks and herds and camels, into two companies, 8thinking, "If Esau comes to the one company and destroys it, then the company that is left will escape."

9 And Jacob said, "O God of my father Abraham and God of my father Isaac, O LORD who said to me, 'Return to your country and to your kindred, and I will do you good,' 10I am not worthy of the least of all the steadfast love and all the faithfulness that you have shown to your servant, for with only my staff I crossed this Jordan; and now I have become two companies. 11Deliver me, please, from the hand of my brother, from the hand of Esau, for I am afraid of him; he may come and kill us all, the mothers with the children. 12Yet you have said, 'I will surely do you good, and make your offspring as the sand of the sea, which cannot be counted because of their number.' "

13 So he spent that night there, and from what he had with him he took a present for his brother Esau, 14two hundred female goats and twenty male goats, two hundred ewes and twenty rams, 15thirty milch camels and their colts, forty cows and ten bulls, twenty female donkeys and ten male donkeys. 16These he delivered into the hand of his servants, every drove by itself, and said to his servants, "Pass on ahead of me, and put a space between drove and drove." 17He instructed the foremost, "When Esau my brother meets you, and asks you, 'To whom do you belong? Where are you going? And whose are these ahead of you?' 18then you shall say, 'They belong to your servant Jacob; they are a present sent to my lord Esau; and moreover he is behind us.' " 19He likewise instructed the second and the third and all who followed the droves, "You shall say the same thing to Esau when you meet him, 20and you shall say, 'Moreover your servant Jacob is behind us.' " For he thought, "I may appease him with the present that goes

a Meaning of Heb uncertain   *b* Ch 32.1 in Heb
c Here taken to mean *Two camps*

ahead of me, and afterwards I shall see his face; perhaps he will accept me." ²¹ So the present passed on ahead of him; and he himself spent that night in the camp.

32.1–21: Jacob prepares to meet his brother Esau. After twenty years of separation, the reader recalls that the last words we heard from Esau were, "I will kill my brother Jacob" (27.41). Jacob's preparations to meet Esau exhibit great anxiety about whether Esau still carries this threat with him (v. 11). **1–2:** *Angels of God* again meet Jacob as he enters Canaan, just as the angels visited him when he left Canaan (28.12). Jacob names the place *Mahanaim*, "two camps," because it is *God's camp*. Bethel, "house of God," was the place name of the previous encounter with angels (28.19). **3–8:** Jacob sends gifts to appease his brother Esau. Jacob hears the ominous news that Esau is coming to meet him with an army of *four hundred men* (v. 6). Jacob has good reason to be *greatly afraid and distressed* (v. 7).

22 The same night he got up and took his two wives, his two maids, and his eleven children, and crossed the ford of the Jabbok. ²³ He took them and sent them across the stream, and likewise everything that he had. ²⁴ Jacob was left alone; and a man wrestled with him until daybreak. ²⁵ When the man saw that he did not prevail against Jacob, he struck him on the hip socket; and Jacob's hip was put out of joint as he wrestled with him. ²⁶ Then he said, "Let me go, for the day is breaking." But Jacob said, "I will not let you go, unless you bless me." ²⁷ So he said to him, "What is your name?" And he said, "Jacob." ²⁸ Then the man^a said, "You shall no longer be called Jacob, but Israel,^b for you have striven with God and with humans,^c and have prevailed." ²⁹ Then Jacob asked him, "Please tell me your name." But he said, "Why is it that you ask my name?" And there he blessed him. ³⁰ So Jacob called the place Peniel,^d saying, "For I have seen God face to face, and yet my life is preserved." ³¹ The sun rose upon him as he passed Penuel, limping because of his hip. ³² Therefore to this day the Israelites do not eat the thigh muscle that is on the hip socket, because he struck Jacob on the hip socket at the thigh muscle.

32.22–32: Jacob wrestles with God. This is an ancient story that has played several roles in its long history. The story explained the reason for the place name, *Peniel* ("Face of God," v. 30). It also explained the reason for the dietary law that Israelites do not eat the thigh muscle of any animal (v. 32) and the reason for the change of Jacob's name to Israel (v. 28). Jacob's life as an individual becomes a portrait of Israel's life as a nation. Israel as a people will struggle with God and limp away with a blessing. **24:** The sudden and unexplained appearance of *a man* in the night suggests a mysterious or supernatural figure. **25:** Jacob was winning the wrestling match until he was crippled by a wrestler's trick that dislocated his hip. **28:** The identity of the "man" is now revealed: Jacob has *striven with God*. **30:** Jacob's experience is remarkable in light of a prevailing Old Testament tradition that no human can see *God face to face* and live (Ex 33.11–23; Judg 6.22–23).

33 Now Jacob looked up and saw Esau coming, and four hundred men with him. So he divided the children among Leah and Rachel and the two maids. ² He put the maids with their children in front, then Leah with her children, and Rachel and Joseph last of all. ³ He himself went on ahead of them, bowing himself to the ground seven times, until he came near his brother.

4 But Esau ran to meet him, and embraced him, and fell on his neck and kissed him, and they wept. ⁵ When Esau looked up and saw the women and children, he said, "Who are these with you?" Jacob said, "The children whom God has graciously given your servant." ⁶ Then the maids drew near, they and their children, and bowed down; ⁷ Leah likewise and her children drew near and bowed down; and finally Joseph and Rachel drew near, and they bowed down. ⁸ Esau said, "What do you mean by all this company that I met?" Jacob answered, "To find favor with my lord." ⁹ But Esau said, "I have enough, my brother; keep what you have for yourself." ¹⁰ Jacob said, "No, please; if I find favor with you, then accept my present from

a Heb *he*   b That is *The one who strives with God* or *God strives*   c Or *with divine and human beings*
d That is *The face of God*

my hand; for truly to see your face is like seeing the face of God—since you have received me with such favor. [11] Please accept my gift that is brought to you, because God has dealt graciously with me, and because I have everything I want." So he urged him, and he took it.

12 Then Esau said, "Let us journey on our way, and I will go alongside you." [13] But Jacob said to him, "My lord knows that the children are frail and that the flocks and herds, which are nursing, are a care to me; and if they are overdriven for one day, all the flocks will die. [14] Let my lord pass on ahead of his servant, and I will lead on slowly, according to the pace of the cattle that are before me and according to the pace of the children, until I come to my lord in Seir."

15 So Esau said, "Let me leave with you some of the people who are with me." But he said, "Why should my lord be so kind to me?" [16] So Esau returned that day on his way to Seir. [17] But Jacob journeyed to Succoth,[a] and built himself a house, and made booths for his cattle; therefore the place is called Succoth.

33.1–17: Jacob reconciles with Esau. 10: Jacob's words link his encounter with God in ch. 32 with his encounter with Esau: *To see your face is like seeing the face of God* (see 32.30). 11: Jacob's offer of a *gift* ("berakah") to Esau in effect returns the "blessing" ("berakah") Jacob had stolen from Esau twenty years earlier (27.36). 12–16: Although Jacob and Esau reconcile with one another, Jacob is still wary of his brother. Jacob tries diplomatically to keep a distance between himself and Esau, although Esau wants them to stay together. 17: *Succoth* means "booths" and is a name of a town just across the Jordan River and east of Canaan (Josh 13.27).

18 Jacob came safely to the city of Shechem, which is in the land of Canaan, on his way from Paddan-aram; and he camped before the city. [19] And from the sons of Hamor, Shechem's father, he bought for one hundred pieces of money[b] the plot of land on which he had pitched his tent. [20] There he erected an altar and called it El-Elohe-Israel.[c]

34 Now Dinah the daughter of Leah, whom she had borne to Jacob, went out to visit the women of the region. [2] When Shechem son of Hamor the Hivite, prince of the region, saw her, he seized her and lay with her by force. [3] And his soul was drawn to Dinah daughter of Jacob; he loved the girl, and spoke tenderly to her. [4] So Shechem spoke to his father Hamor, saying, "Get me this girl to be my wife."

5 Now Jacob heard that Shechem[d] had defiled his daughter Dinah; but his sons were with his cattle in the field, so Jacob held his peace until they came. [6] And Hamor the father of Shechem went out to Jacob to speak with him, [7] just as the sons of Jacob came in from the field. When they heard of it, the men were indignant and very angry, because he had committed an outrage in Israel by lying with Jacob's daughter, for such a thing ought not to be done.

8 But Hamor spoke with them, saying, "The heart of my son Shechem longs for your daughter; please give her to him in marriage. [9] Make marriages with us; give your daughters to us, and take our daughters for yourselves. [10] You shall live with us; and the land shall be open to you; live and trade in it, and get property in it." [11] Shechem also said to her father and to her brothers, "Let me find favor with you, and whatever you say to me I will give. [12] Put the marriage present and gift as high as you like, and I will give whatever you ask me; only give me the girl to be my wife."

13 The sons of Jacob answered Shechem and his father Hamor deceitfully, because he had defiled their sister Dinah. [14] They said to them, "We cannot do this thing, to give our sister to one who is uncircumcised, for that would be a disgrace to us. [15] Only on this condition will we consent to you: that you will become as we are and every male among you be circumcised. [16] Then we will give our daughters to you, and we will take your daughters for ourselves, and we will live among you and become one people. [17] But if

---

a That is *Booths*   b Heb *one hundred qesitah*
c That is *God, the God of Israel*   d Heb *he*

you will not listen to us and be circumcised, then we will take our daughter and be gone."

18 Their words pleased Hamor and Hamor's son Shechem. [19]And the young man did not delay to do the thing, because he was delighted with Jacob's daughter. Now he was the most honored of all his family. [20]So Hamor and his son Shechem came to the gate of their city and spoke to the men of their city, saying, [21]"These people are friendly with us; let them live in the land and trade in it, for the land is large enough for them; let us take their daughters in marriage, and let us give them our daughters. [22]Only on this condition will they agree to live among us, to become one people: that every male among us be circumcised as they are circumcised. [23]Will not their livestock, their property, and all their animals be ours? Only let us agree with them, and they will live among us." [24]And all who went out of the city gate heeded Hamor and his son Shechem; and every male was circumcised, all who went out of the gate of his city.

25 On the third day, when they were still in pain, two of the sons of Jacob, Simeon and Levi, Dinah's brothers, took their swords and came against the city unawares, and killed all the males. [26]They killed Hamor and his son Shechem with the sword, and took Dinah out of Shechem's house, and went away. [27]And the other sons of Jacob came upon the slain, and plundered the city, because their sister had been defiled. [28]They took their flocks and their herds, their donkeys, and whatever was in the city and in the field. [29]All their wealth, all their little ones and their wives, all that was in the houses, they captured and made their prey. [30]Then Jacob said to Simeon and Levi, "You have brought trouble on me by making me odious to the inhabitants of the land, the Canaanites and the Perizzites; my numbers are few, and if they gather themselves against me and attack me, I shall be destroyed, both I and my household." [31]But they said, "Should our sister be treated like a whore?"

33.18–34.31: The rape of Jacob's daughter, Dinah. This story of rape and revenge is the first example of violence in the interaction of Israelites and Canaanites.

Their relationships up to this point in Genesis have been cordial and peaceful. **33.18–19:** *Shechem* is both the name of the city and the name of the son of Hamor, the "prince of the region" (34.2). **20:** *El-Elohe-Israel* means "God, the God of Israel." The ancient divine name "El" appears elsewhere in Genesis, usually combined with another word: El Elyon (14.19), El Shaddai (17.1), El Olam (21.33), and El-bethel (35.7). **34.2–3:** The story reports that Shechem raped Dinah and then *loved* and *spoke tenderly to her*. Dinah's response or feelings are not given. **15:** To be *circumcised* involves cutting off the foreskin of the male penis. Circumcision* was a physical sign of a male's belonging to the covenant* people of Israel (17.9–14). **25–29:** The violence of the revenge (killing all males, taking all their possessions, and capturing their wives and children) seems excessive. That is especially true if the self-interests of the brothers rather than the interests of Dinah are being served. The story seems intentionally ambiguous at key points in order to draw the reader into wrestling with the moral dilemmas and issues raised by the narrative.* **26:** The reader is suddenly aware that Dinah has been staying in *Shechem's house*. Was she there because she wanted to be? Or was she held there by force? Again, we do not know Dinah's feelings. **30–31:** The ethical debate between Jacob (concerned with pragmatic realities) and his sons (concerned with moral principle) ends without resolution.

35 God said to Jacob, "Arise, go up to Bethel, and settle there. Make an altar there to the God who appeared to you when you fled from your brother Esau." [2]So Jacob said to his household and to all who were with him, "Put away the foreign gods that are among you, and purify yourselves, and change your clothes; [3]then come, let us go up to Bethel, that I may make an altar there to the God who answered me in the day of my distress and has been with me wherever I have gone." [4]So they gave to Jacob all the foreign gods that they had, and the rings that were in their ears; and Jacob hid them under the oak that was near Shechem.

5 As they journeyed, a terror from God fell upon the cities all around them, so that no one pursued them. [6]Jacob came to Luz (that is, Bethel), which is in the land of Canaan, he and all the people who were with

him, [7]and there he built an altar and called the place El-bethel,[a] because it was there that God had revealed himself to him when he fled from his brother. [8]And Deborah, Rebekah's nurse, died, and she was buried under an oak below Bethel. So it was called Allon-bacuth.[b]

[9] God appeared to Jacob again when he came from Paddan-aram, and he blessed him. [10]God said to him, "Your name is Jacob; no longer shall you be called Jacob, but Israel shall be your name." So he was called Israel. [11]God said to him, "I am God Almighty:[c] be fruitful and multiply; a nation and a company of nations shall come from you, and kings shall spring from you. [12]The land that I gave to Abraham and Isaac I will give to you, and I will give the land to your offspring after you." [13]Then God went up from him at the place where he had spoken with him. [14]Jacob set up a pillar in the place where he had spoken with him, a pillar of stone; and he poured out a drink offering on it, and poured oil on it. [15]So Jacob called the place where God had spoken with him Bethel.

35.1–15: Jacob returns to Bethel. After many years, Jacob returns to Bethel where God had first encountered and blessed Jacob when he was fleeing from his brother Esau (28.10–22). **2:** *The foreign gods that are among you* probably included the household gods or idols that Rachel had stolen from her father Laban when they fled from him (31.19). **7:** *El-bethel* means "God of Bethel" or "God of the house of God." *God had revealed himself* to Jacob there at Bethel in 28.10–22. **14:** As elsewhere in Genesis (28.18), setting up *a pillar of stone* and *pouring oil on it* marks the location as a holy site at which the deity was worshipped. **15:** *Bethel* means "house of God."

[16] Then they journeyed from Bethel; and when they were still some distance from Ephrath, Rachel was in childbirth, and she had hard labor. [17]When she was in her hard labor, the midwife said to her, "Do not be afraid; for now you will have another son." [18]As her soul was departing (for she died), she named him Ben-oni;[d] but his father called him Benjamin.[e] [19]So Rachel died, and she was buried on the way to Ephrath

(that is, Bethlehem), [20]and Jacob set up a pillar at her grave; it is the pillar of Rachel's tomb, which is there to this day. [21]Israel journeyed on, and pitched his tent beyond the tower of Eder.

[22] While Israel lived in that land, Reuben went and lay with Bilhah his father's concubine; and Israel heard of it.

Now the sons of Jacob were twelve. [23]The sons of Leah: Reuben (Jacob's firstborn), Simeon, Levi, Judah, Issachar, and Zebulun. [24]The sons of Rachel: Joseph and Benjamin. [25]The sons of Bilhah, Rachel's maid: Dan and Naphtali. [26]The sons of Zilpah, Leah's maid: Gad and Asher. These were the sons of Jacob who were born to him in Paddan-aram.

[27] Jacob came to his father Isaac at Mamre, or Kiriath-arba (that is, Hebron), where Abraham and Isaac had resided as aliens. [28]Now the days of Isaac were one hundred eighty years. [29]And Isaac breathed his last; he died and was gathered to his people, old and full of days; and his sons Esau and Jacob buried him.

35.16–29: Benjamin is born and Rachel dies. 18: *Ben-oni* means "son of my sorrow," reflecting Rachel's suffering in childbirth. Jacob changes the name slightly to *Benjamin,* "son of the right hand." Sitting at the right hand of a ruler or elder is a position of honor. Benjamin is the son of Jacob's favored wife (29.30) and thus Jacob's favored son (see 42.36–38). **22:** Jacob's firstborn son Reuben had sexual relations *with Bilhah his father's concubine,** a grievous offense. This incident is the reason Reuben's status as firstborn son will be diminished in Jacob's blessing of his twelve sons (49.3–4). **27–29:** The last days of Isaac provide an occasion for reconciliation between Jacob and his father (v. 27; see 27.35). The two sons, Esau and Jacob, join together in burying their father, Isaac (v. 29), just as earlier the brothers Isaac and Ishmael had joined together to bury their father, Abraham (25.9).

36 These are the <u>descendants of Esau</u> (that is, Edom). [2]Esau took his wives from the Canaanites: Adah daughter of Elon

---

a That is *God of Bethel*   b That is *Oak of weeping*
c Traditional rendering of Heb *El Shaddai*   d That is *Son of my sorrow*   e That is *Son of the right hand* or *Son of the South*

the Hittite, Oholibamah daughter of Anah son*a* of Zibeon the Hivite, ³and <u>Basemath, Ishmael's daughter</u>, sister of Nebaioth. ⁴Adah bore Eliphaz to Esau; Basemath bore Reuel; ⁵and Oholibamah bore Jeush, Jalam, and Korah. These are the sons of Esau who were born to him in the land of Canaan.

6 Then Esau took his wives, his sons, his daughters, and all the members of his household, his cattle, all his livestock, and all the property he had acquired in the land of Canaan; and he moved to a land some distance from his brother Jacob. ⁷For their possessions were too great for them to live together; the land where they were staying could not support them because of their livestock. ⁸So Esau settled in the hill country of Seir; Esau is Edom.

9 These are the descendants of Esau, ancestor of the Edomites, in the hill country of Seir. ¹⁰These are the names of Esau's sons: Eliphaz son of Adah the wife of Esau; Reuel, the son of Esau's wife Basemath. ¹¹The sons of Eliphaz were Teman, Omar, Zepho, Gatam, and Kenaz. ¹²(Timna was a concubine of Eliphaz, Esau's son; she bore Amalek to Eliphaz.) These were the sons of Adah, Esau's wife. ¹³These were the sons of Reuel: Nahath, Zerah, Shammah, and Mizzah. These were the sons of Esau's wife, Basemath. ¹⁴These were the sons of Esau's wife Oholibamah, daughter of Anah son*b* of Zibeon: she bore to Esau Jeush, Jalam, and Korah.

15 These are the clans*c* of the sons of Esau. The sons of Eliphaz the firstborn of Esau: the clans*c* Teman, Omar, Zepho, Kenaz, ¹⁶Korah, Gatam, and Amalek; these are the clans*c* of Eliphaz in the land of Edom; they are the sons of Adah. ¹⁷These are the sons of Esau's son Reuel: the clans*c* Nahath, Zerah, Shammah, and Mizzah; these are the clans*c* of Reuel in the land of Edom; they are the sons of Esau's wife Basemath. ¹⁸These are the sons of Esau's wife Oholibamah: the clans*c* Jeush, Jalam, and Korah; these are the clans*c* born of Esau's wife Oholibamah, the daughter of Anah. ¹⁹These are the sons of Esau (that is, Edom), and these are their clans.*c*

20 These are the sons of Seir the Horite, the inhabitants of the land: Lotan, Shobal, Zibeon, Anah, ²¹Dishon, Ezer, and Dishan; these are the clans*c* of the Horites, the sons of Seir in the land of Edom. ²²The sons of Lotan were Hori and Heman; and Lotan's sister was Timna. ²³These are the sons of Shobal: Alvan, Manahath, Ebal, Shepho, and Onam. ²⁴These are the sons of Zibeon: Aiah and Anah; he is the Anah who found the springs*d* in the wilderness, as he pastured the donkeys of his father Zibeon. ²⁵These are the children of Anah: Dishon and Oholibamah daughter of Anah. ²⁶These are the sons of Dishon: Hemdan, Eshban, Ithran, and Cheran. ²⁷These are the sons of Ezer: Bilhan, Zaavan, and Akan. ²⁸These are the sons of Dishan: Uz and Aran. ²⁹These are the clans*c* of the Horites: the clans*c* Lotan, Shobal, Zibeon, Anah, ³⁰Dishon, Ezer, and Dishan; these are the clans*c* of the Horites, clan by clan*e* in the land of Seir.

31 These are the kings who reigned in the land of Edom, before any king reigned over the Israelites. ³²Bela son of Beor reigned in Edom, the name of his city being Dinhabah. ³³Bela died, and Jobab son of Zerah of Bozrah succeeded him as king. ³⁴Jobab died, and Husham of the land of the Temanites succeeded him as king. ³⁵Husham died, and Hadad son of Bedad, who defeated Midian in the country of Moab, succeeded him as king, the name of his city being Avith. ³⁶Hadad died, and Samlah of Masrekah succeeded him as king. ³⁷Samlah died, and Shaul of Rehoboth on the Euphrates succeeded him as king. ³⁸Shaul died, and Baal-hanan son of Achbor succeeded him as king. ³⁹Baal-hanan son of Achbor died, and Hadar succeeded him as king, the name of his city being Pau; his wife's name was Mehetabel, the daughter of Matred, daughter of Me-zahab.

40 These are the names of the clans*c* of Esau, according to their families and their localities by their names: the clans*c* Timna, Alvah, Jetheth, ⁴¹Oholibamah, Elah, Pinon, ⁴²Kenaz, Teman, Mibzar, ⁴³Magdiel, and Iram; these are the clans*c* of Edom (that is,

a Sam Gk Syr: Heb *daughter*   *b* Gk Syr: Heb *daughter*
c Or *chiefs*   *d* Meaning of Heb uncertain
e Or *chief by chief*

Esau, the father of Edom), according to their settlements in the land that they held.

36.1–43: Esau's descendants. The list here of Esau's descendants and the list of Jacob's twelve sons in 35.22–26 represent a partial fulfillment of the promises of many descendants made to Abraham (15.5), Isaac (26.4), and Jacob (28.14). **1:** Jacob's brother *Esau* is the ancestor of the nation of *Edom.* Edom lies just south and east of Canaan. The land of Canaan will later become the nation of Israel, whose ancestor is Jacob (25.23, 30). **31:** This list of *kings who reigned in the land of Edom* precedes the time of Israel's King David, who conquered and ruled over Edom (2 Sam 8.13–14).

THE STORY OF JOSEPH

Chs. 37–50: The story about Jacob's son, Joseph, is the longest continuous narrative* in Genesis. The story runs from ch. 37 to ch. 50. It is interrupted by an inserted story about Judah and Tamar in ch. 38, although even this story has thematic connections to the Joseph narrative. The Joseph story provides a fitting conclusion to the Genesis ancestor stories as the family grows larger to become the people or nation of Israel. The story also functions as a literary bridge to the events in Egypt in the book of Exodus. Joseph will be the first of the Israelites to be enslaved in Egypt and then rescued, a fate all Israel will eventually share.

37 Jacob settled in the land where his father had lived as an alien, the land of Canaan. ²This is the story of the family of Jacob.

Joseph, being seventeen years old, was shepherding the flock with his brothers; he was a helper to the sons of Bilhah and Zilpah, his father's wives; and Joseph brought a bad report of them to their father. ³Now Israel loved Joseph more than any other of his children, because he was the son of his old age; and he had made him a long robe with sleeves.ᵃ ⁴But when his brothers saw that their father loved him more than all his brothers, they hated him, and could not speak peaceably to him.

5 Once Joseph had a dream, and when he told it to his brothers, they hated him even more. ⁶He said to them, "Listen to this dream that I dreamed. ⁷There we were,

binding sheaves in the field. Suddenly my sheaf rose and stood upright; then your sheaves gathered around it, and bowed down to my sheaf." ⁸His brothers said to him, "Are you indeed to reign over us? Are you indeed to have dominion over us?" So they hated him even more because of his dreams and his words.

9 He had another dream, and told it to his brothers, saying, "Look, I have had another dream: the sun, the moon, and eleven stars were bowing down to me." ¹⁰But when he told it to his father and to his brothers, his father rebuked him, and said to him, "What kind of dream is this that you have had? Shall we indeed come, I and your mother and your brothers, and bow to the ground before you?" ¹¹So his brothers were jealous of him, but his father kept the matter in mind.

12 Now his brothers went to pasture their father's flock near Shechem. ¹³And Israel said to Joseph, "Are not your brothers pasturing the flock at Shechem? Come, I will send you to them." He answered, "Here I am." ¹⁴So he said to him, "Go now, see if it is well with your brothers and with the flock; and bring word back to me." So he sent him from the valley of Hebron.

He came to Shechem, ¹⁵and a man found him wandering in the fields; the man asked him, "What are you seeking?" ¹⁶"I am seeking my brothers," he said; "tell me, please, where they are pasturing the flock." ¹⁷The man said, "They have gone away, for I heard them say, 'Let us go to Dothan.' " So Joseph went after his brothers, and found them at Dothan. ¹⁸They saw him from a distance, and before he came near to them, they conspired to kill him. ¹⁹They said to one another, "Here comes this dreamer. ²⁰Come now, let us kill him and throw him into one of the pits; then we shall say that a wild animal has devoured him, and we shall see what will become of his dreams." ²¹But when Reuben heard it, he delivered him out of their hands, saying, "Let us not take his life." ²²Reuben said to them, "Shed no blood; throw him into this pit here in the

---

ᵃ Traditional rendering (compare Gk): *a coat of many colors;* Meaning of Heb uncertain

wilderness, but lay no hand on him"—that he might rescue him out of their hand and restore him to his father. 23So when Joseph came to his brothers, they stripped him of his robe, the long robe with sleeves*a* that he wore; 24and they took him and threw him into a pit. The pit was empty; there was no water in it.

25 Then they sat down to eat; and looking up they saw a caravan of Ishmaelites coming from Gilead, with their camels carrying gum, balm, and resin, on their way to carry it down to Egypt. 26Then Judah said to his brothers, "What profit is it if we kill our brother and conceal his blood? 27Come, let us sell him to the Ishmaelites, and not lay our hands on him, for he is our brother, our own flesh." And his brothers agreed. 28When some Midianite traders passed by, they drew Joseph up, lifting him out of the pit, and sold him to the Ishmaelites for twenty pieces of silver. And they took Joseph to Egypt.

29 When Reuben returned to the pit and saw that Joseph was not in the pit, he tore his clothes. 30He returned to his brothers, and said, "The boy is gone; and I, where can I turn?" 31Then they took Joseph's robe, slaughtered a goat, and dipped the robe in the blood. 32They had the long robe with sleeves*a* taken to their father, and they said, "This we have found; see now whether it is your son's robe or not." 33He recognized it, and said, "It is my son's robe! A wild animal has devoured him; Joseph is without doubt torn to pieces." 34Then Jacob tore his garments, and put sackcloth on his loins, and mourned for his son many days. 35All his sons and all his daughters sought to comfort him; but he refused to be comforted, and said, "No, I shall go down to Sheol to my son, mourning." Thus his father bewailed him. 36Meanwhile the Midianites had sold him in Egypt to Potiphar, one of Pharaoh's officials, the captain of the guard.

voring of one child over another and the conflict that results is an important theme in Genesis (4.4–5; 21.10; 25.28). *A long robe with sleeves,* since it is impossible to do manual labor while wearing it, suggests a life of leisure for Joseph, who seems prone to sleep and dreams (vv. 5, 9). **5–11:** Dreams will play a role throughout the Joseph story. Each of the three dream sequences (37.5–11; 40.5–23; 41.1–36) contains two paired dreams. The story assumes that these dreams allow one to know the future, which is part of a divine plan. Jacob had some experience with dreams and divine plans in the episode at Bethel (28.10–22), so he *kept the matter in mind* (v. 11). *Binding sheaves* refers to tying newly cut stalks of grain into bundles; these stand in the field for a time to dry (v. 7). **15–28:** The changing of Joseph's clothes, here the stripping of his robe, will mark major transitions in his life throughout the story. Joseph moves from being a favored son to a hired slave. Joseph's brothers first plot to kill him, but *Reuben* (v. 21) and *Judah* (vv. 26–27) intervene to restrain them. Instead, they sell Joseph as a slave to some passing *Midianite traders* and *Ishmaelites.* Both of these groups were descended from Abraham and one of two women slaves, Hagar (16.15) and Keturah (25.1–4). Those whom Israel had formerly enslaved turn around and enslave an Israelite, Joseph. **33:** The brothers show the bloodied robe to their father Jacob without explanation. Jacob himself draws the conclusion that *a wild animal has devoured* Joseph. **34:** Jacob *tore his garments* and wore coarse *sackcloth,** both traditional acts of anguish and mourning the dead (v. 29). **35:** *Sheol** is a dry, dusty pit under the earth where the dead go at the end of their earthly existence.

~~~~~~~~~~~~~~~~~~~~~~~~~~~~~~~~~~~~~

38 It happened at that time that Judah went down from his brothers and settled near a certain Adullamite whose name was Hirah. 2There Judah saw the daughter of a certain Canaanite whose name was Shua; he married her and went in to her. 3She conceived and bore a son; and he named him Er. 4Again she conceived and bore a son whom she named Onan. 5Yet again she bore a son, and she named him Shelah. She*b* was in Chezib when she bore him. 6Judah took a wife for Er his firstborn; her name was Tamar. 7But Er, Judah's firstborn, was wicked in the sight of the LORD,

---

37.1–36: Joseph's dreams and his brothers' schemes. 2: *This is the story of the family of* is a formula that literally in Hebrew reads, "These are the generations of." This formula occurs throughout Genesis as a heading for major new sections; examples include Gen 2.4; 6.9; 10.1; 11.27; 25.19. **3–4:** The fa-

a See note on 37.3   *b* Gk: Heb He

and the LORD put him to death. 8Then Judah said to Onan, "Go in to your brother's wife and perform the duty of a brother-in-law to her; raise up offspring for your brother." 9But since Onan knew that the offspring would not be his, he spilled his semen on the ground whenever he went in to his brother's wife, so that he would not give offspring to his brother. 10What he did was displeasing in the sight of the LORD, and he put him to death also. 11Then Judah said to his daughter-in-law Tamar, "Remain a widow in your father's house until my son Shelah grows up"—for he feared that he too would die, like his brothers. So Tamar went to live in her father's house.

12 In course of time the wife of Judah, Shua's daughter, died; when Judah's time of mourning was over,ᵃ he went up to Timnah to his sheepshearers, he and his friend Hirah the Adullamite. 13When Tamar was told, "Your father-in-law is going up to Timnah to shear his sheep," 14she put off her widow's garments, put on a veil, wrapped herself up, and sat down at the entrance to Enaim, which is on the road to Timnah. She saw that Shelah was grown up, yet she had not been given to him in marriage. 15When Judah saw her, he thought her to be a prostitute, for she had covered her face. 16He went over to her at the roadside, and said, "Come, let me come in to you," for he did not know that she was his daughter-in-law. She said, "What will you give me, that you may come in to me?" 17He answered, "I will send you a kid from the flock." And she said, "Only if you give me a pledge, until you send it." 18He said, "What pledge shall I give you?" She replied, "Your signet and your cord, and the staff that is in your hand." So he gave them to her, and went in to her, and she conceived by him. 19Then she got up and went away, and taking off her veil she put on the garments of her widowhood.

20 When Judah sent the kid by his friend the Adullamite, to recover the pledge from the woman, he could not find her. 21He asked the townspeople, "Where is the temple prostitute who was at Enaim by the wayside?" But they said, "No prostitute has been here." 22So he returned to Judah, and said,

"I have not found her; moreover the towns-people said, 'No prostitute has been here.' " 23Judah replied, "Let her keep the things as her own, otherwise we will be laughed at; you see, I sent this kid, and you could not find her."

24 About three months later Judah was told, "Your daughter-in-law Tamar has played the whore; moreover she is pregnant as a result of whoredom." And Judah said, "Bring her out, and let her be burned." 25As she was being brought out, she sent word to her father-in-law, "It was the owner of these who made me pregnant." And she said, "Take note, please, whose these are, the signet and the cord and the staff." 26Then Judah acknowledged them and said, "She is more in the right than I, since I did not give her to my son Shelah." And he did not lie with her again.

27 When the time of her delivery came, there were twins in her womb. 28While she was in labor, one put out a hand; and the midwife took and bound on his hand a crimson thread, saying, "This one came out first." 29But just then he drew back his hand, and out came his brother; and she said, "What a breach you have made for yourself!" Therefore he was named Perez.ᵇ 30Afterward his brother came out with the crimson thread on his hand; and he was named Zerah.ᶜ

38.1–30: Tamar and Judah. This story interrupts the Joseph narrative* which runs from ch. 37 to ch. 50. However, some of its themes and images are related to images and themes in the larger Joseph narrative. Examples include the function of the goat (37.31 and 38.17, 20), recognizing and deceiving with clothes (37.31–33 and 38.13–17, 26), and irregular sexual activity (38.14–18 and 39.7–18). The climax* of the Tamar-Judah story is the birth of Perez and Zerah. Perez becomes an ancestor of Israel's great King David (Ruth 4.18–22). The long road of the divine promise to David included this irregular detour through Tamar and Judah. This irregularity ties in with the larger theme of the Joseph story as a whole: God manages to bless Joseph and his brothers in spite of and through the many detours of sibling rivalry, deception, slavery, im-

a Heb when Judah was comforted   b That is A breach
c That is Brightness; perhaps alluding to the crimson thread

prisonment, and famine. **7:** The story does not explain the way in which Er was *wicked* nor precisely how *the LORD put him to death*. The details are not necessary to the plot. **8:** *The duty of a brother-in-law* involves the custom of a levirate marriage.* The levirate obligation requires the brother of a married man who has died childless to have sexual intercourse with the dead man's wife. The brother must do so until she becomes pregnant and has a child who will carry on the dead man's name (Deut 25.5–10). **9–10:** *Onan spilled his semen on the ground. . . . What he did was displeasing.* This is not meant as a generalized judgment against masturbation or birth control. It involves only a specialized case of failure to fulfill the levirate obligation. **11:** Judah has no intention of allowing Shelah to perform the levirate duty of a brother-in-law with Tamar. He apparently assumes association with Tamar somehow caused the death of his other sons. He does not want the same to happen to his only remaining son, Shelah (v. 14). **14:** In light of Tamar's deception and Judah's blindness to what is actually going on, the meanings of the place names are significant. *Entrance to Enaim* means "opening of the eyes." *Timnah* means "conceal." **16:** *Let me come in to you* is a request to have sexual intercourse. **18:** *The signet* was a ring with a distinctive design or stamp which could be used as a personal signature on official or commercial documents. It was often tied to a *cord* and worn around the neck. The *staff* was a walking stick, often with a distinctive family emblem carved on it. The modern-day equivalent of your signet, cord, and staff would be your driver's license and all your credit cards. **21–22:** Judah's messenger asks for the *temple prostitute* ("kedeshah," literally "holy woman," v. 21). The story assumes the presence of prostitutes associated with fertility rituals at Canaanite temples. The term "temple prostitute" is more dignified than the term for an ordinary *prostitute* ("zonah," v. 22). **28–30:** The twin boys repeat the experience of the twins Jacob and Esau. The second-born son comes out ahead of the first-born son (25.22–24). The name *Perez* means "breach" or "breaking forth" out of the womb ahead of his older brother. *Zerah* means "brightness," perhaps in reference to the bright red or crimson thread. Perez is an ancestor of the great King David (Ruth 4.18–22). Like Perez, David was also the youngest among his brothers (1 Sam 16.1–13).

39 Now Joseph was taken down to Egypt, and Potiphar, an officer of Pharaoh, the captain of the guard, an Egyptian, bought him from the Ishmaelites who had brought him down there. ²The LORD was with Joseph, and he became a successful man; he was in the house of his Egyptian master. ³His master saw that the LORD was with him, and that the LORD caused all that he did to prosper in his hands. ⁴So Joseph found favor in his sight and attended him; he made him overseer of his house and put him in charge of all that he had. ⁵From the time that he made him overseer in his house and over all that he had, the LORD blessed the Egyptian's house for Joseph's sake; the blessing of the LORD was on all that he had, in house and field. ⁶So he left all that he had in Joseph's charge; and, with him there, he had no concern for anything but the food that he ate.

Now Joseph was handsome and good-looking. ⁷And after a time his master's wife cast her eyes on Joseph and said, "Lie with me." ⁸But he refused and said to his master's wife, "Look, with me here, my master has no concern about anything in the house, and he has put everything that he has in my hand. ⁹He is not greater in this house than I am, nor has he kept back anything from me except yourself, because you are his wife. How then could I do this great wickedness, and sin against God?" ¹⁰And although she spoke to Joseph day after day, he would not consent to lie beside her or to be with her. ¹¹One day, however, when he went into the house to do his work, and while no one else was in the house, ¹²she caught hold of his garment, saying, "Lie with me!" But he left his garment in her hand, and fled and ran outside. ¹³When she saw that he had left his garment in her hand and had fled outside, ¹⁴she called out to the members of her household and said to them, "See, my husband*a* has brought among us a Hebrew to insult us! He came in to me to lie with me, and I cried out with a loud voice; ¹⁵and when he heard me raise my voice and cry out, he left his garment beside me, and fled outside." ¹⁶Then she kept his garment by her until his master came home, ¹⁷and she told him the same story, saying, "The Hebrew servant, whom

a Heb *he*

you have brought among us, came in to me to insult me; [18]but as soon as I raised my voice and cried out, he left his garment beside me, and fled outside."

19 When his master heard the words that his wife spoke to him, saying, "This is the way your servant treated me," he became enraged. [20]And Joseph's master took him and put him into the prison, the place where the king's prisoners were confined; he remained there in prison. [21]But the LORD was with Joseph and showed him steadfast love; he gave him favor in the sight of the chief jailer. [22]The chief jailer committed to Joseph's care all the prisoners who were in the prison, and whatever was done there, he was the one who did it. [23]The chief jailer paid no heed to anything that was in Joseph's care, because the LORD was with him; and whatever he did, the LORD made it prosper.

39.1–23: Joseph and Potiphar's wife. The story of Joseph resumes after the interlude with Tamar and Judah. **1:** *Pharaoh* is the title for the king of Egypt. **2:** The refrain *the LORD was with Joseph* begins and concludes this episode (vv. 21, 23). **7–20:** Some parallels exist between this scene and an ancient Egyptian story entitled "A Tale of Two Brothers." A man resists the sexual invitations of his brother's wife but then is falsely accused.

40 Some time after this, the cupbearer of the king of Egypt and his baker offended their lord the king of Egypt. [2]Pharaoh was angry with his two officers, the chief cupbearer and the chief baker, [3]and he put them in custody in the house of the captain of the guard, in the prison where Joseph was confined. [4]The captain of the guard charged Joseph with them, and he waited on them; and they continued for some time in custody. [5]One night they both dreamed—the cupbearer and the baker of the king of Egypt, who were confined in the prison—each his own dream, and each dream with its own meaning. [6]When Joseph came to them in the morning, he saw that they were troubled. [7]So he asked Pharaoh's officers, who were with him in custody in his master's house, "Why are your faces downcast today?" [8]They said to him, "We have had dreams, and there is no one to interpret them." And Joseph said to them, "Do not interpretations belong to God? Please tell them to me."

9 So the chief cupbearer told his dream to Joseph, and said to him, "In my dream there was a vine before me, [10]and on the vine there were three branches. As soon as it budded, its blossoms came out and the clusters ripened into grapes. [11]Pharaoh's cup was in my hand; and I took the grapes and pressed them into Pharaoh's cup, and placed the cup in Pharaoh's hand." [12]Then Joseph said to him, "This is its interpretation: the three branches are three days; [13]within three days Pharaoh will lift up your head and restore you to your office; and you shall place Pharaoh's cup in his hand, just as you used to do when you were his cupbearer. [14]But remember me when it is well with you; please do me the kindness to make mention of me to Pharaoh, and so get me out of this place. [15]For in fact I was stolen out of the land of the Hebrews; and here also I have done nothing that they should have put me into the dungeon."

16 When the chief baker saw that the interpretation was favorable, he said to Joseph, "I also had a dream: there were three cake baskets on my head, [17]and in the uppermost basket there were all sorts of baked food for Pharaoh, but the birds were eating it out of the basket on my head." [18]And Joseph answered, "This is its interpretation: the three baskets are three days; [19]within three days Pharaoh will lift up your head—from you!—and hang you on a pole; and the birds will eat the flesh from you."

20 On the third day, which was Pharaoh's birthday, he made a feast for all his servants, and lifted up the head of the chief cupbearer and the head of the chief baker among his servants. [21]He restored the chief cupbearer to his cupbearing, and he placed the cup in Pharaoh's hand; [22]but the chief baker he hanged, just as Joseph had interpreted to them. [23]Yet the chief cupbearer did not remember Joseph, but forgot him.

40.1–23: Joseph interprets the dreams of two prisoners. 5: This is the second of three dream sequences in the Joseph narrative* (37.5–11; 40.5–23; 41.1–36).

The dreams always occur in pairs, here with quite different futures predicted. Joseph shifts his role from the dreamer of dreams to an interpreter of others' dreams. **13:** The phrase *Pharaoh will lift up your head* has a positive meaning of exaltation for the cupbearer. The same phrase in v. 19 has a very negative meaning of execution by hanging for the baker (vv. 20–22).

41 After two whole years, Pharaoh dreamed that he was standing by the Nile, 2and there came up out of the Nile seven sleek and fat cows, and they grazed in the reed grass. 3Then seven other cows, ugly and thin, came up out of the Nile after them, and stood by the other cows on the bank of the Nile. 4The ugly and thin cows ate up the seven sleek and fat cows. And Pharaoh awoke. 5Then he fell asleep and dreamed a second time; seven ears of grain, plump and good, were growing on one stalk. 6Then seven ears, thin and blighted by the east wind, sprouted after them. 7The thin ears swallowed up the seven plump and full ears. Pharaoh awoke, and it was a dream. 8In the morning his spirit was troubled; so he sent and called for all the magicians of Egypt and all its wise men. Pharaoh told them his dreams, but there was no one who could interpret them to Pharaoh.

9 Then the chief cupbearer said to Pharaoh, "I remember my faults today. 10Once Pharaoh was angry with his servants, and put me and the chief baker in custody in the house of the captain of the guard. 11We dreamed on the same night, he and I, each having a dream with its own meaning. 12A young Hebrew was there with us, a servant of the captain of the guard. When we told him, he interpreted our dreams to us, giving an interpretation to each according to his dream. 13As he interpreted to us, so it turned out; I was restored to my office, and the baker was hanged."

14 Then Pharaoh sent for Joseph, and he was hurriedly brought out of the dungeon. When he had shaved himself and changed his clothes, he came in before Pharaoh. 15And Pharaoh said to Joseph, "I have had a dream, and there is no one who can interpret it. I have heard it said of you that when you hear a dream you can interpret it." 16Joseph answered Pharaoh, "It is not I; God will give Pharaoh a favorable answer." 17Then Pharaoh said to Joseph, "In my dream I was standing on the banks of the Nile; 18and seven cows, fat and sleek, came up out of the Nile and fed in the reed grass. 19Then seven other cows came up after them, poor, very ugly, and thin. Never had I seen such ugly ones in all the land of Egypt. 20The thin and ugly cows ate up the first seven fat cows, 21but when they had eaten them no one would have known that they had done so, for they were still as ugly as before. Then I awoke. 22I fell asleep a second time*a* and I saw in my dream seven ears of grain, full and good, growing on one stalk, 23and seven ears, withered, thin, and blighted by the east wind, sprouting after them; 24and the thin ears swallowed up the seven good ears. But when I told it to the magicians, there was no one who could explain it to me."

25 Then Joseph said to Pharaoh, "Pharaoh's dreams are one and the same; God has revealed to Pharaoh what he is about to do. 26The seven good cows are seven years, and the seven good ears are seven years; the dreams are one. 27The seven lean and ugly cows that came up after them are seven years, as are the seven empty ears blighted by the east wind. They are seven years of famine. 28It is as I told Pharaoh; God has shown to Pharaoh what he is about to do. 29There will come seven years of great plenty throughout all the land of Egypt. 30After them there will arise seven years of famine, and all the plenty will be forgotten in the land of Egypt; the famine will consume the land. 31The plenty will no longer be known in the land because of the famine that will follow, for it will be very grievous. 32And the doubling of Pharaoh's dream means that the thing is fixed by God, and God will shortly bring it about. 33Now therefore let Pharaoh select a man who is discerning and wise, and set him over the land of Egypt. 34Let Pharaoh proceed to appoint overseers over the land, and take one-fifth of the produce of the land of Egypt during the seven plenteous years. 35Let them gather all the food of these

a Gk Syr Vg: Heb lacks *I fell asleep a second time*

good years that are coming, and lay up grain under the authority of Pharaoh for food in the cities, and let them keep it. ³⁶That food shall be a reserve for the land against the seven years of famine that are to befall the land of Egypt, so that the land may not perish through the famine."

37 The proposal pleased Pharaoh and all his servants. ³⁸Pharaoh said to his servants, "Can we find anyone else like this—one in whom is the spirit of God?" ³⁹So Pharaoh said to Joseph, "Since God has shown you all this, there is no one so discerning and wise as you. ⁴⁰You shall be over my house, and all my people shall order themselves as you command; only with regard to the throne will I be greater than you." ⁴¹And Pharaoh said to Joseph, "See, I have set you over all the land of Egypt." ⁴²Removing his signet ring from his hand, Pharaoh put it on Joseph's hand; he arrayed him in garments of fine linen, and put a gold chain around his neck. ⁴³He had him ride in the chariot of his second-in-command; and they cried out in front of him, "Bow the knee!"ᵃ Thus he set him over all the land of Egypt. ⁴⁴Moreover Pharaoh said to Joseph, "I am Pharaoh, and without your consent no one shall lift up hand or foot in all the land of Egypt." ⁴⁵Pharaoh gave Joseph the name Zaphenath-paneah; and he gave him Asenath daughter of Potiphera, priest of On, as his wife. Thus Joseph gained authority over the land of Egypt.

46 Joseph was thirty years old when he entered the service of Pharaoh king of Egypt. And Joseph went out from the presence of Pharaoh, and went through all the land of Egypt. ⁴⁷During the seven plenteous years the earth produced abundantly. ⁴⁸He gathered up all the food of the seven years when there was plentyᵇ in the land of Egypt, and stored up food in the cities; he stored up in every city the food from the fields around it. ⁴⁹So Joseph stored up grain in such abundance—like the sand of the sea—that he stopped measuring it; it was beyond measure.

50 Before the years of famine came, Joseph had two sons, whom Asenath daughter of Potiphera, priest of On, bore to him. ⁵¹Joseph named the firstborn Manasseh,ᶜ "For,"

he said, "God has made me forget all my hardship and all my father's house." ⁵²The second he named Ephraim,ᵈ "For God has made me fruitful in the land of my misfortunes."

53 The seven years of plenty that prevailed in the land of Egypt came to an end; ⁵⁴and the seven years of famine began to come, just as Joseph had said. There was famine in every country, but throughout the land of Egypt there was bread. ⁵⁵When all the land of Egypt was famished, the people cried to Pharaoh for bread. Pharaoh said to all the Egyptians, "Go to Joseph; what he says to you, do." ⁵⁶And since the famine had spread over all the land, Joseph opened all the storehouses,ᵉ and sold to the Egyptians, for the famine was severe in the land of Egypt. ⁵⁷Moreover, all the world came to Joseph in Egypt to buy grain, because the famine became severe throughout the world.

41.1–57: Joseph interprets the dreams of Pharaoh. This story marks the key turning point in Joseph's fortunes: His ability as a dream interpreter elevates him to second in command of all Egypt. **1–7:** This is the third of the three dream sequences in the Joseph story. The dreams again appear as a pair, one about *cows* (vv. 2–4) and one about *grain* (vv. 5–7). The *Nile River* that runs through the otherwise dry landscape is Egypt's primary source of water, fertility, and life (vv. 1–4). **14:** Joseph's change of clothes marks major transitions in his life throughout the story (37.23; 39.12; 41.42). **32:** Joseph explains why all of the dreams have been doubled throughout the story (37.5–11; 40.5–23; 41.1–36). The doubling demonstrates that God has predetermined the events that are soon to happen. **42:** Pharaoh's *signet ring* has the Pharaoh's official stamp or "signature." He gives it to Joseph as a sign of his elevation to power as Pharaoh's representative. Joseph's new *garments of fine linen* mark yet another transition in his life (see v. 14). **51–52:** The two names of Joseph's sons, *Manasseh* ("making to forget") and *Ephraim* ("to be fruitful"), celebrate Jo-

---

a *Abrek*, apparently an Egyptian word similar in sound to the Hebrew word meaning *to kneel*   b Sam Gk: MT *the seven years that were*   c That is *Making to forget*
d From a Hebrew word meaning *to be fruitful*
e Gk Vg Compare Syr: Heb *opened all that was in* (or, *among*) *them*

seph's elevation out of slavery and prison. **57:** The material benefit of providing food in the midst of famine *throughout the world* is another example of the fulfillment of the promise to Abraham that his family would be a blessing "to all the families of the earth" (12.3). The verse also provides a transition to the famine in Canaan and explains why Joseph's brothers will come to Egypt seeking food.

42 When Jacob learned that there was grain in Egypt, he said to his sons, "Why do you keep looking at one another? ²I have heard," he said, "that there is grain in Egypt; go down and buy grain for us there, that we may live and not die." ³So ten of Joseph's brothers went down to buy grain in Egypt. ⁴But Jacob did not send Joseph's brother Benjamin with his brothers, for he feared that harm might come to him. ⁵Thus the sons of Israel were among the other people who came to buy grain, for the famine had reached the land of Canaan.

6 Now Joseph was governor over the land; it was he who sold to all the people of the land. And Joseph's brothers came and bowed themselves before him with their faces to the ground. ⁷When Joseph saw his brothers, he recognized them, but he treated them like strangers and spoke harshly to them. "Where do you come from?" he said. They said, "From the land of Canaan, to buy food." ⁸Although Joseph had recognized his brothers, they did not recognize him. ⁹Joseph also remembered the dreams that he had dreamed about them. He said to them, "You are spies; you have come to see the nakedness of the land!" ¹⁰They said to him, "No, my lord; your servants have come to buy food. ¹¹We are all sons of one man; we are honest men; your servants have never been spies." ¹²But he said to them, "No, you have come to see the nakedness of the land!" ¹³They said, "We, your servants, are twelve brothers, the sons of a certain man in the land of Canaan; the youngest, however, is now with our father, and one is no more." ¹⁴But Joseph said to them, "It is just as I have said to you; you are spies! ¹⁵Here is how you shall be tested: as Pharaoh lives, you shall not leave this place unless your youngest brother comes here! ¹⁶Let one of you go and bring your

brother, while the rest of you remain in prison, in order that your words may be tested, whether there is truth in you; or else, as Pharaoh lives, surely you are spies." ¹⁷And he put them all together in prison for three days.

18 On the third day Joseph said to them, "Do this and you will live, for I fear God: ¹⁹if you are honest men, let one of your brothers stay here where you are imprisoned. The rest of you shall go and carry grain for the famine of your households, ²⁰and bring your youngest brother to me. Thus your words will be verified, and you shall not die." And they agreed to do so. ²¹They said to one another, "Alas, we are paying the penalty for what we did to our brother; we saw his anguish when he pleaded with us, but we would not listen. That is why this anguish has come upon us." ²²Then Reuben answered them, "Did I not tell you not to wrong the boy? But you would not listen. So now there comes a reckoning for his blood." ²³They did not know that Joseph understood them, since he spoke with them through an interpreter. ²⁴He turned away from them and wept; then he returned and spoke to them. And he picked out Simeon and had him bound before their eyes. ²⁵Joseph then gave orders to fill their bags with grain, to return every man's money to his sack, and to give them provisions for their journey. This was done for them.

42.1–25: Joseph's brothers seek food in Egypt. 4: *Benjamin* is the youngest of Jacob's sons. He is the one full brother that Joseph has since Benjamin and Joseph are the only children of Jacob's favored wife, Rachel. **6:** Joseph's brothers unknowingly fulfill the prediction in Joseph's earlier two dreams in 37.5–11: They *bowed themselves before him.* **22:** *A reckoning for his blood* assumes a moral order in which murder or other wrongful actions will bring inevitable punishment (4.10; 9.5).

26 They loaded their donkeys with their grain, and departed. ²⁷When one of them opened his sack to give his donkey fodder at the lodging place, he saw his money at the top of the sack. ²⁸He said to his brothers, "My money has been put back; here it is in my sack!" At this they lost heart and turned

trembling to one another, saying, "What is this that God has done to us?"

29 When they came to their father Jacob in the land of Canaan, they told him all that had happened to them, saying, 30"The man, the lord of the land, spoke harshly to us, and charged us with spying on the land. 31But we said to him, 'We are honest men, we are not spies. 32We are twelve brothers, sons of our father; one is no more, and the youngest is now with our father in the land of Canaan.' 33Then the man, the lord of the land, said to us, 'By this I shall know that you are honest men: leave one of your brothers with me, take grain for the famine of your households, and go your way. 34Bring your youngest brother to me, and I shall know that you are not spies but honest men. Then I will release your brother to you, and you may trade in the land.' "

35 As they were emptying their sacks, there in each one's sack was his bag of money. When they and their father saw their bundles of money, they were dismayed. 36And their father Jacob said to them, "I am the one you have bereaved of children: Joseph is no more, and Simeon is no more, and now you would take Benjamin. All this has happened to me!" 37Then Reuben said to his father, "You may kill my two sons if I do not bring him back to you. Put him in my hands, and I will bring him back to you." 38But he said, "My son shall not go down with you, for his brother is dead, and he alone is left. If harm should come to him on the journey that you are to make, you would bring down my gray hairs with sorrow to Sheol."

42.38: *Sheol** is a dusty pit under the earth where all the dead go. Jacob does not want to die an old man (*my gray hairs*) consumed by sorrow.

43

Now the famine was severe in the land. 2And when they had eaten up the grain that they had brought from Egypt, their father said to them, "Go again, buy us a little more food." 3But Judah said to him, "The man solemnly warned us, saying, 'You shall not see my face unless your brother is with you.' 4If you will send our brother with us, we will go down and buy you food; 5but if you will not send him, we will not go down, for the man said to us, 'You shall not see my face, unless your brother is with you.' " 6Israel said, "Why did you treat me so badly as to tell the man that you had another brother?" 7They replied, "The man questioned us carefully about ourselves and our kindred, saying, 'Is your father still alive? Have you another brother?' What we told him was in answer to these questions. Could we in any way know that he would say, 'Bring your brother down'?" 8Then Judah said to his father Israel, "Send the boy with me, and let us be on our way, so that we may live and not die—you and we and also our little ones. 9I myself will be surety for him; you can hold me accountable for him. If I do not bring him back to you and set him before you, then let me bear the blame forever. 10If we had not delayed, we would now have returned twice."

11 Then their father Israel said to them, "If it must be so, then do this: take some of the choice fruits of the land in your bags, and carry them down as a present to the man— a little balm and a little honey, gum, resin, pistachio nuts, and almonds. 12Take double the money with you. Carry back with you the money that was returned in the top of your sacks; perhaps it was an oversight. 13Take your brother also, and be on your way again to the man; 14may God Almighty*a* grant you mercy before the man, so that he may send back your other brother and Benjamin. As for me, if I am bereaved of my children, I am bereaved." 15So the men took the present, and they took double the money with them, as well as Benjamin. Then they went on their way down to Egypt, and stood before Joseph.

16 When Joseph saw Benjamin with them, he said to the steward of his house, "Bring the men into the house, and slaughter an animal and make ready, for the men are to dine with me at noon." 17The man did as Joseph said, and brought the men to Joseph's house. 18Now the men were afraid because they were brought to Joseph's house, and they said, "It is because of the money, replaced in our sacks the first time, that we

a Traditional rendering of Heb *El Shaddai*

have been brought in, so that he may have an opportunity to fall upon us, to make slaves of us and take our donkeys." ¹⁹So they went up to the steward of Joseph's house and spoke with him at the entrance to the house. ²⁰They said, "Oh, my lord, we came down the first time to buy food; ²¹and when we came to the lodging place we opened our sacks, and there was each one's money in the top of his sack, our money in full weight. So we have brought it back with us. ²²Moreover we have brought down with us additional money to buy food. We do not know who put our money in our sacks." ²³He replied, "Rest assured, do not be afraid; your God and the God of your father must have put treasure in your sacks for you; I received your money." Then he brought Simeon out to them. ²⁴When the steward[a] had brought the men into Joseph's house, and given them water, and they had washed their feet, and when he had given their donkeys fodder, ²⁵they made the present ready for Joseph's coming at noon, for they had heard that they would dine there.

26 When Joseph came home, they brought him the present that they had carried into the house, and bowed to the ground before him. ²⁷He inquired about their welfare, and said, "Is your father well, the old man of whom you spoke? Is he still alive?" ²⁸They said, "Your servant our father is well; he is still alive." And they bowed their heads and did obeisance. ²⁹Then he looked up and saw his brother Benjamin, his mother's son, and said, "Is this your youngest brother, of whom you spoke to me? God be gracious to you, my son!" ³⁰With that, Joseph hurried out, because he was overcome with affection for his brother, and he was about to weep. So he went into a private room and wept there. ³¹Then he washed his face and came out; and controlling himself he said, "Serve the meal." ³²They served him by himself, and them by themselves, and the Egyptians who ate with him by themselves, because the Egyptians could not eat with the Hebrews, for that is an abomination to the Egyptians. ³³When they were seated before him, the firstborn according to his birthright and the youngest according to his youth, the men looked at one another in amazement. ³⁴Portions were taken to them from Joseph's table, but Benjamin's portion was five times as much as any of theirs. So they drank and were merry with him.

43.1–34: Joseph's brothers return to Egypt with Benjamin. 8–9: Judah puts himself on the line and reassures his father Jacob concerning Benjamin's safe return. Judah's words prepare the reader for his later actions in 44.18–34. **23:** Their brother *Simeon* had been detained in their first journey to Egypt (42.19, 24). He is now freed to return to his brothers. **26:** The prediction of Joseph's earlier dreams is fulfilled a second time when Joseph's brothers *bowed to the ground before him* (37.5–11; 42.6). **29:** Joseph and Benjamin were the only sons of their mother, Rachel. Thus, they are full brothers. **33–34:** The order of honor is typically the firstborn as most honored and the youngest as least honored. But Benjamin as the youngest of the twelve brothers receives preferential treatment. This continues the important theme throughout Genesis of the favored younger son (20.10; 25.23; 37.3, 8).

44 Then he commanded the steward of his house, "Fill the men's sacks with food, as much as they can carry, and put each man's money in the top of his sack. ²Put my cup, the silver cup, in the top of the sack of the youngest, with his money for the grain." And he did as Joseph told him. ³As soon as the morning was light, the men were sent away with their donkeys. ⁴When they had gone only a short distance from the city, Joseph said to his steward, "Go, follow after the men; and when you overtake them, say to them, 'Why have you returned evil for good? Why have you stolen my silver cup?[b] ⁵Is it not from this that my lord drinks? Does he not indeed use it for divination? You have done wrong in doing this.' "

6 When he overtook them, he repeated these words to them. ⁷They said to him, "Why does my lord speak such words as these? Far be it from your servants that they should do such a thing! ⁸Look, the money that we found at the top of our sacks, we brought back to you from the land of Ca-

---

a Heb *the man* *b* Gk Compare Vg: Heb lacks *Why have you stolen my silver cup?*

naan; why then would we steal silver or gold from your lord's house? ⁹Should it be found with any one of your servants, let him die; moreover the rest of us will become my lord's slaves." ¹⁰He said, "Even so; in accordance with your words, let it be: he with whom it is found shall become my slave, but the rest of you shall go free." ¹¹Then each one quickly lowered his sack to the ground, and each opened his sack. ¹²He searched, beginning with the eldest and ending with the youngest; and the cup was found in Benjamin's sack. ¹³At this they tore their clothes. Then each one loaded his donkey, and they returned to the city.

14 Judah and his brothers came to Joseph's house while he was still there; and they fell to the ground before him. ¹⁵Joseph said to them, "What deed is this that you have done? Do you not know that one such as I can practice divination?" ¹⁶And Judah said, "What can we say to my lord? What can we speak? How can we clear ourselves? God has found out the guilt of your servants; here we are then, my lord's slaves, both we and also the one in whose possession the cup has been found." ¹⁷But he said, "Far be it from me that I should do so! Only the one in whose possession the cup was found shall be my slave; but as for you, go up in peace to your father."

18 Then Judah stepped up to him and said, "O my lord, let your servant please speak a word in my lord's ears, and do not be angry with your servant; for you are like Pharaoh himself. ¹⁹My lord asked his servants, saying, 'Have you a father or a brother?' ²⁰And we said to my lord, 'We have a father, an old man, and a young brother, the child of his old age. His brother is dead; he alone is left of his mother's children, and his father loves him.' ²¹Then you said to your servants, 'Bring him down to me, so that I may set my eyes on him.' ²²We said to my lord, 'The boy cannot leave his father, for if he should leave his father, his father would die.' ²³Then you said to your servants, 'Unless your youngest brother comes down with you, you shall see my face no more.' ²⁴When we went back to your servant my father we told him the words of my lord. ²⁵And when

our father said, 'Go again, buy us a little food,' ²⁶we said, 'We cannot go down. Only if our youngest brother goes with us, will we go down; for we cannot see the man's face unless our youngest brother is with us.' ²⁷Then your servant my father said to us, 'You know that my wife bore me two sons; ²⁸one left me, and I said, Surely he has been torn to pieces; and I have never seen him since. ²⁹If you take this one also from me, and harm comes to him, you will bring down my gray hairs in sorrow to Sheol.' ³⁰Now therefore, when I come to your servant my father and the boy is not with us, then, as his life is bound up in the boy's life, ³¹when he sees that the boy is not with us, he will die; and your servants will bring down the gray hairs of your servant our father with sorrow to Sheol. ³²For your servant became surety for the boy to my father, saying, 'If I do not bring him back to you, then I will bear the blame in the sight of my father all my life.' ³³Now therefore, please let your servant remain as a slave to my lord in place of the boy; and let the boy go back with his brothers. ³⁴For how can I go back to my father if the boy is not with me? I fear to see the suffering that would come upon my father."

44.1–34: Joseph puts his brothers to the test. 4: *Why have you returned evil for good?* This question sounds a theme central to the Joseph story as a whole. Joseph's words to his brothers in 50.20 summarize the theme of the interplay of good and evil. **5:** *Divination* is the skill of determining the divine will or plan for the future. This was apparently done by observing the effects created by certain objects placed in the water contained in the sacred *silver cup* (v. 4). **9:** The brothers' words unknowingly put Benjamin under the threat of death since the silver cup was planted in his sack (vv. 2, 12). **13:** *They tore their clothes,* a sign of intense anguish and grief. **14:** The story places *Judah* in the foreground as the leader of his brothers. He is about to play a key role as the hero in this scene. Joseph's earlier dreams in 37.5–11 are again fulfilled as the brothers *fell to the ground before him.* **16:** *Here we are then, my lord's slaves:* Those who once sold Joseph as a slave (37.28) offer themselves as slaves to Joseph. **17:** Joseph offers the other brothers the temptation to save themselves by sacrificing Benjamin. The test is a replay of the brothers' earlier decision to sacrifice their brother Joseph for their own benefit (37.28). **29, 31:** *Sheol** is the place of the dead. **33–34:** Judah offers himself *in place of the boy,* Benjamin. Judah's willingness to sacrifice himself to save Benjamin redeems his earlier involvement in the plot to sell Joseph as a slave (37.26).

45 Then Joseph could no longer control himself before all those who stood by him, and he cried out, "Send everyone away from me." So no one stayed with him when Joseph made himself known to his brothers. 2And he wept so loudly that the Egyptians heard it, and the household of Pharaoh heard it. 3Joseph said to his brothers, "I am Joseph. Is my father still alive?" But his brothers could not answer him, so dismayed were they at his presence.

4 Then Joseph said to his brothers, "Come closer to me." And they came closer. He said, "I am your brother, Joseph, whom you sold into Egypt. 5And now do not be distressed, or angry with yourselves, because you sold me here; for God sent me before you to preserve life. 6For the famine has been in the land these two years; and there are five more years in which there will be neither plowing nor harvest. 7God sent me before you to preserve for you a remnant on earth, and to keep alive for you many survivors. 8So it was not you who sent me here, but God; he has made me a father to Pharaoh, and lord of all his house and ruler over all the land of Egypt. 9Hurry and go up to my father and say to him, 'Thus says your son Joseph, God has made me lord of all Egypt; come down to me, do not delay. 10You shall settle in the land of Goshen, and you shall be near me, you and your children and your children's children, as well as your flocks, your herds, and all that you have. 11I will provide for you there—since there are five more years of famine to come—so that you and your household, and all that you have, will not come to poverty.' 12And now your eyes and the eyes of my brother Benjamin see that it is my own mouth that speaks to you. 13You must tell my father how greatly I am honored in Egypt, and all that you have seen. Hurry and bring my father down here."

14Then he fell upon his brother Benjamin's neck and wept, while Benjamin wept upon his neck. 15And he kissed all his brothers and wept upon them; and after that his brothers talked with him.

16 When the report was heard in Pharaoh's house, "Joseph's brothers have come," Pharaoh and his servants were pleased. 17Pharaoh said to Joseph, "Say to your brothers, 'Do this: load your animals and go back to the land of Canaan. 18Take your father and your households and come to me, so that I may give you the best of the land of Egypt, and you may enjoy the fat of the land.' 19You are further charged to say, 'Do this: take wagons from the land of Egypt for your little ones and for your wives, and bring your father, and come. 20Give no thought to your possessions, for the best of all the land of Egypt is yours.' "

21 The sons of Israel did so. Joseph gave them wagons according to the instruction of Pharaoh, and he gave them provisions for the journey. 22To each one of them he gave a set of garments; but to Benjamin he gave three hundred pieces of silver and five sets of garments. 23To his father he sent the following: ten donkeys loaded with the good things of Egypt, and ten female donkeys loaded with grain, bread, and provision for his father on the journey. 24Then he sent his brothers on their way, and as they were leaving he said to them, "Do not quarrel*a* along the way."

25 So they went up out of Egypt and came to their father Jacob in the land of Canaan. 26And they told him, "Joseph is still alive! He is even ruler over all the land of Egypt." He was stunned; he could not believe them. 27But when they told him all the words of Joseph that he had said to them, and when he saw the wagons that Joseph had sent to carry him, the spirit of their father Jacob revived. 28Israel said, "Enough! My son Joseph is still alive. I must go and see him before I die."

45.1–28: Joseph reveals his true identity to his brothers. 5: Joseph recognizes that his slavery and

a Or *be agitated*

coming to Egypt were part of a larger divine plan *to preserve life* for both his own family and "all the families of the earth" (12.3). **10:** *Goshen* is a fertile pasture land in the delta region of the Nile River in northeast Egypt (47.1–6).

46 When Israel set out on his journey with all that he had and came to Beer-sheba, he offered sacrifices to the God of his father Isaac. ²God spoke to Israel in visions of the night, and said, "Jacob, Jacob." And he said, "Here I am." ³Then he said, "I am God,*a* the God of your father; do not be afraid to go down to Egypt, for I will make of you a great nation there. ⁴I myself will go down with you to Egypt, and I will also bring you up again; and Joseph's own hand shall close your eyes."

5 Then Jacob set out from Beer-sheba; and the sons of Israel carried their father Jacob, their little ones, and their wives, in the wagons that Pharaoh had sent to carry him. ⁶They also took their livestock and the goods that they had acquired in the land of Canaan, and they came into Egypt, Jacob and all his offspring with him, ⁷his sons, and his sons' sons with him, his daughters, and his sons' daughters; all his offspring he brought with him into Egypt.

8 Now these are the names of the Israelites, Jacob and his offspring, who came to Egypt. Reuben, Jacob's firstborn, ⁹and the children of Reuben: Hanoch, Pallu, Hezron, and Carmi. ¹⁰The children of Simeon: Jemuel, Jamin, Ohad, Jachin, Zohar, and Shaul,*b* the son of a Canaanite woman. ¹¹The children of Levi: Gershon, Kohath, and Merari. ¹²The children of Judah: Er, Onan, Shelah, Perez, and Zerah (but Er and Onan died in the land of Canaan); and the children of Perez were Hezron and Hamul. ¹³The children of Issachar: Tola, Puvah, Jashub,*c* and Shimron. ¹⁴The children of Zebulun: Sered, Elon, and Jahleel ¹⁵(these are the sons of Leah, whom she bore to Jacob in Paddan-aram, together with his daughter Dinah; in all his sons and his daughters numbered thirty-three). ¹⁶The children of Gad: Ziphion, Haggi, Shuni, Ezbon, Eri, Arodi, and Areli. ¹⁷The children of Asher: Imnah, Ishvah, Ishvi, Beriah, and their sister Serah.

The children of Beriah: Heber and Malchiel ¹⁸(these are the children of Zilpah, whom Laban gave to his daughter Leah; and these she bore to Jacob—sixteen persons). ¹⁹The children of Jacob's wife Rachel: Joseph and Benjamin. ²⁰To Joseph in the land of Egypt were born Manasseh and Ephraim, whom Asenath daughter of Potiphera, priest of On, bore to him. ²¹The children of Benjamin: Bela, Becher, Ashbel, Gera, Naaman, Ehi, Rosh, Muppim, Huppim, and Ard ²²(these are the children of Rachel, who were born to Jacob—fourteen persons in all). ²³The children of Dan: Hashum.*d* ²⁴The children of Naphtali: Jahzeel, Guni, Jezer, and Shillem ²⁵(these are the children of Bilhah, whom Laban gave to his daughter Rachel, and these she bore to Jacob—seven persons in all). ²⁶All the persons belonging to Jacob who came into Egypt, who were his own offspring, not including the wives of his sons, were sixty-six persons in all. ²⁷The children of Joseph, who were born to him in Egypt, were two; all the persons of the house of Jacob who came into Egypt were seventy.

28 Israel*e* sent Judah ahead to Joseph to lead the way before him into Goshen. When they came to the land of Goshen, ²⁹Joseph made ready his chariot and went up to meet his father Israel in Goshen. He presented himself to him, fell on his neck, and wept on his neck a good while. ³⁰Israel said to Joseph, "I can die now, having seen for myself that you are still alive." ³¹Joseph said to his brothers and to his father's household, "I will go up and tell Pharaoh, and will say to him, 'My brothers and my father's household, who were in the land of Canaan, have come to me. ³²The men are shepherds, for they have been keepers of livestock; and they have brought their flocks, and their herds, and all that they have.' ³³When Pharaoh calls you, and says, 'What is your occupation?' ³⁴you shall say, 'Your servants have been keepers of livestock from our youth even until now, both we and our ancestors'—in order that you may settle in the land of Goshen, be-

a Heb *the God*   *b* Or *Saul*   *c* Compare Sam Gk Num 26.24; 1 Chr 7.1: MT *Iob*   *d* Gk: Heb *Hushim*
e Heb *He*

cause all shepherds are abhorrent to the Egyptians."

46.1–47.31: Jacob moves his family to live with Joseph in Egypt. 46.1–4: Jacob had once before received a vision at night in which God spoke words of assurance and blessing when he had left Canaan (28.10–22). Then as now, God promised Jacob, *"I myself will go down with you* and *bring you up again"* (v. 4; 28.15). **27:** The *seventy* members of *the house of Jacob* are a partial fulfillment of the promise of many descendants repeated throughout Genesis (15.5; 28.14). **34:** *Goshen* is a pasture land in the Nile River delta isolated from the rest of Egypt. *Shepherds are abhorrent to the Egyptians:* Egyptian agriculture was based more on crops and field agriculture that would be endangered by wandering herds of grazing animals.

47 So Joseph went and told Pharaoh, "My father and my brothers, with their flocks and herds and all that they possess, have come from the land of Canaan; they are now in the land of Goshen." ²From among his brothers he took five men and presented them to Pharaoh. ³Pharaoh said to his brothers, "What is your occupation?" And they said to Pharaoh, "Your servants are shepherds, as our ancestors were." ⁴They said to Pharaoh, "We have come to reside as aliens in the land; for there is no pasture for your servants' flocks because the famine is severe in the land of Canaan. Now, we ask you, let your servants settle in the land of Goshen." ⁵Then Pharaoh said to Joseph, "Your father and your brothers have come to you. ⁶The land of Egypt is before you; settle your father and your brothers in the best part of the land; let them live in the land of Goshen; and if you know that there are capable men among them, put them in charge of my livestock."

7 Then Joseph brought in his father Jacob, and presented him before Pharaoh, and Jacob blessed Pharaoh. ⁸Pharaoh said to Jacob, "How many are the years of your life?" ⁹Jacob said to Pharaoh, "The years of my earthly sojourn are one hundred thirty; few and hard have been the years of my life. They do not compare with the years of the life of my ancestors during their long sojourn." ¹⁰Then Jacob blessed Pharaoh, and went out from the presence of Pharaoh. ¹¹Joseph settled his father and his brothers, and granted them a holding in the land of Egypt, in the best part of the land, in the land of Rameses, as Pharaoh had instructed. ¹²And Joseph provided his father, his brothers, and all his father's household with food, according to the number of their dependents.

13 Now there was no food in all the land, for the famine was very severe. The land of Egypt and the land of Canaan languished because of the famine. ¹⁴Joseph collected all the money to be found in the land of Egypt and in the land of Canaan, in exchange for the grain that they bought; and Joseph brought the money into Pharaoh's house. ¹⁵When the money from the land of Egypt and from the land of Canaan was spent, all the Egyptians came to Joseph, and said, "Give us food! Why should we die before your eyes? For our money is gone." ¹⁶And Joseph answered, "Give me your livestock, and I will give you food in exchange for your livestock, if your money is gone." ¹⁷So they brought their livestock to Joseph; and Joseph gave them food in exchange for the horses, the flocks, the herds, and the donkeys. That year he supplied them with food in exchange for all their livestock. ¹⁸When that year was ended, they came to him the following year, and said to him, "We can not hide from my lord that our money is all spent; and the herds of cattle are my lord's. There is nothing left in the sight of my lord but our bodies and our lands. ¹⁹Shall we die before your eyes, both we and our land? Buy us and our land in exchange for food. We with our land will become slaves to Pharaoh; just give us seed, so that we may live and not die, and that the land may not become desolate."

20 So Joseph bought all the land of Egypt for Pharaoh. All the Egyptians sold their fields, because the famine was severe upon them; and the land became Pharaoh's. ²¹As for the people, he made slaves of them*a* from one end of Egypt to the other. ²²Only the land of the priests he did not buy; for the

---

a Sam Gk Compare Vg: MT *He removed them to the cities*

priests had a fixed allowance from Pharaoh, and lived on the allowance that Pharaoh gave them; therefore they did not sell their land. 23Then Joseph said to the people, "Now that I have this day bought you and your land for Pharaoh, here is seed for you; sow the land. 24And at the harvests you shall give one-fifth to Pharaoh, and four-fifths shall be your own, as seed for the field and as food for yourselves and your households, and as food for your little ones." 25They said, "You have saved our lives; may it please my lord, we will be slaves to Pharaoh." 26So Joseph made it a statute concerning the land of Egypt, and it stands to this day, that Pharaoh should have the fifth. The land of the priests alone did not become Pharaoh's.

27 Thus Israel settled in the land of Egypt, in the region of Goshen; and they gained possessions in it, and were fruitful and multiplied exceedingly. 28Jacob lived in the land of Egypt seventeen years; so the days of Jacob, the years of his life, were one hundred forty-seven years.

29 When the time of Israel's death drew near, he called his son Joseph and said to him, "If I have found favor with you, put your hand under my thigh and promise to deal loyally and truly with me. Do not bury me in Egypt. 30When I lie down with my ancestors, carry me out of Egypt and bury me in their burial place." He answered, "I will do as you have said." 31And he said, "Swear to me"; and he swore to him. Then Israel bowed himself on the head of his bed.

47.1–31. 11: *The land of Rameses* is another name for Goshen. Rameses was the name of a pharaoh in Egypt (Ex 1.11). **13–26:** The severity of the famine in Egypt forces the population gradually to give up their money, livestock, land, and freedom to the authority of Pharaoh. The program is managed by Joseph. Joseph's role in making slaves of the Egyptians (v. 25) will be reversed in Ex 1.8–14 when a new pharaoh will enslave the Israelites. **29:** Jacob's instruction to Joseph to *put your hand under my thigh,* near the male reproductive organs, is a ritual of making an intimate and solemn oath or promise (see 24.2). **30:** *Their burial place* is the cave at Machpelah, which Abraham had purchased from the Hittites (23.1–20).

48 After this Joseph was told, "Your father is ill." So he took with him his two sons, Manasseh and Ephraim. 2When Jacob was told, "Your son Joseph has come to you," he[a] summoned his strength and sat up in bed. 3And Jacob said to Joseph, "God Almighty[b] appeared to me at Luz in the land of Canaan, and he blessed me, 4and said to me, 'I am going to make you fruitful and increase your numbers; I will make of you a company of peoples, and will give this land to your offspring after you for a perpetual holding.' 5Therefore your two sons, who were born to you in the land of Egypt before I came to you in Egypt, are now mine; Ephraim and Manasseh shall be mine, just as Reuben and Simeon are. 6As for the offspring born to you after them, they shall be yours. They shall be recorded under the names of their brothers with regard to their inheritance. 7For when I came from Paddan, Rachel, alas, died in the land of Canaan on the way, while there was still some distance to go to Ephrath; and I buried her there on the way to Ephrath" (that is, Bethlehem).

8 When Israel saw Joseph's sons, he said, "Who are these?" 9Joseph said to his father, "They are my sons, whom God has given me here." And he said, "Bring them to me, please, that I may bless them." 10Now the eyes of Israel were dim with age, and he could not see well. So Joseph brought them near him; and he kissed them and embraced them. 11Israel said to Joseph, "I did not expect to see your face; and here God has let me see your children also." 12Then Joseph removed them from his father's knees,[c] and he bowed himself with his face to the earth. 13Joseph took them both, Ephraim in his right hand toward Israel's left, and Manasseh in his left hand toward Israel's right, and brought them near him. 14But Israel stretched out his right hand and laid it on the head of Ephraim, who was the younger, and his left hand on the head of Manasseh, crossing his hands, for Manasseh was the firstborn. 15He blessed Joseph, and said,

---

a Heb *Israel*   *b* Traditional rendering of Heb *El Shaddai*   *c* Heb *from his knees*

"The God before whom my ancestors
    Abraham and Isaac walked,
the God who has been my shepherd all
    my life to this day,
16 the angel who has redeemed me from
    all harm, bless the boys;
and in them let my name be
    perpetuated, and the name of my
    ancestors Abraham and Isaac;
and let them grow into a multitude on
    the earth."

17 When Joseph saw that his father laid his right hand on the head of Ephraim, it displeased him; so he took his father's hand, to remove it from Ephraim's head to Manasseh's head. 18 Joseph said to his father, "Not so, my father! Since this one is the firstborn, put your right hand on his head." 19 But his father refused, and said, "I know, my son, I know; he also shall become a people, and he also shall be great. Nevertheless his younger brother shall be greater than he, and his offspring shall become a multitude of nations." 20 So he blessed them that day, saying,

"By you*a* Israel will invoke blessings,
    saying,
'God make you*a* like Ephraim and like
    Manasseh.'"

So he put Ephraim ahead of Manasseh. 21 Then Israel said to Joseph, "I am about to die, but God will be with you and will bring you again to the land of your ancestors. 22 I now give to you one portion*b* more than to your brothers, the portion*b* that I took from the hand of the Amorites with my sword and with my bow."

48.1–22: Jacob blesses Joseph's two sons. 3: Jacob refers to God's first blessing given to him at Bethel (also known as Luz) in 28.10–22. **5–6:** Jacob adopts his two grandsons, *Ephraim and Manasseh*, as his own sons on a par with the oldest sons, Reuben and Simeon. This action explains why Manasseh and Ephraim will be listed in place of Joseph in later lists of the twelve tribes of Israel (Num 1.32–35; Josh 17.17). These tribes were dominant in certain periods of Israel's history. **13–14:** The blessing by Jacob (also known as Israel) with the *right hand* would imply a more favored status than a blessing with the left hand. The firstborn son would normally receive the right-hand blessing, but Jacob lays his right hand on

Ephraim, who was the younger (v. 14). **19:** Old blind Jacob (v. 10) refuses Joseph's request to give the favored right-hand blessing to the elder Manasseh. The scene is a replay of the elderly and blind Isaac blessing the younger Jacob in place of Esau (27.1–40). **22:** Jacob gives to Joseph *the portion that I took from the hand of the Amorites* in battle. The word for *portion* ("shekem") is a wordplay on the Canaanite or Amorite town of Shechem, which Jacob and his sons captured in a violent raid (34.25–29). Shechem was located on the border between Ephraim and Manasseh, the two Joseph tribes.

49 Then Jacob called his sons, and said: "Gather around, that I may tell you what will happen to you in days to come.
2 Assemble and hear, O sons of Jacob;
    listen to Israel your father.

3 Reuben, you are my firstborn,
    my might and the first fruits of my
      vigor,
    excelling in rank and excelling in
      power.
4 Unstable as water, you shall no longer
      excel
    because you went up onto your
      father's bed;
    then you defiled it—you*c* went up
      onto my couch!

5 Simeon and Levi are brothers;
    weapons of violence are their swords.
6 May I never come into their council;
    may I not be joined to their
      company—
for in their anger they killed men,
    and at their whim they hamstrung
      oxen.
7 Cursed be their anger, for it is fierce,
    and their wrath, for it is cruel!
I will divide them in Jacob,
    and scatter them in Israel.

8 Judah, your brothers shall praise you;
    your hand shall be on the neck of
      your enemies;

a you here is singular in Heb   *b* Or *mountain slope* (Heb *shekem*, a play on the name of the town and district of Shechem)   *c* Gk Syr Tg: Heb *he*

your father's sons shall bow down
  before you.
9 Judah is a lion's whelp;
  from the prey, my son, you have gone
    up.
He crouches down, he stretches out like
    a lion,
  like a lioness—who dares rouse him
    up?
10 The scepter shall not depart from
    Judah,
  nor the ruler's staff from between his
    feet,
until tribute comes to him;ª
  and the obedience of the peoples is
    his.
11 Binding his foal to the vine
  and his donkey's colt to the choice
    vine,
he washes his garments in wine
  and his robe in the blood of grapes;
12 his eyes are darker than wine,
  and his teeth whiter than milk.

13 Zebulun shall settle at the shore of the
    sea;
  he shall be a haven for ships,
  and his border shall be at Sidon.

14 Issachar is a strong donkey,
  lying down between the sheepfolds;
15 he saw that a resting place was good,
  and that the land was pleasant;
so he bowed his shoulder to the
    burden,
  and became a slave at forced labor.

16 Dan shall judge his people
  as one of the tribes of Israel.
17 Dan shall be a snake by the roadside,
  a viper along the path,
that bites the horse's heels
  so that its rider falls backward.

18 I wait for your salvation, O LORD.

19 Gad shall be raided by raiders,
  but he shall raid at their heels.

20 Asher'sᵇ food shall be rich,
  and he shall provide royal delicacies.

21 Naphtali is a doe let loose
  that bears lovely fawns.ᶜ

22 Joseph is a fruitful bough,
  a fruitful bough by a spring;
  his branches run over the wall.ᵈ
23 The archers fiercely attacked him;
  they shot at him and pressed him
    hard.
24 Yet his bow remained taut,
  and his armsᵉ were made agile
by the hands of the Mighty One of
    Jacob,
  by the name of the Shepherd, the
    Rock of Israel,
25 by the God of your father, who will help
    you,
  by the Almightyᶠ who will bless you
with blessings of heaven above,
blessings of the deep that lies beneath,
  blessings of the breasts and of the
    womb.
26 The blessings of your father
  are stronger than the blessings of the
    eternal mountains,
  the bountiesᵍ of the everlasting hills;
may they be on the head of Joseph,
  on the brow of him who was set apart
    from his brothers.

27 Benjamin is a ravenous wolf,
  in the morning devouring the prey,
  and at evening dividing the spoil."

28 All these are the twelve tribes of Israel,
and this is what their father said to them
when he blessed them, blessing each one of
them with a suitable blessing.

29 Then he charged them, saying to
them, "I am about to be gathered to my people. Bury me with my ancestors—in the cave
in the field of Ephron the Hittite, 30in the
cave in the field at Machpelah, near Mamre,
in the land of Canaan, in the field that Abra-

---

a Or until Shiloh comes or until he comes to Shiloh or
(with Syr) until he comes to whom it belongs
b Gk Vg Syr: Heb From Asher   c Or that gives
beautiful words   d Meaning of Heb uncertain
e Heb the arms of his hands   f Traditional rendering of
Heb Shaddai   g Cn Compare Gk: Heb of my progenitors
to the boundaries

ham bought from Ephro[n]e Hittite as a burial site. 31There Abra[m] and his wife Sarah were buried; there [I]c and his wife Rebekah were buried; an[d] here I buried Leah— 32the field and th[e c]ve that is in it were purchased from the [H]ites." 33When Jacob ended his charge to sons, he drew up his feet into the bed, [brea]thed his last, and was gathered to his pe[ople].

49.1–33: Jacob's last words t[o] sons. Jacob's deathbed blessing of his sons is a[ncie]nt Hebrew poetry, although the varied blessin[g a]nd condemnations may reflect later historical fo[rc]es (v. 28). **3–4:** *Reuben* should be exalted as Jacob's[fir]stborn son, but he will be demoted in status beca[use] he *defiled* his *father's bed.* Reuben had sexual rel[atio]ns with one of Jacob's concubines* (35.22). **5–7:** [Jac]ob's condemnation of Simeon and Levi stems fro[m th]eir leadership in the violent killing of the men of [Shec]hem (34.25–26, 30). Jacob's pledge to *divide* a[nd] *scatter* them points to Simeon's absorption into t[he]ribe of Judah (Josh 19.9) and Levi's becoming a [lan]dless priestly tribe (Num 18.6–7, 20). **8–12:** The na[me] *Judah* puns on the phrase *shall praise you* ("y[ı]ka"). These verses anticipate the preeminence an[d]prosperity of the royal line of King David, who aros[e o]ut of the tribe of Judah. **16:** The name *Dan* plays on[the] verb *judge* ("yadin"). **19:** The name *Gad* plays [on] the words *raided, raiders,* and *raid* ("gad"). **22–[27:]** This large section celebrates the future fertility a[nd]strength of the tribe of Joseph. **29–30:** Abraham's p[ur]chase of the burial cave is recounted in 23.1–20.

50 Then Joseph threw himse[lf o]n his father's face and wept over [h]im and kissed him. 2Joseph commanded [th]e physicians in his service to embalm his [fa]ther. So the physicians embalmed Israel; 3[th]ey spent forty days in doing this, for that i[s t]he time required for embalming. And the [Eg]yptians wept for him seventy days.

4 When the days of weeping for [hi]m were past, Joseph addressed the hous[eh]old of Pharaoh, "If now I have found fav[or] with you, please speak to Pharaoh as follo[ws]: 5My father made me swear an oath; he sa[id], 'I am about to die. In the tomb that I he[w]d out for myself in the land of Canaan, the[re] you shall bury me.' Now therefore let m[e g]o up, so that I may bury my father; then I [wi]ll re-

turn." 6Pharaoh answered, "Go up, and bury your father, as he made you swear to do."

7 So Joseph went up to bury his father. With him went up all the servants of Pharaoh, the elders of his household, and all the elders of the land of Egypt, 8as well as all the household of Joseph, his brothers, and his father's household. Only their children, their flocks, and their herds were left in the land of Goshen. 9Both chariots and charioteers went up with him. It was a very great company. 10When they came to the threshing floor of Atad, which is beyond the Jordan, they held there a very great and sorrowful lamentation; and he observed a time of mourning for his father seven days. 11When the Canaanite inhabitants of the land saw the mourning on the threshing floor of Atad, they said, "This is a grievous mourning on the part of the Egyptians." Therefore the place was named Abel-mizraim;[a] it is beyond the Jordan. 12Thus his sons did for him as he had instructed them. 13They carried him to the land of Canaan and buried him in the cave of the field at Machpelah, the field near Mamre, which Abraham bought as a burial site from Ephron the Hittite. 14After he had buried his father, Joseph returned to Egypt with his brothers and all who had gone up with him to bury his father.

50.1–14: Jacob is embalmed and buried. 2: *To embalm* the dead body of Jacob was an Egyptian custom of treating the corpse so that it would be preserved. The preservation would allow Joseph to return the body to Canaan and bury it there as Jacob had requested.

15 Realizing that their father was dead, Joseph's brothers said, "What if Joseph still bears a grudge against us and pays us back in full for all the wrong that we did to him?" 16So they approached[b] Joseph, saying, "Your father gave this instruction before he died, 17'Say to Joseph: I beg you, forgive the crime of your brothers and the wrong they did in harming you.' Now therefore please forgive the crime of the servants of the God

a That is mourning (or meadow) of Egypt   *b Gk Syr: Heb they commanded*

of your father." Joseph wept when they spoke to him. 18Then his brothers also wept,ᵃ fell down before him, and said, "We are here as your slaves." 19But Joseph said to them, "Do not be afraid! Am I in the place of God? 20Even though you intended to do harm to me, God intended it for good, in order to preserve a numerous people, as he is doing today. 21So have no fear; I myself will provide for you and your little ones." In this way he reassured them, speaking kindly to them.

22 So Joseph remained in Egypt, he and his father's household; and Joseph lived one hundred ten years. 23Joseph saw Ephraim's children of the third generation; the children of Machir son of Manasseh were also born on Joseph's knees.

24 Then Joseph said to his brothers, "I am about to die; but God will surely come to you, and bring you up out of this land to the land that he swore to Abraham, to Isaac, and

to Jacob." 25Joseph made the Israelites swear, saying, "When God comes to you, you shall carry my bones from here." 26And Joseph died, being one hundred ten years old; he was embalmed and placed in a coffin in Egypt.

50.15–26: Joseph once again forgives his brothers. 18: The brothers' words, *we are here as your slaves*, unintentionally anticipate the slavery of the Israelites in Egypt in Ex 1–14. 19–21: Joseph's words sound the overriding theme of the Joseph story: the divine ability to guide events and to turn evil into good. 25: The book of Genesis ends with the promise to Joseph that his body would be buried in the land of Canaan. The Israelites fulfill the promise in Ex 13.19 and Josh 24.32.

a Cn: Heb *came*

EXODUS

Introduction

The book of Exodus is a book about freedom and obligation, telling one of the Old Testament's central stories. It is the story of the liberation of Israel out of slavery in Egypt (chs. 1–15). But the book of Exodus is not only about Israel's freedom. It is also about the people of Israel's entering into a formal covenant* relationship of laws and obligations with God on their way to the promised land of Canaan (chs. 16–40). Exodus contains diverse forms of literature: narratives,* poetry, commandments, and laws. Among these diverse literatures, the poetic Song of the Sea in ch. 15 is probably one of the oldest texts within the entire Bible. The book of Exodus began its long history of development with early traditions like ch. 15, the Ten Commandments in ch. 20, and the earliest collection of laws in the Bible, the "Covenant Code" in chs. 21–23. Later writers and editors added many narratives, laws, and traditions over hundreds of years as the book of Exodus reached its final form, sometime in the sixth or fifth century BCE. The many traditions and laws of Exodus are joined together into a coherent story with a central human character, Moses, who led Israel out of slavery and into its covenant relationship with God.

The story of Israel's exodus out of Egypt forms one of the most important, influential narratives of the Bible. The Passover* festival celebrates the event as an annual ritual (ch. 12). Israel's experience of slavery in Egypt shaped many Old Testament laws designed to protect the disadvantaged (23.9; Lev 19.33–34). The Old Testament prophets* used the exodus from Egypt as a continuing model of God's saving power when Israel was in crisis (Isa 51.10). The Ten Commandments in ch. 20 and the other laws in Exodus formed the basis for ongoing ethical and legal reflection in Israel's life as a nation and people. The story of Israel's worship of the golden calf and the breaking of the formal relationship of exclusive loyalty to God resonated with the Israelites in exile in Babylon in the sixth century BCE. Most important, God's resolve to remain present in the midst of this sinful people in spite of their sin provided a word of hope to exiles who wondered if the Exile* marked an end or a new beginning in their relationship with God.

READING GUIDE

Three critical moments punctuate the book of Exodus. Each moment is marked by a buildup of tension, suspense, and preparation. The first critical moment is Israel's crossing the Red Sea into the safety and freedom of the other side. God sends ten plagues against Egypt, each time demanding that the Egyptian leader, Pharaoh, set Israel free. Only after the tenth and final plague, including the death of the firstborn sons of Egypt, does Pharaoh finally set Israel free (chs. 12–15). The second key moment in Exodus is the establishment of the formal relationship or covenant between God and Israel at Mount Sinai. After witnessing the dramatic display of God's power and presence on Mount Sinai, the Israelites pledge to enter a special relationship with God and to obey God's laws and commandments (chs. 19–24). The third critical moment in Exodus comes when Israel worships the golden calf and jeopardizes the exclusive relationship with God. God nevertheless continues to lead the Israelites in their wilderness journey to Canaan, even though they are a rebellious and sinful people (chs. 32–34). These three moments—freedom, obligation, and the renewal of a relationship—define the primary turning points in the story of Israel in Exodus.

1 These are the names of the sons of Israel who came to Egypt with Jacob, each with his household: 2Reuben, Simeon, Levi, and Judah, 3Issachar, Zebulun, and Benjamin, 4Dan and Naphtali, Gad and Asher. 5The total number of people born to Jacob was seventy. Joseph was already in Egypt. 6Then Joseph died, and all his brothers, and that whole generation. 7But the Israelites were fruitful and prolific; they multiplied and grew exceedingly strong, so that the land was filled with them.

8 Now a new king arose over Egypt, who did not know Joseph. 9He said to his people, "Look, the Israelite people are more numerous and more powerful than we. 10Come, let us deal shrewdly with them, or they will increase and, in the event of war, join our enemies and fight against us and escape from the land." 11Therefore they set taskmasters over them to oppress them with forced labor. They built supply cities, Pithom and Rameses, for Pharaoh. 12But the more they were oppressed, the more they multiplied and spread, so that the Egyptians came to dread the Israelites. 13The Egyptians became ruthless in imposing tasks on the Israelites, 14and made their lives bitter with hard service in mortar and brick and in every kind of field labor. They were ruthless in all the tasks that they imposed on them.

15 The king of Egypt said to the Hebrew midwives, one of whom was named Shiphrah and the other Puah, 16"When you act as midwives to the Hebrew women, and see them on the birthstool, if it is a boy, kill him; but if it is a girl, she shall live." 17But the midwives feared God; they did not do as the king of Egypt commanded them, but they let the boys live. 18So the king of Egypt summoned the midwives and said to them, "Why have you done this, and allowed the boys to live?" 19The midwives said to Pharaoh, "Because the Hebrew women are not like the Egyptian women; for they are vigorous and give birth before the midwife comes to them." 20So God dealt well with the midwives; and the people multiplied and became very strong. 21And because the midwives feared God, he gave them families. 22Then Pharaoh commanded all his people, "Every boy that is born to the Hebrews*a* you shall throw into the Nile, but you shall let every girl live."

1.1–22: A new king arises in Egypt and forces the Israelites to become slaves. Exodus continues the story of the family of Jacob in Egypt which concluded the book of Genesis. Israel's turn in fortunes from a people of honor to a people of slavery fulfills God's words to Abraham in Gen 15.12–16: Israel will go to a land not theirs and become slaves for four hundred years. **7:** The growing number and strength of the Israelites fulfills the promises of many descendants made to the ancestors in Genesis (Gen 13.16; 32.12). **8:** The *new king* of Egypt is not named, but some identify him as Rameses II (13th century BCE) in light of 1.11 and the building of a city called Rameses. The new ruler did not have the same high regard for Joseph and his family as had the previous ruler (Gen 47.1–12). **9:** The claim that the Israelites are *more numerous and more powerful* than the Egyptians may well be an exaggeration that shows the paranoia of the Egyptian ruler. **15:** It is not clear whether these two midwives are *Hebrew midwives* or Egyptians who act as midwives for the Hebrew women. The names of these heroic women, Shiphrah and Puah, suggest they may be Hebrew in origin. On the other hand, the information in vv. 17 and 21 that they *feared God* can refer to non-Israelites who acknowledge or obey Israel's God (Gen 20.1–11). **16:** Killing all the baby boys would cut off all the male lines of descent and thus eventually kill off

a Sam Gk Tg: Heb lacks *to the Hebrews*

the whole people. **19:** The midwives' deceptive claim that Hebrew women give birth more quickly is a way to cover up their refusal to obey the ruler's command to kill the Israelite babies. **22:** The Egyptian ruler or Pharaoh expands the command to kill Israelite boys to *all his people,* not just the midwives. All Egyptians are now guilty and will be subject to God's judgment.

2 Now a man from the house of Levi went and married a Levite woman. ²The woman conceived and bore a son; and when she saw that he was a fine baby, she hid him three months. ³When she could hide him no longer she got a papyrus basket for him, and plastered it with bitumen and pitch; she put the child in it and placed it among the reeds on the bank of the river. ⁴His sister stood at a distance, to see what would happen to him.

5 The daughter of Pharaoh came down to bathe at the river, while her attendants walked beside the river. She saw the basket among the reeds and sent her maid to bring it. ⁶When she opened it, she saw the child. He was crying, and she took pity on him. "This must be one of the Hebrews' children," she said. ⁷Then his sister said to Pharaoh's daughter, "Shall I go and get you a nurse from the Hebrew women to nurse the child for you?" ⁸Pharaoh's daughter said to her, "Yes." So the girl went and called the child's mother. ⁹Pharaoh's daughter said to her, "Take this child and nurse it for me, and I will give you your wages." So the woman took the child and nursed it. ¹⁰When the child grew up, she brought him to Pharaoh's daughter, and she took him as her son. She named him Moses,ᵃ "because," she said, "I drew him outᵇ of the water."

2.1–10: Moses is born and saved from the Nile River. This story of Moses' birth and rescue from the river includes parallels to other birth stories of heroes, especially the Legend* of King Sargon of Akkad (8th century BCE). **1:** Moses is born of parents from the Israelite tribe of *Levi*. The Levite tribe became a tribe of priests or servants dedicated to the worship of God (32.25–29). The family tree for the tribe of Levi in 6.14–27 names Moses' parents as Amran and Jochebed (6.20). Moses' brother is Aaron. **3:** The Bible uses this rare word for *basket* only one other time. It is the same word used for Noah's "ark" in Gen 6.14, another

story of dramatic rescue from water. **4:** Moses' *sister* is not named here. Later we will discover that she is Miriam, a sister to Aaron (15.20) and to Moses (Num 26.59). Micah 6.4 lists these three siblings—Moses, Aaron, and Miriam—as the leaders of Israel in their wilderness trek from Egypt to the promised land of Canaan. **9:** Pharaoh's own daughter conspires with Hebrew women to resist her father's vicious program against Israelite children. In a satisfying twist of fate, Pharaoh's daughter will pay *wages* to Moses' mother for nursing the mother's own child. **10:** The name *Moses* ("Mosheh") plays on the verb "to draw out" ("mashah").

11 One day, after Moses had grown up, he went out to his people and saw their forced labor. He saw an Egyptian beating a Hebrew, one of his kinsfolk. ¹²He looked this way and that, and seeing no one he killed the Egyptian and hid him in the sand. ¹³When he went out the next day, he saw two Hebrews fighting; and he said to the one who was in the wrong, "Why do you strike your fellow Hebrew?" ¹⁴He answered, "Who made you a ruler and judge over us? Do you mean to kill me as you killed the Egyptian?" Then Moses was afraid and thought, "Surely the thing is known." ¹⁵When Pharaoh heard of it, he sought to kill Moses.

But Moses fled from Pharaoh. He settled in the land of Midian, and sat down by a well. ¹⁶The priest of Midian had seven daughters. They came to draw water, and filled the troughs to water their father's flock. ¹⁷But some shepherds came and drove them away. Moses got up and came to their defense and watered their flock. ¹⁸When they returned to their father Reuel, he said, "How is it that you have come back so soon today?" ¹⁹They said, "An Egyptian helped us against the shepherds; he even drew water for us and watered the flock." ²⁰He said to his daughters, "Where is he? Why did you leave the man? Invite him to break bread." ²¹Moses agreed to stay with the man, and he gave Moses his daughter Zipporah in marriage. ²²She bore a son, and he named him Gershom; for he said, "I have been an alienᶜ residing in a foreign land."

a Heb *Mosheh*   *b* Heb *mashah*   *c* Heb *ger*

Moses and the Legend of Sargon

The story of the infant Moses in a basket floating in the river resembles other ancient Near Eastern stories about the birth and infancy of a hero. For example, there are some striking parallels between the Legend★ of Sargon and the biblical account. Sargon was the king of the nation of Akkad in Mesopotamia and reigned around 2600 BCE. The legend recounts how Sargon's mother gave birth to a child in secrecy. She placed the baby "in a basket of rushes; with bitumen she sealed the lid." She placed the basket in a river. A person named Akki saw the baby in the river, rescued him, and raised him as his own son. Eventually the baby became a leader and king of the people of Akkad. The story about Moses in ch. 2 seems to draw from a tradition similar to this legend.

23 After a long time the king of Egypt died. The Israelites groaned under their slavery, and cried out. Out of the slavery their cry for help rose up to God. 24God heard their groaning, and God remembered his covenant with Abraham, Isaac, and Jacob. 25God looked upon the Israelites, and God took notice of them.

2.11–25: Moses kills an Egyptian and flees to Midian. 11: The story moves immediately from Moses as a baby (2.1–10) to Moses as an adult. **13:** The Hebrew verb for *strike* ("nakah") is the same verb used in v. 12 when Moses *killed* the Egyptian, in v. 11 when the Egyptian was *beating* the Hebrew, and the word used as God "strikes" Egypt with the plagues later in the story (3.20; 12.12–13). **15:** Genesis 25.2 portrays the people of *Midian* as descended from Abraham and Keturah. They are a wandering people associated with the Sinai Peninsula south of Canaan and with northern Arabia, which lies east and north of Canaan. **18:** The name of Moses' father-in-law is *Reuel* here, but the name varies in other biblical traditions. His name is sometimes Jethro (3.1; 18.1) or Hobab (Num 10.29; Judg 4.11). **22:** Moses gives his son the name *Gershom* as a wordplay on the word for *alien* ("ger"). In a sense, Moses is an alien or stranger in every land. The Midianites consider him an "Egyptian" (2.19). The Egyptians seek to kill him as a Hebrew sympathizer (2.15). The Hebrews reject him as not one of their own (2.14). **23–24:** God *heard* Israel's cry of distress and God *remembered his covenant*★ or promise made to Israel's ancestors in Genesis (*Abraham*—Gen 15.12–16; *Isaac*—26.24; *Jacob*—35.11–12).

God calls Moses to lead Israel out of Egypt

3.1–4.31: Moses encounters God veiled in a burning bush at Mount Horeb, otherwise known as Mount Sinai. God calls Moses to leave Midian and return to Egypt to lead Israel out of slavery to freedom. Moses responds with five objections or reasons why he should not lead Israel (3.11, 13; 4. 1, 10, 13). However, God patiently responds to each objection and insists that Moses go. Finally, Moses obeys (4.18–20).

3 Moses was keeping the flock of his father-in-law Jethro, the priest of Midian; he led his flock beyond the wilderness, and came to Horeb, the mountain of God. 2There the angel of the LORD appeared to him in a flame of fire out of a bush; he looked, and the bush was blazing, yet it was not consumed. 3Then Moses said, "I must turn aside and look at this great sight, and see why the bush is not burned up." 4When the LORD saw that he had turned aside to see, God called to him out of the bush, "Moses, Moses!" And he said, "Here I am." 5Then he said, "Come no closer! Remove the sandals from your feet, for the place on which you are standing is holy ground." 6He said further, "I am the God of your father, the God of Abraham, the God of Isaac, and the God of Jacob." And Moses hid his face, for he was afraid to look at God.

7 Then the LORD said, "I have observed the misery of my people who are in Egypt; I

have heard their cry on account of their taskmasters. Indeed, I know their sufferings, 8and I have come down to deliver them from the Egyptians, and to bring them up out of that land to a good and broad land, a land flowing with milk and honey, to the country of the Canaanites, the Hittites, the Amorites, the Perizzites, the Hivites, and the Jebusites. 9The cry of the Israelites has now come to me; I have also seen how the Egyptians oppress them. 10So come, I will send you to Pharaoh to bring my people, the Israelites, out of Egypt." 11But Moses said to God, "Who am I that I should go to Pharaoh, and bring the Israelites out of Egypt?" 12He said, "I will be with you; and this shall be the sign for you that it is I who sent you: when you have brought the people out of Egypt, you shall worship God on this mountain."

13 But Moses said to God, "If I come to the Israelites and say to them, 'The God of your ancestors has sent me to you,' and they ask me, 'What is his name?' what shall I say to them?" 14God said to Moses, "I AM WHO I AM."*a* He said further, "Thus you shall say to the Israelites, 'I AM has sent me to you.'" 15God also said to Moses, "Thus you shall say to the Israelites, 'The LORD,*b* the God of your ancestors, the God of Abraham, the God of Isaac, and the God of Jacob, has sent me to you':

This is my name forever,

and this my title for all generations.

16Go and assemble the elders of Israel, and say to them, 'The LORD, the God of your ancestors, the God of Abraham, of Isaac, and of Jacob, has appeared to me, saying: I have given heed to you and to what has been done to you in Egypt. 17I declare that I will bring you up out of the misery of Egypt, to the land of the Canaanites, the Hittites, the Amorites, the Perizzites, the Hivites, and the Jebusites, a land flowing with milk and honey.' 18They will listen to your voice; and you and the elders of Israel shall go to the king of Egypt and say to him, 'The LORD, the God of the Hebrews, has met with us; let us now go a three days' journey into the wilderness, so that we may sacrifice to the LORD our God.' 19I know, however, that the king of Egypt will not let you go unless compelled by a mighty hand.*c* 20So I will stretch out my hand and strike Egypt with all my wonders that I will perform in it; after that he will let you go. 21I will bring this people into such favor with the Egyptians that, when you go, you will not go empty-handed; 22each woman shall ask her neighbor and any woman living in the neighbor's house for jewelry of silver and of gold, and clothing, and you shall put them on your sons and on your daughters; and so you shall plunder the Egyptians."

3.1–22. 1: *Jethro* is an alternate name for Moses' father-in-law, who is otherwise known as Reuel (2.18) or Hobab (Num 10.29). Mount *Horeb* is an alternate name for Mount Sinai (19.11). *The mountain of God* reflects a common notion in the ancient Near East that mountain tops were the special dwelling places of the divine. **2:** *Fire* is a frequent biblical image for the deity's presence (Gen 15.17). **4:** *The LORD* is considered interchangeable with *the angel of the LORD* in v. 2. **6:** *To look at God* was a fearful thing because it could mean instant death (33.20; Isa 6.5). **8:** This is the first of many biblical examples in which the phrase *a land flowing with milk and honey* describes the goodness and fertility of the promised land of Canaan (13.5; Num 13.27). This list of peoples—*the Canaanites, the Hittites, the Amorites, the Perizzites, the Hivites, and the Jebusites*—is the traditional listing of the native inhabitants of the land of Canaan (Gen 15.19–21; Deut 7.1). **11–12:** This is the first of a series of five objections which Moses raises to God's call to lead Israel out of Egypt. Moses feels inadequate for the mission, but God assures him that God will be with him. As a sign, God promises that Moses and the Israelites will return to worship *on this mountain* of Horeb or Sinai (19.11). **13–15:** Moses' second objection is a request for God's name. God reveals the new divine name as *I AM WHO I AM* ("ehyeh asher ehyeh") or *I WILL BE WHO I WILL BE*. This name is a wordplay on the divine name "yhwh," usually pronounced "Yahweh." The name "Yahweh" derives from the verb "to be" ("hayah") and may be translated "he causes to be" or "he creates." Ancient Jewish practice considered the divine name "Yahweh" so holy and special that it should never be pro-

a Or I AM WHAT I AM or I WILL BE WHAT I WILL BE
b The word "LORD" when spelled with capital letters stands for the divine name, YHWH, which is here connected with the verb *hayah*, "to be"   *c* Gk Vg: Heb *no, not by a mighty hand*

nounced. Wherever the name occurred, the reader used instead the Hebrew word for "the Lord" ("adonai"). This NRSV translation follows this ancient practice, substituting "the LORD" for every occurrence of "Yahweh" in the Hebrew text. The divine name, *I AM WHO I AM*, reveals God's intention to be present with Israel. At the same time, the name hides some of God's character until a later time of disclosure (33.19; 34.6–7). Moreover, the text underscores the identification of *the God of Abraham, the God of Isaac, and the God of Jacob* from the book of Genesis with the same God whose new name is revealed as *the LORD* ("Yahweh"). **18:** *Sacrifice* involves the killing of an animal and offering part of it to the deity as an act of worship and devotion. **22:** God's pressure on the Egyptians to release the Israelites will eventually become so strong that the Egyptians will be anxious to send them away with gold, silver, and fine clothing. In this way, Israel will *plunder the Egyptians* and take their war booty as a sign that God has won the victory in the battle with Pharaoh and the Egyptians. The promise is fulfilled in 12.33–36.

4 Then Moses answered, "But suppose they do not believe me or listen to me, but say, 'The LORD did not appear to you.'" ²The LORD said to him, "What is that in your hand?" He said, "A staff." ³And he said, "Throw it on the ground." So he threw the staff on the ground, and it became a snake; and Moses drew back from it. ⁴Then the LORD said to Moses, "Reach out your hand, and seize it by the tail"—so he reached out his hand and grasped it, and it became a staff in his hand— ⁵"so that they may believe that the LORD, the God of their ancestors, the God of Abraham, the God of Isaac, and the God of Jacob, has appeared to you."

6 Again, the LORD said to him, "Put your hand inside your cloak." He put his hand into his cloak; and when he took it out, his hand was leprous,ᵃ as white as snow. ⁷Then God said, "Put your hand back into your cloak"—so he put his hand back into his cloak, and when he took it out, it was restored like the rest of his body— ⁸"If they will not believe you or heed the first sign, they may believe the second sign. ⁹If they will not believe even these two signs or heed you, you shall take some water from the Nile and pour it on the dry ground; and the water

that you shall take from the Nile will become blood on the dry ground."

10 But Moses said to the LORD, "O my Lord, I have never been eloquent, neither in the past nor even now that you have spoken to your servant; but I am slow of speech and slow of tongue." ¹¹Then the LORD said to him, "Who gives speech to mortals? Who makes them mute or deaf, seeing or blind? Is it not I, the LORD? ¹²Now go, and I will be with your mouth and teach you what you are to speak." ¹³But he said, "O my Lord, please send someone else." ¹⁴Then the anger of the LORD was kindled against Moses and he said, "What of your brother Aaron the Levite? I know that he can speak fluently; even now he is coming out to meet you, and when he sees you his heart will be glad. ¹⁵You shall speak to him and put the words in his mouth; and I will be with your mouth and with his mouth, and will teach you what you shall do. ¹⁶He indeed shall speak for you to the people; he shall serve as a mouth for you, and you shall serve as God for him. ¹⁷Take in your hand this staff, with which you shall perform the signs."

18 Moses went back to his father-in-law Jethro and said to him, "Please let me go back to my kindred in Egypt and see whether they are still living." And Jethro said to Moses, "Go in peace." ¹⁹The LORD said to Moses in Midian, "Go back to Egypt; for all those who were seeking your life are dead." ²⁰So Moses took his wife and his sons, put them on a donkey, and went back to the land of Egypt; and Moses carried the staff of God in his hand.

21 And the LORD said to Moses, "When you go back to Egypt, see that you perform before Pharaoh all the wonders that I have put in your power; but I will harden his heart, so that he will not let the people go. ²²Then you shall say to Pharaoh, 'Thus says the LORD: Israel is my firstborn son. ²³I said to you, "Let my son go that he may worship me." But you refused to let him go; now I will kill your firstborn son.'"

24 On the way, at a place where they

ᵃ A term for several skin diseases; precise meaning uncertain

spent the night, the LORD met him and tried to kill him. 25 But Zipporah took a flint and cut off her son's foreskin, and touched Moses'[a] feet with it, and said, "Truly you are a bridegroom of blood to me!" 26 So he let him alone. It was then she said, "A bridegroom of blood by circumcision."

27 The LORD said to Aaron, "Go into the wilderness to meet Moses." So he went; and he met him at the mountain of God and kissed him. 28 Moses told Aaron all the words of the LORD with which he had sent him, and all the signs with which he had charged him. 29 Then Moses and Aaron went and assembled all the elders of the Israelites. 30 Aaron spoke all the words that the LORD had spoken to Moses, and performed the signs in the sight of the people. 31 The people believed; and when they heard that the LORD had given heed to the Israelites and that he had seen their misery, they bowed down and worshiped.

4.1–31. 1: Moses raises a third objection. God responds by offering three signs to be performed to bolster the people's confidence in Moses (vv. 2–9). Moses and his brother Aaron perform the signs in 4.30. Moses' brother Aaron will use the sign of the staff's turning into a serpent (vv. 2–5) as a means to try to convince Pharaoh (7.8–13). The third sign, the Nile River's turning into blood (v. 9), will become the first plague against Egypt (7.14–25). **10:** Moses' fourth objection is his inability as a speaker: *slow of speech and slow of tongue.* **13:** In a final desperate objection, Moses asks that God *send someone else.* **14:** For the first time, *the anger of the LORD* appears after much patience with Moses. God promises to send Moses' brother Aaron as his mouthpiece (vv. 14–17). **21:** The theme of God's *hardening the heart* of Pharaoh plays an important role throughout the story of Israel's exodus out of Egypt. Ancient Israel understood the *heart* as the intersecting point of human intellect and the human will. God repeatedly stiffens or hardens the heart or will of Pharaoh against letting Israel go (9.12; 14.8). This emphasis on God's control of Pharaoh ensures that Egypt will finally come to acknowledge God's power. On the other hand, the texts also repeatedly declare that Pharaoh hardens his own heart or will (7.13–14; 9.7, 34–35). Thus, Pharaoh can also be held morally responsible for his own willful actions. Pharaoh even confesses his own sin and responsibility for wrongdoing (9.27–28). The story holds together affir-

mations of divine guidance and control along with human freedom and responsibility. **23:** The threat to Pharaoh to *kill your firstborn son* will be accomplished in the tenth and final plague (12.29–32). In this way, God will reclaim Israel as God's *firstborn son* (v. 22). **24–26:** This story of the deity's attack and circumcision's* role as a defense against the deity is difficult to understand. We have lost some of the historical context that underlies the original story. However, the mention of Pharaoh's "firstborn son" in the preceding verse (v. 23) suggests a connection to the final plague when the deity killed all the Egyptian firstborn. The protective power of the blood on the doorposts of the Israelites' houses caused the LORD to pass over their houses and not kill the Israelites' firstborn (12.12, 22–23). In the same way, the protective blood of circumcision here protects either Moses or his son (the pronoun "him" in vv. 24–26 is ambiguous). Circumcision is a ritual involving cutting off the foreskin of the male penis. A *flint* is a sharpened stone used in the ritual. *Moses' feet* is probably an alternate way of saying his genitals. *A bridegroom of blood* may reflect the practice of some cultures that called the circumcised male "a bridegroom." The theme of the deity's attack against those whom the deity has chosen for a special mission occurs elsewhere in the Bible (Gen 32.22–32; Num 22.22–35; Josh 5.13–15; Judg 2.1–5). **27:** *The mountain of God* is Mount Horeb, also known as Mount Sinai (3.1).

~~~~~~~~~~~~~~~~~~~~~~~~~~~~~~~~~~~~~

5 Afterward Moses and Aaron went to Pharaoh and said, "Thus says the LORD, the God of Israel, 'Let my people go, so that they may celebrate a festival to me in the wilderness.' " 2 But Pharaoh said, "Who is the LORD, that I should heed him and let Israel go? I do not know the LORD, and I will not let Israel go." 3 Then they said, "The God of the Hebrews has revealed himself to us; let us go a three days' journey into the wilderness to sacrifice to the LORD our God, or he will fall upon us with pestilence or sword." 4 But the king of Egypt said to them, "Moses and Aaron, why are you taking the people away from their work? Get to your labors!" 5 Pharaoh continued, "Now they are more numerous than the people of the land[b] and yet you want them to stop working!"

a Heb *his*   *b* Sam: Heb *The people of the land are now many*

6That same day Pharaoh commanded the taskmasters of the people, as well as their supervisors, 7"You shall no longer give the people straw to make bricks, as before; let them go and gather straw for themselves. 8But you shall require of them the same quantity of bricks as they have made previously; do not diminish it, for they are lazy; that is why they cry, 'Let us go and offer sacrifice to our God.' 9Let heavier work be laid on them; then they will labor at it and pay no attention to deceptive words."

10 So the taskmasters and the supervisors of the people went out and said to the people, "Thus says Pharaoh, 'I will not give you straw. 11Go and get straw yourselves, wherever you can find it; but your work will not be lessened in the least.'" 12So the people scattered throughout the land of Egypt, to gather stubble for straw. 13The taskmasters were urgent, saying, "Complete your work, the same daily assignment as when you were given straw." 14And the supervisors of the Israelites, whom Pharaoh's taskmasters had set over them, were beaten, and were asked, "Why did you not finish the required quantity of bricks yesterday and today, as you did before?"

15 Then the Israelite supervisors came to Pharaoh and cried, "Why do you treat your servants like this? 16No straw is given to your servants, yet they say to us, 'Make bricks!' Look how your servants are beaten! You are unjust to your own people."a 17He said, "You are lazy, lazy; that is why you say, 'Let us go and sacrifice to the LORD.' 18Go now, and work; for no straw shall be given you, but you shall still deliver the same number of bricks." 19The Israelite supervisors saw that they were in trouble when they were told, "You shall not lessen your daily number of bricks." 20As they left Pharaoh, they came upon Moses and Aaron who were waiting to meet them. 21They said to them, "The LORD look upon you and judge! You have brought us into bad odor with Pharaoh and his officials, and have put a sword in their hand to kill us."

22 Then Moses turned again to the LORD and said, "O LORD, why have you mistreated this people? Why did you ever send me?

23Since I first came to Pharaoh to speak in your name, he has mistreated this people, and you have done nothing at all to deliver your people."

5.1–23: Moses and Aaron confront Pharaoh for the first time. 2: Pharaoh's words, *I do not know the LORD*, introduce a major theme of knowing the LORD, which plays a role throughout this section of Exodus (7.5, 17; 8.10; 9.14; 14.18). **3:** The threat of *pestilence or sword* points indirectly to the plagues that will begin soon. **5:** The claim that the number of Israelites exceeds that of the Egyptians is probably an exaggeration of a paranoid Pharaoh (1.9). The need *to stop working* in order to worship the LORD will become a defining practice of the Israelite community with the commandment concerning the sabbath (20.8–11; Deut 5.12–15). **21:** *Bad odor with Pharaoh* foreshadows the bad odor that will accompany the first two plagues (7.21; 8.13–14). **22–23:** This is another example of Moses' boldness to speak words of resistance, correction, or complaint to God (chs. 3–4; 32.11–14; 33.12–23).

6 Then the LORD said to Moses, "Now you shall see what I will do to Pharaoh: Indeed, by a mighty hand he will let them go; by a mighty hand he will drive them out of his land."

2 God also spoke to Moses and said to him: "I am the LORD. 3I appeared to Abraham, Isaac, and Jacob as God Almighty,b but by my name 'The LORD'c I did not make myself known to them. 4I also established my covenant with them, to give them the land of Canaan, the land in which they resided as aliens. 5I have also heard the groaning of the Israelites whom the Egyptians are holding as slaves, and I have remembered my covenant. 6Say therefore to the Israelites, 'I am the LORD, and I will free you from the burdens of the Egyptians and deliver you from slavery to them. I will redeem you with an outstretched arm and with mighty acts of judgment. 7I will take you as my people, and I will be your God. You shall know that I am the LORD your God, who has freed you from the burdens of the Egyptians. 8I will bring you into the land that I swore to give to Abra-

---

a Gk Compare Syr Vg: Heb *beaten, and the sin of your people*   b Traditional rendering of Heb *El Shaddai*
c Heb *YHWH*; see note at 3.15

ham, Isaac, and Jacob; I will give it to you for a possession. I am the LORD.' " 9Moses told this to the Israelites; but they would not listen to Moses, because of their broken spirit and their cruel slavery.

10 Then the LORD spoke to Moses, 11"Go and tell Pharaoh king of Egypt to let the Israelites go out of his land." 12But Moses spoke to the LORD, "The Israelites have not listened to me; how then shall Pharaoh listen to me, poor speaker that I am?"*a* 13Thus the LORD spoke to Moses and Aaron, and gave them orders regarding the Israelites and Pharaoh king of Egypt, charging them to free the Israelites from the land of Egypt.

The LORD reaffirms the mission of Moses and Aaron

6.1–7.7: The LORD responds to the complaints of Israel (5.21) and of Moses (5.22–23). God reaffirms the role of Moses and Aaron as leaders of Israel and the divine intention to rescue Israel as God's chosen people from slavery. This section provides an alternate version to chs. 3–4 and is often attributed to the later Priestly tradition (see sidebar, "Two Different Creation Stories, p. 4). 6.1: *By a mighty hand* refers to Pharaoh's power and authority. 2–3: On the significance of the divine name *the LORD*, see the comment on 3.13–15. The name *God Almighty* (*El Shaddai*) literally means "God of the Mountain" which is an appropriate name for this deity who appears on Mount Horeb/Sinai. The claim here that the ancestors in Genesis did not know the name *the LORD* ("Yahweh") contradicts an alternate tradition that Abraham, Isaac, and Jacob did know and use the name *the LORD* (Gen 12.8; 26.22; 32.9). 6: To *redeem* means to pay a ransom in order to set free and regain possession of a family member or plot of land that has been taken over by another person or owner (Lev 25.25–28, 47–49). *With an outstretched arm* refers to the extension of God's power against the Egyptians. The promise is literally fulfilled when Moses "stretched out his hand" and God parted the Red Sea (14.21) and then allowed the water to rush back upon the Egyptians (14.26–28). 7: *You shall know* continues the important theme concerning the purpose of the exodus out of Egypt: the knowledge of God by both Egyptians and Israelites (see comment on 5.2). 8: God *swore* or made a promise to each of the ancestors in Genesis: Abraham (Gen 13.14–15), Isaac (Gen 26.3), and Jacob (Gen 28.13).

14 The following are the heads of their ancestral houses: the sons of Reuben, the firstborn of Israel: Hanoch, Pallu, Hezron, and Carmi; these are the families of Reuben. 15The sons of Simeon: Jemuel, Jamin, Ohad, Jachin, Zohar, and Shaul,*b* the son of a Canaanite woman; these are the families of Simeon. 16The following are the names of the sons of Levi according to their genealogies: Gershon,*c* Kohath, and Merari, and the length of Levi's life was one hundred thirty-seven years. 17The sons of Gershon:*c* Libni and Shimei, by their families. 18The sons of Kohath: Amram, Izhar, Hebron, and Uzziel, and the length of Kohath's life was one hundred thirty-three years. 19The sons of Merari: Mahli and Mushi. These are the families of the Levites according to their genealogies. 20Amram married Jochebed his father's sister and she bore him Aaron and Moses, and the length of Amram's life was one hundred thirty-seven years. 21The sons of Izhar: Korah, Nepheg, and Zichri. 22The sons of Uzziel: Mishael, Elzaphan, and Sithri. 23Aaron married Elisheba, daughter of Amminadab and sister of Nahshon, and she bore him Nadab, Abihu, Eleazar, and Ithamar. 24The sons of Korah: Assir, Elkanah, and Abiasaph; these are the families of the Korahites. 25Aaron's son Eleazar married one of the daughters of Putiel, and she bore him Phinehas. These are the heads of the ancestral houses of the Levites by their families.

6.14–25: This genealogy* or family tree traces the family line of Jacob's three oldest sons: Reuben (v. 14), Simeon (v. 15), and Levi (vv. 16–25). The focus is clearly on the descendants of Levi, a family of priests. The family tree of Levi has two functions: to identify Moses and Aaron as Levites and brothers, and to trace the priestly line through Aaron to his son Eleazar (vv. 23–24) and his grandson Phinehas (v. 25). Eleazar takes over Aaron's role as high priest in Num 20.22–29. God commissions Phinehas and his descendants as priests in Num 25.6–13.

26 It was this same Aaron and Moses to whom the LORD said, "Bring the Israelites

---

a Heb *me? I am uncircumcised of lips*   *b* Or *Saul*
c Also spelled *Gershom*; see 2.22

out of the land of Egypt, company by company." [27]It was they who spoke to Pharaoh king of Egypt to bring the Israelites out of Egypt, the same Moses and Aaron.

28 On the day when the LORD spoke to Moses in the land of Egypt, [29]he said to him, "I am the LORD; tell Pharaoh king of Egypt all that I am speaking to you." [30]But Moses said in the LORD's presence, "Since I am a poor speaker,*a* why would Pharaoh listen to me?"

7 The LORD said to Moses, "See, I have made you like God to Pharaoh, and your brother Aaron shall be your prophet. [2]You shall speak all that I command you, and your brother Aaron shall tell Pharaoh to let the Israelites go out of his land. [3]But I will harden Pharaoh's heart, and I will multiply my signs and wonders in the land of Egypt. [4]When Pharaoh does not listen to you, I will lay my hand upon Egypt and bring my people the Israelites, company by company, out of the land of Egypt by great acts of judgment. [5]The Egyptians shall know that I am the LORD, when I stretch out my hand against Egypt and bring the Israelites out from among them." [6]Moses and Aaron did so; they did just as the LORD commanded them. [7]Moses was eighty years old and Aaron eighty-three when they spoke to Pharaoh.

6.26–7.7. 1: The relationship between Moses and Aaron as his mouthpiece will be similar to the relationship between God and Moses. Just as Moses is God's *prophet** or messenger, so Aaron will be Moses' *prophet* or spokesperson. 3: *Harden Pharaoh's heart:* See comment on 4.21. 5: *Stretch out my hand:* See comment on 6.6. 7: Contrary to expectations, the younger brother Moses is superior to the older brother Aaron. This is a frequent motif* in biblical narratives* (Gen 25.23; 37.5–11).

8 The LORD said to Moses and Aaron, [9]"When Pharaoh says to you, 'Perform a wonder,' then you shall say to Aaron, 'Take your staff and throw it down before Pharaoh, and it will become a snake.'" [10]So Moses and Aaron went to Pharaoh and did as the LORD had commanded; Aaron threw down his staff before Pharaoh and his officials, and it became a snake. [11]Then Pharaoh

summoned the wise men and the sorcerers; and they also, the magicians of Egypt, did the same by their secret arts. [12]Each one threw down his staff, and they became snakes; but Aaron's staff swallowed up theirs. [13]Still Pharaoh's heart was hardened, and he would not listen to them, as the LORD had said.

7.8–13: **Aaron's staff turns into a snake before Pharaoh.** Aaron uses the same miraculous sign to try to convince Pharaoh of God's power that he had earlier used to convince the Israelites (4.1–5; 30). **12:** The word *snake* is the same word translated as "dragon" in Ezek 29.3, where it describes the Egyptian Pharaoh: "Thus says the Lord GOD: I am against you, Pharaoh king of Egypt, the great dragon." Aaron's snake swallowing the Egyptians' snakes foreshadows the future victory of Israel's God over Pharaoh. **13:** *Pharaoh's heart was hardened:* See comment on 4.21.

14 Then the LORD said to Moses, "Pharaoh's heart is hardened; he refuses to let the people go. [15]Go to Pharaoh in the morning, as he is going out to the water; stand by at the river bank to meet him, and take in your hand the staff that was turned into a snake. [16]Say to him, 'The LORD, the God of the Hebrews, sent me to you to say, "Let my people go, so that they may worship me in the wilderness." But until now you have not listened. [17]Thus says the LORD, "By this you shall know that I am the LORD." See, with the staff that is in my hand I will strike the water that is in the Nile, and it shall be turned to blood. [18]The fish in the river shall die, the river itself shall stink, and the Egyptians shall be unable to drink water from the Nile.'" [19]The LORD said to Moses, "Say to Aaron, 'Take your staff and stretch out your hand over the waters of Egypt—over its rivers, its canals, and its ponds, and all its pools of water—so that they may become blood; and there shall be blood throughout the whole land of Egypt, even in vessels of wood and in vessels of stone.'"

20 Moses and Aaron did just as the LORD commanded. In the sight of Pharaoh and of his officials he lifted up the staff and struck

a Heb *am uncircumcised of lips*; see 6.12

the water in the river, and all the water in the river was turned into blood, 21and the fish in the river died. The river stank so that the Egyptians could not drink its water, and there was blood throughout the whole land of Egypt. 22But the magicians of Egypt did the same by their secret arts; so Pharaoh's heart remained hardened, and he would not listen to them, as the LORD had said. 23Pharaoh turned and went into his house, and he did not take even this to heart. 24And all the Egyptians had to dig along the Nile for water to drink, for they could not drink the water of the river.

25 Seven days passed after the LORD had struck the Nile.

7.14–25: The first plague: The Nile turns to blood. The Nile River was the primary source of water and life for Egypt. However, the Egyptians had earlier used the Nile as an instrument of death when Pharaoh ordered every Hebrew baby boy to be thrown into the river (1.22). This first plague, the river's turning to blood, recalls that previous atrocity. The plague also recalls one of the first miraculous signs God gave to Moses to convince the Israelites of God's power (4.9). **14:** *Pharaoh's heart is hardened:* See comment on 4.21. See also 7.22. **19:** The same phrase, *pools of water*, appears in the creation story in Gen 1.10 translated, "waters that were gathered together." Pharaoh's unjust enslavement of Israel prompts this series of ecological disasters. In effect, the plagues undo the life-giving order and structure of creation in Gen 1. **22:** A progression is evident in the experience of *the magicians of Egypt* throughout the ten plagues. They are able to duplicate the first and second plagues (7.14; 8.7). However, they cannot duplicate the third plague (8.18–19). In the fifth plague, not only do the magicians fail to duplicate the plague of boils, they themselves suffer its effects (9.11). The Egyptian magicians disappear entirely during the last five plagues.

8 ^aThen the LORD said to Moses, "Go to Pharaoh and say to him, 'Thus says the LORD: Let my people go, so that they may worship me. 2If you refuse to let them go, I will plague your whole country with frogs. 3The river shall swarm with frogs; they shall come up into your palace, into your bedchamber and your bed, and into the houses of your officials and of your people,^b and

into your ovens and your kneading bowls. 4The frogs shall come up on you and on your people and on all your officials.' " 5c And the LORD said to Moses, "Say to Aaron, 'Stretch out your hand with your staff over the rivers, the canals, and the pools, and make frogs come up on the land of Egypt.' 6So Aaron stretched out his hand over the waters of Egypt; and the frogs came up and covered the land of Egypt. 7But the magicians did the same by their secret arts, and brought frogs up on the land of Egypt.

8 Then Pharaoh called Moses and Aaron, and said, "Pray to the LORD to take away the frogs from me and my people, and I will let the people go to sacrifice to the LORD." 9Moses said to Pharaoh, "Kindly tell me when I am to pray for you and for your officials and for your people, that the frogs may be removed from you and your houses and be left only in the Nile." 10And he said, "Tomorrow." Moses said, "As you say! So that you may know that there is no one like the LORD our God, 11the frogs shall leave you and your houses and your officials and your people; they shall be left only in the Nile." 12Then Moses and Aaron went out from Pharaoh; and Moses cried out to the LORD concerning the frogs that he had brought upon Pharaoh.^d 13And the LORD did as Moses requested: the frogs died in the houses, the courtyards, and the fields. 14And they gathered them together in heaps, and the land stank. 15But when Pharaoh saw that there was a respite, he hardened his heart, and would not listen to them, just as the LORD had said.

8.1–15: The second plague: Swarms of frogs invade the land. The second plague involves the rupture of the created boundary that separates creatures of the water (frogs) and the dry land of Egypt. **3:** The same word, *swarm*, occurs in the creation story in Gen 1.20 to describe the creatures of the waters. **7:** On *the magicians*, see comment on 7.22. **8:** This is the first of several times when Pharaoh will seem to surrender but then quickly harden his heart and refuse to let the Israelites go (v. 15; see 8.28, 32; 9.27–28, 34–35;

a Ch 7.26 in Heb　　*b* Gk: Heb *upon your people*
c Ch 8.1 in Heb　　*d* Or *frogs, as he had agreed with Pharaoh*

10.16–17, 20, 24, 27). **15:** On Pharaoh's *hardened heart,* see comment on 4.21.

16 Then the LORD said to Moses, "Say to Aaron, 'Stretch out your staff and strike the dust of the earth, so that it may become gnats throughout the whole land of Egypt.' " [17]And they did so; Aaron stretched out his hand with his staff and struck the dust of the earth, and gnats came on humans and animals alike; all the dust of the earth turned into gnats throughout the whole land of Egypt. [18]The magicians tried to produce gnats by their secret arts, but they could not. There were gnats on both humans and animals. [19]And the magicians said to Pharaoh, "This is the finger of God!" But Pharaoh's heart was hardened, and he would not listen to them, just as the LORD had said.

8.16–19: The third plague: Dust turns into gnats. 18: For the first time, the Egyptian *magicians* are unable to duplicate the plague. See comment on 7.22. **19:** On Pharaoh's *hardened heart,* see comment on 4.21.

20 Then the LORD said to Moses, "Rise early in the morning and present yourself before Pharaoh, as he goes out to the water, and say to him, 'Thus says the LORD: Let my people go, so that they may worship me. [21]For if you will not let my people go, I will send swarms of flies on you, your officials, and your people, and into your houses; and the houses of the Egyptians shall be filled with swarms of flies; so also the land where they live. [22]But on that day I will set apart the land of Goshen, where my people live, so that no swarms of flies shall be there, that you may know that I the LORD am in this land. [23]Thus I will make a distinction*a* between my people and your people. This sign shall appear tomorrow.' " [24]The LORD did so, and great swarms of flies came into the house of Pharaoh and into his officials' houses; in all of Egypt the land was ruined because of the flies.

25 Then Pharaoh summoned Moses and Aaron, and said, "Go, sacrifice to your God within the land." [26]But Moses said, "It would not be right to do so; for the sacrifices

that we offer to the LORD our God are offensive to the Egyptians. If we offer in the sight of the Egyptians sacrifices that are offensive to them, will they not stone us? [27]We must go a three days' journey into the wilderness and sacrifice to the LORD our God as he commands us." [28]So Pharaoh said, "I will let you go to sacrifice to the LORD your God in the wilderness, provided you do not go very far away. Pray for me." [29]Then Moses said, "As soon as I leave you, I will pray to the LORD that the swarms of flies may depart tomorrow from Pharaoh, from his officials, and from his people; only do not let Pharaoh again deal falsely by not letting the people go to sacrifice to the LORD."

30 So Moses went out from Pharaoh and prayed to the LORD. [31]And the LORD did as Moses asked: he removed the swarms of flies from Pharaoh, from his officials, and from his people; not one remained. [32]But Pharaoh hardened his heart this time also, and would not let the people go.

8.20–32: The fourth plague: Swarms of flies invade Egyptian but not Israelite houses. 22: Israel had lived apart from the Egyptians in *the land of Goshen,* a fertile area in the delta region of the Nile River, since the days of Joseph (Gen 45.10). Israelite shepherds offended the Egyptians (Gen 43.32; 46.34). This offense and subsequent separation from other Egyptians proves to be advantageous, since the people of Israel are untouched by the plagues that terrorize Egypt (9.4, 26; 10.23). The tenth plague, with its blood on the doorpost of each individual Israelite house, seems to reflect another tradition in which the Israelites lived not apart from but among the other Egyptian homes (11.7; 12.23). **26:** The *sacrifices* probably involved sheep (12.1–10), and Egyptians found shepherds and sheep *offensive* (Gen 46.34). **28:** See v. 32 and the comment on 8.8. **32:** See comment on 4.21.

9 Then the LORD said to Moses, "Go to Pharaoh, and say to him, 'Thus says the LORD, the God of the Hebrews: Let my people go, so that they may worship me. [2]For if you refuse to let them go and still hold them, [3]the hand of the LORD will strike with a deadly pestilence your livestock in the field:

a Gk Vg: Heb *will set redemption*

the horses, the donkeys, the camels, the herds, and the flocks. 4But the LORD will make a distinction between the livestock of Israel and the livestock of Egypt, so that nothing shall die of all that belongs to the Israelites.'" 5The LORD set a time, saying, "Tomorrow the LORD will do this thing in the land." 6And on the next day the LORD did so; all the livestock of the Egyptians died, but of the livestock of the Israelites not one died. 7Pharaoh inquired and found that not one of the livestock of the Israelites was dead. But the heart of Pharaoh was hardened, and he would not let the people go.

9.1–7: The fifth plague: Disease kills Egyptian but not Israelite animals. 6: The claim that *all the live-stock of the Egyptians died* is in some tension with the later plagues, when more Egyptian livestock are repeatedly involved (9.10, 19–21; 11.5; 12.29). **7:** On Pharaoh's *hardened heart,* see comment on 4.21.

8 Then the LORD said to Moses and Aaron, "Take handfuls of soot from the kiln, and let Moses throw it in the air in the sight of Pharaoh. 9It shall become fine dust all over the land of Egypt, and shall cause festering boils on humans and animals throughout the whole land of Egypt." 10So they took soot from the kiln, and stood before Pharaoh, and Moses threw it in the air, and it caused festering boils on humans and animals. 11The magicians could not stand before Moses because of the boils, for the boils afflicted the magicians as well as all the Egyptians. 12But the LORD hardened the heart of Pharaoh, and he would not listen to them, just as the LORD had spoken to Moses.

9.8–12: The sixth plague: Soot and ashes cause boils on humans and animals. 10: This is the first plague in which *humans* are directly affected along with the *animals*. **11:** On the *magicians,* see comment on 7.22. **12:** On Pharaoh's *hardened heart,* see comment on 4.21. This is the first time *the LORD* explicitly *hardened his heart.*

13 Then the LORD said to Moses, "Rise up early in the morning and present yourself before Pharaoh, and say to him, 'Thus says the LORD, the God of the Hebrews: Let my people go, so that they may worship me. 14For this time I will send all my plagues upon you yourself, and upon your officials, and upon your people, so that you may know that there is no one like me in all the earth. 15For by now I could have stretched out my hand and struck you and your people with pestilence, and you would have been cut off from the earth. 16But this is why I have let you live: to show you my power, and to make my name resound through all the earth. 17You are still exalting yourself against my people, and will not let them go. 18Tomorrow at this time I will cause the heaviest hail to fall that has ever fallen in Egypt from the day it was founded until now. 19Send, therefore, and have your livestock and everything that you have in the open field brought to a secure place; every human or animal that is in the open field and is not brought under shelter will die when the hail comes down upon them.'" 20Those officials of Pharaoh who feared the word of the LORD hurried their slaves and livestock off to a secure place. 21Those who did not regard the word of the LORD left their slaves and livestock in the open field.

22 The LORD said to Moses, "Stretch out your hand toward heaven so that hail may fall on the whole land of Egypt, on humans and animals and all the plants of the field in the land of Egypt." 23Then Moses stretched out his staff toward heaven, and the LORD sent thunder and hail, and fire came down on the earth. And the LORD rained hail on the land of Egypt; 24there was hail with fire flashing continually in the midst of it, such heavy hail as had never fallen in all the land of Egypt since it became a nation. 25The hail struck down everything that was in the open field throughout all the land of Egypt, both human and animal; the hail also struck down all the plants of the field, and shattered every tree in the field. 26Only in the land of Goshen, where the Israelites were, there was no hail.

27 Then Pharaoh summoned Moses and Aaron, and said to them, "This time I have sinned; the LORD is in the right, and I and my people are in the wrong. 28Pray to the LORD! Enough of God's thunder and hail! I

will let you go; you need stay no longer." ²⁹Moses said to him, "As soon as I have gone out of the city, I will stretch out my hands to the LORD; the thunder will cease, and there will be no more hail, so that you may know that the earth is the LORD's. ³⁰But as for you and your officials, I know that you do not yet fear the LORD God." ³¹(Now the flax and the barley were ruined, for the barley was in the ear and the flax was in bud. ³²But the wheat and the spelt were not ruined, for they are late in coming up.) ³³So Moses left Pharaoh, went out of the city, and stretched out his hands to the LORD; then the thunder and the hail ceased, and the rain no longer poured down on the earth. ³⁴But when Pharaoh saw that the rain and the hail and the thunder had ceased, he sinned once more and hardened his heart, he and his officials. ³⁵So the heart of Pharaoh was hardened, and he would not let the Israelites go, just as the LORD had spoken through Moses.

9.13–35: The seventh plague: Thunder, hail, and fire pour out of the skies. 20–21: The story acknowledges for the first time a distinction between some Egyptians *who feared the word of the LORD* and *those who did not regard the word of the LORD*. **22:** The plagues' disruption of the order established by God at creation now extends to the *plants* as well as animals and humans (Gen 1.11–12, 2.5). **26:** On the separation of Israelites *in the land of Goshen*, see comment on 8.22. **27:** This is the first time Pharaoh confesses, *"I have sinned."* He will do so one more time in 10.16. **32:** Some plants survive, only to be devoured in the next plague (10.12, 15). **34–35:** On Pharaoh's *hardened heart,* see comment on 4.21.

10 Then the LORD said to Moses, "Go to Pharaoh; for I have hardened his heart and the heart of his officials, in order that I may show these signs of mine among them, ²and that you may tell your children and grandchildren how I have made fools of the Egyptians and what signs I have done among them—so that you may know that I am the LORD."

3 So Moses and Aaron went to Pharaoh, and said to him, "Thus says the LORD, the God of the Hebrews, 'How long will you refuse to humble yourself before me? Let my people go, so that they may worship me. ⁴For if you refuse to let my people go, tomorrow I will bring locusts into your country. ⁵They shall cover the surface of the land, so that no one will be able to see the land. They shall devour the last remnant left you after the hail, and they shall devour every tree of yours that grows in the field. ⁶They shall fill your houses, and the houses of all your officials and of all the Egyptians—something that neither your parents nor your grandparents have seen, from the day they came on earth to this day.' " Then he turned and went out from Pharaoh.

7 Pharaoh's officials said to him, "How long shall this fellow be a snare to us? Let the people go, so that they may worship the LORD their God; do you not yet understand that Egypt is ruined?" ⁸So Moses and Aaron were brought back to Pharaoh, and he said to them, "Go, worship the LORD your God! But which ones are to go?" ⁹Moses said, "We will go with our young and our old; we will go with our sons and daughters and with our flocks and herds, because we have the LORD's festival to celebrate." ¹⁰He said to them, "The LORD indeed will be with you, if ever I let your little ones go with you! Plainly, you have some evil purpose in mind. ¹¹No, never! Your men may go and worship the LORD, for that is what you are asking." And they were driven out from Pharaoh's presence.

12 Then the LORD said to Moses, "Stretch out your hand over the land of Egypt, so that the locusts may come upon it and eat every plant in the land, all that the hail has left." ¹³So Moses stretched out his staff over the land of Egypt, and the LORD brought an east wind upon the land all that day and all that night; when morning came, the east wind had brought the locusts. ¹⁴The locusts came upon all the land of Egypt and settled on the whole country of Egypt, such a dense swarm of locusts as had never been before, nor ever shall be again. ¹⁵They covered the surface of the whole land, so that the land was black; and they ate all the plants in the land and all the fruit of the trees that the hail had left; nothing green was left, no tree, no plant in the field, in all

the land of Egypt. [16]Pharaoh hurriedly summoned Moses and Aaron and said, "I have sinned against the LORD your God, and against you. [17]Do forgive my sin just this once, and pray to the LORD your God that at the least he remove this deadly thing from me." [18]So he went out from Pharaoh and prayed to the LORD. [19]The LORD changed the wind into a very strong west wind, which lifted the locusts and drove them into the Red Sea;[a] not a single locust was left in all the country of Egypt. [20]But the LORD hardened Pharaoh's heart, and he would not let the Israelites go.

10.1–20: The eighth plague: An east wind brings swarms of locusts. 7: This is the first time Pharaoh's own *officials* seek to persuade him to *let the people go.* **13:** The blowing of *the east wind* and the duration *all that night* anticipates the parallel events when "a strong east wind" blows back the waters of the Red Sea "all night" (14.21) to expose dry land so that the Israelites can cross safely. **15:** The land *black* with locusts anticipates the next plague of darkness (vv. 21–22). **16:** This is the second and last time Pharaoh confesses his guilt, *"I have sinned"* (see 9.27). **19:** The mention of the *wind* and the *Red Sea* foreshadows the Red Sea crossing (14.21, 28). **20:** On Pharaoh's *hardened heart,* see comment on 4.21.

---

21 Then the LORD said to Moses, "Stretch out your hand toward heaven so that there may be darkness over the land of Egypt, a darkness that can be felt." [22]So Moses stretched out his hand toward heaven, and there was dense darkness in all the land of Egypt for three days. [23]People could not see one another, and for three days they could not move from where they were; but all the Israelites had light where they lived. [24]Then Pharaoh summoned Moses, and said, "Go, worship the LORD. Only your flocks and your herds shall remain behind. Even your children may go with you." [25]But Moses said, "You must also let us have sacrifices and burnt offerings to sacrifice to the LORD our God. [26]Our livestock also must go with us; not a hoof shall be left behind, for we must choose some of them for the worship of the LORD our God, and we will not know what to use to worship the LORD until

we arrive there." [27]But the LORD hardened Pharaoh's heart, and he was unwilling to let them go. [28]Then Pharaoh said to him, "Get away from me! Take care that you do not see my face again, for on the day you see my face you shall die." [29]Moses said, "Just as you say! I will never see your face again."

10.21–29: The ninth plague: A dense darkness sweeps over all Egypt. 23: The Israelites again are separated and thus do not suffer the effects of the plagues on the Egyptians. See comment on 8.22. **27:** On Pharaoh's *hardened heart,* see comment on 4.21. **28–29:** Moses pledges not to seek an audience with Pharaoh again, but Pharaoh will in fact summon Moses one more time during the tenth and final plague (12.31). Moses' words may also hint at the death of Pharaoh and his army at the Red Sea crossing (14.13, 26–29).

---

11 The LORD said to Moses, "I will bring one more plague upon Pharaoh and upon Egypt; afterwards he will let you go from here; indeed, when he lets you go, he will drive you away. [2]Tell the people that every man is to ask his neighbor and every woman is to ask her neighbor for objects of silver and gold." [3]The LORD gave the people favor in the sight of the Egyptians. Moreover, Moses himself was a man of great importance in the land of Egypt, in the sight of Pharaoh's officials and in the sight of the people.

4 Moses said, "Thus says the LORD: About midnight I will go out through Egypt. [5]Every firstborn in the land of Egypt shall die, from the firstborn of Pharaoh who sits on his throne to the firstborn of the female slave who is behind the handmill, and all the firstborn of the livestock. [6]Then there will be a loud cry throughout the whole land of Egypt, such as has never been or will ever be again. [7]But not a dog shall growl at any of the Israelites—not at people, not at animals—so that you may know that the LORD makes a distinction between Egypt and Israel. [8]Then all these officials of yours shall come down to me, and bow low to me, saying, 'Leave us, you and all the people who

a Or Sea of Reeds

follow you.' After that I will leave." And in hot anger he left Pharaoh.

9 The LORD said to Moses, "Pharaoh will not listen to you, in order that my wonders may be multiplied in the land of Egypt." 10Moses and Aaron performed all these wonders before Pharaoh; but the LORD hardened Pharaoh's heart, and he did not let the people of Israel go out of his land.

11.1–10: Moses warns Pharaoh about the tenth and final plague. 1–2: The horror of the final plague will cause Pharaoh and the other Egyptians to plead with Israel to leave their land. The Egyptians will voluntarily surrender *objects of silver and gold* (v. 2) as predicted in 3.22 and fulfilled in 12.35–36. This plundering of the Egyptians signifies Egypt's defeat in the battle with Israel's God. Israel will carry away the spoils of war. **5:** The coming death of *every firstborn in the land of Egypt* expands the earlier judgment of 4.22–23, which predicted the death only of Pharaoh's firstborn son. Part of the background to this judgment is the deity's claim to all firstborn among humans and animals as God's rightful possession (13.1–2). **10:** On Pharaoh's *hardened heart,* see comment on 4.21.

12 The LORD said to Moses and Aaron in the land of Egypt: 2This month shall mark for you the beginning of months; it shall be the first month of the year for you. 3Tell the whole congregation of Israel that on the tenth of this month they are to take a lamb for each family, a lamb for each household. 4If a household is too small for a whole lamb, it shall join its closest neighbor in obtaining one; the lamb shall be divided in proportion to the number of people who eat of it. 5Your lamb shall be without blemish, a year-old male; you may take it from the sheep or from the goats. 6You shall keep it until the fourteenth day of this month; then the whole assembled congregation of Israel shall slaughter it at twilight. 7They shall take some of the blood and put it on the two doorposts and the lintel of the houses in which they eat it. 8They shall eat the lamb that same night; they shall eat it roasted over the fire with unleavened bread and bitter herbs. 9Do not eat any of it raw or boiled in water, but roasted over the fire, with its head, legs, and inner organs. 10You shall let none of it

remain until the morning; anything that remains until the morning you shall burn. 11This is how you shall eat it: your loins girded, your sandals on your feet, and your staff in your hand; and you shall eat it hurriedly. It is the passover of the LORD. 12For I will pass through the land of Egypt that night, and I will strike down every firstborn in the land of Egypt, both human beings and animals; on all the gods of Egypt I will execute judgments: I am the LORD. 13The blood shall be a sign for you on the houses where you live: when I see the blood, I will pass over you, and no plague shall destroy you when I strike the land of Egypt.

14 This day shall be a day of remembrance for you. You shall celebrate it as a festival to the LORD; throughout your generations you shall observe it as a perpetual ordinance. 15Seven days you shall eat unleavened bread; on the first day you shall remove leaven from your houses, for whoever eats leavened bread from the first day until the seventh day shall be cut off from Israel. 16On the first day you shall hold a solemn assembly, and on the seventh day a solemn assembly; no work shall be done on those days; only what everyone must eat, that alone may be prepared by you. 17You shall observe the festival of unleavened bread, for on this very day I brought your companies out of the land of Egypt: you shall observe this day throughout your generations as a perpetual ordinance. 18In the first month, from the evening of the fourteenth day until the evening of the twenty-first day, you shall eat unleavened bread. 19For seven days no leaven shall be found in your houses; for whoever eats what is leavened shall be cut off from the congregation of Israel, whether an alien or a native of the land. 20You shall eat nothing leavened; in all your settlements you shall eat unleavened bread.

21 Then Moses called all the elders of Israel and said to them, "Go, select lambs for your families, and slaughter the passover lamb. 22Take a bunch of hyssop, dip it in the blood that is in the basin, and touch the lintel and the two doorposts with the blood in the basin. None of you shall go outside the door of your house until morning. 23For the

LORD will pass through to strike down the Egyptians; when he sees the blood on the lintel and on the two doorposts, the LORD will pass over that door and will not allow the destroyer to enter your houses to strike you down. 24You shall observe this rite as a perpetual ordinance for you and your children. 25When you come to the land that the LORD will give you, as he has promised, you shall keep this observance. 26And when your children ask you, 'What do you mean by this observance?' 27you shall say, 'It is the passover sacrifice to the LORD, for he passed over the houses of the Israelites in Egypt, when he struck down the Egyptians but spared our houses.'" And the people bowed down and worshiped.

28 The Israelites went and did just as the LORD had commanded Moses and Aaron.

12.1–28: The LORD provides instructions for the annual festivals of Passover* and Unleavened Bread. The flow of the exodus story is interrupted by instructions for celebrating the two festivals of Passover and Unleavened Bread. The immediate purpose of the Passover is to mark every Israelite home with blood so that it will be protected from the effects of the tenth plague, the death of all Egyptian firstborn. After Israel leaves Egypt, the annual festivals of Passover and Unleavened Bread will enable future generations to remember and identify the story of the Exodus as their own (vv. 14–17). **2:** *This month* begins the new year. It occurs in the springtime (March—April) and is called either Abib (13.4; Deut 16.1) or Nisan (Esth 3.7) in later biblical traditions. Older biblical traditions begin the new year in the fall (23.16; 34.22). **7:** The smearing of the lamb's blood on the doorposts and lintel or upper door frame will mark the house as Israelite and thus protect it from the plague, which will kill all the Egyptian firstborn (vv. 12–13, 21–23). **8:** *Unleavened bread,* or biscuits without yeast, is quickly baked bread. Verses 33–34 provide the connection with the Exodus: The Israelites had to hurry out of Egypt and so could not wait for their bread dough to rise. The *bitter herbs* recall the bitterness of Israel's slavery. **9:** The lamb is to be *roasted* rather than eaten *raw or boiled* to ensure all of its blood is drained. The blood is the essence of life and must be returned to the deity and not eaten in recognition that life belongs to God (Gen 9.4; Lev 17.10–14). **13:** The verb *pass over* ("pasah," also in vv. 23, 27) is the basis for the festival's

name, Passover ("pesah," v. 11). **22:** *Hyssop** is an aromatic plant or bush that is used for ritual purification (Lev 14.4; Num 19.6). **23:** *The destroyer* is an agent that brings death and is here distinguished from *the LORD.*

29 At midnight the LORD struck down all the firstborn in the land of Egypt, from the firstborn of Pharaoh who sat on his throne to the firstborn of the prisoner who was in the dungeon, and all the firstborn of the livestock. 30Pharaoh arose in the night, he and all his officials and all the Egyptians; and there was a loud cry in Egypt, for there was not a house without someone dead. 31Then he summoned Moses and Aaron in the night, and said, "Rise up, go away from my people, both you and the Israelites! Go, worship the LORD, as you said. 32Take your flocks and your herds, as you said, and be gone. And bring a blessing on me too!"

33 The Egyptians urged the people to hasten their departure from the land, for they said, "We shall all be dead." 34So the people took their dough before it was leavened, with their kneading bowls wrapped up in their cloaks on their shoulders. 35The Israelites had done as Moses told them; they had asked the Egyptians for jewelry of silver and gold, and for clothing, 36and the LORD had given the people favor in the sight of the Egyptians, so that they let them have what they asked. And so they plundered the Egyptians.

37 The Israelites journeyed from Rameses to Succoth, about six hundred thousand men on foot, besides children. 38A mixed crowd also went up with them, and livestock in great numbers, both flocks and herds. 39They baked unleavened cakes of the dough that they had brought out of Egypt; it was not leavened, because they were driven out of Egypt and could not wait, nor had they prepared any provisions for themselves.

40 The time that the Israelites had lived in Egypt was four hundred thirty years. 41At the end of four hundred thirty years, on that very day, all the companies of the LORD went out from the land of Egypt. 42That was for the LORD a night of vigil, to bring them out of the land of Egypt. That same night is a

vigil to be kept for the LORD by all the Israelites throughout their generations.

43 The LORD said to Moses and Aaron: This is the ordinance for the passover: no foreigner shall eat of it, 44but any slave who has been purchased may eat of it after he has been circumcised; 45no bound or hired servant may eat of it. 46It shall be eaten in one house; you shall not take any of the animal outside the house, and you shall not break any of its bones. 47The whole congregation of Israel shall celebrate it. 48If an alien who resides with you wants to celebrate the passover to the LORD, all his males shall be circumcised; then he may draw near to celebrate it; he shall be regarded as a native of the land. But no uncircumcised person shall eat of it; 49there shall be one law for the native and for the alien who resides among you.

50 All the Israelites did just as the LORD had commanded Moses and Aaron. 51That very day the LORD brought the Israelites out of the land of Egypt, company by company.

12.29–51: Egypt's firstborn die and Israel departs from Egypt. 34: The haste to leave Egypt provides a rationale for the haste in eating the Passover✶ meal (vv. 8, 11) and for celebrating the festival of Unleavened Bread (v. 39; 13.3–10). **35–36:** The people of Israel *plundered* Egypt as they received *silver and gold* from their former oppressors. The plundered jewelry is Israel's war booty and implies the victory of Israel's God over Pharaoh. **37:** *Six hundred thousand men* apart from women, children, and elderly would mean an amazing total population of about two million Israelites. This large number appears again in the census list in Num 1.46 (603,550 Israelite warriors). A typical large army in this ancient period would be 15,000–20,000 warriors. **38:** A *mixed crowd* suggests an ethnically mixed group that joins the Israelites in fleeing Egypt (see Num 11.4). **41:** Gen 15.13 predicted 400 years of slavery in Egypt. Gen 15.16 predicted four generations or about 160 years (assuming 40 years per generation). **43–49:** The LORD provides further instructions about the Passover as it applies to *an alien who resides with you.* The instructions follow appropriately the earlier mention of the "mixed crowd" that joined Israel's exodus (v. 38).

13 The LORD said to Moses: 2Consecrate to me all the firstborn; what-ever is the first to open the womb among the Israelites, of human beings and animals, is mine.

3 Moses said to the people, "Remember this day on which you came out of Egypt, out of the house of slavery, because the LORD brought you out from there by strength of hand; no leavened bread shall be eaten. 4Today, in the month of Abib, you are going out. 5When the LORD brings you into the land of the Canaanites, the Hittites, the Amorites, the Hivites, and the Jebusites, which he swore to your ancestors to give you, a land flowing with milk and honey, you shall keep this observance in this month. 6Seven days you shall eat unleavened bread, and on the seventh day there shall be a festival to the LORD. 7Unleavened bread shall be eaten for seven days; no leavened bread shall be seen in your possession, and no leaven shall be seen among you in all your territory. 8You shall tell your child on that day, 'It is because of what the LORD did for me when I came out of Egypt.' 9It shall serve for you as a sign on your hand and as a reminder on your forehead, so that the teaching of the LORD may be on your lips; for with a strong hand the LORD brought you out of Egypt. 10You shall keep this ordinance at its proper time from year to year.

11 "When the LORD has brought you into the land of the Canaanites, as he swore to you and your ancestors, and has given it to you, 12you shall set apart to the LORD all that first opens the womb. All the firstborn of your livestock that are males shall be the LORD's. 13But every firstborn donkey you shall redeem with a sheep; if you do not redeem it, you must break its neck. Every firstborn male among your children you shall redeem. 14When in the future your child asks you, 'What does this mean?' you shall answer, 'By strength of hand the LORD brought us out of Egypt, from the house of slavery. 15When Pharaoh stubbornly refused to let us go, the LORD killed all the firstborn in the land of Egypt, from human firstborn to the firstborn of animals. Therefore I sacrifice to the LORD every male that first opens the womb, but every firstborn of my sons I redeem.' 16It shall serve as a sign on your hand

and as an emblem*a* on your forehead that by strength of hand the LORD brought us out of Egypt."

13.1–16: Unleavened Bread and the firstborn: God provides instructions for life in Canaan. The death of Egypt's firstborn (12.29) prompts the LORD to instruct Israel concerning the dedication or consecration of Israel's firstborn to God (vv. 1–2, 11–16). The instructions for Passover* (12.1–28, 43–51) also prompt God to provide laws for celebrating a closely related festival, the festival of Unleavened Bread (vv. 3–10). Both obligations will begin later, *when the LORD brings you into the land of the Canaanites* (vv. 5, 11). As such, the laws function as a promise for the future. **4:** On *the month of Abib*, see comment on 12.2. **5:** This listing of peoples—*the Canaanites, the Hittites, the Amorites, the Hivites, and the Jebusites*—is a traditional list of the native inhabitants of the promised land of Canaan (Gen 15.19–21; Deut 7.1). **9:** *Sign on your hand* and *reminder on your forehead* indicate ornaments that came to be worn in worship in remembrance of the Exodus. In Jewish practice, they are called phylacteries. See v. 16 and Deut 6.8. **13:** The *donkey* is ritually unclean (Lev 11.3). Therefore, a ritually clean animal (a sheep) must be offered to *redeem* or purchase back the firstborn donkey from God. If the owner does not redeem the donkey with a sheep, the owner *must break its neck* and kill it since it cannot be ritually slaughtered as a clean animal. The firstborn donkey belongs to God and cannot be used by humans without redeeming it. *Every firstborn male* child must be redeemed or purchased back from God, either with money (Num 18.16; five shekels*) or the substitution of a member of the priestly tribe of Levi (Num 3.11–13). On the meaning of *redeem*, see comment on 6.6. **16:** See comment on v. 9.

17 When Pharaoh let the people go, God did not lead them by way of the land of the Philistines, although that was nearer; for God thought, "If the people face war, they may change their minds and return to Egypt." 18So God led the people by the roundabout way of the wilderness toward the Red Sea.*b* The Israelites went up out of the land of Egypt prepared for battle. 19And Moses took with him the bones of Joseph who had required a solemn oath of the Israelites, saying, "God will surely take notice of you, and then you must carry my bones with you

from here." 20They set out from Succoth, and camped at Etham, on the edge of the wilderness. 21The LORD went in front of them in a pillar of cloud by day, to lead them along the way, and in a pillar of fire by night, to give them light, so that they might travel by day and by night. 22Neither the pillar of cloud by day nor the pillar of fire by night left its place in front of the people.

13.17–22: Led by the pillars of cloud and fire, Israel begins to leave Egypt. 17: *The Philistines* were a people who lived on the western border of Canaan near the shores of the Mediterranean Sea. Their territory would have been the most direct route from Goshen (the Nile Delta region of Egypt) to Canaan. However, the reference to *the Philistines* here may represent a later tradition since the Philistines settled this region sometime later than the traditional date for Israel's exodus (after 1200 BCE). **18:** Some scholars argue that the *Red Sea* ("yam suf") is too far south and too large a body of water to have been the sea Israel would eventually cross (14.21–28). Thus, some prefer to call it the "Sea of Reeds" and assume it was a shallow body of water farther north in Egypt near the Mediterranean Sea. However, later readers in ancient Israel may have known only about the larger Red Sea. **19:** See Gen 50.24–26. **20:** The place name *Succoth* in Hebrew means "Booths" or temporary shelters. The locations of Succoth and Ethan are uncertain, except that they are on the eastern border of Egypt. **21:** The two pillars or columns of cloud and fire are apparently one and the same (14.24–25). The cloud by itself is visible by day. At night, only the fire within the cloud is visible. The cloud and fire are visible signs of God's presence among the Israelites.

14 Then the LORD said to Moses: 2Tell the Israelites to turn back and camp in front of Pi-hahiroth, between Migdol and the sea, in front of Baal-zephon; you shall camp opposite it, by the sea. 3Pharaoh will say of the Israelites, "They are wandering aimlessly in the land; the wilderness has closed in on them." 4I will harden Pharaoh's heart, and he will pursue them, so that I will gain glory for myself over Pharaoh and all his

a Or *as a frontlet*; Meaning of Heb uncertain
b Or *Sea of Reeds*

army; and the Egyptians shall know that I am the LORD. And they did so.

5 When the king of Egypt was told that the people had fled, the minds of Pharaoh and his officials were changed toward the people, and they said, "What have we done, letting Israel leave our service?" [6]So he had his chariot made ready, and took his army with him; [7]he took six hundred picked chariots and all the other chariots of Egypt with officers over all of them. [8]The LORD hardened the heart of Pharaoh king of Egypt and he pursued the Israelites, who were going out boldly. [9]The Egyptians pursued them, all Pharaoh's horses and chariots, his chariot drivers and his army; they overtook them camped by the sea, by Pi-hahiroth, in front of Baal-zephon.

10 As Pharaoh drew near, the Israelites looked back, and there were the Egyptians advancing on them. In great fear the Israelites cried out to the LORD. [11]They said to Moses, "Was it because there were no graves in Egypt that you have taken us away to die in the wilderness? What have you done to us, bringing us out of Egypt? [12]Is this not the very thing we told you in Egypt, 'Let us alone and let us serve the Egyptians'? For it would have been better for us to serve the Egyptians than to die in the wilderness." [13]But Moses said to the people, "Do not be afraid, stand firm, and see the deliverance that the LORD will accomplish for you today; for the Egyptians whom you see today you shall never see again. [14]The LORD will fight for you, and you have only to keep still."

15 Then the LORD said to Moses, "Why do you cry out to me? Tell the Israelites to go forward. [16]But you lift up your staff, and stretch out your hand over the sea and divide it, that the Israelites may go into the sea on dry ground. [17]Then I will harden the hearts of the Egyptians so that they will go in after them; and so I will gain glory for myself over Pharaoh and all his army, his chariots, and his chariot drivers. [18]And the Egyptians shall know that I am the LORD, when I have gained glory for myself over Pharaoh, his chariots, and his chariot drivers."

19 The angel of God who was going before the Israelite army moved and went behind them; and the pillar of cloud moved from in front of them and took its place behind them. [20]It came between the army of Egypt and the army of Israel. And so the cloud was there with the darkness, and it lit up the night; one did not come near the other all night.

21 Then Moses stretched out his hand over the sea. The LORD drove the sea back by a strong east wind all night, and turned the sea into dry land; and the waters were divided. [22]The Israelites went into the sea on dry ground, the waters forming a wall for them on their right and on their left. [23]The Egyptians pursued, and went into the sea after them, all of Pharaoh's horses, chariots, and chariot drivers. [24]At the morning watch the LORD in the pillar of fire and cloud looked down upon the Egyptian army, and threw the Egyptian army into panic. [25]He clogged[a] their chariot wheels so that they turned with difficulty. The Egyptians said, "Let us flee from the Israelites, for the LORD is fighting for them against Egypt."

26 Then the LORD said to Moses, "Stretch out your hand over the sea, so that the water may come back upon the Egyptians, upon their chariots and chariot drivers." [27]So Moses stretched out his hand over the sea, and at dawn the sea returned to its normal depth. As the Egyptians fled before it, the LORD tossed the Egyptians into the sea. [28]The waters returned and covered the chariots and the chariot drivers, the entire army of Pharaoh that had followed them into the sea; not one of them remained. [29]But the Israelites walked on dry ground through the sea, the waters forming a wall for them on their right and on their left.

30 Thus the LORD saved Israel that day from the Egyptians; and Israel saw the Egyptians dead on the seashore. [31]Israel saw the great work that the LORD did against the Egyptians. So the people feared the LORD and believed in the LORD and in his servant Moses.

14.1–31: Israel crosses the Red Sea, and God defeats the Egyptians. As Pharaoh had tried to drown

a Sam Gk Syr: MT *removed*

The Red Sea Crossing and Creation Stories

The *dividing* of *the sea* and the drying up of the sea to clear *dry ground* (14.16, 21–22; 15.8) contain echoes of some accounts of the world's creation in the ancient world, including Israel. Creation occurs as the LORD splits or cuts into pieces the primeval sea monster or dragon named Rahab or Leviathan.★ Alternatively, the LORD defeats the watery primeval chaos by drying up the sea. In this regard, Isa 51.9–10 addresses the LORD: "Was it not you who cut Rahab in pieces, who pierced the dragon? Was it not you who dried up the sea, the waters of the great deep?" Psalm 74.12–15 speaks in a similar vein: "You divided the sea by your might; you broke the heads of the dragons in the waters. You crushed the heads of Leviathan . . . You dried up ever-flowing streams." These creation themes help to interpret the larger significance of Israel's exodus out of Egypt as the deity's defeat of the primal forces of evil and chaos in the world.

Israel's children in the Nile River (1.22), so Pharaoh and his army will drown in the Red Sea. The sea crossing is one of the central events in ancient Israel's collective memory. **2:** *Pi-hahiroth, Migdol,* and *Baal-zephon* appear here as sites on the eastern boundary of Egypt, just before Israel crosses into the wilderness of the Sinai Peninsula. **4:** On Pharaoh's *hardened heart,* see comment on 4.21. **8:** On Pharaoh's *hardened heart,* see v. 4 and comment on 4.21. **13:** *The Egyptians . . . you shall never see again* recalls Moses' words to Pharaoh in 10.28–29. **14:** The image of *the LORD* as a divine warrior★ who *will fight for you* is a frequent biblical theme (15.3; Ps 24.8; Isa 42.13). **17:** On the *hardening of the heart,* see comment on 4.21. **19:** The *angel* is an alternate way of describing the presence of the LORD (v. 24).

Moses and Miriam sing songs of victory
15.1–21: These songs of Moses and Miriam represent some of the earliest traditions of the Bible. The elevated language of Hebrew poetry in the songs contains many examples of parallelism,★ or doubling of thoughts and images in consecutive lines. A recurring image in the poem is the stone. Israel's enemy sinks or freezes in fear like a lead stone (vv. 5, 10, 16) in contrast to the eternal security of God's stone mountain sanctuary (vv. 17–18). The Song of Moses (vv. 1–18) retells the story of ch. 14 with some differences in details. For example, Israel's crossing the sea on dry land (14.22) is not described in the song.

15 Then Moses and the Israelites sang this song to the LORD:

"I will sing to the LORD, for he has
    triumphed gloriously;
  horse and rider he has thrown into
    the sea.
2 The LORD is my strength and my might,ᵃ
    and he has become my salvation;
  this is my God, and I will praise him,
    my father's God, and I will exalt him.
3 The LORD is a warrior;
    the LORD is his name.

4 "Pharaoh's chariots and his army he
    cast into the sea;
  his picked officers were sunk in the
    Red Sea.ᵇ
5 The floods covered them;
    they went down into the depths like a
    stone.
6 Your right hand, O LORD, glorious in
    power—
  your right hand, O LORD, shattered
    the enemy.
7 In the greatness of your majesty you
    overthrew your adversaries;
  you sent out your fury, it consumed
    them like stubble.
8 At the blast of your nostrils the waters
    piled up,
  the floods stood up in a heap;
    the deeps congealed in the heart of
    the sea.

a Or *song*   *b* Or *Sea of Reeds*

9 The enemy said, 'I will pursue, I will
        overtake,
    I will divide the spoil, my desire shall
        have its fill of them.
    I will draw my sword, my hand shall
        destroy them.'
10 You blew with your wind, the sea
        covered them;
    they sank like lead in the mighty
        waters.

11 "Who is like you, O LORD, among the
        gods?
    Who is like you, majestic in holiness,
        awesome in splendor, doing wonders?
12 You stretched out your right hand,
    the earth swallowed them.

13 "In your steadfast love you led the
        people whom you redeemed;
    you guided them by your strength to
        your holy abode.
14 The peoples heard, they trembled;
    pangs seized the inhabitants of
        Philistia.
15 Then the chiefs of Edom were
        dismayed;
    trembling seized the leaders of Moab;
    all the inhabitants of Canaan melted
        away.
16 Terror and dread fell upon them;
    by the might of your arm, they
        became still as a stone
    until your people, O LORD, passed by,
    until the people whom you acquired
        passed by.
17 You brought them in and planted them
        on the mountain of your own
        possession,
    the place, O LORD, that you made
        your abode,
    the sanctuary, O LORD, that your
        hands have established.
18 The LORD will reign forever and ever."

19 When the horses of Pharaoh with his
chariots and his chariot drivers went into the
sea, the LORD brought back the waters of the
sea upon them; but the Israelites walked
through the sea on dry ground.

20 Then the prophet Miriam, Aaron's sister, took a tambourine in her hand; and all
the women went out after her with tambourines and with dancing. 21 And Miriam sang
to them:
    "Sing to the LORD, for he has
        triumphed gloriously;
    horse and rider he has thrown into the
        sea."

15.1–21. 3: *The* LORD *is a warrior:* see comment on
14.14. **4:** On *the Red Sea,* see comment on 13.18. **11:**
Who is like you, O LORD *, among the gods?* This question assumes that the LORD is the one superior god
above a number of other lesser gods gathered in a
heavenly council. This theme occurs in other ancient
biblical poems (Ps 86.8; 89.6–8). **13:** The poem turns
from the victory against the Egyptians and describes
God leading Israel to the land of Canaan. **14–16:** *Philistia* (v. 14), *Edom, Moab,* and *Canaan* (v. 15) are
nations in and around the promised land of Canaan
whom Israel will encounter on the way there. **17:** *The
mountain* may be a reference to the much later establishment of the LORD's Temple* on Mount Zion* in
the city of Jerusalem (Ps 48.1–3) or to the hill country
of Canaan in general (Ps 78.54). **20–21:** *The prophet*
Miriam may have been the original bard or singer in
an earlier version of the tradition. It was women who
typically sang victory songs after military victories in
ancient Israel (Judg 11.34; 1 Sam 18.6–7).

Israel complains and God responds
15.22–17.7: God provides water and food in response
to the legitimate complaints of Israel as they enter into
the dry desert of the Sinai Peninsula. Similar complaints about food and water later (see Num 11.1–9,
31–35; 20.1–13) provoke God's anger and punishment.

---

22 Then Moses ordered Israel to set out
from the Red Sea,ᵃ and they went into the
wilderness of Shur. They went three days in
the wilderness and found no water. 23 When
they came to Marah, they could not drink
the water of Marah because it was bitter.
That is why it was called Marah.ᵇ 24 And the
people complained against Moses, saying,
"What shall we drink?" 25 He cried out to the
LORD; and the LORD showed him a piece of
wood;ᶜ he threw it into the water, and the
water became sweet.

a Or *Sea of Reeds*   *b* That is *Bitterness*   *c* Or *a tree*

There the LORD[a] made for them a statute and an ordinance and there he put them to the test. 26He said, "If you will listen carefully to the voice of the LORD your God, and do what is right in his sight, and give heed to his commandments and keep all his statutes, I will not bring upon you any of the diseases that I brought upon the Egyptians; for I am the LORD who heals you."

27 Then they came to Elim, where there were twelve springs of water and seventy palm trees; and they camped there by the water.

16 The whole congregation of the Israelites set out from Elim; and Israel came to the wilderness of Sin, which is between Elim and Sinai, on the fifteenth day of the second month after they had departed from the land of Egypt. 2The whole congregation of the Israelites complained against Moses and Aaron in the wilderness. 3The Israelites said to them, "If only we had died by the hand of the LORD in the land of Egypt, when we sat by the fleshpots and ate our fill of bread; for you have brought us out into this wilderness to kill this whole assembly with hunger."

4 Then the LORD said to Moses, "I am going to rain bread from heaven for you, and each day the people shall go out and gather enough for that day. In that way I will test them, whether they will follow my instruction or not. 5On the sixth day, when they prepare what they bring in, it will be twice as much as they gather on other days." 6So Moses and Aaron said to all the Israelites, "In the evening you shall know that it was the LORD who brought you out of the land of Egypt, 7and in the morning you shall see the glory of the LORD, because he has heard your complaining against the LORD. For what are we, that you complain against us?" 8And Moses said, "When the LORD gives you meat to eat in the evening and your fill of bread in the morning, because the LORD has heard the complaining that you utter against him—what are we? Your complaining is not against us but against the LORD."

25: Traditional cultures believed that certain kinds of *wood* or trees had the ability to "heal" poisonous water and make it *sweet* or drinkable. **16.1:** *The wilderness of Sin* is in the Sinai Peninsula just east of Egypt. **5:** They will gather *twice as much* on the *sixth day* in order that they may rest on the seventh day. The seventh day is the day of sabbath rest when no work is to be done (vv. 22–30; see the commandment in 20.8–11).

9 Then Moses said to Aaron, "Say to the whole congregation of the Israelites, 'Draw near to the LORD, for he has heard your complaining.'" 10And as Aaron spoke to the whole congregation of the Israelites, they looked toward the wilderness, and the glory of the LORD appeared in the cloud. 11The LORD spoke to Moses and said, 12"I have heard the complaining of the Israelites; say to them, 'At twilight you shall eat meat, and in the morning you shall have your fill of bread; then you shall know that I am the LORD your God.'"

13 In the evening quails came up and covered the camp; and in the morning there was a layer of dew around the camp. 14When the layer of dew lifted, there on the surface of the wilderness was a fine flaky substance, as fine as frost on the ground. 15When the Israelites saw it, they said to one another, "What is it?"[b] For they did not know what it was. Moses said to them, "It is the bread that the LORD has given you to eat. 16This is what the LORD has commanded: 'Gather as much of it as each of you needs, an omer to a person according to the number of persons, all providing for those in their own tents.'" 17The Israelites did so, some gathering more, some less. 18But when they measured it with an omer, those who gathered much had nothing over, and those who gathered little had no shortage; they gathered as much as each of them needed. 19And Moses said to them, "Let no one leave any of it over until morning." 20But they did not listen to Moses; some left part of it until morning, and it bred worms and became foul. And Moses was angry with them. 21Morning by morning

---

15.22–16.8. 23: The place name *Marah* means "Bitterness," a wordplay on the *bitter* water there.

a Heb *he*　　*b* Or *"It is manna"* (Heb *man hu*, see verse 31)

they gathered it, as much as each needed; but when the sun grew hot, it melted.

22 On the sixth day they gathered twice as much food, two omers apiece. When all the leaders of the congregation came and told Moses, 23 he said to them, "This is what the LORD has commanded: 'Tomorrow is a day of solemn rest, a holy sabbath to the LORD; bake what you want to bake and boil what you want to boil, and all that is left over put aside to be kept until morning.'" 24 So they put it aside until morning, as Moses commanded them; and it did not become foul, and there were no worms in it. 25 Moses said, "Eat it today, for today is a sabbath to the LORD; today you will not find it in the field. 26 Six days you shall gather it; but on the seventh day, which is a sabbath, there will be none."

27 On the seventh day some of the people went out to gather, and they found none. 28 The LORD said to Moses, "How long will you refuse to keep my commandments and instructions? 29 See! The LORD has given you the sabbath, therefore on the sixth day he gives you food for two days; each of you stay where you are; do not leave your place on the seventh day." 30 So the people rested on the seventh day.

31 The house of Israel called it manna; it was like coriander seed, white, and the taste of it was like wafers made with honey. 32 Moses said, "This is what the LORD has commanded: 'Let an omer of it be kept throughout your generations, in order that they may see the food with which I fed you in the wilderness, when I brought you out of the land of Egypt.'" 33 And Moses said to Aaron, "Take a jar, and put an omer of manna in it, and place it before the LORD, to be kept throughout your generations." 34 As the LORD commanded Moses, so Aaron placed it before the covenant,a for safekeeping. 35 The Israelites ate manna forty years, until they came to a habitable land; they ate manna, until they came to the border of the land of Canaan. 36 An omer is a tenth of an ephah.

17 From the wilderness of Sin the whole congregation of the Israelites journeyed by stages, as the LORD com-

manded. They camped at Rephidim, but there was no water for the people to drink. 2 The people quarreled with Moses, and said, "Give us water to drink." Moses said to them, "Why do you quarrel with me? Why do you test the LORD?" 3 But the people thirsted there for water; and the people complained against Moses and said, "Why did you bring us out of Egypt, to kill us and our children and livestock with thirst?" 4 So Moses cried out to the LORD, "What shall I do with this people? They are almost ready to stone me." 5 The LORD said to Moses, "Go on ahead of the people, and take some of the elders of Israel with you; take in your hand the staff with which you struck the Nile, and go. 6 I will be standing there in front of you on the rock at Horeb. Strike the rock, and water will come out of it, so that the people may drink." Moses did so, in the sight of the elders of Israel. 7 He called the place Massahb and Meribah,c because the Israelites quarreled and tested the LORD, saying, "Is the LORD among us or not?"

16.9–17.7. 15: The phrase *What is it?* ("man hu") is a pun on the name of the food "manna" (v. 31). 16: *An omer* is a unit of dry measure, less than a gallon. See v. 36 where the *omer* is defined as one-tenth of an "ephah." An "ephah" is about 20 liters. 34: *The covenant*★ refers to the two stone tablets on which the Ten Commandments were written. The tablets were carried in an ornate container called the "ark" or "ark of the covenant" (25.16). Aaron placed the jar of manna into the same ark. 35: The transition from *manna* to the produce of *Canaan* occurs in Josh 5.12. 17.7: *Massah* means "Test," and *Meribah* means "Quarrel."

---

8 Then Amalek came and fought with Israel at Rephidim. 9 Moses said to Joshua, "Choose some men for us and go out, fight with Amalek. Tomorrow I will stand on the top of the hill with the staff of God in my hand." 10 So Joshua did as Moses told him, and fought with Amalek, while Moses, Aaron, and Hur went up to the top of the hill. 11 Whenever Moses held up his hand,

a Or *treaty* or *testimony*; Heb *eduth*   b That is *Test*
c That is *Quarrel*

Israel prevailed; and whenever he lowered his hand, Amalek prevailed. 12But Moses' hands grew weary; so they took a stone and put it under him, and he sat on it. Aaron and Hur held up his hands, one on one side, and the other on the other side; so his hands were steady until the sun set. 13And Joshua defeated Amalek and his people with the sword.

14 Then the LORD said to Moses, "Write this as a reminder in a book and recite it in the hearing of Joshua: I will utterly blot out the remembrance of Amalek from under heaven." 15And Moses built an altar and called it, The LORD is my banner. 16He said, "A hand upon the banner of the LORD!a The LORD will have war with Amalek from generation to generation."

17.8–16: Amalek attacks Israel, but Israel defeats them. 8: *Amalek* is a desert tribe from the nation of Edom (Gen 36.12) that lives in the wilderness around Kadesh (Num 13.29). **9:** This is the first mention of *Joshua.* Joshua is Moses' young assistant (24.13; 33.11) and Israel's military commander. Joshua becomes leader of all Israel after Moses' death (Num 27.12–23; Josh 1.1–11). **10:** *Hur* is a leader in the Israelite tribe of Judah (24.14; 31.2). **11–12:** Moses' raised hands are a sign of divine power that aids the Israelites in their battle against Amalek. **14:** *Write . . . in a book:* This is the first reference to Moses' writing in a book or scroll. 1 Chronicles 4.41–43 recounts the final defeat of Amalek during the reign of Hezekiah, king of Judah. **15:** The word *banner* ("nas") puns on the verb "test" ("nasah," v. 7). **16:** *War with Amalek* continues for many generations (1 Sam 15.1–9; 30.1–20).

Jethro gives administrative advice

18.1–27: Alternate versions of this story in which Jethro is not involved occur in Num 11.10–30 and Deut 1.9–18.

---

18 Jethro, the priest of Midian, Moses' father-in-law, heard of all that God had done for Moses and for his people Israel, how the LORD had brought Israel out of Egypt. 2After Moses had sent away his wife Zipporah, his father-in-law Jethro took her back, 3along with her two sons. The name of the one was Gershom (for he said, "I have

been an alienb in a foreign land"), 4and the name of the other, Eliezerc (for he said, "The God of my father was my help, and delivered me from the sword of Pharaoh"). 5Jethro, Moses' father-in-law, came into the wilderness where Moses was encamped at the mountain of God, bringing Moses' sons and wife to him. 6He sent word to Moses, "I, your father-in-law Jethro, am coming to you, with your wife and her two sons." 7Moses went out to meet his father-in-law; he bowed down and kissed him; each asked after the other's welfare, and they went into the tent. 8Then Moses told his father-in-law all that the LORD had done to Pharaoh and to the Egyptians for Israel's sake, all the hardship that had beset them on the way, and how the LORD had delivered them. 9Jethro rejoiced for all the good that the LORD had done to Israel, in delivering them from the Egyptians.

10 Jethro said, "Blessed be the LORD, who has delivered you from the Egyptians and from Pharaoh. 11Now I know that the LORD is greater than all gods, because he delivered the people from the Egyptians,d when they dealt arrogantly with them." 12And Jethro, Moses' father-in-law, brought a burnt offering and sacrifices to God; and Aaron came with all the elders of Israel to eat bread with Moses' father-in-law in the presence of God.

13 The next day Moses sat as judge for the people, while the people stood around him from morning until evening. 14When Moses' father-in-law saw all that he was doing for the people, he said, "What is this that you are doing for the people? Why do you sit alone, while all the people stand around you from morning until evening?" 15Moses said to his father-in-law, "Because the people come to me to inquire of God. 16When they have a dispute, they come to me and I decide between one person and another, and I make known to them the statutes and instructions of God." 17Moses' father-in-law said to him, "What you are doing is not good. 18You will surely wear yourself out, both you and these

a Cn: Meaning of Heb uncertain   b Heb ger
c Heb Eli, my God; ezer, help   d The clause
because . . . Egyptians has been transposed from verse 10

people with you. For the task is too heavy for you; you cannot do it alone. ¹⁹Now listen to me. I will give you counsel, and God be with you! You should represent the people before God, and you should bring their cases before God; ²⁰teach them the statutes and instructions and make known to them the way they are to go and the things they are to do. ²¹You should also look for able men among all the people, men who fear God, are trustworthy, and hate dishonest gain; set such men over them as officers over thousands, hundreds, fifties and tens. ²²Let them sit as judges for the people at all times; let them bring every important case to you, but decide every minor case themselves. So it will be easier for you, and they will bear the burden with you. ²³If you do this, and God so commands you, then you will be able to endure, and all these people will go to their home in peace."

24 So Moses listened to his father-in-law and did all that he had said. ²⁵Moses chose able men from all Israel and appointed them as heads over the people, as officers over thousands, hundreds, fifties, and tens. ²⁶And they judged the people at all times;

■▬▬▬▬▬▬▬▬▬▬▬▬▬▬▬▬▬▬▬▬▬▬▬▬▬▬▬▬▬▬▬▬▬▬▬▬■

Map Israel's exodus out of Egypt and wilderness journey

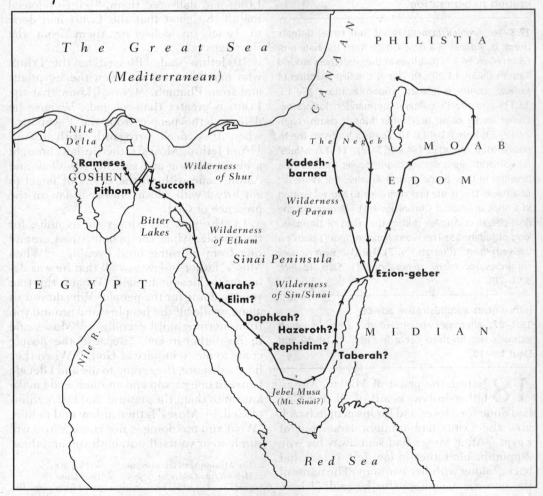

hard cases they brought to Moses, but any minor case they decided themselves. ²⁷Then Moses let his father-in-law depart, and he went off to his own country.

18.1–27. 1: The name of Moses' father-in-law is *Jethro* here, but the name varies in other biblical traditions. His name is sometimes Reuel (2.18) or Hobab (Num 10.29; Judg 4.11). **2:** Moses' Midianite wife Zipporah (2.21–22) went with Moses from Midian to Egypt (4.20). At some point, *Moses had sent away his wife.* Now Jethro brings her and the two sons back to join Moses (vv. 5–6). **3:** On *Gershom*, see comment on 2.22. **4:** The name *Eliezer* means "my God [is] help." **5:** *The mountain of God* is Mount Horeb, otherwise known as Mount Sinai (3.1). **21:** These numbered divisions of the population most often appear in military contexts (2 Sam 18.1).

Israel prepares for the covenant with the LORD 19.1–25: This chapter begins a major new section within the book of Exodus, 19.1–24.18. God initiates a formal relationship or covenant agreement with Israel. This covenant includes lists of obligations for Israel in the form of the Ten Commandments (20.1–17) and the laws in the Book of the Covenant (20.22–23.19). Israel will remain encamped in this area at Sinai until Num 10.11–12.

---

19 On the third new moon after the Israelites had gone out of the land of Egypt, on that very day, they came into the wilderness of Sinai. ²They had journeyed from Rephidim, entered the wilderness of Sinai, and camped in the wilderness; Israel camped there in front of the mountain. ³Then Moses went up to God; the LORD called to him from the mountain, saying, "Thus you shall say to the house of Jacob, and tell the Israelites: ⁴You have seen what I did to the Egyptians, and how I bore you on eagles' wings and brought you to myself. ⁵Now therefore, if you obey my voice and keep my covenant, you shall be my treasured possession out of all the peoples. Indeed, the whole earth is mine, ⁶but you shall be for me a priestly kingdom and a holy nation. These are the words that you shall speak to the Israelites."

7 So Moses came, summoned the elders of the people, and set before them all these words that the LORD had commanded him. ⁸The people all answered as one: "Everything that the LORD has spoken we will do." Moses reported the words of the people to the LORD. ⁹Then the LORD said to Moses, "I am going to come to you in a dense cloud, in order that the people may hear when I speak with you and so trust you ever after."

When Moses had told the words of the people to the LORD, ¹⁰the LORD said to Moses: "Go to the people and consecrate them today and tomorrow. Have them wash their clothes ¹¹and prepare for the third day, because on the third day the LORD will come down upon Mount Sinai in the sight of all the people. ¹²You shall set limits for the people all around, saying, 'Be careful not to go up the mountain or to touch the edge of it. Any who touch the mountain shall be put to death. ¹³No hand shall touch them, but they shall be stoned or shot with arrows;*ᵃ* whether animal or human being, they shall not live.' When the trumpet sounds a long blast, they may go up on the mountain." ¹⁴So Moses went down from the mountain to the people. He consecrated the people, and they washed their clothes. ¹⁵And he said to the people, "Prepare for the third day; do not go near a woman."

16 On the morning of the third day there was thunder and lightning, as well as a thick cloud on the mountain, and a blast of a trumpet so loud that all the people who were in the camp trembled. ¹⁷Moses brought the people out of the camp to meet God. They took their stand at the foot of the mountain. ¹⁸Now Mount Sinai was wrapped in smoke, because the LORD had descended upon it in fire; the smoke went up like the smoke of a kiln, while the whole mountain shook violently. ¹⁹As the blast of the trumpet grew louder and louder, Moses would speak and God would answer him in thunder. ²⁰When the LORD descended upon Mount Sinai, to the top of the mountain, the LORD summoned Moses to the top of the mountain, and Moses went up. ²¹Then the LORD said to Moses, "Go down and warn the people not to break through to the LORD to look; oth-

a Heb lacks *with arrows*

erwise many of them will perish. 22 Even the priests who approach the LORD must consecrate themselves or the LORD will break out against them." 23 Moses said to the LORD, "The people are not permitted to come up to Mount Sinai; for you yourself warned us, saying, 'Set limits around the mountain and keep it holy.' " 24 The LORD said to him, "Go down, and come up bringing Aaron with you; but do not let either the priests or the people break through to come up to the LORD; otherwise he will break out against them." 25 So Moses went down to the people and told them.

19.1–25. 1: *The wilderness of Sinai* in the Sinai Peninsula east of Egypt contains many mountains. The exact location of Mount Sinai is not known. The mountain is traditionally located in the south-central area of the Sinai Peninsula. 4: The image of God leading Israel out of Egypt like an eagle is expanded in Deut 32.11. 6: Israel as *a priestly kingdom and a holy nation* implies that God has set Israel apart from other nations. Israel has a higher standard of holiness and a mission to mediate between God and other nations. 12–13: The mountain is holy because of God's presence. Holiness and ritual impurity cannot mix. Unless a person is properly prepared, any human contact with the realm of God's holiness leads to death (vv. 21–24). 15: Sexual relations rendered a person ritually unclean for a day (1 Sam 21.4). 16: Ancient Israel and its neighboring cultures often portrayed the appearance of the deity with an accompanying storm of *thunder, lightning,* and a *thick cloud* (Ps 29; 68). 21–24: On the danger of crossing the boundary of holiness, see comment on vv. 12–13.

The Ten Commandments
20.1–21: These ten rules form the core of Israel's obligation in its relationship with God. Moses repeats these Ten Commandments in slightly altered form to a new generation in Deut 5.6–21. God is the one who writes the Ten Commandments on two stone tablets (31.18). The commandments are a central element of the faith of Judaism and Christianity.

20 Then God spoke all these words: 2 I am the LORD your God, who brought you out of the land of Egypt, out of the house of slavery; 3 you shall have no other gods before*a* me.

4 You shall not make for yourself an idol, whether in the form of anything that is in heaven above, or that is on the earth beneath, or that is in the water under the earth. 5 You shall not bow down to them or worship them; for I the LORD your God am a jealous God, punishing children for the iniquity of parents, to the third and the fourth generation of those who reject me, 6 but showing steadfast love to the thousandth generation*b* of those who love me and keep my commandments.

7 You shall not make wrongful use of the name of the LORD your God, for the LORD will not acquit anyone who misuses his name.

8 Remember the sabbath day, and keep it holy. 9 Six days you shall labor and do all your work. 10 But the seventh day is a sabbath to the LORD your God; you shall not do any work—you, your son or your daughter, your male or female slave, your livestock, or the alien resident in your towns. 11 For in six days the LORD made heaven and earth, the sea, and all that is in them, but rested the seventh day; therefore the LORD blessed the sabbath day and consecrated it.

12 Honor your father and your mother, so that your days may be long in the land that the LORD your God is giving you.

13 You shall not murder.*c*

14 You shall not commit adultery.

15 You shall not steal.

16 You shall not bear false witness against your neighbor.

17 You shall not covet your neighbor's house; you shall not covet your neighbor's wife, or male or female slave, or ox, or donkey, or anything that belongs to your neighbor.

18 When all the people witnessed the thunder and lightning, the sound of the trumpet, and the mountain smoking, they were afraid*d* and trembled and stood at a distance, 19 and said to Moses, "You speak to us, and we will listen; but do not let God speak to us, or we will die." 20 Moses said to

a Or *besides*   b Or *to thousands*   c Or *kill*
d Sam Gk Syr Vg: MT *they saw*

the people, "Do not be afraid; for God has come only to test you and to put the fear of him upon you so that you do not sin." 21Then the people stood at a distance, while Moses drew near to the thick darkness where God was.

20.1–21. 4: The description assumes a three-level universe: *heaven above, earth beneath,* and *water under the earth.* See Gen 1.6–10. **7:** The prohibition against the *wrongful use of the name of the* LORD is aimed particularly at violating oaths made in the deity's name (Lev 19.12). **8:** The root meaning of the *sabbath* is "to stop, to rest." To *keep it holy* signifies setting the seventh day apart as different from all other days of the week. **11:** In the creation story in Gen 1, God created the world in six days and rested on the seventh (Gen 2.1–3). **12:** The commandment concerning parents may have originally been aimed especially at the care of elderly parents. **13:** *Murder* refers to any killing not sanctioned by the community, including personal acts of revenge. **16:** The prohibition of *false witness* involves false testimony in judicial cases and disputes. **17:** To *covet* refers to the inner yearning and strong desire to take something that rightfully belongs to others, especially the poor and less powerful.

Additional laws in the Book of the Covenant
20.22–23.19: Most scholars consider this group of laws to be the oldest of all the legal collections of the Bible. These biblical laws have several parallels in subject matter and form to ancient Babylonian law codes. The laws alternate between religious concerns and criminal, social, and economic matters.

22 The LORD said to Moses: Thus you shall say to the Israelites: "You have seen for yourselves that I spoke with you from heaven. 23You shall not make gods of silver alongside me, nor shall you make for yourselves gods of gold. 24You need make for me only an altar of earth and sacrifice on it your burnt offerings and your offerings of well-being, your sheep and your oxen; in every place where I cause my name to be remembered I will come to you and bless you. 25But if you make for me an altar of stone, do not build it of hewn stones; for if you use a chisel upon it you profane it. 26You shall not go up by steps to my altar, so that your nakedness may not be exposed on it."

21 These are the ordinances that you shall set before them:
2 When you buy a male Hebrew slave, he shall serve six years, but in the seventh he shall go out a free person, without debt. 3If he comes in single, he shall go out single; if he comes in married, then his wife shall go out with him. 4If his master gives him a wife and she bears him sons or daughters, the wife and her children shall be her master's and he shall go out alone. 5But if the slave declares, "I love my master, my wife, and my children; I will not go out a free person," 6then his master shall bring him before God.ᵃ He shall be brought to the door or the doorpost; and his master shall pierce his ear with an awl; and he shall serve him for life.
7 When a man sells his daughter as a slave, she shall not go out as the male slaves do. 8If she does not please her master, who designated her for himself, then he shall let her be redeemed; he shall have no right to sell her to a foreign people, since he has dealt unfairly with her. 9If he designates her for his son, he shall deal with her as with a daughter. 10If he takes another wife to himself, he shall not diminish the food, clothing, or marital rights of the first wife.ᵇ 11And if he does not do these three things for her, she shall go out without debt, without payment of money.
12 Whoever strikes a person mortally shall be put to death. 13If it was not premeditated, but came about by an act of God, then I will appoint for you a place to which the killer may flee. 14But if someone willfully attacks and kills another by treachery, you shall take the killer from my altar for execution.

20.22–21.14. 20.26: The concern for stairs and the exposure of *nakedness* implies that those doing the sacrificing at the altar wore robes that were open at the bottom. **21.6:** The blood on the doorpost from the *pierced ear* was a sign of the permanent attachment of the slave to the household. **8:** The case deals with a husband's taking a slave as a wife or concubine* through whom he might have children (Gen 21.10–13). **13–14:** Accidental killers could flee to designated

a Or *to the judges*   *b* Heb *of her*

"cities of refuge" where they could live protected from family members of the victim who would seek revenge (Num 35.9–28).

〜〜〜〜〜〜〜〜〜〜〜〜〜〜〜〜

15 Whoever strikes father or mother shall be put to death.

16 Whoever kidnaps a person, whether that person has been sold or is still held in possession, shall be put to death.

17 Whoever curses father or mother shall be put to death.

18 When individuals quarrel and one strikes the other with a stone or fist so that the injured party, though not dead, is confined to bed, 19but recovers and walks around outside with the help of a staff, then the assailant shall be free of liability, except to pay for the loss of time, and to arrange for full recovery.

20 When a slaveowner strikes a male or female slave with a rod and the slave dies immediately, the owner shall be punished. 21But if the slave survives a day or two, there is no punishment; for the slave is the owner's property.

22 When people who are fighting injure a pregnant woman so that there is a miscarriage, and yet no further harm follows, the one responsible shall be fined what the woman's husband demands, paying as much as the judges determine. 23If any harm follows, then you shall give life for life, 24eye for eye, tooth for tooth, hand for hand, foot for foot, 25burn for burn, wound for wound, stripe for stripe.

26 When a slaveowner strikes the eye of a male or female slave, destroying it, the owner shall let the slave go, a free person, to compensate for the eye. 27If the owner knocks out a tooth of a male or female slave, the slave shall be let go, a free person, to compensate for the tooth.

28 When an ox gores a man or a woman to death, the ox shall be stoned, and its flesh shall not be eaten; but the owner of the ox shall not be liable. 29If the ox has been accustomed to gore in the past, and its owner has been warned but has not restrained it, and it kills a man or a woman, the ox shall be stoned, and its owner also shall be put to death. 30If a ransom is imposed on the owner, then the owner shall pay whatever is imposed for the redemption of the victim's life. 31If it gores a boy or a girl, the owner shall be dealt with according to this same rule. 32If the ox gores a male or female slave, the owner shall pay to the slaveowner thirty shekels of silver, and the ox shall be stoned.

33 If someone leaves a pit open, or digs a pit and does not cover it, and an ox or a donkey falls into it, 34the owner of the pit shall make restitution, giving money to its owner, but keeping the dead animal.

35 If someone's ox hurts the ox of another, so that it dies, then they shall sell the live ox and divide the price of it; and the dead animal they shall also divide. 36But if it was known that the ox was accustomed to gore in the past, and its owner has not restrained it, the owner shall restore ox for ox, but keep the dead animal.

21.15–36. 23–24: The principle of *life for life* seeks to limit the extent of any revenge. The principle also means that simply paying money to a victim or victim's family cannot compensate for the loss of a priceless life or limb. **28:** The *ox shall be stoned* and *not eaten* because it has become ritually impure by causing the death of a human.

〜〜〜〜〜〜〜〜〜〜〜〜〜〜〜〜

22 *a*When someone steals an ox or a sheep, and slaughters it or sells it, the thief shall pay five oxen for an ox, and four sheep for a sheep. *b* The thief shall make restitution, but if unable to do so, shall be sold for the theft. 4When the animal, whether ox or donkey or sheep, is found alive in the thief's possession, the thief shall pay double.

2*c* If a thief is found breaking in, and is beaten to death, no bloodguilt is incurred; 3but if it happens after sunrise, bloodguilt is incurred.

5 When someone causes a field or vineyard to be grazed over, or lets livestock loose to graze in someone else's field, restitution shall be made from the best in the owner's field or vineyard.

6 When fire breaks out and catches in

a Ch 21.37 in Heb *b* Verses 2, 3, and 4 rearranged thus: 3b, 4, 2, 3a *c* Ch 22.1 in Heb

thorns so that the stacked grain or the standing grain or the field is consumed, the one who started the fire shall make full restitution.

7 When someone delivers to a neighbor money or goods for safekeeping, and they are stolen from the neighbor's house, then the thief, if caught, shall pay double. 8If the thief is not caught, the owner of the house shall be brought before God,*a* to determine whether or not the owner had laid hands on the neighbor's goods.

9 In any case of disputed ownership involving ox, donkey, sheep, clothing, or any other loss, of which one party says, "This is mine," the case of both parties shall come before God;*a* the one whom God condemns*b* shall pay double to the other.

10 When someone delivers to another a donkey, ox, sheep, or any other animal for safekeeping, and it dies or is injured or is carried off, without anyone seeing it, 11an oath before the LORD shall decide between the two of them that the one has not laid hands on the property of the other; the owner shall accept the oath, and no restitution shall be made. 12But if it was stolen, restitution shall be made to its owner. 13If it was mangled by beasts, let it be brought as evidence; restitution shall not be made for the mangled remains.

14 When someone borrows an animal from another and it is injured or dies, the owner not being present, full restitution shall be made. 15If the owner was present, there shall be no restitution; if it was hired, only the hiring fee is due.

16 When a man seduces a virgin who is not engaged to be married, and lies with her, he shall give the bride-price for her and make her his wife. 17But if her father refuses to give her to him, he shall pay an amount equal to the bride-price for virgins.

18 You shall not permit a female sorcerer to live.

19 Whoever lies with an animal shall be put to death.

20 Whoever sacrifices to any god, other than the LORD alone, shall be devoted to destruction.

21 You shall not wrong or oppress a resident alien, for you were aliens in the land of Egypt. 22You shall not abuse any widow or orphan. 23If you do abuse them, when they cry out to me, I will surely heed their cry; 24my wrath will burn, and I will kill you with the sword, and your wives shall become widows and your children orphans.

25 If you lend money to my people, to the poor among you, you shall not deal with them as a creditor; you shall not exact interest from them. 26If you take your neighbor's cloak in pawn, you shall restore it before the sun goes down; 27for it may be your neighbor's only clothing to use as cover; in what else shall that person sleep? And if your neighbor cries out to me, I will listen, for I am compassionate.

28 You shall not revile God, or curse a leader of your people.

29 You shall not delay to make offerings from the fullness of your harvest and from the outflow of your presses.*c*

The firstborn of your sons you shall give to me. 30You shall do the same with your oxen and with your sheep: seven days it shall remain with its mother; on the eighth day you shall give it to me.

22.21–30. 21–24: Israel's experience of being *aliens in the land of Egypt* motivated these laws against oppressing *a resident alien** or other marginal people in the community (see 23.9). Israel also knew firsthand the power of the oppressed who *cry out* to arouse God's saving action (see 2.23–25). **30:** The *seven days* of waiting is the time required for the mother and the baby to become ritually clean after the birth (Lev 12.2–3).

31 You shall be people consecrated to me; therefore you shall not eat any meat that is mangled by beasts in the field; you shall throw it to the dogs.

23 You shall not spread a false report. You shall not join hands with the wicked to act as a malicious witness. 2You shall not follow a majority in wrongdoing; when you bear witness in a lawsuit, you shall not side with the majority so as to pervert

a Or before the judges   b Or the judges condemn

justice; ³nor shall you be partial to the poor in a lawsuit.

4 When you come upon your enemy's ox or donkey going astray, you shall bring it back.

5 When you see the donkey of one who hates you lying under its burden and you would hold back from setting it free, you must help to set it free.ᵃ

6 You shall not pervert the justice due to your poor in their lawsuits. ⁷Keep far from a false charge, and do not kill the innocent and those in the right, for I will not acquit the guilty. ⁸You shall take no bribe, for a bribe blinds the officials, and subverts the cause of those who are in the right.

9 You shall not oppress a resident alien; you know the heart of an alien, for you were aliens in the land of Egypt.

10 For six years you shall sow your land and gather in its yield; ¹¹but the seventh year you shall let it rest and lie fallow, so that the poor of your people may eat; and what they leave the wild animals may eat. You shall do the same with your vineyard, and with your olive orchard.

12 Six days you shall do your work, but on the seventh day you shall rest, so that your ox and your donkey may have relief, and your homeborn slave and the resident alien may be refreshed. ¹³Be attentive to all that I have said to you. Do not invoke the names of other gods; do not let them be heard on your lips.

14 Three times in the year you shall hold a festival for me. ¹⁵You shall observe the festival of unleavened bread; as I commanded you, you shall eat unleavened bread for seven days at the appointed time in the month of Abib, for in it you came out of Egypt.

No one shall appear before me empty-handed.

16 You shall observe the festival of harvest, of the first fruits of your labor, of what you sow in the field. You shall observe the festival of ingathering at the end of the year, when you gather in from the field the fruit of your labor. ¹⁷Three times in the year all your males shall appear before the Lord GOD.

18 You shall not offer the blood of my sacrifice with anything leavened, or let the fat of my festival remain until the morning.

19 The choicest of the first fruits of your ground you shall bring into the house of the LORD your God.

You shall not boil a kid in its mother's milk.

23.15–19. 15: On *the festival of unleavened bread*, see 13.3–10. 19: The prohibition against boiling a young goat or *kid in its mother's milk* involves the ritual impurity of crossing the boundary between life and death. The mother's milk gives life, but using it to boil meat mixes it with death.

---

20 I am going to send an angel in front of you, to guard you on the way and to bring you to the place that I have prepared. ²¹Be attentive to him and listen to his voice; do not rebel against him, for he will not pardon your transgression; for my name is in him.

22 But if you listen attentively to his voice and do all that I say, then I will be an enemy to your enemies and a foe to your foes.

23 When my angel goes in front of you, and brings you to the Amorites, the Hittites, the Perizzites, the Canaanites, the Hivites, and the Jebusites, and I blot them out, ²⁴you shall not bow down to their gods, or worship them, or follow their practices, but you shall utterly demolish them and break their pillars in pieces. ²⁵You shall worship the LORD your God, and Iᵇ will bless your bread and your water; and I will take sickness away from among you. ²⁶No one shall miscarry or be barren in your land; I will fulfill the number of your days. ²⁷I will send my terror in front of you, and will throw into confusion all the people against whom you shall come, and I will make all your enemies turn their backs to you. ²⁸And I will send the pestilenceᶜ in front of you, which shall drive out the Hivites, the Canaanites, and the Hittites from before you. ²⁹I will not drive them out from before you in one year, or the land would become desolate and the wild animals would multiply against you. ³⁰Little by little I will

ᵃ Meaning of Heb uncertain   ᵇ Gk Vg: Heb *he*
ᶜ Or *hornets:* Meaning of Heb uncertain

drive them out from before you, until you have increased and possess the land. 31I will set your borders from the Red Sea*a* to the sea of the Philistines, and from the wilderness to the Euphrates; for I will hand over to you the inhabitants of the land, and you shall drive them out before you. 32You shall make no covenant with them and their gods. 33They shall not live in your land, or they will make you sin against me; for if you worship their gods, it will surely be a snare to you.

23.20–33: God gives promises and instructions regarding Israel's future entry into Canaan. 20: The LORD promises to send *an angel* as a divine representative to protect and fight for the Israelites (see v. 23 and 14.19). Discussion about the angel continues in 32.34 and 33.2. The angel will reappear in Josh 5.13–15 and Judg 2.1–5. **31:** *The sea of the Philistines* is the Mediterranean Sea to the west of Canaan. *The wilderness* is probably the Negev region south of Canaan. The boundaries correspond roughly to the size of Israel under King Solomon (1 Kings 4.21).

24 Then he said to Moses, "Come up to the LORD, you and Aaron, Nadab, and Abihu, and seventy of the elders of Israel, and worship at a distance. 2Moses alone shall come near the LORD; but the others shall not come near, and the people shall not come up with him."

3 Moses came and told the people all the words of the LORD and all the ordinances; and all the people answered with one voice, and said, "All the words that the LORD has spoken we will do." 4And Moses wrote down all the words of the LORD. He rose early in the morning, and built an altar at the foot of the mountain, and set up twelve pillars, corresponding to the twelve tribes of Israel. 5He sent young men of the people of Israel, who offered burnt offerings and sacrificed oxen as offerings of well-being to the LORD. 6Moses took half of the blood and put it in basins, and half of the blood he dashed against the altar. 7Then he took the book of the covenant, and read it in the hearing of the people; and they said, "All that the LORD has spoken we will do, and we will be obedient." 8Moses took the blood and dashed it on the people, and said, "See the blood of the covenant that

the LORD has made with you in accordance with all these words."

9 Then Moses and Aaron, Nadab, and Abihu, and seventy of the elders of Israel went up, 10and they saw the God of Israel. Under his feet there was something like a pavement of sapphire stone, like the very heaven for clearness. 11God*b* did not lay his hand on the chief men of the people of Israel; also they beheld God, and they ate and drank.

12 The LORD said to Moses, "Come up to me on the mountain, and wait there; and I will give you the tablets of stone, with the law and the commandment, which I have written for their instruction." 13So Moses set out with his assistant Joshua, and Moses went up into the mountain of God. 14To the elders he had said, "Wait here for us, until we come to you again; for Aaron and Hur are with you; whoever has a dispute may go to them."

15 Then Moses went up on the mountain, and the cloud covered the mountain. 16The glory of the LORD settled on Mount Sinai, and the cloud covered it for six days; on the seventh day he called to Moses out of the cloud. 17Now the appearance of the glory of the LORD was like a devouring fire on the top of the mountain in the sight of the people of Israel. 18Moses entered the cloud, and went up on the mountain. Moses was on the mountain for forty days and forty nights.

24.1–18: The LORD, Moses, and the people formally enter into a covenant* relationship. 1: Nadab and Abihu are two sons of Aaron who serve as priests (see 6.23). **6–8:** *The altar* represents God's presence (v. 6). Sprinkling blood on the altar and then the people signifies their binding together in relationship. *The book of the covenant* is presumably some form of the laws and commandments in chs. 20–23. **9:** On *Nadab and Abihu,* see comment on v. 1. **14:** *Hur* is a leader from the Israelite tribe of Judah (17.10; 31.2).

Furnishings for the tabernacle
25.1–40: This unit begins an extended section of instructions for building and furnishing the portable sanctuary or shrine called the tabernacle* (25.1–

a Or *Sea of Reeds*   *b* Heb *He*

31.18). The tabernacle is to be the vehicle of God's presence as they leave God's dwelling place of Mount Sinai and set off on the journey through the wilderness to the promised land. The tabernacle will not be built until after the golden calf rebellion (ch. 32) and the renewal of the covenant* (chs. 33–34).

25

The LORD said to Moses: ²Tell the Israelites to take for me an offering; from all whose hearts prompt them to give you shall receive the offering for me. ³This is the offering that you shall receive from them: gold, silver, and bronze, ⁴blue, purple, and crimson yarns and fine linen, goats' hair, ⁵tanned rams' skins, fine leather,ᵃ acacia wood, ⁶oil for the lamps, spices for the anointing oil and for the fragrant incense, ⁷onyx stones and gems to be set in the ephod and for the breastpiece. ⁸And have them make me a sanctuary, so that I may dwell among them. ⁹In accordance with all that I show you concerning the pattern of the tabernacle and of all its furniture, so you shall make it.

10 They shall make an ark of acacia wood; it shall be two and a half cubits long, a cubit and a half wide, and a cubit and a half high. ¹¹You shall overlay it with pure gold, inside and outside you shall overlay it, and you shall make a molding of gold upon it all around. ¹²You shall cast four rings of gold for it and put them on its four feet, two rings on the one side of it, and two rings on the other side. ¹³You shall make poles of acacia wood, and overlay them with gold. ¹⁴And you shall put the poles into the rings on the sides of the ark, by which to carry the ark. ¹⁵The poles shall remain in the rings of the ark; they shall not be taken from it. ¹⁶You shall put into the ark the covenantᵇ that I shall give you.

17 Then you shall make a mercy seatᶜ of pure gold; two cubits and a half shall be its length, and a cubit and a half its width. ¹⁸You shall make two cherubim of gold; you shall make them of hammered work, at the two ends of the mercy seat.ᵈ ¹⁹Make one cherub at the one end, and one cherub at the other; of one piece with the mercy seatᵈ you shall make the cherubim at its two ends. ²⁰The cherubim shall spread out their wings above, overshadowing the mercy seatᵈ with their wings. They shall face one to another; the faces of the cherubim shall be turned toward the mercy seat.ᵈ ²¹You shall put the mercy seatᵈ on the top of the ark; and in the ark you shall put the covenantᵇ that I shall give you. ²²There I will meet with you, and from above the mercy seat,ᵈ from between the two cherubim that are on the ark of the covenant,ᵇ I will deliver to you all my commands for the Israelites.

23 You shall make a table of acacia wood, two cubits long, one cubit wide, and a cubit and a half high. ²⁴You shall overlay it with pure gold, and make a molding of gold around it. ²⁵You shall make around it a rim a handbreadth wide, and a molding of gold around the rim. ²⁶You shall make for it four rings of gold, and fasten the rings to the four corners at its four legs. ²⁷The rings that hold the poles used for carrying the table shall be close to the rim. ²⁸You shall make the poles of acacia wood, and overlay them with gold, and the table shall be carried with these. ²⁹You shall make its plates and dishes for incense, and its flagons and bowls with which to pour drink offerings; you shall make them of pure gold. ³⁰And you shall set the bread of the Presence on the table before me always.

25.1–30. 3: The *gold* and *silver* and other finery derive presumably from what the Egyptians gave to the Israelites as they fled Egypt (12.35–36). **7:** On the *ephod,*★ see comment on 28.6. **10:** The wooden *ark* is a container that functions as a throne or footstool for the divine presence. **16:** The two tablets of stone that contain the Ten Commandments are *the covenant* that will be carried in the ark. **17–22:** *Cherubim*★ are half-human and half-animal creatures with wings. The head is human, and the body is usually a lion or bull. They guard holy areas as well as kings. The *mercy seat* is the throne for the deity's presence. **21:** On *the covenant,* see comment on v. 16. **30:** *The bread of the Presence* is set out *on the table* as a sign of hospitality to the deity, but the priests actually eat the bread (Lev 24.5–9).

---

a Meaning of Heb uncertain   *b* Or *treaty,* or *testimony;* Heb *eduth*   *c* Or *a cover*   *d* Or *the cover*

31 You shall make a lampstand of pure gold. The base and the shaft of the lampstand shall be made of hammered work; its cups, its calyxes, and its petals shall be of one piece with it; 32and there shall be six branches going out of its sides, three branches of the lampstand out of one side of it and three branches of the lampstand out of the other side of it; 33three cups shaped like almond blossoms, each with calyx and petals, on one branch, and three cups shaped like almond blossoms, each with calyx and petals, on the other branch—so for the six branches going out of the lampstand. 34On the lampstand itself there shall be four cups shaped like almond blossoms, each with its calyxes and petals. 35There shall be a calyx of one piece with it under the first pair of branches, a calyx of one piece with it under the next pair of branches, and a calyx of one piece with it under the last pair of branches—so for the six branches that go out of the lampstand. 36Their calyxes and their branches shall be of one piece with it, the whole of it one hammered piece of pure gold. 37You shall make the seven lamps for it; and the lamps shall be set up so as to give light on the space in front of it. 38Its snuffers and trays shall be of pure gold. 39It, and all these utensils, shall be made from a talent of pure gold. 40And see that you make them according to the pattern for them, which is being shown you on the mountain.

Instructions concerning the tabernacle's frame and curtains

26.1–37: The description of the tabernacle includes some parallels to the description of Solomon's Temple* in Jerusalem (1 Kings 6) and the vision of the new Temple in Ezek 40–43.

26 Moreover you shall make the tabernacle with ten curtains of fine twisted linen, and blue, purple, and crimson yarns; you shall make them with cherubim skillfully worked into them. 2The length of each curtain shall be twenty-eight cubits, and the width of each curtain four cubits; all the curtains shall be of the same size. 3Five curtains shall be joined to one another; and the other five curtains shall be joined to one another. 4You shall make loops of blue on the edge of the outermost curtain in the first set; and likewise you shall make loops on the edge of the outermost curtain in the second set. 5You shall make fifty loops on the one curtain, and you shall make fifty loops on the edge of the curtain that is in the second set; the loops shall be opposite one another. 6You shall make fifty clasps of gold, and join the curtains to one another with the clasps, so that the tabernacle may be one whole.

7 You shall also make curtains of goats' hair for a tent over the tabernacle; you shall make eleven curtains. 8The length of each curtain shall be thirty cubits, and the width of each curtain four cubits; the eleven curtains shall be of the same size. 9You shall join five curtains by themselves, and six curtains by themselves, and the sixth curtain you shall double over at the front of the tent. 10You shall make fifty loops on the edge of the curtain that is outermost in one set, and fifty loops on the edge of the curtain that is outermost in the second set.

11 You shall make fifty clasps of bronze, and put the clasps into the loops, and join the tent together, so that it may be one whole. 12The part that remains of the curtains of the tent, the half curtain that remains, shall hang over the back of the tabernacle. 13The cubit on the one side, and the cubit on the other side, of what remains in the length of the curtains of the tent, shall hang over the sides of the tabernacle, on this side and that side, to cover it. 14You shall make for the tent a covering of tanned rams' skins and an outer covering of fine leather.*a*

15 You shall make upright frames of acacia wood for the tabernacle. 16Ten cubits shall be the length of a frame, and a cubit and a half the width of each frame. 17There shall be two pegs in each frame to fit the frames together; you shall make these for all the frames of the tabernacle. 18You shall make the frames for the tabernacle: twenty frames for the south side; 19and you shall make forty bases of silver under the twenty frames, two bases under the first frame for its two pegs, and two bases under the next

a Meaning of Heb uncertain

frame for its two pegs; 20and for the second side of the tabernacle, on the north side twenty frames, 21and their forty bases of silver, two bases under the first frame, and two bases under the next frame; 22and for the rear of the tabernacle westward you shall make six frames. 23You shall make two frames for corners of the tabernacle in the rear; 24they shall be separate beneath, but joined at the top, at the first ring; it shall be the same with both of them; they shall form the two corners. 25And so there shall be eight frames, with their bases of silver, sixteen bases; two bases under the first frame, and two bases under the next frame.

26 You shall make bars of acacia wood, five for the frames of the one side of the tabernacle, 27and five bars for the frames of the other side of the tabernacle, and five bars for the frames of the side of the tabernacle at the rear westward. 28The middle bar, halfway up the frames, shall pass through from end to end. 29You shall overlay the frames with gold, and shall make their rings of gold to hold the bars; and you shall overlay the bars with gold. 30Then you shall erect the tabernacle according to the plan for it that you were shown on the mountain.

31 You shall make a curtain of blue, purple, and crimson yarns, and of fine twisted linen; it shall be made with cherubim skillfully worked into it. 32You shall hang it on four pillars of acacia overlaid with gold, which have hooks of gold and rest on four bases of silver. 33You shall hang the curtain under the clasps, and bring the ark of the covenant*a* in there, within the curtain; and the curtain shall separate for you the holy place from the most holy. 34You shall put the mercy seat*b* on the ark of the covenant*a* in the most holy place. 35You shall set the table outside the curtain, and the lampstand on the south side of the tabernacle opposite the table; and you shall put the table on the north side.

36 You shall make a screen for the entrance of the tent, of blue, purple, and crimson yarns, and of fine twisted linen, embroidered with needlework. 37You shall make for the screen five pillars of acacia, and overlay them with gold; their hooks shall be of gold,

and you shall cast five bases of bronze for them.

Constructing the altar, the court, and the lamps
27.1–21: These instructions pertain to items and areas outside and surrounding the tabernacle* itself.

27 You shall make the altar of acacia wood, five cubits long and five cubits wide; the altar shall be square, and it shall be three cubits high. 2You shall make horns for it on its four corners; its horns shall be of one piece with it, and you shall overlay it with bronze. 3You shall make pots for it to receive its ashes, and shovels and basins and forks and firepans; you shall make all its utensils of bronze. 4You shall also make for it a grating, a network of bronze; and on the net you shall make four bronze rings at its four corners. 5You shall set it under the ledge of the altar so that the net shall extend halfway down the altar. 6You shall make poles for the altar, poles of acacia wood, and overlay them with bronze; 7the poles shall be put through the rings, so that the poles shall be on the two sides of the altar when it is carried. 8You shall make it hollow, with boards. They shall be made just as you were shown on the mountain.

9 You shall make the court of the tabernacle. On the south side the court shall have hangings of fine twisted linen one hundred cubits long for that side; 10its twenty pillars and their twenty bases shall be of bronze, but the hooks of the pillars and their bands shall be of silver. 11Likewise for its length on the north side there shall be hangings one hundred cubits long, their pillars twenty and their bases twenty, of bronze, but the hooks of the pillars and their bands shall be of silver. 12For the width of the court on the west side there shall be fifty cubits of hangings, with ten pillars and ten bases. 13The width of the court on the front to the east shall be fifty cubits. 14There shall be fifteen cubits of hangings on the one side, with three pillars and three bases. 15There shall be fifteen cubits of hangings on the other side, with three pillars and three bases. 16For the gate of the

a Or *treaty,* or *testimony;* Heb *eduth*   *b* Or *the cover* court there shall be a screen twenty cubits long, of blue, purple, and crimson yarns, and of fine twisted linen, embroidered with needlework; it shall have four pillars and with them four bases. 17All the pillars around the court shall be banded with silver; their hooks shall be of silver, and their bases of bronze. 18The length of the court shall be one hundred cubits, the width fifty, and the height five cubits, with hangings of fine twisted linen and bases of bronze. 19All the utensils of the tabernacle for every use, and all its pegs and all the pegs of the court, shall be of bronze.

20 You shall further command the Israelites to bring you pure oil of beaten olives for the light, so that a lamp may be set up to burn regularly. 21In the tent of meeting, outside the curtain that is before the covenant,*a* Aaron and his sons shall tend it from evening to morning before the LORD. It shall be a perpetual ordinance to be observed throughout their generations by the Israelites.

28 Then bring near to you your brother Aaron, and his sons with him, from among the Israelites, to serve me as priests—Aaron and Aaron's sons, Nadab and Abihu, Eleazar and Ithamar. 2You shall make sacred vestments for the glorious adornment of your brother Aaron. 3And you shall speak to all who have ability, whom I have endowed with skill, that they make Aaron's vestments to consecrate him for my priesthood. 4These are the vestments that they shall make: a breastpiece, an ephod, a robe, a checkered tunic, a turban, and a sash. When they make these sacred vestments for your brother Aaron and his sons to serve me as priests, 5they shall use gold, blue, purple, and crimson yarns, and fine linen.

6 They shall make the ephod of gold, of blue, purple, and crimson yarns, and of fine twisted linen, skillfully worked. 7It shall have two shoulder-pieces attached to its two edges, so that it may be joined together. 8The decorated band on it shall be of the same workmanship and materials, of gold, of blue, purple, and crimson yarns, and of fine twisted linen. 9You shall take two onyx stones, and engrave on them the names of the sons of Israel, 10six of their names on the one stone, and the names of the remaining six on the other stone, in the order of their birth. 11As a gem-cutter engraves signets, so you shall engrave the two stones with the names of the sons of Israel; you shall mount them in settings of gold filigree. 12You shall set the two stones on the shoulder-pieces of the ephod, as stones of remembrance for the sons of Israel; and Aaron shall bear their names before the LORD on his two shoulders for remembrance. 13You shall make settings of gold filigree, 14and two chains of pure gold, twisted like cords; and you shall attach the corded chains to the settings.

15 You shall make a breastpiece of judgment, in skilled work; you shall make it in the style of the ephod; of gold, of blue and purple and crimson yarns, and of fine twisted linen you shall make it. 16It shall be square and doubled, a span in length and a span in width. 17You shall set in it four rows of stones. A row of carnelian,*b* chrysolite, and emerald shall be the first row; 18and the second row a turquoise, a sapphire*c* and a moonstone; 19and the third row a jacinth, an agate, and an amethyst; 20and the fourth row a beryl, an onyx, and a jasper; they shall be set in gold filigree. 21There shall be twelve stones with names corresponding to the names of the sons of Israel; they shall be like signets, each engraved with its name, for the twelve tribes. 22You shall make for the breastpiece chains of pure gold, twisted like cords; 23and you shall make for the breastpiece two rings of gold, and put the two rings on the two edges of the breastpiece. 24You shall put the two cords of gold in the two rings at the edges of the breastpiece; 25the two ends of the two cords you shall attach to the two settings, and so attach it in front to the shoulder-pieces of the ephod. 26You shall make two rings of gold, and put them at the two ends of the breastpiece, on its inside edge next to the ephod. 27You shall make two rings of gold, and attach them in front to the lower part of the two shoulder-pieces of the ephod, at its joining above the

a Or *treaty*, or *testimony*; Heb *eduth*　*b* The identity of several of these stones is uncertain　*c* Or *lapis lazuli*

decorated band of the ephod. 28The breast-piece shall be bound by its rings to the rings of the ephod with a blue cord, so that it may lie on the decorated band of the ephod, and so that the breastpiece shall not come loose from the ephod. 29So Aaron shall bear the names of the sons of Israel in the breastpiece of judgment on his heart when he goes into the holy place, for a continual remembrance before the LORD. 30In the breastpiece of judgment you shall put the Urim and the Thummim, and they shall be on Aaron's heart when he goes in before the LORD; thus Aaron shall bear the judgment of the Isra-elites on his heart before the LORD continually.

31 You shall make the robe of the ephod all of blue. 32It shall have an opening for the head in the middle of it, with a woven bind-ing around the opening, like the opening in a coat of mail,ª so that it may not be torn. 33On its lower hem you shall make pome-granates of blue, purple, and crimson yarns, all around the lower hem, with bells of gold between them all around— 34a golden bell and a pomegranate alternating all around the lower hem of the robe. 35Aaron shall wear it when he ministers, and its sound shall be heard when he goes into the holy place before the LORD, and when he comes out, so that he may not die.

36 You shall make a rosette of pure gold, and engrave on it, like the engraving of a sig-net, "Holy to the LORD." 37You shall fasten it on the turban with a blue cord; it shall be on the front of the turban. 38It shall be on Aaron's forehead, and Aaron shall take on himself any guilt incurred in the holy offer-ing that the Israelites consecrate as their sa-cred donations; it shall always be on his fore-head, in order that they may find favor before the LORD.

39 You shall make the checkered tunic of fine linen, and you shall make a turban of fine linen, and you shall make a sash em-broidered with needlework.

40 For Aaron's sons you shall make tunics and sashes and headdresses; you shall make them for their glorious adornment. 41You shall put them on your brother Aaron, and on his sons with him, and shall anoint them

and ordain them and consecrate them, so that they may serve me as priests. 42You shall make for them linen undergarments to cover their naked flesh; they shall reach from the hips to the thighs; 43Aaron and his sons shall wear them when they go into the tent of meeting, or when they come near the altar to minister in the holy place; or they will bring guilt on themselves and die. This shall be a perpetual ordinance for him and for his descendants after him.

28.1–43: The LORD gives guidelines for making the priestly garments. 6: *The ephod** is a long priestly robe; it was sometimes used to obtain an oracle* or message from the deity (1 Sam 23.9–12). 15–30: The *breastpiece of judgment* functioned as a means to ob-tain divine messages and guidance. It was a pouch containing the *Urim and Thummim,* light and dark stones used to determine the deity's will in a given situation (v. 30).

Instructions for the ordination of the priests
29.1–46: These instructions for ordination* are carried out when Aaron and his sons are formally set apart as priests in Lev 8–9. Blood is considered a sacred sub-stance with power to purify and make holy (Lev 17.11). Thus, blood plays an important role in purify-ing the priests and the altar throughout this section.

29 Now this is what you shall do to them to consecrate them, so that they may serve me as priests. Take one young bull and two rams without blemish, 2and unleavened bread, unleavened cakes mixed with oil, and unleavened wafers spread with oil. You shall make them of choice wheat flour. 3You shall put them in one basket and bring them in the basket, and bring the bull and the two rams. 4You shall bring Aaron and his sons to the entrance of the tent of meeting, and wash them with water. 5Then you shall take the vestments, and put on Aaron the tunic and the robe of the ephod, and the ephod, and the breastpiece, and gird him with the decorated band of the ephod; 6and you shall set the turban on his head, and put the holy diadem on the turban. 7You shall take the anointing oil, and pour it on his head and

a Meaning of Heb uncertain

anoint him. [8]Then you shall bring his sons, and put tunics on them, [9]and you shall gird them with sashes[a] and tie headdresses on them; and the priesthood shall be theirs by a perpetual ordinance. You shall then ordain Aaron and his sons.

10 You shall bring the bull in front of the tent of meeting. Aaron and his sons shall lay their hands on the head of the bull, [11]and you shall slaughter the bull before the LORD, at the entrance of the tent of meeting, [12]and shall take some of the blood of the bull and put it on the horns of the altar with your finger, and all the rest of the blood you shall pour out at the base of the altar. [13]You shall take all the fat that covers the entrails, and the appendage of the liver, and the two kidneys with the fat that is on them, and turn them into smoke on the altar. [14]But the flesh of the bull, and its skin, and its dung, you shall burn with fire outside the camp; it is a sin offering.

15 Then you shall take one of the rams, and Aaron and his sons shall lay their hands on the head of the ram, [16]and you shall slaughter the ram, and shall take its blood and dash it against all sides of the altar. [17]Then you shall cut the ram into its parts, and wash its entrails and its legs, and put them with its parts and its head, [18]and turn the whole ram into smoke on the altar; it is a burnt offering to the LORD; it is a pleasing odor, an offering by fire to the LORD.

19 You shall take the other ram; and Aaron and his sons shall lay their hands on the head of the ram, [20]and you shall slaughter the ram, and take some of its blood and put it on the lobe of Aaron's right ear and on the lobes of the right ears of his sons, and on the thumbs of their right hands, and on the big toes of their right feet, and dash the rest of the blood against all sides of the altar. [21]Then you shall take some of the blood that is on the altar, and some of the anointing oil, and sprinkle it on Aaron and his vestments and on his sons and his sons' vestments with him; then he and his vestments shall be holy, as well as his sons and his sons' vestments.

22 You shall also take the fat of the ram, the fat tail, the fat that covers the entrails, the appendage of the liver, the two kidneys with the fat that is on them, and the right thigh (for it is a ram of ordination), [23]and one loaf of bread, one cake of bread made with oil, and one wafer, out of the basket of unleavened bread that is before the LORD; [24]and you shall place all these on the palms of Aaron and on the palms of his sons, and raise them as an elevation offering before the LORD. [25]Then you shall take them from their hands, and turn them into smoke on the altar on top of the burnt offering of pleasing odor before the LORD; it is an offering by fire to the LORD.

26 You shall take the breast of the ram of Aaron's ordination and raise it as an elevation offering before the LORD; and it shall be your portion. [27]You shall consecrate the breast that was raised as an elevation offering and the thigh that was raised as an elevation offering from the ram of ordination, from that which belonged to Aaron and his sons. [28]These things shall be a perpetual ordinance for Aaron and his sons from the Israelites, for this is an offering; and it shall be an offering by the Israelites from their sacrifice of offerings of well-being, their offering to the LORD.

29 The sacred vestments of Aaron shall be passed on to his sons after him; they shall be anointed in them and ordained in them. [30]The son who is priest in his place shall wear them seven days, when he comes into the tent of meeting to minister in the holy place.

31 You shall take the ram of ordination, and boil its flesh in a holy place; [32]and Aaron and his sons shall eat the flesh of the ram and the bread that is in the basket, at the entrance of the tent of meeting. [33]They themselves shall eat the food by which atonement is made, to ordain and consecrate them, but no one else shall eat of them, because they are holy. [34]If any of the flesh for the ordination, or of the bread, remains until the morning, then you shall burn the remainder with fire; it shall not be eaten, because it is holy.

35 Thus you shall do to Aaron and to his sons, just as I have commanded you; through

a Gk: Heb *sashes, Aaron and his sons*

seven days you shall ordain them. 36Also every day you shall offer a bull as a sin offering for atonement. Also you shall offer a sin offering for the altar, when you make atonement for it, and shall anoint it, to consecrate it. 37Seven days you shall make atonement for the altar, and consecrate it, and the altar shall be most holy; whatever touches the altar shall become holy.

38 Now this is what you shall offer on the altar: two lambs a year old regularly each day. 39One lamb you shall offer in the morning, and the other lamb you shall offer in the evening; 40and with the first lamb one-tenth of a measure of choice flour mixed with one-fourth of a hin of beaten oil, and one-fourth of a hin of wine for a drink offering. 41And the other lamb you shall offer in the evening, and shall offer with it a grain offering and its drink offering, as in the morning, for a pleasing odor, an offering by fire to the LORD. 42It shall be a regular burnt offering throughout your generations at the entrance of the tent of meeting before the LORD, where I will meet with you, to speak to you there. 43I will meet with the Israelites there, and it shall be sanctified by my glory; 44I will consecrate the tent of meeting and the altar; Aaron also and his sons I will consecrate, to serve me as priests. 45I will dwell among the Israelites, and I will be their God. 46And they shall know that I am the LORD their God, who brought them out of the land of Egypt that I might dwell among them; I am the LORD their God.

29.33–40. 33–37: *To consecrate* the priests means to set them apart in a formal ceremony for special service. **40:** *A measure* is an ephah, which is equivalent to about 20 liters. A *hin* is one-sixth of an ephah, about 3 liters.

30 You shall make an altar on which to offer incense; you shall make it of acacia wood. 2It shall be one cubit long, and one cubit wide; it shall be square, and shall be two cubits high; its horns shall be of one piece with it. 3You shall overlay it with pure gold, its top, and its sides all around and its horns; and you shall make for it a molding of gold all around. 4And you shall make two golden rings for it; under its molding on two opposite sides of it you shall make them, and they shall hold the poles with which to carry it. 5You shall make the poles of acacia wood, and overlay them with gold. 6You shall place it in front of the curtain that is above the ark of the covenant,*a* in front of the mercy seat*b* that is over the covenant,*a* where I will meet with you. 7Aaron shall offer fragrant incense on it; every morning when he dresses the lamps he shall offer it, 8and when Aaron sets up the lamps in the evening, he shall offer it, a regular incense offering before the LORD throughout your generations. 9You shall not offer unholy incense on it, or a burnt offering, or a grain offering; and you shall not pour a drink offering on it. 10Once a year Aaron shall perform the rite of atonement on its horns. Throughout your generations he shall perform the atonement for it once a year with the blood of the atoning sin offering. It is most holy to the LORD.

11 The LORD spoke to Moses: 12When you take a census of the Israelites to register them, at registration all of them shall give a ransom for their lives to the LORD, so that no plague may come upon them for being registered. 13This is what each one who is registered shall give: half a shekel according to the shekel of the sanctuary (the shekel is twenty gerahs), half a shekel as an offering to the LORD. 14Each one who is registered, from twenty years old and upward, shall give the LORD's offering. 15The rich shall not give more, and the poor shall not give less, than the half shekel, when you bring this offering to the LORD to make atonement for your lives. 16You shall take the atonement money from the Israelites and shall designate it for the service of the tent of meeting; before the LORD it will be a reminder to the Israelites of the ransom given for your lives.

17 The LORD spoke to Moses: 18You shall make a bronze basin with a bronze stand for washing. You shall put it between the tent of meeting and the altar, and you shall put water in it; 19with the water*c* Aaron and his sons shall wash their hands and their feet.

a Or *treaty,* or *testimony;* Heb *eduth*　　*b* Or *the cover*
c Heb *it*

20When they go into the tent of meeting, or when they come near the altar to minister, to make an offering by fire to the LORD, they shall wash with water, so that they may not die. 21They shall wash their hands and their feet, so that they may not die: it shall be a perpetual ordinance for them, for him and for his descendants throughout their generations.

22 The LORD spoke to Moses: 23Take the finest spices: of liquid myrrh five hundred shekels, and of sweet-smelling cinnamon half as much, that is, two hundred fifty, and two hundred fifty of aromatic cane, 24and five hundred of cassia—measured by the sanctuary shekel—and a hin of olive oil; 25and you shall make of these a sacred anointing oil blended as by the perfumer; it shall be a holy anointing oil. 26With it you shall anoint the tent of meeting and the ark of the covenant,*a* 27and the table and all its utensils, and the lampstand and its utensils, and the altar of incense, 28and the altar of burnt offering with all its utensils, and the basin with its stand; 29you shall consecrate them, so that they may be most holy; whatever touches them will become holy. 30You shall anoint Aaron and his sons, and consecrate them, in order that they may serve me as priests. 31You shall say to the Israelites, "This shall be my holy anointing oil throughout your generations. 32It shall not be used in any ordinary anointing of the body, and you shall make no other like it in composition; it is holy, and it shall be holy to you. 33Whoever compounds any like it or whoever puts any of it on an unqualified person shall be cut off from the people."

34 The LORD said to Moses: Take sweet spices, stacte, and onycha, and galbanum, sweet spices with pure frankincense (an equal part of each), 35and make an incense blended as by the perfumer, seasoned with salt, pure and holy; 36and you shall beat some of it into powder, and put part of it before the covenant*a* in the tent of meeting where I shall meet with you; it shall be for you most holy. 37When you make incense according to this composition, you shall not make it for yourselves; it shall be regarded by you as holy to the LORD. 38Whoever makes any like it to use as perfume shall be cut off from the people.

31 The LORD spoke to Moses: 2See, I have called by name Bezalel son of Uri son of Hur, of the tribe of Judah: 3and I have filled him with divine spirit,*b* with ability, intelligence, and knowledge in every kind of craft, 4to devise artistic designs, to work in gold, silver, and bronze, 5in cutting stones for setting, and in carving wood, in every kind of craft. 6Moreover, I have appointed with him Oholiab son of Ahisamach, of the tribe of Dan; and I have given skill to all the skillful, so that they may make all that I have commanded you: 7the tent of meeting, and the ark of the covenant,*a* and the mercy seat*c* that is on it, and all the furnishings of the tent, 8the table and its utensils, and the pure lampstand with all its utensils, and the altar of incense, 9and the altar of burnt offering with all its utensils, and the basin with its stand, 10and the finely worked vestments, the holy vestments for the priest Aaron and the vestments of his sons, for their service as priests, 11and the anointing oil and the fragrant incense for the holy place. They shall do just as I have commanded you.

30.1–31.11: The LORD gives instructions for other matters related to the priests and the worship sanctuary. 30.10: *Once a year* would be the Day of Atonement* as specified in greater detail in Lev 16. 11–13: The act of taking *a census* or counting the people for military or administrative purposes was believed to arouse the deity's anger, thereby bringing on *a plague* (2 Sam 24.10). Thus, each person had to pay a *ransom* or fee of *half a shekel** in order to ward off the plague. Numbers 1.17–47 records the first census taken of the Israelites in the wilderness. 31.2–6: The *divine spirit* (v. 3) fills the two skilled workers, *Bezalel* (v. 2) and *Oholiab* (v. 6), with *ability, intelligence, and knowledge* in their particular skills of artistry and construction.

12 The LORD said to Moses: 13You yourself are to speak to the Israelites: "You shall keep my sabbaths, for this is a sign between me and you throughout your generations,

a Or *treaty,* or *testimony;* Heb *eduth*   *b* Or *with the spirit of God*   *c* Or *the cover* given in order that you may know that I, the LORD, sanctify you. ¹⁴You shall keep the sabbath, because it is holy for you; everyone who profanes it shall be put to death; whoever does any work on it shall be cut off from among the people. ¹⁵Six days shall work be done, but the seventh day is a sabbath of solemn rest, holy to the LORD; whoever does any work on the sabbath day shall be put to death. ¹⁶Therefore the Israelites shall keep the sabbath, observing the sabbath throughout their generations, as a perpetual covenant. ¹⁷It is a sign forever between me and the people of Israel that in six days the LORD made heaven and earth, and on the seventh day he rested, and was refreshed."

18 When God*a* finished speaking with Moses on Mount Sinai, he gave him the two tablets of the covenant,*b* tablets of stone, written with the finger of God.

31.12–18: God gives a concluding reminder of the sabbath commandment. Reference to work on the tabernacle* in the preceding section (31.1–11) occasions the reminder about the regular need to rest from work on the sabbath day (20.8–11). Like the tabernacle that sets apart a sacred space in the community, the sabbath sets apart sacred time in the ongoing life of the community. **18:** This action fulfills the promise God made to Moses in 24.12. The two *tablets of stone* will figure prominently in the next story of the golden calf. They will become signs of the breaking of the old covenant* (32.15–16, 19) and the making of a new covenant (34.1, 4).

Israel worships a golden calf
32.1–35: Israel makes an idol in the form of a golden calf and worships it. This deed violates the important prohibition in the Ten Commandments against worshipping other gods and making idols (20.3–4). The story has a parallel in a later account about King Jeroboam, who sets up golden calves at two worship sites in northern Israel (1 Kings 12.25–33).

32 When the people saw that Moses delayed to come down from the mountain, the people gathered around Aaron, and said to him, "Come, make gods for us, who shall go before us; as for this Moses, the man who brought us up out of the land of Egypt, we do not know what has become of him."

²Aaron said to them, "Take off the gold rings that are on the ears of your wives, your sons, and your daughters, and bring them to me." ³So all the people took off the gold rings from their ears, and brought them to Aaron. ⁴He took the gold from them, formed it in a mold,*c* and cast an image of a calf; and they said, "These are your gods, O Israel, who brought you up out of the land of Egypt!" ⁵When Aaron saw this, he built an altar before it; and Aaron made proclamation and said, "Tomorrow shall be a festival to the LORD." ⁶They rose early the next day, and offered burnt offerings and brought sacrifices of well-being; and the people sat down to eat and drink, and rose up to revel.

7 The LORD said to Moses, "Go down at once! Your people, whom you brought up out of the land of Egypt, have acted perversely; ⁸they have been quick to turn aside from the way that I commanded them; they have cast for themselves an image of a calf, and have worshiped it and sacrificed to it, and said, 'These are your gods, O Israel, who brought you up out of the land of Egypt!' " ⁹The LORD said to Moses, "I have seen this people, how stiff-necked they are. ¹⁰Now let me alone, so that my wrath may burn hot against them and I may consume them; and of you I will make a great nation."

11 But Moses implored the LORD his God, and said, "O LORD, why does your wrath burn hot against your people, whom you brought out of the land of Egypt with great power and with a mighty hand? ¹²Why should the Egyptians say, 'It was with evil intent that he brought them out to kill them in the mountains, and to consume them from the face of the earth'? Turn from your fierce wrath; change your mind and do not bring disaster on your people. ¹³Remember Abraham, Isaac, and Israel, your servants, how you swore to them by your own self, saying to them, 'I will multiply your descendants like the stars of heaven, and all this land that I have promised I will give to your descendants, and they shall inherit it forever.' " ¹⁴And the LORD changed his mind about the

b Heb *he*   *a* Or *treaty,* or *testimony;* Heb *eduth*
c Or *fashioned it with a graving tool;* Meaning of Heb uncertain

disaster that he planned to bring on his people.

32.1–14. 2–3: The *gold rings* presumably come from the gold jewelry given to the Israelites by the Egyptians when they fled Egypt (12.35–36). **4:** The *calf* or young bull was a common image for certain Canaanite gods. **7:** The LORD tells Moses that now the Israelites are *your people*. They are no longer God's people. **10:** The LORD plans to *consume* or completely destroy the Israelites for their disobedience. The LORD will then take Moses alone and make of him *a great nation*. That is the same promise God first made to Abraham (Gen 12.2). **11– 14:** Moses pleads to God on behalf of the Israelites. Moses reminds God that they are *your people* (vv. 11, 12; see 33.13). To destroy Israel would do harm to the LORD's international reputation (v. 12). It would also violate God's promise to Abraham, Isaac, and Jacob (v. 13; see 6.2–8). God *swore* or made a promise to each of the ancestors in Genesis: Abraham (Gen 13.14–15), Isaac (Gen 26.3), and Jacob/Israel (Gen 28.13). Remarkably, Moses succeeds. *The LORD* changed his *mind* about destroying Israel.

15 Then Moses turned and went down from the mountain, carrying the two tablets of the covenant*a* in his hands, tablets that were written on both sides, written on the front and on the back. 16 The tablets were the work of God, and the writing was the writing of God, engraved upon the tablets. 17 When Joshua heard the noise of the people as they shouted, he said to Moses, "There is a noise of war in the camp." 18 But he said,

"It is not the sound made by victors,
 or the sound made by losers;
it is the sound of revelers that I hear."

19 As soon as he came near the camp and saw the calf and the dancing, Moses' anger burned hot, and he threw the tablets from his hands and broke them at the foot of the mountain. 20 He took the calf that they had made, burned it with fire, ground it to powder, scattered it on the water, and made the Israelites drink it.

21 Moses said to Aaron, "What did this people do to you that you have brought so great a sin upon them?" 22 And Aaron said, "Do not let the anger of my lord burn hot; you know the people, that they are bent on evil. 23 They said to me, 'Make us gods, who shall go before us; as for this Moses, the man who brought us up out of the land of Egypt, we do not know what has become of him.' 24 So I said to them, 'Whoever has gold, take it off'; so they gave it to me, and I threw it into the fire, and out came this calf!"

25 When Moses saw that the people were running wild (for Aaron had let them run wild, to the derision of their enemies), 26 then Moses stood in the gate of the camp, and said, "Who is on the LORD's side? Come to me!" And all the sons of Levi gathered around him. 27 He said to them, "Thus says the LORD, the God of Israel, 'Put your sword on your side, each of you! Go back and forth from gate to gate throughout the camp, and each of you kill your brother, your friend, and your neighbor.'" 28 The sons of Levi did as Moses commanded, and about three thousand of the people fell on that day. 29 Moses said, "Today you have ordained yourselves*b* for the service of the LORD, each one at the cost of a son or a brother, and so have brought a blessing on yourselves this day."

30 On the next day Moses said to the people, "You have sinned a great sin. But now I will go up to the LORD; perhaps I can make atonement for your sin." 31 So Moses returned to the LORD and said, "Alas, this people has sinned a great sin; they have made for themselves gods of gold. 32 But now, if you will only forgive their sin—but if not, blot me out of the book that you have written." 33 But the LORD said to Moses, "Whoever has sinned against me I will blot out of my book. 34 But now go, lead the people to the place about which I have spoken to you; see, my angel shall go in front of you. Nevertheless, when the day comes for punishment, I will punish them for their sin."

35 Then the LORD sent a plague on the people, because they made the calf—the one that Aaron made.

32.15–35. 15: On *the two tablets of the covenant,*＊ see comment on 31.18. **17:** *Joshua* is Moses' young assistant (24.13). **19:** Moses *broke* the stone *tablets* on

---

a Or *treaty,* or *testimony;* Heb *eduth* *b* Gk Vg
Compare Tg: Heb *Today ordain yourselves*

which God had written the Ten Commandments (vv. 15–16). The act dramatized Israel's severe disobedience, which broke the formal relationship between God and the people. **21–23:** In contrast to Moses, who takes responsibility and pleads to God on behalf of the people, Aaron blames the people in order to escape his own responsibility for the rebellion. **24:** Aaron's version of the story suggests that the golden calf emerged by itself miraculously out of the fire. The earlier account clearly tells the real story: Aaron himself was the one responsible for making the golden calf (v. 4; see vv. 25, 35). **26–29:** The members of the tribe of *Levi* obey Moses. Thus, Moses *ordained* or set them apart *for the service of the LORD* as priests. The ordination* of the Levites occurs in Num 8. Numbers 16–18 suggests that the Levites will be subordinate to Aaron and the priests in his line. **34:** The LORD promises to send *my angel*, a subordinate divine messenger and commander, to lead Israel into Canaan (23.20, 23). The question will become whether, in addition to the angel, God's own divine presence will go in the midst of Israel to lead them (33.2–3).

33 The LORD said to Moses, "Go, leave this place, you and the people whom you have brought up out of the land of Egypt, and go to the land of which I swore to Abraham, Isaac, and Jacob, saying, 'To your descendants I will give it.' ²I will send an angel before you, and I will drive out the Canaanites, the Amorites, the Hittites, the Perizzites, the Hivites, and the Jebusites. ³Go up to a land flowing with milk and honey; but I will not go up among you, or I would consume you on the way, for you are a stiff-necked people."

4 When the people heard these harsh words, they mourned, and no one put on ornaments. ⁵For the LORD had said to Moses, "Say to the Israelites, 'You are a stiff-necked people; if for a single moment I should go up among you, I would consume you. So now take off your ornaments, and I will decide what to do to you.' " ⁶Therefore the Israelites stripped themselves of their ornaments, from Mount Horeb onward.

7 Now Moses used to take the tent and pitch it outside the camp, far off from the camp; he called it the tent of meeting. And everyone who sought the LORD would go out to the tent of meeting, which was outside the camp. ⁸Whenever Moses went out to the tent, all the people would rise and stand, each of them, at the entrance of their tents and watch Moses until he had gone into the tent. ⁹When Moses entered the tent, the pillar of cloud would descend and stand at the entrance of the tent, and the LORD would speak with Moses. ¹⁰When all the people saw the pillar of cloud standing at the entrance of the tent, all the people would rise and bow down, all of them, at the entrance of their tent. ¹¹Thus the LORD used to speak to Moses face to face, as one speaks to a friend. Then he would return to the camp; but his young assistant, Joshua son of Nun, would not leave the tent.

12 Moses said to the LORD, "See, you have said to me, 'Bring up this people'; but you have not let me know whom you will send with me. Yet you have said, 'I know you by name, and you have also found favor in my sight.' ¹³Now if I have found favor in your sight, show me your ways, so that I may know you and find favor in your sight. Consider too that this nation is your people." ¹⁴He said, "My presence will go with you, and I will give you rest." ¹⁵And he said to him, "If your presence will not go, do not carry us up from here. ¹⁶For how shall it be known that I have found favor in your sight, I and your people, unless you go with us? In this way, we shall be distinct, I and your people, from every people on the face of the earth."

17 The LORD said to Moses, "I will do the very thing that you have asked; for you have found favor in my sight, and I know you by name." ¹⁸Moses said, "Show me your glory, I pray." ¹⁹And he said, "I will make all my goodness pass before you, and will proclaim before you the name, 'The LORD';ᵃ and I will be gracious to whom I will be gracious, and will show mercy on whom I will show mercy. ²⁰But," he said, "you cannot see my face; for no one shall see me and live." ²¹And the LORD continued, "See, there is a place by me where you shall stand on the rock; ²²and while my glory passes by I will put you in a cleft of the rock, and I will cover you with my hand until I have passed by; ²³then I will

a Heb YHWH; see note at 3.15

take away my hand, and you shall see my back; but my face shall not be seen."

33.1–23: Moses seeks assurance of God's presence with Israel. 2–3: The LORD promises to *send an angel,* a subordinate divine messenger. However, God's own presence cannot go with Israel lest God's own holiness come in contact with and *consume* the *stiff-necked* people of Israel. **5–6:** The *stripping* of Israel's *ornaments* involves letting go of the jewelry Israel had stripped from the Egyptians (12.35–36). **7:** *The tent of meeting* reflects an older tradition of a tent or shrine in which the deity delivers oracles.* Although the tent of meeting probably preceded the tabernacle* tradition, the two came to be associated with one another (27.19–21). Moses pitches the tent of meeting *far off from the camp* rather than at its center in this interim time while God decides what to do with Israel (v. 5). The tent will eventually be located in the middle of the Israelite camp (Num 2.2). **14:** God's words in Hebrew are literally *"My presence will go"* (not "with you"). God will go to Canaan but not "with" or "in the midst of" Israel because of its sin. **16:** Moses asks that God not only *go* to Canaan (v. 14), but Moses insists that God go *with us* or "in our midst." In v. 17, God relents and agrees to Moses' request. **19:** On the divine name *LORD,* see comment on 3.13–15. This verse and God's character revealed to Moses in 34.6–7 add new dimensions by accenting God's compassion and mercy. In 3.13–15, the LORD's name is "I will be who I will be." Here the name is *I will be gracious to whom I will be gracious.* **20–23:** A human could not look directly into the deity's face, for it would cause death (v. 20; see 3.6; Isa 6.5). However, Moses will see more of God than before; he will see God's *back* (v. 23).

God reveals the divine character and makes a new covenant

34.1–35: This chapter represents a significant turning point in Exodus. Worship of the golden calf threatened Israel's relationship with God. However, Moses urges God to provide a deeper revelation of God's character. This deeper revelation (vv. 6–7) enabled a new covenant to be restored (vv. 10–11, 27–28). The new covenant repeats a number of laws given earlier in Exodus with an emphasis on not worshipping other gods and laws relating to the exodus and the sabbath (vv. 12–26).

34 The LORD said to Moses, "Cut two tablets of stone like the former ones,

and I will write on the tablets the words that were on the former tablets, which you broke. ²Be ready in the morning, and come up in the morning to Mount Sinai and present yourself there to me, on the top of the mountain. ³No one shall come up with you, and do not let anyone be seen throughout all the mountain; and do not let flocks or herds graze in front of that mountain." ⁴So Moses cut two tablets of stone like the former ones; and he rose early in the morning and went up on Mount Sinai, as the LORD had commanded him, and took in his hand the two tablets of stone. ⁵The LORD descended in the cloud and stood with him there, and proclaimed the name, "The LORD."*ᵃ* ⁶The LORD passed before him, and proclaimed,

"The LORD, the LORD,
a God merciful and gracious,
slow to anger,
and abounding in steadfast love and
faithfulness,
⁷ keeping steadfast love for the
thousandth generation,*ᵇ*
forgiving iniquity and transgression and
sin,
yet by no means clearing the guilty,
but visiting the iniquity of the parents
upon the children
and the children's children,
to the third and the fourth generation."

⁸And Moses quickly bowed his head toward the earth, and worshiped. ⁹He said, "If now I have found favor in your sight, O Lord, I pray, let the Lord go with us. Although this is a stiff-necked people, pardon our iniquity and our sin, and take us for your inheritance."

10 He said: I hereby make a covenant. Before all your people I will perform marvels, such as have not been performed in all the earth or in any nation; and all the people among whom you live shall see the work of the LORD; for it is an awesome thing that I will do with you.

11 Observe what I command you today. See, I will drive out before you the Amorites, the Canaanites, the Hittites, the Perizzites, the Hivites, and the Jebusites. ¹²Take care

a Heb *YHWH*; see note at 3.15   *b* Or *for thousands*

Accenting God's Mercy over God's Judgment

Israel's worship of the golden calf caused its covenant* relationship with God to be broken. The restoration of a new covenant between God and Israel was made possible through a deeper revealing of God's character that accented God's mercy and compassion. This deeper revelation is evident when the reader compares the first description of God's character in 20.5–6 and the second description in 34.6–7.

Exodus 20.5–6

I the LORD your God am a jealous God, punishing children for the iniquity of parents, to the third and the fourth generation of those who reject me, but showing steadfast love to the thousandth generation of those who love me and keep my commandments.

Exodus 34.6–7

The LORD, the LORD, a God merciful and gracious, slow to anger, and abounding in steadfast love and faithfulness, keeping steadfast love for the thousandth generation, forgiving iniquity and transgression and sin, yet by no means clearing the guilty, but visiting the iniquity of parents upon the children and the children's children, to the third and the fourth generation.

A number of differences are evident between the two similar texts. Exodus 20.5–6 places God's punishment as the first element of God's character that is emphasized, whereas 34.6–7 places this punishment as a secondary part of God's nature. The steadfast love, in secondary position in 20.5–6, moves to the front in 34.6–7. Exodus 34.6–7 also expands considerably the description of God's compassionate nature: slowness to anger, abundance of mercy, grace, and faithfulness. The condition that God shows steadfast love to "those who love me and keep my commandments" in 20.5–6 is removed in 34.6–7. Instead, 34.6–7 speaks of God as "forgiving iniquity."

Variations of this important description of God's nature occur in several other texts in the Old Testament: Num 14.18; Neh 9.17; Ps 103.8; Joel 2.13; Jon 4.2. Because of its repeated use, the description appears to have functioned as a creed or confession of faith in ancient Israel.

not to make a covenant with the inhabitants of the land to which you are going, or it will become a snare among you. 13You shall tear down their altars, break their pillars, and cut down their sacred poles[a] 14(for you shall worship no other god, because the LORD, whose name is Jealous, is a jealous God). 15You shall not make a covenant with the inhabitants of the land, for when they prostitute themselves to their gods and sacrifice to their gods, someone among them will invite you, and you will eat of the sacrifice. 16And you will take wives from among their daughters for your sons, and their daughters who prostitute themselves to their gods will make your sons also prostitute themselves to their gods.

34.1–16. 4: Moses had broken the *former tablets of stone* when Israel worshipped the idol of the golden calf. Their idolatry* threatened to destroy their relationship with God (32.19). **6–7:** These verses reflect important differences in the description of God's character when compared to a similar description in

a Heb *Asherim*

20.5–6. The changes place more emphasis on God's mercy, grace, and forgiveness while still retaining the element of God's punishment for disobedience. **13:** *Pillars* of stone and *sacred poles* ("asherim") of wood were used in native Canaanite fertility religion in worshipping the gods Baal★ and Asherah★ (Judg 6.25).

17 You shall not make cast idols.

18 You shall keep the festival of unleavened bread. Seven days you shall eat unleavened bread, as I commanded you, at the time appointed in the month of Abib; for in the month of Abib you came out from Egypt.

19 All that first opens the womb is mine, all your male*ᵃ* livestock, the firstborn of cow and sheep. ²⁰The firstborn of a donkey you shall redeem with a lamb, or if you will not redeem it you shall break its neck. All the firstborn of your sons you shall redeem.

No one shall appear before me empty-handed.

21 Six days you shall work, but on the seventh day you shall rest; even in plowing time and in harvest time you shall rest. ²²You shall observe the festival of weeks, the first fruits of wheat harvest, and the festival of ingathering at the turn of the year. ²³Three times in the year all your males shall appear before the LORD God, the God of Israel. ²⁴For I will cast out nations before you, and enlarge your borders; no one shall covet your land when you go up to appear before the LORD your God three times in the year.

25 You shall not offer the blood of my sacrifice with leaven, and the sacrifice of the festival of the passover shall not be left until the morning.

26 The best of the first fruits of your ground you shall bring to the house of the LORD your God.

You shall not boil a kid in its mother's milk.

27 The LORD said to Moses: Write these words; in accordance with these words I have made a covenant with you and with Israel. ²⁸He was there with the LORD forty days and forty nights; he neither ate bread nor drank water. And he wrote on the tablets the words of the covenant, the ten commandments.*ᵇ*

29 Moses came down from Mount Sinai. As he came down from the mountain with the two tablets of the covenant*ᶜ* in his hand, Moses did not know that the skin of his face shone because he had been talking with God. ³⁰When Aaron and all the Israelites saw Moses, the skin of his face was shining, and they were afraid to come near him. ³¹But Moses called to them; and Aaron and all the leaders of the congregation returned to him, and Moses spoke with them. ³²Afterward all the Israelites came near, and he gave them in commandment all that the LORD had spoken with him on Mount Sinai. ³³When Moses had finished speaking with them, he put a veil on his face; ³⁴but whenever Moses went in before the LORD to speak with him, he would take the veil off, until he came out; and when he came out, and told the Israelites what he had been commanded, ³⁵the Israelites would see the face of Moses, that the skin of his face was shining; and Moses would put the veil on his face again, until he went in to speak with him.

34.17–35. 19–20: On *redeeming the firstborn*, see comment on 13.13. **24:** To *covet* refers to the inner yearning and strong desire to take something that rightfully belongs to others, especially the poor and less powerful. **29:** Moses' unique and close relationship with God caused some of God's divine radiance or light to pass onto Moses. Thus, *the skin of his face shone*. **33:** Just as the cloud veiled the deity's fiery radiance or glory (24.15–18), so Moses *put a veil on his face* to shield the people from his own shining radiance.

Moses prepares to construct the tabernacle
35.1–36.7: This section begins an extensive unit dealing with the actual construction of the tabernacle★ (chs. 35–40). The tabernacle is the tangible and mobile sign of God's presence in the midst of the Israelites as they leave Mount Sinai and travel through the wilderness to Canaan. The instructions for building the tabernacle were first given in chs. 25–31. The golden calf crisis (ch. 32) had endangered the tabernacle project. However, the resolution and new covenant★ in chs. 33–34 enabled the tabernacle construction to move forward. The construction obediently follows the instructions that were previously given. The detailed nature of the instructions and process for building the tabernacle resembles the detailed account of

a Gk Theodotion Vg Tg: Meaning of Heb uncertain
b Heb *words*   *c* Or *treaty*, or *testimony*; Heb *eduth*

the building of Solomon's Temple* (1 Kings 6–8) and the detailed character of Ezekiel's promise of a new Temple in Jerusalem (Ezek 40–43).

---

35 Moses assembled all the congregation of the Israelites and said to them: These are the things that the LORD has commanded you to do:

2 Six days shall work be done, but on the seventh day you shall have a holy sabbath of solemn rest to the LORD; whoever does any work on it shall be put to death. 3You shall kindle no fire in all your dwellings on the sabbath day.

4 Moses said to all the congregation of the Israelites: This is the thing that the LORD has commanded: 5Take from among you an offering to the LORD; let whoever is of a generous heart bring the LORD's offering: gold, silver, and bronze; 6blue, purple, and crimson yarns, and fine linen; goats' hair, 7tanned rams' skins, and fine leather;*ª acacia wood, 8oil for the light, spices for the anointing oil and for the fragrant incense, 9and onyx stones and gems to be set in the ephod and the breastpiece.

10 All who are skillful among you shall come and make all that the LORD has commanded: the tabernacle, 11its tent and its covering, its clasps and its frames, its bars, its pillars, and its bases; 12the ark with its poles, the mercy seat,*ᵇ and the curtain for the screen; 13the table with its poles and all its utensils, and the bread of the Presence; 14the lampstand also for the light, with its utensils and its lamps, and the oil for the light; 15and the altar of incense, with its poles, and the anointing oil and the fragrant incense, and the screen for the entrance, the entrance of the tabernacle; 16the altar of burnt offering, with its grating of bronze, its poles, and all its utensils, the basin with its stand; 17the hangings of the court, its pillars and its bases, and the screen for the gate of the court; 18the pegs of the tabernacle and the pegs of the court, and their cords; 19the finely worked vestments for ministering in the holy place, the holy vestments for the priest Aaron, and the vestments of his sons, for their service as priests.

20 Then all the congregation of the Isra-elites withdrew from the presence of Moses. 21And they came, everyone whose heart was stirred, and everyone whose spirit was willing, and brought the LORD's offering to be used for the tent of meeting, and for all its service, and for the sacred vestments. 22So they came, both men and women; all who were of a willing heart brought brooches and earrings and signet rings and pendants, all sorts of gold objects, everyone bringing an offering of gold to the LORD. 23And everyone who possessed blue or purple or crimson yarn or fine linen or goats' hair or tanned rams' skins or fine leather,*ª brought them. 24Everyone who could make an offering of silver or bronze brought it as the LORD's offering; and everyone who possessed acacia wood of any use in the work, brought it. 25All the skillful women spun with their hands, and brought what they had spun in blue and purple and crimson yarns and fine linen; 26all the women whose hearts moved them to use their skill spun the goats' hair. 27And the leaders brought onyx stones and gems to be set in the ephod and the breastpiece, 28and spices and oil for the light, and for the anointing oil, and for the fragrant incense. 29All the Israelite men and women whose hearts made them willing to bring anything for the work that the LORD had commanded by Moses to be done, brought it as a freewill offering to the LORD.

30 Then Moses said to the Israelites: See, the LORD has called by name Bezalel son of Uri son of Hur, of the tribe of Judah; 31he has filled him with divine spirit,*ᶜ with skill, intelligence, and knowledge in every kind of craft, 32to devise artistic designs, to work in gold, silver, and bronze, 33in cutting stones for setting, and in carving wood, in every kind of craft. 34And he has inspired him to teach, both him and Oholiab son of Ahisamach, of the tribe of Dan. 35He has filled them with skill to do every kind of work done by an artisan or by a designer or by an embroiderer in blue, purple, and crimson yarns, and in fine linen, or by a weaver—by any sort of artisan or skilled designer.

a Meaning of Heb uncertain   *b* Or *the cover*
c Or *the spirit of God*

35.1–35. 2–3: Just as the sabbath law had concluded the instructions for building the tabernacle (31.12–17), the sabbath law now introduces the actual work of construction. **22–29:** The people offer willingly what they have for the tabernacle. Presumably some of it included the gold, silver, jewelry, and clothing that the Egyptians gave to them when they fled Egypt (12.35–36). **30–35:** The passage about *Bezalel* and *Oholiab* elaborates 31.1–5. The *divine spirit* gives them *knowledge in every kind of craft* (v. 31) as in 31.3. Additionally, the spirit of God *inspired* them *to teach* others their skills (v. 34).

36

Bezalel and Oholiab and every skillful one to whom the LORD has given skill and understanding to know how to do any work in the construction of the sanctuary shall work in accordance with all that the LORD has commanded.

2 Moses then called Bezalel and Oholiab and every skillful one to whom the LORD had given skill, everyone whose heart was stirred to come to do the work; ³and they received from Moses all the freewill offerings that the Israelites had brought for doing the work on the sanctuary. They still kept bringing him freewill offerings every morning, ⁴so that all the artisans who were doing every sort of task on the sanctuary came, each from the task being performed, ⁵and said to Moses, "The people are bringing much more than enough for doing the work that the LORD has commanded us to do." ⁶So Moses gave command, and word was proclaimed throughout the camp: "No man or woman is to make anything else as an offering for the sanctuary." So the people were restrained from bringing; ⁷for what they had already brought was more than enough to do all the work.

36.5–7: Pharaoh's oppressive complaint about the laziness of Israelite slave workers at the beginning of the book (5.4–9) contrasts sharply with Israel's eagerness and enthusiasm in working on the tabernacle here at the end of the book.

The ark of the covenant, the tabernacle, and its furnishings
36.8–39.43: The construction of the tabernacle and its contents follows closely and methodically the instruc-

tions first given in chs. 25–31 with some minor omissions. The sequence proceeds from first constructing the outside frames and curtains and then moving inward to make the holiest furnishings and objects inside the tabernacle. This pattern reverses the sequence of the instructions in chs. 25–31, which move from the innermost, holiest furnishings to the outer objects and surroundings.

8 All those with skill among the workers made the tabernacle with ten curtains; they were made of fine twisted linen, and blue, purple, and crimson yarns, with cherubim skillfully worked into them. ⁹The length of each curtain was twenty-eight cubits, and the width of each curtain four cubits; all the curtains were of the same size.

10 He joined five curtains to one another, and the other five curtains he joined to one another. ¹¹He made loops of blue on the edge of the outermost curtain of the first set; likewise he made them on the edge of the outermost curtain of the second set; ¹²he made fifty loops on the one curtain, and he made fifty loops on the edge of the curtain that was in the second set; the loops were opposite one another. ¹³And he made fifty clasps of gold, and joined the curtains one to the other with clasps; so the tabernacle was one whole.

14 He also made curtains of goats' hair for a tent over the tabernacle; he made eleven curtains. ¹⁵The length of each curtain was thirty cubits, and the width of each curtain four cubits; the eleven curtains were of the same size. ¹⁶He joined five curtains by themselves, and six curtains by themselves. ¹⁷He made fifty loops on the edge of the outermost curtain of the one set, and fifty loops on the edge of the other connecting curtain. ¹⁸He made fifty clasps of bronze to join the tent together so that it might be one whole. ¹⁹And he made for the tent a covering of tanned rams' skins and an outer covering of fine leather.ᵃ

20 Then he made the upright frames for the tabernacle of acacia wood. ²¹Ten cubits was the length of a frame, and a cubit and a half the width of each frame. ²²Each frame

a Meaning of Heb uncertain

had two pegs for fitting together; he did this for all the frames of the tabernacle. 23The frames for the tabernacle he made in this way: twenty frames for the south side; 24and he made forty bases of silver under the twenty frames, two bases under the first frame for its two pegs, and two bases under the next frame for its two pegs. 25For the second side of the tabernacle, on the north side, he made twenty frames 26and their forty bases of silver, two bases under the first frame and two bases under the next frame. 27For the rear of the tabernacle westward he made six frames. 28He made two frames for corners of the tabernacle in the rear. 29They were separate beneath, but joined at the top, at the first ring; he made two of them in this way, for the two corners. 30There were eight frames with their bases of silver: sixteen bases, under every frame two bases.

31 He made bars of acacia wood, five for the frames of the one side of the tabernacle, 32and five bars for the frames of the other side of the tabernacle, and five bars for the frames of the tabernacle at the rear westward. 33He made the middle bar to pass through from end to end halfway up the frames. 34And he overlaid the frames with gold, and made rings of gold for them to hold the bars, and overlaid the bars with gold.

35 He made the curtain of blue, purple, and crimson yarns, and fine twisted linen, with cherubim skillfully worked into it. 36For it he made four pillars of acacia, and overlaid them with gold; their hooks were of gold, and he cast for them four bases of silver. 37He also made a screen for the entrance to the tent, of blue, purple, and crimson yarns, and fine twisted linen, embroidered with needle-work; 38and its five pillars with their hooks. He overlaid their capitals and their bases with gold, but their five bases were of bronze.

37 Bezalel made the ark of acacia wood; it was two and a half cubits long, a cubit and a half wide, and a cubit and a half high. 2He overlaid it with pure gold inside and outside, and made a molding of gold around it. 3He cast for it four rings of gold for its four feet, two rings on its one side and two rings on its other side. 4He made poles of acacia wood, and overlaid them with gold, 5and put the poles into the rings on the sides of the ark, to carry the ark. 6He made a mercy seat*a* of pure gold; two cubits and a half was its length, and a cubit and a half its width. 7He made two cherubim of hammered gold; at the two ends of the mercy seat*b* he made them, 8one cherub at the one end, and one cherub at the other end; of one piece with the mercy seat*b* he made the cherubim at its two ends. 9The cherubim spread out their wings above, overshadowing the mercy seat*b* with their wings. They faced one another; the faces of the cherubim were turned toward the mercy seat.*b*

10 He also made the table of acacia wood, two cubits long, one cubit wide, and a cubit and a half high. 11He overlaid it with pure gold, and made a molding of gold around it. 12He made around it a rim a handbreadth wide, and made a molding of gold around the rim. 13He cast for it four rings of gold, and fastened the rings to the four corners at its four legs. 14The rings that held the poles used for carrying the table were close to the rim. 15He made the poles of acacia wood to carry the table, and overlaid them with gold. 16And he made the vessels of pure gold that were to be on the table, its plates and dishes for incense, and its bowls and flagons with which to pour drink offerings.

17 He also made the lampstand of pure gold. The base and the shaft of the lampstand were made of hammered work; its cups, its calyxes, and its petals were of one piece with it. 18There were six branches going out of its sides, three branches of the lampstand out of one side of it and three branches of the lampstand out of the other side of it; 19three cups shaped like almond blossoms, each with calyx and petals, on one branch, and three cups shaped like almond blossoms, each with calyx and petals, on the other branch—so for the six branches going out of the lampstand. 20On the lampstand itself there were four cups shaped like almond blossoms, each with its calyxes and petals. 21There was a calyx of one piece with it under the first pair of branches, a calyx of one piece with it under the next pair of

a Or *a cover*   *b* Or *the cover*

branches, and a calyx of one piece with it under the last pair of branches. 22Their calyxes and their branches were of one piece with it, the whole of it one hammered piece of pure gold. 23He made its seven lamps and its snuffers and its trays of pure gold. 24He made it and all its utensils of a talent of pure gold.

25 He made the altar of incense of acacia wood, one cubit long, and one cubit wide; it was square, and was two cubits high; its horns were of one piece with it. 26He overlaid it with pure gold, its top, and its sides all around, and its horns; and he made for it a molding of gold all around, 27and made two golden rings for it under its molding, on two opposite sides of it, to hold the poles with which to carry it. 28And he made the poles of acacia wood, and overlaid them with gold.

29 He made the holy anointing oil also, and the pure fragrant incense, blended as by the perfumer.

38 He made the altar of burnt offering also of acacia wood; it was five cubits long, and five cubits wide; it was square, and three cubits high. 2He made horns for it on its four corners; its horns were of one piece with it, and he overlaid it with bronze. 3He made all the utensils of the altar, the pots, the shovels, the basins, the forks, and the firepans: all its utensils he made of bronze. 4He made for the altar a grating, a network of bronze, under its ledge, extending halfway down. 5He cast four rings on the four corners of the bronze grating to hold the poles; 6he made the poles of acacia wood, and overlaid them with bronze. 7And he put the poles through the rings on the sides of the altar, to carry it with them; he made it hollow, with boards.

8 He made the basin of bronze with its stand of bronze, from the mirrors of the women who served at the entrance to the tent of meeting.

9 He made the court; for the south side the hangings of the court were of fine twisted linen, one hundred cubits long; 10its twenty pillars and their twenty bases were of bronze, but the hooks of the pillars and their bands were of silver. 11For the north side there were hangings one hundred cubits long; its twenty pillars and their twenty bases were of bronze, but the hooks of the pillars and their bands were of silver. 12For the west side there were hangings fifty cubits long, with ten pillars and ten bases; the hooks of the pillars and their bands were of silver. 13And for the front to the east, fifty cubits. 14The hangings for one side of the gate were fifteen cubits, with three pillars and three bases. 15And so for the other side; on each side of the gate of the court were hangings of fifteen cubits, with three pillars and three bases. 16All the hangings around the court were of fine twisted linen. 17The bases for the pillars were of bronze, but the hooks of the pillars and their bands were of silver; the overlaying of their capitals was also of silver, and all the pillars of the court were banded with silver. 18The screen for the entrance to the court was embroidered with needlework in blue, purple, and crimson yarns and fine twisted linen. It was twenty cubits long and, along the width of it, five cubits high, corresponding to the hangings of the court. 19There were four pillars; their four bases were of bronze, their hooks of silver, and the overlaying of their capitals and their bands of silver. 20All the pegs for the tabernacle and for the court all around were of bronze.

21 These are the records of the tabernacle, the tabernacle of the covenant,[a] which were drawn up at the commandment of Moses, the work of the Levites being under the direction of Ithamar son of the priest Aaron. 22Bezalel son of Uri son of Hur, of the tribe of Judah, made all that the LORD commanded Moses; 23and with him was Oholiab son of Ahisamach, of the tribe of Dan, engraver, designer, and embroiderer in blue, purple, and crimson yarns, and in fine linen.

24 All the gold that was used for the work, in all the construction of the sanctuary, the gold from the offering, was twenty-nine talents and seven hundred thirty shekels, measured by the sanctuary shekel. 25The silver from those of the congregation who were counted was one hundred talents and one thousand seven hundred seventy-five shek-

a Or treaty, or testimony; Heb eduth

els, measured by the sanctuary shekel; 26a beka a head (that is, half a shekel, measured by the sanctuary shekel), for everyone who was counted in the census, from twenty years old and upward, for six hundred three thousand, five hundred fifty men. 27The hundred talents of silver were for casting the bases of the sanctuary, and the bases of the curtain; one hundred bases for the hundred talents, a talent for a base. 28Of the thousand seven hundred seventy-five shekels he made hooks for the pillars, and overlaid their capitals and made bands for them. 29The bronze that was contributed was seventy talents, and two thousand four hundred shekels; 30with it he made the bases for the entrance of the tent of meeting, the bronze altar and the bronze grating for it and all the utensils of the altar, 31the bases all around the court, and the bases of the gate of the court, all the pegs of the tabernacle, and all the pegs around the court.

38.26: The *census* and its total count of 603,550 men reflects the results of the census in Num 1.45–46. The law concerning payment during a census occurs in 30.12–14.

39 Of the blue, purple, and crimson yarns they made finely worked vestments, for ministering in the holy place; they made the sacred vestments for Aaron; as the LORD had commanded Moses.

2 He made the ephod of gold, of blue, purple, and crimson yarns, and of fine twisted linen. 3Gold leaf was hammered out and cut into threads to work into the blue, purple, and crimson yarns and into the fine twisted linen, in skilled design. 4They made for the ephod shoulder-pieces, joined to it at its two edges. 5The decorated band on it was of the same materials and workmanship, of gold, of blue, purple, and crimson yarns, and of fine twisted linen; as the LORD had commanded Moses.

6 The onyx stones were prepared, enclosed in settings of gold filigree and engraved like the engravings of a signet, according to the names of the sons of Israel. 7He set them on the shoulder-pieces of the ephod, to be stones of remembrance for the sons of Israel; as the LORD had commanded Moses.

8 He made the breastpiece, in skilled work, like the work of the ephod, of gold, of blue, purple, and crimson yarns, and of fine twisted linen. 9It was square; the breastpiece was made double, a span in length and a span in width when doubled. 10They set in it four rows of stones. A row of carnelian,*a* chrysolite, and emerald was the first row; 11and the second row, a turquoise, a sapphire,*b* and a moonstone; 12and the third row, a jacinth, an agate, and an amethyst; 13and the fourth row, a beryl, an onyx, and a jasper; they were enclosed in settings of gold filigree. 14There were twelve stones with names corresponding to the names of the sons of Israel; they were like signets, each engraved with its name, for the twelve tribes. 15They made on the breastpiece chains of pure gold, twisted like cords; 16and they made two settings of gold filigree and two gold rings, and put the two rings on the two edges of the breastpiece; 17and they put the two cords of gold in the two rings at the edges of the breastpiece. 18Two ends of the two cords they had attached to the two settings of filigree; in this way they attached it in front to the shoulder-pieces of the ephod. 19Then they made two rings of gold, and put them at the two ends of the breastpiece, on its inside edge next to the ephod. 20They made two rings of gold, and attached them in front to the lower part of the two shoulder-pieces of the ephod, at its joining above the decorated band of the ephod. 21They bound the breastpiece by its rings to the rings of the ephod with a blue cord, so that it should lie on the decorated band of the ephod, and that the breastpiece should not come loose from the ephod; as the LORD had commanded Moses.

22 He also made the robe of the ephod woven all of blue yarn; 23and the opening of the robe in the middle of it was like the opening in a coat of mail,*c* with a binding around the opening, so that it might not be torn.

a The identification of several of these stones is uncertain *b* Or *lapis lazuli* *c* Meaning of Heb uncertain

24On the lower hem of the robe they made pomegranates of blue, purple, and crimson yarns, and of fine twisted linen. 25They also made bells of pure gold, and put the bells between the pomegranates on the lower hem of the robe all around, between the pomegranates; 26a bell and a pomegranate, a bell and a pomegranate all around on the lower hem of the robe for ministering; as the LORD had commanded Moses.

27 They also made the tunics, woven of fine linen, for Aaron and his sons, 28and the turban of fine linen, and the headdresses of fine linen, and the linen undergarments of fine twisted linen, 29and the sash of fine twisted linen, and of blue, purple, and crimson yarns, embroidered with needlework; as the LORD had commanded Moses.

30 They made the rosette of the holy diadem of pure gold, and wrote on it an inscription, like the engraving of a signet, "Holy to the LORD." 31They tied to it a blue cord, to fasten it on the turban above; as the LORD had commanded Moses.

39.1–31: This section recounts the making of Aaron's priestly vestments or clothing. The refrain *as the LORD had commanded Moses* recurs seven times throughout the chapter (vv. 1, 5, 7, 21, 26, 29, 31). This sevenfold refrain mirrors the sevenfold refrain and structure of the seven days of creation in Gen 1.1–2.4.

32 In this way all the work of the tabernacle of the tent of meeting was finished; the Israelites had done everything just as the LORD had commanded Moses. 33Then they brought the tabernacle to Moses, the tent and all its utensils, its hooks, its frames, its bars, its pillars, and its bases; 34the covering of tanned rams' skins and the covering of fine leather,*a* and the curtain for the screen; 35the ark of the covenant*b* with its poles and the mercy seat;*c* 36the table with all its utensils, and the bread of the Presence; 37the pure lampstand with its lamps set on it and all its utensils, and the oil for the light; 38the golden altar, the anointing oil and the fragrant incense, and the screen for the entrance of the tent; 39the bronze altar, and its grating of bronze, its poles, and all its utensils; the basin with its stand; 40the hangings of the court, its pillars, and its bases, and the screen for the gate of the court, its cords, and its pegs; and all the utensils for the service of the tabernacle, for the tent of meeting; 41the finely worked vestments for ministering in the holy place, the sacred vestments for the priest Aaron, and the vestments of his sons to serve as priests. 42The Israelites had done all of the work just as the LORD had commanded Moses. 43When Moses saw that they had done all the work just as the LORD had commanded, he blessed them.

40 The LORD spoke to Moses: 2On the first day of the first month you shall set up the tabernacle of the tent of meeting. 3You shall put in it the ark of the covenant,*b* and you shall screen the ark with the curtain. 4You shall bring in the table, and arrange its setting; and you shall bring in the lampstand, and set up its lamps. 5You shall put the golden altar for incense before the ark of the covenant,*b* and set up the screen for the entrance of the tabernacle. 6You shall set the altar of burnt offering before the entrance of the tabernacle of the tent of meeting, 7and place the basin between the tent of meeting and the altar, and put water in it. 8You shall set up the court all around, and hang up the screen for the gate of the court. 9Then you shall take the anointing oil, and anoint the tabernacle and all that is in it, and consecrate it and all its furniture, so that it shall become holy. 10You shall also anoint the altar of burnt offering and all its utensils, and consecrate the altar, so that the altar shall be most holy. 11You shall also anoint the basin with its stand, and consecrate it. 12Then you shall bring Aaron and his sons to the entrance of the tent of meeting, and shall wash them with water, 13and put on Aaron the sacred vestments, and you shall anoint him and consecrate him, so that he may serve me as priest. 14You shall bring his sons also and put tunics on them, 15and anoint them, as you anointed their father, that they may serve me as priests: and their anointing shall admit them to a perpetual priesthood throughout all generations to come.

a Meaning of Heb uncertain   *b* Or *treaty*, or *testimony*; Heb *eduth*   *c* Or *the cover*

16 Moses did everything just as the LORD had commanded him. 17In the first month in the second year, on the first day of the month, the tabernacle was set up. 18Moses set up the tabernacle; he laid its bases, and set up its frames, and put in its poles, and raised up its pillars; 19and he spread the tent over the tabernacle, and put the covering of the tent over it; as the LORD had commanded Moses. 20He took the covenant[a] and put it into the ark, and put the poles on the ark, and set the mercy seat[b] above the ark; 21and he brought the ark into the tabernacle, and set up the curtain for screening, and screened the ark of the covenant;[a] as the LORD had commanded Moses. 22He put the table in the tent of meeting, on the north side of the tabernacle, outside the curtain, 23and set the bread in order on it before the LORD; as the LORD had commanded Moses. 24He put the lampstand in the tent of meeting, opposite the table on the south side of the tabernacle, 25and set up the lamps before the LORD; as the LORD had commanded Moses. 26He put the golden altar in the tent of meeting before the curtain, 27and offered fragrant incense on it; as the LORD had commanded Moses. 28He also put in place the screen for the entrance of the tabernacle. 29He set the altar of burnt offering at the entrance of the tabernacle of the tent of meeting, and offered on it the burnt offering and the grain offering as the LORD had commanded Moses. 30He set the basin between the tent of meeting and the altar, and put water in it for washing, 31with which Moses and Aaron and his sons washed their hands and their feet. 32When they went into the tent of meeting, and when they approached the altar, they washed; as the LORD had commanded Moses. 33He set up the court around the tabernacle and the altar, and put up the screen at the gate of the court. So Moses finished the work.

40.1–33: Moses completes the work by erecting the tabernacle and arranging its furnishings. 2: The es-tablishment of the tabernacle *on the first day of the first month* marks the beginning of the rhythms, seasons, and festivals of the new cultic year. The construction of the universe (Gen 1.1–2.4) had provided order and structure out of chaos that enabled the beginning of time and of life. In a similar way, Israel's construction of the tabernacle out of the chaos of the golden calf (ch. 32) provides order and structure for the beginning of Israel's worship and cultic life as it journeys through the wilderness. The text again brings together the *tabernacle* tradition and the older tradition of the *tent of meeting* (39.32, 40; 40.6, 22, 24, 29, 35; see comment on 33.7). **17:** Israel had arrived at Mount Sinai in the third month of the first year after going out of Egypt (19.1). Moses sets up the tabernacle nine months later *in the first month in the second year*.

34 Then the cloud covered the tent of meeting, and the glory of the LORD filled the tabernacle. 35Moses was not able to enter the tent of meeting because the cloud settled upon it, and the glory of the LORD filled the tabernacle. 36Whenever the cloud was taken up from the tabernacle, the Israelites would set out on each stage of their journey; 37but if the cloud was not taken up, then they did not set out until the day that it was taken up. 38For the cloud of the LORD was on the tabernacle by day, and fire was in the cloud[c] by night, before the eyes of all the house of Israel at each stage of their journey.

40.34–38: The glory and cloud of God's presence fill the tabernacle. 34–35: The presence of God in the form of the LORD's "glory" and the "cloud" had "covered" and "settled on" Mount Sinai in 24.15–18. The same divine *glory* and *cloud covered* and *settled upon* the *tent of meeting* and the *tabernacle*. **36:** *Each stage of their journey* looks forward to Israel's continuing trek through the wilderness toward the land of Canaan. The departure from Mount Sinai will actually begin in Num 10.11–36. **38:** On the *cloud by day* and the *fire by night*, see comment on 13.21.

a Or *treaty*, or *testimony*; Heb *eduth*   b Or *the cover*
c Heb *it*

LEVITICUS

Introduction

Leviticus is a collection of laws related to worship, priests, sacrifices, and holiness. The title, "Leviticus," derives from the Greek and Latin titles for the book meaning "the book of the Levites." The Levites themselves, a tribe of priests within ancient Israel, are mentioned only once in Leviticus (25.32–34). However, some biblical traditions trace the ancestry of the high priest Aaron to the tribe of Levi (Ex 6.16–20), and Aaron is the focus of many laws in Leviticus. The book underscores the holiness of Israel's God and the need for the priests and people of Israel to reflect that holiness in all aspects of their lives. The LORD repeatedly commands the people of Israel, "Be holy, for I am holy" (11.44–45; 19.2; 20.26).

Leviticus consists almost entirely of laws and commands with only two brief narrative★ sections, 10.1–7 and 24.10–16. The book presents its many laws and instructions as divine commands mediated through Moses and Aaron at Mount Sinai during Israel's wilderness journey from Egypt to the promised land of Canaan (27.34). However, many scholars agree that these laws actually arose later in Israel's history, from the late pre-exilic period (perhaps seventh century BCE) to the Persian period (fifth century BCE). The laws in Leviticus were probably collected over time in at least two major stages, with the earlier material gathered in chs. 1–16 and the later material concentrated in chs. 17–27. These two editorial stages display two different perspectives on matters of holiness. The earlier material in chs. 1–16 restricted its concern for holiness to the tabernacle★ or worship sanctuary, which was the seat of the divine presence in the midst of Israel in the wilderness. This earlier stage of the laws of Leviticus also viewed holiness as a concern primarily of the priests and not the whole people of Israel. In contrast, the later material in Leviticus (especially chs. 17–27) expands its concern for holiness to the land of Israel and to all the people, not just the priests (18.26; 22.32).

Leviticus contains many earlier traditions, but its final form probably emerged in the postexilic period. In the midst of this crisis and transition in its national life, Leviticus helped Israel recover its distinctive identity and mission. Israel was to be a holy community centered in the worship of the LORD who dwelled in its midst. The Exile involved the end of monarchy, the destruction of the Temple, and the need to rebuild the structure of the community. The priestly manual of Leviticus provided one important resource in the reconstitution of Israel's life and identity as a nation and as the people of God.

The place of Leviticus within the Pentateuch★ (the first five books of the Bible) provides an important clue to understanding its laws. The book of Exodus precedes Leviticus and includes an elaborate set of instructions for building the mobile tent of worship or the sanctuary called the tabernacle (chs. 25–31). The tabernacle contains the ark of the covenant,★ an elaborate box, over which God appears in the midst of Israel. In spite of Israel's grave sin of idolatry★ in worshipping the golden calf (Ex 32.1–35), God mercifully allows the Israelites to build the tabernacle (Ex 34.10–40.38). The laws of Leviticus provide guidelines for the conduct of worship and sacrifices connected with this newly constructed tabernacle. The laws also establish boundaries of holiness, order, and purity to preserve the life and well-being of Israel. The observance of these boundaries of holiness and purity ensures that God's holy presence among this sinful people will be not a threat but a blessing as Israel continues its wilderness journey toward the land of Canaan (Numbers—Deuteronomy).

READING GUIDE

Leviticus is a difficult book for modern readers since it contains few narratives and many laws dealing with unfamiliar matters (the sacrifice of animals and grain, the need to maintain ritual purity and cleanness). A first-time reader might begin by reading three shorter sections of Leviticus to sample its concerns. First, the account of the ordination* of the priests and the beginning of the tabernacle worship service in chs. 8–10 provides insights about the priesthood as well as the power and danger of God's holy presence in the midst of Israel. Second, ch. 19 addresses matters related to holiness: from worship to food to the treatment of neighbors, including the famous injunction, "you shall love your neighbor as yourself" (19.18; see Mk 12.28–31). Third, ch. 25 sets forth a set of laws related to the use of land, the treatment of the poor, and the periodic cancellation of debts from which interpreters have drawn implications for environmental and economic policies.

1–7	Laws concerning sacrifices and offerings
8–10	The consecration of priests and inauguration of tabernacle worship
11–15	Laws distinguishing between clean and unclean
16	Ceremony for the Day of Atonement*
17–26	Laws concerning Israel's life as a holy people
27	Laws related to vows and gifts dedicated to God

Burnt offerings

1.1–17: The LORD gives laws to Moses concerning the sacrifice of whole animals as burnt offerings. These laws begin a section of instructions for voluntary offerings to God (Lev 1–3). Such offerings stand in contrast to other sacrifices of animals and produce that are required at certain fixed times and festivals during the year (chs. 16, 23).

1 The LORD summoned Moses and spoke to him from the tent of meeting, saying: ²Speak to the people of Israel and say to them: When any of you bring an offering of livestock to the LORD, you shall bring your offering from the herd or from the flock.

3 If the offering is a burnt offering from the herd, you shall offer a male without blemish; you shall bring it to the entrance of the tent of meeting, for acceptance in your behalf before the LORD. ⁴You shall lay your hand on the head of the burnt offering, and it shall be acceptable in your behalf as atonement for you. ⁵The bull shall be slaughtered before the LORD; and Aaron's sons the

priests shall offer the blood, dashing the blood against all sides of the altar that is at the entrance of the tent of meeting. ⁶The burnt offering shall be flayed and cut up into its parts. ⁷The sons of the priest Aaron shall put fire on the altar and arrange wood on the fire. ⁸Aaron's sons the priests shall arrange the parts, with the head and the suet, on the wood that is on the fire on the altar; ⁹but its entrails and its legs shall be washed with water. Then the priest shall turn the whole into smoke on the altar as a burnt offering, an offering by fire of pleasing odor to the LORD.

10 If your gift for a burnt offering is from the flock, from the sheep or goats, your offering shall be a male without blemish. ¹¹It shall be slaughtered on the north side of the altar before the LORD, and Aaron's sons the priests shall dash its blood against all sides of the altar. ¹²It shall be cut up into its parts, with its head and its suet, and the priest shall arrange them on the wood that is on the fire on the altar; ¹³but the entrails and the legs shall be washed with water. Then the priest

shall offer the whole and turn it into smoke on the altar; it is a burnt offering, an offering by fire of pleasing odor to the LORD.

14 If your offering to the LORD is a burnt offering of birds, you shall choose your offering from turtledoves or pigeons. [15]The priest shall bring it to the altar and wring off its head, and turn it into smoke on the altar; and its blood shall be drained out against the side of the altar. [16]He shall remove its crop with its contents[a] and throw it at the east side of the altar, in the place for ashes. [17]He shall tear it open by its wings without severing it. Then the priest shall turn it into smoke on the altar, on the wood that is on the fire; it is a burnt offering, an offering by fire of pleasing odor to the LORD.

1.1–17. 1: *The tent of meeting* came to be identified with the tabernacle,* the mobile tent of worship in the wilderness. In earlier traditions, it was probably different from the tabernacle. Exodus 33.7–11 mentions the tent of meeting as existing before the tabernacle was constructed (Ex 35.1–40.38). **3:** The *burnt offering* is unique among the many sacrifices in that it was entirely consumed in the fire on the altar. All other types of sacrifices involved only a portion to be burned on the altar; the remainder was given back as food to be eaten by the priests, the poor, other dependent members of the community, or the donor. The requirement that the male animal be *without blemish* means that the animal is not blind, lame, or sick. The prophet* in Mal 1.8 asks, "When you offer blind animals in sacrifice, is that not wrong? And when you offer those that are lame or sick, is that not wrong?" **4:** To *lay your hand on the head* of the sacrificed animal signifies the donor's ownership of the animal that is being offered to God and the donor's receipt of the benefits of the sacrifice. In this case, the benefits include *atonement** for sin, that is, the forgiveness or "covering over" of offenses against God. Burnt offerings especially involved cases of sins of omission or sinful thoughts. Job 1.5 portrays the righteous man named Job who "would rise early in the morning and offer burnt offerings . . . For Job said, 'It may be that my children have sinned, and cursed God in their hearts.' " **5:** Ancient Israelites considered *blood* to carry the sacred essence of life; it had the power to cleanse ritual impurity and sin (17.11; Gen 9.4). The act of *dashing the blood against the altar* signifies God's involvement in the ritual and the reconciliation

with the one who offered the animal (see Ex 24.6–8). The priests who presided at the sacrifices were *Aaron's sons* since the Israelite priesthood was a hereditary office and Aaron was the first high priest (Ex 28.1–5; Num 18.1–7). **9:** The fire of sacrifice transforms the animal into smoke that rises to the heavenly dwelling place of God. The sacrificed animal thus becomes a *pleasing odor to the LORD,* a phrase indicating God's acceptance of the offering; see Gen 8.20–22. **14–17:** The poor who are not able to afford the sacrifice of cattle or sheep have the option of presenting an *offering of birds;* compare 12.2–8.

Grain offerings
2.1–16: The LORD gives instructions for grain offerings. Three different kinds of grain offerings are discussed in these laws: choice flour with olive oil and the spice frankincense (vv. 1–3), unleavened or yeastless cakes mixed with oil (vv. 4–7), and parched or baked grain with oil and frankincense (vv. 14–16).

---

2 When anyone presents a grain offering to the LORD, the offering shall be of choice flour; the worshiper shall pour oil on it, and put frankincense on it, [2]and bring it to Aaron's sons the priests. After taking from it a handful of the choice flour and oil, with all its frankincense, the priest shall turn this token portion into smoke on the altar, an offering by fire of pleasing odor to the LORD. [3]And what is left of the grain offering shall be for Aaron and his sons, a most holy part of the offerings by fire to the LORD.

4 When you present a grain offering baked in the oven, it shall be of choice flour: unleavened cakes mixed with oil, or unleavened wafers spread with oil. [5]If your offering is grain prepared on a griddle, it shall be of choice flour mixed with oil, unleavened; [6]break it in pieces, and pour oil on it; it is a grain offering. [7]If your offering is grain prepared in a pan, it shall be made of choice flour in oil. [8]You shall bring to the LORD the grain offering that is prepared in any of these ways; and when it is presented to the priest, he shall take it to the altar. [9]The priest shall remove from the grain offering its token portion and turn this into smoke on the altar, an offering by fire of pleasing odor to the

a Meaning of Heb uncertain

LORD. ¹⁰And what is left of the grain offering shall be for Aaron and his sons; it is a most holy part of the offerings by fire to the LORD.

11 No grain offering that you bring to the LORD shall be made with leaven, for you must not turn any leaven or honey into smoke as an offering by fire to the LORD. ¹²You may bring them to the LORD as an offering of choice products, but they shall not be offered on the altar for a pleasing odor. ¹³You shall not omit from your grain offerings the salt of the covenant with your God; with all your offerings you shall offer salt.

14 If you bring a grain offering of first fruits to the LORD, you shall bring as the grain offering of your first fruits coarse new grain from fresh ears, parched with fire. ¹⁵You shall add oil to it and lay frankincense on it; it is a grain offering. ¹⁶And the priest shall turn a token portion of it into smoke—some of the coarse grain and oil with all its frankincense; it is an offering by fire to the LORD.

2.11: Any fermented flour or grain product was considered ritually unclean and thus not acceptable as a sacrifice to God. Like leaven or yeast, honey caused flour to ferment and thus could not be part of any grain offering. **13:** In contrast to leaven and honey that ferment and change grain products and thus render them ritually impure, salt is a preservative of food products. Thus, salt was considered a purifying agent. The *salt of the covenant*★ may suggest a traditional association of salt with the enduring preservation of a covenant relationship in a ritual meal of covenant making.

Offerings of well-being

3.1–17: The LORD offers guidelines for offerings of well-being. These laws concern the burnt offering of the fat and kidneys of animals on the altar in order to allow the consumption of the animal's meat by the donor. The procedure is similar to the whole burnt offerings in 1.1–17, except that the meat is not burned on the altar but consumed by worshippers in a covenant★ meal of well-being or peace. The meal binds together the worshippers and the LORD.

---

3 If the offering is a sacrifice of well-being, if you offer an animal of the herd, whether male or female, you shall offer one without blemish before the LORD. ²You shall lay your hand on the head of the offering and slaughter it at the entrance of the tent of meeting; and Aaron's sons the priests shall dash the blood against all sides of the altar. ³You shall offer from the sacrifice of well-being, as an offering by fire to the LORD, the fat that covers the entrails and all the fat that is around the entrails; ⁴the two kidneys with the fat that is on them at the loins, and the appendage of the liver, which he shall remove with the kidneys. ⁵Then Aaron's sons shall turn these into smoke on the altar, with the burnt offering that is on the wood on the fire, as an offering by fire of pleasing odor to the LORD.

6 If your offering for a sacrifice of well-being to the LORD is from the flock, male or female, you shall offer one without blemish. ⁷If you present a sheep as your offering, you shall bring it before the LORD ⁸and lay your hand on the head of the offering. It shall be slaughtered before the tent of meeting, and Aaron's sons shall dash its blood against all sides of the altar. ⁹You shall present its fat from the sacrifice of well-being, as an offering by fire to the LORD: the whole broad tail, which shall be removed close to the backbone, the fat that covers the entrails, and all the fat that is around the entrails; ¹⁰the two kidneys with the fat that is on them at the loins, and the appendage of the liver, which you shall remove with the kidneys. ¹¹Then the priest shall turn these into smoke on the altar as a food offering by fire to the LORD.

12 If your offering is a goat, you shall bring it before the LORD ¹³and lay your hand on its head; it shall be slaughtered before the tent of meeting; and the sons of Aaron shall dash its blood against all sides of the altar. ¹⁴You shall present as your offering from it, as an offering by fire to the LORD, the fat that covers the entrails, and all the fat that is around the entrails; ¹⁵the two kidneys with the fat that is on them at the loins, and the appendage of the liver, which you shall remove with the kidneys. ¹⁶Then the priest shall turn these into smoke on the altar as a food offering by fire for a pleasing odor.

All fat is the LORD's. ¹⁷It shall be a perpetual statute throughout your generations, in all your settlements: you must not eat any fat or any blood.

Purification offerings

4.1–5.13: The LORD gives directives for purification offerings to be given when an individual or group unintentionally sins or becomes ritually unclean. The first group of laws in this section (4.1–35) is organized by the status of the person who sins inadvertently: a priest (4.1–12), the whole congregation of Israel (4.13–21), a ruler (4.22–26), or an ordinary individual (4.27–35). The second group of laws in 5.1–13 also concerns unintentional sins and is organized by the relative financial resources of the offender: a person of some means (5.1–6), a person of lesser means (5.7–10), and a person of minimal means (5.11–13).

---

4 The LORD spoke to Moses, saying, ²Speak to the people of Israel, saying: When anyone sins unintentionally in any of the LORD's commandments about things not to be done, and does any one of them:

3 If it is the anointed priest who sins, thus bringing guilt on the people, he shall offer for the sin that he has committed a bull of the herd without blemish as a sin offering to the LORD. ⁴He shall bring the bull to the entrance of the tent of meeting before the LORD and lay his hand on the head of the bull; the bull shall be slaughtered before the LORD. ⁵The anointed priest shall take some of the blood of the bull and bring it into the tent of meeting. ⁶The priest shall dip his finger in the blood and sprinkle some of the blood seven times before the LORD in front of the curtain of the sanctuary. ⁷The priest shall put some of the blood on the horns of the altar of fragrant incense that is in the tent of meeting before the LORD; and the rest of the blood of the bull he shall pour out at the base of the altar of burnt offering, which is at the entrance of the tent of meeting. ⁸He shall remove all the fat from the bull of sin offering: the fat that covers the entrails and all the fat that is around the entrails; ⁹the two kidneys with the fat that is on them at the loins; and the appendage of the liver, which he shall remove with the kidneys, ¹⁰just as these are removed from the ox of the sacrifice of well-being. The priest

shall turn them into smoke upon the altar of burnt offering. ¹¹But the skin of the bull and all its flesh, as well as its head, its legs, its entrails, and its dung— ¹²all the rest of the bull—he shall carry out to a clean place outside the camp, to the ash heap, and shall burn it on a wood fire; at the ash heap it shall be burned.

13 If the whole congregation of Israel errs unintentionally and the matter escapes the notice of the assembly, and they do any one of the things that by the LORD's commandments ought not to be done and incur guilt; ¹⁴when the sin that they have committed becomes known, the assembly shall offer a bull of the herd for a sin offering and bring it before the tent of meeting. ¹⁵The elders of the congregation shall lay their hands on the head of the bull before the LORD, and the bull shall be slaughtered before the LORD. ¹⁶The anointed priest shall bring some of the blood of the bull into the tent of meeting, ¹⁷and the priest shall dip his finger in the blood and sprinkle it seven times before the LORD, in front of the curtain. ¹⁸He shall put some of the blood on the horns of the altar that is before the LORD in the tent of meeting; and the rest of the blood he shall pour out at the base of the altar of burnt offering that is at the entrance of the tent of meeting. ¹⁹He shall remove all its fat and turn it into smoke on the altar. ²⁰He shall do with the bull just as is done with the bull of sin offering; he shall do the same with this. The priest shall make atonement for them, and they shall be forgiven. ²¹He shall carry the bull outside the camp, and burn it as he burned the first bull; it is the sin offering for the assembly.

4.1–21. 6: Sprinkling blood or oil *seven times* reflects the quality of completeness and wholeness associated with the number seven in the Bible. For example, a whole weekly cycle ends on the sabbath or seventh day of the week (Ex 20.8–11). The seven sprinklings of blood purify the whole sanctuary or place of worship. **8–12:** The holiest portions of the animal, the fat and kidneys, are burned as a sacrifice on the altar. The remainder of the animal, which has symbolically absorbed the unintentional guilt of the offending priest, is carried to a ritually clean *ash heap* outside the camp or city where it is burned. Jeremiah 31.40 refers to such an ash heap of dead animal carcasses outside the city of Jerusalem. This ash heap was probably associated with the purification offerings connected with the Temple* in Jerusalem and performed in accordance with these laws in Leviticus. **15:** *The elders* represent the whole congregation as they *lay their hands on the head of the bull.* This ritual act signifies the transfer of guilt from the community to the animal. The removal of the animal to an area outside the camp symbolizes the removal of the community's guilt and impurity (v. 21).

22 When a ruler sins, doing unintentionally any one of all the things that by commandments of the LORD his God ought not to be done and incurs guilt, 23once the sin that he has committed is made known to him, he shall bring as his offering a male goat without blemish. 24He shall lay his hand on the head of the goat; it shall be slaughtered at the spot where the burnt offering is slaughtered before the LORD; it is a sin offering. 25The priest shall take some of the blood of the sin offering with his finger and put it on the horns of the altar of burnt offering, and pour out the rest of its blood at the base of the altar of burnt offering. 26All its fat he shall turn into smoke on the altar, like the fat of the sacrifice of well-being. Thus the priest shall make atonement on his behalf for his sin, and he shall be forgiven.

27 If anyone of the ordinary people among you sins unintentionally in doing any one of the things that by the LORD's commandments ought not to be done and incurs guilt, 28when the sin that you have committed is made known to you, you shall bring a female goat without blemish as your offering, for the sin that you have committed. 29You shall lay your hand on the head of the sin offering; and the sin offering shall be slaughtered at the place of the burnt offering. 30The priest shall take some of its blood with his finger and put it on the horns of the altar of burnt offering, and he shall pour out the rest of its blood at the base of the altar. 31He shall remove all its fat, as the fat is removed from the offering of well-being, and the priest shall turn it into smoke on the altar for a pleasing odor to the LORD. Thus the

priest shall make atonement on your behalf, and you shall be forgiven.

32 If the offering you bring as a sin offering is a sheep, you shall bring a female without blemish. 33You shall lay your hand on the head of the sin offering; and it shall be slaughtered as a sin offering at the spot where the burnt offering is slaughtered. 34The priest shall take some of the blood of the sin offering with his finger and put it on the horns of the altar of burnt offering, and pour out the rest of its blood at the base of the altar. 35You shall remove all its fat, as the fat of the sheep is removed from the sacrifice of well-being, and the priest shall turn it into smoke on the altar, with the offerings by fire to the LORD. Thus the priest shall make atonement on your behalf for the sin that you have committed, and you shall be forgiven.

5 When any of you sin in that you have heard a public adjuration to testify and—though able to testify as one who has seen or learned of the matter—do not speak up, you are subject to punishment. 2Or when any of you touch any unclean thing—whether the carcass of an unclean beast or the carcass of unclean livestock or the carcass of an unclean swarming thing—and are unaware of it, you have become unclean, and are guilty. 3Or when you touch human uncleanness—any uncleanness by which one can become unclean— and are unaware of it, when you come to know it, you shall be guilty. 4Or when any of you utter aloud a rash oath for a bad or a good purpose, whatever people utter in an oath, and are unaware of it, when you come to know it, you shall in any of these be guilty. 5When you realize your guilt in any of these, you shall confess the sin that you have committed. 6And you shall bring to the LORD, as your penalty for the sin that you have committed, a female from the flock, a sheep or a goat, as a sin offering; and the priest shall make atonement on your behalf for your sin.

7 But if you cannot afford a sheep, you shall bring to the LORD, as your penalty for the sin that you have committed, two turtledoves or two pigeons, one for a sin offering and the other for a burnt offering. 8You shall

bring them to the priest, who shall offer first the one for the sin offering, wringing its head at the nape without severing it. [9]He shall sprinkle some of the blood of the sin offering on the side of the altar, while the rest of the blood shall be drained out at the base of the altar; it is a sin offering. [10]And the second he shall offer for a burnt offering according to the regulation. Thus the priest shall make atonement on your behalf for the sin that you have committed, and you shall be forgiven.

11 But if you cannot afford two turtle-doves or two pigeons, you shall bring as your offering for the sin that you have committed one-tenth of an ephah of choice flour for a sin offering; you shall not put oil on it or lay frankincense on it, for it is a sin offering. [12]You shall bring it to the priest, and the priest shall scoop up a handful of it as its memorial portion, and turn this into smoke on the altar, with the offerings by fire to the LORD; it is a sin offering. [13]Thus the priest shall make atonement on your behalf for whichever of these sins you have committed, and you shall be forgiven. Like the grain of-fering, the rest shall be for the priest.

4.22–5.13. 2–3: For more extensive discussion of ritual cleanness and uncleanness, see 11.1–15.33. **5–6:** To *confess the sin* involves a verbal acknowledgment to the priest of inadvertent guilt. Such confession is a nec-essary complement to the offering of the animal sac-rifice in this ritual of atonement* or forgiveness. **7–13:** Poor persons who *cannot afford a sheep* (v. 7) may offer two birds. Those who cannot even afford two birds may substitute a grain offering for the animal sacrifice in the ritual of forgiveness (vv. 11–13).

Restitution offerings

5.14–6.7: The LORD requires restitution offerings for the misuse of holy sanctuary objects or the LORD's holy name. These laws stipulate certain repayments and pu-rification offerings to those who desecrate holy objects of the sanctuary, fail to fulfill vows to God, or deceive a neighbor by swearing a false oath in the name of God.

---

14 The LORD spoke to Moses, saying: [15]When any of you commit a trespass and sin unintentionally in any of the holy things of the LORD, you shall bring, as your guilt offering to the LORD, a ram without blemish from the flock, convertible into silver by the sanctuary shekel; it is a guilt offering. [16]And you shall make restitution for the holy thing in which you were remiss, and shall add one-fifth to it and give it to the priest. The priest shall make atonement on your behalf with the ram of the guilt offering, and you shall be forgiven.

17 If any of you sin without knowing it, doing any of the things that by the LORD's commandments ought not to be done, you have incurred guilt, and are subject to pun-ishment. [18]You shall bring to the priest a ram without blemish from the flock, or the equivalent, as a guilt offering; and the priest shall make atonement on your behalf for the error that you committed unintentionally, and you shall be forgiven. [19]It is a guilt of-fering; you have incurred guilt before the LORD.

6 [a]The LORD spoke to Moses, saying: [2]When any of you sin and commit a tres-pass against the LORD by deceiving a neigh-bor in a matter of a deposit or a pledge, or by robbery, or if you have defrauded a neigh-bor, [3]or have found something lost and lied about it—if you swear falsely regarding any of the various things that one may do and sin thereby— [4]when you have sinned and real-ize your guilt, and would restore what you took by robbery or by fraud or the deposit that was committed to you, or the lost thing that you found, [5]or anything else about which you have sworn falsely, you shall repay the principal amount and shall add one-fifth to it. You shall pay it to its owner when you realize your guilt. [6]And you shall bring to the priest, as your guilt offering to the LORD, a ram without blemish from the flock, or its equivalent, for a guilt offering. [7]The priest shall make atonement on your behalf before the LORD, and you shall be forgiven for any of the things that one may do and incur guilt thereby.

6.1–7: The previous laws in Leviticus have dealt largely with obligations and sacrifices to God. These laws con-cern injury to a neighbor. The principle is that resti-tution must be made to the neighbor before the of-

a Ch 5.20 in Heb

fender can be reconciled to God through a guilt or purification offering (see Mt 5.23–24).

Supplementary instructions

6.8–7.38: The LORD provides supplementary instructions to the priests concerning a number of different sacrifices.

8[a] The LORD spoke to Moses, saying: 9Command Aaron and his sons, saying: This is the ritual of the burnt offering. The burnt offering itself shall remain on the hearth upon the altar all night until the morning, while the fire on the altar shall be kept burning. 10The priest shall put on his linen vestments after putting on his linen undergarments next to his body; and he shall take up the ashes to which the fire has reduced the burnt offering on the altar, and place them beside the altar. 11Then he shall take off his vestments and put on other garments, and carry the ashes out to a clean place outside the camp. 12The fire on the altar shall be kept burning; it shall not go out. Every morning the priest shall add wood to it, lay out the burnt offering on it, and turn into smoke the fat pieces of the offerings of well-being. 13A perpetual fire shall be kept burning on the altar; it shall not go out.

14 This is the ritual of the grain offering: The sons of Aaron shall offer it before the LORD, in front of the altar. 15They shall take from it a handful of the choice flour and oil of the grain offering, with all the frankincense that is on the offering, and they shall turn its memorial portion into smoke on the altar as a pleasing odor to the LORD. 16Aaron and his sons shall eat what is left of it; it shall be eaten as unleavened cakes in a holy place; in the court of the tent of meeting they shall eat it. 17It shall not be baked with leaven. I have given it as their portion of my offerings by fire; it is most holy, like the sin offering and the guilt offering. 18Every male among the descendants of Aaron shall eat of it, as their perpetual due throughout your generations, from the LORD's offerings by fire; anything that touches them shall become holy.

19 The LORD spoke to Moses, saying: 20This is the offering that Aaron and his sons shall offer to the LORD on the day when he is anointed: one-tenth of an ephah of choice flour as a regular offering, half of it in the morning and half in the evening. 21It shall be made with oil on a griddle; you shall bring it well soaked, as a grain offering of baked[b] pieces, and you shall present it as a pleasing odor to the LORD. 22And so the priest, anointed from among Aaron's descendants as a successor, shall prepare it; it is the LORD's—a perpetual due—to be turned entirely into smoke. 23Every grain offering of a priest shall be wholly burned; it shall not be eaten.

24 The LORD spoke to Moses, saying: 25Speak to Aaron and his sons, saying: This is the ritual of the sin offering. The sin offering shall be slaughtered before the LORD at the spot where the burnt offering is slaughtered; it is most holy. 26The priest who offers it as a sin offering shall eat of it; it shall be eaten in a holy place, in the court of the tent of meeting. 27Whatever touches its flesh shall become holy; and when any of its blood is spattered on a garment, you shall wash the bespattered part in a holy place. 28An earthen vessel in which it was boiled shall be broken; but if it is boiled in a bronze vessel, that shall be scoured and rinsed in water. 29Every male among the priests shall eat of it; it is most holy. 30But no sin offering shall be eaten from which any blood is brought into the tent of meeting for atonement in the holy place; it shall be burned with fire.

6.8–30. 10–11: The special priestly garments are considered holy and worn only when the priests are in the sanctuary or altar area (Ex 28.40–43). Therefore, the priest must change into other clothes whenever he carries the ashes from the altar to a designated area outside the camp. **12–13:** The perpetual *fire on the altar* that cannot go out is probably based on the events recounted in 9.24, the official inauguration of the worship and sacrifices of the tabernacle* in the wilderness. The requirement to maintain a perpetual fire may reflect a tradition to keep this divine fire going so that all sacrifices would be made sacred by its miraculous flame. **24–29:** These laws assume that the

a Ch 6.1 in Heb   *b* Meaning of Heb uncertain

qualities of ritual cleanness and uncleanness can be passed from one object or person to another through contagious touch.

〜〜〜〜〜〜〜〜〜〜〜

7 This is the ritual of the guilt offering. It is most holy; 2at the spot where the burnt offering is slaughtered, they shall slaughter the guilt offering, and its blood shall be dashed against all sides of the altar. 3All its fat shall be offered: the broad tail, the fat that covers the entrails, 4the two kidneys with the fat that is on them at the loins, and the appendage of the liver, which shall be removed with the kidneys. 5The priest shall turn them into smoke on the altar as an offering by fire to the LORD; it is a guilt offering. 6Every male among the priests shall eat of it; it shall be eaten in a holy place; it is most holy.

7 The guilt offering is like the sin offering, there is the same ritual for them; the priest who makes atonement with it shall have it. 8So, too, the priest who offers anyone's burnt offering shall keep the skin of the burnt offering that he has offered. 9And every grain offering baked in the oven, and all that is prepared in a pan or on a griddle, shall belong to the priest who offers it. 10But every other grain offering, mixed with oil or dry, shall belong to all the sons of Aaron equally.

11 This is the ritual of the sacrifice of the offering of well-being that one may offer to the LORD. 12If you offer it for thanksgiving, you shall offer with the thank offering unleavened cakes mixed with oil, unleavened wafers spread with oil, and cakes of choice flour well soaked in oil. 13With your thanksgiving sacrifice of well-being you shall bring your offering with cakes of leavened bread. 14From this you shall offer one cake from each offering, as a gift to the LORD; it shall belong to the priest who dashes the blood of the offering of well-being. 15And the flesh of your thanksgiving sacrifice of well-being shall be eaten on the day it is offered; you shall not leave any of it until morning. 16But if the sacrifice you offer is a votive offering or a freewill offering, it shall be eaten on the day that you offer your sacrifice, and what is left of it shall be eaten the next day; 17but

what is left of the flesh of the sacrifice shall be burned up on the third day. 18If any of the flesh of your sacrifice of well-being is eaten on the third day, it shall not be acceptable, nor shall it be credited to the one who offers it; it shall be an abomination, and the one who eats of it shall incur guilt.

19 Flesh that touches any unclean thing shall not be eaten; it shall be burned up. As for other flesh, all who are clean may eat such flesh. 20But those who eat flesh from the LORD's sacrifice of well-being while in a state of uncleanness shall be cut off from their kin. 21When any one of you touches any unclean thing—human uncleanness or an unclean animal or any unclean creature—and then eats flesh from the LORD's sacrifice of well-being, you shall be cut off from your kin.

22 The LORD spoke to Moses, saying: 23Speak to the people of Israel, saying: You shall eat no fat of ox or sheep or goat. 24The fat of an animal that died or was torn by wild animals may be put to any other use, but you must not eat it. 25If any one of you eats the fat from an animal of which an offering by fire may be made to the LORD, you who eat it shall be cut off from your kin. 26You must not eat any blood whatever, either of bird or of animal, in any of your settlements. 27Any one of you who eats any blood shall be cut off from your kin.

28 The LORD spoke to Moses, saying: 29Speak to the people of Israel, saying: Any one of you who would offer to the LORD your sacrifice of well-being must yourself bring to the LORD your offering from your sacrifice of well-being. 30Your own hands shall bring the LORD's offering by fire; you shall bring the fat with the breast, so that the breast may be raised as an elevation offering before the LORD. 31The priest shall turn the fat into smoke on the altar, but the breast shall belong to Aaron and his sons. 32And the right thigh from your sacrifices of well-being you shall give to the priest as an offering; 33the one among the sons of Aaron who offers the blood and fat of the offering of well-being shall have the right thigh for a portion. 34For I have taken the breast of the elevation offering, and the thigh that is offered, from the

people of Israel, from their sacrifices of well-being, and have given them to Aaron the priest and to his sons, as a perpetual due from the people of Israel. ³⁵This is the portion allotted to Aaron and to his sons from the offerings made by fire to the LORD, once they have been brought forward to serve the LORD as priests; ³⁶these the LORD commanded to be given them, when he anointed them, as a perpetual due from the people of Israel throughout their generations.

37 This is the ritual of the burnt offering, the grain offering, the sin offering, the guilt offering, the offering of ordination, and the sacrifice of well-being, ³⁸which the LORD commanded Moses on Mount Sinai, when he commanded the people of Israel to bring their offerings to the LORD, in the wilderness of Sinai.

7.1–38. 13: The instructions here seem to combine the thanksgiving offering and the offering of well-being into one *thanksgiving sacrifice of well-being*. Elsewhere in Leviticus the two offerings are distinct (22.21, 29). 16: A *votive offering* is a sacrifice offered to God by a person who has successfully fulfilled a vow made to God. An example is Hannah, who vowed to dedicate her son Samuel to the service of God. She and her husband brought the child and left him with the priest Eli and then "they slaughtered the bull" (1 Sam 1.11, 24–25; see Lev 27.1–33). A *freewill offering* is a sacrifice donated to God as a voluntary and spontaneous expression of happiness and gratitude. 19–21: For more detailed laws about which things, conditions, and animals are considered ritually unclean, see 11.1–15.33. 30: The *elevation offering* involves the worshipper's lifting up the sacrifice that is offered and transferring it to the elevated hands of the priest (see Ex 29.24). The transfer signifies the lifting up of the sacrifice to God through the mediation of the priest.

Aaron and his sons ordained

8.1–36: The LORD directs Moses to consecrate or induct Aaron and his sons into the priesthood. The chapter's frequent phrase *as the LORD commanded Moses* (vv. 9, 13, 17, 21, 29, 36) affirms Moses' strict adherence to the procedures for priestly ordination* first outlined in the laws in Ex 29.

---

8 The LORD spoke to Moses, saying: ²Take Aaron and his sons with him, the vestments, the anointing oil, the bull of sin offering, the two rams, and the basket of unleavened bread; ³and assemble the whole congregation at the entrance of the tent of meeting. ⁴And Moses did as the LORD commanded him. When the congregation was assembled at the entrance of the tent of meeting, ⁵Moses said to the congregation, "This is what the LORD has commanded to be done."

6 Then Moses brought Aaron and his sons forward, and washed them with water. ⁷He put the tunic on him, fastened the sash around him, clothed him with the robe, and put the ephod on him. He then put the decorated band of the ephod around him, tying the ephod to him with it. ⁸He placed the breastpiece on him, and in the breastpiece he put the Urim and the Thummim. ⁹And he set the turban on his head, and on the turban, in front, he set the golden ornament, the holy crown, as the LORD commanded Moses.

10 Then Moses took the anointing oil and anointed the tabernacle and all that was in it, and consecrated them. ¹¹He sprinkled some of it on the altar seven times, and anointed the altar and all its utensils, and the basin and its base, to consecrate them. ¹²He poured some of the anointing oil on Aaron's head and anointed him, to consecrate him. ¹³And Moses brought forward Aaron's sons, and clothed them with tunics, and fastened sashes around them, and tied headdresses on them, as the LORD commanded Moses.

14 He led forward the bull of sin offering; and Aaron and his sons laid their hands upon the head of the bull of sin offering, ¹⁵and it was slaughtered. Moses took the blood and with his finger put some on each of the horns of the altar, purifying the altar; then he poured out the blood at the base of the altar. Thus he consecrated it, to make atonement for it. ¹⁶Moses took all the fat that was around the entrails, and the appendage of the liver, and the two kidneys with their fat, and turned them into smoke on the altar. ¹⁷But the bull itself, its skin and flesh and its dung, he burned with fire outside the camp, as the LORD commanded Moses.

18 Then he brought forward the ram of

burnt offering. Aaron and his sons laid their hands on the head of the ram, [19]and it was slaughtered. Moses dashed the blood against all sides of the altar. [20]The ram was cut into its parts, and Moses turned into smoke the head and the parts and the suet. [21]And after the entrails and the legs were washed with water, Moses turned into smoke the whole ram on the altar; it was a burnt offering for a pleasing odor, an offering by fire to the LORD, as the LORD commanded Moses.

22 Then he brought forward the second ram, the ram of ordination. Aaron and his sons laid their hands on the head of the ram, [23]and it was slaughtered. Moses took some of its blood and put it on the lobe of Aaron's right ear and on the thumb of his right hand and on the big toe of his right foot. [24]After Aaron's sons were brought forward, Moses put some of the blood on the lobes of their right ears and on the thumbs of their right hands and on the big toes of their right feet; and Moses dashed the rest of the blood against all sides of the altar. [25]He took the fat—the broad tail, all the fat that was around the entrails, the appendage of the liver, and the two kidneys with their fat—and the right thigh. [26]From the basket of unleavened bread that was before the LORD, he took one cake of unleavened bread, one cake of bread with oil, and one wafer, and placed them on the fat and on the right thigh. [27]He placed all these on the palms of Aaron and on the palms of his sons, and raised them as an elevation offering before the LORD. [28]Then Moses took them from their hands and turned them into smoke on the altar with the burnt offering. This was an ordination offering for a pleasing odor, an offering by fire to the LORD. [29]Moses took the breast and raised it as an elevation offering before the LORD; it was Moses' portion of the ram of ordination, as the LORD commanded Moses.

30 Then Moses took some of the anointing oil and some of the blood that was on the altar and sprinkled them on Aaron and his vestments, and also on his sons and their vestments. Thus he consecrated Aaron and his vestments, and also his sons and their vestments.

31 And Moses said to Aaron and his sons, "Boil the flesh at the entrance of the tent of meeting, and eat it there with the bread that is in the basket of ordination offerings, as I was commanded, 'Aaron and his sons shall eat it'; [32]and what remains of the flesh and the bread you shall burn with fire. [33]You shall not go outside the entrance of the tent of meeting for seven days, until the day when your period of ordination is completed. For it will take seven days to ordain you; [34]as has been done today, the LORD has commanded to be done to make atonement for you. [35]You shall remain at the entrance of the tent of meeting day and night for seven days, keeping the LORD's charge so that you do not die; for so I am commanded." [36]Aaron and his sons did all the things that the LORD commanded through Moses.

8.1–36. 7: *The ephod** is a long and ornate robe or apron hanging as two shoulder pieces on the shoulders of the priest. Stones engraved with the names of the twelve tribes of Israel were attached to the ephod as a remembrance of Israel before the deity (Ex 28.6–14). **8:** *The Urim and the Thummim* were stones used to determine the deity's will or guidance when a decision needed to be made. They were kept in a pouch in the breastpiece worn on the chest of the priest. **10–13:** Pouring *the anointing** oil on the head of a person was a means of designating him or her to a special office in the community such as a prophet,* king, or priest (1 Kings 19.6; Ex 29.7). Objects such as the *tabernacle** (v. 10) and the *altar* (v. 11) were also anointed to set them apart as holy within the community (Ex 40.9–10). On the *tabernacle* (v. 10), see comment on 1.1. On the sprinkling of oil *seven times* (v. 11), see comment on 4.6. **23:** The blood smeared on the body's extremities (*ear*, *thumb*, and *big toe*) purifies Aaron's whole body and protects him from impurities. **33–35:** The seven-day period completes the cycle of transition for Aaron and his sons from service in the common sphere to service in the sacred sphere of worship and the sanctuary.

Aaron as high priest

9.1–24: Aaron commences his work as priest by offering a number of the sacrifices for which instructions have been given in the preceding chapters. Those sacrifices include the *sin offering* (v. 8; see 4.1–35), the *burnt offering* (v. 12; see 1.1–17), the *grain offering*

(v. 17; 2.1–16), the *sacrifice of well-being* (v. 18; see 3.1–17), and the *elevation offering* (v. 21; see 7.30).

9 On the eighth day Moses summoned Aaron and his sons and the elders of Israel. ²He said to Aaron, "Take a bull calf for a sin offering and a ram for a burnt offering, without blemish, and offer them before the LORD. ³And say to the people of Israel, 'Take a male goat for a sin offering; a calf and a lamb, yearlings without blemish, for a burnt offering; ⁴and an ox and a ram for an offering of well-being to sacrifice before the LORD; and a grain offering mixed with oil. For today the LORD will appear to you.'" ⁵They brought what Moses commanded to the front of the tent of meeting; and the whole congregation drew near and stood before the LORD. ⁶And Moses said, "This is the thing that the LORD commanded you to do, so that the glory of the LORD may appear to you." ⁷Then Moses said to Aaron, "Draw near to the altar and sacrifice your sin offering and your burnt offering, and make atonement for yourself and for the people; and sacrifice the offering of the people, and make atonement for them; as the LORD has commanded."

8 Aaron drew near to the altar, and slaughtered the calf of the sin offering, which was for himself. ⁹The sons of Aaron presented the blood to him, and he dipped his finger in the blood and put it on the horns of the altar; and the rest of the blood he poured out at the base of the altar. ¹⁰But the fat, the kidneys, and the appendage of the liver from the sin offering he turned into smoke on the altar, as the LORD commanded Moses; ¹¹and the flesh and the skin he burned with fire outside the camp.

12 Then he slaughtered the burnt offering. Aaron's sons brought him the blood, and he dashed it against all sides of the altar. ¹³And they brought him the burnt offering piece by piece, and the head, which he turned into smoke on the altar. ¹⁴He washed the entrails and the legs and, with the burnt offering, turned them into smoke on the altar.

15 Next he presented the people's offering. He took the goat of the sin offering that was for the people, and slaughtered it, and

presented it as a sin offering like the first one. ¹⁶He presented the burnt offering, and sacrificed it according to regulation. ¹⁷He presented the grain offering, and, taking a handful of it, he turned it into smoke on the altar, in addition to the burnt offering of the morning.

18 He slaughtered the ox and the ram as a sacrifice of well-being for the people. Aaron's sons brought him the blood, which he dashed against all sides of the altar, ¹⁹and the fat of the ox and of the ram—the broad tail, the fat that covers the entrails, the two kidneys and the fat on them,^a and the appendage of the liver. ²⁰They first laid the fat on the breasts, and the fat was turned into smoke on the altar; ²¹and the breasts and the right thigh Aaron raised as an elevation offering before the LORD, as Moses had commanded.

22 Aaron lifted his hands toward the people and blessed them; and he came down after sacrificing the sin offering, the burnt offering, and the offering of well-being. ²³Moses and Aaron entered the tent of meeting, and then came out and blessed the people; and the glory of the LORD appeared to all the people. ²⁴Fire came out from the LORD and consumed the burnt offering and the fat on the altar; and when all the people saw it, they shouted and fell on their faces.

9.1–24. 1: *The eighth day* comes at the end of the seven-day consecration period in 8.33–35. **6:** The purpose of the sacrifices and worship of the people is *that the glory of the LORD may appear to you.* Israel was often reminded that God's presence among them was not an automatic result of their rituals. **22:** Priests lifted up their hands and *blessed* the people. The traditional priestly blessing of Aaron is recorded in Num 6.24–26: "The LORD bless you and keep you; the LORD make his face to shine upon you, and be gracious to you; the LORD lift up his countenance upon you, and give you peace." **23–24:** *The glory of the LORD* appeared to Israel in the wilderness as a pillar of fire shrouded in a cloud (Ex 24.17; 40.38). When *fire came out from the LORD* to light this first fire for the burning of the sacrifices, the fire presumably came from the fiery cloud of the divine presence.

a Gk: Heb *the broad tail, and that which covers, and the kidneys*

Nadab and Abihu

10.1–20: Aaron's sons, Nadab and Abihu, die as a consequence of their improper sacrifice. The chapter explores the dangers associated with priestly duties because of the nearness of the divine presence and the need for strict observance of proper procedures.

10 Now Aaron's sons, Nadab and Abihu, each took his censer, put fire in it, and laid incense on it; and they offered unholy fire before the LORD, such as he had not commanded them. ²And fire came out from the presence of the LORD and consumed them, and they died before the LORD. ³Then Moses said to Aaron, "This is what the LORD meant when he said,

'Through those who are near me
    I will show myself holy,
and before all the people
    I will be glorified.' "
And Aaron was silent.

4 Moses summoned Mishael and Elzaphan, sons of Uzziel the uncle of Aaron, and said to them, "Come forward, and carry your kinsmen away from the front of the sanctuary to a place outside the camp." ⁵They came forward and carried them by their tunics out of the camp, as Moses had ordered. ⁶And Moses said to Aaron and to his sons Eleazar and Ithamar, "Do not dishevel your hair, and do not tear your vestments, or you will die and wrath will strike all the congregation; but your kindred, the whole house of Israel, may mourn the burning that the LORD has sent. ⁷You shall not go outside the entrance of the tent of meeting, or you will die; for the anointing oil of the LORD is on you." And they did as Moses had ordered.

8 And the LORD spoke to Aaron: ⁹Drink no wine or strong drink, neither you nor your sons, when you enter the tent of meeting, that you may not die; it is a statute forever throughout your generations. ¹⁰You are to distinguish between the holy and the common, and between the unclean and the clean; ¹¹and you are to teach the people of Israel all the statutes that the LORD has spoken to them through Moses.

12 Moses spoke to Aaron and to his remaining sons, Eleazar and Ithamar: Take the grain offering that is left from the LORD's offerings by fire, and eat it unleavened beside the altar, for it is most holy; ¹³you shall eat it in a holy place, because it is your due and your sons' due, from the offerings by fire to the LORD; for so I am commanded. ¹⁴But the breast that is elevated and the thigh that is raised, you and your sons and daughters as well may eat in any clean place; for they have been assigned to you and your children from the sacrifices of the offerings of well-being of the people of Israel. ¹⁵The thigh that is raised and the breast that is elevated they shall bring, together with the offerings by fire of the fat, to raise for an elevation offering before the LORD; they are to be your due and that of your children forever, as the LORD has commanded.

10.1–15. 1: A *censer* is a container for burning incense. Nadab and Abihu somehow defied the rules when they offered *unholy fire before the LORD*. The coals may not have been properly prepared or were taken from the altar of another god. See Num 16.36–40. **3:** *Aaron was silent.* In other words, Aaron refrained from the normal cries and lament* of mourning because this was prohibited for the high priest and priests sprinkled with anointing* oil (21.10–12). **6–7:** Moses' prohibition to Aaron and his remaining sons not to *dishevel your hair* or *tear your vestments* is a command not to carry out the normal customs of mourning the death of a family member. Coming near or in contact with a corpse rendered a person ritually unclean or impure for seven days (Num 19.11). Such ritual uncleanness would defile any sacrifices that the priests would perform during the period of seven days. Thus, priests were not allowed to attend a funeral or come near a corpse except that of a close family member (21.1–3). However, the high priest (Aaron) or priests sprinkled with oil (Aaron's other sons, Eleazar and Ithamar) were not even permitted to mourn close family members such as a son or brother as here (21.10–12). **10:** Teaching the distinctions between the *holy and the common* and the *unclean and the clean* involves teaching the subject matter of chs. 11–15.

16 Then Moses made inquiry about the goat of the sin offering, and—it had already been burned! He was angry with Eleazar and Ithamar, Aaron's remaining sons, and said, ¹⁷"Why did you not eat the sin offering in

Ritual Purity and Cleanness

The concern for ritual purity or cleanness was an important aspect of ancient Israelite society that may be unfamiliar to many in our own culture. Purity in ancient Israel meant being free from any physical, moral, or ritual contamination. Impurity or uncleanness came about through such things as contact with a corpse, the involuntary flow of bodily fluids (for example, blood or semen), certain skin diseases (often translated incorrectly in some English versions as "leprosy"), or the eating of prohibited foods. Becoming impure or unclean from various causes was a common occurrence for most people (attending a funeral, unintentionally eating unclean food, menstruation). Thus, rituals of purification were readily available to make oneself clean again. Impurity was not sin and could always be removed through various ritual washings, the passage of time, or specified offerings.

The purity laws functioned as part of a social symbol system that identified certain natural boundaries in order to protect the society from destructive or dangerous powers. When something or someone crossed over or confused these boundaries, the result was uncleanness. For example, unclean animals were those that in some way mixed or crossed over perceived boundaries. Certain sea creatures were unclean because they lacked the fins and scales usually associated with fish who lived in the sea. These unclean sea creatures (for example, clams) did not fit within the boundaries of typical sea animals. The most powerful or dangerous purity boundary was the one between life and death. Purity regulations touched on such matters as food, sex and marriage, family relationships, business practices, physical anomalies, and abhorrent worship practices of other gods by other nations. No single principle or concept can explain all the aspects of the purity laws. However, these laws preserve certain boundaries of holiness and separation within the community of God's people, which is holy or sacred by virtue of God's presence in its midst (26.11–13).

the sacred area? For it is most holy, and God[a] has given it to you that you may remove the guilt of the congregation, to make atonement on their behalf before the LORD. 18Its blood was not brought into the inner part of the sanctuary. You should certainly have eaten it in the sanctuary, as I commanded." 19And Aaron spoke to Moses, "See, today they offered their sin offering and their burnt offering before the LORD; and yet such things as these have befallen me! If I had eaten the sin offering today, would it have been agreeable to the LORD?" 20And when Moses heard that, he agreed.

10.16–20: Moses *was angry* with Aaron's two sons, Eleazar and Ithamar, because they *did not eat the sin offering in the sacred area* (vv. 16–17). Normally, the priests were required to eat the meat of the sin offering

rather than burn it on the altar (6.24–26). In this case, however, Aaron's sons burned the flesh of the goat (the sin offering) rather than eat it. The reason may be that earlier the sacrifice had been defiled by the sin and death of their brothers (vv. 1–2). This reasoning seems implied in Aaron's response to Moses (v. 19), which Moses then accepts (v. 20). The case provides a model for negotiation among conflicting laws and requirements in special circumstances.

Laws regarding purity
11.1–15.33 This section of laws deals with matters of purity and the distinction between clean and unclean. The laws specify four primary sources of uncleanness: animal carcasses (ch. 11), childbirth (ch. 12), skin diseases (chs. 13–14), and genital discharges such as semen or menstrual blood (ch. 15). The fifth and most

a Heb *he*

powerful source of impurity is the human corpse, which is discussed in the laws in Num 19. Ancient Israelites understood many of these sources of impurity to derive from crossing the dangerous and powerful boundary between life and death. (See sidebar, p. 136.)

11 The LORD spoke to Moses and Aaron, saying to them: 2Speak to the people of Israel, saying:

From among all the land animals, these are the creatures that you may eat. 3Any animal that has divided hoofs and is cleft-footed and chews the cud—such you may eat. 4But among those that chew the cud or have divided hoofs, you shall not eat the following: the camel, for even though it chews the cud, it does not have divided hoofs; it is unclean for you. 5The rock badger, for even though it chews the cud, it does not have divided hoofs; it is unclean for you. 6The hare, for even though it chews the cud, it does not have divided hoofs; it is unclean for you. 7The pig, for even though it has divided hoofs and is cleft-footed, it does not chew the cud; it is unclean for you. 8Of their flesh you shall not eat, and their carcasses you shall not touch; they are unclean for you.

9 These you may eat, of all that are in the waters. Everything in the waters that has fins and scales, whether in the seas or in the streams—such you may eat. 10But anything in the seas or the streams that does not have fins and scales, of the swarming creatures in the waters and among all the other living creatures that are in the waters—they are detestable to you 11and detestable they shall remain. Of their flesh you shall not eat, and their carcasses you shall regard as detestable. 12Everything in the waters that does not have fins and scales is detestable to you.

13 These you shall regard as detestable among the birds. They shall not be eaten; they are an abomination: the eagle, the vulture, the osprey, 14the buzzard, the kite of any kind; 15every raven of any kind; 16the ostrich, the nighthawk, the sea gull, the hawk of any kind; 17the little owl, the cormorant, the great owl, 18the water hen, the desert owl,*a* the carrion vulture, 19the stork, the heron of any kind, the hoopoe, and the bat.*b*

20 All winged insects that walk upon all fours are detestable to you. 21But among the winged insects that walk on all fours you may eat those that have jointed legs above their feet, with which to leap on the ground. 22Of them you may eat: the locust according to its kind, the bald locust according to its kind, the cricket according to its kind, and the grasshopper according to its kind. 23But all other winged insects that have four feet are detestable to you.

24 By these you shall become unclean; whoever touches the carcass of any of them shall be unclean until the evening, 25and whoever carries any part of the carcass of any of them shall wash his clothes and be unclean until the evening. 26Every animal that has divided hoofs but is not cleft-footed or does not chew the cud is unclean for you; everyone who touches one of them shall be unclean. 27All that walk on their paws, among the animals that walk on all fours, are unclean for you; whoever touches the carcass of any of them shall be unclean until the evening, 28and the one who carries the carcass shall wash his clothes and be unclean until the evening; they are unclean for you.

29 These are unclean for you among the creatures that swarm upon the earth: the weasel, the mouse, the great lizard according to its kind, 30the gecko, the land crocodile, the lizard, the sand lizard, and the chameleon. 31These are unclean for you among all that swarm; whoever touches one of them when they are dead shall be unclean until the evening. 32And anything upon which any of them falls when they are dead shall be unclean, whether an article of wood or cloth or skin or sacking, any article that is used for any purpose; it shall be dipped into water, and it shall be unclean until the evening, and then it shall be clean. 33And if any of them falls into any earthen vessel, all that is in it shall be unclean, and you shall break the vessel. 34Any food that could be eaten shall be unclean if water from any such vessel comes upon it; and any liquid that could be drunk

a Or *pelican*   *b* Identification of several of the birds in verses 13–19 is uncertain

shall be unclean if it was in any such vessel. ³⁵Everything on which any part of the carcass falls shall be unclean; whether an oven or stove, it shall be broken in pieces; they are unclean, and shall remain unclean for you. ³⁶But a spring or a cistern holding water shall be clean, while whatever touches the carcass in it shall be unclean. ³⁷If any part of their carcass falls upon any seed set aside for sowing, it is clean; ³⁸but if water is put on the seed and any part of their carcass falls on it, it is unclean for you.

39 If an animal of which you may eat dies, anyone who touches its carcass shall be unclean until the evening. ⁴⁰Those who eat of its carcass shall wash their clothes and be unclean until the evening; and those who carry the carcass shall wash their clothes and be unclean until the evening.

41 All creatures that swarm upon the earth are detestable; they shall not be eaten. ⁴²Whatever moves on its belly, and whatever moves on all fours, or whatever has many feet, all the creatures that swarm upon the earth, you shall not eat; for they are detestable. ⁴³You shall not make yourselves detestable with any creature that swarms; you shall not defile yourselves with them, and so become unclean. ⁴⁴For I am the LORD your God; sanctify yourselves therefore, and be holy, for I am holy. You shall not defile yourselves with any swarming creature that moves on the earth. ⁴⁵For I am the LORD who brought you up from the land of Egypt, to be your God; you shall be holy, for I am holy.

46 This is the law pertaining to land animal and bird and every living creature that moves through the waters and every creature that swarms upon the earth, ⁴⁷to make a distinction between the unclean and the clean, and between the living creature that may be eaten and the living creature that may not be eaten.

11.1–47: The LORD gives instructions to Moses and Aaron regarding clean and unclean foods. 7: The biblical tradition came to consider the pig as a particularly unclean animal, associated with rituals of other gods (Isa 65.4; 66.17). 24–25: Ritual uncleanness in matters of food could be removed by bathing the

body, washing the clothes, and waiting the required amount of time (*until the evening*). 32–38: Objects as well as animals and people can be rendered unclean by touching what is unclean. Thus, an earthenware pot (v. 33) or earthenware stove (v. 35) must be broken into pieces and never used again if it becomes ritually contaminated. Unlike metal, impurity cannot be removed from clay or earthenware objects.

12 The LORD spoke to Moses, saying: ²Speak to the people of Israel, saying:

If a woman conceives and bears a male child, she shall be ceremonially unclean seven days; as at the time of her menstruation, she shall be unclean. ³On the eighth day the flesh of his foreskin shall be circumcised. ⁴Her time of blood purification shall be thirty-three days; she shall not touch any holy thing, or come into the sanctuary, until the days of her purification are completed. ⁵If she bears a female child, she shall be unclean two weeks, as in her menstruation; her time of blood purification shall be sixty-six days.

6 When the days of her purification are completed, whether for a son or for a daughter, she shall bring to the priest at the entrance of the tent of meeting a lamb in its first year for a burnt offering, and a pigeon or a turtledove for a sin offering. ⁷He shall offer it before the LORD, and make atonement on her behalf; then she shall be clean from her flow of blood. This is the law for her who bears a child, male or female. ⁸If she cannot afford a sheep, she shall take two turtledoves or two pigeons, one for a burnt offering and the other for a sin offering; and the priest shall make atonement on her behalf, and she shall be clean.

12.1–8: The LORD issues laws concerning the purification of women after childbirth. 2: That the woman is *ceremonially unclean* after childbirth does not imply any moral evil or sin. It is the flow of blood associated with childbirth and the dangerous mixture of life (the birth of a child) and death (the flow of blood) that renders the mother ritually unclean for the specified time period. 6: The *sin offering* is more properly a purification offering since the woman has committed no sin. The birth of a child is a blessing in ancient Israel, but it involves crossing boundaries of life and death and thus creates a condition of ceremonial uncleanness.

Skin diseases

13.1–59: The LORD mandates procedures for dealing with the ritual impurity associated with various skin diseases. The withering and discoloration of human skin often accompanies the process of death. Thus, any skin disease on a living person whose symptoms resemble what happens to a person's skin in death mixes or confuses the boundaries of life and death. Such mixtures or confusions render that person ritually impure. The priest's role in such cases is to determine whether a given skin condition is sufficiently severe to render a person unclean for a shorter or longer time.

13.2–4. 2: The phrase *leprous disease* should be understood not as the particular disease of leprosy but as a variety of skin diseases that are severe enough to render a person ritually impure. This is true of the phrase as it is used throughout the chapter. **4:** Confining the diseased person involves a concern that the person not contaminate another person with ritual impurity. The priest is not a medical doctor, so the process of isolation is for ritual reasons, not medical.

13 The LORD spoke to Moses and Aaron, saying:

2 When a person has on the skin of his body a swelling or an eruption or a spot, and it turns into a leprous*a* disease on the skin of his body, he shall be brought to Aaron the priest or to one of his sons the priests. ³The priest shall examine the disease on the skin of his body, and if the hair in the diseased area has turned white and the disease appears to be deeper than the skin of his body, it is a leprous*a* disease; after the priest has examined him he shall pronounce him ceremonially unclean. ⁴But if the spot is white in the skin of his body, and appears no deeper than the skin, and the hair in it has not turned white, the priest shall confine the diseased person for seven days. ⁵The priest shall examine him on the seventh day, and if he sees that the disease is checked and the disease has not spread in the skin, then the priest shall confine him seven days more. ⁶The priest shall examine him again on the seventh day, and if the disease has abated and the disease has not spread in the skin, the priest shall pronounce him clean; it is only an eruption; and he shall wash his clothes, and be clean. ⁷But if the eruption spreads in the skin after he has shown himself to the priest for his cleansing, he shall appear again before the priest. ⁸The priest shall make an examination, and if the eruption has spread in the skin, the priest shall pronounce him unclean; it is a leprous*a* disease.

9 When a person contracts a leprous*a* disease, he shall be brought to the priest. ¹⁰The priest shall make an examination, and if there is a white swelling in the skin that has turned the hair white, and there is quick raw flesh in the swelling, ¹¹it is a chronic leprous*a* disease in the skin of his body. The priest shall pronounce him unclean; he shall not confine him, for he is unclean. ¹²But if the disease breaks out in the skin, so that it covers all the skin of the diseased person from head to foot, so far as the priest can see, ¹³then the priest shall make an examination, and if the disease has covered all his body, he shall pronounce him clean of the disease; since it has all turned white, he is clean. ¹⁴But if raw flesh ever appears on him, he shall be unclean; ¹⁵the priest shall examine the raw flesh and pronounce him unclean. Raw flesh is unclean, for it is a leprous*a* disease. ¹⁶But if the raw flesh again turns white, he shall come to the priest; ¹⁷the priest shall examine him, and if the disease has turned white, the priest shall pronounce the diseased person clean. He is clean.

18 When there is on the skin of one's body a boil that has healed, ¹⁹and in the place of the boil there appears a white swelling or a reddish-white spot, it shall be shown to the priest. ²⁰The priest shall make an examination, and if it appears deeper than the skin and its hair has turned white, the priest shall pronounce him unclean; this is a leprous*a* disease, broken out in the boil. ²¹But if the priest examines it and the hair on it is not white, nor is it deeper than the skin but has abated, the priest shall confine him

a A term for several skin diseases; precise meaning uncertain

seven days. ²²If it spreads in the skin, the priest shall pronounce him unclean; it is diseased. ²³But if the spot remains in one place and does not spread, it is the scar of the boil; the priest shall pronounce him clean.

24 Or, when the body has a burn on the skin and the raw flesh of the burn becomes a spot, reddish-white or white, ²⁵the priest shall examine it. If the hair in the spot has turned white and it appears deeper than the skin, it is a leprous*a* disease; it has broken out in the burn, and the priest shall pronounce him unclean. This is a leprous*a* disease. ²⁶But if the priest examines it and the hair in the spot is not white, and it is no deeper than the skin but has abated, the priest shall confine him seven days. ²⁷The priest shall examine him the seventh day; if it is spreading in the skin, the priest shall pronounce him unclean. This is a leprous*a* disease. ²⁸But if the spot remains in one place and does not spread in the skin but has abated, it is a swelling from the burn, and the priest shall pronounce him clean; for it is the scar of the burn.

29 When a man or woman has a disease on the head or in the beard, ³⁰the priest shall examine the disease. If it appears deeper than the skin and the hair in it is yellow and thin, the priest shall pronounce him unclean; it is an itch, a leprous*a* disease of the head or the beard. ³¹If the priest examines the itching disease, and it appears no deeper than the skin and there is no black hair in it, the priest shall confine the person with the itching disease for seven days. ³²On the seventh day the priest shall examine the itch; if the itch has not spread, and there is no yellow hair in it, and the itch appears to be no deeper than the skin, ³³he shall shave, but the itch he shall not shave. The priest shall confine the person with the itch for seven days more. ³⁴On the seventh day the priest shall examine the itch; if the itch has not spread in the skin and it appears to be no deeper than the skin, the priest shall pronounce him clean. He shall wash his clothes and be clean. ³⁵But if the itch spreads in the skin after he was pronounced clean, ³⁶the priest shall examine him. If the itch has spread in the skin, the priest need not seek

for the yellow hair; he is unclean. ³⁷But if in his eyes the itch is checked, and black hair has grown in it, the itch is healed, he is clean; and the priest shall pronounce him clean.

38 When a man or a woman has spots on the skin of the body, white spots, ³⁹the priest shall make an examination, and if the spots on the skin of the body are of a dull white, it is a rash that has broken out on the skin; he is clean.

40 If anyone loses the hair from his head, he is bald but he is clean. ⁴¹If he loses the hair from his forehead and temples, he has baldness of the forehead but he is clean. ⁴²But if there is on the bald head or the bald forehead a reddish-white diseased spot, it is a leprous*a* disease breaking out on his bald head or his bald forehead. ⁴³The priest shall examine him; if the diseased swelling is reddish-white on his bald head or on his bald forehead, which resembles a leprous*a* disease in the skin of the body, ⁴⁴he is leprous,*a* he is unclean. The priest shall pronounce him unclean; the disease is on his head.

45 The person who has the leprous*a* disease shall wear torn clothes and let the hair of his head be disheveled; and he shall cover his upper lip and cry out, "Unclean, unclean." ⁴⁶He shall remain unclean as long as he has the disease; he is unclean. He shall live alone; his dwelling shall be outside the camp.

47 Concerning clothing: when a leprous*a* disease appears in it, in woolen or linen cloth, ⁴⁸in warp or woof of linen or wool, or in a skin or in anything made of skin, ⁴⁹if the disease shows greenish or reddish in the garment, whether in warp or woof or in skin or in anything made of skin, it is a leprous*a* disease and shall be shown to the priest. ⁵⁰The priest shall examine the disease, and put the diseased article aside for seven days. ⁵¹He shall examine the disease on the seventh day. If the disease has spread in the cloth, in warp or woof, or in the skin, whatever be the use of the skin, this is a spreading leprous*a* disease; it is unclean. ⁵²He shall burn the cloth-

a A term for several skin diseases; precise meaning uncertain

ing, whether diseased in warp or woof, woolen or linen, or anything of skin, for it is a spreading leprous*a* disease; it shall be burned in fire.

53 If the priest makes an examination, and the disease has not spread in the clothing, in warp or woof or in anything of skin, 54the priest shall command them to wash the article in which the disease appears, and he shall put it aside seven days more. 55The priest shall examine the diseased article after it has been washed. If the diseased spot has not changed color, though the disease has not spread, it is unclean; you shall burn it in fire, whether the leprous*a* spot is on the inside or on the outside.

56 If the priest makes an examination, and the disease has abated after it is washed, he shall tear the spot out of the cloth, in warp or woof, or out of skin. 57If it appears again in the garment, in warp or woof, or in anything of skin, it is spreading; you shall burn with fire that in which the disease appears. 58But the cloth, warp or woof, or anything of skin from which the disease disappears when you have washed it, shall then be washed a second time, and it shall be clean.

59 This is the ritual for a leprous*a* disease in a cloth of wool or linen, either in warp or woof, or in anything of skin, to decide whether it is clean or unclean.

Three purification rituals

14.1–57: The Lord specifies three purification rituals that allow a person healed of skin disease to resume life within the community. The process of progressive reintegration into the society involves one purification ritual on the first day (vv. 2–8), a second ritual on the seventh day (v. 9), and a third ritual on the eighth day (vv. 10–32).

14 The Lord spoke to Moses, saying: 2This shall be the ritual for the leprous*a* person at the time of his cleansing:

He shall be brought to the priest; 3the priest shall go out of the camp, and the priest shall make an examination. If the disease is healed in the leprous*a* person, 4the priest shall command that two living clean birds and cedarwood and crimson yarn and hyssop be brought for the one who is to be cleansed.

5The priest shall command that one of the birds be slaughtered over fresh water in an earthen vessel. 6He shall take the living bird with the cedarwood and the crimson yarn and the hyssop, and dip them and the living bird in the blood of the bird that was slaughtered over the fresh water. 7He shall sprinkle it seven times upon the one who is to be cleansed of the leprous*a* disease; then he shall pronounce him clean, and he shall let the living bird go into the open field. 8The one who is to be cleansed shall wash his clothes, and shave off all his hair, and bathe himself in water, and he shall be clean. After that he shall come into the camp, but shall live outside his tent seven days. 9On the seventh day he shall shave all his hair: of head, beard, eyebrows; he shall shave all his hair. Then he shall wash his clothes, and bathe his body in water, and he shall be clean.

14.1–9. 4: The function of the *cedarwood and crimson yarn* is not clear. Their reddish color may be associated with the color of blood, which is considered a purifying agent. *Hyssop*★ is an aromatic plant associated with rituals of purification. In Ex 12.22, hyssop was the plant used to apply blood on the doorposts during the Passover★ in order to protect the Israelites from death (see also Num 19.6). **6–8:** The *living bird* that is dipped in the blood of another bird and then set free carries away enough of the healed person's uncleanness to allow him or her to *come into the camp* but not yet into *his tent*. **9:** The second round of shaving and bathing on the seventh day allows the person to rejoin his or her family in the tent.

10 On the eighth day he shall take two male lambs without blemish, and one ewe lamb in its first year without blemish, and a grain offering of three-tenths of an ephah of choice flour mixed with oil, and one log*b* of oil. 11The priest who cleanses shall set the person to be cleansed, along with these things, before the Lord, at the entrance of the tent of meeting. 12The priest shall take one of the lambs, and offer it as a guilt offering, along with the log*b* of oil, and raise them as an elevation offering before the

a A term for several skin diseases; precise meaning uncertain　　*b* A liquid measure

LORD. [13]He shall slaughter the lamb in the place where the sin offering and the burnt offering are slaughtered in the holy place; for the guilt offering, like the sin offering, belongs to the priest: it is most holy. [14]The priest shall take some of the blood of the guilt offering and put it on the lobe of the right ear of the one to be cleansed, and on the thumb of the right hand, and on the big toe of the right foot. [15]The priest shall take some of the log*a* of oil and pour it into the palm of his own left hand, [16]and dip his right finger in the oil that is in his left hand and sprinkle some oil with his finger seven times before the LORD. [17]Some of the oil that remains in his hand the priest shall put on the lobe of the right ear of the one to be cleansed, and on the thumb of the right hand, and on the big toe of the right foot, on top of the blood of the guilt offering. [18]The rest of the oil that is in the priest's hand he shall put on the head of the one to be cleansed. Then the priest shall make atonement on his behalf before the LORD: [19]the priest shall offer the sin offering, to make atonement for the one to be cleansed from his uncleanness. Afterward he shall slaughter the burnt offering; [20]and the priest shall offer the burnt offering and the grain offering on the altar. Thus the priest shall make atonement on his behalf and he shall be clean.

21 But if he is poor and cannot afford so much, he shall take one male lamb for a guilt offering to be elevated, to make atonement on his behalf, and one-tenth of an ephah of choice flour mixed with oil for a grain offering and a log*a* of oil; [22]also two turtledoves or two pigeons, such as he can afford, one for a sin offering and the other for a burnt offering. [23]On the eighth day he shall bring them for his cleansing to the priest, to the entrance of the tent of meeting, before the LORD; [24]and the priest shall take the lamb of the guilt offering and the log*a* of oil, and the priest shall raise them as an elevation offering before the LORD. [25]The priest shall slaughter the lamb of the guilt offering and shall take some of the blood of the guilt offering, and put it on the lobe of the right ear of the one to be cleansed, and on the thumb

of the right hand, and on the big toe of the right foot. [26]The priest shall pour some of the oil into the palm of his own left hand, [27]and shall sprinkle with his right finger some of the oil that is in his left hand seven times before the LORD. [28]The priest shall put some of the oil that is in his hand on the lobe of the right ear of the one to be cleansed, and on the thumb of the right hand, and the big toe of the right foot, where the blood of the guilt offering was placed. [29]The rest of the oil that is in the priest's hand he shall put on the head of the one to be cleansed, to make atonement on his behalf before the LORD. [30]And he shall offer, of the turtledoves or pigeons such as he can afford, [31]one*b* for a sin offering and the other for a burnt offering, along with a grain offering; and the priest shall make atonement before the LORD on behalf of the one being cleansed. [32]This is the ritual for the one who has a leprous*c* disease, who cannot afford the offerings for his cleansing.

33 The LORD spoke to Moses and Aaron, saying:

34 When you come into the land of Canaan, which I give you for a possession, and I put a leprous*c* disease in a house in the land of your possession, [35]the owner of the house shall come and tell the priest, saying, "There seems to me to be some sort of disease in my house." [36]The priest shall command that they empty the house before the priest goes to examine the disease, or all that is in the house will become unclean; and afterward the priest shall go in to inspect the house. [37]He shall examine the disease; if the disease is in the walls of the house with greenish or reddish spots, and if it appears to be deeper than the surface, [38]the priest shall go outside to the door of the house and shut up the house seven days. [39]The priest shall come again on the seventh day and make an inspection; if the disease has spread in the walls of the house, [40]the priest shall command that the stones in which the disease appears be taken out and thrown into an unclean place outside the city. [41]He shall have

a A liquid measure   *b* Gk Syr: Heb *afford,* [31]*such as he can afford, one   c* A term for several skin diseases; precise meaning uncertain

the inside of the house scraped thoroughly, and the plaster that is scraped off shall be dumped in an unclean place outside the city. ⁴²They shall take other stones and put them in the place of those stones, and take other plaster and plaster the house.

43 If the disease breaks out again in the house, after he has taken out the stones and scraped the house and plastered it, ⁴⁴the priest shall go and make inspection; if the disease has spread in the house, it is a spreading leprous^a disease in the house; it is unclean. ⁴⁵He shall have the house torn down, its stones and timber and all the plaster of the house, and taken outside the city to an unclean place. ⁴⁶All who enter the house while it is shut up shall be unclean until the evening; ⁴⁷and all who sleep in the house shall wash their clothes; and all who eat in the house shall wash their clothes.

48 If the priest comes and makes an inspection, and the disease has not spread in the house after the house was plastered, the priest shall pronounce the house clean; the disease is healed. ⁴⁹For the cleansing of the house he shall take two birds, with cedarwood and crimson yarn and hyssop, ⁵⁰and shall slaughter one of the birds over fresh water in an earthen vessel, ⁵¹and shall take the cedarwood and the hyssop and the crimson yarn, along with the living bird, and dip them in the blood of the slaughtered bird and the fresh water, and sprinkle the house seven times. ⁵²Thus he shall cleanse the house with the blood of the bird, and with the fresh water, and with the living bird, and with the cedarwood and hyssop and crimson yarn; ⁵³and he shall let the living bird go out of the city into the open field; so he shall make atonement for the house, and it shall be clean.

54 This is the ritual for any leprous^a disease: for an itch, ⁵⁵for leprous^a diseases in clothing and houses, ⁵⁶and for a swelling or an eruption or a spot, ⁵⁷to determine when it is unclean and when it is clean. This is the ritual for leprous^a diseases.

14.10–57. 10–20: These offerings by the healed person on the eighth day are related to the offerings of restitution or repayment for inadvertently causing a

holy object or worship space to become unclean and other unintentional offenses (see 5.1–19). The dabbing of blood (v. 14) and oil (vv. 17–18) on the extremities of the healed person (ear, thumb, big toe) cleanses the entire person (see the cleansing of the priest in 8.30). **33–53:** These instructions involve cleansing or restoring a house that has been infected by an unclean fungus or rot (v. 37). The contagion of an unclean house affects all persons who come under its roof (v. 46). The ritual for reinstating a *healed* house (vv. 48–53) is similar to the first step in reinstating a healed person to the community (vv. 2–8).

Eliminating the uncleanness of bodily discharges
15.1–33: The purity laws concerning bodily emissions treat two different situations: more serious genital emissions of fluid that are irregular or a sign of disease and thus require sacrifices for purification (vv. 2–15, 25–30), and less serious genital emissions that are natural and thus require only bathing for purification (vv. 19–24). Such genital emissions enter into the realm of purity concerns because the flow of blood and semen from the body represents the loss of life. On the other hand, the genitalia are associated with the procreation of life. This mixture of the powerful forces and boundaries of life and death creates impure or unclean conditions that require purification.

15 The LORD spoke to Moses and Aaron, saying: ²Speak to the people of Israel and say to them:

When any man has a discharge from his member,^b his discharge makes him ceremonially unclean. ³The uncleanness of his discharge is this: whether his member^b flows with his discharge, or his member^b is stopped from discharging, it is uncleanness for him. ⁴Every bed on which the one with the discharge lies shall be unclean; and everything on which he sits shall be unclean. ⁵Anyone who touches his bed shall wash his clothes, and bathe in water, and be unclean until the evening. ⁶All who sit on anything on which the one with the discharge has sat shall wash their clothes, and bathe in water, and be unclean until the evening. ⁷All who touch the body of the one with the discharge shall wash their clothes, and bathe in water,

a A term for several skin diseases; precise meaning uncertain　b Heb *flesh* and be unclean until the evening. 8If the one with the discharge spits on persons who are clean, then they shall wash their clothes, and bathe in water, and be unclean until the evening. 9Any saddle on which the one with the discharge rides shall be unclean. 10All who touch anything that was under him shall be unclean until the evening, and all who carry such a thing shall wash their clothes, and bathe in water, and be unclean until the evening. 11All those whom the one with the discharge touches without his having rinsed his hands in water shall wash their clothes, and bathe in water, and be unclean until the evening. 12Any earthen vessel that the one with the discharge touches shall be broken; and every vessel of wood shall be rinsed in water.

13 When the one with a discharge is cleansed of his discharge, he shall count seven days for his cleansing; he shall wash his clothes and bathe his body in fresh water, and he shall be clean. 14On the eighth day he shall take two turtledoves or two pigeons and come before the LORD to the entrance of the tent of meeting and give them to the priest. 15The priest shall offer them, one for a sin offering and the other for a burnt offering; and the priest shall make atonement on his behalf before the LORD for his discharge.

16 If a man has an emission of semen, he shall bathe his whole body in water, and be unclean until the evening. 17Everything made of cloth or of skin on which the semen falls shall be washed with water, and be unclean until the evening. 18If a man lies with a woman and has an emission of semen, both of them shall bathe in water, and be unclean until the evening.

19 When a woman has a discharge of blood that is her regular discharge from her body, she shall be in her impurity for seven days, and whoever touches her shall be unclean until the evening. 20Everything upon which she lies during her impurity shall be unclean; everything also upon which she sits shall be unclean. 21Whoever touches her bed shall wash his clothes, and bathe in water, and be unclean until the evening. 22Whoever touches anything upon which

she sits shall wash his clothes, and bathe in water, and be unclean until the evening; 23whether it is the bed or anything upon which she sits, when he touches it he shall be unclean until the evening. 24If any man lies with her, and her impurity falls on him, he shall be unclean seven days; and every bed on which he lies shall be unclean.

25 If a woman has a discharge of blood for many days, not at the time of her impurity, or if she has a discharge beyond the time of her impurity, all the days of the discharge she shall continue in uncleanness; as in the days of her impurity, she shall be unclean. 26Every bed on which she lies during all the days of her discharge shall be treated as the bed of her impurity; and everything on which she sits shall be unclean, as in the uncleanness of her impurity. 27Whoever touches these things shall be unclean, and shall wash his clothes, and bathe in water, and be unclean until the evening. 28If she is cleansed of her discharge, she shall count seven days, and after that she shall be clean. 29On the eighth day she shall take two turtledoves or two pigeons and bring them to the priest at the entrance of the tent of meeting. 30The priest shall offer one for a sin offering and the other for a burnt offering; and the priest shall make atonement on her behalf before the LORD for her unclean discharge.

31 Thus you shall keep the people of Israel separate from their uncleanness, so that they do not die in their uncleanness by defiling my tabernacle that is in their midst.

32 This is the ritual for those who have a discharge: for him who has an emission of semen, becoming unclean thereby, 33for her who is in the infirmity of her period, for anyone, male or female, who has a discharge, and for the man who lies with a woman who is unclean.

15.1–33. 16–18: The normal act of sexual intercourse and the emission of semen render both the man and the woman unclean with the minor purification of bathing and one day's time required. The Bible does not view sex as evil but as a gift from God (see Song of Solomon). However, sexual union involves powerful forces of life and thus is protected by rituals of purification. **31:** Concern for the holiness of the *tabernacle*★ is at the heart of these purity laws as well as other laws in Leviticus. The tabernacle is the ornate tent of worship that contains the seat of God's presence in the midst of Israel's wilderness camp (see 1.1). The issue is not so much to protect God but to protect the people from coming in contact with the holiness of God *so that they do not die in their uncleanness.*

Rituals for the Day of Atonement★

16.1–34: The function of this annual ritual is two-fold: First, the purification offerings purge the *tabernacle*★ or place of worship from uncleanness (vv. 16–19); second, the priestly confession of sin, the setting free of the scapegoat, and the people's refraining from work and food purge the people from their sin (vv. 21–31). Atonement refers to the forgiveness or "covering over" of human sin and ritual impurity.

16 The LORD spoke to Moses after the death of the two sons of Aaron, when they drew near before the LORD and died. ²The LORD said to Moses:

Tell your brother Aaron not to come just at any time into the sanctuary inside the curtain before the mercy seat*ᵃ* that is upon the ark, or he will die; for I appear in the cloud upon the mercy seat.*ᵃ* ³Thus shall Aaron come into the holy place: with a young bull for a sin offering and a ram for a burnt offering. ⁴He shall put on the holy linen tunic, and shall have the linen undergarments next to his body, fasten the linen sash, and wear the linen turban; these are the holy vestments. He shall bathe his body in water, and then put them on. ⁵He shall take from the congregation of the people of Israel two male goats for a sin offering, and one ram for a burnt offering.

6 Aaron shall offer the bull as a sin offering for himself, and shall make atonement for himself and for his house. ⁷He shall take the two goats and set them before the LORD at the entrance of the tent of meeting; ⁸and Aaron shall cast lots on the two goats, one lot for the LORD and the other lot for Azazel.*ᵇ* ⁹Aaron shall present the goat on which the lot fell for the LORD, and offer it as a sin offering; ¹⁰but the goat on which the lot fell for Azazel*ᵇ* shall be presented alive before the LORD to make atonement over it, that it

may be sent away into the wilderness to Azazel.*ᵇ*

11 Aaron shall present the bull as a sin offering for himself, and shall make atonement for himself and for his house; he shall slaughter the bull as a sin offering for himself. ¹²He shall take a censer full of coals of fire from the altar before the LORD, and two handfuls of crushed sweet incense, and he shall bring it inside the curtain ¹³and put the incense on the fire before the LORD, that the cloud of the incense may cover the mercy seat*ᵃ* that is upon the covenant,*ᶜ* or he will die. ¹⁴He shall take some of the blood of the bull, and sprinkle it with his finger on the front of the mercy seat,*ᵃ* and before the mercy seat*ᵃ* he shall sprinkle the blood with his finger seven times.

16.1–14. 1: The remembrance of the earlier story of the death of *the two sons of Aaron* in 10.1–7 emphasizes the danger of the priestly function of drawing near to God's presence on behalf of the people. The laws concerning purification that have intervened between the story in ch. 10 and the atonement ritual in ch. 16 define the varied conditions of uncleanness that the Day of Atonement may eliminate. **2:** The high priest is allowed to enter the inner sanctuary only at certain times, not *any time.* The instruction appended to the end of the chapter specifies "once in the year" (v. 34). On the *curtain, the mercy seat,* and *the ark,* see Ex 25.17–22; 26.31–35. **7–9:** The *two goats* bear the sins of the people. One goat is killed and sacrificed *as a sin offering* (v. 9). The second goat is kept alive and symbolically carries the sin of the people out of the camp and into the wilderness (v. 10; see vv. 21–22). *Azazel* was the name of a goat-demon who was thought to inhabit desolate places (17.7; Isa 34.14). Here the name simply designates a remote wilderness place to which the goat carries the sins and impurity of the community. **13:** This verse reflects biblical traditions that stipulate that any human who sees God will die (Ex 33.20). The cloud of smoke from the incense veils the deity and also placates the deity with the sweet aroma (1.9).

15 He shall slaughter the goat of the sin offering that is for the people and bring its blood inside the curtain, and do with its

a Or *the cover*   *b* Traditionally rendered *a scapegoat*
c Or *treaty,* or *testament;* Heb *eduth*

blood as he did with the blood of the bull, sprinkling it upon the mercy seat[a] and before the mercy seat.[a] 16Thus he shall make atonement for the sanctuary, because of the uncleannesses of the people of Israel, and because of their transgressions, all their sins; and so he shall do for the tent of meeting, which remains with them in the midst of their uncleannesses. 17No one shall be in the tent of meeting from the time he enters to make atonement in the sanctuary until he comes out and has made atonement for himself and for his house and for all the assembly of Israel. 18Then he shall go out to the altar that is before the LORD and make atonement on its behalf, and shall take some of the blood of the bull and of the blood of the goat, and put it on each of the horns of the altar. 19He shall sprinkle some of the blood on it with his finger seven times, and cleanse it and hallow it from the uncleannesses of the people of Israel.

20 When he has finished atoning for the holy place and the tent of meeting and the altar, he shall present the live goat. 21Then Aaron shall lay both his hands on the head of the live goat, and confess over it all the iniquities of the people of Israel, and all their transgressions, all their sins, putting them on the head of the goat, and sending it away into the wilderness by means of someone designated for the task.[b] 22The goat shall bear on itself all their iniquities to a barren region; and the goat shall be set free in the wilderness.

23 Then Aaron shall enter the tent of meeting, and shall take off the linen vestments that he put on when he went into the holy place, and shall leave them there. 24He shall bathe his body in water in a holy place, and put on his vestments; then he shall come out and offer his burnt offering and the burnt offering of the people, making atonement for himself and for the people. 25The fat of the sin offering he shall turn into smoke on the altar. 26The one who sets the goat free for Azazel[c] shall wash his clothes and bathe his body in water, and afterward may come into the camp. 27The bull of the sin offering and the goat of the sin offering, whose blood was brought in to make atone-

ment in the holy place, shall be taken outside the camp; their skin and their flesh and their dung shall be consumed in fire. 28The one who burns them shall wash his clothes and bathe his body in water, and afterward may come into the camp.

29 This shall be a statute to you forever: In the seventh month, on the tenth day of the month, you shall deny yourselves,[d] and shall do no work, neither the citizen nor the alien who resides among you. 30For on this day atonement shall be made for you, to cleanse you; from all your sins you shall be clean before the LORD. 31It is a sabbath of complete rest to you, and you shall deny yourselves;[d] it is a statute forever. 32The priest who is anointed and consecrated as priest in his father's place shall make atonement, wearing the linen vestments, the holy vestments. 33He shall make atonement for the sanctuary, and he shall make atonement for the tent of meeting and for the altar, and he shall make atonement for the priests and for all the people of the assembly. 34This shall be an everlasting statute for you, to make atonement for the people of Israel once in the year for all their sins. And Moses did as the LORD had commanded him.

16.15–34. 22: All the sin of the people is transferred to *the goat,* which carries their sins outside the camp and into *the wilderness.* 26: On *Azazel,* see comment on vv. 7–9. 30–31: The *day of atonement* is to be a *sabbath,* a day of rest when the people refrain from work (see Ex 20.8–11).

Laws regarding holiness

17.1–26.46: The section of laws in chs. 17–26 once formed an independent collection. These laws (especially chs. 19–23) focus on maintaining the holiness of the whole Israelite community and the holiness of the land of Canaan where they will live. The laws are often called the "Holiness Code." See sidebar, p. 149.

---

17 The LORD spoke to Moses: 2 Speak to Aaron and his sons and to all the people of Israel and say to them:

---

a Or *the cover*   *b* Meaning of Heb uncertain
c Traditionally rendered *a scapegoat*   *d* Or *shall fast*

This is what the LORD has commanded. ³If anyone of the house of Israel slaughters an ox or a lamb or a goat in the camp, or slaughters it outside the camp, ⁴and does not bring it to the entrance of the tent of meeting, to present it as an offering to the LORD before the tabernacle of the LORD, he shall be held guilty of bloodshed; he has shed blood, and he shall be cut off from the people. ⁵This is in order that the people of Israel may bring their sacrifices that they offer in the open field, that they may bring them to the LORD, to the priest at the entrance of the tent of meeting, and offer them as sacrifices of well-being to the LORD. ⁶The priest shall dash the blood against the altar of the LORD at the entrance of the tent of meeting, and turn the fat into smoke as a pleasing odor to the LORD, ⁷so that they may no longer offer their sacrifices for goat-demons, to whom they prostitute themselves. This shall be a statute forever to them throughout their generations.

8 And say to them further: Anyone of the house of Israel or of the aliens who reside among them who offers a burnt offering or sacrifice, ⁹and does not bring it to the entrance of the tent of meeting, to sacrifice it to the LORD, shall be cut off from the people.

10 If anyone of the house of Israel or of the aliens who reside among them eats any blood, I will set my face against that person who eats blood, and will cut that person off from the people. ¹¹For the life of the flesh is in the blood; and I have given it to you for making atonement for your lives on the altar; for, as life, it is the blood that makes atonement. ¹²Therefore I have said to the people of Israel: No person among you shall eat blood, nor shall any alien who resides among you eat blood. ¹³And anyone of the people of Israel, or of the aliens who reside among them, who hunts down an animal or bird that may be eaten shall pour out its blood and cover it with earth.

14 For the life of every creature—its blood is its life; therefore I have said to the people of Israel: You shall not eat the blood of any creature, for the life of every creature is its blood; whoever eats it shall be cut off. ¹⁵All persons, citizens or aliens, who eat what dies of itself or what has been torn by wild animals, shall wash their clothes, and bathe themselves in water, and be unclean until the evening; then they shall be clean. ¹⁶But if they do not wash themselves or bathe their body, they shall bear their guilt.

17.1–16: The LORD issues instructions for slaughtering animals. 5: The implication is that all animal meat used for food must be first offered to the LORD as a sacrifice and then eaten. **7:** The reason for regulating animal slaughter is to prevent sacrifices from being offered to *goat-demons.* The word for *goat-demon* is the same as the word "Azazel" used elsewhere (16.26; Isa 34.14). To *prostitute themselves* is a metaphor* for the worship of other gods or idols (20.5). **11:** On *the blood* and *atonement,** see comments on 1.4 and 1.5.

---

18 The LORD spoke to Moses, saying: 2 Speak to the people of Israel and say to them: I am the LORD your God. ³You shall not do as they do in the land of Egypt, where you lived, and you shall not do as they do in the land of Canaan, to which I am bringing you. You shall not follow their statutes. ⁴My ordinances you shall observe and my statutes you shall keep, following them: I am the LORD your God. ⁵You shall keep my statutes and my ordinances; by doing so one shall live: I am the LORD.

6 None of you shall approach anyone near of kin to uncover nakedness: I am the LORD. ⁷You shall not uncover the nakedness of your father, which is the nakedness of your mother; she is your mother, you shall not uncover her nakedness. ⁸You shall not uncover the nakedness of your father's wife; it is the nakedness of your father. ⁹You shall not uncover the nakedness of your sister, your father's daughter or your mother's daughter, whether born at home or born abroad. ¹⁰You shall not uncover the nakedness of your son's daughter or of your daughter's daughter, for their nakedness is your own nakedness. ¹¹You shall not uncover the nakedness of your father's wife's daughter, begotten by your father, since she is your sister. ¹²You shall not uncover the nakedness of your father's sister; she is your father's flesh. ¹³You shall not uncover the nakedness of your mother's sister, for she is your

mother's flesh. [14]You shall not uncover the nakedness of your father's brother, that is, you shall not approach his wife; she is your aunt. [15]You shall not uncover the nakedness of your daughter-in-law: she is your son's wife; you shall not uncover her nakedness. [16]You shall not uncover the nakedness of your brother's wife; it is your brother's nakedness. [17]You shall not uncover the nakedness of a woman and her daughter, and you shall not take[a] her son's daughter or her daughter's daughter to uncover her nakedness; they are your[b] flesh; it is depravity. [18]And you shall not take[a] a woman as a rival to her sister, uncovering her nakedness while her sister is still alive.

19 You shall not approach a woman to uncover her nakedness while she is in her menstrual uncleanness. [20]You shall not have sexual relations with your kinsman's wife, and defile yourself with her. [21]You shall not give any of your offspring to sacrifice them[c] to Molech, and so profane the name of your God: I am the LORD. [22]You shall not lie with a male as with a woman; it is an abomination. [23]You shall not have sexual relations with any animal and defile yourself with it, nor shall any woman give herself to an animal to have sexual relations with it: it is perversion.

24 Do not defile yourselves in any of these ways, for by all these practices the nations I am casting out before you have defiled themselves. [25]Thus the land became defiled; and I punished it for its iniquity, and the land vomited out its inhabitants. [26]But you shall keep my statutes and my ordinances and commit none of these abominations, either the citizen or the alien who resides among you [27](for the inhabitants of the land, who were before you, committed all of these abominations, and the land became defiled); [28]otherwise the land will vomit you out for defiling it, as it vomited out the nation that was before you. [29]For whoever commits any of these abominations shall be cut off from their people. [30]So keep my charge not to commit any of these abominations that were done before you, and not to defile yourselves by them: I am the LORD your God.

18.1–30: The LORD lays out prohibitions concerning sexual relations. 6: To *approach* and to *uncover nakedness* are euphemisms* for sexual intercourse. **9–18:** A number of earlier biblical characters violated some of these laws. Abraham married his half-sister (v. 11; Gen 20.12). Amram (the father of Moses) married Jochebed, who was the sister of Amram's father (v. 12; Ex 6.20). Judah married Tamar, his daughter-in-law (v. 15; Gen 38). Jacob married the two sisters, Rachel and Leah (v. 18; Gen 29.15–30). These violations, however, occurred before the laws of Leviticus came into force. Moreover, the custom of levirate marriage* in which the brother of a dead husband has an obligation to marry the dead man's widow in order to father children seems to be an exception to v. 16 (see Deut 25.5–10). **21:** *Molech* was the pagan deity of the nation of Ammon, which was located just east of Canaan. The Bible associates the rite of child sacrifice with the god Molech (2 Kings 23.10; Jer 32.35).

19 The LORD spoke to Moses, saying: 2 Speak to all the congregation of the people of Israel and say to them: You shall be holy, for I the LORD your God am holy. [3]You shall each revere your mother and father, and you shall keep my sabbaths: I am the LORD your God. [4]Do not turn to idols or make cast images for yourselves: I am the LORD your God.

5 When you offer a sacrifice of well-being to the LORD, offer it in such a way that it is acceptable in your behalf. [6]It shall be eaten on the same day you offer it, or on the next day; and anything left over until the third day shall be consumed in fire. [7]If it is eaten at all on the third day, it is an abomination; it will not be acceptable. [8]All who eat it shall be subject to punishment, because they have profaned what is holy to the LORD; and any such person shall be cut off from the people.

9 When you reap the harvest of your land, you shall not reap to the very edges of your field, or gather the gleanings of your harvest. [10]You shall not strip your vineyard bare, or gather the fallen grapes of your vineyard; you shall leave them for the poor and the alien: I am the LORD your God.

11 You shall not steal; you shall not deal

a Or *marry*   b Gk: Heb lacks *your*   c Heb *to pass them over*

The Concept of Holiness

Holiness in Leviticus involves two dimensions. The first dimension is holiness as separation. The sacred is separate from the ordinary or common. The holiness of God as a divine being is separate and distinct from humanity. Circles of graduated holiness extend out from the center of Israel's community. The sanctuary in the middle is the holiest part of the Israelite camp because of its association with the presence of God. The priests are separate from the other members of the community because of their service to God and the worship life of the people. Moreover, Israel as God's holy people is distinct from other nations. These boundaries of separation between what is holy and not holy are related to the boundaries of purity and impurity in some of the other laws in Leviticus (ch. 11; see sidebar, "Ritual Purity and Cleanness," p. 136).

A second dimension of holiness in Leviticus is the more positive concept of holiness as a goal toward which Israel should strive. Leviticus is clearly aware of the threat presented by sinfulness and impurity (chs. 16, 26). However, it also holds up the holiness of God as a model to be imitated. "You shall be holy, for I the LORD your God am holy" (19.2). Such holiness is made concrete in specific moral and ethical commands and behaviors outlined in Lev 19. The most comprehensive of these commands is the injunction to love your neighbor (19.18) and to love the alien (19.34). Holiness is not so much an abstract quality or concept but more a set of actions and behaviors that arise out of Israel's unique relationship with a holy God.

falsely; and you shall not lie to one another. 12And you shall not swear falsely by my name, profaning the name of your God: I am the LORD.

13 You shall not defraud your neighbor; you shall not steal; and you shall not keep for yourself the wages of a laborer until morning. 14You shall not revile the deaf or put a stumbling block before the blind; you shall fear your God: I am the LORD.

15 You shall not render an unjust judgment; you shall not be partial to the poor or defer to the great: with justice you shall judge your neighbor. 16You shall not go around as a slanderer[a] among your people, and you shall not profit by the blood[b] of your neighbor: I am the LORD.

17 You shall not hate in your heart anyone of your kin; you shall reprove your neighbor, or you will incur guilt yourself. 18You shall not take vengeance or bear a grudge against any of your people, but you shall love your neighbor as yourself: I am the LORD.

19 You shall keep my statutes. You shall not let your animals breed with a different kind; you shall not sow your field with two kinds of seed; nor shall you put on a garment made of two different materials.

20 If a man has sexual relations with a woman who is a slave, designated for another man but not ransomed or given her freedom, an inquiry shall be held. They shall not be put to death, since she has not been freed; 21but he shall bring a guilt offering for himself to the LORD, at the entrance of the tent of meeting, a ram as guilt offering. 22And the priest shall make atonement for him with the ram of guilt offering before the LORD for his sin that he committed; and the sin he committed shall be forgiven him.

23 When you come into the land and plant all kinds of trees for food, then you shall regard their fruit as forbidden;[c] three years it shall be forbidden[d] to you, it must not be eaten. 24In the fourth year all their fruit shall be set apart for rejoicing in the LORD. 25But in the fifth year you may eat of

a Meaning of Heb uncertain   b Heb stand against the blood   c Heb as their uncircumcision   d Heb uncircumcision

their fruit, that their yield may be increased for you: I am the LORD your God.

26 You shall not eat anything with its blood. You shall not practice augury or witchcraft. 27You shall not round off the hair on your temples or mar the edges of your beard. 28You shall not make any gashes in your flesh for the dead or tattoo any marks upon you: I am the LORD.

29 Do not profane your daughter by making her a prostitute, that the land not become prostituted and full of depravity. 30You shall keep my sabbaths and reverence my sanctuary: I am the LORD.

31 Do not turn to mediums or wizards; do not seek them out, to be defiled by them: I am the LORD your God.

32 You shall rise before the aged, and defer to the old; and you shall fear your God: I am the LORD.

33 When an alien resides with you in your land, you shall not oppress the alien. 34The alien who resides with you shall be to you as the citizen among you; you shall love the alien as yourself, for you were aliens in the land of Egypt: I am the LORD your God.

35 You shall not cheat in measuring length, weight, or quantity. 36You shall have honest balances, honest weights, an honest ephah, and an honest hin: I am the LORD your God, who brought you out of the land of Egypt. 37You shall keep all my statutes and all my ordinances, and observe them: I am the LORD.

19.1–37: The LORD commands holiness in ethical and ritual spheres of life. 2: This verse supplies the central principle, *you shall be holy*, and its primary justification, *for I the LORD your God am holy*, which underlie all the laws that follow. On the concept of holiness, see sidebar on p. 149. **3:** The *sabbath* is the seventh day of every week. On the sabbath day, rest was commanded and work prohibited (Ex 20.8–11). **5:** On *the sacrifice of well-being*, see comment on 3.1–17. **18:** To *love your neighbor as yourself* is cited in Mk 12.31 as one of two laws that summarize all the commandments. The *neighbor* refers to a fellow Israelite. Verses 33–34 extend the same obligation of love to the resident alien.✶ *Love* in this context is less an emotion and more an action of kindness and fairness. **19:** The prohibition of mixing animal species, plant seeds,

or other materials is grounded in God's creation, which set up boundaries of separation between each species (Gen 1). Crossing such boundaries created dangerous situations of impurity, not unlike mixing forces of life and death. Holiness is closely connected to notions of separation and distinctiveness. See sidebar, "Ritual Purity and Cleanness," p. 136. **26:** *Augury or witchcraft* involve pagan rites used in consulting the dead spirits. An example is King Saul, who went to the witch of Endor in order to rouse the dead spirit of the prophet✶ Samuel (1 Sam 28.3–25). **27–28:** These are customs associated with mourning the dead in the pagan worship of other gods. **30:** On the *sabbath*, see comment on v. 3. **36:** The *ephah* and the *hin* were units of measure used in business transactions.

20 The LORD spoke to Moses, saying: 2Say further to the people of Israel:

Any of the people of Israel, or of the aliens who reside in Israel, who give any of their offspring to Molech shall be put to death; the people of the land shall stone them to death. 3I myself will set my face against them, and will cut them off from the people, because they have given of their offspring to Molech, defiling my sanctuary and profaning my holy name. 4And if the people of the land should ever close their eyes to them, when they give of their offspring to Molech, and do not put them to death, 5I myself will set my face against them and against their family, and will cut them off from among their people, them and all who follow them in prostituting themselves to Molech.

6 If any turn to mediums and wizards, prostituting themselves to them, I will set my face against them, and will cut them off from the people. 7Consecrate yourselves therefore, and be holy; for I am the LORD your God. 8Keep my statutes, and observe them; I am the LORD; I sanctify you. 9All who curse father or mother shall be put to death; having cursed father or mother, their blood is upon them.

10 If a man commits adultery with the wife of*a* his neighbor, both the adulterer and the adulteress shall be put to death. 11The man who lies with his father's wife has uncovered his father's nakedness; both of them

a Heb repeats *if a man commits adultery with the wife of*

shall be put to death; their blood is upon them. ¹²If a man lies with his daughter-in-law, both of them shall be put to death; they have committed perversion, their blood is upon them. ¹³If a man lies with a male as with a woman, both of them have committed an abomination; they shall be put to death; their blood is upon them. ¹⁴If a man takes a wife and her mother also, it is depravity; they shall be burned to death, both he and they, that there may be no depravity among you. ¹⁵If a man has sexual relations with an animal, he shall be put to death; and you shall kill the animal. ¹⁶If a woman approaches any animal and has sexual relations with it, you shall kill the woman and the animal; they shall be put to death, their blood is upon them.

17 If a man takes his sister, a daughter of his father or a daughter of his mother, and sees her nakedness, and she sees his nakedness, it is a disgrace, and they shall be cut off in the sight of their people; he has uncovered his sister's nakedness, he shall be subject to punishment. ¹⁸If a man lies with a woman having her sickness and uncovers her nakedness, he has laid bare her flow and she has laid bare her flow of blood; both of them shall be cut off from their people. ¹⁹You shall not uncover the nakedness of your mother's sister or of your father's sister, for that is to lay bare one's own flesh; they shall be subject to punishment. ²⁰If a man lies with his uncle's wife, he has uncovered his uncle's nakedness; they shall be subject to punishment; they shall die childless. ²¹If a man takes his brother's wife, it is impurity; he has uncovered his brother's nakedness; they shall be childless.

22 You shall keep all my statutes and all my ordinances, and observe them, so that the land to which I bring you to settle in may not vomit you out. ²³You shall not follow the practices of the nation that I am driving out before you. Because they did all these things, I abhorred them. ²⁴But I have said to you: You shall inherit their land, and I will give it to you to possess, a land flowing with milk and honey. I am the LORD your God; I have separated you from the peoples. ²⁵You shall therefore make a distinction between the clean animal and the unclean, and between the unclean bird and the clean; you shall not bring abomination on yourselves by animal or by bird or by anything with which the ground teems, which I have set apart for you to hold unclean. ²⁶You shall be holy to me; for I the LORD am holy, and I have separated you from the other peoples to be mine.

27 A man or a woman who is a medium or a wizard shall be put to death; they shall be stoned to death, their blood is upon them.

20.1–27: The chapter largely repeats several laws from chs. 18–19 but adds specific penalties for violations of the laws. **2–5:** *Molech:* See comment on 18.21. **10–21:** The sexual transgressions listed here exhibit varying severity as indicated by the punishments specified: vv. 10–16, death; vv. 17–19, banishment from the community; and vv. 20–21, childlessness. **25:** Descriptions of which animals are clean or unclean appear in ch. 11. On the notions of *clean* and *unclean*, see sidebar, "Ritual Purity and Cleanness," p. 136. **26:** The verse is another statement of the foundational principle of these holiness laws: *You shall be holy . . . for I the LORD am holy* (see 19.2).

The holiness of priests

21.1–22.33: The LORD offers guidelines to protect the holiness of priests and the holiness of the sacrifices they administer. The requirements of holiness are more stringent for priests than for lay persons.

21 The LORD said to Moses: Speak to the priests, the sons of Aaron, and say to them:

No one shall defile himself for a dead person among his relatives, ²except for his nearest kin: his mother, his father, his son, his daughter, his brother; ³likewise, for a virgin sister, close to him because she has had no husband, he may defile himself for her. ⁴But he shall not defile himself as a husband among his people and so profane himself. ⁵They shall not make bald spots upon their heads, or shave off the edges of their beards, or make any gashes in their flesh. ⁶They shall be holy to their God, and not profane the name of their God; for they offer the LORD's offerings by fire, the food of their God; therefore they shall be holy. ⁷They shall not marry a prostitute or a woman who has been defiled; neither shall they marry a woman divorced from her husband. For they are holy to their God, [8]and you shall treat them as holy, since they offer the food of your God; they shall be holy to you, for I the LORD, I who sanctify you, am holy. [9]When the daughter of a priest profanes herself through prostitution, she profanes her father; she shall be burned to death.

10 The priest who is exalted above his fellows, on whose head the anointing oil has been poured and who has been consecrated to wear the vestments, shall not dishevel his hair, nor tear his vestments. [11]He shall not go where there is a dead body; he shall not defile himself even for his father or mother. [12]He shall not go outside the sanctuary and thus profane the sanctuary of his God; for the consecration of the anointing oil of his God is upon him: I am the LORD. [13]He shall marry only a woman who is a virgin. [14]A widow, or a divorced woman, or a woman who has been defiled, a prostitute, these he shall not marry. He shall marry a virgin of his own kin, [15]that he may not profane his offspring among his kin; for I am the LORD; I sanctify him.

21.1–11. 1–3: Contact with or proximity to a human corpse was considered the most severe source of impurity (Num 19). Thus, priests were prohibited from attending funerals for the dead except for close family members. **5:** These disfigurements were associated with mourning rites in neighboring pagan religions (19.27–28). **7:** *A woman who has been defiled* is one who has been involved in sexual activity outside the bonds of marriage (for example, a woman who has been raped). **10–11:** See vv. 1–3.

---

16 The LORD spoke to Moses, saying: [17]Speak to Aaron and say: No one of your offspring throughout their generations who has a blemish may approach to offer the food of his God. [18]For no one who has a blemish shall draw near, one who is blind or lame, or one who has a mutilated face or a limb too long, [19]or one who has a broken foot or a broken hand, [20]or a hunchback, or a dwarf, or a man with a blemish in his eyes or an itching disease or scabs or crushed testicles.

[21]No descendant of Aaron the priest who has a blemish shall come near to offer the LORD's offerings by fire; since he has a blemish, he shall not come near to offer the food of his God. [22]He may eat the food of his God, of the most holy as well as of the holy. [23]But he shall not come near the curtain or approach the altar, because he has a blemish, that he may not profane my sanctuaries; for I am the LORD; I sanctify them. [24]Thus Moses spoke to Aaron and to his sons and to all the people of Israel.

22 The LORD spoke to Moses, saying: [2]Direct Aaron and his sons to deal carefully with the sacred donations of the people of Israel, which they dedicate to me, so that they may not profane my holy name; I am the LORD. [3]Say to them: If anyone among all your offspring throughout your generations comes near the sacred donations, which the people of Israel dedicate to the LORD, while he is in a state of uncleanness, that person shall be cut off from my presence: I am the LORD. [4]No one of Aaron's offspring who has a leprous[a] disease or suffers a discharge may eat of the sacred donations until he is clean. Whoever touches anything made unclean by a corpse or a man who has had an emission of semen, [5]and whoever touches any swarming thing by which he may be made unclean or any human being by whom he may be made unclean—whatever his uncleanness may be— [6]the person who touches any such shall be unclean until evening and shall not eat of the sacred donations unless he has washed his body in water. [7]When the sun sets he shall be clean; and afterward he may eat of the sacred donations, for they are his food. [8]That which died or was torn by wild animals he shall not eat, becoming unclean by it: I am the LORD. [9]They shall keep my charge, so that they may not incur guilt and die in the sanctuary[b] for having profaned it: I am the LORD; I sanctify them.

10 No lay person shall eat of the sacred donations. No bound or hired servant of the priest shall eat of the sacred donations; [11]but

---

a A term for several skin diseases; precise meaning uncertain   b Vg: Heb *incur guilt for it and die in it*

if a priest acquires anyone by purchase, the person may eat of them; and those that are born in his house may eat of his food. 12If a priest's daughter marries a layman, she shall not eat of the offering of the sacred donations; 13but if a priest's daughter is widowed or divorced, without offspring, and returns to her father's house, as in her youth, she may eat of her father's food. No lay person shall eat of it. 14If a man eats of the sacred donation unintentionally, he shall add one-fifth of its value to it, and give the sacred donation to the priest. 15No one shall profane the sacred donations of the people of Israel, which they offer to the LORD, 16causing them to bear guilt requiring a guilt offering, by eating their sacred donations: for I am the LORD; I sanctify them.

22.2–16: The *sacred donations* are the portions of the animal and grain sacrifices that the priest reserves for his own consumption. This is in accord with the laws in 2.3, 6.25–26, and 7.31–32.

17 The LORD spoke to Moses, saying: 18Speak to Aaron and his sons and all the people of Israel and say to them: When anyone of the house of Israel or of the aliens residing in Israel presents an offering, whether in payment of a vow or as a freewill offering that is offered to the LORD as a burnt offering, 19to be acceptable in your behalf it shall be a male without blemish, of the cattle or the sheep or the goats. 20You shall not offer anything that has a blemish, for it will not be acceptable in your behalf.

21 When anyone offers a sacrifice of well-being to the LORD, in fulfillment of a vow or as a freewill offering, from the herd or from the flock, to be acceptable it must be perfect; there shall be no blemish in it. 22Anything blind, or injured, or maimed, or having a discharge or an itch or scabs—these you shall not offer to the LORD or put any of them on the altar as offerings by fire to the LORD. 23An ox or a lamb that has a limb too long or too short you may present for a freewill offering; but it will not be accepted for a vow. 24Any animal that has its testicles bruised or crushed or torn or cut, you shall not offer to the LORD; such you shall not do

within your land, 25nor shall you accept any such animals from a foreigner to offer as food to your God; since they are mutilated, with a blemish in them, they shall not be accepted in your behalf.

26 The LORD spoke to Moses, saying: 27When an ox or a sheep or a goat is born, it shall remain seven days with its mother, and from the eighth day on it shall be acceptable as the LORD's offering by fire. 28But you shall not slaughter, from the herd or the flock, an animal with its young on the same day. 29When you sacrifice a thanksgiving offering to the LORD, you shall sacrifice it so that it may be acceptable in your behalf. 30It shall be eaten on the same day; you shall not leave any of it until morning: I am the LORD. 31 Thus you shall keep my commandments and observe them: I am the LORD. 32You shall not profane my holy name, that I may be sanctified among the people of Israel: I am the LORD; I sanctify you, 33I who brought you out of the land of Egypt to be your God: I am the LORD.

The yearly festivals

23.1–44: These laws apply to all Israelites, especially farmers, since they deal mainly with agricultural matters. Other biblical laws for festivals appear in Ex 23.14–17, 34.21–23, and Deut 16.

23 The LORD spoke to Moses, saying: 2Speak to the people of Israel and say to them: These are the appointed festivals of the LORD that you shall proclaim as holy convocations, my appointed festivals.

3 Six days shall work be done; but the seventh day is a sabbath of complete rest, a holy convocation; you shall do no work: it is a sabbath to the LORD throughout your settlements.

4 These are the appointed festivals of the LORD, the holy convocations, which you shall celebrate at the time appointed for them. 5In the first month, on the fourteenth day of the month, at twilight,*a* there shall be a passover offering to the LORD, 6and on the fifteenth day of the same month is the festival of unleavened bread to the LORD; seven

a Heb *between the two evenings*

days you shall eat unleavened bread. ⁷On the first day you shall have a holy convocation; you shall not work at your occupations. ⁸For seven days you shall present the LORD's offerings by fire; on the seventh day there shall be a holy convocation: you shall not work at your occupations.

23.1–8. 3: On the *sabbath* as a day of *rest*, see Ex 20.8–11. 5–8: The festivals of Passover* and Unleavened Bread are commemorations of Israel's exodus out of Egypt (Ex 12–13). They were originally two different festivals, but they came to be connected and celebrated together (Deut 16.1–8).

9 The LORD spoke to Moses: ¹⁰Speak to the people of Israel and say to them: When you enter the land that I am giving you and you reap its harvest, you shall bring the sheaf of the first fruits of your harvest to the priest. ¹¹He shall raise the sheaf before the LORD, that you may find acceptance; on the day after the sabbath the priest shall raise it. ¹²On the day when you raise the sheaf, you shall offer a lamb a year old, without blemish, as a burnt offering to the LORD. ¹³And the grain offering with it shall be two-tenths of an ephah of choice flour mixed with oil, an offering by fire of pleasing odor to the LORD; and the drink offering with it shall be of wine, one-fourth of a hin. ¹⁴You shall eat no bread or parched grain or fresh ears until that very day, until you have brought the offering of your God: it is a statute forever throughout your generations in all your settlements.

15 And from the day after the sabbath, from the day on which you bring the sheaf of the elevation offering, you shall count off seven weeks; they shall be complete. ¹⁶You shall count until the day after the seventh sabbath, fifty days; then you shall present an offering of new grain to the LORD. ¹⁷You shall bring from your settlements two loaves of bread as an elevation offering, each made of two-tenths of an ephah; they shall be of choice flour, baked with leaven, as first fruits to the LORD. ¹⁸You shall present with the bread seven lambs a year old without blemish, one young bull, and two rams; they shall be a burnt offering to the LORD, along with

their grain offering and their drink offerings, an offering by fire of pleasing odor to the LORD. ¹⁹You shall also offer one male goat for a sin offering, and two male lambs a year old as a sacrifice of well-being. ²⁰The priest shall raise them with the bread of the first fruits as an elevation offering before the LORD, together with the two lambs; they shall be holy to the LORD for the priest. ²¹On that same day you shall make proclamation; you shall hold a holy convocation; you shall not work at your occupations. This is a statute forever in all your settlements throughout your generations.

22 When you reap the harvest of your land, you shall not reap to the very edges of your field, or gather the gleanings of your harvest; you shall leave them for the poor and for the alien: I am the LORD your God.

23 The LORD spoke to Moses, saying: ²⁴Speak to the people of Israel, saying: In the seventh month, on the first day of the month, you shall observe a day of complete rest, a holy convocation commemorated with trumpet blasts. ²⁵You shall not work at your occupations; and you shall present the LORD's offering by fire.

26 The LORD spoke to Moses, saying: ²⁷Now, the tenth day of this seventh month is the day of atonement; it shall be a holy convocation for you: you shall deny yourselves*a* and present the LORD's offering by fire; ²⁸and you shall do no work during that entire day; for it is a day of atonement, to make atonement on your behalf before the LORD your God. ²⁹For anyone who does not practice self-denial*b* during that entire day shall be cut off from the people. ³⁰And anyone who does any work during that entire day, such a one I will destroy from the midst of the people. ³¹You shall do no work: it is a statute forever throughout your generations in all your settlements. ³²It shall be to you a sabbath of complete rest, and you shall deny yourselves;*a* on the ninth day of the month at evening, from evening to evening you shall keep your sabbath.

33 The LORD spoke to Moses, saying: ³⁴Speak to the people of Israel, saying: On

a Or *shall fast*   *b* Or *does not fast*

the fifteenth day of this seventh month, and lasting seven days, there shall be the festival of booths *a* to the LORD. 35 The first day shall be a holy convocation; you shall not work at your occupations. 36 Seven days you shall present the LORD's offerings by fire; on the eighth day you shall observe a holy convocation and present the LORD's offerings by fire; it is a solemn assembly; you shall not work at your occupations.

37 These are the appointed festivals of the LORD, which you shall celebrate as times of holy convocation, for presenting to the LORD offerings by fire—burnt offerings and grain offerings, sacrifices and drink offerings, each on its proper day— 38 apart from the sabbaths of the LORD, and apart from your gifts, and apart from all your votive offerings, and apart from all your freewill offerings, which you give to the LORD.

39 Now, the fifteenth day of the seventh month, when you have gathered in the produce of the land, you shall keep the festival of the LORD, lasting seven days; a complete rest on the first day, and a complete rest on the eighth day. 40 On the first day you shall take the fruit of majestic *b* trees, branches of palm trees, boughs of leafy trees, and willows of the brook; and you shall rejoice before the LORD your God for seven days. 41 You shall keep it as a festival to the LORD seven days in the year; you shall keep it in the seventh month as a statute forever throughout your generations. 42 You shall live in booths for seven days; all that are citizens in Israel shall live in booths, 43 so that your generations may know that I made the people of Israel live in booths when I brought them out of the land of Egypt: I am the LORD your God.

44 Thus Moses declared to the people of Israel the appointed festivals of the LORD.

23.9–44. 9–14: The offering of *first fruits* occurred at the beginning of the barley harvest in the spring of the year. 15–22: The festival of *weeks* is celebrated *seven weeks* (v. 15) or *fifty days* (v. 16) after the festival of Unleavened Bread. The festival is also called "Pentecost"* (from a Greek word meaning "fifty"). The festival marks the harvest of *new grain* (v. 16), namely, wheat. 23–24: The festival of trumpets observes the beginning of the new year in the old agricultural calendar.* *The seventh month* (v. 24) is in the autumn (September—October). 26–32: Details for the *day of atonement*★ occur in ch. 16. 33–36: *The festival of booths* or tabernacles★ was a feast of thanksgiving during the autumn harvest. Additional provisions for this festival are given in vv. 39–43. The festival came to be associated with God's care of Israel in the wilderness journey from Egypt to the promised land (v. 43). 38: On the *sabbath* as a day of rest, see Ex 20.8–11. Numbers 28–29 enumerates further details about the various *offerings by fire* (v. 37) to be given at each festival.

24 The LORD spoke to Moses, saying: 2 Command the people of Israel to bring you pure oil of beaten olives for the lamp, that a light may be kept burning regularly. 3 Aaron shall set it up in the tent of meeting, outside the curtain of the covenant, *c* to burn from evening to morning before the LORD regularly; it shall be a statute forever throughout your generations. 4 He shall set up the lamps on the lampstand of pure gold *d* before the LORD regularly.

5 You shall take choice flour, and bake twelve loaves of it; two-tenths of an ephah shall be in each loaf. 6 You shall place them in two rows, six in a row, on the table of pure gold. *e* 7 You shall put pure frankincense with each row, to be a token offering for the bread, as an offering by fire to the LORD. 8 Every sabbath day Aaron shall set them in order before the LORD regularly as a commitment of the people of Israel, as a covenant forever. 9 They shall be for Aaron and his descendants, who shall eat them in a holy place, for they are most holy portions for him from the offerings by fire to the LORD, a perpetual due.

10 A man whose mother was an Israelite and whose father was an Egyptian came out among the people of Israel; and the Israelite woman's son and a certain Israelite began fighting in the camp. 11 The Israelite woman's son blasphemed the Name in a curse. And they brought him to Moses— now his mother's name was Shelomith,

a Or *tabernacles*: Heb *succoth*   *b* Meaning of Heb uncertain   *c* Or *treaty*, or *testament*; Heb *eduth*   *d* Heb *pure lampstand*   *e* Heb *pure table*

daughter of Dibri, of the tribe of Dan— [12]and they put him in custody, until the decision of the LORD should be made clear to them.

13 The LORD said to Moses, saying: [14]Take the blasphemer outside the camp; and let all who were within hearing lay their hands on his head, and let the whole congregation stone him. [15]And speak to the people of Israel, saying: Anyone who curses God shall bear the sin. [16]One who blasphemes the name of the LORD shall be put to death; the whole congregation shall stone the blasphemer. Aliens as well as citizens, when they blaspheme the Name, shall be put to death. [17]Anyone who kills a human being shall be put to death. [18]Anyone who kills an animal shall make restitution for it, life for life. [19]Anyone who maims another shall suffer the same injury in return: [20]fracture for fracture, eye for eye, tooth for tooth; the injury inflicted is the injury to be suffered. [21]One who kills an animal shall make restitution for it; but one who kills a human being shall be put to death. [22]You shall have one law for the alien and for the citizen: for I am the LORD your God. [23]Moses spoke thus to the people of Israel; and they took the blasphemer outside the camp, and stoned him to death. The people of Israel did as the LORD had commanded Moses.

24.1–23: The LORD issues laws related to the lamp and bread in the sanctuary and the punishment of blasphemy in the camp. 1–4: On the pure oil for the *lamp* in *the tent of meeting*, see Ex 27.20–21. **5–9:** On the *bread* for the sanctuary (v. 7), see Ex 25.23–30. *An ephah* is a unit of measure (v. 5). *Frankincense* is an aromatic spice (v. 7). The *sabbath* (v. 8) is the seventh day of the week and is kept holy by refraining from work (Ex 20.8–11). **11:** To *blaspheme* is to show contempt or lack of reverence for God. *The Name* is the sacred name for God (YHWH) given to Moses and the Israelites in Ex 3.13–15. The offense involves both blaspheming the divine name (see Ex 20.7) and cursing God (Ex 22.28) as indicated in vv. 15–16. **14:** The spoken curse using the powerful divine name contaminates with guilt both the speaker and those who hear it. When the people *lay their hands* on the speaker's head, they transfer their guilt back to the blasphemer (16.21–22). To *stone him* is a communal act of public

execution. Pelting the guilty person with stones until he dies cleanses the community from the evil (Deut 17.2–7). **20:** This principle is the so-called "lex talionis" or "law of retribution," *eye for eye, tooth for tooth*. It is designed to limit the amount of punishment. **22:** Any distinction in the treatment of Israelites versus non-Israelites is prohibited. This principle is occasioned by the previous case of the blasphemer, who was half-Israelite and half-Egyptian (v. 10).

Laws regarding the sabbatical year and the jubilee year

25.1–55: The basic principle behind these laws is that the land is ultimately owned by God (v. 23). Humans have only temporary possession of it. Thus, humans should avoid excessive economic exploitation of the land or other people. Similar laws about the periodic release of land, slaves, and debts occur in Ex 21.2–6, Ex 23.10–11, and Deut 15.1–18.

25 The LORD spoke to Moses on Mount Sinai, saying: [2]Speak to the people of Israel and say to them: When you enter the land that I am giving you, the land shall observe a sabbath for the LORD. [3]Six years you shall sow your field, and six years you shall prune your vineyard, and gather in their yield; [4]but in the seventh year there shall be a sabbath of complete rest for the land, a sabbath for the LORD: you shall not sow your field or prune your vineyard. [5]You shall not reap the aftergrowth of your harvest or gather the grapes of your unpruned vine: it shall be a year of complete rest for the land. [6]You may eat what the land yields during its sabbath—you, your male and female slaves, your hired and your bound laborers who live with you; [7]for your livestock also, and for the wild animals in your land all its yield shall be for food.

8 You shall count off seven weeks[a] of years, seven times seven years, so that the period of seven weeks of years gives forty-nine years. [9]Then you shall have the trumpet sounded loud; on the tenth day of the seventh month—on the day of atonement—you shall have the trumpet sounded throughout all your land. [10]And you shall hallow the fiftieth year and you shall proclaim liberty

a Or *sabbaths*

throughout the land to all its inhabitants. It shall be a jubilee for you: you shall return, every one of you, to your property and every one of you to your family. 11That fiftieth year shall be a jubilee for you: you shall not sow, or reap the aftergrowth, or harvest the unpruned vines. 12For it is a jubilee; it shall be holy to you: you shall eat only what the field itself produces.

13 In this year of jubilee you shall return, every one of you, to your property. 14When you make a sale to your neighbor or buy from your neighbor, you shall not cheat one another. 15When you buy from your neighbor, you shall pay only for the number of years since the jubilee; the seller shall charge you only for the remaining crop years. 16If the years are more, you shall increase the price, and if the years are fewer, you shall diminish the price; for it is a certain number of harvests that are being sold to you. 17You shall not cheat one another, but you shall fear your God; for I am the LORD your God.

18 You shall observe my statutes and faithfully keep my ordinances, so that you may live on the land securely. 19The land will yield its fruit, and you will eat your fill and live on it securely. 20Should you ask, "What shall we eat in the seventh year, if we may not sow or gather in our crop?" 21I will order my blessing for you in the sixth year, so that it will yield a crop for three years. 22When you sow in the eighth year, you will be eating from the old crop; until the ninth year, when its produce comes in, you shall eat the old. 23The land shall not be sold in perpetuity, for the land is mine; with me you are but aliens and tenants. 24Throughout the land that you hold, you shall provide for the redemption of the land.

25.1–24. 2–7: The *sabbath* (v. 2) typically refers to the seventh day of the week, a day of rest from work (Ex 20.8–11). Here the term applies to every *seventh year* (v. 4). The land rests by having no crops planted on it. **8–12:** The *jubilee* year (vv. 11–12) occurs after every seven times seven years (v. 8) or, in other words, every fiftieth year (v. 10). The *return to your property* and *to your family* presupposes a return to the original allocation of the plots of land in Canaan assigned to each Israelite tribe, clan,* and family. This allocation of land occurs after the conquest of Canaan in Josh 13–22. The function of the law is both periodic economic equalization and support of the clan and family social structure. **13–17:** Land may be bought and sold as a temporary lease between each jubilee year. However, the buyer knows that the land will revert to the original owner in the fiftieth year of the jubilee. **23:** The ultimate divine ownership of the land is the theological presupposition behind the sabbatical and jubilee laws of release. *In perpetuity* means forever. In other words, every sale of land must be only temporary so that its ownership may periodically revert to the original owners. **24:** *Redemption* involves a relative or family member's taking back land or persons that originally belonged to the family (see v. 25).

25 If anyone of your kin falls into difficulty and sells a piece of property, then the next of kin shall come and redeem what the relative has sold. 26If the person has no one to redeem it, but then prospers and finds sufficient means to do so, 27the years since its sale shall be computed and the difference shall be refunded to the person to whom it was sold, and the property shall be returned. 28But if there are not sufficient means to recover it, what was sold shall remain with the purchaser until the year of jubilee; in the jubilee it shall be released, and the property shall be returned.

29 If anyone sells a dwelling house in a walled city, it may be redeemed until a year has elapsed since its sale; the right of redemption shall be one year. 30If it is not redeemed before a full year has elapsed, a house that is in a walled city shall pass in perpetuity to the purchaser, throughout the generations; it shall not be released in the jubilee. 31But houses in villages that have no walls around them shall be classed as open country; they may be redeemed, and they shall be released in the jubilee. 32As for the cities of the Levites, the Levites shall forever have the right of redemption of the houses in the cities belonging to them. 33Such property as may be redeemed from the Levites—houses sold in a city belonging to them—shall be released in the jubilee; because the houses in the cities of the Levites are their possession among the people of Israel. 34But the open land around their

cities may not be sold; for that is their possession for all time.

35 If any of your kin fall into difficulty and become dependent on you,[a] you shall support them; they shall live with you as though resident aliens. 36Do not take interest in advance or otherwise make a profit from them, but fear your God; let them live with you. 37You shall not lend them your money at interest taken in advance, or provide them food at a profit. 38I am the LORD your God, who brought you out of the land of Egypt, to give you the land of Canaan, to be your God.

39 If any who are dependent on you become so impoverished that they sell themselves to you, you shall not make them serve as slaves. 40They shall remain with you as hired or bound laborers. They shall serve with you until the year of the jubilee. 41Then they and their children with them shall be free from your authority; they shall go back to their own family and return to their ancestral property. 42For they are my servants, whom I brought out of the land of Egypt; they shall not be sold as slaves are sold. 43You shall not rule over them with harshness, but shall fear your God. 44As for the male and female slaves whom you may have, it is from the nations around you that you may acquire male and female slaves. 45You may also acquire them from among the aliens residing with you, and from their families that are with you, who have been born in your land; and they may be your property. 46You may keep them as a possession for your children after you, for them to inherit as property. These you may treat as slaves, but as for your fellow Israelites, no one shall rule over the other with harshness.

47 If resident aliens among you prosper, and if any of your kin fall into difficulty with one of them and sell themselves to an alien, or to a branch of the alien's family, 48after they have sold themselves they shall have the right of redemption; one of their brothers may redeem them, 49or their uncle or their uncle's son may redeem them, or anyone of their family who is of their own flesh may redeem them; or if they prosper they may redeem themselves. 50They shall compute with the purchaser the total from the year when they sold themselves to the alien until the jubilee year; the price of the sale shall be applied to the number of years: the time they were with the owner shall be rated as the time of a hired laborer. 51If many years remain, they shall pay for their redemption in proportion to the purchase price; 52and if few years remain until the jubilee year, they shall compute thus: according to the years involved they shall make payment for their redemption. 53As a laborer hired by the year they shall be under the alien's authority, who shall not, however, rule with harshness over them in your sight. 54And if they have not been redeemed in any of these ways, they and their children with them shall go free in the jubilee year. 55For to me the people of Israel are servants; they are my servants whom I brought out from the land of Egypt: I am the LORD your God.

25.25–55: These laws deal with four progressively more serious economic situations of need: (1) the need to sell off a part of the family land holdings (vv. 25–34); (2) the need to become dependent on a fellow Israelite (vv. 35–38); (3) the need to sell oneself as a hired laborer to a fellow Israelite (vv. 39–46); and (4) the need to sell oneself as a hired laborer to a resident alien* or non-Israelite (vv. 47–55). On the *right of redemption* (vv. 29, 32), see comment on v. 24. Since the Levites (a priestly tribe within Israel) did not receive an allotment of land as did the other tribes, they received instead a number of cities throughout Israel (Num 18.20–24; 35.1–8). The basic theological conviction behind the laws in vv. 25–55 is that the Israelites should be slaves or servants to no one other than the LORD (vv. 42, 55).

Blessings for obedience and curses for disobedience
26.1–46: The laws of Leviticus conclude with a list of blessings and curses, a typical part of other ancient Near Eastern law codes and treaties. Similar blessings and curses conclude a collection of laws in Ex 23.20–33 and Deut 28.1–68.

---

26 You shall make for yourselves no idols and erect no carved images or

a Meaning of Heb uncertain

pillars, and you shall not place figured stones in your land, to worship at them; for I am the LORD your God. ²You shall keep my sabbaths and reverence my sanctuary: I am the LORD.

26.1–2. 1: The prohibited *idols*, *images*, and *pillars* may refer both to images of Israel's God and to images of foreign gods. **2:** The *sabbaths* include the seventh day of every week as a day of rest (19.3; Ex 20.8–11) and the sabbath years (ch. 25).

3 If you follow my statutes and keep my commandments and observe them faithfully, ⁴I will give you your rains in their season, and the land shall yield its produce, and the trees of the field shall yield their fruit. ⁵Your threshing shall overtake the vintage, and the vintage shall overtake the sowing; you shall eat your bread to the full, and live securely in your land. ⁶And I will grant peace in the land, and you shall lie down, and no one shall make you afraid; I will remove dangerous animals from the land, and no sword shall go through your land. ⁷You shall give chase to your enemies, and they shall fall before you by the sword. ⁸Five of you shall give chase to a hundred, and a hundred of you shall give chase to ten thousand; your enemies shall fall before you by the sword. ⁹I will look with favor upon you and make you fruitful and multiply you; and I will maintain my covenant with you. ¹⁰You shall eat old grain long stored, and you shall have to clear out the old to make way for the new. ¹¹I will place my dwelling in your midst, and I shall not abhor you. ¹²And I will walk among you, and will be your God, and you shall be my people. ¹³I am the LORD your God who brought you out of the land of Egypt, to be their slaves no more; I have broken the bars of your yoke and made you walk erect.

14 But if you will not obey me, and do not observe all these commandments, ¹⁵if you spurn my statutes, and abhor my ordinances, so that you will not observe all my commandments, and you break my covenant, ¹⁶I in turn will do this to you: I will bring terror on you; consumption and fever that waste the eyes and cause life to pine away. You shall sow your seed in vain, for your enemies shall eat it. ¹⁷I will set my face against you, and you shall be struck down by your enemies; your foes shall rule over you, and you shall flee though no one pursues you. ¹⁸And if in spite of this you will not obey me, I will continue to punish you sevenfold for your sins. ¹⁹I will break your proud glory, and I will make your sky like iron and your earth like copper. ²⁰Your strength shall be spent to no purpose: your land shall not yield its produce, and the trees of the land shall not yield their fruit.

21 If you continue hostile to me, and will not obey me, I will continue to plague you sevenfold for your sins. ²²I will let loose wild animals against you, and they shall bereave you of your children and destroy your livestock; they shall make you few in number, and your roads shall be deserted.

23 If in spite of these punishments you have not turned back to me, but continue hostile to me, ²⁴then I too will continue hostile to you: I myself will strike you sevenfold for your sins. ²⁵I will bring the sword against you, executing vengeance for the covenant; and if you withdraw within your cities, I will send pestilence among you, and you shall be delivered into enemy hands. ²⁶When I break your staff of bread, ten women shall bake your bread in a single oven, and they shall dole out your bread by weight; and though you eat, you shall not be satisfied.

27 But if, despite this, you disobey me, and continue hostile to me, ²⁸I will continue hostile to you in fury; I in turn will punish you myself sevenfold for your sins. ²⁹You shall eat the flesh of your sons, and you shall eat the flesh of your daughters. ³⁰I will destroy your high places and cut down your incense altars; I will heap your carcasses on the carcasses of your idols. I will abhor you. ³¹I will lay your cities waste, will make your sanctuaries desolate, and I will not smell your pleasing odors. ³²I will devastate the land, so that your enemies who come to settle in it shall be appalled at it. ³³And you I will scatter among the nations, and I will unsheathe the sword against you; your land shall be a desolation, and your cities a waste.

34 Then the land shall enjoy*a* its sabbath years as long as it lies desolate, while you are in the land of your enemies; then the land shall rest, and enjoy*a* its sabbath years. 35As long as it lies desolate, it shall have the rest it did not have on your sabbaths when you were living on it. 36And as for those of you who survive, I will send faintness into their hearts in the lands of their enemies; the sound of a driven leaf shall put them to flight, and they shall flee as one flees from the sword, and they shall fall though no one pursues. 37They shall stumble over one another, as if to escape a sword, though no one pursues; and you shall have no power to stand against your enemies. 38You shall perish among the nations, and the land of your enemies shall devour you. 39And those of you who survive shall languish in the land of your enemies because of their iniquities; also they shall languish because of the iniquities of their ancestors.

40 But if they confess their iniquity and the iniquity of their ancestors, in that they committed treachery against me and, moreover, that they continued hostile to me— 41so that I, in turn, continued hostile to them and brought them into the land of their enemies; if then their uncircumcised heart is humbled and they make amends for their iniquity, 42then will I remember my covenant with Jacob; I will remember also my covenant with Isaac and also my covenant with Abraham, and I will remember the land. 43For the land shall be deserted by them, and enjoy*a* its sabbath years by lying desolate without them, while they shall make amends for their iniquity, because they dared to spurn my ordinances, and they abhorred my statutes. 44Yet for all that, when they are in the land of their enemies, I will not spurn them, or abhor them so as to destroy them utterly and break my covenant with them; for I am the LORD their God; 45but I will remember in their favor the covenant with their ancestors whom I brought out of the land of Egypt in the sight of the nations, to be their God: I am the LORD.

26.32–45: These descriptions of deportation from the land of Canaan and life in exile in a foreign country recall northern Israel's experience under the Assyrian empire in 722 BCE (2 Kings 17) and southern Judah's later exile to Babylon in 587 BCE (2 Kings 24–25). On the *land* and its *sabbath years*, see 25.1–7. The *uncircumcised** *heart* (v. 41) is a metaphor* for Israel's stubborn and rebellious will (Deut 10.16). Circumcision* is a ritual involving cutting off the foreskin of the penis as a sign of belonging to the covenant* community.

46 These are the statutes and ordinances and laws that the LORD established between himself and the people of Israel on Mount Sinai through Moses.

27 The LORD spoke to Moses, saying: 2Speak to the people of Israel and say to them: When a person makes an explicit vow to the LORD concerning the equivalent for a human being, 3the equivalent for a male shall be: from twenty to sixty years of age the equivalent shall be fifty shekels of silver by the sanctuary shekel. 4If the person is a female, the equivalent is thirty shekels. 5If the age is from five to twenty years of age, the equivalent is twenty shekels for a male and ten shekels for a female. 6If the age is from one month to five years, the equivalent for a male is five shekels of silver, and for a female the equivalent is three shekels of silver. 7And if the person is sixty years old or over, then the equivalent for a male is fifteen shekels, and for a female ten shekels. 8If any cannot afford the equivalent, they shall be brought before the priest and the priest shall assess them; the priest shall assess them according to what each one making a vow can afford.

9 If it concerns an animal that may be brought as an offering to the LORD, any such that may be given to the LORD shall be holy. 10Another shall not be exchanged or substituted for it, either good for bad or bad for good; and if one animal is substituted for another, both that one and its substitute shall be holy. 11If it concerns any unclean animal that may not be brought as an offering to the LORD, the animal shall be presented before the priest. 12The priest shall assess it: whether good or bad, according to the as-

a Or *make up for*

sessment of the priest, so it shall be. 13But if it is to be redeemed, one-fifth must be added to the assessment.

14 If a person consecrates a house to the LORD, the priest shall assess it: whether good or bad, as the priest assesses it, so it shall stand. 15And if the one who consecrates the house wishes to redeem it, one-fifth shall be added to its assessed value, and it shall revert to the original owner.

16 If a person consecrates to the LORD any inherited landholding, its assessment shall be in accordance with its seed requirements: fifty shekels of silver to a homer of barley seed. 17If the person consecrates the field as of the year of jubilee, that assessment shall stand; 18but if the field is consecrated after the jubilee, the priest shall compute the price for it according to the years that remain until the year of jubilee, and the assessment shall be reduced. 19And if the one who consecrates the field wishes to redeem it, then one-fifth shall be added to its assessed value, and it shall revert to the original owner; 20but if the field is not redeemed, or if it has been sold to someone else, it shall no longer be redeemable. 21But when the field is released in the jubilee, it shall be holy to the LORD as a devoted field; it becomes the priest's holding. 22If someone consecrates to the LORD a field that has been purchased, which is not a part of the inherited landholding, 23the priest shall compute for it the proportionate assessment up to the year of jubilee, and the assessment shall be paid as of that day, a sacred donation to the LORD. 24In the year of jubilee the field shall return to the one from whom it was bought, whose holding the land is. 25All assessments shall be by the sanctuary shekel: twenty gerahs shall make a shekel.

26 A firstling of animals, however, which as a firstling belongs to the LORD, cannot be consecrated by anyone; whether ox or sheep, it is the LORD's. 27If it is an unclean animal, it shall be ransomed at its assessment, with one-fifth added; if it is not redeemed, it shall be sold at its assessment.

28 Nothing that a person owns that has been devoted to destruction for the LORD, be it human or animal, or inherited landholding, may be sold or redeemed; every devoted thing is most holy to the LORD. 29No human beings who have been devoted to destruction can be ransomed; they shall be put to death.

30 All tithes from the land, whether the seed from the ground or the fruit from the tree, are the LORD's; they are holy to the LORD. 31If persons wish to redeem any of their tithes, they must add one-fifth to them. 32All tithes of herd and flock, every tenth one that passes under the shepherd's staff, shall be holy to the LORD. 33Let no one inquire whether it is good or bad, or make substitution for it; if one makes substitution for it, then both it and the substitute shall be holy and cannot be redeemed.

34 These are the commandments that the LORD gave to Moses for the people of Israel on Mount Sinai.

27.1–34: The LORD issues rules for those who wish to redeem or buy back special sacrifices or donations previously dedicated to God. Persons often dedicated a gift to the sanctuary in the context of a vow to God made after experiencing a special blessing or deliverance from evil (1 Sam 1.11; Ps 66.13–15). 3: A shekel* is a standard unit of weight. 11, 27: On unclean animals, see ch. 11. 16: A homer is a standard unit of volume. 18: On the year of jubilee, see 25.8–24. 25: Both the shekel and the gerah are standard units of weight. 28–29: Devoted to destruction refers to property or humans taken as booty in holy war.* The booty is dedicated to God and thus could not be kept and used by lay people. Property and animals were given to the priests in the sanctuary, and humans were put to death. 30–33: A tithe is a one-tenth portion of a crop or flock that is given as an offering to God for use by the priests serving in the sanctuary. In Numbers, the tithe offering belongs to the Levites (Num 18.21). In Deuteronomy, the tithe offering reverts to the donor and is shared with the Levites, aliens, orphans, and widows (Deut 12.5–12; 26.10–13).

NUMBERS

Introduction

The book of Numbers, the fourth book of the Old Testament, derives its name from the two census lists that number the people in each of the twelve tribes of Israel (chs. 1, 26). The Hebrew title for the book, "In the Wilderness," comes from the first verse of the book and accurately describes its setting. Numbers is the story of the people of Israel in the wilderness as they travel from Egypt and the wilderness mountain of Sinai toward the promised land of Canaan. The most important transition in the story is the death of the old and rebellious generation of Israelites and the birth of a new generation of Israelites in the wilderness. This new generation of hope stands poised to enter the land of Canaan at the end of the book of Numbers.

An important feature of Numbers is its great variety of literary forms and topics. The reader will encounter a mixture of stories and laws, travel itineraries and census lists, lists of personal names and lists of instructions for worship, reports of military battles and accounts of legal disputes. Some of the material is earlier and some later in origin. However, this diverse collection of literature has been woven together into a coherent story of Israel's holy camp on the move through the wilderness.

The final form of the story of Numbers probably emerged in light of Israel's experience of exile★ in Babylon (587 BCE) and shortly after its return to the homeland of Judah (539 BCE). The passage from an old and rebellious generation that had died in the wilderness and the birth of a generation of hope provided an enduring paradigm for new generations of Israelites who returned home from exile to the promised land of Judah. The struggles, conflicts, and rebellions of Israel in the wilderness provided a mirror for Israel's struggles in exile and in its return to rebuild the Jewish community in Judah.

READING GUIDE

The transition from the old generation of the wilderness to the new generation of hope and promise on the edge of the promised land forms the primary theme and structure for the book of Numbers. This structure is marked by the two census lists of the twelve tribes of Israel in chs. 1 and 26. The first census list in Num 1 introduces the first half of the book, chs. 1–25. Israel's obedient preparations for the march through the wilderness in chs. 1–10 abruptly turn into Israel's disobedient rebellions against God and Moses in chs. 11–25. The climactic rebellion story is the spy story of chs. 13–14, the key narrative★ in Numbers. As a result of this growing rebellion against God, the old generation of Israelites is condemned to die in the wilderness and not allowed to enter the promised land of Canaan (14.20–38). However, the LORD promises to bring a new generation of young Israelites born during the wilderness journey into the land of Canaan (14.31).

The second census list in Num 26 marks the rise of this new generation of hope (26.63–65). This census list introduces the second half of the book, chs. 26–36, which displays a significantly different mood and tone. Whereas the first half of Numbers was dominated by themes of rebellion and death, this second half resonates with new life, hope, obedience, and the resolution of potential conflict through negotiation and dialogue.

The book of Numbers contains many well-known biblical passages and images. Some of them include the priestly benediction or blessing (ch. 6), manna as food for Israel in the wilderness (ch. 11), Miriam's leprosy (ch. 12), water from the rock (ch. 20), the bronze serpent (ch. 21), Balaam's talking donkey (ch. 22), and the bold daughters of Zelophehad (chs. 27, 36).

1–10	Preparations for Israel's march through the wilderness
11–20	The old generation's slide into rebellion and death
21–25	Signs of hope in the midst of the death of the old generation
26–36	The rise of a new generation on the edge of the promised land

A census of the twelve tribes of Israel
1.1–46: The purpose of this numbering of Israelite males over twenty years of age is to determine the number of soldiers who will be *able to go to war* (v. 3) in the upcoming battles for the conquest of Canaan. However, the later rebellions of this generation of Israelites will disqualify them from taking part in the battles for Canaan (chs. 13–14). A similar census in ch. 26 will number an entirely new generation of Israelites whom the LORD will allow to enter the promised land of Canaan (26.63–65).

1 The LORD spoke to Moses in the wilderness of Sinai, in the tent of meeting, on the first day of the second month, in the second year after they had come out of the land of Egypt, saying: ²Take a census of the whole congregation of Israelites, in their clans, by ancestral houses, according to the number of names, every male individually; ³from twenty years old and upward, everyone in Israel able to go to war. You and Aaron shall enroll them, company by company. ⁴A man from each tribe shall be with you, each man the head of his ancestral house. ⁵These are the names of the men who shall assist you:

From Reuben, Elizur son of Shedeur.
6 From Simeon, Shelumiel son of Zurishaddai.
7 From Judah, Nahshon son of Amminadab.
8 From Issachar, Nethanel son of Zuar.
9 From Zebulun, Eliab son of Helon.
10 From the sons of Joseph:
from Ephraim, Elishama son of Ammihud;
from Manasseh, Gamaliel son of Pedahzur.
11 From Benjamin, Abidan son of Gideoni.
12 From Dan, Ahiezer son of Ammishaddai.
13 From Asher, Pagiel son of Ochran.
14 From Gad, Eliasaph son of Deuel.
15 From Naphtali, Ahira son of Enan.
16These were the ones chosen from the congregation, the leaders of their ancestral tribes, the heads of the divisions of Israel.

1.1–16. 1: Israel's camp has been situated in *the wilderness of Sinai* since Ex 19.1–2. The *tent of meeting* covers the tabernacle*, a portable sanctuary or shrine. The tent is the place where Moses, the leader of Israel, receives oracles* and instructions from the LORD. Formerly, the tent of meeting stood outside Israel's camp, but now it will be situated in the middle of the camp (see Ex 33.7–11; Num 2.2). *The first day of the second month* means one month has elapsed since Israel finished constructing the portable tabernacle or shrine (Ex 40.17). **2:** Israel was divided into twelve tribes. Each tribe contained a number of smaller groups called *clans**. Each clan in turn contained a number of smaller family groups called *ancestral houses*. **5–15:** This list of the twelve tribes of Israel largely reflects the sequence of the births of the twelve sons of Jacob in Gen 29.31–30.24 and Gen 35.16–18, grouped according to the status of their mothers. The children of Leah and Rachel (Jacob's favored wives) are listed first. The children born of the servant women (Bilhah and Zilpah) are listed last.

17 Moses and Aaron took these men who had been designated by name, ¹⁸and on the first day of the second month they assembled the whole congregation together. They registered themselves in their clans, by their ancestral houses, according to the number of names from twenty years old and upward,

individually, 19 as the LORD commanded Moses. So he enrolled them in the wilderness of Sinai.

20 The descendants of Reuben, Israel's firstborn, their lineage, in their clans, by their ancestral houses, according to the number of names, individually, every male from twenty years old and upward, everyone able to go to war: 21 those enrolled of the tribe of Reuben were forty-six thousand five hundred.

22 The descendants of Simeon, their lineage, in their clans, by their ancestral houses, those of them that were numbered, according to the number of names, individually, every male from twenty years old and upward, everyone able to go to war: 23 those enrolled of the tribe of Simeon were fifty-nine thousand three hundred.

24 The descendants of Gad, their lineage, in their clans, by their ancestral houses, according to the number of the names, from twenty years old and upward, everyone able to go to war: 25 those enrolled of the tribe of Gad were forty-five thousand six hundred fifty.

26 The descendants of Judah, their lineage, in their clans, by their ancestral houses, according to the number of names, from twenty years old and upward, everyone able to go to war: 27 those enrolled of the tribe of Judah were seventy-four thousand six hundred.

28 The descendants of Issachar, their lineage, in their clans, by their ancestral houses, according to the number of names, from twenty years old and upward, everyone able to go to war: 29 those enrolled of the tribe of Issachar were fifty-four thousand four hundred.

30 The descendants of Zebulun, their lineage, in their clans, by their ancestral houses, according to the number of names, from twenty years old and upward, everyone able to go to war: 31 those enrolled of the tribe of Zebulun were fifty-seven thousand four hundred.

32 The descendants of Joseph, namely, the descendants of Ephraim, their lineage, in their clans, by their ancestral houses, according to the number of names, from twenty years old and upward, everyone able to go to war: 33 those enrolled of the tribe of Ephraim were forty thousand five hundred.

34 The descendants of Manasseh, their lineage, in their clans, by their ancestral houses, according to the number of names, from twenty years old and upward, everyone able to go to war: 35 those enrolled of the tribe of Manasseh were thirty-two thousand two hundred.

36 The descendants of Benjamin, their lineage, in their clans, by their ancestral houses, according to the number of names, from twenty years old and upward, everyone able to go to war: 37 those enrolled of the tribe of Benjamin were thirty-five thousand four hundred.

38 The descendants of Dan, their lineage, in their clans, by their ancestral houses, according to the number of names, from twenty years old and upward, everyone able to go to war: 39 those enrolled of the tribe of Dan were sixty-two thousand seven hundred.

40 The descendants of Asher, their lineage, in their clans, by their ancestral houses, according to the number of names, from twenty years old and upward, everyone able to go to war: 41 those enrolled of the tribe of Asher were forty-one thousand five hundred.

42 The descendants of Naphtali, their lineage, in their clans, by their ancestral houses, according to the number of names, from twenty years old and upward, everyone able to go to war: 43 those enrolled of the tribe of Naphtali were fifty-three thousand four hundred.

44 These are those who were enrolled, whom Moses and Aaron enrolled with the help of the leaders of Israel, twelve men, each representing his ancestral house. 45 So the whole number of the Israelites, by their ancestral houses, from twenty years old and upward, everyone able to go to war in Israel— 46 their whole number was six hundred three thousand five hundred fifty. 47 The Levites, however, were not numbered by their ancestral tribe along with them.

48 The LORD had said to Moses: 49 Only the tribe of Levi you shall not enroll, and you

shall not take a census of them with the other Israelites. ⁵⁰Rather you shall appoint the Levites over the tabernacle of the covenant,ᵃ and over all its equipment, and over all that belongs to it; they are to carry the tabernacle and all its equipment, and they shall tend it, and shall camp around the tabernacle. ⁵¹When the tabernacle is to set out, the Levites shall take it down; and when the tabernacle is to be pitched, the Levites shall set it up. And any outsider who comes near shall be put to death. ⁵²The other Israelites shall camp in their respective regimental camps, by companies; ⁵³but the Levites shall camp around the tabernacle of the covenant,ᵃ that there may be no wrath on the congregation of the Israelites; and the Levites shall perform the guard duty of the tabernacle of the covenant.ᵃ ⁵⁴The Israelites did so; they did just as the LORD commanded Moses.

1.17–54. 17–46: The numbers for each individual tribe as well as the total number of male warriors for all twelve tribes (603,550; vv. 44–46) have seemed impossibly high to many commentators. The number of soldiers assumes a total population of men, women, and children of around two million Israelites. Several solutions have been offered to bring down the number to a more plausible figure. However, the present form of the text assumes the full number of 603,550 Israelite soldiers. As such, the census numbers demonstrate the LORD's partial fulfillment of the promises of innumerable descendants made earlier to Israel's ancestors (Gen 15.5; 22.17). **47–54:** *The tribe of Levi* (v. 49) stands apart as a priestly tribe exempted from military service and dedicated to the care and administration of *the tabernacle of the covenant*⋆ (v. 50). Therefore, the Levites have their own separate census. *The tabernacle* is the portable sanctuary or shrine at which the powerful and holy presence of God could be present in the midst of the Israelites. The Levites camp around the tabernacle as a protective buffer between God's presence and the rest of the Israelite camp so *that there may be no wrath on the congregation of the Israelites* (v. 53). An *outsider* in this case is anyone who is not from the priestly tribe of Levi (v. 51).

2 The LORD spoke to Moses and Aaron, saying: ²The Israelites shall camp each in their respective regiments, under ensigns by their ancestral houses; they shall camp facing the tent of meeting on every side. ³Those to camp on the east side toward the sunrise shall be of the regimental encampment of Judah by companies. The leader of the people of Judah shall be Nahshon son of Amminadab, ⁴with a company as enrolled of seventy-four thousand six hundred. ⁵Those to camp next to him shall be the tribe of Issachar. The leader of the Issacharites shall be Nethanel son of Zuar, ⁶with a company as enrolled of fifty-four thousand four hundred. ⁷Then the tribe of Zebulun: The leader of the Zebulunites shall be Eliab son of Helon, ⁸with a company as enrolled of fifty-seven thousand four hundred. ⁹The total enrollment of the camp of Judah, by companies, is one hundred eighty-six thousand four hundred. They shall set out first on the march.

10 On the south side shall be the regimental encampment of Reuben by companies. The leader of the Reubenites shall be Elizur son of Shedeur, ¹¹with a company as enrolled of forty-six thousand five hundred. ¹²And those to camp next to him shall be the tribe of Simeon. The leader of the Simeonites shall be Shelumiel son of Zurishaddai, ¹³with a company as enrolled of fifty-nine thousand three hundred. ¹⁴Then the tribe of Gad: The leader of the Gadites shall be Eliasaph son of Reuel, ¹⁵with a company as enrolled of forty-five thousand six hundred fifty. ¹⁶The total enrollment of the camp of Reuben, by companies, is one hundred fifty-one thousand four hundred fifty. They shall set out second.

17 The tent of meeting, with the camp of the Levites, shall set out in the center of the camps; they shall set out just as they camp, each in position, by their regiments.

18 On the west side shall be the regimental encampment of Ephraim by companies. The leader of the people of Ephraim shall be Elishama son of Ammihud, ¹⁹with a company as enrolled of forty thousand five hundred. ²⁰Next to him shall be the tribe of Manasseh. The leader of the people of Manasseh shall be Gamaliel son of Pedah-

ᵃ Or *treaty*, or *testimony*; Heb *eduth*

zur, 21with a company as enrolled of thirty-two thousand two hundred. 22Then the tribe of Benjamin: The leader of the Benjaminites shall be Abidan son of Gideoni, 23with a company as enrolled of thirty-five thousand four hundred. 24The total enrollment of the camp of Ephraim, by companies, is one hundred eight thousand one hundred. They shall set out third on the march.

25 On the north side shall be the regimental encampment of Dan by companies. The leader of the Danites shall be Ahiezer son of Ammishaddai, 26with a company as enrolled of sixty-two thousand seven hundred. 27Those to camp next to him shall be the tribe of Asher. The leader of the Asherites shall be Pagiel son of Ochran, 28with a company as enrolled of forty-one thousand five hundred. 29Then the tribe of Naphtali: The leader of the Naphtalites shall be Ahira son of Enan, 30with a company as enrolled of fifty-three thousand four hundred. 31The total enrollment of the camp of Dan is one hundred fifty-seven thousand six hundred. They shall set out last, by companies.a

32 This was the enrollment of the Israelites by their ancestral houses; the total enrollment in the camps by their companies was six hundred three thousand five hundred fifty. 33Just as the LORD had commanded Moses, the Levites were not enrolled among the other Israelites.

34 The Israelites did just as the LORD had commanded Moses: They camped by regiments, and they set out the same way, everyone by clans, according to ancestral houses.

2.1–34: The arrangement of Israel's camp and the order of marching. The tent of meeting, which contains the tabernacle* or portable sanctuary, stands in the middle of the Israelite camp (vv. 2, 17). The Levites form a protective inner circle around the tent of meeting (1.53). In the outer circle of the camp, the twelve tribes divide into four groups of three tribes each. Each group of three tribes camps at one of the four cardinal points (east, south, west, north) relative to the tent of meeting. **2:** *Ensigns* are symbols or flags with unique designs that represent the individual *ancestral houses* or family groups. **3:** The order of march begins with the eastern tribes led by *Judah*, the preeminent tribe

among the twelve. Then the tribes of the south (vv. 10–16), the tent of meeting and Levites (v. 17), the tribes of the west (vv. 18–24), and the tribes of the north (vv. 25–31) follow in order during the march. **32:** On the incredibly large number of Israelites who were counted in the census, see comment on 1.17–46.

---

3 This is the lineage of Aaron and Moses at the time when the LORD spoke with Moses on Mount Sinai. 2These are the names of the sons of Aaron: Nadab the first-born, and Abihu, Eleazar, and Ithamar; 3these are the names of the sons of Aaron, the anointed priests, whom he ordained to minister as priests. 4Nadab and Abihu died before the LORD when they offered unholy fire before the LORD in the wilderness of Sinai, and they had no children. Eleazar and Ithamar served as priests in the lifetime of their father Aaron.

5 Then the LORD spoke to Moses, saying: 6Bring the tribe of Levi near, and set them before Aaron the priest, so that they may assist him. 7They shall perform duties for him and for the whole congregation in front of the tent of meeting, doing service at the tabernacle; 8they shall be in charge of all the furnishings of the tent of meeting, and attend to the duties for the Israelites as they do service at the tabernacle. 9You shall give the Levites to Aaron and his descendants; they are unreservedly given to him from among the Israelites. 10But you shall make a register of Aaron and his descendants; it is they who shall attend to the priesthood, and any outsider who comes near shall be put to death.

11 Then the LORD spoke to Moses, saying: 12I hereby accept the Levites from among the Israelites as substitutes for all the firstborn that open the womb among the Israelites. The Levites shall be mine, 13for all the firstborn are mine; when I killed all the firstborn in the land of Egypt, I consecrated for my own all the firstborn in Israel, both human and animal; they shall be mine. I am the LORD.

14 Then the LORD spoke to Moses in the

---

a Compare verses 9, 16, 24: Heb *by their regiments*

wilderness of Sinai, saying: 15Enroll the Levites by ancestral houses and by clans. You shall enroll every male from a month old and upward. 16So Moses enrolled them according to the word of the LORD, as he was commanded. 17The following were the sons of Levi, by their names: Gershon, Kohath, and Merari. 18These are the names of the sons of Gershon by their clans: Libni and Shimei. 19The sons of Kohath by their clans: Amram, Izhar, Hebron, and Uzziel. 20The sons of Merari by their clans: Mahli and Mushi. These are the clans of the Levites, by their ancestral houses.

21 To Gershon belonged the clan of the Libnites and the clan of the Shimeites; these were the clans of the Gershonites. 22Their enrollment, counting all the males from a month old and upward, was seven thousand five hundred. 23The clans of the Gershonites were to camp behind the tabernacle on the west, 24with Eliasaph son of Lael as head of the ancestral house of the Gershonites. 25The responsibility of the sons of Gershon in the tent of meeting was to be the tabernacle, the tent with its covering, the screen for the entrance of the tent of meeting, 26the hangings of the court, the screen for the entrance of the court that is around the tabernacle and the altar, and its cords—all the service pertaining to these.

27 To Kohath belonged the clan of the Amramites, the clan of the Izharites, the clan of the Hebronites, and the clan of the Uzzielites; these are the clans of the Kohathites. 28Counting all the males, from a month old and upward, there were eight thousand six hundred, attending to the duties of the sanctuary. 29The clans of the Kohathites were to camp on the south side of the tabernacle, 30with Elizaphan son of Uzziel as head of the ancestral house of the clans of the Kohathites. 31Their responsibility was to be the ark, the table, the lampstand, the altars, the vessels of the sanctuary with which the priests minister, and the screen—all the service pertaining to these. 32Eleazar son of Aaron the priest was to be chief over the leaders of the Levites, and to have oversight of those who had charge of the sanctuary.

33 To Merari belonged the clan of the Mahlites and the clan of the Mushites: these are the clans of Merari. 34Their enrollment, counting all the males from a month old and upward, was six thousand two hundred. 35The head of the ancestral house of the clans of Merari was Zuriel son of Abihail; they were to camp on the north side of the tabernacle. 36The responsibility assigned to the sons of Merari was to be the frames of the tabernacle, the bars, the pillars, the bases, and all their accessories—all the service pertaining to these; 37also the pillars of the court all around, with their bases and pegs and cords.

38 Those who were to camp in front of the tabernacle on the east—in front of the tent of meeting toward the east—were Moses and Aaron and Aaron's sons, having charge of the rites within the sanctuary, whatever had to be done for the Israelites; and any outsider who came near was to be put to death. 39The total enrollment of the Levites whom Moses and Aaron enrolled at the commandment of the LORD, by their clans, all the males from a month old and upward, was twenty-two thousand.

3.1–51: The duties, census, and function of the Levites. 1: The two leaders, Aaron and Moses, are listed here because they are brothers and both belong to the tribe of Levi (see Ex 6.23). **3:** *The sons of Aaron* are special *anointed* priests whom the other Levites assist (v. 6). **4:** The story of the death of Nadab and Abihu occurs in Lev 10.1–7. **8:** On *the tent of meeting* and the *tabernacle,* see comment on 1.1. **10:** An *outsider* is anyone who is not from the priestly tribe of Levi (see also v. 38). **11–13:** Earlier laws (Ex 13.2; 22.29–30) commanded that all human firstborn male children should be given to the LORD. This entailed either a lifetime of religious service or being redeemed or bought back through animal sacrifices or monetary offerings. However, this law allows the whole tribe of Levi to function as substitutes for the other Israelite firstborn children. **15:** The earlier census of the twelve tribes had counted all the males twenty years and older (1.3). The census of the Levites counts all the males who are one month and older, since they will be substitutes for all Israelite firstborn males who are one month or older (vv. 40–43). **17–39:** The three clans* of the Levites surround the tabernacle or portable shrine on three sides: the *Gershonites* on the *west* (v. 23), the *Kohath-*

ites on the *south* (v. 29), and the *clans of Merari* on the *north* (v. 35). The prestigious eastern side of the tabernacle is occupied by the families of *Moses and Aaron and Aaron's sons* (v. 38). An *outsider* is any person not from the tribe of Levi (v. 38). On details on the *ark* (v. 31), the furnishings of the *tabernacle* (v. 23), and the *tent of meeting* (v. 25), see Ex 25–27; 30.

40 Then the LORD said to Moses: Enroll all the firstborn males of the Israelites, from a month old and upward, and count their names. 41But you shall accept the Levites for me—I am the LORD—as substitutes for all the firstborn among the Israelites, and the livestock of the Levites as substitutes for all the firstborn among the livestock of the Israelites. 42So Moses enrolled all the firstborn among the Israelites, as the LORD commanded him. 43The total enrollment, all the firstborn males from a month old and upward, counting the number of names, was twenty-two thousand two hundred seventy-three.

44 Then the LORD spoke to Moses, saying: 45Accept the Levites as substitutes for all the firstborn among the Israelites, and the livestock of the Levites as substitutes for their livestock; and the Levites shall be mine. I am the LORD. 46As the price of redemption of the two hundred seventy-three of the firstborn of the Israelites, over and above the number of the Levites, 47you shall accept five shekels apiece, reckoning by the shekel of the sanctuary, a shekel of twenty gerahs. 48Give to Aaron and his sons the money by which the excess number of them is redeemed. 49So Moses took the redemption money from those who were over and above those redeemed by the Levites; 50from the firstborn of the Israelites he took the money, one thousand three hundred sixty-five shekels, reckoned by the shekel of the sanctuary; 51and Moses gave the redemption money to Aaron and his sons, according to the word of the LORD, as the LORD had commanded Moses.

3.40–51: The total number of Levites who could be substitutes for the other Israelite firstborn children was 22,000 (v. 39). The total number of Israelite firstborn was 22,273 (v. 43). The remaining 273 Israelite first-

born could be redeemed or purchased back for *five shekels** each (vv. 46–47). The *shekel* and the *gerah* were standard units of weight used in calculating the monetary value of silver and gold. The *shekel of the sanctuary* was the governing standard for the weight of the shekel (v. 47).

A second census of Levites eligible for priestly duties

4.1–49: The earlier census of the Levites (3.14–39) had determined the number of Levites available to substitute for other Israelite firstborn males. This second levitical census numbers those who are 30–50 years old and thus eligible for priestly service.

4 The LORD spoke to Moses and Aaron, saying: 2Take a census of the Kohathites separate from the other Levites, by their clans and their ancestral houses, 3from thirty years old up to fifty years old, all who qualify to do work relating to the tent of meeting. 4The service of the Kohathites relating to the tent of meeting concerns the most holy things.

5 When the camp is to set out, Aaron and his sons shall go in and take down the screening curtain, and cover the ark of the covenant*a* with it; 6then they shall put on it a covering of fine leather,*b* and spread over that a cloth all of blue, and shall put its poles in place. 7Over the table of the bread of the Presence they shall spread a blue cloth, and put on it the plates, the dishes for incense, the bowls, and the flagons for the drink offering; the regular bread also shall be on it; 8then they shall spread over them a crimson cloth, and cover it with a covering of fine leather,*b* and shall put its poles in place. 9They shall take a blue cloth, and cover the lampstand for the light, with its lamps, its snuffers*, its trays, and all the vessels for oil with which it is supplied; 10and they shall put it with all its utensils in a covering of fine leather,*b* and put it on the carrying frame. 11Over the golden altar they shall spread a blue cloth, and cover it with a covering of fine leather,*b* and shall put its poles in place; 12and they shall take all the utensils of the

a Or *treaty*, or *testimony*; Heb *eduth*   *b* Meaning of Heb uncertain service that are used in the sanctuary, and put them in a blue cloth, and cover them with a covering of fine leather,^a and put them on the carrying frame. ¹³They shall take away the ashes from the altar, and spread a purple cloth over it; ¹⁴and they shall put on it all the utensils of the altar, which are used for the service there, the firepans, the forks, the shovels, and the basins, all the utensils of the altar; and they shall spread on it a covering of fine leather,^a and shall put its poles in place. ¹⁵When Aaron and his sons have finished covering the sanctuary and all the furnishings of the sanctuary, as the camp sets out, after that the Kohathites shall come to carry these, but they must not touch the holy things, or they will die. These are the things of the tent of meeting that the Kohathites are to carry.

16 Eleazar son of Aaron the priest shall have charge of the oil for the light, the fragrant incense, the regular grain offering, and the anointing oil, the oversight of all the tabernacle and all that is in it, in the sanctuary and in its utensils.

17 Then the LORD spoke to Moses and Aaron, saying: ¹⁸You must not let the tribe of the clans of the Kohathites be destroyed from among the Levites. ¹⁹This is how you must deal with them in order that they may live and not die when they come near to the most holy things: Aaron and his sons shall go in and assign each to a particular task or burden. ²⁰But the Kohathites^b must not go in to look on the holy things even for a moment; otherwise they will die.

21 Then the LORD spoke to Moses, saying: ²²Take a census of the Gershonites also, by their ancestral houses and by their clans; ²³from thirty years old up to fifty years old you shall enroll them, all who qualify to do work in the tent of meeting. ²⁴This is the service of the clans of the Gershonites, in serving and bearing burdens: ²⁵They shall carry the curtains of the tabernacle, and the tent of meeting with its covering, and the outer covering of fine leather^a that is on top of it, and the screen for the entrance of the tent of meeting, ²⁶and the hangings of the court, and the screen for the entrance of the gate of the court that is around the tab-

ernacle and the altar, and their cords, and all the equipment for their service; and they shall do all that needs to be done with regard to them. ²⁷All the service of the Gershonites shall be at the command of Aaron and his sons, in all that they are to carry, and in all that they have to do; and you shall assign to their charge all that they are to carry. ²⁸This is the service of the clans of the Gershonites relating to the tent of meeting, and their responsibilities are to be under the oversight of Ithamar son of Aaron the priest.

29 As for the Merarites, you shall enroll them by their clans and their ancestral houses; ³⁰from thirty years old up to fifty years old you shall enroll them, everyone who qualifies to do the work of the tent of meeting. ³¹This is what they are charged to carry, as the whole of their service in the tent of meeting: the frames of the tabernacle, with its bars, pillars, and bases, ³²and the pillars of the court all around with their bases, pegs, and cords, with all their equipment and all their related service; and you shall assign by name the objects that they are required to carry. ³³This is the service of the clans of the Merarites, the whole of their service relating to the tent of meeting, under the hand of Ithamar son of Aaron the priest.

4.4–33: *The ark of the covenant*✶ (v. 5) is a wooden container that contains the stone tablets of the Ten Commandments and also functions as a throne or footstool for the divine presence (Ex 25.10–22). The ark is housed in the inner room of the tabernacle within the tent of meeting. On details of the ark, the tabernacle furnishings, and the tent of meeting, see Ex 25–27; 30. The warning concerning the special danger to the Kohathites (vv. 17–20) stems from their responsibility to handle *the most holy things* (v. 4).

---

34 So Moses and Aaron and the leaders of the congregation enrolled the Kohathites, by their clans and their ancestral houses, ³⁵from thirty years old up to fifty years old, everyone who qualified for work relating to the tent of meeting; ³⁶and their enrollment by clans was two thousand seven hundred fifty. ³⁷This was the enrollment of the clans

a Meaning of Heb uncertain   *b* Heb *they*

of the Kohathites, all who served at the tent of meeting, whom Moses and Aaron enrolled according to the commandment of the LORD by Moses.

38 The enrollment of the Gershonites, by their clans and their ancestral houses, [39]from thirty years old up to fifty years old, everyone who qualified for work relating to the tent of meeting— [40]their enrollment by their clans and their ancestral houses was two thousand six hundred thirty. [41]This was the enrollment of the clans of the Gershonites, all who served at the tent of meeting, whom Moses and Aaron enrolled according to the commandment of the LORD.

42 The enrollment of the clans of the Merarites, by their clans and their ancestral houses, [43]from thirty years old up to fifty years old, everyone who qualified for work relating to the tent of meeting— [44]their enrollment by their clans was three thousand two hundred. [45]This is the enrollment of the clans of the Merarites, whom Moses and Aaron enrolled according to the commandment of the LORD by Moses.

46 All those who were enrolled of the Levites, whom Moses and Aaron and the leaders of Israel enrolled, by their clans and their ancestral houses, [47]from thirty years old up to fifty years old, everyone who qualified to do the work of service and the work of bearing burdens relating to the tent of meeting, [48]their enrollment was eight thousand five hundred eighty. [49]According to the commandment of the LORD through Moses they were appointed to their several tasks of serving or carrying; thus they were enrolled by him, as the LORD commanded Moses.

5 The LORD spoke to Moses, saying: [2]Command the Israelites to put out of the camp everyone who is leprous,[a] or has a discharge, and everyone who is unclean through contact with a corpse; [3]you shall put out both male and female, putting them outside the camp; they must not defile their camp, where I dwell among them. [4]The Israelites did so, putting them outside the camp; as the LORD had spoken to Moses, so the Israelites did.

5 The LORD spoke to Moses, saying: [6]Speak to the Israelites: When a man or a woman wrongs another, breaking faith with the LORD, that person incurs guilt [7]and shall confess the sin that has been committed. The person shall make full restitution for the wrong, adding one-fifth to it, and giving it to the one who was wronged. [8]If the injured party has no next of kin to whom restitution may be made for the wrong, the restitution for wrong shall go to the LORD for the priest, in addition to the ram of atonement with which atonement is made for the guilty party. [9]Among all the sacred donations of the Israelites, every gift that they bring to the priest shall be his. [10]The sacred donations of all are their own; whatever anyone gives to the priest shall be his.

5.1–10: Impurity and sins against the neighbor. This section begins a series of laws in chs. 5–6 designed to preserve the holiness and purity of the Israelite camp. **1–4:** Since the Israelite camp contains the tabernacle where, the LORD says, *I dwell among them,* the ritual purity of the camp and its inhabitants must be preserved. On the concept of ritual purity and defilement, see sidebar, "Ritual Purity and Cleanness," p. 136. Three causes of impurity are named here: *leprous* or diseased skin (see Lev 13), a genital *discharge* (see Lev 15), or *contact with a corpse* (see Num 19.11–13). **5–9:** This legal case is an addition to the law of restitution to injured parties and their families in Lev 6.1–7. The case stipulates procedures when *the injured party has no next of kin to whom restitution may be made* (v. 8). On the *ram of atonement*[*] (v. 8), see Lev 6.6–7.

---

11 The LORD spoke to Moses, saying: [12]Speak to the Israelites and say to them: If any man's wife goes astray and is unfaithful to him, [13]if a man has had intercourse with her but it is hidden from her husband, so that she is undetected though she has defiled herself, and there is no witness against her since she was not caught in the act; [14]if a spirit of jealousy comes on him, and he is jealous of his wife who has defiled herself; or if a spirit of jealousy comes on him, and he is jealous of his wife, though she has not defiled herself; [15]then the man shall bring

a A term for several skin diseases; precise meaning uncertain

his wife to the priest. And he shall bring the offering required for her, one-tenth of an ephah of barley flour. He shall pour no oil on it and put no frankincense on it, for it is a grain offering of jealousy, a grain offering of remembrance, bringing iniquity to remembrance.

16 Then the priest shall bring her near, and set her before the LORD; 17the priest shall take holy water in an earthen vessel, and take some of the dust that is on the floor of the tabernacle and put it into the water. 18The priest shall set the woman before the LORD, dishevel the woman's hair, and place in her hands the grain offering of remembrance, which is the grain offering of jealousy. In his own hand the priest shall have the water of bitterness that brings the curse. 19Then the priest shall make her take an oath, saying, "If no man has lain with you, if you have not turned aside to uncleanness while under your husband's authority, be immune to this water of bitterness that brings the curse. 20But if you have gone astray while under your husband's authority, if you have defiled yourself and some man other than your husband has had intercourse with you," 21—let the priest make the woman take the oath of the curse and say to the woman—"the LORD make you an execration and an oath among your people, when the LORD makes your uterus drop, your womb discharge; 22now may this water that brings the curse enter your bowels and make your womb discharge, your uterus drop!" And the woman shall say, "Amen. Amen."

23 Then the priest shall put these curses in writing, and wash them off into the water of bitterness. 24He shall make the woman drink the water of bitterness that brings the curse, and the water that brings the curse shall enter her and cause bitter pain. 25The priest shall take the grain offering of jealousy out of the woman's hand, and shall elevate the grain offering before the LORD and bring it to the altar; 26and the priest shall take a handful of the grain offering, as its memorial portion, and turn it into smoke on the altar, and afterward shall make the woman drink the water. 27When he has made her drink the water, then, if she has defiled herself and has been unfaithful to her husband, the water that brings the curse shall enter into her and cause bitter pain, and her womb shall discharge, her uterus drop, and the woman shall become an execration among her people. 28But if the woman has not defiled herself and is clean, then she shall be immune and be able to conceive children.

29 This is the law in cases of jealousy, when a wife, while under her husband's authority, goes astray and defiles herself, 30or when a spirit of jealousy comes on a man and he is jealous of his wife; then he shall set the woman before the LORD, and the priest shall apply this entire law to her. 31The man shall be free from iniquity, but the woman shall bear her iniquity.

5.11–31: The case of a woman suspected of adultery. Those convicted of adultery by the evidence of witnesses were subject to the death penalty (Lev 20.10). This supplemental case involves instances in which a husband has a suspicion of adultery or *a spirit of jealousy* (v. 14) but *there is no witness against her* (v. 13). **15:** An *ephah* is a unit of dry measure, roughly half a bushel. Grain offerings were typically accompanied by olive *oil* and *frankincense*, an aromatic spice (Lev 2.1), but this is a special *grain offering of jealousy* and *remembrance*. **17:** The *holy water* is the water used by the priests for ritual washing and purification (Ex 30.17–21, 28–29). **18:** To *dishevel the hair* is a custom associated with mourning (Lev 10.6) or a sign of uncleanness (Lev 13.45). **19–28:** The oath forms the basis for the trial by ordeal, a practice known elsewhere in the ancient world. The woman expresses her acceptance of the trial and the oath by saying, "*Amen, amen*" (v. 22). When the woman drinks the holy *water of bitterness* (v. 19), two results are possible. If she is indeed guilty of adultery as the husband suspected, she will suffer a collapsed uterus and become an *execration* (v. 27), that is, a person under a curse. If she is not guilty, she will be *immune* from the effects of the bitter water and *able to conceive children* (v. 28). **31:** The husband will be *free from iniquity* and not suffer punishment if his wife proves to be innocent through the ordeal. He has the right to request that his wife go through the trial by ordeal.

6 The LORD spoke to Moses, saying: 2Speak to the Israelites and say to them: When either men or women make a special

vow, the vow of a nazirite,[a] to separate themselves to the LORD, [3]they shall separate themselves from wine and strong drink; they shall drink no wine vinegar or other vinegar, and shall not drink any grape juice or eat grapes, fresh or dried. [4]All their days as nazirites[b] they shall eat nothing that is produced by the grapevine, not even the seeds or the skins.

5 All the days of their nazirite vow no razor shall come upon the head; until the time is completed for which they separate themselves to the LORD, they shall be holy; they shall let the locks of the head grow long.

6 All the days that they separate themselves to the LORD they shall not go near a corpse. [7]Even if their father or mother, brother or sister, should die, they may not defile themselves; because their consecration to God is upon the head. [8]All their days as nazirites[b] they are holy to the LORD.

9 If someone dies very suddenly nearby, defiling the consecrated head, then they shall shave the head on the day of their cleansing; on the seventh day they shall shave it. [10]On the eighth day they shall bring two turtledoves or two young pigeons to the priest at the entrance of the tent of meeting, [11]and the priest shall offer one as a sin offering and the other as a burnt offering, and make atonement for them, because they incurred guilt by reason of the corpse. They shall sanctify the head that same day, [12]and separate themselves to the LORD for their days as nazirites,[b] and bring a male lamb a year old as a guilt offering. The former time shall be void, because the consecrated head was defiled.

13 This is the law for the nazirites[b] when the time of their consecration has been completed: they shall be brought to the entrance of the tent of meeting, [14]and they shall offer their gift to the LORD, one male lamb a year old without blemish as a burnt offering, one ewe lamb a year old without blemish as a sin offering, one ram without blemish as an offering of well-being, [15]and a basket of unleavened bread, cakes of choice flour mixed with oil and unleavened wafers spread with oil, with their grain offering and their drink offerings. [16]The priest shall present them before the LORD and offer their sin offering and burnt offering, [17]and shall offer the ram as a sacrifice of well-being to the LORD, with the basket of unleavened bread; the priest also shall make the accompanying grain offering and drink offering. [18]Then the nazirites[b] shall shave the consecrated head at the entrance of the tent of meeting, and shall take the hair from the consecrated head and put it on the fire under the sacrifice of well-being. [19]The priest shall take the shoulder of the ram, when it is boiled, and one unleavened cake out of the basket, and one unleavened wafer, and shall put them in the palms of the nazirites,[b] after they have shaved the consecrated head. [20]Then the priest shall elevate them as an elevation offering before the LORD; they are a holy portion for the priest, together with the breast that is elevated and the thigh that is offered. After that the nazirites[b] may drink wine.

21 This is the law for the nazirites[b] who take a vow. Their offering to the LORD must be in accordance with the nazirite[a] vow, apart from what else they can afford. In accordance with whatever vow they take, so they shall do, following the law for their consecration.

6.1–21: The vow of the nazirites. Nazirites were men and women who took vows to offer themselves for special service to the LORD for a specified time. Biblical examples of lifelong nazirites include Samson (Judg 13.2–14) and Samuel (1 Sam 1.11). The nazirite law here assumes a limited duration of special service, not a lifetime. **7:** *Consecration* means dedication to special service to God. **9–12:** *Suddenly* and unexpectedly coming in contact with a corpse causes the nazirite to become ritually unclean (*defiling the consecrated head*, v. 9). Such defilement requires the nazirite to be ritually cleansed and rededicated. **13–20:** On the background of the various offerings to mark the end of the nazirite's vow, see Lev 1–4. On the *elevation offering*, see Lev 7.32–34.

22 The LORD spoke to Moses, saying: [23]Speak to Aaron and his sons, saying, Thus

---

a That is *one separated* or *one consecrated* b That is *those separated* or *those consecrated* you shall bless the Israelites: You shall say to them,

24 The LORD bless you and keep you;
25 the LORD make his face to shine upon
　　you, and be gracious to you;
26 the LORD lift up his countenance upon
　　you, and give you peace.

27 So they shall put my name on the Israelites, and I will bless them.

6.22–27: The priestly blessing. Priests concluded communal worship with these words of blessing and peace. Two silver cylinders discovered by archaeologists and dated to 600 BCE contain portions of this ancient priestly blessing written in Hebrew. To *shine* the *face* and *lift up* the *countenance* or "face of the LORD" are images of protection, favor, and graciousness (vv. 25–26; see Ps 67.1–2; Job 34.29). *Peace* ("shalom") connotes well-being and wholeness in all aspects of one's life (v. 26). Putting the divine *name on the Israelites* implies that they belong exclusively to the LORD and that the LORD will care for them.

The offerings of the leaders of the twelve tribes
7.1–89: Chapter 7 begins a larger section (chs. 7–10) that is set in a flashback to one month earlier than the time specified at the beginning of Numbers. *The day when Moses had finished setting up the tabernacle** (v. 1) was the first day of the first month (Ex 40.17). In contrast, Num 1.1 begins on the first day of the second month. The time frame will return to the second month in Num 10.11. The long list of offerings in ch. 7 was part of the ceremony consecrating or dedicating the tabernacle and altar. The sequence of the twelve tribes in vv. 12–83 follows the same sequence as in 2.3–31, and the names of the tribal leaders are the same as in 1.5–15. Each tribal leader presents exactly the same offering.

---

7 On the day when Moses had finished setting up the tabernacle, and had anointed and consecrated it with all its furnishings, and had anointed and consecrated the altar with all its utensils, 2the leaders of Israel, heads of their ancestral houses, the leaders of the tribes, who were over those who were enrolled, made offerings. 3They brought their offerings before the LORD, six covered wagons and twelve oxen, a wagon for every two of the leaders, and for each one an ox; they presented them before the taber-

nacle. 4Then the LORD said to Moses: 5Accept these from them, that they may be used in doing the service of the tent of meeting, and give them to the Levites, to each according to his service. 6So Moses took the wagons and the oxen, and gave them to the Levites. 7Two wagons and four oxen he gave to the Gershonites, according to their service; 8and four wagons and eight oxen he gave to the Merarites, according to their service, under the direction of Ithamar son of Aaron the priest. 9But to the Kohathites he gave none, because they were charged with the care of the holy things that had to be carried on the shoulders.

10 The leaders also presented offerings for the dedication of the altar at the time when it was anointed; the leaders presented their offering before the altar. 11The LORD said to Moses: They shall present their offerings, one leader each day, for the dedication of the altar.

12 The one who presented his offering the first day was Nahshon son of Amminadab, of the tribe of Judah; 13his offering was one silver plate weighing one hundred thirty shekels, one silver basin weighing seventy shekels, according to the shekel of the sanctuary, both of them full of choice flour mixed with oil for a grain offering; 14one golden dish weighing ten shekels, full of incense; 15one young bull, one ram, one male lamb a year old, for a burnt offering; 16one male goat for a sin offering; 17and for the sacrifice of well-being, two oxen, five rams, five male goats, and five male lambs a year old. This was the offering of Nahshon son of Amminadab.

7.13: On *the shekel of the sanctuary,* see comment on 3.40–51.

---

18 On the second day Nethanel son of Zuar, the leader of Issachar, presented an offering; 19he presented for his offering one silver plate weighing one hundred thirty shekels, one silver basin weighing seventy shekels, according to the shekel of the sanctuary, both of them full of choice flour mixed with oil for a grain offering; 20one golden dish weighing ten shekels, full of incense;

21one young bull, one ram, one male lamb a year old, as a burnt offering; 22one male goat as a sin offering; 23and for the sacrifice of well-being, two oxen, five rams, five male goats, and five male lambs a year old. This was the offering of Nethanel son of Zuar.

24 On the third day Eliab son of Helon, the leader of the Zebulunites: 25his offering was one silver plate weighing one hundred thirty shekels, one silver basin weighing seventy shekels, according to the shekel of the sanctuary, both of them full of choice flour mixed with oil for a grain offering; 26one golden dish weighing ten shekels, full of incense; 27one young bull, one ram, one male lamb a year old, for a burnt offering; 28one male goat for a sin offering; 29and for the sacrifice of well-being, two oxen, five rams, five male goats, and five male lambs a year old. This was the offering of Eliab son of Helon.

30 On the fourth day Elizur son of Shedeur, the leader of the Reubenites: 31his offering was one silver plate weighing one hundred thirty shekels, one silver basin weighing seventy shekels, according to the shekel of the sanctuary, both of them full of choice flour mixed with oil for a grain offering; 32one golden dish weighing ten shekels, full of incense; 33one young bull, one ram, one male lamb a year old, for a burnt offering; 34one male goat for a sin offering; 35and for the sacrifice of well-being, two oxen, five rams, five male goats, and five male lambs a year old. This was the offering of Elizur son of Shedeur.

36 On the fifth day Shelumiel son of Zurishaddai, the leader of the Simeonites: 37his offering was one silver plate weighing one hundred thirty shekels, one silver basin weighing seventy shekels, according to the shekel of the sanctuary, both of them full of choice flour mixed with oil for a grain offering; 38one golden dish weighing ten shekels, full of incense; 39one young bull, one ram, one male lamb a year old, for a burnt offering; 40one male goat for a sin offering; 41and for the sacrifice of well-being, two oxen, five rams, five male goats, and five male lambs a year old. This was the offering of Shelumiel son of Zurishaddai.

42 On the sixth day Eliasaph son of Deuel, the leader of the Gadites: 43his offering was one silver plate weighing one hundred thirty shekels, one silver basin weighing seventy shekels, according to the shekel of the sanctuary, both of them full of choice flour mixed with oil for a grain offering; 44one golden dish weighing ten shekels, full of incense; 45one young bull, one ram, one male lamb a year old, for a burnt offering; 46one male goat for a sin offering; 47and for the sacrifice of well-being, two oxen, five rams, five male goats, and five male lambs a year old. This was the offering of Eliasaph son of Deuel.

48 On the seventh day Elishama son of Ammihud, the leader of the Ephraimites: 49his offering was one silver plate weighing one hundred thirty shekels, one silver basin weighing seventy shekels, according to the shekel of the sanctuary, both of them full of choice flour mixed with oil for a grain offering; 50one golden dish weighing ten shekels, full of incense; 51one young bull, one ram, one male lamb a year old, for a burnt offering; 52one male goat for a sin offering; 53and for the sacrifice of well-being, two oxen, five rams, five male goats, and five male lambs a year old. This was the offering of Elishama son of Ammihud.

54 On the eighth day Gamaliel son of Pedahzur, the leader of the Manassites: 55his offering was one silver plate weighing one hundred thirty shekels, one silver basin weighing seventy shekels, according to the shekel of the sanctuary, both of them full of choice flour mixed with oil for a grain offering; 56one golden dish weighing ten shekels, full of incense; 57one young bull, one ram, one male lamb a year old, for a burnt offering; 58one male goat for a sin offering; 59and for the sacrifice of well-being, two oxen, five rams, five male goats, and five male lambs a year old. This was the offering of Gamaliel son of Pedahzur.

60 On the ninth day Abidan son of Gideoni, the leader of the Benjaminites: 61his offering was one silver plate weighing one hundred thirty shekels, one silver basin weighing seventy shekels, according to the shekel of the sanctuary, both of them full of

choice flour mixed with oil for a grain offering; 62one golden dish weighing ten shekels, full of incense; 63one young bull, one ram, one male lamb a year old, for a burnt offering; 64one male goat for a sin offering; 65and for the sacrifice of well-being, two oxen, five rams, five male goats, and five male lambs a year old. This was the offering of Abidan son of Gideoni.

66 On the tenth day Ahiezer son of Ammishaddai, the leader of the Danites: 67his offering was one silver plate weighing one hundred thirty shekels, one silver basin weighing seventy shekels, according to the shekel of the sanctuary, both of them full of choice flour mixed with oil for a grain offering; 68one golden dish weighing ten shekels, full of incense; 69one young bull, one ram, one male lamb a year old, for a burnt offering; 70one male goat for a sin offering; 71and for the sacrifice of well-being, two oxen, five rams, five male goats, and five male lambs a year old. This was the offering of Ahiezer son of Ammishaddai.

72 On the eleventh day Pagiel son of Ochran, the leader of the Asherites: 73his offering was one silver plate weighing one hundred thirty shekels, one silver basin weighing seventy shekels, according to the shekel of the sanctuary, both of them full of choice flour mixed with oil for a grain offering; 74one golden dish weighing ten shekels, full of incense; 75one young bull, one ram, one male lamb a year old, for a burnt offering; 76one male goat for a sin offering; 77and for the sacrifice of well-being, two oxen, five rams, five male goats, and five male lambs a year old. This was the offering of Pagiel son of Ochran.

78 On the twelfth day Ahira son of Enan, the leader of the Naphtalites: 79his offering was one silver plate weighing one hundred thirty shekels, one silver basin weighing seventy shekels, according to the shekel of the sanctuary, both of them full of choice flour mixed with oil for a grain offering; 80one golden dish weighing ten shekels, full of incense; 81one young bull, one ram, one male lamb a year old, for a burnt offering; 82one male goat for a sin offering; 83and for the sacrifice of well-being, two oxen, five rams,

five male goats, and five male lambs a year old. This was the offering of Ahira son of Enan.

84 This was the dedication offering for the altar, at the time when it was anointed, from the leaders of Israel: twelve silver plates, twelve silver basins, twelve golden dishes, 85each silver plate weighing one hundred thirty shekels and each basin seventy, all the silver of the vessels two thousand four hundred shekels according to the shekel of the sanctuary, 86the twelve golden dishes, full of incense, weighing ten shekels apiece according to the shekel of the sanctuary, all the gold of the dishes being one hundred twenty shekels; 87all the livestock for the burnt offering twelve bulls, twelve rams, twelve male lambs a year old, with their grain offering; and twelve male goats for a sin offering; 88and all the livestock for the sacrifice of well-being twenty-four bulls, the rams sixty, the male goats sixty, the male lambs a year old sixty. This was the dedication offering for the altar, after it was anointed.

89 When Moses went into the tent of meeting to speak with the LORD,ᵃ he would hear the voice speaking to him from above the mercy seatᵇ that was on the ark of the covenantᶜ from between the two cherubim; thus it spoke to him.

8 The LORD spoke to Moses, saying: 2Speak to Aaron and say to him: When you set up the lamps, the seven lamps shall give light in front of the lampstand. 3Aaron did so; he set up its lamps to give light in front of the lampstand, as the LORD had commanded Moses. 4Now this was how the lampstand was made, out of hammered work of gold. From its base to its flowers, it was hammered work; according to the pattern that the LORD had shown Moses, so he made the lampstand.

8.1–26: The seven lamps and the dedication of the Levites. 1–4: The instructions for the seven lamps in the tabernacle were given in Ex 25.31–40.

5 The LORD spoke to Moses, saying: 6Take the Levites from among the Israelites

a Heb *him*   b Or *the cover*   c Or *treaty,* or *testimony;* Heb *eduth* and cleanse them. 7Thus you shall do to them, to cleanse them: sprinkle the water of purification on them, have them shave their whole body with a razor and wash their clothes, and so cleanse themselves. 8Then let them take a young bull and its grain offering of choice flour mixed with oil, and you shall take another young bull for a sin offering. 9You shall bring the Levites before the tent of meeting, and assemble the whole congregation of the Israelites. 10When you bring the Levites before the LORD, the Israelites shall lay their hands on the Levites, 11and Aaron shall present the Levites before the LORD as an elevation offering from the Israelites, that they may do the service of the LORD. 12The Levites shall lay their hands on the heads of the bulls, and he shall offer the one for a sin offering and the other for a burnt offering to the LORD, to make atonement for the Levites. 13Then you shall have the Levites stand before Aaron and his sons, and you shall present them as an elevation offering to the LORD.

14 Thus you shall separate the Levites from among the other Israelites, and the Levites shall be mine. 15Thereafter the Levites may go in to do service at the tent of meeting, once you have cleansed them and presented them as an elevation offering. 16For they are unreservedly given to me from among the Israelites; I have taken them for myself, in place of all that open the womb, the firstborn of all the Israelites. 17For all the firstborn among the Israelites are mine, both human and animal. On the day that I struck down all the firstborn in the land of Egypt I consecrated them for myself, 18but I have taken the Levites in place of all the firstborn among the Israelites. 19Moreover, I have given the Levites as a gift to Aaron and his sons from among the Israelites, to do the service for the Israelites at the tent of meeting, and to make atonement for the Israelites, in order that there may be no plague among the Israelites for coming too close to the sanctuary.

20 Moses and Aaron and the whole congregation of the Israelites did with the Levites accordingly; the Israelites did with the Levites just as the LORD had commanded Moses concerning them. 21The Levites purified themselves from sin and washed their clothes; then Aaron presented them as an elevation offering before the LORD, and Aaron made atonement for them to cleanse them. 22Thereafter the Levites went in to do their service in the tent of meeting in attendance on Aaron and his sons. As the LORD had commanded Moses concerning the Levites, so they did with them.

23 The LORD spoke to Moses, saying: 24This applies to the Levites: from twenty-five years old and upward they shall begin to do duty in the service of the tent of meeting; 25and from the age of fifty years they shall retire from the duty of the service and serve no more. 26They may assist their brothers in the tent of meeting in carrying out their duties, but they shall perform no service. Thus you shall do with the Levites in assigning their duties.

8.5–26. 6: The Levites must be ritually *cleansed* so that they can handle the holy objects with which they are entrusted. On the concept of ritual purity and cleansing, see the sidebar on p. 136. 10: The Israelites *lay their hands on the Levites* as an act of identification and substitution. The Levites represent all Israel and substitute for Israel's obligation to sacrifice its firstborn to the LORD through the Levites' service in the sanctuary or place of worship (see 3.11–13; 8.16–18). 11: The *elevation offering* signifies the transference of the Levites from the status of a common tribe to a holy tribe dedicated to *the service of the LORD* (see Lev 7.30). 12: Any unintentional guilt or impurity among the Levites is transferred to the bulls when they *lay their hands on the heads of the bulls.* The *sin offering* and the *burnt offering* serve to *make atonement** or remove the impurity or guilt of wrongful actions. See Lev 1.3–9; 4.20–21.

9 The LORD spoke to Moses in the wilderness of Sinai, in the first month of the second year after they had come out of the land of Egypt, saying: 2Let the Israelites keep the passover at its appointed time. 3On the fourteenth day of this month, at twilight,*a* you shall keep it at its appointed time; according to all its statutes and all its regu-

a Heb *between the two evenings*

lations you shall keep it. [4]So Moses told the Israelites that they should keep the passover. [5]They kept the passover in the first month, on the fourteenth day of the month, at twilight,[a] in the wilderness of Sinai. Just as the LORD had commanded Moses, so the Israelites did. [6]Now there were certain people who were unclean through touching a corpse, so that they could not keep the passover on that day. They came before Moses and Aaron on that day, [7]and said to him, "Although we are unclean through touching a corpse, why must we be kept from presenting the LORD's offering at its appointed time among the Israelites?" [8]Moses spoke to them, "Wait, so that I may hear what the LORD will command concerning you."

9 The LORD spoke to Moses, saying: [10]Speak to the Israelites, saying: Anyone of you or your descendants who is unclean through touching a corpse, or is away on a journey, shall still keep the passover to the LORD. [11]In the second month on the fourteenth day, at twilight,[a] they shall keep it; they shall eat it with unleavened bread and bitter herbs. [12]They shall leave none of it until morning, nor break a bone of it; according to all the statute for the passover they shall keep it. [13]But anyone who is clean and is not on a journey, and yet refrains from keeping the passover, shall be cut off from the people for not presenting the LORD's offering at its appointed time; such a one shall bear the consequences for the sin. [14]Any alien residing among you who wishes to keep the passover to the LORD shall do so according to the statute of the passover and according to its regulation; you shall have one statute for both the resident alien and the native.

9.1–14: Celebrating Passover*: uncleanness and resident aliens. 1: On the date of *the first month of the second year,* see comment on 7.1–89. **2–5:** The festival of Passover celebrates the freedom and exodus out of slavery in Egypt (Ex 12.1–28). **6–13:** Becoming *unclean through touching a corpse* (v. 6) represented a severe ritual impurity (see sidebar, "Ritual Purity and Cleanness," p. 136) that would prevent an Israelite from fulfilling the obligation to observe the Passover on the designated date of *the fourteenth day* of *the first month.* Being *away on a journey* (v. 10) would

also prevent observance. Moses consults the LORD in this unprecedented legal case. The decision is made to allow an alternate date one month later for celebrating Passover (*in the second month on the fourteenth day,* v. 11). **14:** An *alien residing among you* is a foreigner who has taken up permanent residence among the Israelites (Ex 12.43–49).

15 On the day the tabernacle was set up, the cloud covered the tabernacle, the tent of the covenant;[b] and from evening until morning it was over the tabernacle, having the appearance of fire. [16]It was always so: the cloud covered it by day[c] and the appearance of fire by night. [17]Whenever the cloud lifted from over the tent, then the Israelites would set out; and in the place where the cloud settled down, there the Israelites would camp. [18]At the command of the LORD the Israelites would set out, and at the command of the LORD they would camp. As long as the cloud rested over the tabernacle, they would remain in camp. [19]Even when the cloud continued over the tabernacle many days, the Israelites would keep the charge of the LORD, and would not set out. [20]Sometimes the cloud would remain a few days over the tabernacle, and according to the command of the LORD they would remain in camp; then according to the command of the LORD they would set out. [21]Sometimes the cloud would remain from evening until morning; and when the cloud lifted in the morning, they would set out, or if it continued for a day and a night, when the cloud lifted they would set out. [22]Whether it was two days, or a month, or a longer time, that the cloud continued over the tabernacle, resting upon it, the Israelites would remain in camp and would not set out; but when it lifted they would set out. [23]At the command of the LORD they would camp, and at the command of the LORD they would set out. They kept the charge of the LORD, at the command of the LORD by Moses.

9.15–23: The fiery cloud veiling the divine presence. 15: *The day the tabernacle* was set up* was the same date as in v. 1, 7.1, and Ex 40.17. *The cloud* that

a Heb *between the two evenings*   b Or *treaty,* or *testimony;* Heb *eduth*   c Gk Syr Vg: Heb lacks *by day*

had *the appearance of fire* veiled the divine presence while also providing visible assurance that the LORD was present and guiding the Israelites in their wilderness journey (Ex 13.21–22; 40.34–35). On the *tabernacle*, the *tent of the covenant* (also known as the tent of meeting), see comments on 1.1 and 1.47–54.

10 The LORD spoke to Moses, saying: ²Make two silver trumpets; you shall make them of hammered work; and you shall use them for summoning the congregation, and for breaking camp. ³When both are blown, the whole congregation shall assemble before you at the entrance of the tent of meeting. ⁴But if only one is blown, then the leaders, the heads of the tribes of Israel, shall assemble before you. ⁵When you blow an alarm, the camps on the east side shall set out; ⁶when you blow a second alarm, the camps on the south side shall set out. An alarm is to be blown whenever they are to set out. ⁷But when the assembly is to be gathered, you shall blow, but you shall not sound an alarm. ⁸The sons of Aaron, the priests, shall blow the trumpets; this shall be a perpetual institution for you throughout your generations. ⁹When you go to war in your land against the adversary who oppresses you, you shall sound an alarm with the trumpets, so that you may be remembered before the LORD your God and be saved from your enemies. ¹⁰Also on your days of rejoicing, at your appointed festivals, and at the beginnings of your months, you shall blow the trumpets over your burnt offerings and over your sacrifices of well-being; they shall serve as a reminder on your behalf before the LORD your God: I am the LORD your God.

10.1–10: The two silver trumpets. The two silver trumpets are sacred instruments blown by priests for four purposes: to call together the whole *congregation* or the *leaders* for an assembly (vv. 3–4), to provide a signal to *set out* from camp on the wilderness sojourn (vv. 5–6), to *sound an alarm* at the time of war (v. 9), and to call a celebration *on your days of rejoicing* (v. 10). According to the ancient Jewish historian Josephus* and as depicted on ancient Jewish coins, the silver trumpets are about twelve inches long with a slender body and wide mouth.

11 In the second year, in the second month, on the twentieth day of the month, the cloud lifted from over the tabernacle of the covenant.ᵃ ¹²Then the Israelites set out by stages from the wilderness of Sinai, and the cloud settled down in the wilderness of Paran. ¹³They set out for the first time at the command of the LORD by Moses. ¹⁴The standard of the camp of Judah set out first, company by company, and over the whole company was Nahshon son of Amminadab. ¹⁵Over the company of the tribe of Issachar was Nethanel son of Zuar; ¹⁶and over the company of the tribe of Zebulun was Eliab son of Helon.

17 Then the tabernacle was taken down, and the Gershonites and the Merarites, who carried the tabernacle, set out. ¹⁸Next the standard of the camp of Reuben set out, company by company; and over the whole company was Elizur son of Shedeur. ¹⁹Over the company of the tribe of Simeon was Shelumiel son of Zurishaddai, ²⁰and over the company of the tribe of Gad was Eliasaph son of Deuel.

21 Then the Kohathites, who carried the holy things, set out; and the tabernacle was set up before their arrival. ²²Next the standard of the Ephraimite camp set out, company by company, and over the whole company was Elishama son of Ammihud. ²³Over the company of the tribe of Manasseh was Gamaliel son of Pedahzur, ²⁴and over the company of the tribe of Benjamin was Abidan son of Gideoni.

25 Then the standard of the camp of Dan, acting as the rear guard of all the camps, set out, company by company, and over the whole company was Ahiezer son of Ammishaddai. ²⁶Over the company of the tribe of Asher was Pagiel son of Ochran, ²⁷and over the company of the tribe of Naphtali was Ahira son of Enan. ²⁸This was the order of march of the Israelites, company by company, when they set out.

29 Moses said to Hobab son of Reuel the Midianite, Moses' father-in-law, "We are setting out for the place of which the LORD said, 'I will give it to you'; come with us, and

a Or *treaty*, or *testimony*; Heb *eduth*

we will treat you well; for the LORD has promised good to Israel." ³⁰But he said to him, "I will not go, but I will go back to my own land and to my kindred." ³¹He said, "Do not leave us, for you know where we should camp in the wilderness, and you will serve as eyes for us. ³²Moreover, if you go with us, whatever good the LORD does for us, the same we will do for you."

33 So they set out from the mount of the LORD three days' journey with the ark of the covenant of the LORD going before them three days' journey, to seek out a resting place for them, ³⁴the cloud of the LORD being over them by day when they set out from the camp.

35 Whenever the ark set out, Moses would say,

"Arise, O LORD, let your enemies be
    scattered,
    and your foes flee before you."
³⁶And whenever it came to rest, he would say,

"Return, O LORD of the ten thousand
    thousands of Israel."ᵃ

10.11–36: The actual beginning of the march of the holy camp of Israel. 11: The date now moves ahead to *the second month, on the twentieth day* which is nineteen days after the census was taken in 1.1 (see comment on 7.1). On *the cloud* and *the tabernacle of the covenant*, see comment on 9.15. **12:** The Israelites move from *the wilderness of Sinai* in the southern part of the Sinai peninsula to *the wilderness of Paran* in the northern part of the Sinai peninsula on their way north to the land of Canaan. **14–28:** On the sequence of the twelve tribes and the Levites as they set out on the march, see chs. 2–3. The list of tribal leaders corresponds to the list in 1.5–15. According to ch. 2, the twelve Israelite tribes are divided into four groups of three tribes each. The four groups of tribes each had their own *standard* (a flag or other symbol, vv. 14, 18, 22, 25). **29:** *Moses' father-in-law* is known here as *Hobab*, but in other biblical traditions he is sometimes known as Jethro (Ex 3.1) or Reuel (Ex 2.18). Hobab is a member of the *Midianite* people, but in Judg 4.11 he is called a Kenite, a group probably related to the Midianites. Israel's relationships with Midianites or Kenites are often positive (Ex 2.11–22), but at times there is conflict (Num 25; 31). **33:** On *the ark of the covenant*, see comment on 1.1. **34:** On *the cloud of*

the LORD, see comment on 9.15. **35–36:** These two ancient battle cries associate the portable *ark* with the presence of the LORD as the Divine Warrior* who fights on Israel's behalf in holy war* against Israel's *enemies*.

11 Now when the people complained in the hearing of the LORD about their misfortunes, the LORD heard it and his anger was kindled. Then the fire of the LORD burned against them, and consumed some outlying parts of the camp. ²But the people cried out to Moses; and Moses prayed to the LORD, and the fire abated. ³So that place was called Taberah,ᵇ because the fire of the LORD burned against them.

4 The rabble among them had a strong craving; and the Israelites also wept again, and said, "If only we had meat to eat! ⁵We remember the fish we used to eat in Egypt for nothing, the cucumbers, the melons, the leeks, the onions, and the garlic; ⁶but now our strength is dried up, and there is nothing at all but this manna to look at."

7 Now the manna was like coriander seed, and its color was like the color of gum resin. ⁸The people went around and gathered it, ground it in mills or beat it in mortars, then boiled it in pots and made cakes of it; and the taste of it was like the taste of cakes baked with oil. ⁹When the dew fell on the camp in the night, the manna would fall with it.

11.1–35: Israel's abrupt turn to rebellion in the wilderness. Chapters 1–10 portrayed Israel as very obedient to the LORD's every command. Suddenly and unexpectedly, Israel begins to complain about the hardships of the wilderness and to rebel against the LORD and Moses. **1:** *The fire of the LORD* presumably originated from the fiery cloud of the divine presence in the midst of the camp (see 9.15–16; Lev 10.1–2). **4:** *The rabble* is a disorderly mob of non-Israelites who traveled with Israel out of Egypt. In Ex 12.38, they are called a "mixed crowd" (see Lev 24.10). **6–9:** *Manna* was a special food from the LORD provided daily in the desert for the Israelites (Ex 16).

10 Moses heard the people weeping throughout their families, all at the en-

---

ᵃ Meaning of Heb uncertain   ᵇ That is *Burning*

trances of their tents. Then the LORD became very angry, and Moses was displeased. [11]So Moses said to the LORD, "Why have you treated your servant so badly? Why have I not found favor in your sight, that you lay the burden of all this people on me? [12]Did I conceive all this people? Did I give birth to them, that you should say to me, 'Carry them in your bosom, as a nurse carries a sucking child,' to the land that you promised on oath to their ancestors? [13]Where am I to get meat to give to all this people? For they come weeping to me and say, 'Give us meat to eat!' [14]I am not able to carry all this people alone, for they are too heavy for me. [15]If this is the way you are going to treat me, put me to death at once—if I have found favor in your sight—and do not let me see my misery."

16 So the LORD said to Moses, "Gather for me seventy of the elders of Israel, whom you know to be the elders of the people and officers over them; bring them to the tent of meeting, and have them take their place there with you. [17]I will come down and talk with you there; and I will take some of the spirit that is on you and put it on them; and they shall bear the burden of the people along with you so that you will not bear it all by yourself. [18]And say to the people: Consecrate yourselves for tomorrow, and you shall eat meat; for you have wailed in the hearing of the LORD, saying, 'If only we had meat to eat! Surely it was better for us in Egypt.' Therefore the LORD will give you meat, and you shall eat. [19]You shall eat not only one day, or two days, or five days, or ten days, or twenty days, [20]but for a whole month—until it comes out of your nostrils and becomes loathsome to you—because you have rejected the LORD who is among you, and have wailed before him, saying, 'Why did we ever leave Egypt?' " [21]But Moses said, "The people I am with number six hundred thousand on foot; and you say, 'I will give them meat, that they may eat for a whole month'! [22]Are there enough flocks and herds to slaughter for them? Are there enough fish in the sea to catch for them?" [23]The LORD said to Moses, "Is the LORD's power limited?[a] Now you shall see whether my word will come true for you or not."

24 So Moses went out and told the people the words of the LORD; and he gathered seventy elders of the people, and placed them all around the tent. [25]Then the LORD came down in the cloud and spoke to him, and took some of the spirit that was on him and put it on the seventy elders; and when the spirit rested upon them, they prophesied. But they did not do so again.

26 Two men remained in the camp, one named Eldad, and the other named Medad, and the spirit rested on them; they were among those registered, but they had not gone out to the tent, and so they prophesied in the camp. [27]And a young man ran and told Moses, "Eldad and Medad are prophesying in the camp." [28]And Joshua son of Nun, the assistant of Moses, one of his chosen men,[b] said, "My lord Moses, stop them!" [29]But Moses said to him, "Are you jealous for my sake? Would that all the LORD's people were prophets, and that the LORD would put his spirit on them!" [30]And Moses and the elders of Israel returned to the camp.

31 Then a wind went out from the LORD, and it brought quails from the sea and let them fall beside the camp, about a day's journey on this side and a day's journey on the other side, all around the camp, about two cubits deep on the ground. [32]So the people worked all that day and night and all the next day, gathering the quails; the least anyone gathered was ten homers; and they spread them out for themselves all around the camp. [33]But while the meat was still between their teeth, before it was consumed, the anger of the LORD was kindled against the people, and the LORD struck the people with a very great plague. [34]So that place was called Kibroth-hattaavah,[c] because there they buried the people who had the craving. [35]From Kibroth-hattaavah the people journeyed to Hazeroth.

11.10–35. 12: Moses' rhetorical* questions imply that the LORD and not Moses is the one who *conceived* and *gave birth* to Israel. Thus, Moses argues, the LORD and

---

a Heb LORD's *hand too short?*   *b* Or *of Moses from his youth*   *c* That is *Graves of craving*

not Moses should be responsible for nursing Israel as *a sucking child*. These female images of mother and wet nurse for the Lord are rare but not unique (Deut 32.18; Isa 66.12–13). **15:** Like Moses, several biblical leaders plead with God to put them to death when caught in desperate circumstances. Examples include the prophets★ Elijah (1 Kings 19.4), Jeremiah (Jer 20.17), and Jonah (Jon 4.3), and the judge Samson (Judg 16.30). **16–17:** In an alternate version of the story, Jethro (the father-in-law of Moses) offers a similar solution of Moses' sharing leadership with seventy elders (Ex 18.13–26). The divine *spirit* (v. 17) is often associated with leaders and prophets in the Bible (Judg 3.10) and can be transferred from one person to another (vv. 24–25; 2 Kings 2.9–10). **18:** The command to the people to *consecrate yourselves* involves ritual purification and preparation before encountering the holy presence of the Lord. **25:** The elders temporarily *prophesied* or mediated messages from the Lord but then ceased. This suggests that Moses remains the one authoritative prophet or mediator of the Lord's words to the people. **26–30:** The scene appears to assume *the tent* of meeting which contains the tabernacle★ and the ark (see 1.1) is located outside *the camp* of Israelite tribes (see Ex 33.7–11). Another tradition in Numbers places the tent and its contents in the middle of the Israelite camp (2.2). **31:** The two scenes of the *spirit* distributed upon the seventy elders (vv. 16–30) and the *wind* bearing the quails share the same key word in Hebrew, "ruaḥ," which can mean either "wind" or "spirit." A similar quails story occurs in Ex 16.13, although in Numbers the quails become a means of judgment and not favor because of the people's rejection of the manna (vv. 4–6). **32:** A *homer* is a unit of dry measure equal to several bushels.

12 While they were at Hazeroth, Miriam and Aaron spoke against Moses because of the Cushite woman whom he had married (for he had indeed married a Cushite woman); ²and they said, "Has the Lord spoken only through Moses? Has he not spoken through us also?" And the Lord heard it. ³Now the man Moses was very humble,[a] more so than anyone else on the face of the earth. ⁴Suddenly the Lord said to Moses, Aaron, and Miriam, "Come out, you three, to the tent of meeting." So the three of them came out. ⁵Then the Lord came down in a pillar of cloud, and stood at the entrance of the tent, and called Aaron and Miriam; and

they both came forward. ⁶And he said, "Hear my words:

When there are prophets among you,
    I the Lord make myself known to
        them in visions;
    I speak to them in dreams.
⁷ Not so with my servant Moses;
    he is entrusted with all my house.
⁸ With him I speak face to face—clearly,
        not in riddles;
    and he beholds the form of the
        Lord.

Why then were you not afraid to speak against my servant Moses?" ⁹And the anger of the Lord was kindled against them, and he departed.

10 When the cloud went away from over the tent, Miriam had become leprous,[b] as white as snow. And Aaron turned towards Miriam and saw that she was leprous. ¹¹Then Aaron said to Moses, "Oh, my lord, do not punish us[c] for a sin that we have so foolishly committed. ¹²Do not let her be like one stillborn, whose flesh is half consumed when it comes out of its mother's womb." ¹³And Moses cried to the Lord, "O God, please heal her." ¹⁴But the Lord said to Moses, "If her father had but spit in her face, would she not bear her shame for seven days? Let her be shut out of the camp for seven days, and after that she may be brought in again." ¹⁵So Miriam was shut out of the camp for seven days; and the people did not set out on the march until Miriam had been brought in again. ¹⁶After that the people set out from Hazeroth, and camped in the wilderness of Paran.

12.1–16: The jealous rebellion of Miriam and Aaron. Israel's rebellion spreads from the "outlying parts of the camp" among "the rabble" (11.1, 4) to the inner circle of leaders. Miriam and Aaron are the sister and brother of Moses (26.59) and co-leaders with him (Mic 6.4). **1:** The region of *Cush* in the Bible usually refers to Ethiopia but at times refers to the Arabian region of Midian. Habakkuk 3.7 names "Cushan" as parallel to Midian. Since Moses' wife Zipporah was from Midian

a Or *devout*   *b* A term for several skin diseases; precise meaning uncertain   *c* Heb *do not lay sin upon us*

(Ex 2.15–21), the charge that she is a *Cushite* probably refers to her Midianite origins. **4–5:** On *the tent of meeting* and *the cloud* that veiled the divine presence, see comments on 1.1 and 9.15. **6–8:** *Prophets*★ may legitimately receive mediated messages from God through *visions* and *dreams* (Joel 2.28). However, such prophets are secondary in authority to Moses who speaks with God *face to face* and directly without the intermediation of visions or dreams (Ex 33.12–34.9). According to Ex 33.23, Moses sees the "back" of God, which may provide the background for the claim that *he beholds the form of the Lord* (v. 8). **10–11:** It is not clear why only Miriam is punished with skin disease. It may be that Aaron could not be allowed to have a leprous skin disease since the resultant ritual impurity would have disqualified him in his priestly duties for a time (Lev 13; 21.16–24). Aaron's reference to Moses as *my lord* and his plea for Moses' help is an ironic★ confirmation of what Aaron and Miriam had earlier denied—Moses' unique relationship to God. **14:** A parent spitting in a child's face is a sign of shame (Deut 25.9; Isa 50.6). God orders Miriam to bear her shame by being shut out of the camp for seven days.

13 The Lord said to Moses, 2"Send men to spy out the land of Canaan, which I am giving to the Israelites; from each of their ancestral tribes you shall send a man, every one a leader among them." 3So Moses sent them from the wilderness of Paran, according to the command of the Lord, all of them leading men among the Israelites. 4These were their names: From the tribe of Reuben, Shammua son of Zaccur; 5from the tribe of Simeon, Shaphat son of Hori; 6from the tribe of Judah, Caleb son of Jephunneh; 7from the tribe of Issachar, Igal son of Joseph; 8from the tribe of Ephraim, Hoshea son of Nun; 9from the tribe of Benjamin, Palti son of Raphu; 10from the tribe of Zebulun, Gaddiel son of Sodi; 11from the tribe of Joseph (that is, from the tribe of Manasseh), Gaddi son of Susi; 12from the tribe of Dan, Ammiel son of Gemalli; 13from the tribe of Asher, Sethur son of Michael; 14from the tribe of Naphtali, Nahbi son of Vophsi; 15from the tribe of Gad, Geuel son of Machi. 16These were the names of the men whom Moses sent to spy out the land. And Moses changed the name of Hoshea son of Nun to Joshua.

17 Moses sent them to spy out the land of Canaan, and said to them, "Go up there into the Negeb, and go up into the hill country, 18and see what the land is like, and whether the people who live in it are strong or weak, whether they are few or many, 19and whether the land they live in is good or bad, and whether the towns that they live in are unwalled or fortified, 20and whether the land is rich or poor, and whether there are trees in it or not. Be bold, and bring some of the fruit of the land." Now it was the season of the first ripe grapes.

21 So they went up and spied out the land from the wilderness of Zin to Rehob, near Lebo-hamath. 22They went up into the Negeb, and came to Hebron; and Ahiman, Sheshai, and Talmai, the Anakites, were there. (Hebron was built seven years before Zoan in Egypt.) 23And they came to the Wadi Eshcol, and cut down from there a branch with a single cluster of grapes, and they carried it on a pole between two of them. They also brought some pomegranates and figs. 24That place was called the Wadi Eshcol,*a* because of the cluster that the Israelites cut down from there.

13.1–33: The spy mission into Canaan. 4–16: The sequence of the twelve tribes is the same as the sequence in 1.5–15, but the names of the tribal leaders who are spies are different. *Caleb* is designated as the representative of the tribe of Judah (v. 6). However, other traditions suggest that Caleb was originally not an Israelite but a Kenizzite (32.12; Josh 14.6, 14). The narrative★ assumes, however, that he was adopted into the tribe of Judah. **17:** *The Negeb* is the region north of the wilderness of Paran and just south of the land of Canaan. **21:** This later addition to an earlier version of the spy story expands the area surveyed by the spies to include the whole land of Canaan from the far south (*wilderness of Zin*) to the far north in what will become the tribal territory of Dan (*Rehob, near Lebo-hamath*). The older version of the spy story (vv. 22–24) focuses only on the area of the *Negeb* and southern Canaan near *Hebron* (v. 22). **22:** *The Anakites* are one of the native groups living within Canaan. They were a people known for their great physical stature (Deut 9.2). According to later biblical accounts,

a That is *Cluster*

remnants of these giants remained west of Canaan in the Philistine regions of Gaza, Gath, and Ashdod (Josh 11.21–22). Four of these giants were killed by David's men (2 Sam 21.18–22), and the giant Goliath of Gath was slain by the young warrior David with a slingshot (1 Sam 17).

25 At the end of forty days they returned from spying out the land. 26And they came to Moses and Aaron and to all the congregation of the Israelites in the wilderness of Paran, at Kadesh; they brought back word to them and to all the congregation, and showed them the fruit of the land. 27And they told him, "We came to the land to which you sent us; it flows with milk and honey, and this is its fruit. 28Yet the people who live in the land are strong, and the towns are fortified and very large; and besides, we saw the descendants of Anak there. 29The Amalekites live in the land of the Negeb; the Hittites, the Jebusites, and the Amorites live in the hill country; and the Canaanites live by the sea, and along the Jordan."

30 But Caleb quieted the people before Moses, and said, "Let us go up at once and occupy it, for we are well able to overcome it." 31Then the men who had gone up with him said, "We are not able to go up against this people, for they are stronger than we." 32So they brought to the Israelites an unfavorable report of the land that they had spied out, saying, "The land that we have gone through as spies is a land that devours its inhabitants; and all the people that we saw in it are of great size. 33There we saw the Nephilim (the Anakites come from the Nephilim); and to ourselves we seemed like grasshoppers, and so we seemed to them."

13.25–33. 26: The desert oasis of *Kadesh* or Kadesh-barnea (32.8) will be the location of the Israelite camp for much of their remaining years in the wilderness (Num 13–20; see 20.1, 22). **27:** *The land flowing with milk and honey* is a frequent biblical phrase that describes the lush fertility of the promised land of Canaan (Ex 3.17; Josh 5.6). **28:** *The descendants of Anak* are the same Anakites mentioned in v. 22. **29:** *The Amalekites* were often involved in hostilities with Israel throughout the biblical story (Ex 17.8–16; 1 Sam 15.1–9). *The Hittites, the Jebusites, the Amorites, and*

the Canaanites constitute the traditional list of Canaan's native inhabitants (Gen 15.19–21; Deut 7.1). **30–31:** In the earlier version of the spy story, Caleb is the only faithful one among the twelve spies; he encourages the people to go ahead with the plan to conquer the land of Canaan. In verses that reflect a later version of the story, Joshua is added as a faithful spy along with Caleb (note the name change in vv. 8, 16 and the inclusion of Joshua with Caleb in 14.6, 38). **32:** Earlier the spies had reported that the land was fertile and good (v. 27), but now the spies change their story. They demonize the land as a monster that *devours its inhabitants*. **33:** The spies continue to exaggerate the dangers of Canaan by invoking the threat of *the Nephilim*, a semi-divine and mythological race of giants. The Nephilim (literally "fallen ones") were purported to be the semi-divine offspring of divine beings who had fallen from the heavens and mated with humans (Gen 6.4).

14 Then all the congregation raised a loud cry, and the people wept that night. 2And all the Israelites complained against Moses and Aaron; the whole congregation said to them, "Would that we had died in the land of Egypt! Or would that we had died in this wilderness! 3Why is the LORD bringing us into this land to fall by the sword? Our wives and our little ones will become booty; would it not be better for us to go back to Egypt?" 4So they said to one another, "Let us choose a captain, and go back to Egypt."

14.1–45: The decisive rebellion: the old generation's refusal to enter the promised land. This key narrative* forms the basis for the overall structure of the book of Numbers, which divides into the death of the old generation of the wilderness (chs. 1–25) and the birth of a new generation of hope on the edge of the promised land (chs. 26–36). The old rebellious generation is condemned to wander for forty years and die in the wilderness (vv. 22–23, 29–30). Only the new generation of *little ones* (along with the two faithful spies Caleb and Joshua) will be allowed to enter the land of Canaan (vv. 24, 30–31; see 26.63–65). **3:** The Israelites' concern that their wives and children *will become booty* means that they believe they will be defeated by the inhabitants of Canaan and their families will be carried off as the spoils of war. They are unwilling to trust the LORD's promise and power to conquer the Canaanites and their gods. **4:** The Israelites had often yearned to go back to Egypt in earlier episodes (Ex 16.3; Num 11.5). However, the Israelites now actually seek a new leader and adopt a plan by which to return to Egypt. The plan to return to Egyptian slavery is an outright rejection of the LORD "who brought you out of the land of Egypt, out of the house of slavery" (Ex 20.2).

5 Then Moses and Aaron fell on their faces before all the assembly of the congregation of the Israelites. 6And Joshua son of Nun and Caleb son of Jephunneh, who were among those who had spied out the land, tore their clothes 7and said to all the congregation of the Israelites, "The land that we went through as spies is an exceedingly good land. 8If the LORD is pleased with us, he will bring us into this land and give it to us, a land that flows with milk and honey. 9Only, do not rebel against the LORD; and do not fear the people of the land, for they are no more than bread for us; their protection is removed from them, and the LORD is with us; do not fear them." 10But the whole congregation threatened to stone them.

Then the glory of the LORD appeared at the tent of meeting to all the Israelites.

Map Canaan at the time of the Conquest

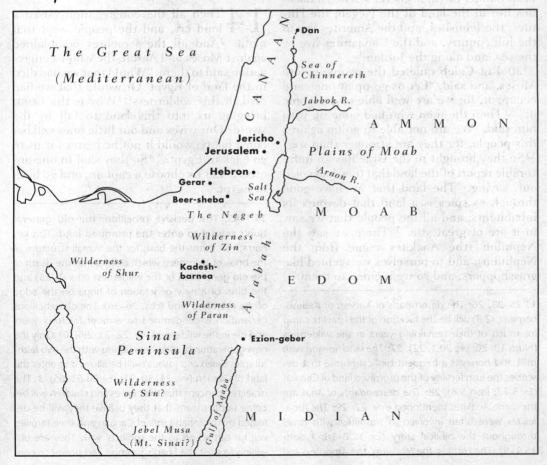

¹¹And the LORD said to Moses, "How long will this people despise me? And how long will they refuse to believe in me, in spite of all the signs that I have done among them? ¹²I will strike them with pestilence and disinherit them, and I will make of you a nation greater and mightier than they."

13 But Moses said to the LORD, "Then the Egyptians will hear of it, for in your might you brought up this people from among them, ¹⁴and they will tell the inhabitants of this land. They have heard that you, O LORD, are in the midst of this people; for you, O LORD, are seen face to face, and your cloud stands over them and you go in front of them, in a pillar of cloud by day and in a pillar of fire by night. ¹⁵Now if you kill this people all at one time, then the nations who have heard about you will say, ¹⁶'It is because the LORD was not able to bring this people into the land he swore to give them that he has slaughtered them in the wilderness.' ¹⁷And now, therefore, let the power of the LORD be great in the way that you promised when you spoke, saying,

¹⁸ 'The LORD is slow to anger,
　　and abounding in steadfast love,
　　forgiving iniquity and transgression,
　　but by no means clearing the guilty,
　　visiting the iniquity of the parents
　　upon the children
　　to the third and the fourth generation.'
¹⁹Forgive the iniquity of this people according to the greatness of your steadfast love, just as you have pardoned this people, from Egypt even until now."

20 Then the LORD said, "I do forgive, just as you have asked; ²¹nevertheless—as I live, and as all the earth shall be filled with the glory of the LORD— ²²none of the people who have seen my glory and the signs that I did in Egypt and in the wilderness, and yet have tested me these ten times and have not obeyed my voice, ²³shall see the land that I swore to give to their ancestors; none of those who despised me shall see it. ²⁴But my servant Caleb, because he has a different spirit and has followed me wholeheartedly, I will bring into the land into which he went, and his descendants shall possess it. ²⁵Now, since the Amalekites and the Canaanites live

in the valleys, turn tomorrow and set out for the wilderness by the way to the Red Sea."ᵃ

14.5–25. 5: *Fell on their faces:* This gesture of Moses and Aaron is an act of humility and request before God to lessen the severity of the divine judgment they know will come. **10:** To *stone them* is to kill them by throwing heavy stones at them. *The glory of the LORD* is associated with the appearance of the fiery cloud of the divine presence (Ex 16.10). On *the tent of meeting,* see comment on 1.1. **12:** The LORD threatens to annihilate all Israel and to start over to form a new nation with Moses alone. A similar threat against Israel and a similar offer to Moses was made when Israel worshipped the golden calf (Ex 32.10). **17–18:** Moses appeals to the promise of the LORD's gracious and forgiving character that was made to him on Mount Sinai after the golden calf incident (Ex 34.1–9). **19–23:** The LORD's response is true to both dimensions of the divine character that Moses cited in v. 18: "abounding in steadfast love" and "by no means clearing the guilty." Thus, the LORD will *forgive the iniquity* and not annihilate all the Israelites (v. 20). *Nevertheless,* none of the old generation *shall see the land* of Canaan (vv. 21–23). Only the children of this old generation, their "little ones" (v. 31), will enter the land of Canaan. **24:** *Caleb* is listed alone as the one faithful member of the old generation who will be allowed to enter the promised land. Joshua will also be included with Caleb (vv. 30, 38). See comment on 13.30–31.

26 And the LORD spoke to Moses and to Aaron, saying: ²⁷How long shall this wicked congregation complain against me? I have heard the complaints of the Israelites, which they complain against me. ²⁸Say to them, "As I live," says the LORD, "I will do to you the very things I heard you say: ²⁹your dead bodies shall fall in this very wilderness; and of all your number, included in the census, from twenty years old and upward, who have complained against me, ³⁰not one of you shall come into the land in which I swore to settle you, except Caleb son of Jephunneh and Joshua son of Nun. ³¹But your little ones, who you said would become booty, I will bring in, and they shall know the land that you have despised. ³²But as for you,

a Or Sea of Reeds

your dead bodies shall fall in this wilderness. 33And your children shall be shepherds in the wilderness for forty years, and shall suffer for your faithlessness, until the last of your dead bodies lies in the wilderness. 34According to the number of the days in which you spied out the land, forty days, for every day a year, you shall bear your iniquity, forty years, and you shall know my displeasure." 35I the LORD have spoken; surely I will do thus to all this wicked congregation gathered together against me: in this wilderness they shall come to a full end, and there they shall die.

36 And the men whom Moses sent to spy out the land, who returned and made all the congregation complain against him by bringing a bad report about the land— 37the men who brought an unfavorable report about the land died by a plague before the LORD. 38But Joshua son of Nun and Caleb son of Jephunneh alone remained alive, of those men who went to spy out the land.

39 When Moses told these words to all the Israelites, the people mourned greatly. 40They rose early in the morning and went up to the heights of the hill country, saying, "Here we are. We will go up to the place that the LORD has promised, for we have sinned." 41But Moses said, "Why do you continue to transgress the command of the LORD? That will not succeed. 42Do not go up, for the LORD is not with you; do not let yourselves be struck down before your enemies. 43For the Amalekites and the Canaanites will confront you there, and you shall fall by the sword; because you have turned back from following the LORD, the LORD will not be with you." 44But they presumed to go up to the heights of the hill country, even though the ark of the covenant of the LORD, and Moses, had not left the camp. 45Then the Amalekites and the Canaanites who lived in that hill country came down and defeated them, pursuing them as far as Hormah.

Canaanites are native inhabitants of the land of Canaan. On *the ark of the covenant,** see comment on 4.5–33. The absence of the ark from among the Israelites in their attack was a visible sign that the LORD was not with them, guaranteeing their defeat. *Hormah* is located south and east of Canaan in the area of Edom.

15 The LORD spoke to Moses, saying: 2Speak to the Israelites and say to them: When you come into the land you are to inhabit, which I am giving you, 3and you make an offering by fire to the LORD from the herd or from the flock—whether a burnt offering or a sacrifice, to fulfill a vow or as a freewill offering or at your appointed festivals—to make a pleasing odor for the LORD, 4then whoever presents such an offering to the LORD shall present also a grain offering, one-tenth of an ephah of choice flour, mixed with one-fourth of a hin of oil. 5Moreover, you shall offer one-fourth of a hin of wine as a drink offering with the burnt offering or the sacrifice, for each lamb. 6For a ram, you shall offer a grain offering, two-tenths of an ephah of choice flour mixed with one-third of a hin of oil; 7and as a drink offering you shall offer one-third of a hin of wine, a pleasing odor to the LORD. 8When you offer a bull as a burnt offering or a sacrifice, to fulfill a vow or as an offering of well-being to the LORD, 9then you shall present with the bull a grain offering, three-tenths of an ephah of choice flour, mixed with half a hin of oil, 10and you shall present as a drink offering half a hin of wine, as an offering by fire, a pleasing odor to the LORD.

11 Thus it shall be done for each ox or ram, or for each of the male lambs or the kids. 12According to the number that you offer, so you shall do with each and every one. 13Every native Israelite shall do these things in this way, in presenting an offering by fire, a pleasing odor to the LORD. 14An alien who lives with you, or who takes up permanent residence among you, and wishes to offer an offering by fire, a pleasing odor to the LORD, shall do as you do. 15As for the assembly, there shall be for both you and the resident alien a single statute, a perpetual statute throughout your generations; you and the

14.26–45. 28: *As I live* is a typical oath formula for making a binding promise or threat; see v. 20. **29:** *The census* of the Israelites is the count taken in ch. 1. **30:** See comment on 13.30–31. **31:** See v. 3. **34:** See 13.25. **43–45:** *The Amalekites* and *the*

alien shall be alike before the LORD. ¹⁶You and the alien who resides with you shall have the same law and the same ordinance.

17 The LORD spoke to Moses, saying: ¹⁸Speak to the Israelites and say to them: After you come into the land to which I am bringing you, ¹⁹whenever you eat of the bread of the land, you shall present a donation to the LORD. ²⁰From your first batch of dough you shall present a loaf as a donation; you shall present it just as you present a donation from the threshing floor. ²¹Throughout your generations you shall give to the LORD a donation from the first of your batch of dough.

22 But if you unintentionally fail to observe all these commandments that the LORD has spoken to Moses— ²³everything that the LORD has commanded you by Moses, from the day the LORD gave commandment and thereafter, throughout your generations— ²⁴then if it was done unintentionally without the knowledge of the congregation, the whole congregation shall offer one young bull for a burnt offering, a pleasing odor to the LORD, together with its grain offering and its drink offering, according to the ordinance, and one male goat for a sin offering. ²⁵The priest shall make atonement for all the congregation of the Israelites, and they shall be forgiven; it was unintentional, and they have brought their offering, an offering by fire to the LORD, and their sin offering before the LORD, for their error. ²⁶All the congregation of the Israelites shall be forgiven, as well as the aliens residing among them, because the whole people was involved in the error.

27 An individual who sins unintentionally shall present a female goat a year old for a sin offering. ²⁸And the priest shall make atonement before the LORD for the one who commits an error, when it is unintentional, to make atonement for the person, who then shall be forgiven. ²⁹For both the native among the Israelites and the alien residing among them—you shall have the same law for anyone who acts in error. ³⁰But whoever acts high-handedly, whether a native or an alien, affronts the LORD, and shall be cut off from among the people. ³¹Because of having despised the word of the LORD and broken his commandment, such a person shall be utterly cut off and bear the guilt.

32 When the Israelites were in the wilderness, they found a man gathering sticks on the sabbath day. ³³Those who found him gathering sticks brought him to Moses, Aaron, and to the whole congregation. ³⁴They put him in custody, because it was not clear what should be done to him. ³⁵Then the LORD said to Moses, "The man shall be put to death; all the congregation shall stone him outside the camp." ³⁶The whole congregation brought him outside the camp and stoned him to death, just as the LORD had commanded Moses.

37 The LORD said to Moses: ³⁸Speak to the Israelites, and tell them to make fringes on the corners of their garments throughout their generations and to put a blue cord on the fringe at each corner. ³⁹You have the fringe so that, when you see it, you will remember all the commandments of the LORD and do them, and not follow the lust of your own heart and your own eyes. ⁴⁰So you shall remember and do all my commandments, and you shall be holy to your God. ⁴¹I am the LORD your God, who brought you out of the land of Egypt, to be your God: I am the LORD your God.

15.1–41: Regulations that reassure a future life in the promised land. These laws interrupt the old generation's downward slide into rebellion with laws which assume that future generations of Israelites will eventually carry on life in the promised land of Canaan: *when you come into the land you are to inhabit* (v. 2). **1–16:** These laws prescribe additional grain and drink offerings to accompany burnt offerings (Lev 1) and offerings of well-being (Lev 3). *A pleasing odor for the LORD* (v. 3) is a phrase indicating the LORD's acceptance of the offering as the aroma arises from the burning of the sacrifice (see Gen 8.20–22). An *ephah* is a unit of dry measure of roughly half a bushel, and a *hin* is a unit of liquid measure somewhere between a quart and a gallon (vv. 4–10). **17–21:** This law about offering the *first batch of dough* supplements the law of offering first fruits in Lev 23.9–14. **22–31:** These laws summarize and supplement the laws for unintentional acts of disobedience in Lev 4–5. To *make atonement** (vv. 25, 28) means to make clean, forgive, or cover over guilt or impurity. To *act high-handedly* (v. 30) is to sin deliberately and boldly as opposed to *unintentional* errors (v. 28). The punishment for high-handed or intentional sin is to *be utterly cut off*, probably meaning the death penalty or expulsion from the community (vv. 30–31). The Israelites' refusal to enter the land of Canaan (chs. 13–14) was probably understood as a "high-handed" and intentional act of disobedience for which the old generation suffered death. **32–36:** The earlier law in the background of this case is one prohibiting lighting a fire on the sabbath in Ex 35.2–3. A man demonstrates the intention to light a fire on the sabbath by *gathering sticks* (v. 32). The case demonstrates that the intention to disobey carries the same penalty and guilt as the actual act of disobedience itself. **37–41:** The royal *blue cord* (v. 38) stands out in color among the white fringes of the garment, just as the commandments of God should stand out in the mind of the worshipper (vv. 38–39). Such fringes, called "tallit," are still worn on traditional Jewish prayer shawls.

16 Now Korah son of Izhar son of Kohath son of Levi, along with Dathan and Abiram sons of Eliab, and On son of Peleth—descendants of Reuben—took ²two hundred fifty Israelite men, leaders of the congregation, chosen from the assembly, well-known men,*ᵃ* and they confronted Moses. ³They assembled against Moses and against Aaron, and said to them, "You have gone too far! All the congregation are holy, every one of them, and the LORD is among them. So why then do you exalt yourselves above the assembly of the LORD?" ⁴When Moses heard it, he fell on his face. ⁵Then he said to Korah and all his company, "In the morning the LORD will make known who is his, and who is holy, and who will be allowed to approach him; the one whom he will choose he will allow to approach him. ⁶Do this: take censers, Korah and all your*ᵇ* company, ⁷and tomorrow put fire in them, and lay incense on them before the LORD; and the man whom the LORD chooses shall be the holy one. You Levites have gone too far!" ⁸Then Moses said to Korah, "Hear now, you Levites! ⁹Is it too little for you that the God of Israel has separated you from the congregation of Israel, to allow you to approach him in order to perform the duties of the LORD's tabernacle, and to stand before the congregation and serve them? ¹⁰He has allowed you to approach him, and all your brother Levites with you; yet you seek the priesthood as well! ¹¹Therefore you and all your company have gathered together against the LORD. What is Aaron that you rail against him?"

12 Moses sent for Dathan and Abiram sons of Eliab; but they said, "We will not come! ¹³Is it too little that you have brought us up out of a land flowing with milk and honey to kill us in the wilderness, that you must also lord it over us? ¹⁴It is clear you have not brought us into a land flowing with milk and honey, or given us an inheritance of fields and vineyards. Would you put out the eyes of these men? We will not come!"

15 Moses was very angry and said to the LORD, "Pay no attention to their offering. I have not taken one donkey from them, and I have not harmed any one of them." ¹⁶And Moses said to Korah, "As for you and all your company, be present tomorrow before the LORD, you and they and Aaron; ¹⁷and let each one of you take his censer, and put incense on it, and each one of you present his censer before the LORD, two hundred fifty censers; you also, and Aaron, each his censer." ¹⁸So each man took his censer, and they put fire in the censers and laid incense on them, and they stood at the entrance of the tent of meeting with Moses and Aaron. ¹⁹Then Korah assembled the whole congregation against them at the entrance of the tent of meeting. And the glory of the LORD appeared to the whole congregation.

20 Then the LORD spoke to Moses and to Aaron, saying: ²¹Separate yourselves from this congregation, so that I may consume them in a moment. ²²They fell on their faces, and said, "O God, the God of the spirits of all flesh, shall one person sin and you become angry with the whole congregation?"

23 And the LORD spoke to Moses, saying: ²⁴Say to the congregation: Get away from the dwellings of Korah, Dathan, and Abiram. ²⁵So Moses got up and went to Dathan and Abiram; the elders of Israel followed him.

---

a Cn: Heb *and they confronted Moses, and two hundred fifty men . . . well-known men*   *b* Heb *his*

26He said to the congregation, "Turn away from the tents of these wicked men, and touch nothing of theirs, or you will be swept away for all their sins." 27So they got away from the dwellings of Korah, Dathan, and Abiram; and Dathan and Abiram came out and stood at the entrance of their tents, together with their wives, their children, and their little ones. 28And Moses said, "This is how you shall know that the LORD has sent me to do all these works; it has not been of my own accord: 29If these people die a natural death, or if a natural fate comes on them, then the LORD has not sent me. 30But if the LORD creates something new, and the ground opens its mouth and swallows them up, with all that belongs to them, and they go down alive into Sheol, then you shall know that these men have despised the LORD."

31 As soon as he finished speaking all these words, the ground under them was split apart. 32The earth opened its mouth and swallowed them up, along with their households—everyone who belonged to Korah and all their goods. 33So they with all that belonged to them went down alive into Sheol; the earth closed over them, and they perished from the midst of the assembly. 34All Israel around them fled at their outcry, for they said, "The earth will swallow us too!" 35And fire came out from the LORD and consumed the two hundred fifty men offering the incense.

36a Then the LORD spoke to Moses, saying: 37Tell Eleazar son of Aaron the priest to take the censers out of the blaze; then scatter the fire far and wide. 38For the censers of these sinners have become holy at the cost of their lives. Make them into hammered plates as a covering for the altar, for they presented them before the LORD and they became holy. Thus they shall be a sign to the Israelites. 39So Eleazar the priest took the bronze censers that had been presented by those who were burned; and they were hammered out as a covering for the altar— 40a reminder to the Israelites that no outsider, who is not of the descendants of Aaron, shall approach to offer incense before the LORD, so as not to become like Korah and his company—just as the LORD had said to him through Moses.

41 On the next day, however, the whole congregation of the Israelites rebelled against Moses and against Aaron, saying, "You have killed the people of the LORD." 42And when the congregation had assembled against them, Moses and Aaron turned toward the tent of meeting; the cloud had covered it and the glory of the LORD appeared. 43Then Moses and Aaron came to the front of the tent of meeting, 44and the LORD spoke to Moses, saying, 45"Get away from this congregation, so that I may consume them in a moment." And they fell on their faces. 46Moses said to Aaron, "Take your censer, put fire on it from the altar and lay incense on it, and carry it quickly to the congregation and make atonement for them. For wrath has gone out from the LORD; the plague has begun." 47So Aaron took it as Moses had ordered, and ran into the middle of the assembly, where the plague had already begun among the people. He put on the incense, and made atonement for the people. 48He stood between the dead and the living; and the plague was stopped. 49Those who died by the plague were fourteen thousand seven hundred, besides those who died in the affair of Korah. 50When the plague was stopped, Aaron returned to Moses at the entrance of the tent of meeting.

16.1–50: The rebellions continue: Levites, leaders, and all the people. Many scholars suggest that this story probably developed out of several stages of editing. The earliest form of the narrative* may have focused only on a revolt against Moses by the leaders Dathan and Abiram from the tribe of Reuben (vv. 12–15). The story was then enlarged to include 250 lay leaders who claimed the right to act as priests and received punishment (vv. 2, 4–7, 18, 35). One of the last stages in the story's formation was the introduction of a rebel leader from the tribe of Levi named Korah (vv. 1, 8–11, 16–17). **1:** The figure of *On son of Peleth* is mentioned only here as one of the Reubenite leaders. *Dathan and Abiram* are the rebel leaders from the tribe of Reuben who will reappear throughout the story. **5:** The question of *who will be allowed to ap-*

a Ch 17.1 in Heb

proach the LORD involves the issue of who can legitimately perform the duties of the priest in offering incense and sacrifices at the central altar. **6:** *Censers* are bowls containing hot coals in which incense could be burned. **7–11:** According to previous sections in Numbers, the *Levites* are a tribe of priests. However, most of the Levites serve and assist the one family among the Levites who may legitimately serve as high priests and preside at all sacrifices—the line of Aaron and his sons (3.1–10). The Levites take care of the objects and structure of the *tabernacle** (v. 9), the portable tent of worship that houses the altar and is the visible sign of the divine presence in the midst of Israel's camp. **12:** Dathan and Abiram are from the tribe of Reuben, not the priestly tribe of Levi. Like Korah and the Levites, they too demand the right to act as high priests like Aaron and his sons. **13:** Dathan and Abiram use the phrase *a land flowing with milk and honey* to refer to the land of Israel's slavery, Egypt, rather than its usual referent, the promised land of Canaan (13.27). **21:** The LORD threatens to *consume* the whole congregation of Israel for the rebellions of its leaders. This generation has already been condemned to die in the wilderness (14.29–30), but the LORD threatens to annihilate them immediately. **22:** *Fell on their faces:* See comment on 14.5. **24:** The LORD responds to Moses and Aaron's gesture of humility and request for forgiveness (falling on their faces, v. 22) by restricting the threat of death to the rebel leaders and their families—Korah, Dathan, and Abiram. **30, 33:** *Sheol** is a dry and dusty place under the surface of the earth where all humans who die were believed to go. Sheol is sometimes personified as a monster who opens its mouth to swallow people (13.32; Isa 5.14). **35:** When *fire came out from the LORD*, the fire presumably came out from the fiery cloud of the divine presence (9.15–16). **37–39:** On *censers*, see comment on v. 6. **42:** On *the glory of the LORD*, see comment on 14.10. On *the tent of meeting*, see comment on 1.1. **45:** The LORD threatens to annihilate all Israel a second time (see v. 21). Again, the action of Moses and Aaron restricts the scope of the LORD's punishment (vv. 46–49). **46–47:** To *make atonement** means to make clean, forgive, or cover over guilt or impurity.

---

17 [a]The LORD spoke to Moses, saying: [2]Speak to the Israelites, and get twelve staffs from them, one for each ancestral house, from all the leaders of their ancestral houses. Write each man's name on his staff, [3]and write Aaron's name on the staff of Levi. For there shall be one staff for the head of each ancestral house. [4]Place them in the tent of meeting before the covenant,[b] where I meet with you. [5]And the staff of the man whom I choose shall sprout; thus I will put a stop to the complaints of the Israelites that they continually make against you. [6]Moses spoke to the Israelites; and all their leaders gave him staffs, one for each leader, according to their ancestral houses, twelve staffs; and the staff of Aaron was among theirs. [7]So Moses placed the staffs before the LORD in the tent of the covenant.[b]

[8] When Moses went into the tent of the covenant[b] on the next day, the staff of Aaron for the house of Levi had sprouted. It put forth buds, produced blossoms, and bore ripe almonds. [9]Then Moses brought out all the staffs from before the LORD to all the Israelites; and they looked, and each man took his staff. [10]And the LORD said to Moses, "Put back the staff of Aaron before the covenant,[b] to be kept as a warning to rebels, so that you may make an end of their complaints against me, or else they will die." [11]Moses did so; just as the LORD commanded him, so he did.

[12] The Israelites said to Moses, "We are perishing; we are lost, all of us are lost! [13]Everyone who approaches the tabernacle of the LORD will die. Are we all to perish?"

17.1–12: Aaron's flowering staff. 2: The *twelve staffs* are specially decorated rods representing each of the twelve Israelite tribes or *ancestral houses*. **3:** The high priest Aaron is a member of the tribe of Levi (Ex 6.16–20). **7–8:** The *tent of the covenant** is also known as the tent of meeting. See comments on 1.1 and 1.47–54. **10:** *Before the covenant* is shorthand for "before the ark of the covenant." See comment on 4.5–33. **13:** On *the tabernacle*, see comment on 1.47–54.

---

18 The LORD said to Aaron: You and your sons and your ancestral house with you shall bear responsibility for offenses connected with the sanctuary, while you and your sons alone shall bear responsibility for

---

a Ch 17.16 in Heb   *b* Or *treaty*, or *testimony;* Heb *eduth*

offenses connected with the priesthood. ²So bring with you also your brothers of the tribe of Levi, your ancestral tribe, in order that they may be joined to you, and serve you while you and your sons with you are in front of the tent of the covenant.ᵃ ³They shall perform duties for you and for the whole tent. But they must not approach either the utensils of the sanctuary or the altar, otherwise both they and you will die. ⁴They are attached to you in order to perform the duties of the tent of meeting, for all the service of the tent; no outsider shall approach you. ⁵You yourselves shall perform the duties of the sanctuary and the duties of the altar, so that wrath may never again come upon the Israelites. ⁶It is I who now take your brother Levites from among the Israelites; they are now yours as a gift, dedicated to the LORD, to perform the service of the tent of meeting. ⁷But you and your sons with you shall diligently perform your priestly duties in all that concerns the altar and the area behind the curtain. I give your priesthood as a gift;ᵇ any outsider who approaches shall be put to death.

8 The LORD spoke to Aaron: I have given you charge of the offerings made to me, all the holy gifts of the Israelites; I have given them to you and your sons as a priestly portion due you in perpetuity. ⁹This shall be yours from the most holy things, reserved from the fire: every offering of theirs that they render to me as a most holy thing, whether grain offering, sin offering, or guilt offering, shall belong to you and your sons. ¹⁰As a most holy thing you shall eat it; every male may eat it; it shall be holy to you. ¹¹This also is yours: I have given to you, together with your sons and daughters, as a perpetual due, whatever is set aside from the gifts of all the elevation offerings of the Israelites; everyone who is clean in your house may eat them. ¹²All the best of the oil and all the best of the wine and of the grain, the choice produce that they give to the LORD, I have given to you. ¹³The first fruits of all that is in their land, which they bring to the LORD, shall be yours; everyone who is clean in your house may eat of it. ¹⁴Every devoted thing in Israel shall be yours. ¹⁵The first issue of the womb of all creatures, human and animal, which is offered to the LORD, shall be yours; but the firstborn of human beings you shall redeem, and the firstborn of unclean animals you shall redeem. ¹⁶Their redemption price, reckoned from one month of age, you shall fix at five shekels of silver, according to the shekel of the sanctuary (that is, twenty gerahs). ¹⁷But the firstborn of a cow, or the firstborn of a sheep, or the firstborn of a goat, you shall not redeem; they are holy. You shall dash their blood on the altar, and shall turn their fat into smoke as an offering by fire for a pleasing odor to the LORD; ¹⁸but their flesh shall be yours, just as the breast that is elevated and as the right thigh are yours. ¹⁹All the holy offerings that the Israelites present to the LORD I have given to you, together with your sons and daughters, as a perpetual due; it is a covenant of salt forever before the LORD for you and your descendants as well. ²⁰Then the LORD said to Aaron: You shall have no allotment in their land, nor shall you have any share among them; I am your share and your possession among the Israelites.

18.1–32: The duties and support of the priests and Levites. This chapter makes a crucial distinction between Aaron and his sons as the Levites who serve as high priests and the other members of the tribe of Levi, who serve as assistants to Aaron and his sons (3.5–10). 2, 4: On the tent of the covenant* (v. 2) and its alternate designation as the tent of meeting (v. 4), see comments on 1.1 and 1.47–54. An outsider is any member of the Israelite community who is not from the priestly tribe of Levi or the family of Aaron. 7: On the outsider, see comment on 18.2, 4. The area behind the curtain is the so-called "most holy place," the innermost room of the tabernacle,* which contains the ark of the covenant, the seat of the divine presence (see comment on 4.4–33). 9, 11: On the grain offering, the sin offering, the guilt offering, and the elevation offering, see Lev 2; 4–7. 13: On offering the first fruits of the harvest, see Lev 23.9–14. 14: A devoted thing is something that a worshipper has dedicated to God (Lev 23.21, 28). 15–16: On the offering of the firstborn and their redemption or monetary substitu-

a Or treaty, or testimony; Heb eduth   b Heb as a service of gift

tion, see 3.11–13, 40–51. The *shekel* and the *gerah* were standard measures of weight used to calculate the monetary value of gold and silver. The *shekel of the sanctuary* was the governing standard of weight. **17:** See Lev 27.26. *A pleasing odor to the* LORD signifies the LORD's acceptance of the burnt offering. **19:** A *covenant of salt* derives its significance from the use of salt as a long-term preservative; salt was used in meals that celebrated the making of covenants or agreements in the ancient Near East. A *covenant of salt* was an unbreakable and enduring agreement. According to Lev 2.13, salt accompanied all offerings and sacrifices. **20:** Aaron and his priestly descendants will not be allowed to own any land in Canaan. They will rely only on donations and offerings to the LORD presented by worshippers.

21 To the Levites I have given every tithe in Israel for a possession in return for the service that they perform, the service in the tent of meeting. 22From now on the Israelites shall no longer approach the tent of meeting, or else they will incur guilt and die. 23But the Levites shall perform the service of the tent of meeting, and they shall bear responsibility for their own offenses; it shall be a perpetual statute throughout your generations. But among the Israelites they shall have no allotment, 24because I have given to the Levites as their portion the tithe of the Israelites, which they set apart as an offering to the LORD. Therefore I have said of them that they shall have no allotment among the Israelites.

25 Then the LORD spoke to Moses, saying: 26You shall speak to the Levites, saying: When you receive from the Israelites the tithe that I have given you from them for your portion, you shall set apart an offering from it to the LORD, a tithe of the tithe. 27It shall be reckoned to you as your gift, the same as the grain of the threshing floor and the fullness of the wine press. 28Thus you also shall set apart an offering to the LORD from all the tithes that you receive from the Israelites; and from them you shall give the LORD's offering to the priest Aaron. 29Out of all the gifts to you, you shall set apart every offering due to the LORD; the best of all of them is the part to be consecrated. 30Say also to them: When you have set apart the

best of it, then the rest shall be reckoned to the Levites as produce of the threshing floor, and as produce of the wine press. 31You may eat it in any place, you and your households; for it is your payment for your service in the tent of meeting. 32You shall incur no guilt by reason of it, when you have offered the best of it. But you shall not profane the holy gifts of the Israelites, on pain of death.

18.21–32: Apart from Aaron and his sons, the other members of the tribe of Levi will be given cities and surrounding pasture land (35.1–8) as well as a portion of the offerings given by the Israelites (vv. 21–32). The *tithe* (vv. 21, 24, 26, 28) is a one-tenth portion of grain or produce that is required as an offering to the LORD (Lev 27.30–32). On *the tent of meeting* (vv. 22, 23, 31), see comment on 1.1. On the duties of the Levites in connection with the tent of meeting, see 3.5–10; 4.1–33.

19 The LORD spoke to Moses and Aaron, saying: 2This is a statute of the law that the LORD has commanded: Tell the Israelites to bring you a red heifer without defect, in which there is no blemish and on which no yoke has been laid. 3You shall give it to the priest Eleazar, and it shall be taken outside the camp and slaughtered in his presence. 4The priest Eleazar shall take some of its blood with his finger and sprinkle it seven times towards the front of the tent of meeting. 5Then the heifer shall be burned in his sight; its skin, its flesh, and its blood, with its dung, shall be burned. 6The priest shall take cedarwood, hyssop, and crimson material, and throw them into the fire in which the heifer is burning. 7Then the priest shall wash his clothes and bathe his body in water, and afterwards he may come into the camp; but the priest shall remain unclean until evening. 8The one who burns the heifer*a* shall wash his clothes in water and bathe his body in water; he shall remain unclean until evening. 9Then someone who is clean shall gather up the ashes of the heifer, and deposit them outside the camp in a clean place; and they shall be kept for the congregation of the Israelites for the water for

a Heb it

cleansing. It is a purification offering. ¹⁰The one who gathers the ashes of the heifer shall wash his clothes and be unclean until evening.

This shall be a perpetual statute for the Israelites and for the alien residing among them. ¹¹Those who touch the dead body of any human being shall be unclean seven days. ¹²They shall purify themselves with the water on the third day and on the seventh day, and so be clean; but if they do not purify themselves on the third day and on the seventh day, they will not become clean. ¹³All who touch a corpse, the body of a human being who has died, and do not purify themselves, defile the tabernacle of the LORD; such persons shall be cut off from Israel. Since water for cleansing was not dashed on them, they remain unclean; their uncleanness is still on them.

14 This is the law when someone dies in a tent: everyone who comes into the tent, and everyone who is in the tent, shall be unclean seven days. ¹⁵And every open vessel with no cover fastened on it is unclean. ¹⁶Whoever in the open field touches one who has been killed by a sword, or who has died naturally,ᵃ or a human bone, or a grave, shall be unclean seven days. ¹⁷For the unclean they shall take some ashes of the burnt purification offering, and running water shall be added in a vessel; ¹⁸then a clean person shall take hyssop, dip it in the water, and sprinkle it on the tent, on all the furnishings, on the persons who were there, and on whoever touched the bone, the slain, the corpse, or the grave. ¹⁹The clean person shall sprinkle the unclean ones on the third day and on the seventh day, thus purifying them on the seventh day. Then they shall wash their clothes and bathe themselves in water, and at evening they shall be clean. ²⁰Any who are unclean but do not purify themselves, those persons shall be cut off from the assembly, for they have defiled the sanctuary of the LORD. Since the water for cleansing has not been dashed on them, they are unclean.

21 It shall be a perpetual statute for them. The one who sprinkles the water for cleansing shall wash his clothes, and whoever touches the water for cleansing shall be

unclean until evening. ²²Whatever the unclean person touches shall be unclean, and anyone who touches it shall be unclean until evening.

19.1–22: The ashes of the red cow and the purification of the unclean. 2: The ritual associated with the ashes of the *red heifer* (better translated as "red cow") treats the severe impurity caused by contact with a human corpse (v. 11). On ritual purity and cleanness, see the sidebar on p. 136. The redness of the cow probably symbolizes the redness of blood, a powerful purifying agent according to biblical tradition. **3:** *Eleazar* is the son of Aaron. The red cow is slaughtered *outside the camp,* unlike other sacrifices that occur at the altar in the middle of the camp. This is likely due to the severity of the impurity of corpse contamination with which the red cow is associated. **6:** The reddish *crimson material* has a color association with blood similar to that of the red cow (see comment on v. 1). This association is also suggested by the unusual burning of the blood (v. 5). *Hyssop✷* is an aromatic plant often associated with purification rituals. **12:** Although a priest (in this case, Eleazar; v. 3) is required when ashes of the red cow are created, the ritual of purification using the ashes mixed with water may be performed by any person in the community. **13:** On the *tabernacle,✷* see comment on 1.47–54. **14–16:** The uncleanness or impurity of corpse contamination is perceived as a contagious condition. This corpse contagion can be transferred to persons and *open vessels* through touch or simply through being under the same roof of a *tent* or dwelling as a corpse. **18:** On *hyssop,* see comment on v. 6.

20 The Israelites, the whole congregation, came into the wilderness of Zin in the first month, and the people stayed in Kadesh. Miriam died there, and was buried there.

2 Now there was no water for the congregation; so they gathered together against Moses and against Aaron. ³The people quarreled with Moses and said, "Would that we had died when our kindred died before the LORD! ⁴Why have you brought the assembly of the LORD into this wilderness for us and our livestock to die here? ⁵Why have you brought us up out of Egypt, to bring us to

ᵃ Heb lacks *naturally*

this wretched place? It is no place for grain, or figs, or vines, or pomegranates; and there is no water to drink." 6Then Moses and Aaron went away from the assembly to the entrance of the tent of meeting; they fell on their faces, and the glory of the LORD appeared to them. 7The LORD spoke to Moses, saying: 8Take the staff, and assemble the congregation, you and your brother Aaron, and command the rock before their eyes to yield its water. Thus you shall bring water out of the rock for them; thus you shall provide drink for the congregation and their livestock.

20.1–29: The waters of Meribah and the deaths of Miriam and Aaron. 1: *Miriam* is the sister of Aaron and Moses (26.59) and a leader with them (Mic 6.4). **2:** A similar story about the people's complaint about the lack of water occurred at Meribah in Ex 17.1–7. **6:** When Moses and Aaron *fell on their faces,* they were humbly seeking the LORD's forgiveness for the people's complaint about the lack of water. On the *tent of meeting,* see comment on 1.1. *The glory of the LORD* is the divine presence veiled in a fiery cloud that traveled with Israel throughout the wilderness (see Ex 16.10; 40.34–38). **8:** *The staff* is presumably the same staff or rod used by Moses during the exodus out of Egypt (Ex 7.20–21) and in the Exodus version of the water at Meribah story (Ex 17.5–6). It may be significant that the LORD's explicit command for Moses to "strike the rock" in Ex 17.6 is absent in the parallel story here.

9 So Moses took the staff from before the LORD, as he had commanded him. 10Moses and Aaron gathered the assembly together before the rock, and he said to them, "Listen, you rebels, shall we bring water for you out of this rock?" 11Then Moses lifted up his hand and struck the rock twice with his staff; water came out abundantly, and the congregation and their livestock drank. 12But the LORD said to Moses and Aaron, "Because you did not trust in me, to show my holiness before the eyes of the Israelites, therefore you shall not bring this assembly into the land that I have given them." 13These are the waters of Meribah,*a* where the people of Israel quarreled with the LORD, and by which he showed his holiness.

14 Moses sent messengers from Kadesh to the king of Edom, "Thus says your brother Israel: You know all the adversity that has befallen us: 15how our ancestors went down to Egypt, and we lived in Egypt a long time; and the Egyptians oppressed us and our ancestors; 16and when we cried to the LORD, he heard our voice, and sent an angel and brought us out of Egypt; and here we are in Kadesh, a town on the edge of your territory. 17Now let us pass through your land. We will not pass through field or vineyard, or drink water from any well; we will go along the King's Highway, not turning aside to the right hand or to the left until we have passed through your territory."

18 But Edom said to him, "You shall not pass through, or we will come out with the sword against you." 19The Israelites said to him, "We will stay on the highway; and if we drink of your water, we and our livestock, then we will pay for it. It is only a small matter; just let us pass through on foot." 20But he said, "You shall not pass through." And Edom came out against them with a large force, heavily armed. 21Thus Edom refused to give Israel passage through their territory; so Israel turned away from them.

22 They set out from Kadesh, and the Israelites, the whole congregation, came to Mount Hor. 23Then the LORD said to Moses and Aaron at Mount Hor, on the border of the land of Edom, 24"Let Aaron be gathered to his people. For he shall not enter the land that I have given to the Israelites, because you rebelled against my command at the waters of Meribah. 25Take Aaron and his son Eleazar, and bring them up Mount Hor; 26strip Aaron of his vestments, and put them on his son Eleazar. But Aaron shall be gathered to his people,*b* and shall die there." 27Moses did as the LORD had commanded; they went up Mount Hor in the sight of the whole congregation. 28Moses stripped Aaron of his vestments, and put them on his son Eleazar; and Aaron died there on the top of the mountain. Moses and Eleazar came down from the mountain. 29When all the congregation saw that Aaron had died, all

a That is *Quarrel*　　*b* Heb lacks *to his people*

the house of Israel mourned for Aaron thirty days.

20.9–29. 9: The staff may also be Aaron's staff, which flowered in Num 17. Aaron's staff was placed before the ark of the covenant* (17.10), an alternative description of the phrase *before the Lord.* **12:** The Lord's angry response and punishment of Moses and Aaron is surprising and difficult to explain. Commentators have offered many possible solutions, but no clear explanation emerges out of the narrative* itself. Did Moses' act of striking the rock disobey the Lord's instruction only to "command the rock" (v. 8)? Did Moses and Aaron in some way take credit themselves and away from the Lord (v. 10)? Did Moses and Aaron in some way imply that the Lord was unable or unwilling to give water to the people (v. 10)? Both Moses and Aaron are condemned to join the old generation in death outside the promised land of Canaan. Aaron's death is recorded in 20.22–29, and Moses' death is recorded in Deut 34.1–8. **13:** The place name *Meribah* is a play on the Hebrew verb meaning *quarrel* ("rib"). **14:** *Edom* is a nation that lies south and east of the land of Canaan. Israel recalled times of both friendly (2 Kings 3.4–27) and hostile (1 Kings 11.14–17) relationships with Edom. The story of Jacob and Esau (Gen 25.22–28; 33.1–17) represents in part the conflict and reconciliation of two brother nations, Israel (Gen 32.28) and Edom (Gen 25.30). This story lies in the background as Moses speaks to the king of Edom of *your brother Israel.* **16:** On the *angel* as an agent of divine guidance, see Ex 14.19 and Num 22.22–35. *Kadesh* is the desert oasis where Israel spent much of its time in the wilderness (13.26; 20.1). **17:** *The King's Highway* was a main route from the Gulf of Aqaba in the south through the nations of Edom, Moab, and Ammon, ending in Syria to the north. The highway ran roughly parallel to the eastern boundary of Canaan. **24:** To *be gathered to his people* means that Aaron will join his ancestors in death. On the events at *the waters of Meribah,* see vv. 2–13. **26:** Aaron's *vestments* are the vestments of the office of high priest (Ex 28; Lev 8.7–9).

21 When the Canaanite, the king of Arad, who lived in the Negeb, heard that Israel was coming by the way of Atharim, he fought against Israel and took some of them captive. ²Then Israel made a vow to the Lord and said, "If you will indeed give this people into our hands, then we will utterly destroy their towns." ³The Lord listened to the voice of Israel, and handed over the Canaanites; and they utterly destroyed them and their towns; so the place was called Hormah.ᵃ

4 From Mount Hor they set out by the way to the Red Sea,ᵇ to go around the land of Edom; but the people became impatient on the way. ⁵The people spoke against God and against Moses, "Why have you brought us up out of Egypt to die in the wilderness? For there is no food and no water, and we detest this miserable food." ⁶Then the Lord sent poisonousᶜ serpents among the people, and they bit the people, so that many Israelites died. ⁷The people came to Moses and said, "We have sinned by speaking against the Lord and against you; pray to the Lord to take away the serpents from us." So Moses prayed for the people. ⁸And the Lord said to Moses, "Make a poisonousᵈ serpent, and set it on a pole; and everyone who is bitten shall look at it and live." ⁹So Moses made a serpent of bronze, and put it upon a pole; and whenever a serpent bit someone, that person would look at the serpent of bronze and live.

21.1–35: Victories and plagues along the journey. 1–3: This account of Israel's obedience and military victory against a southern Canaanite enemy at *Hormah* ("Destruction") forms a counterpoint to Israel's earlier disobedience and military defeat in southern Canaan at the end of the spy story in 14.39–45 ("pursuing them as far as Hormah," 14.45). **5:** The Israelites typically complained against Moses or Aaron in previous murmuring stories (11.2; 14.2; 16.3). However, this time their rebellion is more serious in that they aim their complaint *against God and against Moses.* **6:** The Hebrew word for "poisonous" literally means "fiery," a reference to the burning pain of a snake bite (see also v. 8). **9:** *A serpent of bronze* is a wordplay in Hebrew, "nehash" ("serpent") and "nehoshet" ("bronze"). Later in Israel's history, King Hezekiah tore down and destroyed what was alleged to be Moses' bronze serpent called "Nehushtan." The sacred object had become an idolatrous object of worship and was thus destroyed (2 Kings 18.4). In the ancient world,

a Heb *Destruction*   b Or *Sea of Reeds*   c Or *fiery;* Heb *seraphim*   d Or *fiery;* Heb *seraph*

the snake was a complex and powerful symbol of evil, conveying death as well as fertility, life, and healing.

10 The Israelites set out, and camped in Oboth. [11]They set out from Oboth, and camped at Iye-abarim, in the wilderness bordering Moab toward the sunrise. [12]From there they set out, and camped in the Wadi Zered. [13]From there they set out, and camped on the other side of the Arnon, in[a] the wilderness that extends from the boundary of the Amorites; for the Arnon is the boundary of Moab, between Moab and the Amorites. [14]Wherefore it is said in the Book of the Wars of the LORD,

"Waheb in Suphah and the wadis.
The Arnon [15]and the slopes of the
 wadis
that extend to the seat of Ar,
and lie along the border of Moab."[b]

16 From there they continued to Beer;[c] that is the well of which the LORD said to Moses, "Gather the people together, and I will give them water." [17]Then Israel sang this song:

"Spring up, O well!—Sing to it!—
[18] the well that the leaders sank,
 that the nobles of the people dug,
 with the scepter, with the staff."

From the wilderness to Mattanah, [19]from Mattanah to Nahaliel, from Nahaliel to Bamoth, [20]and from Bamoth to the valley lying in the region of Moab by the top of Pisgah that overlooks the wasteland.[d]

21 Then Israel sent messengers to King Sihon of the Amorites, saying, [22]"Let me pass through your land; we will not turn aside into field or vineyard; we will not drink the water of any well; we will go by the King's Highway until we have passed through your territory." [23]But Sihon would not allow Israel to pass through his territory. Sihon gathered all his people together, and went out against Israel to the wilderness; he came to Jahaz, and fought against Israel. [24]Israel put him to the sword, and took possession of his land from the Arnon to the Jabbok, as far as to the Ammonites; for the boundary of the Ammonites was strong. [25]Israel took all these towns, and Israel settled in all the towns of the Amorites, in Heshbon, and in

all its villages. [26]For Heshbon was the city of King Sihon of the Amorites, who had fought against the former king of Moab and captured all his land as far as the Arnon. [27]Therefore the ballad singers say,

"Come to Heshbon, let it be built;
 let the city of Sihon be established.
[28] For fire came out from Heshbon,
 flame from the city of Sihon.
It devoured Ar of Moab,
 and swallowed up[e] the heights of the
 Arnon.
[29] Woe to you, O Moab!
 You are undone, O people of
 Chemosh!
He has made his sons fugitives,
 and his daughters captives,
 to an Amorite king, Sihon.
[30] So their posterity perished
 from Heshbon[f] to Dibon,
 and we laid waste until fire spread to
 Medeba."[g]

31 Thus Israel settled in the land of the Amorites. [32]Moses sent to spy out Jazer; and they captured its villages, and dispossessed the Amorites who were there.

33 Then they turned and went up the road to Bashan; and King Og of Bashan came out against them, he and all his people, to battle at Edrei. [34]But the LORD said to Moses, "Do not be afraid of him; for I have given him into your hand, with all his people, and all his land. You shall do to him as you did to King Sihon of the Amorites, who ruled in Heshbon." [35]So they killed him, his sons, and all his people, until there was no survivor left; and they took possession of his land.

21.10–33. 10–13: The locations mentioned center around the land of Moab on the eastern boundary of Canaan. 14: This one biblical reference to *the Book of the Wars of the LORD* suggests it is an ancient poetic collection describing Israel's early military conquests. Another such collection is mentioned in Josh 10.13 and 2 Sam 1.18 ("Book of Jashar"). The content of these works is otherwise unknown. 15: *Ar* is apparently

a Gk: Heb *which is in* b Meaning of Heb uncertain c That is *Well* d Or *Jeshimon* e Gk: Heb *and the lords of* f Gk: Heb *we have shot at them; Heshbon has perished* g Compare Sam Gk: Meaning of MT uncertain

an important city in Moab (see v. 28). **16:** The place name *Beer* is the Hebrew word for a *well* of water. **19–20:** Several of these place names are otherwise unknown. Moab is a nation that lies on the eastern boundary of Canaan. *Pisgah* is a high plateau that looks out to the west over a *wasteland*, the Jordan River valley, and on to the land of Canaan (Deut 34.1–4). **21:** *The Amorites* occupy a small nation just north of Moab. **22:** On *the King's Highway*, see comment on 20.17. **24:** Israel captured the land between two rivers or wadis,* the *Arnon* to the south and the *Jabbok* to the north. **27–30:** This ancient poem is a taunt song that celebrates an earlier Amorite conquest of a part of Moab's territory. *Chemosh* (v. 29) is the god of the Moabites. **33:** *Bashan* is another small Amorite nation just north of the Jabbok river.

22 The Israelites set out, and camped in the plains of Moab across the Jordan from Jericho. ²Now Balak son of Zippor saw all that Israel had done to the Amorites. ³Moab was in great dread of the people, because they were so numerous; Moab was overcome with fear of the people of Israel. ⁴And Moab said to the elders of Midian, "This horde will now lick up all that is around us, as an ox licks up the grass of the field." Now Balak son of Zippor was king of Moab at that time. ⁵He sent messengers to Balaam son of Beor at Pethor, which is on the Euphrates, in the land of Amaw,ᵃ to summon him, saying, "A people has come out of Egypt; they have spread over the face of the earth, and they have settled next to me. ⁶Come now, curse this people for me, since they are stronger than I; perhaps I shall be able to defeat them and drive them from the land; for I know that whomever you bless is blessed, and whomever you curse is cursed."

7 So the elders of Moab and the elders of Midian departed with the fees for divination in their hand; and they came to Balaam, and gave him Balak's message. ⁸He said to them, "Stay here tonight, and I will bring back word to you, just as the LORD speaks to me"; so the officials of Moab stayed with Balaam. ⁹God came to Balaam and said, "Who are these men with you?" ¹⁰Balaam said to God, "King Balak son of Zippor of Moab, has sent me this message: ¹¹'A people has come out

of Egypt and has spread over the face of the earth; now come, curse them for me; perhaps I shall be able to fight against them and drive them out.'" ¹²God said to Balaam, "You shall not go with them; you shall not curse the people, for they are blessed." ¹³So Balaam rose in the morning, and said to the officials of Balak, "Go to your own land, for the LORD has refused to let me go with you." ¹⁴So the officials of Moab rose and went to Balak, and said, "Balaam refuses to come with us."

22.1–40: The prophet* Balaam, King Balak, and three encounters with the angel of the LORD. Balak, king of Moab, hears of the Israelite victories against the Amorites and becomes afraid. He hires a prophet or seer from Mesopotamia named Balaam to come and place a curse on Israel. Balaam, however, ends up becoming an instrument of the LORD, blessing Israel rather than cursing it. **2:** On *all that Israel had done to the Amorites*, see 21.21–35. **4:** On the connections between Moab, Midian, and Balaam the prophet, see chs. 25 and 31. **5:** *The Euphrates* is a major river in Mesopotamia. **6:** A prophet's spoken words of *curse* or *blessing* were believed to unleash either negative or positive powers that would shape the outcome of future events. **7:** Balaam is a hired prophet* who charged *fees for divination*. *Divination* was an ancient means of finding information about future events by interpreting some object such as the configuration of spots on the liver of a sacrificed animal. **8:** Surprisingly, although Balaam is a non-Israelite prophet, he says he will obey Israel's God, the LORD (see vv. 18, 20).

15 Once again Balak sent officials, more numerous and more distinguished than these. ¹⁶They came to Balaam and said to him, "Thus says Balak son of Zippor: 'Do not let anything hinder you from coming to me; ¹⁷for I will surely do you great honor, and whatever you say to me I will do; come, curse this people for me.'" ¹⁸But Balaam replied to the servants of Balak, "Although Balak were to give me his house full of silver and gold, I could not go beyond the command of the LORD my God, to do less or more. ¹⁹You remain here, as the others did, so that I may learn what more the LORD may say to me."

a Or land of his kinsfolk

The Prophet Balaam

In the history of biblical interpretation,★ the prophet★ or seer named Balaam has received mixed reviews. Some commentators have viewed Balaam as a true and obedient prophet of God. Others have labeled him an evil and false prophet. The variation in evaluating Balaam's character is due in part to the complexity of the biblical record itself. The figure of Balaam emerges from Num 22–24 in a largely positive light. Although Balaam is lampooned in the donkey episode in 22.22–35, he ends up obediently speaking God's word of blessing rather than curse. The prophet Micah affirms the way Balaam turned back the evil scheme of King Balak (Mic 6.5). On the other hand, Deut 23.3–6 portrays Balaam negatively and uses his association with Moab as a reason for prohibiting Moabites and Ammonites from entering the assembly of God's people. Later Balaam is killed for having counseled the Midianite women to lead Israel astray in the worship of a false god named Baal★ of Peor (see Num 25; 31.8, 16).

This ambivalence toward the character of Balaam reflects a long history. Stories about a legendary prophet named Balaam circulated not only in Israel but also among its Near Eastern neighbors. Archaeologists have discovered plaster panels in a non-Israelite temple at Deir 'Allah in modern-day Jordan that include the name of a famed prophet named Balaam. The inscription, which is dated to the eighth century BCE, recounts Balaam's vision from the gods at night. The vision includes a message from a council of gods called the "shaddai" gods. Interestingly, the Hebrew word "Shaddai" (translated as "the Almighty") is used as a title for Israel's God in the biblical oracles★ of Balaam. Balaam is described as the one "who sees the vision of the Almighty ('Shaddai')" in Num 24.4, 16. In the inscription at Deir 'Allah, the gods inform Balaam that a drought is about to come on the land and the order of nature is about to be overturned. Balaam prays to the gods to reverse their decision and avoid such a calamity. The character of Balaam portrayed in Num 22–24 is probably built upon a legendary prophet who was known in the area near Moab and the Jordan River where the biblical story of Balaam is set.

20That night God came to Balaam and said to him, "If the men have come to summon you, get up and go with them; but do only what I tell you to do." 21So Balaam got up in the morning, saddled his donkey, and went with the officials of Moab.

22 God's anger was kindled because he was going, and the angel of the LORD took his stand in the road as his adversary. Now he was riding on the donkey, and his two servants were with him. 23The donkey saw the angel of the LORD standing in the road, with a drawn sword in his hand; so the donkey turned off the road, and went into the field; and Balaam struck the donkey, to turn it back onto the road. 24Then the angel of the LORD stood in a narrow path between the vineyards, with a wall on either side. 25When the donkey saw the angel of the LORD, it scraped against the wall, and scraped Balaam's foot against the wall; so he struck it again. 26Then the angel of the LORD went ahead, and stood in a narrow place, where there was no way to turn either to the right or to the left. 27When the donkey saw the angel of the LORD, it lay down under Balaam; and Balaam's anger was kindled, and he struck the donkey with his staff. 28Then the LORD opened the mouth of the donkey, and it said to Balaam, "What have I done to

you, that you have struck me these three times?" 29 Balaam said to the donkey, "Because you have made a fool of me! I wish I had a sword in my hand! I would kill you right now!" 30 But the donkey said to Balaam, "Am I not your donkey, which you have ridden all your life to this day? Have I been in the habit of treating you this way?" And he said, "No."

31 Then the LORD opened the eyes of Balaam, and he saw the angel of the LORD standing in the road, with his drawn sword in his hand; and he bowed down, falling on his face. 32 The angel of the LORD said to him, "Why have you struck your donkey these three times? I have come out as an adversary, because your way is perverse*a* before me. 33 The donkey saw me, and turned away from me these three times. If it had not turned away from me, surely just now I would have killed you and let it live." 34 Then Balaam said to the angel of the LORD, "I have sinned, for I did not know that you were standing in the road to oppose me. Now therefore, if it is displeasing to you, I will return home." 35 The angel of the LORD said to Balaam, "Go with the men; but speak only what I tell you to speak." So Balaam went on with the officials of Balak.

36 When Balak heard that Balaam had come, he went out to meet him at Ir-moab, on the boundary formed by the Arnon, at the farthest point of the boundary. 37 Balak said to Balaam, "Did I not send to summon you? Why did you not come to me? Am I not able to honor you?" 38 Balaam said to Balak, "I have come to you now, but do I have power to say just anything? The word God puts in my mouth, that is what I must say." 39 Then Balaam went with Balak, and they came to Kiriath-huzoth. 40 Balak sacrificed oxen and sheep, and sent them to Balaam and to the officials who were with him.

22.15–40. 22: Although the LORD had just commanded Balaam to go to King Balak (v. 20), the LORD becomes angry at Balaam *because he was going.* As a result, *the angel of the LORD* blocks Balaam's way. The threat of an angel contending against a person whom God has just commanded to go on a mission is a motif★ that occurs elsewhere in the Bible. Moses is

threatened by the LORD when he begins his mission to lead Israel out of Egypt (Ex 4.24–26). Joshua encounters an angelic commander of the LORD's army with a drawn sword as he begins his mission to conquer Canaan (Josh 5.13–15). Jacob wrestles with God as he returns home to Canaan (Gen 22–32). These stories emphasize that even those sent by God remain subject to God's will and are not immune from correction or judgment. **23:** Balaam is supposed to be a professional diviner and prophet. However, his own *donkey* is able to see what he does not see, *the angel of the LORD* standing in front of him. **28:** The talking donkey gives this scene the character of a fable,★ which makes fun of Balaam. Just as *the LORD opened the mouth of the donkey,* so the LORD will need to open the eyes of Balaam (v. 31). Verbs of "seeing" and "looking" are key words throughout the Balaam story of chs. 22–24. **32, 35:** The LORD's commands to go (v. 20), to stop (v. 32), and to go again (v. 35) demonstrate to Balaam that the LORD is in sole command of him. The LORD will be ready to attack Balaam if he does not do God's will and bless Israel. **36:** The *Arnon* river is the northern boundary of the nation of Moab. **40:** The sacrifices of oxen and sheep were likely part of the ritual of divination (see comment on v. 7).

Balaam's four oracles of blessing

22.41–24.25: The contents of Balaam's first two oracles★ or pronouncements of blessing (23.7–10 and 23.18–24) are intricately related to and dependent on the surrounding narrative★ about Balaam and Balak. In contrast, the contents of Balaam's third and fourth oracles of blessing (24.3–9 and 24.15–24) are less tied to the narrative. Thus, they may have had an independent life prior to being incorporated into the present story.

---

41 On the next day Balak took Balaam and brought him up to Bamoth-baal; and from there he could see part of the people of Israel.*b* 1 Then Balaam said to Balak, "Build me seven altars here, and prepare seven bulls and seven rams for me." 2 Balak did as Balaam had said; and Balak and Balaam offered a bull and a ram on each altar. 3 Then Balaam said to Balak, "Stay here beside your burnt offerings while I go aside. Perhaps the LORD will come to meet

---

a Meaning of Heb uncertain　　*b* Heb lacks *of Israel*

me. Whatever he shows me I will tell you."
And he went to a bare height.

4 Then God met Balaam; and Balaam
said to him, "I have arranged the seven altars, and have offered a bull and a ram on
each altar." 5The LORD put a word in Balaam's mouth, and said, "Return to Balak,
and this is what you must say." 6So he returned to Balak,*a* who was standing beside
his burnt offerings with all the officials of
Moab. 7Then Balaam*b* uttered his oracle,
saying:

"Balak has brought me from Aram,
    the king of Moab from the eastern
        mountains:
'Come, curse Jacob for me;
    Come, denounce Israel!'
8 How can I curse whom God has not
        cursed?
    How can I denounce those whom the
        LORD has not denounced?
9 For from the top of the crags I see him,
    from the hills I behold him;
    Here is a people living alone,
        and not reckoning itself among the
            nations!
10 Who can count the dust of Jacob,
        or number the dust-cloud*c* of Israel?
    Let me die the death of the upright,
        and let my end be like his!"

11 Then Balak said to Balaam, "What
have you done to me? I brought you to curse
my enemies, but now you have done nothing
but bless them." 12He answered, "Must I not
take care to say what the LORD puts into my
mouth?"

13 So Balak said to him, "Come with me
to another place from which you may see
them; you shall see only part of them, and
shall not see them all; then curse them for
me from there." 14So he took him to the field
of Zophim, to the top of Pisgah. He built
seven altars, and offered a bull and a ram on
each altar. 15Balaam said to Balak, "Stand
here beside your burnt offerings, while I
meet the LORD over there." 16The LORD met
Balaam, put a word into his mouth, and said,
"Return to Balak, and this is what you shall
say." 17When he came to him, he was standing beside his burnt offerings with the officials of Moab. Balak said to him, "What has

the LORD said?" 18Then Balaam uttered his
oracle, saying:

"Rise, Balak, and hear;
    listen to me, O son of Zippor:
19 God is not a human being, that he
        should lie,
    or a mortal, that he should change his
        mind.
    Has he promised, and will he not do it?
    Has he spoken, and will he not
        fulfill it?
20 See, I received a command to bless;
    he has blessed, and I cannot revoke it.
21 He has not beheld misfortune in Jacob;
    nor has he seen trouble in Israel.
    The LORD their God is with them,
        acclaimed as a king among them.
22 God, who brings them out of Egypt,
    is like the horns of a wild ox for them.
23 Surely there is no enchantment against
        Jacob,
    no divination against Israel;
    now it shall be said of Jacob and Israel,
        'See what God has done!'
24 Look, a people rising up like a lioness,
    and rousing itself like a lion!
    It does not lie down until it has eaten
        the prey
    and drunk the blood of the slain."

25 Then Balak said to Balaam, "Do not
curse them at all, and do not bless them at
all." 26But Balaam answered Balak, "Did I
not tell you, 'Whatever the LORD says, that
is what I must do'?"

27 So Balak said to Balaam, "Come now,
I will take you to another place; perhaps it
will please God that you may curse them for
me from there." 28So Balak took Balaam to
the top of Peor, which overlooks the wasteland.*d* 29Balaam said to Balak, "Build me
seven altars here, and prepare seven bulls
and seven rams for me." 30So Balak did as
Balaam had said, and offered a bull and a
ram on each altar.

22.41–23.30. 7: *Aram* is the biblical name for the nation of Syria, which lies north and east of Moab. **10:**
The dust of Jacob is a reference to God's promises in

a Heb *him*   *b* Heb *he*   *c* Or *fourth part*
d Or *overlooks Jeshimon*

Genesis that the descendants of Abraham and Jacob would be as numerous as the dust of the earth (Gen 13.16; 28.14). **14:** On *Pisgah,* see comment on 21.19–20. **19:** God does not *change his mind* about promises of blessing and good fortune. On the other hand, God can sometimes be swayed to alter divine decisions about threatened judgments and punishments (Gen 18.16–33; Ex 32.1–14). **24:** On the images of the *rising lion* and *lioness,* see comment on 24.17. **28:** *Peor* is located east of the Jordan river near Pisgah (21.20).

24

Now Balaam saw that it pleased the LORD to bless Israel, so he did not go, as at other times, to look for omens, but set his face toward the wilderness. ²Balaam looked up and saw Israel camping tribe by tribe. Then the spirit of God came upon him, ³and he uttered his oracle, saying:

"The oracle of Balaam son of Beor,
    the oracle of the man whose eye is
    clear,*
⁴ the oracle of one who hears the words
        of God,
    who sees the vision of the Almighty,*
    who falls down, but with eyes
        uncovered:
⁵ how fair are your tents, O Jacob,
    your encampments, O Israel!
⁶ Like palm groves that stretch far away,
    like gardens beside a river,
    like aloes that the LORD has planted,
    like cedar trees beside the waters.
⁷ Water shall flow from his buckets,
    and his seed shall have abundant
        water,
    his king shall be higher than Agag,
    and his kingdom shall be exalted.
⁸ God who brings him out of Egypt,
    is like the horns of a wild ox
        for him;
    he shall devour the nations that are his
        foes
    and break their bones.
    He shall strike with his arrows.*
⁹ He crouched, he lay down like a lion,
    and like a lioness; who will rouse
        him up?
    Blessed is everyone who blesses you,
        and cursed is everyone who curses
        you."

10 Then Balak's anger was kindled against Balaam, and he struck his hands together. Balak said to Balaam, "I summoned you to curse my enemies, but instead you have blessed them these three times. ¹¹Now be off with you! Go home! I said, 'I will reward you richly,' but the LORD has denied you any reward." ¹²And Balaam said to Balak, "Did I not tell your messengers whom you sent to me, ¹³'If Balak should give me his house full of silver and gold, I would not be able to go beyond the word of the LORD, to do either good or bad of my own will; what the LORD says, that is what I will say'? ¹⁴So now, I am going to my people; let me advise you what this people will do to your people in days to come."

15 So he uttered his oracle, saying:
"The oracle of Balaam son of Beor,
    the oracle of the man whose eye is
    clear,*
16 the oracle of one who hears the words
        of God,
    and knows the knowledge of the Most
        High,*
    who sees the vision of the Almighty,*
    who falls down, but with his eyes
        uncovered:
17 I see him, but not now;
    I behold him, but not near—
    a star shall come out of Jacob,
    and a scepter shall rise out of Israel;
    it shall crush the borderlands* of Moab,
    and the territory* of all the Shethites.
18 Edom will become a possession,
    Seir a possession of its enemies,*
    while Israel does valiantly.
19 One out of Jacob shall rule,
    and destroy the survivors of Ir."

20 Then he looked on Amalek, and uttered his oracle, saying:
"First among the nations was Amalek,
    but its end is to perish forever."
21 Then he looked on the Kenite, and uttered his oracle, saying:
"Enduring is your dwelling place,
    and your nest is set in the rock;

a Or *closed* or *open*   b Traditional rendering of Heb *Shaddai*   c Meaning of Heb uncertain   d Or *of Elyon*   e Or *forehead*   f Some Mss read *skull*   g Heb *Seir, its enemies, a possession*

22 yet Kain is destined for burning.
    How long shall Asshur take you away
        captive?"
23 Again he uttered his oracle, saying:
    "Alas, who shall live when God does this?
24   But ships shall come from Kittim
    and shall afflict Asshur and Eber;
        and he also shall perish forever."
25 Then Balaam got up and went back to his place, and Balak also went his way.

24.1–25. 1: An *omen* is information derived from divination (see comment on 22.7). 2: That *the spirit of God came upon* Balaam suggests a more direct mode of divine inspiration and guidance than reliance on omens (v. 1). 4: *The Almighty* (Heb., "Shaddai") is an ancient divine name applied to the LORD (Gen 17.1; Ex 6.3). The Balaam inscription found by archaeologists at Deir 'Allah includes mention of "Shaddai" gods (see the sidebar on p. 198). 7: Some commentators link this *Agag* to King Agag of the Amalekites whom the Israelite king Saul defeated in 1 Sam 15. 9: On the images of the roused *lion* and *lioness,* see comment on 24.17. 13: See 22.18. 16: *The Most High* (Heb., "Elyon") is an ancient divine name used for the LORD in other biblical contexts (Gen 14.18–24; Deut 32.8). On *the Almighty* as a divine name, see comment on 24.4. 17: The image of *a star* could be used as a metaphor★ for a king (Isa 14.12). The *scepter* or royal staff symbolized royal authority, much like the staffs of Moses and Aaron represented their authority as leader and priest of Israel (17.10; 20.8). Many commentators understand these images of a future royal figure as pointing to King David and his victories over Moab and Edom (2 Sam 8.2, 11–14). The blessing of Jacob in Gen 49.9–10 uses the image of the crouching lion and lioness waiting to be roused for the tribe of Judah (the tribe of King David). These same images appear in Balaam's oracles★ (23.24; 24.9). The *Sheth-ites* may be an ethnic group within the nation of Moab. 18: The nation of *Edom* is also known as *Seir* (Gen 32.3). 19: *Ir* is apparently a town in Moab (see 22.36). 20: On *Amalek* and the Amalekites, see comment on 13.29. 21–22: On *the Kenites,* see comment on 10.29. The mention of *Kain* with the Kenites suggests a link to the Genesis ancestors, Cain and Tubal-cain (Gen 4.1–22). 22, 24: These final verses of the oracle are somewhat obscure. *Asshur* (v. 22, 24) is the biblical name for the empire of Assyria. *Kittim* (v. 24) is usually another name for Cyprus. *Eber* is uncertain.

25 While Israel was staying at Shittim, the people began to have sexual relations with the women of Moab. 2These invited the people to the sacrifices of their gods, and the people ate and bowed down to their gods. 3Thus Israel yoked itself to the Baal of Peor, and the LORD's anger was kindled against Israel. 4The LORD said to Moses, "Take all the chiefs of the people, and impale them in the sun before the LORD, in order that the fierce anger of the LORD may turn away from Israel." 5And Moses said to the judges of Israel, "Each of you shall kill any of your people who have yoked themselves to the Baal of Peor."

6 Just then one of the Israelites came and brought a Midianite woman into his family, in the sight of Moses and in the sight of the whole congregation of the Israelites, while they were weeping at the entrance of the tent of meeting. 7When Phinehas son of Eleazar, son of Aaron the priest, saw it, he got up and left the congregation. Taking a spear in his hand, 8he went after the Israelite man into the tent, and pierced the two of them, the Israelite and the woman, through the belly. So the plague was stopped among the people of Israel. 9Nevertheless those that died by the plague were twenty-four thousand.

10 The LORD spoke to Moses, saying: 11"Phinehas son of Eleazar, son of Aaron the priest, has turned back my wrath from the Israelites by manifesting such zeal among them on my behalf that in my jealousy I did not consume the Israelites. 12Therefore say, 'I hereby grant him my covenant of peace. 13It shall be for him and for his descendants after him a covenant of perpetual priesthood, because he was zealous for his God, and made atonement for the Israelites.' "

14 The name of the slain Israelite man, who was killed with the Midianite woman, was Zimri son of Salu, head of an ancestral house belonging to the Simeonites. 15The name of the Midianite woman who was killed was Cozbi daughter of Zur, who was the head of a clan, an ancestral house in Midian.

16 The LORD said to Moses, 17"Harass the Midianites, and defeat them; 18for they have harassed you by the trickery with which

they deceived you in the affair of Peor, and in the affair of Cozbi, the daughter of a leader of Midian, their sister; she was killed on the day of the plague that resulted from Peor."

25.1–18: The final rebellion: Israel's worship of a foreign god and entanglements with foreign women. The chapter combines two incidents in which the old wilderness generation of Israelites rebel against God's commands. One incident involves Israelite men having sexual relations with women from Moab, which leads them to worship the Moabite god Baal* of Peor (vv. 1–5). A second incident involves an Israelite from the tribe of Simeon who has sexual relations with a woman from Midian (vv. 6–15). Intermarriage with foreign peoples was feared since it was believed to lead to the worship of foreign gods (Deut 7.1–5). Yet other biblical traditions do not condemn intermarriage. Moses himself was married to a Midianite woman (Ex 2.15–22), and the book of Ruth portrays an Israelite man's marriage to a Moabite woman named Ruth in a very favorable light. The LORD sends a plague as punishment that kills 24,000 Israelites (v. 9). Those who are killed are presumably the last remnants of the old generation, which had been condemned to die in the wilderness in the spy story of Num 13–14 (see 14.28–30). This old generation had been counted in the first census list in Num 1. The new census list in Num 26 will mark the emergence of an entirely new generation of Israelites, who will be allowed to enter the promised land of Canaan (see 26.63–65). **1:** *Shittim* may be the same as Abelshittim, which is located on the plains of Moab (33.49). The Hebrew verb "znh," translated here as *to have sexual relations with,* may also mean "to prostitute themselves with." The same verb can also be used for the forbidden worship of foreign gods (Ex 34.12–16: "your sons also prostitute themselves to their gods," v. 16). **3:** *Baal* means "lord," but the title is used here for the name of a non-Israelite god, *Baal of Peor.* **6:** On *the tent of meeting,* see comment on 1.1. **7:** *Phinehas* is the grandson of the high priest Aaron (see Ex 6.23–25). **12–13:** A *covenant* of peace is a promise of well-being (Ezek 37.26). The *perpetual priesthood* offered to Phinehas is an extension of the perpetual priesthood first given to Aaron and his sons (Ex 40.12–15). **16–18:** The military defeat of *the Midianites* commanded here will be carried out by the new generation of Israelites in Num 31. The earlier incident involving the Moabite women and the god Baal of Peor (vv. 1–5) is joined together with the Midianite incident (vv. 6–15) as essentially one episode.

A second census of a new generation of Israelites 26.1–65: The first census list in Num 1 had counted the twelve tribes of Israel who had been born in Egypt and experienced the exodus out of Egypt. This old generation rebelled against the LORD; hence the LORD condemned them to die in the wilderness without entering the promised land of Canaan (14.28–35). However, the LORD promised to bring the new generation of Israelites into the land of Canaan. This second census list in Num 26 marks the beginning of the story of this new generation of Israelites who will enter the land of Canaan (26.63–65).

---

26 After the plague the LORD said to Moses and to Eleazar son of Aaron the priest, ²"Take a census of the whole congregation of the Israelites, from twenty years old and upward, by their ancestral houses, everyone in Israel able to go to war." ³Moses and Eleazar the priest spoke with them in the plains of Moab by the Jordan opposite Jericho, saying, ⁴"Take a census of the people,ᵃ from twenty years old and upward," as the LORD commanded Moses.

The Israelites, who came out of the land of Egypt, were:

5 Reuben, the firstborn of Israel. The descendants of Reuben: of Hanoch, the clan of the Hanochites; of Pallu, the clan of the Palluites; ⁶of Hezron, the clan of the Hezronites; of Carmi, the clan of the Carmites. ⁷These are the clans of the Reubenites; the number of those enrolled was forty-three thousand seven hundred thirty. ⁸And the descendants of Pallu: Eliab. ⁹The descendants of Eliab: Nemuel, Dathan, and Abiram. These are the same Dathan and Abiram, chosen from the congregation, who rebelled against Moses and Aaron in the company of Korah, when they rebelled against the LORD, ¹⁰and the earth opened its mouth and swallowed them up along with Korah, when that company died, when the fire devoured two hundred fifty men; and they became a warning. ¹¹Notwithstanding, the sons of Korah did not die.

a Heb lacks *take a census of the people:* Compare verse 2

12 The descendants of Simeon by their clans: of Nemuel, the clan of the Nemuelites; of Jamin, the clan of the Jaminites; of Jachin, the clan of the Jachinites; 13 of Zerah, the clan of the Zerahites; of Shaul, the clan of the Shaulites.*a* 14 These are the clans of the Simeonites, twenty-two thousand two hundred.

15 The children of Gad by their clans: of Zephon, the clan of the Zephonites; of Haggi, the clan of the Haggites; of Shuni, the clan of the Shunites; 16 of Ozni, the clan of the Oznites; of Eri, the clan of the Erites; 17 of Arod, the clan of the Arodites; of Areli, the clan of the Arelites. 18 These are the clans of the Gadites: the number of those enrolled was forty thousand five hundred.

19 The sons of Judah: Er and Onan; Er and Onan died in the land of Canaan. 20 The descendants of Judah by their clans were: of Shelah, the clan of the Shelanites; of Perez, the clan of the Perezites; of Zerah, the clan of the Zerahites. 21 The descendants of Perez were: of Hezron, the clan of the Hezronites; of Hamul, the clan of the Hamulites. 22 These are the clans of Judah: the number of those enrolled was seventy-six thousand five hundred.

23 The descendants of Issachar by their clans: of Tola, the clan of the Tolaites; of Puvah, the clan of the Punites; 24 of Jashub, the clan of the Jashubites; of Shimron, the clan of the Shimronites. 25 These are the clans of Issachar: sixty-four thousand three hundred enrolled.

26 The descendants of Zebulun by their clans: of Sered, the clan of the Seredites; of Elon, the clan of the Elonites; of Jahleel, the clan of the Jahleelites. 27 These are the clans of the Zebulunites; the number of those enrolled was sixty thousand five hundred.

28 The sons of Joseph by their clans: Manasseh and Ephraim. 29 The descendants of Manasseh: of Machir, the clan of the Machirites; and Machir was the father of Gilead; of Gilead, the clan of the Gileadites. 30 These are the descendants of Gilead: of Iezer, the clan of the Iezerites; of Helek, the clan of the Helekites; 31 and of Asriel, the clan of the Asrielites; and of Shechem, the clan of the Shechemites; 32 and of She-

mida, the clan of the Shemidaites; and of Hepher, the clan of the Hepherites. 33 Now Zelophehad son of Hepher had no sons, but daughters: and the names of the daughters of Zelophehad were Mahlah, Noah, Hoglah, Milcah, and Tirzah. 34 These are the clans of Manasseh; the number of those enrolled was fifty-two thousand seven hundred.

35 These are the descendants of Ephraim according to their clans: of Shuthelah, the clan of the Shuthelahites; of Becher, the clan of the Becherites; of Tahan, the clan of the Tahanites. 36 And these are the descendants of Shuthelah: of Eran, the clan of the Eranites. 37 These are the clans of the Ephraimites: the number of those enrolled was thirty-two thousand five hundred. These are the descendants of Joseph by their clans.

38 The descendants of Benjamin by their clans: of Bela, the clan of the Belaites; of Ashbel, the clan of the Ashbelites; of Ahiram, the clan of the Ahiramites; 39 of Shephupham, the clan of the Shuphamites; of Hupham, the clan of the Huphamites. 40 And the sons of Bela were Ard and Naaman: of Ard, the clan of the Ardites; of Naaman, the clan of the Naamites. 41 These are the descendants of Benjamin by their clans; the number of those enrolled was forty-five thousand six hundred.

42 These are the descendants of Dan by their clans: of Shuham, the clan of the Shuhamites. These are the clans of Dan by their clans. 43 All the clans of the Shuhamites: sixty-four thousand four hundred enrolled.

44 The descendants of Asher by their families: of Imnah, the clan of the Imnites; of Ishvi, the clan of the Ishvites; of Beriah, the clan of the Beriites. 45 Of the descendants of Beriah: of Heber, the clan of the Heberites; of Malchiel, the clan of the Malchielites. 46 And the name of the daughter of Asher was Serah. 47 These are the clans of the Asherites: the number of those enrolled was fifty-three thousand four hundred.

48 The descendants of Naphtali by their clans: of Jahzeel, the clan of the Jahzeelites; of Guni, the clan of the Gunites; 49 of Jezer,

a Or Saul . . . Saulites

the clan of the Jezerites; of Shillem, the clan of the Shillemites. ⁵⁰These are the Naphtalites*a* by their clans: the number of those enrolled was forty-five thousand four hundred.

51 This was the number of the Israelites enrolled: six hundred and one thousand seven hundred thirty.

52 The LORD spoke to Moses, saying: ⁵³To these the land shall be apportioned for inheritance according to the number of names. ⁵⁴To a large tribe you shall give a large inheritance, and to a small tribe you shall give a small inheritance; every tribe shall be given its inheritance according to its enrollment. ⁵⁵But the land shall be apportioned by lot; according to the names of their ancestral tribes they shall inherit. ⁵⁶Their inheritance shall be apportioned according to lot between the larger and the smaller.

57 This is the enrollment of the Levites by their clans: of Gershon, the clan of the Gershonites; of Kohath, the clan of the Kohathites; of Merari, the clan of the Merarites. ⁵⁸These are the clans of Levi: the clan of the Libnites, the clan of the Hebronites, the clan of the Mahlites, the clan of the Mushites, the clan of the Korahites. Now Kohath was the father of Amram. ⁵⁹The name of Amram's wife was Jochebed daughter of Levi, who was born to Levi in Egypt; and she bore to Amram: Aaron, Moses, and their sister Miriam. ⁶⁰To Aaron were born Nadab, Abihu, Eleazar, and Ithamar. ⁶¹But Nadab and Abihu died when they offered unholy fire before the LORD. ⁶²The number of those enrolled was twenty-three thousand, every male one month old and upward; for they were not enrolled among the Israelites because there was no allotment given to them among the Israelites.

63 These were those enrolled by Moses and Eleazar the priest, who enrolled the Israelites in the plains of Moab by the Jordan opposite Jericho. ⁶⁴Among these there was not one of those enrolled by Moses and Aaron the priest, who had enrolled the Israelites in the wilderness of Sinai. ⁶⁵For the LORD had said of them, "They shall die in the wilderness." Not one of them was left, except Caleb son of Jephunneh and Joshua son of Nun.

26.1–65. 1: *After the plague* is a reference to the plague in 25.8–9. *Eleazar* is the son of Aaron who became the high priest at Aaron's death (20.22–29). **5–50:** This second census list is similar in form to the census list in Num 1, but there are some notable differences. The total numbers for each of the twelve tribes are different. The tribe of Simeon sustained the greatest loss of numbers, perhaps as a result of the Simeonite's sin in 25.14 (compare 26.12–14 and 1.23). The sequence of the twelve tribes is slightly different from Num 1 and closer to the order of the tribes in Num 2. Another difference between Num 1 and 26 is that various sub-clans* are added in Num 26 under each tribe as a sign of the birth of a new generation. These clan names are similar to those listed in Gen 46.8–27. **51:** The total here of 601,730 Israelites is slightly less than the first census total of 603,550 in 1.46. **52–56:** In addition to the need to determine the number of warriors who are able to go to war (v. 2), this new census has a second purpose. The numbers will determine the relative sizes of the allotments of land necessary for each tribe when Israel conquers the land of Canaan (see Josh 13–19). **57–62:** As in the first census (3.14–39), the Levites have a separate census. The death of *Nadab and Abihu* (v. 61) is recounted in Lev 10.1–2. **64–65:** The enrollment in *the wilderness of Sinai* was the census in Num 1. Everyone of the old generation counted in Num 1 was condemned to *die in the wilderness* because of their refusal to go and conquer Canaan (14.20–25, 28–35). Because of their faithfulness, only *Caleb* and *Joshua* would live to enter the promised land (14.30, 38).

27 Then the daughters of Zelophehad came forward. Zelophehad was son of Hepher son of Gilead son of Machir son of Manasseh son of Joseph, a member of the Manassite clans. The names of his daughters were: Mahlah, Noah, Hoglah, Milcah, and Tirzah. ²They stood before Moses, Eleazar the priest, the leaders, and all the congregation, at the entrance of the tent of meeting, and they said, ³"Our father died in the wilderness; he was not among the company of those who gathered themselves together against the LORD in the company of Korah, but died for his own sin; and he had no sons. ⁴Why should the name of our father be taken away from his clan because he had no

a Heb *clans of Naphtali*

son? Give to us a possession among our father's brothers."

5 Moses brought their case before the LORD. 6And the LORD spoke to Moses, saying: 7The daughters of Zelophehad are right in what they are saying; you shall indeed let them possess an inheritance among their father's brothers and pass the inheritance of their father on to them. 8You shall also say to the Israelites, "If a man dies, and has no son, then you shall pass his inheritance on to his daughter. 9If he has no daughter, then you shall give his inheritance to his brothers. 10If he has no brothers, then you shall give his inheritance to his father's brothers. 11And if his father has no brothers, then you shall give his inheritance to the nearest kinsman of his clan, and he shall possess it. It shall be for the Israelites a statute and ordinance, as the LORD commanded Moses."

27.1–11: The daughters of Zelophehad and the inheritance of land. This legal case involves the conflict between two principles. On one hand, Israelite land normally passed from father to son and not to daughters. On the other hand, a high priority was given to maintaining a given land allotment within a particular family or clan* in order to maintain a fair distribution of the land among family groups. On the basis of the priority of this latter principle, the five daughters of a man named Zelophehad argue that they ought to receive their father's allotment of land as an inheritance. In the end, the LORD and Moses agree. In Num 36, the case is taken up again with some restrictions on whom the daughters of Zelophehad can marry in order to preserve the land in the family group. **1:** Zelophehad's death and a report about his children is cited in the census in 26.33. **2:** On *the tent of meeting*, see 1.1. **3:** The daughters deny their father's involvement in the rebellion of Korah in Num 16. **4:** *The name of our father* is a reference to the family name and the inheritance of land to which it is attached.

12 The LORD said to Moses, "Go up this mountain of the Abarim range, and see the land that I have given to the Israelites. 13When you have seen it, you also shall be gathered to your people, as your brother Aaron was, 14because you rebelled against my word in the wilderness of Zin when the congregation quarreled with me.*ª You did

not show my holiness before their eyes at the waters." (These are the waters of Meribath-kadesh in the wilderness of Zin.) 15Moses spoke to the LORD, saying, 16"Let the LORD, the God of the spirits of all flesh, appoint someone over the congregation 17who shall go out before them and come in before them, who shall lead them out and bring them in, so that the congregation of the LORD may not be like sheep without a shepherd." 18So the LORD said to Moses, "Take Joshua son of Nun, a man in whom is the spirit, and lay your hand upon him; 19have him stand before Eleazar the priest and all the congregation, and commission him in their sight. 20You shall give him some of your authority, so that all the congregation of the Israelites may obey. 21But he shall stand before Eleazar the priest, who shall inquire for him by the decision of the Urim before the LORD; at his word they shall go out, and at his word they shall come in, both he and all the Israelites with him, the whole congregation." 22So Moses did as the LORD commanded him. He took Joshua and had him stand before Eleazar the priest and the whole congregation; 23he laid his hands on him and commissioned him—as the LORD had directed through Moses.

27.12–23: The succession of leadership from Moses to Joshua. 13: Aaron's death is recorded in 20.22–29. **14:** Moses sinned in the incident in Num 20.2–13. **18:** The divine *spirit* is often associated with leaders and prophets* in the Bible (Judg 3.10) and can be transferred from one person to another (Num 11.24–25; 2 Kings 2.9–10). See the distribution of the spirit among the leaders of Israel in 11.16–17. To *lay your hand* on another involves the transfer of a power or status from one person to another. In this case, Moses' authority transfers in part to Joshua. **20:** Moses' leadership remains unique and unrepeatable so that Joshua receives only a part or *some* of Moses' *authority* (see Deut 34.9–10). **21:** Joshua's leadership will be supplemented by the priest Eleazar, who will seek guidance from the LORD through *the Urim. The Urim* are objects (perhaps light and dark stones) used by Israelite priests in determining the deity's will in a given situation (Ex 28.30; 1 Sam 14.41).

a Heb lacks *with me*

Appointed offerings for various festivals and times

28.1–29.40: Other biblical lists of offerings at festivals include Lev 23 and Deut 16.1–17. The *ephah* and *hin* are frequently mentioned in these laws as measurements of grain and oil. An *ephah* is a unit of dry measure of roughly half a bushel, and a *hin* is a unit of liquid measure somewhere between a quart and a gallon. Another frequent phrase among these laws, *a pleasing odor to the* Lord, indicates a divinely accepted offering as the aroma arises from the burning of the sacrifice (see Gen 8.20–22).

28 The Lord spoke to Moses, saying: 2Command the Israelites, and say to them: My offering, the food for my offerings by fire, my pleasing odor, you shall take care to offer to me at its appointed time. 3And you shall say to them, This is the offering by fire that you shall offer to the Lord: two male lambs a year old without blemish, daily, as a regular offering. 4One lamb you shall offer in the morning, and the other lamb you shall offer at twilight;*a* 5also one-tenth of an ephah of choice flour for a grain offering, mixed with one-fourth of a hin of beaten oil. 6It is a regular burnt offering, ordained at Mount Sinai for a pleasing odor, an offering by fire to the Lord. 7Its drink offering shall be one-fourth of a hin for each lamb; in the sanctuary you shall pour out a drink offering of strong drink to the Lord. 8The other lamb you shall offer at twilight*a* with a grain offering and a drink offering like the one in the morning; you shall offer it as an offering by fire, a pleasing odor to the Lord.

9 On the sabbath day: two male lambs a year old without blemish, and two-tenths of an ephah of choice flour for a grain offering, mixed with oil, and its drink offering— 10this is the burnt offering for every sabbath, in addition to the regular burnt offering and its drink offering.

11 At the beginnings of your months you shall offer a burnt offering to the Lord: two young bulls, one ram, seven male lambs a year old without blemish; 12also three-tenths of an ephah of choice flour for a grain offering, mixed with oil, for each bull; and two-tenths of choice flour for a grain offering,

mixed with oil, for the one ram; 13and one-tenth of choice flour mixed with oil as a grain offering for every lamb—a burnt offering of pleasing odor, an offering by fire to the Lord. 14Their drink offerings shall be half a hin of wine for a bull, one-third of a hin for a ram, and one-fourth of a hin for a lamb. This is the burnt offering of every month throughout the months of the year. 15And there shall be one male goat for a sin offering to the Lord; it shall be offered in addition to the regular burnt offering and its drink offering.

16 On the fourteenth day of the first month there shall be a passover offering to the Lord. 17And on the fifteenth day of this month is a festival; seven days shall unleavened bread be eaten. 18On the first day there shall be a holy convocation. You shall not work at your occupations. 19You shall offer an offering by fire, a burnt offering to the Lord: two young bulls, one ram, and seven male lambs a year old; see that they are without blemish. 20Their grain offering shall be of choice flour mixed with oil: three-tenths of an ephah shall you offer for a bull, and two-tenths for a ram; 21one-tenth shall you offer for each of the seven lambs; 22also one male goat for a sin offering, to make atonement for you. 23You shall offer these in addition to the burnt offering of the morning, which belongs to the regular burnt offering. 24In the same way you shall offer daily, for seven days, the food of an offering by fire, a pleasing odor to the Lord; it shall be offered in addition to the regular burnt offering and its drink offering. 25And on the seventh day you shall have a holy convocation; you shall not work at your occupations.

26 On the day of the first fruits, when you offer a grain offering of new grain to the Lord at your festival of weeks, you shall have a holy convocation; you shall not work at your occupations. 27You shall offer a burnt offering, a pleasing odor to the Lord: two young bulls, one ram, seven male lambs a year old. 28Their grain offering shall be of choice flour mixed with oil, three-tenths of

a Heb *between the two evenings*

an ephah for each bull, two-tenths for one ram, 29one-tenth for each of the seven lambs; 30with one male goat, to make atonement for you. 31In addition to the regular burnt offering with its grain offering, you shall offer them and their drink offering. They shall be without blemish.

28.1–31. 9: *The sabbath day* is every seventh day. The sabbath, a day of rest and no work, is holy to the LORD (see Ex 20.8–11). 16: *Passover** is a springtime festival that celebrates Israel's exodus out of Egypt (Ex 12.1–13.10). 17: *Unleavened bread* is a yeastless bread that does not rise during baking. It is associated with Passover since the Israelites hurriedly left Egypt and could not wait for their bread to rise when baking it (Ex 12.33–34). 26: The *festival of weeks* or Pentecost* marks the beginning of the wheat harvest (Lev 23.15–21).

29 On the first day of the seventh month you shall have a holy convocation; you shall not work at your occupations. It is a day for you to blow the trumpets, 2and you shall offer a burnt offering, a pleasing odor to the LORD: one young bull, one ram, seven male lambs a year old without blemish. 3Their grain offering shall be of choice flour mixed with oil, three-tenths of one ephah for the bull, two-tenths for the ram, 4and one-tenth for each of the seven lambs; 5with one male goat for a sin offering, to make atonement for you. 6These are in addition to the burnt offering of the new moon and its grain offering, and the regular burnt offering and its grain offering, and their drink offerings, according to the ordinance for them, a pleasing odor, an offering by fire to the LORD.

7 On the tenth day of this seventh month you shall have a holy convocation, and deny yourselves;*a* you shall do no work. 8You shall offer a burnt offering to the LORD, a pleasing odor: one young bull, one ram, seven male lambs a year old. They shall be without blemish. 9Their grain offering shall be of choice flour mixed with oil, three-tenths of an ephah for the bull, two-tenths for the one ram, 10one-tenth for each of the seven lambs; 11with one male goat for a sin offering, in addition to the sin offering of atonement, and the regular burnt offering and its grain offering, and their drink offerings.

12 On the fifteenth day of the seventh month you shall have a holy convocation; you shall not work at your occupations. You shall celebrate a festival to the LORD seven days. 13You shall offer a burnt offering, an offering by fire, a pleasing odor to the LORD: thirteen young bulls, two rams, fourteen male lambs a year old. They shall be without blemish. 14Their grain offering shall be of choice flour mixed with oil, three-tenths of an ephah for each of the thirteen bulls, two-tenths for each of the two rams, 15and one-tenth for each of the fourteen lambs; 16also one male goat for a sin offering, in addition to the regular burnt offering, its grain offering and its drink offering.

17 On the second day: twelve young bulls, two rams, fourteen male lambs a year old without blemish, 18with the grain offering and the drink offerings for the bulls, for the rams, and for the lambs, as prescribed in accordance with their number; 19also one male goat for a sin offering, in addition to the regular burnt offering and its grain offering, and their drink offerings.

20 On the third day: eleven bulls, two rams, fourteen male lambs a year old without blemish, 21with the grain offering and the drink offerings for the bulls, for the rams, and for the lambs, as prescribed in accordance with their number; 22also one male goat for a sin offering, in addition to the regular burnt offering and its grain offering and its drink offering.

23 On the fourth day: ten bulls, two rams, fourteen male lambs a year old without blemish, 24with the grain offering and the drink offerings for the bulls, for the rams, and for the lambs, as prescribed in accordance with their number; 25also one male goat for a sin offering, in addition to the regular burnt offering, its grain offering and its drink offering.

26 On the fifth day: nine bulls, two rams, fourteen male lambs a year old without blemish, 27with the grain offering and the drink offerings for the bulls, for the rams,

a Or *and fast*

and for the lambs, as prescribed in accordance with their number; 28also one male goat for a sin offering, in addition to the regular burnt offering and its grain offering and its drink offering.

29 On the sixth day: eight bulls, two rams, fourteen male lambs a year old without blemish, 30with the grain offering and the drink offerings for the bulls, for the rams, and for the lambs, as prescribed in accordance with their number; 31also one male goat for a sin offering, in addition to the regular burnt offering, its grain offering, and its drink offerings.

32 On the seventh day: seven bulls, two rams, fourteen male lambs a year old without blemish, 33with the grain offering and the drink offerings for the bulls, for the rams, and for the lambs, as prescribed in accordance with their number; 34also one male goat for a sin offering, besides the regular burnt offering, its grain offering, and its drink offering.

35 On the eighth day you shall have a solemn assembly; you shall not work at your occupations. 36You shall offer a burnt offering, an offering by fire, a pleasing odor to the LORD: one bull, one ram, seven male lambs a year old without blemish, 37and the grain offering and the drink offerings for the bull, for the ram, and for the lambs, as prescribed in accordance with their number; 38also one male goat for a sin offering, in addition to the regular burnt offering and its grain offering and its drink offering.

39 These you shall offer to the LORD at your appointed festivals, in addition to your votive offerings and your freewill offerings, as your burnt offerings, your grain offerings, your drink offerings, and your offerings of well-being.

40a So Moses told the Israelites everything just as the LORD had commanded Moses.

29.1–40. 1: *The first day of the seventh month* is New Year's Day (Rosh Hashanah, "head of the year,") and occurs in the autumn of the year. 7: *The tenth day of the seventh month* is the Day of Atonement* or Yom Kippur (Lev 23.26–32). 12: *The fifteenth day of the*

seventh month is the festival of booths or Sukkot (Lev 23.33–36). It was a feast of thanksgiving during the autumn harvest and a remembrance of God's care over Israel during its wilderness journey from Egypt to Canaan.

30 Then Moses said to the heads of the tribes of the Israelites: This is what the LORD has commanded. 2When a man makes a vow to the LORD, or swears an oath to bind himself by a pledge, he shall not break his word; he shall do according to all that proceeds out of his mouth.

3 When a woman makes a vow to the LORD, or binds herself by a pledge, while within her father's house, in her youth, 4and her father hears of her vow or her pledge by which she has bound herself, and says nothing to her; then all her vows shall stand, and any pledge by which she has bound herself shall stand. 5But if her father expresses disapproval to her at the time that he hears of it, no vow of hers, and no pledge by which she has bound herself, shall stand; and the LORD will forgive her, because her father had expressed to her his disapproval.

6 If she marries, while obligated by her vows or any thoughtless utterance of her lips by which she has bound herself, 7and her husband hears of it and says nothing to her at the time that he hears, then her vows shall stand, and her pledges by which she has bound herself shall stand. 8But if, at the time that her husband hears of it, he expresses disapproval to her, then he shall nullify the vow by which she was obligated, or the thoughtless utterance of her lips, by which she bound herself; and the LORD will forgive her. 9(But every vow of a widow or of a divorced woman, by which she has bound herself, shall be binding upon her.) 10And if she made a vow in her husband's house, or bound herself by a pledge with an oath, 11and her husband heard it and said nothing to her, and did not express disapproval to her, then all her vows shall stand, and any pledge by which she bound herself shall stand. 12But if her husband nullifies them at the time that he hears them, then whatever

a Ch 30.1 in Heb

proceeds out of her lips concerning her vows, or concerning her pledge of herself, shall not stand. Her husband has nullified them, and the LORD will forgive her. [13]Any vow or any binding oath to deny herself,[a] her husband may allow to stand, or her husband may nullify. [14]But if her husband says nothing to her from day to day,[b] then he validates all her vows, or all her pledges, by which she is obligated; he has validated them, because he said nothing to her at the time that he heard of them. [15]But if he nullifies them some time after he has heard of them, then he shall bear her guilt.

16 These are the statutes that the LORD commanded Moses concerning a husband and his wife, and a father and his daughter while she is still young and in her father's house.

30.1–16: Men, women, and the fulfillment of vows. These laws concerning vows by men and women reflect an ancient society in which young women or married women were normally under the responsibility and supervision of men, whether fathers or husbands. **9:** *A widow* or *a divorced woman* is not under the supervision or care of a man and thus has full responsibility for her own vow. **15:** Under certain circumstances, the husband *shall bear* the wife's *guilt,* meaning that he is responsible for fulfilling the vow she made.

31

The LORD spoke to Moses, saying, [2]"Avenge the Israelites on the Midianites; afterward you shall be gathered to your people." [3]So Moses said to the people, "Arm some of your number for the war, so that they may go against Midian, to execute the LORD's vengeance on Midian. [4]You shall send a thousand from each of the tribes of Israel to the war." [5]So out of the thousands of Israel, a thousand from each tribe were conscripted, twelve thousand armed for battle. [6]Moses sent them to the war, a thousand from each tribe, along with Phinehas son of Eleazar the priest,[c] with the vessels of the sanctuary and the trumpets for sounding the alarm in his hand. [7]They did battle against Midian, as the LORD had commanded Moses, and killed every male. [8]They killed the kings of Midian: Evi, Rekem, Zur, Hur, and Reba, the five kings of Midian, in addition to others who were slain by them; and they also killed Balaam son of Beor with the sword. [9]The Israelites took the women of Midian and their little ones captive; and they took all their cattle, their flocks, and all their goods as booty. [10]All their towns where they had settled, and all their encampments, they burned, [11]but they took all the spoil and all the booty, both people and animals. [12]Then they brought the captives and the booty and the spoil to Moses, to Eleazar the priest, and to the congregation of the Israelites, at the camp on the plains of Moab by the Jordan at Jericho.

13 Moses, Eleazar the priest, and all the leaders of the congregation went to meet them outside the camp. [14]Moses became angry with the officers of the army, the commanders of thousands and the commanders of hundreds, who had come from service in the war. [15]Moses said to them, "Have you allowed all the women to live? [16]These women here, on Balaam's advice, made the Israelites act treacherously against the LORD in the affair of Peor, so that the plague came among the congregation of the LORD. [17]Now therefore, kill every male among the little ones, and kill every woman who has known a man by sleeping with him. [18]But all the young girls who have not known a man by sleeping with him, keep alive for yourselves. [19]Camp outside the camp seven days; whoever of you has killed any person or touched a corpse, purify yourselves and your captives on the third and on the seventh day. [20]You shall purify every garment, every article of skin, everything made of goats' hair, and every article of wood."

21 Eleazar the priest said to the troops who had gone to battle: "This is the statute of the law that the LORD has commanded Moses: [22]gold, silver, bronze, iron, tin, and lead— [23]everything that can withstand fire, shall be passed through fire, and it shall be clean. Nevertheless it shall also be purified with the water for purification; and whatever cannot withstand fire, shall be passed

---

a Or *to fast*   *b* Or *from that day to the next*
c Gk: Heb adds *to the war*

through the water. 24You must wash your clothes on the seventh day, and you shall be clean; afterward you may come into the camp."

25 The LORD spoke to Moses, saying, 26"You and Eleazar the priest and the heads of the ancestral houses of the congregation make an inventory of the booty captured, both human and animal. 27Divide the booty into two parts, between the warriors who went out to battle and all the congregation. 28From the share of the warriors who went out to battle, set aside as tribute for the LORD, one item out of every five hundred, whether persons, oxen, donkeys, sheep, or goats. 29Take it from their half and give it to Eleazar the priest as an offering to the LORD. 30But from the Israelites' half you shall take one out of every fifty, whether persons, oxen, donkeys, sheep, or goats—all the animals—and give them to the Levites who have charge of the tabernacle of the LORD."

31 Then Moses and Eleazar the priest did as the LORD had commanded Moses:

32 The booty remaining from the spoil that the troops had taken totaled six hundred seventy-five thousand sheep, 33seventy-two thousand oxen, 34sixty-one thousand donkeys, 35and thirty-two thousand persons in all, women who had not known a man by sleeping with him.

36 The half-share, the portion of those who had gone out to war, was in number three hundred thirty-seven thousand five hundred sheep and goats, 37and the LORD's tribute of sheep and goats was six hundred seventy-five. 38The oxen were thirty-six thousand, of which the LORD's tribute was seventy-two. 39The donkeys were thirty thousand five hundred, of which the LORD's tribute was sixty-one. 40The persons were sixteen thousand, of which the LORD's tribute was thirty-two persons. 41Moses gave the tribute, the offering for the LORD, to Eleazar the priest, as the LORD had commanded Moses.

42 As for the Israelites' half, which Moses separated from that of the troops, 43the congregation's half was three hundred thirty-seven thousand five hundred sheep and goats, 44thirty-six thousand oxen, 45thirty

thousand five hundred donkeys, 46and sixteen thousand persons. 47From the Israelites' half Moses took one of every fifty, both of persons and of animals, and gave them to the Levites who had charge of the tabernacle of the LORD; as the LORD had commanded Moses.

48 Then the officers who were over the thousands of the army, the commanders of thousands and the commanders of hundreds, approached Moses, 49and said to Moses, "Your servants have counted the warriors who are under our command, and not one of us is missing. 50And we have brought the LORD's offering, what each of us found, articles of gold, armlets and bracelets, signet rings, earrings, and pendants, to make atonement for ourselves before the LORD." 51Moses and Eleazar the priest received the gold from them, all in the form of crafted articles. 52And all the gold of the offering that they offered to the LORD, from the commanders of thousands and the commanders of hundreds, was sixteen thousand seven hundred fifty shekels. 53(The troops had all taken plunder for themselves.) 54So Moses and Eleazar the priest received the gold from the commanders of thousands and of hundreds, and brought it into the tent of meeting as a memorial for the Israelites before the LORD.

31.1–54: Holy war* against Midian. 2: The LORD's command to *avenge the Israelites on the Midianites* stems from the Midianites' role in drawing Israel into the worship of a god other than the LORD in the incident at Peor (25.1–18). Moses will soon die and *be gathered to* and join his *people*, namely, his dead ancestors (Deut 34). 6: *The trumpets for sounding the alarm* were first introduced in 10.9. The involvement of the priest and objects from the tabernacle* or mobile worship *sanctuary* indicate that this is a holy war. In a holy war, the LORD fights with Israel; every adult male is to be killed; women and children may be taken as captives; and a percentage of all items of value are to be offered to the LORD and given to the priests (Deut 20.1–18). 8: The Israelites kill the prophet* Balaam. Balaam had spoken words of blessing on Israel (chs. 22–24). However, Balaam had also urged the Midianite women to entice the Israelites to worship a foreign god and thus abandon the LORD (v. 16). 16: Although *Balaam* is never mentioned in the story of

Israel's sin at Peor in ch. 25, this verse condemns *Balaam's* secret involvement *in the affair of Peor.* **17:** Young Midianite males are killed in order to ensure that they will not become part of that country's army. However, Midianites will reappear as Israel's enemy in Judg 6–8. **18:** Any Midianite women who may have had illicit sexual relations with Israelite men are killed. All Midianite virgins are allowed to live. **19–24:** On the concept of ritual purification and cleanness, see sidebar on p. 136. On the ritual contamination of those who *killed a person* or *touched a corpse* (v. 19), see the purification ritual with water and the ashes of the red cow in ch. 19. **52:** A *shekel* is a standard unit of weight used to calculate the monetary value of gold and silver. **54:** On *the tent of meeting,* see 1.1.

Reuben and Gad's request

32.1–42: Two of the Israelite tribes, Reuben and Gad, request permission from Moses to settle outside Canaan in the area just east of the Jordan River in the plains of Moab. Israel had captured this land from King Sihon and King Og in 21.21–35. Moses eventually grants the request, and the land is actually distributed to these two tribes along with a portion to the half-tribe of Manasseh (v. 33) in Josh 13.8–32; 22.

---

32 Now the Reubenites and the Gadites owned a very great number of cattle. When they saw that the land of Jazer and the land of Gilead was a good place for cattle, 2the Gadites and the Reubenites came and spoke to Moses, to Eleazar the priest, and to the leaders of the congregation, saying, 3"Ataroth, Dibon, Jazer, Nimrah, Heshbon, Elealeh, Sebam, Nebo, and Beon— 4the land that the LORD subdued before the congregation of Israel—is a land for cattle; and your servants have cattle." 5They continued, "If we have found favor in your sight, let this land be given to your servants for a possession; do not make us cross the Jordan."

6 But Moses said to the Gadites and to the Reubenites, "Shall your brothers go to war while you sit here? 7Why will you discourage the hearts of the Israelites from going over into the land that the LORD has given them? 8Your fathers did this, when I sent them from Kadesh-barnea to see the land. 9When they went up to the Wadi Eshcol and saw the land, they discouraged the hearts of the Israelites from going into the land that the LORD had given them. 10The LORD's anger was kindled on that day and he swore, saying, 11'Surely none of the people who came up out of Egypt, from twenty years old and upward, shall see the land that I swore to give to Abraham, to Isaac, and to Jacob, because they have not unreservedly followed me— 12none except Caleb son of Jephunneh the Kenizzite and Joshua son of Nun, for they have unreservedly followed the LORD.' 13And the LORD's anger was kindled against Israel, and he made them wander in the wilderness for forty years, until all the generation that had done evil in the sight of the LORD had disappeared. 14And now you, a brood of sinners, have risen in place of your fathers, to increase the LORD's fierce anger against Israel! 15If you turn away from following him, he will again abandon them in the wilderness; and you will destroy all this people."

16 Then they came up to him and said, "We will build sheepfolds here for our flocks, and towns for our little ones, 17but we will take up arms as a vanguard*a* before the Israelites, until we have brought them to their place. Meanwhile our little ones will stay in the fortified towns because of the inhabitants of the land. 18We will not return to our homes until all the Israelites have obtained their inheritance. 19We will not inherit with them on the other side of the Jordan and beyond, because our inheritance has come to us on this side of the Jordan to the east."

20 So Moses said to them, "If you do this—if you take up arms to go before the LORD for the war, 21and all those of you who bear arms cross the Jordan before the LORD, until he has driven out his enemies from before him 22and the land is subdued before the LORD—then after that you may return and be free of obligation to the LORD and to Israel, and this land shall be your possession before the LORD. 23But if you do not do this, you have sinned against the LORD; and be sure your sin will find you out. 24Build towns for your little ones, and folds for your flocks; but do what you have promised."

a Cn: Heb *hurrying*

25 Then the Gadites and the Reubenites said to Moses, "Your servants will do as my lord commands. 26 Our little ones, our wives, our flocks, and all our livestock shall remain there in the towns of Gilead; 27 but your servants will cross over, everyone armed for war, to do battle for the LORD, just as my lord orders."

28 So Moses gave command concerning them to Eleazar the priest, to Joshua son of Nun, and to the heads of the ancestral houses of the Israelite tribes. 29 And Moses said to them, "If the Gadites and the Reubenites, everyone armed for battle before the LORD, will cross over the Jordan with you and the land shall be subdued before you, then you shall give them the land of Gilead for a possession; 30 but if they will not cross over with you armed, they shall have possessions among you in the land of Canaan." 31 The Gadites and the Reubenites answered, "As the LORD has spoken to your servants, so we will do. 32 We will cross over armed before the LORD into the land of Canaan, but the possession of our inheritance shall remain with us on this side of*a* the Jordan."

33 Moses gave to them—to the Gadites and to the Reubenites and to the half-tribe of Manasseh son of Joseph—the kingdom of King Sihon of the Amorites and the kingdom of King Og of Bashan, the land and its towns, with the territories of the surrounding towns. 34 And the Gadites rebuilt Dibon, Ataroth, Aroer, 35 Atroth-shophan, Jazer, Jogbehah, 36 Beth-nimrah, and Beth-haran, fortified cities, and folds for sheep. 37 And the Reubenites rebuilt Heshbon, Elealeh, Kiriathaim, 38 Nebo, and Baal-meon (some names being changed), and Sibmah; and they gave names to the towns that they rebuilt. 39 The descendants of Machir son of Manasseh went to Gilead, captured it, and dispossessed the Amorites who were there; 40 so Moses gave Gilead to Machir son of Manasseh, and he settled there. 41 Jair son of Manasseh went and captured their villages, and renamed them Havvoth-jair.*b* 42 And Nobah went and captured Kenath and its villages, and renamed it Nobah after himself.

32.1–42. 1: *Jazer* is part of the territory captured from King Sihon of the Amorites (21.32). *Gilead* is the lush hill country east of the Jordan River (Gen 31.21). **2:** *Eleazar* has taken over his father Aaron's role as high priest (20.22–29). **8–15:** Moses recalls the disastrous events of the spy story in chs. 13–14. Moses is afraid that the Israelites may again be discouraged from entering the land of Canaan if the two tribes of Reuben and Gad do not join Israel's army in crossing the Jordan River and conquering Canaan. **16–32:** Reuben and Gad offer a compromise in response to Moses' objections. They will be allowed to settle in the territory east of the Jordan River, but they will first join with the other Israelites in fighting the Canaanites and capturing the land west of the Jordan River in Canaan. Moses accepts their compromise solution. **33:** *The half-tribe of Manasseh* unexpectedly appears as it joins Reuben and Gad in settling in the territory east of the Jordan River outside Canaan. The other half of the tribe of Manasseh eventually settled west of the Jordan River in Canaan near Shechem (Josh 13.29–31; 17.1–13). On Israel's conquest of the territory of King Sihon and Og, see 21.21–35. **34–42:** The actual settlement of these territories occurs in Josh 13.8–32.

33 These are the stages by which the Israelites went out of the land of Egypt in military formation under the leadership of Moses and Aaron. 2 Moses wrote down their starting points, stage by stage, by command of the LORD; and these are their stages according to their starting places. 3 They set out from Rameses in the first month, on the fifteenth day of the first month; on the day after the passover the Israelites went out boldly in the sight of all the Egyptians, 4 while the Egyptians were burying all their firstborn, whom the LORD had struck down among them. The LORD executed judgments even against their gods.

5 So the Israelites set out from Rameses, and camped at Succoth. 6 They set out from Succoth, and camped at Etham, which is on the edge of the wilderness. 7 They set out from Etham, and turned back to Pi-hahiroth, which faces Baal-zephon; and they camped before Migdol. 8 They set out from Pi-hahiroth, passed through the sea into the wilder-

a Heb *beyond*   *b* That is *the villages of Jair*

ness, went a three days' journey in the wilderness of Etham, and camped at Marah. [9]They set out from Marah and came to Elim; at Elim there were twelve springs of water and seventy palm trees, and they camped there. [10]They set out from Elim and camped by the Red Sea.[a] [11]They set out from the Red Sea[a] and camped in the wilderness of Sin. [12]They set out from the wilderness of Sin and camped at Dophkah. [13]They set out from Dophkah and camped at Alush. [14]They set out from Alush and camped at Rephidim, where there was no water for the people to drink. [15]They set out from Rephidim and camped in the wilderness of Sinai. [16]They set out from the wilderness of Sinai and camped at Kibroth-hattaavah. [17]They set out from Kibroth-hattaavah and camped at Hazeroth. [18]They set out from Hazeroth and camped at Rithmah. [19]They set out from Rithmah and camped at Rimmon-perez. [20]They set out from Rimmon-perez and camped at Libnah. [21]They set out from Libnah and camped at Rissah. [22]They set out from Rissah and camped at Kehelathah. [23]They set out from Kehelathah and camped at Mount Shepher. [24]They set out from Mount Shepher and camped at Haradah. [25]They set out from Haradah and camped at Makheloth. [26]They set out from Makheloth and camped at Tahath. [27]They set out from Tahath and camped at Terah. [28]They set out from Terah and camped at Mithkah. [29]They set out from Mithkah and camped at Hashmonah. [30]They set out from Hashmonah and camped at Moseroth. [31]They set out from Moseroth and camped at Bene-jaakan. [32]They set out from Bene-jaakan and camped at Hor-haggidgad. [33]They set out from Hor-haggidgad and camped at Jotbathah. [34]They set out from Jotbathah and camped at Abronah. [35]They set out from Abronah and camped at Ezion-geber. [36]They set out from Ezion-geber and camped in the wilderness of Zin (that is, Kadesh). [37]They set out from Kadesh and camped at Mount Hor, on the edge of the land of Edom.

[38] Aaron the priest went up Mount Hor at the command of the LORD and died there in the fortieth year after the Israelites had come out of the land of Egypt, on the first day of the fifth month. [39]Aaron was one hundred twenty-three years old when he died on Mount Hor.

[40] The Canaanite, the king of Arad, who lived in the Negeb in the land of Canaan, heard of the coming of the Israelites.

[41] They set out from Mount Hor and camped at Zalmonah. [42]They set out from Zalmonah and camped at Punon. [43]They set out from Punon and camped at Oboth. [44]They set out from Oboth and camped at Iye-abarim, in the territory of Moab. [45]They set out from Iyim and camped at Dibon-gad. [46]They set out from Dibon-gad and camped at Almon-diblathaim. [47]They set out from Almon-diblathaim and camped in the mountains of Abarim, before Nebo. [48]They set out from the mountains of Abarim and camped in the plains of Moab by the Jordan at Jericho; [49]they camped by the Jordan from Beth-jeshimoth as far as Abel-shittim in the plains of Moab.

[50] In the plains of Moab by the Jordan at Jericho, the LORD spoke to Moses, saying: [51]Speak to the Israelites, and say to them: When you cross over the Jordan into the land of Canaan, [52]you shall drive out all the inhabitants of the land from before you, destroy all their figured stones, destroy all their cast images, and demolish all their high places. [53]You shall take possession of the land and settle in it, for I have given you the land to possess. [54]You shall apportion the land by lot according to your clans; to a large one you shall give a large inheritance, and to a small one you shall give a small inheritance; the inheritance shall belong to the person on whom the lot falls; according to your ancestral tribes you shall inherit. [55]But if you do not drive out the inhabitants of the land from before you, then those whom you let remain shall be as barbs in your eyes and thorns in your sides; they shall trouble you in the land where you are settling. [56]And I will do to you as I thought to do to them.

33.1–56: The stages of Israel's wilderness journey from Egypt to Canaan. 3–5: On the death of Egypt's

a Or *Sea of Reeds*

firstborn and Israel's travel from *Rameses* to *Succoth*, see Ex 12.29–37. **6–15:** Israel's travel *from Succoth* (v. 6) to *the wilderness of Sinai* (v. 15) is recounted in Ex 13.17–19.1. **16–49:** Israel's journey *from the wilderness of Sinai* (v. 16) to *the plains of Moab* (vv. 49–50) is narrated in 10.11–22.1. The death of *Aaron the priest* (vv. 38–39) is recounted in 20.22–29. **50–56:** The LORD commands Moses to *speak to the Israelites* (v. 51) and warn them about the need to *drive out all the inhabitants of the land* of Canaan and all their gods (v. 52). Otherwise, the LORD says to Israel, *I will do to you as I thought to do to them* [the Canaanites] (v. 56). Moses fulfills this divine command to speak to Israel in the book of Deuteronomy with a series of instructional speeches. In the end, however, Israel will not drive out the Canaanites from the land. As a result, Israel will suffer difficulty and oppression during the period of the judges (Judg 1.1–3.6).

34 The LORD spoke to Moses, saying: ²Command the Israelites, and say to them: When you enter the land of Canaan (this is the land that shall fall to you for an inheritance, the land of Canaan, defined by its boundaries), ³your south sector shall extend from the wilderness of Zin along the side of Edom. Your southern boundary shall begin from the end of the Dead Sea*a* on the east; ⁴your boundary shall turn south of the ascent of Akrabbim, and cross to Zin, and its outer limit shall be south of Kadesh-barnea; then it shall go on to Hazar-addar, and cross to Azmon; ⁵the boundary shall turn from Azmon to the Wadi of Egypt, and its termination shall be at the Sea.

6 For the western boundary, you shall have the Great Sea and its*b* coast; this shall be your western boundary.

7 This shall be your northern boundary: from the Great Sea you shall mark out your line to Mount Hor; ⁸from Mount Hor you shall mark it out to Lebo-hamath, and the outer limit of the boundary shall be at Zedad; ⁹then the boundary shall extend to Ziphron, and its end shall be at Hazar-enan; this shall be your northern boundary.

10 You shall mark out your eastern boundary from Hazar-enan to Shepham; ¹¹and the boundary shall continue down from Shepham to Riblah on the east side of Ain; and the boundary shall go down, and reach the eastern slope of the sea of Chinnereth; ¹²and the boundary shall go down to the Jordan, and its end shall be at the Dead Sea.*a* This shall be your land with its boundaries all around.

13 Moses commanded the Israelites, saying: This is the land that you shall inherit by lot, which the LORD has commanded to give to the nine tribes and to the half-tribe; ¹⁴for the tribe of the Reubenites by their ancestral houses and the tribe of the Gadites by their ancestral houses have taken their inheritance, and also the half-tribe of Manasseh; ¹⁵the two tribes and the half-tribe have taken their inheritance beyond the Jordan at Jericho eastward, toward the sunrise.

16 The LORD spoke to Moses, saying: ¹⁷These are the names of the men who shall apportion the land to you for inheritance: the priest Eleazar and Joshua son of Nun. ¹⁸You shall take one leader of every tribe to apportion the land for inheritance. ¹⁹These are the names of the men: Of the tribe of Judah, Caleb son of Jephunneh. ²⁰Of the tribe of the Simeonites, Shemuel son of Ammihud. ²¹Of the tribe of Benjamin, Elidad son of Chislon. ²²Of the tribe of the Danites a leader, Bukki son of Jogli. ²³Of the Josephites: of the tribe of the Manassites a leader, Hanniel son of Ephod, ²⁴and of the tribe of the Ephraimites a leader, Kemuel son of Shiphtan. ²⁵Of the tribe of the Zebulunites a leader, Eli-zaphan son of Parnach. ²⁶Of the tribe of the Issacharites a leader, Paltiel son of Azzan. ²⁷And of the tribe of the Asherites a leader, Ahihud son of Shelomi. ²⁸Of the tribe of the Naphtalites a leader, Pedahel son of Ammihud. ²⁹These were the ones whom the LORD commanded to apportion the inheritance for the Israelites in the land of Canaan.

34.1–29: The boundaries of Canaan and tribal supervisors for dividing the land. 1–12: This delineation of the boundaries of the promised land follows closely the description of the area covered by the spies in chs. 13–14. The southern boundary is the wilderness of Zin (13.21; see v. 3), and the northern boundary

a Heb *Salt Sea*   *b* Syr: Heb lacks *its*

reaches to Lebo-hamath (13.21; see v. 8). The Jordan River forms the eastern boundary of Canaan, and "the Sea" or "Great Sea" (the Mediterranean) forms the western border (13.29; see vv. 6, 12). These are ideal boundaries since Israel's historical boundaries never actually extended as far west as the Mediterranean Sea in the biblical period. Israel reached its greatest territorial size under King David and King Solomon (2 Sam 8.1–14; 1 Kings 8.65). Israel's settlement of the land is recounted in Josh 13–19. **13–15:** The story of *the Reubenites, the Gadites,* and *the half-tribe of Manasseh* settling east of the Jordan River outside Canaan is narrated in ch. 32. **17:** *Eleazar* has already taken over the role of high priest from his father Aaron (20.22–29). *Joshua* will replace Moses as leader of the people when the Israelites cross the Jordan River into Canaan (27.12–23). Moses' sin at Meribah prevented him from entering Canaan (20.2–13). **18–29:** These names of tribal leaders appear here for the first time with the exception of *Caleb,* the leader of *the tribe of Judah* (v. 19; see 13.6, 30; 14.30).

35

In the plains of Moab by the Jordan at Jericho, the LORD spoke to Moses, saying: 2Command the Israelites to give, from the inheritance that they possess, towns for the Levites to live in; you shall also give to the Levites pasture lands surrounding the towns. 3The towns shall be theirs to live in, and their pasture lands shall be for their cattle, for their livestock, and for all their animals. 4The pasture lands of the towns, which you shall give to the Levites, shall reach from the wall of the town outward a thousand cubits all around. 5You shall measure, outside the town, for the east side two thousand cubits, for the south side two thousand cubits, for the west side two thousand cubits, and for the north side two thousand cubits, with the town in the middle; this shall belong to them as pasture land for their towns.

6 The towns that you give to the Levites shall include the six cities of refuge, where you shall permit a slayer to flee, and in addition to them you shall give forty-two towns. 7The towns that you give to the Levites shall total forty-eight, with their pasture lands. 8And as for the towns that you shall give from the possession of the Israelites, from the larger tribes you shall take many, and from the smaller tribes you shall take few; each, in proportion to the inheritance that it obtains, shall give of its towns to the Levites.

9 The LORD spoke to Moses, saying: 10Speak to the Israelites, and say to them: When you cross the Jordan into the land of Canaan, 11then you shall select cities to be cities of refuge for you, so that a slayer who kills a person without intent may flee there. 12The cities shall be for you a refuge from the avenger, so that the slayer may not die until there is a trial before the congregation.

13 The cities that you designate shall be six cities of refuge for you: 14you shall designate three cities beyond the Jordan, and three cities in the land of Canaan, to be cities of refuge. 15These six cities shall serve as refuge for the Israelites, for the resident or transient alien among them, so that anyone who kills a person without intent may flee there.

16 But anyone who strikes another with an iron object, and death ensues, is a murderer; the murderer shall be put to death. 17Or anyone who strikes another with a stone in hand that could cause death, and death ensues, is a murderer; the murderer shall be put to death. 18Or anyone who strikes another with a weapon of wood in hand that could cause death, and death ensues, is a murderer; the murderer shall be put to death. 19The avenger of blood is the one who shall put the murderer to death; when they meet, the avenger of blood shall execute the sentence. 20Likewise, if someone pushes another from hatred, or hurls something at another, lying in wait, and death ensues, 21or in enmity strikes another with the hand, and death ensues, then the one who struck the blow shall be put to death; that person is a murderer; the avenger of blood shall put the murderer to death, when they meet.

22 But if someone pushes another suddenly without enmity, or hurls any object without lying in wait, 23or, while handling any stone that could cause death, unintentionally*a* drops it on another and death en-

a Heb *without seeing*

sues, though they were not enemies, and no harm was intended, 24then the congregation shall judge between the slayer and the avenger of blood, in accordance with these ordinances; 25and the congregation shall rescue the slayer from the avenger of blood. Then the congregation shall send the slayer back to the original city of refuge. The slayer shall live in it until the death of the high priest who was anointed with the holy oil. 26But if the slayer shall at any time go outside the bounds of the original city of refuge, 27and is found by the avenger of blood outside the bounds of the city of refuge, and is killed by the avenger, no bloodguilt shall be incurred. 28For the slayer must remain in the city of refuge until the death of the high priest; but after the death of the high priest the slayer may return home.

29 These things shall be a statute and ordinance for you throughout your generations wherever you live.

30 If anyone kills another, the murderer shall be put to death on the evidence of witnesses; but no one shall be put to death on the testimony of a single witness. 31Moreover you shall accept no ransom for the life of a murderer who is subject to the death penalty; a murderer must be put to death. 32Nor shall you accept ransom for one who has fled to a city of refuge, enabling the fugitive to return to live in the land before the death of the high priest. 33You shall not pollute the land in which you live; for blood pollutes the land, and no expiation can be made for the land, for the blood that is shed in it, except by the blood of the one who shed it. 34You shall not defile the land in which you live, in which I also dwell; for I the LORD dwell among the Israelites.

35.1–34: Cities for the Levites, cities of refuge, and borderline cases involving murder and blood revenge. 1–8: *The plains of Moab* lie just east of the *Jordan* River. *Jericho* is the town that lies just west of the Jordan River inside the land of Canaan (v. 1). The priestly tribe of *Levites* is unique among the tribes of Israel. They will receive *towns to live in* rather than an allotment of tribal land when Israel conquers Canaan (v. 2; see 18.20–24; Josh 21). A *cubit* is a unit of length, approximately one and a half feet. Thus, a *thousand*

cubits is about 1,500 feet. On *the cities of refuge*, see 35.9–15. 9–15: The *cities of refuge* (v. 11) provide a safe place for those who have accidentally or unintentionally killed someone. The *avenger* (v. 12), a member of the dead victim's family, would exact revenge for the person's death by killing the murderer. *Beyond the Jordan* (v. 14) is the area east of the Jordan River just outside Canaan where Reuben, Gad, and the half-tribe of Manasseh settled (Num 32). 16–34: The laws distinguish between intentional or negligent murder versus accidental killing. In intentional murders but not accidental killings, the community allows the *avenger of blood* (vv. 19, 21) to kill the murderer in revenge for the death of a family member (see comment on vv. 9–15). The spilling of human blood *pollutes the land* (v. 33), even if it is an unintentional killing. The killer is made clean from the impurity or pollution through the atoning *death of the high priest* in the city of refuge (vv. 25–28). A *ransom* (vv. 31–32) is a payment of money or other items of value that repay and wipe out the impurity caused by an unclean act or condition. In this case, the loss of a human's life cannot be repaid or atoned through money or property but only through the death of the murderer or (in the case of accidental killings) through *the death of the high priest* (v. 32).

36 The heads of the ancestral houses of the clans of the descendants of Gilead son of Machir son of Manasseh, of the Josephite clans, came forward and spoke in the presence of Moses and the leaders, the heads of the ancestral houses of the Israelites; 2they said, "The LORD commanded my lord to give the land for inheritance by lot to the Israelites; and my lord was commanded by the LORD to give the inheritance of our brother Zelophehad to his daughters. 3But if they are married into another Israelite tribe, then their inheritance will be taken from the inheritance of our ancestors and added to the inheritance of the tribe into which they marry; so it will be taken away from the allotted portion of our inheritance. 4And when the jubilee of the Israelites comes, then their inheritance will be added to the inheritance of the tribe into which they have married; and their inheritance will be taken from the inheritance of our ancestral tribe."

5 Then Moses commanded the Israelites according to the word of the LORD, saying,

"The descendants of the tribe of Joseph are right in what they are saying. 6This is what the LORD commands concerning the daughters of Zelophehad, 'Let them marry whom they think best; only it must be into a clan of their father's tribe that they are married, 7so that no inheritance of the Israelites shall be transferred from one tribe to another; for all Israelites shall retain the inheritance of their ancestral tribes. 8Every daughter who possesses an inheritance in any tribe of the Israelites shall marry one from the clan of her father's tribe, so that all Israelites may continue to possess their ancestral inheritance. 9No inheritance shall be transferred from one tribe to another; for each of the tribes of the Israelites shall retain its own inheritance.' "

10 The daughters of Zelophehad did as the LORD had commanded Moses. 11Mahlah, Tirzah, Hoglah, Milcah, and Noah, the daughters of Zelophehad, married sons of their father's brothers. 12They were married into the clans of the descendants of Manasseh son of Joseph, and their inheritance remained in the tribe of their father's clan.

13 These are the commandments and the ordinances that the LORD commanded through Moses to the Israelites in the plains of Moab by the Jordan at Jericho.

36.1–13: The daughters of Zelophehad revisited: maintaining the fair distribution of tribal lands. This legal judgment provides a supplement to the earlier case involving the daughters of Zelophehad in 27.1–11. The daughters are required to marry within their own tribe so that the land they have inherited will not pass into the hands of another tribe and thus upset the balanced distribution of Canaan's land among the Israelite tribes. **2:** On the prior decision about the daughters' being allowed to inherit the land of their father Zelophehad, see 27.4–8. **3–4:** This complaint about the possibility of the daughters' land being transferred from one tribe to another tribe assumes that any land the new bride owns passes into the possession of her husband at marriage. *The jubilee* occurs every fifty years. It involves the free return of all tribal lands that have been bought or sold during the previous fifty-year period back to the original tribal owners of the land (Lev 25.8–55). However, in this case the potential transfer of the land did not occur through buying or selling but through marriage. Therefore, the land would not be returned to the first tribe who originally owned it, since the jubilee involves only land that has been bought and sold. This practice would adversely affect the original balance and distribution of land among the tribes. Thus, any Israelite daughters who receive an inheritance of land can marry only within their own tribe. **13:** On *the plains of Moab, the Jordan* River, and *Jericho*, see comments on 35.1–8.

DEUTERONOMY

Introduction

Deuteronomy presents itself as an address by Moses to Israel just before the invasion of the promised land. Moses proclaims the law by which Israel is to shape its life in the land as God's faithful people. This law (Deut 12–26) calls on Israel to reform itself. It urges exclusive loyalty to the LORD by demanding that all sacrificial worship be centralized in a single location. It also seeks to make Israel a just and humane society by advocating concern for the poor and disadvantaged. Moses prefaces this law by reviewing the history of the last generation (chs. 1–4) and motivating Israel to careful obedience (chs. 5–11). After teaching the law, Moses refers to the future implications of the covenant★ that God has established (chs. 27–30) and recites two poems (chs. 32–33). Narratives★ about the transition of leadership and the death of Moses (chs. 31, 34) lead into the upcoming narratives about Israel's conquest (Joshua) and life in the land (Judges, 1–2 Samuel, 1–2 Kings).

The law of reform in Deuteronomy was originally produced in a time of religious, political, and social crisis. Religious loyalty was being undermined by the worship of other gods and an unfaithful monarchy. Some classes of society had fallen into poverty. There are indications that Deuteronomy was originally directed to the northern kingdom of Israel rather than to Judah. Deuteronomy was later expanded to serve as the introduction to the Deuteronomistic★ History (see the introduction to Joshua). The distinctive theology, style, and language of Deuteronomy strongly influenced that later work.

READING GUIDE

Deuteronomy contains both narrative and law. Readers may follow the story of Israel under the leadership of Moses by concentrating on Deut 1–3, 9–10, 31, and 34. Those interested in Deuteronomy's distinctive guidelines for Israel's religious and social life will want to begin with chs. 12–18 and 20. Deuteronomy offers updates or revisions of older laws found in Ex 21–23. Readers can discover Deuteronomy's special outlook by comparing these chapters in Exodus and the laws in Deuteronomy.

1–4	Moses reviews Israel's history
5–11	Moses preaches about the law
12–26	Moses proclaims the law
27–30	Moses makes a covenant in Moab
31–34	Moses concludes with warnings and blessings

1 These are the words that Moses spoke to all Israel beyond the Jordan—in the wilderness, on the plain opposite Suph, between Paran and Tophel, Laban, Hazeroth, and Di-zahab. ²(By the way of Mount Seir it takes eleven days to reach Kadesh-barnea from Horeb.) ³In the fortieth year, on the first day of the eleventh month, Moses spoke to the Israelites just as the LORD had commanded him to speak to them. ⁴This was after he had defeated King Sihon of the Amorites, who reigned in Heshbon, and King Og of Bashan, who reigned in Ashtaroth and*a* in Edrei. ⁵Beyond the Jordan in the

a Gk Syr Vg Compare Josh 12.4: Heb lacks *and*

land of Moab, Moses undertook to expound this law as follows:

6 The LORD our God spoke to us at Horeb, saying, "You have stayed long enough at this mountain. 7 Resume your journey, and go into the hill country of the Amorites as well as into the neighboring regions—the Arabah, the hill country, the Shephelah, the Negeb, and the seacoast—the land of the Canaanites and the Lebanon, as far as the great river, the river Euphrates. 8 See, I have set the land before you; go in and take possession of the land that I* swore to your ancestors, to Abraham, to Isaac, and to Jacob, to give to them and to their descendants after them."

1.1–8: Setting the scene. 1–3: Moses addresses Israel just before they invade the promised land. He speaks to a new generation born in the wilderness. **5:** Israel will soon cross the *Jordan* westward into Canaan from *Moab*. **6:** *Horeb* is Deuteronomy's name for Mount Sinai. **7:** The promised land is envisioned as extending north to *the river Euphrates,* although Israel actually occupied a much smaller area.

9 At that time I said to you, "I am unable by myself to bear you. 10 The LORD your God has multiplied you, so that today you are as numerous as the stars of heaven. 11 May the LORD, the God of your ancestors, increase you a thousand times more and bless you, as he has promised you! 12 But how can I bear the heavy burden of your disputes all by myself? 13 Choose for each of your tribes individuals who are wise, discerning, and reputable to be your leaders." 14 You answered me, "The plan you have proposed is a good one." 15 So I took the leaders of your tribes, wise and reputable individuals, and installed them as leaders over you, commanders of thousands, commanders of hundreds, commanders of fifties, commanders of tens, and officials, throughout your tribes. 16 I charged your judges at that time: "Give the members of your community a fair hearing, and judge rightly between one person and another, whether citizen or resident alien. 17 You must not be partial in judging: hear out the small and the great alike; you shall not be intimidated by anyone, for the judgment is God's.

Any case that is too hard for you, bring to me, and I will hear it." 18 So I charged you at that time with all the things that you should do.

1.9–18: Judicial leaders. 10–11: Moses' overwork has been caused by Israel's population growth, a fulfillment of the LORD's promise to Abraham (Gen 15.5). **15–16:** This justice system is comprehensive, reaching down to the level of *commanders of tens.* It is to be fair, even when a disdained *resident alien** is involved. **17:** Fair decisions are ensured by impartiality and appeals to Moses' special expertise.

19 Then, just as the LORD our God had ordered us, we set out from Horeb and went through all that great and terrible wilderness that you saw, on the way to the hill country of the Amorites, until we reached Kadesh-barnea. 20 I said to you, "You have reached the hill country of the Amorites, which the LORD our God is giving us. 21 See, the LORD your God has given the land to you; go up, take possession, as the LORD, the God of your ancestors, has promised you; do not fear or be dismayed."

22 All of you came to me and said, "Let us send men ahead of us to explore the land for us and bring back a report to us regarding the route by which we should go up and the cities we will come to." 23 The plan seemed good to me, and I selected twelve of you, one from each tribe. 24 They set out and went up into the hill country, and when they reached the Valley of Eshcol they spied it out 25 and gathered some of the land's produce, which they brought down to us. They brought back a report to us, and said, "It is a good land that the LORD our God is giving us."

26 But you were unwilling to go up. You rebelled against the command of the LORD your God; 27 you grumbled in your tents and said, "It is because the LORD hates us that he has brought us out of the land of Egypt, to hand us over to the Amorites to destroy us. 28 Where are we headed? Our kindred have made our hearts melt by reporting, 'The people are stronger and taller than we; the cities are large and fortified up to heaven!

a Sam Gk: MT *the* LORD

Related Nations

Israel thought of *Edom, Moab, and Ammon* as kindred peoples and expressed this in terms of lineage. The ancestor of Edom was Esau the brother to Jacob. Moab and Ammon were understood to be sons of Abraham's nephew Lot. Like Israel, these nations had dispossessed the previous inhabitants of their territory (2.20–23).

We actually saw there the offspring of the Anakim!'" 29I said to you, "Have no dread or fear of them. 30The LORD your God, who goes before you, is the one who will fight for you, just as he did for you in Egypt before your very eyes, 31and in the wilderness, where you saw how the LORD your God carried you, just as one carries a child, all the way that you traveled until you reached this place. 32But in spite of this, you have no trust in the LORD your God, 33who goes before you on the way to seek out a place for you to camp, in fire by night, and in the cloud by day, to show you the route you should take."

34 When the LORD heard your words, he was wrathful and swore: 35"Not one of these—not one of this evil generation—shall see the good land that I swore to give to your ancestors, 36except Caleb son of Jephunneh. He shall see it, and to him and to his descendants I will give the land on which he set foot, because of his complete fidelity to the LORD." 37Even with me the LORD was angry on your account, saying, "You also shall not enter there. 38Joshua son of Nun, your assistant, shall enter there; encourage him, for he is the one who will secure Israel's possession of it. 39And as for your little ones, who you thought would become booty, your children, who today do not yet know right from wrong, they shall enter there; to them I will give it, and they shall take possession of it. 40But as for you, journey back into the wilderness, in the direction of the Red Sea."[a]

41 You answered me, "We have sinned against the LORD! We are ready to go up and fight, just as the LORD our God commanded us." So all of you strapped on your battle gear, and thought it easy to go up into the hill country. 42The LORD said to me, "Say to them, 'Do not go up and do not fight, for I am not in the midst of you; otherwise you will be defeated by your enemies.'" 43Although I told you, you would not listen. You rebelled against the command of the LORD and presumptuously went up into the hill country. 44The Amorites who lived in that hill country then came out against you and chased you as bees do. They beat you down in Seir as far as Hormah. 45When you returned and wept before the LORD, the LORD would neither heed your voice nor pay you any attention.

1.19–45: A failed attempt at conquest. 19: *Amorites* is a general term for the inhabitants of the land, but especially for those in the hills. *Kadesh-barnea* is a southern oasis in the Negeb. **22:** Sending out advance scouts was standard practice (Josh 2; Judg 18.1–10). **24–25:** *Eshcol* means "cluster of grapes," underscoring the land's fruitfulness. At first, only the positive aspects of the scouts' report are mentioned (contrast v. 28), which adds to the surprise when Israel proves unwilling to attack. **28:** The fabled* *Anakim* were reputed to be of gigantic size. **29–33:** Moses gives three reasons why they should *have no dread or fear* (v. 29): The LORD has already fought for them (v. 30), carried them like a child (v. 31), and guided them on their journey (v. 33). **34–38:** All the adults of that generation were to die outside the land except for *Caleb* (v. 36) and *Joshua* (v. 38). According to Num 13–14, these two were the only spies who urged Israel to attack. The exclusion of Moses from the land is seen here as the people's fault (contrast 32.51). **39:** These *little ones* are the new generation to whom Moses is now speaking the words of Deuteronomy. **41–45:** When-

a Or *Sea of Reeds*

ever it fought as the LORD's army, Israel prevailed, but in this case it defiantly fought on its own.

~~~~~~

2 46 After you had stayed at Kadesh as many days as you did, [1] we journeyed back into the wilderness, in the direction of the Red Sea,[a] as the LORD had told me and skirted Mount Seir for many days. [2] Then the LORD said to me: [3] "You have been skirting this hill country long enough. Head north, [4] and charge the people as follows: You are about to pass through the territory of your kindred, the descendants of Esau, who live in Seir. They will be afraid of you, so, be very careful [5] not to engage in battle with them, for I will not give you even so much as a foot's length of their land, since I have given Mount Seir to Esau as a possession. [6] You shall purchase food from them for money, so that you may eat; and you shall also buy water from them for money, so that you may drink. [7] Surely the LORD your God has blessed you in all your undertakings; he knows your going through this great wilderness. These forty years the LORD your God has been with you; you have lacked nothing." [8] So we passed by our kin, the descendants of Esau who live in Seir, leaving behind the route of the Arabah, and leaving behind Elath and Ezion-geber.

When we had headed out along the route of the wilderness of Moab, [9] the LORD said to me: "Do not harass Moab or engage them in battle, for I will not give you any of its land as a possession, since I have given Ar as a possession to the descendants of Lot." [10] (The Emim—a large and numerous people, as tall as the Anakim—had formerly inhabited it. [11] Like the Anakim, they are usually reckoned as Rephaim, though the Moabites call them Emim. [12] Moreover, the Horim had formerly inhabited Seir, but the descendants of Esau dispossessed them, destroying them and settling in their place, as Israel has done in the land that the LORD gave them as a possession.) [13] "Now then, proceed to cross over the Wadi Zered."

So we crossed over the Wadi Zered. [14] And the length of time we had traveled from Kadesh-barnea until we crossed the Wadi Zered was thirty-eight years, until the entire generation of warriors had perished from the camp, as the LORD had sworn concerning them. [15] Indeed, the LORD's own hand was against them, to root them out from the camp, until all had perished.

[16] Just as soon as all the warriors had died off from among the people, [17] the LORD spoke to me, saying, [18] "Today you are going to cross the boundary of Moab at Ar. [19] When you approach the frontier of the Ammonites, do not harass them or engage them in battle, for I will not give the land of the Ammonites to you as a possession, because I have given it to the descendants of Lot." [20] (It also is usually reckoned as a land of Rephaim. Rephaim formerly inhabited it, though the Ammonites call them Zamzummim, [21] a strong and numerous people, as tall as the Anakim. But the LORD destroyed them from before the Ammonites so that they could dispossess them and settle in their place. [22] He did the same for the descendants of Esau, who live in Seir, by destroying the Horim before them so that they could dispossess them and settle in their place even to this day. [23] As for the Avvim, who had lived in settlements in the vicinity of Gaza, the Caphtorim, who came from Caphtor, destroyed them and settled in their place.) [24] "Proceed on your journey and cross the Wadi Arnon. See, I have handed over to you King Sihon the Amorite of Heshbon, and his land. Begin to take possession by engaging him in battle. [25] This day I will begin to put the dread and fear of you upon the peoples everywhere under heaven; when they hear report of you, they will tremble and be in anguish because of you."

1.46–2.25: Through Edom and Moab. 1.46: Numbers 20.14–21 and 21.10–20 report another version of this story. *Many days* covers thirty-eight years and the death of the first generation (2.14). **2.1:** *Mount Seir* refers to Edom's territory. **8:** *Elath and Ezion-geber* were located on the shore of the Red Sea, south of Edom. **9:** Here *Ar* indicates the territory of Moab in general, while in v. 18 it refers to a specific city. **10–12:** Details about fabled* and extinct peoples (compare

a Or *Sea of Reeds*

vv. 20–23) were of interest to ancient readers. **13:** The *Wadi* Zered* marked the boundary between Edom and Moab. **14–16:** The death of the last of the previous generation means that conquest can begin. **18:** To move north out of Moab means that war with King Sihon is inevitable. **19:** Ammonite territory lay just to the east of Israel's line of advance. **24–25:** *Wadi Arnon* was the border between Moab and the territory of King Sihon. The language of divine warrior* theology indicates certain victory: *I have handed over*. The LORD as divine warrior uses the weapons of *dread and fear.*

26 So I sent messengers from the wilderness of Kedemoth to King Sihon of Heshbon with the following terms of peace: ²⁷"If you let me pass through your land, I will travel only along the road; I will turn aside neither to the right nor to the left. ²⁸You shall sell me food for money, so that I may eat, and supply me water for money, so that I may drink. Only allow me to pass through on foot— ²⁹just as the descendants of Esau who live in Seir have done for me and likewise the Moabites who live in Ar—until I cross the Jordan into the land that the LORD our God is giving us." ³⁰But King Sihon of Heshbon was not willing to let us pass through, for the LORD your God had hardened his spirit and made his heart defiant in order to hand him over to you, as he has now done.

31 The LORD said to me, "See, I have begun to give Sihon and his land over to you. Begin now to take possession of his land." ³²So when Sihon came out against us, he and all his people for battle at Jahaz, ³³the LORD our God gave him over to us; and we struck him down, along with his offspring and all his people. ³⁴At that time we captured all his towns, and in each town we utterly destroyed men, women, and children. We left not a single survivor. ³⁵Only the livestock we kept as spoil for ourselves, as well as the plunder of the towns that we had captured. ³⁶From Aroer on the edge of the Wadi Arnon (including the town that is in the wadi itself) as far as Gilead, there was no citadel too high for us. The LORD our God gave everything to us. ³⁷You did not encroach, however, on the land of the Ammonites, avoiding

the whole upper region of the Wadi Jabbok as well as the towns of the hill country, just as*ᵃ* the LORD our God had charged.

2.26–37: Defeating King Sihon. 27–29: Moses asks for safe passage as a way of luring Sihon into battle. Sihon's rejection of this apparently reasonable request justifies Israel's attack. **30:** *Hardened his spirit* indicates that the LORD was behind Sihon's resistance. God's ultimate control of the events that follow is shown by the expression *hand over* (v. 30) and the repetition of "give" (vv. 31, 33, 36). **34–35:** *Utterly destroyed* indicates that the entire population of each captured town fell under the ban* (see 20.16–18; Josh 6.21). The *livestock* and other *plunder* were not destroyed, but kept for Israel's use. **36:** The line *from Aroer* northward *as far as Gilead* encompasses all of Sihon's territory.

3 When we headed up the road to Bashan, King Og of Bashan came out against us, he and all his people, for battle at Edrei. ²The LORD said to me, "Do not fear him, for I have handed him over to you, along with his people and his land. Do to him as you did to King Sihon of the Amorites, who reigned in Heshbon." ³So the LORD our God also handed over to us King Og of Bashan and all his people. We struck him down until not a single survivor was left. ⁴At that time we captured all his towns; there was no citadel that we did not take from them—sixty towns, the whole region of Argob, the kingdom of Og in Bashan. ⁵All these were fortress towns with high walls, double gates, and bars, besides a great many villages. ⁶And we utterly destroyed them, as we had done to King Sihon of Heshbon, in each city utterly destroying men, women, and children. ⁷But all the livestock and the plunder of the towns we kept as spoil for ourselves.

3.1–7: Defeating King Og. 1: *Bashan* designates the territory north of Gilead. **4–5:** This emphasizes the extent and marvel of Israel's victory. **6–7:** The practice of *utterly destroying* (banning*) the population testifies that it is the LORD as divine warrior* who is responsible for Israel's triumph (compare 2.34–35).

---

a Gk Tg: Heb *and all*

8 So at that time we took from the two kings of the Amorites the land beyond the Jordan, from the Wadi Arnon to Mount Hermon 9(the Sidonians call Hermon Sirion, while the Amorites call it Senir), 10all the towns of the tableland, the whole of Gilead, and all of Bashan, as far as Salecah and Edrei, towns of Og's kingdom in Bashan. 11(Now only King Og of Bashan was left of the remnant of the Rephaim. In fact his bed, an iron bed, can still be seen in Rabbah of the Ammonites. By the common cubit it is nine cubits long and four cubits wide.) 12As for the land that we took possession of at that time, I gave to the Reubenites and Gadites the territory north of Aroer,a that is on the edge of the Wadi Arnon, as well as half the hill country of Gilead with its towns, 13and I gave to the half-tribe of Manasseh the rest of Gilead and all of Bashan, Og's kingdom. (The whole region of Argob: all that portion of Bashan used to be called a land of Rephaim; 14Jair the Manassite acquired the whole region of Argob as far as the border of the Geshurites and the Maacathites, and he named them—that is, Bashan—after himself, Havvoth-jair,b as it is to this day.) 15To Machir I gave Gilead. 16And to the Reubenites and the Gadites I gave the territory from Gilead as far as the Wadi Arnon, with the middle of the wadi as a boundary, and up to the Jabbok, the wadi being boundary of the Ammonites; 17the Arabah also, with the Jordan and its banks, from Chinnereth down to the sea of the Arabah, the Dead Sea,c with the lower slopes of Pisgah on the east.

18 At that time, I charged you as follows: "Although the LORD your God has given you this land to occupy, all your troops shall cross over armed as the vanguard of your Israelite kin. 19Only your wives, your children, and your livestock—I know that you have much livestock—shall stay behind in the towns that I have given to you. 20When the LORD gives rest to your kindred, as to you, and they too have occupied the land that the LORD your God is giving them beyond the Jordan, then each of you may return to the property that I have given to you." 21And I charged Joshua as well at that time, saying: "Your own eyes have seen everything that the LORD your God has done to these two kings; so the LORD will do to all the kingdoms into which you are about to cross. 22Do not fear them, for it is the LORD your God who fights for you."

3.8–22: Moses assigns land east of the Jordan. 8–11: *At that time* (vv. 8, 12, 18, 21, 23) marks off a series of topics. Geographic description emphasizes the size of the territory captured. Og's fabled* size as one of the *Rephaim* (mythic giants; v. 11) increases the wonder of the victory. His *bed* was probably a rock formation linked to him by local tradition. **12–17:** Reuben and Gad receive the southern part of the territory and Manasseh the northern part. Because Manasseh settled on both sides of the Jordan, it is called *the half-tribe of Manasseh* (v. 13). The territories of two important clans* of Manasseh are described as land grants to their founding ancestors: *Jair* (v. 14) and *Machir* (v. 15). **18–20:** Moses' speech reflects Deuteronomy's characteristic emphasis on community solidarity. *Rest* (v. 20) means the complete achievement of God's plans and a peaceful life enjoyed in the land. **21–22:** Moses urges Joshua to have confidence in the upcoming conquest, based on the past victories of the divine warrior* *who fights for you.*

---

23 At that time, too, I entreated the LORD, saying: 24"O Lord GOD, you have only begun to show your servant your greatness and your might; what god in heaven or on earth can perform deeds and mighty acts like yours! 25Let me cross over to see the good land beyond the Jordan, that good hill country and the Lebanon." 26But the LORD was angry with me on your account and would not heed me. The LORD said to me, "Enough from you! Never speak to me of this matter again! 27Go up to the top of Pisgah and look around you to the west, to the north, to the south, and to the east. Look well, for you shall not cross over this Jordan. 28But charge Joshua, and encourage and strengthen him, because it is he who shall cross over at the head of this people and who shall secure their possession of the land that you will see." 29So we remained in the valley opposite Beth-peor.

a Heb territory from Aroer   b That is Settlement of Jair
c Heb Salt Sea

3.23–29: Moses is forbidden to enter Canaan. 26: The LORD's anger at Moses refers to what is said in 1.37, but the reason for this anger is never entirely explained. **27:** Moses will climb Mount *Pisgah* just before his death (ch. 34). **29:** Moses' review of history stops at this point. The narrative* action will not resume until ch. 31. *Beth-peor* is a more precise designation for the place where Moses is delivering his speech (1.5; 4.46).

4 So now, Israel, give heed to the statutes and ordinances that I am teaching you to observe, so that you may live to enter and occupy the land that the LORD, the God of your ancestors, is giving you. 2You must neither add anything to what I command you nor take away anything from it, but keep the commandments of the LORD your God with which I am charging you. 3You have seen for yourselves what the LORD did with regard to the Baal of Peor—how the LORD your God destroyed from among you everyone who followed the Baal of Peor, 4while those of you who held fast to the LORD your God are all alive today.

5 See, just as the LORD my God has charged me, I now teach you statutes and ordinances for you to observe in the land that you are about to enter and occupy. 6You must observe them diligently, for this will show your wisdom and discernment to the peoples, who, when they hear all these statutes, will say, "Surely this great nation is a wise and discerning people!" 7For what other great nation has a god so near to it as the LORD our God is whenever we call to him? 8And what other great nation has statutes and ordinances as just as this entire law that I am setting before you today?

9 But take care and watch yourselves closely, so as neither to forget the things that your eyes have seen nor to let them slip from your mind all the days of your life; make them known to your children and your children's children— 10how you once stood before the LORD your God at Horeb, when the LORD said to me, "Assemble the people for me, and I will let them hear my words, so that they may learn to fear me as long as they live on the earth, and may teach their chil-

dren so"; 11you approached and stood at the foot of the mountain while the mountain was blazing up to the very heavens, shrouded in dark clouds. 12Then the LORD spoke to you out of the fire. You heard the sound of words but saw no form; there was only a voice. 13He declared to you his covenant, which he charged you to observe, that is, the ten commandments;[a] and he wrote them on two stone tablets. 14And the LORD charged me at that time to teach you statutes and ordinances for you to observe in the land that you are about to cross into and occupy.

15 Since you saw no form when the LORD spoke to you at Horeb out of the fire, take care and watch yourselves closely, 16so that you do not act corruptly by making an idol for yourselves, in the form of any figure— the likeness of male or female, 17the likeness of any animal that is on the earth, the likeness of any winged bird that flies in the air, 18the likeness of anything that creeps on the ground, the likeness of any fish that is in the water under the earth. 19And when you look up to the heavens and see the sun, the moon, and the stars, all the host of heaven, do not be led astray and bow down to them and serve them, things that the LORD your God has allotted to all the peoples everywhere under heaven. 20But the LORD has taken you and brought you out of the iron-smelter, out of Egypt, to become a people of his very own possession, as you are now.

21 The LORD was angry with me because of you, and he vowed that I should not cross the Jordan and that I should not enter the good land that the LORD your God is giving for your possession. 22For I am going to die in this land without crossing over the Jordan, but you are going to cross over to take possession of that good land. 23So be careful not to forget the covenant that the LORD your God made with you, and not to make for yourselves an idol in the form of anything that the LORD your God has forbidden you. 24For the LORD your God is a devouring fire, a jealous God.

a Heb the ten words

4.1–24: A summons to obedience. 1–2: Moses shifts from reviewing history to encouraging obedience to the law he is about to proclaim (vv. 5, 14). **3–4:** The *Baal* of Peor* incident is recounted in Num 25.1–13. It reflects a basic tenet of Deuteronomy: If you disobey you will be destroyed (v. 24); if you obey you will live (v. 1). **6–8:** An appeal to ethnic pride motivates obedience, along with a reminder of the saving acts of the LORD (v. 7; also v. 20). **9:** Teaching the next generation is a central concern of Deuteronomy (6.20–25). **15–19:** According to Deuteronomy, idolatry* and the worship of other gods were the most serious sins Israel could commit. **20:** The image of an *iron-smelter* emphasizes the brutality of slavery in Egypt. **23–24:** *A jealous God* means a God who is zealously committed to *the covenant** made with Israel.

25 When you have had children and children's children, and become complacent in the land, if you act corruptly by making an idol in the form of anything, thus doing what is evil in the sight of the LORD your God, and provoking him to anger, 26 I call heaven and earth to witness against you today that you will soon utterly perish from the land that you are crossing the Jordan to occupy; you will not live long on it, but will be utterly destroyed. 27 The LORD will scatter you among the peoples; only a few of you will be left among the nations where the LORD will lead you. 28 There you will serve other gods made by human hands, objects of wood and stone that neither see, nor hear, nor eat, nor smell. 29 From there you will seek the LORD your God, and you will find him if you search after him with all your heart and soul. 30 In your distress, when all these things have happened to you in time to come, you will return to the LORD your God and heed him. 31 Because the LORD your God is a merciful God, he will neither abandon you nor destroy you; he will not forget the covenant with your ancestors that he swore to them.

32 For ask now about former ages, long before your own, ever since the day that God created human beings on the earth; ask from one end of heaven to the other: has anything so great as this ever happened or has its like ever been heard of? 33 Has any people ever heard the voice of a god speaking out of a fire, as you have heard, and lived? 34 Or has any god ever attempted to go and take a nation for himself from the midst of another nation, by trials, by signs and wonders, by war, by a mighty hand and an outstretched arm, and by terrifying displays of power, as the LORD your God did for you in Egypt before your very eyes? 35 To you it was shown so that you would acknowledge that the LORD is God; there is no other besides him. 36 From heaven he made you hear his voice to discipline you. On earth he showed you his great fire, while you heard his words coming out of the fire. 37 And because he loved your ancestors, he chose their descendants after them. He brought you out of Egypt with his own presence, by his great power, 38 driving out before you nations greater and mightier than yourselves, to bring you in, giving you their land for a possession, as it is still today. 39 So acknowledge today and take to heart that the LORD is God in heaven above and on the earth beneath; there is no other. 40 Keep his statutes and his commandments, which I am commanding you today for your own well-being and that of your descendants after you, so that you may long remain in the land that the LORD your God is giving you for all time.

4.25–40. 25–31: A look to the future. 27–28: What Moses foresees as Israel's possible future (idolatry,* national destruction, exile into pagan lands) would already have been contemporary reality for some of Deuteronomy's early readers. **29–30:** Readers enduring exile are challenged to repent and *return to the LORD.* **31:** Exiles are to rely on the LORD's character as *a merciful God* who would *not forget the covenant.** **32–40: Israel's unique experience of God. 32:** Moses motivates obedience and loyalty by highlighting Israel's unique experience with the LORD. **33:** The sound and fire of the Mount Horeb revelation taught discipline (v. 36). **34:** The exodus from Egypt and its aftermath revealed God's love (vv. 37–38).

41 Then Moses set apart on the east side of the Jordan three cities 42 to which a homicide could flee, someone who unintentionally kills another person, the two not having been at enmity before; the homicide could flee to one of these cities and live:

43Bezer in the wilderness on the tableland belonging to the Reubenites, Ramoth in Gilead belonging to the Gadites, and Golan in Bashan belonging to the Manassites.

44 This is the law that Moses set before the Israelites. 45These are the decrees and the statutes and ordinances that Moses spoke to the Israelites when they had come out of Egypt, 46beyond the Jordan in the valley opposite Beth-peor, in the land of King Sihon of the Amorites, who reigned at Heshbon, whom Moses and the Israelites defeated when they came out of Egypt. 47They occupied his land and the land of King Og of Bashan, the two kings of the Amorites on the eastern side of the Jordan: 48from Aroer, which is on the edge of the Wadi Arnon, as far as Mount Sirion*a* (that is, Hermon), 49together with all the Arabah on the east side of the Jordan as far as the Sea of the Arabah, under the slopes of Pisgah.

4.41–49. 41–43: Cities of refuge. To shelter the unintentional killer from vengeful relatives (19.1–13). Joshua will set up three other cities west of the Jordan (Josh 20). **44–49: Introduction to the law. 45–46:** This sets the scene for Moses' proclamation of the law (compare 1.1–5). **49:** *The Arabah on the east side of the Jordan* describes the Jordan valley running south to the Dead Sea (*Sea of the Arabah*).

5 Moses convened all Israel, and said to them:

Hear, O Israel, the statutes and ordinances that I am addressing to you today; you shall learn them and observe them diligently. 2The LORD our God made a covenant with us at Horeb. 3Not with our ancestors did the LORD make this covenant, but with us, who are all of us here alive today. 4The LORD spoke with you face to face at the mountain, out of the fire. 5(At that time I was standing between the LORD and you to declare to you the words *b* of the LORD; for you were afraid because of the fire and did not go up the mountain.) And he said:

6 I am the LORD your God, who brought you out of the land of Egypt, out of the house of slavery; 7you shall have no other gods before*c* me.

8 You shall not make for yourself an idol, whether in the form of anything that is in heaven above, or that is on the earth beneath, or that is in the water under the earth. 9You shall not bow down to them or worship them; for I the LORD your God am a jealous God, punishing children for the iniquity of parents, to the third and fourth generation of those who reject me, 10but showing steadfast love to the thousandth generation*d* of those who love me and keep my commandments.

11 You shall not make wrongful use of the name of the LORD your God, for the LORD will not acquit anyone who misuses his name.

12 Observe the sabbath day and keep it holy, as the LORD your God commanded you. 13Six days you shall labor and do all your work. 14But the seventh day is a sabbath to the LORD your God; you shall not do any work—you, or your son or your daughter, or your male or female slave, or your ox or your donkey, or any of your livestock, or the resident alien in your towns, so that your male and female slave may rest as well as you. 15Remember that you were a slave in the land of Egypt, and the LORD your God brought you out from there with a mighty hand and an outstretched arm; therefore the LORD your God commanded you to keep the sabbath day.

16 Honor your father and your mother, as the LORD your God commanded you, so that your days may be long and that it may go well with you in the land that the LORD your God is giving you.

17 You shall not murder.*e*

18 Neither shall you commit adultery.

19 Neither shall you steal.

20 Neither shall you bear false witness against your neighbor.

21 Neither shall you covet your neighbor's wife.

Neither shall you desire your neighbor's house, or field, or male or female slave, or ox, or donkey, or anything that belongs to your neighbor.

a Syr: Heb *Sion*　　b Q Mss Sam Gk Syr Vg Tg: MT *word*　　c Or *besides*　　d Or *to thousands*　
e Or *kill*

5.1–21: The ten commandments. 3: The ten words (the Hebrew expression, see note *a* at 4.13) epitomize the *covenant** God has made with every new generation of readers (*with us*). **4–5:** There is tension between the tradition that the LORD spoke directly to the people (*face to face*) and the notion that Moses served as go-between or mediator. **6–7:** The LORD's self-identification as the one who delivered Israel *out of the land of Egypt* justifies a claim on Israel's obedience and encourages Israel's exclusive loyalty. The translation *before me* implies that no other god should take priority over the LORD or appear in the LORD's presence. The translation *besides me* (note *c*) emphasizes exclusive allegiance. **8–10:** The prohibition of idols is based on the LORD's jealous intolerance that demands absolute fidelity. The threat to three or four generations of those who repudiate the LORD is numerically overwhelmed by God's covenant* loyalty (*steadfast love;* v. 10) shown to thousands of generations (or perhaps individuals, note *d*). **11:** God's personal name "Yahweh" is not to be used to swear false oaths or do harmful magic. **15:** In contrast to Ex 20.11, Deuteronomy motivates sabbath rest by reference to slavery in Egypt. **16:** This addresses the situation of adult children living in extended family units under the authority of aged parents. **17:** Outright murder, death by careless accident, and unauthorized blood vengeance are forbidden. The translation *murder* is too narrow, but *kill* (note *e*) is too broad. **21:** Moral concern extends beyond outward action to internal attitude.

22 These words the LORD spoke with a loud voice to your whole assembly at the mountain, out of the fire, the cloud, and the thick darkness, and he added no more. He wrote them on two stone tablets, and gave them to me. 23When you heard the voice out of the darkness, while the mountain was burning with fire, you approached me, all the heads of your tribes and your elders; 24and you said, "Look, the LORD our God has shown us his glory and greatness, and we have heard his voice out of the fire. Today we have seen that God may speak to someone and the person may still live. 25So now why should we die? For this great fire will consume us; if we hear the voice of the LORD our God any longer, we shall die. 26For who is there of all flesh that has heard the voice of the living God speaking out of fire, as we

have, and remained alive? 27Go near, you yourself, and hear all that the LORD our God will say. Then tell us everything that the LORD our God tells you, and we will listen and do it."

28 The LORD heard your words when you spoke to me, and the LORD said to me: "I have heard the words of this people, which they have spoken to you; they are right in all that they have spoken. 29If only they had such a mind as this, to fear me and to keep all my commandments always, so that it might go well with them and with their children forever! 30Go say to them, 'Return to your tents.' 31But you, stand here by me, and I will tell you all the commandments, the statutes and the ordinances, that you shall teach them, so that they may do them in the land that I am giving them to possess." 32You must therefore be careful to do as the LORD your God has commanded you; you shall not turn to the right or to the left. 33You must follow exactly the path that the LORD your God has commanded you, so that you may live, and that it may go well with you, and that you may live long in the land that you are to possess.

5.22–33: Moses as intermediary. 23–26: It was commonly assumed that to be near the deity was to risk mortal danger. **27:** In other words, Deuteronomy is nothing less than the authentic voice of God as mediated by Moses (compare v. 31). **32–33:** Emphasizing the rewards of obedience motivates readers *to follow exactly the path* commanded in Deuteronomy.

6 Now this is the commandment—the statutes and the ordinances—that the LORD your God charged me to teach you to observe in the land that you are about to cross into and occupy, 2so that you and your children and your children's children may fear the LORD your God all the days of your life, and keep all his decrees and his commandments that I am commanding you, so that your days may be long. 3Hear therefore, O Israel, and observe them diligently, so that it may go well with you, and so that you may multiply greatly in a land flowing with milk and honey, as the LORD, the God of your ancestors, has promised you.

4 Hear, O Israel: The LORD is our God, the LORD alone.[a] 5You shall love the LORD your God with all your heart, and with all your soul, and with all your might. 6Keep these words that I am commanding you today in your heart. 7Recite them to your children and talk about them when you are at home and when you are away, when you lie down and when you rise. 8Bind them as a sign on your hand, fix them as an emblem[b] on your forehead, 9and write them on the doorposts of your house and on your gates.

6.1–9: The essence of the law. 1–3: Obedience to the law *in the land* (v. 1) is rewarded by long life, prosperity, and population growth in that same land (v. 3). *Flowing with milk and honey* (v. 3) is a conventional description of material abundance. 4–5: The LORD is unique in power and unity and thus has an exclusive claim on Israel's love and loyalty. The translation *alone* accents the LORD's incomparability. The translations offered in note *a* emphasize the LORD's unity in contrast to belief in a multiplicity of gods. 6–9: Striking metaphors* call on Israel to internalize the law (*in your heart*, v. 6) and take it personally (*bind them*, v. 8), so that it pervades every aspect of life (*talk about them*, v. 7; *write them*, v. 9). *Recite* (v. 7) literally means to "sharpen up" for instruction.

10 When the LORD your God has brought you into the land that he swore to your ancestors, to Abraham, to Isaac, and to Jacob, to give you—a land with fine, large cities that you did not build, 11houses filled with all sorts of goods that you did not fill, hewn cisterns that you did not hew, vineyards and olive groves that you did not plant—and when you have eaten your fill, 12take care that you do not forget the LORD, who brought you out of the land of Egypt, out of the house of slavery. 13The LORD your God you shall fear; him you shall serve, and by his name alone you shall swear. 14Do not follow other gods, any of the gods of the peoples who are all around you, 15because the LORD your God, who is present with you, is a jealous God. The anger of the LORD your God would be kindled against you and he would destroy you from the face of the earth. 16 Do not put the LORD your God to the test, as you tested him at Massah. 17You

must diligently keep the commandments of the LORD your God, and his decrees, and his statutes that he has commanded you. 18Do what is right and good in the sight of the LORD, so that it may go well with you, and so that you may go in and occupy the good land that the LORD swore to your ancestors to give you, 19thrusting out all your enemies from before you, as the LORD has promised.

20 When your children ask you in time to come, "What is the meaning of the decrees and the statutes and the ordinances that the LORD our God has commanded you?" 21then you shall say to your children, "We were Pharaoh's slaves in Egypt, but the LORD brought us out of Egypt with a mighty hand. 22The LORD displayed before our eyes great and awesome signs and wonders against Egypt, against Pharaoh and all his household. 23He brought us out from there in order to bring us in, to give us the land that he promised on oath to our ancestors. 24Then the LORD commanded us to observe all these statutes, to fear the LORD our God, for our lasting good, so as to keep us alive, as is now the case. 25If we diligently observe this entire commandment before the LORD our God, as he has commanded us, we will be in the right."

6.10–25: Keep this law in the new land. 10–12: That the LORD is the source of these good things undercuts any pride Israel might feel in its prosperity. 15: Israel's loyalty is motivated by the LORD's basic nature as *a jealous God*, one who is so passionately concerned with Israel's exclusive allegiance that national destruction is a real possibility. 16: See Ex 17.1–7. 20–25: Deuteronomy is regularly concerned with the instruction of the next generation (vv. 3, 7). This retelling of the story of salvation includes each succeeding generation by repeatedly using *we* and *us*.

7 When the LORD your God brings you into the land that you are about to enter and occupy, and he clears away many nations before you—the Hittites, the Girgashites, the Amorites, the Canaanites, the

a Or *The LORD our God is one LORD*, or *The LORD our God, the LORD is one*, or *The LORD is our God, the LORD is one*   b Or *as a frontlet*

Perizzites, the Hivites, and the Jebusites, seven nations mightier and more numerous than you— 2and when the LORD your God gives them over to you and you defeat them, then you must utterly destroy them. Make no covenant with them and show them no mercy. 3Do not intermarry with them, giving your daughters to their sons or taking their daughters for your sons, 4for that would turn away your children from following me, to serve other gods. Then the anger of the LORD would be kindled against you, and he would destroy you quickly. 5But this is how you must deal with them: break down their altars, smash their pillars, hew down their sacred poles,ᵃ and burn their idols with fire. 6For you are a people holy to the LORD your God; the LORD your God has chosen you out of all the peoples on earth to be his people, his treasured possession.

7 It was not because you were more numerous than any other people that the LORD set his heart on you and chose you—for you were the fewest of all peoples. 8It was because the LORD loved you and kept the oath that he swore to your ancestors, that the LORD has brought you out with a mighty hand, and redeemed you from the house of slavery, from the hand of Pharaoh king of Egypt. 9Know therefore that the LORD your God is God, the faithful God who maintains covenant loyalty with those who love him and keep his commandments, to a thousand generations, 10and who repays in their own person those who reject him. He does not delay but repays in their own person those who reject him. 11Therefore, observe diligently the commandment—the statutes and the ordinances—that I am commanding you today.

12 If you heed these ordinances, by diligently observing them, the LORD your God will maintain with you the covenant loyalty that he swore to your ancestors; 13he will love you, bless you, and multiply you; he will bless the fruit of your womb and the fruit of your ground, your grain and your wine and your oil, the increase of your cattle and the issue of your flock, in the land that he swore to your ancestors to give you. 14You shall be the most blessed of peoples, with neither ste-

rility nor barrenness among you or your livestock. 15The LORD will turn away from you every illness; all the dread diseases of Egypt that you experienced, he will not inflict on you, but he will lay them on all who hate you. 16You shall devour all the peoples that the LORD your God is giving over to you, showing them no pity; you shall not serve their gods, for that would be a snare to you.

7.1–16: Keep yourself separate. 2: Israel must *utterly destroy* the foreign population by enforcing the ban★ of 20.16–18 (see 2.34; Josh 6.21). **3–4**: Marriage forms social and religious affiliations between families and would lead the Israelite partner to worship or *serve other gods*. Isolation is not motivated by ethnic pride, but is needed to keep Israel loyal. **5**: The temptation of idolatry★ is suppressed by destroying shrines and equipment. **13–14**: The LORD's promise of fruitfulness in family, field, and flock discredits the claims of Canaanite fertility religion.

17 If you say to yourself, "These nations are more numerous than I; how can I dispossess them?" 18do not be afraid of them. Just remember what the LORD your God did to Pharaoh and to all Egypt, 19the great trials that your eyes saw, the signs and wonders, the mighty hand and the outstretched arm by which the LORD your God brought you out. The LORD your God will do the same to all the peoples of whom you are afraid. 20Moreover, the LORD your God will send the pestilenceᵇ against them, until even the survivors and the fugitives are destroyed. 21Have no dread of them, for the LORD your God, who is present with you, is a great and awesome God. 22The LORD your God will clear away these nations before you little by little; you will not be able to make a quick end of them, otherwise the wild animals would become too numerous for you. 23But the LORD your God will give them over to you, and throw them into great panic, until they are destroyed. 24He will hand their kings over to you and you shall blot out their name from under heaven; no one will be able to stand against you, until you have de-

a Heb *Asherim*   b Or *hornets*: Meaning of Heb uncertain

stroyed them. 25The images of their gods you shall burn with fire. Do not covet the silver or the gold that is on them and take it for yourself, because you could be ensnared by it; for it is abhorrent to the LORD your God. 26Do not bring an abhorrent thing into your house, or you will be set apart for destruction like it. You must utterly detest and abhor it, for it is set apart for destruction.

7.17–26: Do not fear, remember the Exodus. 20: *Pestilence* echoes the plagues against Egypt. The translation *hornets* (note *b*) may be a metaphor* for panic or a swarming invader. **23:** *Great panic* is the classic weapon of the divine warrior* (Judg 7.19–22). **25–26:** The total eradication called for by the holy war* ban* must be rigorously applied, lest Israel itself fall into the category of what is banned or *set apart for destruction* (see Josh 6.18; 7.12).

8 This entire commandment that I command you today you must diligently observe, so that you may live and increase, and go in and occupy the land that the LORD promised on oath to your ancestors. 2Remember the long way that the LORD your God has led you these forty years in the wilderness, in order to humble you, testing you to know what was in your heart, whether or not you would keep his commandments. 3He humbled you by letting you hunger, then by feeding you with manna, with which neither you nor your ancestors were acquainted, in order to make you understand that one does not live by bread alone, but by every word that comes from the mouth of the LORD.ᵃ 4The clothes on your back did not wear out and your feet did not swell these forty years. 5Know then in your heart that as a parent disciplines a child so the LORD your God disciplines you. 6Therefore keep the commandments of the LORD your God, by walking in his ways and by fearing him. 7For the LORD your God is bringing you into a good land, a land with flowing streams, with springs and underground waters welling up in valleys and hills, 8a land of wheat and barley, of vines and fig trees and pomegranates, a land of olive trees and honey, 9a land where you may eat bread without scarcity, where you will lack nothing, a land whose stones are

iron and from whose hills you may mine copper. 10You shall eat your fill and bless the LORD your God for the good land that he has given you.

11 Take care that you do not forget the LORD your God, by failing to keep his commandments, his ordinances, and his statutes, which I am commanding you today. 12When you have eaten your fill and have built fine houses and live in them, 13and when your herds and flocks have multiplied, and your silver and gold is multiplied, and all that you have is multiplied, 14then do not exalt yourself, forgetting the LORD your God, who brought you out of the land of Egypt, out of the house of slavery, 15who led you through the great and terrible wilderness, an arid wasteland with poisonousᵇ snakes and scorpions. He made water flow for you from flint rock, 16and fed you in the wilderness with manna that your ancestors did not know, to humble you and to test you, and in the end to do you good. 17Do not say to yourself, "My power and the might of my own hand have gotten me this wealth." 18But remember the LORD your God, for it is he who gives you power to get wealth, so that he may confirm his covenant that he swore to your ancestors, as he is doing today. 19If you do forget the LORD your God and follow other gods to serve and worship them, I solemnly warn you today that you shall surely perish. 20Like the nations that the LORD is destroying before you, so shall you perish, because you would not obey the voice of the LORD your God.

8.1–20: Remember the LORD's saving acts. 2–6: The story of *manna* (v. 3) is reported in Ex 16. The wilderness experience (vv. 2–4) educated and disciplined Israel to keep the law in the new land (vv. 5–6). **7–20:** Israel's good life in the land (vv. 7–10) would be jeopardized by forgetfulness and pride (vv. 11–14, 17, 19–20). The remedy is to remember the LORD's saving deeds and wilderness lessons (vv. 14–16, 18).

9 Hear, O Israel! You are about to cross the Jordan today, to go in and dispossess

a Or *by anything that the LORD decrees*   *b* Or *fiery;* Heb *seraph* nations larger and mightier than you, great cities, fortified to the heavens, 2a strong and tall people, the offspring of the Anakim, whom you know. You have heard it said of them, "Who can stand up to the Anakim?" 3Know then today that the LORD your God is the one who crosses over before you as a devouring fire; he will defeat them and subdue them before you, so that you may dispossess and destroy them quickly, as the LORD has promised you.

4 When the LORD your God thrusts them out before you, do not say to yourself, "It is because of my righteousness that the LORD has brought me in to occupy this land"; it is rather because of the wickedness of these nations that the LORD is dispossessing them before you. 5It is not because of your righteousness or the uprightness of your heart that you are going in to occupy their land; but because of the wickedness of these nations the LORD your God is dispossessing them before you, in order to fulfill the promise that the LORD made on oath to your ancestors, to Abraham, to Isaac, and to Jacob.

9.1–5: Do not be smug or self-righteous. 1–3: The reader is reminded of the circumstances behind Moses' speech (1.1–5). Moses is imitating the address typically given to encourage warriors before a battle (see 20.2–4). 4–5: Do not be self-satisfied. The conquest is not a confirmation of your *righteousness,* but of Canaanite *wickedness.*

6 Know, then, that the LORD your God is not giving you this good land to occupy because of your righteousness; for you are a stubborn people. 7Remember and do not forget how you provoked the LORD your God to wrath in the wilderness; you have been rebellious against the LORD from the day you came out of the land of Egypt until you came to this place.

8 Even at Horeb you provoked the LORD to wrath, and the LORD was so angry with you that he was ready to destroy you. 9When I went up the mountain to receive the stone tablets, the tablets of the covenant that the LORD made with you, I remained on the mountain forty days and forty nights; I neither ate bread nor drank water. 10And the LORD gave me the two stone tablets written with the finger of God; on them were all the words that the LORD had spoken to you at the mountain out of the fire on the day of the assembly. 11At the end of forty days and forty nights the LORD gave me the two stone tablets, the tablets of the covenant. 12Then the LORD said to me, "Get up, go down quickly from here, for your people whom you have brought from Egypt have acted corruptly. They have been quick to turn from the way that I commanded them; they have cast an image for themselves." 13Furthermore the LORD said to me, "I have seen that this people is indeed a stubborn people. 14Let me alone that I may destroy them and blot out their name from under heaven; and I will make of you a nation mightier and more numerous than they."

15 So I turned and went down from the mountain, while the mountain was ablaze; the two tablets of the covenant were in my two hands. 16Then I saw that you had indeed sinned against the LORD your God, by casting for yourselves an image of a calf; you had been quick to turn from the way that the LORD had commanded you. 17So I took hold of the two tablets and flung them from my two hands, smashing them before your eyes. 18Then I lay prostrate before the LORD as before, forty days and forty nights; I neither ate bread nor drank water, because of all the sin you had committed, provoking the LORD by doing what was evil in his sight. 19For I was afraid that the anger that the LORD bore against you was so fierce that he would destroy you. But the LORD listened to me that time also. 20The LORD was so angry with Aaron that he was ready to destroy him, but I interceded also on behalf of Aaron at that same time. 21Then I took the sinful thing you had made, the calf, and burned it with fire and crushed it, grinding it thoroughly, until it was reduced to dust; and I threw the dust of it into the stream that runs down the mountain.

22 At Taberah also, and at Massah, and at Kibroth-hattaavah, you provoked the LORD to wrath. 23And when the LORD sent you from Kadesh-barnea, saying, "Go up and occupy the land that I have given you," you

rebelled against the command of the LORD your God, neither trusting him nor obeying him. 24You have been rebellious against the LORD as long as he has*a* known you.

9.6–24: Remember your rebellion and God's pardon. 7: A repetition of *you have been rebellious against the LORD* encloses this section (see v. 24). **12:** The LORD's words carry a message of rejection: They are *your people*, Moses, not mine. **14:** *Let me alone* indicates that Moses should not intercede for Israel. The LORD proposes restarting the process of forming a chosen people from the beginning. **17:** *Smashing* the tablets symbolizes that the covenant* has itself been shattered. **22–24:** Moses cites history to prove that Israel has always *been rebellious* (v. 24). The incident at *Taberah* is reported in Num 11.1–3, *Massah* in Ex 17.1–7, and *Kibroth-hattaavah* in Num 11.31–34. The rebellion at *Kadesh-barnea* is recounted in Deut 1.19–33.

~~~~~~~~~~~~~~~~~~~~~~~~~~~~~~~~~~~~~~~

25 Throughout the forty days and forty nights that I lay prostrate before the LORD when the LORD intended to destroy you, 26I prayed to the LORD and said, "Lord GOD, do not destroy the people who are your very own possession, whom you redeemed in your greatness, whom you brought out of Egypt with a mighty hand. 27Remember your servants, Abraham, Isaac, and Jacob; pay no attention to the stubbornness of this people, their wickedness and their sin, 28otherwise the land from which you have brought us might say, 'Because the LORD was not able to bring them into the land that he promised them, and because he hated them, he has brought them out to let them die in the wilderness.' 29For they are the people of your very own possession, whom you brought out by your great power and by your outstretched arm."

10 At that time the LORD said to me, "Carve out two tablets of stone like the former ones, and come up to me on the mountain, and make an ark of wood. 2I will write on the tablets the words that were on the former tablets, which you smashed, and you shall put them in the ark." 3So I made an ark of acacia wood, cut two tablets of stone like the former ones, and went up the mountain with the two tablets in my hand.

4Then he wrote on the tablets the same words as before, the ten commandments*b* that the LORD had spoken to you on the mountain out of the fire on the day of the assembly; and the LORD gave them to me. 5So I turned and came down from the mountain, and put the tablets in the ark that I had made; and there they are, as the LORD commanded me.

6 (The Israelites journeyed from Beeroth-bene-jaakan*c* to Moserah. There Aaron died, and there he was buried; his son Eleazar succeeded him as priest. 7From there they journeyed to Gudgodah, and from Gudgodah to Jotbathah, a land with flowing streams. 8At that time the LORD set apart the tribe of Levi to carry the ark of the covenant of the LORD, to stand before the LORD to minister to him, and to bless in his name, to this day. 9Therefore Levi has no allotment or inheritance with his kindred; the LORD is his inheritance, as the LORD your God promised him.)

10 I stayed on the mountain forty days and forty nights, as I had done the first time. And once again the LORD listened to me. The LORD was unwilling to destroy you. 11The LORD said to me, "Get up, go on your journey at the head of the people, that they may go in and occupy the land that I swore to their ancestors to give them."

9.25–10.11: Intercession and forgiveness. 9.25: Moses returns to the incident described in 9.18–19. The flashback is enclosed by the phrase *forty days and forty nights* (see 10.10). **10.1–4:** Israel is back to where it started in 9.10. **10.10:** *The first time* refers to 9.11.

~~~~~~~~~~~~~~~~~~~~~~~~~~~~~~~~~~~~~~~

12 So now, O Israel, what does the LORD your God require of you? Only to fear the LORD your God, to walk in all his ways, to love him, to serve the LORD your God with all your heart and with all your soul, 13and to keep the commandments of the LORD your God*d* and his decrees that I am commanding you today, for your own well-being. 14Although heaven and the heaven of heav-

---

a Sam Gk: MT *I have*   *b* Heb *the ten words*
c Or *the wells of the Bene-jaakan*   *d* Q Ms Gk Syr: MT lacks *your God*

ens belong to the LORD your God, the earth with all that is in it, [15]yet the LORD set his heart in love on your ancestors alone and chose you, their descendants after them, out of all the peoples, as it is today. [16]Circumcise, then, the foreskin of your heart, and do not be stubborn any longer. [17]For the LORD your God is God of gods and Lord of lords, the great God, mighty and awesome, who is not partial and takes no bribe, [18]who executes justice for the orphan and the widow, and who loves the strangers, providing them food and clothing. [19]You shall also love the stranger, for you were strangers in the land of Egypt. [20]You shall fear the LORD your God; him alone you shall worship; to him you shall hold fast, and by his name you shall swear. [21]He is your praise; he is your God, who has done for you these great and awesome things that your own eyes have seen. [22]Your ancestors went down to Egypt seventy persons; and now the LORD your God has made you as numerous as the stars in heaven.

10.12–22: What the LORD requires of you. 12: *To fear* is to be reverent and obedient (also v. 20). *To love* God is part of a mutual circle that begins with the LORD's elective love for Israel's ancestors (v. 15) and culminates in the love that both God and Israel have for the needy stranger (vv. 18–19). *To serve* is to worship. **16:** *Circumcise . . . the foreskin of your heart* means to remove any obstacle to willing obedience. **21:** *He is your praise* means either that God is the true object of Israel's praise or the reason they are praised by others.

11 You shall love the LORD your God, therefore, and keep his charge, his decrees, his ordinances, and his commandments always. [2]Remember today that it was not your children (who have not known or seen the discipline of the LORD your God), but it is you who must acknowledge his greatness, his mighty hand and his outstretched arm, [3]his signs and his deeds that he did in Egypt to Pharaoh, the king of Egypt, and to all his land; [4]what he did to the Egyptian army, to their horses and chariots, how he made the water of the Red Sea[a] flow over them as they pursued you, so that the LORD has destroyed them to this day;

[5]what he did to you in the wilderness, until you came to this place; [6]and what he did to Dathan and Abiram, sons of Eliab son of Reuben, how in the midst of all Israel the earth opened its mouth and swallowed them up, along with their households, their tents, and every living being in their company; [7]for it is your own eyes that have seen every great deed that the LORD did.

8 Keep, then, this entire commandment that I am commanding you today, so that you may have strength to go in and occupy the land that you are crossing over to occupy, [9]and so that you may live long in the land that the LORD swore to your ancestors to give them and to their descendants, a land flowing with milk and honey. [10]For the land that you are about to enter to occupy is not like the land of Egypt, from which you have come, where you sow your seed and irrigate by foot like a vegetable garden. [11]But the land that you are crossing over to occupy is a land of hills and valleys, watered by rain from the sky, [12]a land that the LORD your God looks after. The eyes of the LORD your God are always on it, from the beginning of the year to the end of the year.

13 If you will only heed his every commandment[b] that I am commanding you today—loving the LORD your God, and serving him with all your heart and with all your soul— [14]then he[c] will give the rain for your land in its season, the early rain and the later rain, and you will gather in your grain, your wine, and your oil; [15]and he[c] will give grass in your fields for your livestock, and you will eat your fill. [16]Take care, or you will be seduced into turning away, serving other gods and worshiping them, [17]for then the anger of the LORD will be kindled against you and he will shut up the heavens, so that there will be no rain and the land will yield no fruit; then you will perish quickly off the good land that the LORD is giving you.

18 You shall put these words of mine in your heart and soul, and you shall bind them as a sign on your hand, and fix them as an emblem[d] on your forehead. [19]Teach them

a Or *Sea of Reeds*   b Compare Gk: Heb *my commandments*   c Sam Gk Vg: MT *I*   d Or *as a frontlet*

to your children, talking about them when you are at home and when you are away, when you lie down and when you rise. [20]Write them on the doorposts of your house and on your gates, [21]so that your days and the days of your children may be multiplied in the land that the LORD swore to your ancestors to give them, as long as the heavens are above the earth.

22 If you will diligently observe this entire commandment that I am commanding you, loving the LORD your God, walking in all his ways, and holding fast to him, [23]then the LORD will drive out all these nations before you, and you will dispossess nations larger and mightier than yourselves. [24]Every place on which you set foot shall be yours; your territory shall extend from the wilderness to the Lebanon and from the River, the river Euphrates, to the Western Sea. [25]No one will be able to stand against you; the LORD your God will put the fear and dread of you on all the land on which you set foot, as he promised you.

11.1–25: Three reasons to obey. 2–7: The first is God's past discipline. For *Dathan and Abiram* (v. 6), see Num 16. **9–12:** Israel's second motive is the richness of the land. Rainless Egypt demanded that farmers *irrigate by foot* (v. 10), a tedious procedure using a foot-powered device. In contrast, Canaan is watered by God's trustworthy providence (vv. 11–12). **14:** *Early rain and later rain* are showers that fall in October and then in April. **18–21:** Concentration on the law is to be intense and personal (compare 6.4–9). **22–25:** Israel's third reason to obey is God's promise of an extensive and easy conquest. The optimistic territorial claim of v. 24 (see 1.7) corresponds to the jurisdiction of David and Solomon (1 Kings 4.21, 24).

26 See, I am setting before you today a blessing and a curse: [27]the blessing, if you obey the commandments of the LORD your God that I am commanding you today; [28]and the curse, if you do not obey the commandments of the LORD your God, but turn from the way that I am commanding you today, to follow other gods that you have not known.

29 When the LORD your God has brought you into the land that you are entering to occupy, you shall set the blessing on Mount Gerizim and the curse on Mount Ebal. [30]As you know, they are beyond the Jordan, some distance to the west, in the land of the Canaanites who live in the Arabah, opposite Gilgal, beside the oak[a] of Moreh.

31 When you cross the Jordan to go in to occupy the land that the LORD your God is giving you, and when you occupy it and live in it, [32]you must diligently observe all the statutes and ordinances that I am setting before you today.

11.26–32: Choose either blessing or curse. 26–28: A section of blessings and curses concludes Deuteronomy (ch. 28). **29:** Chapter 27 gives detailed instructions for this ceremony, which Joshua will eventually perform (Josh 8.30–35). **30:** The geography is confusing. *Gilgal* is nowhere near these two mountains. **32:** Moses concludes his introduction with a final appeal for obedience.

12 These are the statutes and ordinances that you must diligently observe in the land that the LORD, the God of your ancestors, has given you to occupy all the days that you live on the earth.

2 You must demolish completely all the places where the nations whom you are about to dispossess served their gods, on the mountain heights, on the hills, and under every leafy tree. [3]Break down their altars, smash their pillars, burn their sacred poles[b] with fire, and hew down the idols of their gods, and thus blot out their name from their places. [4]You shall not worship the LORD your God in such ways. [5]But you shall seek the place that the LORD your God will choose out of all your tribes as his habitation to put his name there. You shall go there, [6]bringing there your burnt offerings and your sacrifices, your tithes and your donations, your votive gifts, your freewill offerings, and the firstlings of your herds and flocks. [7]And you shall eat there in the presence of the LORD your God, you and your households together, rejoicing in all the undertakings in which the LORD your God has blessed you.

a Gk Syr: Compare Gen 12.6; Heb *oaks* or *terebinths*
b Heb *Asherim*

Worship at a Central Sanctuary

The centralization of sacrifice is Deuteronomy's most distinctive demand. Sacrificial worship was to take place only at a single, central sanctuary at a location to be chosen by the LORD (12.5, 11, 14, 18, 26). Earlier practice had permitted sacrifice at many local altars scattered around the country (Ex 20.24). Deuteronomy never identifies the site of this central sanctuary. This radical reform was imposed on Judah by King Josiah, who considered Jerusalem to be the LORD's chosen place (2 Kings 23.4–20).

8 You shall not act as we are acting here today, all of us according to our own desires, 9for you have not yet come into the rest and the possession that the LORD your God is giving you. 10When you cross over the Jordan and live in the land that the LORD your God is allotting to you, and when he gives you rest from your enemies all around so that you live in safety, 11then you shall bring everything that I command you to the place that the LORD your God will choose as a dwelling for his name: your burnt offerings and your sacrifices, your tithes and your donations, and all your choice votive gifts that you vow to the LORD. 12And you shall rejoice before the LORD your God, you together with your sons and your daughters, your male and female slaves, and the Levites who reside in your towns (since they have no allotment or inheritance with you).

13 Take care that you do not offer your burnt offerings at any place you happen to see. 14But only at the place that the LORD will choose in one of your tribes—there you shall offer your burnt offerings and there you shall do everything I command you.

15 Yet whenever you desire you may slaughter and eat meat within any of your towns, according to the blessing that the LORD your God has given you; the unclean and the clean may eat of it, as they would of gazelle or deer. 16The blood, however, you must not eat; you shall pour it out on the ground like water. 17Nor may you eat within your towns the tithe of your grain, your wine, and your oil, the firstlings of your herds and your flocks, any of your votive gifts that you vow, your freewill offerings, or your dona-

tions; 18these you shall eat in the presence of the LORD your God at the place that the LORD your God will choose, you together with your son and your daughter, your male and female slaves, and the Levites resident in your towns, rejoicing in the presence of the LORD your God in all your undertakings. 19Take care that you do not neglect the Levite as long as you live in your land.

20 When the LORD your God enlarges your territory, as he has promised you, and you say, "I am going to eat some meat," because you wish to eat meat, you may eat meat whenever you have the desire. 21If the place where the LORD your God will choose to put his name is too far from you, and you slaughter as I have commanded you any of your herd or flock that the LORD has given you, then you may eat within your towns whenever you desire. 22Indeed, just as gazelle or deer is eaten, so you may eat it; the unclean and the clean alike may eat it. 23Only be sure that you do not eat the blood; for the blood is the life, and you shall not eat the life with the meat. 24Do not eat it; you shall pour it out on the ground like water. 25Do not eat it, so that all may go well with you and your children after you, because you do what is right in the sight of the LORD. 26But the sacred donations that are due from you, and your votive gifts, you shall bring to the place that the LORD will choose. 27You shall present your burnt offerings, both the meat and the blood, on the altar of the LORD your God; the blood of your other sacrifices shall be poured out beside*a* the al-

a Or *on*

tar of the LORD your God, but the meat you may eat.

28 Be careful to obey all these words that I command you today,[a] so that it may go well with you and with your children after you forever, because you will be doing what is good and right in the sight of the LORD your God.

12.1–28: Centralize all sacrifice. 2–3: Israel's local worship sites were often also used for Canaanite worship. *Sacred poles* (*Asherim,* note b) were wooden symbols of the goddess Asherah.* **5:** The LORD is not present there directly, but in the form of *his name.* The central sanctuary is to be a focus of pilgrimage (*go there*). **6:** Every sacrifice and offering must be taken there (vv. 11, 13–14, 17, 26–27). **7:** Most sacrifices culminated in a joyous meal. **12:** The worship assembly is to be inclusive, including women and marginalized groups (also vv. 18–19). **15:** All animal slaughter was potentially a religious act. Centralizing sacrifice meant that killing animals locally would now be a purely secular affair. Those who ate such non-sacrificial meat could be in a state of ritual uncleanness (also vv. 21–22). **16:** *Blood* was dangerous and powerful and could never be eaten. It must be disposed of in a completely non-sacrificial manner, poured on the ground *like water* (also vv. 23–25).

---

29 When the LORD your God has cut off before you the nations whom you are about to enter to dispossess them, when you have dispossessed them and live in their land, [30]take care that you are not snared into imitating them, after they have been destroyed before you: do not inquire concerning their gods, saying, "How did these nations worship their gods? I also want to do the same." [31]You must not do the same for the LORD your God, because every abhorrent thing that the LORD hates they have done for their gods. They would even burn their sons and their daughters in the fire to their gods. [32][b]You must diligently observe everything that I command you; do not add to it or take anything from it.

13 [c]If prophets or those who divine by dreams appear among you and promise you omens or portents, [2]and the omens or the portents declared by them take place, and they say, "Let us follow other gods"

(whom you have not known) "and let us serve them," [3]you must not heed the words of those prophets or those who divine by dreams; for the LORD your God is testing you, to know whether you indeed love the LORD your God with all your heart and soul. [4]The LORD your God you shall follow, him alone you shall fear, his commandments you shall keep, his voice you shall obey, him you shall serve, and to him you shall hold fast. [5]But those prophets or those who divine by dreams shall be put to death for having spoken treason against the LORD your God— who brought you out of the land of Egypt and redeemed you from the house of slavery—to turn you from the way in which the LORD your God commanded you to walk. So you shall purge the evil from your midst.

6 If anyone secretly entices you—even if it is your brother, your father's son or[d] your mother's son, or your own son or daughter, or the wife you embrace, or your most intimate friend—saying, "Let us go worship other gods," whom neither you nor your ancestors have known, [7]any of the gods of the peoples that are around you, whether near you or far away from you, from one end of the earth to the other, [8]you must not yield to or heed any such persons. Show them no pity or compassion and do not shield them. [9]But you shall surely kill them; your own hand shall be first against them to execute them, and afterwards the hand of all the people. [10]Stone them to death for trying to turn you away from the LORD your God, who brought you out of the land of Egypt, out of the house of slavery. [11]Then all Israel shall hear and be afraid, and never again do any such wickedness.

12 If you hear it said about one of the towns that the LORD your God is giving you to live in, [13]that scoundrels from among you have gone out and led the inhabitants of the town astray, saying, "Let us go and worship other gods," whom you have not known, [14]then you shall inquire and make a thorough investigation. If the charge is estab-

---

a Gk Sam Syr: MT lacks *today*   b Ch 13.1 in Heb
c Ch 13.2 in Heb   d Sam Gk Compare Tg: MT lacks *your father's son or*

lished that such an abhorrent thing has been done among you, 15you shall put the inhabitants of that town to the sword, utterly destroying it and everything in it—even putting its livestock to the sword. 16All of its spoil you shall gather into its public square; then burn the town and all its spoil with fire, as a whole burnt offering to the LORD your God. It shall remain a perpetual ruin, never to be rebuilt. 17Do not let anything devoted to destruction stick to your hand, so that the LORD may turn from his fierce anger and show you compassion, and in his compassion multiply you, as he swore to your ancestors, 18if you obey the voice of the LORD your God by keeping all his commandments that I am commanding you today, doing what is right in the sight of the LORD your God.

12.29–13.18: Do not be enticed by other gods. 12.30: One source of temptation is curiosity and a desire to imitate. **13.1–5:** False prophets* are another lure. Their message would be especially tempting if they could authenticate it with *omens* and *portents* (v. 2; contrast 18.22). **6–11:** Temptation could also come *secretly* (v. 6) from someone very close. In contrast to its long history with the LORD during the Exodus (vv. 5, 10), Israel has had no experience with these *other gods* (vv. 6, 13). **12–18:** An apostate town is to be treated as the object of holy war* (20.16–18). In this case, not only are humans *utterly destroyed* (v. 15), but cattle, all moveable property, and the town itself are to be *devoted to destruction* (vv. 16–17; compare Josh 6.21, 24).

14 You are children of the LORD your God. You must not lacerate yourselves or shave your forelocks for the dead. 2For you are a people holy to the LORD your God; it is you the LORD has chosen out of all the peoples on earth to be his people, his treasured possession.

3 You shall not eat any abhorrent thing. 4These are the animals you may eat: the ox, the sheep, the goat, 5the deer, the gazelle, the roebuck, the wild goat, the ibex, the antelope, and the mountain-sheep. 6Any animal that divides the hoof and has the hoof cleft in two, and chews the cud, among the animals, you may eat. 7Yet of those that chew the cud or have the hoof cleft you shall not eat these: the camel, the hare, and the rock badger, because they chew the cud but do not divide the hoof; they are unclean for you. 8And the pig, because it divides the hoof but does not chew the cud, is unclean for you. You shall not eat their meat, and you shall not touch their carcasses.

9 Of all that live in water you may eat these: whatever has fins and scales you may eat. 10And whatever does not have fins and scales you shall not eat; it is unclean for you.

11 You may eat any clean birds. 12But these are the ones that you shall not eat: the eagle, the vulture, the osprey, 13the buzzard, the kite of any kind; 14every raven of any kind; 15the ostrich, the nighthawk, the sea gull, the hawk of any kind; 16the little owl and the great owl, the water hen 17and the desert owl,*a* the carrion vulture and the cormorant, 18the stork, the heron of any kind; the hoopoe and the bat.*b* 19And all winged insects are unclean for you; they shall not be eaten. 20You may eat any clean winged creature.

21 You shall not eat anything that dies of itself; you may give it to aliens residing in your towns for them to eat, or you may sell it to a foreigner. For you are a people holy to the LORD your God.

You shall not boil a kid in its mother's milk.

14.1–21: Clean and unclean foods. 1: These mourning rituals may have been part of Canaanite worship. **3:** Any *abhorrent thing* would damage one's relationship with God (see 7.26; 12.31). **6–7:** Domestic animals provide the standard for what may be eaten. **8:** The *pig* may have been used in Canaanite rituals. **9–10:** Ordinary fish are the standard for what is clean. **21:** Whatever died a natural death would contain forbidden blood. These dietary rules do not apply to non-Israelites. Boiling a baby goat in its own *mother's milk* may have been a Canaanite ritual.

22 Set apart a tithe of all the yield of your seed that is brought in yearly from the field. 23In the presence of the LORD your God, in the place that he will choose as a dwelling

a Or *pelican*   *b* Identification of several of the birds in verses 12–18 is uncertain

Ritual Purity

Israel's purity system categorized persons, objects, and foods. It had nothing to do with modern notions of hygiene. Those who ate unclean food became ritually unclean. They were excluded from social contact and the worship assembly until their impurity was removed. A similar list of clean and unclean animals is given in Lev 11.

for his name, you shall eat the tithe of your grain, your wine, and your oil, as well as the firstlings of your herd and flock, so that you may learn to fear the LORD your God always. 24But if, when the LORD your God has blessed you, the distance is so great that you are unable to transport it, because the place where the LORD your God will choose to set his name is too far away from you, 25then you may turn it into money. With the money secure in hand, go to the place that the LORD your God will choose; 26spend the money for whatever you wish—oxen, sheep, wine, strong drink, or whatever you desire. And you shall eat there in the presence of the LORD your God, you and your household rejoicing together. 27As for the Levites resident in your towns, do not neglect them, because they have no allotment or inheritance with you.

28 Every third year you shall bring out the full tithe of your produce for that year, and store it within your towns; 29the Levites, because they have no allotment or inheritance with you, as well as the resident aliens, the orphans, and the widows in your towns, may come and eat their fill so that the LORD your God may bless you in all the work that you undertake.

14.22–29: Set apart tithes. 22–23: Ten percent of one's crop, along with firstborn animals, are taken to the central sanctuary and eaten as a sacrificial meal (12.17–18). 24–26: If transportation is a problem, the tithe may be converted to cash to buy a joyful banquet at the central sanctuary. 27–29: Every three years, a second tenth is stored up to provide for the needy. Apparently this practice took place on the third and sixth year of every seven-year cycle (15.1).

15 Every seventh year you shall grant a remission of debts. 2And this is the manner of the remission: every creditor shall remit the claim that is held against a neighbor, not exacting it of a neighbor who is a member of the community, because the LORD's remission has been proclaimed. 3Of a foreigner you may exact it, but you must remit your claim on whatever any member of your community owes you. 4There will, however, be no one in need among you, because the LORD is sure to bless you in the land that the LORD your God is giving you as a possession to occupy, 5if only you will obey the LORD your God by diligently observing this entire commandment that I command you today. 6When the LORD your God has blessed you, as he promised you, you will lend to many nations, but you will not borrow; you will rule over many nations, but they will not rule over you.

7 If there is among you anyone in need, a member of your community in any of your towns within the land that the LORD your God is giving you, do not be hard-hearted or tight-fisted toward your needy neighbor. 8You should rather open your hand, willingly lending enough to meet the need, whatever it may be. 9Be careful that you do not entertain a mean thought, thinking, "The seventh year, the year of remission, is near," and therefore view your needy neighbor with hostility and give nothing; your neighbor might cry to the LORD against you, and you would incur guilt. 10Give liberally and be ungrudging when you do so, for on this account the LORD your God will bless you in all your work and in all that you undertake. 11Since there will never cease to be some in need on the earth, I therefore command you, "Open

your hand to the poor and needy neighbor in your land."

15.1–11: Remit debts every seventh year. 1: This is a revision of Ex 23.10–11. *A remission of debts* prevents the creation of a permanent debtor class. **4–5:** The ideal result of perfect obedience (*no one in need*) stands in tension with v. 11. **8–9:** Generous lending is understood as a form of social service. **11:** The permanent reality of poverty provides an opportunity for generosity.

12 If a member of your community, whether a Hebrew man or a Hebrew woman, is sold*ᵃ* to you and works for you six years, in the seventh year you shall set that person free. ¹³And when you send a male slave*ᵇ* out from you a free person, you shall not send him out empty-handed. ¹⁴Provide liberally out of your flock, your threshing floor, and your wine press, thus giving to him some of the bounty with which the LORD your God has blessed you. ¹⁵Remember that you were a slave in the land of Egypt, and the LORD your God redeemed you; for this reason I lay this command upon you today. ¹⁶But if he says to you, "I will not go out from you," because he loves you and your household, since he is well off with you, ¹⁷then you shall take an awl and thrust it through his earlobe into the door, and he shall be your slave*ᶜ* forever.

You shall do the same with regard to your female slave.*ᵈ*

18 Do not consider it a hardship when you send them out from you free persons, because for six years they have given you services worth the wages of hired laborers; and the LORD your God will bless you in all that you do.

19 Every firstling male born of your herd and flock you shall consecrate to the LORD your God; you shall not do work with your firstling ox nor shear the firstling of your flock. ²⁰You shall eat it, you together with your household, in the presence of the LORD your God year by year at the place that the LORD will choose. ²¹But if it has any defect—any serious defect, such as lameness or blindness—you shall not sacrifice it to the LORD your God; ²²within your towns you

may eat it, the unclean and the clean alike, as you would a gazelle or deer. ²³Its blood, however, you must not eat; you shall pour it out on the ground like water.

15.12–23. 12–18: Hebrew slaves. 12: This fellow *Hebrew* would have been *sold* (but see note *a*) to meet unpaid debts. Release comes on the *seventh year* of service (not the seven-year cycle of vv. 1–11). **14–15:** This law is a revision of Ex 21.2–6. Its socially compassionate provisions are typical of Deuteronomy, as is the motivating reference to the Exodus (compare 5.15). **17:** Explicit concern for a *female slave* is typical of Deuteronomy (21.10–17). **19–23: Consecrate firstborn male animals. 19–20:** This is a revision of Ex 22.30. Because the animal belongs to the LORD, no economic benefit may be derived from it. It is to be eaten as a sacrifice at the central sanctuary. **21–23:** If too defective to sacrifice, it becomes a secular meal at home (compare 12.15–16, 20–25).

16 Observe the month*ᵉ* of Abib by keeping the passover to the LORD your God, for in the month of Abib the LORD your God brought you out of Egypt by night. ²You shall offer the passover sacrifice to the LORD your God, from the flock and the herd, at the place that the LORD will choose as a dwelling for his name. ³You must not eat with it anything leavened. For seven days you shall eat unleavened bread with it—the bread of affliction—because you came out of the land of Egypt in great haste, so that all the days of your life you may remember the day of your departure from the land of Egypt. ⁴No leaven shall be seen with you in all your territory for seven days; and none of the meat of what you slaughter on the evening of the first day shall remain until morning. ⁵You are not permitted to offer the passover sacrifice within any of your towns that the LORD your God is giving you. ⁶But at the place that the LORD your God will choose as a dwelling for his name, only there shall you offer the passover sacrifice, in the evening at sunset, the time of day when you departed from Egypt. ⁷You shall cook it and eat it at the place that the LORD your God will

---

a Or *sells himself or herself*   *b* Heb *him*
c Or *bondman*   *d* Or *bondwoman*   *e* Or *new moon*

choose; the next morning you may go back to your tents. 8For six days you shall continue to eat unleavened bread, and on the seventh day there shall be a solemn assembly for the LORD your God, when you shall do no work.

9 You shall count seven weeks; begin to count the seven weeks from the time the sickle is first put to the standing grain. 10Then you shall keep the festival of weeks to the LORD your God, contributing a freewill offering in proportion to the blessing that you have received from the LORD your God. 11Rejoice before the LORD your God—you and your sons and your daughters, your male and female slaves, the Levites resident in your towns, as well as the strangers, the orphans, and the widows who are among you—at the place that the LORD your God will choose as a dwelling for his name. 12Remember that you were a slave in Egypt, and diligently observe these statutes.

13 You shall keep the festival of booths*a* for seven days, when you have gathered in the produce from your threshing floor and your wine press. 14Rejoice during your festival, you and your sons and your daughters, your male and female slaves, as well as the Levites, the strangers, the orphans, and the widows resident in your towns. 15Seven days you shall keep the festival to the LORD your God at the place that the LORD will choose; for the LORD your God will bless you in all your produce and in all your undertakings, and you shall surely celebrate.

16 Three times a year all your males shall appear before the LORD your God at the place that he will choose: at the festival of unleavened bread, at the festival of weeks, and at the festival of booths.*a* They shall not appear before the LORD empty-handed; 17all shall give as they are able, according to the blessing of the LORD your God that he has given you.

16.1–17: Celebrate three pilgrimage festivals. 1: *Passover** takes place in *Abib,* when the first grain is harvested. **2:** Deuteronomy's revision of Ex 23.14–17 turns previously local observances into festivals at the central sanctuary (also vv. 11, 15). **5–6:** The former practice of offering the Passover sacrifice *within any of*

your towns is replaced by a centralized festival. This centralization was instituted in Judah by King Josiah (2 Kings 23.21–23). Passover reverted to a domestic celebration when the destruction of the Temple* by Rome made sacrifice impossible. **9–10:** Seven weeks later in early summer is the *festival of weeks.* **11:** Including society's marginalized groups is typical of Deuteronomy (v. 14). **13–14:** The autumn grape harvest marks the end of the agricultural year and the *festival of booths.* Deuteronomy fails to mention this festival's most distinctive feature, residence in temporary shelters or *booths,* but emphasizes all-inclusive merrymaking.

---

18 You shall appoint judges and officials throughout your tribes, in all your towns that the LORD your God is giving you, and they shall render just decisions for the people. 19You must not distort justice; you must not show partiality; and you must not accept bribes, for a bribe blinds the eyes of the wise and subverts the cause of those who are in the right. 20Justice, and only justice, you shall pursue, so that you may live and occupy the land that the LORD your God is giving you.

21 You shall not plant any tree as a sacred pole*b* beside the altar that you make for the LORD your God; 22nor shall you set up a stone pillar—things that the LORD your God hates.

17 You must not sacrifice to the LORD your God an ox or a sheep that has a defect, anything seriously wrong; for that is abhorrent to the LORD your God.

2 If there is found among you, in one of your towns that the LORD your God is giving you, a man or woman who does what is evil in the sight of the LORD your God, and transgresses his covenant 3by going to serve other gods and worshiping them—whether the sun or the moon or any of the host of heaven, which I have forbidden— 4and if it is reported to you or you hear of it, and you make a thorough inquiry, and the charge is proved true that such an abhorrent thing has occurred in Israel, 5then you shall bring out to your gates that man or that woman who has committed this crime and you shall stone the

---

a Or *tabernacles;* Heb *succoth*   *b* Heb *Asherah*

man or woman to death. 6On the evidence of two or three witnesses the death sentence shall be executed; a person must not be put to death on the evidence of only one witness. 7The hands of the witnesses shall be the first raised against the person to execute the death penalty, and afterward the hands of all the people. So you shall purge the evil from your midst.

8 If a judicial decision is too difficult for you to make between one kind of bloodshed and another, one kind of legal right and another, or one kind of assault and another— any such matters of dispute in your towns—then you shall immediately go up to the place that the LORD your God will choose, 9where you shall consult with the levitical priests and the judge who is in office in those days; they shall announce to you the decision in the case. 10Carry out exactly the decision that they announce to you from the place that the LORD will choose, diligently observing everything they instruct you. 11You must carry out fully the law that they interpret for you or the ruling that they announce to you; do not turn aside from the decision that they announce to you, either to the right or to the left. 12As for anyone who presumes to disobey the priest appointed to minister there to the LORD your God, or the judge, that person shall die. So you shall purge the evil from Israel. 13All the people will hear and be afraid, and will not act presumptuously again.

16.18–17.13: Maintain a fair justice system. 16.19: The phrase beginning *a bribe blinds the eyes* quotes a proverb (Ex 23.8). **16.21–17.1:** Three short laws forbid improper ritual practices. A *sacred pole* (16.21) was a symbol of the goddess Asherah★ (note *b*). **2–6:** The sample case of someone who worships *other gods* (v. 3) illustrates a fair and rigorous judicial procedure. Fairness requires a *thorough inquiry* (v. 4) and more than one eyewitness to the crime (v. 6). **7:** *Witnesses* cast the first stones in order to affirm the truth of their testimony (Jn 8.7; Acts 7.58). **8–13:** Before sanctuary centralization, priests of the local shrines advised on legal fine points. Deuteronomy instead establishes a centralized court of appeal, staffed by both civil and priestly judges (vv. 9, 12).

14 When you have come into the land that the LORD your God is giving you, and have taken possession of it and settled in it, and you say, "I will set a king over me, like all the nations that are around me," 15you may indeed set over you a king whom the LORD your God will choose. One of your own community you may set as king over you; you are not permitted to put a foreigner over you, who is not of your own community. 16Even so, he must not acquire many horses for himself, or return the people to Egypt in order to acquire more horses, since the LORD has said to you, "You must never return that way again." 17And he must not acquire many wives for himself, or else his heart will turn away; also silver and gold he must not acquire in great quantity for himself. 18When he has taken the throne of his kingdom, he shall have a copy of this law written for him in the presence of the levitical priests. 19It shall remain with him and he shall read in it all the days of his life, so that he may learn to fear the LORD his God, diligently observing all the words of this law and these statutes, 20neither exalting himself above other members of the community nor turning aside from the commandment, either to the right or to the left, so that he and his descendants may reign long over his kingdom in Israel.

17.14–20: The king. 16–17: Deuteronomy has a low opinion of kingship and restricts its usual perquisites. The grandeur of King Solomon serves as a negative example (compare 1 Kings 10–11). **18–19:** Monarchy is brought under the control of the law. **20:** The king is to be an obedient "constitutional monarch" on the same level with ordinary citizens.

18 The levitical priests, the whole tribe of Levi, shall have no allotment or inheritance within Israel. They may eat the sacrifices that are the LORD's portion*a* 2but they shall have no inheritance among the other members of the community; the LORD is their inheritance, as he promised them.

3 This shall be the priests' due from the people, from those offering a sacrifice,

a Meaning of Heb uncertain

whether an ox or a sheep: they shall give to the priest the shoulder, the two jowls, and the stomach. [4]The first fruits of your grain, your wine, and your oil, as well as the first of the fleece of your sheep, you shall give him. [5]For the LORD your God has chosen Levi[a] out of all your tribes, to stand and minister in the name of the LORD, him and his sons for all time.

[6] If a Levite leaves any of your towns, from wherever he has been residing in Israel, and comes to the place that the LORD will choose (and he may come whenever he wishes), [7]then he may minister in the name of the LORD his God, like all his fellow-Levites who stand to minister there before the LORD. [8]They shall have equal portions to eat, even though they have income from the sale of family possessions.[b]

[9] When you come into the land that the LORD your God is giving you, you must not learn to imitate the abhorrent practices of those nations. [10]No one shall be found among you who makes a son or daughter pass through fire, or who practices divination, or is a soothsayer, or an augur, or a sorcerer, [11]or one who casts spells, or who consults ghosts or spirits, or who seeks oracles from the dead. [12]For whoever does these things is abhorrent to the LORD; it is because of such abhorrent practices that the LORD your God is driving them out before you. [13]You must remain completely loyal to the LORD your God. [14]Although these nations that you are about to dispossess do give heed to soothsayers and diviners, as for you, the LORD your God does not permit you to do so.

[15] The LORD your God will raise up for you a prophet[c] like me from among your own people; you shall heed such a prophet.[d] [16]This is what you requested of the LORD your God at Horeb on the day of the assembly when you said: "If I hear the voice of the LORD my God any more, or ever again see this great fire, I will die." [17]Then the LORD replied to me: "They are right in what they have said. [18]I will raise up for them a prophet[e] like you from among their own people; I will put my words in the mouth of the prophet,[e] who shall speak to them everything that I command. [19]Anyone who does

not heed the words that the prophet[f] shall speak in my name, I myself will hold accountable. [20]But any prophet who speaks in the name of other gods, or who presumes to speak in my name a word that I have not commanded the prophet to speak—that prophet shall die." [21]You may say to yourself, "How can we recognize a word that the LORD has not spoken?" [22]If a prophet speaks in the name of the LORD but the thing does not take place or prove true, it is a word that the LORD has not spoken. The prophet has spoken it presumptuously; do not be frightened by it.

18.1–22. 1–8: The levitical priests. 1: Deuteronomy does not make any sharp distinction between *levitical priests* and other members of the *tribe of Levi*. **3–4:** Although priests may have income from other sources (v. 8), they are supported by designated portions of the sacrifices. **6–8:** This provision blunts the devastating economic impact that sanctuary centralization would have on local priests. Any Levite who relocates to the central sanctuary is to receive a priestly appointment. **9–22: True and false prophets.** * **10–11:** Various methods of divination and practitioners of secret arts are listed and labeled as abominations. Seeking *oracles* * *from the dead* is illustrated by 1 Sam 28.6–19. **15:** A series of *prophets* like Moses is intended, rather than only a single one (notes *c, d, e*). **20–22:** Prophecy in the name of another god is easily rejected, but false prophecy in the name of the LORD poses a more difficult problem. The suggested practical standard (*the thing does not take place*, v. 22) could be applied to a prophet's overall message, but not to individual oracles.

---

19 When the LORD your God has cut off the nations whose land the LORD your God is giving you, and you have dispossessed them and settled in their towns and in their houses, [2]you shall set apart three cities in the land that the LORD your God is giving you to possess. [3]You shall calculate the distances[g] and divide into three regions the land that the LORD your God gives you as a possession, so that any homicide can flee to one of them.

---

a Heb *him*   *b* Meaning of Heb uncertain
c Or *prophets*   *d* Or *such prophets*   *e* Or *mouths of the prophets*   *f* Heb *he*   *g* Or *prepare roads to them*

4 Now this is the case of a homicide who might flee there and live, that is, someone who has killed another person unintentionally when the two had not been at enmity before: 5Suppose someone goes into the forest with another to cut wood, and when one of them swings the ax to cut down a tree, the head slips from the handle and strikes the other person who then dies; the killer may flee to one of these cities and live. 6But if the distance is too great, the avenger of blood in hot anger might pursue and overtake and put the killer to death, although a death sentence was not deserved, since the two had not been at enmity before. 7Therefore I command you: You shall set apart three cities.

8 If the LORD your God enlarges your territory, as he swore to your ancestors—and he will give you all the land that he promised your ancestors to give you, 9provided you diligently observe this entire commandment that I command you today, by loving the LORD your God and walking always in his ways—then you shall add three more cities to these three, 10so that the blood of an innocent person may not be shed in the land that the LORD your God is giving you as an inheritance, thereby bringing bloodguilt upon you.

11 But if someone at enmity with another lies in wait and attacks and takes the life of that person, and flees into one of these cities, 12then the elders of the killer's city shall send to have the culprit taken from there and handed over to the avenger of blood to be put to death. 13Show no pity; you shall purge the guilt of innocent blood from Israel, so that it may go well with you.

14 You must not move your neighbor's boundary marker, set up by former generations, on the property that will be allotted to you in the land that the LORD your God is giving you to possess.

15 A single witness shall not suffice to convict a person of any crime or wrongdoing in connection with any offense that may be committed. Only on the evidence of two or three witnesses shall a charge be sustained. 16If a malicious witness comes forward to accuse someone of wrongdoing, 17then both parties to the dispute shall appear before the LORD, before the priests and the judges who are in office in those days, 18and the judges shall make a thorough inquiry. If the witness is a false witness, having testified falsely against another, 19then you shall do to the false witness just as the false witness had meant to do to the other. So you shall purge the evil from your midst. 20The rest shall hear and be afraid, and a crime such as this shall never again be committed among you. 21Show no pity: life for life, eye for eye, tooth for tooth, hand for hand, foot for foot.

19.1–21. 1–13: **Cities of asylum. 3:** Intentional murder was punished by retaliation from the victim's family. Before sanctuary centralization, someone who had killed accidentally (vv. 4–5) could find asylum at a local altar (Ex 21.12–14). Fairness requires easy approach to the three places of asylum, either in regard to *the distances* or the quality of access roads (note *g*). **6:** The *avenger of blood,* a close relative designated by custom to hunt down the killer, would not weigh the claims of the accused fairly. **8–9:** Moses set up three cities east of the Jordan (4.41–43), and Joshua three on the west (Josh 20). **11–12:** This case contrasts with that of vv. 4–6, so the right of asylum does not apply. **14–21: Boundary markers and witnesses. 14:** This could be done openly through economic pressure against poor landowners as well as in secret (27.17). Ancestral land is a gift from the LORD and not to be alienated from the family that owns it. **16–19:** This law restates Ex 23.1 in light of the central court of 17.8–13. **21:** Justice in Israel depended almost entirely on eyewitness testimony, so stern punishment is in order.

20 When you go out to war against your enemies, and see horses and chariots, an army larger than your own, you shall not be afraid of them; for the LORD your God is with you, who brought you up from the land of Egypt. 2Before you engage in battle, the priest shall come forward and speak to the troops, 3and shall say to them: "Hear, O Israel! Today you are drawing near to do battle against your enemies. Do not lose heart, or be afraid, or panic, or be in dread of them; 4for it is the LORD your God who goes with you, to fight for you against your enemies, to give you victory." 5Then the officials shall address the troops, saying, "Has anyone built a new house but not dedicated

it? He should go back to his house, or he might die in the battle and another dedicate it. 6Has anyone planted a vineyard but not yet enjoyed its fruit? He should go back to his house, or he might die in the battle and another be first to enjoy its fruit? 7Has anyone become engaged to a woman but not yet married her? He should go back to his house, or he might die in the battle and another marry her." 8The officials shall continue to address the troops, saying, "Is anyone afraid or disheartened? He should go back to his house, or he might cause the heart of his comrades to melt like his own." 9When the officials have finished addressing the troops, then the commanders shall take charge of them.

10 When you draw near to a town to fight against it, offer it terms of peace. 11If it accepts your terms of peace and surrenders to you, then all the people in it shall serve you at forced labor. 12If it does not submit to you peacefully, but makes war against you, then you shall besiege it; 13and when the LORD your God gives it into your hand, you shall put all its males to the sword. 14You may, however, take as your booty the women, the children, livestock, and everything else in the town, all its spoil. You may enjoy the spoil of your enemies, which the LORD your God has given you. 15Thus you shall treat all the towns that are very far from you, which are not towns of the nations here. 16But as for the towns of these peoples that the LORD your God is giving you as an inheritance, you must not let anything that breathes remain alive. 17You shall annihilate them—the Hittites and the Amorites, the Canaanites and the Perizzites, the Hivites and the Jebusites—just as the LORD your God has commanded, 18so that they may not teach you to do all the abhorrent things that they do for their gods, and you thus sin against the LORD your God.

19 If you besiege a town for a long time, making war against it in order to take it, you must not destroy its trees by wielding an ax against them. Although you may take food from them, you must not cut them down. Are trees in the field human beings that they should come under siege from you? 20You may destroy only the trees that you know do not produce food; you may cut them down for use in building siegeworks against the town that makes war with you, until it falls.

20.1–20: Holy war.* **1:** In holy war confident faith is a prerequisite for victory. **2–4:** First comes a priestly war sermon. **5–8:** Exemptions are provided for any who deserve to enjoy some new venture and those whose fear might undercut the army's courage. **10–15:** Besieged cities outside the promised land (far from you, v. 15) are to be offered terms. If they resist, all potential warriors are to be killed, but women and children may be enslaved and everything else plundered. **16–18:** By contrast, the entire population of an enemy city inside the promised land is to be put to the ban* and devoted to destruction (you shall annihilate them, v. 17). **19–20:** This limits the devastation of siege warfare.

21 If, in the land that the LORD your God is giving you to possess, a body is found lying in open country, and it is not known who struck the person down, 2then your elders and your judges shall come out to measure the distances to the towns that are near the body. 3The elders of the town nearest the body shall take a heifer that has never been worked, one that has not pulled in the yoke; 4the elders of that town shall bring the heifer down to a wadi with running water, which is neither plowed nor sown, and shall break the heifer's neck there in the wadi. 5Then the priests, the sons of Levi, shall come forward, for the LORD your God has chosen them to minister to him and to pronounce blessings in the name of the LORD, and by their decision all cases of dispute and assault shall be settled. 6All the elders of that town nearest the body shall wash their hands over the heifer whose neck was broken in the wadi, 7and they shall declare: "Our hands did not shed this blood, nor were we witnesses to it. 8Absolve, O LORD, your people Israel, whom you redeemed; do not let the guilt of innocent blood remain in the midst of your people Israel." Then they will be absolved of bloodguilt. 9So you shall purge the guilt of innocent blood from your midst, because you must do what is right in the sight of the LORD.

21.1–9: Unsolved murder. 1–2: The objective reality of bloodguilt endangers the nearest community. **3–4:** Guilt is eliminated by the death of a heifer and a symbolic ritual of hand washing. That the heifer *has never been worked* and the land *neither plowed nor sown* indicates that no human benefit has been derived from them. **6:** Washing hands *over the heifer* dramatically declares innocence and perhaps conveys the guilt to the carcass.

10 When you go out to war against your enemies, and the LORD your God hands them over to you and you take them captive, ¹¹suppose you see among the captives a beautiful woman whom you desire and want to marry, ¹²and so you bring her home to your house: she shall shave her head, pare her nails, ¹³discard her captive's garb, and shall remain in your house a full month, mourning for her father and mother; after that you may go in to her and be her husband, and she shall be your wife. ¹⁴But if you are not satisfied with her, you shall let her go free and not sell her for money. You must not treat her as a slave, since you have dishonored her.

15 If a man has two wives, one of them loved and the other disliked, and if both the loved and the disliked have borne him sons, the firstborn being the son of the one who is disliked, ¹⁶then on the day when he wills his possessions to his sons, he is not permitted to treat the son of the loved as the firstborn in preference to the son of the disliked, who is the firstborn. ¹⁷He must acknowledge as firstborn the son of the one who is disliked, giving him a double portion*a* of all that he has; since he is the first issue of his virility, the right of the firstborn is his.

18 If someone has a stubborn and rebellious son who will not obey his father and mother, who does not heed them when they discipline him, ¹⁹then his father and his mother shall take hold of him and bring him out to the elders of his town at the gate of that place. ²⁰They shall say to the elders of his town, "This son of ours is stubborn and rebellious. He will not obey us. He is a glutton and a drunkard." ²¹Then all the men of the town shall stone him to death. So you

shall purge the evil from your midst; and all Israel will hear, and be afraid.

21.10–21: Laws for family life. 10–14: A female captive desired as a wife would have no male relatives to safeguard her rights. She is protected from a later reduction to slave status. Their sexual relationship (*you have dishonored her,* v. 14) establishes the husband's obligation. **15–17:** The law giving the oldest son a larger inheritance cannot be set aside because of favoritism. *Double portion* (v. 17) points to the custom of dividing an inheritance into shares equal to the number of sons plus one and giving the eldest two shares (but compare note *a*). **18–21:** Disrespect for both *father and mother* is the issue, and both parents must agree to take action. The seriousness of this offense is revealed by the extreme punishment, intended to be a public deterrent.

22 When someone is convicted of a crime punishable by death and is executed, and you hang him on a tree, ²³his corpse must not remain all night upon the tree; you shall bury him that same day, for anyone hung on a tree is under God's curse. You must not defile the land that the LORD your God is giving you for possession.

22 You shall not watch your neighbor's ox or sheep straying away and ignore them; you shall take them back to their owner. ²If the owner does not reside near you or you do not know who the owner is, you shall bring it to your own house, and it shall remain with you until the owner claims it; then you shall return it. ³You shall do the same with a neighbor's donkey; you shall do the same with a neighbor's garment; and you shall do the same with anything else that your neighbor loses and you find. You may not withhold your help.

4 You shall not see your neighbor's donkey or ox fallen on the road and ignore it; you shall help to lift it up.

5 A woman shall not wear a man's apparel, nor shall a man put on a woman's garment; for whoever does such things is abhorrent to the LORD your God.

6 If you come on a bird's nest, in any tree or on the ground, with fledglings or eggs,

a Heb *two-thirds*

with the mother sitting on the fledglings or on the eggs, you shall not take the mother with the young. 7 Let the mother go, taking only the young for yourself, in order that it may go well with you and you may live long.

8 When you build a new house, you shall make a parapet for your roof; otherwise you might have bloodguilt on your house, if anyone should fall from it.

9 You shall not sow your vineyard with a second kind of seed, or the whole yield will have to be forfeited, both the crop that you have sown and the yield of the vineyard itself.

10 You shall not plow with an ox and a donkey yoked together.

11 You shall not wear clothes made of wool and linen woven together.

12 You shall make tassels on the four corners of the cloak with which you cover yourself.

21.22–22.12: Laws of purity and community life. 21.22–23: Extended exposure of a hanged body would *defile the land,* putting it into a state of ritual impurity. **22.1–4:** This law revises Ex 23.4–5, widening the circle of neighborly responsibility. **5:** Impurity results from a blurring of culturally defined gender boundaries. **6–7:** This hints at good conservation practices and a respect for parental relationships even among animals (compare 14.21b). **8:** Houses had flat roofs used as living and working space. **9–11:** Forbidden mixtures cause impurity by violating distinctions made in creation. **12:** According to Num 15.38–40, *tassels* serve as reminders to obey the law.

13 Suppose a man marries a woman, but after going in to her, he dislikes her 14 and makes up charges against her, slandering her by saying, "I married this woman; but when I lay with her, I did not find evidence of her virginity." 15 The father of the young woman and her mother shall then submit the evidence of the young woman's virginity to the elders of the city at the gate. 16 The father of the young woman shall say to the elders: "I gave my daughter in marriage to this man but he dislikes her; 17 now he has made up charges against her, saying, 'I did not find evidence of your daughter's virginity.' But here is the evidence of my daughter's virgin-

ity." Then they shall spread out the cloth before the elders of the town. 18 The elders of that town shall take the man and punish him; 19 they shall fine him one hundred shekels of silver (which they shall give to the young woman's father) because he has slandered a virgin of Israel. She shall remain his wife; he shall not be permitted to divorce her as long as he lives.

20 If, however, this charge is true, that evidence of the young woman's virginity was not found, 21 then they shall bring the young woman out to the entrance of her father's house and the men of her town shall stone her to death, because she committed a disgraceful act in Israel by prostituting herself in her father's house. So you shall purge the evil from your midst.

22 If a man is caught lying with the wife of another man, both of them shall die, the man who lay with the woman as well as the woman. So you shall purge the evil from Israel.

23 If there is a young woman, a virgin already engaged to be married, and a man meets her in the town and lies with her, 24 you shall bring both of them to the gate of that town and stone them to death, the young woman because she did not cry for help in the town and the man because he violated his neighbor's wife. So you shall purge the evil from your midst.

25 But if the man meets the engaged woman in the open country, and the man seizes her and lies with her, then only the man who lay with her shall die. 26 You shall do nothing to the young woman; the young woman has not committed an offense punishable by death, because this case is like that of someone who attacks and murders a neighbor. 27 Since he found her in the open country, the engaged woman may have cried for help, but there was no one to rescue her.

28 If a man meets a virgin who is not engaged, and seizes her and lies with her, and they are caught in the act, 29 the man who lay with her shall give fifty shekels of silver to the young woman's father, and she shall become his wife. Because he violated her he shall not be permitted to divorce her as long as he lives.

30[a] A man shall not marry his father's wife, thereby violating his father's rights.[b]

22.13–30: Laws about sex and marriage. 13–19: Rather than simply exercising his right of divorce, the husband viciously slanders his unwanted wife. The *evidence of her virginity* (v. 14) is the bloodstain on the *cloth* (v. 17) on which the couple consummated their marriage. Both parents defend their daughter, but the father alone addresses the elders. The space around *the gate* (v. 15) was the standard location for legal business. **20–21:** *Disgraceful act* refers to outrageous behavior that violates community standards. **22:** Because she is the *wife of another man,* the adultery is seen as a violation of his rights. **23–27:** Engagement is the equivalent of marriage. Again it is only the husband's rights that are at issue (v. 24). The second case is rape: *The man seizes her* (v. 25). Fairness requires that she be given the benefit of the doubt. **28–29:** If the raped woman is not married or engaged, it is a crime against her father, who has suffered the loss of her bride price. The victim's respectable status as wife is permanently protected. **30:** Forbidding marriage to one's father's former wife protects the integrity of the extended family.

23 No one whose testicles are crushed or whose penis is cut off shall be admitted to the assembly of the LORD.

2 Those born of an illicit union shall not be admitted to the assembly of the LORD. Even to the tenth generation, none of their descendants shall be admitted to the assembly of the LORD.

3 No Ammonite or Moabite shall be admitted to the assembly of the LORD. Even to the tenth generation, none of their descendants shall be admitted to the assembly of the LORD, [4]because they did not meet you with food and water on your journey out of Egypt, and because they hired against you Balaam son of Beor, from Pethor of Mesopotamia, to curse you. [5](Yet the LORD your God refused to heed Balaam; the LORD your God turned the curse into a blessing for you, because the LORD your God loved you.) [6]You shall never promote their welfare or their prosperity as long as you live.

7 You shall not abhor any of the Edomites, for they are your kin. You shall not abhor any of the Egyptians, because you were an alien residing in their land. [8]The children of the third generation that are born to them may be admitted to the assembly of the LORD.

9 When you are encamped against your enemies you shall guard against any impropriety.

10 If one of you becomes unclean because of a nocturnal emission, then he shall go outside the camp; he must not come within the camp. [11]When evening comes, he shall wash himself with water, and when the sun has set, he may come back into the camp.

12 You shall have a designated area outside the camp to which you shall go. [13]With your utensils you shall have a trowel; when you relieve yourself outside, you shall dig a hole with it and then cover up your excrement. [14]Because the LORD your God travels along with your camp, to save you and to hand over your enemies to you, therefore your camp must be holy, so that he may not see anything indecent among you and turn away from you.

23.1–14: Laws guarding community purity. 1–6: As a sacral gathering, the *assembly of the LORD* must exclude anyone who would be ritually impure on a permanent basis. Any lack of bodily wholeness or being the offspring of an *illicit union* (v. 2) would cause this. Ammonites and Moabites had a history of intractable hostility to Israel (vv. 3–4). Moreover, Israel viewed both nations as deriving from incestuous relationships (Gen 19.30–38). **9–14:** The LORD as divine warrior* is present in the war camp (v. 14), so ritual impurity must be prevented.

15 Slaves who have escaped to you from their owners shall not be given back to them. [16]They shall reside with you, in your midst, in any place they choose in any one of your towns, wherever they please; you shall not oppress them.

17 None of the daughters of Israel shall be a temple prostitute; none of the sons of Israel shall be a temple prostitute. [18]You shall not bring the fee of a prostitute or the

a Ch 23.1 in Heb   *b* Heb *uncovering his father's skirt*

wages of a male prostitute*a* into the house of the LORD your God in payment for any vow, for both of these are abhorrent to the LORD your God.

19 You shall not charge interest on loans to another Israelite, interest on money, interest on provisions, interest on anything that is lent. 20On loans to a foreigner you may charge interest, but on loans to another Israelite you may not charge interest, so that the LORD your God may bless you in all your undertakings in the land that you are about to enter and possess.

21 If you make a vow to the LORD your God, do not postpone fulfilling it; for the LORD your God will surely require it of you, and you would incur guilt. 22But if you refrain from vowing, you will not incur guilt. 23Whatever your lips utter you must diligently perform, just as you have freely vowed to the LORD your God with your own mouth.

24 If you go into your neighbor's vineyard, you may eat your fill of grapes, as many as you wish, but you shall not put any in a container. 25 If you go into your neighbor's standing grain, you may pluck the ears with your hand, but you shall not put a sickle to your neighbor's standing grain.

23.15–25: Laws about harmony in relationships. **15–16:** Asylum is granted to slaves who have fled from a foreign master. **17:** The words translated *temple prostitute* refer to prohibited female and male religious personnel of some kind, but not necessarily to any involvement with sex. **18:** Temple obligations must not be paid with money derived from ordinary prostitution or the earnings of "a dog" (note *a*), usually assumed to be a homosexual *male prostitute*. **19–20:** This law restates Ex 22.25. The wealthy are to assist poor Israelites with interest-free loans. **21–23:** A *vow* was a sacrifice promised in expectation of divine assistance. **24–25:** The landowner is protected from unfair exploitation by the poor, who were permitted to gather food in this way (24.19–22).

24 Suppose a man enters into marriage with a woman, but she does not please him because he finds something objectionable about her, and so he writes her a certificate of divorce, puts it in her hand, and sends her out of his house; she then leaves his house 2and goes off to become another man's wife. 3Then suppose the second man dislikes her, writes her a bill of divorce, puts it in her hand, and sends her out of his house (or the second man who married her dies); 4her first husband, who sent her away, is not permitted to take her again to be his wife after she has been defiled; for that would be abhorrent to the LORD, and you shall not bring guilt on the land that the LORD your God is giving you as a possession.

5 When a man is newly married, he shall not go out with the army or be charged with any related duty. He shall be free at home one year, to be happy with the wife whom he has married.

6 No one shall take a mill or an upper millstone in pledge, for that would be taking a life in pledge.

7 If someone is caught kidnaping another Israelite, enslaving or selling the Israelite, then that kidnaper shall die. So you shall purge the evil from your midst.

8 Guard against an outbreak of a leprous*b* skin disease by being very careful; you shall carefully observe whatever the levitical priests instruct you, just as I have commanded them. 9Remember what the LORD your God did to Miriam on your journey out of Egypt.

10 When you make your neighbor a loan of any kind, you shall not go into the house to take the pledge. 11You shall wait outside, while the person to whom you are making the loan brings the pledge out to you. 12If the person is poor, you shall not sleep in the garment given you as*c* the pledge. 13You shall give the pledge back by sunset, so that your neighbor may sleep in the cloak and bless you; and it will be to your credit before the LORD your God.

14 You shall not withhold the wages of poor and needy laborers, whether other Israelites or aliens who reside in your land in one of your towns. 15You shall pay them their wages daily before sunset, because they

a Heb *a dog*　　*b* A term for several skin diseases; precise meaning uncertain　　*c* Heb lacks *the garment given you as*

are poor and their livelihood depends on them; otherwise they might cry to the LORD against you, and you would incur guilt.

16 Parents shall not be put to death for their children, nor shall children be put to death for their parents; only for their own crimes may persons be put to death.

17 You shall not deprive a resident alien or an orphan of justice; you shall not take a widow's garment in pledge. 18Remember that you were a slave in Egypt and the LORD your God redeemed you from there; therefore I command you to do this.

19 When you reap your harvest in your field and forget a sheaf in the field, you shall not go back to get it; it shall be left for the alien, the orphan, and the widow, so that the LORD your God may bless you in all your undertakings. 20When you beat your olive trees, do not strip what is left; it shall be for the alien, the orphan, and the widow.

21 When you gather the grapes of your vineyard, do not glean what is left; it shall be for the alien, the orphan, and the widow. 22Remember that you were a slave in the land of Egypt; therefore I am commanding you to do this.

24.1–22: Laws protecting social harmony. 1–4: Divorce was the sole prerogative of the husband, who could initiate it for even trivial reasons (vv. 1, 3). The woman receives a *certificate* or *bill of divorce* (the Hebrew phrase in vv. 1 and 3 is identical), clarifying her freedom to remarry. **6:** The household *mill* ground daily bread needed for *life*. **7:** This law restates Ex 21.16. **8–9:** *Leprous skin disease* covers a wide range of ailments (note *b*). The Miriam incident is reported in Num 12.10–15. **10–13:** These rules, restating Ex 22.26–27, defend the dignity of poor people who have defaulted on a loan and forfeited their collateral. **14–15:** Workers who live from hand to mouth are protected from oppression, while employers are protected from guilt. **17–22:** Israel's own experience of slavery motivates compassion for impoverished groups.

25 Suppose two persons have a dispute and enter into litigation, and the judges decide between them, declaring one to be in the right and the other to be in the wrong. 2If the one in the wrong deserves to be flogged, the judge shall make that person lie down and be beaten in his presence with the number of lashes proportionate to the offense. 3Forty lashes may be given but not more; if more lashes than these are given, your neighbor will be degraded in your sight.

4 You shall not muzzle an ox while it is treading out the grain.

5 When brothers reside together, and one of them dies and has no son, the wife of the deceased shall not be married outside the family to a stranger. Her husband's brother shall go in to her, taking her in marriage, and performing the duty of a husband's brother to her, 6and the firstborn whom she bears shall succeed to the name of the deceased brother, so that his name may not be blotted out of Israel. 7But if the man has no desire to marry his brother's widow, then his brother's widow shall go up to the elders at the gate and say, "My husband's brother refuses to perpetuate his brother's name in Israel; he will not perform the duty of a husband's brother to me." 8Then the elders of his town shall summon him and speak to him. If he persists, saying, "I have no desire to marry her," 9then his brother's wife shall go up to him in the presence of the elders, pull his sandal off his foot, spit in his face, and declare, "This is what is done to the man who does not build up his brother's house." 10Throughout Israel his family shall be known as "the house of him whose sandal was pulled off."

11 If men get into a fight with one another, and the wife of one intervenes to rescue her husband from the grip of his opponent by reaching out and seizing his genitals, 12you shall cut off her hand; show no pity.

13 You shall not have in your bag two kinds of weights, large and small. 14You shall not have in your house two kinds of measures, large and small. 15You shall have only a full and honest weight; you shall have only a full and honest measure, so that your days may be long in the land that the LORD your God is giving you. 16For all who do such things, all who act dishonestly, are abhorrent to the LORD your God.

17 Remember what Amalek did to you on your journey out of Egypt, 18how he attacked you on the way, when you were faint and

weary, and struck down all who lagged behind you; he did not fear God. ¹⁹Therefore when the LORD your God has given you rest from all your enemies on every hand, in the land that the LORD your God is giving you as an inheritance to possess, you shall blot out the remembrance of Amalek from under heaven; do not forget.

25.1–19: Laws protecting members of society. 1–3: The dignity of the offender is preserved by proper supervision of punishment and limits to its severity. **4:** Even domestic animals have rights (compare 22.10). **5–10:** This custom (levirate marriage*) protects the deceased by ensuring him a son to inherit his property and carry on his name. It also protects the widow from the calamities of poverty and childlessness. It presupposes that these brothers *reside together* (v. 5) in an extended family. The living brother may refuse to perform his duty, but must then endure public shame. **11–12:** Her punishment is severe, perhaps because she has compromised the man's fertility. **13–16:** Commercial dishonesty undermines Israel's relationship with the LORD. **17–19:** This is reported in Ex 17.8–16.

26 When you have come into the land that the LORD your God is giving you as an inheritance to possess, and you possess it, and settle in it, ²you shall take some of the first of all the fruit of the ground, which you harvest from the land that the LORD your God is giving you, and you shall put it in a basket and go to the place that the LORD your God will choose as a dwelling for his name. ³You shall go to the priest who is in office at that time, and say to him, "Today I declare to the LORD your God that I have come into the land that the LORD swore to our ancestors to give us." ⁴When the priest takes the basket from your hand and sets it down before the altar of the LORD your God, ⁵you shall make this response before the LORD your God: "A wandering Aramean was my ancestor; he went down into Egypt and lived there as an alien, few in number, and there he became a great nation, mighty and populous. ⁶When the Egyptians treated us harshly and afflicted us, by imposing hard labor on us, ⁷we cried to the LORD, the God of our ancestors; the LORD heard our voice and saw our affliction, our toil, and our op-

pression. ⁸The LORD brought us out of Egypt with a mighty hand and an outstretched arm, with a terrifying display of power, and with signs and wonders; ⁹and he brought us into this place and gave us this land, a land flowing with milk and honey. ¹⁰So now I bring the first of the fruit of the ground that you, O LORD, have given me." You shall set it down before the LORD your God and bow down before the LORD your God. ¹¹Then you, together with the Levites and the aliens who reside among you, shall celebrate with all the bounty that the LORD your God has given to you and to your house.

12 When you have finished paying all the tithe of your produce in the third year (which is the year of the tithe), giving it to the Levites, the aliens, the orphans, and the widows, so that they may eat their fill within your towns, ¹³then you shall say before the LORD your God: "I have removed the sacred portion from the house, and I have given it to the Levites, the resident aliens, the orphans, and the widows, in accordance with your entire commandment that you commanded me; I have neither transgressed nor forgotten any of your commandments: ¹⁴I have not eaten of it while in mourning; I have not removed any of it while I was unclean; and I have not offered any of it to the dead. I have obeyed the LORD my God, doing just as you commanded me. ¹⁵Look down from your holy habitation, from heaven, and bless your people Israel and the ground that you have given us, as you swore to our ancestors—a land flowing with milk and honey."

26.1–15: First fruits and tithes. 4: The first symbolic presentation is made by the priest, who has access to the *altar of the LORD.* **5–9:** This creedal prayer reviews the history of salvation. *A wandering Aramean* refers to Jacob, linked in tradition with Syria ("Aram"; Gen 29–31). **10:** The farmer makes a second presentation of the basket. **11:** It is characteristic of Deuteronomy that impoverished social groups share in the feast. **12:** The tithe of the *third year* is distributed to the poor, not taken to the central sanctuary (14.28–29). **13–14:** As a *sacred portion,* the tithe must be kept from contact with *unclean* persons or forbidden activities.

16 This very day the LORD your God is commanding you to observe these statutes and ordinances; so observe them diligently with all your heart and with all your soul. 17Today you have obtained the LORD's agreement: to be your God; and for you to walk in his ways, to keep his statutes, his commandments, and his ordinances, and to obey him. 18Today the LORD has obtained your agreement: to be his treasured people, as he promised you, and to keep his commandments; 19for him to set you high above all nations that he has made, in praise and in fame and in honor; and for you to be a people holy to the LORD your God, as he promised.

26.16–19: Conclusion to the law. 17–18: *Today* refers to the day on which Deuteronomy was spoken (compare 15.5; 19.9). The LORD and Israel have agreed to abide by the principles of a covenant* relationship.

27 Then Moses and the elders of Israel charged all the people as follows: Keep the entire commandment that I am commanding you today. 2On the day that you cross over the Jordan into the land that the LORD your God is giving you, you shall set up large stones and cover them with plaster. 3You shall write on them all the words of this law when you have crossed over, to enter the land that the LORD your God is giving you, a land flowing with milk and honey, as the LORD, the God of your ancestors, promised you. 4So when you have crossed over the Jordan, you shall set up these stones, about which I am commanding you today, on Mount Ebal, and you shall cover them with plaster. 5And you shall build an altar there to the LORD your God, an altar of stones on which you have not used an iron tool. 6You must build the altar of the LORD your God of unhewn*a* stones. Then offer up burnt offerings on it to the LORD your God, 7make sacrifices of well-being, and eat them there, rejoicing before the LORD your God. 8You shall write on the stones all the words of this law very clearly.

9 Then Moses and the levitical priests spoke to all Israel, saying: Keep silence and hear, O Israel! This very day you have be-come the people of the LORD your God. 10Therefore obey the LORD your God, observing his commandments and his statutes that I am commanding you today.

11 The same day Moses charged the people as follows: 12When you have crossed over the Jordan, these shall stand on Mount Gerizim for the blessing of the people: Simeon, Levi, Judah, Issachar, Joseph, and Benjamin. 13And these shall stand on Mount Ebal for the curse: Reuben, Gad, Asher, Zebulun, Dan, and Naphtali. 14Then the Levites shall declare in a loud voice to all the Israelites:

27.1–13: The covenant* ceremony at Shechem. 4: *Mount Ebal* stands just north of Shechem, and Mount Gerizim (v. 12) rises to the south. **8:** These *stones* are the ones referred to in vv. 2–4, not the altar stones. **12–13:** The two groups are either receiving a blessing and curse spoken by the Levites (compare v. 14) or are proclaiming the blessing and curse themselves.

15 "Cursed be anyone who makes an idol or casts an image, anything abhorrent to the LORD, the work of an artisan, and sets it up in secret." All the people shall respond, saying, "Amen!"

16 "Cursed be anyone who dishonors father or mother." All the people shall say, "Amen!"

17 "Cursed be anyone who moves a neighbor's boundary marker." All the people shall say, "Amen!"

18 "Cursed be anyone who misleads a blind person on the road." All the people shall say, "Amen!"

19 "Cursed be anyone who deprives the alien, the orphan, and the widow of justice." All the people shall say, "Amen!"

20 "Cursed be anyone who lies with his father's wife, because he has violated his father's rights."*b* All the people shall say, "Amen!"

21 "Cursed be anyone who lies with any animal." All the people shall say, "Amen!"

22 "Cursed be anyone who lies with his sister, whether the daughter of his father or the daughter of his mother." All the people shall say, "Amen!"

a Heb *whole*   *b* Heb *uncovered his father's skirt*

23 "Cursed be anyone who lies with his mother-in-law." All the people shall say, "Amen!"

24 "Cursed be anyone who strikes down a neighbor in secret." All the people shall say, "Amen!"

25 "Cursed be anyone who takes a bribe to shed innocent blood." All the people shall say, "Amen!"

26 "Cursed be anyone who does not uphold the words of this law by observing them." All the people shall say, "Amen!"

27.14–26: Twelve curses. 15: Curses are powerful words that bring on unavoidable misfortune. The people's *amen* turns the destructive potential of each curse upon themselves. Most of these curses deal with actions committed *in secret* (also v. 24) that could not be controlled by public sanctions. **26:** This last summary curse motivates obedience to the entire law of Deuteronomy.

28 If you will only obey the LORD your God, by diligently observing all his commandments that I am commanding you today, the LORD your God will set you high above all the nations of the earth; 2all these blessings shall come upon you and overtake you, if you obey the LORD your God:

3 Blessed shall you be in the city, and blessed shall you be in the field.

4 Blessed shall be the fruit of your womb, the fruit of your ground, and the fruit of your livestock, both the increase of your cattle and the issue of your flock.

5 Blessed shall be your basket and your kneading bowl.

6 Blessed shall you be when you come in, and blessed shall you be when you go out.

7 The LORD will cause your enemies who rise against you to be defeated before you; they shall come out against you one way, and flee before you seven ways. 8The LORD will command the blessing upon you in your barns, and in all that you undertake; he will bless you in the land that the LORD your God is giving you. 9The LORD will establish you as his holy people, as he has sworn to you, if you keep the commandments of the LORD your God and walk in his ways. 10All the peoples of the earth shall see that you are called by the name of the LORD, and they shall be afraid of you. 11The LORD will make you abound in prosperity, in the fruit of your womb, in the fruit of your livestock, and in the fruit of your ground in the land that the LORD swore to your ancestors to give you. 12The LORD will open for you his rich storehouse, the heavens, to give the rain of your land in its season and to bless all your undertakings. You will lend to many nations, but you will not borrow. 13The LORD will make you the head, and not the tail; you shall be only at the top, and not at the bottom— if you obey the commandments of the LORD your God, which I am commanding you today, by diligently observing them, 14and if you do not turn aside from any of the words that I am commanding you today, either to the right or to the left, following other gods to serve them.

28.1–14: Blessings for obedience. 1: Israel's high status among the nations is a repeated theme (vv. 9–10, 13). **2:** A blessing is an effective power-laden word that brings about well-being and prosperity. These are conditional blessings, dependent on Israel's obedience (vv. 13–14). **4–5:** Israel often associated fertility (vv. 8, 11) and rain (v. 12) with the gods of Canaan, but here they are affirmed as blessings from the LORD.

15 But if you will not obey the LORD your God by diligently observing all his commandments and decrees, which I am commanding you today, then all these curses shall come upon you and overtake you:

16 Cursed shall you be in the city, and cursed shall you be in the field.

17 Cursed shall be your basket and your kneading bowl.

18 Cursed shall be the fruit of your womb, the fruit of your ground, the increase of your cattle and the issue of your flock.

19 Cursed shall you be when you come in, and cursed shall you be when you go out.

20 The LORD will send upon you disaster, panic, and frustration in everything you attempt to do, until you are destroyed and perish quickly, on account of the evil of your deeds, because you have forsaken me. 21The LORD will make the pestilence cling to you until it has consumed you off the land that

you are entering to possess. 22The LORD will afflict you with consumption, fever, inflammation, with fiery heat and drought, and with blight and mildew; they shall pursue you until you perish. 23The sky over your head shall be bronze, and the earth under you iron. 24The LORD will change the rain of your land into powder, and only dust shall come down upon you from the sky until you are destroyed.

25 The LORD will cause you to be defeated before your enemies; you shall go out against them one way and flee before them seven ways. You shall become an object of horror to all the kingdoms of the earth. 26Your corpses shall be food for every bird of the air and animal of the earth, and there shall be no one to frighten them away. 27The LORD will afflict you with the boils of Egypt, with ulcers, scurvy, and itch, of which you cannot be healed. 28The LORD will afflict you with madness, blindness, and confusion of mind; 29you shall grope about at noon as blind people grope in darkness, but you shall be unable to find your way; and you shall be continually abused and robbed, without anyone to help. 30You shall become engaged to a woman, but another man shall lie with her. You shall build a house, but not live in it. You shall plant a vineyard, but not enjoy its fruit. 31Your ox shall be butchered before your eyes, but you shall not eat of it. Your donkey shall be stolen in front of you, and shall not be restored to you. Your sheep shall be given to your enemies, without anyone to help you. 32Your sons and daughters shall be given to another people, while you look on; you will strain your eyes looking for them all day but be powerless to do anything. 33A people whom you do not know shall eat up the fruit of your ground and of all your labors; you shall be continually abused and crushed, 34and driven mad by the sight that your eyes shall see. 35The LORD will strike you on the knees and on the legs with grievous boils of which you cannot be healed, from the sole of your foot to the crown of your head. 36The LORD will bring you, and the king whom you set over you, to a nation that neither you nor your ancestors have known, where you shall serve other gods, of wood and stone. 37You shall become an object of horror, a proverb, and a byword among all the peoples where the LORD will lead you.

38 You shall carry much seed into the field but shall gather little in, for the locust shall consume it. 39You shall plant vineyards and dress them, but you shall neither drink the wine nor gather the grapes, for the worm shall eat them. 40You shall have olive trees throughout all your territory, but you shall not anoint yourself with the oil, for your olives shall drop off. 41You shall have sons and daughters, but they shall not remain yours, for they shall go into captivity. 42All your trees and the fruit of your ground the cicada shall take over. 43Aliens residing among you shall ascend above you higher and higher, while you shall descend lower and lower. 44They shall lend to you but you shall not lend to them; they shall be the head and you shall be the tail.

45 All these curses shall come upon you, pursuing and overtaking you until you are destroyed, because you did not obey the LORD your God, by observing the commandments and the decrees that he commanded you. 46They shall be among you and your descendants as a sign and a portent forever.

47 Because you did not serve the LORD your God joyfully and with gladness of heart for the abundance of everything, 48therefore you shall serve your enemies whom the LORD will send against you, in hunger and thirst, in nakedness and lack of everything. He will put an iron yoke on your neck until he has destroyed you. 49The LORD will bring a nation from far away, from the end of the earth, to swoop down on you like an eagle, a nation whose language you do not understand, 50a grim-faced nation showing no respect to the old or favor to the young. 51It shall consume the fruit of your livestock and the fruit of your ground until you are destroyed, leaving you neither grain, wine, and oil, nor the increase of your cattle and the issue of your flock, until it has made you perish. 52It shall besiege you in all your towns until your high and fortified walls, in which you trusted, come down throughout your land; it shall besiege you in all your towns

throughout the land that the LORD your God has given you. ⁵³In the desperate straits to which the enemy siege reduces you, you will eat the fruit of your womb, the flesh of your own sons and daughters whom the LORD your God has given you. ⁵⁴Even the most refined and gentle of men among you will begrudge food to his own brother, to the wife whom he embraces, and to the last of his remaining children, ⁵⁵giving to none of them any of the flesh of his children whom he is eating, because nothing else remains to him, in the desperate straits to which the enemy siege will reduce you in all your towns. ⁵⁶She who is the most refined and gentle among you, so gentle and refined that she does not venture to set the sole of her foot on the ground, will begrudge food to the husband whom she embraces, to her own son, and to her own daughter, ⁵⁷begrudging even the afterbirth that comes out from between her thighs, and the children that she bears, because she is eating them in secret for lack of anything else, in the desperate straits to which the enemy siege will reduce you in your towns.

58 If you do not diligently observe all the words of this law that are written in this book, fearing this glorious and awesome name, the LORD your God, ⁵⁹then the LORD will overwhelm both you and your offspring with severe and lasting afflictions and grievous and lasting maladies. ⁶⁰He will bring back upon you all the diseases of Egypt, of which you were in dread, and they shall cling to you. ⁶¹Every other malady and affliction, even though not recorded in the book of this law, the LORD will inflict on you until you are destroyed. ⁶²Although once you were as numerous as the stars in heaven, you shall be left few in number, because you did not obey the LORD your God. ⁶³And just as the LORD took delight in making you prosperous and numerous, so the LORD will take delight in bringing you to ruin and destruction; you shall be plucked off the land that you are entering to possess. ⁶⁴The LORD will scatter you among all peoples, from one end of the earth to the other; and there you shall serve other gods, of wood and stone, which neither you nor your ancestors have known.

⁶⁵Among those nations you shall find no ease, no resting place for the sole of your foot. There the LORD will give you a trembling heart, failing eyes, and a languishing spirit. ⁶⁶Your life shall hang in doubt before you; night and day you shall be in dread, with no assurance of your life. ⁶⁷In the morning you shall say, "If only it were evening!" and at evening you shall say, "If only it were morning!"—because of the dread that your heart shall feel and the sights that your eyes shall see. ⁶⁸The LORD will bring you back in ships to Egypt, by a route that I promised you would never see again; and there you shall offer yourselves for sale to your enemies as male and female slaves, but there will be no buyer.

28.15–68: Curses for disobedience. 15: The preponderance of curses over blessings emphasizes the urgent need to reform. **16–19:** These curses correspond to the blessings of vv. 3–6. **23–24:** These curses oppose the blessing of v. 12. **25:** This malediction corresponds to v. 7. **43–44:** These curses counter vv. 12–13. **45–46:** A temporary conclusion is reached, but even more curses follow. **47–57:** In this second section, Israel's disobedience seems to be an inescapable certainty. The curses focus on the horrors of invasion and siege. **58–68:** This third section describes a systematic reversal of the LORD's saving acts.

29 ᵃThese are the words of the covenant that the LORD commanded Moses to make with the Israelites in the land of Moab, in addition to the covenant that he had made with them at Horeb.

2ᵇ Moses summoned all Israel and said to them: You have seen all that the LORD did before your eyes in the land of Egypt, to Pharaoh and to all his servants and to all his land, ³the great trials that your eyes saw, the signs, and those great wonders. ⁴But to this day the LORD has not given you a mind to understand, or eyes to see, or ears to hear. ⁵I have led you forty years in the wilderness. The clothes on your back have not worn out, and the sandals on your feet have not worn out; ⁶you have not eaten bread, and you have not drunk wine or strong drink—so that you

a Ch 28.69 in Heb   *b* Ch 29.1 in Heb

may know that I am the LORD your God. 7When you came to this place, King Sihon of Heshbon and King Og of Bashan came out against us for battle, but we defeated them. 8We took their land and gave it as an inheritance to the Reubenites, the Gadites, and the half-tribe of Manasseh. 9Therefore diligently observe the words of this covenant, in order that you may succeed*a* in everything that you do.

10 You stand assembled today, all of you, before the LORD your God—the leaders of your tribes,*b* your elders, and your officials, all the men of Israel, 11your children, your women, and the aliens who are in your camp, both those who cut your wood and those who draw your water— 12to enter into the covenant of the LORD your God, sworn by an oath, which the LORD your God is making with you today; 13in order that he may establish you today as his people, and that he may be your God, as he promised you and as he swore to your ancestors, to Abraham, to Isaac, and to Jacob. 14I am making this covenant, sworn by an oath, not only with you who stand here with us today before the LORD our God, 15but also with those who are not here with us today. 16You know how we lived in the land of Egypt, and how we came through the midst of the nations through which you passed. 17You have seen their detestable things, the filthy idols of wood and stone, of silver and gold, that were among them. 18It may be that there is among you a man or woman, or a family or tribe, whose heart is already turning away from the LORD our God to serve the gods of those nations. It may be that there is among you a root sprouting poisonous and bitter growth. 19All who hear the words of this oath and bless themselves, thinking in their hearts, "We are safe even though we go our own stubborn ways" (thus bringing disaster on moist and dry alike)*c*— 20the LORD will be unwilling to pardon them, for the LORD's anger and passion will smoke against them. All the curses written in this book will descend on them, and the LORD will blot out their names from under heaven. 21The LORD will single them out from all the tribes of Israel for calamity, in accordance with all the curses of the covenant written in this book of the law. 22The next generation, your children who rise up after you, as well as the foreigner who comes from a distant country, will see the devastation of that land and the afflictions with which the LORD has afflicted it— 23all its soil burned out by sulfur and salt, nothing planted, nothing sprouting, unable to support any vegetation, like the destruction of Sodom and Gomorrah, Admah and Zeboiim, which the LORD destroyed in his fierce anger— 24they and indeed all the nations will wonder, "Why has the LORD done thus to this land? What caused this great display of anger?" 25They will conclude, "It is because they abandoned the covenant of the LORD, the God of their ancestors, which he made with them when he brought them out of the land of Egypt. 26They turned and served other gods, worshiping them, gods whom they had not known and whom he had not allotted to them; 27so the anger of the LORD was kindled against that land, bringing on it every curse written in this book. 28The LORD uprooted them from their land in anger, fury, and great wrath, and cast them into another land, as is now the case." 29The secret things belong to the LORD our God, but the revealed things belong to us and to our children forever, to observe all the words of this law.

29.1–29: The covenant★ made in Moab. 1: The covenant once made *at Horeb* (compare 5.2) is renewed *in the land of Moab,* just before Israel crosses into its new land (compare 1.5). **2–8:** The LORD's providence has been revealed through past events, but it is only now that these lessons can be understood (v. 4). **10–11:** The covenant community is all-inclusive, incorporating even resident *aliens★* and menial servants. **14–15:** Deuteronomy's readers are also part of this covenant community. **19:** The obscure *moist and dry alike* (note *c*) means that all will suffer, innocent or guilty. **24–28:** An imagined dialogue warns of destruction and exile if the covenant is violated (compare 1 Kings 9.8–9). **29:** The LORD's ways will always remain a mystery★ best left to God, but Israel's task is to obey *revealed things,* that is *the words of this law.*

a Or *deal wisely*   *b* Gk Syr: Heb *your leaders, your tribes*   *c* Meaning of Heb uncertain

30 When all these things have happened to you, the blessings and the curses that I have set before you, if you call them to mind among all the nations where the LORD your God has driven you, ²and return to the LORD your God, and you and your children obey him with all your heart and with all your soul, just as I am commanding you today, ³then the LORD your God will restore your fortunes and have compassion on you, gathering you again from all the peoples among whom the LORD your God has scattered you. ⁴Even if you are exiled to the ends of the world,ᵃ from there the LORD your God will gather you, and from there he will bring you back. ⁵The LORD your God will bring you into the land that your ancestors possessed, and you will possess it; he will make you more prosperous and numerous than your ancestors.

6 Moreover, the LORD your God will circumcise your heart and the heart of your descendants, so that you will love the LORD your God with all your heart and with all your soul, in order that you may live. ⁷The LORD your God will put all these curses on your enemies and on the adversaries who took advantage of you. ⁸Then you shall again obey the LORD, observing all his commandments that I am commanding you today, ⁹and the LORD your God will make you abundantly prosperous in all your undertakings, in the fruit of your body, in the fruit of your livestock, and in the fruit of your soil. For the LORD will again take delight in prospering you, just as he delighted in prospering your ancestors, ¹⁰when you obey the LORD your God by observing his commandments and decrees that are written in this book of the law, because you turn to the LORD your God with all your heart and with all your soul.

11 Surely, this commandment that I am commanding you today is not too hard for you, nor is it too far away. ¹²It is not in heaven, that you should say, "Who will go up to heaven for us, and get it for us so that we may hear it and observe it?" ¹³Neither is it beyond the sea, that you should say, "Who will cross to the other side of the sea for us, and get it for us so that we may hear it and observe it?" ¹⁴No, the word is very near to you; it is in your mouth and in your heart for you to observe.

15 See, I have set before you today life and prosperity, death and adversity. ¹⁶If you obey the commandments of the LORD your Godᵇ that I am commanding you today, by loving the LORD your God, walking in his ways, and observing his commandments, decrees, and ordinances, then you shall live and become numerous, and the LORD your God will bless you in the land that you are entering to possess. ¹⁷But if your heart turns away and you do not hear, but are led astray to bow down to other gods and serve them, ¹⁸I declare to you today that you shall perish; you shall not live long in the land that you are crossing the Jordan to enter and possess. ¹⁹I call heaven and earth to witness against you today that I have set before you life and death, blessings and curses. Choose life so that you and your descendants may live, ²⁰loving the LORD your God, obeying him, and holding fast to him; for that means life to you and length of days, so that you may live in the land that the LORD swore to give to your ancestors, to Abraham, to Isaac, and to Jacob.

30.1–20. 1–10: Repentance leads to restoration. 1–5: Even exile will not mean the end of Israel's peoplehood if they repent (compare 4.29–31). **6:** In contrast to the demand of 10.16 that Israel do this, here it is the LORD who will remove all obstacles to wholehearted devotion (*circumcise your heart*). Love for the LORD will become second nature. **7–9:** Then the *curses* will fall on the *enemies* (v. 7), while Israel will enjoy the blessings (v. 9). **11–20: Choose life. 11–14:** This law is "user-friendly," easy to grasp and easy to accomplish. The impossibility of climbing up to *heaven* (v. 12) and the difficulty of crossing *the sea* (v. 13) were both proverbial. **15:** Israel's choice is simplicity itself: Obey and live, or disobey by worshipping other gods and perish. **19:** Ancient covenants* were witnessed by the gods of the parties involved. Here the witnesses are *heaven and earth*.

---

a Heb *of heaven*　　*b* Gk: Heb lacks *If you obey the commandments of the LORD your God*

31 When Moses had finished speaking all[a] these words to all Israel, [2]he said to them: "I am now one hundred twenty years old. I am no longer able to get about, and the LORD has told me, 'You shall not cross over this Jordan.' [3]The LORD your God himself will cross over before you. He will destroy these nations before you, and you shall dispossess them. Joshua also will cross over before you, as the LORD promised. [4]The LORD will do to them as he did to Sihon and Og, the kings of the Amorites, and to their land, when he destroyed them. [5]The LORD will give them over to you and you shall deal with them in full accord with the command that I have given to you. [6]Be strong and bold; have no fear or dread of them, because it is the LORD your God who goes with you; he will not fail you or forsake you."

[7] Then Moses summoned Joshua and said to him in the sight of all Israel: "Be strong and bold, for you are the one who will go with this people into the land that the LORD has sworn to their ancestors to give them; and you will put them in possession of it. [8]It is the LORD who goes before you. He will be with you; he will not fail you or forsake you. Do not fear or be dismayed."

[9] Then Moses wrote down this law, and gave it to the priests, the sons of Levi, who carried the ark of the covenant of the LORD, and to all the elders of Israel. [10]Moses commanded them: "Every seventh year, in the scheduled year of remission, during the festival of booths,[b] [11]when all Israel comes to appear before the LORD your God at the place that he will choose, you shall read this law before all Israel in their hearing. [12]Assemble the people—men, women, and children, as well as the aliens residing in your towns—so that they may hear and learn to fear the LORD your God and to observe diligently all the words of this law, [13]and so that their children, who have not known it, may hear and learn to fear the LORD your God, as long as you live in the land that you are crossing over the Jordan to possess."

[14] The LORD said to Moses, "Your time to die is near; call Joshua and present yourselves in the tent of meeting, so that I may commission him." So Moses and Joshua went and presented themselves in the tent of meeting, [15]and the LORD appeared at the tent in a pillar of cloud; the pillar of cloud stood at the entrance to the tent.

31.1–15: Preparing for the future. 1: The narrative* action picks up from where it stopped in 3.23–29. **3–8:** Attention shifts to Israel's future under Joshua (also vv. 14–15) and in the land (also vv. 9–13). **10:** The *year of remission* is described in 15.1–11 and the *festival of booths* in 16.13–15. **12–13:** No distinction is made between men and women; both need to *hear and learn* the law. Concern for the education of *children* is typical of Deuteronomy (6.2, 7). **14–15:** The LORD came to communicate with Israel from time to time at *the tent of meeting* (Ex 33.7–11).

〰〰〰〰〰〰〰〰〰〰〰〰〰〰〰〰〰〰〰

[16] The LORD said to Moses, "Soon you will lie down with your ancestors. Then this people will begin to prostitute themselves to the foreign gods in their midst, the gods of the land into which they are going; they will forsake me, breaking my covenant that I have made with them. [17]My anger will be kindled against them in that day. I will forsake them and hide my face from them; they will become easy prey, and many terrible troubles will come upon them. In that day they will say, 'Have not these troubles come upon us because our God is not in our midst?' [18]On that day I will surely hide my face on account of all the evil they have done by turning to other gods. [19]Now therefore write this song, and teach it to the Israelites; put it in their mouths, in order that this song may be a witness for me against the Israelites. [20]For when I have brought them into the land flowing with milk and honey, which I promised on oath to their ancestors, and they have eaten their fill and grown fat, they will turn to other gods and serve them, despising me and breaking my covenant. [21]And when many terrible troubles come upon them, this song will confront them as a witness, because it will not be lost from the mouths of their descendants. For I know what they are inclined to do even now, before I have brought them into the land that

---

a Q Ms Gk: MT *Moses went and spoke*
b Or *tabernacles*; Heb *succoth*

I promised them on oath." 22That very day Moses wrote this song and taught it to the Israelites.

23 Then the LORD commissioned Joshua son of Nun and said, "Be strong and bold, for you shall bring the Israelites into the land that I promised them; I will be with you."

24 When Moses had finished writing down in a book the words of this law to the very end, 25Moses commanded the Levites who carried the ark of the covenant of the LORD, saying, 26"Take this book of the law and put it beside the ark of the covenant of the LORD your God; let it remain there as a witness against you. 27For I know well how rebellious and stubborn you are. If you already have been so rebellious toward the LORD while I am still alive among you, how much more after my death! 28Assemble to me all the elders of your tribes and your officials, so that I may recite these words in their hearing and call heaven and earth to witness against them. 29For I know that after my death you will surely act corruptly, turning aside from the way that I have commanded you. In time to come trouble will befall you, because you will do what is evil in the sight of the LORD, provoking him to anger through the work of your hands."

31.16–30: The song and the law as witnesses. 16: Moses predicts a disobedient future during which the song of Moses (vv. 19, 21) and the written law (v. 26) will serve as witnesses against Israel. Prostitution is a powerful metaphor* for Israel's disloyalty. **17–18:** *Hide my face* describes the removal of God's presence (compare 32.20). **19:** *Put it in their mouths* means to make them memorize it. **26:** The *book of the law* (Deuteronomy) is to be a concrete *witness* that Israel agreed to the terms of the covenant* they have broken (vv. 16, 20).

---

30 Then Moses recited the words of this song, to the very end, in the hearing of the whole assembly of Israel:

32 Give ear, O heavens, and I will speak;
 let the earth hear the words of my mouth.
2 May my teaching drop like the rain,
 my speech condense like the dew;

like gentle rain on grass,
 like showers on new growth.
3 For I will proclaim the name of the LORD;
 ascribe greatness to our God!

4 The Rock, his work is perfect,
 and all his ways are just.
A faithful God, without deceit,
 just and upright is he;
5 yet his degenerate children have dealt falsely with him,[a]
 a perverse and crooked generation.
6 Do you thus repay the LORD,
 O foolish and senseless people?
Is not he your father, who created you,
 who made you and established you?
7 Remember the days of old,
 consider the years long past;
ask your father, and he will inform you;
 your elders, and they will tell you.
8 When the Most High[b] apportioned the nations,
 when he divided humankind,
he fixed the boundaries of the peoples
 according to the number of the gods;[c]
9 the LORD's own portion was his people,
 Jacob his allotted share.

10 He sustained[d] him in a desert land,
 in a howling wilderness waste;
he shielded him, cared for him,
 guarded him as the apple of his eye.
11 As an eagle stirs up its nest,
 and hovers over its young;
as it spreads its wings, takes them up,
 and bears them aloft on its pinions,
12 the LORD alone guided him;
 no foreign god was with him.
13 He set him atop the heights of the land,
 and fed him with[e] produce of the field;
he nursed him with honey from the crags,
 with oil from flinty rock;

a Meaning of Heb uncertain b Traditional rendering of Heb *Elyon* c Q Ms Compare Gk Tg: MT *the Israelites* d Sam Gk Compare Tg: MT *found* e Sam Gk Syr Tg: MT *he ate*

14 curds from the herd, and milk from the
  flock,
  with fat of lambs and rams;
  Bashan bulls and goats,
  together with the choicest wheat—
  you drank fine wine from the blood of
  grapes.

15 Jacob ate his fill;[a]
  Jeshurun grew fat, and kicked.
  You grew fat, bloated, and gorged!
  He abandoned God who made him,
  and scoffed at the Rock of his
  salvation.

16 They made him jealous with strange
  gods,
  with abhorrent things they provoked
  him.

17 They sacrificed to demons, not God,
  to deities they had never known,
  to new ones recently arrived,
  whom your ancestors had not feared.

18 You were unmindful of the Rock that
  bore you;[b]
  you forgot the God who gave you
  birth.

19 The LORD saw it, and was jealous;[c]
  he spurned[d] his sons and daughters.

20 He said: I will hide my face from them,
  I will see what their end will be;
  for they are a perverse generation,
  children in whom there is no
  faithfulness.

21 They made me jealous with what is no
  god,
  provoked me with their idols.
  So I will make them jealous with what
  is no people,
  provoke them with a foolish nation.

22 For a fire is kindled by my anger,
  and burns to the depths of Sheol;
  it devours the earth and its increase,
  and sets on fire the foundations of
  the mountains.

23 I will heap disasters upon them,
  spend my arrows against them:

24 wasting hunger,
  burning consumption,
  bitter pestilence.
  The teeth of beasts I will send against
  them,

with venom of things crawling in the
  dust.

25 In the street the sword shall bereave,
  and in the chambers terror,
  for young man and woman alike,
  nursing child and old gray head.

26 I thought to scatter them[e]
  and blot out the memory of them
  from humankind;

27 but I feared provocation by the enemy,
  for their adversaries might
  misunderstand
  and say, "Our hand is triumphant;
  it was not the LORD who did all this."

28 They are a nation void of sense;
  there is no understanding in them.

29 If they were wise, they would
  understand this;
  they would discern what the end
  would be.

30 How could one have routed a thousand,
  and two put a myriad to flight,
  unless their Rock had sold them,
  the LORD had given them up?

31 Indeed their rock is not like our Rock;
  our enemies are fools.[e]

32 Their vine comes from the vinestock of
  Sodom,
  from the vineyards of Gomorrah;
  their grapes are grapes of poison,
  their clusters are bitter;

33 their wine is the poison of serpents,
  the cruel venom of asps.

34 Is not this laid up in store with me,
  sealed up in my treasuries?

35 Vengeance is mine, and recompense,
  for the time when their foot shall slip;
  because the day of their calamity is at
  hand,
  their doom comes swiftly.

36 Indeed the LORD will vindicate his
  people,
  have compassion on his servants,

a Q Mss Sam Gk: MT lacks *Jacob ate his fill*
b Or *that begot you*   c Q Mss Gk: MT lacks *was jealous*
d Cn: Heb *he spurned because of provocation*
e Gk: Meaning of Heb uncertain

when he sees that their power is gone,
　　neither bond nor free remaining.
37 Then he will say: Where are their gods,
　　the rock in which they took refuge,
38 who ate the fat of their sacrifices,
　　and drank the wine of their libations?
　Let them rise up and help you,
　　let them be your protection!

39 See now that I, even I, am he;
　　there is no god besides me.
　I kill and I make alive;
　　I wound and I heal;
　　and no one can deliver from my
　　　hand.
40 For I lift up my hand to heaven,
　　and swear: As I live forever,
41 when I whet my flashing sword,
　　and my hand takes hold on judgment;
　I will take vengeance on my adversaries,
　　and will repay those who hate me.
42 I will make my arrows drunk with blood,
　　and my sword shall devour flesh—
　with the blood of the slain and the
　　　captives,
　　from the long-haired enemy.
43 Praise, O heavens,ᵃ his people,
　　worship him, all you gods!ᵇ
　For he will avenge the blood of his
　　　children,ᶜ
　　and take vengeance on his
　　　adversaries;
　he will repay those who hate him,ᵇ
　　and cleanse the land for his people.ᵈ

32.1–43: The song of Moses. 1: God employs the format of a lawsuit to charge Israel with infidelity. The *heavens* and *earth* are called as witnesses to the lawsuit. **4:** The dominant poetic image is God as *Rock,* symbolizing strength and security (vv. 15, 18, 30, 31). **7–14:** Israel's story begins with their election as God's people. While dividing up the nations among the lesser gods (v. 8; note *c*), the LORD chose Israel as a personal inheritance (v. 9). **15–18:** The next stage is disobedience. *Jeshurun* (v. 15) is a poetic name for Israel, meaning "the upright one." God is portrayed as a mother *Rock* who gave birth to Israel (v. 18). **19–27:** Israel's treachery leads to punishment. The LORD moderates this punishment out of self-concern, not because Israel deserves it (vv. 26–27). **28–30:** The song concludes with God's vindication. The foolish enemy

cannot understand that their earlier victories were the result of the LORD's abandonment of Israel. **35:** *Vengeance* (see vv. 41, 43) implies vindication of the LORD's rights as Israel's God and the restoration of Israel's status. **37–39:** In contrast to false gods, the LORD is the only one worthy of the designation "God." **40–42:** The LORD takes a war oath to be vindicated against all enemies. **43:** The poet calls upon the gods to praise the LORD as the victorious divine warrior* (restored text; notes *a–d*).

44 Moses came and recited all the words of this song in the hearing of the people, he and Joshuaᵉ son of Nun. ⁴⁵When Moses had finished reciting all these words to all Israel, ⁴⁶he said to them: "Take to heart all the words that I am giving in witness against you today; give them as a command to your children, so that they may diligently observe all the words of this law. ⁴⁷This is no trifling matter for you, but rather your very life; through it you may live long in the land that you are crossing over the Jordan to possess."

48 On that very day the LORD addressed Moses as follows: ⁴⁹"Ascend this mountain of the Abarim, Mount Nebo, which is in the land of Moab, across from Jericho, and view the land of Canaan, which I am giving to the Israelites for a possession; ⁵⁰you shall die there on the mountain that you ascend and shall be gathered to your kin, as your brother Aaron died on Mount Hor and was gathered to his kin; ⁵¹because both of you broke faith with me among the Israelites at the waters of Meribath-kadesh in the wilderness of Zin, by failing to maintain my holiness among the Israelites. ⁵²Although you may view the land from a distance, you shall not enter it—the land that I am giving to the Israelites."

32.44–52: Transition to the death of Moses. 46: *All the words* refers to the song and *this law.* Both will serve as future *witnesses* against Israel (31.19, 21, 26). **51:** According to Num 20.10–13, 24 and 27.12–14, Moses and Aaron sinned while securing water from the rock at *Meribath-kadesh* (Meribah).

a Q Ms Gk: MT *nations*   *b* Q Ms Gk: MT lacks this line   *c* Q Ms Gk: MT *his servants*   *d* Q Ms Sam Gk Vg: MT *his land his people*   *e* Sam Gk Syr Vg: MT *Hoshea*

33

This is the blessing with which Moses, the man of God, blessed the Israelites before his death. ²He said:

The LORD came from Sinai,
and dawned from Seir upon us;[a]
he shone forth from Mount Paran.
With him were myriads of holy ones;[b]
at his right, a host of his own.[c]
³ Indeed, O favorite among[d] peoples,
all his holy ones were in your charge;
they marched at your heels,
accepted direction from you.
⁴ Moses charged us with the law,
as a possession for the assembly of
Jacob.
⁵ There arose a king in Jeshurun,
when the leaders of the people
assembled—
the united tribes of Israel.

⁶ May Reuben live, and not die out,
even though his numbers are few.

⁷And this he said of Judah:
O LORD, give heed to Judah,
and bring him to his people;
strengthen his hands for him,[e]
and be a help against his adversaries.

⁸And of Levi he said:
Give to Levi[f] your Thummim,
and your Urim to your loyal one,
whom you tested at Massah,
with whom you contended at the
waters of Meribah;
⁹ who said of his father and mother,
"I regard them not";
he ignored his kin,
and did not acknowledge his children.
For they observed your word,
and kept your covenant.
¹⁰ They teach Jacob your ordinances,
and Israel your law;
they place incense before you,
and whole burnt offerings on your
altar.
¹¹ Bless, O LORD, his substance,
and accept the work of his hands;
crush the loins of his adversaries,
of those that hate him, so that they
do not rise again.

¹²Of Benjamin he said:
The beloved of the LORD rests in
safety—
the High God[g] surrounds him all day
long—
the beloved[h] rests between his
shoulders.

¹³And of Joseph he said:
Blessed by the LORD be his land,
with the choice gifts of heaven
above,
and of the deep that lies beneath;
¹⁴ with the choice fruits of the sun,
and the rich yield of the months;
¹⁵ with the finest produce of the ancient
mountains,
and the abundance of the everlasting
hills;
¹⁶ with the choice gifts of the earth and its
fullness,
and the favor of the one who dwells
on Sinai.[i]
Let these come on the head of Joseph,
on the brow of the prince among his
brothers.
¹⁷ A firstborn[j] bull—majesty is his!
His horns are the horns of a wild ox;
with them he gores the peoples,
driving them to[k] the ends of the
earth;
such are the myriads of Ephraim,
such the thousands of Manasseh.

¹⁸And of Zebulun he said:
Rejoice, Zebulun, in your going out;
and Issachar, in your tents.
¹⁹ They call peoples to the mountain;
there they offer the right sacrifices;
for they suck the affluence of the seas
and the hidden treasures of the
sand.

a Gk Syr Vg Compare Tg: Heb *upon them*
b Cn Compare Gk Sam Syr Vg: MT *He came from Ribeboth-kodesh*,   c Cn Compare Gk: meaning of Heb uncertain   d Or *O lover of the*   e Cn: Heb *with his hands he contended*   f Q Ms Gk: MT lacks *Give to Levi*
g Heb *above him*   h Heb *he*   i Cn: Heb *in the bush*
j Q Ms Gk Syr Vg: MT *His firstborn*   k Cn: Heb *the peoples, together*

20And of Gad he said:
  Blessed be the enlargement of Gad!
  Gad lives like a lion;
    he tears at arm and scalp.
21 He chose the best for himself,
    for there a commander's allotment
        was reserved;
  he came at the head of the people,
  he executed the justice of the LORD,
    and his ordinances for Israel.

22And of Dan he said:
  Dan is a lion's whelp
    that leaps forth from Bashan.

23And of Naphtali he said:
  O Naphtali, sated with favor,
    full of the blessing of the LORD,
    possess the west and the south.

24And of Asher he said:
  Most blessed of sons be Asher;
    may he be the favorite of his brothers,
    and may he dip his foot in oil.
25 Your bars are iron and bronze;
    and as your days, so is your strength.

26 There is none like God, O Jeshurun,
    who rides through the heavens to
        your help,
    majestic through the skies.
27 He subdues the ancient gods,*a*
    shatters*b* the forces of old;*c*
  he drove out the enemy before you,
    and said, "Destroy!"
28 So Israel lives in safety,
    untroubled is Jacob's abode*d*
  in a land of grain and wine,
    where the heavens drop down dew.
29 Happy are you, O Israel! Who is like
        you,
    a people saved by the LORD,
  the shield of your help,
    and the sword of your triumph!
  Your enemies shall come fawning to
        you,
    and you shall tread on their backs.

heavenly beings (*holy ones;* but see note *b*). There are similar descriptions in Judg 5.4–5 and Hab 3.3–15. **5:** This *king* is Israel's triumphant God. *Jeshurun* (v. 26; 32.15) is a poetic name for Israel. **6:** Verses 6–25 form a collection of traditional sayings and wishes about the tribes similar to Gen 49. *Reuben* has dwindled and is struggling. **7:** A northern perspective is indicated by the absence of Simeon and a reference to the separation of Judah (*bring him to his people*). **8–11:** Several traditions describe the proverbial loyalty of *Levi* (Ex 17.1–7; 32.26–29; Num 25.1–13). *Thummim* and *Urim* (v. 8) were the sacred lots through which the LORD's will could be learned. Teaching God's *law* and offering sacrifice were basic priestly prerogatives (v. 10). **12:** *Benjamin* is protected by *shoulders,* either those of God or the slopes of their hills. **13–17:** *Ephraim* and *Manasseh* (v. 17; descended from *Joseph,* Gen 48) are extolled for their military prowess, using the image of an aggressive bull. The tradition of the LORD as *one who dwells on Sinai* or "in the bush" (note *i*) is reflected in Ex 3.1–3. **18–19:** *Zebulun* and *Issachar* are known for their tribal sanctuary (probably on Mount Tabor) and the riches they enjoy from access to the Mediterranean Sea. **20–21:** *Gad* requested the rich territory east of the Jordan (Num 32.1–5, 16–19), thus choosing *the best for himself.* **22:** *Dan* is aggressive, like a lion *from Bashan.* **23–25:** *Naphtali* and *Asher* are acclaimed for their territory's fertility. To dip one's *foot in oil* (v. 24) is a metaphor* for enjoying abundance. **26–29:** The poem returns to the theme of the divine warrior (compare vv. 1–5), whose victory benefits Israel with a secure life in a rich land. Verse 27 is perplexing and suggested translations vary widely (notes *a–c*).

34 Then Moses went up from the plains of Moab to Mount Nebo, to the top of Pisgah, which is opposite Jericho, and the LORD showed him the whole land: Gilead as far as Dan, 2all Naphtali, the land of Ephraim and Manasseh, all the land of Judah as far as the Western Sea, 3the Negeb, and the Plain—that is, the valley of Jericho, the city of palm trees—as far as Zoar. 4The LORD said to him, "This is the land of which I swore to Abraham, to Isaac, and to Jacob, saying, 'I will give it to your descendants'; I

33.1–29: The blessing of Moses. 2–3: The LORD as divine warrior* advances into battle from the mountains of the southern wilderness, leading an army of

a Or *The eternal God is a dwelling place*   *b* Cn: Heb *from underneath*   *c* Or *the everlasting arms*
d Or *fountain*

have let you see it with your eyes, but you shall not cross over there." 5 Then Moses, the servant of the LORD, died there in the land of Moab, at the LORD's command. 6 He was buried in a valley in the land of Moab, opposite Beth-peor, but no one knows his burial place to this day. 7 Moses was one hundred twenty years old when he died; his sight was unimpaired and his vigor had not abated. 8 The Israelites wept for Moses in the plains of Moab thirty days; then the period of mourning for Moses was ended.

9 Joshua son of Nun was full of the spirit of wisdom, because Moses had laid his hands on him; and the Israelites obeyed him, doing as the LORD had commanded Moses.

10 Never since has there arisen a prophet in Israel like Moses, whom the LORD knew face to face. 11 He was unequaled for all the signs and wonders that the LORD sent him to perform in the land of Egypt, against Pharaoh and all his servants and his entire land, 12 and for all the mighty deeds and all the terrifying displays of power that Moses performed in the sight of all Israel.

34.1–12: The death of Moses. 1–3: The narrative* continues directly from 32.52. From *Mount Nebo,* east of the north shore of the Dead Sea, Moses is shown a westward panorama from north (*Dan*) to south (*the Negeb* and *Zoar*). **4:** The reason that Moses had to die outside the land is never clearly stated (1.37; 4.21–22; 32.50–51). **7:** *One hundred twenty years* is the maximum life span according to Gen 6.3. A long and vigorous life was the expected reward for righteousness. **10:** Moses was a *prophet,* speaking to the people for God (5.27) and interceding for them (9.18–20, 25–29; 10.10–11). *Face to face* implies direct and unmediated communication.

JOSHUA

Introduction

Joshua consists of three types of material. Narratives* of conquest under the leadership of the LORD, who fought for Israel as a warrior, make up Josh 2–11. Chapters 12–21 consist of geography in the form of lists and descriptions. Theological addresses constitute the book's introduction (ch. 1) and conclusions (chs. 23–24). Narrative, geography, and address all claim the land of promise for Israel. The individual stories in Joshua, which began as folktales about local victories, were written down and gathered into a connected narrative as the triumphs of a unified Israel (chs. 2–11). Later this story was re-edited (growing to chs. 1–12, 23) to form part of a history of Israel in the land told from the perspective of Deuteronomy's theology. Scholars call this larger work (Deuteronomy through 2 Kings except for Ruth) the Deuteronomistic* History. It was written just before or just after the end of the monarchy in Judah (late seventh or early sixth century BCE). Finally, the geographical material of chs. 13–21, the story of ch. 22, and a second conclusion in ch. 24 were added.

Israel's possession of the land was almost always endangered by outside attack or foreign rule. The threat came first from their local neighbors, but later from the major world empires of Assyria, Babylon, and Persia. The book of Joshua served generation after generation as a call to obedient loyalty to God and as a claim on the land God had promised them.

[margin handwriting: Kingdom of God]

READING GUIDE

The narrative portions of Joshua, chs. 1–11, 22–24, are the most interesting. They may be read straight through as a connected story beginning with the death of Moses and ending with the death of Joshua. The reader should look for the interconnections among the individual stories: Rahab (ch. 2) leads to Jericho (ch. 6), which leads to Achan (ch. 7), which leads in turn to the capture of Ai (ch. 8), and so forth. It is a good idea to keep a map or Bible atlas open in order to follow the action. The geography of conquest falls into three campaigns: central (chs. 6–8), south (ch. 10), and north (ch. 11). In addition, it is helpful to read the battle reports from the perspective of holy war,* as presented in Deut 20.

1–12	Joshua conquers the land
13–21	Joshua divides the land
22–24	Warnings about the future

1 After the death of Moses the servant of the LORD, the LORD spoke to Joshua son of Nun, Moses' assistant, saying, 2"My servant Moses is dead. Now proceed to cross the Jordan, you and all this people, into the land that I am giving to them, to the Israelites. 3Every place that the sole of your foot will tread upon I have given to you, as I promised to Moses. 4From the wilderness and the Lebanon as far as the great river, the river Euphrates, all the land of the Hittites, to the Great Sea in the west shall be your territory. 5No one shall be able to stand against you all the days of your life. As I was with Moses, so I will be with you; I will not fail you or forsake you. 6Be strong and courageous; for you shall put this people in possession of the land that I swore to their ancestors to give them. 7Only be strong and very courageous, being careful to act in ac-

cordance with all the law that my servant Moses commanded you; do not turn from it to the right hand or to the left, so that you may be successful wherever you go. 8This book of the law shall not depart out of your mouth; you shall meditate on it day and night, so that you may be careful to act in accordance with all that is written in it. For then you shall make your way prosperous, and then you shall be successful. 9I hereby command you: Be strong and courageous; do not be frightened or dismayed, for the LORD your God is with you wherever you go."

1.1–9: The LORD commissions Joshua. 2: Joshua is to move westward across the river in order to give Israel possession of the land (v. 6). **3:** To walk over land was a way of legally claiming it. **4:** The idea that the land of promise extends to *the river Euphrates* reflects Deut 11.24 and royal ideology (Ps 72.8). **5:** The LORD as divine warrior* promises Joshua military success (see v. 3) and a supportive presence (v. 9). **7–8:** The theology reflects Deuteronomy: Undeviating obedience to the *book of the law* produces prosperity and success. Joshua is to be like the ideal king of Deut 17.18–20.

10 Then Joshua commanded the officers of the people, 11"Pass through the camp, and command the people: 'Prepare your provisions; for in three days you are to cross over the Jordan, to go in to take possession of the land that the LORD your God gives you to possess.' "

12 To the Reubenites, the Gadites, and the half-tribe of Manasseh Joshua said, 13"Remember the word that Moses the servant of the LORD commanded you, saying, 'The LORD your God is providing you a place of rest, and will give you this land.' 14Your wives, your little ones, and your livestock shall remain in the land that Moses gave you beyond the Jordan. But all the warriors among you shall cross over armed before your kindred and shall help them, 15until the LORD gives rest to your kindred as well as to you, and they too take possession of the land that the LORD your God is giving them. Then you shall return to your own land and take possession of it, the land that Moses the servant of the LORD gave you beyond the Jordan to the east."

16 They answered Joshua: "All that you have commanded us we will do, and wherever you send us we will go. 17Just as we obeyed Moses in all things, so we will obey you. Only may the LORD your God be with you, as he was with Moses! 18Whoever rebels against your orders and disobeys your words, whatever you command, shall be put to death. Only be strong and courageous."

1.10–18: Joshua commands the people. 11: These *three days* are concluded by 3.2. **12–15:** These tribes have already occupied land east of the Jordan. The command of Moses is reported in Deut 3.18–20. *Rest* (vv. 13, 15) is security in the land established by defeat of the enemy (21.44; 23.1). **17–18:** The eastern tribes agree with enthusiasm, but their double use of *only* introduces some tension into the plot. Will the LORD *be with* Joshua? Will Joshua *be strong and courageous?*

2 Then Joshua son of Nun sent two men secretly from Shittim as spies, saying, "Go, view the land, especially Jericho." So they went, and entered the house of a prostitute whose name was Rahab, and spent the night there. 2The king of Jericho was told, "Some Israelites have come here tonight to search out the land." 3Then the king of Jericho sent orders to Rahab, "Bring out the men who have come to you, who entered your house, for they have come only to search out the whole land." 4But the woman took the two men and hid them. Then she said, "True, the men came to me, but I did not know where they came from. 5And when it was time to close the gate at dark, the men went out. Where the men went I do not know. Pursue them quickly, for you can overtake them." 6She had, however, brought them up to the roof and hidden them with the stalks of flax that she had laid out on the roof. 7So the men pursued them on the way to the Jordan as far as the fords. As soon as the pursuers had gone out, the gate was shut.

8 Before they went to sleep, she came up to them on the roof 9and said to the men: "I know that the LORD has given you the land, and that dread of you has fallen on us, and that all the inhabitants of the land melt in fear before you. 10For we have heard how

the LORD dried up the water of the Red Sea[a] before you when you came out of Egypt, and what you did to the two kings of the Amorites that were beyond the Jordan, to Sihon and Og, whom you utterly destroyed. 11As soon as we heard it, our hearts melted, and there was no courage left in any of us because of you. The LORD your God is indeed God in heaven above and on earth below. 12Now then, since I have dealt kindly with you, swear to me by the LORD that you in turn will deal kindly with my family. Give me a sign of good faith 13that you will spare my father and mother, my brothers and sisters, and all who belong to them, and deliver our lives from death." 14The men said to her, "Our life for yours! If you do not tell this business of ours, then we will deal kindly and faithfully with you when the LORD gives us the land."

2.1–14: Rahab outsmarts the spies. 1: Rahab is a legally independent woman with her own *house,* where the presence of strangers would not be questioned. The spies apparently think this is a good place to gather information. **3:** *Come to you* (also v. 4) has a double meaning. Understood as "come into you" it can imply sexual intercourse. **6–7:** Although she saves them from the king, they find themselves trapped on her roof with the city gate shut. Their situation gives her leverage to negotiate an agreement. *The pursuers* block their route back, deepening their predicament. **8:** Rahab takes the initiative in the negotiations. **9–11:** She provides the content of the spies' eventual report (v. 24) and confesses that the LORD is the universal God (echoing Deut 4.39). Sihon and Og were *utterly destroyed* (v. 10), that is, devoted to destruction in holy war.＊ This is the fate Rahab seeks to avoid. **12–14:** She suggests a pact of reciprocal protection, and the spies agree. She has *dealt kindly* (v. 12) by showing faithfulness to the relationship between host and guest. In return they are to *deal kindly* by honoring an agreement to protect her extended family.

15 Then she let them down by a rope through the window, for her house was on the outer side of the city wall and she resided within the wall itself. 16She said to them, "Go toward the hill country, so that the pursuers may not come upon you. Hide yourselves there three days, until the pursuers

have returned; then afterward you may go your way." 17The men said to her, "We will be released from this oath that you have made us swear to you 18if we invade the land and you do not tie this crimson cord in the window through which you let us down, and you do not gather into your house your father and mother, your brothers, and all your family. 19If any of you go out of the doors of your house into the street, they shall be responsible for their own death, and we shall be innocent; but if a hand is laid upon any who are with you in the house, we shall bear the responsibility for their death. 20But if you tell this business of ours, then we shall be released from this oath that you made us swear to you." 21She said, "According to your words, so be it." She sent them away and they departed. Then she tied the crimson cord in the window.

22 They departed and went into the hill country and stayed there three days, until the pursuers returned. The pursuers had searched all along the way and found nothing. 23Then the two men came down again from the hill country. They crossed over, came to Joshua son of Nun, and told him all that had happened to them. 24They said to Joshua, "Truly the LORD has given all the land into our hands; moreover all the inhabitants of the land melt in fear before us."

2.15–24: The spies renegotiate. 15: It is difficult to reconcile the location of Rahab's house with the collapse of Jericho's wall in Josh 6. **16:** She is still in charge. These *three days* are difficult to correlate with the three days of 1.11 and 3.2. **17–20:** Once they are safely out of Rahab's trap, the spies seek to clarify their obligations in order to avoid violating them unintentionally. They insist on a conspicuous means of identification, strict concentration of Rahab's family in one place, and that their secret be kept. **24:** The spies report only what Rahab has told them (vv. 9, 11).

3 Early in the morning Joshua rose and set out from Shittim with all the Israelites, and they came to the Jordan. They camped there before crossing over. 2At the end of three days the officers went through the

a Or *Sea of Reeds*

camp ³and commanded the people, "When you see the ark of the covenant of the LORD your God being carried by the levitical priests, then you shall set out from your place. Follow it, ⁴so that you may know the way you should go, for you have not passed this way before. Yet there shall be a space between you and it, a distance of about two thousand cubits; do not come any nearer to it." ⁵Then Joshua said to the people, "Sanctify yourselves; for tomorrow the LORD will do wonders among you." ⁶To the priests Joshua said, "Take up the ark of the covenant, and pass on in front of the people." So they took up the ark of the covenant and went in front of the people.

7 The LORD said to Joshua, "This day I will begin to exalt you in the sight of all Israel, so that they may know that I will be with you as I was with Moses. ⁸You are the one who shall command the priests who bear the ark of the covenant, 'When you come to the edge of the waters of the Jordan, you shall stand still in the Jordan.' " ⁹Joshua then said to the Israelites, "Draw near and hear the words of the LORD your God." ¹⁰Joshua said, "By this you shall know that among you is the living God who without fail will drive out from before you the Canaanites, Hittites, Hivites, Perizzites, Girgashites, Amorites, and Jebusites: ¹¹the ark of the covenant of the Lord of all the earth is going to pass before you into the Jordan. ¹²So now select twelve men from the tribes of Israel, one from each tribe. ¹³When the soles of the feet of the priests who bear the ark of the LORD, the Lord of all the earth, rest in the waters of the Jordan, the waters of the Jordan flowing from above shall be cut off; they shall stand in a single heap."

14 When the people set out from their tents to cross over the Jordan, the priests bearing the ark of the covenant were in front of the people. ¹⁵Now the Jordan overflows all its banks throughout the time of harvest. So when those who bore the ark had come to the Jordan, and the feet of the priests bearing the ark were dipped in the edge of the water, ¹⁶the waters flowing from above stood still, rising up in a single heap far off at Adam, the city that is beside Zarethan,

while those flowing toward the sea of the Arabah, the Dead Sea,ᵃ were wholly cut off. Then the people crossed over opposite Jericho. ¹⁷While all Israel were crossing over on dry ground, the priests who bore the ark of the covenant of the LORD stood on dry ground in the middle of the Jordan, until the entire nation finished crossing over the Jordan.

3.1–17: Crossing the Jordan. 3: The crossing is described as a religious procession led by the ark. 4: Because the ark is dangerously holy (compare 2 Sam 6.6–7), the people must keep their distance. 5: To be ready for a miraculous event, the people are to perform a ceremony to make themselves holy. 7: The concern raised by 1.17 is resolved here and in 6.27: The LORD is indeed *with* Joshua. 10: As *the living God,* the LORD will be alive and active in the upcoming conquest. 12: The selection of twelve men anticipates 4.2. 15: That the Jordan *overflows all its banks* increases the wonder of the miracle and makes it possible for the priests' feet to touch *the edge of the water.* 16: Because the flow *stood still* sixteen miles (twenty-five kilometers) upstream at *Adam,* the water that would have flowed downstream was *cut off.*

4 When the entire nation had finished crossing over the Jordan, the LORD said to Joshua: ²"Select twelve men from the people, one from each tribe, ³and command them, 'Take twelve stones from here out of the middle of the Jordan, from the place where the priests' feet stood, carry them over with you, and lay them down in the place where you camp tonight.' " ⁴Then Joshua summoned the twelve men from the Israelites, whom he had appointed, one from each tribe. ⁵Joshua said to them, "Pass on before the ark of the LORD your God into the middle of the Jordan, and each of you take up a stone on his shoulder, one for each of the tribes of the Israelites, ⁶so that this may be a sign among you. When your children ask in time to come, 'What do those stones mean to you?' ⁷then you shall tell them that the waters of the Jordan were cut off in front of the ark of the covenant of the LORD. When it crossed over the Jordan, the waters of the

a Heb *Salt Sea*

Jordan were cut off. So these stones shall be to the Israelites a memorial forever."

8 The Israelites did as Joshua commanded. They took up twelve stones out of the middle of the Jordan, according to the number of the tribes of the Israelites, as the LORD told Joshua, carried them over with them to the place where they camped, and laid them down there. 9(Joshua set up twelve stones in the middle of the Jordan, in the place where the feet of the priests bearing the ark of the covenant had stood; and they are there to this day.)

4.1–9: Commemorative stones. 1: Verse 11 repeats words from this verse and 3.17 to indicate that vv. 2–10 happened while the crossing was still going on. **3:** The stones are temporarily deposited in the camp, but will be set up permanently at Gilgal (v. 20). **6–7:** The stones memorialize the crossing for future generations (compare Deut 6.20–25). This answer highlights the role of the *ark* and that the water was *cut off* (in contrast to vv. 22–24). **9:** What is apparently a second group of stones is installed in the river itself.

10 The priests who bore the ark remained standing in the middle of the Jordan, until everything was finished that the LORD commanded Joshua to tell the people, according to all that Moses had commanded Joshua. The people crossed over in haste. 11As soon as all the people had finished crossing over, the ark of the LORD, and the priests, crossed over in front of the people. 12The Reubenites, the Gadites, and the half-tribe of Manasseh crossed over armed before the Israelites, as Moses had ordered them. 13About forty thousand armed for war crossed over before the LORD to the plains of Jericho for battle.

14 On that day the LORD exalted Joshua in the sight of all Israel; and they stood in awe of him, as they had stood in awe of Moses, all the days of his life.

15 The LORD said to Joshua, 16"Command the priests who bear the ark of the covenant,ᵃ to come up out of the Jordan." 17Joshua therefore commanded the priests, "Come up out of the Jordan." 18When the priests bearing the ark of the covenant of the LORD came up from the middle of the Jor-

dan, and the soles of the priests' feet touched dry ground, the waters of the Jordan returned to their place and overflowed all its banks, as before.

19 The people came up out of the Jordan on the tenth day of the first month, and they camped in Gilgal on the east border of Jericho. 20Those twelve stones, which they had taken out of the Jordan, Joshua set up in Gilgal, 21saying to the Israelites, "When your children ask their parents in time to come, 'What do these stones mean?' 22then you shall let your children know, 'Israel crossed over the Jordan here on dry ground.' 23For the LORD your God dried up the waters of the Jordan for you until you crossed over, as the LORD your God did to the Red Sea,ᵇ which he dried up for us until we crossed over, 24so that all the peoples of the earth may know that the hand of the LORD is mighty, and so that you may fear the LORD your God forever."

4.10–24: The crossing completed. 11: The action of crossing is picked up again from v. 1. **12–13:** Particular mention of the eastern tribes emphasizes that all Israel engaged in the conquest together, a motif* also present in Deut 3.18–20. **14:** This exaltation fulfills the pledge of 3.7. **18:** The events of 3.15–16 are reversed item by item. **19:** The date points forward to Passover* in 5.10. **22–24:** This answer (in contrast to vv. 6–7) focuses on similarities to crossing the Red Sea on *dry ground* (Ex 14.22).

5 When all the kings of the Amorites beyond the Jordan to the west, and all the kings of the Canaanites by the sea, heard that the LORD had dried up the waters of the Jordan for the Israelites until they had crossed over, their hearts melted, and there was no longer any spirit in them, because of the Israelites.

2 At that time the LORD said to Joshua, "Make flint knives and circumcise the Israelites a second time." 3So Joshua made flint knives, and circumcised the Israelites at Gibeath-haaraloth.ᶜ 4This is the reason why Joshua circumcised them: all the males of

a Or *treaty*, or *testimony*; Heb *eduth*   b Or *Sea of Reeds*   c That is *the Hill of the Foreskins*

the people who came out of Egypt, all the warriors, had died during the journey through the wilderness after they had come out of Egypt. 5Although all the people who came out had been circumcised, yet all the people born on the journey through the wilderness after they had come out of Egypt had not been circumcised. 6For the Israelites traveled forty years in the wilderness, until all the nation, the warriors who came out of Egypt, perished, not having listened to the voice of the LORD. To them the LORD swore that he would not let them see the land that he had sworn to their ancestors to give us, a land flowing with milk and honey. 7So it was their children, whom he raised up in their place, that Joshua circumcised; for they were uncircumcised, because they had not been circumcised on the way.

8 When the circumcising of all the nation was done, they remained in their places in the camp until they were healed. 9The LORD said to Joshua, "Today I have rolled away from you the disgrace of Egypt." And so that place is called Gilgal a to this day.

10 While the Israelites were camped in Gilgal they kept the passover in the evening on the fourteenth day of the month in the plains of Jericho. 11On the day after the passover, on that very day, they ate the produce of the land, unleavened cakes and parched grain. 12The manna ceased on the day they ate the produce of the land, and the Israelites no longer had manna; they ate the crops of the land of Canaan that year.

5.1–12: A new start in a new land. 1: Enemy fear repeats Rahab's observations (2.9–11) and will motivate enemy strategy (9.1–2; 10.1–5; 11.1–5). 2: The use of flint knives demonstrates the conservatism of ritual. Israel's circumcised generation had died in the wilderness. Circumcision* a second time applies to the men of the post-exodus generation. 3: Apparently this explains the name of a hill near Gilgal (note c). 9: The disgrace of Egypt may refer to Israel's former status as slaves or insults suffered from the Egyptians. Probably Gilgal originally referred to a circle of stones, but here it is explained by reference to Joshua's circumcision (note a). 11–12: The end of manna coordinates with the first Passover* in the land. It signifies that Israel has moved from the wilderness into an agriculturally pro-

ductive land. Unleavened cakes and parched grain could be prepared quickly and would be appropriate foods for the first day of this new situation.

13 Once when Joshua was by Jericho, he looked up and saw a man standing before him with a drawn sword in his hand. Joshua went to him and said to him, "Are you one of us, or one of our adversaries?" 14He replied, "Neither; but as commander of the army of the LORD I have now come." And Joshua fell on his face to the earth and worshiped, and he said to him, "What do you command your servant, my lord?" 15The commander of the army of the LORD said to Joshua, "Remove the sandals from your feet, for the place where you stand is holy." And Joshua did so.

5.13–15: The commander of the LORD's army. 13: By Jericho must be understood as "in the general vicinity of Jericho." The drawn sword indicates that war is imminent. Apparently assuming that the man is a human soldier, Joshua challenges him. 14: The commander is not part of either human army, but a visible sign that the LORD's supernatural forces will be fighting for Israel. 15: A quotation from Ex 3.5 draws a parallel between Joshua and Moses.

6 Now Jericho was shut up inside and out because of the Israelites; no one came out and no one went in. 2The LORD said to Joshua, "See, I have handed Jericho over to you, along with its king and soldiers. 3You shall march around the city, all the warriors circling the city once. Thus you shall do for six days, 4with seven priests bearing seven trumpets of rams' horns before the ark. On the seventh day you shall march around the city seven times, the priests blowing the trumpets. 5When they make a long blast with the ram's horn, as soon as you hear the sound of the trumpet, then all the people shall shout with a great shout; and the wall of the city will fall down flat, and all the people shall charge straight ahead." 6So Joshua son of Nun summoned the priests and said to them, "Take up the ark of the covenant, and have seven priests carry seven trumpets

a Related to Heb galal to roll

of rams' horns in front of the ark of the LORD." 7To the people he said, "Go forward and march around the city; have the armed men pass on before the ark of the LORD."

8 As Joshua had commanded the people, the seven priests carrying the seven trumpets of rams' horns before the LORD went forward, blowing the trumpets, with the ark of the covenant of the LORD following them. 9And the armed men went before the priests who blew the trumpets; the rear guard came after the ark, while the trumpets blew continually. 10To the people Joshua gave this command: "You shall not shout or let your voice be heard, nor shall you utter a word, until the day I tell you to shout. Then you shall shout." 11So the ark of the LORD went around the city, circling it once; and they came into the camp, and spent the night in the camp.

12 Then Joshua rose early in the morning, and the priests took up the ark of the LORD. 13The seven priests carrying the seven trumpets of rams' horns before the ark of the LORD passed on, blowing the trumpets continually. The armed men went before them, and the rear guard came after the ark of the LORD, while the trumpets blew continually. 14On the second day they marched around the city once and then returned to the camp. They did this for six days.

15 On the seventh day they rose early, at dawn, and marched around the city in the same manner seven times. It was only on that day that they marched around the city seven times. 16And at the seventh time, when the priests had blown the trumpets, Joshua said to the people, "Shout! For the LORD has given you the city. 17The city and all that is in it shall be devoted to the LORD for destruction. Only Rahab the prostitute and all who are with her in her house shall live because she hid the messengers we sent. 18As for you, keep away from the things devoted to destruction, so as not to covet*a* and take any of the devoted things and make the camp of Israel an object for destruction, bringing trouble upon it. 19But all silver and gold, and vessels of bronze and iron, are sacred to the LORD; they shall go into the treasury of the LORD." 20So the people shouted,

and the trumpets were blown. As soon as the people heard the sound of the trumpets, they raised a great shout, and the wall fell down flat; so the people charged straight ahead into the city and captured it. 21Then they devoted to destruction by the edge of the sword all in the city, both men and women, young and old, oxen, sheep, and donkeys.

6.1–21: The capture of Jericho. 1: The problem facing Israel is Jericho's impregnable defensive wall. **2:** An assurance of victory was part of holy war* tradition (8.1; 10.8). **3:** Israel is to engage in a ceremonial siege. **5:** A *long blast* on a trumpet will signal the attack, and *a great shout* will initiate it (vv. 16, 20). Both are part of holy war tradition. **8–9:** The order of march is: *armed men* followed by *seven priests* with trumpets, then *the ark,* and finally *the rear guard.* **18:** To *take any of the devoted things* would put Israel itself under the ban* (*an object for destruction*) by the principle of contagion. This will be Achan's crime (7.21). **20:** Israel makes an assault from all sides at once.

---

22 Joshua said to the two men who had spied out the land, "Go into the prostitute's house, and bring the woman out of it and all who belong to her, as you swore to her." 23So the young men who had been spies went in and brought Rahab out, along with her father, her mother, her brothers, and all who belonged to her—they brought all her kindred out—and set them outside the camp of Israel. 24They burned down the city, and everything in it; only the silver and gold, and the vessels of bronze and iron, they put into the treasury of the house of the LORD. 25But Rahab the prostitute, with her family and all who belonged to her, Joshua spared. Her family*b* has lived in Israel ever since. For she hid the messengers whom Joshua sent to spy out Jericho.

26 Joshua then pronounced this oath, saying,

"Cursed before the LORD be anyone
who tries
to build this city—this Jericho!

---

a Gk: Heb *devote to destruction* Compare 7.21
b Heb *She*

The Spoils of Holy War

Because it was the divine warrior* who achieved Israel's victories, booty won in holy war* belonged partly or entirely to the LORD. Such booty fell under the ban* (Heb., "herem"; NRSV "devote to destruction," "utterly destroy," "annihilate"). It belonged irrevocably to the LORD and had to be kept from human use. As potential slaves, the entire enemy population routinely fell under the ban and was to be killed (Deut 20.16–17). Normally, non-living booty and cattle did not come under the ban (8.2; 11.14), but Jericho is a special case. Its domestic animals are killed along with its people (v. 21), and valuable metals are deposited in the sanctuary (vv. 19, 24).

At the cost of his firstborn he shall lay
its foundation,
and at the cost of his youngest he
shall set up its gates!"
27 So the LORD was with Joshua; and his fame was in all the land.

6.22–27: The aftermath of Jericho's fall. 23: Rahab's family stays *outside the camp* because the holy war* encampment must remain ritually clean (Deut 23.9–14). **25:** The Rahab story explains and justifies the existence of a foreign group still living *in Israel*. **26:** Joshua caps Jericho's state of being banned* (devoted to destruction; v. 21) with a curse blocking its reconstruction (compare Deut 13.16). 1 Kings 16.34 reports the consequences of this curse.

7 But the Israelites broke faith in regard to the devoted things: Achan son of Carmi son of Zabdi son of Zerah, of the tribe of Judah, took some of the devoted things; and the anger of the LORD burned against the Israelites.

2 Joshua sent men from Jericho to Ai, which is near Beth-aven, east of Bethel, and said to them, "Go up and spy out the land." And the men went up and spied out Ai. ³Then they returned to Joshua and said to him, "Not all the people need go up; about two or three thousand men should go up and attack Ai. Since they are so few, do not make the whole people toil up there." ⁴So about three thousand of the people went up there; and they fled before the men of Ai. ⁵The men of Ai killed about thirty-six of them, chasing them from outside the gate as far as Sheb-

arim and killing them on the slope. The hearts of the people melted and turned to water.

6 Then Joshua tore his clothes, and fell to the ground on his face before the ark of the LORD until the evening, he and the elders of Israel; and they put dust on their heads. ⁷Joshua said, "Ah, Lord GOD! Why have you brought this people across the Jordan at all, to hand us over to the Amorites so as to destroy us? Would that we had been content to settle beyond the Jordan! ⁸O Lord, what can I say, now that Israel has turned their backs to their enemies! ⁹The Canaanites and all the inhabitants of the land will hear of it, and surround us, and cut off our name from the earth. Then what will you do for your great name?"

10 The LORD said to Joshua, "Stand up! Why have you fallen upon your face? ¹¹Israel has sinned; they have transgressed my covenant that I imposed on them. They have taken some of the devoted things; they have stolen, they have acted deceitfully, and they have put them among their own belongings. ¹²Therefore the Israelites are unable to stand before their enemies; they turn their backs to their enemies, because they have become a thing devoted for destruction themselves. I will be with you no more, unless you destroy the devoted things from among you. ¹³Proceed to sanctify the people, and say, 'Sanctify yourselves for tomorrow; for thus says the LORD, the God of Israel, "There are devoted things among you, O Israel; you will be unable to stand before

your enemies until you take away the devoted things from among you." ¹⁴In the morning therefore you shall come forward tribe by tribe. The tribe that the LORD takes shall come near by clans, the clan that the LORD takes shall come near by households, and the household that the LORD takes shall come near one by one. ¹⁵And the one who is taken as having the devoted things shall be burned with fire, together with all that he has, for having transgressed the covenant of the LORD, and for having done an outrageous thing in Israel.' "

7.1–15: The consequences of Achan's sin. 1: Achan, a man of impeccable ancestry, has ignored Joshua's explicit warning concerning the ban* (6.18). He acted alone, but the principle of corporate responsibility means that all *the Israelites broke faith* (also v. 11). Thus *the anger of the LORD* is directed against the entire nation. **2:** Sending spies was a typical first step in a campaign (2.1; Judg 1.23). **5:** Such a great panic associated with only *thirty-six* deaths indicates something is seriously amiss. Israel experiences the fear their enemies have felt: *The hearts of the people melted* (contrast 2.11; 5.1). **7–9:** Joshua follows the pattern of typical lament* prayers such as Ps 44 or 74. He questions the LORD's motives and seeks to provoke a response by highlighting the potential damage to the LORD's reputation (*great name*). **11:** As a violation of the *covenant** (also v. 15), Achan's crime endangers Israel's relationship with the LORD in a fundamental way. **12:** The contagious effect of items *devoted for destruction* (compare 6.18) means that the entire nation has fallen under the ban. **13:** The people must engage in a ceremony to make themselves holy in order to prepare for contact with God's action (compare 3.5). **14:** The procedure for discovering the culprit involves the use of the sacred lot (1 Sam 14.40–42). **15:** An *outrageous thing in Israel* means a heinous crime against society that endangers the whole nation.

16 So Joshua rose early in the morning, and brought Israel near tribe by tribe, and the tribe of Judah was taken. ¹⁷He brought near the clans of Judah, and the clan of the Zerahites was taken; and he brought near the clan of the Zerahites, family by family,ᵃ and Zabdi was taken. ¹⁸And he brought near his household one by one, and Achan son of Carmi son of Zabdi son of Zerah, of the tribe of Judah, was taken. ¹⁹Then Joshua said to Achan, "My son, give glory to the LORD God of Israel and make confession to him. Tell me now what you have done; do not hide it from me." ²⁰And Achan answered Joshua, "It is true; I am the one who sinned against the LORD God of Israel. This is what I did: ²¹when I saw among the spoil a beautiful mantle from Shinar, and two hundred shekels of silver, and a bar of gold weighing fifty shekels, then I coveted them and took them. They now lie hidden in the ground inside my tent, with the silver underneath."

22 So Joshua sent messengers, and they ran to the tent; and there it was, hidden in his tent with the silver underneath. ²³They took them out of the tent and brought them to Joshua and all the Israelites; and they spread them out before the LORD. ²⁴Then Joshua and all Israel with him took Achan son of Zerah, with the silver, the mantle, and the bar of gold, with his sons and daughters, with his oxen, donkeys, and sheep, and his tent and all that he had; and they brought them up to the Valley of Achor. ²⁵Joshua said, "Why did you bring trouble on us? The LORD is bringing trouble on you today." And all Israel stoned him to death; they burned them with fire, cast stones on them, ²⁶and raised over him a great heap of stones that remains to this day. Then the LORD turned from his burning anger. Therefore that place to this day is called the Valley of Achor.ᵇ

7.16–26: Discovery and punishment. 16–18: That *Joshua rose early in the morning* signals obedient zeal (3.1; 6.12). The sacred lot gave only a yes or no answer, so the discovery process moves down through smaller and smaller social units: *tribe, clan,** *family* (household). **19:** Because confession acknowledges God's justice, it is the equivalent of giving *glory to the LORD*. **21:** Cloth, silver, and gold are typical items of plunder (2 Kings 7.8). The *mantle from Shinar* would be a costly outer robe imported from Babylon. **22:** Discovery of *the silver underneath* (v. 21) communicates the complete accuracy of Achan's confession. **25–26:** The *trouble* (better: "state of ritual isolation"; 6.18) brought on by Achan connects to the *Valley of Achor*

---

a Mss Syr: MT *man by man*   *b* That is *Trouble*

(note b), where later generations could view the stone pile that marked his grave.

〰〰〰〰〰〰〰〰〰〰〰〰〰〰〰〰〰〰〰〰

8 Then the LORD said to Joshua, "Do not fear or be dismayed; take all the fighting men with you, and go up now to Ai. See, I have handed over to you the king of Ai with his people, his city, and his land. 2You shall do to Ai and its king as you did to Jericho and its king; only its spoil and its livestock you may take as booty for yourselves. Set an ambush against the city, behind it."

3 So Joshua and all the fighting men set out to go up against Ai. Joshua chose thirty thousand warriors and sent them out by night 4with the command, "You shall lie in ambush against the city, behind it; do not go very far from the city, but all of you stay alert. 5I and all the people who are with me will approach the city. When they come out against us, as before, we shall flee from them. 6They will come out after us until we have drawn them away from the city; for they will say, 'They are fleeing from us, as before.' While we flee from them, 7you shall rise up from the ambush and seize the city; for the LORD your God will give it into your hand. 8And when you have taken the city, you shall set the city on fire, doing as the LORD has ordered; see, I have commanded you." 9So Joshua sent them out; and they went to the place of ambush, and lay between Bethel and Ai, to the west of Ai; but Joshua spent that night in the camp.ᵃ

10 In the morning Joshua rose early and mustered the people, and went up, with the elders of Israel, before the people to Ai. 11All the fighting men who were with him went up, and drew near before the city, and camped on the north side of Ai, with a ravine between them and Ai. 12Taking about five thousand men, he set them in ambush between Bethel and Ai, to the west of the city. 13So they stationed the forces, the main encampment that was north of the city and its rear guard west of the city. But Joshua spent that night in the valley. 14When the king of Ai saw this, he and all his people, the inhabitants of the city, hurried out early in the morning to the meeting place facing the Arabah to meet Israel in battle; but he did not know that there was an ambush against him behind the city. 15And Joshua and all Israel made a pretense of being beaten before them, and fled in the direction of the wilderness. 16So all the people who were in the city were called together to pursue them, and as they pursued Joshua they were drawn away from the city. 17There was not a man left in Ai or Bethel who did not go out after Israel; they left the city open, and pursued Israel.

8.1–13: Setting the trap at Ai. 2: From now on, Israel is to follow the more usual pattern of killing all potential slaves, but keeping the other spoils of war. Even though ultimate victory is given by the LORD (vv. 1, 7, 18), human strategy (*an ambush*) is still required. **3:** Here the ambush is *thirty thousand* strong; in v. 12 it will number only five thousand. Such irregularities resulted when different narrative* versions were blended together. **8:** The tactical purpose of setting *the city on fire* is not revealed until v. 20. Unanswered questions boost reader interest.

〰〰〰〰〰〰〰〰〰〰〰〰〰〰〰〰〰〰〰〰

18 Then the LORD said to Joshua, "Stretch out the sword that is in your hand toward Ai; for I will give it into your hand." And Joshua stretched out the sword that was in his hand toward the city. 19As soon as he stretched out his hand, the troops in ambush rose quickly out of their place and rushed forward. They entered the city, took it, and at once set the city on fire. 20So when the men of Ai looked back, the smoke of the city was rising to the sky. They had no power to flee this way or that, for the people who fled to the wilderness turned back against the pursuers. 21When Joshua and all Israel saw that the ambush had taken the city and that the smoke of the city was rising, then they turned back and struck down the men of Ai. 22And the others came out from the city against them; so they were surrounded by Israelites, some on one side, and some on the other; and Israel struck them down until no one was left who survived or escaped. 23But the king of Ai was taken alive and brought to Joshua.

24 When Israel had finished slaughtering

a Heb *among the people*

all the inhabitants of Ai in the open wilderness where they pursued them, and when all of them to the very last had fallen by the edge of the sword, all Israel returned to Ai, and attacked it with the edge of the sword. 25The total of those who fell that day, both men and women, was twelve thousand—all the people of Ai. 26For Joshua did not draw back his hand, with which he stretched out the sword, until he had utterly destroyed all the inhabitants of Ai. 27Only the livestock and the spoil of that city Israel took as their booty, according to the word of the LORD that he had issued to Joshua. 28So Joshua burned Ai, and made it forever a heap of ruins, as it is to this day. 29And he hanged the king of Ai on a tree until evening; and at sunset Joshua commanded, and they took his body down from the tree, threw it down at the entrance of the gate of the city, and raised over it a great heap of stones, which stands there to this day.

been used"; and they offered on it burnt offerings to the LORD, and sacrificed offerings of well-being. 32And there, in the presence of the Israelites, Joshua[b] wrote on the stones a copy of the law of Moses, which he had written. 33All Israel, alien as well as citizen, with their elders and officers and their judges, stood on opposite sides of the ark in front of the levitical priests who carried the ark of the covenant of the LORD, half of them in front of Mount Gerizim and half of them in front of Mount Ebal, as Moses the servant of the LORD had commanded at the first, that they should bless the people of Israel. 34And afterward he read all the words of the law, blessings and curses, according to all that is written in the book of the law. 35There was not a word of all that Moses commanded that Joshua did not read before all the assembly of Israel, and the women, and the little ones, and the aliens who resided among them.

8.14–29: Victory at Ai. 14–15: The sight of Israel's main army draws the forces of Ai out to the north. Israel's withdrawal pulls them farther away from the city *in the direction of the wilderness,* that is, eastward away from the ambush on the west (vv. 12–13). **19:** Joshua's extended sword signals the ambush to overrun the undefended (v. 17) city. **20–21:** *The smoke of the city* both disheartens the defenders and signals the Israelite main body to turn and attack. Biblical narratives* are not always in strict chronological order: v. 21 overlaps with the last part of v. 20. **22:** The Israelite ambush comes out of Ai to attack the enemy's rear, *so they were surrounded by Israelites.* **25–27:** Devoting the enemy population to destruction (*utterly destroyed;* v. 26) but sparing the booty follows the pattern set by v. 2. **28:** Joshua's action explains the name of *Ai,* which means "the ruin." **29:** Exposing an enemy's body was a great insult (1 Sam 31.10). Joshua is careful not to violate Deut 21.22–23. This *great heap of stones* was presumably a well-known landmark (compare 7.26; 10.27).

8.30–35: Building an altar, reading the law. 30–31: Joshua obeys Mosaic ordinance (Deut 11.29–30; 27.2–13) by building an altar for sacrifice, writing on stones (v. 32), and arranging the people for blessing and cursing (v. 33). Deuteronomy 27.5 is quoted directly. **32:** These are not the altar stones, but others set up in accordance with Deut 27.4. **34–35:** In obedience to Deut 31.10–12, Joshua reads *the book of the law* (Deuteronomy), including the *blessings and curses* of Deut 28. There is an emphasis on totality: *All the words* and *all that is written* are read to *all the assembly.*

---

30 Then Joshua built on Mount Ebal an altar to the LORD, the God of Israel, 31just as Moses the servant of the LORD had commanded the Israelites, as it is written in the book of the law of Moses, "an altar of unhewn[a] stones, on which no iron tool has

9 Now when all the kings who were beyond the Jordan in the hill country and in the lowland all along the coast of the Great Sea toward Lebanon—the Hittites, the Amorites, the Canaanites, the Perizzites, the Hivites, and the Jebusites—heard of this, 2they gathered together with one accord to fight Joshua and Israel.

3 But when the inhabitants of Gibeon heard what Joshua had done to Jericho and to Ai, 4they on their part acted with cunning: they went and prepared provisions,[c] and took worn-out sacks for their donkeys, and

a Heb *whole*　　*b* Heb *he*　　*c* Cn: Meaning of Heb uncertain wineskins, worn-out and torn and mended, [5]with worn-out, patched sandals on their feet, and worn-out clothes; and all their provisions were dry and moldy. [6]They went to Joshua in the camp at Gilgal, and said to him and to the Israelites, "We have come from a far country; so now make a treaty with us." [7]But the Israelites said to the Hivites, "Perhaps you live among us; then how can we make a treaty with you?" [8]They said to Joshua, "We are your servants." And Joshua said to them, "Who are you? And where do you come from?" [9]They said to him, "Your servants have come from a very far country, because of the name of the LORD your God; for we have heard a report of him, of all that he did in Egypt, [10]and of all that he did to the two kings of the Amorites who were beyond the Jordan, King Sihon of Heshbon, and King Og of Bashan who lived in Ashtaroth. [11]So our elders and all the inhabitants of our country said to us, 'Take provisions in your hand for the journey; go to meet them, and say to them, "We are your servants; come now, make a treaty with us."' [12]Here is our bread; it was still warm when we took it from our houses as our food for the journey, on the day we set out to come to you, but now, see, it is dry and moldy; [13]these wineskins were new when we filled them, and see, they are burst; and these garments and sandals of ours are worn out from the very long journey." [14]So the leaders[a] partook of their provisions, and did not ask direction from the LORD. [15]And Joshua made peace with them, guaranteeing their lives by a treaty; and the leaders of the congregation swore an oath to them.

9.1–15: The Gibeonite deception. 1–4: There are two contrasting reactions to the news about Israel's victories. The kings of the various peoples *gathered . . . to fight* (v. 2). But the citizens of Gibeon *acted with cunning* (v. 4). **6:** Their argument rests on being from *a far country* (also v. 9), exempting them from the extermination required by Deut 20.16–18. **7:** In reality they are *Hivites,* one of the nations to be destroyed (9.1; Deut. 20.17). A *treaty* with any who *live among* Israel was forbidden (Deut 7.2). **8:** Their language about being *servants* is respectful, but it is also ironic* in light of vv. 21, 23, 27. **9–10:** Their speech is similar

to Rahab's confession (2.10–11), but is hypocritical. **15:** All three Israelite parties fall for the ruse. The ordinary Israelites of vv. 6 and 7 ("men" is the better reading, note *a*) taste the evidence. Joshua makes *peace.* The *leaders of the congregation* swear *an oath.* Gibeonites retained their special status as a foreign enclave down to the reign of David (2 Sam 21.1–6).

〜〜〜〜〜〜〜

[16] But when three days had passed after they had made a treaty with them, they heard that they were their neighbors and were living among them. [17]So the Israelites set out and reached their cities on the third day. Now their cities were Gibeon, Chephirah, Beeroth, and Kiriath-jearim. [18]But the Israelites did not attack them, because the leaders of the congregation had sworn to them by the LORD, the God of Israel. Then all the congregation murmured against the leaders. [19]But all the leaders said to all the congregation, "We have sworn to them by the LORD, the God of Israel, and now we must not touch them. [20]This is what we will do to them: We will let them live, so that wrath may not come upon us, because of the oath that we swore to them." [21]The leaders said to them, "Let them live." So they became hewers of wood and drawers of water for all the congregation, as the leaders had decided concerning them.

[22] Joshua summoned them, and said to them, "Why did you deceive us, saying, 'We are very far from you,' while in fact you are living among us? [23]Now therefore you are cursed, and some of you shall always be slaves, hewers of wood and drawers of water for the house of my God." [24]They answered Joshua, "Because it was told to your servants for a certainty that the LORD your God had commanded his servant Moses to give you all the land, and to destroy all the inhabitants of the land before you; so we were in great fear for our lives because of you, and did this thing. [25]And now we are in your hand: do as it seems good and right in your sight to do to us." [26]This is what he did for them: he saved them from the Israelites; and they did not kill them. [27]But on that day Joshua made them hewers of wood and drawers of water for the

[a] Gk: Heb *men*

congregation and for the altar of the LORD, to continue to this day, in the place that he should choose.

9.16–27: Discovery and punishment. 16: The fears of v. 7 are realized; the Gibeonites indeed are *living among them.* **20–21:** The sanctity of the oath must be preserved, but this deception has endangered the community and must be punished. The expression *hewers of wood and drawers of water* indicates a subservient servant class (Deut 29.11). **22:** Joshua summarizes their deceit by contrasting *very far* (see vv. 6, 9) with *living among us* (see vv. 7, 16). **23:** Some Gibeonites are to be servants of the *house of my God,* that is, the Temple.*

10 When King Adoni-zedek of Jerusalem heard how Joshua had taken Ai, and had utterly destroyed it, doing to Ai and its king as he had done to Jericho and its king, and how the inhabitants of Gibeon had made peace with Israel and were among them, ²he*ᵃ* became greatly frightened, because Gibeon was a large city, like one of the royal cities, and was larger than Ai, and all its men were warriors. ³So King Adoni-zedek of Jerusalem sent a message to King Hoham of Hebron, to King Piram of Jarmuth, to King Japhia of Lachish, and to King Debir of Eglon, saying, ⁴"Come up and help me, and let us attack Gibeon; for it has made peace with Joshua and with the Israelites." ⁵Then the five kings of the Amorites—the king of Jerusalem, the king of Hebron, the king of Jarmuth, the king of Lachish, and the king of Eglon—gathered their forces, and went up with all their armies and camped against Gibeon, and made war against it.

6 And the Gibeonites sent to Joshua at the camp in Gilgal, saying, "Do not abandon your servants; come up to us quickly, and save us, and help us; for all the kings of the Amorites who live in the hill country are gathered against us." ⁷So Joshua went up from Gilgal, he and all the fighting force with him, all the mighty warriors. ⁸The LORD said to Joshua, "Do not fear them, for I have handed them over to you; not one of them shall stand before you." ⁹So Joshua came upon them suddenly, having marched up all night from Gilgal. ¹⁰And the LORD threw

them into a panic before Israel, who inflicted a great slaughter on them at Gibeon, chased them by the way of the ascent of Beth-horon, and struck them down as far as Azekah and Makkedah. ¹¹As they fled before Israel, while they were going down the slope of Beth-horon, the LORD threw down huge stones from heaven on them as far as Azekah, and they died; there were more who died because of the hailstones than the Israelites killed with the sword.

10.1–11: Victory at Gibeon. 1: News of Israel's success motivates enemy action (compare 5.1; 9.1–2; 11.1–3). **2:** Israel's treaty with *Gibeon* threatened Jerusalem's northern approaches. **3:** These four cities are south and west of Jerusalem. **6:** *All the kings of the Amorites* is an exaggeration to motivate Israel's response. **10:** *Panic* is a standard weapon of the divine warrior* (Ex 14.24; Judg 7.21–22). The pursuit extends westward from Gibeon, down through the pass at *the ascent of Beth-horon,* then far southward. **11:** Weather phenomena are also weapons of the divine warrior (Isa 30.30).

12 On the day when the LORD gave the Amorites over to the Israelites, Joshua spoke to the LORD; and he said in the sight of Israel,

"Sun, stand still at Gibeon,
    and Moon, in the valley of Aijalon."
¹³ And the sun stood still, and the moon stopped,
    until the nation took vengeance on
        their enemies.

Is this not written in the Book of Jashar? The sun stopped in midheaven, and did not hurry to set for about a whole day. ¹⁴There has been no day like it before or since, when the LORD heeded a human voice; for the LORD fought for Israel.

15 Then Joshua returned, and all Israel with him, to the camp at Gilgal.

10.12–15: The sun stands still. 12–13: A prose framework encloses and reinterprets an older poetic text from *the Book of Jashar* (see 2 Sam 1.18). According to the framework, Joshua's request *to the LORD* (v. 12) for extended daylight causes the sun to stop in its noon

a Heb *they*

position (*in midheaven*, v. 13) and delay its setting. The poem itself actually addresses the moon and sun, not God. The poet calls upon them to freeze in stunned amazement at the scope of Israel's victory (compare Ex 15.16; Hab 3.11). **14:** That *the LORD fought for Israel* perfectly summarizes the divine warrior* tradition.

16 Meanwhile, these five kings fled and hid themselves in the cave at Makkedah. [17]And it was told Joshua, "The five kings have been found, hidden in the cave at Makkedah." [18]Joshua said, "Roll large stones against the mouth of the cave, and set men by it to guard them; [19]but do not stay there yourselves; pursue your enemies, and attack them from the rear. Do not let them enter their towns, for the LORD your God has given them into your hand." [20]When Joshua and the Israelites had finished inflicting a very great slaughter on them, until they were wiped out, and when the survivors had entered into the fortified towns, [21]all the people returned safe to Joshua in the camp at Makkedah; no one dared to speak*a* against any of the Israelites.

22 Then Joshua said, "Open the mouth of the cave, and bring those five kings out to me from the cave." [23]They did so, and brought the five kings out to him from the cave, the king of Jerusalem, the king of Hebron, the king of Jarmuth, the king of Lachish, and the king of Eglon. [24]When they brought the kings out to Joshua, Joshua summoned all the Israelites, and said to the chiefs of the warriors who had gone with him, "Come near, put your feet on the necks of these kings." Then they came near and put their feet on their necks. [25]And Joshua said to them, "Do not be afraid or dismayed; be strong and courageous; for thus the LORD will do to all the enemies against whom you fight." [26]Afterward Joshua struck them down and put them to death, and he hung them on five trees. And they hung on the trees until evening. [27]At sunset Joshua commanded, and they took them down from the trees and threw them into the cave where they had hidden themselves; they set large stones against the mouth of the cave, which remain to this very day.

10.16–27: Executing the five kings. 16: *Makkedah* was the southernmost limit of the enemy's flight (v. 10) and the starting point for the final phase of the campaign (v. 28). **20:** In spite of Joshua's energetic pursuit (v. 19), *survivors* do escape to *the fortified towns*, thus setting up the need for attacks on Lachish, Eglon, and Hebron (vv. 31, 34, 36). **24:** *Feet on the necks* of enemy kings symbolizes total victory (Ps 110.1). **26–27:** Exposing enemy bodies was a humiliating insult (1 Sam 31.10; 2 Sam 4.12). Joshua obeys Deut 21.22–23. These *large stones* were presumably a well-known landmark (compare 7.26; 8.29).

28 Joshua took Makkedah on that day, and struck it and its king with the edge of the sword; he utterly destroyed every person in it; he left no one remaining. And he did to the king of Makkedah as he had done to the king of Jericho.

29 Then Joshua passed on from Makkedah, and all Israel with him, to Libnah, and fought against Libnah. [30]The LORD gave it also and its king into the hand of Israel; and he struck it with the edge of the sword, and every person in it; he left no one remaining in it; and he did to its king as he had done to the king of Jericho.

31 Next Joshua passed on from Libnah, and all Israel with him, to Lachish, and laid siege to it, and assaulted it. [32]The LORD gave Lachish into the hand of Israel, and he took it on the second day, and struck it with the edge of the sword, and every person in it, as he had done to Libnah.

33 Then King Horam of Gezer came up to help Lachish; and Joshua struck him and his people, leaving him no survivors.

34 From Lachish Joshua passed on with all Israel to Eglon; and they laid siege to it, and assaulted it; [35]and they took it that day, and struck it with the edge of the sword; and every person in it he utterly destroyed that day, as he had done to Lachish.

36 Then Joshua went up with all Israel from Eglon to Hebron; they assaulted it, [37]and took it, and struck it with the edge of the sword, and its king and its towns, and every person in it; he left no one remaining,

a Heb *moved his tongue*

just as he had done to Eglon, and utterly destroyed it with every person in it.

38 Then Joshua, with all Israel, turned back to Debir and assaulted it, ³⁹ and he took it with its king and all its towns; they struck them with the edge of the sword, and utterly destroyed every person in it; he left no one remaining; just as he had done to Hebron, and, as he had done to Libnah and its king, so he did to Debir and its king.

40 So Joshua defeated the whole land, the hill country and the Negeb and the lowland and the slopes, and all their kings; he left no one remaining, but utterly destroyed all that breathed, as the LORD God of Israel commanded. ⁴¹ And Joshua defeated them from Kadesh-barnea to Gaza, and all the country of Goshen, as far as Gibeon. ⁴² Joshua took all these kings and their land at one time, because the LORD God of Israel fought for Israel. ⁴³ Then Joshua returned, and all Israel with him, to the camp at Gilgal.

10.28–43: Capturing five cities. 31: Three cites (*Lachish*, Eglon, and Hebron) were part of the earlier coalition, but Jerusalem and Jarmuth (v. 3) are not attacked. No mention is made of the kings of Lachish or Eglon; they have already been killed (vv. 23, 26). **33:** *Gezer* is not captured. It did not become part of Israel until the reign of Solomon (1 Kings 9.16–17). **37:** Mention of a king of Hebron seems to contradict vv. 23, 26. **41:** This describes the land conquered so far: The south boundary runs east to west from *Kadesh-barnea to Gaza*. Northward it extends *as far as Gibeon*. The extent of *the country of Goshen* (11.16; perhaps 15.51) is unknown.

11 When King Jabin of Hazor heard of this, he sent to King Jobab of Madon, to the king of Shimron, to the king of Achshaph, ² and to the kings who were in the northern hill country, and in the Arabah south of Chinneroth, and in the lowland, and in Naphoth-dor on the west, ³ to the Canaanites in the east and the west, the Amorites, the Hittites, the Perizzites, and the Jebusites in the hill country, and the Hivites under Hermon in the land of Mizpah. ⁴ They came out, with all their troops, a great army, in number like the sand on the seashore, with very many horses and chariots. ⁵ All these kings joined their forces, and came and camped together at the waters of Merom, to fight with Israel.

6 And the LORD said to Joshua, "Do not be afraid of them, for tomorrow at this time I will hand over all of them, slain, to Israel; you shall hamstring their horses, and burn their chariots with fire." ⁷ So Joshua came suddenly upon them with all his fighting force, by the waters of Merom, and fell upon them. ⁸ And the LORD handed them over to Israel, who attacked them and chased them as far as Great Sidon and Misrephoth-maim, and eastward as far as the valley of Mizpeh. They struck them down, until they had left no one remaining. ⁹ And Joshua did to them as the LORD commanded him; he hamstrung their horses, and burned their chariots with fire.

10 Joshua turned back at that time, and took Hazor, and struck its king down with the sword. Before that time Hazor was the head of all those kingdoms. ¹¹ And they put to the sword all who were in it, utterly destroying them; there was no one left who breathed, and he burned Hazor with fire. ¹² And all the towns of those kings, and all their kings, Joshua took, and struck them with the edge of the sword, utterly destroying them, as Moses the servant of the LORD had commanded. ¹³ But Israel burned none of the towns that stood on mounds except Hazor, which Joshua did burn. ¹⁴ All the spoil of these towns, and the livestock, the Israelites took for their booty; but all the people they struck down with the edge of the sword, until they had destroyed them, and they did not leave any who breathed. ¹⁵ As the LORD had commanded his servant Moses, so Moses commanded Joshua, and so Joshua did; he left nothing undone of all that the LORD had commanded Moses.

11.1–15: Conquests in the north. 1–3: Deborah and Barak also confront a *King Jabin of Hazor* in Judg 4–5. *Jabin* may have been a dynastic name for Hazor's kings. Separate folk traditions about Hazor simply used this well-known name. Jabin's response parallels the pattern of 10.1–5. **4:** Israel's enemies had the advantage of *horses and chariots,* a sophisticated and expensive weapons system. **6:** To *hamstring* a horse means to cut its rear leg tendons so that it could no longer be used in war (2 Sam 8.4). Israel was unable to support and use chariots until the reign of Solomon. **8:** The LORD is always the real victor in holy war* tradition. **11:** The language for the holy war ban,* *no one left who breathed* (also v. 14), is taken from Deut 20.16. **13:** Israel did not destroy most captured cities, but took them over in accordance with the principle of Deut 6.10–11.

~~~

16 So Joshua took all that land: the hill country and all the Negeb and all the land of Goshen and the lowland and the Arabah and the hill country of Israel and its lowland, 17from Mount Halak, which rises toward Seir, as far as Baal-gad in the valley of Lebanon below Mount Hermon. He took all their kings, struck them down, and put them to death. 18Joshua made war a long time with all those kings. 19There was not a town that made peace with the Israelites, except the Hivites, the inhabitants of Gibeon; all were taken in battle. 20For it was the LORD's doing to harden their hearts so that they would come against Israel in battle, in order that they might be utterly destroyed, and might receive no mercy, but be exterminated, just as the LORD had commanded Moses.

21 At that time Joshua came and wiped out the Anakim from the hill country, from Hebron, from Debir, from Anab, and from all the hill country of Judah, and from all the hill country of Israel; Joshua utterly destroyed them with their towns. 22None of the Anakim was left in the land of the Israelites; some remained only in Gaza, in Gath, and in Ashdod. 23So Joshua took the whole land, according to all that the LORD had spoken to Moses; and Joshua gave it for an inheritance to Israel according to their tribal allotments. And the land had rest from war.

11.16–23: Culmination of the conquest. 16: The description parallels 10.40. **17:** A line of territorial extent reaches from *Mount Halak* in the south on the border with Edom to *Baal-gad* somewhere near *Mount Hermon* on Israel's north (12.7; 13.5–6). **20:** The stubborn hostility and incessant attacks of the enemy were *the LORD's doing,* part of a divine plan to wipe them out. **21–22:** In Israelite folklore, *the Anakim* were an ancient

indigenous race of unusual stature. **23:** The LORD has kept the promise made in 1.3–5, and Joshua has completed the task assigned in 1.6. With the words *the land had rest from war,* the conquest draws to a close.

~~~

12 Now these are the kings of the land, whom the Israelites defeated, whose land they occupied beyond the Jordan toward the east, from the Wadi Arnon to Mount Hermon, with all the Arabah eastward: 2King Sihon of the Amorites who lived at Heshbon, and ruled from Aroer, which is on the edge of the Wadi Arnon, and from the middle of the valley as far as the river Jabbok, the boundary of the Ammonites, that is, half of Gilead, 3and the Arabah to the Sea of Chinneroth eastward, and in the direction of Beth-jeshimoth, to the sea of the Arabah, the Dead Sea,[a] southward to the foot of the slopes of Pisgah; 4and King Og[b] of Bashan, one of the last of the Rephaim, who lived at Ashtaroth and at Edrei 5and ruled over Mount Hermon and Salecah and all Bashan to the boundary of the Geshurites and the Maacathites, and over half of Gilead to the boundary of King Sihon of Heshbon. 6Moses, the servant of the LORD, and the Israelites defeated them; and Moses the servant of the LORD gave their land for a possession to the Reubenites and the Gadites and the half-tribe of Manasseh.

7 The following are the kings of the land whom Joshua and the Israelites defeated on the west side of the Jordan, from Baal-gad in the valley of Lebanon to Mount Halak, that rises toward Seir (and Joshua gave their land to the tribes of Israel as a possession according to their allotments, 8in the hill country, in the lowland, in the Arabah, in the slopes, in the wilderness, and in the Negeb, the land of the Hittites, Amorites, Canaanites, Perizzites, Hivites, and Jebusites):

9 the king of Jericho	one
the king of Ai, which is next to Bethel	one
10 the king of Jerusalem	one
the king of Hebron	one
11 the king of Jarmuth	one
the king of Lachish	one

a Heb *Salt Sea*   *b* Gk: Heb *the boundary of King Og*

12 the king of Eglon — one
the king of Gezer — one
13 the king of Debir — one
the king of Geder — one
14 the king of Hormah — one
the king of Arad — one
15 the king of Libnah — one
the king of Adullam — one
16 the king of Makkedah — one
the king of Bethel — one
17 the king of Tappuah — one
the king of Hepher — one
18 the king of Aphek — one
the king of Lasharon — one
19 the king of Madon — one
the king of Hazor — one
20 the king of Shimron-meron — one
the king of Achshaph — one
21 the king of Taanach — one
the king of Megiddo — one
22 the king of Kedesh — one
the king of Jokneam in Carmel — one
23 the king of Dor in Naphath-dor — one
the king of Goiim in Galilee,^{a} — one
24 the king of Tirzah — one
thirty-one kings in all.

12.1–24: A list of defeated kings. 1–6: Moses defeated two kings east of the Jordan. The territories seized from *Sihon* are delineated in vv. 2–3 and those taken from *Og* in vv. 4–5. **7–8:** Joshua seized territory from thirty-one kings (v. 24). This description mirrors 11.16–17. **9–24:** *Jericho* and *Ai* naturally come first (v. 9). The five cities of 10.3 are listed in vv. 10–12a. The four cities of 11.1 are listed in vv. 19–20.

13 Now Joshua was old and advanced in years; and the LORD said to him, "You are old and advanced in years, and very much of the land still remains to be possessed. 2This is the land that still remains: all the regions of the Philistines, and all those of the Geshurites 3(from the Shihor, which is east of Egypt, northward to the boundary of Ekron, it is reckoned as Canaanite; there are five rulers of the Philistines, those of Gaza, Ashdod, Ashkelon, Gath, and Ekron), and those of the Avvim 4in the south; all the land of the Canaanites, and Mearah that belongs to the Sidonians, to Aphek, to the boundary of the Amorites, 5and the land of the Gebalites, and all Lebanon, toward the east, from Baal-gad below Mount Hermon to Lebo-hamath, 6all the inhabitants of the hill country from Lebanon to Misrephoth-maim, even all the Sidonians. I will myself drive them out from before the Israelites; only allot the land to Israel for an inheritance, as I have commanded you. 7Now therefore divide this land for an inheritance to the nine tribes and the half-tribe of Manasseh."

13.1–7: The land that remains. 1: Joshua's advanced age prompts the distribution of territory west of the Jordan (v. 7). **2–6:** A parenthetical digression describes Philistine territory and areas to the north in Phoenicia and Lebanon as land yet to be conquered. The LORD will eventually drive these peoples out, but for now Joshua is to allot the land already conquered (v. 6).

8 With the other half-tribe of Manasseh^b the Reubenites and the Gadites received their inheritance, which Moses gave them, beyond the Jordan eastward, as Moses the servant of the LORD gave them: 9from Aroer, which is on the edge of the Wadi Arnon, and the town that is in the middle of the valley, and all the tableland from^c Medeba as far as Dibon; 10and all the cities of King Sihon of the Amorites, who reigned in Heshbon, as far as the boundary of the Ammonites; 11and Gilead, and the region of the Geshurites and Maacathites, and all Mount Hermon, and all Bashan to Salecah; 12all the kingdom of Og in Bashan, who reigned in Ashtaroth and in Edrei (he alone was left of the survivors of the Rephaim); these Moses had defeated and driven out. 13Yet the Israelites did not drive out the Geshurites or the Maacathites; but Geshur and Maacath live within Israel to this day.

14 To the tribe of Levi alone Moses gave no inheritance; the offerings by fire to the LORD God of Israel are their inheritance, as he said to them.

15 Moses gave an inheritance to the tribe of the Reubenites according to their clans. 16Their territory was from Aroer, which is on

a Gk: Heb *Gilgal*   *b* Cn: Heb *With it*   *c* Compare Gk: Heb lacks *from*

Dividing Up the Promised Land

The geographical information in Josh 13–19 comes in two forms: tribal boundary descriptions and town lists. The town lists are mostly derived from administrative sources from a period later than the events described in Joshua. The difference between tribal and town lists is particularly clear for 15.20–62 and 18.21–28.

the edge of the Wadi Arnon, and the town that is in the middle of the valley, and all the tableland by Medeba; 17 with Heshbon, and all its towns that are in the tableland; Dibon, and Bamoth-baal, and Beth-baal-meon, 18 and Jahaz, and Kedemoth, and Mephaath, 19 and Kiriathaim, and Sibmah, and Zereth-shahar on the hill of the valley, 20 and Beth-peor, and the slopes of Pisgah, and Beth-jeshimoth, 21 that is, all the towns of the tableland, and all the kingdom of King Sihon of the Amorites, who reigned in Heshbon, whom Moses defeated with the leaders of Midian, Evi and Rekem and Zur and Hur and Reba, as princes of Sihon, who lived in the land. 22 Along with the rest of those they put to death, the Israelites also put to the sword Balaam son of Beor, who practiced divination. 23 And the border of the Reubenites was the Jordan and its banks. This was the inheritance of the Reubenites according to their families, with their towns and villages.

24 Moses gave an inheritance also to the tribe of the Gadites, according to their families. 25 Their territory was Jazer, and all the towns of Gilead, and half the land of the Ammonites, to Aroer, which is east of Rabbah, 26 and from Heshbon to Ramath-mizpeh and Betonim, and from Mahanaim to the territory of Debir,[a] 27 and in the valley Beth-haram, Beth-nimrah, Succoth, and Zaphon, the rest of the kingdom of King Sihon of Heshbon, the Jordan and its banks, as far as the lower end of the Sea of Chinnereth, eastward beyond the Jordan. 28 This is the inheritance of the Gadites according to their clans, with their towns and villages.

29 Moses gave an inheritance to the half-tribe of Manasseh; it was allotted to the half-tribe of the Manassites according to their families. 30 Their territory extended from Mahanaim, through all Bashan, the whole kingdom of King Og of Bashan, and all the settlements of Jair, which are in Bashan, sixty towns, 31 and half of Gilead, and Ashtaroth, and Edrei, the towns of the kingdom of Og in Bashan; these were allotted to the people of Machir son of Manasseh according to their clans—for half the Machirites.

32 These are the inheritances that Moses distributed in the plains of Moab, beyond the Jordan east of Jericho. 33 But to the tribe of Levi Moses gave no inheritance; the LORD God of Israel is their inheritance, as he said to them.

13.8–33: East of the Jordan. 8–14: A general outline moves from south to north. *Aroer* on the edge of the *Wadi★ Arnon* (v. 9) forms the boundary with Moab on the south. *Mount Hermon* and the former *kingdom of Og in Bashan* mark off the north (vv. 11–12). There are two exceptions: *Geshur and Maacath* remain as alien enclaves (v. 13) and *the tribe of Levi* receives no allotment (vv. 14, 33). **15–23:** Reuben's territory is described by a line of extent drawn north *from Aroer* (v. 16) and a list of towns (vv. 17–20). **24–28:** Gad lies to the north of Reuben. Two boundary lines run northward *from Heshbon* and *from Mahanaim* (v. 26). There is a short list of four towns in the first part of v. 27. **29–31:** The clans★ of Manasseh east of the Jordan occupy territory north and east of Gad.

14 These are the inheritances that the Israelites received in the land of Canaan, which the priest Eleazar, and Joshua son of Nun, and the heads of the families of the tribes of the Israelites distributed to

a Gk Syr Vg: Heb *Lidebir*

them. [2]Their inheritance was by lot, as the LORD had commanded Moses for the nine and one-half tribes. [3]For Moses had given an inheritance to the two and one-half tribes beyond the Jordan; but to the Levites he gave no inheritance among them. [4]For the people of Joseph were two tribes, Manasseh and Ephraim; and no portion was given to the Levites in the land, but only towns to live in, with their pasture lands for their flocks and herds. [5]The Israelites did as the LORD commanded Moses; they allotted the land.

6 Then the people of Judah came to Joshua at Gilgal; and Caleb son of Jephunneh the Kenizzite said to him, "You know what the LORD said to Moses the man of God in Kadesh-barnea concerning you and me. [7]I was forty years old when Moses the servant of the LORD sent me from Kadesh-barnea to spy out the land; and I brought him an honest report. [8]But my companions who went up with me made the heart of the people melt; yet I wholeheartedly followed the LORD my God. [9]And Moses swore on that day, saying, 'Surely the land on which your foot has trodden shall be an inheritance for you and your children forever, because you have wholeheartedly followed the LORD my God.' [10]And now, as you see, the LORD has kept me alive, as he said, these forty-five years since the time that the LORD spoke this word to Moses, while Israel was journeying through the wilderness; and here I am today, eighty-five years old. [11]I am still as strong today as I was on the day that Moses sent me; my strength now is as my strength was then, for war, and for going and coming. [12]So now give me this hill country of which the LORD spoke on that day; for you heard on that day how the Anakim were there, with great fortified cities; it may be that the LORD will be with me, and I shall drive them out, as the LORD said."

13 Then Joshua blessed him, and gave Hebron to Caleb son of Jephunneh for an inheritance. [14]So Hebron became the inheritance of Caleb son of Jephunneh the Kenizzite to this day, because he wholeheartedly followed the LORD, the God of Israel. [15]Now the name of Hebron formerly was Kiriath-arba;[a] this Arba was[b] the greatest man among the Anakim. And the land had rest from war.

14.1–15: Prelude to land distribution. 1: Joshua is joined by *the priest Eleazar* because casting the sacred lot was a priestly monopoly (Deut 33.8). **2:** Distribution *by lot* confirms that the results are in accordance with divine will. **4:** The total number of allotments comes out to twelve because Joseph gave rise to two tribes and Levi received no territory. **6–12:** *Caleb* claims a special grant of territory based on his honest and loyal behavior as a spy (vv. 7–8; Num 13) and the promise of Moses (v. 9). He supports his case by reference to his great age and warlike vigor (vv. 10–11). It was Israel's fear of the *Anakim* (vv. 12, 15) that had caused the original problem (Num 13.28).

15 The lot for the tribe of the people of Judah according to their families reached southward to the boundary of Edom, to the wilderness of Zin at the farthest south. [2]And their south boundary ran from the end of the Dead Sea,[c] from the bay that faces southward; [3]it goes out southward of the ascent of Akrabbim, passes along to Zin, and goes up south of Kadesh-barnea, along by Hezron, up to Addar, makes a turn to Karka, [4]passes along to Azmon, goes out by the Wadi of Egypt, and comes to its end at the sea. This shall be your south boundary. [5]And the east boundary is the Dead Sea,[c] to the mouth of the Jordan. And the boundary on the north side runs from the bay of the sea at the mouth of the Jordan; [6]and the boundary goes up to Beth-hoglah, and passes along north of Beth-arabah; and the boundary goes up to the Stone of Bohan, Reuben's son; [7]and the boundary goes up to Debir from the Valley of Achor, and so northward, turning toward Gilgal, which is opposite the ascent of Adummim, which is on the south side of the valley; and the boundary passes along to the waters of En-shemesh, and ends at En-rogel; [8]then the boundary goes up by the valley of the son of Hinnom at the southern slope of the Jebusites (that is, Jerusalem); and the boundary goes up to the top of

a That is *the city of Arba*   *b* Heb lacks *this Arba was*
c Heb *Salt Sea*

the mountain that lies over against the valley of Hinnom, on the west, at the northern end of the valley of Rephaim; [9]then the boundary extends from the top of the mountain to the spring of the Waters of Nephtoah, and from there to the towns of Mount Ephron; then the boundary bends around to Baalah (that is, Kiriath-jearim); [10]and the boundary circles west of Baalah to Mount Seir, passes along to the northern slope of Mount Jearim (that is, Chesalon), and goes down to Beth-shemesh, and passes along by Timnah; [11]the boundary goes out to the slope of the hill north of Ekron, then the boundary bends around to Shikkeron, and passes along to Mount Baalah, and goes out to Jabneel; then the boundary comes to an end at the sea. [12]And the west boundary was the Mediterranean with its coast. This is the boundary surrounding the people of Judah according to their families.

15.1–12: The boundaries of Judah. 1–4: Judah's south border (running east to west) is similar to Num 34.3–6. 5–11: The north border with Benjamin is reported in great detail from east to west and coincides with 18.15–19.

13 According to the commandment of the LORD to Joshua, he gave to Caleb son of Jephunneh a portion among the people of Judah, Kiriath-arba,[a] that is, Hebron (Arba was the father of Anak). [14]And Caleb drove out from there the three sons of Anak: Sheshai, Ahiman, and Talmai, the descendants of Anak. [15]From there he went up against the inhabitants of Debir; now the name of Debir formerly was Kiriath-sepher. [16]And Caleb said, "Whoever attacks Kiriath-sepher and takes it, to him I will give my daughter Achsah as wife." [17]Othniel son of Kenaz, the brother of Caleb, took it; and he gave him his daughter Achsah as wife. [18]When she came to him, she urged him to ask her father for a field. As she dismounted from her donkey, Caleb said to her, "What do you wish?" [19]She said to him, "Give me a present; since you have set me in the land of the Negeb, give me springs of water as well." So Caleb gave her the upper springs and the lower springs.

15.13–19: A land grant for Achsah. 13–15: This parallels the account given in 14.6–15. 17–18: Although Achsah prods her husband to ask for a field, nothing of this sort apparently happens. 19: Instead she herself goes on to request springs of water from her father. Because her land is arid she calls it land of the Negeb (the Negeb is arid territory). Achsah's story (paralleled in Judg 1.10–15) explains why the Othniel clan* controlled both Debir and two springs associated with Hebron.

20 This is the inheritance of the tribe of the people of Judah according to their families. [21]The towns belonging to the tribe of the people of Judah in the extreme south, toward the boundary of Edom, were Kabzeel, Eder, Jagur, [22]Kinah, Dimonah, Adadah, [23]Kedesh, Hazor, Ithnan, [24]Ziph, Telem, Bealoth, [25]Hazor-hadattah, Kerioth-hezron (that is, Hazor), [26]Amam, Shema, Moladah, [27]Hazar-gaddah, Heshmon, Beth-pelet, [28]Hazar-shual, Beer-sheba, Biziothiah, [29]Baalah, Iim, Ezem, [30]Eltolad, Chesil, Hormah, [31]Ziklag, Madmannah, Sansannah, [32]Lebaoth, Shilhim, Ain, and Rimmon: in all, twenty-nine towns, with their villages.

33 And in the lowland, Eshtaol, Zorah, Ashnah, [34]Zanoah, En-gannim, Tappuah, Enam, [35]Jarmuth, Adullam, Socoh, Azekah, [36]Shaaraim, Adithaim, Gederah, Gederothaim: fourteen towns with their villages.

37 Zenan, Hadashah, Migdal-gad, [38]Dilan, Mizpeh, Jokthe-el, [39]Lachish, Bozkath, Eglon, [40]Cabbon, Lahmam, Chitlish, [41]Gederoth, Beth-dagon, Naamah, and Makkedah: sixteen towns with their villages.

42 Libnah, Ether, Ashan, [43]Iphtah, Ashnah, Nezib, [44]Keilah, Achzib, and Mareshah: nine towns with their villages.

45 Ekron, with its dependencies and its villages; [46]from Ekron to the sea, all that were near Ashdod, with their villages.

47 Ashdod, its towns and its villages; Gaza, its towns and its villages; to the Wadi of Egypt, and the Great Sea with its coast.

48 And in the hill country, Shamir, Jattir, Socoh, [49]Dannah, Kiriath-sannah (that is, Debir), [50]Anab, Eshtemoh, Anim, [51]Go-

a That is the city of Arba

shen, Holon, and Giloh: eleven towns with their villages.

52 Arab, Dumah, Eshan, 53Janim, Beth-tappuah, Aphekah, 54Humtah, Kiriath-arba (that is, Hebron), and Zior: nine towns with their villages.

55 Maon, Carmel, Ziph, Juttah, 56Jezreel, Jokdeam, Zanoah, 57Kain, Gibeah, and Timnah: ten towns with their villages.

58 Halhul, Beth-zur, Gedor, 59Maarath, Beth-anoth, and Eltekon: six towns with their villages.

60 Kiriath-baal (that is, Kiriath-jearim) and Rabbah: two towns with their villages.

61 In the wilderness, Beth-arabah, Middin, Secacah, 62Nibshan, the City of Salt, and En-gedi: six towns with their villages.

63 But the people of Judah could not drive out the Jebusites, the inhabitants of Jerusalem; so the Jebusites live with the people of Judah in Jerusalem to this day.

15.20–63: The towns of Judah. 20: This description was taken from an authentic source cataloging the administrative districts of the kingdom of Judah. The remainder of this list was used to portray Benjamin (18.21–28). 21–32: Districts are grouped and labeled geographically. This first district is in the *south* (v. 21; Heb., "the Negeb"). Each district concludes with an enumeration of *towns, with their villages* (v. 32). 33–44: Three districts are in the *lowland* (Heb., "Shephelah"). 45–47: This district of Philistine towns does not follow the pattern and was not part of the original source document. 48–60: Other districts are in the *hill country*. 61–62: One district is in the *wilderness*. 63: Jerusalem became part of Israel only under David (2 Sam 5.6–9).

16 The allotment of the Josephites went from the Jordan by Jericho, east of the waters of Jericho, into the wilderness, going up from Jericho into the hill country to Bethel; 2then going from Bethel to Luz, it passes along to Ataroth, the territory of the Archites; 3then it goes down westward to the territory of the Japhletites, as far as the territory of Lower Beth-horon, then to Gezer, and it ends at the sea.

4 The Josephites—Manasseh and Ephraim—received their inheritance.

5 The territory of the Ephraimites by their families was as follows: the boundary of their inheritance on the east was Ataroth-addar as far as Upper Beth-horon, 6and the boundary goes from there to the sea; on the north is Michmethath; then on the east the boundary makes a turn toward Taanath-shiloh, and passes along beyond it on the east to Janoah, 7then it goes down from Janoah to Ataroth and to Naarah, and touches Jericho, ending at the Jordan. 8From Tappuah the boundary goes westward to the Wadi Kanah, and ends at the sea. Such is the inheritance of the tribe of the Ephraimites by their families, 9together with the towns that were set apart for the Ephraimites within the inheritance of the Manassites, all those towns with their villages. 10They did not, however, drive out the Canaanites who lived in Gezer: so the Canaanites have lived within Ephraim to this day but have been made to do forced labor.

16.1–10: Ephraim. 1–3: As sons of Joseph, Ephraim and Manasseh together make up *the Josephites*. Their south boundary is also the north boundary of Benjamin (18.12–13). 5–9: Ephraim's north boundary is traced from its center point, first eastward and southward from *Michmethath* (vv. 6–7), then westward from nearby *Tappuah* (v. 8). 10: *Gezer* remained Canaanite until the reign of Solomon (1 Kings 9.16–17).

17 Then allotment was made to the tribe of Manasseh, for he was the firstborn of Joseph. To Machir the firstborn of Manasseh, the father of Gilead, were allotted Gilead and Bashan, because he was a warrior. 2And allotments were made to the rest of the tribe of Manasseh, by their families, Abiezer, Helek, Asriel, Shechem, Hepher, and Shemida; these were the male descendants of Manasseh son of Joseph, by their families.

3 Now Zelophehad son of Hepher son of Gilead son of Machir son of Manasseh had no sons, but only daughters; and these are the names of his daughters: Mahlah, Noah, Hoglah, Milcah, and Tirzah. 4They came before the priest Eleazar and Joshua son of Nun and the leaders, and said, "The LORD commanded Moses to give us an inheritance

along with our male kin." So according to the commandment of the LORD he gave them an inheritance among the kinsmen of their father. 5Thus there fell to Manasseh ten portions, besides the land of Gilead and Bashan, which is on the other side of the Jordan, 6because the daughters of Manasseh received an inheritance along with his sons. The land of Gilead was allotted to the rest of the Manassites.

7 The territory of Manasseh reached from Asher to Michmethath, which is east of Shechem; then the boundary goes along southward to the inhabitants of En-tappuah. 8The land of Tappuah belonged to Manasseh, but the town of Tappuah on the boundary of Manasseh belonged to the Ephraimites. 9Then the boundary went down to the Wadi Kanah. The towns here, to the south of the wadi, among the towns of Manasseh, belong to Ephraim. Then the boundary of Manasseh goes along the north side of the wadi and ends at the sea. 10The land to the south is Ephraim's and that to the north is Manasseh's, with the sea forming its boundary; on the north Asher is reached, and on the east Issachar. 11Within Issachar and Asher, Manasseh had Beth-shean and its villages, Ibleam and its villages, the inhabitants of Dor and its villages, the inhabitants of En-dor and its villages, the inhabitants of Taanach and its villages, and the inhabitants of Megiddo and its villages (the third is Naphath).*a* 12Yet the Manassites could not take possession of those towns; but the Canaanites continued to live in that land. 13But when the Israelites grew strong, they put the Canaanites to forced labor, but did not utterly drive them out.

17.1–13: Manasseh. 1: Elements of Manasseh tracing descent from *Machir* occupied territory east of the Jordan. 2: Six clans* traced descent through Manasseh's male heirs. 3–6: Five other clans descended from the female heirs of Manasseh, the daughters of *Zelophehad.* Joshua fulfills the command of Moses reported in Num 27.1–11. 7–9: The south boundary parallels Ephraim's north boundary (16.6, 8). 11–12: Idealized boundaries did not always match the reality of tribal affiliation (compare 16.9).

14 The tribe of Joseph spoke to Joshua, saying, "Why have you given me but one lot and one portion as an inheritance, since we are a numerous people, whom all along the LORD has blessed?" 15And Joshua said to them, "If you are a numerous people, go up to the forest, and clear ground there for yourselves in the land of the Perizzites and the Rephaim, since the hill country of Ephraim is too narrow for you." 16The tribe of Joseph said, "The hill country is not enough for us; yet all the Canaanites who live in the plain have chariots of iron, both those in Beth-shean and its villages and those in the Valley of Jezreel." 17Then Joshua said to the house of Joseph, to Ephraim and Manasseh, "You are indeed a numerous people, and have great power; you shall not have one lot only, 18but the hill country shall be yours, for though it is a forest, you shall clear it and possess it to its farthest borders; for you shall drive out the Canaanites, though they have chariots of iron, and though they are strong."

17.14–18: More territory for Joseph. 14–15: Ephraim and Manasseh together as *the tribe of Joseph* complain that they have too little land. Joshua points out that their size gives them the resources to clear the highland forests. 16: Unsatisfied, they go on to lament* that the military strength of the Canaanites keeps them from settling the plains. 17–18: The large population of Ephraim and Manasseh is actually not a problem, but an opportunity for an expansive future. In addition to clearing the forests, they will eventually *drive out the Canaanites.*

18 Then the whole congregation of the Israelites assembled at Shiloh, and set up the tent of meeting there. The land lay subdued before them.

2 There remained among the Israelites seven tribes whose inheritance had not yet been apportioned. 3So Joshua said to the Israelites, "How long will you be slack about going in and taking possession of the land that the LORD, the God of your ancestors, has given you? 4Provide three men from each tribe, and I will send them out that they

a Meaning of Heb uncertain

may begin to go throughout the land, writing a description of it with a view to their inheritances. Then come back to me. 5They shall divide it into seven portions, Judah continuing in its territory on the south, and the house of Joseph in their territory on the north. 6You shall describe the land in seven divisions and bring the description here to me; and I will cast lots for you here before the LORD our God. 7The Levites have no portion among you, for the priesthood of the LORD is their heritage; and Gad and Reuben and the half-tribe of Manasseh have received their inheritance beyond the Jordan eastward, which Moses the servant of the LORD gave them."

8 So the men started on their way; and Joshua charged those who went to write the description of the land, saying, "Go throughout the land and write a description of it, and come back to me; and I will cast lots for you here before the LORD in Shiloh." 9So the men went and traversed the land and set down in a book a description of it by towns in seven divisions; then they came back to Joshua in the camp at Shiloh, 10and Joshua cast lots for them in Shiloh before the LORD; and there Joshua apportioned the land to the Israelites, to each a portion.

18.1–10: Dividing the land into seven portions. 1: So far the process of dividing the land has taken place at Gilgal (14.6). Now it abruptly moves to the sanctuary of *Shiloh,* where the LORD is present in the *tent of meeting.* **4–5:** The remaining seven tribes will engage in a lottery for territory. In preparation, the land is divided into equitable allotments by a representative commission. **6:** The division is conducted fairly by sacred lot under the LORD's supervision (compare v. 10). **9:** The result of the commission's work is a document (NRSV: *book*) delineating the divisions *by towns.* This seems to describe the source used to create chs. 18–19, in which town lists play an important part.

11 The lot of the tribe of Benjamin according to its families came up, and the territory allotted to it fell between the tribe of Judah and the tribe of Joseph. 12On the north side their boundary began at the Jordan; then the boundary goes up to the slope of Jericho on the north, then up through the hill country westward; and it ends at the wilderness of Beth-aven. 13From there the boundary passes along southward in the direction of Luz, to the slope of Luz (that is, Bethel), then the boundary goes down to Ataroth-addar, on the mountain that lies south of Lower Beth-horon. 14Then the boundary goes in another direction, turning on the western side southward from the mountain that lies to the south, opposite Beth-horon, and it ends at Kiriath-baal (that is, Kiriath-jearim), a town belonging to the tribe of Judah. This forms the western side. 15The southern side begins at the outskirts of Kiriath-jearim; and the boundary goes from there to Ephron,ᵃ to the spring of the Waters of Nephtoah; 16then the boundary goes down to the border of the mountain that overlooks the valley of the son of Hinnom, which is at the north end of the valley of Rephaim; and it then goes down the valley of Hinnom, south of the slope of the Jebusites, and downward to En-rogel; 17then it bends in a northerly direction going on to En-shemesh, and from there goes to Geliloth, which is opposite the ascent of Adummim; then it goes down to the Stone of Bohan, Reuben's son; 18and passing on to the north of the slope of Beth-arabahᵇ it goes down to the Arabah; 19then the boundary passes on to the north of the slope of Beth-hoglah; and the boundary ends at the northern bay of the Dead Sea,ᶜ at the south end of the Jordan: this is the southern border. 20The Jordan forms its boundary on the eastern side. This is the inheritance of the tribe of Benjamin, according to its families, boundary by boundary all around.

21 Now the towns of the tribe of Benjamin according to their families were Jericho, Beth-hoglah, Emek-keziz, 22Beth-arabah, Zemaraim, Bethel, 23Avvim, Parah, Ophrah, 24Chephar-ammoni, Ophni, and Geba— twelve towns with their villages: 25Gibeon, Ramah, Beeroth, 26Mizpeh, Chephirah, Mozah, 27Rekem, Irpeel, Taralah, 28Zela, Haeleph, Jebusᵈ (that is, Jerusalem), Gib-

---

a Cn See 15.9. Heb *westward*   b Gk: Heb *to the slope over against the Arabah*   c Heb *Salt Sea*   d Gk Syr Vg: Heb *the Jebusite* eah*a* and Kiriath-jearim*b*—fourteen towns with their villages. This is the inheritance of the tribe of Benjamin according to its families.

18.11–28: The lot for Benjamin. 12–13: Its boundaries are described in a counter-clockwise direction (vv. 11–20). The north border parallels that of Ephraim (16.1–3). **15–19:** The south border parallels 15.5–9 (Judah's north border) but is given in the reverse direction (west to east). **21–24:** Benjamin's two districts come from the same source as those of Judah (15.21–62). Benjamin was split by the breakup of Israel after Solomon's death (1 Kings 12). This district describes towns located in the northern kingdom. **25–28:** This district consists of towns located in the kingdom of Judah.

19 The second lot came out for Simeon, for the tribe of Simeon, according to its families; its inheritance lay within the inheritance of the tribe of Judah. 2It had for its inheritance Beer-sheba, Sheba, Moladah, 3Hazar-shual, Balah, Ezem, 4Eltolad, Bethul, Hormah, 5Ziklag, Beth-marcaboth, Hazar-susah, 6Beth-lebaoth, and Sharuhen—thirteen towns with their villages; 7Ain, Rimmon, Ether, and Ashan—four towns with their villages; 8together with all the villages all around these towns as far as Baalath-beer, Ramah of the Negeb. This was the inheritance of the tribe of Simeon according to its families. 9The inheritance of the tribe of Simeon formed part of the territory of Judah; because the portion of the tribe of Judah was too large for them, the tribe of Simeon obtained an inheritance within their inheritance.

10 The third lot came up for the tribe of Zebulun, according to its families. The boundary of its inheritance reached as far as Sarid; 11then its boundary goes up westward, and on to Maralah, and touches Dabbesheth, then the wadi that is east of Jokneam; 12from Sarid it goes in the other direction eastward toward the sunrise to the boundary of Chisloth-tabor; from there it goes to Daberath, then up to Japhia; 13from there it passes along on the east toward the sunrise to Gath-hepher, to Eth-kazin, and going on to Rimmon it bends toward Neah; 14then on

the north the boundary makes a turn to Hannathon, and it ends at the valley of Iphtah-el; 15and Kattath, Nahalal, Shimron, Idalah, and Bethlehem—twelve towns with their villages. 16This is the inheritance of the tribe of Zebulun, according to its families—these towns with their villages.

17 The fourth lot came out for Issachar, for the tribe of Issachar, according to its families. 18Its territory included Jezreel, Chesulloth, Shunem, 19Hapharaim, Shion, Anaharath, 20Rabbith, Kishion, Ebez, 21Remeth, En-gannim, En-haddah, Beth-pazzez; 22the boundary also touches Tabor, Shahazumah, and Beth-shemesh, and its boundary ends at the Jordan—sixteen towns with their villages. 23This is the inheritance of the tribe of Issachar, according to its families—the towns with their villages.

24 The fifth lot came out for the tribe of Asher according to its families. 25Its boundary included Helkath, Hali, Beten, Achshaph, 26Allammelech, Amad, and Mishal; on the west it touches Carmel and Shihor-libnath, 27then it turns eastward, goes to Beth-dagon, and touches Zebulun and the valley of Iphtah-el northward to Beth-emek and Neiel; then it continues in the north to Cabul, 28Ebron, Rehob, Hammon, Kanah, as far as Great Sidon; 29then the boundary turns to Ramah, reaching to the fortified city of Tyre; then the boundary turns to Hosah, and it ends at the sea; Mahalab,*c* Achzib, 30Ummah, Aphek, and Rehob—twenty-two towns with their villages. 31This is the inheritance of the tribe of Asher according to its families—these towns with their villages.

32 The sixth lot came out for the tribe of Naphtali, for the tribe of Naphtali, according to its families. 33And its boundary ran from Heleph, from the oak in Zaanannim, and Adami-nekeb, and Jabneel, as far as Lakkum; and it ended at the Jordan; 34then the boundary turns westward to Aznoth-tabor, and goes from there to Hukkok, touching Zebulun at the south, and Asher on the west, and Judah on the east at the Jordan. 35The fortified towns are Ziddim, Zer, Hammath,

---

a Heb *Gibeath*   *b* Gk: Heb *Kiriath*   *c* Cn Compare Gk: Heb *Mehebel*

Rakkath, Chinnereth, 36Adamah, Ramah, Hazor, 37Kedesh, Edrei, En-hazor, 38Iron, Migdal-el, Horem, Beth-anath, and Beth-shemesh—nineteen towns with their villages. 39This is the inheritance of the tribe of Naphtali according to its families—the towns with their villages.

40 The seventh lot came out for the tribe of Dan, according to its families. 41The territory of its inheritance included Zorah, Eshtaol, Ir-shemesh, 42Shaalabbin, Aijalon, Ithlah, 43Elon, Timnah, Ekron, 44Eltekeh, Gibbethon, Baalath, 45Jehud, Bene-berak, Gath-rimmon, 46Me-jarkon, and Rakkon at the border opposite Joppa. 47When the territory of the Danites was lost to them, the Danites went up and fought against Leshem, and after capturing it and putting it to the sword, they took possession of it and settled in it, calling Leshem, Dan, after their ancestor Dan. 48This is the inheritance of the tribe of Dan, according to their families—these towns with their villages.

49 When they had finished distributing the several territories of the land as inheritances, the Israelites gave an inheritance among them to Joshua son of Nun. 50By command of the LORD they gave him the town that he asked for, Timnath-serah in the hill country of Ephraim; he rebuilt the town, and settled in it.

51 These are the inheritances that the priest Eleazar and Joshua son of Nun and the heads of the families of the tribes of the Israelites distributed by lot at Shiloh before the LORD, at the entrance of the tent of meeting. So they finished dividing the land.

19.1–51: The other six lots. 1–9: Because its territory lies inside that of Judah (vv. 1, 9), *Simeon* has no boundary description. Its towns are listed in two districts (vv. 2–6 and 7). **10–16:** For *Zebulun,* a detailed boundary description (vv. 10–14) is followed by a town list (v. 15). The south border is traced westward from Sarid (vv. 10–11), then eastward from the same town (v. 12). The east border is given in v. 13 and the north border in v. 14. **17–23:** *Issachar* is described by a town list (vv. 18–21) followed by a small portion of north boundary (v. 22). **24–31:** The boundary description for *Asher* is confusingly mingled with items from

a town list. **32–39:** The boundary description for *Naphtali* (vv. 33–34) is followed by a town list (vv. 35–38). **40–48:** *Dan* is described on the basis of a town list (vv. 41–46). Dan's move north to a new home is reported in Judges 18. **51:** *The priest Eleazar* cast the *lot* at the *tent of meeting,* which emphasizes that all was done in accordance with God's will.

20 Then the LORD spoke to Joshua, saying, 2"Say to the Israelites, 'Appoint the cities of refuge, of which I spoke to you through Moses, 3so that anyone who kills a person without intent or by mistake may flee there; they shall be for you a refuge from the avenger of blood. 4The slayer shall flee to one of these cities and shall stand at the entrance of the gate of the city, and explain the case to the elders of that city; then the fugitive shall be taken into the city, and given a place, and shall remain with them. 5And if the avenger of blood is in pursuit, they shall not give up the slayer, because the neighbor was killed by mistake, there having been no enmity between them before. 6The slayer shall remain in that city until there is a trial before the congregation, until the death of the one who is high priest at the time: then the slayer may return home, to the town in which the deed was done.' "

7 So they set apart Kedesh in Galilee in the hill country of Naphtali, and Shechem in the hill country of Ephraim, and Kiriath-arba (that is, Hebron) in the hill country of Judah. 8And beyond the Jordan east of Jericho, they appointed Bezer in the wilderness on the tableland, from the tribe of Reuben, and Ramoth in Gilead, from the tribe of Gad, and Golan in Bashan, from the tribe of Manasseh. 9These were the cities designated for all the Israelites, and for the aliens residing among them, that anyone who killed a person without intent could flee there, so as not to die by the hand of the avenger of blood, until there was a trial before the congregation.

20.1–9: Cities of refuge. 2–3: Murders were avenged by a near relative of the victim, the *avenger of blood* (see v. 5). Easily accessible *cities of refuge* prevented any miscarriage of justice in cases of unintentional manslaughter (Num 35.13–28; Deut 19.1–13). **7–8:**

Cities are designated for six regions, three on each side of the Jordan.

~~~~~~~~~~~~~~~~~~~~~~~~~~~~~~~~~~

21 Then the heads of the families of the Levites came to the priest Eleazar and to Joshua son of Nun and to the heads of the families of the tribes of the Israelites; 2they said to them at Shiloh in the land of Canaan, "The LORD commanded through Moses that we be given towns to live in, along with their pasture lands for our livestock." 3So by command of the LORD the Israelites gave to the Levites the following towns and pasture lands out of their inheritance.

4 The lot came out for the families of the Kohathites. So those Levites who were descendants of Aaron the priest received by lot thirteen towns from the tribes of Judah, Simeon, and Benjamin.

5 The rest of the Kohathites received by lot ten towns from the families of the tribe of Ephraim, from the tribe of Dan, and the half-tribe of Manasseh.

6 The Gershonites received by lot thirteen towns from the families of the tribe of Issachar, from the tribe of Asher, from the tribe of Naphtali, and from the half-tribe of Manasseh in Bashan.

7 The Merarites according to their families received twelve towns from the tribe of Reuben, the tribe of Gad, and the tribe of Zebulun.

8 These towns and their pasture lands the Israelites gave by lot to the Levites, as the LORD had commanded through Moses.

9 Out of the tribe of Judah and the tribe of Simeon they gave the following towns mentioned by name, 10which went to the descendants of Aaron, one of the families of the Kohathites who belonged to the Levites, since the lot fell to them first. 11They gave them Kiriath-arba (Arba being the father of Anak), that is Hebron, in the hill country of Judah, along with the pasture lands around it. 12But the fields of the town and its villages had been given to Caleb son of Jephunneh as his holding.

13 To the descendants of Aaron the priest they gave Hebron, the city of refuge for the slayer, with its pasture lands, Libnah with its pasture lands, 14Jattir with its pasture lands, Eshtemoa with its pasture lands, 15Holon with its pasture lands, Debir with its pasture lands, 16Ain with its pasture lands, Juttah with its pasture lands, and Beth-shemesh with its pasture lands—nine towns out of these two tribes. 17Out of the tribe of Benjamin: Gibeon with its pasture lands, Geba with its pasture lands, 18Anathoth with its pasture lands, and Almon with its pasture lands—four towns. 19The towns of the descendants of Aaron—the priests—were thirteen in all, with their pasture lands.

20 As to the rest of the Kohathites belonging to the Kohathite families of the Levites, the towns allotted to them were out of the tribe of Ephraim. 21To them were given Shechem, the city of refuge for the slayer, with its pasture lands in the hill country of Ephraim, Gezer with its pasture lands, 22Kibzaim with its pasture lands, and Beth-horon with its pasture lands—four towns. 23Out of the tribe of Dan: Elteke with its pasture lands, Gibbethon with its pasture lands, 24Aijalon with its pasture lands, Gath-rimmon with its pasture lands—four towns. 25Out of the half-tribe of Manasseh: Taanach with its pasture lands, and Gath-rimmon with its pasture lands—two towns. 26The towns of the families of the rest of the Kohathites were ten in all, with their pasture lands.

27 To the Gershonites, one of the families of the Levites, were given out of the half-tribe of Manasseh, Golan in Bashan with its pasture lands, the city of refuge for the slayer, and Beeshterah with its pasture lands—two towns. 28Out of the tribe of Issachar: Kishion with its pasture lands, Daberath with its pasture lands, 29Jarmuth with its pasture lands, En-gannim with its pasture lands—four towns. 30Out of the tribe of Asher: Mishal with its pasture lands, Abdon with its pasture lands, 31Helkath with its pasture lands, and Rehob with its pasture lands—four towns. 32Out of the tribe of Naphtali: Kedesh in Galilee with its pasture lands, the city of refuge for the slayer, Hammoth-dor with its pasture lands, and Kartan with its pasture lands— three towns. 33The towns of the several families of the Gershonites were in all thirteen, with their pasture lands.

34 To the rest of the Levites—the Mera-rite families—were given out of the tribe of Zebulun: Jokneam with its pasture lands, Kartah with its pasture lands, ³⁵Dimnah with its pasture lands, Nahalal with its pasture lands—four towns. ³⁶Out of the tribe of Reuben: Bezer with its pasture lands, Jahzah with its pasture lands, ³⁷Kedemoth with its pasture lands, and Mephaath with its pasture lands—four towns. ³⁸Out of the tribe of Gad: Ramoth in Gilead with its pasture lands, the city of refuge for the slayer, Mahanaim with its pasture lands, ³⁹Heshbon with its pasture lands, Jazer with its pasture lands—four towns in all. ⁴⁰As for the towns of the several Merarite families, that is, the remainder of the families of the Levites, those allotted to them were twelve in all.

41 The towns of the Levites within the holdings of the Israelites were in all forty-eight towns with their pasture lands. ⁴²Each of these towns had its pasture lands around it; so it was with all these towns.

43 Thus the LORD gave to Israel all the land that he swore to their ancestors that he would give them; and having taken possession of it, they settled there. ⁴⁴And the LORD gave them rest on every side just as he had sworn to their ancestors; not one of all their enemies had withstood them, for the LORD had given all their enemies into their hands. ⁴⁵Not one of all the good promises that the LORD had made to the house of Israel had failed; all came to pass.

21.1–45. 1–42: Cities for the Levites. 2: Although Levi receives no allotment for agriculture, the tribe is assigned residence towns and grazing land. For this command, see Num 35.2–8. **4–7:** The levitical cities appear in four divisions. Levi was divided into three clans,* and the *Kohathites* were further subdivided into the *descendants of Aaron* (v. 4; the priests) and those not of priestly descent. **13–19:** The thirteen towns for *the descendants of Aaron* reflect an older source list. The other three lists were created by collecting names from Joshua 13, 16–17, 19, and 20. **32:** Because the source list (vv. 13–19) contained thirteen towns, *Naphtali* contributes only *three towns* instead of the usual four in order to achieve the ideal total of forty-eight (v. 41). **43–45:** All has been achieved (v. 43) and all promises fulfilled (v. 45). *Rest on every side* (v. 44) means war has been replaced by peace (1.13, 15; 22.4).

~~~~~~~~~~~~~~~~

22 Then Joshua summoned the Reubenites, the Gadites, and the half-tribe of Manasseh, ²and said to them, "You have observed all that Moses the servant of the LORD commanded you, and have obeyed me in all that I have commanded you; ³you have not forsaken your kindred these many days, down to this day, but have been careful to keep the charge of the LORD your God. ⁴And now the LORD your God has given rest to your kindred, as he promised them; therefore turn and go to your tents in the land where your possession lies, which Moses the servant of the LORD gave you on the other side of the Jordan. ⁵Take good care to observe the commandment and instruction that Moses the servant of the LORD commanded you, to love the LORD your God, to walk in all his ways, to keep his commandments, and to hold fast to him, and to serve him with all your heart and with all your soul." ⁶So Joshua blessed them and sent them away, and they went to their tents.

7 Now to the one half of the tribe of Manasseh Moses had given a possession in Bashan; but to the other half Joshua had given a possession beside their fellow Israelites in the land west of the Jordan. And when Joshua sent them away to their tents and blessed them, ⁸he said to them, "Go back to your tents with much wealth, and with very much livestock, with silver, gold, bronze, and iron, and with a great quantity of clothing; divide the spoil of your enemies with your kindred." ⁹So the Reubenites and the Gadites and the half-tribe of Manasseh returned home, parting from the Israelites at Shiloh, which is in the land of Canaan, to go to the land of Gilead, their own land of which they had taken possession by command of the LORD through Moses.

22.1–9: The eastern tribes return home. 4: Because *rest* has been achieved (21.44), the commitments made in 1.13, 15 can now be fulfilled. *Go to your tents* reflects traditional language for the dispersal of the national assembly (1 Kings 12.16) or tribal militia. **7:** Manasseh's situation is unique, with territory both east and west of the Jordan. **8:** Sharing out the *spoil* of conquest corresponds to Israel's traditional custom (1 Sam 30.21–25).

~~~~~~~~~~~~~~~~~~~~

10 When they came to the region*a* near the Jordan that lies in the land of Canaan, the Reubenites and the Gadites and the half-tribe of Manasseh built there an altar by the Jordan, an altar of great size. 11The Israelites heard that the Reubenites and the Gadites and the half-tribe of Manasseh had built an altar at the frontier of the land of Canaan, in the region*b* near the Jordan, on the side that belongs to the Israelites. 12And when the people of Israel heard of it, the whole assembly of the Israelites gathered at Shiloh, to make war against them.

13 Then the Israelites sent the priest Phinehas son of Eleazar to the Reubenites and the Gadites and the half-tribe of Manasseh, in the land of Gilead, 14and with him ten chiefs, one from each of the tribal families of Israel, every one of them the head of a family among the clans of Israel. 15They came to the Reubenites, the Gadites, and the half-tribe of Manasseh, in the land of Gilead, and they said to them, 16"Thus says the whole congregation of the LORD, 'What is this treachery that you have committed against the God of Israel in turning away today from following the LORD, by building yourselves an altar today in rebellion against the LORD? 17Have we not had enough of the sin at Peor from which even yet we have not cleansed ourselves, and for which a plague came upon the congregation of the LORD, 18that you must turn away today from following the LORD! If you rebel against the LORD today, he will be angry with the whole congregation of Israel tomorrow. 19But now, if your land is unclean, cross over into the LORD's land where the LORD's tabernacle now stands, and take for yourselves a possession among us; only do not rebel against the LORD, or rebel against us*c* by building yourselves an altar other than the altar of the LORD our God. 20Did not Achan son of Zerah break faith in the matter of the devoted things, and wrath fell upon all the congregation of Israel? And he did not perish alone for his iniquity!' "

21 Then the Reubenites, the Gadites, and the half-tribe of Manasseh said in answer to the heads of the families of Israel, 22"The LORD, God of gods! The LORD, God of gods! He knows; and let Israel itself know! If it was in rebellion or in breach of faith toward the LORD, do not spare us today 23for building an altar to turn away from following the LORD; or if we did so to offer burnt offerings or grain offerings or offerings of well-being on it, may the LORD himself take vengeance. 24No! We did it from fear that in time to come your children might say to our children, 'What have you to do with the LORD, the God of Israel? 25For the LORD has made the Jordan a boundary between us and you, you Reubenites and Gadites; you have no portion in the LORD.' So your children might make our children cease to worship the LORD. 26Therefore we said, 'Let us now build an altar, not for burnt offering, nor for sacrifice, 27but to be a witness between us and you, and between the generations after us, that we do perform the service of the LORD in his presence with our burnt offerings and sacrifices and offerings of well-being; so that your children may never say to our children in time to come, "You have no portion in the LORD." ' 28And we thought, If this should be said to us or to our descendants in time to come, we could say, 'Look at this copy of the altar of the LORD, which our ancestors made, not for burnt offerings, nor for sacrifice, but to be a witness between us and you.' 29Far be it from us that we should rebel against the LORD, and turn away this day from following the LORD by building an altar for burnt offering, grain offering, or sacrifice, other than the altar of the LORD our God that stands before his tabernacle!"

30 When the priest Phinehas and the chiefs of the congregation, the heads of the families of Israel who were with him, heard the words that the Reubenites and the Gadites and the Manassites spoke, they were satisfied. 31The priest Phinehas son of Eleazar said to the Reubenites and the Gadites and

a Or *to Geliloth*   *b* Or *at Geliloth*   *c* Or *make rebels of us*

the Manassites, "Today we know that the LORD is among us, because you have not committed this treachery against the LORD; now you have saved the Israelites from the hand of the LORD."

32 Then the priest Phinehas son of Eleazar and the chiefs returned from the Reubenites and the Gadites in the land of Gilead to the land of Canaan, to the Israelites, and brought back word to them. 33The report pleased the Israelites; and the Israelites blessed God and spoke no more of making war against them, to destroy the land where the Reubenites and the Gadites were settled. 34The Reubenites and the Gadites called the altar Witness;*a* "For," said they, "it is a witness between us that the LORD is God."

22.10–34: The altar of witness. 10: The story presupposes that only one altar for sacrifice is permissible. Dissension focuses on whether this *altar by the Jordan* is evidence of apostasy (vv. 16–20) or actually a token of loyalty (vv. 22–29). Its *great size* relates to its intended function as a visible witness (vv. 27–28, 34). 12: The story is told from the perspective of the western tribes, describing them as *the Israelites* to the exclusion of the eastern tribes (also vv. 32, 33). 17: The incident at *Peor* is reported in Num 25. 18: The principle of collective responsibility means the whole nation is endangered by the rebellion of some (compare v. 20). 19: Territory outside of Canaan might be ritually *unclean,* a place where loyalty to the LORD would be impossible. 22: The eastern tribes begin with a confessional exclamation (compare 1 Kings 18.39) and a hypothetical self-condemnation that asserts their fidelity in the strongest terms. 27: The eastern tribes repeatedly cite lists of sacrifices (vv. 23, 26, 29) to deny that they intend to offer them at the newly built altar. Here they use a similar catalog to affirm their loyalty. 28: The altar's purpose is finally revealed. It is only a *copy,* a replica pointing to loyal service at the legitimate altar at Shiloh. 34: The altar's name does not appear in the Hebrew text (note *a*). What is important is its function as a *witness between us,* that is, between the eastern and western tribes.

23 A long time afterward, when the LORD had given rest to Israel from all their enemies all around, and Joshua was old and well advanced in years, 2Joshua summoned all Israel, their elders and heads,

their judges and officers, and said to them, "I am now old and well advanced in years; 3and you have seen all that the LORD your God has done to all these nations for your sake, for it is the LORD your God who has fought for you. 4I have allotted to you as an inheritance for your tribes those nations that remain, along with all the nations that I have already cut off, from the Jordan to the Great Sea in the west. 5The LORD your God will push them back before you, and drive them out of your sight; and you shall possess their land, as the LORD your God promised you. 6Therefore be very steadfast to observe and do all that is written in the book of the law of Moses, turning aside from it neither to the right nor to the left, 7so that you may not be mixed with these nations left here among you, or make mention of the names of their gods, or swear by them, or serve them, or bow yourselves down to them, 8but hold fast to the LORD your God, as you have done to this day. 9For the LORD has driven out before you great and strong nations; and as for you, no one has been able to withstand you to this day. 10One of you puts to flight a thousand, since it is the LORD your God who fights for you, as he promised you. 11Be very careful, therefore, to love the LORD your God. 12For if you turn back, and join the survivors of these nations left here among you, and intermarry with them, so that you marry their women and they yours, 13know assuredly that the LORD your God will not continue to drive out these nations before you; but they shall be a snare and a trap for you, a scourge on your sides, and thorns in your eyes, until you perish from this good land that the LORD your God has given you.

14 "And now I am about to go the way of all the earth, and you know in your hearts and souls, all of you, that not one thing has failed of all the good things that the LORD your God promised concerning you; all have come to pass for you, not one of them has failed. 15But just as all the good things that the LORD your God promised concerning you have been fulfilled for you, so the LORD

a Cn Compare Syr: Heb lacks *Witness*

will bring upon you all the bad things, until he has destroyed you from this good land that the LORD your God has given you. 16If you transgress the covenant of the LORD your God, which he enjoined on you, and go and serve other gods and bow down to them, then the anger of the LORD will be kindled against you, and you shall perish quickly from the good land that he has given to you."

23.1–16: Joshua's farewell. 1: Joshua's great age (13.1) motivates an exhortation* to faithfulness and a warning about the future. *Rest* signals the end of the conquest (21.44; 22.4). **4:** In spite of many victories, some enemy nations still *remain.* They represent both opportunities for further success (v. 5) and dangerous enticements to infidelity (vv. 7, 12–13). **6:** Future success requires that the whole nation show the same undeviating obedience to *the book of the law* (Deuteronomy) that was enjoined on Joshua in 1.7–8. **12:** Intermarriage would establish complex relationships between families resulting in religious disloyalty (Deut 7.3–4). **13:** The metaphors* of *a snare and a trap* signify loss of freedom, and *a scourge* communicates political oppression (1 Kings 12.11). Exile *from this good land* is threatened three times (vv. 13, 15, 16). **14–15:** The LORD has been trustworthy in keeping past promises (see 21.45), but this means that the LORD's threatened punishments are equally certain to take place.

24 Then Joshua gathered all the tribes of Israel to Shechem, and summoned the elders, the heads, the judges, and the officers of Israel; and they presented themselves before God. 2And Joshua said to all the people, "Thus says the LORD, the God of Israel: Long ago your ancestors—Terah and his sons Abraham and Nahor—lived beyond the Euphrates and served other gods. 3Then I took your father Abraham from beyond the River and led him through all the land of Canaan and made his offspring many. I gave him Isaac; 4and to Isaac I gave Jacob and Esau. I gave Esau the hill country of Seir to possess, but Jacob and his children went down to Egypt. 5Then I sent Moses and Aaron, and I plagued Egypt with what I did in its midst; and afterwards I brought you out. 6When I brought your ancestors out of Egypt, you came to the sea; and the Egyptians pursued your ancestors with chariots

and horsemen to the Red Sea.*a* 7When they cried out to the LORD, he put darkness between you and the Egyptians, and made the sea come upon them and cover them; and your eyes saw what I did to Egypt. Afterwards you lived in the wilderness a long time. 8Then I brought you to the land of the Amorites, who lived on the other side of the Jordan; they fought with you, and I handed them over to you, and you took possession of their land, and I destroyed them before you. 9Then King Balak son of Zippor of Moab, set out to fight against Israel. He sent and invited Balaam son of Beor to curse you, 10but I would not listen to Balaam; therefore he blessed you; so I rescued you out of his hand. 11When you went over the Jordan and came to Jericho, the citizens of Jericho fought against you, and also the Amorites, the Perizzites, the Canaanites, the Hittites, the Girgashites, the Hivites, and the Jebusites; and I handed them over to you. 12I sent the hornet*b* ahead of you, which drove out before you the two kings of the Amorites; it was not by your sword or by your bow. 13I gave you a land on which you had not labored, and towns that you had not built, and you live in them; you eat the fruit of vineyards and olive-yards that you did not plant.

24.1–13: The saving acts of God. 1: A long list of participants emphasizes that *all the tribes of Israel* appeared *before God,* that is, at the sanctuary of *Shechem.* **2:** *Thus says the LORD* indicates that Joshua is speaking as a prophet.* **3:** The *River* is the Euphrates. **7:** This protective *darkness* is mentioned in Ex 14.20. **9–10:** The story of Balaam is reported in Num 22–24. **11:** The detail that *the citizens of Jericho fought* relies on a tradition different from that of Joshua 6. **12:** *Hornet* (note *b;* Deut 7.20) may be a metaphor* for panic (compare 10.10). **13:** This description of the land reflects Deut 6.10–11.

14 "Now therefore revere the LORD, and serve him in sincerity and in faithfulness; put away the gods that your ancestors served beyond the River and in Egypt, and serve the LORD. 15Now if you are unwilling to serve the LORD, choose this day whom you will

a Or *Sea of Reeds*   *b* Meaning of Heb uncertain

serve, whether the gods your ancestors served in the region beyond the River or the gods of the Amorites in whose land you are living; but as for me and my household, we will serve the LORD."

16 Then the people answered, "Far be it from us that we should forsake the LORD to serve other gods; 17for it is the LORD our God who brought us and our ancestors up from the land of Egypt, out of the house of slavery, and who did those great signs in our sight. He protected us along all the way that we went, and among all the peoples through whom we passed; 18and the LORD drove out before us all the peoples, the Amorites who lived in the land. Therefore we also will serve the LORD, for he is our God."

19 But Joshua said to the people, "You cannot serve the LORD, for he is a holy God. He is a jealous God; he will not forgive your transgressions or your sins. 20If you forsake the LORD and serve foreign gods, then he will turn and do you harm, and consume you, after having done you good." 21And the people said to Joshua, "No, we will serve the LORD!" 22Then Joshua said to the people, "You are witnesses against yourselves that you have chosen the LORD, to serve him." And they said, "We are witnesses." 23He said, "Then put away the foreign gods that are among you, and incline your hearts to the LORD, the God of Israel." 24The people said to Joshua, "The LORD our God we will serve, and him we will obey." 25So Joshua made a covenant with the people that day, and made statutes and ordinances for them at Shechem. 26Joshua wrote these words in the book of the law of God; and he took a large stone, and set it up there under the oak in the sanctuary of the LORD. 27Joshua said to all the people, "See, this stone shall be a witness against us; for it has heard all the words of the LORD that he spoke to us; therefore it shall be a witness against you, if you deal falsely with your God." 28So Joshua sent the people away to their inheritances.

24.14–28: Joshua insists on religious fidelity. 14–15: Three types of gods had proven to be ineffective. Abraham was taken away from the territory of the *gods beyond the River* (v. 3), and the gods of *Egypt* and of

the Amorites could not protect their worshippers (vv. 5–7 and 8–13). **19–20:** With a rhetorical* jolt, Joshua warns Israel of the difficulties and dangers implicit in their commitment: *You cannot serve the LORD.* The obstacle is God's basic nature as a *jealous God,* one who is passionately determined to be Israel's only God. **23:** *Incline your heart* calls for personal conviction, not just outward conformity (1 Kings 8.58). The demand to *put away the foreign gods* may reflect a ceremony of burying idols at Shechem (compare Gen 35.2–4). **25–26:** Joshua performed three actions to give structure and effectiveness to Israel's commitment: He *made a covenant,** wrote down its rules in *the book of the law,* and set up a witness stone *under the oak* (see Judg 9.6). **27:** The stone is a witness in the sense of being a visible public reminder (compare 22.27, 34), but also because it was present when *all the words of the LORD* (that is, vv. 2–13) were proclaimed.

29 After these things Joshua son of Nun, the servant of the LORD, died, being one hundred ten years old. 30They buried him in his own inheritance at Timnath-serah, which is in the hill country of Ephraim, north of Mount Gaash.

31 Israel served the LORD all the days of Joshua, and all the days of the elders who outlived Joshua and had known all the work that the LORD did for Israel.

32 The bones of Joseph, which the Israelites had brought up from Egypt, were buried at Shechem, in the portion of ground that Jacob had bought from the children of Hamor, the father of Shechem, for one hundred pieces of money;[a] it became an inheritance of the descendants of Joseph.

33 Eleazar son of Aaron died; and they buried him at Gibeah, the town of his son Phinehas, which had been given him in the hill country of Ephraim.

24.29–33: Burial traditions. 29–30: Great age is a sign of exceptional faithfulness (Gen 50.26; Deut 34.7). *Timnath-serah* was granted to Joshua in 19.49–50. **31:** This looks forward to the book of Judges (compare Judg 2.9). **32:** These traditions are reported in Gen 33.18–20; 50.24–25; Ex 13.19. **33:** *Eleazar* has played an important role in Joshua (14.1; 17.4; 19.51; 21.1).

a Heb *one hundred qesitah*

JUDGES

Introduction

Judges continues the story of the Deuteronomistic* History (see the introduction to Joshua) from the death of Joshua (Judg 2.8) to just before the birth of Samuel (1 Sam 1). After an incomplete conquest that leaves much in the hands of Israel's foes (ch. 1), Israel's life in the land follows a recurring pattern of disloyalty to God followed by oppression by enemies. When Israel cries out in repentance, the LORD sends deliverers (judges). Most of these judges are military leaders (chs. 2–12). In contrast, the judge Samson is a solitary champion (chs. 13–16). Finally Israel is described as descending into idolatry,* violence, and civil war, as a result of not yet having a king (chs. 17–21). The stories of the six judges were originally individual tales of local heroes, but were gathered together and converted into a succession of leaders of national importance. Judges illustrates the principle that disloyalty to God leads to national catastrophe, while repentance and obedience can lead to deliverance.

Israel's hold on the land of promise was often insecure. The two kingdoms that made up Israel eventually collapsed (2 Kings 17, 24, 25), and many inhabitants were taken into exile. Judges is one answer to what went wrong. Israel had not always been loyal to God, and this tendency for disobedience began early. Yet the cyclical pattern of Judges also offered hope in times of national distress. To cry to the LORD might once again lead to deliverance.

READING GUIDE

Judges may be read theologically as a cautionary tale about disloyalty to God and its consequences. It can also be enjoyed as great literature about improbable heroes. The reader might choose to compare the characters' contrasting personality traits as revealed by their words and actions. Readers may also wish to explore issues of oppression and patriarchal power by comparing the dreadful stories about Jephthah's daughter (11.29–40), the Levite's concubine* (ch. 19), and the efforts made to get replacement wives for the decimated tribe of Benjamin (ch. 21).

1	Incomplete conquest
2–12	The cycle of the judges
13–16	Samson the lone hero
17–21	Disorder and infidelity

1 After the death of Joshua, the Israelites inquired of the LORD, "Who shall go up first for us against the Canaanites, to fight against them?" ²The LORD said, "Judah shall go up. I hereby give the land into his hand." ³Judah said to his brother Simeon, "Come up with me into the territory allotted to me, that we may fight against the Canaanites; then I too will go with you into the territory allotted to you." So Simeon went with him. ⁴Then Judah went up and the LORD gave the Canaanites and the Perizzites into their hand; and they defeated ten thousand of them at Bezek. ⁵They came upon Adoni-bezek at Bezek, and fought against him, and defeated the Canaanites and the Perizzites. ⁶Adoni-bezek fled; but they pursued him, and caught him, and cut off his thumbs and big toes. ⁷Adoni-bezek said, "Seventy kings with their thumbs and big toes cut off used to pick up scraps under my table; as I have done, so God has paid me

back." They brought him to Jerusalem, and he died there.

8 Then the people of Judah fought against Jerusalem and took it. They put it to the sword and set the city on fire. 9Afterward the people of Judah went down to fight against the Canaanites who lived in the hill country, in the Negeb, and in the lowland. 10Judah went against the Canaanites who lived in Hebron (the name of Hebron was formerly Kiriath-arba); and they defeated Sheshai and Ahiman and Talmai.

11 From there they went against the inhabitants of Debir (the name of Debir was formerly Kiriath-sepher). 12Then Caleb said, "Whoever attacks Kiriath-sepher and takes it, I will give him my daughter Achsah as wife." 13And Othniel son of Kenaz, Caleb's younger brother, took it; and he gave him his daughter Achsah as wife. 14When she came to him, she urged him to ask her father for a field. As she dismounted from her donkey, Caleb said to her, "What do you wish?" 15She said to him, "Give me a present; since you have set me in the land of the Negeb, give me also Gulloth-mayim."*a* So Caleb gave her Upper Gulloth and Lower Gulloth.

16 The descendants of Hobab*b* the Kenite, Moses' father-in-law, went up with the people of Judah from the city of palms into the wilderness of Judah, which lies in the Negeb near Arad. Then they went and settled with the Amalekites.*c* 17Judah went with his brother Simeon, and they defeated the Canaanites who inhabited Zephath, and devoted it to destruction. So the city was called Hormah. 18Judah took Gaza with its territory, Ashkelon with its territory, and Ekron with its territory. 19The LORD was with Judah, and he took possession of the hill country, but could not drive out the inhabitants of the plain, because they had chariots of iron. 20Hebron was given to Caleb, as Moses had said; and he drove out from it the three sons of Anak. 21But the Benjaminites did not drive out the Jebusites who lived in Jerusalem; so the Jebusites have lived in Jerusalem among the Benjaminites to this day.

1.1–21: Successful conquests by Judah and Simeon. 1: In contrast to the complete conquest described in Joshua (Josh 11.23; 21.43–45), Judg 1 portrays an ongoing conquest that continued *after the death of Joshua*. **2:** Judah's successes contrast with the comparative failures of the northern tribes (vv. 22–36). Divine guidance in tactics and an assurance of victory were elements of holy war* tradition. **3:** The tribes *Judah* and *Simeon* are personified as individuals. **8:** This assertion is in tension with v. 21. Jerusalem first became Israelite under David (2 Sam 5.6–9). **10:** These accomplishments are credited to Caleb in v. 20 (and Josh 15.14). **11–15:** The story of Achsah is duplicated in Josh 15.13–19. She argues that she needs pools (note *a*) because she has received arid land (metaphorically,* *land of the Negeb*). **16:** The Kenites were a foreign group associated with Israel (5.24; 1 Sam 15.6). They *settled* with the "people" Israel (the better reading, note *c*). **17:** *Hormah* is a wordplay on the Hebrew word "herem," the holy war ban* inflicted on it when Judah and Simeon *devoted it to destruction*. **19:** *Chariots* with *iron* fittings gave battlefield superiority outside the broken terrain of *the hill country*. **21:** Native *Jebusites* remained a distinct group in *Jerusalem* even after David's capture of the city (2 Sam 24.18).

22 The house of Joseph also went up against Bethel; and the LORD was with them. 23The house of Joseph sent out spies to Bethel (the name of the city was formerly Luz). 24When the spies saw a man coming out of the city, they said to him, "Show us the way into the city, and we will deal kindly with you." 25So he showed them the way into the city; and they put the city to the sword, but they let the man and all his family go. 26So the man went to the land of the Hittites and built a city, and named it Luz; that is its name to this day.

27 Manasseh did not drive out the inhabitants of Beth-shean and its villages, or Taanach and its villages, or the inhabitants of Dor and its villages, or the inhabitants of Ibleam and its villages, or the inhabitants of Megiddo and its villages; but the Canaanites continued to live in that land. 28When Israel grew strong, they put the Canaanites to forced labor, but did not in fact drive them out.

29 And Ephraim did not drive out the

a That is *Basins of Water*   *b* Gk: Heb lacks *Hobab*
c See 1 Sam 15.6: Heb *people*

Canaanites who lived in Gezer; but the Canaanites lived among them in Gezer.

30 Zebulun did not drive out the inhabitants of Kitron, or the inhabitants of Nahalol; but the Canaanites lived among them, and became subject to forced labor.

31 Asher did not drive out the inhabitants of Acco, or the inhabitants of Sidon, or of Ahlab, or of Achzib, or of Helbah, or of Aphik, or of Rehob; 32 but the Asherites lived among the Canaanites, the inhabitants of the land; for they did not drive them out.

33 Naphtali did not drive out the inhabitants of Beth-shemesh, or the inhabitants of Beth-anath, but lived among the Canaanites, the inhabitants of the land; nevertheless the inhabitants of Beth-shemesh and of Beth-anath became subject to forced labor for them.

34 The Amorites pressed the Danites back into the hill country; they did not allow them to come down to the plain. 35 The Amorites continued to live in Har-heres, in Aijalon, and in Shaalbim, but the hand of the house of Joseph rested heavily on them, and they became subject to forced labor. 36 The border of the Amorites ran from the ascent of Akrabbim, from Sela and upward.

1.22–36: Failures of the northern tribes. 22–26: The capture of Bethel is the only success reported. **27–29:** This information is duplicated in Josh 16.10; 17.11–13. These cities did not become part of Israel until the reigns of David and Solomon. **34:** For the saga of the *Danites,* see Judg 18.

2 Now the angel of the LORD went up from Gilgal to Bochim, and said, "I brought you up from Egypt, and brought you into the land that I had promised to your ancestors. I said, 'I will never break my covenant with you. 2 For your part, do not make a covenant with the inhabitants of this land; tear down their altars.' But you have not obeyed my command. See what you have done! 3 So now I say, I will not drive them out before you; but they shall become adversaries*a* to you, and their gods shall be a snare to you." 4 When the angel of the LORD spoke these words to all the Israelites, the people lifted up their voices and wept. 5 So they

named that place Bochim,*b* and there they sacrificed to the LORD.

2.1–5: The angel of the LORD appears. 1: *The angel of the LORD* is a manifestation by which the LORD appears directly to humans (6.11; 13.3). The Hebrew word "mal'ak" can also be translated "messenger." *Gilgal,* Joshua's former headquarters, abruptly reappears without explanation. **2–3:** Because Israel has failed to keep aloof from the native population (Ex 34.12–13; Deut 7.2, 5), the LORD has implemented the punishment anticipated in Josh 23.13. **5:** This tradition originally explained the name of a sanctuary (note *b*).

6 When Joshua dismissed the people, the Israelites all went to their own inheritances to take possession of the land. 7 The people worshiped the LORD all the days of Joshua, and all the days of the elders who outlived Joshua, who had seen all the great work that the LORD had done for Israel. 8 Joshua son of Nun, the servant of the LORD, died at the age of one hundred ten years. 9 So they buried him within the bounds of his inheritance in Timnath-heres, in the hill country of Ephraim, north of Mount Gaash. 10 Moreover, that whole generation was gathered to their ancestors, and another generation grew up after them, who did not know the LORD or the work that he had done for Israel.

11 Then the Israelites did what was evil in the sight of the LORD and worshiped the Baals; 12 and they abandoned the LORD, the God of their ancestors, who had brought them out of the land of Egypt; they followed other gods, from among the gods of the peoples who were all around them, and bowed down to them; and they provoked the LORD to anger. 13 They abandoned the LORD, and worshiped Baal and the Astartes. 14 So the anger of the LORD was kindled against Israel, and he gave them over to plunderers who plundered them, and he sold them into the power of their enemies all around, so that they could no longer withstand their enemies. 15 Whenever they marched out, the hand of the LORD was against them to bring misfortune, as the LORD had warned them

a OL Vg Compare Gk: Heb *sides*   *b* That is *Weepers*

and sworn to them; and they were in great distress. 16 Then the LORD raised up judges, who delivered them out of the power of those who plundered them. [17]Yet they did not listen even to their judges; for they lusted after other gods and bowed down to them. They soon turned aside from the way in which their ancestors had walked, who had obeyed the commandments of the LORD; they did not follow their example. [18]Whenever the LORD raised up judges for them, the LORD was with the judge, and he delivered them from the hand of their enemies all the days of the judge; for the LORD would be moved to pity by their groaning because of those who persecuted and oppressed them. [19]But whenever the judge died, they would relapse and behave worse than their ancestors, following other gods, worshiping them and bowing down to them. They would not drop any of their practices or their stubborn ways. [20]So the anger of the LORD was kindled against Israel; and he said, "Because this people have transgressed my covenant that I commanded their ancestors, and have not obeyed my voice, [21]I will no longer drive out before them any of the nations that Joshua left when he died." [22]In order to test Israel, whether or not they would take care to walk in the way of the LORD as their ancestors did, [23]the LORD had left those nations, not driving them out at once, and had not handed them over to Joshua.

3 Now these are the nations that the LORD left to test all those in Israel who had no experience of any war in Canaan [2](it was only that successive generations of Israelites might know war, to teach those who had no experience of it before): [3]the five lords of the Philistines, and all the Canaanites, and the Sidonians, and the Hivites who lived on Mount Lebanon, from Mount Baal-hermon as far as Lebo-hamath. [4]They were for the testing of Israel, to know whether Israel would obey the commandments of the LORD, which he commanded their ancestors by Moses. [5]So the Israelites lived among the Canaanites, the Hittites, the Amorites, the Perizzites, the Hivites, and the Jebusites; [6]and they took their daughters as wives for themselves, and their own daughters they gave to their sons; and they worshiped their gods.

2.6–3.6. 2.6–19: The cyclical pattern. 6–9: This statement is duplicated in Josh 24.28–31. The dismissal seems to close the assembly described in Josh 24.1–27, thereby skipping back over Judg 1.1–2.5. **10:** In contrast to the elders of v. 7, the ignorance of *another generation* sets in motion a repeated pattern of events. **11–13:** First Israel would abandon the LORD for other gods. *Baals** (vv. 11, 13) and *the Astartes** (v. 13) represent Canaanite religion as a whole (10.6). **14–15:** This would in turn lead to the LORD's anger and oppression by enemies. **16–18:** The LORD would then send *judges* (military leaders) to deliver Israel. **19:** But each time, the people would revert to the worship of other gods and begin the cycle again. **2.20–3.6: The nations left in the land. 2.20–23:** Israel's failure to complete the conquest was both a punishment (vv. 20–21) and a test of obedience (vv. 22–23; 3.1, 4). **3.2:** Another explanation is offered: They remained to train Israel for war. **3.6:** Intermarriage unavoidably entangled Israel in idolatry* (Deut 7.3–4).

~~~~~~~~~~~~~~~~~~~~~~~~~~~~

7 The Israelites did what was evil in the sight of the LORD, forgetting the LORD their God, and worshiping the Baals and the Asherahs. [8]Therefore the anger of the LORD was kindled against Israel, and he sold them into the hand of King Cushan-rishathaim of Aram-naharaim; and the Israelites served Cushan-rishathaim eight years. [9]But when the Israelites cried out to the LORD, the LORD raised up a deliverer for the Israelites, who delivered them, Othniel son of Kenaz, Caleb's younger brother. [10]The spirit of the LORD came upon him, and he judged Israel; he went out to war, and the LORD gave King Cushan-rishathaim of Aram into his hand; and his hand prevailed over Cushan-rishathaim. [11]So the land had rest forty years. Then Othniel son of Kenaz died.

3.7–11: Othniel. 7: Apostasy begins the cyclical pattern set forth in 2.11–19. The plural *Baals** and *Asherahs** denotes the worship of these divinities at multiple local shrines. Asherah was worshiped as the consort of Baal* or Yahweh and represented by a wooden pole (6.25). **8:** Subjugation follows. *Cushan-rishathaim* is otherwise unknown and sounds like a feature of folklore rather than history ("Cushan of Double Wickedness"). *Aram-naharaim* refers to northwestern Mesopotamia. **9:** The pattern is completed by Israel's cry to the LORD and deliverance. **10:** *The spirit of the LORD* is a force that empowers chosen heroes to perform extraordinary deeds of strength and leadership. **11:** The individual judges are unified by a chronological structure (see also v. 8) that reaches to 1 Kings 6.1.

12 The Israelites again did what was evil in the sight of the LORD; and the LORD strengthened King Eglon of Moab against Israel, because they had done what was evil in the sight of the LORD. ¹³In alliance with the Ammonites and the Amalekites, he went and defeated Israel; and they took possession of the city of palms. ¹⁴So the Israelites served King Eglon of Moab eighteen years.

15 But when the Israelites cried out to the LORD, the LORD raised up for them a deliverer, Ehud son of Gera, the Benjaminite, a left-handed man. The Israelites sent tribute by him to King Eglon of Moab. ¹⁶Ehud made for himself a sword with two edges, a cubit in length; and he fastened it on his right thigh under his clothes. ¹⁷Then he presented the tribute to King Eglon of Moab. Now Eglon was a very fat man. ¹⁸When Ehud had finished presenting the tribute, he sent the people who carried the tribute on their way. ¹⁹But he himself turned back at the sculptured stones near Gilgal, and said, "I have a secret message for you, O king." So the king said,*ᵃ* "Silence!" and all his attendants went out from his presence. ²⁰Ehud came to him, while he was sitting alone in his cool roof chamber, and said, "I have a message from God for you." So he rose from his seat. ²¹Then Ehud reached with his left hand, took the sword from his right thigh, and thrust it into Eglon's*ᵇ* belly; ²²the hilt also went in after the blade, and the fat closed over the blade, for he did not draw the sword out of his belly; and the dirt came out.*ᶜ* ²³Then Ehud went out into the vestibule,*ᵈ* and closed the doors of the roof chamber on him, and locked them.

24 After he had gone, the servants came. When they saw that the doors of the roof chamber were locked, they thought, "He must be relieving himself*ᵉ* in the cool chamber." ²⁵So they waited until they were embarrassed. When he still did not open the doors of the roof chamber, they took the key and opened them. There was their lord lying dead on the floor.

26 Ehud escaped while they delayed, and passed beyond the sculptured stones, and escaped to Seirah. ²⁷When he arrived, he sounded the trumpet in the hill country of Ephraim; and the Israelites went down with him from the hill country, having him at their head. ²⁸He said to them, "Follow after me; for the LORD has given your enemies the Moabites into your hand." So they went down after him, and seized the fords of the Jordan against the Moabites, and allowed no one to cross over. ²⁹At that time they killed about ten thousand of the Moabites, all strong, able-bodied men; no one escaped. ³⁰So Moab was subdued that day under the hand of Israel. And the land had rest eighty years.

31 After him came Shamgar son of Anath, who killed six hundred of the Philistines with an oxgoad. He too delivered Israel.

3.12–31. 12–30: Ehud. 13: *The city of palms* is Jericho. **15–16:** That Ehud was *left-handed* lets him hide his short sword (*with two edges* for stabbing) in an unexpected place on his *right thigh.* **20:** Eglon *rose from his seat,* expecting to hear a divine oracle.★ **24:** Readers would enjoy rough humor at the expense of their enemies. The delay gives Ehud time to escape and raise a rebellion. **28:** Holding *the fords of the Jordan* prevented the enemy from escaping back across to Moab. **31: Shamgar.** Since 4.1 refers to Ehud, this mysterious figure (compare 5.6) is not part of the book's system of judges. Since *son of* indicates membership in a group or class and *Anath* was a war goddess, Shamgar may have been a mercenary.

4 The Israelites again did what was evil in the sight of the LORD, after Ehud died. ²So the LORD sold them into the hand of King Jabin of Canaan, who reigned in Hazor; the commander of his army was Sisera, who

---

a Heb *he said*   *b* Heb *his*   *c* With Tg Vg: Meaning of Heb uncertain   *d* Meaning of Heb uncertain   *e* Heb *covering his feet*

lived in Harosheth-ha-goiim. ³Then the Is-raelites cried out to the LORD for help; for he had nine hundred chariots of iron, and had oppressed the Israelites cruelly twenty years.

4 At that time Deborah, a prophetess, wife of Lappidoth, was judging Israel. ⁵She used to sit under the palm of Deborah be-tween Ramah and Bethel in the hill country of Ephraim; and the Israelites came up to her for judgment. ⁶She sent and summoned Barak son of Abinoam from Kedesh in Naph-tali, and said to him, "The LORD, the God of Israel, commands you, 'Go, take position at Mount Tabor, bringing ten thousand from the tribe of Naphtali and the tribe of Zebu-lun. ⁷I will draw out Sisera, the general of Jabin's army, to meet you by the Wadi Kishon with his chariots and his troops; and I will give him into your hand.'" ⁸Barak said to her, "If you will go with me, I will go; but if you will not go with me, I will not go." ⁹And she said, "I will surely go with you; nev-ertheless, the road on which you are going will not lead to your glory, for the LORD will sell Sisera into the hand of a woman." Then Deborah got up and went with Barak to Ke-desh. ¹⁰Barak summoned Zebulun and Naphtali to Kedesh; and ten thousand war-riors went up behind him; and Deborah went up with him.

11 Now Heber the Kenite had separated from the other Kenites,ᵃ that is, the descen-dants of Hobab the father-in-law of Moses, and had encamped as far away as Elon-be-zaanannim, which is near Kedesh.

4.1–11: Deborah and Barak prepare for battle. 2: *Jabin* is also named as king of *Hazor* in Josh 11.1–11. **3:** *Chariots* with *iron* fittings gave a decisive tactical advantage. **4:** Here *judging* refers to settling disputes, but the verb also means to serve as military leader (3.10). As a *prophetess*★ Deborah delivers messages from the LORD (vv. 6–7, 14). **6–7:** In accord with holy war★ tradition, the LORD dictates tactics and gives an assurance of victory. The territories of *Naphtali* and *Zebulun* touched at *Mount Tabor*. **9:** Barak is penal-ized for his fainthearted response. The reader who as-sumes that *the hand of a woman* refers to Deborah is in for a surprise.

12 When Sisera was told that Barak son of Abinoam had gone up to Mount Tabor, ¹³Sisera called out all his chariots, nine hun-dred chariots of iron, and all the troops who were with him, from Harosheth-ha-goiim to the Wadi Kishon. ¹⁴Then Deborah said to Barak, "Up! For this is the day on which the LORD has given Sisera into your hand. The LORD is indeed going out before you." So Barak went down from Mount Tabor with ten thousand warriors following him. ¹⁵And the LORD threw Sisera and all his chariots and all his army into a panicᵇ before Barak; Sisera got down from his chariot and fled away on foot, ¹⁶while Barak pursued the chariots and the army to Harosheth-ha-goiim. All the army of Sisera fell by the sword; no one was left.

17 Now Sisera had fled away on foot to the tent of Jael wife of Heber the Kenite; for there was peace between King Jabin of Ha-zor and the clan of Heber the Kenite. ¹⁸Jael came out to meet Sisera, and said to him, "Turn aside, my lord, turn aside to me; have no fear." So he turned aside to her into the tent, and she covered him with a rug. ¹⁹Then he said to her, "Please give me a little water to drink; for I am thirsty." So she opened a skin of milk and gave him a drink and cov-ered him. ²⁰He said to her, "Stand at the entrance of the tent, and if anybody comes and asks you, 'Is anyone here?' say, 'No.'" ²¹But Jael wife of Heber took a tent peg, and took a hammer in her hand, and went softly to him and drove the peg into his temple, until it went down into the ground—he was lying fast asleep from weariness—and he died. ²²Then, as Barak came in pursuit of Sisera, Jael went out to meet him, and said to him, "Come, and I will show you the man whom you are seeking." So he went into her tent; and there was Sisera lying dead, with the tent peg in his temple.

23 So on that day God subdued King Ja-bin of Canaan before the Israelites. ²⁴Then the hand of the Israelites bore harder and harder on King Jabin of Canaan, until they destroyed King Jabin of Canaan.

ᵃ Heb *from the Kain*   ᵇ Heb adds *to the sword*; compare verse 16

4.12–24: Sisera's defeat and Jael's exploit. 13: The battle takes place in the plain of the *Wadi* ✶ *Kishon,* west of Mount Tabor. **15:** *Panic* is a standard weapon of the divine warrior✶ (Josh 10.10). The circumstances behind this panic are not described (but see 5.20–21). **16:** *Barak pursued the chariots,* but Sisera has abandoned his and run off (vv. 15, 17). **17:** This *peace* explains why Sisera feels comfortable seeking refuge with Jael. **18–19:** *Jael* takes the initiative, going out to invite him in. The *rug* and *milk* sound like courteous hospitality, but by encouraging sleep, Jael is setting him up for the kill. **20:** Sisera's request reveals both his unmanly fear and his misplaced confidence in Jael. **21:** Hammering tent pegs would have been a routine task for a woman in this culture.

5 Then Deborah and Barak son of Abinoam sang on that day, saying:
2 "When locks are long in Israel,
  when the people offer themselves
    willingly—
  bless *a* the LORD!

3 "Hear, O kings; give ear, O princes;
  to the LORD I will sing,
  I will make melody to the LORD, the
    God of Israel.

4 "LORD, when you went out from Seir,
  when you marched from the region of
    Edom,
  the earth trembled,
  and the heavens poured,
  the clouds indeed poured water.
5 The mountains quaked before the
    LORD, the One of Sinai,
  before the LORD, the God of
    Israel.

6 "In the days of Shamgar son of Anath,
  in the days of Jael, caravans ceased
  and travelers kept to the byways.
7 The peasantry prospered in Israel,
  they grew fat on plunder,
  because you arose, Deborah,
  arose as a mother in Israel.
8 When new gods were chosen,
  then war was in the gates.
  Was shield or spear to be seen
  among forty thousand in Israel?

9 My heart goes out to the commanders
    of Israel
  who offered themselves willingly
    among the people.
  Bless the LORD.

5.1–31: The song of Deborah. 2: Archaic language makes this poem difficult to interpret (notes *a, b, d*). *Locks are long* may refer to vows of military dedication, similar to Samson's long hair. **4–5:** The poetic format of a "theophany"✶ describes the awe-inspiring approach of the divine warrior✶ (compare Deut 33.2–3). **6–8:** Israel's precarious situation before the victory (vv. 6, 8), is contrasted with the good fortune that followed (v. 7). *Mother in Israel* (v. 7) is an honorific title signifying authority and leadership.

10 "Tell of it, you who ride on white
    donkeys,
  you who sit on rich carpets *b*
  and you who walk by the way.
11 To the sound of musicians *b* at the
    watering places,
  there they repeat the triumphs of the
    LORD,
  the triumphs of his peasantry in
    Israel.

"Then down to the gates marched the
    people of the LORD.

12 "Awake, awake, Deborah!
  Awake, awake, utter a song!
  Arise, Barak, lead away your captives,
  O son of Abinoam.
13 Then down marched the remnant of the
    noble;
  the people of the LORD marched
    down for him *c* against the
    mighty.
14 From Ephraim they set out *d* into the
    valley, *e*
  following you, Benjamin, with your
    kin;
  from Machir marched down the
    commanders,

a Or *You who offer yourselves willingly among the people, bless*   *b* Meaning of Heb uncertain   *c* Gk: Heb *me*
d Cn: Heb *From Ephraim their root*   *e* Gk: Heb *in Amalek*

and from Zebulun those who bear the
marshal's staff;

15 the chiefs of Issachar came with
Deborah,
and Issachar faithful to Barak;
into the valley they rushed out at his
heels.
Among the clans of Reuben
there were great searchings of heart.

16 Why did you tarry among the sheepfolds,
to hear the piping for the flocks?
Among the clans of Reuben
there were great searchings of heart.

17 Gilead stayed beyond the Jordan;
and Dan, why did he abide with the
ships?
Asher sat still at the coast of the sea,
settling down by his landings.

18 Zebulun is a people that scorned death;
Naphtali too, on the heights of the
field.

5.10–18: Everyone is to celebrate, both aristocrats who *ride* and *sit on rich carpets* and ordinary folk who *walk*. *Watering places* were customary spots for social interaction. 14–18: Reflecting a stage of tribal affinity earlier than the conventional twelve-tribe system, the poem alludes to ten groups and censures four of them for not participating. *Machir* (v. 14) and *Gilead* (v. 17) appear in place of Manasseh and Gad. Judah, Simeon, and Levi are not mentioned at all.

---

19 "The kings came, they fought;
then fought the kings of Canaan,
at Taanach, by the waters of Megiddo;
they got no spoils of silver.

20 The stars fought from heaven,
from their courses they fought against
Sisera.

21 The torrent Kishon swept them away,
the onrushing torrent, the torrent
Kishon.
March on, my soul, with might!

22 "Then loud beat the horses' hoofs
with the galloping, galloping of his
steeds.

23 "Curse Meroz, says the angel of the
LORD,
curse bitterly its inhabitants,

because they did not come to the help
of the LORD,
to the help of the LORD against the
mighty.

24 "Most blessed of women be Jael,
the wife of Heber the Kenite,
of tent-dwelling women most blessed.

25 He asked water and she gave him milk,
she brought him curds in a lordly bowl.

26 She put her hand to the tent peg
and her right hand to the workmen's
mallet;
she struck Sisera a blow,
she crushed his head,
she shattered and pierced his temple.

27 He sank, he fell,
he lay still at her feet;
at her feet he sank, he fell;
where he sank, there he fell dead.

5.19–27. 20–21: The heavenly forces of the divine warrior* fight, and the Kishon River overwhelms the enemy. 22: The escaping chariot horses are vividly described. 23: Both the town *Meroz* and the incident cited are otherwise unknown. 26–27: In this version Sisera seems to be standing when attacked (contrast 4.21). The penetrating tent peg and his fall "between her feet" (NRSV: *at her feet*) probably have sexual implications. This scene may be a reversal of the customary rape alluded to in v. 30.

---

28 "Out of the window she peered,
the mother of Sisera gazed[a] through
the lattice:
'Why is his chariot so long in coming?
Why tarry the hoofbeats of his
chariots?'

29 Her wisest ladies make answer,
indeed, she answers the question
herself:

30 'Are they not finding and dividing the
spoil?—
A girl or two for every man;
spoil of dyed stuffs for Sisera,
spoil of dyed stuffs embroidered,
two pieces of dyed work embroidered
for my neck as spoil?'

a Gk Compare Tg: Heb *exclaimed*

5.28–30: With delicious sarcasm, the poet describes Sisera's mother waiting in vain. Her reference to *hoofbeats* (v. 28) is ironic* in light of v. 22. Her son is not ravishing captive women (v. 30), but has been ravished himself.

31 "So perish all your enemies, O LORD!
    But may your friends be like the sun
        as it rises in its might."

And the land had rest forty years.

6 The Israelites did what was evil in the sight of the LORD, and the LORD gave them into the hand of Midian seven years. ²The hand of Midian prevailed over Israel; and because of Midian the Israelites provided for themselves hiding places in the mountains, caves and strongholds. ³For whenever the Israelites put in seed, the Midianites and the Amalekites and the people of the east would come up against them. ⁴They would encamp against them and destroy the produce of the land, as far as the neighborhood of Gaza, and leave no sustenance in Israel, and no sheep or ox or donkey. ⁵For they and their livestock would come up, and they would even bring their tents, as thick as locusts; neither they nor their camels could be counted; so they wasted the land as they came in. ⁶Thus Israel was greatly impoverished because of Midian; and the Israelites cried out to the LORD for help.

7 When the Israelites cried to the LORD on account of the Midianites, ⁸the LORD sent a prophet to the Israelites; and he said to them, "Thus says the LORD, the God of Israel: I led you up from Egypt, and brought you out of the house of slavery; ⁹and I delivered you from the hand of the Egyptians, and from the hand of all who oppressed you, and drove them out before you, and gave you their land; ¹⁰and I said to you, 'I am the LORD your God; you shall not pay reverence to the gods of the Amorites, in whose land you live.' But you have not given heed to my voice."

6.1–10: Oppression by Midian. 3–4: Nomadic raiders are devastating the local food supply. **7–10:** These accusations reflect the indictment delivered at Bochim

(2.1–5). To *give heed* to the LORD's *voice* (v. 10) means to obey.

11 Now the angel of the LORD came and sat under the oak at Ophrah, which belonged to Joash the Abiezrite, as his son Gideon was beating out wheat in the wine press, to hide it from the Midianites. ¹²The angel of the LORD appeared to him and said to him, "The LORD is with you, you mighty warrior." ¹³Gideon answered him, "But sir, if the LORD is with us, why then has all this happened to us? And where are all his wonderful deeds that our ancestors recounted to us, saying, 'Did not the LORD bring us up from Egypt?' But now the LORD has cast us off, and given us into the hand of Midian." ¹⁴Then the LORD turned to him and said, "Go in this might of yours and deliver Israel from the hand of Midian; I hereby commission you." ¹⁵He responded, "But sir, how can I deliver Israel? My clan is the weakest in Manasseh, and I am the least in my family." ¹⁶The LORD said to him, "But I will be with you, and you shall strike down the Midianites, every one of them." ¹⁷Then he said to him, "If now I have found favor with you, then show me a sign that it is you who speak with me. ¹⁸Do not depart from here until I come to you, and bring out my present, and set it before you." And he said, "I will stay until you return."

19 So Gideon went into his house and prepared a kid, and unleavened cakes from an ephah of flour; the meat he put in a basket, and the broth he put in a pot, and brought them to him under the oak and presented them. ²⁰The angel of God said to him, "Take the meat and the unleavened cakes, and put them on this rock, and pour out the broth." And he did so. ²¹Then the angel of the LORD reached out the tip of the staff that was in his hand, and touched the meat and the unleavened cakes; and fire sprang up from the rock and consumed the meat and the unleavened cakes; and the angel of the LORD vanished from his sight. ²²Then Gideon perceived that it was the angel of the LORD; and Gideon said, "Help me, Lord GOD! For I have seen the angel of the LORD face to face." ²³But the LORD

said to him, "Peace be to you; do not fear, you shall not die." 24Then Gideon built an altar there to the LORD, and called it, The LORD is peace. To this day it still stands at Ophrah, which belongs to the Abiezrites.

6.11–24: The call of Gideon. 11: *The angel of the LORD* is a visible manifestation of the LORD's presence (compare v. 14). *Wheat* would normally be beaten or threshed* on a windy hilltop, not in the confined space of a *wine press.* **15:** Objections are a standard element of call stories (Ex 3.10–12). **24:** One purpose of this traditional story was to authenticate a local altar of sacrifice.

25 That night the LORD said to him, "Take your father's bull, the second bull seven years old, and pull down the altar of Baal that belongs to your father, and cut down the sacred pole*a* that is beside it; 26and build an altar to the LORD your God on the top of the stronghold here, in proper order; then take the second bull, and offer it as a burnt offering with the wood of the sacred pole*a* that you shall cut down." 27So Gideon took ten of his servants, and did as the LORD had told him; but because he was too afraid of his family and the townspeople to do it by day, he did it by night.

28 When the townspeople rose early in the morning, the altar of Baal was broken down, and the sacred pole*a* beside it was cut down, and the second bull was offered on the altar that had been built. 29So they said to one another, "Who has done this?" After searching and inquiring, they were told, "Gideon son of Joash did it." 30Then the townspeople said to Joash, "Bring out your son, so that he may die, for he has pulled down the altar of Baal and cut down the sacred pole*a* beside it." 31But Joash said to all who were arrayed against him, "Will you contend for Baal? Or will you defend his cause? Whoever contends for him shall be put to death by morning. If he is a god, let him contend for himself, because his altar has been pulled down." 32Therefore on that day Gideon*b* was called Jerubbaal, that is to say, "Let Baal contend against him," because he pulled down his altar.

6.25–32: Gideon pulls down Baal's★ altar. 25–26: The *sacred pole* was a symbol of the goddess Asherah★ (note *a*). Using it as firewood would be a calculated desecration. **27:** Gideon is an ambivalent hero (v. 15, 17); he prefers to act *by night.* **31:** *If he is a god:* A god unable to defend its own interests is not really a god at all. **32:** Gideon's other name, *Jerubbaal* ("let Baal contend"), would have been offensive to later believers. Here it receives an orthodox interpretation★ as a reminder of Baal's humiliation.

33 Then all the Midianites and the Amalekites and the people of the east came together, and crossing the Jordan they encamped in the Valley of Jezreel. 34But the spirit of the LORD took possession of Gideon; and he sounded the trumpet, and the Abiezrites were called out to follow him. 35He sent messengers throughout all Manasseh, and they too were called out to follow him. He also sent messengers to Asher, Zebulun, and Naphtali, and they went up to meet them.

36 Then Gideon said to God, "In order to see whether you will deliver Israel by my hand, as you have said, 37I am going to lay a fleece of wool on the threshing floor; if there is dew on the fleece alone, and it is dry on all the ground, then I shall know that you will deliver Israel by my hand, as you have said." 38And it was so. When he rose early next morning and squeezed the fleece, he wrung enough dew from the fleece to fill a bowl with water. 39Then Gideon said to God, "Do not let your anger burn against me, let me speak one more time; let me, please, make trial with the fleece just once more; let it be dry only on the fleece, and on all the ground let there be dew." 40And God did so that night. It was dry on the fleece only, and on all the ground there was dew.

6.33–40: Assembling troops and seeking a sign. 34–35: The dynamic power of *the spirit of the LORD* inspires an unexpected act of leadership. Beginning with his own clan,★ *the Abiezrites,* Gideon attracts his own tribe and three neighboring ones. **36–40:** Gideon's repeated quest for certainty corresponds to his ambivalent character (6.15, 17, 27), but is not actually

a Heb *Asherah*   *b* Heb *he*

condemned in the narrative.* Assurance of victory was an important element in holy war* tradition.

7 Then Jerubbaal (that is, Gideon) and all the troops that were with him rose early and encamped beside the spring of Harod; and the camp of Midian was north of them, below[a] the hill of Moreh, in the valley.

2 The LORD said to Gideon, "The troops with you are too many for me to give the Midianites into their hand. Israel would only take the credit away from me, saying, 'My own hand has delivered me.' 3 Now therefore proclaim this in the hearing of the troops, 'Whoever is fearful and trembling, let him return home.' " Thus Gideon sifted them out;[b] twenty-two thousand returned, and ten thousand remained.

4 Then the LORD said to Gideon, "The troops are still too many; take them down to the water and I will sift them out for you there. When I say, 'This one shall go with you,' he shall go with you; and when I say, 'This one shall not go with you,' he shall not go." 5 So he brought the troops down to the water; and the LORD said to Gideon, "All those who lap the water with their tongues, as a dog laps, you shall put to one side; all those who kneel down to drink, putting their hands to their mouths,[c] you shall put to the other side." 6 The number of those that lapped was three hundred; but all the rest of the troops knelt down to drink water. 7 Then the LORD said to Gideon, "With the three hundred that lapped I will deliver you, and give the Midianites into your hand. Let all the others go to their homes." 8 So he took the jars of the troops from their hands,[d] and their trumpets; and he sent all the rest of Israel back to their own tents, but retained the three hundred. The camp of Midian was below him in the valley.

9 That same night the LORD said to him, "Get up, attack the camp; for I have given it into your hand. 10 But if you fear to attack, go down to the camp with your servant Purah; 11 and you shall hear what they say, and afterward your hands shall be strengthened to attack the camp." Then he went down with his servant Purah to the outposts of the armed men that were in the camp.

12 The Midianites and the Amalekites and all the people of the east lay along the valley as thick as locusts; and their camels were without number, countless as the sand on the seashore. 13 When Gideon arrived, there was a man telling a dream to his comrade; and he said, "I had a dream, and in it a cake of barley bread tumbled into the camp of Midian, and came to the tent, and struck it so that it fell; it turned upside down, and the tent collapsed." 14 And his comrade answered, "This is no other than the sword of Gideon son of Joash, a man of Israel; into his hand God has given Midian and all the army."

7.1–14: Preparing for battle. 2: In holy war,* the LORD alone wins the victory. **3:** Sending home the *fearful* accords with Deut 20.8. **4–6:** The Hebrew text of the second test is perplexing (note *c*), and the point of preferring *those who lap* over *those who kneel* (v. 5) is baffling. Few Israelites lap water, so that only a tiny fraction of the original ten thousand remain. **8:** Those who stay take the provisions of those who are leaving (retaining the Hebrew text, note *d*). **10:** That Gideon would still *fear to attack* after the LORD's word of assurance in v. 9 typifies his character. **13–14:** Dreams were regarded as premonitions of the future. The symbols are appropriate: a *tent* for Midianite nomads and *barley bread* for Israelite farmers.

15 When Gideon heard the telling of the dream and its interpretation, he worshiped; and he returned to the camp of Israel, and said, "Get up; for the LORD has given the army of Midian into your hand." 16 After he divided the three hundred men into three companies, and put trumpets into the hands of all of them, and empty jars, with torches inside the jars, 17 he said to them, "Look at me, and do the same; when I come to the outskirts of the camp, do as I do. 18 When I blow the trumpet, I and all who are with me, then you also blow the trumpets around the whole camp, and shout, 'For the LORD and for Gideon!' "

19 So Gideon and the hundred who were

a Heb *from*   *b* Cn: Heb *home, and depart from Mount Gilead' "*   *c* Heb places the words *putting their hands to their mouths* after the word *lapped* in verse 6
d Cn: Heb *So the people took provisions in their hands*

with him came to the outskirts of the camp at the beginning of the middle watch, when they had just set the watch; and they blew the trumpets and smashed the jars that were in their hands. 20So the three companies blew the trumpets and broke the jars, holding in their left hands the torches, and in their right hands the trumpets to blow; and they cried, "A sword for the LORD and for Gideon!" 21Every man stood in his place all around the camp, and all the men in camp ran; they cried out and fled. 22When they blew the three hundred trumpets, the LORD set every man's sword against his fellow and against all the army; and the army fled as far as Beth-shittah toward Zererah,ᵃ as far as the border of Abel-meholah, by Tabbath. 23And the men of Israel were called out from Naphtali and from Asher and from all Manasseh, and they pursued after the Midianites.

24 Then Gideon sent messengers throughout all the hill country of Ephraim, saying, "Come down against the Midianites and seize the waters against them, as far as Beth-barah, and also the Jordan." So all the men of Ephraim were called out, and they seized the waters as far as Beth-barah, and also the Jordan. 25They captured the two captains of Midian, Oreb and Zeeb; they killed Oreb at the rock of Oreb, and Zeeb they killed at the wine press of Zeeb, as they pursued the Midianites. They brought the heads of Oreb and Zeeb to Gideon beyond the Jordan.

8 Then the Ephraimites said to him, "What have you done to us, not to call us when you went to fight against the Midianites?" And they upbraided him violently. 2So he said to them, "What have I done now in comparison with you? Is not the gleaning of the grapes of Ephraim better than the vintage of Abiezer? 3God has given into your hands the captains of Midian, Oreb and Zeeb; what have I been able to do in comparison with you?" When he said this, their anger against him subsided.

logically appropriate moment to attack. **21–22:** The result is panic, the classic weapon of the divine warrior* (4.15). This victory became a proverbial example (Ps 83.9–11; Isa 9.4). **8.1–2:** *The Ephraimites resent being left out of the original summons (6.35; 7.23), but Gideon responds wisely with a soothing compliment: The dregs of Ephraim are better than the very best my clan* has to offer.*

4 Then Gideon came to the Jordan and crossed over, he and the three hundred who were with him, exhausted and famished.ᵇ 5So he said to the people of Succoth, "Please give some loaves of bread to my followers, for they are exhausted, and I am pursuing Zebah and Zalmunna, the kings of Midian." 6But the officials of Succoth said, "Do you already have in your possession the hands of Zebah and Zalmunna, that we should give bread to your army?" 7Gideon replied, "Well then, when the LORD has given Zebah and Zalmunna into my hand, I will trample your flesh on the thorns of the wilderness and on briers." 8From there he went up to Penuel, and made the same request of them; and the people of Penuel answered him as the people of Succoth had answered. 9So he said to the people of Penuel, "When I come back victorious, I will break down this tower."

10 Now Zebah and Zalmunna were in Karkor with their army, about fifteen thousand men, all who were left of all the army of the people of the east; for one hundred twenty thousand men bearing arms had fallen. 11So Gideon went up by the caravan route east of Nobah and Jogbehah, and attacked the army; for the army was off its guard. 12Zebah and Zalmunna fled; and he pursued them and took the two kings of Midian, Zebah and Zalmunna, and threw all the army into a panic.

13 When Gideon son of Joash returned from the battle by the ascent of Heres, 14he caught a young man, one of the people of Succoth, and questioned him; and he listed for him the officials and elders of Succoth, seventy-seven people. 15Then he came to the people of Succoth, and said, "Here are Zebah and Zalmunna, about whom you taunted

7.15–8.3: Victory over Midian. 7.16: The *torches* remain *inside the jars* to preserve the element of surprise. **19:** The *beginning of the middle watch* is a psycho-

ᵃ Another reading is *Zeredah*   ᵇ Gk: Heb *pursuing*

me, saying, 'Do you already have in your possession the hands of Zebah and Zalmunna, that we should give bread to your troops who are exhausted?' " 16 So he took the elders of the city and he took thorns of the wilderness and briers and with them he trampled*a* the people of Succoth. 17 He also broke down the tower of Penuel, and killed the men of the city.

18 Then he said to Zebah and Zalmunna, "What about the men whom you killed at Tabor?" They answered, "As you are, so were they, every one of them; they resembled the sons of a king." 19 And he replied, "They were my brothers, the sons of my mother; as the LORD lives, if you had saved them alive, I would not kill you." 20 So he said to Jether his firstborn, "Go kill them!" But the boy did not draw his sword, for he was afraid, because he was still a boy. 21 Then Zebah and Zalmunna said, "You come and kill us; for as the man is, so is his strength." So Gideon proceeded to kill Zebah and Zalmunna; and he took the crescents that were on the necks of their camels.

8.4–21: Pursuit and vengeance. 5: *Zebah and Zalmunna* represent a different story-telling tradition from that featuring Oreb and Zeeb (7.25). **6:** The *hands* of the enemy could be cut off to serve as evidence of their capture or death. **19:** Gideon demands personal blood vengeance. *Sons of my mother* indicates these were his full brothers, an important consideration in a polygamous society. **20–21:** To have a mere *boy* kill them would be a grave insult.

---

22 Then the Israelites said to Gideon, "Rule over us, you and your son and your grandson also; for you have delivered us out of the hand of Midian." 23 Gideon said to them, "I will not rule over you, and my son will not rule over you; the LORD will rule over you." 24 Then Gideon said to them, "Let me make a request of you; each of you give me an earring he has taken as booty." (For the enemy*b* had golden earrings, because they were Ishmaelites.) 25 "We will willingly give them," they answered. So they spread a garment, and each threw into it an earring he had taken as booty. 26 The weight of the golden earrings that he requested was one

thousand seven hundred shekels of gold (apart from the crescents and the pendants and the purple garments worn by the kings of Midian, and the collars that were on the necks of their camels). 27 Gideon made an ephod of it and put it in his town, in Ophrah; and all Israel prostituted themselves to it there, and it became a snare to Gideon and to his family. 28 So Midian was subdued before the Israelites, and they lifted up their heads no more. So the land had rest forty years in the days of Gideon.

29 Jerubbaal son of Joash went to live in his own house. 30 Now Gideon had seventy sons, his own offspring, for he had many wives. 31 His concubine who was in Shechem also bore him a son, and he named him Abimelech. 32 Then Gideon son of Joash died at a good old age, and was buried in the tomb of his father Joash at Ophrah of the Abiezrites.

33 As soon as Gideon died, the Israelites relapsed and prostituted themselves with the Baals, making Baal-berith their god. 34 The Israelites did not remember the LORD their God, who had rescued them from the hand of all their enemies on every side; 35 and they did not exhibit loyalty to the house of Jerubbaal (that is, Gideon) in return for all the good that he had done to Israel.

8.22–35: Israel offers Gideon hereditary rule. 23: *The LORD will rule over you* expresses the traditional notion that choosing human kings violates the LORD's kingship (1 Sam 8.7). **24:** *Ishmaelites* were similar in culture to the Midianites, but these were distinct nationalities (Gen 16; 25.1–4). **27:** *Ephod** usually describes a priestly vestment, which could be used for divination. Perhaps this gold ephod was used to robe an idol. **31:** A *concubine** was a subordinate wife with lower legal status. **33:** *Baal-berith* (Baal* of the Covenant; 9.4) was a god worshipped in Shechem, probably the same as El-berith (9.46).

---

9 Now Abimelech son of Jerubbaal went to Shechem to his mother's kinsfolk and said to them and to the whole clan of his mother's family, 2 "Say in the hearing of all

a With verse 7, Compare Gk: Heb *he taught*
b Heb *they*

the lords of Shechem, 'Which is better for you, that all seventy of the sons of Jerubbaal rule over you, or that one rule over you?' Remember also that I am your bone and your flesh." 3So his mother's kinsfolk spoke all these words on his behalf in the hearing of all the lords of Shechem; and their hearts inclined to follow Abimelech, for they said, "He is our brother." 4They gave him seventy pieces of silver out of the temple of Baal-berith with which Abimelech hired worthless and reckless fellows, who followed him. 5He went to his father's house at Ophrah, and killed his brothers the sons of Jerubbaal, seventy men, on one stone; but Jotham, the youngest son of Jerubbaal, survived, for he hid himself. 6Then all the lords of Shechem and all Beth-millo came together, and they went and made Abimelech king, by the oak of the pillar*a* at Shechem.

9.1–6: Abimelech seizes royal power. 1–3: Abimelech's mother belonged to a clan* of Shechem (8.31). **5:** *On one stone* may indicate a parody of sacrifice (1 Sam 14.33–34), but clearly communicates that the killing was deliberate and cold-blooded. **6:** *Beth-millo* indicates a building (literally "House on Filled-Up Ground"), but here must refer to a group in Shechem's system of government (v. 20; compare "White House").

7 When it was told to Jotham, he went and stood on the top of Mount Gerizim, and cried aloud and said to them, "Listen to me, you lords of Shechem, so that God may listen to you.
8 The trees once went out
　　to anoint a king over themselves.
　So they said to the olive tree,
　　'Reign over us.'
9 The olive tree answered them,
　　'Shall I stop producing my rich oil
　　　by which gods and mortals are
　　　　honored,
　　and go to sway over the trees?'
10 Then the trees said to the fig tree,
　　'You come and reign over us.'
11 But the fig tree answered them,
　　'Shall I stop producing my sweetness
　　　and my delicious fruit,
　　and go to sway over the trees?'

12 Then the trees said to the vine,
　　'You come and reign over us.'
13 But the vine said to them,
　　'Shall I stop producing my wine
　　　that cheers gods and mortals,
　　and go to sway over the trees?'
14 So all the trees said to the bramble,
　　'You come and reign over us.'
15 And the bramble said to the trees,
　　'If in good faith you are anointing me
　　　king over you,
　　then come and take refuge in my
　　　shade;
　　but if not, let fire come out of the
　　　bramble
　　and devour the cedars of
　　　Lebanon.'

16 "Now therefore, if you acted in good faith and honor when you made Abimelech king, and if you have dealt well with Jerubbaal and his house, and have done to him as his actions deserved— 17for my father fought for you, and risked his life, and rescued you from the hand of Midian; 18but you have risen up against my father's house this day, and have killed his sons, seventy men on one stone, and have made Abimelech, the son of his slave woman, king over the lords of Shechem, because he is your kinsman— 19if, I say, you have acted in good faith and honor with Jerubbaal and with his house this day, then rejoice in Abimelech, and let him also rejoice in you; 20but if not, let fire come out from Abimelech, and devour the lords of Shechem, and Beth-millo; and let fire come out from the lords of Shechem, and from Beth-millo, and devour Abimelech." 21Then Jotham ran away and fled, going to Beer, where he remained for fear of his brother Abimelech.

9.7–21: Jotham's fable.* 8–13: This fable displays a cynicism about kingship similar to 1 Samuel 8. The useful plants (representing Gideon; 8.22–23) refuse kingship as a waste of their valuable aptitudes. **14–15:** The worthless *bramble* (Abimelech) accepts. But beware! The bramble's *shade* is prickly and meager, and its potential for *fire* threatens danger. **16:** The rest of

a Cn: Meaning of Heb uncertain

Jotham's speech is an extended curse that culminates in vv. 19–20. **17–18:** The curse is interrupted to demonstrate that the leaders of Shechem have not acted fairly. **20:** *Fire* represents the dissension that is soon to unfold. Jotham's curse reaches fulfillment in vv. 56–57.

22 Abimelech ruled over Israel three years. ²³But God sent an evil spirit between Abimelech and the lords of Shechem; and the lords of Shechem dealt treacherously with Abimelech. ²⁴This happened so that the violence done to the seventy sons of Jerubbaal might be avenged*a* and their blood be laid on their brother Abimelech, who killed them, and on the lords of Shechem, who strengthened his hands to kill his brothers. ²⁵So, out of hostility to him, the lords of Shechem set ambushes on the mountain tops. They robbed all who passed by them along that way; and it was reported to Abimelech.

26 When Gaal son of Ebed moved into Shechem with his kinsfolk, the lords of Shechem put confidence in him. ²⁷They went out into the field and gathered the grapes from their vineyards, trod them, and celebrated. Then they went into the temple of their god, ate and drank, and ridiculed Abimelech. ²⁸Gaal son of Ebed said, "Who is Abimelech, and who are we of Shechem, that we should serve him? Did not the son of Jerubbaal and Zebul his officer serve the men of Hamor father of Shechem? Why then should we serve him? ²⁹If only this people were under my command! Then I would remove Abimelech; I would say*b* to him, 'Increase your army, and come out.' "

30 When Zebul the ruler of the city heard the words of Gaal son of Ebed, his anger was kindled. ³¹He sent messengers to Abimelech at Arumah,*c* saying, "Look, Gaal son of Ebed and his kinsfolk have come to Shechem, and they are stirring up*d* the city against you. ³²Now therefore, go by night, you and the troops that are with you, and lie in wait in the fields. ³³Then early in the morning, as soon as the sun rises, get up and rush on the city; and when he and the troops that are with him come out against you, you may deal with them as best you can."

9.22–33: The plot against Abimelech. 23: *An evil spirit* creates a relationship of mutual distrust (1 Sam 16.14). **24:** Israel believed that evil deeds spontaneously brought on their own appropriate penalty. *Violence* and *blood* (bloodshed) would naturally rebound on the culprits. **25:** A breakdown in civil order (compare 5.6) undermines Abimelech's authority and diminishes the collection of royal tolls. **26:** *Gaal* and his relatives relocate to Shechem, but his nationalistic rhetoric* (vv. 28–29) indicates that he has ethnic ties there. **27:** Talk would be loose and emotions would run high at this celebration of the wine harvest. **28:** Gaal's argument appeals to ethnic pride: Abimelech is an upstart outsider. Both Jerubbaal and *Zebul* (Abimelech's deputy, v. 30) once served the authentic native leadership of Shechem, *the men of Hamor.* Hamor was a renowned character from Shechem's past (Gen 33.19). **33:** Zebul intends to make sure that Gaal and his troops *come out against* Abimelech (v. 38).

34 So Abimelech and all the troops with him got up by night and lay in wait against Shechem in four companies. ³⁵When Gaal son of Ebed went out and stood in the entrance of the gate of the city, Abimelech and the troops with him rose from the ambush. ³⁶And when Gaal saw them, he said to Zebul, "Look, people are coming down from the mountain tops!" And Zebul said to him, "The shadows on the mountains look like people to you." ³⁷Gaal spoke again and said, "Look, people are coming down from Tabbur-erez, and one company is coming from the direction of Elon-meonenim."*e* ³⁸Then Zebul said to him, "Where is your boast*f* now, you who said, 'Who is Abimelech, that we should serve him?' Are not these the troops you made light of? Go out now and fight with them." ³⁹So Gaal went out at the head of the lords of Shechem, and fought with Abimelech. ⁴⁰Abimelech chased him, and he fled before him. Many fell wounded, up to the entrance of the gate. ⁴¹So Abimelech resided at Arumah; and Zebul drove out Gaal and his kinsfolk, so that they could not live on at Shechem.

a Heb *might come*   b Gk: Heb *and he said*
c Cn See 9.41. Heb *Tormah*   d Cn: Heb *are besieging*
e That is *Diviners' Oak*   f Heb *mouth*

42 On the following day the people went out into the fields. When Abimelech was told, [43]he took his troops and divided them into three companies, and lay in wait in the fields. When he looked and saw the people coming out of the city, he rose against them and killed them. [44]Abimelech and the company that was[a] with him rushed forward and stood at the entrance of the gate of the city, while the two companies rushed on all who were in the fields and killed them. [45]Abimelech fought against the city all that day; he took the city, and killed the people that were in it; and he razed the city and sowed it with salt.

46 When all the lords of the Tower of Shechem heard of it, they entered the stronghold of the temple of El-berith. [47]Abimelech was told that all the lords of the Tower of Shechem were gathered together. [48]So Abimelech went up to Mount Zalmon, he and all the troops that were with him. Abimelech took an ax in his hand, cut down a bundle of brushwood, and took it up and laid it on his shoulder. Then he said to the troops with him, "What you have seen me do, do quickly, as I have done." [49]So every one of the troops cut down a bundle and following Abimelech put it against the stronghold, and they set the stronghold on fire over them, so that all the people of the Tower of Shechem also died, about a thousand men and women.

9.34–49: Abimelech defeats Shechem. 34: By dividing his troops into *four companies,* Abimelech improves their chance of approaching unobserved. **39:** Gaal leads out Shechem's aristocrats (*the lords of Shechem*), who are driven back into the city with heavy losses. **41:** Although Abimelech does not storm the city at this point, Zebul is able to expel Gaal and his supporters. **42:** The ordinary farmers go out to work in the fields, perhaps to harvest (v. 27). **44:** The detachment under Abimelech's direct command blocks escape back into Shechem, while the other two contingents trap and slaughter the common folk. **45:** This is total war. Abimelech pulls down buildings and blocks resettlement by sowing Shechem with salt as a symbolic curse. **46:** Although the identity of *the lords of the Tower of Shechem* is unclear, they are an aristocratic group who seek safety in the city's last

citadel. Ancient temples were often constructed as strongholds.

50 Then Abimelech went to Thebez, and encamped against Thebez, and took it. [51]But there was a strong tower within the city, and all the men and women and all the lords of the city fled to it and shut themselves in; and they went to the roof of the tower. [52]Abimelech came to the tower, and fought against it, and came near to the entrance of the tower to burn it with fire. [53]But a certain woman threw an upper millstone on Abimelech's head, and crushed his skull. [54]Immediately he called to the young man who carried his armor and said to him, "Draw your sword and kill me, so people will not say about me, 'A woman killed him.'" So the young man thrust him through, and he died. [55]When the Israelites saw that Abimelech was dead, they all went home. [56]Thus God repaid Abimelech for the crime he committed against his father in killing his seventy brothers; [57]and God also made all the wickedness of the people of Shechem fall back on their heads, and on them came the curse of Jotham son of Jerubbaal.

9.50–57: The death of Abimelech. 51–52: This narrative* begins as a replay of his assault on Shechem. **53:** *An upper millstone* was commonly used by women. It was of a size to be picked up in two hands and thrown. **54:** Although Abimelech seeks to avoid the notoriety of being killed by a woman (compare 4.9), he became a proverbial example of such a death (2 Sam 11.21). **56–57:** God's retributive justice (v. 24) and Jotham's curse (v. 20) have worked together to achieve a satisfying conclusion.

10 After Abimelech, Tola son of Puah son of Dodo, a man of Issachar, who lived at Shamir in the hill country of Ephraim, rose to deliver Israel. [2]He judged Israel twenty-three years. Then he died, and was buried at Shamir.

3 After him came Jair the Gileadite, who judged Israel twenty-two years. [4]He had thirty sons who rode on thirty donkeys; and they had thirty towns, which are in the land

a Vg and some Gk Mss: Heb *companies that were*

The Judges of Israel

In addition to the six so-called major judges, tradition preserved a concise list of others who "judged Israel" (10.1–5; 12.7–15). Family details (10.4; 12.9, 14) glorify their wealth and eminence. These minor judges seem to have been civil officials rather than military leaders.

of Gilead, and are called Havvoth-jair to this day. [5]Jair died, and was buried in Kamon.

6 The Israelites again did what was evil in the sight of the LORD, worshiping the Baals and the Astartes, the gods of Aram, the gods of Sidon, the gods of Moab, the gods of the Ammonites, and the gods of the Philistines. Thus they abandoned the LORD, and did not worship him. [7]So the anger of the LORD was kindled against Israel, and he sold them into the hand of the Philistines and into the hand of the Ammonites, [8]and they crushed and oppressed the Israelites that year. For eighteen years they oppressed all the Israelites that were beyond the Jordan in the land of the Amorites, which is in Gilead. [9]The Ammonites also crossed the Jordan to fight against Judah and against Benjamin and against the house of Ephraim; so that Israel was greatly distressed.

10 So the Israelites cried to the LORD, saying, "We have sinned against you, because we have abandoned our God and have worshiped the Baals." [11]And the LORD said to the Israelites, "Did I not deliver you[a] from the Egyptians and from the Amorites, from the Ammonites and from the Philistines? [12]The Sidonians also, and the Amalekites, and the Maonites, oppressed you; and you cried to me, and I delivered you out of their hand. [13]Yet you have abandoned me and worshiped other gods; therefore I will deliver you no more. [14]Go and cry to the gods whom you have chosen; let them deliver you in the time of your distress." [15]And the Israelites said to the LORD, "We have sinned; do to us whatever seems good to you; but deliver us this day!" [16]So they put away the foreign gods from among them and worshiped the LORD; and he could no longer bear to see Israel suffer.

17 Then the Ammonites were called to arms, and they encamped in Gilead; and the Israelites came together, and they encamped at Mizpah. [18]The commanders of the people of Gilead said to one another, "Who will begin the fight against the Ammonites? He shall be head over all the inhabitants of Gilead."

10.1–18. 1–5: Minor judges: Tola and Jair. 1–2: *Tola* is the only minor judge credited with a military role (*rose to deliver Israel*). Tradition preserves the names *Tola* and *Puah* (as Puvah) as clans* of *Issachar* (Gen 46.13). **3–5:** *Jair* was remembered as a pioneer in the settlement of Gilead (Josh 13.30; 1 Kings 4.13). *Havvoth-jair* means "tent villages of Jair." **6–18: Oppression by Ammon. 6:** A long catalog of gods emphasizes the magnitude of Israel's infidelity. **7–8:** *The Ammonites* lived to the east and south of Israel's territory in *Gilead*. **12:** Traditions of deliverance from *the Sidonians* or the otherwise unknown *Maonites* are not preserved elsewhere. **13:** The LORD has fulfilled the threat made in 2.3. **16:** To *put away the foreign gods* may reflect an established ceremony (Gen 35.2–4; Josh 24.23). The LORD's relationship to Israel is described as an emotional attachment.

---

11 Now Jephthah the Gileadite, the son of a prostitute, was a mighty warrior. Gilead was the father of Jephthah. [2]Gilead's wife also bore him sons; and when his wife's sons grew up, they drove Jephthah away, saying to him, "You shall not inherit anything in our father's house; for you are the son of another woman." [3]Then Jephthah fled from his brothers and lived in the land of Tob. Outlaws collected around Jephthah and went raiding with him.

a Heb lacks *Did I not deliver you*

4 After a time the Ammonites made war against Israel. [5]And when the Ammonites made war against Israel, the elders of Gilead went to bring Jephthah from the land of Tob. [6]They said to Jephthah, "Come and be our commander, so that we may fight with the Ammonites." [7]But Jephthah said to the elders of Gilead, "Are you not the very ones who rejected me and drove me out of my father's house? So why do you come to me now when you are in trouble?" [8]The elders of Gilead said to Jephthah, "Nevertheless, we have now turned back to you, so that you may go with us and fight with the Ammonites, and become head over us, over all the inhabitants of Gilead." [9]Jephthah said to the elders of Gilead, "If you bring me home again to fight with the Ammonites, and the LORD gives them over to me, I will be your head." [10]And the elders of Gilead said to Jephthah, "The LORD will be witness between us; we will surely do as you say." [11]So Jephthah went with the elders of Gilead, and the people made him head and commander over them; and Jephthah spoke all his words before the LORD at Mizpah.

11.1–11: Jephthah becomes leader of Gilead. 3: Jephthah's career as a brigand parallels David's early history (1 Sam 22.2). **6:** The elders first offer the apparently temporary position of military *commander*. **8:** Jephthah holds out for a better offer: permanent *head* or ruler *over all the inhabitants of Gilead* (10.18). **11:** He validates the agreement by reciting it in the witnessing presence of the LORD at the shrine *at Mizpah.*

12 Then Jephthah sent messengers to the king of the Ammonites and said, "What is there between you and me, that you have come to me to fight against my land?" [13]The king of the Ammonites answered the messengers of Jephthah, "Because Israel, on coming from Egypt, took away my land from the Arnon to the Jabbok and to the Jordan; now therefore restore it peaceably." [14]Once again Jephthah sent messengers to the king of the Ammonites [15]and said to him: "Thus says Jephthah: Israel did not take away the land of Moab or the land of the Ammonites, [16]but when they came up from Egypt, Israel went through the wilderness to the Red Sea[a] and came to Kadesh. [17]Israel then sent messengers to the king of Edom, saying, 'Let us pass through your land'; but the king of Edom would not listen. They also sent to the king of Moab, but he would not consent. So Israel remained at Kadesh. [18]Then they journeyed through the wilderness, went around the land of Edom and the land of Moab, arrived on the east side of the land of Moab, and camped on the other side of the Arnon. They did not enter the territory of Moab, for the Arnon was the boundary of Moab. [19]Israel then sent messengers to King Sihon of the Amorites, king of Heshbon; and Israel said to him, 'Let us pass through your land to our country.' [20]But Sihon did not trust Israel to pass through his territory; so Sihon gathered all his people together, and encamped at Jahaz, and fought with Israel. [21]Then the LORD, the God of Israel, gave Sihon and all his people into the hand of Israel, and they defeated them; so Israel occupied all the land of the Amorites, who inhabited that country. [22]They occupied all the territory of the Amorites from the Arnon to the Jabbok and from the wilderness to the Jordan. [23]So now the LORD, the God of Israel, has conquered the Amorites for the benefit of his people Israel. Do you intend to take their place? [24]Should you not possess what your god Chemosh gives you to possess? And should we not be the ones to possess everything that the LORD our God has conquered for our benefit? [25]Now are you any better than King Balak son of Zippor of Moab? Did he ever enter into conflict with Israel, or did he ever go to war with them? [26]While Israel lived in Heshbon and its villages, and in Aroer and its villages, and in all the towns that are along the Arnon, three hundred years, why did you not recover them within that time? [27]It is not I who have sinned against you, but you are the one who does me wrong by making war on me. Let the LORD, who is judge, decide today for the Israelites or for the Ammonites." [28]But the king of the Ammonites did not heed the message that Jephthah sent him.

a Or *Sea of Reeds*

11.12–28: Jephthah's diplomacy fails. 13: The king asserts that Israel has unlawfully occupied land north of *the Arnon* River and south of the *Jabbok,* directly west of the Ammonite homeland. Later statements indicate that Ammon is claiming this territory on the basis that it once belonged to Moab. **15:** Jephthah's position is that Israel did not take this territory from either *Moab* or *the Ammonites,* but rather obtained it 300 years ago (v. 26) by conquering the Amorite king Sihon (vv. 21–22). **18:** He emphasizes that Israel did not go into Moab. Even at that time *the Arnon was the boundary of Moab.* **24:** Early Israel believed that the gods of other nations existed and legitimately guarded the interests of their own people. *Chemosh,* the god of Moab, was associated with the territory under dispute.

29 Then the spirit of the LORD came upon Jephthah, and he passed through Gilead and Manasseh. He passed on to Mizpah of Gilead, and from Mizpah of Gilead he passed on to the Ammonites. ³⁰And Jephthah made a vow to the LORD, and said, "If you will give the Ammonites into my hand, ³¹then whoever comes out of the doors of my house to meet me, when I return victorious from the Ammonites, shall be the LORD's, to be offered up by me as a burnt offering." ³²So Jephthah crossed over to the Ammonites to fight against them; and the LORD gave them into his hand. ³³He inflicted a massive defeat on them from Aroer to the neighborhood of Minnith, twenty towns, and as far as Abel-keramim. So the Ammonites were subdued before the people of Israel.

34 Then Jephthah came to his home at Mizpah; and there was his daughter coming out to meet him with timbrels and with dancing. She was his only child; he had no son or daughter except her. ³⁵When he saw her, he tore his clothes, and said, "Alas, my daughter! You have brought me very low; you have become the cause of great trouble to me. For I have opened my mouth to the LORD, and I cannot take back my vow." ³⁶She said to him, "My father, if you have opened your mouth to the LORD, do to me according to what has gone out of your mouth, now that the LORD has given you vengeance against your enemies, the Ammonites." ³⁷And she

said to her father, "Let this thing be done for me: Grant me two months, so that I may go and wanderᵃ on the mountains, and bewail my virginity, my companions and I." ³⁸"Go," he said and sent her away for two months. So she departed, she and her companions, and bewailed her virginity on the mountains. ³⁹At the end of two months, she returned to her father, who did with her according to the vow he had made. She had never slept with a man. So there arose an Israelite custom that ⁴⁰for four days every year the daughters of Israel would go out to lament the daughter of Jephthah the Gileadite.

11.29–40: Jephthah's vow. 29: Only now *the spirit of the LORD* empowers Jephthah, perhaps reflecting the LORD's earlier reluctance to deliver Israel (10.13–16). **30:** Another example of a war vow can be found in Num 21.2. **31:** His vow is rash, careless, and egocentric. The language does not necessarily specify that this will be a human sacrifice (NRSV *whoever* could also be "whatever"). Israelites shared their houses with farm animals. *Burnt offering* suggests an animal, although human sacrifice was not unknown in Israel. **34:** She is doing an expected and predictable thing. Israelite women customarily celebrated victories *with timbrels and with dancing* (Ex 15.20–21; 1 Sam 18.6–7). **35:** He is distraught (*tore his clothes*), but also sounds as though he is blaming her. Every ancient reader would agree that his vow was irrevocable. **36–37:** She is courageous and suitably devout, but also seizes control of how she will spend the last months of her life. *Bewail my virginity:* To die without the possibility of motherhood was a dreadful tragedy in Israelite culture (reemphasized in v. 39). Jephthah too is now childless (v. 34). **40:** This annual commemoration may have preserved her story for later generations.

12 The men of Ephraim were called to arms, and they crossed to Zaphon and said to Jephthah, "Why did you cross over to fight against the Ammonites, and did not call us to go with you? We will burn your house down over you!" ²Jephthah said to them, "My people and I were engaged in conflict with the Ammonites who oppressed usᵇ severely. But when I called you, you did

ᵃ Cn: Heb *go down*   ᵇ Gk OL, Syr H: Heb lacks *who oppressed us*

not deliver me from their hand. ³When I saw that you would not deliver me, I took my life in my hand, and crossed over against the Ammonites, and the LORD gave them into my hand. Why then have you come up to me this day, to fight against me?" ⁴Then Jephthah gathered all the men of Gilead and fought with Ephraim; and the men of Gilead defeated Ephraim, because they said, "You are fugitives from Ephraim, you Gileadites—in the heart of Ephraim and Manasseh."ᵃ ⁵Then the Gileadites took the fords of the Jordan against the Ephraimites. Whenever one of the fugitives of Ephraim said, "Let me go over," the men of Gilead would say to him, "Are you an Ephraimite?" When he said, "No," ⁶they said to him, "Then say Shibboleth," and he said, "Sibboleth," for he could not pronounce it right. Then they seized him and killed him at the fords of the Jordan. Forty-two thousand of the Ephraimites fell at that time.

7 Jephthah judged Israel six years. Then Jephthah the Gileadite died, and was buried in his town in Gilead.ᵇ

8 After him Ibzan of Bethlehem judged Israel. ⁹He had thirty sons. He gave his thirty daughters in marriage outside his clan and brought in thirty young women from outside for his sons. He judged Israel seven years. ¹⁰Then Ibzan died, and was buried at Bethlehem.

11 After him Elon the Zebulunite judged Israel; and he judged Israel ten years. ¹²Then Elon the Zebulunite died, and was buried at Aijalon in the land of Zebulun.

13 After him Abdon son of Hillel the Pirathonite judged Israel. ¹⁴He had forty sons and thirty grandsons, who rode on seventy donkeys; he judged Israel eight years. ¹⁵Then Abdon son of Hillel the Pirathonite died, and was buried at Pirathon in the land of Ephraim, in the hill country of the Amalekites.

12.1–15. 1–7: War between Ephraim and Gilead. 1–3: The reader does not know which side to believe. No such appeal to Ephraim by Jephthah has been reported. **4:** Ephraim insults Gilead as being nothing but *fugitives* or refugees from Ephraim, insisting that Gilead is really only a part *of Ephraim and Manasseh* (but

see note *a*). **5:** Gilead blocks the way back across the Jordan and uses a difference in local dialect as a password. The phrase *fugitives of Ephraim* grimly echoes their earlier taunt (v. 4). **7:** This information seems to derive from the list of minor judges (10.1–5; 12.8–15). **8–15: Minor judges: Ibzan, Elon, and Abdon. 12:** *Elon* is remembered as a clan* ancestor in Zebulun (Gen 46.14).

13 The Israelites again did what was evil in the sight of the LORD, and the LORD gave them into the hand of the Philistines forty years.

2 There was a certain man of Zorah, of the tribe of the Danites, whose name was Manoah. His wife was barren, having borne no children. ³And the angel of the LORD appeared to the woman and said to her, "Although you are barren, having borne no children, you shall conceive and bear a son. ⁴Now be careful not to drink wine or strong drink, or to eat anything unclean, ⁵for you shall conceive and bear a son. No razor is to come on his head, for the boy shall be a naziriteᶜ to God from birth. It is he who shall begin to deliver Israel from the hand of the Philistines." ⁶Then the woman came and told her husband, "A man of God came to me, and his appearance was like that of an angelᵈ of God, most awe-inspiring; I did not ask him where he came from, and he did not tell me his name; ⁷but he said to me, 'You shall conceive and bear a son. So then drink no wine or strong drink, and eat nothing unclean, for the boy shall be a naziriteᶜ to God from birth to the day of his death.'"

13.1–7: Samson's birth foretold. 3: *The angel of the LORD* represents the LORD's visible presence. **4:** *Wine or strong drink* (Num 6.3) were forbidden to a nazirite. She is to keep away from these because her unborn son must be untouched by them. **5:** A *nazirite* lived a special lifestyle dedicated to God's purposes (see note *c;* Num 6.1–21; 1 Sam 1.11). Normally nazirites took a temporary vow of dedication; Samson was to be a permanent nazirite *from birth*. **6:** She supposes she has encountered *a man of God*, that is, a prophet,* but

a Meaning of Heb uncertain: Gk omits *because . . . Manasseh*   *b* Gk: Heb *in the towns of Gilead*   *c* That is *one separated* or *one consecrated*   *d* Or *the angel*

from his striking appearance she comes close to sensing the actual truth—that he was a divine messenger.

8 Then Manoah entreated the LORD, and said, "O LORD, I pray, let the man of God whom you sent come to us again and teach us what we are to do concerning the boy who will be born." ⁹God listened to Manoah, and the angel of God came again to the woman as she sat in the field; but her husband Manoah was not with her. ¹⁰So the woman ran quickly and told her husband, "The man who came to me the other day has appeared to me." ¹¹Manoah got up and followed his wife, and came to the man and said to him, "Are you the man who spoke to this woman?" And he said, "I am." ¹²Then Manoah said, "Now when your words come true, what is to be the boy's rule of life; what is he to do?" ¹³The angel of the LORD said to Manoah, "Let the woman give heed to all that I said to her. ¹⁴She may not eat of anything that comes from the vine. She is not to drink wine or strong drink, or eat any unclean thing. She is to observe everything that I commanded her."

15 Manoah said to the angel of the LORD, "Allow us to detain you, and prepare a kid for you." ¹⁶The angel of the LORD said to Manoah, "If you detain me, I will not eat your food; but if you want to prepare a burnt offering, then offer it to the LORD." (For Manoah did not know that he was the angel of the LORD.) ¹⁷Then Manoah said to the angel of the LORD, "What is your name, so that we may honor you when your words come true?" ¹⁸But the angel of the LORD said to him, "Why do you ask my name? It is too wonderful."

19 So Manoah took the kid with the grain offering, and offered it on the rock to the LORD, to him who works^a wonders.^{b} ²⁰When the flame went up toward heaven from the altar, the angel of the LORD ascended in the flame of the altar while Manoah and his wife looked on; and they fell on their faces to the ground. ²¹The angel of the LORD did not appear again to Manoah and his wife. Then Manoah realized that it was the angel of the LORD. ²²And Manoah said to his wife, "We shall surely die, for we have

seen God." ²³But his wife said to him, "If the LORD had meant to kill us, he would not have accepted a burnt offering and a grain offering at our hands, or shown us all these things, or now announced to us such things as these."

24 The woman bore a son, and named him Samson. The boy grew, and the LORD blessed him. ²⁵The spirit of the LORD began to stir him in Mahaneh-dan, between Zorah and Eshtaol.

13.8–25: The angel reappears. 13–14: Manoah discovers nothing new from the second appearance for which he has prayed. **15–16:** Manoah offers the customary hospitality for important visitors (6.19; Gen 18.3–5). He still has no idea who this is. **18:** *Wonderful* implies that the name is beyond human understanding. **19–20:** Gideon's experience was similar (6.20–21). **22:** This is the standard reaction after experiencing a visible manifestation of God (6.22). **23:** Throughout the narrative,* she is more perceptive than her husband. **25:** At this point, *the spirit of the LORD* is only a latent stirring or agitation (contrast 14.6).

---

14 Once Samson went down to Timnah, and at Timnah he saw a Philistine woman. ²Then he came up, and told his father and mother, "I saw a Philistine woman at Timnah; now get her for me as my wife." ³But his father and mother said to him, "Is there not a woman among your kin, or among all our^c people, that you must go to take a wife from the uncircumcised Philistines?" But Samson said to his father, "Get her for me, because she pleases me." ⁴His father and mother did not know that this was from the LORD; for he was seeking a pretext to act against the Philistines. At that time the Philistines had dominion over Israel.

5 Then Samson went down with his father and mother to Timnah. When he came to the vineyards of Timnah, suddenly a young lion roared at him. ⁶The spirit of the LORD rushed on him, and he tore the lion apart barehanded as one might tear apart a kid. But he did not tell his father or his mother what he had done. ⁷Then he went

---

a Gk Vg: Heb *and working* b Heb *wonders, while Manoah and his wife looked on* c Cn: Heb *my*

down and talked with the woman, and she pleased Samson. 8After a while he returned to marry her, and he turned aside to see the carcass of the lion, and there was a swarm of bees in the body of the lion, and honey. 9He scraped it out into his hands, and went on, eating as he went. When he came to his father and mother, he gave some to them, and they ate it. But he did not tell them that he had taken the honey from the carcass of the lion.

10 His father went down to the woman, and Samson made a feast there as the young men were accustomed to do. 11When the people saw him, they brought thirty companions to be with him. 12Samson said to them, "Let me now put a riddle to you. If you can explain it to me within the seven days of the feast, and find it out, then I will give you thirty linen garments and thirty festal garments. 13But if you cannot explain it to me, then you shall give me thirty linen garments and thirty festal garments." So they said to him, "Ask your riddle; let us hear it." 14He said to them,

"Out of the eater came something to eat.
Out of the strong came something sweet."

But for three days they could not explain the riddle.

15 On the fourth*a* day they said to Samson's wife, "Coax your husband to explain the riddle to us, or we will burn you and your father's house with fire. Have you invited us here to impoverish us?" 16So Samson's wife wept before him, saying, "You hate me; you do not really love me. You have asked a riddle of my people, but you have not explained it to me." He said to her, "Look, I have not told my father or my mother. Why should I tell you?" 17She wept before him the seven days that their feast lasted; and because she nagged him, on the seventh day he told her. Then she explained the riddle to her people. 18The men of the town said to him on the seventh day before the sun went down,

"What is sweeter than honey?
What is stronger than a lion?"

And he said to them,

"If you had not plowed with my heifer, you would not have found out my riddle."

19Then the spirit of the LORD rushed on him, and he went down to Ashkelon. He killed thirty men of the town, took their spoil, and gave the festal garments to those who had explained the riddle. In hot anger he went back to his father's house. 20And Samson's wife was given to his companion, who had been his best man.

14.1–20: Samson's riddle. 3: Their hesitation is fitting, for intermarriage often leads to apostasy (Deut 7.3–4). **4:** God works behind ordinary human events (compare 9.24). **5:** The first trip to *Timnah* is for parental negotiations and a meeting of the couple (v. 7). **6:** *The spirit of the* LORD gave other judges the ability to serve as military leaders (3.10; 6.34; 11.29), but infuses Samson with physical strength (v. 19). **8–9:** Samson's second trip was *to marry her.* Does he discover the honey on his way back from Timnah? **10:** Now *his father* arrives in Timnah, and Samson gives *a feast.* **11:** *Companions* were a standard feature of marriage celebrations (Ps 45.14). **14:** Proposing and solving *riddles* was a favorite intellectual exercise in the ancient world. **16–17:** Her persistence is akin to Delilah's (16.6–17; compare *you do not really love me* with 16.15). **18:** Their solution sounds like a riddle itself. Is "love" a more profound answer to their question? Samson's response also occurs in riddle form. By exploiting his wife, they have *plowed with* his *heifer.* **19:** The people of *Ashkelon* were also Philistines. Samson can pay off his wager and still not really lose.

---

15 After a while, at the time of the wheat harvest, Samson went to visit his wife, bringing along a kid. He said, "I want to go into my wife's room." But her father would not allow him to go in. 2Her father said, "I was sure that you had rejected her; so I gave her to your companion. Is not her younger sister prettier than she? Why not take her instead?" 3Samson said to them, "This time, when I do mischief to the Philistines, I will be without blame." 4So Samson went and caught three hundred foxes, and took some torches; and he turned the foxes*b* tail to tail, and put a torch between

a Gk Syr: Heb *seventh*   *b* Heb *them*

each pair of tails. 5When he had set fire to the torches, he let the foxes go into the standing grain of the Philistines, and burned up the shocks and the standing grain, as well as the vineyards and*a* olive groves. 6Then the Philistines asked, "Who has done this?" And they said, "Samson, the son-in-law of the Timnite, because he has taken Samson's wife and given her to his companion." So the Philistines came up, and burned her and her father. 7Samson said to them, "If this is what you do, I swear I will not stop until I have taken revenge on you." 8He struck them down hip and thigh with great slaughter; and he went down and stayed in the cleft of the rock of Etam.

15.1–8: Samson's revenge. 1: This may have been a form of marriage in which the woman continued to live with her parents. **2:** That he had *rejected her* (divorced her) was a reasonable conclusion in light of 14.19. Ancient readers would have seen the offer of *her younger sister* as a sensible compromise. **4:** The *foxes* are a way of spreading the fire widely and quickly. **6:** This was precisely the fate Samson's wife had hoped to avoid (14.15). **8:** The meaning of *hip and thigh* is uncertain, but implies ferocious physical combat.

9 Then the Philistines came up and encamped in Judah, and made a raid on Lehi. 10The men of Judah said, "Why have you come up against us?" They said, "We have come up to bind Samson, to do to him as he did to us." 11Then three thousand men of Judah went down to the cleft of the rock of Etam, and they said to Samson, "Do you not know that the Philistines are rulers over us? What then have you done to us?" He replied, "As they did to me, so I have done to them." 12They said to him, "We have come down to bind you, so that we may give you into the hands of the Philistines." Samson answered them, "Swear to me that you yourselves will not attack me." 13They said to him, "No, we will only bind you and give you into their hands; we will not kill you." So they bound him with two new ropes, and brought him up from the rock.

14 When he came to Lehi, the Philistines came shouting to meet him; and the spirit of the LORD rushed on him, and the ropes that were on his arms became like flax that has caught fire, and his bonds melted off his hands. 15Then he found a fresh jawbone of a donkey, reached down and took it, and with it he killed a thousand men. 16And Samson said,

"With the jawbone of a donkey,
heaps upon heaps,
with the jawbone of a donkey
I have slain a thousand men."

17When he had finished speaking, he threw away the jawbone; and that place was called Ramath-lehi.*b*

18 By then he was very thirsty, and he called on the LORD, saying, "You have granted this great victory by the hand of your servant. Am I now to die of thirst, and fall into the hands of the uncircumcised?" 19So God split open the hollow place that is at Lehi, and water came from it. When he drank, his spirit returned, and he revived. Therefore it was named En-hakkore,*c* which is at Lehi to this day. 20And he judged Israel in the days of the Philistines twenty years.

15.9–20: Samson retaliates at Lehi. 11: The dispatch of *three thousand men* to capture a single individual is humorous. **13:** That these are *two new ropes* adds to the wonder of his escape. **14:** *Shouting* (Heb., "yelling a war cry") conveys their triumph and jubilation. Two vivid images communicate the strength infused by the *spirit of the LORD*. **16:** The words for *donkey* and *heap* are the same in Hebrew. **17:** The story of Samson's exploit was preserved by its attachment to two landmarks (notes *b, c*). **19:** His *spirit returned,* that is, his vigor and positive attitude.

16 Once Samson went to Gaza, where he saw a prostitute and went in to her. 2The Gazites were told,*d* "Samson has come here." So they circled around and lay in wait for him all night at the city gate. They kept quiet all night, thinking, "Let us wait until the light of the morning; then we will kill him." 3But Samson lay only until midnight. Then at midnight he rose up, took

---

a Gk Tg Vg: Heb lacks *and*   *b* That is *The Hill of the Jawbone*   *c* That is *The Spring of the One who Called*   *d* Gk: Heb lacks *were told*

hold of the doors of the city gate and the two posts, pulled them up, bar and all, put them on his shoulders, and carried them to the top of the hill that is in front of Hebron.

4 After this he fell in love with a woman in the valley of Sorek, whose name was Delilah. 5 The lords of the Philistines came to her and said to her, "Coax him, and find out what makes his strength so great, and how we may overpower him, so that we may bind him in order to subdue him; and we will each give you eleven hundred pieces of silver." 6 So Delilah said to Samson, "Please tell me what makes your strength so great, and how you could be bound, so that one could subdue you." 7 Samson said to her, "If they bind me with seven fresh bowstrings that are not dried out, then I shall become weak, and be like anyone else." 8 Then the lords of the Philistines brought her seven fresh bowstrings that had not dried out, and she bound him with them. 9 While men were lying in wait in an inner chamber, she said to him, "The Philistines are upon you, Samson!" But he snapped the bowstrings, as a strand of fiber snaps when it touches the fire. So the secret of his strength was not known.

10 Then Delilah said to Samson, "You have mocked me and told me lies; please tell me how you could be bound." 11 He said to her, "If they bind me with new ropes that have not been used, then I shall become weak, and be like anyone else." 12 So Delilah took new ropes and bound him with them, and said to him, "The Philistines are upon you, Samson!" (The men lying in wait were in an inner chamber.) But he snapped the ropes off his arms like a thread.

13 Then Delilah said to Samson, "Until now you have mocked me and told me lies; tell me how you could be bound." He said to her, "If you weave the seven locks of my head with the web and make it tight with the pin, then I shall become weak, and be like anyone else." 14 So while he slept, Delilah took the seven locks of his head and wove them into the web,[a] and made them tight with the pin. Then she said to him, "The Philistines are upon you, Samson!" But he awoke from his sleep, and pulled away the pin, the loom, and the web.

15 Then she said to him, "How can you say, 'I love you,' when your heart is not with me? You have mocked me three times now and have not told me what makes your strength so great." 16 Finally, after she had nagged him with her words day after day, and pestered him, he was tired to death. 17 So he told her his whole secret, and said to her, "A razor has never come upon my head; for I have been a nazirite[b] to God from my mother's womb. If my head were shaved, then my strength would leave me; I would become weak, and be like anyone else."

18 When Delilah realized that he had told her his whole secret, she sent and called the lords of the Philistines, saying, "This time come up, for he has told his whole secret to me." Then the lords of the Philistines came up to her, and brought the money in their hands. 19 She let him fall asleep on her lap; and she called a man, and had him shave off the seven locks of his head. He began to weaken,[c] and his strength left him. 20 Then she said, "The Philistines are upon you, Samson!" When he awoke from his sleep, he thought, "I will go out as at other times, and shake myself free." But he did not know that the LORD had left him. 21 So the Philistines seized him and gouged out his eyes. They brought him down to Gaza and bound him with bronze shackles; and he ground at the mill in the prison. 22 But the hair of his head began to grow again after it had been shaved.

16.1–22: Delilah betrays Samson. 1–3: *Gaza* was one of the five Philistine cities. *Hebron* is about forty miles (sixty kilometers) uphill from Gaza. **4:** Because she lives in *the valley of Sorek,* she is probably a Philistine. **7:** *Bowstrings* were made of animal tendons. They are to be *fresh* because new things were thought to have magical powers. **11:** Specifying *new ropes* again points to magical notions. **13:** *The web* and *the pin* were parts of a loom (v. 14). Perhaps to entangle Samson in something so domestic as weaving would magically drain his warrior powers. By involving his hair, Samson has revealed part of his secret. **20:** The loss of his nazirite status (13.5) means *the LORD had left him,* so that the spirit would no longer empower his mighty

a Compare Gk: in verses 13–14, Heb lacks *and make it tight . . . into the web*   *b* That is *one separated* or *one consecrated*   *c* Gk: Heb *She began to torment him*

feats (14.6, 19; 15.14). **21:** Samson grinds grain with a hand mill, a menial task performed by women and slaves (compare Lam 5.13).

23 Now the lords of the Philistines gathered to offer a great sacrifice to their god Dagon, and to rejoice; for they said, "Our god has given Samson our enemy into our hand." 24When the people saw him, they praised their god; for they said, "Our god has given our enemy into our hand, the ravager of our country, who has killed many of us." 25And when their hearts were merry, they said, "Call Samson, and let him entertain us." So they called Samson out of the prison, and he performed for them. They made him stand between the pillars; 26and Samson said to the attendant who held him by the hand, "Let me feel the pillars on which the house rests, so that I may lean against them." 27Now the house was full of men and women; all the lords of the Philistines were there, and on the roof there were about three thousand men and women, who looked on while Samson performed.

28 Then Samson called to the LORD and said, "Lord GOD, remember me and strengthen me only this once, O God, so that with this one act of revenge I may pay back the Philistines for my two eyes."[a] 29And Samson grasped the two middle pillars on which the house rested, and he leaned his weight against them, his right hand on the one and his left hand on the other. 30Then Samson said, "Let me die with the Philistines." He strained with all his might; and the house fell on the lords and all the people who were in it. So those he killed at his death were more than those he had killed during his life. 31Then his brothers and all his family came down and took him and brought him up and buried him between Zorah and Eshtaol in the tomb of his father Manoah. He had judged Israel twenty years.

16.23–31: Samson's retaliation. 23: *Dagon* was a Canaanite grain god adopted by the Philistines (1 Sam 5.1–5). **26:** *The house* is either Dagon's temple or a large hall. **28:** This *one act* will avenge two wrongs (but see note *a*).

17 There was a man in the hill country of Ephraim whose name was Micah. 2He said to his mother, "The eleven hundred pieces of silver that were taken from you, about which you uttered a curse, and even spoke it in my hearing,—that silver is in my possession; I took it; but now I will return it to you."[b] And his mother said, "May my son be blessed by the LORD!" 3Then he returned the eleven hundred pieces of silver to his mother; and his mother said, "I consecrate the silver to the LORD from my hand for my son, to make an idol of cast metal." 4So when he returned the money to his mother, his mother took two hundred pieces of silver, and gave it to the silversmith, who made it into an idol of cast metal; and it was in the house of Micah. 5This man Micah had a shrine, and he made an ephod and teraphim, and installed one of his sons, who became his priest. 6In those days there was no king in Israel; all the people did what was right in their own eyes.

7 Now there was a young man of Bethlehem in Judah, of the clan of Judah. He was a Levite residing there. 8This man left the town of Bethlehem in Judah, to live wherever he could find a place. He came to the house of Micah in the hill country of Ephraim to carry on his work.[c] 9Micah said to him, "From where do you come?" He replied, "I am a Levite of Bethlehem in Judah, and I am going to live wherever I can find a place." 10Then Micah said to him, "Stay with me, and be to me a father and a priest, and I will give you ten pieces of silver a year, a set of clothes, and your living."[d] 11The Levite agreed to stay with the man; and the young man became to him like one of his sons. 12So Micah installed the Levite, and the young man became his priest, and was in the house of Micah. 13Then Micah said, "Now I know that the LORD will prosper me, because the Levite has become my priest."

a Or *so that I may be avenged upon the Philistines for one of my two eyes*   *b* The words *but now I will return it to you* are transposed from the end of verse 3 in Heb   *c* Or *Ephraim, continuing his journey*   *d* Heb *living, and the Levite went*

17.1–13: Micah builds a shrine and hires a priest. 2: Micah confesses to a theft that has put him under *a curse*. His mother seeks to counteract the curse with a blessing. NRSV considers the text scrambled and re-arranges it (note *b*). **3–4:** She takes further action to nullify the curse, using part of the consecrated silver for an *idol of cast metal*. **5:** This is a private, family sanctuary (Heb., "house of God"). The *ephod** (a priestly garment) and *teraphim* (figurines) were uti-lized to discover God's will. **6:** This editorial refrain (18.1; 19.1; 21.25) approves of kingship and com-municates displeasure with Micah's actions. **7:** He was *of the clan* of Judah* in the sense of living with them as a resident alien.* **10:** *Father* is an honorific title (compare 5.7). **13:** By virtue of his lineage, *the Levite* is preferable as priest to Micah's son (v. 5).

18 In those days there was no king in Israel. And in those days the tribe of the Danites was seeking for itself a territory to live in; for until then no territory among the tribes of Israel had been allotted to them. ²So the Danites sent five valiant men from the whole number of their clan, from Zorah and from Eshtaol, to spy out the land and to explore it; and they said to them, "Go, ex-plore the land." When they came to the hill country of Ephraim, to the house of Micah, they stayed there. ³While they were at Mi-cah's house, they recognized the voice of the young Levite; so they went over and asked him, "Who brought you here? What are you doing in this place? What is your business here?" ⁴He said to them, "Micah did such and such for me, and he hired me, and I have become his priest." ⁵Then they said to him, "Inquire of God that we may know whether the mission we are undertaking will suc-ceed." ⁶The priest replied, "Go in peace. The mission you are on is under the eye of the LORD."

7 The five men went on, and when they came to Laish, they observed the people who were there living securely, after the manner of the Sidonians, quiet and unsuspecting, lacking[a] nothing on earth, and possessing wealth.[b] Furthermore, they were far from the Sidonians and had no dealings with Aram.[c] ⁸When they came to their kinsfolk at Zorah and Eshtaol, they said to them,

"What do you report?" ⁹They said, "Come, let us go up against them; for we have seen the land, and it is very good. Will you do nothing? Do not be slow to go, but enter in and possess the land. ¹⁰When you go, you will come to an unsuspecting people. The land is broad—God has indeed given it into your hands—a place where there is no lack of anything on earth."

18.1–10: Dan searches for a new home. 2: Conquest stories typically begin with the dispatch of spies (1.24; Josh 2). **3:** Apparently they recognized his regional ac-cent. **5:** Part of a priest's job was to discover God's will.

11 Six hundred men of the Danite clan, armed with weapons of war, set out from Zo-rah and Eshtaol, ¹²and went up and en-camped at Kiriath-jearim in Judah. On this account that place is called Mahaneh-dan[d] to this day; it is west of Kiriath-jearim. ¹³From there they passed on to the hill country of Ephraim, and came to the house of Micah.

14 Then the five men who had gone to spy out the land (that is, Laish) said to their comrades, "Do you know that in these build-ings there are an ephod, teraphim, and an idol of cast metal? Now therefore consider what you will do." ¹⁵So they turned in that direction and came to the house of the young Levite, at the home of Micah, and greeted him. ¹⁶While the six hundred men of the Danites, armed with their weapons of war, stood by the entrance of the gate, ¹⁷the five men who had gone to spy out the land pro-ceeded to enter and take the idol of cast metal, the ephod, and the teraphim.[e] The priest was standing by the entrance of the gate with the six hundred men armed with weapons of war. ¹⁸When the men went into Micah's house and took the idol of cast metal, the ephod, and the teraphim, the priest said to them, "What are you doing?" ¹⁹They said to him, "Keep quiet! Put your hand over your mouth, and come with us,

a Cn Compare 18.10: Meaning of Heb uncertain
b Meaning of Heb uncertain   *c* Symmachus: Heb *with anyone*   *d* That is *Camp of Dan*   *e* Compare 17.4, 5; 18.14: Heb *teraphim and the cast metal*

and be to us a father and a priest. Is it better for you to be priest to the house of one person, or to be priest to a tribe and clan in Israel?" ²⁰Then the priest accepted the offer. He took the ephod, the teraphim, and the idol, and went along with the people.

21 So they resumed their journey, putting the little ones, the livestock, and the goods in front of them. ²²When they were some distance from the home of Micah, the men who were in the houses near Micah's house were called out, and they overtook the Danites. ²³They shouted to the Danites, who turned around and said to Micah, "What is the matter that you come with such a company?" ²⁴He replied, "You take my gods that I made, and the priest, and go away, and what have I left? How then can you ask me, 'What is the matter?' " ²⁵And the Danites said to him, "You had better not let your voice be heard among us or else hot-tempered fellows will attack you, and you will lose your life and the lives of your household." ²⁶Then the Danites went their way. When Micah saw that they were too strong for him, he turned and went back to his home.

27 The Danites, having taken what Micah had made, and the priest who belonged to him, came to Laish, to a people quiet and unsuspecting, put them to the sword, and burned down the city. ²⁸There was no deliverer, because it was far from Sidon and they had no dealings with Aram.^a It was in the valley that belongs to Beth-rehob. They rebuilt the city, and lived in it. ²⁹They named the city Dan, after their ancestor Dan, who was born to Israel; but the name of the city was formerly Laish. ³⁰Then the Danites set up the idol for themselves. Jonathan son of Gershom, son of Moses,^b and his sons were priests to the tribe of the Danites until the time the land went into captivity. ³¹So they maintained as their own Micah's idol that he had made, as long as the house of God was at Shiloh.

became a national shrine of the northern kingdom (1 Kings 12.29–30). *Jonathan* is presumably the previously unnamed Levite. The priestly family in charge of Dan descended from *Moses* (but see note b). *Captivity* refers to the results of the Assyrian conquests (2 Kings 15.29; 17.5–6). **31:** The true *house of God* was at Shiloh (1 Sam 1–2). The illegitimate background of the sanctuary of Dan has been emphasized at every turn: pilfered silver (17.2–3), stolen illicit image (17.5–6; 18.16–18, 24), opportunistic priest (17.9; 18.19–20).

19 In those days, when there was no king in Israel, a certain Levite, residing in the remote parts of the hill country of Ephraim, took to himself a concubine from Bethlehem in Judah. ²But his concubine became angry with^c him, and she went away from him to her father's house at Bethlehem in Judah, and was there some four months. ³Then her husband set out after her, to speak tenderly to her and bring her back. He had with him his servant and a couple of donkeys. When he reached^d her father's house, the girl's father saw him and came with joy to meet him. ⁴His father-in-law, the girl's father, made him stay, and he remained with him three days; so they ate and drank, and he^e stayed there. ⁵On the fourth day they got up early in the morning, and he prepared to go; but the girl's father said to his son-in-law, "Fortify yourself with a bit of food, and after that you may go." ⁶So the two men sat and ate and drank together; and the girl's father said to the man, "Why not spend the night and enjoy yourself?" ⁷When the man got up to go, his father-in-law kept urging him until he spent the night there again. ⁸On the fifth day he got up early in the morning to leave; and the girl's father said, "Fortify yourself." So they lingered^f until the day declined, and the two of them ate and drank.^g ⁹When the man with his concubine and his servant got up to leave, his father-in-law, the girl's father, said to him, "Look, the day has worn on until it is almost evening.

18.11–31: Dan establishes a sanctuary. 21: The most vulnerable members of the party are protected from pursuit. **25:** *Hot-tempered fellows:* Dan had a reputation for belligerence (Gen 49.17; Deut 33.22). **30:** Dan

a Cn Compare verse 7: Heb *with anyone*   *b* Another reading is *son of Manasseh*   *c* Gk OL: Heb *prostituted herself against*   *d* Gk: Heb *she brought him*
e Compare verse 7 and Gk: Heb *they*   *f* Cn: Heb *Linger*   *g* Gk: Heb lacks *and drank*

Spend the night. See, the day has drawn to a close. Spend the night here and enjoy yourself. Tomorrow you can get up early in the morning for your journey, and go home."

10 But the man would not spend the night; he got up and departed, and arrived opposite Jebus (that is, Jerusalem). He had with him a couple of saddled donkeys, and his concubine was with him. ¹¹When they were near Jebus, the day was far spent, and the servant said to his master, "Come now, let us turn aside to this city of the Jebusites, and spend the night in it." ¹²But his master said to him, "We will not turn aside into a city of foreigners, who do not belong to the people of Israel; but we will continue on to Gibeah." ¹³Then he said to his servant, "Come, let us try to reach one of these places, and spend the night at Gibeah or at Ramah." ¹⁴So they passed on and went their way; and the sun went down on them near Gibeah, which belongs to Benjamin. ¹⁵They turned aside there, to go in and spend the night at Gibeah. He went in and sat down in the open square of the city, but no one took them in to spend the night.

16 Then at evening there was an old man coming from his work in the field. The man was from the hill country of Ephraim, and he was residing in Gibeah. (The people of the place were Benjaminites.) ¹⁷When the old man looked up and saw the wayfarer in the open square of the city, he said, "Where are you going and where do you come from?" ¹⁸He answered him, "We are passing from Bethlehem in Judah to the remote parts of the hill country of Ephraim, from which I come. I went to Bethlehem in Judah; and I am going to my home.ᵃ Nobody has offered to take me in. ¹⁹We your servants have straw and fodder for our donkeys, with bread and wine for me and the woman and the young man along with us. We need nothing more." ²⁰The old man said, "Peace be to you. I will care for all your wants; only do not spend the night in the square." ²¹So he brought him into his house, and fed the donkeys; they washed their feet, and ate and drank.

that a king would make such horrifying lawlessness unlikely. As *a concubine*⋆ she is a recognized wife with inferior legal status. **2:** She returns to her family of origin (*father's house*), but the circumstances are unclear (note *c*). **4–9:** The point of this prolonged account is that they left much later in the afternoon than was wise. **12:** The *irony*⋆ is sharp. Jerusalem as *a city of foreigners* is rejected as inhospitable in favor of shelter with *the people of Israel*. **15:** That *no one took them in* would be considered outrageous; hospitality was an important civic virtue. **16:** The *old man* is a fellow countryman (*hill country of Ephraim;* v. 1) living as a resident alien⋆ *in Gibeah.*

22 While they were enjoying themselves, the men of the city, a perverse lot, surrounded the house, and started pounding on the door. They said to the old man, the master of the house, "Bring out the man who came into your house, so that we may have intercourse with him." ²³And the man, the master of the house, went out to them and said to them, "No, my brothers, do not act so wickedly. Since this man is my guest, do not do this vile thing. ²⁴Here are my virgin daughter and his concubine; let me bring them out now. Ravish them and do whatever you want to them; but against this man do not do such a vile thing." ²⁵But the men would not listen to him. So the man seized his concubine, and put her out to them. They wantonly raped her, and abused her all through the night until the morning. And as the dawn began to break, they let her go. ²⁶As morning appeared, the woman came and fell down at the door of the man's house where her master was, until it was light.

27 In the morning her master got up, opened the doors of the house, and when he went out to go on his way, there was his concubine lying at the door of the house, with her hands on the threshold. ²⁸"Get up," he said to her, "we are going." But there was no answer. Then he put her on the donkey; and the man set out for his home. ²⁹When he had entered his house, he took a knife, and grasping his concubine he cut her into twelve pieces, limb by limb, and sent her throughout all the territory of Israel. ³⁰Then

19.1–21: Spending the night in Gibeah. 1: *In those days . . . Israel:* This refrain (17.6; 18.1; 21.25) suggests

a Gk Compare 19.29. Heb *to the house of the LORD*

he commanded the men whom he sent, saying, "Thus shall you say to all the Israelites, 'Has such a thing ever happened[a] since the day that the Israelites came up from the land of Egypt until this day? Consider it, take counsel, and speak out.'"

19.22–30: The rape of the Levite's concubine.* **22:** Their threat of homosexual rape is the polar opposite of suitable hospitality. It parallels the behavior of the men of Sodom (Gen 19.5). **23–24:** For *the master of the house,* the obligations of hospitality take precedence over family loyalties. However, he does not extend the protection of hospitality to the concubine. *Vile thing* denotes a loathsome and foolish act, especially a sexual crime. **25–26:** The cowardly Levite acts to save himself. The powerful description of rape and the poignant final scene at the door fuel the reader's outrage against Gibeah. Her husband (v. 3) is now called *her master;* he has treated her as a disposable object. **27–28:** The affecting image of *her hands on the threshold* provides a sharp contrast to his brusque unconcern. **29:** Her body is treated as an object, a signal to rally the nation (compare 1 Sam 11.7).

20 Then all the Israelites came out, from Dan to Beer-sheba, including the land of Gilead, and the congregation assembled in one body before the LORD at Mizpah. ²The chiefs of all the people, of all the tribes of Israel, presented themselves in the assembly of the people of God, four hundred thousand foot-soldiers bearing arms. ³(Now the Benjaminites heard that the people of Israel had gone up to Mizpah.) And the Israelites said, "Tell us, how did this criminal act come about?" ⁴The Levite, the husband of the woman who was murdered, answered, "I came to Gibeah that belongs to Benjamin, I and my concubine, to spend the night. ⁵The lords of Gibeah rose up against me, and surrounded the house at night. They intended to kill me, and they raped my concubine until she died. ⁶Then I took my concubine and cut her into pieces, and sent her throughout the whole extent of Israel's territory; for they have committed a vile outrage in Israel. ⁷So now, you Israelites, all of you, give your advice and counsel here."

8 All the people got up as one, saying, "We will not any of us go to our tents, nor will any of us return to our houses. ⁹But now this is what we will do to Gibeah: we will go up[b] against it by lot. ¹⁰We will take ten men of a hundred throughout all the tribes of Israel, and a hundred of a thousand, and a thousand of ten thousand, to bring provisions for the troops, who are going to repay[c] Gibeah of Benjamin for all the disgrace that they have done in Israel." ¹¹So all the men of Israel gathered against the city, united as one.

12 The tribes of Israel sent men through all the tribe of Benjamin, saying, "What crime is this that has been committed among you? ¹³Now then, hand over those scoundrels in Gibeah, so that we may put them to death, and purge the evil from Israel." But the Benjaminites would not listen to their kinsfolk, the Israelites. ¹⁴The Benjaminites came together out of the towns to Gibeah, to go out to battle against the Israelites. ¹⁵On that day the Benjaminites mustered twenty-six thousand armed men from their towns, besides the inhabitants of Gibeah. ¹⁶Of all this force, there were seven hundred picked men who were left-handed; every one could sling a stone at a hair, and not miss. ¹⁷And the Israelites, apart from Benjamin, mustered four hundred thousand armed men, all of them warriors.

20.1–17: Israel assembles to attack Benjamin. **1:** *From Dan to Beer-sheba* designates the north and south limits of Israel. **3:** Because Gibeah is Benjaminite (19.16), the Ephraimite Levite's personal quarrel escalates into intertribal conflict. **5:** The Levite's version omits important details in order to magnify the threat to himself and conceal his own culpability. **6:** *Vile outrage* signifies an intentional affront to Israel's core values. **9:** *By lot* refers to the way the ten percent of the next verse are to be chosen. **15–17:** Although Israel has an overwhelming numerical advantage, Benjamin's contingent of crack marksmen (v. 16) suggests that things will not be so simple.

18 The Israelites proceeded to go up to Bethel, where they inquired of God, "Which

a Compare Gk: Heb ³⁰*And all who saw it said, "Such a thing has not happened or been seen* b Gk: Heb lacks *we will go up* c Compare Gk: Meaning of Heb uncertain

of us shall go up first to battle against the Benjaminites?" And the LORD answered, "Judah shall go up first."

19 Then the Israelites got up in the morning, and encamped against Gibeah. 20 The Israelites went out to battle against Benjamin; and the Israelites drew up the battle line against them at Gibeah. 21 The Benjaminites came out of Gibeah, and struck down on that day twenty-two thousand of the Israelites. 23[a] The Israelites went up and wept before the LORD until the evening; and they inquired of the LORD, "Shall we again draw near to battle against our kinsfolk the Benjaminites?" And the LORD said, "Go up against them." 22 The Israelites took courage, and again formed the battle line in the same place where they had formed it on the first day.

24 So the Israelites advanced against the Benjaminites the second day. 25 Benjamin moved out against them from Gibeah the second day, and struck down eighteen thousand of the Israelites, all of them armed men. 26 Then all the Israelites, the whole army, went back to Bethel and wept, sitting there before the LORD; they fasted that day until evening. Then they offered burnt offerings and sacrifices of well-being before the LORD. 27 And the Israelites inquired of the LORD (for the ark of the covenant of God was there in those days, 28 and Phinehas son of Eleazar, son of Aaron, ministered before it in those days), saying, "Shall we go out once more to battle against our kinsfolk the Benjaminites, or shall we desist?" The LORD answered, "Go up, for tomorrow I will give them into your hand."

20.18–28: Benjamin's initial victories. 18: Nearby *Bethel* was the chief sanctuary of central Israel. The answer comes either by the sacred lots or through an oracle* delivered by a priest. **23–24:** *Before the LORD* indicates that they returned to the sanctuary of Bethel to weep (v. 26). **28:** Only this third answer includes a promise of victory (contrast vv. 18, 23).

29 So Israel stationed men in ambush around Gibeah. 30 Then the Israelites went up against the Benjaminites on the third day, and set themselves in array against Gibeah,

as before. 31 When the Benjaminites went out against the army, they were drawn away from the city. As before they began to inflict casualties on the troops, along the main roads, one of which goes up to Bethel and the other to Gibeah, as well as in the open country, killing about thirty men of Israel. 32 The Benjaminites thought, "They are being routed before us, as previously." But the Israelites said, "Let us retreat and draw them away from the city toward the roads." 33 The main body of the Israelites drew back its battle line to Baal-tamar, while those Israelites who were in ambush rushed out of their place west[b] of Geba. 34 There came against Gibeah ten thousand picked men out of all Israel, and the battle was fierce. But the Benjaminites did not realize that disaster was close upon them.

35 The LORD defeated Benjamin before Israel; and the Israelites destroyed twenty-five thousand one hundred men of Benjamin that day, all of them armed.

36 Then the Benjaminites saw that they were defeated.[c]

The Israelites gave ground to Benjamin, because they trusted to the troops in ambush that they had stationed against Gibeah. 37 The troops in ambush rushed quickly upon Gibeah. Then they put the whole city to the sword. 38 Now the agreement between the main body of Israel and the men in ambush was that when they sent up a cloud of smoke out of the city 39 the main body of Israel should turn in battle. But Benjamin had begun to inflict casualties on the Israelites, killing about thirty of them; so they thought, "Surely they are defeated before us, as in the first battle." 40 But when the cloud, a column of smoke, began to rise out of the city, the Benjaminites looked behind them—and there was the whole city going up in smoke toward the sky! 41 Then the main body of Israel turned, and the Benjaminites were dismayed, for they saw that disaster was close upon them. 42 Therefore they turned away from the Israelites in the direction of the wilderness; but the battle overtook them, and

---

a Verses 22 and 23 are transposed   *b* Gk Vg: Heb *in the plain*   *c* This sentence is continued by verse 45.

those who came out of the city^a were slaughtering them in between.^b ⁴³Cutting down^c the Benjaminites, they pursued them from Nohah^d and trod them down as far as a place east of Gibeah. ⁴⁴Eighteen thousand Benjaminites fell, all of them courageous fighters. ⁴⁵When they turned and fled toward the wilderness to the rock of Rimmon, five thousand of them were cut down on the main roads, and they were pursued as far as Gidom, and two thousand of them were slain. ⁴⁶So all who fell that day of Benjamin were twenty-five thousand arms-bearing men, all of them courageous fighters. ⁴⁷But six hundred turned and fled toward the wilderness to the rock of Rimmon, and remained at the rock of Rimmon for four months. ⁴⁸Meanwhile, the Israelites turned back against the Benjaminites, and put them to the sword— the city, the people, the animals, and all that remained. Also the remaining towns they set on fire.

20.29–48: Israel crushes Benjamin. 33: The tactics of *ambush* and simulated retreat parallel Josh 8.3–23. **35:** The magnitude of the disaster is clear when the number killed (v. 46) is compared with Benjamin's starting total (v. 15). **36:** The course of the battle is recounted twice in overlapping parallel stories: vv. 29–36 (as far as note *c*) and vv. 36–43. **40–41:** The role of the *smoke* is the same as in Josh 8.20–21. **42:** Benjamin is trapped and butchered between the main army (*the Israelites*) and the ambush (*those who came out of the city*). **47–48:** These *six hundred* are the only survivors. Near total annihilation of the Benjaminites sets up the situation for the next chapter.

21 Now the Israelites had sworn at Mizpah, "No one of us shall give his daughter in marriage to Benjamin." ²And the people came to Bethel, and sat there until evening before God, and they lifted up their voices and wept bitterly. ³They said, "O Lord, the God of Israel, why has it come to pass that today there should be one tribe lacking in Israel?" ⁴On the next day, the people got up early, and built an altar there, and offered burnt offerings and sacrifices of well-being. ⁵Then the Israelites said, "Which of all the tribes of Israel did not come up in the assembly to the Lord?" For a solemn oath

had been taken concerning whoever did not come up to the Lord to Mizpah, saying, "That one shall be put to death." ⁶But the Israelites had compassion for Benjamin their kin, and said, "One tribe is cut off from Israel this day. ⁷What shall we do for wives for those who are left, since we have sworn by the Lord that we will not give them any of our daughters as wives?"

8 Then they said, "Is there anyone from the tribes of Israel who did not come up to the Lord to Mizpah?" It turned out that no one from Jabesh-gilead had come to the camp, to the assembly. ⁹For when the roll was called among the people, not one of the inhabitants of Jabesh-gilead was there. ¹⁰So the congregation sent twelve thousand soldiers there and commanded them, "Go, put the inhabitants of Jabesh-gilead to the sword, including the women and the little ones. ¹¹This is what you shall do; every male and every woman that has lain with a male you shall devote to destruction." ¹²And they found among the inhabitants of Jabesh-gilead four hundred young virgins who had never slept with a man and brought them to the camp at Shiloh, which is in the land of Canaan.

13 Then the whole congregation sent word to the Benjaminites who were at the rock of Rimmon, and proclaimed peace to them. ¹⁴Benjamin returned at that time; and they gave them the women whom they had saved alive of the women of Jabesh-gilead; but they did not suffice for them.

21.1–14: Wives for Benjamin from Jabesh-gilead. 1: This oath is considered unbreakable (v. 5). **8:** Although others from Gilead had participated (20.1), *Jabesh-gilead* did not. **10–11:** As a result of their vow, they treat this as a holy war* and *devote to destruction* everyone not useful for their plan. **14:** This tradition may explain why Jabesh-gilead and King Saul (a Benjaminite from Gibeah) had friendly relations (1 Sam 11.1–11; 31.11–13). Four hundred women are not enough for the six hundred surviving men.

---

a Compare Vg and some Gk Mss: Heb *cities*
b Compare Syr: Meaning of Heb uncertain
c Gk: Heb *Surrounding*   *d* Gk: Heb *pursued them at their resting place*

15 The people had compassion on Benjamin because the LORD had made a breach in the tribes of Israel. 16 So the elders of the congregation said, "What shall we do for wives for those who are left, since there are no women left in Benjamin?" 17 And they said, "There must be heirs for the survivors of Benjamin, in order that a tribe may not be blotted out from Israel. 18 Yet we cannot give any of our daughters to them as wives." For the Israelites had sworn, "Cursed be anyone who gives a wife to Benjamin." 19 So they said, "Look, the yearly festival of the LORD is taking place at Shiloh, which is north of Bethel, on the east of the highway that goes up from Bethel to Shechem, and south of Lebonah." 20 And they instructed the Benjaminites, saying, "Go and lie in wait in the vineyards, 21 and watch; when the young women of Shiloh come out to dance in the dances, then come out of the vineyards and each of you carry off a wife for himself from the young women of Shiloh, and go to the land of Benjamin. 22 Then if their fathers or their brothers come to complain to us, we will say to them, 'Be generous and allow us to have them; because we did not capture in battle a wife for each man. But neither did you incur guilt by giving your daughters to them.' " 23 The Benjaminites did so; they took wives for each of them from the dancers whom they abducted. Then they went and returned to their territory, and rebuilt the towns, and lived in them. 24 So the Israelites departed from there at that time by tribes and families, and they went out from there to their own territories.

25 In those days there was no king in Israel; all the people did what was right in their own eyes.

21.15–25: Capturing wives at Shiloh. 17: Although not *blotted out,* Benjamin remained one of the smaller tribes. **21:** This may reflect an on-going custom of obtaining wives by ritualized capture at the annual festival at Shiloh. **22:** *Brothers* are the natural protectors of their unmarried sisters (Song 8.8–9), and *fathers* would lose financially if marriage bypassed the usual negotiations. **25:** Rape, civil war, genocide—all resulted because Israel had *no king.*

RUTH

Introduction

The book of Ruth opens with a crisis: While living in Moab, an Israelite woman named Naomi loses her husband and sons. In a society in which property is passed down through males, she thus is left destitute in a foreign land. The book works toward this problem's solution, as her Moabite daughter-in-law Ruth secures for both women land and offspring, with the help of a wealthy Judean landowner named Boaz. The genealogy★ that closes the book reveals that the child born to Ruth and Boaz is the ancestor of none other than King David.

Scholars who focus on the narrative★ quality of the book (calling it an "idyll" or a "novella" or a "short story") believe the genealogy was added to the book to encourage the book's acceptance into the canon.★ Other interpreters see the genealogy as a key to the purpose of its composition: to celebrate David or to give Davidic authority to marriage between Judeans and non-Judeans. If the genealogy is original, then the book was likely written close to the time of the Davidic monarchy. If the primary concern is to authorize intermarriage, then the book may have been part of the larger discussion of intermarriage in the time of Ezra and Nehemiah (Ezra 8).

In the Jewish canon, the book is found in The Writings,★ at the close of the Bible. There, Ruth is clustered with Esther, Ecclesiastes, Song of Solomon, and Lamentations, and together they are called the megillot (singular, "megillah"★)—the scrolls read in annual Jewish festivals. Because of its agricultural setting and concerns, Ruth is linked with the festival of Shavuot★ (also called The Feast of Weeks,★ or Pentecost★), a harvest celebration. At least by the eighth century CE, Shavuot was also identified as the time during which Moses received the Torah★ at Mt. Sinai. The compilers of the Christian canon grouped Ruth with the historical books, putting it there because of its chronological setting "when the judges ruled" (Ruth 1.1).

Both explicit allusions and similarities in theme link Ruth with other narratives of the Hebrew Bible. Like Tamar (Gen 38), Ruth goes to extraordinary measures to procure a son; like Abraham (Gen 12), she leaves her family to go to a foreign land; like Sarah and Rachel (Gen 12–30), she and Naomi struggle with the absence of sons in a society in which land and authority are male prerogatives.

READING GUIDE

Because of its brevity, the book of Ruth is easily read in its entirety, allowing readers the luxury of reading it multiple times. After understanding the story's basic plot, the reader can subsequently ask: Are the characters portrayed as models of perfect behavior or are they complex personalities? What are their motives? How does the strong focus on women fit with the book's "happy ending" of the birth of a male? How often is God mentioned in this book and in what contexts?

1 The problem: famine, death and childlessness
2 Ruth temporarily provides for Naomi and herself
3 Ruth, Naomi, and Boaz work toward more permanent arrangements
4 Resolution: Ruth and Boaz marry and a child is born

1 In the days when the judges ruled, there was a famine in the land, and a certain man of Bethlehem in Judah went to live in the country of Moab, he and his wife and two sons. ²The name of the man was Elimelech and the name of his wife Naomi, and the names of his two sons were Mahlon and Chilion; they were Ephrathites from Bethlehem in Judah. They went into the country of Moab and remained there. ³But Elimelech, the husband of Naomi, died, and she was left with her two sons. ⁴These took Moabite wives; the name of the one was Orpah and the name of the other Ruth. When they had lived there about ten years, ⁵both Mahlon and Chilion also died, so that the woman was left without her two sons and her husband.

1.1–5: Famine and death. 1: *When the judges ruled* sets the story of Ruth before the rise of kingship, when charismatic leaders led Israel against its foes. The book of Judges portrays this period as one of instability, when faithfulness to God led to success, but idolatry* led to failure (see Judg 3.10). When, ironically,* *Bethlehem* (literally "house of bread") becomes a place of *famine,* a *man, his wife,* and his *two sons* move to *Moab,* a suspect place in biblical tradition (Gen 19.37; Deut 23.3). **2:** *Elimelech:* "My god is king." The rhyming names *Mahlon* and *Chilion* mean "weakness" and "consumption." *Ephrathites:* Elsewhere, Ephratha is linked with *Bethlehem* (Mic 5.2; 1 Sam 17.12) and may refer to the large clan* in which Bethlehem was located. **3:** In a sudden reversal, Naomi takes center stage. *Elimelech* (now called Naomi's husband) dies and, after ten years, so do Mahlon and Chilion, leaving Naomi without *her husband* and *her two sons.*

6 Then she started to return with her daughters-in-law from the country of Moab, for she had heard in the country of Moab that the LORD had considered his people and given them food. ⁷So she set out from the place where she had been living, she and her two daughters-in-law, and they went on their way to go back to the land of Judah. ⁸But Naomi said to her two daughters-in-law, "Go back each of you to your mother's house. May the LORD deal kindly with you, as you have dealt with the dead and with me. ⁹The LORD grant that you may find security, each of you in the house of your husband." Then she kissed them, and they wept aloud. ¹⁰They said to her, "No, we will return with you to your people." ¹¹But Naomi said, "Turn back, my daughters, why will you go with me? Do I still have sons in my womb that they may become your husbands? ¹²Turn back, my daughters, go your way, for I am too old to have a husband. Even if I thought there was hope for me, even if I should have a husband tonight and bear sons, ¹³would you then wait until they were grown? Would you then refrain from marrying? No, my daughters, it has been far more bitter for me than for you, because the hand of the LORD has turned against me." ¹⁴Then they wept aloud again. Orpah kissed her mother-in-law, but Ruth clung to her.

15 So she said, "See, your sister-in-law has gone back to her people and to her gods; return after your sister-in-law." ¹⁶But Ruth said,

"Do not press me to leave you
    or to turn back from following you!
Where you go, I will go;
    where you lodge, I will lodge;
your people shall be my people,
    and your God my God.
17 Where you die, I will die—
    there will I be buried.
May the LORD do thus and so to me,
    and more as well,
if even death parts me from you!"

¹⁸When Naomi saw that she was determined to go with her, she said no more to her.

19 So the two of them went on until they came to Bethlehem. When they came to Bethlehem, the whole town was stirred because of them; and the women said, "Is this Naomi?" ²⁰She said to them,

"Call me no longer Naomi,ᵃ
    call me Mara,ᵇ
for the Almightyᶜ has dealt bitterly
    with me.
21 I went away full,
    but the LORD has brought me back
        empty;

---

a That is *Pleasant*   *b* That is *Bitter*   *c* Traditional rendering of Heb *Shaddai*

why call me Naomi
  when the LORD has dealt harshly with[a]
    me,
  and the Almighty[b] has brought
    calamity upon me?"

22 So Naomi returned together with Ruth the Moabite, her daughter-in-law, who came back with her from the country of Moab. They came to Bethlehem at the beginning of the barley harvest.

1.6–22: Two return to Bethlehem. Naomi decides to return to Bethlehem (reversing Elimelech's decision to go to Moab). Her impassioned speech assumes that if she cannot offer Orpah and Ruth husbands then they have no future with her. **8–14:** Told to return to the house of their mothers ("house of the father" is more common), Orpah obeys Naomi, but Ruth *clings* to her (in Gen 1.24, this verb describes marital union). **16–17:** Ruth's beautiful poem of loyalty states her willingness to exchange her gods, family, and land in order to be with Naomi. *May the LORD do thus and so* is a typical oath formula. **19–22:** Naomi's silence, her insistence on being called *Mara* ("bitter") upon her entry into Bethlehem, and her reference to returning *empty* indicate that Naomi is not initially comforted by the presence of her Moabite daughter-in-law.

2 Now Naomi had a kinsman on her husband's side, a prominent rich man, of the family of Elimelech, whose name was Boaz. [2]And Ruth the Moabite said to Naomi, "Let me go to the field and glean among the ears of grain, behind someone in whose sight I may find favor." She said to her, "Go, my daughter." [3]So she went. She came and gleaned in the field behind the reapers. As it happened, she came to the part of the field belonging to Boaz, who was of the family of Elimelech. [4]Just then Boaz came from Bethlehem. He said to the reapers, "The LORD be with you." They answered, "The LORD bless you." [5]Then Boaz said to his servant who was in charge of the reapers, "To whom does this young woman belong?" [6]The servant who was in charge of the reapers answered, "She is the Moabite who came back with Naomi from the country of Moab. [7]She said, 'Please, let me glean and gather among the sheaves behind the reapers.' So she came, and she has been on her feet from early this

morning until now, without resting even for a moment."[c]

8 Then Boaz said to Ruth, "Now listen, my daughter, do not go to glean in another field or leave this one, but keep close to my young women. [9]Keep your eyes on the field that is being reaped, and follow behind them. I have ordered the young men not to bother you. If you get thirsty, go to the vessels and drink from what the young men have drawn." [10]Then she fell prostrate, with her face to the ground, and said to him, "Why have I found favor in your sight, that you should take notice of me, when I am a foreigner?" [11]But Boaz answered her, "All that you have done for your mother-in-law since the death of your husband has been fully told me, and how you left your father and mother and your native land and came to a people that you did not know before. [12]May the LORD reward you for your deeds, and may you have a full reward from the LORD, the God of Israel, under whose wings you have come for refuge!" [13]Then she said, "May I continue to find favor in your sight, my lord, for you have comforted me and spoken kindly to your servant, even though I am not one of your servants."

14 At mealtime Boaz said to her, "Come here, and eat some of this bread, and dip your morsel in the sour wine." So she sat beside the reapers, and he heaped up for her some parched grain. She ate until she was satisfied, and she had some left over. [15]When she got up to glean, Boaz instructed his young men, "Let her glean even among the standing sheaves, and do not reproach her. [16]You must also pull out some handfuls for her from the bundles, and leave them for her to glean, and do not rebuke her."

17 So she gleaned in the field until evening. Then she beat out what she had gleaned, and it was about an ephah of barley. [18]She picked it up and came into the town, and her mother-in-law saw how much she had gleaned. Then she took out and gave her what was left over after she herself had been

---

a Or *has testified against*   b Traditional rendering of Heb *Shaddai*   c Compare Gk Vg: Meaning of Heb uncertain

satisfied. [19]Her mother-in-law said to her, "Where did you glean today? And where have you worked? Blessed be the man who took notice of you." So she told her mother-in-law with whom she had worked, and said, "The name of the man with whom I worked today is Boaz." [20]Then Naomi said to her daughter-in-law, "Blessed be he by the LORD, whose kindness has not forsaken the living or the dead!" Naomi also said to her, "The man is a relative of ours, one of our nearest kin."[a] [21]Then Ruth the Moabite said, "He even said to me, 'Stay close by my servants, until they have finished all my harvest.'" [22]Naomi said to Ruth, her daughter-in-law, "It is better, my daughter, that you go out with his young women, otherwise you might be bothered in another field." [23]So she stayed close to the young women of Boaz, gleaning until the end of the barley and wheat harvests; and she lived with her mother-in-law.

2.1–23: Ruth in Boaz's field. Although the reader is told about the relationship between Boaz and Naomi, Ruth seems unaware of this information (it was *as it happened* that she arrived in Boaz's field, v. 3). **4:** As she arrived, *just then Boaz came*. These felicitous "coincidences" hold a key to the theology of Ruth, demonstrating a God who works behind the scenes and through human action. **7:** Ruth's request to *glean★ among the sheaves* is beyond the scope of common gleaning privileges (Lev 19.9; 23.22; Deut 24.19), and thereby requires the consent of the landowner. Boaz not only approves Ruth's request, but grants her more favors in the field. He offers her protection and the familial privileges of sharing water and the common meal. **15–18:** Boaz extends Ruth's gleaning privileges even further. She gathers an *ephah* of grain, variously calculated at 29–50 pounds. Ruth shares the grain, as well as her lunch leftovers, with Naomi. **19–22:** Naomi reveals to Ruth what the reader already knows: Boaz is a *relative,* one obligated to keep land within the family (Lev 25.25). Ruth alters Boaz's words in her report to Naomi (*stay close by my servants,* v. 21; *keep close to my young women,* v. 8). **23:** As both the barley and wheat harvests draw to a close, the women face difficult months ahead.

3 Naomi her mother-in-law said to her, "My daughter, I need to seek some se-

curity for you, so that it may be well with you. [2]Now here is our kinsman Boaz, with whose young women you have been working. See, he is winnowing barley tonight at the threshing floor. [3]Now wash and anoint yourself, and put on your best clothes and go down to the threshing floor; but do not make yourself known to the man until he has finished eating and drinking. [4]When he lies down, observe the place where he lies; then, go and uncover his feet and lie down; and he will tell you what to do." [5]She said to her, "All that you tell me I will do."

6 So she went down to the threshing floor and did just as her mother-in-law had instructed her. [7]When Boaz had eaten and drunk, and he was in a contented mood, he went to lie down at the end of the heap of grain. Then she came stealthily and uncovered his feet, and lay down. [8]At midnight the man was startled, and turned over, and there, lying at his feet, was a woman! [9]He said, "Who are you?" And she answered, "I am Ruth, your servant; spread your cloak over your servant, for you are next-of-kin."[a] [10]He said, "May you be blessed by the LORD, my daughter; this last instance of your loyalty is better than the first; you have not gone after young men, whether poor or rich. [11]And now, my daughter, do not be afraid, I will do for you all that you ask, for all the assembly of my people know that you are a worthy woman. [12]But now, though it is true that I am a near kinsman, there is another kinsman more closely related than I. [13]Remain this night, and in the morning, if he will act as next-of-kin[a] for you, good; let him do it. If he is not willing to act as next-of-kin[a] for you, then, as the LORD lives, I will act as next-of-kin[a] for you. Lie down until the morning."

14 So she lay at his feet until morning, but got up before one person could recognize another; for he said, "It must not be known that the woman came to the threshing floor." [15]Then he said, "Bring the cloak you are wearing and hold it out." So she held it, and he measured out six measures of barley, and put it on her back; then he went into the city.

a Or *one with the right to redeem*

16She came to her mother-in-law, who said, "How did things go with you,[a] my daughter?" Then she told her all that the man had done for her, 17saying, "He gave me these six measures of barley, for he said, 'Do not go back to your mother-in-law empty-handed.' " 18She replied, "Wait, my daughter, until you learn how the matter turns out, for the man will not rest, but will settle the matter today."

3.1–18: At the threshing★ floor. 2–3: At Naomi's initiative, Ruth *washes and anoints*★ herself and goes to the *threshing floor*, where grain is winnowed★ in the early evening breeze. An important man like Boaz might not personally winnow or protect the grain; some believe that he was performing religious responsibilities. **4:** *Uncover his feet and lie down:* The instructions of Naomi are provocative. The word for *feet* ("margelot") is related to the more common word "regel," which often in the Bible refers to sexual organs. **6–11:** Ruth requests not only that Boaz act as *next-of-kin* but also that he *spread* his *cloak* over her, suggesting marriage. **12–13:** *Another kinsman more related than I:* The complication of a closer relative is often seen as referring to the practice of levirate marriage,★ in which the brother of a deceased man is expected to have sexual relations with his widow in order to sire an heir for the dead man (Deut 25.5–10). The situation in Ruth does not fit the levirate marriage, since Boaz was not brother to Mahlon or Chilion. Hence, Boaz's speech may indicate that two issues are at stake in Ruth's proposition: marriage and the redemption of Elimelech's land. **14–18:** Ruth's visit must be kept secret until the encounter with the other relative, so she leaves in the darkness. Boaz gives her an unidentified *six measures of barley.* Ruth's report, unlike Boaz's speech, mentions Naomi.

---

4 No sooner had Boaz gone up to the gate and sat down there than the next-of-kin,[b] of whom Boaz had spoken, came passing by. So Boaz said, "Come over, friend; sit down here." And he went over and sat down. 2Then Boaz took ten men of the elders of the city, and said, "Sit down here"; so they sat down. 3He then said to the next-of-kin,[b] "Naomi, who has come back from the country of Moab, is selling the parcel of land that belonged to our kinsman Elimelech. 4So I thought I would tell you of it, and say: Buy it in the presence of those sitting here, and in the presence of the elders of my people. If you will redeem it, redeem it; but if you will not, tell me, so that I may know; for there is no one prior to you to redeem it, and I come after you." So he said, "I will redeem it." 5Then Boaz said, "The day you acquire the field from the hand of Naomi, you are also acquiring Ruth[c] the Moabite, the widow of the dead man, to maintain the dead man's name on his inheritance." 6At this, the next-of-kin[b] said, "I cannot redeem it for myself without damaging my own inheritance. Take my right of redemption yourself, for I cannot redeem it."

7 Now this was the custom in former times in Israel concerning redeeming and exchanging: to confirm a transaction, the one took off a sandal and gave it to the other; this was the manner of attesting in Israel. 8So when the next-of-kin[b] said to Boaz, "Acquire it for yourself," he took off his sandal. 9Then Boaz said to the elders and all the people, "Today you are witnesses that I have acquired from the hand of Naomi all that belonged to Elimelech and all that belonged to Chilion and Mahlon. 10I have also acquired Ruth the Moabite, the wife of Mahlon, to be my wife, to maintain the dead man's name on his inheritance, in order that the name of the dead may not be cut off from his kindred and from the gate of his native place; today you are witnesses." 11Then all the people who were at the gate, along with the elders, said, "We are witnesses. May the LORD make the woman who is coming into your house like Rachel and Leah, who together built up the house of Israel. May you produce children in Ephrathah and bestow a name in Bethlehem; 12and, through the children that the LORD will give you by this young woman, may your house be like the house of Perez, whom Tamar bore to Judah."

13 So Boaz took Ruth and she became his wife. When they came together, the LORD made her conceive, and she bore a son. 14Then the women said to Naomi, "Blessed be the LORD, who has not left you this day without next-of-kin;[b] and may his name be

---

a Or *"Who are you,*   *b* Or *one with the right to redeem*
c OL Vg: Heb *from the hand of Naomi and from Ruth*

renowned in Israel! 15He shall be to you a restorer of life and a nourisher of your old age; for your daughter-in-law who loves you, who is more to you than seven sons, has borne him." 16Then Naomi took the child and laid him in her bosom, and became his nurse. 17The women of the neighborhood gave him a name, saying, "A son has been born to Naomi." They named him Obed; he became the father of Jesse, the father of David.

18 Now these are the descendants of Perez: Perez became the father of Hezron, 19Hezron of Ram, Ram of Amminadab, 20Amminadab of Nahshon, Nahshon of Salmon, 21Salmon of Boaz, Boaz of Obed, 22Obed of Jesse, and Jesse of David.

4.1–22: At the city gate. 1–2: In ancient Israel, business was transacted at the city *gate* and was witnessed by *elders*. 3–6: Boaz offers to buy Naomi's land (implying that she owned the property) if the other man does not wish to do so. The next-of-kin retracts his offer when Boaz links land redemption to the marriage of Ruth. If the man begets a child with Ruth, the land will revert to Naomi. 7: The removing of a *sandal* to seal a business deal differs from the practice in Deut 25.9, in which a man who refuses to perform levirate marriage* is shamed by the dead man's widow. 9–10: Boaz announces his intention both to redeem the land and to marry Ruth. 11–12: The crowds link Ruth with other biblical characters: with *Rachel and Leah,* two sisters who struggled for love and children (Gen 30); and with *Perez,* born after *Tamar* tricked *Judah* into fulfilling the duties of the levirate marriage (Gen 38). 13–17: Naomi's security is sealed by the birth of a male child, whom Boaz designates as the redeemer of her land. In a story that assumes the inheritance rights of men, the praise that Ruth is more to Naomi *than seven sons* is striking. 18–22: Boaz, like many other important biblical figures, appears in seventh place in the genealogy* traced from Perez (4.12). While the book began with a man's decision and ends with a list of male names, the women Ruth and Naomi remain solidly in the heart of the story.

1 SAMUEL

Introduction

The books of 1 and 2 Samuel were originally a single book recounting the beginning of the monarchy and the reigns of its first two kings, Saul and David. The book was named after Samuel because he plays a prominent role in its beginning section, which was even attributed to his authorship. The name is not entirely appropriate, however, since Samuel dies well before 1 Samuel ends (25.1). This book was also part of a larger unit known as the Deuteronomistic★ History, which incorporates the present books of Deuteronomy, Joshua, Judges, 1–2 Samuel, and 1–2 Kings. The Deuteronomistic History is the central history of Israel in the Hebrew Bible, or Old Testament. It relates Israel's history from their conquest of the land under Joshua (related in Josh 1–12) to the end of the kingdoms of Israel (2 Kings 17) and Judah (2 Kings 24–25). It evaluates that history according to the laws and theology of the book of Deuteronomy, with which it begins. The Deuteronomistic History as a whole stresses such matters as obedience to the law, God's choice of Jerusalem as a central place of worship for Israel, and the kingship of David. This history was composed by one or more authors whose names have not come down to us, and who are therefore referred to as "deuteronomists." It was probably written during the Exile★ (after 586 BCE) as a way of collecting Israel's traditions and editing them into a single, running historical account. The collectors or editors occasionally inserted commentary, some-times in the form of speeches and always in their own distinctive deuteronomistic style. First Samuel 8, with its reference to the Exodus (v. 8) and the people crying out (v. 18), and 1 Sam 12, with its review of Israel's history and its command to "heed the voice of the LORD" (vv. 14–15), give examples of deuteronomistic style.

While the book of Samuel may contain older source material, its final composition as part of the Deuteronomistic History took place in the Exile (after 586 BCE). This was hundreds of years after the events described in Samuel (David reigned around 1000 BCE). The author/editor was attempting to offer a theological explanation for the great crisis of the Exile and perhaps some hope and even a model for restoration in David. Hence, David is the central character not only in 1–2 Samuel but in the entire Deuteronomistic History.

READING GUIDE

As the outline below shows, 1 Samuel falls into three main sections, each organized around one of its principal characters, Samuel, Saul, and David. Samuel and Saul both prepare the way for David. Samuel is a transitional figure—the last of the judges and the prophet★ who anoints★ Saul and then announces his rejection by the LORD and anoints David in his place. Saul is a tragic figure—plucked from obscurity and thrust into a position of power for which he is unfit. Everything he does is a mistake. His rapid decline is balanced by David's meteoric rise. David can do no wrong. Like Saul, he is presented as humble and without personal ambition for king-ship. But unlike Saul, "the LORD was with David"—a major theme in the book. David, for his part, consistently trusts in the LORD to guide his movements and actions. While Samuel is a literary masterpiece, the reader may draw closer to actual history by asking whether Saul was really so bad and David so innocent as their portraits in 1 Samuel indicate.

1 There was a certain man of Ramathaim, a Zuphite[a] from the hill country of Ephraim, whose name was Elkanah son of Jeroham son of Elihu son of Tohu son of Zuph, an Ephraimite. [2]He had two wives; the name of the one was Hannah, and the name of the other Peninnah. Peninnah had children, but Hannah had no children.

3 Now this man used to go up year by year from his town to worship and to sacrifice to the LORD of hosts at Shiloh, where the two sons of Eli, Hophni and Phinehas, were priests of the LORD. [4]On the day when Elkanah sacrificed, he would give portions to his wife Peninnah and to all her sons and daughters; [5]but to Hannah he gave a double portion,[b] because he loved her, though the LORD had closed her womb. [6]Her rival used to provoke her severely, to irritate her, because the LORD had closed her womb. [7]So it went on year by year; as often as she went up to the house of the LORD, she used to provoke her. Therefore Hannah wept and would not eat. [8]Her husband Elkanah said to her, "Hannah, why do you weep? Why do you not eat? Why is your heart sad? Am I not more to you than ten sons?"

9 After they had eaten and drunk at Shiloh, Hannah rose and presented herself before the LORD.[c] Now Eli the priest was sitting on the seat beside the doorpost of the temple of the LORD. [10]She was deeply distressed and prayed to the LORD, and wept bitterly. [11]She made this vow: "O LORD of hosts, if only you will look on the misery of your servant, and remember me, and not forget your servant, but will give to your servant a male child, then I will set him before you as a nazirite[d] until the day of his death. He shall drink neither wine nor intoxicants,[e] and no razor shall touch his head."

12 As she continued praying before the LORD, Eli observed her mouth. [13]Hannah was praying silently; only her lips moved, but her voice was not heard; therefore Eli thought she was drunk. [14]So Eli said to her, "How long will you make a drunken spectacle of yourself? Put away your wine." [15]But Hannah answered, "No, my lord, I am a woman deeply troubled; I have drunk neither wine nor strong drink, but I have been pouring out my soul before the LORD. [16]Do not regard your servant as a worthless woman, for I have been speaking out of my great anxiety and vexation all this time." [17]Then Eli answered, "Go in peace; the God of Israel grant the petition you have made to him." [18]And she said, "Let your servant find favor in your sight." Then the woman went to her quarters,[f] ate and drank with her husband,[g] and her countenance was sad no longer.[h]

1.1–18: Hannah's request. 3: Elkanah's annual pilgrimage to the temple of Yahweh or *house of the LORD* (v. 7) in Shiloh shows him to be a righteous man. *LORD of hosts* or "armies" (Hebrew "sebaoth") describes the LORD's leadership in wars both divine and on behalf of Israel. **5–8:** The value of a woman's ability to bear children in ancient Israel lies behind Hannah's depression. Her barrenness is comparable to that of Sarah, Rebekah, and Rachel in Genesis and of Samson's mother in Judg 13. **11:** *Nazirites* were "devoted" to the LORD for some special purpose and were prohibited from drinking alcohol or eating grapes, cutting their hair or beards, and approaching a dead body (Num 6.1–21). *Intoxicants* refers to a form of beer. **13:** *Eli thought she was drunk* either because his eyesight was poor (3.2) or because he had lost the capacity to discern the sacred from the secular, and therefore could not tell that Hannah was praying.

19 They rose early in the morning and worshiped before the LORD; then they went

a Compare Gk and 1 Chr 6.35–36: Heb *Ramathaim-zophim*   b Syr: Meaning of Heb uncertain
c Gk: Heb lacks *and presented herself before the LORD*
d That is *one separated* or *one consecrated*
e Cn Compare Gk Q Ms 1.22: MT *then I will give him to the LORD all the days of his life*   f Gk: Heb *went her way*   g Gk: Heb lacks *and drank with her husband*
h Gk: Meaning of Heb uncertain

back to their house at Ramah. Elkanah knew his wife Hannah, and the LORD remembered her. 20In due time Hannah conceived and bore a son. She named him Samuel, for she said, "I have asked him of the LORD."

21 The man Elkanah and all his household went up to offer to the LORD the yearly sacrifice, and to pay his vow. 22But Hannah did not go up, for she said to her husband, "As soon as the child is weaned, I will bring him, that he may appear in the presence of the LORD, and remain there forever; I will offer him as a nazirite*a* for all time."*b* 23Her husband Elkanah said to her, "Do what seems best to you, wait until you have weaned him; only—may the LORD establish his word."*c* So the woman remained and nursed her son, until she weaned him. 24When she had weaned him, she took him up with her, along with a three-year-old bull,*d* an ephah of flour, and a skin of wine. She brought him to the house of the LORD at Shiloh; and the child was young. 25Then they slaughtered the bull, and they brought the child to Eli. 26And she said, "Oh, my lord! As you live, my lord, I am the woman who was standing here in your presence, praying to the LORD. 27For this child I prayed; and the LORD has granted me the petition that I made to him. 28Therefore I have lent him to the LORD; as long as he lives, he is given to the LORD."

She left him there for*e* the LORD.

1.19–28: **Samuel's birth.** The gift of a son to Hannah shows God's favor toward the disadvantaged and indicates that Samuel is chosen for a special purpose. **19:** *Elkanah knew his wife:* An idiom for sexual relations. **20:** *Samuel's* name ostensibly means "God has heard," so the reader expects Hannah to say that she named her son Samuel because "God heard" her prayer. Her statement that she *asked him of the LORD* is a pun on the name of Saul instead. **28:** *Given* is another pun on Saul's name. This is exactly the same as Saul's name in Hebrew ("sha'ul"). It might even be translated, "He is Saul to the LORD." These puns may indicate that this story was originally about Saul's birth rather than Samuel's, or they may simply be the author's way of alluding to Saul as Israel's first king.

2 Hannah prayed and said,
"My heart exults in the LORD;
    my strength is exalted in my God.*f*
My mouth derides my enemies,
    because I rejoice in my*g* victory.

2 "There is no Holy One like the LORD,
    no one besides you;
    there is no Rock like our God.
3 Talk no more so very proudly,
    let not arrogance come from your
        mouth;
for the LORD is a God of knowledge,
    and by him actions are weighed.
4 The bows of the mighty are broken,
    but the feeble gird on strength.
5 Those who were full have hired
        themselves out for bread,
    but those who were hungry are fat
        with spoil.
The barren has borne seven,
    but she who has many children is
        forlorn.
6 The LORD kills and brings to life;
    he brings down to Sheol and raises
        up.
7 The LORD makes poor and makes rich;
    he brings low, he also exalts.
8 He raises up the poor from the dust;
    he lifts the needy from the ash
        heap,
to make them sit with princes
    and inherit a seat of honor.*h*
For the pillars of the earth are the
        LORD's,
    and on them he has set the world.

9 "He will guard the feet of his faithful
        ones,
    but the wicked shall be cut off in
        darkness;
    for not by might does one prevail.

a That is *one separated* or *one consecrated*
b Cn Compare Q Ms: MT lacks *I will offer him as a nazirite for all time*   *c* MT: Q Ms Gk Compare Syr *that which goes out of your mouth*   *d* Q Ms and Gk Syr: MT *three bulls*   *e* Gk (Compare Q Ms) and Gk at 2.11: MT *And he (that is, Elkanah) worshiped there before*
f Gk: Heb *the LORD*   *g* Q Ms: MT *your*
h Gk (Compare Q Ms) adds *He grants the vow of the one who vows, and blesses the years of the just*

10. The LORD! His adversaries shall be
        shattered;
    the Most High[a] will thunder in
        heaven.
    The LORD will judge the ends of the
        earth;
    he will give strength to his king,
    and exalt the power of his anointed."

2.1–10: The song of Hannah. This is a psalm of thanksgiving for a national victory that has been placed in Hannah's mouth. **1:** *Strength*, literally, "horn," seems to make use of the image of a proud animal. **5:** *The barren has borne seven:* This line probably led to the psalm's insertion. Hannah had only six children (2.21). **6:** *Sheol* was the place of the dead, the underworld. **10:** The reference to *his king* shows that the psalm was written later than Hannah since there was no king of Israel yet in her time. *Anointed,* (Heb., "mashiah") was a title for the king and the source of the term "messiah."*

---

11 Then Elkanah went home to Ramah, while the boy remained to minister to the LORD, in the presence of the priest Eli.

12 Now the sons of Eli were scoundrels; they had no regard for the LORD 13 or for the duties of the priests to the people. When anyone offered sacrifice, the priest's servant would come, while the meat was boiling, with a three-pronged fork in his hand, 14 and he would thrust it into the pan, or kettle, or caldron, or pot; all that the fork brought up the priest would take for himself.[b] This is what they did at Shiloh to all the Israelites who came there. 15 Moreover, before the fat was burned, the priest's servant would come and say to the one who was sacrificing, "Give meat for the priest to roast; for he will not accept boiled meat from you, but only raw." 16 And if the man said to him, "Let them burn the fat first, and then take whatever you wish," he would say, "No, you must give it now; if not, I will take it by force." 17 Thus the sin of the young men was very great in the sight of the LORD; for they treated the offerings of the LORD with contempt.

18 Samuel was ministering before the LORD, a boy wearing a linen ephod. 19 His mother used to make for him a little robe and take it to him each year, when she went up

with her husband to offer the yearly sacrifice. 20 Then Eli would bless Elkanah and his wife, and say, "May the LORD repay[c] you with children by this woman for the gift that she made to[d] the LORD"; and then they would return to their home.

21 And[e] the LORD took note of Hannah; she conceived and bore three sons and two daughters. And the boy Samuel grew up in the presence of the LORD.

22 Now Eli was very old. He heard all that his sons were doing to all Israel, and how they lay with the women who served at the entrance to the tent of meeting. 23 He said to them, "Why do you do such things? For I hear of your evil dealings from all these people. 24 No, my sons; it is not a good report that I hear the people of the LORD spreading abroad. 25 If one person sins against another, someone can intercede for the sinner with the LORD;[f] but if someone sins against the LORD, who can make intercession?" But they would not listen to the voice of their father; for it was the will of the LORD to kill them.

26 Now the boy Samuel continued to grow both in stature and in favor with the LORD and with the people.

2.11–26: The wicked sons of Eli. Samuel's faithful service contrasts with the evil deeds of Eli's sons and hints that he will replace Eli. **12–17:** Priests made their living by receiving a portion of the sacrifices. The custom in Shiloh (vv. 13–14), which is different from that prescribed elsewhere (Lev 7.28–36; Deut 18.3), was for the priest to get whatever the fork brought up while the meat was boiling. By demanding the fat portion, which properly belonged to God, and taking it first, before the sacrifice was made, Eli's sons were sinning directly against the LORD (v. 25) by treating him with contempt (vv. 12, 17). Moreover, they threatened violence against worshippers who tried to do right (v. 16). **18:** The *linen ephod** was a kind of apron worn by priests. **22:** The *tent of meeting* is another name for the tabernacle,* a moveable shrine. Apparently the temple of the LORD at Shiloh (1.3) was actually a tent shrine. **25:** *It was the will of the LORD to kill them:* This

---

a Cn Heb *against him he*   b Gk Syr Vg: Heb *with it*
c Q Ms Gk: MT *give*   d Q Ms Gk: MT *for the petition that she asked of*   e Q Ms Gk: MT *When*
f Gk Compare Q Ms: MT *another, God will mediate for him*

explanation of the obstinacy of Eli's sons is like God's hardening of Pharaoh's heart in Ex 4–12.

~~~~~~~~~~

27 A man of God came to Eli and said to him, "Thus the LORD has said, 'I revealed[a] myself to the family of your ancestor in Egypt when they were slaves[b] to the house of Pharaoh. 28 I chose him out of all the tribes of Israel to be my priest, to go up to my altar, to offer incense, to wear an ephod before me; and I gave to the family of your ancestor all my offerings by fire from the people of Israel. 29 Why then look with greedy eye[c] at my sacrifices and my offerings that I commanded, and honor your sons more than me by fattening yourselves on the choicest parts of every offering of my people Israel?' 30 Therefore the LORD the God of Israel declares: 'I promised that your family and the family of your ancestor should go in and out before me forever'; but now the LORD declares: 'Far be it from me; for those who honor me I will honor, and those who despise me shall be treated with contempt. 31 See, a time is coming when I will cut off your strength and the strength of your ancestor's family, so that no one in your family will live to old age. 32 Then in distress you will look with greedy eye[d] on all the prosperity that shall be bestowed upon Israel; and no one in your family shall ever live to old age. 33 The only one of you whom I shall not cut off from my altar shall be spared to weep out his[e] eyes and grieve his[f] heart; all the members of your household shall die by the sword.[g] 34 The fate of your two sons, Hophni and Phinehas, shall be the sign to you—both of them shall die on the same day. 35 I will raise up for myself a faithful priest, who shall do according to what is in my heart and in my mind. I will build him a sure house, and he shall go in and out before my anointed one forever. 36 Everyone who is left in your family shall come to implore him for a piece of silver or a loaf of bread, and shall say, Please put me in one of the priest's places, that I may eat a morsel of bread.' "

2.27–36: The oracle* against Eli. This was probably written by the deuteronomistic* editor. **27:** *Your ancestor* may allude to Moses, to whom Eli's family

traced their ancestry, rather than the tribe of Levi. The names of Eli's sons, Hophni and Phinehas (1.3; 2.34), are actually Egyptian, which is consistent with the phrase *in Egypt*. **28:** *To go up to my altar, to offer incense, to wear an ephod** refer to three principal duties of priests. Going up to the altar refers to making animal sacrifices. **31–33:** The cutting off of Eli's household refers not to the death of Eli and his sons in 1 Sam 4 but to Saul's annihilation of the priests of Nob in 1 Sam 22. Abiathar is the one spared. **35–36:** The *faithful priest* is Zadok, who came to prominence when Abiathar was banished by Solomon (1 Kings 1–2). The Zadokites were Aaron's descendants, and this passage may reflect a rivalry between the descendants of Moses and Aaron for the priesthood.

~~~~~~~~~~

3 Now the boy Samuel was ministering to the LORD under Eli. The word of the LORD was rare in those days; visions were not widespread.

2 At that time Eli, whose eyesight had begun to grow dim so that he could not see, was lying down in his room; 3 the lamp of God had not yet gone out, and Samuel was lying down in the temple of the LORD, where the ark of God was. 4 Then the LORD called, "Samuel! Samuel!"[h] and he said, "Here I am!" 5 and ran to Eli, and said, "Here I am, for you called me." But he said, "I did not call; lie down again." So he went and lay down. 6 The LORD called again, "Samuel!" Samuel got up and went to Eli, and said, "Here I am, for you called me." But he said, "I did not call, my son; lie down again." 7 Now Samuel did not yet know the LORD, and the word of the LORD had not yet been revealed to him. 8 The LORD called Samuel again, a third time. And he got up and went to Eli, and said, "Here I am, for you called me." Then Eli perceived that the LORD was calling the boy. 9 Therefore Eli said to Samuel, "Go, lie down; and if he calls you, you shall say, 'Speak, LORD, for your servant is listening.' " So Samuel went and lay down in his place.

10 Now the LORD came and stood there,

---

a Gk Tg Syr: Heb *Did I reveal*   b Q Ms Gk: MT lacks *slaves*   c Q Ms Gk: MT *then kick*   d Q Ms Gk: MT *will kick*   e Q Ms Gk: MT *your*   f Q Ms Gk: Heb *your*   g Q Ms See Gk: MT *die like mortals*   h Q Ms Gk See 3.10: MT *the* LORD *called Samuel*

calling as before, "Samuel! Samuel!" And Samuel said, "Speak, for your servant is listening." 11Then the LORD said to Samuel, "See, I am about to do something in Israel that will make both ears of anyone who hears of it tingle. 12On that day I will fulfill against Eli all that I have spoken concerning his house, from beginning to end. 13For I have told him that I am about to punish his house forever, for the iniquity that he knew, because his sons were blaspheming God,*a* and he did not restrain them. 14Therefore I swear to the house of Eli that the iniquity of Eli's house shall not be expiated by sacrifice or offering forever."

15 Samuel lay there until morning; then he opened the doors of the house of the LORD. Samuel was afraid to tell the vision to Eli. 16But Eli called Samuel and said, "Samuel, my son." He said, "Here I am." 17Eli said, "What was it that he told you? Do not hide it from me. May God do so to you and more also, if you hide anything from me of all that he told you." 18So Samuel told him everything and hid nothing from him. Then he said, "It is the LORD; let him do what seems good to him."

19 As Samuel grew up, the LORD was with him and let none of his words fall to the ground. 20And all Israel from Dan to Beer-sheba knew that Samuel was a trustworthy prophet of the LORD. 21The LORD continued to appear at Shiloh, for the LORD revealed himself to Samuel at Shiloh by the word of the LORD. 4 1And the word of Samuel came to all Israel.

a typical oath formula. Eli adjures Samuel, forcing him to reveal his conversation with the LORD. 19–21: All of Samuel's prophecies come true (none *fall to the ground*), and this is known *from Dan to Beer-sheba*, the traditional northern and southern boundaries of Israel. All Israel recognizes Samuel as a reliable prophet of the LORD.

In those days the Philistines mustered for war against Israel,*b* and Israel went out to battle against them;*c* they encamped at Ebenezer, and the Philistines encamped at Aphek. 2The Philistines drew up in line against Israel, and when the battle was joined,*d* Israel was defeated by the Philistines, who killed about four thousand men on the field of battle. 3When the troops came to the camp, the elders of Israel said, "Why has the LORD put us to rout today before the Philistines? Let us bring the ark of the covenant of the LORD here from Shiloh, so that he may come among us and save us from the power of our enemies." 4So the people sent to Shiloh, and brought from there the ark of the covenant of the LORD of hosts, who is enthroned on the cherubim. The two sons of Eli, Hophni and Phinehas, were there with the ark of the covenant of God.

5 When the ark of the covenant of the LORD came into the camp, all Israel gave a mighty shout, so that the earth resounded. 6When the Philistines heard the noise of the shouting, they said, "What does this great shouting in the camp of the Hebrews mean?" When they learned that the ark of the LORD had come to the camp, 7the Philistines were afraid; for they said, "Gods have*e* come into the camp." They also said, "Woe to us! For nothing like this has happened before. 8Woe to us! Who can deliver us from the power of these mighty gods? These are the gods who struck the Egyptians with every sort of plague in the wilderness. 9Take courage, and be men, O Philistines, in order not to become slaves to the Hebrews as they have been to you; be men and fight."

3.1–4.1a: Samuel's call. 1: *Word of the LORD . . . visions* are means of prophetic* revelation. **3:** The lamp in the temple was to burn at night (Ex 27.21). Since *the lamp of God had not yet gone out,* it must have been just before dawn. Samuel's bed was in the temple near the inner sanctuary where the *ark of God* was kept. **7:** *Samuel did not yet know the LORD:* Samuel's role as a prophet had not yet been established since *the word of the LORD had not yet been revealed to him.* That he would "know" the LORD provides a further contrast to Eli's sons, who did not regard or "know" the LORD (2.12). **14:** Eli's sons are guilty of profaning the sacrifices that might otherwise have atoned for their sins. **17:** *May God do so to you and more also* is

a Another reading is *for themselves*   *b* Gk: Heb lacks *In those days the Philistines mustered for war against Israel* *c* Gk: Heb *against the Philistines*   *d* Meaning of Heb uncertain   *e* Or *A god has*

10 So the Philistines fought; Israel was defeated, and they fled, everyone to his home. There was a very great slaughter, for there fell of Israel thirty thousand foot soldiers. 11The ark of God was captured; and the two sons of Eli, Hophni and Phinehas, died.

12 A man of Benjamin ran from the battle line, and came to Shiloh the same day, with his clothes torn and with earth upon his head. 13When he arrived, Eli was sitting upon his seat by the road watching, for his heart trembled for the ark of God. When the man came into the city and told the news, all the city cried out. 14When Eli heard the sound of the outcry, he said, "What is this uproar?" Then the man came quickly and told Eli. 15Now Eli was ninety-eight years old and his eyes were set, so that he could not see. 16The man said to Eli, "I have just come from the battle; I fled from the battle today." He said, "How did it go, my son?" 17The messenger replied, "Israel has fled before the Philistines, and there has also been a great slaughter among the troops; your two sons also, Hophni and Phinehas, are dead, and the ark of God has been captured." 18When he mentioned the ark of God, Eli*a* fell over backward from his seat by the side of the gate; and his neck was broken and he died, for he was an old man, and heavy. He had judged Israel forty years.

19 Now his daughter-in-law, the wife of Phinehas, was pregnant, about to give birth. When she heard the news that the ark of God was captured, and that her father-in-law and her husband were dead, she bowed and gave birth; for her labor pains overwhelmed her. 20As she was about to die, the women attending her said to her, "Do not be afraid, for you have borne a son." But she did not answer or give heed. 21She named the child Ichabod, meaning, "The glory has departed from Israel," because the ark of God had been captured and because of her father-in-law and her husband. 22She said, "The glory has departed from Israel, for the ark of God has been captured."

an old "ark narrative"* which described the capture and return of the ark. **1b:** The *Philistines* came from the northwestern Mediterranean area (especially the island of Crete) and entered Palestine (which is derived from "Philistine") in approximately 1200 BCE, about the same time the Israelites were emerging in the central highlands. In this period they were Israel's traditional enemy. **4:** *Cherubim** were mythical griffin-like creatures with body parts from different creatures, often including wings and human heads. They were commonly depicted in palaces and temples. The ark is described as the throne of "the LORD of hosts who sits *enthroned on the cherubim*," and the Israelites believe that the LORD is therefore present with them in battle. **6:** *Hebrews* is a term commonly used in the Bible by foreigners speaking of the Israelites. It may designate a socioeconomic group rather than an ethnic or family unit. **7–8:** *Gods:* The Philistines assume that the Israelites, like themselves, are polytheists. **18:** *Forty years* in the Bible is a round number for a single generation. **21–22:** *Ichabod* probably means "Where is the glory?" Phinehas's wife gives her son this name in lamentation* for the capture of the ark, which represents the LORD's presence or glory.

5 When the Philistines captured the ark of God, they brought it from Ebenezer to Ashdod; 2then the Philistines took the ark of God and brought it into the house of Dagon and placed it beside Dagon. 3When the people of Ashdod rose early the next day, there was Dagon, fallen on his face to the ground before the ark of the LORD. So they took Dagon and put him back in his place. 4But when they rose early on the next morning, Dagon had fallen on his face to the ground before the ark of the LORD, and the head of Dagon and both his hands were lying cut off upon the threshold; only the trunk of*b* Dagon was left to him. 5This is why the priests of Dagon and all who enter the house of Dagon do not step on the threshold of Dagon in Ashdod to this day.

6 The hand of the LORD was heavy upon the people of Ashdod, and he terrified and struck them with tumors, both in Ashdod and in its territory. 7And when the inhabitants of Ashdod saw how things were, they said, "The ark of the God of Israel must not

---

4.1b–22: The capture of the ark. Many scholars believe that 4.1–7.1 and possibly 2 Sam 6 are based on

a Heb *he*   *b* Heb lacks *the trunk of*

remain with us; for his hand is heavy on us and on our god Dagon." [8]So they sent and gathered together all the lords of the Philistines, and said, "What shall we do with the ark of the God of Israel?" The inhabitants of Gath replied, "Let the ark of God be moved on to us."[a] So they moved the ark of the God of Israel to Gath.[b] [9]But after they had brought it to Gath,[c] the hand of the LORD was against the city, causing a very great panic; he struck the inhabitants of the city, both young and old, so that tumors broke out on them. [10]So they sent the ark of the God of Israel[d] to Ekron. But when the ark of God came to Ekron, the people of Ekron cried out, "Why[e] have they brought around to us[f] the ark of the God of Israel to kill us[f] and our[g] people?" [11]They sent therefore and gathered together all the lords of the Philistines, and said, "Send away the ark of the God of Israel, and let it return to its own place, that it may not kill us and our people." For there was a deathly panic[h] throughout the whole city. The hand of God was very heavy there; [12]those who did not die were stricken with tumors, and the cry of the city went up to heaven.

5.1–12: The LORD's triumph. In the ancient Near East, wars between nations were interpreted as contests between their respective gods. This story explains that even though the Philistines defeated Israel, the LORD was superior to Dagon, a Philistine god. **1:** *Ashdod* was one of five principal Philistine cities. The other four were Ashkelon, Ekron, Gath, and Gaza. **2:** *Beside Dagon* means beside the idol or statue of Dagon in his temple or *house.* Dagon was a Canaanite fertility god adopted by the Philistines. **3:** After the first night the Philistines find the idol of Dagon bowing prostrate before the ark. **4–5:** This is an etiology★ for the practice of jumping over thresholds in order to avoid offending the spirits of a particular building or space (compare Zeph 1.9). **6–12:** The tumors and mice (in the next chapter) have led to the identification of this outbreak as bubonic plague, which was common in coastal areas. According to this story, however, the plague is the LORD's doing. **8:** The *lords of the Philistines* are the rulers of the five Philistine cities. The word for *lord* here ("seren") is Philistine and cognate with the Greek word "tyrannos," or tyrant.

6 The ark of the LORD was in the country of the Philistines seven months. [2]Then the Philistines called for the priests and the diviners and said, "What shall we do with the ark of the LORD? Tell us what we should send with it to its place." [3]They said, "If you send away the ark of the God of Israel, do not send it empty, but by all means return him a guilt offering. Then you will be healed and will be ransomed;[i] will not his hand then turn from you?" [4]And they said, "What is the guilt offering that we shall return to him?" They answered, "Five gold tumors and five gold mice, according to the number of the lords of the Philistines; for the same plague was upon all of you and upon your lords. [5]So you must make images of your tumors and images of your mice that ravage the land, and give glory to the God of Israel; perhaps he will lighten his hand on you and your gods and your land. [6]Why should you harden your hearts as the Egyptians and Pharaoh hardened their hearts? After he had made fools of them, did they not let the people go, and they departed? [7]Now then, get ready a new cart and two milch cows that have never borne a yoke, and yoke the cows to the cart, but take their calves home, away from them. [8]Take the ark of the LORD and place it on the cart, and put in a box at its side the figures of gold, which you are returning to him as a guilt offering. Then send it off, and let it go its way. [9]And watch; if it goes up on the way to its own land, to Beth-shemesh, then it is he who has done us this great harm; but if not, then we shall know that it is not his hand that struck us; it happened to us by chance."

10 The men did so; they took two milch cows and yoked them to the cart, and shut up their calves at home. [11]They put the ark of the LORD on the cart, and the box with the gold mice and the images of their tu-

---

a Gk Compare Q Ms: MT *They answered, "Let the ark of the God of Israel be brought around to Gath."*
b Gk: Heb lacks *to Gath*   *c* Q Ms: MT lacks *to Gath*
d Q Ms Gk: MT lacks *of Israel*   *e* Q Ms Gk: MT lacks *Why*   *f* Heb *me*   *g* Heb *my*   *h* Q Ms reads *a panic from the LORD*   *i* Q Ms Gk: MT *and it will be known to you*

mors. ¹²The cows went straight in the direction of Beth-shemesh along one highway, lowing as they went; they turned neither to the right nor to the left, and the lords of the Philistines went after them as far as the border of Beth-shemesh.

13 Now the people of Beth-shemesh were reaping their wheat harvest in the valley. When they looked up and saw the ark, they went with rejoicing to meet it.ᵃ ¹⁴The cart came into the field of Joshua of Beth-shemesh, and stopped there. A large stone was there; so they split up the wood of the cart and offered the cows as a burnt offering to the LORD. ¹⁵The Levites took down the ark of the LORD and the box that was beside it, in which were the gold objects, and set them upon the large stone. Then the people of Beth-shemesh offered burnt offerings and presented sacrifices on that day to the LORD. ¹⁶When the five lords of the Philistines saw it, they returned that day to Ekron.

17 These are the gold tumors, which the Philistines returned as a guilt offering to the LORD: one for Ashdod, one for Gaza, one for Ashkelon, one for Gath, one for Ekron; ¹⁸also the gold mice, according to the number of all the cities of the Philistines belonging to the five lords, both fortified cities and unwalled villages. The great stone, beside which they set down the ark of the LORD, is a witness to this day in the field of Joshua of Beth-shemesh.

19 The descendants of Jeconiah did not rejoice with the people of Beth-shemesh when they greetedᵇ the ark of the LORD; and he killed seventy men of them.ᶜ The people mourned because the LORD had made a great slaughter among the people. ²⁰Then the people of Beth-shemesh said, "Who is able to stand before the LORD, this holy God? To whom shall he go so that we may be rid of him?" ²¹So they sent messengers to the inhabitants of Kiriath-jearim, saying, "The Philistines have returned the ark of the LORD. Come down and take it up to you."

7 ¹And the people of Kiriath-jearim came and took up the ark of the LORD, and brought it to the house of Abinadab on the hill. They consecrated his son, Eleazar, to have charge of the ark of the LORD.

6.1–7.1: The return of the ark. Suspecting that the ark is the source of their problems, the Philistines decide to send it back to Israel. They include with it a *guilt offering* (v. 3), which should probably be understood as compensation for having taken the ark and in hopes of appeasing the LORD and avoiding further punishment from him. There is one gold tumor and one gold mouse for each of the five Philistine cities (vv. 4, 17–18). **7:** The cart is new and therefore ritually pure. The two cows have never been yoked and are therefore fit to be sacrificed (compare Num 19.2; Deut 21.3). They are also *milch cows,* meaning that they have young calves. This is part of the test described in v. 9. **9:** Unaccustomed to pulling a cart, these two cows would be expected to wander aimlessly in search of their calves. If, contrary to this expectation, the cows headed straight for Israelite territory, the Philistines would know that their sufferings had indeed been sent by the LORD. **12:** The cows take the most direct route into Israelite territory. **15:** This verse is likely a later addition by a scribe* concerned to have the Levites, the priestly tribe, handle the ark. **20:** *Who is able to stand before the LORD* is apparently a technical expression for priestly service. The people are asking whether there is a priest who can handle the ark.

2 From the day that the ark was lodged at Kiriath-jearim, a long time passed, some twenty years, and all the house of Israel lamentedᵈ after the LORD.

3 Then Samuel said to all the house of Israel, "If you are returning to the LORD with all your heart, then put away the foreign gods and the Astartes from among you. Direct your heart to the LORD, and serve him only, and he will deliver you out of the hand of the Philistines." ⁴So Israel put away the Baals and the Astartes, and they served the LORD only.

5 Then Samuel said, "Gather all Israel at Mizpah, and I will pray to the LORD for you." ⁶So they gathered at Mizpah, and drew water and poured it out before the LORD. They fasted that day, and said, "We have sinned against the LORD." And Samuel judged the people of Israel at Mizpah.

a Gk: Heb *rejoiced to see it*   *b* Gk: Heb *And he killed some of the people of Beth-shemesh, because they looked into*   *c* Heb *killed seventy men, fifty thousand men*   *d* Meaning of Heb uncertain

7 When the Philistines heard that the people of Israel had gathered at Mizpah, the lords of the Philistines went up against Israel. And when the people of Israel heard of it they were afraid of the Philistines. 8The people of Israel said to Samuel, "Do not cease to cry out to the LORD our God for us, and pray that he may save us from the hand of the Philistines." 9So Samuel took a sucking lamb and offered it as a whole burnt offering to the LORD; Samuel cried out to the LORD for Israel, and the LORD answered him. 10As Samuel was offering up the burnt offering, the Philistines drew near to attack Israel; but the LORD thundered with a mighty voice that day against the Philistines and threw them into confusion; and they were routed before Israel. 11And the men of Israel went out of Mizpah and pursued the Philistines, and struck them down as far as beyond Beth-car.

12 Then Samuel took a stone and set it up between Mizpah and Jeshanah,*a* and named it Ebenezer;*b* for he said, "Thus far the LORD has helped us." 13So the Philistines were subdued and did not again enter the territory of Israel; the hand of the LORD was against the Philistines all the days of Samuel. 14The towns that the Philistines had taken from Israel were restored to Israel, from Ekron to Gath; and Israel recovered their territory from the hand of the Philistines. There was peace also between Israel and the Amorites.

15 Samuel judged Israel all the days of his life. 16He went on a circuit year by year to Bethel, Gilgal, and Mizpah; and he judged Israel in all these places. 17Then he would come back to Ramah, for his home was there; he administered justice there to Israel, and built there an altar to the LORD.

7.2–17: Samuel judges Israel. Samuel is described as a transitional figure between the era of the judges and the monarchy. He embodies the roles of priest, prophet,* and now judge. **2:** *Twenty years* is a way of designating half a generation. The phrase fits Samuel into the structure of the book of Judges in which a period of foreign oppression precedes Israel's repentance. **3–4:** The call for *returning to the LORD with all your heart* from the sin of idolatry* marks these verses

as an addition by the deuteronomistic* editor. *Baal** and *Astarte** were the leading male and female fertility gods of Canaan. **5:** *Mizpah* became the administrative and religious capital after Jerusalem's destruction in 586 BCE. The setting of this story in Mizpah may indicate a late date of composition. **6:** The libations and fasting described here are part of a community purification ritual, perhaps in preparation for war. **8–9:** Samuel is depicted as an intercessor for the people in the tradition of Moses and Jeremiah. **10:** The first part of this verse is parenthetical; Yahweh's answer is the thunder. **12:** An etiology* for the name *Ebenezer*, whose original meaning was religious and military: "stone of the helper/warrior." **13–14:** The typical deuteronomistic formulas for the judges are here applied to Samuel (compare Judg 3.30; 8.28; 11.33). **15–17:** The book of Judges describes two types of judges: military leaders and legal figures. This chapter ascribes both roles to Samuel. The towns of *Bethel, Gilgal, Mizpah,* and *Ramah* were all within the territories of the tribes of Ephraim and Benjamin.

CHOOSING A KING

Chs. 8–12: Chapters 9–11 contain three accounts of Saul's being chosen king that have been bound together editorially and surrounded by Samuel's convocations of the people in chs. 8 and 12.

---

8 When Samuel became old, he made his sons judges over Israel. 2The name of his firstborn son was Joel, and the name of his second, Abijah; they were judges in Beer-sheba. 3Yet his sons did not follow in his ways, but turned aside after gain; they took bribes and perverted justice.

4 Then all the elders of Israel gathered together and came to Samuel at Ramah, 5and said to him, "You are old and your sons do not follow in your ways; appoint for us, then, a king to govern us, like other nations." 6But the thing displeased Samuel when they said, "Give us a king to govern us." Samuel prayed to the LORD, 7and the LORD said to Samuel, "Listen to the voice of the people in all that they say to you; for they have not rejected you, but they have rejected me from being king over them. 8Just as they have

a Gk Syr: Heb *Shen*   *b* That is *Stone of Help*

done to me,[a] from the day I brought them up out of Egypt to this day, forsaking me and serving other gods, so also they are doing to you. 9Now then, listen to their voice; only—you shall solemnly warn them, and show them the ways of the king who shall reign over them."

10 So Samuel reported all the words of the LORD to the people who were asking him for a king. 11He said, "These will be the ways of the king who will reign over you: he will take your sons and appoint them to his chariots and to be his horsemen, and to run before his chariots; 12and he will appoint for himself commanders of thousands and commanders of fifties, and some to plow his ground and to reap his harvest, and to make his implements of war and the equipment of his chariots. 13He will take your daughters to be perfumers and cooks and bakers. 14He will take the best of your fields and vineyards and olive orchards and give them to his courtiers. 15He will take one-tenth of your grain and of your vineyards and give it to his officers and his courtiers. 16He will take your male and female slaves, and the best of your cattle[b] and donkeys, and put them to his work. 17He will take one-tenth of your flocks, and you shall be his slaves. 18And in that day you will cry out because of your king, whom you have chosen for yourselves; but the LORD will not answer you in that day."

19 But the people refused to listen to the voice of Samuel; they said, "No! but we are determined to have a king over us, 20so that we also may be like other nations, and that our king may govern us and go out before us and fight our battles." 21When Samuel had heard all the words of the people, he repeated them in the ears of the LORD. 22The LORD said to Samuel, "Listen to their voice and set a king over them." Samuel then said to the people of Israel, "Each of you return home."

8.1–22: Israel demands a king. 1–3: *Beer-sheba* was the southernmost city in Judah and far outside of Samuel's jurisdiction in 7.15–17. It became an administrative center during the period of the monarchy of Judah. These facts suggest 8.1–3 may have been written

against the practice of hereditary leadership. Like Eli's sons, Samuel's sons are evil. **4–9:** Both Samuel and the LORD are displeased by the people's request for a king. This does not necessarily mean that monarchy itself is bad but only that the people's request demonstrates a lack of faith in the LORD. **8:** The review of Israel's history as one of forsaking the LORD is indicative of the deuteronomistic* narrator's view. **10:** *Asking* is a play on the name "Saul." **11–17:** These verses preview the social consequences of monarchy by detailing *the ways of the king.* The Hebrew word translated *ways* means "custom" or "judgment." Ironically,* the king to whom the people look for justice will follow the typical ancient Near Eastern practices of taxation and conscription of workers for his service. The items in this list appear to be based on Solomon's reign. **18:** The language of this verse is characteristic of the deuteronomistic narrator and resembles that of the framework of the book of Judges. **20:** *Govern,* or "judge." **22:** The LORD permits the people to have a king even though he does not approve of their demand.

9 There was a man of Benjamin whose name was Kish son of Abiel son of Zeror son of Becorath son of Aphiah, a Benjaminite, a man of wealth. 2He had a son whose name was Saul, a handsome young man. There was not a man among the people of Israel more handsome than he; he stood head and shoulders above everyone else.

3 Now the donkeys of Kish, Saul's father, had strayed. So Kish said to his son Saul, "Take one of the boys with you; go and look for the donkeys." 4He passed through the hill country of Ephraim and passed through the land of Shalishah, but they did not find them. And they passed through the land of Shaalim, but they were not there. Then he passed through the land of Benjamin, but they did not find them.

5 When they came to the land of Zuph, Saul said to the boy who was with him, "Let us turn back, or my father will stop worrying about the donkeys and worry about us." 6But he said to him, "There is a man of God in this town; he is a man held in honor. Whatever he says always comes true. Let us go

a Gk: Heb lacks *to me*   *b* Gk: Heb *young men*

there now; perhaps he will tell us about the journey on which we have set out." 7Then Saul replied to the boy, "But if we go, what can we bring the man? For the bread in our sacks is gone, and there is no present to bring to the man of God. What have we?" 8The boy answered Saul again, "Here, I have with me a quarter shekel of silver; I will give it to the man of God, to tell us our way." 9(Formerly in Israel, anyone who went to inquire of God would say, "Come, let us go to the seer"; for the one who is now called a prophet was formerly called a seer.) 10Saul said to the boy, "Good; come, let us go." So they went to the town where the man of God was.

9.1–10.16: Saul's anointing.* 9.2: Saul's height and handsomeness are qualities typically attributed to a king. **3:** *Donkeys* were ridden by kings (Zech 9.9; Mt 21.1–9), so that the story already hints at Saul's kingship. *One of the boys* refers to a servant who may or may not have been young. **6:** *Man of God* is a title for a prophet.* This prophet turns out to be Samuel (v. 14). But the identification is secondary, since Saul and his servant do not initially seem to know who Samuel is. In the original tale, Saul's encounter was with an anonymous seer. The *town* would have been understood as Ramah, Samuel's home. **7:** The *present* was necessary as a sort of payment to the man of God for divining the whereabouts of the donkeys. **8:** A *shekel** was not a coin but a measure of weight of less than half an ounce. **9:** This is an obvious editorial comment identifying a *seer* as a *prophet.*

11 As they went up the hill to the town, they met some girls coming out to draw water, and said to them, "Is the seer here?" 12They answered, "Yes, there he is just ahead of you. Hurry; he has come just now to the town, because the people have a sacrifice today at the shrine. 13As soon as you enter the town, you will find him, before he goes up to the shrine to eat. For the people will not eat until he comes, since he must bless the sacrifice; afterward those eat who are invited. Now go up, for you will meet him immediately." 14So they went up to the town. As they were entering the town, they saw Samuel coming out toward them on his way up to the shrine.

9.11–14. 11: Cities were built on hills for protection. Drawing water was typically done by women, usually in the morning or evening when it was cooler. This suggests that it was around sundown. **12:** The *shrine* or "high place" was a hill or raised platform where worship, especially sacrifices, took place. Since deuteronomistic* literature generally condemns the high places,* this reference is probably part of the original tale. **13:** Some sacrifices provided occasions for feasting after the portion of the animal designated for God was burned.

15 Now the day before Saul came, the LORD had revealed to Samuel: 16"Tomorrow about this time I will send to you a man from the land of Benjamin, and you shall anoint him to be ruler over my people Israel. He shall save my people from the hand of the Philistines; for I have seen the suffering of[a] my people, because their outcry has come to me." 17When Samuel saw Saul, the LORD told him, "Here is the man of whom I spoke to you. He it is who shall rule over my people." 18Then Saul approached Samuel inside the gate, and said, "Tell me, please, where is the house of the seer?" 19Samuel answered Saul, "I am the seer; go up before me to the shrine, for today you shall eat with me, and in the morning I will let you go and will tell you all that is on your mind. 20As for your donkeys that were lost three days ago, give no further thought to them, for they have been found. And on whom is all Israel's desire fixed, if not on you and on all your ancestral house?" 21Saul answered, "I am only a Benjaminite, from the least of the tribes of Israel, and my family is the humblest of all the families of the tribe of Benjamin. Why then have you spoken to me in this way?"

9.15–21. 16: Anointing* involved smearing a person's head with scented olive oil as a way of designating the person for a particular office. *Ruler* in Hebrew is "nagid," which means "king designate" in this verse. **18:** The *gate* of a city was a well-fortified entrance to a walled city. It was the site of commerce and the place where trials were held. **19–20:** In the original tale, the seer consulted God overnight in order to address

a Gk: Heb lacks *the suffering of*

Saul's need. But the old tale has been transformed editorially so that Samuel has been told to expect Saul (vv. 15–17) and now goes ahead and tells him *all that is on* his *mind* by assuring him that the donkeys have been found (v. 20). The next morning is reserved for Saul's anointing. **21:** Saul's objection is typical of people who receive a divine call in the Bible, such as Moses (Ex 4.10–17) and Jeremiah (Jer 1.6). It also shows Saul's humility and God's preference for the small and weak.

22 Then Samuel took Saul and his servant-boy and brought them into the hall, and gave them a place at the head of those who had been invited, of whom there were about thirty. 23 And Samuel said to the cook, "Bring the portion I gave you, the one I asked you to put aside." 24 The cook took up the thigh and what went with it *a* and set them before Saul. Samuel said, "See, what was kept is set before you. Eat; for it is set *b* before you at the appointed time, so that you might eat with the guests." *c*

So Saul ate with Samuel that day. 25 When they came down from the shrine into the town, a bed was spread for Saul *d* on the roof, and he lay down to sleep. *e* 26 Then at the break of dawn *f* Samuel called to Saul upon the roof, "Get up, so that I may send you on your way." Saul got up, and both he and Samuel went out into the street.

9.22–26. 22–24: Saul is treated as a highly honored guest. He is given *the thigh,* which is usually reserved for the deity or the priests. **25:** Saul sleeps *on the roof,* which was flat and where there was a cool breeze, indicating that the story is set in the summer.

27 As they were going down to the outskirts of the town, Samuel said to Saul, "Tell the boy to go on before us, and when he has passed on, stop here yourself for a while, that I may make known to you the word of God."

10 1 Samuel took a vial of oil and poured it on his head, and kissed him; he said, "The LORD has anointed you ruler over his people Israel. You shall reign over the people of the LORD and you will save them from the hand of their enemies all around. Now this shall be the sign to you that the LORD has anointed you ruler *g* over his her-

itage: 2 When you depart from me today you will meet two men by Rachel's tomb in the territory of Benjamin at Zelzah; they will say to you, 'The donkeys that you went to seek are found, and now your father has stopped worrying about them and is worrying about you, saying: What shall I do about my son?' 3 Then you shall go on from there further and come to the oak of Tabor; three men going up to God at Bethel will meet you there, one carrying three kids, another carrying three loaves of bread, and another carrying a skin of wine. 4 They will greet you and give you two loaves of bread, which you shall accept from them. 5 After that you shall come to Gibeath-elohim, *h* at the place where the Philistine garrison is; there, as you come to the town, you will meet a band of prophets coming down from the shrine with harp, tambourine, flute, and lyre playing in front of them; they will be in a prophetic frenzy. 6 Then the spirit of the LORD will possess you, and you will be in a prophetic frenzy along with them and be turned into a different person. 7 Now when these signs meet you, do whatever you see fit to do, for God is with you. 8 And you shall go down to Gilgal ahead of me; then I will come down to you to present burnt offerings and offer sacrifices of well-being. Seven days you shall wait, until I come to you and show you what you shall do."

9 As he turned away to leave Samuel, God gave him another heart; and all these signs were fulfilled that day. 10 When they were going from there *i* to Gibeah, *j* a band of prophets met him; and the spirit of God possessed him, and he fell into a prophetic frenzy along with them. 11 When all who knew him before saw how he prophesied with the prophets, the people said to one another, "What has come over the son of Kish? Is Saul also among the prophets?" 12 A man of the place answered, "And who is their fa-

a Meaning of Heb uncertain   *b* Q Ms Gk: MT *it was kept*   *c* Cn: Heb *it was kept for you, saying, I have invited the people*   *d* Gk: Heb *and he spoke with Saul*   *e* Gk: Heb lacks *and he lay down to sleep*   *f* Gk: Heb *and they arose early and at break of dawn*   *g* Gk: Heb lacks *over his people Israel. You shall . . . anointed you ruler*   *h* Or *the Hill of God*   *i* Gk: Heb *they came there*   *j* Or *the hill*

ther?" Therefore it became a proverb, "Is Saul also among the prophets?" [13]When his prophetic frenzy had ended, he went home.[a]

14 Saul's uncle said to him and to the boy, "Where did you go?" And he replied, "To seek the donkeys; and when we saw they were not to be found, we went to Samuel." [15]Saul's uncle said, "Tell me what Samuel said to you." [16]Saul said to his uncle, "He told us that the donkeys had been found." But about the matter of the kingship, of which Samuel had spoken, he did not tell him anything.

9.27–10.16. 1: The LORD's *heritage* is the land of Israel. The original idea behind this expression is that every nation is the inheritance of the god it worships. **3–4:** The *three men going up to God at Bethel* are carrying items for sacrifice. They give *two loaves of bread* to Saul, one for him and one for his servant. A better reading, found in the Greek translation known as the Septuagint,* is "two offerings of bread." Thus, Saul again receives the portion of a priest. **5–7:** Music was often used to induce an ecstasy in which prophets* uttered their oracles* (2 Kings 3.15–16). The judges were also moved to action by the spirit of the LORD. Saul's instruction to *do whatever you see fit to do* is a military commission. **8:** This verse connects this story to 13.7b–15. **10–13:** These verses describe the fulfillment of the third sign. The description is also an etiology* for the proverb, *Is Saul also among the prophets?* (v. 11). A different explanation occurs in 19.19–24. Whatever its origin, the proverb seems to have a positive meaning in this context. The LORD's spirit empowers Saul both to prophesy and to rule. The *father* of a group of prophets (v. 12) is their leader. **14–16:** It is surprising that Saul's uncle rather than his father questions him, since the uncle has not been mentioned before in the story. These verses are editorial and set the stage for the following story (10.17–27a). Since Saul's anointing* was private, there is a need for a public proclamation that he is king.

17 Samuel summoned the people to the LORD at Mizpah [18]and said to them,[b] "Thus says the LORD, the God of Israel, 'I brought up Israel out of Egypt, and I rescued you from the hand of the Egyptians and from the hand of all the kingdoms that were oppressing you.' [19]But today you have rejected your God, who saves you from all your calamities and your distresses; and you have said, 'No! but set a king over us.' Now therefore present yourselves before the LORD by your tribes and by your clans."

20 Then Samuel brought all the tribes of Israel near, and the tribe of Benjamin was taken by lot. [21]He brought the tribe of Benjamin near by its families, and the family of the Matrites was taken by lot. Finally he brought the family of the Matrites near man by man,[c] and Saul the son of Kish was taken by lot. But when they sought him, he could not be found. [22]So they inquired again of the LORD, "Did the man come here?"[d] and the LORD said, "See, he has hidden himself among the baggage." [23]Then they ran and brought him from there. When he took his stand among the people, he was head and shoulders taller than any of them. [24]Samuel said to all the people, "Do you see the one whom the LORD has chosen? There is no one like him among all the people." And all the people shouted, "Long live the king!"

25 Samuel told the people the rights and duties of the kingship; and he wrote them in a book and laid it up before the LORD. Then Samuel sent all the people back to their homes. [26]Saul also went to his home at Gibeah, and with him went warriors whose hearts God had touched. [27]But some worthless fellows said, "How can this man save us?" They despised him and brought him no present. But he held his peace.

10.17–27a: Saul is chosen by lot. 18–19: These verses offer another example of deuteronomistic* language. **20–21:** Israelite society was structured according to a hierarchy: tribe, clan,* family ("house of the father"), and individual. Elsewhere in the Bible (Josh 7.14; 1 Sam 14.41) the lot is used to find a person guilty of breaking a law or vow. Some scholars believe that two stories are combined at this point, one in which Saul was present and chosen by lot and another in which he was chosen by oracle* or because of his height. **22:** *Inquired* is another pun on Saul's name. **25:** *The rights and duties of the kingship* probably set out the responsibilities of king and people to each other. The

a Cn: Heb *he came to the shrine*   *b* Heb *to the people of Israel*   *c* Gk: Heb lacks *Finally . . . man by man*   *d* Gk: Heb *Is there yet a man to come here?*

expression here is nearly identical to "the ways of the king" in 8.9, 11, although the two passages seem to refer to two different lists or documents. **26–27a:** Saul's return to Gibeah and the doubts of the *worthless fellows* prepare the way for the subsequent story in which Saul will prove his ability to save Israel.

Now Nahash, king of the Ammonites, had been grievously oppressing the Gadites and the Reubenites. He would gouge out the right eye of each of them and would not grant Israel a deliverer. No one was left of the Israelites across the Jordan whose right eye Nahash, king of the Ammonites, had not gouged out. But there were seven thousand men who had escaped from the Ammonites and had entered Jabesh-gilead.*ᵃ*

11 About a month later,*ᵇ* Nahash the Ammonite went up and besieged Jabesh-gilead; and all the men of Jabesh said to Nahash, "Make a treaty with us, and we will serve you." 2But Nahash the Ammonite said to them, "On this condition I will make a treaty with you, namely that I gouge out everyone's right eye, and thus put disgrace upon all Israel." 3The elders of Jabesh said to him, "Give us seven days' respite that we may send messengers through all the territory of Israel. Then, if there is no one to save us, we will give ourselves up to you." 4When the messengers came to Gibeah of Saul, they reported the matter in the hearing of the people; and all the people wept aloud.

5 Now Saul was coming from the field behind the oxen; and Saul said, "What is the matter with the people, that they are weeping?" So they told him the message from the inhabitants of Jabesh. 6And the spirit of God came upon Saul in power when he heard these words, and his anger was greatly kindled. 7He took a yoke of oxen, and cut them in pieces and sent them throughout all the territory of Israel by messengers, saying, "Whoever does not come out after Saul and Samuel, so shall it be done to his oxen!" Then the dread of the LORD fell upon the people, and they came out as one. 8When he mustered them at Bezek, those from Israel were three hundred thousand, and those from Judah seventy*ᶜ* thousand. 9They said

to the messengers who had come, "Thus shall you say to the inhabitants of Jabesh-gilead: 'Tomorrow, by the time the sun is hot, you shall have deliverance.'" When the messengers came and told the inhabitants of Jabesh, they rejoiced. 10So the inhabitants of Jabesh said, "Tomorrow we will give ourselves up to you, and you may do to us whatever seems good to you." 11The next day Saul put the people in three companies. At the morning watch they came into the camp and cut down the Ammonites until the heat of the day; and those who survived were scattered, so that no two of them were left together.

12 The people said to Samuel, "Who is it that said, 'Shall Saul reign over us?' Give them to us so that we may put them to death." 13But Saul said, "No one shall be put to death this day, for today the LORD has brought deliverance to Israel."

14 Samuel said to the people, "Come, let us go to Gilgal and there renew the kingship." 15So all the people went to Gilgal, and there they made Saul king before the LORD in Gilgal. There they sacrificed offerings of well-being before the LORD, and there Saul and all the Israelites rejoiced greatly.

10.27b–11.15: Saul defeats the Ammonites. 10.27b: This paragraph was lost from the Hebrew text but can now be restored from a Dead Sea Scroll fragment of Samuel, as the translator's note indicates. The missing material explains the reason for the conflict in ch. 11. *The Gadites and the Reubenites* were Israelites living east of the Jordan River in territory which the Ammonite king, Nahash, considered his, but which Israel also claimed. The city of Jabesh in Gilead was farther north and outside of the disputed area, but Nahash threatened it because some of the Israelites from Gad and Reuben had fled there. **11.3:** The messengers are not sent directly to Saul but *through all the territory of Israel.* **4–5:** Even in Gibeah the messengers do not seek out Saul, but he learns of their mission because of the weeping of the people as he returns from the field.

a Q Ms Compare Josephus, *Antiquities* VI.v.1 (68–71): MT lacks *Now Nahash . . . entered Jabesh-gilead.*
b Q Ms Gk: MT lacks *About a month later*   *c* Q Ms Gk: MT *thirty*

Thus, the story does not seem to assume that Saul is king. **6:** The *spirit of God* spurs Saul to military action as it had some of the deliverers in the book of Judges. **7:** Saul's action symbolizes a threat against the animals and perhaps the people themselves who do not join in the war. References to dismemberment occur in ancient treaties, so that Saul's actions assume a covenant* relationship among the tribes. **8:** The division between Israel and Judah is reflected here though it did not occur until after Solomon's reign. **10:** *We will give ourselves up to you* means literally, "we will come out to you." What sounds to Nahash like a surrender cleverly masks a threat. The people of Jabesh will come out to fight! **11:** *The next day* actually began at sunset according to Israelite reckoning, and *the morning watch* was in the early hours before sunrise. This was a surprise attack before dawn. **12–14:** These verses are editorial and bind 10.17–27a with 10.27b–11.15. It was the "worthless fellows" in 10.27a who asked, *Shall Saul reign over us?* The editor adds Samuel to the story at this point even though he plays no role in the battle account. The editor also speaks of *renew(ing) the kingship.* **15:** The original story did not assume that Saul was already king but explained that the people *made Saul king* as a result of his victory on this occasion.

12 Samuel said to all Israel, "I have listened to you in all that you have said to me, and have set a king over you. ²See, it is the king who leads you now; I am old and gray, but my sons are with you. I have led you from my youth until this day. ³Here I am; testify against me before the LORD and before his anointed. Whose ox have I taken? Or whose donkey have I taken? Or whom have I defrauded? Whom have I oppressed? Or from whose hand have I taken a bribe to blind my eyes with it? Testify against me*ᵃ* and I will restore it to you." ⁴They said, "You have not defrauded us or oppressed us or taken anything from the hand of anyone." ⁵He said to them, "The LORD is witness against you, and his anointed is witness this day, that you have not found anything in my hand." And they said, "He is witness."

6 Samuel said to the people, "The LORD is witness, who*ᵇ* appointed Moses and Aaron and brought your ancestors up out of the land of Egypt. ⁷Now therefore take your stand, so that I may enter into judgment with

you before the LORD, and I will declare to you*ᶜ* all the saving deeds of the LORD that he performed for you and for your ancestors. ⁸When Jacob went into Egypt and the Egyptians oppressed them,*ᵈ* then your ancestors cried to the LORD and the LORD sent Moses and Aaron, who brought forth your ancestors out of Egypt, and settled them in this place. ⁹But they forgot the LORD their God; and he sold them into the hand of Sisera, commander of the army of King Jabin of*ᵉ* Hazor, and into the hand of the Philistines, and into the hand of the king of Moab; and they fought against them. ¹⁰Then they cried to the LORD, and said, 'We have sinned, because we have forsaken the LORD, and have served the Baals and the Astartes; but now rescue us out of the hand of our enemies, and we will serve you.' ¹¹And the LORD sent Jerubbaal and Barak,*ᶠ* and Jephthah, and Samson,*ᵍ* and rescued you out of the hand of your enemies on every side; and you lived in safety. ¹²But when you saw that King Nahash of the Ammonites came against you, you said to me, 'No, but a king shall reign over us,' though the LORD your God was your king. ¹³See, here is the king whom you have chosen, for whom you have asked; see, the LORD has set a king over you. ¹⁴If you will fear the LORD and serve him and heed his voice and not rebel against the commandment of the LORD, and if both you and the king who reigns over you will follow the LORD your God, it will be well; ¹⁵but if you will not heed the voice of the LORD, but rebel against the commandment of the LORD, then the hand of the LORD will be against you and your king.*ʰ* ¹⁶Now therefore take your stand and see this great thing that the LORD will do before your eyes. ¹⁷Is it not the wheat harvest today? I will call upon the LORD, that he may send thunder and rain; and you shall know and see that the wick-

a Gk: Heb lacks *Testify against me*
b Gk: Heb lacks *is witness, who*
c Gk: Heb lacks *and I will declare to you*
d Gk: Heb lacks *and the Egyptians oppressed them*
e Gk: Heb lacks *King Jabin of*   *f* Gk Syr: Heb *Bedan*   *g* Gk: Heb *Samuel*   *h* Gk: Heb *and your ancestors*

edness that you have done in the sight of the LORD is great in demanding a king for yourselves." 18So Samuel called upon the LORD, and the LORD sent thunder and rain that day; and all the people greatly feared the LORD and Samuel.

12.1–25: Samuel's farewell. 3: Samuel's words are reminiscent of Moses' in Num 16.15 and contrast with the "ways of the king" that he listed in 1 Sam 8. **6–12:** This long retrospective on Israel's history expresses the opinions and concerns of the deuteronomistic* editor. **13–15:** Even though the people's request for a king evinced a lack of faith, they and their king can still prosper as long as they will serve the LORD. **16–18:** The *wheat harvest* was in early summer. The lack of rain was a threat to the crops. Thus, this miracle shows the LORD's response to Samuel and hints at his displeasure with the people.

---

19 All the people said to Samuel, "Pray to the LORD your God for your servants, so that we may not die; for we have added to all our sins the evil of demanding a king for ourselves." 20And Samuel said to the people, "Do not be afraid; you have done all this evil, yet do not turn aside from following the LORD, but serve the LORD with all your heart; 21and do not turn aside after useless things that cannot profit or save, for they are useless. 22For the LORD will not cast away his people, for his great name's sake, because it has pleased the LORD to make you a people for himself. 23Moreover as for me, far be it from me that I should sin against the LORD by ceasing to pray for you; and I will instruct you in the good and the right way. 24Only fear the LORD, and serve him faithfully with all your heart; for consider what great things he has done for you. 25But if you still do wickedly, you shall be swept away, both you and your king."

12.19–25: Samuel is again described as an intercessor on behalf of the people. The language of these verses, especially vv. 24–25, underlines the main themes of the Deuteronomistic* History. *For his great name's sake* in v. 22 means that Yahweh's own reputation might be damaged if he were not patient with his people but destroyed them too readily.

---

13 Saul was . . .*a* years old when he began to reign; and he reigned . . . and two*b* years over Israel.

2 Saul chose three thousand out of Israel; two thousand were with Saul in Michmash and the hill country of Bethel, and a thousand were with Jonathan in Gibeah of Benjamin; the rest of the people he sent home to their tents. 3Jonathan defeated the garrison of the Philistines that was at Geba; and the Philistines heard of it. And Saul blew the trumpet throughout all the land, saying, "Let the Hebrews hear!" 4When all Israel heard that Saul had defeated the garrison of the Philistines, and also that Israel had become odious to the Philistines, the people were called out to join Saul at Gilgal.

5 The Philistines mustered to fight with Israel, thirty thousand chariots, and six thousand horsemen, and troops like the sand on the seashore in multitude; they came up and encamped at Michmash, to the east of Beth-aven. 6When the Israelites saw that they were in distress (for the troops were hard pressed), the people hid themselves in caves and in holes and in rocks and in tombs and in cisterns. 7Some Hebrews crossed the Jordan to the land of Gad and Gilead. Saul was still at Gilgal, and all the people followed him trembling.

8 He waited seven days, the time appointed by Samuel; but Samuel did not come to Gilgal, and the people began to slip away from Saul.*c* 9So Saul said, "Bring the burnt offering here to me, and the offerings of well-being." And he offered the burnt offering. 10As soon as he had finished offering the burnt offering, Samuel arrived; and Saul went out to meet him and salute him. 11Samuel said, "What have you done?" Saul replied, "When I saw that the people were slipping away from me, and that you did not come within the days appointed, and that the Philistines were mustering at Michmash, 12I said, 'Now the Philistines will come down upon me at Gilgal, and I have not entreated the favor of the LORD'; so I forced myself,

---

a The number is lacking in the Heb text (the verse is lacking in the Septuagint).   *b* *Two* is not the entire number; something has dropped out.   *c* Heb *him*

and offered the burnt offering." 13Samuel said to Saul, "You have done foolishly; you have not kept the commandment of the LORD your God, which he commanded you. The LORD would have established your kingdom over Israel forever, 14but now your kingdom will not continue; the LORD has sought out a man after his own heart; and the LORD has appointed him to be ruler over his people, because you have not kept what the LORD commanded you." 15And Samuel left and went on his way from Gilgal.*a* The rest of the people followed Saul to join the army; they went up from Gilgal toward Gibeah of Benjamin.*b*

13.1–14.52: Saul's wars with the Philistines. 13.1: Saul's age at his accession* is unknown. The Hebrew text actually says he was one year old, which is, of course, impossible. It also says that he reigned two years, but the events recounted for his reign indicate a much longer period. **3–4:** *Jonathan,* Saul's son, is mentioned here for the first time. Since he is a grown man, this story is substantially later than 9.1–10.16, where Saul appears as a young man. Both Jonathan and Saul are credited with defeating the Philistine garrison. This may indicate the composite nature of this account, or Saul, as king, may have received the credit for his son's victory. *Geba* and Gibeah are very similar in Hebrew and appear to be confused here. **7b–15a:** This story of Saul's rejection alludes to Samuel's order in 10.8. Both passages refer to an interval of *seven days* between them, but the intervening events in chs. 10–12 would require a much longer time. The nature of Saul's sin is not altogether clear. Perhaps he is condemned for trying to usurp Samuel's role of religious leadership. The *man after [Yahweh's] own heart* is an allusion to David. It does not imply any special quality of David but is simply a way of saying that he is chosen by the LORD.

Saul counted the people who were present with him, about six hundred men. 16Saul, his son Jonathan, and the people who were present with them stayed in Geba of Benjamin; but the Philistines encamped at Michmash. 17And raiders came out of the camp of the Philistines in three companies; one company turned toward Ophrah, to the land of Shual, 18another company turned toward Bethhoron, and another company turned toward the mountain*c* that looks down upon the valley of Zeboim toward the wilderness.

19 Now there was no smith to be found throughout all the land of Israel; for the Philistines said, "The Hebrews must not make swords or spears for themselves"; 20so all the Israelites went down to the Philistines to sharpen their plowshares, mattocks, axes, or sickles;*d* 21The charge was two-thirds of a shekel*e* for the plowshares and for the mattocks, and one-third of a shekel for sharpening the axes and for setting the goads.*f* 22So on the day of the battle neither sword nor spear was to be found in the possession of any of the people with Saul and Jonathan; but Saul and his son Jonathan had them.

13.15b–22: These verses set the stage for the battle account in the next chapter. *Geba* and *Michmash* (v. 16) were across from each other on opposite sides of a valley. The Philistine *raiders* (vv. 17–18) customarily went north, west, and east from Michmash to attack Israelite settlements and keep them subdued. The Philistines also controlled the Israelites by maintaining a monopoly on iron working (vv. 19–22).

23 Now a garrison of the Philistines had gone out to the pass of Michmash. 14 1One day Jonathan son of Saul said to the young man who carried his armor, "Come, let us go over to the Philistine garrison on the other side." But he did not tell his father. 2Saul was staying in the outskirts of Gibeah under the pomegranate tree that is at Migron; the troops that were with him were about six hundred men, 3along with Ahijah son of Ahitub, Ichabod's brother, son of Phinehas son of Eli, the priest of the LORD in Shiloh, carrying an ephod. Now the people did not know that Jonathan had gone. 4In the pass,*g* by which Jonathan tried to go over to the Philistine garrison, there was a rocky crag on one side and a rocky crag on the other; the name of the one was Bozez, and the name of the other

a Gk: Heb *went up from Gilgal to Gibeah of Benjamin*
b Gk: Heb lacks *The rest . . . of Benjamin*
c Cn Compare Gk: Heb *toward the border*   *d* Gk: Heb *plowshare*   *e* Heb *was a pim*   *f* Cn: Meaning of Heb uncertain   *g* Heb *Between the passes*

Seneh. [5] One crag rose on the north in front of Michmash, and the other on the south in front of Geba.

6 Jonathan said to the young man who carried his armor, "Come, let us go over to the garrison of these uncircumcised; it may be that the Lord will act for us; for nothing can hinder the Lord from saving by many or by few." [7] His armor-bearer said to him, "Do all that your mind inclines to.[a] I am with you; as your mind is, so is mine."[b] [8] Then Jonathan said, "Now we will cross over to those men and will show ourselves to them. [9] If they say to us, 'Wait until we come to you,' then we will stand still in our place, and we will not go up to them. [10] But if they say, 'Come up to us,' then we will go up; for the Lord has given them into our hand. That will be the sign for us." [11] So both of them showed themselves to the garrison of the Philistines; and the Philistines said, "Look, Hebrews are coming out of the holes where they have hidden themselves." [12] The men of the garrison hailed Jonathan and his armor-bearer, saying, "Come up to us, and we will show you something." Jonathan said to his armor-bearer, "Come up after me; for the Lord has given them into the hand of Israel." [13] Then Jonathan climbed up on his hands and feet, with his armor-bearer following after him. The Philistines[c] fell before Jonathan, and his armor-bearer, coming after him, killed them. [14] In that first slaughter Jonathan and his armor-bearer killed about twenty men within an area about half a furrow long in an acre[d] of land. [15] There was a panic in the camp, in the field, and among all the people; the garrison and even the raiders trembled; the earth quaked; and it became a very great panic.

16 Saul's lookouts in Gibeah of Benjamin were watching as the multitude was surging back and forth.[e] [17] Then Saul said to the troops that were with him, "Call the roll and see who has gone from us." When they had called the roll, Jonathan and his armor-bearer were not there. [18] Saul said to Ahijah, "Bring the ark[f] of God here." For at that time the ark[f] of God went with the Israelites. [19] While Saul was talking to the priest, the tumult in the camp of the Philistines in-creased more and more; and Saul said to the priest, "Withdraw your hand." [20] Then Saul and all the people who were with him rallied and went into the battle; and every sword was against the other, so that there was very great confusion. [21] Now the Hebrews who previously had been with the Philistines and had gone up with them into the camp turned and joined the Israelites who were with Saul and Jonathan. [22] Likewise, when all the Israelites who had gone into hiding in the hill country of Ephraim heard that the Philistines were fleeing, they too followed closely after them in the battle. [23] So the Lord gave Israel the victory that day.

13.23–14.23a. 13.23: The battle begins with the Philistines' movement to the pass on their side of the valley. 14.1: The *young man who carried his armor:* The armor-bearer was a formidable soldier as the involvement of this man in the battle shows. 3: This *ephod*⋆ was an object that was carried by priests and used to divine the will of God. It was carried in priestly garments, which may explain why the same word was used for both (1 Sam 2.18). *The people* is often used to mean the army. 6: *These uncircumcised*⋆ is a derogatory term for the Philistines. 13: Jonathan wounded the Philistines, and his armor-bearer finished them off. 19: *Withdraw your hand:* Saul had called Ahijah the priest with the intention of consulting the Lord through him (the Greek text reads "ephod" instead of "ark"). Before receiving an answer to his inquiry, Saul decided to attack. 21: The *Hebrews* here are distinguished from the *Israelites*. They are first allied with the Philistines and then turn against them. They may have been mercenaries of some kind.

The battle passed beyond Beth-aven, and the troops with Saul numbered altogether about ten thousand men. The battle spread out over the hill country of Ephraim.

24 Now Saul committed a very rash act on that day.[g] He had laid an oath on the troops, saying, "Cursed be anyone who eats food before it is evening and I have been avenged on my enemies." So none of the

a Gk: Heb *Do all that is in your mind. Turn*
b Gk: Heb lacks *so is mine*   c Heb *They*   d Heb *yoke*
e Gk: Heb *they went and there*   f Gk *the ephod*
g Gk: Heb *The Israelites were distressed that day*

troops tasted food. 25All the troops*a* came upon a honeycomb; and there was honey on the ground. 26When the troops came upon the honeycomb, the honey was dripping out; but they did not put their hands to their mouths, for they feared the oath. 27But Jonathan had not heard his father charge the troops with the oath; so he extended the staff that was in his hand, and dipped the tip of it in the honeycomb, and put his hand to his mouth; and his eyes brightened. 28Then one of the soldiers said, "Your father strictly charged the troops with an oath, saying, 'Cursed be anyone who eats food this day.' And so the troops are faint." 29Then Jonathan said, "My father has troubled the land; see how my eyes have brightened because I tasted a little of this honey. 30How much better if today the troops had eaten freely of the spoil taken from their enemies; for now the slaughter among the Philistines has not been great."

31 After they had struck down the Philistines that day from Michmash to Aijalon, the troops were very faint; 32so the troops flew upon the spoil, and took sheep and oxen and calves, and slaughtered them on the ground; and the troops ate them with the blood. 33Then it was reported to Saul, "Look, the troops are sinning against the LORD by eating with the blood." And he said, "You have dealt treacherously; roll a large stone before me here."*b* 34Saul said, "Disperse yourselves among the troops, and say to them, 'Let all bring their oxen or their sheep, and slaughter them here, and eat; and do not sin against the LORD by eating with the blood.'" So all of the troops brought their oxen with them that night, and slaughtered them there. 35And Saul built an altar to the LORD; it was the first altar that he built to the LORD.

be slaughtered upon the stone, thereby allowing the blood to be drained before the meat was cooked and eaten.

~~~~~~~~~~~~~~~~~~~~~~~~~~~~~~~~

36 Then Saul said, "Let us go down after the Philistines by night and despoil them until the morning light; let us not leave one of them." They said, "Do whatever seems good to you." But the priest said, "Let us draw near to God here." 37So Saul inquired of God, "Shall I go down after the Philistines? Will you give them into the hand of Israel?" But he did not answer him that day. 38Saul said, "Come here, all you leaders of the people; and let us find out how this sin has arisen today. 39For as the LORD lives who saves Israel, even if it is in my son Jonathan, he shall surely die!" But there was no one among all the people who answered him. 40He said to all Israel, "You shall be on one side, and I and my son Jonathan will be on the other side." The people said to Saul, "Do what seems good to you." 41Then Saul said, "O LORD God of Israel, why have you not answered your servant today? If this guilt is in me or in my son Jonathan, O LORD God of Israel, give Urim; but if this guilt is in your people Israel,*c* give Thummim." And Jonathan and Saul were indicated by the lot, but the people were cleared. 42Then Saul said, "Cast the lot between me and my son Jonathan." And Jonathan was taken.

43 Then Saul said to Jonathan, "Tell me what you have done." Jonathan told him, "I tasted a little honey with the tip of the staff that was in my hand; here I am, I will die." 44Saul said, "God do so to me and more also; you shall surely die, Jonathan!" 45Then the people said to Saul, "Shall Jonathan die, who has accomplished this great victory in Israel? Far from it! As the LORD lives, not one hair of his head shall fall to the ground; for he has worked with God today." So the people ransomed Jonathan, and he did not die. 46Then Saul withdrew from pursuing the Philistines; and the Philistines went to their own place.

14.23b–35. 24–30: Saul's foolish oath caused his troops to be faint and prevented them from gaining a complete victory. 31–35: A further result of Saul's oath was that it led his hungry soldiers to commit a ritual offense by slaughtering animals *on the ground* so that the blood did not drain out. Hence, they ate meat cooked *with the blood.* Saul then commanded them to *roll a large stone* to the site so that animals could

a Heb *land*　　*b* Gk: Heb *me this day*　　*c* Vg Compare Gk: Heb 41*Saul said to the* LORD, *the God of Israel*

14.36–46: Finally, Saul's oath nearly cost the life of Jonathan. The inquiry through the priest (v. 37) involves yes/no questions, with the additional possibility that no answer will be forthcoming. Verses 40–42 illustrate at least one method of divination or lot casting. Neither the mechanism nor the meaning of the Urim and Thummim are known, but they functioned to answer yes/no questions or to choose between two alternatives. **45:** It is not clear exactly how *the people ransomed Jonathan.* Perhaps this situation foreshadows Jonathan's death before he can succeed Saul.

47 When Saul had taken the kingship over Israel, he fought against all his enemies on every side—against Moab, against the Ammonites, against Edom, against the kings of Zobah, and against the Philistines; wherever he turned he routed them. ⁴⁸He did valiantly, and struck down the Amalekites, and rescued Israel out of the hands of those who plundered them.

49 Now the sons of Saul were Jonathan, Ishvi, and Malchishua; and the names of his two daughters were these: the name of the firstborn was Merab, and the name of the younger, Michal. ⁵⁰The name of Saul's wife was Ahinoam daughter of Ahimaaz. And the name of the commander of his army was Abner son of Ner, Saul's uncle; ⁵¹Kish was the father of Saul, and Ner the father of Abner was the son of Abiel.

52 There was hard fighting against the Philistines all the days of Saul; and when Saul saw any strong or valiant warrior, he took him into his service.

14.47–52. 47–48: These verses indicate Saul's military success as king. *Moab, the Ammonites,* and *Edom* were the three countries on the other side of the Jordan from Israel. *Zobah* was an important Aramean (Syrian) city-state. The *Amalekites* were a nomadic tribe south of Judah. This reference to Saul's defeat of them is contradicted by the story in ch. 15. **49:** *Ishvi* may be the same as Ishbaal, Saul's successor, who is otherwise not named in this list. **52:** The reference to Saul's draft of *any strong or valiant warrior* is an appropriate introduction to the story of David beginning in 16.14.

15 Samuel said to Saul, "The LORD sent me to anoint you king over his people Israel; now therefore listen to the words of the LORD. ²Thus says the LORD of hosts, 'I will punish the Amalekites for what they did in opposing the Israelites when they came up out of Egypt. ³Now go and attack Amalek, and utterly destroy all that they have; do not spare them, but kill both man and woman, child and infant, ox and sheep, camel and donkey.' "

4 So Saul summoned the people, and numbered them in Telaim, two hundred thousand foot soldiers, and ten thousand soldiers of Judah. ⁵Saul came to the city of the Amalekites and lay in wait in the valley. ⁶Saul said to the Kenites, "Go! Leave! Withdraw from among the Amalekites, or I will destroy you with them; for you showed kindness to all the people of Israel when they came up out of Egypt." So the Kenites withdrew from the Amalekites. ⁷Saul defeated the Amalekites, from Havilah as far as Shur, which is east of Egypt. ⁸He took King Agag of the Amalekites alive, but utterly destroyed all the people with the edge of the sword. ⁹Saul and the people spared Agag, and the best of the sheep and of the cattle and of the fatlings, and the lambs, and all that was valuable, and would not utterly destroy them; all that was despised and worthless they utterly destroyed.

15.1–35: Another rejection of Saul. 2: An allusion to the story in Ex 17.8–16, which is also recalled in Deut 25.17–19. **3:** The order to *utterly destroy* the Amalekites reflects the practice of the "ban"* or "devotion to destruction" (Heb., "herem"), used by Israel and other peoples in the ancient Middle East. When it was implemented, the enemy and all their property were annihilated as a kind of sacrifice to the deity. **4:** Saul's army is unbelievably large. Either the figures have been exaggerated or the Hebrew word translated "thousand" actually refers to a military unit much smaller than a thousand men. **6:** The precise event in which the Kenites *showed kindness* is unknown.

10 The word of the LORD came to Samuel: ¹¹"I regret that I made Saul king, for he has turned back from following me, and has not carried out my commands." Samuel was

angry; and he cried out to the LORD all night. ¹²Samuel rose early in the morning to meet Saul, and Samuel was told, "Saul went to Carmel, where he set up a monument for himself, and on returning he passed on down to Gilgal." ¹³When Samuel came to Saul, Saul said to him, "May you be blessed by the LORD; I have carried out the command of the LORD." ¹⁴But Samuel said, "What then is this bleating of sheep in my ears, and the lowing of cattle that I hear?" ¹⁵Saul said, "They have brought them from the Amalekites; for the people spared the best of the sheep and the cattle, to sacrifice to the LORD your God; but the rest we have utterly destroyed." ¹⁶Then Samuel said to Saul, "Stop! I will tell you what the LORD said to me last night." He replied, "Speak."

17 Samuel said, "Though you are little in your own eyes, are you not the head of the tribes of Israel? The LORD anointed you king over Israel. ¹⁸And the LORD sent you on a mission, and said, 'Go, utterly destroy the sinners, the Amalekites, and fight against them until they are consumed.' ¹⁹Why then did you not obey the voice of the LORD? Why did you swoop down on the spoil, and do what was evil in the sight of the LORD?" ²⁰Saul said to Samuel, "I have obeyed the voice of the LORD, I have gone on the mission on which the LORD sent me, I have brought Agag the king of Amalek, and I have utterly destroyed the Amalekites. ²¹But from the spoil the people took sheep and cattle, the best of the things devoted to destruction, to sacrifice to the LORD your God in Gilgal." ²²And Samuel said,

"Has the LORD as great delight in burnt
　　offerings and sacrifices,
　as in obedience to the voice of the
　　LORD?
Surely, to obey is better than sacrifice,
　and to heed than the fat of rams.
23 For rebellion is no less a sin than
　　divination,
　and stubbornness is like iniquity and
　　idolatry.
Because you have rejected the word of
　　the LORD,
　he has also rejected you from being
　　king."

15.10–23. 15: Saul defends himself by blaming his troops (*the people*) for sparing the best of the sheep and cattle, though he is implicated in v. 9. He also says that the animals were spared for sacrifice, and this is the ground for Samuel's subsequent rebuke. **22:** *The fat of rams* was the part of the animal burned in sacrifice to the LORD. **23:** The kind of *divination* prohibited here is related to foreign idolatry* and does not include divination through a legitimate priest of the LORD. *Rebellion* and *stubbornness* are like *divination* and *idolatry* because they involve turning away from the LORD.

24 Saul said to Samuel, "I have sinned; for I have transgressed the commandment of the LORD and your words, because I feared the people and obeyed their voice. ²⁵Now therefore, I pray, pardon my sin, and return with me, so that I may worship the LORD." ²⁶Samuel said to Saul, "I will not return with you; for you have rejected the word of the LORD, and the LORD has rejected you from being king over Israel." ²⁷As Samuel turned to go away, Saul caught hold of the hem of his robe, and it tore. ²⁸And Samuel said to him, "The LORD has torn the kingdom of Israel from you this very day, and has given it to a neighbor of yours, who is better than you. ²⁹Moreover the Glory of Israel will not recant[a] or change his mind; for he is not a mortal, that he should change his mind." ³⁰Then Saul[b] said, "I have sinned; yet honor me now before the elders of my people and before Israel, and return with me, so that I may worship the LORD your God." ³¹So Samuel turned back after Saul; and Saul worshiped the LORD.

32 Then Samuel said, "Bring Agag king of the Amalekites here to me." And Agag came to him haltingly.[c] Agag said, "Surely this is the bitterness of death."[d] ³³But Samuel said,

"As your sword has made women
　　childless,
　so your mother shall be childless
　　among women."

And Samuel hewed Agag in pieces before the LORD in Gilgal.

a Q Ms Gk: MT *deceive*　　*b* Heb *he*　　*c* Cn Compare Gk: Meaning of Heb uncertain　　*d* Q Ms Gk: MT *Surely the bitterness of death is past*

34 Then Samuel went to Ramah; and Saul went up to his house in Gibeah of Saul. [35] Samuel did not see Saul again until the day of his death, but Samuel grieved over Saul. And the LORD was sorry that he had made Saul king over Israel.

15.24–35. 27: Grasping the *hem* of a person's garment was a way of submitting or pleading. **28:** Samuel uses the torn hem as an object lesson. The LORD *has torn the kingdom* from Saul and given it to his *neighbor,* an allusion to David. **29:** The point of this verse is that the LORD will not *change his mind,* so Saul's further pleading is futile. *The Glory of Israel* is an epithet* for the LORD not used elsewhere in the Hebrew Bible. The general message of the verse seems to contradict the larger context in which the LORD has changed his mind about allowing Saul to be king. Some scholars address this contradiction by positing v. 29 as a later addition. **33:** Agag's dismemberment *before the LORD* at the hands of Samuel was a ritual execution as punishment either for war crimes or for violation of an unknown treaty. **35:** The statement that *Samuel did not see Saul again until the day of his death* anticipates the story in 1 Sam 28 but stands in tension with 1 Sam 19.18–24.

16 The LORD said to Samuel, "How long will you grieve over Saul? I have rejected him from being king over Israel. Fill your horn with oil and set out; I will send you to Jesse the Bethlehemite, for I have provided for myself a king among his sons." [2] Samuel said, "How can I go? If Saul hears of it, he will kill me." And the LORD said, "Take a heifer with you, and say, 'I have come to sacrifice to the LORD.' [3] Invite Jesse to the sacrifice, and I will show you what you shall do; and you shall anoint for me the one whom I name to you." [4] Samuel did what the LORD commanded, and came to Bethlehem. The elders of the city came to meet him trembling, and said, "Do you come peaceably?" [5] He said, "Peaceably; I have come to sacrifice to the LORD; sanctify yourselves and come with me to the sacrifice." And he sanctified Jesse and his sons and invited them to the sacrifice.

6 When they came, he looked on Eliab and thought, "Surely the LORD's anointed is now before the LORD."[a] [7] But the LORD said

to Samuel, "Do not look on his appearance or on the height of his stature, because I have rejected him; for the LORD does not see as mortals see; they look on the outward appearance, but the LORD looks on the heart." [8] Then Jesse called Abinadab, and made him pass before Samuel. He said, "Neither has the LORD chosen this one." [9] Then Jesse made Shammah pass by. And he said, "Neither has the LORD chosen this one." [10] Jesse made seven of his sons pass before Samuel, and Samuel said to Jesse, "The LORD has not chosen any of these." [11] Samuel said to Jesse, "Are all your sons here?" And he said, "There remains yet the youngest, but he is keeping the sheep." And Samuel said to Jesse, "Send and bring him; for we will not sit down until he comes here." [12] He sent and brought him in. Now he was ruddy, and had beautiful eyes, and was handsome. The LORD said, "Rise and anoint him; for this is the one." [13] Then Samuel took the horn of oil, and anointed him in the presence of his brothers; and the spirit of the LORD came mightily upon David from that day forward. Samuel then set out and went to Ramah.

16.1–13: David's anointing. **4–5:** The *elders of the city* were nobles who functioned as a council of civic leaders. Jesse seems to be among the elders of Bethlehem. **6–7:** Like Saul, Eliab is tall and handsome. Samuel is impressed but is warned that the LORD regards the inner qualities or *heart* as more important than outer appearance. The writer is building a contrast between Saul and David. **8–9:** David's brothers are rejected one by one. Samuel is probably using some device like the Urim and Thummim to determine whether each of the sons is the one chosen by the LORD. **10:** This verse agrees with 17.12 in crediting Jesse with eight sons, but 1 Chr 2.13–15 mentions only seven with David as the youngest. Since the number seven had special meaning as a symbol for completeness or for largeness, the seventh son may have been seen as specially blessed. Perhaps David was originally the seventh son and the tradition became altered over time. Or perhaps he is described as the eighth son as a way of highlighting his humble origins. **11:** The word translated *the youngest* may also mean "the smallest" and again contrasts David with Saul. David is also

a Heb *him*

keeping the sheep. The image of a shepherd was a common metaphor* for kings (2 Sam 5.2). **12:** *Ruddy* means "reddish" of hair and complexion (Gen 25.25).

14 Now the spirit of the LORD departed from Saul, and an evil spirit from the LORD tormented him. 15And Saul's servants said to him, "See now, an evil spirit from God is tormenting you. 16Let our lord now command the servants who attend you to look for someone who is skillful in playing the lyre; and when the evil spirit from God is upon you, he will play it, and you will feel better." 17So Saul said to his servants, "Provide for me someone who can play well, and bring him to me." 18One of the young men answered, "I have seen a son of Jesse the Bethlehemite who is skillful in playing, a man of valor, a warrior, prudent in speech, and a man of good presence; and the LORD is with him." 19So Saul sent messengers to Jesse, and said, "Send me your son David who is with the sheep." 20Jesse took a donkey loaded with bread, a skin of wine, and a kid, and sent them by his son David to Saul. 21And David came to Saul, and entered his service. Saul loved him greatly, and he became his armor-bearer. 22Saul sent to Jesse, saying, "Let David remain in my service, for he has found favor in my sight." 23And whenever the evil spirit from God came upon Saul, David took the lyre and played it with his hand, and Saul would be relieved and feel better, and the evil spirit would depart from him.

16.14–23: David comes to Saul's court. 14: The contrast between David and Saul continues. The *spirit of the LORD* came upon David (v. 13) but left Saul. In its place Saul is tormented by an *evil spirit from the LORD.* This may be an ancient way of describing mental illness. The theological point is that the LORD has abandoned Saul. **16:** The *lyre* was a hand-held instrument. Musicians were used in the ancient world to ward off evil spirits. **18:** *A man of valor* is a "nobleman." In 9.1 the same expression is translated "a man of wealth." *Prudent in speech* or "skilled of speech" implies both eloquence and cleverness. *The LORD is with him* expresses a central theme of the David story, which has its beginning in this text. **19:** David's role as a shepherd again hints at his future as king. **21:** The

word "love" expressed not only affection but also loyalty. Because *Saul loved [David] greatly* he established a relationship with him and made a commitment to him, appointing him as his *armor-bearer*, which indicates David's skill as a warrior.

17 Now the Philistines gathered their armies for battle; they were gathered at Socoh, which belongs to Judah, and encamped between Socoh and Azekah, in Ephes-dammim. 2Saul and the Israelites gathered and encamped in the valley of Elah, and formed ranks against the Philistines. 3The Philistines stood on the mountain on the one side, and Israel stood on the mountain on the other side, with a valley between them. 4And there came out from the camp of the Philistines a champion named Goliath, of Gath, whose height was six*a* cubits and a span. 5He had a helmet of bronze on his head, and he was armed with a coat of mail; the weight of the coat was five thousand shekels of bronze. 6He had greaves of bronze on his legs and a javelin of bronze slung between his shoulders. 7The shaft of his spear was like a weaver's beam, and his spear's head weighed six hundred shekels of iron; and his shield-bearer went before him. 8He stood and shouted to the ranks of Israel, "Why have you come out to draw up for battle? Am I not a Philistine, and are you not servants of Saul? Choose a man for yourselves, and let him come down to me. 9If he is able to fight with me and kill me, then we will be your servants; but if I prevail against him and kill him, then you shall be our servants and serve us." 10And the Philistine said, "Today I defy the ranks of Israel! Give me a man, that we may fight together." 11When Saul and all Israel heard these words of the Philistine, they were dismayed and greatly afraid.

17.1–58: David defeats the Philistine champion. An initial version of this story in vv. 1–11, 32–49, 51–54 has been extensively supplemented in the Hebrew text by vv. 12–31, 50, 55–58; 18.1–5. The supplementary material does not occur in the old Greek translation (known as the Septuagint* and abbreviated as LXX*).

a MT: Q Ms Gk *four*

Its addition has caused a series of tensions within the story relating to David's presence in Saul's army, the way in which the Philistine died, and Saul's acquaintance with David (see below). **4:** *Goliath* is a genuine Philistine name. But it occurs only here and in v. 23, which is supplemental. Otherwise, David's opponent is simply called "the Philistine." The name has come into the story under the influence of 2 Sam 21.19, which says that a man named Elhanan killed Goliath. *Six cubits and a span* was about nine and one-half feet. The Greek reading, "four cubits and a span," about six and one-half feet, is more realistic and probably original. **5–7:** The armor described here is not genuinely Philistine but reflects items from different armies at different times. It is designed to paint a very imposing picture of the Philistine. *Five thousand shekels** was almost 126 pounds. **6:** The *javelin* was more likely a curved sword or scimitar. **7:** The spear's description is borrowed from 2 Sam 21.19. The comparison of the shaft with *a weaver's beam* is obscure. It may refer to size or to a leather thong attached to some spears to facilitate hurling. *Six hundred shekels of iron* was more than 15 pounds.

12 Now David was the son of an Ephrathite of Bethlehem in Judah, named Jesse, who had eight sons. In the days of Saul the man was already old and advanced in years.*a* ¹³The three eldest sons of Jesse had followed Saul to the battle; the names of his three sons who went to the battle were Eliab the firstborn, and next to him Abinadab, and the third Shammah. ¹⁴David was the youngest; the three eldest followed Saul, ¹⁵but David went back and forth from Saul to feed his father's sheep at Bethlehem. ¹⁶For forty days the Philistine came forward and took his stand, morning and evening.

17 Jesse said to his son David, "Take for your brothers an ephah of this parched grain and these ten loaves, and carry them quickly to the camp to your brothers; ¹⁸also take these ten cheeses to the commander of their thousand. See how your brothers fare, and bring some token from them."

19 Now Saul, and they, and all the men of Israel, were in the valley of Elah, fighting with the Philistines. ²⁰David rose early in the morning, left the sheep with a keeper, took the provisions, and went as Jesse had commanded him. He came to the encampment

as the army was going forth to the battle line, shouting the war cry. ²¹Israel and the Philistines drew up for battle, army against army. ²²David left the things in charge of the keeper of the baggage, ran to the ranks, and went and greeted his brothers. ²³As he talked with them, the champion, the Philistine of Gath, Goliath by name, came up out of the ranks of the Philistines, and spoke the same words as before. And David heard him.

24 All the Israelites, when they saw the man, fled from him and were very much afraid. ²⁵The Israelites said, "Have you seen this man who has come up? Surely he has come up to defy Israel. The king will greatly enrich the man who kills him, and will give him his daughter and make his family free in Israel." ²⁶David said to the men who stood by him, "What shall be done for the man who kills this Philistine, and takes away the reproach from Israel? For who is this uncircumcised Philistine that he should defy the armies of the living God?" ²⁷The people answered him in the same way, "So shall it be done for the man who kills him."

17.12–27. 12: The *Ephrathite*s were a subgroup within the Calebite clan,* which was part of Judah. **14–15:** Here, David is a shepherd boy running errands for his father rather than a warrior already in the army as in 16.14–23. **16:** In this supplementary version of the story, the Philistine had been challenging the Israelites *for forty days*, while in the initial version David fights him the first time he comes out. **17:** *An ephah* was about half a bushel. **18:** *Some token* refers to a personal effect that would indicate that the brothers had received the gift from their father and that they were well. **25:** *Free* meant exempt from slavery and from taxes and conscription. **26:** David's courage comes from his recognition that the LORD will help him because the Philistine has reproached the *living God*.

28 His eldest brother Eliab heard him talking to the men; and Eliab's anger was kindled against David. He said, "Why have you come down? With whom have you left those few sheep in the wilderness? I know your presumption and the evil of your heart;

a Gk Syr: Heb *among men*

for you have come down just to see the battle." ²⁹David said, "What have I done now? It was only a question." ³⁰He turned away from him toward another and spoke in the same way; and the people answered him again as before.

31 When the words that David spoke were heard, they repeated them before Saul; and he sent for him. ³²David said to Saul, "Let no one's heart fail because of him; your servant will go and fight with this Philistine." ³³Saul said to David, "You are not able to go against this Philistine to fight with him; for you are just a boy, and he has been a warrior from his youth." ³⁴But David said to Saul, "Your servant used to keep sheep for his father; and whenever a lion or a bear came, and took a lamb from the flock, ³⁵I went after it and struck it down, rescuing the lamb from its mouth; and if it turned against me, I would catch it by the jaw, strike it down, and kill it. ³⁶Your servant has killed both lions and bears; and this uncircumcised Philistine shall be like one of them, since he has defied the armies of the living God." ³⁷David said, "The LORD, who saved me from the paw of the lion and from the paw of the bear, will save me from the hand of this Philistine." So Saul said to David, "Go, and may the LORD be with you!"

38 Saul clothed David with his armor; he put a bronze helmet on his head and clothed him with a coat of mail. ³⁹David strapped Saul's sword over the armor, and he tried in vain to walk, for he was not used to them. Then David said to Saul, "I cannot walk with these; for I am not used to them." So David removed them. ⁴⁰Then he took his staff in his hand, and chose five smooth stones from the wadi, and put them in his shepherd's bag, in the pouch; his sling was in his hand, and he drew near to the Philistine.

17.28–40. 33–37: While David has experience fighting wild animals as a shepherd, he is still not the warrior described in 16.18. This tension results from the addition to the originally independent story in ch. 17. **38–39:** David's inability to move in Saul's armor emphasizes his lack of experience as a soldier. But it also shows Saul's failure to understand that David's advantage lay in his mobility. **40:** *His staff* was a shepherd's

staff, little more than a stick. The *sling* was not a shepherd's toy but a deadly weapon of war wielded by entire divisions of armies. It consisted of two cords attached to a pouch from which a stone was hurled, potentially with great accuracy (Judg 20.16).

41 The Philistine came on and drew near to David, with his shield-bearer in front of him. ⁴²When the Philistine looked and saw David, he disdained him, for he was only a youth, ruddy and handsome in appearance. ⁴³The Philistine said to David, "Am I a dog, that you come to me with sticks?" And the Philistine cursed David by his gods. ⁴⁴The Philistine said to David, "Come to me, and I will give your flesh to the birds of the air and to the wild animals of the field." ⁴⁵But David said to the Philistine, "You come to me with sword and spear and javelin; but I come to you in the name of the LORD of hosts, the God of the armies of Israel, whom you have defied. ⁴⁶This very day the LORD will deliver you into my hand, and I will strike you down and cut off your head; and I will give the dead bodies of the Philistine army this very day to the birds of the air and to the wild animals of the earth, so that all the earth may know that there is a God in Israel, ⁴⁷and that all this assembly may know that the LORD does not save by sword and spear; for the battle is the LORD's and he will give you into our hand."

17.41–47: An element of ancient warfare involved taunting the opponent and boasting of one's own superiority. The Philistine is distracted by David's staff (v. 43) and overlooks his real weapon, the sling. David's reply (vv. 45–47) is religious in nature and promises retribution for the Philistine's defiance of the LORD. David does not need the Philistine's arms because the LORD fights for him.

48 When the Philistine drew nearer to meet David, David ran quickly toward the battle line to meet the Philistine. ⁴⁹David put his hand in his bag, took out a stone, slung it, and struck the Philistine on his forehead; the stone sank into his forehead, and he fell face down on the ground.

50 So David prevailed over the Philistine with a sling and a stone, striking down the

Philistine and killing him; there was no sword in David's hand. [51]Then David ran and stood over the Philistine; he grasped his sword, drew it out of its sheath, and killed him; then he cut off his head with it.

When the Philistines saw that their champion was dead, they fled. [52]The troops of Israel and Judah rose up with a shout and pursued the Philistines as far as Gath[a] and the gates of Ekron, so that the wounded Philistines fell on the way from Shaaraim as far as Gath and Ekron. [53]The Israelites came back from chasing the Philistines, and they plundered their camp. [54]David took the head of the Philistine and brought it to Jerusalem; but he put his armor in his tent.

[55] When Saul saw David go out against the Philistine, he said to Abner, the commander of the army, "Abner, whose son is this young man?" Abner said, "As your soul lives, O king, I do not know." [56]The king said, "Inquire whose son the stripling is." [57]On David's return from killing the Philistine, Abner took him and brought him before Saul, with the head of the Philistine in his hand. [58]Saul said to him, "Whose son are you, young man?" And David answered, "I am the son of your servant Jesse the Bethlehemite."

17.48–58. 49: It is not by chance that David's stone strikes the Philistine in a spot where he is vulnerable. David's speech shows that this is understood as God's doing. 50: This supplemental verse is a summary of the action. It causes some tension with v. 51, which says that David killed the Philistine with his own sword after felling him with the sling and then beheaded him. 54: This verse contains an anachronism,* since *Jerusalem* was not conquered until David became king of Israel (2 Sam 5). *His tent:* Goliath's sword later surfaces among the priests at Nob (21.9), suggesting that this phrase should be read as "the tent (shrine) of Yahweh." 55: *Whose son is this young man?* is idiomatic. Saul is not asking who David's father is. Again, this question indicates the story's originally independent nature, since according to 16.14–23 Saul and David already had a close relationship.

18 When David[b] had finished speaking to Saul, the soul of Jonathan was bound to the soul of David, and Jonathan

loved him as his own soul. [2]Saul took him that day and would not let him return to his father's house. [3]Then Jonathan made a covenant with David, because he loved him as his own soul. [4]Jonathan stripped himself of the robe that he was wearing, and gave it to David, and his armor, and even his sword and his bow and his belt. [5]David went out and was successful wherever Saul sent him; as a result, Saul set him over the army. And all the people, even the servants of Saul, approved.

18.1–30: Saul's jealousy of David. 1–5: These verses interrupt the initial narrative,* which continues in v. 6 with the return home after David's victory. They continue the supplemental material from ch. 17. 2–3: Jonathan's love for David implies political loyalty in addition to personal affection. 4: Jonathan's act is highly symbolic. By giving his royal robe and armor to David, Jonathan, in effect, hands over the succession to the throne. 5: This verse is also supplemental. In the initial narrative David is promoted for quite a different reason (vv. 12–13).

[6] As they were coming home, when David returned from killing the Philistine, the women came out of all the towns of Israel, singing and dancing, to meet King Saul, with tambourines, with songs of joy, and with musical instruments.[c] [7]And the women sang to one another as they made merry,

"Saul has killed his thousands,
    and David his ten thousands."

[8]Saul was very angry, for this saying displeased him. He said, "They have ascribed to David ten thousands, and to me they have ascribed thousands; what more can he have but the kingdom?" [9]So Saul eyed David from that day on.

[10] The next day an evil spirit from God rushed upon Saul, and he raved within his house, while David was playing the lyre, as he did day by day. Saul had his spear in his hand; [11]and Saul threw the spear, for he thought, "I will pin David to the wall." But David eluded him twice.

[12] Saul was afraid of David, because the

a Gk Syr: Heb *Gai*   *b* Heb *he*   *c* Or *triangles, or three-stringed instruments*

LORD was with him but had departed from Saul. 13 So Saul removed him from his presence, and made him a commander of a thousand; and David marched out and came in, leading the army. 14 David had success in all his undertakings; for the LORD was with him. 15 When Saul saw that he had great success, he stood in awe of him. 16 But all Israel and Judah loved David; for it was he who marched out and came in leading them.

17 Then Saul said to David, "Here is my elder daughter Merab; I will give her to you as a wife; only be valiant for me and fight the LORD's battles." For Saul thought, "I will not raise a hand against him; let the Philistines deal with him." 18 David said to Saul, "Who am I and who are my kinsfolk, my father's family in Israel, that I should be son-in-law to the king?" 19 But at the time when Saul's daughter Merab should have been given to David, she was given to Adriel the Meholathite as a wife.

18.6–19.9: *Saul eyed David* means that Saul kept a wary eye on him. **10–11:** These verses are also supplemental. In the initial story, Saul's attempt to kill David with his spear (19.8–10) provides the climax* to a series of subtle moves against David. *He raved* is the same word translated "prophesy" elsewhere. It refers to ecstatic (irrational) behavior. **13–14:** Saul promotes David because he is afraid to have David near him. He also hopes that David will be killed in battle. *Marched out and came in* is an idiom for "went to war." **16:** *All Israel and Judah loved David* again expresses political loyalty, thus giving Saul all the more reason to fear. **17–19:** These verses are supplemental as they are not included in the original Greek or Septuagint* version (LXX*). If these verses are related to 17.25, Saul has changed the conditions of his promise. David's response in v. 18 shows his humility and lack of ambition to be king. The *son-in-law to the king* was an important political position, since he was potentially an heir to the throne. In the end (v. 19), Saul goes back on his promise despite David's heroic deeds.

20 Now Saul's daughter Michal loved David. Saul was told, and the thing pleased him. 21 Saul thought, "Let me give her to him that she may be a snare for him and that the hand of the Philistines may be against him."

Therefore Saul said to David a second time,[a] "You shall now be my son-in-law." 22 Saul commanded his servants, "Speak to David in private and say, 'See, the king is delighted with you, and all his servants love you; now then, become the king's son-in-law.'" 23 So Saul's servants reported these words to David in private. And David said, "Does it seem to you a little thing to become the king's son-in-law, seeing that I am a poor man and of no repute?" 24 The servants of Saul told him, "This is what David said." 25 Then Saul said, "Thus shall you say to David, 'The king desires no marriage present except a hundred foreskins of the Philistines, that he may be avenged on the king's enemies.'" Now Saul planned to make David fall by the hand of the Philistines. 26 When his servants told David these words, David was well pleased to be the king's son-in-law. Before the time had expired, 27 David rose and went, along with his men, and killed one hundred[b] of the Philistines; and David brought their foreskins, which were given in full number to the king, that he might become the king's son-in-law. Saul gave him his daughter Michal as a wife. 28 But when Saul realized that the LORD was with David, and that Saul's daughter Michal loved him, 29 Saul was still more afraid of David. So Saul was David's enemy from that time forward.

30 Then the commanders of the Philistines came out to battle; and as often as they came out, David had more success than all the servants of Saul, so that his fame became very great.

18.20–30. 20: *Michal* was Saul's younger daughter. **21:** This plan of Saul's is slightly more direct than his hope that David's promotion over the army would lead to his death. **23–25:** The *marriage present* or "bride price" was set by the bride's father and paid to him by the groom. **26:** *David was well pleased to be the king's son-in-law*, despite his claim to lack of ambition. **28:** *Michal loved him:* Even Saul's own daughter was loyal to David, as she would shortly demonstrate.

a Heb *by two*   b Gk Compare 2 Sam 3.14: Heb *two hundred*

19 Saul spoke with his son Jonathan and with all his servants about killing David. But Saul's son Jonathan took great delight in David. [2]Jonathan told David, "My father Saul is trying to kill you; therefore be on guard tomorrow morning; stay in a secret place and hide yourself. [3]I will go out and stand beside my father in the field where you are, and I will speak to my father about you; if I learn anything I will tell you." [4]Jonathan spoke well of David to his father Saul, saying to him, "The king should not sin against his servant David, because he has not sinned against you, and because his deeds have been of good service to you; [5]for he took his life in his hand when he attacked the Philistine, and the LORD brought about a great victory for all Israel. You saw it, and rejoiced; why then will you sin against an innocent person by killing David without cause?" [6]Saul heeded the voice of Jonathan; Saul swore, "As the LORD lives, he shall not be put to death." [7]So Jonathan called David and related all these things to him. Jonathan then brought David to Saul, and he was in his presence as before.

8 Again there was war, and David went out to fight the Philistines. He launched a heavy attack on them, so that they fled before him. [9]Then an evil spirit from the LORD came upon Saul, as he sat in his house with his spear in his hand, while David was playing music. [10]Saul sought to pin David to the wall with the spear; but he eluded Saul, so that he struck the spear into the wall. David fled and escaped that night.

11 Saul sent messengers to David's house to keep watch over him, planning to kill him in the morning. David's wife Michal told him, "If you do not save your life tonight, tomorrow you will be killed." [12]So Michal let David down through the window; he fled away and escaped. [13]Michal took an idol[a] and laid it on the bed; she put a net[b] of goats' hair on its head, and covered it with the clothes. [14]When Saul sent messengers to take David, she said, "He is sick." [15]Then Saul sent the messengers to see David for themselves. He said, "Bring him up to me in the bed, that I may kill him." [16]When the messengers came in, the idol[c] was in the bed, with the covering[b] of goats' hair on its head. [17]Saul said to Michal, "Why have you deceived me like this, and let my enemy go, so that he has escaped?" Michal answered Saul, "He said to me, 'Let me go; why should I kill you?'"

18 Now David fled and escaped; he came to Samuel at Ramah, and told him all that Saul had done to him. He and Samuel went and settled at Naioth. [19]Saul was told, "David is at Naioth in Ramah." [20]Then Saul sent messengers to take David. When they saw the company of the prophets in a frenzy, with Samuel standing in charge of[b] them, the spirit of God came upon the messengers of Saul, and they also fell into a prophetic frenzy. [21]When Saul was told, he sent other messengers, and they also fell into a frenzy. Saul sent messengers again the third time, and they also fell into a frenzy. [22]Then he himself went to Ramah. He came to the great well that is in Secu;[d] he asked, "Where are Samuel and David?" And someone said, "They are at Naioth in Ramah." [23]He went there, toward Naioth in Ramah; and the spirit of God came upon him. As he was going, he fell into a prophetic frenzy, until he came to Naioth in Ramah. [24]He too stripped off his clothes, and he too fell into a frenzy before Samuel. He lay naked all that day and all that night. Therefore it is said, "Is Saul also among the prophets?"

19.1–24: More attempts on David's life. 5: Killing an innocent person was a serious crime that could taint an entire nation and bring the wrath of God. **11–17:** This was originally the continuation of the story of David's marriage in 18.20–29 and took place on the couple's wedding night. **12:** The house was evidently built into the city wall, so that David went *through the window* and escaped the city. **13:** *An idol:* The Hebrew word, "teraphim," refers to household gods like those that Rachel took from her father (Gen 31.33–35). The one used by Michal must have been close to life-size. **17:** Michal lies to protect herself. A threat from David could not explain her ruse with the bed after his de-

a Heb *took the teraphim*   b Meaning of Heb uncertain
c Heb *the teraphim*   d Gk reads *to the well of the threshing floor on the bare height*

parture. **18:** *Ramah*, Samuel's hometown, was about two miles north of Gibeah, while David's home, Bethlehem and Judah, lay to the south. David would hardly have fled north. The story is included here for literary and theological reasons. *Naioth* may be not a proper name but a word meaning "camps" or "huts" where the prophets* lived near their leader Samuel. **23–24:** The saying *Is Saul also among the prophets?* has a different explanation here from the one offered in 10.10–12. The perspective on Saul in this latter case is negative. The depiction of him lying *naked* is degrading. The fact that the LORD's spirit comes upon him to prevent him from arresting David clearly shows that God is on David's side against Saul.

20 David fled from Naioth in Ramah. He came before Jonathan and said, "What have I done? What is my guilt? And what is my sin against your father that he is trying to take my life?" ²He said to him, "Far from it! You shall not die. My father does nothing either great or small without disclosing it to me; and why should my father hide this from me? Never!" ³But David also swore, "Your father knows well that you like me; and he thinks, 'Do not let Jonathan know this, or he will be grieved.' But truly, as the LORD lives and as you yourself live, there is but a step between me and death." ⁴Then Jonathan said to David, "Whatever you say, I will do for you." ⁵David said to Jonathan, "Tomorrow is the new moon, and I should not fail to sit with the king at the meal; but let me go, so that I may hide in the field until the third evening. ⁶If your father misses me at all, then say, 'David earnestly asked leave of me to run to Bethlehem his city; for there is a yearly sacrifice there for all the family.' ⁷If he says, 'Good!' it will be well with your servant; but if he is angry, then know that evil has been determined by him. ⁸Therefore deal kindly with your servant, for you have brought your servant into a sacred covenant*ᵃ* with you. But if there is guilt in me, kill me yourself; why should you bring me to your father?" ⁹Jonathan said, "Far be it from you! If I knew that it was decided by my father that evil should come upon you, would I not tell you?" ¹⁰Then David said to Jonathan, "Who will tell me if your father answers you harshly?" ¹¹Jona-

than replied to David, "Come, let us go out into the field." So they both went out into the field.

12 Jonathan said to David, "By the LORD, the God of Israel! When I have sounded out my father, about this time tomorrow, or on the third day, if he is well disposed toward David, shall I not then send and disclose it to you? ¹³But if my father intends to do you harm, the LORD do so to Jonathan, and more also, if I do not disclose it to you, and send you away, so that you may go in safety. May the LORD be with you, as he has been with my father. ¹⁴If I am still alive, show me the faithful love of the LORD; but if I die,*ᵇ* ¹⁵never cut off your faithful love from my house, even if the LORD were to cut off every one of the enemies of David from the face of the earth." ¹⁶Thus Jonathan made a covenant with the house of David, saying, "May the LORD seek out the enemies of David." ¹⁷Jonathan made David swear again by his love for him; for he loved him as he loved his own life.

20.1–42: The covenant* of David and Jonathan. 2: Jonathan is unaware that Saul has tried to kill David and still believes that his father would not act without first consulting him. **5:** The *new moon** in ancient Israel was a day of sacrificing and feasting. **8:** Jonathan asks David to *deal kindly* or "loyally" with him. The term implies faithfulness to a treaty, and Jonathan goes on to mention the covenant between them. **13:** *The LORD do so to Jonathan, and more also:* Jonathan swears that he will warn David. Jonathan's wish that the LORD be with David as he was with Saul suggests that David will be king. **14–15:** *Faithful love* also means "loyalty." *My house* means Jonathan's descendants. David's oath of loyalty to Jonathan's house anticipates the account of his treatment of Jonathan's son in 2 Sam 9. **16:** *The enemies of David* include Saul. **17:** *Love* again expresses political loyalty.

18 Jonathan said to him, "Tomorrow is the new moon; you will be missed, because your place will be empty. ¹⁹On the day after tomorrow, you shall go a long way down; go

a Heb *a covenant of the LORD*   *b* Meaning of Heb uncertain

to the place where you hid yourself earlier, and remain beside the stone there.ª ²⁰I will shoot three arrows to the side of it, as though I shot at a mark. ²¹Then I will send the boy, saying, 'Go, find the arrows.' If I say to the boy, 'Look, the arrows are on this side of you, collect them,' then you are to come, for, as the LORD lives, it is safe for you and there is no danger. ²²But if I say to the young man, 'Look, the arrows are beyond you,' then go; for the LORD has sent you away. ²³As for the matter about which you and I have spoken, the LORD is witnessᵇ between you and me forever."

24 So David hid himself in the field. When the new moon came, the king sat at the feast to eat. ²⁵The king sat upon his seat, as at other times, upon the seat by the wall. Jonathan stood, while Abner sat by Saul's side; but David's place was empty.

26 Saul did not say anything that day; for he thought, "Something has befallen him; he is not clean, surely he is not clean." ²⁷But on the second day, the day after the new moon, David's place was empty. And Saul said to his son Jonathan, "Why has the son of Jesse not come to the feast, either yesterday or today?" ²⁸Jonathan answered Saul, "David earnestly asked leave of me to go to Bethlehem; ²⁹he said, 'Let me go; for our family is holding a sacrifice in the city, and my brother has commanded me to be there. So now, if I have found favor in your sight, let me get away, and see my brothers.' For this reason he has not come to the king's table."

30 Then Saul's anger was kindled against Jonathan. He said to him, "You son of a perverse, rebellious woman! Do I not know that you have chosen the son of Jesse to your own shame, and to the shame of your mother's nakedness? ³¹For as long as the son of Jesse lives upon the earth, neither you nor your kingdom shall be established. Now send and bring him to me, for he shall surely die." ³²Then Jonathan answered his father Saul, "Why should he be put to death? What has he done?" ³³But Saul threw his spear at him to strike him; so Jonathan knew that it was the decision of his father to put David to death. ³⁴Jonathan rose from the table in

fierce anger and ate no food on the second day of the month, for he was grieved for David, and because his father had disgraced him.

35 In the morning Jonathan went out into the field to the appointment with David, and with him was a little boy. ³⁶He said to the boy, "Run and find the arrows that I shoot." As the boy ran, he shot an arrow beyond him. ³⁷When the boy came to the place where Jonathan's arrow had fallen, Jonathan called after the boy and said, "Is the arrow not beyond you?" ³⁸Jonathan called after the boy, "Hurry, be quick, do not linger." So Jonathan's boy gathered up the arrows and came to his master. ³⁹But the boy knew nothing; only Jonathan and David knew the arrangement. ⁴⁰Jonathan gave his weapons to the boy and said to him, "Go and carry them to the city." ⁴¹As soon as the boy had gone, David rose from beside the stone heapᶜ and prostrated himself with his face to the ground. He bowed three times, and they kissed each other, and wept with each other; David wept the more.ᵈ ⁴²Then Jonathan said to David, "Go in peace, since both of us have sworn in the name of the LORD, saying, 'The LORD shall be between me and you, and between my descendants and your descendants, forever.' " He got up and left; and Jonathan went into the city.ᵉ

20.18–42. 30: *Nakedness* is a euphemism* for the genitals. Saul's remark is coarse and insulting. He accuses Jonathan of treason and says that he is a shame to his mother's genitals. 31: Saul perceives that David will be king if he is not killed. 33: Saul tries to kill Jonathan with his spear just as he tried to kill David. 41–42a: This is an addition emphasizing the affection and loyalty between David and Jonathan. If the two had been able to meet openly like this, the sign in the previous verses would be unnecessary.

21 ᶠDavid came to Nob to the priest Ahimelech. Ahimelech came trembling to meet David, and said to him, "Why are you alone, and no one with you?" ²David

a Meaning of Heb uncertain *b* Gk: Heb lacks *witness* *c* Gk: Heb *from beside the south* *d* Vg: Meaning of Heb uncertain *e* This sentence is 21.1 in Heb *f* Ch 21.2 in Heb

said to the priest Ahimelech, "The king has charged me with a matter, and said to me, 'No one must know anything of the matter about which I send you, and with which I have charged you.' I have made an appointment*a* with the young men for such and such a place. ³Now then, what have you at hand? Give me five loaves of bread, or whatever is here." ⁴The priest answered David, "I have no ordinary bread at hand, only holy bread—provided that the young men have kept themselves from women." ⁵David answered the priest, "Indeed women have been kept from us as always when I go on an expedition; the vessels of the young men are holy even when it is a common journey; how much more today will their vessels be holy?" ⁶So the priest gave him the holy bread; for there was no bread there except the bread of the Presence, which is removed from before the LORD, to be replaced by hot bread on the day it is taken away.

7 Now a certain man of the servants of Saul was there that day, detained before the LORD; his name was Doeg the Edomite, the chief of Saul's shepherds.

8 David said to Ahimelech, "Is there no spear or sword here with you? I did not bring my sword or my weapons with me, because the king's business required haste." ⁹The priest said, "The sword of Goliath the Philistine, whom you killed in the valley of Elah, is here wrapped in a cloth behind the ephod; if you will take that, take it, for there is none here except that one." David said, "There is none like it; give it to me."

10 David rose and fled that day from Saul; he went to King Achish of Gath. ¹¹The servants of Achish said to him, "Is this not David the king of the land? Did they not sing to one another of him in dances,

'Saul has killed his thousands,
    and David his ten thousands'?"

¹²David took these words to heart and was very much afraid of King Achish of Gath. ¹³So he changed his behavior before them; he pretended to be mad when in their presence.*b* He scratched marks on the doors of the gate, and let his spittle run down his beard. ¹⁴Achish said to his servants, "Look, you see the man is mad; why then have you

brought him to me? ¹⁵Do I lack madmen, that you have brought this fellow to play the madman in my presence? Shall this fellow come into my house?"

21.1–15: David visits Nob. 1: *Ahimelech* was the brother of Ahijah, Saul's chaplain, and the great-grandson of Eli. He *came trembling to meet David* perhaps because David was alone, and Ahimelech suspected something was wrong. **4–5:** Sexual abstinence, as expressed in the phrase *have kept themselves from women*, was practiced by soldiers preparing for war and by worshippers. David affirms that he and his men are on a holy mission and so have been abstinent. Although *vessels* can refer to tools, weapons, or other implements, here it is a euphemism* for the sexual organs. **7:** The fact that *Doeg* was *detained before the LORD* probably means that he had a vow to fulfill. *Shepherds* may be a mistake for "runners"; the words are very similar in Hebrew. Kings were often escorted by runners. **9:** David had placed *the sword of Goliath* in his own tent according to 17.54, but see the comment on that verse. The *ephod** mentioned here seems to be an idol (Judg 8.27) rather than a priestly garment. **10:** *Achish,* like Goliath, is a genuine Philistine name. **11:** If it is not a simple anachronism,* the Philistines recognize David already as *the king of the land.* **13–15:** *To be mad* was seen in the ancient world as being divinely "touched." Hence, the Philistines, fearing divine wrath, leave David alone. The story also jabs fun at the Philistines who cannot tell madness from sanity and who, by their own admission, have plenty of *madmen.*

---

22 David left there and escaped to the cave of Adullam; when his brothers and all his father's house heard of it, they went down there to him. ²Everyone who was in distress, and everyone who was in debt, and everyone who was discontented gathered to him; and he became captain over them. Those who were with him numbered about four hundred.

3 David went from there to Mizpeh of Moab. He said to the king of Moab, "Please let my father and mother come*c* to you, until I know what God will do for me." ⁴He left them with the king of Moab, and they stayed

a Q Ms Vg Compare Gk: Meaning of MT uncertain
b Heb *in their hands*   *c* Syr Vg: Heb *come out*

with him all the time that David was in the stronghold. 5 Then the prophet Gad said to David, "Do not remain in the stronghold; leave, and go into the land of Judah." So David left, and went into the forest of Hereth.

22.1–23: David gains a following. 1–5: The account of David's travels related here delays the continuation of the story of the priests of Nob, but it also shows David building an army. *Adullam* was in Judah and served as David's headquarters. The *cave* may be an error for *stronghold;* the two words are similar in Hebrew. This suggests that the otherwise unknown stronghold in v. 4 is also Adullam. **2:** David's army consists of those who are unhappy with Saul. Many of these people may have fled earlier to the wilderness of Judah to escape Saul's reach. **3–4:** The connection of David's family with Moab is attested by Ruth 4.17–22. **5:** The image of a king sitting in council under a sacred tree was a common one in the ancient Near East.

6 Saul heard that David and those who were with him had been located. Saul was sitting at Gibeah, under the tamarisk tree on the height, with his spear in his hand, and all his servants were standing around him. 7 Saul said to his servants who stood around him, "Hear now, you Benjaminites; will the son of Jesse give every one of you fields and vineyards, will he make you all commanders of thousands and commanders of hundreds? 8 Is that why all of you have conspired against me? No one discloses to me when my son makes a league with the son of Jesse, none of you is sorry for me or discloses to me that my son has stirred up my servant against me, to lie in wait, as he is doing today." 9 Doeg the Edomite, who was in charge of Saul's servants, answered, "I saw the son of Jesse coming to Nob, to Ahimelech son of Ahitub; 10 he inquired of the LORD for him, gave him provisions, and gave him the sword of Goliath the Philistine."

22.6–10. 7: *The son of Jesse* is a disparaging reference to David. It was common for the king to reward his loyal servants. David may have been making promises of rewards to his followers. But Saul is saying that because they are not from Judah, David's tribe, the Benjaminites can expect no such rewards if David becomes king. **10:** Chapter 21 does not mention that

Ahimelech *inquired of the* LORD *for [David],* but this plays an important role in the confrontation to follow.

11 The king sent for the priest Ahimelech son of Ahitub and for all his father's house, the priests who were at Nob; and all of them came to the king. 12 Saul said, "Listen now, son of Ahitub." He answered, "Here I am, my lord." 13 Saul said to him, "Why have you conspired against me, you and the son of Jesse, by giving him bread and a sword, and by inquiring of God for him, so that he has risen against me, to lie in wait, as he is doing today?"

14 Then Ahimelech answered the king, "Who among all your servants is so faithful as David? He is the king's son-in-law, and is quick*a* to do your bidding, and is honored in your house. 15 Is today the first time that I have inquired of God for him? By no means! Do not let the king impute anything to his servant or to any member of my father's house; for your servant has known nothing of all this, much or little." 16 The king said, "You shall surely die, Ahimelech, you and all your father's house." 17 The king said to the guard who stood around him, "Turn and kill the priests of the LORD, because their hand also is with David; they knew that he fled, and did not disclose it to me." But the servants of the king would not raise their hand to attack the priests of the LORD. 18 Then the king said to Doeg, "You, Doeg, turn and attack the priests." Doeg the Edomite turned and attacked the priests; on that day he killed eighty-five who wore the linen ephod. 19 Nob, the city of the priests, he put to the sword; men and women, children and infants, oxen, donkeys, and sheep, he put to the sword.

20 But one of the sons of Ahimelech son of Ahitub, named Abiathar, escaped and fled after David. 21 Abiathar told David that Saul had killed the priests of the LORD. 22 David said to Abiathar, "I knew on that day, when Doeg the Edomite was there, that he would surely tell Saul. I am responsible*b* for the

---

a Heb *and turns aside*　*b* Gk Vg: Meaning of Heb uncertain

lives of all your father's house. 23Stay with me, and do not be afraid; for the one who seeks my life seeks your life; you will be safe with me."

22.11–23. 13: Saul accuses Ahimelech of treason. 14–15: Ahimelech's eloquent defense makes the point that David is Saul's most loyal servant and son-in-law and that he (Ahimelech) was unaware of any change in their relationship. 16–17: These reminders only infuriate Saul more, and he orders the death of the priests. 18: Only Doeg, who is an Edomite, dares to attack the LORD's priests. 19: Saul devotes Nob to destruction. Ironically,* this is what he failed to do against the Amalekites in ch. 15. 20–23: The one escapee is Abiathar in fulfillment of the oracle* against the house of Eli in 2.27–36. He will prove a useful asset to David.

23 Now they told David, "The Philistines are fighting against Keilah, and are robbing the threshing floors." 2David inquired of the LORD, "Shall I go and attack these Philistines?" The LORD said to David, "Go and attack the Philistines and save Keilah." 3But David's men said to him, "Look, we are afraid here in Judah; how much more then if we go to Keilah against the armies of the Philistines?" 4Then David inquired of the LORD again. The LORD answered him, "Yes, go down to Keilah; for I will give the Philistines into your hand." 5So David and his men went to Keilah, fought with the Philistines, brought away their livestock, and dealt them a heavy defeat. Thus David rescued the inhabitants of Keilah.

6 When Abiathar son of Ahimelech fled to David at Keilah, he came down with an ephod in his hand. 7Now it was told Saul that David had come to Keilah. And Saul said, "God has given[a] him into my hand; for he has shut himself in by entering a town that has gates and bars." 8Saul summoned all the people to war, to go down to Keilah, to besiege David and his men. 9When David learned that Saul was plotting evil against him, he said to the priest Abiathar, "Bring the ephod here." 10David said, "O LORD, the God of Israel, your servant has heard that Saul seeks to come to Keilah, to destroy the city on my account. 11And now, will[b] Saul

come down as your servant has heard? O LORD, the God of Israel, I beseech you, tell your servant." The LORD said, "He will come down." 12Then David said, "Will the men of Keilah surrender me and my men into the hand of Saul?" The LORD said, "They will surrender you." 13Then David and his men, who were about six hundred, set out and left Keilah; they wandered wherever they could go. When Saul was told that David had escaped from Keilah, he gave up the expedition. 14David remained in the strongholds in the wilderness, in the hill country of the Wilderness of Ziph. Saul sought him every day, but the LORD[c] did not give him into his hand.

23.1–29: Narrow escapes. 1–6: This episode illustrates the importance of Abiathar's ability to divine through the ephod* as explained in v. 6. Keilah was an independent city within Philistine territory. Both times when David inquired his questions required an answer of yes or no, which could be determined through casting lots. Abiathar's ephod (v. 6) was just such an instrument. 7–14: Although David was hoping to cultivate the loyalty of the people of Keilah, they were willing to betray him to Saul. The ephod forewarned him and allowed him to escape Saul.

15 David was in the Wilderness of Ziph at Horesh when he learned that[d] Saul had come out to seek his life. 16Saul's son Jonathan set out and came to David at Horesh; there he strengthened his hand through the LORD.[e] 17He said to him, "Do not be afraid; for the hand of my father Saul shall not find you; you shall be king over Israel, and I shall be second to you; my father Saul also knows that this is so." 18Then the two of them made a covenant before the LORD; David remained at Horesh, and Jonathan went home.

19 Then some Ziphites went up to Saul at Gibeah and said, "David is hiding among us in the strongholds of Horesh, on the hill of Hachilah, which is south of Jeshimon. 20Now, O king, whenever you wish to come

a Gk Tg: Heb made a stranger of   b Q Ms Compare Gk: MT Will the men of Keilah surrender me into his hand? Will   c Q Ms Gk: MT God   d Or saw that   e Compare Q Ms Gk: MT God

down, do so; and our part will be to surrender him into the king's hand." 21 Saul said, "May you be blessed by the LORD for showing me compassion! 22 Go and make sure once more; find out exactly where he is, and who has seen him there; for I am told that he is very cunning. 23 Look around and learn all the hiding places where he lurks, and come back to me with sure information. Then I will go with you; and if he is in the land, I will search him out among all the thousands of Judah." 24 So they set out and went to Ziph ahead of Saul.

David and his men were in the wilderness of Maon, in the Arabah to the south of Jeshimon. 25 Saul and his men went to search for him. When David was told, he went down to the rock and stayed in the wilderness of Maon. When Saul heard that, he pursued David into the wilderness of Maon. 26 Saul went on one side of the mountain, and David and his men on the other side of the mountain. David was hurrying to get away from Saul, while Saul and his men were closing in on David and his men to capture them. 27 Then a messenger came to Saul, saying, "Hurry and come; for the Philistines have made a raid on the land." 28 So Saul stopped pursuing David, and went against the Philistines; therefore that place was called the Rock of Escape.[a] 29[b] David then went up from there, and lived in the strongholds of En-gedi.

23.15–29. 17: The recognition that David will be king and Jonathan the second in command is extraordinary in the mouth of Jonathan himself, the crown prince. **19–29:** Saul is frustrated that David stays one jump ahead of him, which he is able to do because of the ephod (v. 22). This time (v. 26) David is trapped on one side of a hill which Saul's force is circling from both directions. The last-minute notice about the Philistines (v. 27) shows Yahweh's protection of David. Either meaning for the etiology* in v. 28 ("rock of escape" or "rock of division") is appropriate in the context of this story.

24 When Saul returned from following the Philistines, he was told, "David is in the wilderness of En-gedi." 2 Then Saul took three thousand chosen men out of all

Israel, and went to look for David and his men in the direction of the Rocks of the Wild Goats. 3 He came to the sheepfolds beside the road, where there was a cave; and Saul went in to relieve himself.[c] Now David and his men were sitting in the innermost parts of the cave. 4 The men of David said to him, "Here is the day of which the LORD said to you, 'I will give your enemy into your hand, and you shall do to him as it seems good to you.'" Then David went and stealthily cut off a corner of Saul's cloak. 5 Afterward David was stricken to the heart because he had cut off a corner of Saul's cloak. 6 He said to his men, "The LORD forbid that I should do this thing to my lord, the LORD's anointed, to raise my hand against him; for he is the LORD's anointed." 7 So David scolded his men severely and did not permit them to attack Saul. Then Saul got up and left the cave, and went on his way.

24.1–22: David spares Saul. 3: *To relieve himself* (literally, "to cover his feet") is a euphemism* for defecation. The portrait of Saul at this point is particularly degrading. **4a:** The prophecy to which David's men refer here is not recorded. **4b–5:** These verses probably originally were located after v. 7a. David's cutting off Saul's hem may be seen as symbolic emasculation or a symbol of his taking Saul's kingdom. This may be why David's conscience bothered him. **6:** To attack Saul, the LORD's anointed,* was to attack the LORD. **7a:** David scolds his men for their suggestion in v. 4a that he kill Saul.

8 Afterwards David also rose up and went out of the cave and called after Saul, "My lord the king!" When Saul looked behind him, David bowed with his face to the ground, and did obeisance. 9 David said to Saul, "Why do you listen to the words of those who say, 'David seeks to do you harm'? 10 This very day your eyes have seen how the LORD gave you into my hand in the cave; and some urged me to kill you, but I spared[d] you. I said, 'I will not raise my hand against my lord; for he is the LORD's anointed.' 11 See,

a Or *Rock of Division*; Meaning of Heb uncertain
b Ch 24.1 in Heb   c Heb *to cover his feet*   d Gk Syr
Tg Vg: Heb *it* (my eye) *spared*

my father, see the corner of your cloak in my hand; for by the fact that I cut off the corner of your cloak, and did not kill you, you may know for certain that there is no wrong or treason in my hands. I have not sinned against you, though you are hunting me to take my life. 12May the LORD judge between me and you! May the LORD avenge me on you; but my hand shall not be against you. 13As the ancient proverb says, 'Out of the wicked comes forth wickedness'; but my hand shall not be against you. 14Against whom has the king of Israel come out? Whom do you pursue? A dead dog? A single flea? 15May the LORD therefore be judge, and give sentence between me and you. May he see to it, and plead my cause, and vindicate me against you."

16 When David had finished speaking these words to Saul, Saul said, "Is this your voice, my son David?" Saul lifted up his voice and wept. 17He said to David, "You are more righteous than I; for you have repaid me good, whereas I have repaid you evil. 18Today you have explained how you have dealt well with me, in that you did not kill me when the LORD put me into your hands. 19For who has ever found an enemy, and sent the enemy safely away? So may the LORD reward you with good for what you have done to me this day. 20Now I know that you shall surely be king, and that the kingdom of Israel shall be established in your hand. 21Swear to me therefore by the LORD that you will not cut off my descendants after me, and that you will not wipe out my name from my father's house." 22So David swore this to Saul. Then Saul went home; but David and his men went up to the stronghold.

24.8–22. 11: *My father* is a respectful address from the younger David to the older Saul; it may also imply David's right to inherit Saul's kingdom. 14: *A dead dog? A single flea?* These terms of self-disparagement may be read in two ways. David could be saying he is insignificant or that Saul is mistaken if he thinks David is insignificant. 20: Even Saul recognizes that David will succeed him. 21–22: David's oath not to wipe out Saul's descendants anticipates his treatment of Jonathan's son, Mephibosheth, in 2 Sam 9.

25 Now Samuel died; and all Israel assembled and mourned for him. They buried him at his home in Ramah.

Then David got up and went down to the wilderness of Paran.

2 There was a man in Maon, whose property was in Carmel. The man was very rich; he had three thousand sheep and a thousand goats. He was shearing his sheep in Carmel. 3Now the name of the man was Nabal, and the name of his wife Abigail. The woman was clever and beautiful, but the man was surly and mean; he was a Calebite. 4David heard in the wilderness that Nabal was shearing his sheep. 5So David sent ten young men; and David said to the young men, "Go up to Carmel, and go to Nabal, and greet him in my name. 6Thus you shall salute him: 'Peace be to you, and peace be to your house, and peace be to all that you have. 7I hear that you have shearers; now your shepherds have been with us, and we did them no harm, and they missed nothing, all the time they were in Carmel. 8Ask your young men, and they will tell you. Therefore let my young men find favor in your sight; for we have come on a feast day. Please give whatever you have at hand to your servants and to your son David.' "

9 When David's young men came, they said all this to Nabal in the name of David; and then they waited. 10But Nabal answered David's servants, "Who is David? Who is the son of Jesse? There are many servants today who are breaking away from their masters. 11Shall I take my bread and my water and the meat that I have butchered for my shearers, and give it to men who come from I do not know where?" 12So David's young men turned away, and came back and told him all this. 13David said to his men, "Every man strap on his sword!" And every one of them strapped on his sword; David also strapped on his sword; and about four hundred men went up after David, while two hundred remained with the baggage.

14 But one of the young men told Abigail, Nabal's wife, "David sent messengers out of the wilderness to salute our master; and he shouted insults at them. 15Yet the men were very good to us, and we suffered no harm,

and we never missed anything when we were in the fields, as long as we were with them; [16]they were a wall to us both by night and by day, all the while we were with them keeping the sheep. [17]Now therefore know this and consider what you should do; for evil has been decided against our master and against all his house; he is so ill-natured that no one can speak to him."

18 Then Abigail hurried and took two hundred loaves, two skins of wine, five sheep ready dressed, five measures of parched grain, one hundred clusters of raisins, and two hundred cakes of figs. She loaded them on donkeys [19]and said to her young men, "Go on ahead of me; I am coming after you." But she did not tell her husband Nabal. [20]As she rode on the donkey and came down under cover of the mountain, David and his men came down toward her; and she met them. [21]Now David had said, "Surely it was in vain that I protected all that this fellow has in the wilderness, so that nothing was missed of all that belonged to him; but he has returned me evil for good. [22]God do so to David[a] and more also, if by morning I leave so much as one male of all who belong to him."

25.1–43: Nabal and Abigail. The placement of this story between the two accounts of David's chances to kill Saul (chs. 24 and 26) is significant. While David avoids shedding Saul's blood, he is almost guilty of killing many innocent people in Nabal's household. **2–3:** *Nabal* is like Saul in many ways. He is "rich as a king" and was probably an important figure, perhaps the chieftain, among the *Calebite*s, one of the leading clans* of Judah. The name Nabal means "fool" or "brute." It was probably not the man's real name but represents his character. His wife, *Abigail*, on the other hand, is his complete opposite. The only other Abigail in the Bible is David's sister (1 Chr 2.16). **4–8:** *Shearing sheep* was a festival time in Israel. David requests a gift, hoping that Nabal, in the spirit of the festival, will be generous. The gift David expects is more or less obligatory as payment for not harming or "protecting" Nabal's shepherds. The *ten young men* whom David sends should give Nabal an idea of the size of gift David is expecting, namely, as much as ten men can carry. **10–11:** Nabal's reply is insulting. His questions, *Who is David? Who is the son of Jesse?*, are a way of

saying that David is insignificant and do not mean that Nabal does not know who David is. Nabal calls David, in effect, a runaway slave and a vagabond. **14–17:** Nabal's own servants recognize that he is *ill-natured* and untrustworthy. In this emergency they go to Abigail. **18:** *Five measures:* The Hebrew word is "se'ah." Five se'ahs was about a bushel. *Cakes of figs* were clumps rather than a bakery product. **22:** David vows to annihilate every *male* in Nabal's household. This sets the stage for the arrival of Abigail, who, as a female, is the only person who can prevent a tragedy.

---

23 When Abigail saw David, she hurried and alighted from the donkey, and fell before David on her face, bowing to the ground. [24]She fell at his feet and said, "Upon me alone, my lord, be the guilt; please let your servant speak in your ears, and hear the words of your servant. [25]My lord, do not take seriously this ill-natured fellow, Nabal; for as his name is, so is he; Nabal[b] is his name, and folly is with him; but I, your servant, did not see the young men of my lord, whom you sent.

26 "Now then, my lord, as the LORD lives, and as you yourself live, since the LORD has restrained you from bloodguilt and from taking vengeance with your own hand, now let your enemies and those who seek to do evil to my lord be like Nabal. [27]And now let this present that your servant has brought to my lord be given to the young men who follow my lord. [28]Please forgive the trespass of your servant; for the LORD will certainly make my lord a sure house, because my lord is fighting the battles of the LORD; and evil shall not be found in you so long as you live. [29]If anyone should rise up to pursue you and to seek your life, the life of my lord shall be bound in the bundle of the living under the care of the LORD your God; but the lives of your enemies he shall sling out as from the hollow of a sling. [30]When the LORD has done to my lord according to all the good that he has spoken concerning you, and has appointed you prince over Israel, [31]my lord shall have no cause of grief, or pangs of conscience, for having shed blood without cause or for hav-

---

a Gk Compare Syr: Heb *the enemies of David*
b That is *Fool*

ing saved himself. And when the LORD has dealt well with my lord, then remember your servant."

32 David said to Abigail, "Blessed be the LORD, the God of Israel, who sent you to meet me today! 33 Blessed be your good sense, and blessed be you, who have kept me today from bloodguilt and from avenging myself by my own hand! 34 For as surely as the LORD the God of Israel lives, who has restrained me from hurting you, unless you had hurried and come to meet me, truly by morning there would not have been left to Nabal so much as one male." 35 Then David received from her hand what she had brought him; he said to her, "Go up to your house in peace; see, I have heeded your voice, and I have granted your petition."

36 Abigail came to Nabal; he was holding a feast in his house, like the feast of a king. Nabal's heart was merry within him, for he was very drunk; so she told him nothing at all until the morning light. 37 In the morning, when the wine had gone out of Nabal, his wife told him these things, and his heart died within him; he became like a stone. 38 About ten days later the LORD struck Nabal, and he died.

39 When David heard that Nabal was dead, he said, "Blessed be the LORD who has judged the case of Nabal's insult to me, and has kept back his servant from evil; the LORD has returned the evildoing of Nabal upon his own head." Then David sent and wooed Abigail, to make her his wife. 40 When David's servants came to Abigail at Carmel, they said to her, "David has sent us to you to take you to him as his wife." 41 She rose and bowed down, with her face to the ground, and said, "Your servant is a slave to wash the feet of the servants of my lord." 42 Abigail got up hurriedly and rode away on a donkey; her five maids attended her. She went after the messengers of David and became his wife.

43 David also married Ahinoam of Jezreel; both of them became his wives. 44 Saul had given his daughter Michal, David's wife, to Palti son of Laish, who was from Gallim.

speech is the model of eloquence and tact. She refers to herself as David's *servant* (v. 24) and begs him to ignore the *ill-natured fellow, Nabal.* Verse 26 seems to anticipate the conclusion of the story, according to which Nabal died, but not by David's hand. Abigail diplomatically refers to the supplies she brings to David as a *present* for his men (v. 27). Her reference to the LORD's giving David a *sure house* means she knows he will be king. The mention of anyone who *should rise up to pursue [David] and to seek [his] life* (v. 29) alludes to Saul. The *bundle of the living* is the list of those who live. Abigail's wish that God *sling out* David's enemies is reminiscent of David's victory in ch. 17 and anticipates Nabal's death in v. 37. Abigail closes her speech by gently suggesting that shedding innocent blood would be an obstacle to his kingship (vv. 30–31). *When the LORD has dealt well with my lord* could refer to David's becoming king or, in an ironic* way, to Nabal's death. *Remember your servant* is a marriage proposal. **34–35:** David perceives that it is the LORD, through Abigail, who has prevented him from committing a great offense. **37:** Nabal's *heart became like a stone* may refer to a coma. **43:** Saul's wife was also named *Ahinoam* (14.50).

26

Then the Ziphites came to Saul at Gibeah, saying, "David is in hiding on the hill of Hachilah, which is opposite Jeshimon."ᵃ 2 So Saul rose and went down to the Wilderness of Ziph, with three thousand chosen men of Israel, to seek David in the Wilderness of Ziph. 3 Saul encamped on the hill of Hachilah, which is opposite Jeshimonᵃ beside the road. But David remained in the wilderness. When he learned that Saul had come after him into the wilderness, 4 David sent out spies, and learned that Saul had indeed arrived. 5 Then David set out and came to the place where Saul had encamped; and David saw the place where Saul lay, with Abner son of Ner, the commander of his army. Saul was lying within the encampment, while the army was encamped around him.

6 Then David said to Ahimelech the Hittite, and to Joab's brother Abishai son of Zeruiah, "Who will go down with me into the camp to Saul?" Abishai said, "I will go down with you." 7 So David and Abishai went to the

---

25.23–43. 23: Unlike Nabal, Abigail is very respectful toward David, treating him as a king. 24–31: Abigail's

---

a Or *opposite the wasteland*

army by night; there Saul lay sleeping within the encampment, with his spear stuck in the ground at his head; and Abner and the army lay around him. 8Abishai said to David, "God has given your enemy into your hand today; now therefore let me pin him to the ground with one stroke of the spear; I will not strike him twice." 9But David said to Abishai, "Do not destroy him; for who can raise his hand against the LORD's anointed, and be guiltless?" 10David said, "As the LORD lives, the LORD will strike him down; or his day will come to die; or he will go down into battle and perish. 11The LORD forbid that I should raise my hand against the LORD's anointed; but now take the spear that is at his head, and the water jar, and let us go." 12So David took the spear that was at Saul's head and the water jar, and they went away. No one saw it, or knew it, nor did anyone awake; for they were all asleep, because a deep sleep from the LORD had fallen upon them.

26.1–25: A second opportunity to kill Saul. This story is very similar to the one in ch. 24, and the two may be variants of a single original. **6:** *Joab* was David's nephew (1 Chr 2.16) and would become the commander of his army. **8:** David can kill Saul with the same *spear* Saul once used against David. **12:** The LORD is again protecting David.

13 Then David went over to the other side, and stood on top of a hill far away, with a great distance between them. 14David called to the army and to Abner son of Ner, saying, "Abner! Will you not answer?" Then Abner replied, "Who are you that calls to the king?" 15David said to Abner, "Are you not a man? Who is like you in Israel? Why then have you not kept watch over your lord the king? For one of the people came in to destroy your lord the king. 16This thing that you have done is not good. As the LORD lives, you deserve to die, because you have not kept watch over your lord, the LORD's anointed. See now, where is the king's spear, or the water jar that was at his head?"

17 Saul recognized David's voice, and said, "Is this your voice, my son David?" David said, "It is my voice, my lord, O king." 18And he added, "Why does my lord pursue

his servant? For what have I done? What guilt is on my hands? 19Now therefore let my lord the king hear the words of his servant. If it is the LORD who has stirred you up against me, may he accept an offering; but if it is mortals, may they be cursed before the LORD, for they have driven me out today from my share in the heritage of the LORD, saying, 'Go, serve other gods.' 20Now therefore, do not let my blood fall to the ground, away from the presence of the LORD; for the king of Israel has come out to seek a single flea, like one who hunts a partridge in the mountains."

21 Then Saul said, "I have done wrong; come back, my son David, for I will never harm you again, because my life was precious in your sight today; I have been a fool, and have made a great mistake." 22David replied, "Here is the spear, O king! Let one of the young men come over and get it. 23The LORD rewards everyone for his righteousness and his faithfulness; for the LORD gave you into my hand today, but I would not raise my hand against the LORD's anointed. 24As your life was precious today in my sight, so may my life be precious in the sight of the LORD, and may he rescue me from all tribulation." 25Then Saul said to David, "Blessed be you, my son David! You will do many things and will succeed in them." So David went his way, and Saul returned to his place.

26.13–25. 13: *David went over to the other side* so that if Saul pursues him he can lead the army away from his unsuspecting men. **16:** *You deserve to die* hints at Abner's assassination (2 Sam 3). **19:** David curses any persons who have caused Saul to pursue him because this has driven him from the land of Israel, which is the LORD's *heritage*. The *other gods* are the gods of countries outside of Israel where David says he has been driven. **20:** *A partridge* is literally "the caller" or "calling bird." The comparison is apt since David is calling to Saul from a mountain. **25:** Saul's blessing subtly indicates that David will be king.

27 David said in his heart, "I shall now perish one day by the hand of Saul; there is nothing better for me than to escape to the land of the Philistines; then Saul will despair of seeking me any longer within the

borders of Israel, and I shall escape out of his hand." ²So David set out and went over, he and the six hundred men who were with him, to King Achish son of Maoch of Gath. ³David stayed with Achish at Gath, he and his troops, every man with his household, and David with his two wives, Ahinoam of Jezreel, and Abigail of Carmel, Nabal's widow. ⁴When Saul was told that David had fled to Gath, he no longer sought for him.

5 Then David said to Achish, "If I have found favor in your sight, let a place be given me in one of the country towns, so that I may live there; for why should your servant live in the royal city with you?" ⁶So that day Achish gave him Ziklag; therefore Ziklag has belonged to the kings of Judah to this day. ⁷The length of time that David lived in the country of the Philistines was one year and four months.

8 Now David and his men went up and made raids on the Geshurites, the Girzites, and the Amalekites; for these were the landed settlements from Telam\[a\] on the way to Shur and on to the land of Egypt. ⁹David struck the land, leaving neither man nor woman alive, but took away the sheep, the oxen, the donkeys, the camels, and the clothing, and came back to Achish. ¹⁰When Achish asked, "Against whom\[b\] have you made a raid today?" David would say, "Against the Negeb of Judah," or "Against the Negeb of the Jerahmeelites," or, "Against the Negeb of the Kenites." ¹¹David left neither man nor woman alive to be brought back to Gath, thinking, "They might tell about us, and say, 'David has done so and so.'" Such was his practice all the time he lived in the country of the Philistines. ¹²Achish trusted David, thinking, "He has made himself utterly abhorrent to his people Israel; therefore he shall always be my servant."

28 In those days the Philistines gathered their forces for war, to fight against Israel. Achish said to David, "You know, of course, that you and your men are to go out with me in the army." ²David said to Achish, "Very well, then you shall know what your servant can do." Achish said to David, "Very well, I will make you my bodyguard for life."

27.1–28.2: David with the Philistines. 1–4: David is driven by Saul's pursuits to flee to the Philistines. *Achish* is the same character as in 21.10. But the two passages are in tension, since David would not have gone to Achish after pretending to be mad in 21.10–15. **6:** It was common for kings to give grants of land to faithful servants. In this case Achish also benefited because *Ziklag* guarded the southern frontier of Philistine territory. **8:** The mention of the *Amalekites* stands in tension with ch. 15 where they are all killed. **10:** *The Negeb* is the southern wilderness area of Palestine. *Kenites* should be read as "Kenizzites." They and the *Jerahmeelites* were clans* within Judah. David was attacking other peoples and then fooling Achish by telling him that he had attacked parts of Judah. **12:** Achish felt confident of David's loyalty because he thought David had alienated himself from his own people. **28.2:** *Then you shall know what your servant can do* has a double meaning. Achish thinks David is saying that he will show his potential against Israel. David is actually saying that in the heat of battle Achish will find out how David remains loyal to Israel.

3 Now Samuel had died, and all Israel had mourned for him and buried him in Ramah, his own city. Saul had expelled the mediums and the wizards from the land. ⁴The Philistines assembled, and came and encamped at Shunem. Saul gathered all Israel, and they encamped at Gilboa. ⁵When Saul saw the army of the Philistines, he was afraid, and his heart trembled greatly. ⁶When Saul inquired of the LORD, the LORD did not answer him, not by dreams, or by Urim, or by prophets. ⁷Then Saul said to his servants, "Seek out for me a woman who is a medium, so that I may go to her and inquire of her." His servants said to him, "There is a medium at Endor."

28.3–25: Saul consults a ghost. 3: *Mediums and wizards* are often used in conjunction and refer to devices used to communicate with the dead. Such practices are condemned by the law in Deut 18.10. **4:** *Shunem* and *Gilboa* locate the site of the battle near the Jezreel Valley, far north of the Negeb where the previous stories were set. **6:** Three means of divining were *dreams,*

---

a Compare Gk 15.4: Heb *from of old*   b Q Ms Gk Vg: MT lacks *whom*

or incubation, in which one expected the answer to an inquiry to be given at night, in a dream, often when one slept at a holy place; *Urim,* or lots, which have been used earlier in 1 Samuel; and *prophets,** like the man of God in 9.1–10.16. **7:** *A woman who is a medium* literally means "a woman of (who deals with) spirits," using the word translated "medium" in v. 3.

8 So Saul disguised himself and put on other clothes and went there, he and two men with him. They came to the woman by night. And he said, "Consult a spirit for me, and bring up for me the one whom I name to you." ⁹The woman said to him, "Surely you know what Saul has done, how he has cut off the mediums and the wizards from the land. Why then are you laying a snare for my life to bring about my death?" ¹⁰But Saul swore to her by the LORD, "As the LORD lives, no punishment shall come upon you for this thing." ¹¹Then the woman said, "Whom shall I bring up for you?" He answered, "Bring up Samuel for me." ¹²When the woman saw Samuel, she cried out with a loud voice; and the woman said to Saul, "Why have you deceived me? You are Saul!" ¹³The king said to her, "Have no fear; what do you see?" The woman said to Saul, "I see a divine being*ᵃ* coming up out of the ground." ¹⁴He said to her, "What is his appearance?" She said, "An old man is coming up; he is wrapped in a robe." So Saul knew that it was Samuel, and he bowed with his face to the ground, and did obeisance.

15 Then Samuel said to Saul, "Why have you disturbed me by bringing me up?" Saul answered, "I am in great distress, for the Philistines are warring against me, and God has turned away from me and answers me no more, either by prophets or by dreams; so I have summoned you to tell me what I should do." ¹⁶Samuel said, "Why then do you ask me, since the LORD has turned from you and become your enemy? ¹⁷The LORD has done to you just as he spoke by me; for the LORD has torn the kingdom out of your hand, and given it to your neighbor, David. ¹⁸Because you did not obey the voice of the LORD, and did not carry out his fierce wrath against Amalek, therefore the LORD has

done this thing to you today. ¹⁹Moreover the LORD will give Israel along with you into the hands of the Philistines; and tomorrow you and your sons shall be with me; the LORD will also give the army of Israel into the hands of the Philistines."

20 Immediately Saul fell full length on the ground, filled with fear because of the words of Samuel; and there was no strength in him, for he had eaten nothing all day and all night. ²¹The woman came to Saul, and when she saw that he was terrified, she said to him, "Your servant has listened to you; I have taken my life in my hand, and have listened to what you have said to me. ²²Now therefore, you also listen to your servant; let me set a morsel of bread before you. Eat, that you may have strength when you go on your way." ²³He refused, and said, "I will not eat." But his servants, together with the woman, urged him; and he listened to their words. So he got up from the ground and sat on the bed. ²⁴Now the woman had a fatted calf in the house. She quickly slaughtered it, and she took flour, kneaded it, and baked unleavened cakes. ²⁵She put them before Saul and his servants, and they ate. Then they rose and went away that night.

28.8–25. 8: *Saul disguised himself* because he was breaking his own law (v. 3) by visiting the woman. **11–12a:** These verses are an insertion identifying Samuel as the ghost. Originally, the woman recognized Saul because of his oath in v. 10 not to punish her. **13:** *The ground* can also mean "the underworld." *Divine being* can refer to a god or to a ghost or spirit. **14:** The *robe* was Samuel's characteristic garment and the apparent means by which Saul recognized him. **17–18:** These verses refer to the story in ch. 15. **19:** *Tomorrow you and your sons shall be with me:* They will be dead. **24:** *A fatted calf in the house:* Livestock were typically kept on the ground floor of Israelite houses with sleeping quarters above them on a second floor.

29 Now the Philistines gathered all their forces at Aphek, while the Israelites were encamped by the fountain that is in Jezreel. ²As the lords of the Philistines

a Or *a god;* or *gods*

were passing on by hundreds and by thousands, and David and his men were passing on in the rear with Achish, 3the commanders of the Philistines said, "What are these Hebrews doing here?" Achish said to the commanders of the Philistines, "Is this not David, the servant of King Saul of Israel, who has been with me now for days and years? Since he deserted to me I have found no fault in him to this day." 4But the commanders of the Philistines were angry with him; and the commanders of the Philistines said to him, "Send the man back, so that he may return to the place that you have assigned to him; he shall not go down with us to battle, or else he may become an adversary to us in the battle. For how could this fellow reconcile himself to his lord? Would it not be with the heads of the men here? 5Is this not David, of whom they sing to one another in dances,

'Saul has killed his thousands,
     and David his ten thousands'?"

6 Then Achish called David and said to him, "As the LORD lives, you have been honest, and to me it seems right that you should march out and in with me in the campaign; for I have found nothing wrong in you from the day of your coming to me until today. Nevertheless the lords do not approve of you. 7So go back now; and go peaceably; do nothing to displease the lords of the Philistines." 8David said to Achish, "But what have I done? What have you found in your servant from the day I entered your service until now, that I should not go and fight against the enemies of my lord the king?" 9Achish replied to David, "I know that you are as blameless in my sight as an angel of God; nevertheless, the commanders of the Philistines have said, 'He shall not go up with us to the battle.' 10Now then rise early in the morning, you and the servants of your lord who came with you, and go to the place that I appointed for you. As for the evil report, do not take it to heart, for you have done well before me.*a* Start early in the morning, and leave as soon as you have light." 11So David set out with his men early in the morning, to return to the land of the Philistines. But the Philistines went up to Jezreel.

29.1–11: The Philistines reject David. 2: *The lords of the Philistines* are the rulers of the five main Philistine cities. **3:** The *commanders* of the Philistine army who will actually be in battle object to the presence of David and his men, whom they refer to as *Hebrews*, possibly a term for mercenaries. **6:** It is surprising that *Achish,* the Philistine, swears here by the LORD, that is, Yahweh, the God of Israel. **8:** David's wish to *fight against the enemies of my lord the king* is ambiguous. David's "lord" is Saul, but Achish takes it as a reference to himself. **10:** *The place that I appointed for you* is Ziklag.

30 Now when David and his men came to Ziklag on the third day, the Amalekites had made a raid on the Negeb and on Ziklag. They had attacked Ziklag, burned it down, 2and taken captive the women and all*b* who were in it, both small and great; they killed none of them, but carried them off, and went their way. 3When David and his men came to the city, they found it burned down, and their wives and sons and daughters taken captive. 4Then David and the people who were with him raised their voices and wept, until they had no more strength to weep. 5David's two wives also had been taken captive, Ahinoam of Jezreel, and Abigail the widow of Nabal of Carmel. 6David was in great danger; for the people spoke of stoning him, because all the people were bitter in spirit for their sons and daughters. But David strengthened himself in the LORD his God.

30.1–31: David defeats the Amalekites. 1: *On the third day:* Ziklag is over 50 miles from Aphek. The journey took three days. The writer emphasizes David's distance from the battle where Saul is killed. The Amalekite *raid* on Ziklag may have been in retaliation for David's raids against the Amalekites (27.8). This story stands in tension with ch. 15 where the Amalekites were supposedly all destroyed. **2:** *The women and all:* The men were all with David. *Both small and great* is a figure of speech referring to two extremes and everything in the middle. Here, the terms describe poverty or wealth and obscurity or social prominence. **6:**

---

a Gk: Heb lacks *and go to the place . . . done well before me*   *b* Gk: Heb lacks *and all*

Stoning as a type of execution implies that David had been accused of failing as a leader to provide adequate protection. *Strengthened himself* may mean summoning courage as well as gathering support within the army. David is here depicted as an ideal ruler.

7 David said to the priest Abiathar son of Ahimelech, "Bring me the ephod." So Abiathar brought the ephod to David. 8 David inquired of the LORD, "Shall I pursue this band? Shall I overtake them?" He answered him, "Pursue; for you shall surely overtake and shall surely rescue." 9 So David set out, he and the six hundred men who were with him. They came to the Wadi Besor, where those stayed who were left behind. 10 But David went on with the pursuit, he and four hundred men; two hundred stayed behind, too exhausted to cross the Wadi Besor.

11 In the open country they found an Egyptian, and brought him to David. They gave him bread and he ate; they gave him water to drink; 12 they also gave him a piece of fig cake and two clusters of raisins. When he had eaten, his spirit revived; for he had not eaten bread or drunk water for three days and three nights. 13 Then David said to him, "To whom do you belong? Where are you from?" He said, "I am a young man of Egypt, servant to an Amalekite. My master left me behind because I fell sick three days ago. 14 We had made a raid on the Negeb of the Cherethites and on that which belongs to Judah and on the Negeb of Caleb; and we burned Ziklag down." 15 David said to him, "Will you take me down to this raiding party?" He said, "Swear to me by God that you will not kill me, or hand me over to my master, and I will take you down to them."

16 When he had taken him down, they were spread out all over the ground, eating and drinking and dancing, because of the great amount of spoil they had taken from the land of the Philistines and from the land of Judah. 17 David attacked them from twilight until the evening of the next day. Not one of them escaped, except four hundred young men, who mounted camels and fled. 18 David recovered all that the Amalekites had taken; and David rescued his two wives. 19 Nothing was missing, whether small or great, sons or daughters, spoil or anything that had been taken; David brought back everything. 20 David also captured all the flocks and herds, which were driven ahead of the other cattle; people said, "This is David's spoil."

21 Then David came to the two hundred men who had been too exhausted to follow David, and who had been left at the Wadi Besor. They went out to meet David and to meet the people who were with him. When David drew near to the people he saluted them. 22 Then all the corrupt and worthless fellows among the men who had gone with David said, "Because they did not go with us, we will not give them any of the spoil that we have recovered, except that each man may take his wife and children, and leave." 23 But David said, "You shall not do so, my brothers, with what the LORD has given us; he has preserved us and handed over to us the raiding party that attacked us. 24 Who would listen to you in this matter? For the share of the one who goes down into the battle shall be the same as the share of the one who stays by the baggage; they shall share alike." 25 From that day forward he made it a statute and an ordinance for Israel; it continues to the present day.

26 When David came to Ziklag, he sent part of the spoil to his friends, the elders of Judah, saying, "Here is a present for you from the spoil of the enemies of the LORD"; 27 it was for those in Bethel, in Ramoth of the Negeb, in Jattir, 28 in Aroer, in Siphmoth, in Eshtemoa, 29 in Racal, in the towns of the Jerahmeelites, in the towns of the Kenites, 30 in Hormah, in Bor-ashan, in Athach, 31 in Hebron, all the places where David and his men had roamed.

30.7–31. 7–8: The *ephod** was used by priests to divine the answers to yes/no questions such as those in v. 8. **12:** *Fig cake* was a clump of figs. **14:** *The Cherethites* were mercenaries from the island of Crete who were closely associated with the Philistines. **23–25:** This is an etiology* for a custom in the writer's day. David's decree of *a statute and an ordinance for Israel* shows his kingly decisiveness and authority. **26–31:** The cities listed here were all in southern Judah. David's gifts to the *elders* of these cities would cause them to look favorably upon him when the time came to choose a king over Judah.

31

Now the Philistines fought against Israel; and the men of Israel fled before the Philistines, and many fell[a] on Mount Gilboa. 2The Philistines overtook Saul and his sons; and the Philistines killed Jonathan and Abinadab and Malchishua, the sons of Saul. 3The battle pressed hard upon Saul; the archers found him, and he was badly wounded by them. 4Then Saul said to his armor-bearer, "Draw your sword and thrust me through with it, so that these uncircumcised may not come and thrust me through, and make sport of me." But his armor-bearer was unwilling; for he was terrified. So Saul took his own sword and fell upon it. 5When his armor-bearer saw that Saul was dead, he also fell upon his sword and died with him. 6So Saul and his three sons and his armor-bearer and all his men died together on the same day. 7When the men of Israel who were on the other side of the valley and those beyond the Jordan saw that the men of Israel had fled and that Saul and his sons were dead, they forsook their towns and fled; and the Philistines came and occupied them.

8 The next day, when the Philistines came to strip the dead, they found Saul and his three sons fallen on Mount Gilboa. 9They cut off his head, stripped off his armor, and sent messengers throughout the land of the Philistines to carry the good news to the houses of their idols and to the people. 10They put his armor in the temple of Astarte;[b] and they fastened his body to the wall of Beth-shan. 11But when the inhabitants of Jabesh-gilead heard what the Philistines had done to Saul, 12all the valiant men set out, traveled all night long, and took the body of Saul and the bodies of his sons from the wall of Beth-shan. They came to Jabesh and burned them there. 13Then they took their bones and buried them under the tamarisk tree in Jabesh, and fasted seven days.

31.1–13: Saul's death. 1 Chronicles 10 contains a parallel account. **4:** *These uncircumcised** are the Philistines. Saul does not want to suffer humiliation and torture at their hands, so he asks his armor-bearer to finish him off. The armor-bearer refuses, perhaps out of respect for the LORD's anointed.* **11–13:** The men of Jabesh rescue Saul's body. They are moved to do this because of Saul's rescue of their city at the beginning of his reign (10.27b–11.15). It is unusual that they burned the bodies of Saul and his sons (v. 12), since cremation was not practiced by the Israelites.

a Heb *and they fell slain*   *b* Heb plural

2 SAMUEL

Introduction

The book of 2 Samuel is the continuation of 1 Samuel in the Deuteronomistic History★ (see the introduction to 1 Samuel). The first half of the book relates how David, after Saul's death (2 Sam 1), became king of Judah (ch. 2) and then Israel (ch. 5). It tells how he built a small empire through military conquest and how he established a capital and a dynasty★ in Jerusalem. The LORD's promise to David of an eternal dynasty (ch. 7) is a key passage in the Deuteronomistic History. It brings together the themes of Jerusalem as the divinely chosen center for worship and the Davidic line as the chosen family of kings in Judah. The second half of the book describes David's problems, which are all political problems within Israel and arise from within David's extended family. These include his adultery with Bathsheba (chs. 11–12), the rape of Tamar and murder of Amnon (ch. 13), and the revolts of Absalom and Sheba (chs. 13–20). This last section at least has been judged by scholars to have been an independent unit known as the "Succession Narrative" or "Court History." It lacks signs of deuteronomistic style and seems therefore to have been separate in some way from the Deuteronomistic History. There is no consensus about where it begins, however (some say ch. 9, others 2.8–4.12), and the once widely held view that the "Succession Narrative" represented realistic history can no longer be sustained.

The date and setting of 2 Samuel are, of course, the same as for 1 Samuel. Scholars are of two minds, however, about how the message of the book addresses its context. Some believe that the book, especially its second half, continues the defense of David evident in 1 Samuel as a way of promoting at least the hope in the restoration of the monarchy. Others, however, see it as strongly anti-Davidic, in opposition to any attempt to reinstitute kingship in Israel. A great deal hinges on how the story in 2 Sam 11–12 is understood.

READING GUIDE

The ambiguity of 2 Samuel is a mark of its literary sophistication. The mixture of praise for David with hints of cynical political calculation renders interpretation of the book open-ended. 2 Samuel recounts many deaths as David attains and retains power: Abner, Ishbosheth, Amnon, Absalom, Amasa. Is the writer attempting to defend David against charges of murder and usurpation? Does the book continue the contrast between Saul and David, showing how the annihilation of Saul's house and the rise of David took place according to the will of the LORD? Or is the author more cynical and subtle, contending that abuse of power is inherent with monarchs? Close attention to the interaction of the characters in 2 Samuel will help readers to answer these questions for themselves. The reader may also benefit from an awareness of the literary depth of the material. The story of Absalom's revolt, for example, may originally have been independent, with its own set of social and political causes. As it now stands, however, it is explained theologically as a consequence of David's sin with Bathsheba.

1–10	David's reign over Judah, then over Israel
11–12	David's sin with Bathsheba
13–20	Absalom's revolt
21–24	Miscellaneous materials about David's reign

1 After the death of Saul, when David had returned from defeating the Amalekites, David remained two days in Ziklag. ²On the third day, a man came from Saul's camp, with his clothes torn and dirt on his head. When he came to David, he fell to the ground and did obeisance. ³David said to him, "Where have you come from?" He said to him, "I have escaped from the camp of Israel." ⁴David said to him, "How did things go? Tell me!" He answered, "The army fled from the battle, but also many of the army fell and died; and Saul and his son Jonathan also died." ⁵Then David asked the young man who was reporting to him, "How do you know that Saul and his son Jonathan died?" ⁶The young man reporting to him said, "I happened to be on Mount Gilboa; and there was Saul leaning on his spear, while the chariots and the horsemen drew close to him. ⁷When he looked behind him, he saw me, and called to me. I answered, 'Here sir.' ⁸And he said to me, 'Who are you?' I answered him, 'I am an Amalekite.' ⁹He said to me, 'Come, stand over me and kill me; for convulsions have seized me, and yet my life still lingers.' ¹⁰So I stood over him, and killed him, for I knew that he could not live after he had fallen. I took the crown that was on his head and the armlet that was on his arm, and I have brought them here to my lord."

11 Then David took hold of his clothes and tore them; and all the men who were with him did the same. ¹²They mourned and wept, and fasted until evening for Saul and for his son Jonathan, and for the army of the LORD and for the house of Israel, because they had fallen by the sword. ¹³David said to the young man who had reported to him, "Where do you come from?" He answered, "I am the son of a resident alien, an Amalekite." ¹⁴David said to him, "Were you not afraid to lift your hand to destroy the LORD's anointed?" ¹⁵Then David called one of the young men and said, "Come here and strike him down." So he struck him down and he died. ¹⁶David said to him, "Your blood be on your head; for your own mouth has testified against you, saying, 'I have killed the LORD's anointed.' "

1.1–16: David learns of Saul's death. 2: *With his clothes torn and dirt on his head:* Conventional signs of grief. **5–10:** The Amalekite who brings the news to David tells a different version of Saul's death from the one in 1 Sam 31. His casual attitude (*I happened to be on Mount Gilboa,* v. 6) in the heat of battle suggests that he is lying in hopes of gaining David's favor. The fact that he is an *Amalekite* (v. 8) does not endear him to David and his men, who have just come from fighting the Amalekites. The account of this battle is difficult to reconcile with 1 Sam 15, where Saul's army killed all the Amalekites except their king. But it also provides an ironic* view of Saul's sin: Saul is condemned for failing to annihilate the Amalekites completely, and now one of those Amalekites claims to have killed him. David's predicament is clear: Although he presumably wanted Saul to be dead, he cannot even seem to have anything to do with killing Saul, since that would leave him open to charges of usurping the throne. The *crown* and *armlet* (v. 10) were Saul's royal insignia. David's possession of them would have to be explained. **13–16:** A *resident alien** is a non-Israelite who lives in Israel, which may also explain how this Amalekite escaped being slaughtered by Saul's army in 1 Sam 15. It also gives David the opening he needs: Since the Amalekite would have been responsible for following Israelite laws and customs, David judges him guilty of the capital offense of having killed the LORD's anointed.*

17 David intoned this lamentation over Saul and his son Jonathan. ¹⁸(He ordered that The Song of the Bow*ᵃ* be taught to the people of Judah; it is written in the Book of Jashar.) He said:

¹⁹ Your glory, O Israel, lies slain upon your
　　high places!
　　How the mighty have fallen!
²⁰ Tell it not in Gath,
　　proclaim it not in the streets of
　　　Ashkelon;
　or the daughters of the Philistines will
　　rejoice,
　　the daughters of the uncircumcised
　　　will exult.

²¹ You mountains of Gilboa,
　　let there be no dew or rain upon you,
　　nor bounteous fields!*ᵇ*

a Heb *that The Bow*   *b* Meaning of Heb uncertain

For there the shield of the mighty was
defiled,
the shield of Saul, anointed with oil
no more.

22 From the blood of the slain,
from the fat of the mighty,
the bow of Jonathan did not turn back,
nor the sword of Saul return empty.

23 Saul and Jonathan, beloved and lovely!
In life and in death they were not
divided;
they were swifter than eagles,
they were stronger than lions.

24 O daughters of Israel, weep over Saul,
who clothed you with crimson, in
luxury,
who put ornaments of gold on your
apparel.

25 How the mighty have fallen
in the midst of the battle!

Jonathan lies slain upon your high
places.
26 I am distressed for you, my brother
Jonathan;
greatly beloved were you to me;
your love to me was wonderful,
passing the love of women.

27 How the mighty have fallen,
and the weapons of war perished!

**1.17–27: David's lament* over Saul and Jonathan.
18:** The title, *The Song of the Bow,* may reflect a textual error. If original, it refers to the tune to which the
lament was sung. *The Book of Jashar* was a collection
of poems that no longer exists. *20: Gath* and *Ashkelon*
were Philistine cities. The poem pleads that the news
of Saul's and Jonathan's deaths not be proclaimed in
Philistine cities, where there would be rejoicing over it.
21: *Gilboa* was the mountain where Saul and Jonathan
died in battle. It is being cursed along with the surrounding hills because of this tragedy. Shields were
made of leather and *anointed* with oil* in preparation
for battle. Saul's shield now lies *defiled* from bloody
battle and unused because its owner is dead. **24:** The

poem calls upon the Israelites to mourn because they
prospered under Saul's rule.

2 After this David inquired of the LORD,
"Shall I go up into any of the cities of
Judah?" The LORD said to him, "Go up." David said, "To which shall I go up?" He said,
"To Hebron." 2So David went up there,
along with his two wives, Ahinoam of Jezreel,
and Abigail the widow of Nabal of Carmel.
3David brought up the men who were with
him, every one with his household; and they
settled in the towns of Hebron. 4Then the
people of Judah came, and there they
anointed David king over the house of Judah.

When they told David, "It was the people
of Jabesh-gilead who buried Saul," 5David
sent messengers to the people of Jabesh-
gilead, and said to them, "May you be
blessed by the LORD, because you showed
this loyalty to Saul your lord, and buried him!
6Now may the LORD show steadfast love and
faithfulness to you! And I too will reward you
because you have done this thing. 7There-
fore let your hands be strong, and be valiant;
for Saul your lord is dead, and the house of
Judah has anointed me king over them."

2.1–32: Civil war. 1: David *inquired of the LORD* by
means of some device, like lots, which could provide
answers to yes/no questions. Hence, his question
about going to *any of the cities of Judah* received a yes
answer. By process of elimination he then determined
that *Hebron* was the chosen city. Hebron was the capital of Judah. **2:** David's two wives, *Ahinoam* and *Abigail,* were both from the area around Hebron and were
therefore important political assets for his assumption
of the throne of Judah. Through his marriage to Abigail, David had assumed the wealth and position of a
prominent Calebite leader, perhaps their chieftain
(1 Sam 25). The Calebites were a prominent clan* in
Judah. **4a:** *The people of Judah* may be the same as
the elders of Judah to whom David distributed the
spoil from his defeat of the Amalekites (1 Sam
30.26–31). They *anointed** David by smearing oil on
his head. This was a symbol of election. "Messiah" is
a transliteration of the Hebrew word for anointed.
4b–7: The people of *Jabesh* in the region of *Gilead*
were among Saul's most loyal supporters. He had rescued them at the beginning of his reign (1 Sam
10.27b–11.15), and they had returned the favor by

rescuing his corpse from the Philistines (1 Sam 31.11–13). David congratulates them for their loyalty (v. 5) and then invites them to join with him as Saul's replacement (vv. 6–7). By making overtures to the enclaves of Saul's strongest support he forces the hand of Saul's successor, Ishbaal, whereupon civil war between Israel and Judah ensues.

8 But Abner son of Ner, commander of Saul's army, had taken Ishbaal[a] son of Saul, and brought him over to Mahanaim. 9He made him king over Gilead, the Ashurites, Jezreel, Ephraim, Benjamin, and over all Israel. 10Ishbaal,[a] Saul's son, was forty years old when he began to reign over Israel, and he reigned two years. But the house of Judah followed David. 11The time that David was king in Hebron over the house of Judah was seven years and six months.

2.8–11: *Abner* was Saul's cousin or uncle (1 Sam 14.50). He is obviously the power behind *Ishbaal*'s throne. The Hebrew text reads "Ish-bosheth" instead of "Ishbaal." Later scribes* substituted the word "bosheth," meaning "abomination," for the name of the Canaanite god Baal.* The word "baal" means "lord;" rather than indicating that Saul worshipped Baal, it may have been used as a title for the LORD (Yahweh). *Mahanaim* was east of the Jordan. Abner took Ishbaal there for protection because the Philistines had captured most of the Israelite territory. Thus, the description of Ishbaal's domain in v. 9 was more ideal than real at this point. *Ashurites* or "Assyrians" is impossible. A better reading is "Geshurites," who lived east of the Sea of Galilee. *Forty years* (v. 10) is a round number for a generation. If Ishbaal reigned *two years* over Israel during David's *seven years and six months* over Judah, five and a half years remain unaccounted for. Either there was an interregnum* in Israel after Saul's death before Ishbaal came to power, or David became king of Judah while Saul was still alive.

12 Abner son of Ner, and the servants of Ishbaal[a] son of Saul, went out from Mahanaim to Gibeon. 13Joab son of Zeruiah, and the servants of David, went out and met them at the pool of Gibeon. One group sat on one side of the pool, while the other sat on the other side of the pool. 14Abner said to Joab, "Let the young men come forward and have a contest before us." Joab said, "Let

them come forward." 15So they came forward and were counted as they passed by, twelve for Benjamin and Ishbaal[a] son of Saul, and twelve of the servants of David. 16Each grasped his opponent by the head, and thrust his sword in his opponent's side; so they fell down together. Therefore that place was called Helkath-hazzurim,[b] which is at Gibeon. 17The battle was very fierce that day; and Abner and the men of Israel were beaten by the servants of David.

18 The three sons of Zeruiah were there, Joab, Abishai, and Asahel. Now Asahel was as swift of foot as a wild gazelle. 19Asahel pursued Abner, turning neither to the right nor to the left as he followed him. 20Then Abner looked back and said, "Is it you, Asahel?" He answered, "Yes, it is." 21Abner said to him, "Turn to your right or to your left, and seize one of the young men, and take his spoil." But Asahel would not turn away from following him. 22Abner said again to Asahel, "Turn away from following me; why should I strike you to the ground? How then could I show my face to your brother Joab?" 23But he refused to turn away. So Abner struck him in the stomach with the butt of his spear, so that the spear came out at his back. He fell there, and died where he lay. And all those who came to the place where Asahel had fallen and died, stood still.

24 But Joab and Abishai pursued Abner. As the sun was going down they came to the hill of Ammah, which lies before Giah on the way to the wilderness of Gibeon. 25The Benjaminites rallied around Abner and formed a single band; they took their stand on the top of a hill. 26Then Abner called to Joab, "Is the sword to keep devouring forever? Do you not know that the end will be bitter? How long will it be before you order your people to turn from the pursuit of their kinsmen?" 27Joab said, "As God lives, if you had not spoken, the people would have continued to pursue their kinsmen, not stopping until morning." 28Joab sounded the trumpet and all the people stopped; they no longer pursued Israel or engaged in battle any further.

a Gk Compare 1 Chr 8.33; 9.39: Heb *Ish-bosheth*, "man of shame"   b That is *Field of Sword-edges*

29 Abner and his men traveled all that night through the Arabah; they crossed the Jordan, and, marching the whole forenoon,[a] they came to Mahanaim. 30 Joab returned from the pursuit of Abner; and when he had gathered all the people together, there were missing of David's servants nineteen men besides Asahel. 31 But the servants of David had killed of Benjamin three hundred sixty of Abner's men. 32 They took up Asahel and buried him in the tomb of his father, which was at Bethlehem. Joab and his men marched all night, and the day broke upon them at Hebron.

2.12–32: 12: According to 2 Sam 21.1–9, the people of *Gibeon* held a grudge against Saul and may have helped David. 13: *Zeruiah* was David's sister and *Joab* his cousin, according to 1 Chr 2.16. Joab was also the commander of David's army. The *pool of Gibeon* may refer to an enormous pit that has been discovered at the site of the ancient city. The pit descended to the city's water supply. 14–16: The *contest* here is a representative combat: a tournament between a small group from each side, rather than a full battle involving everyone. It provides an etiology* for the name in v. 16—*Helkath-hazzurim* means "field of the flint swords," or field of sword-edges. Since the contest is indecisive, a full battle breaks out (v. 17). 18–23: The death of *Asahel* gives his brother, Joab, a personal incentive for killing Abner (3.26–30). 26: *People* often means the army. 29: The *Arabah* is the geological depression from the Sea of Galilee to the Gulf of Aqabah. Here it refers to the Jordan Valley north of the Dead Sea.

3 There was a long war between the house of Saul and the house of David; David grew stronger and stronger, while the house of Saul became weaker and weaker.

2 Sons were born to David at Hebron: his firstborn was Amnon, of Ahinoam of Jezreel; 3 his second, Chileab, of Abigail the widow of Nabal of Carmel; the third, Absalom son of Maacah, daughter of King Talmai of Geshur; 4 the fourth, Adonijah son of Haggith; the fifth, Shephatiah son of Abital; 5 and the sixth, Ithream, of David's wife Eglah. These were born to David in Hebron.

6 While there was war between the house of Saul and the house of David, Abner was making himself strong in the house of Saul. 7 Now Saul had a concubine whose name was Rizpah daughter of Aiah. And Ishbaal[b] said to Abner, "Why have you gone in to my father's concubine?" 8 The words of Ishbaal[c] made Abner very angry; he said, "Am I a dog's head for Judah? Today I keep showing loyalty to the house of your father Saul, to his brothers, and to his friends, and have not given you into the hand of David; and yet you charge me now with a crime concerning this woman. 9 So may God do to Abner and so may he add to it! For just what the LORD has sworn to David, that will I accomplish for him, 10 to transfer the kingdom from the house of Saul, and set up the throne of David over Israel and over Judah, from Dan to Beer-sheba." 11 And Ishbaal[b] could not answer Abner another word, because he feared him.

12 Abner sent messengers to David at Hebron,[d] saying, "To whom does the land belong? Make your covenant with me, and I will give you my support to bring all Israel over to you." 13 He said, "Good; I will make a covenant with you. But one thing I require of you: you shall never appear in my presence unless you bring Saul's daughter Michal when you come to see me." 14 Then David sent messengers to Saul's son Ishbaal,[e] saying, "Give me my wife Michal, to whom I became engaged at the price of one hundred foreskins of the Philistines." 15 Ishbaal[e] sent and took her from her husband Paltiel the son of Laish. 16 But her husband went with her, weeping as he walked behind her all the way to Bahurim. Then Abner said to him, "Go back home!" So he went back.

17 Abner sent word to the elders of Israel, saying, "For some time past you have been seeking David as king over you. 18 Now then bring it about; for the LORD has promised David: Through my servant David I will save my people Israel from the hand of the Philistines, and from all their enemies." 19 Abner also spoke directly to the Benjaminites; then Abner went to tell David at Hebron all that

a Meaning of Heb uncertain   b Heb *And he*
c Gk Compare 1 Chr 8.33; 9.39: Heb *Ish-bosheth*,
"man of shame"   d Gk: Heb *where he was*
e Heb *Ish-bosheth*

Israel and the whole house of Benjamin were ready to do.

3.1–39: The assassination of Abner. 2–5: A similar list of David's sons born in Hebron occurs in 1 Chr 3.1–4. *Chileab* is there called Daniel. His name is uncertain and, like *Shephatiah* and *Ithream*, is not mentioned again. He may have died as a child. David's marriage to *Maacah* probably sealed a treaty with her father, the king of Geshur. **7:** A *concubine** was a female slave used for sexual purposes. To sleep with a member of the harem was to stake a claim to the throne. Thus, Ishbaal's question accuses Abner of treason. **8:** Abner responds angrily because the power is in his hands and he has been loyal to Saul and Ishbaal. He says Ishbaal is treating him as a *dog's head*. This expression is unique but obviously reproachful. **9–10:** *So may God do . . . and so may he add* is an oath formula. Abner swears that he will join David, and since he holds the true power, he will thereby *transfer the kingdom* of Israel to David. *From Dan to Beer-sheba* marks the traditional boundaries, north and south, of the united kingdom of Israel. **13–16:** David requires the return of his wife Michal since, as Saul's daughter, she is the basis for his claim to Saul's throne (1 Sam 20–29). *Ishbaal* may have been legally obligated to return Michal to her first husband. *Paltiel* or ''Palti'' was Michal's second husband after she was taken from David (1 Sam 25.44). **17:** The *elders of Israel* were the leaders of the tribes. **19:** *Benjamin* was the native tribe of both Saul and Abner.

20 When Abner came with twenty men to David at Hebron, David made a feast for Abner and the men who were with him. [21]Abner said to David, "Let me go and rally all Israel to my lord the king, in order that they may make a covenant with you, and that you may reign over all that your heart desires." So David dismissed Abner, and he went away in peace.

22 Just then the servants of David arrived with Joab from a raid, bringing much spoil with them. But Abner was not with David at Hebron, for David[a] had dismissed him, and he had gone away in peace. [23]When Joab and all the army that was with him came, it was told Joab, "Abner son of Ner came to the king, and he has dismissed him, and he has gone away in peace." [24]Then Joab went to the king and said, "What have you done? Abner came to you; why did you dismiss him, so that he got away? [25]You know that Abner son of Ner came to deceive you, and to learn your comings and goings and to learn all that you are doing."

26 When Joab came out from David's presence, he sent messengers after Abner, and they brought him back from the cistern of Sirah; but David did not know about it. [27]When Abner returned to Hebron, Joab took him aside in the gateway to speak with him privately, and there he stabbed him in the stomach. So he died for shedding[b] the blood of Asahel, Joab's[c] brother. [28]Afterward, when David heard of it, he said, "I and my kingdom are forever guiltless before the LORD for the blood of Abner son of Ner. [29]May the guilt[d] fall on the head of Joab, and on all his father's house; and may the house of Joab never be without one who has a discharge, or who is leprous,[e] or who holds a spindle, or who falls by the sword, or who lacks food!" [30]So Joab and his brother Abishai murdered Abner because he had killed their brother Asahel in the battle at Gibeon.

31 Then David said to Joab and to all the people who were with him, "Tear your clothes, and put on sackcloth, and mourn over Abner." And King David followed the bier. [32]They buried Abner at Hebron. The king lifted up his voice and wept at the grave of Abner, and all the people wept. [33]The king lamented for Abner, saying,

"Should Abner die as a fool dies?
[34] Your hands were not bound,
  your feet were not fettered;
 as one falls before the wicked
  you have fallen."
And all the people wept over him again. [35]Then all the people came to persuade David to eat something while it was still day; but David swore, saying, "So may God do to me, and more, if I taste bread or anything else before the sun goes down!" [36]All the people took notice of it, and it pleased them; just as everything the king did pleased all the people. [37]So all the people and all Israel un-

---

a Heb *he*   *b* Heb lacks *shedding*   *c* Heb *his*
d Heb *May it*   *e* A term for several skin diseases; precise meaning uncertain

derstood that day that the king had no part in the killing of Abner son of Ner. 38And the king said to his servants, "Do you not know that a prince and a great man has fallen this day in Israel? 39Today I am powerless, even though anointed king; these men, the sons of Zeruiah, are too violent for me. The LORD pay back the one who does wickedly in accordance with his wickedness!"

3.20–39. 21–23: The story repeats that Abner left David *in peace* as a way of emphasizing David's innocence in Abner's death. Joab's return after Abner had left (v. 22) suggests that David had sent Joab away in order to avoid a confrontation. 25: *Comings and goings* are military maneuvers. Joab is accusing Abner of spying. 27: Joab kills Abner in revenge for Abner's killing Asahel (2.18–23). The story hints that Joab may also have acted to preserve his place as army commander. 29: David curses Joab's descendants with illness because of his act. A *spindle* may also mean a crutch. 30: *Abishai* is not mentioned in the story but may have been involved with Joab in planning Abner's murder. 31: *Sackcloth* was an unknown kind of material worn by mourners. 33: *Fool* is a translation of the Hebrew "nabal" and is reminiscent of the story in 1 Sam 25.

4 When Saul's son Ishbaal*a* heard that Abner had died at Hebron, his courage failed, and all Israel was dismayed. 2Saul's son had two captains of raiding bands; the name of the one was Baanah, and the name of the other Rechab. They were sons of Rimmon a Benjaminite from Beeroth—for Beeroth is considered to belong to Benjamin. 3(Now the people of Beeroth had fled to Gittaim and are there as resident aliens to this day).

4 Saul's son Jonathan had a son who was crippled in his feet. He was five years old when the news about Saul and Jonathan came from Jezreel. His nurse picked him up and fled; and, in her haste to flee, it happened that he fell and became lame. His name was Mephibosheth.*b*

5 Now the sons of Rimmon the Beerothite, Rechab and Baanah, set out, and about the heat of the day they came to the house of Ishbaal,*c* while he was taking his noonday rest. 6They came inside the house as though

to take wheat, and they struck him in the stomach; then Rechab and his brother Baanah escaped.*d* 7Now they had come into the house while he was lying on his couch in his bedchamber; they attacked him, killed him, and beheaded him. Then they took his head and traveled by way of the Arabah all night long. 8They brought the head of Ishbaal*c* to David at Hebron and said to the king, "Here is the head of Ishbaal,*c* son of Saul, your enemy, who sought your life; the LORD has avenged my lord the king this day on Saul and on his offspring."

9 David answered Rechab and his brother Baanah, the sons of Rimmon the Beerothite, "As the LORD lives, who has redeemed my life out of every adversity, 10when the one who told me, 'See, Saul is dead,' thought he was bringing good news, I seized him and killed him at Ziklag—this was the reward I gave him for his news. 11How much more then, when wicked men have killed a righteous man on his bed in his own house! And now shall I not require his blood at your hand, and destroy you from the earth?" 12So David commanded the young men, and they killed them; they cut off their hands and feet, and hung their bodies beside the pool at Hebron. But the head of Ishbaal*c* they took and buried in the tomb of Abner at Hebron.

4.1–12: The assassination of Ishbaal. 2–3: *Beeroth* was one of the Gibeonite cities that joined Israel (Josh 9.17). Its residents fled and were presumably replaced by Israelites from Benjamin. 4: *Mephibosheth:* The original form of the name was Meribbaal as in 1 Chr 8.34; 9.40. The notice in this verse interrupts the narrative* but makes the point that there is no other suitable candidate for king in Saul's line after Ishbaal, a situation that prepares the way for the events narrated in 5.1. 7: *The Arabah* here refers to the Jordan Valley. 11: David refers to Ishbaal as a *righteous man* rather than as Yahweh's anointed,* suggesting that he does not recognize Ishbaal's kingship. 12: The kind of ritual execution described in this verse was reserved for traitors.

a Heb lacks *Ishbaal*   b In 1 Chr 8.34 and 9.40, *Merib-baal*   c Heb *Ish-bosheth*   d Meaning of Heb of verse 6 uncertain

5 Then all the tribes of Israel came to David at Hebron, and said, "Look, we are your bone and flesh. ²For some time, while Saul was king over us, it was you who led out Israel and brought it in. The LORD said to you: It is you who shall be shepherd of my people Israel, you who shall be ruler over Israel." ³So all the elders of Israel came to the king at Hebron; and King David made a covenant with them at Hebron before the LORD, and they anointed David king over Israel. ⁴David was thirty years old when he began to reign, and he reigned forty years. ⁵At Hebron he reigned over Judah seven years and six months; and at Jerusalem he reigned over all Israel and Judah thirty-three years.

6 The king and his men marched to Jerusalem against the Jebusites, the inhabitants of the land, who said to David, "You will not come in here, even the blind and the lame will turn you back"—thinking, "David cannot come in here." ⁷Nevertheless David took the stronghold of Zion, which is now the city of David. ⁸David had said on that day, "Whoever would strike down the Jebusites, let him get up the water shaft to attack the lame and the blind, those whom David hates."ᵃ Therefore it is said, "The blind and the lame shall not come into the house." ⁹David occupied the stronghold, and named it the city of David. David built the city all around from the Millo inward. ¹⁰And David became greater and greater, for the LORD, the God of hosts, was with him.

11 King Hiram of Tyre sent messengers to David, along with cedar trees, and carpenters and masons who built David a house. ¹²David then perceived that the LORD had established him king over Israel, and that he had exalted his kingdom for the sake of his people Israel.

13 In Jerusalem, after he came from Hebron, David took more concubines and wives; and more sons and daughters were born to David. ¹⁴These are the names of those who were born to him in Jerusalem: Shammua, Shobab, Nathan, Solomon, ¹⁵Ibhar, Elishua, Nepheg, Japhia, ¹⁶Elishama, Eliada, and Eliphelet.

5.1–16: David becomes king of Israel. 1–2: These verses are probably an editorial addition as they anticipate the action of the elders in v. 3. *Bone and flesh* means blood kinship. The people of Israel claim David as one of their own even though he was from Judah. *Led out* and *brought in* are idioms for military leadership. *Shepherd* is a common metaphor* for *ruler* or king. **3:** The *elders* were the senior leaders of the tribes. **4:** *Forty years* is a round number for a generation. **6–8:** The exact meaning of these verses is not clear. 1 Chr 11.5–6 differs, indicating that even the Chronicler found these verses confusing. The important point is that David conquered Jerusalem, which provided him a neutral capital in his effort to unite Israel and Judah. **9:** *Millo* means "fill" and apparently refers to a landfill or artificial platform created near the *stronghold*. **10:** The *hosts* are the armies, heavenly and earthly. **11:** *Tyre* was the capital of Phoenicia, the country north of Israel. Its *cedar* was a luxury item in the ancient Near East.

17 When the Philistines heard that David had been anointed king over Israel, all the Philistines went up in search of David; but David heard about it and went down to the stronghold. ¹⁸Now the Philistines had come and spread out in the valley of Rephaim. ¹⁹David inquired of the LORD, "Shall I go up against the Philistines? Will you give them into my hand?" The LORD said to David, "Go up; for I will certainly give the Philistines into your hand." ²⁰So David came to Baal-perazim, and David defeated them there. He said, "The LORD has burst forth againstᵇ my enemies before me, like a bursting flood." Therefore that place is called Baal-perazim.ᶜ ²¹The Philistines abandoned their idols there, and David and his men carried them away.

22 Once again the Philistines came up, and were spread out in the valley of Rephaim. ²³When David inquired of the LORD, he said, "You shall not go up; go around to their rear, and come upon them opposite the balsam trees. ²⁴When you hear the sound of marching in the tops of the balsam trees, then be on the alert; for then the LORD has gone out before you to strike down the army

a Another reading is *those who hate David*
b Heb *paraz*   *c* That is *Lord of Bursting Forth*

of the Philistines." 25David did just as the LORD had commanded him; and he struck down the Philistines from Geba all the way to Gezer.

5.17–25: David defeats the Philistines. 17: David's defeat of the Philistines probably preceded his conquest of Jerusalem, since they stood between Hebron and Jerusalem and would have resisted the unification of Israel and Judah. David's *stronghold* here is probably Adullam, not Jerusalem. **19:** *David inquired of the LORD* by means of some device that provided answers to yes/no questions. **20:** This verse is an etiology* for the name *Baal-perazim*, which means "Lord of bursting forth." **21:** A victorious army typically captured the idols that its opponent brought to the battlefield to show the superiority of its own gods. **22–25:** David's victory on this occasion is divinely directed.

6 David again gathered all the chosen men of Israel, thirty thousand. 2David and all the people with him set out and went from Baale-judah, to bring up from there the ark of God, which is called by the name of the LORD of hosts who is enthroned on the cherubim. 3They carried the ark of God on a new cart, and brought it out of the house of Abinadab, which was on the hill. Uzzah and Ahio,*a* the sons of Abinadab, were driving the new cart 4with the ark of God;*b* and Ahio*a* went in front of the ark. 5David and all the house of Israel were dancing before the LORD with all their might, with songs*c* and lyres and harps and tambourines and castanets and cymbals.

6 When they came to the threshing floor of Nacon, Uzzah reached out his hand to the ark of God and took hold of it, for the oxen shook it. 7The anger of the LORD was kindled against Uzzah; and God struck him there because he reached out his hand to the ark;*d* and he died there beside the ark of God. 8David was angry because the LORD had burst forth with an outburst upon Uzzah; so that place is called Perez-uzzah,*e* to this day. 9David was afraid of the LORD that day; he said, "How can the ark of the LORD come into my care?" 10So David was unwilling to take the ark of the LORD into his care in the city of David; instead David took it to the house of Obed-edom the Gittite. 11The

ark of the LORD remained in the house of Obed-edom the Gittite three months; and the LORD blessed Obed-edom and all his household.

12 It was told King David, "The LORD has blessed the household of Obed-edom and all that belongs to him, because of the ark of God." So David went and brought up the ark of God from the house of Obed-edom to the city of David with rejoicing; 13and when those who bore the ark of the LORD had gone six paces, he sacrificed an ox and a fatling. 14David danced before the LORD with all his might; David was girded with a linen ephod. 15So David and all the house of Israel brought up the ark of the LORD with shouting, and with the sound of the trumpet.

16 As the ark of the LORD came into the city of David, Michal daughter of Saul looked out of the window, and saw King David leaping and dancing before the LORD; and she despised him in her heart.

17 They brought in the ark of the LORD, and set it in its place, inside the tent that David had pitched for it; and David offered burnt offerings and offerings of well-being before the LORD. 18When David had finished offering the burnt offerings and the offerings of well-being, he blessed the people in the name of the LORD of hosts, 19and distributed food among all the people, the whole multitude of Israel, both men and women, to each a cake of bread, a portion of meat,*f* and a cake of raisins. Then all the people went back to their homes.

20 David returned to bless his household. But Michal the daughter of Saul came out to meet David, and said, "How the king of Israel honored himself today, uncovering himself today before the eyes of his servants' maids, as any vulgar fellow might shamelessly uncover himself!" 21David said to Michal, "It was before the LORD, who chose me in place of your father and all his household, to appoint me as prince over Israel, the

a Or *and his brother*   *b* Compare Gk: Heb *and brought it out of the house of Abinadab, which was on the hill with the ark of God*   *c* Q Ms Gk 1 Chr 13.8: Heb *fir trees*
d 1 Chr 13.10 Compare Q Ms: Meaning of Heb uncertain   *e* That is *Bursting Out Against Uzzah*
f Vg: Meaning of Heb uncertain

people of the LORD, that I have danced before the LORD. 22I will make myself yet more contemptible than this, and I will be abased in my own eyes; but by the maids of whom you have spoken, by them I shall be held in honor." 23And Michal the daughter of Saul had no child to the day of her death.

6.1–23: David brings the ark to Jerusalem. 1: The word translated "thousand" designates a military unit of much smaller size. Then, *thirty thousand* would be thirty units. **2:** *Baale-judah* is another name for Kiriath-jearim, according to Josh 15.9. This is where the ark was left in 1 Sam 7.1. The *ark* was viewed as the throne of the LORD. *Cherubim* were mythical griffins that often guarded temples and palaces. **6–8:** *Uzzah*'s death shows the awesome holiness of the ark. The story also provides an etiological★ explanation for the name Perez-uzzah (see note *e*). **10:** *Obed-edom* was from Gath (*the Gittite*) and was apparently among the Philistines who followed David from his days with the Philistines. **14:** A *linen ephod*★ was an apron typically worn by priests (1 Sam 2.18). **20:** Michal accuses David of fraternizing with the lowest element of society, thus implying that he is not dignified enough to be king. **21–22:** David replies that the LORD made him king in place of her father, Saul. **23:** Michal had no children either because the LORD prevented it or because David had no relations with her. Her children would have been Saul's heirs and therefore a threat to David's rule.

7 Now when the king was settled in his house, and the LORD had given him rest from all his enemies around him, 2the king said to the prophet Nathan, "See now, I am living in a house of cedar, but the ark of God stays in a tent." 3Nathan said to the king, "Go, do all that you have in mind; for the LORD is with you."

4 But that same night the word of the LORD came to Nathan: 5Go and tell my servant David: Thus says the LORD: Are you the one to build me a house to live in? 6I have not lived in a house since the day I brought up the people of Israel from Egypt to this day, but I have been moving about in a tent and a tabernacle. 7Wherever I have moved about among all the people of Israel, did I ever speak a word with any of the tribal leaders*a* of Israel, whom I commanded to shep-

herd my people Israel, saying, "Why have you not built me a house of cedar?" 8Now therefore thus you shall say to my servant David: Thus says the LORD of hosts: I took you from the pasture, from following the sheep to be prince over my people Israel; 9and I have been with you wherever you went, and have cut off all your enemies from before you; and I will make for you a great name, like the name of the great ones of the earth. 10And I will appoint a place for my people Israel and will plant them, so that they may live in their own place, and be disturbed no more; and evildoers shall afflict them no more, as formerly, 11from the time that I appointed judges over my people Israel; and I will give you rest from all your enemies. Moreover the LORD declares to you that the LORD will make you a house. 12When your days are fulfilled and you lie down with your ancestors, I will raise up your offspring after you, who shall come forth from your body, and I will establish his kingdom. 13He shall build a house for my name, and I will establish the throne of his kingdom forever. 14I will be a father to him, and he shall be a son to me. When he commits iniquity, I will punish him with a rod such as mortals use, with blows inflicted by human beings. 15But I will not take*b* my steadfast love from him, as I took it from Saul, whom I put away from before you. 16Your house and your kingdom shall be made sure forever before me;*c* your throne shall be established forever. 17In accordance with all these words and with all this vision, Nathan spoke to David.

18 Then King David went in and sat before the LORD, and said, "Who am I, O Lord GOD, and what is my house, that you have brought me thus far? 19And yet this was a small thing in your eyes, O Lord GOD; you have spoken also of your servant's house for a great while to come. May this be instruction for the people,*d* O Lord GOD! 20And what more can David say to you? For you know your servant, O Lord GOD! 21Because of your promise, and according to your own

a Or *any of the tribes*   *b* Gk Syr Vg 1 Chr 17.13: Heb *shall not depart*   *c* Gk Heb Mss: MT *before you;* Compare 2 Sam 7.26, 29   *d* Meaning of Heb uncertain

heart, you have wrought all this greatness, so that your servant may know it. 22Therefore you are great, O LORD God; for there is no one like you, and there is no God besides you, according to all that we have heard with our ears. 23Who is like your people, like Israel? Is there another*a* nation on earth whose God went to redeem it as a people, and to make a name for himself, doing great and awesome things for them,*b* by driving out*c* before his people nations and their gods?*d* 24And you established your people Israel for yourself to be your people forever; and you, O LORD, became their God. 25And now, O LORD God, as for the word that you have spoken concerning your servant and concerning his house, confirm it forever; do as you have promised. 26Thus your name will be magnified forever in the saying, 'The LORD of hosts is God over Israel'; and the house of your servant David will be established before you. 27For you, O LORD of hosts, the God of Israel, have made this revelation to your servant, saying, 'I will build you a house'; therefore your servant has found courage to pray this prayer to you. 28And now, O Lord GOD, you are God, and your words are true, and you have promised this good thing to your servant; 29now therefore may it please you to bless the house of your servant, so that it may continue forever before you; for you, O Lord GOD, have spoken, and with your blessing shall the house of your servant be blessed forever."

7.1–29: A dynasty* for David. 1: The second half of this verse, about the LORD giving David rest, is not in the parallel version in 1 Chr 17.1. It is also contradicted by the subsequent accounts of David's wars and by the statement in 1 Kings 5.3–4 that rest came only to Solomon. **5–7:** There is a play throughout the chapter on the word "house." The *house* David proposes to build is a temple. But the LORD declines David's offer and says instead that he will build David a house, that is, a dynasty. The claim in vv. 6–7 that the LORD has never had a *house* (temple) seems to overlook the temple in Shiloh (1 Sam 1–3). **10:** The *place* mentioned here is probably a place of worship, namely the Jerusalem Temple. **11–12:** The *house* that the LORD promises David is a dynasty. **13:** It is David's son who will build the Temple. **16:** David's dynasty will be per-

manent and *established forever.* **23:** David here refers to the exodus from Egypt and the conquest of Canaan.

8 Some time afterward, David attacked the Philistines and subdued them; David took Metheg-ammah out of the hand of the Philistines.

2 He also defeated the Moabites and, making them lie down on the ground, measured them off with a cord; he measured two lengths of cord for those who were to be put to death, and one length*e* for those who were to be spared. And the Moabites became servants to David and brought tribute.

3 David also struck down King Hadadezer son of Rehob of Zobah, as he went to restore his monument*f* at the river Euphrates. 4David took from him one thousand seven hundred horsemen, and twenty thousand foot soldiers. David hamstrung all the chariot horses, but left enough for a hundred chariots. 5When the Arameans of Damascus came to help King Hadadezer of Zobah, David killed twenty-two thousand men of the Arameans. 6Then David put garrisons among the Arameans of Damascus; and the Arameans became servants to David and brought tribute. The LORD gave victory to David wherever he went. 7David took the gold shields that were carried by the servants of Hadadezer, and brought them to Jerusalem. 8From Betah and from Berothai, towns of Hadadezer, King David took a great amount of bronze.

9 When King Toi of Hamath heard that David had defeated the whole army of Hadadezer, 10Toi sent his son Joram to King David, to greet him and to congratulate him because he had fought against Hadadezer and defeated him. Now Hadadezer had often been at war with Toi. Joram brought with him articles of silver, gold, and bronze; 11these also King David dedicated to the LORD, together with the silver and gold that he dedicated from all the nations he subdued, 12from Edom, Moab, the Ammonites,

a Gk: Heb *one*   *b* Heb *you*   *c* Gk 1 Chr 17.21: Heb *for your land*   *d* Cn: Heb *before your people, whom you redeemed for yourself from Egypt, nations and its gods*   *e* Heb *one full length*   *f* Compare 1 Sam 15.12 and 2 Sam 18.18

the Philistines, Amalek, and from the spoil of King Hadadezer son of Rehob of Zobah.

13 David won a name for himself. When he returned, he killed eighteen thousand Edomites*a* in the Valley of Salt. 14He put garrisons in Edom; throughout all Edom he put garrisons, and all the Edomites became David's servants. And the LORD gave victory to David wherever he went.

15 So David reigned over all Israel; and David administered justice and equity to all his people. 16Joab son of Zeruiah was over the army; Jehoshaphat son of Ahilud was recorder; 17Zadok son of Ahitub and Ahimelech son of Abiathar were priests; Seraiah was secretary; 18Benaiah son of Jehoiada was over*b* the Cherethites and the Pelethites; and David's sons were priests.

8.1–18: David's wars. 1: The meaning of *Methegammah* is uncertain. **2:** The *Moabites* lived on the other side of the Dead Sea from Israel. **3:** *Zobah* was an Aramean (Syrian) city-state. The word *restore* may also be read as "leave." Thus, David, rather than *Hadadezer,* may have been traveling to the Euphrates to erect a monument. **4:** David *hamstrung* the horses he could not use to keep someone else from using them against him. Joshua was commanded to do the same thing with the chariot horses he captured (Josh 11.6). This suggests that the Israelites did not yet use chariots extensively in battle. **5:** *Twenty-two thousand* may be twenty-two military units, which numbered much less than a thousand. **9:** *Hamath* was an important city-state north of Syria. **10:** *Joram,* the son of *King Toi,* has an Israelite name! **13–14:** *Edom* was the southernmost country east of the Jordan. **15–17:** The exact functions of the *recorder* and the *secretary* in David's administration are unknown. **18:** The *Cherethites and Pelethites* were the royal bodyguard (23.23) and were related to if not identical with the Philistines. Apparently, in David's day the king and his sons could serve as priests.

9 David asked, "Is there still anyone left of the house of Saul to whom I may show kindness for Jonathan's sake?" 2Now there was a servant of the house of Saul whose name was Ziba, and he was summoned to David. The king said to him, "Are you Ziba?" And he said, "At your service!" 3The king said, "Is there anyone remaining of the

house of Saul to whom I may show the kindness of God?" Ziba said to the king, "There remains a son of Jonathan; he is crippled in his feet." 4The king said to him, "Where is he?" Ziba said to the king, "He is in the house of Machir son of Ammiel, at Lo-debar." 5Then King David sent and brought him from the house of Machir son of Ammiel, at Lo-debar. 6Mephibosheth*c* son of Jonathan son of Saul came to David, and fell on his face and did obeisance. David said, "Mephibosheth!"*c* He answered, "I am your servant." 7David said to him, "Do not be afraid, for I will show you kindness for the sake of your father Jonathan; I will restore to you all the land of your grandfather Saul, and you yourself shall eat at my table always." 8He did obeisance and said, "What is your servant, that you should look upon a dead dog such as I?"

9 Then the king summoned Saul's servant Ziba, and said to him, "All that belonged to Saul and to all his house I have given to your master's grandson. 10You and your sons and your servants shall till the land for him, and shall bring in the produce, so that your master's grandson may have food to eat; but your master's grandson Mephibosheth*e* shall always eat at my table." Now Ziba had fifteen sons and twenty servants. 11Then Ziba said to the king, "According to all that my lord the king commands his servant, so your servant will do." Mephibosheth*c* ate at David's*d* table, like one of the king's sons. 12Mephibosheth*c* had a young son whose name was Mica. And all who lived in Ziba's house became Mephibosheth's*e* servants. 13Mephibosheth*c* lived in Jerusalem, for he always ate at the king's table. Now he was lame in both his feet.

9.1–13: Jonathan's son. 1: The story in 21.1–14 originally preceded this one. It tells of the execution of a group of Saul's sons and grandsons, which provides background to David's question, *Is there still anyone left of the house of Saul?* David's *kindness for Jonathan's sake* fulfills the promise of loyalty that he made

a Gk: Heb *returned from striking down eighteen thousand Arameans*   *b* Syr Tg Vg 20.23; 1 Chr 18.17: Heb lacks *was over*   *c* Or *Merib-baal:* See 4.4 note   *d* Gk: Heb *my*   *e* Or *Merib-baal's:* See 4.4 note

to Jonathan in several places in 1 Sam. **3:** *Crippled in his feet:* See comment on 4.4. This handicap made him unable to go to war and therefore unsuitable to be king. **4:** *Machir* became a loyal supporter of David (17.27). *Lo-debar* was a northern Israelite city east of the Jordan. **6:** *Mephibosheth's* name was originally Merib-baal. **7:** Eating at the king's table was a sign of favor. It also gave David the chance to keep a close watch on Merib-baal, who was still heir to Saul's kingdom. **8:** *Dead dog* was a term of self-reproach. **9–13:** While he lived in Jerusalem with David, Merib-baal would receive the income from Saul's lands, which Ziba and his family would work.

10 Some time afterward, the king of the Ammonites died, and his son Hanun succeeded him. ²David said, "I will deal loyally with Hanun son of Nahash, just as his father dealt loyally with me." So David sent envoys to console him concerning his father. When David's envoys came into the land of the Ammonites, ³the princes of the Ammonites said to their lord Hanun, "Do you really think that David is honoring your father just because he has sent messengers with condolences to you? Has not David sent his envoys to you to search the city, to spy it out, and to overthrow it?" ⁴So Hanun seized David's envoys, shaved off half the beard of each, cut off their garments in the middle at their hips, and sent them away. ⁵When David was told, he sent to meet them, for the men were greatly ashamed. The king said, "Remain at Jericho until your beards have grown, and then return."

6 When the Ammonites saw that they had become odious to David, the Ammonites sent and hired the Arameans of Beth-rehob and the Arameans of Zobah, twenty thousand foot soldiers, as well as the king of Maacah, one thousand men, and the men of Tob, twelve thousand men. ⁷When David heard of it, he sent Joab and all the army with the warriors. ⁸The Ammonites came out and drew up in battle array at the entrance of the gate; but the Arameans of Zobah and of Rehob, and the men of Tob and Maacah, were by themselves in the open country.

9 When Joab saw that the battle was set against him both in front and in the rear, he chose some of the picked men of Israel, and

arrayed them against the Arameans; ¹⁰the rest of his men he put in the charge of his brother Abishai, and he arrayed them against the Ammonites. ¹¹He said, "If the Arameans are too strong for me, then you shall help me; but if the Ammonites are too strong for you, then I will come and help you. ¹²Be strong, and let us be courageous for the sake of our people, and for the cities of our God; and may the LORD do what seems good to him." ¹³So Joab and the people who were with him moved forward into battle against the Arameans; and they fled before him. ¹⁴When the Ammonites saw that the Arameans fled, they likewise fled before Abishai, and entered the city. Then Joab returned from fighting against the Ammonites, and came to Jerusalem.

15 But when the Arameans saw that they had been defeated by Israel, they gathered themselves together. ¹⁶Hadadezer sent and brought out the Arameans who were beyond the Euphrates; and they came to Helam, with Shobach the commander of the army of Hadadezer at their head. ¹⁷When it was told David, he gathered all Israel together, and crossed the Jordan, and came to Helam. The Arameans arrayed themselves against David and fought with him. ¹⁸The Arameans fled before Israel; and David killed of the Arameans seven hundred chariot teams, and forty thousand horsemen,ᵃ and wounded Shobach the commander of their army, so that he died there. ¹⁹When all the kings who were servants of Hadadezer saw that they had been defeated by Israel, they made peace with Israel, and became subject to them. So the Arameans were afraid to help the Ammonites any more.

10.1–19: The Ammonite war. 2: *Nahash* was Saul's enemy in 1 Sam 10.27b–11.15. He and David had a treaty. *Hanun's* actions here indicate that Israel was the superior partner in the treaty or that David was trying to make Israel the superior partner. **4:** *Hanun's* treatment of the *envoys* is symbolic emasculation. The *beard* was a symbol of masculinity. Cutting off *their garments* below the waist was a symbolic castration. **5:** *Jericho* was the closest Israelite city west of the Jor-

a 1 Chr 19.18 and some Gk Mss read *foot soldiers*

dan opposite Ammon. **6:** *Beth-rehob* and *Zobah* were Aramean (Syrian) city-states. The word for *thousand* may refer to a much smaller military unit. *Maacah* and *Tob* were states in northern Palestine east of the Jordan. **9:** *Joab* made a tactical mistake that led to having enemies on two opposing sides. **12:** Joab encouraged his men to fight for the *cities* that Israel claimed east of the Jordan.

11 In the spring of the year, the time when kings go out to battle, David sent Joab with his officers and all Israel with him; they ravaged the Ammonites, and besieged Rabbah. But David remained at Jerusalem.

2 It happened, late one afternoon, when David rose from his couch and was walking about on the roof of the king's house, that he saw from the roof a woman bathing; the woman was very beautiful. ³David sent someone to inquire about the woman. It was reported, "This is Bathsheba daughter of Eliam, the wife of Uriah the Hittite." ⁴So David sent messengers to get her, and she came to him, and he lay with her. (Now she was purifying herself after her period.) Then she returned to her house. ⁵The woman conceived; and she sent and told David, "I am pregnant."

6 So David sent word to Joab, "Send me Uriah the Hittite." And Joab sent Uriah to David. ⁷When Uriah came to him, David asked how Joab and the people fared, and how the war was going. ⁸Then David said to Uriah, "Go down to your house, and wash your feet." Uriah went out of the king's house, and there followed him a present from the king. ⁹But Uriah slept at the entrance of the king's house with all the servants of his lord, and did not go down to his house. ¹⁰When they told David, "Uriah did not go down to his house," David said to Uriah, "You have just come from a journey. Why did you not go down to your house?" ¹¹Uriah said to David, "The ark and Israel and Judah remain in booths;ᵃ and my lord Joab and the servants of my lord are camping in the open field; shall I then go to my house, to eat and to drink, and to lie with my wife? As you live, and as your soul lives, I will not do such a thing." ¹²Then David said to Uriah, "Remain here today also, and tomorrow I will send you back." So Uriah remained in Jerusalem that day. On the next day, ¹³David invited him to eat and drink in his presence and made him drunk; and in the evening he went out to lie on his couch with the servants of his lord, but he did not go down to his house.

14 In the morning David wrote a letter to Joab, and sent it by the hand of Uriah. ¹⁵In the letter he wrote, "Set Uriah in the forefront of the hardest fighting, and then draw back from him, so that he may be struck down and die." ¹⁶As Joab was besieging the city, he assigned Uriah to the place where he knew there were valiant warriors. ¹⁷The men of the city came out and fought with Joab; and some of the servants of David among the people fell. Uriah the Hittite was killed as well. ¹⁸Then Joab sent and told David all the news about the fighting; ¹⁹and he instructed the messenger, "When you have finished telling the king all the news about the fighting, ²⁰then, if the king's anger rises, and if he says to you, 'Why did you go so near the city to fight? Did you not know that they would shoot from the wall? ²¹Who killed Abimelech son of Jerubbaal?ᵇ Did not a woman throw an upper millstone on him from the wall, so that he died at Thebez? Why did you go so near the wall?' then you shall say, 'Your servant Uriah the Hittite is dead too.' "

22 So the messenger went, and came and told David all that Joab had sent him to tell. ²³The messenger said to David, "The men gained an advantage over us, and came out against us in the field; but we drove them back to the entrance of the gate. ²⁴Then the archers shot at your servants from the wall; some of the king's servants are dead; and your servant Uriah the Hittite is dead also." ²⁵David said to the messenger, "Thus you shall say to Joab, 'Do not let this matter trouble you, for the sword devours now one and now another; press your attack on the city, and overthrow it.' And encourage him."

26 When the wife of Uriah heard that her husband was dead, she made lamentation for

a Or *at Succoth*   *b* Gk Syr Judg 7.1: Heb *Jerubbesheth*

him. 27When the mourning was over, David sent and brought her to his house, and she became his wife, and bore him a son.

11.1–27: David and Bathsheba. 1: This story is set a year after the events in the previous chapter. It is not clear why *David remained at Jerusalem,* but the story in 21.15–17 may lie in the background. **2:** David had been taking an afternoon nap on *the roof of the king's house* where it was cool. From there he was able to look down into the courtyard of surrounding houses where he saw the *woman bathing. Uriah* was one of David's best soldiers, according to 23.39. **4:** Bathsheba *was purifying herself after her period* by bathing according to Lev 15.19–28. She was at the most fertile time of her cycle when she slept with David. This also makes it clear that her child must be David's, not Uriah's. **7:** It must have seemed strange to Uriah to be called back from battle for a personal audience with the king only to be asked the most general questions. Perhaps this raised his suspicions and caused him to be on his best behavior. The *people* are the army. **8:** *Wash your feet* is a euphemism* for sexual intercourse. In Hebrew idiom, the *feet* often refer to the genitals. **9:** As a pious soldier who is consecrated for war (see 1 Sam 21.5), Uriah refuses to sleep with his wife. **14:** David has confidence enough in Uriah's loyalty to send his death warrant by his own hand knowing that Uriah, even if he could read, would not read it. **16–21:** Joab also uses Uriah's death to cover up his mistake in drawing too close to the city wall. The story of *Abimelech* (v. 21) is in Judg 9. **27:** This verse provides a transition to the continuation of the story in the next chapter.

---

12 But the thing that David had done displeased the LORD, 1and the LORD sent Nathan to David. He came to him, and said to him, "There were two men in a certain city, the one rich and the other poor. 2The rich man had very many flocks and herds; 3but the poor man had nothing but one little ewe lamb, which he had bought. He brought it up, and it grew up with him and with his children; it used to eat of his meager fare, and drink from his cup, and lie in his bosom, and it was like a daughter to him. 4Now there came a traveler to the rich man, and he was loath to take one of his own flock or herd to prepare for the wayfarer who had come to him, but he took the poor

man's lamb, and prepared that for the guest who had come to him." 5Then David's anger was greatly kindled against the man. He said to Nathan, "As the LORD lives, the man who has done this deserves to die; 6he shall restore the lamb fourfold, because he did this thing, and because he had no pity."

7 Nathan said to David, "You are the man! Thus says the LORD, the God of Israel: I anointed you king over Israel, and I rescued you from the hand of Saul; 8I gave you your master's house, and your master's wives into your bosom, and gave you the house of Israel and of Judah; and if that had been too little, I would have added as much more. 9Why have you despised the word of the LORD, to do what is evil in his sight? You have struck down Uriah the Hittite with the sword, and have taken his wife to be your wife, and have killed him with the sword of the Ammonites. 10Now therefore the sword shall never depart from your house, for you have despised me, and have taken the wife of Uriah the Hittite to be your wife. 11Thus says the LORD: I will raise up trouble against you from within your own house; and I will take your wives before your eyes, and give them to your neighbor, and he shall lie with your wives in the sight of this very sun. 12For you did it secretly; but I will do this thing before all Israel, and before the sun." 13David said to Nathan, "I have sinned against the LORD." Nathan said to David, "Now the LORD has put away your sin; you shall not die. 14Nevertheless, because by this deed you have utterly scorned the LORD,*a* the child that is born to you shall die." 15Then Nathan went to his house.

The LORD struck the child that Uriah's wife bore to David, and it became very ill. 16David therefore pleaded with God for the child; David fasted, and went in and lay all night on the ground. 17The elders of his house stood beside him, urging him to rise from the ground; but he would not, nor did he eat food with them. 18On the seventh day the child died. And the servants of David were afraid to tell him that the child was

---

a Ancient scribal tradition: Compare 1 Sam 25.22 note: Heb *scorned the enemies of the* LORD

dead; for they said, "While the child was still alive, we spoke to him, and he did not listen to us; how then can we tell him the child is dead? He may do himself some harm." 19 But when David saw that his servants were whispering together, he perceived that the child was dead; and David said to his servants, "Is the child dead?" They said, "He is dead."

20 Then David rose from the ground, washed, anointed himself, and changed his clothes. He went into the house of the LORD, and worshiped; he then went to his own house; and when he asked, they set food before him and he ate. 21 Then his servants said to him, "What is this thing that you have done? You fasted and wept for the child while it was alive; but when the child died, you rose and ate food." 22 He said, "While the child was still alive, I fasted and wept; for I said, 'Who knows? The LORD may be gracious to me, and the child may live.' 23 But now he is dead; why should I fast? Can I bring him back again? I shall go to him, but he will not return to me."

24 Then David consoled his wife Bathsheba, and went to her, and lay with her; and she bore a son, and he named him Solomon. The LORD loved him, 25 and sent a message by the prophet Nathan; so he named him Jedidiah,ᵃ because of the LORD.

26 Now Joab fought against Rabbah of the Ammonites, and took the royal city. 27 Joab sent messengers to David, and said, "I have fought against Rabbah; moreover, I have taken the water city. 28 Now, then, gather the rest of the people together, and encamp against the city, and take it; or I myself will take the city, and it will be called by my name." 29 So David gathered all the people together and went to Rabbah, and fought against it and took it. 30 He took the crown of Milcomᵇ from his head; the weight of it was a talent of gold, and in it was a precious stone; and it was placed on David's head. He also brought forth the spoil of the city, a very great amount. 31 He brought out the people who were in it, and set them to work with saws and iron picks and iron axes, or sent them to the brickworks. Thus he did to all the cities of the Ammonites. Then David and all the people returned to Jerusalem.

12.1–31: David's punishment. 1–6: Nathan brings a legal case before David. As king he was responsible for ensuring the rights of the poor. The fourfold restoration mentioned in v. 6 is prescribed in Ex 22.1. Other textual witnesses have "sevenfold." **8:** There is some textual support for reading "daughter(s)" instead of *house* in this verse. The point in any case is that David had many women as wives and concubines.* But like the rich man in Nathan's parable,* he stole what belonged to his poor neighbor. The mention of *your master's wives* assumes that David took over Saul's harem. **11–12:** These verses allude to Absalom's revolt, specifically his deed in 16.20–23. **13–18:** David's sin is transferred to his newborn son, who then dies because of it. **20:** The *house of the LORD* is the Temple* in Jerusalem, which had not yet been built. This appears, therefore, to be an anachronism.* **24–25:** *Solomon* means "his replacement." He was a replacement for the dead child. But his name *Jedidiah* ("beloved of Yahweh"), which does not occur for Solomon anywhere else, hints that he will replace David (whose name means "beloved") as king. **26–29:** Joab captured the citadel and the water supply of Rabbah, the Ammonite capital, so that David's conquest of the rest of the city was fairly simple. **30:** *Milcom* was the national god of the Ammonites. *A talent* was about 75 pounds.

13 Some time passed. David's son Absalom had a beautiful sister whose name was Tamar; and David's son Amnon fell in love with her. 2 Amnon was so tormented that he made himself ill because of his sister Tamar, for she was a virgin and it seemed impossible to Amnon to do anything to her. 3 But Amnon had a friend whose name was Jonadab, the son of David's brother Shimeah; and Jonadab was a very crafty man. 4 He said to him, "O son of the king, why are you so haggard morning after morning? Will you not tell me?" Amnon said to him, "I love Tamar, my brother Absalom's sister." 5 Jonadab said to him, "Lie down on your bed, and pretend to be ill; and when your father comes to see you, say to him, 'Let my sister Tamar come and give me something to eat, and prepare the food in my sight, so that I may see it and eat it from her

ᵃ That is *Beloved of the* LORD   ᵇ Gk See 1 Kings 11.5, 33: Heb *their kings* hand.' " 6So Amnon lay down, and pretended to be ill; and when the king came to see him, Amnon said to the king, "Please let my sister Tamar come and make a couple of cakes in my sight, so that I may eat from her hand."

7 Then David sent home to Tamar, saying, "Go to your brother Amnon's house, and prepare food for him." 8So Tamar went to her brother Amnon's house, where he was lying down. She took dough, kneaded it, made cakes in his sight, and baked the cakes. 9Then she took the pan and set them*a* out before him, but he refused to eat. Amnon said, "Send out everyone from me." So everyone went out from him. 10Then Amnon said to Tamar, "Bring the food into the chamber, so that I may eat from your hand." So Tamar took the cakes she had made, and brought them into the chamber to Amnon her brother. 11But when she brought them near him to eat, he took hold of her, and said to her, "Come, lie with me, my sister." 12She answered him, "No, my brother, do not force me; for such a thing is not done in Israel; do not do anything so vile! 13As for me, where could I carry my shame? And as for you, you would be as one of the scoundrels in Israel. Now therefore, I beg you, speak to the king; for he will not withhold me from you." 14But he would not listen to her; and being stronger than she, he forced her and lay with her.

15 Then Amnon was seized with a very great loathing for her; indeed, his loathing was even greater than the lust he had felt for her. Amnon said to her, "Get out!" 16But she said to him, "No, my brother;*b* for this wrong in sending me away is greater than the other that you did to me." But he would not listen to her. 17He called the young man who served him and said, "Put this woman out of my presence, and bolt the door after her." 18(Now she was wearing a long robe with sleeves; for this is how the virgin daughters of the king were clothed in earlier times.*c*) So his servant put her out, and bolted the door after her. 19But Tamar put ashes on her head, and tore the long robe that she was wearing; she put her hand on her head, and went away, crying aloud as she went.

20 Her brother Absalom said to her, "Has Amnon your brother been with you? Be quiet for now, my sister; he is your brother; do not take this to heart." So Tamar remained, a desolate woman, in her brother Absalom's house. 21When King David heard of all these things, he became very angry, but he would not punish his son Amnon, because he loved him, for he was his firstborn.*d* 22But Absalom spoke to Amnon neither good nor bad; for Absalom hated Amnon, because he had raped his sister Tamar.

13.1–22: The rape of Tamar. 1: Tamar was Absalom's full *sister* but Amnon's half-sister. David was the father of all three, but Tamar's and Absalom's mother was different from Amnon's. **2:** As a virgin daughter of the king, Tamar was probably guarded and therefore it *seemed impossible to Amnon to do anything to her.* **6:** The word for *cakes* is similar to the Hebrew word for "heart." This may describe their shape. It also suggests Amnon's love. **11:** The term *my sister* reflects the kinship of Amnon to Tamar. It is also common in ancient love poetry and expresses his sexual desire (compare Song 4.9–10; 5.1). **12:** *Such a thing* may refer to incest or rape or both. **13:** Tamar suggests that David would allow their marriage despite its incestuous nature. In part, at least, she is trying to buy time. **16:** Exodus 22.16 and Deut 22.28–29 required marriage in similar cases. Tamar may have such laws in mind when she says that in sending her away Amnon is committing a *greater* wrong than the rape itself. **17:** Having robbed Tamar of her virginity, Amnon takes her identity as well, contemptuously calling her *this woman.* **18:** The exact nature of the *long robe with sleeves* is unknown. The same expression is used for Joseph's garment in Gen 37.3. **19:** Putting ashes on the head and tearing the clothes were signs of grief, though Tamar may also have torn *the long robe* worn by the king's virgin daughters because it was no longer appropriate. **20:** By *desolate* is meant unmarried. **22:** *Neither good nor bad* means not at all. It indicates Absalom's silence and his self-restraint.

23 After two full years Absalom had sheepshearers at Baal-hazor, which is near Ephraim, and Absalom invited all the king's

a Heb *and poured*   *b* Cn Compare Gk Vg: Meaning of Heb uncertain   *c* Cn: Heb *were clothed in robes*   *d* Q Ms Gk: MT lacks *but he would not punish . . . firstborn*

sons. 24Absalom came to the king, and said, "Your servant has sheepshearers; will the king and his servants please go with your servant?" 25But the king said to Absalom, "No, my son, let us not all go, or else we will be burdensome to you." He pressed him, but he would not go but gave him his blessing. 26Then Absalom said, "If not, please let my brother Amnon go with us." The king said to him, "Why should he go with you?" 27But Absalom pressed him until he let Amnon and all the king's sons go with him. Absalom made a feast like a king's feast.*a* 28Then Absalom commanded his servants, "Watch when Amnon's heart is merry with wine, and when I say to you, 'Strike Amnon,' then kill him. Do not be afraid; have I not myself commanded you? Be courageous and valiant." 29So the servants of Absalom did to Amnon as Absalom had commanded. Then all the king's sons rose, and each mounted his mule and fled.

30　While they were on the way, the report came to David that Absalom had killed all the king's sons, and not one of them was left. 31The king rose, tore his garments, and lay on the ground; and all his servants who were standing by tore their garments. 32But Jonadab, the son of David's brother Shimeah, said, "Let not my lord suppose that they have killed all the young men the king's sons; Amnon alone is dead. This has been determined by Absalom from the day Amnon*b* raped his sister Tamar. 33Now therefore, do not let my lord the king take it to heart, as if all the king's sons were dead; for Amnon alone is dead."

34　But Absalom fled. When the young man who kept watch looked up, he saw many people coming from the Horonaim road*c* by the side of the mountain. 35Jonadab said to the king, "See, the king's sons have come; as your servant said, so it has come about." 36As soon as he had finished speaking, the king's sons arrived, and raised their voices and wept; and the king and all his servants also wept very bitterly.

37　But Absalom fled, and went to Talmai son of Ammihud, king of Geshur. David mourned for his son day after day. 38Absalom, having fled to Geshur, stayed there

three years. 39And the heart of*d* the king went out, yearning for Absalom; for he was now consoled over the death of Amnon.

13.23–39: Amnon's murder. 23: Sheepshearing was a time of celebration. **27:** The *feast* was a drinking bout. **29:** David and his sons rode on *mules* (18.9; 1 Kings 1.33). **30–33:** David initially thought that Absalom had killed all the king's sons, which would make sense if he were attempting a coup. But his intention at this point is purely revenge against Amnon. The clever *Jonadab* appears as a false friend to Amnon. **37:** *Talmai*, the *king of Geshur*, was Absalom's maternal grandfather (3.3). **39:** The first part of this verse may mean that David was tired of marching out in pursuit of Absalom rather than that he yearned for him. This would explain David's reluctance in the next chapter to allow Absalom back into his presence.

14 Now Joab son of Zeruiah perceived that the king's mind was on Absalom. 2Joab sent to Tekoa and brought from there a wise woman. He said to her, "Pretend to be a mourner; put on mourning garments, do not anoint yourself with oil, but behave like a woman who has been mourning many days for the dead. 3Go to the king and speak to him as follows." And Joab put the words into her mouth.

4　When the woman of Tekoa came to the king, she fell on her face to the ground and did obeisance, and said, "Help, O king!" 5The king asked her, "What is your trouble?" She answered, "Alas, I am a widow; my husband is dead. 6Your servant had two sons, and they fought with one another in the field; there was no one to part them, and one struck the other and killed him. 7Now the whole family has risen against your servant. They say, 'Give up the man who struck his brother, so that we may kill him for the life of his brother whom he murdered, even if we destroy the heir as well.' Thus they would quench my one remaining ember, and leave to my husband neither name nor remnant on the face of the earth."

8　Then the king said to the woman, "Go to your house, and I will give orders con-

---

a Gk Compare Q Ms: MT lacks *Absalom made a feast like a king's feast*　*b* Heb *he*　*c* Cn Compare Gk: Heb *the road behind him*　*d* Q Ms Gk: MT *And David*

cerning you." 9The woman of Tekoa said to the king, "On me be the guilt, my lord the king, and on my father's house; let the king and his throne be guiltless." 10The king said, "If anyone says anything to you, bring him to me, and he shall never touch you again." 11Then she said, "Please, may the king keep the LORD your God in mind, so that the avenger of blood may kill no more, and my son not be destroyed." He said, "As the LORD lives, not one hair of your son shall fall to the ground."

14.1–33: Absalom's return. 1: The fact that *the king's mind was on Absalom* does not mean that he was now favorably inclined toward Absalom, as this story makes clear. 2: *Tekoa* was a village south of Bethlehem. Perhaps David took an interest in this case because the woman was from his home territory. *Wise* also means skilled. This woman was a skilled actress. 8–11: David grants the woman's request and swears by the LORD that her one remaining son will not be harmed. The woman will urge David to apply this oath to his situation with Absalom. Since David's ruling is contrary to the customary punishment, the woman accepts any guilt that David may incur (v. 9).

12 Then the woman said, "Please let your servant speak a word to my lord the king." He said, "Speak." 13The woman said, "Why then have you planned such a thing against the people of God? For in giving this decision the king convicts himself, inasmuch as the king does not bring his banished one home again. 14We must all die; we are like water spilled on the ground, which cannot be gathered up. But God will not take away a life; he will devise plans so as not to keep an outcast banished forever from his presence.*a* 15Now I have come to say this to my lord the king because the people have made me afraid; your servant thought, 'I will speak to the king; it may be that the king will perform the request of his servant. 16For the king will hear, and deliver his servant from the hand of the man who would cut both me and my son off from the heritage of God.' 17Your servant thought, 'The word of my lord the king will set me at rest'; for my lord the king is like the angel of God, discerning good and evil. The LORD your God be with you!"

18 Then the king answered the woman, "Do not withhold from me anything I ask you." The woman said, "Let my lord the king speak." 19The king said, "Is the hand of Joab with you in all this?" The woman answered and said, "As surely as you live, my lord the king, one cannot turn right or left from anything that my lord the king has said. For it was your servant Joab who commanded me; it was he who put all these words into the mouth of your servant. 20In order to change the course of affairs your servant Joab did this. But my lord has wisdom like the wisdom of the angel of God to know all things that are on the earth."

21 Then the king said to Joab, "Very well, I grant this; go, bring back the young man Absalom." 22Joab prostrated himself with his face to the ground and did obeisance, and blessed the king; and Joab said, "Today your servant knows that I have found favor in your sight, my lord the king, in that the king has granted the request of his servant." 23So Joab set off, went to Geshur, and brought Absalom to Jerusalem. 24The king said, "Let him go to his own house; he is not to come into my presence." So Absalom went to his own house, and did not come into the king's presence.

25 Now in all Israel there was no one to be praised so much for his beauty as Absalom; from the sole of his foot to the crown of his head there was no blemish in him. 26When he cut the hair of his head (for at the end of every year he used to cut it; when it was heavy on him, he cut it), he weighed the hair of his head, two hundred shekels by the king's weight. 27There were born to Absalom three sons, and one daughter whose name was Tamar; she was a beautiful woman.

28 So Absalom lived two full years in Jerusalem, without coming into the king's presence. 29Then Absalom sent for Joab to send him to the king; but Joab would not come to him. He sent a second time, but Joab would not come. 30Then he said to his servants, "Look, Joab's field is next to mine,

a Meaning of Heb uncertain

and he has barley there; go and set it on fire." So Absalom's servants set the field on fire. 31Then Joab rose and went to Absalom at his house, and said to him, "Why have your servants set my field on fire?" 32Absalom answered Joab, "Look, I sent word to you: Come here, that I may send you to the king with the question, 'Why have I come from Geshur? It would be better for me to be there still.' Now let me go into the king's presence; if there is guilt in me, let him kill me!" 33Then Joab went to the king and told him; and he summoned Absalom. So he came to the king and prostrated himself with his face to the ground before the king; and the king kissed Absalom.

14.12–33. 14: Amnon is dead and cannot be brought to life again, but David can accept Absalom, who is still alive. **15–17:** These verses are out of place; the woman continues to plead for her son, but David has already rendered his decision. They probably originally went after v. 7. *The man who would cut both me and my son off* is the blood avenger, a member of the clan* appointed to avenge the death of the murdered son. *The heritage of God* refers not only to the land of Israel but to its people. **21–24:** David allows Absalom to return but refuses to see him personally. **26:** *Two hundred shekels** would be over five pounds, an extraordinary amount of hair. **27:** Absalom named his daughter after his sister, *Tamar* (ch. 13). **28–33:** This episode shows Absalom's rash nature and suggests that Joab may have held a grudge against him.

15 After this Absalom got himself a chariot and horses, and fifty men to run ahead of him. 2Absalom used to rise early and stand beside the road into the gate; and when anyone brought a suit before the king for judgment, Absalom would call out and say, "From what city are you?" When the person said, "Your servant is of such and such a tribe in Israel," 3Absalom would say, "See, your claims are good and right; but there is no one deputed by the king to hear you." 4Absalom said moreover, "If only I were judge in the land! Then all who had a suit or cause might come to me, and I would give them justice." 5Whenever people came near to do obeisance to him, he would put out his hand and take hold of them, and kiss them. 6Thus Absalom did to every Israelite who came to the king for judgment; so Absalom stole the hearts of the people of Israel.

7 At the end of four*a* years Absalom said to the king, "Please let me go to Hebron and pay the vow that I have made to the LORD. 8For your servant made a vow while I lived at Geshur in Aram: If the LORD will indeed bring me back to Jerusalem, then I will worship the LORD in Hebron."*b* 9The king said to him, "Go in peace." So he got up, and went to Hebron. 10But Absalom sent secret messengers throughout all the tribes of Israel, saying, "As soon as you hear the sound of the trumpet, then shout: Absalom has become king at Hebron!" 11Two hundred men from Jerusalem went with Absalom; they were invited guests, and they went in their innocence, knowing nothing of the matter. 12While Absalom was offering the sacrifices, he sent for*c* Ahithophel the Gilonite, David's counselor, from his city Giloh. The conspiracy grew in strength, and the people with Absalom kept increasing.

15.1–12: The revolt begins. 1: The *chariot and horses* and *fifty men to run ahead* were trappings of kingship (1 Kings 1.5). The fifty men were probably a royal bodyguard. **5:** Absalom would not allow anyone to bow or *do obeisance to him* but fashioned himself as a "man of the people." **6:** *Stole the hearts* is translated "deceived" in Gen 31.20 and is appropriate here also. **7–10:** *Hebron* was the capital of Judah, where David had been made king of both Judah and Israel and had ruled Judah for seven years. Absalom was mirroring his father's rise by declaring himself king in Hebron. His revolt, however, was not limited to Judah but spread *throughout all the tribes of Israel* (v. 10). **8:** *Geshur* was the Aramean city-state where Absalom fled after killing Amnon (13.37–39). **12:** On the great wisdom of *David's counselor, Ahithophel,* see 16.15–23.

13 A messenger came to David, saying, "The hearts of the Israelites have gone after Absalom." 14Then David said to all his officials who were with him at Jerusalem, "Get up! Let us flee, or there will be no escape for us from Absalom. Hurry, or he will soon

a Gk Syr: Heb *forty*   *b* Gk Mss: Heb lacks *in Hebron*
c Or *he sent*

overtake us, and bring disaster down upon us, and attack the city with the edge of the sword." 15The king's officials said to the king, "Your servants are ready to do whatever our lord the king decides." 16So the king left, followed by all his household, except ten concubines whom he left behind to look after the house. 17The king left, followed by all the people; and they stopped at the last house. 18All his officials passed by him; and all the Cherethites, and all the Pelethites, and all the six hundred Gittites who had followed him from Gath, passed on before the king.

19 Then the king said to Ittai the Gittite, "Why are you also coming with us? Go back, and stay with the king; for you are a foreigner, and also an exile from your home. 20You came only yesterday, and shall I today make you wander about with us, while I go wherever I can? Go back, and take your kinsfolk with you; and may the LORD show[a] steadfast love and faithfulness to you." 21But Ittai answered the king, "As the LORD lives, and as my lord the king lives, wherever my lord the king may be, whether for death or for life, there also your servant will be." 22David said to Ittai, "Go then, march on." So Ittai the Gittite marched on, with all his men and all the little ones who were with him. 23The whole country wept aloud as all the people passed by; the king crossed the Wadi Kidron, and all the people moved on toward the wilderness.

24 Abiathar came up, and Zadok also, with all the Levites, carrying the ark of the covenant of God. They set down the ark of God, until the people had all passed out of the city. 25Then the king said to Zadok, "Carry the ark of God back into the city. If I find favor in the eyes of the LORD, he will bring me back and let me see both it and the place where it stays. 26But if he says, 'I take no pleasure in you,' here I am, let him do to me what seems good to him." 27The king also said to the priest Zadok, "Look,[b] go back to the city in peace, you and Abiathar,[c] with your two sons, Ahimaaz your son, and Jonathan son of Abiathar. 28See, I will wait at the fords of the wilderness until word comes from you to inform me." 29So Zadok and Abi-

athar carried the ark of God back to Jerusalem, and they remained there.

30 But David went up the ascent of the Mount of Olives, weeping as he went, with his head covered and walking barefoot; and all the people who were with him covered their heads and went up, weeping as they went. 31David was told that Ahithophel was among the conspirators with Absalom. And David said, "O LORD, I pray you, turn the counsel of Ahithophel into foolishness."

32 When David came to the summit, where God was worshiped, Hushai the Archite came to meet him with his coat torn and earth on his head. 33David said to him, "If you go on with me, you will be a burden to me. 34But if you return to the city and say to Absalom, 'I will be your servant, O king; as I have been your father's servant in time past, so now I will be your servant,' then you will defeat for me the counsel of Ahithophel. 35The priests Zadok and Abiathar will be with you there. So whatever you hear from the king's house, tell it to the priests Zadok and Abiathar. 36Their two sons are with them there, Zadok's son Ahimaaz and Abiathar's son Jonathan; and by them you shall report to me everything you hear." 37So Hushai, David's friend, came into the city, just as Absalom was entering Jerusalem.

15.13–16.14: David flees Jerusalem. 15.16: Concubines were female slaves used for sexual purposes. 17: The last house refers to the last house on the outskirts of Jerusalem. 18: The Cherethites and Pelethites were related to or identical with Philistines who served as the royal bodyguard. Gittites were Philistines from Gath. All of these groups had followed David from his days with the Philistines. 23: The Wadi Kidron is the valley between Jerusalem and the Mount of Olives. David is heading east toward the Jordan. 24: Abiathar and Zadok were David's two priests. 31–34: David was disheartened to learn that his wise adviser, Ahithophel (see 16.15–23) had joined Absalom. As he walked up the Mount of Olives (v. 30), he prayed for help against Ahithophel. His prayer was answered at the summit when he met Hushai, who would help him defeat

a Gk Compare 2.6: Heb lacks may the LORD show
b Gk: Heb Are you a seer or Do you see? c Cn: Heb lacks and Abiathar

Ahithophel's advice. **37:** *David's friend* may have been a title for an intimate adviser or "best man."

16 When David had passed a little beyond the summit, Ziba the servant of Mephibosheth*a* met him, with a couple of donkeys saddled, carrying two hundred loaves of bread, one hundred bunches of raisins, one hundred of summer fruits, and one skin of wine. ²The king said to Ziba, "Why have you brought these?" Ziba answered, "The donkeys are for the king's household to ride, the bread and summer fruit for the young men to eat, and the wine is for those to drink who faint in the wilderness." ³The king said, "And where is your master's son?" Ziba said to the king, "He remains in Jerusalem; for he said, 'Today the house of Israel will give me back my grandfather's kingdom.' " ⁴Then the king said to Ziba, "All that belonged to Mephibosheth*a* is now yours." Ziba said, "I do obeisance; let me find favor in your sight, my lord the king."

5 When King David came to Bahurim, a man of the family of the house of Saul came out whose name was Shimei son of Gera; he came out cursing. ⁶He threw stones at David and at all the servants of King David; now all the people and all the warriors were on his right and on his left. ⁷Shimei shouted while he cursed, "Out! Out! Murderer! Scoundrel! ⁸The LORD has avenged on all of you the blood of the house of Saul, in whose place you have reigned; and the LORD has given the kingdom into the hand of your son Absalom. See, disaster has overtaken you; for you are a man of blood."

9 Then Abishai son of Zeruiah said to the king, "Why should this dead dog curse my lord the king? Let me go over and take off his head." ¹⁰But the king said, "What have I to do with you, you sons of Zeruiah? If he is cursing because the LORD has said to him, 'Curse David,' who then shall say, 'Why have you done so?' " ¹¹David said to Abishai and to all his servants, "My own son seeks my life; how much more now may this Benjaminite! Let him alone, and let him curse; for the LORD has bidden him. ¹²It may be that the LORD will look on my distress,*b* and the LORD will repay me with good for this curs-

ing of me today." ¹³So David and his men went on the road, while Shimei went along on the hillside opposite him and cursed as he went, throwing stones and flinging dust at him. ¹⁴The king and all the people who were with him arrived weary at the Jordan;*c* and there he refreshed himself.

16.1–14. 3–4: *Your master's son* is Merib-baal. His grandfather was Saul, and Ziba claims that he is hoping to take over his grandfather's place as king. But Ziba may be lying (19.24–30). David rewards Ziba by giving him Saul's property. There is some question about whether David has the legal right to do this. **5:** *Shimei* belonged not only to Saul's tribe (Benjamin) but also to his *family* or clan.* **6–8:** Shimei accused David of murdering members of Saul's family and usurping the throne. He may have in mind the deaths of Abner and Ishbaal or those of Saul's sons and grandsons in 21.1–14. **9:** *Abishai* was Joab's brother. Both are recognized in 2 Samuel as violent men. He calls Shimei a *dead dog,* a term of reproach.

15 Now Absalom and all the Israelites*d* came to Jerusalem; Ahithophel was with him. ¹⁶When Hushai the Archite, David's friend, came to Absalom, Hushai said to Absalom, "Long live the king! Long live the king!" ¹⁷Absalom said to Hushai, "Is this your loyalty to your friend? Why did you not go with your friend?" ¹⁸Hushai said to Absalom, "No; but the one whom the LORD and this people and all the Israelites have chosen, his I will be, and with him I will remain. ¹⁹Moreover, whom should I serve? Should it not be his son? Just as I have served your father, so I will serve you."

20 Then Absalom said to Ahithophel, "Give us your counsel; what shall we do?" ²¹Ahithophel said to Absalom, "Go in to your father's concubines, the ones he has left to look after the house; and all Israel will hear that you have made yourself odious to your father, and the hands of all who are with you will be strengthened." ²²So they pitched a tent for Absalom upon the roof; and Absalom went in to his father's concubines in the sight of all Israel. ²³Now in those days the

a Or *Merib-baal:* See 4.4 note   *b* Gk Vg: Heb *iniquity*
c Gk: Heb lacks *at the Jordan*   *d* Gk: Heb *all the people, the men of Israel*

counsel that Ahithophel gave was as if one consulted the oracle*a* of God; so all the counsel of Ahithophel was esteemed, both by David and by Absalom.

17 Moreover Ahithophel said to Absalom, "Let me choose twelve thousand men, and I will set out and pursue David tonight. 2I will come upon him while he is weary and discouraged, and throw him into a panic; and all the people who are with him will flee. I will strike down only the king, 3and I will bring all the people back to you as a bride comes home to her husband. You seek the life of only one man,*b* and all the people will be at peace." 4The advice pleased Absalom and all the elders of Israel.

16.15–17.29: Overcoming Ahithophel. 16.16–19: Hushai's words are duplicitous. When he says, *Long live the king* (v. 16), he means David. Similarly, when he affirms his loyalty to *the one whom the Lord and this people* have chosen, he also means David. In both cases, Absalom takes these statements as a reference to himself. **20–22:** By sleeping with David's concubines,★ Absalom makes his claim to the throne emphatic. His deed fulfills Nathan's oracle★ (12.12). **23:** The *counsel that Ahithophel gave* was very highly prized. His motive for joining Absalom is not certain, but it is possible that he was Bathsheba's grandfather (compare 11.3 and 23.34) and may have held a grudge against David for his treatment of Bathsheba and Uriah. **17.1–4:** *Ahithophel's* advice is to attack while David's forces are weak from fleeing.

---

5 Then Absalom said, "Call Hushai the Archite also, and let us hear too what he has to say." 6When Hushai came to Absalom, Absalom said to him, "This is what Ahithophel has said; shall we do as he advises? If not, you tell us." 7Then Hushai said to Absalom, "This time the counsel that Ahithophel has given is not good." 8Hushai continued, "You know that your father and his men are warriors, and that they are enraged, like a bear robbed of her cubs in the field. Besides, your father is expert in war; he will not spend the night with the troops. 9Even now he has hidden himself in one of the pits, or in some other place. And when some of our troops*c* fall at the first attack, whoever hears it will say, 'There has been a slaughter among the troops who follow Absalom.' 10Then even the valiant warrior, whose heart is like the heart of a lion, will utterly melt with fear; for all Israel knows that your father is a warrior, and that those who are with him are valiant warriors. 11But my counsel is that all Israel be gathered to you, from Dan to Beer-sheba, like the sand by the sea for multitude, and that you go to battle in person. 12So we shall come upon him in whatever place he may be found, and we shall light on him as the dew falls on the ground; and he will not survive, nor will any of those with him. 13If he withdraws into a city, then all Israel will bring ropes to that city, and we shall drag it into the valley, until not even a pebble is to be found there." 14Absalom and all the men of Israel said, "The counsel of Hushai the Archite is better than the counsel of Ahithophel." For the Lord had ordained to defeat the good counsel of Ahithophel, so that the Lord might bring ruin on Absalom.

15 Then Hushai said to the priests Zadok and Abiathar, "Thus and so did Ahithophel counsel Absalom and the elders of Israel; and thus and so I have counseled. 16Therefore send quickly and tell David, 'Do not lodge tonight at the fords of the wilderness, but by all means cross over; otherwise the king and all the people who are with him will be swallowed up.' " 17Jonathan and Ahimaaz were waiting at En-rogel; a servant-girl used to go and tell them, and they would go and tell King David; for they could not risk being seen entering the city. 18But a boy saw them, and told Absalom; so both of them went away quickly, and came to the house of a man at Bahurim, who had a well in his courtyard; and they went down into it. 19The man's wife took a covering, stretched it over the well's mouth, and spread out grain on it; and nothing was known of it. 20When Absalom's servants came to the woman at the house, they said, "Where are Ahimaaz and Jonathan?" The woman said to them, "They have crossed over the brook*d* of water." And when they had searched and could not find them, they returned to Jerusalem.

a Heb *word*   *b* Gk: Heb *like the return of the whole (is) the man whom you seek*   *c* Gk Mss: Heb *some of them*
d Meaning of Heb uncertain

21 After they had gone, the men came up out of the well, and went and told King David. They said to David, "Go and cross the water quickly; for thus and so has Ahithophel counseled against you." 22 So David and all the people who were with him set out and crossed the Jordan; by daybreak not one was left who had not crossed the Jordan.

23 When Ahithophel saw that his counsel was not followed, he saddled his donkey and went off home to his own city. He set his house in order, and hanged himself; he died and was buried in the tomb of his father.

24 Then David came to Mahanaim, while Absalom crossed the Jordan with all the men of Israel. 25 Now Absalom had set Amasa over the army in the place of Joab. Amasa was the son of a man named Ithra the Ishmaelite,[a] who had married Abigal daughter of Nahash, sister of Zeruiah, Joab's mother. 26 The Israelites and Absalom encamped in the land of Gilead.

27 When David came to Mahanaim, Shobi son of Nahash from Rabbah of the Ammonites, and Machir son of Ammiel from Lo-debar, and Barzillai the Gileadite from Rogelim, 28 brought beds, basins, and earthen vessels, wheat, barley, meal, parched grain, beans and lentils,[b] 29 honey and curds, sheep, and cheese from the herd, for David and the people with him to eat; for they said, "The troops are hungry and weary and thirsty in the wilderness."

17.5–29. 5–14: *Hushai* advises that Absalom wait and then attack David with the full force of *all Israel* (v. 11). Of course, Hushai is trying to give David time to recuperate and reorganize. He also plays on Absalom's ego, saying that all the people will follow him, and he can lead them into battle (v. 12). Even though Ahithophel's advice is obviously better than Hushai's, *the* LORD *had ordained* that Absalom would be persuaded to follow Hushai. **15–16:** *Hushai* sends word to David through the priests and their sons. He has bought David some time but urges him to cross the Jordan quickly and escape. **18–19:** The *well* was a simple pit; its opening could be covered with a blanket and *grain* spread over it for perfect camouflage. **23:** *Ahithophel* committed suicide perhaps because he knew that the end of Absalom's reign was imminent. **24:** *Mahanaim* was a site east of the Jordan that was easily defensible.

25: *Amasa* was David's nephew, the son of his sister *Zeruiah*. She is called the daughter of *Nahash* here rather than the daughter of Jesse. This may be a scribal error (Nahash occurs in v. 27), or Abigail may have been David's half-sister. **27:** This *Nahash* is the Ammonite king with whom David had a treaty (10.1–2). His son, *Shobi*, loyal to the treaty, now helps David in exile.

18 Then David mustered the men who were with him, and set over them commanders of thousands and commanders of hundreds. 2 And David divided the army into three groups:[c] one third under the command of Joab, one third under the command of Abishai son of Zeruiah, Joab's brother, and one third under the command of Ittai the Gittite. The king said to the men, "I myself will also go out with you." 3 But the men said, "You shall not go out. For if we flee, they will not care about us. If half of us die, they will not care about us. But you are worth ten thousand of us;[d] therefore it is better that you send us help from the city." 4 The king said to them, "Whatever seems best to you I will do." So the king stood at the side of the gate, while all the army marched out by hundreds and by thousands. 5 The king ordered Joab and Abishai and Ittai, saying, "Deal gently for my sake with the young man Absalom." And all the people heard when the king gave orders to all the commanders concerning Absalom.

6 So the army went out into the field against Israel; and the battle was fought in the forest of Ephraim. 7 The men of Israel were defeated there by the servants of David, and the slaughter there was great on that day, twenty thousand men. 8 The battle spread over the face of all the country; and the forest claimed more victims that day than the sword.

9 Absalom happened to meet the servants of David. Absalom was riding on his mule, and the mule went under the thick branches of a great oak. His head caught fast in the oak, and he was left hanging[e] between

a 1 Chr 2.17: Heb *Israelite*　　*b* Heb *and lentils and parched grain*　　*c* Gk: Heb *sent forth the army* *d* Gk Vg Symmachus: Heb *for now there are ten thousand such as we*　　*e* Gk Syr Tg: Heb *was put*

heaven and earth, while the mule that was under him went on. 10A man saw it, and told Joab, "I saw Absalom hanging in an oak." 11Joab said to the man who told him, "What, you saw him! Why then did you not strike him there to the ground? I would have been glad to give you ten pieces of silver and a belt." 12But the man said to Joab, "Even if I felt in my hand the weight of a thousand pieces of silver, I would not raise my hand against the king's son; for in our hearing the king commanded you and Abishai and Ittai, saying: For my sake protect the young man Absalom! 13On the other hand, if I had dealt treacherously against his life*a* (and there is nothing hidden from the king), then you yourself would have stood aloof." 14Joab said, "I will not waste time like this with you." He took three spears in his hand, and thrust them into the heart of Absalom, while he was still alive in the oak. 15And ten young men, Joab's armor-bearers, surrounded Absalom and struck him, and killed him.

16 Then Joab sounded the trumpet, and the troops came back from pursuing Israel, for Joab restrained the troops. 17They took Absalom, threw him into a great pit in the forest, and raised over him a very great heap of stones. Meanwhile all the Israelites fled to their homes. 18Now Absalom in his lifetime had taken and set up for himself a pillar that is in the King's Valley, for he said, "I have no son to keep my name in remembrance"; he called the pillar by his own name. It is called Absalom's Monument to this day.

18.1–19.10: The defeat and death of Absalom.
18.1–8: By following Hushai's advice to delay in Jerusalem, Absalom gave David the opportunity to regroup his forces and to choose the battle site. David and his men used the rugged *forest of Ephraim* to counter the larger numbers of Absalom's army. **9:** The *mule* was the royal mount for King David and his sons. Thus, Absalom's unseating from the mule symbolizes his loss of the kingdom. His predicament, being caught by the head, reminds one of his glorious hair (14.26) and suggests that his pride was his downfall. **14:** *Spears* may also be translated "sticks." Apparently, Joab stabbed or struck Absalom with them in order to dislodge him from the tree and finish him off (v. 15).

17: Burial under a *heap of stones* was a sign of a cursed person (Josh 7.26).

19 Then Ahimaaz son of Zadok said, "Let me run, and carry tidings to the king that the LORD has delivered him from the power of his enemies." 20Joab said to him, "You are not to carry tidings today; you may carry tidings another day, but today you shall not do so, because the king's son is dead." 21Then Joab said to a Cushite, "Go, tell the king what you have seen." The Cushite bowed before Joab, and ran. 22Then Ahimaaz son of Zadok said again to Joab, "Come what may, let me also run after the Cushite." And Joab said, "Why will you run, my son, seeing that you have no reward*b* for the tidings?" 23"Come what may," he said, "I will run." So he said to him, "Run." Then Ahimaaz ran by the way of the Plain, and outran the Cushite.

24 Now David was sitting between the two gates. The sentinel went up to the roof of the gate by the wall, and when he looked up, he saw a man running alone. 25The sentinel shouted and told the king. The king said, "If he is alone, there are tidings in his mouth." He kept coming, and drew near. 26Then the sentinel saw another man running; and the sentinel called to the gatekeeper and said, "See, another man running alone!" The king said, "He also is bringing tidings." 27The sentinel said, "I think the running of the first one is like the running of Ahimaaz son of Zadok." The king said, "He is a good man, and comes with good tidings."

28 Then Ahimaaz cried out to the king, "All is well!" He prostrated himself before the king with his face to the ground, and said, "Blessed be the LORD your God, who has delivered up the men who raised their hand against my lord the king." 29The king said, "Is it well with the young man Absalom?" Ahimaaz answered, "When Joab sent your servant,*c* I saw a great tumult, but I do not know what it was." 30The king said, "Turn aside, and stand here." So he turned aside, and stood still.

a Another reading is *at the risk of my life* *b* Meaning of Heb uncertain *c* Heb *the king's servant, your servant*

31 Then the Cushite came; and the Cushite said, "Good tidings for my lord the king! For the LORD has vindicated you this day, delivering you from the power of all who rose up against you." 32The king said to the Cushite, "Is it well with the young man Absalom?" The Cushite answered, "May the enemies of my lord the king, and all who rise up to do you harm, be like that young man."

33ª The king was deeply moved, and went up to the chamber over the gate, and wept; and as he went, he said, "O my son Absalom, my son, my son Absalom! Would I had died instead of you, O Absalom, my son, my son!"

19 It was told Joab, "The king is weeping and mourning for Absalom." 2So the victory that day was turned into mourning for all the troops; for the troops heard that day, "The king is grieving for his son." 3The troops stole into the city that day as soldiers steal in who are ashamed when they flee in battle. 4The king covered his face, and the king cried with a loud voice, "O my son Absalom, O Absalom, my son, my son!" 5Then Joab came into the house to the king, and said, "Today you have covered with shame the faces of all your officers who have saved your life today, and the lives of your sons and your daughters, and the lives of your wives and your concubines, 6for love of those who hate you and for hatred of those who love you. You have made it clear today that commanders and officers are nothing to you; for I perceive that if Absalom were alive and all of us were dead today, then you would be pleased. 7So go out at once and speak kindly to your servants; for I swear by the LORD, if you do not go, not a man will stay with you this night; and this will be worse for you than any disaster that has come upon you from your youth until now."

8Then the king got up and took his seat in the gate. The troops were all told, "See, the king is sitting in the gate"; and all the troops came before the king.

Meanwhile, all the Israelites had fled to their homes. 9All the people were disputing throughout all the tribes of Israel, saying, "The king delivered us from the hand of our enemies, and saved us from the hand of the Philistines; and now he has fled out of the land because of Absalom. 10But Absalom, whom we anointed over us, is dead in battle. Now therefore why do you say nothing about bringing the king back?"

11 King David sent this message to the priests Zadok and Abiathar, "Say to the elders of Judah, 'Why should you be the last to bring the king back to his house? The talk of all Israel has come to the king.ᵇ 12You are my kin, you are my bone and my flesh; why then should you be the last to bring back the king?' 13And say to Amasa, 'Are you not my bone and my flesh? So may God do to me, and more, if you are not the commander of my army from now on, in place of Joab.'" 14Amasaᶜ swayed the hearts of all the people of Judah as one, and they sent word to the king, "Return, both you and all your servants." 15So the king came back to the Jordan; and Judah came to Gilgal to meet the king and to bring him over the Jordan.

a Ch 19.1 in Heb   b Gk: Heb *to the king, to his house*
c Heb *He*

16 Shimei son of Gera, the Benjaminite, from Bahurim, hurried to come down with the people of Judah to meet King David; 17 with him were a thousand people from Benjamin. And Ziba, the servant of the house of Saul, with his fifteen sons and his twenty servants, rushed down to the Jordan ahead of the king, 18 while the crossing was taking place,^a to bring over the king's household, and to do his pleasure.

Shimei son of Gera fell down before the king, as he was about to cross the Jordan, 19 and said to the king, "May my lord not hold me guilty or remember how your servant did wrong on the day my lord the king left Jerusalem; may the king not bear it in mind. 20 For your servant knows that I have sinned; therefore, see, I have come this day, the first of all the house of Joseph to come down to meet my lord the king." 21 Abishai son of Zeruiah answered, "Shall not Shimei be put to death for this, because he cursed the LORD's anointed?" 22 But David said, "What have I to do with you, you sons of Zeruiah, that you should today become an adversary to me? Shall anyone be put to death in Israel this day? For do I not know that I am this day king over Israel?" 23 The king said to Shimei, "You shall not die." And the king gave him his oath.

19.16–23: *Shimei* and those with him were from the tribe of *Benjamin,* Saul's tribe. Shimei had ridiculed David when he fled from Jerusalem (16.5–13). Now that David is victorious, he asks forgiveness. He and the Benjaminites are the first of the Israelites or the *house of Joseph* (v. 20) to welcome David back. *Abishai* still wants to kill Shimei (16.9), but David refuses. It may have been customary for a new king to pardon criminals on the day of his coronation (see 1 Sam 11.13).

24 Mephibosheth^b grandson of Saul came down to meet the king; he had not taken care of his feet, or trimmed his beard, or washed his clothes, from the day the king left until the day he came back in safety. 25 When he came from Jerusalem to meet the king, the king said to him, "Why did you not go with me, Mephibosheth?"^b 26 He answered, "My lord, O king, my servant de-

ceived me; for your servant said to him, 'Saddle a donkey for me,^c so that I may ride on it and go with the king.' For your servant is lame. 27 He has slandered your servant to my lord the king. But my lord the king is like the angel of God; do therefore what seems good to you. 28 For all my father's house were doomed to death before my lord the king; but you set your servant among those who eat at your table. What further right have I, then, to appeal to the king?" 29 The king said to him, "Why speak any more of your affairs? I have decided: you and Ziba shall divide the land." 30 Mephibosheth^b said to the king, "Let him take it all, since my lord the king has arrived home safely."

19.24–30. 24: *Taken care of his feet* may mean trimmed his toenails, since the writer cites it as evidence that Merib-baal (*Mephibosheth*) had been mourning David's exile. **26–30:** *Ziba* had accused Merib-baal of plotting to take the throne (16.1–4). Merib-baal here defends himself, saying that Ziba refused to help him to flee with David, and he could not leave on his own accord because he is crippled. David's decision (v. 29) indicates that he does not know which of them is telling the truth.

31 Now Barzillai the Gileadite had come down from Rogelim; he went on with the king to the Jordan, to escort him over the Jordan. 32 Barzillai was a very aged man, eighty years old. He had provided the king with food while he stayed at Mahanaim, for he was a very wealthy man. 33 The king said to Barzillai, "Come over with me, and I will provide for you in Jerusalem at my side." 34 But Barzillai said to the king, "How many years have I still to live, that I should go up with the king to Jerusalem? 35 Today I am eighty years old; can I discern what is pleasant and what is not? Can your servant taste what he eats or what he drinks? Can I still listen to the voice of singing men and singing women? Why then should your servant be an added burden to my lord the king? 36 Your servant will go a little way over the Jordan with the king. Why should the king recom-

a Cn: Heb *the ford crossed*   *b* Or *Merib-baal:* See 4.4 note   *c* Gk Syr Vg: Heb *said, 'I will saddle a donkey for myself*

pense me with such a reward? 37Please let your servant return, so that I may die in my own town, near the graves of my father and my mother. But here is your servant Chimham; let him go over with my lord the king; and do for him whatever seems good to you." 38The king answered, "Chimham shall go over with me, and I will do for him whatever seems good to you; and all that you desire of me I will do for you." 39Then all the people crossed over the Jordan, and the king crossed over; the king kissed Barzillai and blessed him, and he returned to his own home. 40The king went on to Gilgal, and Chimham went on with him; all the people of Judah, and also half the people of Israel, brought the king on his way.

19.31–40: *Barzillai* had helped to provide for David in exile (17.27). David now invites him to come live in his palace in Jerusalem. Barzillai replies that he is too old to enjoy it but arranges for the king to take his son *Chimham* instead.

41 Then all the people of Israel came to the king, and said to him, "Why have our kindred the people of Judah stolen you away, and brought the king and his household over the Jordan, and all David's men with him?" 42All the people of Judah answered the people of Israel, "Because the king is near of kin to us. Why then are you angry over this matter? Have we eaten at all at the king's expense? Or has he given us any gift?" 43But the people of Israel answered the people of Judah, "We have ten shares in the king, and in David also we have more than you. Why then did you despise us? Were we not the first to speak of bringing back our king?" But the words of the people of Judah were fiercer than the words of the people of Israel.

19.41–43. 41: Because of David's invitation (vv. 11–12) the army (*people*) of Judah welcomes David back before the army of Israel. 42: The army of Judah denies that it has received any special favors or bribes from David. 43: The *ten shares* are the ten northern tribes of Israel.

20 Now a scoundrel named Sheba son of Bichri, a Benjaminite, happened to be there. He sounded the trumpet and cried out,

"We have no portion in David,
 no share in the son of Jesse!
Everyone to your tents, O Israel!"

2So all the people of Israel withdrew from David and followed Sheba son of Bichri; but the people of Judah followed their king steadfastly from the Jordan to Jerusalem.

3 David came to his house at Jerusalem; and the king took the ten concubines whom he had left to look after the house, and put them in a house under guard, and provided for them, but did not go in to them. So they were shut up until the day of their death, living as if in widowhood.

20.1–26: Sheba's revolt. 1: *Everyone to your tents* is an idiom for military demobilization. Sheba is calling for the army of Israel to withdraw from David. 2: *All the people of Israel* refers only to the northern tribes, as the rest of the verse shows. The phrase probably exaggerates the extent of the northern disaffection with David (see v. 21). 3: David no longer had sexual relations with the *ten concubines** he had left behind because Absalom had slept with them (16.20–22).

4 Then the king said to Amasa, "Call the men of Judah together to me within three days, and be here yourself." 5So Amasa went to summon Judah; but he delayed beyond the set time that had been appointed him. 6David said to Abishai, "Now Sheba son of Bichri will do us more harm than Absalom; take your lord's servants and pursue him, or he will find fortified cities for himself, and escape from us." 7Joab's men went out after him, along with the Cherethites, the Pelethites, and all the warriors; they went out from Jerusalem to pursue Sheba son of Bichri. 8When they were at the large stone that is in Gibeon, Amasa came to meet them. Now Joab was wearing a soldier's garment and over it was a belt with a sword in its sheath fastened at his waist; as he went forward it fell out. 9Joab said to Amasa, "Is it well with you, my brother?" And Joab took Amasa by the beard with his right hand to kiss him. 10But Amasa did not notice the sword in Joab's hand; Joab struck him in the belly so that his entrails poured out on the

ground, and he died. He did not strike a second blow.

Then Joab and his brother Abishai pursued Sheba son of Bichri. 11And one of Joab's men took his stand by Amasa, and said, "Whoever favors Joab, and whoever is for David, let him follow Joab." 12Amasa lay wallowing in his blood on the highway, and the man saw that all the people were stopping. Since he saw that all who came by him were stopping, he carried Amasa from the highway into a field, and threw a garment over him. 13Once he was removed from the highway, all the people went on after Joab to pursue Sheba son of Bichri.

20.4–13. 7: *The Cherethites* and *Pelethites* were the royal bodyguard. They were closely related to if not identical with the Philistines. 8–10: *Joab*'s assassination of *Amasa* is similar to his murder of Abner (3.26–39). His motive is not explained but presumably had to do with the fact that Amasa had taken Joab's place as army commander.

~~~

14 Sheba*a* passed through all the tribes of Israel to Abel of Beth-maacah;*b* and all the Bichrites*c* assembled, and followed him inside. 15Joab's forces*d* came and besieged him in Abel of Beth-maacah; they threw up a siege ramp against the city, and it stood against the rampart. Joab's forces were battering the wall to break it down. 16Then a wise woman called from the city, "Listen! Listen! Tell Joab, 'Come here, I want to speak to you.'" 17He came near her; and the woman said, "Are you Joab?" He answered, "I am." Then she said to him, "Listen to the words of your servant." He answered, "I am listening." 18Then she said, "They used to say in the old days, 'Let them inquire at Abel'; and so they would settle a matter. 19I am one of those who are peaceable and faithful in Israel; you seek to destroy a city that is a mother in Israel; why will you swallow up the heritage of the LORD?" 20Joab answered, "Far be it from me, far be it, that I should swallow up or destroy! 21That is not the case! But a man of the hill country of Ephraim, called Sheba son of Bichri, has lifted up his hand against King David; give him up alone, and I will withdraw from the

city." The woman said to Joab, "His head shall be thrown over the wall to you." 22Then the woman went to all the people with her wise plan. And they cut off the head of Sheba son of Bichri, and threw it out to Joab. So he blew the trumpet, and they dispersed from the city, and all went to their homes, while Joab returned to Jerusalem to the king.

23 Now Joab was in command of all the army of Israel;*e* Benaiah son of Jehoiada was in command of the Cherethites and the Pelethites; 24Adoram was in charge of the forced labor; Jehoshaphat son of Ahilud was the recorder; 25Sheva was secretary; Zadok and Abiathar were priests; 26and Ira the Jairite was also David's priest.

20.14–26. 14: *Abel* is at the northern extreme of Israel. 15: Ancient Israelite cities were surrounded by thick walls that had to be broken through with battering rams. 16: This *wise woman* is both intelligent and eloquent. She may have been a city official. 18–19: The woman says that *Abel* is one of Israel's original cities and should not be destroyed. 21: The woman does not know about Sheba, indicating that his revolt did not reach to all Israel but included only part of Benjamin and *the hill country of Ephraim*. 23–26: This cabinet list is very similar to the one in 8.16–18. It probably came to this location by attachment to 21.1–14. The *forced labor* was conscripted from the northern tribes by David and Solomon. Its leader, *Adoram* or Adoniram, was later stoned when the Israelites rebelled against the Davidic dynasty* (1 Kings 12.18).

~~~

21 Now there was a famine in the days of David for three years, year after year; and David inquired of the LORD. The LORD said, "There is bloodguilt on Saul and on his house, because he put the Gibeonites to death." 2So the king called the Gibeonites and spoke to them. (Now the Gibeonites were not of the people of Israel, but of the remnant of the Amorites; although the people of Israel had sworn to spare them, Saul had tried to wipe them out in his zeal for the people of Israel and Judah.) 3David said to the Gibeonites, "What shall I do for you?

---

a Heb *He*   *b* Compare 20.15: Heb *and Beth-maacah*
c Compare Gk Vg: Heb *Berites*   *d* Heb *They*
e Cn: Heb *Joab to all the army, Israel*

How shall I make expiation, that you may bless the heritage of the LORD?" 4The Gibeonites said to him, "It is not a matter of silver or gold between us and Saul or his house; neither is it for us to put anyone to death in Israel." He said, "What do you say that I should do for you?" 5They said to the king, "The man who consumed us and planned to destroy us, so that we should have no place in all the territory of Israel— 6let seven of his sons be handed over to us, and we will impale them before the LORD at Gibeon on the mountain of the LORD."*a* The king said, "I will hand them over."

7 But the king spared Mephibosheth,*b* the son of Saul's son Jonathan, because of the oath of the LORD that was between them, between David and Jonathan son of Saul. 8The king took the two sons of Rizpah daughter of Aiah, whom she bore to Saul, Armoni and Mephibosheth;*b* and the five sons of Merab*c* daughter of Saul, whom she bore to Adriel son of Barzillai the Meholathite; 9he gave them into the hands of the Gibeonites, and they impaled them on the mountain before the LORD. The seven of them perished together. They were put to death in the first days of harvest, at the beginning of barley harvest.

10 Then Rizpah the daughter of Aiah took sackcloth, and spread it on a rock for herself, from the beginning of harvest until rain fell on them from the heavens; she did not allow the birds of the air to come on the bodies*d* by day, or the wild animals by night. 11When David was told what Rizpah daughter of Aiah, the concubine of Saul, had done, 12David went and took the bones of Saul and the bones of his son Jonathan from the people of Jabesh-gilead, who had stolen them from the public square of Beth-shan, where the Philistines had hung them up, on the day the Philistines killed Saul on Gilboa. 13He brought up from there the bones of Saul and the bones of his son Jonathan; and they gathered the bones of those who had been impaled. 14They buried the bones of Saul and of his son Jonathan in the land of Benjamin in Zela, in the tomb of his father Kish; they did all that the king commanded. After that, God heeded supplications for the land.

21.1–14: The execution of Saul's heirs. 1–2: The *Gibeonites* had a special treaty with Israel (Josh 9). This story assumes that the violation of that treaty brought divine wrath. The Bible nowhere recounts Saul's attempted extermination of the Gibeonites. **3:** The LORD's *heritage* is both the land and the people of Israel. **4:** This is a matter for blood vengeance, but as resident aliens* in Israel the Gibeonites do not have that right. **5–9:** It was typical for the founder of a new dynasty* to annihilate the potential claimants from the previous dynasty. David does this here. Saul's alleged offense provides a religious legitimation for this political act. Only Merib-baal is spared (v. 7), probably because he was crippled and could not therefore be king, though this may also reflect David's affection for Jonathan. This story originally came before 9.1, in which David asks if anyone is left in Saul's house. The event took place early in David's reign over Israel. *Sons* (v. 6) may also include grandsons. *Mephibosheth* or Mephibaal in v. 8 is the proper reading. This was not Jonathan's son, Merib-baal, who was spared. The *barley harvest* was in April—May. **10:** *Rizpah* was Saul's concubine.* **11–14:** As a result of Rizpah's action, David tries to honor the memory of Saul and Jonathan. According to 1 Sam 31.12, their *bones* were burned. This is either a contradiction, or David gathered only their ashes.

15 The Philistines went to war again with Israel, and David went down together with his servants. They fought against the Philistines, and David grew weary. 16Ishbi-benob, one of the descendants of the giants, whose spear weighed three hundred shekels of bronze, and who was fitted out with new weapons,*e* said he would kill David. 17But Abishai son of Zeruiah came to his aid, and attacked the Philistine and killed him. Then David's men swore to him, "You shall not go out with us to battle any longer, so that you do not quench the lamp of Israel."

18 After this a battle took place with the Philistines, at Gob; then Sibbecai the Hushathite killed Saph, who was one of the descendants of the giants. 19Then there was another battle with the Philistines at Gob;

a Cn Compare Gk and 21.9: Heb *at Gibeah of Saul, the chosen of the* LORD   *b* Or *Merib-baal*: See 4.4 note
c Two Heb Mss Syr Compare Gk: MT *Michal*
d Heb *them*   *e* Heb *was belted anew*

and Elhanan son of Jaare-oregim, the Bethlehemite, killed Goliath the Gittite, the shaft of whose spear was like a weaver's beam. 20There was again war at Gath, where there was a man of great size, who had six fingers on each hand, and six toes on each foot, twenty-four in number; he too was descended from the giants. 21When he taunted Israel, Jonathan son of David's brother Shimei, killed him. 22These four were descended from the giants in Gath; they fell by the hands of David and his servants.

21.16–19. 16: *Three hundred shekels** was almost eight pounds. 19: Some of the information in this verse has been secondarily added to the story in 1 Sam 17.

22 David spoke to the LORD the words of this song on the day when the LORD delivered him from the hand of all his enemies, and from the hand of Saul. 2He said:

The LORD is my rock, my fortress, and
    my deliverer,
3   my God, my rock, in whom I take
      refuge,
my shield and the horn of my salvation,
    my stronghold and my refuge,
    my savior; you save me from violence.
4 I call upon the LORD, who is worthy to
    be praised,
    and I am saved from my enemies.

5 For the waves of death encompassed
    me,
    the torrents of perdition assailed me;
6 the cords of Sheol entangled me,
    the snares of death confronted me.

7 In my distress I called upon the LORD;
    to my God I called.
From his temple he heard my voice,
    and my cry came to his ears.

22.1–51: **A psalm of praise**. This psalm, which is the same as Psalm 18, was written long after David's time but is inserted here as appropriate to David's sentiments. 2–3: The image of the LORD as a protective *rock* is common in the Bible. 5–6: *Perdition* is a reference to the underworld, the abode of the dead, known in the Bible as *Sheol*. 7: The mention of the *temple* is an

indication that this psalm was written after David, since the Temple was built by Solomon.

---

8 Then the earth reeled and rocked;
    the foundations of the heavens
      trembled
    and quaked, because he was angry.
9 Smoke went up from his nostrils,
    and devouring fire from his mouth;
    glowing coals flamed forth from him.
10 He bowed the heavens, and came
      down;
    thick darkness was under his feet.
11 He rode on a cherub, and flew;
    he was seen upon the wings of the
      wind.
12 He made darkness around him a
      canopy,
    thick clouds, a gathering of water.
13 Out of the brightness before him
    coals of fire flamed forth.
14 The LORD thundered from heaven;
    the Most High uttered his voice.
15 He sent out arrows, and scattered them
    —lightning, and routed them.
16 Then the channels of the sea were
      seen,
    the foundations of the world were laid
      bare
at the rebuke of the LORD,
    at the blast of the breath of his
      nostrils.

22.8–16. 8: The LORD's appearance is accompanied by an earthquake. 9: The LORD is pictured here as a fire-breathing dragon. 11–16: The LORD is depicted here as the storm God. A *cherub* (v. 11) was a mythical, griffin-like creature. God's *voice* (v. 14) is thunder, and he throws lightning bolts at his enemies (v. 15). The psalmist envisions the world as flat and is trapped in the underworld beneath *the foundations of the world*, which the LORD's roar uncovers (v. 16).

---

17 He reached from on high, he took me,
    he drew me out of mighty waters.
18 He delivered me from my strong enemy,
    from those who hated me;
    for they were too mighty for me.
19 They came upon me in the day of my
    calamity,
    but the LORD was my stay.

20 He brought me out into a broad place;
 he delivered me, because he delighted
  in me.

21 The LORD rewarded me according to my
 righteousness;
 according to the cleanness of my
  hands he recompensed me.
22 For I have kept the ways of the LORD,
 and have not wickedly departed from
  my God.
23 For all his ordinances were before me,
 and from his statutes I did not turn
  aside.
24 I was blameless before him,
 and I kept myself from guilt.
25 Therefore the LORD has recompensed
 me according to my
  righteousness,
 according to my cleanness in his
  sight.

26 With the loyal you show yourself loyal;
 with the blameless you show yourself
  blameless;
27 with the pure you show yourself pure,
 and with the crooked you show
  yourself perverse.
28 You deliver a humble people,
 but your eyes are upon the haughty to
  bring them down.
29 Indeed, you are my lamp, O LORD,
 the LORD lightens my darkness.
30 By you I can crush a troop,
 and by my God I can leap over a
  wall.
31 This God—his way is perfect;
 the promise of the LORD proves true;
 he is a shield for all who take refuge
  in him.

32 For who is God, but the LORD?
 And who is a rock, except our God?
33 The God who has girded me with
 strength*a*
 has opened wide my path.*b*
34 He made my*c* feet like the feet of deer,
 and set me secure on the heights.
35 He trains my hands for war,
 so that my arms can bend a bow of
  bronze.

36 You have given me the shield of your
 salvation,
 and your help*d* has made me great.
37 You have made me stride freely,
 and my feet do not slip;
38 I pursued my enemies and destroyed
 them,
 and did not turn back until they were
  consumed.
39 I consumed them; I struck them down,
 so that they did not rise;
 they fell under my feet.
40 For you girded me with strength for the
 battle;
 you made my assailants sink under
  me.
41 You made my enemies turn their backs
 to me,
 those who hated me, and I destroyed
  them.
42 They looked, but there was no one to
 save them;
 they cried to the LORD, but he did
  not answer them.
43 I beat them fine like the dust of the
 earth,
 I crushed them and stamped them
  down like the mire of the streets.

22.32–37. 32: This is a monotheistic claim; the LORD
(Yahweh) alone is God. **33–37:** The LORD equips the
psalmist for battle.

~~~~~~~~~~~~~~~~~~~~~~~~~~~~~~~~~~~

44 You delivered me from strife with the
 peoples;*e*
 you kept me as the head of the
  nations;
 people whom I had not known served
  me.
45 Foreigners came cringing to me;
 as soon as they heard of me, they
  obeyed me.
46 Foreigners lost heart,
 and came trembling out of their
  strongholds.

a Q Ms Gk Syr Vg Compare Ps 18.32: MT *God is my
strong refuge* *b* Meaning of Heb uncertain
c Another reading is *his* *d* Q Ms: MT *your answering*
e Gk: Heb *from strife with my people*

47 The LORD lives! Blessed be my rock,
    and exalted be my God, the rock of
      my salvation,
48 the God who gave me vengeance
    and brought down peoples under
      me,
49 who brought me out from my enemies;
    you exalted me above my adversaries,
    you delivered me from the violent.

50 For this I will extol you, O LORD,
    among the nations,
    and sing praises to your name.
51 He is a tower of salvation for his king,
    and shows steadfast love to his
      anointed,
    to David and his descendants
      forever.

22.51: *Steadfast love* can also mean loyalty. *Anointed*⋆ was a title for the king; it is the word "messiah."⋆ The reference to *David and his descendants,* if original to the psalm, would indicate that it comes from royal circles in Judah.

23

Now these are the last words of David:
  The oracle of David, son of Jesse,
    the oracle of the man whom God
      exalted,ᵃ
  the anointed of the God of Jacob,
    the favorite of the Strong One of
      Israel:

2 The spirit of the LORD speaks through
    me,
    his word is upon my tongue.
3 The God of Israel has spoken,
    the Rock of Israel has said to me:
  One who rules over people justly,
    ruling in the fear of God,
4 is like the light of morning,
    like the sun rising on a cloudless
      morning,
    gleaming from the rain on the grassy
      land.

5 Is not my house like this with God?
    For he has made with me an
      everlasting covenant,

ordered in all things and secure.
  Will he not cause to prosper
    all my help and my desire?
6 But the godless areᵇ all like thorns that
    are thrown away;
    for they cannot be picked up with the
      hand;
7 to touch them one uses an iron bar
    or the shaft of a spear.
  And they are entirely consumed in
    fire on the spot.ᶜ

23.1–7: The last words of David. This is another poem attributed to David. Its date is uncertain. **3–4:** The image of the king as the sun was common in the ancient Near East, especially in Egypt, though it was less common in Israel. **5:** The *house* of the king is his dynasty.⋆ The *everlasting covenant*⋆ refers to the LORD's promise of an eternal dynasty for David in 2 Sam 7. **6–7:** These verses continue the image of vv. 3–4. The *godless* are like *thorns* consumed by the sun's heat.

8 These are the names of the warriors whom David had: Josheb-basshebeth a Tahchemonite; he was chief of the Three;ᵈ he wielded his spearᵉ against eight hundred whom he killed at one time.

9 Next to him among the three warriors was Eleazar son of Dodo son of Ahohi. He was with David when they defied the Philistines who were gathered there for battle. The Israelites withdrew, 10but he stood his ground. He struck down the Philistines until his arm grew weary, though his hand clung to the sword. The LORD brought about a great victory that day. Then the people came back to him—but only to strip the dead.

11 Next to him was Shammah son of Agee, the Hararite. The Philistines gathered together at Lehi, where there was a plot of ground full of lentils; and the army fled from the Philistines. 12But he took his stand in the middle of the plot, defended it, and killed the Philistines; and the LORD brought about a great victory.

ᵃ Q Ms: MT *who was raised on high*   ᵇ Heb *But worthlessness*   ᶜ Heb *in sitting*   ᵈ Gk Vg Compare 1 Chr 11.11: Meaning of Heb uncertain   ᵉ 1 Chr 11.11: Meaning of Heb uncertain

13 Towards the beginning of harvest three of the thirty[a] chiefs went down to join David at the cave of Adullam, while a band of Philistines was encamped in the valley of Rephaim. [14]David was then in the stronghold; and the garrison of the Philistines was then at Bethlehem. [15]David said longingly, "O that someone would give me water to drink from the well of Bethlehem that is by the gate!" [16]Then the three warriors broke through the camp of the Philistines, drew water from the well of Bethlehem that was by the gate, and brought it to David. But he would not drink of it; he poured it out to the LORD, [17]for he said, "The LORD forbid that I should do this. Can I drink the blood of the men who went at the risk of their lives?" Therefore he would not drink it. The three warriors did these things.

18 Now Abishai son of Zeruiah, the brother of Joab, was chief of the Thirty.[b] With his spear he fought against three hundred men and killed them, and won a name beside the Three. [19]He was the most renowned of the Thirty,[c] and became their commander; but he did not attain to the Three.

20 Benaiah son of Jehoiada was a valiant warrior[d] from Kabzeel, a doer of great deeds; he struck down two sons of Ariel[e] of Moab. He also went down and killed a lion in a pit on a day when snow had fallen. [21]And he killed an Egyptian, a handsome man. The Egyptian had a spear in his hand; but Benaiah went against him with a staff, snatched the spear out of the Egyptian's hand, and killed him with his own spear. [22]Such were the things Benaiah son of Jehoiada did, and won a name beside the three warriors. [23]He was renowned among the Thirty, but he did not attain to the Three. And David put him in charge of his bodyguard.

24 Among the Thirty were Asahel brother of Joab; Elhanan son of Dodo of Bethlehem; [25]Shammah of Harod; Elika of Harod; [26]Helez the Paltite; Ira son of Ikkesh of Tekoa; [27]Abiezer of Anathoth; Mebunnai the Hushathite; [28]Zalmon the Ahohite; Maharai of Netophah; [29]Heleb son of Baanah of Netophah; Ittai son of Ribai of Gibeah of the Ben-jaminites; [30]Benaiah of Pirathon; Hiddai of the torrents of Gaash; [31]Abi-albon the Arbathite; Azmaveth of Bahurim; [32]Eliahba of Shaalbon; the sons of Jashen: Jonathan [33]son of[f] Shammah the Hararite; Ahiam son of Sharar the Hararite; [34]Eliphelet son of Ahasbai of Maacah; Eliam son of Ahithophel the Gilonite; [35]Hezro[g] of Carmel; Paarai the Arbite; [36]Igal son of Nathan of Zobah; Bani the Gadite; [37]Zelek the Ammonite; Naharai of Beeroth, the armor-bearer of Joab son of Zeruiah; [38]Ira the Ithrite; Gareb the Ithrite; [39]Uriah the Hittite—thirty-seven in all.

23.8–39: David's heroes. 8–12: Nothing more is known about *the three* greatest warriors in David's army besides what is reported here. **13–17:** The story in these verses is not about the three warriors just listed but about three anonymous members of the honor guard of *the thirty*. At *the beginning of the harvest* (v. 13) the weather was hot and dry, which is why David became thirsty. The *stronghold* (v. 14) was the fortress at Adullam. Since a *garrison of the Philistines was then at Bethlehem,* this must have been early in David's reign. Bethlehem was David's hometown, which accounts for his fond remembrance of the water there. **16–17:** Pouring out the water was a way of honoring the three men. Water was often poured out as a libation or sacrifice to God. **20:** *Benaiah* was the commander of David's bodyguard and later of the army under Solomon. **24:** It is strange to find *Asahel* in this list since he seems to be a young warrior aspiring to greatness at the time of his death (2.18–23). *Elhanan* killed Goliath (21.19). **30:** This is a different *Benaiah* from the one in vv. 20–23. **39:** *Uriah* was Bathsheba's husband (ch. 11). It is uncertain how the count of *thirty-seven* is achieved. The addition of the "Three" plus Abishai and Benaiah brings the number to thirty-five. Joab may have been counted as a member of this elite group, though his name is not specifically mentioned. The list in vv. 24–39 has thirty names in it. But there are textual variations where an additional name may have been read.

~~~~~~~~~~~~~~~~~~~~~~~~~~~~~~~~~~~

a Heb adds *head*　　*b* Two Heb Mss Syr: MT *Three*　*c* Syr Compare 1 Chr 11.25: Heb *Was he the most renowned of the Three?*　　*d* Another reading is *the son of Ish-hai*　　*e* Gk: Heb lacks *sons of*　　*f* Gk: Heb lacks *son of*　　*g* Another reading is *Hezrai*

24 Again the anger of the LORD was kindled against Israel, and he incited David against them, saying, "Go, count the people of Israel and Judah." 2So the king said to Joab and the commanders of the army,[a] who were with him, "Go through all the tribes of Israel, from Dan to Beer-sheba, and take a census of the people, so that I may know how many there are." 3But Joab said to the king, "May the LORD your God increase the number of the people a hundredfold, while the eyes of my lord the king can still see it! But why does my lord the king want to do this?" 4But the king's word prevailed against Joab and the commanders of the army. So Joab and the commanders of the army went out from the presence of the king to take a census of the people of Israel. 5They crossed the Jordan, and began from[b] Aroer and from the city that is in the middle of the valley, toward Gad and on to Jazer. 6Then they came to Gilead, and to Kadesh in the land of the Hittites;[c] and they came to Dan, and from Dan[d] they went around to Sidon, 7and came to the fortress of Tyre and to all the cities of the Hivites and Canaanites; and they went out to the Negeb of Judah at Beer-sheba. 8So when they had gone through all the land, they came back to Jerusalem at the end of nine months and twenty days. 9Joab reported to the king the number of those who had been recorded: in Israel there were eight hundred thousand soldiers able to draw the sword, and those of Judah were five hundred thousand.

24.1–25: David's census. 1: *Again* implies that this story is the sequel to an earlier one, perhaps 21.1–14. This same story is found in 1 Chr 21, where v.1 says that Satan rather than the LORD *incited* David. A census provided the basis for conscription and taxation. The fact that a plague ensued suggests that some ritual taboo was broken. **2:** *From Dan to Beer-sheba* were the traditional northern and southern boundaries of Israel. **9:** The count is limited to men of military age. The Hebrew word translated *thousand* may refer to a much smaller military unit. Israel and Judah are numbered separately because Judah was exempted from taxation.

---

10 But afterward, David was stricken to the heart because he had numbered the people. David said to the LORD, "I have sinned greatly in what I have done. But now, O LORD, I pray you, take away the guilt of your servant; for I have done very foolishly." 11When David rose in the morning, the word of the LORD came to the prophet Gad, David's seer, saying, 12"Go and say to David: Thus says the LORD: Three things I offer[e] you; choose one of them, and I will do it to you." 13So Gad came to David and told him; he asked him, "Shall three[f] years of famine come to you on your land? Or will you flee three months before your foes while they pursue you? Or shall there be three days' pestilence in your land? Now consider, and decide what answer I shall return to the one who sent me." 14Then David said to Gad, "I am in great distress; let us fall into the hand of the LORD, for his mercy is great; but let me not fall into human hands."

15 So the LORD sent a pestilence on Israel from that morning until the appointed time; and seventy thousand of the people died, from Dan to Beer-sheba. 16But when the angel stretched out his hand toward Jerusalem to destroy it, the LORD relented concerning the evil, and said to the angel who was bringing destruction among the people, "It is enough; now stay your hand." The angel of the LORD was then by the threshing floor of Araunah the Jebusite. 17When David saw the angel who was destroying the people, he said to the LORD, "I alone have sinned, and I alone have done wickedly; but these sheep, what have they done? Let your hand, I pray, be against me and against my father's house."

18 That day Gad came to David and said to him, "Go up and erect an altar to the LORD on the threshing floor of Araunah the Jebusite." 19Following Gad's instructions, David went up, as the LORD had commanded. 20When Araunah looked down, he saw the king and his servants coming toward him; and Araunah went out and prostrated

---

a 1 Chr 21.2 Gk: Heb *to Joab the commander of the army* *b* Gk Mss: Heb *encamped in Aroer south of* *c* Gk: Heb *to the land of Tahtim-hodshi* *d* Cn Compare Gk: Heb *they came to Dan-jaan and* *e* Or *hold over* *f* 1 Chr 21.12 Gk: Heb *seven*

himself before the king with his face to the ground. 21Araunah said, "Why has my lord the king come to his servant?" David said, "To buy the threshing floor from you in order to build an altar to the LORD, so that the plague may be averted from the people." 22Then Araunah said to David, "Let my lord the king take and offer up what seems good to him; here are the oxen for the burnt offering, and the threshing sledges and the yokes of the oxen for the wood. 23All this, O king, Araunah gives to the king." And Araunah said to the king, "May the LORD your God respond favorably to you."

24 But the king said to Araunah, "No, but I will buy them from you for a price; I will not offer burnt offerings to the LORD my God that cost me nothing." So David bought the threshing floor and the oxen for fifty shekels of silver. 25David built there an altar to the LORD, and offered burnt offerings and offerings of well-being. So the LORD answered his supplication for the land, and the plague was averted from Israel.

24.10–25. 10–14: David is given a choice of three punishments. He chooses *the hand of the LORD*, an idiom for plague, trusting in the LORD's mercy. **15–16:** David's strategy works. The plague is stopped after only one day. *The appointed time* (v. 15) may be the time of the evening meal. *Evil* (v. 16) is not moral evil but destruction. *Araunah* is called Ornan in 1 Chr 21. A *threshing* floor* was a flat, high area where grain was separated from the chaff.* In the Bible, God often appears to people at threshing floors (Judg 6.11–12). **17:** The *sheep* are the people of Jerusalem. The image is of David, the king, as their shepherd. **18–25:** These verses indicate that the plague was stopped after David built his altar and made his offerings rather than by the LORD's free will as in v. 16. The site of David's altar is the location of the later altar of burnt offering of Solomon's Temple. *Fifty shekels** (v. 24) was about one and a quarter pounds.

1 KINGS

Introduction

The book of 1 Kings continues the narrative* of 1–2 Samuel. It begins with the account of David's death and the (unexpected) succession of his son Solomon (chs. 1–11). The deuteronomistic* author/editor gives a theological explanation (Solomon's sin) for the subsequent division of the kingdom. The account then alternates between kings of Israel and Judah. The Israelite kings are all wicked and continue in the "sin of Jeroboam," which the writer believes is the idolatry* at Bethel and other places of worship outside Jerusalem. Hence, one dynasty* after another falls. The kings of Judah fare slightly better, but this is mainly because of David's faithfulness and the LORD's promise to him of an enduring "house." The central part of the book (chs. 12–16), therefore, is a little like a list of kings that has been expanded by anecdotes. The final chapters, however, are filled with the fantastic exploits of prophets,* especially of the legendary* Elijah as he confronts his archenemy, Jezebel, the wife of King Ahab.

As with 1–2 Samuel, the final version of 1 Kings was produced in the Exile,* the writer trying to account theologically for the events of Israel's history. The division of the kingdom is the result of Solomon's sin (11.32–37). The kingdom of Judah lasted longer and was more stable than the kingdom of Israel because of David's loyalty and the LORD's promise. The standard practice whereby the founder of a new dynasty would annihilate the male rivals of the old is also given a theological framework by the author of 1 Kings in a series of prophecies and fulfillments. The stories of the prophets, including most of the ones about Elijah, do not reflect deuteronomistic editing and may have been added later. More than preachers or even oracle* givers, these prophets are miracle-working "men of God" whose stories are comparable to the legends surrounding early Christian saints.

READING GUIDE

The reader should be aware that the criteria by which the deuteronomistic historian evaluates the kings of Israel and Judah arose at a much later date. For instance, the idea that Jerusalem was the only legitimate place of worship (centralization) comes from the period of the final kings of Judah, at the earliest. 1 Kings, therefore, is primarily a work of theology, not of history. The history it conveys is interpreted through the eyes of a theologian. Nowhere is this clearer than with the presentation of the reign of Omri (16.21–28). Although he was likely the most important king of Israel, his reign is treated in very cursory fashion. The reign of his son Ahab, in contrast, receives a great deal of attention—but only because it is the setting of the great religious conflict between Elijah and Jezebel.

1–11   The reign of Solomon
12–16   The Israelite dynasties of Jeroboam and Baasha and their individual counterparts in Judah
17–22   The reign of Ahab and Jezebel and stories of Elijah and other prophets

1 King David was old and advanced in years; and although they covered him with clothes, he could not get warm. ²So his servants said to him, "Let a young virgin be sought for my lord the king, and let her wait on the king, and be his attendant; let her lie in your bosom, so that my lord the king may be warm." ³So they searched for a beautiful girl throughout all the territory of Israel, and found Abishag the Shunammite, and brought her to the king. ⁴The girl was very beautiful. She became the king's attendant and served him, but the king did not know her sexually.

5 Now Adonijah son of Haggith exalted himself, saying, "I will be king"; he prepared for himself chariots and horsemen, and fifty men to run before him. ⁶His father had never at any time displeased him by asking, "Why have you done thus and so?" He was also a very handsome man, and he was born next after Absalom. ⁷He conferred with Joab son of Zeruiah and with the priest Abiathar, and they supported Adonijah. ⁸But the priest Zadok, and Benaiah son of Jehoiada, and the prophet Nathan, and Shimei, and Rei, and David's own warriors did not side with Adonijah.

9 Adonijah sacrificed sheep, oxen, and fatted cattle by the stone Zoheleth, which is beside En-rogel, and he invited all his brothers, the king's sons, and all the royal officials of Judah, ¹⁰but he did not invite the prophet Nathan or Benaiah or the warriors or his brother Solomon.

1.1–53: Solomon succeeds David. 1–4: The choice of *Abishag* (v. 3) to *serve* David (v. 4) is a test of his virility. The fact that *he did not know her sexually* (v. 4) indicates that he is impotent and therefore no longer fit to be king. **5:** The knowledge of David's impotence spurs *Adonijah* to declare himself king. The *chariots and horsemen, and fifty men to run before him* were trappings of kingship (2 Sam 15.1). **6:** As the *next after Absalom*, Adonijah was David's oldest living son (see 2 Sam 3.2–5; nothing is known about Chileab, and many scholars assume he died in infancy). Therefore, he was by all rights the heir to the throne. **7–8:** The court is divided between those who support Adonijah for king (Joab and Abiathar, v. 7) and those who support Solomon (Zadok, Benaiah, and Nathan, among

others, v. 8). Since Adonijah was the rightful heir, it must be explained how Solomon came to succeed David. That is the topic of the rest of the chapter. **9–10:** Adonijah holds a sacrifice to celebrate his coronation. Such sacrifices were like banquets because the meat from the sacrificed animals was eaten. Adonijah recognized Solomon as his rival and did not invite him or those who supported him to the sacrifice.

11 Then Nathan said to Bathsheba, Solomon's mother, "Have you not heard that Adonijah son of Haggith has become king and our lord David does not know it? ¹²Now therefore come, let me give you advice, so that you may save your own life and the life of your son Solomon. ¹³Go in at once to King David, and say to him, 'Did you not, my lord the king, swear to your servant, saying: Your son Solomon shall succeed me as king, and he shall sit on my throne? Why then is Adonijah king?' ¹⁴Then while you are still there speaking with the king, I will come in after you and confirm your words."

15 So Bathsheba went to the king in his room. The king was very old; Abishag the Shunammite was attending the king. ¹⁶Bathsheba bowed and did obeisance to the king, and the king said, "What do you wish?" ¹⁷She said to him, "My lord, you swore to your servant by the LORD your God, saying: Your son Solomon shall succeed me as king, and he shall sit on my throne. ¹⁸But now suddenly Adonijah has become king, though you, my lord the king, do not know it. ¹⁹He has sacrificed oxen, fatted cattle, and sheep in abundance, and has invited all the children of the king, the priest Abiathar, and Joab the commander of the army; but your servant Solomon he has not invited. ²⁰But you, my lord the king—the eyes of all Israel are on you to tell them who shall sit on the throne of my lord the king after him. ²¹Otherwise it will come to pass, when my lord the king sleeps with his ancestors, that my son Solomon and I will be counted offenders."

1.11–21. 11: It is surprising to find Nathan and Bathsheba in cahoots; when they were mentioned together previously (2 Sam 11–12), Nathan was condemning David for his adultery with Bathsheba and murder of her husband. **12:** Nathan advises Bathsheba on how

to *save your own life and the life of your son Solomon.*
The lives of Bathsheba and Solomon were in danger if
Adonijah became king, since new kings customarily
killed off all their potential rivals (compare v. 21).
17: The promise Bathsheba cites here is not recorded
elsewhere and may be fictional. She may be taking
advantage of David's senility in order to have Solomon
declared king.

22 While she was still speaking with the
king, the prophet Nathan came in. 23 The
king was told, "Here is the prophet Nathan."
When he came in before the king, he did
obeisance to the king, with his face to the
ground. 24 Nathan said, "My lord the king,
have you said, 'Adonijah shall succeed me as
king, and he shall sit on my throne'? 25 For
today he has gone down and has sacrificed
oxen, fatted cattle, and sheep in abundance,
and has invited all the king's children, Joab
the commander*a* of the army, and the priest
Abiathar, who are now eating and drinking
before him, and saying, 'Long live King
Adonijah!' 26 But he did not invite me, your
servant, and the priest Zadok, and Benaiah
son of Jehoiada, and your servant Solomon.
27 Has this thing been brought about by my
lord the king and you have not let your servants know who should sit on the throne of
my lord the king after him?"

28 King David answered, "Summon
Bathsheba to me." So she came into the
king's presence, and stood before the king.
29 The king swore, saying, "As the LORD lives,
who has saved my life from every adversity,
30 as I swore to you by the LORD, the God of
Israel, 'Your son Solomon shall succeed me
as king, and he shall sit on my throne in my
place,' so will I do this day." 31 Then Bathsheba bowed with her face to the ground,
and did obeisance to the king, and said,
"May my lord King David live forever!"

32 King David said, "Summon to me the
priest Zadok, the prophet Nathan, and Benaiah son of Jehoiada." When they came before the king, 33 the king said to them, "Take
with you the servants of your lord, and have
my son Solomon ride on my own mule, and
bring him down to Gihon. 34 There let the
priest Zadok and the prophet Nathan anoint
him king over Israel; then blow the trumpet,

and say, 'Long live King Solomon!' 35 You
shall go up following him. Let him enter and
sit on my throne; he shall be king in my
place; for I have appointed him to be ruler
over Israel and over Judah." 36 Benaiah son
of Jehoiada answered the king, "Amen! May
the LORD, the God of my lord the king, so
ordain. 37 As the LORD has been with my lord
the king, so may he be with Solomon, and
make his throne greater than the throne of
my lord King David."

1.22–37. 28–32: The movements of Bathsheba and
Nathan are confusing and may indicate editorial work
of some sort. As it stands, the reader must assume that
each of them leaves the king's presence when he interviews the other. **33:** The *mule* was the royal mount
(2 Sam 18.9). The *Gihon* spring was the water source
for the city of Jerusalem.

38 So the priest Zadok, the prophet Nathan, and Benaiah son of Jehoiada, and the
Cherethites and the Pelethites, went down
and had Solomon ride on King David's mule,
and led him to Gihon. 39 There the priest Zadok took the horn of oil from the tent and
anointed Solomon. Then they blew the
trumpet, and all the people said, "Long live
King Solomon!" 40 And all the people went
up following him, playing on pipes and rejoicing with great joy, so that the earth
quaked at their noise.

41 Adonijah and all the guests who were
with him heard it as they finished feasting.
When Joab heard the sound of the trumpet,
he said, "Why is the city in an uproar?"
42 While he was still speaking, Jonathan son
of the priest Abiathar arrived. Adonijah said,
"Come in, for you are a worthy man and
surely you bring good news." 43 Jonathan answered Adonijah, "No, for our lord King David has made Solomon king; 44 the king has
sent with him the priest Zadok, the prophet
Nathan, and Benaiah son of Jehoiada, and
the Cherethites and the Pelethites; and they
had him ride on the king's mule; 45 the priest
Zadok and the prophet Nathan have
anointed him king at Gihon; and they have
gone up from there rejoicing, so that the city

a Gk: Heb *the commanders*

is in an uproar. This is the noise that you heard. ⁴⁶Solomon now sits on the royal throne. ⁴⁷Moreover the king's servants came to congratulate our lord King David, saying, 'May God make the name of Solomon more famous than yours, and make his throne greater than your throne.' The king bowed in worship on the bed ⁴⁸and went on to pray thus, 'Blessed be the LORD, the God of Israel, who today has granted one of my offspring^a to sit on my throne and permitted me to witness it.' "

49 Then all the guests of Adonijah got up trembling and went their own ways. ⁵⁰Adonijah, fearing Solomon, got up and went to grasp the horns of the altar. ⁵¹Solomon was informed, "Adonijah is afraid of King Solomon; see, he has laid hold of the horns of the altar, saying, 'Let King Solomon swear to me first that he will not kill his servant with the sword.' " ⁵²So Solomon responded, "If he proves to be a worthy man, not one of his hairs shall fall to the ground; but if wickedness is found in him, he shall die." ⁵³Then King Solomon sent to have him brought down from the altar. He came to do obeisance to King Solomon; and Solomon said to him, "Go home."

1.38–53. 38: *The Cherethites and Pelethites* were the royal bodyguard; they were Philistines or associated with the Philistines. **39:** Anointing⋆ was a way of designating a person for some special office. It involved dripping or smearing fine olive oil on the person's head. **50:** The *horns of the altar* were projections from each corner of a sacrificial altar. Since the altar was holy, grasping the horns was a way of seeking sanctuary from execution.

2 When David's time to die drew near, he charged his son Solomon, saying: ²"I am about to go the way of all the earth. Be strong, be courageous, ³and keep the charge of the LORD your God, walking in his ways and keeping his statutes, his commandments, his ordinances, and his testimonies, as it is written in the law of Moses, so that you may prosper in all that you do and wherever you turn. ⁴Then the LORD will establish his word that he spoke concerning me: 'If your heirs take heed to their way, to walk before me in faithfulness with all their heart and with all their soul, there shall not fail you a successor on the throne of Israel.'

5 "Moreover you know also what Joab son of Zeruiah did to me, how he dealt with the two commanders of the armies of Israel, Abner son of Ner, and Amasa son of Jether, whom he murdered, retaliating in time of peace for blood that had been shed in war, and putting the blood of war on the belt around his waist, and on the sandals on his feet. ⁶Act therefore according to your wisdom, but do not let his gray head go down to Sheol in peace. ⁷Deal loyally, however, with the sons of Barzillai the Gileadite, and let them be among those who eat at your table; for with such loyalty they met me when I fled from your brother Absalom. ⁸There is also with you Shimei son of Gera, the Benjaminite from Bahurim, who cursed me with a terrible curse on the day when I went to Mahanaim; but when he came down to meet me at the Jordan, I swore to him by the LORD, 'I will not put you to death with the sword.' ⁹Therefore do not hold him guiltless, for you are a wise man; you will know what you ought to do to him, and you must bring his gray head down with blood to Sheol."

2.1–46: Solomon deals with his rivals. 1–4: David's charge to Solomon is in deuteronomistic⋆ style and is typical of the charges that one leader gives to another in the Deuteronomistic History, especially Moses' charge to Joshua and the people (Deut 4.40; 32.23). **5–9:** David's orders justify Solomon's actions in the rest of the chapter. He is told to execute Joab because of Joab's murders of Abner (2 Sam 3.26–30) and Amasa (2 Sam 20.4–10). However, these murders were committed years earlier, so that punishing Joab at this point makes little sense. Solomon's true motive for Joab's execution was political—Joab had supported Adonijah. *Sheol*⋆ (v. 6) was the abode of the dead. *Barzillai* had helped David when he fled from Absalom (2 Sam 17.27), and David had promised to take care of Barzillai's son as a reward (2 Sam 19.31–40). *Shimei* had cursed David when he fled from Absalom (2 Sam 16.5–8) and then apologized when David returned victorious (2 Sam 19.16–23).

a Gk: Heb *one*

10 Then David slept with his ancestors, and was buried in the city of David. [11] The time that David reigned over Israel was forty years; he reigned seven years in Hebron, and thirty-three years in Jerusalem. [12] So Solomon sat on the throne of his father David; and his kingdom was firmly established.

13 Then Adonijah son of Haggith came to Bathsheba, Solomon's mother. She asked, "Do you come peaceably?" He said, "Peaceably." [14] Then he said, "May I have a word with you?" She said, "Go on." [15] He said, "You know that the kingdom was mine, and that all Israel expected me to reign; however, the kingdom has turned about and become my brother's, for it was his from the LORD. [16] And now I have one request to make of you; do not refuse me." She said to him, "Go on." [17] He said, "Please ask King Solomon—he will not refuse you—to give me Abishag the Shunammite as my wife." [18] Bathsheba said, "Very well; I will speak to the king on your behalf."

19 So Bathsheba went to King Solomon, to speak to him on behalf of Adonijah. The king rose to meet her, and bowed down to her; then he sat on his throne, and had a throne brought for the king's mother, and she sat on his right. [20] Then she said, "I have one small request to make of you; do not refuse me." And the king said to her, "Make your request, my mother; for I will not refuse you." [21] She said, "Let Abishag the Shunammite be given to your brother Adonijah as his wife." [22] King Solomon answered his mother, "And why do you ask Abishag the Shunammite for Adonijah? Ask for him the kingdom as well! For he is my elder brother; ask not only for him but also for the priest Abiathar and for Joab son of Zeruiah!" [23] Then King Solomon swore by the LORD, "So may God do to me, and more also, for Adonijah has devised this scheme at the risk of his life! [24] Now therefore as the LORD lives, who has established me and placed me on the throne of my father David, and who has made me a house as he promised, today Adonijah shall be put to death." [25] So King Solomon sent Benaiah son of Jehoiada; he struck him down, and he died.

2.10–25. 10–12: David's death and burial. *Forty years* (v. 11) is often a round number for a generation in the Bible. **12–25:** The story of Adonijah's request is not very believable. To take a member of the harem, such as Abishag, would be a blatant play for the throne. Adonijah would hardly have been foolish enough to make such a request with Solomon in power. Besides, he could not have chosen a worse advocate than the king's own mother. Solomon's true motive for having Adonijah killed was again political; he was removing his rival for kingship.

26 The king said to the priest Abiathar, "Go to Anathoth, to your estate; for you deserve death. But I will not at this time put you to death, because you carried the ark of the Lord GOD before my father David, and because you shared in all the hardships my father endured." [27] So Solomon banished Abiathar from being priest to the LORD, thus fulfilling the word of the LORD that he had spoken concerning the house of Eli in Shiloh.

2.26–27: Abiathar was the only supporter Adonijah had not killed, apparently because he was a priest. He was banished instead. The prophecy *concerning the house of Eli in Shiloh* is in 1 Sam 2.27–36. This story also explains the dominance of the Zadokite priests in Jerusalem at the expense of their rivals in the line of Eli.

28 When the news came to Joab—for Joab had supported Adonijah though he had not supported Absalom—Joab fled to the tent of the LORD and grasped the horns of the altar. [29] When it was told King Solomon, "Joab has fled to the tent of the LORD and now is beside the altar," Solomon sent Benaiah son of Jehoiada, saying, "Go, strike him down." [30] So Benaiah came to the tent of the LORD and said to him, "The king commands, 'Come out.'" But he said, "No, I will die here." Then Benaiah brought the king word again, saying, "Thus said Joab, and thus he answered me." [31] The king replied to him, "Do as he has said, strike him down and bury him; and thus take away from me and from my father's house the guilt for the blood that Joab shed without cause. [32] The LORD will bring back his bloody deeds on his own

head, because, without the knowledge of my father David, he attacked and killed with the sword two men more righteous and better than himself, Abner son of Ner, commander of the army of Israel, and Amasa son of Jether, commander of the army of Judah. 33 So shall their blood come back on the head of Joab and on the head of his descendants forever; but to David, and to his descendants, and to his house, and to his throne, there shall be peace from the LORD forevermore." 34 Then Benaiah son of Jehoiada went up and struck him down and killed him; and he was buried at his own house near the wilderness. 35 The king put Benaiah son of Jehoiada over the army in his place, and the king put the priest Zadok in the place of Abiathar.

36 Then the king sent and summoned Shimei, and said to him, "Build yourself a house in Jerusalem, and live there, and do not go out from there to any place whatever. 37 For on the day you go out, and cross the Wadi Kidron, know for certain that you shall die; your blood shall be on your own head." 38 And Shimei said to the king, "The sentence is fair; as my lord the king has said, so will your servant do." So Shimei lived in Jerusalem many days.

39 But it happened at the end of three years that two of Shimei's slaves ran away to King Achish son of Maacah of Gath. When it was told Shimei, "Your slaves are in Gath," 40 Shimei arose and saddled a donkey, and went to Achish in Gath, to search for his slaves; Shimei went and brought his slaves from Gath. 41 When Solomon was told that Shimei had gone from Jerusalem to Gath and returned, 42 the king sent and summoned Shimei, and said to him, "Did I not make you swear by the LORD, and solemnly adjure you, saying, 'Know for certain that on the day you go out and go to any place whatever, you shall die'? And you said to me, 'The sentence is fair; I accept.' 43 Why then have you not kept your oath to the LORD and the commandment with which I charged you?" 44 The king also said to Shimei, "You know in your own heart all the evil that you did to my father David; so the LORD will bring back your evil on your own head. 45 But King Sol-

omon shall be blessed, and the throne of David shall be established before the LORD forever." 46 Then the king commanded Benaiah son of Jehoiada; and he went out and struck him down, and he died.

So the kingdom was established in the hand of Solomon.

2.28–46. 28–35: Joab is executed, ostensibly at David's command, despite his plea for sanctuary at the *horns of the altar* (v. 28; see 1.50). **36–46a:** Solomon confined Shimei to Jerusalem, perhaps to prevent him from causing any trouble in his home tribe of Benjamin (also Saul's tribe). When he violated his confinement, Solomon had him executed. **46b:** *The kingdom was established in the hand of Solomon* because all his rivals were removed.

---

3 Solomon made a marriage alliance with Pharaoh king of Egypt; he took Pharaoh's daughter and brought her into the city of David, until he had finished building his own house and the house of the LORD and the wall around Jerusalem. 2 The people were sacrificing at the high places, however, because no house had yet been built for the name of the LORD.

3 Solomon loved the LORD, walking in the statutes of his father David; only, he sacrificed and offered incense at the high places. 4 The king went to Gibeon to sacrifice there, for that was the principal high place; Solomon used to offer a thousand burnt offerings on that altar. 5 At Gibeon the LORD appeared to Solomon in a dream by night; and God said, "Ask what I should give you." 6 And Solomon said, "You have shown great and steadfast love to your servant my father David, because he walked before you in faithfulness, in righteousness, and in uprightness of heart toward you; and you have kept for him this great and steadfast love, and have given him a son to sit on his throne today. 7 And now, O LORD my God, you have made your servant king in place of my father David, although I am only a little child; I do not know how to go out or come in. 8 And your servant is in the midst of the people whom you have chosen, a great people, so numerous they cannot be numbered or counted. 9 Give your servant therefore an un-

derstanding mind to govern your people, able to discern between good and evil; for who can govern this your great people?"

10 It pleased the Lord that Solomon had asked this. 11God said to him, "Because you have asked this, and have not asked for yourself long life or riches, or for the life of your enemies, but have asked for yourself understanding to discern what is right, 12I now do according to your word. Indeed I give you a wise and discerning mind; no one like you has been before you and no one like you shall arise after you. 13I give you also what you have not asked, both riches and honor all your life; no other king shall compare with you. 14If you will walk in my ways, keeping my statutes and my commandments, as your father David walked, then I will lengthen your life."

15 Then Solomon awoke; it had been a dream. He came to Jerusalem where he stood before the ark of the covenant of the LORD. He offered up burnt offerings and offerings of well-being, and provided a feast for all his servants.

3.1–15: Solomon's gift of wisdom. 1: A *marriage alliance* was a treaty sealed with a marriage, a common practice in the ancient Near East. This verse anticipates 11.1, where foreign women prove to be Solomon's undoing. **2–4:** *High places* were raised platforms where worship took place. They are usually condemned in the Bible. But these verses explain that the use of them during Solomon's early reign, especially his use of the one at Gibeon, was permissible since the Temple* had not yet been built. Solomon's actions here may be a dream incubation—a way of seeking divine revelation through a dream by petitioning a deity and then sleeping at that god's shrine. **5–9:** Solomon's reference to himself as *a little child* (v. 7) expresses his feelings of being overwhelmed by his responsibility as king and is not to be taken literally. He requests *an understanding mind* in order to *govern* (lit., "judge") the numerous people of Israel. **10–14:** The LORD grants Solomon's request and promises him wealth as well. Thus, Solomon's traditional wisdom and magnificence are explained as gifts from God.

---

16 Later, two women who were prostitutes came to the king and stood before him.

17The one woman said, "Please, my lord, this woman and I live in the same house; and I gave birth while she was in the house. 18Then on the third day after I gave birth, this woman also gave birth. We were together; there was no one else with us in the house, only the two of us were in the house. 19Then this woman's son died in the night, because she lay on him. 20She got up in the middle of the night and took my son from beside me while your servant slept. She laid him at her breast, and laid her dead son at my breast. 21When I rose in the morning to nurse my son, I saw that he was dead; but when I looked at him closely in the morning, clearly it was not the son I had borne." 22But the other woman said, "No, the living son is mine, and the dead son is yours." The first said, "No, the dead son is yours, and the living son is mine." So they argued before the king.

23 Then the king said, "The one says, 'This is my son that is alive, and your son is dead'; while the other says, 'Not so! Your son is dead, and my son is the living one.'" 24So the king said, "Bring me a sword," and they brought a sword before the king. 25The king said, "Divide the living boy in two; then give half to the one, and half to the other." 26But the woman whose son was alive said to the king—because compassion for her son burned within her—"Please, my lord, give her the living boy; certainly do not kill him!" The other said, "It shall be neither mine nor yours; divide it." 27Then the king responded: "Give the first woman the living boy; do not kill him. She is his mother." 28All Israel heard of the judgment that the king had rendered; and they stood in awe of the king, because they perceived that the wisdom of God was in him, to execute justice.

3.16–28: An illustration of Solomon's wisdom. The king served as a kind of "supreme court," and it was his responsibility to see that justice was equitably disbursed in the land. This seemingly impossible case shows Solomon's great wisdom in judgment.

---

4 King Solomon was king over all Israel, 2and these were his high officials: Azariah son of Zadok was the priest; 3Elihoreph

and Ahijah sons of Shisha were secretaries; Jehoshaphat son of Ahilud was recorder; [4]Benaiah son of Jehoiada was in command of the army; Zadok and Abiathar were priests; [5]Azariah son of Nathan was over the officials; Zabud son of Nathan was priest and king's friend; [6]Ahishar was in charge of the palace; and Adoniram son of Abda was in charge of the forced labor.

7 Solomon had twelve officials over all Israel, who provided food for the king and his household; each one had to make provision for one month in the year. [8]These were their names: Ben-hur, in the hill country of Ephraim; [9]Ben-deker, in Makaz, Shaalbim, Beth-shemesh, and Elon-beth-hanan; [10]Ben-hesed, in Arubboth (to him belonged Socoh and all the land of Hepher); [11]Benabinadab, in all Naphath-dor (he had Taphath, Solomon's daughter, as his wife); [12]Baana son of Ahilud, in Taanach, Megiddo, and all Beth-shean, which is beside Zarethan below Jezreel, and from Bethshean to Abel-meholah, as far as the other side of Jokmeam; [13]Ben-geber, in Ramothgilead (he had the villages of Jair son of Manasseh, which are in Gilead, and he had the region of Argob, which is in Bashan, sixty great cities with walls and bronze bars); [14]Ahinadab son of Iddo, in Mahanaim; [15]Ahimaaz, in Naphtali (he had taken Basemath, Solomon's daughter, as his wife); [16]Baana son of Hushai, in Asher and Bealoth; [17]Jehoshaphat son of Paruah, in Issachar; [18]Shimei son of Ela, in Benjamin; [19]Geber son of Uri, in the land of Gilead, the country of King Sihon of the Amorites and of King Og of Bashan. And there was one official in the land of Judah.

20 Judah and Israel were as numerous as the sand by the sea; they ate and drank and were happy. [21]ᵃSolomon was sovereign over all the kingdoms from the Euphrates to the land of the Philistines, even to the border of Egypt; they brought tribute and served Solomon all the days of his life.

ince had to provide for the king one month in the year (v. 7). Judah is listed separately (v. 19) because it was exempted from taxation as David's and Solomon's home tribe. **20–21:** This is an idealized statement, as the revolt immediately after Solomon's death indicates. The extent of his actual rule may also be exaggerated here.

22 Solomon's provision for one day was thirty cors of choice flour, and sixty cors of meal, [23]ten fat oxen, and twenty pasture-fed cattle, one hundred sheep, besides deer, gazelles, roebucks, and fatted fowl. [24]For he had dominion over all the region west of the Euphrates from Tiphsah to Gaza, over all the kings west of the Euphrates; and he had peace on all sides. [25]During Solomon's lifetime Judah and Israel lived in safety, from Dan even to Beer-sheba, all of them under their vines and fig trees. [26]Solomon also had forty thousand stalls of horses for his chariots, and twelve thousand horsemen. [27]Those officials supplied provisions for King Solomon and for all who came to King Solomon's table, each one in his month; they let nothing be lacking. [28]They also brought to the required place barley and straw for the horses and swift steeds, each according to his charge.

29 God gave Solomon very great wisdom, discernment, and breadth of understanding as vast as the sand on the seashore, [30]so that Solomon's wisdom surpassed the wisdom of all the people of the east, and all the wisdom of Egypt. [31]He was wiser than anyone else, wiser than Ethan the Ezrahite, and Heman, Calcol, and Darda, children of Mahol; his fame spread throughout all the surrounding nations. [32]He composed three thousand proverbs, and his songs numbered a thousand and five. [33]He would speak of trees, from the cedar that is in the Lebanon to the hyssop that grows in the wall; he would speak of animals, and birds, and reptiles, and fish. [34]People came from all the nations to hear the wisdom of Solomon; they came from all the kings of the earth who had heard of his wisdom.

4.1–34: Solomon's administration. 1–6: Similar lists are found for David's cabinet in 2 Sam 8.15–18; 20.23–26. **7–19:** Solomon reorganized Israel into twelve provinces for purposes of taxation. Each prov-

a Ch 5.1 in Heb

4.22–34. 22–28: A *cor* (v. 22) was about eleven bushels. *From Dan to Beer-sheba* (v. 25) marked the traditional boundaries of Israel and Judah. The expression *all of them under their vine and fig trees* was an idiom for tranquillity and agricultural prosperity. **29–34:** Solomon's legendary* wisdom is said to exceed that of *the people of the east,* which is probably a reference to Mesopotamia (roughly modern Iraq), and *of Egypt* (v. 30), the two great civilizations of the ancient Near East. Wisdom in the sense used here involved not only wise judgment but also the composition of wisdom literature,* such as proverbs, and the observation of the natural world (vv. 32–33).

5 *a* Now King Hiram of Tyre sent his servants to Solomon, when he heard that they had anointed him king in place of his father; for Hiram had always been a friend to David. 2 Solomon sent word to Hiram, saying, 3 "You know that my father David could not build a house for the name of the LORD his God because of the warfare with which his enemies surrounded him, until the LORD put them under the soles of his feet. *b* 4 But now the LORD my God has given me rest on every side; there is neither adversary nor misfortune. 5 So I intend to build a house for the name of the LORD my God, as the LORD said to my father David, 'Your son, whom I will set on your throne in your place, shall build the house for my name.' 6 Therefore command that cedars from the Lebanon be cut for me. My servants will join your servants, and I will give you whatever wages you set for your servants; for you know that there is no one among us who knows how to cut timber like the Sidonians."

7 When Hiram heard the words of Solomon, he rejoiced greatly, and said, "Blessed be the LORD today, who has given to David a wise son to be over this great people." 8 Hiram sent word to Solomon, "I have heard the message that you have sent to me; I will fulfill all your needs in the matter of cedar and cypress timber. 9 My servants shall bring it down to the sea from the Lebanon; I will make it into rafts to go by sea to the place you indicate. I will have them broken up there for you to take away. And you shall meet my needs by providing food for my household." 10 So Hiram supplied Solomon's every need for timber of cedar and cypress. 11 Solomon in turn gave Hiram twenty thousand cors of wheat as food for his household, and twenty cors of fine oil. Solomon gave this to Hiram year by year. 12 So the LORD gave Solomon wisdom, as he promised him. There was peace between Hiram and Solomon; and the two of them made a treaty.

13 King Solomon conscripted forced labor out of all Israel; the levy numbered thirty thousand men. 14 He sent them to the Lebanon, ten thousand a month in shifts; they would be a month in the Lebanon and two months at home; Adoniram was in charge of the forced labor. 15 Solomon also had seventy thousand laborers and eighty thousand stonecutters in the hill country, 16 besides Solomon's three thousand three hundred supervisors who were over the work, having charge of the people who did the work. 17 At the king's command, they quarried out great, costly stones in order to lay the foundation of the house with dressed stones. 18 So Solomon's builders and Hiram's builders and the Gebalites did the stonecutting and prepared the timber and the stone to build the house.

5.1–18: Solomon prepares to build the Temple.* 1: *Tyre* was a Phoenician city-state on the Mediterranean coast north of Israel, essentially modern Lebanon. The trees from this area were highly valued in antiquity. King Hiram provided building materials to David for his palace in Jerusalem (2 Sam 5.11–12). In the ancient Near East a god's house was his temple. **3:** The *house for the name of the LORD* is the temple of Yahweh. Since the LORD does not actually reside in the Temple, it is built for his "name." **4:** *Rest* is an important theme in the Deuteronomistic* History (see 2 Sam 7.1). The LORD promised the people rest when they had entered the promised land and come to the "place" where he would make his name dwell (Deut 12.10–11). With Solomon the promise of rest is fulfilled so that the Temple can now be built in Jerusalem. This emphasis on rest may be a play on Solomon's name, which sounds like the Hebrew word "shalom," meaning peace (see 1 Chr 22.9). **6:** The *Sidonians* were people from Sidon,

a Ch 5.15 in Heb   *b* Gk Tg Vg: Heb *my feet* or *his feet*

another Phoenician city-state. Here, however, it seems to refer to Phoenicians in general. **13:** Solomon's labor force was conscripted from *Israel* as distinguished from Judah. It is clear from ch. 12 that the use of this conscripted labor continued after the Temple was completed. **18:** *Gebalites* were people from the Phoenician city-state of Byblos (also known as Gebal).

6 In the four hundred eightieth year after the Israelites came out of the land of Egypt, in the fourth year of Solomon's reign over Israel, in the month of Ziv, which is the second month, he began to build the house of the LORD. ²The house that King Solomon built for the LORD was sixty cubits long, twenty cubits wide, and thirty cubits high. ³The vestibule in front of the nave of the house was twenty cubits wide, across the width of the house. Its depth was ten cubits in front of the house. ⁴For the house he made windows with recessed frames.ᵃ ⁵He also built a structure against the wall of the house, running around the walls of the house, both the nave and the inner sanctuary; and he made side chambers all around. ⁶The lowest storyᵇ was five cubits wide, the middle one was six cubits wide, and the third was seven cubits wide; for around the outside of the house he made offsets on the wall in order that the supporting beams should not be inserted into the walls of the house.

7 The house was built with stone finished at the quarry, so that neither hammer nor ax nor any tool of iron was heard in the temple while it was being built.

8 The entrance for the middle story was on the south side of the house: one went up by winding stairs to the middle story, and from the middle story to the third. ⁹So he built the house, and finished it; he roofed the house with beams and planks of cedar. ¹⁰He built the structure against the whole house, each storyᶜ five cubits high, and it was joined to the house with timbers of cedar.

11 Now the word of the LORD came to Solomon, ¹²"Concerning this house that you are building, if you will walk in my statutes, obey my ordinances, and keep all my commandments by walking in them, then I will establish my promise with you, which I made to your father David. ¹³I will dwell among

the children of Israel, and will not forsake my people Israel."

6.1–38: The Temple* building. 1: *The fourth year of Solomon's reign* would be about 960 BCE, placing the date of the Exodus at 1440. But *the four hundred eightieth year* is probably an artificial number, perhaps representing twelve generations using the traditional round number of forty years for a generation. *The month of Ziv* was in the spring (April—May). **2:** A *cubit* was about eighteen inches. **3–5:** The basic design of the building with its three main parts—here translated the *vestibule, nave,* and *inner sanctuary*—was typical of the style of temples in ancient Syria and Phoenicia. **7:** Iron tools were forbidden for the construction of altars (Deut 27.5; Josh 8.31). Something of this same prohibition may have been at work in the Temple building. **11–13:** These verses are in typical deuteronomistic* language. They make the promise to David and Yahweh's presence among the people conditional upon Solomon's obedience.

14 So Solomon built the house, and finished it. ¹⁵He lined the walls of the house on the inside with boards of cedar; from the floor of the house to the rafters of the ceiling, he covered them on the inside with wood; and he covered the floor of the house with boards of cypress. ¹⁶He built twenty cubits of the rear of the house with boards of cedar from the floor to the rafters, and he built this within as an inner sanctuary, as the most holy place. ¹⁷The house, that is, the nave in front of the inner sanctuary, was forty cubits long. ¹⁸The cedar within the house had carvings of gourds and open flowers; all was cedar, no stone was seen. ¹⁹The inner sanctuary he prepared in the innermost part of the house, to set there the ark of the covenant of the LORD. ²⁰The interior of the inner sanctuary was twenty cubits long, twenty cubits wide, and twenty cubits high; he overlaid it with pure gold. He also overlaid the altar with cedar.ᵈ ²¹Solomon overlaid the inside of the house with pure gold, then he drew chains of gold across, in front of the inner sanctuary, and overlaid it with gold. ²²Next

---

a Gk: Meaning of Heb uncertain   *b* Gk: Heb *structure*
c Heb lacks *each story*   *d* Meaning of Heb uncertain

he overlaid the whole house with gold, in order that the whole house might be perfect; even the whole altar that belonged to the inner sanctuary he overlaid with gold.

23 In the inner sanctuary he made two cherubim of olivewood, each ten cubits high. ²⁴Five cubits was the length of one wing of the cherub, and five cubits the length of the other wing of the cherub; it was ten cubits from the tip of one wing to the tip of the other. ²⁵The other cherub also measured ten cubits; both cherubim had the same measure and the same form. ²⁶The height of one cherub was ten cubits, and so was that of the other cherub. ²⁷He put the cherubim in the innermost part of the house; the wings of the cherubim were spread out so that a wing of one was touching the one wall, and a wing of the other cherub was touching the other wall; their other wings toward the center of the house were touching wing to wing. ²⁸He also overlaid the cherubim with gold.

29 He carved the walls of the house all around about with carved engravings of cherubim, palm trees, and open flowers, in the inner and outer rooms. ³⁰The floor of the house he overlaid with gold, in the inner and outer rooms.

31 For the entrance to the inner sanctuary he made doors of olivewood; the lintel and the doorposts were five-sided.*a* ³²He covered the two doors of olivewood with carvings of cherubim, palm trees, and open flowers; he overlaid them with gold, and spread gold on the cherubim and on the palm trees.

33 So also he made for the entrance to the nave doorposts of olivewood, four-sided each, ³⁴and two doors of cypress wood; the two leaves of the one door were folding, and the two leaves of the other door were folding. ³⁵He carved cherubim, palm trees, and open flowers, overlaying them with gold evenly applied upon the carved work. ³⁶He built the inner court with three courses of dressed stone to one course of cedar beams.

37 In the fourth year the foundation of the house of the LORD was laid, in the month of Ziv. ³⁸In the eleventh year, in the month of Bul, which is the eighth month, the house was finished in all its parts, and according to

all its specifications. He was seven years in building it.

6.14–38. 14–36: The interior of the Temple* was lavishly decorated. The various designs of plants and fruits were likely symbols of fertility. The *cherubim*★ (plural of *cherub,* vv. 23–29) were mythical griffin-like creatures whose statues often guarded the entrances to temples and palaces in the ancient Near East. **37:** This verse refers to v. 1. **38:** The month of *Bul* was in the fall (October–November).

7 Solomon was building his own house thirteen years, and he finished his entire house.

2 He built the House of the Forest of the Lebanon one hundred cubits long, fifty cubits wide, and thirty cubits high, built on four rows of cedar pillars, with cedar beams on the pillars. ³It was roofed with cedar on the forty-five rafters, fifteen in each row, which were on the pillars. ⁴There were window frames in the three rows, facing each other in the three rows. ⁵All the doorways and doorposts had four-sided frames, opposite, facing each other in the three rows.

6 He made the Hall of Pillars fifty cubits long and thirty cubits wide. There was a porch in front with pillars, and a canopy in front of them.

7 He made the Hall of the Throne where he was to pronounce judgment, the Hall of Justice, covered with cedar from floor to floor.

8 His own house where he would reside, in the other court back of the hall, was of the same construction. Solomon also made a house like this hall for Pharaoh's daughter, whom he had taken in marriage.

9 All these were made of costly stones, cut according to measure, sawed with saws, back and front, from the foundation to the coping, and from outside to the great court. ¹⁰The foundation was of costly stones, huge stones, stones of eight and ten cubits. ¹¹There were costly stones above, cut to measure, and cedarwood. ¹²The great court had three courses of dressed stone to one

a Meaning of Heb uncertain

layer of cedar beams all around; so had the inner court of the house of the LORD, and the vestibule of the house.

7.1–12: Solomon's palace complex. 1: Solomon spent *thirteen* years on his own palace and only seven on the Temple* (7.38). But the writer of 1 Kings stresses the Temple by spending much more time on it. Also, in the Hebrew (Masoretic*) text the material about Solomon's palace is sandwiched between accounts dealing with the Temple (6.1–38 and 7.13–51). The order of the Greek or Septuagint* (LXX*) text is different. Whichever placement is original, both Hebrew and Greek versions show that, for the author of 1 Kings, the Temple was of greater importance. **2–5:** The *House of the Forest of the Lebanon* may have derived its name from its rows of cedar pillars.

〰〰〰〰〰〰〰〰〰〰〰〰

13 Now King Solomon invited and received Hiram from Tyre. 14 He was the son of a widow of the tribe of Naphtali, whose father, a man of Tyre, had been an artisan in bronze; he was full of skill, intelligence, and knowledge in working bronze. He came to King Solomon, and did all his work.

15 He cast two pillars of bronze. Eighteen cubits was the height of the one, and a cord of twelve cubits would encircle it; the second pillar was the same.*a* 16 He also made two capitals of molten bronze, to set on the tops of the pillars; the height of the one capital was five cubits, and the height of the other capital was five cubits. 17 There were nets of checker work with wreaths of chain work for the capitals on the tops of the pillars; seven*b* for the one capital, and seven*b* for the other capital. 18 He made the columns with two rows around each latticework to cover the capitals that were above the pomegranates; he did the same with the other capital. 19 Now the capitals that were on the tops of the pillars in the vestibule were of lily-work, four cubits high. 20 The capitals were on the two pillars and also above the rounded projection that was beside the latticework; there were two hundred pomegranates in rows all around; and so with the other capital. 21 He set up the pillars at the vestibule of the temple; he set up the pillar on the south and called it Jachin; and he set up the pillar on the north and called it Boaz. 22 On the tops

of the pillars was lily-work. Thus the work of the pillars was finished.

23 Then he made the molten sea; it was round, ten cubits from brim to brim, and five cubits high. A line of thirty cubits would encircle it completely. 24 Under its brim were panels all around it, each of ten cubits, surrounding the sea; there were two rows of panels, cast when it was cast. 25 It stood on twelve oxen, three facing north, three facing west, three facing south, and three facing east; the sea was set on them. The hindquarters of each were toward the inside. 26 Its thickness was a handbreadth; its brim was made like the brim of a cup, like the flower of a lily; it held two thousand baths.*c*

7.13–51: The bronze furnishings of the Temple.* 13–14: This *Hiram* is not the king but a craftsman. 2 Chronicles 2.12–13 calls him Huram-Abi. *Skill,* literally "wisdom." This word may also mean skill at a particular craft, and that is doubtless its nuance here. **15–22:** The *two pillars* had some symbolic meaning that is no longer clear. Their names, *Jachin* ("he establishes") and *Boaz* ("in him is strength") may represent the LORD's foundation of the earth or sacred trees (v. 21). **23–26:** The *molten sea* probably represented the primeval chaos which the LORD had defeated before making the world, in one version of creation. Another possibility is that the *molten sea* represents the primeval deep out of which the LORD created the universe, according to Gen 1. The *twelve oxen* on which it stood (v. 25) were fertility symbols.

〰〰〰〰〰〰〰〰〰〰〰〰

27 He also made the ten stands of bronze; each stand was four cubits long, four cubits wide, and three cubits high. 28 This was the construction of the stands: they had borders; the borders were within the frames; 29 on the borders that were set in the frames were lions, oxen, and cherubim. On the frames, both above and below the lions and oxen, there were wreaths of beveled work. 30 Each stand had four bronze wheels and axles of bronze; at the four corners were supports for a basin. The supports were cast with wreaths at the side of each. 31 Its opening was within the crown whose height was one cubit; its

a Cn: Heb *and a cord of twelve cubits encircled the second pillar*; Compare Jer 52.21   *b* Heb: Gk *a net*   *c* A Heb measure of volume

opening was round, as a pedestal is made; it was a cubit and a half wide. At its opening there were carvings; its borders were four-sided, not round. 32The four wheels were underneath the borders; the axles of the wheels were in the stands; and the height of a wheel was a cubit and a half. 33The wheels were made like a chariot wheel; their axles, their rims, their spokes, and their hubs were all cast. 34There were four supports at the four corners of each stand; the supports were of one piece with the stands. 35On the top of the stand there was a round band half a cubit high; on the top of the stand, its stays and its borders were of one piece with it. 36On the surfaces of its stays and on its borders he carved cherubim, lions, and palm trees, where each had space, with wreaths all around. 37In this way he made the ten stands; all of them were cast alike, with the same size and the same form.

38 He made ten basins of bronze; each basin held forty baths,*a* each basin measured four cubits; there was a basin for each of the ten stands. 39He set five of the stands on the south side of the house, and five on the north side of the house; he set the sea on the southeast corner of the house.

40 Hiram also made the pots, the shovels, and the basins. So Hiram finished all the work that he did for King Solomon on the house of the LORD: 41the two pillars, the two bowls of the capitals that were on the tops of the pillars, the two latticeworks to cover the two bowls of the capitals that were on the tops of the pillars; 42the four hundred pomegranates for the two latticeworks, two rows of pomegranates for each latticework, to cover the two bowls of the capitals that were on the pillars; 43the ten stands, the ten basins on the stands; 44the one sea, and the twelve oxen underneath the sea.

45 The pots, the shovels, and the basins, all these vessels that Hiram made for King Solomon for the house of the LORD were of burnished bronze. 46In the plain of the Jordan the king cast them, in the clay ground between Succoth and Zarethan. 47Solomon left all the vessels unweighed, because there were so many of them; the weight of the bronze was not determined.

48 So Solomon made all the vessels that were in the house of the LORD: the golden altar, the golden table for the bread of the Presence, 49the lampstands of pure gold, five on the south side and five on the north, in front of the inner sanctuary; the flowers, the lamps, and the tongs, of gold; 50the cups, snuffers, basins, dishes for incense, and fire-pans, of pure gold; the sockets for the doors of the innermost part of the house, the most holy place, and for the doors of the nave of the temple, of gold.

51 Thus all the work that King Solomon did on the house of the LORD was finished. Solomon brought in the things that his father David had dedicated, the silver, the gold, and the vessels, and stored them in the treasuries of the house of the LORD.

7.27–51. 27–39: The *ten stands* and *ten lavers* were also richly decorated with symbols of fertility and divine power. **48:** The *golden altar* was apparently for burning incense. On the *bread of the Presence,* see Lev 24.5–9. **49:** The *lampstands* were made to hold lamps consisting of a container for oil and a wick. They were not candlesticks.

8 Then Solomon assembled the elders of Israel and all the heads of the tribes, the leaders of the ancestral houses of the Israelites, before King Solomon in Jerusalem, to bring up the ark of the covenant of the LORD out of the city of David, which is Zion. 2All the people of Israel assembled to King Solomon at the festival in the month Ethanim, which is the seventh month. 3And all the elders of Israel came, and the priests carried the ark. 4So they brought up the ark of the LORD, the tent of meeting, and all the holy vessels that were in the tent; the priests and the Levites brought them up. 5King Solomon and all the congregation of Israel, who had assembled before him, were with him before the ark, sacrificing so many sheep and oxen that they could not be counted or numbered. 6Then the priests brought the ark of the covenant of the LORD to its place, in the inner sanctuary of the house, in the most holy

a A Heb measure of volume

place, underneath the wings of the cherubim. ⁷For the cherubim spread out their wings over the place of the ark, so that the cherubim made a covering above the ark and its poles. ⁸The poles were so long that the ends of the poles were seen from the holy place in front of the inner sanctuary; but they could not be seen from outside; they are there to this day. ⁹There was nothing in the ark except the two tablets of stone that Moses had placed there at Horeb, where the LORD made a covenant with the Israelites, when they came out of the land of Egypt. ¹⁰And when the priests came out of the holy place, a cloud filled the house of the LORD, ¹¹so that the priests could not stand to minister because of the cloud; for the glory of the LORD filled the house of the LORD.

12 Then Solomon said,
"The LORD has said that he would dwell in thick darkness.
13 I have built you an exalted house,
a place for you to dwell in forever."

14 Then the king turned around and blessed all the assembly of Israel, while all the assembly of Israel stood. ¹⁵He said, "Blessed be the LORD, the God of Israel, who with his hand has fulfilled what he promised with his mouth to my father David, saying, ¹⁶'Since the day that I brought my people Israel out of Egypt, I have not chosen a city from any of the tribes of Israel in which to build a house, that my name might be there; but I chose David to be over my people Israel.' ¹⁷My father David had it in mind to build a house for the name of the LORD, the God of Israel. ¹⁸But the LORD said to my father David, 'You did well to consider building a house for my name; ¹⁹nevertheless you shall not build the house, but your son who shall be born to you shall build the house for my name.' ²⁰Now the LORD has upheld the promise that he made; for I have risen in the place of my father David; I sit on the throne of Israel, as the LORD promised, and have built the house for the name of the LORD, the God of Israel. ²¹There I have provided a place for the ark, in which is the covenant of the LORD that he made with our ancestors when he brought them out of the land of Egypt."

8.1–66: The dedication of the Temple.* 2: *The month* of *Ethanim,* also called Tishri, was in the fall (September—October). This means that the dedication of the Temple occurred nearly a year after its completion, perhaps to coincide with the autumn new year celebration. **7–8:** The ark was carried by *poles* inside of rings on either side of the box that was the ark proper. The expression *to this day* may indicate that the writer lived while the Temple was still standing. **11:** The *glory of the LORD* was the thick cloud that symbolized the LORD's presence. **15–21:** Solomon's speech beginning in this verse is a deuteronomistic* composition. It links the promise to David of a dynasty* (2 Sam 7) with that of rest for Israel (Deut 12.11–12). It therefore identifies the "place" described in Deuteronomy with Solomon's Temple.

22 Then Solomon stood before the altar of the LORD in the presence of all the assembly of Israel, and spread out his hands to heaven. ²³He said, "O LORD, God of Israel, there is no God like you in heaven above or on earth beneath, keeping covenant and steadfast love for your servants who walk before you with all their heart, ²⁴the covenant that you kept for your servant my father David as you declared to him; you promised with your mouth and have this day fulfilled with your hand. ²⁵Therefore, O LORD, God of Israel, keep for your servant my father David that which you promised him, saying, 'There shall never fail you a successor before me to sit on the throne of Israel, if only your children look to their way, to walk before me as you have walked before me.' ²⁶Therefore, O God of Israel, let your word be confirmed, which you promised to your servant my father David.

27 "But will God indeed dwell on the earth? Even heaven and the highest heaven cannot contain you, much less this house that I have built! ²⁸Regard your servant's prayer and his plea, O LORD my God, heeding the cry and the prayer that your servant prays to you today; ²⁹that your eyes may be open night and day toward this house, the place of which you said, 'My name shall be there,' that you may heed the prayer that your servant prays toward this place. ³⁰Hear the plea of your servant and of your people

Israel when they pray toward this place; O hear in heaven your dwelling place; heed and forgive.

31 "If someone sins against a neighbor and is given an oath to swear, and comes and swears before your altar in this house, 32then hear in heaven, and act, and judge your servants, condemning the guilty by bringing their conduct on their own head, and vindicating the righteous by rewarding them according to their righteousness.

33 "When your people Israel, having sinned against you, are defeated before an enemy but turn again to you, confess your name, pray and plead with you in this house, 34then hear in heaven, forgive the sin of your people Israel, and bring them again to the land that you gave to their ancestors.

35 "When heaven is shut up and there is no rain because they have sinned against you, and then they pray toward this place, confess your name, and turn from their sin, because you punish*a* them, 36then hear in heaven, and forgive the sin of your servants, your people Israel, when you teach them the good way in which they should walk; and grant rain on your land, which you have given to your people as an inheritance.

37 "If there is famine in the land, if there is plague, blight, mildew, locust, or caterpillar; if their enemy besieges them in any*b* of their cities; whatever plague, whatever sickness there is; 38whatever prayer, whatever plea there is from any individual or from all your people Israel, all knowing the afflictions of their own hearts so that they stretch out their hands toward this house; 39then hear in heaven your dwelling place, forgive, act, and render to all whose hearts you know— according to all their ways, for only you know what is in every human heart— 40so that they may fear you all the days that they live in the land that you gave to our ancestors.

41 "Likewise when a foreigner, who is not of your people Israel, comes from a distant land because of your name 42—for they shall hear of your great name, your mighty hand, and your outstretched arm—when a foreigner comes and prays toward this house, 43then hear in heaven your dwelling place, and do according to all that the foreigner

calls to you, so that all the peoples of the earth may know your name and fear you, as do your people Israel, and so that they may know that your name has been invoked on this house that I have built.

44 "If your people go out to battle against their enemy, by whatever way you shall send them, and they pray to the LORD toward the city that you have chosen and the house that I have built for your name, 45then hear in heaven their prayer and their plea, and maintain their cause.

46 "If they sin against you—for there is no one who does not sin—and you are angry with them and give them to an enemy, so that they are carried away captive to the land of the enemy, far off or near; 47yet if they come to their senses in the land to which they have been taken captive, and repent, and plead with you in the land of their captors, saying, 'We have sinned, and have done wrong; we have acted wickedly'; 48if they repent with all their heart and soul in the land of their enemies, who took them captive, and pray to you toward their land, which you gave to their ancestors, the city that you have chosen, and the house that I have built for your name; 49then hear in heaven your dwelling place their prayer and their plea, maintain their cause 50and forgive your people who have sinned against you, and all their transgressions that they have committed against you; and grant them compassion in the sight of their captors, so that they may have compassion on them 51(for they are your people and heritage, which you brought out of Egypt, from the midst of the iron-smelter). 52Let your eyes be open to the plea of your servant, and to the plea of your people Israel, listening to them whenever they call to you. 53For you have separated them from among all the peoples of the earth, to be your heritage, just as you promised through Moses, your servant, when you brought our ancestors out of Egypt, O Lord GOD."

8.22–53: Solomon's prayer contains seven petitions, which address various future problems and ask the LORD to heed the prayers made in and toward the

a Or *when you answer*   *b* Gk Syr: Heb *in the land*

Temple.* Scholars debate whether this prayer or part of it comes before the Exile* or after it. Verses 44–53, in particular, are often considered a later expansion of the prayer. The idea behind the word *heritage* in v. 53 is that each nation has its own god and each god his own people; the LORD's heritage is Israel.

54 Now when Solomon finished offering all this prayer and this plea to the LORD, he arose from facing the altar of the LORD, where he had knelt with hands outstretched toward heaven; ⁵⁵he stood and blessed all the assembly of Israel with a loud voice:

56 "Blessed be the LORD, who has given rest to his people Israel according to all that he promised; not one word has failed of all his good promise, which he spoke through his servant Moses. ⁵⁷The LORD our God be with us, as he was with our ancestors; may he not leave us or abandon us, ⁵⁸but incline our hearts to him, to walk in all his ways, and to keep his commandments, his statutes, and his ordinances, which he commanded our ancestors. ⁵⁹Let these words of mine, with which I pleaded before the LORD, be near to the LORD our God day and night, and may he maintain the cause of his servant and the cause of his people Israel, as each day requires; ⁶⁰so that all the peoples of the earth may know that the LORD is God; there is no other. ⁶¹Therefore devote yourselves completely to the LORD our God, walking in his statutes and keeping his commandments, as at this day."

8.54–61: The benediction mentions *[the LORD's] commandments, his statutes, and his ordinances* (v. 58), which is a way of referring to the law of Moses. The confession that *the LORD is God; there is no other* (v. 60) is very similar to the traditional confession of Judaism known as the "shema" (Deut 6.4).

62 Then the king, and all Israel with him, offered sacrifice before the LORD. ⁶³Solomon offered as sacrifices of well-being to the LORD twenty-two thousand oxen and one hundred twenty thousand sheep. So the king and all the people of Israel dedicated the house of the LORD. ⁶⁴The same day the king consecrated the middle of the court that was in front of the house of the LORD; for there

he offered the burnt offerings and the grain offerings and the fat pieces of the sacrifices of well-being, because the bronze altar that was before the LORD was too small to receive the burnt offerings and the grain offerings and the fat pieces of the sacrifices of well-being.

65 So Solomon held the festival at that time, and all Israel with him—a great assembly, people from Lebo-hamath to the Wadi of Egypt—before the LORD our God, seven days.ᵃ ⁶⁶On the eighth day he sent the people away; and they blessed the king, and went to their tents, joyful and in good spirits because of all the goodness that the LORD had shown to his servant David and to his people Israel.

8.62–66: These verses describe Solomon's great sacrifices and celebration at the Temple* dedication. The *bronze altar* (v. 64) was the altar of burnt offering, which, oddly, was not described among the bronze works of Hiram in ch. 7. *The festival* was the Feast of Tabernacles* or Booths ("sukkot") described in Lev 23.33–43; Num 29.12–38. *From Lebo-hamath to the Wadi* of Egypt* describes the idealized boundaries of Israel during the reigns of David and Solomon, from northern Syria to the Egyptian border.

9 When Solomon had finished building the house of the LORD and the king's house and all that Solomon desired to build, ²the LORD appeared to Solomon a second time, as he had appeared to him at Gibeon. ³The LORD said to him, "I have heard your prayer and your plea, which you made before me; I have consecrated this house that you have built, and put my name there forever; my eyes and my heart will be there for all time. ⁴As for you, if you will walk before me, as David your father walked, with integrity of heart and uprightness, doing according to all that I have commanded you, and keeping my statutes and my ordinances, ⁵then I will establish your royal throne over Israel forever, as I promised your father David, saying, 'There shall not fail you a successor on the throne of Israel.'

a Compare Gk: Heb *seven days and seven days, fourteen days*

6 "If you turn aside from following me, you or your children, and do not keep my commandments and my statutes that I have set before you, but go and serve other gods and worship them, 7 then I will cut Israel off from the land that I have given them; and the house that I have consecrated for my name I will cast out of my sight; and Israel will become a proverb and a taunt among all peoples. 8 This house will become a heap of ruins;[a] everyone passing by it will be astonished, and will hiss; and they will say, 'Why has the LORD done such a thing to this land and to this house?' 9 Then they will say, 'Because they have forsaken the LORD their God, who brought their ancestors out of the land of Egypt, and embraced other gods, worshiping them and serving them; therefore the LORD has brought this disaster upon them.' "

9.1–9: The LORD appears to Solomon again. The promise to David of an eternal dynasty* is extended to Solomon, but only on the condition of his obedience. Verses 6–9 anticipate the disobedience of Solomon and other kings, as well as the Exile.*

10 At the end of twenty years, in which Solomon had built the two houses, the house of the LORD and the king's house, 11 King Hiram of Tyre having supplied Solomon with cedar and cypress timber and gold, as much as he desired, King Solomon gave to Hiram twenty cities in the land of Galilee. 12 But when Hiram came from Tyre to see the cities that Solomon had given him, they did not please him. 13 Therefore he said, "What kind of cities are these that you have given me, my brother?" So they are called the land of Cabul[b] to this day. 14 But Hiram had sent to the king one hundred twenty talents of gold.

9.10–28: Other activities of Solomon. 10–14: Solomon seems to be in financial difficulties and is forced to sell land, though his bargaining appears shrewd. *Cabul* (v. 13) is explained as meaning "as nothing." This is a popular etymology or even an etiology* (a story or report that explains something's origin). The real meaning of the name is unknown. The *talent* was a measure of weight. Its amount varied, but it could be as much as 130 pounds.

15 This is the account of the forced labor that King Solomon conscripted to build the house of the LORD and his own house, the Millo and the wall of Jerusalem, Hazor, Megiddo, Gezer 16 (Pharaoh king of Egypt had gone up and captured Gezer and burned it down, had killed the Canaanites who lived in the city, and had given it as dowry to his daughter, Solomon's wife; 17 so Solomon rebuilt Gezer), Lower Beth-horon, 18 Baalath, Tamar in the wilderness, within the land, 19 as well as all of Solomon's storage cities, the cities for his chariots, the cities for his cavalry, and whatever Solomon desired to build, in Jerusalem, in Lebanon, and in all the land of his dominion. 20 All the people who were left of the Amorites, the Hittites, the Perizzites, the Hivites, and the Jebusites, who were not of the people of Israel— 21 their descendants who were still left in the land, whom the Israelites were unable to destroy completely—these Solomon conscripted for slave labor, and so they are to this day. 22 But of the Israelites Solomon made no slaves; they were the soldiers, they were his officials, his commanders, his captains, and the commanders of his chariotry and cavalry.

23 These were the chief officers who were over Solomon's work: five hundred fifty, who had charge of the people who carried on the work.

24 But Pharaoh's daughter went up from the city of David to her own house that Solomon had built for her; then he built the Millo.

25 Three times a year Solomon used to offer up burnt offerings and sacrifices of well-being on the altar that he built for the LORD, offering incense[c] before the LORD. So he completed the house.

26 King Solomon built a fleet of ships at Ezion-geber, which is near Eloth on the shore of the Red Sea,[d] in the land of Edom. 27 Hiram sent his servants with the fleet, sailors who were familiar with the sea, together with the servants of Solomon. 28 They went

a Syr Old Latin: Heb *will become high*   b Perhaps meaning *a land good for nothing*   c Gk: Heb *offering incense with it that was*   d Or *Sea of Reeds*

to Ophir, and imported from there four hundred twenty talents of gold, which they delivered to King Solomon.

9.15–28. 15–22: The *Millo*, probably meaning "fill," seems to have been earthwork connecting the Temple* area to the palace complex on the south. *Hazor, Megiddo,* and *Gezer* (v. 15) were all important administrative centers for Solomon. The *Amorites, Hittites, Perizzites, Hivites, and Jebusites* (v. 20) are names the Bible uses for different native Canaanite peoples. They are familiar from the book of Genesis (Gen 15.19–20). The claim (v. 22) that Solomon did not force Israelites to work in his levy of slaves seems contradicted by 5.13; 11.28; and the events in ch. 12. **24:** *Pharaoh's daughter* is a subtheme in chs. 1–11 (see 3.1; 9.16) that leads up to the report of his sin in ch. 11. **26–28:** The location of *Ophir* is unknown; it may have been in southern Arabia. On the weight of a *talent,* see comment on v. 14.

10 When the queen of Sheba heard of the fame of Solomon (fame due to*a* the name of the LORD), she came to test him with hard questions. ²She came to Jerusalem with a very great retinue, with camels bearing spices, and very much gold, and precious stones; and when she came to Solomon, she told him all that was on her mind. ³Solomon answered all her questions; there was nothing hidden from the king that he could not explain to her. ⁴When the queen of Sheba had observed all the wisdom of Solomon, the house that he had built, ⁵the food of his table, the seating of his officials, and the attendance of his servants, their clothing, his valets, and his burnt offerings that he offered at the house of the LORD, there was no more spirit in her.

6 So she said to the king, "The report was true that I heard in my own land of your accomplishments and of your wisdom, 7but I did not believe the reports until I came and my own eyes had seen it. Not even half had been told me; your wisdom and prosperity far surpass the report that I had heard. ⁸Happy are your wives!*b* Happy are these your servants, who continually attend you and hear your wisdom! ⁹Blessed be the LORD your God, who has delighted in you and set you on the throne of Israel! Because the LORD

loved Israel forever, he has made you king to execute justice and righteousness." ¹⁰Then she gave the king one hundred twenty talents of gold, a great quantity of spices, and precious stones; never again did spices come in such quantity as that which the queen of Sheba gave to King Solomon.

11 Moreover, the fleet of Hiram, which carried gold from Ophir, brought from Ophir a great quantity of almug wood and precious stones. ¹²From the almug wood the king made supports for the house of the LORD, and for the king's house, lyres also and harps for the singers; no such almug wood has come or been seen to this day.

13 Meanwhile King Solomon gave to the queen of Sheba every desire that she expressed, as well as what he gave her out of Solomon's royal bounty. Then she returned to her own land, with her servants.

10.1–13: The queen of Sheba visits. *Sheba* was in Arabia, perhaps modern Yemen. The *queen* may have come on a trade mission from one of the tribes living in that area. The story has been greatly elaborated as a display of Solomon's wealth and wisdom. **5:** *Spirit* may also mean "breath." **9:** It is rather surprising that a foreigner blesses by the name of Israel's God, Yahweh. This may be what the writer thinks she must have said. **10:** On the weight of a *talent,* see comment on 9.14. **12:** The reference to *almug wood* occurs only here in the Bible; the exact species is unknown.

14 The weight of gold that came to Solomon in one year was six hundred sixty-six talents of gold, ¹⁵besides that which came from the traders and from the business of the merchants, and from all the kings of Arabia and the governors of the land. ¹⁶King Solomon made two hundred large shields of beaten gold; six hundred shekels of gold went into each large shield. ¹⁷He made three hundred shields of beaten gold; three minas of gold went into each shield; and the king put them in the House of the Forest of Lebanon. ¹⁸The king also made a great ivory throne, and overlaid it with the finest gold. ¹⁹The throne had six steps. The top of the throne was rounded in the back, and on each

a Meaning of Heb uncertain   *b* Gk Syr: Heb *men*

side of the seat were arm rests and two lions standing beside the arm rests, 20while twelve lions were standing, one on each end of a step on the six steps. Nothing like it was ever made in any kingdom. 21All King Solomon's drinking vessels were of gold, and all the vessels of the House of the Forest of Lebanon were of pure gold; none were of silver—it was not considered as anything in the days of Solomon. 22For the king had a fleet of ships of Tarshish at sea with the fleet of Hiram. Once every three years the fleet of ships of Tarshish used to come bringing gold, silver, ivory, apes, and peacocks.*a*

23 Thus King Solomon excelled all the kings of the earth in riches and in wisdom. 24The whole earth sought the presence of Solomon to hear his wisdom, which God had put into his mind. 25Every one of them brought a present, objects of silver and gold, garments, weaponry, spices, horses, and mules, so much year by year.

26 Solomon gathered together chariots and horses; he had fourteen hundred chariots and twelve thousand horses, which he stationed in the chariot cities and with the king in Jerusalem. 27The king made silver as common in Jerusalem as stones, and he made cedars as numerous as the sycamores of the Shephelah. 28Solomon's import of horses was from Egypt and Kue, and the king's traders received them from Kue at a price. 29A chariot could be imported from Egypt for six hundred shekels of silver, and a horse for one hundred fifty; so through the king's traders they were exported to all the kings of the Hittites and the kings of Aram.

10.14–29: More on Solomon's wealth and activities.
14: *Six hundred sixty-six talents of gold* would be an enormous sum—between thirty and eighty-five tons! See comment on 9.14. **16–17:** There were 50 *shekels** in a mina and 60 *minas* in a talent, which could weigh between 45 and 130 pounds. Thus the large shields would have weighed between 9 and 26 pounds and the small ones half as much. **22:** *Ships of Tarshish* were probably large ships capable of making a long voyage. Tarshish was a site in southern Spain that represented the western extreme of the world known to the biblical writers. **27:** The *Shephelah* is the lowland area in southern Palestine between the Mediterranean coast-

land and the central highlands. **28:** *Kue* was in southeastern Anatolia (Turkey) near Cilicia. *Egypt* (Heb., "Misrayim") may be a mistake for Musri, also in Anatolia north of Kue.

~~~~~~~~~~

11 King Solomon loved many foreign women along with the daughter of Pharaoh: Moabite, Ammonite, Edomite, Sidonian, and Hittite women, 2from the nations concerning which the LORD had said to the Israelites, "You shall not enter into marriage with them, neither shall they with you; for they will surely incline your heart to follow their gods"; Solomon clung to these in love. 3Among his wives were seven hundred princesses and three hundred concubines; and his wives turned away his heart. 4For when Solomon was old, his wives turned away his heart after other gods; and his heart was not true to the LORD his God, as was the heart of his father David. 5For Solomon followed Astarte the goddess of the Sidonians, and Milcom the abomination of the Ammonites. 6So Solomon did what was evil in the sight of the LORD, and did not completely follow the LORD, as his father David had done. 7Then Solomon built a high place for Chemosh the abomination of Moab, and for Molech the abomination of the Ammonites, on the mountain east of Jerusalem. 8He did the same for all his foreign wives, who offered incense and sacrificed to their gods.

9 Then the LORD was angry with Solomon, because his heart had turned away from the LORD, the God of Israel, who had appeared to him twice, 10and had commanded him concerning this matter, that he should not follow other gods; but he did not observe what the LORD commanded. 11Therefore the LORD said to Solomon, "Since this has been your mind and you have not kept my covenant and my statutes that I have commanded you, I will surely tear the kingdom from you and give it to your servant. 12Yet for the sake of your father David I will not do it in your lifetime; I will tear it out of the hand of your son. 13I will not, however, tear away the entire kingdom; I will give one

a Or *baboons*

tribe to your son, for the sake of my servant David and for the sake of Jerusalem, which I have chosen."

14 Then the LORD raised up an adversary against Solomon, Hadad the Edomite; he was of the royal house in Edom. [15]For when David was in Edom, and Joab the commander of the army went up to bury the dead, he killed every male in Edom [16](for Joab and all Israel remained there six months, until he had eliminated every male in Edom); [17]but Hadad fled to Egypt with some Edomites who were servants of his father. He was a young boy at that time. [18]They set out from Midian and came to Paran; they took people with them from Paran and came to Egypt, to Pharaoh king of Egypt, who gave him a house, assigned him an allowance of food, and gave him land. [19]Hadad found great favor in the sight of Pharaoh, so that he gave him his sister-in-law for a wife, the sister of Queen Tahpenes. [20]The sister of Tahpenes gave birth by him to his son Genubath, whom Tahpenes weaned in Pharaoh's house; Genubath was in Pharaoh's house among the children of Pharaoh. [21]When Hadad heard in Egypt that David slept with his ancestors and that Joab the commander of the army was dead, Hadad said to Pharaoh, "Let me depart, that I may go to my own country." [22]But Pharaoh said to him, "What do you lack with me that you now seek to go to your own country?" And he said, "No, do let me go."

23 God raised up another adversary against Solomon,[a] Rezon son of Eliada, who had fled from his master, King Hadadezer of Zobah. [24]He gathered followers around him and became leader of a marauding band, after the slaughter by David; they went to Damascus, settled there, and made him king in Damascus. [25]He was an adversary of Israel all the days of Solomon, making trouble as Hadad did; he despised Israel and reigned over Aram.

11.1–43: Solomon's troubles. The writer has divided the account of Solomon's reign into two parts for theological reasons. The first part (chs. 1–10) told of his successes, the greatest of which was the building of the Temple.* But the division of the kingdom after

Solomon required an explanation, which the writer furnishes in the account of Solomon's religious failures in ch. 11. 1: Solomon's many foreign wives were partly the result of treaties with other nations. 2: See Deut 7.1–4 for the law prohibiting foreign marriages. 3: A large harem was also a symbol of royal grandeur. The *princesses* were not all of royal birth but had gained royal status through marriage. *Concubines,** on the other hand, had no royal status but were female slaves used for sexual purposes. 4: The statement that Solomon's *heart was not true* is a pun on his name. The word "true" in Hebrew is "shalem," which sounds like "Shelomoh," Solomon in Hebrew. 5: *Astarte** was a prominent Phoenician and Canaanite goddess. The Hebrew text deliberately distorts her name to "Ashtoreth" to rhyme with the word "bosheth," meaning "abomination." *Milcom* was the chief god of the Ammonites, who lived in the area of modern northern Jordan. 7: *Chemosh* was the chief god of the Moabites in central Jordan. *Molech* is a distortion of the name Milcom. 11–13: The announcement of Solomon's punishment anticipates the story of the division of the kingdom under Rehoboam in the next chapter. 14–25: Solomon's first two adversaries are foreign. The word *adversary* is "satan," which does not imply any supernatural force in this case. The fact that both *Hadad the Edomite* and *Rezon* began their careers during David's reign indicates that they caused trouble for Solomon early in his reign. However, the writer has placed their stories here because of the partitioning of the account of Solomon into "positive" and "negative" sections.

26 Jeroboam son of Nebat, an Ephraimite of Zeredah, a servant of Solomon, whose mother's name was Zeruah, a widow, rebelled against the king. [27]The following was the reason he rebelled against the king. Solomon built the Millo, and closed up the gap in the wall[b] of the city of his father David. [28]The man Jeroboam was very able, and when Solomon saw that the young man was industrious he gave him charge over all the forced labor of the house of Joseph. [29]About that time, when Jeroboam was leaving Jerusalem, the prophet Ahijah the Shilonite found him on the road. Ahijah had clothed himself with a new garment. The two of

a Heb *him*   b Heb lacks *in the wall*

them were alone in the open country ³⁰when Ahijah laid hold of the new garment he was wearing and tore it into twelve pieces. ³¹He then said to Jeroboam: Take for yourself ten pieces; for thus says the LORD, the God of Israel, "See, I am about to tear the kingdom from the hand of Solomon, and will give you ten tribes. ³²One tribe will remain his, for the sake of my servant David and for the sake of Jerusalem, the city that I have chosen out of all the tribes of Israel. ³³This is because he hasᵃ forsaken me, worshiped Astarte the goddess of the Sidonians, Chemosh the god of Moab, and Milcom the god of the Ammonites, and hasᵃ not walked in my ways, doing what is right in my sight and keeping my statutes and my ordinances, as his father David did. ³⁴Nevertheless I will not take the whole kingdom away from him but will make him ruler all the days of his life, for the sake of my servant David whom I chose and who did keep my commandments and my statutes; ³⁵but I will take the kingdom away from his son and give it to you—that is, the ten tribes. ³⁶Yet to his son I will give one tribe, so that my servant David may always have a lamp before me in Jerusalem, the city where I have chosen to put my name. ³⁷I will take you, and you shall reign over all that your soul desires; you shall be king over Israel. ³⁸If you will listen to all that I command you, walk in my ways, and do what is right in my sight by keeping my statutes and my commandments, as David my servant did, I will be with you, and will build you an enduring house, as I built for David, and I will give Israel to you. ³⁹For this reason I will punish the descendants of David, but not forever." ⁴⁰Solomon sought therefore to kill Jeroboam; but Jeroboam promptly fled to Egypt, to King Shishak of Egypt, and remained in Egypt until the death of Solomon.

41 Now the rest of the acts of Solomon, all that he did as well as his wisdom, are they not written in the Book of the Acts of Solomon? ⁴²The time that Solomon reigned in Jerusalem over all Israel was forty years. ⁴³Solomon slept with his ancestors and was buried in the city of his father David; and his son Rehoboam succeeded him.

11.26–43. 26: *Jeroboam* was Solomon's third adversary. **27:** The *reason he rebelled* against Solomon was Ahijah's oracle⋆ (vv. 29–39) promising him kingship over the northern tribes. **29–32:** One tribe is either missing or presumed in Ahijah's symbolic division of the kingdom, since Jeroboam receives *ten pieces* and only one of the twelve pieces is kept for David. Different scholars have proposed that the tribes of Benjamin, Simeon, or Levi are assumed to accompany Judah. **36:** The word translated *lamp* can refer to a "fiefdom" or minor domain. **37–38:** Jeroboam receives the same promise of an enduring dynasty⋆ that was given to David if he will be obedient to Yahweh. **40:** It is not clear how Solomon found out about Ahijah's oracle to Jeroboam. **41–43:** This is typical of the concluding notices the deuteronomist⋆ supplies for the reigns of kings. The *Book of the Acts of Solomon* is no longer extant. *Forty years* (v. 42) is a round number for the length of a generation. That *Solomon slept with his ancestors* is an idiomatic way of saying that he died.

12 Rehoboam went to Shechem, for all Israel had come to Shechem to make him king. ²When Jeroboam son of Nebat heard of it (for he was still in Egypt, where he had fled from King Solomon), then Jeroboam returned fromᵇ Egypt. ³And they sent and called him; and Jeroboam and all the assembly of Israel came and said to Rehoboam, ⁴"Your father made our yoke heavy. Now therefore lighten the hard service of your father and his heavy yoke that he placed on us, and we will serve you." ⁵He said to them, "Go away for three days, then come again to me." So the people went away.

6 Then King Rehoboam took counsel with the older men who had attended his father Solomon while he was still alive, saying, "How do you advise me to answer this people?" ⁷They answered him, "If you will be a servant to this people today and serve them, and speak good words to them when you answer them, then they will be your servants forever." ⁸But he disregarded the advice that the older men gave him, and consulted with the young men who had grown up with him and now attended him. ⁹He said to them, "What do you advise that we answer this peo-

a Gk Syr Vg: Heb *they have*   b Gk Vg Compare 2 Chr 10.2: Heb *lived in*

ple who have said to me, 'Lighten the yoke that your father put on us'?" [10]The young men who had grown up with him said to him, "Thus you should say to this people who spoke to you, 'Your father made our yoke heavy, but you must lighten it for us'; thus you should say to them, 'My little finger is thicker than my father's loins. [11]Now, whereas my father laid on you a heavy yoke, I will add to your yoke. My father disciplined you with whips, but I will discipline you with scorpions.' "

12 So Jeroboam and all the people came to Rehoboam the third day, as the king had said, "Come to me again the third day." [13]The king answered the people harshly. He disregarded the advice that the older men had given him [14]and spoke to them according to the advice of the young men, "My father made your yoke heavy, but I will add to your yoke; my father disciplined you with whips, but I will discipline you with scorpions." [15]So the king did not listen to the people, because it was a turn of affairs brought about by the LORD that he might fulfill his word, which the LORD had spoken by Ahijah the Shilonite to Jeroboam son of Nebat.

12.1–24: The division of the kingdom. 2–3a: These verses are contradicted by v. 20, in which Jeroboam does not return until after the secession of the northern tribes. Verses 2–3a are not in the Greek (Septuagint,⋆ LXX⋆) version of 1 Kings and are probably a secondary scribal gloss. **10:** *My father's loins* is a euphemism.⋆ Rehoboam is saying that he is more of a man than his father so that the people can expect harsher treatment from him than from Solomon. **11:** Rehoboam makes the same point here, where *scorpions* may refer to a particularly vicious kind of whip. **12:** *Jeroboam*'s name is secondary here, having been added under the influence of vv. 2–3a. **15:** The author interprets the events in explicitly theological terms as the LORD's doing to fulfill Ahijah's oracle⋆ in 11.29–39.

〰〰〰〰〰〰〰〰〰〰〰〰〰〰

16 When all Israel saw that the king would not listen to them, the people answered the king,

"What share do we have in David?
    We have no inheritance in the son of
        Jesse.
To your tents, O Israel!

Look now to your own house,
    O David."

So Israel went away to their tents. [17]But Rehoboam reigned over the Israelites who were living in the towns of Judah. [18]When King Rehoboam sent Adoram, who was taskmaster over the forced labor, all Israel stoned him to death. King Rehoboam then hurriedly mounted his chariot to flee to Jerusalem. [19]So Israel has been in rebellion against the house of David to this day.

20 When all Israel heard that Jeroboam had returned, they sent and called him to the assembly and made him king over all Israel. There was no one who followed the house of David, except the tribe of Judah alone.

21 When Rehoboam came to Jerusalem, he assembled all the house of Judah and the tribe of Benjamin, one hundred eighty thousand chosen troops to fight against the house of Israel, to restore the kingdom to Rehoboam son of Solomon. [22]But the word of God came to Shemaiah the man of God: [23]Say to King Rehoboam of Judah, son of Solomon, and to all the house of Judah and Benjamin, and to the rest of the people, [24]"Thus says the LORD, You shall not go up or fight against your kindred the people of Israel. Let everyone go home, for this thing is from me." So they heeded the word of the LORD and went home again, according to the word of the LORD.

12.16–24. 16: *To your tents, O Israel* is a summons to military demobilization. The people, especially the army, of Israel is withdrawing from Rehoboam. A similar cry went up at Sheba's revolt in 2 Sam 20.1. **18:** *Adoram* is mentioned in 2 Sam 20.24 and 1 Kings 4.6 (Adoniram) as the head of the forced labor for David and Solomon. His presence was a particularly bitter and insulting reminder to the Israelite people of the burden of labor they had been forced to endure under Solomon. Hence, they stoned him. **19:** Even though the bulk of Israel left the house of David and sided with Rehoboam, the writer speaks of Israel's being *in rebellion*, indicating that his perspective is that of a citizen of Judah. In addition, the phrase *to this day* shows that the writer lived at a considerably later date. **21–24:** *Shemaiah*'s oracle expresses the view of v. 15 that the division was the LORD's doing. It addresses *Judah and Benjamin* (v. 23), while v. 20 speaks of Judah alone as the southern kingdom. Benjamin was probably divided between the two countries.

~~~~~~~~~~~~~~~

25 Then Jeroboam built Shechem in the hill country of Ephraim, and resided there; he went out from there and built Penuel. 26Then Jeroboam said to himself, "Now the kingdom may well revert to the house of David. 27If this people continues to go up to offer sacrifices in the house of the LORD at Jerusalem, the heart of this people will turn again to their master, King Rehoboam of Judah; they will kill me and return to King Rehoboam of Judah." 28So the king took counsel, and made two calves of gold. He said to the people,*a* "You have gone up to Jerusalem long enough. Here are your gods, O Israel, who brought you up out of the land of Egypt." 29He set one in Bethel, and the other he put in Dan. 30And this thing became a sin, for the people went to worship before the one at Bethel and before the other as far as Dan.*b* 31He also made houses*c* on high places, and appointed priests from among all the people, who were not Levites. 32Jeroboam appointed a festival on the fifteenth day of the eighth month like the festival that was in Judah, and he offered sacrifices on the altar; so he did in Bethel, sacrificing to the calves that he had made. And he placed in Bethel the priests of the high places that he had made. 33He went up to the altar that he had made in Bethel on the fifteenth day in the eighth month, in the month that he alone had devised; he appointed a festival for the people of Israel, and he went up to the altar to offer incense.

12.25–33: The sin of Jeroboam. 25: *Jeroboam built Shechem* and *Penuel* not in the sense of building them from the ground up but in the sense of fortifying already existing sites. **28:** Images of calves and bulls were commonly used in the ancient Near East to represent deities, especially fertility gods like Baal.★ The *golden calves* and Jeroboam's words to the people about them are reminiscent of the golden calf built by Aaron in Ex 32 and his words in 32.4. **29:** *Dan* was regarded as the northernmost city in Israel. *Bethel* was near the border between Israel and Judah. **31:** The *houses on the high places*★ were temples at various local shrines. Besides the royal sanctuaries at Dan and

Bethel, making it unnecessary to make a pilgrimage to Jerusalem, the writer accuses Jeroboam of setting up temples throughout his land. These were probably shrines to the LORD, but the writer regards Jerusalem as the only legitimate place to worship the LORD. Another aspect of Jeroboam's apostasy, in the writer's view, was his appointment of non-Levites as priests at the local shrines. **32:** Jeroboam is also accused of changing the religious calendar★ by establishing a festival in the eighth month to rival the Feast of Tabernacles★ in the seventh month in Jerusalem when the Temple★ there was dedicated (see 8.65).

~~~~~~~~~~~~~~~

13 While Jeroboam was standing by the altar to offer incense, a man of God came out of Judah by the word of the LORD to Bethel 2and proclaimed against the altar by the word of the LORD, and said, "O altar, altar, thus says the LORD: 'A son shall be born to the house of David, Josiah by name; and he shall sacrifice on you the priests of the high places who offer incense on you, and human bones shall be burned on you.' " 3He gave a sign the same day, saying, "This is the sign that the LORD has spoken: 'The altar shall be torn down, and the ashes that are on it shall be poured out.' " 4When the king heard what the man of God cried out against the altar at Bethel, Jeroboam stretched out his hand from the altar, saying, "Seize him!" But the hand that he stretched out against him withered so that he could not draw it back to himself. 5The altar also was torn down, and the ashes poured out from the altar, according to the sign that the man of God had given by the word of the LORD. 6The king said to the man of God, "Entreat now the favor of the LORD your God, and pray for me, so that my hand may be restored to me." So the man of God entreated the LORD; and the king's hand was restored to him, and became as it was before. 7Then the king said to the man of God, "Come home with me and dine, and I will give you a gift." 8But the man of God said to the king, "If you give me half your kingdom, I will not go in with you; nor will I eat food or drink water in this place. 9For thus I was

a Gk: Heb *to them*   *b* Compare Gk: Heb *went to the one as far as Dan*   *c* Gk Vg Compare 13.32: Heb *a house*

commanded by the word of the LORD: You shall not eat food, or drink water, or return by the way that you came." ¹⁰So he went another way, and did not return by the way that he had come to Bethel.

13.1–10: The oracle* against the altar at Bethel. The prophetic* legend* in this chapter was probably inserted here after the completion of the Deuteronomistic* History. Its setting, however, is Jeroboam's ascent to the altar at Bethel, apparently at its dedication (see 12.33). **2:** This story probably arose after the time of *Josiah* (640–609 BCE), who is credited with destroying the shrine at Bethel (2 Kings 23.15–18), some 300 years after Jeroboam. **3:** *Sign* here implies an unusual or miraculous occurrence. It looks ahead to v. 5, though it is not clear there how the altar was torn down. **4:** Jeroboam's withered *hand* or arm is miraculous, but it is not called a sign. **9:** Eating and drinking at Bethel would have indicated approval of the shrine there.

11 Now there lived an old prophet in Bethel. One of his sons came and told him all that the man of God had done that day in Bethel; the words also that he had spoken to the king, they told to their father. ¹²Their father said to them, "Which way did he go?" And his sons showed him the way that the man of God who came from Judah had gone. ¹³Then he said to his sons, "Saddle a donkey for me." So they saddled a donkey for him, and he mounted it. ¹⁴He went after the man of God, and found him sitting under an oak tree. He said to him, "Are you the man of God who came from Judah?" He answered, "I am." ¹⁵Then he said to him, "Come home with me and eat some food." ¹⁶But he said, "I cannot return with you, or go in with you; nor will I eat food or drink water with you in this place; ¹⁷for it was said to me by the word of the LORD: You shall not eat food or drink water there, or return by the way that you came." ¹⁸Then the other*ᵃ* said to him, "I also am a prophet as you are, and an angel spoke to me by the word of the LORD: Bring him back with you into your house so that he may eat food and drink water." But he was deceiving him. ¹⁹Then the man of God*ᵃ* went back with him, and ate food and drank water in his house.

13.11–34: The young man of God and the old prophet.★ This is the main part of the story. It has nothing to do with Jeroboam but concerns obedience to the prophetic word and has affinities with other prophetic legends* such as 1 Kings 20 and the stories about Elijah and Elisha. **18:** The motive of the old prophet in lying to his younger colleague is not explained.

20 As they were sitting at the table, the word of the LORD came to the prophet who had brought him back; ²¹and he proclaimed to the man of God who came from Judah, "Thus says the LORD: Because you have disobeyed the word of the LORD, and have not kept the commandment that the LORD your God commanded you, ²²but have come back and have eaten food and drunk water in the place of which he said to you, 'Eat no food, and drink no water,' your body shall not come to your ancestral tomb." ²³After the man of God*ᵃ* had eaten food and had drunk, they saddled for him a donkey belonging to the prophet who had brought him back. ²⁴Then as he went away, a lion met him on the road and killed him. His body was thrown in the road, and the donkey stood beside it; the lion also stood beside the body. ²⁵People passed by and saw the body thrown in the road, with the lion standing by the body. And they came and told it in the town where the old prophet lived.

26 When the prophet who had brought him back from the way heard of it, he said, "It is the man of God who disobeyed the word of the LORD; therefore the LORD has given him to the lion, which has torn him and killed him according to the word that the LORD spoke to him." ²⁷Then he said to his sons, "Saddle a donkey for me." So they saddled one, ²⁸and he went and found the body thrown in the road, with the donkey and the lion standing beside the body. The lion had not eaten the body or attacked the donkey. ²⁹The prophet took up the body of the man of God, laid it on the donkey, and brought it back to the city,*ᵇ* to mourn and to bury him. ³⁰He laid the body in his own grave; and

a Heb *he*   *b* Gk: Heb *he came to the town of the old prophet* they mourned over him, saying, "Alas, my brother!" 31After he had buried him, he said to his sons, "When I die, bury me in the grave in which the man of God is buried; lay my bones beside his bones. 32For the saying that he proclaimed by the word of the LORD against the altar in Bethel, and against all the houses of the high places that are in the cities of Samaria, shall surely come to pass."

33 Even after this event Jeroboam did not turn from his evil way, but made priests for the high places again from among all the people; any who wanted to be priests he consecrated for the high places. 34This matter became sin to the house of Jeroboam, so as to cut it off and to destroy it from the face of the earth.

13.20–34. 20–25: The harsh judgment is meant to teach a lesson. The young man of God should have obeyed the LORD rather than trusting another prophet. 31–32: The oracle* is fulfilled in the purge of Josiah (2 Kings 23.15–18), who saves the bones of the old prophet. The reference to the *cities of Samaria* can be no earlier than 721 BCE, when Israel was annexed by the Assyrians and turned into an Assyrian province. 33–34: After the prophetic legend, the narrative* returns to the topic of Jeroboam's apostasy.

14 At that time Abijah son of Jeroboam fell sick. 2Jeroboam said to his wife, "Go, disguise yourself, so that it will not be known that you are the wife of Jeroboam, and go to Shiloh; for the prophet Ahijah is there, who said of me that I should be king over this people. 3Take with you ten loaves, some cakes, and a jar of honey, and go to him; he will tell you what shall happen to the child."

4 Jeroboam's wife did so; she set out and went to Shiloh, and came to the house of Ahijah. Now Ahijah could not see, for his eyes were dim because of his age. 5But the LORD said to Ahijah, "The wife of Jeroboam is coming to inquire of you concerning her son; for he is sick. Thus and thus you shall say to her."

When she came, she pretended to be another woman. 6But when Ahijah heard the sound of her feet, as she came in at the door, he said, "Come in, wife of Jeroboam; why do you pretend to be another? For I am charged with heavy tidings for you. 7Go, tell Jeroboam, 'Thus says the LORD, the God of Israel: Because I exalted you from among the people, made you leader over my people Israel, 8and tore the kingdom away from the house of David to give it to you; yet you have not been like my servant David, who kept my commandments and followed me with all his heart, doing only that which was right in my sight, 9but you have done evil above all those who were before you and have gone and made for yourself other gods, and cast images, provoking me to anger, and have thrust me behind your back; 10therefore, I will bring evil upon the house of Jeroboam. I will cut off from Jeroboam every male, both bond and free in Israel, and will consume the house of Jeroboam, just as one burns up dung until it is all gone. 11Anyone belonging to Jeroboam who dies in the city, the dogs shall eat; and anyone who dies in the open country, the birds of the air shall eat; for the LORD has spoken.' 12Therefore set out, go to your house. When your feet enter the city, the child shall die. 13All Israel shall mourn for him and bury him; for he alone of Jeroboam's family shall come to the grave, because in him there is found something pleasing to the LORD, the God of Israel, in the house of Jeroboam. 14Moreover the LORD will raise up for himself a king over Israel, who shall cut off the house of Jeroboam today, even right now!*a*

15 "The LORD will strike Israel, as a reed is shaken in the water; he will root up Israel out of this good land that he gave to their ancestors, and scatter them beyond the Euphrates, because they have made their sacred poles,*b* provoking the LORD to anger. 16He will give Israel up because of the sins of Jeroboam, which he sinned and which he caused Israel to commit."

17 Then Jeroboam's wife got up and went away, and she came to Tirzah. As she came to the threshold of the house, the child died. 18All Israel buried him and mourned for him, according to the word of the LORD,

a Meaning of Heb uncertain   *b* Heb *Asherim*

which he spoke by his servant the prophet Ahijah.

14.1–18: The oracle* against Jeroboam. 3: The *ten loaves, some cakes, and a jar of honey* are payment to a seer for revealing the future. **6:** *Ahijah,* as a true man of God, knows that his visitor is the *wife of Jeroboam* despite his blindness (v. 4) and her disguise (vv. 2, 5). **7–11:** These verses, a deuteronomistic* insertion, focus on the fate of Jeroboam's royal house rather than on that of his ill son. Jeroboam had the opportunity to establish a dynasty* like David's (v. 8), but his sin will prevent that from happening. All of Jeroboam's *male* heirs (v. 10, male is literally "one who urinates on a wall") will be killed by a usurper. The threat in v. 11 is drawn from a curse of non-burial. **12–14:** The original oracle told of the impending death of Jeroboam's son and mentioned the coming of a new royal house, but without elaboration. **15:** *Sacred poles* were fertility symbols used in the worship of the Canaanite goddess, Asherah.* **17–18:** The fulfillment of Ahijah's prophecy.

19 Now the rest of the acts of Jeroboam, how he warred and how he reigned, are written in the Book of the Annals of the Kings of Israel. 20The time that Jeroboam reigned was twenty-two years; then he slept with his ancestors, and his son Nadab succeeded him.

21 Now Rehoboam son of Solomon reigned in Judah. Rehoboam was forty-one years old when he began to reign, and he reigned seventeen years in Jerusalem, the city that the LORD had chosen out of all the tribes of Israel, to put his name there. His mother's name was Naamah the Ammonite. 22Judah did what was evil in the sight of the LORD; they provoked him to jealousy with their sins that they committed, more than all that their ancestors had done. 23For they also built for themselves high places, pillars, and sacred poles*a* on every high hill and under every green tree; 24there were also male temple prostitutes in the land. They committed all the abominations of the nations that the LORD drove out before the people of Israel.

25 In the fifth year of King Rehoboam, King Shishak of Egypt came up against Jerusalem; 26he took away the treasures of the house of the LORD and the treasures of the

king's house; he took everything. He also took away all the shields of gold that Solomon had made; 27so King Rehoboam made shields of bronze instead, and committed them to the hands of the officers of the guard, who kept the door of the king's house. 28As often as the king went into the house of the LORD, the guard carried them and brought them back to the guardroom.

29 Now the rest of the acts of Rehoboam, and all that he did, are they not written in the Book of the Annals of the Kings of Judah? 30There was war between Rehoboam and Jeroboam continually. 31Rehoboam slept with his ancestors and was buried with his ancestors in the city of David. His mother's name was Naamah the Ammonite. His son Abijam succeeded him.

14.19–31: The reigns of Jeroboam and Rehoboam. Most of these verses are the standard deuteronomistic formulas for kings. **19:** The *Book of the Annals of the Kings of Israel* no longer exists, so its exact nature is unknown. **20:** *Slept with his ancestors* is an idiom for death. **21–24:** The typical beginning formula for a king of Judah included the name of the "queen mother," the mother of the king. *High places** were shrines used for worship. *Pillars* were standing stones used in worship. The biblical writers connect them especially with service to other gods. On *sacred poles,* see comment on v. 15. **25–26:** *Shishak* (also called Shoshenq or Sheshonk) invaded Palestine around 922 BCE. His annals mention sites in Israel but not Jerusalem, apparently because Rehoboam paid him off. **29:** The *Book of the Annals of the Kings of Judah* also no longer exists. **31:** *Ancestors* is literally "fathers." Rehoboam is buried with the previous kings of Judah, as are subsequent kings as well, *in the city of David.* The location of these tombs is not known, but it was probably not within the walls of Jerusalem.

15 Now in the eighteenth year of King Jeroboam son of Nebat, Abijam began to reign over Judah. 2He reigned for three years in Jerusalem. His mother's name was Maacah daughter of Abishalom. 3He committed all the sins that his father did before him; his heart was not true to the LORD his God, like the heart of his father David.

a Heb *Asherim*

4Nevertheless for David's sake the LORD his God gave him a lamp in Jerusalem, setting up his son after him, and establishing Jerusalem; 5because David did what was right in the sight of the LORD, and did not turn aside from anything that he commanded him all the days of his life, except in the matter of Uriah the Hittite. 6The war begun between Rehoboam and Jeroboam continued all the days of his life. 7The rest of the acts of Abijam, and all that he did, are they not written in the Book of the Annals of the Kings of Judah? There was war between Abijam and Jeroboam. 8Abijam slept with his ancestors, and they buried him in the city of David. Then his son Asa succeeded him.

15.1–8: Abijam of Judah. 1: *Abijam* is called Abijah in 2 Chr 13.1 and is judged in Chronicles to be good. **2:** *Abishalom* is apparently Absalom, David's rebellious son (2 Sam 13–19). If so, *Maacah* would have been David's granddaughter. **4:** *A lamp* may also mean a fiefdom or minor domain. **6:** This verse is repetitive; see 14.30.

9 In the twentieth year of King Jeroboam of Israel, Asa began to reign over Judah; 10he reigned forty-one years in Jerusalem. His mother's name was Maacah daughter of Abishalom. 11Asa did what was right in the sight of the LORD, as his father David had done. 12He put away the male temple prostitutes out of the land, and removed all the idols that his ancestors had made. 13He also removed his mother Maacah from being queen mother, because she had made an abominable image for Asherah; Asa cut down her image and burned it at the Wadi Kidron. 14But the high places were not taken away. Nevertheless the heart of Asa was true to the LORD all his days. 15He brought into the house of the LORD the votive gifts of his father and his own votive gifts—silver, gold, and utensils.

16 There was war between Asa and King Baasha of Israel all their days. 17King Baasha of Israel went up against Judah, and built Ramah, to prevent anyone from going out or coming in to King Asa of Judah. 18Then Asa took all the silver and the gold that were left in the treasures of the house of the LORD and the treasures of the king's house, and gave them into the hands of his servants. King Asa sent them to King Ben-hadad son of Tabrimmon son of Hezion of Aram, who resided in Damascus, saying, 19"Let there be an alliance between me and you, like that between my father and your father: I am sending you a present of silver and gold; go, break your alliance with King Baasha of Israel, so that he may withdraw from me." 20Ben-hadad listened to King Asa, and sent the commanders of his armies against the cities of Israel. He conquered Ijon, Dan, Abel-beth-maacah, and all Chinneroth, with all the land of Naphtali. 21When Baasha heard of it, he stopped building Ramah and lived in Tirzah. 22Then King Asa made a proclamation to all Judah, none was exempt: they carried away the stones of Ramah and its timber, with which Baasha had been building; with them King Asa built Geba of Benjamin and Mizpah. 23Now the rest of all the acts of Asa, all his power, all that he did, and the cities that he built, are they not written in the Book of the Annals of the Kings of Judah? But in his old age he was diseased in his feet. 24Then Asa slept with his ancestors, and was buried with his ancestors in the city of his father David; his son Jehoshaphat succeeded him.

15.9–24: Asa of Judah. 12: The term for *idols* is a disparaging one and sounds like the word for "dung" in 14.10. **13:** The nature of Maacah's *abominable image* is not known; it may have been related to *Asherah*'s★ role as a Canaanite fertility goddess. **14:** The *high places*★ were shrines. Here, they were apparently used for the worship of the LORD, not of other gods. **17:** *Ramah* was in Benjamin on the main road between north and south. **20:** The places listed in this verse are all in northern Israel. Thus, Asa used Ben-hadad to divert Baasha's attention from his southern border with Judah. **22:** *None was exempt* means that Asa conscripted a labor force of all the men of Judah for this project. *Geba* and *Mizpah* were on opposite sides of a pass along the north-south road a little north of Ramah. Asa was, therefore, extending his northern border. **23:** *Feet* is probably a euphemism for the sexual organs; Asa likely died of a venereal disease. This verse implies that the disease was punishment for some unnamed sin.

25 Nadab son of Jeroboam began to reign over Israel in the second year of King Asa of Judah; he reigned over Israel two years. 26 He did what was evil in the sight of the LORD, walking in the way of his ancestor and in the sin that he caused Israel to commit.

27 Baasha son of Ahijah, of the house of Issachar, conspired against him; and Baasha struck him down at Gibbethon, which belonged to the Philistines; for Nadab and all Israel were laying siege to Gibbethon. 28 So Baasha killed Nadab*a* in the third year of King Asa of Judah, and succeeded him. 29 As soon as he was king, he killed all the house of Jeroboam; he left to the house of Jeroboam not one that breathed, until he had destroyed it, according to the word of the LORD that he spoke by his servant Ahijah the Shilonite— 30 because of the sins of Jeroboam that he committed and that he caused Israel to commit, and because of the anger to which he provoked the LORD, the God of Israel.

31 Now the rest of the acts of Nadab, and all that he did, are they not written in the Book of the Annals of the Kings of Israel? 32 There was war between Asa and King Baasha of Israel all their days.

15.25–32: Nadab of Israel. 25: *Nadab* marks the end of the royal house of Jeroboam. 26: *His ancestor* is literally "his father," Jeroboam. 27: *Baasha* was an army general who led a government takeover. 29–30: After assassinating Nadab, Baasha killed all of Jeroboam's male heirs because they were potential rivals for the throne. This was a customary practice for the founders of new royal houses. The deuteronomist,* however, sees this as punishment for Jeroboam as prophesied by Ahijah (14.7–11).

33 In the third year of King Asa of Judah, Baasha son of Ahijah began to reign over all Israel at Tirzah; he reigned twenty-four years. 34 He did what was evil in the sight of the LORD, walking in the way of Jeroboam and in the sin that he caused Israel to commit.

16 The word of the LORD came to Jehu son of Hanani against Baasha, saying, 2 "Since I exalted you out of the dust and made you leader over my people Israel, and

you have walked in the way of Jeroboam, and have caused my people Israel to sin, provoking me to anger with their sins, 3 therefore, I will consume Baasha and his house, and I will make your house like the house of Jeroboam son of Nebat. 4 Anyone belonging to Baasha who dies in the city the dogs shall eat; and anyone of his who dies in the field the birds of the air shall eat."

5 Now the rest of the acts of Baasha, what he did, and his power, are they not written in the Book of the Annals of the Kings of Israel? 6 Baasha slept with his ancestors, and was buried at Tirzah; and his son Elah succeeded him. 7 Moreover the word of the LORD came by the prophet Jehu son of Hanani against Baasha and his house, both because of all the evil that he did in the sight of the LORD, provoking him to anger with the work of his hands, in being like the house of Jeroboam, and also because he destroyed it.

15.33–16.7: Baasha of Israel. 15.34: *The sin that [Jeroboam] caused Israel to commit* was the worship at the shrines of Dan and Bethel (12.25–33). 16.1–4: This oracle* predicts the demise of the house of Baasha in terms very similar to the one against Jeroboam in 14.7–11. Both are likely the work of the deuteronomist. 7: This verse seems secondary because it is repetitive of vv. 1–4 and because it follows the closing formula for Baasha in vv. 5–6. The last clause, *and also because he destroyed it,* has been understood by some as "even though he destroyed [the house of Jeroboam]."

8 In the twenty-sixth year of King Asa of Judah, Elah son of Baasha began to reign over Israel in Tirzah; he reigned two years. 9 But his servant Zimri, commander of half his chariots, conspired against him. When he was at Tirzah, drinking himself drunk in the house of Arza, who was in charge of the palace at Tirzah, 10 Zimri came in and struck him down and killed him, in the twenty-seventh year of King Asa of Judah, and succeeded him.

11 When he began to reign, as soon as he had seated himself on his throne, he killed all the house of Baasha; he did not leave him

a Heb *him*

a single male of his kindred or his friends. ¹²Thus Zimri destroyed all the house of Baasha, according to the word of the LORD, which he spoke against Baasha by the prophet Jehu— ¹³because of all the sins of Baasha and the sins of his son Elah that they committed, and that they caused Israel to commit, provoking the LORD God of Israel to anger with their idols. ¹⁴Now the rest of the acts of Elah, and all that he did, are they not written in the Book of the Annals of the Kings of Israel?

16.8–14: Elah of Israel. 9: Like Baasha, *Zimri* was a general in the army who led a revolt. **11–13:** Zimri follows the standard practice of wiping out all the male heirs of the previous royal house. Again, the deuteronomist explains this theologically as punishment from the LORD as predicted by a prophet.⋆

15 In the twenty-seventh year of King Asa of Judah, Zimri reigned seven days in Tirzah. Now the troops were encamped against Gibbethon, which belonged to the Philistines, ¹⁶and the troops who were encamped heard it said, "Zimri has conspired, and he has killed the king"; therefore all Israel made Omri, the commander of the army, king over Israel that day in the camp. ¹⁷So Omri went up from Gibbethon, and all Israel with him, and they besieged Tirzah. ¹⁸When Zimri saw that the city was taken, he went into the citadel of the king's house; he burned down the king's house over himself with fire, and died— ¹⁹because of the sins that he committed, doing evil in the sight of the LORD, walking in the way of Jeroboam, and for the sin that he committed, causing Israel to sin. ²⁰Now the rest of the acts of Zimri, and the conspiracy that he made, are they not written in the Book of the Annals of the Kings of Israel?

16.15–20: Zimri of Israel. The formulaic nature of the deuteronomistic⋆ evaluation is clear in this case from the fact that Zimri reigned only *seven days* (v. 15), yet he is still condemned for all the sins of his predecessors (v. 19).

21 Then the people of Israel were divided into two parts; half of the people followed Tibni son of Ginath, to make him king, and half followed Omri. ²²But the people who followed Omri overcame the people who followed Tibni son of Ginath; so Tibni died, and Omri became king. ²³In the thirty-first year of King Asa of Judah, Omri began to reign over Israel; he reigned for twelve years, six of them in Tirzah.

24 He bought the hill of Samaria from Shemer for two talents of silver; he fortified the hill, and called the city that he built, Samaria, after the name of Shemer, the owner of the hill.

25 Omri did what was evil in the sight of the LORD; he did more evil than all who were before him. ²⁶For he walked in all the way of Jeroboam son of Nebat, and in the sins that he caused Israel to commit, provoking the LORD, the God of Israel, to anger by their idols. ²⁷Now the rest of the acts of Omri that he did, and the power that he showed, are they not written in the Book of the Annals of the Kings of Israel? ²⁸Omri slept with his ancestors, and was buried in Samaria; his son Ahab succeeded him.

16.21–28: Omri of Israel. 21–22: The civil war described here was between two other military commanders, *Omri* and *Tibni*, with Omri eventually being victorious. **24:** Omri's acquisition of *Samaria* and his designation of it as his capital was similar to David's acquisition and establishment of Jerusalem as his capital. **25–28:** Historically, Omri was one of the most powerful and important kings of Israel. He founded a dynasty⋆ that lasted through five kings. Israel was known by other countries as the "house of Omri" for generations after Omri's death. The fact that the deuteronomist disposes of Omri in just a few verses using the same formulas as for all other kings indicates that his interests are primarily theological rather than historical.

29 In the thirty-eighth year of King Asa of Judah, Ahab son of Omri began to reign over Israel; Ahab son of Omri reigned over Israel in Samaria twenty-two years. ³⁰Ahab son of Omri did evil in the sight of the LORD more than all who were before him.

31 And as if it had been a light thing for him to walk in the sins of Jeroboam son of Nebat, he took as his wife Jezebel daughter

of King Ethbaal of the Sidonians, and went and served Baal, and worshiped him. ³²He erected an altar for Baal in the house of Baal, which he built in Samaria. ³³Ahab also made a sacred pole.ᵃ Ahab did more to provoke the anger of the LORD, the God of Israel, than had all the kings of Israel who were before him. ³⁴In his days Hiel of Bethel built Jericho; he laid its foundation at the cost of Abiram his firstborn, and set up its gates at the cost of his youngest son Segub, according to the word of the LORD, which he spoke by Joshua son of Nun.

16.29–34: The beginning of Ahab's reign. Like his father, Ahab was also a powerful king. His prominence in the Bible, however, is due to religious reasons. He is regarded as the most wicked king of Israel (v. 33), largely because of his wife, Jezebel (v. 32). His reign also stands out in 1 Kings as the setting of the Elijah stories. **31:** *Jezebel* means "Where is the prince?" and comes from ritual lamentation* in the worship of Baal.* *Ethbaal* means "Baal exists." These names set the stage for the conflict between the LORD (Yahweh) and Baal in the following stories. Ethbaal was king of Tyre, a city-state of the Phoenicians, who are here called *Sidonians*. **34:** This verse alludes to the curse in Josh 6.26. It is unclear whether *at the cost of* implies accidental death of the sons or a deliberate sacrifice. The practice of burying children in the foundation of buildings to bring good fortune is known from elsewhere in the ancient Near East.

17 Now Elijah the Tishbite, of Tishbeᵇ in Gilead, said to Ahab, "As the LORD the God of Israel lives, before whom I stand, there shall be neither dew nor rain these years, except by my word." ²The word of the LORD came to him, saying, ³"Go from here and turn eastward, and hide yourself by the Wadi Cherith, which is east of the Jordan. ⁴You shall drink from the wadi, and I have commanded the ravens to feed you there." ⁵So he went and did according to the word of the LORD; he went and lived by the Wadi Cherith, which is east of the Jordan. ⁶The ravens brought him bread and meat in the morning, and bread and meat in the evening; and he drank from the wadi. ⁷But after a while the wadi dried up, because there was no rain in the land.

⁸ Then the word of the LORD came to him, saying, ⁹"Go now to Zarephath, which belongs to Sidon, and live there; for I have commanded a widow there to feed you." ¹⁰So he set out and went to Zarephath. When he came to the gate of the town, a widow was there gathering sticks; he called to her and said, "Bring me a little water in a vessel, so that I may drink." ¹¹As she was going to bring it, he called to her and said, "Bring me a morsel of bread in your hand." ¹²But she said, "As the LORD your God lives, I have nothing baked, only a handful of meal in a jar, and a little oil in a jug; I am now gathering a couple of sticks, so that I may go home and prepare it for myself and my son, that we may eat it, and die." ¹³Elijah said to her, "Do not be afraid; go and do as you have said; but first make me a little cake of it and bring it to me, and afterwards make something for yourself and your son. ¹⁴For thus says the LORD the God of Israel: The jar of meal will not be emptied and the jug of oil will not fail until the day that the LORD sends rain on the earth." ¹⁵She went and did as Elijah said, so that she as well as he and her household ate for many days. ¹⁶The jar of meal was not emptied, neither did the jug of oil fail, according to the word of the LORD that he spoke by Elijah.

17.1–24: Elijah and the drought. 1: *Elijah* means "Yahweh is (my) God," and it sets the theme for the following chapters. The cessation of rain shows that it is the LORD (Yahweh), not Baal,* who controls the elements and therefore fertility. **3:** A *Wadi* was a stream bed with or without water rather than a brook, as it has been translated. **9:** Elijah is sent north into Phoenician territory. The two stories that follow show Elijah's status as a miracle-working man of God.

¹⁷ After this the son of the woman, the mistress of the house, became ill; his illness was so severe that there was no breath left in him. ¹⁸She then said to Elijah, "What have you against me, O man of God? You have come to me to bring my sin to remembrance, and to cause the death of my son!"

ᵃ Heb *Asherah*   ᵇ Gk: Heb *of the settlers*

19But he said to her, "Give me your son." He took him from her bosom, carried him up into the upper chamber where he was lodging, and laid him on his own bed. 20He cried out to the LORD, "O LORD my God, have you brought calamity even upon the widow with whom I am staying, by killing her son?" 21Then he stretched himself upon the child three times, and cried out to the LORD, "O LORD my God, let this child's life come into him again." 22The LORD listened to the voice of Elijah; the life of the child came into him again, and he revived. 23Elijah took the child, brought him down from the upper chamber into the house, and gave him to his mother; then Elijah said, "See, your son is alive." 24So the woman said to Elijah, "Now I know that you are a man of God, and that the word of the LORD in your mouth is truth."

17.17–24. 17: The woman who was previously described as destitute is here called *the mistress of the house*. This is one indication that the story in vv. 17–24 has been adapted from or influenced by the story about Elisha in 2 Kings 4.11–37. **18:** The woman implies that her son's death is divine punishment for some sin. **19:** *The upper chamber* is another element drawn from the story in 2 Kings 4, which explains how the chamber was built for the prophet.★ **21–22:** Elijah's actions suggest that *life* or "breath" went from Elijah's body into the boy's so that he revived. Examples of this kind of contactual magic are found elsewhere from the ancient Near East. The point of the story, however, is that this was the LORD's doing.

18 After many days the word of the LORD came to Elijah, in the third year of the drought,ᵃ saying, "Go, present yourself to Ahab; I will send rain on the earth." 2So Elijah went to present himself to Ahab. The famine was severe in Samaria. 3Ahab summoned Obadiah, who was in charge of the palace. (Now Obadiah revered the LORD greatly; 4when Jezebel was killing off the prophets of the LORD, Obadiah took a hundred prophets, hid them fifty to a cave, and provided them with bread and water.) 5Then Ahab said to Obadiah, "Go through the land to all the springs of water and to all the wadis; perhaps we may find grass to keep the horses and mules alive, and not lose some of the animals." 6So they divided the land between them to pass through it; Ahab went in one direction by himself, and Obadiah went in another direction by himself.

7 As Obadiah was on the way, Elijah met him; Obadiah recognized him, fell on his face, and said, "Is it you, my lord Elijah?" 8He answered him, "It is I. Go, tell your lord that Elijah is here." 9And he said, "How have I sinned, that you would hand your servant over to Ahab, to kill me? 10As the LORD your God lives, there is no nation or kingdom to which my lord has not sent to seek you; and when they would say, 'He is not here,' he would require an oath of the kingdom or nation, that they had not found you. 11But now you say, 'Go, tell your lord that Elijah is here.' 12As soon as I have gone from you, the spirit of the LORD will carry you I know not where; so, when I come and tell Ahab and he cannot find you, he will kill me, although I your servant have revered the LORD from my youth. 13Has it not been told my lord what I did when Jezebel killed the prophets of the LORD, how I hid a hundred of the LORD's prophets fifty to a cave, and provided them with bread and water? 14Yet now you say, 'Go, tell your lord that Elijah is here'; he will surely kill me." 15Elijah said, "As the LORD of hosts lives, before whom I stand, I will surely show myself to him today." 16So Obadiah went to meet Ahab, and told him; and Ahab went to meet Elijah.

18.1–46: Contest on Mount Carmel. 3: *Obadiah* is loyal to Yahweh; his name means "servant of Yahweh." **4:** There is no story preserved about Jezebel *killing off the prophets*★ of the LORD. **5:** *Ahab* is more concerned about saving his animals than about his wife's slaughter of the LORD's prophets. **7–8:** Obadiah calls Elijah *my lord*, but Elijah refers to Ahab as *your lord*, thus hinting that he is not pleased about Obadiah being a servant to such a wicked king. **12:** Obadiah's fear about Elijah's disappearance shows the aura of mystery★ and power that surrounded the prophet. **15:** *LORD of hosts* is a title for Yahweh indicating his authority over the armies or hosts of both heaven and earth.

a Heb lacks *of the drought*

17 When Ahab saw Elijah, Ahab said to him, "Is it you, you troubler of Israel?" ¹⁸He answered, "I have not troubled Israel; but you have, and your father's house, because you have forsaken the commandments of the LORD and followed the Baals. ¹⁹Now therefore have all Israel assemble for me at Mount Carmel, with the four hundred fifty prophets of Baal and the four hundred prophets of Asherah, who eat at Jezebel's table."

20 So Ahab sent to all the Israelites, and assembled the prophets at Mount Carmel. ²¹Elijah then came near to all the people, and said, "How long will you go limping with two different opinions? If the LORD is God, follow him; but if Baal, then follow him." The people did not answer him a word. ²²Then Elijah said to the people, "I, even I only, am left a prophet of the LORD; but Baal's prophets number four hundred fifty. ²³Let two bulls be given to us; let them choose one bull for themselves, cut it in pieces, and lay it on the wood, but put no fire to it; I will prepare the other bull and lay it on the wood, but put no fire to it. ²⁴Then you call on the name of your god and I will call on the name of the LORD; the god who answers by fire is indeed God." All the people answered, "Well spoken!" ²⁵Then Elijah said to the prophets of Baal, "Choose for yourselves one bull and prepare it first, for you are many; then call on the name of your god, but put no fire to it." ²⁶So they took the bull that was given them, prepared it, and called on the name of Baal from morning until noon, crying, "O Baal, answer us!" But there was no voice, and no answer. They limped about the altar that they had made. ²⁷At noon Elijah mocked them, saying, "Cry aloud! Surely he is a god; either he is meditating, or he has wandered away, or he is on a journey, or perhaps he is asleep and must be awakened." ²⁸Then they cried aloud and, as was their custom, they cut themselves with swords and lances until the blood gushed out over them. ²⁹As midday passed, they raved on until the time of the offering of the oblation, but there was no voice, no answer, and no response.

18.17–29. 17–18: Ahab blames Elijah for the drought and calls him the *troubler of Israel*, but Elijah points out that it is Ahab's apostasy that has brought trouble to Israel. **19:** *Baal** and *Asherah** were the leading male and female deities, respectively, in the fertility religion of ancient Canaan. *Carmel* means "vineyard of (the god) El" and implies affiliation with Canaanite fertility religion. Mount Carmel is near the Mediterranean coast in northern Israel and held a place for worship near its summit. **21:** *Elijah* accuses the people of *limping with two different opinions* or "straddling the fence" between the worship of Yahweh and that of Baal. The word "limping" is echoed later (v. 26) in referring to the ritual dance of the prophets of Baal. **22:** *Elijah* is overstating the case when he says, *I, even I only, am left a prophet of the LORD* since there are at least the 150 prophets of the LORD saved by Obadiah. **23–24:** Elijah proposes a decisive test to determine whether the LORD (Yahweh) or Baal truly controls the storm. The *fire* for which each of them prays is lightning. **26:** *No voice* or "sound" means that there was no thunder. When the prophets *limped about the altar* they were apparently engaged in a ritual dance. **27:** *He is meditating* may mean that he is relieving himself (see Gen 24.63), which would certainly fit with Elijah's mocking. **28:** This kind of blood-letting was common in ritual as a sign of fervency or perhaps sympathetic magic. **29:** The verb for *raved on* also means "prophesy" and implies trance behavior or some other loss of self-control. The *time of the offering of the oblation,* about 3 p.m. Second Kings 3.20 also mentions a morning oblation. The practice of two daily oblations may have arisen first in the Exile* or later. The reference to the oblation also implies the existence of a central sanctuary and therefore a southern author.

30 Then Elijah said to all the people, "Come closer to me"; and all the people came closer to him. First he repaired the altar of the LORD that had been thrown down; ³¹Elijah took twelve stones, according to the number of the tribes of the sons of Jacob, to whom the word of the LORD came, saying, "Israel shall be your name"; ³²with the stones he built an altar in the name of the LORD. Then he made a trench around the altar, large enough to contain two measures of seed. ³³Next he put the wood in order, cut the bull in pieces, and laid it on the wood. He said, "Fill four jars with water and pour it on the

burnt offering and on the wood." 34Then he said, "Do it a second time"; and they did it a second time. Again he said, "Do it a third time"; and they did it a third time, 35so that the water ran all around the altar, and filled the trench also with water.

36 At the time of the offering of the oblation, the prophet Elijah came near and said, "O LORD, God of Abraham, Isaac, and Israel, let it be known this day that you are God in Israel, that I am your servant, and that I have done all these things at your bidding. 37Answer me, O LORD, answer me, so that this people may know that you, O LORD, are God, and that you have turned their hearts back." 38Then the fire of the LORD fell and consumed the burnt offering, the wood, the stones, and the dust, and even licked up the water that was in the trench. 39When all the people saw it, they fell on their faces and said, "The LORD indeed is God; the LORD indeed is God." 40Elijah said to them, "Seize the prophets of Baal; do not let one of them escape." Then they seized them; and Elijah brought them down to the Wadi Kishon, and killed them there.

41 Elijah said to Ahab, "Go up, eat and drink; for there is a sound of rushing rain." 42So Ahab went up to eat and to drink. Elijah went up to the top of Carmel; there he bowed himself down upon the earth and put his face between his knees. 43He said to his servant, "Go up now, look toward the sea." He went up and looked, and said, "There is nothing." Then he said, "Go again seven times." 44At the seventh time he said, "Look, a little cloud no bigger than a person's hand is rising out of the sea." Then he said, "Go say to Ahab, 'Harness your chariot and go down before the rain stops you.'" 45In a little while the heavens grew black with clouds and wind; there was a heavy rain. Ahab rode off and went to Jezreel. 46But the hand of the LORD was on Elijah; he girded up his loins and ran in front of Ahab to the entrance of Jezreel.

18.30–46. 30–32: *Elijah's* repair and use of an altar away from Jerusalem would not have been approved by the deuteronomistic* historian and is one indication that the stories in chs. 17–19 are a later insertion.

32: *Two measures* (Heb., two "se'ahs") *of seed* was about three pecks or seven gallons, though this seems too small for the amount indicated in the story. Some have suggested that it refers to the amount of land that could be planted by two measures of seed. But this seems inappropriately large. 33–35: The point of drenching the sacrifice is to make clear that the fire is not accidental and does not originate on the earth. It also makes the test all the more difficult in order to impress the audience with the LORD's power, especially during a drought. 36–39: The LORD answers by sending lightning onto the altar, and the people recognize that Yahweh is the true God, who controls the storm and fertility. 40: The slaughter of the *prophets* of *Baal* counters Jezebel's slaughter of the LORD's prophets. 41: *Elijah* tells *Ahab* to *eat and drink.* Ahab may have been fasting for ritual purposes before and during the contest. 42–45: Elijah's call for the end of the drought is yet one more sign of the LORD's control over the elements and of Elijah's prowess as a man of God. 46: *Jezreel* was about 17 miles away! Elijah was able to outrun Ahab's chariot because *the hand of the LORD was on [him]; hand* often signifies power.

19 Ahab told Jezebel all that Elijah had done, and how he had killed all the prophets with the sword. 2Then Jezebel sent a messenger to Elijah, saying, "So may the gods do to me, and more also, if I do not make your life like the life of one of them by this time tomorrow." 3Then he was afraid; he got up and fled for his life, and came to Beer-sheba, which belongs to Judah; he left his servant there.

4 But he himself went a day's journey into the wilderness, and came and sat down under a solitary broom tree. He asked that he might die: "It is enough; now, O LORD, take away my life, for I am no better than my ancestors." 5Then he lay down under the broom tree and fell asleep. Suddenly an angel touched him and said to him, "Get up and eat." 6He looked, and there at his head was a cake baked on hot stones, and a jar of water. He ate and drank, and lay down again. 7The angel of the LORD came a second time, touched him, and said, "Get up and eat, otherwise the journey will be too much for you." 8He got up, and ate and drank; then he went in the strength of that food forty days and forty nights to Horeb the mount of God. 9At

that place he came to a cave, and spent the night there.

Then the word of the LORD came to him, saying, "What are you doing here, Elijah?" [10] He answered, "I have been very zealous for the LORD, the God of hosts; for the Israelites have forsaken your covenant, thrown down your altars, and killed your prophets with the sword. I alone am left, and they are seeking my life, to take it away."

11 He said, "Go out and stand on the mountain before the LORD, for the LORD is about to pass by." Now there was a great wind, so strong that it was splitting mountains and breaking rocks in pieces before the LORD, but the LORD was not in the wind; and after the wind an earthquake, but the LORD was not in the earthquake; [12] and after the earthquake a fire, but the LORD was not in the fire; and after the fire a sound of sheer silence. [13] When Elijah heard it, he wrapped his face in his mantle and went out and stood at the entrance of the cave. Then there came a voice to him that said, "What are you doing here, Elijah?" [14] He answered, "I have been very zealous for the LORD, the God of hosts; for the Israelites have forsaken your covenant, thrown down your altars, and killed your prophets with the sword. I alone am left, and they are seeking my life, to take it away." [15] Then the LORD said to him, "Go, return on your way to the wilderness of Damascus; when you arrive, you shall anoint Hazael as king over Aram. [16] Also you shall anoint Jehu son of Nimshi as king over Israel; and you shall anoint Elisha son of Shaphat of Abel-meholah as prophet in your place. [17] Whoever escapes from the sword of Hazael, Jehu shall kill; and whoever escapes from the sword of Jehu, Elisha shall kill. [18] Yet I will leave seven thousand in Israel, all the knees that have not bowed to Baal, and every mouth that has not kissed him."

19 So he set out from there, and found Elisha son of Shaphat, who was plowing. There were twelve yoke of oxen ahead of him, and he was with the twelfth. Elijah passed by him and threw his mantle over him. [20] He left the oxen, ran after Elijah, and said, "Let me kiss my father and my mother, and then I will follow you." Then Elijah[a]

said to him, "Go back again; for what have I done to you?" [21] He returned from following him, took the yoke of oxen, and slaughtered them; using the equipment from the oxen, he boiled their flesh, and gave it to the people, and they ate. Then he set out and followed Elijah, and became his servant.

19.1–21: Elijah on Mount Horeb. 1–3: *Elijah* flees south some 130 miles to *Beer-sheba* out of fear of Jezebel. **8:** Like Moses, Elijah fasts *forty days and forty nights*. Elijah goes to *Horeb the mount of God,* which is called Sinai at other places in the Bible. It is the place where Moses received the law. **9:** The Hebrew text reads "the" *cave,* apparently the same cave where Moses hid when the LORD passed by (Ex 33.17–23). **11–12:** The LORD does not appear in any of these violent forms, which might be associated with the storm god, Baal. Rather, the LORD appears quietly. **13:** Elijah *wrapped his face in his mantle,* apparently because he was afraid. **14:** Again, Elijah is overstating matters when he says *I alone am left.* **15–18:** The LORD evidently accepts Elijah's "resignation." Elijah is assured that he is not alone (v. 18), but he is told to *anoint** or designate Elisha ("my God saves") as his replacement. The other two commissions in these verses are actually carried out by Elisha (2 Kings 8–9). **19:** The introduction of *Elisha* is abrupt. We know nothing of his background except what is narrated here. The *twelve yoke of oxen* (v. 19) suggests that he is from a wealthy family. The *mantle* was a token of the prophetic office. When he *threw his mantle over him,* Elijah was designating Elisha as his replacement. **20:** Elijah's response to Elisha's request in v. 20 is obscure. By asking *What have I done to you?* he may be asking Elisha to keep in mind that he has received an important call. **21:** Elisha's feast is a way of bidding goodbye to his former life.

---

20 King Ben-hadad of Aram gathered all his army together; thirty-two kings were with him, along with horses and chariots. He marched against Samaria, laid siege to it, and attacked it. [2] Then he sent messengers into the city to King Ahab of Israel, and said to him: "Thus says Ben-hadad: [3] Your silver and gold are mine; your fairest wives and children also are mine." [4] The king of Israel answered, "As you say, my lord,

a Heb *he*

O king, I am yours, and all that I have." ⁵The messengers came again and said: "Thus says Ben-hadad: I sent to you, saying, 'Deliver to me your silver and gold, your wives and children'; ⁶nevertheless I will send my servants to you tomorrow about this time, and they shall search your house and the houses of your servants, and lay hands on whatever pleases them,ᵃ and take it away."

7 Then the king of Israel called all the elders of the land, and said, "Look now! See how this man is seeking trouble; for he sent to me for my wives, my children, my silver, and my gold; and I did not refuse him." ⁸Then all the elders and all the people said to him, "Do not listen or consent." ⁹So he said to the messengers of Ben-hadad, "Tell my lord the king: All that you first demanded of your servant I will do; but this thing I cannot do." The messengers left and brought him word again. ¹⁰Ben-hadad sent to him and said, "The gods do so to me, and more also, if the dust of Samaria will provide a handful for each of the people who follow me." ¹¹The king of Israel answered, "Tell him: One who puts on armor should not brag like one who takes it off." ¹²When Ben-hadad heard this message—now he had been drinking with the kings in the booths—he said to his men, "Take your positions!" And they took their positions against the city.

13 Then a certain prophet came up to King Ahab of Israel and said, "Thus says the LORD, Have you seen all this great multitude? Look, I will give it into your hand today; and you shall know that I am the LORD." ¹⁴Ahab said, "By whom?" He said, "Thus says the LORD, By the young men who serve the district governors." Then he said, "Who shall begin the battle?" He answered, "You." ¹⁵Then he mustered the young men who served the district governors, two hundred thirty-two; after them he mustered all the people of Israel, seven thousand.

20.1–43: Tales of other prophets.* This chapter probably went originally with ch. 22 as in the Greek (Septuagint*) version of 1 Kings, which has chs. 20 and 21 in reverse order. The stories in chs. 20 and 22 are out of place historically, since they assume a setting

in which Israel was dominated by Aram (Syria), which was not the case during Ahab's reign. **1:** The *thirty-two kings* were rulers not of nations but of city-states or chieftains dominated by Damascus. **2:** The king of Israel is here identified as *Ahab,* but this identification is likely secondary. For most of the chapter he is called simply "the king of Israel." **12:** *The booths* probably refer to the army's tents. However, it might also be read as "Sukkoth," a site east of the Jordan. **14:** The *young men who serve the district governors* seems to be a special rank or division within the military, but we no longer know exactly what it means.

16 They went out at noon, while Ben-hadad was drinking himself drunk in the booths, he and the thirty-two kings allied with him. ¹⁷The young men who served the district governors went out first. Ben-hadad had sent out scouts,ᵇ and they reported to him, "Men have come out from Samaria." ¹⁸He said, "If they have come out for peace, take them alive; if they have come out for war, take them alive."

19 But these had already come out of the city: the young men who served the district governors, and the army that followed them. ²⁰Each killed his man; the Arameans fled and Israel pursued them, but King Ben-hadad of Aram escaped on a horse with the cavalry. ²¹The king of Israel went out, attacked the horses and chariots, and defeated the Arameans with a great slaughter.

22 Then the prophet approached the king of Israel and said to him, "Come, strengthen yourself, and consider well what you have to do; for in the spring the king of Aram will come up against you."

23 The servants of the king of Aram said to him, "Their gods are gods of the hills, and so they were stronger than we; but let us fight against them in the plain, and surely we shall be stronger than they. ²⁴Also do this: remove the kings, each from his post, and put commanders in place of them; ²⁵and muster an army like the army that you have lost, horse for horse, and chariot for chariot; then we will fight against them in the plain, and surely we shall be stronger than they." He heeded their voice, and did so.

a Gk Syr Vg: Heb *you*   *b* Heb lacks *scouts*

26 In the spring Ben-hadad mustered the Arameans and went up to Aphek to fight against Israel. 27After the Israelites had been mustered and provisioned, they went out to engage them; the people of Israel encamped opposite them like two little flocks of goats, while the Arameans filled the country. 28A man of God approached and said to the king of Israel, "Thus says the LORD: Because the Arameans have said, 'The LORD is a god of the hills but he is not a god of the valleys,' therefore I will give all this great multitude into your hand, and you shall know that I am the LORD." 29They encamped opposite one another seven days. Then on the seventh day the battle began; the Israelites killed one hundred thousand Aramean foot soldiers in one day. 30The rest fled into the city of Aphek; and the wall fell on twenty-seven thousand men that were left.

Ben-hadad also fled, and entered the city to hide. 31His servants said to him, "Look, we have heard that the kings of the house of Israel are merciful kings; let us put sackcloth around our waists and ropes on our heads, and go out to the king of Israel; perhaps he will spare your life." 32So they tied sackcloth around their waists, put ropes on their heads, went to the king of Israel, and said, "Your servant Ben-hadad says, 'Please let me live.' " And he said, "Is he still alive? He is my brother." 33Now the men were watching for an omen; they quickly took it up from him and said, "Yes, Ben-hadad is your brother." Then he said, "Go and bring him." So Ben-hadad came out to him; and he had him come up into the chariot. 34Ben-hadad[a] said to him, "I will restore the towns that my father took from your father; and you may establish bazaars for yourself in Damascus, as my father did in Samaria." The king of Israel responded,[b] "I will let you go on those terms." So he made a treaty with him and let him go.

much fewer than a thousand men. **31:** *Sackcloth*★ (Heb., "saq") refers to some type of clothing that was worn to show sorrow. **32–33:** The servants of *Ben-hadad* refer to him as the *servant* of the *king of Israel*. But the king of Israel calls him a *brother*, thus making him an equal. This is also treaty language and indicates that the king of Israel wants to be treaty partners with Ben-hadad. This indication is the sign or *omen* the servants of Ben-hadad were awaiting.

35 At the command of the LORD a certain member of a company of prophets[c] said to another, "Strike me!" But the man refused to strike him. 36Then he said to him, "Because you have not obeyed the voice of the LORD, as soon as you have left me, a lion will kill you." And when he had left him, a lion met him and killed him. 37Then he found another man and said, "Strike me!" So the man hit him, striking and wounding him. 38Then the prophet departed, and waited for the king along the road, disguising himself with a bandage over his eyes. 39As the king passed by, he cried to the king and said, "Your servant went out into the thick of the battle; then a soldier turned and brought a man to me, and said, 'Guard this man; if he is missing, your life shall be given for his life, or else you shall pay a talent of silver.' 40While your servant was busy here and there, he was gone." The king of Israel said to him, "So shall your judgment be; you yourself have decided it." 41Then he quickly took the bandage away from his eyes. The king of Israel recognized him as one of the prophets. 42Then he said to him, "Thus says the LORD, 'Because you have let the man go whom I had devoted to destruction, therefore your life shall be for his life, and your people for his people.' " 43The king of Israel set out toward home, resentful and sullen, and came to Samaria.

20.16–34. 22: *In the spring* is literally "at the turn of the year," which may mean "next year." **23–25:** A *chariot* force would be more useful on flat ground than in hilly or mountainous territory. **30:** *Twenty-seven thousand* may be a simple exaggeration, or the word translated "thousand" may refer to a military unit of

20.35–43. 39: A *talent* was a measure of weight between 45 and 130 pounds. **42:** Devotion to *destruction* was an aspect of holy war★ in which the enemy was killed as a kind of sacrifice. The *king of Israel* is condemned for not carrying out Yahweh's command,

a Heb *He*   *b* Heb lacks *The king of Israel responded*
c Heb *of the sons of the prophets*

much the same as Saul is condemned in 1 Sam 15 for the same offense.

〜〜〜〜〜〜〜〜〜〜〜〜〜〜〜〜〜〜〜

21 Later the following events took place: Naboth the Jezreelite had a vineyard in Jezreel, beside the palace of King Ahab of Samaria. ²And Ahab said to Naboth, "Give me your vineyard, so that I may have it for a vegetable garden, because it is near my house; I will give you a better vineyard for it; or, if it seems good to you, I will give you its value in money." ³But Naboth said to Ahab, "The Lord forbid that I should give you my ancestral inheritance." ⁴Ahab went home resentful and sullen because of what Naboth the Jezreelite had said to him; for he had said, "I will not give you my ancestral inheritance." He lay down on his bed, turned away his face, and would not eat.

5 His wife Jezebel came to him and said, "Why are you so depressed that you will not eat?" ⁶He said to her, "Because I spoke to Naboth the Jezreelite and said to him, 'Give me your vineyard for money; or else, if you prefer, I will give you another vineyard for it'; but he answered, 'I will not give you my vineyard.' " ⁷His wife Jezebel said to him, "Do you now govern Israel? Get up, eat some food, and be cheerful; I will give you the vineyard of Naboth the Jezreelite."

8 So she wrote letters in Ahab's name and sealed them with his seal; she sent the letters to the elders and the nobles who lived with Naboth in his city. ⁹She wrote in the letters, "Proclaim a fast, and seat Naboth at the head of the assembly; ¹⁰seat two scoundrels opposite him, and have them bring a charge against him, saying, 'You have cursed God and the king.' Then take him out, and stone him to death." ¹¹The men of his city, the elders and the nobles who lived in his city, did as Jezebel had sent word to them. Just as it was written in the letters that she had sent to them, ¹²they proclaimed a fast and seated Naboth at the head of the assembly. ¹³The two scoundrels came in and sat opposite him; and the scoundrels brought a charge against Naboth, in the presence of the people, saying, "Naboth cursed God and the king." So they took him outside the city, and stoned him to death. ¹⁴Then they sent to Jez-

ebel, saying, "Naboth has been stoned; he is dead."

─────────────────────

21.1–29: Naboth's vineyard. 1: Naboth's vineyard was in *Jezreel,* while the royal palace was in Samaria. The phrase *of Samaria* was probably added later by a scribe* who was influenced by the David and Bathsheba story in 2 Sam 11–12. The story is set in Jezreel where Ahab had another palace. **3:** Israelite law forbade the sale of one's *ancestral inheritance* in perpetuity (Lev 25.23–28). **8–14:** Jezebel's actions show a keen awareness of Israelite law, which required two witnesses in capital cases (Deut 17.6) and condemned blasphemy (Lev 24.10–23) and speaking against the king (Ex 22.28). Her plot against Naboth is not done in ignorance of Israelite tradition but in spite of it.

〜〜〜〜〜〜〜〜〜〜〜〜〜〜〜〜〜〜〜

15 As soon as Jezebel heard that Naboth had been stoned and was dead, Jezebel said to Ahab, "Go, take possession of the vineyard of Naboth the Jezreelite, which he refused to give you for money; for Naboth is not alive, but dead." ¹⁶As soon as Ahab heard that Naboth was dead, Ahab set out to go down to the vineyard of Naboth the Jezreelite, to take possession of it.

17 Then the word of the Lord came to Elijah the Tishbite, saying: ¹⁸Go down to meet King Ahab of Israel, who rules*ᵃ* in Samaria; he is now in the vineyard of Naboth, where he has gone to take possession. ¹⁹You shall say to him, "Thus says the Lord: Have you killed, and also taken possession?" You shall say to him, "Thus says the Lord: In the place where dogs licked up the blood of Naboth, dogs will also lick up your blood."

20 Ahab said to Elijah, "Have you found me, O my enemy?" He answered, "I have found you. Because you have sold yourself to do what is evil in the sight of the Lord, ²¹I will bring disaster on you; I will consume you, and will cut off from Ahab every male, bond or free, in Israel; ²²and I will make your house like the house of Jeroboam son of Nebat, and like the house of Baasha son of Ahijah, because you have provoked me to anger and have caused Israel to sin. ²³Also concerning Jezebel the Lord said, 'The dogs shall eat Jezebel within the bounds of Jez-

a Heb *who is*

reel.' 24Anyone belonging to Ahab who dies in the city the dogs shall eat; and anyone of his who dies in the open country the birds of the air shall eat."

25 (Indeed, there was no one like Ahab, who sold himself to do what was evil in the sight of the LORD, urged on by his wife Jezebel. 26He acted most abominably in going after idols, as the Amorites had done, whom the LORD drove out before the Israelites.)

27 When Ahab heard those words, he tore his clothes and put sackcloth over his bare flesh; he fasted, lay in the sackcloth, and went about dejectedly. 28Then the word of the LORD came to Elijah the Tishbite: 29"Have you seen how Ahab has humbled himself before me? Because he has humbled himself before me, I will not bring the disaster in his days; but in his son's days I will bring the disaster on his house."

21.15–29. 18: Again, the phrase *in Samaria* is an addition. **20–24:** The oracle* against Ahab has been turned into a prophecy about the fall of the entire dynasty,* similar to those against the houses of Jeroboam (14.7–11) and Baasha (16.1–4). Verse 23, however, is new and is directed specifically against Jezebel. **27–29:** Ahab's repentance delays the fall of the dynasty until after his reign. These verses were likely written by a different author from the one responsible for vv. 25–26, which view Ahab as the worst of all Israelite kings.

22 For three years Aram and Israel continued without war. 2But in the third year King Jehoshaphat of Judah came down to the king of Israel. 3The king of Israel said to his servants, "Do you know that Ramoth-gilead belongs to us, yet we are doing nothing to take it out of the hand of the king of Aram?" 4He said to Jehoshaphat, "Will you go with me to battle at Ramoth-gilead?" Jehoshaphat replied to the king of Israel, "I am as you are; my people are your people, my horses are your horses."

5 But Jehoshaphat also said to the king of Israel, "Inquire first for the word of the LORD." 6Then the king of Israel gathered the prophets together, about four hundred of them, and said to them, "Shall I go to battle against Ramoth-gilead, or shall I refrain?"

They said, "Go up; for the LORD will give it into the hand of the king." 7But Jehoshaphat said, "Is there no other prophet of the LORD here of whom we may inquire?" 8The king of Israel said to Jehoshaphat, "There is still one other by whom we may inquire of the LORD, Micaiah son of Imlah; but I hate him, for he never prophesies anything favorable about me, but only disaster." Jehoshaphat said, "Let the king not say such a thing." 9Then the king of Israel summoned an officer and said, "Bring quickly Micaiah son of Imlah." 10Now the king of Israel and King Jehoshaphat of Judah were sitting on their thrones, arrayed in their robes, at the threshing floor at the entrance of the gate of Samaria; and all the prophets were prophesying before them. 11Zedekiah son of Chenaanah made for himself horns of iron, and he said, "Thus says the LORD: With these you shall gore the Arameans until they are destroyed." 12All the prophets were prophesying the same and saying, "Go up to Ramoth-gilead and triumph; the LORD will give it into the hand of the king."

22.1–53: The prophecy of Micaiah. 2: As in ch. 20, the *king of Israel* in this story was originally not identified. The identification as Ahab is secondary and probably incorrect. **3:** *Ramoth-gilead* was an important site east of the Jordan river. **5:** The fact that *Jehoshaphat* wants to inquire of the LORD reflects the author's positive view of him. The *king of Israel* is depicted as an enemy of the true prophet,* Micaiah. **6:** The *prophets* are probably court prophets who were sustained by the king. It is not clear whether they are even worshippers of the LORD (Yahweh). In fact, the number *four hundred* recalls the prophets of Baal* in 18.19. Their oracle* appears favorable to *the king*, but it could be ambiguous since they do not say which king will be given victory. **7:** *Jehoshaphat* is skeptical of the quick answer and the unanimity of the 400 prophets, so he requests another *prophet of the LORD*, one who is a true prophet of Yahweh but not associated with the 400 court prophets. **8:** The fact that *Micaiah . . . never prophesies anything favorable* about the king *but only disaster* is an indication that Micaiah is a true prophet, since prophets often opposed kings. **10:** A *threshing* floor* was a broad, flat area where grain was separated from the hull. Kings are often pictured in the Bible as sitting enthroned outside in similar settings (1 Sam 14.2; 22.6). **11:** Prophets in the Bible often carried out symbolic acts like the one described here (Jer 13; Ezek 4). Nothing is known outside of this story about this *Zedekiah*. But his name ("the righteousness of Yahweh") indicates that he was a worshipper of the LORD (Yahweh).

〰〰〰〰〰〰〰〰〰〰

13 The messenger who had gone to summon Micaiah said to him, "Look, the words of the prophets with one accord are favorable to the king; let your word be like the word of one of them, and speak favorably." ¹⁴But Micaiah said, "As the LORD lives, whatever the LORD says to me, that I will speak."

15 When he had come to the king, the king said to him, "Micaiah, shall we go to Ramoth-gilead to battle, or shall we refrain?" He answered him, "Go up and triumph; the LORD will give it into the hand of the king." ¹⁶But the king said to him, "How many times must I make you swear to tell me nothing but the truth in the name of the LORD?" ¹⁷Then Micaiah*ᵃ* said, "I saw all Israel scattered on the mountains, like sheep that have no shepherd; and the LORD said, 'These have no master; let each one go home in peace.'" ¹⁸The king of Israel said to Jehoshaphat, "Did I not tell you that he would not prophesy anything favorable about me, but only disaster?"

19 Then Micaiah*ᵃ* said, "Therefore hear the word of the LORD: I saw the LORD sitting on his throne, with all the host of heaven standing beside him to the right and to the left of him. ²⁰And the LORD said, 'Who will entice Ahab, so that he may go up and fall at Ramoth-gilead?' Then one said one thing, and another said another, ²¹until a spirit came forward and stood before the LORD, saying, 'I will entice him.' ²²'How?' the LORD asked him. He replied, 'I will go out and be a lying spirit in the mouth of all his prophets.' Then the LORD*ᵃ* said, 'You are to entice him, and you shall succeed; go out and do it.' ²³So you see, the LORD has put a lying spirit in the mouth of all these your prophets; the LORD has decreed disaster for you."

caiah's first response agrees completely with that of the court prophets. He may, in fact, be mimicking them. **16:** The *king* of Israel recognizes Micaiah's insincerity and adjures him to speak *the truth in the name of the LORD*. **17:** The image of a king as a *shepherd* was common in the ancient Near East (2 Sam 5.2). The sheep are without a shepherd in *Micaiah*'s vision because the king has died. **19:** The LORD is depicted as a king *sitting on his throne* surrounded by his council of advisers, here called the *host of heaven*. **20:** This is the only time in the story proper that the king of Israel is identified as *Ahab*. The council deliberates how to *entice* him to go to *Ramoth-gilead* where he will *fall*, that is, be killed. **21–23:** A *spirit* or "breath" steps forward and volunteers to deceive Ahab as a *lying spirit in the mouth of his prophets.*

〰〰〰〰〰〰〰〰〰〰

24 Then Zedekiah son of Chenaanah came up to Micaiah, slapped him on the cheek, and said, "Which way did the spirit of the LORD pass from me to speak to you?" ²⁵Micaiah replied, "You will find out on that day when you go in to hide in an inner chamber." ²⁶The king of Israel then ordered, "Take Micaiah, and return him to Amon the governor of the city and to Joash the king's son, ²⁷and say, 'Thus says the king: Put this fellow in prison, and feed him on reduced rations of bread and water until I come in peace.'" ²⁸Micaiah said, "If you return in peace, the LORD has not spoken by me." And he said, "Hear, you peoples, all of you!"

29 So the king of Israel and King Jehoshaphat of Judah went up to Ramoth-gilead. ³⁰The king of Israel said to Jehoshaphat, "I will disguise myself and go into battle, but you wear your robes." So the king of Israel disguised himself and went into battle. ³¹Now the king of Aram had commanded the thirty-two captains of his chariots, "Fight with no one small or great, but only with the king of Israel." ³²When the captains of the chariots saw Jehoshaphat, they said, "It is surely the king of Israel." So they turned to fight against him; and Jehoshaphat cried out. ³³When the captains of the chariots saw that it was not the king of Israel, they turned back from pursuing him. ³⁴But a certain man

---

22.13–23. 13–14: *Micaiah*, unlike the court prophets, cannot speak what he wishes or what the king wants to hear, but only what the LORD says to him. **15:** *Mi-*

a Heb *he*

drew his bow and unknowingly struck the king of Israel between the scale armor and the breastplate; so he said to the driver of his chariot, "Turn around, and carry me out of the battle, for I am wounded." 35The battle grew hot that day, and the king was propped up in his chariot facing the Arameans, until at evening he died; the blood from the wound had flowed into the bottom of the chariot. 36Then about sunset a shout went through the army, "Every man to his city, and every man to his country!"

37 So the king died, and was brought to Samaria; they buried the king in Samaria. 38They washed the chariot by the pool of Samaria; the dogs licked up his blood, and the prostitutes washed themselves in it,ᵃ according to the word of the LORD that he had spoken. 39Now the rest of the acts of Ahab, and all that he did, and the ivory house that he built, and all the cities that he built, are they not written in the Book of the Annals of the Kings of Israel? 40So Ahab slept with his ancestors; and his son Ahaziah succeeded him.

41 Jehoshaphat son of Asa began to reign over Judah in the fourth year of King Ahab of Israel. 42Jehoshaphat was thirty-five years old when he began to reign, and he reigned twenty-five years in Jerusalem. His mother's name was Azubah daughter of Shilhi. 43He walked in all the way of his father Asa; he did not turn aside from it, doing what was right in the sight of the LORD; yet the high places were not taken away, and the people still sacrificed and offered incense on the high places. 44Jehoshaphat also made peace with the king of Israel.

king of Israel believed Micaiah enough so that he *disguised himself* in order to avoid being a target of the enemy. This probably means that he did not wear his royal *robes* as did *Jehoshaphat*. **32–33:** Something about *Jehoshaphat*'s cry, perhaps his accent, alerted the Arameans that he was not the king of Israel. **36:** *Every man to his city, and every man to his country* is a cry to military demobilization. See 2 Sam 20.1; 1 Kings 12.16. **38:** The fact that *the dogs licked up [Ahab's] blood* is evidently meant as a fulfillment of Elijah's word in 21.19. **40:** The idiom *slept with his ancestors* is not used anywhere else of a king who suffered a violent death. Thus the closing formula for Ahab's reign seems to ignore his death in battle. **43:** The *high places*✱ were places for worship outside of Jerusalem.

45 Now the rest of the acts of Jehoshaphat, and his power that he showed, and how he waged war, are they not written in the Book of the Annals of the Kings of Judah? 46The remnant of the male temple prostitutes who were still in the land in the days of his father Asa, he exterminated.

47 There was no king in Edom; a deputy was king. 48Jehoshaphat made ships of the Tarshish type to go to Ophir for gold; but they did not go, for the ships were wrecked at Ezion-geber. 49Then Ahaziah son of Ahab said to Jehoshaphat, "Let my servants go with your servants in the ships," but Jehoshaphat was not willing. 50Jehoshaphat slept with his ancestors and was buried with his ancestors in the city of his father David; his son Jehoram succeeded him.

51 Ahaziah son of Ahab began to reign over Israel in Samaria in the seventeenth year of King Jehoshaphat of Judah; he reigned two years over Israel. 52He did what was evil in the sight of the LORD, and walked in the way of his father and mother, and in the way of Jeroboam son of Nebat, who caused Israel to sin. 53He served Baal and worshiped him; he provoked the LORD, the God of Israel, to anger, just as his father had done.

22.24–44. 24: *Zedekiah* claims that the lying spirit is actually in *Micaiah*. **25:** *Micaiah*'s point is not entirely clear. Apparently, he foresees Zedekiah trying to *hide in an inner chamber* after Israel's defeat. Another possible interpretation would take Micaiah's meaning to be coarsely sarcastic: You will know the answer to your question (v. 24) the next time you relieve yourself (taking *hide in an inner chamber* to be a euphemism✱). **27–28:** *In peace* means alive and unharmed. **30:** The

a Heb lacks *in it*

2 KINGS

Introduction

The book of 2 Kings is the continuation of 1 Kings and the final biblical book of the Deuteronomistic★ History (see the introduction to 1 Samuel). In some ways the hand of the deuteronomistic author appears more clearly in 2 Kings than in the previous books of the History, partly because the contents of the book are closer to the author's time than is the case with the previous books. Deuteronomistic editing is especially apparent in the evaluations of the kings. The kings of Israel are all condemned for perpetuating the sin of Jeroboam in the shrines he built at Dan and Bethel. Several of the kings of Judah, on the other hand, are viewed favorably, although most of them are accused of failing to do away with the "high places,"★ shrines other than the Jerusalem Temple,★ which is considered the only legitimate place for worship. The author obviously had access to a king list or perhaps royal annals for information about the kings. In addition, a significant portion of 2 Kings consists of stories about prophets.★ There is reason to believe that many of these stories were inserted by a later writer or editor into the already completed Deuteronomistic History.

The Deuteronomistic History was composed in the Exile.★ 2 Kings recounts the destruction of Jerusalem and the beginning of the Babylonian captivity. The author struggles to explain the cause for the Exile, blaming it on both Manasseh (21.10–15) and Zedekiah and his contemporaries (24.20). Curiously, no attempt is made to explain how the promise of an eternal Davidic dynasty★ is to be understood in the light of the Exile. Indeed, the book ends on an ambiguous note. On the one hand, it offers no explicit hope for restoration. On the other hand, the final four verses mention the release from prison of Jehoiachin, the next-to-last king of Judah, and his elevation in the Babylonian court. They therefore hint at a possible restoration of the Davidic monarchy.

READING GUIDE

The reader may find the names of the kings unfamiliar and the alternation between Israel and Judah difficult to track. What is more important than knowing the details of this history is understanding the author's overall perspective, which entails trying to explain Israel's history theologically. Thus, Judah outlasts Israel because of the LORD's reward of a dynasty for David's faithfulness. Israel's destruction is due to its apostasy, as is Judah's captivity. But in Judah's case there may still be hope for the future. The stories about Elisha and the prophets add another dimension to this narrative.★ While they emphasize the supremacy of the LORD in contrast to other gods, they also display a legendary★ quality in describing the deeds of the prophets, which does not correspond to the deuteronomistic outlook.

1–8	Stories about Elisha and the prophets
9–10	Jehu's revolt
11–16	Various kings; focus on Judah
17	The fall of Israel
18–20	Hezekiah
21	Manasseh and Amon
22–23	Josiah
24–25	The final kings and fall of Judah

1

After the death of Ahab, Moab rebelled against Israel.

2 Ahaziah had fallen through the lattice in his upper chamber in Samaria, and lay injured; so he sent messengers, telling them, "Go, inquire of Baal-zebub, the god of Ekron, whether I shall recover from this injury." ³But the angel of the LORD said to Elijah the Tishbite, "Get up, go to meet the messengers of the king of Samaria, and say to them, 'Is it because there is no God in Israel that you are going to inquire of Baal-zebub, the god of Ekron?' ⁴Now therefore thus says the LORD, 'You shall not leave the bed to which you have gone, but you shall surely die.'" So Elijah went.

5 The messengers returned to the king, who said to them, "Why have you returned?" ⁶They answered him, "There came a man to meet us, who said to us, 'Go back to the king who sent you, and say to him: Thus says the LORD: Is it because there is no God in Israel that you are sending to inquire of Baal-zebub, the god of Ekron? Therefore you shall not leave the bed to which you have gone, but shall surely die.'" ⁷He said to them, "What sort of man was he who came to meet you and told you these things?" ⁸They answered him, "A hairy man, with a leather belt around his waist." He said, "It is Elijah the Tishbite."

9 Then the king sent to him a captain of fifty with his fifty men. He went up to Elijah, who was sitting on the top of a hill, and said to him, "O man of God, the king says, 'Come down.'" ¹⁰But Elijah answered the captain of fifty, "If I am a man of God, let fire come down from heaven and consume you and your fifty." Then fire came down from heaven, and consumed him and his fifty.

11 Again the king sent to him another captain of fifty with his fifty. He went up[a] and said to him, "O man of God, this is the king's order: Come down quickly!" ¹²But Elijah answered them, "If I am a man of God, let fire come down from heaven and consume you and your fifty." Then the fire of God came down from heaven and consumed him and his fifty.

13 Again the king sent the captain of a third fifty with his fifty. So the third captain of fifty went up, and came and fell on his knees before Elijah, and entreated him, "O man of God, please let my life, and the life of these fifty servants of yours, be precious in your sight. ¹⁴Look, fire came down from heaven and consumed the two former captains of fifty men with their fifties; but now let my life be precious in your sight." ¹⁵Then the angel of the LORD said to Elijah, "Go down with him; do not be afraid of him." So he set out and went down with him to the king, ¹⁶and said to him, "Thus says the LORD: Because you have sent messengers to inquire of Baal-zebub, the god of Ekron,—is it because there is no God in Israel to inquire of his word?—therefore you shall not leave the bed to which you have gone, but you shall surely die."

17 So he died according to the word of the LORD that Elijah had spoken. His brother,[b] Jehoram succeeded him as king in the second year of King Jehoram son of Jehoshaphat of Judah, because Ahaziah had no son. ¹⁸Now the rest of the acts of Ahaziah that he did, are they not written in the Book of the Annals of the Kings of Israel?

1.1–18: The death of Ahaziah. 1: This verse anticipates the story in 3.4–27 and may be out of place here. **2:** The *lattice* was decorative, but also functional in the sense of admitting light and air while providing some privacy. It was not strong enough to keep a person from falling, as this story shows. Ahaziah sent messengers to *inquire,* a technical term for divination. *Baal-zebub,*★ meaning "lord of the fly," is a deliberate mocking distortion of the name Baal-zebul,★ "Baal★ the prince." **3:** The Hebrew word for *angel* also means messenger. **8:** A *hairy man,* literally "a man of hair," may refer to a coarse garment that was the mantle of prophets★ (Zech 13.4). **10, 12:** The *fire of God from heaven* was probably lightning.

2

Now when the LORD was about to take Elijah up to heaven by a whirlwind, Elijah and Elisha were on their way from Gilgal. ²Elijah said to Elisha, "Stay here; for the LORD has sent me as far as Bethel." But Elisha said, "As the LORD lives, and as you your-

a Gk Compare verses 9, 13: Heb *He answered*
b Gk Syr: Heb lacks *His brother*

self live, I will not leave you." So they went down to Bethel. ³The company of prophets*a* who were in Bethel came out to Elisha, and said to him, "Do you know that today the LORD will take your master away from you?" And he said, "Yes, I know; keep silent."

4 Elijah said to him, "Elisha, stay here; for the LORD has sent me to Jericho." But he said, "As the LORD lives, and as you yourself live, I will not leave you." So they came to Jericho. ⁵The company of prophets*a* who were at Jericho drew near to Elisha, and said to him, "Do you know that today the LORD will take your master away from you?" And he answered, "Yes, I know; be silent."

6 Then Elijah said to him, "Stay here; for the LORD has sent me to the Jordan." But he said, "As the LORD lives, and as you yourself live, I will not leave you." So the two of them went on. ⁷Fifty men of the company of prophets*a* also went, and stood at some distance from them, as they both were standing by the Jordan. ⁸Then Elijah took his mantle and rolled it up, and struck the water; the water was parted to the one side and to the other, until the two of them crossed on dry ground.

9 When they had crossed, Elijah said to Elisha, "Tell me what I may do for you, before I am taken from you." Elisha said, "Please let me inherit a double share of your spirit." ¹⁰He responded, "You have asked a hard thing; yet, if you see me as I am being taken from you, it will be granted you; if not, it will not." ¹¹As they continued walking and talking, a chariot of fire and horses of fire separated the two of them, and Elijah ascended in a whirlwind into heaven. ¹²Elisha kept watching and crying out, "Father, father! The chariots of Israel and its horsemen!" But when he could no longer see him, he grasped his own clothes and tore them in two pieces.

2.1–12: The translation of Elijah. The stories in this chapter fall outside of the standard wording that marks the beginning and ending of the reigns of the kings, called regnal formulas (1.17–18; 3.1), which may indicate that they, along with other stories about the prophets,⋆ are later additions to the Deuteronomistic⋆ History. **1:** The only other person in the Bible

who was taken *up to heaven* without dying was Enoch (Gen 5.24). **3:** The *company of prophets*, literally "the sons of the prophets," were followers of prophets, perhaps even a guild or school of prophets. They were also aware, perhaps through prophetic agency, that *the LORD will take* Elijah away. **8:** Elijah's *mantle* is a symbol of his power as a prophet (see 1.8; Zech 13.4), which Elisha will inherit (2.13). His division of the Jordan here is reminiscent of Moses' division of the Red Sea (Ex 14.21–22) and of Joshua's division of the Jordan (Josh 3.13–17). **9:** *Double share* does not mean twice as much as Elijah but the portion of the first-born son (Deut 21.17), or two-thirds. **12:** Elisha calls Elijah his *father* out of respect for his teacher, not because there is a blood relationship between them. *The chariots of Israel and its horsemen* may allude to the image of the LORD as commander of the heavenly armies ("Yahweh sebaoth," "the LORD of hosts"; see 6.17).

~~~~~~~~~~~~~~~~~~~~~~~~~~~~~

13 He picked up the mantle of Elijah that had fallen from him, and went back and stood on the bank of the Jordan. ¹⁴He took the mantle of Elijah that had fallen from him, and struck the water, saying, "Where is the LORD, the God of Elijah?" When he had struck the water, the water was parted to the one side and to the other, and Elisha went over.

15 When the company of prophets*a* who were at Jericho saw him at a distance, they declared, "The spirit of Elijah rests on Elisha." They came to meet him and bowed to the ground before him. ¹⁶They said to him, "See now, we have fifty strong men among your servants; please let them go and seek your master; it may be that the spirit of the LORD has caught him up and thrown him down on some mountain or into some valley." He responded, "No, do not send them." ¹⁷But when they urged him until he was ashamed, he said, "Send them." So they sent fifty men who searched for three days but did not find him. ¹⁸When they came back to him (he had remained at Jericho), he said to them, "Did I not say to you, Do not go?"

19 Now the people of the city said to Elisha, "The location of this city is good, as my

a Heb *sons of the prophets*

lord sees; but the water is bad, and the land is unfruitful." 20He said, "Bring me a new bowl, and put salt in it." So they brought it to him. 21Then he went to the spring of water and threw the salt into it, and said, "Thus says the LORD, I have made this water wholesome; from now on neither death nor miscarriage shall come from it." 22So the water has been wholesome to this day, according to the word that Elisha spoke.

23 He went up from there to Bethel; and while he was going up on the way, some small boys came out of the city and jeered at him, saying, "Go away, baldhead! Go away, baldhead!" 24When he turned around and saw them, he cursed them in the name of the LORD. Then two she-bears came out of the woods and mauled forty-two of the boys. 25From there he went on to Mount Carmel, and then returned to Samaria.

2.13–25: Elisha as Elijah's successor. The stories here show that Elisha has inherited Elijah's power as a man of God. 13–14: Elisha *picked up the mantle of Elijah*, which was the symbol of his prophetic★ power (1.8; Zech 13.4). He then *struck the water* of the Jordan with it and *parted* it just as Elijah had done (2.8) and much as Joshua did when he succeeded Moses (Ex 14.21–22; Josh 3.13–17). 15: The *company of prophets* (see comment on 2.3) recognize Elisha as Elijah's successor. 16–18: Elisha knows that Elijah has been taken up and will not be found, but he acquiesces to a search at the insistence of the other prophets. 19–22: Elisha's miraculous purification of the spring also shows that he has the power of Elijah. This story offers an etiological★ explanation for the renowned spring at Jericho that is still active today. 23–25: This legend★ was preserved not for its high ethical quality but to show the power now vested in Elisha and to teach that one should have respect for prophets.

3 In the eighteenth year of King Jehoshaphat of Judah, Jehoram son of Ahab became king over Israel in Samaria; he reigned twelve years. 2He did what was evil in the sight of the LORD, though not like his father and mother, for he removed the pillar of Baal that his father had made. 3Nevertheless he clung to the sin of Jeroboam son of Nebat, which he caused Israel to commit; he did not depart from it.

4 Now King Mesha of Moab was a sheep breeder, who used to deliver to the king of Israel one hundred thousand lambs, and the wool of one hundred thousand rams. 5But when Ahab died, the king of Moab rebelled against the king of Israel. 6So King Jehoram marched out of Samaria at that time and mustered all Israel. 7As he went he sent word to King Jehoshaphat of Judah, "The king of Moab has rebelled against me; will you go with me to battle against Moab?" He answered, "I will; I am with you, my people are your people, my horses are your horses." 8Then he asked, "By which way shall we march?" Jehoram answered, "By the way of the wilderness of Edom."

9 So the king of Israel, the king of Judah, and the king of Edom set out; and when they had made a roundabout march of seven days, there was no water for the army or for the animals that were with them. 10Then the king of Israel said, "Alas! The LORD has summoned us, three kings, only to be handed over to Moab." 11But Jehoshaphat said, "Is there no prophet of the LORD here, through whom we may inquire of the LORD?" Then one of the servants of the king of Israel answered, "Elisha son of Shaphat, who used to pour water on the hands of Elijah, is here." 12Jehoshaphat said, "The word of the LORD is with him." So the king of Israel and Jehoshaphat and the king of Edom went down to him.

3.1–27: The independence of Moab. 1: The information here about the beginning of Jehoram's reign disagrees with that of 1.17. The two verses may be based on two distinct chronologies. 2: A *pillar* was often used, much as an idol would be, as a symbol for a god in worship. 3: *The sin of Jeroboam* was the two shrines at Dan and Bethel (1 Kings 12.25–33). 4: *Moab* was the country across the Dead Sea from Israel. The *lambs* and *wool* that *King Mesha* sent to Israel were the yearly payment of tribute of a subject state to its overlord. 8: *Edom* was east of Judah and south of Moab. It was apparently controlled at this time by Judah. *Jehoram* plans to attack Moab from the south. 11: As in 1 Kings 22.7, it is the righteous King *Jehoshaphat* of Judah who asks for a prophet★ of the LORD. To *inquire* is a technical term for divination or seeking an oracle★ from God. *Elisha* is here recognized as *Elijah's* servant *who used to pour water* on his hands.

13 Elisha said to the king of Israel, "What have I to do with you? Go to your father's prophets or to your mother's." But the king of Israel said to him, "No; it is the LORD who has summoned us, three kings, only to be handed over to Moab." 14Elisha said, "As the LORD of hosts lives, whom I serve, were it not that I have regard for King Jehoshaphat of Judah, I would give you neither a look nor a glance. 15But get me a musician." And then, while the musician was playing, the power of the LORD came on him. 16And he said, "Thus says the LORD, 'I will make this wadi full of pools.' 17For thus says the LORD, 'You shall see neither wind nor rain, but the wadi shall be filled with water, so that you shall drink, you, your cattle, and your animals.' 18This is only a trifle in the sight of the LORD, for he will also hand Moab over to you. 19You shall conquer every fortified city and every choice city; every good tree you shall fell, all springs of water you shall stop up, and every good piece of land you shall ruin with stones." 20The next day, about the time of the morning offering, suddenly water began to flow from the direction of Edom, until the country was filled with water.

3.13–20. 13: *What have I to do with you?* means "We have nothing in common"; Elisha wants nothing to do with the king of Israel. Jehoram's *father* was Ahab and his *mother* Jezebel. Their *prophets* were worshippers of Baal★ and Asherah★ (1 Kings 18.19). 15: Music was used to induce the prophet's ecstatic experience in which he would give his oracle★ (compare 1 Sam. 10.5, 9–13). 19: The measures described in this verse would ruin a piece of land for agriculture. 20: The *morning offering* or oblation was made at dawn. 1 Kings 18.29 refers to a second oblation at about 3 p.m. The practice of two oblations may have begun in the Exile★ or later. This is an indication that this story was written at a later date.

21 When all the Moabites heard that the kings had come up to fight against them, all who were able to put on armor, from the youngest to the oldest, were called out and were drawn up at the frontier. 22When they rose early in the morning, and the sun shone upon the water, the Moabites saw the water opposite them as red as blood. 23They said, "This is blood; the kings must have fought together, and killed one another. Now then, Moab, to the spoil!" 24But when they came

The Mesha Stele

The Mesha stele (a stele, pronounced "steely," is an inscribed pillar) or Moabite stone was discovered in 1868 in what is now the country of Jordan. It is the only inscription known to exist from the ancient country of Moab and in the language of that country. While it was discovered intact, subsequent feuding over it, especially by Western powers, led the Bedouin Arabs who possessed it to destroy it. Only about half of the original stele remains today in fragmentary form. The rest has been reconstructed. The stele was erected by King Mesha of Moab (2 Kings 3.4) sometime in the second half of the ninth century (850–800) BCE. In it, Mesha claims to have broken free of the domination of Israel under Omri and Ahab. The inscription mentions the LORD (Yahweh) as well as the institution of the ban,★ or devotion to destruction, which is also found in the Bible (for example, 1 Sam 15.3). According to this practice, everything of the enemy's that can breathe—men, women, children, animals—is killed as a sacrifice to the deity. The Mesha stele, therefore, makes it clear that holy war★ was not unique to Israel but was an institution common in the ancient Near East.

to the camp of Israel, the Israelites rose up and attacked the Moabites, who fled before them; as they entered Moab they continued the attack.[a] 25 The cities they overturned, and on every good piece of land everyone threw a stone, until it was covered; every spring of water they stopped up, and every good tree they felled. Only at Kir-hareseth did the stone walls remain, until the slingers surrounded and attacked it. 26 When the king of Moab saw that the battle was going against him, he took with him seven hundred swordsmen to break through, opposite the king of Edom; but they could not. 27 Then he took his firstborn son who was to succeed him, and offered him as a burnt offering on the wall. And great wrath came upon Israel, so they withdrew from him and returned to their own land.

3.21–27. 22: The *red* color of the water is appropriate to Edom, which comes from the word for red and which was known for its red sandstone (see Gen 25.25, 30). **27:** Child sacrifice was practiced in the ancient Near East. Here the king of Moab sacrifices his son to Chemosh, Moab's god. It is not clear what is meant by *great wrath came upon Israel*. Perhaps it means that the Israelites became afraid when they witnessed this desperate act, though the most natural interpretation would seem to be that Chemosh's wrath was directed against Israel in some form.

4 Now the wife of a member of the company of prophets[b] cried to Elisha, "Your servant my husband is dead; and you know that your servant feared the LORD, but a creditor has come to take my two children as slaves." 2 Elisha said to her, "What shall I do for you? Tell me, what do you have in the house?" She answered, "Your servant has nothing in the house, except a jar of oil." 3 He said, "Go outside, borrow vessels from all your neighbors, empty vessels and not just a few. 4 Then go in, and shut the door behind you and your children, and start pouring into all these vessels; when each is full, set it aside." 5 So she left him and shut the door behind her and her children; they kept bringing vessels to her, and she kept pouring. 6 When the vessels were full, she said to her son, "Bring me another vessel." But he said

to her, "There are no more." Then the oil stopped flowing. 7 She came and told the man of God, and he said, "Go sell the oil and pay your debts, and you and your children can live on the rest."

4.1–44: Elisha's wonders. 1–7: This story is similar to the one about Elijah in 1 Kings 17.8–16. The sale of oneself or one's family members to pay debts was permitted on a temporary basis by Israelite law (Lev 25.39–42; Deut 15.1–17).

8 One day Elisha was passing through Shunem, where a wealthy woman lived, who urged him to have a meal. So whenever he passed that way, he would stop there for a meal. 9 She said to her husband, "Look, I am sure that this man who regularly passes our way is a holy man of God. 10 Let us make a small roof chamber with walls, and put there for him a bed, a table, a chair, and a lamp, so that he can stay there whenever he comes to us."

11 One day when he came there, he went up to the chamber and lay down there. 12 He said to his servant Gehazi, "Call the Shunammite woman." When he had called her, she stood before him. 13 He said to him, "Say to her, Since you have taken all this trouble for us, what may be done for you? Would you have a word spoken on your behalf to the king or to the commander of the army?" She answered, "I live among my own people." 14 He said, "What then may be done for her?" Gehazi answered, "Well, she has no son, and her husband is old." 15 He said, "Call her." When he had called her, she stood at the door. 16 He said, "At this season, in due time, you shall embrace a son." She replied, "No, my lord, O man of God; do not deceive your servant."

17 The woman conceived and bore a son at that season, in due time, as Elisha had declared to her.

18 When the child was older, he went out one day to his father among the reapers. 19 He complained to his father, "Oh, my head, my head!" The father said to his ser-

---

a Compare Gk Syr: Meaning of Heb uncertain
b Heb *the sons of the prophets*

vant, "Carry him to his mother." 20He carried him and brought him to his mother; the child sat on her lap until noon, and he died. 21She went up and laid him on the bed of the man of God, closed the door on him, and left. 22Then she called to her husband, and said, "Send me one of the servants and one of the donkeys, so that I may quickly go to the man of God and come back again." 23He said, "Why go to him today? It is neither new moon nor sabbath." She said, "It will be all right." 24Then she saddled the donkey and said to her servant, "Urge the animal on; do not hold back for me unless I tell you." 25So she set out, and came to the man of God at Mount Carmel.

When the man of God saw her coming, he said to Gehazi his servant, "Look, there is the Shunammite woman; 26run at once to meet her, and say to her, Are you all right? Is your husband all right? Is the child all right?" She answered, "It is all right." 27When she came to the man of God at the mountain, she caught hold of his feet. Gehazi approached to push her away. But the man of God said, "Let her alone, for she is in bitter distress; the LORD has hidden it from me and has not told me." 28Then she said, "Did I ask my lord for a son? Did I not say, Do not mislead me?" 29He said to Gehazi, "Gird up your loins, and take my staff in your hand, and go. If you meet anyone, give no greeting, and if anyone greets you, do not answer; and lay my staff on the face of the child." 30Then the mother of the child said, "As the LORD lives, and as you yourself live, I will not leave without you." So he rose up and followed her. 31Gehazi went on ahead and laid the staff on the face of the child, but there was no sound or sign of life. He came back to meet him and told him, "The child has not awakened."

32 When Elisha came into the house, he saw the child lying dead on his bed. 33So he went in and closed the door on the two of them, and prayed to the LORD. 34Then he got up on the bed*a* and lay upon the child, putting his mouth upon his mouth, his eyes upon his eyes, and his hands upon his hands; and while he lay bent over him, the flesh of the child became warm. 35He got down, walked once to and fro in the room, then got

up again and bent over him; the child sneezed seven times, and the child opened his eyes. 36Elisha*b* summoned Gehazi and said, "Call the Shunammite woman." So he called her. When she came to him, he said, "Take your son." 37She came and fell at his feet, bowing to the ground; then she took her son and left.

4.8–37: This story is also similar to one about Elijah in 1 Kings 17.17–24, which it has influenced (see comments on 1 Kings 17). *Mount Carmel* (v. 25) was a holy site and the location of Elijah's victory in 1 Kings 18. It has apparently become Elisha's residence. *Gehazi*, Elisha's servant, is mentioned here (v. 25), without introduction, for the first time. As in 1 Kings 17, Elisha's resuscitation of the boy involves contactual magic (v. 34), though the miracle is clearly seen as the LORD's doing (v. 33). The boy's sneezing (v. 35) is a sign of life.

---

38 When Elisha returned to Gilgal, there was a famine in the land. As the company of prophets was*c* sitting before him, he said to his servant, "Put the large pot on, and make some stew for the company of prophets."*d* 39One of them went out into the field to gather herbs; he found a wild vine and gathered from it a lapful of wild gourds, and came and cut them up into the pot of stew, not knowing what they were. 40They served some for the men to eat. But while they were eating the stew, they cried out, "O man of God, there is death in the pot!" They could not eat it. 41He said, "Then bring some flour." He threw it into the pot, and said, "Serve the people and let them eat." And there was nothing harmful in the pot.

42 A man came from Baal-shalishah, bringing food from the first fruits to the man of God: twenty loaves of barley and fresh ears of grain in his sack. Elisha said, "Give it to the people and let them eat." 43But his servant said, "How can I set this before a hundred people?" So he repeated, "Give it to the people and let them eat, for thus says the LORD, 'They shall eat and have some left.'"

---

a Heb lacks *on the bed*   *b* Heb *he*   *c* Heb *sons of the prophets were*   *d* Heb *sons of the prophets*

⁴⁴He set it before them, they ate, and had some left, according to the word of the LORD.

4.38–44. 38–41: This story is similar to the one in 2.19–22. **42–44:** Compare the New Testament stories of Jesus' multiplication of the loaves (Mt 14.13–21; 15.32–38; and their parallels in the other Gospels).

〜〜〜〜〜〜〜〜〜〜〜〜〜〜〜〜〜〜〜〜

5 Naaman, commander of the army of the king of Aram, was a great man and in high favor with his master, because by him the LORD had given victory to Aram. The man, though a mighty warrior, suffered from leprosy.ᵃ ²Now the Arameans on one of their raids had taken a young girl captive from the land of Israel, and she served Naaman's wife. ³She said to her mistress, "If only my lord were with the prophet who is in Samaria! He would cure him of his leprosy."ᵃ ⁴So Naamanᵇ went in and told his lord just what the girl from the land of Israel had said. ⁵And the king of Aram said, "Go then, and I will send along a letter to the king of Israel."

He went, taking with him ten talents of silver, six thousand shekels of gold, and ten sets of garments. ⁶He brought the letter to the king of Israel, which read, "When this letter reaches you, know that I have sent to you my servant Naaman, that you may cure him of his leprosy."ᵃ ⁷When the king of Israel read the letter, he tore his clothes and said, "Am I God, to give death or life, that this man sends word to me to cure a man of his leprosy?ᵃ Just look and see how he is trying to pick a quarrel with me."

8 But when Elisha the man of God heard that the king of Israel had torn his clothes, he sent a message to the king, "Why have you torn your clothes? Let him come to me, that he may learn that there is a prophet in Israel." ⁹So Naaman came with his horses and chariots, and halted at the entrance of Elisha's house. ¹⁰Elisha sent a messenger to him, saying, "Go, wash in the Jordan seven times, and your flesh shall be restored and you shall be clean." ¹¹But Naaman became angry and went away, saying, "I thought that for me he would surely come out, and stand and call on the name of the LORD his God,

and would wave his hand over the spot, and cure the leprosy!ᵃ ¹²Are not Abanaᶜ and Pharpar, the rivers of Damascus, better than all the waters of Israel? Could I not wash in them, and be clean?" He turned and went away in a rage. ¹³But his servants approached and said to him, "Father, if the prophet had commanded you to do something difficult, would you not have done it? How much more, when all he said to you was, 'Wash, and be clean'?" ¹⁴So he went down and immersed himself seven times in the Jordan, according to the word of the man of God; his flesh was restored like the flesh of a young boy, and he was clean.

15 Then he returned to the man of God, he and all his company; he came and stood before him and said, "Now I know that there is no God in all the earth except in Israel; please accept a present from your servant." ¹⁶But he said, "As the LORD lives, whom I serve, I will accept nothing!" He urged him to accept, but he refused. ¹⁷Then Naaman said, "If not, please let two mule-loads of earth be given to your servant; for your servant will no longer offer burnt offering or sacrifice to any god except the LORD. ¹⁸But may the LORD pardon your servant on one count: when my master goes into the house of Rimmon to worship there, leaning on my arm, and I bow down in the house of Rimmon, when I do bow down in the house of Rimmon, may the LORD pardon your servant on this one count." ¹⁹He said to him, "Go in peace."

But when Naaman had gone from him a short distance, ²⁰Gehazi, the servant of Elisha the man of God, thought, "My master has let that Aramean Naaman off too lightly by not accepting from him what he offered. As the LORD lives, I will run after him and get something out of him." ²¹So Gehazi went after Naaman. When Naaman saw someone running after him, he jumped down from the chariot to meet him and said, "Is everything all right?" ²²He replied, "Yes, but my master has sent me to say, 'Two members of a com-

---

a A term for several skin diseases; precise meaning uncertain   *b* Heb *he*   *c* Another reading is *Amana*

pany of prophets[a] have just come to me from the hill country of Ephraim; please give them a talent of silver and two changes of clothing.' " 23Naaman said, "Please accept two talents." He urged him, and tied up two talents of silver in two bags, with two changes of clothing, and gave them to two of his servants, who carried them in front of Gehazi.[b] 24When he came to the citadel, he took the bags[c] from them, and stored them inside; he dismissed the men, and they left.

25 He went in and stood before his master; and Elisha said to him, "Where have you been, Gehazi?" He answered, "Your servant has not gone anywhere at all." 26But he said to him, "Did I not go with you in spirit when someone left his chariot to meet you? Is this a time to accept money and to accept clothing, olive orchards and vineyards, sheep and oxen, and male and female slaves? 27Therefore the leprosy[d] of Naaman shall cling to you, and to your descendants forever." So he left his presence leprous,[d] as white as snow.

5.1–27: The healing of Naaman. 1: The story presupposes a time when *Aram* (Syria) dominates Israel. This was the case during the Jehu dynasty★ (see 10.32) but not during the Omri dynasty where this story is set, according to its current placement in 2 Kings. However, neither the *king of Aram* nor the king of Israel (v. 5) is named. *Leprosy* is a broad term for some skin diseases. It was greatly feared because it was regarded as incurable, disfiguring, fatal, and highly contagious. **3:** *The prophet*★ is later identified as Elisha. The story shows how his fame reached beyond the borders of Israel. **5:** A *talent* could weigh from 45 to 130 pounds. A shekel weighed less than half an ounce. *Six thousand shekels* was probably about 150 pounds. **13:** *Father* is a title of respect here and does not indicate any blood relationship. **15:** Naaman's statement is very similar to Israel's confession of faith (Deut 6.4). **17:** The idea behind *Naaman's* request for *two mule-loads of earth* was that the LORD (Yahweh) could only be worshipped on Israelite soil. **18:** *Rimmon* ("pomegranate") is a mocking distortion of Ramman, a title for the Syrian god Hadad. Naaman continues to worship the deity of his native land only because he is forced to do so; he no longer believes in Hadad. **19b–27:** This episode shows the danger of trying to deceive a prophet.

6 Now the company of prophets[a] said to Elisha, "As you see, the place where we live under your charge is too small for us. 2Let us go to the Jordan, and let us collect logs there, one for each of us, and build a place there for us to live." He answered, "Do so." 3Then one of them said, "Please come with your servants." And he answered, "I will." 4So he went with them. When they came to the Jordan, they cut down trees. 5But as one was felling a log, his ax head fell into the water; he cried out, "Alas, master! It was borrowed." 6Then the man of God said, "Where did it fall?" When he showed him the place, he cut off a stick, and threw it in there, and made the iron float. 7He said, "Pick it up." So he reached out his hand and took it.

8 Once when the king of Aram was at war with Israel, he took counsel with his officers. He said, "At such and such a place shall be my camp." 9But the man of God sent word to the king of Israel, "Take care not to pass this place, because the Arameans are going down there." 10The king of Israel sent word to the place of which the man of God spoke. More than once or twice he warned such a place[e] so that it was on the alert.

6.1–23: More wonders of Elisha. 1–7: This story, in which Elisha makes an *ax head* float, is set near the Jordan River where trees grow because of the abundance of water. **8–10:** Elisha's strategic importance for the Israelites is invaluable, since he is able to warn them of the impeding actions of their enemies, *the Arameans* (Syrians).

11 The mind of the king of Aram was greatly perturbed because of this; he called his officers and said to them, "Now tell me who among us sides with the king of Israel?" 12Then one of his officers said, "No one, my lord king. It is Elisha, the prophet in Israel, who tells the king of Israel the words that you speak in your bedchamber." 13He said, "Go and find where he is; I will send and seize him." He was told, "He is in Dothan." 14So he sent horses and chariots there and

a Heb *sons of the prophets*   *b* Heb *him*   *c* Heb lacks *the bags*   *d* A term for several skin diseases; precise meaning uncertain   *e* Heb *warned it*

a great army; they came by night, and surrounded the city.

15 When an attendant of the man of God rose early in the morning and went out, an army with horses and chariots was all around the city. His servant said, "Alas, master! What shall we do?" 16He replied, "Do not be afraid, for there are more with us than there are with them." 17Then Elisha prayed: "O LORD, please open his eyes that he may see." So the LORD opened the eyes of the servant, and he saw; the mountain was full of horses and chariots of fire all around Elisha. 18When the Arameans*a* came down against him, Elisha prayed to the LORD, and said, "Strike this people, please, with blindness." So he struck them with blindness as Elisha had asked. 19Elisha said to them, "This is not the way, and this is not the city; follow me, and I will bring you to the man whom you seek." And he led them to Samaria.

20 As soon as they entered Samaria, Elisha said, "O LORD, open the eyes of these men so that they may see." The LORD opened their eyes, and they saw that they were inside Samaria. 21When the king of Israel saw them he said to Elisha, "Father, shall I kill them? Shall I kill them?" 22He answered, "No! Did you capture with your sword and your bow those whom you want to kill? Set food and water before them so that they may eat and drink; and let them go to their master." 23So he prepared for them a great feast; after they ate and drank, he sent them on their way, and they went to their master. And the Arameans no longer came raiding into the land of Israel.

24 Some time later King Ben-hadad of Aram mustered his entire army; he marched against Samaria and laid siege to it. 25As the siege continued, famine in Samaria became so great that a donkey's head was sold for eighty shekels of silver, and one-fourth of a kab of dove's dung for five shekels of silver. 26Now as the king of Israel was walking on the city wall, a woman cried out to him, "Help, my lord king!" 27He said, "No! Let the LORD help you. How can I help you? From the threshing floor or from the wine press?" 28But then the king asked her, "What is your complaint?" She answered, "This woman said to me, 'Give up your son; we will eat him today, and we will eat my son tomorrow.' 29So we cooked my son and ate him. The next day I said to her, 'Give up your son and we will eat him.' But she has hidden her son." 30When the king heard the words of the woman he tore his clothes—now since he was walking on the city wall, the people could see that he had sackcloth on his body underneath— 31and he said, "So may God do to me, and more, if the head of Elisha son of Shaphat stays on his shoulders today." 32So he dispatched a man from his presence.

Now Elisha was sitting in his house, and the elders were sitting with him. Before the messenger arrived, Elisha said to the elders, "Are you aware that this murderer has sent someone to take off my head? When the messenger comes, see that you shut the door and hold it closed against him. Is not the sound of his master's feet behind him?" 33While he was still speaking with them, the king*b* came down to him and said, "This trouble is from the LORD! Why should I hope in the LORD any longer?" 1But Elisha said, "Hear the word of the LORD: thus says the LORD, Tomorrow about this time a measure of choice meal shall be sold for a shekel, and two measures of barley for a shekel, at the gate of Samaria." 2Then the captain on whose hand the king leaned said to the man of God, "Even if the LORD were to make windows in the sky, could such a thing happen?" But he said, "You shall see it

---

6.11–23: 12: The Aramean officer tells his king that Elisha knows even the most intimate words spoken by the king in his *bedchamber*. Though this is certainly an exaggeration, it is quite disconcerting to the king. 13–14: The story stresses Elisha's importance since he is the reason for an invasion by the Arameans. 17: This verse vividly illustrates the title "the LORD of hosts" ("Yahweh sebaoth"), since the LORD controls both earthly and heavenly armies (see 2.11). 21: *Father* is a term of respect for a superior. Thus, in this story the king was subject to the prophet.*

a Heb *they*   *b* See 7.2: Heb *messenger*

with your own eyes, but you shall not eat from it."

6.24–7.20: The siege of Samaria. 6.24–25: In a *siege*, a city was surrounded and its food supply cut off in order to starve out the inhabitants. Thus, food prices within the city soared. A *shekel*★ was a measure of weight of just less than half an ounce. A *kab* was slightly more than a quart. **27:** The *threshing*★ *floor* was a flat, raised area where grain was separated from the hull. A *wine press* was where grapes were squeezed for their juice to make wine. The king is replying that he has no more access to food supplies than does the woman who is asking for his help. His wish, *Let the LORD help you*, seems sarcastic in this context, as he likely blames the LORD for the predicament of the city. **28–29:** The woman's *complaint* is a legal case, since *the king* is, in effect, the supreme court of the land. The case she brings reflects the desperate straits of the city, where people have resorted to cannibalism. It also recalls, in a distorted way, the case of Solomon's judgment in 1 Kings 3.16–28. **30:** *Sackcloth*★ is a transliteration of the Hebrew "saq," which refers to some kind of garment worn to symbolize mourning. **31:** It is not clear why the king holds *Elisha* responsible for the siege, but it seems to be a classic case of blaming the messenger for the message. The LORD has sent the trouble (v. 33), and Elisha is the LORD's messenger. **33:** *The king* may be asking why he *should hope in the Lord any longer* or what more (punishment) he can expect from *the LORD* if he kills Elisha. **7.1:** Compare 6.25. Elisha predicts that the availability of food will dramatically increase and hence the prices be drastically reduced within a day. **2:** *On whose hand the king leaned* was a title for a special assistant to the king.

3 Now there were four leprous*a* men outside the city gate, who said to one another, "Why should we sit here until we die? 4If we say, 'Let us enter the city,' the famine is in the city, and we shall die there; but if we sit here, we shall also die. Therefore, let us desert to the Aramean camp; if they spare our lives, we shall live; and if they kill us, we shall but die." 5So they arose at twilight to go to the Aramean camp; but when they came to the edge of the Aramean camp, there was no one there at all. 6For the Lord had caused the Aramean army to hear the sound of chariots, and of horses, the sound of a great army, so that they said to one another, "The king of Israel has hired the kings of the Hittites and the kings of Egypt to fight against us." 7So they fled away in the twilight and abandoned their tents, their horses, and their donkeys leaving the camp just as it was, and fled for their lives. 8When these leprous*a* men had come to the edge of the camp, they went into a tent, ate and drank, carried off silver, gold, and clothing, and went and hid them. Then they came back, entered another tent, carried off things from it, and went and hid them.

9 Then they said to one another, "What we are doing is wrong. This is a day of good news; if we are silent and wait until the morning light, we will be found guilty; therefore let us go and tell the king's household." 10So they came and called to the gatekeepers of the city, and told them, "We went to the Aramean camp, but there was no one to be seen or heard there, nothing but the horses tied, the donkeys tied, and the tents as they were." 11Then the gatekeepers called out and proclaimed it to the king's household. 12The king got up in the night, and said to his servants, "I will tell you what the Arameans have prepared against us. They know that we are starving; so they have left the camp to hide themselves in the open country, thinking, 'When they come out of the city, we shall take them alive and get into the city.'" 13One of his servants said, "Let some men take five of the remaining horses, since those left here will suffer the fate of the whole multitude of Israel that have perished already;*b* let us send and find out." 14So they took two mounted men, and the king sent them after the Aramean army, saying, "Go and find out." 15So they went after them as far as the Jordan; the whole way was littered with garments and equipment that the Arameans had thrown away in their haste. So the messengers returned, and told the king.

16 Then the people went out, and plundered the camp of the Arameans. So a measure of choice meal was sold for a shekel,

---

a A term for several skin diseases; precise meaning uncertain   *b* Compare Gk Syr Vg: Meaning of Heb uncertain

and two measures of barley for a shekel, according to the word of the LORD. [17]Now the king had appointed the captain on whose hand he leaned to have charge of the gate; the people trampled him to death in the gate, just as the man of God had said when the king came down to him. [18]For when the man of God had said to the king, "Two measures of barley shall be sold for a shekel, and a measure of choice meal for a shekel, about this time tomorrow in the gate of Samaria," [19]the captain had answered the man of God, "Even if the LORD were to make windows in the sky, could such a thing happen?" And he had answered, "You shall see it with your own eyes, but you shall not eat from it." [20]It did indeed happen to him; the people trampled him to death in the gate.

7.3–20. 3: On leprosy, see comment on 5.1. People with skin diseases were isolated from society because leprosy was contagious. Hence, these *four leprous men* are *outside the city gate*. 4: The four men surrender to the Arameans because they have nothing to lose. 6: *Egypt* (Heb., "Misrayim") may be a mistake for Musri, an area in Anatolia (modern Turkey), which was also the home of the *Hittites*. 17–20: These verses explain the fulfillment of the oracle* in v. 2.

8 Now Elisha had said to the woman whose son he had restored to life, "Get up and go with your household, and settle wherever you can; for the LORD has called for a famine, and it will come on the land for seven years." [2]So the woman got up and did according to the word of the man of God; she went with her household and settled in the land of the Philistines seven years. [3]At the end of the seven years, when the woman returned from the land of the Philistines, she set out to appeal to the king for her house and her land. [4]Now the king was talking with Gehazi the servant of the man of God, saying, "Tell me all the great things that Elisha has done." [5]While he was telling the king how Elisha had restored a dead person to life, the woman whose son he had restored to life appealed to the king for her house and her land. Gehazi said, "My lord king, here is the woman, and here is her son whom Elisha restored to life." [6]When the king questioned the woman, she told him. So the king appointed an official for her, saying, "Restore all that was hers, together with all the revenue of the fields from the day that she left the land until now."

8.1–6: Elisha and the Shunammite woman. These verses refer to and may continue the stories in 4.8–37. 1: *Seven years* is a round number for completeness, indicating that the *famine* was severe and long-lasting. 2: The *land of the Philistines* was along the southern coast of Palestine near the area known today as the Gaza strip. 3: It is not clear who is trying to take the woman's land, but they are more than squatters, for they are making a legal claim. 4–5: The miraculous part of this tale is the timing. The woman appeared just as the fascinated *king* was hearing the story of her involvement with Elisha. *Gehazi* appears here without reference to his leprosy. Either this episode is connected with 4.8–37 or comes from a source completely apart from the story in ch. 5. However, the fact that Gehazi alone is speaking with the king may indicate that this story arose after Elisha's death.

[7] Elisha went to Damascus while King Ben-hadad of Aram was ill. When it was told him, "The man of God has come here," [8]the king said to Hazael, "Take a present with you and go to meet the man of God. Inquire of the LORD through him, whether I shall recover from this illness." [9]So Hazael went to meet him, taking a present with him, all kinds of goods of Damascus, forty camel loads. When he entered and stood before him, he said, "Your son King Ben-hadad of Aram has sent me to you, saying, 'Shall I recover from this illness?'" [10]Elisha said to him, "Go, say to him, 'You shall certainly recover'; but the LORD has shown me that he shall certainly die." [11]He fixed his gaze and stared at him, until he was ashamed. Then the man of God wept. [12]Hazael asked, "Why does my lord weep?" He answered, "Because I know the evil that you will do to the people of Israel; you will set their fortresses on fire, you will kill their young men with the sword, dash in pieces their little ones, and rip up their pregnant women." [13]Hazael said, "What is your servant, who is a mere dog, that he should do this great thing?" Elisha answered, "The LORD has shown me that

you are to be king over Aram." 14Then he left Elisha, and went to his master Ben-hadad,[a] who said to him, "What did Elisha say to you?" And he answered, "He told me that you would certainly recover." 15But the next day he took the bed-cover and dipped it in water and spread it over the king's face, until he died. And Hazael succeeded him.

8.7–15: The designation of Hazael. Elisha here apparently carries out the commission given to Elijah in 1 Kings 19.15. **8:** *Inquire* is a technical term for divination. Stories of inquiry through a prophet* in the case of illness are found also in 1 Kings 14.1–14; 2 Kings 1.2–17. **9:** *Forty camel loads* would be an enormous sum. That this is exaggeration is also clear from the fact that forty is a round number for a large quantity. *Your son* is an expression of humility and self-effacement. *Ben-hadad* is placing Elisha above him. **11:** The subject of these verbs is apparently Elisha. Perhaps Elisha *stared* at Hazael until Hazael *was ashamed.* Another possibility is that Elisha *stared* in a kind of trance until he himself became *ashamed.* **12:** Elisha foresees that Hazael will be the LORD's instrument to punish Israel. **13:** *Hazael* refers to himself as *a mere dog,* not because he sees violent acts described by Elisha as despicable but because he is of low social status and does not have the power to carry out such deeds. Elisha explains, however, that he is to be *king over Aram.* **15:** *Until he died* suggests that *Hazael* is responsible for Ben-hadad's death. The Hebrew is more ambiguous, however. Placing the wet *bed-cover over the king's face* may have been simply a way of cooling him off, and this verse may only explain the time of his death.

16 In the fifth year of King Joram son of Ahab of Israel,[b] Jehoram son of King Jehoshaphat of Judah began to reign. 17He was thirty-two years old when he became king, and he reigned eight years in Jerusalem. 18He walked in the way of the kings of Israel, as the house of Ahab had done, for the daughter of Ahab was his wife. He did what was evil in the sight of the LORD. 19Yet the LORD would not destroy Judah, for the sake of his servant David, since he had promised to give a lamp to him and to his descendants forever.

20 In his days Edom revolted against the rule of Judah, and set up a king of their own. 21Then Joram crossed over to Zair with all his chariots. He set out by night and attacked the Edomites and their chariot commanders who had surrounded him;[c] but his army fled home. 22So Edom has been in revolt against the rule of Judah to this day. Libnah also revolted at the same time. 23Now the rest of the acts of Joram, and all that he did, are they not written in the Book of the Annals of the Kings of Judah? 24So Joram slept with his ancestors, and was buried with them in the city of David; his son Ahaziah succeeded him.

25 In the twelfth year of King Joram son of Ahab of Israel, Ahaziah son of King Jehoram of Judah began to reign. 26Ahaziah was twenty-two years old when he began to reign; he reigned one year in Jerusalem. His mother's name was Athaliah, a granddaughter of King Omri of Israel. 27He also walked in the way of the house of Ahab, doing what was evil in the sight of the LORD, as the house of Ahab had done, for he was son-in-law to the house of Ahab.

28 He went with Joram son of Ahab to wage war against King Hazael of Aram at Ramoth-gilead, where the Arameans wounded Joram. 29King Joram returned to be healed in Jezreel of the wounds that the Arameans had inflicted on him at Ramah, when he fought against King Hazael of Aram. King Ahaziah son of Jehoram of Judah went down to see Joram son of Ahab in Jezreel, because he was wounded.

8.16–29: Regnal formulas for Joram and Ahaziah. 20: The *king* of *Edom* referred to in 3.9 may have been only a "deputy" under the king of Judah (1 Kings 22.47). **28:** *Ramoth-gilead* was east of the Jordan in territory disputed between Israel and Aram.

9 Then the prophet Elisha called a member of the company of prophets[d] and said to him, "Gird up your loins; take this flask of oil in your hand, and go to Ramoth-gilead. 2When you arrive, look there

---

a Heb lacks *Ben-hadad*   *b* Gk Syr: Heb adds *Jehoshaphat being king of Judah,*   *c* Meaning of Heb uncertain   *d* Heb *sons of the prophets*

for Jehu son of Jehoshaphat, son of Nimshi; go in and get him to leave his companions, and take him into an inner chamber. [3]Then take the flask of oil, pour it on his head, and say, 'Thus says the LORD: I anoint you king over Israel.' Then open the door and flee; do not linger."

4 So the young man, the young prophet, went to Ramoth-gilead. [5]He arrived while the commanders of the army were in council, and he announced, "I have a message for you, commander." "For which one of us?" asked Jehu. "For you, commander." [6]So Jehu[a] got up and went inside; the young man poured the oil on his head, saying to him, "Thus says the LORD the God of Israel: I anoint you king over the people of the LORD, over Israel. [7]You shall strike down the house of your master Ahab, so that I may avenge on Jezebel the blood of my servants the prophets, and the blood of all the servants of the LORD. [8]For the whole house of Ahab shall perish; I will cut off from Ahab every male, bond or free, in Israel. [9]I will make the house of Ahab like the house of Jeroboam son of Nebat, and like the house of Baasha son of Ahijah. [10]The dogs shall eat Jezebel in the territory of Jezreel, and no one shall bury her." Then he opened the door and fled.

11 When Jehu came back to his master's officers, they said to him, "Is everything all right? Why did that madman come to you?" He answered them, "You know the sort and how they babble." [12]They said, "Liar! Come on, tell us!" So he said, "This is just what he said to me: 'Thus says the LORD, I anoint you king over Israel.' " [13]Then hurriedly they all took their cloaks and spread them for him on the bare[b] steps; and they blew the trumpet, and proclaimed, "Jehu is king."

9.1–10.36: Jehu's revolt. 9.1–3: The revolt is begun by Elisha. Again, the anointing* of Jehu is apparently meant as a carrying out of the commission to Elijah (1 Kings 19.16). **7–10a:** These verses are an addition by the deuteronomistic* editor. They violate Elisha's order to anoint Jehu and flee (v. 3). They are also comparable to the prophetic oracles* against the houses of Jeroboam (1 Kings 14.7–11), Baasha (1 Kings 16.2–4), and Ahab (1 Kings 21.21–24). As in 1 Kings

21.21–24, the dynasty* here is referred to as the *house of Ahab* (vv. 8–9), even though it is actually the "house of Omri." The reason is the focal role of Ahab's reign in 1–2 Kings and his reputation as the worst king of Israel (1 Kings 21.25). **11:** In part because of such ecstatic experiences, a prophet* was sometimes called a *madman* (Jer 29.26; Hos 9.7). **13:** By spreading their *cloaks* before him, the other commanders signal their submission to Jehu as their king (Mt 21.8).

---

14 Thus Jehu son of Jehoshaphat son of Nimshi conspired against Joram. Joram with all Israel had been on guard at Ramoth-gilead against King Hazael of Aram; [15]but King Joram had returned to be healed in Jezreel of the wounds that the Arameans had inflicted on him, when he fought against King Hazael of Aram. So Jehu said, "If this is your wish, then let no one slip out of the city to go and tell the news in Jezreel." [16]Then Jehu mounted his chariot and went to Jezreel, where Joram was lying ill. King Ahaziah of Judah had come down to visit Joram.

17 In Jezreel, the sentinel standing on the tower spied the company of Jehu arriving, and said, "I see a company." Joram said, "Take a horseman; send him to meet them, and let him say, 'Is it peace?' " [18]So the horseman went to meet him; he said, "Thus says the king, 'Is it peace?' " Jehu responded, "What have you to do with peace? Fall in behind me." The sentinel reported, saying, "The messenger reached them, but he is not coming back." [19]Then he sent out a second horseman, who came to them and said, "Thus says the king, 'Is it peace?' " Jehu answered, "What have you to do with peace? Fall in behind me." [20]Again the sentinel reported, "He reached them, but he is not coming back. It looks like the driving of Jehu son of Nimshi; for he drives like a maniac."

21 Joram said, "Get ready." And they got his chariot ready. Then King Joram of Israel and King Ahaziah of Judah set out, each in his chariot, and went to meet Jehu; they met him at the property of Naboth the Jezreelite. [22]When Joram saw Jehu, he said, "Is it

---

a Heb *he*   *b* Meaning of Heb uncertain

peace, Jehu?" He answered, "What peace can there be, so long as the many whoredoms and sorceries of your mother Jezebel continue?" 23Then Joram reined about and fled, saying to Ahaziah, "Treason, Ahaziah!" 24Jehu drew his bow with all his strength, and shot Joram between the shoulders, so that the arrow pierced his heart; and he sank in his chariot. 25Jehu said to his aide Bidkar, "Lift him out, and throw him on the plot of ground belonging to Naboth the Jezreelite; for remember, when you and I rode side by side behind his father Ahab how the LORD uttered this oracle against him: 26'For the blood of Naboth and for the blood of his children that I saw yesterday, says the LORD, I swear I will repay you on this very plot of ground.' Now therefore lift him out and throw him on the plot of ground, in accordance with the word of the LORD."

27 When King Ahaziah of Judah saw this, he fled in the direction of Beth-haggan. Jehu pursued him, saying, "Shoot him also!" And they shot him*a* in the chariot at the ascent to Gur, which is by Ibleam. Then he fled to Megiddo, and died there. 28His officers carried him in a chariot to Jerusalem, and buried him in his tomb with his ancestors in the city of David.

29 In the eleventh year of Joram son of Ahab, Ahaziah began to reign over Judah.

30 When Jehu came to Jezreel, Jezebel heard of it; she painted her eyes, and adorned her head, and looked out of the window. 31As Jehu entered the gate, she said, "Is it peace, Zimri, murderer of your master?" 32He looked up to the window and said, "Who is on my side? Who?" Two or three eunuchs looked out at him. 33He said, "Throw her down." So they threw her down; some of her blood spattered on the wall and on the horses, which trampled on her. 34Then he went in and ate and drank; he said, "See to that cursed woman and bury her; for she is a king's daughter." 35But when they went to bury her, they found no more of her than the skull and the feet and the palms of her hands. 36When they came back and told him, he said, "This is the word of the LORD, which he spoke by his servant Elijah the Tishbite, 'In the territory of Jezreel

the dogs shall eat the flesh of Jezebel; 37the corpse of Jezebel shall be like dung on the field in the territory of Jezreel, so that no one can say, This is Jezebel.' "

9.14–37. 21, 25–26: Either the story of Jehu's revolt has been tailored as a fulfillment of Elijah's oracle* in 1 Kings 21 in punishment for the murder of Naboth, or these verses reflect the original setting of the oracle against Ahab and Jezebel, which has been changed in order to attribute it to Elijah in 1 Kings 21. 22: *Whoredoms* probably refers to the worship of other gods, as is frequently the case in the Bible (compare the book of Hosea). *Sorceries* may also refer to other practices (divination and the like) associated with the worship of other gods. 30: It is not clear why *Jezebel* dresses up. It may be that she is described this way in order to fit the image of a prostitute. 31: Jezebel calls Jehu *Zimri* because Zimri led a revolt and was the *murderer of [his] master*. Zimri's subsequent reign lasted only seven days, so that Jezebel is also implying that Jehu's kingship will be unsuccessful (1 Kings 16.9–20). 32–33: *Eunuchs* were used to guard the harem. Jezebel was thrown from the second story of the building. 34–37: *Jezebel*'s death is described as the fulfillment, though elaborated, of *Elijah*'s prophecy in 1 Kings 21.23. Her gruesome end fulfills the threat of non-burial in 1 Kings 21.24 (compare 2 Kings 9.10).

10 Now Ahab had seventy sons in Samaria. So Jehu wrote letters and sent them to Samaria, to the rulers of Jezreel,*b* to the elders, and to the guardians of the sons of*c* Ahab, saying, 2"Since your master's sons are with you and you have at your disposal chariots and horses, a fortified city, and weapons, 3select the son of your master who is the best qualified, set him on his father's throne, and fight for your master's house." 4But they were utterly terrified and said, "Look, two kings could not withstand him; how then can we stand?" 5So the steward of the palace, and the governor of the city, along with the elders and the guardians, sent word to Jehu: "We are your servants; we will do anything you say. We will not make anyone king; do whatever you think right."

a Syr Vg Compare Gk: Heb lacks *and they shot him*
b Or *of the city*; Vg Compare Gk   c Gk: Heb lacks *of the sons of*

6Then he wrote them a second letter, saying, "If you are on my side, and if you are ready to obey me, take the heads of your master's sons and come to me at Jezreel tomorrow at this time." Now the king's sons, seventy persons, were with the leaders of the city, who were charged with their upbringing. 7When the letter reached them, they took the king's sons and killed them, seventy persons; they put their heads in baskets and sent them to him at Jezreel. 8When the messenger came and told him, "They have brought the heads of the king's sons," he said, "Lay them in two heaps at the entrance of the gate until the morning." 9Then in the morning when he went out, he stood and said to all the people, "You are innocent. It was I who conspired against my master and killed him; but who struck down all these? 10Know then that there shall fall to the earth nothing of the word of the LORD, which the LORD spoke concerning the house of Ahab; for the LORD has done what he said through his servant Elijah." 11So Jehu killed all who were left of the house of Ahab in Jezreel, all his leaders, close friends, and priests, until he left him no survivor.

12 Then he set out and went to Samaria. On the way, when he was at Beth-eked of the Shepherds, 13Jehu met relatives of King Ahaziah of Judah and said, "Who are you?" They answered, "We are kin of Ahaziah; we have come down to visit the royal princes and the sons of the queen mother." 14He said, "Take them alive." They took them alive, and slaughtered them at the pit of Beth-eked, forty-two in all; he spared none of them.

15 When he left there, he met Jehonadab son of Rechab coming to meet him; he greeted him, and said to him, "Is your heart as true to mine as mine is to yours?"[a] Jehonadab answered, "It is." Jehu said,[b] "If it is, give me your hand." So he gave him his hand. Jehu took him up with him into the chariot. 16He said, "Come with me, and see my zeal for the LORD." So he[c] had him ride in his chariot. 17When he came to Samaria, he killed all who were left to Ahab in Samaria, until he had wiped them out, according to the word of the LORD that he spoke to Elijah.

18 Then Jehu assembled all the people and said to them, "Ahab offered Baal small service; but Jehu will offer much more. 19Now therefore summon to me all the prophets of Baal, all his worshipers, and all his priests; let none be missing, for I have a great sacrifice to offer to Baal; whoever is missing shall not live." But Jehu was acting with cunning in order to destroy the worshipers of Baal. 20Jehu decreed, "Sanctify a solemn assembly for Baal." So they proclaimed it. 21Jehu sent word throughout all Israel; all the worshipers of Baal came, so that there was no one left who did not come. They entered the temple of Baal, until the temple of Baal was filled from wall to wall. 22He said to the keeper of the wardrobe, "Bring out the vestments for all the worshipers of Baal." So he brought out the vestments for them. 23Then Jehu entered the temple of Baal with Jehonadab son of Rechab; he said to the worshipers of Baal, "Search and see that there is no worshiper of the LORD here among you, but only worshipers of Baal." 24Then they proceeded to offer sacrifices and burnt offerings.

Now Jehu had stationed eighty men outside, saying, "Whoever allows any of those to escape whom I deliver into your hands shall forfeit his life." 25As soon as he had finished presenting the burnt offering, Jehu said to the guards and to the officers, "Come in and kill them; let no one escape." So they put them to the sword. The guards and the of-

---

10.1–14. 1: *Sons* probably means descendants, that is, sons and grandsons, although Ahab may have had a large enough harem to produce seventy sons. 9–10: The exact meaning of Jehu's words in v. 9 is unclear. However, he seems to be suggesting that his revolt is more than a rebellion by a single individual and that the LORD is behind it. Hence, the prophecies against Ahab's house will be fulfilled (v. 10). 14: *Forty-two* was also the number of boys killed by bears in 2.24. This may indicate that it was a conventional number for disaster.

---

a Gk: Heb *Is it right with your heart, as my heart is with your heart?*   *b* Gk: Heb lacks *Jehu said*   *c* Gk Syr Tg: Heb *they*

ficers threw them out, and then went into the citadel of the temple of Baal. 26They brought out the pillar*a* that was in the temple of Baal, and burned it. 27Then they demolished the pillar of Baal, and destroyed the temple of Baal, and made it a latrine to this day.

28 Thus Jehu wiped out Baal from Israel. 29But Jehu did not turn aside from the sins of Jeroboam son of Nebat, which he caused Israel to commit—the golden calves that were in Bethel and in Dan. 30The LORD said to Jehu, "Because you have done well in carrying out what I consider right, and in accordance with all that was in my heart have dealt with the house of Ahab, your sons of the fourth generation shall sit on the throne of Israel." 31But Jehu was not careful to follow the law of the LORD the God of Israel with all his heart; he did not turn from the sins of Jeroboam, which he caused Israel to commit.

32 In those days the LORD began to trim off parts of Israel. Hazael defeated them throughout the territory of Israel: 33from the Jordan eastward, all the land of Gilead, the Gadites, the Reubenites, and the Manassites, from Aroer, which is by the Wadi Arnon, that is, Gilead and Bashan. 34Now the rest of the acts of Jehu, all that he did, and all his power, are they not written in the Book of the Annals of the Kings of Israel? 35So Jehu slept with his ancestors, and they buried him in Samaria. His son Jehoahaz succeeded him. 36The time that Jehu reigned over Israel in Samaria was twenty-eight years.

11 Now when Athaliah, Ahaziah's mother, saw that her son was dead, she set about to destroy all the royal family. 2But Jehosheba, King Joram's daughter, Ahaziah's sister, took Joash son of Ahaziah, and stole him away from among the king's children who were about to be killed; she put*b* him and his nurse in a bedroom. Thus she*c* hid him from Athaliah, so that he was not killed; 3he remained with her six years, hidden in the house of the LORD, while Athaliah reigned over the land.

4 But in the seventh year Jehoiada summoned the captains of the Carites and of the guards and had them come to him in the house of the LORD. He made a covenant with them and put them under oath in the house of the LORD; then he showed them the king's son. 5He commanded them, "This is what you are to do: one-third of you, those who go off duty on the sabbath and guard the king's house 6(another third being at the gate Sur and a third at the gate behind the guards), shall guard the palace; 7and your two divisions that come on duty in force on the sabbath and guard the house of the LORD*d* 8shall surround the king, each with weapons in hand; and whoever approaches the ranks is to be killed. Be with the king in his comings and goings."

11.1–21: The reign of Athaliah and revolt of Jehoash. 1–3: *Athaliah* was the daughter of Ahab and Jezebel who had married Joram king of Judah in a treaty between Israel and Judah (8.18). After the death of her son, *Ahaziah*, she seized power. No regnal formula is reported for her because the writer of 2 Kings did not consider her a legitimate ruler. **4:** *Jehoiada* was a priest. Since the new king, Jehoash (or Joash), was only seven years old, Jehoiada was really in charge of the kingdom. The *Carites* were apparently the royal bodyguard, and this may be an error for Cherethites, the name for the bodyguard under David and Solomon (2 Sam 8.18). **5–7:** The parenthetical statement in v. 6 is probably a late gloss or explanatory addition, trying to identify the other two divisions. The *gate Sur* is unknown. Jehoiada chooses the change of the guard

10.15–36. 15: *Son of Rechab* designates *Jehonadab's* clan* rather than his father. The Rechabites were ascetics and strict devotees of the LORD (Yahweh). See Jer 35. **24–25:** Hosea 1.4 seems to condemn Jehu's bloodshed. **26:** The *pillar* was an important element in the worship of Baal;* it represented him much like an idol. **32:** The reigns of Jehu and his descendants were marked by the subjugation of Israel to Aram (Syria). See also 13.3. Many of the stories about prophets* earlier in 1–2 Kings seem to presuppose this political situation, which was not true under the Omri dynasty.*

a Gk Vg Syr Tg: Heb *pillars*   *b* With 2 Chr 22.11: Heb lacks *she put*   *c* Gk Syr Vg Compare 2 Chr 22.11: Heb *they*   *d* Heb *the* LORD *to the king*

on the *sabbath* as the time for the revolt. This made all the troops available to him in order to protect Jehoash. It was also a time when troop movements would not be suspicious.

~~~~~~~~~~~~~~~~~~~~

9 The captains did according to all that the priest Jehoiada commanded; each brought his men who were to go off duty on the sabbath, with those who were to come on duty on the sabbath, and came to the priest Jehoiada. [10]The priest delivered to the captains the spears and shields that had been King David's, which were in the house of the LORD; [11]the guards stood, every man with his weapons in his hand, from the south side of the house to the north side of the house, around the altar and the house, to guard the king on every side. [12]Then he brought out the king's son, put the crown on him, and gave him the covenant;*a* they proclaimed him king, and anointed him; they clapped their hands and shouted, "Long live the king!"

13 When Athaliah heard the noise of the guard and of the people, she went into the house of the LORD to the people; [14]when she looked, there was the king standing by the pillar, according to custom, with the captains and the trumpeters beside the king, and all the people of the land rejoicing and blowing trumpets. Athaliah tore her clothes and cried, "Treason! Treason!" [15]Then the priest Jehoiada commanded the captains who were set over the army, "Bring her out between the ranks, and kill with the sword anyone who follows her." For the priest said, "Let her not be killed in the house of the LORD." [16]So they laid hands on her; she went through the horses' entrance to the king's house, and there she was put to death.

17 Jehoiada made a covenant between the LORD and the king and people, that they should be the LORD's people; also between the king and the people. [18]Then all the people of the land went to the house of Baal, and tore it down; his altars and his images they broke in pieces, and they killed Mattan, the priest of Baal, before the altars. The priest posted guards over the house of the LORD. [19]He took the captains, the Carites, the guards, and all the people of the land;

then they brought the king down from the house of the LORD, marching through the gate of the guards to the king's house. He took his seat on the throne of the kings. [20]So all the people of the land rejoiced; and the city was quiet after Athaliah had been killed with the sword at the king's house.

21[b] Jehoash[c] was seven years old when he began to reign.

11.9–21. 10: The *spears and shields* mentioned here were originally of gold and dedicated by David (2 Sam 8.7). But they had been replaced by Rehoboam with bronze articles after Shishak's invasion (1 Kings 14.26–27). **12:** The *covenant** would have been a written document, perhaps laws or a contract between the people and the king. However, the word may be an error for armlet, associated with the crown in 2 Sam 1.10. See comment on 11.17. **14:** The *pillar* in front of the Temple* is meant here. **17:** Only after Athaliah's removal is the covenant made. It appears to be an agreement between the people and the king to follow the LORD, but its exact nature and its relationship to the laws in the Bible are unknown. **20:** The exact identity of the *people of the land* is disputed. They may have been the landholders or leading citizens of Judah.

~~~~~~~~~~~~~~~~~~~~

12 In the seventh year of Jehu, Jehoash began to reign; he reigned forty years in Jerusalem. His mother's name was Zibiah of Beer-sheba. [2]Jehoash did what was right in the sight of the LORD all his days, because the priest Jehoiada instructed him. [3]Nevertheless the high places were not taken away; the people continued to sacrifice and make offerings on the high places.

4 Jehoash said to the priests, "All the money offered as sacred donations that is brought into the house of the LORD, the money for which each person is assessed—the money from the assessment of persons—and the money from the voluntary offerings brought into the house of the LORD, [5]let the priests receive from each of the donors; and let them repair the house wherever any need of repairs is discovered." [6]But by the twenty-third year of King Jehoash the priests had made no repairs on the house.

a Or *treaty* or *testimony*; Heb *eduth*   *b* Ch 12.1 in Heb
c Another spelling is *Joash*; see verse 19

⁷Therefore King Jehoash summoned the priest Jehoiada with the other priests and said to them, "Why are you not repairing the house? Now therefore do not accept any more money from your donors but hand it over for the repair of the house." ⁸So the priests agreed that they would neither accept more money from the people nor repair the house.

9 Then the priest Jehoiada took a chest, made a hole in its lid, and set it beside the altar on the right side as one entered the house of the LORD; the priests who guarded the threshold put in it all the money that was brought into the house of the LORD. ¹⁰Whenever they saw that there was a great deal of money in the chest, the king's secretary and the high priest went up, counted the money that was found in the house of the LORD, and tied it up in bags. ¹¹They would give the money that was weighed out into the hands of the workers who had the oversight of the house of the LORD; then they paid it out to the carpenters and the builders who worked on the house of the LORD, ¹²to the masons and the stonecutters, as well as to buy timber and quarried stone for making repairs on the house of the LORD, as well as for any outlay for repairs of the house. ¹³But for the house of the LORD no basins of silver, snuffers, bowls, trumpets, or any vessels of gold, or of silver, were made from the money that was brought into the house of the LORD, ¹⁴for that was given to the workers who were repairing the house of the LORD with it. ¹⁵They did not ask an accounting from those into whose hand they delivered the money to pay out to the workers, for they dealt honestly. ¹⁶The money from the guilt offerings and the money from the sin offerings was not brought into the house of the LORD; it belonged to the priests.

17 At that time King Hazael of Aram went up, fought against Gath, and took it. But when Hazael set his face to go up against Jerusalem, ¹⁸King Jehoash of Judah took all the votive gifts that Jehoshaphat, Jehoram, and Ahaziah, his ancestors, the kings of Judah, had dedicated, as well as his own votive gifts, all the gold that was found in the trea-

suries of the house of the LORD and of the king's house, and sent these to King Hazael of Aram. Then Hazael withdrew from Jerusalem.

19 Now the rest of the acts of Joash, and all that he did, are they not written in the Book of the Annals of the Kings of Judah? ²⁰His servants arose, devised a conspiracy, and killed Joash in the house of Millo, on the way that goes down to Silla. ²¹It was Jozacar son of Shimeath and Jehozabad son of Shomer, his servants, who struck him down, so that he died. He was buried with his ancestors in the city of David; then his son Amaziah succeeded him.

12.1–21: The reign of Jehoash. 1: *Forty years* is probably a round number for a generation. **3:** The *high places** were shrines other than the Temple* of Jerusalem. **4–16:** Jehoash repairs the Temple. Jehoash has to admonish the priests (v. 7), who are slow to carry out the repairs. *Money* is literally "silver." Parts of this account, however, seem to assume that the contributions were in the form of coins, which would be an anachronism* since coins began to be used widely in Palestine no earlier than the late sixth century BCE. **18:** *Votive gifts* were special items of value that the kings of Judah had dedicated to the Temple. By paying these to Hazael as tribute, Jehoash capitulated to him and in effect bribed him to prevent him from attacking Jerusalem. **19:** The *Annals of the Kings of Judah* may have been official records of the monarchy of Judah. They no longer exist. **20:** *Millo* means "fill"; it probably refers to the earthwork done by David to fill in the saddle between the Temple area and the palace area south of it (2 Sam 5.9). **21:** The motive behind Jehoash's assassination is not explained in 2 Kings. See 2 Chr 24.20–27.

---

13 In the twenty-third year of King Joash son of Ahaziah of Judah, Jehoahaz son of Jehu began to reign over Israel in Samaria; he reigned seventeen years. ²He did what was evil in the sight of the LORD, and followed the sins of Jeroboam son of Nebat, which he caused Israel to sin; he did not depart from them. ³The anger of the LORD was kindled against Israel, so that he gave them repeatedly into the hand of King Hazael of Aram, then into the hand of Benhadad son of Hazael. ⁴But Jehoahaz en-

treated the LORD, and the LORD heeded him; for he saw the oppression of Israel, how the king of Aram oppressed them. 5Therefore the LORD gave Israel a savior, so that they escaped from the hand of the Arameans; and the people of Israel lived in their homes as formerly. 6Nevertheless they did not depart from the sins of the house of Jeroboam, which he caused Israel to sin, but walked[a] in them; the sacred pole[b] also remained in Samaria. 7So Jehoahaz was left with an army of not more than fifty horsemen, ten chariots and ten thousand footmen; for the king of Aram had destroyed them and made them like the dust at threshing. 8Now the rest of the acts of Jehoahaz and all that he did, including his might, are they not written in the Book of the Annals of the Kings of Israel? 9So Jehoahaz slept with his ancestors, and they buried him in Samaria; then his son Joash succeeded him.

10 In the thirty-seventh year of King Joash of Judah, Jehoash son of Jehoahaz began to reign over Israel in Samaria; he reigned sixteen years. 11He also did what was evil in the sight of the LORD; he did not depart from all the sins of Jeroboam son of Nebat, which he caused Israel to sin, but walked in them. 12Now the rest of the acts of Joash, and all that he did, as well as the might with which he fought against King Amaziah of Judah, are they not written in the Book of the Annals of the Kings of Israel? 13So Joash slept with his ancestors, and Jeroboam sat upon his throne; Joash was buried in Samaria with the kings of Israel.

13.1–13: The reigns of Jehoahaz and Joash. 1: *Joash* and *Jehoash* are two versions of the same name. **2:** *The sins of Jeroboam* are the shrines at Dan and Bethel (1 Kings 12.25–33). **3:** Like the rest of the regnal formulas, this verse is deuteronomistic* and sounds much like part of the deuteronomistic formula found in the book of Judges (Judg 2.14; 4.1–2; 6.1). **5:** The idea and language are also borrowed from the book of Judges. The identity of this *savior* is not clear, but it may be a reference to Elisha (vv. 14–21). **6:** *The sins of the house of Jeroboam* are the same as the sins of Jeroboam (v. 2). The *sacred pole* was used in the worship of the Canaanite goddess Asherah.* **7:** *Like the*

dust at threshing* means that the army had scattered. **10:** While they bear the same name, *Joash* king of Judah and *Jehoash* king of Israel are two different people. **13:** This Jeroboam is distinct from the one in 1 Kings 12–14 and is often called Jeroboam II.

14 Now when Elisha had fallen sick with the illness of which he was to die, King Joash of Israel went down to him, and wept before him, crying, "My father, my father! The chariots of Israel and its horsemen!" 15Elisha said to him, "Take a bow and arrows"; so he took a bow and arrows. 16Then he said to the king of Israel, "Draw the bow"; and he drew it. Elisha laid his hands on the king's hands. 17Then he said, "Open the window eastward"; and he opened it. Elisha said, "Shoot"; and he shot. Then he said, "The LORD's arrow of victory, the arrow of victory over Aram! For you shall fight the Arameans in Aphek until you have made an end of them." 18He continued, "Take the arrows"; and he took them. He said to the king of Israel, "Strike the ground with them"; he struck three times, and stopped. 19Then the man of God was angry with him, and said, "You should have struck five or six times; then you would have struck down Aram until you had made an end of it, but now you will strike down Aram only three times."

20 So Elisha died, and they buried him. Now bands of Moabites used to invade the land in the spring of the year. 21As a man was being buried, a marauding band was seen and the man was thrown into the grave of Elisha; as soon as the man touched the bones of Elisha, he came to life and stood on his feet.

22 Now King Hazael of Aram oppressed Israel all the days of Jehoahaz. 23But the LORD was gracious to them and had compassion on them; he turned toward them, because of his covenant with Abraham, Isaac, and Jacob, and would not destroy them; nor has he banished them from his presence until now.

24 When King Hazael of Aram died, his son Ben-hadad succeeded him. 25Then Jehoash son of Jehoahaz took again from

a Gk Syr Tg Vg: Heb *he walked*   *b* Heb *Asherah*

Ben-hadad son of Hazael the towns that he had taken from his father Jehoahaz in war. Three times Joash defeated him and recovered the towns of Israel.

13.14–25: Elisha's death. This story lies outside of the framework of the regnal formulas. That is, it follows the closing formula for Joash (vv. 12–13) but precedes the beginning formula for Jeroboam II (14.23–24). Since the deuteronomistic* editor regularly uses these formulas as the framework for the history, this story may be either out of place or a later addition. **14:** *My father* is a term of respect showing the king's subordination to the prophet.* The exact sense of *the chariots of Israel and its horsemen* here is uncertain. It recalls previous episodes in the Elisha stories (2.12; 6.17) and may have become a kind of nickname for him because of these episodes. **15–17:** Symbolic acts like this one are frequently carried out by prophets in the Bible, especially by Ezekiel and Jeremiah. In this case, the LORD's *arrow of victory* is shot *eastward* (v. 17), toward *Aram* (Syria), to represent victory over the Arameans. **18–19:** This is an example of bellomancy, the use of weapons of war to foretell the future, which was common in the ancient Near East. **20–21:** Elisha's miraculous powers continue even after his death. **22–23:** While these verses were certainly written after the fall of Israel in 721 BCE, the writer still appeals to the people of the north in stating that the LORD has not ultimately abandoned them. **24–25:** These verses fulfill Elisha's prediction in v. 19.

14 In the second year of King Joash son of Joahaz of Israel, King Amaziah son of Joash of Judah, began to reign. ²He was twenty-five years old when he began to reign, and he reigned twenty-nine years in Jerusalem. His mother's name was Jehoaddin of Jerusalem. ³He did what was right in the sight of the LORD, yet not like his ancestor David; in all things he did as his father Joash had done. ⁴But the high places were not removed; the people still sacrificed and made offerings on the high places. ⁵As soon as the royal power was firmly in his hand he killed his servants who had murdered his father the king. ⁶But he did not put to death the children of the murderers; according to what is written in the book of the law of Moses, where the LORD commanded, "The parents shall not be put to death for the children, or

the children be put to death for the parents; but all shall be put to death for their own sins."

7 He killed ten thousand Edomites in the Valley of Salt and took Sela by storm; he called it Jokthe-el, which is its name to this day.

8 Then Amaziah sent messengers to King Jehoash son of Jehoahaz, son of Jehu, of Israel, saying, "Come, let us look one another in the face." ⁹King Jehoash of Israel sent word to King Amaziah of Judah, "A thornbush on Lebanon sent to a cedar on Lebanon, saying, 'Give your daughter to my son for a wife'; but a wild animal of Lebanon passed by and trampled down the thornbush. ¹⁰You have indeed defeated Edom, and your heart has lifted you up. Be content with your glory, and stay at home; for why should you provoke trouble so that you fall, you and Judah with you?"

14.1–29: The reigns of Amaziah of Judah and Jeroboam II of Israel. 4: The *high places** were shrines other than the Temple* of Jerusalem. **6:** The *law* referred to here is Deut 24.16. **7:** The location of the *Valley of Salt* is uncertain, but most scholars locate it south of the Dead Sea in the same depression in which the Dead Sea or Salt Sea lies. *Sela* means "rock" or "crag." The meaning of *Jokthe-el* is uncertain. One suggestion is that it means "God destroys." **8:** *Let us look one another in the face* is a challenge to battle (v. 11). **9:** The *fable** does not imply any marriage treaty or relationship between Amaziah and Joash. Its point, rather, is that Amaziah is trying to make himself more important than he is and that he will be *trampled down* if he continues.

11 But Amaziah would not listen. So King Jehoash of Israel went up; he and King Amaziah of Judah faced one another in battle at Beth-shemesh, which belongs to Judah. ¹²Judah was defeated by Israel; everyone fled home. ¹³King Jehoash of Israel captured King Amaziah of Judah son of Jehoash, son of Ahaziah, at Beth-shemesh; he came to Jerusalem, and broke down the wall of Jerusalem from the Ephraim Gate to the Corner Gate, a distance of four hundred cubits. ¹⁴He seized all the gold and silver, and all the vessels that were found in the house of

the LORD and in the treasuries of the king's house, as well as hostages; then he returned to Samaria.

15 Now the rest of the acts that Jehoash did, his might, and how he fought with King Amaziah of Judah, are they not written in the Book of the Annals of the Kings of Israel? [16]Jehoash slept with his ancestors, and was buried in Samaria with the kings of Israel; then his son Jeroboam succeeded him.

17 King Amaziah son of Joash of Judah lived fifteen years after the death of King Jehoash son of Jehoahaz of Israel. [18]Now the rest of the deeds of Amaziah, are they not written in the Book of the Annals of the Kings of Judah? [19]They made a conspiracy against him in Jerusalem, and he fled to Lachish. But they sent after him to Lachish, and killed him there. [20]They brought him on horses; he was buried in Jerusalem with his ancestors in the city of David. [21]All the people of Judah took Azariah, who was sixteen years old, and made him king to succeed his father Amaziah. [22]He rebuilt Elath and restored it to Judah, after King Amaziah[a] slept with his ancestors.

23 In the fifteenth year of King Amaziah son of Joash of Judah, King Jeroboam son of Joash of Israel began to reign in Samaria; he reigned forty-one years. [24]He did what was evil in the sight of the LORD; he did not depart from all the sins of Jeroboam son of Nebat, which he caused Israel to sin. [25]He restored the border of Israel from Lebo-hamath as far as the Sea of the Arabah, according to the word of the LORD, the God of Israel, which he spoke by his servant Jonah son of Amittai, the prophet, who was from Gath-hepher. [26]For the LORD saw that the distress of Israel was very bitter; there was no one left, bond or free, and no one to help Israel. [27]But the LORD had not said that he would blot out the name of Israel from under heaven, so he saved them by the hand of Jeroboam son of Joash.

28 Now the rest of the acts of Jeroboam, and all that he did, and his might, how he fought, and how he recovered for Israel Damascus and Hamath, which had belonged to Judah, are they not written in the Book of the Annals of the Kings of Israel? [29]Jeroboam slept with his ancestors, the kings of Israel; his son Zechariah succeeded him.

14.11–29. 13: A *cubit* was about 18 inches, so 400 cubits is about 200 yards. The *wall* of a city was essential for its protection. 19: *Lachish* was an important fortress and city about 25 miles southwest of Jerusalem. 22: *Elath* was an important port city at the tip of the Gulf of Aqaba. Amaziah was able to *rebuild and restore it* to Judah after he had defeated Edom (v. 7). 25: *Lebo-hamath* represented the idealized northern border of Israel in northern Syria as described for Solomon (1 Kings 8.65). The *Sea of the Arabah* was the Dead Sea. *Jonah* was the prophet* about whom the book of Jonah was written. The oracles* referred to here, however, are not recorded. 28: *Jeroboam*'s reign was a prosperous one, but he did not restore *Damascus and Hamath* to Israel, nor had they once *belonged to Judah*. The text has been damaged in transmission, and the original reading is uncertain.

15 In the twenty-seventh year of King Jeroboam of Israel King Azariah son of Amaziah of Judah began to reign. [2]He was sixteen years old when he began to reign, and he reigned fifty-two years in Jerusalem. His mother's name was Jecoliah of Jerusalem. [3]He did what was right in the sight of the LORD, just as his father Amaziah had done. [4]Nevertheless the high places were not taken away; the people still sacrificed and made offerings on the high places. [5]The LORD struck the king, so that he was leprous[b] to the day of his death, and lived in a separate house. Jotham the king's son was in charge of the palace, governing the people of the land. [6]Now the rest of the acts of Azariah, and all that he did, are they not written in the Book of the Annals of the Kings of Judah? [7]Azariah slept with his ancestors; they buried him with his ancestors in the city of David; his son Jotham succeeded him.

8 In the thirty-eighth year of King Azariah of Judah, Zechariah son of Jeroboam reigned over Israel in Samaria six months. [9]He did what was evil in the sight of the LORD, as his ancestors had done. He did not depart from the sins of Jeroboam son of Nebat, which he

---

a Heb *the king*   b A term for several skin diseases; precise meaning uncertain

caused Israel to sin. ¹⁰Shallum son of Jabesh conspired against him, and struck him down in public and killed him, and reigned in place of him. ¹¹Now the rest of the deeds of Zechariah are written in the Book of the Annals of the Kings of Israel. ¹²This was the promise of the LORD that he gave to Jehu, "Your sons shall sit on the throne of Israel to the fourth generation." And so it happened.

13 Shallum son of Jabesh began to reign in the thirty-ninth year of King Uzziah of Judah; he reigned one month in Samaria. ¹⁴Then Menahem son of Gadi came up from Tirzah and came to Samaria; he struck down Shallum son of Jabesh in Samaria and killed him; he reigned in place of him. ¹⁵Now the rest of the deeds of Shallum, including the conspiracy that he made, are written in the Book of the Annals of the Kings of Israel. ¹⁶At that time Menahem sacked Tiphsah, all who were in it and its territory from Tirzah on; because they did not open it to him, he sacked it. He ripped open all the pregnant women in it.

17 In the thirty-ninth year of King Azariah of Judah, Menahem son of Gadi began to reign over Israel; he reigned ten years in Samaria. ¹⁸He did what was evil in the sight of the LORD; he did not depart all his days from any of the sins of Jeroboam son of Nebat, which he caused Israel to sin. ¹⁹King Pul of Assyria came against the land; Menahem gave Pul a thousand talents of silver, so that he might help him confirm his hold on the royal power. ²⁰Menahem exacted the money from Israel, that is, from all the wealthy, fifty shekels of silver from each one, to give to the king of Assyria. So the king of Assyria turned back, and did not stay there in the land. ²¹Now the rest of the deeds of Menahem, and all that he did, are they not written in the Book of the Annals of the Kings of Israel? ²²Menahem slept with his ancestors, and his son Pekahiah succeeded him.

15.1–38: Azariah and Jotham of Judah; Zechariah, Shallum, Menahem, and Pekahiah of Israel. 1: *Azariah* is also known as Uzziah (2 Chr 26). 4: *High places** were shrines other than the Temple* of Jerusalem. 5: *Leprosy* was a word used for a variety of skin diseases.

It was greatly feared because it was regarded as fatal and incurable. Lepers were isolated because the disease was contagious. Hence, Azariah and his son Jotham were co-regents, that is, they ruled together. **12:** The prophecy about the duration of the Jehu dynasty* occurs in 10.30. The rapid succession of contenders to the throne at the end of the Jehu dynasty is reminiscent of the last days of Baasha's house in 1 Kings 16. **15:** *The rest of the deeds* is part of the standard deuteronomistic* formula. Since he reigned only one month (v. 13), *Shallum* did not have time to accomplish many deeds. **16:** *Tiphsah* was a town on the Euphrates, quite out of *Menahem's* reach. A better reading is Tappuah (as in the Septuagint*), which was within Israel. The practice of *rip[ping] open pregnant women* is mentioned elsewhere in the Bible in the context of wars with other countries (2 Kings 8.12; Hos 13.16; Am 1.13). The reason for Menahem's brutality against the town of Tappuah is unknown, but it has been suggested that this was Shallum's hometown. **19:** *Pul* was another name for Tiglath-pileser III, one of the greatest kings of the Assyrian empire (see v. 29). A *talent* was between 45 and 130 pounds. *A thousand talents of silver* was an enormous sum. **20:** A *shekel* was slightly less than half an ounce.

23 In the fiftieth year of King Azariah of Judah, Pekahiah son of Menahem began to reign over Israel in Samaria; he reigned two years. ²⁴He did what was evil in the sight of the LORD; he did not turn away from the sins of Jeroboam son of Nebat, which he caused Israel to sin. ²⁵Pekah son of Remaliah, his captain, conspired against him with fifty of the Gileadites, and attacked him in Samaria, in the citadel of the palace along with Argob and Arieh; he killed him, and reigned in place of him. ²⁶Now the rest of the deeds of Pekahiah, and all that he did, are written in the Book of the Annals of the Kings of Israel.

27 In the fifty-second year of King Azariah of Judah, Pekah son of Remaliah began to reign over Israel in Samaria; he reigned twenty years. ²⁸He did what was evil in the sight of the LORD; he did not depart from the sins of Jeroboam son of Nebat, which he caused Israel to sin.

29 In the days of King Pekah of Israel, King Tiglath-pileser of Assyria came and captured Ijon, Abel-beth-maacah, Janoah, Kedesh, Hazor, Gilead, and Galilee, all the

land of Naphtali; and he carried the people captive to Assyria. ³⁰Then Hoshea son of Elah made a conspiracy against Pekah son of Remaliah, attacked him, and killed him; he reigned in place of him, in the twentieth year of Jotham son of Uzziah. ³¹Now the rest of the acts of Pekah, and all that he did, are written in the Book of the Annals of the Kings of Israel.

32 In the second year of King Pekah son of Remaliah of Israel, King Jotham son of Uzziah of Judah began to reign. ³³He was twenty-five years old when he began to reign and reigned sixteen years in Jerusalem. His mother's name was Jerusha daughter of Zadok. ³⁴He did what was right in the sight of the LORD, just as his father Uzziah had done. ³⁵Nevertheless the high places were not removed; the people still sacrificed and made offerings on the high places. He built the upper gate of the house of the LORD. ³⁶Now the rest of the acts of Jotham, and all that he did, are they not written in the Book of the Annals of the Kings of Judah? ³⁷In those days the LORD began to send King Rezin of Aram and Pekah son of Remaliah against Judah. ³⁸Jotham slept with his ancestors, and was buried with his ancestors in the city of David, his ancestor; his son Ahaz succeeded him.

15.23–38: 27: *Twenty years* is difficult to fit into a chronology for Israel. If it is not a simple error or exaggeration, it may indicate that Israel was divided and that *Pekah* reigned over a splinter section of it before becoming king over the entire country. 29: The sites listed in this verse are all in northern Israel which, along with Damascus and Syria, was ravaged in 733–732 BCE. 30: Tiglath-pileser helped *Hoshea* to overthrow *Pekah*. The overthrow and Hoshea's pro-Assyrian policy kept Israel from meeting the same fate as Syria in 732. Hoshea's kingdom, however, was only a part of the former state, since the northern part of the country was made into an Assyrian province. 37: *Pekah* and *Rezin* wanted to force Judah to join them in a coalition to resist Tiglath-Pileser of Assyria. The matter came to a head during the reign of Ahaz. See 16.5.

16 In the seventeenth year of Pekah son of Remaliah, King Ahaz son of Jotham of Judah began to reign. ²Ahaz was twenty years old when he began to reign; he reigned sixteen years in Jerusalem. He did not do what was right in the sight of the LORD his God, as his ancestor David had done, ³but he walked in the way of the kings of Israel. He even made his son pass through fire, according to the abominable practices of the nations whom the LORD drove out before the people of Israel. ⁴He sacrificed and made offerings on the high places, on the hills, and under every green tree.

5 Then King Rezin of Aram and King Pekah son of Remaliah of Israel came up to wage war on Jerusalem; they besieged Ahaz but could not conquer him. ⁶At that time the king of Edom*ᵃ* recovered Elath for Edom,*ᵇ* and drove the Judeans from Elath; and the Edomites came to Elath, where they live to this day. ⁷Ahaz sent messengers to King Tiglath-pileser of Assyria, saying, "I am your servant and your son. Come up, and rescue me from the hand of the king of Aram and from the hand of the king of Israel, who are attacking me." ⁸Ahaz also took the silver and gold found in the house of the LORD and in the treasures of the king's house, and sent a present to the king of Assyria. ⁹The king of Assyria listened to him; the king of Assyria marched up against Damascus, and took it, carrying its people captive to Kir; then he killed Rezin.

10 When King Ahaz went to Damascus to meet King Tiglath-pileser of Assyria, he saw the altar that was at Damascus. King Ahaz sent to the priest Uriah a model of the altar, and its pattern, exact in all its details. ¹¹The priest Uriah built the altar; in accordance with all that King Ahaz had sent from Damascus, just so did the priest Uriah build it, before King Ahaz arrived from Damascus. ¹²When the king came from Damascus, the king viewed the altar. Then the king drew near to the altar, went up on it, ¹³and offered his burnt offering and his grain offering, poured his drink offering, and dashed the blood of his offerings of well-being against the altar. ¹⁴The bronze altar that was before the LORD he removed from the front of the

a Cn: Heb *King Rezin of Aram*   *b* Cn: Heb *Aram*

house, from the place between his altar and the house of the LORD, and put it on the north side of his altar. ¹⁵King Ahaz commanded the priest Uriah, saying, "Upon the great altar offer the morning burnt offering, and the evening grain offering, and the king's burnt offering, and his grain offering, with the burnt offering of all the people of the land, their grain offering, and their drink offering; then dash against it all the blood of the burnt offering, and all the blood of the sacrifice; but the bronze altar shall be for me to inquire by." ¹⁶The priest Uriah did everything that King Ahaz commanded.

17 Then King Ahaz cut off the frames of the stands, and removed the laver from them; he removed the sea from the bronze oxen that were under it, and put it on a pediment of stone. ¹⁸The covered portal for use on the sabbath that had been built inside the palace, and the outer entrance for the king he removed from*a* the house of the LORD. He did this because of the king of Assyria. ¹⁹Now the rest of the acts of Ahaz that he did, are they not written in the Book of the Annals of the Kings of Judah? ²⁰Ahaz slept with his ancestors, and was buried with his ancestors in the city of David; his son Hezekiah succeeded him.

16.1–20: The reign of Ahaz. 3: Making *his son pass through fire* is a reference to child sacrifice (see 3.27). **5:** This verse refers to the "Syro-Ephraimitic crisis" of 734 BCE. See comment on 15.37. The oracle* of Isaiah in Isa 7 is directed to this situation. **6:** Judah's problems with Syria and Israel weakened its hold on *Elath* (see 14.22), and the Edomites took advantage. **7–9:** These verses continue with the Syro-Ephraimitic crisis. According to Isa 7, Isaiah counseled Ahaz against seeking the help of the Assyrians. These verses indicate that Ahaz chose to ignore that advice and purchased the aid of *Tiglath-pileser* against Syria and Israel. This placed Judah in a subject relationship to Assyria that would be the source of future problems. *Kir* is the place of the Syrians' origin, according to Am 9.7. It is also mentioned as the place of Syrian exile in Am 1.5. It is obviously in Mesopotamia though its exact location is unknown. **10–16:** This story is apparently meant as condemnation of Ahaz to illustrate his importation of foreign elements into the worship of the LORD. It may be, however, that Ahaz intended the new altar to

honor the LORD. *Uriah the priest* is likely the same figure mentioned in Isa 8.2. **17–18:** Ahaz was forced to remove some of the *bronze* from the Temple* in order to make his payment of tribute to the Assyrian king. For descriptions of the *bronze oxen* under the sea and the *laver stands,* see 1 Kings 7.23–37. The meaning and nature of *the covered portal for use on the sabbath* (v. 18) is not certain.

〜〜〜〜〜〜〜〜〜

17 In the twelfth year of King Ahaz of Judah, Hoshea son of Elah began to reign in Samaria over Israel; he reigned nine years. ²He did what was evil in the sight of the LORD, yet not like the kings of Israel who were before him. ³King Shalmaneser of Assyria came up against him; Hoshea became his vassal, and paid him tribute. ⁴But the king of Assyria found treachery in Hoshea; for he had sent messengers to King So of Egypt, and offered no tribute to the king of Assyria, as he had done year by year; therefore the king of Assyria confined him and imprisoned him.

5 Then the king of Assyria invaded all the land and came to Samaria; for three years he besieged it. ⁶In the ninth year of Hoshea the king of Assyria captured Samaria; he carried the Israelites away to Assyria. He placed them in Halah, on the Habor, the river of Gozan, and in the cities of the Medes.

17.1–41: The fall of Israel. 2: It is not clear why Hoshea is judged to be less evil than his predecessors. **4:** Hosea 7.11 may reflect the prophet* Hosea's judgment of the foolishness of *Hoshea's* revolt against Assyria. **5:** The fact that Samaria held out for *three years* is a tribute to its defenses. **6:** This verse marks the end of the northern kingdom of Israel. The places listed here to which the people of Israel were deported were all close to the Assyrian homeland.

〜〜〜〜〜〜〜〜〜

7 This occurred because the people of Israel had sinned against the LORD their God, who had brought them up out of the land of Egypt from under the hand of Pharaoh king of Egypt. They had worshiped other gods ⁸and walked in the customs of the nations whom the LORD drove out before the people

a Cn: Heb lacks from

of Israel, and in the customs that the kings of Israel had introduced.[a] 9The people of Israel secretly did things that were not right against the LORD their God. They built for themselves high places at all their towns, from watchtower to fortified city; 10they set up for themselves pillars and sacred poles[b] on every high hill and under every green tree; 11there they made offerings on all the high places, as the nations did whom the LORD carried away before them. They did wicked things, provoking the LORD to anger; 12they served idols, of which the LORD had said to them, "You shall not do this." 13Yet the LORD warned Israel and Judah by every prophet and every seer, saying, "Turn from your evil ways and keep my commandments and my statutes, in accordance with all the law that I commanded your ancestors and that I sent to you by my servants the prophets." 14They would not listen but were stubborn, as their ancestors had been, who did not believe in the LORD their God. 15They despised his statutes, and his covenant that he made with their ancestors, and the warnings that he gave them. They went after false idols and became false; they followed the nations that were around them, concerning whom the LORD had commanded them that they should not do as they did. 16They rejected all the commandments of the LORD their God and made for themselves cast images of two calves; they made a sacred pole,[c] worshiped all the host of heaven, and served Baal. 17They made their sons and their daughters pass through fire; they used divination and augury; and they sold themselves to do evil in the sight of the LORD, provoking him to anger. 18Therefore the LORD was very angry with Israel and removed them out of his sight; none was left but the tribe of Judah alone.

stars). Making *their sons and their daughters pass through fire* is child sacrifice.

19 Judah also did not keep the commandments of the LORD their God but walked in the customs that Israel had introduced. 20The LORD rejected all the descendants of Israel; he punished them and gave them into the hand of plunderers, until he had banished them from his presence.

21 When he had torn Israel from the house of David, they made Jeroboam son of Nebat king. Jeroboam drove Israel from following the LORD and made them commit great sin. 22The people of Israel continued in all the sins that Jeroboam committed; they did not depart from them 23until the LORD removed Israel out of his sight, as he had foretold through all his servants the prophets. So Israel was exiled from their own land to Assyria until this day.

24 The king of Assyria brought people from Babylon, Cuthah, Avva, Hamath, and Sepharvaim, and placed them in the cities of Samaria in place of the people of Israel; they took possession of Samaria, and settled in its cities. 25When they first settled there, they did not worship the LORD; therefore the LORD sent lions among them, which killed some of them. 26So the king of Assyria was told, "The nations that you have carried away and placed in the cities of Samaria do not know the law of the god of the land; therefore he has sent lions among them; they are killing them, because they do not know the law of the god of the land." 27Then the king of Assyria commanded, "Send there one of the priests whom you carried away from there; let him[d] go and live there, and teach them the law of the god of the land." 28So one of the priests whom they had carried away from Samaria came and lived in Bethel; he taught them how they should worship the LORD.

17.7–18: Many scholars regard these verses as a later addition, in deuteronomistic* style, to the initial Deuteronomistic History, since they explain Israel's fall as the result of idolatry,* as opposed to the explanation in vv. 21–23, which culminates the theme of the sin of Jeroboam. *Pillars* and *sacred poles* (vv. 10, 16) were trappings of the worship of Canaanite gods. The *host of heaven* (v. 16) refers to astral deities (sun, moon,

17.19–28. 19–20: These verses are also an addition, perhaps part of the addition in vv. 7–18. They make it clear that Judah was guilty of the same offenses as Is-

---

a Meaning of Heb uncertain   *b* Heb *Asherim*
c Heb *Asherah*   *d* Syr Vg: Heb *them*

rael. They were apparently written in the Exile* (after 586 BCE) as indicated in v. 20, where *all the descendants of Israel* would include both Israel and Judah. **21–23:** These verses conclude the theme of the *sin(s) of Jeroboam,* which refers to the shrines at Dan and Bethel (1 Kings 12.25–33) and which every king of Israel is accused of perpetuating. **24:** In addition to deporting the people of Israel, the Assyrians settled captives from other countries in the former land of Israel. They also renamed the area the Assyrian province of Samaria (Samerina). **25–28:** A widely accepted idea in the ancient Near East was that each country had its own god and each god its own country. It was therefore considered important by the Assyrians that the people whom they had imported into Israel learn the *law of the god of the land* (v. 26), and the attacks by lions were blamed on the failure to do this.

29 But every nation still made gods of its own and put them in the shrines of the high places that the people of Samaria had made, every nation in the cities in which they lived; ³⁰the people of Babylon made Succothbenoth, the people of Cuth made Nergal, the people of Hamath made Ashima; ³¹the Avites made Nibhaz and Tartak; the Sepharvites burned their children in the fire to Adrammelech and Anammelech, the gods of Sepharvaim. ³²They also worshiped the LORD and appointed from among themselves all sorts of people as priests of the high places, who sacrificed for them in the shrines of the high places. ³³So they worshiped the LORD but also served their own gods, after the manner of the nations from among whom they had been carried away. ³⁴To this day they continue to practice their former customs.

They do not worship the LORD and they do not follow the statutes or the ordinances or the law or the commandment that the LORD commanded the children of Jacob, whom he named Israel. ³⁵The LORD had made a covenant with them and commanded them, "You shall not worship other gods or bow yourselves to them or serve them or sacrifice to them, ³⁶but you shall worship the LORD, who brought you out of the land of Egypt with great power and with an outstretched arm; you shall bow yourselves to him, and to him you shall sacrifice. ³⁷The

statutes and the ordinances and the law and the commandment that he wrote for you, you shall always be careful to observe. You shall not worship other gods; ³⁸you shall not forget the covenant that I have made with you. You shall not worship other gods, ³⁹but you shall worship the LORD your God; he will deliver you out of the hand of all your enemies." ⁴⁰They would not listen, however, but they continued to practice their former custom.

41 So these nations worshiped the LORD, but also served their carved images; to this day their children and their children's children continue to do as their ancestors did.

17.29–41. 29–34a: The newcomers, however, also retained the gods of their homelands and worshiped them along with the LORD. The names of the gods in vv. 30–31 are distortions or misspellings of the names of gods from different parts of the ancient Near East. However, the errors do not seem to be intentional. Rather, they betray an author (probably the deuteronomist) who is unfamiliar with these different gods and who also writes at a later date, as indicated by the *to this day* statement in v. 34a. **34b–40:** These verses were added by a later writer who viewed the religion of the Samaritans (the residents of the province of Samaria) as illegitimate. Verse 34b, therefore, directly contradicts v. 33. Many faithful Jews hated the Samaritans in part because of their religious practice, which mixed elements from other religions into Jewish observances. Samaritans were also regarded as practicing a form of Judaism, however, particularly at later periods. The animosity between the two groups surfaces in Ezra 4.1–3 and is clearly reflected in stories in the New Testament Gospels (Lk 10.29–37; Jn 4.7–42). **41:** This verse summarizes vv. 29–34a and may have been their original conclusion. It agrees with the viewpoint that the settlers worshipped both the LORD and other gods.

18 In the third year of King Hoshea son of Elah of Israel, Hezekiah son of King Ahaz of Judah began to reign. ²He was twenty-five years old when he began to reign; he reigned twenty-nine years in Jerusalem. His mother's name was Abi daughter of Zechariah. ³He did what was right in the sight of the LORD just as his ancestor David had done. ⁴He removed the high places,

broke down the pillars, and cut down the sacred pole.[a] He broke in pieces the bronze serpent that Moses had made, for until those days the people of Israel had made offerings to it; it was called Nehushtan. 5He trusted in the LORD the God of Israel; so that there was no one like him among all the kings of Judah after him, or among those who were before him. 6For he held fast to the LORD; he did not depart from following him but kept the commandments that the LORD commanded Moses. 7The LORD was with him; wherever he went, he prospered. He rebelled against the king of Assyria and would not serve him. 8He attacked the Philistines as far as Gaza and its territory, from watchtower to fortified city.

18.1–19.37: Hezekiah and the invasion of Sennacherib. The invasion of Sennacherib, king of Assyria, which is recounted in these chapters, took place in 701 BCE and is documented both in the Bible and in Assyrian records. Similar versions of the story are found in 2 Chr 32 and Isa 36. The Assyrian version was recorded in Sennacherib's annals and in a famous relief of the defeat of Lachish on his palace wall in Nineveh. **18.4:** The *high places**★* were shrines other than the Jerusalem Temple.★ They could be used for the worship of the LORD or of other gods. Here it appears to be the latter that is envisioned, since *pillars* and *sacred poles* were used in the worship of Canaanite gods. The *bronze serpent that Moses had made* was to save the people from poisonous snakes (Num 21.6–9). **5:** Statements of incomparability like this one are made also for Moses as a prophet★ (Deut 34.10), for Solomon for wisdom (1 Kings 3.12), and for Josiah for obedience (2 Kings 23.25). **8:** The *Philistines* had remained more or less independent in their land since the time of David. Hezekiah subjugated them to Judah, probably to strengthen the resistance to the Assyrians.

9 In the fourth year of King Hezekiah, which was the seventh year of King Hoshea son of Elah of Israel, King Shalmaneser of Assyria came up against Samaria, besieged it, 10and at the end of three years, took it. In the sixth year of Hezekiah, which was the ninth year of King Hoshea of Israel, Samaria was taken. 11The king of Assyria carried the Israelites away to Assyria, settled them in Halah, on the Habor, the river of Gozan, and in the cities of the Medes, 12because they did not obey the voice of the LORD their God but transgressed his covenant—all that Moses the servant of the LORD had commanded; they neither listened nor obeyed.

13 In the fourteenth year of King Hezekiah, King Sennacherib of Assyria came up against all the fortified cities of Judah and captured them. 14King Hezekiah of Judah sent to the king of Assyria at Lachish, saying, "I have done wrong; withdraw from me; whatever you impose on me I will bear." The king of Assyria demanded of King Hezekiah of Judah three hundred talents of silver and thirty talents of gold. 15Hezekiah gave him all the silver that was found in the house of the LORD and in the treasuries of the king's house. 16At that time Hezekiah stripped the gold from the doors of the temple of the LORD, and from the doorposts that King Hezekiah of Judah had overlaid and gave it to the king of Assyria. 17The king of Assyria sent the Tartan, the Rabsaris, and the Rabshakeh with a great army from Lachish to King Hezekiah at Jerusalem. They went up and came to Jerusalem. When they arrived, they came and stood by the conduit of the upper pool, which is on the highway to the Fuller's Field. 18When they called for the king, there came out to them Eliakim son of Hilkiah, who was in charge of the palace, and Shebnah the secretary, and Joah son of Asaph, the recorder.

19 The Rabshakeh said to them, "Say to Hezekiah: Thus says the great king, the king of Assyria: On what do you base this confidence of yours? 20Do you think that mere words are strategy and power for war? On whom do you now rely, that you have rebelled against me? 21See, you are relying now on Egypt, that broken reed of a staff, which will pierce the hand of anyone who leans on it. Such is Pharaoh king of Egypt to all who rely on him. 22But if you say to me, 'We rely on the LORD our God,' is it not he whose high places and altars Hezekiah has removed, saying to Judah and to Jerusalem, 'You shall worship before this altar in Jerusalem'? 23Come now, make a wager with my

a Heb *Asherah*

master the king of Assyria: I will give you two thousand horses, if you are able on your part to set riders on them. 24How then can you repulse a single captain among the least of my master's servants, when you rely on Egypt for chariots and for horsemen? 25Moreover, is it without the LORD that I have come up against this place to destroy it? The LORD said to me, Go up against this land, and destroy it."

26 Then Eliakim son of Hilkiah, and Shebnah, and Joah said to the Rabshakeh, "Please speak to your servants in the Aramaic language, for we understand it; do not speak to us in the language of Judah within the hearing of the people who are on the wall." 27But the Rabshakeh said to them, "Has my master sent me to speak these words to your master and to you, and not to the people sitting on the wall, who are doomed with you to eat their own dung and to drink their own urine?"

18.9–27. 9–12: These verses reiterate the information about the fall of Israel in ch. 17. 14: A *talent* could weigh between 45 and 130 pounds. 17: *Tartan, Rabsaris,* and *Rabshakeh* are all titles for Assyrian military officers. The exact location of the *conduit of the upper pool* is unknown. 18: The three Assyrians meet with three officials of the court of Judah—*Eliakim, Shebnah,* and *Joah.* The precise functions of their offices as the one *in charge of the palace, secretary,* and *recorder* are uncertain. 19–25: Part of the tactics of ancient warfare involved speeches like this one designed to discourage the enemy. The Rabshakeh makes the point that the Assyrians greatly outnumber the forces of Judah (vv. 23–24) and asks who else the people of Judah are relying on. He observes, quite correctly, that the Egyptians to whom Hezekiah may have looked for help (v. 24), are powerless compared with the Assyrian army. His comparison of Egypt to a *broken reed of a staff* in v. 21 is found also in Ezek 29.6 and may have been a proverb. The other possibility he raises is that they are dependent on the LORD. To counter this, he states that Hezekiah *removed* the LORD's *high places** *and altars* (v. 22), which may have been true in a sense. That is, in his effort to centralize the government and religion of Judah, Hezekiah may have outlawed all shrines outside of Jerusalem. The Rabshakeh also claims that the LORD sent the Assyrians against Jerusalem. This claim may also have had a measure of truth

to the extent that Hezekiah or his predecessors likely swore an oath by the LORD to be loyal to their Assyrian overlord. 26: *Aramaic** was the language of diplomacy of that time. *The language of Judah* was Hebrew. 27: The fates described here refer to the conditions of starvation of a city under siege.

28 Then the Rabshakeh stood and called out in a loud voice in the language of Judah, "Hear the word of the great king, the king of Assyria! 29Thus says the king: 'Do not let Hezekiah deceive you, for he will not be able to deliver you out of my hand. 30Do not let Hezekiah make you rely on the LORD by saying, The LORD will surely deliver us, and this city will not be given into the hand of the king of Assyria.' 31Do not listen to Hezekiah; for thus says the king of Assyria: 'Make your peace with me and come out to me; then every one of you will eat from your own vine and your own fig tree, and drink water from your own cistern, 32until I come and take you away to a land like your own land, a land of grain and wine, a land of bread and vineyards, a land of olive oil and honey, that you may live and not die. Do not listen to Hezekiah when he misleads you by saying, The LORD will deliver us. 33Has any of the gods of the nations ever delivered its land out of the hand of the king of Assyria? 34Where are the gods of Hamath and Arpad? Where are the gods of Sepharvaim, Hena, and Ivvah? Have they delivered Samaria out of my hand? 35Who among all the gods of the countries have delivered their countries out of my hand, that the LORD should deliver Jerusalem out of my hand?' "

18.28–35: The Rabshakeh's second speech is in Hebrew (*the language of Judah,* v. 28), is directed to the common defenders of the city, and is designed to effect a mutiny. He calls on them to surrender, promising prosperity first in their homeland (v. 31) and then in exile (v. 32). The part of the speech regarded as blasphemy by the biblical writers is vv. 33–35, where the Rabshakeh compares the LORD to the gods of other nations, none of whom has been able to save their people from the Assyrian assault.

36 But the people were silent and answered him not a word, for the king's com-

mand was, "Do not answer him." [37]Then Eliakim son of Hilkiah, who was in charge of the palace, and Shebna the secretary, and Joah son of Asaph, the recorder, came to Hezekiah with their clothes torn and told him the words of the Rabshakeh.

19 When King Hezekiah heard it, he tore his clothes, covered himself with sackcloth, and went into the house of the LORD. [2]And he sent Eliakim, who was in charge of the palace, and Shebna the secretary, and the senior priests, covered with sackcloth, to the prophet Isaiah son of Amoz. [3]They said to him, "Thus says Hezekiah, This day is a day of distress, of rebuke, and of disgrace; children have come to the birth, and there is no strength to bring them forth. [4]It may be that the LORD your God heard all the words of the Rabshakeh, whom his master the king of Assyria has sent to mock the living God, and will rebuke the words that the LORD your God has heard; therefore lift up your prayer for the remnant that is left." [5]When the servants of King Hezekiah came to Isaiah, [6]Isaiah said to them, "Say to your master, 'Thus says the LORD: Do not be afraid because of the words that you have heard, with which the servants of the king of Assyria have reviled me. [7]I myself will put a spirit in him, so that he shall hear a rumor and return to his own land; I will cause him to fall by the sword in his own land.' "

[8] The Rabshakeh returned, and found the king of Assyria fighting against Libnah; for he had heard that the king had left Lachish. [9]When the king[a] heard concerning King Tirhakah of Ethiopia,[b] "See, he has set out to fight against you," he sent messengers again to Hezekiah, saying, [10]"Thus shall you speak to King Hezekiah of Judah: Do not let your God on whom you rely deceive you by promising that Jerusalem will not be given into the hand of the king of Assyria. [11]See, you have heard what the kings of Assyria have done to all lands, destroying them utterly. Shall you be delivered? [12]Have the gods of the nations delivered them, the nations that my predecessors destroyed, Gozan, Haran, Rezeph, and the people of Eden who were in Telassar? [13]Where is the king of Hamath, the king of Arpad, the king

of the city of Sepharvaim, the king of Hena, or the king of Ivvah?"

18.36–19.13. 18.37; 19.1–2: Wearing *torn clothes* and *sackcloth* (Heb., "saq") were signs of great sorrow or distress. *Isaiah, son of Amoz,* is also the prophet* behind the book of Isaiah. **3:** *Children have come to the birth, and there is no strength to bring them forth* may be a proverb. It alludes to great pain and suffering associated with labor. Here, it expresses frustration because the people of Judah do not have the strength to carry out the rebellion against the Assyrians. **4:** It was in his second speech (18.28–35) that the Rabshakeh *mock(ed) the living God.* **8:** *Libnah* was southwest of Jerusalem and north of Lachish. **9:** *Tirhaka* (Tarhaka) was from Nubia *(Ethiopia)* and did not become king of Egypt until around 690 BCE. His name here is probably an error made by the much later biblical writer. **11–13:** The Rabshakeh's letter here is very similar to his speech in 18.33–35.

---

[14] Hezekiah received the letter from the hand of the messengers and read it; then Hezekiah went up to the house of the LORD and spread it before the LORD. [15]And Hezekiah prayed before the LORD, and said: "O LORD the God of Israel, who are enthroned above the cherubim, you are God, you alone, of all the kingdoms of the earth; you have made heaven and earth. [16]Incline your ear, O LORD, and hear; open your eyes, O LORD, and see; hear the words of Sennacherib, which he has sent to mock the living God. [17]Truly, O LORD, the kings of Assyria have laid waste the nations and their lands, [18]and have hurled their gods into the fire, though they were no gods but the work of human hands—wood and stone—and so they were destroyed. [19]So now, O LORD our God, save us, I pray you, from his hand, so that all the kingdoms of the earth may know that you, O LORD, are God alone."

19.14–19. 15: The *cherubim* is a reference to the ark, which had two cherubim depicted on its lid. These were mythical, griffin-like creatures whose statues often adorned temples and palaces in the ancient Near East. **16–19:** Hezekiah's prayer addresses the Rab-

---

a Heb *he*　　*b* Or *Nubia;* Heb *Cush*

The Siege of Lachish

The city of Lachish, southwest of Jerusalem, was an important and well-fortified outpost of Judah during the reign of King Hezekiah. When the Assyrian emperor Sennacherib came to Palestine in 701 BCE, he besieged and conquered Lachish and then set up his headquarters there, from which he threatened Jerusalem (2 Kings 18.14). In addition to the Bible's accounts of the events of 701 (2 Kings 18–19; 2 Chr 32; Isa 36), we possess Sennacherib's own annals. Unfortunately, these versions of the story do not always agree. For example, Sennacherib claims to have conquered Jerusalem, while the Bible indicates that he never reached Jerusalem. Sennacherib's annals say nothing about the plague which, according to the Bible (2 Kings 19.35), forced him to withdraw from Judah. All accounts agree that Sennacherib left Hezekiah on the throne of Judah, which seems extraordinary considering Hezekiah's rebellion. They also agree that Hezekiah paid tribute to Sennacherib, though they differ about the amount. Sennacherib was so proud of his conquest of Lachish that he had a relief (a raised carving) of the battle included in the decorations of his palace wall in Nineveh. The relief graphically depicts the tactics and weapons used in ancient Near Eastern warfare. The site of ancient Lachish has recently been excavated, and the discoveries there confirm the basic accuracy of the relief.

shakeh's claim that the gods of the nations had not saved them and neither could the LORD save Judah. Through Hezekiah the author makes the point that those gods were not real but only idols. Hence, Hezekiah calls on the LORD for deliverance as a way of showing the world that the LORD (Yahweh) is *God alone.*

20 Then Isaiah son of Amoz sent to Hezekiah, saying, "Thus says the LORD, the God of Israel: I have heard your prayer to me about King Sennacherib of Assyria. 21 This is the word that the LORD has spoken concerning him:
She despises you, she scorns you—
　virgin daughter Zion;
she tosses her head—behind your back,
　daughter Jerusalem.

22 "Whom have you mocked and reviled?
　Against whom have you raised your
　　voice
and haughtily lifted your eyes?
　Against the Holy One of Israel!
23 By your messengers you have mocked
　the Lord,

and you have said, 'With my many
　chariots
I have gone up the heights of the
　mountains,
　to the far recesses of Lebanon;
I felled its tallest cedars,
　its choicest cypresses;
I entered its farthest retreat,
　its densest forest.
24 I dug wells
　and drank foreign waters,
I dried up with the sole of my foot
　all the streams of Egypt.'

25 "Have you not heard
　that I determined it long ago?
I planned from days of old
　what now I bring to pass,
that you should make fortified cities
　crash into heaps of ruins,
26 while their inhabitants, shorn of
　strength,
　are dismayed and confounded;
they have become like plants of the
　field
　and like tender grass,

like grass on the housetops,
    blighted before it is grown.

27 "But I know your rising*a* and your
      sitting,
    your going out and coming in,
    and your raging against me.
28 Because you have raged against me
    and your arrogance has come to my
      ears,
    I will put my hook in your nose
    and my bit in your mouth;
    I will turn you back on the way
    by which you came.

29 "And this shall be the sign for you: This year you shall eat what grows of itself, and in the second year what springs from that; then in the third year sow, reap, plant vineyards, and eat their fruit. 30 The surviving remnant of the house of Judah shall again take root downward, and bear fruit upward; 31 for from Jerusalem a remnant shall go out, and from Mount Zion a band of survivors. The zeal of the LORD of hosts will do this.

32 "Therefore thus says the LORD concerning the king of Assyria: He shall not come into this city, shoot an arrow there, come before it with a shield, or cast up a siege ramp against it. 33 By the way that he came, by the same he shall return; he shall not come into this city, says the LORD. 34 For I will defend this city to save it, for my own sake and for the sake of my servant David."

35 That very night the angel of the LORD set out and struck down one hundred eighty-five thousand in the camp of the Assyrians; when morning dawned, they were all dead bodies. 36 Then King Sennacherib of Assyria left, went home, and lived at Nineveh. 37 As he was worshiping in the house of his god Nisroch, his sons Adrammelech and Sharezer killed him with the sword, and they escaped into the land of Ararat. His son Esarhaddon succeeded him.

19.20–37. 21: *She* is the *virgin daughter Zion,*★ a reference to Jerusalem. *Toss(ing) her head* was a way of showing contempt. The idea is that the city of Jerusalem disdains the Assyrian king Sennacherib. 22–24: Sennacherib is caricatured as arrogant and boastful to the point that he has *reviled* the LORD. The speaker in vv. 23–24 is Sennacherib. See Isa 10.12–19; 14.24–27. 25–28: Now, the LORD speaks. The message in these verses is that it is the LORD who determined Sennacherib's victories and who will now bring him down because of his pride. 29–31: This oracle★ is considered more realistic and thus more original than the surrounding material. The *sign* it describes is a three-year period before agriculture returns to its normal cycle and the Assyrian threat is finally removed (v. 29). The oracle also describes the survival of a *remnant* in the city of *Jerusalem* from which the countryside will be repopulated after the Assyrian devastation (vv. 30–31). 32–33: These verses reflect the doctrine of the inviolability of Jerusalem, that is, the belief that the LORD would never allow the city of Jerusalem to be captured. The idea may have arisen as a result of the city's survival in 701. It was later countered by the prophet★ Jeremiah (Jer 7). 35: This verse describes a plague that devastated Sennacherib's army and forced him to return in shame to Nineveh. The historical veracity of the event cannot be confirmed or denied. 36–37: Sennacherib's assassination did not take place until 20 years later in 681 BCE. *Ararat* (v. 37) is modern Armenia north of Assyria.

20 In those days Hezekiah became sick and was at the point of death. The prophet Isaiah son of Amoz came to him, and said to him, "Thus says the LORD: Set your house in order, for you shall die; you shall not recover." 2 Then Hezekiah turned his face to the wall and prayed to the LORD: 3 "Remember now, O LORD, I implore you, how I have walked before you in faithfulness with a whole heart, and have done what is good in your sight." Hezekiah wept bitterly. 4 Before Isaiah had gone out of the middle court, the word of the LORD came to him: 5 "Turn back, and say to Hezekiah prince of my people, Thus says the LORD, the God of your ancestor David: I have heard your prayer, I have seen your tears; indeed, I will heal you; on the third day you shall go up to the house of the LORD. 6 I will add fifteen years to your life. I will deliver you and this city out of the hand of the king of Assyria; I will defend this city for my own sake and for my servant David's sake." 7 Then Isaiah said,

a Gk Compare Isa 37.27 Q Ms: MT lacks *rising*

"Bring a lump of figs. Let them take it and apply it to the boil, so that he may recover."

8 Hezekiah said to Isaiah, "What shall be the sign that the LORD will heal me, and that I shall go up to the house of the LORD on the third day?" 9 Isaiah said, "This is the sign to you from the LORD, that the LORD will do the thing that he has promised: the shadow has now advanced ten intervals; shall it retreat ten intervals?" 10 Hezekiah answered, "It is normal for the shadow to lengthen ten intervals; rather let the shadow retreat ten intervals." 11 The prophet Isaiah cried to the LORD; and he brought the shadow back the ten intervals, by which the sun*a* had declined on the dial of Ahaz.

12 At that time King Merodach-baladan son of Baladan of Babylon sent envoys with letters and a present to Hezekiah, for he had heard that Hezekiah had been sick. 13 Hezekiah welcomed them;*b* he showed them all his treasure house, the silver, the gold, the spices, the precious oil, his armory, all that was found in his storehouses; there was nothing in his house or in all his realm that Hezekiah did not show them. 14 Then the prophet Isaiah came to King Hezekiah, and said to him, "What did these men say? From where did they come to you?" Hezekiah answered, "They have come from a far country, from Babylon." 15 He said, "What have they seen in your house?" Hezekiah answered, "They have seen all that is in my house; there is nothing in my storehouses that I did not show them."

16 Then Isaiah said to Hezekiah, "Hear the word of the LORD: 17 Days are coming when all that is in your house, and that which your ancestors have stored up until this day, shall be carried to Babylon; nothing shall be left, says the LORD. 18 Some of your own sons who are born to you shall be taken away; they shall be eunuchs in the palace of the king of Babylon." 19 Then Hezekiah said to Isaiah, "The word of the LORD that you have spoken is good." For he thought, "Why not, if there will be peace and security in my days?"

20 The rest of the deeds of Hezekiah, all his power, how he made the pool and the conduit and brought water into the city, are they not written in the Book of the Annals of the Kings of Judah? 21 Hezekiah slept with his ancestors; and his son Manasseh succeeded him.

20.1–21: Hezekiah's illness and the Babylonian envoy. The stories in this chapter are probably out of order and originally preceded the invasion of Sennacherib in 701 BCE, since v. 6 promises defense of Jerusalem, and the visit of Merodach-baladan must have preceded Hezekiah's revolt against Assyria. **7:** The *lump of figs* served as a poultice, a medicinal substance applied directly to the skin, to draw out the boil. **8–11:** Comparable to Josh 10.12–13, where the sun stood still, here it retreated 10 hours. **12–19:** *Merodach-baladan* is Marduk-apal-iddina, who ruled in Babylon 720–709 and again in 702 and opposed Assyria. His visit to Jerusalem would have involved plotting for Hezekiah's revolt against Assyria. In this context, however, it has been used to foreshadow the Babylonian Exile.* *Eunuchs* (v. 18) were castrated males who were often employed as guardians and servants in the royal harem. However, the Hebrew word may simply mean a palace servant or official. **20:** The *conduit* by which Hezekiah *brought water into the city* probably refers to the Siloam tunnel in Jerusalem, which contained an inscription describing its construction. **21:** There is no notice about Hezekiah's burial "in the city of David" as there is for his predecessors. The reason is unclear, though it may reflect an actual change in practice. 2 Chr 32.33 says he was buried "on the ascent to the tombs of the descendants of David," which may suggest that the royal tombs of Judah were full.

21 Manasseh was twelve years old when he began to reign; he reigned fifty-five years in Jerusalem. His mother's name was Hephzibah. 2 He did what was evil in the sight of the LORD, following the abominable practices of the nations that the LORD drove out before the people of Israel. 3 For he rebuilt the high places that his father Hezekiah had destroyed; he erected altars for Baal, made a sacred pole,*c* as King Ahab of Israel had done, worshiped all the host of heaven, and served them. 4 He built altars in the house of the LORD, of which the LORD had said, "In Jerusalem I will put my name." 5 He

a Syr See Isa 38.8 and Tg: Heb *it When Hezekiah heard about them* *b* Gk Vg Syr: Heb *c* Heb *Asherah*

built altars for all the host of heaven in the two courts of the house of the LORD. [6]He made his son pass through fire; he practiced soothsaying and augury, and dealt with mediums and with wizards. He did much evil in the sight of the LORD, provoking him to anger. [7]The carved image of Asherah that he had made he set in the house of which the LORD said to David and to his son Solomon, "In this house, and in Jerusalem, which I have chosen out of all the tribes of Israel, I will put my name forever; [8]I will not cause the feet of Israel to wander any more out of the land that I gave to their ancestors, if only they will be careful to do according to all that I have commanded them, and according to all the law that my servant Moses commanded them." [9]But they did not listen; Manasseh misled them to do more evil than the nations had done that the LORD destroyed before the people of Israel.

10 The LORD said by his servants the prophets, [11]"Because King Manasseh of Judah has committed these abominations, has done things more wicked than all that the Amorites did, who were before him, and has caused Judah also to sin with his idols; [12]therefore thus says the LORD, the God of Israel, I am bringing upon Jerusalem and Judah such evil that the ears of everyone who hears of it will tingle. [13]I will stretch over Jerusalem the measuring line for Samaria, and the plummet for the house of Ahab; I will wipe Jerusalem as one wipes a dish, wiping it and turning it upside down. [14]I will cast off the remnant of my heritage, and give them into the hand of their enemies; they shall become a prey and a spoil to all their enemies, [15]because they have done what is evil in my sight and have provoked me to anger, since the day their ancestors came out of Egypt, even to this day."

16 Moreover Manasseh shed very much innocent blood, until he had filled Jerusalem from one end to another, besides the sin that he caused Judah to sin so that they did what was evil in the sight of the LORD.

17 Now the rest of the acts of Manasseh, all that he did, and the sin that he committed, are they not written in the Book of the Annals of the Kings of Judah? [18]Manasseh slept with his ancestors, and was buried in the garden of his house, in the garden of Uzza. His son Amon succeeded him.

19 Amon was twenty-two years old when he began to reign; he reigned two years in Jerusalem. His mother's name was Meshullemeth daughter of Haruz of Jotbah. [20]He did what was evil in the sight of the LORD, as his father Manasseh had done. [21]He walked in all the way in which his father walked, served the idols that his father served, and worshiped them; [22]he abandoned the LORD, the God of his ancestors, and did not walk in the way of the LORD. [23]The servants of Amon conspired against him, and killed the king in his house. [24]But the people of the land killed all those who had conspired against King Amon, and the people of the land made his son Josiah king in place of him. [25]Now the rest of the acts of Amon that he did, are they not written in the Book of the Annals of the Kings of Judah? [26]He was buried in his tomb in the garden of Uzza; then his son Josiah succeeded him.

21.1–26: Manasseh and Amon. 1: Manasseh is credited with the longest reign, *fifty-five years*, of any king of Israel or Judah. **3:** A *sacred pole* was an important part of the worship of the Canaanite goddess Asherah.* The *host of heaven* refers to the astral gods—sun, moon, and stars. These practices were outlawed by Deuteronomy (12.29–31; 17.3). **6:** *He made his son pass through fire* refers to child sacrifice. *Mediums and wizards* are often used in conjunction and refer to devices used to communicate with the dead. Such practices are condemned by the law in Deuteronomy (18.10). See 1 Sam 28. **7–8:** Here the promise of the central "place" chosen by Yahweh (Deut 12.5) is combined with the promise of a dynasty* to *David* (2 Sam 7). **11:** *Amorites* is a general name for the inhabitants of Canaan before the Israelites. **13:** The *measuring line* and *plummet* suggest that Judah will be judged by the same standards by which *Samaria* and its worst kings, *the house of Ahab*, were condemned. Compare Am 7.7–9. To *wipe Jerusalem as one wipes a dish* means to empty it completely. **14:** The LORD's *heritage* is the nation of Israel. Since the northern kingdom is no more, Judah is the *remnant* of that heritage. These verses, therefore, predict the Babylonian Exile* and blame it on Manasseh. Quite a different story is told in

2 Chr 33.10–13. **16:** This verse may be an addition, since it does not seem to relate well to the surrounding context. **18:** *Manasseh* also is not *buried* in the city of David but *in the garden of Uzza.* Both the identity of Uzza and the location of this garden are unknown. **24:** The *people of the land* may be the landowning nobility, but their identity is disputed. **26:** *Amon* is also buried in the *garden of Uzza.*

22 Josiah was eight years old when he began to reign; he reigned thirty-one years in Jerusalem. His mother's name was Jedidah daughter of Adaiah of Bozkath. ²He did what was right in the sight of the LORD, and walked in all the way of his father David; he did not turn aside to the right or to the left.

3 In the eighteenth year of King Josiah, the king sent Shaphan son of Azaliah, son of Meshullam, the secretary, to the house of the LORD, saying, ⁴"Go up to the high priest Hilkiah, and have him count the entire sum of the money that has been brought into the house of the LORD, which the keepers of the threshold have collected from the people; ⁵let it be given into the hand of the workers who have the oversight of the house of the LORD; let them give it to the workers who are at the house of the LORD, repairing the house, ⁶that is, to the carpenters, to the builders, to the masons; and let them use it to buy timber and quarried stone to repair the house. ⁷But no accounting shall be asked from them for the money that is delivered into their hand, for they deal honestly."

8 The high priest Hilkiah said to Shaphan the secretary, "I have found the book of the law in the house of the LORD." When Hilkiah gave the book to Shaphan, he read it. ⁹Then Shaphan the secretary came to the king, and reported to the king, "Your servants have emptied out the money that was found in the house, and have delivered it into the hand of the workers who have oversight of the house of the LORD." ¹⁰Shaphan the secretary informed the king, "The priest Hilkiah has given me a book." Shaphan then read it aloud to the king.

22.1–23.30: The reign and reform of Josiah. Josiah, along with Hezekiah, is one of the good kings of Judah

and one of the heroes of the Deuteronomistic* History. He is renowned for his obedience (22.2; 23.25) to the law book found during his reign. **22.3–10:** The Temple* repairs made by Josiah lead to the discovery of a copy of the *book of the law,* which has long been identified as a form of the book of Deuteronomy.

11 When the king heard the words of the book of the law, he tore his clothes. ¹²Then the king commanded the priest Hilkiah, Ahikam son of Shaphan, Achbor son of Micaiah, Shaphan the secretary, and the king's servant Asaiah, saying, ¹³"Go, inquire of the LORD for me, for the people, and for all Judah, concerning the words of this book that has been found; for great is the wrath of the LORD that is kindled against us, because our ancestors did not obey the words of this book, to do according to all that is written concerning us."

14 So the priest Hilkiah, Ahikam, Achbor, Shaphan, and Asaiah went to the prophetess Huldah the wife of Shallum son of Tikvah, son of Harhas, keeper of the wardrobe; she resided in Jerusalem in the Second Quarter, where they consulted her. ¹⁵She declared to them, "Thus says the LORD, the God of Israel: Tell the man who sent you to me, ¹⁶Thus says the LORD, I will indeed bring disaster on this place and on its inhabitants—all the words of the book that the king of Judah has read. ¹⁷Because they have abandoned me and have made offerings to other gods, so that they have provoked me to anger with all the work of their hands, therefore my wrath will be kindled against this place, and it will not be quenched. ¹⁸But as to the king of Judah, who sent you to inquire of the LORD, thus shall you say to him, Thus says the LORD, the God of Israel: Regarding the words that you have heard, ¹⁹because your heart was penitent, and you humbled yourself before the LORD, when you heard how I spoke against this place, and against its inhabitants, that they should become a desolation and a curse, and because you have torn your clothes and wept before me, I also have heard you, says the LORD. ²⁰Therefore, I will gather you to your ancestors, and you shall be gathered to your grave in peace; your eyes shall not see all the di-

saster that I will bring on this place." They took the message back to the king.

22.11–20. 11: Tearing *clothes* is a sign of repentance and distress. Josiah is worried because of the punishments threatened in the law for disobedience, since the people of Judah have not kept the law. **13:** *Inquire* is a technical term for divining or seeking an oracle✶ from God. **14:** *The prophetess*✶ *Huldah* is one of the few women in the Bible so designated (Miriam, Ex 15.20; Deborah, Judg 4.4; and Isaiah's wife[?], Isa 8.3). The *Second Quarter* was apparently an expansion of the city of Jerusalem that had taken place, perhaps during Hezekiah's day, in part to accommodate the influx of refugees from Israel. **15–17:** *The man who sent you to me* is Josiah. *This place* is Jerusalem. This part of Huldah's oracle anticipates the destruction of Jerusalem and the Babylonian Exile.✶ **20:** Most scholars believe at least the second half of Huldah's oracle to be genuine because it seems to be contradicted by history. Josiah did not in fact go to his grave peacefully, if this is what *in peace* means. Rather, he was killed in battle (23.29).

23 Then the king directed that all the elders of Judah and Jerusalem should be gathered to him. ²The king went up to the house of the LORD, and with him went all the people of Judah, all the inhabitants of Jerusalem, the priests, the prophets, and all the people, both small and great; he read in their hearing all the words of the book of the covenant that had been found in the house of the LORD. ³The king stood by the pillar and made a covenant before the LORD, to follow the LORD, keeping his commandments, his decrees, and his statutes, with all his heart and all his soul, to perform the words of this covenant that were written in this book. All the people joined in the covenant.

4 The king commanded the high priest Hilkiah, the priests of the second order, and the guardians of the threshold, to bring out of the temple of the LORD all the vessels made for Baal, for Asherah, and for all the host of heaven; he burned them outside Jerusalem in the fields of the Kidron, and carried their ashes to Bethel. ⁵He deposed the idolatrous priests whom the kings of Judah had ordained to make offerings in the high

places at the cities of Judah and around Jerusalem; those also who made offerings to Baal, to the sun, the moon, the constellations, and all the host of the heavens. ⁶He brought out the image of[a] Asherah from the house of the LORD, outside Jerusalem, to the Wadi Kidron, burned it at the Wadi Kidron, beat it to dust and threw the dust of it upon the graves of the common people. ⁷He broke down the houses of the male temple prostitutes that were in the house of the LORD, where the women did weaving for Asherah. ⁸He brought all the priests out of the towns of Judah, and defiled the high places where the priests had made offerings, from Geba to Beer-sheba; he broke down the high places of the gates that were at the entrance of the gate of Joshua the governor of the city, which were on the left at the gate of the city. ⁹The priests of the high places, however, did not come up to the altar of the LORD in Jerusalem, but ate unleavened bread among their kindred. ¹⁰He defiled Topheth, which is in the valley of Ben-hinnom, so that no one would make a son or a daughter pass through fire as an offering to Molech. ¹¹He removed the horses that the kings of Judah had dedicated to the sun, at the entrance to the house of the LORD, by the chamber of the eunuch Nathan-melech, which was in the precincts;[b] then he burned the chariots of the sun with fire. ¹²The altars on the roof of the upper chamber of Ahaz, which the kings of Judah had made, and the altars that Manasseh had made in the two courts of the house of the LORD, he pulled down from there and broke in pieces, and threw the rubble into the Wadi Kidron. ¹³The king defiled the high places that were east of Jerusalem, to the south of the Mount of Destruction, which King Solomon of Israel had built for Astarte the abomination of the Sidonians, for Chemosh the abomination of Moab, and for Milcom the abomination of the Ammonites. ¹⁴He broke the pillars in pieces, cut down the sacred poles,[c] and covered the sites with human bones.

a Heb lacks *image of*   *b* Meaning of Heb uncertain
c Heb *Asherim*

23.1–14. 1–3: Huldah's original oracle* may not have been so bleak, or at least it may have been conditional, since it motivated Josiah to try to carry out reforms so as to avoid disaster. On the language of v. 3, compare 23.25 and Deut 6.5. 4–5: Josiah's reforms included purging the Temple* of the trappings of the worship of other gods. The *Kidron* was the valley between the city of Jerusalem and the Mount of Olives. 6: Throwing the *dust* from the *image of Asherah* upon the *graves* would defile the image all the more. 7: The word translated *male temple prostitutes* may actually include both male and female prostitutes who served in the fertility rituals of the worship of Baal* and Asherah. 8: In bringing the *priests out of the towns of Judah* and destroying the *high places* Josiah was executing the deuteronomic* ideal of centralization, according to which the Temple in Jerusalem was the only legitimate place to worship the LORD. *From Geba to Beer-sheba* was the extent of the kingdom of Judah. 9: The *priests of the high places*, however, refused to go to Jerusalem. Eating *unleavened bread* accompanied sacrifices (Lev 6.14–18), which apparently continued outside of Jerusalem despite Josiah's efforts. 10: *Topheth* was a valley that marked Jerusalem's western border. Also known as the valley of (the son of) Hinnom (Heb., "ge' hinnom"), it became Jerusalem's trash dump and was used by Jesus as the image for hell (Gehenna,* see Mt 10.28). It was despised because it had served as a place of child sacrifice to the Ammonite god Molech (a distortion of the name Milcom made by borrowing the vowels from the word "bosheth," meaning "abomination"). 11: This verse suggests that *horses* were an important part of the worship of the sun, which was imagined as being drawn daily across the sky in a *chariot*. 12: Offerings from *altars on the roof* are mentioned in Jer 32.29. The *altars that Manasseh had made* are mentioned in 21.5. 13: *Mount of Destruction* is probably a play on the Hebrew name for the Mount of Olives ("Mount of Anointing") because of the altars to foreign gods erected there. 14: *Pillars* and *sacred poles* were used in the worship of the Canaanite gods. *Cover(ing) the sites with human bones* would further defile them.

15 Moreover, the altar at Bethel, the high place erected by Jeroboam son of Nebat, who caused Israel to sin—he pulled down that altar along with the high place. He burned the high place, crushing it to dust; he also burned the sacred pole.*a* 16As Josiah turned, he saw the tombs there on the mount; and he sent and took the bones out of the tombs, and burned them on the altar, and defiled it, according to the word of the LORD that the man of God proclaimed,*b* when Jeroboam stood by the altar at the festival; he turned and looked up at the tomb of the man of God who had predicted these things. 17Then he said, "What is that monument that I see?" The people of the city told him, "It is the tomb of the man of God who came from Judah and predicted these things that you have done against the altar at Bethel." 18He said, "Let him rest; let no one move his bones." So they let his bones alone, with the bones of the prophet who came out of Samaria. 19Moreover, Josiah removed all the shrines of the high places that were in the towns of Samaria, which kings of Israel had made, provoking the LORD to anger; he did to them just as he had done at Bethel. 20He slaughtered on the altars all the priests of the high places who were there, and burned human bones on them. Then he returned to Jerusalem.

21 The king commanded all the people, "Keep the passover to the LORD your God as prescribed in this book of the covenant." 22No such passover had been kept since the days of the judges who judged Israel, even during all the days of the kings of Israel and of the kings of Judah; 23but in the eighteenth year of King Josiah this passover was kept to the LORD in Jerusalem.

24 Moreover Josiah put away the mediums, wizards, teraphim,*c* idols, and all the abominations that were seen in the land of Judah and in Jerusalem, so that he established the words of the law that were written in the book that the priest Hilkiah had found in the house of the LORD. 25Before him there was no king like him, who turned to the LORD with all his heart, with all his soul, and with all his might, according to all the law of Moses; nor did any like him arise after him.

26 Still the LORD did not turn from the fierceness of his great wrath, by which his

a Heb *Asherah*   b Gk: Heb *proclaimed, who had predicted these things*   c Or *household gods*

anger was kindled against Judah, because of all the provocations with which Manasseh had provoked him. 27The LORD said, "I will remove Judah also out of my sight, as I have removed Israel; and I will reject this city that I have chosen, Jerusalem, and the house of which I said, My name shall be there."

28 Now the rest of the acts of Josiah, and all that he did, are they not written in the Book of the Annals of the Kings of Judah? 29In his days Pharaoh Neco king of Egypt went up to the king of Assyria to the river Euphrates. King Josiah went to meet him; but when Pharaoh Neco met him at Megiddo, he killed him. 30His servants carried him dead in a chariot from Megiddo, brought him to Jerusalem, and buried him in his own tomb. The people of the land took Jehoahaz son of Josiah, anointed him, and made him king in place of his father.

23.15–30. 15: On *Jeroboam*'s *altar at Bethel,* see 1 Kings 12.25–33. 16–18: The story of the *man of God* from Bethel is found in 1 Kings 13. 19–20: According to these verses, Josiah's reforms reached as far as Samaria. He may have annexed at least part of the territory of the former northern kingdom as his own. 21–23: On the *passover** see Ex 12.1–32 and Deut 16.1–8. 24: On *mediums* and *wizards,* see 21.6. *Teraphim* or "household idols" play a role in stories in Gen 31.33–35 and 1 Sam 19.11–16. 25: Josiah was incomparably obedient (22.2; Deut 6.5) as Moses was an incomparable prophet* (Deut 34.10), Solomon incomparably wise (1 Kings 3.12), and Hezekiah incomparably faithful (2 Kings 18.5). 26: This statement is curious because 23.4–14 makes it clear that Josiah corrected *Manasseh*'s apostasies. The writer is apparently struggling to find a theological reason for the Exile* and ends up blaming it on Manasseh. 27: This verse is a reversal of the doctrine in Deuteronomy of a *chosen* place. 29: *King Josiah*'s sudden death came as a shock to those who had placed trust in his reforms.

---

31 Jehoahaz was twenty-three years old when he began to reign; he reigned three months in Jerusalem. His mother's name was Hamutal daughter of Jeremiah of Libnah. 32He did what was evil in the sight of the LORD, just as his ancestors had done. 33Pharaoh Neco confined him at Riblah in the land of Hamath, so that he might not reign in Jerusalem, and imposed tribute on the land of one hundred talents of silver and a talent of gold. 34Pharaoh Neco made Eliakim son of Josiah king in place of his father Josiah, and changed his name to Jehoiakim. But he took Jehoahaz away; he came to Egypt, and died there. 35Jehoiakim gave the silver and the gold to Pharaoh, but he taxed the land in order to meet Pharaoh's demand for money. He exacted the silver and the gold from the people of the land, from all according to their assessment, to give it to Pharaoh Neco.

23.31–35: The reign of Jehoahaz. 32: The judgment that Jehoahaz *did what was evil in the sight of the* LORD is clearly formulaic, since Jehoahaz reigned only three months. 33: *Pharaoh Neco* apparently deposed Jehoahaz on the way back to Egypt. Jehoahaz, also known as Shallum (Jer 22.11), had evidently been chosen by the people, but Neco did not believe he would be favorable to Egypt and so replaced him. A *talent* varied in weight from 45 to 130 pounds. 34: *Eliakim* was *Jehoahaz*'s older brother. *Neco* found him more suitable. His name, *Jehoiakim*, means "Yahweh establishes" and may have been intended by Neco to remind Jehoiakim that he had sworn an oath of loyalty to Egypt by the LORD (Yahweh).

---

36 Jehoiakim was twenty-five years old when he began to reign; he reigned eleven years in Jerusalem. His mother's name was Zebidah daughter of Pedaiah of Rumah. 37He did what was evil in the sight of the LORD, just as all his ancestors had done.

24 In his days King Nebuchadnezzar of Babylon came up; Jehoiakim became his servant for three years; then he turned and rebelled against him. 2The LORD sent against him bands of the Chaldeans, bands of the Arameans, bands of the Moabites, and bands of the Ammonites; he sent them against Judah to destroy it, according to the word of the LORD that he spoke by his servants the prophets. 3Surely this came upon Judah at the command of the LORD, to remove them out of his sight, for the sins of Manasseh, for all that he had committed, 4and also for the innocent blood that he had shed; for he filled Jerusalem with innocent blood, and the LORD was not willing to par-

don. 5Now the rest of the deeds of Jehoiakim, and all that he did, are they not
written in the Book of the Annals of the
Kings of Judah? 6So Jehoiakim slept with his
ancestors; then his son Jehoiachin succeeded him. 7The king of Egypt did not come
again out of his land, for the king of Babylon
had taken over all that belonged to the king
of Egypt from the Wadi of Egypt to the River
Euphrates.

23.36–24.7: The reign of Jehoiakim. 24.1: The new
power at the end of the seventh century BCE was *Babylon* (see v. 7). Judah came under Babylonian control
around 605 BCE and *rebelled* three years later. **2:** *Chaldeans* is another name for Babylonians. **3–4:** As in
23.26, the Exile* is blamed on *Manasseh*. **7:** Nebuchadnezzar, king of Babylon, had defeated the Egyptians in the battle of Carchemish in 605 BCE, so Egypt
no longer controlled Judah.

8 Jehoiachin was eighteen years old when
he began to reign; he reigned three months
in Jerusalem. His mother's name was Ne-
hushta daughter of Elnathan of Jerusalem.
9He did what was evil in the sight of the
LORD, just as his father had done.
10 At that time the servants of King Nebuchadnezzar of Babylon came up to Jerusalem, and the city was besieged. 11King Nebuchadnezzar of Babylon came to the city,
while his servants were besieging it; 12King
Jehoiachin of Judah gave himself up to the
king of Babylon, himself, his mother, his servants, his officers, and his palace officials.
The king of Babylon took him prisoner in the
eighth year of his reign.
13 He carried off all the treasures of the
house of the LORD, and the treasures of the
king's house; he cut in pieces all the vessels
of gold in the temple of the LORD, which
King Solomon of Israel had made, all this as
the LORD had foretold. 14He carried away all
Jerusalem, all the officials, all the warriors,
ten thousand captives, all the artisans and
the smiths; no one remained, except the
poorest people of the land. 15He carried
away Jehoiachin to Babylon; the king's
mother, the king's wives, his officials, and
the elite of the land, he took into captivity

from Jerusalem to Babylon. 16The king of
Babylon brought captive to Babylon all the
men of valor, seven thousand, the artisans
and the smiths, one thousand, all of them
strong and fit for war. 17The king of Babylon
made Mattaniah, Jehoiachin's uncle, king
in his place, and changed his name to
Zedekiah.

**24.8–17: Jehoiachin and the Babylonian incursion.
8–9:** Again, since *Jehoiachin* reigned only *three
months*, the judgment that he did *evil in the sight of
the LORD* is a stereotypical formula. **10–12:** Jehoiakim
died after his rebellion but before the Babylonians
reached Jerusalem. That, plus the fact that Jehoiachin
surrendered himself, may be the reason the Babylonians did not destroy the city in the invasion of 597.
Jehoiachin, also called Jeconiah (1 Chr 3.16) and Coniah (Jer 22.24) was the son of Jehoiakim. **14:** The
statement that *all Jerusalem* was taken captive is an
obvious exaggeration. Evidently, the upper class was
exiled. **15:** This wave of captives included King Jehoiachin. The prophet* Ezekiel was also among them (Ezek
1.1). **17:** *Mattaniah* means "gift of Yahweh." Nebuchadnezzar changed it to *Zedekiah*, "the judgment of
Yahweh," perhaps as a reminder that the LORD would
bring judgment upon him if he broke his oath of loyalty, sworn by the LORD, to Babylon.

18 Zedekiah was twenty-one years old
when he began to reign; he reigned eleven
years in Jerusalem. His mother's name was
Hamutal daughter of Jeremiah of Libnah. 19He did what was evil in the sight
of the LORD, just as Jehoiakim had done.
20Indeed, Jerusalem and Judah so angered
the LORD that he expelled them from his
presence.
Zedekiah rebelled against the king of
25 Babylon. 1And in the ninth year of
his reign, in the tenth month, on the
tenth day of the month, King Nebuchadnezzar of Babylon came with all his army against
Jerusalem, and laid siege to it; they built
siegeworks against it all around. 2So the city
was besieged until the eleventh year of King
Zedekiah. 3On the ninth day of the fourth
month the famine became so severe in the
city that there was no food for the people of
the land. 4Then a breach was made in the

city wall;[a] the king with all the soldiers fled[b] by night by the way of the gate between the two walls, by the king's garden, though the Chaldeans were all around the city. They went in the direction of the Arabah. [5]But the army of the Chaldeans pursued the king, and overtook him in the plains of Jericho; all his army was scattered, deserting him. [6]Then they captured the king and brought him up to the king of Babylon at Riblah, who passed sentence on him. [7]They slaughtered the sons of Zedekiah before his eyes, then put out the eyes of Zedekiah; they bound him in fetters and took him to Babylon.

8 In the fifth month, on the seventh day of the month—which was the nineteenth year of King Nebuchadnezzar, king of Babylon—Nebuzaradan, the captain of the bodyguard, a servant of the king of Babylon, came to Jerusalem. [9]He burned the house of the LORD, the king's house, and all the houses of Jerusalem; every great house he burned down. [10]All the army of the Chaldeans who were with the captain of the guard broke down the walls around Jerusalem. [11]Nebuzaradan the captain of the guard carried into exile the rest of the people who were left in the city and the deserters who had defected to the king of Babylon—all the rest of the population. [12]But the captain of the guard left some of the poorest people of the land to be vinedressers and tillers of the soil.

13 The bronze pillars that were in the house of the LORD, as well as the stands and the bronze sea that were in the house of the LORD, the Chaldeans broke in pieces, and carried the bronze to Babylon. [14]They took away the pots, the shovels, the snuffers, the dishes for incense, and all the bronze vessels used in the temple service, [15]as well as the firepans and the basins. What was made of gold the captain of the guard took away for the gold, and what was made of silver, for the silver. [16]As for the two pillars, the one sea, and the stands, which Solomon had made for the house of the LORD, the bronze of all these vessels was beyond weighing. [17]The height of the one pillar was eighteen cubits, and on it was a bronze capital; the height of the capital was three cubits; lat-

ticework and pomegranates, all of bronze, were on the capital all around. The second pillar had the same, with the latticework.

18 The captain of the guard took the chief priest Seraiah, the second priest Zephaniah, and the three guardians of the threshold; [19]from the city he took an officer who had been in command of the soldiers, and five men of the king's council who were found in the city; the secretary who was the commander of the army who mustered the people of the land; and sixty men of the people of the land who were found in the city. [20]Nebuzaradan the captain of the guard took them, and brought them to the king of Babylon at Riblah. [21]The king of Babylon struck them down and put them to death at Riblah in the land of Hamath. So Judah went into exile out of its land.

24.18–25.21: The reign of Zedekiah and the fall of Jerusalem. This section is very similar to Jer 52, and the first part of it to Jer 39.1–10. 24.20: Here the Exile* is blamed mostly on Zedekiah and his generation. 25.2–3: The city of Jerusalem fell to the Babylonians in 587 or 586 BCE. 4: The Arabah means the Jordan valley north of the Dead Sea. 11: Jeremiah 52.29 gives the number of captives from this deportation as 832. 13–17: On the items taken from the Temple,* see 1 Kings 7.15–50; Jer 52.17–23. 18–21: The other leaders of the city who were considered responsible for fostering the rebellion were executed.

22 He appointed Gedaliah son of Ahikam son of Shaphan as governor over the people who remained in the land of Judah, whom King Nebuchadnezzar of Babylon had left. [23]Now when all the captains of the forces and their men heard that the king of Babylon had appointed Gedaliah as governor, they came with their men to Gedaliah at Mizpah, namely, Ishmael son of Nethaniah, Johanan son of Kareah, Seraiah son of Tanhumeth the Netophathite, and Jaazaniah son of the Maacathite. [24]Gedaliah swore to them and their men, saying, "Do not be afraid because of the Chaldean officials; live in the land, serve the king of Babylon, and it shall be well

a Heb lacks wall   b Gk Compare Jer 39.4; 52.7: Heb lacks the king and lacks fled

with you." 25 But in the seventh month, Ishmael son of Nethaniah son of Elishama, of the royal family, came with ten men; they struck down Gedaliah so that he died, along with the Judeans and Chaldeans who were with him at Mizpah. 26 Then all the people, high and low,ᵃ and the captains of the forces set out and went to Egypt; for they were afraid of the Chaldeans.

25.22–26: The rule and assassination of Gedaliah. 22: The word *governor* does not actually appear in the Hebrew text. Gedaliah is not given any title. **23:** The administrative capital was moved from Jerusalem to *Mizpah*. **25:** Perhaps because he was not a descendant of David, *Gedaliah* was regarded as an illegitimate ruler and was assassinated by members of the *royal family.*

27 In the thirty-seventh year of the exile of King Jehoiachin of Judah, in the twelfth month, on the twenty-seventh day of the month, King Evil-merodach of Babylon, in the year that he began to reign, released King Jehoiachin of Judah from prison; 28 he spoke kindly to him, and gave him a seat above the other seats of the kings who were with him in Babylon. 29 So Jehoiachin put aside his prison clothes. Every day of his life he dined regularly in the king's presence. 30 For his allowance, a regular allowance was given him by the king, a portion every day, as long as he lived.

25.27–30: The elevation of Jehoiachin. The year is around 562, so that there is a gap of about 25 years between the events described in these verses and those in the verses immediately preceding. This may indicate that these verses are a later addition. Their purpose is not clear, but some have suggested that they subtly express the possibility that God may again restore the Davidic monarchy. **27–28:** *Evil-merodach* was Awil-Marduk. His reason for releasing Jehoiachin from prison is not made clear. **29–30:** Even though he remained a captive, probably until he died, Jehoiachin's status was enhanced and his life made more comfortable.

a Or *young and old*

1 CHRONICLES

Introduction to 1, 2 Chronicles

The Chronicler offers his readers a history of what was important from the community's (namely Judah's) past, something quite different from the earlier narratives* of 1 and 2 Samuel and 1 and 2 Kings. While the Deuteronomistic* History (Judges through 2 Kings) tries to justify the destruction of both the northern kingdom of Israel and the southern kingdom of Judah by showing how both communities turned their backs on God by practicing idolatry,* the Chronicler is more concerned to present a positive model from Israel's past. Starting with David as an example, the narratives that stand out in the Chronicler's history are those in which the community or king respond faithfully to God, finding unity and security in response. Good kings are those who "seek the LORD," and in return they experience military and economic success, and their subjects experience great joy in gathering before the Temple* in Jerusalem for worship. These positive models are intended to speak to the Chronicler's readers, to convince them that in "seeking the LORD" at the Temple in their own day, they will find their fullest sense of purpose and community.

The narratives of the Chronicler's history abound with historical problems from the view of a modern reader. David makes provision for the use of marble in building the Temple (1 Chr 29.2); however, marble was not used in Jerusalem until the Hellenistic* age seven hundred years later. David collects "10,000 darics" (1 Chr 29.7) for the Temple, a coin of the Persian empire 500 years after the Davidic period. Impossibly large numbers of military forces are mustered in the field (300,000 from Judah, 280,000 from Benjamin, facing a "million" from Egypt; 2 Chr 14.8–9), and stock numbers are often used (for example, Shishak of Egypt attacks with "1,200 chariots and 60,000 chariots," playing on the number 12 and its multiples; 2 Chr 12.3). The Chronicler never mentions David's transgression in taking Bathsheba as wife (2 Sam 11–12), nor for that matter Solomon's fall into idolatry (1 Kings 11). These tendencies are similar to Hellenistic historians of the same general period, suggesting the Chronicler is simply writing about the past with commonly accepted, perhaps even expected, conventions.

Part of the dilemma over the historical value of 1 and 2 Chronicles involves what potential sources the author had at his disposal. The author cites a number of sources that are otherwise unknown; however, the general stylistic uniformity between narratives where sources are mentioned and where none are indicated raises the suspicion that such sources may not have existed. There is no conclusive evidence to support the Chronicler's use of any sources other than 1 Samuel through 2 Kings.

In its original form, the Hebrew Chronicles would have filled one single scroll. Its division into two parts was accomplished when the codex or book-form of transmitting literature became the standard, probably in the early centuries CE.

While numerous proposals have been offered for the date of the Chronicler's composition, perhaps the most telling points are the interest in military matters and the result of "peace" when the community "seeks the LORD." Following the death of Alexander the Great (around 330 BCE), his successors fought incessantly with each other, often across the landscape of Palestine. Archaeological evidence demonstrates that in the last decades of the fourth century BCE nearly every urban center in Palestine suffered military destruction. It was not until the Ptolemaic★ rulers of Egypt suppressed their Syrian rivals that peace came to Palestine in the early second century BCE. In the midst of such turmoil, a message focusing on the peace that "seeking the LORD" might bring would have been particularly powerful.

The author focuses almost exclusively on the events affecting Jerusalem and the Temple. With regard to the Temple, the author shows particular interest in the activities of the priesthood and individuals given prominence in Temple affairs. Many scholars conclude that the author was a member of the Temple priesthood.

READING GUIDE

When recounting a story of Israel's past, the Chronicler skillfully weaves personal encounters and community responses. A characteristic narrative is the account of the reign of Judah's King Asa (2 Chr 14–16). It opens with the land having "rest," in part because Asa "did what was good and right" in God's view and "commanded Judah to seek the LORD" (2 Chr 14.4). He orders his people to build fortifications around the urban areas since "the land is still ours because we have sought the LORD our God . . . and he has given us peace on every side" (2 Chr 14.7). This sense of security is challenged by Zerah the "Ethiopian," who comes with a million-man army to attack Judah. Asa offers a simple petition for help, and "the LORD defeated the Ethiopians" (2 Chr 14.12). Fresh from this great victory, the Chronicler has an otherwise unattested prophet★ confront the king in a decisive way. This is similar to the style of the Greek historian Herodotus, who uses the figures of various wise counselors to present a ruler with a choice to follow wisdom or pride. In Asa's case, it is "Azariah the son of Oded" who gives voice to the central theological theme of the Chronicler: "The LORD is with you, while you are with him. If you seek him, he will be found by you, but if you abandon him, he will abandon you" (2 Chr 15.2). Taking heart from the prophet's message, Asa convenes all his subjects (Judah and Benjamin) as well as those faithful from the northern kingdom who had joined with Judah (2 Chr 15.9–10). After sacrificing to God, the assembled populace "entered into covenant★ to seek the LORD, the God of their ancestors, with all their heart and with all their soul" (v. 12), an echo of Israel's basic credo of Deut 6.4–5. To emphasize the seriousness of this act, the Chronicler adds that whoever did not join with the covenant "should be put to death" (v. 13). Not wanting to close on a negative note, the Chronicler portrays the community enthusiastically embracing this arrangement: "All Judah rejoiced over the oath; for they had sworn with all their heart, and had sought him with their whole desire, and he was found by them, and the LORD gave them rest all around" (v. 15). This is a paradigm that the Chronicler uses frequently: the king being presented with the need to "seek" God and then the community actively and joyously embracing God.

1 Chronicles
1–9   Genealogical★ prologue
10–20 David's reign
21–29 Transition (centrality of the Temple)
2 Chronicles
1–9   Solomon's rule
10–36 Dissolution of Judah

THE GENEALOGICAL* PROLOGUE

Chs. 1–9: The Chronicler begins his history in a way similar to a number of ancient Greek histories by trying to show the internal connectedness of the nation. After tracing the nation's descent from a common stock of ancestors, the historian focuses on the tribe of Judah and the family line of David, which is of central importance to the destiny of Jerusalem.

1 Adam, Seth, Enosh; 2Kenan, Mahalalel, Jared; 3Enoch, Methuselah, Lamech; 4Noah, Shem, Ham, and Japheth.

5 The descendants of Japheth: Gomer, Magog, Madai, Javan, Tubal, Meshech, and Tiras. 6The descendants of Gomer: Ashkenaz, Diphath,*a* and Togarmah. 7The descendants of Javan: Elishah, Tarshish, Kittim, and Rodanim.*b*

8 The descendants of Ham: Cush, Egypt, Put, and Canaan. 9The descendants of Cush: Seba, Havilah, Sabta, Raama, and Sabteca. The descendants of Raamah: Sheba and Dedan. 10Cush became the father of Nimrod; he was the first to be a mighty one on the earth.

11 Egypt became the father of Ludim, Anamim, Lehabim, Naphtuhim, 12Pathrusim, Casluhim, and Caphtorim, from whom the Philistines come.*c*

13 Canaan became the father of Sidon his firstborn, and Heth, 14and the Jebusites, the Amorites, the Girgashites, 15the Hivites, the Arkites, the Sinites, 16the Arvadites, the Zemarites, and the Hamathites.

17 The descendants of Shem: Elam, Asshur, Arpachshad, Lud, Aram, Uz, Hul, Gether, and Meshech.*d* 18Arpachshad became the father of Shelah; and Shelah became the father of Eber. 19To Eber were born two sons: the name of the one was Peleg (for in his days the earth was divided), and the name of his brother Joktan. 20Joktan became the father of Almodad, Sheleph, Hazarmaveth, Jerah, 21Hadoram, Uzal, Diklah, 22Ebal, Abimael, Sheba, 23Ophir, Havilah, and Jobab; all these were the descendants of Joktan.

24 Shem, Arpachshad, Shelah; 25Eber, Peleg, Reu; 26Serug, Nahor, Terah; 27Abram, that is, Abraham.

28 The sons of Abraham: Isaac and Ishmael. 29These are their genealogies: the firstborn of Ishmael, Nebaioth; and Kedar, Adbeel, Mibsam, 30Mishma, Dumah, Massa, Hadad, Tema, 31Jetur, Naphish, and Kedemah. These are the sons of Ishmael. 32The sons of Keturah, Abraham's concubine: she bore Zimran, Jokshan, Medan, Midian, Ishbak, and Shuah. The sons of Jokshan: Sheba and Dedan. 33The sons of Midian: Ephah, Epher, Hanoch, Abida, and Eldaah. All these were the descendants of Keturah.

34 Abraham became the father of Isaac. The sons of Isaac: Esau and Israel. 35The sons of Esau: Eliphaz, Reuel, Jeush, Jalam, and Korah. 36The sons of Eliphaz: Teman, Omar, Zephi, Gatam, Kenaz, Timna, and Amalek. 37The sons of Reuel: Nahath, Zerah, Shammah, and Mizzah.

38 The sons of Seir: Lotan, Shobal, Zibeon, Anah, Dishon, Ezer, and Dishan. 39The sons of Lotan: Hori and Homam; and Lotan's sister was Timna. 40The sons of Shobal: Alian, Manahath, Ebal, Shephi, and Onam. The sons of Zibeon: Aiah and Anah. 41The sons of Anah: Dishon. The sons of Dishon: Hamran, Eshban, Ithran, and Cheran. 42The sons of Ezer: Bilhan, Zaavan, and Jaakan.*e* The sons of Dishan:*f* Uz and Aran.

43 These are the kings who reigned in the land of Edom before any king reigned over the Israelites: Bela son of Beor, whose city was called Dinhabah. 44When Bela died, Jobab son of Zerah of Bozrah succeeded him. 45When Jobab died, Husham of the land of the Temanites succeeded him. 46When Husham died, Hadad son of Bedad, who defeated Midian in the country of Moab, succeeded him; and the name of his city was Avith. 47When Hadad died, Samlah of Masrekah succeeded him. 48When Samlah died, Shaul*g* of Rehoboth on the Euphrates succeeded him. 49When Shaul*g* died, Baal-

a Gen 10.3 *Ripath;* See Gk Vg   *b* Gen 10.4 *Dodanim;* See Syr Vg   *c* Heb *Casluhim, from which the Philistines come, Caphtorim;* See Am 9.7, Jer 47.4   *d Mash* in Gen 10.23   *e* Or *and Akan;* See Gen 36.27   *f* See 1.38: Heb *Dishon*   *g* Or *Saul*

hanan son of Achbor succeeded him. [50]When Baal-hanan died, Hadad succeeded him; the name of his city was Pai, and his wife's name Mehetabel daughter of Matred, daughter of Me-zahab. [51]And Hadad died.

The clans[a] of Edom were: clans[a] Timna, Aliah,[b] Jetheth, [52]Oholibamah, Elah, Pinon, [53]Kenaz, Teman, Mibzar, [54]Magdiel, and Iram; these are the clans[a] of Edom.

1.1–54: Genealogy* of the ancestors. Summarizing much information from Genesis, the Chronicler starts with Adam and takes the sequence down to Jacob (also known as Israel). **43:** *These are the kings who reigned in the land of Edom:* Located to the southeast of the land of Judah and on the other side of the Jordan valley, Edom was always recognized as having a close relationship to Judah. Israel also recognized that Edom had adopted a monarchic form of political organization before Israel had embraced monarchy. **51:** *The clans* of Edom:* In Hebrew the word for "clans" is normally translated as "chiefs." Prior to the emergence of David and the Judean monarchy, Edom was an independent kingdom; however, David was able to assert control over Edom and reduce its leaders to "chiefs."

2 These are the sons of Israel: Reuben, Simeon, Levi, Judah, Issachar, Zebulun, [2]Dan, Joseph, Benjamin, Naphtali, Gad, and Asher. [3]The sons of Judah: Er, Onan, and Shelah; these three the Canaanite woman Bath-shua bore to him. Now Er, Judah's firstborn, was wicked in the sight of the LORD, and he put him to death. [4]His daughter-in-law Tamar also bore him Perez and Zerah. Judah had five sons in all.

[5] The sons of Perez: Hezron and Hamul. [6]The sons of Zerah: Zimri, Ethan, Heman, Calcol, and Dara,[c] five in all. [7]The sons of Carmi: Achar, the troubler of Israel, who transgressed in the matter of the devoted thing; [8]and Ethan's son was Azariah.

2.1–4.23: The tribe of Judah and the line of David. The Chronicler writes from a Judean perspective, emphasizing the events of the southern kingdom as though they were decisive for the larger fate of "all Israel." Accordingly, the lineage of the tribe of Judah and the line of David were of special concern. Their priority for the author is apparent by their placement

first in the lineage of Israel. **2.4:** *His daughter-in-law Tamar also bore him Perez* alludes to the narrative* in Gen 38 where Tamar must seduce Judah by deceit to gain her legitimate rights. David comes from the "Perez" line of the clan.* **7:** *The sons of Carmi: Achar, the troubler of Israel:* Carmi was a descendant of Zerah's line. Achan (for which the Chronicler uses Achar) appears in Josh 7.1–26, where he violates the command to destroy all the possessions of the inhabitants of Jericho. The notice of Zerah's line may have brought to the author's mind the incident with Achar. *Troubler* is a Hebrew pun, a word sounding similar to Achar (see Jn 7.24).

[9] The sons of Hezron, who were born to him: Jerahmeel, Ram, and Chelubai. [10]Ram became the father of Amminadab, and Amminadab became the father of Nahshon, prince of the sons of Judah. [11]Nahshon became the father of Salma, Salma of Boaz, [12]Boaz of Obed, Obed of Jesse. [13]Jesse became the father of Eliab his firstborn, Abinadab the second, Shimea the third, [14]Nethanel the fourth, Raddai the fifth, [15]Ozem the sixth, David the seventh; [16]and their sisters were Zeruiah and Abigail. The sons of Zeruiah: Abishai, Joab, and Asahel, three. [17]Abigail bore Amasa, and the father of Amasa was Jether the Ishmaelite.

[18] Caleb son of Hezron had children by his wife Azubah, and by Jerioth; these were her sons: Jesher, Shobab, and Ardon. [19]When Azubah died, Caleb married Ephrath, who bore him Hur. [20]Hur became the father of Uri, and Uri became the father of Bezalel.

[21] Afterward Hezron went in to the daughter of Machir father of Gilead, whom he married when he was sixty years old; and she bore him Segub; [22]and Segub became the father of Jair, who had twenty-three towns in the land of Gilead. [23]But Geshur and Aram took from them Havvoth-jair, Kenath and its villages, sixty towns. All these were descendants of Machir, father of Gilead. [24]After the death of Hezron, in Calebephrathah, Abijah wife of Hezron bore him Ashhur, father of Tekoa.

a Or *chiefs*   *b* Or *Alvah*; See Gen 36.40
c Or *Darda*; Compare Syr Tg some Gk Mss; See
1 Kings 4.31

2.9–24. 10: *Nahshon, prince of the sons of Judah:* The term for "prince" (Heb., "nasi") had a variety of meanings in antiquity. Nahshon may be described in this way to highlight the line of David, since Nahshon's sister married Moses' brother Aaron (Ex 6.23) and thus helped form the primary line of Israel's priesthood. Such a connection would tie the royal and priestly family lines together. **13:** *Jesse became the father of:* The narrative posits ten generations from Judah to Jesse, directly tying the ancestry of David's father to a founder of the nation. **21:** *Machir father of Gilead:* The genealogies* use the term "father" to refer to a person or family lineage that made up a portion of the population of a specific place.

~~~~~~~~~~~~~~~~~~~~~~~~~~~~~~~~~~~~~~

25 The sons of Jerahmeel, the firstborn of Hezron: Ram his firstborn, Bunah, Oren, Ozem, and Ahijah. 26Jerahmeel also had another wife, whose name was Atarah; she was the mother of Onam. 27The sons of Ram, the firstborn of Jerahmeel: Maaz, Jamin, and Eker. 28The sons of Onam: Shammai and Jada. The sons of Shammai: Nadab and Abishur. 29The name of Abishur's wife was Abihail, and she bore him Ahban and Molid. 30The sons of Nadab: Seled and Appaim; and Seled died childless. 31The son*a* of Appaim: Ishi. The son*a* of Ishi: Sheshan. The son*a* of Sheshan: Ahlai. 32The sons of Jada, Shammai's brother: Jether and Jonathan; and Jether died childless. 33The sons of Jonathan: Peleth and Zaza. These were the descendants of Jerahmeel. 34Now Sheshan had no sons, only daughters; but Sheshan had an Egyptian slave, whose name was Jarha. 35So Sheshan gave his daughter in marriage to his slave Jarha; and she bore him Attai. 36Attai became the father of Nathan, and Nathan of Zabad. 37Zabad became the father of Ephlal, and Ephlal of Obed. 38Obed became the father of Jehu, and Jehu of Azariah. 39Azariah became the father of Helez, and Helez of Eleasah. 40Eleasah became the father of Sismai, and Sismai of Shallum. 41Shallum became the father of Jekamiah, and Jekamiah of Elishama.

42 The sons of Caleb brother of Jerahmeel: Mesha*b* his firstborn, who was father of Ziph. The sons of Mareshah father of Hebron. 43The sons of Hebron: Korah, Tap-

puah, Rekem, and Shema. 44Shema became father of Raham, father of Jorkeam; and Rekem became the father of Shammai. 45The son of Shammai: Maon; and Maon was the father of Beth-zur. 46Ephah also, Caleb's concubine, bore Haran, Moza, and Gazez; and Haran became the father of Gazez. 47The sons of Jahdai: Regem, Jotham, Geshan, Pelet, Ephah, and Shaaph. 48Maacah, Caleb's concubine, bore Sheber and Tirhanah. 49She also bore Shaaph father of Madmannah, Sheva father of Machbenah and father of Gibea; and the daughter of Caleb was Achsah. 50These were the descendants of Caleb.

The sons*c* of Hur the firstborn of Ephrathah: Shobal father of Kiriath-jearim, 51Salma father of Bethlehem, and Hareph father of Beth-gader. 52Shobal father of Kiriath-jearim had other sons: Haroeh, half of the Menuhoth. 53And the families of Kiriath-jearim: the Ithrites, the Puthites, the Shumathites, and the Mishraites; from these came the Zorathites and the Eshtaolites. 54The sons of Salma: Bethlehem, the Netophathites, Atroth-beth-joab, and half of the Manahathites, the Zorites. 55The families also of the scribes that lived at Jabez: the Tirathites, the Shimeathites, and the Sucathites. These are the Kenites who came from Hammath, father of the house of Rechab.

3 These are the sons of David who were born to him in Hebron: the firstborn Amnon, by Ahinoam the Jezreelite; the second Daniel, by Abigail the Carmelite; 2the third Absalom, son of Maacah, daughter of King Talmai of Geshur; the fourth Adonijah, son of Haggith; 3the fifth Shephatiah, by Abital; the sixth Ithream, by his wife Eglah; 4six were born to him in Hebron, where he reigned for seven years and six months. And he reigned thirty-three years in Jerusalem. 5These were born to him in Jerusalem: Shimea, Shobab, Nathan, and Solomon, four by Bath-shua, daughter of Ammiel; 6then Ibhar, Elishama, Eliphelet, 7Nogah, Nepheg, Japhia, 8Elishama, Eliada, and

---

a Heb *sons*   *b* Gk reads *Mareshah*   *c* Gk Vg: Heb *son*

Eliphelet, nine. [9] All these were David's sons, besides the sons of the concubines; and Tamar was their sister.

10 The descendants of Solomon: Rehoboam, Abijah his son, Asa his son, Jehoshaphat his son, [11] Joram his son, Ahaziah his son, Joash his son, [12] Amaziah his son, Azariah his son, Jotham his son, [13] Ahaz his son, Hezekiah his son, Manasseh his son, [14] Amon his son, Josiah his son. [15] The sons of Josiah: Johanan the firstborn, the second Jehoiakim, the third Zedekiah, the fourth Shallum. [16] The descendants of Jehoiakim: Jeconiah his son, Zedekiah his son; [17] and the sons of Jeconiah, the captive: Shealtiel his son, [18] Malchiram, Pedaiah, Shenazzar, Jekamiah, Hoshama, and Nedabiah; [19] The sons of Pedaiah: Zerubbabel and Shimei; and the sons of Zerubbabel: Meshullam and Hananiah, and Shelomith was their sister; [20] and Hashubah, Ohel, Berechiah, Hasadiah, and Jushab-hesed, five. [21] The sons of Hananiah: Pelatiah and Jeshaiah, his son[a] Rephaiah, his son[a] Arnan, his son[a] Obadiah, his son[a] Shecaniah. [22] The son[b] of Shecaniah: Shemaiah. And the sons of Shemaiah: Hattush, Igal, Bariah, Neariah, and Shaphat, six. [23] The sons of Neariah: Elioenai, Hizkiah, and Azrikam, three. [24] The sons of Elioenai: Hodaviah, Eliashib, Pelaiah, Akkub, Johanan, Delaiah, and Anani, seven.

3.1–24. 1: *These are the sons of David:* This unit begins with the notice of the sons born to David while he reigned as king in Hebron, a time quickly skipped over by the author in the subsequent narratives.* Much of the material is rearranged from several places in 2 Samuel. 10: *The descendants of Solomon* introduces a new listing highlighting the royal succession of the southern kingdom. Of particular interest are the lines extending into the period of the Exile* and beyond, ending sometime in the fourth century BCE. 19: *The sons of Pedaiah: Zerubbabel:* Presumably the author means the same Zerubbabel who acted as governor of the province of Yehud (post-exilic Judah) for the Persians (see Hag 1.1, Ezra 3.2). The Greek Old Testament has a reading of "the sons of Shealtiel" here, which may reflect an effort to harmonize the genealogical* information here with that in other biblical sources such as Ezra. *And Shelomith was their sister:* Shelomith, the only female mentioned in the course of the royal lineage, is prominently featured in a post-exilic seal impression as the "noble wife" of Elnathan, a Persian period governor who served sometime after Zerubbabel. Elnathan may have been using his marriage to a member of the Davidic lineage to help legitimate his political authority.

4 The sons of Judah: Perez, Hezron, Carmi, Hur, and Shobal. [2] Reaiah son of Shobal became the father of Jahath, and Jahath became the father of Ahumai and Lahad. These were the families of the Zorathites. [3] These were the sons[c] of Etam: Jezreel, Ishma, and Idbash; and the name of their sister was Hazzelelponi, [4] and Penuel was the father of Gedor, and Ezer the father of Hushah. These were the sons of Hur, the firstborn of Ephrathah, the father of Bethlehem. [5] Ashhur father of Tekoa had two wives, Helah and Naarah; [6] Naarah bore him Ahuzzam, Hepher, Temeni, and Haahashtari.[d] These were the sons of Naarah. [7] The sons of Helah: Zereth, Izhar,[e] and Ethnan. [8] Koz became the father of Anub, Zobebah, and the families of Aharhel son of Harum. [9] Jabez was honored more than his brothers; and his mother named him Jabez, saying, "Because I bore him in pain." [10] Jabez called on the God of Israel, saying, "Oh that you would bless me and enlarge my border, and that your hand might be with me, and that you would keep me from hurt and harm!" And God granted what he asked. [11] Chelub the brother of Shuhah became the father of Mehir, who was the father of Eshton. [12] Eshton became the father of Beth-rapha, Paseah, and Tehinnah the father of Ir-nahash. These are the men of Recah. [13] The sons of Kenaz: Othniel and Seraiah; and the sons of Othniel: Hathath and Meonothai.[f] [14] Meonothai became the father of Ophrah; and Seraiah became the father of Joab father of Ge-harashim,[g] so-called because they were artisans. [15] The sons of Caleb son of Jephunneh: Iru, Elah, and Naam; and the son[b] of

a Gk Compare Syr Vg: Heb *sons of*   b Heb *sons*
c Gk Compare Vg: Heb *the father*   d Or *Ahashtari*
e Another reading is *Zohar*   f Gk Vg: Heb lacks *and Meonothai*   g That is *Valley of artisans*

Elah: Kenaz. [16]The sons of Jehallelel: Ziph, Ziphah, Tiria, and Asarel. [17]The sons of Ezrah: Jether, Mered, Epher, and Jalon. These are the sons of Bithiah, daughter of Pharaoh, whom Mered married;[a] and she conceived and bore[b] Miriam, Shammai, and Ishbah father of Eshtemoa. [18]And his Judean wife bore Jered father of Gedor, Heber father of Soco, and Jekuthiel father of Zanoah. [19]The sons of the wife of Hodiah, the sister of Naham, were the fathers of Keilah the Garmite and Eshtemoa the Maacathite. [20]The sons of Shimon: Amnon, Rinnah, Ben-hanan, and Tilon. The sons of Ishi: Zoheth and Ben-zoheth. [21]The sons of Shelah son of Judah: Er father of Lecah, Laadah father of Mareshah, and the families of the guild of linen workers at Beth-ashbea; [22]and Jokim, and the men of Cozeba, and Joash, and Saraph, who married into Moab but returned to Lehem[c] (now the records[d] are ancient). [23]These were the potters and inhabitants of Netaim and Gederah; they lived there with the king in his service.

4.1–23. 1: *The sons of Judah:* With this phrase the author returns to the point with which the list began (at 2.3), now with the intent of tracing the other branches of this clan.* This material has proven to be very difficult to interpret since the genealogies* are not fully integrated. The author may be compiling material from several different sources. 4: *The father of Bethlehem:* The author again uses family terminology to indicate a portion of the clan that had been responsible for settling well-known locales. 9: *Jabez was honored more than his brothers:* Unattested otherwise in the Old Testament, this notice reflects extraordinary efforts to justify a name. The name "Jabez" means "pain" in Hebrew, even though this individual was honored. Being "honored" more than his brothers may mean that he received a bigger portion of the family inheritance. He also appealed to God for protection that none would cause him pain, ensuring that his name would not lead to harm. 22: *Now the records are ancient:* The term for "records" is more openended, usually translated "matters." The author may simply be indicating he knows nothing beyond the bare facts that these named individuals went to Moab and returned. It is such a scenario that underlies the opening of the book of Ruth.

24 The sons of Simeon: Nemuel, Jamin, Jarib, Zerah, Shaul;[e] [25]Shallum was his son, Mibsam his son, Mishma his son. [26]The sons of Mishma: Hammuel his son, Zaccur his son, Shimei his son. [27]Shimei had sixteen sons and six daughters; but his brothers did not have many children, nor did all their family multiply like the Judeans. [28]They lived in Beer-sheba, Moladah, Hazar-shual, [29]Bilhah, Ezem, Tolad, [30]Bethuel, Hormah, Ziklag, [31]Beth-marcaboth, Hazar-susim, Beth-biri, and Shaaraim. These were their towns until David became king. [32]And their villages were Etam, Ain, Rimmon, Tochen, and Ashan, five towns, [33]along with all their villages that were around these towns as far as Baal. These were their settlements. And they kept a genealogical record.

34 Meshobab, Jamlech, Joshah son of Amaziah, [35]Joel, Jehu son of Joshibiah son of Seraiah son of Asiel, [36]Elioenai, Jaakobah, Jeshohaiah, Asaiah, Adiel, Jesimiel, Benaiah, [37]Ziza son of Shiphi son of Allon son of Jedaiah son of Shimri son of Shemaiah— [38]these mentioned by name were leaders in their families, and their clans increased greatly. [39]They journeyed to the entrance of Gedor, to the east side of the valley, to seek pasture for their flocks, [40]where they found rich, good pasture, and the land was very broad, quiet, and peaceful; for the former inhabitants there belonged to Ham. [41]These, registered by name, came in the days of King Hezekiah of Judah, and attacked their tents and the Meunim who were found there, and exterminated them to this day, and settled in their place, because there was pasture there for their flocks. [42]And some of them, five hundred men of the Simeonites, went to Mount Seir, having as their leaders Pelatiah, Neariah, Rephaiah, and Uzziel, sons of Ishi; [43]they destroyed the remnant of the Amalekites that had escaped, and they have lived there to this day.

4.24–43: **The tribe of Simeon.** Since the author has begun with Judah, it makes some sense to continue the examination of Israel by turning to the family

---

a The clause: *These are . . . married* is transposed from verse 18   b Heb lacks *and bore*   c Vg Compare Gk: Heb *and Jashubi-lahem*   d Or *matters*   e Or *Saul*

group of Simeon, a tribe connected with Judah both by birth (Judah and Simeon were Jacob's sons by the same mother) and by proximity. **28:** *They lived in Beer-sheba:* These places all lie along the extreme southern edge of Judean settlements fringing the Negev desert. **31:** *Until David became king may* mean that these were self-governing cities until they became part of the Davidic kingdom. **39:** *They journeyed to the entrance of Gedor:* The Greek version has "Gerar," which some believe is a more appropriate setting for the story. Gedor is a common place name; either name would place the valley to the west of the Judean heartland. **43:** *They destroyed the remnant of the Amalekites,* one of the peoples inhabiting Canaan prior to Israel's taking of the land. Mt. Seir is normally located on the other side of the Jordan valley in territory controlled by Edom. This territorial claim may indicate some expansion of clan* elements into the southeastern regions outside of Judah.

5 The sons of Reuben the firstborn of Israel. (He was the firstborn, but because he defiled his father's bed his birthright was given to the sons of Joseph son of Israel, so that he is not enrolled in the genealogy according to the birthright; ²though Judah became prominent among his brothers and a ruler came from him, yet the birthright belonged to Joseph.) ³The sons of Reuben, the firstborn of Israel: Hanoch, Pallu, Hezron, and Carmi. ⁴The sons of Joel: Shemaiah his son, Gog his son, Shimei his son, ⁵Micah his son, Reaiah his son, Baal his son, ⁶Beerah his son, whom King Tilgath-pilneser of Assyria carried away into exile; he was a chieftain of the Reubenites. ⁷And his kindred by their families, when the genealogy of their generations was reckoned: the chief, Jeiel, and Zechariah, ⁸and Bela son of Azaz, son of Shema, son of Joel, who lived in Aroer, as far as Nebo and Baal-meon. ⁹He also lived to the east as far as the beginning of the desert this side of the Euphrates, because their cattle had multiplied in the land of Gilead. ¹⁰And in the days of Saul they made war on the Hagrites, who fell by their hand; and they lived in their tents throughout all the region east of Gilead.

5.1–10: The tribe of Reuben. The Chronicler begins a consideration of the tribes of Israel that settled on

the other side of the Jordan. Reference to Simeon's taking territory near Mt. Seir in the preceding chapter may have been intended as the bridge to this block of material. Otherwise, there is no apparent explanation for moving to the traditions of Reuben, the "firstborn" of Jacob. **1:** *Because he defiled his father's bed* is a reference to Reuben's encounter with Bilhah, one of his father's concubines* (Gen 35.22). **6:** *Whom King Tilgath-pilneser of Assyria carried away into exile* is a reference to Tiglath-pilesar III, the Assyrian king most responsible for the westward expansion of Assyria. In 733–732 BCE, he led a campaign into Galilee and the eastern side of the Jordan, which would fit with the author's comment.

11 The sons of Gad lived beside them in the land of Bashan as far as Salecah: ¹²Joel the chief, Shapham the second, Janai, and Shaphat in Bashan. ¹³And their kindred according to their clans: Michael, Meshullam, Sheba, Jorai, Jacan, Zia, and Eber, seven. ¹⁴These were the sons of Abihail son of Huri, son of Jaroah, son of Gilead, son of Michael, son of Jeshishai, son of Jahdo, son of Buz; ¹⁵Ahi son of Abdiel, son of Guni, was chief in their clan; ¹⁶and they lived in Gilead, in Bashan and in its towns, and in all the pasture lands of Sharon to their limits. ¹⁷All of these were enrolled by genealogies in the days of King Jotham of Judah, and in the days of King Jeroboam of Israel.

5.11–17: The tribe of Gad. Following the pattern of reviewing the tribes that settled on the eastern side of the Jordan Valley, the author provides an overview of Gad, usually the eleventh son of Jacob. Structurally, this section is very similar to the previous section on Reuben, and seems unrelated to any other biblical records of the Gadites. **16:** *And in all the pasture lands of Sharon:* This is not the "Sharon" south of the Carmel range along the coastal plain of Israel, but a region north of Moab. All the place names in this narrative* point to a location near the modern Golan.

18 The Reubenites, the Gadites, and the half-tribe of Manasseh had valiant warriors, who carried shield and sword, and drew the bow, expert in war, forty-four thousand seven hundred sixty, ready for service. ¹⁹They made war on the Hagrites, Jetur, Naphish, and Nodab; ²⁰and when they received

help against them, the Hagrites and all who were with them were given into their hands, for they cried to God in the battle, and he granted their entreaty because they trusted in him. 21 They captured their livestock: fifty thousand of their camels, two hundred fifty thousand sheep, two thousand donkeys, and one hundred thousand captives. 22 Many fell slain, because the war was of God. And they lived in their territory until the exile.

5.18–22: The Transjordan war. In the process of reviewing those tribes of Israel who settled in the Transjordan, the Chronicler includes a brief battle narrative★ that features all of the tribes to the east of the Jordan cooperating in a major military campaign. The language and theme are characteristic of the Chronicler, suggesting that if a source was used, the Chronicler has thoroughly reworked it. **18:** *Who carried shield and sword, and drew the bow:* This string of descriptive terms indicates a professional, trained military force as opposed to the more common citizen militia. The author is deeply concerned with military matters. **19:** *They made war on the Hagrites, Jetur, Naphish, and Nodab:* These are groups identified in Genesis as descendants of Ishamael. **20:** *For they cried to God in the battle, and he granted their entreaty:* For the Chronicler, military success depends upon seeking divine assistance.

23 The members of the half-tribe of Manasseh lived in the land; they were very numerous from Bashan to Baal-hermon, Senir, and Mount Hermon. 24 These were the heads of their clans: Epher,[a] Ishi, Eliel, Azriel, Jeremiah, Hodaviah, and Jahdiel, mighty warriors, famous men, heads of their clans. 25 But they transgressed against the God of their ancestors, and prostituted themselves to the gods of the peoples of the land, whom God had destroyed before them. 26 So the God of Israel stirred up the spirit of King Pul of Assyria, the spirit of King Tilgath-pilneser of Assyria, and he carried them away, namely, the Reubenites, the Gadites, and the half-tribe of Manasseh, and brought them to Halah, Habor, Hara, and the river Gozan, to this day.

5.23–26: The half-tribe of Manasseh. While a portion of this tribe settled in the central hill country of Sa-

maria, a portion also settled in the Transjordan. The place names indicate an impossibly large area for effective control; the author may mean that members of this tribe were scattered throughout this extensive area. **25:** *But they transgressed against the God of their ancestors:* Following on the Deuteronomistic★ History's judgment against the northern kingdom on account of idolatry,★ the Chronicler sees idolatry—"prostituting themselves"—as the fundamental reason for their subsequent exile by the Assyrians. There is an ironic★ contrast intended here: Just as their common seeking of divine assistance in battle had led to their success, their common departure from God by committing idolatry caused the Transjordanian tribes to be exiled.

6 [b]The sons of Levi: Gershom,[c] Kohath, and Merari. 2 The sons of Kohath: Amram, Izhar, Hebron, and Uzziel. 3 The children of Amram: Aaron, Moses, and Miriam. The sons of Aaron: Nadab, Abihu, Eleazar, and Ithamar. 4 Eleazar became the father of Phinehas, Phinehas of Abishua, 5 Abishua of Bukki, Bukki of Uzzi, 6 Uzzi of Zerahiah, Zerahiah of Meraioth, 7 Meraioth of Amariah, Amariah of Ahitub, 8 Ahitub of Zadok, Zadok of Ahimaaz, 9 Ahimaaz of Azariah, Azariah of Johanan, 10 and Johanan of Azariah (it was he who served as priest in the house that Solomon built in Jerusalem). 11 Azariah became the father of Amariah, Amariah of Ahitub, 12 Ahitub of Zadok, Zadok of Shallum, 13 Shallum of Hilkiah, Hilkiah of Azariah, 14 Azariah of Seraiah, Seraiah of Jehozadak; 15 and Jehozadak went into exile when the LORD sent Judah and Jerusalem into exile by the hand of Nebuchadnezzar.

16[d] The sons of Levi: Gershom, Kohath, and Merari. 17 These are the names of the sons of Gershom: Libni and Shimei. 18 The sons of Kohath: Amram, Izhar, Hebron, and Uzziel. 19 The sons of Merari: Mahli and Mushi. These are the clans of the Levites according to their ancestry. 20 Of Gershom: Libni his son, Jahath his son, Zimmah his son, 21 Joah his son, Iddo his son, Zerah his son, Jeatherai his son. 22 The sons of Kohath:

---

a Gk Vg: Heb *and Epher*   b Ch 5.27 in Heb
c Heb *Gershon,* variant of *Gershom;* See 6.16
d Ch 6.1 in Heb

Amminadab his son, Korah his son, Assir his son, 23Elkanah his son, Ebiasaph his son, Assir his son, 24Tahath his son, Uriel his son, Uzziah his son, and Shaul his son. 25The sons of Elkanah: Amasai and Ahimoth, 26Elkanah his son, Zophai his son, Nahath his son, 27Eliab his son, Jeroham his son, Elkanah his son. 28The sons of Samuel: Joel*a* his firstborn, the second Abijah.*b* 29The sons of Merari: Mahli, Libni his son, Shimei his son, Uzzah his son, 30Shimea his son, Haggiah his son, and Asaiah his son.

31 These are the men whom David put in charge of the service of song in the house of the LORD, after the ark came to rest there. 32They ministered with song before the tabernacle of the tent of meeting, until Solomon had built the house of the LORD in Jerusalem; and they performed their service in due order. 33These are the men who served; and their sons were: Of the Kohathites: Heman, the singer, son of Joel, son of Samuel, 34son of Elkanah, son of Jeroham, son of Eliel, son of Toah, 35son of Zuph, son of Elkanah, son of Mahath, son of Amasai, 36son of Elkanah, son of Joel, son of Azariah, son of Zephaniah, 37son of Tahath, son of Assir, son of Ebiasaph, son of Korah, 38son of Izhar, son of Kohath, son of Levi, son of Israel; 39and his brother Asaph, who stood on his right, namely, Asaph son of Berechiah, son of Shimea, 40son of Michael, son of Baaseiah, son of Malchijah, 41son of Ethni, son of Zerah, son of Adaiah, 42son of Ethan, son of Zimmah, son of Shimei, 43son of Jahath, son of Gershom, son of Levi. 44On the left were their kindred the sons of Merari: Ethan son of Kishi, son of Abdi, son of Malluch, 45son of Hashabiah, son of Amaziah, son of Hilkiah, 46son of Amzi, son of Bani, son of Shemer, 47son of Mahli, son of Mushi, son of Merari, son of Levi; 48and their kindred the Levites were appointed for all the service of the tabernacle of the house of God.

ical importance for Israel's destiny. By the time of the Chronicler's history, the priesthood of Israel had been segmented into various family lines with differing responsibilities and social standings. Those who belonged to the sons of Aaron were eligible for the high priesthood, the chief administrative office of the Temple.* Those who belonged to the various lines of the Levites other than Aaron's had lesser roles in the Temple. The Chronicler begins consideration of this important family group by tracing the line of Aaron, but with several omissions and rearrangements. **3:** *The children of Amram: Aaron, Moses, and Miriam:* This remarkable family group, which by tradition had offered significant leadership in Israel's early history, is linked to the Levitical tribe. Miriam is the only female in this lineage. **28:** *The sons of Samuel:* With the judgment against Elkanah's line for abuse of their office (1 Sam 2.27–36), Samuel takes on the role of chief priest, thus the Chronicler's interest in his line. **31:** *These are the men whom David put in charge of the service of song:* Although David's son Solomon is the one who built the Temple, the Chronicler asserts that all the main elements of Temple worship were put in place by David. He justifies this perspective by noting that such worship was instigated "after the ark came to rest there," assuming that once the ark had been brought into Jerusalem, regular formal worship would be required. While it is not historically implausible that David would have authorized the formation of dedicated musicians for worship prior to the foundation of the Temple, this elaborate form of the organization suggests the Chronicler is referring to the form of Temple music professionals of his own day.

49 But Aaron and his sons made offerings on the altar of burnt offering and on the altar of incense, doing all the work of the most holy place, to make atonement for Israel, according to all that Moses the servant of God had commanded. 50These are the sons of Aaron: Eleazar his son, Phinehas his son, Abishua his son, 51Bukki his son, Uzzi his son, Zerahiah his son, 52Meraioth his son, Amariah his son, Ahitub his son, 53Zadok his son, Ahimaaz his son.

54 These are their dwelling places according to their settlements within their bor-

---

6.1–66: Priests—Levites and Aaronides. This section, along with that devoted to the tribe of Judah, represents the most elaborate portion of the genealogical* prologue. From the Chronicler's viewpoint, the tribe of Levi and the formal Temple* service responsibilities that only this family can undertake for Israel are of crit-

---

a Gk Syr Compare verse 33 and 1 Sam 8.2: Heb lacks *Joel*　　*b* Heb reads *Vashni, and Abijah* for *the second Abijah*, taking *the second* as a proper name

ders: to the sons of Aaron of the families of Kohathites—for the lot fell to them first—[55]to them they gave Hebron in the land of Judah and its surrounding pasture lands, [56]but the fields of the city and its villages they gave to Caleb son of Jephunneh. [57]To the sons of Aaron they gave the cities of refuge: Hebron, Libnah with its pasture lands, Jattir, Eshtemoa with its pasture lands, [58]Hilen[a] with its pasture lands, Debir with its pasture lands, [59]Ashan with its pasture lands, and Beth-shemesh with its pasture lands. [60]From the tribe of Benjamin, Geba with its pasture lands, Alemeth with its pasture lands, and Anathoth with its pasture lands. All their towns throughout their families were thirteen.

61 To the rest of the Kohathites were given by lot out of the family of the tribe, out of the half-tribe, the half of Manasseh, ten towns. [62]To the Gershomites according to their families were allotted thirteen towns out of the tribes of Issachar, Asher, Naphtali, and Manasseh in Bashan. [63]To the Merarites according to their families were allotted twelve towns out of the tribes of Reuben, Gad, and Zebulun. [64]So the people of Israel gave the Levites the towns with their pasture lands. [65]They also gave them by lot out of the tribes of Judah, Simeon, and Benjamin these towns that are mentioned by name.

66 And some of the families of the sons of Kohath had towns of their territory out of the tribe of Ephraim. [67]They were given the cities of refuge: Shechem with its pasture lands in the hill country of Ephraim, Gezer with its pasture lands, [68]Jokmeam with its pasture lands, Beth-horon with its pasture lands, [69]Aijalon with its pasture lands, Gath-rimmon with its pasture lands; [70]and out of the half-tribe of Manasseh, Aner with its pasture lands, and Bileam with its pasture lands, for the rest of the families of the Kohathites.

6.49–66. 49: *But Aaron and his sons made offerings on the altar:* One of the prime distinctions between the line of Aaron and the other members of the tribe of Levi is that the sons of Aaron could offer the sacrifices to atone for sin and purify the worshipper. Ac-

cording to all that *Moses the servant of God had commanded:* The Chronicler presents both Moses and David as sources of the customs that govern Temple service. Efforts to reconstruct the form of the Pentateuch* that the Chronicler used by comparing the regulations he attributed to Moses to the present contents of the Pentateuch have yielded conflicting results. Often the Chronicler freely adapts the regulations of the Pentateuch to fit the circumstances of his narrative.* **54**: *These are their dwelling places:* Drawing largely from the list in Josh 21.5–39, the Chronicler may be including this register to show how the Levites were distributed throughout the territory of Israel, emphasizing their importance to the well-being of the nation.

---

71 To the Gershomites: out of the half-tribe of Manasseh: Golan in Bashan with its pasture lands and Ashtaroth with its pasture lands; [72]and out of the tribe of Issachar: Kedesh with its pasture lands, Daberath[b] with its pasture lands, [73]Ramoth with its pasture lands, and Anem with its pasture lands; [74]out of the tribe of Asher: Mashal with its pasture lands, Abdon with its pasture lands, [75]Hukok with its pasture lands, and Rehob with its pasture lands; [76]and out of the tribe of Naphtali: Kedesh in Galilee with its pasture lands, Hammon with its pasture lands, and Kiriathaim with its pasture lands. [77]To the rest of the Merarites out of the tribe of Zebulun: Rimmono with its pasture lands, Tabor with its pasture lands, [78]and across the Jordan from Jericho, on the east side of the Jordan, out of the tribe of Reuben: Bezer in the steppe with its pasture lands, Jahzah with its pasture lands, [79]Kedemoth with its pasture lands, and Mephaath with its pasture lands; [80]and out of the tribe of Gad: Ramoth in Gilead with its pasture lands, Mahanaim with its pasture lands, [81]Heshbon with its pasture lands, and Jazer with its pasture lands.

7 The sons[c] of Issachar: Tola, Puah, Jashub, and Shimron, four. [2]The sons of Tola: Uzzi, Rephaiah, Jeriel, Jahmai, Ibsam, and Shemuel, heads of their ancestral houses, namely of Tola, mighty warriors of

---

a Other readings *Hilez, Holon*; See Josh 21.15
b Or *Dobrath*   c Syr Compare Vg: Heb And to the sons

their generations, their number in the days of David being twenty-two thousand six hundred. ³The son*a* of Uzzi: Izrahiah. And the sons of Izrahiah: Michael, Obadiah, Joel, and Isshiah, five, all of them chiefs; ⁴and along with them, by their generations, according to their ancestral houses, were units of the fighting force, thirty-six thousand, for they had many wives and sons. ⁵Their kindred belonging to all the families of Issachar were in all eighty-seven thousand mighty warriors, enrolled by genealogy.

6 The sons of Benjamin: Bela, Becher, and Jediael, three. ⁷The sons of Bela: Ezbon, Uzzi, Uzziel, Jerimoth, and Iri, five, heads of ancestral houses, mighty warriors; and their enrollment by genealogies was twenty-two thousand thirty-four. ⁸The sons of Becher: Zemirah, Joash, Eliezer, Elioenai, Omri, Jeremoth, Abijah, Anathoth, and Alemeth. All these were the sons of Becher; ⁹and their enrollment by genealogies, according to their generations, as heads of their ancestral houses, mighty warriors, was twenty thousand two hundred. ¹⁰The sons of Jediael: Bilhan. And the sons of Bilhan: Jeush, Benjamin, Ehud, Chenaanah, Zethan, Tarshish, and Ahishahar. ¹¹All these were the sons of Jediael according to the heads of their ancestral houses, mighty warriors, seventeen thousand two hundred, ready for service in war. ¹²And Shuppim and Huppim were the sons of Ir, Hushim the son*a* of Aher.

13 The descendants of Naphtali: Jahziel, Guni, Jezer, and Shallum, the descendants of Bilhah.

7.1–13. 1–5: The tribe of Issachar. The Chronicler had limited knowledge of this northern tribe. His characteristic interest in military factors is evident throughout. **6–12: The tribe of Benjamin.** This is the first of two sections dealing with this important tribe. In this section, the Chronicler's military interests predominate. **13: The tribe of Naphtali.** The brevity of this section indicates how little the Chronicler knew in his day of this northern tribe.

14 The sons of Manasseh: Asriel, whom his Aramean concubine bore; she bore Machir the father of Gilead. ¹⁵And Machir took a wife for Huppim and for Shuppim. The name of his sister was Maacah. And the name of the second was Zelophehad; and Zelophehad had daughters. ¹⁶Maacah the wife of Machir bore a son, and she named him Peresh; the name of his brother was Sheresh; and his sons were Ulam and Rekem. ¹⁷The son*a* of Ulam: Bedan. These were the sons of Gilead son of Machir, son of Manasseh. ¹⁸And his sister Hammolecheth bore Ishhod, Abiezer, and Mahlah. ¹⁹The sons of Shemida were Ahian, Shechem, Likhi, and Aniam.

7.14–19: The tribe of Manasseh. This section recounts the lineage of the tribe that settled in the central Samarian hill country, as opposed to the portion that settled in the Transjordan. This section has a number of grammatical and textual difficulties, suggesting that the received form has been corrupted. **15:** *And Zelophehad had daughters:* This is a reference to a significant question concerning the inheritance of property in the absence of a male heir (Num 26.33; 27.1–11; 36.1–12).

20 The sons of Ephraim: Shuthelah, and Bered his son, Tahath his son, Eleadah his son, Tahath his son, ²¹Zabad his son, Shuthelah his son, and Ezer and Elead. Now the people of Gath, who were born in the land, killed them, because they came down to raid their cattle. ²²And their father Ephraim mourned many days, and his brothers came to comfort him. ²³Ephraim*b* went in to his wife, and she conceived and bore a son; and he named him Beriah, because disaster*c* had befallen his house. ²⁴His daughter was Sheerah, who built both Lower and Upper Beth-horon, and Uzzen-sheerah. ²⁵Rephah was his son, Resheph his son, Telah his son, Tahan his son, ²⁶Ladan his son, Ammihud his son, Elishama his son, ²⁷Nun*d* his son, Joshua his son. ²⁸Their possessions and settlements were Bethel and its towns, and eastward Naaran, and westward Gezer and its towns, Shechem and its towns, as far as Ayyah and its towns; ²⁹also along the borders of the Manassites, Beth-shean and its towns, Taanach and its towns, Megiddo and its

---

a Heb *sons*   *b* Heb *He*   *c* Heb *beraah*
d Here spelled *Non*; see Ex 33.11

towns, Dor and its towns. In these lived the sons of Joseph son of Israel.

7.20–29: The tribe of Ephraim. Manasseh and Ephraim were the two sons of Joseph, which may account for the placement of this section. **21:** *Now the people of Gath, who were born in the land:* Gath was normally associated with the Philistines (1 Sam 7.14) and was said to have been the giant Goliath's home (1 Sam 17.4). Being born in the land would mark them as part of the population of Canaan as opposed to the Philistines who, like the Israelites, had come from another place to settle in the land. **24:** *His daughter was Sheerah:* Although founders of cities or other settlements are often noted, this is the only woman credited with founding cities. Upper and Lower Beth-horon were important centers in ancient Israel; Uzzensheerah is otherwise unmentioned in the Bible.

30 The sons of Asher: Imnah, Ishvah, Ishvi, Beriah, and their sister Serah. [31] The sons of Beriah: Heber and Malchiel, who was the father of Birzaith. [32] Heber became the father of Japhlet, Shomer, Hotham, and their sister Shua. [33] The sons of Japhlet: Pasach, Bimhal, and Ashvath. These are the sons of Japhlet. [34] The sons of Shemer: Ahi, Rohgah, Hubbah, and Aram. [35] The sons of Helem[a] his brother: Zophah, Imna, Shelesh, and Amal. [36] The sons of Zophah: Suah, Harnepher, Shual, Beri, Imrah, [37] Bezer, Hod, Shamma, Shilshah, Ithran, and Beera. [38] The sons of Jether: Jephunneh, Pispa, and Ara. [39] The sons of Ulla: Arah, Hanniel, and Rizia. [40] All of these were men of Asher, heads of ancestral houses, select mighty warriors, chief of the princes. Their number enrolled by genealogies, for service in war, was twenty-six thousand men.

7.30–40: The tribe of Asher. This concise section raises a number of questions: Many of the names are not Hebrew; the list only follows the lineage of Heber; and the number of warriors is low compared to the other tribes. Some suggest the "Heberites" were a mixed group of Israelites and Canaanites who settled on the western fringes of the Samarian hill country.

8 Benjamin became the father of Bela his firstborn, Ashbel the second, Aharah the third, [2] Nohah the fourth, and Rapha the fifth. [3] And Bela had sons: Addar, Gera, Abihud,[b] [4] Abishua, Naaman, Ahoah, [5] Gera, Shephuphan, and Huram. [6] These are the sons of Ehud (they were heads of ancestral houses of the inhabitants of Geba, and they were carried into exile to Manahath): [7] Naaman,[c] Ahijah, and Gera, that is, Heglam,[d] who became the father of Uzza and Ahihud. [8] And Shaharaim had sons in the country of Moab after he had sent away his wives Hushim and Baara. [9] He had sons by his wife Hodesh: Jobab, Zibia, Mesha, Malcam, [10] Jeuz, Sachia, and Mirmah. These were his sons, heads of ancestral houses. [11] He also had sons by Hushim: Abitub and Elpaal. [12] The sons of Elpaal: Eber, Misham, and Shemed, who built Ono and Lod with its towns, [13] and Beriah and Shema (they were heads of ancestral houses of the inhabitants of Aijalon, who put to flight the inhabitants of Gath); [14] and Ahio, Shashak, and Jeremoth. [15] Zebadiah, Arad, Eder, [16] Michael, Ishpah, and Joha were sons of Beriah. [17] Zebadiah, Meshullam, Hizki, Heber, [18] Ishmerai, Izliah, and Jobab were the sons of Elpaal. [19] Jakim, Zichri, Zabdi, [20] Elienai, Zillethai, Eliel, [21] Adaiah, Beraiah, and Shimrath were the sons of Shimei. [22] Ishpan, Eber, Eliel, [23] Abdon, Zichri, Hanan, [24] Hananiah, Elam, Anthothijah, [25] Iphdeiah, and Penuel were the sons of Shashak. [26] Shamsherai, Shehariah, Athaliah, [27] Jaareshiah, Elijah, and Zichri were the sons of Jeroham. [28] These were the heads of ancestral houses, according to their generations, chiefs. These lived in Jerusalem.

29 Jeiel[e] the father of Gibeon lived in Gibeon, and the name of his wife was Maacah. [30] His firstborn son: Abdon, then Zur, Kish, Baal,[f] Nadab, [31] Gedor, Ahio, Zecher, [32] and Mikloth, who became the father of Shimeah. Now these also lived opposite their kindred in Jerusalem, with their kindred. [33] Ner became the father of Kish, Kish of Saul,[g] Saul[g] of Jonathan, Malchishua, Abinadab, and Esh-baal; [34] and the son of Jona-

---

a Or *Hotham*; see 7.32   b Or *father of Ehud*; see 8.6
c Heb *and Naaman*   d Or *he carried them into exile*
e Compare 9.35: Heb lacks *Jeiel*   f Gk Ms adds *Ner*;
Compare 8.33 and 9.36   g Or *Shaul*

than was Merib-baal; and Merib-baal became the father of Micah. ³⁵The sons of Micah: Pithon, Melech, Tarea, and Ahaz. ³⁶Ahaz became the father of Jehoaddah; and Jehoaddah became the father of Alemeth, Azmaveth, and Zimri; Zimri became the father of Moza. ³⁷Moza became the father of Binea; Raphah was his son, Eleasah his son, Azel his son. ³⁸Azel had six sons, and these are their names: Azrikam, Bocheru, Ishmael, Sheariah, Obadiah, and Hanan; all these were the sons of Azel. ³⁹The sons of his brother Eshek: Ulam his firstborn, Jeush the second, and Eliphelet the third. ⁴⁰The sons of Ulam were mighty warriors, archers, having many children and grandchildren, one hundred fifty. All these were Benjaminites.

8.1–40: The tribe of Benjamin. This is the second listing of the Benjaminite tribe. The Chronicler may have needed this additional material to weave several strands of his narrative* together—the relationship of the Benjaminite and Judean tribes; the lineage of Saul, the first king of Israel; and the centrality of Jerusalem. 33: Saul of Jonathan, Malchishua, Abinadab, and Eshbaal: Of note among the family of Saul are several persons bearing names with the Canaanite god Baal's* name. Eshbaal means "man of Baal."

9 So all Israel was enrolled by genealogies; and these are written in the Book of the Kings of Israel. And Judah was taken into exile in Babylon because of their unfaithfulness. ²Now the first to live again in their possessions in their towns were Israelites, priests, Levites, and temple servants.

3 And some of the people of Judah, Benjamin, Ephraim, and Manasseh lived in Jerusalem: ⁴Uthai son of Ammihud, son of Omri, son of Imri, son of Bani, from the sons of Perez son of Judah. ⁵And of the Shilonites: Asaiah the firstborn, and his sons. ⁶Of the sons of Zerah: Jeuel and their kin, six hundred ninety. ⁷Of the Benjaminites: Sallu son of Meshullam, son of Hodaviah, son of Hassenuah, ⁸Ibneiah son of Jeroham, Elah son of Uzzi, son of Michri, and Meshullam son of Shephatiah, son of Reuel, son of Ibnijah; ⁹and their kindred according to their

generations, nine hundred fifty-six. All these were heads of families according to their ancestral houses.

9.1–34: The organization of the post-exilic community. This section opens with a summary of what has gone before (vv. 1–2) and moves on to a detailed listing of those responsible for Jerusalem after the return from exile. The Chronicler places characteristic emphasis on the role of the Levites in maintaining proper worship. 2: Now the first . . . were Israelites, priests, Levites, and temple servants: This is a description in brief of the basic social structure, according to the Chronicler, of post-exilic Yehud. The Israelites are all those in the population with no formal Temple* function; the priests are the sons of Aaron, those entitled to offer the sacrifices on behalf of the worshippers; the Levites are those with non-sacrificial responsibilities in the Temple; and the temple servants are a class of persons assigned to assist in the mundane functions of the Temple. The Chronicler spends a large portion of this section on those with a connection to the Temple to underscore its importance. 3: And some of the people of Judah, Benjamin, Ephraim, and Manasseh lived in Jerusalem: Sitting on the boundary of the territories settled by Judah and Benjamin, the presence of these family groups is expected. Ephraim and Manasseh, being northern tribes, would not have been expected to appear in this group. However, the Chronicler includes a theme to be developed in the historical narratives:* The participation of elements of Ephraim and Manasseh confirms the ideal of "all Israel" coming together to seek God.

10 Of the priests: Jedaiah, Jehoiarib, Jachin, ¹¹and Azariah son of Hilkiah, son of Meshullam, son of Zadok, son of Meraioth, son of Ahitub, the chief officer of the house of God; ¹²and Adaiah son of Jeroham, son of Pashhur, son of Malchijah, and Maasai son of Adiel, son of Jahzerah, son of Meshullam, son of Meshillemith, son of Immer; ¹³besides their kindred, heads of their ancestral houses, one thousand seven hundred sixty, qualified for the work of the service of the house of God.

14 Of the Levites: Shemaiah son of Hasshub, son of Azrikam, son of Hashabiah, of the sons of Merari; ¹⁵and Bakbakkar, Heresh, Galal, and Mattaniah son of Mica, son

of Zichri, son of Asaph; [16]and Obadiah son of Shemaiah, son of Galal, son of Jeduthun, and Berechiah son of Asa, son of Elkanah, who lived in the villages of the Netophathites.

17 The gatekeepers were: Shallum, Akkub, Talmon, Ahiman; and their kindred Shallum was the chief, [18]stationed previously in the king's gate on the east side. These were the gatekeepers of the camp of the Levites. [19]Shallum son of Kore, son of Ebiasaph, son of Korah, and his kindred of his ancestral house, the Korahites, were in charge of the work of the service, guardians of the thresholds of the tent, as their ancestors had been in charge of the camp of the LORD, guardians of the entrance. [20]And Phinehas son of Eleazar was chief over them in former times; the LORD was with him. [21]Zechariah son of Meshelemiah was gatekeeper at the entrance of the tent of meeting. [22]All these, who were chosen as gatekeepers at the thresholds, were two hundred twelve. They were enrolled by genealogies in their villages. David and the seer Samuel established them in their office of trust. [23]So they and their descendants were in charge of the gates of the house of the LORD, that is, the house of the tent, as guards. [24]The gatekeepers were on the four sides, east, west, north, and south; [25]and their kindred who were in their villages were obliged to come in every seven days, in turn, to be with them; [26]for the four chief gatekeepers, who were Levites, were in charge of the chambers and the treasures of the house of God. [27]And they would spend the night near the house of God; for on them lay the duty of watching, and they had charge of opening it every morning.

28 Some of them had charge of the utensils of service, for they were required to count them when they were brought in and taken out. [29]Others of them were appointed over the furniture, and over all the holy utensils, also over the choice flour, the wine, the oil, the incense, and the spices. [30]Others, of the sons of the priests, prepared the mixing of the spices, [31]and Mattithiah, one of the Levites, the firstborn of Shallum the Korahite, was in charge of making the flat cakes. [32]Also some of their kindred of the Kohathites had charge of the rows of bread, to prepare them for each sabbath.

33 Now these are the singers, the heads of ancestral houses of the Levites, living in the chambers of the temple free from other service, for they were on duty day and night. [34]These were heads of ancestral houses of the Levites, according to their generations; these leaders lived in Jerusalem.

9.10–34. 20: *And Phineas . . . was chief over them in former times:* This notice refers to Num 25.1–13, where Phineas kills an Israelite and his Midianite wife for defiling the tent of meeting. It suggests that the *gatekeepers at the entrance* may have had a role in determining who could enter the Levitical orders and who could not. 22: *David and the seer Samuel established them in their office of trust* is a curious connection of persons since David had little, in fact, to do with Samuel. The text probably recalls Samuel's condemnation of the priest Eli's line for abuse of office (1 Sam 3.10–18) which, in the Chronicler's view, received royal approval by David's founding of the Temple functionaries.

---

35 In Gibeon lived the father of Gibeon, Jeiel, and the name of his wife was Maacah. [36]His firstborn son was Abdon, then Zur, Kish, Baal, Ner, Nadab, [37]Gedor, Ahio, Zechariah, and Mikloth; [38]and Mikloth became the father of Shimeam; and these also lived opposite their kindred in Jerusalem, with their kindred. [39]Ner became the father of Kish, Kish of Saul, Saul of Jonathan, Malchishua, Abinadab, and Esh-baal; [40]and the son of Jonathan was Merib-baal; and Merib-baal became the father of Micah. [41]The sons of Micah: Pithon, Melech, Tahrea, and Ahaz;[a] [42]and Ahaz became the father of Jarah, and Jarah of Alemeth, Azmaveth, and Zimri; and Zimri became the father of Moza. [43]Moza became the father of Binea; and Rephaiah was his son, Eleasah his son, Azel his son. [44]Azel had six sons, and these are their names: Azrikam, Bocheru, Ishmael, Sheariah, Obadiah, and Hanan; these were the sons of Azel.

a Compare 8.35: Heb lacks *and Ahaz*

ACCOUNT OF DAVID'S REIGN

Chs. 10–20: These chapters sometimes repeat, and on occasion summarize, portions of the narratives* of David's reign in 2 Sam 5 through 1 Kings 2. Many of these earlier accounts are completely left out by the Chronicler, and others are rewritten so thoroughly as to bear little resemblance to the earlier account. In these narratives, the Chronicler highlights David's success as king and his role in selecting Jerusalem as the capital, along with preparing for the construction and staffing of the Temple.*

10 Now the Philistines fought against Israel; and the men of Israel fled before the Philistines, and fell slain on Mount Gilboa. 2 The Philistines overtook Saul and his sons; and the Philistines killed Jonathan and Abinadab and Malchishua, sons of Saul. 3 The battle pressed hard on Saul; and the archers found him, and he was wounded by the archers. 4 Then Saul said to his armor-bearer, "Draw your sword, and thrust me through with it, so that these uncircumcised may not come and make sport of me." But his armor-bearer was unwilling, for he was terrified. So Saul took his own sword and fell on it. 5 When his armor-bearer saw that Saul was dead, he also fell on his sword and died. 6 Thus Saul died; he and his three sons and all his house died together. 7 When all the men of Israel who were in the valley saw that the army*a* had fled and that Saul and his sons were dead, they abandoned their towns and fled; and the Philistines came and occupied them.

8 The next day when the Philistines came to strip the dead, they found Saul and his sons fallen on Mount Gilboa. 9 They stripped him and took his head and his armor, and sent messengers throughout the land of the Philistines to carry the good news to their idols and to the people. 10 They put his armor in the temple of their gods, and fastened his head in the temple of Dagon. 11 But when all Jabesh-gilead heard everything that the Philistines had done to Saul, 12 all the valiant warriors got up and took away the body of Saul and the bodies of his sons, and brought them to Jabesh. Then they buried their bones under the oak in Jabesh, and fasted seven days.

13 So Saul died for his unfaithfulness; he was unfaithful to the LORD in that he did not keep the command of the LORD; moreover, he had consulted a medium, seeking guidance, 14 and did not seek guidance from the LORD. Therefore the LORD*b* put him to death and turned the kingdom over to David son of Jesse.

10.1–14: The death of Saul. As Israel's first king, Saul was of particular interest to the writer of 1 and 2 Samuel. In contrast, the Chronicler gives him little notice. **13:** *So Saul died for his unfaithfulness* is the Chronicler's sad commentary on Saul's moral failure, particularly his seeking instruction from someone other than a prophet* of the LORD.

11 Then all Israel gathered together to David at Hebron and said, "See, we are your bone and flesh. 2 For some time now, even while Saul was king, it was you who commanded the army of Israel. The LORD your God said to you: It is you who shall be shepherd of my people Israel, you who shall be ruler over my people Israel." 3 So all the elders of Israel came to the king at Hebron, and David made a covenant with them at Hebron before the LORD. And they anointed David king over Israel, according to the word of the LORD by Samuel.

11.1–3: David is chosen king. 1: *All Israel* is a variation on "all the tribes of Israel" in 2 Sam 5. In the Chronicler's time, tribal identity may no longer be certain. **3:** *According to the word of the LORD by Samuel:* The Chronicler betrays his use of 1 and 2 Samuel here since he has not previously mentioned Samuel's anointing* David as king.

4 David and all Israel marched to Jerusalem, that is Jebus, where the Jebusites were, the inhabitants of the land. 5 The inhabitants of Jebus said to David, "You will not come in here." Nevertheless David took the stronghold of Zion, now the city of David. 6 David had said, "Whoever attacks the Jebusites first shall be chief and com-

a Heb *they*   *b* Heb *he*

mander." And Joab son of Zeruiah went up first, so he became chief. [7]David resided in the stronghold; therefore it was called the city of David. [8]He built the city all around, from the Millo in complete circuit; and Joab repaired the rest of the city. [9]And David became greater and greater, for the LORD of hosts was with him.

11.4–9: David captures Jerusalem. The Chronicler omits his source's mention that David reigned in Hebron for 7 years (2 Sam 5.5) to make it look as though David's first action after becoming king was to conquer Jerusalem. **6:** *Whoever attacks the Jebusites first shall be chief and commander* is a challenge to his men very different from the account in 2 Sam 5.8. **9:** *David became greater and greater, for the LORD of Hosts was with him:* For the Chronicler, the measure of success was expressed in terms of the king's closeness to God. This phrase highlights the reason for David's great success as king as recounted in the following narratives.*

---

10 Now these are the chiefs of David's warriors, who gave him strong support in his kingdom, together with all Israel, to make him king, according to the word of the LORD concerning Israel. [11]This is an account of David's mighty warriors: Jashobeam, son of Hachmoni,[a] was chief of the Three;[b] he wielded his spear against three hundred whom he killed at one time.

12 And next to him among the three warriors was Eleazar son of Dodo, the Ahohite. [13]He was with David at Pas-dammim when the Philistines were gathered there for battle. There was a plot of ground full of barley. Now the people had fled from the Philistines, [14]but he and David took their stand in the middle of the plot, defended it, and killed the Philistines; and the LORD saved them by a great victory.

15 Three of the thirty chiefs went down to the rock to David at the cave of Adullam, while the army of Philistines was encamped in the valley of Rephaim. [16]David was then in the stronghold; and the garrison of the Philistines was then at Bethlehem. [17]David said longingly, "O that someone would give me water to drink from the well of Bethlehem that is by the gate!" [18]Then the Three broke through the camp of the Philistines, and drew water from the well of Bethlehem that was by the gate, and they brought it to David. But David would not drink of it; he poured it out to the LORD, [19]and said, "My God forbid that I should do this. Can I drink the blood of these men? For at the risk of their lives they brought it." Therefore he would not drink it. The three warriors did these things.

20 Now Abishai,[c] the brother of Joab, was chief of the Thirty.[d] With his spear he fought against three hundred and killed them, and won a name beside the Three. [21]He was the most renowned[e] of the Thirty,[d] and became their commander; but he did not attain to the Three.

22 Benaiah son of Jehoiada was a valiant man[f] of Kabzeel, a doer of great deeds; he struck down two sons of[g] Ariel of Moab. He also went down and killed a lion in a pit on a day when snow had fallen. [23]And he killed an Egyptian, a man of great stature, five cubits tall. The Egyptian had in his hand a spear like a weaver's beam; but Benaiah went against him with a staff, snatched the spear out of the Egyptian's hand, and killed him with his own spear. [24]Such were the things Benaiah son of Jehoiada did, and he won a name beside the three warriors. [25]He was renowned among the Thirty, but he did not attain to the Three. And David put him in charge of his bodyguard.

11.10–25: David's mighty men. Generally a repetition of 2 Sam 23.8–39 with few minor variations.

---

26 The warriors of the armies were Asahel brother of Joab, Elhanan son of Dodo of Bethlehem, [27]Shammoth of Harod,[h] Helez the Pelonite, [28]Ira son of Ikkesh of Tekoa, Abiezer of Anathoth, [29]Sibbecai the Hushathite, Ilai the Ahohite, [30]Maharai of Netophah, Heled son of Baanah of Netophah,

a Or *a Hachmonite*   *b* Compare 2 Sam 23.8: Heb *Thirty* or *captains*   *c* Gk Vg Tg Compare 2 Sam 23.18: Heb *Abshai*   *d* Syr: Heb *Three*   *e* Compare 2 Sam 23.19: Heb *more renowned among the two*   *f* Syr: Heb *the son of a valiant man*   *g* See 2 Sam 23.20: Heb lacks *sons of*   *h* Compare 2 Sam 23.25: Heb *the Harorite*

31Ithai son of Ribai of Gibeah of the Benjaminites, Benaiah of Pirathon, 32Hurai of the wadis of Gaash, Abiel the Arbathite, 33Azmaveth of Baharum, Eliahba of Shaalbon, 34Hashem*a* the Gizonite, Jonathan son of Shagee the Hararite, 35Ahiam son of Sachar the Hararite, Eliphal son of Ur, 36Hepher the Mecherathite, Ahijah the Pelonite, 37Hezro of Carmel, Naarai son of Ezbai, 38Joel the brother of Nathan, Mibhar son of Hagri, 39Zelek the Ammonite, Naharai of Beeroth, the armor-bearer of Joab son of Zeruiah, 40Ira the Ithrite, Gareb the Ithrite, 41Uriah the Hittite, Zabad son of Ahlai, 42Adina son of Shiza the Reubenite, a leader of the Reubenites, and thirty with him, 43Hanan son of Maacah, and Joshaphat the Mithnite, 44Uzzia the Ashterathite, Shama and Jeiel sons of Hotham the Aroerite, 45Jediael son of Shimri, and his brother Joha the Tizite, 46Eliel the Mahavite, and Jeribai and Joshaviah sons of Elnaam, and Ithmah the Moabite, 47Eliel, and Obed, and Jaasiel the Mezobaite.

12 The following are those who came to David at Ziklag, while he could not move about freely because of Saul son of Kish; they were among the mighty warriors who helped him in war. 2They were archers, and could shoot arrows and sling stones with either the right hand or the left; they were Benjaminites, Saul's kindred. 3The chief was Ahiezer, then Joash, both sons of Shemaah of Gibeah; also Jeziel and Pelet sons of Azmaveth; Beracah, Jehu of Anathoth, 4Ishmaiah of Gibeon, a warrior among the Thirty and a leader over the Thirty; Jeremiah,*b* Jahaziel, Johanan, Jozabad of Gederah, 5Eluzai,*c* Jerimoth, Bealiah, Shemariah, Shephatiah the Haruphite; 6Elkanah, Isshiah, Azarel, Joezer, and Jashobeam, the Korahites; 7and Joelah and Zebadiah, sons of Jeroham of Gedor.

8 From the Gadites there went over to David at the stronghold in the wilderness mighty and experienced warriors, expert with shield and spear, whose faces were like the faces of lions, and who were swift as gazelles on the mountains: 9Ezer the chief, Obadiah second, Eliab third, 10Mishmannah fourth, Jeremiah fifth, 11Attai sixth, Eliel seventh, 12Johanan eighth, Elzabad ninth, 13Jeremiah tenth, Machbannai eleventh. 14These Gadites were officers of the army, the least equal to a hundred and the greatest to a thousand. 15These are the men who crossed the Jordan in the first month, when it was overflowing all its banks, and put to flight all those in the valleys, to the east and to the west.

16 Some Benjaminites and Judahites came to the stronghold to David. 17David went out to meet them and said to them, "If you have come to me in friendship, to help me, then my heart will be knit to you; but if you have come to betray me to my adversaries, though my hands have done no wrong, then may the God of our ancestors see and give judgment." 18Then the spirit came upon Amasai, chief of the Thirty, and he said,

"We are yours, O David;
    and with you, O son of Jesse!
Peace, peace to you,
    and peace to the one who helps you!
For your God is the one who helps
    you."

Then David received them, and made them officers of his troops.

19 Some of the Manassites deserted to David when he came with the Philistines for the battle against Saul. (Yet he did not help them, for the rulers of the Philistines took counsel and sent him away, saying, "He will desert to his master Saul at the cost of our heads.") 20As he went to Ziklag these Manassites deserted to him: Adnah, Jozabad, Jediael, Michael, Jozabad, Elihu, and Zillethai, chiefs of the thousands in Manasseh. 21They helped David against the band of raiders,*d* for they were all warriors and commanders in the army. 22Indeed from day to day people kept coming to David to help him, until there was a great army, like an army of God.

12.1–22: David's loyal forces. To emphasize the prowess of David's forces, the Chronicler refers to the time when David was trying to keep away from Saul.

a Compare Gk and 2 Sam 23.32: Heb *the sons of Hashem*   *b* Heb verse 5   *c* Heb verse 6
d Or *as officers of his troops*

During this time, experienced and skilled warriors join with David's cause. There is almost no parallel material to these narratives* in 1 Samuel. **18:** *"Peace, peace to you":* Despite the Chronicler's interest in military matters, one of the marks that the community is on the right path is God's granting of peace. This may also be a wordplay on "Jerusalem," "City of Peace," reminding the audience of Jerusalem's highest goal. **19:** *Some of the Manassites:* The tribe of Manasseh was one of the primary population groups in the central portion of the northern district of Israel. Specific reference to these individuals as well as other northern tribal groups emphasizes the unanimity of support for David as opposed to Saul, the legitimate king of the nation.

23 These are the numbers of the divisions of the armed troops who came to David in Hebron to turn the kingdom of Saul over to him, according to the word of the LORD. 24The people of Judah bearing shield and spear numbered six thousand eight hundred armed troops. 25Of the Simeonites, mighty warriors, seven thousand one hundred. 26Of the Levites four thousand six hundred. 27Jehoiada, leader of the house of Aaron, and with him three thousand seven hundred. 28Zadok, a young warrior, and twenty-two commanders from his own ancestral house. 29Of the Benjaminites, the kindred of Saul, three thousand, of whom the majority had continued to keep their allegiance to the house of Saul. 30Of the Ephraimites, twenty thousand eight hundred, mighty warriors, notables in their ancestral houses. 31Of the half-tribe of Manasseh, eighteen thousand, who were expressly named to come and make David king. 32Of Issachar, those who had understanding of the times, to know what Israel ought to do, two hundred chiefs, and all their kindred under their command. 33Of Zebulun, fifty thousand seasoned troops, equipped for battle with all the weapons of war, to help David*a* with singleness of purpose. 34Of Naphtali, a thousand commanders, with whom there were thirty-seven thousand armed with shield and spear. 35Of the Danites, twenty-eight thousand six hundred equipped for battle. 36Of Asher, forty thousand seasoned troops ready for battle. 37Of the Reubenites and Gadites and the half-tribe of Manasseh from beyond the Jordan, one hundred twenty thousand armed with all the weapons of war.

12.23: *These are the numbers:* This listing of troop strength seems grossly inflated. Some believe the author has misunderstood terms for "unit" and has understood it as a word for "thousand." Others have argued the numbers are symbolic rather than real.

38 All these, warriors arrayed in battle order, came to Hebron with full intent to make David king over all Israel; likewise all the rest of Israel were of a single mind to make David king. 39They were there with David for three days, eating and drinking, for their kindred had provided for them. 40And also their neighbors, from as far away as Issachar and Zebulun and Naphtali, came bringing food on donkeys, camels, mules, and oxen—abundant provisions of meal, cakes of figs, clusters of raisins, wine, oil, oxen, and sheep, for there was joy in Israel.

12.38: *All the rest of Israel were of a single mind to make David king:* The Chronicler emphasizes that the community acts as one throughout the book. Of particular importance to the author is the idea of "all Israel," even though the history focuses almost exclusively on events impacting the region or tribe of Judah only.

13 David consulted with the commanders of the thousands and of the hundreds, with every leader. 2David said to the whole assembly of Israel, "If it seems good to you, and if it is the will of the LORD our God, let us send abroad to our kindred who remain in all the land of Israel, including the priests and Levites in the cities that have pasture lands, that they may come together to us. 3Then let us bring again the ark of our God to us; for we did not turn to it in the days of Saul." 4The whole assembly agreed to do so, for the thing pleased all the people.

5 So David assembled all Israel from the Shihor of Egypt to Lebo-hamath, to bring the ark of God from Kiriath-jearim. 6And David and all Israel went up to Baalah, that is, to Kiriath-jearim, which belongs to Judah,

a Gk: Heb lacks *David*

to bring up from there the ark of God, the LORD, who is enthroned on the cherubim, which is called by his*a* name. 7They carried the ark of God on a new cart, from the house of Abinadab, and Uzzah and Ahio*b* were driving the cart. 8David and all Israel were dancing before God with all their might, with song and lyres and harps and tambourines and cymbals and trumpets.

9 When they came to the threshing floor of Chidon, Uzzah put out his hand to hold the ark, for the oxen shook it. 10The anger of the LORD was kindled against Uzzah; he struck him down because he put out his hand to the ark; and he died there before God. 11David was angry because the LORD had burst out against Uzzah; so that place is called Perez-uzzah*c* to this day. 12David was afraid of God that day; he said, "How can I bring the ark of God into my care?" 13So David did not take the ark into his care into the city of David; he took it instead to the house of Obed-edom the Gittite. 14The ark of God remained with the household of Obed-edom in his house three months, and the LORD blessed the household of Obed-edom and all that he had.

13.1–14: Moving the ark into Jerusalem. An important prelude to David's effectual rule from Jerusalem was bringing the ark of the covenant* into what will be the "chosen city" of Jerusalem. Rearranging the order of his source (2 Sam 6.1–11), the Chronicler has David acting to bring the divine presence as symbolized by the ark (Num 10.33–36) into the capital city even before beginning his own palace. The Chronicler's deliberate reformatting of the sequence of events highlights the importance the narrative* will give to honoring God's presence in Jerusalem. **2:** *David said to the whole assembly of Israel:* In 2 Samuel, David simply makes the decision to bring the ark into the city; here, the Chronicler has David act on the basis of community consensus and divine will. **3:** *We did not turn to it in the days of Saul:* The ark served as a physical manifestation of God's presence. As such, it could ensure that a prophet* was receiving a message from God himself. This comment also serves to underscore the Chronicler's condemnation of Saul for having failed to consult authorized prophets. **5:** *All Israel from the Shihor of Egypt to Lebo-hamath* is probably the largest amount of territory attributed to Israel in the

Old Testament. Shihor of Egypt was the furthest eastern branch of the Nile in Egypt; Lebo-hamath may have been a divide within the Beqa' Valley of modern Lebanon. **6:** *The ark of God, the LORD, who is enthroned on the cherubim,* which is called by his name:* This is an elaborated title for the ark, though of uncertain meaning, possibly emphasizing the uniqueness of this object. **9:** *Threshing* floor of Chidon:* The owner's name was "Nacon" in 2 Sam 6.6. The Chronicler offers no explanation for the change in name.

14

King Hiram of Tyre sent messengers to David, along with cedar logs, and masons and carpenters to build a house for him. 2David then perceived that the LORD had established him as king over Israel, and that his kingdom was highly exalted for the sake of his people Israel.

3 David took more wives in Jerusalem, and David became the father of more sons and daughters. 4These are the names of the children whom he had in Jerusalem: Shammua, Shobab, and Nathan; Solomon, 5Ibhar, Elishua, and Elpelet; 6Nogah, Nepheg, and Japhia; 7Elishama, Beeliada, and Eliphelet.

8 When the Philistines heard that David had been anointed king over all Israel, all the Philistines went up in search of David; and David heard of it and went out against them. 9Now the Philistines had come and made a raid in the valley of Rephaim. 10David inquired of God, "Shall I go up against the Philistines? Will you give them into my hand?" The LORD said to him, "Go up, and I will give them into your hand." 11So he went up to Baal-perazim, and David defeated them there. David said, "God has burst out*d* against my enemies by my hand, like a bursting flood." Therefore that place is called Baal-perazim.*e* 12They abandoned their gods there, and at David's command they were burned.

13 Once again the Philistines made a raid in the valley. 14When David again inquired of God, God said to him, "You shall not go up after them; go around and come on them

a Heb lacks *his*   *b* Or *and his brother*   *c* That is *Bursting Out Against Uzzah*   *d* Heb *paraz*   *e* That is *Lord of Bursting Out*

opposite the balsam trees. ¹⁵When you hear the sound of marching in the tops of the balsam trees, then go out to battle; for God has gone out before you to strike down the army of the Philistines." ¹⁶David did as God had commanded him, and they struck down the Philistine army from Gibeon to Gezer. ¹⁷The fame of David went out into all lands, and the LORD brought the fear of him on all nations.

14.1–17: Consolidation of David's rule. As the prelude to the movement of the ark into Jerusalem, David's claim on Jerusalem is solidified. **1:** *King Hiram of Tyre sent messengers to David, along with cedar logs:* The cedars of Lebanon were prized in antiquity as a prime building material. Cedar, which is naturally resistant to rot, symbolized eternity in the ancient Near East. **10:** *David inquired of God* is the technical language for consulting with a prophet* to seek God's will. **12:** *They abandoned their gods there and at David's command they were burned:* In the Chronicler's source (2 Sam 5.21), David and his forces "carry away" the idols. Here, the Chronicler has David following more explicitly the Pentateuchal* regulations for the disposal of idols (Deut 12.3). **16:** *They struck down the Philistine army from Gibeon to Gezer:* Gibeon was slightly north of Jerusalem; Gezer lay at the boundary of the hill country and the coastal plain. Essentially this description would confine the Philistines to the strip of land that constitutes the coastal plain. There is some archaeological evidence that at the time of David's reign, Philistine expansion into the hill country was reversed.

15 David*ᵃ* built houses for himself in the city of David, and he prepared a place for the ark of God and pitched a tent for it. ²Then David commanded that no one but the Levites were to carry the ark of God, for the LORD had chosen them to carry the ark of the LORD and to minister to him forever. ³David assembled all Israel in Jerusalem to bring up the ark of the LORD to its place, which he had prepared for it. ⁴Then David gathered together the descendants of Aaron and the Levites: ⁵of the sons of Kohath, Uriel the chief, with one hundred twenty of his kindred; ⁶of the sons of Merari, Asaiah the chief, with two hundred twenty of his kindred; ⁷of the sons of Gershom, Joel

the chief, with one hundred thirty of his kindred; ⁸of the sons of Elizaphan, Shemaiah the chief, with two hundred of his kindred; ⁹of the sons of Hebron, Eliel the chief, with eighty of his kindred; ¹⁰of the sons of Uzziel, Amminadab the chief, with one hundred twelve of his kindred.

15.1–16.43: The ark is installed in Jerusalem. Unlike Saul, David had properly consulted with, and obeyed, the messages he received from God. With Jerusalem secured as the capital of the nascent kingdom, David was ready to bring the ark into the city. Much of this chapter is the Chronicler's elaboration on his source, 2 Sam 6.12–16. Characteristic of the Chronicler's revision is the emphasis on the proper order for such ritual actions. **15.2:** *Then David commanded that no one but the Levites:* The Chronicler conceives that David established some of the regulations governing worship. Here, though there were no preexisting requirements as to who could carry the ark, David sets down the rule that only Levites can carry the ark. *Forever* as the length of such responsibility is in keeping with other charges to the priesthood (see Num 25.13).

11 David summoned the priests Zadok and Abiathar, and the Levites Uriel, Asaiah, Joel, Shemaiah, Eliel, and Amminadab. ¹²He said to them, "You are the heads of families of the Levites; sanctify yourselves, you and your kindred, so that you may bring up the ark of the LORD, the God of Israel, to the place that I have prepared for it. ¹³Because you did not carry it the first time,*ᵇ* the LORD our God burst out against us, because we did not give it proper care." ¹⁴So the priests and the Levites sanctified themselves to bring up the ark of the LORD, the God of Israel. ¹⁵And the Levites carried the ark of God on their shoulders with the poles, as Moses had commanded according to the word of the LORD.

16 David also commanded the chiefs of the Levites to appoint their kindred as the singers to play on musical instruments, on harps and lyres and cymbals, to raise loud sounds of joy. ¹⁷So the Levites appointed Heman son of Joel; and of his kindred Asaph son of Berechiah; and of the sons of Merari,

a Heb *He*   *b* Meaning of Heb uncertain

their kindred, Ethan son of Kushaiah; 18and with them their kindred of the second order, Zechariah, Jaaziel, Shemiramoth, Jehiel, Unni, Eliab, Benaiah, Maaseiah, Mattithiah, Eliphelehu, and Mikneiah, and the gatekeepers Obed-edom and Jeiel. 19The singers Heman, Asaph, and Ethan were to sound bronze cymbals; 20Zechariah, Aziel, Shemiramoth, Jehiel, Unni, Eliab, Maaseiah, and Benaiah were to play harps according to Alamoth; 21but Mattithiah, Eliphelehu, Mikneiah, Obed-edom, Jeiel, and Azaziah were to lead with lyres according to the Sheminith. 22Chenaniah, leader of the Levites in music, was to direct the music, for he understood it. 23Berechiah and Elkanah were to be gatekeepers for the ark. 24Shebaniah, Joshaphat, Nethanel, Amasai, Zechariah, Benaiah, and Eliezer, the priests, were to blow the trumpets before the ark of God. Obed-edom and Jehiah also were to be gatekeepers for the ark.

25 So David and the elders of Israel, and the commanders of the thousands, went to bring up the ark of the covenant of the LORD from the house of Obed-edom with rejoicing. 26And because God helped the Levites who were carrying the ark of the covenant of the LORD, they sacrificed seven bulls and seven rams. 27David was clothed with a robe of fine linen, as also were all the Levites who were carrying the ark, and the singers, and Chenaniah the leader of the music of the singers; and David wore a linen ephod. 28So all Israel brought up the ark of the covenant of the LORD with shouting, to the sound of the horn, trumpets, and cymbals, and made loud music on harps and lyres.

29 As the ark of the covenant of the LORD came to the city of David, Michal daughter of Saul looked out of the window, and saw King David leaping and dancing; and she despised him in her heart.

15.11–29. 12: *He said to them:* The Chronicler typically interspersed speeches by the main figures of the narratives,* underlining his particular concerns at critical points. This same technique was often employed by ancient Greek historians as a way of enabling the reader to see what the historian believed were the crucial elements behind decisive actions. Here David un-

derscores the lineage of those to whom he is entrusting the ritual of moving the ark. This depiction stands in contrast to the earlier effort to move the ark, which ended in failure because *we did not give it proper care* (v. 13). For the Chronicler, maintenance of the community's relationship to God is directly related to the degree of care taken in approaching or handing holy things. **16:** *To raise loud sounds of joy:* For the Chronicler, events in which the community is united in worship are marked by joy and celebration. **22:** *Chenaniah . . . was to direct the music, for he understood it:* The word translated "music" here is difficult. This translation may well reflect the proper understanding of the passage, or the text may relate to the carrying or transporting of the ark. The emphasis is on having someone direct the process either of singing or carrying the ark because they know how to give it "proper care." **28:** *So all Israel brought up the ark of the covenant* of the LORD: Again the Chronicler's emphasis is on the unity of the community in undertaking a critical effort. **29:** *Michal daughter of Saul . . . saw King David leaping and dancing; and she despised him in her heart:* This is an abridged version of 2 Sam 6.20–23, but without the observation that David's nakedness disturbed Michal. The Chronicler may be trying to draw another contrast between Saul and David by portraying Michal's displeasure at David's joy in bringing the ark to Jerusalem.

16 They brought in the ark of God, and set it inside the tent that David had pitched for it; and they offered burnt offerings and offerings of well-being before God. 2When David had finished offering the burnt offerings and the offerings of well-being, he blessed the people in the name of the LORD; 3and he distributed to every person in Israel—man and woman alike—to each a loaf of bread, a portion of meat,*a* and a cake of raisins.

4 He appointed certain of the Levites as ministers before the ark of the LORD, to invoke, to thank, and to praise the LORD, the God of Israel. 5Asaph was the chief, and second to him Zechariah, Jeiel, Shemiramoth, Jehiel, Mattithiah, Eliab, Benaiah, Obed-edom, and Jeiel, with harps and lyres; Asaph was to sound the cymbals, 6and the priests

a Compare Gk Syr Vg: Meaning of Heb uncertain

Benaiah and Jahaziel were to blow trumpets regularly, before the ark of the covenant of God.

7 Then on that day David first appointed the singing of praises to the LORD by Asaph and his kindred.

16.1–7. 2: *When David had finished offering:* David is the only royal figure the Chronicler portrays positively when he acts in a priestly manner. He offers sacrifices and blesses the people, both priestly actions. **4:** *To invoke, to thank, and to praise the LORD, the God of Israel:* Each action is related to a specific type of Psalm: To invoke God's actions by the psalms of lament,* to thank God by a psalm of thanksgiving, and to praise God by one of the hymns in the Psalter. Through the offering of music before the ark these Levites act on behalf of the community. **7:** *The singing of praises to the LORD by Asaph and his kindred:* What follows is a psalm constructed from portions of several of the canonical* Psalms (96, 105, and 106), illustrating the praising, thanking, and invoking of God. It reflects the form of hymn composition common in the Chronicler's own day.

8 O give thanks to the LORD, call on his name,
    make known his deeds among the peoples.
9 Sing to him, sing praises to him,
    tell of all his wonderful works.
10 Glory in his holy name;
    let the hearts of those who seek the LORD rejoice.
11 Seek the LORD and his strength,
    seek his presence continually.
12 Remember the wonderful works he has done,
    his miracles, and the judgments he uttered,
13 O offspring of his servant Israel,ᵃ
    children of Jacob, his chosen ones.

14 He is the LORD our God;
    his judgments are in all the earth.
15 Remember his covenant forever,
    the word that he commanded, for a thousand generations,
16 the covenant that he made with Abraham,
    his sworn promise to Isaac,

17 which he confirmed to Jacob as a statute,
    to Israel as an everlasting covenant,
18 saying, "To you I will give the land of Canaan
    as your portion for an inheritance."

19 When they were few in number,
    of little account, and strangers in the land,ᵇ
20 wandering from nation to nation,
    from one kingdom to another people,
21 he allowed no one to oppress them;
    he rebuked kings on their account,
22 saying, "Do not touch my anointed ones;
    do my prophets no harm."

23 Sing to the LORD, all the earth.
    Tell of his salvation from day to day.
24 Declare his glory among the nations,
    his marvelous works among all the peoples.
25 For great is the LORD, and greatly to be praised;
    he is to be revered above all gods.
26 For all the gods of the peoples are idols,
    but the LORD made the heavens.
27 Honor and majesty are before him;
    strength and joy are in his place.

28 Ascribe to the LORD, O families of the peoples,
    ascribe to the LORD glory and strength.
29 Ascribe to the LORD the glory due his name;
    bring an offering, and come before him.
    Worship the LORD in holy splendor;
30   tremble before him, all the earth.
    The world is firmly established; it shall never be moved.
31 Let the heavens be glad, and let the earth rejoice,
    and let them say among the nations, "The LORD is king!"

a Another reading is *Abraham* (compare Ps 105.6)
b Heb *in it*

32 Let the sea roar, and all that fills it;
    let the field exult, and everything in
      it.
33 Then shall the trees of the forest sing
      for joy
    before the LORD, for he comes to
      judge the earth.
34 O give thanks to the LORD, for he is
      good;
    for his steadfast love endures forever.

35 Say also:
  "Save us, O God of our salvation,
    and gather and rescue us from among
      the nations,
  that we may give thanks to your holy
      name,
    and glory in your praise.
36 Blessed be the LORD, the God of Israel,
    from everlasting to everlasting."
Then all the people said "Amen!" and praised
the LORD.

37 David left Asaph and his kinsfolk there
before the ark of the covenant of the LORD
to minister regularly before the ark as each
day required, 38and also Obed-edom and
his*a* sixty-eight kinsfolk; while Obed-edom
son of Jeduthun and Hosah were to be gatekeepers. 39And he left the priest Zadok and
his kindred the priests before the tabernacle
of the LORD in the high place that was at
Gibeon, 40to offer burnt offerings to the
LORD on the altar of burnt offering regularly,
morning and evening, according to all that is
written in the law of the LORD that he commanded Israel. 41With them were Heman
and Jeduthun, and the rest of those chosen
and expressly named to render thanks to the
LORD, for his steadfast love endures forever.
42Heman and Jeduthun had with them
trumpets and cymbals for the music, and instruments for sacred song. The sons of Jeduthun were appointed to the gate.

16.39: *He left the priest Zadok . . . before the
tabernacle* of the LORD in the high place* that was at
Gibeon:* Since no permanent structure had been
erected in Jerusalem for the ark, sacrifices continue to
be offered at Gibeon. The author understands this activity to be in accord with God's wishes. This assessment is in contrast to the Deuteronomistic* History,

which sees any place of offering outside of Jerusalem
as problematical (1 Kings 3.3–4).

43 Then all the people departed to their
homes, and David went home to bless his
household.

17 Now when David settled in his
house, David said to the prophet Nathan, "I am living in a house of cedar, but
the ark of the covenant of the LORD is under
a tent." 2Nathan said to David, "Do all that
you have in mind, for God is with you."

17.1–27: The Davidic covenant.* Though he follows
his source (2 Sam 7.1–29) fairly closely, the Chronicler
makes a few adjustments to subtly shift the meaning
of several passages. These changes emphasize both
Solomon's coming kingdom as the fulfillment of the
promises to David and God's eternal rule over Israel.
1: *Now when David settled in his house:* The setting
of the promises to David in the Chronicler's history
makes much more sense than in 2 Samuel. Here, David
has just returned to his home, and in this opening David realizes how well-provided his own palace is in contrast to the tent that houses the ark.

3 But that same night the word of the
LORD came to Nathan, saying: 4Go and tell
my servant David: Thus says the LORD: You
shall not build me a house to live in. 5For I
have not lived in a house since the day I
brought out Israel to this very day, but I have
lived in a tent and a tabernacle.*b* 6Wherever
I have moved about among all Israel, did I
ever speak a word with any of the judges of
Israel, whom I commanded to shepherd my
people, saying, Why have you not built me a
house of cedar? 7Now therefore thus you
shall say to my servant David: Thus says the
LORD of hosts: I took you from the pasture,
from following the sheep, to be ruler over my
people Israel; 8and I have been with you
wherever you went, and have cut off all your
enemies before you; and I will make for you
a name, like the name of the great ones of
the earth. 9I will appoint a place for my people Israel, and will plant them, so that they
may live in their own place, and be disturbed

a Gk Syr Vg: Heb *their*   *b* Gk 2 Sam 7.6: Heb *but I
have been from tent to tent and from tabernacle*

no more; and evildoers shall wear them down no more, as they did formerly, ¹⁰from the time that I appointed judges over my people Israel; and I will subdue all your enemies.

Moreover I declare to you that the LORD will build you a house. ¹¹When your days are fulfilled to go to be with your ancestors, I will raise up your offspring after you, one of your own sons, and I will establish his kingdom. ¹²He shall build a house for me, and I will establish his throne forever. ¹³I will be a father to him, and he shall be a son to me. I will not take my steadfast love from him, as I took it from him who was before you, ¹⁴but I will confirm him in my house and in my kingdom forever, and his throne shall be established forever. ¹⁵In accordance with all these words and all this vision, Nathan spoke to David.

16 Then King David went in and sat before the LORD, and said, "Who am I, O LORD God, and what is my house, that you have brought me thus far? ¹⁷And even this was a small thing in your sight, O God; you have also spoken of your servant's house for a great while to come. You regard me as someone of high rank,ᵃ O LORD God! ¹⁸And what more can David say to you for honoring your servant? You know your servant. ¹⁹For your servant's sake, O LORD, and according to your own heart, you have done all these great deeds, making known all these great things. ²⁰There is no one like you, O LORD, and there is no God besides you, according to all that we have heard with our ears. ²¹Who is like your people Israel, one nation on the earth whom God went to redeem to be his people, making for yourself a name for great and terrible things, in driving out nations before your people whom you redeemed from Egypt? ²²And you made your people Israel to be your people forever; and you, O LORD, became their God.

23 "And now, O LORD, as for the word that you have spoken concerning your servant and concerning his house, let it be established forever, and do as you have promised. ²⁴Thus your name will be established and magnified forever in the saying, 'The LORD of hosts, the God of Israel, is Israel's God'; and the house of your servant David

will be established in your presence. ²⁵For you, my God, have revealed to your servant that you will build a house for him; therefore your servant has found it possible to pray before you. ²⁶And now, O LORD, you are God, and you have promised this good thing to your servant; ²⁷therefore may it please you to bless the house of your servant, that it may continue forever before you. For you, O LORD, have blessed and are blessedᵇ forever."

17.3–27. 10: *And I will subdue all your enemies:* Unlike 2 Samuel where this statement is in the past tense, the Chronicler places it in the future, anticipating the conditions that will make it possible to build the Temple.★ **14:** *I will confirm him in my house and in my kingdom:* In 2 Samuel, the promise is that David's house (dynasty★) and kingdom will be established forever. The Chronicler here affirms a strongly theocratic perspective: The kingdom belongs to God, not some successor from David's line. **16:** *Then King David went in and sat before the LORD:* David's response of overwhelming gratitude to God is taken without major alteration from 2 Samuel.

David's military success
18.1–20.8: A precondition of God's promise to David was that God would subdue all the king's enemies. This motif★ becomes the primary point of these closing chapters on David's reign, recounting his great success against a variety of the surrounding peoples. While many of the individual sections closely follow their sources in 2 Samuel, the Chronicler has lifted them from several different settings to combine them for a more dramatic effect.

18 Some time afterward, David attacked the Philistines and subdued them; he took Gath and its villages from the Philistines.

2 He defeated Moab, and the Moabites became subject to David and brought tribute.

3 David also struck down King Hadadezer of Zobah, toward Hamath,ᵃ as he went to set up a monument at the river Euphrates. ⁴David took from him one thousand chariots, seven thousand cavalry, and twenty

ᵃ Meaning of Heb uncertain   ᵇ Or *and it is blessed*

thousand foot soldiers. David hamstrung all the chariot horses, but left one hundred of them. 5 When the Arameans of Damascus came to help King Hadadezer of Zobah, David killed twenty-two thousand Arameans. 6 Then David put garrisons*a* in Aram of Damascus; and the Arameans became subject to David, and brought tribute. The LORD gave victory to David wherever he went. 7 David took the gold shields that were carried by the servants of Hadadezer, and brought them to Jerusalem. 8 From Tibhath and from Cun, cities of Hadadezer, David took a vast quantity of bronze; with it Solomon made the bronze sea and the pillars and the vessels of bronze.

18.6–8. 6: *The LORD gave victory to David wherever he went:* For the Chronicler, it is God's support, not David's skill as a warrior, that ensures the victory. **8:** *David took a vast quantity of bronze:* Not in the Chronicler's source, this aside underlies the author's concern to show that the fabrication of the Temple* was the combined work of both David and Solomon.

9 When King Tou of Hamath heard that David had defeated the whole army of King Hadadezer of Zobah, 10 he sent his son Hadoram to King David, to greet him and to congratulate him, because he had fought against Hadadezer and defeated him. Now Hadadezer had often been at war with Tou. He sent all sorts of articles of gold, of silver, and of bronze; 11 these also King David dedicated to the LORD, together with the silver and gold that he had carried off from all the nations, from Edom, Moab, the Ammonites, the Philistines, and Amalek.

18.11: *These also King David dedicated to the LORD, together with the silver and gold that he carried off:* Though this information is present in 2 Samuel, here the emphasis is on David's setting aside these items for God to prepare for construction of the Temple.

12 Abishai son of Zeruiah killed eighteen thousand Edomites in the Valley of Salt. 13 He put garrisons in Edom; and all the Edomites became subject to David. And the LORD gave victory to David wherever he went.

14 So David reigned over all Israel; and he administered justice and equity to all his people. 15 Joab son of Zeruiah was over the army; Jehoshaphat son of Ahilud was recorder; 16 Zadok son of Ahitub and Ahimelech son of Abiathar were priests; Shavsha was secretary; 17 Benaiah son of Jehoiada was over the Cherethites and the Pelethites; and David's sons were the chief officials in the service of the king.

19 Some time afterward, King Nahash of the Ammonites died, and his son succeeded him. 2 David said, "I will deal loyally with Hanun son of Nahash, for his father dealt loyally with me." So David sent messengers to console him concerning his father. When David's servants came to Hanun in the land of the Ammonites, to console him, 3 the officials of the Ammonites said to Hanun, "Do you think, because David has sent consolers to you, that he is honoring your father? Have not his servants come to you to search and to overthrow and to spy out the land?" 4 So Hanun seized David's servants, shaved them, cut off their garments in the middle at their hips, and sent them away; 5 and they departed. When David was told about the men, he sent messengers to them, for they felt greatly humiliated. The king said, "Remain at Jericho until your beards have grown, and then return."

6 When the Ammonites saw that they had made themselves odious to David, Hanun and the Ammonites sent a thousand talents of silver to hire chariots and cavalry from Mesopotamia, from Aram-maacah and from Zobah. 7 They hired thirty-two thousand chariots and the king of Maacah with his army, who came and camped before Medeba. And the Ammonites were mustered from their cities and came to battle. 8 When David heard of it, he sent Joab and all the army of the warriors. 9 The Ammonites came out and drew up in battle array at the entrance of the city, and the kings who had come were by themselves in the open country.

10 When Joab saw that the line of battle was set against him both in front and in the

a Gk Vg 2 Sam 8.6 Compare Syr: Heb lacks *garrisons*

rear, he chose some of the picked men of Israel and arrayed them against the Arameans; [11] the rest of his troops he put in the charge of his brother Abishai, and they were arrayed against the Ammonites. [12] He said, "If the Arameans are too strong for me, then you shall help me; but if the Ammonites are too strong for you, then I will help you. [13] Be strong, and let us be courageous for our people and for the cities of our God; and may the LORD do what seems good to him." [14] So Joab and the troops who were with him advanced toward the Arameans for battle; and they fled before him. [15] When the Ammonites saw that the Arameans fled, they likewise fled before Abishai, Joab's brother, and entered the city. Then Joab came to Jerusalem.

16 But when the Arameans saw that they had been defeated by Israel, they sent messengers and brought out the Arameans who were beyond the Euphrates, with Shophach the commander of the army of Hadadezer at their head. [17] When David was informed, he gathered all Israel together, crossed the Jordan, came to them, and drew up his forces against them. When David set the battle in array against the Arameans, they fought with him. [18] The Arameans fled before Israel; and David killed seven thousand Aramean charioteers and forty thousand foot soldiers, and also killed Shophach the commander of their army. [19] When the servants of Hadadezer saw that they had been defeated by Israel, they made peace with David, and became subject to him. So the Arameans were not willing to help the Ammonites any more.

19.18: *David killed seven thousand Aramean charioteers and forty thousand foot soldiers:* In 2 Sam 10.18, the number of charioteers is given as seven hundred. The Chronicler has a pronounced tendency to prefer larger numbers, which may be the result of misunderstanding the numbers of his source, or a deliberate revision in light of military practices of his own day. David's slaughter of so many during his military campaigns comes back to haunt him as a reason that he cannot build the Temple★ (1 Chr 22.8).

20 In the spring of the year, the time when kings go out to battle, Joab led out the army, ravaged the country of the Ammonites, and came and besieged Rabbah. But David remained at Jerusalem. Joab attacked Rabbah, and overthrew it. [2] David took the crown of Milcom[a] from his head; he found that it weighed a talent of gold, and in it was a precious stone; and it was placed on David's head. He also brought out the booty of the city, a very great amount. [3] He brought out the people who were in it, and set them to work[b] with saws and iron picks and axes.[c] Thus David did to all the cities of the Ammonites. Then David and all the people returned to Jerusalem.

4 After this, war broke out with the Philistines at Gezer; then Sibbecai the Hushathite killed Sippai, who was one of the descendants of the giants; and the Philistines were subdued. [5] Again there was war with the Philistines; and Elhanan son of Jair killed Lahmi the brother of Goliath the Gittite, the shaft of whose spear was like a weaver's beam. [6] Again there was war at Gath, where there was a man of great size, who had six fingers on each hand, and six toes on each foot, twenty-four in number; he also was descended from the giants. [7] When he taunted Israel, Jonathan son of Shimea, David's brother, killed him. [8] These were descended from the giants in Gath; they fell by the hand of David and his servants.

20.5: *Elhanan son of Jair killed Lahmi the brother of Goliath:* It appears the Chronicler is deliberately trying to harmonize two different traditions in 1 and 2 Samuel—that David killed Goliath (1 Sam 17) and that Elhanan the Bethlehemite killed Goliath (2 Sam 21.19).

TRANSITION IN REIGNS

Chs. 21–29: While David is still clearly on the throne, this section provides a number of points of continuity between David's reign, which is ending, and Solomon's, which is beginning. Along the way, David makes all the necessary provisions to ensure the successful completion of the Temple★ and the continuing

a Gk Vg See 1 Kings 11.5, 33: MT *of their king*
b Compare 2 Sam 12.31: Heb *and he sawed*
c Compare 2 Sam 12.31: Heb *saws*

growth of Jerusalem. The Chronicler's version is in marked contrast to the opening chapters of 1 Kings where Solomon apparently gains the throne at the last minute thanks to the resourceful intervention of the prophet* Nathan and Solomon's mother Bathsheba. While palace infighting and splits among the influential court officials are evident in the account of 1 Kings, Chronicles has "all Israel" along with all the royal household and high court officials enthusiastically support Solomon as David's successor. This revision of the process by which Solomon gains the throne underlines the Chronicler's concern about presenting a positive model of community unity as a way of preparing to "seek God." It also shows that the completion of the Temple was accomplished by the legitimate heir of David's throne, who fulfilled David's intention to build the Temple.

21 Satan stood up against Israel, and incited David to count the people of Israel. ²So David said to Joab and the commanders of the army, "Go, number Israel, from Beer-sheba to Dan, and bring me a report, so that I may know their number." ³But Joab said, "May the LORD increase the number of his people a hundredfold! Are they not, my lord the king, all of them my lord's servants? Why then should my lord require this? Why should he bring guilt on Israel?" ⁴But the king's word prevailed against Joab. So Joab departed and went throughout all Israel, and came back to Jerusalem. ⁵Joab gave the total count of the people to David. In all Israel there were one million one hundred thousand men who drew the sword, and in Judah four hundred seventy thousand who drew the sword. ⁶But he did not include Levi and Benjamin in the numbering, for the king's command was abhorrent to Joab.

21.1–27: The plague against Israel. Following on the heels of David's string of military victories, disaster strikes in the form of a plague triggered by David's taking of a census. While the Chronicler has closely followed his source in 2 Sam 24, the author has also made significant alterations to bring into strong relief several critical themes. **1:** *Satan stood up against Israel:* This is the only place in the Hebrew Bible where Satan appears as a proper name. In Job and Zech 3 "the Satan" appears as an agent of God, but here Satan acts as an agent opposed to God. Why a census of the peo-

ple would be considered such a grievous offense is unclear. Possibly the Chronicler thought such a census presumed human ownership of the kingdom that in reality was God's, thus inciting God's anger. **5:** *In all Israel there were one million one hundred thousand men who drew the sword:* 2 Samuel has 800,000, but the Chronicler may have been thinking the numbers in 2 Samuel did not include some of the other tribes, hence his assumption of a larger number.

7 But God was displeased with this thing, and he struck Israel. ⁸David said to God, "I have sinned greatly in that I have done this thing. But now, I pray you, take away the guilt of your servant; for I have done very foolishly." ⁹The LORD spoke to Gad, David's seer, saying, ¹⁰"Go and say to David, 'Thus says the LORD: Three things I offer you; choose one of them, so that I may do it to you.'" ¹¹So Gad came to David and said to him, "Thus says the LORD, 'Take your choice: ¹²either three years of famine; or three months of devastation by your foes, while the sword of your enemies overtakes you; or three days of the sword of the LORD, pestilence on the land, and the angel of the LORD destroying throughout all the territory of Israel.' Now decide what answer I shall return to the one who sent me." ¹³Then David said to Gad, "I am in great distress; let me fall into the hand of the LORD, for his mercy is very great; but let me not fall into human hands."

21.7–13. 7: *God was displeased with this thing, and he struck Israel:* This is an addition by the Chronicler. In 2 Sam 24, following Joab's report David realizes his sin and repents before God. For the Chronicler, the realization of sin most often follows on some direct word or action. The author offers no suggestion as to what is meant by God *struck* Israel. **13:** *David said to Gad, "I am in great distress; let me fall into the hand of the LORD":* The Chronicler's source has "let us," putting the emphasis on the welfare of the community. The Chronicler has instead subtly shifted the focus onto David.

14 So the LORD sent a pestilence on Israel; and seventy thousand persons fell in Israel. ¹⁵And God sent an angel to Jerusalem to destroy it; but when he was about to de-

stroy it, the LORD took note and relented concerning the calamity; he said to the destroying angel, "Enough! Stay your hand." The angel of the LORD was then standing by the threshing floor of Ornan the Jebusite. [16]David looked up and saw the angel of the LORD standing between earth and heaven, and in his hand a drawn sword stretched out over Jerusalem. Then David and the elders, clothed in sackcloth, fell on their faces. [17]And David said to God, "Was it not I who gave the command to count the people? It is I who have sinned and done very wickedly. But these sheep, what have they done? Let your hand, I pray, O LORD my God, be against me and against my father's house; but do not let your people be plagued!"

21.15: *And God sent an angel to Jerusalem to destroy it:* As the center of David's human reign, special judgment was reserved for Jerusalem. God's recognition of the impeding disaster triggered the mercy that David had hoped for. *The angel of the LORD was then standing by the threshing* ★ *floor of Ornan the Jebusite:* A threshing floor was usually located on an exposed height where a steady wind would be available to allow the separation of the chaff ★ from the grain. When David and the elders of Israel see the angel, they repent immediately.

18 Then the angel of the LORD commanded Gad to tell David that he should go up and erect an altar to the LORD on the threshing floor of Ornan the Jebusite. [19]So David went up following Gad's instructions, which he had spoken in the name of the LORD. [20]Ornan turned and saw the angel; and while his four sons who were with him hid themselves, Ornan continued to thresh wheat. [21]As David came to Ornan, Ornan looked and saw David; he went out from the threshing floor, and did obeisance to David with his face to the ground. [22]David said to Ornan, "Give me the site of the threshing floor that I may build on it an altar to the LORD—give it to me at its full price—so that the plague may be averted from the people." [23]Then Ornan said to David, "Take it; and let my lord the king do what seems good to him; see, I present the oxen for burnt offerings, and the threshing sledges for the wood,

and the wheat for a grain offering. I give it all." [24]But King David said to Ornan, "No; I will buy them for the full price. I will not take for the LORD what is yours, nor offer burnt offerings that cost me nothing." [25]So David paid Ornan six hundred shekels of gold by weight for the site. [26]David built there an altar to the LORD and presented burnt offerings and offerings of well-being. He called upon the LORD, and he answered him with fire from heaven on the altar of burnt offering. [27]Then the LORD commanded the angel, and he put his sword back into its sheath.

21.18–27. 18: *Then the angel of the LORD commanded Gad to tell David that he should go up and erect an altar to the LORD on the threshing floor:* In 2 Samuel Gad goes directly to David without prompting. The Chronicler wants the reader to understand more clearly that the foundation of the Temple ★ is the result of divine initiative, so an angel prompts Gad to pass along the command to build an altar. There is a tradition in the Bible of marking places of divine disclosure by building altars. **26:** *He called upon the LORD, and he answered him with fire from heaven on the altar of burnt offering:* In 2 Samuel God hears David's appeal and averts the plague. The Chronicler has reworked this simpler report into a miraculous affirmation of God's choice of the location, with echoes of the inauguration of Aaron's priesthood (Lev 9.24) and Elijah's victory over the prophets ★ of Baal ★ (1 Kings 18.38).

28 At that time, when David saw that the LORD had answered him at the threshing floor of Ornan the Jebusite, he made his sacrifices there. [29]For the tabernacle of the LORD, which Moses had made in the wilderness, and the altar of burnt offering were at that time in the high place at Gibeon; [30]but David could not go before it to inquire of God, for he was afraid of the sword of the angel of the LORD. [1]Then David said, "Here shall be the house of the LORD God and here the altar of burnt offering for Israel."

2 David gave orders to gather together the aliens who were residing in the land of Israel, and he set stonecutters to prepare dressed stones for building the house of God. [3]David

also provided great stores of iron for nails for the doors of the gates and for clamps, as well as bronze in quantities beyond weighing, ⁴and cedar logs without number—for the Sidonians and Tyrians brought great quantities of cedar to David. ⁵For David said, "My son Solomon is young and inexperienced, and the house that is to be built for the LORD must be exceedingly magnificent, famous and glorified throughout all lands; I will therefore make preparation for it." So David provided materials in great quantity before his death.

21.28–22.19: Preparations for the Temple. * While 2 Sam 24 does not explicitly draw the connection between the resolution of the plague and the selection of the site for the Temple, the Chronicler makes certain the connection is clear. The Chronicler also makes the connection with David explicit by having David make extraordinary provision for a building his son will actually build. Using the device of a major speech, this section ends with David giving voice to some of the most characteristic themes of the Chronicler's history. Most of this material does not appear in 2 Samuel. **21.28:** *He made his sacrifices there* refers to David's own personal sacrifices in contrast to the sacrifices made to stay the plague. **29:** *The high place* * at Gibeon:* While Gibeon was an important religious center, only the Chronicler attests a tradition that the tabernacle* and altar were present there (16.39). **30:** *For he was afraid of the sword of the angel:* Though the plague had been stayed, just prior to the vision of the angel over Jerusalem David had offered himself and his lineage in place of the larger community (21.17). To go into the presence of God at a location other than the one where God had stayed his judgment, in the Chronicler's view, would have exposed David to potential harm. **22.1:** *Here shall be the house of the LORD God and here the altar of burnt offering for Israel:* The house of the LORD is the standard title for the Temple. The altar of burnt offering for Israel is the place where the annual sacrifice for the atonement* of the community's sins could be made. **5:** *The house that is to be built for the LORD must be exceedingly magnificent, famous and glorified throughout all lands:* The Chronicler wants the Temple to be a stunning accomplishment not for the glory of David or Solomon, but to bring the world's attention to Israel's god.

⁶ Then he called for his son Solomon and charged him to build a house for the LORD, the God of Israel. ⁷David said to Solomon, "My son, I had planned to build a house to the name of the LORD my God. ⁸But the word of the LORD came to me, saying, 'You have shed much blood and have waged great wars; you shall not build a house to my name, because you have shed so much blood in my sight on the earth. ⁹See, a son shall be born to you; he shall be a man of peace. I will give him peace from all his enemies on every side; for his name shall be Solomon,^a and I will give peace^b and quiet to Israel in his days. ¹⁰He shall build a house for my name. He shall be a son to me, and I will be a father to him, and I will establish his royal throne in Israel forever.' ¹¹Now, my son, the LORD be with you, so that you may succeed in building the house of the LORD your God, as he has spoken concerning you. ¹²Only, may the LORD grant you discretion and understanding, so that when he gives you charge over Israel you may keep the law of the LORD your God. ¹³Then you will prosper if you are careful to observe the statutes and the ordinances that the LORD commanded Moses for Israel. Be strong and of good courage. Do not be afraid or dismayed. ¹⁴With great pains I have provided for the house of the LORD one hundred thousand talents of gold, one million talents of silver, and bronze and iron beyond weighing, for there is so much of it; timber and stone too I have provided. To these you must add more. ¹⁵You have an abundance of workers: stonecutters, masons, carpenters, and all kinds of artisans without number, skilled in working ¹⁶gold, silver, bronze, and iron. Now begin the work, and the LORD be with you."

¹⁷ David also commanded all the leaders of Israel to help his son Solomon, saying, ¹⁸"Is not the LORD your God with you? Has he not given you peace on every side? For he has delivered the inhabitants of the land into my hand; and the land is subdued before the LORD and his people. ¹⁹Now set your mind and heart to seek the LORD your God. Go and build the sanctuary of the LORD God so

a Heb *Shelomoh*   *b* Heb *shalom*

that the ark of the covenant of the LORD and the holy vessels of God may be brought into a house built for the name of the LORD."

22.6–19. 6: *He called for his son Solomon and charged him to build a house for the LORD:* Given the conditions of the promise made to David and his line in ch. 17, David's charge to Solomon carries the strong implication that Solomon will succeed his father on the throne. **8:** *But the word of the LORD came to me, saying, "You have shed much blood":* The opening wording of this verse suggests a message from a prophet.* The shedding of blood is not, in and of itself, an offense that would make one ritually impure. The Chronicler is seeking a larger purpose here, to connect the Temple* and Jerusalem—City of Peace. Solomon, because his name can be understood as "Man of peace," will be the builder of the Temple; David, man of war, cannot build it. **12:** *Only, may the LORD grant you discretion and understanding, so that . . . you may keep the law of the LORD:* This is a reflection of 1 Kings 3 where God grants Solomon an understanding mind and the ability to discern between good and evil. The Chronicler's version narrows the scope of Solomon's fabled* wisdom by defining its purpose as directing one in the law. **13:** *Be strong and of good courage. Do not be afraid or be dismayed:* The thing feared is not specified. This is the language of "holy war,"* used prominently in Joshua (see Josh 1.9). **19:** *Now set your mind and heart to seek the LORD your God:* David's call for the leaders of Israel to help Solomon is also a tacit call for them to recognize his legitimacy as king. For the Chronicler, part of maintaining a relationship with God involves the willful seeking after God, as David calls on the leadership to do.

23 When David was old and full of days, he made his son Solomon king over Israel.

2 David assembled all the leaders of Israel and the priests and the Levites. ³The Levites, thirty years old and upward, were counted, and the total was thirty-eight thousand. ⁴"Twenty-four thousand of these," David said, "shall have charge of the work in the house of the LORD, six thousand shall be officers and judges, ⁵four thousand gatekeepers, and four thousand shall offer praises to the LORD with the instruments that I have made for praise." ⁶And David organized them in divisions corresponding to

the sons of Levi: Gershon,ᵃ Kohath, and Merari.

7 The sons of Gershonᵇ were Ladan and Shimei. ⁸The sons of Ladan: Jehiel the chief, Zetham, and Joel, three. ⁹The sons of Shimei: Shelomoth, Haziel, and Haran, three. These were the heads of families of Ladan. ¹⁰And the sons of Shimei: Jahath, Zina, Jeush, and Beriah. These four were the sons of Shimei. ¹¹Jahath was the chief, and Zizah the second; but Jeush and Beriah did not have many sons, so they were enrolled as a single family.

12 The sons of Kohath: Amram, Izhar, Hebron, and Uzziel, four. ¹³The sons of Amram: Aaron and Moses. Aaron was set apart to consecrate the most holy things, so that he and his sons forever should make offerings before the LORD, and minister to him and pronounce blessings in his name forever; ¹⁴but as for Moses the man of God, his sons were to be reckoned among the tribe of Levi. ¹⁵The sons of Moses: Gershom and Eliezer. ¹⁶The sons of Gershom: Shebuel the chief. ¹⁷The sons of Eliezer: Rehabiah the chief; Eliezer had no other sons, but the sons of Rehabiah were very numerous. ¹⁸The sons of Izhar: Shelomith the chief. ¹⁹The sons of Hebron: Jeriah the chief, Amariah the second, Jahaziel the third, and Jekameam the fourth. ²⁰The sons of Uzziel: Micah the chief and Isshiah the second.

21 The sons of Merari: Mahli and Mushi. The sons of Mahli: Eleazar and Kish. ²²Eleazar died having no sons, but only daughters; their kindred, the sons of Kish, married them. ²³The sons of Mushi: Mahli, Eder, and Jeremoth, three.

24 These were the sons of Levi by their ancestral houses, the heads of families as they were enrolled according to the number of the names of the individuals from twenty years old and upward who were to do the work for the service of the house of the LORD. ²⁵For David said, "The LORD, the God of Israel, has given rest to his people; and he resides in Jerusalem forever. ²⁶And so the Levites no longer need to carry the

---

a Or *Gershom*; See 1 Chr 6.1, note, and 23.15
b Vg Compare Gk Syr: Heb *to the Gershonite*

tabernacle or any of the things for its service"— 27for according to the last words of David these were the number of the Levites from twenty years old and upward— 28"but their duty shall be to assist the descendants of Aaron for the service of the house of the LORD, having the care of the courts and the chambers, the cleansing of all that is holy, and any work for the service of the house of God; 29to assist also with the rows of bread, the choice flour for the grain offering, the wafers of unleavened bread, the baked offering, the offering mixed with oil, and all measures of quantity or size. 30And they shall stand every morning, thanking and praising the LORD, and likewise at evening, 31and whenever burnt offerings are offered to the LORD on sabbaths, new moons, and appointed festivals, according to the number required of them, regularly before the LORD. 32Thus they shall keep charge of the tent of meeting and the sanctuary, and shall attend the descendants of Aaron, their kindred, for the service of the house of the LORD."

23.1–32: The appointment of the Levites. By the Chronicler's day, the personnel involved in the administration of formal religious observance were divided broadly into two groups. The priests were those of the tribe of Levi who came from the line of Aaron, the brother of Moses. From the ranks of the priests the High Priest was chosen, and the priests were the only ones who could offer sacrifices in the Temple.* The larger group of Temple personnel consisted of members of the tribe of Levi who had lineages different from Aaron's line. These were apparently organized in a variety of guilds with various forms of service within the Temple and/or the formal religious life of the community. **3:** *The Levites, thirty years old and upward, were counted* following the general date when they could begin official duties (Num 4.3). **6:** *David organized them in divisions corresponding to the sons of Levi:* This wording may mean David simply organized them into three divisions and used the traditional names of Levi's sons as a way to delineate them. **25:** *He resides in Jerusalem forever:* One of the Chronicler's chief purposes is to convince his readers of the importance of Jerusalem despite the disasters it has experienced in the past. The divine presence residing in Jerusalem meant that no other religious center held the same importance for worship that Jerusalem now held,

thus diminishing Gibeon, where the Chronicler places the tabernacle* and the altar of burnt offering.

〰〰〰〰〰〰〰

24 The divisions of the descendants of Aaron were these. The sons of Aaron: Nadab, Abihu, Eleazar, and Ithamar. 2But Nadab and Abihu died before their father, and had no sons; so Eleazar and Ithamar became the priests. 3Along with Zadok of the sons of Eleazar, and Ahimelech of the sons of Ithamar, David organized them according to the appointed duties in their service. 4Since more chief men were found among the sons of Eleazar than among the sons of Ithamar, they organized them under sixteen heads of ancestral houses of the sons of Eleazar, and eight of the sons of Ithamar. 5They organized them by lot, all alike, for there were officers of the sanctuary and officers of God among both the sons of Eleazar and the sons of Ithamar. 6The scribe Shemaiah son of Nethanel, a Levite, recorded them in the presence of the king, and the officers, and Zadok the priest, and Ahimelech son of Abiathar, and the heads of ancestral houses of the priests and of the Levites; one ancestral house being chosen for Eleazar and one chosen for Ithamar.

7 The first lot fell to Jehoiarib, the second to Jedaiah, 8the third to Harim, the fourth to Seorim, 9the fifth to Malchijah, the sixth to Mijamin, 10the seventh to Hakkoz, the eighth to Abijah, 11the ninth to Jeshua, the tenth to Shecaniah, 12the eleventh to Eliashib, the twelfth to Jakim, 13the thirteenth to Huppah, the fourteenth to Jeshebeab, 14the fifteenth to Bilgah, the sixteenth to Immer, 15the seventeenth to Hezir, the eighteenth to Happizzez, 16the nineteenth to Pethahiah, the twentieth to Jehezkel, 17the twenty-first to Jachin, the twenty-second to Gamul, 18the twenty-third to Delaiah, the twenty-fourth to Maaziah. 19These had as their appointed duty in their service to enter the house of the LORD according to the procedure established for them by their ancestor Aaron, as the LORD God of Israel had commanded him.

24.1–19: The appointment of the priests. The priests held the foremost position within the Temple.* Their service in the Temple was divided into a sequence of twenty-four divisions, each of which was on duty for half a month out of the year.

~~~~~~

20 And of the rest of the sons of Levi: of the sons of Amram, Shubael; of the sons of Shubael, Jehdeiah. 21 Of Rehabiah: of the sons of Rehabiah, Isshiah the chief. 22 Of the Izharites, Shelomoth; of the sons of Shelomoth, Jahath. 23 The sons of Hebron:ᵃ Jeriah the chief,ᵇ Amariah the second, Jahaziel the third, Jekameam the fourth. 24 The sons of Uzziel, Micah; of the sons of Micah, Shamir. 25 The brother of Micah, Isshiah; of the sons of Isshiah, Zechariah. 26 The sons of Merari: Mahli and Mushi. The sons of Jaaziah: Beno.ᶜ 27 The sons of Merari: of Jaaziah, Beno,ᶜ Shoham, Zaccur, and Ibri. 28 Of Mahli: Eleazar, who had no sons. 29 Of Kish, the sons of Kish: Jerahmeel. 30 The sons of Mushi: Mahli, Eder, and Jerimoth. These were the sons of the Levites according to their ancestral houses. 31 These also cast lots corresponding to their kindred, the descendants of Aaron, in the presence of King David, Zadok, Ahimelech, and the heads of ancestral houses of the priests and of the Levites, the chief as well as the youngest brother.

24.20–31: Updating the appointments of Levites. This section fits very poorly in its present setting. There is no introduction to the section, and the material largely repeats 1 Chr 23.6–23, but with additions to the various family lines, suggesting that the narrative* has been revised to provide an updating of the listing of the Levites, ending with twenty-four courses of Levites to match the twenty-four courses of the priests.

~~~~~~

25 David and the officers of the army also set apart for the service the sons of Asaph, and of Heman, and of Jeduthun, who should prophesy with lyres, harps, and cymbals. The list of those who did the work and of their duties was: 2 Of the sons of Asaph: Zaccur, Joseph, Nethaniah, and Asarelah, sons of Asaph, under the direction of Asaph, who prophesied under the direction of the king. 3 Of Jeduthun, the sons of Jeduthun: Gedaliah, Zeri, Jeshaiah, Shimei,ᵈ Hashabiah, and Mattithiah, six, under the direction of their father Jeduthun, who prophesied with the lyre in thanksgiving and praise to the LORD. 4 Of Heman, the sons of Heman: Bukkiah, Mattaniah, Uzziel, Shebuel, and Jerimoth, Hananiah, Hanani, Eliathah, Giddalti, and Romamti-ezer, Joshbekashah, Mallothi, Hothir, Mahazioth. 5 All these were the sons of Heman the king's seer, according to the promise of God to exalt him; for God had given Heman fourteen sons and three daughters. 6 They were all under the direction of their father for the music in the house of the LORD with cymbals, harps, and lyres for the service of the house of God. Asaph, Jeduthun, and Heman were under the order of the king. 7 They and their kindred, who were trained in singing to the LORD, all of whom were skillful, numbered two hundred eighty-eight. 8 And they cast lots for their duties, small and great, teacher and pupil alike.

9 The first lot fell for Asaph to Joseph; the second to Gedaliah, to him and his brothers and his sons, twelve; 10 the third to Zaccur, his sons and his brothers, twelve; 11 the fourth to Izri, his sons and his brothers, twelve; 12 the fifth to Nethaniah, his sons and his brothers, twelve; 13 the sixth to Bukkiah, his sons and his brothers, twelve; 14 the seventh to Jesarelah,ᵉ his sons and his brothers, twelve; 15 the eighth to Jeshaiah, his sons and his brothers, twelve; 16 the ninth to Mattaniah, his sons and his brothers, twelve; 17 the tenth to Shimei, his sons and his brothers, twelve; 18 the eleventh to Azarel, his sons and his brothers, twelve; 19 the twelfth to Hashabiah, his sons and his brothers, twelve; 20 to the thirteenth, Shubael, his sons and his brothers, twelve; 21 to the fourteenth, Mattithiah, his sons and his brothers, twelve; 22 to the fifteenth, to Jeremoth, his sons and his brothers, twelve; 23 to the sixteenth, to Hananiah, his sons and his brothers, twelve; 24 to the seventeenth, to Joshbekashah, his sons and his brothers, twelve; 25 to the eighteenth, to Hanani, his sons and his brothers, twelve; 26 to the nine-

---

a See 23.19: Heb lacks *Hebron*   *b* See 23.19: Heb lacks *the chief*   *c* Or *his son*: Meaning of Heb uncertain   *d* One Ms: Gk: MT lacks *Shimei*   *e* Or *Asarelah*; see 25.2

teenth, to Mallothi, his sons and his brothers, twelve; 27to the twentieth, to Eliathah, his sons and his brothers, twelve; 28to the twenty-first, to Hothir, his sons and his brothers, twelve; 29to the twenty-second, to Giddalti, his sons and his brothers, twelve; 30to the twenty-third, to Mahazioth, his sons and his brothers, twelve; 31to the twenty-fourth, to Romamti-ezer, his sons and his brothers, twelve.

25.1–31: The appointment of musical service. Music as a part of the formal worship conducted in the Temple* almost certainly predates the Exile.* However, the intricacy of the musical arrangements for Temple service reflected in Chronicles more likely represents the forms known by the Chronicler.

---

26 As for the divisions of the gatekeepers: of the Korahites, Meshelemiah son of Kore, of the sons of Asaph. 2Meshelemiah had sons: Zechariah the firstborn, Jediael the second, Zebadiah the third, Jathniel the fourth, 3Elam the fifth, Jehohanan the sixth, Eliehoenai the seventh. 4Obed-edom had sons: Shemaiah the firstborn, Jehozabad the second, Joah the third, Sachar the fourth, Nethanel the fifth, 5Ammiel the sixth, Issachar the seventh, Peullethai the eighth; for God blessed him. 6Also to his son Shemaiah sons were born who exercised authority in their ancestral houses, for they were men of great ability. 7The sons of Shemaiah: Othni, Rephael, Obed, and Elzabad, whose brothers were able men, Elihu and Semachiah. 8All these, sons of Obed-edom with their sons and brothers, were able men qualified for the service; sixty-two of Obed-edom. 9Meshelemiah had sons and brothers, able men, eighteen. 10Hosah, of the sons of Merari, had sons: Shimri the chief (for though he was not the firstborn, his father made him chief), 11Hilkiah the second, Tebaliah the third, Zechariah the fourth: all the sons and brothers of Hosah totaled thirteen.

12 These divisions of the gatekeepers, corresponding to their leaders, had duties, just as their kindred did, ministering in the house of the LORD; 13and they cast lots by ancestral houses, small and great alike, for their gates. 14The lot for the east fell to Shelemiah. They cast lots also for his son Zechariah, a prudent counselor, and his lot came out for the north. 15Obed-edom's came out for the south, and to his sons was allotted the storehouse. 16For Shuppim and Hosah it came out for the west, at the gate of Shallecheth on the ascending road. Guard corresponded to guard. 17On the east there were six Levites each day,a on the north four each day, on the south four each day, as well as two and two at the storehouse; 18and for the colonnadeb on the west there were four at the road and two at the colonnade.b 19These were the divisions of the gatekeepers among the Korahites and the sons of Merari.

26.1–19: The appointment of the gatekeepers. The Temple* precincts were entered by means of a series of gateways, with each gate guarded by Levites. In David's day, there would have been no reason to have such officials appointed, but the Chronicler wants to present all major Temple assignments as coming from David to emphasize the importance of the Temple.

---

20 And of the Levites, Ahijah had charge of the treasuries of the house of God and the treasuries of the dedicated gifts. 21The sons of Ladan, the sons of the Gershonites belonging to Ladan, the heads of families belonging to Ladan the Gershonite: Jehieli.c

22 The sons of Jehieli, Zetham and his brother Joel, were in charge of the treasuries of the house of the LORD. 23Of the Amramites, the Izharites, the Hebronites, and the Uzzielites: 24Shebuel son of Gershom, son of Moses, was chief officer in charge of the treasuries. 25His brothers: from Eliezer were his son Rehabiah, his son Jeshaiah, his son Joram, his son Zichri, and his son Shelomoth. 26This Shelomoth and his brothers were in charge of all the treasuries of the dedicated gifts that King David, and the heads of families, and the officers of the thousands and the hundreds, and the commanders of the army, had dedicated. 27From booty won in battles they dedicated gifts for

---

a Gk: Heb lacks *each day*   b Heb *parbar*: meaning uncertain   c The Hebrew text of verse 21 is confused

the maintenance of the house of the LORD. 28Also all that Samuel the seer, and Saul son of Kish, and Abner son of Ner, and Joab son of Zeruiah had dedicated—all dedicated gifts were in the care of Shelomoth*a* and his brothers.

26.20–28: The appointment of financial overseers. David and his warriors had already been reported as making substantial donations from their military booty to the Temple.* Keeping watch over these resources as well as future revenues was a responsibility of one of the Levitical orders.

29 Of the Izharites, Chenaniah and his sons were appointed to outside duties for Israel, as officers and judges. 30Of the Hebronites, Hashabiah and his brothers, one thousand seven hundred men of ability, had the oversight of Israel west of the Jordan for all the work of the LORD and for the service of the king. 31Of the Hebronites, Jerijah was chief of the Hebronites. (In the fortieth year of David's reign search was made, of whatever genealogy or family, and men of great ability among them were found at Jazer in Gilead.) 32King David appointed him and his brothers, two thousand seven hundred men of ability, heads of families, to have the oversight of the Reubenites, the Gadites, and the half-tribe of the Manassites for everything pertaining to God and for the affairs of the king.

26.29–32: The appointment of judicial officials. One of the Chronicler's themes is the responsibility of royal figures for ensuring the proper observance of religious regulations. The appointment of Levitical groups for this responsibility accords with other evidence that the Levites explained the meaning of the law to worshippers (see Neh 8.7–8). **32:** *Everything pertaining to God and for the affairs of the king:* As royal appointees, though their primary duties may relate to religious matters, they could also be called upon to administer royal regulations.

27 This is the list of the people of Israel, the heads of families, the commanders of the thousands and the hundreds, and their officers who served the king in all matters concerning the divisions that came and went, month after month throughout the year, each division numbering twenty-four thousand:

2 Jashobeam son of Zabdiel was in charge of the first division in the first month; in his division were twenty-four thousand. 3He was a descendant of Perez, and was chief of all the commanders of the army for the first month. 4Dodai the Ahohite was in charge of the division of the second month; Mikloth was the chief officer of his division. In his division were twenty-four thousand. 5The third commander, for the third month, was Benaiah son of the priest Jehoiada, as chief; in his division were twenty-four thousand. 6This is the Benaiah who was a mighty man of the Thirty and in command of the Thirty; his son Ammizabad was in charge of his division.*b* 7Asahel brother of Joab was fourth, for the fourth month, and his son Zebadiah after him; in his division were twenty-four thousand. 8The fifth commander, for the fifth month, was Shamhuth, the Izrahite; in his division were twenty-four thousand. 9Sixth, for the sixth month, was Ira son of Ikkesh the Tekoite; in his division were twenty-four thousand. 10Seventh, for the seventh month, was Helez the Pelonite, of the Ephraimites; in his division were twenty-four thousand. 11Eighth, for the eighth month, was Sibbecai the Hushathite, of the Zerahites; in his division were twenty-four thousand. 12Ninth, for the ninth month, was Abiezer of Anathoth, a Benjaminite; in his division were twenty-four thousand. 13Tenth, for the tenth month, was Maharai of Netophah, of the Zerahites; in his division were twenty-four thousand. 14Eleventh, for the eleventh month, was Benaiah of Pirathon, of the Ephraimites; in his division were twenty-four thousand. 15Twelfth, for the twelfth month, was Heldai the Netophathite, of Othniel; in his division were twenty-four thousand.

16 Over the tribes of Israel, for the Reubenites, Eliezer son of Zichri was chief officer; for the Simeonites, Shephatiah son of Maacah; 17for Levi, Hashabiah son of

a Gk Compare 26.28: Heb *Shelomith* *b* Gk Vg: Heb *Ammizabad was his division*

Kemuel; for Aaron, Zadok; 18for Judah, Elihu, one of David's brothers; for Issachar, Omri son of Michael; 19for Zebulun, Ishmaiah son of Obadiah; for Naphtali, Jerimoth son of Azriel; 20for the Ephraimites, Hoshea son of Azaziah; for the half-tribe of Manasseh, Joel son of Pedaiah; 21for the half-tribe of Manasseh in Gilead, Iddo son of Zechariah; for Benjamin, Jaasiel son of Abner; 22for Dan, Azarel son of Jeroham. These were the leaders of the tribes of Israel. 23David did not count those below twenty years of age, for the LORD had promised to make Israel as numerous as the stars of heaven. 24Joab son of Zeruiah began to count them, but did not finish; yet wrath came upon Israel for this, and the number was not entered into the account of the Annals of King David.

27.1–24: The military organization of the kingdom. The Chronicler believes national security depends on seeking God in the proper way. Having arrayed the various levels of priests and Levites, and thus having arranged for the proper seeking of God, the Chronicler posits David attending to the ordering of military affairs. The overall description is of a conscripted army that would be called together in the event of national emergency. Each tribe presents 24,000 men (twice 12,000), to be available for service each month of the year, on a parallel with the priestly service. The names of the various commanders seem to be largely drawn from the list of David's heroes found in 1 Chr 11. **23:** *David did not count those below twenty years of age, for the LORD had promised to make Israel as numerous as the stars of heaven:* Twenty years of age was the point at which most men would have already been married and had children (Num 1.3). The reference to God's promise refers to the time of Abraham, when God promised his descendants would be as numerous as the stars (Gen 15.5; 22.17).

~~~~~~~

25 Over the king's treasuries was Azmaveth son of Adiel. Over the treasuries in the country, in the cities, in the villages and in the towers, was Jonathan son of Uzziah. 26Over those who did the work of the field, tilling the soil, was Ezri son of Chelub. 27Over the vineyards was Shimei the Ramathite. Over the produce of the vineyards for the wine cellars was Zabdi the Shiphmite.

28Over the olive and sycamore trees in the Shephelah was Baal-hanan the Gederite. Over the stores of oil was Joash. 29Over the herds that pastured in Sharon was Shitrai the Sharonite. Over the herds in the valleys was Shaphat son of Adlai. 30Over the camels was Obil the Ishmaelite. Over the donkeys was Jehdeiah the Meronothite. Over the flocks was Jaziz the Hagrite. 31All these were stewards of King David's property.

32 Jonathan, David's uncle, was a counselor, being a man of understanding and a scribe; Jehiel son of Hachmoni attended the king's sons. 33Ahithophel was the king's counselor, and Hushai the Archite was the king's friend. 34After Ahithophel came Jehoiada son of Benaiah, and Abiathar. Joab was commander of the king's army.

27.25–34: Miscellaneous royal officials. Just as the military affairs were placed in proper order by David, the Chronicler notes David's efforts at organizing the affairs of the royal administration. Stewards were needed for the various royal properties that were part of the king's wealth.

~~~~~~~

28 David assembled at Jerusalem all the officials of Israel, the officials of the tribes, the officers of the divisions that served the king, the commanders of the thousands, the commanders of the hundreds, the stewards of all the property and cattle of the king and his sons, together with the palace officials, the mighty warriors, and all the warriors. 2Then King David rose to his feet and said: "Hear me, my brothers and my people. I had planned to build a house of rest for the ark of the covenant of the LORD, for the footstool of our God; and I made preparations for building. 3But God said to me, 'You shall not build a house for my name, for you are a warrior and have shed blood.' 4Yet the LORD God of Israel chose me from all my ancestral house to be king over Israel forever; for he chose Judah as leader, and in the house of Judah my father's house, and among my father's sons he took delight in making me king over all Israel. 5And of all my sons, for the LORD has given me many, he has chosen my son Solomon to sit upon the throne of the kingdom of the

LORD over Israel. 6He said to me, 'It is your son Solomon who shall build my house and my courts, for I have chosen him to be a son to me, and I will be a father to him. 7I will establish his kingdom forever if he continues resolute in keeping my commandments and my ordinances, as he is today.' 8Now therefore in the sight of all Israel, the assembly of the LORD, and in the hearing of our God, observe and search out all the commandments of the LORD your God; that you may possess this good land, and leave it for an inheritance to your children after you forever.

9 "And you, my son Solomon, know the God of your father, and serve him with single mind and willing heart; for the LORD searches every mind, and understands every plan and thought. If you seek him, he will be found by you; but if you forsake him, he will abandon you forever. 10Take heed now, for the LORD has chosen you to build a house as the sanctuary; be strong, and act."

11 Then David gave his son Solomon the plan of the vestibule of the temple, and of its houses, its treasuries, its upper rooms, and its inner chambers, and of the room for the mercy seat;ᵃ 12and the plan of all that he had in mind: for the courts of the house of the LORD, all the surrounding chambers, the treasuries of the house of God, and the treasuries for dedicated gifts; 13for the divisions of the priests and of the Levites, and all the work of the service in the house of the LORD; for all the vessels for the service in the house of the LORD, 14the weight of gold for all golden vessels for each service, the weight of silver vessels for each service, 15the weight of the golden lampstands and their lamps, the weight of gold for each lampstand and its lamps, the weight of silver for a lampstand and its lamps, according to the use of each in the service, 16the weight of gold for each table for the rows of bread, the silver for the silver tables, 17and pure gold for the forks, the basins, and the cups; for the golden bowls and the weight of each; for the silver bowls and the weight of each; 18for the altar of incense made of refined gold, and its weight; also his plan for the golden chariot of the cherubim that spread their wings and covered the ark of the covenant of the LORD.

19 "All this, in writing at the LORD's direction, he made clear to me—the plan of all the works."

20 David said further to his son Solomon, "Be strong and of good courage, and act. Do not be afraid or dismayed; for the LORD God, my God, is with you. He will not fail you or forsake you, until all the work for the service of the house of the LORD is finished. 21Here are the divisions of the priests and the Levites for all the service of the house of God; and with you in all the work will be every volunteer who has skill for any kind of service; also the officers and all the people will be wholly at your command."

28.1–21: David's charge to Solomon. Employing again the royal speech as a means of giving voice to his own concerns, the Chronicler has David offer this important charge at the conclusion of organizing the community for the future. **2:** *A house of rest for the ark of the covenant* of the LORD, for the footstool of our God:* These are terms found in Ps 132, which praises God for having chosen Jerusalem as his eternal dwelling place. **8:** *In the sight of all Israel, the assembly of the LORD, and in the hearing of our God:* The whole community is proclaimed to be the "assembly" or corporate entity of God. As with other settings, it is "all Israel" that receives the unified resolve of the leadership. **9:** *If you seek him, he will be found by you; but if you forsake him, he will abandon you forever:* In brief, this is the Chronicler's primary theology. **11:** *Then David gave his son Solomon the plan,* as in the design and manner of ordering. **19:** *All this, in writing at the LORD's direction, he made clear to me:* David functions as a prophetic* figure, receiving the ordering of the Temple* just as Moses received the law from God. In effect, the Chronicler places the commands of David and the commands of Moses on equal footing, making the proper order of the Temple rituals as essential as the Mosaic regulations for what one may eat.

29 King David said to the whole assembly, "My son Solomon, whom alone God has chosen, is young and inexperienced, and the work is great; for the templeᵇ will not be for mortals but for the LORD God. 2So

ᵃ Or *the cover*   ᵇ Heb *fortress*

I have provided for the house of my God, so far as I was able, the gold for the things of gold, the silver for the things of silver, and the bronze for the things of bronze, the iron for the things of iron, and wood for the things of wood, besides great quantities of onyx and stones for setting, antimony, colored stones, all sorts of precious stones, and marble in abundance. ³Moreover, in addition to all that I have provided for the holy house, I have a treasure of my own of gold and silver, and because of my devotion to the house of my God I give it to the house of my God: ⁴three thousand talents of gold, of the gold of Ophir, and seven thousand talents of refined silver, for overlaying the walls of the house, ⁵and for all the work to be done by artisans, gold for the things of gold and silver for the things of silver. Who then will offer willingly, consecrating themselves today to the LORD?"

6 Then the leaders of ancestral houses made their freewill offerings, as did also the leaders of the tribes, the commanders of the thousands and of the hundreds, and the officers over the king's work. ⁷They gave for the service of the house of God five thousand talents and ten thousand darics of gold, ten thousand talents of silver, eighteen thousand talents of bronze, and one hundred thousand talents of iron. ⁸Whoever had precious stones gave them to the treasury of the house of the LORD, into the care of Jehiel the Gershonite. ⁹Then the people rejoiced because these had given willingly, for with single mind they had offered freely to the LORD; King David also rejoiced greatly.

10 Then David blessed the LORD in the presence of all the assembly; David said: "Blessed are you, O LORD, the God of our ancestor Israel, forever and ever. ¹¹Yours, O LORD, are the greatness, the power, the glory, the victory, and the majesty; for all that is in the heavens and on the earth is yours; yours is the kingdom, O LORD, and you are exalted as head above all. ¹²Riches and honor come from you, and you rule over all. In your hand are power and might; and it is in your hand to make great and to give

strength to all. ¹³And now, our God, we give thanks to you and praise your glorious name.

29.1–22a: Provision of offerings for construction. Having made arrangements for the funding of the building of the Temple,* it now remains for David to make one last gesture of his devotion to God. **3:** *I have a treasure of my own of gold and silver, and because of my devotion to the house of my God I give it to the house of my God:* David gives of his own personal wealth to accomplish the building of the Temple. **9:** *Then the people rejoiced because these had given willingly, for with single mind they had offered freely to the LORD:* The assembled company of people are touched by this demonstration of personal commitment. The Chronicler highlights the unity of purpose. **11:** *Yours is the kingdom, O LORD:* This underscores the concept that the kingdom of Israel is God's, not the line of David's.

---

14 "But who am I, and what is my people, that we should be able to make this freewill offering? For all things come from you, and of your own have we given you. ¹⁵For we are aliens and transients before you, as were all our ancestors; our days on the earth are like a shadow, and there is no hope. ¹⁶O LORD our God, all this abundance that we have provided for building you a house for your holy name comes from your hand and is all your own. ¹⁷I know, my God, that you search the heart, and take pleasure in uprightness; in the uprightness of my heart I have freely offered all these things, and now I have seen your people, who are present here, offering freely and joyously to you. ¹⁸O LORD, the God of Abraham, Isaac, and Israel, our ancestors, keep forever such purposes and thoughts in the hearts of your people, and direct their hearts toward you. ¹⁹Grant to my son Solomon that with single mind he may keep your commandments, your decrees, and your statutes, performing all of them, and that he may build the temple*ᵃ* for which I have made provision."

20 Then David said to the whole assembly, "Bless the LORD your God." And all the assembly blessed the LORD, the God of their

---

a Heb *fortress*

ancestors, and bowed their heads and prostrated themselves before the LORD and the king. 21On the next day they offered sacrifices and burnt offerings to the LORD, a thousand bulls, a thousand rams, and a thousand lambs, with their libations, and sacrifices in abundance for all Israel; 22and they ate and drank before the LORD on that day with great joy.

29.14–22a. 18: *Keep forever such purposes and thoughts in the hearts of your people:* The Chronicler uses David's prayer to remind his audience of the need for proper piety. **22:** *And they ate and drank before the LORD on that day with great joy:* When the community is unified in purpose and commitment, then worship results in great joy for all Israel, a recurring motif★ in the Chronicler's history.

They made David's son Solomon king a second time; they anointed him as the LORD's prince, and Zadok as priest. 23Then Solomon sat on the throne of the LORD, succeeding his father David as king; he prospered, and all Israel obeyed him. 24All the leaders and the mighty warriors, and also all the sons of King David, pledged their allegiance to King Solomon. 25The LORD highly exalted Solomon in the sight of all Israel, and bestowed upon him such royal majesty as had not been on any king before him in Israel.

26 Thus David son of Jesse reigned over all Israel. 27The period that he reigned over Israel was forty years; he reigned seven years in Hebron, and thirty-three years in Jerusalem. 28He died in a good old age, full of days, riches, and honor; and his son Solomon succeeded him. 29Now the acts of King David, from first to last, are written in the records of the seer Samuel, and in the records of the prophet Nathan, and in the records of the seer Gad, 30with accounts of all his rule and his might and of the events that befell him and Israel and all the kingdoms of the earth.

29.22b–30: Summary of the transition. This section accomplishes two main tasks: providing the reader with a preview of Solomon's successful reign, and closing out the narratives★ on David. **22b:** *They made David's son Solomon king a second time:* "They" refers to the assembled officialdom and people of Israel, who had already affirmed Solomon as king in ch. 22. The appointment of Solomon as *the LORD's prince* underscores the Chronicler's point that the kingdom is God's, and the line of David rules not by divine right but by permission of God. **24:** *All the leaders . . . pledged their allegiance to King Solomon:* This revises the account of courtly dissension in 1 Kings 1. Unity of the community is an important theme to the Chronicler's presentation. **28:** *His son Solomon succeeded him* is a further affirmation of the legitimacy of Solomon's rule. **29:** *Written in the records of the seer Samuel:* It is uncertain if the Chronicler is referring to the canonical★ books of 1 and 2 Samuel by this title. The *records of the prophet★ Nathan* and *records of the seer Gad* are unknown outside of Chronicles and may constitute literary devices designed to lend authenticity to the narrative.

2 CHRONICLES

Introduction

The Access Bible treats 1 and 2 Chronicles as a single work; for convenience the introductory material from 1 Chronicles is repeated here.

The Chronicler offers his readers a history of what was important from the community's (namely Judah's) past, something quite different from the earlier narratives* of 1 and 2 Samuel and 1 and 2 Kings. While the Deuteronomistic* History (Judges through 2 Kings) tries to justify the destruction of both the northern kingdom of Israel and the southern kingdom of Judah by showing how both communities turned their backs on God by practicing idolatry,* the Chronicler is more concerned to present a positive model from Israel's past. Starting with David as an example, the narratives that stand out in the Chronicler's history are those in which the community or king respond faithfully to God, finding unity and security in response. Good kings are those who "seek the LORD," and in return they experience military and economic success, and their subjects experience great joy in gathering before the Temple* in Jerusalem for worship. These positive models are intended to speak to the Chronicler's readers, to convince them that in "seeking the LORD" at the Temple in their own day, they will find their fullest sense of purpose and community.

The narratives of the Chronicler's history abound with historical problems from the view of a modern reader. David makes provision for the use of marble in building the Temple (1 Chr 29.2); however, marble was not used in Jerusalem until the Hellenistic* age seven hundred years later. David collects "10,000 darics" (1 Chr 29.7) for the Temple, a coin of the Persian empire 500 years after the Davidic period. Impossibly large numbers of military forces are mustered in the field (300,000 from Judah, 280,000 from Benjamin, facing a "million" from Egypt; 2 Chr 14.8–9), and stock numbers are often used (for example, Shishak of Egypt attacks with "1,200 chariots and 60,000 chariots," playing on the number 12 and its multiples; 2 Chr 12.3). The Chronicler never mentions David's transgression in taking Bathsheba as wife (2 Sam 11–12), nor for that matter Solomon's fall into idolatry (1 Kings 11). These tendencies are similar to Hellenistic historians of the same general period, suggesting the Chronicler is simply writing about the past with commonly accepted, perhaps even expected, conventions.

Part of the dilemma over the historical value of 1 and 2 Chronicles involves what potential sources the author had at his disposal. The author cites a number of sources that are otherwise unknown; however, the general stylistic uniformity between narratives where sources are mentioned and where none are indicated raises the suspicion that such sources may not have existed. There is no conclusive evidence to support the Chronicler's use of any sources other than 1 Samuel through 2 Kings.

In its original form, the Hebrew Chronicles would have filled one single scroll. Its division into two parts was accomplished when the codex or book-form of transmitting literature became the standard, probably in the early centuries CE.

While numerous proposals have been offered for the date of the Chronicler's composition, perhaps the most telling points are the interest in military matters and the result of "peace" when the community "seeks the LORD." Following the death of Alexander the Great (around 330 BCE), his successors fought incessantly with each other, often across the landscape of Palestine. Archaeological evidence demonstrates that in the last decades of the fourth century BCE nearly every urban center in Palestine suffered military destruction. It was not until the Ptolemaic✶ rulers of Egypt suppressed their Syrian rivals that peace came to Palestine in the early second century BCE. In the midst of such turmoil, a message focusing on the peace that "seeking the LORD" might bring would have been particularly powerful.

The author focuses almost exclusively on the events affecting Jerusalem and the Temple. With regard to the Temple, the author shows particular interest in the activities of the priesthood and individuals given prominence in Temple affairs. Many scholars conclude that the author was a member of the Temple priesthood.

READING GUIDE

When recounting a story of Israel's past, the Chronicler skillfully weaves personal encounters and community responses. A characteristic narrative is the account of the reign of Judah's King Asa (2 Chr 14–16). It opens with the land having "rest," in part because Asa "did what was good and right" in God's view and "commanded Judah to seek the LORD" (2 Chr 14.4). He orders his people to build fortifications around the urban areas since "the land is still ours because we have sought the LORD our God . . . and he has given us peace on every side" (2 Chr 14.7). This sense of security is challenged by Zerah the "Ethiopian," who comes with a million-man army to attack Judah. Asa offers a simple petition for help, and "the LORD defeated the Ethiopians" (2 Chr 14.12). Fresh from this great victory, the Chronicler has an otherwise unattested prophet✶ confront the king in a decisive way. This is similar to the style of the Greek historian Herodotus, who uses the figures of various wise counselors to present a ruler with a choice to follow wisdom or pride. In Asa's case, it is "Azariah the son of Oded" who gives voice to the central theological theme of the Chronicler: "The LORD is with you, while you are with him. If you seek him, he will be found by you, but if you abandon him, he will abandon you" (2 Chr 15.2). Taking heart from the prophet's message, Asa convenes all his subjects (Judah and Benjamin) as well as those faithful from the northern kingdom who had joined with Judah (2 Chr 15.9–10). After sacrificing to God, the assembled populace "entered into covenant✶ to seek the LORD, the God of their ancestors, with all their heart and with all their soul" (v. 12), an echo of Israel's basic credo of Deut 6.4–5. To emphasize the seriousness of this act, the Chronicler adds that whoever did not join with the covenant "should be put to death" (v. 13). Not wanting to close on a negative note, the Chronicler portrays the community enthusiastically embracing this arrangement: "All Judah rejoiced over the oath; for they had sworn with all their heart, and had sought him with their whole desire, and he was found by them, and the LORD gave them rest all around" (v. 15). This is a paradigm that the Chronicler uses frequently: the king being presented with the need to "seek" God and then the community actively and joyously embracing God.

1 Chronicles

1–9   Genealogical✶ prologue

10–20   David's reign

21–29   Transition (centrality of the Temple)

2 Chronicles

1–9   Solomon's rule

10–36   Dissolution of Judah

SOLOMON'S REIGN

Chs. 1–9: These chapters emphasize the success of Solomon as king over Israel. They attribute that success to Solomon's careful fulfillment of all that David had planned, particularly with regard to the Temple* and the conduct of proper worship. One of the basic points made in this section is that the Temple is the result of the combined efforts of David and Solomon. The Chronicler closely follows his source in 1 Kings 1–11, but by selective editing and rearranging, he creates his own distinctive understanding of Solomon's importance.

1 Solomon son of David established himself in his kingdom; the LORD his God was with him and made him exceedingly great. 2 Solomon summoned all Israel, the commanders of the thousands and of the hundreds, the judges, and all the leaders of all Israel, the heads of families. ³Then Solomon, and the whole assembly with him, went to the high place that was at Gibeon; for God's tent of meeting, which Moses the servant of the LORD had made in the wilderness, was there. ⁴(But David had brought the ark of God up from Kiriath-jearim to the place that David had prepared for it; for he had pitched a tent for it in Jerusalem.) ⁵Moreover the bronze altar that Bezalel son of Uri, son of Hur, had made, was there in front of the tabernacle of the LORD. And Solomon and the assembly inquired at it. ⁶Solomon went up there to the bronze altar before the LORD, which was at the tent of meeting, and offered a thousand burnt offerings on it.

7 That night God appeared to Solomon, and said to him, "Ask what I should give you." ⁸Solomon said to God, "You have shown great and steadfast love to my father David, and have made me succeed him as king. ⁹O LORD God, let your promise to my father David now be fulfilled, for you have made me king over a people as numerous as the dust of the earth. ¹⁰Give me now wisdom and knowledge to go out and come in before this people, for who can rule this great people of yours?" ¹¹God answered Solomon,

"Because this was in your heart, and you have not asked for possessions, wealth, honor, or the life of those who hate you, and have not even asked for long life, but have asked for wisdom and knowledge for yourself that you may rule my people over whom I have made you king, ¹²wisdom and knowledge are granted to you. I will also give you riches, possessions, and honor, such as none of the kings had who were before you, and none after you shall have the like." ¹³So Solomon came from*ᵃ the high place at Gibeon, from the tent of meeting, to Jerusalem. And he reigned over Israel.

14 Solomon gathered together chariots and horses; he had fourteen hundred chariots and twelve thousand horses, which he stationed in the chariot cities and with the king in Jerusalem. ¹⁵The king made silver and gold as common in Jerusalem as stone, and he made cedar as plentiful as the sycamore of the Shephelah. ¹⁶Solomon's horses were imported from Egypt and Kue; the king's traders received them from Kue at the prevailing price. ¹⁷They imported from Egypt, and then exported, a chariot for six hundred shekels of silver, and a horse for one hundred fifty; so through them these were exported to all the kings of the Hittites and the kings of Aram.

1.1–17: Solomon's wisdom. This section sets the stage for the following narratives,* which develop Solomon's concern with building the Temple.* **1:** *Solomon son of David established himself in his kingdom:* It is not clear when the Chronicler understood this to be happening; he may conceive of Solomon's sacrifice occurring just after David's death. **2:** *Solomon summoned all Israel:* The community is unified in worship. **3:** *The high place* that was at Gibeon:* In 1 Kings 3, Solomon's going to Gibeon was viewed negatively since the Deuteronomistic* Historian saw any worship center outside of Jerusalem as heretical. For the Chronicler, Gibeon is the place where the tabernacle* and the altar of burnt offering are situated, and going there to worship is thereby acceptable. **10:** *Give me now wisdom and knowledge to go out and come in before this people* is a rephrasing of the Chronicler's source (1 Kings 3.9), where Solomon requests wisdom to

a Gk Vg: Heb *to*

know good and evil in order to be able to govern. In this rephrasing, Solomon is asking for wisdom to know how to conduct his life as king, a broader goal. **13:** *So Solomon came from the high place at Gibeon:* The Chronicler leaves out the narrative in his source (1 Kings 3.16–28) of Solomon's deciding between two prostitutes claiming the same child. In Kings, the story illustrates how Solomon's wisdom allows him to discern where justice lay and how to execute it. Since the Chronicler sees Solomon's wisdom as leading him to build the Temple, such a powerful story would be distracting. **15:** *The king made silver and gold as common in Jerusalem as stone:* The overview of Solomon's achievements serves to confirm how shrewdly he could conduct himself.

2 ^aSolomon decided to build a temple for the name of the LORD, and a royal palace for himself. 2^bSolomon conscripted seventy thousand laborers and eighty thousand stonecutters in the hill country, with three thousand six hundred to oversee them.

3 Solomon sent word to King Huram of Tyre: "Once you dealt with my father David and sent him cedar to build himself a house to live in. 4I am now about to build a house for the name of the LORD my God and dedicate it to him for offering fragrant incense before him, and for the regular offering of the rows of bread, and for burnt offerings morning and evening, on the sabbaths and the new moons and the appointed festivals of the LORD our God, as ordained forever for Israel. 5The house that I am about to build will be great, for our God is greater than other gods. 6But who is able to build him a house, since heaven, even highest heaven, cannot contain him? Who am I to build a house for him, except as a place to make offerings before him? 7So now send me an artisan skilled to work in gold, silver, bronze, and iron, and in purple, crimson, and blue fabrics, trained also in engraving, to join the skilled workers who are with me in Judah and Jerusalem, whom my father David provided. 8Send me also cedar, cypress, and algum timber from Lebanon, for I know that your servants are skilled in cutting Lebanon timber. My servants will work with your servants 9to prepare timber for me in abundance, for the house I am about to build will

be great and wonderful. 10I will provide for your servants, those who cut the timber, twenty thousand cors of crushed wheat, twenty thousand cors of barley, twenty thousand baths^c of wine, and twenty thousand baths of oil."

11 Then King Huram of Tyre answered in a letter that he sent to Solomon, "Because the LORD loves his people he has made you king over them." 12Huram also said, "Blessed be the LORD God of Israel, who made heaven and earth, who has given King David a wise son, endowed with discretion and understanding, who will build a temple for the LORD, and a royal palace for himself.

13 "I have dispatched Huram-abi, a skilled artisan, endowed with understanding, 14the son of one of the Danite women, his father a Tyrian. He is trained to work in gold, silver, bronze, iron, stone, and wood, and in purple, blue, and crimson fabrics and fine linen, and to do all sorts of engraving and execute any design that may be assigned him, with your artisans, the artisans of my lord, your father David. 15Now, as for the wheat, barley, oil, and wine, of which my lord has spoken, let him send them to his servants. 16We will cut whatever timber you need from Lebanon, and bring it to you as rafts by sea to Joppa; you will take it up to Jerusalem."

17 Then Solomon took a census of all the aliens who were residing in the land of Israel, after the census that his father David had taken; and there were found to be one hundred fifty-three thousand six hundred. 18Seventy thousand of them he assigned as laborers, eighty thousand as stonecutters in the hill country, and three thousand six hundred as overseers to make the people work.

2.1–18: Preparation for building the Temple. ✻ The Chronicler now turns to Solomon's actively putting into place the pieces for assembling the Temple. Much of this portion has used 1 Kings 5.1–18, but the rearranging and supplementation has created a very different narrative. ✻ **1:** *Solomon decided to build a tem-*

a Ch 1.18 in Heb   *b* Ch 2.1 in Heb   *c* A Hebrew measure of volume

ple for the name of the LORD: Taken by itself, this statement seems odd given all the earlier commands David had given Solomon. However, these verses introduce what follows; *decided* means Solomon has resolved on his own to undertake the Temple. **4:** *I am now about to build a house for the name of the LORD my God:* Clarifying the meaning of v. 1, Solomon is ready to put the preparations for the Temple into action. *As ordained forever for Israel:* The Chronicler understands the regular appointed festivals to be an eternal obligation for Israel. The offerings specified prior to this conclusion are drawn from several different places in the Pentateuch.* **11:** *Because the LORD loves his people he has made you king over them:* Solomon, in the author's view, does not rule because of the promise God made to David, but because of God's great love for the community. **12:** *Blessed be the LORD God of Israel, who made heaven and earth:* Spoken by Huram of Tyre, this is the classic expression for those outside Israel about Israel's unique faith (see Jon 1.9). It is the only place where the Chronicler makes such a clear statement concerning creation. **13:** *I have dispatched Huram-abi, a skilled artisan, endowed with understanding:* In the original source (1 Kings 7.14) the artisan is identified as a specialist only in bronze. The Chronicler expands this description to create a parallel between Huram-abi and the figure of Bezalel, who assisted Moses in fabricating the tabernacle* (Ex 31.1–5), thus creating a parallel between the tabernacle in the wilderness and the Temple in Jerusalem. Solomon's census of the aliens was intended to support Temple construction, not to assess military strength, so it was not objectionable to God as David's had been. The term "aliens" relates to residual Canaanite groups still inhabiting the land. For the Chronicler, they cannot be considered part of Israel.

3 Solomon began to build the house of the LORD in Jerusalem on Mount Moriah, where the LORD had appeared to his father David, at the place that David had designated, on the threshing floor of Ornan the Jebusite. ²He began to build on the second day of the second month of the fourth year of his reign. ³These are Solomon's measurements*a* for building the house of God: the length, in cubits of the old standard, was sixty cubits, and the width twenty cubits. ⁴The vestibule in front of the nave of the house was twenty cubits long, across the width of the house;*b* and its height was one

hundred twenty cubits. He overlaid it on the inside with pure gold. ⁵The nave he lined with cypress, covered it with fine gold, and made palms and chains on it. ⁶He adorned the house with settings of precious stones. The gold was gold from Parvaim. ⁷So he lined the house with gold—its beams, its thresholds, its walls, and its doors; and he carved cherubim on the walls.

3.1–5.1: Construction of the Temple. * In this elaborate section, the Chronicler relies mainly on 1 Kings but adds points and elements of his own. **3.1:** *Solomon began to build the house of the LORD in Jerusalem on Mount Moriah:* Only in Chronicles is the Temple mount identified as the place where Abraham nearly sacrificed his son Isaac before God (Gen 22). **3:** *In cubits of the old standard,* possibly before the cubit was standardized in Judean practice. The cubit was a measure of linear size; the older standard was more than 17 inches. **6:** *The gold was gold from Parvaim,* an unknown place that may have produced highly refined gold.

---

8 He made the most holy place; its length, corresponding to the width of the house, was twenty cubits, and its width was twenty cubits; he overlaid it with six hundred talents of fine gold. ⁹The weight of the nails was fifty shekels of gold. He overlaid the upper chambers with gold.

10 In the most holy place he made two carved cherubim and overlaid*c* them with gold. ¹¹The wings of the cherubim together extended twenty cubits: one wing of the one, five cubits long, touched the wall of the house, and its other wing, five cubits long, touched the wing of the other cherub; ¹²and of this cherub, one wing, five cubits long, touched the wall of the house, and the other wing, also five cubits long, was joined to the wing of the first cherub. ¹³The wings of these cherubim extended twenty cubits; the cherubim*d* stood on their feet, facing the nave. ¹⁴And Solomon*e* made the curtain of blue and purple and crimson fabrics and fine linen, and worked cherubim into it.

a Syr: Heb *foundations*   *b* Compare 1 Kings 6.3: Meaning of Heb uncertain   *c* Heb *they overlaid*   *d* Heb *they*   *e* Heb *he*

3.14: *And Solomon made the curtain of blue and purple and crimson fabrics:* The term for "curtain" has more the sense of "veil." In Solomon's Temple a door separated the inner chamber from the rest of the building. In the rebuilt Temple of the post-exilic period, a veil served the same purpose, but the description the Chronicler offers is more like the veil in the tabernacle* (Ex 26.31–32).

15 In front of the house he made two pillars thirty-five cubits high, with a capital of five cubits on the top of each. 16He made encircling*a* chains and put them on the tops of the pillars; and he made one hundred pomegranates, and put them on the chains. 17He set up the pillars in front of the temple, one on the right, the other on the left; the one on the right he called Jachin, and the one on the left, Boaz.

4 He made an altar of bronze, twenty cubits long, twenty cubits wide, and ten cubits high. 2Then he made the molten sea; it was round, ten cubits from rim to rim, and five cubits high. A line of thirty cubits would encircle it completely. 3Under it were panels all around, each of ten cubits, surrounding the sea; there were two rows of panels, cast when it was cast. 4It stood on twelve oxen, three facing north, three facing west, three facing south, and three facing east; the sea was set on them. The hindquarters of each were toward the inside. 5Its thickness was a handbreadth; its rim was made like the rim of a cup, like the flower of a lily; it held three thousand baths.*b* 6He also made ten basins in which to wash, and set five on the right side, and five on the left. In these they were to rinse what was used for the burnt offering. The sea was for the priests to wash in.

7 He made ten golden lampstands as prescribed, and set them in the temple, five on the south side and five on the north. 8He also made ten tables and placed them in the temple, five on the right side and five on the left. And he made one hundred basins of gold. 9He made the court of the priests, and the great court, and doors for the court; he overlaid their doors with bronze. 10He set the sea at the southeast corner of the house.

11 And Huram made the pots, the shovels, and the basins. Thus Huram finished the work that he did for King Solomon on the house of God: 12the two pillars, the bowls, and the two capitals on the top of the pillars; and the two latticeworks to cover the two bowls of the capitals that were on the top of the pillars; 13the four hundred pomegranates for the two latticeworks, two rows of pomegranates for each latticework, to cover the two bowls of the capitals that were on the pillars. 14He made the stands, the basins on the stands, 15the one sea, and the twelve oxen underneath it. 16The pots, the shovels, the forks, and all the equipment for these Huram-abi made of burnished bronze for King Solomon for the house of the LORD. 17In the plain of the Jordan the king cast them, in the clay ground between Succoth and Zeredah. 18Solomon made all these things in great quantities, so that the weight of the bronze was not determined.

19 So Solomon made all the things that were in the house of God: the golden altar, the tables for the bread of the Presence, 20the lampstands and their lamps of pure gold to burn before the inner sanctuary, as prescribed; 21the flowers, the lamps, and the tongs, of purest gold; 22the snuffers, basins, ladles, and firepans, of pure gold. As for the entrance to the temple: the inner doors to the most holy place and the doors of the nave of the temple were of gold.

5 Thus all the work that Solomon did for the house of the LORD was finished. Solomon brought in the things that his father David had dedicated, and stored the silver, the gold, and all the vessels in the treasuries of the house of God.

5.1: *Thus all the work that Solomon did for the house of the LORD was finished:* The Chronicler concludes his descriptions with this formal ending.

2 Then Solomon assembled the elders of Israel and all the heads of the tribes, the leaders of the ancestral houses of the people

a Cn: Heb *in the inner sanctuary*   *b* A Hebrew measure of volume

of Israel, in Jerusalem, to bring up the ark of the covenant of the LORD out of the city of David, which is Zion. 3And all the Israelites assembled before the king at the festival that is in the seventh month. 4And all the elders of Israel came, and the Levites carried the ark. 5So they brought up the ark, the tent of meeting, and all the holy vessels that were in the tent; the priests and the Levites brought them up. 6King Solomon and all the congregation of Israel, who had assembled before him, were before the ark, sacrificing so many sheep and oxen that they could not be numbered or counted. 7Then the priests brought the ark of the covenant of the LORD to its place, in the inner sanctuary of the house, in the most holy place, underneath the wings of the cherubim. 8For the cherubim spread out their wings over the place of the ark, so that the cherubim made a covering above the ark and its poles. 9The poles were so long that the ends of the poles were seen from the holy place in front of the inner sanctuary; but they could not be seen from outside; they are there to this day. 10There was nothing in the ark except the two tablets that Moses put there at Horeb, where the LORD made a covenant*a* with the people of Israel after they came out of Egypt.

11 Now when the priests came out of the holy place (for all the priests who were present had sanctified themselves, without regard to their divisions), 12all the levitical singers, Asaph, Heman, and Jeduthun, their sons and kindred, arrayed in fine linen, with cymbals, harps, and lyres, stood east of the altar with one hundred twenty priests who were trumpeters. 13It was the duty of the trumpeters and singers to make themselves heard in unison in praise and thanksgiving to the LORD, and when the song was raised, with trumpets and cymbals and other musical instruments, in praise to the LORD,

"For he is good,
    for his steadfast love endures
        forever,"

the house, the house of the LORD, was filled with a cloud, 14so that the priests could not stand to minister because of the cloud; for the glory of the LORD filled the house of God.

5.2–14: Installing the ark. Now that the structure of the Temple* has been completed, the Chronicler turns to the final act of centralizing worship at the Temple by narrating the entry of the ark into the structure. Alterations to his source in 1 Kings 8 are relatively minor. **5:** *So they brought up the ark, the tent of meeting, and all the holy vessels that were in the tent underscores the Chronicler's sense that all the essential elements for formal worship are being brought into the Temple. The priests and the Levites brought them up:* In 1 Kings 8.4 most translations note only the Levites, though the wording is the same as here. The phrase is normally understood to mean "levitical priests," used most often in the book of Deuteronomy and a very unusual expression for the Chronicler. His understanding of the term may have been different from Deuteronomy, since for the Chronicler it is not certain that Levites could carry the holy vessels. **11:** *(For all the priests who were present had sanctified themselves):* This parenthetical insert is not found in 1 Kings 8 and reflects the Chronicler's concern for proper ritual order. **13:** *It was the duty of the trumpeters and singers to make themselves heard in unison* reflects the Temple worship of the Chronicler's day and his concern with unified expressions of worship. *And when the song was raised . . . the house, the house of the LORD, was filled with a cloud:* Significantly, the Chronicler has God's presence, symbolized by the cloud, inhabit the Temple in response to the unified worship of the priests and Levites, who had taken the proper care to fulfill all the ritual requirements.

6 Then Solomon said, "The LORD has said that he would reside in thick darkness. 2I have built you an exalted house, a place for you to reside in forever."

3 Then the king turned around and blessed all the assembly of Israel, while all the assembly of Israel stood. 4And he said, "Blessed be the LORD, the God of Israel, who with his hand has fulfilled what he promised with his mouth to my father David, saying, 5'Since the day that I brought my people out of the land of Egypt, I have not chosen a city from any of the tribes of Israel in which to build a house, so that my name might be there, and I chose no one as ruler over my people Israel; 6but I have chosen Jerusalem

a Heb lacks *a covenant*

in order that my name may be there, and I have chosen David to be over my people Israel.' 7My father David had it in mind to build a house for the name of the LORD, the God of Israel. 8But the LORD said to my father David, 'You did well to consider building a house for my name; 9nevertheless you shall not build the house, but your son who shall be born to you shall build the house for my name.' 10Now the LORD has fulfilled his promise that he made; for I have succeeded my father David, and sit on the throne of Israel, as the LORD promised, and have built the house for the name of the LORD, the God of Israel. 11There I have set the ark, in which is the covenant of the LORD that he made with the people of Israel."

12 Then Solomon[a] stood before the altar of the LORD in the presence of the whole assembly of Israel, and spread out his hands. 13Solomon had made a bronze platform five cubits long, five cubits wide, and three cubits high, and had set it in the court; and he stood on it. Then he knelt on his knees in the presence of the whole assembly of Israel, and spread out his hands toward heaven. 14He said, "O LORD, God of Israel, there is no God like you, in heaven or on earth, keeping covenant in steadfast love with your servants who walk before you with all their heart— 15you who have kept for your servant, my father David, what you promised to him. Indeed, you promised with your mouth and this day have fulfilled with your hand. 16Therefore, O LORD, God of Israel, keep for your servant, my father David, that which you promised him, saying, 'There shall never fail you a successor before me to sit on the throne of Israel, if only your children keep to their way, to walk in my law as you have walked before me.' 17Therefore, O LORD, God of Israel, let your word be confirmed, which you promised to your servant David.

6.1–7.11: Dedication of the Temple. * Now that God's presence dwells within the Temple, the Chronicler offers two prayers by Solomon, each emphasizing different aspects of the Temple's dedication. This section marks the mid-point of the Chronicler's history. **6.6:** *I have chosen Jerusalem in order that my name may be there, and I have chosen David to be over my people Israel:* This prayer links the building of the Temple with Solomon's legitimacy as a ruler. The Chronicler draws a strong contrast between God's previous actions and the "new order" now that God dwells in the Temple. Just as God's presence in the Temple demonstrates he has chosen Jerusalem, having one of the line of David build the Temple demonstrates God has chosen that line to be the legitimate rulers of Israel. **13:** *Then he knelt on his knees in the presence of the whole assembly of Israel:* In 1 Kings 8 Solomon stands throughout his prayer. While the Chronicler has him begin by standing, he portrays Solomon as humbled by the honor that has been bestowed on him. **16:** *If only your children keep to their way, to walk in my law as you have walked before me:* This phrase adds a conditionality to the succession of the Davidic line promised in 1 Chr 17. A ruler from the line of David is assured only if *they walk in my law,* possibly reflecting the larger role of the Pentateuch* in regulating daily life in the time of the Chronicler.

18 "But will God indeed reside with mortals on earth? Even heaven and the highest heaven cannot contain you, how much less this house that I have built! 19Regard your servant's prayer and his plea, O LORD my God, heeding the cry and the prayer that your servant prays to you. 20May your eyes be open day and night toward this house, the place where you promised to set your name, and may you heed the prayer that your servant prays toward this place. 21And hear the plea of your servant and of your people Israel, when they pray toward this place; may you hear from heaven your dwelling place; hear and forgive.

22 "If someone sins against another and is required to take an oath and comes and swears before your altar in this house, 23may you hear from heaven, and act, and judge your servants, repaying the guilty by bringing their conduct on their own head, and vindicating those who are in the right by rewarding them in accordance with their righteousness.

24 "When your people Israel, having sinned against you, are defeated before an

a Heb *he*

enemy but turn again to you, confess your name, pray and plead with you in this house, 25 may you hear from heaven, and forgive the sin of your people Israel, and bring them again to the land that you gave to them and to their ancestors.

26 "When heaven is shut up and there is no rain because they have sinned against you, and then they pray toward this place, confess your name, and turn from their sin, because you punish them, 27 may you hear in heaven, forgive the sin of your servants, your people Israel, when you teach them the good way in which they should walk; and send down rain upon your land, which you have given to your people as an inheritance.

28 "If there is famine in the land, if there is plague, blight, mildew, locust, or caterpillar; if their enemies besiege them in any of the settlements of the lands; whatever suffering, whatever sickness there is; 29 whatever prayer, whatever plea from any individual or from all your people Israel, all knowing their own suffering and their own sorrows so that they stretch out their hands toward this house; 30 may you hear from heaven, your dwelling place, forgive, and render to all whose heart you know, according to all their ways, for only you know the human heart. 31 Thus may they fear you and walk in your ways all the days that they live in the land that you gave to our ancestors.

32 "Likewise when foreigners, who are not of your people Israel, come from a distant land because of your great name, and your mighty hand, and your outstretched arm, when they come and pray toward this house, 33 may you hear from heaven your dwelling place, and do whatever the foreigners ask of you, in order that all the peoples of the earth may know your name and fear you, as do your people Israel, and that they may know that your name has been invoked on this house that I have built.

34 "If your people go out to battle against their enemies, by whatever way you shall send them, and they pray to you toward this city that you have chosen and the house that I have built for your name, 35 then hear from heaven their prayer and their plea, and maintain their cause.

36 "If they sin against you—for there is no one who does not sin—and you are angry with them and give them to an enemy, so that they are carried away captive to a land far or near; 37 then if they come to their senses in the land to which they have been taken captive, and repent, and plead with you in the land of their captivity, saying, 'We have sinned, and have done wrong; we have acted wickedly'; 38 if they repent with all their heart and soul in the land of their captivity, to which they were taken captive, and pray toward their land, which you gave to their ancestors, the city that you have chosen, and the house that I have built for your name, 39 then hear from heaven your dwelling place their prayer and their pleas, maintain their cause and forgive your people who have sinned against you. 40 Now, O my God, let your eyes be open and your ears attentive to prayer from this place.

41 "Now rise up, O LORD God, and go to
    your resting place,
        you and the ark of your might.
Let your priests, O LORD God, be
    clothed with salvation,
        and let your faithful rejoice in your
        goodness.
42 O LORD God, do not reject your
    anointed one.
    Remember your steadfast love for
    your servant David."

6.18–42. 39: *Then hear from heaven your dwelling place their prayer and their pleas, maintain their cause and forgive your people:* As the Chronicler prepares to close Solomon's prayer, he departs significantly from the source in 1 Kings 8. Although in Kings Solomon requests that God act to grant Israel compassion in the sight of their captors (Kings was written while many Israelites lived in captivity in Babylon), the Chronicler makes no mention of captivity or captors. Rather, the appeal is more general, that God forgive. **40**: *Let your eyes be open and your ears attentive to prayer from this place:* God's dwelling in the Temple makes it a place of special "connectedness" to heaven, and prayers uttered at the Temple were understood to be particularly effective. **41**: *Now rise up, O LORD God, and go to your resting place:* The Chronicler closes with portions of Psalm 132, which reaffirms God's choice of the line of David and of Jerusalem, both appropriate themes to highlight the potential for Israel that is available under Solomon.

7 When Solomon had ended his prayer, fire came down from heaven and consumed the burnt offering and the sacrifices; and the glory of the LORD filled the temple. ²The priests could not enter the house of the LORD, because the glory of the LORD filled the LORD's house. ³When all the people of Israel saw the fire come down and the glory of the LORD on the temple, they bowed down on the pavement with their faces to the ground, and worshiped and gave thanks to the LORD, saying,

"For he is good,
　　for his steadfast love endures forever."

4 Then the king and all the people offered sacrifice before the LORD. ⁵King Solomon offered as a sacrifice twenty-two thousand oxen and one hundred twenty thousand sheep. So the king and all the people dedicated the house of God. ⁶The priests stood at their posts; the Levites also, with the instruments for music to the LORD that King David had made for giving thanks to the LORD—for his steadfast love endures forever—whenever David offered praises by their ministry. Opposite them the priests sounded trumpets; and all Israel stood.

7 Solomon consecrated the middle of the court that was in front of the house of the LORD; for there he offered the burnt offerings and the fat of the offerings of well-being because the bronze altar Solomon had made could not hold the burnt offering and the grain offering and the fat parts.

8 At that time Solomon held the festival for seven days, and all Israel with him, a very great congregation, from Lebo-hamath to the Wadi of Egypt. ⁹On the eighth day they held a solemn assembly; for they had observed the dedication of the altar seven days and the festival seven days. ¹⁰On the twenty-third day of the seventh month he sent the people away to their homes, joyful and in good spirits because of the goodness that the LORD had shown to David and to Solomon and to his people Israel.

11 Thus Solomon finished the house of the LORD and the king's house; all that Sol-omon had planned to do in the house of the LORD and in his own house he successfully accomplished.

7.1–11. 1: *Fire came down from heaven and consumed the burnt offering and the sacrifices:* Not present in 1 Kings 8, this allusion connects the dedication of the Temple with the altar of burnt offering in the wilderness (Lev 9.24) and with the affirmation of the reality of Israel's God by the prophet* Elijah on Mount Carmel (1 Kings 18.38). **3:** *For he is good, for his steadfast love endures forever:* This affirmation by the people echoes the praise offered God by the Levites (5.13). **6:** *Opposite them the priests sounded trumpets; and all Israel stood:* This depiction of the service of dedication is not in the Chronicler's source (1 Kings 8.62–63). Characteristic of the Chronicler's depiction of worship is the maintenance of proper order, the offering of praise, and the unified spirit of all the people.

12 Then the LORD appeared to Solomon in the night and said to him: "I have heard your prayer, and have chosen this place for myself as a house of sacrifice. ¹³When I shut up the heavens so that there is no rain, or command the locust to devour the land, or send pestilence among my people, ¹⁴if my people who are called by my name humble themselves, pray, seek my face, and turn from their wicked ways, then I will hear from heaven, and will forgive their sin and heal their land. ¹⁵Now my eyes will be open and my ears attentive to the prayer that is made in this place. ¹⁶For now I have chosen and consecrated this house so that my name may be there forever; my eyes and my heart will be there for all time. ¹⁷As for you, if you walk before me, as your father David walked, doing according to all that I have commanded you and keeping my statutes and my ordinances, ¹⁸then I will establish your royal throne, as I made covenant with your father David saying, 'You shall never lack a successor to rule over Israel.'

19 "But if you*ᵃ* turn aside and forsake my statutes and my commandments that I have set before you, and go and serve other gods and worship them, ²⁰then I will pluck you*ᵇ* up from the land that I have given you;*ᵇ* and

a The word *you* in this verse is plural　　*b* Heb *them*

this house, which I have consecrated for my name, I will cast out of my sight, and will make it a proverb and a byword among all peoples. 21And regarding this house, now exalted, everyone passing by will be astonished, and say, 'Why has the LORD done such a thing to this land and to this house?' 22Then they will say, 'Because they abandoned the LORD the God of their ancestors who brought them out of the land of Egypt, and they adopted other gods, and worshiped them and served them; therefore he has brought all this calamity upon them.' "

7.12–22: God's second appearance. God first appeared to Solomon at Gibeon, shortly after the death of David. In this account, God communicates two basic points to Solomon. One is the uniqueness of the Temple,* the second is the conditionality of the rule of the line of David over Israel. While he has supplemented it at points, the Chronicler has generally followed his source (1 Kings 9.1–9). **12:** *I have heard your prayer and have chosen this place for myself as a house of sacrifice:* For the Chronicler, the Temple is important because God has consecrated the place by choosing it for himself. This interpretation* by the Chronicler is related to the idea in Deuteronomy of God's choosing a place for his name to dwell (Deut 12.11, 14). The concept of a *house of sacrifice* places emphasis on the ritual aspects of Temple service and its role as a place of mediation between God and the community. **14:** *If my people . . . humble themselves, pray, seek my face, and turn from their wicked ways* is a classic expression of the Chronicler's theology. When under divine judgment, the community must initiate its contact with God and seek God's face. **16:** *My name may be there forever; my eyes and my heart will be there for all time:* This underscores the finality of God's choice of the Temple.

8 At the end of twenty years, during which Solomon had built the house of the LORD and his own house, 2Solomon rebuilt the cities that Huram had given to him, and settled the people of Israel in them.

3 Solomon went to Hamath-zobah, and captured it. 4He built Tadmor in the wilderness and all the storage towns that he built in Hamath. 5He also built Upper Beth-horon and Lower Beth-horon, fortified cities, with walls, gates, and bars, 6and Baalath, as well as all Solomon's storage towns, and all the towns for his chariots, the towns for his cavalry, and whatever Solomon desired to build, in Jerusalem, in Lebanon, and in all the land of his dominion. 7All the people who were left of the Hittites, the Amorites, the Perizzites, the Hivites, and the Jebusites, who were not of Israel, 8from their descendants who were still left in the land, whom the people of Israel had not destroyed—these Solomon conscripted for forced labor, as is still the case today. 9But of the people of Israel Solomon made no slaves for his work; they were soldiers, and his officers, the commanders of his chariotry and cavalry. 10These were the chief officers of King Solomon, two hundred fifty of them, who exercised authority over the people.

8.1–17: Highlights of Solomon's reign. The Chronicler now offers a series of brief reports, each reflecting Solomon's success and personal piety. Most of these reports touch on some aspect of the Temple.* **6:** *Whatever Solomon desired to build, in Jerusalem, in Lebanon, and in all the land of his dominion:* Having built the Temple first, the way was now open for Solomon to engage in great public works projects.

11 Solomon brought Pharaoh's daughter from the city of David to the house that he had built for her, for he said, "My wife shall not live in the house of King David of Israel, for the places to which the ark of the LORD has come are holy."

12 Then Solomon offered up burnt offerings to the LORD on the altar of the LORD that he had built in front of the vestibule, 13as the duty of each day required, offering according to the commandment of Moses for the sabbaths, the new moons, and the three annual festivals—the festival of unleavened bread, the festival of weeks, and the festival of booths. 14According to the ordinance of his father David, he appointed the divisions of the priests for their service, and the Levites for their offices of praise and ministry alongside the priests as the duty of each day required, and the gatekeepers in their divisions for the several gates; for so David the man of God had commanded. 15They did not turn away from what the king had com-

manded the priests and Levites regarding anything at all, or regarding the treasuries.

16 Thus all the work of Solomon was accomplished from[a] the day the foundation of the house of the LORD was laid until the house of the LORD was finished completely.

8.11–16. 11: *My wife shall not live in the house of King David of Israel:* The Chronicler presumes throughout that his readers are familiar with 1 Kings 7.8, which notes Solomon's marriage to an Egyptian princess. The Chronicler's wording is ambiguous in Hebrew, but it seems to refer not to the places but to the people and things surrounding the ark. As a non-Israelite, Solomon's Egyptian wife could not fit the category of holy persons. **13:** *Offering according to the commandment of Moses:* The Chronicler is concerned with proper ritual. The regulations for such sacrifices are in Num 28. **14:** *According to the ordinance of his father David:* Just as Moses is recognized as a source of authority for the rules of worship, David occupies an esteemed position as source of proper ritual. **16:** *Thus all the work of Solomon was accomplished:* With this formal closure, the Chronicler has described as much of Solomon's activity as he felt was necessary.

---

17 Then Solomon went to Ezion-geber and Eloth on the shore of the sea, in the land of Edom. 18Huram sent him, in the care of his servants, ships and servants familiar with the sea. They went to Ophir, together with the servants of Solomon, and imported from there four hundred fifty talents of gold and brought it to King Solomon.

9 When the queen of Sheba heard of the fame of Solomon, she came to Jerusalem to test him with hard questions, having a very great retinue and camels bearing spices and very much gold and precious stones. When she came to Solomon, she discussed with him all that was on her mind. 2Solomon answered all her questions; there was nothing hidden from Solomon that he could not explain to her. 3When the queen of Sheba had observed the wisdom of Solomon, the house that he had built, 4the food of his table, the seating of his officials, and the attendance of his servants, and their clothing, his valets, and their clothing, and his burnt offerings[b] that he offered at the house of the LORD, there was no more spirit left in her.

5 So she said to the king, "The report was true that I heard in my own land of your accomplishments and of your wisdom, 6but I did not believe the[c] reports until I came and my own eyes saw it. Not even half of the greatness of your wisdom had been told to me; you far surpass the report that I had heard. 7Happy are your people! Happy are these your servants, who continually attend you and hear your wisdom! 8Blessed be the LORD your God, who has delighted in you and set you on his throne as king for the LORD your God. Because your God loved Israel and would establish them forever, he has made you king over them, that you may execute justice and righteousness." 9Then she gave the king one hundred twenty talents of gold, a very great quantity of spices, and precious stones: there were no spices such as those that the queen of Sheba gave to King Solomon.

10 Moreover the servants of Huram and the servants of Solomon who brought gold from Ophir brought algum wood and precious stones. 11From the algum wood, the king made steps[d] for the house of the LORD and for the king's house, lyres also and harps for the singers; there never was seen the like of them before in the land of Judah.

12 Meanwhile King Solomon granted the queen of Sheba every desire that she expressed, well beyond what she had brought to the king. Then she returned to her own land, with her servants.

13 The weight of gold that came to Solomon in one year was six hundred sixty-six talents of gold, 14besides that which the traders and merchants brought; and all the kings of Arabia and the governors of the land brought gold and silver to Solomon. 15King Solomon made two hundred large shields of beaten gold; six hundred shekels of beaten gold went into each large shield. 16He made three hundred shields of beaten gold; three hundred shekels of gold went into each shield; and the king put them in the House of the Forest of Lebanon. 17The king also

---

a Gk Syr Vg: Heb *to*　　*b* Gk Syr Vg 1 Kings 10.5: Heb *ascent*　　*c* Heb *their*　　*d* Gk Vg: Meaning of Heb uncertain

made a great ivory throne, and overlaid it with pure gold. 18The throne had six steps and a footstool of gold, which were attached to the throne, and on each side of the seat were arm rests and two lions standing beside the arm rests, 19while twelve lions were standing, one on each end of a step on the six steps. The like of it was never made in any kingdom. 20All King Solomon's drinking vessels were of gold, and all the vessels of the House of the Forest of Lebanon were of pure gold; silver was not considered as anything in the days of Solomon. 21For the king's ships went to Tarshish with the servants of Huram; once every three years the ships of Tarshish used to come bringing gold, silver, ivory, apes, and peacocks.*

22 Thus King Solomon excelled all the kings of the earth in riches and in wisdom. 23All the kings of the earth sought the presence of Solomon to hear his wisdom, which God had put into his mind. 24Every one of them brought a present, objects of silver and gold, garments, weaponry, spices, horses, and mules, so much year by year. 25Solomon had four thousand stalls for horses and chariots, and twelve thousand horses, which he stationed in the chariot cities and with the king in Jerusalem. 26He ruled over all the kings from the Euphrates to the land of the Philistines, and to the border of Egypt. 27The king made silver as common in Jerusalem as stone, and cedar as plentiful as the sycamore of the Shephelah. 28Horses were imported for Solomon from Egypt and from all lands.

29 Now the rest of the acts of Solomon, from first to last, are they not written in the history of the prophet Nathan, and in the prophecy of Ahijah the Shilonite, and in the visions of the seer Iddo concerning Jeroboam son of Nebat? 30Solomon reigned in Jerusalem over all Israel forty years. 31Solomon slept with his ancestors and was buried in the city of his father David; and his son Rehoboam succeeded him.

9.1–31: Evidence of Solomon's greatness. These narratives* are offered by the Chronicler as a way of affirming the extraordinary reign of Solomon. They relate the concepts of Solomon's great wisdom, received from God, and his immense wealth, built in part by his wisdom. Generally, the Chronicler follows his source in 1 Kings closely. The Chronicler contends that having lavished his own wealth on the Temple,* Solomon (and the kingdom) receives great reward for such devotion. 2: *Solomon answered all her questions:* Part of the plot of the story of the queen of Sheba's visit is that she came prepared with "hard questions," ready to present a test to Solomon. His success in answering her questions led to her honoring him with extravagant gifts. 16: *The king put them in the House of the Forest of Lebanon,* part of the royal palace complex. 22: *King Solomon excelled all the kings of the earth in riches and in wisdom:* Having built the Temple as soon as he was able, Solomon demonstrated his personal commitment to God's plans for Israel. As a result, he has military success, economic prosperity, and the recognition of powerful persons outside Israel. 29: *Are they not written in the history of the prophet* Nathan, *and in the prophecy of Ahijah the Shilonite, and in the visions of the seer Iddo concerning Jeroboam son of Nebat?* These are figures from the Deuteronomistic* History, but there are no other indications that these individuals wrote accounts of Solomon's reign.

THE DISSOLUTION OF JUDAH

Chs. 10–36: Having described the high point of Israel under David and Solomon, the Chronicler now turns his attention to the flow of Israel's history after the division of the kingdom into two parts. Writing in Jerusalem during the post-exilic period, the Chronicler wants to present positive models for his own readership from Israel's past. These models share with David and Solomon a desire to ensure the proper worship of God in the Temple* and to instill in the community the ideal of seeking God. Focused on the Temple in Jerusalem, the Chronicler recounts the historical ebb and flow of the Davidic line that ruled Judah, only rarely incorporating any of the northern kingdom's history into his narrative.* When handling a positive model, the Chronicler follows a set pattern in which a prophet* brings a message to the king, offering a choice between God's way and a human way. The king chooses to obey God, does something good for the Temple, and all the community joins him in joyful obedience. The king goes on to enjoy military success and a positive rule. The figures from Israel's past particularly attractive to the Chronicler are Asa

a Or baboons

(14.1–16.14), Jehoshaphat (17.1–20.37), Joash (22.10–24.27), Hezekiah (29.1–32.33) and Josiah (34.1–35.27). In the case of the last two royal figures, the Chronicler is particularly lavish in praising the positive aspects of their rule. In general, the Chronicler adapts large portions of the narratives of 1 and 2 Kings in constructing his account, but there are extensive blocks of material that seem to have been generated by the Chronicler himself. Whether there were any sources for these materials is a debated issue.

10 Rehoboam went to Shechem, for all Israel had come to Shechem to make him king. 2When Jeroboam son of Nebat heard of it (for he was in Egypt, where he had fled from King Solomon), then Jeroboam returned from Egypt. 3They sent and called him; and Jeroboam and all Israel came and said to Rehoboam, 4"Your father made our yoke heavy. Now therefore lighten the hard service of your father and his heavy yoke that he placed on us, and we will serve you." 5He said to them, "Come to me again in three days." So the people went away.

6 Then King Rehoboam took counsel with the older men who had attended his father Solomon while he was still alive, saying, "How do you advise me to answer this people?" 7They answered him, "If you will be kind to this people and please them, and speak good words to them, then they will be your servants forever." 8But he rejected the advice that the older men gave him, and consulted the young men who had grown up with him and now attended him. 9He said to them, "What do you advise that we answer this people who have said to me, 'Lighten the yoke that your father put on us'?" 10The young men who had grown up with him said to him, "Thus should you speak to the people who said to you, 'Your father made our yoke heavy, but you must lighten it for us'; tell them, 'My little finger is thicker than my father's loins. 11Now, whereas my father laid on you a heavy yoke, I will add to your yoke. My father disciplined you with whips, but I will discipline you with scorpions.'"

12 So Jeroboam and all the people came to Rehoboam the third day, as the king had said, "Come to me again the third day." 13The king answered them harshly. King Rehoboam rejected the advice of the older men; 14he spoke to them in accordance with the advice of the young men, "My father made your yoke heavy, but I will add to it; my father disciplined you with whips, but I will discipline you with scorpions." 15So the king did not listen to the people, because it was a turn of affairs brought about by God so that the LORD might fulfill his word, which he had spoken by Ahijah the Shilonite to Jeroboam son of Nebat.

16 When all Israel saw that the king would not listen to them, the people answered the king,

"What share do we have in David?
     We have no inheritance in the son of Jesse.
Each of you to your tents, O Israel!
     Look now to your own house,
         O David."

So all Israel departed to their tents. 17But Rehoboam reigned over the people of Israel who were living in the cities of Judah. 18When King Rehoboam sent Hadoram, who was taskmaster over the forced labor, the people of Israel stoned him to death. King Rehoboam hurriedly mounted his chariot to flee to Jerusalem. 19So Israel has been in rebellion against the house of David to this day.

10.1–19: Revolt of the north. Jumping quickly into the reign of Rehoboam, Solomon's son, the Chronicler presents the root causes of the division between north and south as stemming from Solomon's excesses, in general following his source (1 Kings 12.1–19). However, he does have a basic problem, since he has excised from his narrative* the report of Solomon's failure to maintain sole allegiance to Israel's god (1 Kings 11). As a result, the division of the kingdom appears to result from arbitrary factors of human politics rather than God's rule. This he handles by a quick gesture to the narrative in 1 Kings, assuming his readers are familiar with the account. 4: *Your father made our yoke heavy* is a reference to the burden of taxation to support public building projects, as well as labor gangs that each region was obligated to supply to the court. 15: *It was a turn of affairs brought about by God so that the LORD might fulfill his word:* Not content to portray the affairs of Israel as subject only to human political ambition, the Chronicler notes that the revolt of the northern tribes triggered by Rehoboam's insensitivity was God's doing. The word *spoken by Ahijah the Shilonite* condemned Solomon for committing idolatry* (1 Kings 11.26–40) and fulfilled the promise that Jeroboam would rule over the larger part of the nation. **19:** *So Israel has been in rebellion against the house of David to this day,* using "Israel" in the formal sense of the northern kingdom formed from the tribes that objected to Rehoboam's policies. The loss of the greater portion of the nation's population and the more economically productive portion of the land must have been seen as a great disaster by Rehoboam.

scheme to make the reader and the protagonist aware of an important decision that must be made. Here the dilemma is clear: follow God's word and allow the division of the community and the diminishment of the Davidic kingdom, or attack quickly and try to regain the kingdom. *So they heeded the word of the LORD:* No motivation is offered, but Rehoboam makes the right decision and follows God's desires. **12:** *So he held Judah and Benjamin:* Having followed God's desires, Rehoboam is able to achieve his military goals of fortifying the northern border and creating strongholds to defend his realm.

11 When Rehoboam came to Jerusalem, he assembled one hundred eighty thousand chosen troops of the house of Judah and Benjamin to fight against Israel, to restore the kingdom to Rehoboam. ²But the word of the LORD came to Shemaiah the man of God: ³Say to King Rehoboam of Judah, son of Solomon, and to all Israel in Judah and Benjamin, ⁴"Thus says the LORD: You shall not go up or fight against your kindred. Let everyone return home, for this thing is from me." So they heeded the word of the LORD and turned back from the expedition against Jeroboam.

5 Rehoboam resided in Jerusalem, and he built cities for defense in Judah. ⁶He built up Bethlehem, Etam, Tekoa, ⁷Beth-zur, Soco, Adullam, ⁸Gath, Mareshah, Ziph, ⁹Adoraim, Lachish, Azekah, ¹⁰Zorah, Aijalon, and Hebron, fortified cities that are in Judah and in Benjamin. ¹¹He made the fortresses strong, and put commanders in them, and stores of food, oil, and wine. ¹²He also put large shields and spears in all the cities, and made them very strong. So he held Judah and Benjamin.

13 The priests and the Levites who were in all Israel presented themselves to him from all their territories. ¹⁴The Levites had left their common lands and their holdings and had come to Judah and Jerusalem, because Jeroboam and his sons had prevented them from serving as priests of the LORD, ¹⁵and had appointed his own priests for the high places, and for the goat-demons, and for the calves that he had made. ¹⁶Those who had set their hearts to seek the LORD God of Israel came after them from all the tribes of Israel to Jerusalem to sacrifice to the LORD, the God of their ancestors. ¹⁷They strengthened the kingdom of Judah, and for three years they made Rehoboam son of Solomon secure, for they walked for three years in the way of David and Solomon.

11.1–12.16: The reign of Rehoboam. Given the division of the kingdom, the Chronicler now turns to consider Rehoboam's rule. Rehoboam is seen in both positive and negative terms by the Chronicler. **11.1:** *When Rehoboam came to Jerusalem, he assembled . . . troops of the house of Judah and Benjamin to fight against Israel, to restore the kingdom:* A normal response to revolt against his rule would be to attack before the new kingdom can organize itself. **4:** *Thus says the LORD: You shall not go up or fight against your kindred:* Prophets* function in the Chronicler's

11.13–17. 13: *The priests and Levites who were in all Israel presented themselves to him:* Rehoboam's following the word from God brings additional support from those devoted to serving God by worship. **16:** *Those who had set their hearts to seek the LORD God of Israel came after them:* In addition to receiving the support of priests and Levites from "all Israel," all those who truly sought God came and joined Rehoboam's kingdom.

18 Rehoboam took as his wife Mahalath daughter of Jerimoth son of David, and of Abihail daughter of Eliab son of Jesse. ¹⁹She bore him sons: Jeush, Shemariah, and Zaham. ²⁰After her he took Maacah daughter of Absalom, who bore him Abijah, Attai, Ziza, and Shelomith. ²¹Rehoboam loved Maacah daughter of Absalom more than all his other wives and concubines (he took

eighteen wives and sixty concubines, and became the father of twenty-eight sons and sixty daughters). 22Rehoboam appointed Abijah son of Maacah as chief prince among his brothers, for he intended to make him king. 23He dealt wisely, and distributed some of his sons through all the districts of Judah and Benjamin, in all the fortified cities; he gave them abundant provisions, and found many wives for them.

12 When the rule of Rehoboam was established and he grew strong, he abandoned the law of the LORD, he and all Israel with him. 2In the fifth year of King Rehoboam, because they had been unfaithful to the LORD, King Shishak of Egypt came up against Jerusalem 3with twelve hundred chariots and sixty thousand cavalry. A countless army came with him from Egypt—Libyans, Sukkiim, and Ethiopians.*a* 4He took the fortified cities of Judah and came as far as Jerusalem. 5Then the prophet Shemaiah came to Rehoboam and to the officers of Judah, who had gathered at Jerusalem because of Shishak, and said to them, "Thus says the LORD: You abandoned me, so I have abandoned you to the hand of Shishak." 6Then the officers of Israel and the king humbled themselves and said, "The LORD is in the right." 7When the LORD saw that they humbled themselves, the word of the LORD came to Shemaiah, saying: "They have humbled themselves; I will not destroy them, but I will grant them some deliverance, and my wrath shall not be poured out on Jerusalem by the hand of Shishak. 8Nevertheless they shall be his servants, so that they may know the difference between serving me and serving the kingdoms of other lands."

12.1–8. 1: *When the rule of Rehoboam was established and he grew strong, he abandoned the law of the LORD, he and all Israel with him:* Having emphasized the positive elements of Rehoboam's rule, the historian now turns to the downside. The *law* (Torah*) refers to the Pentateuchal* regulations for bringing everyday life into accord with God's ways. 2: *Because they had been unfaithful to the LORD:* Historical experience is shaped by the degree to which the community seeks God. Since the people have abandoned the law, God now abandons the community and allows

an enemy to gain the upper hand. 5: *You abandoned me, so I have abandoned you to the hand of Shishak:* This is a classic expression of the Chronicler's sense of immediate retribution, that God repays the community for good or ill depending on the community's action toward God. While the Chronicler is using some of the materials in 1 Kings 14.21–28, in this source the connection is not explicitly drawn between the community's actions and Shishak's campaign. 7: *They have humbled themselves; I will not destroy them, but I will grant them some deliverance:* The second word from God by the prophet* Shemaiah contains God's immediate response to Israel's leaders who have humbled themselves. Though the community will not be destroyed, they will be "humbled" by having to serve the Egyptian king.

9 So King Shishak of Egypt came up against Jerusalem; he took away the treasures of the house of the LORD and the treasures of the king's house; he took everything. He also took away the shields of gold that Solomon had made; 10but King Rehoboam made in place of them shields of bronze, and committed them to the hands of the officers of the guard, who kept the door of the king's house. 11Whenever the king went into the house of the LORD, the guard would come along bearing them, and would then bring them back to the guardroom. 12Because he humbled himself the wrath of the LORD turned from him, so as not to destroy them completely; moreover, conditions were good in Judah.

13 So King Rehoboam established himself in Jerusalem and reigned. Rehoboam was forty-one years old when he began to reign; he reigned seventeen years in Jerusalem, the city that the LORD had chosen out of all the tribes of Israel to put his name there. His mother's name was Naamah the Ammonite. 14He did evil, for he did not set his heart to seek the LORD.

15 Now the acts of Rehoboam, from first to last, are they not written in the records of the prophet Shemaiah and of the seer Iddo, recorded by genealogy? There were continual wars between Rehoboam and Jeroboam.

a Or *Nubians*; Heb *Cushites*

16 Rehoboam slept with his ancestors and was buried in the city of David; and his son Abijah succeeded him.

12.9–16. 9: *So King Shishak of Egypt came up against Jerusalem:* In the Chronicler's view, the historical experience of the community is determined by the community's action toward God. In Egyptian temple wall reliefs at Thebes, there are fragmentary scenes showing Shishak's (Sheshonq I) campaign into Syria-Palestine around the year 930 BCE. Shishak was apparently trying to reassert Egyptian control over the weaker nation-states in the region. **12:** *Moreover, conditions were good in Judah:* The Chronicler softens the impact of this humiliation by noting Judah did well despite Egyptian control. **14:** *He did evil, for he did not set his heart to seek the LORD:* In the summary of Rehoboam's reign, the Chronicler adds this evaluation, expressing his judgment that "seeking" or "abandoning" God depends on a human's willingness to act in a proper way.

13 In the eighteenth year of King Jeroboam, Abijah began to reign over Judah. ²He reigned for three years in Jerusalem. His mother's name was Micaiah daughter of Uriel of Gibeah.

Now there was war between Abijah and Jeroboam. ³Abijah engaged in battle, having an army of valiant warriors, four hundred thousand picked men; and Jeroboam drew up his line of battle against him with eight hundred thousand picked mighty warriors. ⁴Then Abijah stood on the slope of Mount Zemaraim that is in the hill country of Ephraim, and said, "Listen to me, Jeroboam and all Israel! ⁵Do you not know that the LORD God of Israel gave the kingship over Israel forever to David and his sons by a covenant of salt? ⁶Yet Jeroboam son of Nebat, a servant of Solomon son of David, rose up and rebelled against his lord; ⁷and certain worthless scoundrels gathered around him and defied Rehoboam son of Solomon, when Rehoboam was young and irresolute and could not withstand them.

13.1–22: The reign of Abijah. After Rehoboam's checkered rule, Abijah appears as a defender of Davidic prerogatives. The Chronicler has greatly expanded the brief account in his source (1 Kings 15.1–8), using the dramatic setting of assembled armies and stirring speeches. While the deuteronomistic* historian saw Abijah as evil, the Chronicler rehabilitates the figure of Abijah into a positive example for his readers. **5:** *Do you not know that the LORD God of Israel gave the kingship over Israel forever to David and his sons:* In 1 and 2 Kings, the Davidic privilege of rule over all Israel was removed because of Solomon's idolatrous actions (1 Kings 11.9–13), but the Chronicler has excised this incident from his recounting of Solomon's reign. In the Chronicler's narrative,* God's covenant* with David is still in effect; the northern tribes are in revolt against the Davidic line and God. **7:** *Certain worthless scoundrels gathered around him and defied Rehoboam* constitutes a revision of sorts from his earlier account of the split in the kingdom (10.1–19). It is not Rehoboam's disdain for the request of the northern tribes for economic relief that motivated the split, but unsavory types who have backed Jeroboam's revolt.

8 "And now you think that you can withstand the kingdom of the LORD in the hand of the sons of David, because you are a great multitude and have with you the golden calves that Jeroboam made as gods for you. ⁹Have you not driven out the priests of the LORD, the descendants of Aaron, and the Levites, and made priests for yourselves like the peoples of other lands? Whoever comes to be consecrated with a young bull or seven rams becomes a priest of what are no gods. ¹⁰But as for us, the LORD is our God, and we have not abandoned him. We have priests ministering to the LORD who are descendants of Aaron, and Levites for their service. ¹¹They offer to the LORD every morning and every evening burnt offerings and fragrant incense, set out the rows of bread on the table of pure gold, and care for the golden lampstand so that its lamps may burn every evening; for we keep the charge of the LORD our God, but you have abandoned him. ¹²See, God is with us at our head, and his priests have their battle trumpets to sound the call to battle against you. O Israelites, do not fight against the LORD, the God of your ancestors; for you cannot succeed."

13.8–12. 9: *Have you not driven out the priests of the LORD, the descendants of Aaron, and the Levites:* This is a slight recasting of the Chronicler's earlier account (11.13–15) where the religious personnel had simply been prevented from officiating. The more serious charge, *made priests for yourselves like the peoples of other lands,* indicates that the northern kingdom had abandoned their distinctiveness as a people of God and had reduced themselves to being like any other human political entity. **10:** *As for us, the LORD is our God, and we have not abandoned him:* For the Chronicler this is the ultimate statement of community fidelity, expressed most clearly in concern for proper worship and Temple* service. *We have priests ministering to the LORD who are descendants of Aaron, and Levites for their service:* By maintaining the proper order for worship and approach to God, the community expresses its desire to seek him. **12:** *Do not fight against the LORD, the God of your ancestors; for you cannot succeed:* Military success depends upon the community's relationship to God, whether "seeking" him or "abandoning" him. With God beside them, the Chronicler cannot imagine a military defeat.

13.13–22. 14: *They cried out to the LORD, and the priests blew the trumpets:* Sensing the battle was turning in the northern kingdom's favor, the armies of Judah call on God for assistance. **15:** *God defeated Jeroboam and all Israel before Abijah and Judah:* The victory is not won by military strategy but by God's direct intervention. **21:** *Abijah grew strong,* in contrast to Jeroboam and the northern kingdom. Abijah's success is the result of his, and Judah's, reliance on the proper means of worship and the offering of continual service to God. Taking such care to maintain the right relationship to God provided the community with its security and well-being, a model for the Chronicler's reader.

14 [c] So Abijah slept with his ancestors, and they buried him in the city of David. His son Asa succeeded him. In his days the land had rest for ten years. 2 [d] Asa did what was good and right in the sight of the LORD his God. 3 He took away the foreign altars and the high places, broke down the pillars, hewed down the sacred poles,[e] 4 and commanded Judah to seek the LORD, the God of their ancestors, and to keep the law and the commandment. 5 He also removed from all the cities of Judah the high places and the incense altars. And the kingdom had rest under him. 6 He built fortified cities in Judah while the land had rest. He had no war in those years, for the LORD gave him peace. 7 He said to Judah, "Let us build these cities, and surround them with walls and towers, gates and bars; the land is still ours because we have sought the LORD our God; we have sought him, and he has given us peace on every side." So they built and prospered. 8 Asa had an army of three hundred thousand from Judah, armed with large shields and spears, and two hundred eighty thousand troops from Benjamin who carried shields and drew bows; all these were mighty warriors.

13 Jeroboam had sent an ambush around to come on them from behind; thus his troops[a] were in front of Judah, and the ambush was behind them. 14 When Judah turned, the battle was in front of them and behind them. They cried out to the LORD, and the priests blew the trumpets. 15 Then the people of Judah raised the battle shout. And when the people of Judah shouted, God defeated Jeroboam and all Israel before Abijah and Judah. 16 The Israelites fled before Judah, and God gave them into their hands. 17 Abijah and his army defeated them with great slaughter; five hundred thousand picked men of Israel fell slain. 18 Thus the Israelites were subdued at that time, and the people of Judah prevailed, because they relied on the LORD, the God of their ancestors. 19 Abijah pursued Jeroboam, and took cities from him: Bethel with its villages and Jeshanah with its villages and Ephron[b] with its villages. 20 Jeroboam did not recover his power in the days of Abijah; the LORD struck him down, and he died. 21 But Abijah grew strong. He took fourteen wives, and became the father of twenty-two sons and sixteen daughters. 22 The rest of the acts of Abijah, his behavior and his deeds, are written in the story of the prophet Iddo.

14.1–16.14: The reign of Asa. In this classic expansion of his source in 1 Kings, the Chronicler takes a mere

---

a Heb *they*   *b* Another reading is *Ephrain*
c Ch 13.23 in Heb   *d* Ch 14.1 in Heb
e Heb *Asherim*

seven verses on the reign of Asa and develops three chapters with complex plots and a rich theological content. The Chronicler portrays Asa as a model ruler who succeeds in bringing the community into peace, security, and joy by his devotion to God. **2:** *Asa did what was good and right in the sight of the LORD:* The first evaluation the reader receives of Asa is that he acted to suppress idolatry.* **4:** *And commanded Judah to seek the LORD, the God of their ancestors, and to keep the law and the commandment:* In his office as king, Asa also served as the chief legal authority in the realm. The Chronicler has him legislate the observance of Pentateuchal* law, presumably enforced by royal agents.

9 Zerah the Ethiopian*ᵃ* came out against them with an army of a million men and three hundred chariots, and came as far as Mareshah. ¹⁰Asa went out to meet him, and they drew up their lines of battle in the valley of Zephathah at Mareshah. ¹¹Asa cried to the LORD his God, "O LORD, there is no difference for you between helping the mighty and the weak. Help us, O LORD our God, for we rely on you, and in your name we have come against this multitude. O LORD, you are our God; let no mortal prevail against you." ¹²So the LORD defeated the Ethiopians*ᵇ* before Asa and before Judah, and the Ethiopians*ᵇ* fled. ¹³Asa and the army with him pursued them as far as Gerar, and the Ethiopians*ᵇ* fell until no one remained alive; for they were broken before the LORD and his army. The people of Judah*ᶜ* carried away a great quantity of booty. ¹⁴They defeated all the cities around Gerar, for the fear of the LORD was on them. They plundered all the cities; for there was much plunder in them. ¹⁵They also attacked the tents of those who had livestock,*ᵈ* and carried away sheep and goats in abundance, and camels. Then they returned to Jerusalem.

14.9–15. **9:** *Zerah the Ethiopian came out against them with an army of a million men:* Zerah may have been a general of Osorkon I, who ruled Egypt in the opening decades of the ninth century BCE. The figure of a million men may be a of convention for expressing a large massed force rather than a specific number. **13:** *The Ethiopians fell until no one remained alive; for they were broken before the LORD and his army:* Since God

was fighting on behalf of Judah, the Chronicler envisions this as a compelling victory. God's army is the Judean force of Asa.

15 The spirit of God came upon Azariah son of Oded. ²He went out to meet Asa and said to him, "Hear me, Asa, and all Judah and Benjamin: The LORD is with you, while you are with him. If you seek him, he will be found by you, but if you abandon him, he will abandon you. ³For a long time Israel was without the true God, and without a teaching priest, and without law; ⁴but when in their distress they turned to the LORD, the God of Israel, and sought him, he was found by them. ⁵In those times it was not safe for anyone to go or come, for great disturbances afflicted all the inhabitants of the lands. ⁶They were broken in pieces, nation against nation and city against city, for God troubled them with every sort of distress. ⁷But you, take courage! Do not let your hands be weak, for your work shall be rewarded."

8 When Asa heard these words, the prophecy of Azariah son of Oded,*ᵉ* he took courage, and put away the abominable idols from all the land of Judah and Benjamin and from the towns that he had taken in the hill country of Ephraim. He repaired the altar of the LORD that was in front of the vestibule of the house of the LORD.*ᶠ* ⁹He gathered all Judah and Benjamin, and those from Ephraim, Manasseh, and Simeon who were residing as aliens with them, for great numbers had deserted to him from Israel when they saw that the LORD his God was with him. ¹⁰They were gathered at Jerusalem in the third month of the fifteenth year of the reign of Asa. ¹¹They sacrificed to the LORD on that day, from the booty that they had brought, seven hundred oxen and seven thousand sheep. ¹²They entered into a covenant to seek the LORD, the God of their ancestors, with all their heart and with all their soul. ¹³Whoever would not seek the LORD, the God of Israel, should be put to death,

a Or *Nubian;* Heb *Cushite*　　*b* Or *Nubians;* Heb *Cushites*　　*c* Heb *They*　　*d* Meaning of Heb uncertain　　*e* Compare Syr Vg: Heb *the prophecy, the prophet Obed*　　*f* Heb *the vestibule of the* LORD

whether young or old, man or woman. [14]They took an oath to the LORD with a loud voice, and with shouting, and with trumpets, and with horns. [15]All Judah rejoiced over the oath; for they had sworn with all their heart, and had sought him with their whole desire, and he was found by them, and the LORD gave them rest all around.

15.1–15. 2: *The LORD is with you, while you are with him. If you seek him, he will be found by you, but if you abandon him, he will abandon you:* This is a succinct expression of the Chronicler's understanding of God's relationship to Israel. The entire message brought by Azariah is intended to present Asa with an opportunity to act further on behalf of God. **3:** *Israel was without the true God and without a teaching priest and without law:* This indefinite reference possibly relates to the period before Moses, the period of the judges, or some period of anarchy, though perhaps no specific period is intended. The Chronicler noted these items to help his readers appreciate what was present in their own time: the inheritance of God, teaching priests, and law. **9:** *For great numbers had deserted to him:* Asa's actions in response to Azariah's word receive affirmation from others who come to Judah to join with Asa. **12:** *They entered into a covenant* to seek the LORD, the God of their ancestors, with all their heart and all their soul:* This echoes Deut 6.5, which calls on Israel to love God with complete commitment. **15:** *All Judah rejoiced over the oath; for they had sworn with all their heart, and had sought him with their whole desire, and he was found by them, and the LORD gave them rest all around:* When the community is unified in intent, then God will respond. The "seeking" of God had been committed without reservation, and as the result of finding God, the community enjoyed peace.

---

[16] King Asa even removed his mother Maacah from being queen mother because she had made an abominable image for Asherah. Asa cut down her image, crushed it, and burned it at the Wadi Kidron. [17]But the high places were not taken out of Israel. Nevertheless the heart of Asa was true all his days. [18]He brought into the house of God the votive gifts of his father and his own votive gifts—silver, gold, and utensils. [19]And there was no more war until the thirty-fifth year of the reign of Asa.

16 In the thirty-sixth year of the reign of Asa, King Baasha of Israel went up against Judah, and built Ramah, to prevent anyone from going out or coming into the territory of[a] King Asa of Judah. [2]Then Asa took silver and gold from the treasures of the house of the LORD and the king's house, and sent them to King Ben-hadad of Aram, who resided in Damascus, saying, [3]"Let there be an alliance between me and you, like that between my father and your father; I am sending to you silver and gold; go, break your alliance with King Baasha of Israel, so that he may withdraw from me." [4]Ben-hadad listened to King Asa, and sent the commanders of his armies against the cities of Israel. They conquered Ijon, Dan, Abel-maim, and all the store-cities of Naphtali. [5]When Baasha heard of it, he stopped building Ramah, and let his work cease. [6]Then King Asa brought all Judah, and they carried away the stones of Ramah and its timber, with which Baasha had been building, and with them he built up Geba and Mizpah.

[7] At that time the seer Hanani came to King Asa of Judah, and said to him, "Because you relied on the king of Aram, and did not rely on the LORD your God, the army of the king of Aram has escaped you. [8]Were not the Ethiopians[b] and the Libyans a huge army with exceedingly many chariots and cavalry? Yet because you relied on the LORD, he gave them into your hand. [9]For the eyes of the LORD range throughout the entire earth, to strengthen those whose heart is true to him. You have done foolishly in this; for from now on you will have wars." [10]Then Asa was angry with the seer, and put him in the stocks, in prison, for he was in a rage with him because of this. And Asa inflicted cruelties on some of the people at the same time.

[11] The acts of Asa, from first to last, are written in the Book of the Kings of Judah and Israel. [12]In the thirty-ninth year of his reign Asa was diseased in his feet, and his disease became severe; yet even in his disease he did not seek the LORD, but sought help from physicians. [13]Then Asa slept with his ances-

---

a Heb lacks *the territory of*   b Or *Nubians*; Heb *Cushites*

tors, dying in the forty-first year of his reign. [14]They buried him in the tomb that he had hewn out for himself in the city of David. They laid him on a bier that had been filled with various kinds of spices prepared by the perfumer's art; and they made a very great fire in his honor.

15.16–16.14. 16.7: *Because you relied on the king of Aram, and did not rely on the LORD your God:* Asa's use of Temple* treasures to bribe the king of Aram into attacking the northern kingdom was a breech of faith in the ability of God to act on Judah's behalf. The penalty for this breech is continuing military conflict. **14:** *They made a very great fire in his honor:* The Chronicler alone records the custom of making a "great fire" in honor of a deceased ruler, a custom found on the island of Cyprus, among other cultures.

17 His son Jehoshaphat succeeded him, and strengthened himself against Israel. [2]He placed forces in all the fortified cities of Judah, and set garrisons in the land of Judah, and in the cities of Ephraim that his father Asa had taken. [3]The LORD was with Jehoshaphat, because he walked in the earlier ways of his father;[a] he did not seek the Baals, [4]but sought the God of his father and walked in his commandments, and not according to the ways of Israel. [5]Therefore the LORD established the kingdom in his hand. All Judah brought tribute to Jehoshaphat, and he had great riches and honor. [6]His heart was courageous in the ways of the LORD; and furthermore he removed the high places and the sacred poles[b] from Judah.

17.1–20.37: The reign of Jehoshaphat. This is another of the Chronicler's expansions of limited material in the narratives* of 1 and 2 Kings. The Chronicler takes an initially positive assessment of Jehoshaphat and expands his role into a model of bringing the community into accord with God. **4:** *Sought the God of his father and walked in his commandments and not according to the ways of Israel:* Israel was the formal name for the northern kingdom. A prime motif* in this narrative is the danger the idolatrous north presented to the faithful southern kingdom, Judah. The Chronicler begins early in this narrative to underscore the contrast. **6:** *His heart was courageous in the ways*

of the LORD: The *heart* was often seen as the intellectual center or seat of the will in ancient Israel. The expression here conveys Jehoshaphat's desire to conform to the will of God despite the opposition he may encounter.

---

7 In the third year of his reign he sent his officials, Ben-hail, Obadiah, Zechariah, Nethanel, and Micaiah, to teach in the cities of Judah. [8]With them were the Levites, Shemaiah, Nethaniah, Zebadiah, Asahel, Shemiramoth, Jehonathan, Adonijah, Tobijah, and Tob-adonijah; and with these Levites, the priests Elishama and Jehoram. [9]They taught in Judah, having the book of the law of the LORD with them; they went around through all the cities of Judah and taught among the people.

10 The fear of the LORD fell on all the kingdoms of the lands around Judah, and they did not make war against Jehoshaphat. [11]Some of the Philistines brought Jehoshaphat presents, and silver for tribute; and the Arabs also brought him seven thousand seven hundred rams and seven thousand seven hundred male goats. [12]Jehoshaphat grew steadily greater. He built fortresses and storage cities in Judah. [13]He carried out great works in the cities of Judah. He had soldiers, mighty warriors, in Jerusalem. [14]This was the muster of them by ancestral houses: Of Judah, the commanders of the thousands: Adnah the commander, with three hundred thousand mighty warriors, [15]and next to him Jehohanan the commander, with two hundred eighty thousand, [16]and next to him Amasiah son of Zichri, a volunteer for the service of the LORD, with two hundred thousand mighty warriors. [17]Of Benjamin: Eliada, a mighty warrior, with two hundred thousand armed with bow and shield, [18]and next to him Jehozabad with one hundred eighty thousand armed for war. [19]These were in the service of the king, besides those whom the king had placed in the fortified cities throughout all Judah.

17.7–19. 7–9: *They taught in Judah, having the book of the law of the LORD with them:* This extensive teach-

a Another reading is *his father David* 　　*b* Heb *Asherim*

ing mission is undertaken with representatives of the court (*officials*), the central religious authorities (*priests*), and those entrusted with the task of teaching the religious traditions of the community (*Levites*). The *book of the law of the LORD* may refer to the present book of Deuteronomy. **12:** *Jehoshaphat grew steadily greater:* The reward for his faithfulness was peace and prosperity, allowing the king to build stronger fortifications and an ever stronger military force.

18 Now Jehoshaphat had great riches and honor; and he made a marriage alliance with Ahab. ²After some years he went down to Ahab in Samaria. Ahab slaughtered an abundance of sheep and oxen for him and for the people who were with him, and induced him to go up against Ramoth-gilead. ³King Ahab of Israel said to King Jehoshaphat of Judah, "Will you go with me to Ramoth-gilead?" He answered him, "I am with you, my people are your people. We will be with you in the war."

4 But Jehoshaphat also said to the king of Israel, "Inquire first for the word of the LORD." ⁵Then the king of Israel gathered the prophets together, four hundred of them, and said to them, "Shall we go to battle against Ramoth-gilead, or shall I refrain?" They said, "Go up; for God will give it into the hand of the king." ⁶But Jehoshaphat said, "Is there no other prophet of the LORD here of whom we may inquire?" ⁷The king of Israel said to Jehoshaphat, "There is still one other by whom we may inquire of the LORD, Micaiah son of Imlah; but I hate him, for he never prophesies anything favorable about me, but only disaster." Jehoshaphat said, "Let the king not say such a thing." ⁸Then the king of Israel summoned an officer and said, "Bring quickly Micaiah son of Imlah." ⁹Now the king of Israel and King Jehoshaphat of Judah were sitting on their thrones, arrayed in their robes; and they were sitting at the threshing floor at the entrance of the gate of Samaria; and all the prophets were prophesying before them. ¹⁰Zedekiah son of Chenaanah made for himself horns of iron, and he said, "Thus says the LORD: With these you shall gore the Arameans until they are destroyed." ¹¹All the prophets were prophesying the same and saying, "Go up to

Ramoth-gilead and triumph; the LORD will give it into the hand of the king."

12 The messenger who had gone to summon Micaiah said to him, "Look, the words of the prophets with one accord are favorable to the king; let your word be like the word of one of them, and speak favorably." ¹³But Micaiah said, "As the LORD lives, whatever my God says, that I will speak."

18.1–13. 1: *He made a marriage alliance with Ahab:* The Chronicler assumes throughout that his readers know the evils Omri and his son Ahab had brought on the north by idolatrous worship. Closely following his source (1 Kings 22.1–28), the Chronicler also uses his source's anti-Ahab stance to make his own points. Ahab had engaged in extensive trade and hence an alliance may have been economically beneficial to Jehoshaphat. **9:** *They were sitting at the threshing* floor at the entrance of the gate of Samaria; and all the prophets* were prophesying before them:* Threshing floors were associated with activities of importance to the community. Being on a height to catch prevailing winds, such clear, open areas would be more suitable for a large gathering than small spaces within the defensive city walls. **13:** *But Micaiah said, "As the LORD lives, whatever my God says, that I will speak":* Despite the pressure to go along with the words of the other prophets, Micaiah offers a classic statement of the prophet's obligation to be obedient to God alone. The expression is very close to that of the pagan prophet Balaam (Num 22.38).

14 When he had come to the king, the king said to him, "Micaiah, shall we go to Ramoth-gilead to battle, or shall I refrain?" He answered, "Go up and triumph; they will be given into your hand." ¹⁵But the king said to him, "How many times must I make you swear to tell me nothing but the truth in the name of the LORD?" ¹⁶Then Micaiah*ᵃ* said, "I saw all Israel scattered on the mountains, like sheep without a shepherd; and the LORD said, 'These have no master; let each one go home in peace.'" ¹⁷The king of Israel said to Jehoshaphat, "Did I not tell you that he would not prophesy anything favorable about me, but only disaster?"

18 Then Micaiah*ᵃ* said, "Therefore hear

a Heb *he*

the word of the LORD: I saw the LORD sitting on his throne, with all the host of heaven standing to the right and to the left of him. [19]And the LORD said, 'Who will entice King Ahab of Israel, so that he may go up and fall at Ramoth-gilead?' Then one said one thing, and another said another, [20]until a spirit came forward and stood before the LORD, saying, 'I will entice him.' The LORD asked him, 'How?' [21]He replied, 'I will go out and be a lying spirit in the mouth of all his prophets.' Then the LORD[a] said, 'You are to entice him, and you shall succeed; go out and do it.' [22]So you see, the LORD has put a lying spirit in the mouth of these your prophets; the LORD has decreed disaster for you."

23 Then Zedekiah son of Chenaanah came up to Micaiah, slapped him on the cheek, and said, "Which way did the spirit of the LORD pass from me to speak to you?" [24]Micaiah replied, "You will find out on that day when you go in to hide in an inner chamber." [25]The king of Israel then ordered, "Take Micaiah, and return him to Amon the governor of the city and to Joash the king's son; [26]and say, 'Thus says the king: Put this fellow in prison, and feed him on reduced rations of bread and water until I return in peace.' " [27]Micaiah said, "If you return in peace, the LORD has not spoken by me." And he said, "Hear, you peoples, all of you!"

28 So the king of Israel and King Jehoshaphat of Judah went up to Ramoth-gilead. [29]The king of Israel said to Jehoshaphat, "I will disguise myself and go into battle, but you wear your robes." So the king of Israel disguised himself, and they went into battle. [30]Now the king of Aram had commanded the captains of his chariots, "Fight with no one small or great, but only with the king of Israel." [31]When the captains of the chariots saw Jehoshaphat, they said, "It is the king of Israel." So they turned to fight against him; and Jehoshaphat cried out, and the LORD helped him. God drew them away from him, [32]for when the captains of the chariots saw that it was not the king of Israel, they turned back from pursuing him. [33]But a certain man drew his bow and unknowingly struck the king of Israel between the scale armor and the breastplate; so he said to the driver of his chariot, "Turn around, and carry me out of the battle, for I am wounded." [34]The battle grew hot that day, and the king of Israel propped himself up in his chariot facing the Arameans until evening; then at sunset he died.

19 King Jehoshaphat of Judah returned in safety to his house in Jerusalem. [2]Jehu son of Hanani the seer went out to meet him and said to King Jehoshaphat, "Should you help the wicked and love those who hate the LORD? Because of this, wrath has gone out against you from the LORD. [3]Nevertheless, some good is found in you, for you destroyed the sacred poles[b] out of the land, and have set your heart to seek God."

4 Jehoshaphat resided at Jerusalem; then he went out again among the people, from Beer-sheba to the hill country of Ephraim, and brought them back to the LORD, the God of their ancestors. [5]He appointed judges in the land in all the fortified cities of Judah, city by city, [6]and said to the judges, "Consider what you are doing, for you judge not on behalf of human beings but on the LORD's behalf; he is with you in giving judgment. [7]Now, let the fear of the LORD be upon you; take care what you do, for there is no perversion of justice with the LORD our God, or partiality, or taking of bribes."

8 Moreover in Jerusalem Jehoshaphat appointed certain Levites and priests and heads of families of Israel, to give judgment for the LORD and to decide disputed cases. They had their seat at Jerusalem. [9]He charged them: "This is how you shall act: in the fear of the LORD, in faithfulness, and with your whole heart; [10]whenever a case comes to you from your kindred who live in their cities, concerning bloodshed, law or commandment, statutes or ordinances, then you shall instruct them, so that they may not incur guilt before the LORD and wrath may not come on you and your kindred. Do so, and you will not incur guilt. [11]See, Amariah the chief priest is over you in all matters of the LORD; and Zebadiah son of Ishmael, the governor of the house of Judah, in all the

a Heb he   b Heb Asheroth

king's matters; and the Levites will serve you as officers. Deal courageously, and may the LORD be with the good!"

18.14–19.11. 19.2: *Should you help the wicked and love those who hate the LORD?* Following on the disastrous outcome of the battle with the Arameans, this word from the prophet* Jehu serves as the incentive for Jehoshaphat's renewed efforts at bringing the community into accord with God's law. **4:** *Then he went out again among the people . . . and brought them back to the LORD:* Whereas earlier he sent his officials and other representatives, now the king himself undertakes an itinerant mission to teach the law to the people. **9:** *This is how you shall act: in the fear of the LORD, in faithfulness, and with your whole heart:* He lists a unique combination of elements from various portions of the Hebrew Bible. *Fear of the LORD* is necessary to ensure wisdom (Prov 1.7), *faithfulness* to adhere to the traditions and commandments of God, and *whole heart* to ensure full commitment of mind and will to administer justice.

20 After this the Moabites and Ammonites, and with them some of the Meunites,*ᵃ* came against Jehoshaphat for battle. ²Messengers*ᵇ* came and told Jehoshaphat, "A great multitude is coming against you from Edom,*ᶜ* from beyond the sea; already they are at Hazazon-tamar" (that is, En-gedi). ³Jehoshaphat was afraid; he set himself to seek the LORD, and proclaimed a fast throughout all Judah. ⁴Judah assembled to seek help from the LORD; from all the towns of Judah they came to seek the LORD.

5 Jehoshaphat stood in the assembly of Judah and Jerusalem, in the house of the LORD, before the new court, ⁶and said, "O LORD, God of our ancestors, are you not God in heaven? Do you not rule over all the kingdoms of the nations? In your hand are power and might, so that no one is able to withstand you. ⁷Did you not, O our God, drive out the inhabitants of this land before your people Israel, and give it forever to the descendants of your friend Abraham? ⁸They have lived in it, and in it have built you a sanctuary for your name, saying, ⁹'If disaster comes upon us, the sword, judgment,*ᵈ* or pestilence, or famine, we will stand before this house, and before you, for your name is

in this house, and cry to you in our distress, and you will hear and save.' ¹⁰See now, the people of Ammon, Moab, and Mount Seir, whom you would not let Israel invade when they came from the land of Egypt, and whom they avoided and did not destroy— ¹¹they reward us by coming to drive us out of your possession that you have given us to inherit. ¹²O our God, will you not execute judgment upon them? For we are powerless against this great multitude that is coming against us. We do not know what to do, but our eyes are on you."

13 Meanwhile all Judah stood before the LORD, with their little ones, their wives, and their children. ¹⁴Then the spirit of the LORD came upon Jahaziel son of Zechariah, son of Benaiah, son of Jeiel, son of Mattaniah, a Levite of the sons of Asaph, in the middle of the assembly. ¹⁵He said, "Listen, all Judah and inhabitants of Jerusalem, and King Jehoshaphat: Thus says the LORD to you: 'Do not fear or be dismayed at this great multitude; for the battle is not yours but God's. ¹⁶Tomorrow go down against them; they will come up by the ascent of Ziz; you will find them at the end of the valley, before the wilderness of Jeruel. ¹⁷This battle is not for you to fight; take your position, stand still, and see the victory of the LORD on your behalf, O Judah and Jerusalem.' Do not fear or be dismayed; tomorrow go out against them, and the LORD will be with you."

20.1–17. 1: *The Moabites and Ammonites, and with them some of the Meunites came against Jehoshaphat:* Presumably these are all peoples across the Jordan River to the east, though it would not be expected for Judah to face a challenge from these peoples. **15:** *Do not fear or be dismayed at this great multitude; for the battle is not yours but God's:* Jehoshaphat's reward for his renewed efforts to bring the nation into compliance with God is God's protection against this invasion. The implication in the Chronicler's narrative* is that no matter what the transgression, renewed seeking of God can renew the right relationship with him.

---

a Compare 26.7: Heb *Ammonites*   *b* Heb *They*
c One Ms: MT *Aram*   *d* Or *the sword of judgment*

18 Then Jehoshaphat bowed down with his face to the ground, and all Judah and the inhabitants of Jerusalem fell down before the LORD, worshiping the LORD. 19And the Levites, of the Kohathites and the Korahites, stood up to praise the LORD, the God of Israel, with a very loud voice.

20 They rose early in the morning and went out into the wilderness of Tekoa; and as they went out, Jehoshaphat stood and said, "Listen to me, O Judah and inhabitants of Jerusalem! Believe in the LORD your God and you will be established; believe his prophets." 21When he had taken counsel with the people, he appointed those who were to sing to the LORD and praise him in holy splendor, as they went before the army, saying,

"Give thanks to the LORD,
 for his steadfast love endures
  forever."

22As they began to sing and praise, the LORD set an ambush against the Ammonites, Moab, and Mount Seir, who had come against Judah, so that they were routed. 23For the Ammonites and Moab attacked the inhabitants of Mount Seir, destroying them utterly; and when they had made an end of the inhabitants of Seir, they all helped to destroy one another.

24 When Judah came to the watchtower of the wilderness, they looked toward the multitude; they were corpses lying on the ground; no one had escaped. 25When Jehoshaphat and his people came to take the booty from them, they found livestock*a* in great numbers, goods, clothing, and precious things, which they took for themselves until they could carry no more. They spent three days taking the booty, because of its abundance. 26On the fourth day they assembled in the Valley of Beracah, for there they blessed the LORD; therefore that place has been called the Valley of Beracah*b* to this day. 27Then all the people of Judah and Jerusalem, with Jehoshaphat at their head, returned to Jerusalem with joy, for the LORD had enabled them to rejoice over their enemies. 28They came to Jerusalem, with harps and lyres and trumpets, to the house of the LORD. 29The fear of God came on all the kingdoms of the countries when they heard that the LORD had fought against the enemies of Israel. 30And the realm of Jehoshaphat was quiet, for his God gave him rest all around.

31 So Jehoshaphat reigned over Judah. He was thirty-five years old when he began to reign; he reigned twenty-five years in Jerusalem. His mother's name was Azubah daughter of Shilhi. 32He walked in the way of his father Asa and did not turn aside from it, doing what was right in the sight of the LORD. 33Yet the high places were not removed; the people had not yet set their hearts upon the God of their ancestors.

34 Now the rest of the acts of Jehoshaphat, from first to last, are written in the Annals of Jehu son of Hanani, which are recorded in the Book of the Kings of Israel.

35 After this King Jehoshaphat of Judah joined with King Ahaziah of Israel, who did wickedly. 36He joined him in building ships to go to Tarshish; they built the ships in Ezion-geber. 37Then Eliezer son of Dodavahu of Mareshah prophesied against Jehoshaphat, saying, "Because you have joined with Ahaziah, the LORD will destroy what you have made." And the ships were wrecked and were not able to go to Tarshish.

20.18–37. 27: *Then all the people of Judah and Jerusalem, with Jehoshaphat at their head, returned to Jerusalem with joy:* The total destruction and looting of their enemies allowed the people of Judah to experience the joy of being "found" by God. **37:** *Because you have joined with Ahaziah, the LORD will destroy what you have made:* For apparently seeking a commercial alliance again with the idolatrous northern kingdom, Jehoshaphat's punishment was limited simply to the destruction of the means of the alliance, the ships prepared for the venture.

21 Jehoshaphat slept with his ancestors and was buried with his ancestors in the city of David; his son Jehoram succeeded him. 2He had brothers, the sons of Jehoshaphat: Azariah, Jehiel, Zechariah, Azariah, Michael, and Shephatiah; all these were the

a Gk: Heb *among them*   *b* That is *Blessing*

sons of King Jehoshaphat of Judah.[a] 3Their father gave them many gifts, of silver, gold, and valuable possessions, together with fortified cities in Judah; but he gave the kingdom to Jehoram, because he was the firstborn. 4When Jehoram had ascended the throne of his father and was established, he put all his brothers to the sword, and also some of the officials of Israel. 5Jehoram was thirty-two years old when he began to reign; he reigned eight years in Jerusalem. 6He walked in the way of the kings of Israel, as the house of Ahab had done; for the daughter of Ahab was his wife. He did what was evil in the sight of the LORD. 7Yet the LORD would not destroy the house of David because of the covenant that he had made with David, and since he had promised to give a lamp to him and to his descendants forever.

8 In his days Edom revolted against the rule of Judah and set up a king of their own. 9Then Jehoram crossed over with his commanders and all his chariots. He set out by night and attacked the Edomites, who had surrounded him and his chariot commanders. 10So Edom has been in revolt against the rule of Judah to this day. At that time Libnah also revolted against his rule, because he had forsaken the LORD, the God of his ancestors.

11 Moreover he made high places in the hill country of Judah, and led the inhabitants of Jerusalem into unfaithfulness, and made Judah go astray. 12A letter came to him from the prophet Elijah, saying: "Thus says the LORD, the God of your father David: Because you have not walked in the ways of your father Jehoshaphat or in the ways of King Asa of Judah, 13but have walked in the way of the kings of Israel, and have led Judah and the inhabitants of Jerusalem into unfaithfulness, as the house of Ahab led Israel into unfaithfulness, and because you also have killed your brothers, members of your father's house, who were better than yourself, 14see, the LORD will bring a great plague on your people, your children, your wives, and all your possessions, 15and you yourself will have a severe sickness with a disease of your bowels, until your bowels come out, day after day, because of the disease."

16 The LORD aroused against Jehoram the anger of the Philistines and of the Arabs who are near the Ethiopians.[b] 17They came up against Judah, invaded it, and carried away all the possessions they found that belonged to the king's house, along with his sons and his wives, so that no son was left to him except Jehoahaz, his youngest son.

18 After all this the LORD struck him in his bowels with an incurable disease. 19In course of time, at the end of two years, his bowels came out because of the disease, and he died in great agony. His people made no fire in his honor, like the fires made for his ancestors. 20He was thirty-two years old when he began to reign; he reigned eight years in Jerusalem. He departed with no one's regret. They buried him in the city of David, but not in the tombs of the kings.

21.1–20: The reign of Jehoram. The Chronicler expands the limited information available in his source (2 Kings 8.16–19). This is the first king of Judah whom the Chronicler evaluates as uniformly evil: The personal disaster unfaithfulness brings is clearly highlighted. **4:** *He put all his brothers to the sword,* removing any potential rivals to the throne and probably taking control of their wealth. This aside quickly establishes Jehoram as an unjust individual. **6:** *He walked in the way of the kings of Israel* by encouraging idolatry* if not directly engaging in it himself. **10:** *So Edom has been in revolt against the rule of Judah to this day:* Edom, located to the east of Judah on the other side of the Jordan, had been subject to Judah since the reign of David. The loss of Edom was one of the consequences of Jehoram's sin. **12:** *A letter came to him from the prophet* Elijah:* In 1 and 2 Kings, Elijah's prophetic ministry, largely located in the northern kingdom, offered a clear condemnation of idolatry. He also attacked the religious policies of Ahab, the king of Israel to whom Jehoram was related by marriage. The letter's contents and language are strongly colored with the Chronicler's style. The letter condemns Jehoram for killing his brothers and promoting idolatry. **20:** *He departed with no one's regret:* The Chronicler makes an ironic* comment on Jehoram's utter failure as king. The decease of the king was not marked by

a Gk Syr: Heb *Israel*   *b* Or *Nubians;* Heb *Cushites* the ceremonial fire, and in the final insult, he was not buried with the other kings of the line of David.

~~~~~~~~~~

22 The inhabitants of Jerusalem made his youngest son Ahaziah king as his successor; for the troops who came with the Arabs to the camp had killed all the older sons. So Ahaziah son of Jehoram reigned as king of Judah. ²Ahaziah was forty-two years old when he began to reign; he reigned one year in Jerusalem. His mother's name was Athaliah, a granddaughter of Omri. ³He also walked in the ways of the house of Ahab, for his mother was his counselor in doing wickedly. ⁴He did what was evil in the sight of the LORD, as the house of Ahab had done; for after the death of his father they were his counselors, to his ruin. ⁵He even followed their advice, and went with Jehoram son of King Ahab of Israel to make war against King Hazael of Aram at Ramoth-gilead. The Arameans wounded Joram, ⁶and he returned to be healed in Jezreel of the wounds that he had received at Ramah, when he fought King Hazael of Aram. And Ahaziah son of King Jehoram of Judah went down to see Joram son of Ahab in Jezreel, because he was sick.

7 But it was ordained by God that the downfall of Ahaziah should come about through his going to visit Joram. For when he came there he went out with Jehoram to meet Jehu son of Nimshi, whom the LORD had anointed to destroy the house of Ahab. ⁸When Jehu was executing judgment on the house of Ahab, he met the officials of Judah and the sons of Ahaziah's brothers, who attended Ahaziah, and he killed them. ⁹He searched for Ahaziah, who was captured while hiding in Samaria and was brought to Jehu, and put to death. They buried him, for they said, "He is the grandson of Jehoshaphat, who sought the LORD with all his heart." And the house of Ahaziah had no one able to rule the kingdom.

22.1–9: The reign of Ahaziah. The Chronicler greatly reduces the narrative* from his source (2 Kings 8.25–29; 9.14–16, 27–29). The historian is not interested in negative examples for their own sake, but only as examples or warnings of the community's relationship to God. This account provides a brief transition to

Athaliah's seizing of the throne. **3:** *He also walked in the ways of the house of Ahab,* that is, he promoted idolatry.* **8:** *When Jehu was executing judgment on the house of Ahab:* The Chronicler assumes his readers are familiar with the account in 2 Kings 9–10 where God anoints* Jehu to take the throne of the northern kingdom from the line of Ahab. **9:** *They buried him, for they said, "He is the grandson of Jehoshaphat, who sought the LORD with all his heart":* In his source, the Chronicler simply had the statement that Ahaziah was taken back to Jerusalem and buried. He expanded this simple statement to create a contrast between the faithful example of Jehoshaphat and the disastrous reigns of Jehoram and Ahaziah.

~~~~~~~~~~

10 Now when Athaliah, Ahaziah's mother, saw that her son was dead, she set about to destroy all the royal family of the house of Judah. ¹¹But Jehoshabeath, the king's daughter, took Joash son of Ahaziah, and stole him away from among the king's children who were about to be killed; she put him and his nurse in a bedroom. Thus Jehoshabeath, daughter of King Jehoram and wife of the priest Jehoiada—because she was a sister of Ahaziah—hid him from Athaliah, so that she did not kill him; ¹²he remained with them six years, hidden in the house of God, while Athaliah reigned over the land.

23 But in the seventh year Jehoiada took courage, and entered into a compact with the commanders of the hundreds, Azariah son of Jeroham, Ishmael son of Jehohanan, Azariah son of Obed, Maaseiah son of Adaiah, and Elishaphat son of Zichri. ²They went around through Judah and gathered the Levites from all the towns of Judah, and the heads of families of Israel, and they came to Jerusalem. ³Then the whole assembly made a covenant with the king in the house of God. Jehoiadaᵃ said to them, "Here is the king's son! Let him reign, as the LORD promised concerning the sons of David. ⁴This is what you are to do: one-third of you, priests and Levites, who come on duty on the sabbath, shall be gatekeepers, ⁵one-third shall be at the king's house, and one-third at the Gate of the Foundation; and

a Heb *He*

all the people shall be in the courts of the house of the LORD. ⁶Do not let anyone enter the house of the LORD except the priests and ministering Levites; they may enter, for they are holy, but all the other*ᵃ* people shall observe the instructions of the LORD. ⁷The Levites shall surround the king, each with his weapons in his hand; and whoever enters the house shall be killed. Stay with the king in his comings and goings."

22.10–24.27: The reign of Joash. Although at points following closely his source in 2 Kings 11–12, the Chronicler has expanded selected parts of the account to incorporate his own concerns and has added an entire phase of Joash's later rule, marked by apostasy. The focus of the first part of the narrative* is not so much on Joash as on the figure of the high priest Jehoiada, who functions as the model of faithfulness and the example of seeking God. **22.10:** *She set about to destroy all the royal family of the house of Judah,* possibly in revenge for Jehu's killing of the house of Ahab, to which she belonged. **11:** *Jehoshabeath, daughter of King Jehoram and wife of the priest Jehoiada . . . hid him from Athaliah:* 2 Kings presents Jehoshabeath's royal lineage, but not her marriage to Jehoiada. Her heroic action in sheltering the Davidic heir is motivated in several ways, from familial loyalty to her brother to self-interested preservation of the privileges of the Temple* in Jerusalem. **23.2:** *They went around through Judah and gathered the Levites:* While 2 Kings presents the effort to put Joash on the throne as the combined effort of military commanders and Jehoiada, the Chronicler places the conspiracy squarely among the religious personnel, the priests and Levites. The elaborate preparations were designed to conceal the assembly of such a large company of armed Levites.

8 The Levites and all Judah did according to all that the priest Jehoiada commanded; each brought his men, who were to come on duty on the sabbath, with those who were to go off duty on the sabbath; for the priest Jehoiada did not dismiss the divisions. ⁹The priest Jehoiada delivered to the captains the spears and the large and small shields that had been King David's, which were in the house of God; ¹⁰and he set all the people as a guard for the king, everyone with weapon in hand, from the south side of the house to the north side of the house, around the altar and the house. ¹¹Then he brought out the king's son, put the crown on him, and gave him the covenant;*ᵇ* they proclaimed him king, and Jehoiada and his sons anointed him; and they shouted, "Long live the king!"

12 When Athaliah heard the noise of the people running and praising the king, she went into the house of the LORD to the people; ¹³and when she looked, there was the king standing by his pillar at the entrance, and the captains and the trumpeters beside the king, and all the people of the land rejoicing and blowing trumpets, and the singers with their musical instruments leading in the celebration. Athaliah tore her clothes, and cried, "Treason! Treason!" ¹⁴Then the priest Jehoiada brought out the captains who were set over the army, saying to them, "Bring her out between the ranks; anyone who follows her is to be put to the sword." For the priest said, "Do not put her to death in the house of the LORD." ¹⁵So they laid hands on her; she went into the entrance of the Horse Gate of the king's house, and there they put her to death.

16 Jehoiada made a covenant between himself and all the people and the king that they should be the LORD's people. ¹⁷Then all the people went to the house of Baal, and tore it down; his altars and his images they broke in pieces, and they killed Mattan, the priest of Baal, in front of the altars. ¹⁸Jehoiada assigned the care of the house of the LORD to the levitical priests whom David had organized to be in charge of the house of the LORD, to offer burnt offerings to the LORD, as it is written in the law of Moses, with rejoicing and with singing, according to the order of David. ¹⁹He stationed the gatekeepers at the gates of the house of the LORD so that no one should enter who was in any way unclean. ²⁰And he took the captains, the nobles, the governors of the people, and all the people of the land, and they brought the king down from the house of the LORD, marching through the upper gate to the king's house. They set the king on the royal throne. ²¹So

a Heb lacks *other*   *b* Or *treaty,* or *testimony;* Heb *eduth* all the people of the land rejoiced, and the city was quiet after Athaliah had been killed with the sword.

23.8–21. 16: *Jehoiada made a covenant* between himself and all the people and the king that they should be the LORD's people,* thus committing themselves to the exclusive worship of the God of Israel. **18:** *Jehoiada assigned the care of the house of the LORD to the levitical priests whom David had organized to be in charge of the house of the LORD, to offer burnt offerings to the LORD, as it is written in the law of Moses, with rejoicing and with singing, according to the order of David:* This is confusing since only priests, the sons of Aaron, could offer burnt offerings to the LORD. There may be a textual confusion, and the term "levitical priests" may have read "priest and Levites," which would resolve the confusion. The reinstallation of these responsibilities by Jehoiada implies that under Athaliah normal Temple functions were disrupted and now needed to be restored. **19:** *So that no one should enter who was in any way unclean:* This means unclean in a ritual sense, that is, unacceptable to come into God's presence. Such a protection preserves the holiness of the Temple precinct.

24 Joash was seven years old when he began to reign; he reigned forty years in Jerusalem; his mother's name was Zibiah of Beer-sheba. ²Joash did what was right in the sight of the LORD all the days of the priest Jehoiada. ³Jehoiada got two wives for him, and he became the father of sons and daughters.

4 Some time afterward Joash decided to restore the house of the LORD. ⁵He assembled the priests and the Levites and said to them, "Go out to the cities of Judah and gather money from all Israel to repair the house of your God, year by year; and see that you act quickly." But the Levites did not act quickly. ⁶So the king summoned Jehoiada the chief, and said to him, "Why have you not required the Levites to bring in from Judah and Jerusalem the tax levied by Moses, the servant of the LORD, on*ᵃ* the congregation of Israel for the tent of the covenant?"*ᵇ* ⁷For the children of Athaliah, that wicked woman, had broken into the house of God, and had even used all the dedicated things of the house of the LORD for the Baals.

8 So the king gave command, and they made a chest, and set it outside the gate of the house of the LORD. ⁹A proclamation was made throughout Judah and Jerusalem to bring in for the LORD the tax that Moses the servant of God laid on Israel in the wilderness. ¹⁰All the leaders and all the people rejoiced and brought their tax and dropped it into the chest until it was full. ¹¹Whenever the chest was brought to the king's officers by the Levites, when they saw that there was a large amount of money in it, the king's secretary and the officer of the chief priest would come and empty the chest and take it and return it to its place. So they did day after day, and collected money in abundance. ¹²The king and Jehoiada gave it to those who had charge of the work of the house of the LORD, and they hired masons and carpenters to restore the house of the LORD, and also workers in iron and bronze to repair the house of the LORD. ¹³So those who were engaged in the work labored, and the repairing went forward at their hands, and they restored the house of God to its proper condition and strengthened it. ¹⁴When they had finished, they brought the rest of the money to the king and Jehoiada, and with it were made utensils for the house of the LORD, utensils for the service and for the burnt offerings, and ladles, and vessels of gold and silver. They offered burnt offerings in the house of the LORD regularly all the days of Jehoiada.

15 But Jehoiada grew old and full of days, and died; he was one hundred thirty years old at his death. ¹⁶And they buried him in the city of David among the kings, because he had done good in Israel, and for God and his house.

17 Now after the death of Jehoiada the officials of Judah came and did obeisance to the king; then the king listened to them. ¹⁸They abandoned the house of the LORD, the God of their ancestors, and served the sacred poles*ᶜ* and the idols. And wrath came upon Judah and Jerusalem for this guilt of theirs. ¹⁹Yet he sent prophets among them

a Compare Vg: Heb *and*   *b* Or *treaty,* or *testimony;* Heb *eduth*   *c* Heb *Asherim*

to bring them back to the LORD; they testified against them, but they would not
listen.

20 Then the spirit of God took possession
of[a] Zechariah son of the priest Jehoiada; he
stood above the people and said to them,
"Thus says God: Why do you transgress the
commandments of the LORD, so that you
cannot prosper? Because you have forsaken
the LORD, he has also forsaken you." 21 But
they conspired against him, and by command of the king they stoned him to death
in the court of the house of the LORD.
22 King Joash did not remember the kindness
that Jehoiada, Zechariah's father, had shown
him, but killed his son. As he was dying, he
said, "May the LORD see and avenge!"

23 At the end of the year the army of
Aram came up against Joash. They came to
Judah and Jerusalem, and destroyed all the
officials of the people from among them, and
sent all the booty they took to the king of
Damascus. 24 Although the army of Aram
had come with few men, the LORD delivered
into their hand a very great army, because
they had abandoned the LORD, the God of
their ancestors. Thus they executed judgment on Joash.

25 When they had withdrawn, leaving
him severely wounded, his servants conspired against him because of the blood of
the son[b] of the priest Jehoiada, and they
killed him on his bed. So he died; and they
buried him in the city of David, but they did
not bury him in the tombs of the kings.
26 Those who conspired against him were Zabad son of Shimeath the Ammonite, and Jehozabad son of Shimrith the Moabite. 27 Accounts of his sons, and of the many oracles
against him, and of the rebuilding[c] of the
house of God are written in the Commentary
on the Book of the Kings. And his son Amaziah succeeded him.

24.1–27. 10: *All the leaders and all the people rejoiced
and brought their tax and dropped it into the chest:*
Having come on the throne with the support of the
priests and Levites and "all the people," Joash reaffirms
his faithfulness by seeking to repair and restore the
Temple.* By having the Levites fail to go out and collect the tax for the Temple, the Chronicler can portray

the people coming in joy to pay their obligation and
note that the money came in abundantly. **16:** *They
buried him in the city of David among the kings,* a
remarkable honor for Jehoiada. The Chronicler underscores Jehoiada's contributions by depicting him as the
restorer of the legitimate heir to the throne of David,
and as the restorer of proper worship to the Temple.
18: *They abandoned the house of the LORD:* As in the
Chronicler's earlier statements, if Israel abandons
God, God abandons the community. This is the message of the prophet* Zechariah, son of Jehoiada,
which only succeeds in earning his murder. Joash's
reign ends in military disaster and conspiracy against
the king.

~~~~~~

25 Amaziah was twenty-five years old
when he began to reign, and he
reigned twenty-nine years in Jerusalem. His
mother's name was Jehoaddan of Jerusalem.
2 He did what was right in the sight of the
LORD, yet not with a true heart. 3 As soon as
the royal power was firmly in his hand he
killed his servants who had murdered his father the king. 4 But he did not put their children to death, according to what is written
in the law, in the book of Moses, where the
LORD commanded, "The parents shall not be
put to death for the children, or the children
be put to death for the parents; but all shall
be put to death for their own sins."

5 Amaziah assembled the people of Judah, and set them by ancestral houses under
commanders of the thousands and of the
hundreds for all Judah and Benjamin. He
mustered those twenty years old and upward,
and found that they were three hundred
thousand picked troops fit for war, able to
handle spear and shield. 6 He also hired one
hundred thousand mighty warriors from Israel for one hundred talents of silver. 7 But a
man of God came to him and said, "O king,
do not let the army of Israel go with you, for
the LORD is not with Israel—all these
Ephraimites. 8 Rather, go by yourself and act;
be strong in battle, or God will fling you
down before the enemy; for God has power
to help or to overthrow." 9 Amaziah said to
the man of God, "But what shall we do about

---

a Heb *clothed itself with*   *b* Gk Vg: Heb *sons*
c Heb *founding*

the hundred talents that I have given to the army of Israel?" The man of God answered, "The LORD is able to give you much more than this." ¹⁰Then Amaziah discharged the army that had come to him from Ephraim, letting them go home again. But they became very angry with Judah, and returned home in fierce anger.

25.1–28: The reign of Amaziah. Expanding considerably on his source in 2 Kings 14.1–22, the Chronicler elaborates several characteristic themes in recounting Amaziah's rule. In several ways it is similar to the reign of Joash, starting off on the right moral ground but declining into idolatry* with the inescapable judgment against the king and the community. **2:** *He did what was right in the sight of the LORD, yet not with a true heart:* Though technically Amaziah was in the right, the commitment of will and intellect the Chronicler sees as essential was not present. **4:** *According to what is written in the law, in the book of Moses:* This indicates how important the written collection of the Pentateuch* was becoming. Deuteronomy 24.16 provides the specific reference. **7:** *O king, do not let the army of Israel go with you, for the LORD is not with Israel:* Having conducted himself correctly, Amaziah is assured of military success. His hiring of mercenaries from the northern kingdom does not meet with God's approval. The unnamed prophet* (*man of God*) offers him a chance to return to God's favor, an opportunity that Amaziah takes. The result is a great victory for Judah.

11 Amaziah took courage, and led out his people; he went to the Valley of Salt, and struck down ten thousand men of Seir. ¹²The people of Judah captured another ten thousand alive, took them to the top of Sela, and threw them down from the top of Sela, so that all of them were dashed to pieces. ¹³But the men of the army whom Amaziah sent back, not letting them go with him to battle, fell on the cities of Judah from Samaria to Beth-horon; they killed three thousand people in them, and took much booty.

14 Now after Amaziah came from the slaughter of the Edomites, he brought the gods of the people of Seir, set them up as his gods, and worshiped them, making offerings to them. ¹⁵The LORD was angry with Amaziah and sent to him a prophet, who said to

him, "Why have you resorted to a people's gods who could not deliver their own people from your hand?" ¹⁶But as he was speaking the king*ᵃ* said to him, "Have we made you a royal counselor? Stop! Why should you be put to death?" So the prophet stopped, but said, "I know that God has determined to destroy you, because you have done this and have not listened to my advice."

25.11–16. 14: *He brought the gods of the people of Seir, set them up as his gods, and worshiped them:* Having begun his rule correctly, Amaziah now succumbs to idolatry. **16:** *I know that God has determined to destroy you, because you have done this and have not listened to my advice:* The prophet's offer of an opportunity for repentance is abruptly halted by Amaziah, and the prophet gives voice to the Chronicler's view of what such pride leads to. His reign ends in dishonor as conspirators murder him.

17 Then King Amaziah of Judah took counsel and sent to King Joash son of Jehoahaz son of Jehu of Israel, saying, "Come, let us look one another in the face." ¹⁸King Joash of Israel sent word to King Amaziah of Judah, "A thornbush on Lebanon sent to a cedar on Lebanon, saying, 'Give your daughter to my son for a wife'; but a wild animal of Lebanon passed by and trampled down the thornbush. ¹⁹You say, 'See, I have defeated Edom,' and your heart has lifted you up in boastfulness. Now stay at home; why should you provoke trouble so that you fall, you and Judah with you?"

20 But Amaziah would not listen—it was God's doing, in order to hand them over, because they had sought the gods of Edom. ²¹So King Joash of Israel went up; he and King Amaziah of Judah faced one another in battle at Beth-shemesh, which belongs to Judah. ²²Judah was defeated by Israel; everyone fled home. ²³King Joash of Israel captured King Amaziah of Judah, son of Joash, son of Ahaziah, at Beth-shemesh; he brought him to Jerusalem, and broke down the wall of Jerusalem from the Ephraim Gate to the Corner Gate, a distance of four hundred cubits. ²⁴He seized all the gold and silver, and

a Heb *he*

all the vessels that were found in the house of God, and Obed-edom with them; he seized also the treasuries of the king's house, also hostages; then he returned to Samaria.

25 King Amaziah son of Joash of Judah, lived fifteen years after the death of King Joash son of Jehoahaz of Israel. 26 Now the rest of the deeds of Amaziah, from first to last, are they not written in the Book of the Kings of Judah and Israel? 27 From the time that Amaziah turned away from the LORD they made a conspiracy against him in Jerusalem, and he fled to Lachish. But they sent after him to Lachish, and killed him there. 28 They brought him back on horses; he was buried with his ancestors in the city of David.

26 Then all the people of Judah took Uzziah, who was sixteen years old, and made him king to succeed his father Amaziah. 2 He rebuilt Eloth and restored it to Judah, after the king slept with his ancestors. 3 Uzziah was sixteen years old when he began to reign, and he reigned fifty-two years in Jerusalem. His mother's name was Jecoliah of Jerusalem. 4 He did what was right in the sight of the LORD, just as his father Amaziah had done. 5 He set himself to seek God in the days of Zechariah, who instructed him in the fear of God; and as long as he sought the LORD, God made him prosper.

6 He went out and made war against the Philistines, and broke down the wall of Gath and the wall of Jabneh and the wall of Ashdod; he built cities in the territory of Ashdod and elsewhere among the Philistines. 7 God helped him against the Philistines, against the Arabs who lived in Gur-baal, and against the Meunites. 8 The Ammonites paid tribute to Uzziah, and his fame spread even to the border of Egypt, for he became very strong. 9 Moreover Uzziah built towers in Jerusalem at the Corner Gate, at the Valley Gate, and at the Angle, and fortified them. 10 He built towers in the wilderness and hewed out many cisterns, for he had large herds, both in the Shephelah and in the plain, and he had farmers and vinedressers in the hills and in the fertile lands, for he loved the soil. 11 Moreover Uzziah had an army of soldiers, fit for war, in divisions according to the number in the muster made by the secretary Jeiel and the officer Maaseiah, under the direction of Hananiah, one of the king's commanders. 12 The whole number of the heads of ancestral houses of mighty warriors was two thousand six hundred. 13 Under their command was an army of three hundred seven thousand five hundred, who could make war with mighty power, to help the king against the enemy. 14 Uzziah provided for all the army the shields, spears, helmets, coats of mail, bows, and stones for slinging. 15 In Jerusalem he set up machines, invented by skilled workers, on the towers and the corners for shooting arrows and large stones. And his fame spread far, for he was marvelously helped until he became strong.

16 But when he had become strong he grew proud, to his destruction. For he was false to the LORD his God, and entered the temple of the LORD to make offering on the altar of incense. 17 But the priest Azariah went in after him, with eighty priests of the LORD who were men of valor; 18 they withstood King Uzziah, and said to him, "It is not for you, Uzziah, to make offering to the LORD, but for the priests the descendants of Aaron, who are consecrated to make offering. Go out of the sanctuary; for you have done wrong, and it will bring you no honor from the LORD God." 19 Then Uzziah was angry. Now he had a censer in his hand to make offering, and when he became angry with the priests a leprous[b] disease broke out on his forehead, in the presence of the priests in the house of the LORD, by the altar of incense. 20 When the chief priest Azariah, and all the priests, looked at him, he was leprous[a] in his forehead. They hurried him out, and he himself hurried to get out, because the LORD had struck him. 21 King Uzziah was leprous[a] to the day of his death, and being leprous[a] lived in a separate house, for he was excluded from the house of the LORD. His son Jotham was in charge of the palace of the king, governing the people of the land.

22 Now the rest of the acts of Uzziah, from first to last, the prophet Isaiah son of

---

a A term for several skin diseases; precise meaning uncertain

Amoz wrote. 23Uzziah slept with his ancestors; they buried him near his ancestors in the burial field that belonged to the kings, for they said, "He is leprous."*a* His son Jotham succeeded him.

26.1–23: The reign of Uzziah. Greatly expanding on his source (2 Kings 14.21–22; 15.1–3), the Chronicler presents another cycle of good beginnings that end in dishonor. Of particular interest is the incident of Uzziah's taking on the prerogatives of the priesthood. **5:** *He set himself to seek God in the days of Zechariah, who instructed him in the fear of God:* The identity of this Zechariah is uncertain; possibly he is a member of the family of the high priest Jehoiada, whose son was named Zechariah. Uzziah's intent to seek God is highlighted. Being on the right path early in his reign, Uzziah has military and economic success. **16:** *But when he had become strong he grew proud, to his destruction:* Despite his good start, Uzziah moved apart from the law of God. **18:** *It is not for you, Uzziah, to make offering to the LORD, but for the priests the descendants of Aaron:* The intercessory role of the priesthood is understood by the Chronicler to be ordained by God (see Num 16). The priests act as the prophets* do in other settings, bringing an offer to the protagonist to make the right moral choice. **19:** *When he became angry with the priests a leprous disease broke out on his forehead:* His anger at the priests was, indirectly, anger at God's chosen means of regulating worship. Being struck with leprosy made Uzziah unclean, unable to approach the Temple* precinct and unable to conduct normal commerce with those who observed the Mosaic rules regulating ritual cleanliness. **23:** *They buried him near his ancestors,* but because of his uncleanness, he could not be buried with the other kings of the line of David.

---

27 Jotham was twenty-five years old when he began to reign; he reigned sixteen years in Jerusalem. His mother's name was Jerushah daughter of Zadok. 2He did what was right in the sight of the LORD just as his father Uzziah had done—only he did not invade the temple of the LORD. But the people still followed corrupt practices. 3He built the upper gate of the house of the LORD, and did extensive building on the wall of Ophel. 4Moreover he built cities in the hill country of Judah, and forts and towers on the wooded hills. 5He fought with the king of the

Ammonites and prevailed against them. The Ammonites gave him that year one hundred talents of silver, ten thousand cors of wheat and ten thousand of barley. The Ammonites paid him the same amount in the second and the third years. 6So Jotham became strong because he ordered his ways before the LORD his God. 7Now the rest of the acts of Jotham, and all his wars and his ways, are written in the Book of the Kings of Israel and Judah. 8He was twenty-five years old when he began to reign; he reigned sixteen years in Jerusalem. 9Jotham slept with his ancestors, and they buried him in the city of David; and his son Ahaz succeeded him.

27.1–9: The reign of Jotham. Of not much interest to the Chronicler, Jotham's rule receives very short notice. **2:** His main attribute is that *he did not invade the temple,* the primary failing of his father Uzziah.

---

28 Ahaz was twenty years old when he began to reign; he reigned sixteen years in Jerusalem. He did not do what was right in the sight of the LORD, as his ancestor David had done, 2but he walked in the ways of the kings of Israel. He even made cast images for the Baals; 3and he made offerings in the valley of the son of Hinnom, and made his sons pass through fire, according to the abominable practices of the nations whom the LORD drove out before the people of Israel. 4He sacrificed and made offerings on the high places, on the hills, and under every green tree.

5 Therefore the LORD his God gave him into the hand of the king of Aram, who defeated him and took captive a great number of his people and brought them to Damascus. He was also given into the hand of the king of Israel, who defeated him with great slaughter. 6Pekah son of Remaliah killed one hundred twenty thousand in Judah in one day, all of them valiant warriors, because they had abandoned the LORD, the God of their ancestors. 7And Zichri, a mighty warrior of Ephraim, killed the king's son Maaseiah, Azrikam the commander of the palace,

---

a A term for several skin diseases; precise meaning uncertain

and Elkanah the next in authority to the king.

8 The people of Israel took captive two hundred thousand of their kin, women, sons, and daughters; they also took much booty from them and brought the booty to Samaria. 9But a prophet of the LORD was there, whose name was Oded; he went out to meet the army that came to Samaria, and said to them, "Because the LORD, the God of your ancestors, was angry with Judah, he gave them into your hand, but you have killed them in a rage that has reached up to heaven. 10Now you intend to subjugate the people of Judah and Jerusalem, male and female, as your slaves. But what have you except sins against the LORD your God? 11Now hear me, and send back the captives whom you have taken from your kindred, for the fierce wrath of the LORD is upon you." 12Moreover, certain chiefs of the Ephraimites, Azariah son of Johanan, Berechiah son of Meshillemoth, Jehizkiah son of Shallum, and Amasa son of Hadlai, stood up against those who were coming from the war, 13and said to them, "You shall not bring the captives in here, for you propose to bring on us guilt against the LORD in addition to our present sins and guilt. For our guilt is already great, and there is fierce wrath against Israel." 14So the warriors left the captives and the booty before the officials and all the assembly. 15Then those who were mentioned by name got up and took the captives, and with the booty they clothed all that were naked among them; they clothed them, gave them sandals, provided them with food and drink, and anointed them; and carrying all the feeble among them on donkeys, they brought them to their kindred at Jericho, the city of palm trees. Then they returned to Samaria.

16 At that time King Ahaz sent to the king*a* of Assyria for help. 17For the Edomites had again invaded and defeated Judah, and carried away captives. 18And the Philistines had made raids on the cities in the Shephelah and the Negeb of Judah, and had taken Beth-shemesh, Aijalon, Gederoth, Soco with its villages, Timnah with its villages, and Gimzo with its villages; and they settled

there. 19For the LORD brought Judah low because of King Ahaz of Israel, for he had behaved without restraint in Judah and had been faithless to the LORD. 20So King Tilgath-pilneser of Assyria came against him, and oppressed him instead of strengthening him. 21For Ahaz plundered the house of the LORD and the houses of the king and of the officials, and gave tribute to the king of Assyria; but it did not help him.

22 In the time of his distress he became yet more faithless to the LORD—this same King Ahaz. 23For he sacrificed to the gods of Damascus, which had defeated him, and said, "Because the gods of the kings of Aram helped them, I will sacrifice to them so that they may help me." But they were the ruin of him, and of all Israel. 24Ahaz gathered together the utensils of the house of God, and cut in pieces the utensils of the house of God. He shut up the doors of the house of the LORD and made himself altars in every corner of Jerusalem. 25In every city of Judah he made high places to make offerings to other gods, provoking to anger the LORD, the God of his ancestors. 26Now the rest of his acts and all his ways, from first to last, are written in the Book of the Kings of Judah and Israel. 27Ahaz slept with his ancestors, and they buried him in the city, in Jerusalem; but they did not bring him into the tombs of the kings of Israel. His son Hezekiah succeeded him.

28.1–27: The reign of Ahaz. Having portrayed how serious a violation of the Temple* was in the case of Uzziah, the Chronicler has led his readers to one of the turning points in Judean history, the rule of Ahaz. While relying closely on his source (2 Kings 16.1–20), the Chronicler has expanded his materials considerably. **5:** *Therefore the LORD his God gave him into the hand of the king of Aram:* Ahaz's pattern of idolatry* had inescapable consequences in the Chronicler's view. **6:** *Pekah son of Remaliah killed one hundred twenty thousand in Judah in one day . . . because they had abandoned the LORD:* The Chronicler sees Ahaz's apostasy as representative of a more general abandonment of God by the people under his rule. **9:** *But you have killed them in a rage that has reached up to heaven:* With a large body of captives in tow that will

a Gk Syr Vg Compare 2 Kings 16.7: Heb *kings*

be enslaved, the warriors confront the prophet* Oded, who makes clear the choice before them. They choose wisely, and the captives are returned to Jericho. **24:** *He shut up the doors of the house of the LORD:* Ahaz's closure of the doors meant the suspension of the normal daily rituals of the Temple, the very offerings that David and Solomon had taken such care to ensure were performed properly. The Chronicler is stating that Ahaz had undone all the good that David and Solomon had accomplished. **27:** *They did not bring him into the tombs of the kings of Israel:* Like Uzziah, Ahaz was unclean because of his open participation in idolatry and his closure of the Temple. His burial with the other kings would have rendered their tombs unclean.

29 Hezekiah began to reign when he was twenty-five years old; he reigned twenty-nine years in Jerusalem. His mother's name was Abijah daughter of Zechariah. ²He did what was right in the sight of the LORD, just as his ancestor David had done.

29.1–32.33: The reign of Hezekiah. One of the great narratives* of the Chronicler's history is the account of Hezekiah. Incorporating large portions of his source in 2 Kings 18–20, he adds considerable materials concerning Hezekiah's reforms and the great worshipping assemblies, in which the king tries to bring the community back into alignment with God. A number of literary forms are employed, including dramatic speeches, sweeping descriptions, and detailed lists of personnel. **29.2:** *He did what was right in the sight of the LORD, just as his ancestor David had done:* This is an unusual opening for the Chronicler, linking Hezekiah's rule to David's.

3 In the first year of his reign, in the first month, he opened the doors of the house of the LORD and repaired them. ⁴He brought in the priests and the Levites and assembled them in the square on the east. ⁵He said to them, "Listen to me, Levites! Sanctify yourselves, and sanctify the house of the LORD, the God of your ancestors, and carry out the filth from the holy place. ⁶For our ancestors have been unfaithful and have done what was evil in the sight of the LORD our God; they have forsaken him, and have turned away their faces from the dwelling of the LORD, and turned their backs. ⁷They also

shut the doors of the vestibule and put out the lamps, and have not offered incense or made burnt offerings in the holy place to the God of Israel. ⁸Therefore the wrath of the LORD came upon Judah and Jerusalem, and he has made them an object of horror, of astonishment, and of hissing, as you see with your own eyes. ⁹Our fathers have fallen by the sword and our sons and our daughters and our wives are in captivity for this. ¹⁰Now it is in my heart to make a covenant with the LORD, the God of Israel, so that his fierce anger may turn away from us. ¹¹My sons, do not now be negligent, for the LORD has chosen you to stand in his presence to minister to him, and to be his ministers and make offerings to him."

29.3–11. 3: *In the first year of his reign, in the first month, he opened the doors of the house of the LORD,* demonstrating by the priority assigned to this task his dedication to God. **5:** *Sanctify yourselves, and sanctify the house of the LORD . . . and carry out the filth from the holy place:* The closure of the Temple* had dangerously imperiled its sanctity. There are also suggestions that Ahaz had cultivated idolatrous* worship in the Temple precinct itself (2 Kings 16.11–16). To set the Temple service back on the proper course, all the elements of idolatrous worship needed to be removed, and all the proper worship implements and utensils restored to their places.

12 Then the Levites arose, Mahath son of Amasai, and Joel son of Azariah, of the sons of the Kohathites; and of the sons of Merari, Kish son of Abdi, and Azariah son of Jehallelel; and of the Gershonites, Joah son of Zimmah, and Eden son of Joah; ¹³and of the sons of Elizaphan, Shimri and Jeuel; and of the sons of Asaph, Zechariah and Mattaniah; ¹⁴and of the sons of Heman, Jehuel and Shimei; and of the sons of Jeduthun, Shemaiah and Uzziel. ¹⁵They gathered their brothers, sanctified themselves, and went in as the king had commanded, by the words of the LORD, to cleanse the house of the LORD. ¹⁶The priests went into the inner part of the house of the LORD to cleanse it, and they brought out all the unclean things that they found in the temple of the LORD into the court of the house of the LORD; and the Le-

vites took them and carried them out to the Wadi Kidron. [17]They began to sanctify on the first day of the first month, and on the eighth day of the month they came to the vestibule of the LORD; then for eight days they sanctified the house of the LORD, and on the sixteenth day of the first month they finished. [18]Then they went inside to King Hezekiah and said, "We have cleansed all the house of the LORD, the altar of burnt offering and all its utensils, and the table for the rows of bread and all its utensils. [19]All the utensils that King Ahaz repudiated during his reign when he was faithless, we have made ready and sanctified; see, they are in front of the altar of the LORD."

20 Then King Hezekiah rose early, assembled the officials of the city, and went up to the house of the LORD. [21]They brought seven bulls, seven rams, seven lambs, and seven male goats for a sin offering for the kingdom and for the sanctuary and for Judah. He commanded the priests the descendants of Aaron to offer them on the altar of the LORD. [22]So they slaughtered the bulls, and the priests received the blood and dashed it against the altar; they slaughtered the rams and their blood was dashed against the altar; they also slaughtered the lambs and their blood was dashed against the altar. [23]Then the male goats for the sin offering were brought to the king and the assembly; they laid their hands on them, [24]and the priests slaughtered them and made a sin offering with their blood at the altar, to make atonement for all Israel. For the king commanded that the burnt offering and the sin offering should be made for all Israel.

25 He stationed the Levites in the house of the LORD with cymbals, harps, and lyres, according to the commandment of David and of Gad the king's seer and of the prophet Nathan, for the commandment was from the LORD through his prophets. [26]The Levites stood with the instruments of David, and the priests with the trumpets. [27]Then Hezekiah commanded that the burnt offering be offered on the altar. When the burnt offering began, the song to the LORD began also, and the trumpets, accompanied by the instruments of King David of Israel. [28]The whole assembly worshiped, the singers sang, and the trumpeters sounded; all this continued until the burnt offering was finished. [29]When the offering was finished, the king and all who were present with him bowed down and worshiped. [30]King Hezekiah and the officials commanded the Levites to sing praises to the LORD with the words of David and of the seer Asaph. They sang praises with gladness, and they bowed down and worshiped.

31 Then Hezekiah said, "You have now consecrated yourselves to the LORD; come near, bring sacrifices and thank offerings to the house of the LORD." The assembly brought sacrifices and thank offerings; and all who were of a willing heart brought burnt offerings. [32]The number of the burnt offerings that the assembly brought was seventy bulls, one hundred rams, and two hundred lambs; all these were for a burnt offering to the LORD. [33]The consecrated offerings were six hundred bulls and three thousand sheep. [34]But the priests were too few and could not skin all the burnt offerings, so, until other priests had sanctified themselves, their kindred, the Levites, helped them until the work was finished—for the Levites were more conscientious[a] than the priests in sanctifying themselves. [35]Besides the great number of burnt offerings there was the fat of the offerings of well-being, and there were the drink offerings for the burnt offerings. Thus the service of the house of the LORD was restored. [36]And Hezekiah and all the people rejoiced because of what God had done for the people; for the thing had come about suddenly.

29.12–36. 21: *For a sin offering for the kingdom and for the sanctuary and for Judah:* Once the Temple is cleansed, Hezekiah moves quickly to restore the Temple services. To initiate normal services, the king and the community leaders offer a sequence of offerings to atone for sins by the community. 27: *When the burnt offering began, the song to the LORD began also:* Restarting the Temple sacrifices was accompanied by the reinstitution of choral praise to God that David had initiated. 36: *Hezekiah and all the people rejoiced be-*

a Heb *upright in heart*

cause of what God had done for the people: Having been able to restore the Temple service, the assembly sensed that a reversal of God's judgment against Judah was also beginning.

30 Hezekiah sent word to all Israel and Judah, and wrote letters also to Ephraim and Manasseh, that they should come to the house of the LORD at Jerusalem, to keep the passover to the LORD the God of Israel. 2For the king and his officials and all the assembly in Jerusalem had taken counsel to keep the passover in the second month 3(for they could not keep it at its proper time because the priests had not sanctified themselves in sufficient number, nor had the people assembled in Jerusalem). 4The plan seemed right to the king and all the assembly. 5So they decreed to make a proclamation throughout all Israel, from Beer-sheba to Dan, that the people should come and keep the passover to the LORD the God of Israel, at Jerusalem; for they had not kept it in great numbers as prescribed. 6So couriers went throughout all Israel and Judah with letters from the king and his officials, as the king had commanded, saying, "O people of Israel, return to the LORD, the God of Abraham, Isaac, and Israel, so that he may turn again to the remnant of you who have escaped from the hand of the kings of Assyria. 7Do not be like your ancestors and your kindred, who were faithless to the LORD God of their ancestors, so that he made them a desolation, as you see. 8Do not now be stiff-necked as your ancestors were, but yield yourselves to the LORD and come to his sanctuary, which he has sanctified forever, and serve the LORD your God, so that his fierce anger may turn away from you. 9For as you return to the LORD, your kindred and your children will find compassion with their captors, and return to this land. For the LORD your God is gracious and merciful, and will not turn away his face from you, if you return to him."

10 So the couriers went from city to city through the country of Ephraim and Manasseh, and as far as Zebulun; but they laughed them to scorn, and mocked them. 11Only a few from Asher, Manasseh, and Zebulun

humbled themselves and came to Jerusalem. 12The hand of God was also on Judah to give them one heart to do what the king and the officials commanded by the word of the LORD.

30.1–12. 5: *So they decreed to make a proclamation throughout all Israel, from Beer-sheba to Dan, that the people should come and keep the passover*:* These boundaries are the traditional southern and northern points of Israel. The inclusion of both northern and southern portions of the country may be a deliberate effort to connect Hezekiah with the first "united" rule over north and south since the time of Solomon. It is doubtful that Judean rule under Hezekiah could have been extended very far to the north. **12:** *The hand of God was also on Judah to give them one heart to do what the king and the officials commanded by the word of the LORD:* The unity of the people is an important theme to the Chronicler's history.

13 Many people came together in Jerusalem to keep the festival of unleavened bread in the second month, a very large assembly. 14They set to work and removed the altars that were in Jerusalem, and all the altars for offering incense they took away and threw into the Wadi Kidron. 15They slaughtered the passover lamb on the fourteenth day of the second month. The priests and the Levites were ashamed, and they sanctified themselves and brought burnt offerings into the house of the LORD. 16They took their accustomed posts according to the law of Moses the man of God; the priests dashed the blood that they received*a* from the hands of the Levites. 17For there were many in the assembly who had not sanctified themselves; therefore the Levites had to slaughter the passover lamb for everyone who was not clean, to make it holy to the LORD. 18For a multitude of the people, many of them from Ephraim, Manasseh, Issachar, and Zebulun, had not cleansed themselves, yet they ate the passover otherwise than as prescribed. But Hezekiah prayed for them, saying, "The good LORD pardon all 19who set their hearts to seek God, the LORD the God of their ancestors, even though not in accordance with the

a Heb lacks *that they received*

sanctuary's rules of cleanness." 20The LORD heard Hezekiah, and healed the people. 21The people of Israel who were present at Jerusalem kept the festival of unleavened bread seven days with great gladness; and the Levites and the priests praised the LORD day by day, accompanied by loud instruments for the LORD. 22Hezekiah spoke encouragingly to all the Levites who showed good skill in the service of the LORD. So the people ate the food of the festival for seven days, sacrificing offerings of well-being and giving thanks to the LORD the God of their ancestors.

23 Then the whole assembly agreed together to keep the festival for another seven days; so they kept it for another seven days with gladness. 24For King Hezekiah of Judah gave the assembly a thousand bulls and seven thousand sheep for offerings, and the officials gave the assembly a thousand bulls and ten thousand sheep. The priests sanctified themselves in great numbers. 25The whole assembly of Judah, the priests and the Levites, and the whole assembly that came out of Israel, and the resident aliens who came out of the land of Israel, and the resident aliens who lived in Judah, rejoiced. 26There was great joy in Jerusalem, for since the time of Solomon son of King David of Israel there had been nothing like this in Jerusalem. 27Then the priests and the Levites stood up and blessed the people, and their voice was heard; their prayer came to his holy dwelling in heaven.

30.13–27. 18–19: *The good LORD pardon all who set their hearts to seek God:* Since some had come from the north to worship in Jerusalem, they had not subscribed to the proper forms of purity to approach the Temple* precinct. Hezekiah's successful intercession on their behalf is remarkable. 26: *There was great joy in Jerusalem, for since the time of Solomon son of King David of Israel there had been nothing like this in Jerusalem:* Hezekiah's actions serve to reverse the policies not only of Ahaz, but also of other kings who had aided the division of Israel into northern and southern states. The Chronicler envisions a unified community in which the old divisions are overwhelmed by consciousness of an even older unity.

31 Now when all this was finished, all Israel who were present went out to the cities of Judah and broke down the pillars, hewed down the sacred poles,[a] and pulled down the high places and the altars throughout all Judah and Benjamin, and in Ephraim and Manasseh, until they had destroyed them all. Then all the people of Israel returned to their cities, all to their individual properties.

2 Hezekiah appointed the divisions of the priests and of the Levites, division by division, everyone according to his service, the priests and the Levites, for burnt offerings and offerings of well-being, to minister in the gates of the camp of the LORD and to give thanks and praise. 3The contribution of the king from his own possessions was for the burnt offerings: the burnt offerings of morning and evening, and the burnt offerings for the sabbaths, the new moons, and the appointed festivals, as it is written in the law of the LORD. 4He commanded the people who lived in Jerusalem to give the portion due to the priests and the Levites, so that they might devote themselves to the law of the LORD. 5As soon as the word spread, the people of Israel gave in abundance the first fruits of grain, wine, oil, honey, and of all the produce of the field; and they brought in abundantly the tithe of everything. 6The people of Israel and Judah who lived in the cities of Judah also brought in the tithe of cattle and sheep, and the tithe of the dedicated things that had been consecrated to the LORD their God, and laid them in heaps. 7In the third month they began to pile up the heaps, and finished them in the seventh month. 8When Hezekiah and the officials came and saw the heaps, they blessed the LORD and his people Israel. 9Hezekiah questioned the priests and the Levites about the heaps. 10The chief priest Azariah, who was of the house of Zadok, answered him, "Since they began to bring the contributions into the house of the LORD, we have had enough to eat and have plenty to spare; for the LORD has blessed his people, so that we have this great supply left over."

a Heb *Asherim*

31.4: *He commanded the people who lived in Jerusalem to give the portion due to the priests and the Levites, so that they might devote themselves to the law of the LORD:* As recipients of blessing from God's having chosen Jerusalem, the inhabitants were obligated to make extra provision to ensure the Temple* personnel were free to pursue their study and teaching of the law.

11 Then Hezekiah commanded them to prepare store-chambers in the house of the LORD; and they prepared them. 12 Faithfully they brought in the contributions, the tithes and the dedicated things. The chief officer in charge of them was Conaniah the Levite, with his brother Shimei as second; 13 while Jehiel, Azaziah, Nahath, Asahel, Jerimoth, Jozabad, Eliel, Ismachiah, Mahath, and Benaiah were overseers assisting Conaniah and his brother Shimei, by the appointment of King Hezekiah and of Azariah the chief officer of the house of God. 14 Kore son of Imnah the Levite, keeper of the east gate, was in charge of the freewill offerings to God, to apportion the contribution reserved for the LORD and the most holy offerings. 15 Eden, Miniamin, Jeshua, Shemaiah, Amariah, and Shecaniah were faithfully assisting him in the cities of the priests, to distribute the portions to their kindred, old and young alike, by divisions, 16 except those enrolled by genealogy, males from three years old and upwards, all who entered the house of the LORD as the duty of each day required, for their service according to their offices, by their divisions. 17 The enrollment of the priests was according to their ancestral houses; that of the Levites from twenty years old and upwards was according to their offices, by their divisions. 18 The priests were enrolled with all their little children, their wives, their sons, and their daughters, the whole multitude; for they were faithful in keeping themselves holy. 19 And for the descendants of Aaron, the priests, who were in the fields of common land belonging to their towns, town by town, the people designated by name were to distribute portions to every male among the priests and to everyone among the Levites who was enrolled.

20 Hezekiah did this throughout all Judah; he did what was good and right and faithful before the LORD his God. 21 And every work that he undertook in the service of the house of God, and in accordance with the law and the commandments, to seek his God, he did with all his heart; and he prospered.

32 After these things and these acts of faithfulness, King Sennacherib of Assyria came and invaded Judah and encamped against the fortified cities, thinking to win them for himself. 2 When Hezekiah saw that Sennacherib had come and intended to fight against Jerusalem, 3 he planned with his officers and his warriors to stop the flow of the springs that were outside the city; and they helped him. 4 A great many people were gathered, and they stopped all the springs and the wadi that flowed through the land, saying, "Why should the Assyrian kings come and find water in abundance?" 5 Hezekiah*a* set to work resolutely and built up the entire wall that was broken down, and raised towers on it,*b* and outside it he built another wall; he also strengthened the Millo in the city of David, and made weapons and shields in abundance. 6 He appointed combat commanders over the people, and gathered them together to him in the square at the gate of the city and spoke encouragingly to them, saying, 7 "Be strong and of good courage. Do not be afraid or dismayed before the king of Assyria and all the horde that is with him; for there is one greater with us than with him. 8 With him is an arm of flesh; but with us is the LORD our God, to help us and to fight our battles." The people were encouraged by the words of King Hezekiah of Judah.

9 After this, while King Sennacherib of Assyria was at Lachish with all his forces, he sent his servants to Jerusalem to King Hezekiah of Judah and to all the people of Judah that were in Jerusalem, saying, 10 "Thus says King Sennacherib of Assyria: On what are you relying, that you undergo the siege of Jerusalem? 11 Is not Hezekiah misleading

a Heb *He*   *b* Vg: Heb *and raised on the towers*

you, handing you over to die by famine and by thirst, when he tells you, 'The LORD our God will save us from the hand of the king of Assyria'? 12Was it not this same Hezekiah who took away his high places and his altars and commanded Judah and Jerusalem, saying, 'Before one altar you shall worship, and upon it you shall make your offerings'? 13Do you not know what I and my ancestors have done to all the peoples of other lands? Were the gods of the nations of those lands at all able to save their lands out of my hand? 14Who among all the gods of those nations that my ancestors utterly destroyed was able to save his people from my hand, that your God should be able to save you from my hand? 15Now therefore do not let Hezekiah deceive you or mislead you in this fashion, and do not believe him, for no god of any nation or kingdom has been able to save his people from my hand or from the hand of my ancestors. How much less will your God save you out of my hand!"

16 His servants said still more against the Lord GOD and against his servant Hezekiah. 17He also wrote letters to throw contempt on the LORD the God of Israel and to speak against him, saying, "Just as the gods of the nations in other lands did not rescue their people from my hands, so the God of Hezekiah will not rescue his people from my hand." 18They shouted it with a loud voice in the language of Judah to the people of Jerusalem who were on the wall, to frighten and terrify them, in order that they might take the city. 19They spoke of the God of Jerusalem as if he were like the gods of the peoples of the earth, which are the work of human hands.

32.19: *They spoke of the God of Jerusalem as if he were like the gods of the peoples of the earth:* Sennacherib came against Judah because Hezekiah had ceased to pay his annual tribute as a vassal of Assyria. The Chronicler understands this invasion as a test of God's ability to defend his people and to avoid being viewed simply as one of hundreds of national deities in the ancient world.

20 Then King Hezekiah and the prophet Isaiah son of Amoz prayed because of this and cried to heaven. 21And the LORD sent an angel who cut off all the mighty warriors and commanders and officers in the camp of the king of Assyria. So he returned in disgrace to his own land. When he came into the house of his god, some of his own sons struck him down there with the sword. 22So the LORD saved Hezekiah and the inhabitants of Jerusalem from the hand of King Sennacherib of Assyria and from the hand of all his enemies; he gave them rest*a* on every side. 23Many brought gifts to the LORD in Jerusalem and precious things to King Hezekiah of Judah, so that he was exalted in the sight of all nations from that time onward.

32.23: *Many brought gifts to the LORD in Jerusalem and precious things to King Hezekiah:* Just as Solomon had received such honors in his time, Hezekiah's rule is affirmed by recognition from outside Israel. The Chronicler concludes his narrative* by drawing a picture of a prosperous and powerful monarch, in much the same way as Solomon was depicted.

24 In those days Hezekiah became sick and was at the point of death. He prayed to the LORD, and he answered him and gave him a sign. 25But Hezekiah did not respond according to the benefit done to him, for his heart was proud. Therefore wrath came upon him and upon Judah and Jerusalem. 26Then Hezekiah humbled himself for the pride of his heart, both he and the inhabitants of Jerusalem, so that the wrath of the LORD did not come upon them in the days of Hezekiah.

27 Hezekiah had very great riches and honor; and he made for himself treasuries for silver, for gold, for precious stones, for spices, for shields, and for all kinds of costly objects; 28storehouses also for the yield of grain, wine, and oil; and stalls for all kinds of cattle, and sheepfolds.*b* 29He likewise provided cities for himself, and flocks and herds in abundance; for God had given him very great possessions. 30This same Hezekiah closed the upper outlet of the waters of

a Gk Vg: Heb *guided them*   *b* Gk Vg: Heb *flocks for folds*

Gihon and directed them down to the west side of the city of David. Hezekiah prospered in all his works. ³¹So also in the matter of the envoys of the officials of Babylon, who had been sent to him to inquire about the sign that had been done in the land, God left him to himself, in order to test him and to know all that was in his heart.

32 Now the rest of the acts of Hezekiah, and his good deeds, are written in the vision of the prophet Isaiah son of Amoz in the Book of the Kings of Judah and Israel. ³³Hezekiah slept with his ancestors, and they buried him on the ascent to the tombs of the descendants of David; and all Judah and the inhabitants of Jerusalem did him honor at his death. His son Manasseh succeeded him.

33 Manasseh was twelve years old when he began to reign; he reigned fifty-five years in Jerusalem. ²He did what was evil in the sight of the LORD, according to the abominable practices of the nations whom the LORD drove out before the people of Israel. ³For he rebuilt the high places that his father Hezekiah had pulled down, and erected altars to the Baals, made sacred poles,ᵃ worshiped all the host of heaven, and served them. ⁴He built altars in the house of the LORD, of which the LORD had said, "In Jerusalem shall my name be forever." ⁵He built altars for all the host of heaven in the two courts of the house of the LORD. ⁶He made his son pass through fire in the valley of the son of Hinnom, practiced soothsaying and augury and sorcery, and dealt with mediums and with wizards. He did much evil in the sight of the LORD, provoking him to anger. ⁷The carved image of the idol that he had made he set in the house of God, of which God said to David and to his son Solomon, "In this house, and in Jerusalem, which I have chosen out of all the tribes of Israel, I will put my name forever; ⁸I will never again remove the feet of Israel from the land that I appointed for your ancestors, if only they will be careful to do all that I have commanded them, all the law, the statutes, and the ordinances given through Moses." ⁹Manasseh misled Judah and the in-

habitants of Jerusalem, so that they did more evil than the nations whom the LORD had destroyed before the people of Israel.

10 The LORD spoke to Manasseh and to his people, but they gave no heed. ¹¹Therefore the LORD brought against them the commanders of the army of the king of Assyria, who took Manasseh captive in manacles, bound him with fetters, and brought him to Babylon. ¹²While he was in distress he entreated the favor of the LORD his God and humbled himself greatly before the God of his ancestors. ¹³He prayed to him, and God received his entreaty, heard his plea, and restored him again to Jerusalem and to his kingdom. Then Manasseh knew that the LORD indeed was God.

14 Afterward he built an outer wall for the city of David west of Gihon, in the valley, reaching the entrance at the Fish Gate; he carried it around Ophel, and raised it to a very great height. He also put commanders of the army in all the fortified cities in Judah. ¹⁵He took away the foreign gods and the idol from the house of the LORD, and all the altars that he had built on the mountain of the house of the LORD and in Jerusalem, and he threw them out of the city. ¹⁶He also restored the altar of the LORD and offered on it sacrifices of well-being and of thanksgiving; and he commanded Judah to serve the LORD the God of Israel. ¹⁷The people, however, still sacrificed at the high places, but only to the LORD their God.

18 Now the rest of the acts of Manasseh, his prayer to his God, and the words of the seers who spoke to him in the name of the LORD God of Israel, these are in the Annals of the Kings of Israel. ¹⁹His prayer, and how God received his entreaty, all his sin and his faithlessness, the sites on which he built high places and set up the sacred polesᵇ and the images, before he humbled himself, these are written in the records of the seers.ᶜ ²⁰So Manasseh slept with his ancestors, and they buried him in his house. His son Amon succeeded him.

a Heb *Asheroth*   b Heb *Asherim*   c One Ms Gk: MT *of Hozai*

33.1–20: The reign of Manasseh. The Chronicler follows his source closely (2 Kings 21), though the account of Manasseh's repentance is unique to the Chronicler. While he is presented as the paradigm of wickedness in 2 Kings, the Chronicler leaves his readers with a portrait of the repentant person whose seeking God brings him back to Jerusalem. Some believe this is pure fiction by the Chronicler, an effort to create a parallel between the repentant Manasseh and the exilic community. **13:** *Then Manasseh knew that the* LORD *indeed was God:* This echoes a recurring expression in the prophet* Ezekiel.

21 Amon was twenty-two years old when he began to reign; he reigned two years in Jerusalem. 22 He did what was evil in the sight of the LORD, as his father Manasseh had done. Amon sacrificed to all the images that his father Manasseh had made, and served them. 23 He did not humble himself before the LORD, as his father Manasseh had humbled himself, but this Amon incurred more and more guilt. 24 His servants conspired against him and killed him in his house. 25 But the people of the land killed all those who had conspired against King Amon; and the people of the land made his son Josiah king to succeed him.

33.21–25: The reign of Amon. Of little interest to the Chronicler, Amon simply serves to show what would have happened if Manasseh had not repented.

34 Josiah was eight years old when he began to reign; he reigned thirty-one years in Jerusalem. 2 He did what was right in the sight of the LORD, and walked in the ways of his ancestor David; he did not turn aside to the right or to the left. 3 For in the eighth year of his reign, while he was still a boy, he began to seek the God of his ancestor David, and in the twelfth year he began to purge Judah and Jerusalem of the high places, the sacred poles,ª and the carved and the cast images. 4 In his presence they pulled down the altars of the Baals; he demolished the incense altars that stood above them. He broke down the sacred polesª and the carved and the cast images; he made dust of them

and scattered it over the graves of those who had sacrificed to them. 5 He also burned the bones of the priests on their altars, and purged Judah and Jerusalem. 6 In the towns of Manasseh, Ephraim, and Simeon, and as far as Naphtali, in their ruinsᵇ all around, 7 he broke down the altars, beat the sacred polesª and the images into powder, and demolished all the incense altars throughout all the land of Israel. Then he returned to Jerusalem.

8 In the eighteenth year of his reign, when he had purged the land and the house, he sent Shaphan son of Azaliah, Maaseiah the governor of the city, and Joah son of Joahaz, the recorder, to repair the house of the LORD his God. 9 They came to the high priest Hilkiah and delivered the money that had been brought into the house of God, which the Levites, the keepers of the threshold, had collected from Manasseh and Ephraim and from all the remnant of Israel and from all Judah and Benjamin and from the inhabitants of Jerusalem. 10 They delivered it to the workers who had the oversight of the house of the LORD, and the workers who were working in the house of the LORD gave it for repairing and restoring the house. 11 They gave it to the carpenters and the builders to buy quarried stone, and timber for binders, and beams for the buildings that the kings of Judah had let go to ruin. 12 The people did the work faithfully. Over them were appointed the Levites Jahath and Obadiah, of the sons of Merari, along with Zechariah and Meshullam, of the sons of the Kohathites, to have oversight. Other Levites, all skillful with instruments of music, 13 were over the burden bearers and directed all who did work in every kind of service; and some of the Levites were scribes, and officials, and gatekeepers.

14 While they were bringing out the money that had been brought into the house of the LORD, the priest Hilkiah found the book of the law of the LORD given through Moses. 15 Hilkiah said to the secretary Shaphan, "I have found the book of the law in

a Heb *Asherim*   *b* Meaning of Heb uncertain

the house of the LORD"; and Hilkiah gave the book to Shaphan. ¹⁶Shaphan brought the book to the king, and further reported to the king, "All that was committed to your servants they are doing. ¹⁷They have emptied out the money that was found in the house of the LORD and have delivered it into the hand of the overseers and the workers." ¹⁸The secretary Shaphan informed the king, "The priest Hilkiah has given me a book." Shaphan then read it aloud to the king.

19 When the king heard the words of the law he tore his clothes. ²⁰Then the king commanded Hilkiah, Ahikam son of Shaphan, Abdon son of Micah, the secretary Shaphan, and the king's servant Asaiah: ²¹"Go, inquire of the LORD for me and for those who are left in Israel and in Judah, concerning the words of the book that has been found; for the wrath of the LORD that is poured out on us is great, because our ancestors did not keep the word of the LORD, to act in accordance with all that is written in this book."

22 So Hilkiah and those whom the king had sent went to the prophet Huldah, the wife of Shallum son of Tokhath son of Hasrah, keeper of the wardrobe (who lived in Jerusalem in the Second Quarter) and spoke to her to that effect. ²³She declared to them, "Thus says the LORD, the God of Israel: Tell the man who sent you to me, ²⁴Thus says the LORD: I will indeed bring disaster upon this place and upon its inhabitants, all the curses that are written in the book that was read before the king of Judah. ²⁵Because they have forsaken me and have made offerings to other gods, so that they have provoked me to anger with all the works of their hands, my wrath will be poured out on this place and will not be quenched. ²⁶But as to the king of Judah, who sent you to inquire of the LORD, thus shall you say to him: Thus says the LORD, the God of Israel: Regarding the words that you have heard, ²⁷because your heart was penitent and you humbled yourself before God when you heard his words against this place and its inhabitants, and you have humbled yourself before me, and have torn your clothes and wept before

me, I also have heard you, says the LORD. ²⁸I will gather you to your ancestors and you shall be gathered to your grave in peace; your eyes shall not see all the disaster that I will bring on this place and its inhabitants." They took the message back to the king.

29 Then the king sent word and gathered together all the elders of Judah and Jerusalem. ³⁰The king went up to the house of the LORD, with all the people of Judah, the inhabitants of Jerusalem, the priests and the Levites, all the people both great and small; he read in their hearing all the words of the book of the covenant that had been found in the house of the LORD. ³¹The king stood in his place and made a covenant before the LORD, to follow the LORD, keeping his commandments, his decrees, and his statutes, with all his heart and all his soul, to perform the words of the covenant that were written in this book. ³²Then he made all who were present in Jerusalem and in Benjamin pledge themselves to it. And the inhabitants of Jerusalem acted according to the covenant of God, the God of their ancestors. ³³Josiah took away all the abominations from all the territory that belonged to the people of Israel, and made all who were in Israel worship the LORD their God. All his days they did not turn away from following the LORD the God of their ancestors.

35 Josiah kept a passover to the LORD in Jerusalem; they slaughtered the passover lamb on the fourteenth day of the first month. ²He appointed the priests to their offices and encouraged them in the service of the house of the LORD. ³He said to the Levites who taught all Israel and who were holy to the LORD, "Put the holy ark in the house that Solomon son of David, king of Israel, built; you need no longer carry it on your shoulders. Now serve the LORD your God and his people Israel. ⁴Make preparations by your ancestral houses by your divisions, following the written directions of King David of Israel and the written directions of his son Solomon. ⁵Take position in the holy place according to the groupings of the ancestral houses of your kindred the people, and let there be Levites for each division

of an ancestral house.*ᵃ* ⁶Slaughter the passover lamb, sanctify yourselves, and on behalf of your kindred make preparations, acting according to the word of the LORD by Moses."

7 Then Josiah contributed to the people, as passover offerings for all that were present, lambs and kids from the flock to the number of thirty thousand, and three thousand bulls; these were from the king's possessions. ⁸His officials contributed willingly to the people, to the priests, and to the Levites. Hilkiah, Zechariah, and Jehiel, the chief officers of the house of God, gave to the priests for the passover offerings two thousand six hundred lambs and kids and three hundred bulls. ⁹Conaniah also, and his brothers Shemaiah and Nethanel, and Hashabiah and Jeiel and Jozabad, the chiefs of the Levites, gave to the Levites for the passover offerings five thousand lambs and kids and five hundred bulls.

10 When the service had been prepared for, the priests stood in their place, and the Levites in their divisions according to the king's command. ¹¹They slaughtered the passover lamb, and the priests dashed the blood that they received*ᵇ* from them, while the Levites did the skinning. ¹²They set aside the burnt offerings so that they might distribute them according to the groupings of the ancestral houses of the people, to offer to the LORD, as it is written in the book of Moses. And they did the same with the bulls. ¹³They roasted the passover lamb with fire according to the ordinance; and they boiled the holy offerings in pots, in caldrons, and in pans, and carried them quickly to all the people. ¹⁴Afterward they made preparations for themselves and for the priests, because the priests the descendants of Aaron were occupied in offering the burnt offerings and the fat parts until night; so the Levites made preparations for themselves and for the priests, the descendants of Aaron. ¹⁵The singers, the descendants of Asaph, were in their place according to the command of David, and Asaph, and Heman, and the king's seer Jeduthun. The gatekeepers were at each gate; they did not need to interrupt their ser-

vice, for their kindred the Levites made preparations for them.

16 So all the service of the LORD was prepared that day, to keep the passover and to offer burnt offerings on the altar of the LORD, according to the command of King Josiah. ¹⁷The people of Israel who were present kept the passover at that time, and the festival of unleavened bread seven days. ¹⁸No passover like it had been kept in Israel since the days of the prophet Samuel; none of the kings of Israel had kept such a passover as was kept by Josiah, by the priests and the Levites, by all Judah and Israel who were present, and by the inhabitants of Jerusalem. ¹⁹In the eighteenth year of the reign of Josiah this passover was kept.

20 After all this, when Josiah had set the temple in order, King Neco of Egypt went up to fight at Carchemish on the Euphrates, and Josiah went out against him. ²¹But Neco*ᶜ* sent envoys to him, saying, "What have I to do with you, king of Judah? I am not coming against you today, but against the house with which I am at war; and God has commanded me to hurry. Cease opposing God, who is with me, so that he will not destroy you." ²²But Josiah would not turn away from him, but disguised himself in order to fight with him. He did not listen to the words of Neco from the mouth of God, but joined battle in the plain of Megiddo. ²³The archers shot King Josiah; and the king said to his servants, "Take me away, for I am badly wounded." ²⁴So his servants took him out of the chariot and carried him in his second chariot*ᵈ* and brought him to Jerusalem. There he died, and was buried in the tombs of his ancestors. All Judah and Jerusalem mourned for Josiah. ²⁵Jeremiah also uttered a lament for Josiah, and all the singing men and singing women have spoken of Josiah in their laments to this day. They made these a custom in Israel; they are recorded in the Laments. ²⁶Now the rest of the acts of Josiah and his faithful deeds in accordance with what is written in the law of the LORD, ²⁷and

---

a Meaning of Heb uncertain   *b* Heb lacks *that they received*   *c* Heb *he*   *d* Or *the chariot of his deputy*

his acts, first and last, are written in the Book of the Kings of Israel and Judah.

34.1–35.27: The reign of Josiah. Though a king of interest to the Chronicler, Josiah does not have the same prominence in the Chronicler's history that he was accorded in Kings. The Chronicler follows closely his source (2 Kings 22–23) but does not praise him in the same superlatives as Hezekiah. **34.3:** *In the twelfth year he began to purge Judah and Jerusalem of the high places*:* The Chronicler places Josiah's efforts at suppressing idolatry* before the "Book of the Law" is found in the Temple,* the reverse of the narrative* in 2 Kings. For the Chronicler, if a king truly sought God, he would not tolerate rampant idolatry.

36 The people of the land took Jehoahaz son of Josiah and made him king to succeed his father in Jerusalem. 2Jehoahaz was twenty-three years old when he began to reign; he reigned three months in Jerusalem. 3Then the king of Egypt deposed him in Jerusalem and laid on the land a tribute of one hundred talents of silver and one talent of gold. 4The king of Egypt made his brother Eliakim king over Judah and Jerusalem, and changed his name to Jehoiakim; but Neco took his brother Jehoahaz and carried him to Egypt.

5 Jehoiakim was twenty-five years old when he began to reign; he reigned eleven years in Jerusalem. He did what was evil in the sight of the LORD his God. 6Against him King Nebuchadnezzar of Babylon came up, and bound him with fetters to take him to Babylon. 7Nebuchadnezzar also carried some of the vessels of the house of the LORD to Babylon and put them in his palace in Babylon. 8Now the rest of the acts of Jehoiakim, and the abominations that he did, and what was found against him, are written in the Book of the Kings of Israel and Judah; and his son Jehoiachin succeeded him.

9 Jehoiachin was eight years old when he began to reign; he reigned three months and ten days in Jerusalem. He did what was evil in the sight of the LORD. 10In the spring of the year King Nebuchadnezzar sent and brought him to Babylon, along with the precious vessels of the house of the LORD, and

made his brother Zedekiah king over Judah and Jerusalem.

36.1–10. 1–4: The reign of Jehoahaz. The Chronicler says little about the short reign of this minor figure in Judah's history. **5–8: The reign of Jehoiakim.** Apart from his doing evil and suffering disaster because of it, the Chronicler offers no details of Jehoiakim's reign. **9–10: The reign of Jehoiachin.** Another of the minor figures at the close of Judean history, the Chronicler asserts he did evil, though he was only *eight years old.*

11 Zedekiah was twenty-one years old when he began to reign; he reigned eleven years in Jerusalem. 12He did what was evil in the sight of the LORD his God. He did not humble himself before the prophet Jeremiah who spoke from the mouth of the LORD. 13He also rebelled against King Nebuchadnezzar, who had made him swear by God; he stiffened his neck and hardened his heart against turning to the LORD, the God of Israel. 14All the leading priests and the people also were exceedingly unfaithful, following all the abominations of the nations; and they polluted the house of the LORD that he had consecrated in Jerusalem.

15 The LORD, the God of their ancestors, sent persistently to them by his messengers, because he had compassion on his people and on his dwelling place; 16but they kept mocking the messengers of God, despising his words, and scoffing at his prophets, until the wrath of the LORD against his people became so great that there was no remedy.

17 Therefore he brought up against them the king of the Chaldeans, who killed their youths with the sword in the house of their sanctuary, and had no compassion on young man or young woman, the aged or the feeble; he gave them all into his hand. 18All the vessels of the house of God, large and small, and the treasures of the house of the LORD, and the treasures of the king and of his officials, all these he brought to Babylon. 19They burned the house of God, broke down the wall of Jerusalem, burned all its palaces with fire, and destroyed all its precious vessels. 20He took into exile in Babylon those who had escaped from the sword, and they be-

came servants to him and to his sons until the establishment of the kingdom of Persia, 21to fulfill the word of the LORD by the mouth of Jeremiah, until the land had made up for its sabbaths. All the days that it lay desolate it kept sabbath, to fulfill seventy years.

22 In the first year of King Cyrus of Persia, in fulfillment of the word of the LORD spoken by Jeremiah, the LORD stirred up the spirit of King Cyrus of Persia so that he sent a herald throughout all his kingdom and also declared in a written edict: 23"Thus says King Cyrus of Persia: The LORD, the God of heaven, has given me all the kingdoms of the earth, and he has charged me to build him a house at Jerusalem, which is in Judah. Whoever is among you of all his people, may the LORD his God be with him! Let him go up."

36.11–23: The fall of Jerusalem. With a string of bad kings following on Josiah's death, the kingdom was doomed. Zedekiah comes to the throne, and the Chronicler regards him as evil because of his opposition to the prophets* and his rebellion against Nebuchadnezzar. **14:** Lest the king be held the only one at fault, the Chronicler sees the *leading priests and people* as sharing in the blame, particularly for desecrating the Temple.* **21:** The Chronicler ends his history with a word of promise: The land *made up for its sabbaths* by being vacant, and Cyrus, king of Persia, called for a new Temple to be built in Jerusalem. The community can once again enjoy finding and being found by God at the new Temple, if they take to heart the examples of devotion and faithfulness from Israel's past.

EZRA

Introduction to Ezra, Nehemiah

In the form found in most English Bibles, Ezra and Nehemiah are divided into two separate books. This format follows a tradition established in the early centuries of the Christian church, when the Vulgate* (the Bible in Latin) divided these two works. It was only in the fifteenth century CE that Hebrew manuscripts adopted the same custom. In actuality, the most ancient tradition we can trace kept these two works together as one. Most of the ancient lists of books of the Hebrew Bible list them together. Moreover, the two share a number of literary elements, suggesting that they are related.

It has become commonplace in scholarship to see Ezra-Nehemiah as a continuation of the same narrative* as 1 and 2 Chronicles, all these works having been written by the same hand. The reasons are many, but some of the main points are that Ezra-Nehemiah opens with a repetition of 2 Chr 36.22–23, that Ezra-Nehemiah and 1 and 2 Chronicles share vocabulary for Temple* personnel and objects that are not found elsewhere in the Hebrew Bible, and that both 1 and 2 Chronicles and Ezra-Nehemiah have extended genealogical* lists. While this view may still predominate, the last two decades have seen the emergence of a serious challenge from scholars who argue for the independence of Ezra-Nehemiah and 1 and 2 Chronicles. They have sought to base this conclusion on a number of differences in vocabulary, theology, and ideology between the two works. The issue is complex, but here we will look at Ezra-Nehemiah as if it is an independent composition on its own terms.

In literary form, Ezra-Nehemiah is difficult to characterize. The author has employed citations of documents, lists of personnel or community members, historical narratives, and first-person narratives that are often termed "memoirs." Some of the more notable portions are Rehum's correspondence with King Artaxerxes (Ezra 4.7–22), Tattenai's correspondence with King Darius (5.6–17; 6.6–12), a list of those who returned from Babylon (Ezra 2.1–67, repeated in Neh 7.6–68), the "Ezra memoir" (Ezra 7–10), and the "Nehemiah memoir" (mainly Neh 1.1–7.5).

The normal approach to the work has been to read it as a historical narrative, but throughout the work elements appear dislocated and far off the mark for history writing. Given the lack of chronological flow to the work, it would be better to consider it a historical apologetic,* or a defense of a particular position or viewpoint, loosely using the events of the community to support a theological perspective.

Squarely set in the midst of the Persian empire, the work focuses on two imperial functionaries, Ezra and Nehemiah, and the reforms they attempted. If Ezra is placed before Nehemiah, as seems the intent of the author, then Ezra came to Jerusalem in 458 BCE, and Nehemiah's first stint as governor was in 445 BCE. When scholars examine the lists of names, they can determine that the latest names on some lists date from a generation or so after the time of the mid fifth century. They therefore conclude that the work was written around 400 BCE.

Both Ezra and Nehemiah as literary figures are portrayed as disturbed by intermarriage with "foreigners" in the community, and both condemn this activity using a language loaded with religious connotations. This concern hardly seems to fit with Ezra 1–6, where the struggle to rebuild the Temple in Jerusalem almost a century earlier dominates.

Linking the various parts of the work together is the theme of the "house of God." Beginning with the rebuilding of the physical structure of the Temple, the work moves through to the reformation of the community as the "house of God." A subsidiary theme is the rebuilding of the walls of Jerusalem, which would separate the community from the surrounding region, both physically and religiously. These themes are cast in highly religious language, leading the reader to the inevitable assessment of the righteousness of this redefinition of the community.

The Persian empire faced troubled conditions in the mid fifth century as a serious revolt in Egypt, coupled with the assistance of the Greek city-states, openly challenged the empire's control of the Mediterranean. The territory of Yehud, as the region of Jerusalem and the surrounding area was called, suddenly had strategic importance for the empire. One of the techniques the Persian empire used to control subject populations was controlling their access to the land. Since most of the population was engaged in farming or farming-related employment, access to the land was essential for survival, and thus the empire maintained control over the peoples they had conquered. The ability to control land access was threatened when adjacent communities began to intermarry, since this blurred the definition of who had access to what lands. The narratives of Ezra-Nehemiah present two individuals who are charged directly by the Persian king to undertake vaguely described missions, the result of which is the strengthening of the community boundaries by directly attacking the practice of intermarriage. Such a redefinition of the community probably met with strong opposition, and the present literary work of Ezra-Nehemiah sought to provide a theological rationale for accepting what was essentially an imperial dictate.

READING GUIDE

Given the complicated mixture of literary forms in Ezra-Nehemiah, it is difficult to follow all the elements of the narrative. Readers should watch for the "house of God" theme in the various sections; how does the author want us to understand the "house of God"? Also, it is helpful to notice who is allowed to participate in the community, and who is being excluded.

A useful place to begin reading is Ezra 9 where an important transfer takes place, moving from the sanctity of the Temple to the general population of the region. Running throughout the chapter is the consciousness of the Exile* as a punishment and a lesson from the past to serve as an incentive to follow the ways of God more closely in the future.

Ezra

1–2	Prologue
3–6	Rebuilding the house of God
7–10	Ezra's inquiry

Nehemiah

1.1–7.5	Nehemiah's mission
7.6–13.3	Forming the house of God
13.4–30	Postlogue

PROLOGUE

Chs. 1–2 The beginning of Ezra-Nehemiah seeks to establish the legitimacy of rebuilding the house of God, the Temple.* This is expressed by opening with the imperial order to return to Jerusalem and rebuild the Temple, immediately jumping to a listing of those who did return, and concluding with the tangible signs of devotion among them. The repetition of Cyrus's decree (Ezra 1.1–4 and 2 Chr 36.22–23) introduces the theme of Ezra and is not a direct link to the end of 2 Chronicles.

1 In the first year of King Cyrus of Persia, in order that the word of the LORD by the mouth of Jeremiah might be accomplished, the LORD stirred up the spirit of King Cyrus of Persia so that he sent a herald throughout all his kingdom, and also in a written edict declared:

2 "Thus says King Cyrus of Persia: The LORD, the God of heaven, has given me all the kingdoms of the earth, and he has charged me to build him a house at Jerusalem in Judah. 3 Any of those among you who are of his people—may their God be with them!—are now permitted to go up to Jerusalem in Judah, and rebuild the house of the LORD, the God of Israel—he is the God who is in Jerusalem; 4 and let all survivors, in whatever place they reside, be assisted by the people of their place with silver and gold, with goods and with animals, besides freewill offerings for the house of God in Jerusalem."

5 The heads of the families of Judah and Benjamin, and the priests and the Levites—everyone whose spirit God had stirred—got ready to go up and rebuild the house of the LORD in Jerusalem. 6 All their neighbors aided them with silver vessels, with gold, with goods, with animals, and with valuable gifts, besides all that was freely offered. 7 King Cyrus himself brought out the vessels of the house of the LORD that Nebuchadnezzar had carried away from Jerusalem and placed in the house of his gods. 8 King Cyrus of Persia had them released into the charge of Mithredath the treasurer, who counted them out to Sheshbazzar the prince

of Judah. 9 And this was the inventory: gold basins, thirty; silver basins, one thousand; knives,ᵃ twenty-nine; 10 gold bowls, thirty; other silver bowls, four hundred ten; other vessels, one thousand; 11 the total of the gold and silver vessels was five thousand four hundred. All these Sheshbazzar brought up, when the exiles were brought up from Babylonia to Jerusalem.

1.1–11: The decree of Cyrus and its results. The legitimation pattern is opened by having Cyrus, the dominant founder of the Persian empire as Israel experienced it, decree that all those from Jerusalem should return and *rebuild the house of the LORD*. **1–2:** *In order that the word of the LORD by the mouth of Jeremiah might be accomplished:* Jeremiah had claimed the Exile* in Babylon would last 70 years (Jer 29.10). The *first year* of Cyrus is probably a reference to his first year over the Babylonian empire, which he captured in 539 BCE. The decree that follows is substantially the one that closes 2 Chr 36. *Charged me to build him a house at Jerusalem* is not the confession of Cyrus's belief in Israel's God, but rather a balanced polytheistic way of claiming that all subjugated peoples' gods have empowered Persian rule. Thus the Persian king, by virtue of having rule, should honor the gods who have permitted it. In other ancient sources, Cyrus claims the same divine approval from Marduk, the chief Babylonian god. **3:** *He is the God who is in Jerusalem* reflects the common ancient Near Eastern concept that gods and goddesses are specially present and should be worshipped in particular locations. **4:** *For the house of God in Jerusalem* is an expansion of the decree in 2 Chr 36 that allows for the collection of offerings for the Temple* in Jerusalem by all those living outside the city. **5:** *The heads of the families of Judah and Benjamin, and the priests and the Levites:* The primary tribes populating the southern kingdom of Judah were Judah and Benjamin. The priests and Levites were usually counted separately from the tribes. **7:** *King Cyrus himself brought out the vessels of the house of the LORD that Nebuchadnezzar had carried away from Jerusalem:* When Jerusalem and the Temple were destroyed in 587 BCE, the Babylonians looted the Temple precinct, including the gold and silver vessels used in the Temple service. The return of these vessels links the Temple of Solomon that had

a Vg: Meaning of Heb uncertain

been destroyed by the Babylonians with the Temple that will be built after the Exile. **8:** *Sheshbazzar the prince of Judah:* There is no consensus on what this title may have meant in this time period. In Ezra 5.14 Sheshbazzar is called a "governor" of the province, so it may be that the author is using "prince" to indicate a leading citizen. **9:** *And this was the inventory:* This list possibly has been copied from an authentic inventory of the returned vessels.

2 Now these were the people of the province who came from those captive exiles whom King Nebuchadnezzar of Babylon had carried captive to Babylonia; they returned to Jerusalem and Judah, all to their own towns. ²They came with Zerubbabel, Jeshua, Nehemiah, Seraiah, Reelaiah, Mordecai, Bilshan, Mispar, Bigvai, Rehum, and Baanah.

The number of the Israelite people: ³the descendants of Parosh, two thousand one hundred seventy-two. ⁴Of Shephatiah, three hundred seventy-two. ⁵Of Arah, seven hundred seventy-five. ⁶Of Pahath-moab, namely the descendants of Jeshua and Joab, two thousand eight hundred twelve. ⁷Of Elam, one thousand two hundred fifty-four. ⁸Of Zattu, nine hundred forty-five. ⁹Of Zaccai, seven hundred sixty. ¹⁰Of Bani, six hundred forty-two. ¹¹Of Bebai, six hundred twenty-three. ¹²Of Azgad, one thousand two hundred twenty-two. ¹³Of Adonikam, six hundred sixty-six. ¹⁴Of Bigvai, two thousand fifty-six. ¹⁵Of Adin, four hundred fifty-four. ¹⁶Of Ater, namely of Hezekiah, ninety-eight. ¹⁷Of Bezai, three hundred twenty-three. ¹⁸Of Jorah, one hundred twelve. ¹⁹Of Hashum, two hundred twenty-three. ²⁰Of Gibbar, ninety-five. ²¹Of Bethlehem, one hundred twenty-three. ²²The people of Netophah, fifty-six. ²³Of Anathoth, one hundred twenty-eight. ²⁴The descendants of Azmaveth, forty-two. ²⁵Of Kiriatharim, Chephirah, and Beeroth, seven hundred forty-three. ²⁶Of Ramah and Geba, six hundred twenty-one. ²⁷The people of Michmas, one hundred twenty-two. ²⁸Of Bethel and Ai, two hundred twenty-three. ²⁹The descendants of Nebo, fifty-two. ³⁰Of Magbish, one hundred fifty-six. ³¹Of the other Elam, one thousand two hundred fifty-four. ³²Of Harim, three hundred twenty. ³³Of Lod, Hadid, and Ono, seven hundred twenty-five. ³⁴Of Jericho, three hundred forty-five. ³⁵Of Senaah, three thousand six hundred thirty.

2.1–70: The list of those who returned from Babylon. At first glance, the list would seem to be a well-organized, coherent presentation broken into sections by category of occupations. A closer examination reveals that some persons are identified by their family lineage, others by their place of residence. This and other differences suggest the list is a composite product, possibly listing returnees from several different stages of the formation of the community in Jerusalem. From what meager records have survived, the usual conclusion drawn is that following Cyrus's decree several different groups left Babylon for Jerusalem at different times. The list is repeated with some variations in Neh 7.6–73. From a close comparison of the two lists, the list here in Ezra 2 appears to summarize the information in Neh 7, and consequently may be derived from that list. The use of duplicate lists in Ezra-Nehemiah is a deliberate framing device by the author, directing the reader's attention to the level of the individuals who form the "house of God." **2:** *They came with Zerubbabel, Jeshua, Nehemiah, Seraiah, Reelaiah . . . :* Several of these names are well-known governors of Yehud, the Persian province centered in Jerusalem, who were in office at various times from the sixth century onward. Others, such as *Jeshua,* were among the high priests. Some of the individuals were contemporaries of Nehemiah, bringing the close of the list to the mid fifth century. The incorporation of persons over such a range of time shows the essentially nonhistorical interests of the author. *The number of the Israelite people:* The term for *number* is more appropriately "listing," since a formal census does not follow. The first section (vv. 2b–20) lists names by clan* group, the second (vv. 21–35) mainly by location, the third (vv. 36–39) lists priestly clans, the fourth (vv. 40–42) Levitical groups, and the fifth (vv. 43–58) various orders of Temple* servants. These are followed by a miscellaneous group that could not demonstrate a connection to known family lineages (vv. 59–63). A numerical summary of the primary attributes of the community follows (vv. 64–67), then there is a report of the devotion of these groups to the Temple (vv. 68–70). The various numbers given are possible in some cases, though some of the amounts may be artificial, such as 666 (v. 13).

36 The priests: the descendants of Jedaiah, of the house of Jeshua, nine hundred seventy-three. [37]Of Immer, one thousand fifty-two. [38]Of Pashhur, one thousand two hundred forty-seven. [39]Of Harim, one thousand seventeen.

40 The Levites: the descendants of Jeshua and Kadmiel, of the descendants of Hodaviah, seventy-four. [41]The singers: the descendants of Asaph, one hundred twenty-eight. [42]The descendants of the gatekeepers: of Shallum, of Ater, of Talmon, of Akkub, of Hatita, and of Shobai, in all one hundred thirty-nine.

43 The temple servants: the descendants of Ziha, Hasupha, Tabbaoth, [44]Keros, Siaha, Padon, [45]Lebanah, Hagabah, Akkub, [46]Hagab, Shamlai, Hanan, [47]Giddel, Gahar, Reaiah, [48]Rezin, Nekoda, Gazzam, [49]Uzza, Paseah, Besai, [50]Asnah, Meunim, Nephisim, [51]Bakbuk, Hakupha, Harhur, [52]Bazluth, Mehida, Harsha, [53]Barkos, Sisera, Temah, [54]Neziah, and Hatipha.

55 The descendants of Solomon's servants: Sotai, Hassophereth, Peruda, [56]Jaalah, Darkon, Giddel, [57]Shephatiah, Hattil, Pochereth-hazzebaim, and Ami.

58 All the temple servants and the descendants of Solomon's servants were three hundred ninety-two.

59 The following were those who came up from Tel-melah, Tel-harsha, Cherub, Addan, and Immer, though they could not prove their families or their descent, whether they belonged to Israel: [60]the descendants of Delaiah, Tobiah, and Nekoda, six hundred fifty-two. [61]Also, of the descendants of the priests: the descendants of Habaiah, Hakkoz, and Barzillai (who had married one of the daughters of Barzillai the Gileadite, and was called by their name). [62]These looked for their entries in the genealogical records, but they were not found there, and so they were excluded from the priesthood as unclean; [63]the governor told them that they were not to partake of the most holy food, until there should be a priest to consult Urim and Thummim.

64 The whole assembly together was forty-two thousand three hundred sixty, [65]besides their male and female servants, of whom there were seven thousand three hundred thirty-seven; and they had two hundred male and female singers. [66]They had seven hundred thirty-six horses, two hundred forty-five mules, [67]four hundred thirty-five camels, and six thousand seven hundred twenty donkeys.

68 As soon as they came to the house of the LORD in Jerusalem, some of the heads of families made freewill offerings for the house of God, to erect it on its site. [69]According to their resources they gave to the building fund sixty-one thousand darics of gold, five thousand minas of silver, and one hundred priestly robes.

70 The priests, the Levites, and some of the people lived in Jerusalem and its vicinity;[a] and the singers, the gatekeepers, and the temple servants lived in their towns, and all Israel in their towns.

2.36–70. 36: *The priests: the descendants of Jedaiah, of the house of Jeshua: Jedaiah* is named as one of the first priestly figures to return to Jerusalem after the Exile★ (1 Chr 9.10), and *Jeshua* was an important chief priest under the administration of Zerubbabel in the late sixth century (Ezra 3.8). Apparently, Jedaiah was regarded as the founder of a renewed line for the chief priesthood. **43:** *The temple servants* is a technical name for a group devoted to serving the Levites. **55:** *Solomon's servants* appear to have been a similar group. **59:** *Tel-melah, Tel-harsha, Cherub, Addan, and Immer* are place names of uncertain identification.

REBUILDING THE HOUSE OF GOD

Chs. 3–6: This section, in the form of historical narrative,★ includes citations from various documents designed to authenticate the contents. There are disruptions in the chronological order of the narrative, however, and in ch. 4 there is a sudden shift from Hebrew to the Aramaic★ language. Recounting events in chronological order is therefore probably not the intention of this section. Rather, the author is interweaving two actions by the community: the rebuilding of the Temple★ and the reconstitution of the community as the "house of God." The first happens within a gen-

---

a 1 Esdras 5.46: Heb lacks *lived in Jerusalem and its vicinity*

eration of the return to Jerusalem from the Exile,* but the second can take place only several generations later, after the Jerusalem community is separated by its walls and its covenant* to refrain from intermarriage.

3 When the seventh month came, and the Israelites were in the towns, the people gathered together in Jerusalem. 2 Then Jeshua son of Jozadak, with his fellow priests, and Zerubbabel son of Shealtiel with his kin set out to build the altar of the God of Israel, to offer burnt offerings on it, as prescribed in the law of Moses the man of God. 3 They set up the altar on its foundation, because they were in dread of the neighboring peoples, and they offered burnt offerings upon it to the LORD, morning and evening. 4 And they kept the festival of booths,ᵃ as prescribed, and offered the daily burnt offerings by number according to the ordinance, as required for each day, 5 and after that the regular burnt offerings, the offerings at the new moon and at all the sacred festivals of the LORD, and the offerings of everyone who made a freewill offering to the LORD. 6 From the first day of the seventh month they began to offer burnt offerings to the LORD. But the foundation of the temple of the LORD was not yet laid. 7 So they gave money to the masons and the carpenters, and food, drink, and oil to the Sidonians and the Tyrians to bring cedar trees from Lebanon to the sea, to Joppa, according to the grant that they had from King Cyrus of Persia.

3.1–7: The reinstitution of worship. This section describes the resumption of worship at the site of the ruined Temple* as a prelude to the effort to rebuild the Temple, as decreed by the Persian king Cyrus in the opening of the book. **1:** *When the seventh month came* is an enigmatic reference since the year is not disclosed. It may be the seventh month of the earlier date formula of 1.1, that is, the first year of Cyrus (around 539 BCE), though this presents a problem with what follows. The notices of *Jeshua* and *Zerubbabel* (v 2.) focus on two individuals who are usually dated to the early years of the reign of Darius (522–486 BCE). The *seventh month* may refer to the second year of Darius's rule, when a renewed commitment to rebuild-

ing the Temple was made (Hag 2.1). **2:** *As prescribed in the law of Moses the man of God* relates to rules on the composition of the altar found in Ex 20.25. **4:** *And they kept the festival of booths, as prescribed,* reflecting perhaps a concern to follow the rules found in Lev 23.33–43, where the fifteenth day of the seventh month is reserved for the beginning of this important festival. **6:** *But the foundation of the temple of the LORD was not yet laid* distinguishes the resumption of worship from the beginning of rebuilding the physical Temple.

8 In the second year after their arrival at the house of God at Jerusalem, in the second month, Zerubbabel son of Shealtiel and Jeshua son of Jozadak made a beginning, together with the rest of their people, the priests and the Levites and all who had come to Jerusalem from the captivity. They appointed the Levites, from twenty years old and upward, to have the oversight of the work on the house of the LORD. 9 And Jeshua with his sons and his kin, and Kadmiel and his sons, Binnui and Hodaviahᵇ along with the sons of Henadad, the Levites, their sons and kin, together took charge of the workers in the house of God.

10 When the builders laid the foundation of the temple of the LORD, the priests in their vestments were stationed to praise the LORD with trumpets, and the Levites, the sons of Asaph, with cymbals, according to the directions of King David of Israel; 11 and they sang responsively, praising and giving thanks to the LORD,

"For he is good,
    for his steadfast love endures forever
        toward Israel."

And all the people responded with a great shout when they praised the LORD, because the foundation of the house of the LORD was laid. 12 But many of the priests and Levites and heads of families, old people who had seen the first house on its foundations, wept with a loud voice when they saw this house, though many shouted aloud for joy, 13 so that the people could not distinguish the sound of the joyful shout from the sound of the

a Or *tabernacles;* Heb *succoth*　　*b* Compare 2.40; Neh 7.43; 1 Esdras 5.58: Heb *sons of Judah*

people's weeping, for the people shouted so loudly that the sound was heard far away.

3.8–13: Laying the foundation of the Temple. The author highlights the momentous beginning of rebuilding the Temple, emphasizing the devotion of the community. **8:** *In the second year after their arrival at the house of God at Jerusalem* may relate to the third year of Darius, around 519 BCE if the earlier reference was to a time in the reign of Darius. The community arrived at Jerusalem to find the Temple in ruins, hence the need to begin rebuilding. But the author, wanting to connect the Jerusalem community with the sanctified dwelling place of God, has the exiles arriving *at the house of God. They appointed the Levites:* Most likely, Zerubbabel and Jeshua appointed them. **10:** *The priests in their vestments were stationed to praise the LORD with trumpets* recalls the priestly trumpeters in 2 Chr 5.12 at the dedication of the first Temple in the days of Solomon. *According to the directions of King David* emphasizes the continuity between this Second Temple and the worship conducted in the First Temple. Despite the trauma of the destruction of Jerusalem and the Temple, and the Exile* in Babylon, nothing has changed in the way the community worships God. **11:** *They sang responsively:* The leaders sang first, and the assembly responded. Another possible meaning is "antiphonally," with one part of the choir initiating a verse and the other part completing it. The hymn that is sung appears as part of a number of Psalms (for example, Ps 106.1; 107.1; 136.1). **12:** *Old people who had seen the first house:* Sixty-eight years had elapsed since the destruction of the first Temple. *Wept with a loud voice when they saw this house:* Presumably what was planned for the rebuilt Temple was less in size and/or grandeur than that of the Temple of Solomon (as in Hag 2.3). The weeping over what had been lost was drowned out by those who *shouted aloud for joy,* shifting the focus to what could be anticipated for the future.

4 When the adversaries of Judah and Benjamin heard that the returned exiles were building a temple to the LORD, the God of Israel, ²they approached Zerubbabel and the heads of families and said to them, "Let us build with you, for we worship your God as you do, and we have been sacrificing to him ever since the days of King Esar-haddon of Assyria who brought us here." ³But Zerubbabel, Jeshua, and the rest of the heads of families in Israel said to them, "You shall have no part with us in building a house to our God; but we alone will build to the LORD, the God of Israel, as King Cyrus of Persia has commanded us."

4 Then the people of the land discouraged the people of Judah, and made them afraid to build, ⁵and they bribed officials to frustrate their plan throughout the reign of King Cyrus of Persia and until the reign of King Darius of Persia.

4.1–5: Opposition to rebuilding the Temple. This section shows the surrounding peoples opposing the rebuilding of the Temple, just as the following section will detail opposition by surrounding peoples to the rebuilding of the walls of Jerusalem over half a century later. Such opposition to sacred actions furthers the prohibition of intermarriage with the surrounding peoples. **1:** *The adversaries of Judah and Benjamin:* By characterizing these persons as *adversaries,* the author makes their subsequent request less than truthful. **2:** *We worship your God as you do:* As deportees who had been settled in the land by the Assyrians, the "adversaries" would not have known the Pentateuch* nor the orders for Temple service attributed to King David. Consequently, they could not approach God in the same way as the returned exiles. **3:** *We alone will build to the LORD, . . . as King Cyrus of Persia has commanded us:* The community determines to show its devotion on its own, and claims this is required by Cyrus's orders. There is nothing in the decree that restricts who can participate in the rebuilding. **4:** *The people of the land discouraged the people of Judah:* Here *people of the land* is defined by what preceded it, namely they are the deportees who were brought into the land by the Assyrians. However, the author will use the term simply as a generic label for those who are not of Judah. The Hebrew term translated as *discouraged* is better rendered "undermined."

6 In the reign of Ahasuerus, in his accession year, they wrote an accusation against the inhabitants of Judah and Jerusalem.

4.6–24: Opposition to rebuilding Jerusalem. The author now moves from opposition to the Temple rebuilding to opposition to building a wall around Jerusalem. After a brief effort at a chronological transition, there is an exchange of memoranda between several imperial officials and King Artaxerxes I of Persia. As a result, the king orders the suspension of any rebuilding of the city, which the author then ties to opposition to the Temple. While there is no way to authenticate these memos, they have the form and general structure of known imperial memos from the Persian empire, although some elements may have been introduced to carry forward the larger purposes of the book. **6:** *In the reign of Ahasuerus, in his accession**year:* Ahasuerus is the Hebrew version of the name of the Persian king the Greeks called Xerxes. The main royal figure in the book of Esther, Xerxes came to the Persian throne late in the year 486 BCE. The contents of the *accusation* are not specified, nor the consequences of the report. This notice serves to bring the narrative* through a chronological sequence of Persian kings (Cyrus, Darius, Xerxes) to the communications with Artaxerxes.

7 And in the days of Artaxerxes, Bishlam and Mithredath and Tabeel and the rest of their associates wrote to King Artaxerxes of Persia; the letter was written in Aramaic and translated.ᵃ ⁸Rehum the royal deputy and Shimshai the scribe wrote a letter against Jerusalem to King Artaxerxes as follows ⁹(then Rehum the royal deputy, Shimshai the scribe, and the rest of their associates, the judges, the envoys, the officials, the Persians, the people of Erech, the Babylonians, the people of Susa, that is, the Elamites, ¹⁰and the rest of the nations whom the great and noble Osnappar deported and settled in the cities of Samaria and in the rest of the province Beyond the River wrote—and now ¹¹this is a copy of the letter that they sent):

"To King Artaxerxes: Your servants, the people of the province Beyond the River, send greeting. And now ¹²may it be known to the king that the Jews who came up from you to us have gone to Jerusalem. They are rebuilding that rebellious and wicked city; they are finishing the walls and repairing the foundations. ¹³Now may it be known to the king that, if this city is rebuilt and the walls finished, they will not pay tribute, custom, or toll, and the royal revenue will be reduced. ¹⁴Now because we share the salt of the palace and it is not fitting for us to witness the king's dishonor, therefore we send and inform the king, ¹⁵so that a search may be

made in the annals of your ancestors. You will discover in the annals that this is a rebellious city, hurtful to kings and provinces, and that sedition was stirred up in it from long ago. On that account this city was laid waste. ¹⁶We make known to the king that, if this city is rebuilt and its walls finished, you will then have no possession in the province Beyond the River."

───────────

4.7–16. 7: *And in the days of Artaxerxes:* He came to the throne in 465 BCE and remained in power until 423 BCE. The names of the officials sending the memo are Aramaic* and Persian. *The letter was written in Aramaic:* The normal language for conducting official business in the Persian empire was Aramaic. By making note of this detail, the author affirms the seriousness of this exchange. It was *translated* so that the Jerusalem community could understand it. The footnote points out that the Hebrew text goes on to read *in Aramaic,* indicating that the author is quoting from the Aramaic original as opposed to the translation. From this point until 6.18, the narrative is in Aramaic. **8:** *Wrote a letter against Jerusalem* identifies the city with the house of God. **10:** *The rest of the nations . . . deported and settled* refers to vv. 1–2, where the deportees settled to the north of Jerusalem were the "adversaries" seeking to join in rebuilding the Temple. Here, they oppose the rebuilding of Jerusalem's walls. *Osnapper* is a variant name for the Assyrian king Asshurbanipal (669–633 BCE). *Beyond the River* was the official name of the administrative unit of Syria-Palestine (in Aramaic, "Abarnahara"). From the perspective of Mesopotamia and Persia, the territories of Syria-Palestine were across or "beyond" the river Jordan, terminating at the coast of the Mediterranean. **12:** *They are rebuilding that rebellious and wicked city:* The neighboring peoples charge that Jerusalem, with its history of rebellion against empires, should not be rebuilt. Persian imperial practice was to decentralize populations. Only where security or economic concerns were of central importance were cities rebuilt. **13:** *If this city is rebuilt and the walls finished, they will not pay tribute:* A renewed and refortified Jerusalem will follow its earlier history and will revolt against the taxes and dues that provided the economic lifeblood of the empire. **14:** *We share the salt of the palace:* An

a Heb adds *in Aramaic,* indicating that 4.8–6.18 is in Aramaic. Another interpretation is *The letter was written in the Aramaic script and set forth in the Aramaic language*

expression, exact meaning unclear, perhaps saying that the writers are paid in part directly by the palace in the form of salt, a more valued commodity in antiquity than now. **16:** *You will then have no possession in the province Beyond the River:* With hyperbole (exaggeration to make a point) the opponents imply that Jerusalem's revolt would lead to the loss of the whole province.

17 The king sent an answer: "To Rehum the royal deputy and Shimshai the scribe and the rest of their associates who live in Samaria and in the rest of the province Beyond the River, greeting. And now ¹⁸the letter that you sent to us has been read in translation before me. ¹⁹So I made a decree, and someone searched and discovered that this city has risen against kings from long ago, and that rebellion and sedition have been made in it. ²⁰Jerusalem has had mighty kings who ruled over the whole province Beyond the River, to whom tribute, custom, and toll were paid. ²¹Therefore issue an order that these people be made to cease, and that this city not be rebuilt, until I make a decree. ²²Moreover, take care not to be slack in this matter; why should damage grow to the hurt of the king?"

23 Then when the copy of King Artaxerxes' letter was read before Rehum and the scribe Shimshai and their associates, they hurried to the Jews in Jerusalem and by force and power made them cease. ²⁴At that time the work on the house of God in Jerusalem stopped and was discontinued until the second year of the reign of King Darius of Persia.

4.17–24. 19: *I made a decree, and someone searched:* The command was to investigate the charge that Jerusalem had a history of rebellion. Brief accounts of major events were kept for administrative purposes, such as the Babylonian Chronicles, which record the successive revolts of Jerusalem against the Babylonian empire until the city's destruction. **20:** *Jerusalem has had mighty kings who ruled over the whole province Beyond the River:* This would seem to refer to either David or Solomon, who exercised control over a large territory. This makes little sense, however, either in the context or in the kinds of records available to the Persian monarch. The same wording could be translated,

"Moreover, there have been powerful kings over Jerusalem who also ruled over the whole province . . . ,'" placing Artaxerxes in a series of imperial rulers who had successfully controlled Jerusalem and Beyond the River. **21:** *This city not be rebuilt, until I make a decree:* By stopping the rebuilding, Artaxerxes was not making a permanent decision. A future royal decree is exactly what the narrative concerning Nehemiah envisions. **23:** *By force and power made them cease:* The prompt response of Rehum and Shimshai is accompanied by terms that may refer to infantry and cavalry units whose presence would underscore the imperial concern over the rebuilding effort. **24:** *At that time the work on the house of God in Jerusalem stopped:* If read as a historical narrative, the phrase *at that time* makes little sense. Artaxerxes I makes the decision to have the work halted sometime after 465 BCE, but later the note *until the second year of the reign of King Darius* would have to be 521 BCE. Either the author is hopelessly confused regarding chronology, or the purpose of the narrative is not historical but thematic. The notation here returns the narrative to the issue of rebuilding the Temple, bringing it back to v. 5.

5 Now the prophets, Haggai^a and Zechariah son of Iddo, prophesied to the Jews who were in Judah and Jerusalem, in the name of the God of Israel who was over them. ²Then Zerubbabel son of Shealtiel and Jeshua son of Jozadak set out to rebuild the house of God in Jerusalem; and with them were the prophets of God, helping them.

3 At the same time Tattenai the governor of the province Beyond the River and Shethar-bozenai and their associates came to them and spoke to them thus, "Who gave you a decree to build this house and to finish this structure?" ⁴They^b also asked them this, "What are the names of the men who are building this building?" ⁵But the eye of their God was upon the elders of the Jews, and they did not stop them until a report reached Darius and then answer was returned by letter in reply to it.

5.1–6.18: Overcoming opposition and rebuilding the Temple. ⋆ This section of the book highlights the continued commitment of the community to rebuild-

a Aram adds *the prophet*   *b* Gk Syr: Aram *We*

ing the house of God, understood as both the physical Temple and the renewed city of Jerusalem. The section is in Aramaic* and, as in the earlier sections, carries the narrative* forward by extensive quotation from various official documents. **5.1:** *Haggai and Zechariah:* The section opens at the end of the sixth century, where ch. 4 ended, with a mention of two prophets* who, along with Zerubbabel the governor and Joshua the high priest, directed a new effort to rebuild the Temple. These are probably the prophets behind the canonical* books bearing their names. **3:** *Who gave you a decree:* The officials who are inquiring about imperial permission may not be opposing the rebuilding of the Temple as much as showing concern that all is being done in accord with imperial sanction.

6 The copy of the letter that Tattenai the governor of the province Beyond the River and Shethar-bozenai and his associates the envoys who were in the province Beyond the River sent to King Darius; 7they sent him a report, in which was written as follows: "To Darius the king, all peace! 8May it be known to the king that we went to the province of Judah, to the house of the great God. It is being built of hewn stone, and timber is laid in the walls; this work is being done diligently and prospers in their hands. 9Then we spoke to those elders and asked them, 'Who gave you a decree to build this house and to finish this structure?' 10We also asked them their names, for your information, so that we might write down the names of the men at their head. 11This was their reply to us: 'We are the servants of the God of heaven and earth, and we are rebuilding the house that was built many years ago, which a great king of Israel built and finished. 12But because our ancestors had angered the God of heaven, he gave them into the hand of King Nebuchadnezzar of Babylon, the Chaldean, who destroyed this house and carried away the people to Babylonia. 13However, King Cyrus of Babylon, in the first year of his reign, made a decree that this house of God should be rebuilt. 14Moreover, the gold and silver vessels of the house of God, which Nebuchadnezzar had taken out of the temple in Jerusalem and had brought into the temple of Babylon, these King Cyrus took out of the temple of Babylon, and they were deliv-

ered to a man named Sheshbazzar, whom he had made governor. 15He said to him, "Take these vessels; go and put them in the temple in Jerusalem, and let the house of God be rebuilt on its site." 16Then this Sheshbazzar came and laid the foundations of the house of God in Jerusalem; and from that time until now it has been under construction, and it is not yet finished.' 17And now, if it seems good to the king, have a search made in the royal archives there in Babylon, to see whether a decree was issued by King Cyrus for the rebuilding of this house of God in Jerusalem. Let the king send us his pleasure in this matter."

5.6–17. 6: *The copy of the letter:* The author offers extracts from official memoranda to fill out the story line. While there can be no certainty, it appears the author was working from actual documents, which may have been modified slightly to fit the narrative. **12:** *But because our ancestors had angered the God of heaven, he gave them into the hand of King Nebuchadnezzar:* The case for rebuilding the Temple depends in part on the assertion that the Temple was destroyed not because the southern kingdom rebelled against Nebuchadnezzar, an imperial king, but because God was angry. **13:** *King Cyrus . . . made a decree:* See 1.1–4.

6 Then King Darius made a decree, and they searched the archives where the documents were stored in Babylon. 2But it was in Ecbatana, the capital in the province of Media, that a scroll was found on which this was written: "A record. 3In the first year of his reign, King Cyrus issued a decree: Concerning the house of God at Jerusalem, let the house be rebuilt, the place where sacrifices are offered and burnt offerings are brought;*a* its height shall be sixty cubits and its width sixty cubits, 4with three courses of hewn stones and one course of timber; let the cost be paid from the royal treasury. 5Moreover, let the gold and silver vessels of the house of God, which Nebuchadnezzar took out of the temple in Jerusalem and brought to Babylon, be restored and brought back to the temple in Jerusalem, each to its

a Meaning of Aram uncertain

place; you shall put them in the house of God."

6 "Now you, Tattenai, governor of the province Beyond the River, Shethar-bozenai, and you, their associates, the envoys in the province Beyond the River, keep away; 7let the work on this house of God alone; let the governor of the Jews and the elders of the Jews rebuild this house of God on its site. 8Moreover I make a decree regarding what you shall do for these elders of the Jews for the rebuilding of this house of God: the cost is to be paid to these people, in full and without delay, from the royal revenue, the tribute of the province Beyond the River. 9Whatever is needed—young bulls, rams, or sheep for burnt offerings to the God of heaven, wheat, salt, wine, or oil, as the priests in Jerusalem require—let that be given to them day by day without fail, 10so that they may offer pleasing sacrifices to the God of heaven, and pray for the life of the king and his children. 11Furthermore I decree that if anyone alters this edict, a beam shall be pulled out of the house of the perpetrator, who then shall be impaled on it. The house shall be made a dunghill. 12May the God who has established his name there overthrow any king or people that shall put forth a hand to alter this, or to destroy this house of God in Jerusalem. I, Darius, make a decree; let it be done with all diligence."

13 Then, according to the word sent by King Darius, Tattenai, the governor of the province Beyond the River, Shethar-bozenai, and their associates did with all diligence what King Darius had ordered. 14So the elders of the Jews built and prospered, through the prophesying of the prophet Haggai and Zechariah son of Iddo. They finished their building by command of the God of Israel and by decree of Cyrus, Darius, and King Artaxerxes of Persia; 15and this house was finished on the third day of the month of Adar, in the sixth year of the reign of King Darius.

16 The people of Israel, the priests and the Levites, and the rest of the returned exiles, celebrated the dedication of this house of God with joy. 17They offered at the dedication of this house of God one hundred bulls, two hundred rams, four hundred lambs, and as a sin offering for all Israel, twelve male goats, according to the number of the tribes of Israel. 18Then they set the priests in their divisions and the Levites in their courses for the service of God at Jerusalem, as it is written in the book of Moses.

6.1–12. 2: *Ecbatana, the capital of the province of Media:* The search began in Babylon since important royal decrees would be archived there. Ecbatana, at a higher elevation than the main capital of Persepolis, was the location of the Persian kings' summer palace. 4: *Let the cost be paid from the royal treasury:* Cyrus's detailed specifications of the size and form of construction limit how much the rebuilding would cost, since imperial funds were paying for it. 10: *So they may offer pleasing sacrifices . . . and pray for the life of the king and his children:* Persian imperial support for local religious centers is well attested. It was part of a larger policy of bringing local customs into a framework of loyalty to the empire. Darius probably did not worship Israel's God, but that did not prevent him from seeking to convince those who did that Israel's God was concerned with the king's well-being.

6.13–18. 14: *They finished their building by command of the God of Israel and by decree of Cyrus, Darius, and King Artaxerxes of Persia:* In a literal historical reading this makes no sense, since the physical Temple was completed in the reign of Darius, and Artaxerxes had nothing to do with it. However, the formation of the "house of God" involved not only rebuilding the Temple, but also rebuilding the city and separating the community from the surrounding peoples by prohibiting intermarriage. These later steps, under the reformers Ezra and Nehemiah, occurred in the time of Artaxerxes. 15: *The third day of the month of Adar, in the sixth year of the reign of King Darius:* 515 BCE. Some believe the day was originally the twenty-third day of Adar, which would put the completed rebuilding near the anniversary of Solomon's celebration of the completion of the original Temple (2 Chr 7.10) and approximately 70 years after the destruction of that Temple. 17: *As a sin offering for all Israel, twelve male goats, according to the number of the tribes of Israel:* Without a functioning Temple, it was not possible for the priesthood to maintain the regular purification offering for the nation. The offering may be indebted to the vision of a renewed Temple by the prophet Ezekiel (Ezek 43.22–27) in which the sin of-fering purifies the Temple from the pollutions of Is-rael's past. **18:** *As it is written in the book of Moses:* In 1 Chr 23–26 it is David who sets up the courses of the priests and the Levites for the worship in the Temple. There is no prescription for these orders as described in the Pentateuch,* normally what the author means by the *book of Moses.* With the arrangements for the offerings and who would be responsible for them, the Temple is now fully functioning.

19 On the fourteenth day of the first month the returned exiles kept the passover. ²⁰For both the priests and the Levites had purified themselves; all of them were clean. So they killed the passover lamb for all the returned exiles, for their fellow priests, and for themselves. ²¹It was eaten by the people of Israel who had returned from exile, and also by all who had joined them and sepa-rated themselves from the pollutions of the nations of the land to worship the LORD, the God of Israel. ²²With joy they celebrated the festival of unleavened bread seven days; for the LORD had made them joyful, and had turned the heart of the king of Assyria to them, so that he aided them in the work on the house of God, the God of Israel.

6.19–22: The first Passover* in the rebuilt Temple.*
The shift back to Hebrew from Aramaic* draws atten-tion to this central festival. Just as Israel was not a phys-ical nation until they could worship God following their escape from Egypt, celebrated in the Passover, so the exilic community could not be considered a nation until the house of God was fully functioning. With the Temple in place, the Passover celebration had a re-newed importance for the community as a sign of their coming into a new status. The author skillfully con-nects this with the physical separation of the com-munity from the surrounding peoples, a point that Ezra will hammer on as the centerpiece of his reforms. **20:** *The priests and the Levites had purified them-selves:* Following the return from exile, there was a new emphasis on the purity regulations of the Pentateuch* and on extending the areas of life they affected. Before undertaking the Passover, the ritual purity of the priests and Levites had to be assured. **21:** *The people of Israel who had returned from exile, and . . . all who had joined them and separated themselves from the pollutions of the nations:* As a celebration of

God's miraculous deliverance and the formation of the people into a nation, Passover was a powerful symbol of identity. Those who had been exiled and returned clearly would be recognized as part of Israel. The pop-ulation that remained behind joined the Exile* com-munity by separating from the surrounding peoples. *Pollutions:* a term normally reserved for severe viola-tions of the sacral order. It was because of their pol-lutions, according to some parts of the Hebrew Bible, that God removed the Canaanites from the land (Lev 20.22–24). **22:** *Had turned the heart of the king of Assyria to them, so that he aided them in the work:* An echo of Ezra 1.1–4. The use of the title *king of Assyria* is unclear, though the Persian king did adopt this title since the former Assyrian territory was under his rule. It may be a deliberate reference to King Esarhaddon of Assyria (Ezra 4.2); some of the peoples he trans-ported to the territory north of Jerusalem had indeed "come over" to the side of the returning exiles in op-position to their fellow countryfolk, who opposed the Temple.

EZRA'S INQUIRY

Chs. 7–10: With little in the way of transition, a first-person narrative* recounts the conditions under which Ezra was authorized to undertake a trip to Je-rusalem, and his initial concerns once there. The use of a first-person narrative may be the result of the au-thor's use of an authentic source (an "Ezra memoir") or may be a literary device intended to give immediacy and emotional power to the narrative.

7 After this, in the reign of King Artaxerxes of Persia, Ezra son of Seraiah, son of Azariah, son of Hilkiah, ²son of Shallum, son of Zadok, son of Ahitub, ³son of Amariah, son of Azariah, son of Meraioth, ⁴son of Zer-ahiah, son of Uzzi, son of Bukki, ⁵son of Abishua, son of Phinehas, son of Eleazar, son of the chief priest Aaron— ⁶this Ezra went up from Babylonia. He was a scribe skilled in the law of Moses that the LORD the God of Israel had given; and the king granted him all that he asked, for the hand of the LORD his God was upon him.

7 Some of the people of Israel, and some of the priests and Levites, the singers and gatekeepers, and the temple servants also went up to Jerusalem, in the seventh year of King Artaxerxes. ⁸They came to Jerusalem in

the fifth month, which was in the seventh year of the king. [9]On the first day of the first month the journey up from Babylon was begun, and on the first day of the fifth month he came to Jerusalem, for the gracious hand of his God was upon him. [10]For Ezra had set his heart to study the law of the LORD, and to do it, and to teach the statutes and ordinances in Israel.

7.1–10: Introduction to the mission of Ezra. The purpose of this third-person narration is to give the reader a sense of who Ezra was and what was significant about his role in relation to the community. **5:** *Son of Eleazar, son of the chief priest Aaron:* Ezra is given a distinguished lineage, concluding with the most important aspect of his family line, that he was a descendant of the primary line of priests in ancient Israel. **6:** *A scribe* skilled in the law:* The ability to read and write led people to expect that scribes could also explain legal issues. *Law of Moses:* apparently the Pentateuch* in some form. *The king granted him all that he asked, for the hand of the LORD his God was upon him:* There is no explanation of how a person who was a specialist in a religious tradition whose followers were a small minority within the empire could get repeated access to the king. *Hand of the LORD . . . was upon him:* A common expression of the presence of God in some sense guiding the person's career. **7:** *Some of the people of Israel:* Presumably only a small portion of the Jewish community in Babylonia chose to return to Jerusalem. Life in exile was more than likely not too difficult, and the prospect of returning to a land devastated by warfare and economic ruin not very attractive. The *seventh year of King Artaxerxes* would be 458 BCE if this was Artaxerxes I of Persia. Since Ezra's opposition to intermarriage receives no mention in the account of Nehemiah, and Nehemiah addresses the same issues as if they had never been raised before, some have argued Ezra really came under Artaxerxes II (the seventh year being 398 BCE). The confusion over Ezra's chronological relation to Nehemiah comes about from trying to read Ezra-Nehemiah as straight history rather than as an apologetic.* The author intends the reader to believe that Ezra came first. **10:** *Ezra had set his heart to study the law of the LORD, and to do it:* Not only was Ezra a student of the law, but he sought to observe its requirements in his everyday life. Out of this study and experience, Ezra would teach the people.

[11]This is a copy of the letter that King Artaxerxes gave to the priest Ezra, the scribe, a scholar of the text of the commandments of the LORD and his statutes for Israel: [12]"Artaxerxes, king of kings, to the priest Ezra, the scribe of the law of the God of heaven: Peace.[a] And now [13]I decree that any of the people of Israel or their priests or Levites in my kingdom who freely offers to go to Jerusalem may go with you. [14]For you are sent by the king and his seven counselors to make inquiries about Judah and Jerusalem according to the law of your God, which is in your hand, [15]and also to convey the silver and gold that the king and his counselors have freely offered to the God of Israel, whose dwelling is in Jerusalem, [16]with all the silver and gold that you shall find in the whole province of Babylonia, and with the freewill offerings of the people and the priests, given willingly for the house of their God in Jerusalem. [17]With this money, then, you shall with all diligence buy bulls, rams, and lambs, and their grain offerings and their drink offerings, and you shall offer them on the altar of the house of your God in Jerusalem. [18]Whatever seems good to you and your colleagues to do with the rest of the silver and gold, you may do, according to the will of your God. [19]The vessels that have been given you for the service of the house of your God, you shall deliver before the God of Jerusalem. [20]And whatever else is required for the house of your God, which you are responsible for providing, you may provide out of the king's treasury.

7.11–28: King Artaxerxes' commission to Ezra. The letter that Artaxerxes purportedly gave to Ezra elevates Ezra from a religious teacher to an imperial official, undertaking an important mission at the request of the king. While portions of the letter may well be genuine, there are serious questions about the authenticity of other sections, and the author seems to have taken some significant liberties in editing the document. **12:** *Artaxerxes, king of kings:* Persian kings did refer to themselves this way, suggesting part of an authentic Persian letter. **14:** *You are sent by the king and his seven counselors:* Persian monarchs had a high council

a Syr Vg 1 Esdras 8.9: Aram *Perfect*

of seven trusted advisers who were called upon to help with significant decisions. Ezra is instructed *to make inquiries about Judah and Jerusalem,* a vague task. *According to the law of your God* may suggest that Ezra is ensuring that the worship in the Temple* is being properly conducted. *Which is in your hand* has been variously interpreted. On its simplest level, it means that Ezra is physically carrying a copy of the Pentateuch* from Babylon to Jerusalem, although in Hebrew there are more direct ways to express this. The phrase *in your hand* is attested in several Persian period documents as meaning "in your power" or "in your sphere of authority." In this understanding, Artaxerxes is directing Ezra to conduct his inquiry in terms of the laws that are relevant to the inquiry, laws that apply to Ezra's task. **19:** *The vessels that have been given you:* Like the vessels Nebuchadnezzar had taken and Cyrus had returned to the Temple (1.7–11), these vessels are a royal gift bestowed on the Temple as a sign of gratitude for God's granting Artaxerxes' rule.

21 "I, King Artaxerxes, decree to all the treasurers in the province Beyond the River: Whatever the priest Ezra, the scribe of the law of the God of heaven, requires of you, let it be done with all diligence, 22 up to one hundred talents of silver, one hundred cors of wheat, one hundred baths*ᵃ* of wine, one hundred baths*ᵃ* of oil, and unlimited salt. 23 Whatever is commanded by the God of heaven, let it be done with zeal for the house of the God of heaven, or wrath will come upon the realm of the king and his heirs. 24 We also notify you that it shall not be lawful to impose tribute, custom, or toll on any of the priests, the Levites, the singers, the doorkeepers, the temple servants, or other servants of this house of God.

25 "And you, Ezra, according to the God-given wisdom you possess, appoint magistrates and judges who may judge all the people in the province Beyond the River who know the laws of your God; and you shall teach those who do not know them. 26 All who will not obey the law of your God and the law of the king, let judgment be strictly executed on them, whether for death or for banishment or for confiscation of their goods or for imprisonment."

27 Blessed be the LORD, the God of our ancestors, who put such a thing as this into the heart of the king to glorify the house of the LORD in Jerusalem, 28 and who extended to me steadfast love before the king and his counselors, and before all the king's mighty officers. I took courage, for the hand of the LORD my God was upon me, and I gathered leaders from Israel to go up with me.

7.21–28. 22: *Up to one hundred talents of silver:* Instructions for the imperial treasurers to support Ezra within limits. The quantities for most of the commodities are not unreasonable, but the amount of silver is almost a third of the total annual taxation of the province Beyond the River. **24:** *It shall not be lawful to impose tribute, custom, or toll:* The exemption of professionals involved in staffing temples from any taxation is attested in other parts of the Persian empire, so it would not be out of character for such an exemption to be extended to the Temple personnel in Jerusalem. **25:** *Appoint magistrates and judges:* Ezra is charged to reform the judiciary. *God-given wisdom:* Though it is unlikely that a Persian king would have credited Ezra's wisdom to God, this connection appears in several places in the book of Deuteronomy (Deut 4.6; 16.19–20). **26:** *All who will not obey the law of your God* refers not to all peoples of any cultural heritage living in the province, but to those who *know the laws* of God, that is, other Jews. **27:** *To glorify the house of the LORD in Jerusalem:* Since Ezra's official mission has little to do with the physical Temple, it is likely that the "house of God" is not the Temple as such, but the community's adherence to the distinctive customs of Israel.

8 These are their family heads, and this is the genealogy of those who went up with me from Babylonia, in the reign of King Artaxerxes: 2 Of the descendants of Phinehas, Gershom. Of Ithamar, Daniel. Of David, Hattush, 3 of the descendants of Shecaniah. Of Parosh, Zechariah, with whom were registered one hundred fifty males. 4 Of the descendants of Pahath-moab, Eliehoenai son of Zerahiah, and with him two hundred males. 5 Of the descendants of Zattu,*ᵇ* Shecaniah son of Jahaziel, and with him three hundred males. 6 Of the descendants of

a A Heb measure of volume   *b* Gk 1 Esdras 8.32; Heb lacks *of Zattu*

Adin, Ebed son of Jonathan, and with him fifty males. [7]Of the descendants of Elam, Jeshaiah son of Athaliah, and with him seventy males. [8]Of the descendants of Shephatiah, Zebadiah son of Michael, and with him eighty males. [9]Of the descendants of Joab, Obadiah son of Jehiel, and with him two hundred eighteen males. [10]Of the descendants of Bani,[a] Shelomith son of Josiphiah, and with him one hundred sixty males. [11]Of the descendants of Bebai, Zechariah son of Bebai, and with him twenty-eight males. [12]Of the descendants of Azgad, Johanan son of Hakkatan, and with him one hundred ten males. [13]Of the descendants of Adonikam, those who came later, their names being Eliphelet, Jeuel, and Shemaiah, and with them sixty males. [14]Of the descendants of Bigvai, Uthai and Zaccur, and with them seventy males.

8.1–14: Listing of those returning with Ezra. Presented in the form of a list, this section has a very artificial structure, leading many to question its authenticity. **2:** *Of the descendants of Phineas:* The list begins with priests first, followed by the descendants of David. The list of David's descendants in 1 Chr 3 carries the list three or four generations after these individuals. **3:** *Of Parosh, Zechariah:* What follows are twelve distinct family groups of persons with no specified occupations. Given the figures for the number of males in each family group, a total of 1,500 men, and an estimated total of 5,000 men, women, and children would have been part of this group.

15 I gathered them by the river that runs to Ahava, and there we camped three days. As I reviewed the people and the priests, I found there none of the descendants of Levi. [16]Then I sent for Eliezer, Ariel, Shemaiah, Elnathan, Jarib, Elnathan, Nathan, Zechariah, and Meshullam, who were leaders, and for Joiarib and Elnathan, who were wise, [17]and sent them to Iddo, the leader at the place called Casiphia, telling them what to say to Iddo and his colleagues the temple servants at Casiphia, namely, to send us ministers for the house of our God. [18]Since the gracious hand of our God was upon us, they brought us a man of discretion, of the descendants of Mahli son of Levi son of Israel,

namely Sherebiah, with his sons and kin, eighteen; [19]also Hashabiah and with him Jeshaiah of the descendants of Merari, with his kin and their sons, twenty; [20]besides two hundred twenty of the temple servants, whom David and his officials had set apart to attend the Levites. These were all mentioned by name.

8.15–20: An aside concerning the Levites. In the list above (vv. 1–14), although there are priests, there are no Levites. Yet Levites were necessary for the proper functioning of the Temple* since certain duties were exclusively theirs. This section explains how Ezra was able to solve this problem. **15:** *The river that runs to Ahava:* An unknown place in Babylonia. **17:** *The place called Casiphia:* Another unknown place, though the presence of Temple servants there suggests some form of formal worship may have been conducted in this location.

21 Then I proclaimed a fast there, at the river Ahava, that we might deny ourselves[b] before our God, to seek from him a safe journey for ourselves, our children, and all our possessions. [22]For I was ashamed to ask the king for a band of soldiers and cavalry to protect us against the enemy on our way, since we had told the king that the hand of our God is gracious to all who seek him, but his power and his wrath are against all who forsake him. [23]So we fasted and petitioned our God for this, and he listened to our entreaty.

24 Then I set apart twelve of the leading priests: Sherebiah, Hashabiah, and ten of their kin with them. [25]And I weighed out to them the silver and the gold and the vessels, the offering for the house of our God that the king, his counselors, his lords, and all Israel there present had offered; [26]I weighed out into their hand six hundred fifty talents of silver, and one hundred silver vessels worth . . . talents,[c] and one hundred talents of gold, [27]twenty gold bowls worth a thousand darics, and two vessels of fine polished bronze as precious as gold. [28]And I said to them, "You are holy to the LORD, and the

a Gk 1 Esdras 8.36: Heb lacks *Bani*   b Or *might fast*
c The number of talents is lacking

vessels are holy; and the silver and the gold are a freewill offering to the LORD, the God of your ancestors. 29Guard them and keep them until you weigh them before the chief priests and the Levites and the heads of families in Israel at Jerusalem, within the chambers of the house of the LORD." 30So the priests and the Levites took over the silver, the gold, and the vessels as they were weighed out, to bring them to Jerusalem, to the house of our God.

8.21–30: Preparations for the journey to Jerusalem. There are two distinct parts to this section: a concern about physical dangers (vv. 21–23) and some details on the precious metals being carried for the Temple* (vv. 24–30). In the author's view, it may be that carrying so much gold and silver made the expedition a target for robbers, leading to the concerns for security. **21:** *Then I proclaimed a fast there:* Following the Exile,* fasting seems to have become a more common practice to affirm to God and the community the seriousness with which appeals to God were being made. In this case, the fast underscores the community's desire for God to protect them. **23:** *And he listened to our entreaty* anticipates what the reader is told later, that the journey was made safely. **24:** *Then I set apart twelve of the leading priests:* In Ezra-Nehemiah various groupings of twelve appear frequently, possibly as a way of retaining some sense of the twelve-tribe organization that traditionally made up the members of Israel, even though most of the persons in these groups are from the tribe of Judah. **28:** *You are holy to the LORD, and the vessels are holy* summarizes several Pentateuchal* rules regarding priests (Ex 29.1; Lev 21.6) and vessels used in worship (Ex 29.44; 30.29). Only Temple personnel decreed as holy could transport holy objects (Lev 3.31; 4.12–15).

31 Then we left the river Ahava on the twelfth day of the first month, to go to Jerusalem; the hand of our God was upon us, and he delivered us from the hand of the enemy and from ambushes along the way. 32We came to Jerusalem and remained there three days. 33On the fourth day, within the house of our God, the silver, the gold, and the vessels were weighed into the hands of the priest Meremoth son of Uriah, and with him was Eleazar son of Phinehas, and with them were the Levites, Jozabad son of Jeshua

and Noadiah son of Binnui. 34The total was counted and weighed, and the weight of everything was recorded.

35 At that time those who had come from captivity, the returned exiles, offered burnt offerings to the God of Israel, twelve bulls for all Israel, ninety-six rams, seventy-seven lambs, and as a sin offering twelve male goats; all this was a burnt offering to the LORD. 36They also delivered the king's commissions to the king's satraps and to the governors of the province Beyond the River; and they supported the people and the house of God.

8.31–36: The return to Jerusalem. This section provides a clean closure to the basic duties of the party returning with Ezra: the delivery of the Temple* treasures being donated by the Persian monarchy and the initiation of newly endowed sacrifices. **31:** *The hand of our God was upon us:* The same concept of divine empowerment is found in 7.28. **33:** *On the fourth day:* Possibly the party needed the time to rest before engaging in their business. The gifts were *weighed* out in order to ensure the quantities entrusted to Ezra and his group were fully delivered. **35:** *Those who had come from captivity, the returned exiles:* This enigmatic reference may mean just the group that has returned with Ezra or the entire Jerusalem community. Most likely, given the end of v. 36, the reference is intended to be the group that has just returned. The sacrifices that are offered bear symbolic numbers representative of all Israel. Verses 35–36 are related in a third-person form, leading several to suggest they are the work of a later editor. **36:** *They supported the people and the house of God,* the ultimate commendation of those who came with Ezra.

9 After these things had been done, the officials approached me and said, "The people of Israel, the priests, and the Levites have not separated themselves from the peoples of the lands with their abominations, from the Canaanites, the Hittites, the Perizzites, the Jebusites, the Ammonites, the Moabites, the Egyptians, and the Amorites. 2For they have taken some of their daughters as wives for themselves and for their sons. Thus the holy seed has mixed itself with the peoples of the lands, and in this faithlessness the officials and leaders have led the way."

3When I heard this, I tore my garment and my mantle, and pulled hair from my head and beard, and sat appalled. 4Then all who trembled at the words of the God of Israel, because of the faithlessness of the returned exiles, gathered around me while I sat appalled until the evening sacrifice.

9.1–15: Acknowledgment of intermarriage and Ezra's response. The narrative* dealing with Ezra comes to a dramatic point in this chapter. Portions of the community reveal that intermarriage has taken place, and Ezra offers a long prayer of confession trusting that God will not destroy the community because of this sin. The entire framework is expressed in graphic terms, in which intermarriage is colored by terms associated with the most severe violations of God's sanctity. The aura of holiness and purity which must surround the Temple* as God's dwelling place is now transferred to the community as a whole. The community becomes the house of God. **1:** *After these things:* Ezra has disposed of some of the formalities of his mission, and then is confronted by the issue of intermarriage. The list of peoples contains the seven stock enemies of Israel that appear in a number of places in the Hebrew Bible. While marriage with foreigners was not prohibited, marriage with any of these enemies was considered unacceptable because of the danger of idolatry* (for example, Deut 7.1–4). There is no evidence that such peoples would still have been identifiable in the time of Ezra. **2:** *The holy seed has mixed itself* extends language from the "holiness code" of Lev 19 to the population. In Lev 19.19, mixing different seeds is prohibited as an affront to God's holiness. Such action is characterized as *faithlessness* in this narrative, or acting without regard for God's holiness. The entire condemnation of intermarriage here is a process of creatively combining ideas and themes into a new teaching. **3:** *I tore my garment and my mantle, and pulled hair from my head and beard:* These are traditional signs of deeply felt grief. **4:** *All who trembled at the words of the God of Israel* is a reference to those who took seriously the commandments of God, reflecting the original awe of the people when God first revealed his law upon the mountain (Ex 19.16–20).

~~~~~~

5 At the evening sacrifice I got up from my fasting, with my garments and my mantle torn, and fell on my knees, spread out my hands to the LORD my God, 6and said,

"O my God, I am too ashamed and embarrassed to lift my face to you, my God, for our iniquities have risen higher than our heads, and our guilt has mounted up to the heavens. 7From the days of our ancestors to this day we have been deep in guilt, and for our iniquities we, our kings, and our priests have been handed over to the kings of the lands, to the sword, to captivity, to plundering, and to utter shame, as is now the case. 8But now for a brief moment favor has been shown by the LORD our God, who has left us a remnant, and given us a stake in his holy place, in order that he*a* may brighten our eyes and grant us a little sustenance in our slavery. 9For we are slaves; yet our God has not forsaken us in our slavery, but has extended to us his steadfast love before the kings of Persia, to give us new life to set up the house of our God, to repair its ruins, and to give us a wall in Judea and Jerusalem.

9.5–9.6: *Our iniquities . . . and our guilt* are references to the practice of intermarriage; both terms are often used for severe transgressions of the law. **7:** *To utter shame, as is now the case:* Though the Persian monarchs have generally been supportive, there is still the sense of a diminished community because of the need to rely on Persian support. **8:** *Who has left us a remnant, and given us a stake in his holy place:* God's recent gracious acts are reviewed, including allowing the community to survive at all and providing a point of security in Jerusalem. **9:** *For we are slaves:* Despite the favor the monarchy has granted, the community is still in servitude to the empire. The expression will be echoed in Neh 9.36. *To set up the house of our God* serves as the general heading, the specific actions being to *repair its ruins* and to provide *a wall in Judea and Jerusalem.* The *wall* is a metaphor,* standing for a boundary or separation from the surrounding region by staying away from intermarriage. To violate this *wall* becomes all the more serious, a rejection of God's gift intended to help establish the house of God.

~~~~~~

10 "And now, our God, what shall we say after this? For we have forsaken your commandments, 11which you commanded by your servants the prophets, saying, 'The land that you are entering to possess is a land un-

a Heb *our God*

clean with the pollutions of the peoples of the lands, with their abominations. They have filled it from end to end with their uncleanness. ¹²Therefore do not give your daughters to their sons, neither take their daughters for your sons, and never seek their peace or prosperity, so that you may be strong and eat the good of the land and leave it for an inheritance to your children forever.' ¹³After all that has come upon us for our evil deeds and for our great guilt, seeing that you, our God, have punished us less than our iniquities deserved and have given us such a remnant as this, ¹⁴shall we break your commandments again and intermarry with the peoples who practice these abominations? Would you not be angry with us until you destroy us without remnant or survivor? ¹⁵O LORD, God of Israel, you are just, but we have escaped as a remnant, as is now the case. Here we are before you in our guilt, though no one can face you because of this."

9.10–15. 10–11: *For we have forsaken your commandments, which you commanded by your servants the prophets:* The quotation comes from fragments of various texts pieced together, notably Deut 7.1–4; 11.8; 23.6; Isa 1.19; and Lev 18.24–30. 13: *After all that has come upon us* relates to the destruction of Jerusalem and the subsequent exile of a number of leading citizens under the Babylonians. 14: *Shall we break your commandments again and intermarry:* This phrasing equates the idolatry of the late Judean kingdom with the practice of intermarriage in Ezra's day. 15: *You are just:* Despite God's character as a just god (which would mean the community should have been obliterated), the community has survived, yet *guilt* has again come on the community from its intermarriage with the surrounding peoples. The implication is that the community must remove the guilt (that is, intermarriage) or face certain destruction at the hands of a just and holy God.

10 While Ezra prayed and made confession, weeping and throwing himself down before the house of God, a very great assembly of men, women, and children gathered to him out of Israel; the people also wept bitterly. ²Shecaniah son of Jehiel, of the descendants of Elam, addressed Ezra,

saying, "We have broken faith with our God and have married foreign women from the peoples of the land, but even now there is hope for Israel in spite of this. ³So now let us make a covenant with our God to send away all these wives and their children, according to the counsel of my lord and of those who tremble at the commandment of our God; and let it be done according to the law. ⁴Take action, for it is your duty, and we are with you; be strong, and do it." ⁵Then Ezra stood up and made the leading priests, the Levites, and all Israel swear that they would do as had been said. So they swore.

10.1–5: **The people's response.** The narrative* now returns briefly to a third-person form to describe the community's reaction to Ezra's sermon in prayer form. The function of this brief notice is to empower Ezra to act on behalf of the community's own request. 1: *A very great assembly of men, women, and children gathered to him out of Israel:* One of the keys to this section is the idea of an *assembly*. A large number of persons heard Ezra's prayer and *wept bitterly,* indicating their deep grief. 3: *Now let us make a covenant:* Recognizing the gravity of their situation, the assembly calls for action to remove the foreign wives from the community's midst as a sacred act, to be done as dictated by Ezra and *those who tremble at the commandment of our God,* the members of the community particularly concerned with obedience to the law. 5: *The leading priests, the Levites, and all Israel:* Reversing the order of the report from the "officials" in 9.1, the account ensures that the community as a whole observes the new covenant.

6 Then Ezra withdrew from before the house of God, and went to the chamber of Jehohanan son of Eliashib, where he spent the night.ᵃ He did not eat bread or drink water, for he was mourning over the faithlessness of the exiles. ⁷They made a proclamation throughout Judah and Jerusalem to all the returned exiles that they should assemble at Jerusalem, ⁸and that if any did not come within three days, by order of the officials and the elders all their property should be forfeited, and they themselves banned from the congregation of the exiles.

a 1 Esdras 9.2: Heb *where he went*

9 Then all the people of Judah and Benjamin assembled at Jerusalem within the three days; it was the ninth month, on the twentieth day of the month. All the people sat in the open square before the house of God, trembling because of this matter and because of the heavy rain. [10]Then Ezra the priest stood up and said to them, "You have trespassed and married foreign women, and so increased the guilt of Israel. [11]Now make confession to the LORD the God of your ancestors, and do his will; separate yourselves from the peoples of the land and from the foreign wives." [12]Then all the assembly answered with a loud voice, "It is so; we must do as you have said. [13]But the people are many, and it is a time of heavy rain; we cannot stand in the open. Nor is this a task for one day or for two, for many of us have transgressed in this matter. [14]Let our officials represent the whole assembly, and let all in our towns who have taken foreign wives come at appointed times, and with them the elders and judges of every town, until the fierce wrath of our God on this account is averted from us." [15]Only Jonathan son of Asahel and Jahzeiah son of Tikvah opposed this, and Meshullam and Shabbethai the Levites supported them.

10.6–15: Ezra's decree against intermarriage. Rather than issue a proclamation in his role as imperial representative, Ezra convenes an assembly of the community to deliver the regulation to separate themselves from the peoples of the lands. The narrative* underscores the willingness of the community to reform itself, with few exceptions. **6:** *Ezra withdrew:* Having interceded on behalf of the community, Ezra could now retire to another less public place to plan how the community would enact its reforms. His fasting is a traditional means of expressing sorrow for sin. **7:** *A proclamation:* The call to convene an assembly goes to the *returned exiles*, perhaps to differentiate the community from non-Israelite populations that may have moved into the region after the fall of the Judean kingdom. **8:** *Property . . . forfeited:* a penalty that presupposes community control over each individual's possessions. There is evidence that the Persian empire organized some districts into economic collectives in which the individual had wealth only as a part of the collective. Being excluded from the collective would

have dire economic consequences. *Congregation:* the same word in Hebrew as "assembly" in 10.1. **9:** *The ninth month:* Kislev, approximately December of the modern calendar,* a time of cold rains in Palestine. In a human touch, the author notes the people were *trembling* from the awesomeness of the matter at hand, and the cold rains. **10:** *Trespassed:* The violation of separateness has not only caused individual alienation from God, but has affected the community's relationship to God. **11:** *Separate yourselves:* It is not clear if the order to separate is a general one, for which sending away *the foreign wives* is the specific action, or if an additional issue is involved. **14:** The *whole assembly* agrees to Ezra's proposal but makes a series of practical suggestions for its implementation. The work of sorting through those marriages that needed to be dissolved would continue until intermarriage was no longer the guilt of the community.

〰〰〰〰〰〰〰〰〰〰〰

16 Then the returned exiles did so. Ezra the priest selected men,[a] heads of families, according to their families, each of them designated by name. On the first day of the tenth month they sat down to examine the matter. [17]By the first day of the first month they had come to the end of all the men who had married foreign women.

18 There were found of the descendants of the priests who had married foreign women, of the descendants of Jeshua son of Jozadak and his brothers: Maaseiah, Eliezer, Jarib, and Gedaliah. [19]They pledged themselves to send away their wives, and their guilt offering was a ram of the flock for their guilt. [20]Of the descendants of Immer: Hanani and Zebadiah. [21]Of the descendants of Harim: Maaseiah, Elijah, Shemaiah, Jehiel, and Uzziah. [22]Of the descendants of Pashhur: Elioenai, Maaseiah, Ishmael, Nethanel, Jozabad, and Elasah.

23 Of the Levites: Jozabad, Shimei, Kelaiah (that is, Kelita), Pethahiah, Judah, and Eliezer. [24]Of the singers: Eliashib. Of the gatekeepers: Shallum, Telem, and Uri.

25 And of Israel: of the descendants of Parosh: Ramiah, Izziah, Malchijah, Mijamin, Eleazar, Hashabiah,[b] and Benaiah. [26]Of the descendants of Elam: Mattaniah,

a 1 Esdras 9.16: Syr: Heb *And there were selected Ezra,*
b 1 Esdras 9.26 Gk: Heb *Malchijah*

Zechariah, Jehiel, Abdi, Jeremoth, and Elijah. 27 Of the descendants of Zattu: Elioenai, Eliashib, Mattaniah, Jeremoth, Zabad, and Aziza. 28 Of the descendants of Bebai: Jehohanan, Hananiah, Zabbai, and Athlai. 29 Of the descendants of Bani: Meshullam, Malluch, Adaiah, Jashub, Sheal, and Jeremoth. 30 Of the descendants of Pahath-moab: Adna, Chelal, Benaiah, Maaseiah, Mattaniah, Bezalel, Binnui, and Manasseh. 31 Of the descendants of Harim: Eliezer, Isshijah, Malchijah, Shemaiah, Shimeon, 32 Benjamin, Malluch, and Shemariah. 33 Of the descendants of Hashum: Mattenai, Mattattah, Zabad, Eliphelet, Jeremai, Manasseh, and Shimei. 34 Of the descendants of Bani: Maadai, Amram, Uel, 35 Benaiah, Bedeiah, Cheluhi, 36 Vaniah, Meremoth, Eliashib, 37 Mattaniah, Mattenai, and Jaasu. 38 Of the descendants of Binnui: *a* Shimei, 39 Shelemiah, Nathan, Adaiah, 40 Machnadebai, Shashai, Sharai, 41 Azarel, Shelemiah, Shemariah, 42 Shallum, Amariah, and Joseph. 43 Of the descendants of Nebo: Jeiel, Mattithiah, Zabad, Zebina, Jaddai, Joel, and Benaiah. 44 All these had married foreign women, and they sent them away with their children. *b*

10.16–44: The listing of men who had married foreign wives. Moving back to a third-person narrative, ★ the account now describes the process by which the community was examined, and the results of that examination are listed. The emphasis on the actual persons who willingly sent away their foreign wives underscores the community's willingness to take on this level of separation, forming a distinct, "holy" community. **17:** *By the first day of the first month:* The process took three months. **18:** The list is ordered along three lines—the priests, the Levites, and Israel—considering the small enclave of Jerusalem and its surroundings as the totality of the community. **44:** The Hebrew text here is difficult and the translation follows the Greek of 1 Esdras. The Hebrew suggests the children stayed and only the foreign wives were sent away, the children being counted as legitimate members of the community.

---

a Gk: Heb *Bani, Binnui*   *b* 1 Esdras 9.36; Meaning of Heb uncertain

NEHEMIAH

Introduction

The Access Bible treats Ezra-Nehemiah as a single work; for convenience the introductory material from Ezra is repeated here.

In the form found in most English Bibles, Ezra and Nehemiah are divided into two separate books. This format follows a tradition established in the early centuries of the Christian church, when the Vulgate☆ (the Bible in Latin) divided these two works. It was only in the fifteenth century CE that Hebrew manuscripts adopted the same custom. In actuality, the most ancient tradition we can trace kept these two works together as one. Most of the ancient lists of books of the Hebrew Bible list them together. Moreover, the two share a number of literary elements, suggesting that they are related.

It has become commonplace in scholarship to see Ezra-Nehemiah as a continuation of the same narrative☆ as 1 and 2 Chronicles, all these works having been written by the same hand. The reasons are many, but some of the main points are that Ezra-Nehemiah opens with a repetition of 2 Chr 36.22–23, that Ezra-Nehemiah and 1 and 2 Chronicles share vocabulary for Temple☆ personnel and objects that are not found elsewhere in the Hebrew Bible, and that both 1 and 2 Chronicles and Ezra-Nehemiah have extended genealogical☆ lists. While this view may still predominate, the last two decades have seen the emergence of a serious challenge from scholars who argue for the independence of Ezra-Nehemiah and 1 and 2 Chronicles. They have sought to base this conclusion on a number of differences in vocabulary, theology, and ideology between the two works. The issue is complex, but here we will look at Ezra-Nehemiah as if it is an independent composition on its own terms.

In literary form, Ezra-Nehemiah is difficult to characterize. The author has employed citations of documents, lists of personnel or community members, historical narratives, and first-person narratives that are often termed "memoirs." Some of the more notable portions are Rehum's correspondence with King Artaxerxes (Ezra 4.7–22), Tattenai's correspondence with King Darius (5.6–17; 6.6–12), a list of those who returned from Babylon (Ezra 2.1–67, repeated in Neh 7.6–68), the "Ezra memoir" (Ezra 7–10), and the "Nehemiah memoir" (mainly Neh 1.1–7.5).

The normal approach to the work has been to read it as a historical narrative, but throughout the work elements appear dislocated and far off the mark for history writing. Given the lack of chronological flow to the work, it would be better to consider it a historical apologetic,☆ or a defense of a particular position or viewpoint, loosely using the events of the community to support a theological perspective.

Squarely set in the midst of the Persian empire, the work focuses on two imperial functionaries, Ezra and Nehemiah, and the reforms they attempted. If Ezra is placed before Nehemiah, as seems the intent of the author, then Ezra came to Jerusalem in 458 BCE, and Nehemiah's first stint as governor was in 445 BCE. When scholars examine the lists of names, they can determine that the latest names on some lists date from a generation or so after the time of the mid fifth century. They therefore conclude that the work was written around 400 BCE.

Both Ezra and Nehemiah as literary figures are portrayed as disturbed by intermarriage with "foreigners" in the community, and both condemn this activity using a language loaded with religious connotations. This concern hardly seems to fit with Ezra 1–6, where the struggle to rebuild the Temple in Jerusalem almost a century earlier dominates.

Linking the various parts of the work together is the theme of the "house of God." Beginning with the rebuilding of the physical structure of the Temple, the work moves through to the reformation of the community as the "house of God." A subsidiary theme is the rebuilding of the walls of Jerusalem, which would separate the community from the surrounding region, both physically and religiously. These themes are cast in highly religious language, leading the reader to the inevitable assessment of the righteousness of this redefinition of the community.

The Persian empire faced troubled conditions in the mid fifth century as a serious revolt in Egypt, coupled with the assistance of the Greek city-states, openly challenged the empire's control of the Mediterranean. The territory of Yehud, as the region of Jerusalem and the surrounding area was called, suddenly had strategic importance for the empire. One of the techniques the Persian empire used to control subject populations was controlling their access to the land. Since most of the population was engaged in farming or farming-related employment, access to the land was essential for survival, and thus the empire maintained control over the peoples they had conquered. The ability to control land access was threatened when adjacent communities began to intermarry, since this blurred the definition of who had access to what lands. The narratives of Ezra-Nehemiah present two individuals who are charged directly by the Persian king to undertake vaguely described missions, the result of which is the strengthening of the community boundaries by directly attacking the practice of intermarriage. Such a redefinition of the community probably met with strong opposition, and the present literary work of Ezra-Nehemiah sought to provide a theological rationale for accepting what was essentially an imperial dictate.

READING GUIDE

Given the complicated mixture of literary forms in Ezra-Nehemiah, it is difficult to follow all the elements of the narrative. Readers should watch for the "house of God" theme in the various sections; how does the author want us to understand the "house of God"? Also, it is helpful to notice who is allowed to participate in the community, and who is being excluded.

NEHEMIAH'S MISSION

1.1–7.5: Nehemiah opens with a first-person narrative* relating his concerns over Jerusalem and the Persian monarch's appointment of himself as governor over the province. The bulk of the account covers the various incidents of Nehemiah's rule as governor as he attempted to rebuild the walls of Jerusalem. The narrative must constantly balance Nehemiah's leadership of the community and the active opposition of leaders in the surrounding areas. There are several points of connection (as noted in the comments) with the first-person narratives of the book of Ezra.

1 The words of Nehemiah son of Hacaliah. In the month of Chislev, in the twentieth year, while I was in Susa the capital, ²one of my brothers, Hanani, came with certain men from Judah; and I asked them about the Jews that survived, those who had escaped the captivity, and about Jerusalem. ³They replied, "The survivors there in the province who escaped captivity are in great trouble and shame; the wall of Jerusalem is broken down, and its gates have been destroyed by fire."

4 When I heard these words I sat down and wept, and mourned for days, fasting and praying before the God of heaven. ⁵I said, "O Lᴏʀᴅ God of heaven, the great and awesome God who keeps covenant and steadfast love with those who love him and keep his commandments; ⁶let your ear be attentive and your eyes open to hear the prayer of your servant that I now pray before you day and night for your servants, the people of Israel, confessing the sins of the people of Israel, which we have sinned against you. Both I and my family have sinned. ⁷We have offended you deeply, failing to keep the commandments, the statutes, and the ordinances that you commanded your servant Moses. ⁸Remember the word that you commanded your servant Moses, 'If you are unfaithful, I will scatter you among the peoples; ⁹but if you return to me and keep my commandments and do them, though your outcasts are under the farthest skies, I will gather them from there and bring them to the place at which I have chosen to establish

my name.' ¹⁰They are your servants and your people, whom you redeemed by your great power and your strong hand. ¹¹O Lord, let your ear be attentive to the prayer of your servant, and to the prayer of your servants who delight in revering your name. Give success to your servant today, and grant him mercy in the sight of this man!"

At the time, I was cupbearer to the king.

1.1–11: Nehemiah's concern over Jerusalem. The opening explains Nehemiah's appointment as governor and his relentless pursuit of the rebuilding of the city walls. The section ends with a lengthy prayer that gives voice to the author's concept of the proper approach to God. **1:** *The words of Nehemiah:* The Hebrew term for *words* can also be rendered "matters." The opening does not necessarily support the existence of a "Nehemiah memoir." *In the twentieth year:* Apparently the twentieth year of King Artaxerxes (see 2.1). *Susa* was a seasonal palace for the Persian monarchs, though Artaxerxes seemed to have favored it and spent protracted periods there. **2:** *One of my brothers* may indicate a family member (see 7.2) or may simply mean a colleague. *The Jews that survived:* It is unclear what specific group or groups Nehemiah is asking about, but the main point is his concern with the entire community's welfare as well as the city's. **3:** *The wall of Jerusalem is broken down:* This should have been well known, following on the destruction of the city by the Babylonians in 587 ʙᴄᴇ. Some believe the report must relate to a more recent event, and suggest that the events of Ezra 4.23 may provide the background, though nothing in that account would suggest a destruction of the work that had been accomplished. Possibly the report is taken as a sign of the royal disapproval of Ezra 4.23: The wall of Jerusalem is still broken down, and thus Nehemiah must try a different means to aid Jerusalem. Given the use of terms such as *great trouble and shame,* another possibility is that the *wall* and *gates* are metaphors* for the separation that Ezra was trying to achieve. **4:** *I sat down and wept, and mourned for days:* This is a sign of grief, and also a sign of the literary character of the account, since it is hard to conceive of a figure as forceful as Nehemiah acting so victimized for several months. **5:** *God of heaven* was a characteristic title for God in the Persian period (see Ezra 7.12, 23). **10:** *They are your servants and your people:* After confessing his own guilt, Nehemiah calls on God to remember his people since Nehemiah's prayer is on their behalf. **11:** *Give* *success to your servant today, and grant him mercy in the sight of this man:* Nehemiah apparently has formed a plan to address the misfortunes of Jerusalem, but the reader does not yet know what it is. *Man* is clearly a reference to Artaxerxes. In the Persian court, *cupbearer* was a formal office, with responsibility for ensuring the safety of the king's wine supply as well as acting as a royal adviser.

2 In the month of Nisan, in the twentieth year of King Artaxerxes, when wine was served him, I carried the wine and gave it to the king. Now, I had never been sad in his presence before. ²So the king said to me, "Why is your face sad, since you are not sick? This can only be sadness of the heart." Then I was very much afraid. ³I said to the king, "May the king live forever! Why should my face not be sad, when the city, the place of my ancestors' graves, lies waste, and its gates have been destroyed by fire?" ⁴Then the king said to me, "What do you request?" So I prayed to the God of heaven. ⁵Then I said to the king, "If it pleases the king, and if your servant has found favor with you, I ask that you send me to Judah, to the city of my ancestors' graves, so that I may rebuild it." ⁶The king said to me (the queen also was sitting beside him), "How long will you be gone, and when will you return?" So it pleased the king to send me, and I set him a date. ⁷Then I said to the king, "If it pleases the king, let letters be given me to the governors of the province Beyond the River, that they may grant me passage until I arrive in Judah; ⁸and a letter to Asaph, the keeper of the king's forest, directing him to give me timber to make beams for the gates of the temple fortress, and for the wall of the city, and for the house that I shall occupy." And the king granted me what I asked, for the gracious hand of my God was upon me.

2.1–8: Artaxerxes' grant to Nehemiah. Just as Ezra's mission was the result of a gracious act by Artaxerxes, so Nehemiah's appointment as governor is by the favor of the same king. This account shows the conditions of Nehemiah's appointment and underscores God's working through both Artaxerxes and Nehemiah. **1:** *In the month of Nisan, in the twentieth year:* Nisan, is in early Spring, roughly March—April in our

calendar, some three months after receiving the report of 1.3. The *twentieth year of Artaxerxes* would place this in 445 BCE, about 13 years after Ezra's mission. **3:** *The city, the place of my ancestors' graves, lies waste* is a somewhat exaggerated description, though it is probable that sections of the city remained uninhabitable from the ruins of the Babylonian conquest. **6:** *How long will you be gone, and when will you return?* Artaxerxes's reply assumes the granting of Nehemiah's request to rebuild Jerusalem, and the value of Nehemiah to the court. **8:** *To give me timber to make beams for the gates of the temple fortress, and for the wall of the city:* Nehemiah's task in rebuilding the city will include refortification, something the Persian empire would not allow without royal dispensation. Since the beams over the gateways need to be of larger and stronger wood than is readily available in the region, Nehemiah asks for timber from the imperially controlled sources, probably the cedar forests of Lebanon. The granting of timber supplies was also the empowering of Nehemiah to refortify the city, an act undertaken because of troubled conditions in the Egyptian holdings of the empire. *The gracious hand of my God was upon me* parallels Ezra's claim of divine support (Ezra 7.6, 28).

9 Then I came to the governors of the province Beyond the River, and gave them the king's letters. Now the king had sent officers of the army and cavalry with me. ¹⁰When Sanballat the Horonite and Tobiah the Ammonite official heard this, it displeased them greatly that someone had come to seek the welfare of the people of Israel.

11 So I came to Jerusalem and was there for three days. ¹²Then I got up during the night, I and a few men with me; I told no one what my God had put into my heart to do for Jerusalem. The only animal I took was the animal I rode. ¹³I went out by night by the Valley Gate past the Dragon's Spring and to the Dung Gate, and I inspected the walls of Jerusalem that had been broken down and its gates that had been destroyed by fire. ¹⁴Then I went on to the Fountain Gate and to the King's Pool; but there was no place for the animal I was riding to continue. ¹⁵So I went up by way of the valley by night and inspected the wall. Then I turned back and entered by the Valley Gate, and so returned. ¹⁶The officials did not know where I had

gone or what I was doing; I had not yet told the Jews, the priests, the nobles, the officials, and the rest that were to do the work.

2.9–16: Nehemiah's coming to Jerusalem. As with the account of Ezra, there are few details of the lengthy journey from Persia to Jerusalem. The focus is on significant opposition to Nehemiah's task and his consequent need to be cautious in his planning. **9:** *Gave them the king's letters:* Since Nehemiah came directly from the imperial court, it would be convenient for him to carry vital dispatches as well as official declarations of his office. *The king had sent officers of the army and cavalry with me* highlights both the military nature of Nehemiah's commission and the importance the imperial court placed on his success. **10:** *Sanballat the Horonite and Tobiah the Ammonite official: Sanballat* is a Babylonian name and is known from Aramaic* documents of the Persian period to have been the name of the governor of the Persian district of Samaria. *Horonite* probably means his family was from Beth-horon, two Israelite cities located some 12 miles north of Jerusalem (2 Chr 8.5) and controlling a strategic pass. *Tobiah* is a Hebrew name; his exact role is less certain. *The Ammonite official* is perhaps a reference to his region of administrative responsibility. Some have linked him to a powerful family of the same name of a later period that had significant interests in the Transjordan. Others have suggested he is the same as the *Tabeel* of Ezra 4.7, apparently a junior official in the regional administration. As an *Ammonite* (if this is a reference to family origin), Tobiah would be excluded from the "assembly" of Israel (Deut 23.3–6). *It displeased them:* Perhaps because of the new preference the imperial court is showing to Jerusalem, which will bring new revenues and prestige to the city. **11:** The account of the rest of the *three days* parallels Ezra's account (Ezra 8.32). **13:** *I went out by night by the Valley Gate:* Nehemiah's inspection of the city's fortifications, had it been observed, might have raised objections that could be communicated to the king and cause a delay in the project. His inspection tour seems to follow the area known as the "City of David," a spur of land that lies along the western edge of the Kidron Valley south of the Temple* area. Nehemiah moves from the northwest corner of this region along the city walls, which stretched southeastward until they turned and went back north above the Kidron.

17 Then I said to them, "You see the trouble we are in, how Jerusalem lies in ruins with its gates burned. Come, let us rebuild the wall of Jerusalem, so that we may no longer suffer disgrace." 18I told them that the hand of my God had been gracious upon me, and also the words that the king had spoken to me. Then they said, "Let us start building!" So they committed themselves to the common good. 19But when Sanballat the Horonite and Tobiah the Ammonite official, and Geshem the Arab heard of it, they mocked and ridiculed us, saying, "What is this that you are doing? Are you rebelling against the king?" 20Then I replied to them, "The God of heaven is the one who will give us success, and we his servants are going to start building; but you have no share or claim or historic right in Jerusalem."

2.17–20: Nehemiah's decree to the people, and opposition to the project. Just as the previous section introduced Nehemiah's determination to fulfill the commission given him, and introduced the main personalities who would oppose him, this section brings the community into the picture by Nehemiah's leadership, yet notes the opposition. **17:** *Then I said to them:* The whole community, as defined in v. 16. *Disgrace* was a term often associated with the Exile* as God's punishment of the community; in other words, the refortification of the city would finally put to an end the negative results of God's punishment of the community. **18:** *They committed themselves to the common good:* Just as Ezra had found a willingness to undertake the difficult task of separation from the surrounding peoples, Nehemiah finds the community ready to undertake rebuilding the walls. **19:** *Geshem the Arab* is a new figure among the opponents, thought to be the governor of a region in the Shephelah with an administrative center at Lachish. *Are you rebelling against the king?* would be the normal assumption about an effort to rebuild a city's fortifications since it would provide the means to defy imperial power. It is a hollow taunt since Nehemiah was directly commissioned by the imperial court. **20:** *You have no share or claim or historic right in Jerusalem* was a stinging rebuke to his opponents that essentially undercut their intrusion into Nehemiah's administrative affairs. The expression strongly parallels the rejection of help from "adversaries" in rebuilding the Temple* (Ezra 4.3), joining the theme of reestablishing the "house of God" to the rebuilding of the walls.

~~~~~~~~~~

3 Then the high priest Eliashib set to work with his fellow priests and rebuilt the Sheep Gate. They consecrated it and set up its doors; they consecrated it as far as the Tower of the Hundred and as far as the Tower of Hananel. 2And the men of Jericho built next to him. And next to them*a* Zaccur son of Imri built.

3 The sons of Hassenaah built the Fish Gate; they laid its beams and set up its doors, its bolts, and its bars. 4Next to them Meremoth son of Uriah son of Hakkoz made repairs. Next to them Meshullam son of Berechiah son of Meshezabel made repairs. Next to them Zadok son of Baana made repairs. 5Next to them the Tekoites made repairs; but their nobles would not put their shoulders to the work of their Lord.*b*

6 Joiada son of Paseah and Meshullam son of Besodeiah repaired the Old Gate; they laid its beams and set up its doors, its bolts, and its bars. 7Next to them repairs were made by Melatiah the Gibeonite and Jadon the Meronothite—the men of Gibeon and of Mizpah—who were under the jurisdiction of*c* the governor of the province Beyond the River. 8Next to them Uzziel son of Harhaiah, one of the goldsmiths, made repairs. Next to him Hananiah, one of the perfumers, made repairs; and they restored Jerusalem as far as the Broad Wall. 9Next to them Rephaiah son of Hur, ruler of half the district of*d* Jerusalem, made repairs. 10Next to them Jedaiah son of Harumaph made repairs opposite his house; and next to him Hattush son of Hashabneiah made repairs. 11Malchijah son of Harim and Hasshub son of Pahath-moab repaired another section and the Tower of the Ovens. 12Next to him Shallum son of Hallohesh, ruler of half the district of*d* Jerusalem, made repairs, he and his daughters.

13 Hanun and the inhabitants of Zanoah repaired the Valley Gate; they rebuilt it and set up its doors, its bolts, and its bars, and repaired a thousand cubits of the wall, as far as the Dung Gate.

14 Malchijah son of Rechab, ruler of the district of*e* Beth-haccherem, repaired the Dung Gate; he rebuilt it and set up its doors, its bolts, and its bars.

15 And Shallum son of Col-hozeh, ruler of the district of*e* Mizpah, repaired the Fountain Gate; he rebuilt it and covered it and set up its doors, its bolts, and its bars; and he built the wall of the Pool of Shelah of the king's garden, as far as the stairs that go down from the City of David. 16After him Nehemiah son of Azbuk, ruler of half the district of*d* Beth-zur, repaired from a point opposite the graves of David, as far as the artificial pool and the house of the warriors. 17After him the Levites made repairs: Rehum son of Bani; next to him Hashabiah, ruler of half the district of*d* Keilah, made repairs for his district. 18After him their kin made repairs: Binnui,*f* son of Henadad, ruler of half the district of*d* Keilah; 19next to him Ezer son of Jeshua, ruler*g* of Mizpah, repaired another section opposite the ascent to the armory at the Angle. 20After him Baruch son of Zabbai repaired another section from the Angle to the door of the house of the high priest Eliashib. 21After him Meremoth son of Uriah son of Hakkoz repaired another section from the door of the house of Eliashib to the end of the house of Eliashib. 22After him the priests, the men of the surrounding area, made repairs. 23After them Benjamin and Hasshub made repairs opposite their house. After them Azariah son of Maaseiah son of Ananiah made repairs beside his own house. 24After him Binnui son of Henadad repaired another section, from the house of Azariah to the Angle and to the corner. 25Palal son of Uzai repaired opposite the Angle and the tower projecting from the upper house of the king at the court of the guard. After him Pedaiah son of Parosh 26and the temple servants living*h* on Ophel made repairs up to a point opposite the Water Gate on the east and the projecting tower. 27After him the Tekoites repaired another section opposite the great projecting tower as far as the wall of Ophel.

a Heb him   b Or lords   c Meaning of Heb uncertain   d Or supervisor of half the portion assigned to   e Or supervisor of the portion assigned to   f Gk Syr Compare verse 24, 10.9: Heb Bavvai   g Or supervisor   h Cn: Heb were living

28 Above the Horse Gate the priests made repairs, each one opposite his own house. ²⁹After them Zadok son of Immer made repairs opposite his own house. After him Shemaiah son of Shecaniah, the keeper of the East Gate, made repairs. ³⁰After him Hananiah son of Shelemiah and Hanun sixth son of Zalaph repaired another section. After him Meshullam son of Berechiah made repairs opposite his living quarters. ³¹After him Malchijah, one of the goldsmiths, made repairs as far as the house of the temple servants and of the merchants, opposite the Muster Gate,ᵃ and to the upper room of the corner. ³²And between the upper room of the corner and the Sheep Gate the goldsmiths and the merchants made repairs.

3.1–32: The community organizes to rebuild the walls. This section marks the centerpoint of the combined work Ezra-Nehemiah and places the emphasis squarely on the community's efforts. While Ezra and Nehemiah are marked by having "the hand of God" on them, the heroes of the narrative* are the community members, elaborated in various lists, who willingly undertake the formation of the "house of God." The historical value of this list has been under discussion, and many believe it reflects an authentic, if only partial, record of the organization of the rebuilding effort. **1:** *Then the high priest . . . with his fellow priests . . . rebuilt the Sheep Gate:* This gate was located in the northeast corner of the city adjacent to the Temple* precinct and was the principal entry for animals brought for sacrifice. Perhaps because of this, the section of wall is *consecrated* or "made holy." Another possibility is that this section was most vulnerable to attack, and consecrating the wall in effect called on God to help defend it. **5:** *Tekoites:* Tekoa was on the fringe of the Judean desert to the south of Jerusalem. It was the traditional village of the prophet* Amos (Am 1.1). The common people's willingness is contrasted with the *nobles,* whose reasons for opposing Nehemiah are not given. It is possible that Tekoa lay near the boundary between Yehud's administrative area and Gershem's, and the nobles may have feared their involvement would bring difficulties with Gershem. *Their Lord* is a probable reference to Nehemiah. **7:** *Gibeon and of Mizpah . . . under the jurisdiction of the governor of the province Beyond the River:* The Hebrew phrasing is difficult, but it may be that Miz-

pah, and the city of Gibeon which lies slightly south of it, were under some special status. Mizpah was not destroyed by the Babylonians, and it became the administrative center for their rule over the devastated Judean kingdom (Jer 40.7–10). It may have retained some special status as a provincial center as Jerusalem reemerged as the regional capital.

4 ᵇNow when Sanballat heard that we were building the wall, he was angry and greatly enraged, and he mocked the Jews. ²He said in the presence of his associates and of the army of Samaria, "What are these feeble Jews doing? Will they restore things? Will they sacrifice? Will they finish it in a day? Will they revive the stones out of the heaps of rubbish—and burned ones at that?" ³Tobiah the Ammonite was beside him, and he said, "That stone wall they are building—any fox going up on it would break it down!" ⁴Hear, O our God, for we are despised; turn their taunt back on their own heads, and give them over as plunder in a land of captivity. ⁵Do not cover their guilt, and do not let their sin be blotted out from your sight; for they have hurled insults in the face of the builders.

6 So we rebuilt the wall, and all the wall was joined together to half its height; for the people had a mind to work.

7ᶜ But when Sanballat and Tobiah and the Arabs and the Ammonites and the Ashdodites heard that the repairing of the walls of Jerusalem was going forward and the gaps were beginning to be closed, they were very angry, ⁸and all plotted together to come and fight against Jerusalem and to cause confusion in it. ⁹So we prayed to our God, and set a guard as a protection against them day and night.

4.1–23: Opposition and the community's response. Though written as a first-person narrative,* presumably from Nehemiah's view, the focus is on the community. The account alternates between the scorn and plots of the adversaries of the rebuilding, and the community's determination to rebuild the walls of Jerusalem. **2:** *Will they restore things? Will they sacrifice? Will*

ᵃ Or *Hammiphkad Gate*   ᵇ Ch 3.33 in Heb
ᶜ Ch 4.1 in Heb

they finish it in a day? The taunt relates to restoring Jerusalem to its former glory, a task that would take a great deal of time. The community's enthusiasm may be strong at the moment, but as time passes, Sanballat believes they will give up the task. The issue of *sacrifice* relates to dedicating the walls at the completion of the project (see 12.43). **6:** *All the wall was joined together to half its height:* It is unclear if this was half its original height, or half of its planned height (which may have been considerably less, given the restricted resources). **8:** *All plotted together to come and fight,* maybe not as an "official" military force, but perhaps in a series of raids designed to destabilize the building project.

10 But Judah said, "The strength of the burden bearers is failing, and there is too much rubbish so that we are unable to work on the wall." ¹¹And our enemies said, "They will not know or see anything before we come upon them and kill them and stop the work." ¹²When the Jews who lived near them came, they said to us ten times, "From all the places where they live*ᵃ* they will come up against us."*ᵇ* ¹³So in the lowest parts of the space behind the wall, in open places, I stationed the people according to their families,*ᶜ* with their swords, their spears, and their bows. ¹⁴After I looked these things over, I stood up and said to the nobles and the officials and the rest of the people, "Do not be afraid of them. Remember the LORD, who is great and awesome, and fight for your kin, your sons, your daughters, your wives, and your homes."

15 When our enemies heard that their plot was known to us, and that God had frustrated it, we all returned to the wall, each to his work. ¹⁶From that day on, half of my servants worked on construction, and half held the spears, shields, bows, and body-armor; and the leaders posted themselves behind the whole house of Judah, ¹⁷who were building the wall. The burden bearers carried their loads in such a way that each labored on the work with one hand and with the other held a weapon. ¹⁸And each of the builders had his sword strapped at his side while he built. The man who sounded the trumpet was beside me. ¹⁹And I said to the nobles, the officials, and the rest of the people, "The work is great and widely spread out, and we are separated far from one another on the wall. ²⁰Rally to us wherever you hear the sound of the trumpet. Our God will fight for us."

21 So we labored at the work, and half of them held the spears from break of dawn until the stars came out. ²²I also said to the people at that time, "Let every man and his servant pass the night inside Jerusalem, so that they may be a guard for us by night and may labor by day." ²³So neither I nor my brothers nor my servants nor the men of the guard who followed me ever took off our clothes; each kept his weapon in his right hand.*ᵈ*

4.10–23. 10: *But Judah said, "The strength of the burden bearers is failing":* Facing not only external pressure to cease, Nehemiah now had to contend with wavering resolve among the builders. *Judah* is a metaphor* for the whole community. The *burden bearers* hauled materials up to the points on the wall where they were needed. **12:** *They said to us ten times* is an idiom for "repeatedly." These informants want to be sure the community understands that rebuilding may provoke a general raid. **13:** *So in the lowest parts of the space behind the wall, in open places:* Nehemiah's strategy was to place the people where they would be ready to respond to an attack anywhere along the wall line. The *lowest parts* may have been chosen to conceal the force from any attacker. **14:** *Do not be afraid . . . Remember the LORD:* In the biblical tradition of the holy war* the armed force is promised that God will fight on their behalf. **15:** *We all returned to the wall:* The immediate threat of military challenge having passed, the community could now return to the task of rebuilding the wall. Nehemiah's subsequent orders are designed to maximize the work on the wall while demonstrating a preparedness for defense. **16:** *Half of my servants:* Probably a chosen group of individuals under direct employ of Nehemiah and whose loyalty he could count on. With such careful provisions, the danger of general military action against the community was stymied.

5 Now there was a great outcry of the people and of their wives against their Jew-

a Cn: Heb *you return*   *b* Compare Gk Syr: Meaning of Heb uncertain   *c* Meaning of Heb uncertain   *d* Cn: Heb *each his weapon the water*

ish kin. ²For there were those who said, "With our sons and our daughters, we are many; we must get grain, so that we may eat and stay alive." ³There were also those who said, "We are having to pledge our fields, our vineyards, and our houses in order to get grain during the famine." ⁴And there were those who said, "We are having to borrow money on our fields and vineyards to pay the king's tax. ⁵Now our flesh is the same as that of our kindred; our children are the same as their children; and yet we are forcing our sons and daughters to be slaves, and some of our daughters have been ravished; we are powerless, and our fields and vineyards now belong to others."

6 I was very angry when I heard their outcry and these complaints. ⁷After thinking it over, I brought charges against the nobles and the officials; I said to them, "You are all taking interest from your own people." And I called a great assembly to deal with them, ⁸and said to them, "As far as we were able, we have bought back our Jewish kindred who had been sold to other nations; but now you are selling your own kin, who must then be bought back by us!" They were silent, and could not find a word to say. ⁹So I said, "The thing that you are doing is not good. Should you not walk in the fear of our God, to prevent the taunts of the nations our enemies? ¹⁰Moreover I and my brothers and my servants are lending them money and grain. Let us stop this taking of interest. ¹¹Restore to them, this very day, their fields, their vineyards, their olive orchards, and their houses, and the interest on money, grain, wine, and oil that you have been exacting from them." ¹²Then they said, "We will restore everything and demand nothing more from them. We will do as you say." And I called the priests, and made them take an oath to do as they had promised. ¹³I also shook out the fold of my garment and said, "So may God shake out everyone from house and from property who does not perform this promise. Thus may they be shaken out and emptied." And all the assembly said, "Amen," and praised the LORD. And the people did as they had promised.

5.1–13: Economic crisis and Nehemiah's solutions. Told in a first-person fashion, this section recounts a grave economic crisis made worse by the profiteering of some members of the community. Faced with a possible revolt, Nehemiah forcefully takes dramatic steps to alleviate the crisis. **1:** *Now there was a great outcry:* The implication of the placement of this account is that the work of rebuilding was continuing when the crisis reached its potential breaking point. Three different issues are raised by the crowd, all the result of a periodic famine (v. 3). The first issue is the difficulty in getting grain for food (v. 2); the second, the use of fields as collateral to obtain loans for purchasing grain (v. 4); and most seriously, the use of the labor of children as collateral on borrowing money to pay *the king's tax* (v. 5). Normally, taxes were paid in grains in the Persian empire, but when grain was not available, taxes could be paid in the monetary equivalent (usually in terms of weight, such as "so many mina of silver") of the amount of grain owed. In a famine, as the cost of grain escalated, so would the relative value of the taxes owed to the empire. Also, famine was usually triggered by drought, making it difficult for farmers to raise the necessary crop yield to repay a debt. Brokers could loan grains or silver in return for receiving pledges on the future yields of the land or on the available labor in the family group. If the loan was not repaid in the time frame agreed to, the broker could seize all the yield of a given crop, or take members of the family into indentured servitude, often exacting interest on the remaining balance due until the whole loan plus accrued interest was repaid. Nehemiah attempts to address this situation by first calling a *great assembly* (v. 7), announcing the release of new resources into the markets (v. 10). He also requires that productive lands be returned to the debtors so that they will have some means of raising capital to make the debt good (v. 11). The call to *stop this taking of interest* (v. 10) is most likely a reference to the additional interest on the loan when the original repayment schedule cannot be met. This seems to be what the brokers agree to in pledging they will *demand nothing more from them* (v. 12). **13:** *May God shake out everyone from house and from property:* Having forced the brokers to take a solemn oath before the priests (v. 12), Nehemiah engages in a symbolic action, placing a curse on all who violate the pledge. The brokers, being people of means, would take seriously the possibility of losing their wealth. *The people* *did as they had promised* suggests Nehemiah's solutions worked.

14 Moreover from the time that I was appointed to be their governor in the land of Judah, from the twentieth year to the thirty-second year of King Artaxerxes, twelve years, neither I nor my brothers ate the food allowance of the governor. 15The former governors who were before me laid heavy burdens on the people, and took food and wine from them, besides forty shekels of silver. Even their servants lorded it over the people. But I did not do so, because of the fear of God. 16Indeed, I devoted myself to the work on this wall, and acquired no land; and all my servants were gathered there for the work. 17Moreover there were at my table one hundred fifty people, Jews and officials, besides those who came to us from the nations around us. 18Now that which was prepared for one day was one ox and six choice sheep; also fowls were prepared for me, and every ten days skins of wine in abundance; yet with all this I did not demand the food allowance of the governor, because of the heavy burden of labor on the people. 19Remember for my good, O my God, all that I have done for this people.

5.14–19: Nehemiah's refusal to collect the food tax. Having highlighted his generosity in making his own wealth available to those struggling in the famine crisis, in this section Nehemiah shows his refusal to place additional burdens on the populace, despite his right to collect a "food allowance." **14:** *From the twentieth year to the thirty-second year of King Artaxerxes,* or from 445 to 434 BCE. The *food allowance* was apparently the privilege of the local imperial officials to draw their living support from a taxation surcharge. **15:** *Former governors* suggests that Yehud (as the region around Jerusalem was known) had been politically independent for some time prior to Nehemiah. **16:** *I . . . acquired no land:* Imperial privileges included the ability to amass land holdings. Nehemiah's single-mindedness excluded a concern to build wealth. **17:** *There were at my table one hundred fifty people:* Apparently they were all members of his entourage and lesser officials for whom the governor was expected to provide food rations, thereby showing that Nehemiah had every reason to exact the food allowance. **19:** *Remem-*

ber for my good, O my God, all that I have done for this people: This is the first of five separate appeals for God to bear in mind some particular action by, or against, Nehemiah. These appeals make it difficult to assess the character of the so-called "Nehemiah memoir," since such pietistic asides would not be expected in an official report. They do, however, provide insight into the emotions and faith of Nehemiah.

6 Now when it was reported to Sanballat and Tobiah and to Geshem the Arab and to the rest of our enemies that I had built the wall and that there was no gap left in it (though up to that time I had not set up the doors in the gates), 2Sanballat and Geshem sent to me, saying, "Come and let us meet together in one of the villages in the plain of Ono." But they intended to do me harm. 3So I sent messengers to them, saying, "I am doing a great work and I cannot come down. Why should the work stop while I leave it to come down to you?" 4They sent to me four times in this way, and I answered them in the same manner. 5In the same way Sanballat for the fifth time sent his servant to me with an open letter in his hand. 6In it was written, "It is reported among the nations—and Geshem[a] also says it—that you and the Jews intend to rebel; that is why you are building the wall; and according to this report you wish to become their king. 7You have also set up prophets to proclaim in Jerusalem concerning you, 'There is a king in Judah!' And now it will be reported to the king according to these words. So come, therefore, and let us confer together." 8Then I sent to him, saying, "No such things as you say have been done; you are inventing them out of your own mind" 9—for they all wanted to frighten us, thinking, "Their hands will drop from the work, and it will not be done." But now, O God, strengthen my hands.

10 One day when I went into the house of Shemaiah son of Delaiah son of Mehetabel, who was confined to his house, he said, "Let us meet together in the house of God, within the temple, and let us close the doors of the temple, for they are coming to kill you;

a Heb *Gashmu*

indeed, tonight they are coming to kill you." [11]But I said, "Should a man like me run away? Would a man like me go into the temple to save his life? I will not go in!" [12]Then I perceived and saw that God had not sent him at all, but he had pronounced the prophecy against me because Tobiah and Sanballat had hired him. [13]He was hired for this purpose, to intimidate me and make me sin by acting in this way, and so they could give me a bad name, in order to taunt me. [14]Remember Tobiah and Sanballat, O my God, according to these things that they did, and also the prophetess Noadiah and the rest of the prophets who wanted to make me afraid.

6.1–14: Nehemiah's life is threatened. While the account of ch. 4 deals with threats against the community, this section continues a focus on Nehemiah as an individual, revealing a series of plots by the "adversaries" to destroy him. Nehemiah's persistence in directing the rebuilding effort preserved him from being entrapped by their plots. **2:** *The plain of Ono* lay to the northwest of Jerusalem. It may have been in a boundary area between Sanballat's district and Nehemiah's. *They intended to do me harm:* The account provides no reason for this conclusion. **6:** *You and the Jews intend to rebel:* In general, walled cities were not built in the Persian empire. The refortification of Jerusalem would provide an opportunity to defy the empire. Sanballat uses the threat of reporting this to the king (v. 7) to draw Nehemiah out. **10:** *Shemaiah . . . was confined to his house:* Though the account is not clear on the timing, there seems to be some time between Sanballat's efforts to get Nehemiah to meet with him, and this plot. It is not certain why Shemaiah was closed in his house, nor why Nehemiah went to see him. *Tonight they are coming to kill you:* Perhaps Shemaiah had sent word to Nehemiah that he had an important message to convey. His advice to meet in the Temple★ and *close the doors* because the adversaries were coming to kill Nehemiah would have made the governor look cowardly. **13:** *He was hired for this purpose:* It takes Nehemiah time to see through the plot, but Shemaiah may have been a reputable prophet,★ making the deception difficult to detect. **14:** *Remember . . . O my God:* one of Nehemiah's direct appeals to God to keep something before him. Here Nehemiah wants his opponents be repaid according to their deeds, as well as *the prophetess Noadiah and the rest of the prophets*

who may have engaged in the same kinds of deceit as Shemaiah.

15 So the wall was finished on the twenty-fifth day of the month Elul, in fifty-two days. [16]And when all our enemies heard of it, all the nations around us were afraid[a] and fell greatly in their own esteem; for they perceived that this work had been accomplished with the help of our God. [17]Moreover in those days the nobles of Judah sent many letters to Tobiah, and Tobiah's letters came to them. [18]For many in Judah were bound by oath to him, because he was the son-in-law of Shecaniah son of Arah: and his son Jehohanan had married the daughter of Meshullam son of Berechiah. [19]Also they spoke of his good deeds in my presence, and reported my words to him. And Tobiah sent letters to intimidate me.

6.15–7.5: The walls are completed. This section, which recounts the completion of the physical work of refortifying the city, ends with a note on the relatively few people in the city. The rebuilding of the walls is not the final completion of the formation of the "house of God." **6.17:** *The nobles of Judah* are an indefinite group, but presumably related to a traditional aristocracy. **18:** *For many in Judah were bound by oath to him:* The reasons are not specified. Presumably their support of Tobiah results not from opposition to Nehemiah as much as being bound by their oaths.

7 Now when the wall had been built and I had set up the doors, and the gatekeepers, the singers, and the Levites had been appointed, [2]I gave my brother Hanani charge over Jerusalem, along with Hananiah the commander of the citadel—for he was a faithful man and feared God more than many. [3]And I said to them, "The gates of Jerusalem are not to be opened until the sun is hot; while the gatekeepers[b] are still standing guard, let them shut and bar the doors. Appoint guards from among the inhabitants of Jerusalem, some at their watch posts, and others before their own houses." [4]The city was wide and large, but the people within it were few and no houses had been built.

a Another reading is *saw* *b* Heb *while they*

5 Then my God put it into my mind to assemble the nobles and the officials and the people to be enrolled by genealogy. And I found the book of the genealogy of those who were the first to come back, and I found the following written in it:

7.1–5. 1: *The gatekeepers, the singers, and the Levites:* The addition of the singers and Levites is unexpected, though since these groups were well organized they may have served as supplementary help to the gatekeepers, who would have to undertake their duties without prior experience. **3:** *The gates of Jerusalem are not to be opened until the sun is hot,* perhaps as an additional security measure. **5:** *The book of the genealogy:*✶ There is no explanation for where or how the book was found. *Those who were the first to come back:* Perhaps those who first returned from the Exile,✶ or those who first returned with one of the subsequent waves of exiled persons who migrated to Jerusalem.

FORMING THE HOUSE OF GOD

7.6–13.3: This section drops the first-person style of the "Nehemiah memoir" and the concern with opponents to the rebuilding efforts. Instead, the focus is on the community's concerns and corporate commitments. These are presented by means of several large gatherings of the "assembly" of the people interspersed with lengthy lists of the people involved. The culmination is an extended description of the dedication of the city walls and the separation of "Israel" from all those of "foreign descent," thus paralleling the physical separation of the city from the surrounding peoples.

---

6 These are the people of the province who came up out of the captivity of those exiles whom King Nebuchadnezzar of Babylon had carried into exile; they returned to Jerusalem and Judah, each to his town. 7They came with Zerubbabel, Jeshua, Nehemiah, Azariah, Raamiah, Nahamani, Mordecai, Bilshan, Mispereth, Bigvai, Nehum, Baanah.

The number of the Israelite people: 8the descendants of Parosh, two thousand one hundred seventy-two. 9Of Shephatiah, three hundred seventy-two. 10Of Arah, six hundred fifty-two. 11Of Pahath-moab, namely the descendants of Jeshua and Joab, two thousand eight hundred eighteen. 12Of Elam, one thousand two hundred fifty-four. 13Of Zattu, eight hundred forty-five. 14Of Zaccai, seven hundred sixty. 15Of Binnui, six hundred forty-eight. 16Of Bebai, six hundred twenty-eight. 17Of Azgad, two thousand three hundred twenty-two. 18Of Adonikam, six hundred sixty-seven. 19Of Bigvai, two thousand sixty-seven. 20Of Adin, six hundred fifty-five. 21Of Ater, namely of Hezekiah, ninety-eight. 22Of Hashum, three hundred twenty-eight. 23Of Bezai, three hundred twenty-four. 24Of Hariph, one hundred twelve. 25Of Gibeon, ninety-five. 26The people of Bethlehem and Netophah, one hundred eighty-eight. 27Of Anathoth, one hundred twenty-eight. 28Of Beth-azmaveth, forty-two. 29Of Kiriath-jearim, Chephirah, and Beeroth, seven hundred forty-three. 30Of Ramah and Geba, six hundred twenty-one. 31Of Michmas, one hundred twenty-two. 32Of Bethel and Ai, one hundred twenty-three. 33Of the other Nebo, fifty-two. 34The descendants of the other Elam, one thousand two hundred fifty-four. 35Of Harim, three hundred twenty. 36Of Jericho, three hundred forty-five. 37Of Lod, Hadid, and Ono, seven hundred twenty-one. 38Of Senaah, three thousand nine hundred thirty.

39 The priests: the descendants of Jedaiah, namely the house of Jeshua, nine hundred seventy-three. 40Of Immer, one thousand fifty-two. 41Of Pashhur, one thousand two hundred forty-seven. 42Of Harim, one thousand seventeen.

43 The Levites: the descendants of Jeshua, namely of Kadmiel of the descendants of Hodevah, seventy-four. 44The singers: the descendants of Asaph, one hundred forty-eight. 45The gatekeepers: the descendants of Shallum, of Ater, of Talmon, of Akkub, of Hatita, of Shobai, one hundred thirty-eight.

46 The temple servants: the descendants of Ziha, of Hasupha, of Tabbaoth, 47of Keros, of Sia, of Padon, 48of Lebana, of Hagaba, of Shalmai, 49of Hanan, of Giddel, of Gahar, 50of Reaiah, of Rezin, of Nekoda, 51of Gazzam, of Uzza, of Paseah, 52of Besai, of Meunim, of Nephushesim, 53of Bakbuk,

of Hakupha, of Harhur, 54of Bazlith, of Mehida, of Harsha, 55of Barkos, of Sisera, of Temah, 56of Neziah, of Hatipha.

57 The descendants of Solomon's servants: of Sotai, of Sophereth, of Perida, 58of Jaala, of Darkon, of Giddel, 59of Shephatiah, of Hattil, of Pochereth-hazzebaim, of Amon.

60 All the temple servants and the descendants of Solomon's servants were three hundred ninety-two.

61 The following were those who came up from Tel-melah, Tel-harsha, Cherub, Addon, and Immer, but they could not prove their ancestral houses or their descent, whether they belonged to Israel: 62the descendants of Delaiah, of Tobiah, of Nekoda, six hundred forty-two. 63Also, of the priests: the descendants of Hobaiah, of Hakkoz, of Barzillai (who had married one of the daughters of Barzillai the Gileadite and was called by their name). 64These sought their registration among those enrolled in the genealogies, but it was not found there, so they were excluded from the priesthood as unclean; 65the governor told them that they were not to partake of the most holy food, until a priest with Urim and Thummim should come.

66 The whole assembly together was forty-two thousand three hundred sixty, 67besides their male and female slaves, of whom there were seven thousand three hundred thirty-seven; and they had two hundred forty-five singers, male and female. 68They had seven hundred thirty-six horses, two hundred forty-five mules,[a] 69four hundred thirty-five camels, and six thousand seven hundred twenty donkeys.

70 Now some of the heads of ancestral houses contributed to the work. The governor gave to the treasury one thousand darics of gold, fifty basins, and five hundred thirty priestly robes. 71And some of the heads of ancestral houses gave into the building fund twenty thousand darics of gold and two thousand two hundred minas of silver. 72And what the rest of the people gave was twenty thousand darics of gold, two thousand minas of silver, and sixty-seven priestly robes.

73 So the priests, the Levites, the gatekeepers, the singers, some of the people, the temple servants, and all Israel settled in their towns.

7.6–73a: The list of those who returned from Babylon. 6: *These are the people of the province:* Largely repeats the list found in Ezra 2.1–70. Variations between the two lists are minor, but often this list represents a slightly fuller version of the list in Ezra 2. The focus is clearly on *the people,* and the reduplication of the lists shows the author's concern to focus on the community's efforts. **7:** *Nehemiah:* Notice that this is in the third person, rather than the first-person accounts of the "Nehemiah memoir."

~~~~~~

When the seventh month came—the people of Israel being settled in their towns—

8 1all the people gathered together into the square before the Water Gate. They told the scribe Ezra to bring the book of the law of Moses, which the LORD had given to Israel. 2Accordingly, the priest Ezra brought the law before the assembly, both men and women and all who could hear with understanding. This was on the first day of the seventh month. 3He read from it facing the square before the Water Gate from early morning until midday, in the presence of the men and the women and those who could understand; and the ears of all the people were attentive to the book of the law. 4The scribe Ezra stood on a wooden platform that had been made for the purpose; and beside him stood Mattithiah, Shema, Anaiah, Uriah, Hilkiah, and Maaseiah on his right hand; and Pedaiah, Mishael, Malchijah, Hashum, Hash-baddanah, Zechariah, and Meshullam on his left hand. 5And Ezra opened the book in the sight of all the people, for he was standing above all the people; and when he opened it, all the people stood up. 6Then Ezra blessed the LORD, the great God, and all the people answered, "Amen, Amen," lifting up their hands. Then they bowed their heads and worshiped the LORD with their faces to the ground. 7Also Jeshua, Bani, Sherebiah, Jamin, Akkub, Shabbethai, Hodiah, Maaseiah, Kelita, Azariah, Jozabad,

---

a Ezra 2.66 and the margins of some Hebrew Mss: MT lacks *They had . . . forty-five mules*

Hanan, Pelaiah, the Levites,[a] helped the people to understand the law, while the people remained in their places. 8So they read from the book, from the law of God, with interpretation. They gave the sense, so that the people understood the reading.

9 And Nehemiah, who was the governor, and Ezra the priest and scribe, and the Levites who taught the people said to all the people, "This day is holy to the LORD your God; do not mourn or weep." For all the people wept when they heard the words of the law. 10Then he said to them, "Go your way, eat the fat and drink sweet wine and send portions of them to those for whom nothing is prepared, for this day is holy to our LORD; and do not be grieved, for the joy of the LORD is your strength." 11So the Levites stilled all the people, saying, "Be quiet, for this day is holy; do not be grieved." 12And all the people went their way to eat and drink and to send portions and to make great rejoicing, because they had understood the words that were declared to them.

7.73b–8.12: The community gathers to hear the law. This section brings back into the narrative* the figure of Ezra, of whom nothing has been said since the close of the book of Ezra. This sudden reemergence of Ezra and the focus on the importance of the law has led many scholars to conclude that this narrative was originally part of the account of Ezra and was moved to its present position by the editor who has brought Ezra-Nehemiah into its present form. The focus, however, remains on the community's request for the reading of the law, and the way the section is placed makes it clear that the goal is to reform itself into a more obedient community on the eve of the dedication of the city walls. This ceremony also forms the backdrop to the conclusion of this larger section in 13.1–3. **73b:** *When the seventh month came:* The walls were completed in the month of Elul (6.15), the sixth month of the year. A rough chronological sequence is maintained by the placement, though there is some question if enough time is allowed for the people to return to be *settled in their towns* before reassembling in Jerusalem. The *seventh month* was traditionally the time of the Day of Atonement* (on the tenth day) and the Feast of Tabernacles (for a week starting on the fifteenth day). Several scholars have noted that this was also the month specified in Deut

31.10–13 for an assembly of the people to hear a reading of the law every seven years. This is apparently the model on which the account is structured. **8.1:** *They told the scribe* Ezra to bring the book:* The way Ezra is portrayed as subservient to the wishes of the "assembly," rather than the forceful leader of the community as in the book of Ezra tends to weigh against the idea that this narrative* was originally part of the book of Ezra. In the account of this gathering, Ezra is variously termed *the scribe* (vv. 1, 4), *the priest* (v. 2), and *the priest and scribe* (v. 9), both being roles attributed to him in the book of Ezra. **7:** *The Levites helped the people to understand:* One of the traditional roles of the Levites was to teach the meaning of the law to Israel (Deut 33.10), and this may have involved a brief exposition of the passage. The Levites may have moved about the crowd answering queries since *the people remained in their places.* **9:** *Nehemiah . . . and Ezra:* This is one of only two places in the Hebrew text of Ezra-Nehemiah where the two reformers appear together. *This day is holy:* The day of the assembly is a specific sacred occasion. While the specified time of the reading of the law could be considered a holy day, the account may imply that the day is the Feast of Trumpets, set on the first day of the seventh month, which was a sacred day (Lev 23.23–25), although no reading of the law is connected with the Feast of Trumpets. Possibly recognizing how far they had strayed from the law, *the people wept.* **10:** *Then he said to them:* The *he* may be Ezra. The specified foods are typical of a festive meal celebrating a sacred occasion. The phrase *the joy of the LORD is your strength* uses an unusual term for *joy,* one that occurs here and in 1 Chr 16.27, where "strength and joy are in his place." **12:** *All the people went their way . . . to make great rejoicing:* Unlike 1 and 2 Chronicles, where the rejoicing takes place in great corporate scenes, this account portrays the people retiring to their homes to rejoice. Their ability to understand the law provides the opportunity to live in accord with the divine will (Ps 119.34–35).

---

13 On the second day the heads of ancestral houses of all the people, with the priests and the Levites, came together to the scribe Ezra in order to study the words of the law. 14And they found it written in the law, which the LORD had commanded by Moses, that the people of Israel should live in

---

a 1 Esdras 9.48 Vg: Heb *and the Levites*

booths[a] during the festival of the seventh month, 15and that they should publish and proclaim in all their towns and in Jerusalem as follows, "Go out to the hills and bring branches of olive, wild olive, myrtle, palm, and other leafy trees to make booths,[a] as it is written." 16So the people went out and brought them, and made booths[a] for themselves, each on the roofs of their houses, and in their courts and in the courts of the house of God, and in the square at the Water Gate and in the square at the Gate of Ephraim. 17And all the assembly of those who had returned from the captivity made booths[a] and lived in them; for from the days of Jeshua son of Nun to that day the people of Israel had not done so. And there was very great rejoicing. 18And day by day, from the first day to the last day, he read from the book of the law of God. They kept the festival seven days; and on the eighth day there was a solemn assembly, according to the ordinance.

8.13–18: The community keeps the Festival of Booths. One of the specified holy times of the seventh month was the Festival of Booths (Lev 23.33–43), slated to be observed for a week beginning on the fifteenth day of the month. Along with the celebration of the deliverance from Egypt that is the prime focus of the festival, this account continues the reading, and presumably explanation, of the law. **13:** *On the second day* keeps the chronology of 8.2, even though it technically does not observe the festival specifications of the law. This may be an indication that the precise limits of the festival had not been set in the Persian period. In place of the community as a whole, this gathering consists only of the leadership. **17:** *All the assembly . . . made booths:* The whole community is involved. *From the days of Jeshua* is a reference to the period of conquest and Israel's inheritance of the land. The completion of the city walls and the reformation of the community are parallel to Israel's beginnings.

9 Now on the twenty-fourth day of this month the people of Israel were assembled with fasting and in sackcloth, and with earth on their heads.[b] 2Then those of Israelite descent separated themselves from all foreigners, and stood and confessed their sins and the iniquities of their ancestors.

3They stood up in their place and read from the book of the law of the LORD their God for a fourth part of the day, and for another fourth they made confession and worshiped the LORD their God. 4Then Jeshua, Bani, Kadmiel, Shebaniah, Bunni, Sherebiah, Bani, and Chenani stood on the stairs of the Levites and cried out with a loud voice to the LORD their God. 5Then the Levites, Jeshua, Kadmiel, Bani, Hashabneiah, Sherebiah, Hodiah, Shebaniah, and Pethahiah, said, "Stand up and bless the LORD your God from everlasting to everlasting. Blessed be your glorious name, which is exalted above all blessing and praise."

6 And Ezra said:[c] "You are the LORD, you alone; you have made heaven, the heaven of heavens, with all their host, the earth and all that is on it, the seas and all that is in them. To all of them you give life, and the host of heaven worships you. 7You are the LORD, the God who chose Abram and brought him out of Ur of the Chaldeans and gave him the name Abraham; 8and you found his heart faithful before you, and made with him a covenant to give to his descendants the land of the Canaanite, the Hittite, the Amorite, the Perizzite, the Jebusite, and the Girgashite; and you have fulfilled your promise, for you are righteous.

9.1–10.27: A day of community confession. This account explains a solemn covenant* to which the community will bind itself. Most of the section is a lengthy prayer, possibly offered by Ezra, which implores God to see the sufferings of the community in the present. The people hope that seeing how they have suffered, God will spare them any additional hardship in spite of their failure to observe the law. The account closes with the names of those who affirmed the covenant. Many have suggested that all or parts of the account fit best after the materials of Ezra 10. **9.1:** *The twenty-fourth day of this month:* Following the author's chronology, the Feast of Weeks,* lasting eight days, would have ended on the tenth day of the month. The community had clearly prepared for the expression of grief by *fasting* and being dressed in *sackcloth.* * **2:** *Separated themselves:* Possibly a reflec-

---

a Or *tabernacles*; Heb *succoth*   *b* Heb *on them*
c Gk: Heb lacks *And Ezra said*

tion of the "sending away" of the foreign wives of Ezra 10, though the wording here clearly relates to foreign men as well. Since the confession is rooted in the particular experiences of Israel, the wording may simply mean that only those who have continuity with pre-exilic Israel continued with the confession, while converts to Judaism did not participate. **6:** *Ezra said:* This reading follows the Greek translation of Nehemiah (see note *c*). The Hebrew text implies the prayer is offered by the congregation as a whole. The prayer goes on to recount God's special kindness to Israel and the coming into the land of Israel. The prayer also notes the problem of idolatry* that led to judgment, though characterizing these transgressions by the more general casting of the "law behind their backs" (v. 26). Of particular note is the emphasis on God as a "gracious and merciful God" (v. 31).

9 "And you saw the distress of our ancestors in Egypt and heard their cry at the Red Sea.*a* 10You performed signs and wonders against Pharaoh and all his servants and all the people of his land, for you knew that they acted insolently against our ancestors. You made a name for yourself, which remains to this day. 11And you divided the sea before them, so that they passed through the sea on dry land, but you threw their pursuers into the depths, like a stone into mighty waters. 12Moreover, you led them by day with a pillar of cloud, and by night with a pillar of fire, to give them light on the way in which they should go. 13You came down also upon Mount Sinai, and spoke with them from heaven, and gave them right ordinances and true laws, good statutes and commandments, 14and you made known your holy sabbath to them and gave them commandments and statutes and a law through your servant Moses. 15For their hunger you gave them bread from heaven, and for their thirst you brought water for them out of the rock, and you told them to go in to possess the land that you swore to give them.

16 "But they and our ancestors acted presumptuously and stiffened their necks and did not obey your commandments; 17they refused to obey, and were not mindful of the wonders that you performed among them; but they stiffened their necks and determined to return to their slavery in Egypt. But

you are a God ready to forgive, gracious and merciful, slow to anger and abounding in steadfast love, and you did not forsake them. 18Even when they had cast an image of a calf for themselves and said, 'This is your God who brought you up out of Egypt,' and had committed great blasphemies, 19you in your great mercies did not forsake them in the wilderness; the pillar of cloud that led them in the way did not leave them by day, nor the pillar of fire by night that gave them light on the way by which they should go. 20You gave your good spirit to instruct them, and did not withhold your manna from their mouths, and gave them water for their thirst. 21Forty years you sustained them in the wilderness so that they lacked nothing; their clothes did not wear out and their feet did not swell. 22And you gave them kingdoms and peoples, and allotted to them every corner,*b* so they took possession of the land of King Sihon of Heshbon and the land of King Og of Bashan. 23You multiplied their descendants like the stars of heaven, and brought them into the land that you had told their ancestors to enter and possess. 24So the descendants went in and possessed the land, and you subdued before them the inhabitants of the land, the Canaanites, and gave them into their hands, with their kings and the peoples of the land, to do with them as they pleased. 25And they captured fortress cities and a rich land, and took possession of houses filled with all sorts of goods, hewn cisterns, vineyards, olive orchards, and fruit trees in abundance; so they ate, and were filled and became fat, and delighted themselves in your great goodness.

26 "Nevertheless they were disobedient and rebelled against you and cast your law behind their backs and killed your prophets, who had warned them in order to turn them back to you, and they committed great blasphemies. 27Therefore you gave them into the hands of their enemies, who made them suffer. Then in the time of their suffering they cried out to you and you heard them from heaven, and according to your great mercies you gave them saviors who saved them from

a Or *Sea of Reeds*   *b* Meaning of Heb uncertain

the hands of their enemies. 28But after they had rest, they again did evil before you, and you abandoned them to the hands of their enemies, so that they had dominion over them; yet when they turned and cried to you, you heard from heaven, and many times you rescued them according to your mercies. 29And you warned them in order to turn them back to your law. Yet they acted presumptuously and did not obey your commandments, but sinned against your ordinances, by the observance of which a person shall live. They turned a stubborn shoulder and stiffened their neck and would not obey. 30Many years you were patient with them, and warned them by your spirit through your prophets; yet they would not listen. Therefore you handed them over to the peoples of the lands. 31Nevertheless, in your great mercies you did not make an end of them or forsake them, for you are a gracious and merciful God.

32 "Now therefore, our God—the great and mighty and awesome God, keeping covenant and steadfast love—do not treat lightly all the hardship that has come upon us, upon our kings, our officials, our priests, our prophets, our ancestors, and all your people, since the time of the kings of Assyria until today. 33You have been just in all that has come upon us, for you have dealt faithfully and we have acted wickedly; 34our kings, our officials, our priests, and our ancestors have not kept your law or heeded the commandments and the warnings that you gave them. 35Even in their own kingdom, and in the great goodness you bestowed on them, and in the large and rich land that you set before them, they did not serve you and did not turn from their wicked works. 36Here we are, slaves to this day—slaves in the land that you gave to our ancestors to enjoy its fruit and its good gifts. 37Its rich yield goes to the kings whom you have set over us because of our sins; they have power also over our bodies and over our livestock at their pleasure, and we are in great distress."

38ᵃ Because of all this we make a firm agreement in writing, and on that sealed document are inscribed the names of our officials, our Levites, and our priests.

9.9–38. 32: *Keeping covenant* and steadfast love* emphasizes God's enduring relationship with Israel. *Do not treat lightly all the hardship that has come upon us* is an appeal that God not add to the community's burden but accept the deep contrition being expressed. **36:** *Here we are, slaves to this day:* Though overly dramatic, the community most likely did find itself in a bound condition under imperial constraints. **38:** *We make a firm agreement:* The confession has noted the community's present predicament, which now calls for a response that takes the law very seriously, not repeating the sins of the past. To commit to the agreement *in writing* further affirms the serious intent here. The author has made this intent more apparent by listing the names of the community leadership affirming this covenant in 10.1–27. Surprisingly, Ezra is absent from the list.

10 ᵇUpon the sealed document are the names of Nehemiah the governor, son of Hacaliah, and Zedekiah; 2Seraiah, Azariah, Jeremiah, 3Pashhur, Amariah, Malchijah, 4Hattush, Shebaniah, Malluch, 5Harim, Meremoth, Obadiah, 6Daniel, Ginnethon, Baruch, 7Meshullam, Abijah, Mijamin, 8Maaziah, Bilgai, Shemaiah; these are the priests. 9And the Levites: Jeshua son of Azaniah, Binnui of the sons of Henadad, Kadmiel; 10and their associates, Shebaniah, Hodiah, Kelita, Pelaiah, Hanan, 11Mica, Rehob, Hashabiah, 12Zaccur, Sherebiah, Shebaniah, 13Hodiah, Bani, Beninu. 14The leaders of the people: Parosh, Pahath-moab, Elam, Zattu, Bani, 15Bunni, Azgad, Bebai, 16Adonijah, Bigvai, Adin, 17Ater, Hezekiah, Azzur, 18Hodiah, Hashum, Bezai, 19Hariph, Anathoth, Nebai, 20Magpiash, Meshullam, Hezir, 21Meshezabel, Zadok, Jaddua, 22Pelatiah, Hanan, Anaiah, 23Hoshea, Hananiah, Hasshub, 24Hallohesh, Pilha, Shobek, 25Rehum, Hashabnah, Maaseiah, 26Ahiah, Hanan, Anan, 27Malluch, Harim, and Baanah.

28 The rest of the people, the priests, the Levites, the gatekeepers, the singers, the temple servants, and all who have separated themselves from the peoples of the lands to adhere to the law of God, their wives, their

a Ch 10.1 in Heb   *b* Ch 10.2 in Heb

sons, their daughters, all who have knowledge and understanding, ²⁹join with their kin, their nobles, and enter into a curse and an oath to walk in God's law, which was given by Moses the servant of God, and to observe and do all the commandments of the LORD our Lord and his ordinances and his statutes. ³⁰We will not give our daughters to the peoples of the land or take their daughters for our sons; ³¹and if the peoples of the land bring in merchandise or any grain on the sabbath day to sell, we will not buy it from them on the sabbath or on a holy day; and we will forego the crops of the seventh year and the exaction of every debt.

32 We also lay on ourselves the obligation to charge ourselves yearly one-third of a shekel for the service of the house of our God: ³³for the rows of bread, the regular grain offering, the regular burnt offering, the sabbaths, the new moons, the appointed festivals, the sacred donations, and the sin offerings to make atonement for Israel, and for all the work of the house of our God. ³⁴We have also cast lots among the priests, the Levites, and the people, for the wood offering, to bring it into the house of our God, by ancestral houses, at appointed times, year by year, to burn on the altar of the LORD our God, as it is written in the law. ³⁵We obligate ourselves to bring the first fruits of our soil and the first fruits of all fruit of every tree, year by year, to the house of the LORD; ³⁶also to bring to the house of our God, to the priests who minister in the house of our God, the firstborn of our sons and of our livestock, as it is written in the law, and the firstlings of our herds and of our flocks; ³⁷and to bring the first of our dough, and our contributions, the fruit of every tree, the wine and the oil, to the priests, to the chambers of the house of our God; and to bring to the Levites the tithes from our soil, for it is the Levites who collect the tithes in all our rural towns. ³⁸And the priest, the descendant of Aaron, shall be with the Levites when the Levites receive the tithes; and the Levites shall bring up a tithe of the tithes to the house of our God, to the chambers of the storehouse. ³⁹For the people of Israel and the sons of Levi shall bring the contribution of grain, wine, and oil to the storerooms where the vessels of the sanctuary are, and where the priests that minister, and the gatekeepers and the singers are. We will not neglect the house of our God.

10.28–39: The terms of the covenant.* Having made an extensive confession before God, the community now offers a solemn covenant that covers a wide range of obligations. All these will reform the community and bring it into accord with the law of God. **28:** *The rest of the people,* that is, other than the named signatories. **30:** *We will not give our daughters . . . take their daughters:* The first major commitment is to oppose intermarriage and cease its practice. The dissolution of existing ethnically mixed marriages is not called for. **31:** *We will not buy . . . on the sabbath or on a holy day:* This involves observing the sabbath with new rigor, since the law does not prohibit buying on the sabbath, though selling on the sabbath may have been customarily forbidden (Am 8.5). *Forego the crops of the seventh year:* Crop land is to receive a sabbath (Lev 25.1–7), combined with rules regarding the release of debts (Deut 15.1–18). These rules had not previously been linked. **32:** *One-third of a shekel:** This was an annual Temple* tax that continued into the Roman period (Mt 17.24–27). The Temple tax was instituted after the Exile* since there was no source of regular royal underwriting of Temple functions. **34:** The community also commits to supply the *wood offering* to support the Temple service. **35:** *First fruits:* While the first cuttings of grain are specified in the law (Deut 26.1–11), no provision is required for the produce of fruit trees. The remaining obligations commit the community to the support of various aspects of Temple service. **39:** The main thrust of this covenant* extends the coverage of the law, placing a larger sphere of life into the realm of the holy as part of service for the *house of our God.*

---

11 Now the leaders of the people lived in Jerusalem; and the rest of the people cast lots to bring one out of ten to live in the holy city Jerusalem, while nine-tenths remained in the other towns. ²And the people blessed all those who willingly offered to live in Jerusalem.

3 These are the leaders of the province who lived in Jerusalem; but in the towns of Judah all lived on their property in their towns: Israel, the priests, the Levites, the

temple servants, and the descendants of Solomon's servants. 4And in Jerusalem lived some of the Judahites and of the Benjaminites. Of the Judahites: Athaiah son of Uzziah son of Zechariah son of Amariah son of Shephatiah son of Mahalalel, of the descendants of Perez; 5and Maaseiah son of Baruch son of Col-hozeh son of Hazaiah son of Adaiah son of Joiarib son of Zechariah son of the Shilonite. 6All the descendants of Perez who lived in Jerusalem were four hundred sixty-eight valiant warriors.

7 And these are the Benjaminites: Sallu son of Meshullam son of Joed son of Pedaiah son of Kolaiah son of Maaseiah son of Ithiel son of Jeshaiah. 8And his brothers*a* Gabbai, Sallai: nine hundred twenty-eight. 9Joel son of Zichri was their overseer; and Judah son of Hassenuah was second in charge of the city.

10 Of the priests: Jedaiah son of Joiarib, Jachin, 11Seraiah son of Hilkiah son of Meshullam son of Zadok son of Meraioth son of Ahitub, officer of the house of God, 12and their associates who did the work of the house, eight hundred twenty-two; and Adaiah son of Jeroham son of Pelaliah son of Amzi son of Zechariah son of Pashhur son of Malchijah, 13and his associates, heads of ancestral houses, two hundred forty-two; and Amashsai son of Azarel son of Ahzai son of Meshillemoth son of Immer, 14and their associates, valiant warriors, one hundred twenty-eight; their overseer was Zabdiel son of Haggedolim.

15 And of the Levites: Shemaiah son of Hasshub son of Azrikam son of Hashabiah son of Bunni; 16and Shabbethai and Jozabad, of the leaders of the Levites, who were over the outside work of the house of God; 17and Mattaniah son of Mica son of Zabdi son of Asaph, who was the leader to begin the thanksgiving in prayer, and Bakbukiah, the second among his associates; and Abda son of Shammua son of Galal son of Jeduthun. 18All the Levites in the holy city were two hundred eighty-four.

19 The gatekeepers, Akkub, Talmon and their associates, who kept watch at the gates, were one hundred seventy-two. 20And the rest of Israel, and of the priests and the Levites, were in all the towns of Judah, all of them in their inheritance. 21But the temple servants lived on Ophel; and Ziha and Gishpa were over the temple servants.

22 The overseer of the Levites in Jerusalem was Uzzi son of Bani son of Hashabiah son of Mattaniah son of Mica, of the descendants of Asaph, the singers, in charge of the work of the house of God. 23For there was a command from the king concerning them, and a settled provision for the singers, as was required every day. 24And Pethahiah son of Meshezabel, of the descendants of Zerah son of Judah, was at the king's hand in all matters concerning the people.

11.1–24: The community repopulates Jerusalem. Further focusing on the community's dedication to the law, this section depicts the repopulation of Jerusalem, ending with another lengthy list of those who moved into Jerusalem. 1: *One out of ten:* This applies the tithe (Deut 12.17) to the community's total population. This is the first time Jerusalem is called *the holy city,* an extension of the Temple* precinct's sacredness to the entire city now that it is marked by the completed walls. 2: *The people blessed . . . live in Jerusalem:* The community's desire to undertake this task is emphasized. The listing that follows offers leaders (divided into those of Judah and Benjamin), priests, Levites, and gatekeepers.

---

25 And as for the villages, with their fields, some of the people of Judah lived in Kiriath-arba and its villages, and in Dibon and its villages, and in Jekabzeel and its villages, 26and in Jeshua and in Moladah and Beth-pelet, 27in Hazar-shual, in Beer-sheba and its villages, 28in Ziklag, in Meconah and its villages, 29in En-rimmon, in Zorah, in Jarmuth, 30Zanoah, Adullam, and their villages, Lachish and its fields, and Azekah and its villages. So they camped from Beer-sheba to the valley of Hinnom. 31The people of Benjamin also lived from Geba onward, at Michmash, Aija, Bethel and its villages, 32Anathoth, Nob, Ananiah, 33Hazor, Ramah, Gittaim, 34Hadid, Zeboim, Neballat, 35Lod, and Ono, the valley of artisans. 36And cer-

a Gk Mss: Heb *And after him*

tain divisions of the Levites in Judah were joined to Benjamin.

11.25–36: A note about villages outside Jerusalem. This brief account touches on some of the settlements outside Jerusalem that constituted the territory of Judah. Several of the places on the list were not settled by Jews until the Hellenistic* period, so this list may be an idealized fiction, approximating the settlements of Judah as described in the tribal allotments of the book of Joshua (Josh 15.1–12). In effect, this makes the same point as the notice of the Festival of Booths earlier (8.17).

12 These are the priests and the Levites who came up with Zerubbabel son of Shealtiel, and Jeshua: Seraiah, Jeremiah, Ezra, ²Amariah, Malluch, Hattush, ³Shecaniah, Rehum, Meremoth, ⁴Iddo, Ginnethoi, Abijah, ⁵Mijamin, Maadiah, Bilgah, ⁶Shemaiah, Joiarib, Jedaiah, ⁷Sallu, Amok, Hilkiah, Jedaiah. These were the leaders of the priests and of their associates in the days of Jeshua.

8 And the Levites: Jeshua, Binnui, Kadmiel, Sherebiah, Judah, and Mattaniah, who with his associates was in charge of the songs of thanksgiving. ⁹And Bakbukiah and Unno their associates stood opposite them in the service. ¹⁰Jeshua was the father of Joiakim, Joiakim the father of Eliashib, Eliashib the father of Joiada, ¹¹Joiada the father of Jonathan, and Jonathan the father of Jaddua.

12 In the days of Joiakim the priests, heads of ancestral houses, were: of Seraiah, Meraiah; of Jeremiah, Hananiah; ¹³of Ezra, Meshullam; of Amariah, Jehohanan; ¹⁴of Malluchi, Jonathan; of Shebaniah, Joseph; ¹⁵of Harim, Adna; of Meraioth, Helkai; ¹⁶of Iddo, Zechariah; of Ginnethon, Meshullam; ¹⁷of Abijah, Zichri; of Miniamin, of Moadiah, Piltai; ¹⁸of Bilgah, Shammua; of Shemaiah, Jehonathan; ¹⁹of Joiarib, Mattenai; of Jedaiah, Uzzi; ²⁰of Sallai, Kallai; of Amok, Eber; ²¹of Hilkiah, Hashabiah; of Jedaiah, Nethanel.

22 As for the Levites, in the days of Eliashib, Joiada, Johanan, and Jaddua, there were recorded the heads of ancestral houses; also the priests until the reign of Darius the Persian. ²³The Levites, heads of ancestral houses, were recorded in the Book of the Annals until the days of Johanan son of Eliashib. ²⁴And the leaders of the Levites: Hashabiah, Sherebiah, and Jeshua son of Kadmiel, with their associates over against them, to praise and to give thanks, according to the commandment of David the man of God, section opposite to section. ²⁵Mattaniah, Bakbukiah, Obadiah, Meshullam, Talmon, and Akkub were gatekeepers standing guard at the storehouses of the gates. ²⁶These were in the days of Joiakim son of Jeshua son of Jozadak, and in the days of the governor Nehemiah and of the priest Ezra, the scribe.

12.1–26: List of priests and Levites. Though the list appears fairly well organized (priests and Levites from the time of the return, vv. 1–9; high priests during the period of the sixth to fifth centuries, vv. 10–11; priests and Levites from the generation after the return, vv. 12–25; and a chronological summary, v. 26), there is evidence the lists have been expanded over time. While the question of sources and historicity are highly debated, the list in its present position serves to emphasize the sacred character of the newly populated holy city. **24:** *According to the commandment of David:* See the account in 1 Chr 23.30, where David sets several families of Levites aside for this purpose.

27 Now at the dedication of the wall of Jerusalem they sought out the Levites in all their places, to bring them to Jerusalem to celebrate the dedication with rejoicing, with thanksgivings and with singing, with cymbals, harps, and lyres. ²⁸The companies of the singers gathered together from the circuit around Jerusalem and from the villages of the Netophathites; ²⁹also from Beth-gilgal and from the region of Geba and Azmaveth; for the singers had built for themselves villages around Jerusalem. ³⁰And the priests and the Levites purified themselves; and they purified the people and the gates and the wall.

31 Then I brought the leaders of Judah up onto the wall, and appointed two great companies that gave thanks and went in procession. One went to the right on the wall to the Dung Gate; ³²and after them went Hoshaiah and half the officials of Judah, ³³and

Azariah, Ezra, Meshullam, 34Judah, Benjamin, Shemaiah, and Jeremiah, 35and some of the young priests with trumpets: Zechariah son of Jonathan son of Shemaiah son of Mattaniah son of Micaiah son of Zaccur son of Asaph; 36and his kindred, Shemaiah, Azarel, Milalai, Gilalai, Maai, Nethanel, Judah, and Hanani, with the musical instruments of David the man of God; and the scribe Ezra went in front of them. 37At the Fountain Gate, in front of them, they went straight up by the stairs of the city of David, at the ascent of the wall, above the house of David, to the Water Gate on the east.

38 The other company of those who gave thanks went to the left,ᵃ and I followed them with half of the people on the wall, above the Tower of the Ovens, to the Broad Wall, 39and above the Gate of Ephraim, and by the Old Gate, and by the Fish Gate and the Tower of Hananel and the Tower of the Hundred, to the Sheep Gate; and they came to a halt at the Gate of the Guard. 40So both companies of those who gave thanks stood in the house of God, and I and half of the officials with me; 41and the priests Eliakim, Maaseiah, Miniamin, Micaiah, Elioenai, Zechariah, and Hananiah, with trumpets; 42and Maaseiah, Shemaiah, Eleazar, Uzzi, Jehohanan, Malchijah, Elam, and Ezer. And the singers sang with Jezrahiah as their leader. 43They offered great sacrifices that day and rejoiced, for God had made them rejoice with great joy; the women and children also rejoiced. The joy of Jerusalem was heard far away.

44 On that day men were appointed over the chambers for the stores, the contributions, the first fruits, and the tithes, to gather into them the portions required by the law for the priests and for the Levites from the fields belonging to the towns; for Judah rejoiced over the priests and the Levites who ministered. 45They performed the service of their God and the service of purification, as did the singers and the gatekeepers, according to the command of David and his son Solomon. 46For in the days of David and Asaph long ago there was a leader of the singers, and there were songs of praise and thanksgiving to God. 47In the days of Zerubbabel and in the days of Nehemiah all Israel gave the daily portions for the singers and the gatekeepers. They set apart that which was for the Levites; and the Levites set apart that which was for the descendants of Aaron.

12.27–43: The dedication of Jerusalem's walls. This section briefly returns to a first-person style, similar to the other sections of the "Nehemiah memoir." It recounts the elaborate dedication ceremony, with the community divided into two large portions processing along the walls until they meet by the Temple.⋆ The dedication is given a religious dimension with priests and Levites actively participating in the ceremony. **27:** *They sought out the Levites in all their places:* The Levites, who lived in common villages, were needed to ensure the full complement of music and praise. **30:** *Purified themselves:* A necessary preparatory step for a religious ceremony. Also necessary was the purification of *the people,* though purifying the *gates and*

walls represents a new level of concern for correctness. Such an act extends the arena of God's presence from the Temple to the entire walled city. **36:** *And the scribe⋆ Ezra went in front* in recognition of the importance of his contributions to the community. **40:** *Both companies . . . stood in the house of God:* No formal entry into the Temple itself has preceded this point. This makes more sense if the entire walled city is being considered the "house of God." **43:** *The joy of Jerusalem was heard:* This offers a conclusion to the rejoicing and jubilation the community had experienced.

12.44–47: The community ensures Temple⋆ service. Shifting back to a third-person narrative, this section recounts efforts the community made to ensure that the contributions to the Temple stores were properly accounted for. The focus is exclusively on the community and its support for the Temple personnel. **44:** *Men were appointed:* The appointment was by the consensus of the community, not by an individual. Being *over* the stores included the inventorying and redistribution of offerings. Such care was taken because *Judah rejoiced over the priests and the Levites who ministered.* Taking care over the offerings that support these persons was an act of thanksgiving for the joy worship provided to the community. **47:** *The daily portions:* The offering that provided daily rations to the Temple personnel. Paralleling *Zerubbabel,* who rebuilt

a Cn: Heb *opposite*

the Temple, and *Nehemiah*, who rebuilt the walls of Jerusalem, serves the same function as Ezra 1–6 served in mixing the two efforts together: The rebuilding of the walls and subsequent solemn covenant* reformed the house of God just as the physical rebuilding of the building did. To speak of Nehemiah in this manner makes it sound like his term as governor is over.

13 On that day they read from the book of Moses in the hearing of the people; and in it was found written that no Ammonite or Moabite should ever enter the assembly of God, 2because they did not meet the Israelites with bread and water, but hired Balaam against them to curse them—yet our God turned the curse into a blessing. 3When the people heard the law, they separated from Israel all those of foreign descent.

13.1–3: The separation of foreigners. Slipping back into a first-person form, this brief notice highlights again the now sacred character of the community as a whole. **1:** *On that day* is unclear, but in context it must mean on the day of the dedication of the walls. *No Ammonite or Moabite should ever enter the assembly of God* refers to Deut 23.3–6, where "the assembly of God" is the worshipping community appearing in the Temple.* **3:** *They separated from Israel all those of foreign descent,* presumably including non-Ammonite and non-Moabite persons. The Deuteronomic law is being extended to the community as a whole, not just the worshipping body, and to all foreigners, not just Ammonites and Moabites. This marks a further redefinition of the community as a sacred body. Note that intermarriage is not raised here.

THE POSTLOGUE

13.4–31: Having described the communal confession of sin, the entry into a solemn covenant,* the dedication of the walls, and the redefinition of the community as the "house of God," it remains for the author to clarify what happened to Nehemiah. This postlogue offers a sort of conclusion to Nehemiah's mission, showing the reformer forcefully addressing a number of wrongs in the community. The section as a whole is based on the covenant contents of ch. 10, but in reverse order. For example, where the covenant begins with a vow to end intermarriage (10.30), the present section ends with the same issue (vv. 23–27).

Nemehiah's efforts are aimed at trying to get the community to live up to its own promises.

4 Now before this, the priest Eliashib, who was appointed over the chambers of the house of our God, and who was related to Tobiah, 5prepared for Tobiah a large room where they had previously put the grain offering, the frankincense, the vessels, and the tithes of grain, wine, and oil, which were given by commandment to the Levites, singers, and gatekeepers, and the contributions for the priests. 6While this was taking place I was not in Jerusalem, for in the thirty-second year of King Artaxerxes of Babylon I went to the king. After some time I asked leave of the king 7and returned to Jerusalem. I then discovered the wrong that Eliashib had done on behalf of Tobiah, preparing a room for him in the courts of the house of God. 8And I was very angry, and I threw all the household furniture of Tobiah out of the room. 9Then I gave orders and they cleansed the chambers, and I brought back the vessels of the house of God, with the grain offering and the frankincense.

10 I also found out that the portions of the Levites had not been given to them; so that the Levites and the singers, who had conducted the service, had gone back to their fields. 11So I remonstrated with the officials and said, "Why is the house of God forsaken?" And I gathered them together and set them in their stations. 12Then all Judah brought the tithe of the grain, wine, and oil into the storehouses. 13And I appointed as treasurers over the storehouses the priest Shelemiah, the scribe Zadok, and Pedaiah of the Levites, and as their assistant Hanan son of Zaccur son of Mattaniah, for they were considered faithful; and their duty was to distribute to their associates. 14Remember me, O my God, concerning this, and do not wipe out my good deeds that I have done for the house of my God and for his service.

15 In those days I saw in Judah people treading wine presses on the sabbath, and bringing in heaps of grain and loading them on donkeys; and also wine, grapes, figs, and all kinds of burdens, which they brought into Jerusalem on the sabbath day; and I warned

them at that time against selling food. 16Tyrians also, who lived in the city, brought in fish and all kinds of merchandise and sold them on the sabbath to the people of Judah, and in Jerusalem. 17Then I remonstrated with the nobles of Judah and said to them, "What is this evil thing that you are doing, profaning the sabbath day? 18Did not your ancestors act in this way, and did not our God bring all this disaster on us and on this city? Yet you bring more wrath on Israel by profaning the sabbath."

19 When it began to be dark at the gates of Jerusalem before the sabbath, I commanded that the doors should be shut and gave orders that they should not be opened until after the sabbath. And I set some of my servants over the gates, to prevent any burden from being brought in on the sabbath day. 20Then the merchants and sellers of all kinds of merchandise spent the night outside Jerusalem once or twice. 21But I warned them and said to them, "Why do you spend the night in front of the wall? If you do so again, I will lay hands on you." From that time on they did not come on the sabbath. 22And I commanded the Levites that they should purify themselves and come and guard the gates, to keep the sabbath day holy. Remember this also in my favor, O my God, and spare me according to the greatness of your steadfast love.

23 In those days also I saw Jews who had married women of Ashdod, Ammon, and Moab; 24and half of their children spoke the language of Ashdod, and they could not speak the language of Judah, but spoke the language of various peoples. 25And I contended with them and cursed them and beat some of them and pulled out their hair; and I made them take an oath in the name of God, saying, "You shall not give your daughters to their sons, or take their daughters for your sons or for yourselves. 26Did not King Solomon of Israel sin on account of such women? Among the many nations there was no king like him, and he was beloved by his God, and God made him king over all Israel; nevertheless, foreign women made even him to sin. 27Shall we then listen to you and do all this great evil and act treacherously against our God by marrying foreign women?"

28 And one of the sons of Jehoiada, son of the high priest Eliashib, was the son-in-law of Sanballat the Horonite; I chased him away from me. 29Remember them, O my God, because they have defiled the priesthood, the covenant of the priests and the Levites.

30 Thus I cleansed them from everything foreign, and I established the duties of the priests and Levites, each in his work; 31and I provided for the wood offering, at appointed times, and for the first fruits. Remember me, O my God, for good.

13.4–31. 5: *Prepared for Tobiah a large room* in the Temple* precinct: Tobiah was not only one of Nehemiah's primary adversaries, but was an Ammonite, a group to be excluded from the Temple (13.1–2). *They had previously put the grain offering* suggests that the offerings are not coming in as they had been, allowing for the room to be put to other uses. 6: *I was not in Jerusalem:* Nehemiah apparently was called back to the court for reasons not directly relating to his governance of the district. The *thirty-second year* of Artaxerxes would be 432 BCE. 8: *I was very angry:* By making such a public show, Nehemiah may have been hoping to bring the priest Eliashib, a relative of Tobiah, under control. This entire incident is a follow-up to the actions of the community in 13.1–3. 10: *The portions of the Levites had not been given to them:* This is contrary to the pledge made in 10.35–39 not to "neglect the house of our God." It also specifically violates the pledges made in 12.44–47 to ensure the singers could remain at their posts. 17: *Profaning the sabbath day?* This is contrary to the pledges made in 10.31 to keep the sabbath, even if foreign merchants come with goods to sell. 19: *I set some of my servants over the gates,* apparently to ensure that Nehemiah's orders to shut the city gates at the beginning of the sabbath were fulfilled. Cordoning off the city on the sabbath makes the entire city a holy precinct on that day. 22: This explains why Nehemiah commands the *Levites that they should purify themselves and come and guard the gates.* With the entire community turned into a "house of God," the Levites should guard the entryways just as they had previously guarded the entrances into the Temple precincts. 27: *This great evil:* Just as in Ezra, the intermarriage of the community with the surrounding peoples is portrayed in graphic terms as a most serious violation of divine order. The discovery of intermarriage was contrary to the pledges of the community in 10.30. While in ch. 10 the community voluntarily takes on an oath, here Nehemiah made them take an oath, with a strong public display of anger. **28:** *One of the sons of Jehoiada:* Just as Tobiah's relationship to certain of the priests presented a problem at the beginning of this section, now Sanballat's relationship to a member of the high priestly family presents another challenge. **30:** *I cleansed them*

from everything foreign: The community, as a "house of God," has been cleansed of patterns that would pull them away from their strict observance of the law. Just as David and Solomon made specific provisions for the care of the Temple personnel, Nehemiah places himself in the same company for establishing *the duties of the priests and Levites, each in his work.* **31:** *For good,* that is, all the good that Nehemiah has accomplished on behalf of the community.

ESTHER

Introduction

Set in the royal court of Persia, the book of Esther recounts how, through a series of dramatic events, a Jewish woman becomes queen and uses her influence to win for her people the right to fight off a threat of genocide. The Jewish holiday of Purim, described at the end of the book, celebrates this victory. The book's festival theme groups it within the five "megilloth"★ (scrolls) of Jewish Scripture (along with Ruth, Lamentations, Song of Solomon, and Ecclesiastes). Esther is found among the historical books of the Christian canon.★

There are three ancient versions of the book of Esther: the Masoretic text★ (MT), a Jewish manuscript tradition from the Middle Ages; the Septuagint,★ a Greek version from an earlier period; and another Greek manuscript tradition called the A (or Alpha) Text. The MT is the shortest of the versions and is printed here. The longer Septuagint version is accepted as canon by Roman Catholic and Orthodox Christians and is found in the Apocryphal★/deuterocanonical★ books.

Because details from the book do not easily fit with historical information about the Persian king Xerxes (called in the MT Ahasuerus and in the Septuagint Artaxerxes), the book is best considered "historical fiction." Its acceptance (mixed with gentle mockery) of foreign rule, along with lack of concern with the land of Israel, suggests that it was written in the Diaspora★ (communities living outside of Israel), perhaps late in the Persian era★ (the fourth or early third century BCE).

READING GUIDE

The reader is well served to notice the exaggerated features of the narrative★—the extended period of banqueting, the wild mood swings of Ahasuerus and Haman, the use of royal edicts to control interpersonal disputes, and Esther's year-long beauty treatment. What image was the author painting of the Persian court? Noting that Esther is one of the few biblical books named for a woman, modern readers often ponder the gender message of the book. Is Esther a passive woman, bowing to her uncle and subordinating her life to that of others? Does she grow into her own power as the book continues? Since the book does not mention the name of God, a key to its theology may be the "coincidences" that work to the benefit of the Jewish people.

1–2	Esther becomes queen instead of Vashti; Mordecai thwarts a plot
3–8	Esther counters Haman's plot to destroy the Jews
9.1–16	The Jews fight their enemies
9.17–10.3	Purim is instituted and decrees are sent

1 This happened in the days of Ahasuerus, the same Ahasuerus who ruled over one hundred twenty-seven provinces from India to Ethiopia.[a] 2In those days when King Ahasuerus sat on his royal throne in the citadel of Susa, 3in the third year of his reign, he gave a banquet for all his officials and ministers. The army of Persia and Media and the nobles and governors of the provinces were present, 4while he displayed the great

a Or Nubia; Heb Cush

wealth of his kingdom and the splendor and pomp of his majesty for many days, one hundred eighty days in all.

5 When these days were completed, the king gave for all the people present in the citadel of Susa, both great and small, a banquet lasting for seven days, in the court of the garden of the king's palace. 6There were white cotton curtains and blue hangings tied with cords of fine linen and purple to silver rings*a* and marble pillars. There were couches of gold and silver on a mosaic pavement of porphyry, marble, mother-of-pearl, and colored stones. 7Drinks were served in golden goblets, goblets of different kinds, and the royal wine was lavished according to the bounty of the king. 8Drinking was by flagons, without restraint; for the king had given orders to all the officials of his palace to do as each one desired. 9Furthermore, Queen Vashti gave a banquet for the women in the palace of King Ahasuerus.

1.1–9: In the royal court. 1: *Ahasuerus* is usually identified with Xerxes I (486–465 BCE). "Satrapies" is the more usual description of Persian administrative units than *provinces. One hundred twenty-seven* does not correspond to any reckoning known outside the Bible. **2:** *Susa,* at the foot of the Zagros mountains, was one of three royal residences. It consisted of a *citadel,* or fortified city (enclosed with gates), and an unfortified lower city. **3:** *Media* was a large province of the Achaemenid *Persian* empire. **4–8:** The extended period of banqueting, as well as the extensive list of furnishings, paints a picture of a lavish, extravagant gentile* (non-Jewish) court. **9:** *Vashti* is not mentioned in Persian literature. Although the Greek historian Herodotus reports that Persian men and women banqueted together, Vashti's separate banquet explains to the reader why she must be summoned, and the heavy drinking of the all-male audience may suggest the danger Vashti faced in appearing before them.

~~~~~~~~~~~~~~~~

10 On the seventh day, when the king was merry with wine, he commanded Mehuman, Biztha, Harbona, Bigtha and Abagtha, Zethar and Carkas, the seven eunuchs who attended him, 11to bring Queen Vashti before the king, wearing the royal crown, in order to show the peoples and the officials her beauty; for she was fair to behold. 12But

Queen Vashti refused to come at the king's command conveyed by the eunuchs. At this the king was enraged, and his anger burned within him.

13 Then the king consulted the sages who knew the laws*b* (for this was the king's procedure toward all who were versed in law and custom, 14and those next to him were Carshena, Shethar, Admatha, Tarshish, Meres, Marsena, and Memucan, the seven officials of Persia and Media, who had access to the king, and sat first in the kingdom): 15"According to the law, what is to be done to Queen Vashti because she has not performed the command of King Ahasuerus conveyed by the eunuchs?" 16Then Memucan said in the presence of the king and the officials, "Not only has Queen Vashti done wrong to the king, but also to all the officials and all the peoples who are in all the provinces of King Ahasuerus. 17For this deed of the queen will be made known to all women, causing them to look with contempt on their husbands, since they will say, 'King Ahasuerus commanded Queen Vashti to be brought before him, and she did not come.' 18This very day the noble ladies of Persia and Media who have heard of the queen's behavior will rebel against*c* the king's officials, and there will be no end of contempt and wrath! 19If it pleases the king, let a royal order go out from him, and let it be written among the laws of the Persians and the Medes so that it may not be altered, that Vashti is never again to come before King Ahasuerus; and let the king give her royal position to another who is better than she. 20So when the decree made by the king is proclaimed throughout all his kingdom, vast as it is, all women will give honor to their husbands, high and low alike."

21 This advice pleased the king and the officials, and the king did as Memucan proposed; 22he sent letters to all the royal provinces, to every province in its own script and to every people in its own language, declaring that every man should be master in his own house.*d*

a Or *rods*   *b* Cn: Heb *times*   *c* Cn: Heb *will tell*
d Heb adds *and speak according to the language of his people*

1.10–22: **Vashti refuses. 10:** Throughout the book, *eunuchs* (royal servants, often castrated) bridge gaps between men and women, royals and commoners, insiders and outsiders. **12:** The author gives neither the reason for Vashti's refusal nor a judgment on her decision. *The king was enraged:* Ahaserus (and later Haman) has a quick temper. **13–19:** The importance and permanence of Persian *laws* are themes of the book. As elsewhere, the king does not make his own decisions but defers to advisers and documents. *Memucan* the eunuch, not the king, makes the Vashti affair into a forum on women's subordination. **19:** While biblical tradition indicates that Persian law could not be altered (Dan 6.8), such a strategy would have been impractical. **22:** *In its own language:* The Persians generally accepted the ethnic diversity of their kingdom.

2 After these things, when the anger of King Ahasuerus had abated, he remembered Vashti and what she had done and what had been decreed against her. ²Then the king's servants who attended him said, "Let beautiful young virgins be sought out for the king. ³And let the king appoint commissioners in all the provinces of his kingdom to gather all the beautiful young virgins to the harem in the citadel of Susa under custody of Hegai, the king's eunuch, who is in charge of the women; let their cosmetic treatments be given them. ⁴And let the girl who pleases the king be queen instead of Vashti." This pleased the king, and he did so.

5 Now there was a Jew in the citadel of Susa whose name was Mordecai son of Jair son of Shimei son of Kish, a Benjaminite. ⁶Kish*ᵃ* had been carried away from Jerusalem among the captives carried away with King Jeconiah of Judah, whom King Nebuchadnezzar of Babylon had carried away. ⁷Mordecai*ᵇ* had brought up Hadassah, that is Esther, his cousin, for she had neither father nor mother; the girl was fair and beautiful, and when her father and her mother died, Mordecai adopted her as his own daughter. ⁸So when the king's order and his edict were proclaimed, and when many young women were gathered in the citadel of Susa in custody of Hegai, Esther also was taken into the king's palace and put in custody of Hegai, who had charge of the women.

⁹The girl pleased him and won his favor, and he quickly provided her with her cosmetic treatments and her portion of food, and with seven chosen maids from the king's palace, and advanced her and her maids to the best place in the harem. ¹⁰Esther did not reveal her people or kindred, for Mordecai had charged her not to tell. ¹¹Every day Mordecai would walk around in front of the court of the harem, to learn how Esther was and how she fared.

2.1–11: **Esther and Mordecai. 2–4:** While according to Herodotus the Persian king could only marry from seven noble families, this account explains how a commoner, a Jewish one at that, could marry into royalty. **5–6:** The name *Mordecai* is similar to that of the Babylonian god Marduk. *Shimei, Kish,* and *Benjaminite* provide verbal links to King Saul (1 Sam 9.1; 2 Sam 16.5–8). The Hebrew reads that Mordecai was carried away by the Babylonians (see note a), making him over 100 years old. The NRSV suggests, instead, that *Kish* was carried into exile. **7:** *Hadassah,* the Jewish name, means "myrtle." *Esther* sounds similar to the Babylonian goddess Ishtar. **8–11:** Like Joseph (Gen 39.3) and Daniel (Dan 1.9), Esther wins favor in the royal court and is aided by a royal servant. Apparently Jewish identity was not obvious, and there is no mention of Esther's attempts at religious observances like kosher✶ food regulations.

12 The turn came for each girl to go in to King Ahasuerus, after being twelve months under the regulations for the women, since this was the regular period of their cosmetic treatment, six months with oil of myrrh and six months with perfumes and cosmetics for women. ¹³When the girl went in to the king she was given whatever she asked for to take with her from the harem to the king's palace. ¹⁴In the evening she went in; then in the morning she came back to the second harem in custody of Shaashgaz, the king's eunuch, who was in charge of the concubines; she did not go in to the king again, unless the king delighted in her and she was summoned by name.

15 When the turn came for Esther daughter of Abihail the uncle of Mordecai,

a Heb *a Benjamite* *ᶜwho* *b* Heb *He*

who had adopted her as his own daughter, to go in to the king, she asked for nothing except what Hegai the king's eunuch, who had charge of the women, advised. Now Esther was admired by all who saw her. ¹⁶When Esther was taken to King Ahasuerus in his royal palace in the tenth month, which is the month of Tebeth, in the seventh year of his reign, ¹⁷the king loved Esther more than all the other women; of all the virgins she won his favor and devotion, so that he set the royal crown on her head and made her queen instead of Vashti. ¹⁸Then the king gave a great banquet to all his officials and ministers—"Esther's banquet." He also granted a holiday*a* to the provinces, and gave gifts with royal liberality.

19 When the virgins were being gathered together,*b* Mordecai was sitting at the king's gate. ²⁰Now Esther had not revealed her kindred or her people, as Mordecai had charged her; for Esther obeyed Mordecai just as when she was brought up by him. ²¹In those days, while Mordecai was sitting at the king's gate, Bigthan and Teresh, two of the king's eunuchs, who guarded the threshold, became angry and conspired to assassinate*c* King Ahasuerus. ²²But the matter came to the knowledge of Mordecai, and he told it to Queen Esther, and Esther told the king in the name of Mordecai. ²³When the affair was investigated and found to be so, both the men were hanged on the gallows. It was recorded in the book of the annals in the presence of the king.

2.12–23: Esther's and Mordecai's successes. The elaborate procedures portray Esther's chances as a long shot. **15–18:** With savvy Esther follows the instructions of the eunuch who has favored her. Her victory is celebrated by the fourth banquet of the book. **19–23:** Mordecai's protection of the king, while not yet rewarded, will serve as his salvation from Haman's plot in ch. 6. **21:** *Threshold:* Of the king's private room. Greek sources relate that Ahasuerus died from this type of conspiracy. Mordecai's access to the eunuchs may indicate that he held some official position.

3 After these things King Ahasuerus promoted Haman son of Hammedatha the Agagite, and advanced him and set his seat

above all the officials who were with him. ²And all the king's servants who were at the king's gate bowed down and did obeisance to Haman; for the king had so commanded concerning him. But Mordecai did not bow down or do obeisance. ³Then the king's servants who were at the king's gate said to Mordecai, "Why do you disobey the king's command?" ⁴When they spoke to him day after day and he would not listen to them, they told Haman, in order to see whether Mordecai's words would avail; for he had told them that he was a Jew. ⁵When Haman saw that Mordecai did not bow down or do obeisance to him, Haman was infuriated. ⁶But he thought it beneath him to lay hands on Mordecai alone. So, having been told who Mordecai's people were, Haman plotted to destroy all the Jews, the people of Mordecai, throughout the whole kingdom of Ahasuerus.

7 In the first month, which is the month of Nisan, in the twelfth year of King Ahasuerus, they cast Pur—which means "the lot"—before Haman for the day and for the month, and the lot fell on the thirteenth day*d* of the twelfth month, which is the month of Adar. ⁸Then Haman said to King Ahasuerus, "There is a certain people scattered and separated among the peoples in all the provinces of your kingdom; their laws are different from those of every other people, and they do not keep the king's laws, so that it is not appropriate for the king to tolerate them. ⁹If it pleases the king, let a decree be issued for their destruction, and I will pay ten thousand talents of silver into the hands of those who have charge of the king's business, so that they may put it into the king's treasuries." ¹⁰So the king took his signet ring from his hand and gave it to Haman son of Hammedatha the Agagite, the enemy of the Jews. ¹¹The king said to Haman, "The money is given to you, and the people as well, to do with them as it seems good to you."

12 Then the king's secretaries were summoned on the thirteenth day of the first

a Or *an amnesty*   *b* Heb adds *a second time*
c Heb *to lay hands on*   *d* Cn Compare Gk and verse 13 below: Heb *the twelfth month*

month, and an edict, according to all that Haman commanded, was written to the king's satraps and to the governors over all the provinces and to the officials of all the peoples, to every province in its own script and every people in its own language; it was written in the name of King Ahasuerus and sealed with the king's ring. 13Letters were sent by couriers to all the king's provinces, giving orders to destroy, to kill, and to annihilate all Jews, young and old, women and children, in one day, the thirteenth day of the twelfth month, which is the month of Adar, and to plunder their goods. 14A copy of the document was to be issued as a decree in every province by proclamation, calling on all the peoples to be ready for that day. 15The couriers went quickly by order of the king, and the decree was issued in the citadel of Susa. The king and Haman sat down to drink; but the city of Susa was thrown into confusion.

3.1–15: Mordecai angers Haman. 1: Haman's *Agagite* identity puts him in tension with the Benjaminite Mordecai (1 Sam 15.7–9). **2:** As in the case of Vashti's refusal, Mordecai's refusal to bow down is not explained. **4–6:** Mordecai having revealed his identity, Haman hatches a plan against all Jews. **7–11:** *Nisan:* As in other post-exilic books, month names are based on the Babylonian calendar.✶ *Pur:* Akkadian for "lot" (singular, unlike the English usage of "lots"). The date chosen for the pogrom✶ is 11 months hence. **8:** Haman does not identify the rebellious people, but argues their danger to the empire. **10:** *Signet ring:* Sign of royal authority. **11:** *As it seems good to you:* As usual, the king lets others decide. **12–15:** The *edict,* which bears all the royal trappings, allows destruction and plunder of the Jewish people. Coldly, the men drink after issuing a decree of death.

4 When Mordecai learned all that had been done, Mordecai tore his clothes and put on sackcloth and ashes, and went through the city, wailing with a loud and bitter cry; 2he went up to the entrance of the king's gate, for no one might enter the king's gate clothed with sackcloth. 3In every province, wherever the king's command and his decree came, there was great mourning among the Jews, with fasting and weeping and lamenting, and most of them lay in sackcloth and ashes.

4 When Esther's maids and her eunuchs came and told her, the queen was deeply distressed; she sent garments to clothe Mordecai, so that he might take off his sackcloth; but he would not accept them. 5Then Esther called for Hathach, one of the king's eunuchs, who had been appointed to attend her, and ordered him to go to Mordecai to learn what was happening and why. 6Hathach went out to Mordecai in the open square of the city in front of the king's gate, 7and Mordecai told him all that had happened to him, and the exact sum of money that Haman had promised to pay into the king's treasuries for the destruction of the Jews. 8Mordecai also gave him a copy of the written decree issued in Susa for their destruction, that he might show it to Esther, explain it to her, and charge her to go to the king to make supplication to him and entreat him for her people.

9 Hathach went and told Esther what Mordecai had said. 10Then Esther spoke to Hathach and gave him a message for Mordecai, saying, 11"All the king's servants and the people of the king's provinces know that if any man or woman goes to the king inside the inner court without being called, there is but one law—all alike are to be put to death. Only if the king holds out the golden scepter to someone, may that person live. I myself have not been called to come in to the king for thirty days." 12When they told Mordecai what Esther had said, 13Mordecai told them to reply to Esther, "Do not think that in the king's palace you will escape any more than all the other Jews. 14For if you keep silence at such a time as this, relief and deliverance will rise for the Jews from another quarter, but you and your father's family will perish. Who knows? Perhaps you have come to royal dignity for just such a time as this." 15Then Esther said in reply to Mordecai, 16"Go, gather all the Jews to be found in Susa, and hold a fast on my behalf, and neither eat nor drink for three days, night or day. I and my maids will also fast as you do. After that I will go to the king, though it is against the law; and if I perish, I perish." 17Mordecai

then went away and did everything as Esther had ordered him.

4.1–17: Mordecai petitions Esther. 1: *Torn clothes, sackcloth,** and *ashes* are typical gestures of mourning and distress. **4–5:** Why Esther was *distressed* is not explained: Did she fear for Mordecai's safety? **11:** Despite her status as queen, Esther remains under the authority of the king and of the ever present Persian law. **12–14:** Mordecai is the face of Esther's Jewishness. His speech reminds her that she shares the fate of her people. *Another quarter* may be a veiled reference to God, who is not named explicitly in the book. *Perhaps . . . for just such a time as this* summarizes the book's theme: Esther rises to power just in time to save the Jewish people. **16–17:** For the first time, Esther commands Mordecai, and he does everything she says (compare 2.20). The *fast* is one of the few religious observances in the book and prepares the people for the danger Esther is to face.

5 On the third day Esther put on her royal robes and stood in the inner court of the king's palace, opposite the king's hall. The king was sitting on his royal throne inside the palace opposite the entrance to the palace. ²As soon as the king saw Queen Esther standing in the court, she won his favor and he held out to her the golden scepter that was in his hand. Then Esther approached and touched the top of the scepter. ³The king said to her, "What is it, Queen Esther? What is your request? It shall be given you, even to the half of my kingdom." ⁴Then Esther said, "If it pleases the king, let the king and Haman come today to a banquet that I have prepared for the king." ⁵Then the king said, "Bring Haman quickly, so that we may do as Esther desires." So the king and Haman came to the banquet that Esther had prepared. ⁶While they were drinking wine, the king said to Esther, "What is your petition? It shall be granted you. And what is your request? Even to the half of my kingdom, it shall be fulfilled." ⁷Then Esther said, "This is my petition and request: ⁸If I have won the king's favor, and if it pleases the king to grant my petition and fulfill my request, let the king and Haman come tomorrow to the banquet that I will prepare for them, and then I will do as the king has said."

5.1–8: Esther requests two banquets. 1: Esther, while bold, shows respect for the king. **3:** *Half of my kingdom:* Another example of Ahasuerus's impulsive style. **4–5:** A clear strategist, Esther feeds the ego of both the king (throwing him a banquet) and Haman (honoring him with an invitation). **6–8:** Esther requests another banquet, the seventh of the book. By postponing her ultimate request, she leaves the reader in suspense and puffs up Haman, preparing him for a yet more dramatic fall.

9 Haman went out that day happy and in good spirits. But when Haman saw Mordecai in the king's gate, and observed that he neither rose nor trembled before him, he was infuriated with Mordecai; ¹⁰nevertheless Haman restrained himself and went home. Then he sent and called for his friends and his wife Zeresh, ¹¹and Haman recounted to them the splendor of his riches, the number of his sons, all the promotions with which the king had honored him, and how he had advanced him above the officials and the ministers of the king. ¹²Haman added, "Even Queen Esther let no one but myself come with the king to the banquet that she prepared. Tomorrow also I am invited by her, together with the king. ¹³Yet all this does me no good so long as I see the Jew Mordecai sitting at the king's gate." ¹⁴Then his wife Zeresh and all his friends said to him, "Let a gallows fifty cubits high be made, and in the morning tell the king to have Mordecai hanged on it; then go with the king to the banquet in good spirits." This advice pleased Haman, and he had the gallows made.

5.9–14: Haman's mood swings. In good spirits after the queen has shown him honor, Haman is infuriated by Mordecai's repeated refusal to bow. **11:** Haman's bragging to people who already know him suggests an ego out of control. **14:** Because the pogrom* is still months from its execution, the plan to kill Mordecai immediately on a *gallows 50 cubits high* (75 ft!) leaves Haman in good spirits once again.

6 On that night the king could not sleep, and he gave orders to bring the book of records, the annals, and they were read to the king. ²It was found written how Mor-

decai had told about Bigthana and Teresh, two of the king's eunuchs, who guarded the threshold, and who had conspired to assassinate[a] King Ahasuerus. ³Then the king said, "What honor or distinction has been bestowed on Mordecai for this?" The king's servants who attended him said, "Nothing has been done for him." ⁴The king said, "Who is in the court?" Now Haman had just entered the outer court of the king's palace to speak to the king about having Mordecai hanged on the gallows that he had prepared for him. ⁵So the king's servants told him, "Haman is there, standing in the court." The king said, "Let him come in." ⁶So Haman came in, and the king said to him, "What shall be done for the man whom the king wishes to honor?" Haman said to himself, "Whom would the king wish to honor more than me?" ⁷So Haman said to the king, "For the man whom the king wishes to honor, ⁸let royal robes be brought, which the king has worn, and a horse that the king has ridden, with a royal crown on its head. ⁹Let the robes and the horse be handed over to one of the king's most noble officials; let him[b] robe the man whom the king wishes to honor, and let him[b] conduct the man on horseback through the open square of the city, proclaiming before him: 'Thus shall it be done for the man whom the king wishes to honor.' " ¹⁰Then the king said to Haman, "Quickly, take the robes and the horse, as you have said, and do so to the Jew Mordecai who sits at the king's gate. Leave out nothing that you have mentioned." ¹¹So Haman took the robes and the horse and robed Mordecai and led him riding through the open square of the city, proclaiming, "Thus shall it be done for the man whom the king wishes to honor."

12 Then Mordecai returned to the king's gate, but Haman hurried to his house, mourning and with his head covered. ¹³When Haman told his wife Zeresh and all his friends everything that had happened to him, his advisers and his wife Zeresh said to him, "If Mordecai, before whom your downfall has begun, is of the Jewish people, you will not prevail against him, but will surely fall before him."

6.1–14: Royal insomnia benefits Mordecai. In a comic scene, the king passes a sleepless night listening to royal annals. In keeping with the theology of the book, "it just happened" to be the same night Haman hatched his plan; Haman "happens" to be in the court; and Haman's desire for royal treatment "happens" to be given to the very man he wished to hang. **10:** *The Jew Mordecai:* The king makes no connection between Mordecai's ethnicity and the people he had condemned to death in ch. 3. **13:** *If Mordecai . . . is of the Jewish people:* Since Haman had already revealed this information in 5.13, the statement is likely intended as a preview of what is to come.

14 While they were still talking with him, the king's eunuchs arrived and hurried Haman off to the banquet that Esther had prepared. ¹So the king and Haman went in to feast with Queen Esther. ²On the second day, as they were drinking wine, the king again said to Esther, "What is your petition, Queen Esther? It shall be granted you. And what is your request? Even to the half of my kingdom, it shall be fulfilled." ³Then Queen Esther answered, "If I have won your favor, O king, and if it pleases the king, let my life be given me—that is my petition—and the lives of my people—that is my request. ⁴For we have been sold, I and my people, to be destroyed, to be killed, and to be annihilated. If we had been sold merely as slaves, men and women, I would have held my peace; but no enemy can compensate for this damage to the king."[c] ⁵Then King Ahasuerus said to Queen Esther, "Who is he, and where is he, who has presumed to do this?" ⁶Esther said, "A foe and enemy, this wicked Haman!" Then Haman was terrified before the king and the queen. ⁷The king rose from the feast in wrath and went into the palace garden, but Haman stayed to beg his life from Queen Esther, for he saw that the king had determined to destroy him. ⁸When the king returned from the palace garden to the banquet hall, Haman had thrown himself on the couch where Esther was reclining; and the king said, "Will he even assault the

---

a Heb *to lay hands on*   b Heb *them*   c Meaning of Heb uncertain

queen in my presence, in my own house?" As the words left the mouth of the king, they covered Haman's face. 9Then Harbona, one of the eunuchs in attendance on the king, said, "Look, the very gallows that Haman has prepared for Mordecai, whose word saved the king, stands at Haman's house, fifty cubits high." And the king said, "Hang him on that." 10So they hanged Haman on the gallows that he had prepared for Mordecai. Then the anger of the king abated.

7.1–10: Haman's downfall. 3–4: Esther strategically heaps up deferential comments to the king and focuses on his loss (*damage to the king*) in her death. **8:** *Reclining* was a common posture for banqueting. Haman's act of supplication is interpreted by Ahasuerus as a sexual attack on Esther. **9:** A eunuch "happens" to be on hand and suggests a "measure for measure" punishment for Haman.

8 On that day King Ahasuerus gave to Queen Esther the house of Haman, the enemy of the Jews; and Mordecai came before the king, for Esther had told what he was to her. 2Then the king took off his signet ring, which he had taken from Haman, and gave it to Mordecai. So Esther set Mordecai over the house of Haman.

3 Then Esther spoke again to the king; she fell at his feet, weeping and pleading with him to avert the evil design of Haman the Agagite and the plot that he had devised against the Jews. 4The king held out the golden scepter to Esther, 5and Esther rose and stood before the king. She said, "If it pleases the king, and if I have won his favor, and if the thing seems right before the king, and I have his approval, let an order be written to revoke the letters devised by Haman son of Hammedatha the Agagite, which he wrote giving orders to destroy the Jews who are in all the provinces of the king. 6For how can I bear to see the calamity that is coming on my people? Or how can I bear to see the destruction of my kindred?" 7Then King Ahasuerus said to Queen Esther and to the Jew Mordecai, "See, I have given Esther the house of Haman, and they have hanged him on the gallows, because he plotted to lay hands on the Jews. 8You may write as you

please with regard to the Jews, in the name of the king, and seal it with the king's ring; for an edict written in the name of the king and sealed with the king's ring cannot be revoked."

9 The king's secretaries were summoned at that time, in the third month, which is the month of Sivan, on the twenty-third day; and an edict was written, according to all that Mordecai commanded, to the Jews and to the satraps and the governors and the officials of the provinces from India to Ethiopia,*a* one hundred twenty-seven provinces, to every province in its own script and to every people in its own language, and also to the Jews in their script and their language. 10He wrote letters in the name of King Ahasuerus, sealed them with the king's ring, and sent them by mounted couriers riding on fast steeds bred from the royal herd.*b* 11By these letters the king allowed the Jews who were in every city to assemble and defend their lives, to destroy, to kill, and to annihilate any armed force of any people or province that might attack them, with their children and women, and to plunder their goods 12on a single day throughout all the provinces of King Ahasuerus, on the thirteenth day of the twelfth month, which is the month of Adar. 13A copy of the writ was to be issued as a decree in every province and published to all peoples, and the Jews were to be ready on that day to take revenge on their enemies. 14So the couriers, mounted on their swift royal steeds, hurried out, urged by the king's command. The decree was issued in the citadel of Susa.

15 Then Mordecai went out from the presence of the king, wearing royal robes of blue and white, with a great golden crown and a mantle of fine linen and purple, while the city of Susa shouted and rejoiced. 16For the Jews there was light and gladness, joy and honor. 17In every province and in every city, wherever the king's command and his edict came, there was gladness and joy among the Jews, a festival and a holiday. Furthermore, many of the peoples of the country

a Or *Nubia;* Heb *Cush*   *b* Meaning of Heb uncertain

professed to be Jews, because the fear of the Jews had fallen upon them.

8.1–17: Esther and Mordecai issue edicts. 1–2: Yet more reversals: Esther receives Haman's house, and the *signet ring* that Ahasuerus gave to Haman to issue a decree (3.10) is now given to Mordecai to issue a counter-decree. **3:** The king has saved Esther and Mordecai, but she now asks that he save the whole Jewish people. **8:** The irrevocability of a royal edict is both the cause and now the solution to the Jews' problem. **9–11:** *Sivan* (Babylonian "Simanu") was still 9 months from the execution of the original edict. Given free reign to draft the decree, Mordecai allows Jews not only to defend themselves but also to take plunder (though they do not, see 9.10). **15:** Mordecai's *blue and white* robes (as in 1.6) link him with royalty, as foreshadowed in 6.11. **17:** Persians *professed to be Jews*, suggesting that Jewish identity could be chosen for oneself.

9 Now in the twelfth month, which is the month of Adar, on the thirteenth day, when the king's command and edict were about to be executed, on the very day when the enemies of the Jews hoped to gain power over them, but which had been changed to a day when the Jews would gain power over their foes, ²the Jews gathered in their cities throughout all the provinces of King Ahasuerus to lay hands on those who had sought their ruin; and no one could withstand them, because the fear of them had fallen upon all peoples. ³All the officials of the provinces, the satraps and the governors, and the royal officials were supporting the Jews, because the fear of Mordecai had fallen upon them. ⁴For Mordecai was powerful in the king's house, and his fame spread throughout all the provinces as the man Mordecai grew more and more powerful. ⁵So the Jews struck down all their enemies with the sword, slaughtering, and destroying them, and did as they pleased to those who hated them. ⁶In the citadel of Susa the Jews killed and destroyed five hundred people. ⁷They killed Parshandatha, Dalphon, Aspatha, ⁸Poratha, Adalia, Aridatha, ⁹Parmashta, Arisai, Aridai, Vaizatha, ¹⁰the ten sons of Haman son of Hammedatha, the enemy of the Jews; but they did not touch the plunder.

11 That very day the number of those killed in the citadel of Susa was reported to the king. ¹²The king said to Queen Esther, "In the citadel of Susa the Jews have killed five hundred people and also the ten sons of Haman. What have they done in the rest of the king's provinces? Now what is your petition? It shall be granted you. And what further is your request? It shall be fulfilled." ¹³Esther said, "If it pleases the king, let the Jews who are in Susa be allowed tomorrow also to do according to this day's edict, and let the ten sons of Haman be hanged on the gallows." ¹⁴So the king commanded this to be done; a decree was issued in Susa, and the ten sons of Haman were hanged. ¹⁵The Jews who were in Susa gathered also on the fourteenth day of the month of Adar and they killed three hundred persons in Susa; but they did not touch the plunder.

16 Now the other Jews who were in the king's provinces also gathered to defend their lives, and gained relief from their enemies, and killed seventy-five thousand of those who hated them; but they laid no hands on the plunder. ¹⁷This was on the thirteenth day of the month of Adar, and on the fourteenth day they rested and made that a day of feasting and gladness.

9.1–17: The events of Adar. 1: *On the very day* underlines the reversal of fates that has taken place in the book. **5–16:** Jewish self-defense begins *in the citadel of Susa* (vv. 6–12). Fighting *in Susa* (vv. 13–15) may refer to the same locale or the unfortified city; fighting then spreads to other Persian provinces (v. 16). The violence of these verses is variously assessed: Is the killing justified resistance to a planned pogrom★? Is it a troublesome commentary on the excesses of revenge? *They did not touch the plunder* (vv. 10, 15, 16), though Mordecai's edict allowed it, suggesting a religious motive for the fighting. In 1 Sam 15, Saul loses kingship because he took plunder and spared Agag.

---

18 But the Jews who were in Susa gathered on the thirteenth day and on the fourteenth, and rested on the fifteenth day, making that a day of feasting and gladness. ¹⁹Therefore the Jews of the villages, who live in the open towns, hold the fourteenth day

of the month of Adar as a day for gladness and feasting, a holiday on which they send gifts of food to one another.

20 Mordecai recorded these things, and sent letters to all the Jews who were in all the provinces of King Ahasuerus, both near and far, 21 enjoining them that they should keep the fourteenth day of the month Adar and also the fifteenth day of the same month, year by year, 22 as the days on which the Jews gained relief from their enemies, and as the month that had been turned for them from sorrow into gladness and from mourning into a holiday; that they should make them days of feasting and gladness, days for sending gifts of food to one another and presents to the poor. 23 So the Jews adopted as a custom what they had begun to do, as Mordecai had written to them.

24 Haman son of Hammedatha the Agagite, the enemy of all the Jews, had plotted against the Jews to destroy them, and had cast Pur—that is "the lot"—to crush and destroy them; 25 but when Esther came before the king, he gave orders in writing that the wicked plot that he had devised against the Jews should come upon his own head, and that he and his sons should be hanged on the gallows. 26 Therefore these days are called Purim, from the word Pur. Thus because of all that was written in this letter, and of what they had faced in this matter, and of what had happened to them, 27 the Jews established and accepted as a custom for themselves and their descendants and all who joined them, that without fail they would continue to observe these two days every year, as it was written and at the time appointed. 28 These days should be remembered and kept throughout every generation, in every family, province, and city; and these days of Purim should never fall into disuse among the Jews, nor should the commemoration of these days cease among their descendants.

29 Queen Esther daughter of Abihail, along with the Jew Mordecai, gave full written authority, confirming this second letter about Purim. 30 Letters were sent wishing peace and security to all the Jews, to the one hundred twenty-seven provinces of the kingdom of Ahasuerus, 31 and giving orders that these days of Purim should be observed at their appointed seasons, as the Jew Mordecai and Queen Esther enjoined on the Jews, just as they had laid down for themselves and for their descendants regulations concerning their fasts and their lamentations. 32 The command of Queen Esther fixed these practices of Purim, and it was recorded in writing.

9.18–32: Purim celebrations. 18–21: The different days on which the fighting took place here explains why Purim is celebrated for two days. 22: In keeping with the book's strong emphasis on banqueting, Purim observances includes *gifts of food*. 24–26: Ironically,* the festival is named after Haman's plot, first begun in 3.7 with the casting of a lot. 27–28: Because Purim is not found in the Torah* (Pentateuch*), its acceptance would have needed explanation and support. 29–32: The titles of *the Jew Mordecai* (as in 8.7) and *Queen Esther* suggest their different, though complementary, authority for sending letters.

10 King Ahasuerus laid tribute on the land and on the islands of the sea. 2 All the acts of his power and might, and the full account of the high honor of Mordecai, to which the king advanced him, are they not written in the annals of the kings of Media and Persia? 3 For Mordecai the Jew was next in rank to King Ahasuerus, and he was powerful among the Jews and popular with his many kindred, for he sought the good of his people and interceded for the welfare of all his descendants.

10.1–3: Mordecai honored. 2: Like other key events of the book of Esther, Mordecai's deeds are recorded in *the annals of the kings of Media and Persia.* 3: The closing tribute to *Mordecai,* as opposed to Esther for whom the book is named, is sometimes considered a later addition to the book, though Purim is called "Mordecai's Day" in 2 Macc 15.35.

JOB

Introduction

The book of Job offers a sustained reflection on a single topic—God's governance of the world of human beings. It asks passionately: Is that governance just? Justice is understood actively as the ability of the gods (or God) to uphold the righteous and put down the wicked. The approach of the book is typically biblical: The question is personalized ("There was once *a man* in the land of Uz whose name was Job") and developed in a narrative.✶ The discursive essay, which reaches a conclusion through rational discussion and which modern theologians would use to explore the topic, did not exist in the literature of the time. Modern readers must therefore immerse themselves in the story and, like the friends (2.13), sit a while with Job.

Job shows the probing and critical side of ancient Near Eastern literature, works that pointed to the miseries and inequities of life and the seeming inability of the gods to manage the world justly and wisely. Of these works, the most relevant to Job is "The Babylonian Theodicy" (written about 1000 BCE), a dialogue between a sufferer and a sage to whom he goes for comfort and wisdom. The sage is scolding and didactic, but at the end he is won over by the sufferer's anguish and arguments, conceding finally that the gods have put evil into the world. The sufferer, having won the sage's sympathy, acknowledges his suppliant state and asks the gods for pity. "The Babylonian Theodicy" helps us to understand Job: The problem of suffering is intensely personal (the speaker is actually suffering); the sufferer seeks not only counsel but acceptance and solace from the sage; the sufferer never gives up his judgment that his lot is miserable and that society is corrupt (it is the sage who changes!). Though similar in genre,✶ Job makes its own vigorous statement. Prior to Job, there is nothing like his explicit and unyielding declaration of innocence. One reason is the biblical confession of one God, supremely wise, powerful, and just; the God of Israel is responsible for *everything* that happens in the world. The problem of evil in Job is thus more pressing and poignant than in other religions. A second distinctive mark of Job is that God is a powerful actor in the drama, initiating the action in chs. 1–2, responding to Job's charges in chs. 39–42, and bringing all to a close in 42.7–17.

The author of Job is not known, but he may have been a palace scribe✶ with exceptional poetic and intellectual gifts and an acquaintance with other skeptical literature. The date of composition is also unknown, for the book contains no historical reference, and its language cannot be fitted into a typology of the Hebrew language. Most estimates of the date are between the seventh and the fifth centuries BCE. A possible hint regarding the date is that Job is an Edomite, which may suggest the book was written before the sixth-century Exile✶ when Edomites were hated for taking advantage of Israel.

READING GUIDE

The best approach to Job is to defer discussion of its grand ideas such as justice and suffering and simply to read the entire book as a story. The book has characters and a plot with a beginning, middle, and end. It begins by introducing Job as a righteous sheik (1.1–5). The drama begins in the heavenly court with a wager between God and Satan on whether Job's piety is genuine (chs. 1–2). God agrees to the testing of Job. The wager and testing remain hidden from Job and his friends, contributing to the pervasive irony★ of the book. Irony is present when the reader knows more than the characters in the story know. Only the reader knows that it is not because of his sins (as the friends think) but because of his righteousness that Job suffers. In the first test, Job loses property and children but accepts it humbly. The second test afflicts his person. Initially accepting even this evil (2.7–13), he ultimately erupts in a curse upon the day of his birth (ch. 3). His friends object and heatedly defend divine justice and wisdom by a variety of traditional arguments: Job must have done some evil, perhaps unthinkingly; we are sinners in any case, fragile creatures of a few short years; a human being cannot know all the rules defining proper behavior; entrust yourself to God in an emotional rather than an intellectual solution. His un- sympathetic friends provoke Job to abandon his passivity and desire for obliteration. He demands to see God; using legal language, he summons God into court for the adjudication of his com- plaint. His dialogue with the friends extends over three cycles (chs. 4–27), ending when com- munication breaks down completely. Alone, Job begins a sustained address to God with an oath of innocence (27.2), continuing it in his summation and final oath in chs. 29–31. In the mean- time, an anonymous poem on the inaccessibility of wisdom (ch. 28) suggests the futility of the previous dialogues and points forward to a divine intervention by insisting that God alone knows the way to wisdom. In chs. 32–37, Elihu appears as an absurd answer to Job's demand for a mediator between himself and God. Dramatically, Elihu's speeches retard the action and heighten the expectation of the LORD's appearance in ch. 38. In a long-awaited intervention, God answers Job out of the whirlwind, demonstrating by examples (rather than by arguments) that the world is indeed governed wisely (chs. 38–39) and justly (40.6–41.34). To each speech Job responds humbly and then withdraws his suit and accepts God's version (40.3–5; 42.1–6). In the epilogue, God declares Job has won the disputation with the friends and restores his family and his place in the community. For details on the dramatic movement, see the commentary.

Some scholars regard the poetic cycles (3.1–42.6) as the original core to which a prose frame- work (chs. 1–2 and 42.7–17) was later added. Many also suggest that the Elihu speeches are secondary. The evidence, however, for the original unity of Job is compelling: Job is the same stalwart man in the dialogues and in the frame; prose and poetry in the Bible are not radically distinct styles; there are verbal cross-references between the poetic cycle and the prose frame; the Elihu speeches make sense in the literary structure.

In Jewish tradition, Job fascinated the rabbis, as is attested by many discussions about him in the Talmud. Interest centered on his status as a gentile★ (some believed he was a Jewish pros- elyte) and on the question whether he was ultimately motivated by love or by fear. Christian tradition remembers the endurance (the translation "patience" is misleading) of Job (Jas 5.11). Job became a type or example of the virtuous and faithful person to church Fathers. The many homilies of St. Gregory the Great (died 604) sum up patristic tradition about Job and point to medieval usage: Job is an image of Christ★ and of the church, and an example of spiritual and moral life.

1–2	Prologue
3–14	First cycle of speeches
15–21	Second cycle of speeches
22–27	Third cycle of speeches
28	Poem on wisdom
29–31	Final speech of Job

PROLOGUE

Chs. 1–2: God decides to test Job. The action of chs. 1–2 unfolds in alternating scenes on earth (1.1–5, 13–22, and 2.7b–10) and in heaven (1.6–12 and 2.1–7a). Each earthly scene ends with a righteous statement or act by Job (1.5, 22; 2.10). Each heavenly scene begins with the courtiers presenting themselves before the LORD and ends with one member of the court, Satan, leaving to take action.

1 There was once a man in the land of Uz whose name was Job. That man was blameless and upright, one who feared God and turned away from evil. ²There were born to him seven sons and three daughters. ³He had seven thousand sheep, three thousand camels, five hundred yoke of oxen, five hundred donkeys, and very many servants; so that this man was the greatest of all the people of the east. ⁴His sons used to go and hold feasts in one another's houses in turn; and they would send and invite their three sisters to eat and drink with them. ⁵And when the feast days had run their course, Job would send and sanctify them, and he would rise early in the morning and offer burnt offerings according to the number of them all; for Job said, "It may be that my children have sinned, and cursed God in their hearts." This is what Job always did.

1.1–5: Earthly scene I: Introduction of Job the just. 1. *Job* is a venerable hero, well known beyond the confines of Israel (Ezek 14.14, 20). His homeland *Uz* is outside the holy land, located to the east, probably in Edom (Lam 4.21), an area south of the Dead Sea on both sides of the Wadi* Arabah. Job was *blameless and upright*, designations important thematically in the dialogues; they are more fully explained by the following phrases, *feared God* and *turned away from evil*. **4–5:** The children are mentioned to illustrate Job's piety on their behalf and to prepare for their loss in v. 19.

6 One day the heavenly beings*ᵃ* came to present themselves before the LORD, and Satan*ᵇ* also came among them. ⁷The LORD said to Satan,*ᵇ* "Where have you come from?" Satan*ᵇ* answered the LORD, "From going to and fro on the earth, and from walking up and down on it." ⁸The LORD said to Satan,*ᵇ* "Have you considered my servant Job? There is no one like him on the earth, a blameless and upright man who fears God and turns away from evil." ⁹Then Satan*ᵇ* answered the LORD, "Does Job fear God for nothing? ¹⁰Have you not put a fence around him and his house and all that he has, on every side? You have blessed the work of his hands, and his possessions have increased in the land. ¹¹But stretch out your hand now, and touch all that he has, and he will curse you to your face." ¹²The LORD said to Satan,*ᵇ* "Very well, all that he has is in your power; only do not stretch out your hand against him!" So Satan*ᵇ* went out from the presence of the LORD.

1.6–12: Heavenly scene I: Conversation of God and Satan. People imagined the heavenly court on the model of an earthly one: Courtiers present themselves before the king and officials report to the LORD. *Satan*, literally, "the Satan" or the adversary, is not the enemy of God as in later biblical books, but a member of the court whose particular task is to watch the actions of human beings and report back to the LORD. **8–10:** God is pleased by the utterly just actions of Job, but Satan cynically intimates that Job is doing it only for the abundant blessings he receives in return. God allows Satan to test Job to see whether he, when "touched," will curse God. The reader now knows two things that the friends of Job do not: Job is genuinely just, and God is testing him.

13 One day when his sons and daughters were eating and drinking wine in the eldest brother's house, ¹⁴a messenger came to Job

a Heb *sons of God*   *b* Or *the Accuser*; Heb *ha-satan*

and said, "The oxen were plowing and the donkeys were feeding beside them, [15]and the Sabeans fell on them and carried them off, and killed the servants with the edge of the sword; I alone have escaped to tell you." [16]While he was still speaking, another came and said, "The fire of God fell from heaven and burned up the sheep and the servants, and consumed them; I alone have escaped to tell you." [17]While he was still speaking, another came and said, "The Chaldeans formed three columns, made a raid on the camels and carried them off, and killed the servants with the edge of the sword; I alone have escaped to tell you." [18]While he was still speaking, another came and said, "Your sons and daughters were eating and drinking wine in their eldest brother's house, [19]and suddenly a great wind came across the desert, struck the four corners of the house, and it fell on the young people, and they are dead; I alone have escaped to tell you."

20 Then Job arose, tore his robe, shaved his head, and fell on the ground and worshiped. [21]He said, "Naked I came from my mother's womb, and naked shall I return there; the LORD gave, and the LORD has taken away; blessed be the name of the LORD."

22 In all this Job did not sin or charge God with wrongdoing.

1.13–22: Earthly scene II: All that Job has is taken away but Job does not curse God. With divine permission, Satan instigates four attacks, by two peoples (Sabeans, Chaldeans) and two natural forces (the fire of God, a great wind), to wipe out Job's animals, servants, and children. **15:** *The Sabeans* lived in southwest Arabia, contemporary Yemen. Here they must be members of a caravan. **17:** *The Chaldeans* were the rulers of the sixth-century Neo-Babylonian Empire, named here probably to characterize the eastern raiders as devastating. **21–22:** Dramatic suspense is built by postponing Job's response. Contrary to Satan's prediction (v. 11), Job does not curse God but worships and blesses in the sense of praising and acknowledging God's power as almighty.

2 One day the heavenly beings[a] came to present themselves before the LORD, and Satan[b] also came among them to present himself before the LORD. [2]The LORD said to Satan,[b] "Where have you come from?" Satan[c] answered the LORD, "From going to and fro on the earth, and from walking up and down on it." [3]The LORD said to Satan,[b] "Have you considered my servant Job? There is no one like him on the earth, a blameless and upright man who fears God and turns away from evil. He still persists in his integrity, although you incited me against him, to destroy him for no reason." [4]Then Satan[b] answered the LORD, "Skin for skin! All that people have they will give to save their lives.[d] [5]But stretch out your hand now and touch his bone and his flesh, and he will curse you to your face." [6]The LORD said to Satan,[b] "Very well, he is in your power; only spare his life."

7 So Satan[b] went out from the presence of the LORD, and inflicted loathsome sores on Job from the sole of his foot to the crown of his head. [8]Job[e] took a potsherd with which to scrape himself, and sat among the ashes.

2.1–7: Heavenly scene II: Conversation of God with Satan. 3: *You incited me against him, to destroy him for no reason*, a seemingly shocking statement made by God. What is happening to Job is the result of a wager in heaven about which he knows nothing. **4:** *Skin for skin!* A proverbial statement apparently meaning that people will only act out of self-interest. **5–6:** Satan will not concede defeat; he moves to a new level. If I can touch Job's very self, *his bone and his flesh*, as opposed to his property and his children, *he will curse you to your face*. The LORD agrees to extend the test to affect Job's person. The LORD will not speak again until ch. 38. **7:** The scene now shifts from heaven to earth.

9 Then his wife said to him, "Do you still persist in your integrity? Curse[f] God, and die." [10]But he said to her, "You speak as any foolish woman would speak. Shall we receive the good at the hand of God, and not receive the bad?" In all this Job did not sin with his lips.

a Heb *sons of God*   b Or *the Accuser*; Heb *ha-satan*
c Or *The Accuser*; Heb *ha-satan*   d Or *All that the man has he will give for his life*   e Heb *He*
f Heb *Bless*

2.8–10: Earthly scene III: Satan strikes Job. Job's *loathsome sores* mean he is seriously ill and isolated from ordinary social relationships. **9–10:** Job's wife has suffered the same losses as he. She unwittingly quotes both God (2.3) and Satan (1.11; 2.5) and unwittingly recognizes that it is Job's integrity that has brought down him and his household.

11 Now when Job's three friends heard of all these troubles that had come upon him, each of them set out from his home—Eliphaz the Temanite, Bildad the Shuhite, and Zophar the Naamathite. They met together to go and console and comfort him. 12When they saw him from a distance, they did not recognize him, and they raised their voices and wept aloud; they tore their robes and threw dust in the air upon their heads. 13They sat with him on the ground seven days and seven nights, and no one spoke a word to him, for they saw that his suffering was very great.

2.11–13: Introduction of Job's three friends and transition to the dialogues. 11: All three proper names and place names have some relationship to Edom; they come from the East, a part of the world known for its wise discourse. Teman is in Edom (Jer 49.7, 20). Naamah seems to be in central or south Arabia. **13:** The friends' extraordinary lengthy silence reflects Job's extraordinary and unmatched suffering.

FIRST CYCLE OF SPEECHES BEGINS

Ch. 3: Job's curse and lament.* Job's wife had said "Curse God, and die" (2.9), and, initially, Job utters a curse and wants to die. In the course of the dialogues, however, he becomes active in pursuit of justice. Job's curse, like his later oath in 27.2–5 and his challenge to God in 31.35–37, provokes a vigorous response in his friends.

3 After this Job opened his mouth and cursed the day of his birth. 2Job said:
3 "Let the day perish in which I was born,
  and the night that said,
  'A man-child is conceived.'
4 Let that day be darkness!
  May God above not seek it,
  or light shine on it.

5 Let gloom and deep darkness claim it.
  Let clouds settle upon it;
  let the blackness of the day terrify it.
6 That night—let thick darkness seize it!
  let it not rejoice among the days of
    the year;
  let it not come into the number of the
    months.
7 Yes, let that night be barren;
  let no joyful cry be heard*a* in it.
8 Let those curse it who curse the Sea,*b*
  those who are skilled to rouse up
    Leviathan.
9 Let the stars of its dawn be dark;
  let it hope for light, but have none;
  may it not see the eyelids of the
    morning—
10 because it did not shut the doors of my
    mother's womb,
  and hide trouble from my eyes.

11 "Why did I not die at birth,
  come forth from the womb and
    expire?
12 Why were there knees to receive me,
  or breasts for me to suck?
13 Now I would be lying down and quiet;
  I would be asleep; then I would be at
    rest
14 with kings and counselors of the earth
  who rebuild ruins for themselves,
15 or with princes who have gold,
  who fill their houses with silver.
16 Or why was I not buried like a stillborn
    child,
  like an infant that never sees the
    light?
17 There the wicked cease from troubling,
  and there the weary are at rest.
18 There the prisoners are at ease together;
  they do not hear the voice of the
    taskmaster.
19 The small and the great are there,
  and the slaves are free from their
    masters.

20 "Why is light given to one in misery,
  and life to the bitter in soul,

a Heb *come*   *b* Cn: Heb *day*

21 who long for death, but it does not
　　　come,
　　and dig for it more than for hidden
　　　treasures;
22 who rejoice exceedingly,
　　and are glad when they find the
　　　grave?
23 Why is light given to one who cannot
　　　see the way,
　　whom God has fenced in?
24 For my sighing comes like[a] my bread,
　　and my groanings are poured out like
　　　water.
25 Truly the thing that I fear comes upon
　　　me,
　　and what I dread befalls me.
26 I am not at ease, nor am I quiet;
　　I have no rest; but trouble comes."

3.1–26. 3–10: Job curses the day of his birth, wishing
he had never been born. **11–26:** *Why* (vv. 11, 12, 16,
20, 23) pervades biblical laments (Ps 10.1, 13; 22.1;
44.23), demanding from God an explanation of an unfair situation. **23:** *Fenced in:* In 1.10 Satan accused God
of fencing in Job in the sense of protecting him, but
Job sees God's fencing him in as a hostile act.

The response of Eliphaz the Temanite

Chs 4–5: Eliphaz rebukes Job for not acting like a sage
and for forgetting that the innocent are cared for (4.2–
11). From a dream Eliphaz has learned just how insignificant human beings are before their *Maker* (4.12–
21). No need for vexation, he assures Job, the universe
will turn against the wicked (5.1–7). Rather, trust God
who acts justly (5.8–16), for you shall be safe as God
effects justice on earth (5.17–27).

4 Then Eliphaz the Temanite answered:
　2 "If one ventures a word with you,
　　will you be offended?
　　But who can keep from speaking?
3 See, you have instructed many;
　　you have strengthened the weak
　　　hands.
4 Your words have supported those who
　　　were stumbling,
　　and you have made firm the feeble
　　　knees.
5 But now it has come to you, and you are
　　　impatient;
　　it touches you, and you are dismayed.

6 Is not your fear of God your confidence,
　　and the integrity of your ways your
　　　hope?
7 "Think now, who that was innocent ever
　　　perished?
　　Or where were the upright cut off?
8 As I have seen, those who plow iniquity
　　and sow trouble reap the same.
9 By the breath of God they perish,
　　and by the blast of his anger they are
　　　consumed.
10 The roar of the lion, the voice of the
　　　fierce lion,
　　and the teeth of the young lions are
　　　broken.
11 The strong lion perishes for lack of prey,
　　and the whelps of the lioness are
　　　scattered.

12 "Now a word came stealing to me,
　　my ear received the whisper of it.
13 Amid thoughts from visions of the
　　　night,
　　when deep sleep falls on mortals,
14 dread came upon me, and trembling,
　　which made all my bones shake.
15 A spirit glided past my face;
　　the hair of my flesh bristled.
16 It stood still,
　　but I could not discern its
　　　appearance.
　A form was before my eyes;
　　there was silence, then I heard a
　　　voice:
17 'Can mortals be righteous before[b]
　　　God?
　　Can human beings be pure before[b]
　　　their Maker?
18 Even in his servants he puts no trust,
　　and his angels he charges with error;
19 how much more those who live in
　　　houses of clay,
　　whose foundation is in the dust,
　　who are crushed like a moth.
20 Between morning and evening they are
　　　destroyed;
　　they perish forever without any
　　　regarding it.

a Heb *before*　　*b* Or *more than*

21 Their tent-cord is plucked up within
them,
and they die devoid of wisdom.'

5 "Call now; is there anyone who will
answer you?
To which of the holy ones will you turn?
2 Surely vexation kills the fool,
and jealousy slays the simple.
3 I have seen fools taking root,
but suddenly I cursed their dwelling.
4 Their children are far from safety,
they are crushed in the gate,
and there is no one to deliver them.
5 The hungry eat their harvest,
and they take it even out of the
thorns;[a]
and the thirsty[b] pant after their
wealth.
6 For misery does not come from the
earth,
nor does trouble sprout from the
ground;
7 but human beings are born to trouble
just as sparks[c] fly upward.

8 "As for me, I would seek God,
and to God I would commit my
cause.
9 He does great things and unsearchable,
marvelous things without number.
10 He gives rain on the earth
and sends waters on the fields;
11 he sets on high those who are lowly,
and those who mourn are lifted to
safety.
12 He frustrates the devices of the crafty,
so that their hands achieve no
success.
13 He takes the wise in their own
craftiness;
and the schemes of the wily are
brought to a quick end.
14 They meet with darkness in the
daytime,
and grope at noonday as in the night.
15 But he saves the needy from the sword
of their mouth,
from the hand of the mighty.
16 So the poor have hope,
and injustice shuts its mouth.

17 "How happy is the one whom God
reproves;
therefore do not despise the discipline
of the Almighty.[d]
18 For he wounds, but he binds up;
he strikes, but his hands heal.
19 He will deliver you from six troubles;
in seven no harm shall touch you.
20 In famine he will redeem you from
death,
and in war from the power of the
sword.
21 You shall be hidden from the scourge of
the tongue,
and shall not fear destruction when it
comes.
22 At destruction and famine you shall
laugh,
and shall not fear the wild animals of
the earth.
23 For you shall be in league with the
stones of the field,
and the wild animals shall be at peace
with you.
24 You shall know that your tent is safe,
you shall inspect your fold and miss
nothing.
25 You shall know that your descendants
will be many,
and your offspring like the grass of
the earth.
26 You shall come to your grave in ripe old
age,
as a shock of grain comes up to the
threshing floor in its season.
27 See, we have searched this out; it is
true.
Hear, and know it for yourself."

4.1–5.27. 4.12–21: Eliphaz's first statement to Job is
based not on traditional lore, as one might expect, but
on a vision in the night, like Abraham's (Gen 15.12).
The content—human beings are insignificant before
their creator—is nonetheless quite traditional. 5.1: To
which of the holy ones will you turn? That human beings are fragile and transient is so obvious that no one,
not even a heavenly being (holy ones), will deny it. 17:

a Meaning of Heb uncertain   b Aquila Symmachus
Syr Vg: Heb snare   c Or birds; Heb sons of Resheph
d Traditional rendering of Heb Shaddai

Discipline ("musar") is the training employed by a wisdom teacher; it may involve chastisement but has as its goal the acquisition of wisdom.

Job's first response

Chs. 6–7: Job explains that his passionate complaint arises from intense suffering (6.2–7), reaffirms his desire that God annihilate him (6.8–13), rebukes and entreats his friends (6.14–30), and reflects on the miserable lot of the human race (7.1–21).

6 Then Job answered:

2 "O that my vexation were weighed,
    and all my calamity laid in the balances!
3 For then it would be heavier than the sand of the sea;
    therefore my words have been rash.
4 For the arrows of the Almighty[a] are in me;
    my spirit drinks their poison;
    the terrors of God are arrayed against me.
5 Does the wild ass bray over its grass,
    or the ox low over its fodder?
6 Can that which is tasteless be eaten without salt,
    or is there any flavor in the juice of mallows?[b]
7 My appetite refuses to touch them;
    they are like food that is loathsome to me.[b]

8 "O that I might have my request,
    and that God would grant my desire;
9 that it would please God to crush me,
    that he would let loose his hand and cut me off!
10 This would be my consolation;
    I would even exult[b] in unrelenting pain;
    for I have not denied the words of the Holy One.
11 What is my strength, that I should wait?
    And what is my end, that I should be patient?
12 Is my strength the strength of stones,
    or is my flesh bronze?
13 In truth I have no help in me,
    and any resource is driven from me.

14 "Those who withhold[c] kindness from a friend
    forsake the fear of the Almighty.[a]
15 My companions are treacherous like a torrent-bed,
    like freshets that pass away,
16 that run dark with ice,
    turbid with melting snow.
17 In time of heat they disappear;
    when it is hot, they vanish from their place.
18 The caravans turn aside from their course;
    they go up into the waste, and perish.
19 The caravans of Tema look,
    the travelers of Sheba hope.
20 They are disappointed because they were confident;
    they come there and are confounded.
21 Such you have now become to me;[d]
    you see my calamity, and are afraid.
22 Have I said, 'Make me a gift'?
    Or, 'From your wealth offer a bribe for me'?
23 Or, 'Save me from an opponent's hand'?
    Or, 'Ransom me from the hand of oppressors'?

24 "Teach me, and I will be silent;
    make me understand how I have gone wrong.
25 How forceful are honest words!
    But your reproof, what does it reprove?
26 Do you think that you can reprove words,
    as if the speech of the desperate were wind?
27 You would even cast lots over the orphan,
    and bargain over your friend.

28 "But now, be pleased to look at me;
    for I will not lie to your face.
29 Turn, I pray, let no wrong be done.
    Turn now, my vindication is at stake.
30 Is there any wrong on my tongue?
    Cannot my taste discern calamity?

a Traditional rendering of Heb *Shaddai*   *b* Meaning of Heb uncertain   *c* Syr Vg Compare Tg: Meaning of Heb uncertain   *d* Cn Compare Gk Syr: Meaning of Heb uncertain

7 "Do not human beings have a hard
service on earth,
and are not their days like the days of
a laborer?
2 Like a slave who longs for the shadow,
and like laborers who look for their
wages,
3 so I am allotted months of emptiness,
and nights of misery are apportioned
to me.
4 When I lie down I say, 'When shall I
rise?'
But the night is long,
and I am full of tossing until dawn.
5 My flesh is clothed with worms and
dirt;
my skin hardens, then breaks out
again.
6 My days are swifter than a weaver's
shuttle,
and come to their end without hope.*a*

7 "Remember that my life is a breath;
my eye will never again see good.
8 The eye that beholds me will see me no
more;
while your eyes are upon me, I shall
be gone.
9 As the cloud fades and vanishes,
so those who go down to Sheol do not
come up;
10 they return no more to their houses,
nor do their places know them any
more.

11 "Therefore I will not restrain my mouth;
I will speak in the anguish of my
spirit;
I will complain in the bitterness of my
soul.
12 Am I the Sea, or the Dragon,
that you set a guard over me?
13 When I say, 'My bed will comfort me,
my couch will ease my complaint,'
14 then you scare me with dreams
and terrify me with visions,
15 so that I would choose strangling
and death rather than this body.
16 I loathe my life; I would not live forever.
Let me alone, for my days are a
breath.

17 What are human beings, that you make
so much of them,
that you set your mind on them,
18 visit them every morning,
test them every moment?
19 Will you not look away from me for a
while,
let me alone until I swallow my
spittle?
20 If I sin, what do I do to you, you
watcher of humanity?
Why have you made me your target?
Why have I become a burden to
you?
21 Why do you not pardon my
transgression
and take away my iniquity?
For now I shall lie in the earth;
you will seek me, but I shall not be."

6.1–7.21. 6.2: *Vexation* is the mark of a fool (5.2), but Job pleads his own terrible suffering as the source of his vexation. If it could be *weighed*, his friends might see and understand. **5–7:** Obscure. Possibly, Job expresses a desire for the "food" of sympathy. See Ps 69.20–21. **8–13:** At this point, Job is overwhelmed and simply wants annihilation. He expressed the same wish in ch. 3. **14–30:** From his bitter depiction of false friends (vv. 14–21), disappointment at their lack of sympathy (vv. 22–27), and touching final plea (vv. 28–30), Job shows how deeply his friends have wounded and disappointed him. **7.1–21:** A lament* in three sections (vv. 1–8, 9–16, 17–21). Instead of following the lament convention of mentioning the brevity and misery of human life as a means of winning God's favor, Job blames God for humanity's (and his own) suffering (7.8, 12–16, 30). **12:** *The Sea, or the Dragon:* In mythological texts of neighboring cultures, the storm god had to defeat a monstrous personified* sea to become the chief god. The Bible adapted the myth to portray the God of Israel as supreme. Job is sarcastic: Why do you hurt me? I am not important to you. **17–18:** Continuing in the sarcastic vein, Job parodies the words of Ps 8.4: "What are human beings that you are mindful of them, / mortals that you care for them?" Instead of caring for human beings, God scrutinizes them, becoming a *watcher of humanity* (7.20).

a Or *as the thread runs out*

8 Then Bildad the Shuhite answered:
2 "How long will you say these things,
 and the words of your mouth be a
 great wind?
3 Does God pervert justice?
 Or does the Almighty* pervert the
 right?
4 If your children sinned against him,
 he delivered them into the power of
 their transgression.
5 If you will seek God
 and make supplication to the
 Almighty,*
6 if you are pure and upright,
 surely then he will rouse himself for
 you
 and restore to you your rightful place.
7 Though your beginning was small,
 your latter days will be very great.

8 "For inquire now of bygone generations,
 and consider what their ancestors
 have found;
9 for we are but of yesterday, and we
 know nothing,
 for our days on earth are but a
 shadow.
10 Will they not teach you and tell you
 and utter words out of their
 understanding?

11 "Can papyrus grow where there is no
 marsh?
 Can reeds flourish where there is no
 water?
12 While yet in flower and not cut down,
 they wither before any other plant.
13 Such are the paths of all who forget
 God;
 the hope of the godless shall perish.
14 Their confidence is gossamer,
 a spider's house their trust.
15 If one leans against its house, it will not
 stand;
 if one lays hold of it, it will not
 endure.
16 The wicked thrive*b* before the sun,
 and their shoots spread over the
 garden.
17 Their roots twine around the stoneheap;
 they live among the rocks.*c*

18 If they are destroyed from their place,
 then it will deny them, saying, 'I have
 never seen you.'
19 See, these are their happy ways,*d*
 and out of the earth still others will
 spring.

20 "See, God will not reject a blameless
 person,
 nor take the hand of evildoers.
21 He will yet fill your mouth with
 laughter,
 and your lips with shouts of joy.
22 Those who hate you will be clothed with
 shame,
 and the tent of the wicked will be no
 more."

8.1–22: The response of Bildad the Shuhite. 3: *Does God pervert justice?* Justice in the biblical sense involves upholding the innocent and punishing the guilty. Bildad is shocked that Job would deny God is just. **4:** *Your children:* Because of his simple understanding of justice (sin deserves punishment, therefore punishment only follows sin), Bildad judges the slaughter of Job's children to be due to their sin. **11–12:** Evidently proverbial: Just as plants need water, so human beings need life. **13–19:** Difficult. Some assume two plants are compared as in Ps 1 and Jer 17.5–8: One plant, symbolizing the wicked, withers quickly (vv. 12–15), whereas the other plant (reading "the other" in place of *the wicked* in v. 16) survives. The example of the two plants is meant to bring Job to repentance.

Job's second response
Chs. 9–10: Job admits the uselessness of entering into litigation with God. He takes the friends' statements about divine justice in a strictly legal sense. For example, Eliphaz asked in 4.17 whether mortals can be righteous before God. Job interprets "righteous" as winning a legal case (9.2). Other instances of legal language are 9.2–3, 14–16, 19–21, 24.

9 Then Job answered:
2 "Indeed I know that this is so;
 but how can a mortal be just before
 God?

a Traditional rendering of Heb *Shaddai*   b Heb *He thrives*   c Gk Vg Meaning of Heb uncertain   d Meaning of Heb uncertain

3 If one wished to contend with him,
   one could not answer him once in a
   thousand.
4 He is wise in heart, and mighty in
   strength
   —who has resisted him, and
   succeeded?—
5 he who removes mountains, and they do
   not know it,
   when he overturns them in his
   anger;
6 who shakes the earth out of its place,
   and its pillars tremble;
7 who commands the sun, and it does not
   rise;
   who seals up the stars;
8 who alone stretched out the heavens
   and trampled the waves of the Sea;ª
9 who made the Bear and Orion,
   the Pleiades and the chambers of the
   south;
10 who does great things beyond
   understanding,
   and marvelous things without
   number.
11 Look, he passes by me, and I do not see
   him;
   he moves on, but I do not perceive
   him.
12 He snatches away; who can stop him?
   Who will say to him, 'What are you
   doing?'
13 "God will not turn back his anger;
   the helpers of Rahab bowed beneath
   him.
14 How then can I answer him,
   choosing my words with him?
15 Though I am innocent, I cannot answer
   him;
   I must appeal for mercy to my
   accuser.ᵇ
16 If I summoned him and he answered
   me,
   I do not believe that he would listen
   to my voice.
17 For he crushes me with a tempest,
   and multiplies my wounds without
   cause;
18 he will not let me get my breath,
   but fills me with bitterness.

19 If it is a contest of strength, he is the
   strong one!
   If it is a matter of justice, who can
   summon him?ᶜ
20 Though I am innocent, my own mouth
   would condemn me;
   though I am blameless, he would
   prove me perverse.
21 I am blameless; I do not know myself;
   I loathe my life.
22 It is all one; therefore I say,
   he destroys both the blameless and
   the wicked.
23 When disaster brings sudden death,
   he mocks at the calamityᵈ of the
   innocent.
24 The earth is given into the hand of the
   wicked;
   he covers the eyes of its judges—
   if it is not he, who then is it?

25 "My days are swifter than a runner;
   they flee away, they see no good.
26 They go by like skiffs of reed,
   like an eagle swooping on the prey.
27 If I say, 'I will forget my complaint;
   I will put off my sad countenance and
   be of good cheer,'
28 I become afraid of all my suffering,
   for I know you will not hold me
   innocent.
29 I shall be condemned;
   why then do I labor in vain?
30 If I wash myself with soap
   and cleanse my hands with lye,
31 yet you will plunge me into filth,
   and my own clothes will abhor me.
32 For he is not a mortal, as I am, that I
   might answer him,
   that we should come to trial together.
33 There is no umpireᵉ between us,
   who might lay his hand on us both.
34 If he would take his rod away from me,
   and not let dread of him terrify me,
35 then I would speak without fear of him,
   for I know I am not what I am
   thought to be.ᶠ

a Or *trampled the back of the sea dragon*   b Or *for my
right*   c Compare Gk: Heb *me*   d Meaning of Heb
uncertain   e Another reading is *Would that there were
an umpire*   f Cn: Heb *for I am not so in myself*

9.1–35. 2–3: *Be just before God . . . contend with him . . . answer him:* Job responds to Bildad's assertion in 8.20 ("God will not reject a blameless person") in a strictly legal sense: God will not be summoned into court so that an accused person can be found guilty (rejected, 8.20) or declared innocent (9.20). **4–13:** God is beyond responding to human requests. **25–35:** Job considers three alternatives to taking God to court, only to reject them as impossible: (1) if he drops charges, God will find him guilty anyway (9.25–29); (2) if he attempts to purge himself as in Ps 51.7, God will make him filthy again (9.30–31); (3) there is no one impartial adjudicator (*umpire;* 9.32–35).

10

"I loathe my life;
I will give free utterance to my
complaint;
I will speak in the bitterness of my
soul.

2 I will say to God, Do not condemn me;
let me know why you contend against
me.

3 Does it seem good to you to oppress,
to despise the work of your hands
and favor the schemes of the wicked?

4 Do you have eyes of flesh?
Do you see as humans see?

5 Are your days like the days of mortals,
or your years like human years,

6 that you seek out my iniquity
and search for my sin,

7 although you know that I am not guilty,
and there is no one to deliver out of
your hand?

8 Your hands fashioned and made me;
and now you turn and destroy me.[a]

9 Remember that you fashioned me like
clay;
and will you turn me to dust again?

10 Did you not pour me out like milk
and curdle me like cheese?

11 You clothed me with skin and flesh,
and knit me together with bones and
sinews.

12 You have granted me life and steadfast
love,
and your care has preserved my
spirit.

13 Yet these things you hid in your heart;
I know that this was your purpose.

14 If I sin, you watch me,
and do not acquit me of my iniquity.

15 If I am wicked, woe to me!
If I am righteous, I cannot lift up my
head,
for I am filled with disgrace
and look upon my affliction.

16 Bold as a lion you hunt me;
you repeat your exploits against me.

17 You renew your witnesses against me,
and increase your vexation toward
me;
you bring fresh troops against me.[b]

10.8–17: Though Job expects no justice, he nonetheless lists his charges against God: You, the one who brought me into being, nonetheless seek to destroy me!

18 "Why did you bring me forth from the
womb?
Would that I had died before any eye
had seen me,

19 and were as though I had not been,
carried from the womb to the grave.

20 Are not the days of my life few?[c]
Let me alone, that I may find a little
comfort[d]

21 before I go, never to return,
to the land of gloom and deep
darkness,

22 the land of gloom[e] and chaos,
where light is like darkness."

The response of Zophar the Naamathite

Ch 11: Zophar accuses Job of malice in maintaining his innocence (vv. 2–12) and urges him to turn to God, an act of repentance that will assure him prosperity (vv. 13–20). There is profound irony* in Zophar's assertion of a hidden dimension in wisdom (vv. 6–12) and of the untroubled existence of the just (v. 20). The reader knows from chs. 1–2 of God's wager, hidden from the actors, and that it is precisely because Job is just that he suffers.

a Cn Compare Gk Syr: Heb *made me together all around, and you destroy me*   *b* Cn Compare Gk: Heb *toward me; changes and a troop are with me*   *c* Cn Compare Gk Syr: Heb *Are not my days few? Let him cease!*   *d* Heb *that I may brighten up a little*   *e* Heb *gloom as darkness, deep darkness*

11

Then Zophar the Naamathite answered:

2 "Should a multitude of words go
unanswered,
and should one full of talk be
vindicated?
3 Should your babble put others to
silence,
and when you mock, shall no one
shame you?
4 For you say, 'My conduct*a* is pure,
and I am clean in God's*b* sight.'
5 But O that God would speak,
and open his lips to you,
6 and that he would tell you the secrets of
wisdom!
For wisdom is many-sided.*c*
Know then that God exacts of you less
than your guilt deserves.

7 "Can you find out the deep things of
God?
Can you find out the limit of the
Almighty?*d*
8 It is higher than heaven*e*—what can
you do?
Deeper than Sheol—what can you
know?
9 Its measure is longer than the earth,
and broader than the sea.
10 If he passes through, and imprisons,
and assembles for judgment, who can
hinder him?
11 For he knows those who are worthless;
when he sees iniquity, will he not
consider it?
12 But a stupid person will get
understanding,
when a wild ass is born human.*c*

13 "If you direct your heart rightly,
you will stretch out your hands
toward him.
14 If iniquity is in your hand, put it far
away,
and do not let wickedness reside in
your tents.
15 Surely then you will lift up your face
without blemish;
you will be secure, and will not fear.

16 You will forget your misery;
you will remember it as waters that
have passed away.
17 And your life will be brighter than the
noonday;
its darkness will be like the morning.
18 And you will have confidence, because
there is hope;
you will be protected*f* and take your
rest in safety.
19 You will lie down, and no one will make
you afraid;
many will entreat your favor.
20 But the eyes of the wicked will fail;
all way of escape will be lost to
them,
and their hope is to breathe their
last."

Job's third response

Chs. 12–14: Job's speech is the climax✶ of the first
cycle. In essence, he denounces the friends for presuming to speak for God who, being all wise and powerful
(12.13, 16), is responsible for everything that takes
place (12.13–13.5). Job wants only to be allowed to
bring his case directly before God (13.6–28). The prospect brings home to Job how fragile is humanity's grip
on life (14.1–22).

12

Then Job answered:
2 "No doubt you are the people,
and wisdom will die with you.
3 But I have understanding as well as
you;
I am not inferior to you.
Who does not know such things as
these?
4 I am a laughingstock to my friends;
I, who called upon God and he
answered me,
a just and blameless man, I am a
laughingstock.
5 Those at ease have contempt for
misfortune,*c*
but it is ready for those whose feet
are unstable.

---

a Gk: Heb *teaching*   *b* Heb *your*   *c* Meaning of
Heb uncertain   *d* Traditional rendering of Heb
Shaddai   *e* Heb *The heights of heaven*   *f* Or *you will
look around*

6 The tents of robbers are at peace,
　　and those who provoke God are
　　　　secure,
　　who bring their god in their hands.*a*

7 "But ask the animals, and they will
　　　　teach you;
　　the birds of the air, and they will tell
　　　　you;
8 ask the plants of the earth,*b* and they
　　　　will teach you;
　　and the fish of the sea will declare to
　　　　you.
9 Who among all these does not know
　　that the hand of the LORD has done
　　　　this?
10 In his hand is the life of every living
　　　　thing
　　and the breath of every human being.
11 Does not the ear test words
　　as the palate tastes food?
12 Is wisdom with the aged,
　　and understanding in length of days?

12.1–12. 1: *You are the people:* Probably, short for
people with land, the elite who believe they alone are
wise. **7:** *Ask the animals:* In ch. 8 Bildad urged inquiring
of "bygone generations" (v. 8), that is, tradition, to
demonstrate a point. Here, Job says that even animals
know that nothing happens without God.

~~~~~~~~~~~~~~~~~

13 "With God*c* are wisdom and strength;
　　he has counsel and understanding.
14 If he tears down, no one can rebuild;
　　if he shuts someone in, no one can
　　　　open up.
15 If he withholds the waters, they dry up;
　　if he sends them out, they overwhelm
　　　　the land.
16 With him are strength and wisdom;
　　the deceived and the deceiver are his.
17 He leads counselors away stripped,
　　and makes fools of judges.
18 He looses the sash of kings,
　　and binds a waistcloth on their loins.
19 He leads priests away stripped,
　　and overthrows the mighty.
20 He deprives of speech those who are
　　　　trusted,
　　and takes away the discernment of
　　　　the elders.

21 He pours contempt on princes,
　　and looses the belt of the strong.
22 He uncovers the deeps out of darkness,
　　and brings deep darkness to light.
23 He makes nations great, then destroys
　　　　them;
　　he enlarges nations, then leads them
　　　　away.
24 He strips understanding from the
　　　　leaders*d* of the earth,
　　and makes them wander in a pathless
　　　　waste.
25 They grope in the dark without light;
　　he makes them stagger like a
　　　　drunkard.

13 "Look, my eye has seen all this,
　　my ear has heard and understood it.
2 What you know, I also know;
　　I am not inferior to you.
3 But I would speak to the Almighty,*e*
　　and I desire to argue my case with
　　　　God.
4 As for you, you whitewash with lies;
　　all of you are worthless physicians.
5 If you would only keep silent,
　　that would be your wisdom!
6 Hear now my reasoning,
　　and listen to the pleadings of my lips.
7 Will you speak falsely for God,
　　and speak deceitfully for him?
8 Will you show partiality toward him,
　　will you plead the case for God?
9 Will it be well with you when he
　　　　searches you out?
　　Or can you deceive him, as one
　　　　person deceives another?
10 He will surely rebuke you
　　if in secret you show partiality.
11 Will not his majesty terrify you,
　　and the dread of him fall upon you?
12 Your maxims are proverbs of ashes,
　　your defenses are defenses of clay.

13.3: *I would speak to the Almighty:* In his earlier
speeches (3.3–26; 6.8–10), Job wanted to disappear,
but a desire to confront God directly has begun to

a Or *whom God brought forth by his hand;* Meaning of
Heb uncertain　　*b* Or *speak to the earth*　　*c* Heb *him*
d Heb adds *of the people*　　*e* Traditional rendering of
Heb *Shaddai*

emerge, probably because of the mockery of the friends (12.4) and their claim that he is unaware of the hidden dimension of wisdom (11.6–12).

〰〰〰〰〰〰〰〰〰〰〰〰〰〰〰

13 "Let me have silence, and I will speak,
and let come on me what may.
14 I will take my flesh in my teeth,
and put my life in my hand.*a*
15 See, he will kill me; I have no hope;*b*
but I will defend my ways to his
face.
16 This will be my salvation,
that the godless shall not come before
him.
17 Listen carefully to my words,
and let my declaration be in your
ears.
18 I have indeed prepared my case;
I know that I shall be vindicated.
19 Who is there that will contend with
me?
For then I would be silent and die.
20 Only grant two things to me,
then I will not hide myself from your
face:
21 withdraw your hand far from me,
and do not let dread of you terrify me.
22 Then call, and I will answer;
or let me speak, and you reply to me.
23 How many are my iniquities and my
sins?
Make me know my transgression and
my sin.
24 Why do you hide your face,
and count me as your enemy?
25 Will you frighten a windblown leaf
and pursue dry chaff?
26 For you write bitter things against me,
and make me reap*c* the iniquities of
my youth.
27 You put my feet in the stocks,
and watch all my paths;
you set a bound to the soles of my
feet.
28 One wastes away like a rotten thing,
like a garment that is moth-eaten.

14 "A mortal, born of woman, few of
days and full of trouble,
2 comes up like a flower and withers,
flees like a shadow and does not last.

3 Do you fix your eyes on such a one?
Do you bring me into judgment with
you?
4 Who can bring a clean thing out of an
unclean?
No one can.
5 Since their days are determined,
and the number of their months is
known to you,
and you have appointed the bounds
that they cannot pass,
6 look away from them, and desist,*d*
that they may enjoy, like laborers,
their days.

7 "For there is hope for a tree,
if it is cut down, that it will sprout
again,
and that its shoots will not cease.
8 Though its root grows old in the
earth,
and its stump dies in the ground,
9 yet at the scent of water it will bud
and put forth branches like a young
plant.
10 But mortals die, and are laid low;
humans expire, and where are they?
11 As waters fail from a lake,
and a river wastes away and dries up,
12 so mortals lie down and do not rise
again;
until the heavens are no more, they
will not awake
or be roused out of their sleep.
13 O that you would hide me in Sheol,
that you would conceal me until your
wrath is past,
that you would appoint me a set time,
and remember me!
14 If mortals die, will they live again?
All the days of my service I would
wait
until my release should come.
15 You would call, and I would answer
you;
you would long for the work of your
hands.

a Gk: Heb *Why should I take . . . in my hand?*
b Or *Though he kill me, yet I will trust in him*
c Heb *inherit*   d Cn: Heb *that they may desist*

16 For then you would not*a* number my
      steps,
   you would not keep watch over my
      sin;
17 my transgression would be sealed up in
      a bag,
   and you would cover over my
      iniquity.

18 "But the mountain falls and crumbles
      away,
   and the rock is removed from its
      place;
19 the waters wear away the stones;
   the torrents wash away the soil of the
      earth;
   so you destroy the hope of mortals.
20 You prevail forever against them, and
      they pass away;
   you change their countenance, and
      send them away.
21 Their children come to honor, and they
      do not know it;
   they are brought low, and it goes
      unnoticed.
22 They feel only the pain of their own
      bodies,
   and mourn only for themselves."

14.1–22: In vv. 1–6, Job underlines the brevity of human life, asking how God can possibly bring such a miserable creature into judgment (vv. 3–4). In vv. 7–22, Job draws a comparison between the brief human life span and trees ever renewed by water (vv. 7–9) and mountains worn slowly away by water (vv. 18–19). In between he entertains the impossible hope that he might escape the constraints of mortality and be enabled to speak with God beyond the grave (vv. 10–17).

THE BEGINNING OF THE SECOND CYCLE OF SPEECHES

Ch. 15: The response of Eliphaz. Job's talk, according to Eliphaz, does away with genuine religion (vv. 4–6), presumes he has access to the divine assembly (vv. 8–9), and fails to reckon with the insignificance of human beings before God (vv. 12–16). The sages teach that the wicked are severely punished and endure frustration (vv. 17–35).

---

15 Then Eliphaz the Temanite answered:
2 "Should the wise answer with windy
      knowledge,
   and fill themselves with the east
      wind?
3 Should they argue in unprofitable
      talk,
   or in words with which they can do
      no good?
4 But you are doing away with the fear of
      God,
   and hindering meditation before God.
5 For your iniquity teaches your mouth,
   and you choose the tongue of the
      crafty.
6 Your own mouth condemns you, and
      not I;
   your own lips testify against you.

7 "Are you the firstborn of the human
      race?
   Were you brought forth before the
      hills?
8 Have you listened in the council of God?
   And do you limit wisdom to yourself?
9 What do you know that we do not
      know?
   What do you understand that is not
      clear to us?
10 The gray-haired and the aged are on our
      side,
   those older than your father.
11 Are the consolations of God too small
      for you,
   or the word that deals gently with
      you?
12 Why does your heart carry you away,
   and why do your eyes flash,*b*
13 so that you turn your spirit against God,
   and let such words go out of your
      mouth?
14 What are mortals, that they can be
      clean?
   Or those born of woman, that they
      can be righteous?
15 God puts no trust even in his holy ones,
   and the heavens are not clean in his
      sight;

---

a Syr: Heb lacks *not*   *b* Meaning of Heb uncertain

16 how much less one who is abominable
and corrupt,
one who drinks iniquity like water!

17 "I will show you; listen to me;
what I have seen I will declare—

18 what sages have told,
and their ancestors have not hidden,

19 to whom alone the land was given,
and no stranger passed among them.

20 The wicked writhe in pain all their days,
through all the years that are laid up
for the ruthless.

21 Terrifying sounds are in their ears;
in prosperity the destroyer will come
upon them.

22 They despair of returning from
darkness,
and they are destined for the sword.

23 They wander abroad for bread, saying,
'Where is it?'
They know that a day of darkness is
ready at hand;

24 distress and anguish terrify them;
they prevail against them, like a king
prepared for battle.

25 Because they stretched out their hands
against God,
and bid defiance to the Almighty,ᵃ

26 running stubbornly against him
with a thick-bossed shield;

27 because they have covered their faces
with their fat,
and gathered fat upon their loins,

28 they will live in desolate cities,
in houses that no one should inhabit,
houses destined to become heaps of
ruins;

29 they will not be rich, and their wealth
will not endure,
nor will they strike root in the earth;ᵇ

30 they will not escape from darkness;
the flame will dry up their shoots,
and their blossomᶜ will be swept
awayᵈ by the wind.

31 Let them not trust in emptiness,
deceiving themselves;
for emptiness will be their
recompense.

32 It will be paid in full before their time,
and their branch will not be green.

33 They will shake off their unripe grape,
like the vine,
and cast off their blossoms, like the
olive tree.

34 For the company of the godless is
barren,
and fire consumes the tents of
bribery.

35 They conceive mischief and bring forth
evil
and their heart prepares deceit."

15.1–35. 2: *Should the wise answer with windy knowledge?* Eliphaz begins with an attack on Job's motives, without bothering to listen to his words. The deterioration of Job's relationship to his friends increases his interest in exploring his relationship to God. **7–10:** Eliphaz refers to a legend* of a primordial human being who had access to divine wisdom. The language is similar to that describing wisdom in Prov 8.22–31. **18:** *What sages have told:* Eliphaz's portrayal of the fate of the wicked is an indirect rebuke of Job, for he judges Job wrong in continuing to assert his innocence.

Job's first response in the second cycle
Chs 16–17: Job complains against God (16.6–17), following it with an expression of hope (16.18–17.1). He next complains against his friends (17.2–10), following it with an expression of despair (17.11–16).

---

16 Then Job answered:
2 "I have heard many such
things;
miserable comforters are you all.

3 Have windy words no limit?
Or what provokes you that you keep
on talking?

4 I also could talk as you do,
if you were in my place;
I could join words together against
you,
and shake my head at you.

5 I could encourage you with my mouth,
and the solace of my lips would
assuage your pain.

---

a Traditional rendering of Heb *Shaddai*
b Vg: Meaning of Heb uncertain
c Gk: Heb *mouth*
d Cn: Heb *will depart*

6 "If I speak, my pain is not assuaged,
    and if I forbear, how much of it
        leaves me?
7 Surely now God has worn me out;
    he has[a] made desolate all my
        company.
8 And he has[a] shriveled me up,
    which is a witness against me;
my leanness has risen up against me,
    and it testifies to my face.
9 He has torn me in his wrath, and hated
        me;
    he has gnashed his teeth at me;
    my adversary sharpens his eyes
        against me.
10 They have gaped at me with their
        mouths;
    they have struck me insolently on the
        cheek;
    they mass themselves together against
        me.
11 God gives me up to the ungodly,
    and casts me into the hands of the
        wicked.
12 I was at ease, and he broke me in two;
    he seized me by the neck and dashed
        me to pieces;
    he set me up as his target;
13   his archers surround me.
He slashes open my kidneys, and shows
        no mercy;
    he pours out my gall on the ground.
14 He bursts upon me again and again;
    he rushes at me like a warrior.
15 I have sewed sackcloth upon my skin,
    and have laid my strength in the dust.
16 My face is red with weeping,
    and deep darkness is on my eyelids,
17 though there is no violence in my hands,
    and my prayer is pure.

18 "O earth, do not cover my blood;
    let my outcry find no resting place.
19 Even now, in fact, my witness is in
        heaven,
    and he that vouches for me is on high.
20 My friends scorn me;
    my eye pours out tears to God,
21 that he would maintain the right of a
        mortal with God,
    as[b] one does for a neighbor.

22 For when a few years have come,
    I shall go the way from which I shall
        not return.
17 My spirit is broken, my days are
        extinct,
    the grave is ready for me.
2 Surely there are mockers around me,
    and my eye dwells on their
        provocation.

3 "Lay down a pledge for me with
        yourself;
    who is there that will give surety for
        me?
4 Since you have closed their minds to
        understanding,
    therefore you will not let them
        triumph.
5 Those who denounce friends for
        reward—
    the eyes of their children will fail.

6 "He has made me a byword of the
        peoples,
    and I am one before whom people
        spit.
7 My eye has grown dim from grief,
    and all my members are like a
        shadow.
8 The upright are appalled at this,
    and the innocent stir themselves up
        against the godless.
9 Yet the righteous hold to their way,
    and they that have clean hands grow
        stronger and stronger.
10 But you, come back now, all of you,
    and I shall not find a sensible person
        among you.
11 My days are past, my plans are broken
        off,
    the desires of my heart.
12 They make night into day;
    'The light,' they say, 'is near to the
        darkness.'[c]
13 If I look for Sheol as my house,
    if I spread my couch in darkness,
14 if I say to the Pit, 'You are my father,'
    and to the worm, 'My mother,' or 'My
        sister,'

a Heb *you have*   b Syr Vg Tg: Heb *and*   c Meaning
of Heb uncertain

15 where then is my hope?
   Who will see my hope?
16 Will it go down to the bars of Sheol?
   Shall we descend together into the
      dust?"

16.8–17.16. 16.8: *It testifies to my face:* Job believes his wretched physical state advertises to others his alienation from God. **18:** *O earth, do not cover my blood:* Job hopes that his blood that God has shed by the cruel attacks of vv. 11–14 will cry out for vindication like the spilled blood of Abel (Gen 4.10), and that it will happen before his death (v. 22). **19:** *My witness is in heaven:* The identity of the witness is disputed. Is it God or some third party? Most likely, the witness is a third party who would arbitrate between God and Job and be a truthful witness. The rich irony* of these verses is apparent to the reader of chs. 1–2, where just such a third party was introduced: Satan, who is Job's enemy! **17.3:** *Lay down a pledge with me for yourself:* Job offers to God a pledge or token of his innocence. The effect is that of an oath of innocence. Another instance of such a pledge is Gen 38.17–18, where Judah gives his signet, cord, and staff in pledge of full payment later.

The response of Bildad

Ch. 18: With far greater harshness than his first response in ch. 8, Bildad states that Job is egotistically making himself the center of the world, whereas he is really among the wicked. The speech upholds a rigid doctrine of punishment for wicked deeds.

18 Then Bildad the Shuhite answered:
2 "How long will you hunt for
      words?
   Consider, and then we shall speak.
3 Why are we counted as cattle?
   Why are we stupid in your sight?
4 You who tear yourself in your anger—
   shall the earth be forsaken because of
      you,
   or the rock be removed out of its
      place?

5 "Surely the light of the wicked is put
      out,
   and the flame of their fire does not
      shine.
6 The light is dark in their tent,
   and the lamp above them is put out.

7 Their strong steps are shortened,
   and their own schemes throw them
      down.
8 For they are thrust into a net by their
      own feet,
   and they walk into a pitfall.
9 A trap seizes them by the heel;
   a snare lays hold of them.
10 A rope is hid for them in the ground,
    a trap for them in the path.
11 Terrors frighten them on every side,
    and chase them at their heels.
12 Their strength is consumed by hunger,*a*
    and calamity is ready for their
       stumbling.
13 By disease their skin is consumed,*b*
    the firstborn of Death consumes their
       limbs.
14 They are torn from the tent in which
       they trusted,
    and are brought to the king of terrors.
15 In their tents nothing remains;
    sulfur is scattered upon their
       habitations.
16 Their roots dry up beneath,
    and their branches wither above.
17 Their memory perishes from the earth,
    and they have no name in the street.
18 They are thrust from light into
       darkness,
    and driven out of the world.
19 They have no offspring or descendant
       among their people,
    and no survivor where they used to
       live.
20 They of the west are appalled at their
       fate,
    and horror seizes those of the east.
21 Surely such are the dwellings of the
       ungodly,
    such is the place of those who do not
       know God."

18.1–21. 2: *How long will you hunt for words?* Literally, "snare with words." Hunting imagery recurs in vv. 7–11, which depict the wicked being hunted and snared. **4:** *Place:* The word appears in the final verse (v. 21), rounding off the thought in an inclusio*: You

a Or *Disaster is hungry for them*   *b* Cn: Heb *It consumes the limbs of his skin*

cannot move the center of the world (*the rock be removed from its place*, v. 4); the place of the punishment of the wicked is arranged (*such is the place of those who do not know God*, v. 21).

Job's second response

Ch. 19: Far from making himself the center of the universe and far from hunting with words (Bildad's accusations in ch. 18), Job is being hunted by God's net (v. 6) and besieged by God (vv. 11–12). His family life is gone (vv. 13–20), and he can only plead with his friends not to pursue him pitilessly as God does (vv. 21–29).

---

19 Then Job answered:

2 "How long will you torment me,
   and break me in pieces with words?
3 These ten times you have cast reproach
      upon me;
   are you not ashamed to wrong me?
4 And even if it is true that I have erred,
   my error remains with me.
5 If indeed you magnify yourselves against
      me,
   and make my humiliation an
      argument against me,
6 know then that God has put me in the
      wrong,
   and closed his net around me.
7 Even when I cry out, 'Violence!' I am
      not answered;
   I call aloud, but there is no justice.
8 He has walled up my way so that I
      cannot pass,
   and he has set darkness upon my
      paths.
9 He has stripped my glory from me,
   and taken the crown from my head.
10 He breaks me down on every side, and I
      am gone,
   he has uprooted my hope like a tree.
11 He has kindled his wrath against me,
   and counts me as his adversary.
12 His troops come on together;
   they have thrown up siegeworks[a]
      against me,
   and encamp around my tent.

13 "He has put my family far from me,
   and my acquaintances are wholly
      estranged from me.
14 My relatives and my close friends have
      failed me;
15   the guests in my house have forgotten
      me;
   my serving girls count me as a
      stranger;
   I have become an alien in their
      eyes.
16 I call to my servant, but he gives me no
      answer;
   I must myself plead with him.
17 My breath is repulsive to my wife;
   I am loathsome to my own family.
18 Even young children despise me;
   when I rise, they talk against me.
19 All my intimate friends abhor me,
   and those whom I loved have turned
      against me.
20 My bones cling to my skin and to my
      flesh,
   and I have escaped by the skin of my
      teeth.
21 Have pity on me, have pity on me,
      O you my friends,
   for the hand of God has touched me!
22 Why do you, like God, pursue me,
   never satisfied with my flesh?

23 "O that my words were written down!
   O that they were inscribed in a
      book!
24 O that with an iron pen and with lead
   they were engraved on a rock forever!
25 For I know that my Redeemer[b] lives,
   and that at the last he[c] will stand
      upon the earth;[d]
26 and after my skin has been thus
      destroyed,
   then in[e] my flesh I shall see God,[f]
27 whom I shall see on my side,[g]
   and my eyes shall behold, and not
      another.
   My heart faints within me!
28 If you say, 'How we will persecute
      him!'
   and, 'The root of the matter is found
      in him';

---

a Cn: Heb *their way*   b Or *Vindicator*   c Or *that he
the Last*   d Heb *dust*   e Or *without*   f Meaning
of Heb of this verse uncertain   g Or *for myself*

29 be afraid of the sword,
  for wrath brings the punishment of
      the sword,
  so that you may know there is a
      judgment."

19.1–29. 13–20: There is no mention of the death of
Job's children. Instead, Job gives a standard portrayal
of a once-great sheik whose household has disappeared. **21:** *Have pity on my, have pity on me, O you
my friends:* Some take Job's pleading as sarcastic, because his friends have been unremittingly harsh. There
is a correlation between the harshness of his friends
and the harshness of God. **23–27:** The Hebrew is difficult. Just as Job expressed the hope for an impartial
umpire in 10.33, for a postmortem trial in 14.12–17,
and for a witness in heaven in 16.19, he now wishes
he could engrave on a stone marker his side of the case
for all to see. He hopes for a redeemer. Who is this
redeemer? Some suggest it is God, but, most likely, it
is the same third party as the witness (16.19) and umpire (9.33). It is a figure of the heavenly council who
would act as his friend and support. **26:** *And after my
skin has been thus destroyed:* Though some suggest
that Job hopes for a judgment this side of the grave,
it is probable that he hopes for some kind of survival
after death. **28:** *The root of the matter is found in him:*
Because the friends have judged Job guilty, they feel
free to persecute him. Job warns them they are attacking an innocent man and hence will experience the
divine wrath.

The response of Zophar
Ch. 20: Making an appeal to ancient tradition as in
8.8–20, Zophar states his topic in v. 5 and illustrates it
in vv. 6–28. The wicked may rise high, but they inevitably fall (vv. 6–11); they ingest wickedness like delicious food, but they will experience misery (vv. 12–
22); God will bring their wickedness upon them (vv.
23–29).

---

20 Then Zophar the Naamathite answered:

2 "Pay attention! My thoughts urge me to
      answer,
  because of the agitation within me.
3 I hear censure that insults me,
      and a spirit beyond my understanding
          answers me.
4 Do you not know this from of old,

ever since mortals were placed on
      earth,
5 that the exulting of the wicked is
      short,
  and the joy of the godless is but for a
      moment?
6 Even though they mount up high as the
      heavens,
  and their head reaches to the
      clouds,
7 they will perish forever like their own
      dung;
  those who have seen them will say,
      'Where are they?'
8 They will fly away like a dream, and not
      be found;
  they will be chased away like a vision
      of the night.
9 The eye that saw them will see them no
      more,
  nor will their place behold them any
      longer.
10 Their children will seek the favor of the
      poor,
  and their hands will give back their
      wealth.
11 Their bodies, once full of youth,
  will lie down in the dust with them.

12 "Though wickedness is sweet in their
      mouth,
  though they hide it under their
      tongues,
13 though they are loath to let it go,
  and hold it in their mouths,
14 yet their food is turned in their
      stomachs;
  it is the venom of asps within them.
15 They swallow down riches and vomit
      them up again;
  God casts them out of their bellies.
16 They will suck the poison of asps;
  the tongue of a viper will kill them.
17 They will not look on the rivers,
  the streams flowing with honey and
      curds.
18 They will give back the fruit of their
      toil,
  and will not swallow it down;
from the profit of their trading
  they will get no enjoyment.

19 For they have crushed and abandoned
      the poor,
   they have seized a house that they did
      not build.

20 "They knew no quiet in their bellies;
   in their greed they let nothing escape.
21 There was nothing left after they had
      eaten;
   therefore their prosperity will not
      endure.
22 In full sufficiency they will be in
      distress;
   all the force of misery will come upon
      them.
23 To fill their belly to the full
   God*a* will send his fierce anger into
      them,
   and rain it upon them as their food.*b*
24 They will flee from an iron weapon;
   a bronze arrow will strike them
      through.
25 It is drawn forth and comes out of their
      body,
   and the glittering point comes out of
      their gall;
   terrors come upon them.
26 Utter darkness is laid up for their
      treasures;
   a fire fanned by no one will devour
      them;
   what is left in their tent will be
      consumed.
27 The heavens will reveal their iniquity,
   and the earth will rise up against
      them.
28 The possessions of their house will be
      carried away,
   dragged off in the day of God's*c*
      wrath.
29 This is the portion of the wicked from
      God,
   the heritage decreed for them by God."

Job's third response

Ch. 21: Job closes the second cycle of speeches (chs. 15–21) by addressing his three friends' arguments.

21

Then Job answered:
2 "Listen carefully to my words,
   and let this be your consolation.

3 Bear with me, and I will speak;
   then after I have spoken, mock on.
4 As for me, is my complaint addressed to
      mortals?
   Why should I not be impatient?
5 Look at me, and be appalled,
   and lay your hand upon your mouth.
6 When I think of it I am dismayed,
   and shuddering seizes my flesh.
7 Why do the wicked live on,
   reach old age, and grow mighty in
      power?
8 Their children are established in their
      presence,
   and their offspring before their eyes.
9 Their houses are safe from fear,
   and no rod of God is upon them.
10 Their bull breeds without fail;
   their cow calves and never miscarries.
11 They send out their little ones like a
      flock,
   and their children dance around.
12 They sing to the tambourine and the
      lyre,
   and rejoice to the sound of the pipe.
13 They spend their days in prosperity,
   and in peace they go down to Sheol.
14 They say to God, 'Leave us alone!
   We do not desire to know your ways.
15 What is the Almighty,*d* that we should
      serve him?
   And what profit do we get if we pray
      to him?'
16 Is not their prosperity indeed their own
      achievement?*e*
   The plans of the wicked are
      repugnant to me.

17 "How often is the lamp of the wicked
      put out?
   How often does calamity come upon
      them?
   How often does God*a* distribute pains
      in his anger?
18 How often are they like straw before the
      wind,
   and like chaff that the storm carries
      away?

a Heb *he*   *b* Cn: Meaning of Heb uncertain
c Heb *his*   *d* Traditional rendering of Heb *Shaddai*
e Heb *in their hand*

19 You say, 'God stores up their iniquity for
   their children.'
   Let it be paid back to them, so that
      they may know it.
20 Let their own eyes see their
      destruction,
   and let them drink of the wrath of the
      Almighty.*a*
21 For what do they care for their
      household after them,
   when the number of their months is
      cut off?
22 Will any teach God knowledge,
   seeing that he judges those that are
      on high?
23 One dies in full prosperity,
   being wholly at ease and secure,
24 his loins full of milk
   and the marrow of his bones moist.
25 Another dies in bitterness of soul,
   never having tasted of good.
26 They lie down alike in the dust,
   and the worms cover them.

27 "Oh, I know your thoughts,
   and your schemes to wrong me.
28 For you say, 'Where is the house of the
      prince?
   Where is the tent in which the
      wicked lived?'
29 Have you not asked those who travel the
      roads,
   and do you not accept their
      testimony,
30 that the wicked are spared in the day of
      calamity,
   and are rescued in the day of wrath?
31 Who declares their way to their face,
   and who repays them for what they
      have done?
32 When they are carried to the grave,
   a watch is kept over their tomb.
33 The clods of the valley are sweet to
      them;
   everyone will follow after,
   and those who went before are
      innumerable.
34 How then will you comfort me with
      empty nothings?
   There is nothing left of your answers
      but falsehood."

21.1–34. 7–16: Job refutes Zophar's assertion (20.5–11) that the joys of the wicked are only temporary. Their children are not impoverished but flourish. **17–26:** Job refutes Bildad (ch. 19). **27–34:** Against the claim that the houses of tyrants are destroyed, travelers (as opposed to pedants like the friends) report their houses flourish and their tombs are honored. **34:** *How then will you comfort me with empty nothings?* Job began his first speech in this second cycle by calling his friends "miserable comforters" (16.2) and ends the cycle by again denouncing their empty comforting.

THE THIRD CYCLE OF SPEECHES

Chs. 22–27: Textual damage makes it impossible to attribute all the speeches to their proper speaker with certainty. Several passages seem to be out of place or attributed to the wrong person: 24.18–25 is attributed to Job but probably best suits Zophar; 26.1–4, which belongs to Job, is in a speech of Bildad (25.1–6 and 26.5–14); 27.13–24 occurs in a speech of Job but is only appropriate to one of the friends. Job's speech in 26.1–4 prefaces his speech in 27.2–12; 27.13–23 may belong to Zophar.

    Ch. 22: The response of Eliphaz. Eliphaz begins the third and final cycle of speeches. In vv. 2–11 he charges Job with wickedness (v. 5). In vv. 12–20 he charges Job with denying God does justice (the probable meaning of *keep to the old way* in v. 15). Eliphaz concludes by exhorting Job to change his ways (vv. 21–25). If Job does so, he will have joy, the assurance of having his prayers heard, success, and the ability to teach others (vv. 26–29). Throughout, Eliphaz assumes Job has sinned. The ironic* statements of this chapter are especially rich.

22 Then Eliphaz the Temanite answered:
2 "Can a mortal be of use to God?
   Can even the wisest be of service to
      him?
3 Is it any pleasure to the Almighty*a* if you
      are righteous,
   or is it gain to him if you make your
      ways blameless?
4 Is it for your piety that he reproves you,
   and enters into judgment with you?
5 Is not your wickedness great?
   There is no end to your iniquities.

a Traditional rendering of Heb *Shaddai*

6 For you have exacted pledges from your
     family for no reason,
   and stripped the naked of their
     clothing.
7 You have given no water to the weary to
     drink,
   and you have withheld bread from the
     hungry.
8 The powerful possess the land,
   and the favored live in it.
9 You have sent widows away empty-
     handed,
   and the arms of the orphans you have
     crushed.*a*
10 Therefore snares are around you,
   and sudden terror overwhelms you,
11 or darkness so that you cannot see;
   a flood of water covers you.

22.4: *Is it for your piety that he reproves you?* This is
meant sarcastically by Eliphaz, but the reader knows
from 1.8 and 2.3 that Job's piety has led to this reproof.

12 "Is not God high in the heavens?
   See the highest stars, how lofty they
     are!
13 Therefore you say, 'What does God know?
   Can he judge through the deep
     darkness?
14 Thick clouds enwrap him, so that he
     does not see,
   and he walks on the dome of heaven.'
15 Will you keep to the old way
   that the wicked have trod?
16 They were snatched away before their
     time;
   their foundation was washed away by
     a flood.
17 They said to God, 'Leave us alone,'
   and 'What can the Almighty*b* do to
     us?'*c*
18 Yet he filled their houses with good
     things—
   but the plans of the wicked are
     repugnant to me.
19 The righteous see it and are glad;
   the innocent laugh them to scorn,
20 saying, 'Surely our adversaries are cut
     off,
   and what they left, the fire has
     consumed.'

21 "Agree with God,*d* and be at peace;
   in this way good will come to you.
22 Receive instruction from his mouth,
   and lay up his words in your heart.
23 If you return to the Almighty,*b* you will
     be restored,
   if you remove unrighteousness from
     your tents,
24 if you treat gold like dust,
   and gold of Ophir like the stones of
     the torrent-bed,
25 and if the Almighty*b* is your gold
   and your precious silver,
26 then you will delight yourself in the
     Almighty,*b*
   and lift up your face to God.
27 You will pray to him, and he will hear
     you,
   and you will pay your vows.
28 You will decide on a matter, and it will
     be established for you,
   and light will shine on your ways.
29 When others are humiliated, you say it
     is pride;
   for he saves the humble.
30 He will deliver even those who are
     guilty;
   they will escape because of the
     cleanness of your hands."*e*

Job's first response in the third cycle

Chs. 23–24: Job characteristically interprets his friends'
persistent exhortations* to seek God (8.5–6; 11.13–
20; 22.21–30) in a legal sense—appearing before God
in a court of law where he could lay out his case (23.2–
7). But Job admits he cannot meet God in a court and
even if he could, he would be struck dumb with terror
(23.8–17). He then asks a rhetorical* question: Why
does God not make public *times* (of judgment, 24.1)?
He describes two types of malicious behavior, neither
of which seems to be punished by God: oppression of
the poor (24.2–12, especially v. 12) and violations of
the prohibitions against murder and adultery (24.13–
17, especially v. 17). The end of ch. 24 (vv. 18–24)
wholly contradicts Job's statements in ch. 21 and
should therefore probably be attributed to one of the
friends, perhaps Zophar.

---

a Gk Syr Tg Vg: Heb *were crushed*   *b* Traditional
rendering of Heb *Shaddai*   *c* Gk Syr: Heb *them*
d Heb *him*   *e* Meaning of Heb uncertain

23

Then Job answered:
² "Today also my complaint is
  bitter;ᵃ
his ᵇ hand is heavy despite my
  groaning.
³ Oh, that I knew where I might find
  him,
  that I might come even to his
  dwelling!
⁴ I would lay my case before him,
  and fill my mouth with arguments.
⁵ I would learn what he would answer
  me,
  and understand what he would say to
  me.
⁶ Would he contend with me in the
  greatness of his power?
  No; but he would give heed to me.
⁷ There an upright person could reason
  with him,
  and I should be acquitted forever by
  my judge.

⁸ "If I go forward, he is not there;
  or backward, I cannot perceive him;
⁹ on the left he hides, and I cannot
  behold him;
  I turnᶜ to the right, but I cannot see
  him.
¹⁰ But he knows the way that I take;
  when he has tested me, I shall come
  out like gold.
¹¹ My foot has held fast to his steps;
  I have kept his way and have not
  turned aside.
¹² I have not departed from the
  commandment of his lips;
  I have treasured inᵈ my bosom the
  words of his mouth.
¹³ But he stands alone and who can
  dissuade him?
  What he desires, that he does.
¹⁴ For he will complete what he appoints
  for me;
  and many such things are in his
  mind.
¹⁵ Therefore I am terrified at his presence;
  when I consider, I am in dread of
  him.
¹⁶ God has made my heart faint;
  the Almightyᵉ has terrified me;

¹⁷ If only I could vanish in darkness,
  and thick darkness would cover my
  face!ᶠ

23.1–17. 3: *Oh, that I knew where I might find him:* Job has persistently sought to find God (to seek answers), though his friends urge him to find God to seek forgiveness. **13:** *But he stands alone:* In the monotheistic perspective of the book there are no other gods who might persuade or dissuade God from a course of action. **15:** *Therefore I am terrified at his presence* (lit., "his face"). Earlier (7.14; 9.34), Job expressed his fear of being overwhelmed by God's majesty.

24

"Why are times not kept by the
  Almighty,ᵉ
  and why do those who know him
  never see his days?
² The wickedᵍ remove landmarks;
  they seize flocks and pasture them.
³ They drive away the donkey of the
  orphan;
  they take the widow's ox for a pledge.
⁴ They thrust the needy off the road;
  the poor of the earth all hide
  themselves.
⁵ Like wild asses in the desert
  they go out to their toil,
  scavenging in the wasteland
  food for their young.
⁶ They reap in a field not their own
  and they glean in the vineyard of the
  wicked.
⁷ They lie all night naked, without
  clothing,
  and have no covering in the cold.
⁸ They are wet with the rain of the
  mountains,
  and cling to the rock for want of
  shelter.

⁹ "There are those who snatch the orphan
  child from the breast,
  and take as a pledge the infant of the
  poor.

---

a Syr Vg Tg: Heb *rebellious*   *b* Gk Syr: Heb *my*
c Syr Vg: Heb *he turns*   *d* Gk Vg: Heb *from*
e Traditional rendering of Heb *Shaddai*   *f* Or *But I am not destroyed by the darkness; he has concealed the thick darkness from me*   *g* Gk: Heb *they*

10 They go about naked, without clothing;
 though hungry, they carry the
  sheaves;
11 between their terraces[a] they press out
  oil;
 they tread the wine presses, but suffer
  thirst.
12 From the city the dying groan,
 and the throat of the wounded cries
  for help;
 yet God pays no attention to their
  prayer.

13 "There are those who rebel against the
  light,
 who are not acquainted with its ways,
 and do not stay in its paths.
14 The murderer rises at dusk
 to kill the poor and needy,
 and in the night is like a thief.
15 The eye of the adulterer also waits for
  the twilight,
 saying, 'No eye will see me';
 and he disguises his face.
16 In the dark they dig through houses;
 by day they shut themselves up;
 they do not know the light.
17 For deep darkness is morning to all of
  them;
 for they are friends with the terrors of
  deep darkness.

18 "Swift are they on the face of the waters;
 their portion in the land is cursed;
 no treader turns toward their vineyards.
19 Drought and heat snatch away the snow
  waters;
 so does Sheol those who have sinned.
20 The womb forgets them;
 the worm finds them sweet;
they are no longer remembered;
 so wickedness is broken like a tree.

21 "They harm[b] the childless woman,
 and do no good to the widow.
22 Yet God[c] prolongs the life of the mighty
  by his power;
 they rise up when they despair of life.
23 He gives them security, and they are
  supported;
 his eyes are upon their ways.

24 They are exalted a little while, and then
  are gone;
 they wither and fade like the
  mallow;[d]
 they are cut off like the heads of
  grain.
25 If it is not so, who will prove me a liar,
 and show that there is nothing in
  what I say?"

24.1–25. 17: *For they are friends with the terrors of
deep darkness:* The imagery of light and darkness permeates 24.13–17. The wicked "overcome" the light.
18–25: A fragment of a friend's (Zophar's?) speech.
The verses strongly affirm that divine retribution
will fall on the two groups described in vv. 1–12 and
13–17. **22–25:** The verses may be read as a conces-
sion: God, it is true, allows the wicked to flourish but
ultimately will cut them off.

The response of Bildad

25.1–6 and 26.5–14: The Hebrew text has suffered
dislocation. Bildad's speech in ch. 25 is too short and
Job's speech in ch. 26 shifts abruptly in v. 5. Probably,
Bildad's speech was originally 25.1–6 and 26.5–14,
because the verses form a coherent whole. Bildad's
speech is largely in hymnic form. Hymns to the creator
God are found in the speeches of Job (9.5–12;
12.13–25) and his friends (5.9–11). In Job's hymns
God's power is portrayed as arbitrary and irrational,
whereas Bildad portrays a God so powerful and splendid that everything else, including human beings, is
nothing (25.1–6). Verses 5–14 form a cosmogony (an
account of creation), which shows how God, like a
master builder and a heroic warrior, easily shaped primordial massive elements into a vast universe. Bildad
concedes his cosmogony gives only a hint of God's
grandeur (26.14). The implication is that Job has no
right to question God.

25 Then Bildad the Shuhite answered:
2 "Dominion and fear are with
  God;[e]
 he makes peace in his high heaven.
3 Is there any number to his armies?
 Upon whom does his light not
  arise?

a Meaning of Heb uncertain   b Gk Tg: Heb *feed on* or
associate with   c Heb *he*   d Gk: Heb *like all others*
e Heb *him*

4 How then can a mortal be righteous
before God?
How can one born of woman be pure?
5 If even the moon is not bright
and the stars are not pure in his sight,
6 how much less a mortal, who is a
maggot,
and a human being, who is a worm!"

~~~~~~~~~~~~~~~~~~~~~~~~~~~~

Job's second response
26.1–4 and 27.1–12: The attributions of the speeches
have been confused in the transmission of the text. This
commentary assumes Job's brief speech in 26.1–4 is the
preface to his speech in 27.2–12. It also assumes 27.13–
23 belongs not to Job but to Zophar, for it contradicts
Job's previous statements and continues themes from
Zophar's speech in ch. 20. Job's speech is extremely
important in the book, since it brings back phrases from
chs. 1–2, concludes the three cycles of speeches, points
forward to Job's climactic words in chs. 29–31, and is
explicitly quoted by God later on (40.8 cites 27.5–6).

---

26 Then Job answered:
2 "How you have helped one who
has no power!
How you have assisted the arm that
has no strength!
3 How you have counseled one who has
no wisdom,
and given much good advice!
4 With whose help have you uttered
words,
and whose spirit has come forth from
you?
5 The shades below tremble,
the waters and their inhabitants.
6 Sheol is naked before God,
and Abaddon has no covering.
7 He stretches out Zaphon*a* over the
void,
and hangs the earth upon nothing.
8 He binds up the waters in his thick
clouds,
and the cloud is not torn open by
them.
9 He covers the face of the full moon,
and spreads over it his cloud.
10 He has described a circle on the face of
the waters,
at the boundary between light and
darkness.

11 The pillars of heaven tremble,
and are astounded at his rebuke.
12 By his power he stilled the Sea;
by his understanding he struck down
Rahab.
13 By his wind the heavens were made fair;
his hand pierced the fleeing serpent.
14 These are indeed but the outskirts of his
ways;
and how small a whisper do we hear
of him!
But the thunder of his power who can
understand?"

26.1–14. 5: *The shades* are inhabitants of the underworld (Ps 88.10; Prov 9.18) who also appear in the
myths of Israel's neighbors. God's power prevails even
in the underworld, the outermost part of the universe.
The waters are those under the earth, such as are referred to in Jonah's psalm (Jon 2.2–6). **7:** *Zaphon:* A
general designation for the north. It is also the name
of a northern mountain, which could be applied to
Mount Zion* (Ps 48.2). Here, apparently, Zaphon is
conceived as the center of the earth. Like a skilled
builder, God easily fits the massive mountain into its
proper place over formless chaos. **12:** *He stilled the
Sea:* Like a victorious warrior, God defeated the forces
of pre-creation chaos, personified* as the dragon Sea.
Rahab is another name for Sea, or for one of Sea's
allies.

~~~~~~~~~~~~~~~~~~~~~~~~~~~~

27 Job again took up his discourse and
said:
2 "As God lives, who has taken away my
right,
and the Almighty,*b* who has made my
soul bitter,
3 as long as my breath is in me
and the spirit of God is in my nostrils,
4 my lips will not speak falsehood,
and my tongue will not utter deceit.
5 Far be it from me to say that you are
right;
until I die I will not put away my
integrity from me.
6 I hold fast my righteousness, and will
not let it go;
my heart does not reproach me for
any of my days.

a Or *the North* *b* Traditional rendering of Heb *Shaddai*

7 "May my enemy be like the wicked,
     and may my opponent be like the
          unrighteous.
8 For what is the hope of the godless
          when God cuts them off,
     when God takes away their lives?
9 Will God hear their cry
     when trouble comes upon them?
10 Will they take delight in the Almighty?[a]
     Will they call upon God at all times?
11 I will teach you concerning the hand of
          God;
     that which is with the Almighty[a] I will
          not conceal.
12 All of you have seen it yourselves;
     why then have you become altogether
          vain?

27.1–12. 2: *As God lives:* Job's great oath, vowing his innocence, marks a turning point in the story. The solemn formula *as God lives* invites God to punish the false swearer as in 1 Sam 14.39, 45; 2 Sam 2.27. Job has created a new legal context and also an unprecedented situation: His oath makes God the guarantor of the oath but he believes the same God is his enemy. Ending the conversation, Job turns irrevocably to God. **7:** *May my enemy be like the wicked:* Job adapts legal language to his unique situation. The enemy (singular) evidently is God, whom Job wishes to be somehow declared to be in the wrong, and be made to suffer the same painful experiences that Job has endured (v. 8). **11:** Job turns to his friends for the last time (*you* is plural), speaking to them as one who has endured at first hand *the hand of God.*

The response of Zophar (?)
27.13–23: Verse 13 states the topic—the trouble the wicked experience—and gives examples of retribution in different spheres, destruction of families, loss of inheritance, devastation of families, unforeseen terrors, and ruin from the east wind. Zophar in ch. 20 spoke about the inevitable disaster awaiting the wicked.

---

13 "This is the portion of the wicked with
          God,
     and the heritage that oppressors
          receive from the Almighty:[a]
14 If their children are multiplied, it is for
          the sword;
     and their offspring have not enough
          to eat.

15 Those who survive them the pestilence
          buries,
     and their widows make no lamentation.
16 Though they heap up silver like dust,
     and pile up clothing like clay—
17 they may pile it up, but the just will
          wear it,
     and the innocent will divide the silver.
18 They build their houses like nests,
     like booths made by sentinels of the
          vineyard.
19 They go to bed with wealth, but will do
          so no more;
     they open their eyes, and it is gone.
20 Terrors overtake them like a flood;
     in the night a whirlwind carries them
          off.
21 The east wind lifts them up and they
          are gone;
     it sweeps them out of their place.
22 It[b] hurls at them without pity;
     they flee from its[c] power in headlong
          flight.
23 It[b] claps its[c] hands at them,
     and hisses at them from its[c] place.

POEM ON WISDOM

Ch. 28: The anonymous poem breaks the cycle of speeches of Job and his three friends that began in ch. 3. Some consider it a later insertion, but it is original to the story, because it heightens the drama by retarding the action and by raising important questions in the reader's mind. For example, by declaring wisdom inaccessible to human beings, the poem suggests what the reader already suspects, the dialogue between Job and his friends cannot provide a satisfactory answer to his problem. It suggests the answer must come from a non-human source, pointing toward the divine response of chs. 39–42. Structurally, the poem has three sections, vv. 1–11, 12–19, and 20–28. In each section, key words (*place, search, way/path, to see*) play an important role.

---

28 "Surely there is a mine for silver,
     and a place for gold to be refined.
2 Iron is taken out of the earth,
     and copper is smelted from ore.

---

a Traditional rendering of Heb *Shaddai*   *b* Or *He* (that is God)   *c* Or *his*

3 Miners put*a* an end to darkness,
  and search out to the farthest bound
  the ore in gloom and deep darkness.
4 They open shafts in a valley away from
      human habitation;
  they are forgotten by travelers,
  they sway suspended, remote from
      people.
5 As for the earth, out of it comes bread;
  but underneath it is turned up as by
      fire.
6 Its stones are the place of sapphires,*b*
  and its dust contains gold.

7 "That path no bird of prey knows,
  and the falcon's eye has not seen it.
8 The proud wild animals have not
      trodden it;
  the lion has not passed over it.

9 "They put their hand to the flinty rock,
  and overturn mountains by the roots.
10 They cut out channels in the rocks,
  and their eyes see every precious
      thing.
11 The sources of the rivers they probe;*c*
  hidden things they bring to light.

12 "But where shall wisdom be found?
  And where is the place of
      understanding?
13 Mortals do not know the way to it,*d*
  and it is not found in the land of the
      living.
14 The deep says, 'It is not in me,'
  and the sea says, 'It is not with me.'
15 It cannot be gotten for gold,
  and silver cannot be weighed out as
      its price.
16 It cannot be valued in the gold of
      Ophir,
  in precious onyx or sapphire.*b*
17 Gold and glass cannot equal it,
  nor can it be exchanged for jewels of
      fine gold.
18 No mention shall be made of coral or of
      crystal;
  the price of wisdom is above pearls.
19 The chrysolite of Ethiopia*e* cannot
      compare with it,
  nor can it be valued in pure gold.

20 "Where then does wisdom come from?
  And where is the place of
      understanding?
21 It is hidden from the eyes of all living,
  and concealed from the birds of the
      air.
22 Abaddon and Death say,
  'We have heard a rumor of it with our
      ears.'

23 "God understands the way to it,
  and he knows its place.
24 For he looks to the ends of the earth,
  and sees everything under the
      heavens.
25 When he gave to the wind its weight,
  and apportioned out the waters by
      measure;
26 when he made a decree for the rain,
  and a way for the thunderbolt;
27 then he saw it and declared it;
  he established it, and searched it out.
28 And he said to humankind,
  'Truly, the fear of the Lord, that is
      wisdom;
  and to depart from evil is
      understanding.' "

28.1–28. 7: *That path no bird of prey knows:* Human beings who excavate precious metals in mines surpass the vision of the keenest-eyed birds, yet wisdom lies beyond the vision of the most intrepid human explorers. **28:** *Truly, the fear of the Lord, that is wisdom:* The phrase was used in Job 1.8 and 2.3.

JOB'S FINAL STATEMENT

Chs. 29–31: Job's final speech, the longest speech in the book until the LORD's twin speeches in chs. 38–42, is a statement continuing the legal argument of the earlier speeches. In ch. 29 Job portrays himself in exalted terms as a heroic and just person, favored by God (29.2–6) and honored by all in the community (29.7–25). But now, Job complains, he is ridiculed by the dregs of society (30.1–8), assaulted and humiliated by others (30.9–15), attacked by God and denied justice (30.16–31). In his great oath he denies any wrongdoing whatsoever and swears he has adhered to heroic

a Heb *He puts* *b* Or *lapis lazuli*
c Gk Vg: Heb *bind* *d* Gk: Heb *its price*
e Or *Nubia*; Heb *Cush*

standards of justice. He ends with a demand to confront God directly (31.35–40).

29

Job again took up his discourse and said:

2 "O that I were as in the months of old,
  as in the days when God watched
  over me;

3 when his lamp shone over my head,
  and by his light I walked through
  darkness;

4 when I was in my prime,
  when the friendship of God was upon
  my tent;

5 when the Almighty[a] was still with me,
  when my children were around me;

6 when my steps were washed with milk,
  and the rock poured out for me
  streams of oil!

7 When I went out to the gate of the city,
  when I took my seat in the square,

8 the young men saw me and withdrew,
  and the aged rose up and stood;

9 the nobles refrained from talking,
  and laid their hands on their mouths;

10 the voices of princes were hushed,
  and their tongues stuck to the roof of
  their mouths.

11 When the ear heard, it commended me,
  and when the eye saw, it approved;

12 because I delivered the poor who cried,
  and the orphan who had no helper.

13 The blessing of the wretched came
  upon me,
  and I caused the widow's heart to
  sing for joy.

14 I put on righteousness, and it clothed
  me;
  my justice was like a robe and a
  turban.

15 I was eyes to the blind,
  and feet to the lame.

16 I was a father to the needy,
  and I championed the cause of the
  stranger.

17 I broke the fangs of the unrighteous,
  and made them drop their prey from
  their teeth.

18 Then I thought, 'I shall die in my nest,
  and I shall multiply my days like the
  phoenix;[b]

19 my roots spread out to the waters,
  with the dew all night on my
  branches;

20 my glory was fresh with me,
  and my bow ever new in my hand.'

21 "They listened to me, and waited,
  and kept silence for my counsel.

22 After I spoke they did not speak again,
  and my word dropped upon them like
  dew.[c]

23 They waited for me as for the rain;
  they opened their mouths as for the
  spring rain.

24 I smiled on them when they had no
  confidence;
  and the light of my countenance they
  did not extinguish.[d]

25 I chose their way, and sat as chief,
  and I lived like a king among his
  troops,
  like one who comforts mourners.

29.1–25: Job's blessed and heroic life. Job yearns to return to his past life, to the time when he was blessed and honored. The review of his life functions as a kind of self-praise, citing himself as the example of noble conduct and status. **11–17:** The centerpiece of his remembrance is himself as a peerless administrator of justice. Job's treatment of the oppressed and the needy contrasts dramatically with God's treatment of the oppressed and needy Job. **14:** The middle verse of vv. 11–17 is set off by the mention of paired body parts in the surrounding verses (v. 11, *ear, eye*; v. 13, *heart*; v. 15, *eyes, feet*; v. 17, *fangs, teeth*). **18:** *Like the phoenix:* A legendary* bird, which, after living up to 500 years, burned itself to ashes and rose to live another long period. Verses 19–20 continue the images of vitality. **21–25:** Job applies to himself phrases normally applied to God: *spring rain* (v. 23; see also Deut 11.14; Hos 6.3) and *the light of my countenance* (v. 24, compare Ps 4.6; 44.3).

30

"But now they make sport of me,
those who are younger than I,
whose fathers I would have disdained
to set with the dogs of my flock.

---

a Traditional rendering of Heb *Shaddai*　　b Or *like sand*　　c Heb lacks *like dew*　　d Meaning of Heb uncertain

2 What could I gain from the strength of
     their hands?
  All their vigor is gone.
3 Through want and hard hunger
     they gnaw the dry and desolate
        ground,
4 they pick mallow and the leaves of
        bushes,
     and to warm themselves the roots of
        broom.
5 They are driven out from society;
     people shout after them as after a
        thief.
6 In the gullies of wadis they must live,
     in holes in the ground, and in the
        rocks.
7 Among the bushes they bray;
     under the nettles they huddle together.
8 A senseless, disreputable brood,
     they have been whipped out of the
        land.

9 "And now they mock me in song;
     I am a byword to them.
10 They abhor me, they keep aloof from me;
     they do not hesitate to spit at the
        sight of me.
11 Because God has loosed my bowstring
        and humbled me,
     they have cast off restraint in my
        presence.
12 On my right hand the rabble rise up;
     they send me sprawling,
     and build roads for my ruin.
13 They break up my path,
     they promote my calamity;
     no one restrains*a* them.
14 As through a wide breach they come;
     amid the crash they roll on.
15 Terrors are turned upon me;
     my honor is pursued as by the wind,
     and my prosperity has passed away
        like a cloud.

16 "And now my soul is poured out within
        me;
     days of affliction have taken hold of
        me.
17 The night racks my bones,
     and the pain that gnaws me takes no
        rest.

18 With violence he seizes my garment;*b*
     he grasps me by*c* the collar of my
        tunic.
19 He has cast me into the mire,
     and I have become like dust and
        ashes.
20 I cry to you and you do not answer me;
     I stand, and you merely look at me.
21 You have turned cruel to me;
     with the might of your hand you
        persecute me.
22 You lift me up on the wind, you make
        me ride on it,
     and you toss me about in the roar of
        the storm.
23 I know that you will bring me to death,
     and to the house appointed for all
        living.

24 "Surely one does not turn against the
        needy,*d*
     when in disaster they cry for help.*e*
25 Did I not weep for those whose day was
        hard?
     Was not my soul grieved for the
        poor?
26 But when I looked for good, evil came;
     and when I waited for light, darkness
        came.
27 My inward parts are in turmoil, and are
        never still;
     days of affliction come to meet me.
28 I go about in sunless gloom;
     I stand up in the assembly and cry for
        help.
29 I am a brother of jackals,
     and a companion of ostriches.
30 My skin turns black and falls from me,
     and my bones burn with heat.
31 My lyre is turned to mourning,
     and my pipe to the voice of those who
        weep.

30.1–31: Job complains he is attacked by human beings and by God, and his cry is not heard. 11: *God
has loosed my bowstring:* God has disarmed Job. 20:
I cry to you: The verb *cry* is repeated in v. 28. Job cries

a Cn: Heb *helps*   *b* Gk: Heb *my garment is disfigured*
c Heb *like*   *d* Heb *ruin*   *e* Cn: Meaning of Heb
uncertain

out in vain for justice, though basic decency would
demand the needy be heard.

~~~~~~~~~~~~~~~~~~~~~~

31

"I have made a covenant with my
  eyes;
  how then could I look upon a virgin?
2 What would be my portion from God
    above,
    and my heritage from the Almighty[a]
    on high?
3 Does not calamity befall the unrighteous,
    and disaster the workers of iniquity?
4 Does he not see my ways,
    and number all my steps?

5 "If I have walked with falsehood,
    and my foot has hurried to deceit—
6 let me be weighed in a just balance,
    and let God know my integrity!—
7 if my step has turned aside from the way,
    and my heart has followed my eyes,
    and if any spot has clung to my
    hands;
8 then let me sow, and another eat;
    and let what grows for me be rooted
    out.

9 "If my heart has been enticed by a
    woman,
    and I have lain in wait at my
    neighbor's door;
10 then let my wife grind for another,
    and let other men kneel over her.
11 For that would be a heinous crime;
    that would be a criminal offense;
12 for that would be a fire consuming
    down to Abaddon,
    and it would burn to the root all my
    harvest.

13 "If I have rejected the cause of my male
    or female slaves,
    when they brought a complaint
    against me;
14 what then shall I do when God rises up?
    When he makes inquiry, what shall I
    answer him?
15 Did not he who made me in the womb
    make them?
    And did not one fashion us in the
    womb?

16 "If I have withheld anything that the
    poor desired,
    or have caused the eyes of the widow
    to fail,
17 or have eaten my morsel alone,
    and the orphan has not eaten from
    it—
18 for from my youth I reared the orphan[b]
    like a father,
    and from my mother's womb I guided
    the widow[c]—
19 if I have seen anyone perish for lack of
    clothing,
    or a poor person without covering,
20 whose loins have not blessed me,
    and who was not warmed with the
    fleece of my sheep;
21 if I have raised my hand against the
    orphan,
    because I saw I had supporters at the
    gate;
22 then let my shoulder blade fall from my
    shoulder,
    and let my arm be broken from its
    socket.
23 For I was in terror of calamity from
    God,
    and I could not have faced his
    majesty.

24 "If I have made gold my trust,
    or called fine gold my confidence;
25 if I have rejoiced because my wealth
    was great,
    or because my hand had gotten much;
26 if I have looked at the sun[d] when it
    shone,
    or the moon moving in splendor,
27 and my heart has been secretly enticed,
    and my mouth has kissed my hand;
28 this also would be an iniquity to be
    punished by the judges,
    for I should have been false to God
    above.

29 "If I have rejoiced at the ruin of those
    who hated me,
    or exulted when evil overtook them—

a Traditional rendering of Heb *Shaddai* b Heb *him*
c Heb *her* d Heb *the light*

30 I have not let my mouth sin
 by asking for their lives with a curse—
31 if those of my tent ever said,
 'O that we might be sated with his
 flesh!'^a—
32 the stranger has not lodged in the
 street;
 I have opened my doors to the
 traveler—
33 if I have concealed my transgressions as
 others do,^b
 by hiding my iniquity in my bosom,
34 because I stood in great fear of the
 multitude,
 and the contempt of families terrified
 me,
 so that I kept silence, and did not go
 out of doors—
35 O that I had one to hear me!
 (Here is my signature! Let the
 Almighty^c answer me!)
 O that I had the indictment written
 by my adversary!
36 Surely I would carry it on my shoulder;
 I would bind it on me like a crown;
37 I would give him an account of all my
 steps;
 like a prince I would approach him.

38 "If my land has cried out against me,
 and its furrows have wept together;
39 if I have eaten its yield without
 payment,
 and caused the death of its owners;
40 let thorns grow instead of wheat,
 and foul weeds instead of barley."

 The words of Job are ended.

31.1–40: In a negative confession, Job swears an oath to clear himself of all charges. Job swears before God that if he has done any of the deeds he describes, then punishment should afflict him. The chapter is structured in "envelope style": vv. 1–3 and 38–40 (the covenant* and its curse) are the outer envelope, vv. 4–6 and 35–37 (the challenge hurled at God) are the inner envelope, and vv. 7–34 are at the center. The central verses list the potential sins and their penalties. Eleven sins are mentioned in vv. 7–34. After each there is a sanction or some comment (except vv. 24–25 and 32). **1:** *How then could I look upon a virgin?* An ex-

ample of hyperbole.* Here and elsewhere in the chapter, Job is swearing to an extraordinary level of righteousness. By the same token, the oaths are an indirect attack on Job's opponent at law. **36–37:** *Oh, that I had one to hear me!* Job calls out one last time for a public trial with an arbiter present (see 9.33; 16.19; 19.25) to mediate between him and his opponent. **38–40:** Job ends his list of oaths by calling upon earth, a primordial element often invoked in ancient legal ceremonies as a witness. If God remains silent now, he will seem to be the guilty party.

THE SPEECHES OF ELIHU

Chs. 32–37: The four Elihu speeches are often judged to have been added later as an attempt to answer Job more effectively than the three friends. The Elihu speeches are most probably original, however: (1) Elihu is a somewhat comic figure, angrily claiming to be wiser than his elders (the mark of a fool) and would hardly be invented to rebut Job definitively; (2) in the book Elihu makes dramatic sense, for he is the comically exaggerated answer to Job's demand for a mediator between himself and God; (3) the omission of his name in the list of friends in the epilogue (42.7, 9) only shows he is not part of the give-and-take of the dialogues; (4) dramatically, he retards the action and prepares for the appearance of the LORD and the cosmic topics in the divine speeches.

 Ch. 32: Elihu introduces himself. Elihu makes an impression opposite to the one he wants to create. Instead of patiently and wisely drawing on the teaching of his elders, he angrily dismisses them, inadvertently giving himself away by comparing himself to a new wineskin ready to burst (v. 19).

---

32 So these three men ceased to answer Job, because he was righteous in his own eyes. 2Then Elihu son of Barachel the Buzite, of the family of Ram, became angry. He was angry at Job because he justified himself rather than God; 3he was angry also at Job's three friends because they had found no answer, though they had declared Job to be in the wrong.^d 4Now Elihu had waited to speak to Job, because they were older than he. 5But when Elihu saw that there was no

---

a Meaning of Heb uncertain *b* Or *as Adam did*
c Traditional rendering of Heb *Shaddai* *d* Another ancient tradition reads *answer, and had put God in the wrong*

answer in the mouths of these three men, he became angry.

32.2: *Buzite:* The name Buz occurs in Gen 22.21 as the brother of Uz, which is the name of Job's homeland (1.1); it is presumably a place in the same area.

~~~~~~~~~~~~~~~~~~~~~~~~~~~~~~~~~~~~~~~

6 Elihu son of Barachel the Buzite answered:
"I am young in years,
and you are aged;
therefore I was timid and afraid
to declare my opinion to you.
7 I said, 'Let days speak,
and many years teach wisdom.'
8 But truly it is the spirit in a mortal,
the breath of the Almighty,*a* that
makes for understanding.
9 It is not the old*b* that are wise,
nor the aged that understand what is
right.
10 Therefore I say, 'Listen to me;
let me also declare my opinion.'

11 "See, I waited for your words,
I listened for your wise sayings,
while you searched out what to say.
12 I gave you my attention,
but there was in fact no one that
confuted Job,
no one among you that answered his
words.
13 Yet do not say, 'We have found wisdom;
God may vanquish him, not a
human.'
14 He has not directed his words against
me,
and I will not answer him with your
speeches.

15 "They are dismayed, they answer no
more;
they have not a word to say.
16 And am I to wait, because they do not
speak,
because they stand there, and answer
no more?
17 I also will give my answer;
I also will declare my opinion.
18 For I am full of words;
the spirit within me constrains me.

19 My heart is indeed like wine that has no
vent;
like new wineskins, it is ready to
burst.
20 I must speak, so that I may find relief;
I must open my lips and answer.
21 I will not show partiality to any person
or use flattery toward anyone.
22 For I do not know how to flatter—
or my Maker would soon put an end
to me!

~~~~~~~~~~~~~~~~~~~~~~~~~~~~~~~~~~~~~~~

Elihu's first speech
Ch. 33: Contrary to Job's assertion that God did not respond to him, Elihu teaches that God indeed responds to people, teaching them through dreams (vv. 15–18), through suffering (vv. 19–22), and through healing (vv. 23–28). *Pit* (Sheol,✶ the underworld) unifies the three sections, appearing in each (vv. 18, 22, 28). Elihu invites Job to allow God to heal him (especially vv. 29–33).

---

33 "But now, hear my speech, O Job,
and listen to all my words.
2 See, I open my mouth;
the tongue in my mouth speaks.
3 My words declare the uprightness of my
heart,
and what my lips know they speak
sincerely.
4 The spirit of God has made me,
and the breath of the Almighty*a* gives
me life.
5 Answer me, if you can;
set your words in order before me;
take your stand.
6 See, before God I am as you are;
I too was formed from a piece of clay.
7 No fear of me need terrify you;
my pressure will not be heavy on you.

8 "Surely, you have spoken in my hearing,
and I have heard the sound of your
words.
9 You say, 'I am clean, without
transgression;
I am pure, and there is no iniquity in
me.

---

a Traditional rendering of Heb *Shaddai*   *b* Gk Syr Vg: Heb *many*

10 Look, he finds occasions against me,
     he counts me as his enemy;
11 he puts my feet in the stocks,
     and watches all my paths.'

33.9: *You say, "I am clean, without transgression":* Elihu makes Job say more than he actually said. Job did not claim to be clean in an absolute sense even in ch. 31; he claimed only to be innocent of the kind of wrongdoing that has caused his present suffering.

12 "But in this you are not right. I will
     answer you:
  God is greater than any mortal.
13 Why do you contend against him,
     saying, 'He will answer none of my*
        words'?
14 For God speaks in one way,
     and in two, though people do not
        perceive it.
15 In a dream, in a vision of the night,
     when deep sleep falls on mortals,
     while they slumber on their beds,
16 then he opens their ears,
     and terrifies them with warnings,
17 that he may turn them aside from their
        deeds,
     and keep them from pride,
18 to spare their souls from the Pit,
     their lives from traversing the River.
19 They are also chastened with pain upon
        their beds,
     and with continual strife in their bones,
20 so that their lives loathe bread,
     and their appetites dainty food.
21 Their flesh is so wasted away that it
        cannot be seen;
     and their bones, once invisible, now
        stick out.
22 Their souls draw near the Pit,
     and their lives to those who bring
        death.
23 Then, if there should be for one of them
        an angel,
     a mediator, one of a thousand,
     one who declares a person upright,
24 and he is gracious to that person, and
        says,
  'Deliver him from going down into
        the Pit;
     I have found a ransom;

25 let his flesh become fresh with youth;
     let him return to the days of his
        youthful vigor';
26 then he prays to God, and is accepted
        by him,
     he comes into his presence with joy,
  and God*b* repays him for his
        righteousness.
27   That person sings to others and says,
  'I sinned, and perverted what was right,
     and it was not paid back to me.
28 He has redeemed my soul from going
        down to the Pit,
     and my life shall see the light.'

29 "God indeed does all these things,
     twice, three times, with mortals,
30 to bring back their souls from the Pit,
     so that they may see the light of life.*c*
31 Pay heed, Job, listen to me;
     be silent, and I will speak.
32 If you have anything to say, answer me;
     speak, for I desire to justify you.
33 If not, listen to me;
     be silent, and I will teach you
        wisdom."

Elihu's second speech
Ch. 34: Elihu defends God's justice (vv. 2–4) by attacking Job's character (vv. 5–9) and upholding God's character (vv. 10–15) and mode of governance (vv. 16–30). Therefore, he calls on Job to repent (vv. 31–33) and gives his own verdict (vv. 34–37).

---

34 Then Elihu continued and said:
   2 "Hear my words, you wise men,
     and give ear to me, you who know;
  3 for the ear tests words
     as the palate tastes food.
  4 Let us choose what is right;
     let us determine among ourselves
        what is good.
  5 For Job has said, 'I am innocent,
     and God has taken away my right;
  6 in spite of being right I am counted a
        liar;
     my wound is incurable, though I am
        without transgression.'

a Compare Gk: Heb *his*   *b* Heb *he*   *c* Syr: Heb *to be lighted with the light of life*

7 Who is there like Job,
     who drinks up scoffing like water,
8 who goes in company with evildoers
     and walks with the wicked?
9 For he has said, 'It profits one nothing
     to take delight in God.'

10 "Therefore, hear me, you who have
        sense,
     far be it from God that he should do
        wickedness,
     and from the Almighty[a] that he
        should do wrong.
11 For according to their deeds he will
        repay them,
     and according to their ways he will
        make it befall them.
12 Of a truth, God will not do wickedly,
     and the Almighty[a] will not pervert
        justice.
13 Who gave him charge over the earth
     and who laid on him[b] the whole
        world?
14 If he should take back his spirit[c] to
        himself,
     and gather to himself his breath,
15 all flesh would perish together,
     and all mortals return to dust.

16 "If you have understanding, hear this;
     listen to what I say.
17 Shall one who hates justice govern?
     Will you condemn one who is
        righteous and mighty,
18 who says to a king, 'You scoundrel!'
     and to princes, 'You wicked men!';
19 who shows no partiality to nobles,
     nor regards the rich more than the
        poor,
     for they are all the work of his hands?
20 In a moment they die;
     at midnight the people are shaken
        and pass away,
     and the mighty are taken away by no
        human hand.

21 "For his eyes are upon the ways of
        mortals,
     and he sees all their steps.
22 There is no gloom or deep darkness
     where evildoers may hide themselves.

23 For he has not appointed a time[d] for
        anyone
     to go before God in judgment.
24 He shatters the mighty without
        investigation,
     and sets others in their place.
25 Thus, knowing their works,
     he overturns them in the night, and
        they are crushed.
26 He strikes them for their wickedness
     while others look on,
27 because they turned aside from
        following him,
     and had no regard for any of his ways,
28 so that they caused the cry of the poor
        to come to him,
     and he heard the cry of the
        afflicted—
29 When he is quiet, who can condemn?
     When he hides his face, who can
        behold him,
     whether it be a nation or an
        individual?—
30 so that the godless should not reign,
     or those who ensnare the people.

31 "For has anyone said to God,
     'I have endured punishment; I will
        not offend any more;
32 teach me what I do not see;
     if I have done iniquity, I will do it no
        more'?
33 Will he then pay back to suit you,
     because you reject it?
     For you must choose, and not I;
     therefore declare what you know.[e]
34 Those who have sense will say to me,
     and the wise who hear me will say,
35 'Job speaks without knowledge,
     his words are without insight.'
36 Would that Job were tried to the limit,
     because his answers are those of the
        wicked.
37 For he adds rebellion to his sin;
     he claps his hands among us,
     and multiplies his words against
        God."

a Traditional rendering of Heb *Shaddai*   b Heb lacks
on him   c Heb *his heart his spirit*   d Cn: Heb *yet*
e Meaning of Heb of verses 29–33 uncertain

34.1–37. 5: *God has taken away my right* is a legal phrase, meaning that God has denied me litigation. 23: *For he has not appointed a time for anyone* has a legal meaning: Human beings cannot force God into court, for God and God's governance are faultless and beyond questioning.

Elihu's third speech

Ch. 35: Elihu assesses Job's claim that one gains no advantage from being just (v. 3). How dare Job expect a divine response to his conduct? God is too far away to be affected by human behavior (vv. 5–8). Moreover, most people's cries for help are insincere in any case (vv. 9–13). Elihu then derides Job (vv. 14–16).

35 Elihu continued and said:
2 "Do you think this to be just?
You say, 'I am in the right before God.'
3 If you ask, 'What advantage have I?
How am I better off than if I had sinned?'
4 I will answer you
and your friends with you.
5 Look at the heavens and see;
observe the clouds, which are higher than you.
6 If you have sinned, what do you accomplish against him?
And if your transgressions are multiplied, what do you do to him?
7 If you are righteous, what do you give to him;
or what does he receive from your hand?
8 Your wickedness affects others like you,
and your righteousness, other human beings.

9 "Because of the multitude of oppressions people cry out;
they call for help because of the arm of the mighty.
10 But no one says, 'Where is God my Maker,
who gives strength in the night,
11 who teaches us more than the animals of the earth,
and makes us wiser than the birds of the air?'
12 There they cry out, but he does not answer,
because of the pride of evildoers.
13 Surely God does not hear an empty cry,
nor does the Almighty[a] regard it.
14 How much less when you say that you do not see him,
that the case is before him, and you are waiting for him!
15 And now, because his anger does not punish,
and he does not greatly heed transgression,[b]
16 Job opens his mouth in empty talk,
he multiplies words without knowledge."

Elihu's fourth and climactic speech

Chs. 36–37: The speech has three parts. Each begins with an address to Job (36.2–4, 16–21; 37.14–22) and then depicts God as just and wise (36.5–15, 22–25; 37.23–24). The depiction of God in the middle section (36.26–37.13) is accomplished by describing God's masterpiece, the storm, which vividly illustrates divine wisdom and power.

36 Elihu continued and said:
2 "Bear with me a little, and I will show you,
for I have yet something to say on God's behalf.
3 I will bring my knowledge from far away,
and ascribe righteousness to my Maker.
4 For truly my words are not false;
one who is perfect in knowledge is with you.

5 "Surely God is mighty and does not despise any;
he is mighty in strength of understanding.
6 He does not keep the wicked alive,
but gives the afflicted their right.

a Traditional rendering of Heb *Shaddai*   *b* Theodotion Symmachus Compare Vg: Meaning of Heb uncertain

7 He does not withdraw his eyes from the
    righteous,
       but with kings on the throne
    he sets them forever, and they are
       exalted.
8 And if they are bound in fetters
    and caught in the cords of affliction,
9 then he declares to them their work
    and their transgressions, that they are
       behaving arrogantly.
10 He opens their ears to instruction,
    and commands that they return from
       iniquity.
11 If they listen, and serve him,
    they complete their days in
       prosperity,
    and their years in pleasantness.
12 But if they do not listen, they shall
       perish by the sword,
    and die without knowledge.

13 "The godless in heart cherish anger;
    they do not cry for help when he
       binds them.
14 They die in their youth,
    and their life ends in shame.*a*
15 He delivers the afflicted by their
       affliction,
    and opens their ear by adversity.
16 He also allured you out of distress
    into a broad place where there was no
       constraint,
    and what was set on your table was
       full of fatness.

17 "But you are obsessed with the case of
       the wicked;
    judgment and justice seize you.
18 Beware that wrath does not entice you
       into scoffing,
    and do not let the greatness of the
       ransom turn you aside.
19 Will your cry avail to keep you from
       distress,
    or will all the force of your strength?
20 Do not long for the night,
    when peoples are cut off in their
       place.
21 Beware! Do not turn to iniquity;
    because of that you have been tried
       by affliction.

22 See, God is exalted in his power;
    who is a teacher like him?
23 Who has prescribed for him his way,
    or who can say, 'You have done
       wrong'?

24 "Remember to extol his work,
    of which mortals have sung.
25 All people have looked on it;
    everyone watches it from far away.
26 Surely God is great, and we do not
       know him;
    the number of his years is
       unsearchable.
27 For he draws up the drops of water;
    he distills*b* his mist in rain,
28 which the skies pour down
    and drop upon mortals abundantly.
29 Can anyone understand the spreading
       of the clouds,
    the thunderings of his pavilion?
30 See, he scatters his lightning around
       him
    and covers the roots of the sea.
31 For by these he governs peoples;
    he gives food in abundance.
32 He covers his hands with the lightning,
    and commands it to strike the mark.
33 Its crashing*c* tells about him;
    he is jealous*c* with anger against
       iniquity.

37 "At this also my heart trembles,
    and leaps out of its place.
2 Listen, listen to the thunder of his voice
    and the rumbling that comes from his
       mouth.
3 Under the whole heaven he lets it loose,
    and his lightning to the corners of the
       earth.
4 After it his voice roars;
    he thunders with his majestic voice
    and he does not restrain the
       lightnings*d* when his voice is
       heard.
5 God thunders wondrously with his voice;
    he does great things that we cannot
       comprehend.

a Heb *ends among the temple prostitutes*   *b* Cn: Heb
they distill   *c* Meaning of Heb uncertain
d Heb *them*

6 For to the snow he says, 'Fall on the
    earth';
    and the shower of rain, his heavy
        shower of rain,

7 serves as a sign on everyone's hand,
    so that all whom he has made may
        know it.*

8 Then the animals go into their lairs
    and remain in their dens.

9 From its chamber comes the whirlwind,
    and cold from the scattering winds.

10 By the breath of God ice is given,
    and the broad waters are frozen fast.

11 He loads the thick cloud with moisture;
    the clouds scatter his lightning.

12 They turn round and round by his
        guidance,
    to accomplish all that he commands
        them
    on the face of the habitable world.

13 Whether for correction, or for his land,
    or for love, he causes it to happen.

14 "Hear this, O Job;
    stop and consider the wondrous
        works of God.

15 Do you know how God lays his
        command upon them,
    and causes the lightning of his cloud
        to shine?

16 Do you know the balancings of the
        clouds,
    the wondrous works of the one whose
        knowledge is perfect,

17 you whose garments are hot
    when the earth is still because of the
        south wind?

18 Can you, like him, spread out the skies,
    hard as a molten mirror?

19 Teach us what we shall say to him;
    we cannot draw up our case because
        of darkness.

20 Should he be told that I want to speak?
    Did anyone ever wish to be swallowed
        up?

21 Now, no one can look on the light
    when it is bright in the skies,
    when the wind has passed and
        cleared them.

22 Out of the north comes golden splendor;
    around God is awesome majesty.

23 The Almighty*—we cannot find him;
    he is great in power and justice,
    and abundant righteousness he will
        not violate.

24 Therefore mortals fear him;
    he does not regard any who are wise
        in their own conceit."

37.1–24. 15: *Do you know how God lays his command upon them?* This challenging question to Job about the operating of the universe, as well as the similar ones in vv. 15–18, foreshadow the Lord's questions to him in the divine speeches. **23:** *The Almighty—we cannot find him:* Elihu's final speech is full of ironies. Job will soon find the Almighty; God is in the storm that Elihu so eloquently described in 36.26–37.13, but differently than Elihu imagines.

GOD'S TWO SPEECHES TO JOB

38.1–42.6: The Lord's sudden appearance in the storm never fails to astonish even though the ground has been laid for it in Job's oaths and demands of chs. 27 and 29–31 and, in an ironic* way, by Elihu's "appearance" and final statement. God answers Job out of the whirlwind in two speeches (chs. 38–39 and 40–41), each evoking a brief response by Job (40.1–5 and 42.1–6). The structure and the meaning of the speeches have puzzled scholars. Some believe the speeches are deliberately incoherent, irrational divine blasts showing there is no answer to Job's questions except inscrutable divine will. Others rearrange the text, but no rearrangement has won wide acceptance. Most, however, find some kind of logic, even though the speeches are also an example of the mysterious communication of creator to creature. The first speech shows that the world has a design (God is wise, is able to govern), and the second demonstrates the world is just (God upholds the righteous and puts down the wicked).

38.1–40.5: The Lord's first speech and Job's response. God treats Job like a rival claimant to deity. God's questions, despite their variety, come down to one: Did you bring the world into being? Job was the one who established the legal context. Now, under God's relentless legal questioning, he cannot give a single answer. The topic of the speech is *counsel*, which Job is accused of obscuring (38.2). *Who is this*

a Meaning of Heb of verse 7 uncertain   *b* Traditional rendering of Heb *Shaddai*

that darkens counsel by words without knowledge? *Counsel* is better rendered "plan, design" (as in Ps 14.6; 20.4; Prov 20.5). An example of Job's charge that the earth was purely random and without design is 9.5–6, where Job accuses God of overturning the primordial mountains and earth, that is, of not knowing how to create. God counters by asking Job if he actually witnessed the foundation of the earth, and then reveals how carefully he built with measuring line, sockets, and cornerstone while a festive chorus sang as at a Temple* dedication (38.4–7). Another example is Job's accusation that God does not distinguish between the wicked and the righteous (9.24). On the contrary, dawn exposes the night deeds of the wicked, which does not, however, necessarily lead to their punishment (38.12–15). Even the proverbial stupid ostrich is stupid by design (39.13–18), a reminder that God creates not for human beings but for his own inscrutable purpose. The world includes the useful, the bizarre, and even the playful, all by God's design. The rhetorical* method of the speech is to list eight items of the inanimate world (38.4–38) and eight items of the animal and bird kingdoms (38.39–39.30). In none of them did Job have any role, a conclusion that is made clear by Job's inability to answer the divine questions. Significantly, the human race is not mentioned in either catalog. The human race—including Job—are not the center of the universe.

---

38 Then the LORD answered Job out of the whirlwind:

2 "Who is this that darkens counsel by
    words without knowledge?
3 Gird up your loins like a man,
    I will question you, and you shall
      declare to me.

4 "Where were you when I laid the
    foundation of the earth?
    Tell me, if you have understanding.
5 Who determined its measurements—
    surely you know!
    Or who stretched the line upon it?
6 On what were its bases sunk,
    or who laid its cornerstone
7 when the morning stars sang together
    and all the heavenly beings[a] shouted
      for joy?

8 "Or who shut in the sea with doors
    when it burst out from the womb?—

9 when I made the clouds its garment,
    and thick darkness its swaddling
      band,
10 and prescribed bounds for it,
    and set bars and doors,
11 and said, 'Thus far shall you come, and
    no farther,
    and here shall your proud waves be
      stopped'?

38.8: *When it burst out from the womb?* A common myth told of sea personified* as a monster whom the storm god defeated in order to create. Here, the monster is reduced to an infant in order to show God's easy control (see Ps 104.26).

~~~~~~

12 "Have you commanded the morning
    since your days began,
    and caused the dawn to know its
      place,
13 so that it might take hold of the skirts of
    the earth,
    and the wicked be shaken out of it?
14 It is changed like clay under the seal,
    and it is dyed[b] like a garment.
15 Light is withheld from the wicked,
    and their uplifted arm is broken.

16 "Have you entered into the springs of
    the sea,
    or walked in the recesses of the deep?
17 Have the gates of death been revealed
    to you,
    or have you seen the gates of deep
      darkness?
18 Have you comprehended the expanse of
    the earth?
    Declare, if you know all this.

19 "Where is the way to the dwelling of
    light,
    and where is the place of darkness,
20 that you may take it to its territory
    and that you may discern the paths to
      its home?
21 Surely you know, for you were born
    then,
    and the number of your days is great!

a Heb *sons of God*   *b* Cn: Heb *and they stand forth*

22 "Have you entered the storehouses of
the snow,
or have you seen the storehouses of
the hail,

23 which I have reserved for the time of
trouble,
for the day of battle and war?

24 What is the way to the place where the
light is distributed,
or where the east wind is scattered
upon the earth?

25 "Who has cut a channel for the torrents
of rain,
and a way for the thunderbolt,

26 to bring rain on a land where no one
lives,
on the desert, which is empty of
human life,

27 to satisfy the waste and desolate land,
and to make the ground put forth
grass?

28 "Has the rain a father,
or who has begotten the drops of
dew?

29 From whose womb did the ice come
forth,
and who has given birth to the
hoarfrost of heaven?

30 The waters become hard like stone,
and the face of the deep is frozen.

31 "Can you bind the chains of the
Pleiades,
or loose the cords of Orion?

32 Can you lead forth the Mazzaroth in
their season,
or can you guide the Bear with its
children?

33 Do you know the ordinances of the
heavens?
Can you establish their rule on the
earth?

38.26–31. 26: *To bring rain on a land where no one
lives:* God cares for areas where no human beings live,
a rebuke to an anthropocentric view of creation. Human beings are not the measure. 31: *The Pleiades . . .
Orion . . . Mazzaroth . . . the Bear:* The Pleiades is the
Greek name for a cluster of six stars in the Taurus con-

stellation, well known to ancient star gazers. *Orion* is
a constellation on the equator east of Taurus imagined
by the Greeks as a hunter with belt and sword. The
identifications of *Mazzaroth* and *the Bear* are
uncertain.

~~~~~~

34 "Can you lift up your voice to the
clouds,
so that a flood of waters may cover
you?

35 Can you send forth lightnings, so that
they may go
and say to you, 'Here we are'?

36 Who has put wisdom in the inward
parts,[a]
or given understanding to the
mind?[a]

37 Who has the wisdom to number the
clouds?
Or who can tilt the waterskins of the
heavens,

38 when the dust runs into a mass
and the clods cling together?

39 "Can you hunt the prey for the lion,
or satisfy the appetite of the young
lions,

40 when they crouch in their dens,
or lie in wait in their covert?

41 Who provides for the raven its prey,
when its young ones cry to God,
and wander about for lack of food?

39 "Do you know when the mountain
goats give birth?
Do you observe the calving of the
deer?

2 Can you number the months that they
fulfill,
and do you know the time when they
give birth,

3 when they crouch to give birth to their
offspring,
and are delivered of their young?

4 Their young ones become strong, they
grow up in the open;
they go forth, and do not return to
them.

---

a Meaning of Heb uncertain

5 "Who has let the wild ass go free?
    Who has loosed the bonds of the
        swift ass,
6 to which I have given the steppe for its
        home,
    the salt land for its dwelling place?
7 It scorns the tumult of the city;
    it does not hear the shouts of the
        driver.
8 It ranges the mountains as its pasture,
    and it searches after every green
        thing.

9 "Is the wild ox willing to serve you?
    Will it spend the night at your crib?
10 Can you tie it in the furrow with ropes,
    or will it harrow the valleys after you?
11 Will you depend on it because its
        strength is great,
    and will you hand over your labor to it?
12 Do you have faith in it that it will return,
    and bring your grain to your threshing
        floor?*a*

13 "The ostrich's wings flap wildly,
    though its pinions lack plumage.*b*
14 For it leaves its eggs to the earth,
    and lets them be warmed on the
        ground,
15 forgetting that a foot may crush them,
    and that a wild animal may trample
        them.
16 It deals cruelly with its young, as if they
        were not its own;
    though its labor should be in vain, yet
        it has no fear;
17 because God has made it forget wisdom,
    and given it no share in understanding.
18 When it spreads its plumes aloft,*b*
    it laughs at the horse and its rider.

19 "Do you give the horse its might?
    Do you clothe its neck with mane?
20 Do you make it leap like the locust?
    Its majestic snorting is terrible.
21 It paws*c* violently, exults mightily;
    it goes out to meet the weapons.
22 It laughs at fear, and is not dismayed;
    it does not turn back from the sword.
23 Upon it rattle the quiver,
    the flashing spear, and the javelin.

24 With fierceness and rage it swallows the
        ground;
    it cannot stand still at the sound of
        the trumpet.
25 When the trumpet sounds, it says 'Aha!'
    From a distance it smells the battle,
    the thunder of the captains, and the
        shouting.

26 "Is it by your wisdom that the hawk
        soars,
    and spreads its wings toward the
        south?
27 Is it at your command that the eagle
        mounts up
    and makes its nest on high?
28 It lives on the rock and makes its home
    in the fastness of the rocky crag.
29 From there it spies the prey;
    its eyes see it from far away.
30 Its young ones suck up blood;
    and where the slain are, there it is."

40 And the LORD said to Job:
2 "Shall a faultfinder contend with
        the Almighty?*d*
    Anyone who argues with God must
        respond."

3 Then Job answered the LORD:
4 "See, I am of small account; what shall
        I answer you?
    I lay my hand on my mouth.
5 I have spoken once, and I will not
        answer;
    twice, but will proceed no further."

40.2: *Shall a faultfinder contend with the Almighty?* God's concluding question to Job is a legal one: Can the one who brought me into court answer my questions?

God's second speech and Job's response
40.6–42.6: The topic of the second speech is God's justice, which was criticized by Job. *Will you even put me in the wrong* (v. 8) is, literally, "Would you impugn my justice?" Justice here, and in the Bible generally, is

---

a Heb *your grain and your threshing floor*   b Meaning of Heb uncertain   c Gk Syr Vg: Heb *they dig*
d Traditional rendering of Heb *Shaddai*

not the Western concept, passive and impartial (hearing out both sides), but the ancient Near Eastern concept, active and partial (upholding the righteous and putting down the wicked). Job accuses God of being unjust in this sense, that is, allowing the unjust to prosper and the righteous (like Job) to suffer. God's response, in the form of a question (*Have you an arm like God?* v. 9), silences Job, for Job can never be just in this sense. The rhetorical★ method of the second speech is surprising in that God simply describes two great animals: *Behemoth*★ (40.15–24) and *Leviathan*★ (41.1–34). Both animals are mythological beasts (though Behemoth may be modeled on the hippopotamus). Behemoth and Leviathan symbolize the two great untamed and chaotic areas, respectively, the immense and lifeless desert and the vast and chaotic sea. The first speech (chs. 38–39) refuted Job's charge that God governs unwisely (without design) by demonstrating God cares for a vast world beyond human knowing. The second speech rebuts the charge that God is unjust by demonstrating God indeed can control ultimate cosmic evil (represented by Behemoth and Leviathan), but does not necessarily exercise control over it for the immediate benefit of human beings. God's mastery over the beasts is shown by 40.24 (Heb., "By [Behemoth's] eyes he is captured, by hooks his nose is pierced") and by 41.12 (Heb., uncertain, "Did I not silence [Leviathan's] boasting, his mighty words and martial deeds?"). The two beasts symbolize fearsome power that is beyond our understanding or control, yet they have a place in God's universe. They fulfill no evident function, cannot be domesticated, and do not serve human beings. God allows them to exist under divine control, despite their potential for evil. The world is God's, not man's (Job's).

---

6 Then the LORD answered Job out of the whirlwind:

7 "Gird up your loins like a man;
   I will question you, and you declare to me.

8 Will you even put me in the wrong?
   Will you condemn me that you may be justified?

9 Have you an arm like God,
   and can you thunder with a voice like his?

10 "Deck yourself with majesty and dignity;
   clothe yourself with glory and splendor.

11 Pour out the overflowings of your anger,
   and look on all who are proud, and abase them.

12 Look on all who are proud, and bring them low;
   tread down the wicked where they stand.

13 Hide them all in the dust together;
   bind their faces in the world below.*a*

14 Then I will also acknowledge to you
   that your own right hand can give you victory.

40.10: *Deck yourself with majesty and dignity:* God challenges Job to be just in the sense of putting down the wicked (vv. 10–14).

~~~~~~~~~~

15 "Look at Behemoth,
   which I made just as I made you;
   it eats grass like an ox.

16 Its strength is in its loins,
   and its power in the muscles of its belly.

17 It makes its tail stiff like a cedar;
   the sinews of its thighs are knit together.

18 Its bones are tubes of bronze,
   its limbs like bars of iron.

19 "It is the first of the great acts of God—
   only its Maker can approach it with the sword.

20 For the mountains yield food for it
   where all the wild animals play.

21 Under the lotus plants it lies,
   in the covert of the reeds and in the marsh.

22 The lotus trees cover it for shade;
   the willows of the wadi surround it.

23 Even if the river is turbulent, it is not frightened;
   it is confident though Jordan rushes against its mouth.

24 Can one take it with hooks*b*
   or pierce its nose with a snare?

41 *c*"Can you draw out Leviathan*d* with a fishhook,
   or press down its tongue with a cord?

a Heb *the hidden place*   *b* Cn: Heb *in his eyes*
c Ch 40.25 in Heb   *d* Or *the crocodile*

2 Can you put a rope in its nose,
  or pierce its jaw with a hook?
3 Will it make many supplications to you?
  Will it speak soft words to you?
4 Will it make a covenant with you
  to be taken as your servant forever?
5 Will you play with it as with a bird,
  or will you put it on leash for your
    girls?
6 Will traders bargain over it?
  Will they divide it up among the
    merchants?
7 Can you fill its skin with harpoons,
  or its head with fishing spears?
8 Lay hands on it;
  think of the battle; you will not do it
    again!
9 [a] Any hope of capturing it[b] will be
    disappointed;
  were not even the gods[c]
    overwhelmed at the sight of it?
10 No one is so fierce as to dare to stir it
    up.
  Who can stand before it?[d]
11 Who can confront it[d] and be safe?[e]
  —under the whole heaven, who?[f]

12 "I will not keep silence concerning its
    limbs,
  or its mighty strength, or its splendid
    frame.
13 Who can strip off its outer garment?
  Who can penetrate its double coat of
    mail?[g]
14 Who can open the doors of its face?
  There is terror all around its teeth.
15 Its back[h] is made of shields in rows,
  shut up closely as with a seal.
16 One is so near to another
  that no air can come between them.
17 They are joined one to another;
  they clasp each other and cannot be
    separated.
18 Its sneezes flash forth light,
  and its eyes are like the eyelids of the
    dawn.
19 From its mouth go flaming torches;
  sparks of fire leap out.
20 Out of its nostrils comes smoke,
  as from a boiling pot and burning
    rushes.

21 Its breath kindles coals,
  and a flame comes out of its mouth.
22 In its neck abides strength,
  and terror dances before it.
23 The folds of its flesh cling together;
  it is firmly cast and immovable.
24 Its heart is as hard as stone,
  as hard as the lower millstone.
25 When it raises itself up the gods are
    afraid;
  at the crashing they are beside
    themselves.
26 Though the sword reaches it, it does not
    avail,
  nor does the spear, the dart, or the
    javelin.
27 It counts iron as straw,
  and bronze as rotten wood.
28 The arrow cannot make it flee;
  slingstones, for it, are turned to
    chaff.
29 Clubs are counted as chaff;
  it laughs at the rattle of javelins.
30 Its underparts are like sharp
    potsherds;
  it spreads itself like a threshing sledge
    on the mire.
31 It makes the deep boil like a pot;
  it makes the sea like a pot of
    ointment.
32 It leaves a shining wake behind it;
  one would think the deep to be white-
    haired.
33 On earth it has no equal,
  a creature without fear.
34 It surveys everything that is lofty;
  it is king over all that are proud."

42

Then Job answered the LORD:
2 "I know that you can do all
    things,
  and that no purpose of yours can be
    thwarted.
3 'Who is this that hides counsel without
    knowledge?'

---

a Ch 41.1 in Heb   b Heb of it   c Cn Compare
Symmachus Syr: Heb one is   d Heb me   e Gk: Heb
that I shall repay   f Heb to me   g Gk: Heb bridle
h Cn Compare Gk Vg: Heb pride

Therefore I have uttered what I did not
   understand,
      things too wonderful for me, which I
         did not know.
4 'Hear, and I will speak;
      I will question you, and you declare
         to me.'
5 I had heard of you by the hearing of the
      ear,
      but now my eye sees you;
6 therefore I despise myself,
      and repent in dust and ashes."

42.1–6. 3: *Who is this that hides counsel without
knowledge?* Job cites God's two questions from the
first speech (38.2, 3) as a preface to his final statement
in this verse and in the next. The reprise of the opening
sentence, called an inclusio,* signals to the reader that
the section is concluding. **5:** *But now my eye sees you:*
Job had demanded to see God (19.26–27) and re-
sented God's hiding his face (13.24). God's thunder-
ous speech was an occasion for Job to "see" God. **6:**
*Therefore I despise myself and repent in dust and
ashes:* The meaning of the verse is uncertain because
no object is specified for the first verb. Is the verb re-
flexive or does it have an external object such as Job's
previous words or dust and ashes as the symbol of a
deprived plaintiff? Given the frequent legal language
of the book, it seems better to render "I retract and
give up my dust and ashes," that is, I give up my lawsuit (without necessarily admitting I was wrong).

EPILOGUE

42.7–17: The reappearance of the name of the LORD
and the resumption of the prose that was used in the
prologue signals the reader that the story is ending.
God declares Job the winner in his lengthy disputation
about divine wisdom and justice. Acting at God's command, Job intercedes for his friends as he interceded
for his children in the prologue (vv. 7–9). God gives
Job twice as much as he had before. His newly enlarged family consoles him (vv. 10–17).

---

7 After the LORD had spoken these words
to Job, the LORD said to Eliphaz the Temanite: "My wrath is kindled against you and
against your two friends; for you have not
spoken of me what is right, as my servant
Job has. 8Now therefore take seven bulls
and seven rams, and go to my servant Job,
and offer up for yourselves a burnt offering; and my servant Job shall pray for you,
for I will accept his prayer not to deal with
you according to your folly; for you have not
spoken of me what is right, as my servant Job
has done." 9So Eliphaz the Temanite and
Bildad the Shuhite and Zophar the Naamathite went and did what the LORD had
told them; and the LORD accepted Job's
prayer.

10 And the LORD restored the fortunes of
Job when he had prayed for his friends; and
the LORD gave Job twice as much as he had
before. 11Then there came to him all his
brothers and sisters and all who had known
him before, and they ate bread with him in
his house; they showed him sympathy and
comforted him for all the evil that the LORD
had brought upon him; and each of them
gave him a piece of money" and a gold ring.
12The LORD blessed the latter days of Job
more than his beginning; and he had fourteen thousand sheep, six thousand camels, a
thousand yoke of oxen, and a thousand donkeys. 13He also had seven sons and three
daughters. 14He named the first Jemimah,
the second Keziah, and the third Keren-
happuch. 15In all the land there were no
women so beautiful as Job's daughters; and
their father gave them an inheritance along
with their brothers. 16After this Job lived one
hundred and forty years, and saw his children, and his children's children, four generations. 17And Job died, old and full of days.

42.7–17. 7: *You have not spoken of me what is right,
as my servant Job has:* Job, who protested and accused
God of attacking an innocent man, is declared to have
told the truth about God, whereas the friends, who
defended God and divine justice and wisdom without
regard for truth, are judged to have acted out of folly
and incur God's anger. Job is once again an effective
intercessor (v. 10; compare 1.5). **11:** *They ate bread
with him in his house:* The meal shows the harmony
of the restored family and Job's reconciliation with his
friends.

---

a Heb *a qesitah*

PSALMS

Introduction

The Psalms is a collection of 150 songs of praise, prayers, and spiritual poems. All or parts of the book may have served as the hymnbook or prayerbook of the First Temple* (952–587 BCE) or Second Temple (515 BCE–70 CE), as well as the synagogues* that emerged in the Persian era.* The five-book arrangement of the Psalms (1–41, 42–72, 73–89, 90–106, 107–150) parallels the five books of the Torah.* It is likely that Books I–III received their final form earlier than IV–V, since three psalms dealing with the Davidic monarchy appear in crucial positions in Books I–III (2, 72, 89). The sequence seems to be intentional, and the probable purpose was to highlight the apparent failure of the Davidic covenant* with the destruction of Jerusalem and the Temple in 587 BCE (89.38–51). Book IV provides an immediate and effective response at the beginning of Ps 90 by calling attention to Moses, who led the people of God before the existence of monarchy, Temple, or land. Furthermore, Ps 93–99 then provide what many scholars identify as the central theme of the Psalms: the proclamation of God's cosmic and eternal reign (as opposed to the transient Davidic monarchy).

Book V continues to affirm the universal sovereignty of God (107, 145–150), but its more complex structure suggests different nuances. The appearance of Davidic collections (108–110, 138–145) redirects attention toward the Davidic monarchy, but the whole people of God now appears to fulfill the royal function of serving as God's earthly agents (see 144, 149). At the heart of the book, two collections featuring the Exodus (113–118) and Zion* (120–137) surround Ps 119, which upholds the central significance of the Torah. Because it no longer possessed either a land or a monarchy, the post-exilic community reorganized itself around the Torah. The prominence of the Torah in the final shape of the Psalms suggests that the character of the collection shifted as it grew to final form. What started out primarily as a hymnbook or prayerbook took on the additional character of something like a catechism or book of instruction, which is what the word "Torah" essentially means.

The English word "psalm" is derived from a Greek word, which in turn translates a Hebrew word meaning "musical praise." This etymology suggests that the original context of most of the psalms was in Israel's and Judah's worship of God. This probability is reinforced by frequent references to singing, shouting, dancing, and musical instruments. In addition, the Temple is often in view, along with its gates, courts, and altar. Exactly how, where, and when the psalms were used is not known. Undoubtedly the songs of praise were sung as part of worship when the people gathered at the three annual pilgrimage feasts, and they may have been used in daily Temple services and on special occasions and celebrations. The prayers may also have been used at these times. In later times, the psalms would have been used in the synagogues. The prayers may have been used in smaller group settings, possibly even in homes.

Further specificity is difficult to attain. The superscriptions, or headings, of many psalms associate them with particular individuals, especially David, but not with the implication that he was their author. "Of David," for instance, could mean "inspired by David" or "in memory of David." The thirteen instances in which the superscriptions associate the psalm with a specific episode in David's life should be understood as later attempts to provide an imagined narrative* context for the psalm. In this translation, these superscriptions appear in smaller italic type before the first verse of some of the psalms. Psalm 3 gives an example of a superscription linking that Psalm to an event in David's life.

The Psalms are difficult to date. The safest conclusion is that they originated in various periods and had a long and varied history of use, even within the biblical period. The collection in its present form shows signs of having been shaped in response to the crisis of the Exile★ and its aftermath. The Psalms as a book of scripture made it especially suited for teaching persons about God, humankind, and the life of faith.

READING GUIDE
There are obvious similarities among psalms, and it is helpful to attend to the traditional means of categorizing them:

Song of praise or hymn. The typical elements are an invitation to praise God, followed by reasons for praise that focus upon God's character (100, 117) or upon God's work as creator (8, 104) or deliverer (103). Usually considered as sub-types are psalms known as the enthronement psalms (29, 47, 93, 95–99—hymns that celebrate God's reign) and the songs of Zion (46, 48, 76, 84, 87, 120—hymns that focus praise on the city of Jerusalem, thus praising God more indirectly).

Prayer for help. The prayers, often known as laments★ or complaints, address God directly. Typical elements include opening address, description of the distress (the lament or complaint proper), petition for help, affirmation of trust, and vow to praise God. Most of the prayers appear to be those of individuals (13, 22), but there are also several communal laments (44, 74). These prayers are the most frequent type of psalm. The situations out of which they arose are unclear. Their language and imagery suggest sickness, persecution by false accusers, and warfare. Reference to foes or enemies appears regularly in the prayers.

Song of thanksgiving. It is helpful to think of these psalms as the expression of the praise that is promised toward the conclusion of the prayers for help. The usual elements include the offering of thanks to God, a description of the former distress, testimony to God's ability to deliver, and an invitation to others to join in praising God (30, 34).

Royal psalms. This category is based more on content than structure. It includes the psalms that mention the king or appear to have been associated with services or rituals involving the monarchy (2, 18, 20, 21, 45, 72, 89, 101, 110, 132, 144).

Wisdom/Torah psalms. Neither songs of praise nor prayers, they are spiritual poems that offer reflections on or advice concerning the faithful life (37, 49, 73) or the Torah (1, 19, 119).

Scholars frequently disagree on the appropriate categorization of particular psalms. Moreover, other psalms do not fit the major categories. They are sometimes given other designations such as entrance liturgies★ (15, 24), prophetic★ exhortations★ (50, 81, 95), psalms of trust (11, 16, 23, 91), and historical psalms (78, 105, 106, 136).

In addition to noticing the features shared by psalms, readers should attend to what is unique in each psalm. The individuality of each psalm is created by the poet's choice of vocabulary and imagery. Also, typical elements are arranged differently to create a certain effect. Thus, readers should attend carefully to the structure of each psalm. The stylistic device of parallelism★ (expressing essentially the same thought in different words) will be obvious, but it should be noted that only rarely does the second part of a line merely repeat or paraphrase the first part. In the second part, the poet often heightens or intensifies an image or concept. Perhaps the most important stylistic device in the Psalms is repetition. Since the repetition in Hebrew is often obscured by the translation, the following annotations will point out important instances of this device.

Most psalms have a superscription. In addition to personal names, the superscriptions often contain what appear to be liturgical information or instructions. The precise meaning of most of the terms is uncertain, but they may indicate an ancient melody or appropriate musical accompaniment or setting for use in worship. Just as mysterious is the term "Selah," which also appears to have had some liturgical significance, perhaps indicating where a response was to be sung or a musical interlude was to appear.

Because the Psalms in their final form have an instructional intent, the reader may want to keep in mind some of the following questions about the meaning of the Psalms:

How is happiness portrayed in the Psalms, and how does this differ from the varied definitions of happiness today?

How do you assess the claim that God rules the world, especially in light of the reality that God is constantly opposed in the Psalms?

Of what significance is it that "the righteous" in the Psalms are those who constantly find themselves to be the afflicted, poor, persecuted, and needy?

How may the Psalms serve as models for prayer?

What is the theological function of violence and vengeance in the Psalms?

Of what significance is it that complaint and praise are constantly juxtaposed in the Psalms?

BOOK ONE

PSALM 1

1 Happy are those
    who do not follow the advice of the
        wicked,
or take the path that sinners tread,
    or sit in the seat of scoffers;
2 but their delight is in the law of the
        LORD,
    and on his law they meditate day and
        night.
3 They are like trees
    planted by streams of water,
which yield their fruit in its season,
    and their leaves do not wither.
In all that they do, they prosper.

4 The wicked are not so,
    but are like chaff that the wind drives
        away.
5 Therefore the wicked will not stand in
        the judgment,
    nor sinners in the congregation of the
        righteous;

6 for the LORD watches over the way of
        the righteous,
    but the way of the wicked will perish.

1.1–6: Happy are those. 1–2: By defining happiness (2.12) over against *the wicked, sinners,* and *scoffers,* the poet heightens the contrast between two different ways or lifestyles. *Scoffers* refuse to accept instruction (Prov 1.22). The *happy* are those who are constantly open to God's instruction (Josh 1.8). The Hebrew word translated here as *law* is "torah," which would be better translated "instruction" or "teaching." "Torah"* can designate particular legal stipulations, but it can also refer more broadly to the entire tradition of God's revelation. **3–4:** These central verses each contain a comparison. What characterizes *trees planted by streams of water* is their stable rootedness (Jer 17.8). Prosperity should not be understood as a reward but rather as the result of being connected to God. Such rootedness is exactly what *the wicked* lack; they are easily blown away. **5–6:** It is unclear whether judgment should be understood as "the final judgment." In any case, the wicked have no foundation. Lack of connection to God means death, the ultimate contrast to happiness.

PSALM 2

1 Why do the nations conspire,
    and the peoples plot in vain?
2 The kings of the earth set themselves,
    and the rulers take counsel together,
    against the LORD and his anointed,
        saying,
3 "Let us burst their bonds asunder,
    and cast their cords from us."

4 He who sits in the heavens laughs;
    the LORD has them in derision.
5 Then he will speak to them in his
        wrath,
    and terrify them in his fury, saying,
6 "I have set my king on Zion, my holy
        hill."

7 I will tell of the decree of the LORD:
He said to me, "You are my son;
    today I have begotten you.
8 Ask of me, and I will make the nations
        your heritage,
    and the ends of the earth your
        possession.
9 You shall break them with a rod of iron,
    and dash them in pieces like a
        potter's vessel."

10 Now therefore, O kings, be wise;
    be warned, O rulers of the earth.
11 Serve the LORD with fear,
    with trembling 12kiss his feet,*a*
or he will be angry, and you will perish
       in the way;
    for his wrath is quickly kindled.

Happy are all who take refuge in him.

2.1–12: The LORD and the anointed. ★ A royal psalm, it may have been used originally at the coronation of Judean kings. Now paired with Ps 1, it introduces the entire collection. It proclaims God's universal reign, a major theme of the Psalms (Ps 93–99). **1–3:** The LORD's *anointed* (Hebrew "meshiach," usually written "messiah"★) is the Judean king, the earthly agent of God's reign (Ps 72). **4–6:** Because God is cosmic ruler, God can laugh at the presumptuous earthly kings (37.13; 59.9). Verse 6 may have been spoken by a priest or prophet.★ *Zion*★ is the mountain that Jerusalem oc-

cupies, God's *holy hill* (3.4; 15.1). **7–9:** The speaker in v. 7 is the king, who was viewed as God's adopted son (2 Sam 7.14). *Today* apparently indicates the day of enthronement. The promises in vv. 8–9 (see 20.2; 21.4) are standard ancient Near Eastern hyperbole.★ The king is to represent God's universal sovereignty (72.8–11). **10–12:** The rebellious *kings* and *rulers* are now admonished to subject themselves to God's rule. The difficult vv. 11b–12a probably are meant to reinforce *serve the LORD* (see 100.2, where NRSV translates the same verb as "worship"). The words *perish* and *way* recall Ps 1, as does *happy*. To *take refuge* is to trust God and to live in fundamental dependence upon God, a theme that pervades the Psalms (5.11; 7.1; 144.2).

~~~~~~~~~~~~~~~~~~~~~~~~~~~~~~~~~~~~~~~

PSALM 3

A Psalm of David, when he fled from his son Absalom.

1 O LORD, how many are my foes!
    Many are rising against me;
2 many are saying to me,
    "There is no help for you*b* in God."
               Selah

3 But you, O LORD, are a shield around
       me,
    my glory, and the one who lifts up my
       head.
4 I cry aloud to the LORD,
    and he answers me from his holy hill.
               Selah

5 I lie down and sleep;
    I wake again, for the LORD sustains
       me.
6 I am not afraid of ten thousands of
       people
    who have set themselves against me
       all around.

7 Rise up, O LORD!
    Deliver me, O my God!
For you strike all my enemies on the
       cheek;
    you break the teeth of the wicked.

---

a Cn: Meaning of Heb of verses 11b and 12a is uncertain   *b* Syr: Heb *him*

8 Deliverance belongs to the LORD;
 may your blessing be on your people!
 Selah

3.1–8: Help belongs to the LORD. The first prayer for help in the psalter. The superscription invites the reader to hear the prayer in conjunction with David's experience in 2 Sam 15–18. **1–2:** The repetition of *many* emphasizes the threat from the *foes*, who contradict 2.12 by advising self-assertion rather than trust in God. The Hebrew for *help* is a form of *deliver* (v. 7) and *deliverance* (v. 8). **3–4:** Deliverance seems to lie in the future (see v. 7), but it is nonetheless sure (v. 8). **5–6:** Such assurance explains how the daily rhythms of life are still possible amid *ten thousands*, which is from the same root as *many* in v. 1. **7–8:** Petition (vv. 7a, 8b) surrounds profession (vv. 7b–8a). As the foes *are rising* (v. 1), God is asked to *rise* (7.6; 9.19) and to *deliver*, which is precisely what the foes said God cannot do. Thus, it is appropriate that the psalmist trusts that God will deliver by aiming at the *cheek* and *teeth* (58.6), organs of speech. *Deliverance* means the opportunity to live fully, a *blessing* (5.12; 28.9) the psalmist desires for others as well.

PSALM 4

To the leader: with stringed instruments.
A Psalm of David.

1 Answer me when I call, O God of my
 right!
 You gave me room when I was in
 distress.
 Be gracious to me, and hear my
 prayer.

2 How long, you people, shall my honor
 suffer shame?
 How long will you love vain words,
 and seek after lies?   *Selah*
3 But know that the LORD has set apart
 the faithful for himself;
 the LORD hears when I call to
 him.

4 When you are disturbed,*a* do not sin;
 ponder it on your beds, and be silent.
 Selah
5 Offer right sacrifices,
 and put your trust in the LORD.

6 There are many who say, "O that we
 might see some good!
 Let the light of your face shine on us,
 O LORD!"
7 You have put gladness in my heart
 more than when their grain and wine
 abound.

8 I will both lie down and sleep in peace;
 for you alone, O LORD, make me lie
 down in safety.

4.1–8: Trust in the LORD. Usually labeled a lament* because of the prayers in vv. 1, 6–8, it also contains the psalmist's questions to others and subsequent counsel (vv. 2–5), which function as a profession of faith. **1:** Three typical pleas surround a remembrance of past help. *Right* signifies that righteousness is a characteristic of God and God's reign (5.8; 9.8; 96.13). **2–3:** The question is apparently addressed to opponents who have injured the psalmist (3.1–2). In response to opposition, the psalmist affirms that he or she belongs to God. **4–5:** The advice to *be silent* has the sense of "Don't worry" or "Be at peace" (v. 8), and prepares for the admonition to *trust*, which is a pervasive theme in the Psalms (9.10; 21.7). It is synonymous with taking refuge in God (2.12; 62.8; 91.2). When the whole self has been yielded to God, *right sacrifices* (51.19) become possible. **6–8:** Verse 7 suggests that what other people prayed for in v. 6 was wealth and possessions. The psalmist is content with a relationship of trust in God. It affords constant *peace* (3.5) as well as *safety*, even amid the opposition and materialism of others.

PSALM 5

To the leader: for the flutes. A Psalm of David.

1 Give ear to my words, O LORD;
 give heed to my sighing.
2 Listen to the sound of my cry,
 my King and my God,
 for to you I pray.
3 O LORD, in the morning you hear my
 voice;
 in the morning I plead my case to
 you, and watch.

a Or *are angry*

4 For you are not a God who delights in
    wickedness;
    evil will not sojourn with you.
5 The boastful will not stand before your
    eyes;
    you hate all evildoers.
6 You destroy those who speak lies;
    the LORD abhors the bloodthirsty and
    deceitful.

7 But I, through the abundance of your
    steadfast love,
    will enter your house,
    I will bow down toward your holy
    temple
    in awe of you.
8 Lead me, O LORD, in your
    righteousness
    because of my enemies;
    make your way straight before me.

9 For there is no truth in their mouths;
    their hearts are destruction;
    their throats are open graves;
    they flatter with their tongues.
10 Make them bear their guilt, O God;
    let them fall by their own counsels;
    because of their many transgressions
    cast them out,
    for they have rebelled against you.

11 But let all who take refuge in you
    rejoice;
    let them ever sing for joy.
    Spread your protection over them,
    so that those who love your name
    may exult in you.
12 For you bless the righteous, O LORD;
    you cover them with favor as with a
    shield.

5.1–12: I will enter your house. In this lament,* appeal to God (vv. 1–3, 7–8, 11–12) alternates with complaint about the enemies (vv. 4–6, 9–10). Verses 7–8 form a structural and theological center. 1–3: The word King is the first time in the psalter that the Hebrew root "mlk" is used of God. As usual God's sovereignty is proclaimed amid opposition. The morning seems to have been an appointed time for prayer (55.17; 59.16). 4–6: Wickedness is followed by six synonyms. The total of seven suggests God's complete

opposition to unrighteousness (1.6; 2.12). 7–8: The psalmist attributes entry into the Temple* not to personal merit but to God's steadfast love, the first occurrence of "hesed," which is virtually a one-word summary of God's character (see Ex 34.6–7; Ps 100.5; 107.1). The request for God to lead me (23.6; 31.7) anticipates vv. 11–12. Entry into the Temple may have been to make a judicial appeal for vindication from the false accusations of the enemies. 9–10: Verse 9 features four anatomical terms, three of which are organs of speech (3.7). Transgressions in v. 10 connotes willful rebellion. The wicked refuse to be led. 11–12: It was the responsibility of a King (v. 2) to protect his people, and refuge (2.12) is what the psalmist requests.

PSALM 6
To the leader: with stringed instruments; according to The Sheminith. A Psalm of David.

1 O LORD, do not rebuke me in your
    anger,
    or discipline me in your wrath.
2 Be gracious to me, O LORD, for I am
    languishing;
    O LORD, heal me, for my bones are
    shaking with terror.
3 My soul also is struck with terror,
    while you, O LORD—how long?

4 Turn, O LORD, save my life;
    deliver me for the sake of your
    steadfast love.
5 For in death there is no remembrance
    of you;
    in Sheol who can give you praise?

6 I am weary with my moaning;
    every night I flood my bed with
    tears;
    I drench my couch with my weeping.
7 My eyes waste away because of grief;
    they grow weak because of all
    my foes.

8 Depart from me, all you workers of evil,
    for the LORD has heard the sound of
    my weeping.
9 The LORD has heard my supplication;
    the LORD accepts my prayer.
10 All my enemies shall be ashamed and
    struck with terror;

they shall turn back, and in a moment
    be put to shame.

6.1–10: Save my life. This lament* may have been prayed originally in a context of sickness, but the language can be heard metaphorically.* It became one of the church's Penitential Psalms* (a grouping of Psalms that derives from the fourth or fifth century and that are traditionally used in seasons of penitence, such as Lent; see Ps 32, 38, 51, 102, 130, 143). **1–3:** Verse 1 reflects the ancient belief that sickness was caused by sin (41.4; Mk 2.1–12). At the same time, the psalmist appeals to God's grace and healing power. *How long?* is a typical question in the laments. **4–5:** The plea for God to *turn,* accompanied by the appeal to God's *steadfast love* (5.7), is reminiscent of Moses' plea for the people's life (see Ex 32.12; Ps 90.13–14, which is attributed to Moses). *Sheol** is the realm of the dead (30.3; 88.3). **6–7:** The central v. 6a recalls vv. 1–3 and introduces vv. 8–10. **8–10:** Trusting that he or she has been *heard,* the psalmist is transformed. The *terror* formerly experienced (vv. 2–3) will become the enemies'. It is not at all clear that the psalmist has been healed, but trust has triumphed over the pervasive weariness articulated in vv. 1–3, 6–7.

PSALM 7

A Shiggaion of David, which he sang to the
LORD concerning Cush, a Benjaminite.

1 O LORD my God, in you I take refuge;
    save me from all my pursuers, and
        deliver me,
2 or like a lion they will tear me apart;
    they will drag me away, with no one
        to rescue.

3 O LORD my God, if I have done this,
    if there is wrong in my hands,
4 if I have repaid my ally with harm
    or plundered my foe without cause,
5 then let the enemy pursue and overtake
    me,
    trample my life to the ground,
    and lay my soul in the dust.   *Selah*

6 Rise up, O LORD, in your anger;
    lift yourself up against the fury of my
        enemies;
    awake, O my God;*a* you have
        appointed a judgment.

7 Let the assembly of the peoples be
    gathered around you,
    and over it take your seat*b* on high.
8 The LORD judges the peoples;
    judge me, O LORD, according to my
        righteousness
    and according to the integrity that is
        in me.

9 O let the evil of the wicked come to an
    end,
    but establish the righteous,
    you who test the minds and hearts,
        O righteous God.
10 God is my shield,
    who saves the upright in heart.
11 God is a righteous judge,
    and a God who has indignation every
        day.

12 If one does not repent, God*c* will whet
    his sword;
    he has bent and strung his bow;
13 he has prepared his deadly weapons,
    making his arrows fiery shafts.
14 See how they conceive evil,
    and are pregnant with mischief,
    and bring forth lies.
15 They make a pit, digging it out,
    and fall into the hole that they have
        made.
16 Their mischief returns upon their own
    heads,
    and on their own heads their violence
        descends.

17 I will give to the LORD the thanks due
    to his righteousness,
    and sing praise to the name of the
        LORD, the Most High.

7.1–17: Establish the righteous. The allusion in the superscription is unclear, since no Cush appears in the Davidic narratives.* This lament* may originally have been prayed by a person falsely accused (Ps 5). **1–2:** Confidence in God as *refuge* (2.12; 5.11) grounds the petitions. The enemies are often described as animals (10.9). **3–5:** With an oath formula, the psalmist de-

a Or *awake for me*   *b* Cn: Heb *return*   *c* Heb *he*

clares innocence. The claim is for innocence in a particular case (see Job 31). **6–8:** *Judgment* (v. 6), *judges*
(v. 8), and *judge* (v. 11) derive from the Hebrew
"shpt," "to judge" or "do justice," a key word in the
psalm. God's commitment to justice follows from
God's sovereignty over all (vv. 6–8). *Integrity* connotes
innocence (Job 31.6). **9–11:** The other key word is
"tsdq," *righteous* (twice in v. 9; see vv. 8, 11, 17), an
attribute of God and God's reign (4.1; 5.8; 96.13). The
psalmist trusts that God's commitment to justice in the
cosmos will also work itself out for individuals. **12–13:**
The subject of the verbs is unclear (see note *c*). The
NRSV casts God in the role of just warrior (38.2; 64.7).
14–17: The subject of the verbs is *the wicked* (v. 9).
Birth imagery dominates v. 14 (Job 15.35). The psalmist trusts that wickedness destroys itself (9.16; 57.6).
The psalmist interprets this as God's *righteousness* and
is grateful (v. 17; see 1.6).

PSALM 8

*To the leader: according to The Gittith. A Psalm
of David.*

1 O Lord, our Sovereign,
  how majestic is your name in all the
    earth!

You have set your glory above the
  heavens.
2   Out of the mouths of babes and
    infants
  you have founded a bulwark because of
    your foes,
    to silence the enemy and the avenger.

3 When I look at your heavens, the work
    of your fingers,
  the moon and the stars that you have
    established;
4 what are human beings that you are
    mindful of them,
  mortals*ᵃ* that you care for them?

5 Yet you have made them a little lower
    than God,*ᵇ*
  and crowned them with glory and
    honor.
6 You have given them dominion over the
    works of your hands;
  you have put all things under their
    feet,

7 all sheep and oxen,
  and also the beasts of the field,
8 the birds of the air, and the fish of the
    sea,
  whatever passes along the paths of
    the seas.

9 O Lord, our Sovereign,
  how majestic is your name in all the
    earth!

8.1–9: How majestic is your name. The first song of
praise in the psalter, its direct address of God is unique.
1a: Framing the psalm, the refrain (vv. 1a, 9) proclaims
God's world-wide reign. **1b–2:** The NRSV takes v. 1b
as a discrete thought, extending the scope of God's
sovereignty to *the heavens*. If the sense of v. 2 is that
God can use even vulnerable infants as a defense
against God's foes, then v. 2 anticipates vv. 3–8 and
the affirmation that God uses insignificant humans to
exercise God's rule. **3:** The only human action in the
psalm is a passive one—to *look*. **4:** The Hebrew behind
what is the same as *how* in vv. 1, 9, linking the central
verse of the psalm to its framework. **5–8:** What is implied by the relationship between vv. 1, 9 and v. 4 is
here made explicit. The sovereign God has *crowned*
humans with the symbols of sovereignty—*glory and
honor*. God's own works are put under the *dominion*
of humanity (see Gen 1.26–28). **9:** The word *all* occurs
for the fourth time (vv. 1, 6, 7). It is now clear that
God's *all*-ness is inextricably bound up with humankind's response.

PSALM 9

*To the leader: according to Muth-labben.
A Psalm of David.*

1 I will give thanks to the Lord with my
    whole heart;
  I will tell of all your wonderful deeds.
2 I will be glad and exult in you;
  I will sing praise to your name,
    O Most High.

3 When my enemies turned back,
  they stumbled and perished before
    you.

---

a Heb *ben adam*, lit. *son of man*   *b* Or *than the divine
beings* or *angels*: Heb *elohim*

4 For you have maintained my just cause;
   you have sat on the throne giving
      righteous judgment.

5 You have rebuked the nations, you have
      destroyed the wicked;
   you have blotted out their name
      forever and ever.
6 The enemies have vanished in
      everlasting ruins;
   their cities you have rooted out;
   the very memory of them has
      perished.

7 But the LORD sits enthroned forever,
   he has established his throne for
      judgment.
8 He judges the world with righteousness;
   he judges the peoples with equity.

9 The LORD is a stronghold for the
      oppressed,
   a stronghold in times of trouble.
10 And those who know your name put
      their trust in you,
   for you, O LORD, have not forsaken
      those who seek you.

11 Sing praises to the LORD, who dwells in
      Zion.
   Declare his deeds among the peoples.
12 For he who avenges blood is mindful of
      them;
   he does not forget the cry of the
      afflicted.

13 Be gracious to me, O LORD.
   See what I suffer from those who
      hate me;
   you are the one who lifts me up from
      the gates of death,
14 so that I may recount all your praises,
   and, in the gates of daughter Zion,
      rejoice in your deliverance.

15 The nations have sunk in the pit that
      they made;
   in the net that they hid has their own
      foot been caught.

16 The LORD has made himself known, he
      has executed judgment;
   the wicked are snared in the work of
      their own hands. *Higgaion. Selah*

17 The wicked shall depart to Sheol,
   all the nations that forget God.

18 For the needy shall not always be
      forgotten,
   nor the hope of the poor perish
      forever.

19 Rise up, O LORD! Do not let mortals
      prevail;
   let the nations be judged before
      you.
20 Put them in fear, O LORD;
   let the nations know that they are
      only human. *Selah*

9.1–10.18: The hope of the poor. Psalms 9 and 10 were probably written as a single acrostic* poem, one in which every other line begins with the succeeding letter of the Hebrew alphabet.* The Septuagint* (the ancient Greek translation of the Hebrew Scriptures*) treats them as one, and Ps 10 has no superscription. Psalm 9 has the characteristics of a song of thanksgiving and focuses on rebellious nations. Psalm 10 is a lament* that focuses on the wicked. **9.1–8:** The *wonderful deeds* for which the psalmist *gives thanks* include personal (vv. 3–4) as well as corporate deliverance (vv. 5–6). Such deliverance testifies to God's justice and righteousness (vv. 4, 7–8; see 7.11). These attributes characterize God's rule, which is articulated by *throne* (vv. 5, 7) and *enthroned* (v. 7). **9–12:** Because of God's justice and righteousness, the *oppressed* (v. 9) and *afflicted* (v. 12) are invited to *trust* (v. 10) and *praise* God (v. 11). The Hebrew root of *afflicted* recurs six times; it is translated *poor* (9.18; 10.2, 9), *oppressed* (10.12) and *meek* (10.17). That God *avenges blood* means that God values and protects human life. **13–14:** The repetition of *gates* expresses trust in God's ability to deliver from death to life. *Zion** is Jerusalem, God's city, and the psalmist will be there. **15–18:** God's "justice" (NRSV *judgment*) will be manifest as the wicked destroy themselves (7.15–16). *Sheol** is the realm of the dead (6.5). **19–20:** Focus on *the nations* continues (see vv. 5, 15, 17).

PSALM 10

1 Why, O LORD, do you stand far off?
　Why do you hide yourself in times of
　　trouble?
2 In arrogance the wicked persecute the
　　poor—
　let them be caught in the schemes
　　they have devised.

3 For the wicked boast of the desires of
　　their heart,
　those greedy for gain curse and
　　renounce the LORD.
4 In the pride of their countenance the
　　wicked say, "God will not seek it
　　out";
　all their thoughts are, "There is no
　　God."

5 Their ways prosper at all times;
　your judgments are on high, out of
　　their sight;
　as for their foes, they scoff at them.
6 They think in their heart, "We shall not
　　be moved;
　throughout all generations we shall
　　not meet adversity."

7 Their mouths are filled with cursing and
　　deceit and oppression;
　under their tongues are mischief and
　　iniquity.
8 They sit in ambush in the villages;
　in hiding places they murder the
　　innocent.

　Their eyes stealthily watch for the
　　helpless;
9 　they lurk in secret like a lion in its
　　covert;
　they lurk that they may seize the poor;
　they seize the poor and drag them off
　　in their net.

10 They stoop, they crouch,
　and the helpless fall by their might.
11 They think in their heart, "God has
　　forgotten,
　he has hidden his face, he will never
　　see it."

12 Rise up, O LORD; O God, lift up your
　　hand;
　do not forget the oppressed.
13 Why do the wicked renounce God,
　and say in their hearts, "You will not
　　call us to account"?

14 But you do see! Indeed you note trouble
　　and grief,
　that you may take it into your hands;
　the helpless commit themselves to you;
　you have been the helper of the
　　orphan.

15 Break the arm of the wicked and
　　evildoers;
　seek out their wickedness until you
　　find none.
16 The LORD is king forever and ever;
　the nations shall perish from his land.

17 O LORD, you will hear the desire of the
　　meek;
　you will strengthen their heart, you
　　will incline your ear
18 to do justice for the orphan and the
　　oppressed,
　so that those from earth may strike
　　terror no more.[a]

10.1–18. 1–11: The questions in v. 1 mark a transition. Verses 2–11 are an extended description of the wicked, including quotations of their arrogant self-sufficiency and self-assertion (vv. 4, 6, 11). Mocking God, they also think that they can exploit *the poor* with impunity. **12–14:** But the psalmist thinks otherwise, as indicated first by petition (v. 12) and then exclamation (v. 14). *See* is repeated in vv. 11, 14. **15–18:** The psalmist prays that God do what *the wicked* said that God could not do. Naming God *king*, v. 16 recalls 9.4, 7–8. A king's primary commitment is *to do justice*, especially for *the afflicted* (72.1–4).

PSALM 11

To the leader. Of David.

1 In the LORD I take refuge; how can you
　　say to me,
　"Flee like a bird to the mountains;[b]

a Meaning of Heb uncertain　　*b* Gk Syr Jerome Tg: Heb *flee to your mountain, O bird*

2 for look, the wicked bend the bow,
   they have fitted their arrow to the
     string,
   to shoot in the dark at the upright in
     heart.
3 If the foundations are destroyed,
   what can the righteous do?"

4 The LORD is in his holy temple;
   the LORD's throne is in heaven.
   His eyes behold, his gaze examines
     humankind.
5 The LORD tests the righteous and the
     wicked,
   and his soul hates the lover of violence.
6 On the wicked he will rain coals of fire
     and sulfur;
   a scorching wind shall be the portion
     of their cup.
7 For the LORD is righteous;
   he loves righteous deeds;
   the upright shall behold his face.

11.1–7: What can the righteous do? This psalm
of trust may have been spoken originally in the Temple*
by a person who had been advised to *flee* from enemies (Ps 5, 7). **1–3:** An initial profession of trust utilizes
the important word *refuge* (2.12; 5.11; 7.1). The
psalmist quotes advisers. The situation seems hopeless
(v. 3). *Foundations* indicates the basic fabric of the social order. **4:** The psalmist responds by asserting God's
rule on earth (*holy temple*) and *in heaven*. Verse 4 is
the center of the psalm. **5–7:** The characters in view in
vv. 2–3 return here. God opposes *the wicked* (v. 5; see
7.16). They will be judged (v. 6; see Gen 19.24; Ps
75.9), because God *is righteous* (7.9; 9.4, 8). Those
who share God's identity, *the righteous* (vv. 3, 5), *shall
behold his face* (17.15). Those who trust God will not
be disappointed.

PSALM 12

To the leader: according to The Sheminith.
A Psalm of David.

1 Help, O LORD, for there is no longer
     anyone who is godly;
   the faithful have disappeared from
     humankind.
2 They utter lies to each other;
   with flattering lips and a double heart
     they speak.

3 May the LORD cut off all flattering
     lips,
   the tongue that makes great boasts,
4 those who say, "With our tongues we
     will prevail;
   our lips are our own—who is our
     master?"

5 "Because the poor are despoiled,
     because the needy groan,
   I will now rise up," says the LORD;
   "I will place them in the safety for
     which they long."
6 The promises of the LORD are promises
     that are pure,
   silver refined in a furnace on the
     ground,
   purified seven times.

7 You, O LORD, will protect us;
   you will guard us from this generation
     forever.
8 On every side the wicked prowl,
   as vileness is exalted among
     humankind.

12.1–8: The promises of the LORD. Usually categorized as a lament,* it has elements of petition (vv. 1,
3), complaint (vv. 2, 4, 8), and trust (vv. 6–7). Unique
is the inclusion of God's response (v. 5) to the worshipper, perhaps spoken originally in the Temple*
by a prophet* or priest. **1–4:** The most basic human
prayer, *help*, is followed by complaint. The situation recalls Ps 11. The quotation in v. 4 indicates the
utter self-centeredness of the wicked (10.4, 6, 11, 13;
14.1). **5:** God's response reveals that the wicked are
deceived. God will *rise up* (3.7; 10.12) on behalf
of the *poor* and *needy* (see Ex 3.7; 22.21–24;
Ps 9.18). **6–8:** Whereas the speech of the wicked is
deceptive (v. 2), God's *promises* are reliable (v. 6).
They are followed appropriately by a profession of
faith (v. 7), which is effective even as *the wicked
prowl* (v. 8).

PSALM 13

To the leader. A Psalm of David.

1 How long, O LORD? Will you forget me
     forever?
   How long will you hide your face
     from me?

2 How long must I bear pain*a* in my soul,
   and have sorrow in my heart all day
      long?
   How long shall my enemy be exalted
      over me?

3 Consider and answer me, O LORD my
      God!
   Give light to my eyes, or I will sleep
      the sleep of death,
4 and my enemy will say, "I have
      prevailed";
   my foes will rejoice because I am
      shaken.

5 But I trusted in your steadfast love;
   my heart shall rejoice in your
      salvation.
6 I will sing to the LORD,
   because he has dealt bountifully with
      me.

13.1–6: How long, O LORD? This prayer for help may have originally been spoken by a sick person. Complaint (vv. 1–2) is followed by petition (vv. 3–4) and an expression of trust (vv. 5–6). **1–2:** The four-fold repetition of *How long* conveys urgency. *Exalted* is supposed to be God's position (18.46; 46.10), but the *enemy* now occupies it. **3–4:** Each of the three petitions is appropriate in light of the complaints. *Consider* calls God to remember and show God's face. *Answer* is appropriate, given the four questions in vv. 1–2. *Give light* recalls the mention of God's *face*, which is often associated with *light* (Num 6.25; Ps 4.6; 31.16). **5–6:** Whereas the *foes* had been about to *rejoice* (v. 4), now the psalmist *shall rejoice*. Uncertainty has become trust (4.5; 9.10) in God's *steadfast love* (5.7; 6.4). Perhaps the psalmist looks back in gratitude for deliverance; perhaps she or he looks forward in trusting hope; or perhaps the simultaneity of complaint and praise represents what the life of faith always involves.

PSALM 14
To the leader. Of David.

1 Fools say in their hearts, "There is no
      God."
   They are corrupt, they do abominable
      deeds;
   there is no one who does good.

2 The LORD looks down from heaven on
      humankind
   to see if there are any who are wise,
   who seek after God.

3 They have all gone astray, they are all
      alike perverse;
   there is no one who does good,
   no, not one.

4 Have they no knowledge, all the
      evildoers
   who eat up my people as they eat
      bread,
   and do not call upon the LORD?

5 There they shall be in great terror,
   for God is with the company of the
      righteous.
6 You would confound the plans of the
      poor,
   but the LORD is their refuge.

7 O that deliverance for Israel would
      come from Zion!
   When the LORD restores the fortunes
      of his people,
   Jacob will rejoice; Israel will be glad.

14.1–7: Foolishness and wisdom. Often categorized as a prophetic* exhortation* (a psalm that recalls prophetic speech by delivering an indictment of or promise to the people), it is almost identical to Ps 53. **1:** Foolishness is not ignorance, but rather the failure to entrust life to God, resulting in wickedness (compare 10.4). **2:** God's position in *heaven* connotes God's sovereignty, which is precisely what the foolish fail to acknowledge. **3:** Recalling v. 1, v. 3 indicts all humanity, setting up an apparent tension with vv. 4–6. **4–6:** By distinguishing between *evildoers* and those called *my people, the righteous* and *the poor*, these verses seem to contradict v. 3. They may reflect a stratified society dominated by a powerful elite (see Mic 3.1–4). God sides with the victims (9.17–18; 10.17–18; 12.5–7). *There* may suggest that efforts at oppression by the wicked will be their own undoing (7.15–16). The oppressed find *refuge* in God (2.12). The tension between vv. 1–3 and 4–6 preserves the insight that corporate evil and its effects leave no one

a Syr: Heb *hold counsels*

uninvolved or untouched. **7:** This verse may be an exilic or post-exilic addition, which makes the psalm relevant to an era when the people were oppressed by other nations.

PSALM 15
A Psalm of David.

1 O LORD, who may abide in your tent?
   Who may dwell on your holy hill?

2 Those who walk blamelessly, and do
       what is right,
   and speak the truth from their
       heart;
3 who do not slander with their tongue,
   and do no evil to their friends,
       nor take up a reproach against their
       neighbors;
4 in whose eyes the wicked are despised,
   but who honor those who fear the
       LORD;
   who stand by their oath even to their
       hurt;
5 who do not lend money at interest,
   and do not take a bribe against the
       innocent.

   Those who do these things shall never
       be moved.

15.1–5: Who may abide in your tent? An entrance liturgy,⋆ it may have originated as a response in a ritual used as worshippers entered the Temple⋆ (see Ps 24). If so, it now portrays the lifestyle of those who have been described previously as "the righteous" (1.5–6; 14.5). **1:** *Tent* (27.5–6; 61.4) refers to the Temple, preserving the memory of the wilderness tabernacle⋆ (Ex 33.7). The *holy hill* is Zion,⋆ the Temple mount (2.6; 3.4). **2:** To *walk blamelessly* is not to be sinless but rather to be devoted fully to God. Elsewhere, it is God who is *right* or "righteous" (7.11), as well as *true* or showing "faithfulness" (Ex 34.6). **3–5a:** Speech and actions that oppress others are to be avoided, in accordance with God's character, values, and activity. **5b:** In the context of the prayers in Book I, the closing promise cannot be understood to affirm that the righteous will be unopposed, but rather that they will have a secure foundation for facing anything.

PSALM 16
A Miktam of David.

1 Protect me, O God, for in you I take
       refuge.
2 I say to the LORD, "You are my Lord;
   I have no good apart from you."[a]

3 As for the holy ones in the land, they
       are the noble,
   in whom is all my delight.

4 Those who choose another god multiply
       their sorrows;[b]
   their drink offerings of blood I will
       not pour out
   or take their names upon my lips.

5 The LORD is my chosen portion and my
       cup;
   you hold my lot.
6 The boundary lines have fallen for me
       in pleasant places;
   I have a goodly heritage.

7 I bless the LORD who gives me counsel;
   in the night also my heart instructs
       me.
8 I keep the LORD always before me;
   because he is at my right hand, I shall
       not be moved.

9 Therefore my heart is glad, and my soul
       rejoices;
   my body also rests secure.
10 For you do not give me up to Sheol,
   or let your faithful one see the Pit.

11 You show me the path of life.
   In your presence there is fullness of
       joy;
   in your right hand are pleasures
       forevermore.

16.1–11: The path of life. A mixture of prayer (vv. 1–2, 9–11) and profession of faith, it is usually classified as a psalm of trust (Ps 11, 23). **1–2:** Petition is followed by an expression of trust (see *refuge* in 2.12;

a Jerome Tg: Meaning of Heb uncertain
b Cn: Meaning of Heb uncertain

11.8; 14.6). LORD asserts God's sovereignty, and casts the psalmist in the role of servant. **3–4:** Verse 3 probably expresses loyalty to God in the form of honoring God's people, and v. 4 expresses loyalty in the form of rejecting idols and their devotees. **5–6:** The vocabulary derives from the book of Joshua and references to the land, of which everyone was to have a *portion* (19.9), determined by *lot* (18.6), as their *heritage* or "inheritance" (14.3; 17.6). **7–8:** *Bless* indicates submission, which includes openness to God's *counsel*. God's accessibility is unfailing, an effective source of stability (15.5). **9–11:** The assurance of security yields joy from the psalmist's whole being. Entrusting the self to God means avoiding *Sheol** and *the Pit*, names for the realm of death (6.5; 88.3–4), traveling instead *the path of life*. The psalmists had no developed doctrine of resurrection, but they anticipate this belief with their poetic assurances of unbroken communion with God.

PSALM 17
A Prayer of David.

1 Hear a just cause, O LORD; attend to
   my cry;
   give ear to my prayer from lips free of
      deceit.
2 From you let my vindication come;
   let your eyes see the right.

3 If you try my heart, if you visit me by
      night,
   if you test me, you will find no
      wickedness in me;
   my mouth does not transgress.
4 As for what others do, by the word of
      your lips
   I have avoided the ways of the violent.
5 My steps have held fast to your paths;
   my feet have not slipped.

6 I call upon you, for you will answer me,
      O God;
   incline your ear to me, hear my
      words.
7 Wondrously show your steadfast love,
   O savior of those who seek refuge
   from their adversaries at your right
      hand.

8 Guard me as the apple of the eye;
   hide me in the shadow of your wings,

9 from the wicked who despoil me,
   my deadly enemies who surround me.
10 They close their hearts to pity;
   with their mouths they speak
      arrogantly.
11 They track me down;[a] now they
      surround me;
   they set their eyes to cast me to the
      ground.
12 They are like a lion eager to tear,
   like a young lion lurking in ambush.

13 Rise up, O LORD, confront them,
      overthrow them!
   By your sword deliver my life from
      the wicked,
14 from mortals—by your hand, O LORD—
   from mortals whose portion in life is
      in this world.
   May their bellies be filled with what you
      have stored up for them;
   may their children have more than
      enough;
   may they leave something over to
      their little ones.

15 As for me, I shall behold your face in
      righteousness;
   when I awake I shall be satisfied,
      beholding your likeness.

17.1–15: Beholding God's face. This prayer for help may originally have been offered in the Temple* by someone who had been falsely accused (see Ps 5). **1–2:** The psalmist is the victim of those whose speech is not *free of deceit*. *Vindication* is more literally "justice." **3–5:** Often known as a protestation of innocence, these verses do not claim sinlessness but rather innocence in a particular case (7.3–5). **6–9:** The psalmist looks to God for *refuge* (2.12; 16.1). The language recalls the Exodus (see *steadfast love* and *right hand* in v. 7 and Ex 15.12–13). The *shadow of your wings* may allude to the wings of the seraphs who accompanied the ark in the Temple (36.7; 57.1; 63.7). **10–12:** The description of the wicked emphasizes their arrogance and violence (5.9; 10.6–11). **13–15:** God is frequently asked to *rise up* (3.7; 10.12) against enemies. The request is more literally "meet their face," anticipating how the psalmist will *behold* God's *face* (11.7). The

a One Ms Compare Syr: MT *Our steps*

wicked may be *filled* (v. 14) by their treachery, but the psalmist *shall be satisfied* by God (16.11).

〰️〰️〰️〰️〰️〰️〰️〰️〰️

P S A L M   1 8

To the leader. A Psalm of David the servant of the LORD, who addressed the words of this song to the LORD on the day when the LORD delivered him from the hand of all his enemies, and from the hand of Saul. He said:

1 I love you, O LORD, my strength.
2 The LORD is my rock, my fortress, and
      my deliverer,
   my God, my rock in whom I take
      refuge,
   my shield, and the horn of my
      salvation, my stronghold.
3 I call upon the LORD, who is worthy to
      be praised,
   so I shall be saved from my enemies.

4 The cords of death encompassed me;
   the torrents of perdition assailed me;
5 the cords of Sheol entangled me;
   the snares of death confronted me.

6 In my distress I called upon the LORD;
      to my God I cried for help.
   From his temple he heard my voice,
      and my cry to him reached his ears.

7 Then the earth reeled and rocked;
      the foundations also of the mountains
         trembled
      and quaked, because he was angry.
8 Smoke went up from his nostrils,
      and devouring fire from his mouth;
      glowing coals flamed forth from him.
9 He bowed the heavens, and came
         down;
      thick darkness was under his feet.
10 He rode on a cherub, and flew;
      he came swiftly upon the wings of the
         wind.
11 He made darkness his covering around
         him,
      his canopy thick clouds dark with
         water.
12 Out of the brightness before him
      there broke through his clouds
      hailstones and coals of fire.

13 The LORD also thundered in the
         heavens,
      and the Most High uttered his
         voice.*a*
14 And he sent out his arrows, and
         scattered them;
      he flashed forth lightnings, and
         routed them.
15 Then the channels of the sea were
         seen,
      and the foundations of the world
         were laid bare
   at your rebuke, O LORD,
      at the blast of the breath of your
         nostrils.

18.1–50: Exalted be the God of my salvation. A royal psalm of thanksgiving, it is nearly identical to 2 Sam 22. Proposed dates range from David's time to the post-exilic era. After the disappearance of the monarchy, it would have fostered hope by recalling the past (see Ps 144). **1–6:** The king's distress is evident. *Sheol** is the realm of the dead (6.5; 16.10), and the king already has one foot in *Sheol* (v. 5). The preponderance of metaphors* for God in vv. 1–2 suggests that the psalm is as much about God as about the king. *Help* (v. 6) will come from God. **7–15:** God's response (vv. 16–19) is preceded by the description of a theophany,* literally, "an appearance of God." Theophanies employ poetic imagery to emphasize God's cosmic power and presence (50.2–3; 68.7–8). They assert God's sovereignty (29.3–9; 97.1–5; 99.1) and often accompany accounts of deliverances (Ex 15.6–10; Judg 5.4–5).

〰️〰️〰️〰️〰️〰️〰️〰️〰️

16 He reached down from on high, he took
         me;
      he drew me out of mighty waters.
17 He delivered me from my strong
         enemy,
      and from those who hated me;
      for they were too mighty for me.
18 They confronted me in the day of my
         calamity;
      but the LORD was my support.
19 He brought me out into a broad place;
      he delivered me, because he delighted
         in me.

a Gk See 2 Sam 22.14: Heb adds *hailstones and coals of fire*

20 The LORD rewarded me according to my
        righteousness;
    according to the cleanness of my
        hands he recompensed me.
21 For I have kept the ways of the LORD,
    and have not wickedly departed from
        my God.
22 For all his ordinances were before me,
    and his statutes I did not put away
        from me.
23 I was blameless before him,
    and I kept myself from guilt.
24 Therefore the LORD has recompensed
        me according to my
        righteousness,
    according to the cleanness of my
        hands in his sight.

25 With the loyal you show yourself loyal;
    with the blameless you show yourself
        blameless;
26 with the pure you show yourself pure;
    and with the crooked you show
        yourself perverse.
27 For you deliver a humble people,
    but the haughty eyes you bring down.
28 It is you who light my lamp;
    the LORD, my God, lights up my
        darkness.
29 By you I can crush a troop,
    and by my God I can leap over a
        wall.
30 This God—his way is perfect;
    the promise of the LORD proves true;
    he is a shield for all who take refuge
        in him.

31 For who is God except the LORD?
    And who is a rock besides our
        God?—
32 the God who girded me with strength,
    and made my way safe.
33 He made my feet like the feet of a deer,
    and set me secure on the heights.
34 He trains my hands for war,
    so that my arms can bend a bow of
        bronze.
35 You have given me the shield of your
        salvation,
    and your right hand has supported
        me;
    your help[a] has made me great.
36 You gave me a wide place for my steps
        under me,
    and my feet did not slip.
37 I pursued my enemies and overtook
        them;
    and did not turn back until they were
        consumed.
38 I struck them down, so that they were
        not able to rise;
    they fell under my feet.
39 For you girded me with strength for the
        battle;
    you made my assailants sink under
        me.
40 You made my enemies turn their backs
        to me,
    and those who hated me I destroyed.
41 They cried for help, but there was no
        one to save them;
    they cried to the LORD, but he did
        not answer them.
42 I beat them fine, like dust before the
        wind;
    I cast them out like the mire of the
        streets.

43 You delivered me from strife with the
        peoples;[b]
    you made me head of the nations;
    people whom I had not known served
        me.
44 As soon as they heard of me they
        obeyed me;
    foreigners came cringing to me.

18.16–30. 16–19: The mention of *mighty waters*,
symbolizing chaos, suggests the cosmic dimension of
the deliverance. The focus is on God's activity. **20–24:**
Attention shifts to the king and to what sounds like
royal boasting. But the focal point of this section is v.
22, which suggests that God's *ordinances* and *statutes*
are the real source of the king's *righteousness* (vv. 20,
25). To be *blameless* is not to be sinless but rather to
depend completely upon God (15.2; 19.13). **25–30:**
These verses sharpen the emphasis on God's power.
God is the real source of the king's life (v. 28; see 2 Sam
21.17), strength (v. 29; see vv. 1, 32), and protection
(v. 30; see v. 2 and 2.12).

a Or *gentleness*   *b* Gk Tg: Heb *people*

45 Foreigners lost heart,
    and came trembling out of their
        strongholds.

46 The LORD lives! Blessed be my rock,
    and exalted be the God of my
        salvation,
47 the God who gave me vengeance
    and subdued peoples under me;
48 who delivered me from my enemies;
    indeed, you exalted me above my
        adversaries;
    you delivered me from the violent.

49 For this I will extol you, O LORD,
        among the nations,
    and sing praises to your name.
50 Great triumphs he gives to his king,
    and shows steadfast love to his
        anointed,
    to David and his descendants forever.

18.31–50: Perhaps originally a victory hymn, these verses function now to express the king's gratitude to God. Both God and king are cast in the role of warrior. While the king claims some credit (vv. 37–38, 42), the victory really belongs to God (vv. 31–32, 40–41, 43–48, 50) and is evidence of God's sovereignty (vv. 43, 47, 49). The military imagery is problematic; it is important to consider the larger context and its claim that God's cause always represents justice, righteousness, and equity (72.1–7, 12–14; 98.7–9). God's victory is the triumph of *steadfast love* (v. 50).

PSALM 19
To the leader. A Psalm of David.

1 The heavens are telling the glory of
        God;
    and the firmament*a* proclaims his
        handiwork.
2 Day to day pours forth speech,
    and night to night declares
        knowledge.
3 There is no speech, nor are there
        words;
    their voice is not heard;
4 yet their voice*b* goes out through all the
        earth,
    and their words to the end of the
        world.

In the heavens*c* he has set a tent for
        the sun,
5 which comes out like a bridegroom from
        his wedding canopy,
    and like a strong man runs its course
        with joy.
6 Its rising is from the end of the heavens,
    and its circuit to the end of them;
    and nothing is hid from its heat.

7 The law of the LORD is perfect,
    reviving the soul;
    the decrees of the LORD are sure,
        making wise the simple;
8 the precepts of the LORD are right,
    rejoicing the heart;
    the commandment of the LORD is
        clear,
        enlightening the eyes;
9 the fear of the LORD is pure,
    enduring forever;
    the ordinances of the LORD are true
    and righteous altogether.
10 More to be desired are they than gold,
    even much fine gold;
    sweeter also than honey,
    and drippings of the honeycomb.

11 Moreover by them is your servant
        warned;
    in keeping them there is great
        reward.
12 But who can detect their errors?
    Clear me from hidden faults.
13 Keep back your servant also from the
        insolent;*d*
    do not let them have dominion over
        me.
    Then I shall be blameless,
    and innocent of great transgression.

14 Let the words of my mouth and the
        meditation of my heart
    be acceptable to you,
    O LORD, my rock and my redeemer.

19.1–14: My rock and redeemer. Scholars often treat Ps 19 as two psalms: 19A (vv. 1–6), a creation hymn,

a Or *dome*   *b* Gk Jerome Compare Syr: Heb *line*
c Heb *In them*   *d* Or *from proud thoughts*

and 19B (vv. 7–14), a meditation on "torah."* However, this psalm is actually a unity that proclaims the all-encompassing importance of God's "torah" (v. 7, NRSV *law;* see Ps 1, 119). **1–6:** It is possible that the psalmist has adopted and modified an ancient hymn to *the sun* (v. 4). But here *the sun* is a created entity which, along with *the heavens,* proclaims God's *glory* (v. 1) in silent but eloquent *speech* (v. 2). **7–10:** The focus shifts to God's "torah," but the transition is a natural one. It affirms that God's "torah," "instruction," is a basic structure of the cosmos. *Perfect* connotes "pervasive" or "all-encompassing." As the sun makes life possible, which is the sense of *reviving the soul,* so does God's instruction. It is responsible for all good things, including wisdom (v. 7), joy (v. 8), vision (v. 8; *enlightening* recalls the work of *the sun*), piety (v. 9a), and order (v. 9b). There is nothing more valuable (v. 10). **11–13:** NRSV *reward* should be translated "consequence." After the psalmist's confession of sin (v. 12), *blameless* must be understood as "forgiven" and *innocent* as "pardoned." **14:** Forgiven by God, the psalmist's *words* (the same Hebrew word as "speech" in vv. 2–3) can be *acceptable. Redeemer* could be translated "next-of-kin." The cosmic God (v. 1–6), by way of God's "torah" (vv. 7–10), has become the psalmist's gracious next-of-kin.

PSALM 20

To the leader. A Psalm of David.

1 The LORD answer you in the day of
    trouble!
  The name of the God of Jacob protect
    you!
2 May he send you help from the
    sanctuary,
  and give you support from Zion.
3 May he remember all your offerings,
  and regard with favor your burnt
    sacrifices.   *Selah*

4 May he grant you your heart's desire,
  and fulfill all your plans.
5 May we shout for joy over your
    victory,
  and in the name of our God set up
    our banners.
  May the LORD fulfill all your petitions.

6 Now I know that the LORD will help his
    anointed;

he will answer him from his holy
    heaven
  with mighty victories by his right hand.
7 Some take pride in chariots, and some
    in horses,
  but our pride is in the name of the
    LORD our God.
8 They will collapse and fall,
  but we shall rise and stand upright.

9 Give victory to the king, O LORD;
  answer us when we call.[a]

20.1–9: The LORD will help. This royal psalm may have been used in the Temple* when Israel prepared for battle. After the demise of the monarchy, it would have expressed hope in God's ability to help. **1–5:** As the people pray for the king, the real focus is on God's activity. *Answer* in v. 1 recurs twice (vv. 6, 9). NRSV often translates *victory* (v. 5) as "deliverance," "salvation," or "help." The root occurs twice in v. 6 (*help, victories*) and again in v. 9. **6–8:** The *anointed** (v. 6) is the king (v. 9; 2.2; 18.50), the earthly agent of God's rule. The people's *pride* or trust is appropriately directed not to the king, but to God (v. 7). **9:** As note *a* suggests, the closing prayer is ambiguous. NRSV construes it as the people's prayer for themselves and *the king.*

PSALM 21

To the leader. A Psalm of David.

1 In your strength the king rejoices,
    O LORD,
  and in your help how greatly he
    exults!
2 You have given him his heart's desire,
  and have not withheld the request of
    his lips.   *Selah*
3 For you meet him with rich blessings;
  you set a crown of fine gold on his
    head.
4 He asked you for life; you gave it to
    him—
  length of days forever and ever.
5 His glory is great through your help;
  splendor and majesty you bestow on
    him.

a Gk: Heb *give victory, O* LORD; *let the King answer us when we call*

6 You bestow on him blessings forever;
  you make him glad with the joy of
     your presence.
7 For the king trusts in the LORD,
  and through the steadfast love of the
     Most High he shall not be
     moved.

8 Your hand will find out all your
     enemies;
  your right hand will find out those
     who hate you.
9 You will make them like a fiery furnace
     when you appear.
  The LORD will swallow them up in his
     wrath,
  and fire will consume them.
10 You will destroy their offspring from the
     earth,
  and their children from among
     humankind.
11 If they plan evil against you,
  if they devise mischief, they will not
     succeed.
12 For you will put them to flight;
  you will aim at their faces with your
     bows.

13 Be exalted, O LORD, in your strength!
  We will sing and praise your power.

21.1–13: The king exults in God's help. Linked to Ps
20 by the continued focus on *the king* (20.9; 21.1), it
may have been used originally upon the king's return
from battle. After the demise of the monarchy, it
would have been used to celebrate God's help for the
people. **1–6:** The psalm is encompassed by references
to God's *strength* (vv. 1, 13). *The king* has received
the divine *help* (vv. 1, 5) requested in Ps 20 (compare
20.4 and 21.2). **7:** The king's power is derived from
God's *strength* (vv. 1, 13), and it is fitting that he *trusts
in the LORD* (2 Kings 18.5). God's *steadfast love* is the
foundation of the Davidic dynasty* (2 Sam 7.15;
1 Kings 3.6). **8–12:** It is not clear whether these words
are addressed to *the king* or to God. Since *the king* is
viewed as God's earthly agent, the ambiguity is appropriate (18.31–50). Verse 10 represents the typical
means of claiming sovereignty or victory (2 Kings 8.12;
Ps 137.8–9). **13:** God is clearly addressed, as the people join the king in praising God.

PSALM 22

*To the leader: according to The Deer
of the Dawn. A Psalm of David.*

1 My God, my God, why have you
     forsaken me?
  Why are you so far from helping me,
     from the words of my groaning?
2 O my God, I cry by day, but you do not
     answer;
  and by night, but find no rest.

3 Yet you are holy,
  enthroned on the praises of Israel.
4 In you our ancestors trusted;
  they trusted, and you delivered them.
5 To you they cried, and were saved;
  in you they trusted, and were not put
     to shame.

6 But I am a worm, and not human;
  scorned by others, and despised by
     the people.
7 All who see me mock at me;
  they make mouths at me, they shake
     their heads;
8 "Commit your cause to the LORD; let
     him deliver—
  let him rescue the one in whom he
     delights!"

9 Yet it was you who took me from the
     womb;
  you kept me safe on my mother's
     breast.
10 On you I was cast from my birth,
  and since my mother bore me you
     have been my God.
11 Do not be far from me,
  for trouble is near
  and there is no one to help.

12 Many bulls encircle me,
  strong bulls of Bashan surround me;
13 they open wide their mouths at me,
  like a ravening and roaring lion.

14 I am poured out like water,
  and all my bones are out of joint;
  my heart is like wax;
  it is melted within my breast;

15 my mouth*a* is dried up like a potsherd,
　　and my tongue sticks to my jaws;
　　you lay me in the dust of death.

16 For dogs are all around me;
　　a company of evildoers encircles me.
　My hands and feet have shriveled;*b*
17 I can count all my bones.
　They stare and gloat over me;
18 they divide my clothes among
　　　themselves,
　　and for my clothing they cast lots.

22.1–31: God rules the nations. The intensity of this lament* is created by its structure. It consists of two complaints (vv. 1–11, 12–21), each with two parts (vv. 1–5, 6–11 and 12–15, 16–21), followed by two sections of praise (vv. 22–26, 27–31). **1–5:** The threefold appearance of the phrase *My God* suggests intimacy that now seems broken (see Mk 15.34). The psalmist cannot understand *why* God is *so far* away (vv. 11, 19). Praise (v. 3) asserts God's sovereign ability to help, which God has done in past times (vv. 4–5). But memory increases misery. **6–11:** Forsakenness by God is accompanied by human abandonment and ridicule (vv. 6–8). The psalmist is utterly dehumanized—a *worm.* **12–18:** Each complaint features animals, symbolizing enemies, which surround the psalmist (vv. 12–13, 16a–b; see 7.2; 10.9). Death threatens, as the anatomical imagery suggests (vv. 14–15, 16c–18). Because they assume death is imminent, the enemies divide the psalmist's possessions (v. 18; see Mk 15.24).

19 But you, O LORD, do not be far away!
　　O my help, come quickly to my aid!
20 Deliver my soul from the sword,
　　my life*c* from the power of the dog!
21 　Save me from the mouth of the lion!

　From the horns of the wild oxen you
　　　have rescued*d* me.
22 I will tell of your name to my brothers
　　　and sisters;*e*
　　in the midst of the congregation I will
　　　praise you:
23 You who fear the LORD, praise him!
　　All you offspring of Jacob, glorify him;
　　stand in awe of him, all you offspring
　　　of Israel!
24 For he did not despise or abhor
　　the affliction of the afflicted;

he did not hide his face from me,*f*
　　but heard when I*g* cried to him.

25 From you comes my praise in the great
　　　congregation;
　　my vows I will pay before those who
　　　fear him.
26 The poor*h* shall eat and be satisfied;
　　those who seek him shall praise the
　　　LORD.
　　May your hearts live forever!

27 All the ends of the earth shall remember
　　and turn to the LORD;
　and all the families of the nations
　　shall worship before him.*i*
28 For dominion belongs to the LORD,
　　and he rules over the nations.

29 To him,*j* indeed, shall all who sleep in*k*
　　　the earth bow down;
　　before him shall bow all who go down
　　　to the dust,
　　and I shall live for him.*l*
30 Posterity will serve him;
　　future generations will be told about
　　　the Lord,
31 and*m* proclaim his deliverance to a
　　　people yet unborn,
　　saying that he has done it.

22.19–31. 19–21: The petitions draw on vocabulary used earlier in the psalm—*far* (vv. 1, 11), *help* (v. 11), *deliver* (v. 8), *save* (see *helping* in v. 1). Through it all, the psalmist still trusts God. Verse 21b marks a transition. To be "answered" (see note d) *from the horns of the wild oxen* suggests that the following *praise* comes in the midst of ongoing suffering. **22–26:** Each verse contains the word *praise* except v. 24, which suggests that God is present among *the afflicted,* a community of which gathers around the psalmist (vv. 25–26). The payment of *vows* was part of a ritual of gratitude (56.12; 61.8), probably involving a sacrificial meal. **27–31:** The psalmist's community achieves

a Cn: Heb *strength*　　*b* Meaning of Heb uncertain
c Heb *my only one*　　*d* Heb *answered*　　*e* Or *kindred*
f Heb *him*　　*g* Heb *he*　　*h* Or *afflicted*　　*i* Gk Syr
Jerome: Heb *you*　　*j* Cn: Heb *They have eaten and*
k Cn: Heb *all the fat ones*　　*l* Compare Gk Syr Vg: Heb
and he who cannot keep himself alive　　*m* Compare Gk:
Heb *it will be told about the Lord to the generation,* *31they*
will come and

world-wide proportions. Even the dead will participate (v. 29), as will people *yet unborn* (v. 31). The God who *rules over the nations* (v. 28) claims a universal following.

〜〜〜〜〜〜〜〜〜〜〜〜〜

PSALM 23
A Psalm of David.

1 The LORD is my shepherd, I shall not
      want.
2   He makes me lie down in green
         pastures;
   he leads me beside still waters;*ᵃ*
3   he restores my soul.*ᵇ*
   He leads me in right paths*ᶜ*
      for his name's sake.

4 Even though I walk through the darkest
         valley,*ᵈ*
   I fear no evil;
   for you are with me;
      your rod and your staff—
      they comfort me.

5 You prepare a table before me
      in the presence of my enemies;
   you anoint my head with oil;
      my cup overflows.
6 Surely*ᵉ* goodness and mercy*ᶠ* shall
         follow me
   all the days of my life,
   and I shall dwell in the house of the
      LORD
      my whole life long.*ᵍ*

─────────────────────

23.1–6: God's love will pursue me. It is a psalm of trust. **1:** *Shepherd* was a royal title in the ancient Near East, and it was the responsibility of kings to provide for their people (Jer 23.1–4; Ezek 34.1–10). The psalmist proclaims loyal submission to God and affirms that God has made complete provision. **2–3:** Details of God's provision are listed: food (*green pastures*), drink (*still waters*), and protection (*right paths*). The result is life; *restores my soul* means "keeps me alive." *For his name's sake* indicates that God keeps people alive because it is God's character to do so. **4:** God's provision endures in the worst of circumstances. The switch to direct address in this central verse heightens the sense of intimate presence, which means no threat is so great as to *fear. Rod* can designate a shepherd's equipment, but it also denotes royal authority. **5–6:**

The image shifts to that of a gracious host, who provides as did the *shepherd*—food (*a table*), drink (*my cup*), and protection (*the house of the LORD*). *Enemies* are no threat. Hospitality abounds, signified by the anointing* *oil.* Abundant life is attributed to God's *goodness* (100.5; 106.1) and *mercy* (usually translated "steadfast love," as in 5.7; 21.7), which "pursue" (rather than *follow*) the psalmist.

〜〜〜〜〜〜〜〜〜〜〜〜〜

PSALM 24
Of David. A Psalm.

1 The earth is the LORD's and all that is
         in it,
   the world, and those who live in it;
2 for he has founded it on the seas,
      and established it on the rivers.

3 Who shall ascend the hill of the LORD?
      And who shall stand in his holy
         place?
4 Those who have clean hands and pure
         hearts,
   who do not lift up their souls to what
         is false,
      and do not swear deceitfully.
5 They will receive blessing from the
      LORD,
   and vindication from the God of their
         salvation.
6 Such is the company of those who seek
         him,
   who seek the face of the God of
      Jacob.*ʰ*   *Selah*

7 Lift up your heads, O gates!
   and be lifted up, O ancient doors!
      that the King of glory may come in.
8 Who is the King of glory?
   The LORD, strong and mighty,
      the LORD, mighty in battle.
9 Lift up your heads, O gates!
   and be lifted up, O ancient doors!
      that the King of glory may come in.
10 Who is this King of glory?
   The LORD of hosts,
      he is the King of glory.   *Selah*

─────────────────────

a Heb *waters of rest*   *b* Or *life*   *c* Or *paths of righteousness*   *d* Or *the valley of the shadow of death* *e* Or *Only*   *f* Or *kindness*   *g* Heb *for length of days* *h* Gk Syr: Heb *your face, O Jacob*

24.1–10: The King of glory. An entrance liturgy* (see Ps 15), it was probably used originally in a procession as worshippers accompanied the ark of the covenant* into the Temple.* **1–2:** The profession of faith anticipates the explicit affirmation of God's sovereignty in vv. 7–10. The *seas* and *rivers* represent the chaotic waters that God ordered into a cosmos. **3:** The questions may have been asked by a priest as worshippers approached the Temple gates (15.1). **4–6:** The worshippers' response follows. *Clean hands* (73.13) and *pure hearts* (73.1) may reflect exterior and interior preparation. *False* is sometimes associated with idolatry,* and to *not swear deceitfully* indicates proper relationship to other persons (see Ex 20.16). Proper relatedness to God and neighbor constitutes *blessing* and *vindication*, a word usually translated as "righteousness." Seeking God's *face* (11.7; 17.15) may have meant entering the Temple, but also indicates submission to God. **7–10:** These verses have the character of a responsorial ritual between priests and worshippers at the Temple gates. *Mighty in battle* may allude to v. 2, since creation was often portrayed as a battle with chaos. *Lord of hosts* may also have a military ring, since *hosts* can mean an army. *Hosts* can also indicate the heavenly beings surrounding God (29.1–2; 82.1). Verses 7–10 offer a ritual enactment of the claims made in vv. 1–2 (5.2; 98.6).

PSALM 25

Of David.

1 To you, O Lord, I lift up my soul.
2 O my God, in you I trust;
    do not let me be put to shame;
    do not let my enemies exult
        over me.
3 Do not let those who wait for you be
        put to shame;
    let them be ashamed who are
        wantonly treacherous.

4 Make me to know your ways, O Lord;
    teach me your paths.
5 Lead me in your truth, and teach me,
    for you are the God of my salvation;
    for you I wait all day long.

6 Be mindful of your mercy, O Lord, and
        of your steadfast love,
    for they have been from of old.

7 Do not remember the sins of my youth
        or my transgressions;
    according to your steadfast love
        remember me,
    for your goodness' sake, O Lord!

8 Good and upright is the Lord;
    therefore he instructs sinners in the
        way.
9 He leads the humble in what is right,
    and teaches the humble his way.
10 All the paths of the Lord are steadfast
        love and faithfulness,
    for those who keep his covenant and
        his decrees.

11 For your name's sake, O Lord,
    pardon my guilt, for it is great.
12 Who are they that fear the Lord?
    He will teach them the way that they
        should choose.
13 They will abide in prosperity,
    and their children shall possess the
        land.
14 The friendship of the Lord is for those
        who fear him,
    and he makes his covenant known to
        them.
15 My eyes are ever toward the Lord,
    for he will pluck my feet out of the
        net.

16 Turn to me and be gracious to me,
    for I am lonely and afflicted.
17 Relieve the troubles of my heart,
    and bring me*a* out of my distress.
18 Consider my affliction and my trouble,
    and forgive all my sins.
19 Consider how many are my foes,
    and with what violent hatred they
        hate me.
20 O guard my life, and deliver me;
    do not let me be put to shame, for I
        take refuge in you.
21 May integrity and uprightness preserve
        me,
    for I wait for you.

a *Or The troubles of my heart are enlarged; bring me*

22 Redeem Israel, O God,
   out of all its troubles.

25.1–22: For you I wait. A lament,* it contains petition (vv. 2b–3, 4–7, 11, 16–18, 19–22), praise (vv. 8–10), and assurance (vv. 12–15). Their unique arrangement may be due to the acrostic* structure (see Ps 9–10). **1–2a:** In keeping with Ps 24.4, the psalmist promises to *lift up my soul* to the LORD (86.4; 143.8). The phrase means to "offer my life," the essence of *trust* (86.2; 143.8). **2b–3:** *Shame* and *wait* become thematic (vv. 5, 20–21). **4–7:** An interest in teaching is introduced (vv. 8–9, 12), as is a focus on God's *way* or *ways* (vv. 4, 8, 9, 12; the same Hebrew root lies behind *leads* in vv. 5, 9). **8–10:** This characterization of God recalls the historic confession in Ex 34.6–7. **11:** This petition is the central line of the psalm; it gives the prayer the character of a confession of sin (see v. 18; Ps 32, 51). **12–15:** The assurance of *prosperity* must be heard in light of ongoing complaint (vv. 16–21). *Prosperity* involves connectedness to God (1.3), which is what God's *friendship* designates. *Fear* (vv. 12, 14) connotes reverence and trust. **16–21:** The psalmist is one of the *afflicted* (v. 16; 22.24) and is opposed by *foes* (v. 19; 3.1). *Refuge* is found in God (2.12; 5.11). *Integrity* results from complete dependence upon God. **22:** Standing outside the acrostic structure, it may have been appended to give the psalm an explicitly corporate orientation.

PSALM 26
Of David.

1 Vindicate me, O LORD,
   for I have walked in my integrity,
   and I have trusted in the LORD
      without wavering.
2 Prove me, O LORD, and try me;
   test my heart and mind.
3 For your steadfast love is before my eyes,
   and I walk in faithfulness to you.*a*

4 I do not sit with the worthless,
   nor do I consort with hypocrites;
5 I hate the company of evildoers,
   and will not sit with the wicked.

6 I wash my hands in innocence,
   and go around your altar, O LORD,
7 singing aloud a song of thanksgiving,
   and telling all your wondrous deeds.

8 O LORD, I love the house in which you
      dwell,
   and the place where your glory
      abides.
9 Do not sweep me away with sinners,
   nor my life with the bloodthirsty,
10 those in whose hands are evil devices,
   and whose right hands are full of
      bribes.

11 But as for me, I walk in my integrity;
   redeem me, and be gracious to me.
12 My foot stands on level ground;
   in the great congregation I will bless
      the LORD.

26.1–12: Vindicate me, O LORD. This lament* may have been prayed originally by a falsely accused person seeking help in the Temple* (see Ps 5, 7, 17). **1–3:** *Vindicate me* could be translated more literally "establish justice for me" (7.8; 17.1–2). *Integrity* (vv. 1, 11; 25.21) denotes complete dependence on God; it is synonymous with *trusted*. The psalmist knows God's ways—*steadfast love* and *faithfulness* (v. 3)—and has nothing to hide (v. 2; 7.9; 17.3). **4–5:** The psalmist asserts that he or she opposes *evil*, just as God does (5.5). The claim is not of sinlessness but rather of innocence in a particular case (7.3–5). **6–8:** The central section focuses on the psalmist and the Temple. Verse 6 describes what priests would have done to prepare themselves for service in the Temple, but it may be heard figuratively. *Love* of the Temple expresses loyalty and trust. **9–10:** As in vv. 4–5, the focus is on *evil* and *evildoers*. **11–12:** Echoing v. 1, the psalmist states with whom he or she *stands*—with God's people, another indication of loyalty and trust. *Bless* originally connoted "to kneel," an act of submission.

PSALM 27
Of David.

1 The LORD is my light and my salvation;
   whom shall I fear?
   The LORD is the stronghold*b* of my life;
   of whom shall I be afraid?

2 When evildoers assail me
   to devour my flesh—

a Or *in your faithfulness*   *b* Or *refuge*

my adversaries and foes—
they shall stumble and fall.

3 Though an army encamp against me,
my heart shall not fear;
though war rise up against me,
yet I will be confident.

4 One thing I asked of the LORD,
that will I seek after:
to live in the house of the LORD
all the days of my life,
to behold the beauty of the LORD,
and to inquire in his temple.

5 For he will hide me in his shelter
in the day of trouble;
he will conceal me under the cover of
his tent;
he will set me high on a rock.

6 Now my head is lifted up
above my enemies all around me,
and I will offer in his tent
sacrifices with shouts of joy;
I will sing and make melody to the
LORD.

7 Hear, O LORD, when I cry aloud,
be gracious to me and answer me!
8 "Come," my heart says, "seek his
face!"
Your face, LORD, do I seek.
9   Do not hide your face from me.

Do not turn your servant away in
anger,
you who have been my help.
Do not cast me off, do not forsake me,
O God of my salvation!
10 If my father and mother forsake me,
the LORD will take me up.

11 Teach me your way, O LORD,
and lead me on a level path
because of my enemies.
12 Do not give me up to the will of
my adversaries,
for false witnesses have risen against
me,
and they are breathing out violence.

13 I believe that I shall see the goodness of
the LORD
in the land of the living.
14 Wait for the LORD;
be strong, and let your heart take
courage;
wait for the LORD!

27.1–14: The LORD is my light. Reversing the usual order of a lament,* it begins with assurance (vv. 1–6) and moves to prayer (vv. 7–12) before returning to assurance (vv. 13–14). **1–3:** *Light* symbolizes *life*, which is also what *salvation* means in a context where *life* is threatened (vv. 2–3). *Light* also anticipates vv. 8–9, since God's *face* is often associated with *light* (Num 6.25; Ps 4.6). The military image can be construed metaphorically.* **4–6:** Persecuted by enemies, the psalmist may have literally sought *shelter* in the *temple*, God's *house* or *tent* (15.1). The imagery may be metaphorical for entrusting the self to God. The *temple* mount was a *rock* (Isa 30.29), but God is also addressed as a *rock* (18.2; 28.1). *Behold the beauty* and *to inquire* may refer to unknown rituals. **7–10:** The psalmists regularly *seek* God's *face* or "presence" (11.7; 24.6). To be forsaken by family was to be threatened with death. **11–12:** False accusations and their destructive effects may be the source of the psalmist's complaint (see Ps 7, 17, 26). **13–14:** The opposite of *fear* (v. 1) is faith, and it engenders hope for the self and others (see "wait" in 25.3, 5, 21; 31.24).

PSALM 28
Of David.

1 To you, O LORD, I call;
my rock, do not refuse to hear me,
for if you are silent to me,
I shall be like those who go down to
the Pit.
2 Hear the voice of my supplication,
as I cry to you for help,
as I lift up my hands
toward your most holy sanctuary.*a*

3 Do not drag me away with the wicked,
with those who are workers of evil,
who speak peace with their neighbors,
while mischief is in their hearts.

a Heb *your innermost sanctuary*

4 Repay them according to their work,
　　and according to the evil of their
　　　　deeds;
　　repay them according to the work of
　　　　their hands;
　　render them their due reward.
5 Because they do not regard the works of
　　　　the LORD,
　　or the work of his hands,
　　he will break them down and build
　　　　them up no more.

6 Blessed be the LORD,
　　for he has heard the sound of my
　　　　pleadings.
7 The LORD is my strength and my
　　　　shield;
　　in him my heart trusts;
　　so I am helped, and my heart exults,
　　and with my song I give thanks to
　　　　him.

8 The LORD is the strength of his
　　　　people;
　　he is the saving refuge of his
　　　　anointed.
9 O save your people, and bless your
　　　　heritage;
　　be their shepherd, and carry them
　　　　forever.

28.1–9: With my song I give thanks. Most scholars
assume that vv. 6–7 indicate that the prayer of vv. 1–4
has been answered; hence they classify the psalm as a
song of thanksgiving. Others label it a prayer for help,
or even a royal psalm, due to the phrase *his anointed**
in v. 8 (2.2). **1–2:** The *Pit* is the realm of death
(116.10). In an unstable situation, the psalmist appeals
to *my rock* (27.5). Uplifted *hands* represent the posture of prayer (63.4). Perhaps the psalm was originally
prayed as the psalmist faced the holy of holies, the site
of God's earthly throne (1 Kings 6.5). **3–5:** The prayer
is not so much for revenge as it is for justice, since *the
wicked* pursue their own *work* as opposed to the *works
of the LORD*. **6–7:** The psalmist asked God to *hear* (v. 2),
and God *has heard* (v. 6). God has been a protecting
shield (3.4) and has *helped* (22.19). The appropriate
response is gratitude. **8–9:** Using the word *strength*
from v. 7, v. 8 introduces a corporate dimension by
mentioning God's *people* and the *anointed*, the king.
Even after affirming that God is a *saving refuge*, the

psalmist still prays, *save your people.* God's work is
never done. As v. 1 suggested, God's constant provision is necessary for the people to live (23.1).

PSALM 29
A Psalm of David.

1 Ascribe to the LORD, O heavenly beings, [a]
　　ascribe to the LORD glory and
　　　　strength.
2 Ascribe to the LORD the glory of his
　　　　name;
　　worship the LORD in holy splendor.

3 The voice of the LORD is over the
　　　　waters;
　　the God of glory thunders,
　　the LORD, over mighty waters.
4 The voice of the LORD is powerful;
　　the voice of the LORD is full of
　　　　majesty.

5 The voice of the LORD breaks the
　　　　cedars;
　　the LORD breaks the cedars of
　　　　Lebanon.
6 He makes Lebanon skip like a calf,
　　and Sirion like a young wild ox.

7 The voice of the LORD flashes forth
　　　　flames of fire.
8 The voice of the LORD shakes the
　　　　wilderness;
　　the LORD shakes the wilderness of
　　　　Kadesh.

9 The voice of the LORD causes the oaks
　　　　to whirl, [b]
　　and strips the forest bare;
　　and in his temple all say, "Glory!"

10 The LORD sits enthroned over the
　　　　flood;
　　the LORD sits enthroned as king
　　　　forever.
11 May the LORD give strength to his
　　　　people!
　　May the LORD bless his people with
　　　　peace!

a Heb *sons of gods*　　*b* Or *causes the deer to calve*

29.1–11: The LORD sits enthroned. An enthronement psalm (see v. 10; Ps 93), it may be among the oldest psalms, perhaps an adaptation of a Canaanite hymn to Baal,* the god of the storm. **1–2:** *Ascribe* means to acknowledge. The *heavenly beings*, probably viewed as deposed Canaanite deities (Ps 82), are to yield to God's sovereignty. *Glory* becomes a key word (vv. 1–3, 9; 24.7–10; 96.3). *Holy splendor* may suggest a reverential posture or perhaps appropriate attire. **3–9:** *Voice* occurs seven times, suggesting the complete power of God. In the context, it suggests thunder, since vv. 3–9 describe the effects of a powerful storm hitting the coast of Palestine, complete with gusty winds (vv. 6–7), sharp lightning (v. 7), and thunder (v. 8). Baal's power has been appropriated by the LORD. God's temple may indicate God's heavenly abode (11.4), but the earthly Temple* may also be in view. **10–11:** The *flood* indicates the cosmic waters, over which God is sovereign. The job of a king was to provide for his people. The ultimate goal was "shalom" ("peace"), for which the psalmist prayed in v. 11 (72.7).

PSALM 30

A Psalm. A Song at the dedication of the temple.
Of David.

1 I will extol you, O LORD, for you have
        drawn me up,
    and did not let my foes rejoice over
        me.
2 O LORD my God, I cried to you for
        help,
    and you have healed me.
3 O LORD, you brought up my soul from
        Sheol,
    restored me to life from among those
        gone down to the Pit.*

4 Sing praises to the LORD, O you his
        faithful ones,
    and give thanks to his holy name.
5 For his anger is but for a moment;
        his favor is for a lifetime.
    Weeping may linger for the night,
        but joy comes with the morning.

6 As for me, I said in my prosperity,
    "I shall never be moved."

7 By your favor, O LORD,
    you had established me as a strong
        mountain;
you hid your face;
    I was dismayed.

8 To you, O LORD, I cried,
    and to the LORD I made supplication:
9 "What profit is there in my death,
    if I go down to the Pit?
Will the dust praise you?
    Will it tell of your faithfulness?
10 Hear, O LORD, and be gracious to me!
    O LORD, be my helper!"

11 You have turned my mourning into
        dancing;
    you have taken off my sackcloth
        and clothed me with joy,
12 so that my soul*b* may praise you and not
        be silent.
    O LORD my God, I will give thanks to
        you forever.

30.1–12: I will give thanks to you forever. The superscription associates the psalm with *the dedication of the temple,* and rabbinic sources identity it with the Feast of Dedication (Hanukkah). A song of thanksgiving, it may have been used originally by someone who had been *healed* (v. 2) from illness. **1–3:** *Healed* may be heard metaphorically* (147.3; Hos 6.1). In any case, the threat was deadly, since *Sheol** (6.5) and *the Pit* (28.1) designate the realm of the dead. **4–5:** The psalmist now invites others to join the song of thanksgiving. The two verbs in v. 4 recur in v. 12. *Joy* in v. 5 anticipates v. 11. **6–12:** These verses rehearse the distress (vv. 6–10) and deliverance (vv. 11–12). Verses 9–10 apparently quote a portion of the prayer mentioned in v. 2 (6.5; 88.10–12). A comparison of v. 6 with v. 12 suggests the psalmist's move from misplaced confidence in the self to humble gratitude and *praise* that will endure *forever.*

PSALM 31

To the leader. A Psalm of David.

1 In you, O LORD, I seek refuge;
    do not let me ever be put to shame;
    in your righteousness deliver me.

a Or *that I should not go down to the Pit*   *b* Heb *that glory*

2 Incline your ear to me;
    rescue me speedily.
 Be a rock of refuge for me,
    a strong fortress to save me.

3 You are indeed my rock and my fortress;
    for your name's sake lead me and
        guide me,
4 take me out of the net that is hidden for
        me,
    for you are my refuge.
5 Into your hand I commit my spirit;
    you have redeemed me, O LORD,
        faithful God.

6 You hate^a those who pay regard to
        worthless idols,
    but I trust in the LORD.
7 I will exult and rejoice in your steadfast
        love,
    because you have seen my affliction;
    you have taken heed of my
        adversities,
8 and have not delivered me into the hand
        of the enemy;
    you have set my feet in a broad place.

9 Be gracious to me, O LORD, for I am in
        distress;
    my eye wastes away from grief,
    my soul and body also.
10 For my life is spent with sorrow,
    and my years with sighing;
 my strength fails because of my misery,^{b}
    and my bones waste away.

11 I am the scorn of all my adversaries,
    a horror^c to my neighbors,
 an object of dread to my acquaintances;
    those who see me in the street flee
        from me.
12 I have passed out of mind like one who
        is dead;
    I have become like a broken vessel.
13 For I hear the whispering of many—
        terror all around!—
    as they scheme together against me,
    as they plot to take my life.

14 But I trust in you, O LORD;
    I say, "You are my God."

15 My times are in your hand;
    deliver me from the hand of my
        enemies and persecutors.
16 Let your face shine upon your servant;
    save me in your steadfast love.
17 Do not let me be put to shame,
        O LORD,
    for I call on you;
    let the wicked be put to shame;
    let them go dumbfounded to Sheol.
18 Let the lying lips be stilled
    that speak insolently against the
        righteous
    with pride and contempt.

19 O how abundant is your goodness
    that you have laid up for those who
        fear you,
 and accomplished for those who take
        refuge in you,
    in the sight of everyone!
20 In the shelter of your presence you hide
        them
    from human plots;
 you hold them safe under your shelter
    from contentious tongues.

21 Blessed be the LORD,
    for he has wondrously shown his
        steadfast love to me
    when I was beset as a city under
        siege.
22 I had said in my alarm,
    "I am driven far^d from your sight."
 But you heard my supplications
    when I cried out to you for help.

23 Love the LORD, all you his saints.
    The LORD preserves the faithful,
    but abundantly repays the one who
        acts haughtily.
24 Be strong, and let your heart take
        courage,
    all you who wait for the LORD.

31.1–24: Into your hand I commit my spirit. A prayer
for help, its uniqueness lies in the frequent expressions
of trust that accompany the petitions (see vv. 1a, 3a,

a One Heb Ms Gk Syr Jerome: MT *I hate*   b Gk Syr:
Heb *my iniquity*   c Cn: Heb *exceedingly*   d Another
reading is *cut off*

4b–8, 14–15a, 19–24). **1–5:** *Refuge* (2.12; 18.2) grounds the subsequent petitions and sets the tone for the entire psalm. Verse 5a means "I turn my life over to you" (see Lk 23.46). **6–8:** Verse 6 should begin "I hate" (see note *a*). To show *trust* in God means to oppose those who oppose God (26.5). It also means to embody God's character, which is essentially *steadfast love* (v. 7; see vv. 16, 21). *Broad place* connotes safety and well-being (18.19). **9–13:** In tension with v. 8 is the petition that implies the psalmist's ongoing *distress*, which connotes "narrowness, tight space," the opposite of *broad place*. The distress leads to social abandonment (22. 6–8). *Terror all around* occurs elsewhere only in Jer 20.3, 10; Jeremiah was also abandoned and ridiculed. **14–18:** Returning to *trust*, v. 14 recalls v. 6, and v. 5 is echoed in v. 15, which means, "I turn my future over to you." The psalmist prays for life, symbolized by the light of God's *face* (4.6), and for *the wicked* to be silenced. *Sheol*★ is the realm of the dead (30.3). **19–22:** In view of ongoing complaint and petition, God's *goodness* cannot mean material prosperity nor a carefree existence. Rather it suggests the assurance of turning one's life over fully to God (vv. 5, 15) and of knowing God is not absent (vv. 14, 22). **23–24:** Such assurance leads the people to *love the* L ORD and *wait for the* L ORD (27.14).

PSALM 32

Of David. A Maskil.

1 Happy are those whose transgression is
    forgiven,
        whose sin is covered.
2 Happy are those to whom the L ORD
        imputes no iniquity,
    and in whose spirit there is no deceit.

3 While I kept silence, my body wasted
    away
        through my groaning all day long.
4 For day and night your hand was heavy
        upon me;
    my strength was dried up*a* as by the
        heat of summer. *Selah*

5 Then I acknowledged my sin to you,
    and I did not hide my iniquity;
        I said, "I will confess my transgressions
            to the L ORD,"
    and you forgave the guilt of my sin.
                Selah

6 Therefore let all who are faithful
    offer prayer to you;
        at a time of distress,*b* the rush of
            mighty waters
    shall not reach them.
7 You are a hiding place for me;
    you preserve me from trouble;
        you surround me with glad cries of
            deliverance. *Selah*

8 I will instruct you and teach you the
        way you should go;
    I will counsel you with my eye upon
        you.
9 Do not be like a horse or a mule,
        without understanding,
    whose temper must be curbed with
        bit and bridle,
    else it will not stay near you.

10 Many are the torments of the wicked,
    but steadfast love surrounds those
        who trust in the L ORD.
11 Be glad in the L ORD and rejoice,
        O righteous,
    and shout for joy, all you upright in
        heart.

32.1–11: I will confess my transgressions. Usually classified as a song of thanksgiving because of the account of deliverance in vv. 3–5, it is one of the church's Penitential Psalms★ (see Ps 6). **1–2:** The beatitudes recall 1.1; 2.12. The *righteous* (v. 11) are portrayed as those who have been forgiven rather than those who deserve God's favor (Rom 4.6–8). **3–5:** *Sin* is the most general term, connoting "to miss the mark." *Transgression(s)* connotes intentional rebellion. *Iniquity* includes the destructive effects of disobedience, which are graphically described and which persist until *sin* is confessed. *Forgiven* and *forgive* frame vv. 1–5. **6–7:** The prayer continues, but as a profession of faith focused on God. **8–9:** It is not clear whether the speaker should be understood as God responding to the psalmist (in words originally delivered by a priest or prophet★), or as the psalmist stating the intention to share what he or she has learned (51.13). **10–11:** The psalmist, apparently addressing other worshippers (or readers), invites them into his or her experience. The

---

a Meaning of Heb uncertain   *b* Cn: Heb *at a time of finding only*

psalm associates forgiveness with God's *steadfast love* (see Ex 34.6–7) and suggests that the essence of *trust* and the source of *joy* are found in confession and forgiveness.

PSALM 33

1 Rejoice in the LORD, O you righteous.
  Praise befits the upright.
2 Praise the LORD with the lyre;
  make melody to him with the harp of
    ten strings.
3 Sing to him a new song;
  play skillfully on the strings, with loud
    shouts.

4 For the word of the LORD is upright,
  and all his work is done in
    faithfulness.
5 He loves righteousness and justice;
  the earth is full of the steadfast love
    of the LORD.

6 By the word of the LORD the heavens
    were made,
  and all their host by the breath of his
    mouth.
7 He gathered the waters of the sea as in
    a bottle;
  he put the deeps in storehouses.

8 Let all the earth fear the LORD;
  let all the inhabitants of the world
    stand in awe of him.
9 For he spoke, and it came to be;
  he commanded, and it stood firm.

10 The LORD brings the counsel of the
    nations to nothing;
  he frustrates the plans of the peoples.
11 The counsel of the LORD stands forever,
  the thoughts of his heart to all
    generations.
12 Happy is the nation whose God is the
    LORD,
  the people whom he has chosen as
    his heritage.

13 The LORD looks down from heaven;
  he sees all humankind.

14 From where he sits enthroned he
    watches
  all the inhabitants of the earth—
15 he who fashions the hearts of them all,
  and observes all their deeds.
16 A king is not saved by his great army;
  a warrior is not delivered by his great
    strength.
17 The war horse is a vain hope for victory,
  and by its great might it cannot save.

18 Truly the eye of the LORD is on those
    who fear him,
  on those who hope in his steadfast
    love,
19 to deliver their soul from death,
  and to keep them alive in famine.

20 Our soul waits for the LORD;
  he is our help and shield.
21 Our heart is glad in him,
  because we trust in his holy name.
22 Let your steadfast love, O LORD, be
    upon us,
  even as we hope in you.

33.1–22: The earth is full of the steadfast love of the LORD. This song of praise responds to Ps 32 (compare 32.11 and 33.1), a conclusion reinforced by the lack of a superscription. **1–3:** The *righteous* and *upright* have been portrayed as those whom God forgives (32.11). They owe their lives to God, so *praise befits* them. *Praise* bespeaks submission to God's sovereignty, a concept associated elsewhere with *a new song* (96.1; 98.1). Verses 2–3 are the first references to musical instruments in the body of a psalm (57.8; 71.22). **4–5:** *Righteousness and justice* are attributes of God's reign (89.14; 96.13). Verses 6–22 expound upon the claim that the world is essentially constituted by God's *word* revealed as *steadfast love* (vv. 18, 22; 5.7; 118.1). **6–9:** Repeating *word* from v. 4, the psalmist attributes the universe to God's creative speech (v. 9). The vocabulary recalls Ex 15 and Gen 1. *Fear* (v. 8) means to acknowledge God's sovereignty. **10–12:** The unfolding of history will not thwart God's *counsel* (Prov 19.21). **13–15:** *Enthroned* further sharpens the focus on God's sovereignty (11.4; 14.2). **16–19:** Highly placed persons and their resources offer only the illusion of power (Prov 21.30–31). Only God, implementing divine love (v. 18), will *deliver* (v. 19; 107.4–9). **20–22:** An affirmation of *trust* precedes a final petition, which also bespeaks *hope* (27.14; 31.24) in God's loving *help* (22.19).

PSALM 34

Of David, when he feigned madness before
Abimelech, so that he drove him out, and he
went away.

1 I will bless the LORD at all times;
  his praise shall continually be in my
    mouth.
2 My soul makes its boast in the LORD;
  let the humble hear and be glad.
3 O magnify the LORD with me,
  and let us exalt his name together.

4 I sought the LORD, and he answered
    me,
  and delivered me from all my fears.
5 Look to him, and be radiant;
  so your*a* faces shall never be
    ashamed.
6 This poor soul cried, and was heard by
    the LORD,
  and was saved from every trouble.
7 The angel of the LORD encamps
  around those who fear him, and
    delivers them.
8 O taste and see that the LORD is good;
  happy are those who take refuge in
    him.
9 O fear the LORD, you his holy ones,
  for those who fear him have no want.
10 The young lions suffer want and
    hunger,
  but those who seek the LORD lack no
    good thing.

11 Come, O children, listen to me;
  I will teach you the fear of the LORD.
12 Which of you desires life,
  and covets many days to enjoy good?
13 Keep your tongue from evil,
  and your lips from speaking deceit.
14 Depart from evil, and do good;
  seek peace, and pursue it.

15 The eyes of the LORD are on the
    righteous,
  and his ears are open to their cry.

16 The face of the LORD is against
    evildoers,
  to cut off the remembrance of them
    from the earth.
17 When the righteous cry for help, the
    LORD hears,
  and rescues them from all their
    troubles.
18 The LORD is near to the brokenhearted,
  and saves the crushed in spirit.

19 Many are the afflictions of the righteous,
  but the LORD rescues them from
    them all.
20 He keeps all their bones;
  not one of them will be broken.
21 Evil brings death to the wicked,
  and those who hate the righteous will
    be condemned.
22 The LORD redeems the life of his
    servants;
  none of those who take refuge in him
    will be condemned.

34.1–22: Which of you desires life? An acrostic✻ song of thanksgiving (see Ps 9–10), its concern to *teach . . . the fear of the LORD* (v. 11) leads some to label it a wisdom psalm. The superscription seems related to 1 Sam 21.13, but there are discrepancies. *1–3*: *Praise* is to be overheard, encouraging others to join *together* with the psalmist. *4–10*: Intending to be exemplary (v. 2), the psalmist recounts God's deliverance, interspersed with invitations for others to *look to* and experience (which is the sense of *taste*) God as well (vv. 5, 8–9). *Fear* connotes trust in and dependence upon God; v. 9 fills out what it means to *take refuge in* God (v. 8; see v. 22; 2.12). *11–14*: Wisdom vocabulary predominates, including the address to *children* (Prov 1.8; 3.1), the theme of *fear of the LORD* (Prov 1.7; 9.10), the goal of *life* (Prov 3.2; 10.17), the concern with proper speech (Prov 4.24; 6.17), and the contrast of *good* and *evil* (Prov 2.20; 3.7). *15–22*: God helps *the righteous* (vv. 15, 17, 19) and opposes *evildoers* (v. 16) and *the wicked* (v. 21). That a mechanistic retributional scheme is not operative is indicated *by the afflictions of the righteous* (v. 19). God's nearness (v. 18; 73.28) offers the resources that make *life* (v. 22) possible in the midst of suffering.

a Gk Syr Jerome: Heb *their*

PSALM 35
Of David.

1 Contend, O LORD, with those who
    contend with me;
  fight against those who fight against
    me!
2 Take hold of shield and buckler,
  and rise up to help me!
3 Draw the spear and javelin
    against my pursuers;
  say to my soul,
    "I am your salvation."

4 Let them be put to shame and dishonor
    who seek after my life.
  Let them be turned back and
    confounded
    who devise evil against me.
5 Let them be like chaff before the wind,
    with the angel of the LORD driving
      them on.
6 Let their way be dark and slippery,
    with the angel of the LORD pursuing
      them.

7 For without cause they hid their net[a]
    for me;
  without cause they dug a pit[b] for my
    life.
8 Let ruin come on them unawares.
  And let the net that they hid ensnare
    them;
    let them fall in it—to their ruin.

9 Then my soul shall rejoice in the LORD,
    exulting in his deliverance.
10 All my bones shall say,
    "O LORD, who is like you?
  You deliver the weak
    from those too strong for them,
    the weak and needy from those who
      despoil them."

11 Malicious witnesses rise up;
    they ask me about things I do not
      know.
12 They repay me evil for good;
    my soul is forlorn.
13 But as for me, when they were sick,
    I wore sackcloth;
    I afflicted myself with fasting.

I prayed with head bowed[c] on my
    bosom,
14 as though I grieved for a friend or a
    brother;
  I went about as one who laments for a
    mother,
    bowed down and in mourning.

35.1–28: My soul is forlorn. All the elements of a prayer for help are here, but in no apparent order: petition for help (vv. 1–3, 17, 22–25); petition against the enemies (vv. 4–6, 8, 19, 26); complaint (vv. 7, 11–12, 15–16, 20–21); vow to praise (vv. 9–10, 18, 28); protestation of innocence (vv. 13–14); and an invitation to praise addressed to allies (v. 27). This psalm may have originated as a prayer of one falsely accused (Ps 17, 26) or of one whose sickness (v. 13) was capitalized upon by enemies. **1–3:** *Contend* suggests a legal proceeding, but the legal language is accompanied by military imagery in vv. 2–3. The language can be construed metaphorically.* **4–8:** The petitions against the enemies are motivated not by vengeance but rather by a longing for justice (v. 24), which involves opposition to oppression. The psalmist trusts that *evil* will destroy itself (1.6; 7.15–16). **9–10:** The self-destruction of *evil* represents the activity of God on behalf of *the weak and needy* (v. 10; 9.18). **11–14:** The complaint in vv. 11–12 ends with *forlorn*, a word that may indicate grief over childlessness and anticipates the psalmist's treatment of others as if they were family (vv. 13–14).

---

15 But at my stumbling they gathered in
    glee,
  they gathered together against me;
  ruffians whom I did not know
    tore at me without ceasing;
16 they impiously mocked more and more,[d]
    gnashing at me with their teeth.

17 How long, O LORD, will you look on?
    Rescue me from their ravages,
    my life from the lions!
18 Then I will thank you in the great
    congregation;
    in the mighty throng I will praise you.

---

a Heb *a pit, their net*   b The word *pit* is transposed from the preceding line   c Or *My prayer turned back*   d Cn Compare Gk: Heb *like the profanest of mockers of a cake*

19 Do not let my treacherous enemies
rejoice over me,
or those who hate me without cause
wink the eye.
20 For they do not speak peace,
but they conceive deceitful words
against those who are quiet in the
land.
21 They open wide their mouths against me;
they say, "Aha, Aha,
our eyes have seen it."

22 You have seen, O LORD; do not be
silent!
O Lord, do not be far from me!
23 Wake up! Bestir yourself for my
defense,
for my cause, my God and my Lord!
24 Vindicate me, O LORD, my God,
according to your righteousness,
and do not let them rejoice over me.
25 Do not let them say to themselves,
"Aha, we have our heart's desire."
Do not let them say, "We have
swallowed you*a* up."

26 Let all those who rejoice at my calamity
be put to shame and confusion;
let those who exalt themselves against
me
be clothed with shame and dishonor.

27 Let those who desire my vindication
shout for joy and be glad,
and say evermore,
"Great is the LORD,
who delights in the welfare of his
servant."
28 Then my tongue shall tell of your
righteousness
and of your praise all day long.

35.15–28. 15–18: Unlike the psalmist, the opponents act like ravenous animals (37.12; 58.6). 19–25: Their arrogance is revealed in their speech (vv. 21, 25). They think they have *seen* (v. 21), but the psalmist trusts that God has *seen* (v. 22). Challenging God to *Wake up!*, the psalmist summarizes the issue as one of justice. *My defense* is literally "my justice," and *vindicate me* is literally "establish justice for me" (v. 24; 26.1). The petition is grounded in God's *righteousness* (v. 28;

7.17; 33.5). 26–28: The contrasting of opponents (v. 26) and allies (v. 27) summarizes the essence of God's *righteousness* (v. 28) as "shalom," "peace" (NRSV *welfare*), a contrast to the opponents who *do not speak peace* (v. 20) and whose behavior results in persecution *without cause* (vv. 7, 19).

〜〜〜〜〜〜〜〜〜〜

PSALM 36

To the leader. Of David, the servant of the LORD.

1 Transgression speaks to the wicked
deep in their hearts;
there is no fear of God
before their eyes.
2 For they flatter themselves in their own
eyes
that their iniquity cannot be found
out and hated.
3 The words of their mouths are mischief
and deceit;
they have ceased to act wisely and do
good.
4 They plot mischief while on their beds;
they are set on a way that is not good;
they do not reject evil.

5 Your steadfast love, O LORD, extends to
the heavens,
your faithfulness to the clouds.
6 Your righteousness is like the mighty
mountains,
your judgments are like the great
deep;
you save humans and animals alike,
O LORD.

7 How precious is your steadfast love,
O God!
All people may take refuge in the
shadow of your wings.
8 They feast on the abundance of your
house,
and you give them drink from the
river of your delights.
9 For with you is the fountain of life;
in your light we see light.

10 O continue your steadfast love to those
who know you,

a Heb *him*

and your salvation to the upright of
heart!
11 Do not let the foot of the arrogant tread
on me,
or the hand of the wicked drive me
away.
12 There the evildoers lie prostrate;
they are thrust down, unable to rise.

36.1–12: The fountain of life. It is usually categorized as a lament,* but petition occurs only in vv. 10–11. The repetition of "ḥesed" (vv. 5, 7, 10) gives it the character of a celebration of God's *steadfast love*. **1–4:** The word *speaks* in v. 1 is used almost exclusively elsewhere of God's speech, but *the wicked* hear only their own rebellious thoughts. Therefore, loyalty to or *fear of God* is replaced by self-assertion, for which the wicked envision no accountability (vv. 2–3; Mic 2.1). **5–6:** *Steadfast love* and *faithfulness* communicate the character of God (Ex 34.6), while *righteousness* and *judgment* (or "acts of justice") summarize God's will (33.4–5; 89.14). Cosmological features, appearing in descending order, suggest that God's *steadfast love* permeates the cosmos. **7–9:** The promise of *refuge in the shadow of your wings* (17.8; 57.1) and the mention of *your house* may suggest an original Temple* setting. The language is probably metaphorical.* God is the *fountain* (68.26) or source of *life*, which *light* symbolizes (4.6). **10–12:** The focus on *the wicked* (v. 11) and *the evildoers* (v. 12) is a reminder of their constant opposition to God and God's people, but the psalmist trusts that God renders ineffective such opposition.

PSALM 37
Of David.

1 Do not fret because of the wicked;
do not be envious of wrongdoers,
2 for they will soon fade like the grass,
and wither like the green herb.

3 Trust in the LORD, and do good;
so you will live in the land, and enjoy
security.
4 Take delight in the LORD,
and he will give you the desires of
your heart.

5 Commit your way to the LORD;
trust in him, and he will act.

6 He will make your vindication shine like
the light,
and the justice of your cause like the
noonday.

7 Be still before the LORD, and wait
patiently for him;
do not fret over those who prosper in
their way,
over those who carry out evil devices.

8 Refrain from anger, and forsake wrath.
Do not fret—it leads only to evil.
9 For the wicked shall be cut off,
but those who wait for the LORD shall
inherit the land.

10 Yet a little while, and the wicked will be
no more;
though you look diligently for their
place, they will not be there.
11 But the meek shall inherit the land,
and delight themselves in abundant
prosperity.

12 The wicked plot against the righteous,
and gnash their teeth at them;
13 but the LORD laughs at the wicked,
for he sees that their day is coming.

14 The wicked draw the sword and bend
their bows
to bring down the poor and needy,
to kill those who walk uprightly;
15 their sword shall enter their own heart,
and their bows shall be broken.

16 Better is a little that the righteous
person has
than the abundance of many wicked.
17 For the arms of the wicked shall be
broken,
but the LORD upholds the righteous.

18 The LORD knows the days of the
blameless,
and their heritage will abide forever;
19 they are not put to shame in evil times,
in the days of famine they have
abundance.

20 But the wicked perish,
   and the enemies of the LORD are like
      the glory of the pastures;
   they vanish—like smoke they vanish
      away.

37.1–40: The LORD loves justice. This acrostic* poem (see Ps 9–10) is usually categorized as a wisdom psalm. It confronts the issue of theodicy* (literally, "the justice of God"), which is raised by the prosperity of *the wicked* (v. 1, plus fourteen more times) and their apparent success in opposing *the righteous* (v. 12, plus eight more times). **1–11:** The advice to the faithful (vv. 1, 3–5, 7–8), to which promises are attached (vv. 2, 6, 9–11), is *Do not fret* (vv. 1, 7, 8). Positively stated, it is *Trust in the LORD* (v. 3; see v. 5). Verse 6 identifies the issue as *justice* (v. 28), and v. 9 introduces the pervading themes: *the wicked shall be cut off* (vv. 22, 28, 34, 38) and *the righteous will inherit the land* (vv. 11, 22, 29, 34). The promise was probably meant figuratively to communicate the assurance of life and future. **12–20:** After vv. 1–11, advice is infrequent (vv. 27, 34). It is replaced by observations that support the promises of vv. 2, 6, 10–11. The *LORD laughs at the wicked*, because they do not threaten divine sovereignty (v. 13; see 2.4). *The wicked* effect their own undoing (vv. 14–15; Ps 7.15–16).

---

21 The wicked borrow, and do not pay
      back,
   but the righteous are generous and
      keep giving;
22 for those blessed by the LORD shall
      inherit the land,
   but those cursed by him shall be cut
      off.

23 Our steps[a] are made firm by the LORD,
   when he delights in our[b] way;
24 though we stumble,[c] we[d] shall not fall
      headlong,
   for the LORD holds us[e] by the hand.

25 I have been young, and now am old,
   yet I have not seen the righteous
      forsaken
   or their children begging bread.
26 They are ever giving liberally and
      lending,
   and their children become a
      blessing.

27 Depart from evil, and do good;
   so you shall abide forever.
28 For the LORD loves justice;
   he will not forsake his faithful ones.

   The righteous shall be kept safe
      forever,
   but the children of the wicked shall
      be cut off.
29 The righteous shall inherit the land,
   and live in it forever.

30 The mouths of the righteous utter
      wisdom,
   and their tongues speak justice.
31 The law of their God is in their hearts;
   their steps do not slip.

32 The wicked watch for the righteous,
   and seek to kill them.
33 The LORD will not abandon them to
      their power,
   or let them be condemned when they
      are brought to trial.

34 Wait for the LORD, and keep to his way,
   and he will exalt you to inherit the
      land;
   you will look on the destruction of
      the wicked.

35 I have seen the wicked oppressing,
   and towering like a cedar of
      Lebanon.[f]
36 Again I[g] passed by, and they were no
      more;
   though I sought them, they could not
      be found.

37 Mark the blameless, and behold the
      upright,
   for there is posterity for the
      peaceable.
38 But transgressors shall be altogether
      destroyed;
   the posterity of the wicked shall be
      cut off.

a Heb *A man's steps*   *b* Heb *his*   *c* Heb *he stumbles*
d Heb *he*   *e* Heb *him*   *f* Gk: Meaning of Heb
uncertain   *g* Gk Syr Jerome: Heb *he*

39 The salvation of the righteous is from
        the LORD;
    he is their refuge in the time of
        trouble.
40 The LORD helps them and rescues
        them;
    he rescues them from the wicked,
        and saves them,
    because they take refuge in him.

37.21–40. 21–26: The concepts of *borrow* and *lend-ing* frame this section. Generosity is its own reward (Prov 14.31; 19.17). **27–29:** Verse 27 recalls v. 3; and v. 28 recalls vv. 5–6, highlighting God's *justice.* **30–31:** *The righteous* are oriented to God, reflecting God's *justice* and appropriating God's "torah," "instruction" (NRSV *law;* 1.1–2). **32–38:** A final exhortation* (v. 34) accompanies further assurance that evil is fleeting and that righteousness will endure. **39–40:** Two different Hebrew words for *refuge* highlight the concept (2.12). That the assurances do not constitute a mechanistic doctrine of retribution is indicated by the recognition that *the righteous* will still experience *the time of trouble.*

PSALM 38

A Psalm of David, for the memorial offering.

1 O LORD, do not rebuke me in your
        anger,
    or discipline me in your wrath.
2 For your arrows have sunk into me,
    and your hand has come down
        on me.

3 There is no soundness in my flesh
    because of your indignation;
    there is no health in my bones
    because of my sin.
4 For my iniquities have gone over my
        head;
    they weigh like a burden too heavy for
        me.

5 My wounds grow foul and fester
    because of my foolishness;
6 I am utterly bowed down and prostrate;
    all day long I go around mourning.
7 For my loins are filled with burning,
    and there is no soundness in my
        flesh.

8 I am utterly spent and crushed;
    I groan because of the tumult of my
        heart.

9 O Lord, all my longing is known
        to you;
    my sighing is not hidden from you.
10 My heart throbs, my strength fails me;
    as for the light of my eyes—it also
        has gone from me.
11 My friends and companions stand aloof
        from my affliction,
    and my neighbors stand far off.

12 Those who seek my life lay their snares;
    those who seek to hurt me speak of
        ruin,
    and meditate treachery all day long.

13 But I am like the deaf, I do not hear;
    like the mute, who cannot speak.
14 Truly, I am like one who does not hear,
    and in whose mouth is no retort.

15 But it is for you, O LORD, that I wait;
    it is you, O Lord my God, who will
        answer.
16 For I pray, "Only do not let them rejoice
        over me,
    those who boast against me when my
        foot slips."

17 For I am ready to fall,
    and my pain is ever with me.
18 I confess my iniquity;
    I am sorry for my sin.
19 Those who are my foes without cause*a*
        are mighty,
    and many are those who hate me
        wrongfully.
20 Those who render me evil for good
    are my adversaries because I follow
        after good.

21 Do not forsake me, O LORD;
    O my God, do not be far from me;
22 make haste to help me,
    O Lord, my salvation.

a Q Ms: MT *my living foes*

38.1–22: My pain is ever with me. A prayer for help, it may have originally been used by sick persons (Ps 6). It is one of the church's Penitential Psalms* (Ps 6). **1–4:** The opening petition (6.1) implies that the distress represents punishment, and vv. 2–4 make this explicit (see v. 18). Verse 3a is repeated in v. 7b. **5–8:** *Grow foul and fester* could suggest that the psalmist suffered from leprosy, but the language can be heard metaphorically.* **9–10:** Apparently near death (v. 10), the psalmist is confident that the dire situation is *known* by God (v. 9). This ray of hope anticipates vv. 15–16, 21–22. **11–12:** Constant opposition from enemies may be bad enough (v. 12), but the psalmist has also been abandoned by those who should have offered support (v. 11; 27.10; 55.12–14; 88.8, 18). **13–14:** It is not clear whether the psalmist pretends not to hear, or whether the situation is so irredeemable that there is nothing left to say. **15–16:** The only hope is God. The psalmist petitions not for healing but for vindication. **17–20:** The psalmist is repentant (vv. 18, 20) but still in constant *pain* (v. 17). **21–22:** Recalling Ps 22.1, 11, 19, these verses undercut the notion of retribution implied by the psalmist's earlier linkage of sin and sickness. The psalmist anticipates that ultimately God will respond compassionately to *pain* (see vv. 9, 15).

PSALM 39

To the leader: to Jeduthun. A Psalm of David.

1 I said, "I will guard my ways
    that I may not sin with my tongue;
I will keep a muzzle on my mouth
    as long as the wicked are in my
        presence."
2 I was silent and still;
    I held my peace to no avail;
my distress grew worse,
3   my heart became hot within me.
While I mused, the fire burned;
    then I spoke with my tongue:

4 "LORD, let me know my end,
    and what is the measure of my days;
    let me know how fleeting my life is.
5 You have made my days a few
        handbreadths,
    and my lifetime is as nothing in your
        sight.
Surely everyone stands as a mere
    breath.   *Selah*

6 Surely everyone goes about like a
    shadow.
Surely for nothing they are in turmoil;
    they heap up, and do not know who
        will gather.

7 "And now, O Lord, what do I wait for?
    My hope is in you.
8 Deliver me from all my transgressions.
    Do not make me the scorn of the
        fool.
9 I am silent; I do not open my mouth,
    for it is you who have done it.
10 Remove your stroke from me;
    I am worn down by the blows[a] of
        your hand.

11 "You chastise mortals
    in punishment for sin,
consuming like a moth what is dear to
        them;
    surely everyone is a mere breath.
        Selah

12 "Hear my prayer, O LORD,
    and give ear to my cry;
    do not hold your peace at my tears.
For I am your passing guest,
    an alien, like all my forebears.
13 Turn your gaze away from me, that I
        may smile again,
    before I depart and am no more."

39.1–13: I am your passing guest. Like a prayer for help, it contains complaint (vv. 4–6), petition (vv. 8, 10, 12–13), and assurance (v. 7). But the generalized nature of the complaint and the puzzling final petition give the psalm the character of a wisdom meditation on the transience of life (Ps 90). **1–3:** The psalmist vows to remain silent, but is compelled to speak (Jer 20.9). **4–6:** Surprisingly, the actual speech is not offensive. It begins with a polite request (v. 4) to *know* something which the psalmist apparently knew well—the transience of human life (vv. 5–6). *Shadow* connotes *fleeting*, as does *breath*, which occurs often in Ecclesiastes (1.2, 14; 2.1; NRSV "vanity"). **7–11:** Again surprisingly, the apparently hopeless psalmist expresses *hope*, and addresses God with pious petitions (vv. 8, 10) which imply a confession of *sin*, a condition af-

a Heb *hostility*

fecting *everyone* (v. 11). **12–13:** While v. 11 sounds hopeless again, the psalmist has at least enough *hope* to continue to pray (v. 12). To be a *passing guest* and *an alien* elsewhere opens one to God's compassion and serves as a basis for petition (Lev 25.23; 1 Chr 29.15). So, it is surprising again that the psalmist ends by asking God to *turn . . . away*. The surprising juxtapositions portray hope and despair as simultaneous realities in the life of the faithful.

P S A L M 4 0

To the leader. Of David. A Psalm.

1 I waited patiently for the LORD;
    he inclined to me and heard my cry.
2 He drew me up from the desolate pit,ᵃ
    out of the miry bog,
and set my feet upon a rock,
    making my steps secure.
3 He put a new song in my mouth,
    a song of praise to our God.
Many will see and fear,
    and put their trust in the LORD.

4 Happy are those who make
    the LORD their trust,
who do not turn to the proud,
    to those who go astray after false
        gods.
5 You have multiplied, O LORD my God,
    your wondrous deeds and your
        thoughts toward us;
    none can compare with you.
Were I to proclaim and tell of them,
    they would be more than can be
        counted.

6 Sacrifice and offering you do not desire,
    but you have given me an open ear.ᵇ
Burnt offering and sin offering
    you have not required.
7 Then I said, "Here I am;
    in the scroll of the book it is written
        of me.ᶜ
8 I delight to do your will, O my God;
    your law is within my heart."

9 I have told the glad news of deliverance
    in the great congregation;
see, I have not restrained my lips,
    as you know, O LORD.

10 I have not hidden your saving help
    within my heart,
    I have spoken of your faithfulness and
        your salvation;
    I have not concealed your steadfast love
        and your faithfulness
    from the great congregation.

11 Do not, O LORD, withhold
    your mercy from me;
    let your steadfast love and your
        faithfulness
    keep me safe forever.
12 For evils have encompassed me
    without number;
my iniquities have overtaken me,
    until I cannot see;
they are more than the hairs of my
        head,
    and my heart fails me.

13 Be pleased, O LORD, to deliver me;
    O LORD, make haste to help me.
14 Let all those be put to shame and
        confusion
    who seek to snatch away my life;
let those be turned back and brought to
        dishonor
    who desire my hurt.
15 Let those be appalled because of their
        shame
    who say to me, "Aha, Aha!"

16 But may all who seek you
    rejoice and be glad in you;
may those who love your salvation
    say continually, "Great is the LORD!"
17 As for me, I am poor and needy,
    but the Lord takes thought for me.
You are my help and my deliverer;
    do not delay, O my God.

40.1–17: Your steadfast love and faithfulness will keep me safe forever. It is often treated as two separate psalms: a song of thanksgiving (vv. 1–10) and a prayer for help (vv. 11–17). Verses 13–17 are nearly identical to Ps 70. **1–3:** The psalmist recalls past faithfulness (v. 1a; 27.14; 31.24) and deliverance. The *new song* suggests grateful recognition of God's sover-

a Cn: Heb *pit of tumult*   *b* Heb *ears you have dug for me*   *c* Meaning of Heb uncertain eignty (33.3; 96.1). The psalmist's response serves as a witness to others to *trust* God (v. 3; see v. 4; 4.5; 33.21). **4–8:** *Trust* in God causes us to be what the Psalms call *happy* (2.12). *Trust* involves offering the whole self to God (v. 7), which is what God wants instead of sacrifice (v. 6; Hos 6.6; Am 5.21–24). God's "torah," "instruction" (NRSV *law*), should be internalized (v. 8; 1.1–2; 37.31). **9–10:** Externally, "trust" means sharing *glad news. Deliverance* (v. 9) and *saving help* (v. 10) represent the same Hebrew root, usually translated "righteousness"; it summarizes what God wills. *Faithfulness* and *steadfast love* summarize God's character (Ex 34.6). **11–12:** Verse 11b can be heard as an indicative: "Your steadfast love and your faithfulness will keep me safe forever." Hope is grounded in God's character. **13–17:** The word *help* frames the section of petition. The *poor and needy* (v. 17) are precisely those whom God wills to *help* (9.18; 12.5).

PSALM 41

To the leader. A Psalm of David.

1 Happy are those who consider the poor;[a]
  the LORD delivers them in the day of trouble.
2 The LORD protects them and keeps them alive;
  they are called happy in the land.
  You do not give them up to the will of their enemies.
3 The LORD sustains them on their sickbed;
  in their illness you heal all their infirmities.[b]

4 As for me, I said, "O LORD, be gracious to me;
  heal me, for I have sinned against you."
5 My enemies wonder in malice
  when I will die, and my name perish.
6 And when they come to see me, they utter empty words,
  while their hearts gather mischief;
  when they go out, they tell it abroad.
7 All who hate me whisper together about me;
  they imagine the worst for me.

8 They think that a deadly thing has fastened on me,
that I will not rise again from where I lie.
9 Even my bosom friend in whom I trusted,
  who ate of my bread, has lifted the heel against me.
10 But you, O LORD, be gracious to me,
  and raise me up, that I may repay them.

11 By this I know that you are pleased with me;
  because my enemy has not triumphed over me.
12 But you have upheld me because of my integrity,
  and set me in your presence forever.

13 Blessed be the LORD, the God of Israel,
  from everlasting to everlasting.
    Amen and Amen.

41.1–13: In your presence forever. It is either a song of thanksgiving or a prayer for help, depending upon whether one concludes that deliverance has already occurred. In either case, it probably originated in a context of illness (vv. 3–4; Ps 38), although the language can be heard metaphorically. ★ **1–3:** The beatitude (v. 1) and repetition of *happy* recall 1.1–2. Here, however, happiness is defined as openness to others rather than openness to God. **4–10:** Identical petitions in v. 4a surround a complaint about *enemies* who clearly disregard the beatitude of v. 1a, as do the psalmist's former friends (v. 9; 38.11). **11–12:** Regardless of whether healing has already occurred, the psalmist is *upheld* by trusting God, which is what *integrity* means (26.1, 11). The psalmist remains in God's *presence forever*, because God always considers *the poor* (v. 1a; 9.18; 40.17). **13:** The doxology concludes Book I (compare 72.19; 89.52; 106.48).

BOOK TWO

PSALM 42

To the leader. A Maskil of the Korahites.

1 As a deer longs for flowing streams,
  so my soul longs for you, O God.

a Or *weak*   b Heb *you change all his bed*

2 My soul thirsts for God,
 for the living God.
When shall I come and behold
 the face of God?
3 My tears have been my food
 day and night,
while people say to me continually,
 "Where is your God?"

4 These things I remember,
 as I pour out my soul:
how I went with the throng,*a*
 and led them in procession to the
  house of God,
with glad shouts and songs of
  thanksgiving,
 a multitude keeping festival.
5 Why are you cast down, O my soul,
 and why are you disquieted within
  me?
Hope in God; for I shall again praise
  him,
 my help 6and my God.

My soul is cast down within me;
 therefore I remember you
from the land of Jordan and of Hermon,
 from Mount Mizar.
7 Deep calls to deep
 at the thunder of your cataracts;
all your waves and your billows
 have gone over me.
8 By day the LORD commands his
  steadfast love,
 and at night his song is with me,
 a prayer to the God of my life.

9 I say to God, my rock,
 "Why have you forgotten me?
Why must I walk about mournfully
 because the enemy oppresses me?"
10 As with a deadly wound in my body,
 my adversaries taunt me,
while they say to me continually,
 "Where is your God?"

11 Why are you cast down, O my soul,
 and why are you disquieted within
  me?
Hope in God; for I shall again praise
  him,
 my help and my God.

42.1–43.5: My help and my God. The two psalms are a unity. A shared refrain concludes each section (42.5, 11; 43.5). Usually classified as a prayer for help, it initiates a collection attributed to *the Korahites*, Levites prominent in the Second Temple* period (Ps 42–49; see also 84–85, 87–88; 1 Chr 9.19). **42.1–5:** The imagery of thirst suggests that God is a necessity of life (63.1; 143.6). It seems that the psalmist was exiled or otherwise prevented from visiting the Temple to *behold the face of God* (11.7; 24.6). Taunting questions (vv. 3, 10) do not help, but the psalmist's own memory is painful also (v. 4). Discouragement is articulated in the refrain, but the final words are *hope* (33.18, 22) and *help*. **6–11:** The psalmist cannot help but *remember* (v. 6; see v. 4). The geographical terms suggest the psalmist may have been in exile; however, the region in view seems to suggest the area where the Jordan River begins, and the terms may simply introduce the water imagery of v. 7. Hope in v. 8 is short-lived, since vv. 9–10 include the psalmist's own questions about God.

PSALM 43

1 Vindicate me, O God, and defend my
  cause
 against an ungodly people;
from those who are deceitful and unjust
 deliver me!
2 For you are the God in whom I take
  refuge;
 why have you cast me off?
Why must I walk about mournfully
 because of the oppression of the
  enemy?

3 O send out your light and your truth;
 let them lead me;
let them bring me to your holy hill
 and to your dwelling.
4 Then I will go to the altar of God,
 to God my exceeding joy;
and I will praise you with the harp,
 O God, my God.

5 Why are you cast down, O my soul,
 and why are you disquieted within
  me?

a Meaning of Heb uncertain

Hope in God; for I shall again praise
   him,
  my help and my God.

43.1–5: *Vindicate me* is literally "establish justice for me." More questions occur in v. 2 before the petition continues in v. 3. *Light* may echo the psalmist's desire to see God's *face,* which is often associated with *light* (4.6). Verses 3–4 voice the trust that the psalmist will indeed revisit the Temple (see *holy hill* in 15.1). The language may be construed literally or figuratively. The confidence expressed in vv. 3–4 accentuates *hope* in the final occurrence of the refrain.

PSALM 44

To the leader. Of the Korahites. A Maskil.

1 We have heard with our ears, O God,
   our ancestors have told us,
what deeds you performed in their days,
   in the days of old:
2 you with your own hand drove out the
     nations,
  but them you planted;
you afflicted the peoples,
  but them you set free;
3 for not by their own sword did they win
   the land,
  nor did their own arm give them
   victory;
but your right hand, and your arm,
   and the light of your countenance,
   for you delighted in them.

4 You are my King and my God;
  you command*a* victories for Jacob.
5 Through you we push down our foes;
   through your name we tread down
   our assailants.
6 For not in my bow do I trust,
  nor can my sword save me.
7 But you have saved us from our foes,
  and have put to confusion those who
   hate us.
8 In God we have boasted continually,
  and we will give thanks to your name
   forever.   *Selah*

9 Yet you have rejected us and abased us,
  and have not gone out with our
   armies.

10 You made us turn back from the foe,
  and our enemies have gotten spoil.
11 You have made us like sheep for
   slaughter,
  and have scattered us among
   the nations.
12 You have sold your people for a trifle,
  demanding no high price for them.

13 You have made us the taunt of our
   neighbors,
  the derision and scorn of those
   around us.
14 You have made us a byword among the
   nations,
  a laughingstock*b* among the peoples.
15 All day long my disgrace is before me,
  and shame has covered my face
16 at the words of the taunters and
   revilers,
  at the sight of the enemy and the
   avenger.

17 All this has come upon us,
  yet we have not forgotten you,
  or been false to your covenant.
18 Our heart has not turned back,
  nor have our steps departed from
   your way,
19 yet you have broken us in the haunt of
   jackals,
  and covered us with deep darkness.

20 If we had forgotten the name of our
   God,
  or spread out our hands to a strange
   god,
21 would not God discover this?
  For he knows the secrets of the heart.
22 Because of you we are being killed all
   day long,
  and accounted as sheep for the
   slaughter.

23 Rouse yourself! Why do you sleep,
   O Lord?
  Awake, do not cast us off forever!

---

a Gk Syr: Heb *You are my King, O God; command*
b Heb *a shaking of the head*

24 Why do you hide your face?
  Why do you forget our affliction and
    oppression?
25 For we sink down to the dust;
  our bodies cling to the ground.
26 Rise up, come to our help.
  Redeem us for the sake of your
    steadfast love.

44.1–26: Why do you sleep, O LORD? It is the first communal lament in the psalter. The historical crisis that precipitated it is unknown. It may have arisen during the monarchy and would have been used as subsequent crises arose, such as the destruction of Jerusalem and the Exile.* **1–8:** The rehearsal of God's *deeds* (78.3–4) leads to an affirmation of God's sovereignty (v. 4a), after which *trust* in God is affirmed (21.7; 22.4–5). **9–16:** The opening profession of faith makes this section of complaint all the more poignant. Not a good shepherd, God is letting the *sheep face slaughter* (vv. 11, 22). **17–22:** The poignancy increases with this protestation of innocence (7.3–5). The people claim not to have broken *covenant** (v. 17) nor to have *forgotten* God (vv. 17, 20). **23–26:** Beginning with a wake-up call (7.6; 35.23), the psalm concludes with biting questions (13.1), a summary of the complaint (v. 25), and one more petition (v. 26), which appeals to God's *steadfast love* (Ex 34.6; Ps 5.7; 33.5, 18, 22).

PSALM 45

To the leader: according to Lilies.
Of the Korahites. A Maskil. A love song.

1 My heart overflows with a goodly
    theme;
  I address my verses to the king;
  my tongue is like the pen of a ready
    scribe.

2 You are the most handsome of men;
  grace is poured upon your lips;
  therefore God has blessed you
    forever.
3 Gird your sword on your thigh,
    O mighty one,
  in your glory and majesty.

4 In your majesty ride on victoriously
  for the cause of truth and to defend[a]
    the right;

let your right hand teach you dread
    deeds.
5 Your arrows are sharp
  in the heart of the king's enemies;
  the peoples fall under you.

6 Your throne, O God,[b] endures forever
    and ever.
  Your royal scepter is a scepter of
    equity;
7 you love righteousness and hate
    wickedness.
Therefore God, your God, has anointed
    you
  with the oil of gladness beyond your
    companions;
8 your robes are all fragrant with myrrh
    and aloes and cassia.
From ivory palaces stringed instruments
    make you glad;
9 daughters of kings are among your
    ladies of honor;
  at your right hand stands the queen
    in gold of Ophir.

10 Hear, O daughter, consider and incline
    your ear;
  forget your people and your father's
    house,
11 and the king will desire your beauty.
Since he is your lord, bow to him;
12 the people[c] of Tyre will seek your
    favor with gifts,
  the richest of the people 13with all
    kinds of wealth.

The princess is decked in her chamber
    with gold-woven robes;[d]
14 in many-colored robes she is led to
    the king;
  behind her the virgins, her
    companions, follow.
15 With joy and gladness they are led along
  as they enter the palace of the king.

16 In the place of ancestors you, O king,[e]
    shall have sons;

a Cn: Heb *and the meekness of*   b Or *Your throne is a throne of God, it*   c Heb *daughter*   d Or *people.*
13*All glorious is the princess within, gold embroidery is her clothing*   e Heb lacks *O king*

you will make them princes in all the
earth.
17 I will cause your name to be celebrated
in all generations;
therefore the peoples will praise you
forever and ever.

45.1–17: **My verses to the king.** The superscription,
A love song, indicates the uniqueness of this royal
psalm, which is addressed not to God but *to the king*
(v. 1). It was probably written in honor of and for use
at the wedding of a Judean or Israelite king. **1–2:** *Grace*
is an attribute of God (Ex 34.6). Verse 2 articulates a
special relationship between *king* and God. **3–5:** God
directs the king's military pursuits (18.31–45), which
are aimed at the fulfillment of God's purposes—*truth*
(or "faithfulness") and the defense of the oppressed
(v. 4; 72.12–14). **6–7:** Verse 6 appears to attribute divinity to the king; but the word in question elsewhere
describes human leaders who have been endowed
with strength by God (Ex 4.16; 7.1), as v. 7 suggests.
The king's job is to enact God's will for *equity* and
righteousness (98.9). **8–9:** The elaborate attire, music,
and attendants suggest a wedding. **10–15:** The *queen*
(v. 9) is addressed with admonitions (vv. 10–11) and
promises (v. 12). A description of her attire (v. 13) precedes the portrayal of the wedding procession. **16–17:**
It is not clear whether these promises should be understood as the poet's or God's (see v. 2).

PSALM 46
To the leader. Of the Korahites.
According to Alamoth. A Song.

1 God is our refuge and strength,
a very present*ᵃ* help in trouble.
2 Therefore we will not fear, though the
earth should change,
though the mountains shake in the
heart of the sea;
3 though its waters roar and foam,
though the mountains tremble with
its tumult. *Selah*

4 There is a river whose streams make
glad the city of God,
the holy habitation of the Most High.
5 God is in the midst of the city;*ᵇ* it shall
not be moved;
God will help it when the morning
dawns.

6 The nations are in an uproar, the
kingdoms totter;
he utters his voice, the earth melts.
7 The LORD of hosts is with us;
the God of Jacob is our refuge.*ᶜ Selah*

8 Come, behold the works of the LORD;
see what desolations he has brought
on the earth.
9 He makes wars cease to the end of the
earth;
he breaks the bow, and shatters the
spear;
he burns the shields with fire.
10 "Be still, and know that I am God!
I am exalted among the nations,
I am exalted in the earth."
11 The LORD of hosts is with us;
the God of Jacob is our refuge.*ᶜ Selah*

46.1–11: **The LORD of hosts is with us.** A song of
Zion,* its focus on Jerusalem (vv. 4–5) is surrounded
by proclamations of God's cosmic sovereignty (vv.
1–3, 8–10), thus anticipating Ps 47. **1–3:** God is a powerful protective presence (v. 1; see vv. 7, 11) and worthy of trust in the worst circumstances (vv. 2–3). For
the mountains to shake meant the world was threatened. **4–6:** *The city of God* is a stable point which *shall
not be moved* (*moved* is the same Hebrew word as
shake in v. 2 and *totter* in v. 6) amid the surrounding
uproar (v. 6; the same Hebrew word as *roar* in v. 3).
The language is symbolic and hyperbolic* (for instance, there is no river in Jerusalem; see Ezek
47.1–12). That the *earth melts* articulates not destruction but submission to God. **7:** *Hosts* accentuates the
emphasis on God's sovereignty (24.10). **8–11:** Verse 8
is sarcastic. God's *desolations* consist of destroying instruments of war. *Be still* suggests "Stop!" It is an order
to acknowledge God's sovereignty.

PSALM 47
To the leader. Of the Korahites. A Psalm.

1 Clap your hands, all you peoples;
shout to God with loud songs of joy.
2 For the LORD, the Most High, is
awesome,
a great king over all the earth.

---

a Or *well proved*   *b* Heb *of it*   *c* Or *fortress*

3 He subdued peoples under us,
and nations under our feet.
4 He chose our heritage for us,
the pride of Jacob whom he loves.
Selah

5 God has gone up with a shout,
the LORD with the sound of a trumpet.
6 Sing praises to God, sing praises;
sing praises to our King, sing praises.
7 For God is the king of all the earth;
sing praises with a psalm.*ᵃ*

8 God is king over the nations;
God sits on his holy throne.
9 The princes of the peoples gather
as the people of the God of Abraham.
For the shields of the earth belong to
God;
he is highly exalted.

47.1–9: God is highly exalted. An enthronement psalm (see Ps 93), it invites recognition of God's sovereignty and describes God's symbolic enthronement in the Temple* (v. 5). **1–4:** In keeping with God's cosmic claim (see Ps 46), *all you peoples* are invited to *clap your hands* (v. 1), a joyful acknowledgment of God's kingship and God's subduing of *peoples* and *nations* (vv. 2–3). *Most High* represents the first occurrence of the psalm's key word, which recurs as *gone up* (v. 5) and *exalted* (v. 9). God shares the benefits of sovereignty with those whom God *loves* (v. 4; 78.68). **5:** Linked to v. 1 by *shout* and v. 9 by *gone up/exalted*, this central verse portrays the enactment of God's enthronement, originally in the context of worship in the Temple. **6–9:** Verse 6 surrounds *God* and *our King* with the invitation to *sing praises*. *King* recurs in vv. 7–8. *Shields* (v. 9) probably designates kings (89.18). All earthly rulers *belong to God*.

PSALM 48

A Song. A Psalm of the Korahites.

1 Great is the LORD and greatly to be
praised
in the city of our God.
His holy mountain, 2beautiful in
elevation,
is the joy of all the earth,
Mount Zion, in the far north,
the city of the great King.

3 Within its citadels God
has shown himself a sure defense.

4 Then the kings assembled,
they came on together.
5 As soon as they saw it, they were
astounded;
they were in panic, they took to flight;
6 trembling took hold of them there,
pains as of a woman in labor,
7 as when an east wind shatters
the ships of Tarshish.

8 As we have heard, so have we seen
in the city of the LORD of hosts,
in the city of our God,
which God establishes forever. *Selah*

9 We ponder your steadfast love, O God,
in the midst of your temple.
10 Your name, O God, like your praise,
reaches to the ends of the earth.
Your right hand is filled with victory.
11 Let Mount Zion be glad,
let the towns*ᵇ* of Judah rejoice
because of your judgments.

12 Walk about Zion, go all around it,
count its towers,
13 consider well its ramparts;
go through its citadels,
that you may tell the next generation
14 that this is God,
our God forever and ever.
He will be our guide forever.

48.1–14: The city of the great King. A song of Zion,* it affirms that Jerusalem symbolizes God's universal sovereignty (see Ps 47). It may have been used originally by pilgrims as they approached and entered Jerusalem. **1–3:** The seven titles for Jerusalem communicate its importance. The word translated *north* is "zaphon," the Canaanite mountain of the gods. The God of *Mount Zion* has displaced the Canaanite deities (see Ps 82). **4–7:** These verses draw on the tradition of Zion's indestructibility, as well as the tradition of the holy war* in which God wins without an actual fight. *East wind* recalls the defeat of the Egyptians in Ex 14, which led to the planting of God's people "on the mountain of your own possession" (Ex 15.17). **8–11:**

a Heb *Maskil*   *b* Heb *daughters*

Just as the sight of Jerusalem had a powerful effect on opposing kings (v. 5), so it also has on pilgrims who approach and enter the *temple*. *Victory* in v. 10 is literally "righteousness," and *judgments* in v. 11 is literally "justices." Entry into the city puts pilgrims in touch with the essence of God's will (97.2), as well as the essence of God's character, *steadfast love* (33.5; 89.14). **12–14:** The city's revelatory power is the rationale for observing its architectural detail. *Count* (v. 12) and *tell* (v. 14) represent the same Hebrew root. Careful observation of the city leads to proclamation about the city's God.

PSALM 49

To the leader. Of the Korahites. A Psalm.

1 Hear this, all you peoples;
    give ear, all inhabitants of the world,
2 both low and high,
    rich and poor together.
3 My mouth shall speak wisdom;
    the meditation of my heart shall be
        understanding.
4 I will incline my ear to a proverb;
    I will solve my riddle to the music of
        the harp.

5 Why should I fear in times of trouble,
    when the iniquity of my persecutors
        surrounds me,
6 those who trust in their wealth
    and boast of the abundance of their
        riches?
7 Truly, no ransom avails for one's life,*a*
    there is no price one can give to God
        for it.
8 For the ransom of life is costly,
    and can never suffice,
9 that one should live on forever
    and never see the grave.*b*

10 When we look at the wise, they die;
    fool and dolt perish together
    and leave their wealth to others.
11 Their graves*c* are their homes forever,
    their dwelling places to all
        generations,
    though they named lands their own.
12 Mortals cannot abide in their pomp;
    they are like the animals that perish.

13 Such is the fate of the foolhardy,
    the end of those*d* who are pleased
        with their lot.   *Selah*
14 Like sheep they are appointed for Sheol;
    Death shall be their shepherd;
    straight to the grave they descend,*e*
    and their form shall waste away;
    Sheol shall be their home.*f*
15 But God will ransom my soul from the
        power of Sheol,
    for he will receive me.   *Selah*

16 Do not be afraid when some become
        rich,
    when the wealth of their houses
        increases.
17 For when they die they will carry
        nothing away;
    their wealth will not go down after
        them.
18 Though in their lifetime they count
        themselves happy
    —for you are praised when you do
        well for yourself—
19 they*g* will go to the company of their
        ancestors,
    who will never again see the light.
20 Mortals cannot abide in their pomp;
    they are like the animals that perish.

49.1–20: Mortals cannot abide in their pomp. This wisdom psalm addresses a *riddle* (v. 4) that can be inferred from the content of its two sections (vv. 5–12, 13–20): How are humans *like the animals* (vv. 12, 20)? **1–4:** *Harp* suggests a setting in worship, but the psalm is ultimately aimed at a universal audience. **5–12:** Persons *who trust in their wealth* (v. 6) live with the illusion that ultimate security can be purchased (vv. 7–9). But death disproves the illusion by sparing no one (vv. 10–11). Humans fare no better than *the animals*, despite their riches, which is what *pomp* means (v. 12). **13–20:** The universality of death is not the final word. *The foolhardy* (v. 13) will permanently reside in *Sheol,*★ the realm of the dead (v. 14; 6.5); but God will *ransom* the psalmist's life in a way that no human can purchase life (vv. 7–8). What is meant by *God* . . .

a Another reading is *no one can ransom a brother*
b Heb *the pit*   *c* Gk Syr Compare Tg: Heb *their inward* (thought)   *d* Tg: Heb *after them*   *e* Cn: Heb *the upright shall have dominion over them in the morning*
f Meaning of Heb uncertain   *g* Cn: Heb *you*

will receive me is unclear, but it pushes beyond the normal view that all persons go to *Sheol* (see 22.19; 73.24; Gen 5.24; 2 Kings 2.1–12). Verse 20 in Hebrew is not identical to v. 12. It should be translated, "Mortals with riches and no understanding are like the animals that perish." For those who understand (v. 3), God offers a hope that no amount of wealth can purchase. Finally then, only *the foolhardy*, who lack understanding and thus fail to *trust* God (see v. 6), die without hope *like the animals.*

PSALM 50

A Psalm of Asaph.

1 The mighty one, God the LORD,
   speaks and summons the earth
   from the rising of the sun to its
      setting.
2 Out of Zion, the perfection of beauty,
   God shines forth.

3 Our God comes and does not keep
      silence,
   before him is a devouring fire,
   and a mighty tempest all around him.
4 He calls to the heavens above
   and to the earth, that he may judge
      his people:
5 "Gather to me my faithful ones,
   who made a covenant with me by
      sacrifice!"
6 The heavens declare his righteousness,
   for God himself is judge.   *Selah*

7 "Hear, O my people, and I will speak,
   O Israel, I will testify against you.
   I am God, your God.
8 Not for your sacrifices do I rebuke you;
   your burnt offerings are continually
      before me.
9 I will not accept a bull from your house,
   or goats from your folds.
10 For every wild animal of the forest is
      mine,
   the cattle on a thousand hills.
11 I know all the birds of the air,[a]
   and all that moves in the field is
      mine.

12 "If I were hungry, I would not tell you,
   for the world and all that is in it is
      mine.

13 Do I eat the flesh of bulls,
   or drink the blood of goats?
14 Offer to God a sacrifice of thanksgiving,[b]
   and pay your vows to the Most High.
15 Call on me in the day of trouble;
   I will deliver you, and you shall glorify
      me."

16 But to the wicked God says:
   "What right have you to recite my
      statutes,
   or take my covenant on your lips?
17 For you hate discipline,
   and you cast my words behind you.
18 You make friends with a thief when you
      see one,
   and you keep company with
      adulterers.

19 "You give your mouth free rein for evil,
   and your tongue frames deceit.
20 You sit and speak against your kin;
   you slander your own mother's child.
21 These things you have done and I have
      been silent;
   you thought that I was one just like
      yourself.
   But now I rebuke you, and lay the
      charge before you.

22 "Mark this, then, you who forget God,
   or I will tear you apart, and there will
      be no one to deliver.
23 Those who bring thanksgiving as their
      sacrifice honor me;
   to those who go the right way[c]
   I will show the salvation of God."

50.1–23: Thanksgiving as sacrifice. A prophetic* exhortation* (see Ps 14), it offers the word of God (vv. 5, 7–23), apparently delivered originally by a prophet or priest during worship. *Asaph* was a Levite appointed by David to be "chief" of several "ministers before the ark of the LORD" (1 Chr 16.4–5; see Ps 73–83). **1–6:** The divine speech is introduced with a theophany,* an appearance of God (vv. 2–3; 18.7–15; 97.2–5). Verses 1–3 assert God's cosmic reign, the attributes of which are justice (see *judge* in vv. 4, 6) and *righteous-*

a Gk Syr Tg: Heb *mountains*   *b* Or *make thanksgiving your sacrifice to God*   *c* Heb *who set a way* ness (98.9). God's people have failed to embody these *covenant** standards (v. 5), and are put on trial (Mic 6.1–2). **7–15:** The first charge involves misunderstanding of *sacrifices.* They are not something God needs (vv. 10–13), but rather are to be a means of expressing gratitude to God (v. 14). God desires the proper understanding (40.6–8; 51.19; Hos 6.6; Am 5.21–24). **16–22:** *The wicked* are what God's people have become, and the second *charge* (v. 21) involves disobedience to *covenant* stipulations. Verses 18–19 allude to the Ten Commandments. God has *been silent* but will be no longer (see v. 3). **23:** The first line summarizes vv. 7–15, and the second summarizes vv. 16–22. *Salvation* or life is the promise for those who participate properly in the *covenant.*

PSALM 51

To the leader. A Psalm of David, when the prophet Nathan came to him, after he had gone in to Bathsheba.

1 Have mercy on me, O God,
    according to your steadfast love;
  according to your abundant mercy
    blot out my transgressions.
2 Wash me thoroughly from my iniquity,
    and cleanse me from my sin.

3 For I know my transgressions,
    and my sin is ever before me.
4 Against you, you alone, have I sinned,
    and done what is evil in your sight,
  so that you are justified in your
      sentence
    and blameless when you pass
      judgment.
5 Indeed, I was born guilty,
    a sinner when my mother conceived
      me.

6 You desire truth in the inward being;[a]
    therefore teach me wisdom in my
      secret heart.
7 Purge me with hyssop, and I shall be
      clean;
    wash me, and I shall be whiter than
      snow.
8 Let me hear joy and gladness;
    let the bones that you have crushed
      rejoice.
9 Hide your face from my sins,
    and blot out all my iniquities.

10 Create in me a clean heart, O God,
     and put a new and right[b] spirit within
       me.
11 Do not cast me away from your
       presence,
     and do not take your holy spirit from
       me.
12 Restore to me the joy of your salvation,
     and sustain in me a willing[c] spirit.

13 Then I will teach transgressors your
       ways,
     and sinners will return to you.
14 Deliver me from bloodshed, O God,
     O God of my salvation,
     and my tongue will sing aloud of your
       deliverance.

15 O Lord, open my lips,
     and my mouth will declare your
       praise.
16 For you have no delight in sacrifice;
     if I were to give a burnt offering, you
       would not be pleased.
17 The sacrifice acceptable to God[d] is a
       broken spirit;
     a broken and contrite heart, O God,
       you will not despise.

18 Do good to Zion in your good pleasure;
     rebuild the walls of Jerusalem,
19 then you will delight in right sacrifices,
     in burnt offerings and whole burnt
       offerings;
     then bulls will be offered on your
       altar.

51.1–19: I know my transgressions. A prayer for help, it became one of the church's Penitential Psalms* (Ps 6). The psalmist's complaint involves personal sinfulness, leading the editors of the psalter to associate it with David (2 Sam 11–12). **1–5:** The focus on God's character recalls Israel's fundamental profession in Ex 34.6–7. *Sin* is a more general term than *transgressions,* which suggests intentional rebellion. *Iniquity* and *guilty* represent the same Hebrew word. Verse 5a is literally, "Indeed, I was born into iniquity." Verse 4 recalls 2 Sam 12.13. **6–12:** *Sin* is not the final reality.

---

a Meaning of Heb uncertain   *b* Or *steadfast*
c Or *generous*   *d* Or *My sacrifice, O God,*

There is a God-given *wisdom* (37.30–31) that yields *truth* or "faithfulness," so the psalmist continues to pray for forgiveness (vv. 7–9) and a new start (vv. 10–12). Specific rituals of cleansing may have been involved (v. 7; Lev 14.49, 52). The repetition of *spirit* reinforces the plea for God to *create* (Gen 1.2). The psalmist anticipates a new creation (Ezek 36.25–27). **13–17:** The forgiven and transformed psalmist will be in a position to *teach* others God's *ways* (32.8–9), although not without opposition (v. 14a). The psalmist promises to make public testimony to God's activity with every organ of speech (vv. 14–15) and by offering God the whole self (vv. 16–17). *Broken* connotes humility and gratitude (50.14, 23). **18–19:** These verses were probably added to ensure that vv. 16–17 not be construed to advocate abolition of *sacrifice.*

PSALM 52

To the leader. A Maskil of David, when Doeg the Edomite came to Saul and said to him, "David has come to the house of Ahimelech."

1 Why do you boast, O mighty one,
  of mischief done against the godly?[a]
  All day long 2you are plotting
    destruction.
  Your tongue is like a sharp razor,
    you worker of treachery.
3 You love evil more than good,
  and lying more than speaking the
    truth.   *Selah*
4 You love all words that devour,
  O deceitful tongue.

5 But God will break you down forever;
  he will snatch and tear you from your
    tent;
  he will uproot you from the land of
    the living.   *Selah*
6 The righteous will see, and fear,
  and will laugh at the evildoer,[b]
    saying,
7 "See the one who would not take
  refuge in God,
  but trusted in abundant riches,
  and sought refuge in wealth!"[c]

8 But I am like a green olive tree
  in the house of God.
  I trust in the steadfast love of God
    forever and ever.

9 I will thank you forever,
  because of what you have done.
In the presence of the faithful
  I will proclaim[d] your name, for it is
    good.

52.1–9: I trust in the steadfast love of God. It is classified as a psalm of trust (vv. 8–9), a prophetic* announcement of judgment (vv. 1–5), and a wisdom psalm to instruct *the righteous* (vv. 6–7). The superscription suggests that the *mighty one* (v. 1) is *Doeg,* who betrayed David and killed the priests of Nob (1 Sam 22.9). **1–4:** The psalm is addressed not to God but to a formidable opponent of God and the psalmist. In view of the occurrence of *steadfast love* in v. 8, it should be retained in v. 1, the second line of which would then read, "the steadfast love of God lasts all the day." The opening verse then lays out the option to *evil* that the *mighty one* has rejected but which the psalmist has embraced. Treacherous speech characterizes wickedness (10.7; 35.20; 38.12). **5–7a:** The destiny of the wicked will be a lesson to *the righteous* concerning the proper source of *refuge.* **7b–9:** Whereas the wicked one *trusted . . . in wealth,* the psalmist places *trust* in God's love (see v. 1) and is solidly rooted there (1.3; 92.12–15). Eternal gratitude contrasts with the greed of the *mighty one* (vv. 2–4, 7).

PSALM 53

To the leader: according to Mahalath. A Maskil of David.

1 Fools say in their hearts, "There is no
    God."
  They are corrupt, they commit
    abominable acts;
  there is no one who does good.

2 God looks down from heaven on
    humankind
  to see if there are any who are wise,
  who seek after God.

3 They have all fallen away, they are all
    alike perverse;
  there is no one who does good,
  no, not one.

a Cn Compare Syr: Heb *the kindness of God*
b Heb *him*   *c* Syr Tg: Heb *in his destruction*
d Cn: Heb *wait for*

4 Have they no knowledge, those
  evildoers,
    who eat up my people as they eat
    bread,
    and do not call upon God?

5 There they shall be in great terror,
    in terror such as has not been.
  For God will scatter the bones of the
    ungodly;[a]
    they will be put to shame,[b] for God
    has rejected them.

6 O that deliverance for Israel would
    come from Zion!
  When God restores the fortunes of
    his people,
    Jacob will rejoice; Israel will be glad.

53.1–6: Terror for the ungodly. It is nearly identical to Ps 14, except for v. 5 (compare 14.5–6). The two versions apparently made their way into the psalter because they existed in separate collections. **5:** While 14.5–6 proclaim God's protective presence with the righteous and the poor, v. 5 elaborates upon the *great terror*, which will involve judgment on those who oppose God. This particular direction is fitting following the judgment described in Ps 52.

PSALM 54

To the leader: with stringed instruments.
A Maskil of David, when the Ziphites went and
told Saul, "David is in hiding among us."

1 Save me, O God, by your name,
    and vindicate me by your might.
2 Hear my prayer, O God;
    give ear to the words of my mouth.

3 For the insolent have risen against me,
    the ruthless seek my life;
    they do not set God before them.
                              Selah

4 But surely, God is my helper;
    the Lord is the upholder of[c] my life.
5 He will repay my enemies for their
    evil.
  In your faithfulness, put an end to
    them.

6 With a freewill offering I will sacrifice
    to you;
  I will give thanks to your name,
    O LORD, for it is good.
7 For he has delivered me from every
    trouble,
    and my eye has looked in triumph on
    my enemies.

54.1–7: Save me, O God, by your name. Usually considered a prayer for help, it is sometimes classified as a song of thanksgiving, since v. 7 may indicate that deliverance has occurred. Originally it may have been used by falsely accused persons seeking sanctuary in the Temple* (see Ps 5, 7). The superscription alludes to 1 Sam 23.19. **1–2:** The opening petitions are typical (17.1; 26.1). *Name* recurs in v. 6; it focuses the issue on God's character as one who is *good* (v. 6) and shows *faithfulness* (v. 5; Ex 34.6). **3–5:** References to opponents encompass the central profession of faith in v. 4 (see 10.14; 22.19). The issue in v. 5 is not so much personal revenge as the establishment of justice. **6–7:** The motive for the psalmist's *freewill offering* (2 Chr 31.14) is gratitude for the actual or anticipated deliverance, which reveals God's character.

PSALM 55

To the leader: with stringed instruments.
A Maskil of David.

1 Give ear to my prayer, O God;
    do not hide yourself from my
    supplication.
2 Attend to me, and answer me;
    I am troubled in my complaint.
  I am distraught 3by the noise of the
    enemy,
    because of the clamor of the wicked.
  For they bring[d] trouble upon me,
    and in anger they cherish enmity
    against me.

4 My heart is in anguish within me,
    the terrors of death have fallen upon
    me.

a Cn Compare Gk Syr: Heb *him who encamps against you*   b Gk: Heb *you have put (them) to shame*   c Gk Syr Jerome: Heb *is of those who uphold* or *is with those who uphold*   d Cn Compare Gk: Heb *they cause to totter*

5 Fear and trembling come upon me,
    and horror overwhelms me.
6 And I say, "O that I had wings like a
    dove!
    I would fly away and be at rest;
7 truly, I would flee far away;
    I would lodge in the wilderness; *Selah*
8 I would hurry to find a shelter for
    myself
    from the raging wind and tempest."

9 Confuse, O Lord, confound their
    speech;
    for I see violence and strife in the
    city.
10 Day and night they go around it
    on its walls,
    and iniquity and trouble are within it;
11   ruin is in its midst;
    oppression and fraud
    do not depart from its marketplace.

12 It is not enemies who taunt me—
    I could bear that;
    it is not adversaries who deal insolently
    with me—
    I could hide from them.
13 But it is you, my equal,
    my companion, my familiar friend,
14 with whom I kept pleasant company;
    we walked in the house of God with
    the throng.
15 Let death come upon them;
    let them go down alive to Sheol;
    for evil is in their homes and in their
    hearts.

16 But I call upon God,
    and the LORD will save me.
17 Evening and morning and at noon
    I utter my complaint and moan,
    and he will hear my voice.
18 He will redeem me unharmed
    from the battle that I wage,
    for many are arrayed against me.
19 God, who is enthroned from of old,
                     Selah
    will hear, and will humble them—
    because they do not change,
    and do not fear God.

20 My companion laid hands on a friend
    and violated a covenant with me[a]
21 with speech smoother than butter,
    but with a heart set on war;
    with words that were softer than oil,
    but in fact were drawn swords.

22 Cast your burden[b] on the LORD,
    and he will sustain you;
    he will never permit
    the righteous to be moved.

23 But you, O God, will cast them down
    into the lowest pit;
    the bloodthirsty and treacherous
    shall not live out half their days.
    But I will trust in you.

55.1–23: But I call upon God. The typical elements of a prayer for help are present—petition (vv. 1–2a, 9a, 15), complaint (vv. 2b–8, 9b–11, 12–14, 20–21), expression of trust (vv. 16–19, 22–23). Their irregular arrangement may symbolize the chaotic conditions facing the psalmist. **1–5:** The *complaint* suggests powerful opposition. *Terrors* and *trembling* are ordinarily what the judgment of God produces (see Ex 15.15–16). **6–8:** Thus, the psalmist wants to escape *like a dove* (11.1; Jer 9.2–3). **9–11:** Recalling Gen 11.1–9, v. 9 suggests that the enemies also oppose God with their *violence* (7.16; 11.5). **12–15:** Societal chaos is accompanied by personal betrayal (35.12–15; 38.11). The psalmist longs for the opponents to go to *Sheol,* * the realm of the dead (6.5). **16–19:** In the midst of *horror* (v. 5), the psalmist looks to God, *enthroned from of old.* Monarchs were responsible for peace, and the psalmist trusts that God will preserve life *unharmed,* literally, "in peace." **20–23:** The psalmist concludes by inviting others to *trust* (v. 23) their life and future to God's care (v. 22).

PSALM 56

To the leader: according to The Dove on Far-off Terebinths. Of David. A Miktam, when the Philistines seized him in Gath.

1 Be gracious to me, O God, for people
    trample on me;
    all day long foes oppress me;

a Heb lacks *with me*   *b* Or *Cast what he has given you*

2 my enemies trample on me all day long,
       for many fight against me.
   O Most High, 3when I am afraid,
       I put my trust in you.
4 In God, whose word I praise,
       in God I trust; I am not afraid;
       what can flesh do to me?

5 All day long they seek to injure my
           cause;
       all their thoughts are against me for
           evil.
6 They stir up strife, they lurk,
       they watch my steps.
   As they hoped to have my life,
7   so repay*a* them for their crime;
       in wrath cast down the peoples,
           O God!

8 You have kept count of my tossings;
       put my tears in your bottle.
   Are they not in your record?
9 Then my enemies will retreat
       in the day when I call.
   This I know, that*b* God is for me.
10 In God, whose word I praise,
       in the LORD, whose word I praise,
11 in God I trust; I am not afraid.
       What can a mere mortal do to me?

12 My vows to you I must perform, O God;
       I will render thank offerings to you.
13 For you have delivered my soul from
           death,
       and my feet from falling,
   so that I may walk before God
       in the light of life.

56.1–13: I am not afraid. Petition and complaint (vv.
1–2, 5–8) suggest this is a prayer for help, but some
consider it a song of thanksgiving, concluding that vv.
12–13 indicate that deliverance has occurred (see Ps
54). The superscription alludes to 1 Sam 21.10–14.
1–2: *Fight* suggests a military context, but *trample*
connotes socioeconomic abuse. The language may be
metaphorical.✶ The threat is enduring: *all day long*
(vv. 1–2, 5). **3–4:** The crucial contrast is between being
afraid and putting *trust* in God (vv. 3, 4, 11). *Praise* for
God's *word* (vv. 4, 10) occurs only here in the Old
Testament; *word* may refer to the whole tradition of
God's saving activity or to an implied promise of de-

liverance. **5–11:** Verses 5–7 describe what others *can
. . . do to* the psalmist (vv. 4, 10). Known by God (v.
8; see 40.7) and trusting that God is *for me* (v. 9; see
118.6), the psalmist is *not afraid.* **12–13:** *Vows* and
thank offerings indicate humble gratitude (50.14;
116.17–18) for *life* in God's presence, an enduring
source of *light* (4.6; 27.1).

PSALM 57

To the leader: Do Not Destroy. Of David.
A Miktam, when he fled from Saul, in the cave.

1 Be merciful to me, O God, be merciful
           to me,
       for in you my soul takes refuge;
   in the shadow of your wings I will take
           refuge,
       until the destroying storms pass by.
2 I cry to God Most High,
       to God who fulfills his purpose for
           me.
3 He will send from heaven and save me,
       he will put to shame those who
           trample on me.   *Selah*
   God will send forth his steadfast love
       and his faithfulness.

4 I lie down among lions
       that greedily devour*c* human prey;
   their teeth are spears and arrows,
       their tongues sharp swords.

5 Be exalted, O God, above the heavens.
       Let your glory be over all the earth.

6 They set a net for my steps;
       my soul was bowed down.
   They dug a pit in my path,
       but they have fallen into it
           themselves.   *Selah*
7 My heart is steadfast, O God,
       my heart is steadfast.
   I will sing and make melody.
8   Awake, my soul!
   Awake, O harp and lyre!
       I will awake the dawn.

---

a Cn: Heb *rescue*   *b* Or *because*   *c* Cn: Heb *are
aflame for*

9 I will give thanks to you, O Lord, among
   the peoples;
   I will sing praises to you among the
   nations.
10 For your steadfast love is as high as the
   heavens;
   your faithfulness extends to the
   clouds.

11 Be exalted, O God, above the heavens.
   Let your glory be over all the earth.

57.1–11: Let your glory be over all the earth. Usually classified as a prayer for help, it could be understood as a song of thanksgiving, depending on the interpretation* of v. 6 (see Ps 54, 56). The superscription alludes to 1 Sam 21.1; 24.3. Verse 4 may indicate the prayer was originally that of a falsely accused person (see Ps 5, 7). **1–3:** An extended expression of trust features *refuge* (2.12; 17.8). The psalmist is confident that God's essential character—*steadfast love* and *faithfulness* (Ex 34.6; Ps 33.5; 89.14)—will enact the divine *purpose*. The repetition of *send* reinforces the point. **4–6:** Complaint in vv. 4, 6 surrounds the first occurrence of the refrain in v. 5 (see v. 11). Typically, the wicked are described as weapon-bearing beasts (7.2; 11.2), who also employ *a net* and *a pit* (9.15). **7–8:** Regardless of whether v. 6 indicates the removal of the threat, the psalmist is confident that security lies with God. The psalmist is eager to greet God's help, originally perhaps at the conclusion of a night vigil in the Temple.* **9–11:** The promise of grateful praise arises from the conviction that God's *steadfast love* and *faithfulness* (see v. 3) pervade the cosmos (36.5). Verses 7–11 recur in nearly identical form as 108.1–5.

~~~~~~~~

P S A L M   5 8

To the leader: Do Not Destroy. Of David.
A Miktam.

1 Do you indeed decree what is right, you
   gods?[a]
   Do you judge people fairly?
2 No, in your hearts you devise wrongs;
   your hands deal out violence on
   earth.

3 The wicked go astray from the womb;
   they err from their birth, speaking
   lies.

4 They have venom like the venom of a
   serpent,
   like the deaf adder that stops its ear,
5 so that it does not hear the voice of
   charmers
   or of the cunning enchanter.

6 O God, break the teeth in their mouths;
   tear out the fangs of the young lions,
   O LORD!
7 Let them vanish like water that runs
   away;
   like grass let them be trodden down[b]
   and wither.
8 Let them be like the snail that dissolves
   into slime;
   like the untimely birth that never sees
   the sun.
9 Sooner than your pots can feel the heat
   of thorns,
   whether green or ablaze, may he
   sweep them away!

10 The righteous will rejoice when they see
   vengeance done;
   they will bathe their feet in the blood
   of the wicked.
11 People will say, "Surely there is a
   reward for the righteous;
   surely there is a God who judges on
   earth."

58.1–11: Violence on earth, justice on earth. A prayer for help, its unusual beginning (vv. 1–4) and conclusion (vv. 10–11) give it a prophetic,* instructional tone. **1–2:** It is unclear whether the opening questions are addressed to the *gods* (Ps 82) or to *wicked* persons (Ps 52). **3–5:** *Wicked* persons are clearly targeted in the complaint. They are deceitful and destructive (5.6; 57.4). **6–11:** Despite v. 10, v. 11 makes it clear that the motivation behind the petition in vv. 6–9 is not personal revenge but the desire for justice to prevail. If the violence is to stop, *the wicked* must be disarmed (see v. 6). *Reward* in v. 11 is literally "fruit." *Judges* could be translated "establishes justice." The psalmist affirms, despite appearances (vv. 1–5), that God's justice *on earth* (v. 11) will ultimately triumph over *violence on earth* (v. 2).

~~~~~~~~

a Or *mighty lords*   *b* Cn: Meaning of Heb uncertain

PSALM 59

To the leader: Do Not Destroy. Of David.
A Miktam, when Saul ordered his house to be
watched in order to kill him.

1 Deliver me from my enemies, O my
   God;
   protect me from those who rise up
      against me.
2 Deliver me from those who work evil;
   from the bloodthirsty save me.

3 Even now they lie in wait for my life;
   the mighty stir up strife against me.
   For no transgression or sin of mine,
      O LORD,
4   for no fault of mine, they run and
      make ready.

   Rouse yourself, come to my help and
      see!
5   You, LORD God of hosts, are God of
      Israel.
   Awake to punish all the nations;
   spare none of those who
      treacherously plot evil.   *Selah*

6 Each evening they come back,
   howling like dogs
   and prowling about the city.
7 There they are, bellowing with their
      mouths,
   with sharp words[a] on their lips—
   for "Who," they think,[b] "will hear
      us?"

8 But you laugh at them, O LORD;
   you hold all the nations in derision.
9 O my strength, I will watch for you;
   for you, O God, are my fortress.
10 My God in his steadfast love will meet
      me;
   my God will let me look in triumph
      on my enemies.

11 Do not kill them, or my people may
      forget;
   make them totter by your power, and
      bring them down,
   O Lord, our shield.

12 For the sin of their mouths, the words
      of their lips,
   let them be trapped in their pride.
   For the cursing and lies that they utter,
13   consume them in wrath;
   consume them until they are no
      more.
   Then it will be known to the ends of the
      earth
   that God rules over Jacob.   *Selah*

14 Each evening they come back,
   howling like dogs
   and prowling about the city.
15 They roam about for food,
   and growl if they do not get their fill.

16 But I will sing of your might;
   I will sing aloud of your steadfast love
      in the morning.
   For you have been a fortress for me
   and a refuge in the day of my distress.
17 O my strength, I will sing praises to you,
   for you, O God, are my fortress,
   the God who shows me steadfast love.

59.1–17: In steadfast love, God will meet me. A
prayer for help, it may have originated as the prayer
of a falsely accused person seeking sanctuary in the
Temple* (Ps 5, 7). The superscription associates it with
Saul's threats on David's life (1 Sam 19.11). **1–5:** Petition anticipates subsequent expressions of assurance,
since *protect* is the same Hebrew root as *fortress* (vv.
9, 16–17). A protestation of innocence (vv. 3c–4a;
7.3–5) is followed by a poetic wake-up call (44.23)
addressed to *God of hosts*, which suggests God is in
for a fight (24.10). **6–7:** To help the psalmist, God
must oppose the enemies who are imaged as ravenous
dogs (22.16, 20) and whose arrogant *words* demonstrate an utter lack of accountability (10.4). **8–10:**
God's laughter indicates divine sovereignty (2.4),
which is the basis of the psalmist's trust that God's
steadfast love (vv. 10, 16, 17) will prevail. **11–13:**
While sounding vindictive, the psalmist's motivation is
God-centered. Defeat of the *enemies* will show *that
God rules*. **14–15:** *Growl* also means "lodge," suggesting the persistence of the enemies (see v. 6). **16–
17:** More persistent is God's *steadfast love*, the endur-

a Heb *with swords*   *b* Heb lacks *they think*

ing source of the psalmist's *strength* (vv. 9, 17) and protection.

PSALM 60

To the leader: according to the Lily
of the Covenant. A Miktam of David;
for instruction; when he struggled with Aram-
naharaim and with Aram-zobah, and when Joab
on his return killed twelve thousand Edomites
in the Valley of Salt.

1 O God, you have rejected us, broken
     our defenses;
   you have been angry; now restore us!
2 You have caused the land to quake; you
     have torn it open;
   repair the cracks in it, for it is
     tottering.
3 You have made your people suffer hard
     things;
   you have given us wine to drink that
     made us reel.

4 You have set up a banner for those who
     fear you,
   to rally to it out of bowshot.[a]   *Selah*
5 Give victory with your right hand, and
     answer us,[b]
   so that those whom you love may be
     rescued.

6 God has promised in his sanctuary:[c]
   "With exultation I will divide up
     Shechem,
   and portion out the Vale of Succoth.
7 Gilead is mine, and Manasseh is mine;
   Ephraim is my helmet;
   Judah is my scepter.
8 Moab is my washbasin;
   on Edom I hurl my shoe;
   over Philistia I shout in triumph."

9 Who will bring me to the fortified city?
   Who will lead me to Edom?
10 Have you not rejected us, O God?
   You do not go out, O God, with our
     armies.
11 O grant us help against the foe,
   for human help is worthless.
12 With God we shall do valiantly;
   it is he who will tread down our foes.

60.1–12: Grant us help against the foe. This communal prayer for help is associated by the editors of the psalter with events described in 2 Sam 8 (see vv. 13–14), although the details of the psalm are not congruent with that narrative.* **1–3:** The complaint attributes the people's misfortune to God's anger (79.5). *Rejected* recurs in v. 10. **4–5:** Verse 4 perhaps should be understood as petition to make it consistent with v. 5. **6–8:** The divine promise locates hope for reversal with God's ownership of all lands and peoples, including Israelite places (vv. 6–7) and enemy territories (v. 8). The images in v. 8a–b may be construed as insults, but the idea may be that *Moab* and *Edom* are God's personal possessions. **9:** *Edom* is singled out as the primary source of the people's problem (137.7). **10–12:** Even so, these verses return to the perspective of vv. 1–5, suggesting God is both the problem and the solution. Only God's *help* (22.19), as opposed to *human help* (146.3), will enable the people to *do valiantly* (118.15–16.)

PSALM 61

To the leader: with stringed instruments.
Of David.

1 Hear my cry, O God;
   listen to my prayer.
2 From the end of the earth I call to you,
   when my heart is faint.

   Lead me to the rock
     that is higher than I;
3 for you are my refuge,
   a strong tower against the enemy.

4 Let me abide in your tent forever,
   find refuge under the shelter of your
     wings.   *Selah*
5 For you, O God, have heard my vows;
   you have given me the heritage of
     those who fear your name.

6 Prolong the life of the king;
   may his years endure to all
     generations!
7 May he be enthroned forever before God;
   appoint steadfast love and
     faithfulness to watch over him!

---

a Gk Syr Jerome: Heb *because of the truth*   *b* Another reading is *me*   *c* Or *by his holiness*

8 So I will always sing praises to your
      name,
   as I pay my vows day after day.

61.1–8: Lead me to the rock. A prayer for help, its
petitions (vv. 1, 2c, 4, 6–7) are juxtaposed with expressions of trust (vv. 3, 5, 8). **1–3:** Verse 2a can be
understood geographically, but it can also be heard
metaphorically* to indicate a serious situation. *Lead
me to the rock* (v. 2; 27.5) may indicate the psalmist
was seeking *refuge* (2.12; 5.11) in the Temple* from
false accusers (see Ps 5, 7). **4–5:** Entrance into the Temple may be indicated by *tent* (15.1), and perhaps too
by *the shelter of your wings* (17.8; 57.1; 63.7). That
the psalmist's *vows* have been heard probably expresses the foundation of the previous petitions rather
than indicating that the distress is over (22.25; 65.1).
6–7: It is not clear whether the psalm was prayed originally by *the king*, but probably not. The petition
would have been heard as a prayer for the nation after
the disappearance of the monarchy . **8:** *Vows* recalls v.
5. *Praises* result from trusting that God will indeed be
the psalmist's *refuge* (vv. 3, 4).

PSALM 62

*To the leader: according to Jeduthun. A Psalm
of David.*

1 For God alone my soul waits in
      silence;
   from him comes my salvation.
2 He alone is my rock and my salvation,
     my fortress; I shall never be shaken.

3 How long will you assail a person,
     will you batter your victim, all
       of you,
     as you would a leaning wall, a
      tottering fence?
4 Their only plan is to bring down a
      person of prominence.
   They take pleasure in falsehood;
   they bless with their mouths,
     but inwardly they curse.   *Selah*

5 For God alone my soul waits in
      silence,
   for my hope is from him.
6 He alone is my rock and my salvation,
     my fortress; I shall not be shaken.

7 On God rests my deliverance and my
      honor;
   my mighty rock, my refuge is in God.

8 Trust in him at all times, O people;
   pour out your heart before him;
   God is a refuge for us.   *Selah*

9 Those of low estate are but a breath,
     those of high estate are a delusion;
  in the balances they go up;
    they are together lighter than a
      breath.
10 Put no confidence in extortion,
     and set no vain hopes on robbery;
  if riches increase, do not set your
      heart on them.

11 Once God has spoken;
     twice have I heard this:
  that power belongs to God,
12   and steadfast love belongs to you,
     O Lord.
  For you repay to all
     according to their work.

62.1–12: God alone is my rock. A psalm of trust, it
recalls Ps 61 (compare 61.2–3 with 62.7). **1–6:** The
similar vv. 1–2, 5–6 surround a description of the enemies. *Alone* (vv. 1–2, 5–6) emphasizes the psalmist's
total dependence upon God. **7:** This central verse is
transitional, summing up the direction of vv. 1–6 (see
rock in vv. 1, 6, 7) and anticipating the instruction in
vv. 8–10. **8–10:** *Trust* (v. 8) and *Put . . . confidence*
(v. 10) represent the same Hebrew verb. The psalmist
invites others to the same *trust* he or she has articulated. **11–12:** Hope rests finally on the foundation of
God's *steadfast love* (59.10, 16–17; 63.3).

PSALM 63

*A Psalm of David, when he was
in the Wilderness of Judah.*

1 O God, you are my God, I seek you,
     my soul thirsts for you;
  my flesh faints for you,
     as in a dry and weary land where
      there is no water.
2 So I have looked upon you in the
      sanctuary,
   beholding your power and glory.

3 Because your steadfast love is better
    than life,
    my lips will praise you.
4 So I will bless you as long as I live;
    I will lift up my hands and call on
    your name.

5 My soul is satisfied as with a rich feast,[a]
    and my mouth praises you with joyful
    lips
6 when I think of you on my bed,
    and meditate on you in the watches
    of the night;
7 for you have been my help,
    and in the shadow of your wings I
    sing for joy.
8 My soul clings to you;
    your right hand upholds me.

9 But those who seek to destroy my life
    shall go down into the depths of the
    earth;
10 they shall be given over to the power of
    the sword,
    they shall be prey for jackals.
11 But the king shall rejoice in God;
    all who swear by him shall exult,
    for the mouths of liars will be
    stopped.

63.1–11: My soul thirsts for you. A song of thanksgiving or psalm of trust, it apparently narrates the experience and results of the psalmist's encounter with God in the Temple* (Ps 17). The editors of the psalter associated it with David in the wilderness (compare v. 9 with 1 Sam 23.4; 24.2). **1–2:** Lack of *water* (42.2) symbolizes the need that the psalmist addresses by entering the Temple where *beholding* God occurs (27.4). **3:** To see God is to comprehend God's character, which is *steadfast love* (Ex 34.6–7; Ps 17.7; 62.12). **4:** The psalmist responds with praise and prayer, indicated by uplifted *hands*. **5–8:** The metaphor* shifts from thirst to hunger, which is also *satisfied* (17.15; 65.4), leading again to *praises* (v. 5), prayerful meditation (v. 6), and a profession of faith in God's *help* and protection (see *shadow of your wings* in 17.8; 57.1). **9–11:** Those who *seek* the psalmist's *life* (38.12; 54.3) will be eaten instead of eating (see v. 5). The prayer may have been prayed originally by *the king*, but probably not (61.6–7).

PSALM 64
To the leader. A Psalm of David.

1 Hear my voice, O God, in my
    complaint;
    preserve my life from the dread
    enemy.
2 Hide me from the secret plots of the
    wicked,
    from the scheming of evildoers,
3 who whet their tongues like swords,
    who aim bitter words like arrows,
4 shooting from ambush at the blameless;
    they shoot suddenly and without fear.
5 They hold fast to their evil purpose;
    they talk of laying snares secretly,
thinking, "Who can see us?[b]
6 Who can search out our crimes?[c]
    We have thought out a cunningly
    conceived plot."
    For the human heart and mind are
    deep.

7 But God will shoot his arrow at them;
    they will be wounded suddenly.
8 Because of their tongue he will bring
    them to ruin;[d]
    all who see them will shake with
    horror.
9 Then everyone will fear;
    they will tell what God has brought
    about,
    and ponder what he has done.

10 Let the righteous rejoice in the LORD
    and take refuge in him.
    Let all the upright in heart glory.

64.1–10: What God has brought about. It is a prayer for help (note *complaint* in v. 1). **1–6:** The *tongues* and *words* of the wicked act as weapons (57.4; 140.3); and they believe that they act with impunity (v. 5) and without accountability (v. 6; 10.4, 6, 11). **7–9:** Verse 7 picks up the vocabulary of vv. 3–4 to affirm God's response, which will serve as a witness and motivation to others (v. 9; 52.5–6). **10:** In the midst of opposition, *the righteous* always have a *refuge* in God (2.12; 62.8).

---

a Heb *with fat and fatness*   b Syr: Heb *them*
c Cn: Heb *They search out crimes*   d Cn: Heb *They
will bring him to ruin, their tongue being against them*

PSALM 65

To the leader. A Psalm of David. A Song.

1 Praise is due to you,
    O God, in Zion;
and to you shall vows be performed,
2   O you who answer prayer!
To you all flesh shall come.
3 When deeds of iniquity overwhelm us,
    you forgive our transgressions.
4 Happy are those whom you choose and
        bring near
    to live in your courts.
We shall be satisfied with the goodness
        of your house,
    your holy temple.

5 By awesome deeds you answer us with
        deliverance,
    O God of our salvation;
you are the hope of all the ends of the
        earth
    and of the farthest seas.
6 By your[a] strength you established the
        mountains;
    you are girded with might.
7 You silence the roaring of the seas,
    the roaring of their waves,
    the tumult of the peoples.
8 Those who live at earth's farthest
        bounds are awed by your signs;
you make the gateways of the morning
        and the evening shout for joy.

9 You visit the earth and water it,
    you greatly enrich it;
the river of God is full of water;
    you provide the people with grain,
    for so you have prepared it.
10 You water its furrows abundantly,
    settling its ridges,
softening it with showers,
    and blessing its growth.
11 You crown the year with your bounty;
    your wagon tracks overflow with
        richness.
12 The pastures of the wilderness
        overflow,
    the hills gird themselves with joy,
13 the meadows clothe themselves with
        flocks,

the valleys deck themselves with
        grain,
    they shout and sing together for joy.

65.1–13: Praise is due to you, O God. A communal song of thanksgiving, it may originally have been used at the autumn harvest festival (Succoth). **1–4:** The three-fold *to you* in vv. 1–2 focuses attention on God, who has *satisfied* the people in the *temple*, perhaps an allusion to the ritual meals that accompanied thanksgiving sacrifices. Forgiveness seems to result from God's initiative rather than the people's. **5–8:** God's *answer* (v. 5; see v. 2) affects not only God's people but all people and all creation. God wills and effects security for the world. **9–13:** An illustration of God-given security is the rain which leads to an abundance of *grain* and *flocks*. Appropriately, the created elements *sing together for joy* (v. 13; see v. 8).

PSALM 66

To the leader. A Song. A Psalm.

1 Make a joyful noise to God, all the
        earth;
2   sing the glory of his name;
    give to him glorious praise.
3 Say to God, "How awesome are your
        deeds!
    Because of your great power, your
        enemies cringe before you.
4 All the earth worships you;
    they sing praises to you,
    sing praises to your name."   *Selah*

5 Come and see what God has done:
    he is awesome in his deeds among
        mortals.
6 He turned the sea into dry land;
    they passed through the river on foot.
There we rejoiced in him,
7   who rules by his might forever,
whose eyes keep watch on the nations—
    let the rebellious not exalt
        themselves.   *Selah*

8 Bless our God, O peoples,
    let the sound of his praise be heard,
9 who has kept us among the living,
    and has not let our feet slip.

a Gk Jerome: Heb *his*

10 For you, O God, have tested us;
  you have tried us as silver is tried.
11 You brought us into the net;
  you laid burdens on our backs;
12 you let people ride over our heads;
  we went through fire and through
    water;
  yet you have brought us out to a
    spacious place.^a

13 I will come into your house with burnt
    offerings;
  I will pay you my vows,
14 those that my lips uttered
  and my mouth promised when I was
    in trouble.
15 I will offer to you burnt offerings of
    fatlings,
  with the smoke of the sacrifice of
    rams;
  I will make an offering of bulls and
    goats.   *Selah*

16 Come and hear, all you who fear God,
  and I will tell what he has done for
    me.
17 I cried aloud to him,
  and he was extolled with my tongue.
18 If I had cherished iniquity in my heart,
  the Lord would not have listened.
19 But truly God has listened;
  he has given heed to the words of my
    prayer.

20 Blessed be God,
  because he has not rejected my
    prayer
  or removed his steadfast love from
    me.

66.1–20: Come and see, come and hear. In this communal song of thanksgiving, the shift to first-person singular language in v. 13 implies that an individual has personally appropriated the communal story of deliverance. **1–4:** *All the earth* (vv. 1, 4) is invited to acknowledge the sovereignty of the cosmic God (100.1). **5–7:** The description of *what God has done* (v. 5; 64.9) recalls the Exodus. **8–12:** Verses 9 and 12 suggest that the people have been *tested* and *tried* (v. 10) in order that they may be vindicated (17.3). **13–19:** Recalling

vv. 5 and 16 suggests that individual deliverance parallels communal deliverance. A personal exodus has occurred, for which the psalmist is thankful and offers appropriate sacrifices (vv. 13–15; 22.25–26; 56.12–13). **20:** The psalmist responds as all peoples have been invited to do in v. 8. What God *has done* (v. 16) reveals God's character—*steadfast love* (Ex 34.6–7; Ps 33.5, 18, 22).

PSALM 67
To the leader: with stringed instruments.
A Psalm. A Song.

1 May God be gracious to us and bless us
  and make his face to shine upon us,
                    Selah
2 that your way may be known upon
    earth,
  your saving power among all nations.
3 Let the peoples praise you, O God;
  let all the peoples praise you.

4 Let the nations be glad and sing for joy,
  for you judge the peoples with
    equity
  and guide the nations upon earth.
                    Selah
5 Let the peoples praise you, O God;
  let all the peoples praise you.

6 The earth has yielded its increase;
  God, our God, has blessed us.
7 May God continue to bless us;
  let all the ends of the earth revere
    him.

67.1–7: Let all peoples praise you. A communal song of thanksgiving, it can also be understood as a prayer for God's blessing (vv. 1, 7). **1–2:** Verse 1 recalls Num 6.22–27 where blessing and *face* are associated 4.6; 31.16). The blessing of the people will involve *all nations* (Gen 12.1–3). **3–5:** A refrain surrounds the central v. 4. Justice (*judge* could be translated "establish justice") and *equity* are attributes of God's reign (98.9). **6–7:** The concept of blessing and the universal perspective recall vv. 1–2.

a Cn Compare Gk Syr Jerome Tg: Heb *to a saturation*

PSALM 68

To the leader. Of David. A Psalm. A Song.

1 Let God rise up, let his enemies be
    scattered;
  let those who hate him flee before
    him.
2 As smoke is driven away, so drive them
    away;
  as wax melts before the fire,
  let the wicked perish before God.
3 But let the righteous be joyful;
  let them exult before God;
  let them be jubilant with joy.

4 Sing to God, sing praises to his name;
  lift up a song to him who rides upon
    the clouds*a*—
  his name is the LORD—
  be exultant before him.

5 Father of orphans and protector of
    widows
  is God in his holy habitation.
6 God gives the desolate a home to live in;
  he leads out the prisoners to
    prosperity,
  but the rebellious live in a parched
    land.

7 O God, when you went out before your
    people,
  when you marched through the
    wilderness,   *Selah*
8 the earth quaked, the heavens poured
    down rain
  at the presence of God, the God of
    Sinai,
  at the presence of God, the God of
    Israel.
9 Rain in abundance, O God, you
    showered abroad;
  you restored your heritage when it
    languished;
10 your flock found a dwelling in it;
  in your goodness, O God, you
    provided for the needy.

11 The Lord gives the command;
  great is the company of those*b* who
    bore the tidings:

12 "The kings of the armies, they flee,
    they flee!"
  The women at home divide the spoil,
13 though they stay among the
    sheepfolds—
  the wings of a dove covered with silver,
    its pinions with green gold.
14 When the Almighty*c* scattered kings
    there,
  snow fell on Zalmon.

15 O mighty mountain, mountain of
    Bashan;
  O many-peaked mountain, mountain
    of Bashan!
16 Why do you look with envy, O many-
    peaked mountain,
  at the mount that God desired for his
    abode,
  where the LORD will reside forever?

17 With mighty chariotry, twice ten
    thousand,
  thousands upon thousands,
  the Lord came from Sinai into the
    holy place.*d*
18 You ascended the high mount,
  leading captives in your train
  and receiving gifts from people,
  even from those who rebel against the
    LORD God's abiding there.
19 Blessed be the Lord,
  who daily bears us up;
  God is our salvation.   *Selah*
20 Our God is a God of salvation,
  and to GOD, the Lord, belongs escape
    from death.

21 But God will shatter the heads of his
    enemies,
  the hairy crown of those who walk in
    their guilty ways.
22 The Lord said,
  "I will bring them back from Bashan,
  I will bring them back from the depths
    of the sea,

a Or *cast up a highway for him who rides through the*
deserts   b Or *company of the women   c* Traditional
rendering of Heb *Shaddai   d* Cn: Heb *The Lord among*
them Sinai in the holy (place)

23 so that you may bathe[a] your feet in
      blood,
   so that the tongues of your dogs may
      have their share from the foe."

68.1–35: The processions of my God. A communal
song of thanksgiving, it depicts a processional celebration of God's reign in the Temple,* perhaps involving
the ark (see Ps 24). **1–3:** Verse 1 recalls Num 10.35,
which suggests that the ark of the covenant* symbolized God's victory over enemies. **4–6:** The Canaanite
god Baal* was known as the one *who rides upon the
clouds.* Israel's God has displaced Baal (see Ps 48, 82).
Verses 5–6 allude to the Exodus, suggesting that what
God wills has occurred. **7–18:** The poem proceeds
with further historical allusions: *wilderness* (v. 7), *Sinai*
(v. 8), and possession of the land (vv. 9–14). God and
the people make their way *from Sinai* (v. 17) to *the
high mount* (v. 18), Zion,* rejecting other locations
(vv. 15–16). **19–23:** Having arrived at Zion, the celebration of God's victory over all *enemies* begins. The
result is life (vv. 19–20).

24 Your solemn processions are seen,[b]
      O God,
   the processions of my God, my King,
      into the sanctuary—
25 the singers in front, the musicians last,
      between them girls playing
         tambourines:
26 "Bless God in the great congregation,
      the LORD, O you who are of Israel's
         fountain!"
27 There is Benjamin, the least of them, in
      the lead,
   the princes of Judah in a body,
   the princes of Zebulun, the princes of
      Naphtali.

28 Summon your might, O God;
      show your strength, O God, as you
         have done for us before.
29 Because of your temple at Jerusalem
      kings bear gifts to you.
30 Rebuke the wild animals that live
      among the reeds,
   the herd of bulls with the calves of
      the peoples.
   Trample[c] under foot those who lust
      after tribute;
   scatter the peoples who delight in war.[d]

31 Let bronze be brought from Egypt;
      let Ethiopia[e] hasten to stretch out its
         hands to God.

32 Sing to God, O kingdoms of the earth;
      sing praises to the Lord,   *Selah*
33 O rider in the heavens, the ancient
      heavens;
   listen, he sends out his voice, his
      mighty voice.
34 Ascribe power to God,
      whose majesty is over Israel;
   and whose power is in the skies.
35 Awesome is God in his[f] sanctuary,
      the God of Israel;
   he gives power and strength to his
      people.

   Blessed be God!

68.24–35. 24–27: God is greeted as *King* (see Ex
15.18; Ps 24.7–10) in a festive procession. These four
tribes seem to represent the whole people. **28–31:**
God's sovereignty is not universally recognized (see Ps
2). A new manifestation of *might* and *strength* is
needed. **32–35:** Verses 32–33 recall v. 4. The Hebrew
behind *might* and *strength* in v. 28 recurs four more
times—*mighty* (v. 33) and *power* (three times in vv.
34–35). Despite opposition, God will prevail; and the
people will share the benefits (vv. 5–6).

PSALM 69
To the leader: according to Lilies. Of David.

1 Save me, O God,
      for the waters have come up to my
         neck.
2 I sink in deep mire,
      where there is no foothold;
   I have come into deep waters,
      and the flood sweeps over me.
3 I am weary with my crying;
      my throat is parched.
   My eyes grow dim
      with waiting for my God.

---

a Gk Syr Tg: Heb *shatter*   *b* Or *have been seen*
c Cn: Heb *Trampling*   *d* Meaning of Heb of verse 30
is uncertain   *e* Or *Nubia*; Heb *Cush*   *f* Gk: Heb
from your

4 More in number than the hairs of my
        head
    are those who hate me without
        cause;
many are those who would destroy me,
    my enemies who accuse me falsely.
What I did not steal
    must I now restore?
5 O God, you know my folly;
    the wrongs I have done are not
        hidden from you.

6 Do not let those who hope in you be put
        to shame because of me,
    O Lord GOD of hosts;
do not let those who seek you be
        dishonored because of me,
    O God of Israel.
7 It is for your sake that I have borne
        reproach,
    that shame has covered my face.
8 I have become a stranger to my
        kindred,
    an alien to my mother's children.

9 It is zeal for your house that has
        consumed me;
    the insults of those who insult you
        have fallen on me.
10 When I humbled my soul with fasting,*a*
    they insulted me for doing so.
11 When I made sackcloth my clothing,
    I became a byword to them.
12 I am the subject of gossip for those who
        sit in the gate,
    and the drunkards make songs about
        me.

13 But as for me, my prayer is to you,
        O LORD.
    At an acceptable time, O God,
    in the abundance of your steadfast
        love, answer me.
With your faithful help 14rescue me
    from sinking in the mire;
    let me be delivered from my enemies
    and from the deep waters.
15 Do not let the flood sweep over me,
    or the deep swallow me up,
    or the Pit close its mouth over me.

16 Answer me, O LORD, for your steadfast
        love is good;
    according to your abundant mercy,
        turn to me.
17 Do not hide your face from your
        servant,
    for I am in distress—make haste to
        answer me.
18 Draw near to me, redeem me,
    set me free because of my enemies.

69.1–36: The LORD hears the needy. In this prayer for
help, the psalmist is convinced that he or she suffers
for God's sake (v. 7). Alternating petition and complaint characterize the first two sections (vv. 1–13b,
13c–29), which are roughly parallel in vocabulary and
imagery. Two sections of praise (vv. 30–33, 34–36)
follow. **1–3:** *Neck* is the original sense of "nephesh,"
usually translated "soul" or "life." **4–5:** The original
situation may have involved *enemies who accuse . . .
falsely* (Ps 5, 7). Verse 5 implies innocence; the persecution is *without cause* (35.7, 19). **6–13b:** The psalmist's isolation (v. 8; 38.11) is for God's sake (vv. 7, 9).
The Hebrew behind *reproach* occurs five more times
as *insult(s)* in vv. 9, 10, 19, 20. In the midst of trouble,
the psalmist prays (v. 13a–b), an act of entrusting life
and future to God. **13c–18:** Paralleling vv. 1–4, these
verses indicate the psalmist takes his or her stand on
God's *steadfast love* (vv. 13, 16), faithfulness (v. 13),
and *mercy* (v. 16). The psalmist trusts that God's
goodness will correspond to the way that God has revealed the divine self (Ex 34.6–7).

19 You know the insults I receive,
    and my shame and dishonor;
    my foes are all known to you.
20 Insults have broken my heart,
    so that I am in despair.
I looked for pity, but there was none;
    and for comforters, but I found
        none.
21 They gave me poison for food,
    and for my thirst they gave me
        vinegar to drink.

22 Let their table be a trap for them,
    a snare for their allies.

a Gk Syr: Heb *I wept, with fasting my soul,* or *I made my
soul mourn with fasting*

23 Let their eyes be darkened so that they
   cannot see,
     and make their loins tremble
       continually.
24 Pour out your indignation upon them,
     and let your burning anger overtake
       them.
25 May their camp be a desolation;
     let no one live in their tents.
26 For they persecute those whom you
     have struck down,
     and those whom you have wounded,
       they attack still more.ᵃ
27 Add guilt to their guilt;
     may they have no acquittal from you.
28 Let them be blotted out of the book of
     the living;
     let them not be enrolled among the
       righteous.
29 But I am lowly and in pain;
     let your salvation, O God, protect me.

30 I will praise the name of God with a
     song;
     I will magnify him with thanksgiving.
31 This will please the LORD more than an
     ox
     or a bull with horns and hoofs.
32 Let the oppressed see it and be glad;
     you who seek God, let your hearts
       revive.
33 For the LORD hears the needy,
     and does not despise his own that are
       in bonds.

34 Let heaven and earth praise him,
     the seas and everything that moves in
       them.
35 For God will save Zion
     and rebuild the cities of Judah;
   and his servants shall liveᵇ there and
       possess it;
36   the children of his servants shall
       inherit it,
     and those who love his name shall
       live in it.

69.19–36. 19–21: Paralleling vv. 5–11 (see *you know*
in vv. 5, 19), these verses focus on the *foes*, preparing
for vv. 22–29. 22–29: Petitions against the enemies
(35.4–8; 58.6–9) are motivated not so much by re-

venge but by a desire for "righteousness," which is
how the Hebrew behind *acquittal* is usually translated.
The psalmist trusts that God stands with the *lowly*
(12.5; 109.22, 31). 30–33: Thus, the *oppressed* and
needy will want to join the psalmist's praise. The
psalmist's life proves to be exemplary (see v. 6).
34–36: Perhaps a post-exilic addition, these verses extend praise throughout space and time (22.27–31).

PSALM 70

*To the leader. Of David, for the
memorial offering.*

1 Be pleased, O God, to deliver me.
     O LORD, make haste to help me!
2 Let those be put to shame and
     confusion
     who seek my life.
   Let those be turned back and brought
     to dishonor
     who desire to hurt me.
3 Let those who say, "Aha, Aha!"
     turn back because of their shame.

4 Let all who seek you
     rejoice and be glad in you.
   Let those who love your salvation
     say evermore, "God is great!"
5 But I am poor and needy;
     hasten to me, O God!
   You are my help and my deliverer;
     O LORD, do not delay!

70.1–5: Make haste to help me. A prayer for help, it
is nearly identical to 40.13–17. The only major difference is between 40.17 and 70.5, which includes the
petition for God to *hasten* (see v. 1). The translation
memorial offering in the superscription is uncertain.
1–3: *Help* recurs in v. 5, framing the psalm, along with
the concept of deliverance. The petition against the
enemies recalls 69.22–29. 4–5: These verses recall
69.29, 33. The psalmists regularly affirm that God
stands with the *poor and needy* (9.18; 10.17–18).

PSALM 71

1 In you, O LORD, I take refuge;
     let me never be put to shame.

a Gk Syr: Heb *recount the pain of*   b Syr: Heb *and
they shall live*

2 In your righteousness deliver me and
    rescue me;
  incline your ear to me and save me.
3 Be to me a rock of refuge,
    a strong fortress,*ᵃ to save me,
  for you are my rock and my fortress.

4 Rescue me, O my God, from the hand
    of the wicked,
  from the grasp of the unjust and
    cruel.
5 For you, O Lord, are my hope,
  my trust, O LORD, from my youth.
6 Upon you I have leaned from my birth;
  it was you who took me from my
    mother's womb.
  My praise is continually of you.

7 I have been like a portent to many,
  but you are my strong refuge.
8 My mouth is filled with your praise,
  and with your glory all day long.
9 Do not cast me off in the time of old
    age;
  do not forsake me when my strength
    is spent.
10 For my enemies speak concerning me,
  and those who watch for my life
    consult together.
11 They say, "Pursue and seize that person
    whom God has forsaken,
  for there is no one to deliver."

12 O God, do not be far from me;
  O my God, make haste to help me!
13 Let my accusers be put to shame and
    consumed;
  let those who seek to hurt me
    be covered with scorn and disgrace.
14 But I will hope continually,
  and will praise you yet more and
    more.
15 My mouth will tell of your righteous
    acts,
  of your deeds of salvation all day long,
    though their number is past my
    knowledge.
16 I will come praising the mighty deeds of
    the Lord GOD,
  I will praise your righteousness, yours
    alone.

17 O God, from my youth you have taught
    me,
  and I still proclaim your wondrous
    deeds.
18 So even to old age and gray hairs,
    O God, do not forsake me,
  until I proclaim your might
    to all the generations to come.ᵇ
  Your power ¹⁹and your righteousness,
    O God,
  reach the high heavens.

  You who have done great things,
    O God, who is like you?
20 You who have made me see many
    troubles and calamities
  will revive me again;
  from the depths of the earth
    you will bring me up again.
21 You will increase my honor,
  and comfort me once again.

22 I will also praise you with the harp
    for your faithfulness, O my God;
  I will sing praises to you with the lyre,
    O Holy One of Israel.
23 My lips will shout for joy
    when I sing praises to you;
  my soul also, which you have rescued.
24 All day long my tongue will talk of your
    righteous help,
  for those who tried to do me harm
    have been put to shame, and
    disgraced.

71.1–24: O God, who is like you? A prayer for help,
its similarities with Ps 22 and 31 suggest that it may
be an anthology of quotations from other psalms.
1–4: Verses 1–3 are nearly identical to 31.1–3a. **5–8:**
Reminiscent of 22.9–10, these verses reinforce the
psalmist's affirmation of dependence upon God (see
refuge in vv. 1, 7). The mention of *youth* in v. 5 prepares for *old age* in v. 9. The themes recur in vv. 17–
18. **9–13:** As in 22.1, the psalmist is *forsaken* (v. 11;
see vv. 9, 18). Verse 12 recalls 22.19. **14–17:** *Righteous
acts* and *righteousness* are the same Hebrew word.
The conviction that God wills to set things right un-

a Gk Compare 31.3: Heb *to come continually you have
commanded*   *b* Gk Compare Syr: Heb *to a generation,
to all that come*

derlies the petition against the enemies (v. 13). **18–24:** The question *who is like you?* focuses attention on God's character. The psalmist affirms that God's *faithfulness* is fundamental (Ex 34.6) and that it is manifest as *righteous help* (v. 24; see the same Hebrew word in vv. 15, 16, 19).

PSALM 72
Of Solomon.

1 Give the king your justice, O God,
  and your righteousness to a king's
  son.
2 May he judge your people with
  righteousness,
  and your poor with justice.
3 May the mountains yield prosperity for
  the people,
  and the hills, in righteousness.
4 May he defend the cause of the poor of
  the people,
  give deliverance to the needy,
  and crush the oppressor.

5 May he live*a* while the sun endures,
  and as long as the moon, throughout
  all generations.
6 May he be like rain that falls on the
  mown grass,
  like showers that water the earth.
7 In his days may righteousness flourish
  and peace abound, until the moon is
  no more.

8 May he have dominion from sea to sea,
  and from the River to the ends of the
  earth.
9 May his foes*b* bow down before him,
  and his enemies lick the dust.
10 May the kings of Tarshish and of the
  isles
  render him tribute,
  may the kings of Sheba and Seba
  bring gifts.
11 May all kings fall down before him,
  all nations give him service.

12 For he delivers the needy when they
  call,
  the poor and those who have no
  helper.

13 He has pity on the weak and the needy,
  and saves the lives of the needy.
14 From oppression and violence he
  redeems their life;
  and precious is their blood in his
  sight.

15 Long may he live!
  May gold of Sheba be given to him.
  May prayer be made for him
  continually,
  and blessings invoked for him all day
  long.
16 May there be abundance of grain in the
  land;
  may it wave on the tops of the
  mountains;
  may its fruit be like Lebanon;
  and may people blossom in the cities
  like the grass of the field.
17 May his name endure forever,
  his fame continue as long as the sun.
  May all nations be blessed in him;*c*
  may they pronounce him happy.

18 Blessed be the LORD, the God of Israel,
  who alone does wondrous things.
19 Blessed be his glorious name forever;
  may his glory fill the whole earth.
      Amen and Amen.

20 The prayers of David son of Jesse are
  ended.

72.1–20: Your justice and righteousness. This royal psalm was probably used originally as a prayer for the Judean king on the day of his coronation (see Ps 2). It may date from the time *of Solomon.* After the disappearance of the monarchy, it would have been heard as a prayer for the enactment of God's will for *justice* and *righteousness.* **1–7:** These two key words appear in v. 1 and are repeated. *The king* was the earthly agent of God's will, which always involves *justice* and *righteousness* (98.9; 99.4). When they are enacted, the result is "shalom" (*prosperity* in v. 3; *peace* in v. 7). The petitions suggest that the cosmos will not operate properly apart from *justice* and *righteousness* (36.5–6; 82.5). **8–11:** God's rule enacted by *the king* is to ex-

a Gk: Heb *may they fear you*   *b* Cn: Heb *those who live in the wilderness*   *c* Or *bless themselves by him*

tend in both time (v. 7) and space (vv. 8–11). *The River* is probably the Euphrates. *Tarshish* and *the isles* indicate Spain and Mediterranean regions, while *Sheba and Seba* occupy the Arabian peninsula. These place names symbolize God's universal rule. **12–14:** *Justice* and *righteousness* exist when the *needy, poor,* and *weak* are protected and empowered. **15–17:** There are cosmic consequences of the king's enactment of *justice* and *righteousness* (see vv. 5–7). Verse 17 recalls Gen 12.1–3. **18–19:** An appropriate conclusion to the psalm, these verses also provide the concluding doxology for Book II (compare 41.13). **20:** The Davidic collection may be Ps 51–72 or Ps 3–72.

BOOK THREE

PSALM 73

A Psalm of Asaph.

1 Truly God is good to the upright,*ᵃ*
  to those who are pure in heart.
2 But as for me, my feet had almost
      stumbled;
  my steps had nearly slipped.
3 For I was envious of the arrogant;
  I saw the prosperity of the wicked.

4 For they have no pain;
  their bodies are sound and sleek.
5 They are not in trouble as others are;
  they are not plagued like other
      people.
6 Therefore pride is their necklace;
  violence covers them like a garment.
7 Their eyes swell out with fatness;
  their hearts overflow with follies.
8 They scoff and speak with malice;
  loftily they threaten oppression.
9 They set their mouths against heaven,
      and their tongues range over the
      earth.

10 Therefore the people turn and praise
      them,*ᵇ*
  and find no fault in them.*ᶜ*
11 And they say, "How can God know?
  Is there knowledge in the
      Most High?"
12 Such are the wicked;
  always at ease, they increase in
      riches.

13 All in vain I have kept my heart clean
  and washed my hands in innocence.
14 For all day long I have been plagued,
  and am punished every morning.

15 If I had said, "I will talk on in this way,"
  I would have been untrue to the
      circle of your children.
16 But when I thought how to understand
      this,
  it seemed to me a wearisome task,
17 until I went into the sanctuary of God;
  then I perceived their end.
18 Truly you set them in slippery places;
  you make them fall to ruin.
19 How they are destroyed in a moment,
  swept away utterly by terrors!
20 They are*ᵈ* like a dream when one
      awakes;
  on awaking you despise their
      phantoms.

21 When my soul was embittered,
  when I was pricked in heart,
22 I was stupid and ignorant;
  I was like a brute beast toward you.
23 Nevertheless I am continually with you;
  you hold my right hand.
24 You guide me with your counsel,
  and afterward you will receive me
      with honor.*ᵉ*
25 Whom have I in heaven but you?
  And there is nothing on earth that I
      desire other than you.
26 My flesh and my heart may fail,
  but God is the strength*ᶠ* of my heart
      and my portion forever.

27 Indeed, those who are far from you will
      perish;
  you put an end to those who are false
      to you.
28 But for me it is good to be near God;
  I have made the Lord GOD my
      refuge,
  to tell of all your works.

a Or *good to Israel*   *b* Cn: Heb *his people return here*
c Cn: Heb *abundant waters are drained by them*
d Cn: Heb *Lord*   *e* Or *to glory*   *f* Heb *rock*

73.1–28: I am continually with you. Often labeled a psalm of trust, its instructional intent suggests it may be a wisdom psalm. It is best divided into three sections (vv. 1–12, 13–17, 18–28), each of which begins with the same Hebrew word, translated *truly* in vv. 1 and 18. It initiates a collection of eleven *Asaph* psalms (see Ps 50). **1–3:** Because of the focus on God's *children* in v. 15, v. 1 should follow the Hebrew to read "Israel" rather than *upright. Pure in heart* characterizes the worshipping community (24.4). The psalmist is pulled toward doubt by the *prosperity of the wicked.* **4–12:** This *prosperity* (vv. 4–5, 7, 12) is accompanied by the denial of accountability to God and others (vv. 6, 8–9, 11). Verse 10 seems to indicate that even arrogance attracts others. **13–17:** Verses 13–14 expand upon the doubt expressed in vv. 2–3. It appears that crime does pay; but the psalmist realizes that such *talk* would lead to alienation from the community of faith. The insight expressed in the pivotal v. 15 is consolidated in vv. 16–17 as the psalmist apparently enters the Temple.✶ **18–20:** Whereas the psalmist *had nearly slipped* (v. 2), now he or she perceives that the wicked are on *slippery* ground. **21–26:** Looking back on former doubt, the psalmist realizes that he or she was and is constantly with God. The key phrase is *with you* (v. 23). Verse 24 probably does not articulate a doctrine of resurrection, but develops typical thinking about the afterlife (22.29; 49.15). **27–28:** *Good* in v. 28 recalls v. 1. Goodness is not the material prosperity the wicked possess, but rather nearness to God. Having found *refuge* in God (2.12; 71.1), the psalmist's *talk* (v. 15) now takes the form of proclamation.

PSALM 74
A Maskil of Asaph.

1 O God, why do you cast us off
        forever?
    Why does your anger smoke against
        the sheep of your pasture?
2 Remember your congregation, which
        you acquired long ago,
    which you redeemed to be the tribe of
        your heritage.
    Remember Mount Zion, where you
        came to dwell.
3 Direct your steps to the perpetual
        ruins;
    the enemy has destroyed everything
        in the sanctuary.

4 Your foes have roared within your holy
        place;
    they set up their emblems there.
5 At the upper entrance they hacked
        the wooden trellis with axes.*a*
6 And then, with hatchets and hammers,
        they smashed all its carved work.
7 They set your sanctuary on fire;
    they desecrated the dwelling place of
        your name,
    bringing it to the ground.
8 They said to themselves, "We will
        utterly subdue them";
    they burned all the meeting places of
        God in the land.

9 We do not see our emblems;
    there is no longer any prophet,
    and there is no one among us who
        knows how long.
10 How long, O God, is the foe to scoff?
    Is the enemy to revile your name
        forever?
11 Why do you hold back your hand;
    why do you keep your hand in*b* your
        bosom?

12 Yet God my King is from of old,
    working salvation in the earth.
13 You divided the sea by your might;
    you broke the heads of the dragons in
        the waters.
14 You crushed the heads of Leviathan;
    you gave him as food*c* for the
        creatures of the wilderness.
15 You cut openings for springs and torrents;
    you dried up ever-flowing streams.
16 Yours is the day, yours also the night;
    you established the luminaries*d* and
        the sun.
17 You have fixed all the bounds of the
        earth;
    you made summer and winter.

18 Remember this, O LORD, how the
        enemy scoffs,
    and an impious people reviles your
        name.

a Cn Compare Gk Syr: Meaning of Heb uncertain
b Cn: Heb *do you consume your right hand from*
c Heb *food for the people*   *d* Or *moon;* Heb *light*

19 Do not deliver the soul of your dove to
the wild animals;
do not forget the life of your poor
forever.

20 Have regard for your*a* covenant,
for the dark places of the land are full
of the haunts of violence.
21 Do not let the downtrodden be put to
shame;
let the poor and needy praise your
name.
22 Rise up, O God, plead your cause;
remember how the impious scoff at
you all day long.
23 Do not forget the clamor of your foes,
the uproar of your adversaries that
goes up continually.

74.1–23: Remember your congregation. This communal prayer for help is usually associated with the destruction of Jerusalem and the Temple* in 587 BCE. **1–11:** The questions in vv. 1, 10–11 frame the section. Verse 2 alludes to the Exodus and entry into the land. *Remember* recurs in vv. 18, 22. Verses 4–8 describe the destruction of the Temple and other holy places. The absence of any sign or word from God (v. 9) leads to the people's questions. **12–17:** That God is *King* is evident in the Exodus (vv. 13–14), the description of which reaches mythic proportions and leads to the affirmation of God's power over *the dragons* and *Leviathan,** symbols of chaotic forces. **18–23:** The Exodus and subsequent *covenant** (Ex 24.1–8; Ps 44.17) at Sinai were evidence of God's concern for the *poor*, *downtrodden*, and *needy*. The people pray that the scoffing of the *impious* will cause God to *remember* and act as God acted *long ago* (v. 2).

PSALM 75

*To the leader: Do Not Destroy. A Psalm
of Asaph. A Song.*

1 We give thanks to you, O God;
we give thanks; your name is near.
People tell of your wondrous deeds.

2 At the set time that I appoint
I will judge with equity.
3 When the earth totters, with all its
inhabitants,
it is I who keep its pillars steady.
Selah

4 I say to the boastful, "Do not boast,"
and to the wicked, "Do not lift up
your horn;
5 do not lift up your horn on high,
or speak with insolent neck."

6 For not from the east or from the west
and not from the wilderness comes
lifting up;
7 but it is God who executes judgment,
putting down one and lifting up
another.
8 For in the hand of the LORD there is a
cup
with foaming wine, well mixed;
he will pour a draught from it,
and all the wicked of the earth
shall drain it down to the dregs.
9 But I will rejoice*b* forever;
I will sing praises to the God of
Jacob.

10 All the horns of the wicked I will cut off,
but the horns of the righteous shall
be exalted.

75.1–10: The righteous shall be exalted. Often classified as a prophetic* judgment oracle* (see especially vv. 2, 7, 10), the first divine speech (vv. 2–5) is preceded by praise (v. 1), and the second (v. 10) by a profession of faith (vv. 6–8) and a promise to praise (v. 9). **1:** Gratitude and proclamation of God's *wondrous deeds* go together (9.1; 26.7). **2–5:** In order to *judge*, or "establish justice" (v. 2), God must oppose *the wicked* and their self-assertion. The key word is *lift up* (vv. 4–5; see also vv. 6–7). **6–9:** Echoing vv. 2–5, the psalmist celebrates God's establishment of justice. Oppressors drink the *cup* of destruction (11.6). **10:** *Horns* (vv. 4–5) symbolize power. The self-assertive are humbled; the *righteous* are *exalted*.

PSALM 76

*To the leader: with stringed instruments.
A Psalm of Asaph. A Song.*

1 In Judah God is known,
his name is great in Israel.
2 His abode has been established in
Salem,
his dwelling place in Zion.

a Gk Syr: Heb *the*   *b* Gk: Heb *declare*

3 There he broke the flashing arrows,
　　the shield, the sword, and the
　　　　weapons of war.   *Selah*

4 Glorious are you, more majestic
　　than the everlasting mountains.*ᵃ*
5 The stouthearted were stripped of their
　　　　spoil;
　　they sank into sleep;
　　none of the troops
　　　was able to lift a hand.
6 At your rebuke, O God of Jacob,
　　both rider and horse lay stunned.

7 But you indeed are awesome!
　　Who can stand before you
　　when once your anger is roused?
8 From the heavens you uttered
　　　　judgment;
　　the earth feared and was still
9 when God rose up to establish
　　　　judgment,
　　to save all the oppressed of the earth.
　　　　　　　　　　　　　Selah

10 Human wrath serves only to praise you,
　　when you bind the last bit of your*ᵇ*
　　　wrath around you.
11 Make vows to the LORD your God, and
　　　perform them;
　　let all who are around him bring gifts
　　to the one who is awesome,
12 who cuts off the spirit of princes,
　　who inspires fear in the kings of the
　　　earth.

76.1–12: The one who is awesome. A song of Zion,*
but its real focus is upon God (vv. 4, 7, 11–12). **1–3:**
Zion symbolizes God's claim on the whole world (vv.
8–9) and God's will for its well-being. *Salem,*
"shalem," is similar to "shalom," "peace," anticipating v. 3 (46.9). **4–9:** Reminiscent of the Exodus, vv.
4–6 prepare for the affirmation that God wills *judgment* or "justice" (vv. 8–9; 75.2, 7) for *all the oppressed. Awesome* (vv. 7, 11) represents the same Hebrew root as *feared/fear* (vv. 8, 12). **10–12:** Verse 10
suggests that all opposition to God is futile. God's
claim preempts the claims of the most powerful
earthly rulers (v. 12).

PSALM 77
To the leader: according to Jeduthun. Of Asaph.
A Psalm.

1 I cry aloud to God,
　　aloud to God, that he may hear me.
2 In the day of my trouble I seek
　　　the Lord;
　　in the night my hand is stretched out
　　　　without wearying;
　　my soul refuses to be comforted.
3 I think of God, and I moan;
　　I meditate, and my spirit faints.   *Selah*

4 You keep my eyelids from closing;
　　I am so troubled that I cannot speak.
5 I consider the days of old,
　　and remember the years of long ago.
6 I commune*ᶜ* with my heart in the night;
　　I meditate and search my spirit:*ᵈ*
7 "Will the Lord spurn forever,
　　and never again be favorable?
8 Has his steadfast love ceased forever?
　　Are his promises at an end for all
　　　　time?
9 Has God forgotten to be gracious?
　　Has he in anger shut up his
　　　　compassion?"   *Selah*
10 And I say, "It is my grief
　　that the right hand of the Most High
　　　has changed."

11 I will call to mind the deeds of the
　　　LORD;
　　I will remember your wonders of old.
12 I will meditate on all your work,
　　and muse on your mighty deeds.
13 Your way, O God, is holy.
　　What god is so great as our God?
14 You are the God who works wonders;
　　you have displayed your might among
　　　the peoples.
15 With your strong arm you redeemed
　　　your people,
　　the descendants of Jacob and Joseph.
　　　　　　　　　　　　　Selah

---

a Gk: Heb *the mountains of prey*   *b* Heb lacks *your*
c Gk Syr: Heb *My music*   *d* Syr Jerome: Heb *my spirit*
searches

16 When the waters saw you, O God,
  when the waters saw you, they were
    afraid;
  the very deep trembled.
17 The clouds poured out water;
  the skies thundered;
  your arrows flashed on every side.
18 The crash of your thunder was in the
    whirlwind;
  your lightnings lit up the world;
  the earth trembled and shook.
19 Your way was through the sea,
  your path, through the mighty
    waters;
  yet your footprints were unseen.
20 You led your people like a flock
  by the hand of Moses and Aaron.

77.1–20: I will remember your wonders of old. Resembling a prayer for help, vv.1–10 report the psalmist's anguished meditations (vv. 1–6), bitter questions (vv. 7–9), and hopeless conclusion (v. 10). While the psalmist continues to *meditate* (v. 12; see vv. 3, 6) in vv. 11–20, the tone and conclusions are remarkably different. **1–6:** The outstretched *hand* indicates prayer, but constant prayer and meditation yield only a faint *spirit* (142.3; 143.4). **7–10:** The psalmist's questions employ words that describe God's fundamental character—*steadfast love*, grace, and *compassion* or mercy (Ex 34.6). But God seems to have *changed*. **11–20:** The switch to direct address in v. 11 creates a more intimate tone. The psalmist's memory (v. 11; see v. 5) of God's *wonders of old* now inspires hope. The language and imagery recall the Exodus. Verse 19 suggests a renewed faith that will be effective even when God's *way* is *unseen*.

PSALM 78
A Maskil of Asaph.

1 Give ear, O my people, to my
    teaching;
  incline your ears to the words of my
    mouth.
2 I will open my mouth in a parable;
  I will utter dark sayings from of old,
3 things that we have heard and known,
  that our ancestors have told us.
4 We will not hide them from their
    children;
  we will tell to the coming generation

the glorious deeds of the LORD, and his
    might,
  and the wonders that he has done.

5 He established a decree in Jacob,
  and appointed a law in Israel,
  which he commanded our ancestors
    to teach to their children;
6 that the next generation might know
    them,
  the children yet unborn,
  and rise up and tell them to their
    children,
7 so that they should set their hope in
    God,
  and not forget the works of God,
  but keep his commandments;
8 and that they should not be like their
    ancestors,
  a stubborn and rebellious generation,
  a generation whose heart was not
    steadfast,
  whose spirit was not faithful to God.

9 The Ephraimites, armed with*a* the bow,
  turned back on the day of battle.
10 They did not keep God's covenant,
  but refused to walk according to his
    law.
11 They forgot what he had done,
  and the miracles that he had shown
    them.
12 In the sight of their ancestors he
    worked marvels
  in the land of Egypt, in the fields of
    Zoan.
13 He divided the sea and let them pass
    through it,
  and made the waters stand like
    a heap.
14 In the daytime he led them with
    a cloud,
  and all night long with a fiery light.
15 He split rocks open in the wilderness,
  and gave them drink abundantly as
    from the deep.
16 He made streams come out of the rock,
  and caused waters to flow down like
    rivers.

a Heb *armed with shooting*

17 Yet they sinned still more against him,
  rebelling against the Most High in
    the desert.
18 They tested God in their heart
  by demanding the food they craved.
19 They spoke against God, saying,
  "Can God spread a table in the
    wilderness?
20 Even though he struck the rock so that
    water gushed out
  and torrents overflowed,
 can he also give bread,
  or provide meat for his people?"

78.1–72: The wonders God has done. Usually classified as a historical psalm (one that rehearses major elements of Israel's story), its aim is to teach (vv. 1, 5) and inspire faithfulness (vv. 6–8). Two parallel sections (vv. 12–39, 40–72) follow the introduction (vv. 1–11). **1–11:** The focus on knowing (vv. 3, 6) and teaching (vv. 1, 5), consistent with the goal of faithfulness to the *covenant** (v. 10) and "torah" (*law*, v. 10), recalls both the wisdom literature* and Deuteronomy (see 6.20–25). **12–16:** The recital begins with God's gracious activity—the Exodus and guidance in the *wilderness* (Ex 13.21–22; 14.21–29; 17.1–6). **17–20:** The recital continues with the people's rebellion (Ex 15.22–25; 16.4–36; 17.1–7).

21 Therefore, when the LORD heard, he
    was full of rage;
  a fire was kindled against Jacob,
    his anger mounted against Israel,
22 because they had no faith in God,
  and did not trust his saving power.
23 Yet he commanded the skies above,
  and opened the doors of heaven;
24 he rained down on them manna to eat,
  and gave them the grain of heaven.
25 Mortals ate of the bread of angels;
  he sent them food in abundance.
26 He caused the east wind to blow in the
    heavens,
  and by his power he led out the south
    wind;
27 he rained flesh upon them like dust,
  winged birds like the sand of the seas;
28 he let them fall within their camp,
  all around their dwellings.
29 And they ate and were well filled,
  for he gave them what they craved.

30 But before they had satisfied their
    craving,
  while the food was still in their
    mouths,
31 the anger of God rose against them
  and he killed the strongest of them,
  and laid low the flower of Israel.
32 In spite of all this they still sinned;
  they did not believe in his wonders.
33 So he made their days vanish like a
    breath,
  and their years in terror.
34 When he killed them, they sought for
    him;
  they repented and sought God
    earnestly.
35 They remembered that God was their
    rock,
  the Most High God their redeemer.
36 But they flattered him with their
    mouths;
  they lied to him with their tongues.
37 Their heart was not steadfast toward
    him;
  they were not true to his covenant.
38 Yet he, being compassionate,
    forgave their iniquity,
  and did not destroy them;
 often he restrained his anger,
  and did not stir up all his wrath.
39 He remembered that they were but
    flesh,
  a wind that passes and does not come
    again.
40 How often they rebelled against him in
    the wilderness
  and grieved him in the desert!
41 They tested God again and again,
  and provoked the Holy One of Israel.
42 They did not keep in mind his power,
  or the day when he redeemed them
    from the foe;
43 when he displayed his signs in Egypt,
  and his miracles in the fields of Zoan.
44 He turned their rivers to blood,
  so that they could not drink of their
    streams.
45 He sent among them swarms of flies,
    which devoured them,
  and frogs, which destroyed them.

46 He gave their crops to the caterpillar,
    and the fruit of their labor to the
        locust.
47 He destroyed their vines with hail,
    and their sycamores with frost.
48 He gave over their cattle to the hail,
    and their flocks to thunderbolts.
49 He let loose on them his fierce anger,
    wrath, indignation, and distress,
    a company of destroying angels.
50 He made a path for his anger;
    he did not spare them from death,
    but gave their lives over to the
        plague.
51 He struck all the firstborn in Egypt,
    the first issue of their strength in the
        tents of Ham.
52 Then he led out his people like sheep,
    and guided them in the wilderness
        like a flock.
53 He led them in safety, so that they were
        not afraid;
    but the sea overwhelmed their
        enemies.
54 And he brought them to his holy hill,
    to the mountain that his right hand
        had won.
55 He drove out nations before them;
    he apportioned them for a possession
    and settled the tribes of Israel in their
        tents.

56 Yet they tested the Most High God,
    and rebelled against him.
    They did not observe his decrees,
57 but turned away and were faithless like
        their ancestors;
    they twisted like a treacherous bow.
58 For they provoked him to anger with
        their high places;
    they moved him to jealousy with their
        idols.
59 When God heard, he was full of wrath,
    and he utterly rejected Israel.
60 He abandoned his dwelling at Shiloh,
    the tent where he dwelt among
        mortals,
61 and delivered his power to captivity,
    his glory to the hand of the foe.
62 He gave his people to the sword,
    and vented his wrath on his heritage.

63 Fire devoured their young men,
    and their girls had no marriage song.
64 Their priests fell by the sword,
    and their widows made no
        lamentation.
65 Then the Lord awoke as from sleep,
    like a warrior shouting because of
        wine.
66 He put his adversaries to rout;
    he put them to everlasting disgrace.

67 He rejected the tent of Joseph,
    he did not choose the tribe of Ephraim;
68 but he chose the tribe of Judah,
    Mount Zion, which he loves.
69 He built his sanctuary like the high
        heavens,
    like the earth, which he has founded
        forever.
70 He chose his servant David,
    and took him from the sheepfolds;
71 from tending the nursing ewes he
        brought him
    to be the shepherd of his people
        Jacob,
    of Israel, his inheritance.
72 With upright heart he tended them,
    and guided them with skillful hand.

78.21–72. 21–32: Rebellion evokes God's *rage* (v. 21) and *anger* (vv. 21, 31), but God still graciously provides (vv. 23–29; Ex 16.4–36). **33–39:** There are consequences for disobedience (vv. 33–34), but God ultimately proves to be *compassionate* (v. 38). **40–72:** This section demonstrates the same pattern found in vv. 12–39: God's gracious activity (vv. 40–55; Ex 7.14–12.30) is followed by the people's rebellion (vv. 56–58), which evokes God's *wrath* (vv. 59–64; vv. 62–64 seem to allude to 1 Sam 4.10–11), which in turn is followed by God's grace (vv. 65–72). Verse 67 may reflect the destruction of the northern kingdom in 722 BCE. The concluding verses reflect the promises to the Davidic dynasty* (2 Sam 7.1–17; Ps 89.19–37).

PSALM 79

A Psalm of Asaph.

1 O God, the nations have come into your
        inheritance;
    they have defiled your holy temple;
    they have laid Jerusalem in ruins.

2 They have given the bodies of your
    servants
    to the birds of the air for food,
    the flesh of your faithful to the wild
    animals of the earth.
3 They have poured out their blood like
    water
    all around Jerusalem,
    and there was no one to bury them.
4 We have become a taunt to our
    neighbors,
    mocked and derided by those around
    us.

5 How long, O LORD? Will you be angry
    forever?
    Will your jealous wrath burn like fire?
6 Pour out your anger on the nations
    that do not know you,
    and on the kingdoms
    that do not call on your name.
7 For they have devoured Jacob
    and laid waste his habitation.

8 Do not remember against us the
    iniquities of our ancestors;
    let your compassion come speedily to
    meet us,
    for we are brought very low.
9 Help us, O God of our salvation,
    for the glory of your name;
    deliver us, and forgive our sins,
    for your name's sake.
10 Why should the nations say,
    "Where is their God?"
    Let the avenging of the outpoured blood
    of your servants
    be known among the nations before
    our eyes.

11 Let the groans of the prisoners come
    before you;
    according to your great power
    preserve those doomed to die.
12 Return sevenfold into the bosom of our
    neighbors
    the taunts with which they taunted
    you, O Lord!
13 Then we your people, the flock of your
    pasture,
    will give thanks to you forever;

from generation to generation we will
    recount your praise.

79.1–13: **Help us, O God.** A communal lament,* it probably originated with the destruction of the *temple* and *Jerusalem* (v. 1) in 587 BCE. **1–5:** Unburied bodies (vv. 2–3) compound the uncleanness represented by the entrance of *the nations* into the *temple* (v. 1). The people's status as a *taunt* (v. 4) anticipates the *taunts* against God (v. 12; 44.13). The questions in v. 5 communicate the people's doubt and fear (80.4). **6–12:** The petitions call for a redirecting of God's *anger* (v. 6) and a display of God's *compassion* (v. 8), despite the people's *sins* (v. 9). The question of *the nations* in v. 10 reflects the people's own doubt (42.10; 115.2). The petitions against the nations are motivated not simply by revenge but by a desire for deliverance from oppression. **13:** The pastoral imagery recalls 78.70–72 and anticipates 80.1.

PSALM 80

To the leader: on Lilies, a Covenant. Of Asaph.
A Psalm.

1 Give ear, O Shepherd of Israel,
    you who lead Joseph like a flock!
    You who are enthroned upon the
    cherubim, shine forth
2   before Ephraim and Benjamin and
    Manasseh.
    Stir up your might,
    and come to save us!

3 Restore us, O God;
    let your face shine, that we may be
    saved.

4 O LORD God of hosts,
    how long will you be angry with your
    people's prayers?
5 You have fed them with the bread of
    tears,
    and given them tears to drink in full
    measure.
6 You make us the scorn[a] of our
    neighbors;
    our enemies laugh among
    themselves.

a Syr: Heb *strife*

7 Restore us, O God of hosts;
    let your face shine, that we may be
        saved.

8 You brought a vine out of Egypt;
    you drove out the nations and planted
        it.
9 You cleared the ground for it;
    it took deep root and filled the land.
10 The mountains were covered with its
        shade,
    the mighty cedars with its branches;
11 it sent out its branches to the sea,
    and its shoots to the River.
12 Why then have you broken down its
        walls,
    so that all who pass along the way
        pluck its fruit?
13 The boar from the forest ravages it,
    and all that move in the field feed on
        it.

14 Turn again, O God of hosts;
    look down from heaven, and see;
have regard for this vine,
15   the stock that your right hand
        planted.[a]
16 They have burned it with fire, they have
        cut it down;[b]
    may they perish at the rebuke of your
        countenance.
17 But let your hand be upon the one at
        your right hand,
    the one whom you made strong for
        yourself.
18 Then we will never turn back from you;
    give us life, and we will call on your
        name.

19 Restore us, O LORD God of hosts;
    let your face shine, that we may be
        saved.

80.1–19: Restore us, O God. A fitting companion to Ps 79, it is also a communal lament.* While *Ephraim* and *Manasseh* in v. 2 suggest a northern origin (they were tribes of the northern kingdom; see 1 Kings 12), the psalm orients these references toward the destruction of Jerusalem. The primary structural feature is the refrain (vv. 3, 7, 19) and a variation thereof (v. 14). **1–3:** Calamity does not prevent the people from af-

firming God's sovereignty. *Shepherd* is a royal title (Ezek 34.1–16), and God is *enthroned. Shine forth* suggests the need for a theophany* (a manifestation of the deity in the natural order), a new appearing of God that will *restore* the people (v. 3; Num 6.24–26; Ps 4.6; 67.1). **4–7:** The question in v. 4 (74.10; 79.5) implies the following complaint. *Shepherd* literally means "feeder," but the food has not been appropriate (v. 5). **8–13:** The vine metaphor* recalls the Exodus, establishment in the land, and subsequent demise. **14–19:** *Turn* represents the same Hebrew as *restore.* God's turning must precede the people's restoration (90.13). The *one at your right hand* (v. 17) may be a future king, but v. 18 suggests that it probably refers to the people as a whole.

PSALM 81

To the leader: according to The Gittith.
Of Asaph.

1 Sing aloud to God our strength;
    shout for joy to the God of Jacob.
2 Raise a song, sound the tambourine,
    the sweet lyre with the harp.
3 Blow the trumpet at the new moon,
    at the full moon, on our festal day.
4 For it is a statute for Israel,
    an ordinance of the God of Jacob.
5 He made it a decree in Joseph,
    when he went out over[c] the land of
        Egypt.

I hear a voice I had not known:
6 "I relieved your[d] shoulder of the
        burden;
    your[d] hands were freed from the
        basket.
7 In distress you called, and I rescued
        you;
    I answered you in the secret place of
        thunder;
    I tested you at the waters of Meribah.
                                    Selah
8 Hear, O my people, while I admonish
        you;
    O Israel, if you would but listen to
        me!

a Heb adds from verse 17 *and upon the one whom you made strong for yourself*   b Cn: Heb *it is cut down*   c Or *against*   d Heb *his*

9 There shall be no strange god among
          you;
     you shall not bow down to a foreign
          god.
10 I am the LORD your God,
     who brought you up out of the land
          of Egypt.
     Open your mouth wide and I will fill it.

11 "But my people did not listen to my
          voice;
     Israel would not submit to me.
12 So I gave them over to their stubborn
          hearts,
     to follow their own counsels.
13 O that my people would listen to me,
     that Israel would walk in my ways!
14 Then I would quickly subdue their
          enemies,
     and turn my hand against their foes.
15 Those who hate the LORD would cringe
          before him,
     and their doom would last forever.
16 I would feed you[a] with the finest of the
          wheat,
     and with honey from the rock I would
          satisfy you."

in the midst of the gods he holds
          judgment:
2 "How long will you judge unjustly
     and show partiality to the wicked?
                                                   Selah
3 Give justice to the weak and the
          orphan;
     maintain the right of the lowly and
          the destitute.
4 Rescue the weak and the needy;
     deliver them from the hand of the
          wicked."

5 They have neither knowledge nor
          understanding,
     they walk around in darkness;
     all the foundations of the earth are
          shaken.

6 I say, "You are gods,
     children of the Most High, all of you;
7 nevertheless, you shall die like mortals,
     and fall like any prince."[b]

8 Rise up, O God, judge the earth;
     for all the nations belong to you!

81.1–16: Hear, O my people. It is usually categorized as a prophetic* exhortation* (see Ps 50). A prophet may have originally spoken vv. 6–16 in a worship service. **1–5b:** The divine speech is introduced by a song of praise. Mention of *the trumpet* (v. 3) suggests a possible association with the festal season in the seventh month (Lev 23.23–24; Num 29.1–6). **5c:** The new *voice* marks the beginning of God's word to the people. **6–10:** The Exodus, Sinai, and wilderness are recalled, including *Meribah* where Israel is said to have *tested* God (Ex 17.7; Ps 95.8). *Hear* and *listen* are the same Hebrew word (v. 8), phraseology recalling Deut 6.4, the "Shema," and anticipating vv. 11, 13. **11–16:** By refusing to *listen* (v. 11), past generations chose their own punishment (v. 12). God desires that the current hearers not repeat their mistake (v. 13), so as to thwart God's will to *feed* and *satisfy* (v. 16).

82.1–8: Give justice to the weak. It is often considered a prophetic* exhortation.* The divine speech (vv. 2–4, 6–7, and perhaps v. 5), however, is addressed to *the gods* rather than the people. The poem recounts a trial in heaven, in which *the gods* are indicted (vv. 2–4), convicted (v. 5), and sentenced to death (vv. 6–7). **1:** Israel's *God* precludes the existence of other *gods* (81.9–10). **2–4:** The exhortations serve as indictments. *The gods* have failed to administer *justice*, the crucial criterion of which is whether the *weak* and *needy* are enabled to live. The Hebrew "shpt," "to judge, do justice," is the key word (vv. 1, 2, 3, 8). **5:** When *justice* is not present, the whole *earth* is destabilized and threatened (Isa 24.18–19; Ps 46.1–3). **6–7:** *The gods* will reap the destruction their policies have advanced. The *divine council* (v. 1; 1 Kings 22.19–23; Ps 58.1–2) is terminated. **8:** The demise of *the gods* opens the way for *God* to *judge*, or better, "establish justice" on *earth*, the role of a true sovereign (72.1–7).

PSALM 82

A Psalm of Asaph.

1 God has taken his place in the divine
          council;

---

a Cn Compare verse 16b: Heb *he would feed him*
b Or *fall as one man, O princes*

PSALM 83
A Song. A Psalm of Asaph.

1 O God, do not keep silence;
  do not hold your peace or be still,
    O God!
2 Even now your enemies are in tumult;
  those who hate you have raised their
    heads.
3 They lay crafty plans against your
    people;
  they consult together against those
    you protect.
4 They say, "Come, let us wipe them out
    as a nation;
  let the name of Israel be remembered
    no more."
5 They conspire with one accord;
  against you they make a covenant—
6 the tents of Edom and the Ishmaelites,
  Moab and the Hagrites,
7 Gebal and Ammon and Amalek,
  Philistia with the inhabitants of Tyre;
8 Assyria also has joined them;
  they are the strong arm of the
    children of Lot.   *Selah*

9 Do to them as you did to Midian,
  as to Sisera and Jabin at the Wadi
    Kishon,
10 who were destroyed at En-dor,
  who became dung for the ground.
11 Make their nobles like Oreb and Zeeb,
  all their princes like Zebah and
    Zalmunna,
12 who said, "Let us take the pastures of
    God
  for our own possession."

13 O my God, make them like whirling
    dust,*a*
  like chaff before the wind.
14 As fire consumes the forest,
  as the flame sets the mountains
    ablaze,
15 so pursue them with your tempest
  and terrify them with your
    hurricane.
16 Fill their faces with shame,
  so that they may seek your name,
    O LORD.

17 Let them be put to shame and dismayed
    forever;
  let them perish in disgrace.
18 Let them know that you alone,
  whose name is the LORD,
  are the Most High over all the earth.

83.1–18: That they may seek your name, O LORD. A communal prayer for help, its naming of the *enemies* (vv. 6–8) culminates with *Assyria*, suggesting an origin in the ninth to seventh centuries BCE. But the psalm itself may derive from a later period. **1:** *O God* begins and ends the verse, suggesting that God's presence is more encompassing than that of the many *enemies* (vv. 2, 6–8). **2–5:** Verses 2–3 recall the opposition to God and God's people in 2.1–3. **6–8:** The list of *enemies* may be hyperbolic,* suggesting pervasive opposition, or the names may be arranged geographically to indicate that the people are surrounded. *Assyria* may function symbolically as a reference to Israel's enemies, and was eventually heard this way. **9–12:** Past deliverance (Judg 4–8) grounds the petitions against the *enemies*. **13–18:** The violent-sounding petitions are motivated not so much by a desire for vengeance as a desire for justice, which will involve reconciliation (vv. 16, 18).

PSALM 84
To the leader: according to The Gittith.
Of the Korahites. A Psalm.

1 How lovely is your dwelling place,
  O LORD of hosts!
2 My soul longs, indeed it faints
  for the courts of the LORD;
  my heart and my flesh sing for joy
    to the living God.

3 Even the sparrow finds a home,
  and the swallow a nest for herself,
  where she may lay her young,
  at your altars, O LORD of hosts,
    my King and my God.
4 Happy are those who live in your house,
  ever singing your praise.   *Selah*

5 Happy are those whose strength is in you,
  in whose heart are the highways to
    Zion.*b*

a Or a tumbleweed   b Heb lacks to Zion

6 As they go through the valley of Baca
    they make it a place of springs;
    the early rain also covers it with
        pools.
7 They go from strength to strength;
    the God of gods will be seen in Zion.

8 O Lord God of hosts, hear my prayer;
    give ear, O God of Jacob!   Selah
9 Behold our shield, O God;
    look on the face of your anointed.

10 For a day in your courts is better
    than a thousand elsewhere.
    I would rather be a doorkeeper in the
        house of my God
    than live in the tents of wickedness.
11 For the Lord God is a sun and shield;
    he bestows favor and honor.
    No good thing does the Lord withhold
    from those who walk uprightly.
12 O Lord of hosts,
    happy is everyone who trusts in you.

84.1–12: Happy are those who live in your house. A song of Zion,★ it was probably used originally by pilgrims as they journeyed toward or visited Jerusalem. The focus finally is upon God (vv. 11–12). **1–4:** *Lord of hosts* (vv. 1, 3; see vv. 8, 12) is a title associated with the ark (24.7–10); it bespeaks God's sovereignty, as does the title, *King*. God's *house* (v. 4), the Temple,★ is envisioned by the psalmist as his or her true *home* (v. 3). **5–7:** *Happy* functions as a theme (vv. 4, 5, 12); the source of happiness is thoroughly God-centered (1.1; 2.12). Verses 5b–6a affirm that the pilgrims receive *strength* from God (v. 5) and transmit it to others (v. 6). If *Baca* is an actual place, the location is unknown. The word is similar to one meaning "tears." **8–12:** In v. 9, the psalmist prays for the king, whose palace adjoined the Temple. *Better* and *good things*, from the same Hebrew root, frame vv. 10–11. God is the source of all goodness (73.28), a conviction held by a pilgrim *who trusts in God.*

PSALM 85

To the leader. Of the Korahites. A Psalm.

1 Lord, you were favorable to your land;
    you restored the fortunes of Jacob.
2 You forgave the iniquity of your people;
    you pardoned all their sin.   Selah

3 You withdrew all your wrath;
    you turned from your hot anger.

4 Restore us again, O God of our
        salvation,
    and put away your indignation toward
        us.
5 Will you be angry with us forever?
    Will you prolong your anger to all
        generations?
6 Will you not revive us again,
    so that your people may rejoice
        in you?
7 Show us your steadfast love, O Lord,
    and grant us your salvation.

8 Let me hear what God the Lord will
        speak,
    for he will speak peace to his people,
    to his faithful, to those who turn to
        him in their hearts.[a]
9 Surely his salvation is at hand for those
        who fear him,
    that his glory may dwell in our land.

10 Steadfast love and faithfulness
        will meet;
    righteousness and peace will kiss
        each other.
11 Faithfulness will spring up from the
        ground,
    and righteousness will look down
        from the sky.
12 The Lord will give what is good,
    and our land will yield its increase.
13 Righteousness will go before him,
    and will make a path for his steps.

85.1–13: Steadfast love and faithfulness will meet. A communal prayer for help, it may have originated amid the disappointing circumstances of the early post-exilic era. **1–3:** *Restored the fortunes* probably denotes the return from exile (126.1; Jer 30.3), which the prophets★ proclaimed was precipitated by God's forgiveness (Isa 40.1–2). **4–7:** But the return was not as glorious as had been hoped. The need for a fuller restoration motivates the petitions, which are framed by *salvation* (vv. 4, 7; see v. 9). **8–13:** While vv. 8–9 sug-

a Gk: Heb *but let them not turn back to folly*

gest the necessity of a response, the promise depicted in vv. 10–13 exceeds what the people could ever deserve. *Steadfast love* and *faithfulness* lie at the essence of God's character, and were revealed preeminently following God's gracious forgiveness of the people (Ex 34.6). *Righteousness* (vv. 10, 11, 13) describes the essence of God's will. Verse 11 suggests the whole earth, from *ground* to *sky*, will be permeated by God's gracious presence and purposes, yielding *what is good* (v. 12; 84.11).

PSALM 86

A Prayer of David.

1 Incline your ear, O LORD, and answer me,
   for I am poor and needy.
2 Preserve my life, for I am devoted to you;
   save your servant who trusts in you.
 You are my God; 3be gracious to me, O Lord,
   for to you do I cry all day long.
4 Gladden the soul of your servant,
   for to you, O Lord, I lift up my soul.
5 For you, O Lord, are good and forgiving,
   abounding in steadfast love to all who call on you.
6 Give ear, O LORD, to my prayer;
   listen to my cry of supplication.
7 In the day of my trouble I call on you,
   for you will answer me.

8 There is none like you among the gods, O Lord,
   nor are there any works like yours.
9 All the nations you have made shall come
   and bow down before you, O Lord,
   and shall glorify your name.
10 For you are great and do wondrous things;
   you alone are God.
11 Teach me your way, O LORD,
   that I may walk in your truth;
   give me an undivided heart to revere your name.
12 I give thanks to you, O Lord my God,
   with my whole heart,
   and I will glorify your name forever.

13 For great is your steadfast love toward me;
   you have delivered my soul from the depths of Sheol.
14 O God, the insolent rise up against me;
   a band of ruffians seeks my life,
   and they do not set you before them.
15 But you, O Lord, are a God merciful and gracious,
   slow to anger and abounding in steadfast love and faithfulness.
16 Turn to me and be gracious to me;
   give your strength to your servant;
   save the child of your serving girl.
17 Show me a sign of your favor,
   so that those who hate me may see it and be put to shame,
   because you, LORD, have helped me and comforted me.

86.1–17: Great is your steadfast love. A prayer for help, its petitions and complaints (vv. 1–7, 14–17) surround a core of praise and affirmation (vv. 8–13) in a unique arrangement that departs from the usual culmination in praise. **1–7:** The psalmist belongs among those whom God especially attends, the *poor and needy* (v. 1; 9.9, 18; 10.12; 82.2–3) who entrust their lives to God (v. 2). To *lift up my soul* means essentially to trust, to offer life to God's keeping (25.1; 143.8). **8–13:** *Name* (vv. 9, 11, 12) focuses attention on God's character, which is unsurpassable (vv. 8, 10). God's essence is *steadfast love* (v. 13; see vv. 5, 15), which evokes the psalmist's gratitude. **14–17:** The renewed petitions are grounded in the conviction that God will act in a way similar to the time when God revealed the divine character to Moses (v. 15; Ex 34.6). Like Moses, the psalmist is God's *servant* (vv. 4, 16; 116.16).

PSALM 87

Of the Korahites. A Psalm. A Song.

1 On the holy mount stands the city he founded;
2   the LORD loves the gates of Zion
   more than all the dwellings of Jacob.
3 Glorious things are spoken of you,
   O city of God. *Selah*

4 Among those who know me I mention Rahab and Babylon;

Philistia too, and Tyre, with
    Ethiopia[a]—
    "This one was born there," they say.

5 And of Zion it shall be said,
    "This one and that one were born in
      it";
    for the Most High himself will
      establish it.
6 The LORD records, as he registers the
      peoples,
    "This one was born there."   *Selah*

7 Singers and dancers alike say,
    "All my springs are in you."

87.1–7: Born in Zion.* A song of *Zion*, it celebrates Jerusalem as God's place (vv. 1–2), but it also suggests that Jerusalem represents God's claim on the whole world and its peoples (vv. 3–7; Ps 48). **1–2:** Jerusalem occupies a *holy mount* or hill (2.6; 48.1). **3–7:** Praise of *Zion* in vv. 3, 7 encompasses the verses that share the word *born*. The speaker in vv. 4–5 could be viewed as God or a personified* *Zion*. It is remarkable that traditional enemies look to Jerusalem as their home, suggesting God's claim on the whole world and its peoples (Gen 12.3; Isa 19.23–25).

PSALM 88

A Song. A Psalm of the Korahites. To the leader:
according to Mahalath Leannoth. A Maskil
of Heman the Ezrahite.

1 O LORD, God of my salvation,
    when, at night, I cry out in your
      presence,
2 let my prayer come before you;
    incline your ear to my cry.

3 For my soul is full of troubles,
    and my life draws near to Sheol.
4 I am counted among those who go
      down to the Pit;
    I am like those who have no help,
5 like those forsaken among the dead,
    like the slain that lie in the grave,
    like those whom you remember
      no more,
    for they are cut off from your hand.
6 You have put me in the depths of the
      Pit,
    in the regions dark and deep.

7 Your wrath lies heavy upon me,
    and you overwhelm me with all your
      waves.   *Selah*

8 You have caused my companions to
      shun me;
    you have made me a thing of horror
      to them.
    I am shut in so that I cannot escape;
9   my eye grows dim through sorrow.
    Every day I call on you, O LORD;
    I spread out my hands to you.
10 Do you work wonders for the dead?
    Do the shades rise up to praise you?
                  Selah
11 Is your steadfast love declared in the
      grave,
    or your faithfulness in Abaddon?
12 Are your wonders known in the
      darkness,
    or your saving help in the land of
      forgetfulness?

13 But I, O LORD, cry out to you;
    in the morning my prayer comes
      before you.
14 O LORD, why do you cast me off?
    Why do you hide your face from me?
15 Wretched and close to death from my
      youth up,
    I suffer your terrors; I am desperate.[b]
16 Your wrath has swept over me;
    your dread assaults destroy me.
17 They surround me like a flood all day
      long;
    from all sides they close in on me.
18 You have caused friend and neighbor to
      shun me;
    my companions are in darkness.

88.1–18: In the darkness. Unique among the prayers for help, it contains no explicit movement toward trust or praise. Three different Hebrew words for *cry out* or *call* mark the beginning of its three sections (vv. 1, 9b, 13); each is accompanied by a chronological reference. **1–9a:** Trust is implied in v. 1 and by the fact that the psalmist continues to pray. *Sheol** and *the Pit*, the realm of the dead, indicate the urgency of the situation. Abandonment by God (vv. 3–7; 22.1) is accom-

a Or *Nubia;* Heb *Cush*   *b* Meaning of Heb uncertain

panied by human isolation (v. 8; 31.11; 38.11). **9b–12:** All the questions in vv. 10–12 are about death, but they imply the psalmist's conviction that God ultimately wills and works for life. **13–18:** Questions continue (v. 14), functioning as in vv. 10–12 as a complaint. Verse 18 recalls v. 8, and the final word of the psalm captures its pervasive mood—*darkness* (see vv. 6, 12).

PSALM 89

A Maskil of Ethan the Ezrahite.

1 I will sing of your steadfast love,
   O LORD,*a* forever;
with my mouth I will proclaim your
   faithfulness to all generations.

2 I declare that your steadfast love is
   established forever;
your faithfulness is as firm as the
   heavens.

3 You said, "I have made a covenant with
   my chosen one,
I have sworn to my servant David:

4 'I will establish your descendants
   forever,
and build your throne for all
   generations.'" *Selah*

5 Let the heavens praise your wonders,
   O LORD,
your faithfulness in the assembly of
   the holy ones.

6 For who in the skies can be compared
   to the LORD?
Who among the heavenly beings is
   like the LORD,

7 a God feared in the council of the holy
   ones,
great and awesome*b* above all that
   are around him?

8 O LORD God of hosts,
   who is as mighty as you, O LORD?
Your faithfulness surrounds you.

9 You rule the raging of the sea;
   when its waves rise, you still them.

10 You crushed Rahab like a carcass;
   you scattered your enemies with your
   mighty arm.

11 The heavens are yours, the earth also is
   yours;

the world and all that is in it—you
   have founded them.

12 The north and the south*c*—you created
   them;
Tabor and Hermon joyously praise
   your name.

13 You have a mighty arm;
strong is your hand, high your right
   hand.

14 Righteousness and justice are the
   foundation of your throne;
steadfast love and faithfulness go
   before you.

15 Happy are the people who know the
   festal shout,
who walk, O LORD, in the light of
   your countenance;

16 they exult in your name all day long,
and extol*d* your righteousness.

17 For you are the glory of their strength;
by your favor our horn is exalted.

18 For our shield belongs to the LORD,
our king to the Holy One of Israel.

89.1–52: Where is your steadfast love of old? A royal psalm, it contains praise (vv. 1–2, 5–18) and complaint (vv. 38–51). Verses 3–4, 19–37 are offered as divine speech. It probably originated in response to the destruction of Jerusalem and disappearance of the monarchy in 587 BCE. **1–4:** The two key words appear twice in vv. 1–2: *steadfast love* (see vv. 14, 24, 28, 33, 49) and *faithfulness* (see vv. 5, 8, 14, 24, 33, 49). The focus on God (vv. 1–2) is continued in vv. 5–18, while the focus on the Davidic *covenant*★ (vv. 3–4) continues in vv. 19–37. **5–18:** Among the *heavenly beings, the LORD* is preeminent (vv. 5–8), for God tamed the chaotic powers (vv. 9–10), claimed the whole world (vv. 11–12), and now rules rightly and lovingly (vv. 13–14; 97.2). The appropriate response is worship (vv. 15–18).

---

19 Then you spoke in a vision to your
   faithful one, and said:
"I have set the crown*e* on one who is
   mighty,
I have exalted one chosen from the
   people.

---

a Gk: Heb *the steadfast love of the* LORD   *b* Gk Syr: Heb *greatly awesome*   *c* Or *Zaphon and Yamin*
d Cn: Heb *are exalted in*   *e* Cn: Heb *help*

20 I have found my servant David;
　　with my holy oil I have anointed
　　　him;
21 my hand shall always remain with him;
　　my arm also shall strengthen him.
22 The enemy shall not outwit him,
　　the wicked shall not humble him.
23 I will crush his foes before him
　　and strike down those who hate him.
24 My faithfulness and steadfast love shall
　　be with him;
　　and in my name his horn shall be
　　　exalted.
25 I will set his hand on the sea
　　and his right hand on the rivers.
26 He shall cry to me, 'You are my Father,
　　my God, and the Rock of my
　　　salvation!'
27 I will make him the firstborn,
　　the highest of the kings of the earth.
28 Forever I will keep my steadfast love for
　　him,
　　and my covenant with him will stand
　　　firm.
29 I will establish his line forever,
　　and his throne as long as the heavens
　　　endure.
30 If his children forsake my law
　　and do not walk according to my
　　　ordinances,
31 if they violate my statutes
　　and do not keep my commandments,
32 then I will punish their transgression
　　with the rod
　　and their iniquity with scourges;
33 but I will not remove from him my
　　steadfast love,
　　or be false to my faithfulness.
34 I will not violate my covenant,
　　or alter the word that went forth from
　　　my lips.
35 Once and for all I have sworn by my
　　holiness;
　　I will not lie to David.
36 His line shall continue forever,
　　and his throne endure before me like
　　　the sun.
37 It shall be established forever like the
　　moon,
　　an enduring witness in the skies."
　　　　　　　　　　　　　　　　Selah

38 But now you have spurned and rejected
　　him;
　　you are full of wrath against your
　　　anointed.
39 You have renounced the covenant with
　　your servant;
　　you have defiled his crown in
　　　the dust.
40 You have broken through all his walls;
　　you have laid his strongholds in ruins.
41 All who pass by plunder him;
　　he has become the scorn of his
　　　neighbors.
42 You have exalted the right hand of his
　　foes;
　　you have made all his enemies
　　　rejoice.
43 Moreover, you have turned back the
　　edge of his sword,
　　and you have not supported him in
　　　battle.
44 You have removed the scepter from his
　　hand,[a]
　　and hurled his throne to the ground.
45 You have cut short the days of his
　　youth;
　　you have covered him with shame.
　　　　　　　　　　　　　　　　Selah

46 How long, O LORD? Will you hide
　　yourself forever?
　　How long will your wrath burn like
　　　fire?
47 Remember how short my time is—[b]
　　for what vanity you have created all
　　　mortals!
48 Who can live and never see death?
　　Who can escape the power of Sheol?
　　　　　　　　　　　　　　　　Selah

49 Lord, where is your steadfast love of
　　old,
　　which by your faithfulness you swore
　　　to David?
50 Remember, O Lord, how your servant is
　　taunted;
　　how I bear in my bosom the insults of
　　　the peoples,[c]

a Cn: Heb *removed his cleanness*　　b Meaning of Heb
uncertain　　c Cn: Heb *bosom all of many peoples*

51 with which your enemies taunt,
    O LORD,
      with which they taunted the footsteps
        of your anointed.

52 Blessed be the LORD forever.
    Amen and Amen.

89.19–52. 19–37: Recalling 2 Sam 7, Nathan's oracle*
to David, these verses rehearse the promises of the
covenant (vv. 28, 34) with *David* and *his children*. The
repetition of *forever* (vv. 28, 29, 35, 36) makes for a
jarring transition at v. 38. **38–51:** The supposedly eternal *covenant* has been *renounced* (v. 39), and God's
*anointed** has been *rejected* (v. 38), precipitating the
questions and petitions summarized in v. 49. **52:** The
doxology closes Book III, leaving the question of v. 49
unanswered and inviting the reader forward into Book
IV (see Introduction).

BOOK FOUR

PSALM 90

A Prayer of Moses, the man of God.

1 Lord, you have been our dwelling place*a*
    in all generations.
2 Before the mountains were brought
    forth,
      or ever you had formed the earth and
        the world,
      from everlasting to everlasting you are
        God.

3 You turn us*b* back to dust,
    and say, "Turn back, you mortals."
4 For a thousand years in your sight
    are like yesterday when it is past,
    or like a watch in the night.

5 You sweep them away; they are like a
    dream,
    like grass that is renewed in the
      morning;
6 in the morning it flourishes and is
    renewed;
    in the evening it fades and withers.

7 For we are consumed by your anger;
    by your wrath we are overwhelmed.

8 You have set our iniquities before you,
    our secret sins in the light of your
      countenance.

9 For all our days pass away under your
    wrath;
    our years come to an end*c* like a sigh.
10 The days of our life are seventy years,
    or perhaps eighty, if we are strong;
even then their span*d* is only toil and
    trouble;
    they are soon gone, and we fly away.

11 Who considers the power of your anger?
    Your wrath is as great as the fear that
      is due you.
12 So teach us to count our days
    that we may gain a wise heart.

13 Turn, O LORD! How long?
    Have compassion on your servants!
14 Satisfy us in the morning with your
    steadfast love,
    so that we may rejoice and be glad all
      our days.
15 Make us glad as many days as you have
    afflicted us,
    and as many years as we have seen
      evil.
16 Let your work be manifest to your
    servants,
    and your glorious power to their
      children.
17 Let the favor of the Lord our God be
    upon us,
    and prosper for us the work of our
      hands—
    O prosper the work of our hands!

90.1–17: Satisfy us with your steadfast love. Often
categorized as a communal prayer for help or a wisdom psalm, it begins Book IV by offering a realistic but
hopeful response to the despairing questions of
89.46–49. In so doing, this psalm responds to the crisis
of exile. This is the only psalm attributed to *Moses* (see
Introduction). **1–2:** In contrast to the transience of human life and the homelessness of exile, God is an eter-

---

a Another reading is *our refuge*   *b* Heb *humankind*
c Syr: Heb *we bring our years to an end*   *d* Cn Compare
Gk Syr Jerome Tg: Heb *pride*

nal *dwelling place.* **3–6:** Both vocabulary (*years, yesterday, night, morning, evening*) and poetic structure (for instance, the movement from night to *morning* to *evening* in vv. 5–6) evoke the passage of time, which reveals human transience. **7–11:** The word *wrath* frames this section. It communicates the way that humans experience finitude. **12:** The psalmist asks, in essence, "Teach us to accept each day as a gift," a request that marks the transition from despair to hope. **13–17:** The plea that God *turn* recalls Moses' intercession in Ex 32.12; v. 13b recalls Deut 32.36; and *steadfast love* (v. 14) recalls Ex 34.6–7. The petitions imply trust in God's forgiveness and God's redemption of human time, words which are now associated with joy and gladness. Human time and transience, when entrusted to God, need not be sources of despair. With God, hope is possible.

PSALM 91

1 You who live in the shelter of the Most
High,
who abide in the shadow of the
Almighty,[a]
2 will say to the LORD, "My refuge and
my fortress;
my God, in whom I trust."
3 For he will deliver you from the snare of
the fowler
and from the deadly pestilence;
4 he will cover you with his pinions,
and under his wings you will find
refuge;
his faithfulness is a shield and
buckler.
5 You will not fear the terror of the night,
or the arrow that flies by day,
6 or the pestilence that stalks in darkness,
or the destruction that wastes at
noonday.

7 A thousand may fall at your side,
ten thousand at your right hand,
but it will not come near you.
8 You will only look with your eyes
and see the punishment of the
wicked.

9 Because you have made the LORD your
refuge,[b]
the Most High your dwelling place,

10 no evil shall befall you,
no scourge come near your tent.

11 For he will command his angels
concerning you
to guard you in all your ways.
12 On their hands they will bear you up,
so that you will not dash your foot
against a stone.
13 You will tread on the lion and the adder,
the young lion and the serpent you
will trample under foot.

14 Those who love me, I will deliver;
I will protect those who know my
name.
15 When they call to me, I will answer
them;
I will be with them in trouble,
I will rescue them and honor them.
16 With long life I will satisfy them,
and show them my salvation.

91.1–16: With long life I will satisfy them. A psalm of trust, it seems to respond to the closing petitions of 90.13–17 (compare 90.14 and 91.16). **1–2:** *Trust* characterizes the whole, and *refuge* becomes thematic (see vv. 4, 9; 2.12; 5.11). **3–13:** An extended profession of faith articulates the reasons to *trust*. In the most threatening of circumstances—persecution (v. 3), disease (vv. 5–6), war (vv. 7–8)—God *will deliver* (v. 3). God's *angels* or "messengers" provide constant protection (Ex 23.20; Lk 4.9–12). **14–16:** Divine speech concludes the psalm in an emphatic manner, reinforcing the reasons to *trust* in vv. 3–13.

PSALM 92

A Psalm. A Song for the Sabbath Day.

1 It is good to give thanks to the LORD,
to sing praises to your name, O Most
High;
2 to declare your steadfast love in the
morning,
and your faithfulness by night,
3 to the music of the lute and the harp,
to the melody of the lyre.

a Traditional rendering of Heb *Shaddai*   b Cn: Heb
Because you, LORD, are my refuge; you have made

4 For you, O LORD, have made me glad
　　　by your work;
　　at the works of your hands I sing for
　　　joy.

5 How great are your works, O LORD!
　　Your thoughts are very deep!
6 The dullard cannot know,
　　the stupid cannot understand this:
7 though the wicked sprout like grass
　　and all evildoers flourish,
　　they are doomed to destruction forever,
8 　　but you, O LORD, are on high forever.
9 For your enemies, O LORD,
　　for your enemies shall perish;
　　all evildoers shall be scattered.

10 But you have exalted my horn like that
　　　of the wild ox;
　　you have poured over me[a] fresh oil.
11 My eyes have seen the downfall of my
　　　enemies;
　　my ears have heard the doom of my
　　　evil assailants.

12 The righteous flourish like the palm
　　　tree,
　　and grow like a cedar in Lebanon.
13 They are planted in the house of the
　　　LORD;
　　they flourish in the courts of our
　　　God.
14 In old age they still produce fruit;
　　they are always green and full of sap,
15 showing that the LORD is upright;
　　he is my rock, and there is no
　　　unrighteousness in him.

92.1–15: How great are your works, O LORD! A song of thanksgiving, it celebrates the experience of *the righteous* (v. 12) in general more than a particular deliverance. This orientation gives it an instructional tone. It is the only psalm assigned *for the Sabbath Day*, though the reason is unclear. **1–4:** Gratitude to God takes the form of constantly celebrating God's character—*steadfast love* and *faithfulness* (v. 2; Ex 34.6)—and God's *work* (v. 4), perhaps a reference to creation, which was also associated with *the sabbath* (Gen 2.1–3; Ex 20.8–11). **5–9:** Repeating *works* from v. 4, the celebration continues in v. 5. References to *the wicked* and God's *enemies* surround the central v. 8,

which asserts God's sovereignty, anticipating 93.4. **10–15:** *Evildoers* may *flourish* briefly (v. 7), but *the righteous* will *flourish* (vv. 12–13) permanently. Their stable rootedness in God's presence assures a vitality and fruitfulness that witnesses to God's righteousness (v. 15; 1.3; 52.8).

PSALM 93

1 The LORD is king, he is robed in
　　　majesty;
　　the LORD is robed, he is girded with
　　　strength.
　He has established the world; it shall
　　　never be moved;
2 　　your throne is established from
　　　　of old;
　　you are from everlasting.

3 The floods have lifted up, O LORD,
　　the floods have lifted up their voice;
　　the floods lift up their roaring.
4 More majestic than the thunders of
　　　mighty waters,
　　more majestic than the waves[b] of the
　　　sea,
　　majestic on high is the LORD!

5 Your decrees are very sure;
　　holiness befits your house,
　　O LORD, forevermore.

93.1–5: The LORD is king. It is the first in a collection (Ps 93, 95–99) which explicitly proclaims that God *is king*. In its present setting following Ps 89 and 90, the collection proclaims the LORD's kingship in response to the crisis of the disappearance of the Davidic monarchy. **1–2:** *Girded* usually suggests dress for battle, and creation (v. 1c) is often depicted as divine conquest of chaos. **3–4:** The floods represent the chaotic forces that the LORD has tamed and ordered, thus demonstrating sovereignty. **5:** Kings were responsible for establishing justice and righteousness (72.1–7; 97.2) by their *decrees*. God's *house* is apparently the Temple.* The enthronement collection returns to the theme of *holiness* as it concludes (99.3, 5, 9).

---

a Syr: Meaning of Heb uncertain　　*b* Cn: Heb *majestic are the waves*

PSALM 94

1 O LORD, you God of vengeance,
   you God of vengeance, shine forth!
2 Rise up, O judge of the earth;
   give to the proud what they deserve!
3 O LORD, how long shall the wicked,
   how long shall the wicked exult?

4 They pour out their arrogant words;
   all the evildoers boast.
5 They crush your people, O LORD,
   and afflict your heritage.
6 They kill the widow and the stranger,
   they murder the orphan,
7 and they say, "The LORD does not see;
   the God of Jacob does not perceive."

8 Understand, O dullest of the people;
   fools, when will you be wise?
9 He who planted the ear, does he not
   hear?
   He who formed the eye, does he
   not see?
10 He who disciplines the nations,
   he who teaches knowledge to
      humankind,
   does he not chastise?
11 The LORD knows our thoughts,[a]
   that they are but an empty breath.

12 Happy are those whom you discipline,
      O LORD,
   and whom you teach out of your law,
13 giving them respite from days of
      trouble,
   until a pit is dug for the wicked.
14 For the LORD will not forsake his
      people;
   he will not abandon his heritage;
15 for justice will return to the righteous,
   and all the upright in heart will follow
      it.

16 Who rises up for me against the
      wicked?
   Who stands up for me against
      evildoers?
17 If the LORD had not been my help,
   my soul would soon have lived in the
      land of silence.

18 When I thought, "My foot is slipping,"
   your steadfast love, O LORD, held me
      up.
19 When the cares of my heart are many,
   your consolations cheer my soul.
20 Can wicked rulers be allied with you,
   those who contrive mischief by
      statute?
21 They band together against the life of
      the righteous,
   and condemn the innocent to death.
22 But the LORD has become my
      stronghold,
   and my God the rock of my refuge.
23 He will repay them for their iniquity
   and wipe them out for their
      wickedness;
   the LORD our God will wipe
      them out.

94.1–23: Your steadfast love, O LORD, held me up.
Starting like a communal prayer for help, it takes on an instructional tone as it addresses *fools* (vv. 8–11) and *the righteous* (vv. 14–15). A final prayer (vv. 18–21) is framed by two professions of faith (vv. 16–17, 22–23). Although it seems to interrupt the enthronement collection, its theme of *justice* (v. 15; see v. 2) is congruent with Ps 93, 95–99. **1–7:** *Vengeance* serves the function of establishing *justice*. To create *justice* for the *widow, stranger,* and *orphan* (v. 6), God must confront oppressors, who view themselves as unaccountable (v. 7; 10.4, 11; 73.11). **8–11:** The questions in vv. 8–9 respond to the evildoers' assertion in v. 7. God does *see* (v. 9; 10.14) and God *knows* (v. 11). **12–15:** Verse 12 recalls 1.1–2. Despite current appearances, *justice* will prevail. **16–17:** The psalmist answers her or his own questions. Without God's *help*, she or he would be dead. **18–21:** God's *steadfast love* (90.14; 92.2) and *consolations* (vv. 18–19) contrast with the ruthlessness of the *wicked* (vv. 20–21; see vv. 5–7). **22–23:** While v. 12 recalls Ps 1, *refuge* recalls 2.12. Entrusting life to God yields hope.

PSALM 95

1 O come, let us sing to the LORD;
   let us make a joyful noise to the rock
      of our salvation!

a Heb *the thoughts of humankind*

2 Let us come into his presence with
    thanksgiving;
    let us make a joyful noise to him with
      songs of praise!
3 For the LORD is a great God,
    and a great King above all gods.
4 In his hand are the depths of the earth;
    the heights of the mountains are his
      also.
5 The sea is his, for he made it,
    and the dry land, which his hands
      have formed.

6 O come, let us worship and bow down,
    let us kneel before the LORD,
      our Maker!
7 For he is our God,
    and we are the people of his pasture,
    and the sheep of his hand.

  O that today you would listen to his
    voice!
8   Do not harden your hearts, as at
      Meribah,
    as on the day at Massah in the
      wilderness,
9 when your ancestors tested me,
    and put me to the proof, though they
      had seen my work.
10 For forty years I loathed that generation
    and said, "They are a people whose
      hearts go astray,
    and they do not regard my ways."
11 Therefore in my anger I swore,
    "They shall not enter my rest."

95.1–11: O that you would listen! Part of the enthronement collection (see Ps 93), its unique ending
with divine speech reflects a prophetic* exhortation*
(see Ps 81). **1–5:** The invitations to *praise* are appropriate for hailing a sovereign, anticipating the title *King*
in v. 3. *Thanksgiving* could designate the offering of a
sacrifice or verbal gratitude (50.23; 100.4). The repetition of *hands* (vv. 4–5) symbolizes God's encompassing ownership of the cosmos. **6–7b:** Further invitations and reasons for praise feature God's ownership
of *the people* (100.3). *Maker* recalls both creation
(104.24) and exodus (see 118.24 where "made"
would be better translated as "acted" and alludes to
the Exodus). **7c:** This line culminates vv. 1–7b and introduces the following divine speech. **8–11:** Recalling

events *in the wilderness* following the Exodus (Ex
17.1–7), the speech calls current hearers (see *today* in
v. 7c) to trust rather than test God.

PSALM 96

1 O sing to the LORD a new song;
    sing to the LORD, all the earth.
2 Sing to the LORD, bless his name;
    tell of his salvation from day to day.
3 Declare his glory among the nations,
    his marvelous works among all the
      peoples.
4 For great is the LORD, and greatly to be
      praised;
    he is to be revered above all gods.
5 For all the gods of the peoples are idols,
    but the LORD made the heavens.
6 Honor and majesty are before him;
    strength and beauty are in his
      sanctuary.

7 Ascribe to the LORD, O families of the
      peoples,
    ascribe to the LORD glory and
      strength.
8 Ascribe to the LORD the glory due his
      name;
    bring an offering, and come into his
      courts.
9 Worship the LORD in holy splendor;
    tremble before him, all the earth.

10 Say among the nations, "The LORD is
      king!
    The world is firmly established; it
      shall never be moved.
    He will judge the peoples with
      equity."
11 Let the heavens be glad, and let the
      earth rejoice;
    let the sea roar, and all that fills it;
12   let the field exult, and everything in
      it.
    Then shall all the trees of the forest
      sing for joy
13   before the LORD; for he is coming,
    for he is coming to judge the earth.
    He will judge the world with
      righteousness,
    and the peoples with his truth.

he rescues them from the hand of the
  wicked.
11 Light dawns^c for the righteous,
  and joy for the upright in heart.
12 Rejoice in the LORD, O you righteous,
  and give thanks to his holy name!

96.1–13: A new song. An enthronement psalm (see Ps 93), its use in Temple* worship is attested in 1 Chr 16.22–33. **1–3:** The *new song* (v. 1; 98.1) recalls the former song, which the people sang in response to the Exodus (Ex 15.1–21). Psalm 96 may have arisen or been used to respond to the return from exile (see Isa 42.10), as well as to anticipate future acts of deliverance (v. 13). **4–6:** Among all supposed authorities— *the gods—the* LORD is preeminent (97.9). **7–10a:** Verses 7–9 reproduce 29.1–2, except here they are addressed to *families of the peoples.* Verse 10a invites the explicit proclamation of God's reign. **10b–c:** The creator (93.1) will also *judge,* or better, "establish justice" (see v. 13). **11–12a:** All the cosmic elements are invited to acknowledge God's reign (98.4, 7–8). **12b–13:** The hallmarks of God's royal policy are justice and *righteousness* (97.1; 98.9; 99.4).

PSALM 97

1 The LORD is king! Let the earth rejoice;
  let the many coastlands be glad!
2 Clouds and thick darkness are all
    around him;
  righteousness and justice are the
    foundation of his throne.
3 Fire goes before him,
  and consumes his adversaries on
    every side.
4 His lightnings light up the world;
  the earth sees and trembles.
5 The mountains melt like wax before the
    LORD,
  before the Lord of all the earth.

6 The heavens proclaim his righteousness;
  and all the peoples behold his glory.
7 All worshipers of images are put
    to shame,
  those who make their boast in
    worthless idols;
  all gods bow down before him.
8 Zion hears and is glad,
  and the towns^a of Judah rejoice,
  because of your judgments, O God.
9 For you, O LORD, are most high over all
    the earth;
  you are exalted far above all gods.

10 The LORD loves those who hate^b evil;
  he guards the lives of his faithful;

97.1–12: Righteousness and justice are the foundations of God's throne. Similar in many ways to the other enthronement psalms (see Ps 93), it is also distinctive, featuring the themes of *joy*/gladness (vv. 1, 8, 11–12) and *righteousness* (vv. 2, 6; see vv. 11–12). **1–5:** The language of theophany,* a description of God's appearing in the natural order (18.7–15; 50.1–6), communicates God's cosmic claim, which is characterized by *righteousness and justice* (89.14; 96.13). **6–9:** Although not all people acknowledge God's sovereignty (v. 7), *the heavens* do and so do *Zion** and *Judah* (v. 8). No other claim can rival God's (v. 9; 96.4–5). **10–12:** Verse 10a should probably be understood as an admonition to God's people (see note b) to *hate evil.* The admonition is followed by promises to the *faithful* (vv. 10b–11) that are in accordance with God's *justice* (see vv. 2, 8). The appropriate response is joy and gratitude (v. 12).

PSALM 98
A Psalm.

1 O sing to the LORD a new song,
  for he has done marvelous things.
  His right hand and his holy arm
    have gotten him victory.
2 The LORD has made known his victory;
  he has revealed his vindication in the
    sight of the nations.
3 He has remembered his steadfast love
    and faithfulness
  to the house of Israel.
  All the ends of the earth have seen
    the victory of our God.

4 Make a joyful noise to the LORD, all the
    earth;
  break forth into joyous song and sing
    praises.
5 Sing praises to the LORD with the lyre,
  with the lyre and the sound of melody.

---

a Heb *daughters*   b Cn: Heb *You who love the* LORD *hate*   c Gk Syr Jerome: Heb *is sown*

6 With trumpets and the sound of the
    horn
      make a joyful noise before the King,
      the LORD.

7 Let the sea roar, and all that fills it;
      the world and those who live in it.
8 Let the floods clap their hands;
      let the hills sing together for joy
9 at the presence of the LORD, for he is
      coming
    to judge the earth.
  He will judge the world with
      righteousness,
      and the peoples with equity.

98.1–9: Make a joyful noise before the King. Part of the enthronement collection (see Ps 93), it recalls especially Ps 96 (compare 96.1 and 98.1). **1–3:** Each of these verses speaks of *victory*, usually translated "salvation." The word recalls the former song, which the people sang after the Exodus (see *salvation* in Ex 15.2). God's gift of life to the people reveals God's *steadfast love and faithfulness* (Ex 34.6; Ps 89.14; 92.2). **4–6:** *Make a joyful noise* frames the invitation to *all the earth* (100.1) to acknowledge God as *King.* **7–9:** People are to be joined by the created order in acknowledging God's reign (96.11–12), which is characterized by justice, *righteousness*, and *equity* (96.10, 13; 97.2).

PSALM 99

1 The LORD is king; let the peoples
      tremble!
  He sits enthroned upon the
      cherubim; let the earth quake!
2 The LORD is great in Zion;
      he is exalted over all the peoples.
3 Let them praise your great and
      awesome name.
  Holy is he!
4 Mighty King,[a] lover of justice,
      you have established equity;
  you have executed justice
    and righteousness in Jacob.
5 Extol the LORD our God;
      worship at his footstool.
  Holy is he!

6 Moses and Aaron were among his
    priests,

Samuel also was among those who
    called on his name.
  They cried to the LORD, and he
      answered them.
7 He spoke to them in the pillar of cloud;
      they kept his decrees,
    and the statutes that he gave them.

8 O LORD our God, you answered them;
      you were a forgiving God to them,
    but an avenger of their wrongdoings.
9 Extol the LORD our God,
      and worship at his holy mountain;
    for the LORD our God is holy.

99.1–9: Holy is the LORD. Culminating the collection of enthronement psalms (see Ps 93), it highlights one of the themes of the collection—holiness (vv. 3, 5, 9; 93.5; 96.9; 97.12; 98.1). **1–3:** Trembling and quaking are consistent with the fundamental sense of holiness, which connotes an overwhelming presence that evokes awe and necessitates separation between God and humans (Ex 19.23). *The cherubim** were mythical creatures who attended the ark (see v. 5). **4–5:** These verses make it clear that the *holy* God does not simply distance the divine self from humanity. God deserves *worship*, because God wills and works for *justice and righteousness* among the people (96.13; 97.2; 98.9). God's *footstool* was the ark, where the heavenly God sat *enthroned* (v. 1) in an earthly location, the Temple,* on God's *holy mountain* (v. 9). **6–9:** Although v. 7 reports that the people obeyed, *Moses, Aaron*, and *Samuel* frequently interceded when the people disobeyed. God proved to be both *forgiving* and *an avenger of their wrongdoings*, a tension reflected also in God's revelation to *Moses* in Ex 34.6–7.

PSALM 100

A Psalm of thanksgiving.

1 Make a joyful noise to the LORD, all the
      earth.
2   Worship the LORD with gladness;
      come into his presence with singing.

3 Know that the LORD is God.
    It is he that made us, and we are his;[b]
  we are his people, and the sheep of
      his pasture.

a Cn: Heb *And a king's strength*   b Another reading is *and not we ourselves*

4 Enter his gates with thanksgiving,
     and his courts with praise.
     Give thanks to him, bless his name.

5 For the LORD is good;
     his steadfast love endures forever,
     and his faithfulness to all generations.

100.1–5: Worship the LORD with gladness. A song of praise, it forms a fitting epilogue to the enthronement psalms (Ps 93, 95–99), recalling especially Ps 95 (compare vv. 1–2, 4 with 95.1–2; v. 3 with 95.7). **1–2:** Three invitations to praise call for a recognition of God's sovereignty. This is especially so of *worship*, which could also be translated "serve" (see 2.11, the only other such invitation). **3–4:** Three more imperative verbs in v. 4 invite grateful praise, and the pattern highlights the central imperative in v. 3, *know*, which is followed by a profession of faith. The people's role as *sheep* suggests that God is the shepherd, a royal title (80.1). **5:** The reasons for praise focus on God's fundamental character—*steadfast love* and *faithfulness*—thus recalling Ex 34.6–7, as does Ps 99 (see 98.3).

PSALM 101
Of David. A Psalm.

1 I will sing of loyalty and of justice;
     to you, O LORD, I will sing.
2 I will study the way that is blameless.
     When shall I attain it?

  I will walk with integrity of heart
     within my house;
3 I will not set before my eyes
     anything that is base.

  I hate the work of those who fall away;
     it shall not cling to me.
4 Perverseness of heart shall be far from
     me;
     I will know nothing of evil.

5 One who secretly slanders a neighbor
     I will destroy.
  A haughty look and an arrogant heart
     I will not tolerate.

6 I will look with favor on the faithful in
     the land,
     so that they may live with me;

whoever walks in the way that is
     blameless
     shall minister to me.

7 No one who practices deceit
     shall remain in my house;
  no one who utters lies
     shall continue in my presence.

8 Morning by morning I will destroy
     all the wicked in the land,
  cutting off all evildoers
     from the city of the LORD.

101.1–8: I will walk with integrity. Often classified as a royal psalm, it perhaps originally functioned as a king's oath of office. After the disappearance of the monarchy (see Ps 89), it may have functioned as an implicit plea for restoration and as a description of the *integrity* which everyone should embody. **1–2a:** *Loyalty* represents the word usually translated "steadfast love." The preceding psalms have suggested that it and *justice* characterize God's reign (98.3, 9). *Blameless* and *integrity* (v. 2b) represent the same Hebrew word (see v. 6). God's ways are *blameless;* and as he was supposed to do, the king vows to embody God's character (18.20–25; 72.1–7). **2b–5:** The word *heart* frames this section. *Integrity* will involve the avoidance of all deceit and arrogance. The list recalls 15.3–5 (see "blamelessly" in 15.2). **6–8:** Repeating several words from vv. 2b–5, the king vows to keep and support good company. The *cutting off* of *evildoers* is usually God's prerogative (54.5; 94.23), but the king was viewed as the embodiment of God's reign (18.40; 72.4, 9).

PSALM 102
A prayer of one afflicted, when faint and pleading before the LORD.

1 Hear my prayer, O LORD;
     let my cry come to you.
2 Do not hide your face from me
     in the day of my distress.
  Incline your ear to me;
     answer me speedily in the day when I
     call.

3 For my days pass away like smoke,
     and my bones burn like a furnace.

4 My heart is stricken and withered like
grass;
   I am too wasted to eat my bread.
5 Because of my loud groaning
   my bones cling to my skin.
6 I am like an owl of the wilderness,
   like a little owl of the waste places.
7 I lie awake;
   I am like a lonely bird on the
     housetop.
8 All day long my enemies taunt me;
   those who deride me use my name for
     a curse.
9 For I eat ashes like bread,
   and mingle tears with my drink,
10 because of your indignation and anger;
   for you have lifted me up and thrown
     me aside.
11 My days are like an evening shadow;
   I wither away like grass.

12 But you, O LORD, are enthroned
     forever;
   your name endures to all generations.
13 You will rise up and have compassion
     on Zion,
   for it is time to favor it;
   the appointed time has come.
14 For your servants hold its stones dear,
   and have pity on its dust.
15 The nations will fear the name of the
     LORD,
   and all the kings of the earth your
     glory.
16 For the LORD will build up Zion;
   he will appear in his glory.
17 He will regard the prayer of the
     destitute,
   and will not despise their prayer.

18 Let this be recorded for a generation to
     come,
   so that a people yet unborn may
     praise the LORD:
19 that he looked down from his holy
     height,
   from heaven the LORD looked at the
     earth,
20 to hear the groans of the prisoners,
   to set free those who were doomed to
     die;

21 so that the name of the LORD may be
     declared in Zion,
   and his praise in Jerusalem,
22 when peoples gather together,
   and kingdoms, to worship the LORD.

23 He has broken my strength in
     midcourse;
   he has shortened my days.
24 "O my God," I say, "do not take
     me away
   at the midpoint of my life,
you whose years endure
   throughout all generations."

25 Long ago you laid the foundation of the
     earth,
   and the heavens are the work of your
     hands.
26 They will perish, but you endure;
   they will all wear out like a garment.
You change them like clothing, and they
     pass away;
27 but you are the same, and your years
     have no end.
28 The children of your servants shall live
     secure;
   their offspring shall be established in
     your presence.

102.1–28: Established in your presence. As the superscription suggests, it is an individual prayer for help, at least in part (vv. 1–11, 23–24). Other verses consist of affirmations of God's sovereignty and divine help for *Zion** and God's people (vv. 12–17, 25–28), as well as an expression of gratitude (or perhaps hope) for the return of the exiles (vv. 18–22). It became one of the church's Penitential Psalms* (Ps 6). **1–11:** Petitions (vv. 1–2) are followed by complaint, which is framed by references to *my days* (vv. 3, 11) and *like grass* (vv. 4, 11). The language and imagery suggest physical illness, but they can be understood metaphorically.* **12–22:** The shift of focus to God, *Zion*, and the return of people to *Zion* suggests that vv. 3–11, 23–24 were indeed heard as a metaphorical description of the distress of exile. **23–28:** Individual complaint recurs (vv. 23–24a) before another shift of focus to God (vv. 24b–28). The eternal God will secure the future of God's people, an assurance applicable to both individuals and the whole people (90.13–17).

PSALM 103

Of David.

1 Bless the LORD, O my soul,
    and all that is within me,
    bless his holy name.
2 Bless the LORD, O my soul,
    and do not forget all his benefits—
3 who forgives all your iniquity,
    who heals all your diseases,
4 who redeems your life from the Pit,
    who crowns you with steadfast love
        and mercy,
5 who satisfies you with good as long as
        you live[a]
    so that your youth is renewed like the
        eagle's.

6 The LORD works vindication
    and justice for all who are oppressed.
7 He made known his ways to Moses,
    his acts to the people of Israel.
8 The LORD is merciful and gracious,
    slow to anger and abounding in
        steadfast love.
9 He will not always accuse,
    nor will he keep his anger forever.
10 He does not deal with us according to
        our sins,
    nor repay us according to our
        iniquities.
11 For as the heavens are high above the
        earth,
    so great is his steadfast love toward
        those who fear him;
12 as far as the east is from the west,
    so far he removes our transgressions
        from us.
13 As a father has compassion for his
        children,
    so the LORD has compassion for
        those who fear him.
14 For he knows how we were made;
    he remembers that we are dust.

15 As for mortals, their days are like grass;
    they flourish like a flower of the
        field;
16 for the wind passes over it, and it is
        gone,
    and its place knows it no more.

17 But the steadfast love of the LORD is
        from everlasting to everlasting
    on those who fear him,
    and his righteousness to children's
        children,
18 to those who keep his covenant
    and remember to do his
        commandments.

19 The LORD has established his throne in
        the heavens,
    and his kingdom rules over all.
20 Bless the LORD, O you his angels,
    you mighty ones who do his bidding,
    obedient to his spoken word.
21 Bless the LORD, all his hosts,
    his ministers that do his will.
22 Bless the LORD, all his works,
    in all places of his dominion.
    Bless the LORD, O my soul.

103.1–22: Bless the LORD. A song of praise, it celebrates God's *benefits* (v. 2) in a comprehensive way as signaled by the repetition of *all* (vv. 1–3, 6, 19, 21–22). **1–2:** The invitation to praise is addressed to the psalmist's own self (v. 1; v. 22; 104.1, 35). *Bless* originally meant "to kneel," so the invitation calls for the recognition of God's sovereignty. **3–6:** The reasons for praise are also comprehensive. God does whatever is needed to enhance life. *Steadfast love* (v. 4) recurs in vv. 8, 11, 17; and the Hebrew translated *mercy* recurs in vv. 8 (*merciful*) and 13 (*compassion*). *Vindication* usually appears as "righteousness"; it and *justice* summarize God's will for humankind (97.2; 98.9). **7–18:** To illustrate God's *justice*, the psalmist recalls the Exodus (v. 7) and the golden calf episode, which concludes with divine forgiveness and God's self-revelation to Moses (see Ex 34.6, which v. 8 quotes). Verses 13, 17, 18 seem to make God's *mercy* depend on *fear* and obedience, a tension also reflected in Ex 34.6–7. **19–22:** Because God *rules over all*, all cosmic beings and features are invited to yield themselves to God's claim.

PSALM 104

1 Bless the LORD, O my soul.
    O LORD my God, you are very great.
    You are clothed with honor and majesty,

---

a Meaning of Heb uncertain

2   wrapped in light as with a garment.
    You stretch out the heavens like a tent,
3   you set the beams of your[a] chambers
        on the waters,
  you make the clouds your[a] chariot,
    you ride on the wings of the wind,
4   you make the winds your[a] messengers,
    fire and flame your[a] ministers.

5 You set the earth on its foundations,
    so that it shall never be shaken.
6 You cover it with the deep as with a
      garment;
    the waters stood above the
      mountains.
7 At your rebuke they flee;
    at the sound of your thunder they
      take to flight.
8 They rose up to the mountains, ran
      down to the valleys
    to the place that you appointed for
      them.
9 You set a boundary that they may not
      pass,
    so that they might not again cover the
      earth.

10 You make springs gush forth in the
      valleys;
    they flow between the hills,
11 giving drink to every wild animal;
    the wild asses quench their thirst.
12 By the streams[b] the birds of the air
      have their habitation;
    they sing among the branches.
13 From your lofty abode you water the
      mountains;
    the earth is satisfied with the fruit of
      your work.

104.1–35: O Lord, how manifold are your works! A song of praise linked to Ps 103 by *Bless the Lord, O my soul*, it seems to a be poetic elaboration of 103.22, *Bless the Lord, all his works* (see *work[s]* in vv. 13, 24, 31 as well as the verbal form *make[s]* or *made* in vv. 4, 9, 24). **1–4:** The attributes of sovereignty belong to *the Lord* (vv. 1–2a), who has built the cosmos *on the waters*, which represent mythic forces of chaos and disorder (74.12–15). In the Canaanite view, Baal* rode *the clouds*, a role now taken by *the Lord*. **5–13:** The focus is on *the earth* (vv. 5, 9, 13), which exists as

a result of God's controlling *the waters* (vv. 6–9; Job 38.8–11). *The waters* now serve to sustain God's creatures (vv. 10–13).

~~~~~~~~~~~~~~~~~~~~

14 You cause the grass to grow for the
      cattle,
    and plants for people to use,[c]
  to bring forth food from the earth,
15   and wine to gladden the human
      heart,
  oil to make the face shine,
    and bread to strengthen the human
      heart.
16 The trees of the Lord are watered
      abundantly,
    the cedars of Lebanon that he
      planted.
17 In them the birds build their nests;
    the stork has its home in the fir trees.
18 The high mountains are for the wild
      goats;
    the rocks are a refuge for the coneys.
19 You have made the moon to mark the
      seasons;
    the sun knows its time for setting.
20 You make darkness, and it is night,
    when all the animals of the forest
      come creeping out.
21 The young lions roar for their prey,
    seeking their food from God.
22 When the sun rises, they withdraw
    and lie down in their dens.
23 People go out to their work
    and to their labor until the evening.

24 O Lord, how manifold are your works!
    In wisdom you have made them all;
    the earth is full of your creatures.
25 Yonder is the sea, great and wide,
    creeping things innumerable are
      there,
  living things both small and great.
26 There go the ships,
    and Leviathan that you formed
      to sport in it.

27 These all look to you
    to give them their food in due season;

a Heb *his*   b Heb *By them*   c Or *to cultivate*

28 when you give to them, they gather it
　　　up;
　　when you open your hand, they are
　　　filled with good things.
29 When you hide your face, they are
　　　dismayed;
　　when you take away their breath, they
　　　die
　　and return to their dust.
30 When you send forth your spirit,*a* they
　　　are created;
　　and you renew the face of the
　　　ground.

31 May the glory of the LORD endure
　　　forever;
　　may the LORD rejoice in his
　　　works—
32 who looks on the earth and it trembles,
　　who touches the mountains and they
　　　smoke.
33 I will sing to the LORD as long as I live;
　　I will sing praise to my God while I
　　　have being.
34 May my meditation be pleasing to him,
　　for I rejoice in the LORD.
35 Let sinners be consumed from the
　　　earth,
　　and let the wicked be no more.
　　Bless the LORD, O my soul.
　　Praise the LORD!

104.14–35. 14–23: This section is bounded by references to *people* (vv. 14, 23), for whom God also provides, along with *trees, birds,* and other *animals.*
24–27: Indeed, all *creatures* and other elements in the
created order belong to God and reveal God's *wisdom*
(Prov 3.19; 8.22–31; Jer 10.12). *Sea* creatures, especially *Leviathan** (Job 41.1–11; Ps 74.14), were associated with chaos; but they too are subject to God.
28–30: *Breath* (v. 29) and *spirit* (v. 30) represent the
Hebrew word "ruach," recalling Gen 1.2 and suggesting that creation is ongoing. 31–35: After wishing
for the eternity of God's reign (v. 31) and acknowledging God's power in the language of theophany*
(v. 32; 97.2–5), the psalmist pledges his or her loyalty
(v. 33). *My meditation* (v. 34) probably refers to the
preceding verses. Requesting the disappearance of *the
wicked* is another way of acknowledging God's
sovereignty.

PSALM 105

1 O give thanks to the LORD, call on his
　　　name,
　　make known his deeds among the
　　　peoples.
2 Sing to him, sing praises to him;
　　tell of all his wonderful works.
3 Glory in his holy name;
　　let the hearts of those who seek the
　　　LORD rejoice.
4 Seek the LORD and his strength;
　　seek his presence continually.
5 Remember the wonderful works he has
　　　done,
　　his miracles, and the judgments he
　　　has uttered,
6 O offspring of his servant Abraham,*b*
　　children of Jacob, his chosen ones.

7 He is the LORD our God;
　　his judgments are in all the earth.
8 He is mindful of his covenant forever,
　　of the word that he commanded, for a
　　　thousand generations,
9 the covenant that he made with
　　　Abraham,
　　his sworn promise to Isaac,
10 which he confirmed to Jacob as a
　　　statute,
　　to Israel as an everlasting covenant,
11 saying, "To you I will give the land of
　　　Canaan
　　as your portion for an inheritance."

12 When they were few in number,
　　of little account, and strangers in it,
13 wandering from nation to nation,
　　from one kingdom to another people,
14 he allowed no one to oppress them;
　　he rebuked kings on their account,
15 saying, "Do not touch my anointed
　　　ones;
　　do my prophets no harm."

16 When he summoned famine against the
　　　land,
　　and broke every staff of bread,

---

a Or *your breath*　　*b* Another reading is *Israel* (compare
1 Chr 16.13)

17 he had sent a man ahead of them,
 Joseph, who was sold as a slave.
18 His feet were hurt with fetters,
 his neck was put in a collar of iron;
19 until what he had said came to pass,
 the word of the LORD kept testing
 him.
20 The king sent and released him;
 the ruler of the peoples set him free.
21 He made him lord of his house,
 and ruler of all his possessions,
22 to instruct*a* his officials at his pleasure,
 and to teach his elders wisdom.

23 Then Israel came to Egypt;
 Jacob lived as an alien in the land of
 Ham.
24 And the LORD made his people very
 fruitful,
 and made them stronger than their
 foes,
25 whose hearts he then turned to hate his
 people,
 to deal craftily with his servants.

105.1–45: Tell of all God's wonderful works. Often
classified as a historical psalm (see Ps 78, 106), its recital of God's saving acts is offered in the form of a
song of praise. **1–6:** Invitations to grateful praise and
remembrance focus on what God *has done*, which will
be recounted in the rest of the psalm. **7–11:** The *covenant,** a word that occurs in each of vv. 8–10, is
traced back to *Abraham* and his descendants (Gen
12.1–3; 15.1–19; 17.1–14). **12–25:** This section features the *wandering* (v. 13) of the matriarchs and pa-
triarchs, which left the people in *Egypt* (v. 23). That
the people are designated *anointed** ones, a royal
term, may suggest a post-exilic origin (see Ps 149).

26 He sent his servant Moses,
 and Aaron whom he had chosen.
27 They performed his signs among
 them,
 and miracles in the land of Ham.
28 He sent darkness, and made the land
 dark;
 they rebelled*b* against his words.
29 He turned their waters into blood,
 and caused their fish to die.
30 Their land swarmed with frogs,
 even in the chambers of their kings.

31 He spoke, and there came swarms of
 flies,
 and gnats throughout their country.
32 He gave them hail for rain,
 and lightning that flashed through
 their land.
33 He struck their vines and fig trees,
 and shattered the trees of their
 country.
34 He spoke, and the locusts came,
 and young locusts without number;
35 they devoured all the vegetation in their
 land,
 and ate up the fruit of their ground.
36 He struck down all the firstborn in their
 land,
 the first issue of all their strength.

37 Then he brought Israel*c* out with silver
 and gold,
 and there was no one among their
 tribes who stumbled.
38 Egypt was glad when they departed,
 for dread of them had fallen upon it.
39 He spread a cloud for a covering,
 and fire to give light by night.
40 They asked, and he brought quails,
 and gave them food from heaven in
 abundance.
41 He opened the rock, and water gushed
 out;
 it flowed through the desert like a
 river.
42 For he remembered his holy promise,
 and Abraham, his servant.

43 So he brought his people out with joy,
 his chosen ones with singing.
44 He gave them the lands of the nations,
 and they took possession of the
 wealth of the peoples,
45 that they might keep his statutes
 and observe his laws.
 Praise the LORD!

105.26–45. 26–38: The rehearsal of the Exodus features the plagues (Ex 7.14–12.32). **39–44:** The story
continues with God's provision for the people in the

---

a Gk Syr Jerome: Heb *to bind* *b* Cn Compare Gk Syr:
Heb *they did not rebel* *c* Heb *them*

wilderness and the possession of the land. *Chosen* recurs for the third time (vv. 6, 26, 43). **45:** The final invitation to praise recalls vv. 1–6, and it points forward to Ps 106, which will highlight the people's failure to *observe* God's *laws.*

PSALM 106

1 Praise the LORD!
   O give thanks to the LORD, for he is
      good;
   for his steadfast love endures forever.
2 Who can utter the mighty doings of the
      LORD,
   or declare all his praise?
3 Happy are those who observe justice,
   who do righteousness at all times.

4 Remember me, O LORD, when you
      show favor to your people;
   help me when you deliver them;
5 that I may see the prosperity of your
      chosen ones,
   that I may rejoice in the gladness of
      your nation,
   that I may glory in your heritage.

6 Both we and our ancestors have sinned;
   we have committed iniquity, have
      done wickedly.
7 Our ancestors, when they were in
      Egypt,
   did not consider your wonderful
      works;
   they did not remember the abundance
      of your steadfast love,
   but rebelled against the Most High*a*
      at the Red Sea.*b*
8 Yet he saved them for his name's sake,
   so that he might make known his
      mighty power.
9 He rebuked the Red Sea,*b* and it
      became dry;
   he led them through the deep as
      through a desert.
10 So he saved them from the hand of the
      foe,
   and delivered them from the hand of
      the enemy.
11 The waters covered their adversaries;
   not one of them was left.

12 Then they believed his words;
   they sang his praise.

13 But they soon forgot his works;
   they did not wait for his counsel.
14 But they had a wanton craving in the
      wilderness,
   and put God to the test in the desert;
15 he gave them what they asked,
   but sent a wasting disease among
      them.

16 They were jealous of Moses in
      the camp,
   and of Aaron, the holy one of
      the LORD.
17 The earth opened and swallowed
      up Dathan,
   and covered the faction of Abiram.
18 Fire also broke out in their company;
   the flame burned up the wicked.

19 They made a calf at Horeb
   and worshiped a cast image.
20 They exchanged the glory of God*c*
   for the image of an ox that eats grass.
21 They forgot God, their Savior,
   who had done great things in Egypt,
22 wondrous works in the land of Ham,
   and awesome deeds by the Red Sea.*b*
23 Therefore he said he would destroy
      them—
   had not Moses, his chosen one,
   stood in the breach before him,
   to turn away his wrath from
      destroying them.

106.1–48: Save us, O LORD. Another historical psalm, it covers the same territory as Ps 105; but it tells the story not from the perspective of God's deeds but rather of the people's misdeeds. **1–5:** *Steadfast love* (v. 1) will be the people's only hope (v. 45), even though they regularly forget it (v. 7). The petition in vv. 4–5 anticipates v. 47. **6–12:** Verse 6 summarizes the content of the psalm, introducing the initial focus on the Exodus (Ex 14–15). **13–15:** As v. 13 suggests, the Song of the Sea (Ex 15.1–21) is followed immediately by

---

a Cn Compare 78.17, 56: Heb *rebelled at the sea*
b Or *Sea of Reeds*   *c* Compare Gk Mss: Heb *exchanged their glory*

the people's complaining (Ex 15.24), which persisted throughout the wilderness era (Ex 17.1–7; Num 11.4–34). **16–18:** The episode occurs in Num 16.1–35. **19–23:** The golden calf incident is in view (Ex 32.1–14).

24 Then they despised the pleasant land,
   having no faith in his promise.
25 They grumbled in their tents,
   and did not obey the voice of
   the LORD.
26 Therefore he raised his hand and swore
   to them
   that he would make them fall in the
   wilderness,
27 and would disperse*a* their descendants
   among the nations,
   scattering them over the lands.

28 Then they attached themselves to the
   Baal of Peor,
   and ate sacrifices offered to the dead;
29 they provoked the LORD to anger with
   their deeds,
   and a plague broke out among them.
30 Then Phinehas stood up and interceded,
   and the plague was stopped.
31 And that has been reckoned to him as
   righteousness
   from generation to generation forever.

32 They angered the LORD *b* at the waters
   of Meribah,
   and it went ill with Moses on their
   account;
33 for they made his spirit bitter,
   and he spoke words that were rash.

34 They did not destroy the peoples,
   as the LORD commanded them,
35 but they mingled with the nations
   and learned to do as they did.
36 They served their idols,
   which became a snare to them.
37 They sacrificed their sons
   and their daughters to the demons;
38 they poured out innocent blood,
   the blood of their sons and daughters,
   whom they sacrificed to the idols of
   Canaan;
   and the land was polluted with blood.

39 Thus they became unclean by their acts,
   and prostituted themselves in their
   doings.
40 Then the anger of the LORD was
   kindled against his people,
   and he abhorred his heritage;
41 he gave them into the hand of the
   nations,
   so that those who hated them ruled
   over them.
42 Their enemies oppressed them,
   and they were brought into subjection
   under their power.
43 Many times he delivered them,
   but they were rebellious in their
   purposes,
   and were brought low through their
   iniquity.
44 Nevertheless he regarded their distress
   when he heard their cry.
45 For their sake he remembered his
   covenant,
   and showed compassion according to
   the abundance of his steadfast
   love.
46 He caused them to be pitied
   by all who held them captive.

47 Save us, O LORD our God,
   and gather us from among the
   nations,
   that we may give thanks to your holy
   name
   and glory in your praise.

48 Blessed be the LORD, the God of Israel,
   from everlasting to everlasting.
   And let all the people say, "Amen."
   Praise the LORD!

106.24–48. 24–27: The people's failure to trust the spies sent into Canaan is reviewed (Num 14.1–25). **28–31:** See Num 25.1–13. **32–33:** See Ex 17.1–7. **34–39:** Faithlessness and disobedience continued after entry into the land. **40–47:** The pattern described in vv. 40–46 recalls the book of Judges, but might also apply to Israel's whole history, including the Exile* and

a Syr Compare Ezek 20.23: Heb *cause to fall*
b Heb *him*

dispersion, which is in view in v. 47. Verse 47 reinforces the conclusion that Book IV offers a response
to the Exile (see Introduction; Ps 90). **48:** This doxology concludes Book IV.

~~~~~~~~~~~~~~~~~~

BOOK FIVE

PSALM 107

1 O give thanks to the LORD, for he is
 good;
  for his steadfast love endures forever.
2 Let the redeemed of the LORD say so,
  those he redeemed from trouble
3 and gathered in from the lands,
  from the east and from the west,
  from the north and from the south.*a*

4 Some wandered in desert wastes,
  finding no way to an inhabited town;
5 hungry and thirsty,
  their soul fainted within them.
6 Then they cried to the LORD in their
 trouble,
  and he delivered them from their
 distress;
7 he led them by a straight way,
  until they reached an inhabited town.
8 Let them thank the LORD for his
 steadfast love,
  for his wonderful works to
 humankind.
9 For he satisfies the thirsty,
  and the hungry he fills with good
 things.

10 Some sat in darkness and in gloom,
  prisoners in misery and in irons,
11 for they had rebelled against the words
 of God,
  and spurned the counsel of the Most
 High.
12 Their hearts were bowed down with
 hard labor;
  they fell down, with no one to help.
13 Then they cried to the LORD in their
 trouble,
  and he saved them from their distress;
14 he brought them out of darkness and
 gloom,
  and broke their bonds asunder.

15 Let them thank the LORD for his
 steadfast love,
  for his wonderful works to
 humankind.
16 For he shatters the doors of bronze,
  and cuts in two the bars of iron.

17 Some were sick*b* through their sinful
 ways,
  and because of their iniquities
 endured affliction;
18 they loathed any kind of food,
  and they drew near to the gates of
 death.
19 Then they cried to the LORD in their
 trouble,
  and he saved them from their
 distress;
20 he sent out his word and healed them,
  and delivered them from destruction.
21 Let them thank the LORD for his
 steadfast love,
  for his wonderful works to
 humankind.
22 And let them offer thanksgiving
 sacrifices,
  and tell of his deeds with songs
 of joy.

107.1–43: God delivered them from their distress.
A song of thanksgiving, it begins Book V with what
seems to be a direct response to Ps 106 (compare
107.2–3 with 106.47). **1–3:** Recalling 106.1, v. 1 introduces the theme of *steadfast love* (see the refrain in
vv. 8, 15, 21, 31; plus v. 43). The contrasting theme,
trouble, is introduced in v. 2 and recurs in another
refrain (vv. 6, 13, 19, 28). **4–9:** The *trouble* is stated
generally enough to be widely applicable, but it especially recalls the experiences of wilderness and exile.
Deliverance typically occurs after needy persons have
cried to the LORD (Ex 3.7, 9; Ps 106.44). **10–16:** Again,
the *trouble* can be understood generally, but *darkness*
recalls the Exile★ (Isa 42.7), as does *prisoners* (Isa
49.9). Typically, God helps those *with no one to help*
them (v. 12; 9.18). **17–22:** The *trouble* seems to be
sickness (although see note *b* in v. 17), from which
people are *healed* (v. 20). This imagery may be
metaphorical★ (Isa 57.18–19).

~~~~~~~~~~~~~~~~~~

a Cn: Heb *sea*   *b* Cn: Heb *fools*

23 Some went down to the sea in ships,
    doing business on the mighty
        waters;
24 they saw the deeds of the LORD,
    his wondrous works in the deep.
25 For he commanded and raised the
        stormy wind,
    which lifted up the waves of
        the sea.
26 They mounted up to heaven, they went
        down to the depths;
    their courage melted away in their
        calamity;
27 they reeled and staggered like
        drunkards,
    and were at their wits' end.
28 Then they cried to the LORD in their
        trouble,
    and he brought them out from their
        distress;
29 he made the storm be still,
    and the waves of the sea were
        hushed.
30 Then they were glad because they had
        quiet,
    and he brought them to their desired
        haven.
31 Let them thank the LORD for his
        steadfast love,
    for his wonderful works to
        humankind.
32 Let them extol him in the congregation
        of the people,
    and praise him in the assembly of the
        elders.

33 He turns rivers into a desert,
    springs of water into thirsty ground,
34 a fruitful land into a salty waste,
    because of the wickedness of its
        inhabitants.
35 He turns a desert into pools of water,
    a parched land into springs of
        water.
36 And there he lets the hungry live,
    and they establish a town to live in;
37 they sow fields, and plant vineyards,
    and get a fruitful yield.
38 By his blessing they multiply greatly,
    and he does not let their cattle
        decrease.

39 When they are diminished and brought
        low
    through oppression, trouble,
        and sorrow,
40 he pours contempt on princes
    and makes them wander in trackless
        wastes;
41 but he raises up the needy out of
        distress,
    and makes their families like flocks.
42 The upright see it and are glad;
    and all wickedness stops its mouth.
43 Let those who are wise give heed to
        these things,
    and consider the steadfast love of the
        LORD.

107.23–43. 23–32: Deliverance from distress at *sea* is unique (see Jon 1–2). *The sea, the mighty waters,* and *the depths* may symbolize cosmic chaotic forces (93.3–4). *Wits'* (v. 27) is literally "wisdom," anticipating v. 43. **33–43:** A summary recalling vv. 4–9, this section may have been added to an original vv. 4–32. **43:** Those who heed the preceding instances of deliverance will be taught dependence upon God's *steadfast love,* and such is the essence of wisdom.

PSALM 108

A Song. A Psalm of David.

1 My heart is steadfast, O God, my heart
        is steadfast;[a]
    I will sing and make melody.
    Awake, my soul![b]
2 Awake, O harp and lyre!
    I will awake the dawn.
3 I will give thanks to you, O LORD,
        among the peoples,
    and I will sing praises to you among
        the nations.
4 For your steadfast love is higher than
        the heavens,
    and your faithfulness reaches to the
        clouds.

5 Be exalted, O God, above the heavens,
    and let your glory be over all the
        earth.

a Heb Mss Gk Syr: MT lacks *my heart is steadfast*
b Compare 57.8: Heb *also my soul*

6 Give victory with your right hand, and
    answer me,
  so that those whom you love may be
    rescued.

7 God has promised in his sanctuary:[a]
  "With exultation I will divide up
    Shechem,
  and portion out the Vale of Succoth.
8 Gilead is mine; Manasseh is mine;
  Ephraim is my helmet;
  Judah is my scepter.
9 Moab is my washbasin;
  on Edom I hurl my shoe;
  over Philistia I shout in triumph."

10 Who will bring me to the fortified city?
  Who will lead me to Edom?
11 Have you not rejected us, O God?
  You do not go out, O God, with our
    armies.
12 O grant us help against the foe,
  for human help is worthless.
13 With God we shall do valiantly;
  it is he who will tread down
    our foes.

108.1–13: Human help is worthless. Formed
from combining 57.7–11 (108.1–5) and 60.5–12
(108.6–13), it moves from praise (vv. 1–4) to petition
(vv. 5–6) to divine speech (vv. 7–9) to complaint (vv.
10–11) to petition (v. 12) to expression of trust (v. 13).
The reasons for combining portions of Ps 57 and 60
are unclear. In their present context, vv. 1–4 supply
the grateful praise repeatedly called for in Ps 107 (vv.
1, 8, 15, 21, 31). If this praise is a response to the return
from exile, the movement to petition and complaint
may reflect the reality that the return did not solve all
the people's problems. They still found themselves in
need of *help against the foe* (v. 12).

PSALM 109
To the leader. Of David. A Psalm.

1 Do not be silent, O God of my praise.
2 For wicked and deceitful mouths are
    opened against me,
  speaking against me with lying
    tongues.
3 They beset me with words of hate,
  and attack me without cause.

4 In return for my love they accuse me,
  even while I make prayer for them.[b]
5 So they reward me evil for good,
  and hatred for my love.

6 They say,[c] "Appoint a wicked man
    against him;
  let an accuser stand on his right.
7 When he is tried, let him be found
    guilty;
  let his prayer be counted as sin.
8 May his days be few;
  may another seize his position.
9 May his children be orphans,
  and his wife a widow.
10 May his children wander about and beg;
  may they be driven out of[d] the ruins
    they inhabit.
11 May the creditor seize all that he has;
  may strangers plunder the fruits of
    his toil.
12 May there be no one to do him a
    kindness,
  nor anyone to pity his orphaned
    children.
13 May his posterity be cut off;
  may his name be blotted out in the
    second generation.
14 May the iniquity of his father[e] be
    remembered before the LORD,
  and do not let the sin of his mother
    be blotted out.
15 Let them be before the LORD
    continually,
  and may his[f] memory be cut off from
    the earth.
16 For he did not remember to show
    kindness,
  but pursued the poor and needy
  and the brokenhearted to their death.
17 He loved to curse; let curses come on
    him.
  He did not like blessing; may it be far
    from him.
18 He clothed himself with cursing as his
    coat,
  may it soak into his body like water,
  like oil into his bones.

---

a Or *by his holiness*   b Syr: Heb *I prayer*
c Heb lacks *They say*   d Gk: Heb *and seek*
e Cn: Heb *fathers*   f Gk: Heb *their*

19 May it be like a garment that he wraps
  around himself,
  like a belt that he wears every day."

109.1–31: God stands at the right hand of the needy. Because it contains petition (vv. 1a, 20–21, 26–29), complaint (vv. 1b–5, 22–25), and an expression of praise and trust (vv. 30–31), this psalm is usually classified as a prayer for help of a person falsely accused (see Ps 5, 7). The extended request for revenge in vv. 6–19 is unique. **1–5:** The psalmist is a victim, despite his or her goodness toward others. **6–19:** The addition of *they say*, which is not in the Hebrew text (see note c), attributes the desire for revenge to the psalmist's enemies. The passage should instead be seen as expressing the psalmist's wishes. The charges involve the failure to show *kindness,* thus contributing to the *death* of *poor and needy* persons (v. 16).

20 May that be the reward of my accusers
  from the LORD,
  of those who speak evil against my
  life.
21 But you, O LORD my Lord,
  act on my behalf for your name's
  sake;
  because your steadfast love is good,
  deliver me.
22 For I am poor and needy,
  and my heart is pierced within me.
23 I am gone like a shadow at evening;
  I am shaken off like a locust.
24 My knees are weak through fasting;
  my body has become gaunt.
25 I am an object of scorn to my
  accusers;
  when they see me, they shake their
  heads.

26 Help me, O LORD my God!
  Save me according to your steadfast
  love.
27 Let them know that this is your hand;
  you, O LORD, have done it.
28 Let them curse, but you will bless.
  Let my assailants be put to shame;*a*
  may your servant be glad.
29 May my accusers be clothed with
  dishonor;
  may they be wrapped in their own
  shame as in a mantle.

30 With my mouth I will give great thanks
  to the LORD;
  I will praise him in the midst of the
  throng.
31 For he stands at the right hand of the
  needy,
  to save them from those who would
  condemn them to death.

109.20–31: Even if vv. 6–19 are the words of the enemies, the psalmist claims them (v. 20). The psalmist appeals to God's *steadfast love* (vv. 21, 26; the same Hebrew word was translated *kindness* in vv. 12, 16). The appeal is grounded in the conviction that God loves and favors the *needy* (v. 31; 9.18), among whom is the psalmist (v. 22).

PSALM 110

Of David. A Psalm.

1 The LORD says to my lord,
  "Sit at my right hand
  until I make your enemies your
  footstool."

2 The LORD sends out from Zion
  your mighty scepter.
  Rule in the midst of your foes.
3 Your people will offer themselves
  willingly
  on the day you lead your forces
  on the holy mountains.*b*
  From the womb of the morning,
  like dew, your youth*c* will come to
  you.
4 The LORD has sworn and will not
  change his mind,
  "You are a priest forever according to
  the order of Melchizedek."*d*

5 The Lord is at your right hand;
  he will shatter kings on the day of his
  wrath.
6 He will execute judgment among the
  nations,
  filling them with corpses;

a Gk: Heb *They have risen up and have been put to shame*   b Another reading is *in holy splendor*
c Cn: Heb *the dew of your youth*   d Or *forever, a rightful king by my edict*

he will shatter heads
　　over the wide earth.
7 He will drink from the stream by the
　　　path;
　　therefore he will lift up his head.

110.1–7: The LORD is at your right hand. A royal psalm, it may have been used originally at the coronation of Judean kings (see Ps 2). After the disappearance of the monarchy (see Ps 89), it would have served as a profession of trust in God's continued involvement with the people, to whom Ps 149 attributes the role formerly reserved for kings. **1–3:** Divine speech promises victory over *enemies* (v. 1; 2.1–5, 8–11). The promise is reinforced in v. 2, and probably in v. 3 as well, although its meaning is unclear. **4:** Divine speech resumes in v. 4. *Melchizedek* shared the titles king and priest (Gen 14.18). **5:** *Right hand* designates the position of help (109.31). **6:** Justice will be achieved by God's defeat of oppressors (v. 6; 149.9). The graphic imagery is typical of ancient battle descriptions (2 Kings 8.12; Ps 137.9). **7:** *He* now refers to the king. An uplifted *head* seems to signify deliverance (3.3; 27.6).

PSALM 111

1 Praise the LORD!
　I will give thanks to the LORD with my
　　　whole heart,
　　in the company of the upright, in the
　　　congregation.
2 Great are the works of the LORD,
　　studied by all who delight in them.
3 Full of honor and majesty is his work,
　　and his righteousness endures
　　　forever.
4 He has gained renown by his wonderful
　　　deeds;
　　the LORD is gracious and merciful.
5 He provides food for those who fear him;
　　he is ever mindful of his covenant.
6 He has shown his people the power of
　　　his works,
　　in giving them the heritage of the
　　　nations.
7 The works of his hands are faithful and
　　　just;
　　all his precepts are trustworthy.
8 They are established forever and ever,
　　to be performed with faithfulness and
　　　uprightness.

9 He sent redemption to his people;
　　he has commanded his covenant
　　　forever.
　　Holy and awesome is his name.
10 The fear of the LORD is the beginning
　　　of wisdom;
　　all those who practice it[a] have a good
　　　understanding.
　　His praise endures forever.

111.1–10: The works of the LORD. An acrostic* poem (see Ps 25) to be read in conjunction with Ps 112, it is often categorized as a song of praise. An opening invitation (v. 1a) is followed by the psalmist's own response (v. 1b–c) and reasons for praise that focus on God's *works* (vv. 2, 6–7). **1:** The psalmist's wholehearted response (86.12) is offered publicly. **2–3:** God's *works* include actions (vv. 4–6) and words (vv. 7–9). **4–6:** God's *wonderful deeds,* motivated by God's *gracious and merciful* character (Ex 34.6; Ps 112.4), include the Exodus, provision in the wilderness (v. 5), and gift of the land (v. 6). **7–9:** Established by God's action, the *covenant** (vv. 5, 9) involved *precepts* intended to establish justice among the people. **10:** *Fear of the LORD* involves trust and obedience. It is the essence of *praise* and the evidence of true *wisdom* (Job 28.28; Prov 1.7; 9.10).

PSALM 112

1 Praise the LORD!
　Happy are those who fear the LORD,
　　who greatly delight in his
　　　commandments.
2 Their descendants will be mighty in the
　　　land;
　　the generation of the upright will be
　　　blessed.
3 Wealth and riches are in their houses,
　　and their righteousness endures
　　　forever.
4 They rise in the darkness as a light for
　　　the upright;
　　they are gracious, merciful, and
　　　righteous.
5 It is well with those who deal
　　　generously and lend,
　　who conduct their affairs with justice.

a Gk Syr: Heb *them*

6 For the righteous will never be moved;
   they will be remembered forever.
7 They are not afraid of evil tidings;
   their hearts are firm, secure in the
   LORD.
8 Their hearts are steady, they will not be
   afraid;
   in the end they will look in triumph
   on their foes.
9 They have distributed freely, they have
   given to the poor;
   their righteousness endures forever;
   their horn is exalted in honor.
10 The wicked see it and are angry;
   they gnash their teeth and melt away;
   the desire of the wicked comes
   to nothing.

112.1–10: Happy are those who fear the LORD. An acrostic* poem (see Ps 25), it belongs with Ps 111. It begins like Ps 111, and it features *those who fear the LORD* (v. 1; 111.10). **1–3:** *Happy* and *delight* in v. 1 recall 1.1–2. *Wealth and riches* need not be understood materialistically. The real reward of *the righteous* is stability (vv. 6, 8) and security grounded *in the LORD* (v. 7; 1.3). Because *the righteous* embody God's will, the same thing is said of them that is said of God in 111.3: *their righteousness endures forever* (vv. 3, 9). **4–6:** Like God also, *the righteous* are a source of *light* for others (27.1); and they are *gracious* and *merciful* (v. 4; 111.4). Their lives reflect *justice*, the essence of God's will (72.1–2; 82.3). **7–10:** Because they trust or *fear the LORD* (v. 1), they do not have to be *afraid of evil tidings* (v. 7). Their generosity also models God's will (v. 9), and it sets them apart from *the wicked*, whose behavior *comes to nothing* (literally "perishes"; 1.6).

~~~

PSALM 113

1 Praise the LORD!
   Praise, O servants of the LORD;
   praise the name of the LORD.

2 Blessed be the name of the LORD
   from this time on and forevermore.
3 From the rising of the sun to its setting
   the name of the LORD is to be
   praised.
4 The LORD is high above all nations,
   and his glory above the heavens.

5 Who is like the LORD our God,
   who is seated on high,
6 who looks far down
   on the heavens and the earth?
7 He raises the poor from the dust,
   and lifts the needy from the ash heap,
8 to make them sit with princes,
   with the princes of his people.
9 He gives the barren woman a home,
   making her the joyous mother of
   children.
Praise the LORD!

113.1–9: The God who looks far down. A song of praise, it introduces the Egyptian "Hallel" ("Praise"; Ps 113–118), a collection which, because of its references to the Exodus from Egypt, was and is used at Passover.* **1–4:** Each of the first three verses contains *name of the LORD*, suggesting the importance of God's identity. Verse 4 affirms God's cosmic sovereignty. **5a:** Each of vv. 1–5a contains the name *LORD*. The question specifically raises the issue of the LORD's identity that will be addressed in vv. 5b–9. **5b–9:** God is known by what God does. The God *on high* is one *who looks far down*, or literally, "causes God's self to be low so as to see." This humbling of the divine self leads to exaltation for *the poor* and *needy* (9.18; 109.31). The same Hebrew root underlies *seated* (v. 5b), *sit* (v. 8), and *gives a . . . home* (v. 9). The repetition makes the point that the will of God is done on earth as in heaven (see *heavens and the earth* in v. 6). This constitutes the ultimate reason to *Praise the LORD!*

~~~

PSALM 114

1 When Israel went out from Egypt,
   the house of Jacob from a people of
   strange language,
2 Judah became God's*a* sanctuary,
   Israel his dominion.

3 The sea looked and fled;
   Jordan turned back.
4 The mountains skipped like rams,
   the hills like lambs.

5 Why is it, O sea, that you flee?
   O Jordan, that you turn back?

a Heb *his*

6 O mountains, that you skip like rams?
    O hills, like lambs?

7 Tremble, O earth, at the presence of the
    LORD,
    at the presence of the God of Jacob,
8 who turns the rock into a pool of
    water,
    the flint into a spring of water.

114.1–8: When Israel went out from Egypt. It is a poetic accounting of the Exodus (vv. 1, 3a, 5a), wilderness (v. 8), the crossing of the *Jordan* into the land (vv. 3b, 5b), and the possession of the land (v. 2). It is part of the Egyptian "Hallel" (Ps 113–118). **1–2:** Like the Song of the Sea (Ex 15.1–18), the movement is from Exodus to God's *sanctuary* (v. 2; Ex 15.17). **3–4:** The crossing of the *Jordan* into Canaan was remembered as an event like the Exodus (Josh 4.23–24). The imagery depicts the effects of God's appearing (29.6). **5–8:** The questions in vv. 5–6 prepare for the climactic vv. 7–8, where the name *LORD* appears for the first time. To *tremble* is the appropriate response to *the presence of the LORD* (77.16; 97.4).

PSALM 115

1 Not to us, O LORD, not to us, but to
    your name give glory,
    for the sake of your steadfast love and
    your faithfulness.
2 Why should the nations say,
    "Where is their God?"

3 Our God is in the heavens;
    he does whatever he pleases.
4 Their idols are silver and gold,
    the work of human hands.
5 They have mouths, but do not speak;
    eyes, but do not see.
6 They have ears, but do not hear;
    noses, but do not smell.
7 They have hands, but do not feel;
    feet, but do not walk;
    they make no sound in their throats.
8 Those who make them are like them;
    so are all who trust in them.

9 O Israel, trust in the LORD!
    He is their help and their shield.

10 O house of Aaron, trust in the LORD!
    He is their help and their shield.
11 You who fear the LORD, trust in
    the LORD!
    He is their help and their shield.

12 The LORD has been mindful of us; he
    will bless us;
    he will bless the house of Israel;
    he will bless the house of Aaron;
13 he will bless those who fear the LORD,
    both small and great.

14 May the LORD give you increase,
    both you and your children.
15 May you be blessed by the LORD,
    who made heaven and earth.

16 The heavens are the LORD's heavens,
    but the earth he has given to human
    beings.
17 The dead do not praise the LORD,
    nor do any that go down into
    silence.
18 But we will bless the LORD
    from this time on and forevermore.
Praise the LORD!

115.1–18: Trust in the LORD! Difficult to classify, it has the character of a song of praise and profession of faith. It is part of the Egyptian "Hallel" (Ps 113–118). **1–2:** The double negation emphasizes God's sovereignty and character, the essence of which are *steadfast love* and *faithfulness* (Ex 34.6; Ps 36.5; 98.3). The question (v. 2; 42.3; 79.10) indicates that not all attribute *glory* to God. **3–8:** Reasserting God's sovereignty, v. 3 suggests not that God is whimsical but rather that he is powerful. This situation contrasts with *idols*, whose devotees are also rendered powerless (v. 8; 97.7; Isa 45.16). **9–11:** The issue is *trust* (vv. 8–11). Those who *trust in the LORD* find *help* and protection (33.20). It is unclear whether different groups are addressed (118.2–4; 135.19–20). **12–15:** God remembers (v. 12; 9.12) and *will bless* (5.12; 107.38). Whereas *idols* are made by their devotees (vv. 4, 8), Israel's God *made heaven and earth* (v. 15; 121.2; 124.8). **16–18:** God has chosen to share dominion of *the earth* (v. 16; 8.5–8). The human vocation is to *bless* and *praise* God (v. 18; see v. 1), which means to acknowledge God's ultimate dominion.

PSALM 116

1 I love the LORD, because he has heard
my voice and my supplications.
2 Because he inclined his ear to me,
therefore I will call on him as long as
I live.
3 The snares of death encompassed me;
the pangs of Sheol laid hold on me;
I suffered distress and anguish.
4 Then I called on the name of
the LORD:
"O LORD, I pray, save my life!"

5 Gracious is the LORD, and righteous;
our God is merciful.
6 The LORD protects the simple;
when I was brought low, he
saved me.
7 Return, O my soul, to your rest,
for the LORD has dealt bountifully
with you.

8 For you have delivered my soul from
death,
my eyes from tears,
my feet from stumbling.
9 I walk before the LORD
in the land of the living.
10 I kept my faith, even when I said,
"I am greatly afflicted";
11 I said in my consternation,
"Everyone is a liar."

12 What shall I return to the LORD
for all his bounty to me?
13 I will lift up the cup of salvation
and call on the name of the LORD,
14 I will pay my vows to the LORD
in the presence of all his people.
15 Precious in the sight of the LORD
is the death of his faithful ones.
16 O LORD, I am your servant;
I am your servant, the child of your
serving girl.
You have loosed my bonds.
17 I will offer to you a thanksgiving
sacrifice
and call on the name of the LORD.
18 I will pay my vows to the LORD
in the presence of all his people,
19 in the courts of the house of the LORD,
in your midst, O Jerusalem.
Praise the LORD!

116.1–19: What shall I return to the LORD? In a song of thanksgiving, the psalmist recalls former distress (vv. 3–4, 6b, 8, 10–11), celebrates deliverance (vv. 1–2, 7, 8–9), and renders thanks (vv. 12–19). It is part of the Egyptian "Hallel" (Ps 113–118). **1–4:** *Sheol** (v. 3), the realm of death, was sometimes viewed less as a place and more as a life-invading power (30.3; 49.15). God has delivered the psalmist from a life-threatening situation. The psalmist responds with *love* (v. 1; 5.11; 31.23) and the promise of life-long commitment (v. 2). **5–7:** The deliverance demonstrates God's character (v. 5; 111.3–4) and characteristic activity on behalf of the lowly (v. 6; 113.7). Verse 7a may state the psalmist's intent to visit the Temple* (see vv. 12–19). **8–11:** Recalling again the deliverance *from death* (v. 8) to *living* (v. 9), the psalmist affirms *faith* in God (v. 10) as opposed to human help (v. 11; 108.12). **12–13:** Recalling v. 7, v. 12 asks the question that is answered in v. 13. The *cup of salvation* may indicate a sacrificial offering of some kind (Ex 29.40). **14–19:** Verses 14 and 18 are identical (22.25). The payment includes verbal gratitude (v. 13) and *a thanksgiving sacrifice* (v. 17; Lev 7.12; Ps 107.22), apparently offered in the Temple (v. 19).

PSALM 117

1 Praise the LORD, all you nations!
Extol him, all you peoples!
2 For great is his steadfast love toward us,
and the faithfulness of the LORD
endures forever.
Praise the LORD!

117.1–2: Praise the LORD! A song of praise, its invitation is followed by reasons for *praise*. It is part of the Egyptian "Hallel" (Ps 113–118). **1:** The invitation typically extends beyond the bounds of God's people (97.1; 99.1; 100.1). A cosmic sovereign gathers a universal congregation. **2:** The reasons feature God's fundamental attributes—*steadfast love* and *faithfulness* (Ex 34.6; Ps 100.5; 115.1).

PSALM 118

1 O give thanks to the LORD, for he is
good;
his steadfast love endures forever!

2 Let Israel say,
   "His steadfast love endures forever."
3 Let the house of Aaron say,
   "His steadfast love endures forever."
4 Let those who fear the LORD say,
   "His steadfast love endures forever."

5 Out of my distress I called on the LORD;
   the LORD answered me and set me in
     a broad place.
6 With the LORD on my side I do not fear.
   What can mortals do to me?
7 The LORD is on my side to help me;
   I shall look in triumph on those who
     hate me.
8 It is better to take refuge in the LORD
   than to put confidence in mortals.
9 It is better to take refuge in the LORD
   than to put confidence in princes.

10 All nations surrounded me;
   in the name of the LORD I cut them
     off!
11 They surrounded me, surrounded me on
     every side;
   in the name of the LORD I cut them
     off!
12 They surrounded me like bees;
   they blazed[a] like a fire of thorns;
   in the name of the LORD I cut them
     off!
13 I was pushed hard,[b] so that I was
     falling,
   but the LORD helped me.
14 The LORD is my strength and my might;
   he has become my salvation.

15 There are glad songs of victory in the
     tents of the righteous:
   "The right hand of the LORD does
     valiantly;
16 the right hand of the LORD is exalted;
   the right hand of the LORD does
     valiantly."
17 I shall not die, but I shall live,
   and recount the deeds of the LORD.
18 The LORD has punished me severely,
   but he did not give me over to death.

19 Open to me the gates of righteousness,
   that I may enter through them
   and give thanks to the LORD.

20 This is the gate of the LORD;
   the righteous shall enter through it.

21 I thank you that you have answered me
   and have become my salvation.
22 The stone that the builders rejected
   has become the chief cornerstone.
23 This is the LORD's doing;
   it is marvelous in our eyes.
24 This is the day that the LORD has made;
   let us rejoice and be glad in it.[c]
25 Save us, we beseech you, O LORD!
   O LORD, we beseech you, give us
     success!

26 Blessed is the one who comes in the
     name of the LORD.[d]
   We bless you from the house of the
     LORD.
27 The LORD is God,
   and he has given us light.
   Bind the festal procession with
     branches,
   up to the horns of the altar.[e]

28 You are my God, and I will give thanks
     to you;
   you are my God, I will extol you.

29 O give thanks to the LORD, for he is
     good,
   for his steadfast love endures forever.

118.1–29: God's steadfast love endures forever. Because of the invitation to and the offering of thanks (vv. 19, 21, 28–29) accompanied by a recounting of deliverance from *distress* (vv. 5–18), it is usually classified as a song of thanksgiving of an individual. But the *distress* seems corporate (vv. 10–12), and the celebration of deliverance recalls the Exodus (v. 14). Furthermore, the speaker shifts to the plural in vv. 23–27, in the midst of which is an unexpected petition (v. 25). Hence the psalm possesses both a past and future orientation that is appropriate for the conclusion of the Egyptian "Hallel" (Ps 113–118), which was and is used at Passover.✶ **1–4:** Each verse contains *steadfast love,*

a Gk: Heb *were extinguished*   *b* Gk Syr Jerome: Heb *You pushed me hard*   *c* Or *in him*   *d* Or *Blessed in the name of the* LORD *is the one who comes*   *e* Meaning of Heb uncertain

a word that frames the psalm (vv. 1, 29; 107.1) and a divine trait that deliverance reveals. Verses 2–4 anticipate the plural voice in vv. 23–27. **5–9:** Deliverance reveals that God is *on my side* or "for me" (56.9). The repetition of *refuge* (vv. 8–9; 2.12) emphasizes the effectiveness of divine *help* (v. 7) and the ineffectiveness of human agency (146.3). **10–14:** After recounting again that God has *helped* (v. 13; v. 7), the psalmist explicitly recalls the Exodus (v. 14; Ex 15.2). **15–18:** *Victory* (v. 15) is the same Hebrew word as *salvation* in v. 14 (see also v. 21). God's *deeds* deliver the psalmist from *death* (v. 18) to life. **19–29:** These verses suggest a public celebration of the deliverance recounted in vv. 5–18. The psalmist enters the Temple* (vv. 19–20), recounts again the deliverance (vv. 21–22), and then is joined by other voices (vv. 23–27) before concluding (vv. 28–29). Verse 24a could also be translated, "This is the day on which the LORD has acted," thus alluding to the deliverance described in vv. 5–18. *Branches* (v. 27) may indicate an original connection to the Feast of Booths (Lev 23.40). Like v. 14, v. 28 echoes Ex 15.2.

PSALM 119

1 Happy are those whose way is blameless,
　who walk in the law of the LORD.
2 Happy are those who keep his decrees,
　who seek him with their whole heart,
3 who also do no wrong,
　but walk in his ways.
4 You have commanded your precepts
　to be kept diligently.
5 O that my ways may be steadfast
　in keeping your statutes!
6 Then I shall not be put to shame,
　having my eyes fixed on all your
　　commandments.
7 I will praise you with an upright heart,
　when I learn your righteous
　　ordinances.
8 I will observe your statutes;
　do not utterly forsake me.

9 How can young people keep their way
　pure?
　By guarding it according to your
　　word.
10 With my whole heart I seek you;
　do not let me stray from your
　　commandments.

11 I treasure your word in my heart,
　so that I may not sin against you.
12 Blessed are you, O LORD;
　teach me your statutes.
13 With my lips I declare
　all the ordinances of your mouth.
14 I delight in the way of your decrees
　as much as in all riches.
15 I will meditate on your precepts,
　and fix my eyes on your ways.
16 I will delight in your statutes;
　I will not forget your word.

17 Deal bountifully with your servant,
　so that I may live and observe your
　　word.
18 Open my eyes, so that I may behold
　wondrous things out of your law.
19 I live as an alien in the land;
　do not hide your commandments
　　from me.
20 My soul is consumed with longing
　for your ordinances at all times.
21 You rebuke the insolent, accursed ones,
　who wander from your
　　commandments;
22 take away from me their scorn and
　　contempt,
　for I have kept your decrees.
23 Even though princes sit plotting against
　　me,
　your servant will meditate on your
　　statutes.
24 Your decrees are my delight,
　they are my counselors.

25 My soul clings to the dust;
　revive me according to your word.
26 When I told of my ways, you answered
　　me;
　teach me your statutes.
27 Make me understand the way of your
　　precepts,
　and I will meditate on your wondrous
　　works.
28 My soul melts away for sorrow;
　strengthen me according to your
　　word.
29 Put false ways far from me;
　and graciously teach me your law.

30 I have chosen the way of faithfulness;
   I set your ordinances before me.
31 I cling to your decrees, O LORD;
   let me not be put to shame.
32 I run the way of your commandments,
   for you enlarge my understanding.

119.1–176: The torah* of the LORD. The poem is an acrostic.* The first word of each of vv. 1–8 begins with an "Aleph"; the first word of each of vv. 9–16 begins with "Beth"; and so on throughout the Hebrew alphabet.* Although this psalm contains all types of material—petition, complaint, praise, trust, instruction, admonition—it is usually classified as a "torah"-psalm (see Ps 1, 19). The word "torah" (NRSV *law*) occurs twenty-five times, including at least once in every section except vv. 9–16. In addition, seven synonyms for "torah" occur repeatedly: *decrees, precepts, statutes, command(ment)s, ordinances, word,* and *promise.* Each verse contains one of the eight, except vv. 3, 37, 90, and 122. The psalm's date and origin are unclear. In its current setting, the psalm attests to the importance of "torah" in the post-exilic era as a central feature of communal life (see Introduction). **1–8:** *Happy* and *law* recall the beginning of the psalter (1.1–2; 2.12). While *law* suggests a written code, as do several of the synonyms, "torah" has a broader meaning: "instruction." *Blameless* cannot mean moral perfection, for the psalmist has sinned (v. 176). It connotes dependence upon God that yields happiness, a condition not incompatible with suffering (vv. 22–23, 84–87). **9–16:** *Word* frames the section (vv. 9, 16). Verse 11 recalls Jer 31.33. The psalmist humbly suggests that there is always more to learn. **17–24:** Petition (vv. 17–18) and complaint (v. 19, 21–23) dominate. Verse 19 anticipates v. 54, and the two would have been particularly meaningful in the post-exilic era. **25–32:** Complaint continues (vv. 25a, 28), in the midst of which the psalmist prays for life (v. 25b).

---

33 Teach me, O LORD, the way of your
      statutes,
   and I will observe it to the end.
34 Give me understanding, that I may keep
      your law
   and observe it with my whole heart.
35 Lead me in the path of your
      commandments,
   for I delight in it.
36 Turn my heart to your decrees,
   and not to selfish gain.

37 Turn my eyes from looking at vanities;
   give me life in your ways.
38 Confirm to your servant your promise,
   which is for those who fear you.
39 Turn away the disgrace that I dread,
   for your ordinances are good.
40 See, I have longed for your precepts;
   in your righteousness give me life.

41 Let your steadfast love come to me,
      O LORD,
   your salvation according to your
      promise.
42 Then I shall have an answer for those
      who taunt me,
   for I trust in your word.
43 Do not take the word of truth utterly
      out of my mouth,
   for my hope is in your ordinances.
44 I will keep your law continually,
   forever and ever.
45 I shall walk at liberty,
   for I have sought your precepts.
46 I will also speak of your decrees before
      kings,
   and shall not be put to shame;
47 I find my delight in your commandments,
   because I love them.
48 I revere your commandments, which I
      love,
   and I will meditate on your statutes.

49 Remember your word to your servant,
   in which you have made me hope.
50 This is my comfort in my distress,
   that your promise gives me life.
51 The arrogant utterly deride me,
   but I do not turn away from your *law.*
52 When I think of your ordinances from
      of old,
   I take comfort, O LORD.
53 Hot indignation seizes me because of
      the wicked,
   those who forsake your law.
54 Your statutes have been my songs
   wherever I make my home.
55 I remember your name in the night,
      O LORD,
   and keep your law.
56 This blessing has fallen to me,
   for I have kept your precepts.

57 The LORD is my portion;
  I promise to keep your words.
58 I implore your favor with all my heart;
  be gracious to me according to your
    promise.
59 When I think of your ways,
  I turn my feet to your decrees;
60 I hurry and do not delay
  to keep your commandments.
61 Though the cords of the wicked ensnare
    me,
  I do not forget your law.
62 At midnight I rise to praise you,
  because of your righteous
    ordinances.
63 I am a companion of all who fear you,
  of those who keep your precepts.
64 The earth, O LORD, is full of your
    steadfast love;
  teach me your statutes.

119.33–64. 33–40: Petition begins each of vv. 33–39,
requesting that the psalmist be completely oriented to
God, the giver of *life* (v. 40). 41–48: Assurance becomes the theme—*trust* (v. 42), *hope* (v. 43), *liberty*
(v. 45), *delight* (v. 47). *Steadfast love* is the first of
seven occurrences (vv. 64, 76, 88, 124, 149, 159).
49–56: Remembering, God's and the psalmist's, is featured (vv. 49, 55; see v. 52). Memory leads to *hope*
(v. 49) and *comfort* (v. 50, 52). 57–64: *Portion* refers
to the tribal shares in the land, so the affirmation in v.
57a (16.5; 73.26) would have been especially meaningful to a homeless, landless people.

65 You have dealt well with your servant,
  O LORD, according to your word.
66 Teach me good judgment and
    knowledge,
  for I believe in your
    commandments.
67 Before I was humbled I went astray,
  but now I keep your word.
68 You are good and do good;
  teach me your statutes.
69 The arrogant smear me with lies,
  but with my whole heart I keep your
    precepts.
70 Their hearts are fat and gross,
  but I delight in your law.
71 It is good for me that I was humbled,
  so that I might learn your statutes.

72 The law of your mouth is better to me
  than thousands of gold and silver
    pieces.
73 Your hands have made and fashioned
    me;
  give me understanding that I may
    learn your commandments.
74 Those who fear you shall see me and
    rejoice,
  because I have hoped in your word.
75 I know, O LORD, that your judgments
    are right,
  and that in faithfulness you have
    humbled me.
76 Let your steadfast love become my
    comfort
  according to your promise to your
    servant.
77 Let your mercy come to me, that I may
    live;
  for your law is my delight.
78 Let the arrogant be put to shame,
  because they have subverted me with
    guile;
  as for me, I will meditate on your
    precepts.
79 Let those who fear you turn to me,
  so that they may know your decrees.
80 May my heart be blameless in your
    statutes,
  so that I may not be put to shame.
81 My soul languishes for your salvation;
  I hope in your word.
82 My eyes fail with watching for your
    promise;
  I ask, "When will you comfort me?"
83 For I have become like a wineskin *in*
    the smoke,
  yet I have not forgotten your
    statutes.
84 How long must your servant endure?
  When will you judge those who
    persecute me?
85 The arrogant have dug pitfalls for me;
  they flout your law.
86 All your commandments are
    enduring;
  I am persecuted without cause; help
    me!

87 They have almost made an end of me
on earth;
but I have not forsaken your precepts.
88 In your steadfast love spare my life,
so that I may keep the decrees of your
mouth.

89 The LORD exists forever;
your word is firmly fixed in heaven.
90 Your faithfulness endures to all
generations;
you have established the earth, and it
stands fast.
91 By your appointment they stand today,
for all things are your servants.
92 If your law had not been my delight,
I would have perished in my misery.
93 I will never forget your precepts,
for by them you have given me life.
94 I am yours; save me,
for I have sought your precepts.
95 The wicked lie in wait to destroy me,
but I consider your decrees.
96 I have seen a limit to all perfection,
but your commandment is
exceedingly broad.

119.65–96. 65–72: The key word is *well/good/better*
(vv. 65, 66, 68, 71, 72). The reward for obedience is
not material (v. 72) but rather the *delight* (v. 70) of
conformity to God's will (1.2–3). 73–80: In the context
(v. 75), *blameless* (v. 80) means being forgiven rather
than being sinless. The forgiven sinner instructs others
(32.8–9; 51.13). 81–88: The extended complaints reveal the psalmist's suffering, in the midst of which the
psalmist pleads for *life* (vv. 86, 88). 89–96: While not
entirely leaving behind complaint and petition (vv.
94–95), this section consists primarily of a hymnic profession of faith that asserts God's cosmic sovereignty
(vv. 89–91).

97 Oh, how I love your law!
It is my meditation all day long.
98 Your commandment makes me wiser
than my enemies,
for it is always with me.
99 I have more understanding than all my
teachers,
for your decrees are my meditation.
100 I understand more than the aged,
for I keep your precepts.

101 I hold back my feet from every evil way,
in order to keep your word.
102 I do not turn away from your ordinances,
for you have taught me.
103 How sweet are your words to my taste,
sweeter than honey to my mouth!
104 Through your precepts I get
understanding;
therefore I hate every false way.

105 Your word is a lamp to my feet
and a light to my path.
106 I have sworn an oath and confirmed it,
to observe your righteous ordinances.
107 I am severely afflicted;
give me life, O LORD, according to
your word.
108 Accept my offerings of praise, O LORD,
and teach me your ordinances.
109 I hold my life in my hand continually,
but I do not forget your law.
110 The wicked have laid a snare for me,
but I do not stray from your precepts.
111 Your decrees are my heritage forever;
they are the joy of my heart.
112 I incline my heart to perform your
statutes
forever, to the end.

113 I hate the double-minded,
but I love your law.
114 You are my hiding place and my shield;
I hope in your word.
115 Go away from me, you evildoers,
that I may keep the commandments
of my God.
116 Uphold me according to your promise,
that I may live,
and let me not be put to shame in my
hope.
117 Hold me up, that I may be safe
and have regard for your statutes
continually.
118 You spurn all who go astray from your
statutes;
for their cunning is in vain.
119 All the wicked of the earth you count as
dross;
therefore I love your decrees.
120 My flesh trembles for fear of you,
and I am afraid of your judgments.

119.97–120. 97–104: The sensual language of vv. 97, 103 conveys the depth of the psalmist's *love* for God's instruction, which yields wisdom and *understanding* (vv. 98–100). **105–112:** Like God's own self, God's *word* is a *light* (v. 105; 4.6; 27.1). The psalmist's affliction is again in view (vv. 107, 110). **113–120:** Amid the affliction, there is also divine protection and *hope* (v. 114). *Afraid* (v. 120) probably suggests awe and reverence rather than fright.

121 I have done what is just and right;
　　do not leave me to my oppressors.
122 Guarantee your servant's well-being;
　　do not let the godless oppress me.
123 My eyes fail from watching for your
　　　salvation,
　　and for the fulfillment of your
　　　righteous promise.
124 Deal with your servant according to
　　　your steadfast love,
　　and teach me your statutes.
125 I am your servant; give me
　　　understanding,
　　so that I may know your decrees.
126 It is time for the LORD to act,
　　for your law has been broken.
127 Truly I love your commandments
　　more than gold, more than fine gold.
128 Truly I direct my steps by all your
　　　precepts;*a*
　　I hate every false way.

129 Your decrees are wonderful;
　　therefore my soul keeps them.
130 The unfolding of your words gives
　　　light;
　　it imparts understanding to the
　　　simple.
131 With open mouth I pant,
　　because I long for your
　　　commandments.
132 Turn to me and be gracious to me,
　　as is your custom toward those who
　　　love your name.
133 Keep my steps steady according to your
　　　promise,
　　and never let iniquity have dominion
　　　over me.
134 Redeem me from human oppression,
　　that I may keep your precepts.

135 Make your face shine upon your
　　　servant,
　　and teach me your statutes.
136 My eyes shed streams of tears
　　because your law is not kept.

137 You are righteous, O LORD,
　　and your judgments are right.
138 You have appointed your decrees in
　　　righteousness
　　and in all faithfulness.
139 My zeal consumes me
　　because my foes forget your words.
140 Your promise is well tried,
　　and your servant loves it.
141 I am small and despised,
　　yet I do not forget your precepts.
142 Your righteousness is an everlasting
　　　righteousness,
　　and your law is the truth.
143 Trouble and anguish have come
　　　upon me,
　　but your commandments are my
　　　delight.
144 Your decrees are righteous forever;
　　give me understanding that I may
　　　live.

145 With my whole heart I cry; answer me,
　　　O LORD.
　　I will keep your statutes.
146 I cry to you; save me,
　　that I may observe your decrees.
147 I rise before dawn and cry for help;
　　I put my hope in your words.
148 My eyes are awake before each watch of
　　　the night,
　　that I may meditate on your promise.
149 In your steadfast love hear my voice;
　　O LORD, in your justice preserve my
　　　life.
150 Those who persecute me with evil
　　　purpose draw near;
　　they are far from your law.
151 Yet you are near, O LORD,
　　and all your commandments are true.
152 Long ago I learned from your decrees
　　that you have established them
　　　forever.

a Gk Jerome: Meaning of Heb uncertain

119.121–152. 121–128: Verse 122 may be the most noticeable in the psalm since it contains none of the eight synonyms for "torah." It highlights the psalmist's *servant* role (see vv. 122, 124–125). 129–136: *Custom* in v. 132 is, more literally, "justice." The psalmist asserts that God's "justice" is finally to *be gracious*. 137–144: The key word here is *righteous(ness)* (vv. 137, 138, 142, 144). 145–152: The opposites *near* and *far* are featured in vv. 150–151. Ultimately, God is *near* (73.28).

〰️〰️〰️〰️〰️〰️〰️〰️〰️〰️〰️〰️〰️〰️〰️

153 Look on my misery and rescue me,
    for I do not forget your law.
154 Plead my cause and redeem me;
    give me life according to your
        promise.
155 Salvation is far from the wicked,
    for they do not seek your statutes.
156 Great is your mercy, O Lord;
    give me life according to your justice.
157 Many are my persecutors and my
        adversaries,
    yet I do not swerve from your
        decrees.
158 I look at the faithless with disgust,
    because they do not keep your
        commands.
159 Consider how I love your precepts;
    preserve my life according to your
        steadfast love.
160 The sum of your word is truth;
    and every one of your righteous
        ordinances endures forever.

161 Princes persecute me without cause,
    but my heart stands in awe of your
        words.
162 I rejoice at your word
    like one who finds great spoil.
163 I hate and abhor falsehood,
    but I love your law.
164 Seven times a day I praise you
    for your righteous ordinances.
165 Great peace have those who love your
        law;
    nothing can make them stumble.
166 I hope for your salvation, O Lord,
    and I fulfill your commandments.
167 My soul keeps your decrees;
    I love them exceedingly.

168 I keep your precepts and decrees,
    for all my ways are before you.

169 Let my cry come before you, O Lord;
    give me understanding according to
        your word.
170 Let my supplication come before you;
    deliver me according to your
        promise.
171 My lips will pour forth praise,
    because you teach me your statutes.
172 My tongue will sing of your promise,
    for all your commandments are
        right.
173 Let your hand be ready to help me,
    for I have chosen your precepts.
174 I long for your salvation, O Lord,
    and your law is my delight.
175 Let me live that I may praise you,
    and let your ordinances help me.
176 I have gone astray like a lost sheep; seek
        out your servant,
    for I do not forget your
        commandments.

119.153–176. 153–160: The petition for *life* occurs throughout but is concentrated here (vv. 154, 156, 159). 161–168: It is not clear whether *seven times* is meant literally or whether, since *seven* is the number of completeness, it connotes continual *praise* (v. 164). 169–176: The psalm concludes with the striking simile⋆ of *a lost sheep. Lost* is more literally "perishing," a word associated with the wicked (1.6). Thus it emphasizes that God's "torah" communicates God's essentially merciful character (vv. 77, 156).

〰️〰️〰️〰️〰️〰️〰️〰️〰️〰️〰️〰️〰️〰️〰️

PSALM 120
A Song of Ascents.

1 In my distress I cry to the Lord,
    that he may answer me:
2 "Deliver me, O Lord,
    from lying lips,
    from a deceitful tongue."

3 What shall be given to you?
    And what more shall be done to you,
        you deceitful tongue?
4 A warrior's sharp arrows,
    with glowing coals of the broom
        tree!

5 Woe is me, that I am an alien in
  Meshech,
    that I must live among the tents of
    Kedar.
6 Too long have I had my dwelling
    among those who hate peace.
7 I am for peace;
    but when I speak,
    they are for war.

___

120.1–7: Peace and war. The first of the Songs of Ascents (Ps 120–134), its opening complaint and petition suggest a prayer for help. But its uniqueness makes it appropriate for beginning the Ascents collection. This psalm locates the speaker outside the land (v. 5), while the next two psalms suggest a journey (Ps 121) that ends in Jerusalem (Ps 122; especially *go up* in v. 4, since Jerusalem is on a hill). The Songs of Ascents probably originated as, or became, a collection used by pilgrims as they traveled to and from Jerusalem. Several of the psalms reflect the daily concerns of ordinary folk (Ps 127, 128, 133), and there are numerous references to Jerusalem (Ps 122, 125, 126, 128, 129, 132–134). Psalm 133 suggests that individual families have gathered as the larger family of God, and the concluding Ps 134 sounds like a benediction. 1–4: The *distress* is a frequent one—deceitful enemies (31.18; 109.2). The *deceitful tongue* is personified* and addressed in v. 3 with questions that are answered in v. 4. In short, justice will be done (140.9–11). 5–7: Since they are not close together, *Meshech* (Ezek 32.26) and *Kedar* (Isa 21.16–17) may stand metaphorically* for all those *who hate peace*. The longing for *peace* (vv. 6–7) may anticipate the journey to Jerusalem (122.6–8). The repetition of *peace* in successive lines produces a stair-like pattern appropriate for a *Song of Ascents* (*Ascents* can also mean "stairs" or "steps").

~~~~

PSALM 121
A Song of Ascents.

1 I lift up my eyes to the hills—
    from where will my help come?
2 My help comes from the LORD,
    who made heaven and earth.

3 He will not let your foot be moved;
    he who keeps you will not slumber.
4 He who keeps Israel
    will neither slumber nor sleep.

5 The LORD is your keeper;
    the LORD is your shade at your right
    hand.
6 The sun shall not strike you by day,
    nor the moon by night.

7 The LORD will keep you from all evil;
    he will keep your life.
8 The LORD will keep
    your going out and your coming in
    from this time on and forevermore.

___

121.1–8: The LORD is your keeper. A psalm of trust and the second *Song of Ascents* (see Ps 120), its unifying motif* is a journey for which the LORD is the psalmist's *keeper* (v. 5). 1–2: The cosmic creator (v. 2; 115.15; 124.8; 134.3) is also the psalmist's personal *help*. The stair-like repetition is characteristic of the collection (120.5–7). In the present context, *hills* probably includes Zion* (125.1–2). 3–4: The stair-like pattern (see 120.5–7) continues with *slumber* and *keeps*, which becomes the key word (vv. 5, 7, 8). 5–6: For travelers, *the sun* could be hazardous (Isa 49.10); and the ancients believed that *the moon* was dangerous (see Mt 17.15 where "epileptic" is literally "moonstruck"). God provides protection. 7–8: Three more occurrences of *keep* extend the promise of God's protection from a particular journey to all of *life* and *forevermore* (Deut 28.6).

~~~~

PSALM 122
A Song of Ascents. Of David.

1 I was glad when they said to me,
    "Let us go to the house of the LORD!"
2 Our feet are standing
    within your gates, O Jerusalem.

3 Jerusalem—built as a city
    that is bound firmly together.
4 To it the tribes go up,
    the tribes of the LORD,
  as was decreed for Israel,
    to give thanks to the name of
    the LORD.
5 For there the thrones for judgment were
    set up,
    the thrones of the house of David.

6 Pray for the peace of Jerusalem:
    "May they prosper who love you.

7 Peace be within your walls,
  and security within your towers."
8 For the sake of my relatives and friends
  I will say, "Peace be within you."
9 For the sake of the house of the LORD
  our God,
  I will seek your good.

122.1–9: Pray for the peace of Jerusalem. The focus on *Jerusalem* (vv. 2, 3, 6), makes it a song of Zion★ (see Ps 48, 84). It is the only actual pilgrimage song among the Songs of Ascents, which was probably a pilgrimage collection (see Ps 120). **1–2:** The psalmist joyfully responds to the invitation to visit the Temple★ (Jer 31.6), and v. 2 locates the pilgrims in *Jerusalem*. **3–5:** The phrase, *bound firmly together*, may celebrate Jerusalem's architecture (48.12–14), but it may also suggest the city's ability to bring people together. Such is the subject of v. 4, where *go up* represents the same Hebrew root as *Ascents*. *Tribes* represents more stair-like repetition (see 120.5–7). *Judgment* could be translated "justice," which was to be enacted by *the house of David* in accordance with God's will (72.1–2). **6–8:** The key word is *peace*, the Hebrew word for which ("shalom") is an element of the name *Jerusalem*. *Peace* is the result of doing justice (72.7). **9:** References to *the house of the LORD* frame the psalm (see v. 1). The visit to the Temple has motivated the psalmist to do the *good* that promotes justice and *peace*.

PSALM 123
A Song of Ascents.

1 To you I lift up my eyes,
  O you who are enthroned in the
  heavens!
2 As the eyes of servants
  look to the hand of their master,
  as the eyes of a maid
  to the hand of her mistress,
  so our eyes look to the LORD our God,
  until he has mercy upon us.

3 Have mercy upon us, O LORD, have
  mercy upon us,
  for we have had more than enough of
  contempt.
4 Our soul has had more than its fill
  of the scorn of those who are at ease,
  of the contempt of the proud.

123.1–4: Have mercy upon us, O LORD. If the Songs of Ascents reflect the experience of pilgrims from hostile environments (see Ps 120), then it makes sense that their prayers for help would express trust in the sovereign God (vv. 1–2; see Ps 121), dependence on God's *mercy* (v. 3a), and the frustration of living amid oppression (vv. 3b–4). **1–2:** The repetition of *eyes* maintains a stair-like pattern (see 120.5–7). The pilgrims appropriately posture themselves as *servants* before a cosmic sovereign. The use of *maid* and *mistress* hints at feminine imagery for God (see Ps 131). **3:** The repeated *have mercy* surrounds the LORD with requests for help. **4:** *Contempt* (see also v. 3) and *scorn* recall the conditions that existed in the post-exilic era (see Neh 2.19 where "mocked" and "ridiculed" represent the same Hebrew words).

PSALM 124
A Song of Ascents. Of David.

1 If it had not been the LORD who was on
  our side
  —let Israel now say—
2 if it had not been the LORD who was on
  our side,
  when our enemies attacked us,
3 then they would have swallowed us up
  alive,
  when their anger was kindled against
  us;
4 then the flood would have swept us
  away,
  the torrent would have gone over us;
5 then over us would have gone
  the raging waters.

6 Blessed be the LORD,
  who has not given us
  as prey to their teeth.
7 We have escaped like a bird
  from the snare of the fowlers;
  the snare is broken,
  and we have escaped.

8 Our help is in the name of the LORD,
  who made heaven and earth.

124.1–8: Our help is in the name of the LORD. A communal song of thanksgiving, it is especially appropriate after the prayer for help in Ps 123. As Ps 123 recalls

120, so Ps 124 recalls 121 (compare 121.2 and 124.8), perhaps suggesting an intentional arranging of the Songs of Ascents (see Ps 120). **1–2:** The two *if*-clauses implicitly affirm the *help* proclaimed explicitly in v. 8. The invitation in v. 1b (see 129.1) implies liturgical* use by the pilgrims assembled in Jerusalem (see Ps 122). **3–5:** Without God's *help* (v. 8), the people would have been overwhelmed by chaotic forces, represented by *flood, torrent,* and *waters.* **6–7:** The repetitions of *We have escaped* and *snare* is another instance of stair-like repetition (see 120.5–7). The order is important. The instruments of enslavement are encompassed by references to freedom. **8:** The community now affirms what an individual voice affirmed in 121.2.

PSALM 125
A Song of Ascents.

¹ Those who trust in the LORD are like
    Mount Zion,
  which cannot be moved, but abides
    forever.
² As the mountains surround Jerusalem,
  so the LORD surrounds his people,
  from this time on and forevermore.
³ For the scepter of wickedness shall not
    rest
  on the land allotted to the
    righteous,
  so that the righteous might not stretch
    out
  their hands to do wrong.
⁴ Do good, O LORD, to those who are
    good,
  and to those who are upright in their
    hearts.
⁵ But those who turn aside to their own
    crooked ways
  the LORD will lead away with
    evildoers.
  Peace be upon Israel!

125.1–5: Trust in the LORD. Like several of the Songs of Ascents (see Ps 120), it focuses on Jerusalem (see Ps 122). **1–2:** Appropriately for pilgrims, their destination—*Mount Zion**—becomes a metaphor* for the faithful life. The surrounding terrain also reminds them of God's eternal protection. **3:** The *land allotted* may have been controlled by the wicked, which may reflect the post-exilic situation. *Trust* (v. 1) must exist

amid opposition, and v. 3 implies the petition that *the righteous* not yield to the temptation to imitate their oppressors (see 141.3–4). **4–5:** Petition becomes explicit in v. 4; whereas v. 5 professes faith in God's ultimate sovereignty, despite *the scepter of wickedness* (v. 3). The sovereign God wills *peace,* and *peace* is what the psalmist proclaims (120.7; 122.6–8; 128.6).

PSALM 126
A Song of Ascents.

¹ When the LORD restored the fortunes of
    Zion,ᵃ
  we were like those who dream.
² Then our mouth was filled with
    laughter,
  and our tongue with shouts of joy;
  then it was said among the nations,
    "The LORD has done great things for
    them."
³ The LORD has done great things for us,
  and we rejoiced.

⁴ Restore our fortunes, O LORD,
  like the watercourses in the Negeb.
⁵ May those who sow in tears
  reap with shouts of joy.
⁶ Those who go out weeping,
  bearing the seed for sowing,
  shall come home with shouts of joy,
  carrying their sheaves.

126.1–6: Bringing in the sheaves. The focus on *Zion** is characteristic of the Songs of Ascents (see Ps 120), as are the petition for help (120.1–2; 123.3) and trust in future deliverance (121.7–8; 123.2; 124.8). **1–3:** The return from exile is cited in v. 1 (Deut 30.3; Jer 30.3; Ps 85.1). The image of a *dream* come true was a source of *joy* and celebration, as even *the nations* recognized (compare v. 2b with 115.2). **4–6:** Because the return from exile brought problems of its own, the people needed to continue to pray for restoration (vv. 4–5). The image of *watercourses* communicates hope, since dry streambeds could suddenly become rivers during the rainy season. Striking a thematic note, v. 6 clearly articulates the hope of further *joy.*

a Or brought back those who returned to Zion

PSALM 127

A Song of Ascents. Of Solomon.

1 Unless the LORD builds the house,
    those who build it labor in vain.
  Unless the LORD guards the city,
    the guard keeps watch in vain.
2 It is in vain that you rise up early
    and go late to rest,
  eating the bread of anxious toil;
    for he gives sleep to his beloved.*a*

3 Sons are indeed a heritage from
      the LORD,
    the fruit of the womb a reward.
4 Like arrows in the hand of a warrior
    are the sons of one's youth.
5 Happy is the man who has
    his quiver full of them.
  He shall not be put to shame
    when he speaks with his enemies in
      the gate.

127.1–5: Unless the LORD builds the house. The focus on daily activities (vv. 1–2) and family (vv. 3–5) may reflect the concerns of ordinary pilgrims who originally used the Songs of Ascents (see Ps 120). The attribution to *Solomon* is in keeping with the collection's interest in Jerusalem and the Davidic dynasty.* **1–2:** The key word is *vain.* It, and the repeated *Unless the LORD,* show the stair-like repetition characteristic of the collection (see 120.5–7). Any and every activity will be purposeless unless oriented to God. **3–5:** Because building a house (v. 1) can refer to the establishment of a family, v. 3 follows vv. 1–2 more logically than it may first appear. Children are to be seen as God's gift. The city *gate* was the site of legal activity, so having many children may have brought power and protection in the public arena.

PSALM 128

A Song of Ascents.

1 Happy is everyone who fears
      the LORD,
    who walks in his ways.
2 You shall eat the fruit of the labor of
      your hands;
    you shall be happy, and it shall go
      well with you.

3 Your wife will be like a fruitful vine
      within your house;
    your children will be like olive shoots
      around your table.
4 Thus shall the man be blessed
    who fears the LORD.

5 The LORD bless you from Zion.
    May you see the prosperity of
      Jerusalem
    all the days of your life.
6 May you see your children's children.
    Peace be upon Israel!

128.1–6: Happy is everyone who fears the LORD. Linked to Ps 127 by the word *happy,* it also shares the interest in daily activities and family matters that is characteristic of the Songs of Ascents (see Ps 120). **1–2:** Fear connotes trust and obedience. To be *happy* involves orienting life fully to God (1.1–2; 112.1). **3–4:** The focus shifts from the realm of work to that of family. As in v. 1, the crucial component is fear of God. **5–6:** *Blessed* (v. 4) and *bless* (v. 5; 134.3) demonstrate the stair-like repetition that characterizes the collection (see 120.5–7). The effect is to put the daily concerns of families in the broader context of the *peace* of God's larger family, *Israel* (122.6–8; 125.5; 133.3).

PSALM 129

A Song of Ascents.

1 "Often have they attacked me from my
      youth"
    —let Israel now say—
2 "often have they attacked me from my
      youth,
    yet they have not prevailed against
      me.
3 The plowers plowed on my back;
    they made their furrows long."
4 The LORD is righteous;
    he has cut the cords of the wicked.
5 May all who hate Zion
    be put to shame and turned
      backward.
6 Let them be like the grass on the
      housetops
    that withers before it grows up,

a Or *for he provides for his beloved during sleep*

7 with which reapers do not fill their
hands
or binders of sheaves their arms,
8 while those who pass by do not say,
"The blessing of the LORD be upon
you!
We bless you in the name of the
LORD!"

129.1–8: They have not prevailed against me. This psalm is categorized either as a communal prayer for help or communal thanksgiving, since it is not clear whether deliverance has occurred (vv. 2–4) or is still awaited (vv. 5–8). The combination of individual voice and communal voice is understandable if the Songs of Ascents were used as pilgrim songs (see Ps 120). **1–4:** Verse 1 recalls 124.1. That the people continue to exist (v. 2b) despite frequent opposition (vv. 1–2a, 3) is evidence that God *is righteous* (v. 4); that is, God is responsible for the people's life. **5–8:** The interest in *Zion* characterizes the collection (122.6–8; 125.1–2). Verse 8 apparently articulates what the opponents of *Zion* will *not* hear or experience (compare 134.3).

~~~

PSALM 130

A Song of Ascents.

1 Out of the depths I cry to you, O LORD.
2 Lord, hear my voice!
Let your ears be attentive
to the voice of my supplications!

3 If you, O LORD, should mark iniquities,
Lord, who could stand?
4 But there is forgiveness with you,
so that you may be revered.

5 I wait for the LORD, my soul waits,
and in his word I hope;
6 my soul waits for the Lord
more than those who watch for the
morning,
more than those who watch for the
morning.

7 O Israel, hope in the LORD!
For with the LORD there is steadfast
love,
and with him is great power to
redeem.

8 It is he who will redeem Israel
from all its iniquities.

130.1–8: Out of the depths. The juxtaposition with Ps 129 is auspicious, for it indicates that opposition to God occurs also within the ranks of God's people. This *Song of Ascents* (see Ps 120) became one of the church's Penitential Psalms* (see Ps 6). **1–2:** *The depths* represent a chaotic situation from which the psalmist pleads for deliverance. **3–4:** The question in v. 3 implies that the psalmist's own sinfulness has contributed to the current distress. God's *forgiveness* provides the foundation for the subsequent expressions of *hope* (vv. 5, 7). **5–6:** To *wait* and to *hope* are essentially synonymous (27.14; 31.24). The repetition in v. 6 is stair-like (see 120.5–7) and creates the effect of waiting. **7–8:** *Hope* is also associated with *steadfast love* in 33.18. God's *forgiveness* (v. 4) of *iniquities* (vv. 3, 8) is evidence of God's *steadfast love.* It recalls Israel's past (Ex 34.6–7), and the memory is a source of *hope* (131.3).

~~~

PSALM 131

A Song of Ascents. Of David.

1 O LORD, my heart is not lifted up,
my eyes are not raised too high;
I do not occupy myself with things
too great and too marvelous for me.
2 But I have calmed and quieted my soul,
like a weaned child with its mother;
my soul is like the weaned child that
is with me.*a*

3 O Israel, hope in the LORD
from this time on and forevermore.

131.1–3: Like a weaned child with its mother. The use of *mother*/child imagery and the likelihood of female authorship (v. 2) fits the pilgrimage context of the Songs of Ascents since whole families may have made the trip to Jerusalem (see Ps 120). The psalm is an expression of humble trust that follows well upon Ps 130, to which Ps 131 is verbally linked (130.7; 131.3). **1:** The psalmist's humility is evident in her attitudes (*heart*), demeanor (*eyes*), and vocation (*occupy*). **2:** Her humility, perhaps forced upon her as a woman in a patriarchal culture, is accompanied by a

a Or *my soul within me is like a weaned child*

sense of peace. *A weaned child* is most likely to return to its *mother* for security, so the phrase *with me* strongly suggests that the author is a woman. **3:** Israel's *hope* is to be based on the same experience described in v. 2. Thus, *the* LORD is portrayed as a loving, nurturing *mother* (see Deut 1.31; Isa 66.13; Jer 31.20).

PSALM 132
A Song of Ascents.

1 O LORD, remember in David's favor
    all the hardships he endured;
2 how he swore to the LORD
    and vowed to the Mighty One of Jacob,
3 "I will not enter my house
    or get into my bed;
4 I will not give sleep to my eyes
    or slumber to my eyelids,
5 until I find a place for the LORD,
    a dwelling place for the Mighty One of Jacob."

6 We heard of it in Ephrathah;
    we found it in the fields of Jaar.
7 "Let us go to his dwelling place;
    let us worship at his footstool."

8 Rise up, O LORD, and go to your resting place,
    you and the ark of your might.
9 Let your priests be clothed with righteousness,
    and let your faithful shout for joy.
10 For your servant David's sake
    do not turn away the face of your anointed one.

11 The LORD swore to David a sure oath
    from which he will not turn back:
"One of the sons of your body
    I will set on your throne.
12 If your sons keep my covenant
    and my decrees that I shall teach them,
    their sons also, forevermore,
    shall sit on your throne."

13 For the LORD has chosen Zion;
    he has desired it for his habitation:

14 "This is my resting place forever;
    here I will reside, for I have desired it.
15 I will abundantly bless its provisions;
    I will satisfy its poor with bread.
16 Its priests I will clothe with salvation,
    and its faithful will shout for joy.
17 There I will cause a horn to sprout up for David;
    I have prepared a lamp for my anointed one.
18 His enemies I will clothe with disgrace,
    but on him, his crown will gleam."

132.1–18: A lamp for my anointed* one. Noticeably longer than the other Songs of Ascents (see Ps 120), it is usually classified as a royal psalm (see Ps 2, 72) or a song of Zion* (see Ps 48, 122). As such, it articulates the reasons that Jerusalem is the pilgrim's destination (v. 13). The use of 132.8–9 is assigned to Solomon's dedication of the Temple* (2 Chr 6.41), but vv. 17–18 suggest the psalm originated after the traumatic disappearance of the monarchy (see Ps 89). **1–5:** The *hardships* (v. 1) of David may refer not so much to the efforts recounted in vv. 3–5, but rather to the eventual loss of the monarchy (see vv. 17–18). David's oath recalls 2 Sam 7.1–2. **6–7:** The identity of *it* is unclear; it could be David's oath (vv. 3–5) or perhaps the ark. *Ephrathah* may indicate the region around Bethlehem, David's home. *Jaar* may be a shortened form of Kiriath-jearim, the location of the ark in 1 Sam 6.19–7.2. If the psalm was used by pilgrims, v. 7 may indicate their intent to retrace David's route in moving the ark to Jerusalem (2 Sam 6). **8–10:** Verse 8 may again recall David's journey with the ark, or it may initiate a prayer for the Temple (v. 8), its officiants and worshippers (v. 9), and the royal house (probably now destroyed). **11–12:** God's oath responds to David's oath (vv. 3–5). It recalls the promises to David in 2 Sam 7, although *covenant** recalls 89.3–4. **13–16:** Corresponding to vv. 6–9, this section indicates God's choice of *Zion* as *my resting place* (v. 14; see v. 8). Verse 16 indicates God's response to the petition in v. 9. **17–18:** These verses respond to the plea of v. 10. *Horn* and *lamp* represent the promise of a future monarch, an *anointed one* (2.2), although this designation could also be applied to the whole people (105.15; see Ps 149).

PSALM 133

A Song of Ascents.

1 How very good and pleasant it is
   when kindred live together in unity!
2 It is like the precious oil on the head,
   running down upon the beard,
 on the beard of Aaron,
   running down over the collar of his
     robes.
3 It is like the dew of Hermon,
   which falls on the mountains of Zion.
 For there the LORD ordained his
     blessing,
 life forevermore.

133.1–3: When kindred live together in unity. Like
other Songs of Ascents (see Ps 120), it features family
imagery (v. 1; Ps 127–128) and focuses finally on
Zion* (v. 3; Ps 122). It thus recalls Ps 132. The word
blessing anticipates Ps 134. Ps 133 may represent a
final celebration of the pilgrims' unity before a parting
blessing. **1:** Perhaps originally a proverbial saying, the
focus here is on an extended biological family. **2:** The
simile* probably is intended to communicate joy and
abundance. The stair-like repetition (see 120.5–7) of
running down recreates the effect of dripping oil. **3:**
Hermon was known for abundant *dew*. The simile
shifts attention from local families to the whole family
of God gathered at *Zion*. It is *there* that the gathered
family experiences God's *blessing* of *life forevermore*.

PSALM 134

A Song of Ascents.

1 Come, bless the LORD, all you servants
   of the LORD,
 who stand by night in the house of
   the LORD!
2 Lift up your hands to the holy place,
   and bless the LORD.

3 May the LORD, maker of heaven and
   earth,
 bless you from Zion.

134.1–3: Blessing from Zion.* It provides a fitting
conclusion to the Songs of Ascents (see Ps 120) by
offering a parting benediction (v. 3) to the pilgrims.
1–2: It may have originally been used at a closing worship service on the *night* before the pilgrims' depar-

ture. Two names for the Temple*—*house of the LORD*
and *holy place*—are surrounded by the invitation to
bless the LORD. **3:** Recalling 121.2 and 124.8, it sends
pilgrims on their way with the hope that God will *bless*
them (128.5).

PSALM 135

1 Praise the LORD!
   Praise the name of the LORD;
   give praise, O servants of the LORD,
2 you that stand in the house of
     the LORD,
   in the courts of the house of
     our God.
3 Praise the LORD, for the LORD is good;
   sing to his name, for he is gracious.
4 For the LORD has chosen Jacob for
     himself,
   Israel as his own possession.

5 For I know that the LORD is great;
   our Lord is above all gods.
6 Whatever the LORD pleases he does,
   in heaven and on earth,
   in the seas and all deeps.
7 He it is who makes the clouds rise at
     the end of the earth;
   he makes lightnings for the rain
   and brings out the wind from his
     storehouses.

8 He it was who struck down the firstborn
     of Egypt,
   both human beings and animals;
9 he sent signs and wonders
   into your midst, O Egypt,
   against Pharaoh and all his servants.
10 He struck down many nations
    and killed mighty kings—
11 Sihon, king of the Amorites,
    and Og, king of Bashan,
    and all the kingdoms of Canaan—
12 and gave their land as a heritage,
    a heritage to his people Israel.

13 Your name, O LORD, endures forever,
    your renown, O LORD, throughout all
      ages.
14 For the LORD will vindicate his people,
    and have compassion on his servants.

15 The idols of the nations are silver and
   gold,
     the work of human hands.
16 They have mouths, but they do not
   speak;
     they have eyes, but they do not see;
17 they have ears, but they do not hear,
     and there is no breath in their
     mouths.
18 Those who make them
     and all who trust them
     shall become like them.

19 O house of Israel, bless the LORD!
     O house of Aaron, bless the LORD!
20 O house of Levi, bless the LORD!
     You that fear the LORD, bless
     the LORD!
21 Blessed be the LORD from Zion,
     he who resides in Jerusalem.
   Praise the LORD!

135.1–21: Praise the name of the LORD. A song of
praise, it locates the *servants of the LORD* (v. 1) in the
same place as 134.1. Some scholars suggest that it,
along with Ps 136 and 137, form an appendix to the
Songs of Ascents (Ps 120–134). **1–4:** *Praise* (vv. 1, 3)
and *name* (vv. 1, 3, 13) are thematic. *Name* suggests
character, and the psalm will describe who God is and
how God is *good* (v. 3) by rehearsing what God has
done. Verse 4 anticipates v. 14. **5–14:** The sovereignty
of God *above all gods* (v. 5; see vv. 15–18) is evident
in the created order (vv. 6–7; 115.3) as well as in the
Exodus (vv. 8–9) and entry into *Canaan* (vv. 10–11;
Num 21.21–35). The gift of land to oppressed persons
demonstrates God's *compassion* (v. 14; Deut 32.36).
15–18: In contrast to God's dynamic activity, *idols* do
nothing (115.4–8). **19–21:** The four-fold occurrence
of *bless* again recalls Ps 134, as does the final focus on
Zion.✶ The different addressees may represent different groups, such as the entire congregation and priests
(115.9–11; 118.2–4).

PSALM 136

1 O give thanks to the LORD, for he is
   good,
     for his steadfast love endures forever.
2 O give thanks to the God of gods,
     for his steadfast love endures
     forever.

3 O give thanks to the Lord of lords,
     for his steadfast love endures forever;
4 who alone does great wonders,
     for his steadfast love endures forever;
5 who by understanding made the
   heavens,
     for his steadfast love endures forever;
6 who spread out the earth on the
   waters,
     for his steadfast love endures forever;
7 who made the great lights,
     for his steadfast love endures forever;
8 the sun to rule over the day,
     for his steadfast love endures forever;
9 the moon and stars to rule over
   the night,
     for his steadfast love endures forever;
10 who struck Egypt through their
   firstborn,
     for his steadfast love endures forever;
11 and brought Israel out from among
   them,
     for his steadfast love endures forever;
12 with a strong hand and an outstretched
   arm,
     for his steadfast love endures forever;
13 who divided the Red Sea[a] in two,
     for his steadfast love endures forever;
14 and made Israel pass through the midst
   of it,
     for his steadfast love endures forever;
15 but overthrew Pharaoh and his army in
   the Red Sea,[a]
     for his steadfast love endures forever;
16 who led his people through the
   wilderness,
     for his steadfast love endures forever;
17 who struck down great kings,
     for his steadfast love endures forever;
18 and killed famous kings,
     for his steadfast love endures forever;
19 Sihon, king of the Amorites,
     for his steadfast love endures forever;
20 and Og, king of Bashan,
     for his steadfast love endures forever;
21 and gave their land as a heritage,
     for his steadfast love endures forever;

a Or Sea of Reeds

22 a heritage to his servant Israel,
    for his steadfast love endures
        forever.

23 It is he who remembered us in our low
        estate,
    for his steadfast love endures
        forever;
24 and rescued us from our foes,
    for his steadfast love endures
        forever;
25 who gives food to all flesh,
    for his steadfast love endures
        forever.

26 O give thanks to the God of heaven,
    for his steadfast love endures
        forever.

136.1–26: God's steadfast love endures forever. A song of praise, it recalls Ps 135 (see *good* in 135.5 and 136.1; compare 136.2–3 with 135.5, 136.5–9 with 135.6–7, and 136.10–22 with 135.8–12). It is also frequently labeled a historical psalm (see Ps 78, 105–106). Its most obvious feature is the refrain that is repeated in every verse, suggesting that God's *steadfast love* pervades Israel's story. The refrain probably represents a sung congregational response. **1–3:** Verse 1 recalls 106.1; 107.1; 118.1, 29. As in Ps 135, God's sovereignty—*God of gods* and *Lord of lords*—is evident by what God has done (vv. 4–25). **4–9:** The focus on creation recalls Gen 1. The refrain suggests that creation was motivated by God's *steadfast love*. **10–22:** Also motivated by God's *steadfast love* is the Exodus (vv. 10–15) and guidance in the wilderness toward entry into the *land* (vv. 16–22). **23–25:** Verses 23–24 seem to refer to the return from exile. The perspective becomes cosmic again in v. 25 (see vv. 4–9) with the mention of *all flesh* (104.27). **26:** Because creation and providence reveal God's *steadfast love*, the appropriate response is gratitude.

PSALM 137

1 By the rivers of Babylon—
    there we sat down and there we wept
        when we remembered Zion.
2 On the willows[a] there
    we hung up our harps.
3 For there our captors
    asked us for songs,

and our tormentors asked for mirth,
        saying,
    "Sing us one of the songs of Zion!"

4 How could we sing the LORD's song
    in a foreign land?
5 If I forget you, O Jerusalem,
    let my right hand wither!
6 Let my tongue cling to the roof of my
        mouth,
    if I do not remember you,
    if I do not set Jerusalem
        above my highest joy.

7 Remember, O LORD, against the
        Edomites
    the day of Jerusalem's fall,
    how they said, "Tear it down! Tear it
        down!
    Down to its foundations!"
8 O daughter Babylon, you devastator![b]
    Happy shall they be who pay
        you back
    what you have done to us!
9 Happy shall they be who take your little
        ones
    and dash them against the rock!

137.1–9: When we remembered Zion. ✴ The focus on *Zion* (vv. 1, 3) and *Jerusalem* (vv. 5–7) recalls the Songs of Ascents, and it is likely that Ps 135–137 form an appendix to that collection. Psalm 137 almost certainly originated during the exile in *Babylon* or shortly after the return. **1–4:** The *rivers of Babylon* refer to the canals between the Tigris and Euphrates Rivers. *Remember* serves as a theme (vv. 1, 6, 7). The *songs of Zion* probably indicate the joyful songs sung by pilgrims visiting the city (Ps 48, 84, 122). Tied closely to the place itself, they cannot be sung elsewhere. **5–6:** Although remembering *Jerusalem* was painful (v. 1), to *forget* the city would mean permanent silence—that is, death. Memory sustains hope. **7–9:** While grief was evident in vv. 1–4, rage is now expressed. The *Edomites* were complicit in *Jerusalem's fall* (Ezek 35.1–15; Obad 1–14), and *Babylon* was directly responsible. Verse 9 reflects the brutality of all warfare (2 Kings 8.12), but requests simply that the punishment fit the crime (see v. 8).

---

a Or *poplars*   *b* Or *you who are devastated*

PSALM 138

Of David.

1 I give you thanks, O LORD, with my
   whole heart;
   before the gods I sing your praise;
2 I bow down toward your holy temple
   and give thanks to your name for your
      steadfast love and your
      faithfulness;
   for you have exalted your name and
      your word
   above everything.*a*
3 On the day I called, you answered me,
   you increased my strength of soul.*b*

4 All the kings of the earth shall praise
      you, O LORD,
   for they have heard the words of your
      mouth.
5 They shall sing of the ways of the LORD,
   for great is the glory of the LORD.
6 For though the LORD is high, he regards
      the lowly;
   but the haughty he perceives from far
      away.

7 Though I walk in the midst of trouble,
   you preserve me against the wrath of
      my enemies;
   you stretch out your hand,
   and your right hand delivers me.
8 The LORD will fulfill his purpose
      for me;
   your steadfast love, O LORD, endures
      forever.
   Do not forsake the work of your
      hands.

138.1–8: **With my whole heart.** A song of thanksgiving, it initiates a final Davidic collection (Ps 138–145), the function of which is to respond to the Exile* (see Ps 137) by suggesting that the whole people now fulfills the function formerly served by the Davidic monarchy (Ps 144; see also Ps 149). **1–3:** With his or her whole being (9.1; 119.2), the psalmist is grateful. Reference to *the gods* recalls 135.5 and 136.2–3. God alone is to be worshipped (v. 2), an act that celebrates God's *steadfast love* and *faithfulness* (Ex 34.6; Ps 5.7; 100.5). Acting in character and according to God's *word* (v. 2), God has delivered the psalmist (v. 3; see

v. 7). **4–6:** The psalmist's deliverance, or at least what it represents, is to be universally acclaimed (2.10). God's *ways* involve exalting *the lowly* (113.7–9) and humbling *the haughty*. **7–8:** While v. 7 rehearses the psalmist's deliverance, v. 8 implies an ongoing need, in the midst of which the psalmist is content to trust God's *steadfast love* (v. 2).

PSALM 139

To the leader. Of David. A Psalm.

1 O LORD, you have searched me and
      known me.
2 You know when I sit down and when I
      rise up;
   you discern my thoughts from
      far away.
3 You search out my path and my lying
      down,
   and are acquainted with all my ways.
4 Even before a word is on my tongue,
   O LORD, you know it completely.
5 You hem me in, behind and before,
   and lay your hand upon me.
6 Such knowledge is too wonderful for
      me;
   it is so high that I cannot attain it.

7 Where can I go from your spirit?
   Or where can I flee from your
      presence?
8 If I ascend to heaven, you are there;
   if I make my bed in Sheol, you are
      there.
9 If I take the wings of the morning
   and settle at the farthest limits of the
      sea,
10 even there your hand shall lead me,
   and your right hand shall hold me
      fast.
11 If I say, "Surely the darkness shall cover
      me,
   and the light around me become
      night,"
12 even the darkness is not dark to you;
   the night is as bright as the day,
   for darkness is as light to you.

a Cn: Heb *you have exalted your word above all your
name*   *b* Syr Compare Gk Tg: Heb *you made me
arrogant in my soul with strength*

13 For it was you who formed my inward
parts;
you knit me together in my mother's
womb.
14 I praise you, for I am fearfully and
wonderfully made.
Wonderful are your works;
that I know very well.
15 My frame was not hidden from you,
when I was being made in secret,
intricately woven in the depths of the
earth.
16 Your eyes beheld my unformed
substance.
In your book were written
all the days that were formed for me,
when none of them as yet existed.
17 How weighty to me are your thoughts,
O God!
How vast is the sum of them!
18 I try to count them—they are more
than the sand;
I come to the end*a*—I am still with
you.

19 O that you would kill the wicked,
O God,
and that the bloodthirsty would
depart from me—
20 those who speak of you maliciously,
and lift themselves up against you for
evil!*b*
21 Do I not hate those who hate you,
O LORD?
And do I not loathe those who rise up
against you?
22 I hate them with perfect hatred;
I count them my enemies.
23 Search me, O God, and know my heart;
test me and know my thoughts.
24 See if there is any wicked*c* way in me,
and lead me in the way everlasting.*d*

139.1–24: You have searched me and known me.
The petitions in vv. 19–20, 23–24 suggest that the
psalmist has been falsely accused and appeals to God
for vindication (see Ps 7, 17). Several forms of *know*
represent the key word (vv. 1–2, 4, 6, 14, 23). **1–6:**
The psalmist asserts that he or she is fully *known*—
actions and thoughts (v. 2), as well as lifestyle (v. 3)
and speech (v. 4). V. 5 implies a vulnerability that

could be threatening, but the psalmist seems to welcome God's *knowledge* (v. 6). **7–12:** God's *spirit* represents God's *presence*, which is inescapable. *Sheol**
is the realm of the dead and was ordinarily understood
to be devoid of God's presence (6.5; 30.3), but not
here (see Am 9.2). God's *light* dispels even utter *darkness* (vv. 11–12). The psalmist is secure everywhere
(v. 10; 73.23–24). **13–18:** The conceptual background
of vv. 15–16 is unclear. Along with *knit* in v. 13, *woven*
suggests the metaphor* of God as creative weaver.
While the psalmist cannot understand God's *thoughts*
(v. 17; compare v. 2), he or she is assured of being
with God (v. 18; see vv. 12–17). **19–24:** The petition
in vv. 19–20 seeks not so much personal revenge as it
does justice (140.9–12). Loyalty and openness to God
(vv. 23–24; see v. 1) include opposing those who oppose God (vv. 21–22).

~~~~~~~~~~~~~~~~~~~~~~~~~~~~~~~~

PSALM 140
To the leader. A Psalm of David.

1 Deliver me, O LORD, from evildoers;
protect me from those who are
violent,
2 who plan evil things in their minds
and stir up wars continually.
3 They make their tongue sharp as a
snake's,
and under their lips is the venom of
vipers. *Selah*

4 Guard me, O LORD, from the hands of
the wicked;
protect me from the violent
who have planned my downfall.
5 The arrogant have hidden a trap for me,
and with cords they have spread a
net,*e*
along the road they have set snares
for me. *Selah*

6 I say to the LORD, "You are my God;
give ear, O LORD, to the voice of my
supplications."
7 O LORD, my Lord, my strong deliverer,
you have covered my head in the day
of battle.

---

a Or *I awake*   *b* Cn: Meaning of Heb uncertain
c Heb *hurtful*   *d* Or *the ancient way.* Compare Jer 6.16
e Or *they have spread cords as a net*

8 Do not grant, O LORD, the desires of
　　the wicked;
　　do not further their evil plot.*　　Selah

9 Those who surround me lift up their
　　heads;*
　　let the mischief of their lips
　　　overwhelm them!

10 Let burning coals fall on them!
　　Let them be flung into pits, no more
　　　to rise!

11 Do not let the slanderer be established
　　in the land;
　　let evil speedily hunt down the
　　　violent!

12 I know that the LORD maintains the
　　cause of the needy,
　　and executes justice for the poor.

13 Surely the righteous shall give thanks to
　　your name;
　　the upright shall live in your
　　　presence.

140.1–13: Protect me from those who are violent.
In this prayer for help, the complaints and petitions
against *the wicked* (vv. 1–5, 8–11) recall 139.19–22,
while the expressions of trust (vv. 6–7, 12–13) recall
139.1–18. **1–5:** Elsewhere too, *the wicked* (v. 4) are
violent (vv. 1, 3; 7.16; 11.5). Verbal abuse (v. 3; 58.4)
accompanies *planned* persecution (vv. 4–5; 9.15;
10.9). **6–7:** In the midst of complaint and petition, the
psalmist professes faith. God has *covered* the psalmist
(5.11; 91.4). **8–13:** The petitions (vv. 8–11) aim not at
personal revenge, but rather at the elimination of violence and oppression. In short, the issue is *justice*
(v. 12), which God wills for all, especially the *needy*
and *poor* (9.18; 82.3–4). Such advocacy is cause for
gratitude (v. 13).

PSALM 141
A Psalm of David.

1 I call upon you, O LORD; come quickly
　　to me;
　　give ear to my voice when I call to
　　　you.

2 Let my prayer be counted as incense
　　before you,
　　and the lifting up of my hands as an
　　　evening sacrifice.

3 Set a guard over my mouth, O LORD;
　　keep watch over the door of my lips.

4 Do not turn my heart to any evil,
　　to busy myself with wicked deeds
　　in company with those who work
　　　iniquity;
　　do not let me eat of their delicacies.

5 Let the righteous strike me;
　　let the faithful correct me.
　　Never let the oil of the wicked anoint
　　　my head,*
　　for my prayer is continually* against
　　　their wicked deeds.

6 When they are given over to those who
　　shall condemn them,
　　then they shall learn that my words
　　　were pleasant.

7 Like a rock that one breaks apart and
　　shatters on the land,
　　so shall their bones be strewn at the
　　　mouth of Sheol.*

8 But my eyes are turned toward you,
　　O GOD, my Lord;
　　in you I seek refuge; do not leave me
　　　defenseless.

9 Keep me from the trap that they have
　　laid for me,
　　and from the snares of evildoers.

10 Let the wicked fall into their own nets,
　　while I alone escape.

141.1–10: Do not leave me defenseless. A prayer for
help, it recalls Ps 140 and anticipates Ps 142 (see *trap*
in 140.5; 141.9; 142.3). It requests deliverance not
only from the persecutions of *the wicked* (v. 10), but
also from the temptation to imitate them (vv. 3–5).
1–2: Uplifted *hands* are the posture of *prayer* (28.2;
63.4). The psalmist probably intends the *prayer* to accompany rather than replace an *evening sacrifice* (Ezra
9.5). **3–7:** The focus here is upon the psalmist and *the
wicked* (v. 5). The psalmist prays for support against
the enticement of *evil* (vv. 3–5a). Then he or she apparently anticipates v. 10 by envisioning the destruction of *the wicked*, but vv. 5–7 are very unclear (see

a Heb adds *they are exalted*　　*b* Cn Compare Gk: Heb
those who surround me are uplifted in head; Heb divides
verses 8 and 9 differently　　*c* Gk: Meaning of Heb
uncertain　　*d* Cn: Heb *for continually and my prayer*
e Meaning of Heb of verses 5–7 is uncertain

note e). **8–10:** Despite the enticement of *evil* and the power of *the wicked*, the psalmist entrusts life to God alone. Amid the threat of being *defenseless* (literally, "naked"), the psalmist looks to God as *refuge* (2.12; 142.5). Protection for *the righteous* (v. 5) must finally mean the demise of *the wicked* (vv. 9–10; 140.9–13).

PSALM 142

A Maskil of David. When he was in the cave.
A Prayer.

1 With my voice I cry to the LORD;
　　with my voice I make supplication to
　　　　the LORD.
2 I pour out my complaint before him;
　　I tell my trouble before him.
3 When my spirit is faint,
　　you know my way.

In the path where I walk
　　they have hidden a trap for me.
4 Look on my right hand and see—
　　there is no one who takes notice of
　　　　me;
no refuge remains to me;
　　no one cares for me.

5 I cry to you, O LORD;
　　I say, "You are my refuge,
　　my portion in the land of the living."
6 Give heed to my cry,
　　for I am brought very low.

Save me from my persecutors,
　　for they are too strong for me.
7 Bring me out of prison,
　　so that I may give thanks to your
　　　　name.
The righteous will surround me,
　　for you will deal bountifully with me.

142.1–7: You are my refuge. *Supplication* (v. 1) and *complaint* (v. 2) indicate a prayer for help. It recalls Ps 141 and anticipates Ps 143 (compare 142.3 and 143.4). The superscription is apparently based upon 1 Sam 22.1; 24.3–4 (see Ps 57). Expressions of trust pervade the psalm (vv. 3a, 5, 7b). **1–3a:** Israel's faith was based on the assurance that God hears the needy when they *cry to the LORD* (v. 1; Ex 2.23; Ps 107.12–13). *Faint* indicates the need (107.5; 143.4), which God will *know*. **3b–5:** The need is indicated fur-

ther in renewed *complaint*. *Trap* recalls 140.5; 141.9. Although apparently abandoned by all, the psalmist again moves from *complaint* to assurance: God is a *refuge* (2.12; 141.8). A *portion* originally indicated a parcel of land and thus access to life; God is the psalmist's access to life (16.5; 73.26). **6–7:** Supplication and complaint recur before a final expression of trust (13.6; 116.7) that anticipates human as well as divine support (see v. 4).

PSALM 143

A Psalm of David.

1 Hear my prayer, O LORD;
　　give ear to my supplications in your
　　　　faithfulness;
　　answer me in your righteousness.
2 Do not enter into judgment with your
　　　　servant,
　　for no one living is righteous before
　　　　you.

3 For the enemy has pursued me,
　　crushing my life to the ground,
　　making me sit in darkness like those
　　　　long dead.
4 Therefore my spirit faints within me;
　　my heart within me is appalled.

5 I remember the days of old,
　　I think about all your deeds,
　　I meditate on the works of your hands.
6 I stretch out my hands to you;
　　my soul thirsts for you like a parched
　　　　land.　　　　　　　　　　*Selah*

7 Answer me quickly, O LORD;
　　my spirit fails.
Do not hide your face from me,
　　or I shall be like those who go down
　　　　to the Pit.
8 Let me hear of your steadfast love in the
　　　　morning,
　　for in you I put my trust.
Teach me the way I should go,
　　for to you I lift up my soul.

9 Save me, O LORD, from my enemies;
　　I have fled to you for refuge.*a*

a One Heb Ms Gk: MT *to you I have hidden*

10 Teach me to do your will,
    for you are my God.
  Let your good spirit lead me
    on a level path.

11 For your name's sake, O LORD, preserve
    my life.
  In your righteousness bring me out of
    trouble.

12 In your steadfast love cut off my
    enemies,
  and destroy all my adversaries,
    for I am your servant.

143.1–12: Answer me in your righteousness. The final in a series of prayers for help (Ps 139–143), it became one of the church's Penitential Psalms✶ (see Ps
6). **1–2:** The opening petitions focus on God's character, which pervades the psalm. The psalmist's future
will depend on God's *faithfulness* (v. 1), *righteousness*
(vv. 2, 11), and *steadfast love* (vv. 8, 12). To so depend
on God is what it means to be God's *servant* (vv. 2,
12). To offer life to those who are not *righteous* is what
it means to be God. **3–6:** The *enemy* (v. 3; see vv. 9,
12) threatens the psalmist's *life* (v. 3; see v. 11). Faintness of *spirit* (77.3; 142.3) leads to recollection of
God's past *deeds* and *works* on behalf of the oppressed (v. 5). Memory yields the hope expressed in
the psalmist's reach toward God (v. 6; 42.1–2; 63.1).
7–9: *Answer* echoes the plea of v. 1 and *spirit* the complaint of v. 4. *The Pit* is the realm of the dead (28.1;
30.3). God's *steadfast love* (v. 8; see v. 12) promises
life. To *lift up* the *soul* (v. 8; 25.1; 86.4) means to offer
one's life to God in *trust* and submission to God's *way*.
9–10: Thus, the psalmist prays not only for life but
for God to *teach me* (vv. 8, 10). **11–12:** God's *name's
sake* indicates God's character, at the heart of which
are *righteousness* and *steadfast love* (Ex 34.6; Ps
36.5–6).

PSALM 144
Of David.

1 Blessed be the LORD, my rock,
    who trains my hands for war, and my
      fingers for battle;
2 my rock[a] and my fortress,
    my stronghold and my deliverer,
  my shield, in whom I take refuge,
    who subdues the peoples[b]
      under me.

3 O LORD, what are human beings that
    you regard them,
  or mortals that you think of them?
4 They are like a breath;
    their days are like a passing
      shadow.

5 Bow your heavens, O LORD, and come
    down;
  touch the mountains so that they
    smoke.
6 Make the lightning flash and scatter
    them;
  send out your arrows and rout
    them.
7 Stretch out your hand from on high;
    set me free and rescue me from the
      mighty waters,
  from the hand of aliens,
8 whose mouths speak lies,
    and whose right hands are false.

9 I will sing a new song to you, O God;
    upon a ten-stringed harp I will play to
      you,
10 the one who gives victory to kings,
    who rescues his servant David.
11 Rescue me from the cruel sword,
    and deliver me from the hand of
      aliens,
  whose mouths speak lies,
    and whose right hands are false.

12 May our sons in their youth
    be like plants full grown,
  our daughters like corner pillars,
    cut for the building of a palace.
13 May our barns be filled,
    with produce of every kind;
  may our sheep increase by thousands,
    by tens of thousands in our fields,
14   and may our cattle be heavy with
      young.
  May there be no breach in the walls,[c]
    no exile,
  and no cry of distress in our streets.

---

a With 18.2 and 2 Sam 22.2: Heb *my steadfast love*
b Heb Mss Syr Aquila Jerome: MT *my people*
c Heb lacks *in the walls*

15 Happy are the people to whom such
   blessings fall;
   happy are the people whose God is
   the LORD.

144.1–15: A new song to you, O God. Because of the reference to *David* (v. 10) and because it recalls Ps 18, Ps 144 is usually categorized as a royal psalm. The label is problematic, however, since it reflects the realities of the post-exilic era when the monarchy had disappeared. By rewriting Ps 18, the psalmist suggests that the whole people have appropriated the former role of the monarchy and are heir to the promises formerly attached to it (see Ps 149; Isa 55.3). **1–2:** Recalling 18.1–2, 34, 46–47, these verses also recall the royal Ps 2 and its reminder that God and his purposes are always opposed. **3–8:** Verse 3 is reminiscent of 8.4. An acute awareness of human transience accompanied the loss of the monarchy (see the royal Ps 89, vv. 46–48). Verses 5–8 have transformed the description of a theophany* in 18.7–15 into a request, indicating a problem precipitated by *the hand of aliens* (v. 7; see v. 11). **9–11:** *A new song* is the appropriate response to God's sovereignty (33.3; 96.1; 98.1). Verse 11 apparently imagines a deposed Davidic monarch praying to the sovereign God for restoration. **12–14:** The shift to the plural *our* indicates the transfer of the Davidic ideology to the whole people. These verses reflect the pain of the *exile* that persisted into the post-exilic era. **15:** Alluding to 33.12, v. 15 leaves the people anticipating the help of God whose sovereignty has been affirmed in vv. 9–11.

PSALM 145
Praise. Of David.

1 I will extol you, my God and King,
   and bless your name forever and
   ever.
2 Every day I will bless you,
   and praise your name forever
   and ever.
3 Great is the LORD, and greatly to be
   praised;
   his greatness is unsearchable.

4 One generation shall laud your works to
   another,
   and shall declare your mighty acts.
5 On the glorious splendor of your
   majesty,

and on your wondrous works, I will
   meditate.
6 The might of your awesome deeds shall
   be proclaimed,
   and I will declare your greatness.
7 They shall celebrate the fame of your
   abundant goodness,
   and shall sing aloud of your
   righteousness.

8 The LORD is gracious and merciful,
   slow to anger and abounding in
   steadfast love.
9 The LORD is good to all,
   and his compassion is over all that he
   has made.

10 All your works shall give thanks to you,
   O LORD,
   and all your faithful shall bless you.
11 They shall speak of the glory of your
   kingdom,
   and tell of your power,
12 to make known to all people your*a*
   mighty deeds,
   and the glorious splendor of your*b*
   kingdom.
13 Your kingdom is an everlasting
   kingdom,
   and your dominion endures
   throughout all generations.

   The LORD is faithful in all his words,
   and gracious in all his deeds.*c*
14 The LORD upholds all who are falling,
   and raises up all who are bowed
   down.
15 The eyes of all look to you,
   and you give them their food in due
   season.
16 You open your hand,
   satisfying the desire of every living
   thing.
17 The LORD is just in all his ways,
   and kind in all his doings.
18 The LORD is near to all who call on him,
   to all who call on him in truth.
19 He fulfills the desire of all who fear him;

a Gk Jerome Syr: Heb *his*   *b* Heb *his*   *c* These two lines supplied by Q Ms Gk Syr

he also hears their cry, and saves
    them.
20 The LORD watches over all who
    love him,
    but all the wicked he will destroy.

21 My mouth will speak the praise of the
    LORD,
    and all flesh will bless his holy name
    forever and ever.

145.1–21: My God and King. An acrostic* poem (see Ps 9–10), it is the only psalm to include *Praise* in the superscription. It concludes the final Davidic collection (Ps 138–145); its celebration of God's sovereignty (see vv. 1, 11–13) follows well upon Ps 144. Psalm 145 anticipates the final outpouring of *praise* that concludes the psalter (Ps 146–150; compare 145.21 and 150.6). **1–2:** Not only will the psalmist *bless* God's *name* (103.1), but so will *all flesh* (v. 21). *Bless* connotes the submission appropriate to one who is *King.* **3–6:** The section is encompassed by God's *greatness* (vv. 3, 6; 48.1; 96.4), which is revealed by what God does and which provides reason for blessing God. **7–9:** God's activity also reveals his essential character. Verse 8 cites Ex 34.6, God's self-revelation to Moses (see 86.15; 103.8). *Merciful* and *compassion* represent the same Hebrew root that connotes God's motherly love (see Ps 131). *All* occurs twice in v. 9, and will recur numerous times. **10–13:** Four occurrences of *kingdom* reinforce the opening focus on God's sovereignty. The addition of a missing Hebrew line (see note *c*) surrounds the assertions of God's sovereignty by a consideration of God's character. **14–20:** Returning the focus to God's activity, these verses describe the results of God's faithful love. The destruction of *the wicked* (v. 20b) results not from God's intent but rather from their failure to respond (1.5–6). **21:** Because of the similarity to 150.6, some scholars suggest this may have been the original end to the psalter.

PSALM 146

1 Praise the LORD!
    Praise the LORD, O my soul!
2 I will praise the LORD as long as I live;
    I will sing praises to my God all my
    life long.

3 Do not put your trust in princes,
    in mortals, in whom there is no help.

4 When their breath departs, they return
    to the earth;
    on that very day their plans perish.

5 Happy are those whose help is the God
    of Jacob,
    whose hope is in the LORD their God,
6 who made heaven and earth,
    the sea, and all that is in them;
who keeps faith forever;
7   who executes justice for the
    oppressed;
    who gives food to the hungry.

The LORD sets the prisoners free;
8   the LORD opens the eyes of the blind.
The LORD lifts up those who are bowed
    down;
    the LORD loves the righteous.
9 The LORD watches over the strangers;
    he upholds the orphan and the
    widow,
    but the way of the wicked he brings
    to ruin.

10 The LORD will reign forever,
    your God, O Zion, for all generations.
Praise the LORD!

146.1–10: The LORD will reign forever. A song of praise, it initiates a concluding series of five psalms, all of which begin and end with *Praise the LORD!* **1–4:** Songs of praise typically start with an invitation, but not usually one addressed to *my soul* (but see 103.1; 104.1). *Praise* indicates entrusting of *life* to God, while vv. 3–4 depict the opposite—to *put* one's *trust* in humans (118.8–9). To do so is ultimately futile (v. 4). **5–9:** The final beatitude in the psalter (v. 5) recalls its opening (1.1; 2.12). To be *happy* means to entrust life to the God who is creator (v. 6a) and redeemer (v. 6b). God's advocacy for all in need is summarized by the word *justice* (v. 7; 82.3–4; 140.12). While *the righteous* seem not to belong in the list, they are regularly afflicted in the Psalms (34.19). Nevertheless, *the righteous* find happiness in God, while *the wicked* choose alienation from God and consequent *ruin* (v. 9; 1.5–6; 145.20; 147.6). **10:** Since *justice* is regularly associated with God's sovereignty (97.2; 99.4), the affirmation of God's *reign* provides an appropriate conclusion (145.1, 10–13; 149.2).

PSALM 147

1 Praise the LORD!
   How good it is to sing praises to our
      God;
   for he is gracious, and a song of
      praise is fitting.
2 The LORD builds up Jerusalem;
   he gathers the outcasts of Israel.
3 He heals the brokenhearted,
   and binds up their wounds.
4 He determines the number of the stars;
   he gives to all of them their names.
5 Great is our Lord, and abundant
      in power;
   his understanding is beyond measure.
6 The LORD lifts up the downtrodden;
   he casts the wicked to the ground.

7 Sing to the LORD with thanksgiving;
   make melody to our God on the lyre.
8 He covers the heavens with clouds,
   prepares rain for the earth,
   makes grass grow on the hills.
9 He gives to the animals their food,
   and to the young ravens when they
      cry.
10 His delight is not in the strength of the
      horse,
   nor his pleasure in the speed of
      a runner;[a]
11 but the LORD takes pleasure in those
      who fear him,
   in those who hope in his steadfast
      love.

12 Praise the LORD, O Jerusalem!
   Praise your God, O Zion!
13 For he strengthens the bars of
      your gates;
   he blesses your children within you.
14 He grants peace[b] within your borders;
   he fills you with the finest of wheat.
15 He sends out his command to the earth;
   his word runs swiftly.
16 He gives snow like wool;
   he scatters frost like ashes.
17 He hurls down hail like crumbs—
   who can stand before his cold?
18 He sends out his word, and melts them;
   he makes his wind blow, and the
      waters flow.

19 He declares his word to Jacob,
   his statutes and ordinances to Israel.
20 He has not dealt thus with any other
      nation;
   they do not know his ordinances.
Praise the LORD!

147.1–20: God's word to Jacob. This song of praise features God's activity in the two realms highlighted in Ps 146.6—creation and redemption. Each of three major sections begins with an imperative invitation to praise (vv. 1–6, 7–11, 12–20). **1–6:** A post-exilic setting is reflected in vv. 2–3 (106.47; 107.2–3). The God who cares for the *brokenhearted* (v. 3; Isa 61.1) and *downtrodden* (v. 6) is the God of all the cosmos (vv. 4–5; Isa 40.26). **7–11:** That vv. 8–9 recall 104.14, 27 and vv. 10–11 recall 33.16–18 suggests the possibility that the psalm has been composed with reference to other psalms. *Fear* indicates a trustful obedience that yields *hope*. **12–20:** *Jerusalem* in v. 12 recalls v. 2. It was the place where people went to seek blessing and *peace* (122.6–8; 134.3). God's *word* (Isa 55.12) is addressed to the created order (vv. 15, 18) as well as *to Jacob* (v. 19), suggesting the conviction that God's *ordinances* (vv. 19–20) were intended to order the life of God's people so as to fulfill God's purposes for the whole creation.

~~~~~~~~~~

PSALM 148

1 Praise the LORD!
   Praise the LORD from the heavens;
      praise him in the heights!
2 Praise him, all his angels;
   praise him, all his host!

3 Praise him, sun and moon;
   praise him, all you shining stars!
4 Praise him, you highest heavens,
   and you waters above the heavens!

5 Let them praise the name of the LORD,
   for he commanded and they
      were created.
6 He established them forever and ever;
   he fixed their bounds, which cannot
      be passed.[c]

---

a Heb *legs of a person*   b Or *prosperity*   c Or *he set a law that cannot pass away*

7 Praise the LORD from the earth,
    you sea monsters and all deeps,
8 fire and hail, snow and frost,
    stormy wind fulfilling his command!

9 Mountains and all hills,
    fruit trees and all cedars!
10 Wild animals and all cattle,
    creeping things and flying birds!

11 Kings of the earth and all peoples,
    princes and all rulers of the earth!
12 Young men and women alike,
    old and young together!

13 Let them praise the name of the LORD,
    for his name alone is exalted;
    his glory is above earth and heaven.
14 He has raised up a horn for his people,
    praise for all his faithful,
    for the people of Israel who are close
        to him.
    Praise the LORD!

148.1–14: Praise from the heavens and the earth.
This psalm is the third in a series of songs of praise that
conclude the psalter. Distinctive are the extended invitations to *praise* (vv. 1–5, 7, 13) and the expansive
inclusivity of those invited. **1–6:** *Praise* is invited first
from the heavens, including heavenly beings (v. 2;
29.1; 103.20–21) and bodies (vv. 3–4). The list of participants recalls Gen 1–2, as does the verb *created* (v.
5). **7–13:** *Praise* is now invited *from the earth*, including chaotic forces (v. 7), meteorological phenomena
(v. 8), inanimate things (v. 9a), plants (v. 9b), *animals*
(v. 10), and finally people of all positions and ages (vv.
11–12). The *all*-inclusive invitation anticipates 150.6.
13–14: As in v. 5, *the name of the LORD* is to be praised
(v. 13; 113.1; 149.3). The final verse narrows the focus
to God's *people*, the *faithful* (149.1, 5, 9). They have
experienced God's help, which the image of the *horn*
suggests (75.10; 92.10).

PSALM 149

1 Praise the LORD!
    Sing to the LORD a new song,
        his praise in the assembly of the
            faithful.
2 Let Israel be glad in its Maker;
    let the children of Zion rejoice in
        their King.

3 Let them praise his name with dancing,
    making melody to him with
        tambourine and lyre.
4 For the LORD takes pleasure in
        his people;
    he adorns the humble with victory.
5 Let the faithful exult in glory;
    let them sing for joy on their couches.
6 Let the high praises of God be in their
        throats
    and two-edged swords in their hands,
7 to execute vengeance on the nations
    and punishment on the peoples,
8 to bind their kings with fetters
    and their nobles with chains of iron,
9 to execute on them the judgment
        decreed.
    This is glory for all his faithful ones.
    Praise the LORD!

149.1–9: Glory for all God's faithful. In many ways a
typical song of praise, it departs from the usual style
in vv. 6–9, which focus on the mission of *the faithful*
(vv. 1, 5; see v. 9). **1–4:** The mention of *a new song*
(96.1; 98.1) and *King* suggests that *praise* involves the
joyful recognition of God's sovereign claim on the
whole world (see Ps 148). The reason for praise in v. 4
may allude to the Exodus. **5:** Renewing the invitation
to *praise*, it is the central verse of the psalm and anticipates the unique vv. 6–9. What *on their couches* indicates is unclear, but perhaps it suggests that *praise*
should continue through the night. **6–9:** *Vengeance*
ordinarily belongs to God (Deut 32.35; Ps 94.1), but
Ps 2 entrusts to the monarchy the task of calling to
account rebellious *kings*. Verses 6–9 recall Ps 2, but the
task of executing *judgment*, or better, "establishing
justice," is now the mission of *all* the *faithful*. The former *glory* of the king (21.5) now belongs to the whole
people, *all* God's *faithful* (see Ps 105, 144).

PSALM 150

1 Praise the LORD!
    Praise God in his sanctuary;
        praise him in his mighty firmament!*a*
2 Praise him for his mighty deeds;
    praise him according to his surpassing
        greatness!

a Or *dome*

3 Praise him with trumpet sound;
    praise him with lute and harp!
4 Praise him with tambourine and dance;
    praise him with strings and pipe!
5 Praise him with clanging cymbals;
    praise him with loud clashing
        cymbals!
6 Let everything that breathes praise the
    LORD!
    Praise the LORD!

150.1–6: Praise the LORD! The final position in the psalter calls for a unique song of praise. It consists almost entirely of invitations to *praise*, although v. 2 implies a reason. **1–2:** God's *sanctuary* suggests the Temple,* but it is clear that God's claim is not limited to earthly places. God's *surpassing greatness* communicates God's cosmic sovereignty. The Hebrew roots of *mighty* (v. 1) and *mighty deeds* (v. 2) occur together in 24.8, which proclaim God to be "King of glory." **3–5:** The *trumpet* elsewhere announces God's reign (47.5–7; 98.6), but it is here to be joined by full instrumentation (33.2–3; 68.24–25). **6:** The symphonic expression of *praise* is to be completed by the participation of *everything that breathes*. The cosmic God invites the response of every creature (145.21) No less a congregation will suffice, and no less a doxology would be appropriate to conclude Book V and the whole book.

PROVERBS

Introduction

The book of Proverbs is an anthology—a collection of instructions plus speeches of Wisdom (chs. 1–9), two large collections of two-line sayings (chs. 10–22 and 25–29), a booklet of counsels (22.17–24.34), and some poems (chs. 30–31). The two chief literary genres* represented in the book are the instruction or lecture and the "proverb" or pithy saying. They are examples of the instruction attested in Mesopotamia, but especially favored in Egypt, where seventeen examples from every historical period are known to exist. In a typical instruction a king, high official, or father instructs his son (or disciple or successor) how to live so as to enjoy the blessings of life and avoid unnecessary trouble. Despite their practical and common-sense approach, instructions were thoroughly religious, for they were written in the assumption that the world yields its blessings to those who respect the gods and direct their lives in accord with the order and rhythms of the divinely fashioned universe. The second genre, the saying or proverb, was also very common in the ancient Near East; Mesopotamian and West Semitic sayings collections are extant. The two-line "proverbs" of Proverbs are broader than the modern proverb, which, in one definition, is "a concise statement of an apparent truth that has currency among the people." Some verses in Proverbs are proverbs in this sense, but there are also witty sayings, paradoxes, and riddles. The sayings are hard to translate; even the best efforts of translators can seem banal. In their original language, however, the sayings are incisive and witty, provoking readers to take a fresh look at life. In the phrase of the great eighteenth-century aphorist, Samuel Johnson, "New things are made familiar, and familiar things are made new."

No single date can be assigned to Proverbs, for its collections arose in different periods. The one datable reference (25.1) suggests that officials of King Hezekiah (715–687 BCE) added a collection of proverbs (chs. 25–29) to an existing Solomonic collection. It is likely that some sayings go back to Solomon (or even earlier), for ancient kings sponsored literature. Moreover, Solomon is remembered as a sage and author (1 Kings 3; 4.29–34, 10). Collections of sayings were arranged through techniques such as catchword ("king," "the LORD"), topic (discretion in speech), or type of parallelism.* (Antithetic* parallelism, where the second line points up the first by expressing its opposite, predominates in chs. 10–15). Exactly when the collections were edited into the present book is difficult to say. Many scholars believe that the latest sections of Proverbs are chs. 1–9 and the poem on the virtuous wife (31.10–31) and that these sections influenced the final shaping of the book, which was edited in the post-exilic period.

Who wrote Proverbs? That question is vigorously debated. Some believe the sayings and instructions originated with scribes* in the royal court (or a hypothetical scribal school), whereas others believe the material originated with tribal elders instructing the young in ancestral traditions and customs, the material being written down later by scribes. Though much material may be ultimately of folk origin, the uniform and sophisticated style of the sayings and the foreign influence on the instructions suggest the book was essentially the work of palace scribes.

READING GUIDE

The instructions in chs. 1–9 on a literal level address a young man at critical points in his life such as leaving his parents' home to found his own (1.8–19), discerning the best course to take

in life (2.1–11; 3.1–12, 13–18; 4.1–9, 10–19, 20–27), and being tempted to betray his family and home by following another woman (5.1–22; 6.20–35; 7.1–27). The new literary setting of the instructions, especially the introduction (1.1–7) and the speeches of Wisdom, creates a metaphorical★ horizon that makes the instruction relevant to any person who desires to live optimally in God's world and seek wisdom amid counterclaims and temptations.

The sayings (chs. 10–22 and 25–29) do not so much provide information as help readers to make decisions and see a dimension in the world that is not immediately apparent. They use antithetical types (the wise and foolish, the righteous and wicked, the religious and the impious) to show how human choices and actions bring with them blessing (such as long life, domestic happiness, honor, and wealth) or misfortune (such as premature death, shame, destitution). The sayings are written with a robust confidence in divine justice and in human freedom. That confidence should not be interpreted in a metaphysical way, as a naive belief that things always work out for the best. This book does not ask the questions posed by Job and Qoheleth.

Proverbs influenced Sirach (ca. 180 BCE), who developed the saying into "essays." Later, Hebrew ethical wills, in which parents handed their wisdom to their children, drew from the instructions. Jesus was a wisdom teacher who used paradoxical and witty sayings to teach his disciples about God's reign. The Gospel of John, especially, borrowed from Prov 1–9 to depict Jesus as incarnate wisdom descended from on high to offer human beings life and truth. Like Woman Wisdom (Prov 1.20–33; 8), Jesus speaks in long discourses and, like her (Prov 9.2–5), he invites people to his banquet: "I am the bread of life" (6.35). Two early Christian hymns, John 1.1–18 and Col 1.15–20, drew on Prov 8 to identify Jesus with God's creative word and heavenly wisdom. The Letter of James is an instruction (in letter form) reprising wisdom themes.

The universal truths of Proverbs remain relevant today. Proverbs proclaims that God's world is good, yielding its full blessings only to those who seek wisdom, do justice, and revere God. To those, however, who do not listen to the wisdom God has placed in the world and who are hostile to their neighbor, the world will prove a dangerous place: Evil comes back upon the wicked. The virtues of wisdom, justice, and piety are acquired through discipline, a process requiring sincerity, persistence, and openness to those more experienced. The book declares that right, wise, and reverent conduct is the only way to happiness, which God is invited to grant as a gift.

The book is difficult for some modern readers to enjoy. Some find the instructions without content and the sayings trite. It must be remembered that the instructions of chs. 1–9 are concerned with forming character—developing an openhearted person who is faithful to the basic relationships of life (to God, spouse, household, and neighbors) and who rejects easy compromises. The aphorisms contain traditional insights that help us to grow in wisdom as we decode and ponder them.

1–9	Collection of wisdom speeches and instructions
10.1–22.16	Proverbs of Solomon
22.17–24.22	The words of the wise
24.23–34	Appendix to words of the wise
25–29	Proverbs of Solomon edited by Hezekiah's scribes
30.1–14	The words of Agur
30.15–33	Numerical sayings
31.1–9	The words of Lemuel king of Massa
31.10–31	Praise of the capable wife

1 The proverbs of Solomon son of David,
king of Israel:

2 For learning about wisdom and
    instruction,
  for understanding words of insight,
3 for gaining instruction in wise dealing,
    righteousness, justice, and equity;
4 to teach shrewdness to the simple,
    knowledge and prudence to the
      young—
5 let the wise also hear and gain in
    learning,
  and the discerning acquire skill,
6 to understand a proverb and a figure,
    the words of the wise and their
      riddles.

7 The fear of the LORD is the beginning
    of knowledge;
  fools despise wisdom and instruction.

8 Hear, my child, your father's
    instruction,
  and do not reject your mother's
    teaching;
9 for they are a fair garland for your head,
    and pendants for your neck.
10 My child, if sinners entice you,
    do not consent.
11 If they say, "Come with us, let us lie in
    wait for blood;
  let us wantonly ambush the innocent;
12 like Sheol let us swallow them alive
    and whole, like those who go down to
      the Pit.
13 We shall find all kinds of costly things;
    we shall fill our houses with booty.
14 Throw in your lot among us;
    we will all have one purse"—
15 my child, do not walk in their way,
    keep your foot from their paths;
16 for their feet run to evil,
    and they hurry to shed blood.
17 For in vain is the net baited
    while the bird is looking on;
18 yet they lie in wait—to kill themselves!
    and set an ambush—for their own
      lives!
19 Such is the end^a of all who are greedy
    for gain;
  it takes away the life of its possessors.

**1.1–9.18: Speeches and instructions. 1.1–7: Intro-
duction and purpose of the book. 1:** Egyptian and
biblical wisdom books, contrary to the customary an-
onymity of ancient literature, give the name of the author, who was normally a king or prominent courtier
advising his son or disciple. Solomon, famed for his
wisdom, is named as the author, or, as we might say,
patron of the entire book. **2–7:** There are fourteen (two
times seven) different nouns for wisdom or wise sayings in order to show totality. Verses 2–3 are concerned with learning, v. 4 with teaching, v. 5 with the
teacher or sage, v. 6 with understanding wisdom writings, and v. 7 (in climactic position) with fear of the
LORD. **4:** *The simple* are naive or uninstructed people,
either because of their youth or, sometimes, because
of their carelessness. In the latter case the term has a
negative connotation. **7:** The verse is the climax* of
the introduction, for the LORD is the source of blessings
for the wise. The phrase *wisdom and instruction* reprises the same phrase in v. 2a. *Fear of the LORD* is the
traditional (and not fully satisfactory) translation of
"yir'at YHWH," literally, "revering the LORD." The
phrase means giving to one's God what is due, knowing and accepting one's place in the universe. It primarily designates neither an emotion (fear) nor general reverence, but rather a conviction that one should
honor and serve a particular god.

1.8–19: Parental advice on leaving home. The opening scene of a youth leaving parents and home to establish his own household sets the scene for the entire
book. Every reader must establish a household in the
sense of learning to live well as an adult, accepting
traditional wisdom and discerning where true life is to
be found. **10–14:** A group of sinners invites the youth
not simply to commit a violent crime but to share in
their violent life (*Come with us. . . . Throw in your lot
among us*). **16–17:** Verse 16 is a gloss from Isa 59.7 to
explain the enigmatic v. 17, which is a parable* about
sinners not seeing the divine retribution that works in-
visibly. The evil they plan for others will come upon
them instead (vv. 18–19).

20 Wisdom cries out in the street;
    in the squares she raises her voice.

a Gk: Heb *are the ways*

21 At the busiest corner she cries out;
   at the entrance of the city gates she
      speaks:
22 "How long, O simple ones, will you love
      being simple?
   How long will scoffers delight in their
      scoffing
   and fools hate knowledge?
23 Give heed to my reproof;
   I will pour out my thoughts to you;
   I will make my words known to you.
24 Because I have called and you refused,
   have stretched out my hand and no
      one heeded,
25 and because you have ignored all my
      counsel
   and would have none of my reproof,
26 I also will laugh at your calamity;
   I will mock when panic strikes you,
27 when panic strikes you like a storm,
   and your calamity comes like a
      whirlwind,
   when distress and anguish come upon
      you.
28 Then they will call upon me, but I will
      not answer;
   they will seek me diligently, but will
      not find me.
29 Because they hated knowledge
   and did not choose the fear of the
      LORD,
30 would have none of my counsel,
   and despised all my reproof,
31 therefore they shall eat the fruit of their
      way
   and be sated with their own devices.
32 For waywardness kills the simple,
   and the complacency of fools destroys
      them;
33 but those who listen to me will be
      secure
   and will live at ease, without dread of
      disaster."

1.20–33: The consequences of not heeding Wisdom. Woman Wisdom warns the simple (who seem to have previously rejected her teaching) that she will not be there when the inevitable disaster comes upon them (vv. 22–32). She nonetheless gives them a last chance to accept her (v. 33). Verses 24–27 and 28–31 are parallel sections. Each gives a reason (because, vv.

25, 29) and announces a disaster; the first section employs the grammatical second person, and the second section employs the grammatical third person. 20–21: *The entrance of the city gates* is the entrance to the upper city, which was the place of business and government. 22–23a: The best solution to the textual confusion is to drop v. 22b–c as a later insertion and to translate *How long, O simple ones, will you love being simple?* Its parallel verse is best rendered (differently from NRSV) "Will you turn away from *my reproof?*" The translation "turn away" is preferable to NRSV *give heed to* and is based on the meaning of the same root in v. 32a (*waywardness*) and on Hebrew idiom.

2 My child, if you accept my words
   and treasure up my commandments
      within you,
2 making your ear attentive to wisdom
   and inclining your heart to
      understanding;
3 if you indeed cry out for insight,
   and raise your voice for
      understanding;
4 if you seek it like silver,
   and search for it as for hidden
      treasures—
5 then you will understand the fear of the
      LORD
   and find the knowledge of God.
6 For the LORD gives wisdom;
   from his mouth come knowledge and
      understanding;
7 he stores up sound wisdom for the
      upright;
   he is a shield to those who walk
      blamelessly,
8 guarding the paths of justice
   and preserving the way of his faithful
      ones.
9 Then you will understand righteousness
      and justice
   and equity, every good path;
10 for wisdom will come into your heart,
   and knowledge will be pleasant to
      your soul;
11 prudence will watch over you;
   and understanding will guard you.
12 It will save you from the way of evil,
   from those who speak perversely,
13 who forsake the paths of uprightness
   to walk in the ways of darkness,

14 who rejoice in doing evil
and delight in the perverseness
of evil;
15 those whose paths are crooked,
and who are devious in their ways.

16 You will be saved from the loose*a*
woman,
from the adulteress with her smooth
words,
17 who forsakes the partner of her youth
and forgets her sacred covenant;
18 for her way*b* leads down to death,
and her paths to the shades;
19 those who go to her never come back,
nor do they regain the paths of life.

20 Therefore walk in the way of the good,
and keep to the paths of the just.
21 For the upright will abide in the land,
and the innocent will remain in it;
22 but the wicked will be cut off from the
land,
and the treacherous will be rooted
out of it.

2.1–22: Seek wisdom and the LORD will keep you safe. The form is an acrostic* poem of twenty-two lines (the number of consonants in the Hebrew alphabet*). The first letter of the Hebrew alphabet ("aleph") dominates the first half (vv. 1–11; "aleph" is the initial letter in vv. 1, 3, 4, 5, and 9). The middle letter of the Hebrew alphabet ("lamed") dominates the second half (vv. 12–22; "lamed" is the initial letter of vv. 12, 16, 20). The main point of the poem is that if you seek wisdom with all your strength, the LORD will give it to you, and wisdom will safeguard you from wicked men and seductive women with the result that you can walk on the blessed path. Wisdom will be given to anyone who earnestly seeks it. However, one cannot directly take it; it must be given as a gift. **16–19:** *The loose woman . . . the adulteress. Loose* is literally "foreign." The figure of the dangerous and seductive woman appears again in 5.1–6; 6.20–35; 7.1–27; 9.13–18. Elsewhere in the Bible, a "foreign woman" can be a woman outside the community who is forbidden as a marriage partner, a prostitute or a woman otherwise dangerous to a man. Proverbs' focus is not only on her sexuality but also on her seductive and deceitful speech.

3 My child, do not forget my teaching,
but let your heart keep my
commandments;
2 for length of days and years of life
and abundant welfare they will give
you.

3 Do not let loyalty and faithfulness
forsake you;
bind them around your neck,
write them on the tablet of your
heart.
4 So you will find favor and good repute
in the sight of God and of people.

5 Trust in the LORD with all your heart,
and do not rely on your own insight.
6 In all your ways acknowledge him,
and he will make straight your paths.
7 Do not be wise in your own eyes;
fear the LORD, and turn away from
evil.
8 It will be a healing for your flesh
and a refreshment for your body.

9 Honor the LORD with your substance
and with the first fruits of all your
produce;
10 then your barns will be filled with
plenty,
and your vats will be bursting with
wine.

11 My child, do not despise the LORD's
discipline
or be weary of his reproof,
12 for the LORD reproves the one he loves,
as a father the son in whom he
delights.

3.1–12: Trust in God makes one prosperous. The lecture consists of six four-line exhortations* of a father (or teacher) to a son (or disciple), in each of which a reward is promised. The teacher invites the disciple to memorize the teaching (vv. 1–2) and to be loyal (vv. 3–4), which leads to trust in God, the great teacher (v. 5). Such trust means not relying on oneself (v. 7), honoring God with due worship, and allowing God to become one's teacher and father (vv. 11–12). Consid-

a Heb *strange*   *b* Cn: Heb *house*

erable trust is necessary, for God *reproves* when educating disciples; there may be suffering.

13 Happy are those who find wisdom,
   and those who get understanding,
14 for her income is better than silver,
   and her revenue better than gold.
15 She is more precious than jewels,
   and nothing you desire can compare
      with her.
16 Long life is in her right hand;
   in her left hand are riches and honor.
17 Her ways are ways of pleasantness,
   and all her paths are peace.
18 She is a tree of life to those who lay
      hold of her;
   those who hold her fast are called
      happy.

19 The LORD by wisdom founded the
      earth;
   by understanding he established the
      heavens;
20 by his knowledge the deeps broke open,
   and the clouds drop down the dew.
21 My child, do not let these escape from
      your sight:
   keep sound wisdom and prudence,
22 and they will be life for your soul
   and adornment for your neck.
23 Then you will walk on your way securely
   and your foot will not stumble.
24 If you sit down,ᵃ you will not be afraid;
   when you lie down, your sleep will be
      sweet.
25 Do not be afraid of sudden panic,
   or of the storm that strikes the
      wicked;
26 for the LORD will be your confidence
   and will keep your foot from being
      caught.
27 Do not withhold good from those to
      whom it is due,ᵇ
   when it is in your power to do it.
28 Do not say to your neighbor, "Go, and
      come again,
   tomorrow I will give it"—when you
      have it with you.
29 Do not plan harm against your neighbor
   who lives trustingly beside you.

30 Do not quarrel with anyone without
      cause,
   when no harm has been done to you.
31 Do not envy the violent
   and do not choose any of their ways;
32 for the perverse are an abomination to
      the LORD,
   but the upright are in his confidence.
33 The LORD's curse is on the house of the
      wicked,
   but he blesses the abode of the
      righteous.
34 Toward the scorners he is scornful,
   but to the humble he shows favor.
35 The wise will inherit honor,
   but stubborn fools, disgrace.

3.13–35. 13–20: Wisdom's benefits and prestige.
Some scholars believe the poem consists of vv. 13–26
rather than 13–20. The poem praises wisdom by listing her benefits to the human race and explains her
power by describing her role in creation. Since the
world is made by wisdom, all those who follow wisdom will live well in the world. 18: *Tree of life:* The tree
of life occurs in the Hebrew Scriptures* only in Proverbs and in Gen 2–3. In both books the tree is associated with wisdom. Its fruit gives life and prosperity. It
is also found in Rev 2.7 and 22.2, 14, 19, where it has
been influenced by the picture of the health-giving
tree in Ezek 47.12. 21–35: Kindness to the neighbor
brings blessing to oneself. Treating others well brings
life to oneself. The blessings are portrayed as accruing
to one's very body—eyes (*sight*), throat (*soul:* The
throat is the source of life-breath), *neck,* and *foot.* To
put wisdom into practice brings her gifts, *life* (v. 22a),
honor (*adornment,* v. 22b), and protection from crime
and violence (vv. 23–25).

4 Listen, children, to a father's instruction,
   and be attentive, that you may gainᶜ
      insight;
2 for I give you good precepts:
   do not forsake my teaching.
3 When I was a son with my father,
   tender, and my mother's favorite,
4 he taught me, and said to me,
   "Let your heart hold fast my words;
   keep my commandments, and live.

a Gk: Heb *lie down*   b Heb *from its owners*
c Heb *know*

5 Get wisdom; get insight: do not forget,
　　　nor turn away
　　from the words of my mouth.
6 Do not forsake her, and she will keep
　　　you;
　　love her, and she will guard you.
7 The beginning of wisdom is this: Get
　　　wisdom,
　　and whatever else you get, get insight.
8 Prize her highly, and she will exalt you;
　　she will honor you if you
　　　embrace her.
9 She will place on your head a fair
　　　garland;
　　she will bestow on you a beautiful
　　　crown."

4.1–9: The teacher's life as an example of wisdom.
The teacher draws a parallel between his teaching his
sons now and his father's teaching him as a youth. The
authority of the teacher comes from the obedience he
showed to *his* father. The teacher now is a model of
the blessings that come with reverence and obedience. **4–9:** *Get wisdom:* In vv. 4–6, the disciple is to
take in the teacher's words and get wisdom. In vv. 6,
8–9 wisdom herself becomes active, guarding and
honoring the disciple.

10 Hear, my child, and accept my words,
　　　that the years of your life may
　　　be many.
11 I have taught you the way of wisdom;
　　　I have led you in the paths of
　　　uprightness.
12 When you walk, your step will not be
　　　hampered;
　　and if you run, you will not stumble.
13 Keep hold of instruction; do not let go;
　　guard her, for she is your life.
14 Do not enter the path of the wicked,
　　　and do not walk in the way of
　　　evildoers.
15 Avoid it; do not go on it;
　　turn away from it and pass on.
16 For they cannot sleep unless they have
　　　done wrong;
　　they are robbed of sleep unless they
　　　have made someone stumble.
17 For they eat the bread of wickedness
　　and drink the wine of violence.

18 But the path of the righteous is like the
　　　light of dawn,
　　which shines brighter and brighter
　　　until full day.
19 The way of the wicked is like deep
　　　darkness;
　　they do not know what they stumble
　　　over.
20 My child, be attentive to my words;
　　incline your ear to my sayings.
21 Do not let them escape from
　　　your sight;
　　keep them within your heart.
22 For they are life to those who
　　　find them,
　　and healing to all their flesh.
23 Keep your heart with all vigilance,
　　for from it flow the springs of life.
24 Put away from you crooked speech,
　　and put devious talk far from you.
25 Let your eyes look directly forward,
　　and your gaze be straight before you.
26 Keep straight the path of your feet,
　　and all your ways will be sure.
27 Do not swerve to the right or to
　　　the left;
　　turn your foot away from evil.

4.10–27. 10–19: The two ways. The process of gaining wisdom is essentially the same in all the instructions: One begins by memorizing the teaching and
putting it into practice, then one receives wisdom as
a gift. The passage develops the doctrine of the two
ways, in which the moral life is dramatized as two competing paths, the way of wisdom and the path of the
wicked. Each has its inherent destiny, represented here
by the symbols of light and darkness (vv. 18–19). The
two ways are not static; one must struggle to stay on
the right path. It is possible to leave one path and walk
on the other. **20–27: Heed my words.** This lecture
emphasizes the vigor and sincerity necessary for the
pursuit of wisdom. The poem offers a psychological
picture of discipleship. One perceives the teacher's examples and words through listening and seeing (vv.
20–22) and stores the perceptions in the heart (by
memorizing them) where they are pondered (v. 23).
One then puts into practice what one "knows," that
which is in one's heart or mind. Practicing wisdom
means always speaking the truth (v. 24) and acting
justly (vv. 25–27).

5 My child, be attentive to my wisdom;
  incline your ear to my understanding,

2 so that you may hold on to prudence,
  and your lips may guard
    knowledge.

3 For the lips of a loose*a* woman drip
    honey,
  and her speech is smoother than oil;

4 but in the end she is bitter as
    wormwood,
  sharp as a two-edged sword.

5 Her feet go down to death;
  her steps follow the path to Sheol.

6 She does not keep straight to the path
    of life;
  her ways wander, and she does not
    know it.

7 And now, my child,*b* listen to me,
  and do not depart from the words of
    my mouth.

8 Keep your way far from her,
  and do not go near the door of her
    house;

9 or you will give your honor to others,
  and your years to the merciless,

10 and strangers will take their fill of your
    wealth,
  and your labors will go to the house
    of an alien;

11 and at the end of your life you will
    groan,
  when your flesh and body are
    consumed,

12 and you say, "Oh, how I hated
    discipline,
  and my heart despised reproof!

13 I did not listen to the voice of my
    teachers
  or incline my ear to my instructors.

14 Now I am at the point of utter ruin
  in the public assembly."

15 Drink water from your own cistern,
  flowing water from your own well.

16 Should your springs be scattered
    abroad,
  streams of water in the streets?

17 Let them be for yourself alone,
  and not for sharing with strangers.

18 Let your fountain be blessed,
  and rejoice in the wife of your youth,

19 a lovely deer, a graceful doe.
  May her breasts satisfy you at all times;
  may you be intoxicated always by her
    love.

20 Why should you be intoxicated, my son,
    by another woman
  and embrace the bosom of an
    adulteress?

21 For human ways are under the eyes of
    the LORD,
  and he examines all their paths.

22 The iniquities of the wicked ensnare
    them,
  and they are caught in the toils of
    their sin.

23 They die for lack of discipline,
  and because of their great folly they
    are lost.

5.1–23: Choose the right woman! The teacher exhorts a youth to avoid adulterous liaisons (the "wrong" woman, vv. 3–14) and to enjoy the company of his wife (the "right" woman, vv. 15–19). The poem has four sections (vv. 1–6, 7–14, 15–19, and 20–23), each of which begins with "my child" (implicit in v. 15). Adulterous consorting with the wrong woman leads to loss of health (v. 9), dissipation of family wealth (v. 10), ruined reputation (vv. 9, 14), and bitter regret (vv. 11–13). The context of Proverbs suggests a metaphorical* level of meaning: Seductive and lying words lead one away from one's primary commitment to the tradition and to wisdom. **16:** *Should your springs be scattered abroad?* A disputed phrase. Most probably, *water* is a metaphor for sexual pleasure, as in Song 4.15. The man should exercise his sexuality exclusively with his wife in the context of the household.

6 My child, if you have given your pledge
    to your neighbor,
  if you have bound yourself to
    another,*c*

2 you are snared by the utterance of your
    lips,*d*
  caught by the words of your mouth.

a Heb *strange*   *b* Gk Vg: Heb *children*   *c* Or *a stranger*   *d* Cn Compare Gk Syr: Heb *the words of your mouth*

3 So do this, my child, and save yourself,
　　for you have come into your
　　　　neighbor's power:
　　go, hurry,[a] and plead with your
　　　　neighbor.
4 Give your eyes no sleep
　　and your eyelids no slumber;
5 save yourself like a gazelle from the
　　　　hunter,[b]
　　like a bird from the hand of the
　　　　fowler.

6 Go to the ant, you lazybones;
　　consider its ways, and be wise.
7 Without having any chief
　　or officer or ruler,
8 it prepares its food in summer,
　　and gathers its sustenance in harvest.
9 How long will you lie there,
　　　　O lazybones?
　　When will you rise from your sleep?
10 A little sleep, a little slumber,
　　a little folding of the hands to rest,
11 and poverty will come upon you like a
　　　　robber,
　　and want, like an armed warrior.

12 A scoundrel and a villain
　　goes around with crooked speech,
13 winking the eyes, shuffling the feet,
　　pointing the fingers,
14 with perverted mind devising evil,
　　continually sowing discord;
15 on such a one calamity will descend
　　　　suddenly;
　　in a moment, damage beyond repair.

16 There are six things that the LORD
　　　　hates,
　　seven that are an abomination to him:
17 haughty eyes, a lying tongue,
　　and hands that shed innocent blood,
18 a heart that devises wicked plans,
　　feet that hurry to run to evil,
19 a lying witness who testifies falsely,
　　and one who sows discord in
　　　　a family.

6.1–19: Four short pieces. The section is often judged
to be an addition on the grounds that its topics and
style are very different from the surrounding instructions. It is possible, however, that the editors wanted
to insert related but miscellaneous material at this
point. Thematically, the section is concerned not with
external obstacles to acquiring wisdom, such as violent
men and seductive women, but with internal obstacles, such as poor judgment (vv. 1–5) and laziness (vv.
6–11). It also sketches an evil character (vv. 12–15),
which is wholly unacceptable to the LORD (vv. 16–19).
1–5: *Pledge:* Proverbs is entirely negative on the legal
custom of a third party guaranteeing a loan (11.15;
17.18; 22.26), probably because it endangers the
guarantor. **6–11:** *Lazybones:* Proverbs looks with disdain, and often humorously, on the lazy person (for
example, 10.4; 12.24; 24.30–34), preferring instead
the energetic and responsible person. **12–15:** *A scoundrel and a villain:* A Proverbs type, who is here described as corrupt externally (mouth or *speech, eyes,
feet, fingers*) and internally (*perverted mind*). An evil
destiny hangs over such a type. **16–19:** Proverbs often
declares certain behavior "an abomination to the
LORD" (see 11.1). *Six* and *seven* are an instance of ascending parallelism* of numbers, like "three" and
"four" in 30.18–19, 21–23. The organ such as the eye
stands for the entire activity of seeing, an example of
metonymy.*

~~~~~~

20 My child, keep your father's
　　　　commandment,
　　and do not forsake your mother's
　　　　teaching.
21 Bind them upon your heart always;
　　tie them around your neck.
22 When you walk, they[c] will lead you;
　　when you lie down, they[c] will watch
　　　　over you;
　　and when you awake, they[c] will talk
　　　　with you.
23 For the commandment is a lamp and
　　　　the teaching a light,
　　and the reproofs of discipline are the
　　　　way of life,
24 to preserve you from the wife of
　　　　another,[d]
　　from the smooth tongue of the
　　　　adulteress.
25 Do not desire her beauty in your heart,
　　and do not let her capture you with
　　　　her eyelashes;

---

a Or *humble yourself*　　*b* Cn: Heb *from the hand*
c Heb *it*　　*d* Gk: MT *the evil woman*

26 for a prostitute's fee is only a loaf of
        bread,*a*
      but the wife of another stalks a man's
        very life.
27 Can fire be carried in the bosom
      without burning one's clothes?
28 Or can one walk on hot coals
      without scorching the feet?
29 So is he who sleeps with his neighbor's
        wife;
      no one who touches her will go
        unpunished.
30 Thieves are not despised who steal only
      to satisfy their appetite when they are
        hungry.
31 Yet if they are caught, they will pay
        sevenfold;
      they will forfeit all the goods of their
        house.
32 But he who commits adultery has no
        sense;
      he who does it destroys himself.
33 He will get wounds and dishonor,
      and his disgrace will not be wiped
        away.
34 For jealousy arouses a husband's fury,
      and he shows no restraint when he
        takes revenge.
35 He will accept no compensation,
      and refuses a bribe no matter how
        great.

6.20–35: The dangers of adultery. The teaching of
one's parents, once memorized, becomes a *lamp* that
exposes the danger of an adulteress (v. 23). Unlike a
liaison with a prostitute, whose hire is only a matter of
money, an affair with a married woman can destroy
one's life, bringing upon one shame, physical beatings, and an enraged husband. The instruction focuses
more on the practical consequences of adultery rather
than on its theoretical immorality. **30:** *Thieves are not
despised:* A comparison is drawn between getting
caught for satisfying one's appetite for food (a
euphemism* for the sexual appetite) and getting
caught for adultery. In the first case, a monetary payment makes things right. In the second, money cannot
repair the loss of one's position in the community or
protect one from the vengeance of a deceived
husband.

7 My child, keep my words
      and store up my commandments with
        you;
2 keep my commandments and live,
      keep my teachings as the apple of
        your eye;
3 bind them on your fingers,
      write them on the tablet of your
        heart.
4 Say to wisdom, "You are my sister,"
      and call insight your intimate friend,
5 that they may keep you from the loose*b*
        woman,
      from the adulteress with her smooth
        words.

6 For at the window of my house
      I looked out through my lattice,
7 and I saw among the simple ones,
      I observed among the youths,
      a young man without sense,
8 passing along the street near her corner,
      taking the road to her house
9 in the twilight, in the evening,
      at the time of night and darkness.

10 Then a woman comes toward him,
      decked out like a prostitute, wily of
        heart.*c*
11 She is loud and wayward;
      her feet do not stay at home;
12 now in the street, now in the squares,
      and at every corner she lies in wait.
13 She seizes him and kisses him,
      and with impudent face she says to
        him:
14 "I had to offer sacrifices,
      and today I have paid my vows;
15 so now I have come out to meet you,
      to seek you eagerly, and I have found
        you!
16 I have decked my couch with coverings,
      colored spreads of Egyptian linen;
17 I have perfumed my bed with myrrh,
      aloes, and cinnamon.
18 Come, let us take our fill of love until
        morning;
      let us delight ourselves with love.

a Cn Compare Gk Syr Vg Tg: Heb *for because of a harlot
to a piece of bread*   *b* Heb *strange*   *c* Meaning of
Heb uncertain

19 For my husband is not at home;
    he has gone on a long journey.
20 He took a bag of money with him;
    he will not come home until full
        moon."

21 With much seductive speech she
        persuades him;
    with her smooth talk she
        compels him.
22 Right away he follows her,
    and goes like an ox to the slaughter,
    or bounds like a stag toward the trap[a]
23 until an arrow pierces its entrails.
    He is like a bird rushing into a snare,
        not knowing that it will cost him his
            life.

24 And now, my children, listen to me,
    and be attentive to the words of my
        mouth.
25 Do not let your hearts turn aside to her
        ways;
    do not stray into her paths.
26 for many are those she has laid low,
    and numerous are her victims.
27 Her house is the way to Sheol,
    going down to the chambers of death.

7.1–27: An example of seduction by words. The
tenth and final instruction is also the fourth of the four
warnings against the seductive woman (2.16–19;
5.1–23; 6.20–35). The preface (vv. 1–5) urges the disciple to become a lover of Wisdom rather than a foolish
victim of the lying woman whose typical wiles are narrated. The woman is active and aware, speaking and
acting decisively, whereas the youth is passive and naive, led in silence like a lamb to slaughter. The images
are darkness and night, animals of sacrifice or the hunt,
and death. **4:** *You are my sister:* A designation for the
beloved used in love poetry (Song 4.9, 10, 12; 5.1, 2).
Other love terms are *let us take our fill of love* (v. 18;
see Song 5.1) and the theme of finding and seeking
(v. 10–15; see Song 3.1–4). **14:** *Today I have paid my
vows:* An ambivalent statement, which the youth takes
as an invitation to a feast of meat offered in fulfillment
of a vow, but which the woman intends as the sacrifice
of the youth. Comparison with Jephthah's vow (Judg
11.30–31) is illuminating, for Jephthah also sacrifices
an unsuspecting victim. **20:** *He took a bag of money
with him:* The wife knows from the amount of money

her husband took that he will be gone long enough
for her to dally with the youth.

8 Does not wisdom call,
    and does not understanding raise her
        voice?
2 On the heights, beside the way,
    at the crossroads she takes her
        stand;
3 beside the gates in front of the town,
    at the entrance of the portals she
        cries out:
4 "To you, O people, I call,
    and my cry is to all that live.
5 O simple ones, learn prudence;
    acquire intelligence, you who lack it.
6 Hear, for I will speak noble things,
    and from my lips will come what is
        right;
7 for my mouth will utter truth;
    wickedness is an abomination to my
        lips.
8 All the words of my mouth are
        righteous;
    there is nothing twisted or crooked in
        them.
9 They are all straight to one who
        understands
    and right to those who find
        knowledge.
10 Take my instruction instead of silver,
    and knowledge rather than choice
        gold;
11 for wisdom is better than jewels,
    and all that you may desire cannot
        compare with her.
12 I, wisdom, live with prudence,[b]
    and I attain knowledge and
        discretion.
13 The fear of the LORD is hatred of evil.
    Pride and arrogance and the way of evil
    and perverted speech I hate.
14 I have good advice and sound wisdom;
    I have insight, I have strength.
15 By me kings reign,
    and rulers decree what is just;
16 by me rulers rule,
    and nobles, all who govern rightly.

a Cn Compare Gk: Meaning of Heb uncertain
b Meaning of Heb uncertain

The Personification of Wisdom

One of the most striking features of Proverbs is its vivid personification★ of wisdom as a woman. Personification is a way of presenting an idea, a natural force, or an abstract concept as if it were a person. Woman Wisdom gives two lengthy speeches in the town square (1.20–33 and 8.1–36), and she invites passers-by to the banquet dedicating her newly built palace (9.1–6). Personification is found in other biblical passages, such as Ps 43.3 ("O send out your light and your truth; let them lead me"), but none have the scale and vigor of Wisdom in Proverbs.

Scholars have sought for parallels to Woman Wisdom in comparable literature. Some believe that personified Wisdom is an example of hypostasis, according to which some quality of a god, such as his anger or wisdom, is considered an entity in itself. Woman would thus be an embodiment of the wisdom of the LORD. Proverbs insists, however, that Wisdom is *distinct* from the LORD. Another suggestion is that Wisdom is an Israelite version of the Egyptian goddess Maat, who symbolizes order in the world and is sometimes personified. There is, however, no exact biblical equivalent to the Egyptian concept of cosmic order. Further, personified Maat is a pale abstraction in comparison with Woman Wisdom. A third suggestion is that Woman Wisdom is modeled on the "apkallu" or "umannu" of Mesopotamian mythology, sages who brought to the human race heavenly wisdom such as metallurgy, writing, and ritual. According to this conception, Wisdom is given to the race by a grand process that begins with the gods, passes through mythic sages, and ends with authoritative human beings such as kings, parents, and teachers. This last antecedent is the most likely for Proverbs for two reasons: first because Wisdom is called an "umannu" (NRSV "master worker") in 8.30, and second because in chs. 1–9, a king (Solomon), parents, and teachers join Wisdom in her task of instructing the human race; they are part of the chain of wisdom.

The book presents a counter-figure to Woman Wisdom—the "loose woman" (2.16–19; 5.1–23; 6.20–35; 7.1–27) and Woman Folly (9.13–18). Ultimately derived from warnings to young men against the wrong kind of women, the loose woman has a metaphorical★ dimension in the book: She seeks to seduce her hearers with words, promising them life but dealing them death. The book thus presents the moral life in dramatic terms; there are two voices (Wisdom and Folly), and there are two ways (the way of the righteous and the way of the wicked). Each person must choose one or the other.

Woman Wisdom's speeches in Proverbs contain no specific advice. Rather, she invites her hearers to become her disciples—to trust and obey her, and even to wait at her gates like a dear friend (8.32–36). She promises to bestow security (1.33), rule, wealth, and success (8.14–21). Her authority rests on her intimacy and honored position with God; she was created before everything and has an intimate relationship with God. In fact, traditional love language is used to describe her relationship to God and to human beings (8.30–31, 34).

Wisdom in Proverbs, and Woman Wisdom in particular, has been interpreted in a variety of ways. Jewish tradition generally views wisdom as the Torah.★ The Jewish sage Ben Sira in the early second century BCE interpreted personified Wisdom as the covenant★ of the Most High God, the law of Moses (Sir 24.23). Early Christians used the concept of personified Wisdom to explain the pre-existence of Christ (Jn 1.1–2; Col 1.15–20). In early Christian controversies about the divinity of Christ, Prov 8.22 ("The LORD created me at the beginning of his work") was used as a proof text.

The personification of wisdom gives Proverbs a metaphorical dimension. The moral life is not simply a series of right actions but a fundamental option—seeking wisdom before all else.

17 I love those who love me,
    and those who seek me diligently find
      me.
18 Riches and honor are with me,
    enduring wealth and prosperity.
19 My fruit is better than gold, even fine
      gold,
    and my yield than choice silver.
20 I walk in the way of righteousness,
    along the paths of justice,
21 endowing with wealth those who love
      me,
    and filling their treasuries.
22 The LORD created me at the beginning^a
      of his work,^b
    the first of his acts of long ago.
23 Ages ago I was set up,
    at the first, before the beginning of
      the earth.
24 When there were no depths I was
      brought forth,
    when there were no springs
      abounding with water.
25 Before the mountains had been shaped,
    before the hills, I was brought forth—
26 when he had not yet made earth and
      fields,^c
    or the world's first bits of soil.
27 When he established the heavens, I was
      there,
    when he drew a circle on the face of
      the deep,
28 when he made firm the skies above,
    when he established the fountains of
      the deep,
29 when he assigned to the sea its limit,
    so that the waters might not
      transgress his command,
    when he marked out the foundations of
      the earth,
30   then I was beside him, like a master
      worker;^d
    and I was daily his^e delight,
    rejoicing before him always,
31 rejoicing in his inhabited world
    and delighting in the human race.

32 "And now, my children, listen to me:
    happy are those who keep my ways.
33 Hear instruction and be wise,
    and do not neglect it.

34 Happy is the one who listens to me,
    watching daily at my gates,
      waiting beside my doors.
35 For whoever finds me finds life
    and obtains favor from the LORD;
36 but those who miss me injure
      themselves;
    all who hate me love death."

8.1–36: Woman Wisdom and her blessings for her loyal disciples. The speech of personified* Wisdom promising blessings balances her first speech (1.20–33) threatening those who left her. She appears in the busiest part of the city (vv. 1–3), and addresses the entire populace there, but singles out the simple (vv. 4–5). She establishes her credibility (vv. 6–11), promises her hearers skill in governing along with riches and honor (vv. 12–21), explains her high status by her closeness to God at creation (vv. 22–31), and asks her followers to wait at her door as disciples (vv. 32–36). Unlike the seductive woman in ch. 7 who speaks to a single youth in the dark of night, Wisdom addresses everyone in broad daylight, speaks trustworthy words, and grants life rather than death. **22–31:** The verses are a cosmogony or creation account, which was used in ancient literature to explain and validate important aspects of reality. The first half of the cosmogony (vv. 22–26) emphasizes the birth of Woman Wisdom *before* all else, thus underlining her unique priority. The second half (vv. 27–31) stresses her presence with God, *I was there* (v. 27) and *I was beside him* (v. 30). **30–31:** *I was daily his delight . . . delighting in the human race:* The repetition of the words *delight* and *rejoicing* establishes a correspondence between Wisdom's delighting in the LORD and her delighting in the human race. She bestows on the human race the wisdom and goodness that God put into creation.

9 Wisdom has built her house,
    she has hewn her seven pillars.
2 She has slaughtered her animals, she
      has mixed her wine,
    she has also set her table.
3 She has sent out her servant-girls, she
      calls
    from the highest places in the town,

---

a Or *me as the beginning*   *b* Heb *way*   *c* Meaning of Heb uncertain   *d* Another reading is *little child*   *e* Gk: Heb lacks *his*

4 "You that are simple, turn in here!"
  To those without sense she says,
5 "Come, eat of my bread
  and drink of the wine I have mixed.
6 Lay aside immaturity,ᵃ and live,
  and walk in the way of insight."

7 Whoever corrects a scoffer wins abuse;
  whoever rebukes the wicked
      gets hurt.
8 A scoffer who is rebuked will only hate
      you;
  the wise, when rebuked, will love you.
9 Give instructionᵇ to the wise, and they
      will become wiser still;
  teach the righteous and they will gain
      in learning.
10 The fear of the LORD is the beginning
      of wisdom,
  and the knowledge of the Holy One is
      insight.
11 For by me your days will be multiplied,
  and years will be added to your life.
12 If you are wise, you are wise for
      yourself;
  if you scoff, you alone will bear it.

13 The foolish woman is loud;
  she is ignorant and knows nothing.
14 She sits at the door of her house,
  on a seat at the high places of the
      town,
15 calling to those who pass by,
  who are going straight on their way,
16 "You who are simple, turn in here!"
  And to those without sense she says,
17 "Stolen water is sweet,
  and bread eaten in secret is pleasant."
18 But they do not know that the deadᶜ
      are there,
  that her guests are in the depths of
      Sheol.

9.1–18: The banquets of the two women, plus some aphorisms. Woman Wisdom completes her palace and issues an invitation to the dedicatory banquet (1–6). In vv. 13–18, Woman Folly issues a counter-invitation. Verses 7–12 are individual sayings, which echo some verses in ch. 1 (compare 1.7, "The fear of the LORD is the beginning of knowledge," and 1.22, "How long, O simple ones, will you love being sim-

ple?") and also point ahead to chs. 10–22, where the same two types, the wise and the righteous, are vividly contrasted. **6:** *Lay aside immaturity, and live:* To partake of the banquet creates a bond between Wisdom and her guests, requiring guests to leave behind *immaturity* and ignorance and to become wise. The imperative verb *live* here implies enjoyment of such gifts from Wisdom as a family, riches, and reputation. **11:** *For by me your days will be multiplied:* Originally, this verse probably immediately followed v. 6, for *by me* has no antecedent in the immediately preceding verses. **16–17:** Folly's invitation begins with the same words as Wisdom's (see v. 16 and v. 4), but in v. 17 diverges radically. **17:** In the phrase *stolen water, water* has the erotic meaning it has in 5.15–16, "Drink water from your own cistern, / flowing water from your own well," that is, sexual relations. *Stolen* implies clandestine and adulterous sex. *In secret* evokes the furtive meeting of ch. 7. **18:** *The dead* inhabit the underworld. As in 2.16–18; 5.3–5; 7.24–27, the woman promises life but kills instead.

THE PROVERBS OF SOLOMON

10.1–22.16: Nearly all of chs. 10–15 are antithetic✶ proverbs, that is, the second line (B) restates the first line (A) in an opposite way. The section contrasts the wicked and the righteous person (treated as types) and emphasizes the consequences of human acts. Chapters 16–22, on the other hand, contain far fewer antitheses and many more exceptions to the rule. A key metaphor✶ throughout all these chapters is founding or maintaining a house, which continues the same image as in chs. 1–9. The chapters contain over fifty references to father, mother, son, house, wife or servant.

---

10 The proverbs of Solomon.

A wise child makes a glad father,
  but a foolish child is a mother's grief.
2 Treasures gained by wickedness do not
      profit,
  but righteousness delivers from death.
3 The LORD does not let the righteous go
      hungry,
  but he thwarts the craving of the
      wicked.

ᵃ Or *simpleness*   ᵇ Heb lacks *instruction*
ᶜ Heb *shades*

4 A slack hand causes poverty,
    but the hand of the diligent makes
        rich.
5 A child who gathers in summer is
        prudent,
    but a child who sleeps in harvest
        brings shame.
6 Blessings are on the head of the
        righteous,
    but the mouth of the wicked conceals
        violence.
7 The memory of the righteous is a
        blessing,
    but the name of the wicked will rot.
8 The wise of heart will heed
        commandments,
    but a babbling fool will come to ruin.
9 Whoever walks in integrity walks
        securely,
    but whoever follows perverse ways
        will be found out.
10 Whoever winks the eye causes trouble,
    but the one who rebukes boldly
        makes peace.*a*
11 The mouth of the righteous is a
        fountain of life,
    but the mouth of the wicked conceals
        violence.
12 Hatred stirs up strife,
    but love covers all offenses.
13 On the lips of one who has
        understanding wisdom is found,
    but a rod is for the back of one who
        lacks sense.
14 The wise lay up knowledge,
    but the babbling of a fool brings ruin
        near.
15 The wealth of the rich is their fortress;
    the poverty of the poor is their ruin.
16 The wage of the righteous leads to life,
    the gain of the wicked to sin.
17 Whoever heeds instruction is on the
        path to life,
    but one who rejects a rebuke goes
        astray.
18 Lying lips conceal hatred,
    and whoever utters slander is a fool.
19 When words are many, transgression is
        not lacking,
    but the prudent are restrained in
        speech.

20 The tongue of the righteous is choice
        silver;
    the mind of the wicked is of
        little worth.
21 The lips of the righteous feed many,
    but fools die for lack of sense.
22 The blessing of the LORD makes rich,
    and he adds no sorrow with it.*b*
23 Doing wrong is like sport to a fool,
    but wise conduct is pleasure to a
        person of understanding.
24 What the wicked dread will come upon
        them,
    but the desire of the righteous will be
        granted.
25 When the tempest passes, the wicked
        are no more,
    but the righteous are established
        forever.
26 Like vinegar to the teeth, and smoke to
        the eyes,
    so are the lazy to their employers.
27 The fear of the LORD prolongs life,
    but the years of the wicked will be
        short.
28 The hope of the righteous ends in
        gladness,
    but the expectation of the wicked
        comes to nothing.
29 The way of the LORD is a stronghold for
        the upright,
    but destruction for evildoers.
30 The righteous will never be removed,
    but the wicked will not remain in the
        land.
31 The mouth of the righteous brings forth
        wisdom,
    but the perverse tongue will be cut
        off.
32 The lips of the righteous know what is
        acceptable,
    but the mouth of the wicked what is
        perverse.

10.1–32. 1–3: The first three sayings represent the
three sides of wisdom, the sapiential (wisdom as right
knowledge, v. 1, *wise*), the ethical (wisdom as right
action, v. 2, *righteousness*), and the religious (wisdom

a Gk: Heb *but a babbling fool will come to ruin*
b Or *and toil adds nothing to it*

as right reverence or worship, v. 3, *the* LORD). **1:** In the opening saying, *child, father,* and *mother* refer to the instructions of chs. 1–9 (see 1.8) and show the continuity between the instructions and the sayings. **6:** Proverbs often plays on two senses of the verb "to cover": "cover" in the sense of "conceal" and in the sense of "fill" (see vv. 11 and 12). Line B can also be translated in a sense opposite to NRSV, "violence covers the mouth of the wicked." **9:** Proverbs frequently uses the metaphors* of walking and path for conduct (also current in English). "To walk" is "to conduct oneself, to live"; "way" is "conduct"; "straight" and "crooked" (*perverted*) are "good" and "evil." *Integrity* is literally "straight, whole." **15:** Though Proverbs praises diligence and ridicules laziness, it does not ordinarily praise the wealthy and criticize the poor, but rather makes neutral observations on the situation of rich and poor, as here. **19:** Ordinarily, abundance is good, as in vv. 4, 21, and 27, and scarcity is bad, as in vv. 15 and 21. But where words are concerned the situation is reversed. Words should be few and well chosen (see 17.27). **26:** A lazy person is a common type in Proverbs (mentioned fourteen times in the book) and is often the object of scorn or humor. The lazy are as sure to pain an employer as *vinegar* and *smoke* are sure to pain taste buds and eyes, by an almost chemical necessity.

11

A false balance is an abomination to the LORD,
   but an accurate weight is his delight.
2 When pride comes, then comes disgrace;
   but wisdom is with the humble.
3 The integrity of the upright guides them,
   but the crookedness of the treacherous destroys them.
4 Riches do not profit in the day of wrath,
   but righteousness delivers from death.
5 The righteousness of the blameless keeps their ways straight,
   but the wicked fall by their own wickedness.
6 The righteousness of the upright saves them,
   but the treacherous are taken captive by their schemes.

7 When the wicked die, their hope perishes,
   and the expectation of the godless comes to nothing.
8 The righteous are delivered from trouble,
   and the wicked get into it instead.
9 With their mouths the godless would destroy their neighbors,
   but by knowledge the righteous are delivered.
10 When it goes well with the righteous, the city rejoices;
   and when the wicked perish, there is jubilation.
11 By the blessing of the upright a city is exalted,
   but it is overthrown by the mouth of the wicked.
12 Whoever belittles another lacks sense,
   but an intelligent person remains silent.
13 A gossip goes about telling secrets,
   but one who is trustworthy in spirit keeps a confidence.
14 Where there is no guidance, a nation[a] falls,
   but in an abundance of counselors there is safety.
15 To guarantee loans for a stranger brings trouble,
   but there is safety in refusing to do so.
16 A gracious woman gets honor,
   but she who hates virtue is covered with shame.[b]
   The timid become destitute,[c]
   but the aggressive gain riches.
17 Those who are kind reward themselves,
   but the cruel do themselves harm.
18 The wicked earn no real gain,
   but those who sow righteousness get a true reward.
19 Whoever is steadfast in righteousness will live,
   but whoever pursues evil will die.
20 Crooked minds are an abomination to the LORD,

a Or *an army* b Compare Gk Syr: Heb lacks *but*
she . . . shame c Gk: Heb lacks *The timid . . . destitute*

but those of blameless ways are his
delight.

21 Be assured, the wicked will not go
unpunished,
but those who are righteous will
escape.

22 Like a gold ring in a pig's snout
is a beautiful woman without good
sense.

23 The desire of the righteous ends only in
good;
the expectation of the wicked in
wrath.

24 Some give freely, yet grow all the richer;
others withhold what is due, and only
suffer want.

25 A generous person will be enriched,
and one who gives water will
get water.

26 The people curse those who hold back
grain,
but a blessing is on the head of those
who sell it.

27 Whoever diligently seeks good seeks
favor,
but evil comes to the one who
searches for it.

28 Those who trust in their riches will
wither,[a]
but the righteous will flourish like
green leaves.

29 Those who trouble their households will
inherit wind,
and the fool will be servant to the
wise.

30 The fruit of the righteous is a tree of
life,
but violence[b] takes lives away.

31 If the righteous are repaid on earth,
how much more the wicked and the
sinner!

11.1–31. 4: *The day of wrath* is any life-threatening
disaster as in Job 21.30 and Ezek 7.19. In such mortal
danger riches are of no use; value attaches only to that
which assures ultimate protection—righteousness. 9:
The difference between impiety and righteousness is
so great that what is expressed by *the godless* harms
others, whereas what is not expressed (*knowledge*
here is what is stored in the heart) by *the righteous*
benefits them. 22: A humorous statement that wisdom

is more important than beauty in evaluating a woman.
Ear and nose rings were common adornments of
women. The comparison to a pig seems to have been
made on the basis of sound as well as humorous in-
congruity, for the consonant "z" predominates in the
first line: "nezem zahab be'ap ḥazir," literally, "a ring
of god in the snout of a pig." 27: The persistent quest
for what is good is ultimately a quest that ends in gaining divine favor, perhaps human favor as well. In other
words, to seek happiness, seek excellence. To seek evil
("ra'â"), on the other hand, means only that trouble
("ra'â") will seek one out. The same Hebrew word can
mean "evil" and "trouble."

12 Whoever loves discipline loves
knowledge,
but those who hate to be rebuked are
stupid.

2 The good obtain favor from the LORD,
but those who devise evil he
condemns.

3 No one finds security by wickedness,
but the root of the righteous will
never be moved.

4 A good wife is the crown of her
husband,
but she who brings shame is like
rottenness in his bones.

5 The thoughts of the righteous are just;
the advice of the wicked is
treacherous.

6 The words of the wicked are a deadly
ambush,
but the speech of the upright delivers
them.

7 The wicked are overthrown and are no
more,
but the house of the righteous will
stand.

8 One is commended for good sense,
but a perverse mind is despised.

9 Better to be despised and have a
servant,
than to be self-important and lack
food.

10 The righteous know the needs of their
animals,
but the mercy of the wicked is cruel.

---

a Cn: Heb *fall*   b Cn Compare Gk Syr: Heb *a wise
man*

11 Those who till their land will have
plenty of food,
but those who follow worthless
pursuits have no sense.
12 The wicked covet the proceeds of
wickedness,[a]
but the root of the righteous bears
fruit.
13 The evil are ensnared by the
transgression of their lips,
but the righteous escape from
trouble.
14 From the fruit of the mouth one is filled
with good things,
and manual labor has its reward.
15 Fools think their own way is right,
but the wise listen to advice.
16 Fools show their anger at once,
but the prudent ignore an insult.
17 Whoever speaks the truth gives honest
evidence,
but a false witness speaks deceitfully.
18 Rash words are like sword thrusts,
but the tongue of the wise brings
healing.
19 Truthful lips endure forever,
but a lying tongue lasts only a
moment.
20 Deceit is in the mind of those who plan
evil,
but those who counsel peace
have joy.
21 No harm happens to the righteous,
but the wicked are filled with
trouble.
22 Lying lips are an abomination to the
LORD,
but those who act faithfully are his
delight.
23 One who is clever conceals knowledge,
but the mind of a fool[b] broadcasts
folly.
24 The hand of the diligent will rule,
while the lazy will be put to forced
labor.
25 Anxiety weighs down the human heart,
but a good word cheers it up.
26 The righteous gives good advice
to friends,[c]
but the way of the wicked leads
astray.

27 The lazy do not roast[d] their game,
but the diligent obtain precious
wealth.[d]
28 In the path of righteousness there is
life,
in walking its path there is no death.

12.1–28. 1: Genuine wisdom is gained through conversation with the wise (*discipline*) and through being criticized (*rebuked*). To reject this educational process is to settle for an animal level of consciousness; the Hebrew word for *stupid* in the second line connotes brutish. **14:** Normally, one's mouth is sated from the fruit of the earth, but in this saying one is sated from the words of one's mouth. Words in Proverbs are the prime instance of human activity. One will enjoy the benefits of one's conduct.

13 A wise child loves discipline,[e]
but a scoffer does not listen to
rebuke.
2 From the fruit of their words good
persons eat good things,
but the desire of the treacherous is
for wrongdoing.
3 Those who guard their mouths preserve
their lives;
those who open wide their lips come
to ruin.
4 The appetite of the lazy craves, and gets
nothing,
while the appetite of the diligent is
richly supplied.
5 The righteous hate falsehood,
but the wicked act shamefully and
disgracefully.
6 Righteousness guards one whose way is
upright,
but sin overthrows the wicked.
7 Some pretend to be rich, yet have
nothing;
others pretend to be poor, yet have
great wealth.
8 Wealth is a ransom for a person's life,
but the poor get no threats.
9 The light of the righteous rejoices,
but the lamp of the wicked goes out.

a Or covet the catch of the wicked   b Heb the heart
of fools   c Syr: Meaning of Heb uncertain
d Meaning of Heb uncertain   e Cn: Heb A wise child
the discipline of his father

10 By insolence the heedless make strife,
   but wisdom is with those who take
     advice.
11 Wealth hastily gotten[a] will dwindle,
   but those who gather little by little
     will increase it.
12 Hope deferred makes the heart sick,
   but a desire fulfilled is a tree of life.
13 Those who despise the word bring
     destruction on themselves,
   but those who respect the
     commandment will be rewarded.
14 The teaching of the wise is a fountain of
     life,
   so that one may avoid the snares of
     death.
15 Good sense wins favor,
   but the way of the faithless is their
     ruin.[b]
16 The clever do all things intelligently,
   but the fool displays folly.
17 A bad messenger brings trouble,
   but a faithful envoy, healing.
18 Poverty and disgrace are for the one
     who ignores instruction,
   but one who heeds reproof is
     honored.
19 A desire realized is sweet to the soul,
   but to turn away from evil is an
     abomination to fools.
20 Whoever walks with the wise becomes
     wise,
   but the companion of fools suffers
     harm.
21 Misfortune pursues sinners,
   but prosperity rewards the righteous.
22 The good leave an inheritance to their
     children's children,
   but the sinner's wealth is laid up for
     the righteous.
23 The field of the poor may yield much
     food,
   but it is swept away through
     injustice.
24 Those who spare the rod hate their
     children,
   but those who love them are diligent
     to discipline them.
25 The righteous have enough to satisfy
     their appetite,
   but the belly of the wicked is empty.

13.1–25. 6: *Righteousness* and *sin* are personified* as forces affecting those who commit themselves to them. Fundamental options determine one's course. **24**: The paradox is that one *hates* one's children by being tender with them and *loves* them by being strict, especially at an early age when children can readily change. What is criticized is indulging one's children. The paradoxical language cannot be invoked to justify harsh treatment of children or corporal punishment. Proverbs often states the need of parental discipline: 19.18; 23.13–14; Sir 7.23; 30.1–13.

14 The wise woman[c] builds her house,
   but the foolish tears it down with
     her own hands.
2 Those who walk uprightly fear the
     LORD,
   but one who is devious in conduct
     despises him.
3 The talk of fools is a rod for their backs,[d]
   but the lips of the wise preserve
     them.
4 Where there are no oxen, there is no
     grain;
   abundant crops come by the strength
     of the ox.
5 A faithful witness does not lie,
   but a false witness breathes out lies.
6 A scoffer seeks wisdom in vain,
   but knowledge is easy for one who
     understands.
7 Leave the presence of a fool,
   for there you do not find words of
     knowledge.
8 It is the wisdom of the clever to
     understand where they go,
   but the folly of fools misleads.
9 Fools mock at the guilt offering,[e]
   but the upright enjoy God's favor.
10 The heart knows its own bitterness,
   and no stranger shares its joy.
11 The house of the wicked is destroyed,
   but the tent of the upright flourishes.
12 There is a way that seems right to a
     person,
   but its end is the way to death.[f]

a Gk Vg: Heb *from vanity*   b Cn Compare Gk Syr Vg
Tg: Heb *is enduring*   c Heb *Wisdom of women*
d Cn: Heb *a rod of pride*   e Meaning of Heb uncertain
f Heb *ways of death*

13 Even in laughter the heart is sad,
    and the end of joy is grief.
14 The perverse get what their ways
        deserve,
    and the good, what their deeds
        deserve.*a*
15 The simple believe everything,
    but the clever consider their steps.
16 The wise are cautious and turn away
        from evil,
    but the fool throws off restraint and is
        careless.
17 One who is quick-tempered acts
        foolishly,
    and the schemer is hated.
18 The simple are adorned with*b* folly,
    but the clever are crowned with
        knowledge.
19 The evil bow down before the good,
    the wicked at the gates of the
        righteous.
20 The poor are disliked even by their
        neighbors,
    but the rich have many friends.
21 Those who despise their neighbors are
        sinners,
    but happy are those who are kind to
        the poor.
22 Do they not err that plan evil?
    Those who plan good find loyalty and
        faithfulness.
23 In all toil there is profit,
    but mere talk leads only to poverty.
24 The crown of the wise is their wisdom,*c*
    but folly is the garland*d* of fools.
25 A truthful witness saves lives,
    but one who utters lies is a betrayer.
26 In the fear of the LORD one has strong
        confidence,
    and one's children will have a refuge.
27 The fear of the LORD is a fountain of
        life,
    so that one may avoid the snares of
        death.
28 The glory of a king is a multitude of
        people;
    without people a prince is ruined.
29 Whoever is slow to anger has great
        understanding,
    but one who has a hasty temper exalts
        folly.

30 A tranquil mind gives life to the flesh,
    but passion makes the bones rot.
31 Those who oppress the poor insult their
        Maker,
    but those who are kind to the needy
        honor him.
32 The wicked are overthrown by their
        evildoing,
    but the righteous find a refuge in
        their integrity.*e*
33 Wisdom is at home in the mind of one
        who has understanding,
    but it is not*f* known in the heart of
        fools.
34 Righteousness exalts a nation,
    but sin is a reproach to any people.
35 A servant who deals wisely has the
        king's favor,
    but his wrath falls on one who acts
        shamefully.

14.1–35. 5: How to assess a *witness* in court is a common concern of the book (6.19; 12.17; 19.28). The best criterion is the character of the witness: How does the person ordinarily act? **13:** As observed in v. 10, external behavior does not always mirror internal thought and feeling. People are too complex to be known completely from their actions. **28:** *The glory of a king* is not absolute but depends, surprisingly, on the people he rules. A witty critique of royal power. **30:** *Passion* can also be rendered "jealousy." Inner calmness has a beneficial effect on health.

15 A soft answer turns away wrath,
    but a harsh word stirs up anger.
2 The tongue of the wise dispenses
        knowledge,*g*
    but the mouths of fools pour
        out folly.
3 The eyes of the LORD are in every
        place,
    keeping watch on the evil and the
        good.
4 A gentle tongue is a tree of life,
    but perverseness in it breaks the
        spirit.

a Cn: Heb *from upon him*   *b* Or *inherit*
c Cn Compare Gk: Heb *riches*   *d* Cn: Heb *is the folly*
e Gk Syr: Heb *in their death*   *f* Gk Syr: Heb *lacks not*
g Cn: Heb *makes knowledge good*

5 A fool despises a parent's instruction,
  but the one who heeds admonition is
    prudent.

6 In the house of the righteous there is
    much treasure,
  but trouble befalls the income of the
    wicked.

7 The lips of the wise spread knowledge;
  not so the minds of fools.

8 The sacrifice of the wicked is an
    abomination to the LORD,
  but the prayer of the upright is his
    delight.

9 The way of the wicked is an
    abomination to the LORD,
  but he loves the one who pursues
    righteousness.

10 There is severe discipline for one who
    forsakes the way,
  but one who hates a rebuke will die.

11 Sheol and Abaddon lie open before the
    LORD,
  how much more human hearts!

12 Scoffers do not like to be rebuked;
  they will not go to the wise.

13 A glad heart makes a cheerful
    countenance,
  but by sorrow of heart the spirit is
    broken.

14 The mind of one who has
    understanding seeks knowledge,
  but the mouths of fools feed on folly.

15 All the days of the poor are hard,
  but a cheerful heart has a continual
    feast.

16 Better is a little with the fear of the
    LORD
  than great treasure and trouble with it.

17 Better is a dinner of vegetables where
    love is
  than a fatted ox and hatred with it.

18 Those who are hot-tempered stir up
    strife,
  but those who are slow to anger calm
    contention.

19 The way of the lazy is overgrown with
    thorns,
  but the path of the upright is a level
    highway.

20 A wise child makes a glad father,
  but the foolish despise their mothers.

21 Folly is a joy to one who has no sense,
  but a person of understanding walks
    straight ahead.

22 Without counsel, plans go wrong,
  but with many advisers they succeed.

23 To make an apt answer is a joy to
    anyone,
  and a word in season, how good it is!

24 For the wise the path of life leads
    upward,
  in order to avoid Sheol below.

25 The LORD tears down the house of the
    proud,
  but maintains the widow's
    boundaries.

26 Evil plans are an abomination to the
    LORD,
  but gracious words are pure.

27 Those who are greedy for unjust gain
    make trouble for their
    households,
  but those who hate bribes will live.

28 The mind of the righteous ponders how
    to answer,
  but the mouth of the wicked pours
    out evil.

29 The LORD is far from the wicked,
  but he hears the prayer of the
    righteous.

30 The light of the eyes rejoices the heart,
  and good news refreshes the body.

31 The ear that heeds wholesome
    admonition
  will lodge among the wise.

32 Those who ignore instruction despise
    themselves,
  but those who heed admonition gain
    understanding.

33 The fear of the LORD is instruction in
    wisdom,
  and humility goes before honor.

15.1–33. 1: In responding to angry people, one might
be tempted to use harsh and violent language. The
verse states the paradox that when one responds to
angry people, *soft* is strong and *harsh* is weak. 14:
Heart (*mind*) and mouth are often contrasted as the
organ of storage-reflection (*mind*) and the organ of
expression (*mouth*). Here, the wise use their minds to
seek even more knowledge, whereas fools use their
mouths only to feed on more folly. 26: *Abomination*,

originally a ritual term for an unacceptable offering, is here used metaphorically.* *Pure* in this usage means acceptable to God. **33:** As one must first be low (*humility*) in order to be raised up (*honor*), so *fear of the* L\ORD comes before wisdom.

16

1 The plans of the mind belong to mortals,
   but the answer of the tongue is from the L\ORD.
2 All one's ways may be pure in one's own eyes,
   but the L\ORD weighs the spirit.
3 Commit your work to the L\ORD,
   and your plans will be established.
4 The L\ORD has made everything for its purpose,
   even the wicked for the day of trouble.
5 All those who are arrogant are an abomination to the L\ORD;
   be assured, they will not go unpunished.
6 By loyalty and faithfulness iniquity is atoned for,
   and by the fear of the L\ORD one avoids evil.
7 When the ways of people please the L\ORD,
   he causes even their enemies to be at peace with them.
8 Better is a little with righteousness than large income with injustice.
9 The human mind plans the way,
   but the L\ORD directs the steps.
10 Inspired decisions are on the lips of a king;
   his mouth does not sin in judgment.
11 Honest balances and scales are the L\ORD's;
   all the weights in the bag are his work.
12 It is an abomination to kings to do evil,
   for the throne is established by righteousness.
13 Righteous lips are the delight of a king,
   and he loves those who speak what is right.
14 A king's wrath is a messenger of death,
   and whoever is wise will appease it.

15 In the light of a king's face there is life,
   and his favor is like the clouds that bring the spring rain.
16 How much better to get wisdom than gold!
   To get understanding is to be chosen rather than silver.
17 The highway of the upright avoids evil;
   those who guard their way preserve their lives.
18 Pride goes before destruction,
   and a haughty spirit before a fall.
19 It is better to be of a lowly spirit among the poor
   than to divide the spoil with the proud.
20 Those who are attentive to a matter will prosper,
   and happy are those who trust in the L\ORD.
21 The wise of heart is called perceptive,
   and pleasant speech increases persuasiveness.
22 Wisdom is a fountain of life to one who has it,
   but folly is the punishment of fools.
23 The mind of the wise makes their speech judicious,
   and adds persuasiveness to their lips.
24 Pleasant words are like a honeycomb,
   sweetness to the soul and health to the body.
25 Sometimes there is a way that seems to be right,
   but in the end it is the way to death.
26 The appetite of workers works for them;
   their hunger urges them on.
27 Scoundrels concoct evil,
   and their speech is like a scorching fire.
28 A perverse person spreads strife,
   and a whisperer separates close friends.
29 The violent entice their neighbors,
   and lead them in a way that is not good.
30 One who winks the eyes plans*a* perverse things;
   one who compresses the lips brings evil to pass.

a Gk Syr Vg Tg: Heb *to plan*

31 Gray hair is a crown of glory;
   it is gained in a righteous life.
32 One who is slow to anger is better than
      the mighty,
   and one whose temper is controlled
      than one who captures a city.
33 The lot is cast into the lap,
   but the decision is the LORD's alone.

16.1–33. 1: The heart (*mind*) is the organ of planning and the *tongue* is the organ of speaking and execution. It is not fully in the power of a human being to put plans into effect or control their course. 16: Tradition declares *wisdom* more precious than *gold* and *silver* (3.14; Job 28). Gold and silver can buy many things, but wisdom invites God to give the priceless gifts of long life, wealth, and honor. 20: The saying declares that success and happiness depend both on God and on our own efforts. It does not explore theological issues arising from such an assertion. 27–30: Sayings on three types of wicked people and their speech and demeanor. The first three verses begin with the Hebrew word "'ish," translated "man" or "individual." The second line of each saying states the particular damage a villain's words inflict on others. The final saying (v. 30) sketches the facial mannerisms common to all the malefactors; compare 6.12–15. 33: A *lot*, similar to dice in giving varying results when thrown, was given a designation "yes" or "no" and cast for its answer. See 1 Sam 10.16–26; Num 26.55; Josh 14.2. The answer was believed to be from God.

17 Better is a dry morsel with quiet
   than a house full of feasting with
      strife.
2 A slave who deals wisely will rule over a
      child who acts shamefully,
   and will share the inheritance as one
      of the family.
3 The crucible is for silver, and the
      furnace is for gold,
   but the LORD tests the heart.
4 An evildoer listens to wicked lips;
   and a liar gives heed to a mischievous
      tongue.
5 Those who mock the poor insult their
      Maker;
   those who are glad at calamity will
      not go unpunished.
6 Grandchildren are the crown of
      the aged,

and the glory of children is their
      parents.
7 Fine speech is not becoming to a fool;
   still less is false speech to a ruler.[a]
8 A bribe is like a magic stone in the eyes
      of those who give it;
   wherever they turn they prosper.
9 One who forgives an affront fosters
      friendship,
   but one who dwells on disputes will
      alienate a friend.
10 A rebuke strikes deeper into a
      discerning person
   than a hundred blows into a fool.
11 Evil people seek only rebellion,
   but a cruel messenger will be sent
      against them.
12 Better to meet a she-bear robbed of its
      cubs
   than to confront a fool immersed in
      folly.
13 Evil will not depart from the house
   of one who returns evil for good.
14 The beginning of strife is like letting out
      water;
   so stop before the quarrel breaks out.
15 One who justifies the wicked and one
      who condemns the righteous
   are both alike an abomination to the
      LORD.
16 Why should fools have a price in hand
      to buy wisdom, when they have no
      mind to learn?
17 A friend loves at all times,
   and kinsfolk are born to share
      adversity.
18 It is senseless to give a pledge,
   to become surety for a neighbor.
19 One who loves transgression loves strife;
   one who builds a high threshold
      invites broken bones.
20 The crooked of mind do not prosper,
   and the perverse of tongue fall into
      calamity.
21 The one who begets a fool gets trouble;
   the parent of a fool has no joy.
22 A cheerful heart is a good medicine,
   but a downcast spirit dries up
      the bones.

a Or *a noble person*

23 The wicked accept a concealed bribe
   to pervert the ways of justice.
24 The discerning person looks to wisdom,
   but the eyes of a fool to the ends of
      the earth.
25 Foolish children are a grief to their
      father
   and bitterness to her who bore them.
26 To impose a fine on the innocent is not
      right,
   or to flog the noble for their integrity.
27 One who spares words is
      knowledgeable;
   one who is cool in spirit has
      understanding.
28 Even fools who keep silent are
      considered wise;
   when they close their lips, they are
      deemed intelligent.

17.1–28. 2: Wisdom surmounts natural boundaries
and limits. Slaves of the time could enter a great
household and their conduct, if prudent and trustworthy, would win everyone's respect. A perversely
foolish child could lose out to such wise servants. 8: A
neutral observation on money. A *bribe* can seem like
a *magic stone* since it opens doors hitherto closed. 9:
A paradox: One finds *friendship* if one loses or hides
(*forgives*) *an affront*, and loses (*alienates*) *a friend* if
one finds or makes public (*dwells on*) *disputes*. Friendship has a price—bearing with the faults of the other.
13: Paradoxically, evil stays in the house of anyone
who tries to inflict it on others. 19: Whoever *loves* an
offense in the sense of dwelling on it is equivalently
asking for a quarrel in the same way that any one who
builds an overly *high threshold* is asking for injury.

18 The one who lives alone is self-
      indulgent,
   showing contempt for all who have
      sound judgment.*ª*
2 A fool takes no pleasure in
      understanding,
   but only in expressing personal
      opinion.
3 When wickedness comes, contempt
      comes also;
   and with dishonor comes disgrace.
4 The words of the mouth are deep
      waters;

the fountain of wisdom is a gushing
      stream.
5 It is not right to be partial to the guilty,
   or to subvert the innocent in
      judgment.
6 A fool's lips bring strife,
   and a fool's mouth invites a flogging.
7 The mouths of fools are their ruin,
   and their lips a snare to themselves.
8 The words of a whisperer are like
      delicious morsels;
   they go down into the inner parts of
      the body.
9 One who is slack in work
   is close kin to a vandal.
10 The name of the LORD is a strong
      tower;
   the righteous run into it and are safe.
11 The wealth of the rich is their strong
      city;
   in their imagination it is like a high
      wall.
12 Before destruction one's heart is
      haughty,
   but humility goes before honor.
13 If one gives answer before hearing,
   it is folly and shame.
14 The human spirit will endure sickness;
   but a broken spirit—who can bear?
15 An intelligent mind acquires knowledge,
   and the ear of the wise seeks
      knowledge.
16 A gift opens doors;
   it gives access to the great.
17 The one who first states a case seems
      right,
   until the other comes and cross-
      examines.
18 Casting the lot puts an end to disputes
   and decides between powerful
      contenders.
19 An ally offended is stronger than a city;*ᵇ*
   such quarreling is like the bars of a
      castle.
20 From the fruit of the mouth one's
      stomach is satisfied;
   the yield of the lips brings
      satisfaction.

a Meaning of Heb uncertain   *b* Gk Syr Vg Tg:
Meaning of Heb uncertain

21 Death and life are in the power of the
   tongue,
      and those who love it will eat
         its fruits.
22 He who finds a wife finds a good thing,
      and obtains favor from the LORD.
23 The poor use entreaties,
      but the rich answer roughly.
24 Some*a* friends play at friendship*b*
      but a true friend sticks closer than
         one's nearest kin.

18.1–24. 1: The probable meaning is that those who
do not listen to others cannot grow wise, for wisdom
comes through interaction with others—a process of
instruction and correction. **4:** The *deep waters* of the
mind are revealed by one's words (20.5). The *waters*
become a *stream* nourishing others. **17:** The first
speaker in a lawsuit seems entirely in the right. Then
the opponent *cross-examines.* The law court experience teaches a valuable lesson: There are two sides to
every question. **19:** *Ally* is a family member, literally,
"brother" or "member of the family." An offended
family member can be more unyielding than a fortress.
21: *Love* has the sense of "choose" as in Deut 4.37;
10.15; Isa 41.8. One chooses either life or death by the
words one speaks. One must *eat* the *fruits* (consequences) of one's acts. For similar vocabulary, see
30.15–20.

19 Better the poor walking in integrity
   than one perverse of speech who is
      a fool.
2 Desire without knowledge is not good,
      and one who moves too hurriedly
         misses the way.
3 One's own folly leads to ruin,
      yet the heart rages against
         the LORD.
4 Wealth brings many friends,
      but the poor are left friendless.
5 A false witness will not go unpunished,
      and a liar will not escape.
6 Many seek the favor of the generous,
      and everyone is a friend to a giver of
         gifts.
7 If the poor are hated even by their kin,
      how much more are they shunned by
         their friends!
   When they call after them, they are not
      there.*c*

8 To get wisdom is to love oneself;
      to keep understanding is to prosper.
9 A false witness will not go unpunished,
      and the liar will perish.
10 It is not fitting for a fool to live
      in luxury,
         much less for a slave to rule over
            princes.
11 Those with good sense are slow
      to anger,
         and it is their glory to overlook an
            offense.
12 A king's anger is like the growling of a
      lion,
         but his favor is like dew on the grass.
13 A stupid child is ruin to a father,
      and a wife's quarreling is a continual
         dripping of rain.
14 House and wealth are inherited from
      parents,
         but a prudent wife is from the LORD.
15 Laziness brings on deep sleep;
      an idle person will suffer hunger.
16 Those who keep the commandment will
      live;
         those who are heedless of their ways
            will die.
17 Whoever is kind to the poor lends to the
      LORD,
         and will be repaid in full.
18 Discipline your children while there is
      hope;
         do not set your heart on their
            destruction.
19 A violent tempered person will pay the
      penalty;
         if you effect a rescue, you will only
            have to do it again.*c*
20 Listen to advice and accept instruction,
      that you may gain wisdom for the
         future.
21 The human mind may devise
      many plans,
         but it is the purpose of the LORD that
            will be established.
22 What is desirable in a person is loyalty,
      and it is better to be poor than a liar.

a Syr Tg: Heb A *man of*   *b* Cn Compare Syr Vg Tg:
Meaning of Heb uncertain   *c* Meaning of Heb
uncertain

23 The fear of the LORD is life indeed;
   filled with it one rests secure
   and suffers no harm.
24 The lazy person buries a hand in the
      dish,
   and will not even bring it back to the
      mouth.
25 Strike a scoffer, and the simple will
      learn prudence;
   reprove the intelligent, and they will
      gain knowledge.
26 Those who do violence to their father
      and chase away their mother
   are children who cause shame and
      bring reproach.
27 Cease straying, my child, from the
      words of knowledge,
   in order that you may hear
      instruction.
28 A worthless witness mocks at justice,
   and the mouth of the wicked devours
      iniquity.
29 Condemnation is ready for scoffers,
   and flogging for the backs of fools.

19.1–29. 2: *Desire* (the internal) and *movement* (the external) without sufficient reflection go nowhere. **13:** Another saying on the household (from the male point of view). The two great causes of domestic unhappiness are foolish children and an angry wife or spouse. Wisdom can help one avoid such unhappiness. **14:** As if to balance the preceding verse on the angry wife, this saying asserts the greatest cause of domestic happiness is a suitable wife.

20 Wine is a mocker, strong drink a
      brawler,
   and whoever is led astray by it is not
      wise.
2 The dread anger of a king is like the
      growling of a lion;
   anyone who provokes him to anger
      forfeits life itself.
3 It is honorable to refrain from strife,
   but every fool is quick to quarrel.
4 The lazy person does not plow in season;
   harvest comes, and there is nothing
      to be found.
5 The purposes in the human mind are
      like deep water,
   but the intelligent will draw them out.

6 Many proclaim themselves loyal,
   but who can find one worthy of trust?
7 The righteous walk in integrity—
   happy are the children who follow
      them!
8 A king who sits on the throne of
      judgment
   winnows all evil with his eyes.
9 Who can say, "I have made my heart
      clean;
   I am pure from my sin"?
10 Diverse weights and diverse measures
   are both alike an abomination to the
      LORD.
11 Even children make themselves known
      by their acts,
   by whether what they do is pure and
      right.
12 The hearing ear and the seeing eye—
   the LORD has made them both.
13 Do not love sleep, or else you will come
      to poverty;
   open your eyes, and you will have
      plenty of bread.
14 "Bad, bad," says the buyer,
   then goes away and boasts.
15 There is gold, and abundance of costly
      stones;
   but the lips informed by knowledge
      are a precious jewel.
16 Take the garment of one who has given
      surety for a stranger;
   seize the pledge given as surety for
      foreigners.
17 Bread gained by deceit is sweet,
   but afterward the mouth will be full
      of gravel.
18 Plans are established by taking advice;
   wage war by following wise guidance.
19 A gossip reveals secrets;
   therefore do not associate with a
      babbler.
20 If you curse father or mother,
   your lamp will go out in utter
      darkness.
21 An estate quickly acquired in the
      beginning
   will not be blessed in the end.
22 Do not say, "I will repay evil";
   wait for the LORD, and he will help
      you.

23 Differing weights are an abomination to
　　the LORD,
　　and false scales are not good.
24 All our steps are ordered by
　　the LORD;
　　how then can we understand our own
　　ways?
25 It is a snare for one to say rashly, "It is
　　holy,"
　　and begin to reflect only after making
　　a vow.
26 A wise king winnows the wicked,
　　and drives the wheel over them.
27 The human spirit is the lamp of the
　　LORD,
　　searching every inmost part.
28 Loyalty and faithfulness preserve the
　　king,
　　and his throne is upheld by
　　righteousness.[a]
29 The glory of youths is their strength,
　　but the beauty of the aged is their
　　gray hair.
30 Blows that wound cleanse away evil;
　　beatings make clean the innermost
　　parts.

20.1–30. 15: *Gold* and *costly stones* must refer to jewelry. The most beautiful adornment of a face is not
jewelry but wise *lips*, that is, wise words that show the
beauty within.

21

The king's heart is a stream of
water in the hand of the LORD;
he turns it wherever he will.
2 All deeds are right in the sight of the
　　doer,
　　but the LORD weighs the heart.
3 To do righteousness and justice
　　is more acceptable to the LORD than
　　sacrifice.
4 Haughty eyes and a proud heart—
　　the lamp of the wicked—are sin.
5 The plans of the diligent lead surely to
　　abundance,
　　but everyone who is hasty comes only
　　to want.
6 The getting of treasures by a lying
　　tongue
　　is a fleeting vapor and a snare[b] of
　　death.

7 The violence of the wicked will sweep
　　them away,
　　because they refuse to do what
　　is just.
8 The way of the guilty is crooked,
　　but the conduct of the pure is right.
9 It is better to live in a corner of the
　　housetop
　　than in a house shared with a
　　contentious wife.
10 The souls of the wicked desire evil;
　　their neighbors find no mercy in their
　　eyes.
11 When a scoffer is punished, the simple
　　become wiser;
　　when the wise are instructed, they
　　increase in knowledge.
12 The Righteous One observes the house
　　of the wicked;
　　he casts the wicked down to ruin.
13 If you close your ear to the cry of the
　　poor,
　　you will cry out and not be heard.
14 A gift in secret averts anger;
　　and a concealed bribe in the bosom,
　　strong wrath.
15 When justice is done, it is a joy to the
　　righteous,
　　but dismay to evildoers.
16 Whoever wanders from the way of
　　understanding
　　will rest in the assembly of the dead.
17 Whoever loves pleasure will suffer
　　want;
　　whoever loves wine and oil will not be
　　rich.
18 The wicked is a ransom for the
　　righteous,
　　and the faithless for the upright.
19 It is better to live in a desert land
　　than with a contentious and fretful
　　wife.
20 Precious treasure remains[c] in the house
　　of the wise,
　　but the fool devours it.
21 Whoever pursues righteousness and
　　kindness
　　will find life[d] and honor.

a Gk: Heb *loyalty*　　*b* Gk: Heb *seekers*　　*c* Gk: Heb
and oil　　*d* Gk: Heb *life and righteousness*

22 One wise person went up against a city
of warriors
and brought down the stronghold in
which they trusted.
23 To watch over mouth and tongue
is to keep out of trouble.
24 The proud, haughty person, named
"Scoffer,"
acts with arrogant pride.
25 The craving of the lazy person is fatal,
for lazy hands refuse to labor.
26 All day long the wicked covet,*a*
but the righteous give and do not
hold back.
27 The sacrifice of the wicked is an
abomination;
how much more when brought with
evil intent.
28 A false witness will perish,
but a good listener will testify
successfully.
29 The wicked put on a bold face,
but the upright give thought to*b* their
ways.
30 No wisdom, no understanding, no
counsel,
can avail against the LORD.
31 The horse is made ready for the day of
battle,
but the victory belongs to the LORD.

21.1–31. 14: The wise know the secret of taming *anger* and *strong wrath*—a gift of money. The strategy implies a certain disdain for anger, for a seemingly strong passion can be assuaged by a little money. **17:** Those who desire the trappings of wealth will never get them, for wealth does not come to the idle and those who *love pleasure* (see 6.6–11; 10.4; 12.24, 27). **19:** Living alone is preferable to living in a house spoiled by a spouse's anger. **29:** *The wicked* are defiant (*put on a bold face*) whereas the *upright*, who give thought to their ways, are willing to conform their actions to the teaching of others. The Hebrew text and the ancient versions transmit another reading in the second line: "the upright person *maintains* a faithful course."

22 A good name is to be chosen rather
than great riches,
and favor is better than silver
or gold.

2 The rich and the poor have this in
common:
the LORD is the maker of them all.
3 The clever see danger and hide;
but the simple go on, and suffer for
it.
4 The reward for humility and fear of the
LORD
is riches and honor and life.
5 Thorns and snares are in the way of the
perverse;
the cautious will keep far from them.
6 Train children in the right way,
and when old, they will not stray.
7 The rich rule over the poor,
and the borrower is the slave of the
lender.
8 Whoever sows injustice will reap
calamity,
and the rod of anger will fail.
9 Those who are generous are blessed,
for they share their bread with the
poor.
10 Drive out a scoffer, and strife
goes out;
quarreling and abuse will cease.
11 Those who love a pure heart and are
gracious in speech
will have the king as a friend.
12 The eyes of the LORD keep watch over
knowledge,
but he overthrows the words of the
faithless.
13 The lazy person says, "There is a lion
outside!
I shall be killed in the streets!"
14 The mouth of a loose*c* woman is a deep
pit;
he with whom the LORD is angry falls
into it.
15 Folly is bound up in the heart of
a boy,
but the rod of discipline drives it far
away.
16 Oppressing the poor in order to enrich
oneself,
and giving to the rich, will lead only
to loss.

a Gk: Heb *all day long one covets covetously*   *b* Another reading is *establish*   *c* Heb *strange*

22.1–16. 8: Both metaphors* are agricultural. In line A, bad actions are seed yielding trouble. In line B, *the rod* is a flail which cannot thresh* grain. Evil will be frustrated; it will bear no fruit.

THE WORDS OF THE WISE

22.17–24.22: An instruction partly modeled on the thirteenth-century BCE Egyptian "Instruction of Amenemope." Like its Egyptian model, it has *thirty sayings* (22.20) and is introduced by a preface (22.17–21); its first two admonitions (22.22–25) resemble the first two in "Amenemope." *The words of the wise* offer a kind of professional ethics, warning against behavior that can destroy one's humanity and religion (22.22–23.11) and urging resistance to the temptations of youth (23.12–35). It concludes with counsels of a general nature (24.1–22).

17   The words of the wise:

Incline your ear and hear my words,*ᵃ*
    and apply your mind to my teaching;
18 for it will be pleasant if you keep them
        within you,
    if all of them are ready on your lips.
19 So that your trust may be in the LORD,
    I have made them known to you
        today—yes, to you.
20 Have I not written for you thirty sayings
    of admonition and knowledge,
21 to show you what is right and true,
    so that you may give a true answer to
        those who sent you?

22 Do not rob the poor because they are
        poor,
    or crush the afflicted at the gate;
23 for the LORD pleads their cause
    and despoils of life those who despoil
        them.
24 Make no friends with those given to
        anger,
    and do not associate with hotheads,
25 or you may learn their ways
    and entangle yourself in a snare.
26 Do not be one of those who give pledges,
    who become surety for debts.
27 If you have nothing with which to pay,
    why should your bed be taken from
        under you?

28 Do not remove the ancient landmark
    that your ancestors set up.
29 Do you see those who are skillful in
        their work?
    They will serve kings;
    they will not serve common people.

22.22–23: *The poor* are dangerous to attack, for God will defend them.

23 When you sit down to eat with
    a ruler,
    observe carefully what*ᵇ* is before you,
2 and put a knife to your throat
    if you have a big appetite.
3 Do not desire the ruler's*ᶜ* delicacies,
    for they are deceptive food.
4 Do not wear yourself out to get rich;
    be wise enough to desist.
5 When your eyes light upon it, it is gone;
    for suddenly it takes wings to itself,
    flying like an eagle toward heaven.
6 Do not eat the bread of the stingy;
    do not desire their delicacies;
7 for like a hair in the throat, so are they.*ᵈ*
    "Eat and drink!" they say to you;
    but they do not mean it.
8 You will vomit up the little you have
        eaten,
    and you will waste your pleasant
        words.
9 Do not speak in the hearing of a fool,
    who will only despise the wisdom of
        your words.
10 Do not remove an ancient landmark
    or encroach on the fields of orphans,
11 for their redeemer is strong;
    he will plead their cause against you.
12 Apply your mind to instruction
    and your ear to words of knowledge.
13 Do not withhold discipline from your
        children;
    if you beat them with a rod, they will
        not die.
14 If you beat them with the rod,
    you will save their lives from Sheol.
15 My child, if your heart is wise,
    my heart too will be glad.

a Cn Compare Gk: Heb *Incline your ear, and hear the words of the wise*   *b* Or *who*   *c* Heb *his*
d Meaning of Heb uncertain

16 My soul will rejoice
  when your lips speak what is right.
17 Do not let your heart envy sinners,
  but always continue in the fear of the
    LORD.
18 Surely there is a future,
  and your hope will not be cut off.

19 Hear, my child, and be wise,
  and direct your mind in the way.
20 Do not be among winebibbers,
  or among gluttonous eaters
    of meat;
21 for the drunkard and the glutton will
    come to poverty,
  and drowsiness will clothe them with
    rags.

22 Listen to your father who begot you,
  and do not despise your mother when
    she is old.
23 Buy truth, and do not sell it;
  buy wisdom, instruction, and
    understanding.
24 The father of the righteous will greatly
    rejoice;
  he who begets a wise son will be glad
    in him.
25 Let your father and mother be glad;
  let her who bore you rejoice.

26 My child, give me your heart,
  and let your eyes observe[a] my ways.
27 For a prostitute is a deep pit;
  an adulteress[b] is a narrow well.
28 She lies in wait like a robber
  and increases the number of the
    faithless.

23.1–23. 1–3: Dining etiquette, especially moderation with food and drink, is a common topic in Egyptian instructions. Banquets were an occasion for young servants to advance themselves, and self-indulgence would leave a bad impression. 1: *Observe carefully what is before you* refers both to the food and the host. 2: *Put a knife to your throat:* Put your knife in your jaws rather than in the food, that is, restrain your appetite. 6–7: Don't go to banquets when you are not invited or wanted. Though courtesy forces the host to say *"Eat and drink!"*, the words are insincere. The result will be indigestion and frustration for the unwelcome guest.

13–14: Hyperbole* and sardonic humor are used to give advice on raising children. It is not disciplinary blows that will kill a child but uncorrected behavior that will lead to fatal consequences. The humor and hyperbole show the admonition does not espouse the corporal punishment of children. 17–18: A warning against peer-group pressure, which is especially applicable to the young. Why envy the wicked, for they have no future, no descendants? The warning is repeated in 24.1 and 19–20. 22–23: The two commands in v. 23, *buy truth* and *do not sell it*, continue on a metaphorical* level in the two commands in v. 22, *listen* and *do not despise*.

29 Who has woe? Who has sorrow?
  Who has strife? Who has
    complaining?
  Who has wounds without cause?
  Who has redness of eyes?
30 Those who linger late over wine,
  those who keep trying mixed wines.
31 Do not look at wine when it is red,
  when it sparkles in the cup
  and goes down smoothly.
32 At the last it bites like a serpent,
  and stings like an adder.
33 Your eyes will see strange things,
  and your mind utter perverse things.
34 You will be like one who lies down in
    the midst of the sea,
  like one who lies on the top of
    a mast.[c]
35 "They struck me," you will say,[d] "but I
    was not hurt;
  they beat me, but I did not feel it.
  When shall I awake?
  I will seek another drink."

24 Do not envy the wicked,
  nor desire to be with them;
2 for their minds devise violence,
  and their lips talk of mischief.

3 By wisdom a house is built,
  and by understanding it is
    established;
4 by knowledge the rooms are filled
  with all precious and pleasant riches.

a Another reading is *delight in*   b Heb *an alien woman*
c Meaning of Heb uncertain   d Gk Syr Vg Tg: Heb
lacks *you will say*

5 Wise warriors are mightier than strong
    ones,[a]
    and those who have knowledge than
       those who have strength;
6 for by wise guidance you can wage your
    war,
    and in abundance of counselors there
       is victory.
7 Wisdom is too high for fools;
    in the gate they do not open
       their mouths.

8 Whoever plans to do evil
    will be called a mischief-maker.
9 The devising of folly is sin,
    and the scoffer is an abomination to
       all.

10 If you faint in the day of adversity,
    your strength being small;
11 if you hold back from rescuing those
       taken away to death,
    those who go staggering to the
       slaughter;
12 if you say, "Look, we did not know this"—
    does not he who weighs the heart
       perceive it?
    Does not he who keeps watch over your
       soul know it?
    And will he not repay all according to
       their deeds?

13 My child, eat honey, for it is good,
    and the drippings of the honeycomb
       are sweet to your taste.
14 Know that wisdom is such to your soul;
    if you find it, you will find a future,
    and your hope will not be cut off.

15 Do not lie in wait like an outlaw against
       the home of the righteous;
    do no violence to the place where the
       righteous live;
16 for though they fall seven times, they
       will rise again;
    but the wicked are overthrown by
       calamity.

17 Do not rejoice when your enemies fall,
    and do not let your heart be glad
       when they stumble,

18 or else the LORD will see it and be
       displeased,
    and turn away his anger from them.

19 Do not fret because of evildoers.
    Do not envy the wicked;
20 for the evil have no future;
    the lamp of the wicked will go out.

21 My child, fear the LORD and the king,
    and do not disobey either of them;[b]
22 for disaster comes from them suddenly,
    and who knows the ruin that both
       can bring?

24.3–22. 10–12: The probable meaning of the obscure admonition is that excuses for not aiding one's neighbor will be useless before the all-seeing God. **17–18:** Divine retribution works mysteriously. Human beings should stand aside and not anticipate its results.

23   These also are sayings of the wise:

    Partiality in judging is not good.
24 Whoever says to the wicked, "You are
       innocent,"
    will be cursed by peoples, abhorred by
       nations;
25 but those who rebuke the wicked will
       have delight,
    and a good blessing will come upon
       them.
26 One who gives an honest answer
    gives a kiss on the lips.

27 Prepare your work outside,
    get everything ready for you in the
       field;
    and after that build your house.

28 Do not be a witness against your
       neighbor without cause,
    and do not deceive with your lips.
29 Do not say, "I will do to others as they
       have done to me;
    I will pay them back for what they
       have done."

a Gk Compare Syr Tg: Heb *A wise man is strength*
b Gk: Heb *do not associate with those who change*

30 I passed by the field of one who was
        lazy,
    by the vineyard of a stupid person;
31 and see, it was all overgrown with
        thorns;
    the ground was covered with nettles,
    and its stone wall was broken down.
32 Then I saw and considered it;
    I looked and received instruction.
33 A little sleep, a little slumber,
    a little folding of the hands to rest,
34 and poverty will come upon you like a
        robber,
    and want, like an armed warrior.

24.23–34. Further words of the wise. A carefully arranged appendix to 22.17–24.22. Two areas of life, law (vv. 23–25, 28–29) and farming (vv. 27, 30–34), are used to illustrate the effects of wisdom in word and action. **30–34:** An illustrative story, like those in 6.9–11, ch. 7, and Ps 37.35–36.

25 These are other proverbs of Solomon that the officials of King Hezekiah of Judah copied.

2 It is the glory of God to conceal things,
    but the glory of kings is to search
        things out.
3 Like the heavens for height, like the
        earth for depth,
    so the mind of kings is unsearchable.
4 Take away the dross from the silver,
    and the smith has material for
        a vessel;
5 take away the wicked from the presence
        of the king,
    and his throne will be established in
        righteousness.
6 Do not put yourself forward in the
        king's presence
    or stand in the place of the great;
7 for it is better to be told, "Come up here,"
    than to be put lower in the presence
        of a noble.

    What your eyes have seen
8   do not hastily bring into court;
    for^a what will you do in the end,
        when your neighbor puts you to
            shame?

9 Argue your case with your neighbor
        directly,
    and do not disclose another's secret;
10 or else someone who hears you will
        bring shame upon you,
    and your ill repute will have no end.
11 A word fitly spoken
    is like apples of gold in a setting of
        silver.
12 Like a gold ring or an ornament
        of gold
    is a wise rebuke to a listening ear.
13 Like the cold of snow in the time
        of harvest
    are faithful messengers to those who
        send them;
    they refresh the spirit of their
        masters.
14 Like clouds and wind without rain
    is one who boasts of a gift never
        given.
15 With patience a ruler may be
        persuaded,
    and a soft tongue can break bones.
16 If you have found honey, eat only
        enough for you,
    or else, having too much, you will
        vomit it.
17 Let your foot be seldom in your
        neighbor's house,
    otherwise the neighbor will become
        weary of you and hate you.
18 Like a war club, a sword, or a sharp
        arrow
    is one who bears false witness against
        a neighbor.
19 Like a bad tooth or a lame foot
    is trust in a faithless person in time of
        trouble.
20 Like vinegar on a wound^b
    is one who sings songs to a heavy
        heart.
    Like a moth in clothing or a worm in
        wood,
    sorrow gnaws at the human heart.^c
21 If your enemies are hungry, give them
        bread to eat;

a Cn: Heb *or else*   b Gk: Heb *Like one who takes off a garment on a cold day, like vinegar on lye*   c Gk Syr Tg: Heb lacks *Like a moth . . . human heart*

and if they are thirsty, give them
    water to drink;
22 for you will heap coals of fire on their
    heads,
    and the LORD will reward you.
23 The north wind produces rain,
    and a backbiting tongue, angry
    looks.
24 It is better to live in a corner of the
    housetop
    than in a house shared with a
    contentious wife.
25 Like cold water to a thirsty soul,
    so is good news from a far country.
26 Like a muddied spring or a polluted
    fountain
    are the righteous who give way before
    the wicked.
27 It is not good to eat much honey,
    or to seek honor on top of honor.
28 Like a city breached, without walls,
    is one who lacks self-control.

Chs. 25–29: Proverbs of Solomon. 25.1–28. 1: An important clue to the composition and date of Proverbs. Hezekiah, who was king of Judah from 715–687 BCE, apparently ordered this collection added to an already existing Solomonic collection (perhaps chs. 10–22). **2–3:** The world is full of conundrums and puzzles, but the king is there to unravel them and lead people to serve the gods. The affinity between divine and royal wisdom is expressed by the repetition of the first and last word of each phrase (*glory* and *things*) and by the rhyme in *God* and *king* ("'elohim" and "melakim"). **7:** See Lk 14.8–10. **21–22:** An enemy's vulnerability should not be made an occasion for settling old scores (so also Ex 23.4). Allow God's justice its proper scope (compare 20.22 and 24.17–18). *Heap coals of fire on their heads* alludes to no known practice. It may be hyperbole* for punishment. Romans 12.20 cites the Greek version.

26 Like snow in summer or rain in
    harvest,
    so honor is not fitting for a fool.
2 Like a sparrow in its flitting, like a
    swallow in its flying,
    an undeserved curse goes nowhere.
3 A whip for the horse, a bridle for the
    donkey,
    and a rod for the back of fools.

4 Do not answer fools according to their
    folly,
    or you will be a fool yourself.
5 Answer fools according to their folly,
    or they will be wise in their own eyes.
6 It is like cutting off one's foot and
    drinking down violence,
    to send a message by a fool.
7 The legs of a disabled person hang
    limp;
    so does a proverb in the mouth of a
    fool.
8 It is like binding a stone in a sling
    to give honor to a fool.
9 Like a thornbush brandished by the
    hand of a drunkard
    is a proverb in the mouth of a fool.
10 Like an archer who wounds everybody
    is one who hires a passing fool or
    drunkard.*a*
11 Like a dog that returns to its vomit
    is a fool who reverts to his folly.
12 Do you see persons wise in their own
    eyes?
    There is more hope for fools than for
    them.
13 The lazy person says, "There is a lion in
    the road!
    There is a lion in the streets!"
14 As a door turns on its hinges,
    so does a lazy person in bed.
15 The lazy person buries a hand in the
    dish,
    and is too tired to bring it back to the
    mouth.
16 The lazy person is wiser in self-esteem
    than seven who can answer
    discreetly.
17 Like somebody who takes a passing dog
    by the ears
    is one who meddles in the quarrel of
    another.
18 Like a maniac who shoots deadly
    firebrands and arrows,
19 so is one who deceives a neighbor
    and says, "I am only joking!"
20 For lack of wood the fire goes out,
    and where there is no whisperer,
    quarreling ceases.

a Meaning of Heb uncertain

21 As charcoal is to hot embers and wood
     to fire,
     so is a quarrelsome person for
         kindling strife.
22 The words of a whisperer are like
         delicious morsels;
     they go down into the inner parts of
         the body.
23 Like the glaze[a] covering an earthen
         vessel
     are smooth[b] lips with an
         evil heart.
24 An enemy dissembles in speaking
     while harboring deceit within;
25 when an enemy speaks graciously, do
         not believe it,
     for there are seven abominations
         concealed within;
26 though hatred is covered with guile,
     the enemy's wickedness will be
         exposed in the assembly.
27 Whoever digs a pit will fall into it,
     and a stone will come back on the
         one who starts it rolling.
28 A lying tongue hates its victims,
     and a flattering mouth works ruin.

26.1–28. 4–5: Each saying makes sense in its own
right. Taken together they show the problem, even the
danger, that *fools* pose to their neighbors. 13–16: Four
sayings on the *lazy person*, whom Proverbs derides on
the grounds that this type of person never acts.

27 Do not boast about tomorrow,
     for you do not know what a day
         may bring.
2 Let another praise you, and not your
         own mouth—
     a stranger, and not your own lips.
3 A stone is heavy, and sand is weighty,
     but a fool's provocation is heavier
         than both.
4 Wrath is cruel, anger is overwhelming,
     but who is able to stand before
         jealousy?
5 Better is open rebuke
     than hidden love.
6 Well meant are the wounds a friend
         inflicts,
     but profuse are the kisses of an
         enemy.

7 The sated appetite spurns honey,
     but to a ravenous appetite even the
         bitter is sweet.
8 Like a bird that strays from its nest
     is one who strays from home.
9 Perfume and incense make the heart
         glad,
     but the soul is torn by trouble.[c]
10 Do not forsake your friend or the friend
         of your parent;
     do not go to the house of your
         kindred in the day of your
         calamity.
     Better is a neighbor who is nearby
         than kindred who are far away.
11 Be wise, my child, and make my heart
         glad,
     so that I may answer whoever
         reproaches me.
12 The clever see danger and hide;
     but the simple go on, and suffer for
         it.
13 Take the garment of one who has given
         surety for a stranger;
     seize the pledge given as surety for
         foreigners.[d]
14 Whoever blesses a neighbor with a loud
         voice,
     rising early in the morning,
     will be counted as cursing.
15 A continual dripping on a rainy day
     and a contentious wife are alike;
16 to restrain her is to restrain the wind
     or to grasp oil in the right hand.[e]
17 Iron sharpens iron,
     and one person sharpens the wits[f] of
         another.
18 Anyone who tends a fig tree will eat its
         fruit,
     and anyone who takes care of a
         master will be honored.
19 Just as water reflects the face,
     so one human heart reflects
         another.
20 Sheol and Abaddon are never satisfied,
     and human eyes are never satisfied.

a Cn: Heb *silver of dross*   b Gk: Heb *burning*
c Gk: Heb *the sweetness of a friend is better than one's
own counsel*   d Vg and 20.16: Heb *for a foreign woman*
e Meaning of Heb uncertain   f Heb *face*

21 The crucible is for silver, and the
        furnace is for gold,
    so a person is tested[a] by being
        praised.
22 Crush a fool in a mortar with a pestle
        along with crushed grain,
    but the folly will not be driven out.

23 Know well the condition of your flocks,
        and give attention to your herds;
24 for riches do not last forever,
        nor a crown for all generations.
25 When the grass is gone, and new
        growth appears,
    and the herbage of the mountains is
        gathered,
26 the lambs will provide your clothing,
        and the goats the price of a field;
27 there will be enough goats' milk for your
        food,
    for the food of your household
    and nourishment for your servant-
        girls.

27.1–27. 5: To correct someone is difficult, but it is
better than passing over a fault in silence out of affection (*hidden love*). **14:** *Blesses* can mean simply
"greets" (1 Sam 13.10; 2 Kings 4.29) but the word
cursing in line C keeps the sense "bless" to the fore.
The saying has been interpreted seriously and humorously. If it is taken humorously, *a loud voice* and *early
in the morning* describe boorish behavior that provokes a hostile reaction. If it is taken seriously, *a loud
voice* refers to an insincere greeting as in v. 6 and
26.23–25, 28, and *early in the morning* means "insis-
tently" as in Jer 7.13. **23–27:** A traditional poem priz-
ing flocks and fields over hoarded treasure on the
grounds that wealth in the form of flocks and fields
ever renews itself. Vegetation comes up annually from
the earth; sheep and goats are transformed into food
and clothing.

28

The wicked flee when no one
        pursues,
    but the righteous are as bold as a lion.
2 When a land rebels
        it has many rulers;
    but with an intelligent ruler
        there is lasting order.[b]
3 A ruler[c] who oppresses the poor
    is a beating rain that leaves no food.

4 Those who forsake the law praise the
        wicked,
    but those who keep the law struggle
        against them.
5 The evil do not understand justice,
    but those who seek the LORD
        understand it completely.
6 Better to be poor and walk in integrity
    than to be crooked in one's ways even
        though rich.
7 Those who keep the law are wise
        children,
    but companions of gluttons shame
        their parents.
8 One who augments wealth by exorbitant
        interest
    gathers it for another who is kind to
        the poor.
9 When one will not listen to the law,
    even one's prayers are an
        abomination.
10 Those who mislead the upright into evil
        ways
    will fall into pits of their own
        making,
    but the blameless will have a goodly
        inheritance.
11 The rich is wise in self-esteem,
    but an intelligent poor person sees
        through the pose.
12 When the righteous triumph, there is
        great glory,
    but when the wicked prevail, people
        go into hiding.
13 No one who conceals transgressions will
        prosper,
    but one who confesses and forsakes
        them will obtain mercy.
14 Happy is the one who is never without
        fear,
    but one who is hard-hearted will fall
        into calamity.
15 Like a roaring lion or a charging bear
    is a wicked ruler over a poor people.
16 A ruler who lacks understanding is a
        cruel oppressor;
    but one who hates unjust gain will
        enjoy a long life.

a Heb lacks *is tested*   *b* Meaning of Heb uncertain
c Cn: Heb A *poor person*

17 If someone is burdened with the blood
      of another,
    let that killer be a fugitive
      until death;
    let no one offer assistance.
18 One who walks in integrity will be safe,
    but whoever follows crooked ways will
      fall into the Pit.[a]
19 Anyone who tills the land will have
      plenty of bread,
    but one who follows worthless
      pursuits will have plenty
      of poverty.
20 The faithful will abound with
      blessings,
    but one who is in a hurry to be rich
      will not go unpunished.
21 To show partiality is not good—
    yet for a piece of bread a person may
      do wrong.
22 The miser is in a hurry to get rich
    and does not know that loss is sure to
      come.
23 Whoever rebukes a person will
      afterward find more favor
    than one who flatters with
      the tongue.
24 Anyone who robs father or mother
    and says, "That is no crime,"
    is partner to a thug.
25 The greedy person stirs up strife,
    but whoever trusts in the LORD will
      be enriched.
26 Those who trust in their own wits are
      fools;
    but those who walk in wisdom come
      through safely.
27 Whoever gives to the poor will lack
      nothing,
    but one who turns a blind eye will get
      many a curse.
28 When the wicked prevail, people go into
      hiding;
    but when they perish, the righteous
      increase.

28.1–28. 4: *The law* ("torah"*) is taken by some as
the Mosaic law but it is better to understand it as the
traditional instruction of teachers and parents. To defy
such teaching is to promote the designs of the wicked,
whereas to heed it is to defeat them. **9**: An example

of poetic justice. Whoever does not listen to the law
(or instruction), which comes ultimately from God, will
not be heard by God. **24**: Children lived in their parents' home until they married, and even after marriage
could remain under the parental roof. If the parents
grew feeble, the children might become domineering
and gradually take over the house and its wealth. The
saying declares such usurpation to constitute simple
theft. The children have no more right to their parents'
property while the latter are living than a brigand does
who is from outside the family.

〰〰〰〰〰〰〰〰〰〰〰〰〰〰〰〰

29 One who is often reproved, yet
      remains stubborn,
    will suddenly be broken beyond
      healing.
2 When the righteous are in authority, the
      people rejoice;
    but when the wicked rule, the people
      groan.
3 A child who loves wisdom makes a
      parent glad,
    but to keep company with prostitutes
      is to squander one's substance.
4 By justice a king gives stability to the
      land,
    but one who makes heavy exactions
      ruins it.
5 Whoever flatters a neighbor
    is spreading a net for the neighbor's
      feet.
6 In the transgression of the evil there is a
      snare,
    but the righteous sing and rejoice.
7 The righteous know the rights of the
      poor;
    the wicked have no such
      understanding.
8 Scoffers set a city aflame,
    but the wise turn away wrath.
9 If the wise go to law with fools,
    there is ranting and ridicule without
      relief.
10 The bloodthirsty hate the blameless,
    and they seek the life of the upright.
11 A fool gives full vent to anger,
    but the wise quietly holds it back.
12 If a ruler listens to falsehood,
    all his officials will be wicked.

a Syr: Heb *fall all at once*

13 The poor and the oppressor have this in
        common:
    the LORD gives light to the eyes of
        both.
14 If a king judges the poor with equity,
        his throne will be established
        forever.
15 The rod and reproof give wisdom,
        but a mother is disgraced by a
        neglected child.
16 When the wicked are in authority,
        transgression increases,
    but the righteous will look upon their
        downfall.
17 Discipline your children, and they will
        give you rest;
    they will give delight to your heart.
18 Where there is no prophecy, the people
        cast off restraint,
    but happy are those who keep
        the law.
19 By mere words servants are not
        disciplined,
    for though they understand, they will
        not give heed.
20 Do you see someone who is hasty
        in speech?
    There is more hope for a fool than for
        anyone like that.
21 A slave pampered from childhood
    will come to a bad end. *a*
22 One given to anger stirs up strife,
    and the hothead causes much
        transgression.
23 A person's pride will bring humiliation,
    but one who is lowly in spirit will
        obtain honor.
24 To be a partner of a thief is to hate
        one's own life;
    one hears the victim's curse, but
        discloses nothing. *b*
25 The fear of others *c* lays a snare,
    but one who trusts in the LORD
        is secure.
26 Many seek the favor of a ruler,
    but it is from the LORD that one gets
        justice.
27 The unjust are an abomination to the
        righteous,
    but the upright are an abomination to
        the wicked.

29.1–27. 1: *Remains stubborn* is, literally, "stiffens the neck." There is a possible play on words: Stiffening one's neck risks having it broken. *Suddenly* suggests an extraordinary, perhaps divine, intervention. **4:** The saying uses the metaphor* "high" and "low" for prosperity and decline in order to differentiate between good and bad governance. A just king *gives stability,* literally, "raises up the land." But a king who raises taxes *ruins,* literally, brings down, a country. **15:** As with domestic animals, a staff ("shebet" as in Lev 27.32; Zech 11.7; Ps 23.4) is needed to train and control children. Children (and animals) allowed to run free cannot learn. **18:** *Prophecy* and *law* are paired in Ezek 7.26 and Lam 2.9. In this saying *prophecy* has to do with the community and *law* with the individual. Though a people may be demoralized without credible national guidance, an individual can still find happiness by heeding the instruction of teachers. **24:** An aphorism derived from the legal adjuration summoning witnesses to a crime, which is described in Lev 5.1. By not coming forward to testify one becomes an accomplice of the criminal. Moreover, to get mixed up with a crime is to destroy oneself.

30 The words of Agur son of Jakeh. An oracle.

    Thus says the man: I am weary, O God,
        I am weary, O God. How can I
        prevail? *d*
2   Surely I am too stupid to be human;
        I do not have human understanding.
3   I have not learned wisdom,
        nor have I knowledge of the
        holy ones. *e*
4   Who has ascended to heaven and come
        down?
    Who has gathered the wind in the
        hollow of the hand?
    Who has wrapped up the waters in a
        garment?
    Who has established all the ends of
        the earth?
    What is the person's name?
    And what is the name of the person's
        child?
    Surely you know!

a Vg: Meaning of Heb uncertain   *b* Meaning of Heb
uncertain   *c* Or *human fear*   *d* Or *I am spent.*
Meaning of Heb uncertain   *e* Or *Holy One*

5 Every word of God proves true;
    he is a shield to those who take
      refuge in him.
6 Do not add to his words,
    or else he will rebuke you, and you
      will be found a liar.

7 Two things I ask of you;
    do not deny them to me before I die:
8 Remove far from me falsehood and
      lying;
    give me neither poverty nor riches;
    feed me with the food that I need,
9 or I shall be full, and deny you,
    and say, "Who is the LORD?"
    or I shall be poor, and steal,
    and profane the name of my God.

10 Do not slander a servant to a master,
    or the servant will curse you, and you
      will be held guilty.

11 There are those who curse their
      fathers
    and do not bless their mothers.
12 There are those who are pure in their
      own eyes
    yet are not cleansed of their
      filthiness.
13 There are those—how lofty are their
      eyes,
    how high their eyelids lift!—
14 there are those whose teeth are swords,
    whose teeth are knives,
    to devour the poor from off the earth,
    the needy from among mortals.

15 The leech*a* has two daughters;
    "Give, give," they cry.
  Three things are never satisfied;
    four never say, "Enough":
16 Sheol, the barren womb,
    the earth ever thirsty for water,
    and the fire that never says,
      "Enough."*a*

17 The eye that mocks a father
    and scorns to obey a mother
  will be pecked out by the ravens of the
      valley
    and eaten by the vultures.

18 Three things are too wonderful for me;
    four I do not understand:
19 the way of an eagle in the sky,
    the way of a snake on a rock,
  the way of a ship on the high seas,
    and the way of a man with a girl.

20 This is the way of an adulteress:
    she eats, and wipes her mouth,
    and says, "I have done no wrong."

21 Under three things the earth trembles;
    under four it cannot bear up:
22 a slave when he becomes king,
    and a fool when glutted with food;
23 an unloved woman when she gets
      a husband,
    and a maid when she succeeds her
      mistress.

24 Four things on earth are small,
    yet they are exceedingly wise:
25 the ants are a people without strength,
    yet they provide their food in
      the summer;
26 the badgers are a people without power,
    yet they make their homes in
      the rocks;
27 the locusts have no king,
    yet all of them march in rank;
28 the lizard*b* can be grasped in the hand,
    yet it is found in kings' palaces.

29 Three things are stately in their stride;
    four are stately in their gait:
30 the lion, which is mightiest among wild
      animals
    and does not turn back before any;
31 the strutting rooster,*c* the he-goat,
    and a king striding before*a* his people.

32 If you have been foolish, exalting
      yourself,
    or if you have been devising evil,
    put your hand on your mouth.
33 For as pressing milk produces curds,
    and pressing the nose produces blood,
    so pressing anger produces strife.

a Meaning of Heb uncertain   *b* Or *spider*   *c* Gk Syr
Tg Compare Vg: Meaning of Heb uncertain

30.1–33. 1–10: This poem is the most puzzling section in Proverbs. Verses 1–6 were the original unit, but later vv. 1–10 were edited to make a new and larger speech. Verses 1–6 evoke old passages such as Ps 18.30 (Prov 30.5), Ps 73.22 (Prov 30.2a), Deut 4.2 (Prov 30.6), Deut 30.11–14 (Prov 30.4a). Also influential are the divine questions beginning with "Who?" in Job 38–41 and Isa 40–45 (see Prov 30.4b–d). In vv. 1–6 Agur delivers an oracle* ("ne'um," v. 1) that did not come from his own efforts, for he is worn out, incapable of wisdom, and does not know God (vv. 2–3). Indeed, no human being can have divine wisdom, for who is capable of bringing it down from heaven (v. 4a)? In fact, no act of wisdom and power is possible for human beings (v. 4b–d)! In the process of acknowledging his own impotence and ignorance, Agur finds the assuring word of God, which is reliable and protects him just as it protected the psalmists in Ps 12 and 18 (v. 5). One should not add to the divine word (v. 6). Agur now prays to speak the truth and to have the basic necessities of life (vv. 7–8) lest he offend the God who has rescued him from exhaustion and ignorance (v. 9). Verse 10 concludes vv. 1–9, for *Do not* reprises v. 6. *Curse* in v. 10b links it to what follows. **11–14:** The poem is united by anaphora.* There seems to be a progression from disdaining parental advice (v. 11), to overestimating one's situation (v. 12), to arrogance (v. 13), resulting finally in cruelty directed toward the lowly (v. 14). **18–20:** Anaphora (the repetition of *way*) unites the piece. Each *way* is wondrous: the effortless flight of the eagle (or vulture), the legless movement of the serpent, the massive progress of a ship. The fourth and climactic* *way* is the course of a man and a woman toward each other, the attraction of the sexes. **32–33:** The syntax is like 6.1–3: If you have done such and such, then you must now do such and such. It is a mark of wisdom to make peace and avoid strife (15.18). There is wordplay in *pressing the nose* ("mits ap") and *pressing anger* ("mits appayim," literally, nostrils; anger).

31

The words of King Lemuel. An oracle that his mother taught him:

2 No, my son! No, son of my womb!
  No, son of my vows!
3 Do not give your strength to women,
  your ways to those who destroy
    kings.

4 It is not for kings, O Lemuel,
  it is not for kings to drink wine,
  or for rulers to desire* strong drink;
5 or else they will drink and forget what
    has been decreed,
  and will pervert the rights of all the
    afflicted.
6 Give strong drink to one who is
    perishing,
  and wine to those in bitter distress;
7 let them drink and forget their poverty,
  and remember their misery no more.
8 Speak out for those who cannot speak,
  for the rights of all the destitute.*
9 Speak out, judge righteously,
  defend the rights of the poor
    and needy.

31.1–9: A queen mother's advice to her son, given with wit and style. The queen mother had an important role in the palace because of her insider's knowledge of palace politics and undoubted loyalty to her son. Verses 3–5 warn the king that abuse of sex and alcohol can lead him to *forget* the *afflicted*. Verses 6–9 counsel rather that alcohol be used to aid the poor so that those who are afflicted (*perishing*) can *forget* their *poverty*. Verses 8–9 urge the king to open his mouth (*speak out*) not to drink alcohol but to speak for the voiceless *poor*. The underlying subject of the poem is the king's duty to bring about justice for the *poor*. The women referred to in v. 3 are the women of his harem. An example of moral callousness from sexual indulgence is David's adultery with Bathsheba and the murder of Uriah (2 Sam 11–12). For the association of liquor with disdain for the poor, see Isa 28.1–8; Am 6.1–7.

10 A capable wife who can find?
  She is far more precious than
    jewels.
11 The heart of her husband trusts in her,
  and he will have no lack of gain.
12 She does him good, and not harm,
  all the days of her life.
13 She seeks wool and flax,
  and works with willing hands.
14 She is like the ships of the merchant,
  she brings her food from far away.

a Cn: Heb *where*   *b* Heb *all children of passing away*

15 She rises while it is still night
    and provides food for her household
    and tasks for her servant-girls.
16 She considers a field and buys it;
    with the fruit of her hands she plants
      a vineyard.
17 She girds herself with strength,
    and makes her arms strong.
18 She perceives that her merchandise is
      profitable.
    Her lamp does not go out at night.
19 She puts her hands to the distaff,
    and her hands hold the spindle.
20 She opens her hand to the poor,
    and reaches out her hands to
      the needy.
21 She is not afraid for her household
      when it snows,
    for all her household are clothed in
      crimson.
22 She makes herself coverings;
    her clothing is fine linen and purple.
23 Her husband is known in the city gates,
    taking his seat among the elders of
      the land.
24 She makes linen garments and sells
      them;
    she supplies the merchant with
      sashes.
25 Strength and dignity are her clothing,
    and she laughs at the time to come.
26 She opens her mouth with wisdom,
    and the teaching of kindness is on her
      tongue.
27 She looks well to the ways of her
      household,
    and does not eat the bread of
      idleness.
28 Her children rise up and call her
      happy;
    her husband too, and he praises her:

29 "Many women have done excellently,
    but you surpass them all."
30 Charm is deceitful, and beauty is vain,
    but a woman who fears the LORD is
      to be praised.
31 Give her a share in the fruit of her
      hands,
    and let her works praise her in the
      city gates.

31.10–31: Praise of the capable wife. An acrostic*
poem of twenty-two lines, each line beginning with a
successive letter of the alphabet.* It is an encomium*
or hymn praising the capable wife. A hymn does not
dwell on the inner feelings or the physical appearance
of its hero but describes the hero's mighty feats of
valor, in this case the wife's extraordinarily wise management of her great household. The narrator first describes the wife's wonderful deeds (vv. 11–27), a description that is completed by her own children and
husband (vv. 28–31). **19–20:** The chiasmus* at the
center of the poem (*hands* ("yad") . . . *hands* ("kap")
// *hand* ("kap") . . . *hands* ("yad") shifts the action
from the domestic to the public sphere in that the
hands that weave cloth (v. 19) now open wide in lar-
gesse to the poor beyond the household gates (v. 20).
She is a blessing not only to her family but to the whole
community. The hymn to the capable wife includes a
metaphorical* dimension. The heroic woman evokes
Woman Wisdom of chs. 1–9. Her abundantly prosperous household illustrates the result of becoming a disciple of Wisdom (ch. 8; 9.6, 11). The book began with
a young person leaving the parental house to found
and maintain a new one. It ends with a splendid
household provided by the wisdom of the capable
wife. Visible within the house are all the blessings of
wisdom—wealth, justice, generosity to the poor, reputation, children, and, most precious of all (compare
19.14), a good wife (or spouse). The pursuit of wisdom
has brought every blessing.

ECCLESIASTES

Introduction

Along with other wisdom literature* of the Hebrew Bible (Proverbs and Job), Ecclesiastes offers observations based on human experience; but while Proverbs optimistically suggests that humans can use what they have learned to their advantage (see Prov 10.4), Ecclesiastes' repeated refrain "vanity of vanities" and its harsh rejection of wisdom's practical value lead some to hear it as a voice of despair. The book does, however, offer some moderately hopeful advice: Enjoyment of life and its pleasures is possible and appropriate, as long as it is informed by the inevitability of death.

The call to enjoyment explains the book's connection to the Jewish festival of Sukkot, a time of celebration, and thus its inclusion in the Jewish canon* within the "megilloth," or festival scrolls.* The Jewish name for the book, Qoheleth, derives from 1.1; a noun derived from the Hebrew "qahal" ("assembly"), it may refer to the one who speaks to a gathering. The English "Ecclesiastes" comes from the Greek translation "ekklesiastes," the one who speaks in the "ekklesia" (later used to designate the church), accounting for the traditional translation, "Preacher" (see note *a*). The NRSV offers "Teacher" as its modern equivalent.

Although the book begins with a reference to King Solomon and includes later references to "the king," scholars tend to date the book much later than the monarchy. The style of its language bears out the suggestion of a late date: Words like "pesher" ("interpretation," 8.1) and "'inyan" ("business," 1.13 and elsewhere) are derived from Aramaic,* the common language of the ancient Near East from the seventh century through much of the Hellenistic* period. The literary motif* of Solomonic authorship, which may have helped the book be canonized, is also found in the Song of Solomon and in the Wisdom of Solomon (Apocrypha*).

READING GUIDE

Both in its style and in its theme, the book engages in dialogue with the optimistic wisdom typical of the book of Proverbs. Traditional-sounding proverbs, such as the famous poem in 3.1–8 ("For everything there is a season") are often followed by the author's more sober judgments (3.9: "What gain have the workers from their toil?"). Because of this "yes, but" style, the reader cannot assume that every statement made is the position of the author. Readers should consider how statements are modified, corrected, or even contradicted by subsequent verses. Where is the author's own voice heard?

For many readers over the centuries, Ecclesiastes has served as a check on human pride. Like similar "cynical" tales from Egypt and Mesopotamia, it reminds humans of the limitations in their understanding of the world and of the divine. Ecclesiastes, however, avoids utter despair, choosing to remain in conversation with traditional wisdom and remaining convinced that God is present, even if not always understandable.

Attempts to determine a clear structure for the book have proven frustrating. The following outline is one of many ways of understanding the book's movements.

1.1–3	Title and theses
1.4–11	Poem: nothing new

1 The words of the Teacher,[a] the son of David, king in Jerusalem.
2 Vanity of vanities, says the Teacher,[a]
   vanity of vanities! All is vanity.
3 What do people gain from all the toil
   at which they toil under the sun?
4 A generation goes, and a generation comes,
   but the earth remains forever.
5 The sun rises and the sun goes down,
   and hurries to the place where
      it rises.
6 The wind blows to the south,
   and goes around to the north;
round and round goes the wind,
   and on its circuits the wind returns.
7 All streams run to the sea,
   but the sea is not full;
to the place where the streams flow,
   there they continue to flow.
8 All things[b] are wearisome;
   more than one can express;
the eye is not satisfied with seeing,
   or the ear filled with hearing.
9 What has been is what will be,
   and what has been done is what will
      be done;
   there is nothing new under the sun.
10 Is there a thing of which it is said,
   "See, this is new"?
It has already been,
   in the ages before us.
11 The people of long ago are not
      remembered,
   nor will there be any remembrance
of people yet to come
   by those who come after them.

vanities is Hebrew superlative: "the most insubstantial thing." **3: The dominant question.** Is there any benefit from life? The reader is introduced to vocabulary that will be repeated throughout the book: *Under the sun* refers to wearisome earthly existence, and *toil* bears a negative connotation. **4–11: Nothing ever changes.** The Teacher laments the inability of human activity to alter the flow of the existence. The *sun, wind,* and *streams* repeat their predictable, "no sum" circuits, just as humans are never satisfied with what they see or hear. **10–11:** Throughout the book, the Teacher grieves that even righteous ones are not remembered after death.

~~~~~~~~~~~~~~~~~~~~~~~~~~~~~~~~~

12 I, the Teacher,[a] when king over Israel in Jerusalem, 13 applied my mind to seek and to search out by wisdom all that is done under heaven; it is an unhappy business that God has given to human beings to be busy with. 14 I saw all the deeds that are done under the sun; and see, all is vanity and a chasing after wind.[c]
15 What is crooked cannot be made
      straight,
   and what is lacking cannot
      be counted.
16 I said to myself, "I have acquired great wisdom, surpassing all who were over Jerusalem before me; and my mind has had great experience of wisdom and knowledge." 17 And I applied my mind to know wisdom and to know madness and folly. I perceived that this also is but a chasing after wind.[c]
18 For in much wisdom is much vexation,
   and those who increase knowledge
      increase sorrow.

1.1–11. 1: Superscription. Like many Psalms, the book begins with an editorial comment; it alludes to Solomon. *Teacher:* Hebrew Qoheleth; a form of "qhl" ("assembly"), its meaning is not clear. **2: The book's theme.** *Vanity:* In Hebrew "hevel," meaning "vapor, wind," things transient and impermanent. *Vanity of*

1.12–18. The Teacher's experiment. Though any king of the southern kingdom would fit this description, Solomon is likely implied. **13:** *Mind:* In Hebrew, "heart," the seat of thinking. *Wisdom* refers to prac-

a Heb Qoheleth, traditionally rendered Preacher
b Or words   c Or a feeding on wind. See Hos 12.1

tical, as well as speculative, knowledge. The Teacher begins an empirical investigation into what is useful in life. **14**: *Chasing after wind:* Literally, "shepherding the wind," a futile exertion of energy. This phrase will be repeated eight more times in Ecclesiastes. **15**: Given the proverbial ring of the statement, some suggest that the Teacher is quoting a well-known saying. **17**: *Wisdom, madness, folly:* The list of items from one extreme to the other suggests the complete range of experience. **18**: A second proverbial statement, likely original to the Teacher.

2 I said to myself, "Come now, I will make a test of pleasure; enjoy yourself." But again, this also was vanity. ²I said of laughter, "It is mad," and of pleasure, "What use is it?" ³I searched with my mind how to cheer my body with wine—my mind still guiding me with wisdom—and how to lay hold on folly, until I might see what was good for mortals to do under heaven during the few days of their life. ⁴I made great works; I built houses and planted vineyards for myself; ⁵I made myself gardens and parks, and planted in them all kinds of fruit trees. ⁶I made myself pools from which to water the forest of growing trees. ⁷I bought male and female slaves, and had slaves who were born in my house; I also had great possessions of herds and flocks, more than any who had been before me in Jerusalem. ⁸I also gathered for myself silver and gold and the treasure of kings and of the provinces; I got singers, both men and women, and delights of the flesh, and many concubines.ᵃ

9 So I became great and surpassed all who were before me in Jerusalem; also my wisdom remained with me. ¹⁰Whatever my eyes desired I did not keep from them; I kept my heart from no pleasure, for my heart found pleasure in all my toil, and this was my reward for all my toil. ¹¹Then I considered all that my hands had done and the toil I had spent in doing it, and again, all was vanity and a chasing after wind,ᵇ and there was nothing to be gained under the sun.

2.1–11: Experiment one: pleasure. The preliminary verdict in vv. 1–2 is followed by the empirical data. **4–10**: The literary fiction of Solomonic authorship would lend credibility to these extravagances. Solo-

mon's building projects (1 Kings 7–10), large number of women (1 Kings 7), and wealth were legendary.* **9**: *My wisdom remained:* An experiment, not sheer indulgence. **11**: Despite the initial pleasure, all the work involved in seeking pleasure was unsatisfying. The three-fold verdict on the experiment is devastating: It is *vanity*, *chasing after wind*, and yet another wearisome matter *under the sun.*

12 So I turned to consider wisdom and madness and folly; for what can the one do who comes after the king? Only what has already been done. ¹³Then I saw that wisdom excels folly as light excels darkness.
¹⁴ The wise have eyes in their head,
        but fools walk in darkness.
Yet I perceived that the same fate befalls all of them. ¹⁵Then I said to myself, "What happens to the fool will happen to me also; why then have I been so very wise?" And I said to myself that this also is vanity. ¹⁶For there is no enduring remembrance of the wise or of fools, seeing that in the days to come all will have been long forgotten. How can the wise die just like fools? ¹⁷So I hated life, because what is done under the sun was grievous to me; for all is vanity and a chasing after wind.ᵇ

2.12–17. Experiment two: being wise. 12: *After the king.* How could the successor of the great King Solomon match his wisdom and wealth? The verse may suggest that others need not repeat the experiment since Solomon has done it all. **13–14**: The Teacher sincerely recognizes the superiority of *wisdom* over *folly*, repeating a traditional saying. **15–16**: And yet, being wise doesn't keep you from dying. As throughout the book, the inevitability of death and its power to erase the memory of a person precipitate the Teacher's despair: *How can the wise die just like fools?* **17**: He repeats his three-fold verdict (2.11).

18 I hated all my toil in which I had toiled under the sun, seeing that I must leave it to those who come after me ¹⁹—and who knows whether they will be wise or foolish? Yet they will be master of all for which I toiled and used my wisdom under the sun. This also is vanity. ²⁰So I turned and gave

ᵃ Meaning of Heb uncertain
ᵇ Or *a feeding on wind.* See Hos 12.1

my heart up to despair concerning all the toil of my labors under the sun, 21 because sometimes one who has toiled with wisdom and knowledge and skill must leave all to be enjoyed by another who did not toil for it. This also is vanity and a great evil. 22 What do mortals get from all the toil and strain with which they toil under the sun? 23 For all their days are full of pain, and their work is a vexation; even at night their minds do not rest. This also is vanity.

24 There is nothing better for mortals than to eat and drink, and find enjoyment in their toil. This also, I saw, is from the hand of God; 25 for apart from him*a* who can eat or who can have enjoyment? 26 For to the one who pleases him God gives wisdom and knowledge and joy; but to the sinner he gives the work of gathering and heaping, only to give to one who pleases God. This also is vanity and a chasing after wind.*b*

2.18–26. Experiment three: work. If humans are destined to die and have no control over who will enjoy the fruits of their labor, why work? The prospect is not only *vanity*, but indeed a *great evil* (v. 21). 23: A grim account of the exhaustion of daily *work*. 24: The Teacher's resulting advice: Enjoy the work itself, and don't make contentment dependent on the outcome of your labor. This ability to enjoy the task itself is seen by the Teacher as a gift *from the hand of God*. 25–26: Though in previous verses the Teacher has attributed a common fate to all humans, here he distinguishes the work of the *sinner* as futile. *Sinner* is synonymous with the fool; it does not refer to the person's moral standards.

3 For everything there is a season, and a time for every matter under heaven:
2 a time to be born, and a time to die;
   a time to plant, and a time to pluck up
      what is planted;
3 a time to kill, and a time to heal;
   a time to break down, and a time to
      build up;
4 a time to weep, and a time to laugh;
   a time to mourn, and a time to dance;
5 a time to throw away stones, and a time
      to gather stones together;
   a time to embrace, and a time to refrain
      from embracing;
6 a time to seek, and a time to lose;
   a time to keep, and a time to
      throw away;
7 a time to tear, and a time to sew;
   a time to keep silence, and a time to
      speak;
8 a time to love, and a time to hate;
   a time for war, and a time for peace.

3.1–8. Poem on times. Contrasting extremes demonstrate that there is proper time for all dimensions of human endeavor. 5: *Throw away stones . . . gather stones*. Interpreted by some early Jewish commentators as a time for sexual relations and a time for abstinence.

9 What gain have the workers from their toil? 10 I have seen the business that God has given to everyone to be busy with. 11 He has made everything suitable for its time; moreover he has put a sense of past and future into their minds, yet they cannot find out what God has done from the beginning to the end. 12 I know that there is nothing better for them than to be happy and enjoy themselves as long as they live; 13 moreover, it is God's gift that all should eat and drink and take pleasure in all their toil. 14 I know that whatever God does endures forever; nothing can be added to it, nor anything taken from it; God has done this, so that all should stand in awe before him. 15 That which is, already has been; that which is to be, already is; and God seeks out what has gone by.*c*

16 Moreover I saw under the sun that in the place of justice, wickedness was there, and in the place of righteousness, wickedness was there as well. 17 I said in my heart, God will judge the righteous and the wicked, for he has appointed a time for every matter, and for every work. 18 I said in my heart with regard to human beings that God is testing them to show that they are but animals. 19 For the fate of humans and the fate of animals is the same; as one dies, so dies the other. They all have the same breath, and humans have no advantage over the animals; for all is vanity. 20 All go to one place; all are

a Gk Syr: Heb *apart from me*   *b* Or *a feeding on wind*. See Hos 12.1   *c* Heb *what is pursued*

from the dust, and all turn to dust again. 21Who knows whether the human spirit goes upward and the spirit of animals goes downward to the earth? 22So I saw that there is nothing better than that all should enjoy their work, for that is their lot; who can bring them to see what will be after them?

3.9–22. 9–15: And yet. The punch line robs the reader of whatever comfort the poem has offered: While indeed all things may have their appointed times, human beings are unable to discern those times, much less use the information to their advantage. **11:** *Sense of past and future:* Other possible translations are "sense of eternity," "sense of the world." While humans have intimations of the cosmic dimensions of existence, their knowledge is limited. **12–15:** While this list of what the Teacher knows does not answer his problem, it counterbalances his sense of life's injustice. **16–22: Injustice.** If God determines the times for all things, then God must set a time for judgment. Clearly, however, the *righteous* and the *wicked* have not yet received what they deserve (v. 17). **19:** *Animals* and *humans* are equal in that they die; they share the *breath* breathed into the human at creation (Gen 2). **20:** *One place:* Sheol,★ the realm of the dead (1 Sam 2.6; Jon 2.2). Early Israel had no concept of the afterlife (either immortality or resurrection), though these such ideas grew in popularity during the Persian★ and Hellenistic★ periods, so that by the turn of the era the resurrection of the body was an article of belief for the Pharisees.★ **21:** *Who knows?* The question implies a negative answer: "No one knows." The possibility that the *human spirit* might survive cannot be verified empirically, so the Teacher returns to his conclusion: Enjoy your work while you are alive (v. 22).

4 Again I saw all the oppressions that are practiced under the sun. Look, the tears of the oppressed—with no one to comfort them! On the side of their oppressors there was power—with no one to comfort them. 2And I thought the dead, who have already died, more fortunate than the living, who are still alive; 3but better than both is the one who has not yet been, and has not seen the evil deeds that are done under the sun.

4 Then I saw that all toil and all skill in work come from one person's envy of another. This also is vanity and a chasing after wind.*

5 Fools fold their hands
  and consume their own flesh.
6 Better is a handful with quiet
  than two handfuls with toil,
  and a chasing after wind.*

7 Again, I saw vanity under the sun: 8the case of solitary individuals, without sons or brothers; yet there is no end to all their toil, and their eyes are never satisfied with riches. "For whom am I toiling," they ask, "and depriving myself of pleasure?" This also is vanity and an unhappy business.

9 Two are better than one, because they have a good reward for their toil. 10For if they fall, one will lift up the other; but woe to one who is alone and falls and does not have another to help. 11Again, if two lie together, they keep warm; but how can one keep warm alone? 12And though one might prevail against another, two will withstand one. A threefold cord is not quickly broken.

13 Better is a poor but wise youth than an old but foolish king, who will no longer take advice. 14One can indeed come out of prison to reign, even though born poor in the kingdom. 15I saw all the living who, moving about under the sun, follow that* youth who replaced the king;* 16there was no end to all those people whom he led. Yet those who come later will not rejoice in him. Surely this also is vanity and a chasing after wind.*

4.1–16. 1–12: Observations on oppression, work, and riches. Three observations and three conclusions. **1–3:** Based on his observation of *oppression*, the Teacher concludes that those who have never experienced the tragedy of life are best. *Better than:* A common phrase in the book (4.6; 4.9; 4.13; 5.1; 5.5) and in traditional wisdom (Prov 15.16–17). **4–6:** Based on his observation of competitive envy and the fate of the lazy, he concludes that more possessions are not worth more strife. **7–9:** Based on his observation of a single person working hard for riches and no one with whom to share, he concludes that companionship is preferable to wealth. **12:** *Threefold cord:* Since the topic has been two, the mention of three is curious; it perhaps refers generically to "strength in numbers."

---

a Or *a feeding on wind.* See Hos 12.1   *b* Heb *the second*   *c* Heb *him*

13–16: Reversals. *Better than:* See comment on 4.3. The *king* and *youth* may allude to specific people (Saul and David; Pharaoh and Joseph), or the Teacher may be telling a story to make a point (see 8.10–11; 9.14–15). The tale demonstrates the power of wisdom, even to overcome social expectations; yet the hero of one age is not remembered in the next.

5 *a*Guard your steps when you go to the house of God; to draw near to listen is better than the sacrifice offered by fools; for they do not know how to keep from doing evil.*b* 2*c*Never be rash with your mouth, nor let your heart be quick to utter a word before God, for God is in heaven, and you upon earth; therefore let your words be few.

3 For dreams come with many cares, and a fool's voice with many words.

4 When you make a vow to God, do not delay fulfilling it; for he has no pleasure in fools. Fulfill what you vow. 5It is better that you should not vow than that you should vow and not fulfill it. 6Do not let your mouth lead you into sin, and do not say before the messenger that it was a mistake; why should God be angry at your words, and destroy the work of your hands?

7 With many dreams come vanities and a multitude of words;*d* but fear God.

8 If you see in a province the oppression of the poor and the violation of justice and right, do not be amazed at the matter; for the high official is watched by a higher, and there are yet higher ones over them. 9But all things considered, this is an advantage for a land: a king for a plowed field.*d*

5.1–9: Guard yourself. These sayings parallel traditional biblical wisdom: Attentiveness is better than sacrifice (1 Sam 15.22); speech is dangerous and should be minimal (Prov 13.3); and vows require fulfillment (Deut 23.21). While the Teacher advises caution in all things, he does not reject the Temple* (*house of God*). **6:** *Messenger:* Likely a servant of the Temple, collecting the payment of a vow. **7:** *Fear God:* A common motif* in wisdom literature,* affirming God's control over all matters. **8–9:** Injustice should surprise no one, since it is part of the structure of society. *King for a plowed field:* Meaning unclear, perhaps "a king is worth his upkeep" or "the benefits of an ordered society are worth the cost of social oppression," a point

of view more likely at the upper end of the social hierarchy.

10 The lover of money will not be satisfied with money; nor the lover of wealth, with gain. This also is vanity.

11 When goods increase, those who eat them increase; and what gain has their owner but to see them with his eyes?

12 Sweet is the sleep of laborers, whether they eat little or much; but the surfeit of the rich will not let them sleep.

13 There is a grievous ill that I have seen under the sun: riches were kept by their owners to their hurt, 14and those riches were lost in a bad venture; though they are parents of children, they have nothing in their hands. 15As they came from their mother's womb, so they shall go again, naked as they came; they shall take nothing for their toil, which they may carry away with their hands. 16This also is a grievous ill: just as they came, so shall they go; and what gain do they have from toiling for the wind? 17Besides, all their days they eat in darkness, in much vexation and sickness and resentment.

18 This is what I have seen to be good: it is fitting to eat and drink and find enjoyment in all the toil with which one toils under the sun the few days of the life God gives us; for this is our lot. 19Likewise all to whom God gives wealth and possessions and whom he enables to enjoy them, and to accept their lot and find enjoyment in their toil—this is the gift of God. 20For they will scarcely brood over the days of their lives, because God keeps them occupied with the joy of their hearts.

5.10–20: Insatiability of greed. One who seeks wealth for its own sake, rather than for what it can provide, cannot be satisfied. **11:** What can one do with possessions other than admire them? **12:** A romantic view of the honest laborer who *sleeps* after great exertion compared to the *rich* person who lies awake worried about acquisitions. **14:** While the Teacher has decried riches, he now considers the unfairness of los-

---

a Ch 4.17 in Heb   *b* Cn: Heb *they do not know how to do evil*   *c* Ch 5.1 in Heb   *d* Meaning of Heb uncertain

ing wealth, especially as a *parent*. **15:** Humans are born *naked* and take nothing with them when they die (Job 1.21). **17:** *Eat in darkness:* Either one is too miserly to use oil, or (metaphorically*) one eats without enjoyment. **18–20:** In light of the foregoing investigation, the Teacher advises: Accept the realities of life and find joy wherever possible.

inclusion here is a bit surprising. *Stillborn child:* The one who has never experienced life's pain (*seen the sun*) is the most fortunate (4.1–3; Job 3.16). **6:** If one does not enjoy life, it is futile. **9:** *Better is sight . . . than the wandering of desire:* It is better to be content with what one has than constantly to desire more. **10:** See ch 1. **12:** A summary.

6 There is an evil that I have seen under the sun, and it lies heavy upon humankind: ²those to whom God gives wealth, possessions, and honor, so that they lack nothing of all that they desire, yet God does not enable them to enjoy these things, but a stranger enjoys them. This is vanity; it is a grievous ill. ³A man may beget a hundred children, and live many years; but however many are the days of his years, if he does not enjoy life's good things, or has no burial, I say that a stillborn child is better off than he. ⁴For it comes into vanity and goes into darkness, and in darkness its name is covered; ⁵moreover it has not seen the sun or known anything; yet it finds rest rather than he. ⁶Even though he should live a thousand years twice over, yet enjoy no good—do not all go to one place?

7 All human toil is for the mouth, yet the appetite is not satisfied. ⁸For what advantage have the wise over fools? And what do the poor have who know how to conduct themselves before the living? ⁹Better is the sight of the eyes than the wandering of desire; this also is vanity and a chasing after wind.ᵃ

10 Whatever has come to be has already been named, and it is known what human beings are, and that they are not able to dispute with those who are stronger. ¹¹The more words, the more vanity, so how is one the better? ¹²For who knows what is good for mortals while they live the few days of their vain life, which they pass like a shadow? For who can tell them what will be after them under the sun?

6.1–12: Frustration. In light of his previous advice, the Teacher considers the greatest evil the inability to enjoy what one has. **3:** In the ancient world, many *children* (Deut 11.21) and long life (Ps 91.16) were greatly valued. *No burial:* While the importance of proper burial is clear in the Old Testament (2 Kings 9.30–37), its

7 A good name is better than precious ointment,
  and the day of death, than the day of birth.
² It is better to go to the house of mourning
  than to go to the house of feasting;
 for this is the end of everyone,
  and the living will lay it to heart.
³ Sorrow is better than laughter,
  for by sadness of countenance the heart is made glad.
⁴ The heart of the wise is in the house of mourning;
  but the heart of fools is in the house of mirth.
⁵ It is better to hear the rebuke of the wise
  than to hear the song of fools.
⁶ For like the crackling of thorns under a pot,
  so is the laughter of fools;
  this also is vanity.
⁷ Surely oppression makes the wise foolish,
  and a bribe corrupts the heart.
⁸ Better is the end of a thing than its beginning;
  the patient in spirit are better than the proud in spirit.
⁹ Do not be quick to anger,
  for anger lodges in the bosom of fools.
¹⁰ Do not say, "Why were the former days better than these?"
  For it is not from wisdom that you ask this.
¹¹ Wisdom is as good as an inheritance,
  an advantage to those who see the sun.

ᵃ Or *a feeding on wind*. See Hos 12.1

12 For the protection of wisdom is like the
    protection of money,
  and the advantage of knowledge is
    that wisdom gives life to the one
    who possesses it.
13 Consider the work of God;
  who can make straight what he has
    made crooked?

14 In the day of prosperity be joyful, and in the day of adversity consider; God has made the one as well as the other, so that mortals may not find out anything that will come after them.

7.1–14: Mixture of the Teacher's ideas and traditional wisdom. Forms of Hebrew "tob" (*good*, and in comparative mode, *better*) occur ten times in this section. **1–4:** *Death* is instructive for the living, revealing the true end of all things and hence life's proper priorities. **3:** *Made glad:* Literally "made good", "improved." **6:** *Crackling . . . vanity:* The words of a fool are loud but bring no long-term benefit. **7:** While the Teacher contrasts wisdom with folly, he also recognizes that they are not permanent conditions; in adversity, wisdom may fail. **11–12:** *Wisdom*, while not stable, is good. **13:** *Crooked:* See 1.15. Since people do not receive their just rewards, one should avoid being overly pious or overly wicked.

~~~~~~~~~~~~~~~~~~~~~~~~~~~~~~~~~~~

15 In my vain life I have seen everything; there are righteous people who perish in their righteousness, and there are wicked people who prolong their life in their evildoing. 16 Do not be too righteous, and do not act too wise; why should you destroy yourself? 17 Do not be too wicked, and do not be a fool; why should you die before your time? 18 It is good that you should take hold of the one, without letting go of the other; for the one who fears God shall succeed with both.

19 Wisdom gives strength to the wise more than ten rulers that are in a city.

20 Surely there is no one on earth so righteous as to do good without ever sinning.

21 Do not give heed to everything that people say, or you may hear your servant cursing you; 22 your heart knows that many times you have yourself cursed others.

23 All this I have tested by wisdom; I said, "I will be wise," but it was far from me.

24 That which is, is far off, and deep, very deep; who can find it out? 25 I turned my mind to know and to search out and to seek wisdom and the sum of things, and to know that wickedness is folly and that foolishness is madness. 26 I found more bitter than death the woman who is a trap, whose heart is snares and nets, whose hands are fetters; one who pleases God escapes her, but the sinner is taken by her. 27 See, this is what I found, says the Teacher,[a] adding one thing to another to find the sum, 28 which my mind has sought repeatedly, but I have not found. One man among a thousand I found, but a woman among all these I have not found. 29 See, this alone I found, that God made human beings straightforward, but they have devised many schemes.

7.15–29: Practical advice. 18: *One . . . other:* Not being too wise and not being too foolish (compare vv. 16–17). **20:** *No one . . . sinning:* See 1 Kings 8.46. **26:** *The woman:* Decries the gossipy, frivolous woman (Prov 7). Few men, but even fewer women, are righteous. Does the book reflect an anti-female bias? **29:** *Human beings:* In Hebrew the word is singular ("adham"); the same word is translated *man* in v. 28. *Humans* (or just males?) were created good (Gen 1) but nonetheless sin.

~~~~~~~~~~~~~~~~~~~~~~~~~~~~~~~~~~~

8 Who is like the wise man?
  And who knows the interpretation of
    a thing?
Wisdom makes one's face shine,
  and the hardness of one's
    countenance is changed.

2 Keep[b] the king's command because of your sacred oath. 3 Do not be terrified; go from his presence, do not delay when the matter is unpleasant, for he does whatever he pleases. 4 For the word of the king is powerful, and who can say to him, "What are you doing?" 5 Whoever obeys a command will meet no harm, and the wise mind will know the time and way. 6 For every matter has its time and way, although the troubles of mortals lie heavy upon them. 7 Indeed, they do not know what is to be, for who can tell them

a Qoheleth, traditionally rendered *Preacher*   *b* Heb I keep

how it will be? ⁸No one has power over the wind^a to restrain the wind,^a or power over the day of death; there is no discharge from the battle, nor does wickedness deliver those who practice it. ⁹All this I observed, applying my mind to all that is done under the sun, while one person exercises authority over another to the other's hurt.

8.1–9: Wisdom's value and limits. 2–5: Practical advice on dealing with a king: Recognize his power and do not challenge him openly. *Sacred oath:* a pledge of loyalty to the king, made in God's name. **6–8:** The repetition of *time and way* from v. 5 allows the Teacher to reiterate the inability of humans to understand the future or to control their fates any more than they can control the *wind.*

10 Then I saw the wicked buried; they used to go in and out of the holy place, and were praised in the city where they had done such things.^b This also is vanity. ¹¹Because sentence against an evil deed is not executed speedily, the human heart is fully set to do evil. ¹²Though sinners do evil a hundred times and prolong their lives, yet I know that it will be well with those who fear God, because they stand in fear before him, ¹³but it will not be well with the wicked, neither will they prolong their days like a shadow, because they do not stand in fear before God.

14 There is a vanity that takes place on earth, that there are righteous people who are treated according to the conduct of the wicked, and there are wicked people who are treated according to the conduct of the righteous. I said that this also is vanity. ¹⁵So I commend enjoyment, for there is nothing better for people under the sun than to eat, and drink, and enjoy themselves, for this will go with them in their toil through the days of life that God gives them under the sun.

16 When I applied my mind to know wisdom, and to see the business that is done on earth, how one's eyes see sleep neither day nor night, ¹⁷then I saw all the work of God, that no one can find out what is happening under the sun. However much they may toil in seeking, they will not find it out; even though those who are wise claim to know, they cannot find it out.

8.10–17: No justice. The public praise given the wicked at their death and the lack of swift, clear punishment encourages people in their evil. **12:** In light of earlier comments, this confidence in God's justice is surprising. **13–14:** One cannot distinguish between the *righteous* and the *wicked* by their rewards. **15–17:** A summary of the book's theme: No one, not even the wise, can understand what happens in life.

9 All this I laid to heart, examining it all, how the righteous and the wise and their deeds are in the hand of God; whether it is love or hate one does not know. Everything that confronts them ²is vanity,^c since the same fate comes to all, to the righteous and the wicked, to the good and the evil,^d to the clean and the unclean, to those who sacrifice and those who do not sacrifice. As are the good, so are the sinners; those who swear are like those who shun an oath. ³This is an evil in all that happens under the sun, that the same fate comes to everyone. Moreover, the hearts of all are full of evil; madness is in their hearts while they live, and after that they go to the dead. ⁴But whoever is joined with all the living has hope, for a living dog is better than a dead lion. ⁵The living know that they will die, but the dead know nothing; they have no more reward, and even the memory of them is lost. ⁶Their love and their hate and their envy have already perished; never again will they have any share in all that happens under the sun.

7 Go, eat your bread with enjoyment, and drink your wine with a merry heart; for God has long ago approved what you do. ⁸Let your garments always be white; do not let oil be lacking on your head. ⁹Enjoy life with the wife whom you love, all the days of your vain life that are given you under the sun, because that is your portion in life and in your toil at which you toil under the sun. ¹⁰Whatever your hand finds to do, do with your might; for there is no work or thought or knowledge or wisdom in Sheol, to which you are going.

a Or *breath*　　b Meaning of Heb uncertain
c Syr Compare Gk: Heb *Everything that confronts them* ²*is everything*　　d Gk Syr Vg: Heb lacks *and the evil*

11 Again I saw that under the sun the race is not to the swift, nor the battle to the strong, nor bread to the wise, nor riches to the intelligent, nor favor to the skillful; but time and chance happen to them all. 12For no one can anticipate the time of disaster. Like fish taken in a cruel net, and like birds caught in a snare, so mortals are snared at a time of calamity, when it suddenly falls upon them.

9.1–12: In God's hands. 2: *Clean and unclean, sacrifice and not sacrifice:* References to ritual practices, verifying that the Teacher is not opposed to traditional religion. *Those who swear* are evil. *Those who shun the oath* are good, avoiding unnecessary words (5.2). **3:** Less a concept of complete sinfulness than a cry of despair in face of human frailty and mortality. **4:** *Dog:* a despised animal in ancient Israel (Prov 26.11). The valuing of life over death is either a contradiction or a development beyond the contrary statements in 6.3–6. **8:** *White:* a color for festivals; contrast 7.3–4. **9:** *Wife:* Literally, "woman." **10:** *Sheol*:* See comment on 3.20.

13 I have also seen this example of wisdom under the sun, and it seemed great to me. 14There was a little city with few people in it. A great king came against it and besieged it, building great siegeworks against it. 15Now there was found in it a poor wise man, and he by his wisdom delivered the city. Yet no one remembered that poor man. 16So I said, "Wisdom is better than might; yet the poor man's wisdom is despised, and his words are not heeded."

17 The quiet words of the wise are more to
   be heeded
      than the shouting of a ruler among
         fools.
18 Wisdom is better than weapons of war,
      but one bungler destroys much
         good.

9.13–18: The goodness and limits of wisdom. The parable-like* story, followed by traditional sayings, makes the Teacher's point: While wisdom is better than folly, it does not guarantee fame or respect. **16:** While the *poor man* apparently saved the city, people did not listen to his advice.

10 Dead flies make the perfumer's
      ointment give off a foul odor;
   so a little folly outweighs wisdom and
      honor.
2 The heart of the wise inclines to the
      right,
   but the heart of a fool to the left.
3 Even when fools walk on the road, they
      lack sense,
   and show to everyone that they are
      fools.
4 If the anger of the ruler rises against
      you, do not leave your post,
   for calmness will undo great
      offenses.
5 There is an evil that I have seen under the sun, as great an error as if it proceeded from the ruler: 6folly is set in many high places, and the rich sit in a low place. 7I have seen slaves on horseback, and princes walking on foot like slaves.
8 Whoever digs a pit will fall into it;
   and whoever breaks through a wall
      will be bitten by a snake.
9 Whoever quarries stones will be hurt by
      them;
   and whoever splits logs will be
      endangered by them.
10 If the iron is blunt, and one does not
      whet the edge,
   then more strength must be
      exerted;
   but wisdom helps one to succeed.
11 If the snake bites before it is charmed,
      there is no advantage in a charmer.

10.1–11.10: Traditional sayings, with the Teacher's own observations. 10.2: Ancient Israel considered the *right* the "proper" side (Ex 15.6) and the *left* inferior. **4:** Advice for dealing with a king (Prov 19.12). **5–7:** The unexpected fates of the foolish and the rich, the latter equated with the wise. **8–11:** Inherent risks. *Digs a pit:* See Prov 26.27; 28.10. *Snake:* See Am 5.19.

12 Words spoken by the wise bring them
      favor,
   but the lips of fools consume them.
13 The words of their mouths begin in
      foolishness,
   and their talk ends in wicked
      madness;

14 yet fools talk on and on.
>   No one knows what is to happen,
>   and who can tell anyone what the
>   future holds?
15 The toil of fools wears them out,
>   for they do not even know the way to
>   town.

16 Alas for you, O land, when your king is
>   a servant,[a]
>   and your princes feast in the
>   morning!
17 Happy are you, O land, when your king
>   is a nobleman,
>   and your princes feast at the proper
>   time—
>   for strength, and not for drunkenness!
18 Through sloth the roof sinks in,
>   and through indolence the house
>   leaks.
19 Feasts are made for laughter;
>   wine gladdens life,
>   and money meets every need.
20 Do not curse the king, even in your
>   thoughts,
>   or curse the rich, even in your
>   bedroom;
>   for a bird of the air may carry your voice,
>   or some winged creature tell
>   the matter.

10.12–20. 12–15: The Teacher's own observation (v. 14) incorporated with traditional views on the *fool*. **16–18:** A country suffers if leaders are foolish and do not know the proper times for *feasting*. **20:** Practical advice about not speaking ill of powerful people.

11 Send out your bread upon the
>   waters,
>   for after many days you will get it
>   back.
2 Divide your means seven ways, or even
>   eight,
>   for you do not know what disaster
>   may happen on earth.
3 When clouds are full,
>   they empty rain on the earth;
>   whether a tree falls to the south or to
>   the north,
>   in the place where the tree falls, there
>   it will lie.

4 Whoever observes the wind will
>   not sow;
>   and whoever regards the clouds will
>   not reap.
5 Just as you do not know how the breath comes to the bones in the mother's womb, so you do not know the work of God, who makes everything.
6 In the morning sow your seed, and at evening do not let your hands be idle; for you do not know which will prosper, this or that, or whether both alike will be good.
7 Light is sweet, and it is pleasant for the eyes to see the sun.
8 Even those who live many years should rejoice in them all; yet let them remember that the days of darkness will be many. All that comes is vanity.
9 Rejoice, young man, while you are young, and let your heart cheer you in the days of your youth. Follow the inclination of your heart and the desire of your eyes, but know that for all these things God will bring you into judgment.
10 Banish anxiety from your mind, and put away pain from your body; for youth and the dawn of life are vanity.

11.1–10. 1–2: Likely refers to a trade venture. See Isa 18.2. **3–6:** Adapt to events that are beyond your control (v. 3) and work while you can (v. 6). **8–10:** Enjoy life when possible, always remaining aware that death awaits.

12 Remember your creator in the days of your youth, before the days of trouble come, and the years draw near when you will say, "I have no pleasure in them"; 2before the sun and the light and the moon and the stars are darkened and the clouds return with[b] the rain; 3in the day when the guards of the house tremble, and the strong men are bent, and the women who grind cease working because they are few, and those who look through the windows see dimly; 4when the doors on the street are shut, and the sound of the grinding is low, and one rises up at the sound of a bird, and all the daughters of song are brought low;

a Or *a child*   *b* Or *after*; Heb *'ahar*

⁵when one is afraid of heights, and terrors are in the road; the almond tree blossoms, the grasshopper drags itself along*a* and desire fails; because all must go to their eternal home, and the mourners will go about the streets; ⁶before the silver cord is snapped,*b* and the golden bowl is broken, and the pitcher is broken at the fountain, and the wheel broken at the cistern, ⁷and the dust returns to the earth as it was, and the breath*c* returns to God who gave it. ⁸Vanity of vanities, says the Teacher;*d* all is vanity.

12.1–8: A vision of aging and death. God as *creator:* Job 38, Prov 20. **2–5:** A description of aging and the approach of death. One option is to read the images allegorically:* *Guards of the house* are arms; *strong men* are legs; *women who grind* are teeth; *daughters of song* are birds; *grasshopper* is the image of one walking on crutches. **6–7:** Human death compared to items at the end of their usefulness; perhaps images of a well (*cord, bowl, cistern*). **7:** *Breath returns:* A contradiction or development beyond 3.21. **8:** The body of the book ends with the same phrase with which it began (1.2).

9 Besides being wise, the Teacher*d* also taught the people knowledge, weighing and studying and arranging many proverbs. ¹⁰The Teacher*d* sought to find pleasing words, and he wrote words of truth plainly.

11 The sayings of the wise are like goads, and like nails firmly fixed are the collected sayings that are given by one shepherd.*e* ¹²Of anything beyond these, my child, beware. Of making many books there is no end, and much study is a weariness of the flesh.

13 The end of the matter; all has been heard. Fear God, and keep his commandments; for that is the whole duty of everyone. ¹⁴For God will bring every deed into judgment, including*f* every secret thing, whether good or evil.

12.9–14: Epilogue. Likely added by an editor, these verses speak in third person and make the book more pious. **13:** *Fear God, keep commandments:* While not the opposite of previous ideas (5.6), this advice ends the book on a traditional note. **14:** The body of the book has been less clear about the distinct rewards of *good* and *evil* (8.13–14).

a Or *is a burden*   *b* Syr Vg Compare Gk: Heb *is removed*   *c* Or *the spirit*   *d* *Qoheleth*, traditionally rendered *Preacher*   *e* Meaning of Heb uncertain   *f* Or *into the judgment on*

THE SONG OF SOLOMON

Introduction

Song of Solomon (Song of Songs or Canticles) is a collection of love poems exchanged between a woman and a man, with occasional remarks by one or more choruses. Throughout, the lovers delight in the tastes, smells, and feel of each other, which they describe in a cascade of comparisons with the world of nature and of urban life. The identity of these lovers has been explained in various ways. (1) Solomonic: Because of references to this famous king of Israel, the poems have been read as describing a wedding between Solomon and a shepherdess. (2) Allegorical: By the turn of the era, some Jewish interpreters read the Song as an allegory★ of God's love for Israel, despite (or perhaps because of) the book's lack of mention of God. Similarly, the Christian tradition of reading the poems as expressing Christ's★ love for the church, or seeing "the bride" as the Virgin Mary, has a long history. (3) Sacred marriage: One school of Hebrew Bible interpretation★ draws parallels between these images and ancient Near Eastern descriptions of the sacred union between a god and goddess. (4) Love poetry: Contemporary scholars tend to accept the book as secular love poetry. The extended description of the lover's body, called a "wasf," and the use of "bride" as a term of endearment are analogous to Egyptian, Arabic, and Syrian love poems.

The allegorical reading explains the book's placement in the Jewish canon★: It appears with the five "megilloth" (or festival scrolls★) and is read at Passover.★ In the Christian canon, Songs appears in the poetical books. Various linguistic features suggest that it was written much later than the tenth century, perhaps in the Persian period;★ the references to Solomon are best read as allusions to the great lover of ancient Israel (1 Kings 11.1–3) rather than as a key to the book's authorship. The book bears a strong women's perspective: The woman speaks more often than the man; the woman's sexuality is celebrated rather than controlled; and mothers rather than fathers are mentioned throughout. Some scholars cite this perspective as evidence that the book was written by or for women.

READING GUIDE

Song of Solomon is not easy to read: The meanings of many words are unknown; the metaphorical★ nature of the language often leaves the referent unclear; and speakers are not clearly marked. One focus for reading is to consider how the author has evoked the feeling of love. How do images of fruit, wine, and flowers allow the lovers to speak provocatively? While the lovers clearly express their affection for one another, they also seem aware of the societal constraints under which they live. What opposition does their love meet and how do they respond? The only references to marriage are a puzzling poem about the wedding procession of King Solomon in 3.6–11 and the woman's description as "bride." Does this celebration of physical love without focus on marriage or procreation surprise you?

1 The Song of Songs, which is Solomon's.

2 Let him kiss me with the kisses of his
        mouth!
   For your love is better than wine,
3   your anointing oils are fragrant,
   your name is perfume poured out;
        therefore the maidens love you.
4 Draw me after you, let us make haste.
      The king has brought me into his
        chambers.
   We will exult and rejoice in you;
      we will extol your love more
        than wine;
      rightly do they love you.

5 I am black and beautiful,
      O daughters of Jerusalem,
   like the tents of Kedar,
      like the curtains of Solomon.
6 Do not gaze at me because I am dark,
      because the sun has gazed on me.
   My mother's sons were angry with me;
      they made me keeper of the
        vineyards,
   but my own vineyard I have not kept!

7 Tell me, you whom my soul loves,
      where you pasture your flock,
      where you make it lie down at noon;
   for why should I be like one who
        is veiled
      beside the flocks of your companions?

8 If you do not know,
      O fairest among women,
   follow the tracks of the flock,
      and pasture your kids
      beside the shepherds' tents.

likely the editor's attempt to link the book with Solomon rather than proof of its authorship. **2–8: The woman speaks of love.** Ancient Near Eastern cultures used many sweet, strong scents on the body as well as in religious ceremonies. Throughout the book, such aromas are compared to the scent of the lovers' bodies. **4:** *The king:* The lovers call each other royal names, indicating their majesty in one another's eyes. **5–6:** *Black and beautiful:* The woman maintains that her sun-darkened skin is beautiful. The verses imply an expectation that women have fair skin, perhaps reflecting an urban perspective. *Kedar:* A mountain range, the name of which means "black." *Mother's sons:* Mothers rather than fathers are mentioned in the book, suggesting a strong female perspective. *Vineyards* throughout the book are connected with sexuality. The first mention is literal: Her brothers required her to work outside. The second reference is metaphorical:✶ She has not been chaste. **7:** *Veiled:* Veiling practices in ancient Israel are difficult to reconstruct. In Gen 38, a prostitute wears a veil, and Gen 29.21–25 may imply that brides wore face coverings. The reference here may be metaphorical: Why should she have difficulty seeing him? **8:** Another voice, the male or a chorus, tells her to follow the sheep to find her lover.

9 I compare you, my love,
      to a mare among Pharaoh's chariots.
10 Your cheeks are comely with
        ornaments,
      your neck with strings of jewels.
11 We will make you ornaments of gold,
      studded with silver.

12 While the king was on his couch,
      my nard gave forth its fragrance.
13 My beloved is to me a bag of myrrh
      that lies between my breasts.
14 My beloved is to me a cluster of henna
        blossoms
      in the vineyards of En-gedi.

1.1–8. 1: Superscription. Like many Psalms, the book begins with background information. *Song of Songs:* Hebrew for "best song." *Which is Solomon's* is more

15 Ah, you are beautiful, my love;
   ah, you are beautiful;
      your eyes are doves.
16 Ah, you are beautiful, my beloved,
      truly lovely.
   Our couch is green;
17   the beams of our house are cedar,
      our rafters*a* are pine.

2 I am a rose*b* of Sharon,
   a lily of the valleys.

2 As a lily among brambles,
   so is my love among maidens.

3 As an apple tree among the trees of the
      wood,
   so is my beloved among young men.
   With great delight I sat in his shadow,
      and his fruit was sweet to my taste.
4 He brought me to the banqueting
      house,
   and his intention toward me was love.
5 Sustain me with raisins,
      refresh me with apples;
   for I am faint with love.
6 O that his left hand were under my
      head,
   and that his right hand embraced me!
7 I adjure you, O daughters of Jerusalem,
      by the gazelles or the wild does:
   do not stir up or awaken love
      until it is ready!

**1.9–2.7: The man and the woman speak of love.
1.9–11:** He uses a wide array of images to describe the
woman. *Mare:* Egyptian sources report the military
strategy of sending a mare out to excite and disturb
the enemy's stallions. **12–17:** The woman likens her
own bodily smells and the delight of her lover between
her breasts to *nard, myrrh* and *henna:* aromatic, precious scents. *En-gedi:* A lush oasis close to the Dead
Sea. **15:** The male speaks. **16–17:** The woman's speech
portrays their trysting place as outdoors. **2.1–2:** The
woman sees herself as one of many common flowers;
but her lover sees her as outstanding in beauty. **3–5:**
Fruit is used as erotic imagery. She compares their
trysting place to a *banqueting house* or "winehouse,"
where they are to take their fill of delicacies. **7:** This
statement, issued as a lesson for others, either suggests
the danger of love or requests that the lovers' intimacy

not be interrupted. *Daughters of Jerusalem* refers to
the young women of the city. In the book, their participation advances the dialogue.

8 The voice of my beloved!
      Look, he comes,
   leaping upon the mountains,
      bounding over the hills.
9 My beloved is like a gazelle
      or a young stag.
   Look, there he stands
      behind our wall,
   gazing in at the windows,
      looking through the lattice.
10 My beloved speaks and says to me:
   "Arise, my love, my fair one,
      and come away;
11 for now the winter is past,
      the rain is over and gone.
12 The flowers appear on the earth;
      the time of singing has come,
   and the voice of the turtledove
      is heard in our land.
13 The fig tree puts forth its figs,
      and the vines are in blossom;
      they give forth fragrance.
   Arise, my love, my fair one,
      and come away.
14 O my dove, in the clefts of the rock,
      in the covert of the cliff,
   let me see your face,
      let me hear your voice;
   for your voice is sweet,
      and your face is lovely.
15 Catch us the foxes,
      the little foxes,
   that ruin the vineyards—
      for our vineyards are in blossom."

16 My beloved is mine and I am his;
      he pastures his flock among the
         lilies.
17 Until the day breathes
      and the shadows flee,
   turn, my beloved, be like a gazelle
      or a young stag on the cleft
         mountains.*c*

a Meaning of Heb uncertain   *b* Heb *crocus*
c Or *on the mountains of Bether:* meaning of Heb
uncertain

2.8–17: She reports his invitation. The man beckons to the woman to join him in the countryside, where springtime has awakened nature and desire. **14:** Their love is expressive, yet secretive. He invites her to private places: *clefts* and the *covert*. **15:** A difficult verse to translate. Some consider it a reference to an ancient riddle, the meaning of which has been lost. If *vineyards* symbolize the woman's sexuality (as elsewhere) then the *foxes* are dangers to their lovemaking. **16:** *Pastures the flock* may either be literal (he is a shepherd) or metaphorical* of their love, since she is called a *lily* (2.1). **17:** *Until the day breathes . . . shadows flee:* Although some interpret the reference as to dawn, it likely refers to sunset. The woman tells the man to depart until later in the evening.

3 Upon my bed at night
  I sought him whom my soul loves;
I sought him, but found him not;
  I called him, but he gave no answer.*

2 "I will rise now and go about the city,
  in the streets and in the squares;
I will seek him whom my soul loves."
  I sought him, but found him not.

3 The sentinels found me,
  as they went about in the city.
"Have you seen him whom my soul
  loves?"

4 Scarcely had I passed them,
  when I found him whom my soul
  loves.
I held him, and would not let him go
  until I brought him into my mother's
  house,
  and into the chamber of her that
  conceived me.

5 I adjure you, O daughters of Jerusalem,
  by the gazelles or the wild does:
  do not stir up or awaken love
  until it is ready!

3.1–5: Her nighttime search. Having been sent away, the man does not return, and the woman seeks him. **2–3:** *Streets* and *sentinels* indicate an urban setting. **4:** The book has a strong feminine orientation, speaking of the *mother's house* instead of the more normal house of the father (1.6; 8.1–2; see also Ruth 1.8). Did she really bring her lover into her mother's house or is this a dream? **5:** Another warning (2.7; 5.8).

6 What is that coming up from the
  wilderness,
  like a column of smoke,
perfumed with myrrh and frankincense,
  with all the fragrant powders of the
  merchant?

7 Look, it is the litter of Solomon!
Around it are sixty mighty men
  of the mighty men of Israel,

8 all equipped with swords
  and expert in war,
each with his sword at his thigh
  because of alarms by night.

9 King Solomon made himself a
  palanquin
  from the wood of Lebanon.

10 He made its posts of silver,
  its back of gold, its seat of purple;
its interior was inlaid with love.*
  Daughters of Jerusalem,

11 come out.
Look, O daughters of Zion,
  at King Solomon,
at the crown with which his mother
  crowned him
  on the day of his wedding,
  on the day of the gladness of
  his heart.

3.6–11: A wedding scene. The book's only description of a wedding and of *Solomon* as present, these verses have been variously assessed (1) as a later insertion, modeled on Ps 45 and intended to strengthen the book's connection with Solomon; or (2) as an extended royal image, in which the woman compares the sight of her lover to that of the extravagant entourage of a king known for his love of women (1 Kings 11.1–3). **7:** *Mighty men of Israel*, translated elsewhere in the NRSV as "warriors" (2 Sam 23.8). **8:** *Sword at his thigh:* For easy access (Judg 3.16). **9:** *Wood of Lebanon:* Famous for its aroma and quality (2 Kings 19.23; 1 Kings 4.33). **11:** Jewish sources indicate that, prior to the Roman destruction of Jerusalem in 70 CE, bride and groom wore a wedding *crown.*

4 How beautiful you are, my love,
  how very beautiful!
Your eyes are doves
  behind your veil.

a Gk: Heb lacks this line   *b* Meaning of Heb uncertain

Your hair is like a flock of goats,
   moving down the slopes of Gilead.
2 Your teeth are like a flock of shorn ewes
   that have come up from the washing,
all of which bear twins,
   and not one among them is bereaved.
3 Your lips are like a crimson thread,
   and your mouth is lovely.
Your cheeks are like halves of a
     pomegranate
   behind your veil.
4 Your neck is like the tower of David,
   built in courses;
on it hang a thousand bucklers,
   all of them shields of warriors.
5 Your two breasts are like two fawns,
   twins of a gazelle,
   that feed among the lilies.
6 Until the day breathes
   and the shadows flee,
I will hasten to the mountain of myrrh
   and the hill of frankincense.
7 You are altogether beautiful, my love;
   there is no flaw in you.
8 Come with me from Lebanon, my bride;
   come with me from Lebanon.
Depart*a* from the peak of Amana,
   from the peak of Senir and Hermon,
from the dens of lions,
   from the mountains of leopards.

4.1–7: The man praises the beauty of his lover. 1:
Veil: See comment on 1.7. *Goats* in Israel are primarily
black, while sheep are white. **2:** Her *teeth* are perfect:
white, proportional. **3:** *Crimson thread* describes the
color of her lips or the part between them. *Pomegranates*, elsewhere connected with sexuality, have a juicy
red pulp. **4:** *Built in courses:* Ancient Near Eastern art
shows women wearing multiple layers of metal neck-
laces. **5:** *Fawns, twins:* Perfectly matched and soft. **6:**
Sunset (See 2.17). *Mountain of myrrh* and *hill of frankincense* refer to parts of the woman's body.

9 You have ravished my heart, my sister,
     my bride,
   you have ravished my heart with a
     glance of your eyes,
   with one jewel of your necklace.
10 How sweet is your love, my sister, my
     bride!

how much better is your love than
   wine,
   and the fragrance of your oils than
     any spice!
11 Your lips distill nectar, my bride;
   honey and milk are under your
     tongue;
   the scent of your garments is like the
     scent of Lebanon.
12 A garden locked is my sister, my bride,
   a garden locked, a fountain sealed.
13 Your channel*b* is an orchard of
     pomegranates
   with all choicest fruits,
   henna with nard,
14 nard and saffron, calamus and
     cinnamon,
   with all trees of frankincense,
myrrh and aloes,
   with all chief spices—
15 a garden fountain, a well of living water,
   and flowing streams from Lebanon.

16 Awake, O north wind,
   and come, O south wind!
Blow upon my garden
   that its fragrance may be wafted
     abroad.
Let my beloved come to his garden,
   and eat its choicest fruits.

5 I come to my garden, my sister,
     my bride;
   I gather my myrrh with my spice,
   I eat my honeycomb with my honey,
   I drink my wine with my milk.

Eat, friends, drink,
   and be drunk with love.

4.8–5.1: The man beckons her closer. While not all
identifiable, the place names are far away and exotic;
he imagines her removed from him. **4.9:** As in ancient
Egyptian poetry, *sister* and *bride* need not be read literally but as a description of the close intimacy of the
pair. **12–13:** *Garden locked* and *fountain sealed* refer
to the woman's chastity (Prov 5.15), though the man
has much knowledge of her *channel*, a more intimate
part of her body. The Hebrew word means "sword"

a Or *Look* *b* Meaning of Heb uncertain

or perhaps "sprout." He compares it to exotic, fragrant, desirable anointments and spices. **16:** The woman accepts the comparison and invites him to partake. **5.1:** The man accepts the invitation and delights in what has been offered to him.

〜〜〜〜〜〜〜〜〜〜〜〜〜〜〜〜

2 I slept, but my heart was awake.
　Listen! my beloved is knocking.
"Open to me, my sister, my love,
　　my dove, my perfect one;
for my head is wet with dew,
　　my locks with the drops of the night."
3 I had put off my garment;
　　how could I put it on again?
I had bathed my feet;
　　how could I soil them?
4 My beloved thrust his hand into the
　　　opening,
　　and my inmost being yearned for him.
5 I arose to open to my beloved,
　　and my hands dripped with myrrh,
my fingers with liquid myrrh,
　　upon the handles of the bolt.
6 I opened to my beloved,
　　but my beloved had turned and was
　　　gone.
My soul failed me when he spoke.
I sought him, but did not find him;
　　I called him, but he gave no answer.
7 Making their rounds in the city
　　the sentinels found me;
they beat me, they wounded me,
　　they took away my mantle,
　　those sentinels of the walls.
8 I adjure you, O daughters of Jerusalem,
　　if you find my beloved,
tell him this:
　　I am faint with love.

5.2–8: A second nighttime search. As in 3.1–4, she may either be on an actual search or dreaming. **3:** Although she has prepared herself for his visit, she is reluctant to go to the door. **4:** While likely referring to the window, *opening* also has a sexual connotation. **5:** Because *myrrh* is expensive, dripping suggests excess and luxury. **7:** The *sentinels* guarding the city at night represent the conventions of society, which frown on a young, unaccompanied woman roaming the streets. She does not elaborate on their beating and stripping her, citing this treatment as an example of the lengths to which she will go to find her lover.

8: It is doubtful that the *daughters of Jerusalem* were present during her search. Here, as elsewhere, the chorus adds dramatic effect.

〜〜〜〜〜〜〜〜〜〜〜〜〜〜〜〜

9 What is your beloved more than another
　　　beloved,
　　O fairest among women?
What is your beloved more than another
　　　beloved,
　　that you thus adjure us?

10 My beloved is all radiant and ruddy,
　　distinguished among ten thousand.
11 His head is the finest gold;
　　his locks are wavy,
　　black as a raven.
12 His eyes are like doves
　　beside springs of water,
bathed in milk,
　　fitly set.*a*
13 His cheeks are like beds of spices,
　　yielding fragrance.
His lips are lilies,
　　distilling liquid myrrh.
14 His arms are rounded gold,
　　set with jewels.
His body is ivory work,*a*
　　encrusted with sapphires.*b*
15 His legs are alabaster columns,
　　set upon bases of gold.
His appearance is like Lebanon,
　　choice as the cedars.
16 His speech is most sweet,
　　and he is altogether desirable.
This is my beloved and this is
　　my friend,
　　O daughters of Jerusalem.

5.9–16: The woman praises her lover. This description offers the Hebrew Bible's only description of a man's body by a woman. **10:** A *ruddy* complexion was considered attractive for men (1 Sam 16.12; Gen 2.7). **11–15:** The description, given from *head* to *legs*, compares the man to conventional ancient Near Eastern statues: head and arms of gold, encrusted with jewels. The mention of *his body* (v. 14) sounds general in a list of specific body parts: Some interpreters suggest "loins" for this reference.

〜〜〜〜〜〜〜〜〜〜〜〜〜〜〜〜

a Meaning of Heb uncertain　　*b* Heb *lapis lazuli*

6 Where has your beloved gone,
　　O fairest among women?
　Which way has your beloved turned,
　　that we may seek him with you?

2　My beloved has gone down to his
　　　garden,
　　to the beds of spices,
　to pasture his flock in the gardens,
　　and to gather lilies.
3　I am my beloved's and my beloved is
　　　mine;
　　he pastures his flock among the lilies.

4　You are beautiful as Tirzah, my love,
　　comely as Jerusalem,
　　terrible as an army with banners.
5　Turn away your eyes from me,
　　for they overwhelm me!
　Your hair is like a flock of goats,
　　moving down the slopes of Gilead.
6　Your teeth are like a flock of ewes,
　　that have come up from the washing;
　all of them bear twins,
　　and not one among them is bereaved.
7　Your cheeks are like halves of a
　　　pomegranate
　　behind your veil.
8　There are sixty queens and eighty
　　　concubines,
　　and maidens without number.
9　My dove, my perfect one, is the only one,
　　the darling of her mother,
　　flawless to her that bore her.
　The maidens saw her and called her
　　　happy;
　　the queens and concubines also, and
　　　they praised her.
10　"Who is this that looks forth like the
　　　dawn,
　　fair as the moon, bright as the sun,
　　terrible as an army with banners?"

6.1–10. 1–3: The lover's whereabouts. A short fragment of a song, in which the woman reiterates earlier
themes. **4–10: The man praises the woman's body.**
While this poem shares many of the agricultural comparisons of 4.1–3 (*hair* like *goats*, *teeth* like *ewes*), it
also introduces regal imagery. The woman is seen as
awe-inspiring. She is compared to important cities (*Tirzah* was the capital of the northern kingdom after the

division; *Jerusalem* of the south), and she would invite
the praise even of *queens* and *concubines*.✻

11　I went down to the nut orchard,
　　to look at the blossoms of the valley,
　to see whether the vines had budded,
　　whether the pomegranates were in
　　　bloom.
12　Before I was aware, my fancy set me
　　in a chariot beside my prince.[a]

13[b]　Return, return, O Shulammite!
　　Return, return, that we may look
　　　upon you.

　Why should you look upon the
　　　Shulammite,
　　as upon a dance before two armies?[c]

6.11–13. 11–12: The woman speaks. The regal imagery continues, as the woman calls her lover *my
prince*. **13: A call to the woman.** *Shulammite:* The
woman is called "the Shulammite," meaning unclear.
It could be a feminine form of the name Solomon,
indicating nobility. An unidentified group asks to gaze
upon her. The man rebuffs the request. *A dance before
two armies* may refer to a specific kind of dance or
perhaps explains that such a display would be as lewd
as a woman dancing in front of two armies of men.

7 How graceful are your feet in sandals,
　　O queenly maiden!
　Your rounded thighs are like jewels,
　　the work of a master hand.
2　Your navel is a rounded bowl
　　that never lacks mixed wine.
　Your belly is a heap of wheat,
　　encircled with lilies.
3　Your two breasts are like two fawns,
　　twins of a gazelle.
4　Your neck is like an ivory tower.
　Your eyes are pools in Heshbon,
　　by the gate of Bath-rabbim.
　Your nose is like a tower of Lebanon,
　　overlooking Damascus.
5　Your head crowns you like Carmel,
　　and your flowing locks are like purple;
　　a king is held captive in the tresses.[a]

a Cn: Meaning of Heb uncertain　　*b* Ch 7.1 in Heb
c Or *dance of Mahanaim*

7.1–5: The man praises the woman's body. In his third description of the beauty of the woman's body, the man reverses his gaze and describes her from foot to head. Greater intimacy is implied by these images: He speaks of her *navel* and *belly*, normally hidden by clothing. **4–7:** The woman is compared to majestic geography and architecture. *Heshbon:* South of Jerusalem, known for its large reservior. *Bath-rabbim:* Literally, "daughter of great ones." *Carmel* is a mountain range in northwestern Israel.

6 How fair and pleasant you are,
    O loved one, delectable maiden!*ᵃ*
7 You are stately*ᵇ* as a palm tree,
    and your breasts are like its
        clusters.
8 I say I will climb the palm tree
    and lay hold of its branches.
  O may your breasts be like clusters of
        the vine,
    and the scent of your breath like
        apples,
9 and your kisses*ᶜ* like the best wine
    that goes down*ᵈ* smoothly,
    gliding over lips and teeth.*ᵉ*

10 I am my beloved's,
    and his desire is for me.
11 Come, my beloved,
    let us go forth into the fields,
    and lodge in the villages;
12 let us go out early to the vineyards,
    and see whether the vines have
        budded,
    whether the grape blossoms have
        opened
    and the pomegranates are in bloom.
  There I will give you my love.
13 The mandrakes give forth fragrance,
    and over our doors are all choice
        fruits,
    new as well as old,
    which I have laid up for you, O my
        beloved.

7.6–13: Dialogue between the lovers. The man expresses his desire to touch the woman: She is as delectable as fruit and as delicious as wine. **10–13:** The woman invites the man into the *fields*: There, where blooms are opening, she will give herself to him. In

many cultures *mandrakes* are considered aphrodisiacs (Gen 30.14–16).

8 O that you were like a brother to me,
    who nursed at my mother's breast!
  If I met you outside, I would kiss you,
    and no one would despise me.
2 I would lead you and bring you
    into the house of my mother,
    and into the chamber of the one who
        bore me.*ᶠ*
  I would give you spiced wine to drink,
    the juice of my pomegranates.
3 O that his left hand were under my
        head,
    and that his right hand embraced me!
4 I adjure you, O daughters of Jerusalem,
    do not stir up or awaken love
    until it is ready!

5 Who is that coming up from the
        wilderness,
    leaning upon her beloved?

  Under the apple tree I awakened you.
  There your mother was in labor with
        you;
    there she who bore you was in labor.

8.1–5: Expressions of desire. The woman is aware of the societal constraints on their expressions of love. She wishes for the same freedom of affection and shared space that she would have with a brother. **2:** As elsewhere, *pomegranates* is a sexual image. **5:** The words of the chorus reveal that the lovers have been together in the countryside, perhaps having consummated their desire. For the third time, the woman connects their intimate moments with events of their own conceptions (3.4; 8.2).

6 Set me as a seal upon your heart,
    as a seal upon your arm;
  for love is strong as death,
    passion fierce as the grave.
  Its flashes are flashes of fire,
    a raging flame.

a Syr: Heb *in delights*   *b* Heb *This your stature is*
c Heb *palate*   *d* Heb *down for my lover*   *e* Gk Syr
Vg: Heb *lips of sleepers*   *f* Gk Syr: Heb *my mother; she
(or you) will teach me*

7 Many waters cannot quench love,
    neither can floods drown it.
If one offered for love
    all the wealth of one's house,
    it would be utterly scorned.

8 We have a little sister,
    and she has no breasts.
What shall we do for our sister,
    on the day when she is spoken for?
9 If she is a wall,
    we will build upon her a battlement
        of silver;
but if she is a door,
    we will enclose her with boards of
        cedar.
10 I was a wall,
    and my breasts were like towers;
then I was in his eyes
    as one who brings*a* peace.
11 Solomon had a vineyard at Baal-hamon;
    he entrusted the vineyard to keepers;
    each one was to bring for its fruit a
        thousand pieces of silver.
12 My vineyard, my very own, is for myself;
    you, O Solomon, may have the
        thousand,
    and the keepers of the fruit two
        hundred!

13 O you who dwell in the gardens,
    my companions are listening for your
        voice;
    let me hear it.

14 Make haste, my beloved,
    and be like a gazelle
or a young stag
    upon the mountains of spices!

8.6–14. 6–7: Sayings on love. Documents were secured with wax, which were then stamped with a *seal* bearing the owner's distinctive symbol. The woman marks the man as her own. **8–14: Miscellaneous poems.** The brothers, mentioned in ch. 1, speak. **9:** If on her wedding day she has been chaste (*a wall*), they will give her silver ornaments. If she has not, then they will guard her. **10:** She maintains that she is chaste, and mature with full *breasts* (*towers*). **11–12:** The man maintains that his *vineyard* (that is, the woman) is better than that of Solomon, where a single piece of fruit was worth *a thousand pieces of silver. Baal-hamon* means "possessor of wealth." The location is unknown. **13:** The woman speaks these final verses.

a Or *finds*

ISAIAH

Introduction

In the second division of the Hebrew Bible canon,✫ the Prophets, Isaiah is the first of the four major books, or collections, of prophecies. The other three are Jeremiah, Ezekiel, and the twelve minor prophets (Hosea—Malachi) formed into one book. Isaiah contains prophecies originating with Isaiah son of Amoz in the eighth century BCE, which have been recorded, added to, and edited during the following three centuries. Its sixty-six chapters, which comprise a "collection of collections," can bewilder the reader because of the complex manner in which the individual units have been structured. Three major themes dominate the book. First is the unity and destiny of Israel as the people of the LORD God as they face the threat posed by imperial domination from Mesopotamia (Assyria, Babylonia, and Persia). Second, Jerusalem is the spiritual center and symbol of Israel's role among the nations of the world. Third, the Davidic dynasty✫ bears a special significance. David, the founder, had first established a united kingdom of Israel, with a capital in Jerusalem. The fate of this royal house plays a dominant role in the prophecies of chs. 6–12, but thereafter the theme appears less prominently. This link with the language and themes associated with the Davidic kingship and its future has made Isaiah the "messianic" prophet of the Old Testament. (Messiah✫ means "anointed✫ one," a key royal title.)

READING GUIDE

Because the book of Isaiah took shape over a period of several centuries, it is helpful to consider its major divisions separately. These divisions are marked by separate headings and provide evidence of the book's final editorial shaping. Six major units make up the scroll of Isaiah.

1–4	General introduction: Warning and promise for Judah and Jerusalem
5–12	Warnings to Jerusalem and its royal house
13–27	Warnings and laments addressed to foreign nations and peoples
28–39	Threats to Jerusalem and its great deliverance
40–55	The renewal of hope for Jerusalem
56–66	The coming of the light

The primary historical context for the book is reflected in chs. 6–9, the period between 740–732 BCE. The people of Israel had become divided into two kingdoms, Israel and Judah (the prophet calls them "houses"). Israel (Ephraim) and Syria were attempting to depose the reigning Davidic king of Judah. However, the Judahite king, Ahaz, retained his throne, but in order to do so bought support from Assyria, thereby involving the entire region in the oppressive control of this Mesopotamian power. Further encounters with Assyria led to the destruction of Israel (see Isa 9.8–10.4). When Judah also later rebelled against Assyria, both its ruler, Hezekiah, and the city of Jerusalem were spared the fate that had overtaken Israel (see Isa 36.1–37.38). This reprieve helped emphasize the importance of the religious foundations of Jerusalem's life: the Temple✫ and the royal dynasty of David.

Soon after Babylon replaced Assyria as the oppressing Mesopotamian power, the Babylonians destroyed Jerusalem and its Temple and removed the surviving Davidic ruler. As a result, Israel

itself was broken apart, with many taken into captivity and others forced to flee. Thereafter, the overthrow of Babylon as the enemy of God's people became a central issue (13.1–14.23; 47.1–15). The rebuilding of Jerusalem, the return of the scattered exiles to form once again a united people, and (with considerable caution) the reestablishing of the covenant✶ with the royal house of David (Isa 55.1–6), are the major subject of the prophecies in the later part (chs. 40–66). The very latest sections (especially chs. 24–27) look to a time when the world will be governed by the direct rule of God, who will come in judgment to punish the wicked and establish peace and justice. This reign will end the oppressive rule of foreign powers and of wrongdoers among God's own people. Only then will peace and justice be established under the Davidic royal house in the city of Jerusalem. Isaiah is therefore uniquely within the Bible the prophet of the Kingdom of God.

The book of Isaiah, which reflects events extending through at least three centuries, was written and edited throughout this extended period. The alternative—that the eighth-century prophet foresaw events of a future time and referred to them as having already occurred—would mean that the prophet was meaninglessly and unrealistically detached from the people he addressed. It was vital to the role of the prophet to influence the minds of his hearers, not only in penitence and faith toward God, but in major political decisions of state leading to war or peace. To understand many of the individual prophecies, it is important to understand their political background.

The book itself develops along thematic, rather than narrowly historical, lines. Central among these are promises of the importance of Jerusalem as the city to which the nations of the world will make pilgrimage (see 2.1–4; 60.1–22), the role of the Davidic monarchy in upholding the just rule of God (11.1–5), and the overthrow of Assyria and Babylon as examples of worldly oppression and violence (14.4–11, 12–21). These prophecies declaring God's purpose for the world express broad themes rather than focusing on specific events. Frequently, earlier prophecies are alluded to in later ones and revised or supplemented (this is called intertextuality✶). Even more significant are instances in which words, names, and word pictures are used and then later reinterpreted in subsequent prophecies (see, for example, the reinterpretation of the word picture of *briers and thorns* from 5.6 in 7.23–25; 9.18; 10.17; 27.4). Such intertextuality attests to the intricate process according to which new prophecies were formed out of earlier ones. In recognizing this process, we begin to understand how prophetic sayings and then scrolls were built into books. Once the biblical scrolls had achieved a fixed form, Jewish scribes used similar techniques to construct entire books, which became commentaries on the original canonical ones.

Prophets were originally speakers rather than writers, but once their words were recorded, the writings were brought together and edited so that their lasting message could be kept alive and understood. To interpret a prophetic book, we must attend both to the original situation and to the need to relate one saying to other sayings and to the outcome of events addressed by the prophet. By linking together the separate parts of the prophetic book, we can expect to discern a coherent and enduring message from God. The prophet was God's messenger, declaring a word that possessed divine authority, both in rebuke for wrongdoing and disobedience and in promise for future salvation of an entire people. The process of making spoken prophecies into books was one in which questions of authorship and time of origin cannot always now be answered with certainty. The primary issue was the unity, consistency, and integrity of God's purpose.

Isaiah 1–4

GENERAL INTRODUCTION: WARNING AND PROMISE FOR JUDAH AND JERUSALEM

Chapters 1–4 present two major themes that integrate the book's separate parts. The first theme is the promise of God that Jerusalem (Zion*) will become a center of pilgrimage for the nations of the world (2.1–4) and will be the center from which the knowledge of God will radiate (4.2–6). The second theme, which reappears repeatedly, is that Jerusalem itself must first be purged of wrongdoers and its citizens must repent and turn to seek God's righteousness (1.1–31). Proof of the city's ungodly ways is found in the greed, idolatry,* love of luxury, and indifference to the plight of the poor that characterize its citizens (2.6–22; 3.13–4.1). It is because of such deeds that the land lies in ruin and desolation (1.7–9; 3.1–12).

The historical situation of chs. 1–4 is that of the fifth century BCE when Jerusalem lay at the center of a community of Jews settled in Judah, but served also as the spiritual center and focus for a far wider number living in various parts of the Persian empire. Many were settled still further away, in Egypt and North Africa. Given Judah's political weakness, the need for a firm and consistent focus for the religious life and loyalty of all Jews was paramount. The written legacy of the eighth-century prophet Isaiah of Jerusalem presented Jerusalem as a central source of authority and leadership and as the place to which all these scattered communities would return to make Israel once again their national homeland. Authentic prophecies from Isaiah were preserved and edited to provide this message of new hope. The message of chs. 1–4 reflects directly that of 56–66, indicating a planned structure to the finished book.

READING GUIDE

The main theme of these introductory chapters is the call to penitence and a renewal of commitment to the LORD (ch. 1). Hope for the future is given in 2.1–4 and 4.2–6 in visions of the new glory and authority of Jerusalem, the city that provides assurance of God's blessing. Between these promises the prophet points to the ills and wrongs of the community which hinder the fulfillment of God's purpose.

1.1–20	The ruin and desolation of the land of Judah
2.1–22	Jerusalem: its destiny and wrongdoing
3.1–4.1	Confusion in Judah and Jerusalem
3.13–4.1	The LORD's case against the people
4.2–6	The glory of the new Jerusalem

1 The vision of Isaiah son of Amoz, which he saw concerning Judah and Jerusalem in the days of Uzziah, Jotham, Ahaz, and Hezekiah, kings of Judah.

2 Hear, O heavens, and listen, O earth;
    for the LORD has spoken:
  I reared children and brought
      them up,
    but they have rebelled against me.

3 The ox knows its owner,
    and the donkey its master's crib;
  but Israel does not know,
    my people do not understand.

4 Ah, sinful nation,
    people laden with iniquity,
  offspring who do evil,
    children who deal corruptly,

who have forsaken the LORD,
    who have despised the Holy One of
        Israel,
    who are utterly estranged!

5 Why do you seek further beatings?
    Why do you continue to rebel?
The whole head is sick,
    and the whole heart faint.
6 From the sole of the foot even to the
        head,
    there is no soundness in it,
but bruises and sores
    and bleeding wounds;
they have not been drained, or bound up,
    or softened with oil.

7 Your country lies desolate,
    your cities are burned with fire;
in your very presence
    aliens devour your land;
    it is desolate, as overthrown by
        foreigners.
8 And daughter Zion is left
    like a booth in a vineyard,
like a shelter in a cucumber field,
    like a besieged city.
9 If the LORD of hosts
    had not left us a few survivors,
we would have been like Sodom,
    and become like Gomorrah.

1.1–20: The ruin and desolation of Jerusalem and the land of Judah. 1–9: The portrayal of the desolation of the land and the isolated situation of Jerusalem probably refers to the events of 701 BCE in which the Assyrian king, Sennacherib, laid siege to the city (see 36.1–37.38). Such attacks were repeated in later times and hence provide a context for the whole book. The prophet's rebuke shows how the people's own wrongdoing had brought about their misfortunes. **8:** The *booth* and *shelter* in *vineyard* and *field* were watchmen's huts set up to protect the vines and crops.

10 Hear the word of the LORD,
    you rulers of Sodom!
Listen to the teaching of our God,
    you people of Gomorrah!
11 What to me is the multitude of your
        sacrifices?
    says the LORD;

I have had enough of burnt offerings of
        rams
    and the fat of fed beasts;
I do not delight in the blood of bulls,
    or of lambs, or of goats.

12 When you come to appear before me,*a*
    who asked this from your hand?
    Trample my courts no more;
13 bringing offerings is futile;
    incense is an abomination to me.
New moon and sabbath and calling of
        convocation—
    I cannot endure solemn assemblies
        with iniquity.
14 Your new moons and your appointed
        festivals
    my soul hates;
they have become a burden to me,
    I am weary of bearing them.
15 When you stretch out your hands,
    I will hide my eyes from you;
even though you make many prayers,
    I will not listen;
    your hands are full of blood.
16 Wash yourselves; make yourselves
        clean;
    remove the evil of your doings
    from before my eyes;
cease to do evil,
17   learn to do good;
seek justice,
    rescue the oppressed,
defend the orphan,
    plead for the widow.

18 Come now, let us argue it out,
    says the LORD:
though your sins are like scarlet,
    they shall be like snow;
though they are red like crimson,
    they shall become like wool.
19 If you are willing and obedient,
    you shall eat the good of the land;
20 but if you refuse and rebel,
    you shall be devoured by the sword;
    for the mouth of the LORD has
        spoken.

a Or *see my face*

1.10–20: Criticisms of the Temple* rituals and prayers show that without justice and compassion they are meaningless to God, who ignores them.

〰〰〰〰〰〰〰〰〰〰〰〰〰

21 How the faithful city
    has become a whore!
  She that was full of justice,
    righteousness lodged in her—
    but now murderers!
22 Your silver has become dross,
    your wine is mixed with water.
23 Your princes are rebels
    and companions of thieves.
  Everyone loves a bribe
    and runs after gifts.
  They do not defend the orphan,
    and the widow's cause does not come
      before them.

24 Therefore says the Sovereign, the Lord
    of hosts, the Mighty One of
    Israel:
  Ah, I will pour out my wrath on my
    enemies,
    and avenge myself on my foes!
25 I will turn my hand against you;
    I will smelt away your dross as with
      lye
    and remove all your alloy.
26 And I will restore your judges as at the
    first,
    and your counselors as at the
      beginning.
  Afterward you shall be called the city of
    righteousness,
    the faithful city.

27 Zion shall be redeemed by justice,
    and those in her who repent, by
      righteousness.
28 But rebels and sinners shall be
    destroyed together,
    and those who forsake the Lord shall
      be consumed.
29 For you shall be ashamed of the oaks
    in which you delighted;
    and you shall blush for the gardens
    that you have chosen.
30 For you shall be like an oak
    whose leaf withers,
    and like a garden without water.

31 The strong shall become like tinder,
    and their work*a* like a spark;
  they and their work shall burn together,
    with no one to quench them.

————————————

1.21–31: As a royal city, Jerusalem was a center for the administration of justice over which the king presided. The failure to uphold such justice allowed the most serious crimes to go unpunished. God would therefore have to take action, not only against the criminal wrongdoers, but also against those whose indifference encouraged evil deeds. **29:** The *oaks* were simple rustic shrines, devoted to fertility and the gods and goddesses who were believed to guarantee life-giving power.

〰〰〰〰〰〰〰〰〰〰〰〰〰

2 The word that Isaiah son of Amoz saw
  concerning Judah and Jerusalem.

2 In days to come
    the mountain of the Lord's house
  shall be established as the highest of the
    mountains,
    and shall be raised above the hills;
  all the nations shall stream to it.
3   Many peoples shall come and say,
  "Come, let us go up to the mountain of
    the Lord,
    to the house of the God of Jacob;
  that he may teach us his ways
    and that we may walk in his paths."
  For out of Zion shall go forth
    instruction,
    and the word of the Lord from
      Jerusalem.
4 He shall judge between the nations,
    and shall arbitrate for many peoples;
  they shall beat their swords into
    plowshares,
    and their spears into pruning hooks;
  nation shall not lift up sword against
    nation,
    neither shall they learn war any more.

————————————

**2.1–22: Jerusalem: its destiny and wrongdoing.
1–4:** From the time of David's adoption of the city as his capital, Jerusalem had been celebrated as the place to which many nations paid homage and brought tribute (see Ps 2.2–11). This memorable prophecy re-

a Or *its makers*

interprets this theme, giving divine assurance that the city will become a center from which God's law will be administered among the nations (the city's name is related to the Hebrew word for peace, "shalom." Peace, God's purpose for all nations (v. 4), can only come when there is justice.

5 O house of Jacob,
come, let us walk
in the light of the LORD!
6 For you have forsaken the ways of^a your
people,
O house of Jacob.
Indeed they are full of diviners^b from
the east
and of soothsayers like the
Philistines,
and they clasp hands with foreigners.
7 Their land is filled with silver and gold,
and there is no end to their treasures;
their land is filled with horses,
and there is no end to their chariots.
8 Their land is filled with idols;
they bow down to the work of their
hands,
to what their own fingers have made.
9 And so people are humbled,
and everyone is brought low—
do not forgive them!
10 Enter into the rock,
and hide in the dust
from the terror of the LORD,
and from the glory of his majesty.
11 The haughty eyes of people shall be
brought low,
and the pride of everyone shall be
humbled;
and the LORD alone will be exalted on
that day.
12 For the LORD of hosts has a day
against all that is proud and lofty,
against all that is lifted up and high;^c
13 against all the cedars of Lebanon,
lofty and lifted up;
and against all the oaks of Bashan;
14 against all the high mountains,
and against all the lofty hills;
15 against every high tower,
and against every fortified wall;
16 against all the ships of Tarshish,
and against all the beautiful craft.^d

17 The haughtiness of people shall be
humbled,
and the pride of everyone shall be
brought low;
and the LORD alone will be exalted on
that day.
18 The idols shall utterly pass away.
19 Enter the caves of the rocks
• and the holes of the ground,
from the terror of the LORD,
and from the glory of his majesty,
when he rises to terrify the earth.
20 On that day people will throw away
to the moles and to the bats
their idols of silver and their idols of
gold,
which they made for themselves to
worship,
21 to enter the caverns of the rocks
and the clefts in the crags,
from the terror of the LORD,
and from the glory of his majesty,
when he rises to terrify the earth.
22 Turn away from mortals,
who have only breath in their
nostrils,
for of what account are they?

2.5–22. 5–11: Jerusalem, seeking commercial prosperity and success, neglected its spiritual foundations. *On that day* (v. 11) points to an indefinite time of God's judgment and comes to refer to the great judgment and renewal for Judah and all nations (see Isa 25.9). **12–22:** The prophet depicts God's punishment of human pride through the image of bringing down natural features such as tall trees and *high mountains* (vv. 12–15). Arrogance is the root of idolatry ✫ (vv. 19–20), the belief that human beings can control the divine realm. The Day of the LORD (v. 11) now points to God's judgment against human violence and disregard of the divine laws. The *ships of Tarshish* (v. 16) were the famed trading ships of the maritime nations of the Mediterranean. In Gen 10.4 Tarshish is a great-grandson of Noah, but the several biblical references to it as a place point to its fame as a source of trade, especially trade in precious metals. It is often located in southwestern Spain, but probably more

a Heb lacks *the ways of*   b Cn: Heb lacks *of diviners*
c Cn Compare Gk: Heb *low*   d Compare Gk: Meaning of Heb uncertain

than one site where mining and metal-refining took place bore such a name.

〰〰〰〰〰〰〰〰〰〰〰〰〰

3 For now the Sovereign, the LORD
    of hosts,
  is taking away from Jerusalem and
    from Judah
support and staff—
  all support of bread,
  and all support of water—
2 warrior and soldier,
  judge and prophet,
  diviner and elder,
3 captain of fifty
  and dignitary,
counselor and skillful magician
  and expert enchanter.
4 And I will make boys their princes,
  and babes shall rule over them.
5 The people will be oppressed,
  everyone by another
  and everyone by a neighbor;
the youth will be insolent to the elder,
  and the base to the honorable.

6 Someone will even seize a relative,
  a member of the clan, saying,
"You have a cloak;
  you shall be our leader,
and this heap of ruins
  shall be under your rule."
7 But the other will cry out on that day,
    saying,
"I will not be a healer;
  in my house there is neither bread
    nor cloak;
you shall not make me
  leader of the people."
8 For Jerusalem has stumbled
  and Judah has fallen,
because their speech and their deeds
  are against the LORD,
  defying his glorious presence.

9 The look on their faces bears witness
  against them;
they proclaim their sin like Sodom,
  they do not hide it.
Woe to them!
  For they have brought evil on
    themselves.

10 Tell the innocent how fortunate they
    are,
  for they shall eat the fruit of their
    labors.
11 Woe to the guilty! How unfortunate
    they are,
  for what their hands have done shall
    be done to them.
12 My people—children are their
    oppressors,
  and women rule over them.
O my people, your leaders mislead you,
  and confuse the course of your paths.

3.1–4.1: Confusion in Judah and Jerusalem. 1–8: The city and land will suffer famine and the loss of their natural resources, bringing confusion and panic. There will be no capable judges and elders (vv. 1–5), bringing economic ruin and social chaos (v. 6) with the breakdown of law and order. The broader context indicates that this is the consequence of oppressive foreign invasions and interference (see chs. 5–12). **9–12:** The readers of that time would know, only too well, the ruined state of Judah and its chief city. Disobedience and indifference to the LORD God had brought such misfortune upon them.

〰〰〰〰〰〰〰〰〰〰〰〰〰

13 The LORD rises to argue his case;
  he stands to judge the peoples.
14 The LORD enters into judgment
  with the elders and princes of his
    people:
It is you who have devoured the
    vineyard;
  the spoil of the poor is in your houses.
15 What do you mean by crushing my
    people,
  by grinding the face of the poor? says
    the Lord GOD of hosts.

16 The LORD said:
Because the daughters of Zion are
    haughty
  and walk with outstretched necks,
  glancing wantonly with their eyes,
mincing along as they go,
  tinkling with their feet;
17 the Lord will afflict with scabs
  the heads of the daughters of Zion,
  and the LORD will lay bare their
    secret parts.

18 In that day the Lord will take away the finery of the anklets, the headbands, and the crescents; [19]the pendants, the bracelets, and the scarfs; [20]the headdresses, the armlets, the sashes, the perfume boxes, and the amulets; [21]the signet rings and nose rings; [22]the festal robes, the mantles, the cloaks, and the handbags; [23]the garments of gauze, the linen garments, the turbans, and the veils.

24 Instead of perfume there will be a
　　　stench;
　　and instead of a sash, a rope;
　　and instead of well-set hair, baldness;
　　and instead of a rich robe, a binding
　　　　of sackcloth;
　　instead of beauty, shame.[a]

25 Your men shall fall by the sword
　　and your warriors in battle.

26 And her gates shall lament and mourn;
　　ravaged, she shall sit upon the
　　　ground.

4 Seven women shall take hold of one man
　in that day, saying,
"We will eat our own bread and wear
　　our own clothes;
just let us be called by your name;
　　take away our disgrace."

3.13–4.1: The Lord's case against the people. The reasons for Judah's misfortunes are detailed in a lawsuit which God is bringing against the people. **15–16:** Oppression of the poor and women who indulge in absurd luxury are outward signs of a spiritual sickness. Accordingly, God's punishment will fit the offense (v. 24): The horrors of warfare will reduce many of the women who had so pampered themselves to a state of destitution (3.25–4.1).

2 On that day the branch of the LORD shall be beautiful and glorious, and the fruit of the land shall be the pride and glory of the survivors of Israel. [3]Whoever is left in Zion and remains in Jerusalem will be called holy, everyone who has been recorded for life in Jerusalem, [4]once the Lord has washed away the filth of the daughters of Zion and cleansed the bloodstains of Jerusalem from its midst by a spirit of judgment and by a spirit of burning. [5]Then the LORD will create over the whole site of Mount Zion and over its places of assembly a cloud by day and smoke and the shining of a flaming fire by night. Indeed over all the glory there will be a canopy. [6]It will serve as a pavilion, a shade by day from the heat, and a refuge and a shelter from the storm and rain.

4.2–6: The glory of the new Jerusalem. 5–6: Judgment is the necessary path to the renewal of hope and to the dawning of a time of justice and world peace. Hence, the opening chapters conclude with the vision of a chastened and glorified Jerusalem in which the presence of God will be evident everywhere (vv. 5–6). The visionary presentation is filled with symbolic word pictures in which the title *the branch of the LORD* (v. 2) refers to the new Davidic king (compare 11.1). As God had led the ancestors of the nation through the desert (see Ex 13.21–22), so now the same presence would indicate the protection and blessing of the favored city. The pictures of *shade* and *shelter* (v. 6) counter the warnings of the sufferings and trials in 3.1–4.1.

a Q Ms: MT lacks *shame*

Isaiah 5-12

WARNINGS TO JERUSALEM AND ITS ROYAL HOUSE

These chapters, the oldest part of the book, contain prophecies from 740–732 BCE. There may be an Isaiah "memoir" in 6.1–8.18, part of which is written in the first person, and in which the prophet recounts his call and the three children's sign-names that contain divine messages. Chapter 5 prepares for this memoir with a general warning that God's "vineyard" (Israel) will soon be destroyed (5.1–7) by a far-away nation (5.26–30), Assyria. Further threats of danger and destruction follow (8.19–22). Fresh hope beyond these warnings comes with the promise of

the birth to the house of David of a new king, who will bring deliverance (9.2–7). Judah's sister kingdom in the north, Ephraim, will not share this deliverance (9.8–21).

The perspective changes with the assurance in 10.5–15 that Assyria also, having been God's instrument of punishment, will itself be punished. A series of warnings in word pictures (10.16–34) reaffirms Assyria's overthrow. Israel's fortunes after the collapse of Assyrian domination with the rise of Babylon are briefly outlined (11.1–16). The glowing hope of 9.2–7, that deliverance will come through the new ruler from the Davidic dynasty,* is developed further in 11.1–5, followed by assurance that the entire world order will be transformed in the new age of salvation (11.6–9). At this time survivors of the kingdoms of Judah and Israel who had become scattered among many nations will return to their homeland (11.10–16). A psalm-like hymn of praise and thanksgiving to God for this great final hope brings the collection to a close in ch. 12.

The memoir of 6.1–8.18 probably belongs to the period of the war between Judah and Ephraim (in alliance with Syria) in the years 735–732 BCE. The death of King Uzziah (6.1) initiated a major political crisis, which threatened the survival of the Davidic dynasty. It brought Assyria onto the scene in a way that proved destructive for the entire region. This memoir has, however, been supplemented by many additions that take account of subsequent events. The impact that Assyria was to have upon Judah and Israel for more than a century colors the prophecies of 10.5–34. Chapter 11 takes into account the subsequent dominance of Babylon when Jerusalem was destroyed (587 BCE).

READING GUIDE

5 Let me sing for my beloved
   my love-song concerning his
        vineyard:
   My beloved had a vineyard
      on a very fertile hill.
2 He dug it and cleared it of stones,
      and planted it with choice vines;
   he built a watchtower in the midst of it,
      and hewed out a wine vat in it;
   he expected it to yield grapes,
      but it yielded wild grapes.

3 And now, inhabitants of Jerusalem
      and people of Judah,

judge between me
      and my vineyard.
4 What more was there to do for my
        vineyard
      that I have not done in it?
   When I expected it to yield grapes,
      why did it yield wild grapes?

5 And now I will tell you
      what I will do to my vineyard.
   I will remove its hedge,
      and it shall be devoured;
   I will break down its wall,
      and it shall be trampled down.

6 I will make it a waste;
    it shall not be pruned or hoed,
    and it shall be overgrown with briers
        and thorns;
I will also command the clouds
    that they rain no rain upon it.

7 For the vineyard of the LORD of hosts
    is the house of Israel,
and the people of Judah
    are his pleasant planting;
he expected justice,
    but saw bloodshed;
righteousness,
    but heard a cry!
8 Ah, you who join house to house,
    who add field to field,
until there is room for no one but you,
    and you are left to live alone
    in the midst of the land!
9 The LORD of hosts has sworn in my
        hearing:
Surely many houses shall be desolate,
    large and beautiful houses, without
        inhabitant.
10 For ten acres of vineyard shall yield but
        one bath,
    and a homer of seed shall yield a
        mere ephah.ª

11 Ah, you who rise early in the morning
    in pursuit of strong drink,
who linger in the evening
    to be inflamed by wine,
12 whose feasts consist of lyre and harp,
    tambourine and flute and wine,
but who do not regard the deeds of the
        LORD,
    or see the work of his hands!
13 Therefore my people go into exile
        without knowledge;
their nobles are dying of hunger,
    and their multitude is parched with
        thirst.
14 Therefore Sheol has enlarged its
        appetite
    and opened its mouth beyond
        measure;
the nobility of Jerusalemᵇ and her
        multitude go down,
    her throng and all who exult in her.

15 People are bowed down, everyone is
        brought low,
    and the eyes of the haughty are
        humbled.
16 But the LORD of hosts is exalted
        by justice,
    and the Holy God shows himself holy
        by righteousness.
17 Then the lambs shall graze as in their
        pasture,
    fatlings and kidsᶜ shall feed among
        the ruins.

18 Ah, you who drag iniquity along with
        cords of falsehood,
    who drag sin along as with cart ropes,
19 who say, "Let him make haste,
    let him speed his work
    that we may see it;
let the plan of the Holy One of Israel
        hasten to fulfillment,
    that we may know it!"
20 Ah, you who call evil good
        and good evil,
who put darkness for light
    and light for darkness,
who put bitter for sweet
    and sweet for bitter!
21 Ah, you who are wise in your own eyes,
    and shrewd in your own sight!
22 Ah, you who are heroes in drinking wine
    and valiant at mixing drink,
23 who acquit the guilty for a bribe,
    and deprive the innocent of their
        rights!
24 Therefore, as the tongue of fire devours
        the stubble,
    and as dry grass sinks down in the
        flame,
so their root will become rotten,
    and their blossom go up like dust;
for they have rejected the instruction of
        the LORD of hosts,
    and have despised the word of the
        Holy One of Israel.

25 Therefore the anger of the LORD was
        kindled against his people,

a The Heb bath, homer, and ephah are measures of
quantity   b Heb her nobility   c Cn Compare Gk:
Heb aliens

and he stretched out his hand against
  them and struck them;
the mountains quaked,
and their corpses were like refuse
  in the streets.
For all this his anger has not turned
  away,
  and his hand is stretched out still.

5.1–30: The song of the vineyard. 1–7: The parable★
of an unfruitful vineyard is an apparently unremarkable
story whose full meaning only becomes clear when the
storyteller reveals that he is describing Israel and Judah.
The verdict of v. 6 is valid also for this larger meaning:
The land must soon suffer utter devastation and ruin.
This is the theme-message which underlies all the
prophecies of chs. 5–12 (see especially 6.11–13). The
parable is made more complex by the opening address
in which the speaker declares: *Let me sing for my beloved my love-song.* As a "friend" of the injured vineyard owner, the speaker is an interested onlooker or
perhaps the owner's supporter at a feast. In this case,
the claim to present a *love-song* suggests that the story
will be about a disappointed lover (see the use of vineyard imagery for courtship in Song 8.11–12). In v. 7
the vineyard represents both *Israel* and *Judah.* **8–24:**
The conduct of the ruling classes in Jerusalem involved
greed, manipulation of justice, violence, and dishonesty. Divine judgment is therefore necessary. The concluding part of this indictment may occur in 10.1–3,
with 5.25 correspondingly misplaced from 9.8–21.

26 He will raise a signal for a nation far
      away,
    and whistle for a people at the ends
      of the earth;
    Here they come, swiftly, speedily!
27 None of them is weary, none
      stumbles,
    none slumbers or sleeps,
    not a loincloth is loose,
    not a sandal-thong broken;
28 their arrows are sharp,
    all their bows bent,
    their horses' hoofs seem like flint,
    and their wheels like the whirlwind.
29 Their roaring is like a lion,
    like young lions they roar;
    they growl and seize their prey,
    they carry it off, and no one
      can rescue.

30 They will roar over it on that day,
    like the roaring of the sea.
   And if one look to the land—
    only darkness and distress;
   and the light grows dark with clouds.

5.26–30: This key prophetic declaration shows clearly
how the judgment will fall upon the land of Israel and
Judah and that, a though a foreign nation will bring
about the devastation, the voice of God has summoned it. The image of God acting against Israel by
raising *a signal for a nation far away* becomes a repeated theme showing how God acts to control human destiny (see 11.10–12; 49.22). Although in this
pronouncement the identity of the distant nation is
not revealed, one quickly discovers that it is Assyria
(see 7.17; 8.4).

6 In the year that King Uzziah died, I saw
the Lord sitting on a throne, high and
lofty; and the hem of his robe filled the temple. 2 Seraphs were in attendance above him;
each had six wings: with two they covered
their faces, and with two they covered their
feet, and with two they flew. 3 And one called
to another and said:
  "Holy, holy, holy is the LORD of hosts;
    the whole earth is full of his glory."
4 The pivots*a* on the thresholds shook at the
voices of those who called, and the house
filled with smoke. 5 And I said: "Woe is me!
I am lost, for I am a man of unclean lips, and
I live among a people of unclean lips; yet my
eyes have seen the King, the LORD of hosts!"
  6 Then one of the seraphs flew to me,
holding a live coal that had been taken from
the altar with a pair of tongs. 7 The seraph*b*
touched my mouth with it and said: "Now
that this has touched your lips, your guilt has
departed and your sin is blotted out." 8 Then
I heard the voice of the Lord saying, "Whom
shall I send, and who will go for us?" And I
said, "Here am I; send me!" 9 And he said,
"Go and say to this people:
  'Keep listening, but do not comprehend;
    keep looking, but do not understand.'
10 Make the mind of this people dull,
    and stop their ears,
    and shut their eyes,

---

a Meaning of Heb uncertain *b* Heb *He*

so that they may not look with their
          eyes,
    and listen with their ears,
    and comprehend with their minds,
    and turn and be healed."
11 Then I said, "How long, O Lord?" And
          he said:
"Until cities lie waste
    without inhabitant,
    and houses without people,
    and the land is utterly desolate;
12 until the LORD sends everyone
          far away,
    and vast is the emptiness in the midst
          of the land.
13 Even if a tenth part remain in it,
    it will be burned again,
    like a terebinth or an oak
    whose stump remains standing
    when it is felled."*a*
The holy seed is its stump.

6.1–13: The prophet's call and commission. 1–8:
The year in which *King Uzziah died* is not precisely
known, but his death occurred sometime between
742 and 736 BCE. The king (also called Azariah, 2 Kings
15.1–7) had been stricken with severe illness (2 Kings
15.5), which meant that his son Jotham served for a
time as co-regent with him before succeeding to the
throne (2 Kings 15.7). This co-regency period must be
included in the sixteen years ascribed Jotham's reign
(2 Kings 15.33). It was in this time that a major conflict
arose between an alliance of Syria-Israel (Ephraim) and
Judah (2 Kings 15. 37). The central issue was resistance
against Assyrian expansion in the region (see 2 Kings
15.17–20). Judah's neighbors intended to remove
Ahaz from his throne and to replace him with an otherwise unknown figure called Tabeel (7.6). Isaiah's call
therefore came at a time when Assyrian interference
was beginning to cause severe political upheaval in the
region. **9–10:** The sharp irony* of the commission
given to Isaiah implies awareness of the popular hostility to his message and the people's refusal to accept
it (see 8.11–15). **11:** One of Isaiah's central warnings
is that the entire land of Israel will be ruined because
of the rejection of God's message. The continuing relevance of these prophecies led to their preservation in
this book. **12–13:** The cruel Assyrian policy of exiling
whole populations (see 36.17) is reflected in this warning. The further threat that, even after severe devastation, the land will be *burned again* reflects later

awareness of depredations by both Assyrian and Babylonian armies.

7 In the days of Ahaz son of Jotham son
of Uzziah, king of Judah, King Rezin of
Aram and King Pekah son of Remaliah of
Israel went up to attack Jerusalem, but could
not mount an attack against it. 2When the
house of David heard that Aram had allied
itself with Ephraim, the heart of Ahaz*b* and
the heart of his people shook as the trees of
the forest shake before the wind.

3 Then the LORD said to Isaiah, Go out
to meet Ahaz, you and your son Shear-jashub,*c* at the end of the conduit of the upper
pool on the highway to the Fuller's Field,
4and say to him, Take heed, be quiet, do not
fear, and do not let your heart be faint because of these two smoldering stumps of
firebrands, because of the fierce anger of Rezin and Aram and the son of Remaliah. 5Be-
cause Aram—with Ephraim and the son of
Remaliah—has plotted evil against you,
saying, 6Let us go up against Judah and cut
off Jerusalem*d* and conquer it for ourselves
and make the son of Tabeel king in it; 7there-
fore thus says the Lord GOD:
It shall not stand,
    and it shall not come to pass.
8 For the head of Aram is Damascus,
    and the head of Damascus is Rezin.
(Within sixty-five years Ephraim will be
shattered, no longer a people.)
9 The head of Ephraim is Samaria,
    and the head of Samaria is the son of
          Remaliah.
If you do not stand firm in faith,
    you shall not stand at all.

**7.1–8.4: The message of the names of three chil-
dren. 7.1–3:** For the political context, see 2 Kings
16.5–9. The threat to depose Ahaz was an attempt to
force Judah into joining the anti-Assyrian coalition. The
king countered by seeking assistance from Assyria
(2 Kings 16.7–9), trying to secure his throne and gain
an advantage over Ephraim in a territorial quarrel (see
2 Kings 14.25). Ahaz's overture to Assyria was disas-

a Meaning of Heb uncertain   *b* Heb *his heart*
c That is *A remnant shall return*
d Heb *cut it off*

trous. Isaiah conveys a message through children's names: Shear-jashub, Immanuel, and Maher-Shalal-hashbaz. The first is already the prophet's infant son, whereas the third had not even been conceived when his name was given and inscribed on a tablet (8.1–2). At the child's birth, witnesses would unveil the prescribed name (8.2). The name of the second child, Immanuel (7.14), may indicate a royal figure, an heir to the throne who would assure the future of the dynasty* to the troubled Ahaz. It is more probable, however, that, like the other two, the child is the prophet's and the unnamed young woman of 7.14 is the prophet's wife. **3:** *Shear-jashub,* "a remnant returns," implies the defeat of the armies threatening Jerusalem and their return home in greatly reduced numbers. It could later be interpreted in other ways (see 10.20–23). **6:** *The son of Tabeel* is not otherwise identified, and it is not even clear that he was from a Judahite family. The prophet's emphatic form of address to the king (v. 13) implies that the future of the royal dynasty was threatened. **8:** The note on the dissolution of *Ephraim* (Israel) reflects an editor's awareness that the veiled threat was fulfilled.

10 Again the LORD spoke to Ahaz, saying, ¹¹Ask a sign of the LORD your God; let it be deep as Sheol or high as heaven. ¹²But Ahaz said, I will not ask, and I will not put the LORD to the test. ¹³Then Isaiah*^a* said: "Hear then, O house of David! Is it too little for you to weary mortals, that you weary my God also? ¹⁴Therefore the Lord himself will give you a sign. Look, the young woman*^b* is with child and shall bear a son, and shall name him Immanuel.*^c* ¹⁵He shall eat curds and honey by the time he knows how to refuse the evil and choose the good. ¹⁶For before the child knows how to refuse the evil and choose the good, the land before whose two kings you are in dread will be deserted. ¹⁷The LORD will bring on you and on your people and on your ancestral house such days as have not come since the day that Ephraim departed from Judah—the king of Assyria."

7.10–17. The king rejects a sign, showing that he had not abandoned his plan to seek help from Assyria. **11:** The *sign* indicated that the prophetic word would, in due course, be fulfilled. *Sheol** was the place to which the spirits of the dead descended and is here used for

poetic emphasis. **14:** In spite of the traditional translation of *the young woman* as "virgin," the Hebrew noun implies no more than a woman of marriageable age. The prophet's right to confer the child's name indicates that she was probably his wife. In the context of concern about the future of the Davidic line, however, the child may be a royal heir, possibly Hezekiah, who succeeded Ahaz on the throne of Judah. The later "messianic*" interpretation of prophecies relating to the Davidic kingship belongs to the period after this royal dynasty ceased to rule in Jerusalem (9.2–7; 11.1–5; 55.3–5). *Immanuel,* "God with us," is an exclamation used in worship to affirm God's presence and protection (see Ps 46.11). Ahaz had no need to seek help from Assyria when God was his true helper. **15–17:** Eating *curds and honey* and refusing *the evil* and choosing *the good* came at the time (1–2 years of age) when the child would begin to take solid food and respond to parental discipline. Within less than two years Judah's present enemies would have been forced to flee home. *The day that Ephraim departed* refers to the time when the united kingdom of Israel, over which David and Solomon had reigned, split over allegiance to the Davidic dynasty* (see 1 Kings 12.1–19).

18 On that day the LORD will whistle for the fly that is at the sources of the streams of Egypt, and for the bee that is in the land of Assyria. ¹⁹And they will all come and settle in the steep ravines, and in the clefts of the rocks, and on all the thornbushes, and on all the pastures.

20 On that day the Lord will shave with a razor hired beyond the River—with the king of Assyria—the head and the hair of the feet, and it will take off the beard as well.

21 On that day one will keep alive a young cow and two sheep, ²²and will eat curds because of the abundance of milk that they give; for everyone that is left in the land shall eat curds and honey.

23 On that day every place where there used to be a thousand vines, worth a thousand shekels of silver, will become briers and thorns. ²⁴With bow and arrows one will go there, for all the land will be briers and

a Heb *he*   *b* Gk *the virgin*
c That is *God is with us*

thorns; 25and as for all the hills that used to be hoed with a hoe, you will not go there for fear of briers and thorns; but they will become a place where cattle are let loose and where sheep tread.

7.18–25: Further interpretations★ of the prophet's words. A series of short statements spells out the message of the prophet. **18–19:** The *fly* and the *bee* symbolize the threat from Egypt and Assyria: Israel and Judah were sandwiched between two major world powers. **20:** The hired *razor* is Assyria, which would ravage and destroy Israel's entire land. **21–22:** A further interpretation is given of the sign in v. 15. **23–25:** Three fresh interpretations are provided of the *briers and thorns* from the parable★ of the vineyard in 5.1–7. **24:** The *briers and thorns* are soldiers with *bows and arrows.*

8 Then the LORD said to me, Take a large tablet and write on it in common characters, "Belonging to Maher-shalal-hash-baz,"*a* 2and have it attested*b* for me by reliable witnesses, the priest Uriah and Zechariah son of Jeberechiah. 3And I went to the prophetess, and she conceived and bore a son. Then the LORD said to me, Name him Maher-shalal-hash-baz; 4for before the child knows how to call "My father" or "My mother," the wealth of Damascus and the spoil of Samaria will be carried away by the king of Assyria.

8.1–4: The sign-name of Maher-shalal-hash-baz. This is the third message attached to the name of a child, which had not yet been conceived when the name was given. The name, "The spoil speeds, the prey hastens," points to the defeat of the forces threatening Judah. The witnesses would confirm that the name was given before the child had been conceived.

5 The LORD spoke to me again: 6Because this people has refused the waters of Shiloah that flow gently, and melt in fear before*c* Rezin and the son of Remaliah; 7therefore, the Lord is bringing up against it the mighty flood waters of the River, the king of Assyria and all his glory; it will rise above all its channels and overflow all its banks; 8it will sweep on into Judah as a flood, and, pouring over, it will reach up to the neck; and its outspread wings will fill the breadth of your land, O Immanuel.

9 Band together, you peoples, and be dismayed;
    listen, all you far countries;
gird yourselves and be dismayed;
    gird yourselves and be dismayed!
10 Take counsel together, but it shall be
    brought to naught;
    speak a word, but it will not stand,
    for God is with us.*d*

11 For the LORD spoke thus to me while his hand was strong upon me, and warned me not to walk in the way of this people, saying: 12Do not call conspiracy all that this people calls conspiracy, and do not fear what it fears, or be in dread. 13But the LORD of hosts, him you shall regard as holy; let him be your fear, and let him be your dread. 14He will become a sanctuary, a stone one strikes against; for both houses of Israel he will become a rock one stumbles over—a trap and a snare for the inhabitants of Jerusalem. 15And many among them shall stumble; they shall fall and be broken; they shall be snared and taken.

16 Bind up the testimony, seal the teaching among my disciples. 17I will wait for the LORD, who is hiding his face from the house of Jacob, and I will hope in him. 18See, I and the children whom the LORD has given me are signs and portents in Israel from the LORD of hosts, who dwells on Mount Zion. 19Now if people say to you, "Consult the ghosts and the familiar spirits that chirp and mutter; should not a people consult their gods, the dead on behalf of the living, 20for teaching and for instruction?" surely, those who speak like this will have no dawn! 21They will pass through the land,*e* greatly distressed and hungry; when they are hungry, they will be enraged and will curse*f* their king and their gods. They will turn their faces upward, 22or they will look to the earth, but will see only distress and darkness,

---

a That is *The spoil speeds, the prey hastens* *b* Q Ms Gk Syr: MT *and I caused to be attested* *c* Cn: Meaning of Heb uncertain *d* Heb *immanu el* *e* Heb *it* *f* Or *curse by*

the gloom of anguish; and they will be thrust into thick darkness.*

8.5–22: The rejection of the prophet's message. 5–8: The message of the names is refused. Isaiah becomes the bearer of a new message: Ahaz will indeed seek military help from Assyria (see 2 Kings 16.7–9), but it would open the floodgates to a torrent that would overwhelm the entire land, immersing Judah as well as the sister kingdom in the north. **9–10:** The prophet proclaims: God will establish justice upon earth (the book's overall message; compare 14.24–27; 17.12–14; and see Introduction to chs. 13–27). **11–22:** The prophet retires from public activity until the truth of his warning is established. Verse 16 refers to the *testimony* of the name inscribed on the tablet in 8.1, so the *disciples* are the witnesses of 8.2. The prophet's written "memoir" would originally have ended at v. 18, reemphasizing the message of his children's names, the message the king had rejected. **12–15:** Isaiah, isolated and spurned, is accused of *conspiracy*, although it was the king who had committed conspiracy against God. **19–22:** Short prophecies warn of the folly of rejecting the true word of God. When, in despair, the people turn to seek assurance and knowledge of the future from the forbidden practice of consulting sorcerers and the spirits of the dead, they will simply plunge themselves into deeper darkness.

9 *ᵇ*But there will be no gloom for those who were in anguish. In the former time he brought into contempt the land of Zebulun and the land of Naphtali, but in the latter time he will make glorious the way of the sea, the land beyond the Jordan, Galilee of the nations.
2 *ᶜ*The people who walked in darkness
        have seen a great light;
    those who lived in a land of deep
            darkness—
        on them light has shined.
3 You have multiplied the nation,
        you have increased its joy;
    they rejoice before you
        as with joy at the harvest,
        as people exult when dividing
            plunder.
4 For the yoke of their burden,
        and the bar across their shoulders,
        the rod of their oppressor,

you have broken as on the day of
        Midian.
5 For all the boots of the tramping
            warriors
        and all the garments rolled in blood
        shall be burned as fuel for the fire.
6 For a child has been born for us,
        a son given to us;
    authority rests upon his shoulders;
        and he is named
    Wonderful Counselor, Mighty God,
        Everlasting Father, Prince of
            Peace.
7 His authority shall grow continually,
        and there shall be endless peace
    for the throne of David and his
            kingdom.
    He will establish and uphold it
    with justice and with righteousness
        from this time onward and
            forevermore.
The zeal of the LORD of hosts will do
        this.

9.1–7: Light in the darkness. A brief editorial note looks ahead to the time when the darkness of Assyrian destruction will end and a new era of peace and hope will dawn. The difficult text anticipates the celebrated prophecy of the new king that follows. **2–7: The coming of a new king.** A coronation hymn celebrates the coming of a new king who would restore the honor, fame, and authority of David's royal house (see Ps 2 for a similar royal coronation hymn). The new ruler would reverse the harm wrought by Ahaz. The new king is probably Hezekiah, Ahaz's successor (2 Kings 16.20). His accession* year is uncertain (perhaps 725 or 715 BCE). His ascent to the throne marked the beginning of new royal policy, which was expected to bring a change in the nation's fortunes. Since Hezekiah was not successful in ending Assyria's rule (Isa 36–39), it may be Josiah (639–609 BCE) whose reforming reign is foretold. Under Josiah, Assyrian control over Judah finally ended. The arrival of the new king is described as a royal birth, which involves divine assurance for the royal dynasty. The "birth" probably refers to the king's coronation, a moment of spiritual rebirth (Ps 2.7).

a Meaning of Heb uncertain   *b* Ch 8.23 in Heb
c Ch 9.1 in Heb

8 The Lord sent a word against Jacob,
    and it fell on Israel;
9 and all the people knew it—
    Ephraim and the inhabitants of
      Samaria—
    but in pride and arrogance of heart
      they said:
10 "The bricks have fallen,
    but we will build with dressed stones;
    the sycamores have been cut down,
    but we will put cedars in their place."
11 So the LORD raised adversaries[a] against
      them,
    and stirred up their enemies,
12 the Arameans on the east and the
      Philistines on the west,
    and they devoured Israel with open
      mouth.
  For all this his anger has not turned
      away,
    his hand is stretched out still.

13 The people did not turn to him who
      struck them,
    or seek the LORD of hosts.
14 So the LORD cut off from Israel head
      and tail,
    palm branch and reed in one day—
15 elders and dignitaries are the head,
    and prophets who teach lies are the
      tail;
16 for those who led this people led them
      astray,
    and those who were led by them were
      left in confusion.
17 That is why the Lord did not have pity
      on[b] their young people,
    or compassion on their orphans and
      widows;
  for everyone was godless and an
      evildoer,
    and every mouth spoke folly.
  For all this his anger has not turned
      away,
    his hand is stretched out still.

18 For wickedness burned like a fire,
    consuming briers and thorns;
  it kindled the thickets of the forest,
    and they swirled upward in a column
      of smoke.

19 Through the wrath of the LORD of hosts
    the land was burned,
  and the people became like fuel for the
      fire;
    no one spared another.
20 They gorged on the right, but still were
      hungry,
    and they devoured on the left, but
      were not satisfied;
  they devoured the flesh of their own
      kindred;[c]
21 Manasseh devoured Ephraim, and
    Ephraim Manasseh,
    and together they were against Judah.
  For all this his anger has not turned
      away,
    his hand is stretched out still.

10 Ah, you who make iniquitous
    decrees,
    who write oppressive statutes,
2 to turn aside the needy from justice
    and to rob the poor of my people of
      their right,
  that widows may be your spoil,
    and that you may make the orphans
      your prey!
3 What will you do on the day of
      punishment,
    in the calamity that will come from
      far away?
  To whom will you flee for help,
    and where will you leave your
      wealth,
4 so as not to crouch among the
      prisoners
    or fall among the slain?
  For all this his anger has not turned
      away,
    his hand is stretched out still.

9.8–10.4: No respite for the land of Ephraim.
9.8–21: The Assyrian intervention proved ruinous.
Judah fared less badly than Ephraim; 2 Kings 17.5–23
tells how Ephraim was destroyed (see also Isa 7.8).
The prophet warns against pride and complacency
(vv. 9–10) in trusting that ruin would be overcome.
During the following half-century, persistent external

a Cn: Heb *the adversaries of Rezin*   b Q Ms: MT
rejoice over   c Or *arm*

interference and internal conflicts ruined the region of Ephraim-Samaria. Not till the reign of Josiah more than a century later were serious attempts made to reunite parts of this land with Judah. **10.1–4:** Verses 1–3 belong to the condemnation of the leaders of Jerusalem in 5.8–24 (note also the use of the refrain from 9.8–21 in 5.25), while 10.4 clearly belongs to the warning against Ephraim (9.8–21).

5 Ah, Assyria, the rod of my anger—
　　the club in their hands is my fury!
6 Against a godless nation I send him,
　　and against the people of my wrath I
　　　　command him,
　　to take spoil and seize plunder,
　　　　and to tread them down like the mire
　　　　　　of the streets.
7 But this is not what he intends,
　　nor does he have this in mind;
　　but it is in his heart to destroy,
　　　　and to cut off nations not a few.
8 For he says:
　　"Are not my commanders all kings?
9 Is not Calno like Carchemish?
　　Is not Hamath like Arpad?
　　Is not Samaria like Damascus?
10 As my hand has reached to the
　　　　kingdoms of the idols
　　whose images were greater than those
　　　　of Jerusalem and Samaria,
11 shall I not do to Jerusalem and
　　　　her idols
　　what I have done to Samaria and her
　　　　images?"

12 When the Lord has finished all his work on Mount Zion and on Jerusalem, he[a] will punish the arrogant boasting of the king of Assyria and his haughty pride. 13 For he says:
　　"By the strength of my hand I have
　　　　done it,
　　and by my wisdom, for I have
　　　　understanding;
　　I have removed the boundaries of
　　　　peoples,
　　and have plundered their treasures;
　　like a bull I have brought down those
　　　　who sat on thrones.
14 My hand has found, like a nest,
　　the wealth of the peoples;

and as one gathers eggs that have been
　　　　forsaken,
　　so I have gathered all the earth;
　　and there was none that moved a wing,
　　　　or opened its mouth, or chirped."

15 Shall the ax vaunt itself over the one
　　　　who wields it,
　　or the saw magnify itself against the
　　　　one who handles it?
　　As if a rod should raise the one who lifts
　　　　it up,
　　or as if a staff should lift the one who
　　　　is not wood!
16 Therefore the Sovereign, the LORD of
　　　　hosts,
　　will send wasting sickness among his
　　　　stout warriors,
　　and under his glory a burning will be
　　　　kindled,
　　like the burning of fire.
17 The light of Israel will become a fire,
　　and his Holy One a flame;
　　and it will burn and devour
　　　　his thorns and briers in one day.
18 The glory of his forest and his fruitful
　　　　land
　　　　the LORD will destroy, both soul and
　　　　　　body,
　　and it will be as when an invalid
　　　　wastes away.
19 The remnant of the trees of his forest
　　　　will be so few
　　　　that a child can write them down.

10.5–34: Assyria will not escape the judgment of God. 5–19: Assyria was the agent of God, but its ministers were arrogant and blasphemous (see 36.13–20). When God judged that the time was ripe (v. 2) Assyria would suffer a severe punishment from God (vv. 15–19), set out in a series of word-pictures related to other sayings. **17–19:** The tree imagery is related to the language of "briers and thorns" in 5.6 (see 7.23–25; 9.18; possibly also relates to the wooden rod of 9.4 and 10.5).

20 On that day the remnant of Israel and the survivors of the house of Jacob will no more lean on the one who struck them, but

a Heb I

will lean on the LORD, the Holy One of Israel, in truth. ²¹A remnant will return, the remnant of Jacob, to the mighty God. ²²For though your people Israel were like the sand of the sea, only a remnant of them will return. Destruction is decreed, overflowing with righteousness. ²³For the Lord GOD of hosts will make a full end, as decreed, in all the earth.^a

24 Therefore thus says the Lord GOD of hosts: O my people, who live in Zion, do not be afraid of the Assyrians when they beat you with a rod and lift up their staff against you as the Egyptians did. ²⁵For in a very little while my indignation will come to an end, and my anger will be directed to their destruction. ²⁶The LORD of hosts will wield a whip against them, as when he struck Midian at the rock of Oreb; his staff will be over the sea, and he will lift it as he did in Egypt. ²⁷On that day his burden will be removed from your shoulder, and his yoke will be destroyed from your neck.

He has gone up from Rimmon,^b
28   he has come to Aiath;
   he has passed through Migron,
      at Michmash he stores his baggage;
29   they have crossed over the pass,
      at Geba they lodge for the night;
   Ramah trembles,
      Gibeah of Saul has fled.
30   Cry aloud, O daughter Gallim!
   Listen, O Laishah!
   Answer her, O Anathoth!
31   Madmenah is in flight,
      the inhabitants of Gebim flee
         for safety.
32   This very day he will halt at Nob,
   he will shake his fist
      at the mount of daughter Zion,
      the hill of Jerusalem.

33   Look, the Sovereign, the LORD of
         hosts,
      will lop the boughs with terrifying
         power;
   the tallest trees will be cut down,
      and the lofty will be brought low.
34   He will hack down the thickets of the
         forest with an ax,

and Lebanon with its majestic trees^c
   will fall.

10.20–34. 20–27a: "Shear-jashub" of 7.3, "a remnant returns," could be understood in more than one way, as the three interpretations of vv. 21–23 show. There would be a future nation, but shaped by suffering and loss. Only some of the nation would survive. Similarly, the interpretations in vv. 24–27a of "the rod of their oppressor" (9.4) show that God would free Judah from foreign domination. **27b–32:** This short passage probably refers to the march on Jerusalem by Sennacherib in 701 BCE, the background for Isaiah's later prophecies (see chs. 28–30 and 36–37). It is out of chronological sequence with the events in chs. 7–9 (the reign of King Ahaz). However, its abrupt ending with the oppressor threatening, but not attacking, Jerusalem (v. 32) fits the Assyrian punitive campaign into Judah during the reign of Hezekiah, whose accession* is foretold in 9.2–7. **33–34:** The outcome of Sennacherib's campaign is presented as the cutting down of the *forest* foretold in vv. 18–19. The failure to complete the punitive attack upon Jerusalem in 701 was a judgment of God upon Assyria's blasphemous boasts. The events in chs. 36–37 are understood to fulfill the punishment on Assyria declared in 10.15–19.

11 A shoot shall come out from the
      stump of Jesse,
   and a branch shall grow out of his
      roots.
2 The spirit of the LORD shall rest
      on him,
   the spirit of wisdom and
      understanding,
   the spirit of counsel and might,
   the spirit of knowledge and the fear
      of the LORD.
3 His delight shall be in the fear of the
   LORD.

He shall not judge by what his eyes see,
   or decide by what his ears hear;
4 but with righteousness he shall judge
      the poor,
   and decide with equity for the meek
      of the earth;

---

a Or land   b Cn: Heb and his yoke from your neck,
and a yoke will be destroyed because of fatness
c Cn Compare Gk Vg: Heb with a majestic one

he shall strike the earth with the rod of
  his mouth,
  and with the breath of his lips he
    shall kill the wicked.
5 Righteousness shall be the belt around
    his waist,
  and faithfulness the belt around his
    loins.

6 The wolf shall live with the lamb,
  the leopard shall lie down with the
    kid,
  the calf and the lion and the fatling
    together,
  and a little child shall lead them.
7 The cow and the bear shall graze,
  their young shall lie down together;
  and the lion shall eat straw like
    the ox.
8 The nursing child shall play over the
    hole of the asp,
  and the weaned child shall put its
    hand on the adder's den.
9 They will not hurt or destroy
  on all my holy mountain;
  for the earth will be full of the
    knowledge of the LORD
  as the waters cover the sea.

10 On that day the root of Jesse shall
stand as a signal to the peoples; the nations
shall inquire of him, and his dwelling shall
be glorious.
11 On that day the Lord will extend his
hand yet a second time to recover the remnant that is left of his people, from Assyria,
from Egypt, from Pathros, from Ethiopia,*a*
from Elam, from Shinar, from Hamath, and
from the coastlands of the sea.
12 He will raise a signal for the nations,
  and will assemble the outcasts of
    Israel,
  and gather the dispersed of Judah
    from the four corners of the earth.
13 The jealousy of Ephraim shall depart,
  the hostility of Judah shall be cut off;
  Ephraim shall not be jealous of Judah,
  and Judah shall not be hostile
    towards Ephraim.
14 But they shall swoop down on the backs
  of the Philistines in the west,

together they shall plunder the people
    of the east.
  They shall put forth their hand against
    Edom and Moab,
  and the Ammonites shall obey them.
15 And the LORD will utterly destroy
  the tongue of the sea of Egypt;
  and will wave his hand over the River
    with his scorching wind;
  and will split it into seven channels,
  and make a way to cross on foot;
16 so there shall be a highway from
    Assyria
  for the remnant that is left of
    his people,
  as there was for Israel
  when they came up from the land of
    Egypt.

11.1–16: The renewal of God's promise. 1–5: The
shoot from *the stump of Jesse* refers to the situation
after the Babylonians had removed the last of the Davidic rulers, Zedekiah (2 Kings 25.1–7). His predecessor and nephew, Jehoiachin, had been taken and held
prisoner in Babylon (2 Kings 24.10–12), and this
prophecy reflects the hope that either he, or one of his
descendants, would return to rule (see 55.1–5; 1 Chr
3.16–24). This hope was not fulfilled, and the promises
of Davidic kingship became a messianic* hope. **6–9:**
An addition that conveys a wider message than one of
government and justice: a time of world peace extending throughout the natural order, witnessing the
end of violence, not simply between nations (see Isa
2.4) but between wild and domestic animals. The violence and disorder that had confounded God's purpose since the beginning would be transformed by the
fashioning of a new heaven and a new earth (66.2–3).
As a prominent, and unique, hope in Isaiah, the message is repeated in 65.25. **10–16:** Chapters 5–12 form
a connected series of prophecies, from the devastation
foretold in 6.11–13 until the return of survivors to re-
populate it and to rebuild Jerusalem. This promise of
return forms a significant feature of the book's overall
message. Detailed promises of this return begin in chs.
40–55. Prophecies fulfilling that hope are included in
chs. 56–66. As God's judgment had been heralded by
a signal to a "nation far away" (5.26), so the ending
of the period of judgment and the dawning of the age

a Or Nubia; Heb Cush

of peace would begin with a further *signal* to all *nations* (11.10–12).

12
You will say in that day:
I will give thanks to you, O LORD,
for though you were angry with me,
your anger turned away,
and you comforted me.

2 Surely God is my salvation;
I will trust, and will not be afraid,
for the LORD GOD *a* is my strength and
my might;
he has become my salvation.

3 With joy you will draw water from the wells of salvation. 4And you will say in that day:

Give thanks to the LORD,
call on his name;
make known his deeds among the
nations;
proclaim that his name is exalted.

5 Sing praises to the LORD, for he has
done gloriously;
let this be known *b* in all the
earth.
6 Shout aloud and sing for joy, O royal *c*
Zion,
for great in your midst is the Holy
One of Israel.

12.1–6: A psalm of thanksgiving. Isaiah has been constructed to form a series of "books within books." A psalm of thanksgiving for the salvation of God which will surely come to Jerusalem concludes the section that began in 5.1. These shorter collections display a broad editorial structure where hope and promise follow threats and warnings. Even the punitive fires of judgment are placed within this larger context of the saving purpose of God.

a Heb *for Yah, the* LORD   *b* Or *this is made known*
c Or *O inhabitant of*

Isaiah 13–27

WARNINGS AND LAMENTS ADDRESSED TO FOREIGN NATIONS AND PEOPLES

This collection contains pronouncements that are predominantly threats to the nations caught up in the world events that had affected Israel and Judah. In chs. 24–27 there is a radical and reassuring promise that these times of trial will end with a new era of God's justice. The prophecies against the nations begin in 13.1–14.23 with oracles★ against Babylon. After returning to the renewed announcement of Assyria's inevitable downfall in 14.24–27, they deal in turn with Philistia, Moab, Syria, Egypt, and Arabia. Prophecies relating to Jerusalem (the "valley of vision") in ch. 22 are followed by a lament★ for Tyre (Phoenicia) in ch. 23. Chapters 24–27 conclude in 27.12–13 with a promise like that in 11.10–16: The survivors will return to their homeland.

The historical background begins with the first instances of Isaiah's prophesying (see comment on 6.1), when the threat from Assyria marked the first step toward the breakup and dismemberment of Israel and Judah. It extends until sometime after the fall of Babylon to a combined Medo-Persian army in 538 BCE. The prophecies of chs. 24–27 probably derive from this late period, when the further overthrow of this Medo-Persian power was awaited, with the expectation that it would begin the direct rule of God on earth. There is little agreement about the origins of the oracles in chs. 13–23. Some of them are dated (see 14.28; 20.1), but the present shape of this part of the book presents an overview of God's purpose for all nations from the perspective of the years of Assyrian and Babylonian rule over Judah. The context thus extends over more than two centuries.

READING GUIDE

The prophecies concerning foreign cities and nations present a variety of feelings and attitudes. In the case of Babylon there is an understandable sense of exultation that a terrifying oppressor has at last received just punishment. In the case of Moab, one confronts the grievous pain and suffering that the people will endure, while in the case of Tyre there is the theme that God humbles human pride and achievement. The prophecies relating to Egypt are of special interest, partly because Egyptian promises of military aid to Judah had repeatedly failed to materialize and had, thereby, proved disastrous for God's people. Yet there is also a profound spiritual message of hope in the belief that Egypt, too, would eventually share in the universal knowledge and blessing of the one LORD (19.18–25).

13 The oracle concerning Babylon that Isaiah son of Amoz saw.

2 On a bare hill raise a signal,
　　cry aloud to them;
　wave the hand for them to enter
　　the gates of the nobles.
3 I myself have commanded my
　　consecrated ones,
　have summoned my warriors, my
　　proudly exulting ones,
　　to execute my anger.

4 Listen, a tumult on the mountains
　　as of a great multitude!
　Listen, an uproar of kingdoms,
　　of nations gathering together!
　The LORD of hosts is mustering
　　an army for battle.

5 They come from a distant land,
　　from the end of the heavens,
　　the LORD and the weapons of his
　　　indignation,
　　to destroy the whole earth.

6 Wail, for the day of the LORD is near;
　　it will come like destruction from the
　　　Almighty![a]
7 Therefore all hands will be feeble,
　　and every human heart will melt,
8 　and they will be dismayed.
　Pangs and agony will seize them;
　　they will be in anguish like a woman
　　　in labor.
　They will look aghast at one another;
　　their faces will be aflame.

a Traditional rendering of Heb *Shaddai*

9 See, the day of the LORD comes,
    cruel, with wrath and fierce anger,
  to make the earth a desolation,
    and to destroy its sinners from it.
10 For the stars of the heavens and their
      constellations
    will not give their light;
  the sun will be dark at its rising,
    and the moon will not shed its light.
11 I will punish the world for its evil,
    and the wicked for their iniquity;
  I will put an end to the pride of
      the arrogant,
    and lay low the insolence of
      tyrants.
12 I will make mortals more rare than fine
      gold,
    and humans than the gold of Ophir.
13 Therefore I will make the heavens
      tremble,
    and the earth will be shaken out of its
      place,
  at the wrath of the LORD of hosts
    in the day of his fierce anger.
14 Like a hunted gazelle,
    or like sheep with no one to gather
      them,
  all will turn to their own people,
    and all will flee to their own lands.
15 Whoever is found will be thrust
      through,
    and whoever is caught will fall by the
      sword.
16 Their infants will be dashed to pieces
      before their eyes;
    their houses will be plundered,
      and their wives ravished.
17 See, I am stirring up the Medes against
      them,
    who have no regard for silver
      and do not delight in gold.
18 Their bows will slaughter the young
      men;
    they will have no mercy on the fruit
      of the womb;
    their eyes will not pity children.
19 And Babylon, the glory of kingdoms,
    the splendor and pride of the
      Chaldeans,
  will be like Sodom and Gomorrah
    when God overthrew them.

20 It will never be inhabited
    or lived in for all generations;
  Arabs will not pitch their tents there,
    shepherds will not make their flocks
      lie down there.
21 But wild animals will lie down there,
    and its houses will be full of howling
      creatures;
  there ostriches will live,
    and there goat-demons will dance.
22 Hyenas will cry in its towers,
    and jackals in the pleasant palaces;
  its time is close at hand,
    and its days will not be prolonged.

13.1–22: The overthrow of Babylon. 1–22: It is a surprise that *Babylon,* rather than Assyria, is the great oppressing power to be punished for its excesses and cruelties. The reason lies in the importance of Babylon for the structure of the book: Chs. 40–55 reflect the period of Babylonian imperial control over the nations dealt with in chs. 13–23. Reference to the attacking *Medes* (v. 17) points to this fierce prophecy as a forewarning of the defeat of Babylon in 538 BCE, later anticipated so eagerly in chs. 46–47. Judah's bitter sufferings at the hands of Babylon explain the vengeful spirit in vv. 14–16 and the longing that such a great kingdom should become a perpetual ruin (vv. 20–22).

14 But the LORD will have compassion on Jacob and will again choose Israel, and will set them in their own land; and aliens will join them and attach themselves to the house of Jacob. 2And the nations will take them and bring them to their place, and the house of Israel will possess the nations*a* as male and female slaves in the LORD's land; they will take captive those who were their captors, and rule over those who oppressed them.

3 When the LORD has given you rest from your pain and turmoil and the hard service with which you were made to serve, 4you will take up this taunt against the king of Babylon:

  How the oppressor has ceased!
  How his insolence*b* has ceased!

a Heb *them*   *b* Q Ms Compare Gk Syr Vg: Meaning of
MT uncertain

5 The LORD has broken the staff of the
wicked,
the scepter of rulers,
6 that struck down the peoples in wrath
with unceasing blows,
that ruled the nations in anger
with unrelenting persecution.
7 The whole earth is at rest and quiet;
they break forth into singing.
8 The cypresses exult over you,
the cedars of Lebanon, saying,
"Since you were laid low,
no one comes to cut us down."
9 Sheol beneath is stirred up
to meet you when you come;
it rouses the shades to greet you,
all who were leaders of the earth;
it raises from their thrones
all who were kings of the nations.
10 All of them will speak
and say to you:
"You too have become as weak as we!
You have become like us!"
11 Your pomp is brought down to Sheol,
and the sound of your harps;
maggots are the bed beneath you,
and worms are your covering.

12 How you are fallen from heaven,
O Day Star, son of Dawn!
How you are cut down to the ground,
you who laid the nations low!
13 You said in your heart,
"I will ascend to heaven;
I will raise my throne
above the stars of God;
I will sit on the mount of assembly
on the heights of Zaphon;*a*
14 I will ascend to the tops of the clouds,
I will make myself like the Most High."
15 But you are brought down to Sheol,
to the depths of the Pit.
16 Those who see you will stare at you,
and ponder over you:
"Is this the man who made the earth
tremble,
who shook kingdoms,
17 who made the world like a desert
and overthrew its cities,
who would not let his prisoners go
home?"

18 All the kings of the nations lie in glory,
each in his own tomb;
19 but you are cast out, away from your
grave,
like loathsome carrion,*b*
clothed with the dead, those pierced by
the sword,
who go down to the stones of the Pit,
like a corpse trampled underfoot.
20 You will not be joined with them
in burial,
because you have destroyed your land,
you have killed your people.

May the descendants of evildoers
nevermore be named!
21 Prepare slaughter for his sons
because of the guilt of their father.*c*
Let them never rise to possess the earth
or cover the face of the world with
cities.

**14.1–23: A mocking lament☆ for the death of the
king of Babylon. 1–2:** The Babylonian threat occupies
most of chs. 40–55, so this great world power takes
on a symbolic role as the supreme example of oppression. This editorial note provides a summary of the
message of hope (chs. 56–66; see also 11.12–16).
3–11: A brilliant, mocking lament for the death of the
king of Babylon ironically contrasts the king's power in
life and powerlessness in death and celebrates the
passing of Babylon as a world power. No ruler is
named, and, apart from the introductory heading in
v. 4, direct identification with Babylon is lacking. The
original subject may be some earlier ruler's death, possibly the Assyrian Shalmaneser V (whose death in 705
occurred during Isaiah's ministry and had major re-
percussions for Judah's political stance). But this passage celebrates the downfall of tyranny rather than the
death of a specific individual. *Sheol*☆ (vv. 11, 15) is the
mysterious underworld to which spirits descended after death. The spirits of other dead persons rise up in
amazement that a figure once so proud and supreme
could be brought so low (vv. 16–20). **12–15:** The *Day
Star, son of Dawn* is the Morning Star (Venus). **16–21:**
In extensive royal households other sons were usually
a threat to a crown prince (see 37.38).

---

a Or *assembly in the far north* *b* Cn Compare Gk:
Heb *like a loathed branch* *c* Syr Compare Gk: Heb
fathers

22 I will rise up against them, says the LORD of hosts, and will cut off from Babylon name and remnant, offspring and posterity, says the LORD. 23And I will make it a possession of the hedgehog, and pools of water, and I will sweep it with the broom of destruction, says the LORD of hosts.

24 The LORD of hosts has sworn:
    As I have designed,
        so shall it be;
    and as I have planned,
        so shall it come to pass:
25 I will break the Assyrian in my land,
    and on my mountains trample him
        under foot;
    his yoke shall be removed from them,
        and his burden from their shoulders.
26 This is the plan that is planned
    concerning the whole earth;
    and this is the hand that is stretched
        out
        over all the nations.
27 For the LORD of hosts has planned,
    and who will annul it?
    His hand is stretched out,
        and who will turn it back?

14.24–27: Assyria will suffer divine judgment (see 10.5–34), and, although out of chronological sequence, this is a warning to all nations who threaten God's people (vv. 26–27; see 8.9–10; 17.12–14). In the literary and historical structure of Isa 13–27, the historical rise and fall of the great imperial powers was a preparation for God's rule.

28In the year that King Ahaz died this oracle came:

29 Do not rejoice, all you Philistines,
    that the rod that struck you
        is broken,
    for from the root of the snake will come
        forth an adder,
    and its fruit will be a flying
        fiery serpent.
30 The firstborn of the poor will graze,
    and the needy lie down in safety;
    but I will make your root die of
        famine,
    and your remnant I[a] will kill.

31 Wail, O gate; cry, O city;
    melt in fear, O Philistia, all of you!
For smoke comes out of the north,
    and there is no straggler in its ranks.

32 What will one answer the messengers of
        the nation?
"The LORD has founded Zion,
    and the needy among his people
        will find refuge in her."

15 An oracle concerning Moab.

Because Ar is laid waste in a night,
    Moab is undone;
because Kir is laid waste in a night,
    Moab is undone.
2 Dibon[b] has gone up to the temple,
    to the high places to weep;
over Nebo and over Medeba
    Moab wails.
On every head is baldness,
    every beard is shorn;
3 in the streets they bind on sackcloth;
    on the housetops and in the squares
    everyone wails and melts in tears.
4 Heshbon and Elealeh cry out,
    their voices are heard as far as
        Jahaz;
therefore the loins of Moab quiver;[c]
    his soul trembles.
5 My heart cries out for Moab;
    his fugitives flee to Zoar,
    to Eglath-shelishiyah.
For at the ascent of Luhith
    they go up weeping;
on the road to Horonaim
    they raise a cry of destruction;
6 the waters of Nimrim
    are a desolation;
the grass is withered, the new growth
        fails,
    the verdure is no more.
7 Therefore the abundance they
        have gained
    and what they have laid up

---

a Q Ms Vg: MT he   b Cn: Heb the house and Dibon
c Cn Compare Gk Syr: Heb the armed men of Moab cry
aloud

they carry away
    over the Wadi of the Willows.
8 For a cry has gone
    around the land of Moab;
the wailing reaches to Eglaim,
    the wailing reaches to Beer-elim.
9 For the waters of Dibon*ᵃ* are full
    of blood;
yet I will bring upon Dibon*ᵃ* even
      more—
a lion for those of Moab who escape,
    for the remnant of the land.

15.1–16.13: Prophecies concerning the downfall of Moab. 15.1–9: *Moab* was one of the smaller kingdoms neighboring Judah in the south and to the east of the River Jordan. It covered much of the territory now occupied by Jordan. Moab, though once a part of David's kingdom (2 Sam 8.2), had broken away and suffered Assyrian and Babylonian exploitation. In the course of one or another campaign, this fearful killing took place.

16 Send lambs
    to the ruler of the land,
from Sela, by way of the desert,
    to the mount of daughter Zion.
2 Like fluttering birds,
    like scattered nestlings,
so are the daughters of Moab
    at the fords of the Arnon.
3 "Give counsel,
    grant justice;
make your shade like night
    at the height of noon;
hide the outcasts,
    do not betray the fugitive;
4 let the outcasts of Moab
    settle among you;
be a refuge to them
    from the destroyer."

When the oppressor is no more,
    and destruction has ceased,
and marauders have vanished from the
    land,
5 then a throne shall be established in
    steadfast love
    in the tent of David,
and on it shall sit in faithfulness
a ruler who seeks justice
    and is swift to do what is right.

6 We have heard of the pride of Moab
    —how proud he is!—
of his arrogance, his pride, and his
      insolence;
    his boasts are false.
7 Therefore let Moab wail,
    let everyone wail for Moab.
Mourn, utterly stricken,
    for the raisin cakes of Kir-hareseth.

8 For the fields of Heshbon languish,
    and the vines of Sibmah,
whose clusters once made drunk
    the lords of the nations,
reached to Jazer
    and strayed to the desert;
their shoots once spread abroad
    and crossed over the sea.
9 Therefore I weep with the weeping of
    Jazer
    for the vines of Sibmah;
I drench you with my tears,
    O Heshbon and Elealeh;
for the shout over your fruit harvest
    and your grain harvest has ceased.
10 Joy and gladness are taken away
    from the fruitful field;
and in the vineyards no songs are sung,
    no shouts are raised;
no treader treads out wine in the presses;
    the vintage-shout is hushed.*ᵇ*
11 Therefore my heart throbs like a harp
    for Moab,
    and my very soul for Kir-heres.

12 When Moab presents himself, when he wearies himself upon the high place, when he comes to his sanctuary to pray, he will not prevail.

13 This was the word that the LORD spoke concerning Moab in the past. 14 But now the LORD says, In three years, like the years of a hired worker, the glory of Moab will be brought into contempt, in spite of all its great multitude; and those who survive will be very few and feeble.

16.1–13. 1–11: The appeal to Jerusalem to offer refuge to fugitives from this disaster is a sign of hope that

---

a Q Ms Vg Compare Syr: MT *Dimon*   *b* Gk: Heb *I have hushed*

Moab would renew allegiance to a Davidic king. This prophecy may allude to the reign of Josiah, a link with the promise of 32.1–8. Verses 6–11 rebuke *the pride of Moab.* **12–13:** Subsequent to the disaster of 586 BCE, the relations between Judah and Moab worsened.

17
An oracle concerning Damascus.

See, Damascus will cease to be a city,
　and will become a heap of ruins.
2 Her towns will be deserted forever;[a]
　they will be places for flocks,
　which will lie down, and no one will
　　make them afraid.
3 The fortress will disappear from
　　Ephraim,
　and the kingdom from Damascus;
and the remnant of Aram will be
　like the glory of the children of Israel,
　　　　　says the LORD of hosts.

4 On that day
　the glory of Jacob will be brought low,
　and the fat of his flesh will
　　grow lean.
5 And it shall be as when reapers gather
　　standing grain
　and their arms harvest the ears,
and as when one gleans the ears
　　of grain
　in the Valley of Rephaim.
6 Gleanings will be left in it,
　as when an olive tree is beaten—
two or three berries
　in the top of the highest bough,
four or five
　on the branches of a fruit tree,
　　　says the LORD God of Israel.

7 On that day people will regard their Maker, and their eyes will look to the Holy One of Israel; 8they will not have regard for the altars, the work of their hands, and they will not look to what their own fingers have made, either the sacred poles[b] or the altars of incense.

9 On that day their strong cities will be like the deserted places of the Hivites and the Amorites,[c] which they deserted because of the children of Israel, and there will be desolation.

10 For you have forgotten the God of your
　　salvation,
　and have not remembered the Rock
　　of your refuge;
therefore, though you plant pleasant
　　plants
　and set out slips of an alien god,
11 though you make them grow on the day
　　that you plant them,
　and make them blossom in the
　　morning that you sow;
yet the harvest will flee away
　in a day of grief and incurable pain.

---

17. 1–11: Prophecies concerning Israel and Damascus. 1–6: The background is that of the alliance of Syria (Damascus) and Ephraim (Israel) against Judah, which is also present in chs. 7–8. The message is that expressed in the name of Isaiah's son Shear-jashub ("a remnant returns," Isa 7.3). Instead of the defeated remnant of an army, this time the image is that of gleanings* after a harvest. **7–9:** The original threat gives only a general reason for the coming disaster (vv. 10–11); this added warning against trust in the power of idols intensifies the threat (see 2.8). **10–11:** Reference to the hyperbolic* growth of plants reflects a form of fertility ritual with religious (and probably also sexual) significance.

12 Ah, the thunder of many peoples,
　they thunder like the thundering of
　　the sea!
Ah, the roar of nations,
　they roar like the roaring of mighty
　　waters!
13 The nations roar like the roaring of
　　many waters,
　but he will rebuke them, and they will
　　flee far away,
chased like chaff on the mountains
　　before the wind
　and whirling dust before the storm.
14 At evening time, lo, terror!
　Before morning, they are no more.
This is the fate of those who
　　despoil us,
　and the lot of those who plunder us.

---

a Cn Compare Gk: Heb *the cities of Aroer are deserted*
b Heb *Asherim*　*c* Cn Compare Gk: Heb *places of the wood and the highest bough*

17.12–14: The defeat of a host of nations when they threaten God's people conforms to the warnings in 8.9–10 and 14.24–27.

18 Ah, land of whirring wings
  beyond the rivers of Ethiopia,[a]
2 sending ambassadors by the Nile
  in vessels of papyrus on the waters!
Go, you swift messengers,
  to a nation tall and smooth,
to a people feared near and far,
  a nation mighty and conquering,
  whose land the rivers divide.

3 All you inhabitants of the world,
  you who live on the earth,
when a signal is raised on the
    mountains, look!
  When a trumpet is blown, listen!
4 For thus the LORD said to me:
I will quietly look from my dwelling
  like clear heat in sunshine,
  like a cloud of dew in the heat
    of harvest.
5 For before the harvest, when the
    blossom is over
  and the flower becomes a ripening
    grape,
he will cut off the shoots with pruning
    hooks,
  and the spreading branches he will
    hew away.
6 They shall all be left
  to the birds of prey of the mountains
  and to the animals of the earth.
And the birds of prey will summer on
    them,
  and all the animals of the earth will
    winter on them.

7 At that time gifts will be brought to the LORD of hosts from[b] a people tall and smooth, from a people feared near and far, a nation mighty and conquering, whose land the rivers divide, to Mount Zion, the place of the name of the LORD of hosts.

18.1–7: A prophecy concerning Ethiopia. 1–6: This oracle* probably refers to the situation described in 2 Kings 17.4: Judah sent ambassadors to Ethiopia

(Cush) to negotiate an alliance against Assyria in 724 BCE. Isaiah warns that the LORD does not support such an alliance; it will fail. **7:** This anticipation of the hope in 45.14 shows how an observant editor has unified the message of the book.

19 An oracle concerning Egypt.

See, the LORD is riding on a swift cloud
    and comes to Egypt;
the idols of Egypt will tremble at his
    presence,
  and the heart of the Egyptians will
    melt within them.
2 I will stir up Egyptians against
    Egyptians,
  and they will fight, one against the
    other,
  neighbor against neighbor,
  city against city, kingdom against
    kingdom;
3 the spirit of the Egyptians within them
    will be emptied out,
  and I will confound their plans;
they will consult the idols and the
    spirits of the dead
  and the ghosts and the familiar spirits;
4 I will deliver the Egyptians
  into the hand of a hard master;
a fierce king will rule over them,
  says the Sovereign, the LORD of hosts.

5 The waters of the Nile will be dried up,
  and the river will be parched and dry;
6 its canals will become foul,
  and the branches of Egypt's Nile will
    diminish and dry up,
  reeds and rushes will rot away.
7 There will be bare places by the Nile,
  on the brink of the Nile;
and all that is sown by the Nile will
    dry up,
  be driven away, and be no more.
8 Those who fish will mourn;
  all who cast hooks in the Nile will
    lament,
  and those who spread nets on the
    water will languish.

a Or Nubia; Heb Cush   b Q Ms Gk Vg: MT of

9 The workers in flax will be in despair,
  and the carders and those at the loom
    will grow pale.
10 Its weavers will be dismayed,
  and all who work for wages will be
    grieved.

11 The princes of Zoan are utterly foolish;
  the wise counselors of Pharaoh give
    stupid counsel.
How can you say to Pharaoh,
  "I am one of the sages,
  a descendant of ancient kings"?
12 Where now are your sages?
  Let them tell you and make known
  what the LORD of hosts has planned
    against Egypt.
13 The princes of Zoan have become
    fools,
  and the princes of Memphis
    are deluded;
those who are the cornerstones of its
    tribes
  have led Egypt astray.
14 The LORD has poured into them[a]
  a spirit of confusion;
and they have made Egypt stagger in all
    its doings
  as a drunkard staggers around
    in vomit.
15 Neither head nor tail, palm branch or
    reed,
  will be able to do anything for
    Egypt.

16 On that day the Egyptians will be like women, and tremble with fear before the hand that the LORD of hosts raises against them. 17And the land of Judah will become a terror to the Egyptians; everyone to whom it is mentioned will fear because of the plan that the LORD of hosts is planning against them.
18 On that day there will be five cities in the land of Egypt that speak the language of Canaan and swear allegiance to the LORD of hosts. One of these will be called the City of the Sun.
19 On that day there will be an altar to the LORD in the center of the land of Egypt, and a pillar to the LORD at its border. 20It will be a sign and a witness to the LORD of hosts in the land of Egypt; when they cry to the LORD because of oppressors, he will send them a savior, and will defend and deliver them. 21The LORD will make himself known to the Egyptians; and the Egyptians will know the LORD on that day, and will worship with sacrifice and burnt offering, and they will make vows to the LORD and perform them. 22The LORD will strike Egypt, striking and healing; they will return to the LORD, and he will listen to their supplications and heal them.
23 On that day there will be a highway from Egypt to Assyria, and the Assyrian will come into Egypt, and the Egyptian into Assyria, and the Egyptians will worship with the Assyrians.
24 On that day Israel will be the third with Egypt and Assyria, a blessing in the midst of the earth, 25whom the LORD of hosts has blessed, saying, "Blessed be Egypt my people, and Assyria the work of my hands, and Israel my heritage."

19.1–25: Threats concerning Egypt. 1–15: Throughout the period when Assyria and Babylon were assaulting Israel and Judah, Egypt repeatedly promised protection, yet consistently failed to carry through. "For Egypt's help is worthless and empty" (Isa 30.7). The people famed throughout antiquity for learning and literary skill could offer no defense against a ruthless invader (vv. 11–15). **16–25:** In spite of these failures, Judah's relations with Egypt were prolonged and often close. The prophet looks beyond the turmoil of Mesopotamian rule to the time when a community would dwell there who *spoke the language of Canaan* (v. 18) and swore *allegiance to the LORD of hosts.* Even Assyria would one day become with Egypt and Israel *a blessing in the midst of the earth* (v. 24). This series of remarkable short prophecies builds on the aftermath of the disasters that befell Jerusalem at the hands of the Assyrians and Babylonians. Many citizens fled to Egypt, and, from the sixth century BCE onwards, substantial settlements of exiled Judeans took refuge there. In this bold look across the spiritual boundaries of the ancient world, a genuine religious universalism begins to ap-

a Gk Compare Tg: Heb *it*

pear (vv. 23–24). The knowledge of God revealed to Israel would be shared among other peoples, replacing the failed learning of the Egyptian sages (v. 11).

20 In the year that the commander-in-chief, who was sent by King Sargon of Assyria, came to Ashdod and fought against it and took it— ²at that time the LORD had spoken to Isaiah son of Amoz, saying, "Go, and loose the sackcloth from your loins and take your sandals off your feet," and he had done so, walking naked and barefoot. ³Then the LORD said, "Just as my servant Isaiah has walked naked and barefoot for three years as a sign and a portent against Egypt and Ethiopia,ᵃ ⁴so shall the king of Assyria lead away the Egyptians as captives and the Ethiopiansᵇ as exiles, both the young and the old, naked and barefoot, with buttocks uncovered, to the shame of Egypt. ⁵And they shall be dismayed and confounded because of Ethiopiaᵃ their hope and of Egypt their boast. ⁶In that day the inhabitants of this coastland will say, 'See, this is what has happened to those in whom we hoped and to whom we fled for help and deliverance from the king of Assyria! And we, how shall we escape?' "

20.1–6: A lesson from the past. A brief narrative⋆ reports an event of 715 BCE: A Philistine rebellion against Assyria led to a campaign against Ashdod, one of the five major cities of the Philistines. The Egyptians promised help for the rebellion and Judah was tempted to join. Isaiah's strange action of appearing *naked and barefoot*, like a prisoner of war being sold into slavery (v. 2), warned against such complicity. Egypt's help would prove to be unreliable and worthless (v. 6). This warning was reaffirmed when Hezekiah trusted Egyptian promises in rebelling against Assyria in 703 BCE.

21 The oracle concerning the wilderness of the sea.

As whirlwinds in the Negeb sweep on,
  it comes from the desert,
  from a terrible land.
² A stern vision is told to me;
  the betrayer betrays,
  and the destroyer destroys.

Go up, O Elam,
  lay siege, O Media;
all the sighing she has caused
  I bring to an end.
³ Therefore my loins are filled
    with anguish;
  pangs have seized me,
  like the pangs of a woman in labor;
I am bowed down so that I cannot hear,
  I am dismayed so that I cannot see.
⁴ My mind reels, horror has appalled me;
  the twilight I longed for
  has been turned for me into
    trembling.
⁵ They prepare the table,
  they spread the rugs,
  they eat, they drink.
Rise up, commanders,
  oil the shield!
⁶ For thus the Lord said to me:
"Go, post a lookout,
  let him announce what he sees.
⁷ When he sees riders, horsemen in pairs,
  riders on donkeys, riders on camels,
let him listen diligently,
  very diligently."
⁸ Then the watcherᶜ called out:
"Upon a watchtower I stand, O Lord,
  continually by day,
and at my post I am stationed
  throughout the night.
⁹ Look, there they come, riders,
  horsemen in pairs!"
Then he responded,
  "Fallen, fallen is Babylon;
and all the images of her gods
  lie shattered on the ground."
¹⁰ O my threshed and winnowed one,
  what I have heard from the LORD of
    hosts,
  the God of Israel, I announce to you.

21.1–17: Prophecies concerning Babylon, Edom, and the southern desert lands. 1–10: This anguished warning concerns the fall of *Babylon* (v. 9). The heading (v. 1) addresses the southern desert of the Negeb, but the content points to Babylon. The oracle⋆ may date from the time of the attack on the city by Elam

a Or *Nubia*; Heb *Cush*   b Or *Nubians*; Heb *Cushites*
c Q Ms: MT *a lion*

and Media (538 BCE), when the Medo-Persian over-throw of Babyon marked its end as a world power. This prophecy would provide a framework for the series of prophecies against the nations that began in ch. 13 with the threat to Babylon. It may also date, however, from 703 BCE when the Assyrian king Sennacherib captured the city of Babylon after it had rebelled against Assyria's rule. At this time, the Babylonian ruler Merodach-baladan sent emissaries to Hezekiah of Judah to coordinate rebellion against Assyria (compare Isa 39.1–8).

11 The oracle concerning Dumah.

One is calling to me from Seir,
  "Sentinel, what of the night?
  Sentinel, what of the night?"
12 The sentinel says:
"Morning comes, and also the night.
  If you will inquire, inquire;
  come back again."

13 The oracle concerning the desert
    plain.

In the scrub of the desert plain you will
    lodge,
  O caravans of Dedanites.
14 Bring water to the thirsty,
  meet the fugitive with bread,
  O inhabitants of the land of Tema.
15 For they have fled from the swords,
  from the drawn sword,
  from the bent bow,
  and from the stress of battle.

16 For thus the Lord said to me: Within a year, according to the years of a hired worker, all the glory of Kedar will come to an end; 17and the remaining bows of Kedar's warriors will be few; for the LORD, the God of Israel, has spoken.

21.11–17. 11–12: In 691–689 the Assyrian king, Sennacherib, extended his campaigns further to the south and west, penetrating to *Dumah* (Edom) and the northwest tip of Arabia where the famed caravan cities of Kedar and Dedan were located. This brief, inconclusive prophecy may be reporting the ineffectual nature of this particular foray. **13–17:** The campaign of Sennacherib to plunder the desert cities of *Dedan* and *Tema* is reflected in vv. 14–15, with vv. 16–17 adding

an additional note reflecting later attempts to exploit the region, probably by Babylonian forces.

22 The oracle concerning the valley of vision.

What do you mean that you have
    gone up,
  all of you, to the housetops,
2 you that are full of shoutings,
  tumultuous city, exultant town?
Your slain are not slain by the sword,
  nor are they dead in battle.
3 Your rulers have all fled together;
  they were captured without the use of
    a bow.*a*
All of you who were found were
    captured,
  though they had fled far away.*b*
4 Therefore I said:
Look away from me,
  let me weep bitter tears;
do not try to comfort me
  for the destruction of my
    beloved people.

5 For the Lord GOD of hosts has a day
  of tumult and trampling and
    confusion
  in the valley of vision,
a battering down of walls
  and a cry for help to the mountains.
6 Elam bore the quiver
  with chariots and cavalry,*c*
  and Kir uncovered the shield.
7 Your choicest valleys were full of
    chariots,
  and the cavalry took their stand at the
    gates.
8 He has taken away the covering
    of Judah.

On that day you looked to the weapons of the House of the Forest, 9and you saw that there were many breaches in the city of David, and you collected the waters of the lower pool. 10You counted the houses of Jerusalem, and you broke down the houses to for-

a Or *without their bows*   *b* Gk Syr Vg: Heb *fled from far away*   *c* Meaning of Heb uncertain

tify the wall. ¹¹You made a reservoir between the two walls for the water of the old pool. But you did not look to him who did it, or have regard for him who planned it long ago.

¹² In that day the Lord GOD of hosts
    called to weeping and mourning,
    to baldness and putting on sackcloth;
¹³ but instead there was joy and festivity,
    killing oxen and slaughtering sheep,
    eating meat and drinking wine.
"Let us eat and drink,
    for tomorrow we die."
¹⁴ The LORD of hosts has revealed himself
    in my ears:
Surely this iniquity will not be forgiven
    you until you die,
    says the Lord GOD of hosts.

15 Thus says the Lord GOD of hosts: Come, go to this steward, to Shebna, who is master of the household, and say to him: ¹⁶What right do you have here? Who are your relatives here, that you have cut out a tomb here for yourself, cutting a tomb on the height, and carving a habitation for yourself in the rock? ¹⁷The LORD is about to hurl you away violently, my fellow. He will seize firm hold on you, ¹⁸whirl you round and round, and throw you like a ball into a wide land; there you shall die, and there your splendid chariots shall lie, O you disgrace to your master's house! ¹⁹I will thrust you from your office, and you will be pulled down from your post.

20 On that day I will call my servant Eliakim son of Hilkiah, ²¹and will clothe him with your robe and bind your sash on him. I will commit your authority to his hand, and he shall be a father to the inhabitants of Jerusalem and to the house of Judah. ²²I will place on his shoulder the key of the house of David; he shall open, and no one shall shut; he shall shut, and no one shall open. ²³I will fasten him like a peg in a secure place, and he will become a throne of honor to his ancestral house. ²⁴And they will hang on him the whole weight of his ancestral house, the offspring and issue, every small vessel, from the cups to all the flagons. ²⁵On that day, says the LORD of hosts, the peg that

was fastened in a secure place will give way; it will be cut down and fall, and the load that was on it will perish, for the LORD has spoken.

22.1–25: Warnings to Jerusalem and its leaders. 1–4: The *valley of vision* is Jerusalem, apparently because Isaiah's call-vision took place there (ch. 6). The prophecies refer to the events described in 2 Kings 18.9–12: The northern Israelite city of Samaria was besieged, captured, and destroyed by the king of Assyria. Jerusalem's escape from a similar fate by the timely, but humiliating, surrender of King Hezekiah (2 Kings 18.13–16) may also be referred to. In celebrating their own escape, the citizens of Jerusalem ignored the suffering of their sister nation. Isaiah strongly believed that both Judah and Israel (Ephraim) were two houses of one people before God (see 8.14; 9.21). 5–8a: The fate that had so recently overtaken their compatriots would also befall the citizens of Jerusalem. A century later Babylonian forces captured Jerusalem in 598, destroying it in 587 BCE. 8b–11: Instead of trusting the LORD, the beleaguered citizens trusted their own human defense system. It would fail them, just as surely as the defenses of Samaria had failed. 15–25: Three short, but related, condemnations (vv. 15–19, 20–23, 24–25) concern *Shebna*, the master of the royal household (v. 15), and *Eliakim son of Hilkiah* (v. 20) who had briefly succeeded him (v. 21). These officials are mentioned in 36.3, 11, 22 and played a prominent role in the negotiations for King Hezekiah's surrender to Assyria (see 2 Kings 18.18). Their personal ambitions and folly, which affected their roles in forming national policy, are condemned. Isaiah also condemned the king for relying upon Egyptian promises of support (see Isa 30).

23 The oracle concerning Tyre.
Wail, O ships of Tarshish,
    for your fortress is destroyed.ª
When they came in from Cyprus
    they learned of it.
² Be still, O inhabitants of the coast,
    O merchants of Sidon,
your messengers crossed over the seaᵇ
³   and were on the mighty waters;

a Cn Compare verse 14: Heb *for it is destroyed, without houses*   b Q Ms: MT *crossing over the sea, they replenished you*

your revenue was the grain of Shihor,
   the harvest of the Nile;
   you were the merchant of the nations.
4 Be ashamed, O Sidon, for the sea has
         spoken,
   the fortress of the sea, saying:
   "I have neither labored nor given birth,
   I have neither reared young men
   nor brought up young women."
5 When the report comes to Egypt,
   they will be in anguish over the report
         about Tyre.
6 Cross over to Tarshish—
   wail, O inhabitants of the coast!
7 Is this your exultant city
   whose origin is from days of old,
   whose feet carried her
   to settle far away?
8 Who has planned this
   against Tyre, the bestower of crowns,
   whose merchants were princes,
   whose traders were the honored of
         the earth?
9 The LORD of hosts has planned it—
   to defile the pride of all glory,
   to shame all the honored of the
         earth.
10 Cross over to your own land,
   O ships of[a] Tarshish;
   this is a harbor[b] no more.
11 He has stretched out his hand over the
         sea,
   he has shaken the kingdoms;
   the LORD has given command
         concerning Canaan
   to destroy its fortresses.
12 He said:
   You will exult no longer,
   O oppressed virgin daughter Sidon;
   rise, cross over to Cyprus—
   even there you will have no rest.

13 Look at the land of the Chaldeans!
This is the people; it was not Assyria. They
destined Tyre for wild animals. They erected
their siege towers, they tore down her palaces, they made her a ruin.[c]
14 Wail, O ships of Tarshish,
   for your fortress is destroyed.
15 From that day Tyre will be forgotten for
seventy years, the lifetime of one king. At the

end of seventy years, it will happen to Tyre
as in the song about the prostitute:
16 Take a harp,
   go about the city,
   you forgotten prostitute!
   Make sweet melody,
   sing many songs,
   that you may be remembered.
17 At the end of seventy years, the LORD will
visit Tyre, and she will return to her trade,
and will prostitute herself with all the
kingdoms of the world on the face of the
earth. 18 Her merchandise and her wages will
be dedicated to the LORD; her profits[d] will
not be stored or hoarded, but her merchandise will supply abundant food and fine
clothing for those who live in the presence
of the LORD.

23.1–18: A prophecy concerning Tyre. 1–12: The
Phoenician cities of *Tyre* and *Sidon* were famous in
antiquity as the seafaring and mercantile trading centers of the Mediterranean world. The pride of Tyre was
its fine buildings, wealth, and honor. In 701 BCE, the
Assyrian ruler Sennacherib laid siege to the Phoenician
cities, forcing Luli, king of Sidon, to flee to the island
of *Cyprus* (v. 12). **13–18:** A brief editorial note (v. 13)
points out that Babylon (from 604 BCE) had replaced
the threat from Assyria (compare the book of Nahum,
which celebrates the fall of Nineveh in 612 BCE). This
succession of Mesopotamian oppressors led the later
compilers to supplement earlier prophecies to provide
a fuller picture of God's purpose. Tyre, like an aging
prostitute (v. 16), will shamelessly pursue wealth (a
reference to the rich merchants for which Tyre was
known). In contrast, the final note (v. 18) recognizes
that wealth, rightly earned, can be used in the service
of God.

**The terror of the day of the LORD and the ensuing
reign of blessedness**
24.1–27.13: Chapters 24–27 contain no clear indications of their time of origin and therefore are difficult
to relate to known events. They contrast a time of fearful judgment upon *the city of chaos* (24.10) with a
new era of blessedness, a spectacular feast on the
mountain of God (25.6–10). These chapters may have

a Cn Compare Gk: Heb *like the Nile, daughter*
b Cn: Heb *restraint*   c Meaning of Heb uncertain
d Heb *it*

been a separate prophetic book, but clear references to earlier themes and pronouncements, most notably the "New Song of the Vineyard" (27.2–6; compare 5.1–7), make it more likely that they are a sequel to the prophecies against foreign cities and nations in chs. 13–23. The great empires will be overtaken by a fearful day of God's judgment, followed by a time of peace and justice. The evocative word pictures of doom and disaster, intermixed with hymns of praise and promises of a new age of great peace and blessedness, lift human history into the realm of a great spiritual "super-history" in which evil is overthrown and the faithful are vindicated.

24 Now the LORD is about to lay
waste the earth and make it
desolate,
and he will twist its surface and
scatter its inhabitants.
2 And it shall be, as with the people, so
with the priest;
as with the slave, so with his master;
as with the maid, so with her
mistress;
as with the buyer, so with the seller;
as with the lender, so with the
borrower;
as with the creditor, so with
the debtor.
3 The earth shall be utterly laid waste and
utterly despoiled;
for the LORD has spoken this word.

4 The earth dries up and withers,
the world languishes and withers;
the heavens languish together with
the earth.
5 The earth lies polluted
under its inhabitants;
for they have transgressed laws,
violated the statutes,
broken the everlasting covenant.
6 Therefore a curse devours the earth,
and its inhabitants suffer for their
guilt;
therefore the inhabitants of the earth
dwindled,
and few people are left.
7 The wine dries up,
the vine languishes,
all the merry-hearted sigh.

8 The mirth of the timbrels is stilled,
the noise of the jubilant has ceased,
the mirth of the lyre is stilled.
9 No longer do they drink wine with
singing;
strong drink is bitter to those who
drink it.
10 The city of chaos is broken down,
every house is shut up so that no one
can enter.
11 There is an outcry in the streets for lack
of wine;
all joy has reached its eventide;
the gladness of the earth is banished.
12 Desolation is left in the city,
the gates are battered into ruins.
13 For thus it shall be on the earth
and among the nations,
as when an olive tree is beaten,
as at the gleaning when the grape
harvest is ended.

14 They lift up their voices, they sing for
joy;
they shout from the west over the
majesty of the LORD.
15 Therefore in the east give glory to the
LORD;
in the coastlands of the sea glorify the
name of the LORD, the God of
Israel.
16 From the ends of the earth we hear
songs of praise,
of glory to the Righteous One.
But I say, I pine away,
I pine away. Woe is me!
For the treacherous deal treacherously,
the treacherous deal very
treacherously.

17 Terror, and the pit, and the snare
are upon you, O inhabitant of the
earth!
18 Whoever flees at the sound of the
terror
shall fall into the pit;
and whoever climbs out of the pit
shall be caught in the snare.
For the windows of heaven are opened,
and the foundations of the earth
tremble.

19 The earth is utterly broken,
   the earth is torn asunder,
   the earth is violently shaken.
20 The earth staggers like a drunkard,
   it sways like a hut;
   its transgression lies heavy upon it,
   and it falls, and will not rise again.

21 On that day the LORD will punish
   the host of heaven in heaven,
   and on earth the kings of the earth.
22 They will be gathered together
   like prisoners in a pit;
   they will be shut up in a prison,
   and after many days they will be
      punished.
23 Then the moon will be abashed,
   and the sun ashamed;
   for the LORD of hosts will reign
   on Mount Zion and in Jerusalem,
   and before his elders he will manifest
      his glory.

24.1–23: The day of terror for the city of chaos. This remarkable picture of a tortured and pain-wracked earth views the sufferings of its inhabitants (vv. 17–20) as a consequence of the curse-ridden state of the earth itself (v. 6). The very order of the world, disturbed and in turmoil, can only be put right by divine punishment of evil in a new era of divine rule (vv. 22–23). Despair for the earth combines with trust that ultimately God will prevail, which explains the praise to God in vv. 14–16. Judgment, as proof of divine justice, is itself a necessary part of God's created order. The *city of chaos* (v. 10) is a symbolic city, like Bunyan's Vanity Fair in *Pilgrim's Progress*. Even though the *host of heaven* rebels against God (v. 21), this prophet believes that God will prevail.

25 O LORD, you are my God;
   I will exalt you, I will praise your
      name;
   for you have done wonderful things,
   plans formed of old, faithful and sure.
2 For you have made the city a heap,
   the fortified city a ruin;
   the palace of aliens is a city no more,
   it will never be rebuilt.
3 Therefore strong peoples will glorify
      you;
   cities of ruthless nations will fear you.

4 For you have been a refuge to the poor,
   a refuge to the needy in their distress,
   a shelter from the rainstorm and a
      shade from the heat.
   When the blast of the ruthless was like
      a winter rainstorm,
5 the noise of aliens like heat in a dry
      place,
   you subdued the heat with the shade of
      clouds;
   the song of the ruthless was stilled.

6 On this mountain the LORD of hosts
   will make for all peoples
   a feast of rich food, a feast of well-
      aged wines,
   of rich food filled with marrow, of
      well-aged wines strained clear.
7 And he will destroy on this mountain
   the shroud that is cast over all
      peoples,
   the sheet that is spread over all
      nations;
8 he will swallow up death forever.
   Then the Lord GOD will wipe away the
      tears from all faces,
   and the disgrace of his people he will
      take away from all the earth,
   for the LORD has spoken.
9 It will be said on that day,
   Lo, this is our God; we have waited
      for him, so that he might save us.
   This is the LORD for whom we have
      waited;
   let us be glad and rejoice in his
      salvation.
10 For the hand of the LORD will rest on
      this mountain.

   The Moabites shall be trodden down in
      their place
   as straw is trodden down in a
      dung-pit.
11 Though they spread out their hands in
      the midst of it,
   as swimmers spread out their hands
      to swim,
   their pride will be laid low despite the
      struggle*a* of their hands.

a Meaning of Heb uncertain

12 The high fortifications of his walls will
          be brought down,
      laid low, cast to the ground, even to
          the dust.

25.1–12: The banquet of the LORD of hosts. The
great festival to be celebrated in Jerusalem on the holy
mountain gives pictorial expression to the praise of
God (vv. 1–5). Even in the most violent trouble, God
is *a refuge to the needy in their distress* (v. 4). The
prophetic vision, however, recognizes that there are
wrongs and sufferings on earth that cannot be put
right by stilling *the blast of the ruthless*. The ultimate
resolution of injustice can come only when God over-
comes the power of death itself (v. 7; compare 26.19).
10–12. The humiliation of Moab. This appears to belong with the other warnings in chs. 15–16.

26 On that day this song will be sung in
      the land of Judah:
  We have a strong city;
      he sets up victory
      like walls and bulwarks.
2 Open the gates,
      so that the righteous nation that
          keeps faith
      may enter in.
3 Those of steadfast mind you keep
          in peace—
      in peace because they trust in you.
4 Trust in the LORD forever,
      for in the LORD GOD *a*
      you have an everlasting rock.
5 For he has brought low
      the inhabitants of the height;
      the lofty city he lays low.
  He lays it low to the ground,
      casts it to the dust.
6 The foot tramples it,
      the feet of the poor,
      the steps of the needy.

7 The way of the righteous is level;
      O Just One, you make smooth the
          path of the righteous.
8 In the path of your judgments,
      O LORD, we wait for you;
  your name and your renown
      are the soul's desire.
9 My soul yearns for you in
          the night,

my spirit within me earnestly seeks
          you.
  For when your judgments are in the
          earth,
      the inhabitants of the world learn
          righteousness.
10 If favor is shown to the wicked,
      they do not learn righteousness;
  in the land of uprightness they deal
          perversely
      and do not see the majesty of
          the LORD.
11 O LORD, your hand is lifted up,
      but they do not see it.
  Let them see your zeal for your people,
      and be ashamed.
  Let the fire for your adversaries
      consume them.
12 O LORD, you will ordain peace for us,
      for indeed, all that we have done, you
          have done for us.
13 O LORD our God,
      other lords besides you have ruled
          over us,
      but we acknowledge your name alone.
14 The dead do not live;
      shades do not rise—
  because you have punished and
          destroyed them,
      and wiped out all memory of them.
15 But you have increased the nation,
          O LORD,
      you have increased the nation; you
          are glorified;
      you have enlarged all the borders of
          the land.
16 O LORD, in distress they sought you,
      they poured out a prayer *b*
      when your chastening was on them.
17 Like a woman with child,
      who writhes and cries out in her pangs
      when she is near her time,
  so were we because of you, O LORD;
18   we were with child, we writhed,
      but we gave birth only to wind.
  We have won no victories on earth,
      and no one is born to inhabit
          the world.

a Heb *in Yah, the LORD*   *b* Meaning of Heb uncertain

¹⁹ Your dead shall live, their corpses^a shall
rise.
O dwellers in the dust, awake and
sing for joy!
For your dew is a radiant dew,
and the earth will give birth to those
long dead.^b

²⁰ Come, my people, enter your chambers,
and shut your doors behind you;
hide yourselves for a little while
until the wrath is past.

²¹ For the LORD comes out from his place
to punish the inhabitants of the earth
for their iniquity;
the earth will disclose the blood shed
on it,
and will no longer cover its slain.

26.1–21: Praise to the God of justice. The hymn of
praise to God for the justice of the divine judgments
upon earth in vv. 1–15 indicates that chs. 24–27, and
probably the entire scroll of Isaiah, were designed to
be read, and prayerfully responded to, in acts of worship. The message of God was a call to penitence and
faith, so that unresolved questions and doubts could
be answered by trust, as in v. 3: *Those of steadfast
mind you keep in peace—in peace because they trust
in you.* It is necessary to accept the purpose of God
and to await salvation without fully understanding the
violent wrongs of human history. This trust is expressed in the remarkable outburst of vv. 16–19: When
the promises of God appear so far from fulfillment, a
new vision breaks in, a vision of life beyond the grave
and of life renewed for those long dead. The only other
passage in the Hebrew Scriptures that compares with
this visionary insight into the world beyond the grave
is Dan 12.2. The prophet is attempting to reconcile
the righteousness of God with the problems of suffering and conflict.

27 On that day the LORD with his cruel
and great and strong sword will punish Leviathan the fleeing serpent, Leviathan
the twisting serpent, and he will kill the
dragon that is in the sea.

² On that day:
A pleasant vineyard, sing about it!
³   I, the LORD, am its keeper;
every moment I water it.

I guard it night and day
so that no one can harm it;
⁴   I have no wrath.
If it gives me thorns and briers,
I will march to battle against it.
I will burn it up.
⁵ Or else let it cling to me for protection,
let it make peace with me,
let it make peace with me.

⁶ In days to come^c Jacob shall take root,
Israel shall blossom and put
forth shoots,
and fill the whole world with fruit.

⁷ Has he struck them down as he struck
down those who struck them?
Or have they been killed as their
killers were killed?
⁸ By expulsion,^d by exile you struggled
against them;
with his fierce blast he removed them
in the day of the east wind.
⁹ Therefore by this the guilt of Jacob will
be expiated,
and this will be the full fruit of the
removal of his sin:
when he makes all the stones of the
altars
like chalkstones crushed to pieces,
no sacred poles^e or incense altars will
remain standing.
¹⁰ For the fortified city is solitary,
a habitation deserted and forsaken,
like the wilderness;
the calves graze there,
there they lie down, and strip its
branches.
¹¹ When its boughs are dry, they
are broken;
women come and make a fire
of them.
For this is a people without
understanding;
therefore he that made them will not
have compassion on them,
he that formed them will show them
no favor.

a Cn Compare Syr Tg: Heb *my corpse*   *b* Heb *to the
shades*   *c* Heb *Those to come*   *d* Meaning of Heb
uncertain   *e* Heb *Asherim*

12 On that day the LORD will thresh from the channel of the Euphrates to the Wadi of Egypt, and you will be gathered one by one, O people of Israel. ¹³And on that day a great trumpet will be blown, and those who were lost in the land of Assyria and those who were driven out to the land of Egypt will come and worship the LORD on the holy mountain at Jerusalem.

27.1–13: The new song of the vineyard. 1: The assurance that the LORD *will punish Leviathan** reflects the ancient belief that the earth was created after a great battle between the creator God and a monster symbolizing chaos. In the Babylonian creation epic, this monster is called Tiamat, but other versions use the name Rahab (compare Isa 51.9). The power of God to impose order is needed not simply in the primary

act of creation but in every natural disaster or historical catastrophe, when God's rule needs to be reestablished. **2:** *A pleasant vineyard, sing about it!* Reference to the vineyard parable* of Isa 5.1–7 shows that this new song marks the end of the period in which the former vineyard (Israel) was reduced to a wasteland. **4:** The *thorns and briers* will at last be removed (see 7.23–25; 9.18; 10.17). **7–11:** The restoration has not yet taken place, and the fields of Jacob still lie desolate and *forsaken* (v. 10). The *people without understanding* (v. 11) are those who hold back God's saving work. **12–13.** The promise of return to their homeland for the scattered survivors remains central to the hope for the future in Isaiah. Here and in 11.12–16 (compare 19.23–24), this return is the prelude to the restoration of Israel to its former glory, the completion of God's saving purpose.

Isaiah 28-39

THREATS TO JERUSALEM AND ITS GREAT DELIVERANCE

Chapters 28–31 present sharp prophetic accusations, first against the leaders of Ephraim (28.1–11) and then against those of Jerusalem (28.14–31.9). They charge that these people are pursuing a national policy contrary to God's will, by looking to Egypt rather than to God to provide deliverance from threatening foreign powers. Chapter 32 presents a new hope, beginning in vv. 1–8, with promises of the coming of a just king and responsible and righteous leaders for the nation. Fresh warnings follow, first to Jerusalem and Judah (32.9–33.16), but then to the wider world of other nations (34.1–17). The hope for Jerusalem's future is not abandoned, but rather intensified, with ch. 35 summarizing the later message of chs. 40–66.

Chapters 36–39, largely identical to 2 Kings 18.13–20.19, concern the threatened siege of Jerusalem by the Assyrian king, Sennacherib, in 701 BCE, followed by the reprieve for the beleaguered King Hezekiah and the city (36.1–37.38). A report of Hezekiah's illness and recovery (38.1–9), for which the king offers a psalm of thanksgiving (38.10–20), is followed in 39.1–8 by a visit of emissaries from the Babylonian ruler Merodach-baladan, along with the prophet's ominous warning of danger from that nation.

The background to the prophecies of chs. 28–31 is the situation of 705–701 BCE, when King Hezekiah of Judah joined a rebellion of eastern Mediterranean states against Assyria, following the death of the Assyrian king, Shalmaneser, in 705 BCE. Egypt was the chief instigator and promised military protection for those foolhardy nations that joined in the revolt. These unreliable assurances provide the background to Isaiah's warnings against Egyptian help (chs. 30–31). The revolt was crushed mercilessly in 701. Research into the events behind the accounts of Hezekiah's surrender to Sennacherib, and the extensive reports of the blasphemous speeches of the Assyrian negotiator (called the Rabshakeh) and their rebuff by Isaiah, include the recovery of clay tablets and palace wall illustrations attesting the capture of Lachish and the humiliations inflicted on Hezekiah. These give a very different picture from that in Isa 36–37. Yet, in contrast

to the fate of Samaria and its king, reported in 2 Kings 18.9–12, Hezekiah retained his throne and his city survived intact. The Assyrian royal records presumably exaggerate the victory to flatter their king.

READING GUIDE

In the rebuff to the blasphemous claims of the Assyrian negotiator (37.22–29) and in several other memorable utterances, Isaiah calls for a complete faith in God (28.16) and insists that only such faith can bring true peace and strength (30.15). Similarly, his call for integrity before God (29.13) and his insistence that God cannot be deceived by human secrecy and subterfuge (29.15–16) are the basis for Jewish and Christian teaching about the limitations of human learning and the necessity for submission to the superior wisdom of God (29.14).

28.1–29	The LORD is a refuge and protection
29.1–24	The siege and deliverance of Jerusalem
30.1–33	In quietness and in trust shall be your strength
31.1–9	The lordship of the God of Mount Zion
32.1–20	A king will reign in righteousness
33.1–24	A miscellany of prophetic themes
34.1–17	The LORD's day of vengeance
35.1–10	The triumph of Zion
36.1–37.38	The wonderful deliverance of Jerusalem
38.1–22	Hezekiah's sickness and recovery
39.1–8	The visit of the Babylonian emissaries

The LORD is a refuge and protection
28.1–29: The four units of this chapter (1–6; 7–13; 14–22; 23–29) condemn the foolishness of the leaders of both Ephraim (Israel) and Judah, who show by their drunken and mocking behavior that they neither understand their problems nor are able to remedy them. In contrast, Isaiah sets out the simple and direct message: *"One who trusts will not panic"* (v. 16).

28 Ah, the proud garland of the
        drunkards of Ephraim,
    and the fading flower of its glorious
        beauty,
    which is on the head of those bloated
        with rich food, of those overcome
        with wine!
2   See, the Lord has one who is mighty
        and strong;
    like a storm of hail, a destroying
        tempest,
    like a storm of mighty, overflowing
        waters;

with his hand he will hurl them down
        to the earth.
3   Trampled under foot will be
    the proud garland of the drunkards of
        Ephraim.
4   And the fading flower of its glorious
        beauty,
    which is on the head of those bloated
        with rich food,
    will be like a first-ripe fig before the
        summer;
    whoever sees it, eats it up
    as soon as it comes to hand.

5   In that day the LORD of hosts will be a
        garland of glory,
    and a diadem of beauty, to the
        remnant of his people;
6   and a spirit of justice to the one who
        sits in judgment,
    and strength to those who turn back
        the battle at the gate.

28.1–6: The folly of Ephraim's leaders. It is surprising that the opening prophecy focuses on Ephraim, rather than Judah, which Isaiah usually addressed. Yet Ephraim suffered first, and more severely, from the depredations of Assyria. Judah should learn the necessary lesson: As a sudden rainstorm (v. 2) ruins the festival of those leaders who had already eaten and drunk too much, so would God's judgment wreck the complacent peace of the kingdom (compare 9.8–10.4). A brief word of hope and relief (vv. 5–6) shows that God's judgment always has a way of escape for a penitent remnant.

7 These also reel with wine
    and stagger with strong drink;
  the priest and the prophet reel with
      strong drink,
    they are confused with wine,
    they stagger with strong drink;
  they err in vision,
    they stumble in giving judgment.
8 All tables are covered with filthy vomit;
    no place is clean.

9 "Whom will he teach knowledge,
    and to whom will he explain
      the message?
  Those who are weaned from milk,
    those taken from the breast?
10 For it is precept upon precept, precept
      upon precept,
    line upon line, line upon line,
    here a little, there a little."*a*

11 Truly, with stammering lip
    and with alien tongue
  he will speak to this people,
12   to whom he has said,
  "This is rest;
    give rest to the weary;
  and this is repose";
    yet they would not hear.
13 Therefore the word of the LORD will be
      to them,
  "Precept upon precept, precept upon
      precept,
    line upon line, line upon line,
    here a little, there a little;"*a*
  in order that they may go, and fall
      backward,

and be broken, and snared,
    and taken.

28.7–13: God cannot be mocked with impunity. It is unclear whether this oracle* is addressed to the revelers in vv. 1–4, or whether it is a rebuke to a group of Jerusalem's leaders (compare v. 14). The signs of excess are evident (v. 8) when they turn to mock the prophet and, by implication, God (vv. 9–10). These leaders accuse the prophet of treating them like little children (v. 10). Instead God will teach them a lesson in the language of foreign invaders (v. 11). By rejecting and mocking the prophet's warnings (v. 12), and choosing rebellion against Assyria, they were playing with their own lives and those of the people and would pay the price (v. 13).

14 Therefore hear the word of the LORD,
      you scoffers
    who rule this people in Jerusalem.
15 Because you have said, "We have made
      a covenant with death,
    and with Sheol we have an
      agreement;
  when the overwhelming scourge passes
      through
    it will not come to us;
  for we have made lies our refuge,
    and in falsehood we have taken
      shelter";
16 therefore thus says the Lord GOD,
  See, I am laying in Zion a foundation
      stone,
    a tested stone,
  a precious cornerstone, a sure
      foundation:
    "One who trusts will not panic."
17 And I will make justice the line,
    and righteousness the plummet;
  hail will sweep away the refuge of lies,
    and waters will overwhelm the
      shelter.
18 Then your covenant with death will be
      annulled,
    and your agreement with Sheol will
      not stand;
  when the overwhelming scourge passes
      through

a Meaning of Heb of this verse uncertain

Assyrian Account of the Siege of Jerusalem

As to Hezekiah, the Jew, he did not submit to my yoke, I laid siege to 46 of his strong cities, walled forts, and to the countless small villages in their vicinity, and conquered (them) by means of well-stamped (earth-) ramps, and battering-rams brought (thus) near (to the walls) (combined with) the attack by foot soldiers, (using) mines, breeches as well as sapper work. I drove out (of them) 200,150 people, young and old, male and female, horses, mules, donkeys, camels, big and small cattle beyond counting, and considered (them) booty. Himself I made a prisoner in Jerusalem, his royal residence, like a bird in a cage. I surrounded him with earthwork in order to molest those who were leaving his city's gate. His towns which I had plundered, I took away from his country and gave them (over) to Mitinti, king of Ashdod, Padi, king of Ekron, and Sillibel, king of Gaza. Thus I reduced his country, but I still increased the tribute and the *katrû* -presents (due) to me (as his) overlord which I imposed (later) upon him beyond the former tribute, to be delivered annually. Hezekiah himself, whom the terror-inspiring splendor of my lordship had overwhelmed and whose irregular and elite troops which he had brought into Jerusalem, his royal residence, in order to strengthen (it), had deserted him, did send me, later, to Nineveh, my lordly city, together with 30 talents of gold, 800 talents of silver, precious stones, antimony, large cuts of red stone, couches (inlaid) with ivory, *nîmedu* -chairs (inlaid) with ivory, elephant-hides, ebony-wood, box-wood (and) all kinds of valuable treasures, his (own) daughters, concubines,✶ male and female musicians. In order to deliver the tribute and to do obeisance as a slave he sent his (personal) messenger. (From *The Ancient Near East: Volume One, An Anthology of Texts and Pictures,* edited by James B. Pritchard, Princeton University Press, 1958, p. 200.)

you will be beaten down by it.

19 As often as it passes through, it will
    take you;
  for morning by morning it will pass
    through,
  by day and by night;
  and it will be sheer terror to understand
    the message.

20 For the bed is too short to stretch
    oneself on it,
  and the covering too narrow to wrap
    oneself in it.

21 For the LORD will rise up as on Mount
    Perazim,
  he will rage as in the valley of
    Gibeon
  to do his deed—strange is his deed!—
  and to work his work—alien is his
    work!

22 Now therefore do not scoff,
  or your bonds will be made stronger;

for I have heard a decree of destruction
  from the Lord GOD of hosts upon the
  whole land.

28.14–22: God's strange work. This powerful prophecy expresses the fundamentals of Isaiah's conviction: God alone is the defense and protector of the people of Jerusalem. Instead of trusting in God, however, these leaders had chosen *a covenant✶ with death* and an *agreement with Sheol✶* (v. 18). These titles may refer to a strange ritual with the god of death to make sure that no harm could come to them. Or more likely, they may be a sharply ironic description of the treaty with Egypt that Judah hoped would protect it against any Assyrian reprisal for rebellion. Egypt is caricatured as the kingdom of death because of its obsession with overcoming death (by constructing great pyramids and embalming national figures). In contrast, Isaiah insists that Judah's actions will simply hasten death's arrival.

23 Listen, and hear my voice;
     Pay attention, and hear my speech.
24 Do those who plow for sowing plow
          continually?
     Do they continually open and harrow
          their ground?
25 When they have leveled its surface,
     do they not scatter dill, sow cummin,
   and plant wheat in rows
     and barley in its proper place,
     and spelt as the border?
26 For they are well instructed;
     their God teaches them.

27 Dill is not threshed with a threshing
          sledge,
     nor is a cart wheel rolled over
          cummin;
   but dill is beaten out with a stick,
     and cummin with a rod.
28 Grain is crushed for bread,
     but one does not thresh it forever;
   one drives the cart wheel and horses
          over it,
     but does not pulverize it.
29 This also comes from the LORD
          of hosts;
     he is wonderful in counsel,
     and excellent in wisdom.

28.23–29: The lesson of the farmer's year. This is one of the most instructive prophetic parables* of the Hebrew Scriptures. The variety of activities that make up the farmer's year illustrate the force of vv. 21–22. To the question, "Would not destroying the city where the Temple* stands be a strange work for God the protector?" the prophet's answer is that, like the farmer, God has many varied tasks to perform—and judging a rebellious people is one of them.

29 Ah, Ariel, Ariel,
        the city where David encamped!
   Add year to year;
     let the festivals run their round.
2 Yet I will distress Ariel,
     and there shall be moaning and
          lamentation,
     and Jerusalem*a* shall be to me like an
          Ariel.*b*
3 And like David*c* I will encamp against
          you;

I will besiege you with towers
     and raise siegeworks against you.
4 Then deep from the earth you
          shall speak,
     from low in the dust your words shall
          come;
   your voice shall come from the ground
          like the voice of a ghost,
     and your speech shall whisper out of
          the dust.

29.1–24: The siege and deliverance of Jerusalem. This chapter centers on the threat to Jerusalem by Sennacherib's campaign in 701 BCE (see chs. 36–37). These oracles* attest to both the danger the city faced and its remarkable escape. Warnings explaining the near catastrophe occur in vv. 9–10, 13–14, and 15–16. Jerusalem's survival demanded further reflection on Isaiah's warnings, and Jerusalem's later destruction (587 BCE) posed further questions. These reflections are in vv. 5–8, with further messages of hope in vv. 17–21 and 22–24. **1–4:** *Ah, Ariel, Ariel, the city where David encamped! Ariel,* "altar hearth," refers to the sacred altar in the city, and the reference to King David recalls the taking of the city in 2 Sam 5.6–10, evoking its unique importance both to God and to Israel.

5 But the multitude of your foes*d* shall be
          like small dust,
     and the multitude of tyrants like
          flying chaff.
   And in an instant, suddenly,
6   you will be visited by the LORD
          of hosts
   with thunder and earthquake and great
          noise,
     with whirlwind and tempest, and the
          flame of a devouring fire.
7 And the multitude of all the nations
          that fight against Ariel,
     all that fight against her and her
          stronghold, and who distress her,
     shall be like a dream, a vision
          of the night.
8 Just as when a hungry person dreams of
          eating
     and wakes up still hungry,

a Heb *she*   *b* Probable meaning, *altar hearth;* compare
Ezek 43.15   *c* Gk: Meaning of Heb uncertain
d Cn: Heb *strangers*

or a thirsty person dreams of drinking
and wakes up faint, still thirsty,
so shall the multitude of all the nations be
that fight against Mount Zion.

9 Stupefy yourselves and be in a stupor,
blind yourselves and be blind!
Be drunk, but not from wine;
stagger, but not from strong drink!
10 For the LORD has poured out upon you
a spirit of deep sleep;
he has closed your eyes, you prophets,
and covered your heads, you seers.

11 The vision of all this has become for you like the words of a sealed document. If it is given to those who can read, with the command, "Read this," they say, "We cannot, for it is sealed." 12And if it is given to those who cannot read, saying, "Read this," they say, "We cannot read."

13 The Lord said:
Because these people draw near with
their mouths
and honor me with their lips,
while their hearts are far from me,
and their worship of me is a human
commandment learned by rote;
14 so I will again do
amazing things with this people,
shocking and amazing.
The wisdom of their wise shall perish,
and the discernment of the discerning
shall be hidden.

15 Ha! You who hide a plan too deep for
the LORD,
whose deeds are in the dark,
and who say, "Who sees us? Who
knows us?"
16 You turn things upside down!
Shall the potter be regarded as the clay?
Shall the thing made say of its maker,
"He did not make me";
or the thing formed say of the one who
formed it,
"He has no understanding"?

29.5–16. 5–8: The visitation of the LORD of hosts. God would intervene to protect Jerusalem, but it is not clear what actually occurred in 701 to explain this report (see comment on 37.36). This assurance may go back to Isaiah, or it may result from subsequent reflection on the deliverance of the city and King Hezekiah's continuing reign. The survival of the Davidic dynasty* in Jerusalem was of great significance when the destruction of Samaria and its royal house was recalled (see 2 Kings 18.10–12). 9–12: The people's inability to discern God's purpose is like drunken staggering. The warning in vv. 11–12 witnesses to the way in which the spoken word of the prophet was preserved to become a part of scripture. The reader of the book takes the place of the hearer of the word. 13–14: *The wisdom of their wise shall perish.* The foolhardy policies of the royal counselors and advisers would prove ruinous. 15–16: The prophet mocks the secrecy and subterfuge by which the royal counselors seek to hide their policy, with its high risk of military disaster, from the people.

17 Shall not Lebanon in a very little while
become a fruitful field,
and the fruitful field be regarded as a
forest?
18 On that day the deaf shall hear
the words of a scroll,
and out of their gloom and darkness
the eyes of the blind shall see.
19 The meek shall obtain fresh joy in the
LORD,
and the neediest people shall exult in
the Holy One of Israel.
20 For the tyrant shall be no more,
and the scoffer shall cease to be;
all those alert to do evil shall be cut
off—
21 those who cause a person to lose a
lawsuit,
who set a trap for the arbiter in the
gate,
and without grounds deny justice to
the one in the right.

22 Therefore thus says the LORD, who redeemed Abraham, concerning the house of Jacob:
No longer shall Jacob be ashamed,
no longer shall his face grow pale.
23 For when he sees his children,
the work of my hands, in his midst,
they will sanctify my name;
they will sanctify the Holy One of
Jacob,

and will stand in awe of the God of
Israel.
24 And those who err in spirit will come to
understanding,
and those who grumble will accept
instruction.

29.17–24. 17–21: The renewal of hope. It is not clear
why this message of hope, and the following one, have
been added at this point. Verse 18 affirms that Israel's
period of blindness (see 6.9–10) will pass, suggesting
a link with the renewed warning of this in 29.9. **22–24:**
And those who err in spirit: Israel's foolishness and lack
of discernment (v. 14) requires a look toward God's
deliverance. All who have forsaken God and the path
of righteousness will come to understand the truth.

30 Oh, rebellious children, says the
LORD,
who carry out a plan, but not mine;
who make an alliance, but against my
will,
adding sin to sin;
2 who set out to go down to Egypt
without asking for my counsel,
to take refuge in the protection of
Pharaoh,
and to seek shelter in the shadow of
Egypt;
3 Therefore the protection of Pharaoh
shall become your shame,
and the shelter in the shadow of
Egypt your humiliation.
4 For though his officials are at Zoan
and his envoys reach Hanes,
5 everyone comes to shame
through a people that cannot profit
them,
that brings neither help nor profit,
but shame and disgrace.

**30.1–33: In quietness and in trust shall be your
strength.** These memorable phrases present a central
teaching: Salvation and peace come through trusting
in God, not through human plans and alliances (v. 15).
The chapter is built up from a number of short prophetic sayings (vv. 1–5; 6–7; 12–14; 15–17) deriving
from the time of King Hezekiah's rebellion against Assyria (703–701 BCE) and the negotiations with Egypt
for protection. Subsequently, admonitions (vv. 8–11)
and assurances (vv. 18–26; 29–33) were added. The

assurance includes a warning: God will judge wrongdoers (vv. 27–28). **1–5:** Isaiah rejects Hezekiah's plan
to rebel against Assyria and to trust Egypt's promises
of help. The sending of royal emissaries from Judah to
Egypt (v. 4) must have prompted the original prophecy. This, along with Isaiah's awareness of secret consultations and plans made in Jerusalem (see 29.15),
suggests that he held a privileged position at court.

6 An oracle concerning the animals of the
Negeb.
Through a land of trouble and distress,
of lioness and roaring*a* lion,
of viper and flying serpent,
they carry their riches on the backs of
donkeys,
and their treasures on the humps of
camels,
to a people that cannot profit them.
7 For Egypt's help is worthless and empty,
therefore I have called her,
"Rahab who sits still."*b*

8 Go now, write it before them on
a tablet,
and inscribe it in a book,
so that it may be for the time to come
as a witness forever.
9 For they are a rebellious people,
faithless children,
children who will not hear
the instruction of the LORD;
10 who say to the seers, "Do not see";
and to the prophets, "Do not
prophesy to us what is right;
speak to us smooth things,
prophesy illusions,
11 leave the way, turn aside from the path,
let us hear no more about the Holy
One of Israel."
12 Therefore thus says the Holy One of
Israel:
Because you reject this word,
and put your trust in oppression and
deceit,
and rely on them;
13 therefore this iniquity shall become
for you

a Cn: Heb *from them*   *b* Meaning of Heb uncertain

like a break in a high wall, bulging
out, and about to collapse,
whose crash comes suddenly, in an
instant;
14 its breaking is like that of a potter's
vessel
that is smashed so ruthlessly
that among its fragments not a sherd is
found
for taking fire from the hearth,
or dipping water out of the cistern.

15 For thus said the Lord GOD, the Holy
One of Israel:
In returning and rest you shall be saved;
in quietness and in trust shall be your
strength.
But you refused 16and said,
"No! We will flee upon horses"—
therefore you shall flee!
and, "We will ride upon swift steeds"—
therefore your pursuers shall be swift!
17 A thousand shall flee at the threat
of one,
at the threat of five you shall flee,
until you are left
like a flagstaff on the top of
a mountain,
like a signal on a hill.

30.6–17. 6–7: Egypt was famous for palaces and monuments, and as the gateway to Africa for the caravans
that brought wealth and luxuries (see 1 Kings 10). The
prophet contrasts such exotic wealth with the worthlessness of the promises of Egyptian help. *Rahab* (v. 7)
was a dragon monster of ancient story comparable to
the Leviathan* creature (27.1). Since Egyptian religion
was well known for its many deities portrayed in mixed
animal/human form, the ironic title *"Rahab who sits
still"* (v. 7) may allude to the sphinx-like images of
Egypt. **8–11:** The command to *inscribe it in a book* is
a remarkably rare recognition that prophecy was written down and read long after the time when it had
originally been given. The writing is to become *a witness forever* to the truth that Israel was *a rebellious
people* (v. 9). The readers would be no more willing
to heed the message than the original hearers (see
29.11–12). **12–14:** *Its breaking is like that of a potter's
vessel* (v. 14) emphasizes the suddenness and completeness of the disaster that was to come. Hezekiah's
attempt to build security through an alliance with

Egypt would prove disastrously misjudged. **15–17:**
The poetry of *returning, rest, quietness, and trust* attests that God alone is the defense of Jerusalem.

18 Therefore the LORD waits to be gracious
to you;
therefore he will rise up to show
mercy to you.
For the LORD is a God of justice;
blessed are all those who wait for
him.

19 Truly, O people in Zion, inhabitants of
Jerusalem, you shall weep no more. He will
surely be gracious to you at the sound of your
cry; when he hears it, he will answer you.
20Though the Lord may give you the bread
of adversity and the water of affliction, yet
your Teacher will not hide himself any more,
but your eyes shall see your Teacher. 21And
when you turn to the right or when you turn
to the left, your ears shall hear a word behind
you, saying, "This is the way; walk in it."
22Then you will defile your silver-covered
idols and your gold-plated images. You will
scatter them like filthy rags; you will say to
them, "Away with you!"

23 He will give rain for the seed with
which you sow the ground, and grain, the
produce of the ground, which will be rich
and plenteous. On that day your cattle will
graze in broad pastures; 24and the oxen and
donkeys that till the ground will eat silage,
which has been winnowed with shovel and
fork. 25On every lofty mountain and every
high hill there will be brooks running with
water—on a day of the great slaughter, when
the towers fall. 26Moreover the light of the
moon will be like the light of the sun, and
the light of the sun will be sevenfold, like the
light of seven days, on the day when the
LORD binds up the injuries of his people, and
heals the wounds inflicted by his blow.

30.18–26: This poetic reminder of future hope counters any criticism that the message of rest and quietness (v. 15) was too submissive and politically inactive
to end foreign oppression. Human acceptance of the
divine plan for the nations may require patience and
fortitude in enduring the present order. A later scribe
has described more fully (vv. 19–26) what this longed-
for future would bring. Only when God's judgment

puts an end to human violence and oppression— *when the towers fall* (v. 25)—will such peace and prosperity come.

27 See, the name of the LORD comes from
    far away,
        burning with his anger, and in thick
        rising smoke;[a]
    his lips are full of indignation,
        and his tongue is like a devouring
        fire;
28 his breath is like an overflowing stream
    that reaches up to the neck—
    to sift the nations with the sieve of
        destruction,
        and to place on the jaws of the
            peoples a bridle that leads them
            astray.

29 You shall have a song as in the night when a holy festival is kept; and gladness of heart, as when one sets out to the sound of the flute to go to the mountain of the LORD, to the Rock of Israel. 30And the LORD will cause his majestic voice to be heard and the descending blow of his arm to be seen, in furious anger and a flame of devouring fire, with a cloudburst and tempest and hailstones. 31The Assyrian will be terror-stricken at the voice of the LORD, when he strikes with his rod. 32And every stroke of the staff of punishment that the LORD lays upon him will be to the sound of timbrels and lyres; battling with brandished arm he will fight with him. 33For his burning place[b] has long been prepared; truly it is made ready for the king,[c] its pyre made deep and wide, with fire and wood in abundance; the breath of the LORD, like a stream of sulfur, kindles it.

30.27–33: A song in the night. The concluding comments, a later development of the original message, elaborate on the theme of God's judgment, which will bring an end to the present unsatisfactory world order and establish in its place the righteous order of God. *The Assyrian* (v. 31) has become symbolic for every oppressor of God's people.

31 Alas for those who go down to
    Egypt for help
    and who rely on horses,

who trust in chariots because they are
    many
    and in horsemen because they are
        very strong,
    but do not look to the Holy One
        of Israel
    or consult the LORD!
2 Yet he too is wise and brings disaster;
    he does not call back his words,
    but will rise against the house of the
        evildoers,
        and against the helpers of those who
            work iniquity.
3 The Egyptians are human, and not God;
    their horses are flesh, and not spirit.
When the LORD stretches out his hand,
    the helper will stumble, and the one
        helped will fall,
    and they will all perish together.

4 For thus the LORD said to me,
As a lion or a young lion growls over its
        prey,
    and—when a band of shepherds is
        called out against it—
    is not terrified by their shouting
        or daunted at their noise,
so the LORD of hosts will come down
    to fight upon Mount Zion and upon
        its hill.
5 Like birds hovering overhead, so the
        LORD of hosts
    will protect Jerusalem;
he will protect and deliver it,
    he will spare and rescue it.

6 Turn back to him whom you[d] have deeply betrayed, O people of Israel. 7For on that day all of you shall throw away your idols of silver and idols of gold, which your hands have sinfully made for you.
8 "Then the Assyrian shall fall by a sword,
        not of mortals;
    and a sword, not of humans, shall
        devour him;
he shall flee from the sword,
    and his young men shall be put to
        forced labor.

a Meaning of Heb uncertain   b Or *Topheth*
c Or *Molech*   d Heb *they*

⁹ His rock shall pass away in terror,
  and his officers desert the standard in
      panic,"
says the LORD, whose fire is in
      Zion,
  and whose furnace is in Jerusalem.

31.1–9: The lordship of the God of Mount Zion. ∗
Isaiah continues to warn against complicity with Egypt
in rebellion against Assyria. The LORD *fighting upon
Mount Zion*∗ *and upon its hill* (v. 4) was perhaps originally a threat that God would fight against, not with,
Jerusalem (compare 29.4). Once again, a rebuke
(vv. 1–3) shifts suddenly to assurance (vv. 4–9), raising
the question at what point this new spiritual direction
arose. Was Isaiah compelled to change his warning
into one of promise, or has the situation that occurred
with King Hezekiah's surrender to the Assyrian forces
(2 Kings 18.13–16) necessitated a revised perspective?
The warning and promise introduce (v. 6) the rebuke
that Israel, a rebellious people, must first reject
idolatry∗ before God's deliverance can come. Threat
and assurance are two aspects of the one consistent,
loving purpose of God, to protect and preserve the
people. The reference to *a sword, not of mortals* (v. 8)
alludes to the angelic slaughter described in 37.36.

32 See, a king will reign in
      righteousness,
  and princes will rule with justice.
² Each will be like a hiding place from
      the wind,
  a covert from the tempest,
like streams of water in a dry place,
  like the shade of a great rock in a
      weary land.
³ Then the eyes of those who have sight
      will not be closed,
  and the ears of those who have
      hearing will listen.
⁴ The minds of the rash will have good
      judgment,
  and the tongues of stammerers will
      speak readily and distinctly.
⁵ A fool will no longer be called noble,
  nor a villain said to be honorable.
⁶ For fools speak folly,
  and their minds plot iniquity:
to practice ungodliness,
  to utter error concerning
      the LORD,

to leave the craving of the hungry
      unsatisfied,
  and to deprive the thirsty of drink.
⁷ The villainies of villains are evil;
  they devise wicked devices
to ruin the poor with lying words,
  even when the plea of the needy is
      right.
⁸ But those who are noble plan noble
      things,
  and by noble things they stand.
⁹ Rise up, you women who are at ease,
      hear my voice;
  you complacent daughters, listen to
      my speech.
¹⁰ In little more than a year
  you will shudder, you complacent
      ones;
for the vintage will fail,
  the fruit harvest will not come.
¹¹ Tremble, you women who are at ease,
  shudder, you complacent ones;
strip, and make yourselves bare,
  and put sackcloth on your loins.
¹² Beat your breasts for the pleasant
      fields,
  for the fruitful vine,
¹³ for the soil of my people
  growing up in thorns and briers;
yes, for all the joyous houses
  in the jubilant city.
¹⁴ For the palace will be forsaken,
  the populous city deserted;
the hill and the watchtower
  will become dens forever,
the joy of wild asses,
  a pasture for flocks;
¹⁵ until a spirit from on high is poured out
      on us,
  and the wilderness becomes a fruitful
      field,
  and the fruitful field is deemed
      a forest.
¹⁶ Then justice will dwell in the
      wilderness,
  and righteousness abide in the
      fruitful field.
¹⁷ The effect of righteousness will be
      peace,
  and the result of righteousness,
      quietness and trust forever.

18 My people will abide in a peaceful
    habitation,
  in secure dwellings, and in quiet
    resting places.
19 The forest will disappear completely,*a*
  and the city will be utterly laid low.
20 Happy will you be who sow beside every
    stream,
  who let the ox and the donkey range
    freely.

32.1–20: A king will reign in righteousness. 1–8: The deliverance of the city in 701 BCE was a dangerous precedent: It implied that God's protection could be relied upon unconditionally. The warning to Hezekiah in ch. 39 on the occasion of the visit of Babylonian emissaries was aimed at countering such false expectations. The Davidic kingship could not survive unless it was founded on just government and compassionate administration. This oracle* may be a portrait of the great reforming king, Josiah, during whose long reign (639–609 BCE) Assyrian rule over Judah ended and the royal administration was reformed (see 2 Kings 22.1–23.25). During this period a substantial part of Isaiah's prophecies was probably compiled. **9–14:** The brief respite of hope and renewal during Josiah's reign ended suddenly and disastrously. Babylonian rule swiftly replaced Assyrian oppression. Israel would suffer devastation once again, as Isaiah had declared (see 6.11–12) and the rampant growth of *thorns and briers* (see 5.6) would return. **15–20:** The outpouring of God's *spirit* (v. 15) and the transformation of the ruined land into farmland once again anticipate the hope of the later chapters, especially 60–62. The *forest* (v. 19) indicates oppressing foreign powers (Assyria and Babylon; see 10.18–19), which will *disappear completely*.

33 Ah, you destroyer,
  who yourself have not been
    destroyed;
you treacherous one,
  with whom no one has dealt
    treacherously!
When you have ceased to destroy,
  you will be destroyed;
and when you have stopped dealing
    treacherously,
  you will be dealt with treacherously.

2 O LORD, be gracious to us; we wait for
    you.

Be our arm every morning,
  our salvation in the time of trouble.
3 At the sound of tumult, peoples fled;
  before your majesty, nations
    scattered.
4 Spoil was gathered as the caterpillar
    gathers;
  as locusts leap, they leaped*b* upon it.
5 The LORD is exalted, he dwells on high;
  he filled Zion with justice and
    righteousness;
6 he will be the stability of your times,
  abundance of salvation, wisdom, and
    knowledge;
  the fear of the LORD is Zion's
    treasure.*c*

7 Listen! the valiant*b* cry in the streets;
  the envoys of peace weep bitterly.
8 The highways are deserted,
  travelers have quit the road.
The treaty is broken,
  its oaths*d* are despised,
  its obligation*e* is disregarded.
9 The land mourns and languishes;
  Lebanon is confounded and withers
    away;
  Sharon is like a desert;
  and Bashan and Carmel shake off
    their leaves.

10 "Now I will arise," says the LORD,
  "now I will lift myself up;
  now I will be exalted.
11 You conceive chaff, you bring
    forth stubble;
  your breath is a fire that will consume
    you.
12 And the peoples will be as if burned to
    lime,
  like thorns cut down, that are burned
    in the fire."

33.1–24. A miscellany of prophetic themes. This chapter, and the following two, are difficult to place in context, but they probably reflect the period after the fall of Babylon when the fulfillment of the glowing

a Cn: Heb *And it will hail when the forest comes down*
b Meaning of Heb uncertain   *c* Heb *his treasure;*
meaning of Heb uncertain   *d* Q Ms: MT *cities*
e Or *everyone*

promises of chs. 40–55 was still awaited. **1–6**: The *destroyer* is not identified, but the general context points to Babylon. Deliverance from oppression is still eagerly awaited, but requires patience and trust in God's purpose (v. 6). **7–12**: The lamentation* of vv. 7–9, revealing the devastated condition of the land, is followed by warnings in vv. 10–16 that the wrongdoing of leaders in Jerusalem now hinders the fulfillment of God's promises.

13 Hear, you who are far away, what I have
        done;
    and you who are near, acknowledge
        my might.
14 The sinners in Zion are afraid;
    trembling has seized the godless:
    "Who among us can live with the
        devouring fire?
    Who among us can live with
        everlasting flames?"
15 Those who walk righteously and speak
        uprightly,
    who despise the gain of oppression,
  who wave away a bribe instead of
        accepting it,
    who stop their ears from hearing of
        bloodshed
    and shut their eyes from looking on
        evil,
16 they will live on the heights;
    their refuge will be the fortresses of
        rocks;
    their food will be supplied, their
        water assured.

17 Your eyes will see the king in his
        beauty;
    they will behold a land that stretches
        far away.
18 Your mind will muse on the terror:
    "Where is the one who counted?
    Where is the one who weighed the
        tribute?
    Where is the one who counted the
        towers?"
19 No longer will you see the insolent
        people,
    the people of an obscure speech that
        you cannot comprehend,
    stammering in a language that you
        cannot understand.

20 Look on Zion, the city of our appointed
        festivals!
    Your eyes will see Jerusalem,
    a quiet habitation, an immovable tent,
  whose stakes will never be pulled up,
    and none of whose ropes will
        be broken.
21 But there the LORD in majesty will be
        for us
    a place of broad rivers and streams,
  where no galley with oars can go,
    nor stately ship can pass.
22 For the LORD is our judge, the LORD is
        our ruler,
    the LORD is our king; he will save us.

23 Your rigging hangs loose;
    it cannot hold the mast firm in its
        place,
    or keep the sail spread out.

    Then prey and spoil in abundance will
        be divided;
    even the lame will fall to plundering.
24 And no inhabitant will say, "I am sick";
    the people who live there will be
        forgiven their iniquity.

33.13–24. 13–16: The reference to those *who are far away* and those *who are near* reflects the divided condition of Israel in the wake of the removal of people into exile. The former nation was in danger of becoming two peoples with some still in the territory of Judah and others scattered among many nations. Isaiah emphasizes the unified purpose of God for both groups and the central significance of Jerusalem as the spiritual capital of all. **17–24:** Babylonian control over Judah and the catastrophes that had befallen Jerusalem had cast doubt on the future of the Davidic kingship. The message of 11.1–5 reveals how eagerly the people awaited a descendant of Judah's royal dynasty, and this hope is further repeated here. Instead of the hated representatives of foreign domination—zealous only for plunder and gain (v. 18)—there would be a king upholding justice and building prosperity (v. 17). Jerusalem would once again become *a quiet habitation* and *an immovable tent* (v. 20). The *broad rivers and streams*, strangely out of place in a city with no major waterways, establish a contrast to the many waterways of Babylon, with their oppressive associations.

34

Draw near, O nations, to hear;
O peoples, give heed!
Let the earth hear, and all that fills it;
  the world, and all that comes from it.
2 For the LORD is enraged against all the
    nations,
  and furious against all their hordes;
he has doomed them, has given them
    over for slaughter.
3 Their slain shall be cast out,
  and the stench of their corpses shall
    rise;
the mountains shall flow with their
    blood.
4 All the host of heaven shall rot away,
  and the skies roll up like a scroll.
All their host shall wither
  like a leaf withering on a vine,
  or fruit withering on a fig tree.

5 When my sword has drunk its fill in the
    heavens,
  lo, it will descend upon Edom,
upon the people I have doomed to
    judgment.
6 The LORD has a sword; it is sated with
    blood,
  it is gorged with fat,
with the blood of lambs and goats,
  with the fat of the kidneys of rams.
For the LORD has a sacrifice in Bozrah,
  a great slaughter in the land of Edom.
7 Wild oxen shall fall with them,
  and young steers with the
    mighty bulls.
Their land shall be soaked with blood,
  and their soil made rich with fat.

8 For the LORD has a day of vengeance,
  a year of vindication by Zion's
    cause.*a*
9 And the streams of Edom*b* shall be
    turned into pitch,
  and her soil into sulfur;
her land shall become burning pitch.
10 Night and day it shall not be quenched;
  its smoke shall go up forever.
From generation to generation it shall
    lie waste;
  no one shall pass through it forever
    and ever.

11 But the hawk*c* and the hedgehog*c* shall
    possess it;
  the owl*c* and the raven shall live in it.
He shall stretch the line of confusion
    over it,
  and the plummet of chaos over*d* its
    nobles.
12 They shall name it No Kingdom There,
  and all its princes shall be nothing.
13 Thorns shall grow over its strongholds,
  nettles and thistles in its fortresses.
It shall be the haunt of jackals,
  an abode for ostriches.
14 Wildcats shall meet with hyenas,
  goat-demons shall call to each other;
there too Lilith shall repose,
  and find a place to rest.
15 There shall the owl nest
  and lay and hatch and brood in its
    shadow;
there too the buzzards shall gather,
  each one with its mate.
16 Seek and read from the book of
    the LORD:
  Not one of these shall be missing;
  none shall be without its mate.
For the mouth of the LORD has
    commanded,
  and his spirit has gathered them.
17 He has cast the lot for them,
  his hand has portioned it out to them
    with the line;
they shall possess it forever,
  from generation to generation they
    shall live in it.

34.1–17: The LORD's day of vengeance. Taken together, chs. 34–35 provide a sequel to the prophecies of chs. 24–27, with which they are closely related both in theme and character. The major exception is the warning of the divine punishment that is to befall the people of Edom (34.5–17), a nation that is unexpectedly absent from the foreign peoples included in chs. 13–23. Their inclusion separately at this point may reflect a sharp condemnation of their treacherous role after the destruction of Jerusalem by Babylonian forces in 587 BCE. **1–4:** The opening addresses all nations and peoples with a fearsome warning of judgment to come

---

a Or *of recompense by Zion's defender* *b* Heb *her streams* *c* Identification uncertain *d* Heb lacks *over*

upon them all, similar to the warning of 24.1–23. **5–17:** The especially fierce and bloodthirsty warning of the judgment that is to befall Edom foretells that this land will be reduced to a total ruin, with all its population annihilated (vv. 9–13). It will become a home for wild animals, instead of a place of human habitation (vv. 14–17).

---

35 The wilderness and the dry land
　　　shall be glad,
　the desert shall rejoice and blossom;
like the crocus ²it shall blossom
　　　abundantly,
　and rejoice with joy and singing.
The glory of Lebanon shall be given
　　　to it,
　the majesty of Carmel and Sharon.
They shall see the glory of the LORD,
　the majesty of our God.

³ Strengthen the weak hands,
　and make firm the feeble knees.
⁴ Say to those who are of a fearful
　　　heart,
　"Be strong, do not fear!
Here is your God.
　He will come with vengeance,
with terrible recompense.
　He will come and save you."

⁵ Then the eyes of the blind shall
　　　be opened,
　and the ears of the deaf unstopped;
⁶ then the lame shall leap like a deer,
　and the tongue of the speechless sing
　　　for joy.
For waters shall break forth in the
　　　wilderness,
　and streams in the desert;
⁷ the burning sand shall become a pool,
　and the thirsty ground springs
　　　of water;
the haunt of jackals shall become
　　　a swamp,ᵃ
　the grass shall become reeds and
　　　rushes.

⁸ A highway shall be there,
　and it shall be called the Holy Way;
the unclean shall not travel on it,ᵇ
　but it shall be for God's people;ᶜ

no traveler, not even fools, shall go
　astray.
⁹ No lion shall be there,
　nor shall any ravenous beast come up
　　　on it;
they shall not be found there,
　but the redeemed shall walk there.
¹⁰ And the ransomed of the LORD shall
　　　return,
　and come to Zion with singing;
everlasting joy shall be upon their
　　　heads;
　they shall obtain joy and gladness,
and sorrow and sighing shall
　　　flee away.

35.1–10: The triumph of Zion. ⋆ **1–4:** In contrast to the grim and forbidding warnings of ch. 34, ch. 35 presents a picture of the hope that awaits the people of God when they rebuild the land of Judah and reestablish Jerusalem as their capital. It will be a fitting place to which all the scattered survivors of Israel can return. This chapter, without a clear historical context, may have been added to link chs. 40–55 with chs. 5–34. **5–10:** The hope for the special eminence that will come to Jerusalem (*Zion*) is consistent with chs. 60–62. The theme of the *highway* by which the scattered survivors of the nation will be enabled to return to their homeland (40.1) is anticipated in v. 8 (see also 19.23). The opening up of pools in the wilderness alludes to the promise of 41.17–18, while the opening of *eyes* and *ears* (v. 5) marks the end of the time of Israel's blindness and deafness (compare 6.9–10). Chapter 35 summarizes and concludes chs. 5–34, with their many threats and warnings, and opens the path to the more consistently hopeful message of chs. 40–66. Chapters 36–39 bridge these two major collections by reporting a triumphant sign of hope for Judah at the close of the eighth century.

The wonderful deliverance of Jerusalem
36.1–37.38: Jerusalem was saved from destruction when threatened by the forces of the Assyrian king, Sennacherib, in 701 BCE. The account is repeated from 2 Kings 18.17–19.37 because it provides the main background to chs. 28–31 and because of the major part that Isaiah played. The account itself is straight-

---

a Cn: Heb *in the haunt of jackals is her resting place*
b Or *pass it by*　　c Cn: Heb *for them*

forward: After the Assyrian forces had captured most of the towns and fortified cities of Judah (36.1), the Assyrian king sent his representative, called the Rabshakeh, to King Hezekiah in Jerusalem, urging him to surrender. This ultimatum is exceedingly dismissive of the LORD as protector of Jerusalem, regarding any god save that of the king of Assyria as worthless (36.13–20). A letter effectively repeats the same charges. The Assyrian ultimatum leaves Hezekiah gravely troubled until Isaiah encourages him to refuse (37.22–35). Isaiah insists that the Assyrian king, who has blasphemed God, will be punished accordingly, and that God will defend Jerusalem. Soon afterwards, the angel of the LORD strikes down 185,000 of the besieging force, compelling Sennacherib to return home (37.36–37).

Any effort to reconstruct the actual event needs to take three issues into account. First, 2 Kings 18.13–16 shows that Hezekiah surrendered to Sennacherib after the capture of Lachish and was forced to pay a heavy indemnity. Second, an Assyrian royal chronicle* of the campaign shows that the Assyrian commander regarded Hezekiah's surrender as a victory. Third, some untoward event (37.36) influenced the Assyrian king's return home in haste without destroying Jerusalem and removing its royal head, perhaps severe plague among the soldiers (see Isa 10.16), or news of an Egyptian counterattack (see Isa 37.7, 9). It is unlikely that Sennacherib campaigned against Jerusalem twice, so that the account of the humiliating withdrawal of the Assyrian forces refers to the second occasion, when no formal surrender from Hezekiah took place. It is more likely that Hezekiah did surrender to Sennacherib in 701 BCE, but the terms were remarkably lenient for unknown reasons. The Assyrian royal chronicle presumably omits all details that are less than flattering to the royal commander. To understand the prophetic significance of the narrative, it is important to recognize the contrast between the deliverance of Jerusalem in 701 BCE, and the grievous collapse and surrender of the city to the Babylonian forces in 598 and again in 587 BCE. This contrast is implied in the response of Isaiah to Hezekiah (39.5–8), when Babylonian emissaries visited Jerusalem.

---

36 In the fourteenth year of King Hezekiah, King Sennacherib of Assyria came up against all the fortified cities of Judah and captured them. ²The king of Assyria sent the Rabshakeh from Lachish to King Hezekiah at Jerusalem, with a great army. He stood by the conduit of the upper pool on the highway to the Fuller's Field. ³And there came out to him Eliakim son of Hilkiah, who was in charge of the palace, and Shebna the secretary, and Joah son of Asaph, the recorder.

4 The Rabshakeh said to them, "Say to Hezekiah: Thus says the great king, the king of Assyria: On what do you base this confidence of yours? ⁵Do you think that mere words are strategy and power for war? On whom do you now rely, that you have rebelled against me? ⁶See, you are relying on Egypt, that broken reed of a staff, which will pierce the hand of anyone who leans on it. Such is Pharaoh king of Egypt to all who rely on him. ⁷But if you say to me, 'We rely on the LORD our God,' is it not he whose high places and altars Hezekiah has removed, saying to Judah and to Jerusalem, 'You shall worship before this altar'? ⁸Come now, make a wager with my master the king of Assyria: I will give you two thousand horses, if you are able on your part to set riders on them. ⁹How then can you repulse a single captain among the least of my master's servants, when you rely on Egypt for chariots and for horsemen? ¹⁰Moreover, is it without the LORD that I have come up against this land to destroy it? The LORD said to me, Go up against this land, and destroy it."

11 Then Eliakim, Shebna, and Joah said to the Rabshakeh, "Please speak to your servants in Aramaic, for we understand it; do not speak to us in the language of Judah within the hearing of the people who are on the wall." ¹²But the Rabshakeh said, "Has my master sent me to speak these words to your master and to you, and not to the people sitting on the wall, who are doomed with you to eat their own dung and drink their own urine?"

13 Then the Rabshakeh stood and called out in a loud voice in the language of Judah, "Hear the words of the great king, the king of Assyria! ¹⁴Thus says the king: 'Do not let Hezekiah deceive you, for he will not be able to deliver you. ¹⁵Do not let Hezekiah make you rely on the LORD by saying, The LORD will surely deliver us; this city will not be given into the hand of the king of Assyria.'

16 Do not listen to Hezekiah; for thus says the king of Assyria: 'Make your peace with me and come out to me; then everyone of you will eat from your own vine and your own fig tree and drink water from your own cistern, 17 until I come and take you away to a land like your own land, a land of grain and wine, a land of bread and vineyards. 18 Do not let Hezekiah mislead you by saying, The LORD will save us. Has any of the gods of the nations saved their land out of the hand of the king of Assyria? 19 Where are the gods of Hamath and Arpad? Where are the gods of Sepharvaim? Have they delivered Samaria out of my hand? 20 Who among all the gods of these countries have saved their countries out of my hand, that the LORD should save Jerusalem out of my hand?' "

21 But they were silent and answered him not a word, for the king's command was, "Do not answer him." 22 Then Eliakim son of Hilkiah, who was in charge of the palace, and Shebna the secretary, and Joah son of Asaph, the recorder, came to Hezekiah with their clothes torn, and told him the words of the Rabshakeh.

37 When King Hezekiah heard it, he tore his clothes, covered himself with sackcloth, and went into the house of the LORD. 2 And he sent Eliakim, who was in charge of the palace, and Shebna the secretary, and the senior priests, covered with sackcloth, to the prophet Isaiah son of Amoz. 3 They said to him, "Thus says Hezekiah, This day is a day of distress, of rebuke, and of disgrace; children have come to the birth, and there is no strength to bring them forth. 4 It may be that the LORD your God heard the words of the Rabshakeh, whom his master the king of Assyria has sent to mock the living God, and will rebuke the words that the LORD your God has heard; therefore lift up your prayer for the remnant that is left."

5 When the servants of King Hezekiah came to Isaiah, 6 Isaiah said to them, "Say to your master, 'Thus says the LORD: Do not be afraid because of the words that you have heard, with which the servants of the king of Assyria have reviled me. 7 I myself will put a spirit in him, so that he shall hear a rumor, and return to his own land; I will cause him to fall by the sword in his own land.' "

36.1–37.7: The report of the speech of the Assyrian Rabshakeh and Isaiah's response. Two closely parallel accounts tell the story of the Assyrian address mocking Hezekiah's God along with Isaiah's reply. In the first account (36.1–37.7), the Rabshakeh speaks in the hearing of all Jerusalem, whereas in the second (37.8–38) the ultimatum is conveyed by letter and a much longer reply is given by Isaiah (37.6–7 compared with 37.22–35). **36.2:** *The king of Assyria sent the Rabshakeh from Lachish.* The siege and capture of Lachish formed the major battle of the Assyrian campaign in Judah and was afterwards extensively illustrated in carved wallpanels that decorated Sennacherib's palace. These have been recovered and are now displayed in the British Museum in London.

〜〜〜〜〜〜〜〜〜〜〜〜〜

8 The Rabshakeh returned, and found the king of Assyria fighting against Libnah; for he had heard that the king had left Lachish. 9 Now the king[a] heard concerning King Tirhakah of Ethiopia,[b] "He has set out to fight against you." When he heard it, he sent messengers to Hezekiah, saying, 10 "Thus shall you speak to King Hezekiah of Judah: Do not let your God on whom you rely deceive you by promising that Jerusalem will not be given into the hand of the king of Assyria. 11 See, you have heard what the kings of Assyria have done to all lands, destroying them utterly. Shall you be delivered? 12 Have the gods of the nations delivered them, the nations that my predecessors destroyed, Gozan, Haran, Rezeph, and the people of Eden who were in Telassar? 13 Where is the king of Hamath, the king of Arpad, the king of the city of Sepharvaim, the king of Hena, or the king of Ivvah?"

14 Hezekiah received the letter from the hand of the messengers and read it; then Hezekiah went up to the house of the LORD and spread it before the LORD. 15 And Hezekiah prayed to the LORD, saying: 16 "O LORD of hosts, God of Israel, who are enthroned above the cherubim, you are God, you alone, of all the kingdoms of the earth;

a Heb *he*   *b* Or *Nubia;* Heb *Cush*

you have made heaven and earth. 17Incline your ear, O LORD, and hear; open your eyes, O LORD, and see; hear all the words of Sennacherib, which he has sent to mock the living God. 18Truly, O LORD, the kings of Assyria have laid waste all the nations and their lands, 19and have hurled their gods into the fire, though they were no gods, but the work of human hands—wood and stone—and so they were destroyed. 20So now, O LORD our God, save us from his hand, so that all the kingdoms of the earth may know that you alone are the LORD."

21 Then Isaiah son of Amoz sent to Hezekiah, saying: "Thus says the LORD, the God of Israel: Because you have prayed to me concerning King Sennacherib of Assyria, 22this is the word that the LORD has spoken concerning him:

She despises you, she scorns you—
    virgin daughter Zion;
she tosses her head—behind
        your back,
    daughter Jerusalem.

23 "Whom have you mocked and
            reviled?
    Against whom have you raised your
            voice
and haughtily lifted your eyes?
    Against the Holy One of Israel!
24 By your servants you have mocked
            the Lord,
    and you have said, 'With my many
            chariots
I have gone up the heights of the
            mountains,
    to the far recesses of Lebanon;
I felled its tallest cedars,
    its choicest cypresses;
I came to its remotest height,
    its densest forest.
25 I dug wells
    and drank waters,
I dried up with the sole of my foot
    all the streams of Egypt.'

26 "Have you not heard
    that I determined it long ago?
I planned from days of old
    what now I bring to pass,

that you should make fortified cities
    crash into heaps of ruins,
27 while their inhabitants, shorn of
            strength,
    are dismayed and confounded;
they have become like plants of
            the field
    and like tender grass,
like grass on the housetops,
    blighted*c* before it is grown.

28 "I know your rising up*b* and your sitting
            down,
    your going out and coming in,
    and your raging against me.
29 Because you have raged against me
    and your arrogance has come to my
            ears,
I will put my hook in your nose
    and my bit in your mouth;
I will turn you back on the way
    by which you came.

30 "And this shall be the sign for you: This year eat what grows of itself, and in the second year what springs from that; then in the third year sow, reap, plant vineyards, and eat their fruit. 31The surviving remnant of the house of Judah shall again take root downward, and bear fruit upward; 32for from Jerusalem a remnant shall go out, and from Mount Zion a band of survivors. The zeal of the LORD of hosts will do this.

33 "Therefore thus says the LORD concerning the king of Assyria: He shall not come into this city, shoot an arrow there, come before it with a shield, or cast up a siege ramp against it. 34By the way that he came, by the same he shall return; he shall not come into this city, says the LORD. 35For I will defend this city to save it, for my own sake and for the sake of my servant David."

36 Then the angel of the LORD set out and struck down one hundred eighty-five

a With 2 Kings 19.26: Heb *field*   *b* Q Ms Gk: MT lacks *your rising up*

thousand in the camp of the Assyrians; when morning dawned, they were all dead bodies. 37Then King Sennacherib of Assyria left, went home, and lived at Nineveh. 38As he was worshiping in the house of his god Nisroch, his sons Adrammelech and Sharezer killed him with the sword, and they escaped into the land of Ararat. His son Esar-haddon succeeded him.

37.8–38. 9: *When he heard it, he sent messengers to Hezekiah:* A repetition of the Assyrian ultimatum. **15–21:** The prayer of Hezekiah demonstrates the trust and piety of the king (see especially v. 21). **21–35:** Isaiah replies to the Assyrian letter with a series of prophetic declarations. Jerusalem survived intact and the king retained his throne. These facts were more central to Isaiah's message than the punishment eventually inflicted on Sennacherib, who is accused of blasphemy (37.38). **36:** The work of *the angel of the LORD* may have been an outbreak of disease among forces camped in unhygienic conditions (as foretold in 10.16). Verse 37.7 declares: "I myself will put a spirit in him, so that he shall hear a rumor and return to his own land." Other possibilities cannot be ruled out, and no precise information is available. **37–38:** Sennacherib's assassination by members of his own family is not reported in Assyrian royal chronicles. The king's death occurred some time after the events of 701, but his insult to the God of Jerusalem was seen to demand personal punishment.

38 In those days Hezekiah became sick and was at the point of death. The prophet Isaiah son of Amoz came to him, and said to him, "Thus says the LORD: Set your house in order, for you shall die; you shall not recover." 2Then Hezekiah turned his face to the wall, and prayed to the LORD: 3"Remember now, O LORD, I implore you, how I have walked before you in faithfulness with a whole heart, and have done what is good in your sight." And Hezekiah wept bitterly.

4 Then the word of the LORD came to Isaiah: 5"Go and say to Hezekiah, Thus says the LORD, the God of your ancestor David: I have heard your prayer, I have seen your tears; I will add fifteen years to your life. 6I will deliver you and this city out of the hand of the king of Assyria, and defend this city.

7 "This is the sign to you from the LORD, that the LORD will do this thing that he has promised: 8See, I will make the shadow cast by the declining sun on the dial of Ahaz turn back ten steps." So the sun turned back on the dial the ten steps by which it had declined.*a*

9 A writing of King Hezekiah of Judah, after he had been sick and had recovered from his sickness:
10 I said: In the noontide of my days
　　I must depart;
　I am consigned to the gates of Sheol
　　for the rest of my years.
11 I said, I shall not see the LORD
　　in the land of the living;
　I shall look upon mortals no more
　　among the inhabitants of the world.
12 My dwelling is plucked up and removed
　　　from me
　　like a shepherd's tent;
　like a weaver I have rolled up my life;
　　he cuts me off from the loom;
　from day to night you bring me to an
　　　end;*a*
13 　I cry for help*b* until morning;
　like a lion he breaks all my bones;
　　from day to night you bring me to an
　　　end.*a*

14 Like a swallow or a crane*a* I clamor,
　I moan like a dove.
　My eyes are weary with looking
　　　upward.
　O Lord, I am oppressed; be my
　　　security!
15 But what can I say? For he has spoken
　　　to me,
　　and he himself has done it.
　All my sleep has fled*c*
　　because of the bitterness of my soul.

16 O Lord, by these things people live,
　　and in all these is the life of
　　　my spirit.*a*
　　Oh, restore me to health and make
　　　me live!

a Meaning of Heb uncertain　　*b* Cn: Meaning of Heb uncertain　　*c* Cn Compare Syr: Heb *I will walk slowly all my years*

17 Surely it was for my welfare
     that I had great bitterness;
but you have held back*a* my life
     from the pit of destruction,
for you have cast all my sins
     behind your back.
18 For Sheol cannot thank you,
     death cannot praise you;
those who go down to the Pit cannot
     hope
     for your faithfulness.
19 The living, the living, they thank you,
     as I do this day;
fathers make known to children
     your faithfulness.

20 The LORD will save me,
     and we will sing to stringed
     instruments*b*
all the days of our lives,
     at the house of the LORD.

21 Now Isaiah had said, "Let them take a lump of figs, and apply it to the boil, so that he may recover." 22 Hezekiah also had said, "What is the sign that I shall go up to the house of the LORD?"

38.1–22: Hezekiah's sickness and recovery. The story of Hezekiah's illness (v. 21) is a further illustration of piety (v. 3): His total submissiveness to the will of the LORD God and his subsequent recovery from the sickness are inseparably related to the wonderful deliverance of Jerusalem from the forces of Assyria (v. 6). Signs were evidence of the validity of a prophetic pronouncement (see Isa 7.10–17). The exact nature of the sign is not clear. **10–20:** This psalm of thanksgiving is not included in 2 Kings 20.1–11, but is added as further evidence of the king's piety. It is a personal psalm of thanksgiving for recovery from serious illness. It includes a lamentation during the time of distress (vv. 10–15) and thanksgiving for recovery (vv. 16–20).

39 At that time King Merodach-baladan son of Baladan of Babylon sent envoys with letters and a present to Hezekiah, for he heard that he had been sick and had recovered. 2 Hezekiah welcomed them; he showed them his treasure house, the silver, the gold, the spices, the precious oil, his whole armory, all that was found in his store-

houses. There was nothing in his house or in all his realm that Hezekiah did not show them. 3 Then the prophet Isaiah came to King Hezekiah and said to him, "What did these men say? From where did they come to you?" Hezekiah answered, "They have come to me from a far country, from Babylon." 4 He said, "What have they seen in your house?" Hezekiah answered, "They have seen all that is in my house; there is nothing in my storehouses that I did not show them."

5 Then Isaiah said to Hezekiah, "Hear the word of the LORD of hosts: 6 Days are coming when all that is in your house, and that which your ancestors have stored up until this day, shall be carried to Babylon; nothing shall be left, says the LORD. 7 Some of your own sons who are born to you shall be taken away; they shall be eunuchs in the palace of the king of Babylon." 8 Then Hezekiah said to Isaiah, "The word of the LORD that you have spoken is good." For he thought, "There will be peace and security in my days."

39.1–8: The visit of the Babylonian emissaries. The book of Isaiah is built around belief in God's concern with the Davidic dynasty* of kings and the city of Jerusalem where God's Temple* stood. The contrast between the fate of the dynasty and the city in 701 BCE, when Isaiah was active as a prophet, and events a century later when the Babylonian forces confronted Jerusalem (in 598 and again in 587 BCE), effectively divides the book between two main periods—the Assyrian and the Babylonian epochs. The visit of Babylonian emissaries to Hezekiah when Sennacherib threatened the king and his city forms a bridge between these two main sections. The events in vv. 6–7 occurred in 598 BCE when Jehoiachin was removed from the throne and taken prisoner to Babylon, with most of his immediate household (2 Kings 24.10–17). God's protection of Jerusalem and its Davidic dynasty was not unconditional, but depended upon the obedience and submission of each ruler. The comment of Hezekiah, *There will be peace and security in my days* (v.8), is not selfish complacency but a submissive acceptance of the conditions under which God's promise was conferred. More than this could not be given.

a Cn Compare Gk Vg: Heb *loved*   *b* Heb *my stringed instruments*

Isaiah 40-55

THE RENEWAL OF HOPE FOR JERUSALEM

In 538 BCE, a combined force of Medes and Persians entered the city of Babylon, having previously defeated the Babylonian military might. During the decade before the collapse of Babylonian rule, the prophecies that make up chs. 40–55 were written. They show a remarkable similarity of mood and character and are, with only minor exceptions, attributed to a single prophet. They express in richly poetic language a message of comfort, addressed primarily to Jerusalem, but also to the scattered remnants of the former Israel. They assure the readers that God is Creator and Lord of history. Israel's past experience proves this; the fulfillment of earlier prophecies bears witness to it; and current events confirm it. The prophet points to the rise of Cyrus, the Persian ruler whose victories put an end to Babylon's domination. Unbelief, despair, and idolatry* are all condemned as neglect of the one true God. This emphatic focus on the sole deity of the LORD God of Israel makes these chapters the most forthright declaration of monotheism in the Hebrew Scriptures.

Combined with this message of comfort and reassurance for Israel is a clear promise that those exiled among the nations will return home. A way will open up in the wilderness for this processional return to Jerusalem, and God will providentially support the weak and distressed who make the journey. The city of Babylon will fall (47.1–15) and Jerusalem will be rebuilt (44.28; 54.11–17). Its future will be even more splendid than its past, and a new age of peace and tranquillity will dawn.

Overall, the message balances the warnings and threats that have colored most of chs. 1–39. Even more, however, these chapters allude to earlier prophecies and carry their message further. Clearly the prophet of chs. 40–55, sometimes referred to as Second Isaiah, was close to the scribes who preserved the sayings of the first part, even being described as a "disciple" of the earlier prophet (50.4–6; compare 8.16). Chapters 40–55 carry forward the message about Jerusalem and its future as the symbolic center of Israel as the people of God. The tragedies of the past will become the triumphs of the future in God's plan.

Explicit references to the Persian ruler Cyrus (44.28; 45.1; compare 41.25) point to the events of 545–538 BCE, a time just before the downfall of Babylon. The prophet addresses Israelite captives held in Babylon (42.7, 8) and recognizes the dispersion of many survivors of Israel and Judah among the nations (49.22–23). The fall of Babylon is foretold as imminent, with an expectation of the subsequent release of the captives from Judah and their return home (55.12). Because the prophet alternately addresses Jerusalem and the scattered remnants, it is not clear where he was located. He was clearly sensitive to the sufferings of captives held in Babylon, so he may have been among them. His frequent explicit addresses to Zion and Jerusalem (40.1, 9; 49.14; 52.1), however, may indicate that he cannot have been far from this city, the undoubted spiritual focus of his thinking. Even with this focus, the prophet looks beyond known national boundaries to the undefined coastlands (41.1, 5; 49.1) and the ends of the earth (41.9).

READING GUIDE

Recent study of these sixteen chapters recognizes their psalm-like quality. The prophet's thought and language were evidently deeply colored by the Hebrew psalms. Jerusalem with its Temple* was his spiritual and intellectual home, even though the Temple itself had been in ruins for half

a century. Moreover, the prophecies concentrate intensely on hope and encouragement, giving them great power. The original audience was presumably either indifferent to God's message or near despair about its relevance. Consequently, the emphasis upon the most basic religious themes—the creation of the world, the idea of purpose and meaning in human history, the oneness of God and of all nations and peoples in the divine plan—has made these chapters unequaled anywhere else in prophecy.

40 Comfort, O comfort my people,
  says your God.
2 Speak tenderly to Jerusalem,
  and cry to her
that she has served her term,
  that her penalty is paid,
that she has received from the LORD's
  hand
double for all her sins.

3 A voice cries out:
"In the wilderness prepare the way of
  the LORD,
  make straight in the desert a highway
  for our God.
4 Every valley shall be lifted up,
  and every mountain and hill be made
  low;
the uneven ground shall become level,
  and the rough places a plain.
5 Then the glory of the LORD shall
  be revealed,
  and all people shall see it together,

for the mouth of the LORD has
  spoken."

6 A voice says, "Cry out!"
  And I said, "What shall I cry?"
All people are grass,
  their constancy is like the flower of
  the field.
7 The grass withers, the flower fades,
  when the breath of the LORD blows
  upon it;
  surely the people are grass.
8 The grass withers, the flower fades;
  but the word of our God will stand
  forever.
9 Get you up to a high mountain,
  O Zion, herald of good tidings;[a]
lift up your voice with strength,
  O Jerusalem, herald of good tidings,[b]
  lift it up, do not fear;

a Or O herald of good tidings to Zion   b Or O herald of good tidings to Jerusalem

say to the cities of Judah,
"Here is your God!"

10 See, the Lord GOD comes with might,
and his arm rules for him;
his reward is with him,
and his recompense before him.
11 He will feed his flock like a shepherd;
he will gather the lambs in his arms,
and carry them in his bosom,
and gently lead the mother sheep.

40.1–31: A highway for our God. 1–11: The prophet begins by calling on the reader to bring a message of *comfort* to Jerusalem. Her period of servitude is now complete and freedom is at hand (v. 2). This message of hope pictures a great *highway* stretching across the desert and leading to Jerusalem (vv. 3–5), providing a way home for those scattered remnants of the former Israel who have been captive among the nations, particularly in Babylon. God will strengthen the weakened survivors who feel that they cannot make the journey (vv. 10–11; 29–31).

12 Who has measured the waters in the
hollow of his hand
and marked off the heavens with a
span,
enclosed the dust of the earth in
a measure,
and weighed the mountains in scales
and the hills in a balance?
13 Who has directed the spirit of the LORD,
or as his counselor has instructed
him?
14 Whom did he consult for his
enlightenment,
and who taught him the path of
justice?
Who taught him knowledge,
and showed him the way of
understanding?
15 Even the nations are like a drop from a
bucket,
and are accounted as dust on
the scales;
see, he takes up the isles like fine
dust.
16 Lebanon would not provide fuel
enough,
nor are its animals enough for a burnt
offering.

17 All the nations are as nothing before
him;
they are accounted by him as less
than nothing and emptiness.

18 To whom then will you liken God,
or what likeness compare with him?
19 An idol? —A workman casts it,
and a goldsmith overlays it with gold,
and casts for it silver chains.
20 As a gift one chooses mulberry wood*a*
—wood that will not rot—
then seeks out a skilled artisan
to set up an image that will
not topple.

21 Have you not known? Have you
not heard?
Has it not been told you from the
beginning?
Have you not understood from the
foundations of the earth?
22 It is he who sits above the circle of the
earth,
and its inhabitants are like
grasshoppers;
who stretches out the heavens like a
curtain,
and spreads them like a tent to
live in;
23 who brings princes to naught,
and makes the rulers of the earth as
nothing.

24 Scarcely are they planted, scarcely
sown,
scarcely has their stem taken root in
the earth,
when he blows upon them, and they
wither,
and the tempest carries them off like
stubble.

25 To whom then will you compare me,
or who is my equal? says the Holy
One.
26 Lift up your eyes on high and see:
Who created these?

a Meaning of Heb uncertain

He who brings out their host and
numbers them,
calling them all by name;
because he is great in strength,
mighty in power,
not one is missing.

27 Why do you say, O Jacob,
and speak, O Israel,
"My way is hidden from the LORD,
and my right is disregarded by my
God"?
28 Have you not known? Have you
not heard?
The LORD is the everlasting God,
the Creator of the ends of the earth.
He does not faint or grow weary;
his understanding is unsearchable.
29 He gives power to the faint,
and strengthens the powerless.
30 Even youths will faint and be weary,
and the young will fall exhausted;
31 but those who wait for the LORD shall
renew their strength,
they shall mount up with wings like
eagles,
they shall run and not be weary,
they shall walk and not faint.

40.12–31. 12–20: Such a message would be unbeliev-
able if God were other than the sovereign creator of
the entire universe (vv. 12–14). Even the multitude of
the nations of the world *are as nothing* before such
immense power (v. 17). 21–28: The very stars adhere
to the divine places set for them at creation (v. 26).
Already vv. 19–20 answer the question posed in v. 18:
False ideas of God lead to false expectations about the
divine purpose. Only by abandoning the absurdities
of idolatry✷ can the people grasp the power of God
(v. 23).

41 Listen to me in silence,
O coastlands;
let the peoples renew their strength;
let them approach, then let
them speak;
let us together draw near for
judgment.

2 Who has roused a victor from the east,
summoned him to his service?

He delivers up nations to him,
and tramples kings under foot;
he makes them like dust with his sword,
like driven stubble with his bow.
3 He pursues them and passes on safely,
scarcely touching the path with his
feet.
4 Who has performed and done this,
calling the generations from the
beginning?
I, the LORD, am first,
and will be with the last.
5 The coastlands have seen and
are afraid,
the ends of the earth tremble;
they have drawn near and come.
6 Each one helps the other,
saying to one another, "Take
courage!"
7 The artisan encourages the goldsmith,
and the one who smooths with the
hammer encourages the one who
strikes the anvil,
saying of the soldering, "It is good";
and they fasten it with nails so that it
cannot be moved.
8 But you, Israel, my servant,
Jacob, whom I have chosen,
the offspring of Abraham, my friend;
9 you whom I took from the ends of the
earth,
and called from its farthest corners,
saying to you, "You are my servant,
I have chosen you and not cast you
off";
10 do not fear, for I am with you,
do not be afraid, for I am your God;
I will strengthen you, I will help you,
I will uphold you with my victorious
right hand.

41.1–29: I am your God. 1–5: The speech of the Assyrian Rabshakeh in 36.20 had asked in complacent
irony:✷ "Who among all the gods of the countries
have saved their countries out of my hand, that the
LORD should save Jerusalem out of my hand?" The
prophecies of ch. 41 provide a magnificent rejoinder
to this question, showing how and why the God of
Jerusalem is different. The Holy One of Israel is creator
and director of human history. Proof of this is first seen
in the victories that Cyrus, king of the Medes and Per-

sians, has already won (vv. 2–5, 25). This ruler is mentioned by name more fully in 44.28; 45.1–4, 13. The *coastlands* (vv. 1, 5) are the most distant parts of the earth, so that all nations may recognize that a divine plan is at work. **6–10:** Again the prophet ridicules the foolish work of the idol maker (see also 23–24, 29). God had already called Israel to be the servant-people who would fulfill God's special purpose on earth (compare 49.6).

11 Yes, all who are incensed against you
    shall be ashamed and disgraced;
  those who strive against you
    shall be as nothing and
      shall perish.
12 You shall seek those who contend
    with you,
  but you shall not find them;
  those who war against you
    shall be as nothing at all.
13 For I, the LORD your God,
    hold your right hand;
  it is I who say to you, "Do not fear,
    I will help you."

14 Do not fear, you worm Jacob,
    you insect*a* Israel!
  I will help you, says the LORD;
    your Redeemer is the Holy One of
      Israel.
15 Now, I will make of you a threshing
    sledge,
  sharp, new, and having teeth;
  you shall thresh the mountains and
    crush them,
  and you shall make the hills
    like chaff.
16 You shall winnow them and the wind
    shall carry them away,
  and the tempest shall scatter them.
  Then you shall rejoice in the LORD;
    in the Holy One of Israel you shall
      glory.

17 When the poor and needy seek water,
    and there is none,
  and their tongue is parched
    with thirst,
  I the LORD will answer them,
    I the God of Israel will not forsake
    them.

18 I will open rivers on the bare heights,*b*
    and fountains in the midst of
      the valleys;
  I will make the wilderness a pool
    of water,
    and the dry land springs of water.
19 I will put in the wilderness the cedar,
    the acacia, the myrtle, and the olive;
  I will set in the desert the cypress,
    the plane and the pine together,
20 so that all may see and know,
    all may consider and understand,
  that the hand of the LORD has done this,
    the Holy One of Israel has created it.

21 Set forth your case, says the LORD;
    bring your proofs, says the King of
      Jacob.
22 Let them bring them, and tell us
    what is to happen.
  Tell us the former things, what they are,
    so that we may consider them,
  and that we may know their outcome;
    or declare to us the things to come.
23 Tell us what is to come hereafter,
    that we may know that you are gods;
  do good, or do harm,
    that we may be afraid and terrified.
24 You, indeed, are nothing
    and your work is nothing at all;
  whoever chooses you is an
    abomination.

25 I stirred up one from the north, and he
    has come,
  from the rising of the sun he was
    summoned by name.*c*
  He shall trample*d* on rulers as on
    mortar,
    as the potter treads clay.
26 Who declared it from the beginning, so
    that we might know,
  and beforehand, so that we might say,
    "He is right"?
  There was no one who declared it, none
    who proclaimed,
    none who heard your words.

a Syr: Heb *men of*   *b* Or *trails*   *c* Cn Compare
Q Ms Gk: MT *and he shall call on my name*
d Cn: Heb *come*

27 I first have declared it to Zion,^a
　　and I give to Jerusalem a herald of
　　　good tidings.
28 But when I look there is no one;
　　among these there is no counselor
　　who, when I ask, gives an answer.
29 No, they are all a delusion;
　　their works are nothing;
　　their images are empty wind.

41.11–29. 11–16: The present weakness of Israel (v. 14) is contrasted with the strength that God will confer upon them (vv. 15–16). **17–24:** Israel's tradition taught that, at the beginning of the nation's history, God had provided sustenance for the journey through the wilderness (see Deut 8.1–4), and now that same care would be repeated.

42

Here is my servant, whom
　　I uphold,
　my chosen, in whom my soul
　　delights;
I have put my spirit upon him;
　　he will bring forth justice to the
　　　nations.
2 He will not cry or lift up his voice,
　　or make it heard in the street;
3 a bruised reed he will not break,
　　and a dimly burning wick he will not
　　　quench;
　he will faithfully bring forth justice.
4 He will not grow faint or be crushed
　　until he has established justice in the
　　　earth;
　and the coastlands wait for his
　　teaching.

5 Thus says God, the LORD,
　　who created the heavens and
　　　stretched them out,
　who spread out the earth and what
　　comes from it,
who gives breath to the people upon it
　and spirit to those who walk in it:
6 I am the LORD, I have called you in
　　righteousness,
　I have taken you by the hand and
　　kept you;
I have given you as a covenant to the
　　people,^b
　a light to the nations,

7 to open the eyes that are blind,
　to bring out the prisoners from the
　　dungeon,
　　from the prison those who sit in
　　　darkness.
8 I am the LORD, that is my name;
　　my glory I give to no other,
　　nor my praise to idols.
9 See, the former things have come
　　to pass,
　and new things I now declare;
before they spring forth,
　I tell you of them.

10 Sing to the LORD a new song,
　　his praise from the end of the earth!
Let the sea roar^c and all that fills it,
　the coastlands and their inhabitants.
11 Let the desert and its towns lift up their
　　voice,
　the villages that Kedar inhabits;
let the inhabitants of Sela sing for joy,
　let them shout from the tops of the
　　mountains.
12 Let them give glory to the LORD,
　　and declare his praise in the
　　coastlands.
13 The LORD goes forth like a soldier,
　　like a warrior he stirs up his fury;
he cries out, he shouts aloud,
　he shows himself mighty against his
　　foes.

42.1–25: The mission of the servant. 1–4: The introduction of the servant (see sidebar, p. 929) follows the pattern of a royal emissary being introduced at court. The authority of the sender is conferred on the deputy who is sent. **5–9:** The servant of God is to bring *a light to the nations* (v. 6). This is the coming of salvation and the ending of Israel's spiritual blindness (v. 7), but is this promise only for the scattered survivors of Israel who dwell among the nations, or is it also for those nations themselves? Verse 49.6 answers this question: It is for everyone, although 45.22 comes very close to anticipating this message. The inescapable force of the argument that the LORD God of Israel is the creator and lord of all nations leads to this larger hope for the

a Cn: Heb First to Zion—Behold, behold them
b Meaning of Heb uncertain   c Cn Compare Ps 96.11;
98.7: Heb Those who go down to the sea

The Servant of God

The theme of the "Servant of God" is developed in a distinctive way in 42.1–4, one of four passages that scholars have come to identify as the four "Servant Songs" (the others are 49.1–6; 50.4–9; 52.13–53.12). Their distinctive nature is shown by the role that they ascribe to the servant as having a mission *to raise up the tribes of Jacob* (49.6), and even more remarkably in the intense range of personal suffering endured by the servant (50.6; 53.3–10). These two features have suggested to many scholars that the servant cannot be identical with the Servant-Israel of 41.8 and that the author of the distinctive "Servant Songs" may be different from the author of the rest of chs. 40–55. Yet this conclusion is unnecessary. Although the idea of God's servant is used in more than one way throughout 40–55 (as indeed throughout the book as a whole), the portrayal is consistently that of Israel, suffering, sometimes rebellious, often scattered and disunited. It is this many-sided nature of Israel's servanthood that is presented by the prophet, who recognizes that the servant's task is one that only some within the nation can fulfill.

nations of the world. **10–13:** The revelation of the new task assigned to Israel, God's servant, calls forth a response of praise in the most distant places.

14 For a long time I have held my peace,
    I have kept still and restrained myself;
now I will cry out like a woman in labor,
    I will gasp and pant.
15 I will lay waste mountains and hills,
    and dry up all their herbage;
I will turn the rivers into islands,
    and dry up the pools.
16 I will lead the blind
    by a road they do not know,
by paths they have not known
    I will guide them.
I will turn the darkness before them
    into light,
    the rough places into level ground.
These are the things I will do,
    and I will not forsake them.
17 They shall be turned back and utterly
        put to shame—
    those who trust in carved images,
who say to cast images,
    "You are our gods."

18 Listen, you that are deaf;
    and you that are blind, look up and
        see!

19 Who is blind but my servant,
    or deaf like my messenger whom I
        send?
Who is blind like my dedicated one,
    or blind like the servant of the LORD?
20 He sees many things, but does[a] not
        observe them;
    his ears are open, but he does not hear.
21 The LORD was pleased, for the sake of
        his righteousness,
    to magnify his teaching and make it
        glorious.
22 But this is a people robbed and
        plundered,
    all of them are trapped in holes
        and hidden in prisons;
they have become a prey with no one to
        rescue,
    a spoil with no one to say, "Restore!"
23 Who among you will give heed to this,
    who will attend and listen for the
        time to come?
24 Who gave up Jacob to the spoiler,
    and Israel to the robbers?
Was it not the LORD, against whom we
        have sinned,
    in whose ways they would not walk,
    and whose law they would not obey?

a Heb *You see many things but do*

25 So he poured upon him the heat of his
    anger
    and the fury of war;
    it set him on fire all around, but he did
        not understand;
    it burned him, but he did not take it
        to heart.

42.14–25: The references to the blind and deaf in vv. 16, 18–19 reverse the threatening aspect of the warnings given in 6.9–10 by the eighth-century Isaiah of Jerusalem (see further 43.8). The descriptions of the weak and distressed state of the prophet's own people in v. 22 (see 41.7) may indicate that he himself was suffering in Babylon. It seems probable, however, that the descriptions are typical of the misfortunes that had befallen the former inhabitants of Judah in many places. The mission of God's servant requires a recollection (v. 24) that Israel's present situation was a consequence of its own wrongdoing.

43 But now thus says the LORD,
    he who created you, O Jacob,
    he who formed you, O Israel:
    Do not fear, for I have redeemed you;
        I have called you by name, you are
            mine.
2 When you pass through the waters, I
        will be with you;
    and through the rivers, they shall not
        overwhelm you;
    when you walk through fire you shall
        not be burned,
    and the flame shall not consume you.
3 For I am the LORD your God,
    the Holy One of Israel, your Savior.
    I give Egypt as your ransom,
        Ethiopia*a* and Seba in exchange
            for you.
4 Because you are precious in my sight,
        and honored, and I love you,
    I give people in return for you,
        nations in exchange for your life.
5 Do not fear, for I am with you;
    I will bring your offspring from the
        east,
    and from the west I will gather you;
6 I will say to the north, "Give them up,"
    and to the south, "Do not
        withhold;
    bring my sons from far away

and my daughters from the end of the
    earth—
7 everyone who is called by my name,
    whom I created for my glory,
    whom I formed and made."

8 Bring forth the people who are blind,
        yet have eyes,
    who are deaf, yet have ears!
9 Let all the nations gather together,
    and let the peoples assemble.
    Who among them declared this,
        and foretold to us the former things?
    Let them bring their witnesses to justify
        them,
    and let them hear and say, "It
        is true."
10 You are my witnesses, says the LORD,
    and my servant whom I have chosen,
    so that you may know and believe me
    and understand that I am he.
    Before me no god was formed,
        nor shall there be any after me.
11 I, I am the LORD,
    and besides me there is no savior.
12 I declared and saved and proclaimed,
    when there was no strange god
        among you;
    and you are my witnesses, says the
        LORD.
13 I am God, and also henceforth I am He;
    there is no one who can deliver from
        my hand;
    I work and who can hinder it?

43.1–28: I will be with you. 1–7: The presence of God with Israel is assured, in spite of the apparently hopeless situation in which many survivors of the nation found themselves. Their widely scattered locations reach far beyond the borders of Judah, or even Babylon. A slave's freedom could be negotiated. God would ensure that the host nations to which Judah's citizens had fled for refuge would grant them freedom to return to their homeland. **8–13:** The foretelling of the *former things* (vv. 9, 18) refers to the fulfillment of earlier prophecies, probably those now preserved in the book of Isaiah, as the allusion (v. 8) to the warning given in 6.9–10 makes clear. The LORD God of Israel providentially controls all world history and is the only

a Or *Nubia;* Heb *Cush*

true God. Verse 10 shows how the title *my servant* could be used to describe a whole community.

~~~~~~~~~~~~~~~~~~~~~~~~~

14 Thus says the LORD,
        your Redeemer, the Holy One
            of Israel:
    For your sake I will send to Babylon
        and break down all the bars,
        and the shouting of the Chaldeans
            will be turned to lamentation.*ᵃ*
15 I am the LORD, your Holy One,
        the Creator of Israel, your King.
16 Thus says the LORD,
        who makes a way in the sea,
        a path in the mighty waters,
17 who brings out chariot and horse,
        army and warrior;
    they lie down, they cannot rise,
        they are extinguished, quenched like
            a wick:
18 Do not remember the former things,
        or consider the things of old.
19 I am about to do a new thing;
        now it springs forth, do you not
            perceive it?
    I will make a way in the wilderness
        and rivers in the desert.
20 The wild animals will honor me,
        the jackals and the ostriches;
    for I give water in the wilderness,
        rivers in the desert,
    to give drink to my chosen people,
21   the people whom I formed for myself
    so that they might declare my praise.

22 Yet you did not call upon me, O Jacob;
        but you have been weary of me,
            O Israel!
23 You have not brought me your sheep for
            burnt offerings,
        or honored me with your sacrifices.
    I have not burdened you with offerings,
        or wearied you with frankincense.
24 You have not bought me sweet cane
            with money,
        or satisfied me with the fat of your
            sacrifices.
    But you have burdened me with your
            sins;
        you have wearied me with your
            iniquities.

25 I, I am He
        who blots out your transgressions for
            my own sake,
        and I will not remember your sins.
26 Accuse me, let us go to trial;
        set forth your case, so that you may
            be proved right.
27 Your first ancestor sinned,
        and your interpreters transgressed
            against me.
28 Therefore I profaned the princes of the
            sanctuary,
        I delivered Jacob to utter destruction,
        and Israel to reviling.

───────────────────────

43.14–28. 14–21: Verses 16–17 refer to crossing the sea and the destruction of the pursuing Egyptians (Ex 14.15–30). The return of Israel from among the nations will constitute a new exodus. **22–28:** Israel is presented on one hand as God's servant and witness to the nations and on the other as a weak and sinful people who have burdened God with their sins. Both portraits are valid. The sufferings were necessary and inevitable (v. 28). Yet the consequences of Israel's wrongdoing had now been fully atoned for (see 40.2).

~~~~~~~~~~~~~~~~~~~~~~~~~

44 But now hear, O Jacob my servant,
        Israel whom I have chosen!
2 Thus says the LORD who made you,
        who formed you in the womb and will
            help you:
    Do not fear, O Jacob my servant,
        Jeshurun whom I have chosen.
3 For I will pour water on the thirsty
            land,
        and streams on the dry ground;
    I will pour my spirit upon your
            descendants,
        and my blessing on your offspring.
4 They shall spring up like a green
            tamarisk,
        like willows by flowing streams.
5 This one will say, "I am the LORD's,"
        another will be called by the name of
            Jacob,
    yet another will write on the hand, "The
            LORD's,"
        and adopt the name of Israel.

a Meaning of Heb uncertain

6 Thus says the LORD, the King of Israel,
　　and his Redeemer, the LORD of
　　　hosts:
　I am the first and I am the last;
　　besides me there is no god.
7 Who is like me? Let them proclaim it,
　　let them declare and set it forth
　　　before me.
　Who has announced from of old the
　　things to come?[a]
　Let them tell us[b] what is yet to be.
8 Do not fear, or be afraid;
　　have I not told you from of old and
　　　declared it?
　You are my witnesses!
　Is there any god besides me?
　　There is no other rock; I know not
　　　one.

9 All who make idols are nothing, and the things they delight in do not profit; their witnesses neither see nor know. And so they will be put to shame. [10]Who would fashion a god or cast an image that can do no good? [11]Look, all its devotees shall be put to shame; the artisans too are merely human. Let them all assemble, let them stand up; they shall be terrified, they shall all be put to shame. 12 The ironsmith fashions it[c] and works it over the coals, shaping it with hammers, and forging it with his strong arm; he becomes hungry and his strength fails, he drinks no water and is faint. [13]The carpenter stretches a line, marks it out with a stylus, fashions it with planes, and marks it with a compass; he makes it in human form, with human beauty, to be set up in a shrine. [14]He cuts down cedars or chooses a holm tree or an oak and lets it grow strong among the trees of the forest. He plants a cedar and the rain nourishes it. [15]Then it can be used as fuel. Part of it he takes and warms himself; he kindles a fire and bakes bread. Then he makes a god and worships it, makes it a carved image and bows down before it. [16]Half of it he burns in the fire; over this half he roasts meat, eats it and is satisfied. He also warms himself and says, "Ah, I am warm, I can feel the fire!" [17]The rest of it he makes into a god, his idol, bows down to it

and worships it; he prays to it and says, "Save me, for you are my god!"

18 They do not know, nor do they comprehend; for their eyes are shut, so that they cannot see, and their minds as well, so that they cannot understand. [19]No one considers, nor is there knowledge or discernment to say, "Half of it I burned in the fire; I also baked bread on its coals, I roasted meat and have eaten. Now shall I make the rest of it an abomination? Shall I fall down before a block of wood?" [20]He feeds on ashes; a deluded mind has led him astray, and he cannot save himself or say, "Is not this thing in my right hand a fraud?"

44.1–28: Do not fear, or be afraid. 1–8: Just as God's rainstorm transforms desert into fertile land (v. 3) , so will God transform scattered and weakened Israel. No other god can prevent this happening, and the gods themselves are nothing (v. 6). They have no witnesses among the nations who can foretell future events (v. 7). **9–20:** A sharp reproof of idolatry: The very fact that human beings make such images demonstrates that they are false, since human beings cannot make gods (v. 20).

21 Remember these things, O Jacob,
　　and Israel, for you are my servant;
　I formed you, you are my servant;
　　O Israel, you will not be forgotten
　　　by me.
22 I have swept away your transgressions
　　like a cloud,
　　and your sins like mist;
　return to me, for I have redeemed you.

23 Sing, O heavens, for the LORD has
　　　done it;
　　shout, O depths of the earth;
　break forth into singing, O mountains,
　　O forest, and every tree in it!
　For the LORD has redeemed Jacob,
　　and will be glorified in Israel.

24 Thus says the LORD, your Redeemer,
　　who formed you in the womb:

a Cn: Heb *from my placing an eternal people and things to come*　b Tg: Heb *them*　c Cn: Heb *an ax*

I am the LORD, who made all things,
who alone stretched out the heavens,
who by myself spread out the earth;
25 who frustrates the omens of liars,
and makes fools of diviners;
who turns back the wise,
and makes their knowledge foolish;
26 who confirms the word of his servant,
and fulfills the prediction of his
messengers;
who says of Jerusalem, "It shall be
inhabited,"
and of the cities of Judah, "They shall
be rebuilt,
and I will raise up their ruins";
27 who says to the deep, "Be dry—
I will dry up your rivers";
28 who says of Cyrus, "He is my shepherd,
and he shall carry out all my purpose";
and who says of Jerusalem, "It shall be
rebuilt,"
and of the temple, "Your foundation
shall be laid."

44.21–28: Jerusalem will be rebuilt, the restored city will be inhabited once again and a new Temple will be constructed (vv. 26–28). The designation of the Persian ruler Cyrus as God's *shepherd* (v. 28) and "anointed" (45.1) includes titles used of Israelite kings (for "shepherd" as a title of kings and rulers, see Jer 23.1–5; Ezek 34.1–24). Even a foreign and pagan ruler who attained world power did so as the agent of the God of Israel who directed the course of history. Jews living outside the land used this language to show due recognition to the rulers of nations among whom they lived. Such an understanding did not, however, entirely rule out a special role for the surviving dynasty of David (see 55.3–5).

45 Thus says the LORD to his
anointed, to Cyrus,
whose right hand I have grasped
to subdue nations before him
and strip kings of their robes,
to open doors before him—
and the gates shall not be closed:
2 I will go before you
and level the mountains,^{a}
I will break in pieces the doors
of bronze
and cut through the bars of iron,

3 I will give you the treasures of darkness
and riches hidden in secret places,
so that you may know that it is I, the
LORD,
the God of Israel, who call you by
your name.
4 For the sake of my servant Jacob,
and Israel my chosen,
I call you by your name,
I surname you, though you do not
know me.
5 I am the LORD, and there is no other;
besides me there is no god.
I arm you, though you do not know
me,
6 so that they may know, from the rising
of the sun
and from the west, that there is no
one besides me;
I am the LORD, and there is no other.
7 I form light and create darkness,
I make weal and create woe;
I the LORD do all these things.

45.1–25: Turn to me and be saved. 1–7: *Cyrus* is the world conqueror whom God had chosen to overthrow the power of Babylon and enable the survivors of Israel to return to their homeland, a reaffirmation of the sovereign power of the LORD God (v. 7). This verse expresses fully the claim that God, as God of all nations, is all-powerful.

8 Shower, O heavens, from above,
and let the skies rain down
righteousness;
let the earth open, that salvation may
spring up,^{b}
and let it cause righteousness to
sprout up also;
I the LORD have created it.

9 Woe to you who strive with your Maker,
earthen vessels with the potter!^{c}
Does the clay say to the one who
fashions it, "What are you
making"?
or "Your work has no handles"?

a Q Ms Gk: MT *the swellings* *b* Q Ms: MT *that they may bring forth salvation* *c* Cn: Heb *with the potsherds,* or *with the potters*

10 Woe to anyone who says to a father,
    "What are you begetting?"
    or to a woman, "With what are you in
        labor?"
11 Thus says the LORD,
    the Holy One of Israel, and its Maker:
Will you question me*a* about my
        children,
    or command me concerning the work
        of my hands?
12 I made the earth,
    and created humankind upon it;
it was my hands that stretched out the
        heavens,
    and I commanded all their host.
13 I have aroused Cyrus*b* in righteousness,
    and I will make all his paths straight;
he shall build my city
    and set my exiles free,
not for price or reward,
    says the LORD of hosts.
14 Thus says the LORD:
The wealth of Egypt and the
        merchandise of Ethiopia,*c*
    and the Sabeans, tall of stature,
shall come over to you and be yours,
    they shall follow you;
    they shall come over in chains and
        bow down to you.
They will make supplication to you,
        saying,
    "God is with you alone, and there is
        no other;
    there is no god besides him."
15 Truly, you are a God who hides himself,
    O God of Israel, the Savior.
16 All of them are put to shame and
        confounded,
    the makers of idols go in confusion
        together.
17 But Israel is saved by the LORD
    with everlasting salvation;
you shall not be put to shame or
        confounded
    to all eternity.

45.8–17: Human beings cannot challenge God's declared purpose any more than *clay* can question a
potter (v. 9). Nor can people question parents as to
the kind of offspring they will bring into the world (vv.
10–11). Even the distant tribes of North Africa will rec-

ognize Israel's God (v. 14). To exchange knowledge of
this true God for the spurious aid of an *idol* would be
utter folly (v. 16).

18 For thus says the LORD,
    who created the heavens
        (he is God!),
    who formed the earth and made it
        (he established it;
    he did not create it a chaos,
        he formed it to be inhabited!):
    I am the LORD, and there is no other.
19 I did not speak in secret,
    in a land of darkness;
I did not say to the offspring of Jacob,
    "Seek me in chaos."
I the LORD speak the truth,
    I declare what is right.

20 Assemble yourselves and come together,
    draw near, you survivors of the
        nations!
They have no knowledge—
    those who carry about their wooden
        idols,
and keep on praying to a god
    that cannot save.
21 Declare and present your case;
    let them take counsel together!
Who told this long ago?
    Who declared it of old?
Was it not I, the LORD?
    There is no other god besides me,
a righteous God and a Savior;
    there is no one besides me.

22 Turn to me and be saved,
    all the ends of the earth!
    For I am God, and there is no other.
23 By myself I have sworn,
    from my mouth has gone forth in
        righteousness
    a word that shall not return:
"To me every knee shall bow,
    every tongue shall swear."

24 Only in the LORD, it shall be said of me,
    are righteousness and strength;

a Cn: Heb *Ask me of things to come*   *b* Heb *him*
c Or *Nubia*; Heb *Cush*

all who were incensed against him
        shall come to him and be ashamed.
25 In the LORD all the offspring of Israel
        shall triumph and glory.

45.18–25: The prophet turns to address the many nations of the world. If God can shape the destiny of Israel, God's purpose is that every nation should know that there is no God but one and worship this one God alone. Those who had once made light of it (see 36.18–20) will be ashamed of their foolishness (v. 24) and confess that Israel was the first of many nations to acknowledge the LORD as God.

46 Bel bows down, Nebo stoops,
        their idols are on beasts and cattle;
    these things you carry are loaded
        as burdens on weary animals.
2 They stoop, they bow down together;
        they cannot save the burden,
    but themselves go into captivity.

3 Listen to me, O house of Jacob,
        all the remnant of the house of Israel,
    who have been borne by me from your
            birth,
        carried from the womb;
4 even to your old age I am he,
        even when you turn gray I will carry
            you.
    I have made, and I will bear;
        I will carry and will save.

5 To whom will you liken me and make
            me equal,
        and compare me, as though we were
            alike?
6 Those who lavish gold from the purse,
        and weigh out silver in the scales—
    they hire a goldsmith, who makes it into
            a god;
        then they fall down and worship!
7 They lift it to their shoulders, they
            carry it,
        they set it in its place, and it stands
            there;
        it cannot move from its place.
    If one cries out to it, it does not answer
        or save anyone from trouble.

8 Remember this and consider,*a*
        recall it to mind, you transgressors,

9 remember the former things of old;
        for I am God, and there is no other;
    I am God, and there is no one like
            me,
10 declaring the end from the beginning
        and from ancient times things not yet
            done,
    saying, "My purpose shall stand,
        and I will fulfill my intention,"
11 calling a bird of prey from the east,
        the man for my purpose from a far
            country.
    I have spoken, and I will bring it
            to pass;
        I have planned, and I will do it.

12 Listen to me, you stubborn of heart,
        you who are far from deliverance:
13 I bring near my deliverance, it is not far
            off,
        and my salvation will not tarry;
    I will put salvation in Zion,
        for Israel my glory.

46.1–13: The uselessness of false gods. 1–7: The theme of idolatry* highlights the helpless situation of the priests and worshippers of Babylon. With Babylon facing imminent capture, those who cared for the images of the gods would soon be forced to flee with them to a place of safety (v. 1). Yet they would not find it. There would be no place to hide, and the absurdity of human beings trying to save their gods shows that they are in reality no gods at all. The true deity is the one who carries, not who is carried (vv. 6–7). **8–11:** The true God shapes the destiny of nations (vv. 10–11). The *bird of prey* is *the man for my purpose from a far country,* none other than Cyrus, who will bring release to Israel. **12–13:** Rebuilding and restoring the ruined Jerusalem is God's *salvation.* God's *deliverance* has a very practical aspect to it.

47 Come down and sit in the dust,
        virgin daughter Babylon!
    Sit on the ground without a throne,
        daughter Chaldea!
    For you shall no more be called
        tender and delicate.
2 Take the millstones and grind meal,
        remove your veil,

---

a Meaning of Heb uncertain

strip off your robe, uncover your legs,
    pass through the rivers.
3 Your nakedness shall be uncovered,
    and your shame shall be seen.
I will take vengeance,
    and I will spare no one.
4 Our Redeemer—the LORD of hosts is
       his name—
    is the Holy One of Israel.

5 Sit in silence, and go into darkness,
    daughter Chaldea!
For you shall no more be called
    the mistress of kingdoms.
6 I was angry with my people,
    I profaned my heritage;
I gave them into your hand,
    you showed them no mercy;
on the aged you made your yoke
    exceedingly heavy.
7 You said, "I shall be mistress forever,"
    so that you did not lay these things to
       heart
    or remember their end.

8 Now therefore hear this, you lover of
       pleasures,
    who sit securely,
who say in your heart,
    "I am, and there is no one besides me;
I shall not sit as a widow
    or know the loss of children"—
9 both these things shall come upon you
    in a moment, in one day:
the loss of children and widowhood
    shall come upon you in full
       measure,
in spite of your many sorceries
    and the great power of your
       enchantments.

10 You felt secure in your wickedness;
    you said, "No one sees me."
Your wisdom and your knowledge
    led you astray,
and you said in your heart,
    "I am, and there is no one besides
       me."
11 But evil shall come upon you,
    which you cannot charm away;
disaster shall fall upon you,

which you will not be able to ward
    off;
and ruin shall come on you suddenly,
    of which you know nothing.

12 Stand fast in your enchantments
    and your many sorceries,
with which you have labored from
       your youth;
perhaps you may be able to
       succeed,
    perhaps you may inspire terror.
13 You are wearied with your many
       consultations;
    let those who study*a* the heavens
stand up and save you,
    those who gaze at the stars,
and at each new moon predict
    what*b* shall befall you.

14 See, they are like stubble,
    the fire consumes them;
they cannot deliver themselves
    from the power of the flame.
No coal for warming oneself is this,
    no fire to sit before!
15 Such to you are those with whom you
       have labored,
who have trafficked with you from
       your youth;
they all wander about in their
       own paths;
    there is no one to save you.

47.1–15: The fall of Babylon. 1–9: Babylon is depicted as a mature young lady, accustomed to pampered luxury, but now suddenly seized, stripped, and humiliated. The empire had absorbed many nations and had plundered their lands and treasures, showing no pity even to the weakest (v. 6). The proud assumption that her power would remain unchecked forever (v. 8) had encouraged the city to revel in its excesses, without pity or compassion. Now the pain she had inflicted on others would be brought home to her. **10–15:** It is by divine authority that such terrible retribution comes. Babylon's elaborate rituals and techniques for uncovering the mysteries of the future could not fend off the disaster. The all-consuming fire rav-

a Meaning of Heb uncertain   *b* Gk Syr Compare Vg:
Heb *from what*

aging the countryside concludes this forewarning of Babylon's imminent downfall. This is not gloating over an enemy so much as the conviction that a divine will for justice ultimately shapes the course of human history.

48 Hear this, O house of Jacob,
  who are called by the name of
    Israel,
  and who came forth from the loins*a*
    of Judah;
who swear by the name of the LORD,
  and invoke the God of Israel,
  but not in truth or right.

2 For they call themselves after the holy
    city,
  and lean on the God of Israel;
  the LORD of hosts is his name.

3 The former things I declared
    long ago,
  they went out from my mouth and I
    made them known;
  then suddenly I did them and they
    came to pass.

4 Because I know that you are obstinate,
  and your neck is an iron sinew
  and your forehead brass,

5 I declared them to you from long ago,
  before they came to pass I announced
    them to you,
  so that you would not say, "My idol did
    them,
  my carved image and my cast image
    commanded them."

6 You have heard; now see all this;
  and will you not declare it?
From this time forward I make you hear
    new things,
  hidden things that you have not
    known.

7 They are created now, not long ago;
  before today you have never heard of
    them,
  so that you could not say, "I already
    knew them."

8 You have never heard, you have never
    known,
  from of old your ear has not been
    opened.

For I knew that you would deal very
    treacherously,
  and that from birth you were called a
    rebel.

48.1–22: Reassurance for God's people. 1–8: A significant change of mood occurs with less attention to the rise of Cyrus, although his imminent defeat of Babylon is still taken for granted (v. 14). Instead the prophet addresses Israel, preparing its survivors to make a positive response to the new message of hope. The high mission of Israel contrasts with the persistent unbelief and self-pity of Israel's response. This ambiguity is clear in the rebuke that is added to the privileged title of Israel: who *invoke the God of Israel, but not in truth or right* (v. 1). Offering fine prayers to God was not in itself proof that they were sincerely meant. The evidence that God is guiding Israel is found in the fulfillment of prophecies (v. 3). Yet if the people had been reluctant to believe and act upon prophecies that had been fulfilled, how would they believe new ones? The failures and rebelliousness of the past are the reason for making sure that such mistakes were not repeated in the present (v. 8).

9 For my name's sake I defer my anger,
  for the sake of my praise I restrain it
    for you,
  so that I may not cut you off.

10 See, I have refined you, but not like*b*
    silver;
  I have tested you in the furnace of
    adversity.

11 For my own sake, for my own sake,
    I do it,
  for why should my name*c* be
    profaned?
  My glory I will not give to another.

12 Listen to me, O Jacob,
  and Israel, whom I called:
I am He; I am the first,
  and I am the last.

13 My hand laid the foundation of the earth,
  and my right hand spread out
    the heavens;
  when I summon them,
  they stand at attention.

a Cn: Heb *waters*   *b* Cn: Heb *with*   *c* Gk Old Latin: Heb *for why should it*

14 Assemble, all of you, and hear!
  Who among them has declared these
    things?
  The LORD loves him;
    he shall perform his purpose on
      Babylon,
    and his arm shall be against the
      Chaldeans.
15 I, even I, have spoken and called him,
  I have brought him, and he will
    prosper in his way.
16 Draw near to me, hear this!
  From the beginning I have not spoken
    in secret,
    from the time it came to be I have
      been there.
  And now the Lord GOD has sent me
    and his spirit.

17 Thus says the LORD,
    your Redeemer, the Holy One
      of Israel:
  I am the LORD your God,
    who teaches you for your own good,
    who leads you in the way you
      should go.
18 O that you had paid attention to my
    commandments!
  Then your prosperity would have
    been like a river,
    and your success like the waves of
      the sea;
19 your offspring would have been like the
    sand,
    and your descendants like its grains;
  their name would never be cut off
    or destroyed from before me.

20 Go out from Babylon, flee from
    Chaldea,
  declare this with a shout of joy,
    proclaim it,
  send it forth to the end of the earth;
    say, "The LORD has redeemed his
      servant Jacob!"
21 They did not thirst when he led them
    through the deserts;
  he made water flow for them from
    the rock;
  he split open the rock and the water
    gushed out.

22 "There is no peace," says the LORD, "for
    the wicked."

48.9–22. 9–16: Because the LORD is forgiving and gracious, even imperfect Israel may, with God's help, fulfill a great purpose (vv. 9–11). What would be impossible for a people left to their own resources was possible with God (vv. 12–16). **17–22:** The concluding command: *Go out from Babylon, flee from Chaldea.* Fleeing from Babylon would be like the flight from Egypt by which Israel had first achieved its freedom (v. 21). So it was appropriate to recall the providential care which had made that beginning possible. Once again God would, if necessary, bring *water from the rock* to sustain the returning exiles (see Ex 17.1–7). A final word of warning (v. 22) is a necessary addition to the message concerning Israel's rebellious nature that echoes through the chapter (vv. 1, 4, 5, 18). From the very beginning Israel had received great promises but had failed to respond (especially v. 18). That could happen again and those who, in the pursuit of peace, shunned the risks and dangers of the journey home would find that they enjoyed a worthless tranquillity.

49 Listen to me, O coastlands,
    pay attention, you peoples from far
      away!
  The LORD called me before I was born,
    while I was in my mother's womb he
      named me.
2 He made my mouth like a sharp sword,
    in the shadow of his hand he hid me;
  he made me a polished arrow,
    in his quiver he hid me away.
3 And he said to me, "You are my servant,
  Israel, in whom I will be glorified."
4 But I said, "I have labored in vain,
  I have spent my strength for nothing
    and vanity;
  yet surely my cause is with the LORD,
    and my reward with my God."

5 And now the LORD says,
    who formed me in the womb to be his
      servant,
  to bring Jacob back to him,
    and that Israel might be gathered to
      him,
  for I am honored in the sight of the LORD,
    and my God has become my
      strength—

6 he says,
  "It is too light a thing that you should
        be my servant
    to raise up the tribes of Jacob
    and to restore the survivors of Israel;
  I will give you as a light to the nations,
    that my salvation may reach to the
        end of the earth."

7 Thus says the LORD,
    the Redeemer of Israel and his
        Holy One,
  to one deeply despised, abhorred by the
        nations,
    the slave of rulers,
  "Kings shall see and stand up,
    princes, and they shall prostrate
        themselves,
  because of the LORD, who is faithful,
    the Holy One of Israel, who has
        chosen you."

8 Thus says the LORD:
  In a time of favor I have answered you,
    on a day of salvation I have helped
        you;
  I have kept you and given you
    as a covenant to the people,[a]
  to establish the land,
    to apportion the desolate heritages;
9 saying to the prisoners, "Come out,"
    to those who are in darkness, "Show
        yourselves."
  They shall feed along the ways,
    on all the bare heights[b] shall be their
        pasture;
10 they shall not hunger or thirst,
    neither scorching wind nor sun shall
        strike them down,
  for he who has pity on them will lead
        them,
    and by springs of water will guide
        them.
11 And I will turn all my mountains into a
        road,
    and my highways shall be raised up.
12 Lo, these shall come from far away,
    and lo, these from the north and from
        the west,
    and these from the land of Syene.[c]

13 Sing for joy, O heavens, and exult,
        O earth;
  break forth, O mountains, into
        singing!
  For the LORD has comforted his people,
    and will have compassion on his
        suffering ones.

49.1–26: The servant's mission to the world. 1–6:
The second of the four Servant Songs (see sidebar, p.
929). Israel's servant mission will reach beyond the survivors of the former Israel, and will bring *light* (salvation) *to the nations* (v. 6). Servant-Israel (v. 3) also has
a mission to Israel, suggesting that *Israel* may have
been added later. More probably, one part of the nation has a mission to the other part. **8–13:** The task of
restoring the *tribes of Jacob* (v. 6) consists of establishing the land, apportioning the desolate heritages, and
releasing the prisoners. Exiles will be able to return.
Syene (perhaps southern Egypt) is an example of the
distant locations to which the people had fled.

14 But Zion said, "The LORD has
        forsaken me,
    my Lord has forgotten me."
15 Can a woman forget her nursing child,
    or show no compassion for the child
        of her womb?
  Even these may forget,
    yet I will not forget you.
16 See, I have inscribed you on the palms
        of my hands;
    your walls are continually before me.
17 Your builders outdo your destroyers,[d]
    and those who laid you waste go away
        from you.
18 Lift up your eyes all around and see;
    they all gather, they come to you.
  As I live, says the LORD,
    you shall put all of them on like an
        ornament,
    and like a bride you shall bind
        them on.

19 Surely your waste and your desolate
        places
    and your devastated land—

---

a Meaning of Heb uncertain   b Or *the trails*
c Q Ms: MT *Sinim*   d Or *Your children come swiftly;*
your destroyers

surely now you will be too crowded for
your inhabitants,
and those who swallowed you up will
be far away.
20 The children born in the time of your
bereavement
will yet say in your hearing:
"The place is too crowded for me;
make room for me to settle."
21 Then you will say in your heart,
"Who has borne me these?
I was bereaved and barren,
exiled and put away—
so who has reared these?
I was left all alone—
where then have these come from?"

22 Thus says the Lord GOD:
I will soon lift up my hand to the
nations,
and raise my signal to the peoples;
and they shall bring your sons in their
bosom,
and your daughters shall be carried
on their shoulders.
23 Kings shall be your foster fathers,
and their queens your nursing
mothers.
With their faces to the ground they
shall bow down to you,
and lick the dust of your feet.
Then you will know that I am the LORD;
those who wait for me shall not be
put to shame.

24 Can the prey be taken from the mighty,
or the captives of a tyrant*a* be
rescued?
25 But thus says the LORD:
Even the captives of the mighty shall be
taken,
and the prey of the tyrant be rescued;
for I will contend with those who
contend with you,
and I will save your children.
26 I will make your oppressors eat their
own flesh,
and they shall be drunk with their
own blood as with wine.
Then all flesh shall know
that I am the LORD your Savior,

and your Redeemer, the Mighty One
of Jacob.

49.14–26. 14–21: The apparent impossibility of the
promised restoration of the ruined city is now possible
due to the compassion and love that God has for it
(vv. 14–16). **22–26:** What might sometimes rarely be
possible in human terms—that a human *tyrant* may
set free his *captives* (v. 25)—is possible with God.

50 Thus says the LORD:
Where is your mother's bill of
divorce
with which I put her away?
Or which of my creditors is it
to whom I have sold you?
No, because of your sins you
were sold,
and for your transgressions your
mother was put away.
2 Why was no one there when I came?
Why did no one answer when I
called?
Is my hand shortened, that it cannot
redeem?
Or have I no power to deliver?
By my rebuke I dry up the sea,
I make the rivers a desert;
their fish stink for lack of water,
and die of thirst.*b*
3 I clothe the heavens with blackness,
and make sackcloth their covering.

4 The Lord GOD has given me
the tongue of a teacher,*c*
that I may know how to sustain
the weary with a word.
Morning by morning he wakens—
wakens my ear
to listen as those who are taught.
5 The Lord GOD has opened my ear,
and I was not rebellious,
I did not turn backward.
6 I gave my back to those who struck me,
and my cheeks to those who pulled
out the beard;
I did not hide my face
from insult and spitting.

a Q Ms Syr Vg: MT *of a righteous person*   *b* Or *die on
the thirsty ground*   *c* Cn: Heb *of those who are taught*

7 The Lord GOD helps me;
    therefore I have not been disgraced;
  therefore I have set my face like flint,
    and I know that I shall not be put to
      shame;
8   he who vindicates me is near.
  Who will contend with me?
    Let us stand up together.
  Who are my adversaries?
    Let them confront me.
9 It is the Lord GOD who helps me;
    who will declare me guilty?
  All of them will wear out like a garment;
    the moth will eat them up.

10 Who among you fears the LORD
    and obeys the voice of his servant,
  who walks in darkness
    and has no light,
  yet trusts in the name of the LORD
    and relies upon his God?
11 But all of you are kindlers of fire,
    lighters of firebrands.[a]
  Walk in the flame of your fire,
    and among the brands that you have
      kindled!
  This is what you shall have from my
      hand:
    you shall lie down in torment.

50.1–11: Israel: servant and rebel. 1–3: The opening
questions highlight the need for choice between a
positive believing response and an unbelieving rejection. These differing responses show the contrast between the submissive and obedient servant and the
mocking and insolent rebels. **4–9:** The third of the four
Servant Songs (see sidebar, p. 929) shows that the servant undergoes humiliation and rejection in the course
of fulfilling his mission. The autobiographical form
shows how wholeheartedly the prophet identifies himself with the mission of servant-Israel. **10–11:** The
prophet contrasts those who seek *light* (salvation) in
order to walk by it, and those who use torches (*firebrands*) to kindle destruction (see 10.17 for a similar
use of the picture of light becoming fire).

51 Listen to me, you that pursue
      righteousness,
    you that seek the LORD.
  Look to the rock from which you were
      hewn,

and to the quarry from which
    you were dug.
2 Look to Abraham your father
    and to Sarah who bore you;
  for he was but one when I called him,
    but I blessed him and made
      him many.
3 For the LORD will comfort Zion;
    he will comfort all her waste places,
  and will make her wilderness like Eden,
    her desert like the garden of
      the LORD;
  joy and gladness will be found in her,
    thanksgiving and the voice of song.

4 Listen to me, my people,
    and give heed to me, my nation;
  for a teaching will go out from me,
    and my justice for a light to
      the peoples.
5 I will bring near my deliverance swiftly,
    my salvation has gone out
    and my arms will rule the peoples;
  the coastlands wait for me,
    and for my arm they hope.
6 Lift up your eyes to the heavens,
    and look at the earth beneath;
  for the heavens will vanish like smoke,
    the earth will wear out like a
      garment,
    and those who live on it will die like
      gnats;[b]
  but my salvation will be forever,
    and my deliverance will never
      be ended.

7 Listen to me, you who know
      righteousness,
    you people who have my teaching in
      your hearts;
  do not fear the reproach of others,
    and do not be dismayed when they
      revile you.
8 For the moth will eat them up like a
      garment,
    and the worm will eat them like wool;
  but my deliverance will be forever,
    and my salvation to all generations.

a Syr: Heb *you gird yourselves with firebrands*   b Or *in
like manner*

51.1–23: Stand up, O Jerusalem. 1–8: A fresh argument strengthens the appeal. *Abraham* was *but one* when God *called him* (v. 2). Yet from this one man a whole nation came into being. How much more certainly is God capable of restoring the scattered remnants of Israel. God's salvation is even more certain and secure than is the sky above.

9 Awake, awake, put on strength,
    O arm of the LORD!
  Awake, as in days of old,
    the generations of long ago!
  Was it not you who cut Rahab in
      pieces,
    who pierced the dragon?
10 Was it not you who dried up the sea,
    the waters of the great deep;
  who made the depths of the sea a way
    for the redeemed to cross over?
11 So the ransomed of the LORD shall
      return,
    and come to Zion with singing;
  everlasting joy shall be upon their
      heads;
    they shall obtain joy and gladness,
    and sorrow and sighing shall
        flee away.

12 I, I am he who comforts you;
    why then are you afraid of a mere
        mortal who must die,
    a human being who fades like grass?
13 You have forgotten the LORD, your
      Maker,
    who stretched out the heavens
    and laid the foundations of the earth.
  You fear continually all day long
    because of the fury of the oppressor,
  who is bent on destruction.
    But where is the fury of the
        oppressor?
14 The oppressed shall speedily be
      released;
    they shall not die and go down to
        the Pit,
    nor shall they lack bread.
15 For I am the LORD your God,
    who stirs up the sea so that its waves
        roar—
    the LORD of hosts is his name.

16 I have put my words in your mouth,
    and hidden you in the shadow of my
        hand,
  stretching out*a* the heavens
    and laying the foundations of
        the earth,
  and saying to Zion, "You are my
      people."

17 Rouse yourself, rouse yourself!
    Stand up. O Jerusalem,
  you who have drunk at the hand of
      the LORD
    the cup of his wrath,
  who have drunk to the dregs
    the bowl of staggering.
18 There is no one to guide her
    among all the children she
        has borne;
  there is no one to take her by the hand
    among all the children she has
        brought up.
19 These two things have befallen you
    —who will grieve with you?—
  devastation and destruction, famine and
      sword—
    who will comfort you?*b*
20 Your children have fainted,
    they lie at the head of every street
    like an antelope in a net;
  they are full of the wrath of the LORD,
    the rebuke of your God.

21 Therefore hear this, you who are
      wounded,*c*
    who are drunk, but not with wine:
22 Thus says your Sovereign, the LORD,
    your God who pleads the cause of his
        people:
  See, I have taken from your hand the
      cup of staggering;
  you shall drink no more
    from the bowl of my wrath.
23 And I will put it into the hand of your
      tormentors,
    who have said to you,
    "Bow down, that we may walk
        on you":

a Syr: Heb *planting*   b Q Ms Gk Syr Vg: MT *how may
I comfort you?*   c Or *humbled*

and you have made your back like the
       ground
   and like the street for them to walk
       on.

51.9–23. 9–16: *Cut Rahab in pieces* refers to the ancient pictorial account of creation in which the earth
was formed by cutting in pieces a great dragon monster, here called Rahab (see Leviathan in 27.1). *Dried
up the sea* (v. 10) combines themes from the creation,
when dry land appeared amid the ocean (see Gen 1.9–
10), and the drying up of the sea in the miraculous
crossing, when the ancestors of the nation fled from
Egypt (see Ex 14.21–22). **17–23:** *Jerusalem* is directly
addressed and its ruined state vividly described (v. 23).

~~~~~~~~~~~~~~~~

52 Awake, awake,
       put on your strength, O Zion!
   Put on your beautiful garments,
       O Jerusalem, the holy city;
   for the uncircumcised and the unclean
       shall enter you no more.
2   Shake yourself from the dust, rise up,
       O captive*a* Jerusalem;
   loose the bonds from your neck,
       O captive daughter Zion!

3   For thus says the LORD: You were sold
for nothing, and you shall be redeemed without money. 4For thus says the Lord GOD:
Long ago, my people went down into Egypt
to reside there as aliens; the Assyrian, too,
has oppressed them without cause. 5Now
therefore what am I doing here, says the
LORD, seeing that my people are taken away
without cause? Their rulers howl, says the
LORD, and continually, all day long, my
name is despised. 6Therefore my people
shall know my name; therefore in that day
they shall know that it is I who speak; here
am I.

7   How beautiful upon the mountains
       are the feet of the messenger who
           announces peace,
   who brings good news,
       who announces salvation,
   who says to Zion, "Your God reigns."
8   Listen! Your sentinels lift up
       their voices,
   together they sing for joy;

for in plain sight they see
       the return of the LORD to Zion.
9   Break forth together into singing,
       you ruins of Jerusalem;
   for the LORD has comforted his people,
       he has redeemed Jerusalem.
10 The LORD has bared his holy arm
       before the eyes of all the nations;
   and all the ends of the earth shall see
       the salvation of our God.

11 Depart, depart, go out from there!
       Touch no unclean thing;
   go out from the midst of it, purify
       yourselves,
   you who carry the vessels of
       the LORD.
12 For you shall not go out in haste,
       and you shall not go in flight;
   for the LORD will go before you,
       and the God of Israel will be your
           rear guard.

52.1–12: Put on your beautiful garments. 1–2: The
uncircumcised and unclean are the foreigners who
ruled over Jerusalem. Once God's people had returned
to take control of their beloved city, then this hated
foreign rule would be at an end. **3–6:** This short prose
digression summarizes Israel's sufferings at the hands
of foreigners. It looks ahead to the time when the
promises and assurances of chs. 40–55 will have been
fulfilled. **7–10:** In this prophetic image watchmen on
the city walls see a *messenger bringing news* of Israel's
deliverance (from the power of Babylon). When God's
people return to *Zion,*★ then God will return to be with
them (v. 8). **11–12:** The command to *depart* is a reference to the many places of exile to which Jerusalem's
citizens had been driven. In contrast to the departure
of Israel's forbears from Egypt—the event that marked
the beginning of the nation's history—this departure
would not be *in haste* (see Ex 12.39); nor would it
include the plundering of their captors (v. 11; see Ex
12.35–36).

~~~~~~~~~~~~~~~~

13 See, my servant shall prosper;
       he shall be exalted and lifted up,
       and shall be very high.
14 Just as there were many who were
           astonished at him*b*

---

a Cn: Heb *rise up, sit*   *b* Syr Tg: Heb *you*

—so marred was his appearance,
    beyond human semblance,
    and his form beyond that of
      mortals—
15 so he shall startle[a] many nations;
    kings shall shut their mouths because
      of him;
    for that which had not been told them
      they shall see,
    and that which they had not heard
      they shall contemplate.

53 Who has believed what we have
      heard?
    And to whom has the arm of the
      LORD been revealed?
2 For he grew up before him like a young
      plant,
    and like a root out of dry ground;
    he had no form or majesty that we
      should look at him,
    nothing in his appearance that we
      should desire him.
3 He was despised and rejected by others;
    a man of suffering[b] and acquainted
      with infirmity;
    and as one from whom others hide their
      faces[c]
    he was despised, and we held him of
      no account.

4 Surely he has borne our infirmities
    and carried our diseases;
    yet we accounted him stricken,
      struck down by God, and afflicted.
5 But he was wounded for our
      transgressions,
    crushed for our iniquities;
    upon him was the punishment that
      made us whole,
    and by his bruises we are healed.
6 All we like sheep have gone astray;
    we have all turned to our own way,
    and the LORD has laid on him
      the iniquity of us all.

7 He was oppressed, and he was afflicted,
    yet he did not open his mouth;
    like a lamb that is led to the slaughter,
    and like a sheep that before its
      shearers is silent,
    so he did not open his mouth.

8 By a perversion of justice he was taken
      away.
    Who could have imagined his future?
    For he was cut off from the land of the
      living,
    stricken for the transgression of my
      people.
9 They made his grave with the wicked
    and his tomb[d] with the rich,[e]
    although he had done no violence,
    and there was no deceit in
      his mouth.

10 Yet it was the will of the LORD to crush
      him with pain.[f]
    When you make his life an offering for
      sin,[a]
    he shall see his offspring, and shall
      prolong his days;
    through him the will of the LORD shall
      prosper.
11 Out of his anguish he shall see light;[g]
    he shall find satisfaction through his
      knowledge.
    The righteous one,[h] my servant, shall
      make many righteous,
    and he shall bear their iniquities.
12 Therefore I will allot him a portion with
      the great,
    and he shall divide the spoil with the
      strong;
    because he poured out himself to death,
      and was numbered with the
      transgressors;
    yet he bore the sin of many,
    and made intercession for the
      transgressors.

52.13–53.12: The suffering servant. One of the most remarkable passages in all prophetic literature, this is the fourth of the distinctive Servant passages, or Songs, which describe the fate of Israel as the servant of God (see sidebar, p. 929). The servant will suffer as a result of his commitment to the task (50.4–9). Now what that suffering entails is spelled out in all its hor-

a Meaning of Heb uncertain   b Or *a man of sorrows*
c Or *as one who hides his face from us*   d Q Ms: MT
and in his death   e Cn: Heb *with a rich person*
f Or *by disease*; meaning of Heb uncertain   g Q Mss:
MT lacks *light*   h Or *and he shall find satisfaction.*
Through his knowledge, the righteous one

rifying detail. This enigmatic passage seems to combine many experiences. Even if the references in
53.8–9 are not to actual death but to an extreme of
suffering, the prophet himself cannot have written it.
It is not the death and torture of one person alone that
is being reported here. The servant mission is divisive
in its challenge. Not all the prophet's hearers respond
to his demands, and many have already shown themselves to be rebellious and unresponsive. It is those
who have identified themselves with this servant task,
who have borne the rebukes, reproaches, and wounds
of their fellows, whose fate is described here. So the
prophet has woven into one tapestry of suffering the
terrifying experiences that many had undergone. It is
a mission portrait of servanthood. There is a positive
and reassuring outlook that sees beyond the immediate pain to the rich reward of such endurance (53.12).
It is not a resurrection of an individual that is described
in *he shall see his offspring, and shall prolong his days*
(53.10–11). Rather it is the fruit that will be borne by
those who assume the servant's task and find that, for
all its pain, it gains *a portion with the great* (v. 12).
Moreover, a remarkable sensitivity to the way in which
the righteous often suffer at the hands of wrongdoers
leads to a new perception of the meaning of suffering.
The righteous individual may bear the sin of the many
who are guilty.

54 Sing, O barren one who did
not bear;
burst into song and shout,
you who have not been in labor!
For the children of the desolate woman
will be more
than the children of her that is
married, says the LORD.
2 Enlarge the site of your tent,
and let the curtains of your
habitations be stretched out;
do not hold back; lengthen your cords
and strengthen your stakes.
3 For you will spread out to the right and
to the left,
and your descendants will possess the
nations
and will settle the desolate towns.

4 Do not fear, for you will not be
ashamed;
do not be discouraged, for you will
not suffer disgrace;

for you will forget the shame of your
youth,
and the disgrace of your widowhood
you will remember no more.
5 For your Maker is your husband,
the LORD of hosts is his name;
the Holy One of Israel is your
Redeemer,
the God of the whole earth he
is called.
6 For the LORD has called you
like a wife forsaken and grieved in
spirit,
like the wife of a man's youth when she
is cast off,
says your God.
7 For a brief moment I abandoned you,
but with great compassion I will
gather you.
8 In overflowing wrath for a moment
I hid my face from you,
but with everlasting love I will have
compassion on you,
says the LORD, your Redeemer.

9 This is like the days of Noah to me:
Just as I swore that the waters
of Noah
would never again go over the
earth,
so I have sworn that I will not be angry
with you
and will not rebuke you.
10 For the mountains may depart
and the hills be removed,
but my steadfast love shall not depart
from you,
and my covenant of peace shall not
be removed,
says the LORD, who has compassion
on you.

11 O afflicted one, storm-tossed, and not
comforted,
I am about to set your stones in
antimony,
and lay your foundations with
sapphires.*a*

a Or *lapis lazuli*

12 I will make your pinnacles of rubies,
       your gates of jewels,
       and all your wall of precious
           stones.
13 All your children shall be taught by the
           LORD,
       and great shall be the prosperity of
           your children.
14 In righteousness you shall be
           established;
       you shall be far from oppression, for
           you shall not fear;
       and from terror, for it shall not come
           near you.
15 If anyone stirs up strife,
       it is not from me;
   whoever stirs up strife with you
       shall fall because of you.
16 See it is I who have created the
           smith
       who blows the fire of coals,
       and produces a weapon fit for
           its purpose;
   I have also created the ravager
       to destroy.
17   No weapon that is fashioned against
           you shall prosper,
       and you shall confute every tongue
           that rises against you in
           judgment.
   This is the heritage of the servants of
       the LORD
       and their vindication from me, says
           the LORD.

54.1–17: Consolation for the new Jerusalem. 1–8:
The city must put behind it the memory of its past,
forgetting its shame and disappointments. It must instead make plans for *enlargement* and growth (vv.
2–3). Using the peaceful imagery of *widowhood,* the
prophet looks ahead to the prosperous and bustling
future that awaits it (vv. 6–7). **9–17:** Another lesson
from the traditions of the past is the lesson of Noah,
who after the ending of the Great Deluge was the recipient of a divine promise that never again would
such a catastrophe overtake humankind (see Gen
9.8–17). So God would ensure that Jerusalem's citizens
were taught the divine way (v. 13), and those who
brought strife (v. 15), or made war against the city,
would fail in their purpose (v. 17).

55 Ho, everyone who thirsts,
       come to the waters;
   and you that have no money,
       come, buy and eat!
   Come, buy wine and milk
       without money and without price.
2 Why do you spend your money for that
           which is not bread,
       and your labor for that which does
           not satisfy?
   Listen carefully to me, and eat what is
           good,
       and delight yourselves in rich food.
3 Incline your ear, and come to me;
       listen, so that you may live.
   I will make with you an everlasting
           covenant,
       my steadfast, sure love for David.
4 See, I made him a witness to
           the peoples,
       a leader and commander for
           the peoples.
5 See, you shall call nations that you do
           not know,
       and nations that do not know you
           shall run to you,
   because of the LORD your God, the
           Holy One of Israel,
       for he has glorified you.

55.1–13: Seek the LORD while he may be found. Although this chapter concludes the work of the prophet
of the return, chs. 54 and 55 form a bridge to 56–66.
Two separate units are in the present chapter. **1–5:** The
first unit concerns God's promise to the royal dynasty★
of David (2 Sam 7.1–17), an *everlasting covenant*★
(v. 3). This covenant is an act of God's love, an unmer-
ited gift. Along with the promises set out in 11.1–5
and 32.1–8, it affirms that God will hold fast to the
unqualified promise that, through the authority entrusted to this royal dynasty of kings, Israel will exercise
leadership over the nations (v. 5). This can mean either
that, although the royal family itself would not return
to the throne, leadership among the nations would be
shared throughout the servant-nation, or that the restoration of the Davidic monarchy is promised here.
The course of events in the following half-century reveals that such an expectation remained alive and exercised a strong political influence, even though it
failed to reach fruition. In later years, a larger "messianic" interpretation★ concerning the coming of a di-

vinely sent savior figure was built on this, and the other royal prophecies, of the book of Isaiah and the Psalms.

6 Seek the LORD while he may be found,
    call upon him while he is near;
7 let the wicked forsake their way,
    and the unrighteous their thoughts;
    let them return to the LORD, that he
        may have mercy on them,
    and to our God, for he will
        abundantly pardon.
8 For my thoughts are not your thoughts,
    nor are your ways my ways, says the
        LORD.
9 For as the heavens are higher than the
        earth,
    so are my ways higher than your ways
    and my thoughts than your thoughts.

10 For as the rain and the snow come
        down from heaven,
    and do not return there until they
        have watered the earth,
    making it bring forth and sprout,
    giving seed to the sower and bread to
        the eater,
11 so shall my word be that goes out from
        my mouth;
    it shall not return to me empty,
    but it shall accomplish that which I
        purpose,

and succeed in the thing for which I
    sent it.

12 For you shall go out in joy,
    and be led back in peace;
    the mountains and the hills before you
        shall burst into song,
    and all the trees of the field shall clap
        their hands.
13 Instead of the thorn shall come up the
        cypress;
    instead of the brier shall come up the
        myrtle;
    and it shall be to the LORD for a
        memorial,
    for an everlasting sign that shall not
        be cut off.

55.6–13: The concluding unit (vv. 6–13) makes a rich and memorable appeal concerning the power of the divine word given through the prophet and the certainty that it will accomplish its purpose. What appeared impossible to the human mind was possible with God (vv. 8–9). As *rain and snow* made the earth fertile and productive, so would God's word prove equally effective in achieving its intended purpose (v. 10). The promise of v. 13 summarizes in pictorial language the message of hope for the future by insisting that the ruination of the vineyard of God (Israel) by *briers* and *thorns* would be a feature of the past (see 5.6).

Isaiah 56–66

THE COMING OF THE LIGHT

These chapters fluctuate sharply between stern rebuke and lyrical reassurance. Disloyalty, a return to idol-worship, and conflicts within the community are the central themes of chs. 56–59. Even the keeping of festivals and holding of fasts is fraudulent and insincere, because those who do so do not practice right-dealing with their fellow citizens. This falsity prevents the fulfillment of God's promises. Yet the coming glory of the new Jerusalem is assured (chs. 60–62), although the time of fulfillment is uncertain. Fresh rebukes challenge the insincerity of worship (ch. 65), and fresh lamentations★ denounce injustice within the community (63.16–19). Only a new heaven and a new earth can bring the fullness of peace and rejoicing which God has promised (66.22–23).

These chapters were most likely compiled later than chs. 40–55, belonging to the period after the first stages of the return and restoration in Judah around 520–500 BCE, or even during the

following half-century. The admonitions in 66.1 appear to refer to the rebuilding of the Jerusalem Temple in 520–516 BCE, but whether they came before or after this event is not clear. There is no mention of attempts to restore a descendant of David to the throne, to which other prophecies of the period certainly testify (see Hag 2.20–23; Zech 4.1–14). Nor are these chapters a unified work. Different prophets addressed the pressing issues that frustrated a community struggling to reestablish its identity. It is unclear whether these prophecies were collected and shaped to provide a conclusion to a "Book of Isaiah" that already existed and that was largely similar to our Isa 1–55. Although chs. 56–59 seem to be integrated, chs. 60–66 appear as individual developments of earlier themes and texts. There does seem, however, to be some deliberate connection between chs. 1–4 and 63–66, which attests to the editorial shaping of the final form of the book.

READING GUIDE

Although appearing to qualify the hope promised in chs. 40–55, these later chapters introduce significant themes such as the nature of community and nationhood, the need for self-critical reflection on worship and self-denial, and the importance of faith in breaking down barriers between hostile groups. Faith is not simply about taking hold of promises, but about compassion, heart-searching, and tolerance, all of which are essential for true religious renewal.

56 Thus says the LORD:
Maintain justice, and do what is
    right,
for soon my salvation will come,
    and my deliverance be revealed.

2 Happy is the mortal who does this,
    the one who holds it fast,
who keeps the sabbath, not profaning it,
    and refrains from doing any evil.

3 Do not let the foreigner joined to the
        LORD say,
    "The LORD will surely separate me
        from his people";
and do not let the eunuch say,
    "I am just a dry tree."

4 For thus says the LORD:
To the eunuchs who keep my
    sabbaths,
    who choose the things that please me
    and hold fast my covenant,
5 I will give, in my house and within my
        walls,
    a monument and a name
    better than sons and daughters;
I will give them an everlasting name
    that shall not be cut off.

6 And the foreigners who join themselves
        to the LORD,
    to minister to him, to love the name
        of the LORD,
    and to be his servants,

all who keep the sabbath, and do not
    profane it,
    and hold fast my covenant—
7 these I will bring to my holy mountain,
    and make them joyful in my house of
        prayer;
    their burnt offerings and their sacrifices
        will be accepted on my altar;
    for my house shall be called a house of
        prayer
    for all peoples.
8 Thus says the Lord GOD,
    who gathers the outcasts of Israel,
    I will gather others to them
    besides those already gathered.^{a}

9 All you wild animals,
    all you wild animals in the forest,
        come to devour!
10 Israel's^b sentinels are blind,
    they are all without knowledge;
    they are all silent dogs
        that cannot bark;
    dreaming, lying down,
        loving to slumber.
11 The dogs have a mighty appetite;
    they never have enough.
    The shepherds also have no
        understanding;
    they have all turned to their own way,
    to their own gain, one and all.
12 "Come," they say, "let us^c get wine;
    let us fill ourselves with strong drink.
    And tomorrow will be like today,
        great beyond measure."

57 The righteous perish,
    and no one takes it to heart;
    the devout are taken away,
        while no one understands.
    For the righteous are taken away from
        calamity,
2   and they enter into peace;
    those who walk uprightly
        will rest on their couches.
3 But as for you, come here,
    you children of a sorceress,
    you offspring of an adulterer and a
        whore.^{d}
4 Whom are you mocking?
    Against whom do you open your
        mouth wide
    and stick out your tongue?
    Are you not children of transgression,
        the offspring of deceit—
5 you that burn with lust among the oaks,
    under every green tree;
    you that slaughter your children in the
        valleys,
    under the clefts of the rocks?
6 Among the smooth stones of the valley
        is your portion;
    they, they, are your lot;
    to them you have poured out a drink
        offering,
    you have brought a grain offering.
    Shall I be appeased for these
        things?
7 Upon a high and lofty mountain
    you have set your bed,
    and there you went up to offer
        sacrifice.
8 Behind the door and the doorpost
    you have set up your symbol;
    for, in deserting me,^{e} you have
        uncovered your bed,
    you have gone up to it,
    you have made it wide;
    and you have made a bargain for
        yourself with them,
    you have loved their bed,
    you have gazed on their nakedness.^{f}

56.1–12: Soon my salvation will come. 1–8: The call
to rebuild Jerusalem had been an open invitation (especially 55.6–7). This openness, however, did not take
into account strong traditional rules concerning who
belonged in God's family (see Deut 23.1–8). Now
these rules were being used to exclude those, such as
foreigners and *eunuchs,* who were treated as outcasts
(v. 3), even though this mocked the Temple* as a
house of prayer (v. 7). **9–12:** This sharp rebuke addressed to the *blind* and *silent dogs* reflects the bitter
divisions that had emerged within the community.
Most likely the presence of returned exiles contributed
to this bitterness with those already holding positions
of power in Jerusalem reluctant to give it up.

a Heb *besides his gathered ones*   *b* Heb *His*
c Q Ms Syr Vg Tg: MT *me*   *d* Heb *an adulterer and*
she plays the whore   *e* Meaning of Heb uncertain
f Or *their phallus;* Heb *the hand*

9 You journeyed to Molech*a* with oil,
   and multiplied your perfumes;
you sent your envoys far away,
   and sent down even to Sheol.
10 You grew weary from your many
      wanderings,
   but you did not say, "It is useless."
You found your desire rekindled,
   and so you did not weaken.

11 Whom did you dread and fear
      so that you lied,
and did not remember me
   or give me a thought?
Have I not kept silent and closed my
      eyes,*b*
   and so you do not fear me?
12 I will concede your righteousness and
      your works,
   but they will not help you.
13 When you cry out, let your collection of
      idols deliver you!
The wind will carry them off,
   a breath will take them away.
But whoever takes refuge in me shall
      possess the land
   and inherit my holy mountain.

14 It shall be said,
"Build up, build up, prepare the way,
   remove every obstruction from my
      people's way."
15 For thus says the high and lofty one
   who inhabits eternity, whose name is
      Holy:
I dwell in the high and holy place,
   and also with those who are contrite
      and humble in spirit,
to revive the spirit of the humble,
   and to revive the heart of the
      contrite.
16 For I will not continually accuse,
   nor will I always be angry;
for then the spirits would grow faint
      before me,
   even the souls that I have made.
17 Because of their wicked covetousness I
      was angry;
I struck them, I hid and was angry;
   but they kept turning back to their
      own ways.

18 I have seen their ways, but I will heal
      them;
   I will lead them and repay them with
      comfort,
   creating for their mourners the fruit
      of the lips.*c*
19 Peace, peace, to the far and the near,
      says the LORD;
   and I will heal them.
20 But the wicked are like the tossing sea
      that cannot keep still;
   its waters toss up mire and mud.
21 There is no peace, says my God, for the
      wicked.

57.1–21: No peace for the wicked. 1–10: The sense of disunity within Jerusalem reveals that the end of the captivity had not brought an end to its troubles. It had simply given rise to new ones. There was injustice and false and immoral worship, tolerated under foreign rule (vv. 5–7). Old customs of gods worshipped for centuries throughout the region (v. 9) had been revived while the Temple* of the LORD lay in ruins. *Molech* is probably one of the titles of Baal,* a god especially linked with child sacrifice. **11–21:** The sharp prophetic critique of wrongdoing within the community that characterizes earlier prophecies reappears here with added vigor (see 5.11–25). The warning of 48.22 that there would be no peace for the wicked receives a dismal confirmation in the vain efforts of those who try to secure it (vv. 19–21). There is a note of both lamentation and despair in the repetition of God's call to build and be patient (vv. 14–19) and the response of vv. 20–21, affirming that the wicked are incapable of creating peace.

58 Shout out, do not hold back!
   Lift up your voice like a trumpet!
Announce to my people their
      rebellion,
   to the house of Jacob their sins.
2 Yet day after day they seek me
   and delight to know my ways,
as if they were a nation that practiced
      righteousness
   and did not forsake the ordinance of
      their God;

a Or *the king*   *b* Gk Vg: Heb *silent even for a long time*
c Meaning of Heb uncertain

they ask of me righteous judgments,
  they delight to draw near to God.
3 "Why do we fast, but you do not see?
  Why humble ourselves, but you do
    not notice?"
Look, you serve your own interest on
    your fast day,
  and oppress all your workers.
4 Look, you fast only to quarrel and to
    fight
  and to strike with a wicked fist.
Such fasting as you do today
  will not make your voice heard on
    high.
5 Is such the fast that I choose,
  a day to humble oneself?
Is it to bow down the head like a
    bulrush,
  and to lie in sackcloth and ashes?
Will you call this a fast,
  a day acceptable to the LORD?

6 Is not this the fast that I choose:
  to loose the bonds of injustice,
  to undo the thongs of the yoke,
to let the oppressed go free,
  and to break every yoke?
7 Is it not to share your bread with the
    hungry,
  and bring the homeless poor into your
    house;
when you see the naked, to cover them,
  and not to hide yourself from your
    own kin?
8 Then your light shall break forth like
    the dawn,
  and your healing shall spring
    up quickly;
your vindicator*a* shall go before you,
  the glory of the LORD shall be your
    rear guard.
9 Then you shall call, and the LORD will
    answer;
  you shall cry for help, and he will say,
    Here I am.

If you remove the yoke from among you,
  the pointing of the finger, the
    speaking of evil,
10 if you offer your food to the hungry
  and satisfy the needs of the afflicted,

then your light shall rise in the darkness
  and your gloom be like the noonday.
11 The LORD will guide you continually,
  and satisfy your needs in parched
    places,
  and make your bones strong;
and you shall be like a watered garden,
  like a spring of water,
  whose waters never fail.
12 Your ancient ruins shall be rebuilt;
  you shall raise up the foundations of
    many generations;
you shall be called the repairer of the
    breach,
  the restorer of streets to live in.

13 If you refrain from trampling the
    sabbath,
  from pursuing your own interests on
    my holy day;
if you call the sabbath a delight
  and the holy day of the LORD
    honorable;
if you honor it, not going your
    own ways,
  serving your own interests, or
    pursuing your own affairs;*b*
14 then you shall take delight in the LORD,
  and I will make you ride upon the
    heights of the earth;
I will feed you with the heritage of your
    ancestor Jacob,
  for the mouth of the LORD has
    spoken.

58.1–14: The fast acceptable to God. 1–10: A fresh problem concerns those who maintain a bold public display of piety, but whose actions and way of life flout the basic requirements of justice and goodness. The central issue is fasting, self-denial aimed at concentrating mind and body on prayer, which was publicly declared by wearing *sackcloth** (a rough garment) and smearing the face and hands with *ashes* (symbol of mortality) (v. 5). Yet such deeds unaccompanied by compassion and concern for those less fortunate were meaningless to God (vv. 6–9). **11–14:** The efforts to restore Jerusalem had focused on externals—restoring ancient buildings and replanting neglected fields—instead of the inner recovery of spiritual health and

a Or *vindication*   *b* Heb *or speaking words*

wholeness. Only a renewal of this inner direction of life could bring about the true rebuilding of the city.

59 See, the LORD's hand is not too
    short to save,
    nor his ear too dull to hear.
2 Rather, your iniquities have been
    barriers
    between you and your God,
  and your sins have hidden his face
    from you
    so that he does not hear.
3 For your hands are defiled with blood,
    and your fingers with iniquity;
  your lips have spoken lies,
    your tongue mutters wickedness.
4 No one brings suit justly,
    no one goes to law honestly;
  they rely on empty pleas, they speak
    lies,
    conceiving mischief and begetting
    iniquity.
5 They hatch adders' eggs,
    and weave the spider's web;
  whoever eats their eggs dies,
    and the crushed egg hatches out a
    viper.
6 Their webs cannot serve as clothing;
    they cannot cover themselves with
    what they make.
  Their works are works of iniquity,
    and deeds of violence are in their
    hands.
7 Their feet run to evil,
    and they rush to shed innocent
    blood;
  their thoughts are thoughts of iniquity,
    desolation and destruction are in
    their highways.
8 The way of peace they do not know,
    and there is no justice in their paths.
  Their roads they have made crooked;
    no one who walks in them knows
    peace.

59.1–21: Why God's face is hidden. 1–8. God's salvation has not come, not because God is weak and powerless, but because the people's wrongdoing creates a barrier between themselves and God (vv. 1–2). The rebukes (vv. 3–8) condemn violence, injustice and brigandage, whether arising from lack of any recog-

nized authority to implement justice, or whether because those who wield power in Jerusalem are themselves the chief culprits.

9 Therefore justice is far from us,
    and righteousness does not reach us;
  we wait for light, and lo! there is
    darkness;
    and for brightness, but we walk in
    gloom.
10 We grope like the blind along a wall,
    groping like those who have no eyes;
  we stumble at noon as in the twilight,
    among the vigorous[a] as though we
    were dead.
11 We all growl like bears;
    like doves we moan mournfully.
  We wait for justice, but there is none;
    for salvation, but it is far from us.
12 For our transgressions before you are
    many,
    and our sins testify against us.
  Our transgressions indeed are with us,
    and we know our iniquities:
13 transgressing, and denying the LORD,
    and turning away from following our
    God,
  talking oppression and revolt,
    conceiving lying words and uttering
    them from the heart.
14 Justice is turned back,
    and righteousness stands at a
    distance;
  for truth stumbles in the public square,
    and uprightness cannot enter.
15 Truth is lacking,
    and whoever turns from evil is
    despoiled.

  The LORD saw it, and it displeased him
    that there was no justice.
16 He saw that there was no one,
    and was appalled that there was no
    one to intervene;
  so his own arm brought him victory,
    and his righteousness upheld him.
17 He put on righteousness like a
    breastplate,
    and a helmet of salvation on his head;

a Meaning of Heb uncertain

he put on garments of vengeance for
    clothing,
    and wrapped himself in fury as in a
        mantle.
18 According to their deeds, so will he repay;
    wrath to his adversaries, requital to
        his enemies;
    to the coastlands he will render
        requital.
19 So those in the west shall fear the
        name of the LORD,
    and those in the east, his glory;
    for he will come like a pent-up stream
    that the wind of the LORD drives on.

20 And he will come to Zion as Redeemer,
    to those in Jacob who turn from
        transgression, says the LORD.
21 And as for me, this is my covenant with
them, says the LORD: my spirit that is upon
you, and my words that I have put in your
mouth, shall not depart out of your mouth,
or out of the mouths of your children, or out
of the mouths of your children's children,
says the LORD, from now on and forever.

59.9–21. 9–15a: The lack of an effective administration of justice allowed violence and corruption to flourish. Those who had won power under foreign masters were now unwilling to relinquish control and to empower a new order of religious leaders. It was not until the work of Ezra and Nehemiah, in the middle of the fifth century BCE, that the situation began to be put right. **15b–21:** Without the protection that God alone can bring, the helplessness described so vividly in vv. 10–11 must continue. The assurance in v. 21 that God's word will prove effective indicates that chs. 56–59, at one time, formed a separate collection to which this section was a conclusion.

Visions of the new Jerusalem
Chs. 60–62: After the setbacks and dissensions in chs. 56–59, chs. 60–62 recover the vision of the future central to chs. 40–55. Jerusalem will be rebuilt, a city of peace and righteousness. These chapters reflect the spiritual reawakening that came with the rebuilding and restoration of the Temple★ in Jerusalem in 520–516 BCE. More broadly, these chapters express a positive, if ideal, portrayal of human beings living in peace, prosperity, and harmony. They reveal a goal to strive for, not a simplistic expectation of a condition of human happiness that will drop down as a gift from heaven.

60 Arise, shine; for your light has come,
    and the glory of the LORD has risen
        upon you.
2 For darkness shall cover the earth,
    and thick darkness the peoples;
    but the LORD will arise upon you,
    and his glory will appear over you.
3 Nations shall come to your light,
    and kings to the brightness of your
        dawn.

4 Lift up your eyes and look around;
    they all gather together, they come
        to you;
    your sons shall come from far away,
    and your daughters shall be carried
        on their nurses' arms.
5 Then you shall see and be radiant;
    your heart shall thrill and rejoice,*a*
    because the abundance of the sea shall
        be brought to you,
    the wealth of the nations shall come
        to you.
6 A multitude of camels shall cover you,
    the young camels of Midian and
        Ephah;
    all those from Sheba shall come.
    They shall bring gold and frankincense,
    and shall proclaim the praise of the
        LORD.
7 All the flocks of Kedar shall be gathered
        to you,
    the rams of Nebaioth shall minister to
        you;
    they shall be acceptable on my altar,
    and I will glorify my glorious house.

8 Who are these that fly like a cloud,
    and like doves to their windows?
9 For the coastlands shall wait for me,
    the ships of Tarshish first,
    to bring your children from far away,
    their silver and gold with them,
    for the name of the LORD your God,
    and for the Holy One of Israel,
    because he has glorified you.

a Heb *be enlarged*

10 Foreigners shall build up your walls,
and their kings shall minister to you;
for in my wrath I struck you down,
but in my favor I have had mercy
on you.

11 Your gates shall always be open;
day and night they shall not be shut,
so that nations shall bring you their
wealth,
with their kings led in procession.

12 For the nation and kingdom
that will not serve you shall perish;
those nations shall be utterly
laid waste.

13 The glory of Lebanon shall come
to you,
the cypress, the plane, and the pine,
to beautify the place of my sanctuary;
and I will glorify where my feet
rest.

14 The descendants of those who
oppressed you
shall come bending low to you,
and all who despised you
shall bow down at your feet;
they shall call you the City of the
LORD,
the Zion of the Holy One of Israel.

15 Whereas you have been forsaken and
hated,
with no one passing through,
I will make you majestic forever,
a joy from age to age.

16 You shall suck the milk of nations,
you shall suck the breasts of kings;
and you shall know that I, the LORD,
am your Savior
and your Redeemer, the Mighty One
of Jacob.

17 Instead of bronze I will bring gold,
instead of iron I will bring silver;
instead of wood, bronze,
instead of stones, iron.
I will appoint Peace as your overseer
and Righteousness as your
taskmaster.

18 Violence shall no more be heard in your
land,
devastation or destruction within your
borders;

you shall call your walls Salvation,
and your gates Praise.

19 The sun shall no longer be
your light by day,
nor for brightness shall the moon
give light to you by night; [a]
but the LORD will be your everlasting
light,
and your God will be your glory.

20 Your sun shall no more go down,
or your moon withdraw itself;
for the LORD will be your everlasting
light,
and your days of mourning shall be
ended.

21 Your people shall all be righteous;
they shall possess the land forever.
They are the shoot that I planted, the
work of my hands,
so that I might be glorified.

22 The least of them shall become a clan,
and the smallest one a mighty nation;
I am the LORD;
in its time I will accomplish
it quickly.

60.1–22: Arise, shine, for your light has come. 1–7: The expected return had not occurred. At best, only token numbers of the former population had come back. The vision of a great return was still a distant dream. A new pattern of Jewish life emerged that established rules of conduct for living as peaceably as possible in alien lands. **8–14:** The high point of the great vision of 45.22–23, that foreigners too would share in the coming salvation and prosperity, is here sharply reduced to granting them the role of being servants and suppliers to the restored Israel. **15–22:** Hope for the future Jerusalem as a city of wealth, learning, and authority contrasts with the revelations of conflict and violence that 59.1–8 has revealed. The need to restore a vision of God's intentions for Jerusalem became urgent as a counterweight to the current difficulties. The Temple* was restored and a new focus provided for those who worshipped the LORD in every land.

61 The spirit of the Lord GOD is
upon me,
because the LORD has anointed me;

a Q Ms Gk Old Latin Tg: MT lacks *by night*

he has sent me to bring good news to
the oppressed,
to bind up the brokenhearted,
to proclaim liberty to the captives,
and release to the prisoners;
2 to proclaim the year of the LORD's
favor,
and the day of vengeance of our God;
to comfort all who mourn;
3 to provide for those who mourn in
Zion—
to give them a garland instead
of ashes,
the oil of gladness instead of mourning,
the mantle of praise instead of a faint
spirit.
They will be called oaks of
righteousness,
the planting of the LORD, to display
his glory.
4 They shall build up the ancient ruins,
they shall raise up the former
devastations;
they shall repair the ruined cities,
the devastations of many generations.

5 Strangers shall stand and feed
your flocks,
foreigners shall till your land and
dress your vines;
6 but you shall be called priests of the
LORD,
you shall be named ministers of our
God;
you shall enjoy the wealth of
the nations,
and in their riches you shall glory.
7 Because their*a* shame was double,
and dishonor was proclaimed as their
lot,
therefore they shall possess a double
portion;
everlasting joy shall be theirs.

8 For I the LORD love justice,
I hate robbery and wrongdoing;*b*
I will faithfully give them their
recompense,
and I will make an everlasting
covenant with them.

9 Their descendants shall be known
among the nations,
and their offspring among the
peoples;
all who see them shall acknowledge
that they are a people whom the
LORD has blessed.
10 I will greatly rejoice in the LORD,
my whole being shall exult in my God;
for he has clothed me with the
garments of salvation,
he has covered me with the robe of
righteousness,
as a bridegroom decks himself with a
garland,
and as a bride adorns herself with her
jewels.
11 For as the earth brings forth its shoots,
and as a garden causes what is sown
in it to spring up,
so the Lord GOD will cause
righteousness and praise
to spring up before all the nations.

61.1–11: The year of the LORD's favor. 1–4: All that
God had promised regarding the rebuilding and restoration of Jerusalem would shortly be fulfilled. **5–9:**
Expectation of God's direct action to overthrow the
present world order becomes a marked feature of the
hope expressed throughout chs. 56–66. Where chs.
40–55 had recognized the hand of God at work in the
rise of Cyrus, king of Persia, to direct the destiny of
Judah, now Israel awaits a more direct divine intervention. **8–11:** Assurance that this transformation will take
place derives from the very nature of God. Love of justice and hatred of all forms of wrongdoing are aspects
of God's rule.

62 For Zion's sake I will not keep
silent,
and for Jerusalem's sake I will not
rest,
until her vindication shines out like the
dawn,
and her salvation like a burning torch.
2 The nations shall see your vindication,
and all the kings your glory;
and you shall be called by a new name
that the mouth of the LORD will give.

a Heb *your*   *b* Or *robbery with a burnt offering*

3 You shall be a crown of beauty in the
    hand of the LORD,
  and a royal diadem in the hand of
    your God.
4 You shall no more be termed
    Forsaken,*
  and your land shall no more be
    termed Desolate;*
  but you shall be called My Delight Is in
    Her,*
  and your land Married;*
  for the LORD delights in you,
    and your land shall be married.
5 For as a young man marries a young
    woman,
  so shall your builder* marry you,
  and as the bridegroom rejoices over the
    bride,
  so shall your God rejoice over you.
6 Upon your walls, O Jerusalem,
    I have posted sentinels;
  all day and all night
    they shall never be silent.
  You who remind the LORD,
    take no rest,
7 and give him no rest
    until he establishes Jerusalem
  and makes it renowned throughout
    the earth.
8 The LORD has sworn by his right hand
    and by his mighty arm:
  I will not again give your grain
    to be food for your enemies,
  and foreigners shall not drink the wine
    for which you have labored;
9 but those who garner it shall eat it
    and praise the LORD,
  and those who gather it shall drink it
    in my holy courts.

10 Go through, go through the gates,
    prepare the way for the people;
  build up, build up the highway,
    clear it of stones,
  lift up an ensign over the peoples.
11 The LORD has proclaimed
    to the end of the earth:
  Say to daughter Zion,
    "See, your salvation comes;
  his reward is with him,
    and his recompense before him."

12 They shall be called, "The Holy People,
    The Redeemed of the LORD";
  and you shall be called, "Sought Out,
    A City Not Forsaken."

62.1–12: A city not forsaken. 1–5: As the situation in
Jerusalem failed to change after the downfall of Babylon, the prophet reassured the people of God's intense love for the city. These are presented here in
terms of the intensity of the divine love for the city (vv.
4–5). **6–9:** The wealth and food that foreigners took
were prime examples of the frustrations and disappointments of the past. The people must pray that
such injustice never again occurs (vv. 8–9). **10–12:** A
note of urgency colors the prophet's insistence that
God's promise will not fail.

63 "Who is this that comes from
      Edom,
  from Bozrah in garments stained
    crimson?
  Who is this so splendidly robed,
    marching in his great might?"

  "It is I, announcing vindication,
    mighty to save."

2 "Why are your robes red,
    and your garments like theirs who
      tread the wine press?"

3 "I have trodden the wine press alone,
    and from the peoples no one was
      with me;
  I trod them in my anger
    and trampled them in my wrath;
  their juice spattered on my garments,
    and stained all my robes.
4 For the day of vengeance was in my
      heart,
  and the year for my redeeming work
      had come.
5 I looked, but there was no helper;
    I stared, but there was no one to
      sustain me;
  so my own arm brought me victory,
    and my wrath sustained me.

a Heb *Azubah*   *b* Heb *Shemamah*   *c* Heb *Hephzibah*
d Heb *Beulah*   *e* Cn: Heb *your sons*

6 I trampled down peoples in my anger,
    I crushed them in my wrath,
    and I poured out their lifeblood on
        the earth."

7 I will recount the gracious deeds of the
        LORD,
    the praiseworthy acts of the LORD,
because of all that the LORD has done
        for us,
    and the great favor to the house of
        Israel
that he has shown them according to
        his mercy,
    according to the abundance of his
        steadfast love.
8 For he said, "Surely they are my people,
    children who will not deal falsely";
and he became their savior
9   in all their distress.
It was no messenger[a] or angel
    but his presence that saved them;[b]
in his love and in his pity he redeemed
        them;
    he lifted them up and carried them
        all the days of old.

10 But they rebelled
    and grieved his holy spirit;
therefore he became their enemy;
    he himself fought against them.
11 Then they[c] remembered the days of
        old,
    of Moses his servant.[d]
Where is the one who brought them
        up out of the sea
    with the shepherds of his flock?
Where is the one who put within them
    his holy spirit,
12 who caused his glorious arm
    to march at the right hand of Moses,
who divided the waters before them
    to make for himself an everlasting
        name,
13   who led them through the depths?
Like a horse in the desert,
    they did not stumble.
14 Like cattle that go down into the valley,
    the spirit of the LORD gave them rest.
Thus you led your people,
    to make for yourself a glorious name.

15 Look down from heaven and see,
    from your holy and glorious
        habitation.
Where are your zeal and your might?
    The yearning of your heart and your
        compassion?
They are withheld from me.
16 For you are our father,
    though Abraham does not know us
    and Israel does not acknowledge us;
you, O LORD, are our father;
    our Redeemer from of old is
        your name.
17 Why, O LORD, do you make us stray
        from your ways
    and harden our heart, so that we do
        not fear you?
Turn back for the sake of your servants,
    for the sake of the tribes that are your
        heritage.
18 Your holy people took possession for a
        little while;
    but now our adversaries have
        trampled down your sanctuary.
19 We have long been like those whom you
        do not rule,
    like those not called by your name.

63.1–19: The day of vengeance. 1–6: In vivid and
frightening imagery, human frustration and longing
for the end of violence calls forth this powerful picture
of God acting alone to pass judgment on the warring
nations. Where no human ruler could impose justice
and peace (v. 5), God had to act directly and decisively
(vv. 5–6). **7–14:** In the past, God's presence had accompanied the people and given them victory over
their enemies (v. 9). In the present, the rebelliousness
of the people grieved the spirit of God, aroused the
divine anger, and led to failure and defeat (v. 10). The
people of Israel had learned this lesson in the past
when failure humbled them (see Josh 7.1–26), and
now they had to relearn it (vv. 11–14). **15–19:** Even
after temporary success had brought about a partial
change in Judah's fortunes (v. 18), new threats and
new oppressions had robbed the people of the justice
and prosperity they sought (v. 19).

---

a Gk: Heb *anguish*   b Or *savior*. [9]*In all their distress he
was distressed; the angel of his presence saved them;*
c Heb *he*   d Cn: Heb *his people*

A Summary of the Message of Isaiah

The protection of Jerusalem and its Temple* from the arrogant threats of the Assyrian king, Sennacherib, (chs. 36–37) form a background to the collection of prophecies in Isa 1–39. The hope of rebuilding the Temple after its destruction by the armies of Babylon in 587 BCE are central to the promises of chs. 40–55. The renewed conflicts that surrounded its rebuilding in the years 520–516 BCE color the mixture of threats and warnings of Isa 56–66. What inner meaning and purpose hold together these changing fortunes of the building which aroused such passionate emotions and expectations? Verses 1–2 of chapter 66 offer a fundamental and comprehensive answer by showing how the Temple could be either a means of understanding the reality of God, or a foolish illusion by which God's real claims were evaded. When rightly understood, the Temple was an aid to the humility, obedience, and contrite spirit that God demands.

64 O that you would tear open the
heavens and come down,
so that the mountains would quake at
your presence—
2ᵃ as when fire kindles brushwood
and the fire causes water to boil—
to make your name known to your
adversaries,
so that the nations might tremble at
your presence!
3 When you did awesome deeds that we
did not expect,
you came down, the mountains
quaked at your presence.
4 From ages past no one has heard,
no ear has perceived,
no eye has seen any God besides you,
who works for those who wait
for him.
5 You meet those who gladly do right,
those who remember you in
your ways.
But you were angry, and we sinned;
because you hid yourself we
transgressed.ᵇ
6 We have all become like one who is
unclean,
and all our righteous deeds are like a
filthy cloth.
We all fade like a leaf,
and our iniquities, like the wind, take
us away.

7 There is no one who calls on
your name,
or attempts to take hold of you;
for you have hidden your face from us,
and have deliveredᶜ us into the hand
of our iniquity.
8 Yet, O LORD, you are our Father;
we are the clay, and you are
our potter;
we are all the work of your hand.
9 Do not be exceedingly angry, O LORD,
and do not remember iniquity forever.
Now consider, we are all your people.
10 Your holy cities have become a
wilderness,
Zion has become a wilderness,
Jerusalem a desolation.
11 Our holy and beautiful house,
where our ancestors praised you,
has been burned by fire,
and all our pleasant places have
become ruins.
12 After all this, will you restrain yourself,
O LORD?
Will you keep silent, and punish us so
severely?

64.1–12: The silence of God. 1–7: The present situation appeared as a contradiction to God's power

---

a Ch 64.1 in Heb   *b* Meaning of Heb uncertain
c Gk Syr Old Latin Tg: Heb *melted*

(v. 4). The reason for this lay with the sins of the present generation, which now came in penitent lamentation to confess their rebelliousness to God (vv. 6–7). **8–12:** Even in its failures, Israel remained God's people and could confess its wrongdoing and return to God. The renewed conflict and destruction (v. 11) had arisen in the wake of the rebuilding of the Temple.

65 I was ready to be sought out by
those who did not ask,
to be found by those who did not seek
me.
I said, "Here I am, here I am,"
to a nation that did not call on my
name.
2 I held out my hands all day long
to a rebellious people,
who walk in a way that is not good,
following their own devices;
3 a people who provoke me
to my face continually,
sacrificing in gardens
and offering incense on bricks;
4 who sit inside tombs,
and spend the night in secret places;
who eat swine's flesh,
with broth of abominable things in
their vessels;
5 who say, "Keep to yourself,
do not come near me, for I am too
holy for you."
These are a smoke in my nostrils,
a fire that burns all day long.
6 See, it is written before me:
I will not keep silent, but I will
repay;
I will indeed repay into their laps
7 their[a] iniquities and their[a] ancestors'
iniquities together,
says the LORD;
because they offered incense on the
mountains
and reviled me on the hills,
I will measure into their laps
full payment for their actions.
8 Thus says the LORD:
As the wine is found in the cluster,
and they say, "Do not destroy it,
for there is a blessing in it,"
so I will do for my servants' sake,
and not destroy them all.

9 I will bring forth descendants[b] from
Jacob,
and from Judah inheritors[c] of my
mountains;
my chosen shall inherit it,
and my servants shall settle there.
10 Sharon shall become a pasture
for flocks,
and the Valley of Achor a place for
herds to lie down,
for my people who have sought me.
11 But you who forsake the LORD,
who forget my holy mountain,
who set a table for Fortune
and fill cups of mixed wine for
Destiny;
12 I will destine you to the sword,
and all of you shall bow down to the
slaughter;
because, when I called, you did
not answer,
when I spoke, you did not listen,
but you did what was evil in my sight,
and chose what I did not delight in.
13 Therefore thus says the Lord GOD:
My servants shall eat,
but you shall be hungry;
my servants shall drink,
but you shall be thirsty;
my servants shall rejoice,
but you shall be put to shame;
14 my servants shall sing for gladness of
heart,
but you shall cry out for pain
of heart,
and shall wail for anguish of spirit.
15 You shall leave your name to my chosen
to use as a curse,
and the Lord GOD will put you
to death;
but to his servants he will give a
different name.
16 Then whoever invokes a blessing in the
land
shall bless by the God of faithfulness,
and whoever takes an oath in the land
shall swear by the God of
faithfulness;

a Gk Syr: Heb *your*   *b* Or *a descendant*   *c* Or *an inheritor*

because the former troubles are
forgotten
and are hidden from my sight.

17 For I am about to create new heavens
and a new earth;
the former things shall not be
remembered
or come to mind.
18 But be glad and rejoice forever
in what I am creating;
for I am about to create Jerusalem as a
joy,
and its people as a delight.
19 I will rejoice in Jerusalem,
and delight in my people;
no more shall the sound of weeping be
heard in it,
or the cry of distress.
20 No more shall there be in it
an infant that lives but a few days,
or an old person who does not live
out a lifetime;
for one who dies at a hundred years will
be considered a youth,
and one who falls short of a hundred
will be considered accursed.
21 They shall build houses and inhabit
them;
they shall plant vineyards and eat
their fruit.
22 They shall not build and another
inhabit;
they shall not plant and another eat;
for like the days of a tree shall the days
of my people be,
and my chosen shall long enjoy the
work of their hands.
23 They shall not labor in vain,
or bear children for calamity;[a]
for they shall be offspring blessed by the
LORD—
and their descendants as well.
24 Before they call I will answer,
while they are yet speaking I
will hear.
25 The wolf and the lamb shall feed
together,
the lion shall eat straw like the ox;
but the serpent—its food shall
be dust!

They shall not hurt or destroy
on all my holy mountain,
says the LORD.

**65.1–25: The promise of new heavens and a new
earth. 1–7:** Chapters 63–66 carry forward the essential
message of Isaiah's prophecies into the new age that
came with the return from exile. Idolatry* marked a
relapse into indifference to God. The strange and
crude rites described in vv. 3–4 were designed to con-
jure up and manipulate magical power. The belief that
human beings could perform symbolic rituals and eat
strange foods (magic potions) to make themselves
holy (v. 5), and thereby gain power to harm or heal
others, represented a very ancient (v. 7) and supersti-
tious tradition. **8–16:** How could God punish the
wrongdoers without destroying the whole community
of Judah? The prophetic answer is that, for the present,
both groups must coexist, but that God has reserved
a future judgment to bless those who are faithful, but
to punish those who are guilty (vv. 8–13). Then the
very different fates allotted to the two groups will
become plain (vv. 13–16). **17–25:** God is still in control
of human history. The prophet was aware of the
promises earlier in Isaiah; v. 25 recalls the promise in
11.6–9.

66 Thus says the LORD:
Heaven is my throne
and the earth is my footstool;
what is the house that you would build
for me,
and what is my resting place?
2 All these things my hand has made,
and so all these things are mine,[b]
says the LORD.
But this is the one to whom I will
look,
to the humble and contrite in spirit,
who trembles at my word.

3 Whoever slaughters an ox is like one
who kills a human being;
whoever sacrifices a lamb, like one
who breaks a dog's neck;
whoever presents a grain offering, like
one who offers swine's blood;[c]

a Or sudden terror   b Gk Syr: Heb these things came
to be   c Meaning of Heb uncertain

whoever makes a memorial offering of
frankincense, like one who
blesses an idol.
These have chosen their own ways,
and in their abominations they take
delight;
4 I also will choose to mock*a* them,
and bring upon them what they fear;
because, when I called, no one
answered,
when I spoke, they did not listen;
but they did what was evil in my sight,
and chose what did not please me.
5 Hear the word of the LORD,
you who tremble at his word:
Your own people who hate you
and reject you for my name's sake
have said, "Let the LORD be glorified,
so that we may see your joy";
but it is they who shall be put
to shame.

6 Listen, an uproar from the city!
A voice from the temple!
The voice of the LORD,
dealing retribution to his enemies!

7 Before she was in labor
she gave birth;
before her pain came upon her
she delivered a son.
8 Who has heard of such a thing?
Who has seen such things?
Shall a land be born in one day?
Shall a nation be delivered in one
moment?
Yet as soon as Zion was in labor
she delivered her children.
9 Shall I open the womb and not
deliver?
says the LORD;
shall I, the one who delivers, shut the
womb?
says your God.

10 Rejoice with Jerusalem, and be glad for
her,
all you who love her;
rejoice with her in joy,
all you who mourn over her—

11 that you may nurse and be satisfied
from her consoling breast;
that you may drink deeply with
delight
from her glorious bosom.
12 For thus says the LORD:
I will extend prosperity to her like a
river,
and the wealth of the nations like an
overflowing stream;
and you shall nurse and be carried on
her arm,
and dandled on her knees.
13 As a mother comforts her child,
so I will comfort you;
you shall be comforted in
Jerusalem.
14 You shall see, and your heart shall
rejoice;
your bodies*b* shall flourish like the
grass;
and it shall be known that the hand
of the LORD is with his
servants,
and his indignation is against
his enemies.
15 For the LORD will come in fire,
and his chariots like the whirlwind,
to pay back his anger in fury,
and his rebuke in flames of fire.
16 For by fire will the LORD execute
judgment,
and by his sword, on all flesh;
and those slain by the LORD shall be
many.

17 Those who sanctify and purify themselves to go into the gardens, following the
one in the center, eating the flesh of pigs,
vermin, and rodents, shall come to an end
together, says the LORD.

18 For I know*c* their works and their
thoughts, and I am*d* coming to gather all
nations and tongues; and they shall come
and shall see my glory, 19and I will set a sign
among them. From them I will send survi-

a Or *to punish*　*b* Heb *bones*　*c* Gk Syr: Heb lacks
know　*d* Gk Syr Vg Tg: Heb *it is*

vors to the nations, to Tarshish, Put,^a and Lud—which draw the bow—to Tubal and Javan, to the coastlands far away that have not heard of my fame or seen my glory; and they shall declare my glory among the nations. ²⁰They shall bring all your kindred from all the nations as an offering to the LORD, on horses, and in chariots, and in litters, and on mules, and on dromedaries, to my holy mountain Jerusalem, says the LORD, just as the Israelites bring a grain offering in a clean vessel to the house of the LORD. ²¹And I will also take some of them as priests and as Levites, says the LORD.

²² For as the new heavens and the new
　　　earth,
　　which I will make,
　shall remain before me, says the LORD;
　　so shall your descendants and your
　　　name remain.
²³ From new moon to new moon,
　　and from sabbath to sabbath,
　all flesh shall come to worship before me,
　says the LORD.

24 And they shall go out and look at the dead bodies of the people who have rebelled against me; for their worm shall not die, their fire shall not be quenched, and they shall be an abhorrence to all flesh.

66.1–24: Final warnings and consolations for Jerusalem. 1–5: The final chapter of the book of Isaiah sets out afresh several of the basic themes that have appeared and reappeared throughout the book. Of primary importance is the demand for truth and sincerity in worship. The public performance of ritual and piety shows loyalty to God, but such outward actions must be matched by an inner spirit (see 1.12–17; 29.13). Verse 1 is not a rejection of the Temple, but rather defines its true purpose (see sidebar, p. 958). **6–11:** In spite of the many conflicts and setbacks that had marred Jerusalem's history, the promises of God for the blessing of Israel as a people remained valid. **12–16:** The message of reassurance and hope for the future of Jerusalem did not mean, however, that wrongdoing would pass without judgment. God's promises required obedience and trust. **17:** Reference to the forbidden foods recalls the warning of 65.4. **18–21:** The return of all those who had been exiled from Judah and Israel would mark the fulfillment of God's promise for the people. **22–23:** The prophecies of Isaiah set a goal for all nations. All humankind (*all flesh*) were bound together in one world and would, therefore, ultimately share a single destiny. **24:** Divine judgment cannot be evaded. God's call is an imperious command, and the disobedient cannot participate in the final glory of God's kingdom.

a Gk: Heb *Pul*

JEREMIAH

Introduction

The book of Jeremiah was written for people in the throes of suffering. A historical tragedy underlies the book. In the sixth century BCE, Babylon invaded the nation of Judah and its capital city Jerusalem. The political structure of the country collapsed and, after resistance broke out, the Babylonians destroyed Jerusalem. Accusation, anguish, and grief run through Jeremiah, but hope and promises of a new future appear as well. The book is an honest, artistic, and sometimes chaotic response to the collapse of the nation during and after the invasion. It seeks to help the community survive that tragedy by retelling it, interpreting it, and imagining a world beyond it.

The book of Jeremiah gathers together a complex collection of poems, stories, and sermons associated with the prophet* Jeremiah as speaker and actor. A quick review of the book reveals a mixture of prose narrative* and poetry. The first chapter alone, for example, contains a brief prose introduction (1.1–3), a poem in which God and Jeremiah speak to one another (1.4–10), followed by a further prose narrative that describes Jeremiah's visions (1.11–19). The poetry is largely made up of prophetic oracles. Oracles are poems of judgment and accusation, and sometimes of healing, spoken by a prophet on behalf of God. There are liturgical poems, laments* by Jeremiah, by God, and by the people. The prose passages include stories about Jeremiah and sermons attributed to Jeremiah. These various literary types are scattered about in the book, except for a few obvious groupings of similar material such as the Oracles against the Nations (chs. 46–51). Both the variety of literary types and their apparent lack of order make reading and interpreting the book difficult.

In the past, scholars have explained this literary disarray as the result of a long process of writing. For most of the twentieth century, interpreters thought that the book contained several levels of material deriving from different historical periods. First was the poetry, thought to be Jeremiah's own words, delivered orally to Judahites in the time before the Exile* in 587 BCE. To this were added stories about Jeremiah recorded by his companion Baruch. Next came sermons that are assigned to Jeremiah but were thought to have come from a later writer, perhaps from a group influenced by the theology and language of the book of Deuteronomy. The value of this theory about the writing of the book is that it explained some difficulties of reading. The book does not move in order because poems, stories, and sermons from different times and places were added to each other without narrative intention. Interpreters who held this view were interested in the history behind each story or poem rather than how the literature fit together.

In a modification of this theory, one commentator proposed that the book was composed through a process that resembles a snowball rolling down a hill. To a core collection of Jeremiah's poems were added more poems, stories, and sermons by later followers of the prophet. From this perspective, little coherence can be found in the book. But more recently, scholars have begun to find order that is more poetic than chronological or thematic. This coherence or unity appears in images, metaphors,* and the interplay of voices.

The book is like a conversation among many people as they struggle to survive the invasion and interpret their situation. Besides the voice of Jeremiah, there are other literary characters or voices in the book. Speeches are assigned to the people, to figures like Baruch, Jeremiah's com-

panion, to the nations, and to the city of Jerusalem, which is portrayed as a woman called "daughter Zion." The most frequent speaker—indeed, the most important and dominant voice—is God.

The book divides into two major sections or "books": chs. 1–25 and 26–52. Within these two larger parts are smaller literary divisions.

Book One: Chs. 1–25: How the nation fell

1–10	Cosmic destruction
11–20	Covenant* destroyed
21–25	Aftermath of invasion

Book Two: Chs. 26–52: How the nation will survive

26–36	Blame and hope
37–45	Baruch's account
46–51	Oracles against the nations
52	The end

As may be obvious from the brief outline of the book, the material contained in it cannot be reduced to a few isolated themes. Instead, there are a number of interwoven themes that appear, fade, and reappear. These include dramatic accusations of the nation for its sins, poetic portrayal of the military battle that will destroy them, accusation of breaking the covenant relation with God, instructions about how to survive the disaster, and promises that God will ultimately reverse their circumstances and turn their suffering to joy.

The book's primary theological concern, however, is to defend God from accusations of injustice. People in the ancient world believed that if disaster occurred, it must be because God or the gods caused it. The book of Jeremiah tries to show that God was not unjust in punishing Israel for its sins. The historical collapse of the nation and the destruction of Jerusalem happened not because God was careless, unfaithful, or cruel, but because the people of Israel turned away and sought other gods. But the story does not end there: There will be a future.

Themes of hope appear throughout the book in surprising positions—for example, juxtaposed with poems of judgment and accusation. These hopeful themes come to a climax* in a section called the "Little Book of Consolation" (chs. 30–33). There restoration and joy replace accusation and judgment; there the future is imagined as a festive garden filled with feasting. It is curious that the book of Jeremiah does not place hope at the end, as modern western writers might do, but just after the middle. This central placement of hope means that hope is still surrounded by themes of tragedy, sorrow, and judgment. Some scholars have suggested that this literary arrangement reflects the psychological and spiritual reality of the book's audience in Exile. In captivity, they are caught between tragedy and a new vision of the future.

"Oracles Against the Nations," prophecies of doom against Israel's enemies, come toward the end the book (chs. 46–51). These poems may provide hope for the exiles, for in these chapters the vanquished nation changes places with its enemies. The book's conclusion offers a low-key description of the invasion of Jerusalem by Babylon (ch. 52). The account of the invasion almost exactly duplicates the depiction in 2 Kings 25. It provides the book of Jeremiah with a sobering last word. Since the chapter, and thus the book, ends with the release of the Judean king from

Babylonian prison, the chapter may also suggest hope for the exiles. In the king's survival, exiles may anticipate their own survival.

Jeremiah's ministry is described as beginning in the thirteenth year of King Josiah (627 BCE) and extending to the "captivity of Jerusalem" in 587 BCE (Jer 1.1–3). These were troubled times. The weakening of control by the Assyrian empire over Israel in the late seventh century BCE led to competition between Egypt and the emerging neo-Babylonian (also called "Chaldean") empire for dominance in the Mediterranean region. Within Judah, leading groups split between support of Egypt or Babylon. Many in the royal governing party were pro-Egyptian, whereas Jeremiah and his followers were pro-Babylonian. In 605, Babylon won a military victory over Egypt and control of Judah, but internal strife among Israel's factions continued.

In 597, Judah revolted against Babylon. In response, Babylon invaded Jerusalem, the capital city, and deported the king and other leaders. The Babylonians installed Zedekiah as a puppet king, but in 587 Judah revolted again. When the Babylonians invaded a second time in 587, they destroyed mercilessly. The Temple,* palace, and parts of the city were razed; more of the leading citizens were deported to Babylon. Gedaliah was made governor of the occupied land, but he was assassinated, and a third invasion and further suffering and deportations occurred in 582.

Some survivors remained in the devastated land; some escaped to Egypt; some settled into exile in Babylon. The Babylonian exiles were not released from captivity until 50 years later (537). It was probably during the aftermath of invasion, destruction, and deportation that the book of Jeremiah was compiled in an effort to help the survivors deal with the tragedy. The book reflects conflicts among various surviving groups. It portrays Jeremiah on the side of Babylon and opposed to Egypt and those who escape there.

The relationship of the book to the prophet Jeremiah is greatly disputed. Until recently most interpreters traced the book's poetry to Jeremiah and saw in ch. 36 an account of the book's dictation to Baruch, who wrote it on a scroll. A few interpreters thought that Jeremiah even wrote prose portions of the book, but that view has not gained much acceptance. More recently, commentators have found it difficult to decide what role Jeremiah and Baruch had in the book's writing, since evidence is limited largely to the book itself. Some of the stories may be symbolic, and the poems attributed to Jeremiah may have been written by others in order to convey theological and political messages to the community at different times during its struggles for survival. Rather than trying to pin all the poems, stories, and sermons directly to events in Jeremiah's own life, current interpreters try to make sense of the book as it stands. Jeremiah's life plays a major symbolic role in the book. The sufferings that happen to him happen to the people. His survival in captivity provides hope to the exiles—that they too will survive if they listen to the voice of God expressed in Jeremiah's book.

Chart Kings of Judah mentioned in Jeremiah

King Josiah	640–609 BCE	Jehoiachin (Coniah)	598–97
Jehoahaz II (Shallum)	609	Zedekiah	597–587
Jehoiakim	609–598	Gedaliah (governor)	587–582

READING GUIDE

To understand the book of Jeremiah, it is probably best first to skim the whole book. Locate the large divisions listed above and get a sense of the book's many voices and kinds of literature. Then it will be helpful to return to the first chapter, Jeremiah's call, and think of it as an introduction to the book's major themes. It is important to recall that the book is not chronologically arranged. Time does not move in a straight line. Events in the past, promises about the future, and appeals to the reader in the present are braided together. Memories about the past shape the present and remain alive in it, just as future hope changes perceptions of the present. This overlapping of time is particularly true for survivors of trauma and loss. The present and the past weave together, and hopeful anticipation for the future can burst in without preparation upon the present.

1 The words of Jeremiah son of Hilkiah, of the priests who were in Anathoth in the land of Benjamin, 2to whom the word of the LORD came in the days of King Josiah son of Amon of Judah, in the thirteenth year of his reign. 3It came also in the days of King Jehoiakim son of Josiah of Judah, and until the end of the eleventh year of King Zedekiah son of Josiah of Judah, until the captivity of Jerusalem in the fifth month.

4 Now the word of the LORD came to me saying,

5 "Before I formed you in the womb I
            knew you,
      and before you were born I consecrated
            you;
      I appointed you a prophet to the
            nations."

6Then I said, "Ah, Lord GOD! Truly I do not know how to speak, for I am only a boy." 7But the LORD said to me,

      "Do not say, 'I am only a boy';
      for you shall go to all to whom I send
            you,
      and you shall speak whatever I
            command you.

8 Do not be afraid of them,
      for I am with you to deliver you,
                              says the LORD."

9Then the LORD put out his hand and touched my mouth; and the LORD said to me,

      "Now I have put my words in your
            mouth.

10 See, today I appoint you over nations
            and over kingdoms,

      to pluck up and to pull down,
      to destroy and to overthrow,
      to build and to plant."

Chs. 1–10: Cosmic destruction. Ch. 1: Jeremiah's call. 1–3: The introductory verse tells who Jeremiah was and when he prophesied. He was from a family of priests from a town outside Jerusalem, *Anathoth*. His call came during the time of *King Josiah* and extended until the fall of Jerusalem to Babylon in 587 BCE, a 40-year period that symbolically links him with Moses' 40 years of leadership in the wilderness. Jeremiah is presented as a prophet* like Moses, as promised in Deut 18.18. **4–10:** In a poetic conversation between God and Jeremiah, Jeremiah receives his mission. His call before birth indicates that his prophecy was not his own invention but given to him by God. His resistance on the grounds that he is *only a boy* and so cannot speak properly also indicates that God has sent him; he has not chosen this task for himself. God tells him not to be afraid, promises to be with him, and touches his mouth. This gesture symbolizes the divine origin of the words Jeremiah speaks and the words recorded in this book. The book claims that Jeremiah's words are from God. **10:** Jeremiah is a prophet to the *nations* and will tear down and build up. This short poem gives Jeremiah and his book authority in the face of opposition.

---

11 The word of the LORD came to me, saying, "Jeremiah, what do you see?" And I said, "I see a branch of an almond tree."[a] 12Then the LORD said to me, "You have seen well, for I am watching[b] over my word to

a Heb *shaqed*   *b* Heb *shoqed*

perform it." [13] The word of the LORD came to me a second time, saying, "What do you see?" And I said, "I see a boiling pot, tilted away from the north."

14 Then the LORD said to me: Out of the north disaster shall break out on all the inhabitants of the land. [15] For now I am calling all the tribes of the kingdoms of the north, says the LORD; and they shall come and all of them shall set their thrones at the entrance of the gates of Jerusalem, against all its surrounding walls and against all the cities of Judah. [16] And I will utter my judgments against them, for all their wickedness in forsaking me; they have made offerings to other gods, and worshiped the works of their own hands. [17] But you, gird up your loins; stand up and tell them everything that I command you. Do not break down before them, or I will break you before them. [18] And I for my part have made you today a fortified city, an iron pillar, and a bronze wall, against the whole land—against the kings of Judah, its princes, its priests, and the people of the land. [19] They will fight against you; but they shall not prevail against you, for I am with you, says the LORD, to deliver you.

1.11–19: Jeremiah's mission gains substance from two visions written in prose. 11–13: Jeremiah sees a branch of an almond tree, a "shaqed" in Hebrew. In a play on words, God replies, *I am watching* ("shoqed") *over my word to perform it*. What God says through Jeremiah will happen. Next Jeremiah sees *a boiling pot, tilted away from the north*. The boiling pot is a symbol of destruction, overflowing and burning. The north may refer to a historical enemy, but more likely the threat from the north refers to a mythic enemy, coming like a superhuman monster. Only in 20.4 will the foe from the *north* be identified as Babylon. 14–18: The tilting pot will spill out an army of invaders who will stream upon the land. God is *calling the kingdoms of the north* to invade Jerusalem. Jeremiah himself should have courage throughout the terror, for God will be with him.

The broken family
Chs. 2–3: A story of a broken family underlies and unifies the poetry and prose of this section. The account of this family functions as a summary of the whole book in symbolic form. God appears as husband and father, betrayed, brokenhearted and in search of reconciliation with his unfaithful wife and children.

2 The word of the LORD came to me, saying: [2] Go and proclaim in the hearing of Jerusalem, Thus says the LORD:
I remember the devotion of your
　　youth,
　　your love as a bride,
how you followed me in the
　　wilderness,
　　in a land not sown.
[3] Israel was holy to the LORD,
　　the first fruits of his harvest.
All who ate of it were held guilty;
　　disaster came upon them,
　　　　　　　　　　　　says the LORD.

2.1–3: God speaks and addresses his wife, remembering how good it was during their honeymoon. Then God addresses male Israel in similar terms. Israel was *holy to the LORD*. Both female and male were set apart and protected.

4 Hear the word of the LORD, O house of Jacob, and all the families of the house of Israel. [5] Thus says the LORD:
What wrong did your ancestors find
　　in me
　　that they went far from me,
and went after worthless things, and
　　became worthless themselves?
[6] They did not say, "Where is the LORD
　　who brought us up from the land of
　　　　Egypt,
who led us in the wilderness,
　　in a land of deserts and pits,
in a land of drought and deep
　　darkness,
in a land that no one passes through,
　　where no one lives?"
[7] I brought you into a plentiful land
　　to eat its fruits and its good things.
But when you entered you defiled my
　　land,
　　and made my heritage an
　　　　abomination.
[8] The priests did not say, "Where is the
　　LORD?"
　　Those who handle the law did not
　　　　know me;

the rulers*a* transgressed against me;
the prophets prophesied by Baal,
and went after things that do
not profit.

9 Therefore once more I accuse you,
says the LORD,
and I accuse your children's children.

10 Cross to the coasts of Cyprus and look,
send to Kedar and examine with care;
see if there has ever been such
a thing.

11 Has a nation changed its gods,
even though they are no gods?
But my people have changed their glory
for something that does not profit.

12 Be appalled, O heavens, at this,
be shocked, be utterly desolate,
says the LORD,

13 for my people have committed two evils:
they have forsaken me,
the fountain of living water,
and dug out cisterns for themselves,
cracked cisterns
that can hold no water.

14 Is Israel a slave? Is he a homeborn
servant?
Why then has he become plunder?

15 The lions have roared against him,
they have roared loudly.
They have made his land a waste;
his cities are in ruins, without
inhabitant.

16 Moreover, the people of Memphis and
Tahpanhes
have broken the crown of your head.

17 Have you not brought this upon yourself
by forsaking the LORD your God,
while he led you in the way?

18 What then do you gain by going to Egypt,
to drink the waters of the Nile?
Or what do you gain by going to Assyria,
to drink the waters of the Euphrates?

19 Your wickedness will punish you,
and your apostasies will convict you.
Know and see that it is evil and bitter
for you to forsake the LORD
your God;
the fear of me is not in you,
says the Lord GOD of hosts.

20 For long ago you broke your yoke
and burst your bonds,
and you said, "I will not serve!"
On every high hill
and under every green tree
you sprawled and played the whore.

21 Yet I planted you as a choice vine,
from the purest stock.
How then did you turn degenerate
and become a wild vine?

22 Though you wash yourself with lye
and use much soap,
the stain of your guilt is still before me,
says the Lord GOD.

23 How can you say, "I am not defiled,
I have not gone after the Baals"?
Look at your way in the valley;
know what you have done—
a restive young camel interlacing her
tracks,

24 a wild ass at home in the wilderness,
in her heat sniffing the wind!
Who can restrain her lust?
None who seek her need weary
themselves;
in her month they will find her.

25 Keep your feet from going unshod
and your throat from thirst.
But you said, "It is hopeless,
for I have loved strangers,
and after them I will go."

26 As a thief is shamed when caught,
so the house of Israel shall be
shamed—
they, their kings, their officials,
their priests, and their prophets,

27 who say to a tree, "You are my father,"
and to a stone, "You gave me birth."
For they have turned their backs to me,
and not their faces.
But in the time of their trouble they say,
"Come and save us!"

28 But where are your gods
that you made for yourself?
Let them come, if they can save you,
in your time of trouble;
for you have as many gods
as you have towns, O Judah.

a Heb *shepherds*

29 Why do you complain against me?
    You have all rebelled against me,
          says the LORD.
30 In vain I have struck down
      your children;
    they accepted no correction.
    Your own sword devoured your
      prophets
    like a ravening lion.
31 And you, O generation, behold the word
      of the LORD![a]
    Have I been a wilderness to Israel,
      or a land of thick darkness?
    Why then do my people say, "We are
      free,
    we will come to you no more"?
32 Can a girl forget her ornaments,
      or a bride her attire?
    Yet my people have forgotten me,
      days without number.

33 How well you direct your course
      to seek lovers!
    So that even to wicked women
      you have taught your ways.
34 Also on your skirts is found
      the lifeblood of the innocent poor,
    though you did not catch them
      breaking in.
    Yet in spite of all these things[a]
35 you say, "I am innocent;
      surely his anger has turned from me."
    Now I am bringing you to judgment
      for saying, "I have not sinned."
36 How lightly you gad about,
      changing your ways!
    You shall be put to shame by Egypt
      as you were put to shame by Assyria.
37 From there also you will come away
      with your hands on your head;
    for the LORD has rejected those in
        whom you trust,
    and you will not prosper through
      them.

3 If[b] a man divorces his wife
    and she goes from him
and becomes another man's wife,
    will he return to her?
Would not such a land be greatly
    polluted?

You have played the whore with many
      lovers;
    and would you return to me?
          says the LORD.
2 Look up to the bare heights,[c] and see!
    Where have you not been lain with?
    By the waysides you have sat waiting for
      lovers,
    like a nomad in the wilderness.
    You have polluted the land
      with your whoring and wickedness.
3 Therefore the showers have been
      withheld,
    and the spring rain has not come;
    yet you have the forehead of a whore,
      you refuse to be ashamed.
4 Have you not just now called to me,
    "My Father, you are the friend of my
      youth—
5 will he be angry forever,
      will he be indignant to the end?"
    This is how you have spoken,
      but you have done all the evil that
      you could.

2.4–3.5: In these poems, the divine speaker alternates in addressing male Israel (2.4–16; 2.26–32) and female Judah, portrayed as God's wife (2.17–25; 2.33–3.5). The effect of this switch from male to female is to accuse both figures of infidelity and of going after other gods or lovers. Male Israel changes its gods (2.11), forsakes God, *the fountain of living water* (2.13), digs its own sources of water (2.13) and worships idols (2.27–28). Wife Judah also betrays God, but in more intimate ways. Though she is GOD's wife, she *played the whore* (2.20), went after other lovers (2.23–25, 33; 3.1), and would not *return* to her husband (3.1). The Hebrew word for return also means "to repent." The divine husband, therefore, divorces her (3.1–5). The relationship between God and his wife, symbolizing all the people of Israel and Judah, is over. The family is broken and there appears to be no future.

---

6 The LORD said to me in the days of King Josiah: Have you seen what she did, that faithless one, Israel, how she went up on

---

[a] Meaning of Heb uncertain   [b] Q Ms Gk Syr: MT
Saying, If   [c] *Or the trails*

every high hill and under every green tree, and played the whore there? 7And I thought, "After she has done all this she will return to me"; but she did not return, and her false sister Judah saw it. 8She*a* saw that for all the adulteries of that faithless one, Israel, I had sent her away with a decree of divorce; yet her false sister Judah did not fear, but she too went and played the whore. 9Because she took her whoredom so lightly, she polluted the land, committing adultery with stone and tree. 10Yet for all this her false sister Judah did not return to me with her whole heart, but only in pretense, says the LORD.

11 Then the LORD said to me: Faithless Israel has shown herself less guilty than false Judah. 12Go, and proclaim these words toward the north, and say:

Return, faithless Israel,
                    says the LORD.
I will not look on you in anger,
    for I am merciful,
                    says the LORD;
I will not be angry forever.
13 Only acknowledge your guilt,
    that you have rebelled against the
        LORD your God,
and scattered your favors among
            strangers under every green tree,
    and have not obeyed my voice,
                    says the LORD.
14 Return, O faithless children,
                    says the LORD,
    for I am your master;
I will take you, one from a city and two
        from a family,
    and I will bring you to Zion.

15 I will give you shepherds after my own heart, who will feed you with knowledge and understanding. 16And when you have multiplied and increased in the land, in those days, says the LORD, they shall no longer say, "The ark of the covenant of the LORD." It shall not come to mind, or be remembered, or missed; nor shall another one be made. 17At that time Jerusalem shall be called the throne of the LORD, and all nations shall gather to it, to the presence of the LORD in Jerusalem, and they shall no longer stub-

bornly follow their own evil will. 18In those days the house of Judah shall join the house of Israel, and together they shall come from the land of the north to the land that I gave your ancestors for a heritage.

3.6–18. 6–10: Jeremiah replaces the husband as speaker and reports that the husband had previously had another wife, Israel, who also betrayed him and whom he had also divorced. In this story of the family, both the northern and southern kingdoms have betrayed God and been cast off. Since the northern kingdom of Israel fell to Assyria in 721 BCE, this story explains that historical tragedy in the symbolic terms of betrayal in marriage. **11–18:** The divine husband sends Jeremiah to speak to the first wife and invite her to return. The text reports no response from her. Then the invitation to return is addressed to the children (v. 14). Their father promises them restoration and reunification of the whole people in Jerusalem (vv. 15–18).

19 I thought
    how I would set you among
        my children,
and give you a pleasant land,
    the most beautiful heritage of all the
        nations.
And I thought you would call me, My
        Father,
    and would not turn from following
        me.
20 Instead, as a faithless wife leaves her
        husband,
    so you have been faithless to me,
        O house of Israel,
                    says the LORD.

21 A voice on the bare heights*b* is heard,
    the plaintive weeping of Israel's
        children,
because they have perverted their way,
    they have forgotten the LORD their
        God:
22 Return, O faithless children,
    I will heal your faithlessness.

"Here we come to you;
    for you are the LORD our God.

a Q Ms Gk Mss Syr: MT I   *b* Or *the trails*

23 Truly the hills are*a* a delusion,
　　the orgies on the mountains.
　Truly in the LORD our God
　　is the salvation of Israel.

24 "But from our youth the shameful thing has devoured all for which our ancestors had labored, their flocks and their herds, their sons and their daughters. 25Let us lie down in our shame, and let our dishonor cover us; for we have sinned against the LORD our God, we and our ancestors, from our youth even to this day; and we have not obeyed the voice of the LORD our God."

3.19–24: Though still nostalgic for his wife (2.19–20), the husband/father again invites the children to "return" and promises to heal them. **22–24:** The children then begin to speak, addressing the father directly and repenting of their infidelity and idolatry.* The family is partially restored. The account of the broken family symbolically retells the entire course of Judah's history up to the Exile.* It is likely that the children symbolize the exiles who were invited to return and promised a renewed future in allegiance to their father. The story of this broken family explains the Exile symbolically. The historical destruction of Judah and Jerusalem was not God's fault but was punishment for idolatry and betrayal. That betrayal by all the people appears the more intimate and wrong because it is like betrayal by a spouse.

THE COSMIC BATTLE

Chs. 4–10: Chapter 4 turns away from the story of the broken family to give prominence to announcements of imminent invasion by the "foe from the north." The material in this section is largely poetic, but there are some prose passages as well (7.1–8.3). Although individual passages probably come from many different times, they are collected here around the theme of cosmic destruction at the hands of the mythic "foe from the north."

4 If you return, O Israel,
　　　　　　　　says the LORD,
　if you return to me,
　if you remove your abominations from
　　my presence,
　　and do not waver,
2 and if you swear, "As the LORD lives!"
　in truth, in justice, and in uprightness,

then nations shall be blessed*b* by him,
　and by him they shall boast.

3 For thus says the LORD to the people of Judah and to the inhabitants of Jerusalem:
　Break up your fallow ground,
　　and do not sow among thorns.
4 Circumcise yourselves to the LORD,
　remove the foreskin of your hearts,
　O people of Judah and inhabitants of
　　Jerusalem,
　or else my wrath will go forth like fire,
　and burn with no one to quench it,
　because of the evil of your doings.

4.1–4: Repent. This poem reaches back to the broken marriage by repeating the invitation to "return," and it extends forward in the book by promising God's wrathful judgment against those who do not repent.

The approaching enemy

Chs. 4–6: No narrative* unifies these poems, but the approaching foe looms over the chapters and gives them menacing drama. The voices of God, Jeremiah, a narrator, the people, daughter Zion, and the foe from the north—all speak and argue about God's role in the coming invasion. The battle poems use great art in portraying war. Scenes of approaching armies appeal to the senses and give the superhuman enemy from the north shape in the imagination. With a few details of sight and sound, the poems place readers in the thick of battle.

5 Declare in Judah, and proclaim in Jerusalem, and say:
　Blow the trumpet through the land;
　　shout aloud*c* and say,
　"Gather together, and let us go
　　into the fortified cities!"
6 Raise a standard toward Zion,
　flee for safety, do not delay,
　for I am bringing evil from the north,
　　and a great destruction.
7 A lion has gone up from its thicket,
　a destroyer of nations has set out;
　he has gone out from his place

a Gk Syr Vg: Heb *Truly from the hills is*
b Or *shall bless themselves*
c Or *shout, take your weapons*: Heb *shout, fill* (your hand)

to make your land a waste;
> your cities will be ruins
> without inhabitant.
8 Because of this put on sackcloth,
> lament and wail:
> "The fierce anger of the LORD
> has not turned away from us."

9 On that day, says the LORD, courage shall fail the king and the officials; the priests shall be appalled and the prophets astounded. 10 Then I said, "Ah, Lord GOD, how utterly you have deceived this people and Jerusalem, saying, 'It shall be well with you,' even while the sword is at the throat!"

11 At that time it will be said to this people and to Jerusalem: A hot wind comes from me out of the bare heights*a* in the desert toward my poor people, not to winnow or cleanse— 12 a wind too strong for that. Now it is I who speak in judgment against them.
13 Look! He comes up like clouds,
> his chariots like the whirlwind;
> his horses are swifter than eagles—
> woe to us, for we are ruined!
14 O Jerusalem, wash your heart clean of
> wickedness
> so that you may be saved.
> How long shall your evil schemes
> lodge within you?
15 For a voice declares from Dan
> and proclaims disaster from Mount
> Ephraim.
16 Tell the nations, "Here they are!"
> Proclaim against Jerusalem,
> "Besiegers come from a distant land;
> they shout against the cities of
> Judah.
17 They have closed in around her like
> watchers of a field,
> because she has rebelled against me,
> says the LORD.
18 Your ways and your doings
> have brought this upon you.
> This is your doom; how bitter it is!
> It has reached your very heart."

19 My anguish, my anguish! I writhe in
> pain!
> Oh, the walls of my heart!
> My heart is beating wildly;
> I cannot keep silent;
> for I*b* hear the sound of the trumpet,
> the alarm of war.
20 Disaster overtakes disaster,
> the whole land is laid waste.
> Suddenly my tents are destroyed,
> my curtains in a moment.
21 How long must I see the standard,
> and hear the sound of the trumpet?
22 "For my people are foolish,
> they do not know me;
> they are stupid children,
> they have no understanding.
> They are skilled in doing evil,
> but do not know how to do good."

4.5–31: The sound of the trumpet and the sight of the standard or flag of the army evoke the battle. 6–7: References to the mythic foe add to the unearthly terror coming upon the nation. The enemy is a *lion*, magnified into *a destroyer of nations*. Since God is the one bringing the foe, supernatural forces are arrayed against the nation. 19–22: Although God brings the enemy, God also witnesses the battle with uncontrollable anguish.

23 I looked on the earth, and lo, it was
> waste and void;
> and to the heavens, and they had no
> light.
24 I looked on the mountains, and lo, they
> were quaking,
> and all the hills moved to and fro.
25 I looked, and lo, there was no one at all,
> and all the birds of the air had fled.
26 I looked, and lo, the fruitful land was a
> desert,
> and all its cities were laid in ruins
> before the LORD, before his fierce
> anger.
27 For thus says the LORD: The whole land shall be a desolation; yet I will not make a full end.
28 Because of this the earth shall mourn,
> and the heavens above grow black;
> for I have spoken, I have purposed;
> I have not relented nor will I turn
> back.

a Or *the trails*   *b* Another reading is *for you, O my soul,*

29 At the noise of horseman and archer
  every town takes to flight;
they enter thickets; they climb among
    rocks;
  all the towns are forsaken,
  and no one lives in them.
30 And you, O desolate one,
  what do you mean that you dress in
    crimson,
  that you deck yourself with
    ornaments of gold,
  that you enlarge your eyes with paint?
In vain you beautify yourself.
  Your lovers despise you;
  they seek your life.
31 For I heard a cry as of a woman
    in labor,
  anguish as of one bringing forth her
    first child,
  the cry of daughter Zion gasping for
    breath,
  stretching out her hands,
  "Woe is me! I am fainting before
    killers!"

4.23–31. 23–28: Creation destroyed. The speaker describes a terrifying vision of destruction that reverses the world's creation in the first chapter of Genesis. This picture of the earth as a devastated landscape, *waste and void*, implies that the cosmic battle somehow overturns the world. The impact of the historical invasion of Judah by Babylon meant the end of their national world, the collapse of daily life in their land. The poem describes the symbolic effects of that invasion. Judah's world has come to an end. **29–31:** The battle draws near as suggested by the noise of the attack and the flight of the inhabitants. The poem portrays the city of Jerusalem as a woman called *daughter Zion*. She is probably God's first wife in 2.1–3.25. Portraying the city as a woman indicates how impossible defense against the advancing army is for her and creates pity in the reader.

5 Run to and fro through the streets of
    Jerusalem,
  look around and take note!
Search its squares and see
  if you can find one person
who acts justly
  and seeks truth—
so that I may pardon Jerusalem.*

2 Although they say, "As the LORD lives,"
  yet they swear falsely.
3 O LORD, do your eyes not look
    for truth?
You have struck them,
  but they felt no anguish;
you have consumed them,
  but they refused to take correction.
They have made their faces harder than
    rock;
  they have refused to turn back.

4 Then I said, "These are only the poor,
  they have no sense;
for they do not know the way of
    the LORD,
  the law of their God.
5 Let me go to the rich*b*
  and speak to them;
surely they know the way of the LORD,
  the law of their God."
But they all alike had broken the yoke,
  they had burst the bonds.

6 Therefore a lion from the forest shall
    kill them,
  a wolf from the desert shall destroy
    them.
A leopard is watching against
    their cities;
  everyone who goes out of them shall
    be torn in pieces—
because their transgressions are many,
    their apostasies are great.

5.1–31: God's reluctance to send the attackers. These loosely connected poems show that God does not wish to destroy the nation. Instead, the people are at fault because they will not act justly or repent. God is neither arbitrary nor whimsical in orchestrating the attack on the nation. **1–6:** God will not destroy the nation if Jeremiah can find one righteous person. Though he runs up and down the streets of Jerusalem to the rich and the poor, Jeremiah's search is unsuccessful. God promises invasion by wild animals, which symbolize the invading enemy.

7 How can I pardon you?
  Your children have forsaken me,

a Heb *it*   b Or *the great*

and have sworn by those who are no
    gods.
When I fed them to the full,
    they committed adultery
and trooped to the houses of
    prostitutes.
8 They were well-fed lusty stallions,
    each neighing for his neighbor's wife.
9 Shall I not punish them for these
    things?
                   says the LORD;
and shall I not bring retribution
    on a nation such as this?

10 Go up through her vine-rows
    and destroy,
    but do not make a full end;
strip away her branches,
    for they are not the LORD's.
11 For the house of Israel and the house of
    Judah
    have been utterly faithless to me,
                 says the LORD.
12 They have spoken falsely of the LORD,
    and have said, "He will do nothing.
No evil will come upon us,
    and we shall not see sword or
    famine."
13 The prophets are nothing but wind,
    for the word is not in them.
Thus shall it be done to them!

14 Therefore thus says the LORD, the God
    of hosts:
Because they*a* have spoken this word,
I am now making my words in your
    mouth a fire,
    and this people wood, and the fire
    shall devour them.
15 I am going to bring upon you
    a nation from far away, O house of
    Israel,
                 says the LORD.
It is an enduring nation,
    it is an ancient nation,
a nation whose language you do
    not know,
    nor can you understand what they
    say.
16 Their quiver is like an open tomb;
    all of them are mighty warriors.

17 They shall eat up your harvest and your
    food;
    they shall eat up your sons and your
    daughters;
    they shall eat up your flocks and your
    herds;
    they shall eat up your vines and your
    fig trees;
they shall destroy with the sword
    your fortified cities in which
    you trust.

18 But even in those days, says the LORD,
I will not make a full end of you. 19And when
your people say, "Why has the LORD our God
done all these things to us?" you shall say to
them, "As you have forsaken me and served
foreign gods in your land, so you shall serve
strangers in a land that is not yours."

5.7–19. 7–11: A question that will be repeated (5.29)
addresses an unnamed female. She is probably daughter Zion and God's unfaithful wife (2.1–3.5). God asks
if there is a way to pardon her, but she and her children
have been adulterous. There is no way to avoid punishment. **12–18:** Further accusations of infidelity introduce another announcement of the approaching invader, a mighty nation, superhuman in its capabilities.
However, a prose comment promises not to completely destroy the nation. If the book's audience is the
people in exile, v. 18 speaks to them directly. They are
the remnant who remain after the invasion.

20 Declare this in the house of Jacob,
    proclaim it in Judah:
21 Hear this, O foolish and senseless
    people,
    who have eyes, but do not see,
    who have ears, but do not hear.
22 Do you not fear me? says the LORD;
    Do you not tremble before me?
I placed the sand as a boundary for the
    sea,
    a perpetual barrier that it cannot
    pass;
though the waves toss, they cannot
    prevail,
    though they roar, they cannot pass
    over it.

a Heb *you*

23 But this people has a stubborn and
    rebellious heart;
  they have turned aside and
    gone away.
24 They do not say in their hearts,
  "Let us fear the LORD our God,
  who gives the rain in its season,
    the autumn rain and the spring rain,
  and keeps for us
    the weeks appointed for the harvest."
25 Your iniquities have turned these away,
    and your sins have deprived you of
    good.
26 For scoundrels are found among
    my people;
  they take over the goods of others.
  Like fowlers they set a trap;[a]
    they catch human beings.
27 Like a cage full of birds,
    their houses are full of treachery;
  therefore they have become great and
    rich,
28   they have grown fat and sleek.
  They know no limits in deeds of
    wickedness;
  they do not judge with justice
  the cause of the orphan, to make
    it prosper,
  and they do not defend the rights of
    the needy.
29 Shall I not punish them for these things?
                    says the LORD,
  and shall I not bring retribution
    on a nation such as this?

5.20–29: God's reluctance to punish is overcome because neither Jacob, the northern kingdom that fell to
Assyria in 721 BCE, nor Judah, the southern kingdom
that falls to Babylon in 587, sees, hears, or fears the
Creator. Unlike the sea and the rains that stay in place
and come at the proper times, the people know no
boundaries in their wickedness.

~~~~~~~~~~~~~~~~~~~~~~~~~~~~~~~~~~

30 An appalling and horrible thing
    has happened in the land:
31 the prophets prophesy falsely,
    and the priests rule as the prophets
    direct;[b]
  my people love to have it so,
    but what will you do when the end
    comes?

6 Flee for safety, O children of
    Benjamin,
  from the midst of Jerusalem!
  Blow the trumpet in Tekoa,
    and raise a signal on Beth-
    haccherem;
  for evil looms out of the north,
    and great destruction.
2 I have likened daughter Zion
    to the loveliest pasture.[c]
3 Shepherds with their flocks shall come
    against her.
  They shall pitch their tents around
    her;
  they shall pasture, all in their places.
4 "Prepare war against her;
    up, and let us attack at noon!"
  "Woe to us, for the day declines,
    the shadows of evening lengthen!"
5 "Up, and let us attack by night,
    and destroy her palaces!"
6 For thus says the LORD of hosts:
  Cut down her trees;
    cast up a siege ramp against
    Jerusalem.
  This is the city that must be
    punished;[d]
    there is nothing but oppression within
    her.
7 As a well keeps its water fresh,
    so she keeps fresh her wickedness;
  violence and destruction are heard
    within her;
  sickness and wounds are ever
    before me.
8 Take warning, O Jerusalem,
    or I shall turn from you in disgust,
  and make you a desolation,
    an uninhabited land.

9 Thus says the LORD of hosts:
  Glean[e] thoroughly as a vine
    the remnant of Israel;
  like a grape-gatherer, pass your hand
    again
    over its branches.

---

a Meaning of Heb uncertain   b Or rule by their own
authority   c Or I will destroy daughter Zion, the loveliest
pasture   d Or the city of license   e Cn: Heb They
shall glean

10 To whom shall I speak and give warning,
   that they may hear?
See, their ears are closed,[a]
   they cannot listen.
The word of the LORD is to them an
   object of scorn;
   they take no pleasure in it.
11 But I am full of the wrath of the LORD;
   I am weary of holding it in.

Pour it out on the children in the street,
   and on the gatherings of young men
   as well;
both husband and wife shall be taken,
   the old folk and the very aged.
12 Their houses shall be turned over to
   others,
   their fields and wives together;
for I will stretch out my hand
   against the inhabitants of the land,
                     says the LORD.

6.1–30: Daughter Zion is attacked. This chapter gathers images of the cosmic battle into a collection of poems from a chorus of speakers. The mythic nature of the battle increases when the text identifies daughter Zion as the object of attack. A ferocious military nation wages war against Jerusalem, portrayed as a weak, wanton woman, defenseless in the face of her foe. **1:** A voice urges the *children of Benjamin,* one of the tribes in Judah, to flee the city *for evil looms out of the north.* **4–7:** The poem quotes the enemies' shouts as they prepare for attack. They believe they are acting under divine orders against a wicked city. **10–12:** Jeremiah laments the people's stubbornness. They are not even capable of hearing the prophet's* warning.

~~~~~~~~~~~~~~~~~~~~~~~~~~~~~~

13 For from the least to the greatest
   of them,
   everyone is greedy for unjust gain;
and from prophet to priest,
   everyone deals falsely.
14 They have treated the wound of my
   people carelessly,
   saying, "Peace, peace,"
   when there is no peace.
15 They acted shamefully, they committed
   abomination;
   yet they were not ashamed,
   they did not know how to blush.

Therefore they shall fall among those
   who fall;
   at the time that I punish them, they
   shall be overthrown,
                     says the LORD.
16 Thus says the LORD:
Stand at the crossroads, and look,
   and ask for the ancient paths,
where the good way lies; and walk in it,
   and find rest for your souls.
But they said, "We will not walk in it."
17 Also I raised up sentinels for you:
   "Give heed to the sound of the
   trumpet!"
But they said, "We will not give heed."
18 Therefore hear, O nations,
   and know, O congregation, what will
   happen to them.
19 Hear, O earth; I am going to bring
   disaster on this people,
   the fruit of their schemes,
because they have not given heed to my
   words;
   and as for my teaching, they have
   rejected it.
20 Of what use to me is frankincense that
   comes from Sheba,
   or sweet cane from a distant land?
Your burnt offerings are not acceptable,
   nor are your sacrifices pleasing to me.
21 Therefore thus says the LORD:
See, I am laying before this people
   stumbling blocks against which they
   shall stumble;
parents and children together,
   neighbor and friend shall perish.

6.13–21. 13–15: A refrain that will reappear in 8.10–13 charges the entire community with guilt—from the people to the leaders. Everyone is greedy and leaders lie; therefore, God is justified in punishing them. **16–21:** God assembles the nations and the earth itself as witnesses against them in a covenant* lawsuit.

~~~~~~~~~~~~~~~~~~~~~~~~~~~~~~

22 Thus says the LORD:
See, a people is coming from the land of
   the north,
   a great nation is stirring from the
   farthest parts of the earth.

a Heb *are uncircumcised*

23 They grasp the bow and the javelin,
　　they are cruel and have no mercy,
　　their sound is like the roaring sea;
　they ride on horses,
　　equipped like a warrior for battle,
　　against you, O daughter Zion!

24 "We have heard news of them,
　　our hands fall helpless;
　anguish has taken hold of us,
　　pain as of a woman in labor.
25 Do not go out into the field,
　　or walk on the road;
　for the enemy has a sword,
　　terror is on every side."

26 O my poor people, put on sackcloth,
　　and roll in ashes;
　make mourning as for an only child,
　　most bitter lamentation:
　for suddenly the destroyer
　　will come upon us.

27 I have made you a tester and a refiner*a*
　　among my people
　　so that you may know and test their
　　ways.
28 They are all stubbornly rebellious,
　　going about with slanders;
　they are bronze and iron,
　　all of them act corruptly.
29 The bellows blow fiercely,
　　the lead is consumed by the fire;
　in vain the refining goes on,
　　for the wicked are not removed.
30 They are called "rejected silver,"
　　for the LORD has rejected them.

6.22–30: The attacking army continues to advance *against you, O daughter Zion* (v. 23). **26:** As the symbol of the city there is nothing for her to do but to lament her fate. **27:** God speaks to Jeremiah to tell him his role is like one who tests the authenticity of silver. **30:** Judah is *rejected silver*.

The Temple sermon

Chs. 7–8: This long prose sermon presented by Jeremiah at the Temple✴ in Jerusalem appears to interrupt the poetry of chs. 1–10. The poetry contains multiple images and voices that intrude upon each other

and, in chs. 4–6, focus on the cosmic battle. The prose sermon, by contrast, contains only the voice of Jeremiah as the divine spokesperson. The sermon's subject is the hypocrisy and arrogance of the people's worship. Rather than completely changing the subject from the poetry, the Temple sermon focuses attention on one more aspect of the people's sinfulness. The people themselves, not God, should be blamed for the destruction of the nation. Judah and its capital city, Jerusalem, fell to Babylon in the sixth century BCE because their worship was false. The sermon must have been immensely shocking for its original audience. Since the time of David, the king and the Temple had been closely bound together in the people's thinking. When David came to the throne, God promised that David's son would build the Temple and that David and his throne would be established forever (1 Sam 7.1–7). A century earlier than Jeremiah, the prophet Isaiah had interpreted the promises to David as unconditional assurance of Jerusalem's safety (Isa 36–37). By the time of Jeremiah, the people of Judah seemed to think they were safe no matter what they did.

7 The word that came to Jeremiah from the LORD: 2 Stand in the gate of the LORD's house, and proclaim there this word, and say, Hear the word of the LORD, all you people of Judah, you that enter these gates to worship the LORD. 3 Thus says the LORD of hosts, the God of Israel: Amend your ways and your doings, and let me dwell with you*b* in this place. 4 Do not trust in these deceptive words: "This is*c* the temple of the LORD, the temple of the LORD, the temple of the LORD."

5 For if you truly amend your ways and your doings, if you truly act justly one with another, 6 if you do not oppress the alien, the orphan, and the widow, or shed innocent blood in this place, and if you do not go after other gods to your own hurt, 7 then I will dwell with you in this place, in the land that I gave of old to your ancestors forever and ever.

7.1–7: Standing at the gates of the Temple,✴ Jeremiah tells the people that they must change their ways to dwell *in this place* (7.3, 7, 10, 11). The "place" prob-

a Or *a fortress*　　*b* Or *and I will let you dwell*
c Heb *They are*

ably refers to the Temple, the land, and the city. To live there, they must stop their false reliance on the place itself. Instead, they must act justly toward one another. They claim God's protection in the Temple even though, by oppressing weak members of their society, they act as if they are not God's people. The threat to the nation stems not only from the invading foe but also from their own behavior.

~~~~~~~~~~~~~~~~~~~~~~

8 Here you are, trusting in deceptive words to no avail. 9Will you steal, murder, commit adultery, swear falsely, make offerings to Baal, and go after other gods that you have not known, 10and then come and stand before me in this house, which is called by my name, and say, "We are safe!"—only to go on doing all these abominations? 11Has this house, which is called by my name, become a den of robbers in your sight? You know, I too am watching, says the LORD. 12Go now to my place that was in Shiloh, where I made my name dwell at first, and see what I did to it for the wickedness of my people Israel. 13And now, because you have done all these things, says the LORD, and when I spoke to you persistently, you did not listen, and when I called you, you did not answer, 14therefore I will do to the house that is called by my name, in which you trust, and to the place that I gave to you and to your ancestors, just what I did to Shiloh. 15And I will cast you out of my sight, just as I cast out all your kinsfolk, all the offspring of Ephraim.

16 As for you, do not pray for this people, do not raise a cry or prayer on their behalf, and do not intercede with me, for I will not hear you. 17Do you not see what they are doing in the towns of Judah and in the streets of Jerusalem? 18The children gather wood, the fathers kindle fire, and the women knead dough, to make cakes for the queen of heaven; and they pour out drink offerings to other gods, to provoke me to anger. 19Is it I whom they provoke? says the LORD. Is it not themselves, to their own hurt? 20Therefore thus says the Lord GOD: My anger and my wrath shall be poured out on this place, on human beings and animals, on the trees of the field and the fruit of the ground; it will burn and not be quenched.

7.8–8.3: The sermon moves in a downward spiral of offenses. **7.9:** The people commit crimes and worship *Baal,* a storm deity, not the God of Israel. **12–15:** For these offenses, Jerusalem will become like *Shiloh,* a shrine in the northern kingdom that was destroyed by the Philistines. The Jerusalem Temple* will meet the same fate if the people of Judah do not repent. **16–17:** Yet the sins of Judah are so great that God prohibits Jeremiah from interceding on behalf of the people. **18–19:** Entire families worship the astral deity called *the queen of heaven.*

~~~~~~~~~~~~~~~~~~~~~~

21 Thus says the LORD of hosts, the God of Israel: Add your burnt offerings to your sacrifices, and eat the flesh. 22For in the day that I brought your ancestors out of the land of Egypt, I did not speak to them or command them concerning burnt offerings and sacrifices. 23But this command I gave them, "Obey my voice, and I will be your God, and you shall be my people; and walk only in the way that I command you, so that it may be well with you." 24Yet they did not obey or incline their ear, but, in the stubbornness of their evil will, they walked in their own counsels, and looked backward rather than forward. 25From the day that your ancestors came out of the land of Egypt until this day, I have persistently sent all my servants the prophets to them, day after day; 26yet they did not listen to me, or pay attention, but they stiffened their necks. They did worse than their ancestors did.

27 So you shall speak all these words to them, but they will not listen to you. You shall call to them, but they will not answer you. 28You shall say to them: This is the nation that did not obey the voice of the LORD their God, and did not accept discipline; truth has perished; it is cut off from their lips.

29 Cut off your hair and throw it away;
      raise a lamentation on the bare
            heights,"
   for the LORD has rejected and forsaken
      the generation that provoked
            his wrath.

30 For the people of Judah have done evil in my sight, says the LORD; they have set

a Or *the trails*

their abominations in the house that is called by my name, defiling it. ³¹And they go on building the high place*a* of Topheth, which is in the valley of the son of Hinnom, to burn their sons and their daughters in the fire— which I did not command, nor did it come into my mind. ³²Therefore, the days are surely coming, says the LORD, when it will no more be called Topheth, or the valley of the son of Hinnom, but the valley of Slaughter: for they will bury in Topheth until there is no more room. ³³The corpses of this people will be food for the birds of the air, and for the animals of the earth; and no one will frighten them away. ³⁴And I will bring to an end the sound of mirth and gladness, the voice of the bride and bridegroom in the cities of Judah and in the streets of Jerusalem; for the land shall become a waste.

7.21–34. 29: A poetic verse urges the people to lament,* for God has rejected their worship. **30–32:** People offer their children in sacrifice on *Topheth in the valley of Hinnom.* **33–34:** For these crimes the nation will be destroyed. Their corpses will be littered about, normal life in the land will cease, and *the land shall become a waste.*

8 At that time, says the LORD, the bones of the kings of Judah, the bones of its officials, the bones of the priests, the bones of the prophets, and the bones of the inhabitants of Jerusalem shall be brought out of their tombs; ²and they shall be spread before the sun and the moon and all the host of heaven, which they have loved and served, which they have followed, and which they have inquired of and worshiped; and they shall not be gathered or buried; they shall be like dung on the surface of the ground. ³Death shall be preferred to life by all the remnant that remains of this evil family in all the places where I have driven them, says the LORD of hosts.

8.1–3: In the horrifying conclusion to the sermon, the kings, who are not only the leaders but also symbolize the nation itself, will die and their corpses will be dishonored. The sermon seeks to bring about obedience and true worship. The people must listen to the voice of God through the prophet.* If the book's audience lives in exile, then the sermon makes clear that only true worship will bring about renewed life in the land.

Weeping and lamentation

8.4–10.25: Poetry resumes in this section that continues to announce the impending cosmic battle and also emphasizes themes of weeping and lamentation.* The only response left in the face of the community's stubbornness and infidelity is to weep at the tragedy that is certain to come. The poems gathered here fall into four groupings: 8.4–17 continues to explain why the cosmic battle must come; 8.18–9.26 begins the weeping as if at a funeral for the nation; 10.1–16 contains a communal prayer of loyalty to God; 10.17–25 announces the Exile* as the enemy from the north comes closer. As in earlier chapters in the book, many voices announce, comment upon, or respond to the approaching disaster. Voices of lamentation and weeping that appeared in 3.21; 4.19; 6.26; and 7.29 burst out here with abundant tears that flow from God, Jeremiah, and the people.

---

⁴ You shall say to them, Thus says the
　　LORD:
　When people fall, do they not get up
　　again?
　　If they go astray, do they not turn
　　　back?
⁵ Why then has this people*b* turned away
　　in perpetual backsliding?
　They have held fast to deceit,
　　they have refused to return.
⁶ I have given heed and listened,
　　but they do not speak honestly;
　no one repents of wickedness,
　　saying, "What have I done!"
　All of them turn to their own course,
　　like a horse plunging headlong into
　　　battle.
⁷ Even the stork in the heavens
　　knows its times;
　and the turtledove, swallow, and crane*c*
　　observe the time of their coming;
　but my people do not know
　　the ordinance of the LORD.

⁸ How can you say, "We are wise,
　　and the law of the LORD is with us,"

---

a Gk Tg: Heb *high places*　　*b* One Ms Gk: MT *this people, Jerusalem,*　　*c* Meaning of Heb uncertain

when, in fact, the false pen of the scribes
    has made it into a lie?
9 The wise shall be put to shame,
    they shall be dismayed and taken;
since they have rejected the word
    of the LORD,
    what wisdom is in them?
10 Therefore I will give their wives
    to others
    and their fields to conquerors,
because from the least to the greatest
    everyone is greedy for unjust gain;
from prophet to priest
    everyone deals falsely.
11 They have treated the wound of my
    people carelessly,
    saying, "Peace, peace,"
    when there is no peace.
12 They acted shamefully, they committed
    abomination;
    yet they were not at all ashamed,
    they did not know how to blush.
Therefore they shall fall among those
    who fall;
    at the time when I punish them, they
    shall be overthrown,
            says the LORD.
13 When I wanted to gather them, says the
    LORD,
    there are[a] no grapes on the vine,
    nor figs on the fig tree;
even the leaves are withered,
    and what I gave them has passed
    away from them.[b]

14 Why do we sit still?
Gather together, let us go into the
    fortified cities
    and perish there;
for the LORD our God has doomed us to
    perish,
    and has given us poisoned water to
    drink,
because we have sinned against
    the LORD.
15 We look for peace, but find no good,
    for a time of healing, but there is
    terror instead.

16 The snorting of their horses is heard
    from Dan;

at the sound of the neighing of their
    stallions
    the whole land quakes.
They come and devour the land and all
    that fills it,
    the city and those who live in it.
17 See, I am letting snakes loose among you,
    adders that cannot be charmed,
    and they shall bite you,
            says the LORD.

8.4–17: Why the attack will come. God speaks to Jeremiah in continued perplexity about the people's failure to repent. **6–7:** They behave like wild animals. **8–9:** Their punishment will be captivity. The aftermath of military attack shows wives and fields captured by others. **10–12:** The refrain of accusation from 6.13–15 is repeated here to explain why the invasion must occur. Everyone is deluded and everyone sins. **14–15:** The people speak in confusion and blame God for failing them. Their voice may reflect the feelings of the book's audience in exile, even though their speech is here set before the recounting of the tragedy. **16–17:** God replies by calling attention to the sound of the approaching battle.

18 My joy is gone, grief is upon me,
    my heart is sick.
19 Hark, the cry of my poor people
    from far and wide in the land:
"Is the LORD not in Zion?
    Is her King not in her?"
("Why have they provoked me to anger
    with their images,
    with their foreign idols?")
20 "The harvest is past, the summer
    is ended,
    and we are not saved."
21 For the hurt of my poor people I am
    hurt,
    I mourn, and dismay has taken hold
    of me.

22 Is there no balm in Gilead?
    Is there no physician there?
Why then has the health of my poor
    people
    not been restored?

a Or *I will make an end of them, says the* LORD. *There are*
b Meaning of Heb uncertain

9 ^{a}O that my head were a spring of
     water,
  and my eyes a fountain of tears,
  so that I might weep day and night
    for the slain of my poor people!
2 ^{b}O that I had in the desert
  a traveler's lodging place,
  that I might leave my people
    and go away from them!
  For they are all adulterers,
    a band of traitors.
3 They bend their tongues like bows;
    they have grown strong in the land for
      falsehood, and not for truth;
  for they proceed from evil to evil,
    and they do not know me, says the
     LORD.

8.18–9.26: Weeping. God, the earth, and official mourning women weep to signify the certainty of the nation's destruction. The poetry of weeping also suggests that God joins with the people and the earth in expressing vulnerability, pain, and grief over the invasion that will destroy life in the land. **8.18–9.3:** There is disagreement among scholars about the identity of the principal speaker in this poem, but it is probably God. **21:** The God who suffered in the story of the broken family (2.1–3.25) is in pain and *dismay* again over the *hurt of my poor people.* The Hebrew text reads "daughter of my people," to suggest that God is still lamenting over the broken family relationship. **9.1:** The divine speaker then expresses a wish: *O that my head were a spring of water, and my eyes a fountain of tears, so that I might weep day and night for the slain of my poor people!* Divine tears, unlike divine anger, create a brief solidarity and empathy with the people. If the audience is Israel during the Exile,* divine tears suggest that God has not rejected them forever but suffers with them. **2:** The speaker's mood changes quickly. God desires to escape from the midst of the sinners, an unfaithful people.

4 Beware of your neighbors,
  and put no trust in any of your kin;^{c}
  for all your kin^d are supplanters,
    and every neighbor goes around like a
     slanderer.
5 They all deceive their neighbors,
  and no one speaks the truth;
  they have taught their tongues to speak
    lies;

  they commit iniquity and are too
    weary to repent.^{e}
6 Oppression upon oppression, deceit^f
    upon deceit!
  They refuse to know me, says
    the LORD.

7 Therefore thus says the LORD of hosts:
  I will now refine and test them,
    for what else can I do with my sinful
     people?^{g}
8 Their tongue is a deadly arrow;
  it speaks deceit through the mouth.
  They all speak friendly words to their
    neighbors,
  but inwardly are planning to lay an
    ambush.
9 Shall I not punish them for these
    things? says the LORD;
  and shall I not bring retribution
    on a nation such as this?

10 Take up^h weeping and wailing for the
    mountains,
  and a lamentation for the pastures of
    the wilderness,
  because they are laid waste so that no
    one passes through,
  and the lowing of cattle is not heard;
  both the birds of the air and the animals
    have fled and are gone.
11 I will make Jerusalem a heap of ruins,
  a lair of jackals;
  and I will make the towns of Judah a
    desolation,
  without inhabitant.

12 Who is wise enough to understand this? To whom has the mouth of the LORD spoken, so that they may declare it? Why is the land ruined and laid waste like a wilderness, so that no one passes through? 13 And the LORD says: Because they have forsaken my law that I set before them, and have not obeyed my voice, or walked in accordance

---

a Ch 8.23 in Heb b Ch 9.1 in Heb c Heb *in a brother* d Heb *for every brother* e Cn Compare Gk: Heb *they weary themselves with iniquity.* ^{6}*Your dwelling* f Cn: Heb *Your dwelling in the midst of deceit* g Or *my poor people* h Gk Syr: Heb *I will take up*

with it, ¹⁴but have stubbornly followed their own hearts and have gone after the Baals, as their ancestors taught them. ¹⁵Therefore thus says the LORD of hosts, the God of Israel: I am feeding this people with wormwood, and giving them poisonous water to drink. ¹⁶I will scatter them among nations that neither they nor their ancestors have known; and I will send the sword after them, until I have consumed them.

9.4–16. 4–8: Accusations against the people include their unfaithfulness to each other as they lie, slander, and deceive. In punishment God will refine them like silver. **9:** But God expresses hesitancy with a question also asked earlier (5.9, 29): How can punishment be avoided? **10–11:** The command to weep indicates that the destruction of the earth and of the city of Jerusalem cannot be turned away. The poem implies the end of the world for the inhabitants of Judah. Invasion by the foe from the north will end normal life. **12–16:** These prose verses interpret further the tragedy about to happen, but which for the audience of the book has already occurred. **13–14:** The people did not keep God's law nor listen to God's voice. Instead, they worshipped the *Baals*.*

17 Thus says the LORD of hosts:
Consider, and call for the mourning
women to come;
send for the skilled women to come;
18 let them quickly raise a dirge over us,
so that our eyes may run down with
tears,
and our eyelids flow with water.
19 For a sound of wailing is heard from
Zion:
"How we are ruined!
We are utterly shamed,
because we have left the land,
because they have cast down our
dwellings."

20 Hear, O women, the word of the LORD,
and let your ears receive the word of
his mouth;
teach to your daughters a dirge,
and each to her neighbor a lament.
21 "Death has come up into our windows,
it has entered our palaces,
to cut off the children from the streets

and the young men from
the squares."
22 Speak! Thus says the LORD:
"Human corpses shall fall
like dung upon the open field,
like sheaves behind the reaper,
and no one shall gather them."

23 Thus says the LORD: Do not let the wise boast in their wisdom, do not let the mighty boast in their might, do not let the wealthy boast in their wealth; ²⁴but let those who boast boast in this, that they understand and know me, that I am the LORD; I act with steadfast love, justice, and righteousness in the earth, for in these things I delight, says the LORD.

25 The days are surely coming, says the LORD, when I will attend to all those who are circumcised only in the foreskin: ²⁶Egypt, Judah, Edom, the Ammonites, Moab, and all those with shaven temples who live in the desert. For all these nations are uncircumcised, and all the house of Israel is uncircumcised in heart.

9.17–25. 17: *Mourning women:* In ancient Israel, official mourning women were called to funerals to lead the community in weeping. **21:** Here they are summoned to weep over the destruction of the nation, for *death has come up into our windows.* The funeral to which the people are invited is their own. **23–26:** A prose comment, which seems to continue from 9.12–16 rather than from the weeping poem, announces that God acts in justice for those who *know me.*

10 Hear the word that the LORD speaks to you, O house of Israel. ²Thus says the LORD:
Do not learn the way of the nations,
or be dismayed at the signs of the
heavens;
for the nations are dismayed at them.
3 For the customs of the peoples are false:
a tree from the forest is cut down,
and worked with an ax by the hands
of an artisan;
4 people deck it with silver and gold;
they fasten it with hammer and nails
so that it cannot move.

5 Their idols[a] are like scarecrows in a
　　cucumber field,
　and they cannot speak;
　they have to be carried,
　　for they cannot walk.
　Do not be afraid of them,
　　for they cannot do evil,
　　nor is it in them to do good.

6 There is none like you, O LORD;
　　you are great, and your name is great
　　　in might.
7 Who would not fear you, O King of the
　　nations?
　For that is your due;
　among all the wise ones of the nations
　　and in all their kingdoms
　　there is no one like you.
8 They are both stupid and foolish;
　　the instruction given by idols
　　is no better than wood![b]
9 Beaten silver is brought from Tarshish,
　　and gold from Uphaz.
　They are the work of the artisan and of
　　　the hands of the goldsmith;
　　their clothing is blue and purple;
　　they are all the product of skilled
　　　workers.
10 But the LORD is the true God;
　　he is the living God and the
　　　everlasting King.
　At his wrath the earth quakes,
　　and the nations cannot endure his
　　　indignation.

11 Thus shall you say to them: The gods
who did not make the heavens and the earth
shall perish from the earth and from under
the heavens.[c]

12 It is he who made the earth by
　　his power,
　who established the world by
　　his wisdom,
　and by his understanding stretched
　　out the heavens.
13 When he utters his voice, there is a
　　tumult of waters in the heavens,
　and he makes the mist rise from the
　　ends of the earth.
　He makes lightnings for the rain,

and he brings out the wind from his
　　storehouses.
14 Everyone is stupid and without
　　knowledge;
　goldsmiths are all put to shame by
　　their idols;
　for their images are false,
　　and there is no breath in them.
15 They are worthless, a work of delusion;
　　at the time of their punishment they
　　　shall perish.
16 Not like these is the LORD,[d] the portion
　　of Jacob,
　for he is the one who formed
　　all things,
　and Israel is the tribe of his inheritance;
　　the LORD of hosts is his name.

10.1–16: Hymn of praise. These verses contain a
hymn that expresses loyalty to the one true God and
makes fun of other gods as worthless idols. The hymn,
which seems to follow 9.22, serves as a model of repentance and reconciliation for the exiles surviving the
nation's collapse. The poem is similar in subject and
worship style to the repentance of the children from
the broken family (3.22–25). **2–5:** The people should
neither become like the nations around them nor
adopt their idolatrous* customs. **6:** Israel's God is the
true king of the nations. **8–11:** By contrast, the gods
of the nations are stupid, human creations. **12–16:**
Only the God of Israel is the Creator whose wisdom
made the world. Israel is God's special inheritance. In
this hymn, creation's harmony is reestablished.

~~~~~~~~~~~~~~~~~~~~~~~~~~~~~~~~~

17 Gather up your bundle from the
　　ground,
　O you who live under siege!
18 For thus says the LORD:
　I am going to sling out the inhabitants
　　of the land
　at this time,
　and I will bring distress on them,
　　so that they shall feel it.

19 Woe is me because of my hurt!
　　My wound is severe.
　But I said, "Truly this is my
　　punishment,

a Heb *They*　　b Meaning of Heb uncertain
c This verse is in Aramaic　　d Heb lacks *the LORD*

and I must bear it."

20 My tent is destroyed,
and all my cords are broken;
my children have gone from me,
and they are no more;
there is no one to spread my tent again,
and to set up my curtains.

21 For the shepherds are stupid,
and do not inquire of the LORD;
therefore they have not prospered,
and all their flock is scattered.

22 Hear, a noise! Listen, it is coming—
a great commotion from the land of
the north
to make the cities of Judah a desolation,
a lair of jackals.

23 I know, O LORD, that the way of human
beings is not in their control,
that mortals as they walk cannot
direct their steps.

24 Correct me, O LORD, but in
just measure;
not in your anger, or you will bring
me to nothing.

25 Pour out your wrath on the nations that
do not know you,
and on the peoples that do not call on
your name;
for they have devoured Jacob;
they have devoured him and
consumed him,
and have laid waste his habitation.

10.17–25: Exile. These verses shift back to the time before the Exile,* and God announces that the attack, expected throughout chs. 4–10, is about to come (vv. 17–18, 22). 19–20: A second voice, probably that of Jerusalem personified* as daughter Zion, laments her fate. She is abandoned and her children are gone. 23–25: She admits her sins and asks for divine justice in punishment of both herself and the nations who *devour Jacob,* another name for Israel.

COVENANT DESTROYED

Chs. 11–20: Like the previous chapters, this section of the book seeks to explain the tragedy that has befallen Judah and to defend God from charges of cruelty. It claims that the people brought the catastrophe upon themselves. These chapters continue the poetic accusations of chs. 2–10, but in addition, Jeremiah himself moves into the foreground as a major character in the book. Stories show Jeremiah engaged in symbolic actions (chs. 13, 18, 19, 20). Symbolic actions are prophetic activities that express the prophetic message in dramatic behavior. In addition, this section also includes poems called the "confessions" or "laments*" of Jeremiah (see sidebar on p. 987). The confessions portray Jeremiah's sufferings as he tries to be faithful to his prophetic mission. The covenant* sermon begins the next ten chapters with a curse whose fulfillment becomes inevitable by ch. 20. No blessings, which usually accompany curses, appear here. Their absence suggests that the curse—defeat of Judah—has already occurred and that the audience in exile is asking why it happened and if it is reversible. The sermon interprets their loss of land as the result of their infidelity. Only obedience to God's voice through this prophetic book can set things right.

11 The word that came to Jeremiah from the LORD: 2 Hear the words of this covenant, and speak to the people of Judah and the inhabitants of Jerusalem. 3 You shall say to them, Thus says the LORD, the God of Israel: Cursed be anyone who does not heed the words of this covenant, 4 which I commanded your ancestors when I brought them out of the land of Egypt, from the iron-smelter, saying, Listen to my voice, and do all that I command you. So shall you be my people, and I will be your God, 5 that I may perform the oath that I swore to your ancestors, to give them a land flowing with milk and honey, as at this day. Then I answered, "So be it, LORD."

6 And the LORD said to me: Proclaim all these words in the cities of Judah, and in the streets of Jerusalem: Hear the words of this covenant and do them. 7 For I solemnly warned your ancestors when I brought them up out of the land of Egypt, warning them persistently, even to this day, saying, Obey my voice. 8 Yet they did not obey or incline their ear, but everyone walked in the stubbornness of an evil will. So I brought upon them all the words of this covenant, which I commanded them to do, but they did not.

9 And the LORD said to me: Conspiracy exists among the people of Judah and the inhabitants of Jerusalem. 10They have turned back to the iniquities of their ancestors of old, who refused to heed my words; they have gone after other gods to serve them; the house of Israel and the house of Judah have broken the covenant that I made with their ancestors. 11Therefore, thus says the LORD, assuredly I am going to bring disaster upon them that they cannot escape; though they cry out to me, I will not listen to them. 12Then the cities of Judah and the inhabitants of Jerusalem will go and cry out to the gods to whom they make offerings, but they will never save them in the time of their trouble. 13For your gods have become as many as your towns, O Judah; and as many as the streets of Jerusalem are the altars to shame you have set up, altars to make offerings to Baal.

14 As for you, do not pray for this people, or lift up a cry or prayer on their behalf, for I will not listen when they call to me in the time of their trouble. 15What right has my beloved in my house, when she has done vile deeds? Can vows*a* and sacrificial flesh avert your doom? Can you then exult? 16The LORD once called you, "A green olive tree, fair with goodly fruit"; but with the roar of a great tempest he will set fire to it, and its branches will be consumed. 17The LORD of hosts, who planted you, has pronounced evil against you, because of the evil that the house of Israel and the house of Judah have done, provoking me to anger by making offerings to Baal.

11.1–17: The covenant* curse. In this prose sermon, similar in style to the Temple* sermon (7.1–8.3), Jeremiah announces a curse upon anyone *who does not heed the words* of the covenant (v. 3). The covenant refers to the relationship of loyalty and love that God made with them at Mount Sinai (Ex 19). This sermon has one point that is presented with great simplicity: To possess the land, the people must obey the covenant. **4:** They must *listen to my voice*. The covenant is a two-way relationship. If they obey, then *so shall you be my people, and I will be your God*. **5:** That obedience is the condition of living in the land *flowing with milk and honey*. **6–13:** Otherwise disaster will fall upon

them. **14–17:** Once again God tells Jeremiah not to intercede for the people because they are so sinful.

~~~~~~~~~~

18 It was the LORD who made it known to
    me, and I knew;
    then you showed me their evil deeds.
19 But I was like a gentle lamb
    led to the slaughter.
And I did not know it was against me
    that they devised schemes, saying,
"Let us destroy the tree with its fruit,
    let us cut him off from the land of the
        living,
    so that his name will no longer be
        remembered!"
20 But you, O LORD of hosts, who judge
        righteously,
    who try the heart and the mind,
let me see your retribution upon them,
    for to you I have committed my cause.

21 Therefore thus says the LORD concerning the people of Anathoth, who seek your life, and say, "You shall not prophesy in the name of the LORD, or you will die by our hand"— 22therefore thus says the LORD of hosts: I am going to punish them; the young men shall die by the sword; their sons and their daughters shall die by famine; 23and not even a remnant shall be left of them. For I will bring disaster upon the people of Anathoth, the year of their punishment.

12 You will be in the right, O LORD,
    when I lay charges against you;
    but let me put my case to you.
Why does the way of the guilty prosper?
    Why do all who are treacherous
        thrive?
2 You plant them, and they take root;
    they grow and bring forth fruit;
you are near in their mouths
    yet far from their hearts.
3 But you, O LORD, know me;
    You see me and test me—my heart is
        with you.
Pull them out like sheep for the
        slaughter,
    and set them apart for the day
        of slaughter.

a Gk: Heb *Can many*

4 How long will the land mourn,
    and the grass of every field wither?
For the wickedness of those who live
      in it
    the animals and the birds are swept
      away,
    and because people said, "He is blind
      to our ways."*a*

5 If you have raced with foot-runners and
      they have wearied you,
    how will you compete with horses?
And if in a safe land you fall down,
    how will you fare in the thickets of
      the Jordan?
6 For even your kinsfolk and your own
      family,
    even they have dealt treacherously
      with you;
    they are in full cry after you;
do not believe them,
    though they speak friendly words
      to you.

11.18–12.6: Jeremiah's first confession. See sidebar on p. 987. **18–19:** Jeremiah complains that he is under attack from unidentified enemies. He quotes their plots to get rid of him. **20:** He appeals to God, the just judge, to take vengeance against them. **21–23:** In a prose comment, God promises to punish the enemies, who are identified as people from Jeremiah's own town of Anathoth. But Jeremiah then accuses the just judge of planting and nourishing wickedness. **12.5–6:** The judge replies that things will get worse; even Jeremiah's family will turn against him.

7 I have forsaken my house,
    I have abandoned my heritage;
I have given the beloved of my heart
    into the hands of her enemies.
8 My heritage has become to me
    like a lion in the forest;
    she has lifted up her voice against me—
      therefore I hate her.
9 Is the hyena greedy*b* for my heritage at
      my command?
    Are the birds of prey all around her?
Go, assemble all the wild animals;
    bring them to devour her.
10 Many shepherds have destroyed
    my vineyard,

    they have trampled down my portion,
    they have made my pleasant portion
      a desolate wilderness.
11 They have made it a desolation;
    desolate, it mourns to me.
The whole land is made desolate,
    but no one lays it to heart.
12 Upon all the bare heights*c* in the desert
      spoilers have come;
for the sword of the LORD devours
    from one end of the land to the other;
    no one shall be safe.
13 They have sown wheat and have reaped
      thorns,
    they have tired themselves out but
      profit nothing.
They shall be ashamed of their*d* harvests
    because of the fierce anger of
      the LORD.

14 Thus says the LORD concerning all my evil neighbors who touch the heritage that I have given my people Israel to inherit: I am about to pluck them up from their land, and I will pluck up the house of Judah from among them. 15And after I have plucked them up, I will again have compassion on them, and I will bring them again to their heritage and to their land, everyone of them. 16And then, if they will diligently learn the ways of my people, to swear by my name, "As the LORD lives," as they taught my people to swear by Baal, then they shall be built up in the midst of my people. 17But if any nation will not listen, then I will completely uproot it and destroy it, says the LORD.

12.7–17: God's lament. ⋆ Using the first person pronoun, I, God laments the infidelity of *the beloved of my heart*. Described as a wild *lion*, God's beloved heritage has provoked divine hate, so punishment will follow. **14–17:** A prose comment reuses language of *plucking up* from Jeremiah's call (1.10). God seems to address the exiles directly by promising that those who destroy God's heritage will be *plucked from their land* and God will *pluck* the people of Judah from where they are and return them home, if they listen.

---

a Gk: Heb *to our future*   *b* Cn: Heb *Is the hyena, the bird of prey*   *c* Or *the trails*   *d* Heb *your*

Jeremiah's Confessions

Five poems in the book of Jeremiah are traditionally referred to as "confessions" or "complaints." They are intensely personal expressions of the prophet's* feelings, both as he speaks for God and as he suffers with his people. The five poems (11.18–12.6; 15.10–21; 17.14–18; 18.18–23; 20.7–13) are similar to psalms of lament,* which always contain complaints. Often they also contain requests for vengeance against enemies, a word of assurance, and a promise of praise. Jeremiah plays with these elements of lament, using some elements and dropping others. In all of his confessions, Jeremiah complains about his failure and rejection as a prophet. He says that he undertook his mission against his will and that it brings him nothing but pain. He prophesies only because God sends him; he is a true prophet (1.4–11), not a lying prophet who sends himself (23.21).

By the end of ch. 20, Jeremiah's sufferings and the sufferings of the nation overlap and mimic each other. Both nation and prophet face captivity. Symbolically, Jeremiah represents God as the prophet who must accuse and warn the nation. Yet he also represents the people, because his fate and his sufferings parallel theirs. The prophet's doubt, anger, and grief embody their sufferings. The people, however, also contribute to his suffering by rejecting his words. Thus they bring tragedy upon themselves—suffering that Jeremiah must also undergo, to the point where he wishes he had never been born.

13 Thus said the LORD to me, "Go and buy yourself a linen loincloth, and put it on your loins, but do not dip it in water." ²So I bought a loincloth according to the word of the LORD, and put it on my loins. ³And the word of the LORD came to me a second time, saying, ⁴"Take the loincloth that you bought and are wearing, and go now to the Euphrates,ᵃ and hide it there in a cleft of the rock." ⁵So I went, and hid it by the Euphrates,ᵇ as the LORD commanded me. ⁶And after many days the LORD said to me, "Go now to the Euphrates,ᵃ and take from there the loincloth that I commanded you to hide there." ⁷Then I went to the Euphrates,ᵃ and dug, and I took the loincloth from the place where I had hidden it. But now the loincloth was ruined; it was good for nothing.

8 Then the word of the LORD came to me: ⁹Thus says the LORD: Just so I will ruin the pride of Judah and the great pride of Jerusalem. ¹⁰This evil people, who refuse to hear my words, who stubbornly follow their own will and have gone after other gods to serve them and worship them, shall be like this loincloth, which is good for nothing. ¹¹For

as the loincloth clings to one's loins, so I made the whole house of Israel and the whole house of Judah cling to me, says the LORD, in order that they might be for me a people, a name, a praise, and a glory. But they would not listen.

13.1–27: The nation's pride. In this chapter Jeremiah performs a symbolic act (vv. 1–11), interprets a symbolic event (vv. 12–14), and in poetry again announces exile (vv. 15–27). The theme of the nation's false pride runs throughout the chapter. **1–11:** Jeremiah receives a divine command to purchase a loincloth and *hide it in a cleft of the rock* (v. 4). The results of his action symbolize his prophetic message. The loincloth is ruined by its exposure to the elements. **8–11:** Jeremiah's words explain the action. Judah is supposed to *cling* to God but instead has been full of pride and has refused to listen; hence, the nation will come to ruin.

---

12 You shall speak to them this word: Thus says the LORD, the God of Israel: Every wine-jar should be filled with wine. And they

a Or *to Parah*; Heb *perath*　　*b* Or *by Parah*; Heb *perath*

will say to you, "Do you think we do not know that every wine-jar should be filled with wine?" 13Then you shall say to them: Thus says the LORD: I am about to fill all the inhabitants of this land—the kings who sit on David's throne, the priests, the prophets, and all the inhabitants of Jerusalem—with drunkenness. 14And I will dash them one against another, parents and children together, says the LORD. I will not pity or spare or have compassion when I destroy them.

13.12–14: In a second symbolic event to occur in the future, God interprets actions to be performed by the people, not by Jeremiah. The filling of *wine-jars* signifies not feasting, as readers might expect, but *drunkenness* that is destructive of the people and the land. These verses seem to provide the punishment for the pride named in Jeremiah's symbolic action of hiding the loincloth. This wine-drinking episode points forward to 25.15–29, when all the nations drink from the cup of destruction.

15 Hear and give ear; do not be haughty,
    for the LORD has spoken.
16 Give glory to the LORD your God
    before he brings darkness,
and before your feet stumble
    on the mountains at twilight;
while you look for light,
    he turns it into gloom
    and makes it deep darkness.
17 But if you will not listen,
    my soul will weep in secret for your
        pride;
my eyes will weep bitterly and run down
        with tears,
    because the LORD's flock has been
        taken captive.

18 Say to the king and the queen mother:
    "Take a lowly seat,
for your beautiful crown
    has come down from your head."*a*
19 The towns of the Negeb are shut up
    with no one to open them;
all Judah is taken into exile,
    wholly taken into exile.

20 Lift up your eyes and see
    those who come from the north.

Where is the flock that was given you,
    your beautiful flock?
21 What will you say when they set as head
        over you
    those whom you have trained
    to be your allies?
Will not pangs take hold of you,
    like those of a woman in labor?
22 And if you say in your heart,
    "Why have these things come upon
        me?"
it is for the greatness of your iniquity
    that your skirts are lifted up,
    and you are violated.
23 Can Ethiopians*b* change their skin
    or leopards their spots?
Then also you can do good
    who are accustomed to do evil.
24 I will scatter you*c* like chaff
    driven by the wind from the desert.
25 This is your lot,
    the portion I have measured out to
        you, says the LORD,
because you have forgotten me
    and trusted in lies.
26 I myself will lift up your skirts over your
        face,
    and your shame will be seen.
27 I have seen your abominations,
    your adulteries and neighings, your
        shameless prostitutions
    on the hills of the countryside.
Woe to you, O Jerusalem!
    How long will it be
    before you are made clean?

13.15–27: Jeremiah warns the people against their pride and urges them to listen. **17:** If they do not, his response will be to *weep* at their captivity as God weeps (9.1). **18–19:** The *queen mother,* that is, the mother of the king, will be brought low because the invasion and exile are already underway. **20:** The enemy from the north is coming. **22–27:** According to the Hebrew text, God addresses Jerusalem, personified* again as female, with charges that her infidelity will result in her violation. God will be the one to lift her skirts, that is, to rape her. This shocking language uses the image of a raped woman to de-

a Gk Syr Vg: Meaning of Heb uncertain
b Or *Nubians;* Heb *Cushites*   *c* Heb *them*

scribe the invasion of the city, directed and accomplished by God.

14 The word of the LORD that came to Jeremiah concerning the drought:

2 Judah mourns
    and her gates languish;
they lie in gloom on the ground,
    and the cry of Jerusalem goes up.
3 Her nobles send their servants
        for water;
    they come to the cisterns,
they find no water,
    they return with their vessels empty.
They are ashamed and dismayed
    and cover their heads,
4   because the ground is cracked.
    Because there has been no rain on
        the land
    the farmers are dismayed;
        they cover their heads.
5 Even the doe in the field forsakes her
        newborn fawn
    because there is no grass.
6 The wild asses stand on the bare
        heights,*
    they pant for air like jackals;
their eyes fail
    because there is no herbage.

7 Although our iniquities testify
        against us,
    act, O LORD, for your name's sake;
our apostasies indeed are many,
    and we have sinned against you.
8 O hope of Israel,
    its savior in time of trouble,
why should you be like a stranger in the
        land,
    like a traveler turning aside for the
        night?
9 Why should you be like someone
        confused,
    like a mighty warrior who cannot give
        help?
Yet you, O LORD, are in the midst of us,
    and we are called by your name;
        do not forsake us!

10 Thus says the LORD concerning
        this people:

Truly they have loved to wander,
    they have not restrained their feet;
therefore the LORD does not
        accept them,
    now he will remember their iniquity
        and punish their sins.

14.1–22: Drought and wound. This chapter contains two poems, one concerning a drought (vv. 1–10) and one concerning the wounds of war (vv. 17–22), with prose comment (vv. 11–16) between them. Though an actual drought may lie behind the first poem, it stands here as a image of the destruction of the creation caused by the nations' sinfulness. **3:** The earth and the animals are affected by the people's idolatry* as they return to empty *cisterns,* instead of to the "fountain of living water" (2.13). **8–9:** The people speak in the language of worship, asking why God has forsaken them. **10:** God describes again their *wandering,* as they turn to other gods.

11 The LORD said to me: Do not pray for the welfare of this people. 12Although they fast, I do not hear their cry, and although they offer burnt offering and grain offering, I do not accept them; but by the sword, by famine, and by pestilence I consume them. 13 Then I said: "Ah, Lord GOD! Here are the prophets saying to them, 'You shall not see the sword, nor shall you have famine, but I will give you true peace in this place.'" 14And the LORD said to me: The prophets are prophesying lies in my name; I did not send them, nor did I command them or speak to them. They are prophesying to you a lying vision, worthless divination, and the deceit of their own minds. 15Therefore thus says the LORD concerning the prophets who prophesy in my name though I did not send them, and who say, "Sword and famine shall not come on this land": By sword and famine those prophets shall be consumed. 16And the people to whom they prophesy shall be thrown out into the streets of Jerusalem, victims of famine and sword. There shall be no one to bury them—themselves, their wives, their sons, and their daughters. For I will pour out their wickedness upon them.

a Or *the trails*

14.11–16: In this prose comment we again hear God commanding Jeremiah not to intercede on behalf of the people because their case is beyond hope. Jeremiah stands in contrast to false prophets who preach lies to the people. This conflict suggests that the audience of the book is offered competing interpretations from its religious leaders. Jeremiah is the only prophet sent by God.

17 You shall say to them this word:
    Let my eyes run down with tears night
        and day,
      and let them not cease,
    for the virgin daughter—my people—is
        struck down with a crushing
        blow,
      with a very grievous wound.
18 If I go out into the field,
      look—those killed by the sword!
    And if I enter the city,
      look—those sick with*a* famine!
    For both prophet and priest ply their
        trade throughout the land,
      and have no knowledge.

19 Have you completely rejected Judah?
      Does your heart loathe Zion?
    Why have you struck us down
      so that there is no healing for us?
    We look for peace, but find no good;
      for a time of healing, but there is
        terror instead.
20 We acknowledge our wickedness,
        O LORD,
      the iniquity of our ancestors,
      for we have sinned against you.
21 Do not spurn us, for your name's sake;
      do not dishonor your glorious
        throne;
    remember and do not break your
        covenant with us.
22 Can any idols of the nations bring rain?
      Or can the heavens give showers?
    Is it not you, O LORD our God?
      We set our hope on you,
      for it is you who do all this.

14.17–22. 17: Jeremiah weeps at the woundedness of the people, portrayed as *the virgin daughter*, grievously wounded by *a crushing blow*. **19–22:** The people

use language of worship to protest God's neglect of them and to ask why there is no *healing* and no *rain*. The people's voice probably represents the voice of the exiles, expressing repentance and hope in the same style as the children in 3.22–25.

15 Then the LORD said to me: Though Moses and Samuel stood before me, yet my heart would not turn toward this people. Send them out of my sight, and let them go! 2And when they say to you, "Where shall we go?" you shall say to them: Thus says the LORD:
    Those destined for pestilence, to
        pestilence,
      and those destined for the sword, to
        the sword;
    those destined for famine, to famine,
      and those destined for captivity, to
        captivity.
3And I will appoint over them four kinds of destroyers, says the LORD: the sword to kill, the dogs to drag away, and the birds of the air and the wild animals of the earth to devour and destroy. 4I will make them a horror to all the kingdoms of the earth because of what King Manasseh son of Hezekiah of Judah did in Jerusalem.

5 Who will have pity on you, O Jerusalem,
      or who will bemoan you?
    Who will turn aside
      to ask about your welfare?
6 You have rejected me, says the LORD,
      you are going backward;
    so I have stretched out my hand against
        you and destroyed you—
      I am weary of relenting.
7 I have winnowed them with a
        winnowing fork
      in the gates of the land;
    I have bereaved them, I have destroyed
        my people;
      they did not turn from their ways.
8 Their widows became more numerous
        than the sand of the seas;
    I have brought against the mothers of
        youths
      a destroyer at noonday;

a Heb *look—the sickness of*

I have made anguish and terror
    fall upon her suddenly.
9 She who bore seven has languished;
    she has swooned away;
her sun went down while it was yet
    day;
    she has been shamed and disgraced.
And the rest of them I will give to the
    sword
    before their enemies,
                says the LORD.

15.1–16.21: No future, yet a future. 15.1: Jeremiah cannot intercede with God for this sinful people because their infidelity places them beyond hope. Even the great mediators of the past, *Moses and Samuel,* could not get God to change the divine mind. These refusals by God to hear the prophet also indicate to the exilic audience that Jeremiah did not fail to prevent the nation's fall. Rather, they had sinned and God had no choice but to punish them. **2–3:** Poetry moves from the mythic description of the foe of the north to a more natural description of invasion and destruction. The culprit in this verse is King Manasseh, (2 Kings 21.10–15), who was famous for his idolatry.* **5–9:** God laments over female Jerusalem, describes the disasters ahead, and accepts full responsibility for bringing calamity upon her. But the poem indicates that God has punished her only after becoming *weary of relenting* (v. 6). The poem defends God from charges of cruelty.

~~~~~~~~~~~~~~~~~~~~~~~~~~~~~~~~~

10 Woe is me, my mother, that you ever bore me, a man of strife and contention to the whole land! I have not lent, nor have I borrowed, yet all of them curse me. 11The LORD said: Surely I have intervened in your life*ᵃ* for good, surely I have imposed enemies on you in a time of trouble and in a time of distress.*ᵇ* 12Can iron and bronze break iron from the north?

13 Your wealth and your treasures I will give as plunder, without price, for all your sins, throughout all your territory. 14I will make you serve your enemies in a land that you do not know, for in my anger a fire is kindled that shall burn forever.
15 O LORD, you know;
    remember me and visit me,
    and bring down retribution for me on
        my persecutors.

In your forbearance do not take
    me away;
    know that on your account I suffer
      insult.
16 Your words were found, and I
    ate them,
and your words became to me a joy
    and the delight of my heart;
for I am called by your name,
    O LORD, God of hosts.
17 I did not sit in the company of
      merrymakers,
    nor did I rejoice;
under the weight of your hand I
    sat alone,
    for you had filled me with
      indignation.
18 Why is my pain unceasing,
    my wound incurable,
    refusing to be healed?
Truly, you are to me like a deceitful
    brook,
    like waters that fail.

19 Therefore thus says the LORD:
If you turn back, I will take you back,
    and you shall stand before me.
If you utter what is precious, and not
      what is worthless,
    you shall serve as my mouth.
It is they who will turn to you,
    not you who will turn to them.
20 And I will make you to this people
    a fortified wall of bronze;
they will fight against you,
    but they shall not prevail over you,
for I am with you
    to save you and deliver you,
                says the LORD.
21 I will deliver you out of the hand of the
    wicked,
    and redeem you from the grasp of the
      ruthless.

15.10–21: Jeremiah's second confession. See sidebar on p. 987. **10:** Jeremiah laments his calling to announce the coming tragedy to the community. **15:** He addresses God directly to complain that he has been faithful, taking the divine words into himself like food.

a Heb *intervened with you*   *b* Meaning of Heb uncertain

17: He stayed away from community life. **18:** Like the people, Jeremiah's wound is *incurable,* for God is unreliable. **19–21:** God replies that Jeremiah must *turn to* God, just as Jeremiah has asked the people to do (4.2). Then God will be with him and rescue him.

16 The word of the LORD came to me: ²You shall not take a wife, nor shall you have sons or daughters in this place. ³For thus says the LORD concerning the sons and daughters who are born in this place, and concerning the mothers who bear them and the fathers who beget them in this land: ⁴They shall die of deadly diseases. They shall not be lamented, nor shall they be buried; they shall become like dung on the surface of the ground. They shall perish by the sword and by famine, and their dead bodies shall become food for the birds of the air and for the wild animals of the earth.

5 For thus says the LORD: Do not enter the house of mourning, or go to lament, or bemoan them; for I have taken away my peace from this people, says the LORD, my steadfast love and mercy. ⁶Both great and small shall die in this land; they shall not be buried, and no one shall lament for them; there shall be no gashing, no shaving of the head for them. ⁷No one shall break bread*ᵃ* for the mourner, to offer comfort for the dead; nor shall anyone give them the cup of consolation to drink for their fathers or their mothers. ⁸You shall not go into the house of feasting to sit with them, to eat and drink. ⁹For thus says the LORD of hosts, the God of Israel: I am going to banish from this place, in your days and before your eyes, the voice of mirth and the voice of gladness, the voice of the bridegroom and the voice of the bride.

16.1–21: Jeremiah's celibacy. Several voices debate the meaning of exile. **1–9:** The first is the voice of God, who commands Jeremiah not to take a wife and not to beget children. Jeremiah's isolation from the community becomes even stronger. Yet his life becomes a symbolic act, a sign of what will happen to the people in exile. Normal life will be over. There will be no marriages, and that means there will be no children. Domestic life is over and the people have no future.

10 And when you tell this people all these words, and they say to you, "Why has the LORD pronounced all this great evil against us? What is our iniquity? What is the sin that we have committed against the LORD our God?" ¹¹then you shall say to them: It is because your ancestors have forsaken me, says the LORD, and have gone after other gods and have served and worshiped them, and have forsaken me and have not kept my law; ¹²and because you have behaved worse than your ancestors, for here you are, every one of you, following your stubborn evil will, refusing to listen to me. ¹³Therefore I will hurl you out of this land into a land that neither you nor your ancestors have known, and there you shall serve other gods day and night, for I will show you no favor.

14 Therefore, the days are surely coming, says the LORD, when it shall no longer be said, "As the LORD lives who brought the people of Israel up out of the land of Egypt," ¹⁵but "As the LORD lives who brought the people of Israel up out of the land of the north and out of all the lands where he had driven them." For I will bring them back to their own land that I gave to their ancestors.

16.10–15. 10–13: God quotes the people, who ask questions at the very heart of the book. Why has this happened? Exile has happened because of their sin and infidelity. **14–15:** Divine promises of a hopeful future addressed to the survivors of the nation's fall interrupt announcements of exile.

16 I am now sending for many fishermen, says the LORD, and they shall catch them; and afterward I will send for many hunters, and they shall hunt them from every mountain and every hill, and out of the clefts of the rocks. ¹⁷For my eyes are on all their ways; they are not hidden from my presence, nor is their iniquity concealed from my sight. ¹⁸And*ᵇ* I will doubly repay their iniquity and their sin, because they have polluted my land with the carcasses of their detestable idols, and have filled my inheritance with their abominations.

a Two Mss Gk: MT *break for them*   *b* Gk: Heb *And first*

19 O LORD, my strength and my
　　　stronghold,
　　my refuge in the day of trouble,
　to you shall the nations come
　　from the ends of the earth and say:
　Our ancestors have inherited nothing
　　　but lies,
　　worthless things in which there is no
　　　profit.
20 Can mortals make for themselves gods?
　　Such are no gods!

21 "Therefore I am surely going to teach
them, this time I am going to teach them my
power and my might, and they shall know
that my name is the LORD."

16.16–21. 16–18: God's punishment here may be
against the enemies who have invaded the land and
polluted it with idols. **19–20:** A worshipping voice addresses God in the style of the children's speech (3.22–
25), expressing loyalty and repentance. This speech
provides a model of piety for the exiles to follow.

17 The sin of Judah is written with an
iron pen; with a diamond point it is
engraved on the tablet of their hearts, and
on the horns of their altars, 2while their children remember their altars and their sacred
poles,*a* beside every green tree, and on the
high hills, 3on the mountains in the open
country. Your wealth and all your treasures
I will give for spoil as the price of your sin*b*
throughout all your territory. 4By your own
act you shall lose the heritage that I gave you,
and I will make you serve your enemies in a
land that you do not know, for in my anger
a fire is kindled*c* that shall burn forever.

5 Thus says the LORD:
Cursed are those who trust in
　　　mere mortals
　　and make mere flesh their strength,
　　whose hearts turn away from
　　　the LORD.
6 They shall be like a shrub in
　　　the desert,
　　and shall not see when relief comes.
　They shall live in the parched places of
　　　the wilderness,
　　in an uninhabited salt land.

7 Blessed are those who trust in
　　　the LORD,
　　whose trust is the LORD.
8 They shall be like a tree planted
　　　by water,
　　sending out its roots by the stream.
　It shall not fear when heat comes,
　　and its leaves shall stay green;
　in the year of drought it is not anxious,
　　and it does not cease to bear fruit.

9 The heart is devious above all else;
　　it is perverse—
　who can understand it?
10 I the LORD test the mind
　　and search the heart,
　to give to all according to their ways,
　　according to the fruit of their doings.

11 Like the partridge hatching what it did
　　　not lay,
　　so are all who amass wealth unjustly;
　in mid-life it will leave them,
　　and at their end they will prove to be
　　　fools.

12 O glorious throne, exalted from the
　　　beginning,
　　shrine of our sanctuary!
13 O hope of Israel! O LORD!
　All who forsake you shall be put to
　　　shame;
　those who turn away from you*d* shall be
　　recorded in the underworld,*e*
　for they have forsaken the fountain of
　　living water, the LORD.

17.1–27: True worship. Many voices combine in this
chapter. **1–4:** In prose accusation, God accuses the
people of Judah of idolatry* and promises that they
will be exiled. **5–8:** In language reminiscent of Ps 1,
God announces the cursed fate of those who trust in
themselves, and the blessed condition of those who
trust in God. **12–13:** The voice of worship addressed
to God reappears and speaks about the foolishness of
abandoning *the fountain of living water* (2.13).

a Heb *Asherim*　　*b* Cn: Heb *spoil your high places for sin*
c Two Mss Theodotion: *you kindled*　　*d* Heb *me*
e Or *in the earth*

14 Heal me, O LORD, and I shall be healed;
     save me, and I shall be saved;
     for you are my praise.
15 See how they say to me,
     "Where is the word of the LORD?
     Let it come!"
16 But I have not run away from being a
          shepherd[a] in your service,
     nor have I desired the fatal day.
     You know what came from my lips;
     it was before your face.
17 Do not become a terror to me;
     you are my refuge in the day
          of disaster;
18 Let my persecutors be shamed,
     but do not let me be shamed;
     let them be dismayed,
     but do not let me be dismayed;
     bring on them the day of disaster;
     destroy them with double destruction!

17.14–18: Jeremiah's third confession. See sidebar on p. 987. Jeremiah is less accusatory of God here than in the previous confession and asks for healing of his wound. **15:** He quotes his enemies, who doubt that he speaks the word of God because it has not yet come true. He asks God to take vengeance against them.

19 Thus said the LORD to me: Go and stand in the People's Gate, by which the kings of Judah enter and by which they go out, and in all the gates of Jerusalem, 20and say to them: Hear the word of the LORD, you kings of Judah, and all Judah, and all the inhabitants of Jerusalem, who enter by these gates. 21Thus says the LORD: For the sake of your lives, take care that you do not bear a burden on the sabbath day or bring it in by the gates of Jerusalem. 22And do not carry a burden out of your houses on the sabbath or do any work, but keep the sabbath day holy, as I commanded your ancestors. 23Yet they did not listen or incline their ear; they stiffened their necks and would not hear or receive instruction.

24 But if you listen to me, says the LORD, and bring in no burden by the gates of this city on the sabbath day, but keep the sabbath day holy and do no work on it, 25then there shall enter by the gates of this city kings[b] who sit on the throne of David, riding in chariots and on horses, they and their officials, the people of Judah and the inhabitants of Jerusalem; and this city shall be inhabited forever. 26And people shall come from the towns of Judah and the places around Jerusalem, from the land of Benjamin, from the Shephelah, from the hill country, and from the Negeb, bringing burnt offerings and sacrifices, grain offerings and frankincense, and bringing thank offerings to the house of the LORD. 27But if you do not listen to me, to keep the sabbath day holy, and to carry in no burden through the gates of Jerusalem on the sabbath day, then I will kindle a fire in its gates; it shall devour the palaces of Jerusalem and shall not be quenched.

17.19–27: Sabbath sermon. In this prose passage, God directs Jeremiah to announce to the leadership the absolute necessity of keeping sabbath law. They are not to carry burdens or do work, and they must heed divine commands. If they fail, then Jerusalem will be destroyed by fire. This sermon explains again that the Exile★ did not occur because of God's cruelty or forgetfulness but resulted from the community's failure to be faithful.

Captivity

Chs. 18–20: These chapters mark a climax★ in the first part of the book and are more closely woven than previous sections. In them the threats of captivity and disaster come to a symbolic fulfillment. After relentless efforts by God and Jeremiah to bring the nation to repentance, punishment comes upon them.

---

18 The word that came to Jeremiah from the LORD: 2"Come, go down to the potter's house, and there I will let you hear my words." 3So I went down to the potter's house, and there he was working at his wheel. 4The vessel he was making of clay was spoiled in the potter's hand, and he reworked it into another vessel, as seemed good to him.

5 Then the word of the LORD came to me: 6Can I not do with you, O house of Israel, just as this potter has done? says the LORD.

a Meaning of Heb uncertain   *b* Cn: Heb *kings and officials*

Just like the clay in the potter's hand, so are you in my hand, O house of Israel. ⁷At one moment I may declare concerning a nation or a kingdom, that I will pluck up and break down and destroy it, ⁸but if that nation, concerning which I have spoken, turns from its evil, I will change my mind about the disaster that I intended to bring on it. ⁹And at another moment I may declare concerning a nation or a kingdom that I will build and plant it, ¹⁰but if it does evil in my sight, not listening to my voice, then I will change my mind about the good that I had intended to do to it. ¹¹Now, therefore, say to the people of Judah and the inhabitants of Jerusalem: Thus says the LORD: Look, I am a potter shaping evil against you and devising a plan against you. Turn now, all of you from your evil way, and amend your ways and your doings.

12 But they say, "It is no use! We will follow our own plans, and each of us will act according to the stubbornness of our evil will."

18.1–12: The potter. Prose narrative* describes Jeremiah's visit to the potter. The potter makes a vessel that he dislikes, so he destroys it and starts again. **11:** This action becomes a symbol of God's plan for Israel and occasions a final invitation to repent. **12:** The people adamantly refuse to repent.

13 Therefore thus says the LORD:
Ask among the nations:
Who has heard the like of this?
The virgin Israel has done
a most horrible thing.
14 Does the snow of Lebanon leave
the crags of Sirion?ᵃ
Do the mountainᵇ waters run dry,ᶜ
the cold flowing streams?
15 But my people have forgotten me,
they burn offerings to a delusion;
they have stumbledᵈ in their ways,
in the ancient roads,
and have gone into bypaths,
not the highway,
16 making their land a horror,
a thing to be hissed at forever.
All who pass by it are horrified
and shake their heads.

17 Like the wind from the east,
I will scatter them before the enemy.
I will show them my back, not my face,
in the day of their calamity.

18.13–17: God's response. God laments their idolatry* and turns from them.

18 Then they said, "Come, let us make plots against Jeremiah—for instruction shall not perish from the priest, nor counsel from the wise, nor the word from the prophet. Come, let us bring charges against him,ᵉ and let us not heed any of his words."

19 Give heed to me, O LORD,
and listen to what my adversaries say!
20 Is evil a recompense for good?
Yet they have dug a pit for my life.
Remember how I stood before you
to speak good for them,
to turn away your wrath from them.
21 Therefore give their children over to famine;
hurl them out to the power of the sword,
let their wives become childless and widowed.
May their men meet death by pestilence,
their youths be slain by the sword in battle.
22 May a cry be heard from their houses,
when you bring the marauder suddenly upon them!
For they have dug a pit to catch me,
and laid snares for my feet.
23 Yet you, O LORD, know
all their plotting to kill me.
Do not forgive their iniquity,
do not blot out their sin from your sight.
Let them be tripped up before you;
deal with them while you are angry.

18.18–23: Jeremiah's fourth confession. See sidebar on p. 987. **18:** Enemies of Jeremiah speak in a prose comment that illustrates the community's failure to re-

a Cn: Heb *of the field*　　*b* Cn: Heb *foreign*
c Cn: Heb *Are . . . plucked up?*　　*d* Gk Syr Vg: Heb *they made them stumble*　　*e* Heb *strike him with the tongue*

pent. **19–20:** Jeremiah reminds God of how faithful Jeremiah has been to his prophetic mission. **21–23:** He asks God to punish the enemies who try to kill him. The prophet's* enemies are the enemies of God because they refuse to hear the divine word that the prophet claims to speak.

19 Thus said the LORD: Go and buy a potter's earthenware jug. Take with you*a* some of the elders of the people and some of the senior priests, 2and go out to the valley of the son of Hinnom at the entry of the Potsherd Gate, and proclaim there the words that I tell you. 3You shall say: Hear the word of the LORD, O kings of Judah and inhabitants of Jerusalem. Thus says the LORD of hosts, the God of Israel: I am going to bring such disaster upon this place that the ears of everyone who hears of it will tingle. 4Because the people have forsaken me, and have profaned this place by making offerings in it to other gods whom neither they nor their ancestors nor the kings of Judah have known, and because they have filled this place with the blood of the innocent, 5and gone on building the high places of Baal to burn their children in the fire as burnt offerings to Baal, which I did not command or decree, nor did it enter my mind; 6therefore the days are surely coming, says the LORD, when this place shall no more be called Topheth, or the valley of the son of Hinnom, but the valley of Slaughter. 7And in this place I will make void the plans of Judah and Jerusalem, and will make them fall by the sword before their enemies, and by the hand of those who seek their life. I will give their dead bodies for food to the birds of the air and to the wild animals of the earth. 8And I will make this city a horror, a thing to be hissed at; everyone who passes by it will be horrified and will hiss because of all its disasters. 9And I will make them eat the flesh of their sons and the flesh of their daughters, and all shall eat the flesh of their neighbors in the siege, and in the distress with which their enemies and those who seek their life afflict them.

10 Then you shall break the jug in the sight of those who go with you, 11and shall say to them: Thus says the LORD of hosts:

So will I break this people and this city, as one breaks a potter's vessel, so that it can never be mended. In Topheth they shall bury until there is no more room to bury. 12Thus will I do to this place, says the LORD, and to its inhabitants, making this city like Topheth. 13And the houses of Jerusalem and the houses of the kings of Judah shall be defiled like the place of Topheth—all the houses upon whose roofs offerings have been made to the whole host of heaven, and libations have been poured out to other gods.

14 When Jeremiah came from Topheth, where the LORD had sent him to prophesy, he stood in the court of the LORD's house and said to all the people: 15Thus says the LORD of hosts, the God of Israel: I am now bringing upon this city and upon all its towns all the disaster that I have pronounced against it, because they have stiffened their necks, refusing to hear my words.

19.1–15: The broken pot. Jeremiah performs a symbolic action in which he breaks an earthenware jug in front of the elders and priests to represent the nation. He summarizes their idolatries, their sins, and their refusals to listen. **15:** Then he announces the fulfillment of the long promised disaster.

20 Now the priest Pashhur son of Immer, who was chief officer in the house of the LORD, heard Jeremiah prophesying these things. 2Then Pashhur struck the prophet Jeremiah, and put him in the stocks that were in the upper Benjamin Gate of the house of the LORD. 3The next morning when Pashhur released Jeremiah from the stocks, Jeremiah said to him, The LORD has named you not Pashhur but "Terror-all-around." 4For thus says the LORD: I am making you a terror to yourself and to all your friends; and they shall fall by the sword of their enemies while you look on. And I will give all Judah into the hand of the king of Babylon; he shall carry them captive to Babylon, and shall kill them with the sword. 5I will give all the wealth of this city, all its gains, all its prized belongings, and all the treasures of the kings of Judah into the hand

a Syr Tg Compare Gk: Heb lacks *take with you*

of their enemies, who shall plunder them, and seize them, and carry them to Babylon. 6And you, Pashhur, and all who live in your house, shall go into captivity, and to Babylon you shall go; there you shall die, and there you shall be buried, you and all your friends, to whom you have prophesied falsely.

20.1–6: Jeremiah's captivity. The book does not yet report the invasion of Jerusalem but, instead, portrays the disaster symbolically. Jeremiah himself is captured in the Temple* by the high priest. **4–6:** That event becomes the occasion for Jeremiah's announcement that *Babylon,* mentioned for the first time in the book, will invade and destroy Judah and that the high priest and his supporters will go into captivity.

---

7 O LORD, you have enticed me,
    and I was enticed;
you have overpowered me,
    and you have prevailed.
I have become a laughingstock all day
      long;
    everyone mocks me.
8 For whenever I speak, I must cry out,
    I must shout, "Violence and
      destruction!"
For the word of the LORD has become
    for me
    a reproach and derision all day long.
9 If I say, "I will not mention him,
    or speak any more in his name,"
then within me there is something like a
      burning fire
    shut up in my bones;
I am weary with holding it in,
    and I cannot.
10 For I hear many whispering:
    "Terror is all around!
Denounce him! Let us denounce him!"
    All my close friends
    are watching for me to stumble.
"Perhaps he can be enticed,
    and we can prevail against him,
    and take our revenge on him."
11 But the LORD is with me like a dread
      warrior;
    therefore my persecutors will stumble,
    and they will not prevail.
They will be greatly shamed,
    for they will not succeed.

Their eternal dishonor
    will never be forgotten.
12 O LORD of hosts, you test the righteous,
    you see the heart and the mind;
let me see your retribution upon them,
    for to you I have committed
      my cause.

13 Sing to the LORD;
    praise the LORD!
For he has delivered the life of
    the needy
    from the hands of evildoers.

20.7–13: Jeremiah's fifth confession. See sidebar on p. 987. Jeremiah blames his captivity on God, who has given him words of terror to announce. **9:** Jeremiah tried to withhold his message of violence, but it was like fire: He could not hold it in. Jeremiah's message is not his own but is from God alone. **11–13:** Jeremiah remembers God is with him and that the word will be accomplished.

---

14 Cursed be the day
    on which I was born!
The day when my mother bore me,
    let it not be blessed!
15 Cursed be the man
    who brought the news to my father,
      saying,
"A child is born to you, a son,"
    making him very glad.
16 Let that man be like the cities
    that the LORD overthrew without pity;
let him hear a cry in the morning
    and an alarm at noon,
17 because he did not kill me in the womb;
    so my mother would have been my
      grave,
    and her womb forever great.
18 Why did I come forth from the womb
    to see toil and sorrow,
    and spend my days in shame?

20.14–18: A curse. Jeremiah curses the day of his birth, like Job (Job 3). This curse closes the section on the covenant's* destruction that was begun by the curse against the nation in ch. 11. Jeremiah's curse speaks of the tragedy of his mission to announce disaster so that he wishes he had never been born. If his life represents that of the people, his captivity, the ful-

fillment of his word, and his curse enact and bring about their captivity.

THE INVASION'S AFTERMATH

Chs. 21–25: These loosely connected chapters assume that the nation has already been invaded by Babylon. So far, the book has presented captivity only in symbolic terms, but the invasion is described more realistically in 21.1–10. These chapters focus on survival in the battle's aftermath. Prose narratives* offer advice to the survivors (21.1–10; 24.1–10). Poems explain how the invasion happened by blaming kings and prophets (21.11–23.40). National survival is promised (25.1–14) and international justice foretold (25.15–38). The voice of a narrator is more prominent than in previous chapters, and these chapters refer more directly to historical dates and persons than do earlier chapters.

21 This is the word that came to Jeremiah from the LORD, when King Zedekiah sent to him Pashhur son of Malchiah and the priest Zephaniah son of Maaseiah, saying, 2"Please inquire of the LORD on our behalf, for King Nebuchadrezzar of Babylon is making war against us; perhaps the LORD will perform a wonderful deed for us, as he has often done, and will make him withdraw from us."

3 Then Jeremiah said to them: 4Thus you shall say to Zedekiah: Thus says the LORD, the God of Israel: I am going to turn back the weapons of war that are in your hands and with which you are fighting against the king of Babylon and against the Chaldeans who are besieging you outside the walls; and I will bring them together into the center of this city. 5I myself will fight against you with outstretched hand and mighty arm, in anger, in fury, and in great wrath. 6And I will strike down the inhabitants of this city, both human beings and animals; they shall die of a great pestilence. 7Afterward, says the LORD, I will give King Zedekiah of Judah, and his servants, and the people in this city—those who survive the pestilence, sword, and famine—into the hands of King Nebuchadrezzar of Babylon, into the hands of their enemies, into the hands of those who seek their lives. He shall strike them down with the edge of

the sword; he shall not pity them, or spare them, or have compassion.

8 And to this people you shall say: Thus says the LORD: See, I am setting before you the way of life and the way of death. 9Those who stay in this city shall die by the sword, by famine, and by pestilence; but those who go out and surrender to the Chaldeans who are besieging you shall live and shall have their lives as a prize of war. 10For I have set my face against this city for evil and not for good, says the LORD: it shall be given into the hands of the king of Babylon, and he shall burn it with fire.

21.1–10: The attack. 1–2: Jeremiah presents a prophecy to messengers sent to him by *King Zedekiah* of Judah. Zedekiah hopes that God will send the Babylonians and their king, Nebuchadrezzar, away as in the past (Isa 36–37). **3–7:** But instead of sending the Babylonians (also called the *Chaldeans*) away, God will bring them into the city and fight against Judah. **8–9:** In language that appears also in Deut 30.11–10, the text urges them to "choose life." To live, they must surrender to Babylon.

Kings and prophets*
21.11–23.8: The leaders, royal and religious, receive blame for corruption, for injustice, and for turning away from God. Earlier chapters focused on failures of the whole community, but here the leaders alone fail and lead the nation to ruin.

---

11 To the house of the king of Judah say: Hear the word of the LORD, 12O house of David! Thus says the LORD:

Execute justice in the morning,
     and deliver from the hand of the
          oppressor
anyone who has been robbed,
or else my wrath will go forth like fire,
     and burn, with no one to quench it,
     because of your evil doings.

13 See, I am against you, O inhabitant of
          the valley,
     O rock of the plain,
                              says the LORD;
you who say, "Who can come down
          against us,
     or who can enter our places of refuge?"

14 I will punish you according to the fruit
of your doings,

says the LORD;
I will kindle a fire in its forest,
and it shall devour all that is
around it.

22 Thus says the LORD: Go down to the house of the king of Judah, and speak there this word, 2and say: Hear the word of the LORD, O King of Judah sitting on the throne of David—you, and your servants, and your people who enter these gates. 3Thus says the LORD: Act with justice and righteousness, and deliver from the hand of the oppressor anyone who has been robbed. And do no wrong or violence to the alien, the orphan, and the widow, or shed innocent blood in this place. 4For if you will indeed obey this word, then through the gates of this house shall enter kings who sit on the throne of David, riding in chariots and on horses, they, and their servants, and their people. 5But if you will not heed these words, I swear by myself, says the LORD, that this house shall become a desolation. 6For thus says the LORD concerning the house of the king of Judah:

21.11–22.6a: Justice. 21.11–14: The poem addresses the kings by the title *house of David*, referring to all the kings who occupied the Davidic throne (1 Sam 7). The role of the king is to administer justice. If the kings fail, then the fire of divine wrath will destroy them. 22.1–6a: A prose passage elaborates on the obligations of the kings to do justice for the afflicted.

You are like Gilead to me,
like the summit of Lebanon;
but I swear that I will make you
a desert,
an uninhabited city.ᵃ
7 I will prepare destroyers against you,
all with their weapons;
they shall cut down your choicest cedars
and cast them into the fire.
8 And many nations will pass by this city, and all of them will say one to another, "Why has the LORD dealt in this way with that great city?" 9And they will answer, "Because they abandoned the covenant of the LORD

their God, and worshiped other gods and served them."

10 Do not weep for him who is dead,
nor bemoan him;
weep rather for him who goes away,
for he shall return no more
to see his native land.

11 For thus says the LORD concerning Shallum son of King Josiah of Judah, who succeeded his father Josiah, and who went away from this place: He shall return here no more, 12but in the place where they have carried him captive he shall die, and he shall never see this land again.

13 Woe to him who builds his house by
unrighteousness,
and his upper rooms by injustice;
who makes his neighbors work for
nothing,
and does not give them their wages;
14 who says, "I will build myself a spacious
house
with large upper rooms,"
and who cuts out windows for it,
paneling it with cedar,
and painting it with vermilion.
15 Are you a king
because you compete in cedar?
Did not your father eat and drink
and do justice and righteousness?
Then it was well with him.
16 He judged the cause of the poor
and needy;
then it was well.
Is not this to know me?
says the LORD.
17 But your eyes and heart
are only on your dishonest gain,
for shedding innocent blood,
and for practicing oppression and
violence.

18 Therefore thus says the LORD concerning King Jehoiakim son of Josiah of Judah:
They shall not lament for him, saying,
"Alas, my brother!" or "Alas, sister!"

---

a Cn: Heb *uninhabited cities*

They shall not lament for him, saying,
  "Alas, lord!" or "Alas, his majesty!"
19 With the burial of a donkey he shall be
    buried—
  dragged off and thrown out beyond
    the gates of Jerusalem.

20 Go up to Lebanon, and cry out,
   and lift up your voice in Bashan;
  cry out from Abarim,
   for all your lovers are crushed.
21 I spoke to you in your prosperity,
   but you said, "I will not listen."
  This has been your way from
    your youth,
   for you have not obeyed my voice.
22 The wind shall shepherd all your
    shepherds,
   and your lovers shall go into
    captivity;
  then you will be ashamed and dismayed
   because of all your wickedness.
23 O inhabitant of Lebanon,
   nested among the cedars,
  how you will groan*a* when pangs come
    upon you,
   pain as of a woman in labor!

24 As I live, says the LORD, even if King Coniah son of Jehoiakim of Judah were the signet ring on my right hand, even from there I would tear you off 25 and give you into the hands of those who seek your life, into the hands of those of whom you are afraid, even into the hands of King Nebuchadrezzar of Babylon and into the hands of the Chaldeans. 26 I will hurl you and the mother who bore you into another country, where you were not born, and there you shall die. 27 But they shall not return to the land to which they long to return.

28 Is this man Coniah a despised broken
    pot,
   a vessel no one wants?
  Why are he and his offspring hurled out
   and cast away in a land that they do
    not know?
29 O land, land, land,
   hear the word of the LORD!
30 Thus says the LORD:
  Record this man as childless,

a man who shall not succeed in
   his days;
  for none of his offspring shall succeed
   in sitting on the throne of David,
   and ruling again in Judah.

22.6b–30: Fate of kings and nation. Verse 6 connects all these poems to kings. **7–9:** Punishment will come upon them and the city will be destroyed. **10–11:** *King Josiah* and his son Jehoahaz, also known as *Shallum,* both meet tragic fates. Josiah dies in battle (2 Kings 23.28–30), but sadder still is the fate of Jehoahaz, who is exiled from the land. **13–19:** This poem contrasts good King Josiah with his son, the bad King Jehoiakim. Josiah is a true king because he does justice; his son exploits the people for his own benefit. **20–23:** These verses address an unidentified female ("you" is feminine in the Hebrew text) who is sent outside Israel to neighboring *Lebanon.* This location is puzzling, but the woman seems to be God's unfaithful wife, who has refused to listen. **24–30:** God promises to hurl into Babylonian exile King Jehoiakim's son, King Jehoiachin, here called *Coniah.* **30:** With him, kingship will end.

23 Woe to the shepherds who destroy and scatter the sheep of my pasture! says the LORD. 2 Therefore thus says the LORD, the God of Israel, concerning the shepherds who shepherd my people: It is you who have scattered my flock, and have driven them away, and you have not attended to them. So I will attend to you for your evil doings, says the LORD. 3 Then I myself will gather the remnant of my flock out of all the lands where I have driven them, and I will bring them back to their fold, and they shall be fruitful and multiply. 4 I will raise up shepherds over them who will shepherd them, and they shall not fear any longer, or be dismayed, nor shall any be missing, says the LORD.

5 The days are surely coming, says the LORD, when I will raise up for David a righteous Branch, and he shall reign as king and deal wisely, and shall execute justice and righteousness in the land. 6 In his days Judah will be saved and Israel will live in safety.

a Gk Vg Syr: Heb *will be pitied*

And this is the name by which he will be called: "The LORD is our righteousness."

7 Therefore, the days are surely coming, says the LORD, when it shall no longer be said, "As the LORD lives who brought the people of Israel up out of the land of Egypt," 8but "As the LORD lives who brought out and led the offspring of the house of Israel out of the land of the north and out of all the lands where he*a* had driven them." Then they shall live in their own land.

23.1–8: Restoration. In these prose verses, God promises restoration to kings, portrayed by the traditional figure of the shepherd. If the readers of the book were already in exile, these promises of future Davidic kingship would not contradict Jeremiah's prophecy of invasion. Those events would already have occurred. The audience awaits a new future promised here. The prophecies of doom explain in a variety of ways why things have come to this tragic situation.

9 Concerning the prophets:
My heart is crushed within me,
   all my bones shake;
I have become like a drunkard,
   like one overcome by wine,
because of the LORD
   and because of his holy words.
10 For the land is full of adulterers;
   because of the curse the land
     mourns,
   and the pastures of the wilderness are
     dried up.
Their course has been evil,
   and their might is not right.
11 Both prophet and priest are ungodly;
   even in my house I have found their
     wickedness,
               says the LORD.
12 Therefore their way shall be to them
   like slippery paths in the darkness,
   into which they shall be driven and
     fall;
for I will bring disaster upon them
   in the year of their punishment,
               says the LORD.
13 In the prophets of Samaria
   I saw a disgusting thing:
they prophesied by Baal
   and led my people Israel astray.

14 But in the prophets of Jerusalem
   I have seen a more shocking thing:
they commit adultery and walk in
     lies;
   they strengthen the hands of
     evildoers,
   so that no one turns from wickedness;
all of them have become like Sodom
     to me,
   and its inhabitants like Gomorrah.
15 Therefore thus says the LORD of hosts
     concerning the prophets:
"I am going to make them eat
     wormwood,
   and give them poisoned water
     to drink;
for from the prophets of Jerusalem
   ungodliness has spread throughout
     the land."

16 Thus says the LORD of hosts: Do not listen to the words of the prophets who prophesy to you; they are deluding you. They speak visions of their own minds, not from the mouth of the LORD. 17They keep saying to those who despise the word of the LORD, "It shall be well with you"; and to all who stubbornly follow their own stubborn hearts, they say, "No calamity shall come upon you."

23.9–40: Prophets. As a group of leaders, the prophets* failed to be true to their calling to speak the word of God. **9–11:** God laments over their infidelity. **13–14:** The prophets of the northern kingdom of *Samaria* were *shocking* in their worship of *Baal,** but the prophets of Judah were even worse, like the two cities destroyed for their sinfulness (Gen 19).

18 For who has stood in the council
     of the LORD
   so as to see and to hear his word?
   Who has given heed to his word
     so as to proclaim it?
19 Look, the storm of the LORD!
   Wrath has gone forth,
a whirling tempest;
   it will burst upon the head of
     the wicked.

a Gk: Heb *I*

20 The anger of the LORD will not
        turn back
    until he has executed and
        accomplished
    the intents of his mind.
    In the latter days you will understand it
        clearly.

21 I did not send the prophets,
        yet they ran;
    I did not speak to them,
        yet they prophesied.
22 But if they had stood in my council,
        then they would have proclaimed my
            words to my people,
    and they would have turned them from
        their evil way,
    and from the evil of their doings.

23.18–22: The true prophet is one who goes before God, *in the council of the LORD.* These prophets God did not send, and they did not speak God's words; they are false prophets. By implication, only Jeremiah is a true prophet.

23 Am I a God near by, says the LORD, and not a God far off? 24Who can hide in secret places so that I cannot see them? says the LORD. Do I not fill heaven and earth? says the LORD. 25I have heard what the prophets have said who prophesy lies in my name, saying, "I have dreamed, I have dreamed!" 26How long? Will the hearts of the prophets ever turn back—those who prophesy lies, and who prophesy the deceit of their own heart? 27They plan to make my people forget my name by their dreams that they tell one another, just as their ancestors forgot my name for Baal. 28Let the prophet who has a dream tell the dream, but let the one who has my word speak my word faithfully. What has straw in common with wheat? says the LORD. 29Is not my word like fire, says the LORD, and like a hammer that breaks a rock in pieces? 30See, therefore, I am against the prophets, says the LORD, who steal my words from one another. 31See, I am against the prophets, says the LORD, who use their own tongues and say, "Says the LORD." 32See, I am against those who prophesy lying dreams, says the LORD, and who tell them, and who lead my people astray by their lies and their recklessness, when I did not send them or appoint them; so they do not profit this people at all, says the LORD.

33 When this people, or a prophet, or a priest asks you, "What is the burden of the LORD?" you shall say to them, "You are the burden,*a* and I will cast you off, says the LORD." 34And as for the prophet, priest, or the people who say, "The burden of the LORD," I will punish them and their households. 35Thus shall you say to one another, among yourselves, "What has the LORD answered?" or "What has the LORD spoken?" 36But "the burden of the LORD" you shall mention no more, for the burden is everyone's own word, and so you pervert the words of the living God, the LORD of hosts, our God. 37Thus you shall ask the prophet, "What has the LORD answered you?" or "What has the LORD spoken?" 38But if you say, "the burden of the LORD," thus says the LORD: Because you have said these words, "the burden of the LORD," when I sent to you, saying, You shall not say, "the burden of the LORD," 39therefore, I will surely lift you up*b* and cast you away from my presence, you and the city that I gave to you and your ancestors. 40And I will bring upon you everlasting disgrace and perpetual shame, which shall not be forgotten.

23.23–40: These prose verses continue to discredit the other prophets who have led the people astray. **33–40:** A play on words makes the same attack on the prophets. The word translated *burden* can also mean "oracle***" or "prophetic poem." The prophets who ask for an oracle or message from God learn that they are God's *burden.*

24 The LORD showed me two baskets of figs placed before the temple of the LORD. This was after King Nebuchadrezzar of Babylon had taken into exile from Jerusalem King Jeconiah son of Jehoiakim of Judah, together with the officials of Judah, the artisans, and the smiths, and had brought them to Babylon. 2One basket had very good

a Gk Vg: Heb *What burden*   *b* Heb Mss Gk Vg: MT *forget you*

figs, like first-ripe figs, but the other basket had very bad figs, so bad that they could not be eaten. ³And the LORD said to me, "What do you see, Jeremiah?" I said, "Figs, the good figs very good, and the bad figs very bad, so bad that they cannot be eaten."

4 Then the word of the LORD came to me: ⁵Thus says the LORD, the God of Israel: Like these good figs, so I will regard as good the exiles from Judah, whom I have sent away from this place to the land of the Chaldeans. ⁶I will set my eyes upon them for good, and I will bring them back to this land. I will build them up, and not tear them down; I will plant them, and not pluck them up. ⁷I will give them a heart to know that I am the LORD; and they shall be my people and I will be their God, for they shall return to me with their whole heart.

8 But thus says the LORD: Like the bad figs that are so bad they cannot be eaten, so will I treat King Zedekiah of Judah, his officials, the remnant of Jerusalem who remain in this land, and those who live in the land of Egypt. ⁹I will make them a horror, an evil thing, to all the kingdoms of the earth—a disgrace, a byword, a taunt, and a curse in all the places where I shall drive them. ¹⁰And I will send sword, famine, and pestilence upon them, until they are utterly destroyed from the land that I gave to them and their ancestors.

24.1–10: Figs. Jerusalem has been invaded, King Jehoiachin is in captivity, and King Zedekiah has been appointed in his place. Jeremiah has a vision of *two baskets of figs.* One symbolizes survivors in Babylon; the other stands for those who have stayed in Judah or escaped to Egypt. The first basket is good; the second is rotten. The message for the survivors is that to survive they must cooperate with Babylon. Only then will they have a future.

Babylon's fall

Ch. 25: This chapter closes off the first major division of the book by reaching back to ch. 1. At last, Jeremiah acts as "prophet to the nations" (1.5, 10).

---

25 The word that came to Jeremiah concerning all the people of Judah, in the fourth year of King Jehoiakim son of Josiah of Judah (that was the first year of King Nebuchadrezzar of Babylon), ²which the prophet Jeremiah spoke to all the people of Judah and all the inhabitants of Jerusalem: ³For twenty-three years, from the thirteenth year of King Josiah son of Amon of Judah, to this day, the word of the LORD has come to me, and I have spoken persistently to you, but you have not listened. ⁴And though the LORD persistently sent you all his servants the prophets, you have neither listened nor inclined your ears to hear ⁵when they said, "Turn now, everyone of you, from your evil way and wicked doings, and you will remain upon the land that the LORD has given to you and your ancestors from of old and forever; ⁶do not go after other gods to serve and worship them, and do not provoke me to anger with the work of your hands. Then I will do you no harm." ⁷Yet you did not listen to me, says the LORD, and so you have provoked me to anger with the work of your hands to your own harm.

8 Therefore thus says the LORD of hosts: Because you have not obeyed my words, ⁹I am going to send for all the tribes of the north, says the LORD, even for King Nebuchadrezzar of Babylon, my servant, and I will bring them against this land and its inhabitants, and against all these nations around; I will utterly destroy them, and make them an object of horror and of hissing, and an everlasting disgrace.ᵃ ¹⁰And I will banish from them the sound of mirth and the sound of gladness, the voice of the bridegroom and the voice of the bride, the sound of the millstones and the light of the lamp. ¹¹This whole land shall become a ruin and a waste, and these nations shall serve the king of Babylon seventy years. ¹²Then after seventy years are completed, I will punish the king of Babylon and that nation, the land of the Chaldeans, for their iniquity, says the LORD, making the land an everlasting waste. ¹³I will bring upon that land all the words that I have uttered against it, everything written in this book, which Jeremiah prophesied against all the nations. ¹⁴For many nations and great

---

ᵃ Gk Compare Syr: Heb *and everlasting desolations*

kings shall make slaves of them also; and I will repay them according to their deeds and the work of their hands.

25.1–14: Invaders will be punished. 1: A narrator dates the chapter to the rules of the Judahite *King Jehoiakim* and the Babylonian *King Nebuchadrezzar.* That date, 605 BCE, indicates that Jeremiah has prophesied the fall of Judah to Babylon well in advance of events. His prophecy of the fall of Babylon will, therefore, prove equally reliable. **3–7:** Jeremiah summarizes his career and the people's refusal to listen to his words. This refusal provoked divine anger. **8–14:** God presents the consequences of not listening. **9:** The *tribes of the north,* now identified as Babylon, will be God's agent of destruction. God calls the Babylonian king *my servant.* As divine agents, the Babylonians will destroy life on an international scale. **11:** Judah will serve Babylon for 70 years. This number may simply mean "a long time," for the Exile* lasted only 50 years. **14:** After that time God will punish Babylon.

~~~~~~~~

15 For thus the LORD, the God of Israel, said to me: Take from my hand this cup of the wine of wrath, and make all the nations to whom I send you drink it. 16They shall drink and stagger and go out of their minds because of the sword that I am sending among them.

17 So I took the cup from the LORD's hand, and made all the nations to whom the LORD sent me drink it: 18Jerusalem and the towns of Judah, its kings and officials, to make them a desolation and a waste, an object of hissing and of cursing, as they are today; 19Pharaoh king of Egypt, his servants, his officials, and all his people; 20all the mixed people;*a* all the kings of the land of Uz; all the kings of the land of the Philistines—Ashkelon, Gaza, Ekron, and the remnant of Ashdod; 21Edom, Moab, and the Ammonites; 22all the kings of Tyre, all the kings of Sidon, and the kings of the coastland across the sea; 23Dedan, Tema, Buz, and all who have shaven temples; 24all the kings of Arabia and all the kings of the mixed peoples*a* that live in the desert; 25all the kings of Zimri, all the kings of Elam, and all the kings of Media; 26all the kings of the north, far and near, one after another, and all the kingdoms of the world that are on the face of the earth. And after them the king of Sheshach*b* shall drink.

27 Then you shall say to them, Thus says the LORD of hosts, the God of Israel: Drink, get drunk and vomit, fall and rise no more, because of the sword that I am sending among you.

28 And if they refuse to accept the cup from your hand to drink, then you shall say to them: Thus says the LORD of hosts: You must drink! 29See, I am beginning to bring disaster on the city that is called by my name, and how can you possibly avoid punishment? You shall not go unpunished, for I am summoning a sword against all the inhabitants of the earth, says the LORD of hosts.

25.15–29: Cup of wrath. A symbolic action makes the prophecy of vv. 8–14 concrete. God commands Jeremiah to act as a wine steward. But instead of serving a joyous feast, Jeremiah serves a cup of wrath to the kings of major nations and city-states around Judah. **26:** The final king to drink is the king of Babylon, here called *Sheshach.* All must drink of God's punishment. In the symbolic sphere, Judah and its enemies have already exchanged places. All that remains is for historical events to unfold.

~~~~~~~~

30 You, therefore, shall prophesy against them all these words, and say to them:
   The LORD will roar from on high,
      and from his holy habitation utter his
         voice;
   he will roar mightily against his fold,
      and shout, like those who tread
         grapes,
      against all the inhabitants of
         the earth.
31 The clamor will resound to the ends of
         the earth,
      for the LORD has an indictment
         against the nations;
   he is entering into judgment with all
         flesh,
      and the guilty he will put to
         the sword,
                     says the LORD.

a Meaning of Heb uncertain   *b* *Sheshach* is a cryptogram for *Babel,* Babylon

32 Thus says the LORD of hosts:
See, disaster is spreading
    from nation to nation,
and a great tempest is stirring
    from the farthest parts of the earth!

33 Those slain by the LORD on that day shall extend from one end of the earth to the other. They shall not be lamented, or gathered, or buried; they shall become dung on the surface of the ground.

34 Wail, you shepherds, and cry out;
    roll in ashes, you lords of the flock,
for the days of your slaughter have
        come—and your dispersions,ᵃ
and you shall fall like a choice vessel.

35 Flight shall fail the shepherds,
    and there shall be no escape for the
        lords of the flock.

36 Hark! the cry of the shepherds,
    and the wail of the lords of the flock!
For the LORD is despoiling their
        pasture,

37   and the peaceful folds are devastated,
    because of the fierce anger of
        the LORD.

38 Like a lion he has left his covert;
    for their land has become a waste
because of the cruel sword,
    and because of his fierce anger.

25.30–38: The lion. God is a roaring *lion* who will devour the nations that have destroyed Judah.

HOW THE NATION WILL SURVIVE

Chs. 26–52: The first "book" (chs. 1–25) accused Judah of infidelity, promised destruction and exile, and defended God from accusations of injustice. The second "book" (chs. 26–52) presents stories and poems that reveal how to survive the period after the nation's fall to Babylon. No longer is repentance to avert the disaster the primary concern. The book's audience lives with the community's failure to repent. They themselves must repent and endure. Jeremiah appears here as a model of faithful endurance. Jeremiah's companion Baruch also appears in this part of the book. Baruch has traditionally been named as the writer of stories about Jeremiah, particularly in chs. 37–45. The exilic period was a time of great conflict about how to survive. This book insists that survival requires continued submission to Babylon, repentance, and obedi-

ence as set out in the book of Jeremiah. **Chs. 26–29: Prophetic discord.** These chapters set forth disputes about which prophetic vision of the future will ensure the nation's survival.

---

26 At the beginning of the reign of King Jehoiakim son of Josiah of Judah, this word came from the LORD: ²Thus says the LORD: Stand in the court of the LORD's house, and speak to all the cities of Judah that come to worship in the house of the LORD; speak to them all the words that I command you; do not hold back a word. ³It may be that they will listen, all of them, and will turn from their evil way, that I may change my mind about the disaster that I intend to bring on them because of their evil doings. ⁴You shall say to them: Thus says the LORD: If you will not listen to me, to walk in my law that I have set before you, ⁵and to heed the words of my servants the prophets whom I send to you urgently—though you have not heeded— ⁶then I will make this house like Shiloh, and I will make this city a curse for all the nations of the earth.

7 The priests and the prophets and all the people heard Jeremiah speaking these words in the house of the LORD. ⁸And when Jeremiah had finished speaking all that the LORD had commanded him to speak to all the people, then the priests and the prophets and all the people laid hold of him, saying, "You shall die! ⁹Why have you prophesied in the name of the LORD, saying, 'This house shall be like Shiloh, and this city shall be desolate, without inhabitant'?" And all the people gathered around Jeremiah in the house of the LORD.

10 When the officials of Judah heard these things, they came up from the king's house to the house of the LORD and took their seat in the entry of the New Gate of the house of the LORD. ¹¹Then the priests and the prophets said to the officials and to all the people, "This man deserves the sentence of death because he has prophesied against this city, as you have heard with your own ears."

12 Then Jeremiah spoke to all the offi-

a Meaning of Heb uncertain

cials and all the people, saying, "It is the LORD who sent me to prophesy against this house and this city all the words you have heard. 13 Now therefore amend your ways and your doings, and obey the voice of the LORD your God, and the LORD will change his mind about the disaster that he has pronounced against you. 14 But as for me, here I am in your hands. Do with me as seems good and right to you. 15 Only know for certain that if you put me to death, you will be bringing innocent blood upon yourselves and upon this city and its inhabitants, for in truth the LORD sent me to you to speak all these words in your ears."

16 Then the officials and all the people said to the priests and the prophets, "This man does not deserve the sentence of death, for he has spoken to us in the name of the LORD our God." 17 And some of the elders of the land arose and said to all the assembled people, 18 "Micah of Moresheth, who prophesied during the days of King Hezekiah of Judah, said to all the people of Judah: 'Thus says the LORD of hosts,

> Zion shall be plowed as a field;
> Jerusalem shall become a heap
> of ruins,
> and the mountain of the house a
> wooded height.'

19 Did King Hezekiah of Judah and all Judah actually put him to death? Did he not fear the LORD and entreat the favor of the LORD, and did not the LORD change his mind about the disaster that he had pronounced against them? But we are about to bring great disaster on ourselves!"

20 There was another man prophesying in the name of the LORD, Uriah son of Shemaiah from Kiriath-jearim. He prophesied against this city and against this land in words exactly like those of Jeremiah. 21 And when King Jehoiakim, with all his warriors and all the officials, heard his words, the king sought to put him to death; but when Uriah heard of it, he was afraid and fled and escaped to Egypt. 22 Then King Jehoiakim sent[a] Elnathan son of Achbor and men with him to Egypt, 23 and they took Uriah from Egypt and brought him to King Jehoiakim, who struck him down with the sword and

threw his dead body into the burial place of the common people.

24 But the hand of Ahikam son of Shaphan was with Jeremiah so that he was not given over into the hands of the people to be put to death.

26.1–24: Jeremiah on trial. This chapter shows that Jeremiah faced great conflict but that he is the true prophet* and, hence, is to be heeded. **1–6:** The chapter refers to Jeremiah's Temple* sermon (7.1–8.3) and summarizes it. What is of interest here, however, is the community's response to the sermon. Some accept it; priests, prophets, and King Jehoiakim reject it. Some of the leaders put Jeremiah on trial. **12:** Jeremiah responds to charges by claiming that it was God *who sent me.* The trial concludes with a declaration of Jeremiah's innocence. **17–23:** Some elders present examples of other prophets who spoke judgments against Jerusalem. **18–23:** *King Hezekiah* received the message of the prophet *Micah,* whereas the current king, Jehoiakim, rejected the words of the prophet *Uriah* and had him killed. **24:** Mysteriously, *Ahikam* rescues Jeremiah from death. The story blames the king for rejecting the prophetic word and invites the book's readers to join Jeremiah's supporters. It presents Jeremiah as a model of fidelity who, while in the hands of captors, remains faithful and is rescued from peril.

Yokes

Chs. 27–28: Jeremiah's conflict with other prophetic groups is the subject of these two chapters. Three stories increasingly narrow the conflict from an international disagreement to a personal dispute between two prophets.

---

27 In the beginning of the reign of King Zedekiah[b] son of Josiah of Judah, this word came to Jeremiah from the LORD. 2 Thus the LORD said to me: Make yourself a yoke of straps and bars, and put them on your neck. 3 Send word[c] to the king of Edom, the king of Moab, the king of the Ammonites, the king of Tyre, and the king of Sidon by the hand of the envoys who have come to Jerusalem to King Zedekiah of Judah. 4 Give them this charge for their masters: Thus says the LORD of hosts, the God of Israel: This is

---

a Heb adds *men to Egypt*   *b* Another reading is *Jehoiakim*   *c* Cn: Heb *send them*

what you shall say to your masters: 5It is I who by my great power and my outstretched arm have made the earth, with the people and animals that are on the earth, and I give it to whomever I please. 6Now I have given all these lands into the hand of King Nebuchadnezzar of Babylon, my servant, and I have given him even the wild animals of the field to serve him. 7All the nations shall serve him and his son and his grandson, until the time of his own land comes; then many nations and great kings shall make him their slave.

8 But if any nation or kingdom will not serve this king, Nebuchadnezzar of Babylon, and put its neck under the yoke of the king of Babylon, then I will punish that nation with the sword, with famine, and with pestilence, says the LORD, until I have completed its*a* destruction by his hand. 9You, therefore, must not listen to your prophets, your diviners, your dreamers,*b* your soothsayers, or your sorcerers, who are saying to you, "You shall not serve the king of Babylon." 10For they are prophesying a lie to you, with the result that you will be removed far from your land; I will drive you out, and you will perish. 11But any nation that will bring its neck under the yoke of the king of Babylon and serve him, I will leave on its own land, says the LORD, to till it and live there.

27.1–11: Jeremiah tells the nations that God has placed their lands under the control of Babylon and Nebuchadnezzar, *my servant* (v. 6). Their prophets have a contrary view. 11: Those who refuse to serve Babylon will be put under the *yoke*.

12 I spoke to King Zedekiah of Judah in the same way: Bring your necks under the yoke of the king of Babylon, and serve him and his people, and live. 13Why should you and your people die by the sword, by famine, and by pestilence, as the LORD has spoken concerning any nation that will not serve the king of Babylon? 14Do not listen to the words of the prophets who are telling you not to serve the king of Babylon, for they are prophesying a lie to you. 15I have not sent them, says the LORD, but they are prophesying

falsely in my name, with the result that I will drive you out and you will perish, you and the prophets who are prophesying to you.

16 Then I spoke to the priests and to all this people, saying, Thus says the LORD: Do not listen to the words of your prophets who are prophesying to you, saying, "The vessels of the LORD's house will soon be brought back from Babylon," for they are prophesying a lie to you. 17Do not listen to them; serve the king of Babylon and live. Why should this city become a desolation? 18If indeed they are prophets, and if the word of the LORD is with them, then let them intercede with the LORD of hosts, that the vessels left in the house of the LORD, in the house of the king of Judah, and in Jerusalem may not go to Babylon. 19For thus says the LORD of hosts concerning the pillars, the sea, the stands, and the rest of the vessels that are left in this city, 20which King Nebuchadnezzar of Babylon did not take away when he took into exile from Jerusalem to Babylon King Jeconiah son of Jehoiakim of Judah, and all the nobles of Judah and Jerusalem— 21thus says the LORD of hosts, the God of Israel, concerning the vessels left in the house of the LORD, in the house of the king of Judah, and in Jerusalem: 22They shall be carried to Babylon, and there they shall stay, until the day when I give attention to them, says the LORD. Then I will bring them up and restore them to this place.

27.12–22: The prophets of Judah also oppose the true word of God in a dispute about the Temple* vessels. These sacred items had been deported to Babylon in 597 BCE, and the prophets expect them to be restored to Judah quickly, implying that Babylonian rule will not last long.

28 In that same year, at the beginning of the reign of King Zedekiah of Judah, in the fifth month of the fourth year, the prophet Hananiah son of Azzur, from Gibeon, spoke to me in the house of the LORD, in the presence of the priests and all the people, saying, 2"Thus says the LORD of hosts, the God of Israel: I have broken the

---

a Heb *their*   *b* Gk Syr Vg: Heb *dreams*

yoke of the king of Babylon. ³Within two years I will bring back to this place all the vessels of the LORD's house, which King Nebuchadnezzar of Babylon took away from this place and carried to Babylon. ⁴I will also bring back to this place King Jeconiah son of Jehoiakim of Judah, and all the exiles from Judah who went to Babylon, says the LORD, for I will break the yoke of the king of Babylon."

5 Then the prophet Jeremiah spoke to the prophet Hananiah in the presence of the priests and all the people who were standing in the house of the LORD; ⁶and the prophet Jeremiah said, "Amen! May the LORD do so; may the LORD fulfill the words that you have prophesied, and bring back to this place from Babylon the vessels of the house of the LORD, and all the exiles. ⁷But listen now to this word that I speak in your hearing and in the hearing of all the people. ⁸The prophets who preceded you and me from ancient times prophesied war, famine, and pestilence against many countries and great kingdoms. ⁹As for the prophet who prophesies peace, when the word of that prophet comes true, then it will be known that the LORD has truly sent the prophet."

10 Then the prophet Hananiah took the yoke from the neck of the prophet Jeremiah, and broke it. ¹¹And Hananiah spoke in the presence of all the people, saying, "Thus says the LORD: This is how I will break the yoke of King Nebuchadnezzar of Babylon from the neck of all the nations within two years." At this, the prophet Jeremiah went his way.

12 Sometime after the prophet Hananiah had broken the yoke from the neck of the prophet Jeremiah, the word of the LORD came to Jeremiah: ¹³Go, tell Hananiah, Thus says the LORD: You have broken wooden bars only to forge iron bars in place of them! ¹⁴For thus says the LORD of hosts, the God of Israel: I have put an iron yoke on the neck of all these nations so that they may serve King Nebuchadnezzar of Babylon, and they shall indeed serve him; I have even given him the wild animals. ¹⁵And the prophet Jeremiah said to the prophet Hananiah, "Listen, Hananiah, the LORD has not sent you, and you made this people trust in a lie. ¹⁶There-

fore thus says the LORD: I am going to send you off the face of the earth. Within this year you will be dead, because you have spoken rebellion against the LORD."

17 In that same year, in the seventh month, the prophet Hananiah died.

28.1–17: The conflict of prophetic messages narrows down to a conflict between two prophets of Judah, *Hananiah* and *Jeremiah*. In competing symbolic actions, the two men wear *yokes* to enact and make concrete the prophetic messages. Jeremiah wears a wooden yoke to signify captivity by Babylon. **10:** Hananiah breaks Jeremiah's yoke as an attempt to say the opposite. **12–14:** Jeremiah returns later with an unbreakable *iron yoke.* **17:** Hananiah's death a year later indicates that he was a false prophet preaching his own word, not divine revelation (Deut 18.20).

29 These are the words of the letter that the prophet Jeremiah sent from Jerusalem to the remaining elders among the exiles, and to the priests, the prophets, and all the people, whom Nebuchadnezzar had taken into exile from Jerusalem to Babylon. ²This was after King Jeconiah, and the queen mother, the court officials, the leaders of Judah and Jerusalem, the artisans, and the smiths had departed from Jerusalem. ³The letter was sent by the hand of Elasah son of Shaphan and Gemariah son of Hilkiah, whom King Zedekiah of Judah sent to Babylon to King Nebuchadnezzar of Babylon. It said: ⁴Thus says the LORD of hosts, the God of Israel, to all the exiles whom I have sent into exile from Jerusalem to Babylon: ⁵Build houses and live in them; plant gardens and eat what they produce. ⁶Take wives and have sons and daughters; take wives for your sons, and give your daughters in marriage, that they may bear sons and daughters; multiply there, and do not decrease. ⁷But seek the welfare of the city where I have sent you into exile, and pray to the LORD on its behalf, for in its welfare you will find your welfare. ⁸For thus says the LORD of hosts, the God of Israel: Do not let the prophets and the diviners who are among you deceive you, and do not listen to the dreams that they dream,^a ⁹for

a Cn: Heb *your dreams that you cause to dream*

it is a lie that they are prophesying to you in my name; I did not send them, says the LORD.

10 For thus says the LORD: Only when Babylon's seventy years are completed will I visit you, and I will fulfill to you my promise and bring you back to this place. [11] For surely I know the plans I have for you, says the LORD, plans for your welfare and not for harm, to give you a future with hope. [12] Then when you call upon me and come and pray to me, I will hear you. [13] When you search for me, you will find me; if you seek me with all your heart, [14] I will let you find me, says the LORD, and I will restore your fortunes and gather you from all the nations and all the places where I have driven you, says the LORD, and I will bring you back to the place from which I sent you into exile.

15 Because you have said, "The LORD has raised up prophets for us in Babylon,"— [16] Thus says the LORD concerning the king who sits on the throne of David, and concerning all the people who live in this city, your kinsfolk who did not go out with you into exile: [17] Thus says the LORD of hosts, I am going to let loose on them sword, famine, and pestilence, and I will make them like rotten figs that are so bad they cannot be eaten. [18] I will pursue them with the sword, with famine, and with pestilence, and will make them a horror to all the kingdoms of the earth, to be an object of cursing, and horror, and hissing, and a derision among all the nations where I have driven them, [19] because they did not heed my words, says the LORD, when I persistently sent to you my servants the prophets, but they[a] would not listen, says the LORD. [20] But now, all you exiles whom I sent away from Jerusalem to Babylon, hear the word of the LORD: [21] Thus says the LORD of hosts, the God of Israel, concerning Ahab son of Kolaiah and Zedekiah son of Maaseiah, who are prophesying a lie to you in my name: I am going to deliver them into the hand of King Nebuchadrezzar of Babylon, and he shall kill them before your eyes. [22] And on account of them this curse shall be used by all the exiles from Judah in Babylon: "The LORD make you like Zedekiah and Ahab, whom the king of Babylon roasted in the fire," [23] because they have perpetrated outrage in Israel and have committed adultery with their neighbors' wives, and have spoken in my name lying words that I did not command them; I am the one who knows and bears witness, says the LORD.

24 To Shemaiah of Nehelam you shall say: [25] Thus says the LORD of hosts, the God of Israel: In your own name you sent a letter to all the people who are in Jerusalem, and to the priest Zephaniah son of Maaseiah, and to all the priests, saying, [26] The LORD himself has made you priest instead of the priest Jehoiada, so that there may be officers in the house of the LORD to control any madman who plays the prophet, to put him in the stocks and the collar. [27] So now why have you not rebuked Jeremiah of Anathoth who plays the prophet for you? [28] For he has actually sent to us in Babylon, saying, "It will be a long time; build houses and live in them, and plant gardens and eat what they produce."

29 The priest Zephaniah read this letter in the hearing of the prophet Jeremiah. [30] Then the word of the LORD came to Jeremiah: [31] Send to all the exiles, saying, Thus says the LORD concerning Shemaiah of Nehelam: Because Shemaiah has prophesied to you, though I did not send him, and has led you to trust in a lie, [32] therefore thus says the LORD: I am going to punish Shemaiah of Nehelam and his descendants; he shall not have anyone living among this people to see[b] the good that I am going to do to my people, says the LORD, for he has spoken rebellion against the LORD.

29.1–32: Letters. From Jerusalem, Jeremiah writes letters to the exiles and responds to a letter about him. The letters to the exiles present Jeremiah as the authority about the exiles' survival. **3:** Supporters of Jeremiah serve as couriers. The exiles are not to resist Babylonian rule, but to live there in normal domestic relations and to seek the welfare of the city where they are held captive. **10:** After 70 years, probably symbolizing a long time, their relationship with God will be

a Syr: Heb *you*   b Gk: Heb *and he shall not see*

restored, and they will return to their land. **21–23:** Two false prophets among the exiles, *Ahab* and *Zedekiah,* will die like Hananiah under the deuteronomistic* curse (Deut 18.20). **24–32:** *Shemaiah,* one of the exiles, writes to the high priest in Jerusalem that he should silence Jeremiah. Jeremiah curses him as a false prophet, one like Hananiah.

Little book of consolation

Chs. 30–33: These chapters combine poetry (chs. 30–31) and prose (chs. 32–33) to depict a harmonious, idealized future for Israel and Judah. The placement of these chapters of hope and healing toward the center of the book is puzzling. Stories and poems of accusation and conflict surround them as if to temper the hope the chapters create. This structure may reflect the situation of the exilic audience, for whom escape from captivity remains a distant possibility. The chapters create a vision of what lies ahead, but they do not present a program for escape. Instead, they create unimagined possibilities that may help the community to endure for a new day.

Chs. 30–31: Restoration. The poems create a vision of a future nation in which northern and southern kingdoms are restored and reunited in Jerusalem. Some of the poems collected address male Jacob/Israel. Jacob is a name used for the northern kingdom of Israel, and also the name of the ancestor of all the twelve tribes (Gen 29–30). Other poems address female figures representing Judah and Zion,* or Rachel, one of Jacob's wives and mother of a northern and southern tribe. These names bring together both northern and southern kingdoms.

30 The word that came to Jeremiah from the LORD: ²Thus says the LORD, the God of Israel: Write in a book all the words that I have spoken to you. ³For the days are surely coming, says the LORD, when I will restore the fortunes of my people, Israel and Judah, says the LORD, and I will bring them back to the land that I gave to their ancestors and they shall take possession of it.

4 These are the words that the LORD spoke concerning Israel and Judah:

⁵ Thus says the LORD:
  We have heard a cry of panic,
    of terror, and no peace.
⁶ Ask now, and see,
    can a man bear a child?

Why then do I see every man
    with his hands on his loins like a
      woman in labor?
  Why has every face turned pale?
⁷ Alas! that day is so great
    there is none like it;
  it is a time of distress for Jacob;
    yet he shall be rescued from it.

8 On that day, says the LORD of hosts, I will break the yoke from off his*a* neck, and I will burst his*a* bonds, and strangers shall no more make a servant of him. ⁹But they shall serve the LORD their God and David their king, whom I will raise up for them.

¹⁰ But as for you, have no fear, my servant
      Jacob, says the LORD,
    and do not be dismayed, O Israel;
  for I am going to save you from
      far away,
    and your offspring from the land of
      their captivity.
  Jacob shall return and have quiet and
      ease,
    and no one shall make him afraid.
¹¹ For I am with you, says the LORD, to
      save you;
  I will make an end of all the nations
      among which I scattered you,
    but of you I will not make an end.
  I will chastise you in just measure,
    and I will by no means leave you
      unpunished.

30.1–11. 2: God's command that Jeremiah write these words in *a book* makes it possible for Jeremiah to communicate with the exiles even though he is not with them. **5–7:** Images of panic and pain describe the *distress for Jacob.* **8–11:** Without explanation, hope replaces terror. God will remove the yoke of servitude from them, restore relationship with them, and raise up a king for them.

¹² For thus says the LORD:
  Your hurt is incurable,
    your wound is grievous.
¹³ There is no one to uphold your cause,
    no medicine for your wound,
    no healing for you.

a Cn: Heb *your*

14 All your lovers have forgotten you;
   they care nothing for you;
for I have dealt you the blow of
   an enemy,
   the punishment of a merciless foe,
because your guilt is great,
   because your sins are so numerous.
15 Why do you cry out over your hurt?
   Your pain is incurable.
Because your guilt is great,
   because your sins are so numerous,
   I have done these things to you.
16 Therefore all who devour you shall be
   devoured,
   and all your foes, everyone of them,
      shall go into captivity;
those who plunder you shall be
   plundered,
   and all who prey on you I will make a
      prey.
17 For I will restore health to you,
   and your wounds I will heal,
                        says the LORD,
because they have called you an outcast:
   "It is Zion; no one cares for her!"

30.12–17: In a poetic movement similar to vv. 5–11, this poem also moves unexpectedly from desperation to salvation, but the images shift from panic to wound-edness and healing. The one addressed is daughter Zion, God's unfaithful wife (2.1–3.25). God now pities her in her abandonment.

18 Thus says the LORD:
   I am going to restore the fortunes of the
      tents of Jacob,
   and have compassion on his
      dwellings;
the city shall be rebuilt upon its mound,
   and the citadel set on its rightful site.
19 Out of them shall come thanksgiving,
   and the sound of merrymakers.
I will make them many, and they shall
   not be few;
   I will make them honored, and they
      shall not be disdained.
20 Their children shall be as of old,
   their congregation shall be
      established before me;
   and I will punish all who oppress
      them.

21 Their prince shall be one of their own,
   their ruler shall come from their
      midst;
I will bring him near, and he shall
   approach me,
   for who would otherwise dare to
      approach me?
                        says the LORD.
22 And you shall be my people,
   and I will be your God.

23 Look, the storm of the LORD!
   Wrath has gone forth,
a whirling*a* tempest;
   it will burst upon the head of
      the wicked.
24 The fierce anger of the LORD will not
      turn back
   until he has executed and
      accomplished
   the intents of his mind.
In the latter days you will understand
      this.

30.18–24. 18–22: God speaks to Jacob and refers also to Jerusalem, the city that will be rebuilt. Both northern and southern kingdoms are reunited in a poetic out-burst concerning thanksgiving and new life. **23–24:** The national tragedy receives a summary interpretation. Divine *wrath* will one day end, and the audience will understand it in the future.

31 At that time, says the LORD, I will be the God of all the families of Israel, and they shall be my people.
2 Thus says the LORD:
   The people who survived the sword
      found grace in the wilderness;
   when Israel sought for rest,
3   the LORD appeared to him*b* from far
         away.*c*
   I have loved you with an everlasting
      love;
   therefore I have continued my
      faithfulness to you.
4 Again I will build you, and you shall be
      built,
   O virgin Israel!

a One Ms: Meaning of MT uncertain   *b* Gk: Heb *me*
c Or *to him long ago*

Again you shall take[a] your tambourines,
and go forth in the dance of the
merrymakers.
5 Again you shall plant vineyards
on the mountains of Samaria;
the planters shall plant,
and shall enjoy the fruit.
6 For there shall be a day when sentinels
will call
in the hill country of Ephraim:
"Come, let us go up to Zion,
to the LORD our God."

7 For thus says the LORD:
Sing aloud with gladness for Jacob,
and raise shouts for the chief of the
nations;
proclaim, give praise, and say,
"Save, O LORD, your people,
the remnant of Israel."
8 See, I am going to bring them from the
land of the north,
and gather them from the farthest
parts of the earth,
among them the blind and the lame,
those with child and those in labor,
together;
a great company, they shall return
here.
9 With weeping they shall come,
and with consolations[b] I will lead
them back,
I will let them walk by brooks
of water,
in a straight path in which they shall
not stumble;
for I have become a father to Israel,
and Ephraim is my firstborn.

10 Hear the word of the LORD, O nations,
and declare it in the coastlands far
away;
say, "He who scattered Israel will
gather him,
and will keep him as a shepherd a
flock."
11 For the LORD has ransomed Jacob,
and has redeemed him from hands
too strong for him.
12 They shall come and sing aloud on the
height of Zion,

and they shall be radiant over the
goodness of the LORD,
over the grain, the wine, and the oil,
and over the young of the flock and
the herd;
their life shall become like a watered
garden,
and they shall never languish again.
13 Then shall the young women rejoice in
the dance,
and the young men and the old shall
be merry.
I will turn their mourning into joy,
I will comfort them, and give them
gladness for sorrow.
14 I will give the priests their fill of fatness,
and my people shall be satisfied with
my bounty,
says the LORD.

31.1–14: Return. All Israel, both north and south, will
be reunited. **3–4:** Survivors will return, covenant* will
be restored, and God will take back wife Israel, now
called a *virgin*, no longer a harlot. She will be like Miriam, leading the dance (Ex 15.20–21). **9:** Echoing the
children's return (3.22–25), God takes them back and
promises to be *a father* to them. **10–14:** Everyone in
the society will participate in life that will be fertile and
joyous on Zion.*

---

15 Thus says the LORD:
A voice is heard in Ramah,
lamentation and bitter weeping.
Rachel is weeping for her children;
she refuses to be comforted for her
children,
because they are no more.
16 Thus says the LORD:
Keep your voice from weeping,
and your eyes from tears;
for there is a reward for your work,
says the LORD:
they shall come back from the land of
the enemy;
17 there is hope for your future,
says the LORD:
your children shall come back to their
own country.

a Or *adorn yourself with*   b Gk Compare Vg Tg: Heb
supplications

18 Indeed I heard Ephraim pleading:
"You disciplined me, and I took the
discipline;
I was like a calf untrained.
Bring me back, let me come back,
for you are the LORD my God.
19 For after I had turned away I repented;
and after I was discovered, I struck
my thigh;
I was ashamed, and I was dismayed
because I bore the disgrace of my
youth."
20 Is Ephraim my dear son?
Is he the child I delight in?
As often as I speak against him,
I still remember him.
Therefore I am deeply moved for him;
I will surely have mercy on him,
says the LORD.

21 Set up road markers for yourself,
make yourself guideposts;
consider well the highway,
the road by which you went.
Return, O virgin Israel,
return to these your cities.
22 How long will you waver,
O faithless daughter?
For the LORD has created a new thing
on the earth:
a woman encompasses[a] a man.

23 Thus says the LORD of hosts, the God
of Israel: Once more they shall use these
words in the land of Judah and in its towns
when I restore their fortunes:
"The LORD bless you, O abode of
righteousness,
O holy hill!"
24 And Judah and all its towns shall live there
together, and the farmers and those who
wander[b] with their flocks.
25 I will satisfy the weary,
and all who are faint I will replenish.
26 Thereupon I awoke and looked, and
my sleep was pleasant to me.
27 The days are surely coming, says the
LORD, when I will sow the house of Israel
and the house of Judah with the seed of humans and the seed of animals. 28 And just as
I have watched over them to pluck up and

break down, to overthrow, destroy, and bring
evil, so I will watch over them to build and
to plant, says the LORD. 29 In those days they
shall no longer say:
"The parents have eaten sour grapes,
and the children's teeth are set on
edge."
30 But all shall die for their own sins; the
teeth of everyone who eats sour grapes shall
be set on edge.

31.15–30: Rachel's comfort. Rachel (Gen 27–35),
perhaps symbolizing God's first wife (3.7–11), weeps
for her lost children and receives the breathtaking
news that they will return. **18–20:** Her son, actually her
grandson, repents like the children (3.22–25), and
God receives him back. **21–22:** God addresses wife Israel and asks how long it will be before she repents.
The poem ends with a puzzling claim that God has
done a new thing: *A woman encompasses a man*, perhaps an image of Rachel embracing her returning
child. **23–26:** The woman may be Jerusalem encompassing the people returning from exile. **27–28:** Perhaps wife Rachel encompasses a man sexually to give
birth to a new generation.

31 The days are surely coming, says the
LORD, when I will make a new covenant with
the house of Israel and the house of Judah.
32 It will not be like the covenant that I made
with their ancestors when I took them by the
hand to bring them out of the land of
Egypt—a covenant that they broke, though
I was their husband,[c] says the LORD. 33 But
this is the covenant that I will make with the
house of Israel after those days, says the
LORD: I will put my law within them, and I
will write it on their hearts; and I will be their
God, and they shall be my people. 34 No
longer shall they teach one another, or say
to each other, "Know the LORD," for they
shall all know me, from the least of them to
the greatest, says the LORD; for I will forgive
their iniquity, and remember their sin no
more.

35 Thus says the LORD,
who gives the sun for light by day

a Meaning of Heb uncertain   *b* Cn Compare Syr Vg
Tg: Heb *and they shall wander*   *c* Or *master*

and the fixed order of the moon and
the stars for light by night,
who stirs up the sea so that its waves
roar—
the LORD of hosts is his name:
36 If this fixed order were ever to cease
from my presence, says the LORD,
then also the offspring of Israel would
cease
to be a nation before me forever.

37 Thus says the LORD:
If the heavens above can be measured,
and the foundations of the earth
below can be explored,
then I will reject all the offspring
of Israel
because of all they have done,
says the LORD.

38 The days are surely coming, says the
LORD, when the city shall be rebuilt for the
LORD from the tower of Hananel to the Corner Gate. 39 And the measuring line shall go
out farther, straight to the hill Gareb, and
shall then turn to Goah. 40 The whole valley
of the dead bodies and the ashes, and all the
fields as far as the Wadi Kidron, to the corner of the Horse Gate toward the east, shall
be sacred to the LORD. It shall never again
be uprooted or overthrown.

31.31–40: New covenant.* The poems about the
restored family are followed by a brief but potent
claim that there will be a new way of relating within
the covenant family. God will make a new covenant
with them. God and Israel will live in renewed fidelity.
34: Everyone *from the least to the greatest* will know
God. 35–40: The cosmos itself and the fixed order of
creation will be a sign of that fidelity, and Jerusalem
will be *rebuilt* and never *overthrown.*

A changed future
Chs. 32–33: In these two narrative chapters, Jeremiah
buys a field and offers prayers that signify a hopeful
future for the exiles. Jeremiah purchases a field during
an imprisonment that occurs while Babylon is invading
Jerusalem. During an invasion, land is worthless.
Helped by his companion Baruch (v. 12), Jeremiah redeems the land of his cousin as expected by law. The
foolishness of that purchase stands as a promise that
life will resume in the land. Jeremiah, captive like the
exilic audience, is a model of obedient hopefulness in
the face of tragedy.

32 The word that came to Jeremiah
from the LORD in the tenth year of
King Zedekiah of Judah, which was the eighteenth year of Nebuchadrezzar. 2 At that time
the army of the king of Babylon was besieging Jerusalem, and the prophet Jeremiah was
confined in the court of the guard that was
in the palace of the king of Judah, 3 where
King Zedekiah of Judah had confined him.
Zedekiah had said, "Why do you prophesy
and say: Thus says the LORD: I am going to
give this city into the hand of the king of
Babylon, and he shall take it; 4 King Zedekiah
of Judah shall not escape out of the hands of
the Chaldeans, but shall surely be given into
the hands of the king of Babylon, and shall
speak with him face to face and see him eye
to eye; 5 and he shall take Zedekiah to Babylon, and there he shall remain until I attend
to him, says the LORD; though you fight
against the Chaldeans, you shall not succeed?"

6 Jeremiah said, The word of the LORD
came to me: 7 Hanamel son of your uncle
Shallum is going to come to you and say,
"Buy my field that is at Anathoth, for the
right of redemption by purchase is yours."
8 Then my cousin Hanamel came to me in
the court of the guard, in accordance with
the word of the LORD, and said to me, "Buy
my field that is at Anathoth in the land of
Benjamin, for the right of possession and redemption is yours; buy it for yourself." Then
I knew that this was the word of the LORD.

9 And I bought the field at Anathoth from
my cousin Hanamel, and weighed out the
money to him, seventeen shekels of silver.
10 I signed the deed, sealed it, got witnesses,
and weighed the money on scales. 11 Then I
took the sealed deed of purchase, containing
the terms and conditions, and the open copy;
12 and I gave the deed of purchase to Baruch
son of Neriah son of Mahseiah, in the presence of my cousin Hanamel, in the presence
of the witnesses who signed the deed of purchase, and in the presence of all the Judeans
who were sitting in the court of the guard.

13In their presence I charged Baruch, saying, 14Thus says the LORD of hosts, the God of Israel: Take these deeds, both this sealed deed of purchase and this open deed, and put them in an earthenware jar, in order that they may last for a long time. 15For thus says the LORD of hosts, the God of Israel: Houses and fields and vineyards shall again be bought in this land.

16 After I had given the deed of purchase to Baruch son of Neriah, I prayed to the LORD, saying: 17Ah Lord GOD! It is you who made the heavens and the earth by your great power and by your outstretched arm! Nothing is too hard for you. 18You show steadfast love to the thousandth generation,*a* but repay the guilt of parents into the laps of their children after them, O great and mighty God whose name is the LORD of hosts, 19great in counsel and mighty in deed; whose eyes are open to all the ways of mortals, rewarding all according to their ways and according to the fruit of their doings. 20You showed signs and wonders in the land of Egypt, and to this day in Israel and among all humankind, and have made yourself a name that continues to this very day. 21You brought your people Israel out of the land of Egypt with signs and wonders, with a strong hand and outstretched arm, and with great terror; 22and you gave them this land, which you swore to their ancestors to give them, a land flowing with milk and honey; 23and they entered and took possession of it. But they did not obey your voice or follow your law; of all you commanded them to do, they did nothing. Therefore you have made all these disasters come upon them. 24See, the siege ramps have been cast up against the city to take it, and the city, faced with sword, famine, and pestilence, has been given into the hands of the Chaldeans who are fighting against it. What you spoke has happened, as you yourself can see. 25Yet you, O Lord GOD, have said to me, "Buy the field for money and get witnesses"—though the city has been given into the hands of the Chaldeans.

26 The word of the LORD came to Jeremiah: 27See, I am the LORD, the God of all flesh; is anything too hard for me? 28Therefore, thus says the LORD: I am going to give this city into the hands of the Chaldeans and into the hand of King Nebuchadrezzar of Babylon, and he shall take it. 29The Chaldeans who are fighting against this city shall come, set it on fire, and burn it, with the houses on whose roofs offerings have been made to Baal and libations have been poured out to other gods, to provoke me to anger. 30For the people of Israel and the people of Judah have done nothing but evil in my sight from their youth; the people of Israel have done nothing but provoke me to anger by the work of their hands, says the LORD. 31This city has aroused my anger and wrath, from the day it was built until this day, so that I will remove it from my sight 32because of all the evil of the people of Israel and the people of Judah that they did to provoke me to anger—they, their kings and their officials, their priests and their prophets, the citizens of Judah and the inhabitants of Jerusalem. 33They have turned their backs to me, not their faces; though I have taught them persistently, they would not listen and accept correction. 34They set up their abominations in the house that bears my name, and defiled it. 35They built the high places of Baal in the valley of the son of Hinnom, to offer up their sons and daughters to Molech, though I did not command them, nor did it enter my mind that they should do this abomination, causing Judah to sin.

36 Now therefore thus says the LORD, the God of Israel, concerning this city of which you say, "It is being given into the hand of the king of Babylon by the sword, by famine, and by pestilence": 37See, I am going to gather them from all the lands to which I drove them in my anger and my wrath and in great indignation; I will bring them back to this place, and I will settle them in safety. 38They shall be my people, and I will be their God. 39I will give them one heart and one way, that they may fear me for all time, for their own good and the good of their children after them. 40I will make an everlasting covenant with them, never to draw back from

a Or to thousands

doing good to them; and I will put the fear of me in their hearts, so that they may not turn from me. ⁴¹I will rejoice in doing good to them, and I will plant them in this land in faithfulness, with all my heart and all my soul.

42 For thus says the LORD: Just as I have brought all this great disaster upon this people, so I will bring upon them all the good fortune that I now promise them. ⁴³Fields shall be bought in this land of which you are saying, It is a desolation, without human beings or animals; it has been given into the hands of the Chaldeans. ⁴⁴Fields shall be bought for money, and deeds shall be signed and sealed and witnessed, in the land of Benjamin, in the places around Jerusalem, and in the cities of Judah, of the hill country, of the Shephelah, and of the Negeb; for I will restore their fortunes, says the LORD.

32.1–44. 16–25: Jeremiah's prayer elaborates on the theme of hopefulness, asking God to see the invasion as it occurs. **26–42:** God replies to Jeremiah that there is a future. **38:** The covenant* will be renewed. **42:** The one who brought the disaster will bring a new future.

33 The word of the LORD came to Jeremiah a second time, while he was still confined in the court of the guard: ²Thus says the LORD who made the earth,ᵃ the LORD who formed it to establish it—the LORD is his name: ³Call to me and I will answer you, and will tell you great and hidden things that you have not known. ⁴For thus says the LORD, the God of Israel, concerning the houses of this city and the houses of the kings of Judah that were torn down to make a defense against the siege ramps and before the sword:ᵇ ⁵The Chaldeans are coming in to fightᶜ and to fill them with the dead bodies of those whom I shall strike down in my anger and my wrath, for I have hidden my face from this city because of all their wickedness. ⁶I am going to bring it recovery and healing; I will heal them and reveal to them abundanceᵇ of prosperity and security. ⁷I will restore the fortunes of Judah and the fortunes of Israel, and rebuild them as they were at first. ⁸I will cleanse them

from all the guilt of their sin against me, and I will forgive all the guilt of their sin and rebellion against me. ⁹And this cityᵈ shall be to me a name of joy, a praise and a glory before all the nations of the earth who shall hear of all the good that I do for them; they shall fear and tremble because of all the good and all the prosperity I provide for it.

10 Thus says the LORD: In this place of which you say, "It is a waste without human beings or animals," in the towns of Judah and the streets of Jerusalem that are desolate, without inhabitants, human or animal, there shall once more be heard ¹¹the voice of mirth and the voice of gladness, the voice of the bridegroom and the voice of the bride, the voices of those who sing, as they bring thank offerings to the house of the LORD:

"Give thanks to the LORD of hosts,
  for the LORD is good,
  for his steadfast love endures
    forever!"

For I will restore the fortunes of the land as at first, says the LORD.

12 Thus says the LORD of hosts: In this place that is waste, without human beings or animals, and in all its towns there shall again be pasture for shepherds resting their flocks. ¹³In the towns of the hill country, of the Shephelah, and of the Negeb, in the land of Benjamin, the places around Jerusalem, and in the towns of Judah, flocks shall again pass under the hands of the one who counts them, says the LORD.

14 The days are surely coming, says the LORD, when I will fulfill the promise I made to the house of Israel and the house of Judah. ¹⁵In those days and at that time I will cause a righteous Branch to spring up for David; and he shall execute justice and righteousness in the land. ¹⁶In those days Judah will be saved and Jerusalem will live in safety. And this is the name by which it will be called: "The LORD is our righteousness."

17 For thus says the LORD: David shall never lack a man to sit on the throne of the house of Israel, ¹⁸and the levitical priests

---

a Gk: Heb *it*   *b* Meaning of Heb uncertain
c Cn: Heb *They are coming in to fight against the Chaldeans*   *d* Heb *And it*

shall never lack a man in my presence to offer burnt offerings, to make grain offerings, and to make sacrifices for all time.

19 The word of the LORD came to Jeremiah: 20Thus says the LORD: If any of you could break my covenant with the day and my covenant with the night, so that day and night would not come at their appointed time, 21only then could my covenant with my servant David be broken, so that he would not have a son to reign on his throne, and my covenant with my ministers the Levites. 22Just as the host of heaven cannot be numbered and the sands of the sea cannot be measured, so I will increase the offspring of my servant David, and the Levites who minister to me.

23 The word of the LORD came to Jeremiah: 24Have you not observed how these people say, "The two families that the LORD chose have been rejected by him," and how they hold my people in such contempt that they no longer regard them as a nation? 25Thus says the LORD: Only if I had not established my covenant with day and night and the ordinances of heaven and earth, 26would I reject the offspring of Jacob and of my servant David and not choose any of his descendants as rulers over the offspring of Abraham, Isaac, and Jacob. For I will restore their fortunes, and will have mercy upon them.

33.1–26: Restoration. The restored relationship between God and the people is illustrated here. **3:** God invites Jeremiah to make requests. **6:** God assures the people of *healing* and *prosperity*. **14–16:** God promises to restore the kingship and the priesthood and to reunite the peoples of Israel and Judah.

A good king and a bad community
Chs. 34–35: These two chapters contrast the failure of the king and people to obey God's word (ch. 34) with the exemplary fidelity of a small group of people called Rechabites (ch. 35). The former group faces the dire consequences of infidelity, and the latter group gains a future because of fidelity. Both stories are set during the Babylonian invasion, but the behavior they describe concerns consequences in the exilic present.

34 The word that came to Jeremiah from the LORD, when King Nebuchadrezzar of Babylon and all his army and all the kingdoms of the earth and all the peoples under his dominion were fighting against Jerusalem and all its cities: 2Thus says the LORD, the God of Israel: Go and speak to King Zedekiah of Judah and say to him: Thus says the LORD: I am going to give this city into the hand of the king of Babylon, and he shall burn it with fire. 3And you yourself shall not escape from his hand, but shall surely be captured and handed over to him; you shall see the king of Babylon eye to eye and speak with him face to face; and you shall go to Babylon. 4Yet hear the word of the LORD, O King Zedekiah of Judah! Thus says the LORD concerning you: You shall not die by the sword; 5you shall die in peace. And as spices were burned*a* for your ancestors, the earlier kings who preceded you, so they shall burn spices*b* for you and lament for you, saying, "Alas, lord!" For I have spoken the word, says the LORD.

6 Then the prophet Jeremiah spoke all these words to Zedekiah king of Judah, in Jerusalem, 7when the army of the king of Babylon was fighting against Jerusalem and against all the cities of Judah that were left, Lachish and Azekah; for these were the only fortified cities of Judah that remained.

8 The word that came to Jeremiah from the LORD, after King Zedekiah had made a covenant with all the people in Jerusalem to make a proclamation of liberty to them— 9that all should set free their Hebrew slaves, male and female, so that no one should hold another Judean in slavery. 10And they obeyed, all the officials and all the people who had entered into the covenant that all would set free their slaves, male or female, so that they would not be enslaved again; they obeyed and set them free. 11But afterward they turned around and took back the male and female slaves they had set free, and brought them again into subjection as slaves. 12The word of the LORD came to Jeremiah from the LORD: 13Thus says the LORD, the God of Israel: I myself made a covenant with

a Heb *as there was burning*   *b* Heb *shall burn*

your ancestors when I brought them out of the land of Egypt, out of the house of slavery, saying, ¹⁴"Every seventh year each of you must set free any Hebrews who have been sold to you and have served you six years; you must set them free from your service." But your ancestors did not listen to me or incline their ears to me. ¹⁵You yourselves recently repented and did what was right in my sight by proclaiming liberty to one another, and you made a covenant before me in the house that is called by my name; ¹⁶but then you turned around and profaned my name when each of you took back your male and female slaves, whom you had set free according to their desire, and you brought them again into subjection to be your slaves. ¹⁷Therefore, thus says the LORD: You have not obeyed me by granting a release to your neighbors and friends; I am going to grant a release to you, says the LORD—a release to the sword, to pestilence, and to famine. I will make you a horror to all the kingdoms of the earth. ¹⁸And those who transgressed my covenant and did not keep the terms of the covenant that they made before me, I will make like*a* the calf when they cut it in two and passed between its parts: ¹⁹the officials of Judah, the officials of Jerusalem, the eunuchs, the priests, and all the people of the land who passed between the parts of the calf ²⁰shall be handed over to their enemies and to those who seek their lives. Their corpses shall become food for the birds of the air and the wild animals of the earth. ²¹And as for King Zedekiah of Judah and his officials, I will hand them over to their enemies and to those who seek their lives, to the army of the king of Babylon, which has withdrawn from you. ²²I am going to command, says the LORD, and will bring them back to this city; and they will fight against it, and take it, and burn it with fire. The towns of Judah I will make a desolation without inhabitant.

34.1–22: Jerusalem is under attack. **6–7:** Only the fortress cities of *Lachish* and *Azekah* have not fallen to the Babylonians. The times are dire. **8–10:** Zedekiah proclaims the freedom of Judean slaves, according to the law and God's command (Deut 15.12–14). At first all

the people followed, but then they changed their minds, so they will go into slavery. **18–20:** They will be cut up like a sacrificial animal in a covenant* offering.

~~~~~~~~~~~

35 The word that came to Jeremiah from the LORD in the days of King Jehoiakim son of Josiah of Judah: ²Go to the house of the Rechabites, and speak with them, and bring them to the house of the LORD, into one of the chambers; then offer them wine to drink. ³So I took Jaazaniah son of Jeremiah son of Habazziniah, and his brothers, and all his sons, and the whole house of the Rechabites. ⁴I brought them to the house of the LORD into the chamber of the sons of Hanan son of Igdaliah, the man of God, which was near the chamber of the officials, above the chamber of Maaseiah son of Shallum, keeper of the threshold. ⁵Then I set before the Rechabites pitchers full of wine, and cups; and I said to them, "Have some wine." ⁶But they answered, "We will drink no wine, for our ancestor Jonadab son of Rechab commanded us, 'You shall never drink wine, neither you nor your children; ⁷nor shall you ever build a house, or sow seed; nor shall you plant a vineyard, or even own one; but you shall live in tents all your days, that you may live many days in the land where you reside.' ⁸We have obeyed the charge of our ancestor Jonadab son of Rechab in all that he commanded us, to drink no wine all our days, ourselves, our wives, our sons, or our daughters, ⁹and not to build houses to live in. We have no vineyard or field or seed; ¹⁰but we have lived in tents, and have obeyed and done all that our ancestor Jonadab commanded us. ¹¹But when King Nebuchadrezzar of Babylon came up against the land, we said, 'Come, and let us go to Jerusalem for fear of the army of the Chaldeans and the army of the Arameans.' That is why we are living in Jerusalem."

12 Then the word of the LORD came to Jeremiah: ¹³Thus says the LORD of hosts, the God of Israel: Go and say to the people of Judah and the inhabitants of Jerusalem, Can you not learn a lesson and obey my words?

a Cn: Heb lacks *like*

says the LORD. ¹⁴The command has been carried out that Jonadab son of Rechab gave to his descendants to drink no wine; and they drink none to this day, for they have obeyed their ancestor's command. But I myself have spoken to you persistently, and you have not obeyed me. ¹⁵I have sent to you all my servants the prophets, sending them persistently, saying, "Turn now everyone of you from your evil way, and amend your doings, and do not go after other gods to serve them, and then you shall live in the land that I gave to you and your ancestors." But you did not incline your ear or obey me. ¹⁶The descendants of Jonadab son of Rechab have carried out the command that their ancestor gave them, but this people has not obeyed me. ¹⁷Therefore, thus says the LORD, the God of hosts, the God of Israel: I am going to bring on Judah and on all the inhabitants of Jerusalem every disaster that I have pronounced against them; because I have spoken to them and they have not listened, I have called to them and they have not answered.

18 But to the house of the Rechabites Jeremiah said: Thus says the LORD of hosts, the God of Israel: Because you have obeyed the command of your ancestor Jonadab, and kept all his precepts, and done all that he commanded you, ¹⁹therefore thus says the LORD of hosts, the God of Israel: Jonadab son of Rechab shall not lack a descendant to stand before me for all time.

35.1–19: The *Rechabites,* by contrast, are faithful to their traditions. Little is certain about the identity of the Rechabites. 8–10: They refrained from drinking wine and owning houses or land in the tradition of their ancestor, *Jonadab son of Rechab.* They exemplify true obedience, as shown in 2 Kings 10.15–27, where Jonadab assists King Jehu in purging Baal worship from the land.

36 In the fourth year of King Jehoiakim son of Josiah of Judah, this word came to Jeremiah from the LORD: ²Take a scroll and write on it all the words that I have spoken to you against Israel and Judah and all the nations, from the day I spoke to you, from the days of Josiah until today. ³It may be that when the house of Judah hears of all the disasters that I intend to do to them, all of them may turn from their evil ways, so that I may forgive their iniquity and their sin.

4 Then Jeremiah called Baruch son of Neriah, and Baruch wrote on a scroll at Jeremiah's dictation all the words of the LORD that he had spoken to him. ⁵And Jeremiah ordered Baruch, saying, "I am prevented from entering the house of the LORD; ⁶so you go yourself, and on a fast day in the hearing of the people in the LORD's house you shall read the words of the LORD from the scroll that you have written at my dictation. You shall read them also in the hearing of all the people of Judah who come up from their towns. ⁷It may be that their plea will come before the LORD, and that all of them will turn from their evil ways, for great is the anger and wrath that the LORD has pronounced against this people." ⁸And Baruch son of Neriah did all that the prophet Jeremiah ordered him about reading from the scroll the words of the LORD in the LORD's house.

9 In the fifth year of King Jehoiakim son of Josiah of Judah, in the ninth month, all the people in Jerusalem and all the people who came from the towns of Judah to Jerusalem proclaimed a fast before the LORD. ¹⁰Then, in the hearing of all the people, Baruch read the words of Jeremiah from the scroll, in the house of the LORD, in the chamber of Gemariah son of Shaphan the secretary, which was in the upper court, at the entry of the New Gate of the LORD's house.

11 When Micaiah son of Gemariah son of Shaphan heard all the words of the LORD from the scroll, ¹²he went down to the king's house, into the secretary's chamber; and all the officials were sitting there: Elishama the secretary, Delaiah son of Shemaiah, Elnathan son of Achbor, Gemariah son of Shaphan, Zedekiah son of Hananiah, and all the officials. ¹³And Micaiah told them all the words that he had heard, when Baruch read the scroll in the hearing of the people. ¹⁴Then all the officials sent Jehudi son of Nethaniah son of Shelemiah son of Cushi to say to Baruch, "Bring the scroll that you read in the hearing of the people, and come." So Baruch son of Neriah took the scroll in his

hand and came to them. 15And they said to him, "Sit down and read it to us." So Baruch read it to them. 16When they heard all the words, they turned to one another in alarm, and said to Baruch, "We certainly must report all these words to the king." 17Then they questioned Baruch, "Tell us now, how did you write all these words? Was it at his dictation?" 18Baruch answered them, "He dictated all these words to me, and I wrote them with ink on the scroll." 19Then the officials said to Baruch, "Go and hide, you and Jeremiah, and let no one know where you are."

20 Leaving the scroll in the chamber of Elishama the secretary, they went to the court of the king; and they reported all the words to the king. 21Then the king sent Jehudi to get the scroll, and he took it from the chamber of Elishama the secretary; and Jehudi read it to the king and all the officials who stood beside the king. 22Now the king was sitting in his winter apartment (it was the ninth month), and there was a fire burning in the brazier before him. 23As Jehudi read three or four columns, the king*a* would cut them off with a penknife and throw them into the fire in the brazier, until the entire scroll was consumed in the fire that was in the brazier. 24Yet neither the king, nor any of his servants who heard all these words, was alarmed, nor did they tear their garments. 25Even when Elnathan and Delaiah and Gemariah urged the king not to burn the scroll, he would not listen to them. 26And the king commanded Jerahmeel the king's son and Seraiah son of Azriel and Shelemiah son of Abdeel to arrest the secretary Baruch and the prophet Jeremiah. But the LORD hid them.

27 Now, after the king had burned the scroll with the words that Baruch wrote at Jeremiah's dictation, the word of the LORD came to Jeremiah: 28Take another scroll and write on it all the former words that were in the first scroll, which King Jehoiakim of Judah has burned. 29And concerning King Jehoiakim of Judah you shall say: Thus says the LORD, You have dared to burn this scroll, saying, Why have you written in it that the king of Babylon will certainly come and destroy this land, and will cut off from it hu-

man beings and animals? 30Therefore thus says the LORD concerning King Jehoiakim of Judah: He shall have no one to sit upon the throne of David, and his dead body shall be cast out to the heat by day and the frost by night. 31And I will punish him and his offspring and his servants for their iniquity; I will bring on them, and on the inhabitants of Jerusalem, and on the people of Judah, all the disasters with which I have threatened them—but they would not listen.

32 Then Jeremiah took another scroll and gave it to the secretary Baruch son of Neriah, who wrote on it at Jeremiah's dictation all the words of the scroll that King Jehoiakim of Judah had burned in the fire; and many similar words were added to them.

36.1–32: Two scrolls. This chapter has many parallels with ch. 26, including strong indictments of King Jehoiakim. Baruch, Jeremiah's scribe,* continues the prophet's* message by writing it and by proclaiming it. **2–8:** *Baruch* is a reliable proclaimer of Jeremiah's message of repentance, written by divine command on a *scroll.* **9–19:** Supporters of Jeremiah hear Baruch's reading of the scroll and send him and Jeremiah into hiding. **20–26:** In a dramatic scene, the scroll is read to the king, who cuts it up and burns it as it is being read. The king's action is a symbolic attempt to destroy the uncontrollable power of the word by making it disappear. **27–32:** But the prophetic word cannot be erased; Jeremiah dictates another version and adds more words to it. Jehoiakim, therefore, is responsible for the fall of the nation, for he would not listen.

BARUCH'S ACCOUNT

Chs. 37–45: Baruch is described as the author of these stories about Jeremiah and other survivors of the Babylonian invasion (45.1). Perhaps these chapters represent the additional words of the second scroll (36.32). The chapters show the exilic audience how to survive suffering brought on by invasion and its aftermath. They describe how the prophetic word was rejected, was fulfilled, and how it created conflict among survivors. Jeremiah himself appears as an example of fidelity. He is imprisoned and rescued twice, escapes with his life, and becomes a model of faithful survival.

a Heb *he*

Prison and release

Chs. 37–39: These chapters are all set during the reign of Zedekiah, who is as unaccepting of the prophetic word as his predecessor Jehoiakim.

37 Zedekiah son of Josiah, whom King Nebuchadrezzar of Babylon made king in the land of Judah, succeeded Coniah son of Jehoiakim. ²But neither he nor his servants nor the people of the land listened to the words of the LORD that he spoke through the prophet Jeremiah.

3 King Zedekiah sent Jehucal son of Shelemiah and the priest Zephaniah son of Maaseiah to the prophet Jeremiah saying, "Please pray for us to the LORD our God." ⁴Now Jeremiah was still going in and out among the people, for he had not yet been put in prison. ⁵Meanwhile, the army of Pharaoh had come out of Egypt; and when the Chaldeans who were besieging Jerusalem heard news of them, they withdrew from Jerusalem.

6 Then the word of the LORD came to the prophet Jeremiah: ⁷Thus says the LORD, God of Israel: This is what the two of you shall say to the king of Judah, who sent you to me to inquire of me: Pharaoh's army, which set out to help you, is going to return to its own land, to Egypt. ⁸And the Chaldeans shall return and fight against this city; they shall take it and burn it with fire. ⁹Thus says the LORD: Do not deceive yourselves, saying, "The Chaldeans will surely go away from us," for they will not go away. ¹⁰Even if you defeated the whole army of Chaldeans who are fighting against you, and there remained of them only wounded men in their tents, they would rise up and burn this city with fire.

11 Now when the Chaldean army had withdrawn from Jerusalem at the approach of Pharaoh's army, ¹²Jeremiah set out from Jerusalem to go to the land of Benjamin to receive his share of property*a* among the people there. ¹³When he reached the Benjamin Gate, a sentinel there named Irijah son of Shelemiah son of Hananiah arrested the prophet Jeremiah saying, "You are deserting to the Chaldeans." ¹⁴And Jeremiah said, "That is a lie; I am not deserting to the Chaldeans." But Irijah would not listen to him, and arrested Jeremiah and brought him to the officials. ¹⁵The officials were enraged at Jeremiah, and they beat him and imprisoned him in the house of the secretary Jonathan, for it had been made a prison. ¹⁶Thus Jeremiah was put in the cistern house, in the cells, and remained there many days.

17 Then King Zedekiah sent for him, and received him. The king questioned him secretly in his house, and said, "Is there any word from the LORD?" Jeremiah said, "There is!" Then he said, "You shall be handed over to the king of Babylon." ¹⁸Jeremiah also said to King Zedekiah, "What wrong have I done to you or your servants or this people, that you have put me in prison? ¹⁹Where are your prophets who prophesied to you, saying, 'The king of Babylon will not come against you and against this land'? ²⁰Now please hear me, my lord king: be good enough to listen to my plea, and do not send me back to the house of the secretary Jonathan to die there." ²¹So King Zedekiah gave orders, and they committed Jeremiah to the court of the guard; and a loaf of bread was given him daily from the bakers' street, until all the bread of the city was gone. So Jeremiah remained in the court of the guard.

37.1–21: In ch. 37, the king consults with Jeremiah twice, at the beginning and end of the chapter. The consultations frame Jeremiah's imprisonment. This arrangement suggests that the king is attempting to squeeze a favorable word from Jeremiah. **37.3–10:** Zedekiah's hope is that the power struggles between Egypt and Pharaoh will reduce Babylonian power and avert disaster. Jeremiah says no. **11–16:** In a series of abusive acts toward the prophet, officials imprison him, as if they could imprison the word. **17–21:** Secretly, the king tries to persuade Jeremiah to give him hope, but the prophet faithfully repeats his message of doom and escapes with his life.

38 Now Shephatiah son of Mattan, Gedaliah son of Pashhur, Jucal son of Shelemiah, and Pashhur son of Malchiah heard the words that Jeremiah was saying to all the people, ²Thus says the LORD, Those

a Meaning of Heb uncertain

who stay in this city shall die by the sword, by famine, and by pestilence; but those who go out to the Chaldeans shall live; they shall have their lives as a prize of war, and live. ³Thus says the LORD, This city shall surely be handed over to the army of the king of Babylon and be taken. ⁴Then the officials said to the king, "This man ought to be put to death, because he is discouraging the soldiers who are left in this city, and all the people, by speaking such words to them. For this man is not seeking the welfare of this people, but their harm." ⁵King Zedekiah said, "Here he is; he is in your hands; for the king is powerless against you." ⁶So they took Jeremiah and threw him into the cistern of Malchiah, the king's son, which was in the court of the guard, letting Jeremiah down by ropes. Now there was no water in the cistern, but only mud, and Jeremiah sank in the mud.

7 Ebed-melech the Ethiopian,ᵃ a eunuch in the king's house, heard that they had put Jeremiah into the cistern. The king happened to be sitting at the Benjamin Gate, ⁸So Ebed-melech left the king's house and spoke to the king, ⁹"My lord king, these men have acted wickedly in all they did to the prophet Jeremiah by throwing him into the cistern to die there of hunger, for there is no bread left in the city." ¹⁰Then the king commanded Ebed-melech the Ethiopian,ᵃ "Take three men with you from here, and pull the prophet Jeremiah up from the cistern before he dies." ¹¹So Ebed-melech took the men with him and went to the house of the king, to a wardrobe ofᵇ the storehouse, and took from there old rags and worn-out clothes, which he let down to Jeremiah in the cistern by ropes. ¹²Then Ebed-melech the Ethiopianᵃ said to Jeremiah, "Just put the rags and clothes between your armpits and the ropes." Jeremiah did so. ¹³Then they drew Jeremiah up by the ropes and pulled him out of the cistern. And Jeremiah remained in the court of the guard.

38.1–28: This story does not flow smoothly from the previous chapter. There Jeremiah was in prison, but here he is preaching freely to the people. 1–6: He urges the people to surrender to Babylon to save their lives *as the prize of war* (v. 2). The king again allows

Jeremiah's imprisonment because he will not offer a hopeful message. Jeremiah sinks into the mud. 7–13: An African, Ebed-melech, whose name means "servant of the king," dramatically rescues Jeremiah from death. In contrast to the king and his advisers, Ebed-melech shows true obedience.

14 King Zedekiah sent for the prophet Jeremiah and received him at the third entrance of the temple of the LORD. The king said to Jeremiah, "I have something to ask you; do not hide anything from me." ¹⁵Jeremiah said to Zedekiah, "If I tell you, you will put me to death, will you not? And if I give you advice, you will not listen to me." ¹⁶So King Zedekiah swore an oath in secret to Jeremiah, "As the LORD lives, who gave us our lives, I will not put you to death or hand you over to these men who seek your life."

17 Then Jeremiah said to Zedekiah, "Thus says the LORD, the God of hosts, the God of Israel, If you will only surrender to the officials of the king of Babylon, then your life shall be spared, and this city shall not be burned with fire, and you and your house shall live. ¹⁸But if you do not surrender to the officials of the king of Babylon, then this city shall be handed over to the Chaldeans, and they shall burn it with fire, and you yourself shall not escape from their hand." ¹⁹King Zedekiah said to Jeremiah, "I am afraid of the Judeans who have deserted to the Chaldeans, for I might be handed over to them and they would abuse me." ²⁰Jeremiah said, "That will not happen. Just obey the voice of the LORD in what I say to you, and it shall go well with you, and your life shall be spared. ²¹But if you are determined not to surrender, this is what the LORD has shown me— ²²a vision of all the women remaining in the house of the king of Judah being led out to the officials of the king of Babylon and saying,

'Your trusted friends have seduced you
    and have overcome you;
Now that your feet are stuck in
    the mud,
    they desert you.'

a Or Nubian; Heb Cushite   *b* Cn: Heb *to under*

23All your wives and your children shall be led out to the Chaldeans, and you yourself shall not escape from their hand, but shall be seized by the king of Babylon; and this city shall be burned with fire."

24 Then Zedekiah said to Jeremiah, "Do not let anyone else know of this conversation, or you will die. 25If the officials should hear that I have spoken with you, and they should come and say to you, 'Just tell us what you said to the king; do not conceal it from us, or we will put you to death. What did the king say to you?' 26then you shall say to them, 'I was presenting my plea to the king not to send me back to the house of Jonathan to die there.' " 27All the officials did come to Jeremiah and questioned him; and he answered them in the very words the king had commanded. So they stopped questioning him, for the conversation had not been overheard. 28And Jeremiah remained in the court of the guard until the day that Jerusalem was taken.

38.14–28: The king again consults with Jeremiah, who proclaims the king's capture. In this vision, the king changes places with Jeremiah: The king is *stuck in the mud.*

39 In the ninth year of King Zedekiah of Judah, in the tenth month, King Nebuchadrezzar of Babylon and all his army came against Jerusalem and besieged it; 2in the eleventh year of Zedekiah, in the fourth month, on the ninth day of the month, a breach was made in the city. 3When Jerusalem was taken,ᵃ all the officials of the king of Babylon came and sat in the middle gate: Nergal-sharezer, Samgar-nebo, Sarsechim the Rabsaris, Nergal-sharezer the Rabmag, with all the rest of the officials of the king of Babylon. 4When King Zedekiah of Judah and all the soldiers saw them, they fled, going out of the city at night by way of the king's garden through the gate between the two walls; and they went toward the Arabah. 5But the army of the Chaldeans pursued them, and overtook Zedekiah in the plains of Jericho; and when they had taken him, they brought him up to King Nebuchadrezzar of Babylon, at Riblah, in the land of Hamath; and he

passed sentence on him. 6The king of Babylon slaughtered the sons of Zedekiah at Riblah before his eyes; also the king of Babylon slaughtered all the nobles of Judah. 7He put out the eyes of Zedekiah, and bound him in fetters to take him to Babylon. 8The Chaldeans burned the king's house and the houses of the people, and broke down the walls of Jerusalem. 9Then Nebuzaradan the captain of the guard exiled to Babylon the rest of the people who were left in the city, those who had deserted to him, and the people who remained. 10Nebuzaradan the captain of the guard left in the land of Judah some of the poor people who owned nothing, and gave them vineyards and fields at the same time.

11 King Nebuchadrezzar of Babylon gave command concerning Jeremiah through Nebuzaradan, the captain of the guard, saying, 12"Take him, look after him well and do him no harm, but deal with him as he may ask you." 13So Nebuzaradan the captain of the guard, Nebushazban the Rabsaris, Nergal-sharezer the Rabmag, and all the chief officers of the king of Babylon sent 14and took Jeremiah from the court of the guard. They entrusted him to Gedaliah son of Ahikam son of Shaphan to be brought home. So he stayed with his own people.

15 The word of the LORD came to Jeremiah while he was confined in the court of the guard: 16Go and say to Ebed-melech the Ethiopian:ᵇ Thus says the LORD of hosts, the God of Israel: I am going to fulfill my words against this city for evil and not for good, and they shall be accomplished in your presence on that day. 17But I will save you on that day, says the LORD, and you shall not be handed over to those whom you dread. 18For I will surely save you, and you shall not fall by the sword; but you shall have your life as a prize of war, because you have trusted in me, says the LORD.

39.1–18: In straightforward prose, this chapter recounts the Babylonian invasion of Jerusalem and its

---

a This clause has been transposed from 38.28
b Or *Nubian;* Heb *Cushite*

consequences for Zedekiah and Jeremiah. The narrative's major interest is not the siege but the king's cowardice, escape, and capture, and Jeremiah's release. **3:** Babylonian officials have taken possession of the city and sit at the gate to govern. **9:** After Zedekiah and his family meet a horrible fate, the Babylonian captain distributes occupied land to the poor, perhaps to gain their support. **11–18:** Jeremiah gains Babylonian favor and is released to the protection of Gedaliah, the Judean governor appointed by Babylonians to replace the king. Jeremiah's release has symbolic meaning. He is a model of obedience in captivity, and he returns home as exiles hope to do. **18:** Because he trusts, he gains his life *as a prize of war.*

Chaos

Chs. 40–41: These chapters describe events in Judah after the invasion.

40 The word that came to Jeremiah from the LORD after Nebuzaradan the captain of the guard had let him go from Ramah, when he took him bound in fetters along with all the captives of Jerusalem and Judah who were being exiled to Babylon. ²The captain of the guard took Jeremiah and said to him, "The LORD your God threatened this place with this disaster; ³and now the LORD has brought it about, and has done as he said, because all of you sinned against the LORD and did not obey his voice. Therefore this thing has come upon you. ⁴Now look, I have just released you today from the fetters on your hands. If you wish to come with me to Babylon, come, and I will take good care of you; but if you do not wish to come with me to Babylon, you need not come. See, the whole land is before you; go wherever you think it good and right to go. ⁵If you remain,ᵃ then return to Gedaliah son of Ahikam son of Shaphan, whom the king of Babylon appointed governor of the towns of Judah, and stay with him among the people; or go wherever you think it right to go." So the captain of the guard gave him an allowance of food and a present, and let him go. ⁶Then Jeremiah went to Gedaliah son of Ahikam at Mizpah, and stayed with him among the people who were left in the land.

7 When all the leaders of the forces in the open country and their troops heard that the king of Babylon had appointed Gedaliah son of Ahikam governor in the land, and had committed to him men, women, and children, those of the poorest of the land who had not been taken into exile to Babylon, ⁸they went to Gedaliah at Mizpah—Ishmael son of Nethaniah, Johanan son of Kareah, Seraiah son of Tanhumeth, the sons of Ephai the Netophathite, Jezaniah son of the Maacathite, they and their troops. ⁹Gedaliah son of Ahikam son of Shaphan swore to them and their troops, saying, "Do not be afraid to serve the Chaldeans. Stay in the land and serve the king of Babylon, and it shall go well with you. ¹⁰As for me, I am staying at Mizpah to represent you before the Chaldeans who come to us; but as for you, gather wine and summer fruits and oil, and store them in your vessels, and live in the towns that you have taken over." ¹¹Likewise, when all the Judeans who were in Moab and among the Ammonites and in Edom and in other lands heard that the king of Babylon had left a remnant in Judah and had appointed Gedaliah son of Ahikam son of Shaphan as governor over them, ¹²then all the Judeans returned from all the places to which they had been scattered and came to the land of Judah, to Gedaliah at Mizpah; and they gathered wine and summer fruits in great abundance.

13 Now Johanan son of Kareah and all the leaders of the forces in the open country came to Gedaliah at Mizpah ¹⁴and said to him, "Are you at all aware that Baalis king of the Ammonites has sent Ishmael son of Nethaniah to take your life?" But Gedaliah son of Ahikam would not believe them. ¹⁵Then Johanan son of Kareah spoke secretly to Gedaliah at Mizpah, "Please let me go and kill Ishmael son of Nethaniah, and no one else will know. Why should he take your life, so that all the Judeans who are gathered around you would be scattered, and the remnant of Judah would perish?" ¹⁶But Gedaliah son of Ahikam said to Johanan son of Kareah, "Do not do such a thing, for you are telling a lie about Ishmael."

a Syr: Meaning of Heb uncertain

40.1–16. **1–6:** The Babylonian captain allows Jeremiah to remain in the land, even though Jeremiah had described those who stayed in Judah as bad figs (ch. 24). **7–12:** Under Gedaliah's governance there is peace in the land, and survivors are urged to submit to Babylon. **13–16:** A plot against Gedaliah is reported to him, but Gedaliah cannot believe that Ishmael, a member of the royal family, would be capable of such disloyalty.

41 In the seventh month, Ishmael son of Nethaniah son of Elishama, of the royal family, one of the chief officers of the king, came with ten men to Gedaliah son of Ahikam, at Mizpah. As they ate bread together there at Mizpah, ²Ishmael son of Nethaniah and the ten men with him got up and struck down Gedaliah son of Ahikam son of Shaphan with the sword and killed him, because the king of Babylon had appointed him governor in the land. ³Ishmael also killed all the Judeans who were with Gedaliah at Mizpah, and the Chaldean soldiers who happened to be there.

4 On the day after the murder of Gedaliah, before anyone knew of it, ⁵eighty men arrived from Shechem and Shiloh and Samaria, with their beards shaved and their clothes torn, and their bodies gashed, bringing grain offerings and incense to present at the temple of the LORD. ⁶And Ishmael son of Nethaniah came out from Mizpah to meet them, weeping as he came. As he met them, he said to them, "Come to Gedaliah son of Ahikam." ⁷When they reached the middle of the city, Ishmael son of Nethaniah and the men with him slaughtered them, and threw them*a* into a cistern. ⁸But there were ten men among them who said to Ishmael, "Do not kill us, for we have stores of wheat, barley, oil, and honey hidden in the fields." So he refrained, and did not kill them along with their companions.

9 Now the cistern into which Ishmael had thrown all the bodies of the men whom he had struck down was the large cistern*b* that King Asa had made for defense against King Baasha of Israel; Ishmael son of Nethaniah filled that cistern with those whom he had killed. ¹⁰Then Ishmael took captive all the rest of the people who were in Mizpah, the king's daughters and all the people who were left at Mizpah, whom Nebuzaradan, the captain of the guard, had committed to Gedaliah son of Ahikam. Ishmael son of Nethaniah took them captive and set out to cross over to the Ammonites.

11 But when Johanan son of Kareah and all the leaders of the forces with him heard of all the crimes that Ishmael son of Nethaniah had done, ¹²they took all their men and went to fight against Ishmael son of Nethaniah. They came upon him at the great pool that is in Gibeon. ¹³And when all the people who were with Ishmael saw Johanan son of Kareah and all the leaders of the forces with him, they were glad. ¹⁴So all the people whom Ishmael had carried away captive from Mizpah turned around and came back, and went to Johanan son of Kareah. ¹⁵But Ishmael son of Nethaniah escaped from Johanan with eight men, and went to the Ammonites. ¹⁶Then Johanan son of Kareah and all the leaders of the forces with him took all the rest of the people whom Ishmael son of Nethaniah had carried away captive*c* from Mizpah after he had slain Gedaliah son of Ahikam—soldiers, women, children, and eunuchs, whom Johanan brought back from Gibeon.*d* ¹⁷And they set out, and stopped at Geruth Chimham near Bethlehem, intending to go to Egypt ¹⁸because of the Chaldeans; for they were afraid of them, because Ishmael son of Nethaniah had killed Gedaliah son of Ahikam, whom the king of Babylon had made governor over the land.

41.1–18: During a meal, Ishmael and ten men massacre Gedaliah and everyone with him, as well as pilgrims on their way to the Temple.* They desecrate their bodies by dumping them into a cistern and take the remaining survivors as hostages. Johanan, one of the Judeans, gathers forces and rescues the hostages. The bloodbath gives the Judeans reason to fear the Chaldeans and sets off the events narrated in the next chapters.

a Syr: Heb lacks *and threw them;* compare verse 9
b Gk: Heb *whom he had killed by the hand of Gedaliah*
c Cn: Heb *whom he recovered from Ishmael son of Nethaniah*   d Meaning of Heb uncertain

Emigration to Egypt

Chs. 42–44: Jeremiah is an ally of Babylon and an opponent of Egypt in the international power struggles that afflict Judah at this time. These chapters reflect anti-Egyptian viewpoints. They accuse survivors who go to Egypt of refusing to listen and engaging in idolatry.* Paradoxically, Jeremiah and his scribe* Baruch are also forced into exile.

42 Then all the commanders of the forces, and Johanan son of Kareah and Azariah*a* son of Hoshaiah, and all the people from the least to the greatest, approached ²the prophet Jeremiah and said, "Be good enough to listen to our plea, and pray to the LORD your God for us—for all this remnant. For there are only a few of us left out of many, as your eyes can see. ³Let the LORD your God show us where we should go and what we should do." ⁴The prophet Jeremiah said to them, "Very well: I am going to pray to the LORD your God as you request, and whatever the LORD answers you I will tell you; I will keep nothing back from you." ⁵They in their turn said to Jeremiah, "May the LORD be a true and faithful witness against us if we do not act according to everything that the LORD your God sends us through you. ⁶Whether it is good or bad, we will obey the voice of the LORD our God to whom we are sending you, in order that it may go well with us when we obey the voice of the LORD our God."

7 At the end of ten days the word of the LORD came to Jeremiah. ⁸Then he summoned Johanan son of Kareah and all the commanders of the forces who were with him, and all the people from the least to the greatest, ⁹and said to them, "Thus says the LORD, the God of Israel, to whom you sent me to present your plea before him: ¹⁰If you will only remain in this land, then I will build you up and not pull you down; I will plant you, and not pluck you up; for I am sorry for the disaster that I have brought upon you. ¹¹Do not be afraid of the king of Babylon, as you have been; do not be afraid of him, says the LORD, for I am with you, to save you and to rescue you from his hand. ¹²I will grant you mercy, and he will have mercy on you and restore you to your native soil. ¹³But if you continue to say, 'We will not stay in this land,' thus disobeying the voice of the LORD your God ¹⁴and saying, 'No, we will go to the land of Egypt, where we shall not see war, or hear the sound of the trumpet, or be hungry for bread, and there we will stay,' ¹⁵then hear the word of the LORD, O remnant of Judah. Thus says the LORD of hosts, the God of Israel: If you are determined to enter Egypt and go to settle there, ¹⁶then the sword that you fear shall overtake you there, in the land of Egypt; and the famine that you dread shall follow close after you into Egypt; and there you shall die. ¹⁷All the people who have determined to go to Egypt to settle there shall die by the sword, by famine, and by pestilence; they shall have no remnant or survivor from the disaster that I am bringing upon them.

18 "For thus says the LORD of hosts, the God of Israel: Just as my anger and my wrath were poured out on the inhabitants of Jerusalem, so my wrath will be poured out on you when you go to Egypt. You shall become an object of execration and horror, of cursing and ridicule. You shall see this place no more. ¹⁹The LORD has said to you, O remnant of Judah, Do not go to Egypt. Be well aware that I have warned you today ²⁰that you have made a fatal mistake. For you yourselves sent me to the LORD your God, saying, 'Pray for us to the LORD our God, and whatever the LORD our God says, tell us and we will do it.' ²¹So I have told you today, but you have not obeyed the voice of the LORD your God in anything that he sent me to tell you. ²²Be well aware, then, that you shall die by the sword, by famine, and by pestilence in the place where you desire to go and settle."

42.1–22: Survivors of Ishmael's attack go to Jeremiah to make intercession on their behalf. Should they go to Egypt? They promise to obey his word. **10:** Jeremiah replies that they must *remain* in Judah. Then God will *rebuild* them after the *disaster,* for which God has repented. **18–22:** There is no escape from Babylon.

a Gk: Heb *Jezanian*

43

When Jeremiah finished speaking to all the people all these words of the LORD their God, with which the LORD their God had sent him to them, ²Azariah son of Hoshaiah and Johanan son of Kareah and all the other insolent men said to Jeremiah, "You are telling a lie. The LORD our God did not send you to say, 'Do not go to Egypt to settle there'; ³but Baruch son of Neriah is inciting you against us, to hand us over to the Chaldeans, in order that they may kill us or take us into exile in Babylon." ⁴So Johanan son of Kareah and all the commanders of the forces and all the people did not obey the voice of the LORD, to stay in the land of Judah. ⁵But Johanan son of Kareah and all the commanders of the forces took all the remnant of Judah who had returned to settle in the land of Judah from all the nations to which they had been driven— ⁶the men, the women, the children, the princesses, and everyone whom Nebuzaradan the captain of the guard had left with Gedaliah son of Ahikam son of Shaphan; also the prophet Jeremiah and Baruch son of Neriah. ⁷And they came into the land of Egypt, for they did not obey the voice of the LORD. And they arrived at Tahpanhes.

8 Then the word of the LORD came to Jeremiah in Tahpanhes: ⁹Take some large stones in your hands, and bury them in the clay pavement*a* that is at the entrance to Pharaoh's palace in Tahpanhes. Let the Judeans see you do it, ¹⁰and say to them, Thus says the LORD of hosts, the God of Israel: I am going to send and take my servant King Nebuchadrezzar of Babylon, and he*b* will set his throne above these stones that I have buried, and he will spread his royal canopy over them. ¹¹He shall come and ravage the land of Egypt, giving

> those who are destined for pestilence, to pestilence,
> and those who are destined for captivity, to captivity,
> and those who are destined for the sword, to the sword.

¹²He*c* shall kindle a fire in the temples of the gods of Egypt; and he shall burn them and carry them away captive; and he shall pick clean the land of Egypt, as a shepherd picks his cloak clean of vermin; and he shall depart from there safely. ¹³He shall break the obelisks of Heliopolis, which is in the land of Egypt; and the temples of the gods of Egypt he shall burn with fire.

43.1–13: *Johanan,* the hero of ch. 42, turns insolent and accuses Jeremiah of lying and Baruch of inciting him. Both are forced into Egyptian exile against their will. They escape none of the pain of the exiles in Babylon, for they too leave their homeland as captives. **8–13:** Jeremiah directs a symbolic action of burying stones. Nebuchadrezzar will come and set up his rule there and destroy Egyptian deities.

44

The word that came to Jeremiah for all the Judeans living in the land of Egypt, at Migdol, at Tahpanhes, at Memphis, and in the land of Pathros, ²Thus says the LORD of hosts, the God of Israel: You yourselves have seen all the disaster that I have brought on Jerusalem and on all the towns of Judah. Look at them; today they are a desolation, without an inhabitant in them, ³because of the wickedness that they committed, provoking me to anger, in that they went to make offerings and serve other gods that they had not known, neither they, nor you, nor your ancestors. ⁴Yet I persistently sent to you all my servants the prophets, saying, "I beg you not to do this abominable thing that I hate!" ⁵But they did not listen or incline their ear, to turn from their wickedness and make no offerings to other gods. ⁶So my wrath and my anger were poured out and kindled in the towns of Judah and in the streets of Jerusalem; and they became a waste and a desolation, as they still are today. ⁷And now thus says the LORD God of hosts, the God of Israel: Why are you doing such great harm to yourselves, to cut off man and woman, child and infant, from the midst of Judah, leaving yourselves without a remnant? ⁸Why do you provoke me to anger with the works of your hands, making offerings to other gods in the land of Egypt where you have come to settle? Will you be

a Meaning of Heb uncertain *b* Gk Syr: Heb I
c Gk Syr Vg: Heb I

cut off and become an object of cursing and ridicule among all the nations of the earth? ⁹Have you forgotten the crimes of your ancestors, of the kings of Judah, of their*ᵃ* wives, your own crimes and those of your wives, which they committed in the land of Judah and in the streets of Jerusalem? ¹⁰They have shown no contrition or fear to this day, nor have they walked in my law and my statutes that I set before you and before your ancestors.

44.1–30: Idolatry. ✱ Jeremiah delivers a final prophetic message to Judeans living in Egypt. **1–6:** The fall of Judah and Jerusalem was caused by the people's failure to listen. Those who escaped to Egypt will suffer a similar fate, if they do not leave idolatry aside.

11 Therefore thus says the Lord of hosts, the God of Israel: I am determined to bring disaster on you, to bring all Judah to an end. ¹²I will take the remnant of Judah who are determined to come to the land of Egypt to settle, and they shall perish, everyone; in the land of Egypt they shall fall; by the sword and by famine they shall perish; from the least to the greatest, they shall die by the sword and by famine; and they shall become an object of execration and horror, of cursing and ridicule. ¹³I will punish those who live in the land of Egypt, as I have punished Jerusalem, with the sword, with famine, and with pestilence, ¹⁴so that none of the remnant of Judah who have come to settle in the land of Egypt shall escape or survive or return to the land of Judah. Although they long to go back to live there, they shall not go back, except some fugitives.

15 Then all the men who were aware that their wives had been making offerings to other gods, and all the women who stood by, a great assembly, all the people who lived in Pathros in the land of Egypt, answered Jeremiah: ¹⁶"As for the word that you have spoken to us in the name of the Lord, we are not going to listen to you. ¹⁷Instead, we will do everything that we have vowed, make offerings to the queen of heaven and pour out libations to her, just as we and our ancestors, our kings and our officials, used to do in the towns of Judah and in the streets of Jerusa-

lem. We used to have plenty of food, and prospered, and saw no misfortune. ¹⁸But from the time we stopped making offerings to the queen of heaven and pouring out libations to her, we have lacked everything and have perished by the sword and by famine." ¹⁹And the women said,*ᵇ* "Indeed we will go on making offerings to the queen of heaven and pouring out libations to her; do you think that we made cakes for her, marked with her image, and poured out libations to her without our husbands' being involved?"

20 Then Jeremiah said to all the people, men and women, all the people who were giving him this answer: ²¹"As for the offerings that you made in the towns of Judah and in the streets of Jerusalem, you and your ancestors, your kings and your officials, and the people of the land, did not the Lord remember them? Did it not come into his mind? ²²The Lord could no longer bear the sight of your evil doings, the abominations that you committed; therefore your land became a desolation and a waste and a curse, without inhabitant, as it is to this day. ²³It is because you burned offerings, and because you sinned against the Lord and did not obey the voice of the Lord or walk in his law and in his statutes and in his decrees, that this disaster has befallen you, as is still evident today."

24 Jeremiah said to all the people and all the women, "Hear the word of the Lord, all you Judeans who are in the land of Egypt, ²⁵Thus says the Lord of hosts, the God of Israel: You and your wives have accomplished in deeds what you declared in words, saying, 'We are determined to perform the vows that we have made, to make offerings to the queen of heaven and to pour out libations to her.' By all means, keep your vows and make your libations! ²⁶Therefore hear the word of the Lord, all you Judeans who live in the land of Egypt: Lo, I swear by my great name, says the Lord, that my name shall no longer be pronounced on the lips of

a Heb *his*   *b* Compare Syr: Heb lacks *And the women said*

any of the people of Judah in all the land of Egypt, saying, 'As the Lord GOD lives.' ²⁷I am going to watch over them for harm and not for good; all the people of Judah who are in the land of Egypt shall perish by the sword and by famine, until not one is left. ²⁸And those who escape the sword shall return from the land of Egypt to the land of Judah, few in number; and all the remnant of Judah, who have come to the land of Egypt to settle, shall know whose words will stand, mine or theirs! ²⁹This shall be the sign to you, says the LORD, that I am going to punish you in this place, in order that you may know that my words against you will surely be carried out: ³⁰Thus says the LORD, I am going to give Pharaoh Hophra, king of Egypt, into the hands of his enemies, those who seek his life, just as I gave King Zedekiah of Judah into the hand of King Nebuchadrezzar of Babylon, his enemy who sought his life."

44.15–30: Worship of the queen of heaven exemplifies the idolatry of the exiles. Jeremiah had accused the Judean families of worshiping this astral deity in the Temple sermon (7.1–8.3). Here Jeremiah accuses the women as central participants in this worship. The women, however, speak from their experience. When they stopped worshipping the goddess, their world fell apart. **26:** Because of its idolatry, the believing community will disappear in Egypt. They have no future because they turned from God.

45 The word that the prophet Jeremiah spoke to Baruch son of Neriah, when he wrote these words in a scroll at the dictation of Jeremiah, in the fourth year of King Jehoiakim son of Josiah of Judah: ²Thus says the LORD, the God of Israel, to you, O Baruch: ³You said, "Woe is me! The LORD has added sorrow to my pain; I am weary with my groaning, and I find no rest." ⁴Thus you shall say to him, "Thus says the LORD: I am going to break down what I have built, and pluck up what I have planted—that is, the whole land. ⁵And you, do you seek great things for yourself? Do not seek them; for I am going to bring disaster upon all flesh, says the LORD; but I will give you your life as a prize of war in every place to which you may go."

45.1–5: Baruch's role. Chapter 45 brings the Baruch account to a close and also concludes chs. 26–44. **2–3:** Baruch utters a lament* of sorrow, pain, and weariness that follows curses upon his own people in ch. 44. **4:** God replies through Jeremiah with language used frequently throughout the book, *I am going to break down and pluck up the whole land.* **5:** Suffering cannot be avoided, but Baruch will survive. He will gain *his life as a prize of war.* With Baruch's lament and the divine response to it, the main part of the book ends on a somber note. Baruch is a weary survivor who is promised only his life. The idealized vision of chs. 30–33 is far from sight. But according to chs. 37–45, Jeremiah, Baruch, Ebed-melech, and a remnant survive. Survivors must obey Jeremiah's prophetic message as conveyed in this book.

ORACLES* AGAINST THE NATIONS

Chs. 46–51: These poems, confirming the survival of those who wait in obedient faithfulness, consist of a collection of prophetic poems in judgment against Israel's enemies. Their location at the end of the book gives meaning to Jeremiah's title "prophet* to the nations" (1.5, 10). God's voice in these poems announces that foreign nations had been instruments of divine punishment of Israel and Judah, but soon tables will turn to create a new future. These oracles address Israel's neighbors first (chs. 46–49) and close with oracles against Babylon (chs. 50–51).

46 The word of the LORD that came to the prophet Jeremiah concerning the nations.

2 Concerning Egypt, about the army of Pharaoh Neco, king of Egypt, which was by the river Euphrates at Carchemish and which King Nebuchadrezzar of Babylon defeated in the fourth year of King Jehoiakim son of Josiah of Judah:

³ Prepare buckler and shield,
    and advance for battle!
⁴ Harness the horses;
    mount the steeds!
Take your stations with your helmets,
    whet your lances,
    put on your coats of mail!
⁵ Why do I see them terrified?
    They have fallen back;
    their warriors are beaten down,

and have fled in haste.
They do not look back—
   terror is all around!
          says the LORD.

6 The swift cannot flee away,
   nor can the warrior escape;
in the north by the river Euphrates
   they have stumbled and fallen.

7 Who is this, rising like the Nile,
   like rivers whose waters surge?
8 Egypt rises like the Nile,
   like rivers whose waters surge.
It said, Let me rise, let me cover the
     earth,
   let me destroy cities and their
     inhabitants.
9 Advance, O horses,
   and dash madly, O chariots!
Let the warriors go forth:
   Ethiopia^a and Put who carry
     the shield,
   the Ludim, who draw^b the bow.
10 That day is the day of the Lord GOD of
     hosts,
   a day of retribution,
   to gain vindication from his foes.
The sword shall devour and be sated,
   and drink its fill of their blood.
For the Lord GOD of hosts holds
     a sacrifice
   in the land of the north by the river
     Euphrates.
11 Go up to Gilead, and take balm,
   O virgin daughter Egypt!
In vain you have used many
     medicines;
   there is no healing for you.
12 The nations have heard of your shame,
   and the earth is full of your cry;
for warrior has stumbled against
     warrior;
   both have fallen together.

46.1–25: Against Egypt. These poems bring to poetic fulfillment Jeremiah's prophecies to the Judean remnant that escaped to Egypt (chs. 43–44). Babylon will destroy their safe haven. **2:** The date of the first poem in the *fourth year of Jehoiakim* sets this prophecy in the years when Babylon destroyed Egyptian power in the region. This means that Jeremiah's word of the de-

struction of Egypt came much earlier than the events themselves. For survivors in exile, the date indicates that God's plans have long been in place and that there is hope for the future. **3–12:** A battle scene, similar to scenes of the cosmic battle with the foe from the north in chs. 4–6 and 8–10, opens the poem. God calls troops to prepare for war. **7–12:** The Nile River, famous for its flooding, resembles the rise and fall of Egypt. Egypt cannot possible defend itself since, in this poetic vision, the enemy is divine.

~~~~~~~~~~

13 The word that the LORD spoke to the prophet Jeremiah about the coming of King Nebuchadrezzar of Babylon to attack the land of Egypt:
14 Declare in Egypt, and proclaim
     in Migdol;
   proclaim in Memphis and Tahpanhes;
Say, "Take your stations and be ready,
   for the sword shall devour those
     around you."
15 Why has Apis fled?^c
   Why did your bull not stand?
   —because the LORD thrust
     him down.
16 Your multitude stumbled^d and fell,
   and one said to another,^e
"Come, let us go back to our
     own people
   and to the land of our birth,
   because of the destroying sword."
17 Give Pharaoh, king of Egypt, the name
   "Braggart who missed his chance."

18 As I live, says the King,
   whose name is the LORD of hosts,
one is coming
   like Tabor among the mountains,
   and like Carmel by the sea.
19 Pack your bags for exile,
   sheltered daughter Egypt!
For Memphis shall become a waste,
   a ruin, without inhabitant.

20 A beautiful heifer is Egypt—
   a gadfly from the north lights upon
     her.

a Or *Nubia;* Heb *Cush*   *b* Cn: Heb *who grasp, who draw*   *c* Gk: Heb *Why was it swept away*   *d* Gk: Meaning of Heb uncertain   *e* Gk: Heb *and fell one to another and they said*

21 Even her mercenaries in her midst
    are like fatted calves;
they too have turned and fled
        together,
    they did not stand;
for the day of their calamity has come
        upon them,
    the time of their punishment.

22 She makes a sound like a snake gliding
        away;
    for her enemies march in force,
and come against her with axes,
    like those who fell trees.
23 They shall cut down her forest,
                    says the LORD,
    though it is impenetrable,
because they are more numerous
    than locusts;
    they are without number.
24 Daughter Egypt shall be put to shame;
    she shall be handed over to a people
        from the north.

    25 The LORD of hosts, the God of Israel,
said: See, I am bringing punishment upon
Amon of Thebes, and Pharaoh, and Egypt
and her gods and her kings, upon Pharaoh
and those who trust in him. 26I will hand
them over to those who seek their life, to
King Nebuchadrezzar of Babylon and his officers. Afterward Egypt shall be inhabited as
in the days of old, says the LORD.

27 But as for you, have no fear, my servant
        Jacob,
    and do not be dismayed, O Israel;
for I am going to save you from
        far away,
    and your offspring from the land of
        their captivity.
Jacob shall return and have quiet and
        ease,
    and no one shall make him afraid.
28 As for you, have no fear, my servant
        Jacob,
                    says the LORD,
    for I am with you.
I will make an end of all the nations
    among which I have banished you,
but I will not make an end of you!

I will chastise you in just measure,
    and I will by no means leave you
        unpunished.

46.13–28. 13: A prose comment identifies the human enemy as Nebuchadrezzar, King of Babylon. **14–25:** The battle, however, is really between *Apis,* the bull-god of Egypt, and the God of Israel. **17:** Egypt's king is here called *Braggart* because he boasts about power he never really had. **20–24:** Female metaphors* describe Egypt's vulnerability and shame. Egypt's crimes are pride and false claims to power, but the poem assures the exiles that its God rules the nations. **27–28:** God addresses Israel with words of comfort. Israel is to put aside fear. In their exile God will sustain them and punish their enemies.

47 The word of the LORD that came to
    the prophet Jeremiah concerning the
Philistines, before Pharaoh attacked Gaza:
2 Thus says the LORD:
See, waters are rising out of the north
    and shall become an overflowing
        torrent;
they shall overflow the land and all that
        fills it,
    the city and those who live in it.
People shall cry out,
    and all the inhabitants of the land
        shall wail.
3 At the noise of the stamping of the
        hoofs of his stallions,
    at the clatter of his chariots, at the
        rumbling of their wheels,
parents do not turn back for children,
    so feeble are their hands,
4 because of the day that is coming
    to destroy all the Philistines,
to cut off from Tyre and Sidon
    every helper that remains.
For the LORD is destroying the
        Philistines,
    the remnant of the coastland
        of Caphtor.
5 Baldness has come upon Gaza,
    Ashkelon is silenced.
O remnant of their power!*a*
    How long will you gash yourselves?

a Gk: Heb *their valley*

6 Ah, sword of the LORD!
　　How long until you are quiet?
　　Put yourself into your scabbard,
　　　rest and be still!
7 How can it[a] be quiet,
　　when the LORD has given it
　　　an order?
　　Against Ashkelon and against the
　　　seashore—
　　there he has appointed it.

47.1–7: Against the Philistines. There are historical difficulties with this poem, since Philistia was not a major enemy of Israel during this time. Though its city-states along the seacoast continued for a long time, they ceased to exist as a larger unity during the Babylonian period. In the poetic world of this poem, however, God is the enemy bringing an attacker. **6–7:** The poem ends with the "song of the sword" in which the poet addresses God's weapon and begs it to be still, but the sword is unable to deny God's commands.

48 Concerning Moab.

Thus says the LORD of hosts, the God of Israel:
　　Alas for Nebo, it is laid waste!
　　　Kiriathaim is put to shame, it
　　　　is taken;
　　the fortress is put to shame and broken
　　　down;
2　　the renown of Moab is no more.
　　In Heshbon they planned evil against
　　　her:
　　　"Come, let us cut her off from being
　　　　a nation!"
　　You also, O Madmen, shall be brought
　　　to silence;[b]
　　the sword shall pursue you.
3 Hark! a cry from Horonaim,
　　"Desolation and great destruction!"
4 "Moab is destroyed!"
　　her little ones cry out.
5 For at the ascent of Luhith
　　they go[c] up weeping bitterly;
　　for at the descent of Horonaim
　　　they have heard the distressing cry of
　　　　anguish.
6 Flee! Save yourselves!
　　Be like a wild ass[d] in the desert!

7 Surely, because you trusted in your
　　　strongholds[e] and your treasures,
　　you also shall be taken;
　　Chemosh shall go out into exile,
　　　with his priests and his attendants.
8 The destroyer shall come upon every
　　　town,
　　and no town shall escape;
　　the valley shall perish,
　　　and the plain shall be destroyed,
　　　as the LORD has spoken.

9 Set aside salt for Moab,
　　for she will surely fall;
　　her towns shall become a desolation,
　　　with no inhabitant in them.

10 Accursed is the one who is slack in doing the work of the LORD; and accursed is the one who keeps back the sword from bloodshed.

11 Moab has been at ease from his youth,
　　settled like wine[f] on its dregs;
　　he has not been emptied from vessel to
　　　vessel,
　　nor has he gone into exile;
　　therefore his flavor has remained
　　　and his aroma is unspoiled.
12 Therefore, the time is surely coming, says the LORD, when I shall send to him decanters to decant him, and empty his vessels, and break his[g] jars in pieces. 13 Then Moab shall be ashamed of Chemosh, as the house of Israel was ashamed of Bethel, their confidence.

48.1–47: Against Moab. This long poem concerns a traditional and bitter enemy and neighbor of Israel. **1–2:** God announces an invasion of Moab, whereupon a voice cries in alarm. Moab's sin is arrogance arising from its wealth and power. **7:** *Chemosh* was the chief God of Moab. **11–12:** Because Moab was known for its production of grapes, the poem describes Moab's complacency in terms of *wine* about to be poured out.

14 How can you say, "We are heroes
　　and mighty warriors"?

a Gk Vg: Heb *you*　　*b* The place-name *Madmen* sounds like the Hebrew verb *to be silent*　　*c* Cn: Heb *he goes* *d* Gk Aquila: Heb *like Aroer*　　*e* Gk: Heb *works* *f* Heb lacks *like wine*　　*g* Gk Aquila: Heb *their*

15 The destroyer of Moab and his towns
	has come up,
	and the choicest of his young men
		have gone down to slaughter,
	says the King, whose name is the
		LORD of hosts.
16 The calamity of Moab is near at hand
	and his doom approaches swiftly.
17 Mourn over him, all you his neighbors,
	and all who know his name;
	say, "How the mighty scepter is broken,
		the glorious staff!"

18 Come down from glory,
	and sit on the parched ground,
		enthroned daughter Dibon!
	For the destroyer of Moab has come up
		against you;
	he has destroyed your strongholds.
19 Stand by the road and watch,
	you inhabitant of Aroer!
	Ask the man fleeing and the woman
		escaping;
	say, "What has happened?"
20 Moab is put to shame, for it is broken
		down;
	wail and cry!
	Tell it by the Arnon,
		that Moab is laid waste.

21 Judgment has come upon the tableland, upon Holon, and Jahzah, and Mephaath, 22and Dibon, and Nebo, and Beth-diblathaim, 23and Kiriathaim, and Beth-gamul, and Beth-meon, 24and Kerioth, and Bozrah, and all the towns of the land of Moab, far and near. 25The horn of Moab is cut off, and his arm is broken, says the LORD.

26 Make him drunk, because he magnified himself against the LORD; let Moab wallow in his vomit; he too shall become a laughingstock. 27Israel was a laughingstock for you, though he was not caught among thieves; but whenever you spoke of him you shook your head!

48.14–27. 18–20: God warns the capital city, *Dibon*, addressed as a woman, that she too is under attack. 21–27: The cities of Moab are about to be destroyed.

28 Leave the towns, and live on the rock,
	O inhabitants of Moab!
	Be like the dove that nests
		on the sides of the mouth of a gorge.
29 We have heard of the pride of Moab—
		he is very proud—
	of his loftiness, his pride, and his
		arrogance,
	and the haughtiness of his heart.
30 I myself know his insolence, says the
		LORD;
	his boasts are false,
	his deeds are false.
31 Therefore I wail for Moab;
	I cry out for all Moab;
	for the people of Kir-heres I mourn.
32 More than for Jazer I weep for you,
	O vine of Sibmah!
	Your branches crossed over the sea,
		reached as far as Jazer;[a]
	upon your summer fruits and
			your vintage
		the destroyer has fallen.
33 Gladness and joy have been taken away
		from the fruitful land of Moab;
	I have stopped the wine from the wine
			presses;
	no one treads them with shouts of joy;
		the shouting is not the shout of joy.

48.28–33. 28–30: God next addresses the residents of Moab, urging them to flee and accusing them of false pride. 31–33: Surprisingly, God wails for Moab.

34 Heshbon and Elealeh cry out;[b] as far as Jahaz they utter their voice, from Zoar to Horonaim and Eglath-shelishiyah. For even the waters of Nimrim have become desolate. 35And I will bring to an end in Moab, says the LORD, those who offer sacrifice at a high place and make offerings to their gods. 36Therefore my heart moans for Moab like a flute, and my heart moans like a flute for the people of Kir-heres; for the riches they gained have perished.

37 For every head is shaved and every beard cut off; on all the hands there are gashes, and on the loins sackcloth. 38On all

---

a Two Mss and Isa 16.8: MT *the sea of Jazer*
b Cn: Heb *From the cry of Heshbon to Elealeh*

the housetops of Moab and in the squares there is nothing but lamentation; for I have broken Moab like a vessel that no one wants, says the LORD. 39 How it is broken! How they wail! How Moab has turned his back in shame! So Moab has become a derision and a horror to all his neighbors.

40 For thus says the LORD:
Look, he shall swoop down like
an eagle,
and spread his wings against Moab;
41 the towns*a* shall be taken
and the strongholds seized.
The hearts of the warriors of Moab, on
that day,
shall be like the heart of a woman in
labor.
42 Moab shall be destroyed as a people,
because he magnified himself against
the LORD.
43 Terror, pit, and trap
are before you, O inhabitants
of Moab!
says the LORD.
44 Everyone who flees from the terror
shall fall into the pit,
and everyone who climbs out of the pit
shall be caught in the trap.
For I will bring these things*b*
upon Moab
in the year of their punishment,
says the LORD.

45 In the shadow of Heshbon
fugitives stop exhausted;
for a fire has gone out from Heshbon,
a flame from the house of Sihon;
it has destroyed the forehead of Moab,
the scalp of the people of tumult.*c*
46 Woe to you, O Moab!
The people of Chemosh have
perished,
for your sons have been taken captive,
and your daughters into captivity.
47 Yet I will restore the fortunes of Moab
in the latter days, says the LORD.
Thus far is the judgment on Moab.

48.47: Even more surprising, the poem closes with a divine promise to restore Moab.

49 Concerning the Ammonites.

Thus says the LORD:
Has Israel no sons?
Has he no heir?
Why then has Milcom dispossessed
Gad,
and his people settled in its towns?
2 Therefore, the time is surely coming,
says the LORD,
when I will sound the battle alarm
against Rabbah of the Ammonites;
it shall become a desolate mound,
and its villages shall be burned with
fire;
then Israel shall dispossess those who
dispossessed him,
says the LORD.

3 Wail, O Heshbon, for Ai is laid waste!
Cry out, O daughters*d* of Rabbah!
Put on sackcloth,
lament, and slash yourselves with
whips!*e*
For Milcom shall go into exile,
with his priests and his attendants.
4 Why do you boast in your strength?
Your strength is ebbing,
O faithless daughter.
You trusted in your treasures,
saying,
"Who will attack me?"
5 I am going to bring terror upon you,
says the Lord GOD of hosts,
from all your neighbors,
and you will be scattered, each
headlong,
with no one to gather the fugitives.
6 But afterward I will restore the fortunes of the Ammonites, says the LORD.

49.1–39: Against many nations. 1–6: The history of relations between Israel and their neighbors, the *Ammonites*, was bitter (40.13–41.3). They will be punished for land-grabbing, but God will finally restore them as well.

a Or *Kerioth*   *b* Gk Syr: Heb *bring upon it*   *c* Or *of Shaon*   *d* Or *villages*   *e* Cn: Meaning of Heb uncertain

7 Concerning Edom.

Thus says the LORD of hosts:
  Is there no longer wisdom in Teman?
    Has counsel perished from
      the prudent?
    Has their wisdom vanished?
8 Flee, turn back, get down low,
    inhabitants of Dedan!
  For I will bring the calamity of Esau
    upon him,
    the time when I punish him.
9 If grape-gatherers came to you,
    would they not leave gleanings?
  If thieves came by night,
    even they would pillage only what
      they wanted.
10 But as for me, I have stripped
    Esau bare,
  I have uncovered his hiding places,
  and he is not able to conceal himself.
  His offspring are destroyed,
    his kinsfolk
  and his neighbors; and he is
    no more.
11 Leave your orphans, I will keep them
    alive;
  and let your widows trust in me.

12 For thus says the LORD: If those who do not deserve to drink the cup still have to drink it, shall you be the one to go unpunished? You shall not go unpunished; you must drink it. 13 For by myself I have sworn, says the LORD, that Bozrah shall become an object of horror and ridicule, a waste, and an object of cursing; and all her towns shall be perpetual wastes.

14 I have heard tidings from the LORD,
  and a messenger has been sent
    among the nations:
  "Gather yourselves together and come
    against her,
  and rise up for battle!"
15 For I will make you least among the
    nations,
  despised by humankind.
16 The terror you inspire
  and the pride of your heart have
    deceived you,
  you who live in the clefts of the rock, [a]
    who hold the height of the hill.

Although you make your nest as high as
    the eagle's,
  from there I will bring you down,
               says the LORD.

17 Edom shall become an object of horror; everyone who passes by it will be horrified and will hiss because of all its disasters. 18 As when Sodom and Gomorrah and their neighbors were overthrown, says the LORD, no one shall live there, nor shall anyone settle in it. 19 Like a lion coming up from the thickets of the Jordan against a perennial pasture, I will suddenly chase Edom [b] away from it; and I will appoint over it whomever I choose. [c] For who is like me? Who can summon me? Who is the shepherd who can stand before me? 20 Therefore hear the plan that the LORD has made against Edom and the purposes that he has formed against the inhabitants of Teman: Surely the little ones of the flock shall be dragged away; surely their fold shall be appalled at their fate. 21 At the sound of their fall the earth shall tremble; the sound of their cry shall be heard at the Red Sea. [d] 22 Look, he shall mount up and swoop down like an eagle, and spread his wings against Bozrah, and the heart of the warriors of Edom in that day shall be like the heart of a woman in labor.

49.7–22: The Edomites are Israel's neighbors and the descendants of Jacob's brother, Esau (Gen 36). **7–10:** God will bring calamity upon them and leave only a remnant of orphans and widows with no future. Their sin is never named.

---

23 Concerning Damascus.

Hamath and Arpad are confounded,
  for they have heard bad news;
  they melt in fear, they are troubled like
    the sea [e]
    that cannot be quiet.
24 Damascus has become feeble, she
    turned to flee,
  and panic seized her;

*a Or of Sela   b Heb him   c Or and I will single out
the choicest of his rams: Meaning of Heb uncertain
d Or Sea of Reeds   e Cn: Heb there is trouble in the sea*

anguish and sorrows have taken hold of
her,
as of a woman in labor.

25 How the famous city is forsaken,[a]
the joyful town![b]

26 Therefore her young men shall fall in
her squares,
and all her soldiers shall be destroyed
in that day,
says the LORD of hosts.

27 And I will kindle a fire at the wall of
Damascus,
and it shall devour the strongholds of
Ben-hadad.

28 Concerning Kedar and the kingdoms
of Hazor that King Nebuchadrezzar of Babylon defeated.

Thus says the LORD:
Rise up, advance against Kedar!
Destroy the people of the east!

29 Take their tents and their flocks,
their curtains and all their goods;
carry off their camels for yourselves,
and a cry shall go up: "Terror is all
around!"

30 Flee, wander far away, hide in
deep places,
O inhabitants of Hazor!
says the LORD.
For King Nebuchadrezzar of Babylon
has made a plan against you
and formed a purpose against you.

31 Rise up, advance against a nation at ease,
that lives secure,
says the LORD,
that has no gates or bars,
that lives alone.

32 Their camels shall become booty,
their herds of cattle a spoil.
I will scatter to every wind
those who have shaven temples,
and I will bring calamity
against them from every side,
says the LORD.

33 Hazor shall become a lair of jackals,
an everlasting waste;
no one shall live there,
nor shall anyone settle in it.

49.23–33. 23–27: *Damascus,* the capital of Syria, will
be destroyed. Again no sin is identified. **28–33:** *Kedar*
and *Hazor,* cities in the north, will be attacked by Nebuchadrezzar and their people will be dispersed.

34 The word of the LORD that came to
the prophet Jeremiah concerning Elam, at
the beginning of the reign of King Zedekiah
of Judah.

35 Thus says the LORD of hosts: I am going to break the bow of Elam, the mainstay
of their might; 36 and I will bring upon Elam
the four winds from the four quarters of
heaven; and I will scatter them to all these
winds, and there shall be no nation to which
the exiles from Elam shall not come. 37 I will
terrify Elam before their enemies, and before
those who seek their life; I will bring disaster
upon them, my fierce anger, says the LORD.
I will send the sword after them, until I have
consumed them; 38 and I will set my throne
in Elam, and destroy their king and officials,
says the LORD.

39 But in the latter days I will restore the
fortunes of Elam, says the LORD.

49.34–39: Elam will be destroyed in a cosmic upheaval, but God will restore their fortunes.

Against Babylon

Chs. 50–51: These poems form a suitable conclusion
to the book. In them the punisher is punished, the
destroyer is destroyed, and the inflictor of pain receives
pain. Although earlier parts of the book interpreted
Babylon as an agent of God to punish Judah, these
poems see Babylon as the aggressor who oppressed
Israel. They portray God as a warrior who sets right the
world's injustices and restores the victims' well-being.
The exiles receive a vision of a future in which they will
be released from their captivity, but there is not yet
energy for wild hope and dancing (chs. 30–33).

50 The word that the LORD spoke concerning Babylon, concerning the
land of the Chaldeans, by the prophet
Jeremiah:
2 Declare among the nations
and proclaim,

a Vg: Heb *is not forsaken*   b Syr Vg Tg: Heb *the town
of my joy*

set up a banner and proclaim,
   do not conceal it, say:
Babylon is taken,
   Bel is put to shame,
     Merodach is dismayed.
Her images are put to shame,
   her idols are dismayed.

3 For out of the north a nation has come up against her; it shall make her land a desolation, and no one shall live in it; both human beings and animals shall flee away.

4 In those days and in that time, says the LORD, the people of Israel shall come, they and the people of Judah together; they shall come weeping as they seek the LORD their God. ⁵They shall ask the way to Zion, with faces turned toward it, and they shall come and join*ª* themselves to the LORD by an everlasting covenant that will never be forgotten.

6 My people have been lost sheep; their shepherds have led them astray, turning them away on the mountains; from mountain to hill they have gone, they have forgotten their fold. ⁷All who found them have devoured them, and their enemies have said, "We are not guilty, because they have sinned against the LORD, the true pasture, the LORD, the hope of their ancestors."

8 Flee from Babylon, and go out of the land of the Chaldeans, and be like male goats leading the flock. ⁹For I am going to stir up and bring against Babylon a company of great nations from the land of the north; and they shall array themselves against her; from there she shall be taken. Their arrows are like the arrows of a skilled warrior who does not return empty-handed. ¹⁰Chaldea shall be plundered; all who plunder her shall be sated, says the LORD.

11 Though you rejoice, though you exult,
   O plunderers of my heritage,
though you frisk about like a heifer on
     the grass,
   and neigh like stallions,
12 your mother shall be utterly shamed,

   and she who bore you shall
     be disgraced.
Lo, she shall be the last of the nations,
   a wilderness, dry land, and a desert.
13 Because of the wrath of the LORD she
     shall not be inhabited,
   but shall be an utter desolation;
everyone who passes by Babylon shall
     be appalled
   and hiss because of all her wounds.
14 Take up your positions around Babylon,
   all you that bend the bow;
shoot at her, spare no arrows,
   for she has sinned against the LORD.
15 Raise a shout against her from all sides,
   "She has surrendered;
her bulwarks have fallen,
   her walls are thrown down."
For this is the vengeance of the LORD:
   take vengeance on her,
   do to her as she has done.
16 Cut off from Babylon the sower,
   and the wielder of the sickle in time
     of harvest;
because of the destroying sword
   all of them shall return to their own
     people,
   and all of them shall flee to their own
     land.

17 Israel is a hunted sheep driven away by lions. First the king of Assyria devoured it, and now at the end King Nebuchadrezzar of Babylon has gnawed its bones. ¹⁸Therefore, thus says the LORD of hosts, the God of Israel: I am going to punish the king of Babylon and his land, as I punished the king of Assyria. ¹⁹I will restore Israel to its pasture, and it shall feed on Carmel and in Bashan, and on the hills of Ephraim and in Gilead its hunger shall be satisfied. ²⁰In those days and at that time, says the LORD, the iniquity of Israel shall be sought, and there shall be none; and the sins of Judah, and none shall be found; for I will pardon the remnant that I have spared.

50.1–20: God's declaration of celebration opens the poem. The phrases express deep feeling in a few

a Gk: Heb toward it. Come! They shall join

words. Babylon is taken and her gods are shamed. The agent of destruction is the mythic foe from the north. **4–10:** The fate of Babylon is connected to the fate of Israel, for the coming attack on Babylon will signal the return of Israel and Judah. They will come weeping to seal the covenant★ with God. **11–16:** The plunderers will be destroyed; God commands the army to take position. According to this poetry, the victory is already won, so the celebration may begin. **17–20:** God reinterprets Israel's history as a series of attacks upon lost sheep. They are helpless, even if sinners, and they will be pardoned.

21 Go up to the land of Merathaim;*ᵃ*
  go up against her,
and attack the inhabitants of Pekod*ᵇ*
  and utterly destroy the last of them,*ᶜ*
                  says the LORD;
  do all that I have commanded you.
22 The noise of battle is in the land,
  and great destruction!
23 How the hammer of the whole earth
  is cut down and broken!
How Babylon has become
  a horror among the nations!
24 You set a snare for yourself and you
              were caught, O Babylon,
  but you did not know it;
you were discovered and seized,
  because you challenged the LORD.
25 The LORD has opened his armory,
  and brought out the weapons of
              his wrath,
  for the Lord GOD of hosts has a task
              to do
  in the land of the Chaldeans.
26 Come against her from every
              quarter;
  open her granaries;
pile her up like heaps of grain, and
              destroy her utterly;
  let nothing be left of her.
27 Kill all her bulls,
  let them go down to the slaughter.
Alas for them, their day has come,
  the time of their punishment!

28 Listen! Fugitives and refugees from the land of Babylon are coming to declare in Zion the vengeance of the LORD our God, vengeance for his temple.

29 Summon archers against Babylon, all who bend the bow. Encamp all around her; let no one escape. Repay her according to her deeds; just as she has done, do to her—for she has arrogantly defied the LORD, the Holy One of Israel. ³⁰Therefore her young men shall fall in her squares, and all her soldiers shall be destroyed on that day, says the LORD.

31 I am against you, O arrogant one,
    says the Lord GOD of hosts;
  for your day has come,
    the time when I will punish you.
32 The arrogant one shall stumble and fall,
    with no one to raise him up,
  and I will kindle a fire in his cities,
    and it will devour everything around
      him.

33 Thus says the LORD of hosts: The people of Israel are oppressed, and so too are the people of Judah; all their captors have held them fast and refuse to let them go. ³⁴Their Redeemer is strong; the LORD of hosts is his name. He will surely plead their cause, that he may give rest to the earth, but unrest to the inhabitants of Babylon.

50.21–34: The battle preparations continue and become more vivid. **23–24:** Babylon, the *hammer of the whole earth,* will be cut down despite its great power, for the enemy is God. **28:** Fugitives escape from the city and run to Zion★ to announce the changed state of affairs. **31–32:** God accuses Babylon of exceeding its divine commission to punish Judah: Babylon has gone berserk in its violence. Interpretation of international events has turned upside down in this book. Here Israel and Judah are oppressed people, not guilty people. They have a future, and the enemy will be punished for excesses. **34:** *Their Redeemer* will buy back the captives and give rest to the whole earth.

35 A sword against the Chaldeans, says the
              LORD,
    and against the inhabitants of
              Babylon,
    and against her officials and
              her sages!

a Or *of Double Rebellion*   *b* Or *of Punishment*
c Tg: Heb *destroy after them*

36 A sword against the diviners,
   so that they may become fools!
A sword against her warriors,
   so that they may be destroyed!
37 A sword against her*a* horses and against
      her*a* chariots,
   and against all the foreign troops in
      her midst,
   so that they may become women!
A sword against all her treasures,
   that they may be plundered!
38 A drought*b* against her waters,
   that they may be dried up!
For it is a land of images,
   and they go mad over idols.

39 Therefore wild animals shall live with hyenas in Babylon,*c* and ostriches shall inhabit her; she shall never again be peopled, or inhabited for all generations. 40As when God overthrew Sodom and Gomorrah and their neighbors, says the LORD, so no one shall live there, nor shall anyone settle in her.

41 Look, a people is coming from
      the north;
   a mighty nation and many kings
   are stirring from the farthest parts of
      the earth.
42 They wield bow and spear,
   they are cruel and have no mercy.
The sound of them is like the roaring
      sea;
   they ride upon horses,
set in array as a warrior for battle,
   against you, O daughter Babylon!

43 The king of Babylon heard news
      of them,
   and his hands fell helpless;
anguish seized him,
   pain like that of a woman in labor.

44 Like a lion coming up from the thickets of the Jordan against a perennial pasture, I will suddenly chase them away from her; and I will appoint over her whomever I choose.*d* For who is like me? Who can summon me? Who is the shepherd who can

stand before me? 45Therefore hear the plan that the LORD has made against Babylon, and the purposes that he has formed against the land of the Chaldeans: Surely the little ones of the flock shall be dragged away; surely their*e* fold shall be appalled at their fate. 46At the sound of the capture of Babylon the earth shall tremble, and her cry shall be heard among the nations.

50.35–46: A curse-like poem about the *sword* gloats over the reversal of circumstances about to take place. It is as if chanting words about the sword would activate thrusts into the heart of Babylon. Five times the poem brings the sword against some element of Babylonian society. The last verse shifts to drought. The reason for the attack is Babylon's idolatry.* **41–46:** The people from the north approach; they are cruel, noisy, and arrayed for battled against daughter Babylon. The agent of destruction is God, coming like a lion, coming with a plan that will make the earth tremble.

51

Thus says the LORD:
I am going to stir up a destructive
      wind*f*
  against Babylon
  and against the inhabitants of Leb-
      qamai;*g*
2 and I will send winnowers to Babylon,
   and they shall winnow her.
They shall empty her land
   when they come against her from
      every side
  on the day of trouble.
3 Let not the archer bend his bow,
   and let him not array himself in his
      coat of mail.
Do not spare her young men;
   utterly destroy her entire army.
4 They shall fall down slain in the land of
      the Chaldeans,
   and wounded in her streets.
5 Israel and Judah have not been
      forsaken
   by their God, the LORD of hosts,

a Cn: Heb *his*   *b* Another reading is *A sword*   *c* Heb lacks *in Babylon*   *d* Or *and I will single out the choicest of her rams:* Meaning of Heb uncertain   *e* Syr Gk Tg Compare 49.20: Heb lacks *their*   *f* Or *stir up the spirit of a destroyer*   *g* *Leb-qamai* is a cryptogram for *Kasdim,* Chaldea

though their land is full of guilt
    before the Holy One of Israel.

6 Flee from the midst of Babylon,
        save your lives, each of you!
Do not perish because of her guilt,
        for this is the time of the LORD's
            vengeance;
    he is repaying her what is due.
7 Babylon was a golden cup in the LORD's
        hand,
    making all the earth drunken;
the nations drank of her wine,
    and so the nations went mad.
8 Suddenly Babylon has fallen and
        is shattered;
    wail for her!
Bring balm for her wound;
    perhaps she may be healed.
9 We tried to heal Babylon,
    but she could not be healed.
Forsake her, and let each of us go
        to our own country;
for her judgment has reached up
        to heaven
    and has been lifted up even to the
        skies.
10 The LORD has brought forth our
        vindication;
    come, let us declare in Zion
    the work of the LORD our God.

11 Sharpen the arrows!
    Fill the quivers!
The LORD has stirred up the spirit of the
kings of the Medes, because his purpose
concerning Babylon is to destroy it, for that
is the vengeance of the LORD, vengeance for
his temple.
12 Raise a standard against the walls of
        Babylon;
    make the watch strong;
post sentinels;
    prepare the ambushes;
for the LORD has both planned and done
    what he spoke concerning the
        inhabitants of Babylon.
13 You who live by mighty waters,
        rich in treasures,
    your end has come,
    the thread of your life is cut.

14 The LORD of hosts has sworn by himself:
    Surely I will fill you with troops like a
        swarm of locusts,
    and they shall raise a shout of victory
        over you.

51.1–64: Flee. The opposing futures of Babylon and Israel continue to echo each other in this chapter. However, for the first time God orders the exiles to flee from Babylon and return to Zion.* God's power dominates these passages to show that God is the sovereign of history. Out of nothing God will create a future that will overturn systems of domination. **1–5:** Speaking in the first person, God plans the siege of Babylon. *I am going to stir up a . . . wind. . . . I will send winnowers.** God is bringing about cosmic upheaval that will destroy Babylonian power. **5:** Despite their guilt, God has not abandoned Israel and Judah. **6–10:** The exiles must flee. Urgent appeals to them to escape from the vengeance about to engulf Babylon open the poem. **8:** Babylon has been like a golden cup in God's hand but now has fallen. A voice calls for healing balm, but it is too late. **9:** The exiles *tried to heal Babylon* but they could not, so they flee to Zion to declare God's work. **11–14:** War preparations continue. God orders armies to make their weapons ready and to *prepare ambushes*. The *Medes,* an empire of the time, will destroy Babylon.

15 It is he who made the earth by
        his power,
    who established the world by
        his wisdom,
    and by his understanding stretched out
        the heavens.
16 When he utters his voice there is a
        tumult of waters in the heavens,
    and he makes the mist rise from the
        ends of the earth.
He makes lightnings for the rain,
    and he brings out the wind from his
        storehouses.
17 Everyone is stupid and without
        knowledge;
    goldsmiths are all put to shame by
        their idols;
    for their images are false,
    and there is no breath in them.
18 They are worthless, a work of delusion;
    at the time of their punishment they
        shall perish.

19 Not like these is the LORD,ᵃ the portion
      of Jacob,
   for he is the one who formed
      all things,
   and Israel is the tribe of his inheritance;
      the LORD of hosts is his name.

20 You are my war club, my weapon of
      battle:
   with you I smash nations;
      with you I destroy kingdoms;
21 with you I smash the horse and its rider;
      with you I smash the chariot and the
      charioteer;
22 with you I smash man and woman;
      with you I smash the old man and the
      boy;
   with you I smash the young man and
      the girl;
23   with you I smash shepherds and their
      flocks;
   with you I smash farmers and
      their teams;
   with you I smash governors and
      deputies.

51.15–23. 15–19: A hymn, perhaps representing the
voice of the exiles, praises the Creator, wise and understanding, who made the earth and maintains its
natural processes. Compared to the Creator, the *idols*
are worthless. They are the lifeless gods of the *goldsmith.* **20–23:** Eight times the Creator says to his weapons or his armies, *I smash with you,* creating a rhyth-
mic beat of destruction. Smashed will be nations,
peoples, animals, and rulers.

〰〰〰〰〰〰〰〰〰〰〰

24 I will repay Babylon and all the inhabitants of Chaldea before your very eyes for
all the wrong that they have done in Zion,
says the LORD.

25 I am against you, O destroying
      mountain,
                          says the LORD,
   that destroys the whole earth;
   I will stretch out my hand against you,
      and roll you down from the crags,
      and make you a burned-out
      mountain.
26 No stone shall be taken from you for a
      corner

and no stone for a foundation,
   but you shall be a perpetual waste,
      says the LORD.

27 Raise a standard in the land,
   blow the trumpet among the nations;
prepare the nations for war against her,
   summon against her the kingdoms,
      Ararat, Minni, and Ashkenaz;
appoint a marshal against her,
   bring up horses like bristling locusts.
28 Prepare the nations for war against her,
   the kings of the Medes, with their
      governors and deputies,
   and every land under their dominion.
29 The land trembles and writhes,
   for the LORD's purposes against
      Babylon stand,
to make the land of Babylon a
      desolation,
   without inhabitant.
30 The warriors of Babylon have given up
      fighting,
   they remain in their strongholds;
their strength has failed,
   they have become women;
her buildings are set on fire,
   her bars are broken.
31 One runner runs to meet another,
   and one messenger to meet another,
to tell the king of Babylon
   that his city is taken from end to end:
32 the fords have been seized,
   the marshes have been burned with
      fire,
   and the soldiers are in panic.
33 For thus says the LORD of hosts, the
      God of Israel:
Daughter Babylon is like a threshing
      floor
   at the time when it is trodden;
yet a little while
   and the time of her harvest
      will come.

51.24–33: War preparations continue and God promises Babylon, *the destroying mountain,* that it will be
attacked.

〰〰〰〰〰〰〰〰〰〰〰

a Heb lacks *the* LORD

34 "King Nebuchadrezzar of Babylon has
         devoured me,
     he has crushed me;
 he has made me an empty vessel,
     he has swallowed me like a monster;
 he has filled his belly with my
         delicacies,
     he has spewed me out.
35 May my torn flesh be avenged on
         Babylon,"
     the inhabitants of Zion shall say.
 "May my blood be avenged on the
         inhabitants of Chaldea,"
     Jerusalem shall say.
36 Therefore thus says the LORD:
 I am going to defend your cause
     and take vengeance for you.
 I will dry up her sea
     and make her fountain dry;
37 and Babylon shall become a heap
         of ruins,
     a den of jackals,
 an object of horror and of hissing,
     without inhabitant.

38 Like lions they shall roar together;
     they shall growl like lions' whelps.
39 When they are inflamed, I will set out
         their drink
     and make them drunk, until they
         become merry
 and then sleep a perpetual sleep
     and never wake, says the LORD.
40 I will bring them down like lambs to the
         slaughter,
     like rams and goats.

41 How Sheshach[a] is taken,
     the pride of the whole earth seized!
 How Babylon has become
     an object of horror among the
         nations!
42 The sea has risen over Babylon;
     she has been covered by its
         tumultuous waves.
43 Her cities have become an object
         of horror,
     a land of drought and a desert,
 a land in which no one lives,
     and through which no mortal
         passes.

44 I will punish Bel in Babylon,
     and make him disgorge what he has
         swallowed.
 The nations shall no longer stream to him;
     the wall of Babylon has fallen.

51.34–44: More accusations describing Nebuchadrezzar's violence against the people of Zion accumulate.
Babylon and its God, Bel, will be drunk and engorged.
The superpower is ugly and out of control with its destruction of others.

~~~~~~~~~~~~~~~~~~~~~~~~~~~~~~~~~~~~~~~

45 Come out of her, my people!
     Save your lives, each of you,
     from the fierce anger of the LORD!
46 Do not be fainthearted or fearful
     at the rumors heard in the land—
 one year one rumor comes,
     the next year another,
 rumors of violence in the land
     and of ruler against ruler.

47 Assuredly, the days are coming
     when I will punish the images
         of Babylon;
 her whole land shall be put to shame,
     and all her slain shall fall in
         her midst.
48 Then the heavens and the earth,
     and all that is in them,
 shall shout for joy over Babylon;
     for the destroyers shall come against
         them out of the north,
                     says the LORD.
49 Babylon must fall for the slain of Israel,
     as the slain of all the earth have
         fallen because of Babylon.

50 You survivors of the sword,
     go, do not linger!
 Remember the LORD in a distant land,
     and let Jerusalem come into your
         mind:
51 We are put to shame, for we have heard
         insults;
     dishonor has covered our face,
 for aliens have come
     into the holy places of the
         LORD's house.

a *Sheshach* is a cryptogram for *Babel*, Babylon

52 Therefore the time is surely coming,
        says the LORD,
    when I will punish her idols,
and through all her land
    the wounded shall groan.
53 Though Babylon should mount up to
        heaven,
    and though she should fortify her
        strong height,
from me destroyers would come upon
        her,
    says the LORD.

54 Listen!—a cry from Babylon!
    A great crashing from the land of the
        Chaldeans!
55 For the LORD is laying Babylon waste,
    and stilling her loud clamor.
Their waves roar like mighty waters,
    the sound of their clamor resounds;
56 for a destroyer has come against her,
        against Babylon;
    her warriors are taken,
        their bows are broken;
for the LORD is a God of recompense,
    he will repay in full.
57 I will make her officials and her sages
        drunk,
    also her governors, her deputies, and
        her warriors;
they shall sleep a perpetual sleep and
        never wake,
    says the King, whose name is the
        LORD of hosts.

58 Thus says the LORD of hosts:
The broad wall of Babylon
    shall be leveled to the ground,
and her high gates
    shall be burned with fire.
The peoples exhaust themselves for
        nothing,
    and the nations weary themselves
        only for fire.[a]

51.45–58: Again God calls the exiles to depart and save themselves. 46: They must overcome their fears, which are being caused by rumors among them. In the future God will destroy Babylon. 47–48: The cosmos will participate in the celebration. 50: It is urgent that the exiles should *not linger* but remember that God is in Jerusalem. 50–58: An imaginative portrayal of the attack ends the poetry of the book. There is a *cry*, smashing, *crashing*, for the destroyer has come against Babylon. Her leaders will be *drunk, asleep, never to wake.*

59 The word that the prophet Jeremiah commanded Seraiah son of Neriah son of Mahseiah, when he went with King Zedekiah of Judah to Babylon, in the fourth year of his reign. Seraiah was the quartermaster. 60 Jeremiah wrote in a[b] scroll all the disasters that would come on Babylon, all these words that are written concerning Babylon. 61 And Jeremiah said to Seraiah: "When you come to Babylon, see that you read all these words, 62 and say, 'O LORD, you yourself threatened to destroy this place so that neither human beings nor animals shall live in it, and it shall be desolate forever.' 63 When you finish reading this scroll, tie a stone to it, and throw it into the middle of the Euphrates, 64 and say, 'Thus shall Babylon sink, to rise no more, because of the disasters that I am bringing on her.' "[c]

Thus far are the words of Jeremiah.

51.59–64: In a symbolic act written in prose, Baruch's brother, Seraiah, goes to Babylon under Jeremiah's directions. There Seraiah is to read the scroll containing prophecies against Babylon aloud, attach a stone to the scroll, and sink it in the Euphrates River. Like the sinking scroll, so will Babylon sink from its high position. This symbolic act embodies the divine will. It needs only to come to fulfillment.

THE END

Ch. 52: The prose conclusion to the book reports the end of national life in Judah, but neither God nor Jeremiah appear in it. The purpose of this bleak report may be to describe the fulfillment of Jeremiah's prophetic word. The setting is the Exile,* when Babylonian defeat is far from sight. The chapter is nearly identical to the account of Judah's fall that concludes the book of Kings (2 Kings 24.18–25.30). The narrative* divides into six short scenes.

a Gk Syr Compare Hab 2.13: Heb *and the nations for fire, and they are weary*   b Or *one*   c Gk: Heb *on her. And they shall weary themselves*

52 Zedekiah was twenty-one years old when he began to reign; he reigned eleven years in Jerusalem. His mother's name was Hamutal daughter of Jeremiah of Libnah. 2He did what was evil in the sight of the LORD, just as Jehoiakim had done. 3Indeed, Jerusalem and Judah so angered the LORD that he expelled them from his presence.

Zedekiah rebelled against the king of Babylon. 4And in the ninth year of his reign, in the tenth month, on the tenth day of the month, King Nebuchadrezzar of Babylon came with all his army against Jerusalem, and they laid siege to it; they built siegeworks against it all around. 5So the city was besieged until the eleventh year of King Zedekiah. 6On the ninth day of the fourth month the famine became so severe in the city that there was no food for the people of the land. 7Then a breach was made in the city wall;*a* and all the soldiers fled and went out from the city by night by the way of the gate between the two walls, by the king's garden, though the Chaldeans were all around the city. They went in the direction of the Arabah. 8But the army of the Chaldeans pursued the king, and overtook Zedekiah in the plains of Jericho; and all his army was scattered, deserting him. 9Then they captured the king, and brought him up to the king of Babylon at Riblah in the land of Hamath, and he passed sentence on him. 10The king of Babylon killed the sons of Zedekiah before his eyes, and also killed all the officers of Judah at Riblah. 11He put out the eyes of Zedekiah, and bound him in fetters, and the king of Babylon took him to Babylon, and put him in prison until the day of his death.

12 In the fifth month, on the tenth day of the month—which was the nineteenth year of King Nebuchadrezzar, king of Babylon— Nebuzaradan the captain of the bodyguard who served the king of Babylon, entered Jerusalem. 13He burned the house of the LORD, the king's house, and all the houses of Jerusalem; every great house he burned down. 14All the army of the Chaldeans, who were with the captain of the guard, broke down all the walls around Jerusalem. 15Nebuzaradan the captain of the guard carried into exile some of the poorest of the people and the rest of the people who were left in the city and the deserters who had defected to the king of Babylon, together with the rest of the artisans. 16But Nebuzaradan the captain of the guard left some of the poorest people of the land to be vinedressers and tillers of the soil.

52.1–16. 1–3: Kings Jehoiakim and Zedekiah angered God, and Judah and Jerusalem *were expelled from his presence.* 4–11: Zedekiah's failed escape and the tragedy of his capture and imprisonment and death suggest the possible fate awaiting Judah. 12–16: The people are deported and divided with the poor remaining in the land.

17 The pillars of bronze that were in the house of the LORD, and the stands and the bronze sea that were in the house of the LORD, the Chaldeans broke in pieces, and carried all the bronze to Babylon. 18They took away the pots, the shovels, the snuffers, the basins, the ladles, and all the vessels of bronze used in the temple service. 19The captain of the guard took away the small bowls also, the firepans, the basins, the pots, the lampstands, the ladles, and the bowls for libation, both those of gold and those of silver. 20As for the two pillars, the one sea, the twelve bronze bulls that were under the sea, and the stands,*b* which King Solomon had made for the house of the LORD, the bronze of all these vessels was beyond weighing. 21As for the pillars, the height of the one pillar was eighteen cubits, its circumference was twelve cubits; it was hollow and its thickness was four fingers. 22Upon it was a capital of bronze; the height of the capital was five cubits; latticework and pomegranates, all of bronze, encircled the top of the capital. And the second pillar had the same, with pomegranates. 23There were ninety-six pomegranates on the sides; all the pomegranates encircling the latticework numbered one hundred.

24 The captain of the guard took the chief priest Seraiah, the second priest Zeph-

---

a Heb lacks *wall*   *b* Cn: Heb *that were under the stands*

aniah, and the three guardians of the threshold; [25]and from the city he took an officer who had been in command of the soldiers, and seven men of the king's council who were found in the city; the secretary of the commander of the army who mustered the people of the land; and sixty men of the people of the land who were found inside the city. [26]Then Nebuzaradan the captain of the guard took them, and brought them to the king of Babylon at Riblah. [27]And the king of Babylon struck them down, and put them to death at Riblah in the land of Hamath. So Judah went into exile out of its land.

28 This is the number of the people whom Nebuchadrezzar took into exile: in the seventh year, three thousand twenty-three Judeans; [29]in the eighteenth year of Nebuchadrezzar he took into exile from Jerusalem eight hundred thirty-two persons; [30]in the twenty-third year of Nebuchadrezzar, Nebuzaradan the captain of the guard took into exile of the Judeans seven hundred forty-five persons; all the persons were four thousand six hundred.

31 In the thirty-seventh year of the exile of King Jehoiachin of Judah, in the twelfth month, on the twenty-fifth day of the month, King Evil-merodach of Babylon, in the year he began to reign, showed favor to King Jehoiachin of Judah and brought him out of prison; [32]he spoke kindly to him, and gave him a seat above the seats of the other kings who were with him in Babylon. [33]So Jehoiachin put aside his prison clothes, and every day of his life he dined regularly at the king's table. [34]For his allowance, a regular daily allowance was given him by the king of Babylon, as long as he lived, up to the day of his death.

52.17–34. 17–23: The capture of the sacred Temple* vessels by the Babylonians underscores the end of worship life in the land. **28–30:** The numbers of exiles are provided, but their historical accuracy is in doubt. **31–34:** King Jehoiachin, also imprisoned in Babylon, survives and is restored to the table, though not yet released. The scene of the king's survival may offer a glimmer of hope to exiles for whom the king's survival with dignity may show the way to the future. This book has been about survival in the face of overwhelming catastrophe. If Jeremiah's words of judgment were fulfilled, then his words of hope will triumph as well.

LAMENTATIONS

Introduction

In five powerful, moving poems, Lamentations grieves for the destruction of Jerusalem in 586 BCE by the Babylonian armies. It is like many of the Psalms of lament☆ in its mood and style, and it often speaks in general terms of the destruction, using metaphors☆ and images that focus more on the feelings provoked by the calamity than on the events themselves. It shares with the Deuteronomistic☆ History and some of the prophets☆ the dominant conviction that suffering is an indication of God's displeasure, and yet other voices emerge—protests that the community suffers for the sins of its ancestors, that some of those who suffer (especially children) are innocent, and that the punishment may be unjustifiably harsh. The first four poems are acrostics,☆ the first lines or stanzas beginning with the letters of the alphabet☆ in sequence; the last poem has twenty-two lines, one for each letter of the Hebrew alphabet.

After the destruction of the Second Temple☆ in 70 CE, Lamentations became part of the liturgy☆ for the Ninth of Ab, the date of the Temple's fall. Hence, the book is found in the Jewish Bible with the "Megilloth" or festival scrolls.☆ See sidebar on p. 1053. The Christian canon,☆ following the Septuagint,☆ places the book after Jeremiah, whose strong expressions of emotion gained him the reputation of "the weeping prophet." The shifts in voices and styles, as well as the various acrostic techniques, lead most scholars to conclude that the book is a compilation of various materials, brought together to serve as a community liturgy of lament.

READING GUIDE

Lamentations is most helpfully read as an emotional response to suffering. How do these poems evoke our empathy with physical, emotional, and religious trauma—what it is to survive war, famine, the death of children, the rape of women, and the loss of the nation's religious and political center? How do the various voices (Jerusalem, a feminine voice; another individual "I," probably the poet; the community, in the plural "we") respond to tragedy?

1 First lament of the poet and the city
2 Second lament of the poet and the city
3 Miscellaneous laments
4 Third lament of the poet and the city
5 The community laments

1 How lonely sits the city
   that once was full of people!
How like a widow she has become,
   she that was great among the nations!
She that was a princess among the
      provinces
   has become a vassal.

2 She weeps bitterly in the night,
   with tears on her cheeks;

among all her lovers
   she has no one to comfort her;
all her friends have dealt treacherously
      with her,
   they have become her enemies.

3 Judah has gone into exile with suffering
      and hard servitude;
   she lives now among the nations,
      and finds no resting place;

Acrostic Poems

Many of the stylistic elements of ancient Hebrew poetry remain unclear. One formal technique, however, is self-evident: The practice of beginning each line of a poem with the letters of the Hebrew alphabet in order (there are twenty-two letters in the Hebrew alphabet). This formal technique is called an *acrostic*; in English (and other languages) acrostic poems often use the first letters of a line to spell out a word or name, or to create some other pattern. Hebrew acrostics always follow the alphabetical pattern.

In the Bible, the following poems are acrostics: Psalms 9–10, 25, 34, 37, 111, 112, 119, 145; Proverbs 31.10–31; Lamentations; Nahum 1.2–8 (or possibly 2–10—the lines are disordered and the acrostic is incomplete); and Sirach 57.13–30. Of these texts, Psalms 34, 37, 112, 119, Proverbs 31, and Sirach 57 belong to the wisdom traditions of ancient Israel. It is possible that the acrostic pattern was a device used in schools, to aid in the memorization of a lengthy passage.

It might seem that an acrostic would be highly artificial, even possibly incoherent, since the beginning word of each line is in some sense a separate alphabetic entity, chosen for a reason other than meaning. We should compare this pattern, however, to the use of rhyme in English poetry: A rhyme is a pattern based on similarity of sound, and the aesthetic enjoyment of rhymed poetry is partly dependent on our observation of the poet's art in combining patterns of sound and meaning. Acrostic poems might have provided the same kind of pleasure. To test this supposition, try reading Psalms 9–10 or Lamentations 1 or 3. Do they appear to be arbitrary collections of lines, or do they present a strong sense of coherence? At a minimum, we can say that the acrostic form allows the poet an opportunity to work systematically through an idea or form, all the way "from A to Z," as we say in English. In the case of Lamentations, each chapter of which is composed entirely according to the acrostic pattern, the form provides a powerful structure by means of which to express the complaints and laments of the grieving people. In these chapters, the acrostic pattern is far more than a simple device to aid memorization.

The pattern not only structures but also limits and channels the deep feelings of grief and loss. Every society creates forms of behavior that help people to express their sorrow, and to come to terms with it. These forms of behavior put limits, sometimes even time limits, upon a period of mourning. The acrostics in Lamentations function in a similar way: By using the limits and regularity of the alphabet, they create a literary structure that sets boundaries upon the expression of grief and, in doing so, helps the reader move to a discernment of the hopeful words expressed in the center of the book, Lam 3.22–33.

---

her pursuers have all overtaken her
   in the midst of her distress.

4 The roads to Zion mourn,
   for no one comes to the festivals;
all her gates are desolate,
   her priests groan;

her young girls grieve,[a]
   and her lot is bitter.

5 Her foes have become the masters,
   her enemies prosper,

a Meaning of Heb uncertain

because the LORD has made her suffer
for the multitude of her
transgressions;
her children have gone away,
captives before the foe.

6 From daughter Zion has departed
all her majesty.
Her princes have become like stags
that find no pasture;
they fled without strength
before the pursuer.

7 Jerusalem remembers,
in the days of her affliction and
wandering,
all the precious things
that were hers in days of old.
When her people fell into the hand of
the foe,
and there was no one to help her,
the foe looked on mocking
over her downfall.

8 Jerusalem sinned grievously,
so she has become a mockery;
all who honored her despise her,
for they have seen her nakedness;
she herself groans,
and turns her face away.

9 Her uncleanness was in her skirts;
she took no thought of her future;
her downfall was appalling,
with none to comfort her.
"O LORD, look at my affliction,
for the enemy has triumphed!"

10 Enemies have stretched out their hands
over all her precious things;
she has even seen the nations
invade her sanctuary,
those whom you forbade
to enter your congregation.

1.1–11a: A poet laments Jerusalem. As in many prophetic books (Hosea, Jeremiah, Ezekiel), Jerusalem is
personified* as a woman. In a striking series of contrasts, she who was great is now destitute like a *widow*;
once a princess, she is now a *vassal*, the underling in
a political relationship. 2: Political allies are called Je-

rusalem's *lovers* (Hos 2.7). 3: *Exile*, the conquering
strategy of the neo-Babylonian empire, involved moving large groups of people out of their homelands into
new locations. 4: Public activities (*festivals* and *gates*,
where people gather) have ceased. *Priests* and *young
girls* are among the many categories of people that
the book shows as suffering. 5: The book repeatedly
claims that *the LORD has made her suffer*. 8–10: *Nakedness* may have a sexual connotation (Lev 18.6).
Uncleanness refers to menstruation (Lev 15.16–24).
These conditions intensify her shame, considered by
the author to be as significant as physical suffering. The
immediate mention of *precious things* and the invasion of *her sanctuary*, while on the surface referring to
the Temple,* may have sexual connotations as well.

11 All her people groan
as they search for bread;
they trade their treasures for food
to revive their strength.
Look, O LORD, and see
how worthless I have become.

12 Is it nothing to you,ᵃ all you who
pass by?
Look and see
if there is any sorrow like my sorrow,
which was brought upon me,
which the LORD inflicted
on the day of his fierce anger.

13 From on high he sent fire;
it went deep into my bones;
he spread a net for my feet;
he turned me back;
he has left me stunned,
faint all day long.

14 My transgressions were boundᵃ into a
yoke;
by his hand they were fastened
together;
they weigh on my neck,
sapping my strength;
the Lord handed me over
to those whom I cannot withstand.

15 The LORD has rejected
all my warriors in the midst of me;

a Meaning of Heb uncertain

he proclaimed a time against me
  to crush my young men;
the Lord has trodden as in a wine press
  the virgin daughter Judah.

16 For these things I weep;
  my eyes flow with tears;
for a comforter is far from me,
  one to revive my courage;
my children are desolate,
  for the enemy has prevailed.

17 Zion stretches out her hands,
  but there is no one to comfort her;
the LORD has commanded against Jacob
  that his neighbors should become his
    foes;
Jerusalem has become
  a filthy thing among them.

18 The LORD is in the right,
  for I have rebelled against his word;
but hear, all you peoples,
  and behold my suffering;
my young women and young men
  have gone into captivity.

19 I called to my lovers
  but they deceived me;
my priests and elders
  perished in the city
while seeking food
  to revive their strength.

20 See, O LORD, how distressed I am;
  my stomach churns,
my heart is wrung within me,
  because I have been very rebellious.
In the street the sword bereaves;
  in the house it is like death.

21 They heard how I was groaning,
  with no one to comfort me.
All my enemies heard of my trouble;
  they are glad that you have done it.
Bring on the day you have announced,
  and let them be as I am.

22 Let all their evil doing come before you;
  and deal with them

as you have dealt with me
  because of all my transgressions;
for my groans are many
  and my heart is faint.

1.11b–22: Jerusalem herself speaks. The speaker changes at the end of v. 11, as the woman Jerusalem speaks in the first person. She repeats themes of the first speaker: She is shamed, and the devastation is punishment from God. **13–15:** *Net, fire:* Punishments are described generically (Ps 10.9; Isa 63.3). The weight of Israel's sin is compared to a *yoke* worn by captives of war (Isa 9.4). **16:** The lack of a *comforter* is a repeated theme of the book. **17:** The voice shifts back to third person briefly. *Zion** (the mountain on which Jerusalem is set), *Jacob* (the ancestor of the Israelites), and *Jerusalem* are used as synonyms. *Filthy thing* is the menstrual *uncleanness* of 1.9. **18:** The voice of Jerusalem returns, acknowledging her sin yet lamenting the pain she has experienced. **20:** Jerusalem's lament* resembles that of Jeremiah (Jer 8.18–9.1). **21–22:** Again concerned with being shamed in the face of others, Jerusalem asks that they, too, be treated according to their deeds. *Day you have announced* refers to the Day of the LORD, envisioned as a day of vindication against enemies (Isa 13.6–16).

〰〰〰〰〰〰〰〰〰〰〰〰〰

2 How the Lord in his anger
  has humiliated*a* daughter Zion!
He has thrown down from heaven to
    earth
  the splendor of Israel;
he has not remembered his footstool
  in the day of his anger.

2 The Lord has destroyed without mercy
  all the dwellings of Jacob;
in his wrath he has broken down
  the strongholds of daughter Judah;
he has brought down to the ground in
    dishonor
  the kingdom and its rulers.

3 He has cut down in fierce anger
  all the might of Israel;
he has withdrawn his right hand from
    them
  in the face of the enemy;

---

a Meaning of Heb uncertain

he has burned like a flaming fire
in Jacob,
consuming all around.

4 He has bent his bow like an enemy,
with his right hand set like a foe;
he has killed all in whom we
took pride
in the tent of daughter Zion;
he has poured out his fury like fire.

5 The Lord has become like an enemy;
he has destroyed Israel.
He has destroyed all its palaces,
laid in ruins its strongholds,
and multiplied in daughter Judah
mourning and lamentation.

6 He has broken down his booth like a
garden,
he has destroyed his tabernacle;
the LORD has abolished in Zion
festival and sabbath,
and in his fierce indignation has
spurned
king and priest.

7 The Lord has scorned his altar,
disowned his sanctuary;
he has delivered into the hand of the
enemy
the walls of her palaces;
a clamor was raised in the house of the
LORD
as on a day of festival.

8 The LORD determined to lay in ruins
the wall of daughter Zion;
he stretched the line;
he did not withhold his hand from
destroying;
he caused rampart and wall to lament;
they languish together.

9 Her gates have sunk into the ground;
he has ruined and broken her bars;
her king and princes are among
the nations;
guidance is no more,
and her prophets obtain
no vision from the LORD.

10 The elders of daughter Zion
sit on the ground in silence;
they have thrown dust on their heads
and put on sackcloth;
the young girls of Jerusalem
have bowed their heads to
the ground.

2.1–10. The poet on God's great anger. The poet describes the severity of God's punishment: Jerusalem is destroyed and humiliated. **1:** *Footstool:* The Temple (Ps 99.5). **2:** *Without mercy:* Without restraint. In a series of reversals, the great are brought down *to the ground.* **3–5:** God's *right hand,* his weapon hand, does not defend Israel but draws a bow against her like an enemy (Ex 15.6–12). **6–7:** *Booth, tabernacle*:* The Temple, which along with *festival, king,* and *priest* embodies the religious core of the nation, centered in Jerusalem and linked with the monarchy (2 Sam 7). **8–10:** *Stretched the line:* Apparently a step in destroying a building (2 Kings 21.13). God has broken down the very features intended to protect Jerusalem: *wall, gates* and *ramparts* (used for defense during military attacks). The listing of groups within the city underscores the totality of the destruction. *Dust* and *sackcloth** (v. 10) are typical gestures of mourning.

11 My eyes are spent with weeping;
my stomach churns;
my bile is poured out on the ground
because of the destruction of
my people,
because infants and babes faint
in the streets of the city.

12 They cry to their mothers,
"Where is bread and wine?"
as they faint like the wounded
in the streets of the city,
as their life is poured out
on their mothers' bosom.

13 What can I say for you, to what
compare you,
O daughter Jerusalem?
To what can I liken you, that I may
comfort you,
O virgin daughter Zion?
For vast as the sea is your ruin;
who can heal you?

14 Your prophets have seen for you
        false and deceptive visions;
    they have not exposed your iniquity
        to restore your fortunes,
    but have seen oracles for you
        that are false and misleading.

15 All who pass along the way
        clap their hands at you;
    they hiss and wag their heads
        at daughter Jerusalem;
    "Is this the city that was called
        the perfection of beauty,
        the joy of all the earth?"

16 All your enemies
        open their mouths against you;
    they hiss, they gnash their teeth,
        they cry: "We have devoured her!
    Ah, this is the day we longed for;
        at last we have seen it!"

17 The LORD has done what he purposed,
        he has carried out his threat;
    as he ordained long ago,
        he has demolished without pity;
    he has made the enemy rejoice
            over you,
        and exalted the might of your foes.

18 Cry aloud[a] to the Lord!
        O wall of daughter Zion!
    Let tears stream down like a torrent
        day and night!
    Give yourself no rest,
        your eyes no respite!

19 Arise, cry out in the night,
        at the beginning of the watches!
    Pour out your heart like water
        before the presence of the Lord!
    Lift your hands to him
        for the lives of your children,
    who faint for hunger
        at the head of every street.

2.11–19: The poet continues his lament. 11: Both the *stomach* (also 1.20) and *bile* refer to the seat of emotions (Jer 4.19); bile in addition means "bitterness" (from the taste of the digestive substance secreted from the gallbladder). 14: *False prophets** gave

unwarranted messages of comfort (Jer 14.13–16). 15–16: Jerusalem suffers not only the famine of children but also the taunts of enemies (Jer 19.8). 17: *As he ordained long ago* may refer to the teaching of the pre-exilic prophets, for whom destruction of the nation as punishment for sin was a common motif.* 18–19: The poet urges Jerusalem to petition God.

20 Look, O LORD, and consider!
        To whom have you done this?
    Should women eat their offspring,
        the children they have borne?
    Should priest and prophet be killed
        in the sanctuary of the Lord?

21 The young and the old are lying
        on the ground in the streets;
    my young women and my young men
        have fallen by the sword;
    in the day of your anger you have killed
            them,
        slaughtering without mercy.

22 You invited my enemies from all around
        as if for a day of festival;
    and on the day of the anger of the LORD
        no one escaped or survived;
    those whom I bore and reared
        my enemy has destroyed.

2.20–22: Jerusalem petitions God. The stark picture of women eating their own children and the death of the young raises this question: Has God punished too severely?

3 I am one who has seen affliction
        under the rod of God's[b] wrath;
2   he has driven and brought me
        into darkness without any light;
3   against me alone he turns his hand,
        again and again, all day long.

4   He has made my flesh and my skin
            waste away,
        and broken my bones;
5   he has besieged and enveloped me
        with bitterness and tribulation;
6   he has made me sit in darkness
        like the dead of long ago.

a Cn: Heb *Their heart cried*   *b* Heb *his*

7 He has walled me about so that I
cannot escape;
he has put heavy chains on me;

8 though I call and cry for help,
he shuts out my prayer;

9 he has blocked my ways with hewn
stones,
he has made my paths crooked.

10 He is a bear lying in wait for me,
a lion in hiding;

11 he led me off my way and tore me to
pieces;
he has made me desolate;

12 he bent his bow and set me
as a mark for his arrow.

13 He shot into my vitals
the arrows of his quiver;

14 I have become the laughingstock of all
my people,
the object of their taunt-songs all day
long.

15 He has filled me with bitterness,
he has sated me with wormwood.

16 He has made my teeth grind on gravel,
and made me cower in ashes;

17 my soul is bereft of peace;
I have forgotten what happiness is;

18 so I say, "Gone is my glory,
and all that I had hoped for from the
LORD."

19 The thought of my affliction and my
homelessness
is wormwood and gall!

20 My soul continually thinks of it
and is bowed down within me.

21 But this I call to mind,
and therefore I have hope:

22 The steadfast love of the LORD never
ceases,[a]
his mercies never come to an end;

23 they are new every morning;
great is your faithfulness.

24 "The LORD is my portion," says my
soul,
"therefore I will hope in him."

3.1–66: Multiple responses to suffering. Speakers
and moods shift throughout this chapter, making a
neat outline difficult. Has the material been adjusted
to fit the acrostic* pattern? Does the jarring style
mimic the dissociation of trauma? **1–24: An individual
lament.** Like other individual laments (Ps 38; 22), this
section includes nonspecific complaints of suffering
(vv. 1–19) and a statement of confidence in God (vv.
21–24). Identified neither with the poet who has spoken previously nor with Woman Zion, the speaker is
an individual male (Heb., "geber"). He explicitly
blames God for his troubles, comparing God to a wild
animal (v. 10) and an enemy warrior (vv. 12–13). His
troubles are not outlined but are compared to *heavy
chains* (v. 7) and *gravel* to the teeth (v. 16). **15:** *Wormwood* (also v. 19) is a bitter-tasting plant (Jer 9.14).
19: *Gall:* Bile (see comment on 2.1). **21–24:** Statement
of confidence, a feature of the individual lament.

25 The LORD is good to those who wait for
him,
to the soul that seeks him.

26 It is good that one should wait quietly
for the salvation of the LORD.

27 It is good for one to bear
the yoke in youth,

28 to sit alone in silence
when the Lord has imposed it,

29 to put one's mouth to the dust
(there may yet be hope),

30 to give one's cheek to the smiter,
and be filled with insults.

31 For the Lord will not
reject forever.

32 Although he causes grief, he will have
compassion
according to the abundance of his
steadfast love;

33 for he does not willingly afflict
or grieve anyone.

34 When all the prisoners of the land
are crushed under foot,

35 when human rights are perverted
in the presence of the Most High,

36 when one's case is subverted
—does the Lord not see it?

a Syr Tg: Heb LORD, *we are not cut off*

Megilloth in Jewish Liturgy

While Song of Solomon, Ruth, Lamentations, Ecclesiastes, and Esther originated in different times and places, today they are clustered together in the last section of the Jewish canon called the Writings. This arrangement reflects how the books are used: Each is read at one of the five pilgrimage festivals of Judaism, and their organization in the canon follows the order of the festivals.

Song of Solomon. By the turn of the era some Jewish interpreters were reading Song of Solomon as an allegory of God's love for Israel. For that reason, the book was eventually incorporated into the celebration of Passover, a spring festival that commemorates through the eating of symbolic foods the liberation of the Israelites from bondage in Egypt. The book's springtime references also fit appropriately with Passover's March–April setting.

Ruth. Shavuot, also known as the Feast of Weeks or Pentecost, was originally an agricultural festival, celebrating the end of the barley harvest and the beginning of the wheat harvest. Later it was given a historical connection: Based on Ex 19.1, Moses was said to have received the Law on Mt. Sinai at Shavuot. Both the agricultural and historical themes link with Ruth, since the book mentions harvest and since, according to Jewish tradition, Ruth represents a faithful convert.

Lamentations. Because of the book's concern with the destruction of Jerusalem by the Babylonian armies in 586 BCE, it is read at services on the Ninth of Ab, a day of mourning the loss of both the First and Second Temples (the latter destroyed by the Romans in 70 CE), as well as the exile of the Jewish community from Spain in 1492.

Ecclesiastes. Ecclesiastes' connection with its festival is not an obvious one: The book's insistence that persons should enjoy life links it with Sukkot (also Feast of Booths), which the Israelites are commanded to celebrate in Deut 16.15.

Esther. Of all the Megilloth, Esther has the clearest festival connection, since the book itself serves to explain and to encourage the observance of the festival of Purim. In modern Purim festivals, the book is read and children often dress up as its principal characters. The carnival-like atmosphere of modern Purim practices also finds obvious connections with the sumptuous banqueting in the book of Esther.

---

37 Who can command and have it done,
   if the Lord has not ordained it?
38 Is it not from the mouth of the Most
      High
   that good and bad come?
39 Why should any who draw breath
         complain
   about the punishment of their sins?

40 Let us test and examine our ways,
   and return to the LORD.

41 Let us lift up our hearts as well as our
      hands
   to God in heaven.
42 We have transgressed and rebelled,
   and you have not forgiven.

43 You have wrapped yourself with anger
      and pursued us,
   killing without pity;
44 you have wrapped yourself with a cloud
   so that no prayer can pass through.

45 You have made us filth and rubbish
    among the peoples.

46 All our enemies
    have opened their mouths against us;
47 panic and pitfall have come upon us,
    devastation and destruction.
48 My eyes flow with rivers of tears
    because of the destruction of
        my people.

49 My eyes will flow without ceasing,
    without respite,
50 until the LORD from heaven
    looks down and sees.
51 My eyes cause me grief
    at the fate of all the young women in
        my city.

3.25–51. 25–41: A teaching on God's goodness. In a jarring shift, this section at the center of the book offers beautiful statements of God's mercy, faithfulness, and compassion (vv. 22–33) and teaches silence in the face of suffering. Because some passages appear to contradict material that comes before and after (v. 39: Why should anyone complain?), these verses are often considered a later addition to the book. They function, however, to balance the community's expression of suffering with the book's insistent theme that God is justifiably punishing Judah for its sins. **40–41:** Because God has acted justly, Judah must examine its own wrongs. **42–51: A communal lament.** While beginning with recognition of guilt, the section also complains that God has refused to forgive (vv. 42, 44). Further complaints follow. The shame of defeat and enemy taunts, mentioned earlier in the book, is repeated. **48:** While the speaker shifts to ''I'' the theme remains the fate of the city.

52 Those who were my enemies without
        cause
    have hunted me like a bird;
53 they flung me alive into a pit
    and hurled stones on me;
54 water closed over my head;
    I said, "I am lost."

55 I called on your name, O LORD,
    from the depths of the pit;
56 you heard my plea, "Do not close your
        ear

to my cry for help, but give
    me relief!"
57 You came near when I called on you;
    you said, "Do not fear!"

58 You have taken up my cause, O Lord,
    you have redeemed my life.
59 You have seen the wrong done to me,
        O LORD;
    judge my cause.
60 You have seen all their malice,
    all their plots against me.

61 You have heard their taunts, O LORD,
    all their plots against me.
62 The whispers and murmurs of my
        assailants
    are against me all day long.
63 Whether they sit or rise—see,
    I am the object of their taunt-songs.

64 Pay them back for their deeds, O LORD,
    according to the work of their hands!
65 Give them anguish of heart;
    your curse be on them!
66 Pursue them in anger and destroy them
    from under the LORD's heavens.

3.52–66: A psalm of praise. As in 3.1–24, the individual catalogues his complaints generally and metaphorically: *like a bird*, v. 52; *pit*, vv. 53, 55 (Ps 7.15; 9.10). As in a psalm of thanksgiving (Ps 31), God is reported to have answered the prayer. **52:** *Without cause:* Strikingly different from the assumption of guilt (vv. 22–39). **59–66: Complaint about enemies.** Although the preceding verses suggest that God has already responded to the individual's plea, the speaker explicitly calls for God to punish enemies (1.21–22).

4 How the gold has grown dim,
    how the pure gold is changed!
The sacred stones lie scattered
    at the head of every street.

2 The precious children of Zion,
    worth their weight in fine gold—
how they are reckoned as earthen pots,
    the work of a potter's hands!

3 Even the jackals offer the breast
    and nurse their young,

but my people has become cruel,
  like the ostriches in the wilderness.

4 The tongue of the infant sticks
    to the roof of its mouth for thirst;
  the children beg for food,
    but no one gives them anything.

5 Those who feasted on delicacies
    perish in the streets;
  those who were brought up in purple
    cling to ash heaps.

6 For the chastisement*a* of my people has
      been greater
    than the punishment*b* of Sodom,
  which was overthrown in a moment,
    though no hand was laid on it.*c*

7 Her princes were purer than snow,
    whiter than milk;
  their bodies were more ruddy
      than coral,
    their hair*c* like sapphire.*d*

8 Now their visage is blacker than soot;
    they are not recognized in the streets.
  Their skin has shriveled on their bones;
    it has become as dry as wood.

9 Happier were those pierced by
      the sword
    than those pierced by hunger,
  whose life drains away, deprived
    of the produce of the field.

10 The hands of compassionate women
    have boiled their own children;
  they became their food
    in the destruction of my people.

famine (5.10; Job 30.30). **10:** In a dramatic reversal,
once compassionate mothers eat rather than feed their
young.

11 The LORD gave full vent to his wrath;
    he poured out his hot anger,
  and kindled a fire in Zion
    that consumed its foundations.

12 The kings of the earth did not believe,
    nor did any of the inhabitants of the
      world,
  that foe or enemy could enter
    the gates of Jerusalem.

13 It was for the sins of her prophets
    and the iniquities of her priests,
  who shed the blood of the righteous
    in the midst of her.

14 Blindly they wandered through
      the streets,
    so defiled with blood
  that no one was able
    to touch their garments.

15 "Away! Unclean!" people shouted
      at them;
    "Away! Away! Do not touch!"
  So they became fugitives and
      wanderers;
    it was said among the nations,
  "They shall stay here no longer."

16 The LORD himself has scattered them,
    he will regard them no more;
  no honor was shown to the priests,
    no favor to the elders.

4.1–10: Jerusalem's changed fortunes. The poet portrays a world upside down, where all that is normal
has vanished. **2–4:** Children, once treasured, are as
fragile as clay pots, and scarce food is not given to
them. *Ostriches* have the reputation of neglecting
their young (Job 39.13–18). **5–8:** *Purple*, due to the
costliness of its dye, was worn by royalty. The once
privileged class now starves. **6:** *Sodom:* See Gen
19.24–25. **9:** Quick death would be better than the
slow torture of famine. **8:** *Black* skin is a description of

4.11–16: God's anger has debased Zion. ✷ **12:** The
poet assumes that other nations along with Israel
(Ps 48) believed in the invincibility of Jerusalem.
13: *Prophets* and *priests*, as the primary leaders of the
people, are blamed for the bloodshed of war. **14–15:**
Defiled with blood and *unclean* refer to the purity laws
of Leviticus.

a Or *iniquity*   *b* Or *sin*   *c* Meaning of Heb
uncertain   *d* Or *lapis lazuli*

17 Our eyes failed, ever watching
vainly for help;
we were watching eagerly
for a nation that could not save.

18 They dogged our steps
so that we could not walk in
our streets;
our end drew near; our days were
numbered;
for our end had come.

19 Our pursuers were swifter
than the eagles in the heavens;
they chased us on the mountains,
they lay in wait for us in the
wilderness.

20 The LORD's anointed, the breath of our
life,
was taken in their pits—
the one of whom we said, "Under his
shadow
we shall live among the nations."

21 Rejoice and be glad, O daughter Edom,
you that live in the land of Uz;
but to you also the cup shall pass;
you shall become drunk and strip
yourself bare.

22 The punishment of your iniquity,
O daughter Zion, is
accomplished,
he will keep you in exile no longer;
but your iniquity, O daughter Edom, he
will punish,
he will uncover your sins.

4.17–22. 17–20: The final days of the city. The poet
describes the fall of Jerusalem (2 Kings 25), as she loses
any hope of protection. The *nation that could not save*
is likely Egypt (Jer 44.30). *LORD's anointed** is the king,
who is described in exalted terms. **21–22: Call for
punishment of Edom.** Various biblical accounts complain that Edom gloated over Jerusalem's fall (Obadiah; Ps 137). The poet calls for the punishment and
self-humiliation of Edom. **22:** *Punishment . . .
accomplished* may suggest that the book is written
after the traumatic events described.

5 Remember, O LORD, what has
befallen us;
look, and see our disgrace!

2 Our inheritance has been turned over to
strangers,
our homes to aliens.

3 We have become orphans, fatherless;
our mothers are like widows.

4 We must pay for the water we drink;
the wood we get must be bought.

5 With a yoke^a on our necks we are hard
driven;
we are weary, we are given no rest.

6 We have made a pact with^b Egypt and
Assyria,
to get enough bread.

7 Our ancestors sinned; they are
no more,
and we bear their iniquities.

8 Slaves rule over us;
there is no one to deliver us from
their hand.

9 We get our bread at the peril of
our lives,
because of the sword in the
wilderness.

10 Our skin is black as an oven
from the scorching heat of famine.

11 Women are raped in Zion,
virgins in the towns of Judah.

12 Princes are hung up by their hands;
no respect is shown to the elders.

13 Young men are compelled to grind,
and boys stagger under loads
of wood.

14 The old men have left the city gate,
the young men their music.

15 The joy of our hearts has ceased;
our dancing has been turned
to mourning.

16 The crown has fallen from our head;
woe to us, for we have sinned!

17 Because of this our hearts are sick,
because of these things our eyes have
grown dim:

18 because of Mount Zion, which
lies desolate;
jackals prowl over it.

---

a Symmachus: Heb lacks *With a yoke*   *b* Heb *have
given the hand to*

5.1–22: A community lament. This final poem follows the stylistic features of the communal laments of the Psalms (Ps 44; 79). A long description of misery and specific losses offers a glimpse into a conquered country: Babylonian conquerors force young and old into labor (vv. 5, 13); food and water are scarce (vv. 4, 6, 9, 10); *women are raped* (v. 11); and the once civilized city is now a haunt of *jackals* (v. 18). **7:** *We bear their iniquities:* Is the community accepting the guilt of their forebears or complaining that it is punished for sins not its own? **14–18:** All joy (*music, dancing,* public gathering at the *city gate*) has ceased.

19 But you, O LORD, reign forever;
　　your throne endures to all generations.

20 Why have you forgotten us completely?
　　Why have you forsaken us these many
　　　days?

21 Restore us to yourself, O LORD, that we
　　may be restored;
　　renew our days as of old—

22 unless you have utterly rejected us,
　　and are angry with us beyond
　　　measure.

5.19–22: The poem ends on a poignant note. God's power is undisputed, though God's care is questioned. The community asks that its broken relationship with God be healed, but fears that God's anger may be yet too great.

EZEKIEL

Introduction

Ezekiel presents some of the most theologically challenging and dynamic material among the prophetic books of the Hebrew Bible. It wrestles with the problem of the Babylonian exile in a manner not unlike the modern problem of the Shoah or Holocaust: Why did God allow Jerusalem and the Temple★ to be destroyed, and why did God allow the people of Israel to be carried away into exile? In arguing that God made a deliberate decision to destroy the Temple in order to purify Israel, Ezekiel draws upon his own priestly background in which sacrifice at the altar of the Temple is an essential element in self-purification, which aids in restoring one's relationship with God. The book develops its ideas in two major sections: Chs. 1–32 focus on God's plans to punish both Israel (chs. 1–24) and a select group of nations that would fall to Babylon (chs. 25–32); chs. 33–48 focus on God's plans to restore a purified Israel (chs. 33–39) with the Jerusalem Temple at the center of Israel and all creation (chs. 40–48).

Ezekiel was a Zadokite priest, a descendant of Zadok, one of the priests of David (2 Sam 15.24–29) who was also the priest who anointed★ Solomon (1 Kings 1). The Zadokites were priests at the Jerusalem Temple from that point forward until the Exile.★ Ezekiel was exiled to Babylonia together with King Jehoiachin in 597 BCE. He began his prophetic career five years later at the age of thirty (593 BCE) with a vision in which "the glory of the LORD" appeared to him in the form of a divine throne chariot, from which God instructed him to speak. Ezekiel's prophetic career continued for over 20 years and culminated in his vision of the restored Jerusalem Temple. His last oracle★ with a specified date is from 571 BCE (29.17–21). The book was originally written in an effort to explain the Babylonian exile and to prepare the exiled Judahite community for its return to Jerusalem. Ezekiel's "visions of God" prompted the composition of much apocalyptic★ and mystical literature. These kinds of writings—both Jewish and early Christian—were attempts to grapple with persecution and sufferings, such as threats to the Second Temple, its fall in 70 CE, and the destruction of Judea in 132–135 CE. Because Ezekiel attempts to describe God, a dangerous task, the Mishnah (the basic collection of religious and community regulations in Judaism) requires that readers be knowledgeable in Jewish tradition (m Hagigah 2.1). The book was nearly withdrawn from circulation until the rabbinic sage Hananiah ben Hezekiah resolved its contradictions with the Torah★ (b Shabbat 13b; b Hagigah 13a; b Menahot 45a—all references to the Mishnah). The modern city of Tel Aviv is named for Ezekiel's home in Babylonia (3.15), and the prophet's notion of "the hidden face of God" (39.21–29) plays a major role in contemporary discussion of the Holocaust.

READING GUIDE

Ezekiel's visions of "the glory of the LORD" constitute a literary envelope for the book in which God condemns Jerusalem to destruction and departs from the Temple (chs. 1–11) and then returns to the restored Temple once the people and land of Israel and the city of Jerusalem are purified (chs. 40–48). Ezekiel engages in a great deal of symbolic action, such as taking a sword to his own hair (ch. 5), or refusing to mourn at the death of his wife (24.15–27), to illustrate and actualize God's message. He is very familiar with earlier tradition, such as the Exodus and

Wilderness traditions (Exodus; Numbers), the Priestly sacrificial regulations and Holiness Code (Lev 1–16; 17–26), and the prophecies of Isaiah and Jeremiah. He employs them throughout his own writings to discuss Israel's history (chs. 16; 20), Jerusalem's destruction as purifying sacrifice (chs. 9–11), individual moral responsibility (ch. 18), the downfall of Egypt (ch. 31), the character of the Davidic prince (ch. 34), and the restoration of Israel with "a new heart" and "a new spirit" (11.14–21; 36.16–38). He is concerned throughout the book with protecting the sanctity of God's holy name (36.21) and frequently uses a self-identification formula, "I am the Lord" (36.38), to validate his oracles. The prophecy concerning the valley of the dry bones (ch. 37) underlies Jewish and Christian beliefs concerning resurrection, and the oracle concerning Gog of Magog represents an early apocalyptic scenario of judgment against Israel's enemies. Because Ezekiel's vision of the restored Temple does not correspond to the Second Temple (515 BCE–70 CE), it is generally considered in Jewish tradition to be a portrayal of third Temple to be built at the time of the messiah.*

INTRODUCTION TO EZEKIEL'S PROPHECY

1.1–3.15: The introduction includes a superscription in 1.1–3, which identifies the prophet* and his historical context, and an account of his inaugural vision in 1.4–3.15, in which God commissions him to speak. Compare the call narratives* of Moses (Ex 3) or Isaiah (Isa 6).

1 In the thirtieth year, in the fourth month, on the fifth day of the month, as I was among the exiles by the river Chebar, the heavens were opened, and I saw visions of God. ²On the fifth day of the month (it was the fifth year of the exile of King Jehoiachin), ³the word of the LORD came to the priest Ezekiel son of Buzi, in the land of the Chaldeans by the river Chebar; and the hand of the LORD was on him there.

1.1–3: Superscription. See Isa 1.1; Jer 1.3. **1:** Some understand *the thirtieth year* as the thirtieth year after the prophet's call, the thirtieth year after Josiah's reform, the year of Jehoiachin's exile, or the date of the book's composition. It probably refers to Ezekiel's age at the time of his call. Ezekiel is a priest (1.3), and the age of priestly service begins at thirty (Num 4.3, compare Num 8.23–25) and concludes at fifty. Apart from the reference to the twenty-seventh year in 29.17, the dated oracles of the book extend from the fifth (1.2) to the twenty-fifth year of the Exile* (40.1), so that the book correlates Ezekiel's prophetic oracles with the 20 years of active priestly service. *The river Chebar:* A canal by Nippur, a Babylonian city. **2:** *The fifth year of*

the exile of King Jehoiachin: 593 BCE. **3:** *Buzi* is otherwise unknown. Had he not been exiled, Ezekiel would have served as a Zadokite priest in the Temple.*

4 As I looked, a stormy wind came out of the north: a great cloud with brightness around it and fire flashing forth continually, and in the middle of the fire, something like gleaming amber. ⁵In the middle of it was something like four living creatures. This was their appearance: they were of human form. ⁶Each had four faces, and each of them had four wings. ⁷Their legs were straight, and the soles of their feet were like the sole of a calf's foot; and they sparkled like burnished bronze. ⁸Under their wings on their four sides they had human hands. And the four had their faces and their wings thus: ⁹their wings touched one another; each of them moved straight ahead, without turning as they moved. ¹⁰As for the appearance of their faces: the four had the face of a human being, the face of a lion on the right side, the face of an ox on the left side, and the face of an eagle; ¹¹such were their faces. Their wings were spread out above; each creature had two wings, each of which touched the wing of another, while two covered their bodies. ¹²Each moved straight ahead; wherever the spirit would go, they went, without turning as they went. ¹³In the middle of[a] the living creatures there was

a Gk OL: Heb *And the appearance of*

something that looked like burning coals of fire, like torches moving to and fro among the living creatures; the fire was bright, and lightning issued from the fire. ¹⁴The living creatures darted to and fro, like a flash of lightning.

15 As I looked at the living creatures, I saw a wheel on the earth beside the living creatures, one for each of the four of them.ᵃ ¹⁶As for the appearance of the wheels and their construction: their appearance was like the gleaming of beryl; and the four had the same form, their construction being something like a wheel within a wheel. ¹⁷When they moved, they moved in any of the four directions without veering as they moved. ¹⁸Their rims were tall and awesome, for the rims of all four were full of eyes all around. ¹⁹When the living creatures moved, the wheels moved beside them; and when the living creatures rose from the earth, the wheels rose. ²⁰Wherever the spirit would go, they went, and the wheels rose along with them; for the spirit of the living creatures was in the wheels. ²¹When they moved, the others moved; when they stopped, the others stopped; and when they rose from the earth, the wheels rose along with them; for the spirit of the living creatures was in the wheels.

22 Over the heads of the living creatures there was something like a dome, shining like crystal,ᵇ spread out above their heads. ²³Under the dome their wings were stretched out straight, one toward another; and each of the creatures had two wings covering its body. ²⁴When they moved, I heard the sound of their wings like the sound of mighty waters, like the thunder of the Almighty,ᶜ a sound of tumult like the sound of an army; when they stopped, they let down their wings. ²⁵And there came a voice from above the dome over their heads; when they stopped, they let down their wings.

26 And above the dome over their heads there was something like a throne, in appearance like sapphire;ᵈ and seated above the likeness of a throne was something that seemed like a human form. ²⁷Upward from what appeared like the loins I saw something like gleaming amber, something that looked like fire enclosed all around; and downward from what looked like the loins I saw something that looked like fire, and there was a splendor all around. ²⁸Like the bow in a cloud on a rainy day, such was the appearance of the splendor all around. This was the appearance of the likeness of the glory of the LORD.

1.4–28a: The inaugural vision. The imagery of God's throne chariot (compare 1 Chr 28.18; Ps 18.10) is based on the most holy place in the Temple where the ark of the covenant* is kept under the cherubim* (1 Kings 6; see also Ex 25.10–22; 37.1–9). **4:** Wind, cloud, and fire appear frequently in theophanies* (Ex 19; 1 Kings 19). **5–12:** *Like:* The vision is only a proximate human attempt to describe the divine presence. The *four living creatures* are the cherubim that surround the ark. Exodus 25.18–22; 37.7–9; and 1 Kings 6.23–28; 2 Chr 3.10–14 each mentioned only two, but this passage combines the totals. Composite human/animal winged creatures are well represented throughout the ancient Near East as guardians of thrones, city gates, and temples. The number four presupposes the four horns of the Temple altar (Ex 27.2; 38.2; Zech 2.1–4; 1.18–21), which represent the four "winds" or cardinal directions, indicating God's presence in the Temple at the center of creation. The four faces represent the divine qualities of intelligence (human), royalty (lion), strength (ox), and mobility (eagle). **13–14:** The *burning coals of fire:* The sacrificial altar of the Temple (Ex 27.1–8; 38.1–7) or the incense altars (Ex 30.1–10; 37.5–28). **15–21:** The *wheels* contribute to the imagery of divine motion in all four directions. They are based on the image of the cart that carried the ark of the covenant from Philistia to Jerusalem (1 Sam 6; 2 Sam 6) and the rings that held the poles by which the Levites carried the ark (Ex 25.12–15; 30.4–5). The *wheel within a wheel:* A wheel with a hub. **22–25:** *Dome shining like crystal,* see Gen 1.6–8, which uses "firmament" or "dome" to symbolize the distinction between heaven and earth. *The sound of mighty waters:* The vision is both auditory and visual. **26–28a:** Compare 1 Sam 4.4; 2 Sam 6.2; 1 Chr 13.6, "the ark of the covenant of the LORD of Hosts, who is enthroned on the cherubim." *Sapphire:* See Ex 24.10. Ezekiel attempts to describe God in hu-

---

ᵃ Heb *of their faces*   ᵇ Gk: Heb *like the awesome crystal*   ᶜ Traditional rendering of Heb *Shaddai* ᵈ Or *lapis lazuli*

man terms, but the imagery is inadequate. *Gleaming amber* and *fire* convey the power and incorporeality of the divine presence. The rainbow symbolizes God's covenant with creation (Gen 9.8–17). *The glory of the* LORD: God's presence (Ex 16.6–7; 40.34–38).

~~~~~~~~~~~~~~~~~~~~~~~~~~~~~~~~~~~~~~~

When I saw it, I fell on my face, and I heard the voice of someone speaking.

2 He said to me: O mortal,*ª* stand up on your feet, and I will speak with you. ²And when he spoke to me, a spirit entered into me and set me on my feet; and I heard him speaking to me. ³He said to me, Mortal, I am sending you to the people of Israel, to a nation*ᵇ* of rebels who have rebelled against me; they and their ancestors have transgressed against me to this very day. ⁴The descendants are impudent and stubborn. I am sending you to them, and you shall say to them, "Thus says the Lord GOD." ⁵Whether they hear or refuse to hear (for they are a rebellious house), they shall know that there has been a prophet among them. ⁶And you, O mortal, do not be afraid of them, and do not be afraid of their words, though briers and thorns surround you and you live among scorpions; do not be afraid of their words, and do not be dismayed at their looks, for they are a rebellious house. ⁷You shall speak my words to them, whether they hear or refuse to hear; for they are a rebellious house.

8 But you, mortal, hear what I say to you; do not be rebellious like that rebellious house; open your mouth and eat what I give you. ⁹I looked, and a hand was stretched out to me, and a written scroll was in it. ¹⁰He spread it before me; it had writing on the front and on the back, and written on it were words of lamentation and mourning and woe.

3 He said to me, O mortal, eat what is offered to you; eat this scroll, and go, speak to the house of Israel. ²So I opened my mouth, and he gave me the scroll to eat. ³He said to me, Mortal, eat this scroll that I give you and fill your stomach with it. Then I ate it; and in my mouth it was as sweet as honey.

4 He said to me: Mortal, go to the house of Israel and speak my very words to them. ⁵For you are not sent to a people of obscure speech and difficult language, but to the house of Israel— ⁶not to many peoples of obscure speech and difficult language, whose words you cannot understand. Surely, if I sent you to them, they would listen to you. ⁷But the house of Israel will not listen to you, for they are not willing to listen to me; because all the house of Israel have a hard forehead and a stubborn heart. ⁸See, I have made your face hard against their faces, and your forehead hard against their foreheads. ⁹Like the hardest stone, harder than flint, I have made your forehead; do not fear them or be dismayed at their looks, for they are a rebellious house. ¹⁰He said to me: Mortal, all my words that I shall speak to you receive in your heart and hear with your ears; ¹¹then go to the exiles, to your people, and speak to them. Say to them, "Thus says the Lord GOD"; whether they hear or refuse to hear.

12 Then the spirit lifted me up, and as the glory of the LORD rose*ᶜ* from its place, I heard behind me the sound of loud rumbling; ¹³it was the sound of the wings of the living creatures brushing against one another, and the sound of the wheels beside them, that sounded like a loud rumbling. ¹⁴The spirit lifted me up and bore me away; I went in bitterness in the heat of my spirit, the hand of the LORD being strong upon me. ¹⁵I came to the exiles at Tel-abib, who lived by the river Chebar.*ᵈ* And I sat there among them, stunned, for seven days.

─────────────────────────────────────

1.28b–3.15: The commissioning of Ezekiel. 1.28b: *A voice of someone speaking:* Compare 1 Kings 19.12. **2.1–2:** God addresses Ezekiel as *mortal,* literally, "son of adam," ninety-three times in the book. Adam means "human" in Hebrew, and "son of adam" conveys Ezekiel's mortal status in contrast to God. The *spirit* (literally, "wind") of the LORD prepares Ezekiel to serve as a prophet* (see 1 Sam 10.6, 10; 1 Kings 18.12). **2.3–7:** The charge of Israel's rebellion against God is a constant theme throughout the prophets to

a Or *son of man;* Heb *ben adam* (and so throughout the book when Ezekiel is addressed)   *b* Syr: Heb *to nations*
c Cn: Heb *and blessed be the glory of the* LORD
d Two Mss Syr: Heb *Chebar, and to where they lived.*
Another reading is *Chebar, and I sat where they sat*

justify Israel's suffering as an act of divine punishment. Habakkuk and Job question this theology but ultimately defend God's righteousness. The messenger formula, *Thus says the Lord GOD,* indicates Ezekiel's role as God's representative. **2.8–3.3:** Ezekiel eats the scroll to internalize the divine message. The scroll represents the Torah* scroll stored in the ark of the covenant and read to the people (Deut 31.9–13, 24–27; Neh 8–10). Although the scroll is inscribed with *words of lamentation and mourning and woe,* Ezekiel states that it was *as sweet as honey* (compare Jer 15.16). **4–11:** *Many peoples of obscure speech and difficult language:* Many peoples were incorporated into the Assyrian and Babylonian empires (Isa 33.19). God stresses that the message is for Israel, not the nations. **12–15:** *Tel-abib,* "hill of barley," may derive from the Babylonian expression "til abubi," "hill of the flood"; Babylonia is prone to flooding in the spring.

EZEKIEL'S INITIAL ORACLES AND SYMBOLIC ACTIONS

3.16–7.27: These oracles* and symbolic actions are concerned with the destruction of Jerusalem and fall of the land of Israel.

---

16 At the end of seven days, the word of the LORD came to me: 17 Mortal, I have made you a sentinel for the house of Israel; whenever you hear a word from my mouth, you shall give them warning from me. 18 If I say to the wicked, "You shall surely die," and you give them no warning, or speak to warn the wicked from their wicked way, in order to save their life, those wicked persons shall die for their iniquity; but their blood I will require at your hand. 19 But if you warn the wicked, and they do not turn from their wickedness, or from their wicked way, they shall die for their iniquity; but you will have saved your life. 20 Again, if the righteous turn from their righteousness and commit iniquity, and I lay a stumbling block before them, they shall die; because you have not warned them, they shall die for their sin, and their righteous deeds that they have done shall not be remembered; but their blood I will require at your hand. 21 If, however, you warn the righteous not to sin, and they do not sin, they shall surely live, because they took warning; and you will have saved your life.

22 Then the hand of the LORD was upon me there; and he said to me, Rise up, go out into the valley, and there I will speak with you. 23 So I rose up and went out into the valley; and the glory of the LORD stood there, like the glory that I had seen by the river Chebar; and I fell on my face. 24 The spirit entered into me, and set me on my feet; and he spoke with me and said to me: Go, shut yourself inside your house. 25 As for you, mortal, cords shall be placed on you, and you shall be bound with them, so that you cannot go out among the people; 26 and I will make your tongue cling to the roof of your mouth, so that you shall be speechless and unable to reprove them; for they are a rebellious house. 27 But when I speak with you, I will open your mouth, and you shall say to them, "Thus says the Lord GOD"; let those who will hear, hear; and let those who refuse to hear, refuse; for they are a rebellious house.

3.16–27. 16–21: God describes Ezekiel's role as the *sentinel* or "watchman" for Israel, who is responsible for the lives and moral guidance of the people (Jer 6.17; Hos 9.8; compare Isa 21.6). Like sentinels posted on city walls to watch for danger (2 Sam 18.24; 2 Kings 9.17), gatekeepers are appointed from among the priests to guard the Temple (1 Chr 26). This role, which is developed more fully in ch. 33, is consistent with ch. 18. The prophet's responsibility is presented in four cases. **22–27:** Ezekiel's isolation resembles that of Moses, who spoke directly to God in the tent of meeting (Ex 33.7–34.35; Num 11), and the high priest, who appears alone before God and the ark at Yom Kippur or the Day of Atonement* (Lev 16). Ezekiel's dumbness derives from his priestly role. The priests perform their duties on the altar in silence (Lev 16).

---

4 And you, O mortal, take a brick and set it before you. On it portray a city, Jerusalem; 2 and put siegeworks against it, and build a siege wall against it, and cast up a ramp against it; set camps also against it, and plant battering rams against it all around. 3 Then take an iron plate and place it as an iron wall between you and the city; set your face toward it, and let it be in a state of siege, and press the siege against it. This is a sign for the house of Israel.

4 Then lie on your left side, and place the punishment of the house of Israel upon it; you shall bear their punishment for the number of the days that you lie there. 5For I assign to you a number of days, three hundred ninety days, equal to the number of the years of their punishment; and so you shall bear the punishment of the house of Israel. 6When you have completed these, you shall lie down a second time, but on your right side, and bear the punishment of the house of Judah; forty days I assign you, one day for each year. 7You shall set your face toward the siege of Jerusalem, and with your arm bared you shall prophesy against it. 8See, I am putting cords on you so that you cannot turn from one side to the other until you have completed the days of your siege.

4.1–8: Prophets perform symbolic actions to dramatize their statements and enable them to take effect (Isa 20; Jer 13; 19). Ezekiel builds a model of Jerusalem under siege. The action draws upon the imagery of Jer 1.18. The background of *three hundred and ninety* and *forty* is not entirely certain, and the Septuagint* (the Greek version of the Hebrew Bible) contains entirely different figures. If one counts backwards from the destruction of the Temple* in 587 BCE, the total of 430 years points to the time of the establishment of the united monarchy of Israel under Saul in 1017 BCE. Counting forward 390 years from that date takes one to 627 BCE, the twelfth year of Josiah's reign, the year in which his reforms begin (2 Chr 34.3; compare 2 Kings 22.3). Josiah failed in his attempt to reunite Israel and Judah. The remaining 40 years accounts for the time between the beginning of Josiah's reform and the destruction of Jerusalem.

9 And you, take wheat and barley, beans and lentils, millet and spelt; put them into one vessel, and make bread for yourself. During the number of days that you lie on your side, three hundred ninety days, you shall eat it. 10The food that you eat shall be twenty shekels a day by weight; at fixed times you shall eat it. 11And you shall drink water by measure, one-sixth of a hin; at fixed times you shall drink. 12You shall eat it as a barley-cake, baking it in their sight on human dung. 13The LORD said, "Thus shall the people of Israel eat their bread, unclean, among the nations to which I will drive them." 14Then I said, "Ah Lord GOD! I have never defiled myself; from my youth up until now I have never eaten what died of itself or was torn by animals, nor has carrion flesh come into my mouth." 15Then he said to me, "See, I will let you have cow's dung instead of human dung, on which you may prepare your bread."

16 Then he said to me, Mortal, I am going to break the staff of bread in Jerusalem; they shall eat bread by weight and with fearfulness; and they shall drink water by measure and in dismay. 17Lacking bread and water, they will look at one another in dismay, and waste away under their punishment.

4.9–17: Ezekiel uses a variety of grains to demonstrate that there is insufficient grain to make an entire loaf. *Twenty shekels:** About ten ounces. *One-sixth of a hin:* About two-thirds of a quart. In order to demonstrate the difficult conditions of the coming siege, God commands Ezekiel to bake bread using human dung as fuel. When he protests that this is a breach of priestly purity, God allows him to use cow's dung. **16–17:** See Isa 3.1.

5 And you, O mortal, take a sharp sword; use it as a barber's razor and run it over your head and your beard; then take balances for weighing, and divide the hair. 2One third of the hair you shall burn in the fire inside the city, when the days of the siege are completed; one third you shall take and strike with the sword all around the city;*a* and one third you shall scatter to the wind, and I will unsheathe the sword after them. 3Then you shall take from these a small number, and bind them in the skirts of your robe. 4From these, again, you shall take some, throw them into the fire and burn them up; from there a fire will come out against all the house of Israel.

5.1–4: The *sword* or *barber's razor* (Isa 7.20) symbolizes the weapons of the Babylonians. One third of the hair is burned to represent those who die when the city is burned; one third is struck with the sword to symbolize those killed around the city; and one third

a Heb *it*

is scattered to symbolize those who escape only to be pursued by the Babylonians. Some of the hair is burned once again to symbolize the suffering of the people.

5 Thus says the Lord GOD: This is Jerusalem; I have set her in the center of the nations, with countries all around her. 6But she has rebelled against my ordinances and my statutes, becoming more wicked than the nations and the countries all around her, rejecting my ordinances and not following my statutes. 7Therefore thus says the Lord GOD: Because you are more turbulent than the nations that are all around you, and have not followed my statutes or kept my ordinances, but have acted according to the ordinances of the nations that are all around you; 8therefore thus says the Lord GOD: I, I myself, am coming against you; I will execute judgments among you in the sight of the nations. 9And because of all your abominations, I will do to you what I have never yet done, and the like of which I will never do again. 10Surely, parents shall eat their children in your midst, and children shall eat their parents; I will execute judgments on you, and any of you who survive I will scatter to every wind. 11Therefore, as I live, says the Lord GOD, surely, because you have defiled my sanctuary with all your detestable things and with all your abominations—therefore I will cut you down;*a* my eye will not spare, and I will have no pity. 12One third of you shall die of pestilence or be consumed by famine among you; one third shall fall by the sword around you; and one third I will scatter to every wind and will unsheathe the sword after them.

13 My anger shall spend itself, and I will vent my fury on them and satisfy myself; and they shall know that I, the LORD, have spoken in my jealousy, when I spend my fury on them. 14Moreover I will make you a desolation and an object of mocking among the nations around you, in the sight of all that pass by. 15You shall be*b* a mockery and a taunt, a warning and a horror, to the nations around you, when I execute judgments on you in anger and fury, and with furious punishments—I, the LORD, have spoken—

16when I loose against you*c* my deadly arrows of famine, arrows for destruction, which I will let loose to destroy you, and when I bring more and more famine upon you, and break your staff of bread. 17I will send famine and wild animals against you, and they will rob you of your children; pestilence and bloodshed shall pass through you; and I will bring the sword upon you. I, the LORD, have spoken.

5.5–17: God sums up the theology of punishment that Ezekiel's symbolic actions illustrate. Charging that Israel acts like the nations (see 1 Sam 8.4–5) by defiling the Temple, God states that the people will suffer war and exile, and will perish by pestilence, famine, and sword. God's threat to make Israel *a desolation and an object of mocking among the nations* and to unleash famine, wild animals, etc., against the people recalls threats made in Jer 24.9–10 (see also Deut 28.37; 1 Kings 9.7).

Ezekiel's oracles* against the land of Israel Chs. 6–7: Ezekiel does not distinguish between Israel and Judah, but addresses the entire land and people of Israel arrayed around the Temple (Num 2; Ezek 48). The most holy place serves as the sacred center of the Temple, the Jerusalem Temple as the sacred center of Israel, and Israel as sacred center of the world.

6 The word of the LORD came to me: 2O mortal, set your face toward the mountains of Israel, and prophesy against them, 3and say, You mountains of Israel, hear the word of the Lord GOD! Thus says the Lord GOD to the mountains and the hills, to the ravines and the valleys: I, I myself will bring a sword upon you, and I will destroy your high places. 4Your altars shall become desolate, and your incense stands shall be broken; and I will throw down your slain in front of your idols. 5I will lay the corpses of the people of Israel in front of their idols; and I will scatter your bones around your altars. 6Wherever you live, your towns shall be waste and your high places ruined, so that your altars will be waste and ruined,*d* your

a Another reading is *I will withdraw*　　*b* Gk Syr Vg Tg: Heb *It shall be*　　*c* Heb *them*　　*d* Syr Vg Tg: Heb *and be made guilty*

idols broken and destroyed, your incense stands cut down, and your works wiped out. [7]The slain shall fall in your midst; then you shall know that I am the LORD.

8 But I will spare some. Some of you shall escape the sword among the nations and be scattered through the countries. [9]Those of you who escape shall remember me among the nations where they are carried captive, how I was crushed by their wanton heart that turned away from me, and their wanton eyes that turned after their idols. Then they will be loathsome in their own sight for the evils that they have committed, for all their abominations. [10]And they shall know that I am the LORD; I did not threaten in vain to bring this disaster upon them.

6.1–14: Oracle against the mountains of Israel. *The mountains of Israel:* The homeland of Israel in the hills of Samaria and Judah. **1–7:** Ezekiel identifies the cause of punishment in the various altars and high places★ where the people worship, which compromise the sanctity of the land. As a Zadokite priest, Ezekiel holds that legitimate worship of God must take place only in the Jerusalem Temple (Deut 12). The scattering of dead corpses around the altars renders the land impure (Num 19; see also Lev 21.10–12). The prophet★ employs the prophetic "proof saying," *then you shall know that I am the LORD,* throughout the book to identify God as the source of the prophet's words (Ex 20.2; Lev 19.3–4; see also Ex 3.13–22; Deut 5.6). **8–10:** Ezekiel relies on Isaiah's concept of a remnant of Israel (Isa 4.2–6; 6.13; 10.20–23) to demonstrate God's power to destroy and punish.

11 Thus says the Lord GOD: Clap your hands and stamp your foot, and say, Alas for all the vile abominations of the house of Israel! For they shall fall by the sword, by famine, and by pestilence. [12]Those far off shall die of pestilence; those nearby shall fall by the sword; and any who are left and are spared shall die of famine. Thus I will spend my fury upon them. [13]And you shall know that I am the LORD, when their slain lie among their idols around their altars, on every high hill, on all the mountain tops, under every green tree, and under every leafy oak, wherever they offered pleasing odor to all their idols. [14]I will stretch out my hand

against them, and make the land desolate and waste, throughout all their settlements, from the wilderness to Riblah.[a] Then they shall know that I am the LORD.

6.11–14: Ezekiel returns to the imagery of sword, pestilence, and famine (5.1–17) to tie his oracles against Israel to the fate of Jerusalem. *Altars, on every high hill, on all the mountain tops, under every green tree, and under every leafy oak:* A common formulaic description of pagan worship (Deut 12.2; 1 Kings 14.23; Jer 2.20). The *wilderness* designates the Negeb desert in southern Judah, and *Riblah* ("Diblah" in Hebrew; the Hebrew letters "resh" and "dalet" are similar and sometimes confused) is in Syria (2 Kings 23.33).

7 The word of the LORD came to me: [2]You, O mortal, thus says the Lord GOD to the land of Israel:
An end! The end has come
　upon the four corners of the land.
3 　Now the end is upon you,
　　I will let loose my anger upon you;
　I will judge you according to your ways,
　I will punish you for all your
　　abominations.
4 　My eye will not spare you, I will have no
　　pity.
　I will punish you for your ways,
　　while your abominations are among
　　you.
Then you shall know that I am the LORD.
5 　Thus says the Lord GOD:
　Disaster after disaster! See, it comes.
6 　　An end has come, the end has come.
　It has awakened against you; see,
　　it comes!
7 　Your doom[b] has come to you,
　　O inhabitant of the land.
　The time has come, the day is near—
　　of tumult, not of reveling on the
　　mountains.
8 　Soon now I will pour out my wrath
　　upon you;
　I will spend my anger against you.
　I will judge you according to your ways,
　　and punish you for all your
　　abominations.

a Another reading is *Diblah*　*b* Meaning of Heb uncertain

9 My eye will not spare; I will have no
　　pity.
　　I will punish you according to your
　　　ways,
　　while your abominations are among
　　　you.
Then you shall know that it is I the LORD
who strike.

7.1–27: Ezekiel's prophecy of the end. Ezekiel's three
oracles draw upon the "Day of the LORD" traditions to
announce the "end" of Israel (Am 5.18–20; 8.1–14;
Isa 2.6–22; 13). The "Day of the LORD" functioned
originally as an announcement of God's defense of Israel, but various prophets reconfigured it as an announcement of God's punishment of Israel. **7.1–4:** The
first oracle announces the end of Israel. *End* is drawn
from Amos's prophecy against Bethel (Am 8.1–3),
which includes the imagery of dead bodies scattered
about the altar as in 6.1–7. The *four corners of the land*
indicates the complete destruction of the land and rehearses the four cardinal directions that underlie the
symbolism of the four living creatures in ch. 1 (see Isa
11.12). **5–9:** Ezekiel again employs the statement *the
end has come,* but he shifts his language to that of the
"Day of the LORD" traditions.

10 See, the day! See, it comes!
　　Your doom*ᵃ* has gone out.
　　The rod has blossomed, pride has
　　　budded.
11 　Violence has grown into a rod
　　　of wickedness.
　　None of them shall remain,
　　　not their abundance, not their
　　　　wealth;
　　no pre-eminence among them.*ᵃ*
12 The time has come, the day draws near;
　　let not the buyer rejoice, nor the
　　　seller mourn,
　　for wrath is upon all their multitude.
13 For the sellers shall not return to what has
been sold as long as they remain alive. For
the vision concerns all their multitude; it
shall not be revoked. Because of their
iniquity, they cannot maintain their lives.*ᵃ*
14 They have blown the horn and made
　　　everything ready;
　　but no one goes to battle,
　　for my wrath is upon all their
　　　multitude.

15 The sword is outside, pestilence and
　　　famine are inside;
　　those in the field die by the sword;
　　those in the city—famine and
　　　pestilence devour them.
16 If any survivors escape,
　　they shall be found on the mountains
　　　like doves of the valleys,
　　all of them moaning over their iniquity.
17 All hands shall grow feeble,
　　all knees turn to water.
18 They shall put on sackcloth,
　　horror shall cover them.
　　Shame shall be on all faces,
　　baldness on all their heads.
19 They shall fling their silver into the
　　　streets,
　　their gold shall be treated as unclean.
Their silver and gold cannot save them on
the day of the wrath of the LORD. They shall
not satisfy their hunger or fill their stomachs
with it. For it was the stumbling block of
their iniquity. 20 From their*ᵇ* beautiful ornament, in which they took pride, they made
their abominable images, their detestable
things; therefore I will make of it an unclean
thing to them.
21 I will hand it over to strangers
　　　as booty,
　　to the wicked of the earth as plunder;
　　they shall profane it.
22 I will avert my face from them,
　　so that they may profane my
　　　treasured*ᶜ* place;
　　the violent shall enter it,
　　they shall profane it.
23 Make a chain!*ᵃ*
　　For the land is full of bloody crimes;
　　the city is full of violence.
24 I will bring the worst of the nations
　　to take possession of their houses.
　　I will put an end to the arrogance of the
　　　strong,
　　and their holy places shall be
　　　profaned.
25 When anguish comes, they will seek
　　　peace,
　　but there shall be none.

a Meaning of Heb uncertain　　*b* Syr Symmachus:
Heb *its*　　*c* Or *secret*

26 Disaster comes upon disaster,
    rumor follows rumor;
  they shall keep seeking a vision from the
      prophet;
  instruction shall perish from the
      priest,
  and counsel from the elders.
27 The king shall mourn,
    the prince shall be wrapped in despair,
    and the hands of the people of the
      land shall tremble.
  According to their way I will deal with
      them;
    according to their own judgments I
      will judge them.
And they shall know that I am the LORD.

7.10–27: The third oracle elaborates the imagery of the land's destruction in the "Day of the LORD." **10–11:** The blossoming rod represents Aaron's rod, which designates Levi as the priestly tribe (Num 17), but Jeremiah, a priest descended from Eli (1 Sam 1–3), employs it as a sign of Judah's punishment (Jer 1.11–12). The silver almond-shaped cap, recently discovered by archeologists in Jerusalem, once adorned the rod of a priest. The budding *pride* also translates as "insolence," indicating Ezekiel's view that the priestly rod is now employed for the punishment of Israel, just as Moses' rod punished Egypt (Ex 7–11). **12–13:** Normal life will end. **14–17:** Ezekiel again takes up the imagery of sword, pestilence, and famine (chs. 5–6). **18–21:** Compare Isa 2.6–21, which anticipates that people will throw away their silver and gold idols on the "Day of the LORD." **22:** God's intention to hide the divine face raises tremendous theological problems. God's *treasured place* was the most holy place in the Temple. **23–27:** The leaders are responsible for the punishment.

EZEKIEL'S VISION OF JERUSALEM'S DESTRUCTION

Chs. 8–11: Ezekiel portrays the destruction of Jerusalem as a priestly sacrifice that cleanses the city from impurity.

---

8 In the sixth year, in the sixth month, on the fifth day of the month, as I sat in my house, with the elders of Judah sitting before me, the hand of the Lord GOD fell upon me there. 2I looked, and there was a figure that looked like a human being;[a] below what appeared to be its loins it was fire, and above the loins it was like the appearance of brightness, like gleaming amber. 3It stretched out the form of a hand, and took me by a lock of my head; and the spirit lifted me up between earth and heaven, and brought me in visions of God to Jerusalem, to the entrance of the gateway of the inner court that faces north, to the seat of the image of jealousy, which provokes to jealousy. 4And the glory of the God of Israel was there, like the vision that I had seen in the valley.

5 Then God[b] said to me, "O mortal, lift up your eyes now in the direction of the north." So I lifted up my eyes toward the north, and there, north of the altar gate, in the entrance, was this image of jealousy. 6He said to me, "Mortal, do you see what they are doing, the great abominations that the house of Israel are committing here, to drive me far from my sanctuary? Yet you will see still greater abominations."

7 And he brought me to the entrance of the court; I looked, and there was a hole in the wall. 8Then he said to me, "Mortal, dig through the wall"; and when I dug through the wall, there was an entrance. 9He said to me, "Go in, and see the vile abominations that they are committing here." 10So I went in and looked; there, portrayed on the wall all around, were all kinds of creeping things, and loathsome animals, and all the idols of the house of Israel. 11Before them stood seventy of the elders of the house of Israel, with Jaazaniah son of Shaphan standing among them. Each had his censer in his hand, and the fragrant cloud of incense was ascending. 12Then he said to me, "Mortal, have you seen what the elders of the house of Israel are doing in the dark, each in his room of images? For they say, 'The LORD does not see us, the LORD has forsaken the land.'" 13He said also to me, "You will see still greater abominations that they are committing."

8.1–18: The impurity of the Temple.✶ **1–4:** *The sixth year:* 592 BCE. Ezekiel returns to the imagery of his in-

a Gk: Heb *like fire*   *b* Heb *he*

Describing the Indescribable

The book of Ezekiel contains a number of visions: descriptions in imagery, sounds and sights of realities that are outside ordinary experience (like the vision of the divine throne chariot in ch. 1) or of events that the prophet★ did not witness directly (like the vision of worship in the Jerusalem Temple★ in ch. 8). These visions, which go "behind the scenes" to show divine realities in human terms, had a great influence on later writings. Ezekiel may have influenced the book of Daniel in its visions concerning the course and meaning of world history. It also influenced later books, such as 1 Enoch,★ a Jewish pseudepigraphical★ work from the first century BCE that contains visions concerning the hidden secrets of both the divine and earthly realms; the book of Revelation in the New Testament, which uses visions to express the persecution and suffering of the early Christian church and its significance in human history; and the rabbinic "Heikhalot" ("palaces") literature, in which mystics "ascend" through the seven heavenly "palaces" to encounter the presence of God.

All of these works try to describe matters that are beyond normal human experience, but of course they must work within the limits of human language and experience to do this. This may explain why the images and descriptions seem so fanciful and sometimes even bizarre. As we read Ezekiel and these other writings, we should bear in mind that the writers may have been compelled to try to describe things that are indescribable, and that their language—gemstones and fire, scrolls that are eaten, and creatures with the head of a lion and the wings of an eagle—takes human vocabulary close to the breaking point. We are not meant to believe in these word pictures literally, but they function as metaphors★ that stimulate our imaginations and help us recognize that spiritual truths can be as real and as vivid as physical ones.

augural vision to describe a human-like being. The imagery of *fire* and *brightness like gleaming amber* describes a being that cannot be defined in earthly terms. *The entrance of the gateway of the inner court that faces north* places the prophet at the entry of the most sacred areas of the Temple. *The glory of the God of Israel:* The throne chariot of ch. 1 is present. **5–6:** The *image of jealousy:* North of the altar was a pagan idol placed in the Temple precincts. **7–13:** Mention of *the seventy elders of the house of Israel* and *Jaazaniah son of Shaphan* indicates that the highest leadership of the nation is involved in pagan worship inside the Temple. Shaphan played a major role in Josiah's reform (2 Kings 22); his sons Ahikam, Elasah, and Gemariah, and grandson Micaiah supported Jeremiah (Jer 26; 29; 36). The claim that *the LORD has forsaken the land* indicates the belief that God could not protect Jerusalem from Babylon.

14 Then he brought me to the entrance of the north gate of the house of the LORD; women were sitting there weeping for Tammuz. 15 Then he said to me, "Have you seen this, O mortal? You will see still greater abominations than these."

16 And he brought me into the inner court of the house of the LORD; there, at the entrance of the temple of the LORD, between the porch and the altar, were about twenty-five men, with their backs to the temple of the LORD, and their faces toward the east, prostrating themselves to the sun toward the east. 17 Then he said to me, "Have you seen this, O mortal? Is it not bad enough that the house of Judah commits the abominations done here? Must they fill the land with violence, and provoke my anger still further? See, they are putting the branch to their nose! 18 Therefore I will act in wrath; my eye will not spare, nor will I have pity; and though they cry in my hearing with a loud voice, I will not listen to them."

8.14–18. 14–15: Women weep for *Tammuz,* the Babylonian vegetation god who dies at the onset of the dry season and must be brought back to life to inaugurate the rains. **16–18:** Ezekiel sees twenty-five men engaged in sun worship. The sun god Shamash was the Babylonian god of law and justice.

9 Then he cried in my hearing with a loud voice, saying, "Draw near, you executioners of the city, each with his destroying weapon in his hand." ²And six men came from the direction of the upper gate, which faces north, each with his weapon for slaughter in his hand; among them was a man clothed in linen, with a writing case at his side. They went in and stood beside the bronze altar.

3 Now the glory of the God of Israel had gone up from the cherub on which it rested to the threshold of the house. The LORD called to the man clothed in linen, who had the writing case at his side; ⁴and said to him, "Go through the city, through Jerusalem, and put a mark on the foreheads of those who sigh and groan over all the abominations that are committed in it." ⁵To the others he said in my hearing, "Pass through the city after him, and kill; your eye shall not spare, and you shall show no pity. ⁶Cut down old men, young men and young women, little children and women, but touch no one who has the mark. And begin at my sanctuary." So they began with the elders who were in front of the house. ⁷Then he said to them, "Defile the house, and fill the courts with the slain. Go!" So they went out and killed in the city. ⁸While they were killing, and I was left alone, I fell prostrate on my face and cried out, "Ah Lord GOD! will you destroy all who remain of Israel as you pour out your wrath upon Jerusalem?" ⁹He said to me, "The guilt of the house of Israel and Judah is exceedingly great; the land is full of bloodshed and the city full of perversity; for they say, 'The LORD has forsaken the land, and the LORD does not see.' ¹⁰As for me, my eye will not spare, nor will I have pity, but I will bring down their deeds upon their heads."

11 Then the man clothed in linen, with the writing case at his side, brought back

word, saying, "I have done as you commanded me."

9.1–11: The slaughter of Jerusalem. Sacrificial slaughter at the altar of the Temple portrays the killing of the people of Jerusalem. **1–2:** The *six men* come from the upper gate to the north with weapons in their hands to begin the slaughter. The Babylonian army would have entered Judah from the north (see Jer 1.13–16). The *man clothed in linen* wears the apparel of a priest who serves at the altar (Ex 28.39; Lev 6.10) and carries a *writing case* to record the sacrifices. *The bronze altar* had been moved to the north by Ahaz to accommodate an Assyrian altar (2 Kings 16.14). **3–11:** The living beings are now named *cherubim.** God commands that a *mark* (the ancient Hebrew letter "taw," translated "mark," looks like an X) be placed on the foreheads of *those who sigh and groan over all the abominations,* to protect them from death. A mark on the doorpost protects the Israelites from God's plague against the Egyptians (Ex 12.23). All who lack the mark are to die, defiling the sanctuary. Ezekiel attempts to intercede as Moses did (Ex 32.1–14; Num 14), but God states that the people believe that God lacks power.

The LORD's Departure from Jerusalem
Chs. 10–11: God's throne chariot will return in 43.1–12 when the city is purified and the Temple reestablished.

10 Then I looked, and above the dome that was over the heads of the cherubim there appeared above them something like a sapphire,ᵃ in form resembling a throne. ²He said to the man clothed in linen, "Go within the wheelwork underneath the cherubim; fill your hands with burning coals from among the cherubim, and scatter them over the city." He went in as I looked on. ³Now the cherubim were standing on the south side of the house when the man went in; and a cloud filled the inner court. ⁴Then the glory of the LORD rose up from the cherub to the threshold of the house; the house was filled with the cloud, and the court was full of the brightness of the glory of the LORD. ⁵The sound of the wings of the cherubim was heard as far as the outer court,

a Or lapis lazuli

like the voice of God Almighty[a] when he speaks.

6 When he commanded the man clothed in linen, "Take fire from within the wheelwork, from among the cherubim," he went in and stood beside a wheel. 7And a cherub stretched out his hand from among the cherubim to the fire that was among the cherubim, took some of it and put it into the hands of the man clothed in linen, who took it and went out. 8The cherubim appeared to have the form of a human hand under their wings.

9 I looked, and there were four wheels beside the cherubim, one beside each cherub; and the appearance of the wheels was like gleaming beryl. 10And as for their appearance, the four looked alike, something like a wheel within a wheel. 11When they moved, they moved in any of the four directions without veering as they moved; but in whatever direction the front wheel faced, the others followed without veering as they moved. 12Their entire body, their rims, their spokes, their wings, and the wheels—the wheels of the four of them—were full of eyes all around. 13As for the wheels, they were called in my hearing "the wheelwork." 14Each one had four faces: the first face was that of the cherub, the second face was that of a human being, the third that of a lion, and the fourth that of an eagle.

15 The cherubim rose up. These were the living creatures that I saw by the river Chebar. 16When the cherubim moved, the wheels moved beside them; and when the cherubim lifted up their wings to rise up from the earth, the wheels at their side did not veer. 17When they stopped, the others stopped, and when they rose up, the others rose up with them; for the spirit of the living creatures was in them.

18 Then the glory of the LORD went out from the threshold of the house and stopped above the cherubim. 19The cherubim lifted up their wings and rose up from the earth in my sight as they went out with the wheels beside them. They stopped at the entrance of the east gate of the house of the LORD; and the glory of the God of Israel was above them.

20 These were the living creatures that I saw underneath the God of Israel by the river Chebar; and I knew that they were cherubim. 21Each had four faces, each four wings, and underneath their wings something like human hands. 22As for what their faces were like, they were the same faces whose appearance I had seen by the river Chebar. Each one moved straight ahead.

10.1–22: God commands the *man clothed in linen* to take *burning coals from among the cherubim and scatter them over the city.* Much like the sin offerings presented in the Temple (Lev 4–5), the purpose of the sacrifice is to purify Jerusalem from its iniquity and impurity so that it can be reestablished at a later time (chs. 40–48). God's presence is signified by the *cloud* (Ex 19.9; 1 Kings 8.10–11) and *brightness of the glory of the LORD* as it moves about the Temple complex. Because of the sanctity of the throne chariot or ark, the man clothed in linen is unable to approach, and a cherub hands him the fire (2 Sam 6.6–11). Ezekiel's detailed description of the cherubim* and the wheels differs from ch. 1 in that one of their four faces is a cherub rather than an ox. Many medieval commentators speculate that the face of the cherub might encompass the four individual faces. *The glory of the LORD* above *the entrance of the east gate of the house of the LORD* is the main or processional entrance to the Temple (Ps 24.7–9; 118.19–20).

11 The spirit lifted me up and brought me to the east gate of the house of the LORD, which faces east. There, at the entrance of the gateway, were twenty-five men; among them I saw Jaazaniah son of Azzur, and Pelatiah son of Benaiah, officials of the people. 2He said to me, "Mortal, these are the men who devise iniquity and who give wicked counsel in this city; 3they say, 'The time is not near to build houses; this city is the pot, and we are the meat.' 4Therefore prophesy against them; prophesy, O mortal."

5 Then the spirit of the LORD fell upon me, and he said to me, "Say, Thus says the LORD: This is what you think, O house of Israel; I know the things that come into your mind. 6You have killed many in this city, and have filled its streets with the slain. 7There-

a Traditional rendering of Heb El Shaddai

fore thus says the Lord GOD: The slain whom you have placed within it are the meat, and this city is the pot; but you shall be taken out of it. [8]You have feared the sword; and I will bring the sword upon you, says the Lord GOD. [9]I will take you out of it and give you over to the hands of foreigners, and execute judgments upon you. [10]You shall fall by the sword; I will judge you at the border of Israel. And you shall know that I am the LORD. [11]This city shall not be your pot, and you shall not be the meat inside it; I will judge you at the border of Israel. [12]Then you shall know that I am the LORD, whose statutes you have not followed, and whose ordinances you have not kept, but you have acted according to the ordinances of the nations that are around you."

13 Now, while I was prophesying, Pelatiah son of Benaiah died. Then I fell down on my face, cried with a loud voice, and said, "Ah Lord GOD! will you make a full end of the remnant of Israel?"

11.1–25: Ezekiel prophesies both judgment and restoration for the people. **1–4:** The *spirit* or "wind" transports Ezekiel to the east gate of the Temple where he sees twenty-five officials, probably those worshipping the sun in 8.16. Their statement, "*The time is not near to build houses,*" rejects Jeremiah's call to build and to plant (Jer 1.10; 31.28). The statement, "*This city is the pot, and we are the meat,*" indicates their belief that Jerusalem is to be sacrificed (24.1–14). **5–13:** God instructs Ezekiel to hold the twenty-five leaders responsible for the deaths of the people in Jerusalem. In stating that the dead will become the meat, and the city the pot, Ezekiel turns their statement against them, but indicates that they will be excluded because the sacrifice of the city is meant to purify Jerusalem. He alludes to their fear of foreign invaders and again turns their fears against them by stating that they will die at the borders of Israel (see 2 Kings 25.18–21; Jer 52.24–27). The immediate death of *Pelatiah son of Benaiah* confirms Ezekiel's word (compare Am 7.10–17; Jer 27–28).

〜〜〜〜〜〜〜〜〜〜〜〜〜

14 Then the word of the LORD came to me: [15]Mortal, your kinsfolk, your own kin, your fellow exiles,[a] the whole house of Israel, all of them, are those of whom the inhabitants of Jerusalem have said, "They have gone far from the LORD; to us this land is given for a possession." [16]Therefore say: Thus says the Lord GOD: Though I removed them far away among the nations, and though I scattered them among the countries, yet I have been a sanctuary to them for a little while[b] in the countries where they have gone. [17]Therefore say: Thus says the Lord GOD: I will gather you from the peoples, and assemble you out of the countries where you have been scattered, and I will give you the land of Israel. [18]When they come there, they will remove from it all its detestable things and all its abominations. [19]I will give them one[c] heart, and put a new spirit within them; I will remove the heart of stone from their flesh and give them a heart of flesh, [20]so that they may follow my statutes and keep my ordinances and obey them. Then they shall be my people, and I will be their God. [21]But as for those whose heart goes after their detestable things and their abominations,[d] I will bring their deeds upon their own heads, says the Lord GOD.

22 Then the cherubim lifted up their wings, with the wheels beside them; and the glory of the God of Israel was above them. [23]And the glory of the LORD ascended from the middle of the city, and stopped on the mountain east of the city. [24]The spirit lifted me up and brought me in a vision by the spirit of God into Chaldea, to the exiles. Then the vision that I had seen left me. [25]And I told the exiles all the things that the LORD had shown me.

11.14–25. 14–21: God claims to be *a sanctuary to them for a little while:* God's presence in the world, rather than the Temple's presence in Jerusalem, ensures their future. God promises to gather the people from exile, to give them *the land of Israel*, and to purify the people from abominations in a manner characteristic of priestly purification. The promise of *one heart* (some manuscripts read "a new heart") and *a new spirit within them* takes up a theme from Jeremiah (Jer 32.39; see also Ezek 18.31; 36.26) concerning a new

a Gk Syr: Heb *people of your kindred*   b Or *to some extent*   c Another reading is *a new*   d Cn: Heb *And to the heart of their detestable things and their abominations their heart goes*

covenant* in which God's Torah* is written upon their hearts (Jer 31.33–34; see also Ezek 16.59–63). *"They shall be my people, and I will be their God"* is a formulation that characterizes the covenant between God and Israel/Judah (14.11; 36.28; 37.23; Jer 7.23; 31.33; 32.38; Hos 2.23; Zech 8.8). **22–24:** Ezekiel is returned to *Chaldea* (Babylonia) to report to the exiles.

12 The word of the LORD came to me: ²Mortal, you are living in the midst of a rebellious house, who have eyes to see but do not see, who have ears to hear but do not hear; ³for they are a rebellious house. Therefore, mortal, prepare for yourself an exile's baggage, and go into exile by day in their sight; you shall go like an exile from your place to another place in their sight. Perhaps they will understand, though they are a rebellious house. ⁴You shall bring out your baggage by day in their sight, as baggage for exile; and you shall go out yourself at evening in their sight, as those do who go into exile. ⁵Dig through the wall in their sight, and carry the baggage through it. ⁶In their sight you shall lift the baggage on your shoulder, and carry it out in the dark; you shall cover your face, so that you may not see the land; for I have made you a sign for the house of Israel.

7 I did just as I was commanded. I brought out my baggage by day, as baggage for exile, and in the evening I dug through the wall with my own hands; I brought it out in the dark, carrying it on my shoulder in their sight.

8 In the morning the word of the LORD came to me: ⁹Mortal, has not the house of Israel, the rebellious house, said to you, "What are you doing?" ¹⁰Say to them, "Thus says the Lord GOD: This oracle concerns the prince in Jerusalem and all the house of Israel in it." ¹¹Say, "I am a sign for you: as I have done, so shall it be done to them; they shall go into exile, into captivity." ¹²And the prince who is among them shall lift his baggage on his shoulder in the dark, and shall go out; he*a* shall dig through the wall and carry it through; he shall cover his face, so that he may not see the land with his eyes. ¹³I will spread my net over him, and he shall be caught in my snare; and I will bring him

to Babylon, the land of the Chaldeans, yet he shall not see it; and he shall die there. ¹⁴I will scatter to every wind all who are around him, his helpers and all his troops; and I will unsheathe the sword behind them. ¹⁵And they shall know that I am the LORD, when I disperse them among the nations and scatter them through the countries. ¹⁶But I will let a few of them escape from the sword, from famine and pestilence, so that they may tell of all their abominations among the nations where they go; then they shall know that I am the LORD.

17 The word of the LORD came to me: ¹⁸Mortal, eat your bread with quaking, and drink your water with trembling and with fearfulness; ¹⁹and say to the people of the land, Thus says the Lord GOD concerning the inhabitants of Jerusalem in the land of Israel: They shall eat their bread with fearfulness, and drink their water in dismay, because their land shall be stripped of all it contains, on account of the violence of all those who live in it. ²⁰The inhabited cities shall be laid waste, and the land shall become a desolation; and you shall know that I am the LORD.

12.1–20: Symbolic actions concerning the Exile.* **12.1–7:** The first represents the exile of the house of Israel. God calls Israel *a rebellious house,* but adds *who have eyes to see, but do not see, who have ears to hear, but do not hear,* apparently in reference to Isa 6.9–10. Ezekiel is to prepare his baggage, dig through the wall, and depart with his face covered so that all may see that the exile of Israel is taking place. *I have made you a sign for the house of Israel* (compare Isa 7.14; 8.18). **8–16:** Ezekiel's action provokes questions. He relates the symbolic action to the exile of the Davidic king, which strikes at the foundation of Judean identity and the promise of God's protection of Jerusalem and the house of David (2 Sam 7; Ps 89; 132). Some understand *prince* as a reference to Zedekiah, who served as the Babylonian-appointed regent while Jehoiachin was in exile. Ezekiel's scenario of the prince's escape and capture reflects Zedekiah's capture near Jericho and blinding at Riblah prior to imprisonment in Babylon (2 Kings 25.1–7; Jer 52.4–11).

a Gk Syr: Heb *they*

17–20: Eating meals in fear dramatizes the realities of exile.

Oracles concerning prophets* and prophecy
12.21–14.11: Ezekiel's oracles* affirm the imminent fulfillment of God's visions and challenge those prophets and prophetesses who proclaim false messages of peace.

---

21 The word of the LORD came to me: 22 Mortal, what is this proverb of yours about the land of Israel, which says, "The days are prolonged, and every vision comes to nothing"? 23 Tell them therefore, "Thus says the Lord GOD: I will put an end to this proverb, and they shall use it no more as a proverb in Israel." But say to them, The days are near, and the fulfillment of every vision. 24 For there shall no longer be any false vision or flattering divination within the house of Israel. 25 But I the LORD will speak the word that I speak, and it will be fulfilled. It will no longer be delayed; but in your days, O rebellious house, I will speak the word and fulfill it, says the Lord GOD.

26 The word of the LORD came to me: 27 Mortal, the house of Israel is saying, "The vision that he sees is for many years ahead; he prophesies for distant times." 28 Therefore say to them, Thus says the Lord GOD: None of my words will be delayed any longer, but the word that I speak will be fulfilled, says the Lord GOD.

12.21–28. 21–25: Ezekiel responds to those who claim that his visions will not be fulfilled. *Proverb* here refers to a common saying among the people. *Vision* refers to both visual and auditory experience (see Isa 2.1). **26–27:** Ezekiel responds to the charge that his visions will be fulfilled only in the distant future by stating that they are about to be realized.

13 The word of the LORD came to me: 2 Mortal, prophesy against the prophets of Israel who are prophesying; say to those who prophesy out of their own imagination: "Hear the word of the LORD!" 3 Thus says the Lord GOD, Alas for the senseless prophets who follow their own spirit, and have seen nothing! 4 Your prophets have been like jackals among ruins, O Israel. 5 You

have not gone up into the breaches, or repaired a wall for the house of Israel, so that it might stand in battle on the day of the LORD. 6 They have envisioned falsehood and lying divination; they say, "Says the LORD," when the LORD has not sent them, and yet they wait for the fulfillment of their word! 7 Have you not seen a false vision or uttered a lying divination, when you have said, "Says the LORD," even though I did not speak?

8 Therefore thus says the Lord GOD: Because you have uttered falsehood and envisioned lies, I am against you, says the Lord GOD. 9 My hand will be against the prophets who see false visions and utter lying divinations; they shall not be in the council of my people, nor be enrolled in the register of the house of Israel, nor shall they enter the land of Israel; and you shall know that I am the Lord GOD. 10 Because, in truth, because they have misled my people, saying, "Peace," when there is no peace; and because, when the people build a wall, these prophets*a* smear whitewash on it. 11 Say to those who smear whitewash on it that it shall fall. There will be a deluge of rain,*b* great hailstones will fall, and a stormy wind will break out. 12 When the wall falls, will it not be said to you, "Where is the whitewash you smeared on it?" 13 Therefore thus says the Lord GOD: In my wrath I will make a stormy wind break out, and in my anger there shall be a deluge of rain, and hailstones in wrath to destroy it. 14 I will break down the wall that you have smeared with whitewash, and bring it to the ground, so that its foundation will be laid bare; when it falls, you shall perish within it; and you shall know that I am the LORD. 15 Thus I will spend my wrath upon the wall, and upon those who have smeared it with whitewash; and I will say to you, The wall is no more, nor those who smeared it— 16 the prophets of Israel who prophesied concerning Jerusalem and saw visions of peace for it, when there was no peace, says the Lord GOD.

17 As for you, mortal, set your face against the daughters of your people, who prophesy out of their own imagination;

a Heb *they*　　*b* Heb *rain and you*

prophesy against them ¹⁸and say, Thus says the Lord GOD: Woe to the women who sew bands on all wrists, and make veils for the heads of persons of every height, in the hunt for human lives! Will you hunt down lives among my people, and maintain your own lives? ¹⁹You have profaned me among my people for handfuls of barley and for pieces of bread, putting to death persons who should not die and keeping alive persons who should not live, by your lies to my people, who listen to lies.

20 Therefore thus says the Lord GOD: I am against your bands with which you hunt lives;^a I will tear them from your arms, and let the lives go free, the lives that you hunt down like birds. ²¹I will tear off your veils, and save my people from your hands; they shall no longer be prey in your hands; and you shall know that I am the LORD. ²²Because you have disheartened the righteous falsely, although I have not disheartened them, and you have encouraged the wicked not to turn from their wicked way and save their lives; ²³therefore you shall no longer see false visions or practice divination; I will save my people from your hand. Then you will know that I am the LORD.

13.1–23: Ezekiel must condemn prophets who announce peace (compare Jer 27–28). **1–7:** Ezekiel charges the prophets with false prophecy, claiming that they *prophesy out of their own imagination* rather than speak the word of God. He compares them to jackals who live in the ruins of others rather than do something useful. **8–16:** God is against those prophets who announce *"Peace" when there is no peace*. Much like Hananiah in Jer 27–28, prophets of peace would have relied upon the Davidic tradition of God's promise of security for the monarchy and Jerusalem. Ezekiel compares these prophecies to a wall that is *whitewashed* and then destroyed by rain, hail, and wind. Walls made of sun-dried brick are frequently destroyed by heavy rain and wind. **17–23:** Ezekiel then condemns the women who prophesy falsely and practice divination. Miriam (Ex 15.20–21), Deborah (Judg 4–5), and Huldah (2 Kings 22) demonstrate that female prophets appeared in both Israel and Judah. He points to the divinatory side of their activities in which they employ wristbands and veils (see Moses' veil in Ex 34.29–35), and he indicates that they are paid for their

services in barley and bread. Prophecy was a profession in the ancient world (1 Sam 9.7, but contrast Am 7.10–17). The false prophetesses and diviners apparently play a role in deciding capital cases in which a person's life is at stake. God will tear the bands from their hands and let the lives of such people go free like birds. Birds were frequently employed in divination in the ancient world (see Isa 8.19).

14 Certain elders of Israel came to me and sat down before me. ²And the word of the LORD came to me: ³Mortal, these men have taken their idols into their hearts, and placed their iniquity as a stumbling block before them; shall I let myself be consulted by them? ⁴Therefore speak to them, and say to them, Thus says the Lord GOD: Any of those of the house of Israel who take their idols into their hearts and place their iniquity as a stumbling block before them, and yet come to the prophet—I the LORD will answer those who come with the multitude of their idols, ⁵in order that I may take hold of the hearts of the house of Israel, all of whom are estranged from me through their idols.

6 Therefore say to the house of Israel, Thus says the Lord GOD: Repent and turn away from your idols; and turn away your faces from all your abominations. ⁷For any of those of the house of Israel, or of the aliens who reside in Israel, who separate themselves from me, taking their idols into their hearts and placing their iniquity as a stumbling block before them, and yet come to a prophet to inquire of me by him, I the LORD will answer them myself. ⁸I will set my face against them; I will make them a sign and a byword and cut them off from the midst of my people; and you shall know that I am the LORD.

9 If a prophet is deceived and speaks a word, I, the LORD, have deceived that prophet, and I will stretch out my hand against him, and will destroy him from the midst of my people Israel. ¹⁰And they shall bear their punishment—the punishment of the inquirer and the punishment of the prophet shall be the same— ¹¹so that the

---

a Gk Syr: Heb *lives for birds*

house of Israel may no longer go astray from me, nor defile themselves any more with all their transgressions. Then they shall be my people, and I will be their God, says the Lord GOD.

14.1–11: Ezekiel must contend with competition from other prophets. God states that the elders *have taken their idols into their hearts,* apparently a reference to their consulting pagan diviners or a charge that other Judean prophets are false. The coarse term for *idols,* literally "dung balls," demonstrates Ezekiel's disdain for such persons. In response to those who consult idols or false prophets, God states, *"I, the LORD, will answer him myself,"* and claims to deliberately deceive the false prophets so that they will be destroyed (1 Kings 22). The covenant* formula (see comment on 11.14–21) *they shall be my people, and I will be their God* conveys God's intention to convince the people to remain loyal.

12 The word of the LORD came to me: ¹³Mortal, when a land sins against me by acting faithlessly, and I stretch out my hand against it, and break its staff of bread and send famine upon it, and cut off from it human beings and animals, ¹⁴even if Noah, Daniel,ᵃ and Job, these three, were in it, they would save only their own lives by their righteousness, says the Lord GOD. ¹⁵If I send wild animals through the land to ravage it, so that it is made desolate, and no one may pass through because of the animals; ¹⁶even if these three men were in it, as I live, says the Lord GOD, they would save neither sons nor daughters; they alone would be saved, but the land would be desolate. ¹⁷Or if I bring a sword upon that land and say, "Let a sword pass through the land," and I cut off human beings and animals from it; ¹⁸though these three men were in it, as I live, says the Lord GOD, they would save neither sons nor daughters, but they alone would be saved. ¹⁹Or if I send a pestilence into that land, and pour out my wrath upon it with blood, to cut off humans and animals from it; ²⁰even if Noah, Daniel,ᵃ and Job were in it, as I live, says the Lord GOD, they would save neither son nor daughter; they would save only their own lives by their righteousness.

21 For thus says the Lord GOD: How much more when I send upon Jerusalem my four deadly acts of judgment, sword, famine, wild animals, and pestilence, to cut off humans and animals from it! ²²Yet, survivors shall be left in it, sons and daughters who will be brought out; they will come out to you. When you see their ways and their deeds, you will be consoled for the evil that I have brought upon Jerusalem, for all that I have brought upon it. ²³They shall console you, when you see their ways and their deeds; and you shall know that it was not without cause that I did all that I have done in it, says the Lord GOD.

14.12–23: Concerning individual righteousness. After stating that God deceives false prophets and leads them to destruction, Ezekiel claims that people are responsible for their own moral action and safety from punishment. **12–20:** *Noah, Daniel, and Job* were exemplary righteous persons who had the capacity to save others. Noah saved his family during the flood (Gen 6–9), and Job saved his three friends who spoke wrongly about God (Job 42.7–9). Daniel and his friends saved only themselves by their righteousness (Dan 1; 3; 6), but in the Canaanite legend* of Aqhat, the righteous Dan-El saves his son Aqhat from death. Dan-El in Ezekiel is spelled according to the Canaanite pattern (see note *a*). **21–23:** The same punishments are applied to Jerusalem.

15 The word of the LORD came to me:
2 O mortal, how does the wood of
　　the vine surpass all other wood—
　the vine branch that is among the
　　trees of the forest?
3 Is wood taken from it to make
　　anything?
　Does one take a peg from it on which
　　to hang any object?
4 It is put in the fire for fuel;
　when the fire has consumed both
　　ends of it
　and the middle of it is charred,
　　is it useful for anything?
5 When it was whole it was used
　　for nothing;

a Or, as otherwise read, *Danel*

Using Allegory

Allegory* is a form of extended comparison in which familiar objects or persons stand for ideals, concepts, or other ideas that cannot be seen or touched, such as love, faith, or righteousness. Although allegory is not a popular form in most present-day literature, we occasionally encounter allegory in everyday life. One allegorical figure that is familiar to the modern reader is the statue of Justice sometimes seen in courthouses or other settings. This is a sculpture of a beautiful woman, wearing a blindfold and holding balancing scales in one hand and a sword in the other. The woman's beauty symbolizes the appeal of justice to our admiration of what is right and fair. The blindfold symbolizes that justice makes no distinctions between persons, and therefore takes no account of the differences in importance between people seeking justice. The balance scales symbolize the open, public application of the rules of fairness. The sword symbolizes the penalties that justice can impose. These allegorical elements tell us something about our ideals of justice and righteousness in the contemporary world.

When Ezekiel uses the technique of allegorical comparison, as he does many times in this book, he is trying to make the concepts and ideals of faithfulness, purity, and worship real to the imaginations of his hearers or readers. Although some of his ideas and images are strange to us, with a little thought we, too, can see Ezekiel's vision of a just and holy society.

---

how much less—when the fire has
consumed it,
and it is charred—
can it ever be used for anything!
6 Therefore thus says the Lord GOD: Like the wood of the vine among the trees of the forest, which I have given to the fire for fuel, so I will give up the inhabitants of Jerusalem. 7 I will set my face against them; although they escape from the fire, the fire shall still consume them; and you shall know that I am the LORD, when I set my face against them. 8 And I will make the land desolate, because they have acted faithlessly, says the Lord GOD.

16 The word of the LORD came to me: 2 Mortal, make known to Jerusalem her abominations, 3 and say, Thus says the Lord GOD to Jerusalem: Your origin and your birth were in the land of the Canaanites; your father was an Amorite, and your mother a Hittite. 4 As for your birth, on the day you were born your navel cord was not cut, nor were you washed with water to cleanse you, nor rubbed with salt, nor wrapped in cloths. 5 No eye pitied you, to do any of these things for you out of compassion for you; but you were thrown out in the open field, for you were abhorred on the day you were born.

15.1–8: The allegory* of the useless vine. Ezekiel uses rhetorical* questions to compare the inhabitants of Jerusalem to the wood of a vine, which is entirely useless except for burning (see Judg 9.7–21). **2:** The wood of the vine does not surpass any other wood. **3:** It cannot be used to make anything, since vine branches are twisted and weak. **4–5:** Even when burned, the charred ends are useless. **6–8:** Like useless vine branches, Jerusalem will be burned.

16.1–63: The allegory of Jerusalem as God's adulterous wife. Compare Hosea's marriage to Gomer, whom he charged with harlotry to symbolize Israel's unfaithfulness to God (Hos 1–3; compare Jer 2–3). **1–5:** Ezekiel portrays Jerusalem as an unwanted baby who, like many female babies in pre-industrial cultures, is cast off to die as an economic liability. *Your father was an Amorite, and your mother a Hittite:* Ezekiel believes that a mixture of Amorite or Syrian peoples and Hittites or Anatolian peoples populated Canaan before Israel emerged. Jerusalem was in Canaanite (Jebusite)

hands prior to David's conquest. The Jebusite population was never destroyed.

6 I passed by you, and saw you flailing about in your blood. As you lay in your blood, I said to you, "Live! [7]and grow up[a] like a plant of the field." You grew up and became tall and arrived at full womanhood;[b] your breasts were formed, and your hair had grown; yet you were naked and bare.

8 I passed by you again and looked on you; you were at the age for love. I spread the edge of my cloak over you, and covered your nakedness: I pledged myself to you and entered into a covenant with you, says the Lord GOD, and you became mine. [9]Then I bathed you with water and washed off the blood from you, and anointed you with oil. [10]I clothed you with embroidered cloth and with sandals of fine leather; I bound you in fine linen and covered you with rich fabric.[c] [11]I adorned you with ornaments: I put bracelets on your arms, a chain on your neck, [12]a ring on your nose, earrings in your ears, and a beautiful crown upon your head. [13]You were adorned with gold and silver, while your clothing was of fine linen, rich fabric,[c] and embroidered cloth. You had choice flour and honey and oil for food. You grew exceedingly beautiful, fit to be a queen. [14]Your fame spread among the nations on account of your beauty, for it was perfect because of my splendor that I had bestowed on you, says the Lord GOD.

16.6–14: God commands the abandoned infant to live but does nothing to care for her. She grows up like a plant but remains naked. *I spread the edge of my cloak over you, and covered your nakedness* indicates God's intent to marry the young woman (Ruth 3.9). Only after taking Jerusalem in marriage does God wash the blood from her and clothe her. The description of fine clothing, jewelry, and food (see Isa 3.18–23) demonstrates God's generosity to the unwanted Jerusalem.

---

15 But you trusted in your beauty, and played the whore because of your fame, and lavished your whorings on any passer-by.[d] [16]You took some of your garments, and made for yourself colorful shrines, and on them played the whore; nothing like this has ever been or ever shall be.[c] [17]You also took your beautiful jewels of my gold and my silver that I had given you, and made for yourself male images, and with them played the whore; [18]and you took your embroidered garments to cover them, and set my oil and my incense before them. [19]Also my bread that I gave you—I fed you with choice flour and oil and honey—you set it before them as a pleasing odor; and so it was, says the Lord GOD. [20]You took your sons and your daughters, whom you had borne to me, and these you sacrificed to them to be devoured. As if your whorings were not enough! [21]You slaughtered my children and delivered them up as an offering to them. [22]And in all your abominations and your whorings you did not remember the days of your youth, when you were naked and bare, flailing about in your blood.

23 After all your wickedness (woe, woe to you! says the Lord GOD), [24]you built yourself a platform and made yourself a lofty place in every square; [25]at the head of every street you built your lofty place and prostituted your beauty, offering yourself to every passer-by, and multiplying your whoring. [26]You played the whore with the Egyptians, your lustful neighbors, multiplying your whoring, to provoke me to anger. [27]Therefore I stretched out my hand against you, reduced your rations, and gave you up to the will of your enemies, the daughters of the Philistines, who were ashamed of your lewd behavior. [28]You played the whore with the Assyrians, because you were insatiable; you played the whore with them, and still you were not satisfied. [29]You multiplied your whoring with Chaldea, the land of merchants; and even with this you were not satisfied.

30 How sick is your heart, says the Lord GOD, that you did all these things, the deeds of a brazen whore; [31]building your platform at the head of every street, and making your lofty place in every square! Yet you were not like a whore, because you scorned payment.

---

a Gk Syr: Heb *Live! I made you a myriad*   b Cn: Heb *ornament of ornaments*   c Meaning of Heb uncertain   d Heb adds *let it be his*

32Adulterous wife, who receives strangers instead of her husband! 33Gifts are given to all whores; but you gave your gifts to all your lovers, bribing them to come to you from all around for your whorings. 34So you were different from other women in your whorings: no one solicited you to play the whore; and you gave payment, while no payment was given to you; you were different.

16.15–34: God's charge that Jerusalem used the gifts to become a whore is a way to describe religious unfaithfulness. The metaphor* then shifts to political alliances with foreign nations. Israel allied itself with Egypt during the reigns of Solomon (1 Kings 3.1) and later Hoshea (2 Kings 17.4). Following Israel's destruction in 722/1 BCE, Assyria granted Philistia control of Israelite and Judean territory in the coastal plain. Israel made an alliance with Assyria during the reign of Menahem (2 Kings 15.17–22), and Judah turned to Assyria during the reign of Ahaz (2 Kings 16). Hezekiah established relations with Babylon (2 Kings 20; Isa 39). **30–34:** Ezekiel charges that Jerusalem pays her lovers. Ahaz's "bribe" to Tiglath-pileser (2 Kings 16.8) would be a case in point. When Nebuchadnezzar first conquered Jerusalem, he stripped the Temple of its wealth (2 Kings 24.10–17).

35 Therefore, O whore, hear the word of the LORD: 36Thus says the Lord GOD, Because your lust was poured out and your nakedness uncovered in your whoring with your lovers, and because of all your abominable idols, and because of the blood of your children that you gave to them, 37therefore, I will gather all your lovers, with whom you took pleasure, all those you loved and all those you hated; I will gather them against you from all around, and will uncover your nakedness to them, so that they may see all your nakedness. 38I will judge you as women who commit adultery and shed blood are judged, and bring blood upon you in wrath and jealousy. 39I will deliver you into their hands, and they shall throw down your platform and break down your lofty places; they shall strip you of your clothes and take your beautiful objects and leave you naked and bare. 40They shall bring up a mob against you, and they shall stone you and cut you to pieces with their swords. 41They shall burn

your houses and execute judgments on you in the sight of many women; I will stop you from playing the whore, and you shall also make no more payments. 42So I will satisfy my fury on you, and my jealousy shall turn away from you; I will be calm, and will be angry no longer. 43Because you have not remembered the days of your youth, but have enraged me with all these things; therefore, I have returned your deeds upon your head, says the Lord GOD.

16.35–43: God states that all of Jerusalem's lovers, the nations with whom she was allied, will come to punish her. Deuteronomy 22.22–24 requires that an adulteress be stoned to death.

Have you not committed lewdness beyond all your abominations? 44See, everyone who uses proverbs will use this proverb about you, "Like mother, like daughter." 45You are the daughter of your mother, who loathed her husband and her children; and you are the sister of your sisters, who loathed their husbands and their children. Your mother was a Hittite and your father an Amorite. 46Your elder sister is Samaria, who lived with her daughters to the north of you; and your younger sister, who lived to the south of you, is Sodom with her daughters. 47You not only followed their ways, and acted according to their abominations; within a very little time you were more corrupt than they in all your ways. 48As I live, says the Lord GOD, your sister Sodom and her daughters have not done as you and your daughters have done. 49This was the guilt of your sister Sodom: she and her daughters had pride, excess of food, and prosperous ease, but did not aid the poor and needy. 50They were haughty, and did abominable things before me; therefore I removed them when I saw it. 51Samaria has not committed half your sins; you have committed more abominations than they, and have made your sisters appear righteous by all the abominations that you have committed. 52Bear your disgrace, you also, for you have brought about for your sisters a more favorable judgment; because of your sins in which you acted more abominably than they, they are more in the right than

you. So be ashamed, you also, and bear your disgrace, for you have made your sisters appear righteous.

16.44–52: In charging that Jerusalem is like her mother *who loathed her husband and her children*, God points to the sexual *abominations* of the nations who possessed the land before Israel (Lev 18.24–30; 20.23; Gen 15.16). God compares Jerusalem to Samaria, the elder sister to the north, and Sodom, the younger sister to the south. According to biblical tradition (2 Kings 17; Gen 18–19), both cities were destroyed for their sins, but God states that Jerusalem's sins are even worse.

53 I will restore their fortunes, the fortunes of Sodom and her daughters and the fortunes of Samaria and her daughters, and I will restore your own fortunes along with theirs, 54in order that you may bear your disgrace and be ashamed of all that you have done, becoming a consolation to them. 55As for your sisters, Sodom and her daughters shall return to their former state, Samaria and her daughters shall return to their former state, and you and your daughters shall return to your former state. 56Was not your sister Sodom a byword in your mouth in the day of your pride, 57before your wickedness was uncovered? Now you are a mockery to the daughters of Aram*a* and all her neighbors, and to the daughters of the Philistines, those all around who despise you. 58You must bear the penalty of your lewdness and your abominations, says the LORD.

16.53–58: God intends to *restore the fortunes* of both Sodom and Samaria and their *daughters*, a reference to cities allied with each. In addition, God will restore Jerusalem. God intends to punish or cleanse Israel from sins much like sacrifice at the altar. Jerusalem has become a mockery to *Aram* (some manuscripts read "Edom") and Philistia, Judah's surviving neighbors.

59 Yes, thus says the Lord GOD: I will deal with you as you have done, you who have despised the oath, breaking the covenant; 60yet I will remember my covenant with you in the days of your youth, and I will establish with you an everlasting covenant. 61Then you will remember your ways, and be

ashamed when I*b* take your sisters, both your elder and your younger, and give them to you as daughters, but not on account of my*c* covenant with you. 62I will establish my covenant with you, and you shall know that I am the LORD, 63in order that you may remember and be confounded, and never open your mouth again because of your shame, when I forgive you all that you have done, says the Lord GOD.

16.59–63: *The everlasting covenant*✳ with Jerusalem alludes to God's eternal protection for Jerusalem and the house of David (2 Sam 7; Isa 55.3) which may be compared to Jeremiah's new covenant (Jer 31.31–34). God *remembers* the covenant; only Judah is charged with *breaking* (literally, "transgressing") it. Jerusalem, not God, is charged with violating the "eternal covenant," according to which Jerusalem is destroyed. Samaria and Sodom were sisters, but they will become Jerusalem's daughters, indicating Jerusalem's premier status. *I will establish my covenant with you, and you shall know that I am the LORD* restates the covenant formula (compare Hos 2.20).

17 The word of the LORD came to me: 2O mortal, propound a riddle, and speak an allegory to the house of Israel. 3Say: Thus says the Lord GOD:

A great eagle, with great wings and long pinions,
　　rich in plumage of many colors,
　　came to the Lebanon.
He took the top of the cedar,
4　　broke off its topmost shoot;
he carried it to a land of trade,
　　set it in a city of merchants.
5 Then he took a seed from the land,
　　placed it in fertile soil;
a plant*d* by abundant waters,
　　he set it like a willow twig.
6 It sprouted and became a vine
　　spreading out, but low;
its branches turned toward him,
　　its roots remained where it stood.
So it became a vine;
　　it brought forth branches,
　　put forth foliage.

a Another reading is *Edom*　　*b* Syr: Heb *you*
c Heb lacks *my*　　*d* Meaning of Heb uncertain

7 There was another great eagle,
  with great wings and much plumage.
And see! This vine stretched out
  its roots toward him;
it shot out its branches toward him,
  so that he might water it.
From the bed where it was planted
8   it was transplanted
to good soil by abundant waters,
  so that it might produce branches
  and bear fruit
  and become a noble vine.
9 Say: Thus says the Lord GOD:
  Will it prosper?
  Will he not pull up its roots,
    cause its fruit to rot^a and wither,
    its fresh sprouting leaves to fade?
  No strong arm or mighty army will be
    needed
  to pull it from its roots.
10 When it is transplanted, will it thrive?
  When the east wind strikes it,
    will it not utterly wither,
    wither on the bed where it grew?

17.1–24: The allegory* of the eagles, the vine, and the cedar. The allegory describes Jehoiachin's exile to Babylon, the installation of Zedekiah as king, and Zedekiah's demise when he revolted against Babylon. **1–2:** God instructs Ezekiel to speak *a riddle* and *an allegory.* **3–10:** The allegory proceeds in three stages. The first describes an eagle, later identified as Nebuchadnezzar, who breaks off the top shoot of the cedar and carries it *to a land of trade* and *a city of merchants.* Lebanon was known for "the cedars of Lebanon" (Ps 104.16), but the Davidic palace in Jerusalem, since it was built with cedar, is called the "House of the Forest of Lebanon" (1 Kings 7.2; Isa 22.9). The *topmost shoot* therefore symbolizes the Davidic monarch Jehoiachin (Isa 11.1); and the *land of trade* is Babylon (16.29). The seed that becomes a vine is Zedekiah. The *great eagle* is the Egyptian Pharaoh Psammetichus II, to whom Zedekiah turned for support in his revolt against Nebuchadnezzar (Jer 27). The rhetorical questions portray the destruction of the vine.

11 Then the word of the LORD came to me: 12 Say now to the rebellious house: Do you not know what these things mean? Tell them: The king of Babylon came to Jerusalem, took its king and its officials, and brought them back with him to Babylon. 13 He took one of the royal offspring and made a covenant with him, putting him under oath (he had taken away the chief men of the land), 14 so that the kingdom might be humble and not lift itself up, and that by keeping his covenant it might stand. 15 But he rebelled against him by sending ambassadors to Egypt, in order that they might give him horses and a large army. Will he succeed? Can one escape who does such things? Can he break the covenant and yet escape? 16 As I live, says the Lord GOD, surely in the place where the king resides who made him king, whose oath he despised, and whose covenant with him he broke—in Babylon he shall die. 17 Pharaoh with his mighty army and great company will not help him in war, when ramps are cast up and siege walls built to cut off many lives. 18 Because he despised the oath and broke the covenant, because he gave his hand and yet did all these things, he shall not escape. 19 Therefore thus says the Lord GOD: As I live, I will surely return upon his head my oath that he despised, and my covenant that he broke. 20 I will spread my net over him, and he shall be caught in my snare; I will bring him to Babylon and enter into judgment with him there for the treason he has committed against me. 21 All the pick^b of his troops shall fall by the sword, and the survivors shall be scattered to every wind; and you shall know that I, the LORD, have spoken.

17.11–21: The allegory is explained in detail. God identifies with the Babylonian king by referring to Zedekiah's revolt against Babylon as *the treason that he has committed against me.*

22 Thus says the Lord GOD:
  I myself will take a sprig
    from the lofty top of a cedar;
    I will set it out.
  I will break off a tender one
    from the topmost of its young twigs;
  I myself will plant it
    on a high and lofty mountain.

a Meaning of Heb uncertain   *b* Another reading is *fugitives*

23 On the mountain height of Israel
    I will plant it,
  in order that it may produce boughs and
        bear fruit,
    and become a noble cedar.
  Under it every kind of bird will live;
    in the shade of its branches
        will nest
    winged creatures of every kind.
24 All the trees of the field shall know
      that I am the LORD.
  I bring low the high tree,
    I make high the low tree;
  I dry up the green tree
    and make the dry tree flourish.
  I the LORD have spoken;
    I will accomplish it.

17.22–24: God employs the allegory of the cedar to promise the restoration of the Davidic monarchy (Isa 11.1–10; Jer 23.5–6; 33.15).

18 The word of the LORD came to me: 2What do you mean by repeating this proverb concerning the land of Israel, "The parents have eaten sour grapes, and the children's teeth are set on edge"? 3As I live, says the Lord GOD, this proverb shall no more be used by you in Israel. 4Know that all lives are mine; the life of the parent as well as the life of the child is mine: it is only the person who sins that shall die.

18.1–32: Concerning the responsibility of the individual. The prophet* disputes the view that Israel's punishment is due to the sins of past generations (see Ex 20.5). **1–4:** The opposing view is quoted as a proverb, *"The parents have eaten sour grapes, and the children's teeth are set on edge"* (see Jer 31.29–30).

5 If a man is righteous and does what is lawful and right— 6if he does not eat upon the mountains or lift up his eyes to the idols of the house of Israel, does not defile his neighbor's wife or approach a woman during her menstrual period, 7does not oppress anyone, but restores to the debtor his pledge, commits no robbery, gives his bread to the hungry and covers the naked with a garment, 8does not take advance or accrued interest, withholds his hand from iniquity, executes

true justice between contending parties, 9follows my statutes, and is careful to observe my ordinances, acting faithfully—such a one is righteous; he shall surely live, says the Lord GOD.

18.5–9: Ezekiel describes four cases. The first is *a righteous man*, whose actions are described in accordance with provisions from the Holiness Code (Lev 17–26): *eat upon the mountains*, eat meat without disposing of blood properly at the Temple* (Lev 17; 19.26); *lift up his eyes to the idols of the house of Israel*, improper worship of God (see Ex 20.4–6; Lev 19.4); *defile his neighbor's wife*, adultery (Lev 20.10; see also 19.20–22); *approach a woman during her menstrual period* (Lev 15.19–24); *does not oppress anyone*, economic oppression is unholy (Lev 19.13); *restores to the debtor his pledge* and *covers the naked with a garment*, a person's only cloak could be taken in pledge for a loan, but it had to be returned if the debtor needed it (Ex 22.25–27); *does not take advance or accrued interest* (Ex 22.25; Lev 25.35–38); *executes true justice between contending parties*, in a court of law (Lev 19.15–19). The righteous person will live.

10 If he has a son who is violent, a shedder of blood, 11who does any of these things (though his father*a* does none of them), who eats upon the mountains, defiles his neighbor's wife, 12oppresses the poor and needy, commits robbery, does not restore the pledge, lifts up his eyes to the idols, commits abomination, 13takes advance or accrued interest; shall he then live? He shall not. He has done all these abominable things; he shall surely die; his blood shall be upon himself.

14 But if this man has a son who sees all the sins that his father has done, considers, and does not do likewise, 15who does not eat upon the mountains or lift up his eyes to the idols of the house of Israel, does not defile his neighbor's wife, 16does not wrong anyone, exacts no pledge, commits no robbery, but gives his bread to the hungry and covers the naked with a garment, 17withholds his hand from iniquity,*b* takes no advance or accrued interest, observes my ordinances, and

---

a Heb *he*   *b* Gk: Heb *the poor*

follows my statutes; he shall not die for his father's iniquity; he shall surely live. 18As for his father, because he practiced extortion, robbed his brother, and did what is not good among his people, he dies for his iniquity.

19 Yet you say, "Why should not the son suffer for the iniquity of the father?" When the son has done what is lawful and right, and has been careful to observe all my statutes, he shall surely live. 20The person who sins shall die. A child shall not suffer for the iniquity of a parent, nor a parent suffer for the iniquity of a child; the righteousness of the righteous shall be his own, and the wickedness of the wicked shall be his own.

21 But if the wicked turn away from all their sins that they have committed and keep all my statutes and do what is lawful and right, they shall surely live; they shall not die. 22None of the transgressions that they have committed shall be remembered against them; for the righteousness that they have done they shall live. 23Have I any pleasure in the death of the wicked, says the Lord GOD, and not rather that they should turn from their ways and live? 24But when the righteous turn away from their righteousness and commit iniquity and do the same abominable things that the wicked do, shall they live? None of the righteous deeds that they have done shall be remembered; for the treachery of which they are guilty and the sin they have committed, they shall die.

25 Yet you say, "The way of the Lord is unfair." Hear now, O house of Israel: Is my way unfair? Is it not your ways that are unfair? 26When the righteous turn away from their righteousness and commit iniquity, they shall die for it; for the iniquity that they have committed they shall die. 27Again, when the wicked turn away from the wickedness they have committed and do what is lawful and right, they shall save their life. 28Because they considered and turned away from all the transgressions that they had committed, they shall surely live; they shall not die. 29Yet the house of Israel says, "The way of the Lord is unfair." O house of Israel, are my ways unfair? Is it not your ways that are unfair?

30 Therefore I will judge you, O house of Israel, all of you according to your ways, says the Lord GOD. Repent and turn from all your transgressions; otherwise iniquity will be your ruin.*a* 31Cast away from you all the transgressions that you have committed against me, and get yourselves a new heart and a new spirit! Why will you die, O house of Israel? 32For I have no pleasure in the death of anyone, says the Lord GOD. Turn, then, and live.

18.10–32. 10–13: The son of a righteous person who sins is responsible and will die. 14–18: The son of a sinner who does right will be spared. 19–20: Ezekiel's opponents contend that the son is guilty for the sins of the father, but Ezekiel states that only the person who commits sins will be punished for them. 21–24: A new principle enters the debate. Ezekiel contends that a wicked person who repents will be saved, but a righteous person who sins will be condemned. 25–29: Ezekiel restates the preceding principle about repentance. 30–32: *A new heart and a new spirit* (see 11.19; Jer 31.31–34; 32.36–41).

19 As for you, raise up a lamentation for the princes of Israel, 2and say:
What a lioness was your mother
    among lions!
She lay down among young lions,
    rearing her cubs.
3 She raised up one of her cubs;
    he became a young lion,
and he learned to catch prey;
    he devoured humans.
4 The nations sounded an alarm against
    him;
    he was caught in their pit;
and they brought him with hooks
    to the land of Egypt.
5 When she saw that she was
    thwarted,
    that her hope was lost,
she took another of her cubs
    and made him a young lion.
6 He prowled among the lions;
    he became a young lion,
and he learned to catch prey;
    he devoured people.

---

a Or so that they shall not be a stumbling block of iniquity to you

7 And he ravaged their strongholds,*
    and laid waste their towns;
  the land was appalled, and all in it,
    at the sound of his roaring.
8 The nations set upon him
    from the provinces all around;
  they spread their net over him;
    he was caught in their pit.
9 With hooks they put him in a cage,
    and brought him to the king
        of Babylon;
    they brought him into custody,
  so that his voice should be heard
        no more
    on the mountains of Israel.
10 Your mother was like a vine in
        a vineyard*
    transplanted by the water,
  fruitful and full of branches
    from abundant water.
11 Its strongest stem became
        a ruler's scepter;*
  it towered aloft
    among the thick boughs;
  it stood out in its height
    with its mass of branches.
12 But it was plucked up in fury,
    cast down to the ground;
  the east wind dried it up;
    its fruit was stripped off,
  its strong stem was withered;
    the fire consumed it.
13 Now it is transplanted into
        the wilderness,
    into a dry and thirsty land.
14 And fire has gone out from its stem,
    has consumed its branches and fruit,
  so that there remains in it no strong
        stem,
    no scepter for ruling.

This is a lamentation, and it is used as a
lamentation.

**19.1–14: Two allegories concerning the demise of
the monarchy.** Ezekiel laments the demise of the Davidic monarchy with two allegories styled as dirges or
songs of mourning. **1:** *Raise up a lamentation for the
princes of Israel:* Hebrew poetry typically had three
stressed syllables in each line. The lament,* however,
used a three-stress line followed by a two-stress line.

The poems use the 3/2 stress pattern (called "qinah")
of the funeral lament. Ezekiel refers to the kings as
"princes," thereby expressing the king's diminished
status in relation to the priests (34.24; 45.7–8). **2–9:**
The lion symbolizes the tribe of Judah and the royal
house of David (Gen 49.8–12). *A lioness was your
mother* refers to Judah or all Israel. Note the identification of Israel as the bride of God in Hosea (Hos 1–3),
Jeremiah (Jer 2–3), and Ezekiel (ch. 16). The first cub
who is *brought . . . with hooks to the land of Egypt* is
Jehoahaz, who was exiled to Egypt by Pharaoh Necho
after Josiah's death (2 Kings 23.31–34; 2 Chr 36.1–4).
The second cub who *learned to catch prey* and *devoured people* would be Jehoiakim, whom Pharaoh
Necho placed on the throne after exiling Jehoahaz.
Jeremiah condemns Jehoiakim for his injustice (Jer
21.11–22.19). *And brought him to the king of Babylon; they brought him into custody:* Jehoiachin, who
was exiled to Babylon following Jehoiakim's failed revolt (2 Kings 24.8–17; 2 Chr 36.9–10). **10–14:** This
poem employs the imagery of the vine (see chs. 15;
17; compare Isa 5.1–7). It is impossible to identify the
poem's imagery with specific individuals or countries
(see Isa 10.5–11.16; 1.29–31; 6.13). *The east wind
dried it up:* The "Sharab" or "Hamsin," a dry desert
wind like the Santa Ana winds of southern California,
is frequently employed as a symbol of God's power (Ex
14.21; 15.8–10; Isa 11.15). *Now it is transplanted into
the wilderness:* Jehoiachin's exile.

20 In the seventh year, in the fifth
    month, on the tenth day of the
month, certain elders of Israel came to consult the LORD, and sat down before me.
2And the word of the LORD came to me:
3Mortal, speak to the elders of Israel, and say
to them: Thus says the Lord GOD: Why are
you coming? To consult me? As I live, says
the Lord GOD, I will not be consulted by you.
4Will you judge them, mortal, will you judge
them? Then let them know the abominations
of their ancestors, 5and say to them: Thus
says the Lord GOD: On the day when I chose
Israel, I swore to the offspring of the house
of Jacob—making myself known to them in
the land of Egypt—I swore to them, saying,
I am the LORD your God. 6On that day I
swore to them that I would bring them out

---

a Heb *his widows*   *b* Cn: Heb *in your blood*
c Heb *Its strongest stems became rulers' scepters*

of the land of Egypt into a land that I had searched out for them, a land flowing with milk and honey, the most glorious of all lands. 7And I said to them, Cast away the detestable things your eyes feast on, every one of you, and do not defile yourselves with the idols of Egypt; I am the LORD your God. 8But they rebelled against me and would not listen to me; not one of them cast away the detestable things their eyes feasted on, nor did they forsake the idols of Egypt.

Then I thought I would pour out my wrath upon them and spend my anger against them in the midst of the land of Egypt. 9But I acted for the sake of my name, that it should not be profaned in the sight of the nations among whom they lived, in whose sight I made myself known to them in bringing them out of the land of Egypt. 10So I led them out of the land of Egypt and brought them into the wilderness. 11I gave them my statutes and showed them my ordinances, by whose observance everyone shall live. 12Moreover I gave them my sabbaths, as a sign between me and them, so that they might know that I the LORD sanctify them. 13But the house of Israel rebelled against me in the wilderness; they did not observe my statutes but rejected my ordinances, by whose observance everyone shall live; and my sabbaths they greatly profaned.

Then I thought I would pour out my wrath upon them in the wilderness, to make an end of them. 14But I acted for the sake of my name, so that it should not be profaned in the sight of the nations, in whose sight I had brought them out. 15Moreover I swore to them in the wilderness that I would not bring them into the land that I had given them, a land flowing with milk and honey, the most glorious of all lands, 16because they rejected my ordinances and did not observe my statutes, and profaned my sabbaths; for their heart went after their idols. 17Nevertheless my eye spared them, and I did not destroy them or make an end of them in the wilderness.

20.1–44: Ezekiel's assessment of Israel's past and future. Ezekiel's overview of Israel's history in the wilderness provides a basis for projecting a future in

which Israel will be returned to the wilderness and purged. **1–2:** *The seventh year . . . fifth month . . . tenth day:* August 14, 591 BCE. **3–4:** God refuses to answer the elders and instead calls upon Ezekiel to judge them. **5–32:** God rehearses the history of Israel's rebellion during the Exodus and Wilderness periods (see Ps 106). **5–6:** *I chose Israel:* God uses royal language (see 2 Sam 6.21; 1 Kings 8.16) to prepare the reader for God's role as king (v. 33). *I am the LORD your God. . . . I would bring them out of the land of Egypt:* See Ex 20.2. **7–8:** Apostasy in Egypt: Ex 14.10–12; Josh 24.14; Ps 106.7. **9:** *I acted for the sake of my name:* A key issue in Ezekiel (20.14, 22; 36.22; compare Ex 15.3; 32.12). **10–26:** Apostasy in the wilderness: Ex 32–34; Num 14; 25. **11–12:** The sabbath is the foundational sign of the covenant* (Ex 20.8–11; 31.12–17). **13–17:** The rebellion of the first generation is the golden calf incident (Ex 32–34) and the reaction to the report of the spies (Num 13–14) in which Moses persuaded God not to destroy the entire people (Ex 33.12–33; Num 14.13–25).

18 I said to their children in the wilderness, Do not follow the statutes of your parents, nor observe their ordinances, nor defile yourselves with their idols. 19I the LORD am your God; follow my statutes, and be careful to observe my ordinances, 20and hallow my sabbaths that they may be a sign between me and you, so that you may know that I the LORD am your God. 21But the children rebelled against me; they did not follow my statutes, and were not careful to observe my ordinances, by whose observance everyone shall live; they profaned my sabbaths.

Then I thought I would pour out my wrath upon them and spend my anger against them in the wilderness. 22But I withheld my hand, and acted for the sake of my name, so that it should not be profaned in the sight of the nations, in whose sight I had brought them out. 23Moreover I swore to them in the wilderness that I would scatter them among the nations and disperse them through the countries, 24because they had not executed my ordinances, but had rejected my statutes and profaned my sabbaths, and their eyes were set on their ancestors' idols. 25Moreover I gave them statutes that were not good and ordinances by which they could not live. 26I defiled them through their very gifts, in their

offering up all their firstborn, in order that I might horrify them, so that they might know that I am the LORD.

20.18–26: Following Israel's rebellion at the report of the spies, God condemned the people to death in the wilderness (Num 14.26–38). The rebellion of the second generation refers to acts of apostasy following the incident of the spies (Meribah, Num 20; Baal of Peor, Num 25).

27 Therefore, mortal, speak to the house of Israel and say to them, Thus says the Lord GOD: In this again your ancestors blasphemed me, by dealing treacherously with me. ²⁸For when I had brought them into the land that I swore to give them, then wherever they saw any high hill or any leafy tree, there they offered their sacrifices and presented the provocation of their offering; there they sent up their pleasing odors, and there they poured out their drink offerings. ²⁹(I said to them, What is the high place to which you go? So it is called Bamah*ᵃ* to this day.) ³⁰Therefore say to the house of Israel, Thus says the Lord GOD: Will you defile yourselves after the manner of your ancestors and go astray after their detestable things? ³¹When you offer your gifts and make your children pass through the fire, you defile yourselves with all your idols to this day. And shall I be consulted by you, O house of Israel? As I live, says the Lord GOD, I will not be consulted by you.

32 What is in your mind shall never happen—the thought, "Let us be like the nations, like the tribes of the countries, and worship wood and stone."

20.27–32: Apostasy in the land of Israel. 32: *Let us be like the nations:* See Deut 17.14; 1 Sam 8.4–5 concerning the institution of kingship.

33 As I live, says the Lord GOD, surely with a mighty hand and an outstretched arm, and with wrath poured out, I will be king over you. ³⁴I will bring you out from the peoples and gather you out of the countries where you are scattered, with a mighty hand and an outstretched arm, and with wrath poured out; ³⁵and I will bring you into the wilderness of the peoples, and there I will enter into judgment with you face to face. ³⁶As I entered into judgment with your ancestors in the wilderness of the land of Egypt, so I will enter into judgment with you, says the Lord GOD. ³⁷I will make you pass under the staff, and will bring you within the bond of the covenant. ³⁸I will purge out the rebels among you, and those who transgress against me; I will bring them out of the land where they reside as aliens, but they shall not enter the land of Israel. Then you shall know that I am the LORD.

39 As for you, O house of Israel, thus says the Lord GOD: Go serve your idols, everyone of you now and hereafter, if you will not listen to me; but my holy name you shall no more profane with your gifts and your idols.

40 For on my holy mountain, the mountain height of Israel, says the Lord GOD, there all the house of Israel, all of them, shall serve me in the land; there I will accept them, and there I will require your contributions and the choicest of your gifts, with all your sacred things. ⁴¹As a pleasing odor I will accept you, when I bring you out from the peoples, and gather you out of the countries where you have been scattered; and I will manifest my holiness among you in the sight of the nations. ⁴²You shall know that I am the LORD, when I bring you into the land of Israel, the country that I swore to give to your ancestors. ⁴³There you shall remember your ways and all the deeds by which you have polluted yourselves; and you shall loathe yourselves for all the evils that you have committed. ⁴⁴And you shall know that I am the LORD, when I deal with you for my name's sake, not according to your evil ways, or corrupt deeds, O house of Israel, says the Lord GOD.

20.33–44: God returns Israel to the wilderness to purge and restore the nation. **33:** *I will be king over you:* One of God's fundamental claims. **35:** *Wilderness of the peoples* associates Israel's exile among the nations with the wilderness tradition. **37:** *Pass under the staff:* Be counted to determine the offering due to

ᵃ That is *High Place*

God (see Lev 27.32). **40–44:** *My holy mountain:* the Jerusalem Temple.

45*ᵃ* The word of the LORD came to me: 46Mortal, set your face toward the south, preach against the south, and prophesy against the forest land in the Negeb; 47say to the forest of the Negeb, Hear the word of the LORD: Thus says the Lord GOD, I will kindle a fire in you, and it shall devour every green tree in you and every dry tree; the blazing flame shall not be quenched, and all faces from south to north shall be scorched by it. 48All flesh shall see that I the LORD have kindled it; it shall not be quenched. 49Then I said, "Ah Lord GOD! they are saying of me, 'Is he not a maker of allegories?' "

20.45–49: A prophecy against the Negeb. The Negeb is the desert region of southern Judah from which spies were sent into Canaan (Num 13.17, 22) prior to the rebellion in the wilderness. *South* designates the location of the Edomites (25.13), who are condemned for assisting Babylon in Judah's destruction (25.12–14).

21*ᵇ* The word of the LORD came to me: 2Mortal, set your face toward Jerusalem and preach against the sanctuaries; prophesy against the land of Israel 3and say to the land of Israel, Thus says the LORD: I am coming against you, and will draw my sword out of its sheath, and will cut off from you both righteous and wicked. 4Because I will cut off from you both righteous and wicked, therefore my sword shall go out of its sheath against all flesh from south to north; 5and all flesh shall know that I the LORD have drawn my sword out of its sheath; it shall not be sheathed again. 6Moan therefore, mortal; moan with breaking heart and bitter grief before their eyes. 7And when they say to you, "Why do you moan?" you shall say, "Because of the news that has come. Every heart will melt and all hands will be feeble, every spirit will faint and all knees will turn to water. See, it comes and it will be fulfilled," says the Lord GOD.

21.1–32: Oracles concerning God's sword. These oracles* may have accompanied a symbolic action in-

volving a sword (5.1–4; 14.21). **1–7:** Ezekiel speaks toward the Jerusalem sanctuary as the holy center of the nation.

8 And the word of the LORD came to me: 9Mortal, prophesy and say: Thus says the Lord; Say:
A sword, a sword is sharpened,
  it is also polished;
10 it is sharpened for slaughter,
  honed to flash like lightning!
How can we make merry?
  You have despised the rod,
  and all discipline.*ᶜ*
11 The sword*ᵈ* is given to be polished,
  to be grasped in the hand;
it is sharpened, the sword is polished,
  to be placed in the slayer's hand.
12 Cry and wail, O mortal,
  for it is against my people;
it is against all Israel's princes;
  they are thrown to the sword,
  together with my people.
Ah! Strike the thigh!
13For consider: What! If you despise the rod, will it not happen?*ᶜ* says the Lord GOD.
14 And you, mortal, prophesy;
  strike hand to hand.
Let the sword fall twice, thrice;
  it is a sword for killing.
A sword for great slaughter—
  it surrounds them;
15 therefore hearts melt
  and many stumble.
At all their gates I have set
  the point*ᶜ* of the sword.
Ah! It is made for flashing,
  it is polished*ᵉ* for slaughter.
16 Attack to the right!
  Engage to the left!
  —wherever your edge is directed.
17 I too will strike hand to hand,
  I will satisfy my fury;
  I the LORD have spoken.

21.8–17: Ezekiel's song of the sword. *You have despised the rod:* A rod might normally be used for dis-

a Ch 21.1 in Heb   *b* Ch 21.6 in Heb   *c* Meaning of Heb uncertain   *d* Heb *It*   *e* Tg: Heb *wrapped up*

cipline (Prov 10.13; 22.15), but now a deadly instrument is required.

~~~~~~~~~~~~~~

18 The word of the LORD came to me: ¹⁹Mortal, mark out two roads for the sword of the king of Babylon to come; both of them shall issue from the same land. And make a signpost, make it for a fork in the road leading to a city; ²⁰mark out the road for the sword to come to Rabbah of the Ammonites or to Judah and to*ª* Jerusalem the fortified. ²¹For the king of Babylon stands at the parting of the way, at the fork in the two roads, to use divination; he shakes the arrows, he consults the teraphim,*ᵇ* he inspects the liver. ²²Into his right hand comes the lot for Jerusalem, to set battering rams, to call out for slaughter, for raising the battle cry, to set battering rams against the gates, to cast up ramps, to build siege towers. ²³But to them it will seem like a false divination; they have sworn solemn oaths; but he brings their guilt to remembrance, bringing about their capture.

24 Therefore thus says the Lord GOD: Because you have brought your guilt to remembrance, in that your transgressions are uncovered, so that in all your deeds your sins appear—because you have come to remembrance, you shall be taken in hand.*ᶜ*
²⁵ As for you, vile, wicked prince of Israel,
　　you whose day has come,
　　the time of final punishment,
²⁶ thus says the Lord GOD:
　Remove the turban, take off the crown;
　　things shall not remain as they are.
　Exalt that which is low,
　　abase that which is high.
²⁷ A ruin, a ruin, a ruin—
　　I will make it!
　(Such has never occurred.)
　Until he comes whose right it is;
　　to him I will give it.

28 As for you, mortal, prophesy, and say, Thus says the Lord GOD concerning the Ammonites, and concerning their reproach; say:
　A sword, a sword! Drawn for slaughter,
　　polished to consume,*ᵈ* to flash like
　　lightning.
²⁹ Offering false visions for you,
　　divining lies for you,
　　they place you over the necks

of the vile, wicked ones—
　those whose day has come,
　　the time of final punishment.
³⁰ Return it to its sheath!
　In the place where you were created,
　　in the land of your origin,
　　I will judge you.
³¹ I will pour out my indignation upon
　　you,
　with the fire of my wrath
　　I will blow upon you.
　I will deliver you into brutish hands,
　　those skillful to destroy.
³² You shall be fuel for the fire,
　　your blood shall enter the earth;
　you shall be remembered no more,
　　for I the LORD have spoken.

21.18–32: The sword of Babylon. 18–23: When the Babylonian king reaches a fork in the road, he employs divination to decide which route to take. His alternatives are Jerusalem and Rabbah, the capital of Ammon. Ammon is one of Judah's allies in revolt against Babylon (Jer 27.3). Jerusalem is a former ally of Babylon (2 Kings 20.12–19; Isa 39), but Judah's revolt justifies the protracted siege. *He shakes the arrows, he consults the teraphim, he inspects the liver:* Common techniques of divination. *Teraphim* are household or clan★ gods (Gen 31.19; Judg 17.5; 18.17, 20). **24–27:** The *vile, wicked prince* is Zedekiah. **28–32:** The sword will be wielded against Ammon, but it will be destroyed in Babylon where it was created.

~~~~~~~~~~~~~~

22 The word of the LORD came to me: ²You, mortal, will you judge, will you judge the bloody city? Then declare to it all its abominable deeds. ³You shall say, Thus says the Lord GOD: A city! Shedding blood within itself; its time has come; making its idols, defiling itself. ⁴You have become guilty by the blood that you have shed, and defiled by the idols that you have made; you have brought your day near, the appointed time of your years has come. Therefore I have made you a disgrace before the nations, and a mockery to all the countries. ⁵Those who are near and those who are far from you will mock you, you infamous one, full of tumult.

---

a Gk Syr: Heb *Judah in*　　*b* Or *the household gods*
c Or *be taken captive*　　*d* Cn: Heb *to contain*

6 The princes of Israel in you, everyone according to his power, have been bent on shedding blood. 7Father and mother are treated with contempt in you; the alien residing within you suffers extortion; the orphan and the widow are wronged in you. 8You have despised my holy things, and profaned my sabbaths. 9In you are those who slander to shed blood, those in you who eat upon the mountains, who commit lewdness in your midst. 10In you they uncover their fathers' nakedness; in you they violate women in their menstrual periods. 11One commits abomination with his neighbor's wife; another lewdly defiles his daughter-in-law; another in you defiles his sister, his father's daughter. 12In you, they take bribes to shed blood; you take both advance interest and accrued interest, and make gain of your neighbors by extortion; and you have forgotten me, says the Lord GOD.

13 See, I strike my hands together at the dishonest gain you have made, and at the blood that has been shed within you. 14Can your courage endure, or can your hands remain strong in the days when I shall deal with you? I the LORD have spoken, and I will do it. 15I will scatter you among the nations and disperse you through the countries, and I will purge your filthiness out of you. 16And Ia shall be profaned through you in the sight of the nations; and you shall know that I am the LORD.

22.1–31: Oracles against Jerusalem. Compare Isa 1.2–31. 2–16: Ezekiel's preoccupation with blood derives from his role as a priest, which requires the proper treatment of blood since it is sacred (Lev 17). The crimes listed here derive especially from the Holiness Code in Lev 17–26: *shedding blood* (Lev 19.26; Gen 9.1–7); contempt against parents (Lev 20.9; Ex 21.17); extortion of the aliens, orphans, and widows (Lev 19.33–34; Ex 22.21–22; Deut 14.29); *holy things . . . sabbaths* (Lev 19.30); *slander* (Lev 19.16); *uncover father's nakedness* (Lev 18.8; 20.11); relations with menstruating women (Lev 18.19); incest (Lev 18; 20); bribery (Lev 19.15); interest on loans (Lev 25.36–37); extortion of a neighbor (Lev 19.15–18, 35–36).

17 The word of the LORD came to me: 18Mortal, the house of Israel has become dross to me; all of them, silver,b bronze, tin, iron, and lead. In the smelter they have become dross. 19Therefore thus says the Lord GOD: Because you have all become dross, I will gather you into the midst of Jerusalem. 20As one gathers silver, bronze, iron, lead, and tin into a smelter, to blow the fire upon them in order to melt them; so I will gather you in my anger and in my wrath, and I will put you in and melt you. 21I will gather you and blow upon you with the fire of my wrath, and you shall be melted within it. 22As silver is melted in a smelter, so you shall be melted in it; and you shall know that I the LORD have poured out my wrath upon you.

23 The word of the LORD came to me: 24Mortal, say to it: You are a land that is not cleansed, not rained upon in the day of indignation. 25Its princesc within it are like a roaring lion tearing the prey; they have devoured human lives; they have taken treasure and precious things; they have made many widows within it. 26Its priests have done violence to my teaching and have profaned my holy things; they have made no distinction between the holy and the common, neither have they taught the difference between the unclean and the clean, and they have disregarded my sabbaths, so that I am profaned among them. 27Its officials within it are like wolves tearing the prey, shedding blood, destroying lives to get dishonest gain. 28Its prophets have smeared whitewash on their behalf, seeing false visions and divining lies for them, saying, "Thus says the Lord GOD," when the LORD has not spoken. 29The people of the land have practiced extortion and committed robbery; they have oppressed the poor and needy, and have extorted from the alien without redress. 30And I sought for anyone among them who would repair the wall and stand in the breach before me on behalf of the land, so that I would not destroy it; but I found no one. 31Therefore I have poured out my indignation upon them; I have consumed them with the fire of my wrath; I have returned their conduct upon their heads, says the Lord GOD.

a Gk Syr Vg: Heb *you*   b Transposed from the end of the verse; compare verse 20   c Gk: Heb *indignation*.
25A conspiracy of its prophets

22.17–31. 17–22: Just as precious metals are smelted to remove dross, Israel will be purified in fire to remove its sins and impurities (Isa 1.21–26). **23–31:** The prophet* names all classes of people in Jerusalem, including *its princes, its priests, its officials, its prophets,* and *the people of the land.*

23 The word of the LORD came to me: ²Mortal, there were two women, the daughters of one mother; ³they played the whore in Egypt; they played the whore in their youth; their breasts were caressed there, and their virgin bosoms were fondled. ⁴Oholah was the name of the elder and Oholibah the name of her sister. They became mine, and they bore sons and daughters. As for their names, Oholah is Samaria, and Oholibah is Jerusalem.

5 Oholah played the whore while she was mine; she lusted after her lovers the Assyrians, warriors*ᵃ* ⁶clothed in blue, governors and commanders, all of them handsome young men, mounted horsemen. ⁷She bestowed her favors upon them, the choicest men of Assyria all of them; and she defiled herself with all the idols of everyone for whom she lusted. ⁸She did not give up her whorings that she had practiced since Egypt; for in her youth men had lain with her and fondled her virgin bosom and poured out their lust upon her. ⁹Therefore I delivered her into the hands of her lovers, into the hands of the Assyrians, for whom she lusted. ¹⁰These uncovered her nakedness; they seized her sons and her daughters; and they killed her with the sword. Judgment was executed upon her, and she became a byword among women.

under the Jehu dynasty,* specifically, Menahem (2 Kings 15.17–22), and Hoshea (2 Kings 17.1–6). Ezekiel portrays this alliance as harlotry and argues that it led to Israel's destruction.

11 Her sister Oholibah saw this, yet she was more corrupt than she in her lusting and in her whorings, which were worse than those of her sister. ¹²She lusted after the Assyrians, governors and commanders, warriors*ᵃ* clothed in full armor, mounted horsemen, all of them handsome young men. ¹³And I saw that she was defiled; they both took the same way. ¹⁴But she carried her whorings further; she saw male figures carved on the wall, images of the Chaldeans portrayed in vermilion, ¹⁵with belts around their waists, with flowing turbans on their heads, all of them looking like officers—a picture of Babylonians whose native land was Chaldea. ¹⁶When she saw them she lusted after them, and sent messengers to them in Chaldea. ¹⁷And the Babylonians came to her into the bed of love, and they defiled her with their lust; and after she defiled herself with them, she turned from them in disgust. ¹⁸When she carried on her whorings so openly and flaunted her nakedness, I turned in disgust from her, as I had turned from her sister. ¹⁹Yet she increased her whorings, remembering the days of her youth, when she played the whore in the land of Egypt ²⁰and lusted after her paramours there, whose members were like those of donkeys, and whose emission was like that of stallions. ²¹Thus you longed for the lewdness of your youth, when the Egyptians*ᵇ* fondled your bosom and caressed*ᶜ* your young breasts.

23.1–49: Oholah and Oholibah. Presupposing the portrayal of Israel as God's wife (compare Hos 1–3; Jer 2–3), Ezekiel employs the metaphor* of harlotry to describe Samaria and Jerusalem (see ch. 16). *Oholah,* "her tent," refers to Samaria. The name Oholah alludes to the presence of God who dwells in a tent (according to the Exodus and Wilderness traditions; compare 2 Sam 7.6). *Oholibah,* "my tent is in her," refers to Jerusalem and to the presence of the Temple.* **5–10:** Oholah's or Samaria's relations with the officers of Assyria presuppose its earlier alliance with Assyria

23.11–21: Ezekiel charges that Oholibah, Jerusalem, was even worse than her sister in pursuing both the Assyrians and the Chaldeans or Babylonians (see Jer 3.6–10, 11). King Ahaz of Judah requested Assyrian assistance against Israel in the Syro-Ephraimitic War (2 Kings 16), and Hezekiah later made an alliance with Babylon against Assyria (2 Kings 20.11–19; Isa 39). The reference to relations with Egypt may recall Solo-

a Meaning of Heb uncertain   *b* Two Mss: MT *from Egypt*   *c* Cn: Heb *for the sake of*

mon's early alliance with Egypt (1 Kings 3.1) and Jehoiakim's support from Pharaoh Neco prior to his turn
to Babylon (2 Kings 23.31–24.7).

22 Therefore, O Oholibah, thus says the
Lord GOD: I will rouse against you your lovers from whom you turned in disgust, and I
will bring them against you from every side:
²³the Babylonians and all the Chaldeans,
Pekod and Shoa and Koa, and all the Assyrians with them, handsome young men, governors and commanders all of them, officers
and warriors,ᵃ all of them riding on horses.
²⁴They shall come against you from the
northᵇ with chariots and wagons and a host
of peoples; they shall set themselves against
you on every side with buckler, shield, and
helmet, and I will commit the judgment to
them, and they shall judge you according to
their ordinances. ²⁵I will direct my indignation against you, in order that they may deal
with you in fury. They shall cut off your nose
and your ears, and your survivors shall fall
by the sword. They shall seize your sons and
your daughters, and your survivors shall be
devoured by fire. ²⁶They shall also strip you
of your clothes and take away your fine jewels. ²⁷So I will put an end to your lewdness
and your whoring brought from the land of
Egypt; you shall not long for them, or remember Egypt any more. ²⁸For thus says the
Lord GOD: I will deliver you into the hands
of those whom you hate, into the hands of
those from whom you turned in disgust;
²⁹and they shall deal with you in hatred, and
take away all the fruit of your labor, and
leave you naked and bare, and the nakedness
of your whorings shall be exposed. Your
lewdness and your whorings ³⁰have brought
this upon you, because you played the whore
with the nations, and polluted yourself with
their idols. ³¹You have gone the way of your
sister; therefore I will give her cup into your
hand. ³²Thus says the Lord GOD:

You shall drink your sister's cup,
    deep and wide;
you shall be scorned and derided,
    it holds so much.
³³ You shall be filled with drunkenness
        and sorrow.

A cup of horror and desolation

is the cup of your sister Samaria;
³⁴ you shall drink it and drain it out,
    and gnaw its sherds,
    and tear out your breasts;
for I have spoken, says the Lord GOD.
³⁵Therefore thus says the Lord GOD: Because you have forgotten me and cast me behind your back, therefore bear the consequences of your lewdness and whorings.

22.22–35: Ezekiel declares that Oholibah's *lovers,* the
Babylonians and their allies, will conquer Jerusalem.
Pekod (see Jer 50.21), *Shoa,* and *Koa* are Aramean
tribes allied with Babylon. Drinking from the sister's
cup is a common motif* in Judean prophecy (Isa
51.17, 22; Jer 25.15–29; 51.7; Hab 2.16).

36 The LORD said to me: Mortal, will you
judge Oholah and Oholibah? Then declare
to them their abominable deeds. ³⁷For they
have committed adultery, and blood is on
their hands; with their idols they have committed adultery; and they have even offered
up to them for food the children whom they
had borne to me. ³⁸Moreover this they have
done to me: they have defiled my sanctuary
on the same day and profaned my sabbaths.
³⁹For when they had slaughtered their children for their idols, on the same day they
came into my sanctuary to profane it. This is
what they did in my house.

40 They even sent for men to come from
far away, to whom a messenger was sent, and
they came. For them you bathed yourself,
painted your eyes, and decked yourself with
ornaments; ⁴¹you sat on a stately couch,
with a table spread before it on which you
had placed my incense and my oil. ⁴²The
sound of a raucous multitude was around
her, with many of the rabble brought in
drunken from the wilderness; and they put
bracelets on the armsᶜ of the women, and
beautiful crowns upon their heads.

43 Then I said, Ah, she is worn out with
adulteries, but they carry on their sexual acts
with her. ⁴⁴For they have gone in to her, as
one goes in to a whore. Thus they went in to
Oholah and to Oholibah, wanton women.

a Compare verses 6 and 12: Heb *officers and called ones*
b Gk: Meaning of Heb uncertain   c Heb *hands*

45 But righteous judges shall declare them guilty of adultery and of bloodshed; because they are adulteresses and blood is on their hands.

46 For thus says the Lord GOD: Bring up an assembly against them, and make them an object of terror and of plunder. 47 The assembly shall stone them and with their swords they shall cut them down; they shall kill their sons and their daughters, and burn up their houses. 48 Thus will I put an end to lewdness in the land, so that all women may take warning and not commit lewdness as you have done. 49 They shall repay you for your lewdness, and you shall bear the penalty for your sinful idolatry; and you shall know that I am the Lord GOD.

22.36–49: *They have defiled my sanctuary and profaned my sabbaths:* See ch. 8. *They even sent for men to come from far away* is a reference to Judean attempts to find allies (compare Jer 27.3). The sisters' punishment reflects that of an adulterous woman (Lev 20.10) or a person who profanes God (Lev 20.2–5). *So that all women may take warning and not commit lewdness:* Ezekiel is frequently accused of misogyny.

24 In the ninth year, in the tenth month, on the tenth day of the month, the word of the LORD came to me: 2 Mortal, write down the name of this day, this very day. The king of Babylon has laid siege to Jerusalem this very day. 3 And utter an allegory to the rebellious house and say to them, Thus says the Lord GOD:

Set on the pot, set it on,
    pour in water also;
4 put in it the pieces,
    all the good pieces, the thigh and the
       shoulder;
    fill it with choice bones.
5 Take the choicest one of the flock,
    pile the logs[a] under it;
boil its pieces,[b]
    seethe[c] also its bones in it.

6 Therefore thus says the Lord GOD:
Woe to the bloody city,
    the pot whose rust is in it,
    whose rust has not gone out of it!

Empty it piece by piece,
    making no choice at all.[d]
7 For the blood she shed is inside it;
    she placed it on a bare rock;
    she did not pour it out on the ground,
       to cover it with earth.
8 To rouse my wrath, to take vengeance,
    I have placed the blood she shed
       on a bare rock,
    so that it may not be covered.
9 Therefore thus says the Lord GOD:
    Woe to the bloody city!
    I will even make the pile great.
10 Heap up the logs, kindle the fire;
    boil the meat well, mix in the spices,
    let the bones be burned.
11 Stand it empty upon the coals,
    so that it may become hot, its copper
       glow,
    its filth melt in it, its rust
       be consumed.
12 In vain I have wearied myself;[e]
    its thick rust does not depart.
    To the fire with its rust![f]
13 Yet, when I cleansed you in your filthy
       lewdness,
    you did not become clean from your
       filth;
    you shall not again be cleansed
    until I have satisfied my fury upon
       you.
14 I the LORD have spoken; the time is coming, I will act. I will not refrain, I will not spare, I will not relent. According to your ways and your doings I will judge you, says the Lord GOD.

24.1–14: The allegory* of the pot. As a Temple priest, Ezekiel's duties include tending to pots used to cook sacrificial meat (1 Sam 2.12–17). Like Jeremiah (a priest descended from Eli), he employs activities from his own life as symbolic means to express God's word (see Jer 1.13). **1–2:** *The ninth year . . . the tenth month . . . the tenth day:* January 15, 588 BCE, apparently the day on which Nebuchadnezzar begins the siege of Jerusalem. **3–5:** *The thigh and the shoulder,*

---

a Compare verse 10: Heb *the bones*   b Two Mss: Heb *its boilings*   c Cn: Heb *its bones seethe*   d Heb *piece, no lot has fallen on it*   e Cn: Meaning of Heb uncertain   f Meaning of Heb uncertain

the choice offerings (Num 18.12), including the breast and thigh (Ex 29.26–28; Lev 7.28–36; 10.12–15; Num 18.18; Gen 32.32), are given to the priests. **6–8:** The imagery of the corroded bottom of the pot symbolizes the bloody crimes of Jerusalem. Blood is sacred and must be covered when shed (Lev 17.13–16; Gen 9.1–7). **9–14:** As a cauldron is cleansed by fire, Ezekiel calls for the "cleansing" of Jerusalem by fire.

15 The word of the LORD came to me: 16Mortal, with one blow I am about to take away from you the delight of your eyes; yet you shall not mourn or weep, nor shall your tears run down. 17Sigh, but not aloud; make no mourning for the dead. Bind on your turban, and put your sandals on your feet; do not cover your upper lip or eat the bread of mourners.*a* 18So I spoke to the people in the morning, and at evening my wife died. And on the next morning I did as I was commanded.

19 Then the people said to me, "Will you not tell us what these things mean for us, that you are acting this way?" 20Then I said to them: The word of the LORD came to me: 21Say to the house of Israel, Thus says the Lord GOD: I will profane my sanctuary, the pride of your power, the delight of your eyes, and your heart's desire; and your sons and your daughters whom you left behind shall fall by the sword. 22And you shall do as I have done; you shall not cover your upper lip or eat the bread of mourners.*a* 23Your turbans shall be on your heads and your sandals on your feet; you shall not mourn or weep, but you shall pine away in your iniquities and groan to one another. 24Thus Ezekiel shall be a sign to you; you shall do just as he has done. When this comes, then you shall know that I am the Lord GOD.

25 And you, mortal, on the day when I take from them their stronghold, their joy and glory, the delight of their eyes and their heart's affection, and also*b* their sons and their daughters, 26on that day, one who has escaped will come to you to report to you the news. 27On that day your mouth shall be opened to the one who has escaped, and you shall speak and no longer be silent. So you shall be a sign to them; and they shall know that I am the LORD.

24.15–27: The death of Ezekiel's wife. The death of Ezekiel's wife symbolizes the destruction of Jerusalem (see Isa 7; 8; Jer 16; Hos 1–3). **15–18:** Ezekiel's action draws upon priestly sanctity to symbolize the inability of God and the people of Judah to mourn the loss of Jerusalem when in exile. Priests may not come into contact with the dead (Lev 21.1–12), and the high priest may not mourn for the dead (Lev 21.10–12; compare 10.1–7). **19–24:** *I will profane my sanctuary:* Only the priests could enter the most holy place. The people are to be fully dressed, with turbans and sandals, as they go into exile. **25–27:** During the Temple service, the priests officiated in silence. When the Temple is destroyed, Ezekiel will be able to speak again.

EZEKIEL'S ORACLES CONCERNING THE NATIONS

Chs. 25–32: Like other prophetic books (Isa 13–23; Jer 46–51), Ezekiel contains a section of oracles concerning foreign nations, which are intended to demonstrate God's power throughout the world. The nations included here, Ammon, Moab, Edom, Philistia, Tyre, and Egypt, would all be considered as targets of the Babylonian empire, although Egypt was never taken. Ezekiel identifies the projected expansion of Babylonia as an act of God.

25 The word of the LORD came to me: 2Mortal, set your face toward the Ammonites and prophesy against them. 3Say to the Ammonites, Hear the word of the Lord GOD: Thus says the Lord GOD, Because you said, "Aha!" over my sanctuary when it was profaned, and over the land of Israel when it was made desolate, and over the house of Judah when it went into exile; 4therefore I am handing you over to the people of the east for a possession. They shall set their encampments among you and pitch their tents in your midst; they shall eat your fruit, and they shall drink your milk. 5I will make Rabbah a pasture for camels and Ammon a fold for flocks. Then you shall know that I am the LORD. 6For thus says the Lord GOD: Because you have clapped your hands and stamped your feet and rejoiced with all the malice within you against the land of Israel,

a Vg Tg: Heb *of men*   *b* Heb lacks *and also*

7therefore I have stretched out my hand against you, and will hand you over as plunder to the nations. I will cut you off from the peoples and will make you perish out of the countries; I will destroy you. Then you shall know that I am the LORD.

25.1–7: The oracle concerning Ammon. The Babylonians employed Ammonites against Judah (2 Kings 24.1–2). Later, the Ammonites joined Judah in an anti-Babylonian coalition (Jer 27.3). Ammon was located east of the Jordan River. *Rabbah,* the site of present-day Amman, Jordan, was the capital. The Ammonites are condemned in part for mocking the destruction of the Jerusalem Temple. *The people of the east* are nomadic Arab tribes from the northern Arabian desert who moved into Ammon and Moab following their destruction by Babylonia.

8 Thus says the Lord GOD: Because Moab*a* said, The house of Judah is like all the other nations, 9therefore I will lay open the flank of Moab from the towns*b* on its frontier, the glory of the country, Beth-jeshimoth, Baal-meon, and Kiriathaim. 10I will give it along with Ammon to the people of the east as a possession. Thus Ammon shall be remembered no more among the nations, 11and I will execute judgments upon Moab. Then they shall know that I am the LORD.

25.8–11: The oracle concerning Moab. Like Ammon, the Moabites assisted the Babylonians against Judah (2 Kings 24.1–2) and later joined the anti-Babylonian coalition (Jer 27.3). Moab was located east of the southern portion of the Dead Sea.

12 Thus says the Lord GOD: Because Edom acted revengefully against the house of Judah and has grievously offended in taking vengeance upon them, 13therefore thus says the Lord GOD, I will stretch out my hand against Edom, and cut off from it humans and animals, and I will make it desolate; from Teman even to Dedan they shall fall by the sword. 14I will lay my vengeance upon Edom by the hand of my people Israel; and they shall act in Edom according to my anger and according to my wrath; and they shall know my vengeance, says the Lord GOD.

25.12–14: The oracle concerning Edom. Edom symbolizes God's wrath, perhaps because of its role in the destruction of the Jerusalem Temple (Ps 137.7; Lam 4.21–22; Ob 1–14). It was located southeast of the Dead Sea and sometimes encroached upon southern Judean territories. Edom's ancestor, Esau, was Jacob's twin brother (Gen 25–35).

15 Thus says the Lord GOD: Because with unending hostilities the Philistines acted in vengeance, and with malice of heart took revenge in destruction; 16therefore thus says the Lord GOD, I will stretch out my hand against the Philistines, cut off the Cherethites, and destroy the rest of the seacoast. 17I will execute great vengeance on them with wrathful punishments. Then they shall know that I am the LORD, when I lay my vengeance on them.

25.15–17: The oracle concerning Philistia. Philistia was occupied by Assyria during the eighth and seventh centuries BCE and was turned into an industrial center for the production of olive oil. It is not clear what action they took against Judah in the sixth century. Philistia was located along the Mediterranean coast, west and south of the hill country of Judah. *Cherethites,* the Cretans, were ancestors of the Philistines.

Oracles concerning Tyre and its rulers
Chs. 26–28: Tyre, the preeminent maritime power of the ancient world, joined Judah in revolt against Babylon (Jer 27.3). The Phoenician city of Tyre was an island until its conquest in 332 BCE by Alexander the Great, who built an earthen corridor through the water to assault the city by land. Shortly after his conquest of Jerusalem, Nebuchadnezzar laid siege to Tyre for 13 years but was never able to conquer it.

26 In the eleventh year, on the first day of the month, the word of the LORD came to me: 2Mortal, because Tyre said concerning Jerusalem,

"Aha, broken is the gateway of
    the peoples;
  it has swung open to me;
I shall be replenished,
  now that it is wasted,"

a Gk Old Latin: Heb *Moab and Seir*   *b* Heb *towns from its towns*

³therefore, thus says the Lord GOD:

See, I am against you, O Tyre!
I will hurl many nations against you,
as the sea hurls its waves.
⁴ They shall destroy the walls of Tyre
and break down its towers.
I will scrape its soil from it
and make it a bare rock.
⁵ It shall become, in the midst of the sea,
a place for spreading nets.
I have spoken, says the Lord GOD.
It shall become plunder for the nations,
⁶ and its daughter-towns in the country
shall be killed by the sword.
Then they shall know that I am the LORD.

26.1–21: Four oracles concerning the destruction of Tyre. 1: *The eleventh year . . . the first day of the month:* 587 BCE, shortly after the fall of Jerusalem. **2–6:** Ezekiel's indictment and sentencing of Tyre presupposes that the city was a commercial rival to Judah. *Gateway of the peoples,* literally "gateways," indicates Judah's role in controlling inland trade routes. *Bare rock* ("sela'" or "rock" in Hebrew) plays upon the Hebrew name "Sor" (*Tyre*), which means "rock." *Daughter-towns* designates nearby towns that were subsidiary to Tyre.

7 For thus says the Lord GOD: I will bring against Tyre from the north King Nebuchadrezzar of Babylon, king of kings, together with horses, chariots, cavalry, and a great and powerful army.
⁸ Your daughter-towns in the country
he shall put to the sword.
He shall set up a siege wall against you,
cast up a ramp against you,
and raise a roof of shields
against you.
⁹ He shall direct the shock of his
battering rams against
your walls
and break down your towers with his
axes.
¹⁰ His horses shall be so many
that their dust shall cover you.
At the noise of cavalry, wheels,
and chariots
your very walls shall shake,
when he enters your gates
like those entering a breached city.

¹¹ With the hoofs of his horses
he shall trample all your streets.
He shall put your people to
the sword,
and your strong pillars shall fall to the
ground.
¹² They will plunder your riches
and loot your merchandise;
they shall break down your walls
and destroy your fine houses.
Your stones and timber and soil
they shall cast into the water.
¹³ I will silence the music of your songs;
the sound of your lyres shall be
heard no more.
¹⁴ I will make you a bare rock;
you shall be a place for
spreading nets.
You shall never again be rebuilt,
for I the LORD have spoken,
says the Lord GOD.

26.7–14: *Nebuchadrezzar:* The Akkadian (the semitic language of ancient Mesopotamia) name is frequently mispronounced in Hebrew as Nebuchadnezzar (Dan 1.1). Ezekiel's description presupposes the tactics and weapons of land warfare, which were useless against an island state.

15 Thus says the Lord GOD to Tyre: Shall not the coastlands shake at the sound of your fall, when the wounded groan, when slaughter goes on within you? ¹⁶Then all the princes of the sea shall step down from their thrones; they shall remove their robes and strip off their embroidered garments. They shall clothe themselves with trembling, and shall sit on the ground; they shall tremble every moment, and be appalled at you. ¹⁷And they shall raise a lamentation over you, and say to you:

How you have vanished*ᵃ* from the seas,
O city renowned,
once mighty on the sea,
you and your inhabitants,*ᵇ*
who imposed your*ᶜ* terror
on all the mainland!*ᵈ*

a Gk OL Aquila: Heb *have vanished, O inhabited one,*
b Heb *it and its inhabitants*   *c* Heb *their*
d Cn: Heb *its inhabitants*

18 Now the coastlands tremble
    on the day of your fall;
  the coastlands by the sea
    are dismayed at your passing.

19 For thus says the Lord GOD: When I make you a city laid waste, like cities that are not inhabited, when I bring up the deep over you, and the great waters cover you, 20then I will thrust you down with those who descend into the Pit, to the people of long ago, and I will make you live in the world below, among primeval ruins, with those who go down to the Pit, so that you will not be inhabited or have a place*a* in the land of the living. 21I will bring you to a dreadful end, and you shall be no more; though sought for, you will never be found again, says the Lord GOD.

26.15–21. 15–18: *Princes of the sea* is an allusion to Tyre's trading partners and allies. *They shall raise a lamentation:* The poem is composed in the "qinah" meter, characteristic of laments★ (see comment on 19.1). **19–21:** Ezekiel employs mythological language to portray Tyre's fall. *I bring up the deep over you* reverses the imagery of creation in which dry land emerges from the waters (Gen 1). *Descend into the Pit:* Descent into the underworld at death (see 32.17–22; Isa 24.22; Ps 63.9; 139.15) was a characteristic motif★ of Babylonian mythology in which the fertility god Tammuz had to be rescued from the underworld each year by the goddess Ishtar.

27 The word of the LORD came to me: 2Now you, mortal, raise a lamentation over Tyre, 3and say to Tyre, which sits at the entrance to the sea, merchant of the peoples on many coastlands, Thus says the Lord GOD:

  O Tyre, you have said,
    "I am perfect in beauty."
4 Your borders are in the heart of the
      seas;
  your builders made perfect
      your beauty.
5 They made all your planks
    of fir trees from Senir;
  they took a cedar from Lebanon
    to make a mast for you.
6 From oaks of Bashan
    they made your oars;

they made your deck of pines*b*
    from the coasts of Cyprus,
  inlaid with ivory.
7 Of fine embroidered linen from Egypt
    was your sail,
    serving as your ensign;
  blue and purple from the coasts
      of Elishah
    was your awning.
8 The inhabitants of Sidon and Arvad
    were your rowers;
  skilled men of Zemer*c* were within
      you,
    they were your pilots.
9 The elders of Gebal and its artisans
      were within you,
    caulking your seams;
  all the ships of the sea with their
        mariners were within you,
    to barter for your wares.
10 Paras*d* and Lud and Put
    were in your army,
    your mighty warriors;
  they hung shield and helmet in you;
    they gave you splendor.
11 Men of Arvad and Helech*e*
    were on your walls all around;
    men of Gamad were at your towers.
  They hung their quivers all around your
      walls;
    they made perfect your beauty.

27.1–36: Lamentation over Tyre. The "qinah" meter appears in vv. 3–9, 25–36 (see comment on 19.1). **3–9:** Ezekiel portrays Tyre as a well-built ship, which symbolizes the way in which Tyre achieved wealth through maritime trade. *Senir:* Mt. Hermon in northern Israel (Deut 3.9). *Bashan:* The region east of the Sea of Galilee. *Elishah:* Cyprus. *Arvad:* Phoenicia. *Zemer* means "Tyre" in Hebrew. *Gebal:* Byblos. **10–11:** Tyre's defenders include mercenary troops. *Paras:* Persia. *Lud:* Lydia. *Put:* Libya. *Helech* means "your army" in Hebrew. *Gamad* is uncertain.

---

12 Tarshish did business with you out of the abundance of your great wealth; silver, iron, tin, and lead they exchanged for your

---

a Gk: Heb *I will give beauty*   *b* Or *boxwood*
c Cn Compare Gen 10.18: Heb *your skilled men, O Tyre*
d Or *Persia*   *e* Or *and your army*

wares. ¹³Javan, Tubal, and Meshech traded with you; they exchanged human beings and vessels of bronze for your merchandise. ¹⁴Beth-togarmah exchanged for your wares horses, war horses, and mules. ¹⁵The Rhodians^a traded with you; many coastlands were your own special markets; they brought you in payment ivory tusks and ebony. ¹⁶Edom^b did business with you because of your abundant goods; they exchanged for your wares turquoise, purple, embroidered work, fine linen, coral, and rubies. ¹⁷Judah and the land of Israel traded with you; they exchanged for your merchandise wheat from Minnith, millet,^c honey, oil, and balm. ¹⁸Damascus traded with you for your abundant goods—because of your great wealth of every kind—wine of Helbon, and white wool. ¹⁹Vedan and Javan from Uzal^c entered into trade for your wares; wrought iron, cassia, and sweet cane were bartered for your merchandise. ²⁰Dedan traded with you in saddlecloths for riding. ²¹Arabia and all the princes of Kedar were your favored dealers in lambs, rams, and goats; in these they did business with you. ²²The merchants of Sheba and Raamah traded with you; they exchanged for your wares the best of all kinds of spices, and all precious stones, and gold. ²³Haran, Canneh, Eden, the merchants of Sheba, Asshur, and Chilmad traded with you. ²⁴These traded with you in choice garments, in clothes of blue and embroidered work, and in carpets of colored material, bound with cords and made secure; in these they traded with you.^d ²⁵The ships of Tarshish traveled for you in your trade.

27.12–25a: A prose section contains a catalogue of Tyre's extensive commercial relations. *Tarshish:* Tartessos in southern Spain. *Javan:* Ionians or Greeks. *Tubal and Meshech:* Asia Minor. *Beth-togarmah:* Armenia. *Rhodians* (Greek) means Dedanites in Hebrew. *Edom:* Some read "Aram," but v. 14 makes this unlikely. *Turquoise, purple:* Phoenicia was known for trade in purple dye derived from shellfish. Phoenicia (Gk., "Phoinikos") and Canaan mean "purple." *Minnith:* in Ammonite territory (Judg 11.33). *Helbon:* Thirteen miles north of Damascus. *Vedan and Javan from Uzal:* Uzal is Sana in Yemen. *Dedan:* In central Arabia. *Kedar:* In Arabia. *Sheba:* In Arabia or Ethiopia. *Haran,*

Canneh, Eden: Cities in Syria. *Asshur:* Assyria. *Chilmad:* Media.

So you were filled and heavily laden
    in the heart of the seas.
26 Your rowers have brought you
    into the high seas.
The east wind has wrecked you
    in the heart of the seas.
27 Your riches, your wares, your
    merchandise,
    your mariners and your pilots,
your caulkers, your dealers in
    merchandise,
    and all your warriors within you,
with all the company
    that is with you,
sink into the heart of the seas
    on the day of your ruin.
28 At the sound of the cry of your pilots
    the countryside shakes,
29 and down from their ships
    come all that handle the oar.
The mariners and all the pilots
    of the sea
    stand on the shore
30 and wail aloud over you,
    and cry bitterly.
They throw dust on their heads
    and wallow in ashes;
31 they make themselves bald for you,
    and put on sackcloth,
and they weep over you in bitterness of
    soul,
    with bitter mourning.
32 In their wailing they raise a lamentation
    for you,
    and lament over you:
"Who was ever destroyed^e like Tyre
    in the midst of the sea?
33 When your wares came from the seas,
    you satisfied many peoples;
with your abundant wealth and
    merchandise
    you enriched the kings of the earth.
34 Now you are wrecked by the seas,
    in the depths of the waters;

---

a Gk: Heb *The Dedanites*   *b* Another reading is *Aram*
c Meaning of Heb uncertain   *d* Cn: Heb *in your market*   *e* Tg Vg: Heb *like silence*

your merchandise and all your crew
    have sunk with you.
35 All the inhabitants of the coastlands
    are appalled at you;
  and their kings are horribly afraid,
    their faces are convulsed.
36 The merchants among the peoples hiss
        at you;
  you have come to a dreadful end
    and shall be no more forever."

27.25b–36: The lament resumes with a description of Tyre as a ship sinking by *the east wind,* a symbol of God's power (Ex 14.21).

28

The word of the LORD came to me: 2Mortal, say to the prince of Tyre, Thus says the Lord GOD:
  Because your heart is proud
    and you have said, "I am a god;
  I sit in the seat of the gods,
    in the heart of the seas,"
  yet you are but a mortal, and no god,
    though you compare your mind
    with the mind of a god.
3 You are indeed wiser than Daniel;[a]
    no secret is hidden from you;
4 by your wisdom and your
        understanding
    you have amassed wealth
        for yourself,
  and have gathered gold and silver
    into your treasuries.
5 By your great wisdom in trade
    you have increased your wealth,
  and your heart has become proud in
    your wealth.
6 Therefore thus says the Lord GOD:
  Because you compare your mind
    with the mind of a god,
7 therefore, I will bring strangers
        against you,
    the most terrible of the nations;
  they shall draw their swords against the
        beauty of your wisdom
    and defile your splendor.
8 They shall thrust you down to the Pit,
    and you shall die a violent death
    in the heart of the seas.
9 Will you still say, "I am a god,"
    in the presence of those who kill you,

though you are but a mortal, and no god,
    in the hands of those who wound you?
10 You shall die the death of the
        uncircumcised
    by the hand of foreigners;
  for I have spoken, says the Lord GOD.
11 Moreover the word of the LORD came
to me: 12Mortal, raise a lamentation over the
king of Tyre, and say to him, Thus says the
Lord GOD:
  You were the signet of perfection,[b]
    full of wisdom and perfect in beauty.
13 You were in Eden, the garden of God;
    every precious stone was your
        covering,
  carnelian, chrysolite, and moonstone,
    beryl, onyx, and jasper,
  sapphire,[c] turquoise, and emerald;
    and worked in gold were your settings
    and your engravings.[b]
  On the day that you were created
    they were prepared.
14 With an anointed cherub as guardian I
        placed you;[b]
    you were on the holy mountain
        of God;
    you walked among the stones of fire.
15 You were blameless in your ways
    from the day that you were created,
    until iniquity was found in you.
16 In the abundance of your trade
    you were filled with violence, and you
        sinned;
  so I cast you as a profane thing from
        the mountain of God,
  and the guardian cherub drove you
        out
    from among the stones of fire.
17 Your heart was proud because of your
        beauty;
    you corrupted your wisdom for the
        sake of your splendor.
  I cast you to the ground;
    I exposed you before kings,
    to feast their eyes on you.
18 By the multitude of your iniquities,
    in the unrighteousness of your trade,
    you profaned your sanctuaries.

---

a Or, as otherwise read, *Danel*   *b* Meaning of Heb uncertain   *c* Or *lapis lazuli*

So I brought out fire from within you;
it consumed you,
and I turned you to ashes on the earth
in the sight of all who saw you.
19 All who know you among the peoples
are appalled at you;
you have come to a dreadful end
and shall be no more forever.

**28.1–19: Oracles concerning the rulers of Tyre.
1–10:** Self-deification, a frequent claim of ancient
Near Eastern rulers. *You are indeed wiser than Daniel:*
Ezekiel apparently holds the Tyrian king in high regard
and compares him to Daniel (Heb., Dan El), the wise
ruler of Canaanite mythology who stands behind the
figure of Daniel in biblical tradition (14.12–20). Ezekiel
charges that the king has overstepped his bounds. The
mythological language of descent into the sea and the
Pit reappears. *The uncircumcised** are non-Israelites
(see Gen 17). **11–19:** *Signet:* A sign of royal authority.
Ezekiel employs the imagery of the Garden of Eden
story to describe the Tyrian king's downfall. The
prophet* charges the king with corrupt trade practices.

20 The word of the LORD came to me:
21 Mortal, set your face toward Sidon, and
prophesy against it, 22 and say, Thus says the
Lord GOD:

I am against you, O Sidon,
and I will gain glory in your midst.
They shall know that I am the LORD
when I execute judgments in it,
and manifest my holiness in it;
23 for I will send pestilence into it,
and bloodshed into its streets;
and the dead shall fall in its midst,
by the sword that is against it on
every side.
And they shall know that I am the LORD.
24 The house of Israel shall no longer
find a pricking brier or a piercing thorn
among all their neighbors who have treated
them with contempt. And they shall know
that I am the Lord GOD.

28.20–24: Oracle* concerning Sidon. Another Phoenician port city, 25 miles north of Tyre. Sidon joined
the revolt (Jer 27.3) and probably fell to Nebuchadnezzar.

25 Thus says the Lord GOD: When I
gather the house of Israel from the peoples
among whom they are scattered, and manifest my holiness in them in the sight of the
nations, then they shall settle on their own
soil that I gave to my servant Jacob. 26 They
shall live in safety in it, and shall build
houses and plant vineyards. They shall live
in safety, when I execute judgments upon all
their neighbors who have treated them with
contempt. And they shall know that I am the
LORD their God.

28.25–26: Oracle of blessing for Israel. Once the
nations that treated Israel with contempt are destroyed, the exiles will return to the land of Israel sworn
to Jacob (Gen 28; 35) to manifest God's holiness in the
world. *And they shall know that I am the LORD their
God:* The self-identification formula.

**Seven oracles concerning Egypt and its rulers
Chs. 29–32:** Egypt played a major role in instigating
the revolt against its enemy Babylon. When Pharaoh
Hophra attempted to relieve Jerusalem from the Babylonian siege in 588 BCE, he was repulsed (Jer 37;
44.30; see also Jer 32).

29 In the tenth year, in the tenth
month, on the twelfth day of the
month, the word of the LORD came to me:
2 Mortal, set your face against Pharaoh king
of Egypt, and prophesy against him and
against all Egypt; 3 speak, and say, Thus says
the Lord GOD:

I am against you,
Pharaoh king of Egypt,
the great dragon sprawling
in the midst of its channels,
saying, "My Nile is my own;
I made it for myself."
4 I will put hooks in your jaws,
and make the fish of your channels
stick to your scales.
I will draw you up from your channels,
with all the fish of your channels
sticking to your scales.
5 I will fling you into the wilderness,
you and all the fish of your
channels;
you shall fall in the open field,
and not be gathered and buried.

To the animals of the earth and to the
birds of the air
I have given you as food.
6 Then all the inhabitants of Egypt shall
know
that I am the LORD
because you*a* were a staff of reed
to the house of Israel;
7 when they grasped you with the hand,
you broke,
and tore all their shoulders;
and when they leaned on you,
you broke,
and made all their legs unsteady.*b*

8 Therefore, thus says the Lord GOD: I
will bring a sword upon you, and will cut off
from you human being and animal; 9and the
land of Egypt shall be a desolation and a
waste. Then they shall know that I am the
LORD.

Because you*c* said, "The Nile is mine, and
I made it," 10therefore, I am against you, and
against your channels, and I will make the
land of Egypt an utter waste and desolation,
from Migdol to Syene, as far as the border
of Ethiopia.*d* 11No human foot shall pass
through it, and no animal foot shall pass
through it; it shall be uninhabited forty
years. 12I will make the land of Egypt a desolation among desolated countries; and her
cities shall be a desolation forty years among
cities that are laid waste. I will scatter the
Egyptians among the nations, and disperse
them among the countries.

13 Further, thus says the Lord GOD: At
the end of forty years I will gather the Egyptians from the peoples among whom they
were scattered; 14and I will restore the fortunes of Egypt, and bring them back to the
land of Pathros, the land of their origin; and
there they shall be a lowly kingdom. 15It
shall be the most lowly of the kingdoms, and
never again exalt itself above the nations;
and I will make them so small that they will
never again rule over the nations. 16The
Egyptians*e* shall never again be the reliance
of the house of Israel; they will recall their
iniquity, when they turned to them for aid.
Then they shall know that I am the Lord
GOD.

29.1–16: The first oracle concerning Egypt. 1–3a: *In the tenth year . . . tenth month . . . the twelfth day:* January 7, 587 BCE. **3b–7:** Ezekiel addresses Pharaoh, probably Hophra, after his failed attempt to rescue Je-rusalem. *The great dragon:* Egypt is compared to a dragon in Isa 11.15, which employs the imagery of the seven-headed Leviathan* (Lothan) of Canaanite my-thology, and in Isa 30.7 to the sea dragon Rahab (see also Isa 51.9–10; Job 9.13; 26.12–13; Ps 89.9–10). The *Nile* River is the source of Egypt's life. *A staff of reed to the house of Israel* symbolizes an unreliable support (compare Isa 36.6; 2 Kings 18.21). **8–12:** Egypt's judg-ment results from Pharaoh's claim that the Nile is his and not God's (28.2). *From Migdol to Syene:* Cities that define the northern and southern borders of Egypt. *Forty years:* Forty is a common number for a complete and lengthy period of time (Num 14.33; Judg 3.31; 1 Kings 2.11). **13–16:** Like Israel after it had been punished (28.25–26), Egypt will be restored to its land as a minor kingdom. The prophet clearly has in mind Egypt's failure to aid Israel in its time of need. *Pathros:* Upper Egypt, the southern portion of the kingdom. In Egypt, "up" is south (upstream on the Nile) and "down" is north (downstream on the Nile).

17 In the twenty-seventh year, in the first
month, on the first day of the month, the
word of the LORD came to me: 18Mortal,
King Nebuchadrezzar of Babylon made his
army labor hard against Tyre; every head was
made bald and every shoulder was rubbed
bare; yet neither he nor his army got anything from Tyre to pay for the labor that he
had expended against it. 19Therefore thus
says the Lord GOD: I will give the land of
Egypt to King Nebuchadrezzar of Babylon;
and he shall carry off its wealth and despoil
it and plunder it; and it shall be the wages
for his army. 20I have given him the land of
Egypt as his payment for which he labored,
because they worked for me, says the Lord
GOD.

21 On that day I will cause a horn to
sprout up for the house of Israel, and I will
open your lips among them. Then they shall
know that I am the LORD.

a Gk Syr Vg: Heb *they*   *b* Syr: Heb *stand*   *c* Gk Syr
Vg: Heb *he*   *d* Or *Nubia;* Heb *Cush*   *e* Heb *It*

29.17–21: The second oracle concerning Egypt. *The twenty-seventh year . . . the first month . . . the first day:* April 26, 571 BCE. Ezekiel refers to Nebuchadnezzar's failure to conquer Tyre as a basis for his campaign against Egypt. Following the conclusion of his siege against Tyre in 573 BCE, Nebuchadnezzar attacked Egypt in 668 BCE but failed to conquer the land. *A horn . . . for the house of Israel* refers to the restoration of the Davidic monarchy in the aftermath of Egypt's collapse (see Isa 11.1–16; Ps 132.17).

kiel to lament for Egypt and Ethiopia. Egypt was ruled by an Ethiopian dynasty★ during the late seventh and early sixth centuries BCE (see Isa 20). The prophet employs the "Day of the LORD" motif★ (Am 5.18–20; Isa 2.6–21; 13; 34; Zeph 1.2–18; 2.1–3). *Put and Lud:* See comments on 27.10–11. **6–9:** This oracle★ draws on the "Day of the LORD" materials in Isaiah. *Proud might shall come down:* Isa 2.6–21. *Messengers shall go out:* Isa 18.1–2.

30

The word of the LORD came to me: ²Mortal, prophesy, and say, Thus says the Lord GOD:
    Wail, "Alas for the day!"
³   For a day is near,
        the day of the LORD is near;
    it will be a day of clouds,
        a time of doom*a* for the nations.
⁴ A sword shall come upon Egypt,
        and anguish shall be in Ethiopia,*b*
    when the slain fall in Egypt,
        and its wealth is carried away,
        and its foundations are torn down.
⁵Ethiopia,*b* and Put, and Lud, and all Arabia, and Libya,*c* and the people of the allied land*d* shall fall with them by the sword.

⁶ Thus says the LORD:
    Those who support Egypt shall fall,
        and its proud might shall come down;
    from Migdol to Syene
        they shall fall within it by the sword,
    says the Lord GOD.
⁷ They shall be desolated among other
        desolated countries,
    and their cities shall lie among cities
        laid waste.
⁸ Then they shall know that I am
        the LORD,
    when I have set fire to Egypt,
        and all who help it are broken.
 ⁹ On that day, messengers shall go out from me in ships to terrify the unsuspecting Ethiopians;*e* and anguish shall come upon them on the day of Egypt's doom;*f* for it is coming!

10 Thus says the Lord GOD:
    I will put an end to the hordes of Egypt,
        by the hand of King Nebuchadrezzar
            of Babylon.
¹¹ He and his people with him, the most
        terrible of the nations,
    shall be brought in to destroy the land;
    and they shall draw their swords against
            Egypt,
        and fill the land with the slain.
¹² I will dry up the channels,
        and will sell the land into the hand of
            evildoers;
    I will bring desolation upon the land
        and everything in it
        by the hand of foreigners;
    I the LORD have spoken.

13 Thus says the Lord GOD:
    I will destroy the idols
        and put an end to the images
            in Memphis;
    there shall no longer be a prince in the
            land of Egypt;
        so I will put fear in the land of Egypt.
¹⁴ I will make Pathros a desolation,
        and will set fire to Zoan,
        and will execute acts of judgment on
            Thebes.
¹⁵ I will pour my wrath upon Pelusium,
        the stronghold of Egypt,
        and cut off the hordes of Thebes.
¹⁶ I will set fire to Egypt;
    Pelusium shall be in great agony;
    Thebes shall be breached,
        and Memphis face adversaries by day.

30.1–19: The third oracle concerning Egypt. 1: This section contains four oracles. **2–5:** God instructs Eze-

a Heb lacks *of doom*   *b* Or *Nubia*; Heb *Cush*
c Compare Gk Syr Vg: Heb *Cub*   *d* Meaning of Heb
uncertain   *e* Or *Nubians*; Heb *Cush*   *f* Heb *the day of Egypt*

17 The young men of On and of Pi-beseth
shall fall by the sword;
and the cities themselves[a] shall go
into captivity.
18 At Tehaphnehes the day shall be dark,
when I break there the dominion of
Egypt,
and its proud might shall come to an end;
the city[b] shall be covered by a cloud,
and its daughter-towns shall go into
captivity.
19 Thus I will execute acts of judgment on
Egypt.
Then they shall know that I am the
LORD.

30.10–19. 10–12: *Dry up the channels:* Isa 19.1–15.
13–19: Ezekiel cites Egyptian place names to demonstrate that destruction will encompass the entire land. *Memphis:* The early capital south of Cairo. *Zoan:* Also called Rameses, Tanis, and Avaris, the site where the Hebrew slaves worked in the Nile Delta (Ps 78.12, 43; Ex 1.11). *Thebes:* Egypt's capital throughout much of Israel's history. *Pelusium:* Near Zoan in the northeastern Delta. *On:* Heliopolis, six miles northeast of Cairo. *Pi-beseth:* Bubastis in the eastern Delta. *Tehaphnehes:* By the north shore of the Gulf of Suez.

20 In the eleventh year, in the first month, on the seventh day of the month, the word of the LORD came to me: 21Mortal, I have broken the arm of Pharaoh king of Egypt; it has not been bound up for healing or wrapped with a bandage, so that it may become strong to wield the sword. 22Therefore thus says the Lord GOD: I am against Pharaoh king of Egypt, and will break his arms, both the strong arm and the one that was broken; and I will make the sword fall from his hand. 23I will scatter the Egyptians among the nations, and disperse them throughout the lands. 24I will strengthen the arms of the king of Babylon, and put my sword in his hand; but I will break the arms of Pharaoh, and he will groan before him with the groans of one mortally wounded. 25I will strengthen the arms of the king of Babylon, but the arms of Pharaoh shall fall. And they shall know that I am the LORD, when I put my sword into the hand of the king of Babylon. He shall stretch it out against the land of Egypt, 26and I will scatter the Egyptians among the nations and disperse them throughout the countries. Then they shall know that I am the LORD.

30.20–26: The fourth oracle concerning Pharaoh. *In the eleventh year . . . the first month . . . the seventh day:* April 29, 587 BCE. The *broken arm* of Pharaoh refers to Nebuchadnezzar's defeat of Hophra, who attempted to relieve Jerusalem in 588 BCE (Jer 37.5). The prophet anticipates an even more devastating defeat of Egypt.

---

31 In the eleventh year, in the third month, on the first day of the month, the word of the LORD came to me: 2Mortal, say to Pharaoh king of Egypt and to his hordes:

Whom are you like in your greatness?
3   Consider Assyria, a cedar of Lebanon,
with fair branches and forest shade,
and of great height,
its top among the clouds.[c]
4 The waters nourished it,
the deep made it grow tall,
making its rivers flow[d]
around the place it was planted,
sending forth its streams
to all the trees of the field.
5 So it towered high
above all the trees of the field;
its boughs grew large
and its branches long,
from abundant water in its shoots.
6 All the birds of the air
made their nests in its boughs;
under its branches all the animals of the
field
gave birth to their young;
and in its shade
all great nations lived.
7 It was beautiful in its greatness,
in the length of its branches;
for its roots went down
to abundant water.
8 The cedars in the garden of God could
not rival it,
nor the fir trees equal its boughs;

---

a Heb *and they*   *b* Heb *she*   *c* Gk: Heb *thick boughs*
d Gk: Heb *rivers going*

the plane trees were as nothing
  compared with its branches;
no tree in the garden of God
  was like it in beauty.
9 I made it beautiful
  with its mass of branches,
the envy of all the trees of Eden
  that were in the garden of God.

10 Therefore thus says the Lord GOD:
Because it[a] towered high and set its top
among the clouds,[b] and its heart was proud
of its height, 11 I gave it into the hand of the
prince of the nations; he has dealt with it as
its wickedness deserves. I have cast it out.
12 Foreigners from the most terrible of the
nations have cut it down and left it. On the
mountains and in all the valleys its branches
have fallen, and its boughs lie broken in all
the watercourses of the land; and all the peoples of the earth went away from its shade
and left it.
13 On its fallen trunk settle
  all the birds of the air,
and among its boughs lodge
  all the wild animals.
14 All this is in order that no trees by the
waters may grow to lofty height or set their
tops among the clouds,[b] and that no trees
that drink water may reach up to them in
height.
  For all of them are handed over to death,
    to the world below;
  along with all mortals,
    with those who go down to the Pit.
15 Thus says the Lord GOD: On the day
it went down to Sheol I closed the deep over
it and covered it; I restrained its rivers, and
its mighty waters were checked. I clothed
Lebanon in gloom for it, and all the trees of
the field fainted because of it. 16 I made the
nations quake at the sound of its fall, when
I cast it down to Sheol with those who go
down to the Pit; and all the trees of Eden,
the choice and best of Lebanon, all that were
well watered, were consoled in the world below. 17 They also went down to Sheol with it,
to those killed by the sword, along with its
allies,[c] those who lived in its shade among
the nations.
18 Which among the trees of Eden was
like you in glory and in greatness? Now you

shall be brought down with the trees of Eden
to the world below; you shall lie among the
uncircumcised, with those who are killed by
the sword. This is Pharaoh and all his horde,
says the Lord GOD.

31.1–18: The fifth oracle concerning Pharaoh. The
imagery of a fallen cedar of Lebanon portrays Pharaoh's downfall. **1:** *In the eleventh year . . . the third
month . . . the first day:* June 21, 587 BCE. **2–9:** See
Isaiah's portrayal of the Assyrian monarch as a tall tree
that is to be felled (Isa 10.5–34) and the tradition of
the well-watered tree in the Garden of Eden that plays
a role in the downfall of Adam and Eve (Gen 2–3). **10–
14:** Because of its height and arrogance, the tree is cut
down (Isa 2.6–21; 10.5–34). *The prince of the nations:*
Literally, "the ram of the nations," Nebuchadnezzar.
The Babylonians boasted of the trees they took from
Lebanon. *Pit:* The underworld (Isa 14.3–23). **15–18:**
Sheol: The Hebrew name for the underworld.

32 In the twelfth year, in the twelfth
  month, on the first day of the month,
the word of the LORD came to me: 2 Mortal,
raise a lamentation over Pharaoh king of
Egypt, and say to him:
  You consider yourself a lion among the
    nations,
    but you are like a dragon in the seas;
  you thrash about in your streams,
    trouble the water with your feet,
    and foul your[d] streams.
3 Thus says the Lord GOD:
  In an assembly of many peoples
  I will throw my net over you;
  and I[e] will haul you up in
    my dragnet.
4 I will throw you on the ground,
    on the open field I will fling you,
  and will cause all the birds of the air to
    settle on you,
    and I will let the wild animals of the
      whole earth gorge themselves
      with you.
5 I will strew your flesh on the
    mountains;
    and fill the valleys with your carcass.[f]

a Syr Vg: Heb *you*   b Gk: Heb *thick boughs*
c Heb *its arms*   d Heb *their*   e Gk Vg: Heb *they*
f Symmachus Syr Vg: Heb *your height*

6 I will drench the land with your flowing
    blood
      up to the mountains,
    and the watercourses will be filled
      with you.
7 When I blot you out, I will cover the
    heavens,
      and make their stars dark;
    I will cover the sun with a cloud,
      and the moon shall not give its light.
8 All the shining lights of the heavens
      I will darken above you,
    and put darkness on your land,
        says the Lord GOD.
9 I will trouble the hearts of many peoples,
      as I carry you captive*a* among the
      nations,
    into countries you have not known.
10 I will make many peoples appalled at
    you;
      their kings shall shudder because of
      you.
    When I brandish my sword before them,
      they shall tremble every moment
    for their lives, each one of them,
      on the day of your downfall.
11 For thus says the Lord GOD:
    The sword of the king of Babylon shall
      come against you.
12 I will cause your hordes to fall
      by the swords of mighty ones,
    all of them most terrible among the
      nations.
    They shall bring to ruin the pride of
      Egypt,
      and all its hordes shall perish.
13 I will destroy all its livestock
      from beside abundant waters;
    and no human foot shall trouble them
      any more,
      nor shall the hoofs of cattle trouble
      them.
14 Then I will make their waters clear,
      and cause their streams to run like
      oil, says the Lord GOD.
15 When I make the land of Egypt desolate
    and when the land is stripped of all
      that fills it,
    when I strike down all who live in it,
      then they shall know that I am the
    LORD.

16 This is a lamentation; it shall
      be chanted.
    The women of the nations shall chant
      it.
    Over Egypt and all its hordes they shall
      chant it,
      says the Lord GOD.

32.1–16: Ezekiel's sixth oracle concerning Pharaoh and Egypt. 1: *In the twelfth year . . . the twelfth month . . . the first day:* March 3, 586 BCE. **2–15:** The portrayal of Pharaoh's defeat by God draws upon the mythological traditions of God's defeat of the sea dragon Leviathan* at creation (Isa 11.15; 27.1; Ps 74.12–17; 104.7–9; Job 38.8–11; Ex 15). The motif of darkness recalls the plague of darkness against Egypt (Ex 10.21–29) and the "Day of the LORD" traditions (Joel 2.1–2; 3.15; Zeph 1.15). *The sword of the King of Babylon:* Nebuchadnezzar. The nations will witness God's victory (Ex 15.13–18). **16:** Women served as mourners in the ancient Near East (Jer 9.17–18).

17 In the twelfth year, in the first month,*b* on the fifteenth day of the month, the word of the LORD came to me:
18 Mortal, wail over the hordes of Egypt,
    and send them down,
    with Egypt*c* and the daughters of
      majestic nations,
    to the world below,
      with those who go down to the Pit.
19 "Whom do you surpass in beauty?
    Go down! Be laid to rest with the
      uncircumcised!"
20 They shall fall among those who are killed by the sword. Egypt*d* has been handed over to the sword; carry away both it and its hordes. 21 The mighty chiefs shall speak of them, with their helpers, out of the midst of Sheol: "They have come down, they lie still, the uncircumcised, killed by the sword."

22 Assyria is there, and all its company, their graves all around it, all of them killed, fallen by the sword. 23 Their graves are set in the uttermost parts of the Pit. Its company is all around its grave, all of them killed, fallen by the sword, who spread terror in the land of the living.

a Gk: Heb *bring your destruction*   *b* Gk: Heb lacks *in the first month*   *c* Heb *it*   *d* Heb *It*

24 Elam is there, and all its hordes around its grave; all of them killed, fallen by the sword, who went down uncircumcised into the world below, who spread terror in the land of the living. They bear their shame with those who go down to the Pit. 25They have made Elam[a] a bed among the slain with all its hordes, their graves all around it, all of them uncircumcised, killed by the sword; for terror of them was spread in the land of the living, and they bear their shame with those who go down to the Pit; they are placed among the slain.

26 Meshech and Tubal are there, and all their multitude, their graves all around them, all of them uncircumcised, killed by the sword; for they spread terror in the land of the living. 27And they do not lie with the fallen warriors of long ago[b] who went down to Sheol with their weapons of war, whose swords were laid under their heads, and whose shields[c] are upon their bones; for the terror of the warriors was in the land of the living. 28So you shall be broken and lie among the uncircumcised, with those who are killed by the sword.

29 Edom is there, its kings and all its princes, who for all their might are laid with those who are killed by the sword; they lie with the uncircumcised, with those who go down to the Pit.

30 The princes of the north are there, all of them, and all the Sidonians, who have gone down in shame with the slain, for all the terror that they caused by their might; they lie uncircumcised with those who are killed by the sword, and bear their shame with those who go down to the Pit.

31 When Pharaoh sees them, he will be consoled for all his hordes—Pharaoh and all his army, killed by the sword, says the Lord GOD. 32For he[d] spread terror in the land of the living; therefore he shall be laid to rest among the uncircumcised, with those who are slain by the sword—Pharaoh and all his multitude, says the Lord GOD.

32.17–32: Ezekiel's seventh oracle concerning Egypt. 17: In the twelfth year . . . the first month . . . the fifteenth day: April 27, 586 BCE. 18: God instructs Ezekiel to wail for Egypt as its people descend into the

underworld. 19–32: Egypt will join the nations that have been destroyed. *Assyria* was conquered by Babylon and Media during the period 627–609 BCE. *Elam* was destroyed by the Assyrians in the mid seventh century BCE. *Meshech and Tubal:* Two unidentified kingdoms in Asia Minor that perhaps were taken by Assyria. *Edom* was conquered by Babylon. *The princes of the north:* probably the Phoenicians.

ORACLES AND VISIONS OF RESTORATION

Chs. 33–48: After the fall of Jerusalem (33.21–22), the book emphasizes restoration for Israel (chs. 33–39) and the Temple* (chs. 40–48). **Chs. 33–39: Oracles of restoration for Israel.** News of Jerusalem's fall enables Ezekiel to speak (3.22–27). Many attribute Ezekiel's earlier silence to prophetic practice, but his priestly identity calls for him to serve at the altar in silence. After the fall of the Temple, he can speak.

---

33 The word of the LORD came to me: 2O Mortal, speak to your people and say to them, If I bring the sword upon a land, and the people of the land take one of their number as their sentinel; 3and if the sentinel sees the sword coming upon the land and blows the trumpet and warns the people; 4then if any who hear the sound of the trumpet do not take warning, and the sword comes and takes them away, their blood shall be upon their own heads. 5They heard the sound of the trumpet and did not take warning; their blood shall be upon themselves. But if they had taken warning, they would have saved their lives. 6But if the sentinel sees the sword coming and does not blow the trumpet, so that the people are not warned, and the sword comes and takes any of them, they are taken away in their iniquity, but their blood I will require at the sentinel's hand.

7 So you, mortal, I have made a sentinel for the house of Israel; whenever you hear a word from my mouth, you shall give them warning from me. 8If I say to the wicked, "O wicked ones, you shall surely die," and you do not speak to warn the wicked to turn from their ways, the wicked shall die in their

---

a Heb *it* b Gk Old Latin: Heb *of the uncircumcised* c Cn: Heb *iniquities* d Cn: Heb I

iniquity, but their blood I will require at your hand. ⁹But if you warn the wicked to turn from their ways, and they do not turn from their ways, the wicked shall die in their iniquity, but you will have saved your life.

10 Now you, mortal, say to the house of Israel, Thus you have said: "Our transgressions and our sins weigh upon us, and we waste away because of them; how then can we live?" ¹¹Say to them, As I live, says the Lord GOD, I have no pleasure in the death of the wicked, but that the wicked turn from their ways and live; turn back, turn back from your evil ways; for why will you die, O house of Israel? ¹²And you, mortal, say to your people, The righteousness of the righteous shall not save them when they transgress; and as for the wickedness of the wicked, it shall not make them stumble when they turn from their wickedness; and the righteous shall not be able to live by their righteousness*a* when they sin. ¹³Though I say to the righteous that they shall surely live, yet if they trust in their righteousness and commit iniquity, none of their righteous deeds shall be remembered; but in the iniquity that they have committed they shall die. ¹⁴Again, though I say to the wicked, "You shall surely die," yet if they turn from their sin and do what is lawful and right— ¹⁵if the wicked restore the pledge, give back what they have taken by robbery, and walk in the statutes of life, committing no iniquity— they shall surely live, they shall not die. ¹⁶None of the sins that they have committed shall be remembered against them; they have done what is lawful and right, they shall surely live.

17 Yet your people say, "The way of the Lord is not just," when it is their own way that is not just. ¹⁸When the righteous turn from their righteousness, and commit iniquity, they shall die for it.*b* ¹⁹And when the wicked turn from their wickedness, and do what is lawful and right, they shall live by it.*b* ²⁰Yet you say, "The way of the Lord is not just." O house of Israel, I will judge all of you according to your ways!

21 In the twelfth year of our exile, in the tenth month, on the fifth day of the month, someone who had escaped from Jerusalem came to me and said, "The city has fallen." ²²Now the hand of the LORD had been upon me the evening before the fugitive came; but he had opened my mouth by the time the fugitive came to me in the morning; so my mouth was opened, and I was no longer unable to speak.

23 The word of the LORD came to me: ²⁴Mortal, the inhabitants of these waste places in the land of Israel keep saying, "Abraham was only one man, yet he got possession of the land; but we are many; the land is surely given us to possess." ²⁵Therefore say to them, Thus says the Lord GOD: You eat flesh with the blood, and lift up your eyes to your idols, and shed blood; shall you then possess the land? ²⁶You depend on your swords, you commit abominations, and each of you defiles his neighbor's wife; shall you then possess the land? ²⁷Say this to them, Thus says the Lord GOD: As I live, surely those who are in the waste places shall fall by the sword; and those who are in the open field I will give to the wild animals to be devoured; and those who are in strongholds and in caves shall die by pestilence. ²⁸I will make the land a desolation and a waste, and its proud might shall come to an end; and the mountains of Israel shall be so desolate that no one will pass through. ²⁹Then they shall know that I am the LORD, when I have made the land a desolation and a waste because of all their abominations that they have committed.

30 As for you, mortal, your people who talk together about you by the walls, and at the doors of the houses, say to one another, each to a neighbor, "Come and hear what the word is that comes from the LORD." ³¹They come to you as people come, and they sit before you as my people, and they hear your words, but they will not obey them. For flattery is on their lips, but their heart is set on their gain. ³²To them you are like a singer of love songs,*c* one who has a beautiful voice and plays well on an instrument; they hear what you say, but they will not do it. ³³When this comes—and come it will!—

a Heb *by it*   *b* Heb *them*   *c* Cn: Heb *like a love song*

then they shall know that a prophet has been among them.

33.1–33: Ezekiel's responsibilities as Israel's sentinel. In keeping with the role of the priest to observe God's requirements for Temple service, the prophet* now stands as *sentinel* or "watchman" on behalf of the people so that they will observe God's requirements. **1–9:** God establishes the analogy between the role of the prophet and that of a sentinel who stands watch over a city. The sentinel is not responsible for the fate of the people if he warns them, but he is fully responsible if he does not. The passage presupposes that the threat of death for the wicked can be reversed if they change their ways. **10–20:** See 18.21–32 on individual moral responsibility. Ezekiel debates with those who believe that past righteousness can deliver someone who commits sin later in life and vice versa. **21–22:** *In the twelfth year . . . in the tenth month . . . the fifth day:* January 19, 585 BCE. The prophet first receives word of the Temple's fall, and now speaks freely. **23–29:** Ezekiel counters the claim that *the inhabitants of these waste places*, desert nomads, will take control of the land. Ezekiel argues that they will be destroyed because they do not observe God's requirements for holy life in the land (Lev 17–18). **30–33:** God charges that people come to hear Ezekiel but will not do as he says.

34 The word of the LORD came to me: ²Mortal, prophesy against the shepherds of Israel: prophesy, and say to them—to the shepherds: Thus says the Lord GOD: Ah, you shepherds of Israel who have been feeding yourselves! Should not shepherds feed the sheep? ³You eat the fat, you clothe yourselves with the wool, you slaughter the fatlings; but you do not feed the sheep. ⁴You have not strengthened the weak, you have not healed the sick, you have not bound up the injured, you have not brought back the strayed, you have not sought the lost, but with force and harshness you have ruled them. ⁵So they were scattered, because there was no shepherd; and scattered, they became food for all the wild animals. ⁶My sheep were scattered, they wandered over all the mountains and on every high hill; my sheep were scattered over all the face of the earth, with no one to search or seek for them.

7 Therefore, you shepherds, hear the word of the LORD: ⁸As I live, says the Lord GOD, because my sheep have become a prey, and my sheep have become food for all the wild animals, since there was no shepherd; and because my shepherds have not searched for my sheep, but the shepherds have fed themselves, and have not fed my sheep; ⁹therefore, you shepherds, hear the word of the LORD: ¹⁰Thus says the Lord GOD, I am against the shepherds; and I will demand my sheep at their hand, and put a stop to their feeding the sheep; no longer shall the shepherds feed themselves. I will rescue my sheep from their mouths, so that they may not be food for them.

11 For thus says the Lord GOD: I myself will search for my sheep, and will seek them out. ¹²As shepherds seek out their flocks when they are among their scattered sheep, so I will seek out my sheep. I will rescue them from all the places to which they have been scattered on a day of clouds and thick darkness. ¹³I will bring them out from the peoples and gather them from the countries, and will bring them into their own land; and I will feed them on the mountains of Israel, by the watercourses, and in all the inhabited parts of the land. ¹⁴I will feed them with good pasture, and the mountain heights of Israel shall be their pasture; there they shall lie down in good grazing land, and they shall feed on rich pasture on the mountains of Israel. ¹⁵I myself will be the shepherd of my sheep, and I will make them lie down, says the Lord GOD. ¹⁶I will seek the lost, and I will bring back the strayed, and I will bind up the injured, and I will strengthen the weak, but the fat and the strong I will destroy. I will feed them with justice.

17 As for you, my flock, thus says the Lord GOD: I shall judge between sheep and sheep, between rams and goats: ¹⁸Is it not enough for you to feed on the good pasture, but you must tread down with your feet the rest of your pasture? When you drink of clear water, must you foul the rest with your feet? ¹⁹And must my sheep eat what you have trodden with your feet, and drink what you have fouled with your feet?

20 Therefore, thus says the Lord GOD to

them: I myself will judge between the fat sheep and the lean sheep. 21Because you pushed with flank and shoulder, and butted at all the weak animals with your horns until you scattered them far and wide, 22I will save my flock, and they shall no longer be ravaged; and I will judge between sheep and sheep.

23 I will set up over them one shepherd, my servant David, and he shall feed them: he shall feed them and be their shepherd. 24And I, the LORD, will be their God, and my servant David shall be prince among them; I, the LORD, have spoken.

25 I will make with them a covenant of peace and banish wild animals from the land, so that they may live in the wild and sleep in the woods securely. 26I will make them and the region around my hill a blessing; and I will send down the showers in their season; they shall be showers of blessing. 27The trees of the field shall yield their fruit, and the earth shall yield its increase. They shall be secure on their soil; and they shall know that I am the LORD, when I break the bars of their yoke, and save them from the hands of those who enslaved them. 28They shall no more be plunder for the nations, nor shall the animals of the land devour them; they shall live in safety, and no one shall make them afraid. 29I will provide for them a splendid vegetation so that they shall no more be consumed with hunger in the land, and no longer suffer the insults of the nations. 30They shall know that I, the LORD their God, am with them, and that they, the house of Israel, are my people, says the Lord GOD. 31You are my sheep, the sheep of my pasture*a* and I am your God, says the Lord GOD.

34.1–31: **Oracle concerning Israel's leaders or "shepherds":** Ezekiel contends that Israel's leaders have acted improperly and must be replaced. **1–10:** The image of the shepherd commonly portrays monarchs in ancient Near Eastern literature (David, 1 Sam 16.11; 17). God charges that the *shepherds* have not taken care of the "flock" so that they are *scattered* or sent into exile. *Ah:* Literally, "woe!" **11–16:** God acts as the *shepherd* (Ps 23) who will return the people who have been scattered. *The fat and the strong* will

be destroyed because they neglected the people. **17–31:** Ezekiel portrays the leaders as stronger sheep who trample the pasture and dirty the water that others must use. God's rule will be manifested in the establishment of a Davidic *prince. A covenant* of peace:* The idyllic situation for those whom God will return to the land. Contrary to those who assert that "the inhabitants of the waste places" will take over the land (33.23–29), Ezekiel maintains that God will protect the people of Israel. The references to trees and animals together with the threat of enemies (see Lev 26) recall God's role as creator of the natural world and protector in the human world. *You are my sheep . . . and I am your God:* A variation of the covenant formula (11.20; 14.11).

〰〰〰〰〰〰〰〰〰

35 The word of the LORD came to me: 2Mortal, set your face against Mount Seir, and prophesy against it, 3and say to it, Thus says the Lord GOD:

I am against you, Mount Seir;
I stretch out my hand against you
to make you a desolation and a waste.
4 I lay your towns in ruins;
you shall become a desolation,
and you shall know that I am
the LORD.

5Because you cherished an ancient enmity, and gave over the people of Israel to the power of the sword at the time of their calamity, at the time of their final punishment; 6therefore, as I live, says the Lord GOD, I will prepare you for blood, and blood shall pursue you; since you did not hate bloodshed, bloodshed shall pursue you. 7I will make Mount Seir a waste and a desolation; and I will cut off from it all who come and go. 8I will fill its mountains with the slain; on your hills and in your valleys and in all your watercourses those killed with the sword shall fall. 9I will make you a perpetual desolation, and your cities shall never be inhabited. Then you shall know that I am the LORD.

10 Because you said, "These two nations and these two countries shall be mine, and we will take possession of them,"—although the LORD was there— 11therefore, as I live, says the Lord GOD, I will deal with you ac-

a Gk OL: Heb *pasture, you are people*

cording to the anger and envy that you showed because of your hatred against them; and I will make myself known among you,[a] when I judge you. 12You shall know that I, the LORD, have heard all the abusive speech that you uttered against the mountains of Israel, saying, "They are laid desolate, they are given us to devour." 13And you magnified yourselves against me with your mouth, and multiplied your words against me; I heard it. 14Thus says the Lord GOD: As the whole earth rejoices, I will make you desolate. 15As you rejoiced over the inheritance of the house of Israel, because it was desolate, so I will deal with you; you shall be desolate, Mount Seir, and all Edom, all of it. Then they shall know that I am the LORD.

35.1–36. 15: Edom and Israel. Ezekiel delivers contrasting oracles* concerning judgment against Edom (Isa 34; Jer 49.7–22) and restoration for Israel. The oracles presuppose Edom's actions against Jerusalem at the time of the Babylonian assault (Ob 11–14; Ps 137.7–9). **35.1–15:** The prophecy concerning Edom begins with an initial oracle in vv. 3–4, followed by "proof sayings" in vv. 5–9, 10–13 that establish the grounds for punishment. **1–2a:** *Mount Seir:* The mountain range extending south from the Dead Sea and east of the Arabah that was Edom's homeland (Gen 36.8; Num 24.18; compare Gen 33.16). **2b–4:** The initial oracle calls for Edom's destruction. **5–9:** The first "proof saying" indicates that Edom played a role in Israel's destruction. *Ancient enmity* may allude to the feud between Esau and Jacob or the long history of conflict between Israel and Edom (Num 20.14–21). **10–13:** *These two nations and these two countries:* In addition to the conflict between Esau and Jacob, there is a tradition of God's self-revelation from Seir (Deut 33.2; Judg 5.4). **14–15:** Edom disappeared following the sixth century when it was overrun by nomads who later became known as the Nabateans.

36

And you, mortal, prophesy to the mountains of Israel, and say: O mountains of Israel, hear the word of the LORD. 2Thus says the Lord GOD: Because the enemy said of you, "Aha!" and, "The ancient heights have become our possession," 3therefore prophesy, and say: Thus says the Lord GOD: Because they made you desolate indeed, and crushed you from all sides, so

that you became the possession of the rest of the nations, and you became an object of gossip and slander among the people; 4therefore, O mountains of Israel, hear the word of the Lord GOD: Thus says the Lord GOD to the mountains and the hills, the watercourses and the valleys, the desolate wastes and the deserted towns, which have become a source of plunder and an object of derision to the rest of the nations all around; 5therefore thus says the Lord GOD: I am speaking in my hot jealousy against the rest of the nations, and against all Edom, who, with wholehearted joy and utter contempt, took my land as their possession, because of its pasture, to plunder it. 6Therefore prophesy concerning the land of Israel, and say to the mountains and hills, to the watercourses and valleys, Thus says the Lord GOD: I am speaking in my jealous wrath, because you have suffered the insults of the nations; 7therefore thus says the Lord GOD: I swear that the nations that are all around you shall themselves suffer insults.

8 But you, O mountains of Israel, shall shoot out your branches, and yield your fruit to my people Israel; for they shall soon come home. 9See now, I am for you; I will turn to you, and you shall be tilled and sown; 10and I will multiply your population, the whole house of Israel, all of it; the towns shall be inhabited and the waste places rebuilt; 11and I will multiply human beings and animals upon you. They shall increase and be fruitful; and I will cause you to be inhabited as in your former times, and will do more good to you than ever before. Then you shall know that I am the LORD. 12I will lead people upon you—my people Israel—and they shall possess you, and you shall be their inheritance. No longer shall you bereave them of children.

13 Thus says the Lord GOD: Because they say to you, "You devour people, and you bereave your nation of children," 14therefore you shall no longer devour people and no longer bereave your nation of children, says the Lord GOD; 15and no longer will I let you hear the insults of the nations, no longer

a Gk: Heb *them*

shall you bear the disgrace of the peoples; and no longer shall you cause your nation to stumble, says the Lord GOD.

36.1–15: The oracle concerning the restoration of the mountains of Israel is a deliberate contrast with that against Mount Seir. **2:** God begins by citing Edom's intentions to take control of Israel. **3–12:** The oracle presupposes the depopulation and desolation of the entire land, which must now be replenished. *The rest of the nations:* Edom elsewhere is a symbol for nations that threaten Israel (Isa 34; 63.1–6). *They shall increase and be fruitful:* See Gen 1.22, 28; 9.7. **13–15:** The prophet accuses the mountains of devouring people.

16 The word of the LORD came to me: 17 Mortal, when the house of Israel lived on their own soil, they defiled it with their ways and their deeds; their conduct in my sight was like the uncleanness of a woman in her menstrual period. 18 So I poured out my wrath upon them for the blood that they had shed upon the land, and for the idols with which they had defiled it. 19 I scattered them among the nations, and they were dispersed through the countries; in accordance with their conduct and their deeds I judged them. 20 But when they came to the nations, wherever they came, they profaned my holy name, in that it was said of them, "These are the people of the LORD, and yet they had to go out of his land." 21 But I had concern for my holy name, which the house of Israel had profaned among the nations to which they came.

22 Therefore say to the house of Israel, Thus says the Lord GOD: It is not for your sake, O house of Israel, that I am about to act, but for the sake of my holy name, which you have profaned among the nations to which you came. 23 I will sanctify my great name, which has been profaned among the nations, and which you have profaned among them; and the nations shall know that I am the LORD, says the Lord GOD, when through you I display my holiness before their eyes. 24 I will take you from the nations, and gather you from all the countries, and bring you into your own land. 25 I will sprinkle clean water upon you, and you shall be clean from all your uncleannesses, and from

all your idols I will cleanse you. 26 A new heart I will give you, and a new spirit I will put within you; and I will remove from your body the heart of stone and give you a heart of flesh. 27 I will put my spirit within you, and make you follow my statutes and be careful to observe my ordinances. 28 Then you shall live in the land that I gave to your ancestors; and you shall be my people, and I will be your God. 29 I will save you from all your uncleannesses, and I will summon the grain and make it abundant and lay no famine upon you. 30 I will make the fruit of the tree and the produce of the field abundant, so that you may never again suffer the disgrace of famine among the nations. 31 Then you shall remember your evil ways, and your dealings that were not good; and you shall loathe yourselves for your iniquities and your abominable deeds. 32 It is not for your sake that I will act, says the Lord GOD; let that be known to you. Be ashamed and dismayed for your ways, O house of Israel.

33 Thus says the Lord GOD: On the day that I cleanse you from all your iniquities, I will cause the towns to be inhabited, and the waste places shall be rebuilt. 34 The land that was desolate shall be tilled, instead of being the desolation that it was in the sight of all who passed by. 35 And they will say, "This land that was desolate has become like the garden of Eden; and the waste and desolate and ruined towns are now inhabited and fortified." 36 Then the nations that are left all around you shall know that I, the LORD, have rebuilt the ruined places, and replanted that which was desolate; I, the LORD, have spoken, and I will do it.

37 Thus says the Lord GOD: I will also let the house of Israel ask me to do this for them: to increase their population like a flock. 38 Like the flock for sacrifices,*a* like the flock at Jerusalem during her appointed festivals, so shall the ruined towns be filled with flocks of people. Then they shall know that I am the LORD.

36.16–38: The purification of Israel. Ezekiel portrays the restoration of Israel as a process of purifying sacrifice (chs. 8–11). **16–21:** The prophet initially employs

a Heb *flock of holy things*

the imagery of menstrual blood to portray the impurity of the land. According to priestly thought, blood is the seat of life and holiness, and, hence, requires special care (Gen 9.1–6; Lev 17). Like men who have bodily discharges (Lev 15.1–18), menstruating women are considered unclean (Lev 15.19–30) and require purification. The exile of the people profanes God's name. **22–32:** In order to reclaim God's name, Israel must be restored. God intends to purify Israel with clean water, which is the standard procedure for purification in such cases (Lev 15.7, 11–12; see also Lev 14.5–6, 50–52; Num 19.17). Once the land and people are cleansed, God will provide a *new heart* and a *new spirit* (11.19; 18.31; Jer 31.31–34) that will prompt the people to live a holy life in accordance with God's commandments. The covenant formula (v. 28) signifies the restoration of Israel's relationship with God and the fertility of the land. **33–36:** Replenishing of the land to resemble *the garden of Eden* (Gen 2–3) reveals God to the nations (Ex 15.13–18). **37–38:** The imagery of restoration is related to that of the sacrificial sheep that fill Jerusalem during festivals.

37 The hand of the LORD came upon me, and he brought me out by the spirit of the LORD and set me down in the middle of a valley; it was full of bones. ²He led me all around them; there were very many lying in the valley, and they were very dry. ³He said to me, "Mortal, can these bones live?" I answered, "O Lord GOD, you know." ⁴Then he said to me, "Prophesy to these bones, and say to them: O dry bones, hear the word of the LORD. ⁵Thus says the Lord GOD to these bones: I will cause breath*ᵃ* to enter you, and you shall live. ⁶I will lay sinews on you, and will cause flesh to come upon you, and cover you with skin, and put breath*ᵃ* in you, and you shall live; and you shall know that I am the LORD."

7 So I prophesied as I had been commanded; and as I prophesied, suddenly there was a noise, a rattling, and the bones came together, bone to its bone. ⁸I looked, and there were sinews on them, and flesh had come upon them, and skin had covered them; but there was no breath in them. ⁹Then he said to me, "Prophesy to the breath, prophesy, mortal, and say to the breath:*ᵇ* Thus says the Lord GOD: Come from the four winds, O breath,*ᵇ* and breathe

upon these slain, that they may live." ¹⁰I prophesied as he commanded me, and the breath came into them, and they lived, and stood on their feet, a vast multitude.

11 Then he said to me, "Mortal, these bones are the whole house of Israel. They say, 'Our bones are dried up, and our hope is lost; we are cut off completely.' ¹²Therefore prophesy, and say to them, Thus says the Lord GOD: I am going to open your graves, and bring you up from your graves, O my people; and I will bring you back to the land of Israel. ¹³And you shall know that I am the LORD, when I open your graves, and bring you up from your graves, O my people. ¹⁴I will put my spirit within you, and you shall live, and I will place you on your own soil; then you shall know that I, the LORD, have spoken and will act, says the LORD."

37.1–14: The valley of dry bones. Ezekiel's vision of dry bones symbolizes the restoration of the people of Israel. Many assume that it is based upon his observation of a battlefield filled with the bones of dead soldiers. The vision plays upon priestly concepts of purity, in that a priest must have no contact with the dead (Lev 21.1–12; those who do have contact with a corpse are defiled for a period of seven days, Num 19.10b–22). Since such impurity is the epitome of defilement in priestly thought, this image of new life is a very powerful metaphor* for the restoration and purification of Israel. **1–10:** God instructs him to prophesy. *Valley*, or "plain" is the location of his initial visions (1.22–27). *Breath:* Literally "wind." **11–14:** Resurrection symbolizes the restoration of Israel to its own land (see Isa 26.19; Dan 12.1–4).

15 The word of the LORD came to me: ¹⁶Mortal, take a stick and write on it, "For Judah, and the Israelites associated with it"; then take another stick and write on it, "For Joseph (the stick of Ephraim) and all the house of Israel associated with it"; ¹⁷and join them together into one stick, so that they may become one in your hand. ¹⁸And when your people say to you, "Will you not show us what you mean by these?" ¹⁹say to them, Thus says the Lord GOD: I am about to take the stick of Joseph (which is in the hand of Ephraim) and the tribes of Israel associated

a Or *spirit*   *b* Or *wind* or *spirit*

with it; and I will put the stick of Judah upon it,*a* and make them one stick, in order that they may be one in my hand. 20When the sticks on which you write are in your hand before their eyes, 21then say to them, Thus says the Lord GOD: I will take the people of Israel from the nations among which they have gone, and will gather them from every quarter, and bring them to their own land. 22I will make them one nation in the land, on the mountains of Israel; and one king shall be king over them all. Never again shall they be two nations, and never again shall they be divided into two kingdoms. 23They shall never again defile themselves with their idols and their detestable things, or with any of their transgressions. I will save them from all the apostasies into which they have fallen,*b* and will cleanse them. Then they shall be my people, and I will be their God.

24 My servant David shall be king over them; and they shall all have one shepherd. They shall follow my ordinances and be careful to observe my statutes. 25They shall live in the land that I gave to my servant Jacob, in which your ancestors lived; they and their children and their children's children shall live there forever; and my servant David shall be their prince forever. 26I will make a covenant of peace with them; it shall be an everlasting covenant with them; and I will bless*c* them and multiply them, and will set my sanctuary among them forevermore. 27My dwelling place shall be with them; and I will be their God, and they shall be my people. 28Then the nations shall know that I the LORD sanctify Israel, when my sanctuary is among them forevermore.

37.15–28: The two sticks. Ezekiel's symbolic action represents the unification of Israel and Judah under the rule of a Davidic king. See Isa 11, which also employs the image of a growing tree to symbolize the unification of Israel and Judah under a Davidic king. **15–19:** God instructs Ezekiel to write the names *Judah* and *Joseph* on two *sticks* (see Num 17.1–13). *Judah* is the southern kingdom, and *Joseph* is the father of *Ephraim*, the central tribe of the northern kingdom, Israel. *Stick:* Literally "tree" or "wood." **20–27:** Just as one gathers sticks for a fire (Isa 27.11), God will gather the exiles to establish them as one nation. Ezekiel

draws upon the tradition of permanent Davidic rule (2 Sam 7; Ps 89; 132), the eternal *covenant*⋆ *of peace* granted to the priest Phineas the son of Eleazar and grandson of Aaron (Num 25.10–13; see also Ezek 34.25), and the role of the Temple⋆ as the center of both Israel and all creation (Ex 40; see also Gen 2.1–3).

The Gog and Magog oracles
Chs. 38–39 Ezekiel's oracles against Gog, ruler from the land of Magog, express an apocalyptic⋆ drama of God's victory over the nations that threaten Israel. The original identity of *Gog* is uncertain, although some have identified him with Gyges, a seventh-century BCE ruler of Lydia in Asia Minor. The land of *Magog* appears together with *Meshech*, *Tubal*, *Gomer* (Cimmerians in central Asia Minor), and *Togarmah* (compare *Beth-togarmah*, in Armenia), apparently lands in Asia Minor and Greece. Ezekiel's oracles, however, draw upon Isaiah's prophecies concerning the downfall of a Mesopotamian ruler (Isa 14) and Jeremiah's prophecies concerning a "foe from the north" (Jer 2–3). The original identity of Gog matters little as later interpreters have understood him to be a trans-national symbol of evil, much like Edom and Egypt (for example, Isa 34; 63.1–6; Mal 1.2–5; Ex 15) or chaos monsters such as Leviathan⋆ or Behemoth⋆ (Ps 74; 104; Job 38–41).

---

38 The word of the LORD came to me: 2Mortal, set your face toward Gog, of the land of Magog, the chief prince of Meshech and Tubal. Prophesy against him 3and say: Thus says the Lord GOD: I am against you, O Gog, chief prince of Meshech and Tubal; 4I will turn you around and put hooks into your jaws, and I will lead you out with all your army, horses and horsemen, all of them clothed in full armor, a great company, all of them with shield and buckler, wielding swords. 5Persia, Ethiopia,*d* and Put are with them, all of them with buckler and helmet; 6Gomer and all its troops; Beth-togarmah from the remotest parts of the north with all its troops—many peoples are with you.

7 Be ready and keep ready, you and all the companies that are assembled around you,

---

a Heb *I will put them upon it*   *b* Another reading is *from all the settlements in which they have sinned*
c Tg: Heb *give*   *d* Or *Nubia;* Heb *Cush*

and hold yourselves in reserve for them. ⁸After many days you shall be mustered; in the latter years you shall go against a land restored from war, a land where people were gathered from many nations on the mountains of Israel, which had long lain waste; its people were brought out from the nations and now are living in safety, all of them. ⁹You shall advance, coming on like a storm; you shall be like a cloud covering the land, you and all your troops, and many peoples with you.

10 Thus says the Lord GOD: On that day thoughts will come into your mind, and you will devise an evil scheme. ¹¹You will say, "I will go up against the land of unwalled villages; I will fall upon the quiet people who live in safety, all of them living without walls, and having no bars or gates"; ¹²to seize spoil and carry off plunder; to assail the waste places that are now inhabited, and the people who were gathered from the nations, who are acquiring cattle and goods, who live at the center*a* of the earth. ¹³Sheba and Dedan and the merchants of Tarshish and all its young warriors*b* will say to you, "Have you come to seize spoil? Have you assembled your horde to carry off plunder, to carry away silver and gold, to take away cattle and goods, to seize a great amount of booty?"

14 Therefore, mortal, prophesy, and say to Gog: Thus says the Lord GOD: On that day when my people Israel are living securely, you will rouse yourself*c* ¹⁵and come from your place out of the remotest parts of the north, you and many peoples with you, all of them riding on horses, a great horde, a mighty army; ¹⁶you will come up against my people Israel, like a cloud covering the earth. In the latter days I will bring you against my land, so that the nations may know me, when through you, O Gog, I display my holiness before their eyes.

38.1–16. 1–9: God's initial instructions to Ezekiel present Gog as the leader of a host of nations that threaten Israel, a well-known motif* in the tradition about Zion* as an invincible fortress (see Ps 2; 46–48). *Persia, Ethiopia,* and *Put* (Libya) are distant lands from throughout the ancient Near Eastern world. **10–13:** God portrays Gog's intentions to plunder nations.

Sheba: Southern Arabia. *Dedan:* Rhodes. *Tarshish:* Tartessos in Spain. **14–16:** God portrays Gog's advance with a mighty army against Israel. *In the latter days* normally refers to the future, and many believe the expression to have eschatological* meaning. The nations' knowledge of God draws upon earlier traditions (for example, Ex 15; Isa 2.1–4; Mic 4.1–5; Ps 46–48) in which the nations recognize God's power and sovereignty.

---

17 Thus says the Lord GOD: Are you he of whom I spoke in former days by my servants the prophets of Israel, who in those days prophesied for years that I would bring you against them? ¹⁸On that day, when Gog comes against the land of Israel, says the Lord GOD, my wrath shall be aroused. ¹⁹For in my jealousy and in my blazing wrath I declare: On that day there shall be a great shaking in the land of Israel; ²⁰the fish of the sea, and the birds of the air, and the animals of the field, and all creeping things that creep on the ground, and all human beings that are on the face of the earth, shall quake at my presence, and the mountains shall be thrown down, and the cliffs shall fall, and every wall shall tumble to the ground. ²¹I will summon the sword against Gog*d* in*e* all my mountains, says the Lord GOD; the swords of all will be against their comrades. ²²With pestilence and bloodshed I will enter into judgment with him; and I will pour down torrential rains and hailstones, fire and sulfur, upon him and his troops and the many peoples that are with him. ²³So I will display my greatness and my holiness and make myself known in the eyes of many nations. Then they shall know that I am the LORD.

38.17–23: God portrays the defeat of Gog as a cosmic event that was announced by the prophets.* *On that day* is a formula that appears throughout Isaiah 1–39 (Isa 4.2; 7.18, 20, 21, 23). The cosmic dimensions of the defeat appear in the quaking of the land, including *the fish of the sea, the birds of the air, the animals of the field, all creeping things,* and *all human beings,* which alludes to the created order as described in Gen 1. Likewise, the defeat of Gog by the sword and natural

a Heb *navel*   *b* Heb *young lions*   *c* Gk: Heb *will you not know?*   *d* Heb *him*   *e* Heb *to* or *for*

elements, such as *torrential rains, hailstones, fire,* and *sulphur,* appeal to God's role as creator as well as to the tradition about the destruction of Sodom and Gomorrah (Gen 18–19). Recognition by the nations is the object of God's action.

39 And you, mortal, prophesy against Gog, and say: Thus says the Lord GOD: I am against you, O Gog, chief prince of Meshech and Tubal! 2I will turn you around and drive you forward, and bring you up from the remotest parts of the north, and lead you against the mountains of Israel. 3I will strike your bow from your left hand, and will make your arrows drop out of your right hand. 4You shall fall upon the mountains of Israel, you and all your troops and the peoples that are with you; I will give you to birds of prey of every kind and to the wild animals to be devoured. 5You shall fall in the open field; for I have spoken, says the Lord GOD. 6I will send fire on Magog and on those who live securely in the coastlands; and they shall know that I am the LORD.

7 My holy name I will make known among my people Israel; and I will not let my holy name be profaned any more; and the nations shall know that I am the LORD, the Holy One in Israel. 8It has come! It has happened, says the Lord GOD. This is the day of which I have spoken.

9 Then those who live in the towns of Israel will go out and make fires of the weapons and burn them—bucklers and shields, bows and arrows, handpikes and spears—and they will make fires of them for seven years. 10They will not need to take wood out of the field or cut down any trees in the forests, for they will make their fires of the weapons; they will despoil those who despoiled them, and plunder those who plundered them, says the Lord GOD.

11 On that day I will give to Gog a place for burial in Israel, the Valley of the Travelers*a* east of the sea; it shall block the path of the travelers, for there Gog and all his horde will be buried; it shall be called the Valley of Hamon-gog.*b* 12Seven months the house of Israel shall spend burying them, in order to cleanse the land. 13All the people of the land shall bury them; and it will bring

them honor on the day that I show my glory, says the Lord GOD. 14They will set apart men to pass through the land regularly and bury any invaders*c* who remain on the face of the land, so as to cleanse it; for seven months they shall make their search. 15As the searchers*c* pass through the land, anyone who sees a human bone shall set up a sign by it, until the buriers have buried it in the Valley of Hamon-gog.*b* 16(A city Hamonah*d* is there also.) Thus they shall cleanse the land.

39.1–16: Unburied corpses on the mountains recall the imagery of the vision of dry bones (37.1–14), the death of the Babylonian king in the open (Isa 14.3–23), and the defeat of Assyria on the mountains of Israel (Isa 14.24–27). The victory fires that burn for seven years throughout the land recall the seven-year sabbatical agricultural and economic cycle (Lev 25.1–7; Ex 23.10–11; 21.1–6; Deut 15.1–18). The burial of Gog constitutes the final stage of the cleansing of the land of Israel prior to its restoration. *The Valley of the Travelers* or the "Valley of those who pass by" is apparently a wordplay on the Valley of Abarim east of the Dead Sea. Hebrew for "travelers, passersby" is "ha'obrim." *The Valley of Hamon-gog,* "the valley of the horde of Gog," is a wordplay on the Valley of Hinnom, southwest of Jerusalem, which was known for idolatry,* the burning of children, and dead bodies (2 Kings 23.10; Jer 7.30–34). The seven months of burial purify the land so that God's *glory* or presence may appear. *Hamonah:* "horde."

17 As for you, mortal, thus says the Lord GOD: Speak to the birds of every kind and to all the wild animals: Assemble and come, gather from all around to the sacrificial feast that I am preparing for you, a great sacrificial feast on the mountains of Israel, and you shall eat flesh and drink blood. 18You shall eat the flesh of the mighty, and drink the blood of the princes of the earth—of rams, of lambs, and of goats, of bulls, all of them fatlings of Bashan. 19You shall eat fat until you are filled, and drink blood until you are drunk, at the sacrificial feast that I am preparing for you. 20And you shall be filled at

a Or *of the Abarim*   *b* That is, *the Horde of Gog*
c Heb *travelers*   *d* That is *The Horde*

my table with horses and charioteers,[a] with warriors and all kinds of soldiers, says the Lord GOD.

21 I will display my glory among the nations; and all the nations shall see my judgment that I have executed, and my hand that I have laid on them. 22The house of Israel shall know that I am the LORD their God, from that day forward. 23And the nations shall know that the house of Israel went into captivity for their iniquity, because they dealt treacherously with me. So I hid my face from them and gave them into the hand of their adversaries, and they all fell by the sword. 24I dealt with them according to their uncleanness and their transgressions, and hid my face from them.

25 Therefore thus says the Lord GOD: Now I will restore the fortunes of Jacob, and have mercy on the whole house of Israel; and I will be jealous for my holy name. 26They shall forget[b] their shame, and all the treachery they have practiced against me, when they live securely in their land with no one to make them afraid, 27when I have brought them back from the peoples and gathered them from their enemies' lands, and through them have displayed my holiness in the sight of many nations. 28Then they shall know that I am the LORD their God because I sent them into exile among the nations, and then gathered them into their own land. I will leave none of them behind; 29and I will never again hide my face from them, when I pour out my spirit upon the house of Israel, says the Lord GOD.

39.17–29: The feast of the birds and wild animals recalls the covenant* curses (for example, Deut 28.16–44) in which Israel is fed to the birds and animals, but they are now applied to Israel's enemies (Lev 26.22; Deut 28.26). The *sacrificial feast* reverses the imagery of the banquet on Zion* (Isa 25.6–10). These actions enable God to display the divine glory to the nations. *I hid my face from them* raises the question of God's injustice. *Restore the fortunes of Jacob* recalls God's promise to remember the covenant* with Jacob (Lev 26.40–45) if the people confess their iniquity.

The vision of the restored Temple in Jerusalem
Chs. 40–48: See God's promises (37.24–38) to make a covenant of peace with Israel and to place the sanc-

tuary among them forever. This vision provides a literary and conceptual envelope for the book that complements the visions of God's departure and the Temple's destruction in chs. 1–11 with one of the Temple's restorations and God's return. Ezekiel 40.1–43.12 relates instruction concerning the building of the Temple and the return of God's glory; 43.13–47.12 provides instruction concerning the associated structures and activities of the Temple complex; and 47.13–48.35 guides the reestablishment of the land and people of Israel around the Temple.

40 In the twenty-fifth year of our exile, at the beginning of the year, on the tenth day of the month, in the fourteenth year after the city was struck down, on that very day, the hand of the LORD was upon me, and he brought me there. 2He brought me, in visions of God, to the land of Israel, and set me down upon a very high mountain, on which was a structure like a city to the south. 3When he brought me there, a man was there, whose appearance shone like bronze, with a linen cord and a measuring reed in his hand; and he was standing in the gateway. 4The man said to me, "Mortal, look closely and listen attentively, and set your mind upon all that I shall show you, for you were brought here in order that I might show it to you; declare all that you see to the house of Israel."

40.1–43.12: The Temple* and the return of God's glory. 40.1–4: The date in v. 1 is April 28, 573 BCE. Ezekiel's visions began at the age of 30 in the fifth year of the Exile (1.1–3). After 20 years, Ezekiel would be ready to retire from priestly service at the age of 50 (Num 4.3; 8.23–25). Ezekiel is transported to Mt. Zion, the site of the First Temple. The city of Jerusalem is immediately to the south. Ezekiel's guide recalls the bronze-colored creatures that supported God's throne chariot (1.5–14; 8.2). The *linen cord* and the *measuring reed* enable the guide to instruct Ezekiel in the dimensions of the Temple structures.

5 Now there was a wall all around the outside of the temple area. The length of the measuring reed in the man's hand was six long cubits, each being a cubit and a hand-

a Heb *chariots* *b* Another reading is *They shall bear*

breadth in length; so he measured the thickness of the wall, one reed; and the height, one reed. 6Then he went into the gateway facing east, going up its steps, and measured the threshold of the gate, one reed deep.*a* There were 7recesses, and each recess was one reed wide and one reed deep; and the space between the recesses, five cubits; and the threshold of the gate by the vestibule of the gate at the inner end was one reed deep. 8Then he measured the inner vestibule of the gateway, one cubit. 9Then he measured the vestibule of the gateway, eight cubits; and its pilasters, two cubits; and the vestibule of the gate was at the inner end. 10There were three recesses on either side of the east gate; the three were of the same size; and the pilasters on either side were of the same size. 11Then he measured the width of the opening of the gateway, ten cubits; and the width of the gateway, thirteen cubits. 12There was a barrier before the recesses, one cubit on either side; and the recesses were six cubits on either side. 13Then he measured the gate from the back*b* of the one recess to the back*b* of the other, a width of twenty-five cubits, from wall to wall.*c* 14He measured*d* also the vestibule, twenty cubits; and the gate next to the pilaster on every side of the court.*e* 15From the front of the gate at the entrance to the end of the inner vestibule of the gate was fifty cubits. 16The recesses and their pilasters had windows, with shutters*e* on the inside of the gateway all around, and the vestibules also had windows on the inside all around; and on the pilasters were palm trees.

17 Then he brought me into the outer court; there were chambers there, and a pavement, all around the court; thirty chambers fronted on the pavement. 18The pavement ran along the side of the gates, corresponding to the length of the gates; this was the lower pavement. 19Then he measured the distance from the inner front of*f* the lower gate to the outer front of the inner court, one hundred cubits.*g*

20 Then he measured the gate of the outer court that faced north—its depth and width. 21Its recesses, three on either side, and its pilasters and its vestibule were of the same size as those of the first gate; its depth was fifty cubits, and its width twenty-five cubits. 22Its windows, its vestibule, and its palm trees were of the same size as those of the gate that faced toward the east. Seven steps led up to it; and its vestibule was on the inside.*h* 23Opposite the gate on the north, as on the east, was a gate to the inner court; he measured from gate to gate, one hundred cubits.

24 Then he led me toward the south, and there was a gate on the south; and he measured its pilasters and its vestibule; they had the same dimensions as the others. 25There were windows all around in it and in its vestibule, like the windows of the others; its depth was fifty cubits, and its width twenty-five cubits. 26There were seven steps leading up to it; its vestibule was on the inside.*h* It had palm trees on its pilasters, one on either side. 27There was a gate on the south of the inner court; and he measured from gate to gate toward the south, one hundred cubits.

40.5–47: The Temple walls, gates, and courtyards.
5: *Six long cubits:* over ten feet or three meters. A long cubit is about 518 millimeters or 20.68 inches. **5–16:** The *east gate* is the main gate of the Temple complex, which faces east toward the sun. It is built according to the basic pattern of the fortified Solomonic gates at Gezer, Hazor, and Megiddo, with an initial *threshold* built into the wall, followed by three recessed chambers, an inner threshold, and the *vestibule. Pilaster:* A projecting column that may have served as a door jamb. Windows provide light for the recessed chambers and the vestibule.

40.17–27. 17–19: The thirty chambers that line the *outer court* were used by the Levites for various activities (Jer 35.2–4; Neh 13.4–14). **20–27:** The gates for the outer court to the north and south are similar to the east gate. There is no west gate; the Temple occupies the western side of the compound. Each of the

---

a Heb *deep, and one threshold, one reed deep*
b Gk: Heb *roof*   *c* Heb *opening facing opening*
d Heb *made*   *e* Meaning of Heb uncertain
f Compare Gk: Heb *from before*   *g* Heb adds *the east and the north*   *h* Gk: Heb *before them*

three gates faces a corresponding gate to the inner court.

28 Then he brought me to the inner court by the south gate, and he measured the south gate; it was of the same dimensions as the others. ²⁹Its recesses, its pilasters, and its vestibule were of the same size as the others; and there were windows all around in it and in its vestibule; its depth was fifty cubits, and its width twenty-five cubits. ³⁰There were vestibules all around, twenty-five cubits deep and five cubits wide. ³¹Its vestibule faced the outer court, and palm trees were on its pilasters, and its stairway had eight steps.

32 Then he brought me to the inner court on the east side, and he measured the gate; it was of the same size as the others. ³³Its recesses, its pilasters, and its vestibule were of the same dimensions as the others; and there were windows all around in it and in its vestibule; its depth was fifty cubits, and its width twenty-five cubits. ³⁴Its vestibule faced the outer court, and it had palm trees on its pilasters, on either side; and its stairway had eight steps.

35 Then he brought me to the north gate, and he measured it; it had the same dimensions as the others. ³⁶Its recesses, its pilasters, and its vestibule were of the same size as the others;ᵃ and it had windows all around. Its depth was fifty cubits, and its width twenty-five cubits. ³⁷Its vestibuleᵇ faced the outer court, and it had palm trees on its pilasters, on either side; and its stairway had eight steps.

38 There was a chamber with its door in the vestibule of the gate,ᶜ where the burnt offering was to be washed. ³⁹And in the vestibule of the gate were two tables on either side, on which the burnt offering and the sin offering and the guilt offering were to be slaughtered. ⁴⁰On the outside of the vestibuleᵈ at the entrance of the north gate were two tables; and on the other side of the vestibule of the gate were two tables. ⁴¹Four tables were on the inside, and four tables on the outside of the side of the gate, eight tables, on which the sacrifices were to be slaughtered. ⁴²There were also four tables of hewn stone for the burnt offering, a cubit and a half long, and one cubit and a half wide, and one cubit high, on which the instruments were to be laid with which the burnt offerings and the sacrifices were slaughtered. ⁴³There were pegs, one handbreadth long, fastened all around the inside. And on the tables the flesh of the offering was to be laid.

44 On the outside of the inner gateway there were chambers for the singers in the inner court, oneᵉ at the side of the north gate facing south, the other at the side of the east gate facing north. ⁴⁵He said to me, "This chamber that faces south is for the priests who have charge of the temple, ⁴⁶and the chamber that faces north is for the priests who have charge of the altar; these are the descendants of Zadok, who alone among the descendants of Levi may come near to the LORD to minister to him." ⁴⁷He measured the court, one hundred cubits deep, and one hundred cubits wide, a square; and the altar was in front of the temple.

40.28–47. 28–37: The south, east, and north gates to the inner court are similar to those for the outer court. **38–43:** Chambers were built by the vestibule of the gate to prepare sacrificial animals for the *burnt offering* (Lev 1.3–17), the *sin offering* (Lev 4.1–5.13), and the *guilt offering* (Lev 5.14–6.7). **44–47:** Chambers were placed by the sides of the north and east (LXX* reads "south") for the priests who had charge of the Temple and the altar.

48 Then he brought me to the vestibule of the temple and measured the pilasters of the vestibule, five cubits on either side; and the width of the gate was fourteen cubits; and the sidewalls of the gate were three cubitsᶠ on either side. ⁴⁹The depth of the vestibule was twenty cubits, and the width twelveᵍ cubits; ten steps led upʰ to it; and

ᵃ One Ms: Compare verses 29 and 33: MT lacks *were of the same size as the others*   ᵇ Gk Vg Compare verses 26, 31, 34: Heb *pilasters*   ᶜ Cn: Heb *at the pilasters of the gates*   ᵈ Cn: Heb *to him who goes up*   ᵉ Heb lacks *one*   ᶠ Gk: Heb *and the width of the gate was three cubits*   ᵍ Gk: Heb *eleven*   ʰ Gk: Heb *and by steps that went up*

there were pillars beside the pilasters on either side.

41

Then he brought me to the nave, and measured the pilasters; on each side six cubits was the width of the pilasters.[a] [2]The width of the entrance was ten cubits; and the sidewalls of the entrance were five cubits on either side. He measured the length of the nave, forty cubits, and its width, twenty cubits. [3]Then he went into the inner room and measured the pilasters of the entrance, two cubits; and the width of the entrance, six cubits; and the sidewalls[b] of the entrance, seven cubits. [4]He measured the depth of the room, twenty cubits, and its width, twenty cubits, beyond the nave. And he said to me, This is the most holy place.

40.48–41.26: The Temple. 40.48–41.4: The Temple is constructed according to a three-room pattern, like that of Solomon's Temple (1 Kings 6) and other examples of temples and royal palaces from Canaan and Syria. The three rooms are the *vestibule* (35 feet by 21 feet), an entry or reception room; the *nave* (71 feet by 25 feet), the main hall where the Temple furnishings are placed; and the *inner room* (35 feet by 35 feet), also known as the most holy place, God's throne room which houses the ark of the covenant. Ezekiel does not enter the *inner room* since this is restricted to the high priest on Yom Kippur or the Day of Atonement* (Lev 16). *Pillars:* Like those of Solomon's Temple (1 Kings 7.15–22).

---

5 Then he measured the wall of the temple, six cubits thick; and the width of the side chambers, four cubits, all around the temple. [6]The side chambers were in three stories, one over another, thirty in each story. There were offsets[c] all around the wall of the temple to serve as supports for the side chambers, so that they should not be supported by the wall of the temple. [7]The passageway[d] of the side chambers widened from story to story; for the structure was supplied with a stairway all around the temple. For this reason the structure became wider from story to story. One ascended from the bottom story to the uppermost story by way of the middle one. [8]I saw also that the temple had a raised platform all around; the foundations of the side chambers measured a full reed of six long cubits. [9]The thickness of the outer wall of the side chambers was five cubits; and the free space between the side chambers of the temple [10]and the chambers of the court was a width of twenty cubits all around the temple on every side. [11]The side chambers opened onto the area left free, one door toward the north, and another door toward the south; and the width of the part that was left free was five cubits all around.

41.5–11: Three stories of chambers with thirty chambers each line the walls of the Temple. They have an independent support structure so that they are not supported by the Temple itself. A *stairway* provides access to the upper stories. The supports and stairways occupy more space on the lower stories so that each story is progressively larger. *Raised platform:* The "foundations of the earth" (Mic 6.2; Isa 24.18; Jer 31.37; Ps 82.5).

---

12 The building that was facing the temple yard on the west side was seventy cubits wide; and the wall of the building was five cubits thick all around, and its depth ninety cubits.

13 Then he measured the temple, one hundred cubits deep; and the yard and the building with its walls, one hundred cubits deep; [14]also the width of the east front of the temple and the yard, one hundred cubits.

15 Then he measured the depth of the building facing the yard at the west, together with its galleries[e] on either side, one hundred cubits.

The nave of the temple and the inner room and the outer[f] vestibule [16]were paneled,[g] and, all around, all three had windows with recessed[h] frames. Facing the threshold the temple was paneled with wood all around, from the floor up to the windows (now the windows were covered), [17]to the space above the door, even to the inner room, and on the outside. And on all the walls all around in

---

a Compare Gk: Heb *tent*   *b* Gk: Heb *width*
c Gk Compare 1 Kings 6.6: Heb *they entered*
d Cn: Heb *it was surrounded*   *e* Cn: Meaning of Heb uncertain   *f* Gk: Heb *of the court*   *g* Gk: Heb *the thresholds*   *h* Cn Compare Gk 1 Kings 6.4: Meaning of Heb uncertain

the inner room and the nave there was a pattern.[a] 18It was formed of cherubim and palm trees, a palm tree between cherub and cherub. Each cherub had two faces: 19a human face turned toward the palm tree on the one side, and the face of a young lion turned toward the palm tree on the other side. They were carved on the whole temple all around; 20from the floor to the area above the door, cherubim and palm trees were carved on the wall.[b]

21 The doorposts of the nave were square. In front of the holy place was something resembling 22an altar of wood, three cubits high, two cubits long, and two cubits wide;[c] its corners, its base,[d] and its walls were of wood. He said to me, "This is the table that stands before the LORD." 23The nave and the holy place had each a double door. 24The doors had two leaves apiece, two swinging leaves for each door. 25On the doors of the nave were carved cherubim and palm trees, such as were carved on the walls; and there was a canopy of wood in front of the vestibule outside. 26And there were recessed windows and palm trees on either side, on the sidewalls of the vestibule.[e]

41.12–26. 12–15a: The unidentified building is behind the Temple to the west. **41.15b–26:** The interior decoration of the Temple. *Paneled*, Greek (compare v. 16 and 1 Kings 6.9; 7.3, 7). Hebrew reads "thresholds." The *cherubim** and *palm trees* carved into the paneling of the interior walls represent images from the garden of Eden (see 1 Kings 6.29). Unlike the cherubim who bear the throne chariot, these have only two faces, a human and a young lion. *Something resembling an altar of wood:* The table for the presentation of rows of "the bread of the Presence" (Ex 25.23–30; Lev 24.5–9; 1 Kings 7.48).

42 Then he led me out into the outer court, toward the north, and he brought me to the chambers that were opposite the temple yard and opposite the building on the north. 2The length of the building that was on the north side[f] was[g] one hundred cubits, and the width fifty cubits. 3Across the twenty cubits that belonged to the inner court, and facing the pavement that belonged to the outer court, the cham-

bers rose[h] gallery[i] by gallery[i] in three stories. 4In front of the chambers was a passage on the inner side, ten cubits wide and one hundred cubits deep,[j] and its[k] entrances were on the north. 5Now the upper chambers were narrower, for the galleries[i] took more away from them than from the lower and middle chambers in the building. 6For they were in three stories, and they had no pillars like the pillars of the outer[l] court; for this reason the upper chambers were set back from the ground more than the lower and the middle ones. 7There was a wall outside parallel to the chambers, toward the outer court, opposite the chambers, fifty cubits long. 8For the chambers on the outer court were fifty cubits long, while those opposite the temple were one hundred cubits long. 9At the foot of these chambers ran a passage that one entered from the east in order to enter them from the outer court. 10The width of the passage[m] was fixed by the wall of the court.

On the south[n] also, opposite the vacant area and opposite the building, there were chambers 11with a passage in front of them; they were similar to the chambers on the north, of the same length and width, with the same exits[o] and arrangements and doors. 12So the entrances of the chambers to the south were entered through the entrance at the head of the corresponding passage, from the east, along the matching wall.[i]

13 Then he said to me, "The north chambers and the south chambers opposite the vacant area are the holy chambers, where the priests who approach the LORD shall eat the most holy offerings; there they shall deposit the most holy offerings—the grain offering, the sin offering, and the guilt offering—for the place is holy. 14When the priests enter the holy place, they shall not go

a Heb *measures*   b Cn Compare verse 25: Heb *and the wall*   c Gk: Heb lacks *two cubits wide*
d Gk: Heb *length*   e Cn: Heb *vestibule. And the side chambers of the temple and the canopies*   f Gk: Heb *door*   g Gk: Heb *before the length*   h Heb lacks *the chambers rose*   i Meaning of Heb uncertain
j Gk Syr: Heb *a way of one cubit*   k Heb *their*
l Gk: Heb lacks *outer*   m Heb lacks *of the passage*
n Gk: Heb *east*   o Heb *and all their exits*

out of it into the outer court without laying there the vestments in which they minister, for these are holy; they shall put on other garments before they go near to the area open to the people."

42.1–14: Chambers are built in three stories along the walls that define the outer and inner courts. The priests use them to store and eat *the grain offering* (Lev 2.1–16), *the sin offering* (Lev 4.1–5.13), and *the guilt offering* (Lev 5.14–6.7). The priests must leave their holy vestments in these chambers before entering the outer court.

---

15 When he had finished measuring the interior of the temple area, he led me out by the gate that faces east, and measured the temple area all around. [16]He measured the east side with the measuring reed, five hundred cubits by the measuring reed. [17]Then he turned and measured[a] the north side, five hundred cubits by the measuring reed. [18]Then he turned and measured[a] the south side, five hundred cubits by the measuring reed. [19]Then he turned to the west side and measured, five hundred cubits by the measuring reed. [20]He measured it on the four sides. It had a wall around it, five hundred cubits long and five hundred cubits wide, to make a separation between the holy and the common.

42.15–20: The Temple complex is a 500-cubit square (861.63 feet). The outer wall marks the separation between the holy Temple and the profane world.

---

43 Then he brought me to the gate, the gate facing east. [2]And there, the glory of the God of Israel was coming from the east; the sound was like the sound of mighty waters; and the earth shone with his glory. [3]The[b] vision I saw was like the vision that I had seen when he came to destroy the city, and[c] like the vision that I had seen by the river Chebar; and I fell upon my face. [4]As the glory of the LORD entered the temple by the gate facing east, [5]the spirit lifted me up, and brought me into the inner court; and the glory of the LORD filled the temple.

6 While the man was standing beside me, I heard someone speaking to me out of the temple. [7]He said to me: Mortal, this is the place of my throne and the place for the soles of my feet, where I will reside among the people of Israel forever. The house of Israel shall no more defile my holy name, neither they nor their kings, by their whoring, and by the corpses of their kings at their death.[d] [8]When they placed their threshold by my threshold and their doorposts beside my doorposts, with only a wall between me and them, they were defiling my holy name by their abominations that they committed; therefore I have consumed them in my anger. [9]Now let them put away their idolatry and the corpses of their kings far from me, and I will reside among them forever.

10 As for you, mortal, describe the temple to the house of Israel, and let them measure the pattern; and let them be ashamed of their iniquities. [11]When they are ashamed of all that they have done, make known to them the plan of the temple, its arrangement, its exits and its entrances, and its whole form—all its ordinances and its entire plan and all its laws; and write it down in their sight, so that they may observe and follow the entire plan and all its ordinances. [12]This is the law of the temple: the whole territory on the top of the mountain all around shall be most holy. This is the law of the temple.

43.1–12: The Divine Presence (chs. 1; 8–11) returns to the Temple complex through the east gate from which it had earlier departed (10.19). Ezekiel recalls his inaugural vision and reports that he is transported to the inner court where he sees *the glory of the LORD* filling the Temple (Ex 40.34–35; 1 Kings 8.10–13). God informs him that this will be *the place of my throne* (see 1 Chr 28.2; Ps 132.7; Isa 60.13; Lam 2.1). *The corpses of their kings* refers to burials of kings near the Temple (1 Kings 2.10; 11.43; 2 Kings 21.18, 26). God instructs Ezekiel to teach the people the plan for the Temple. *This is the law of the temple:* Law (Hebrew "torah") is more properly translated "instruction"; the statement summarizes God's instructions concerning the Temple.

---

a Gk: Heb *measuring reed all around. He measured*
b Gk: Heb *Like the vision*   c Syr: Heb *and the visions*
d Or *on their high places*

The Temple complex and its activities

43.13–47.12: Instructions concerning structures associated with the Temple and regulations concerning Temple rituals and practice.

13 These are the dimensions of the altar by cubits (the cubit being one cubit and a handbreadth): its base shall be one cubit high,ᵃ and one cubit wide, with a rim of one span around its edge. This shall be the height of the altar: ¹⁴From the base on the ground to the lower ledge, two cubits, with a width of one cubit; and from the smaller ledge to the larger ledge, four cubits, with a width of one cubit; ¹⁵and the altar hearth, four cubits; and from the altar hearth projecting upward, four horns. ¹⁶The altar hearth shall be square, twelve cubits long by twelve wide. ¹⁷The ledge also shall be square, fourteen cubits long by fourteen wide, with a rim around it half a cubit wide, and its surrounding base, one cubit. Its steps shall face east.

18 Then he said to me: Mortal, thus says the Lord GOD: These are the ordinances for the altar: On the day when it is erected for offering burnt offerings upon it and for dashing blood against it, ¹⁹you shall give to the levitical priests of the family of Zadok, who draw near to me to minister to me, says the Lord GOD, a bull for a sin offering. ²⁰And you shall take some of its blood, and put it on the four horns of the altar, and on the four corners of the ledge, and upon the rim all around; thus you shall purify it and make atonement for it. ²¹You shall also take the bull of the sin offering, and it shall be burnt in the appointed place belonging to the temple, outside the sacred area.

22 On the second day you shall offer a male goat without blemish for a sin offering; and the altar shall be purified, as it was purified with the bull. ²³When you have finished purifying it, you shall offer a bull without blemish and a ram from the flock without blemish. ²⁴You shall present them before the LORD, and the priests shall throw salt on them and offer them up as a burnt offering to the LORD. ²⁵For seven days you shall provide daily a goat for a sin offering; also a bull and a ram from the flock, without

blemish, shall be provided. ²⁶Seven days shall they make atonement for the altar and cleanse it, and so consecrate it. ²⁷When these days are over, then from the eighth day onward the priests shall offer upon the altar your burnt offerings and your offerings of well-being; and I will accept you, says the Lord GOD.

43.13–27: The altar is a four-level stepped structure, like a Mesopotamian ziggurat (a type of pyramid). The *base,* literally "bosom of the earth" (signifying the placement of the altar at the center of the earth), is 18 cubits square. The *lower ledge* is 16 cubits square. The upper ledge is 14 cubits square. The *altar hearth* ("ha-harʾel" in Hebrew, "mountain of God" or "God appeared"; compare Ariel of Isa 29.1) has *four horns* (see Ex 27.2; 29.12; 1 Kings 1.50–51; Zech 2.1–4). The height of the structure is 10 cubits. Its steps face toward the east gate. The seven-day consecration of the altar is performed at Sukkot (Booths; 1 Kings 8.65–66; Ezra 3.1–7; but compare Num 7) and is analogous to the ordination⋆ of priests (Ex 29.1–37; Lev 8). The purification of the altar with blood is analogous to the sprinkling of blood on the priests at their ordination (Ex 29.16), on the altar at Yom Kippur to make atonement⋆ for the people (Lev 16.18–19), and on the people to seal the covenant⋆ (Ex 24.1–8). *Salt* is also offered with grain offerings (Lev 2.13; Num 18.19).

44 Then he brought me back to the outer gate of the sanctuary, which faces east; and it was shut. ²The LORD said to me: This gate shall remain shut; it shall not be opened, and no one shall enter by it; for the LORD, the God of Israel, has entered by it; therefore it shall remain shut. ³Only the prince, because he is a prince, may sit in it to eat food before the LORD; he shall enter by way of the vestibule of the gate, and shall go out by the same way.

4 Then he brought me by way of the north gate to the front of the temple; and I looked, and lo! the glory of the LORD filled the temple of the LORD; and I fell upon my face. ⁵The LORD said to me: Mortal, mark well, look closely, and listen attentively to all that I shall tell you concerning all the ordinances

ᵃ Gk: Heb lacks *high*

of the temple of the LORD and all its laws; and mark well those who may be admitted to[a] the temple and all those who are to be excluded from the sanctuary. 6Say to the rebellious house,[b] to the house of Israel, Thus says the Lord GOD: O house of Israel, let there be an end to all your abominations 7in admitting foreigners, uncircumcised in heart and flesh, to be in my sanctuary, profaning my temple when you offer to me my food, the fat and the blood. You[c] have broken my covenant with all your abominations. 8And you have not kept charge of my sacred offerings; but you have appointed foreigners[d] to act for you in keeping my charge in my sanctuary.

9 Thus says the Lord GOD: No foreigner, uncircumcised in heart and flesh, of all the foreigners who are among the people of Israel, shall enter my sanctuary. 10But the Levites who went far from me, going astray from me after their idols when Israel went astray, shall bear their punishment. 11They shall be ministers in my sanctuary, having oversight at the gates of the temple, and serving in the temple; they shall slaughter the burnt offering and the sacrifice for the people, and they shall attend on them and serve them. 12Because they ministered to them before their idols and made the house of Israel stumble into iniquity, therefore I have sworn concerning them, says the Lord GOD, that they shall bear their punishment. 13They shall not come near to me, to serve me as priest, nor come near any of my sacred offerings, the things that are most sacred; but they shall bear their shame, and the consequences of the abominations that they have committed. 14Yet I will appoint them to keep charge of the temple, to do all its chores, all that is to be done in it.

44.1–46.24: Regulations concerning the Temple. 44.1–3: The east gate remains closed because God enters the Temple through the east gate. The king eats here. **4–14:** Those who have engaged in idolatry* or abominations are to be excluded from the Temple. Foreigners shall not enter (Lev 22.25; compare Isa 56.3–8). Deuteronomy 18.6–8 allows Levites to serve at the altar, but they are disenfranchised here for idolatrous behavior and allowed to perform only secondary service. The passage may presuppose the judgment leveled against the house of Eli (1 Sam 2) or inappropriate Levitical service at the high places* mentioned throughout 1–2 Kings.

15 But the levitical priests, the descendants of Zadok, who kept the charge of my sanctuary when the people of Israel went astray from me, shall come near to me to minister to me; and they shall attend me to offer me the fat and the blood, says the Lord GOD. 16It is they who shall enter my sanctuary, it is they who shall approach my table, to minister to me, and they shall keep my charge. 17When they enter the gates of the inner court, they shall wear linen vestments; they shall have nothing of wool on them, while they minister at the gates of the inner court, and within. 18They shall have linen turbans on their heads, and linen undergarments on their loins; they shall not bind themselves with anything that causes sweat. 19When they go out into the outer court to the people, they shall remove the vestments in which they have been ministering, and lay them in the holy chambers; and they shall put on other garments, so that they may not communicate holiness to the people with their vestments. 20They shall not shave their heads or let their locks grow long; they shall only trim the hair of their heads. 21No priest shall drink wine when he enters the inner court. 22They shall not marry a widow, or a divorced woman, but only a virgin of the stock of the house of Israel, or a widow who is the widow of a priest. 23They shall teach my people the difference between the holy and the common, and show them how to distinguish between the unclean and the clean. 24In a controversy they shall act as judges, and they shall decide it according to my judgments. They shall keep my laws and my statutes regarding all my appointed festivals, and they shall keep my sabbaths holy. 25They shall not defile themselves by going near to a dead person; for father or mother, however, and for son or daughter, and for brother or unmarried sister they may defile them-

a Cn: Heb *the entrance of*   b Gk: Heb lacks *house*
c Gk Syr Vg: Heb *They*   d Heb lacks *foreigners*

selves. 26After he has become clean, they shall count seven days for him. 27On the day that he goes into the holy place, into the inner court, to minister in the holy place, he shall offer his sin offering, says the Lord God.

28 This shall be their inheritance: I am their inheritance; and you shall give them no holding in Israel; I am their holding. 29They shall eat the grain offering, the sin offering, and the guilt offering; and every devoted thing in Israel shall be theirs. 30The first of all the first fruits of all kinds, and every offering of all kinds from all your offerings, shall belong to the priests; you shall also give to the priests the first of your dough, in order that a blessing may rest on your house. 31The priests shall not eat of anything, whether bird or animal, that died of itself or was torn by animals.

44.15–31: The Levites of the Zadokite line (1 Kings 2.26–27) shall enter the sanctuary and serve at the altar. They shall wear only linen (Ex 28.39); they shall not wear holy garments outside of the inner court (42.14); they shall trim their hair, but not shave it (Lev 21.5); they shall not drink wine in the inner court (Lev 10.9); they shall marry only virgins or the widows of other priests (Lev 21.7, 13–14); they shall instruct the people concerning holiness and purity (Lev 10.10–11; Deut 33.8–10; Hag 2.10–13); they shall act as judges (Ex 22.9; Deut 17.8–9; 19.17; 21.1–5); they shall observe the festivals (Lev 23; Num 28–29; Deut 16); they shall avoid contact with the dead and mourning, except for parents and siblings (Lev 21.1–3; Num 19); they shall receive no inheritance other than a share of the first fruits and offerings at the Temple (Num 18; Lev 27.28–29); and they shall not eat meat that was not properly slaughtered (Lev 22.8).

45 When you allot the land as an inheritance, you shall set aside for the Lord a portion of the land as a holy district, twenty-five thousand cubits long and twenty*a* thousand cubits wide; it shall be holy throughout its entire extent. 2Of this, a square plot of five hundred by five hundred cubits shall be for the sanctuary, with fifty cubits for an open space around it. 3In the holy district you shall measure off a section twenty-five thousand cubits long and ten thousand wide, in which shall be the sanctuary, the most holy place. 4It shall be a holy portion of the land; it shall be for the priests, who minister in the sanctuary and approach the Lord to minister to him; and it shall be both a place for their houses and a holy place for the sanctuary. 5Another section, twenty-five thousand cubits long and ten thousand cubits wide, shall be for the Levites who minister at the temple, as their holding for cities to live in.*b*

6 Alongside the portion set apart as the holy district you shall assign as a holding for the city an area five thousand cubits wide, and twenty-five thousand cubits long; it shall belong to the whole house of Israel.

7 And to the prince shall belong the land on both sides of the holy district and the holding of the city, alongside the holy district and the holding of the city, on the west and on the east, corresponding in length to one of the tribal portions, and extending from the western to the eastern boundary 8of the land. It is to be his property in Israel. And my princes shall no longer oppress my people; but they shall let the house of Israel have the land according to their tribes.

9 Thus says the Lord God: Enough, O princes of Israel! Put away violence and oppression, and do what is just and right. Cease your evictions of my people, says the Lord God.

10 You shall have honest balances, an honest ephah, and an honest bath.*c* 11The ephah and the bath shall be of the same measure, the bath containing one-tenth of a homer, and the ephah one-tenth of a homer; the homer shall be the standard measure. 12The shekel shall be twenty gerahs. Twenty shekels, twenty-five shekels, and fifteen shekels shall make a mina for you.

45.1–12. 1–9: The size and distribution of the *holy district* in the land for the use of the priests, the Levites, Israel, and the prince. According to the Hebrew text of v. 1 ("ten thousand cubits wide"), the combined land area is a 25,000-cubit square. The priestly portion includes the area for the sanctuary. The Levites' por-

a Gk: Heb *ten*   *b* Gk: Heb *as their holding, twenty chambers*   *c* A Heb measure of volume

tion equals that of the priests, but the portion for the rest of Israel is half of that. The portion of the *prince* is not included in the *holy district* or *city;* he may not evict Israel. **10–12:** Holiness in the Temple requires just, standardized measures (Lev 19.35–36; Deut 25.13–16; compare Am 8.5; Mic 6.10–11; Prov 11.1; 20.10). The *homer* equals 6.524 bushels; the *ephah* is a dry measure that equals 20.878 quarts; the *bath* is a liquid measure that equals 6.073 gallons; the *shekel*★ is a measure of weight equivalent to 176.29 grains; 50 *shekels* constitute a *mina* equivalent to 20.148 ounces.

13 This is the offering that you shall make: one-sixth of an ephah from each homer of wheat, and one-sixth of an ephah from each homer of barley, ¹⁴and as the fixed portion of oil,ᵃ one-tenth of a bath from each cor (the cor,ᵇ like the homer, contains ten baths); ¹⁵and one sheep from every flock of two hundred, from the pastures of Israel. This is the offering for grain offerings, burnt offerings, and offerings of well-being, to make atonement for them, says the Lord GOD. ¹⁶All the people of the land shall join with the prince in Israel in making this offering. ¹⁷But this shall be the obligation of the prince regarding the burnt offerings, grain offerings, and drink offerings, at the festivals, the new moons, and the sabbaths, all the appointed festivals of the house of Israel: he shall provide the sin offerings, grain offerings, the burnt offerings, and the offerings of well-being, to make atonement for the house of Israel.

18 Thus says the Lord GOD: In the first month, on the first day of the month, you shall take a young bull without blemish, and purify the sanctuary. ¹⁹The priest shall take some of the blood of the sin offering and put it on the doorposts of the temple, the four corners of the ledge of the altar, and the posts of the gate of the inner court. ²⁰You shall do the same on the seventh day of the month for anyone who has sinned through error or ignorance; so you shall make atonement for the temple.

21 In the first month, on the fourteenth day of the month, you shall celebrate the festival of the passover, and for seven days unleavened bread shall be eaten. ²²On that day the prince shall provide for himself and all the people of the land a young bull for a sin offering. ²³And during the seven days of the festival he shall provide as a burnt offering to the LORD seven young bulls and seven rams without blemish, on each of the seven days; and a male goat daily for a sin offering. ²⁴He shall provide as a grain offering an ephah for each bull, an ephah for each ram, and a hin of oil to each ephah. ²⁵In the seventh month, on the fifteenth day of the month and for the seven days of the festival, he shall make the same provision for sin offerings, burnt offerings, and grain offerings, and for the oil.

46 Thus says the Lord GOD: The gate of the inner court that faces east shall remain closed on the six working days; but on the sabbath day it shall be opened and on the day of the new moon it shall be opened. ²The prince shall enter by the vestibule of the gate from outside, and shall take his stand by the post of the gate. The priests shall offer his burnt offering and his offer-

ᵃ Cn: Heb *oil, the bath the oil*   ᵇ Vg: Heb *homer*

ings of well-being, and he shall bow down at the threshold of the gate. Then he shall go out, but the gate shall not be closed until evening. 3The people of the land shall bow down at the entrance of that gate before the LORD on the sabbaths and on the new moons. 4The burnt offering that the prince offers to the LORD on the sabbath day shall be six lambs without blemish and a ram without blemish; 5and the grain offering with the ram shall be an ephah, and the grain offering with the lambs shall be as much as he wishes to give, together with a hin of oil to each ephah. 6On the day of the new moon he shall offer a young bull without blemish, and six lambs and a ram, which shall be without blemish; 7as a grain offering he shall provide an ephah with the bull and an ephah with the ram, and with the lambs as much as he wishes, together with a hin of oil to each ephah. 8When the prince enters, he shall come in by the vestibule of the gate, and he shall go out by the same way.

9 When the people of the land come before the LORD at the appointed festivals, whoever enters by the north gate to worship shall go out by the south gate; and whoever enters by the south gate shall go out by the north gate: they shall not return by way of the gate by which they entered, but shall go out straight ahead. 10When they come in, the prince shall come in with them; and when they go out, he shall go out.

46.1–18: Regulations concerning offerings and property for the prince and the people. 1–8: The east gate is opened on sabbaths and new moons so that the prince may enter to present his offerings. The prince *shall take his stand by the post of the gate* (see 2 Kings 11.14) and bow down at the *threshold of the gate.* The people bow down at the same gate entrance. See Num 28.9–15 for sabbath and new moon sacrifices. **9–10:** The people enter by the north and south gates, but exit by the opposite gates for efficient crowd management. *Appointed festivals* in v. 9 should read "appointed times."

11 At the festivals and the appointed seasons the grain offering with a young bull shall be an ephah, and with a ram an ephah, and with the lambs as much as one wishes

to give, together with a hin of oil to an ephah. 12When the prince provides a freewill offering, either a burnt offering or offerings of well-being as a freewill offering to the LORD, the gate facing east shall be opened for him; and he shall offer his burnt offering or his offerings of well-being as he does on the sabbath day. Then he shall go out, and after he has gone out the gate shall be closed.

13 He shall provide a lamb, a yearling, without blemish, for a burnt offering to the LORD daily; morning by morning he shall provide it. 14And he shall provide a grain offering with it morning by morning regularly, one-sixth of an ephah, and one-third of a hin of oil to moisten the choice flour, as a grain offering to the LORD; this is the ordinance for all time. 15Thus the lamb and the grain offering and the oil shall be provided, morning by morning, as a regular burnt offering.

16 Thus says the Lord GOD: If the prince makes a gift to any of his sons out of his inheritance,[a] it shall belong to his sons, it is their holding by inheritance. 17But if he makes a gift out of his inheritance to one of his servants, it shall be his to the year of liberty; then it shall revert to the prince; only his sons may keep a gift from his inheritance. 18The prince shall not take any of the inheritance of the people, thrusting them out of their holding; he shall give his sons their inheritance out of his own holding, so that none of my people shall be dispossessed of their holding.

46.11–18. 11–15: The freewill and *daily* offerings of the prince are specified (Lev 22.18–23, vow or freewill offering; Num 28.3–8, daily offering). **16–18:** The prince may pass property on to his sons, but property passed to servants reverts to the prince at the jubilee year (Lev 25.8–17). The prince may not pass property of the people to his own sons.

19 Then he brought me through the entrance, which was at the side of the gate, to the north row of the holy chambers for the priests; and there I saw a place at the extreme western end of them. 20He said to me, "This is the place where the priests shall boil

a Gk: Heb *it is his inheritance*

the guilt offering and the sin offering, and where they shall bake the grain offering, in order not to bring them out into the outer court and so communicate holiness to the people."

21 Then he brought me out to the outer court, and led me past the four corners of the court; and in each corner of the court there was a court— 22in the four corners of the court were small[a] courts, forty cubits long and thirty wide; the four were of the same size. 23On the inside, around each of the four courts[b] was a row of masonry, with hearths made at the bottom of the rows all around. 24Then he said to me, "These are the kitchens where those who serve at the temple shall boil the sacrifices of the people."

46.19–24: Areas for the preparation of sacrifices for consumption by the priests are located in the northwestern area of the inner court. Kitchens for the people are located at the four corners of the outer court.

4 7 Then he brought me back to the entrance of the temple; there, water was flowing from below the threshold of the temple toward the east (for the temple faced east); and the water was flowing down from below the south end of the threshold of the temple, south of the altar. 2Then he brought me out by way of the north gate, and led me around on the outside to the outer gate that faces toward the east;[c] and the water was coming out on the south side.

3 Going on eastward with a cord in his hand, the man measured one thousand cubits, and then led me through the water; and it was ankle-deep. 4Again he measured one thousand, and led me through the water; and it was knee-deep. Again he measured one thousand, and led me through the water; and it was up to the waist. 5Again he measured one thousand, and it was a river that I could not cross, for the water had risen; it was deep enough to swim in, a river that could not be crossed. 6He said to me, "Mortal, have you seen this?"

Then he led me back along the bank of the river. 7As I came back, I saw on the bank of the river a great many trees on the one side and on the other. 8He said to me, "This water flows toward the eastern region and goes down into the Arabah; and when it enters the sea, the sea of stagnant waters, the water will become fresh. 9Wherever the river goes,[d] every living creature that swarms will live, and there will be very many fish, once these waters reach there. It will become fresh; and everything will live where the river goes. 10People will stand fishing beside the sea[e] from En-gedi to En-eglaim; it will be a place for the spreading of nets; its fish will be of a great many kinds, like the fish of the Great Sea. 11But its swamps and marshes will not become fresh; they are to be left for salt. 12On the banks, on both sides of the river, there will grow all kinds of trees for food. Their leaves will not wither nor their fruit fail, but they will bear fresh fruit every month, because the water for them flows from the sanctuary. Their fruit will be for food, and their leaves for healing."

47.1–12: Once the Temple is reestablished, water streams up from *below the threshold of the temple to the east* to water the land of Israel. This indicates the role of the Temple as the center of creation (the Garden of Eden, Gen 2.10–14; Ps 46.4). The course of the water reflects that of the Gihon spring (compare the Edenic river, Gen 2.10, 13), and emerges east of the city of David where its waters flow south into the Siloam pool (see 1 Kings 1.32–40; Isa 7.3; 2 Chr 32.4). The water flows into the Jordan Valley and eventually into the *Arabah* (the Jordan rift where the Dead Sea is located) to transform the waters of the Dead Sea into fresh water that supports fish and fruit trees (see Gen 2.1–14).

The reestablishment of the land and people of Israel
47.13–48.35: The reconstruction of the Temple and the resulting renewal of creation provide the basis for the reestablishment of the land and people of Israel.

13 Thus says the Lord GOD: These are the boundaries by which you shall divide the

a Gk Syr Vg: Meaning of Heb uncertain   b Heb *the four of them*   c Meaning of Heb uncertain   d Gk Syr Vg Tg: Heb *the two rivers go*   e Heb *it*

land for inheritance among the twelve tribes of Israel. Joseph shall have two portions. [14]You shall divide it equally; I swore to give it to your ancestors, and this land shall fall to you as your inheritance.

15 This shall be the boundary of the land: On the north side, from the Great Sea by way of Hethlon to Lebo-hamath, and on to Zedad,[a] [16]Berothah, Sibraim (which lies between the border of Damascus and the border of Hamath), as far as Hazer-hatticon, which is on the border of Hauran. [17]So the boundary shall run from the sea to Hazarenon, which is north of the border of Damascus, with the border of Hamath to the north.[b] This shall be the north side.

18 On the east side, between Hauran and Damascus; along the Jordan between Gilead and the land of Israel; to the eastern sea and as far as Tamar.[c] This shall be the east side.

19 On the south side, it shall run from Tamar as far as the waters of Meribathkadesh, from there along the Wadi of Egypt[d] to the Great Sea. This shall be the south side.

20 On the west side, the Great Sea shall be the boundary to a point opposite Lebohamath. This shall be the west side.

21 So you shall divide this land among you according to the tribes of Israel. [22]You shall allot it as an inheritance for yourselves and for the aliens who reside among you and have begotten children among you. They shall be to you as citizens of Israel; with you they shall be allotted an inheritance among the tribes of Israel. [23]In whatever tribe aliens reside, there you shall assign them their inheritance, says the Lord GOD.

47.13–23: The boundaries of the land are an idealized portrayal of the greatest extent of the Davidic kingdom and that of Jeroboam II (2 Sam 8.5–12; 2 Kings 14.25; compare Num 34). The northern border runs from the Mediterranean east to *Hazar-enon*, between Hamath (modern Hama) to the north and Damascus to the south (Num 34.7–9); the eastern border runs south through the Jordan Valley to *Tamar* just south of the Dead Sea (Num 34.10–12); the southern border runs through the Negeb to the *Wadi** of Egypt (modern *Wadi el-Arish* in the northeastern Sinai peninsula; see Num 34.3–5); the western border runs along the Mediterranean coast (Num 34.6). *The aliens who reside among you* (Hebrew "gerim," or "sojourners," later considered converts in post-biblical Hebrew) live according to the same laws as Israelites (Lev 19.34; Num 15.29).

〜〜〜〜〜〜〜

48 These are the names of the tribes: Beginning at the northern border, on the Hethlon road,[e] from Lebo-hamath, as far as Hazar-enon (which is on the border of Damascus, with Hamath to the north), and[f] extending from the east side to the west,[g] Dan, one portion. [2]Adjoining the territory of Dan, from the east side to the west, Asher, one portion. [3]Adjoining the territory of Asher, from the east side to the west, Naphtali, one portion. [4]Adjoining the territory of Naphtali, from the east side to the west, Manasseh, one portion. [5]Adjoining the territory of Manasseh, from the east side to the west, Ephraim, one portion. [6]Adjoining the territory of Ephraim, from the east side to the west, Reuben, one portion. [7]Adjoining the territory of Reuben, from the east side to the west, Judah, one portion.

8 Adjoining the territory of Judah, from the east side to the west, shall be the portion that you shall set apart, twenty-five thousand cubits in width, and in length equal to one of the tribal portions, from the east side to the west, with the sanctuary in the middle of it. [9]The portion that you shall set apart for the LORD shall be twenty-five thousand cubits in length, and twenty[h] thousand in width. [10]These shall be the allotments of the holy portion: the priests shall have an allotment measuring twenty-five thousand cubits on the northern side, ten thousand cubits in width on the western side, ten thousand in width on the eastern side, and twenty-five thousand in length on the southern side, with the sanctuary of the LORD in the middle of it. [11]This shall be for the consecrated priests, the descendants[i] of Zadok, who kept my charge, who did not go astray when the

a Gk: Heb *Lebo-zedad*, [16]Hamath   b Meaning of Heb uncertain   c Compare Syr: Heb *you shall measure* d Heb lacks *of Egypt*   e Compare 47.15: Heb *by the side of the way*   f Cn: Heb *and they shall be his* g Gk Compare verses 2–8: Heb *the east side the west* h Compare 45.1: Heb *ten*   i One Ms Gk: Heb *of the descendants*

people of Israel went astray, as the Levites did. 12It shall belong to them as a special portion from the holy portion of the land, a most holy place, adjoining the territory of the Levites. 13Alongside the territory of the priests, the Levites shall have an allotment twenty-five thousand cubits in length and ten thousand in width. The whole length shall be twenty-five thousand cubits and the width twenty*a* thousand. 14They shall not sell or exchange any of it; they shall not transfer this choice portion of the land, for it is holy to the LORD.

15 The remainder, five thousand cubits in width and twenty-five thousand in length, shall be for ordinary use for the city, for dwellings and for open country. In the middle of it shall be the city; 16and these shall be its dimensions: the north side four thousand five hundred cubits, the south side four thousand five hundred, the east side four thousand five hundred, and the west side four thousand five hundred. 17The city shall have open land: on the north two hundred fifty cubits, on the south two hundred fifty, on the east two hundred fifty, on the west two hundred fifty. 18The remainder of the length alongside the holy portion shall be ten thousand cubits to the east, and ten thousand to the west, and it shall be alongside the holy portion. Its produce shall be food for the workers of the city. 19The workers of the city, from all the tribes of Israel, shall cultivate it. 20The whole portion that you shall set apart shall be twenty-five thousand cubits square, that is, the holy portion together with the property of the city.

21 What remains on both sides of the holy portion and of the property of the city shall belong to the prince. Extending from the twenty-five thousand cubits of the holy portion to the east border, and westward from the twenty-five thousand cubits to the west border, parallel to the tribal portions, it shall belong to the prince. The holy portion with the sanctuary of the temple in the middle of it, 22and the property of the Levites and of the city, shall be in the middle of that which belongs to the prince. The portion of the prince shall lie between the territory of Judah and the territory of Benjamin.

48.1–35: The tribes are assigned equal portions of land arrayed along the length of the land from north to south. **1–7:** The northern tribes are listed from north to south as Dan, Asher, Naphtali, Manasseh, Ephraim, Reuben, Judah. **8–22:** The "holy district," or levitical allotment (45.1–9), is defined in detail. The priests are placed in the north, and the sanctuary is assigned to their portion; the Levites are placed to the south of the priests; and the portion reserved for Israel, which contains *the city* (Jerusalem), is placed to the south of the Levites. The portion allotted to the *prince* is on either side of the "holy district."

23 As for the rest of the tribes: from the east side to the west, Benjamin, one portion. 24Adjoining the territory of Benjamin, from the east side to the west, Simeon, one portion. 25Adjoining the territory of Simeon, from the east side to the west, Issachar, one portion. 26Adjoining the territory of Issachar, from the east side to the west, Zebulun, one portion. 27Adjoining the territory of Zebulun, from the east side to the west, Gad, one portion. 28And adjoining the territory of Gad to the south, the boundary shall run from Tamar to the waters of Meribathkadesh, from there along the Wadi of Egypt*b* to the Great Sea. 29This is the land that you shall allot as an inheritance among the tribes of Israel, and these are their portions, says the Lord GOD.

30 These shall be the exits of the city: On the north side, which is to be four thousand five hundred cubits by measure, 31three gates, the gate of Reuben, the gate of Judah, and the gate of Levi, the gates of the city being named after the tribes of Israel. 32On the east side, which is to be four thousand five hundred cubits, three gates, the gate of Joseph, the gate of Benjamin, and the gate of Dan. 33On the south side, which is to be four thousand five hundred cubits by measure, three gates, the gate of Simeon, the gate of Issachar, and the gate of Zebulun. 34On the west side, which is to be four thousand five hundred cubits, three gates,*c* the gate of Gad, the gate of Asher, and the gate of Naphtali. 35The circumference of the city

a Gk: Heb *ten*   *b* Heb lacks *of Egypt*   *c* One Ms Gk Syr: MT *their gates three*

shall be eighteen thousand cubits. And the name of the city from that time on shall be, The LORD is There.

48.23–35. 23–29: The southern tribes are listed from north to south as Benjamin, Simeon, Issachar, Zebulun, and Gad. **30–35:** There are three gates allotted to the tribes on each side of the square city. The northern gates include Reuben, Judah, and Levi; the eastern gates include Joseph, Benjamin, and Dan; the southern gates include Simeon, Issachar, and Zebulun; and the western gates include Gad, Asher, and Naphtali. The name of the city is *The LORD is There* ("yhwh shammah") to signify the return of God's presence (see Isa 60.14; Jer 30.11).

DANIEL

Introduction

Daniel, the only example of an apocalyptic* book in the Hebrew Bible, appears among the Kethubim* ("Writings") of the Tanakh,* the Jewish version of the Bible, and among the Prophetic Books of the Christian First or Old Testament. Apocalyptic books are generally pseudonymous* or anonymous compositions, such as 1 Enoch,* 2 Baruch, or Revelation, in which a heavenly mediator reveals the future to a human being by means of an other-worldly journey or a review of world history. Apocalyptic literature is generally narrative* in form and employs various other-worldly images or motifs,* such as cosmic war, astronomical calculation, angels, mythological beings, and representations of God or other divine figures. Through a series of visions and dreams that provide a sweeping overview of world history from the Babylonian exile to the Hellenistic* period, Daniel is shown the impending downfall of the Seleucid* Syrian tyrant Antiochus IV Epiphanes* (175–163 BCE) and the emergence of God's kingdom, an independent Jewish state centered around the Jerusalem Temple.*

Although Daniel is initially portrayed as a Jewish exile in the court of the Babylonian King Nebuchadnezzar, the book clearly was not written during the sixth century BCE. Daniel is not a historical figure in Judah from this period, but his image is drawn from that of the legendary* sage and ruler of Canaanite mythology, Dan-El, who saves his son Aqhat from death in the fourteenth-century BCE Ugaritic tablets. Apocalyptic literature frequently employs well-known figures from the past, such as Enoch, Moses, or Ezra. Dan-El was known in Judah as early as the sixth century BCE (Ezek 14.14; 28.3). The literary history of the book is complicated and not well understood. It is written in two languages, Hebrew (1.1–2.4a; 8.1–12.13) and Aramaic* (2.4b–7.28), although these two portions do not correspond to its present literary structure. The tales in chs. 1–6 appear to have been composed in wisdom circles during the fourth or third centuries BCE to address the difficulties that Jews faced when living in the Diaspora.* As indicated by the precise historical knowledge conveyed in Daniel's final vision (chs. 10–12), the full form of the book was composed between 167 BCE, when Antiochus IV desecrated the Temple in Jerusalem, and 164 BCE, when Judah the Maccabee and his warriors rededicated the Temple, thereby inaugurating the festival of Hanukkah. The book supports the Maccabean revolt by positing a succession of four world empires, including Babylonia, Media, Persia, and Greece-Macedonia (see Nebuchadnezzar's dream, ch. 2; and the vision of the four beasts, ch. 7). The succession culminates in the emergence of the Seleucid Syrian empire and the rule of Antiochus IV, who is represented by the "little [horn]" with "human eyes . . . and a mouth speaking arrogantly" in 7.8 and "a contemptible person on whom royal majesty had not been conferred" in 11.21. Following his demise in battle, the anticipated Maccabean victory is symbolized by the deliverance of Daniel's people and the bringing of the dead to life (11.40–12.4). In later periods, Daniel has been read as an apocalyptic vision of the end of time. The Greek versions of Daniel in the Septuagint* and Theodotion contain additional chapters within the body of the work or added at the beginning or end of the book. These additional chapters, which appear separately in the Apocrypha* of Protestant Bibles, include the Prayer of Azariah and the Song of the Three Young Jews; Susanna; and Bel and the Dragon.

READING GUIDE

The book of Daniel is made up of two major sections. Chs. 1–6 presents six tales of Daniel and his companions in the Diaspora. Daniel appears as the epitome of a wise man, completely faithful to God and observant of Jewish tradition even in Babylonian exile. His wisdom and piety enable him to understand the will of God, to interpret it correctly to those around him, and to deliver himself and his companions from various threats. The tales employ these motifs to demonstrate that God will support those who adhere to Jewish identity and practice even when living outside of the land of Israel. They thereby establish both God's and Daniel's credibility as the basis for the visions that follow. The four visions of chs. 7–12 convey the major thrust of the book, insofar as the surveys of world history and the chronological calculations are designed to demonstrate the coming downfall of Antiochus IV and the emergence of the kingdom of God as a preordained divine act revealed to Daniel centuries before.

TALES CONCERNING DANIEL IN EXILE

Chs. 1–6: The tales establish Daniel's credibility as a righteous Jew whose God-given wisdom enables him to overcome the challenges of exile and to point to God's redemption of Jews from foreign domination.

1 In the third year of the reign of King Jehoiakim of Judah, King Nebuchadnezzar of Babylon came to Jerusalem and besieged it. ²The Lord let King Jehoiakim of Judah fall into his power, as well as some of the vessels of the house of God. These he brought to the land of Shinar,ᵃ and placed the vessels in the treasury of his gods.

1.1–21: Four young Jews in the Babylonian court. This tale establishes the theme of adherence to Jewish identity and practice by pointing to the success, wisdom, and good health of four young Jewish men who decline the delicacies and wine of the Babylonian king in order to observe Jewish dietary laws. **1–2:** *The third year of the reign of King Jehoiakim* was 606 BCE. Nebuchadnezzar assumed the throne of Babylon in 605 BCE, after he defeated Egypt and brought Judah under his rule. He besieged Jerusalem in 597 BCE during the reign of Jehoiachin (2 Kings 24.1–16) and again in 587 BCE during the regency of Zedekiah (2 Kings 25.1–7). *Shinar:* the location of Babylon (Gen 10.10; 11.2; Zech 5.11).

3 Then the king commanded his palace master Ashpenaz to bring some of the Israelites of the royal family and of the nobility, ⁴young men without physical defect and handsome, versed in every branch of wisdom, endowed with knowledge and insight, and competent to serve in the king's palace; they were to be taught the literature and language of the Chaldeans. ⁵The king assigned them a daily portion of the royal rations of food and wine. They were to be educated for three years, so that at the end of that time they could be stationed in the king's court. ⁶Among them were Daniel, Hananiah, Mishael, and Azariah, from the tribe of Judah. ⁷The palace master gave them other names: Daniel he called Belteshazzar, Hananiah he called Shadrach, Mishael he called Meshach, and Azariah he called Abednego.

1.3–7: The Babylonians trained persons from subject nations to serve in their courts. *Palace master:* Literally, "chief eunuch." *Chaldeans:* Aramaic-speaking Neo-Babylonians, used in Daniel for wise men. Daniel and his companions were given Babylonian names.

8 But Daniel resolved that he would not defile himself with the royal rations of food and wine; so he asked the palace master to allow him not to defile himself. ⁹Now God allowed Daniel to receive favor and compassion from the palace master. ¹⁰The palace master said to Daniel, "I am afraid of my lord the king; he has appointed your food and your drink. If he should see you in poorer condition than the other young men of your

---

a Gk Theodotion: Heb adds *to the house of his own gods*

own age, you would endanger my head with the king." [11]Then Daniel asked the guard whom the palace master had appointed over Daniel, Hananiah, Mishael, and Azariah: [12]"Please test your servants for ten days. Let us be given vegetables to eat and water to drink. [13]You can then compare our appearance with the appearance of the young men who eat the royal rations, and deal with your servants according to what you observe." [14]So he agreed to this proposal and tested them for ten days. [15]At the end of ten days it was observed that they appeared better and fatter than all the young men who had been eating the royal rations. [16]So the guard continued to withdraw their royal rations and the wine they were to drink, and gave them vegetables. [17]To these four young men God gave knowledge and skill in every aspect of literature and wisdom; Daniel also had insight into all visions and dreams.

18 At the end of the time that the king had set for them to be brought in, the palace master brought them into the presence of Nebuchadnezzar, [19]and the king spoke with them. And among them all, no one was found to compare with Daniel, Hananiah, Mishael, and Azariah; therefore they were stationed in the king's court. [20]In every matter of wisdom and understanding concerning which the king inquired of them, he found them ten times better than all the magicians and enchanters in his whole kingdom. [21]And Daniel continued there until the first year of King Cyrus.

1.8–21. 8–17: The *royal rations of food and wine* are not kosher★ and therefore are unsuitable for Jews (Lev 11; Deut 14). Dream interpretation★ is a mark of wisdom (Gen 40–41).**18–21:** God grants *wisdom and understanding* to those who adhere to divine requirements. *The first year of King Cyrus* was 539 BCE.

2 In the second year of Nebuchadnezzar's reign, Nebuchadnezzar dreamed such dreams that his spirit was troubled and his sleep left him. [2]So the king commanded that the magicians, the enchanters, the sorcerers, and the Chaldeans be summoned to tell the king his dreams. When they came in and stood before the king, [3]he said to them, "I

have had such a dream that my spirit is troubled by the desire to understand it." [4]The Chaldeans said to the king (in Aramaic),[a] "O king, live forever! Tell your servants the dream, and we will reveal the interpretation." [5]The king answered the Chaldeans, "This is a public decree: if you do not tell me both the dream and its interpretation, you shall be torn limb from limb, and your houses shall be laid in ruins. [6]But if you do tell me the dream and its interpretation, you shall receive from me gifts and rewards and great honor. Therefore tell me the dream and its interpretation." [7]They answered a second time, "Let the king first tell his servants the dream, then we can give its interpretation." [8]The king answered, "I know with certainty that you are trying to gain time, because you see I have firmly decreed: [9]if you do not tell me the dream, there is but one verdict for you. You have agreed to speak lying and misleading words to me until things take a turn. Therefore, tell me the dream, and I shall know that you can give me its interpretation." [10]The Chaldeans answered the king, "There is no one on earth who can reveal what the king demands! In fact no king, however great and powerful, has ever asked such a thing of any magician or enchanter or Chaldean. [11]The thing that the king is asking is too difficult, and no one can reveal it to the king except the gods, whose dwelling is not with mortals."

12 Because of this the king flew into a violent rage and commanded that all the wise men of Babylon be destroyed. [13]The decree was issued, and the wise men were about to be executed; and they looked for Daniel and his companions, to execute them. [14]Then Daniel responded with prudence and discretion to Arioch, the king's chief executioner, who had gone out to execute the wise men of Babylon; [15]he asked Arioch, the royal official, "Why is the decree of the king so urgent?" Arioch then explained the matter to Daniel. [16]So Daniel went in and requested that the king give him

---

a The text from this point to the end of chapter 7 is in Aramaic

time and he would tell the king the interpretation.

2.1–49: Nebuchadnezzar's dream. This tale demonstrates God's superiority and Daniel's incomparable wisdom. **1–16:** Nebuchadnezzar's impossible demand prepares the reader for Daniel's role as a supremely competent interpreter in chs. 7–12. Dream and omen interpretation were widely practiced in Babylonia. **1:** *The second year of Nebuchadnezzar's reign* was 603 BCE. Daniel appears before his training is complete (1.1, 5). **4:** From 2.4b through 7.28 the text is written in Aramaic.* While Hebrew is a west Semitic language, Aramaic is an east Semitic language, originating in northern Aram (Syria), that was employed extensively throughout the Near East from the seventh or eighth century BCE until the emergence of Islam in the seventh century CE.

17 Then Daniel went to his home and informed his companions, Hananiah, Mishael, and Azariah, 18 and told them to seek mercy from the God of heaven concerning this mystery, so that Daniel and his companions with the rest of the wise men of Babylon might not perish. 19 Then the mystery was revealed to Daniel in a vision of the night, and Daniel blessed the God of heaven.

20 Daniel said:

"Blessed be the name of God from age
to age,
for wisdom and power are his.
21 He changes times and seasons,
deposes kings and sets up kings;
he gives wisdom to the wise
and knowledge to those who have
understanding.
22 He reveals deep and hidden things;
he knows what is in the darkness,
and light dwells with him.
23 To you, O God of my ancestors,
I give thanks and praise,
for you have given me wisdom
and power,
and have now revealed to me what we
asked of you,
for you have revealed to us what the
king ordered."

2.17–23: *A vision of the night:* Compare 1 Sam 3; 2 Sam 7.4. **18:** *The God of heaven:* A Persian title for

the Jewish deity (Ezra 1.2; 5.11; Neh 1.4; 2.4). **20–23:** A song of praise thanking God for the dream (compare Neh 9.5; Hab 3.4).

24 Therefore Daniel went to Arioch, whom the king had appointed to destroy the wise men of Babylon, and said to him, "Do not destroy the wise men of Babylon; bring me in before the king, and I will give the king the interpretation." 25 Then Arioch quickly brought Daniel before the king and said to him: "I have found among the exiles from Judah a man who can tell the king the interpretation." 26 The king said to Daniel, whose name was Belteshazzar, "Are you able to tell me the dream that I have seen and its interpretation?" 27 Daniel answered the king, "No wise men, enchanters, magicians, or diviners can show to the king the mystery that the king is asking, 28 but there is a God in heaven who reveals mysteries, and he has disclosed to King Nebuchadnezzar what will happen at the end of days. Your dream and the visions of your head as you lay in bed were these: 29 To you, O king, as you lay in bed, came thoughts of what would be hereafter, and the revealer of mysteries disclosed to you what is to be. 30 But as for me, this mystery has not been revealed to me because of any wisdom that I have more than any other living being, but in order that the interpretation may be known to the king and that you may understand the thoughts of your mind.

31 "You were looking, O king, and lo! there was a great statue. This statue was huge, its brilliance extraordinary; it was standing before you, and its appearance was frightening. 32 The head of that statue was of fine gold, its chest and arms of silver, its middle and thighs of bronze, 33 its legs of iron, its feet partly of iron and partly of clay. 34 As you looked on, a stone was cut out, not by human hands, and it struck the statue on its feet of iron and clay and broke them in pieces. 35 Then the iron, the clay, the bronze, the silver, and the gold, were all broken in pieces and became like the chaff of the summer threshing floors; and the wind carried them away, so that not a trace of them could be found. But the stone that struck the

statue became a great mountain and filled the whole earth.

36 "This was the dream; now we will tell the king its interpretation. 37You, O king, the king of kings—to whom the God of heaven has given the kingdom, the power, the might, and the glory, 38into whose hand he has given human beings, wherever they live, the wild animals of the field, and the birds of the air, and whom he has established as ruler over them all—you are the head of gold. 39After you shall arise another kingdom inferior to yours, and yet a third kingdom of bronze, which shall rule over the whole earth. 40And there shall be a fourth kingdom, strong as iron; just as iron crushes and smashes everything,*a* it shall crush and shatter all these. 41As you saw the feet and toes partly of potter's clay and partly of iron, it shall be a divided kingdom; but some of the strength of iron shall be in it, as you saw the iron mixed with the clay. 42As the toes of the feet were part iron and part clay, so the kingdom shall be partly strong and partly brittle. 43As you saw the iron mixed with clay, so will they mix with one another in marriage,*b* but they will not hold together, just as iron does not mix with clay. 44And in the days of those kings the God of heaven will set up a kingdom that shall never be destroyed, nor shall this kingdom be left to another people. It shall crush all these kingdoms and bring them to an end, and it shall stand forever; 45just as you saw that a stone was cut from the mountain not by hands, and that it crushed the iron, the bronze, the

clay, the silver, and the gold. The great God has informed the king what shall be hereafter. The dream is certain, and its interpretation trustworthy."

46 Then King Nebuchadnezzar fell on his face, worshiped Daniel, and commanded that a grain offering and incense be offered to him. 47The king said to Daniel, "Truly, your God is God of gods and Lord of kings and a revealer of mysteries, for you have been able to reveal this mystery!" 48Then the king promoted Daniel, gave him many great gifts, and made him ruler over the whole province of Babylon and chief prefect over all the wise men of Babylon. 49Daniel made a request of the king, and he appointed Shadrach, Meshach, and Abednego over the affairs of the province of Babylon. But Daniel remained at the king's court.

3 King Nebuchadnezzar made a golden statue whose height was sixty cubits and whose width was six cubits; he set it up on the plain of Dura in the province of Babylon. 2Then King Nebuchadnezzar sent for the satraps, the prefects, and the governors, the counselors, the treasurers, the justices, the magistrates, and all the officials of the provinces, to assemble and come to the dedication of the statue that King Nebuchadnezzar had set up. 3So the satraps, the prefects, and the governors, the counselors, the treasurers, the justices, the magistrates, and all the officials of the provinces, assembled for the dedication of the statue that King Nebuchadnezzar had set up. When they were standing before the statue that Nebuchadnezzar had set up, 4the herald proclaimed aloud, "You are commanded, O peoples, nations, and languages, 5that when you hear the sound of the horn, pipe, lyre, trigon,

a Gk Theodotion Syr Vg: Aram adds *and like iron that crushes*　　b Aram *by human seed*

harp, drum, and entire musical ensemble, you are to fall down and worship the golden statue that King Nebuchadnezzar has set up. ⁶Whoever does not fall down and worship shall immediately be thrown into a furnace of blazing fire." ⁷Therefore, as soon as all the peoples heard the sound of the horn, pipe, lyre, trigon, harp, drum, and entire musical ensemble, all the peoples, nations, and languages fell down and worshiped the golden statue that King Nebuchadnezzar had set up.

8 Accordingly, at this time certain Chaldeans came forward and denounced the Jews. ⁹They said to King Nebuchadnezzar, "O king, live forever! ¹⁰You, O king, have made a decree, that everyone who hears the sound of the horn, pipe, lyre, trigon, harp, drum, and entire musical ensemble, shall fall down and worship the golden statue, ¹¹and whoever does not fall down and worship shall be thrown into a furnace of blazing fire. ¹²There are certain Jews whom you have appointed over the affairs of the province of Babylon: Shadrach, Meshach, and Abednego. These pay no heed to you, O king. They do not serve your gods and they do not worship the golden statue that you have set up."

13 Then Nebuchadnezzar in furious rage commanded that Shadrach, Meshach, and Abednego be brought in; so they brought those men before the king. ¹⁴Nebuchadnezzar said to them, "Is it true, O Shadrach, Meshach, and Abednego, that you do not serve my gods and you do not worship the golden statue that I have set up? ¹⁵Now if you are ready when you hear the sound of the horn, pipe, lyre, trigon, harp, drum, and entire musical ensemble to fall down and worship the statue that I have made, well and good.ᵃ But if you do not worship, you shall immediately be thrown into a furnace of blazing fire, and who is the god that will deliver you out of my hands?"

16 Shadrach, Meshach, and Abednego answered the king, "O Nebuchadnezzar, we have no need to present a defense to you in this matter. ¹⁷If our God whom we serve is able to deliver us from the furnace of blazing fire and out of your hand, O king, let him deliver us.ᵇ ¹⁸But if not, be it known to you,

O king, that we will not serve your gods and we will not worship the golden statue that you have set up."

3.1–30: The fiery furnace: The narrative* promotes adherence to Jewish identity and religion by demonstrating that God protects the righteous. **1–18:** Antiochus IV (175–163 BCE) erected a statue of Zeus in the Jerusalem Temple* and demanded that Jews worship Greek gods or be put to death (1 Macc 1.41–64; 2 Macc 6.1–11). His nickname, Epiphanes,* "manifest god," indicates that he expected worship as a god. Worship of national gods was generally understood as a sign of loyalty, but Jews are monotheistic and do not worship pagan gods. Charges of disloyalty prompted many anti-Jewish actions in the Greco-Roman and medieval periods and continue to underlie modern anti-Semitism.

19 Then Nebuchadnezzar was so filled with rage against Shadrach, Meshach, and Abednego that his face was distorted. He ordered the furnace heated up seven times more than was customary, ²⁰and ordered some of the strongest guards in his army to bind Shadrach, Meshach, and Abednego and to throw them into the furnace of blazing fire. ²¹So the men were bound, still wearing their tunics,ᶜ their trousers,ᶜ their hats, and their other garments, and they were thrown into the furnace of blazing fire. ²²Because the king's command was urgent and the furnace was so overheated, the raging flames killed the men who lifted Shadrach, Meshach, and Abednego. ²³But the three men, Shadrach, Meshach, and Abednego, fell down, bound, into the furnace of blazing fire.

24 Then King Nebuchadnezzar was astonished and rose up quickly. He said to his counselors, "Was it not three men that we threw bound into the fire?" They answered the king, "True, O king." ²⁵He replied, "But I see four men unbound, walking in the middle of the fire, and they are not hurt; and the fourth has the appearance of a

---

a Aram lacks *well and good*   *b* Or *If our God whom we serve is able to deliver us, he will deliver us from the furnace of blazing fire and out of your hand, O king.*
c Meaning of Aram word uncertain

god."*a* 26Nebuchadnezzar then approached the door of the furnace of blazing fire and said, "Shadrach, Meshach, and Abednego, servants of the Most High God, come out! Come here!" So Shadrach, Meshach, and Abednego came out from the fire. 27And the satraps, the prefects, the governors, and the king's counselors gathered together and saw that the fire had not had any power over the bodies of those men; the hair of their heads was not singed, their tunics*b* were not harmed, and not even the smell of fire came from them. 28Nebuchadnezzar said, "Blessed be the God of Shadrach, Meshach, and Abednego, who has sent his angel and delivered his servants who trusted in him. They disobeyed the king's command and yielded up their bodies rather than serve and worship any god except their own God. 29Therefore I make a decree: Any people, nation, or language that utters blasphemy against the God of Shadrach, Meshach, and Abednego shall be torn limb from limb, and their houses laid in ruins; for there is no other god who is able to deliver in this way." 30Then the king promoted Shadrach, Meshach, and Abednego in the province of Babylon.

3.19–30: The description of the fiery furnace is full of exaggeration, preparing the reader for the great miracle. **25:** The presence of a fourth man who *has the appearance of a god* (literally, *a son of the gods*) signifies divine intervention to save the young men (see v. 28). The pagan king acknowledges God's power and decrees destruction for nations that challenge God.

4*c* King Nebuchadnezzar to all peoples, nations, and languages that live throughout the earth: May you have abundant prosperity! 2The signs and wonders that the Most High God has worked for me I am pleased to recount.
3 How great are his signs,
    how mighty his wonders!
His kingdom is an everlasting kingdom,
    and his sovereignty is from generation
        to generation.

4.1–37: Nebuchadnezzar's madness. Using the form of an epistle or public proclamation, this chapter dem-

onstrates God's power over pagan rulers. **1–2:** A typical epistolary introduction. *All peoples, nations, and languages that live throughout the earth:* Mesopotamian rulers generally claimed rule over the entire world. The motif* prepares the reader to recognize God's universal sovereignty. **3:** Again, Nebuchadnezzar acknowledges God.

4*d* I, Nebuchadnezzar, was living at ease in my home and prospering in my palace. 5I saw a dream that frightened me; my fantasies in bed and the visions of my head terrified me. 6So I made a decree that all the wise men of Babylon should be brought before me, in order that they might tell me the interpretation of the dream. 7Then the magicians, the enchanters, the Chaldeans, and the diviners came in, and I told them the dream, but they could not tell me its interpretation. 8At last Daniel came in before me—he who was named Belteshazzar after the name of my god, and who is endowed with a spirit of the holy gods*e*—and I told him the dream: 9"O Belteshazzar, chief of the magicians, I know that you are endowed with a spirit of the holy gods*e* and that no mystery is too difficult for you. Hear*f* the dream that I saw; tell me its interpretation.
10*g* Upon my bed this is what I saw;
    there was a tree at the center of the
        earth,
    and its height was great.
11 The tree grew great and strong,
    its top reached to heaven,
    and it was visible to the ends of the
        whole earth.
12 Its foliage was beautiful,
    its fruit abundant,
    and it provided food for all.
The animals of the field found shade
        under it,
    the birds of the air nested in
        its branches,
    and from it all living beings
        were fed.

a Aram *a son of the gods* *b* Meaning of Aram word uncertain *c* Ch 3.31 in Aram *d* Ch 4.1 in Aram *e* Or *a holy, divine spirit* *f* Theodotion: Aram *The visions of* *g* Theodotion Syr Compare Gk: Aram adds *The visions of my head*

13 "I continued looking, in the visions of my head as I lay in bed, and there was a holy watcher, coming down from heaven. 14He cried aloud and said:

'Cut down the tree and chop off
     its branches,
     strip off its foliage and scatter its fruit.
Let the animals flee from beneath it
     and the birds from its branches.
15 But leave its stump and roots in the
     ground,
     with a band of iron and bronze,
     in the tender grass of the field.
Let him be bathed with the dew
     of heaven,
     and let his lot be with the animals of
          the field
     in the grass of the earth.
16 Let his mind be changed from that of a
     human,
     and let the mind of an animal be
          given to him.
     And let seven times pass over him.
17 The sentence is rendered by decree of
     the watchers,
     the decision is given by order of the
          holy ones,
     in order that all who live may know
          that the Most High is sovereign over
               the kingdom of mortals;
     he gives it to whom he will
          and sets over it the lowliest of human
               beings.'

18 "This is the dream that I, King Nebuchadnezzar, saw. Now you, Belteshazzar, declare the interpretation, since all the wise men of my kingdom are unable to tell me the interpretation. You are able, however, for you are endowed with a spirit of the holy gods."a

4.4–18: There are no extra-biblical accounts of Nebuchadnezzar's madness. The Babylonian king Nabonidus (556–539 BCE) lived in the Arabian desert while his son Belshazzar ruled in his stead. 8: Named Belteshazzar after the name of my god: Belteshazzar means "protect his life" and is styled to resemble the name Bel, a title for the Babylonian city god, Marduk. 10–17: The tree at the center of the earth: Ancient Near Eastern mythology frequently employs the image of a

cosmic tree (see Gen 2–3). See also Isa 10.5–34; Ezek 31, which portray Assyrian and Egyptian rulers as trees that will be cut down and sent to the netherworld. 13: Holy watcher: A celestial being (1 Enoch* 1.5; 20.1; Jubilees 4.15). 15: Stump and roots in the ground: See Isa 6.13; 11.1. 16: Let his mind be changed: The motif is derived from Nabonidus, but also presupposes Babylonian traditions of Enkidu, the primal man of the Gilgamesh* epic, who lived among the animals before he was civilized by a woman.

19 Then Daniel, who was called Belteshazzar, was severely distressed for a while. His thoughts terrified him. The king said, "Belteshazzar, do not let the dream or the interpretation terrify you." Belteshazzar answered, "My lord, may the dream be for those who hate you, and its interpretation for your enemies! 20The tree that you saw, which grew great and strong, so that its top reached to heaven and was visible to the end of the whole earth, 21whose foliage was beautiful and its fruit abundant, and which provided food for all, under which animals of the field lived, and in whose branches the birds of the air had nests— 22it is you, O king! You have grown great and strong. Your greatness has increased and reaches to heaven, and your sovereignty to the ends of the earth. 23And whereas the king saw a holy watcher coming down from heaven and saying, 'Cut down the tree and destroy it, but leave its stump and roots in the ground, with a band of iron and bronze, in the grass of the field; and let him be bathed with the dew of heaven, and let his lot be with the animals of the field, until seven times pass over him'— 24this is the interpretation, O king, and it is a decree of the Most High that has come upon my lord the king: 25You shall be driven away from human society, and your dwelling shall be with the wild animals. You shall be made to eat grass like oxen, you shall be bathed with the dew of heaven, and seven times shall pass over you, until you have learned that the Most High has sovereignty over the kingdom of mortals, and gives it to whom he will. 26As it was commanded to leave the stump and roots of the tree, your

a Or a holy, divine spirit

kingdom shall be re-established for you from the time that you learn that Heaven is sovereign. 27Therefore, O king, may my counsel be acceptable to you: atone for*a* your sins with righteousness, and your iniquities with mercy to the oppressed, so that your prosperity may be prolonged."

4.19–27: Nebuchadnezzar's greatness, symbolized by his monumental building programs, was well-known throughout the ancient world.

28 All this came upon King Nebuchadnezzar. 29At the end of twelve months he was walking on the roof of the royal palace of Babylon, 30and the king said, "Is this not magnificent Babylon, which I have built as a royal capital by my mighty power and for my glorious majesty?" 31While the words were still in the king's mouth, a voice came from heaven: "O King Nebuchadnezzar, to you it is declared: The kingdom has departed from you! 32You shall be driven away from human society, and your dwelling shall be with the animals of the field. You shall be made to eat grass like oxen, and seven times shall pass over you, until you have learned that the Most High has sovereignty over the kingdom of mortals and gives it to whom he will." 33Immediately the sentence was fulfilled against Nebuchadnezzar. He was driven away from human society, ate grass like oxen, and his body was bathed with the dew of heaven, until his hair grew as long as eagles' feathers and his nails became like birds' claws.

34 When that period was over, I, Nebuchadnezzar, lifted my eyes to heaven, and my reason returned to me.

I blessed the Most High,
> and praised and honored the one who
> > lives forever.
For his sovereignty is an everlasting
> > sovereignty,
> and his kingdom endures from
> > generation to generation.

35 All the inhabitants of the earth are
> > accounted as nothing,
> and he does what he wills with the
> > host of heaven
> and the inhabitants of the earth.

There is no one who can stay his hand
> or say to him, "What are you doing?"
36At that time my reason returned to me; and my majesty and splendor were restored to me for the glory of my kingdom. My counselors and my lords sought me out, I was re-established over my kingdom, and still more greatness was added to me. 37Now I, Nebuchadnezzar, praise and extol and honor the King of heaven,

for all his works are truth,
> and his ways are justice;
and he is able to bring low
> those who walk in pride.

4.28–37. 28–33: The prediction of the dream is fulfilled. **34–37:** Nebuchadnezzar is restored when he acknowledges God's universal sovereignty.

5 King Belshazzar made a great festival for a thousand of his lords, and he was drinking wine in the presence of the thousand.

2 Under the influence of the wine, Belshazzar commanded that they bring in the vessels of gold and silver that his father Nebuchadnezzar had taken out of the temple in Jerusalem, so that the king and his lords, his wives, and his concubines might drink from them. 3So they brought in the vessels of gold and silver*b* that had been taken out of the temple, the house of God in Jerusalem, and the king and his lords, his wives, and his concubines drank from them. 4They drank the wine and praised the gods of gold and silver, bronze, iron, wood, and stone.

5 Immediately the fingers of a human hand appeared and began writing on the plaster of the wall of the royal palace, next to the lampstand. The king was watching the hand as it wrote. 6Then the king's face turned pale, and his thoughts terrified him. His limbs gave way, and his knees knocked together. 7The king cried aloud to bring in the enchanters, the Chaldeans, and the diviners; and the king said to the wise men of Babylon, "Whoever can read this writing and tell me its interpretation shall be clothed in

a Aram *break off*   *b* Theodotion Vg: Aram lacks *and silver*

purple, have a chain of gold around his neck, and rank third in the kingdom." ⁸Then all the king's wise men came in, but they could not read the writing or tell the king the interpretation. ⁹Then King Belshazzar became greatly terrified and his face turned pale, and his lords were perplexed.

10 The queen, when she heard the discussion of the king and his lords, came into the banqueting hall. The queen said, "O king, live forever! Do not let your thoughts terrify you or your face grow pale. ¹¹There is a man in your kingdom who is endowed with a spirit of the holy gods.ᵃ In the days of your father he was found to have enlightenment, understanding, and wisdom like the wisdom of the gods. Your father, King Nebuchadnezzar, made him chief of the magicians, enchanters, Chaldeans, and diviners,ᵇ ¹²because an excellent spirit, knowledge, and understanding to interpret dreams, explain riddles, and solve problems were found in this Daniel, whom the king named Belteshazzar. Now let Daniel be called, and he will give the interpretation."

5.1–31: Belshazzar's feast. This narrative* demonstrates the punishment of arrogant and sacrilegious rulers. **1:** Belshazzar was not king of Babylon, but served as regent in place of his father Nabonidus. **2–4:** Nebuchadnezzar was not Belshazzar's father (see comment on v. 1). Nebuchadnezzar's son Amel-Marduk (Evil-merodach, 2 Kings 25.27–30; Jer 52.31–34) ruled in 562–560 BCE and was assassinated by his brother-in-law. The use of holy Temple* vessels (see 2 Kings 24.13; 2 Chr 36.10) for drinking praise to the gods constitutes sacrilege like that of Antiochus IV (1 Macc 1.41–50; 2 Macc 5.15–6.11). **5–12:** *The fingers of a human hand:* A supernatural response to Belshazzar's sacrilege. Both the servants and the king demonstrate their incompetence until *the queen* reminds them of Daniel.

13 Then Daniel was brought in before the king. The king said to Daniel, "So you are Daniel, one of the exiles of Judah, whom my father the king brought from Judah? ¹⁴I have heard of you that a spirit of the godsᶜ is in you, and that enlightenment, understanding, and excellent wisdom are found in you. ¹⁵Now the wise men, the enchanters, have

been brought in before me to read this writing and tell me its interpretation, but they were not able to give the interpretation of the matter. ¹⁶But I have heard that you can give interpretations and solve problems. Now if you are able to read the writing and tell me its interpretation, you shall be clothed in purple, have a chain of gold around your neck, and rank third in the kingdom."

17 Then Daniel answered in the presence of the king, "Let your gifts be for yourself, or give your rewards to someone else! Nevertheless I will read the writing to the king and let him know the interpretation. ¹⁸O king, the Most High God gave your father Nebuchadnezzar kingship, greatness, glory, and majesty. ¹⁹And because of the greatness that he gave him, all peoples, nations, and languages trembled and feared before him. He killed those he wanted to kill, kept alive those he wanted to keep alive, honored those he wanted to honor, and degraded those he wanted to degrade. ²⁰But when his heart was lifted up and his spirit was hardened so that he acted proudly, he was deposed from his kingly throne, and his glory was stripped from him. ²¹He was driven from human society, and his mind was made like that of an animal. His dwelling was with the wild asses, he was fed grass like oxen, and his body was bathed with the dew of heaven, until he learned that the Most High God has sovereignty over the kingdom of mortals, and sets over it whomever he will. ²²And you, Belshazzar his son, have not humbled your heart, even though you knew all this! ²³You have exalted yourself against the Lord of heaven! The vessels of his temple have been brought in before you, and you and your lords, your wives and your concubines have been drinking wine from them. You have praised the gods of silver and gold, of bronze, iron, wood, and stone, which do not see or hear or know; but the God in whose power is your very breath, and to whom belong all your ways, you have not honored.

24 "So from his presence the hand was sent and this writing was inscribed. ²⁵And

a Or *a holy, divine spirit*   *b* Aram adds *the king your father*   *c* Or *a divine spirit*

this is the writing that was inscribed: MENE, MENE, TEKEL, and PARSIN. 26This is the interpretation of the matter: MENE, God has numbered the days of[a] your kingdom and brought it to an end; 27TEKEL, you have been weighed on the scales and found wanting; 28PERES,[b] your kingdom is divided and given to the Medes and Persians."

29 Then Belshazzar gave the command, and Daniel was clothed in purple, a chain of gold was put around his neck, and a proclamation was made concerning him that he should rank third in the kingdom.

30 That very night Belshazzar, the Chaldean king, was killed. 31cAnd Darius the Mede received the kingdom, being about sixty-two years old.

5.13–31. 13–29: Daniel chides Belshazzar for his arrogance, unlike "his father" Nebuchadnezzar, prior to interpreting the writing. The words are Aramaic* nouns for units of weight: "mené," a mina; "tequel," a shekel;* "parsin," a half mina. Daniel reads them as verbs: "menah," *to number;* "teqal," *to weigh;* and "peras," *to divide.* The root "prs" also serves as the base for the name Persia. 30: Nabonidus fled Babylon at the approach of the Persian army. There is no evidence that Belshazzar was killed. 31: *Darius the Mede* is not historical. Babylon submitted to Cyrus of Persia in 539. A Persian military commander and relative of the royal family, Darius, took the throne when Cyrus's son Cambyses was assassinated in 522 BCE. The Medes were part of the Persian empire, and various prophecies asserted that Babylon would fall to them (Isa 13.17–22; 21.1–10; Jer 51.11, 28).

6 It pleased Darius to set over the kingdom one hundred twenty satraps, stationed throughout the whole kingdom, 2and over them three presidents, including Daniel; to these the satraps gave account, so that the king might suffer no loss. 3Soon Daniel distinguished himself above all the other presidents and satraps because an excellent spirit was in him, and the king planned to appoint him over the whole kingdom. 4So the presidents and the satraps tried to find grounds for complaint against Daniel in connection with the kingdom. But they could find no grounds for complaint or any corruption, because he was faithful, and no negligence or

corruption could be found in him. 5The men said, "We shall not find any ground for complaint against this Daniel unless we find it in connection with the law of his God."

6 So the presidents and satraps conspired and came to the king and said to him, "O King Darius, live forever! 7All the presidents of the kingdom, the prefects and the satraps, the counselors and the governors are agreed that the king should establish an ordinance and enforce an interdict, that whoever prays to anyone, divine or human, for thirty days, except to you, O king, shall be thrown into a den of lions. 8Now, O king, establish the interdict and sign the document, so that it cannot be changed, according to the law of the Medes and the Persians, which cannot be revoked." 9Therefore King Darius signed the document and interdict.

10 Although Daniel knew that the document had been signed, he continued to go to his house, which had windows in its upper room open toward Jerusalem, and to get down on his knees three times a day to pray to his God and praise him, just as he had done previously. 11The conspirators came and found Daniel praying and seeking mercy before his God. 12Then they approached the king and said concerning the interdict, "O king! Did you not sign an interdict, that anyone who prays to anyone, divine or human, within thirty days except to you, O king, shall be thrown into a den of lions?" The king answered, "The thing stands fast, according to the law of the Medes and Persians, which cannot be revoked." 13Then they responded to the king, "Daniel, one of the exiles from Judah, pays no attention to you, O king, or to the interdict you have signed, but he is saying his prayers three times a day."

14 When the king heard the charge, he was very much distressed. He was determined to save Daniel, and until the sun went down he made every effort to rescue him. 15Then the conspirators came to the king and said to him, "Know, O king, that it is a

---

a Aram lacks *the days of*   b The singular of *Parsin*
c Ch 6.1 in Aram

law of the Medes and Persians that no interdict or ordinance that the king establishes can be changed."

16 Then the king gave the command, and Daniel was brought and thrown into the den of lions. The king said to Daniel, "May your God, whom you faithfully serve, deliver you!" 17A stone was brought and laid on the mouth of the den, and the king sealed it with his own signet and with the signet of his lords, so that nothing might be changed concerning Daniel. 18Then the king went to his palace and spent the night fasting; no food was brought to him, and sleep fled from him.

19 Then, at break of day, the king got up and hurried to the den of lions. 20When he came near the den where Daniel was, he cried out anxiously to Daniel, "O Daniel, servant of the living God, has your God whom you faithfully serve been able to deliver you from the lions?" 21Daniel then said to the king, "O king, live forever! 22My God sent his angel and shut the lions' mouths so that they would not hurt me, because I was found blameless before him; and also before you, O king, I have done no wrong." 23Then the king was exceedingly glad and commanded that Daniel be taken up out of the den. So Daniel was taken up out of the den, and no kind of harm was found on him, because he had trusted in his God. 24The king gave a command, and those who had accused Daniel were brought and thrown into the den of lions—they, their children, and their wives. Before they reached the bottom of the den the lions overpowered them and broke all their bones in pieces.

25 Then King Darius wrote to all peoples and nations of every language throughout the whole world: "May you have abundant prosperity! 26I make a decree, that in all my royal dominion people should tremble and fear before the God of Daniel:

For he is the living God,
    enduring forever.
His kingdom shall never be destroyed,
    and his dominion has no end.
27 He delivers and rescues,
    he works signs and wonders in heaven
        and on earth;

for he has saved Daniel
    from the power of the lions."
28So this Daniel prospered during the reign of Darius and the reign of Cyrus the Persian.

6.1–28: Daniel in the lions' den. This narrative demonstrates God's protection of righteous Jews from foreign monarchs who demand worship of pagan gods and themselves. **1–9:** Darius I (522–486 BCE) organized the Persian empire into twenty "satrapies," administered by officials called *satraps*. See Esth 1.1; 8.9. Daniel's success as *president,* an otherwise unknown position, prompts a plot to bring him down by playing upon his religious piety. Darius is persuaded to demand worship of himself as a god, much like Antiochus IV Epiphanes, "manifest god." *So that it cannot be revoked:* Once signed with the royal signet, Persian laws could not be revoked, even by the king. **10–18:** Judaism requires three set times for prayer: morning, afternoon, and evening (see Ps 55.17; Jdt 9.1). The narrative portrays Darius as a victim of the plot since he intended no harm to Daniel. Cyrus authorized the building of the Second Temple* (2 Chr 36.22–23; Ezra 1.1–4), which was completed during the reign of Darius (Ezra 6). Darius calls upon God to save Daniel, and attempts to do so himself. **22:** God sends an *angel* to protect the righteous Daniel from the lions (compare 3.19–30). **24:** The families of criminals are punished as well to deter crime (Num 16.23–33; Josh 7.24; 2 Sam 21.6, 9; Esth 9–13). **25–27:** Darius's announcement of the kingdom of God serves the fundamental purpose of the book: to point to the establishment of an independent Jewish kingdom identified as the kingdom of God. **28:** Cyrus (539–530 BCE) preceded his son Cambyses (530–522 BCE) and Darius I (522–486 BCE) as ruler of Babylon.

DANIEL'S VISIONS CONCERNING THE COMING KINGDOM OF GOD

Chs. 7–12: The visions point to the establishment of the kingdom of God as the primary theme of the book. Scholars generally agree that these chapters were written in the mid second century BCE to support the Maccabean revolt against Seleucid* Syria. With the fall of Seleucid Syria, the kingdom of God would be realized as an independent Jewish state centered around the Jerusalem Temple.*

---

7 In the first year of King Belshazzar of Babylon, Daniel had a dream and visions

of his head as he lay in bed. Then he wrote down the dream:[a] [2]I,[b] Daniel, saw in my vision by night the four winds of heaven stirring up the great sea, [3]and four great beasts came up out of the sea, different from one another. [4]The first was like a lion and had eagles' wings. Then, as I watched, its wings were plucked off, and it was lifted up from the ground and made to stand on two feet like a human being; and a human mind was given to it. [5]Another beast appeared, a second one, that looked like a bear. It was raised up on one side, had three tusks[c] in its mouth among its teeth and was told, "Arise, devour many bodies!" [6]After this, as I watched, another appeared, like a leopard. The beast had four wings of a bird on its back and four heads; and dominion was given to it. [7]After this I saw in the visions by night a fourth beast, terrifying and dreadful and exceedingly strong. It had great iron teeth and was devouring, breaking in pieces, and stamping what was left with its feet. It was different from all the beasts that preceded it, and it had ten horns. [8]I was considering the horns, when another horn appeared, a little one coming up among them; to make room for it, three of the earlier horns were plucked up by the roots. There were eyes like human eyes in this horn, and a mouth speaking arrogantly.

7.1–28: The vision of the four beasts. This narrative* points to God's overthrow of Antiochus IV. **1–8:** *First year of Belshazzar:* Belshazzar's regency began in 554 BCE. Daniel's vision draws upon creation traditions, which portray God's defeat of the sea or a sea dragon as the basis for the created world order (Ps 74.13–17; 89.9–10; Isa 27.1; 51.9–10; compare Gen 1; Ex 15). Here, the chaos monsters emerge from the sea to overturn creation. *The four winds,*[b] refer to the four cardinal directions, the universal context of *the four beasts,* which represent a succession of empires (ch. 2). The *lion* with *eagles' wings* is Babylon, which employed such figures extensively in art. The *bear* with *three tusks* (literally, "ribs") in its mouth is Media. The *leopard* with *four wings* and *four heads* is Persia, which ruled most of the Near Eastern world. The *beast* with *iron teeth* is the Greek-Macedonian empire of Alexander the Great. *The ten horns* represent the ten rulers of the Seleucid empire, who used horns as symbols of

their power. *The little horn* with *eyes . . . and a mouth speaking arrogantly* is Antiochus IV, who claimed to be a god and usurped the throne following the assassination of his brother, Seleucus IV.

[9] As I watched,
   thrones were set in place,
      and an Ancient One[d] took his
         throne,
   his clothing was white as snow,
      and the hair of his head like
         pure wool;
   his throne was fiery flames,
      and its wheels were burning fire.
[10] A stream of fire issued
      and flowed out from his presence.
   A thousand thousands served him,
      and ten thousand times ten thousand
         stood attending him.
   The court sat in judgment,
      and the books were opened.
[11]I watched then because of the noise of the arrogant words that the horn was speaking. And as I watched, the beast was put to death, and its body destroyed and given over to be burned with fire. [12]As for the rest of the beasts, their dominion was taken away, but their lives were prolonged for a season and a time. [13]As I watched in the night visions,
   I saw one like a human being[e]
      coming with the clouds of heaven.
   And he came to the Ancient One[f]
      and was presented before him.
[14] To him was given dominion
      and glory and kingship,
   that all peoples, nations, and languages
      should serve him.
   His dominion is an everlasting dominion
      that shall not pass away,
   and his kingship is one
      that shall never be destroyed.

7.9–14. 9: *An Ancient One* (literally, "One Ancient of Days"): God. The portrayal of the divine court builds upon traditions in 1 Kings 22; Isa 6; Ezek 1; Ps 82;

a Q Ms Theodotion: MT adds *the beginning of the words;* he said   b Theodotion: Aram *Daniel answered and said, "I   c Or ribs   d Aram an Ancient of Days* e Aram *one like a son of man   f Aram the Ancient of Days*

Job 1. **13:** *One like a human being:* Literally, "one like a son of man" (compare "mortal," literally, "son of man/adam," in Ezek 2.1), a designation for a human being, in this case a messiah* figure who will rule the world as king.

15 As for me, Daniel, my spirit was troubled within me,[a] and the visions of my head terrified me. [16]I approached one of the attendants to ask him the truth concerning all this. So he said that he would disclose to me the interpretation of the matter: [17]"As for these four great beasts, four kings shall arise out of the earth. [18]But the holy ones of the Most High shall receive the kingdom and possess the kingdom forever—forever and ever."

19 Then I desired to know the truth concerning the fourth beast, which was different from all the rest, exceedingly terrifying, with its teeth of iron and claws of bronze, and which devoured and broke in pieces, and stamped what was left with its feet; [20]and concerning the ten horns that were on its head, and concerning the other horn, which came up and to make room for which three of them fell out—the horn that had eyes and a mouth that spoke arrogantly, and that seemed greater than the others. [21]As I looked, this horn made war with the holy ones and was prevailing over them, [22]until the Ancient One[b] came; then judgment was given for the holy ones of the Most High, and the time arrived when the holy ones gained possession of the kingdom.

23 This is what he said: "As for the fourth beast,

there shall be a fourth kingdom
on earth
that shall be different from all the
other kingdoms;
it shall devour the whole earth,
and trample it down, and break it to
pieces.
[24] As for the ten horns,
out of this kingdom ten kings
shall arise,
and another shall arise after them.
This one shall be different from the
former ones,
and shall put down three kings.

25 He shall speak words against the Most
High,
shall wear out the holy ones of the
Most High,
and shall attempt to change the
sacred seasons and the law;
and they shall be given into his power
for a time, two times,[c] and half a
time.
26 Then the court shall sit in judgment,
and his dominion shall be taken away,
to be consumed and totally destroyed.
27 The kingship and dominion
and the greatness of the kingdoms
under the whole heaven
shall be given to the people of the
holy ones of the Most High;
their kingdom shall be an everlasting
kingdom,
and all dominions shall serve and
obey them."

28 Here the account ends. As for me, Daniel, my thoughts greatly terrified me, and my face turned pale; but I kept the matter in my mind.

7.15–28. **16:** *One of the attendants:* An angel. **18:** *The holy ones of the Most High* are either angels or human beings, both of whom were believed to be fighting Antiochus. The Judean revolt was led by the Hasmonean* priestly family, and the service of priests in the Temple* was believed to reflect that of the angels in heaven. **25:** *Shall attempt to change the sacred seasons and the law:* Antiochus banned the observance of sabbath and Torah* (1 Macc 1.41–50; 2 Macc 6.1–11), thus challenging the Jewish concept of creation, which is grounded in the sabbath as part of the created world order (Gen 2.1–3; Ex 31.12–17; compare Prov 8.22–36). *A time, two times, and half a time:* Three and a half years. Antiochus's persecution is of limited duration.

8 In the third year of the reign of King Belshazzar a vision appeared to me, Daniel, after the one that had appeared to me at first. [2]In the vision I was looking and saw myself in Susa the capital, in the province of Elam,[d]

a Aram *troubled in its sheath*   b Aram *the Ancient of Days*   c Aram *a time, times*   d Gk Theodotion: MT Q Ms repeat *in the vision I was looking*

and I was by the river Ulai.ᵃ ³I looked up and saw a ram standing beside the river.ᵇ It had two horns. Both horns were long, but one was longer than the other, and the longer one came up second. ⁴I saw the ram charging westward and northward and southward. All beasts were powerless to withstand it, and no one could rescue from its power; it did as it pleased and became strong.

5 As I was watching, a male goat appeared from the west, coming across the face of the whole earth without touching the ground. The goat had a hornᶜ between its eyes. ⁶It came toward the ram with the two horns that I had seen standing beside the river,ᵇ and it ran at it with savage force. ⁷I saw it approaching the ram. It was enraged against it and struck the ram, breaking its two horns. The ram did not have power to withstand it; it threw the ram down to the ground and trampled upon it, and there was no one who could rescue the ram from its power. ⁸Then the male goat grew exceedingly great; but at the height of its power, the great horn was broken, and in its place there came up four prominent horns toward the four winds of heaven.

9 Out of one of them came anotherᵈ horn, a little one, which grew exceedingly great toward the south, toward the east, and toward the beautiful land. ¹⁰It grew as high as the host of heaven. It threw down to the earth some of the host and some of the stars, and trampled on them. ¹¹Even against the prince of the host it acted arrogantly; it took the regular burnt offering away from him and overthrew the place of his sanctuary. ¹²Because of wickedness, the host was given over to it together with the regular burnt offering;ᵉ it cast truth to the ground, and kept prospering in what it did. ¹³Then I heard a holy one speaking, and another holy one said to the one that spoke, "For how long is this vision concerning the regular burnt offering, the transgression that makes desolate, and the giving over of the sanctuary and host to be trampled?"ᵉ ¹⁴And he answered him,ᶠ "For two thousand three hundred evenings and mornings; then the sanctuary shall be restored to its rightful state."

8.1–27: The vision of the ram and the goat. A second vision surveys Greece's defeat of Persia and points to the downfall of Antiochus IV. The language of the book reverts to Hebrew (see 2.4b). **1–4:** *Third year of Belshazzar:* 552 BCE. *Susa,* located in the province of *Elam* by the River *Ulai* in modern Iran, was the winter capital of the Persian empire. The *ram* with *two horns* is the combined Persian-Median empire. **5:** The *male goat* with a *horn* is the empire of Alexander, who swept through Persia in 333–330 BCE. Alexander died in 323 BCE, and his empire split into separate kingdoms. **9–14:** *Another horn, a little one:* Antiochus IV, who attempted to extend his power to the south and east, including *the beautiful land* of Israel. Alexander defiled the Temple* by turning it into a sanctuary for Zeus. *Two thousand three hundred evenings and mornings:* or 1,150 days, approximately three years and two months (see 7.25; 12.7), the time of Antiochus's persecution (1 Macc 1.54–4.52).

15 When I, Daniel, had seen the vision, I tried to understand it. Then someone appeared standing before me, having the appearance of a man, ¹⁶and I heard a human voice by the Ulai, calling, "Gabriel, help this man understand the vision." ¹⁷So he came near where I stood; and when he came, I became frightened and fell prostrate. But he said to me, "Understand, O mortal,ᵍ that the vision is for the time of the end."

18 As he was speaking to me, I fell into a trance, face to the ground; then he touched me and set me on my feet. ¹⁹He said, "Listen, and I will tell you what will take place later in the period of wrath; for it refers to the appointed time of the end. ²⁰As for the ram that you saw with the two horns, these are the kings of Media and Persia. ²¹The male goatʰ is the king of Greece, and the great horn between its eyes is the first king. ²²As for the horn that was broken, in place of which four others arose, four kingdoms shall arise from hisⁱ nation, but not with his power.

ᵃ Or *the Ulai Gate*   ᵇ Or *gate*   ᶜ Theodotion: Gk *one horn*; Heb *a horn of vision*   ᵈ Cn Compare 7.8: Heb *one*   ᵉ Meaning of Heb uncertain   ᶠ Gk Theodotion Syr Vg: Heb *me*   ᵍ Heb *son of man*   ʰ Or *shaggy male goat*   ⁱ Gk Theodotion Vg: Heb *the*

23 At the end of their rule,
  when the transgressions have reached
    their full measure,
  a king of bold countenance shall arise,
    skilled in intrigue.
24 He shall grow strong in power,[a]
  shall cause fearful destruction,
    and shall succeed in what he does.
  He shall destroy the powerful
    and the people of the holy ones.
25 By his cunning
  he shall make deceit prosper under
    his hand,
  and in his own mind he shall
    be great.
  Without warning he shall destroy many
    and shall even rise up against the
      Prince of princes.
  But he shall be broken, and not by
    human hands.

26 The vision of the evenings and the mornings that has been told is true. As for you, seal up the vision, for it refers to many days from now."

27 So I, Daniel, was overcome and lay sick for some days; then I arose and went about the king's business. But I was dismayed by the vision and did not understand it.

8.15–27: The archangel Gabriel serves as the messenger to humanity in 8.15–26; 9.21–27; Lk 1.11–20. In 1 Enoch* 9 he intercedes on behalf of God's people and destroys the wicked. In Islam, he reveals the Quran to Muhammed. **17–18:** *The* (appointed) *time of the end:* The end of Antiochus's persecution. **25:** *Not by human hands:* God will act. **26:** *Seal up the vision:* Although given to Daniel in the sixth century, it will be realized in the second century (compare Isa 8.16; 29.11–12; 30.8; 34.16–17).

9 In the first year of Darius son of Ahasuerus, by birth a Mede, who became king over the realm of the Chaldeans— 2 in the first year of his reign, I, Daniel, perceived in the books the number of years that, according to the word of the LORD to the prophet Jeremiah, must be fulfilled for the devastation of Jerusalem, namely, seventy years.

3 Then I turned to the Lord God, to seek an answer by prayer and supplication with fasting and sackcloth and ashes. 4 I prayed to the LORD my God and made confession, saying,

"Ah, Lord, great and awesome God, keeping covenant and steadfast love with those who love you and keep your commandments, 5 we have sinned and done wrong, acted wickedly and rebelled, turning aside from your commandments and ordinances. 6 We have not listened to your servants the prophets, who spoke in your name to our kings, our princes, and our ancestors, and to all the people of the land.

7 "Righteousness is on your side, O Lord, but open shame, as at this day, falls on us, the people of Judah, the inhabitants of Jerusalem, and all Israel, those who are near and those who are far away, in all the lands to which you have driven them, because of the treachery that they have committed against you. 8 Open shame, O LORD, falls on us, our kings, our officials, and our ancestors, because we have sinned against you. 9 To the Lord our God belong mercy and forgiveness, for we have rebelled against him, 10 and have not obeyed the voice of the LORD our God by following his laws, which he set before us by his servants the prophets.

11 "All Israel has transgressed your law and turned aside, refusing to obey your voice. So the curse and the oath written in the law of Moses, the servant of God, have been poured out upon us, because we have sinned against you. 12 He has confirmed his words, which he spoke against us and against our rulers, by bringing upon us a calamity so great that what has been done against Jerusalem has never before been done under the whole heaven. 13 Just as it is written in the law of Moses, all this calamity has come upon us. We did not entreat the favor of the LORD our God, turning from our iniquities and reflecting on his[b] fidelity. 14 So the LORD kept watch over this calamity until he brought it upon us. Indeed, the LORD our God is right in all that he has done; for we have disobeyed his voice.

a Theodotion and one Gk Ms: Heb repeats (from 8.22) *but not with his power* b Heb *your*

15 "And now, O Lord our God, who brought your people out of the land of Egypt with a mighty hand and made your name renowned even to this day—we have sinned, we have done wickedly. 16O Lord, in view of all your righteous acts, let your anger and wrath, we pray, turn away from your city Jerusalem, your holy mountain; because of our sins and the iniquities of our ancestors, Jerusalem and your people have become a disgrace among all our neighbors. 17Now therefore, O our God, listen to the prayer of your servant and to his supplication, and for your own sake, Lord,[a] let your face shine upon your desolated sanctuary. 18Incline your ear, O my God, and hear. Open your eyes and look at our desolation and the city that bears your name. We do not present our supplication before you on the ground of our righteousness, but on the ground of your great mercies. 19O Lord, hear; O Lord, forgive; O Lord, listen and act and do not delay! For your own sake, O my God, because your city and your people bear your name!"

9.1–27: The seventy weeks. This chapter applies Jeremiah's prophecy of a 70-year exile (Jer 25.11, 12; 29.10) together with the calculation of the jubilee year (Lev 25.8–17; "seven weeks of years") to predict the end of Antiochus's persecution. 1: *Ahasuerus:* The Hebrew name for the Persian ruler Xerxes (see Esth 1.1; Ezra 4.6). Xerxes I (486–465 BCE) was the son of Darius I, and Xerxes II (425 BCE) was the son of Artaxerxes I (465–425 BCE). Darius II (423–405 BCE) was the son of Xerxes II, and Darius III (336–330 BCE), the son of Arses (338–336 BCE), was the last ruler of Persia; he was assassinated shortly after Alexander's final defeat of the Persian army. 2–19: *Prayer and supplication:* Daniel employs a form of communal confession and petition (compare Ezra 9.6–15; Neh 1.5–11; 9.6–37). 11: *The curse and the oath written in the law of Moses:* See Lev 26.14–45; Deut 28.15–68; 29.10–29.

---

20 While I was speaking, and was praying and confessing my sin and the sin of my people Israel, and presenting my supplication before the LORD my God on behalf of the holy mountain of my God— 21while I was speaking in prayer, the man Gabriel, whom I had seen before in a vision, came to me in swift flight at the time of the evening sacrifice. 22He came[b] and said to me, "Daniel, I have now come out to give you wisdom and understanding. 23At the beginning of your supplications a word went out, and I have come to declare it, for you are greatly beloved. So consider the word and understand the vision:

24 "Seventy weeks are decreed for your people and your holy city: to finish the transgression, to put an end to sin, and to atone for iniquity, to bring in everlasting righteousness, to seal both vision and prophet, and to anoint a most holy place.[c] 25Know therefore and understand: from the time that the word went out to restore and rebuild Jerusalem until the time of an anointed prince, there shall be seven weeks; and for sixty-two weeks it shall be built again with streets and moat, but in a troubled time. 26After the sixty-two weeks, an anointed one shall be cut off and shall have nothing, and the troops of the prince who is to come shall destroy the city and the sanctuary. Its[d] end shall come with a flood, and to the end there shall be war. Desolations are decreed. 27He shall make a strong covenant with many for one week, and for half of the week he shall make sacrifice and offering cease; and in their place[e] shall be an abomination that desolates, until the decreed end is poured out upon the desolator."

9.20–27. 24: *Seventy weeks:* Gabriel interprets Jeremiah's 70 years as "70 weeks of years" by applying the calculation of the jubilee year at "seven weeks of years" (Lev 25.8; see also 2 Chr 36.21). From 167 BCE, the total of 490 years would place the beginning of the calculation in 657 BCE during the reign of Manasseh, whose evil deeds prompted God to destroy Jerusalem and the Temple* (2 Kings 21.10–15). Gabriel's interpretation* points to the Maccabean revolt as the time when the punishment of Jerusalem would end. 25–26: *Seven weeks:* Many claim that this is the 49 years that passed from the destruction of the Temple in 587 BCE to 538 BCE when Sheshbazzar laid the foundation for the Second Temple (Ezra 1.1–11; 5.13–16). The remaining *sixty-two weeks* or 434 years points to

---

a Theodotion Vg Compare Syr: Heb *for the Lord's sake*
b Gk Syr: Heb *He made to understand*   c Or *thing or one*   d Or *His*   e Cn: Meaning of Heb uncertain

104 BCE as the time of fulfillment, which goes beyond the period of the Maccabean revolt. *An anointed* one shall be cut off:* Antiochus removed the high priest Onias III, who was subsequently murdered (2 Macc 4.3–34). *The troops of the prince who is to come:* Antiochus sacked Jerusalem in 167 BCE following his humiliating withdrawal from Egypt. **27:** *He shall make a strong covenant* with many for one week:* Antiochus appointed Jason and then Menelaus as high priests in the Temple (2 Macc 4).

Daniel's vision of Antiochus's fall

Chs. 10–12: The culmination of the book describes the onset of the vision in 10.1–11.1; an overview of history from the fall of Persia to the projected fall of Antiochus IV in 11.2–12.4; and a conclusion that attempts to calculate the realization of the vision in 12.5–13. The author's description of historical events is accurate through 11.39, but the portrayal of Antiochus's demise in 11.40–12.4 is fictitious. The author wrote between December, 167 BCE, when the Temple* was desecrated, and December, 164 BCE, when it was rededicated by Judah the Maccabee.

10 In the third year of King Cyrus of Persia a word was revealed to Daniel, who was named Belteshazzar. The word was true, and it concerned a great conflict. He understood the word, having received understanding in the vision.

2 At that time I, Daniel, had been mourning for three weeks. ³I had eaten no rich food, no meat or wine had entered my mouth, and I had not anointed myself at all, for the full three weeks. ⁴On the twenty-fourth day of the first month, as I was standing on the bank of the great river (that is, the Tigris), ⁵I looked up and saw a man clothed in linen, with a belt of gold from Uphaz around his waist. ⁶His body was like beryl, his face like lightning, his eyes like flaming torches, his arms and legs like the gleam of burnished bronze, and the sound of his words like the roar of a multitude. ⁷I, Daniel, alone saw the vision; the people who were with me did not see the vision, though a great trembling fell upon them, and they fled and hid themselves. ⁸So I was left alone to see this great vision. My strength left me, and my complexion grew deathly pale, and I retained no strength. ⁹Then I heard the sound of his words; and when I heard the sound of his words, I fell into a trance, face to the ground.

10.1–11.1: The onset of Daniel's vision. Compare Ezekiel's vision (Ezek 1). **10.1:** *The third year of King Cyrus of Persia:* 536 BCE, 70 years after the date in 1.1 (see 9.24). **2–4:** Acts of self-denial are typical preparations for trances and other forms of mystical experience. **5:** *Twenty-fourth day of the month:* The 24th of Nissan, one day following the conclusion of Passover.* **5–6:** *A man clothed in linen:* An angel dressed as a priest and gleaming like the cherubim* of Ezekiel's vision (see Ezek 9.2; 40.3). *Uphaz:* See Jer 10.9. **7–9:** *Trance:* See Gen 2.21; 15.2.

10 But then a hand touched me and roused me to my hands and knees. ¹¹He said to me, "Daniel, greatly beloved, pay attention to the words that I am going to speak to you. Stand on your feet, for I have now been sent to you." So while he was speaking this word to me, I stood up trembling. ¹²He said to me, "Do not fear, Daniel, for from the first day that you set your mind to gain understanding and to humble yourself before your God, your words have been heard, and I have come because of your words. ¹³But the prince of the kingdom of Persia opposed me twenty-one days. So Michael, one of the chief princes, came to help me, and I left him there with the prince of the kingdom of Persia,ᵃ ¹⁴and have come to help you understand what is to happen to your people at the end of days. For there is a further vision for those days."

15 While he was speaking these words to me, I turned my face toward the ground and was speechless. ¹⁶Then one in human form touched my lips, and I opened my mouth to speak, and said to the one who stood before me, "My lord, because of the vision such pains have come upon me that I retain no strength. ¹⁷How can my lord's servant talk with my lord? For I am shaking,ᵇ no strength remains in me, and no breath is left in me."

18 Again one in human form touched me and strengthened me. ¹⁹He said, "Do not

a Gk Theodotion: Heb *I was left there with the kings of Persia*   *b* Gk: Heb *from now*

fear, greatly beloved, you are safe. Be strong and courageous!" When he spoke to me, I was strengthened and said, "Let my lord speak, for you have strengthened me." [20]Then he said, "Do you know why I have come to you? Now I must return to fight against the prince of Persia, and when I am through with him, the prince of Greece will come. [21]But I am to tell you what is inscribed in the book of truth. There is no one with me who contends against these princes

11 except Michael, your prince. [1]As for me, in the first year of Darius the Mede, I stood up to support and strengthen him.

10.10–11.1. 10–14: In ancient Near Eastern mythology, conflict among the nations often involves conflict among their gods. *The prince of Persia:* The angel or god of Persia. *Twenty-one days:* The duration of Daniel's fasting in v. 3. *Michael:* The archangel who protects the Jewish people (10.21; 12.1; see also Jude 9; Rev 12.7). **15–17:** Daniel speaks after his lips are touched (Isa 6.5–7; Ex 4.10–17; Ezek 3.26–27). *One in human form:* An angel. **10.18–11.1:** The angel, perhaps Michael, points to conflicts with Persia and Greece which are described in detail.

~~~~~~~~~~~~~~~~~~~~~~~~~~~~~

2 "Now I will announce the truth to you. Three more kings shall arise in Persia. The fourth shall be far richer than all of them, and when he has become strong through his riches, he shall stir up all against the kingdom of Greece. [3]Then a warrior king shall arise, who shall rule with great dominion and take action as he pleases. [4]And while still rising in power, his kingdom shall be broken and divided toward the four winds of heaven, but not to his posterity, nor according to the dominion with which he ruled; for his kingdom shall be uprooted and go to others besides these.

5 "Then the king of the south shall grow strong, but one of his officers shall grow stronger than he and shall rule a realm greater than his own realm. [6]After some years they shall make an alliance, and the daughter of the king of the south shall come to the king of the north to ratify the agreement. But she shall not retain her power, and his offspring shall not endure. She shall

be given up, she and her attendants and her child and the one who supported her.

"In those times [7]a branch from her roots shall rise up in his place. He shall come against the army and enter the fortress of the king of the north, and he shall take action against them and prevail. [8]Even their gods, with their idols and with their precious vessels of silver and gold, he shall carry off to Egypt as spoils of war. For some years he shall refrain from attacking the king of the north; [9]then the latter shall invade the realm of the king of the south, but will return to his own land.

11.2–12.4: Daniel's vision of history. Egypt did not attack Antiochus after 167 BCE. He died of tuberculosis in 164 or 163 BCE following campaigns in Armenia and Elymais (Elam). **2:** The three Persian kings are uncertain. **3–4:** Alexander, whose empire was divided after his death in 323 BCE. **5–6:** *The king of the south:* Ptolemy I (305–282 BCE), founder of the Ptolemaic★ dynasty★ of Egypt. *One of his officers:* Seleucus I (305–281 BCE), founder of the Syrian Seleucid★ dynasty. Ptolemy II's (282–246 BCE) daughter Berenice married Antiochus II (261–247 BCE), but the alliance failed after Berenice, her child, and Antiochus II were murdered. **7–9:** Berenice's brother, Ptolemy III (246–222 BCE), invaded Syria to avenge her death, but he was repulsed by Seleucus II (246–225 BCE). **10:** *His sons:* Seleucus III (225–223 BCE) and Antiochus III (223–187 BCE).

~~~~~~~~~~~~~~~~~~~~~~~~~~~~~

10 "His sons shall wage war and assemble a multitude of great forces, which shall advance like a flood and pass through, and again shall carry the war as far as his fortress. [11]Moved with rage, the king of the south shall go out and do battle against the king of the north, who shall muster a great multitude, which shall, however, be defeated by his enemy. [12]When the multitude has been carried off, his heart shall be exalted, and he shall overthrow tens of thousands, but he shall not prevail. [13]For the king of the north shall again raise a multitude, larger than the former, and after some years[a] he shall advance with a great army and abundant supplies.

a Heb *and at the end of the times years*

14 "In those times many shall rise against the king of the south. The lawless among your own people shall lift themselves up in order to fulfill the vision, but they shall fail. 15Then the king of the north shall come and throw up siegeworks, and take a well-fortified city. And the forces of the south shall not stand, not even his picked troops, for there shall be no strength to resist. 16But he who comes against him shall take the actions he pleases, and no one shall withstand him. He shall take a position in the beautiful land, and all of it shall be in his power. 17He shall set his mind to come with the strength of his whole kingdom, and he shall bring terms of peace*a* and perform them. In order to destroy the kingdom,*b* he shall give him a woman in marriage; but it shall not succeed or be to his advantage. 18Afterward he shall turn to the coastlands, and shall capture many. But a commander shall put an end to his insolence; indeed,*c* he shall turn his insolence back upon him. 19Then he shall turn back toward the fortresses of his own land, but he shall stumble and fall, and shall not be found.

11.10–19. 11–12: Ptolemy IV (222–204 BCE) defeated Antiochus III at Raphia but failed to capitalize on his victory. **13–19:** Antiochus III defeated Ptolemy V (204–180 BCE) in 200 BCE, taking control of the Sinai (and Judea). He later gave his daughter Cleopatra I to Ptolemy V in marriage.

20 "Then shall arise in his place one who shall send an official for the glory of the kingdom; but within a few days he shall be broken, though not in anger or in battle. 21In his place shall arise a contemptible person on whom royal majesty had not been conferred; he shall come in without warning and obtain the kingdom through intrigue. 22Armies shall be utterly swept away and broken before him, and the prince of the covenant as well. 23And after an alliance is made with him, he shall act deceitfully and become strong with a small party. 24Without warning he shall come into the richest parts*d* of the province and do what none of his predecessors had ever done, lavishing plunder, spoil, and wealth on them. He shall devise plans against strongholds, but only for a time. 25He shall stir up his power and determination against the king of the south with a great army, and the king of the south shall wage war with a much greater and stronger army. But he shall not succeed, for plots shall be devised against him 26by those who eat of the royal rations. They shall break him, his army shall be swept away, and many shall fall slain. 27The two kings, their minds bent on evil, shall sit at one table and exchange lies. But it shall not succeed, for there remains an end at the time appointed. 28He shall return to his land with great wealth, but his heart shall be set against the holy covenant. He shall work his will, and return to his own land.

11.20–28: The initial reign of Antiochus IV, who usurped the throne following the assassination of his brother Seleucus IV (187–175 BCE). His initial campaigns against Ptolemy VI (180–145 BCE) were successful.

29 "At the time appointed he shall return and come into the south, but this time it shall not be as it was before. 30For ships of Kittim shall come against him, and he shall lose heart and withdraw. He shall be enraged and take action against the holy covenant. He shall turn back and pay heed to those who forsake the holy covenant. 31Forces sent by him shall occupy and profane the temple and fortress. They shall abolish the regular burnt offering and set up the abomination that makes desolate. 32He shall seduce with intrigue those who violate the covenant; but the people who are loyal to their God shall stand firm and take action. 33The wise among the people shall give understanding to many; for some days, however, they shall fall by sword and flame, and suffer captivity and plunder. 34When they fall victim, they shall receive a little help, and many shall join them insincerely. 35Some of the wise shall fall, so that they may be refined, purified, and cleansed,*e* until the time of the

a Gk: Heb *kingdom, and upright ones with him*
b Heb *it*   *c* Meaning of Heb uncertain   *d* Or *among the richest men*   *e* Heb *made them white*

end, for there is still an interval until the time appointed.

36 "The king shall act as he pleases. He shall exalt himself and consider himself greater than any god, and shall speak horrendous things against the God of gods. He shall prosper until the period of wrath is completed, for what is determined shall be done. [37] He shall pay no respect to the gods of his ancestors, or to the one beloved by women; he shall pay no respect to any other god, for he shall consider himself greater than all. [38] He shall honor the god of fortresses instead of these; a god whom his ancestors did not know he shall honor with gold and silver, with precious stones and costly gifts. [39] He shall deal with the strongest fortresses by the help of a foreign god. Those who acknowledge him he shall make more wealthy, and shall appoint them as rulers over many, and shall distribute the land for a price.

11.29–39: Following his forced withdrawal from Egypt, Antiochus sacked and occupied Jerusalem in 167 BCE, profaned the Temple,* and proscribed the practice of Judaism. 30: *Kittim:* Originally Greeks or Cypriots (Gen 10.4; Ezek 27.6), later Romans. 34: *A little help:* The Maccabean revolt. 36: Antiochus called himself Epiphanes,* "manifest god." 37–39: Antiochus set aside the worship of Tammuz-Adonis in favor of Zeus Olympus, whose statue he placed in the Temple (1 Macc 1.54–59).

40 "At the time of the end the king of the south shall attack him. But the king of the north shall rush upon him like a whirlwind, with chariots and horsemen, and with many ships. He shall advance against countries and pass through like a flood. [41] He shall come into the beautiful land, and tens of thousands shall fall victim, but Edom and Moab and the main part of the Ammonites shall escape from his power. [42] He shall stretch out his hand against the countries, and the land of Egypt shall not escape. [43] He shall become ruler of the treasures of gold and of silver, and all the riches of Egypt; and the Libyans and the Ethiopians[a] shall follow in his train. [44] But reports from the east and the north shall alarm him, and he shall go out with great fury to bring ruin and complete destruction to many. [45] He shall pitch his palatial tents between the sea and the beautiful holy mountain. Yet he shall come to his end, with no one to help him.

11.40–45: The scenario presented here did not take place. *The beautiful land:* Israel.

12 "At that time Michael, the great prince, the protector of your people, shall arise. There shall be a time of anguish, such as has never occurred since nations first came into existence. But at that time your people shall be delivered, everyone who is found written in the book. [2] Many of those who sleep in the dust of the earth[b] shall awake, some to everlasting life, and some to shame and everlasting contempt. [3] Those who are wise shall shine like the brightness of the sky,[c] and those who lead many to righteousness, like the stars forever and ever. [4] But you, Daniel, keep the words secret and the book sealed until the time of the end. Many shall be running back and forth, and evil[d] shall increase."

12.1–4: Michael calls upon Daniel to remain silent about the vision until its fulfillment. 2: Resurrection of the righteous (Isa 26.19; Ezek 37). 3: *Like the brightness of the sky:* The Hebrew word "zohar" ("brightness") from this verse serves as the title of the Zohar, the primary mystical work of Judaism.

5 Then I, Daniel, looked, and two others appeared, one standing on this bank of the stream and one on the other. [6] One of them said to the man clothed in linen, who was upstream, "How long shall it be until the end of these wonders?" [7] The man clothed in linen, who was upstream, raised his right hand and his left hand toward heaven. And I heard him swear by the one who lives forever that it would be for a time, two times, and half a time,[e] and that when the shattering of the power of the holy people comes to an end, all these things would be accom-

a Or *Nubians;* Heb *Cushites*   b Or *the land of dust*
c Or *dome*   d Cn Compare Gk: Heb *knowledge*
e Heb *a time, times, and a half*

plished. [8]I heard but could not understand; so I said, "My lord, what shall be the outcome of these things?" [9]He said, "Go your way, Daniel, for the words are to remain secret and sealed until the time of the end. [10]Many shall be purified, cleansed, and refined, but the wicked shall continue to act wickedly. None of the wicked shall understand, but those who are wise shall understand. [11]From the time that the regular burnt offering is taken away and the abomination that desolates is set up, there shall be one thousand two hundred ninety days. [12]Happy are those who persevere and attain the thousand three hundred thirty-five days. [13]But you, go your way,[a] and rest; you shall rise for your reward at the end of the days."

12.5–13: The realization of the vision. This section attempts to calculate the time when the vision will be realized. **5–6:** *Two others:* Angels. **7:** *A time, two times, and half a time:* Three and a half years, the approximate time from the desecration of the Temple* in 167 BCE to its rededication in 164 BCE (see 7.25). **11:** *One thousand two hundred ninety days:* An attempt to specify the figure in v. 7. **12:** *Thousand three hundred thirty-five days:* A second attempt to specify this figure. **13:** *The end of days:* The end of the period outlined in the vision (see 8.17; 9.26; 11.6, 13, 35, 40; 12.4, 9).

a Gk Theodotion: Heb adds *to the end*

HOSEA

Introduction

Hosea's central concern is Israel's loyalty to its God. He denounces Israel for worshipping other gods, in particular the Canaanite god Baal,* and pleads with Israel to return to the faithful worship of its God alone. To gain his audience's attention and to make his message vivid, Hosea used the metaphor* of marriage to describe Israel's relationship to God. God is pictured as a husband and Israel as his faithless and promiscuous wife. Israel, the disloyal wife, is urged to repent and return to her husband. The marriage metaphor is enacted by Hosea himself in chs. 1–3, when Hosea marries Gomer, described as a prostitute (2.2) and an adulteress (3.1). And Hosea uses the marriage metaphor repeatedly in the speeches in chs. 4–14, which make up the bulk of the book. A prophet* fond of metaphors, Hosea also compares Israel's disloyalty to a barren tree (9.13–17), a stubborn heifer (4.16; 10.11–15), and a rebellious son (11.1–7).

Hosea's prophecy can be divided into two parts, the first a collection of narratives* in chs. 1–3 that describes Israel's disloyalty in terms of Hosea's faithless wife. Narratives about prophets, such as these, typically take up less space in a prophetic book than the prophet's speeches themselves, and they frequently describe prophets acting out the message they wish to deliver. The second and larger part of Hosea is a collection of prophetic speeches (chs. 4–14) that condemn Israel's deceit, predict God's punishment, and express hope for Israel's renewal. It is difficult to know where one speech ends and the next begins, but a dominant pattern can be detected in which indictments of sin are followed by sentences of judgment. In the brief speech that begins this collection, for example, an indictment listing Israel's crimes (4.1–2) is followed by a sentence describing God's punishment (4.3). Much less common are speeches predicting Israel's restoration (11.8–11). Hosea's own speeches may have been supplemented at points by later editors who wished to relate Hosea's message to the southern kingdom of Judah or to the Judeans in exile (11.10–11).

Hosea lived and prophesied in the northern kingdom of Israel, also called Ephraim, at the time of the divided monarchy when Israel and Judah were separate kingdoms. Hosea was the only native northerner among the prophets, the rest of whom all lived in or came from Judah. His career covered the last 30 years of the kingdom of Israel (750–721 BCE), when Israel was under the constant threat of Assyrian imperialism and was wracked by a series of violent coups in its own capital, Samaria. Hosea deplores the internal political violence of this period (7.5–7) and Israel's attempt to protect itself by international alliances (7.11), and he believes Israel's impending doom in the face of Assyrian expansion to be God's punishment for its social and religious corruption.

Hosea is especially critical of the religious scene in Israelite society during this period. His frequent references to Baal (2.8, 13, 16) indicate that many Israelites had turned from their own God to worship this Canaanite deity. This attraction to Baal-worship among the Israelites was an old and continual problem, as the contest between Elijah and the prophets of Baal a century earlier shows (2 Kings 17–19). The Israelites believed that Baal, like Israel's own God, could deliver the rains and agricultural productivity on which their economy and survival depended. The calves that Hosea criticizes (8.5–6), though possibly pedestals or throne images for Israel's God, are also associated with Baal in this period, and Hosea regards them as idols of Baal.

Hosea begins a collection of twelve short prophetic books, often called the Minor Prophets because of their brief length when compared to the longer books of Isaiah, Jeremiah, and Ezekiel. These twelve books are arranged roughly in chronological order, starting with eighth-century prophets, as Hosea, Amos, and Micah are explicitly identified. The collection then moves to prophets of the seventh century and concludes with those of the sixth.

READING GUIDE

One key to understanding Hosea involves recognizing the variety of ways in which the image of marital infidelity is employed to picture Israel's religious disloyalty. Catching the basic point of the comparison and its shock value is more important than reconstructing the actual details of Hosea's marriage, which still elude scholars. It is also important to notice how much of Hosea's message of faithlessness is directed against abuses in Israelite religion: its priesthood, its rituals, its sacred sites and altars, and its basic integrity.

1 The word of the LORD that came to Hosea son of Beeri, in the days of Kings Uzziah, Jotham, Ahaz, and Hezekiah of Judah, and in the days of King Jeroboam son of Joash of Israel.

1.1: Title. The reigns of these Judean kings span almost a hundred years (783–687 BCE), while the reign of the single Israelite king mentioned, Jeroboam, lasts for only 41 of these years (786–746). Since Hosea's speeches are directed to Israel in particular and reflect events leading up to its fall to Assyria in 721 BCE, it is peculiar that the six kings who followed Jeroboam to the throne of Israel during this time are not mentioned here.

2 When the LORD first spoke through Hosea, the LORD said to Hosea, "Go, take for yourself a wife of whoredom and have children of whoredom, for the land commits great whoredom by forsaking the LORD." ³So he went and took Gomer daughter of Diblaim, and she conceived and bore him a son. 4 And the LORD said to him, "Name him Jezreel;ᵃ for in a little while I will punish the house of Jehu for the blood of Jezreel, and I will put an end to the kingdom of the house of Israel. ⁵On that day I will break the bow of Israel in the valley of Jezreel."

6 She conceived again and bore a daughter. Then the LORD said to him, "Name her Lo-ruhamah,ᵇ for I will no longer have pity on the house of Israel or forgive them. ⁷But I will have pity on the house of Judah, and I will save them by the LORD their God; I will not save them by bow, or by sword, or by war, or by horses, or by horsemen."

8 When she had weaned Lo-ruhamah, she conceived and bore a son. ⁹Then the LORD said, "Name him Lo-ammi,ᶜ for you are not my people and I am not your God."ᵈ

10ᵉ Yet the number of the people of Israel shall be like the sand of the sea, which can be neither measured nor numbered; and in the place where it was said to them, "You are not my people," it shall be said to them, "Children of the living God." ¹¹The people of Judah and the people of Israel shall be gathered together, and they shall appoint for themselves one head; and they shall take possession ofᶠ the land, for great shall be the day of Jezreel.

2 ᵍSay to your brother,ʰ Ammi,ⁱ and to your sister,ʲ Ruhamah.ᵏ

1.2–2.1: Hosea marries the prostitute Gomer. In chs. 1 and 3 Hosea acts out the message he wishes to convey to Israel: Just as the wife he marries has been promiscuous, seeking out other lovers, so Israel has been unfaithful to its LORD, seeking out other gods to worship. **1.2:** *Whoredom* translates the common Hebrew term for prostitution. **4:** Hosea's first son *Jezreel* is named after the broad valley in northern Israel where

a That is *God sows*   b That is *Not pitied*   c That is *Not my people*   d Heb *I am not yours*   e Ch 2.1 in Heb   f Heb *rise up from*   g Ch 2.3 in Heb   h Gk: Heb *brothers*   i That is *My people*   j Gk Vg: Heb *sisters*   k That is *Pitied*

Jehu led a bloody coup (2 Kings 9.14–10.11), establishing a dynasty* in which Jeroboam, Hosea's contemporary, was the fourth king. The name symbolizes the imminent end of that dynasty, which occurred during Hosea's career when Jeroboam's son Zechariah was assassinated in 745 BCE. **6–9:** The names of Hosea's daughter, *Lo-ruhamah* ("Not pitied"), and second son, *Lo-ammi* ("Not my people"), symbolize

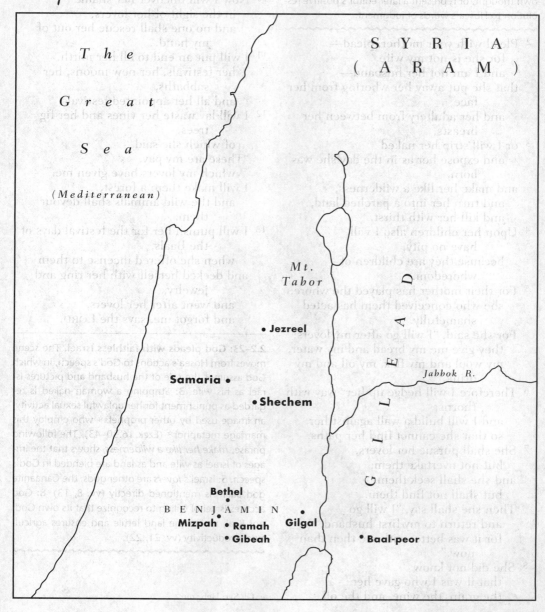

Map Kingdom of Israel in Hosea's time

The

Great

Sea

(Mediterranean)

SYRIA

(ARAM)

Mt. Tabor

Jabbok R.

G I L E A D

• Jezreel

Samaria •

• **Shechem**

Bethel •

B E N J A M I N

Mizpah • • **Ramah**

• **Gibeah**

Gilgal •

• **Baal-peor**

God's rejection of Israel for its faithlessness. **7:** Scholars disagree whether references to the southern kingdom of *Judah* here and elsewhere in Hosea are from Hosea himself or from later Judean editors who wished to relate Hosea's message to their own time and place. **1.10–2.1:** The marked shift to future salvation here, in which the meanings of Hosea's children's names are reversed to their positive counterparts, may either reflect the tension between despair and hope in Hosea's own thought, or represent a later editor's positive resolution to Hosea's words of judgment.

2 Plead with your mother, plead—
  for she is not my wife,
  and I am not her husband—
  that she put away her whoring from her
    face,
  and her adultery from between her
    breasts,
3 or I will strip her naked
  and expose her as in the day she was
    born,
  and make her like a wilderness,
  and turn her into a parched land,
  and kill her with thirst.
4 Upon her children also I will
    have no pity,
  because they are children of
    whoredom.
5 For their mother has played the whore;
  she who conceived them has acted
    shamefully.
  For she said, "I will go after my lovers;
  they give me my bread and my water,
  my wool and my flax, my oil and my
    drink."
6 Therefore I will hedge up her*a* way with
    thorns;
  and I will build a wall against her,
  so that she cannot find her paths.
7 She shall pursue her lovers,
  but not overtake them;
  and she shall seek them,
  but shall not find them.
  Then she shall say, "I will go
  and return to my first husband,
  for it was better with me then than
    now."
8 She did not know
  that it was I who gave her
  the grain, the wine, and the oil,

and who lavished upon her silver
  and gold that they used for Baal.
9 Therefore I will take back
  my grain in its time,
  and my wine in its season;
  and I will take away my wool and my
    flax,
  which were to cover her
    nakedness.
10 Now I will uncover her shame
  in the sight of her lovers,
  and no one shall rescue her out of
    my hand.
11 I will put an end to all her mirth,
  her festivals, her new moons, her
    sabbaths,
  and all her appointed festivals.
12 I will lay waste her vines and her fig
    trees,
  of which she said,
  "These are my pay,
  which my lovers have given me."
  I will make them a forest,
  and the wild animals shall devour
    them.
13 I will punish her for the festival days of
    the Baals,
  when she offered incense to them
  and decked herself with her ring and
    jewelry,
  and went after her lovers,
  and forgot me, says the LORD.

2.2–23: God pleads with faithless Israel. The scene moves from Hosea's actions to God's speech, in which God assumes the role of the husband and pictures Israel as his wife. **3:** Stripping a woman naked is regarded as punishment for her unlawful sexual activity, an image used by other prophets* who employ this marriage metaphor* (Ezek 16.30–43). The following phrase, *make her like a wilderness*, shows that the images of Israel as wife and as land are blended in God's speech. **5:** Israel's *lovers* are other gods; the Canaanite god Baal* is mentioned directly (vv. 8, 13). **8:** God accuses Israel of failing to recognize that its own God, not Baal, makes the land fertile and ensures agricultural productivity (vv. 21, 22).

a Gk Syr: Heb *your*

14 Therefore, I will now allure her,
  and bring her into the wilderness,
  and speak tenderly to her.
15 From there I will give her her
    vineyards,
  and make the Valley of Achor a door
    of hope.
There she shall respond as in the days
    of her youth,
  as at the time when she came out of
    the land of Egypt.
16On that day, says the LORD, you will call me, "My husband," and no longer will you call me, "My Baal."*a* 17For I will remove the names of the Baals from her mouth, and they shall be mentioned by name no more. 18I will make for you*b* a covenant on that day with the wild animals, the birds of the air, and the creeping things of the ground; and I will abolish*c* the bow, the sword, and war from the land; and I will make you lie down in safety. 19And I will take you for my wife forever; I will take you for my wife in righteousness and in justice, in steadfast love, and in mercy. 20I will take you for my wife in faithfulness; and you shall know the LORD.

21 On that day I will answer, says the
    LORD,
  I will answer the heavens
  and they shall answer the earth;
22 and the earth shall answer the grain,
    the wine, and the oil,
  and they shall answer Jezreel;*d*
23   and I will sow him*e* for myself in the
    land.
And I will have pity on Lo-ruhamah,*f*
  and I will say to Lo-ammi,*g* "You are
    my people";
  and he shall say, "You are my God."

2.14–23. 14–15: References to *the wilderness, the Valley of Achor,* and *the land of Egypt* recall Israel's deliverance from slavery in Egypt (Ex 1–15), its journey through the wilderness (Ex 16—Num 36), and its entrance into Canaan (Josh 7.24–26). **16:** Hosea plays on the multiple meanings of the Hebrew word "ba'al": It can be used as a common noun meaning "husband" or "master" or as the name of the Canaanite god Baal.

---

3 The LORD said to me again, "Go, love a woman who has a lover and is an adulteress, just as the LORD loves the people of Israel, though they turn to other gods and love raisin cakes." 2So I bought her for fifteen shekels of silver and a homer of barley and a measure of wine.*h* 3And I said to her, "You must remain as mine for many days; you shall not play the whore, you shall not have intercourse with a man, nor I with you." 4For the Israelites shall remain many days without king or prince, without sacrifice or pillar, without ephod or teraphim. 5Afterward the Israelites shall return and seek the LORD their God, and David their king; they shall come in awe to the LORD and to his goodness in the latter days.

3.1–5: Hosea marries an adulteress. The details of this account are so sketchy that it is difficult to decide whether it describes (1) Hosea's first marriage to Gomer in ch. 1, but from the first- rather than third-person perspective; (2) Hosea's marriage to a second woman; or (3) Hosea's remarriage to Gomer. In any case, the point of his symbolic act is clear: Israel has been an unfaithful wife but God desires her return. **1:** While Hosea connects *raisin cakes* with worship of other gods (as does Isa 16.7), they are also associated with legitimate Israelite worship (2 Sam 6.19). **2:** The nature of Hosea's transaction is unclear. Payment was made in ancient Israel for women slaves (Ex 21.7–11) and for wives (Ex 22.16–17), but this amount is not mentioned elsewhere, and the narrative* does not identify the recipient of the payment. **4:** Hosea predicts a coming judgment in which Israel will lose both political and religious leadership. The *ephod★* (Ex 28.4) and the *teraphim* (Judg 17.5; Zech 10.2) are both associated with priestly activity. **5:** The reference to *David their king* may indicate that Hosea looked forward to the reunification of Israel and Judah under a single king (1.11), since David had once ruled over a united kingdom (2 Sam 5; alternatively, it may represent the perspective of a later editor from the southern kingdom of Judah, over which David's descendants ruled for its entire history.

---

a That is, *"My master"*   *b* Heb *them*   *c* Heb *break*
d That is *God sows*   *e* Cn: Heb *her*   *f* That is *Not pitied*   *g* That is *Not my people*   *h* Gk: Heb *a homer of barley and a lethech of barley*

Prophets and Gender

Hosea's primary image for Israel's disloyalty to God is the wife who is unfaithful to her husband and has become a prostitute. One reason Hosea chose this image is the fact that his audience was primarily male—the men held the power and wealth in ancient patriarchal societies such as biblical Israel. For these men, faithless wives were a stinging shame. And by comparing the men's behavior to faithless wives, Hosea wanted to shock them so they would see the seriousness of their crimes. The image of the faithless wife gave Hosea a forceful means of criticizing the abuses of Israel's male elite. The problem of the image is that it connects disloyalty and sin with women in particular, a connection that must be clearly rejected in order to keep such an image from being used to disparage and mistreat women.

4 Hear the word of the LORD, O people
of Israel;
    for the LORD has an indictment
        against the inhabitants
        of the land.
There is no faithfulness or loyalty,
    and no knowledge of God in the land.
2 Swearing, lying, and murder,
    and stealing and adultery break out;
    bloodshed follows bloodshed.
3 Therefore the land mourns,
    and all who live in it languish;
together with the wild animals
    and the birds of the air,
    even the fish of the sea are perishing.

4 Yet let no one contend,
    and let none accuse,
    for with you is my contention,
        O priest.*a*
5 You shall stumble by day;
    the prophet also shall stumble with
        you by night,
    and I will destroy your mother.
6 My people are destroyed for lack of
        knowledge;
    because you have rejected knowledge,
    I reject you from being a priest to me.
And since you have forgotten the law of
        your God,
    I also will forget your children.

7 The more they increased,
    the more they sinned against me;
    they changed*b* their glory into shame.

8 They feed on the sin of my people;
    they are greedy for their iniquity.
9 And it shall be like people, like priest;
    I will punish them for their ways,
    and repay them for their deeds.
10 They shall eat, but not be satisfied;
    they shall play the whore, but not
        multiply;
    because they have forsaken the LORD
        to devote themselves to
            11whoredom.

4.1–19: God puts Israel on trial. The language of this section puts God's accusations against Israel into the context of a legal proceeding initiated by an *indictment* (v. 1) describing the allegations against Israel. The judicial sentence that will follow (5.1–6.3) is already anticipated here (vv. 3, 6, 9–10). **2:** This list of crimes is similar to those outlawed in the ten commandments (Ex 20.7, 13–16). **4–10:** God prosecutes Israel's priests. **6:** The *law* (Heb., "torah") is the basis for Israel's life and worship.

Wine and new wine
    take away the understanding.
12 My people consult a piece of wood,
    and their divining rod gives
        them oracles.
For a spirit of whoredom has led them
        astray,
    and they have played the whore,
        forsaking their God.

a Cn: Meaning of Heb uncertain   *b* Ancient Heb tradition: MT *I will change*

13 They sacrifice on the tops of the
        mountains,
    and make offerings upon the hills,
    under oak, poplar, and terebinth,
        because their shade is good.

    Therefore your daughters play
        the whore,
        and your daughters-in-law commit
        adultery.
14 I will not punish your daughters when
        they play the whore,
        nor your daughters-in-law when they
        commit adultery;
    for the men themselves go aside with
        whores,
        and sacrifice with temple prostitutes;
    thus a people without understanding
        comes to ruin.

15 Though you play the whore, O Israel,
        do not let Judah become guilty.
    Do not enter into Gilgal,
        or go up to Beth-aven,
    and do not swear, "As the
        LORD lives."
16 Like a stubborn heifer,
        Israel is stubborn;
    can the LORD now feed them
        like a lamb in a broad pasture?

17 Ephraim is joined to idols—
        let him alone.
18 When their drinking is ended, they
        indulge in sexual orgies;
    they love lewdness more than their
        glory.[a]
19 A wind has wrapped them[b] in its wings,
    and they shall be ashamed because of
        their altars.[c]

4.11–19: God prosecutes Israel for heretical worship,
employing the image of prostitution introduced in chs.
1–3. **13:** Since mountains (Mt. Sinai and Mt. Zion*)
and trees (Josh 24.26) are associated with authentic
Israelite worship, Hosea appears to be criticizing the
worship of other gods at these sites (as in Deut 12.2)
rather than these natural features themselves. **14:** The
term *temple prostitutes* translates the Hebrew word
"qedeshot," literally "holy women." Partly because of
the images of prostitution in the context, scholars have

suggested that these women may have been practicing ritual sex in sacred fertility rites. But the Hebrew
term does not suggest this in itself, and there is very
little concrete evidence of such practices in the biblical
world. **15:** *Gilgal* likely refers to a religious sanctuary
marking the site near Jericho where Israel entered Canaan (Josh 4.19–20). *Beth-aven*, literally "house of
worthlessness," appears to be a scornful name for
Bethel ("house of God"), one of the key northern religious shrines (1 Kings 12.26–30).

〰〰〰

5 Hear this, O priests!
    Give heed, O house of Israel!
    Listen, O house of the king!
        For the judgment pertains to you;
    for you have been a snare at Mizpah,
        and a net spread upon Tabor,
2 and a pit dug deep in Shittim;[d]
        but I will punish all of them.

3 I know Ephraim,
        and Israel is not hidden from me;
    for now, O Ephraim, you have played
        the whore;
    Israel is defiled.
4 Their deeds do not permit them
        to return to their God.
    For the spirit of whoredom is within
        them,
    and they do not know the LORD.

5 Israel's pride testifies against him;
        Ephraim[e] stumbles in his guilt;
    Judah also stumbles with them.
6 With their flocks and herds they shall
        go
        to seek the LORD,
    but they will not find him;
        he has withdrawn from them.
7 They have dealt faithlessly with the
        LORD;
        for they have borne illegitimate
        children.
    Now the new moon shall devour them
        along with their fields.

5.1–6.3: God sentences Israel. An extended judgment speech describing God's punishment of Israel

a Cn Compare Gk: Meaning of Heb uncertain
b Heb *her*   *c* Gk Syr: Heb *sacrifices*   *d* Cn: Meaning
of Heb uncertain   *e* Heb *Israel and Ephraim*

follows the indictment of ch. 4. **5.1–7: God reviews Israel's sins. 1:** Hosea does not explain the crimes of *Mizpah*, a town in southern Israel, or of *Tabor*, a mountain in the Jezreel Valley in northern Israel. **7:** The *new moon** marked the beginning of the month and of religious observances in Israel (Isa 1.13, Am 8.5).

8 Blow the horn in Gibeah,
    the trumpet in Ramah.
  Sound the alarm at Beth-aven;
    look behind you, Benjamin!
9 Ephraim shall become a desolation
    in the day of punishment;
  among the tribes of Israel
    I declare what is sure.
10 The princes of Judah have become
    like those who remove the landmark;
  on them I will pour out
    my wrath like water.
11 Ephraim is oppressed, crushed in
      judgment,
    because he was determined to go
      after vanity.ᵃ
12 Therefore I am like maggots to
      Ephraim,
    and like rottenness to the house of
      Judah.
13 When Ephraim saw his sickness,
    and Judah his wound,
  then Ephraim went to Assyria,
    and sent to the great king.ᵇ
  But he is not able to cure you
    or heal your wound.
14 For I will be like a lion to Ephraim,
    and like a young lion to the house of
      Judah.
  I myself will tear and go away;
    I will carry off, and no one shall rescue.
15 I will return again to my place
    until they acknowledge their guilt and
      seek my face.
  In their distress they will beg
    my favor:

6 "Come, let us return to the LORD;
    for it is he who has torn, and he will
      heal us;
  he has struck down, and he will bind
      us up.
2 After two days he will revive us;
    on the third day he will raise us up,
    that we may live before him.

3 Let us know, let us press on to know
      the LORD;
  his appearing is as sure as the dawn;
  he will come to us like the showers,
    like the spring rains that water the
      earth."
4 What shall I do with you, O Ephraim?
    What shall I do with you, O Judah?
  Your love is like a morning cloud,
    like the dew that goes away early.
5 Therefore I have hewn them by the
      prophets,
    I have killed them by the words of my
      mouth,
  and myᶜ judgment goes forth as the
      light.
6 For I desire steadfast love and not
      sacrifice,
    the knowledge of God rather than
      burnt offerings.

5.8–6.3. 5.8–15: God summons the guilty to announce the sentence. **8:** Why Hosea sounds the alarm in *Gibeah, Ramah,* and *Beth-aven,* all cities in the southern part of Israel occupied by the tribe of *Benjamin,* is not entirely clear. **13:** Hosea criticizes Israel for trying to save itself by an alliance with *Assyria,* the imperial power threatening Israel in Hosea's time. Two of Israel's kings, Menahem (2 Kings 15.19–20) and Hoshea (2 Kings 17.3), paid tribute to Assyria to remain in power. **6.1–3:** Hosea anticipates Israel's response to judgment: Only after it is punished will it try to change its ways.

7 But atᵈ Adam they transgressed the
      covenant;
    there they dealt faithlessly with me.
8 Gilead is a city of evildoers,
    tracked with blood.
9 As robbers lie in waitᵉ for someone,
    so the priests are banded together;ᶠ
  they murder on the road to Shechem,
    they commit a monstrous crime.
10 In the house of Israel I have seen a
      horrible thing;

a Gk: Meaning of Heb uncertain
b Cn: Heb *to a king who will contend*
c Gk Syr: Heb *your*   d Cn: Heb *like*
e Cn: Meaning of Heb uncertain
f Syr: Heb *are a company*

Ephraim's whoredom is there, Israel
is defiled.

11 For you also, O Judah, a harvest
is appointed.

6.4–11: Israel's disloyalty. God emphasizes Israel's lack of covenant* loyalty (v. 7), concluding with the image of prostitution (v. 10) that runs through the book. **6:** *Steadfast love* translates the Hebrew word "ḥesed," which describes loyalty to a relationship. Hosea's emphasis on right behavior rather than empty ritual is characteristic of prophetic thought (Am 5.21–24). **7–10:** The violent crime described here cannot be identified. *Adam* may refer to a city near the Jordan River (Josh 3.16). *Gilead*, located east of the Jordan, was the home of a band of men who assassinated Israel's king, Pekahiah (2 Kings 15.25). *Shechem*, Israel's first capital, was one of its most important cities.

When I would restore the fortunes of
my people,

7 ¹when I would heal Israel,
the corruption of Ephraim is revealed,
and the wicked deeds of Samaria;
for they deal falsely,
the thief breaks in,
and the bandits raid outside.
2 But they do not consider
that I remember all their wickedness.
Now their deeds surround them,
they are before my face.
3 By their wickedness they make the king
glad,
and the officials by their treachery.
4 They are all adulterers;
they are like a heated oven,
whose baker does not need to stir the
fire,
from the kneading of the dough until
it is leavened.
5 On the day of our king the officials
became sick with the heat of wine;
he stretched out his hand with
mockers.
6 For they are kindled*a* like an oven, their
heart burns within them;
all night their anger smolders;
in the morning it blazes like a flaming
fire.

7 All of them are hot as an oven,
and they devour their rulers.
All their kings have fallen;
none of them calls upon me.

7.1–16: Israel's political crimes. This speech focuses on the corruption of Israel's ruling elite by criticizing political intrigue at home (vv. 1–7) and alliances abroad (vv. 8–16). **1:** *Samaria* was Israel's capital through most of its history. **4–7:** Employing the image of a blazing oven, Hosea denounces the court officials responsible for numerous assassinations in Samaria. Four of the last six kings of Israel were killed in office.

8 Ephraim mixes himself with
the peoples;
Ephraim is a cake not turned.
9 Foreigners devour his strength,
but he does not know it;
gray hairs are sprinkled upon him,
but he does not know it.
10 Israel's pride testifies against*b* him;
yet they do not return to the LORD
their God,
or seek him, for all this.

11 Ephraim has become like a dove,
silly and without sense;
they call upon Egypt, they go
to Assyria.
12 As they go, I will cast my net over them;
I will bring them down like birds of
the air;
I will discipline them according to the
report made to their assembly.*c*
13 Woe to them, for they have strayed
from me!
Destruction to them, for they have
rebelled against me!
I would redeem them,
but they speak lies against me.

14 They do not cry to me from the heart,
but they wail upon their beds;
they gash themselves for grain
and wine;
they rebel against me.

a Gk Syr: Heb *brought near*   b Or *humbles*
c Meaning of Heb uncertain

Chart   **The politics behind the prophet**

King of Israel	Dates (BCE)	Path to Power	Historical Records
Jeroboam II	786–746	Son of Joash	2 Kings 14.23–29
Zechariah	746–745	Son of Jeroboam II	2 Kings 15.8–12
Shallum	745	Killed Zechariah	2 Kings 15.13–16
Menahem	745–738	Killed Shallum	2 Kings 15.17–22
Pekahiah	738–737	Son of Menahem	2 Kings 15.23–26
Pekah	737–732	Killed Pekahiah	2 Kings 15.25–27

15 It was I who trained and strengthened
　　their arms,
　　yet they plot evil against me.
16 They turn to that which does not profit;[a]
　　they have become like a
　　　defective bow;
　　their officials shall fall by the sword
　　because of the rage of their tongue.
　　So much for their babbling in the land
　　　of Egypt.

7.8–16. 11: Israel's foreign policy appears to have vacillated between alliances with *Egypt* and *Assyria*, the two great superpowers in whose sphere of influence Israel found itself. The history of Israel in 2 Kings mentions Israel's cooperation with Assyria (as explained in the comment on 5.13) and with Egypt (2 Kings 17.4) during Hosea's career. **14:** Gashing the body appears to be associated with earnest appeals to a deity, whether to Israel's God (Jer 41.5) or to Baal★ (1 Kings 18.28).

8 Set the trumpet to your lips!
　　One like a vulture[b] is over the house
　　　of the LORD,
　　because they have broken my covenant,
　　and transgressed my law.
2 Israel cries to me,
　　"My God, we—Israel—know you!"
3 Israel has spurned the good;
　　the enemy shall pursue him.

4 They made kings, but not through me;
　　they set up princes, but without my
　　　knowledge.

With their silver and gold they made
　　idols
　　for their own destruction.
5 Your calf is rejected, O Samaria.
　　My anger burns against them.
　　How long will they be incapable of
　　　innocence?
6 　For it is from Israel,
　an artisan made it;
　　it is not God.
　The calf of Samaria
　　shall be broken to pieces.[c]

8.1–9.9: Israel's religious crimes. Hosea criticizes Israel's religious practices, blaming Israel for worshipping images (8.4–6), participating in empty rituals (8.13), following other gods (9.1), and persecuting the prophets★ (9.7–8). **8.4:** By accusing Israel of making kings without God's knowledge, Hosea may refer to the installation of kings through violent palace uprisings rather than through proper religious and prophetic legitimation (7.1–7). **5–6:** The calf was a prominent religious image in Israel from its beginnings when its first king, Jeroboam I, set up calves in the religious sanctuaries at Bethel and Dan (1 Kings 12.28–30). They may have been considered pedestals or throne images for God, as were the cherubim★ in the Jerusalem Temple★ (1 Kings 6.23–28, 8.10–11), rather than images of God or idols. But both Hosea and Israel's historian (1 Kings 12.28) regard these calves as idols.

a Cn: Meaning of Heb uncertain   *b* Meaning of Heb uncertain   *c* Or *shall go up in flames*

■▪▵▵▵▪■

The Canaanite God Baal

The god Baal,☆ whom Hosea sees as the main rival of Israel's God, was a prominent Canaanite deity. He is known not only from the Bible, where he is presented in a negative light, but also from ancient texts found at Ugarit, a Canaanite city north of Israel where Baal was worshipped. In these texts, Baal is pictured with many of the same attributes as Israel's God. Baal is associated with the storm and with its accompanying phenomena—thunder, lightning, and rain—and is considered the source of the land's fertility, just as Israel's God is (Hosea 2.8–9, 21–23). Baal is described as riding the clouds, just as Israel's God does (Ps 68.4; Deut 33.26). And both deities appear to be associated with calf iconography. Thus, it is not hard to understand why Baal would have had particular appeal to the people of Israel and why Hosea is so insistent that Israel not replace its allegiance to its own God with devotion to Baal.

■▪▵▵▵▪■

7 For they sow the wind,
   and they shall reap the whirlwind.
The standing grain has no heads,
   it shall yield no meal;
if it were to yield,
   foreigners would devour it.
8 Israel is swallowed up;
   now they are among the nations
   as a useless vessel.
9 For they have gone up to Assyria,
   a wild ass wandering alone;
   Ephraim has bargained for lovers.
10 Though they bargain with the
     nations,
   I will now gather them up.
They shall soon writhe
   under the burden of kings
   and princes.

11 When Ephraim multiplied altars to
     expiate sin,
   they became to him altars for
     sinning.
12 Though I write for him the multitude of
     my instructions,
   they are regarded as a strange thing.
13 Though they offer choice sacrifices,*a*
   though they eat flesh,
     the LORD does not accept them.
Now he will remember their iniquity,
   and punish their sins;
   they shall return to Egypt.

14 Israel has forgotten his Maker,
   and built palaces;
and Judah has multiplied fortified
     cities;
   but I will send a fire upon his cities,
   and it shall devour his strongholds.

9 Do not rejoice, O Israel!
   Do not exult*b* as other nations do;
for you have played the whore,
     departing from your God.
You have loved a prostitute's pay
   on all threshing floors.
2 Threshing floor and wine vat shall not
     feed them,
   and the new wine shall fail them.
3 They shall not remain in the land of the
     LORD;
   but Ephraim shall return to Egypt,
   and in Assyria they shall eat unclean
     food.

4 They shall not pour drink offerings of
     wine to the LORD,
   and their sacrifices shall not please
     him.
Such sacrifices shall be like mourners'
     bread;
   all who eat of it shall be defiled;

a Cn: Meaning of Heb uncertain   *b* Gk: Heb *To exultation*

for their bread shall be for their hunger
    only;
    it shall not come to the house of the
      LORD.

8.7–9.4. 8.13: When Hosea describes Israel's punishment as a *return to Egypt,* he reverses the Exodus (2.15; 9.3; Ex 1–15), in which God delivered Israel from slavery. **9.1:** Since *threshing* floors* are sites for worship (2 Sam 24.24–25), Hosea denounces Israel's worship of Baal* there. The *prostitute's pay* to which he refers is likely the grain harvest Israel attributed to Baal rather than to God (2.8). **4:** *Mourners' bread* may be translated literally in two ways: either "bread of sorrow," referring to bread eaten in exile (9.3), or "bread of idolatry,*" referring to Israel's sacrifices that God has rejected.

5 What will you do on the day of
    appointed festival,
    and on the day of the festival of the
      LORD?
6 For even if they escape destruction,
    Egypt shall gather them,
    Memphis shall bury them.
    Nettles shall possess their precious
      things of silver;[a]
    thorns shall be in their tents.

7 The days of punishment have come,
    the days of recompense have come;
    Israel cries,[b]
    "The prophet is a fool,
      the man of the spirit is mad!"
    Because of your great iniquity,
      your hostility is great.
8 The prophet is a sentinel for my God
      over Ephraim,
    yet a fowler's snare is on all his ways,
    and hostility in the house of his God.
9 They have deeply corrupted themselves
    as in the days of Gibeah;
    he will remember their iniquity,
    he will punish their sins.

9.5–9. 6: *Memphis* is a prominent Egyptian city known for its pyramids, tombs, and burial grounds. **9:** Hosea's reference here and in 10.9 to the corruption in *Gibeah* may refer to the intertribal conflict and the crimes that led to it (Judg 19–21).

10 Like grapes in the wilderness,
    I found Israel.
    Like the first fruit on the fig tree,
      in its first season,
    I saw your ancestors.
    But they came to Baal-peor,
      and consecrated themselves to a thing
        of shame,
    and became detestable like the thing
      they loved.
11 Ephraim's glory shall fly away like a
      bird—
    no birth, no pregnancy, no
      conception!
12 Even if they bring up children,
    I will bereave them until no one is
      left.
    Woe to them indeed
      when I depart from them!
13 Once I saw Ephraim as a young palm
      planted in a lovely meadow,[a]
    but now Ephraim must lead out his
      children for slaughter.
14 Give them, O LORD—
    what will you give?
    Give them a miscarrying womb
    and dry breasts.

15 Every evil of theirs began at Gilgal;
    there I came to hate them.
    Because of the wickedness of
      their deeds
    I will drive them out of my house.
    I will love them no more;
      all their officials are rebels.

16 Ephraim is stricken,
    their root is dried up,
    they shall bear no fruit.
    Even though they give birth,
    I will kill the cherished offspring of
      their womb.
17 Because they have not listened to him,
    my God will reject them;
    they shall become wanderers among
      the nations.

9.10–11.7: Images of a rebellious people. With a series of images taken from Israel's agricultural and fam-

a Meaning of Heb uncertain   *b* Cn Compare Gk: Heb *shall know*

ily context—grapes and figs, a young palm tree, a vine, a female calf, a son—Hosea highlights Israel's past potential and present waywardness. **9.10–12:** The comparison of Israel to *grapes* and *figs* begins with images of fertility and a new harvest and concludes with images of infertility and barrenness. **10:** *Baal-peor* is a site east of the Jordan where the Israelites once worshipped Baal (Num 25.1–5). **13–17:** Israel is compared to a *young palm* with great potential (v. 13) whose roots dry up and whose fruit fails (v. 16). **15:** *Gilgal*, the site where Israel entered Canaan (Josh 4.19–20), is criticized by Hosea for its false worship (4.15). **17:** Hosea refers here and elsewhere (5.13–14; 10.14) to Israelites deported by conquering countries, a practice of the Assyrians described also by Israel's historian (2 Kings 15.29; 17.6).

<hr>

10 Israel is a luxuriant vine
that yields its fruit.
The more his fruit increased
the more altars he built;
as his country improved,
he improved his pillars.
2 Their heart is false;
now they must bear their guilt.
The LORD *a* will break down
their altars,
and destroy their pillars.

3 For now they will say:
"We have no king,
for we do not fear the LORD,
and a king—what could he do for us?"
4 They utter mere words;
with empty oaths they make
covenants;
so litigation springs up like poisonous
weeds
in the furrows of the field.
5 The inhabitants of Samaria tremble
for the calf *b* of Beth-aven.
Its people shall mourn for it,
and its idolatrous priests shall wail *c*
over it,
over its glory that has departed from it.
6 The thing itself shall be carried to
Assyria
as tribute to the great king. *d*
Ephraim shall be put to shame,
and Israel shall be ashamed of his
idol. *e*

7 Samaria's king shall perish
like a chip on the face of the waters.
8 The high places of Aven, the sin
of Israel,
shall be destroyed.
Thorn and thistle shall grow up
on their altars.
They shall say to the mountains, Cover
us,
and to the hills, Fall on us.

<hr>

10.1–8: The comparison of Israel to a vine begins with images of bountiful fruit (v. 1) and concludes with images of thorns and thistles (v. 8). **1–2:** *Pillars* were common installations in Israelite sanctuaries (Gen 28.18–22). **3:** The people's words, *"We have no king,"* could anticipate the end of Israel and its kingship; or they could mean that Israel has rejected the rule of God, its divine king (1 Sam 8.4–8), as the following line seems to indicate. **5:** For Hosea's view of Israel's calves, compare 13.2 and 8.5–6 (see comment at 8.5–6). **8:** *The high places* of Aven* (literally, "worthlessness") are the sites of Israel's false worship (4.13).

<hr>

9 Since the days of Gibeah you have
sinned, O Israel;
there they have continued.
Shall not war overtake them in
Gibeah?
10 I will come *f* against the wayward
people to punish them;
and nations shall be gathered against
them
when they are punished *g* for their
double iniquity.

11 Ephraim was a trained heifer
that loved to thresh,
and I spared her fair neck;
but I will make Ephraim break the
ground;
Judah must plow;
Jacob must harrow for himself.
12 Sow for yourselves righteousness;
reap steadfast love;
break up your fallow ground;

a Heb *he*   b Gk Syr: Heb *calves*   c Cn: Heb *exult*
d Cn: Heb *to a king who will contend*   e Cn: Heb
counsel   f Cn Compare Gk: Heb *In my desire*
g Gk: Heb *bound*

for it is time to seek the LORD,
    that he may come and rain
      righteousness upon you.

13 You have plowed wickedness,
    you have reaped injustice,
    you have eaten the fruit of lies.
Because you have trusted in
      your power
    and in the multitude of your
      warriors,
14 therefore the tumult of war shall rise
    against your people,
    and all your fortresses shall
      be destroyed,
as Shalman destroyed Beth-arbel on the
      day of battle
    when mothers were dashed in pieces
      with their children.
15 Thus it shall be done to you, O Bethel,
    because of your great wickedness.
At dawn the king of Israel
    shall be utterly cut off.

11 When Israel was a child, I loved him,
    and out of Egypt I called my son.
2 The more I*a* called them,
    the more they went from me;*b*
they kept sacrificing to the Baals,
    and offering incense to idols.

3 Yet it was I who taught Ephraim to
      walk,
    I took them up in my*c* arms;
    but they did not know that I healed
      them.
4 I led them with cords of human
      kindness,
    with bands of love.
I was to them like those
    who lift infants to their cheeks.*d*
I bent down to them and fed them.

5 They shall return to the land of Egypt,
    and Assyria shall be their king,
    because they have refused to return
      to me.
6 The sword rages in their cities,
    it consumes their oracle-priests,
    and devours because of their
      schemes.

7 My people are bent on turning away
    from me.
To the Most High they call,
    but he does not raise them up at all.*e*

10.9–11.7. 10.9–15: Israel is compared to a female calf (v. 11), once obedient but now plowing wickedness. **9:** For Hosea's criticism of *Gibeah,* see 9.9. **14:** Neither *Shalman* nor *Beth-arbel* can be positively identified, though some have suggested that *Shalman* is a shortened form of Shalmaneser V, who imprisoned Israel's last king, Hoshea, and laid siege to Samaria (2 Kings 17.3–5). **15:** *Bethel* was one of Israel's major religious sanctuaries. **11.1–7:** Israel is compared to a son who, though loved and raised with kindness, is stubborn and rebellious.

8 How can I give you up, Ephraim?
    How can I hand you over, O Israel?
How can I make you like Admah?
    How can I treat you like Zeboiim?
My heart recoils within me;
    my compassion grows warm
      and tender.
9 I will not execute my fierce anger;
    I will not again destroy Ephraim;
for I am God and no mortal,
    the Holy One in your midst,
    and I will not come in wrath.*e*

10 They shall go after the LORD,
    who roars like a lion;
when he roars,
    his children shall come trembling
      from the west.
11 They shall come trembling like birds
      from Egypt,
    and like doves from the land of
      Assyria;
    and I will return them to their homes,
      says the LORD.

11.8–11: A promise of restoration. The tone shifts from judgment to salvation: God shows compassion for Israel and promises to return its people to their homes. **8:** *Admah* and *Zeboiim* are cities which, like Sodom and Gomorrah, symbolize wickedness (Deut

a Gk: Heb *they*   *b* Gk: Heb *them*   *c* Gk Syr Vg: Heb *his*   *d* Or *who ease the yoke on their jaws*
e Meaning of Heb uncertain

29.23). **10:** This image of Israel returning *trembling from the west* assumes an exilic context and suggests that vv. 10–11 may have been added by a later Judean editor.

12[a] Ephraim has surrounded me with lies,
   and the house of Israel with deceit;
but Judah still walks[b] with God,
   and is faithful to the Holy One.

12 Ephraim herds the wind,
   and pursues the east wind all day
      long;
they multiply falsehood and violence;
   they make a treaty with Assyria,
   and oil is carried to Egypt.

2 The LORD has an indictment against
      Judah,
   and will punish Jacob according to his
      ways,
   and repay him according to his deeds.
3 In the womb he tried to supplant his
      brother,
   and in his manhood he strove with
      God.
4 He strove with the angel and prevailed,
   he wept and sought his favor;
he met him at Bethel,
   and there he spoke with him.[c]
5 The LORD the God of hosts,
   the LORD is his name!
6 But as for you, return to your God,
   hold fast to love and justice,
   and wait continually for your God.

7 A trader, in whose hands are false
      balances,
   he loves to oppress.
8 Ephraim has said, "Ah, I am rich,
   I have gained wealth for myself;
in all of my gain
   no offense has been found in me
   that would be sin."[d]
9 I am the LORD your God
   from the land of Egypt;
I will make you live in tents again,
   as in the days of the appointed
      festival.

11.12–13.16: The history of a rebellious people. Hosea recalls major events in Israel's past to illustrate

God's acts of salvation and Israel's acts of rebellion. **12.3a:** Hosea describes the birth of Israel's ancestor Jacob (later renamed Israel) who struggled with *his brother* Esau in their mother's womb (Gen 25.21–26). **3b–4a:** Israel's ancestor Jacob *strove with God* at the Jabbok River when he returned home to meet Esau (Gen 32.22–32). **4b:** God appeared to Israel's ancestor Jacob at *Bethel* in a dream (Gen 28.10–22). **9:** Hosea recalls Israel's deliverance from slavery in *Egypt* and its journey through the wilderness.

10 I spoke to the prophets;
   it was I who multiplied visions,
   and through the prophets I will bring
      destruction.
11 In Gilead[e] there is iniquity,
   they shall surely come to nothing.
In Gilgal they sacrifice bulls,
   so their altars shall be like
      stone heaps
   on the furrows of the field.
12 Jacob fled to the land of Aram,
   there Israel served for a wife,
   and for a wife he guarded sheep.[f]
13 By a prophet the LORD brought Israel
      up from Egypt,
   and by a prophet he was guarded.
14 Ephraim has given bitter offense,
   so his Lord will bring his crimes down
      on him
   and pay him back for his insults.

13 When Ephraim spoke, there was
      trembling;
   he was exalted in Israel;
   but he incurred guilt through Baal
      and died.
2 And now they keep on sinning
   and make a cast image for
      themselves,
   idols of silver made according to their
      understanding,
   all of them the work of artisans.
"Sacrifice to these," they say.[g]
   People are kissing calves!
3 Therefore they shall be like the morning
      mist
   or like the dew that goes away early,

a Ch 12.1 in Heb   *b* Heb *roams* or *rules*   *c* Gk Syr: Heb *us*   *d* Meaning of Heb uncertain   *e* Compare Syr: Heb *Gilead*   *f* Heb lacks *sheep*   *g* Cn Compare Gk: Heb *To these they say sacrifices of people*

like chaff that swirls from the threshing
    floor
  or like smoke from a window.

4 Yet I have been the LORD your God
    ever since the land of Egypt;
you know no God but me,
    and besides me there is no savior.
5 It was I who fed*a* you in the
    wilderness,
    in the land of drought.
6 When I fed*b* them, they were satisfied;
    they were satisfied, and their heart
      was proud;
    therefore they forgot me.
7 So I will become like a lion to them,
    like a leopard I will lurk beside the
      way.
8 I will fall upon them like a bear robbed
    of her cubs,
    and will tear open the covering
      of their heart;
there I will devour them like a lion,
    as a wild animal would mangle them.

9 I will destroy you, O Israel;
    who can help you?*c*
10 Where now is*d* your king, that he may
    save you?
    Where in all your cities are your rulers,
of whom you said,
    "Give me a king and rulers"?
11 I gave you a king in my anger,
    and I took him away in my wrath.

12 Ephraim's iniquity is bound up;
    his sin is kept in store.
13 The pangs of childbirth come for him,
    but he is an unwise son;
for at the proper time he does not
    present himself
    at the mouth of the womb.

14 Shall I ransom them from the power of
    Sheol?
    Shall I redeem them from Death?
O Death, where are*e* your plagues?
O Sheol, where is*e* your destruction?
    Compassion is hidden from my eyes.

15 Although he may flourish among
    rushes,*f*
    the east wind shall come, a blast from
      the LORD,
    rising from the wilderness;
and his fountain shall dry up,
    his spring shall be parched.
It shall strip his treasury
    of every precious thing.
16*g* Samaria shall bear her guilt,
    because she has rebelled against her
      God;
they shall fall by the sword,
    their little ones shall be dashed in
      pieces,
    and their pregnant women
      ripped open.

12.10–13.16. 12.11: For Hosea's view of *Gilead* and
Gilgal, compare 4.15, 6.8. **12:** *The land of Aram* was
the territory to which Israel's ancestor Jacob fled from
his brother Esau's anger (Gen 27.41–45; 29.1–30). **13:**
The prophet to whom Hosea refers is Moses, who led
Israel out of Egypt (Deut 34.10–12). **13.4:** Hosea's idea
that Israel learned to know its God in Egypt appears to
be based on the tradition that the name of God was
revealed to Israel there (Ex 3.13–15). **5–6:** After delivering Israel from Egypt, God fed them manna in the
wilderness (Num 11.7–9). **11:** Hosea may share the
viewpoint of the author of 1 Sam 8.6–8, who saw Israel's request for a king as a rejection of God's rule.
14: *Sheol*✦ was a shadowy realm inhabited by the
dead (Ps 6.5). **16:** Hosea anticipates Israel's end with
a vivid image of the fall of its capital, *Samaria*.

---

14 Return, O Israel, to the LORD your
    God,
    for you have stumbled because of
      your iniquity.
2 Take words with you
    and return to the LORD;
say to him,
    "Take away all guilt;
accept that which is good,
    and we will offer
    the fruit*h* of our lips.

---

a Gk Syr: Heb *knew*   *b* Cn: Heb *according to their*
pasture   *c* Gk Syr: Heb *for in me is your help*
d Gk Syr Vg: Heb *I will be*   *e* Gk Syr: Heb *I will be*
f Or *among brothers*   *g* Ch 14.1 in Heb   *h* Gk Syr:
Heb *bulls*

3 Assyria shall not save us;
  we will not ride upon horses;
  we will say no more, 'Our God,'
  to the work of our hands.
  In you the orphan finds mercy."

14.1–3: A call for repentance. Hosea urges Israel to turn from reliance on other nations to reliance on its God. **3:** To *ride upon horses* is to trust military strength more than God's protection.

~~~~~~

4 I will heal their disloyalty;
  I will love them freely,
  for my anger has turned from them.
5 I will be like the dew to Israel;
  he shall blossom like the lily,
  he shall strike root like the forests of
  Lebanon.[a]
6 His shoots shall spread out;
  his beauty shall be like the olive tree,
  and his fragrance like that of
  Lebanon.
7 They shall again live beneath
  my[b] shadow,
  they shall flourish as a garden;[c]
  they shall blossom like the vine,

their fragrance shall be like the wine
  of Lebanon.

8 O Ephraim, what have I[d] to do with
  idols?
  It is I who answer and look after you.[e]
I am like an evergreen cypress;
  your faithfulness[f] comes from me.
9 Those who are wise understand these
  things;
  those who are discerning know them.
For the ways of the LORD are right,
  and the upright walk in them,
  but transgressors stumble in them.

14.4–9: A second promise of restoration. In the spirit of 11.8–11, God promises to restore Israel to faithfulness and well-being. **5:** The *forests of Lebanon* were legendary★ for their magnificence (Ps 104.16). **9:** The concluding verse in Hosea shares the vocabulary and perspective of the book of Proverbs (10.29) and is likely a conclusion added by Israel's sages.

~~~~~~

a Cn: Heb *like Lebanon*   *b* Heb *his*   *c* Cn: Heb *they shall grow grain*   *d* Or *What more has Ephraim*   *e* Heb *him*   *f* Heb *your fruit*

JOEL

Introduction

Joel is unique among the prophets* in his focus on a natural catastrophe, a widespread and destructive locust plague. Interpreting the plague as divine judgment on Jerusalem, the prophet calls on the people to mourn their predicament (1.5–20) and tells the priests to declare a solemn assembly to repent and ask for God's forgiveness (2.1–17). Then he predicts that God will restore the land to its former prosperity (2.18–27). Two concluding sections that do not mention the locusts, a prediction of the outpouring of God's spirit (2.28–32) and of the political renewal of Jerusalem (3.1–21), are either Joel's visions of the future set in motion by the plague or additions to Joel by a later editor.

No clear historical references in chs. 1–2 connect this plague to a precise period in Jerusalem's history. Such plagues were not uncommon (Am 7.1–3), and understanding the seriousness of these ancient plagues is more important for reading Joel than knowing the exact date of this particular plague. Because the vision of Jerusalem's political renewal in ch. 3 was composed after Jerusalem was destroyed and its citizens exiled, many believe all of Joel was written at this time, perhaps as late as the fourth or fifth centuries BCE. Editors placed Joel between Hosea and Amos, two eighth-century prophets, either because a tradition held that the plague happened in this period or because parts of Joel are so much like Amos (see Joel 3.16a; Amos 1.2a).

READING GUIDE

To appreciate the danger of the crisis Joel faced, the modern reader must recover a sense of the terrible destructiveness of a locust infestation for a pre-industrial agricultural society that lives year to year by its harvests. The key issue for reading the book as a whole is deciding whether the locust plague in 1.1–2.27 is the prelude to the religious and political renewal predicted in 2.28–3.21 or whether these two parts of Joel arise from different experiences in Jerusalem's history.

1 The word of the LORD that came to Joel son of Pethuel:

2 Hear this, O elders,
   give ear, all inhabitants of the land!
   Has such a thing happened in
      your days,
   or in the days of your ancestors?
3 Tell your children of it,
   and let your children tell their
      children,
   and their children another generation.

4 What the cutting locust left,
   the swarming locust has eaten.

What the swarming locust left,
   the hopping locust has eaten,
and what the hopping locust left,
   the destroying locust has eaten.

1.1–4: The locust plague. Joel introduces the locust plague as one unparalleled in the living memory of his people (compare 2.2). **4:** The four terms for locust here and in 2.25 may refer to stages in the growth of the locust. The meanings of the Hebrew terms are unclear, and the translations, *cutting locust*, etc., are only suggestions.

5 Wake up, you drunkards, and weep;
   and wail, all you wine-drinkers,

The Desert Locust

The desert locust, known to scientists as "Schistocerca americana, subspecies gregaria," is a distant cousin of the American grasshopper. It lives and breeds in the great desert stretching from the Sahara in Africa to the Arabian Peninsula, including the Sinai and Judean deserts. In the right conditions, it multiplies rapidly, crowds into dense swarms, and sweeps into neighboring fertile areas, where it eats its own weight in green food each day. A swarm of desert locusts in Somaliland in 1957 was estimated to include 16 billion locusts and to weigh 50,000 tons. The desert locust's threat to Middle Eastern societies is recorded in the earliest human records and continues into the present, where it is monitored and combated by the United Nations Food and Agriculture Organization's Emergency Center for Locust Operations.

over the sweet wine,
for it is cut off from your mouth.
6 For a nation has invaded my land,
powerful and innumerable;
its teeth are lions' teeth,
and it has the fangs of a lioness.
7 It has laid waste my vines,
and splintered my fig trees;
it has stripped off their bark and thrown
it down;
their branches have turned white.

8 Lament like a virgin dressed in
sackcloth
for the husband of her youth.
9 The grain offering and the drink
offering are cut off
from the house of the LORD.
The priests mourn,
the ministers of the LORD.
10 The fields are devastated,
the ground mourns;
for the grain is destroyed,
the wine dries up,
the oil fails.

11 Be dismayed, you farmers,
wail, you vinedressers,
over the wheat and the barley;
for the crops of the field are ruined.
12 The vine withers,
the fig tree droops.
Pomegranate, palm, and apple—
all the trees of the field are dried up;

surely, joy withers away
among the people.

13 Put on sackcloth and lament,
you priests;
wail, you ministers of the altar.
Come, pass the night in sackcloth,
you ministers of my God!
Grain offering and drink offering
are withheld from the house of
your God.

14 Sanctify a fast,
call a solemn assembly.
Gather the elders
and all the inhabitants of the land
to the house of the LORD your God,
and cry out to the LORD.

15 Alas for the day!
For the day of the LORD is near,
and as destruction from the Almighty[a]
it comes.
16 Is not the food cut off
before our eyes,
joy and gladness
from the house of our God?

17 The seed shrivels under the clods,[b]
the storehouses are desolate;

a Traditional rendering of Heb *Shaddai*   b Meaning of Heb uncertain

the granaries are ruined
 because the grain has failed.
18 How the animals groan!
 The herds of cattle wander about
because there is no pasture for them;
 even the flocks of sheep are
  dazed.^a

19 To you, O LORD, I cry.
 For fire has devoured
  the pastures of the wilderness,
and flames have burned
 all the trees of the field.
20 Even the wild animals cry to you
 because the watercourses are
  dried up,
and fire has devoured
 the pastures of the wilderness.

1.5–20: The call to mourning. Joel summons three groups into mourning: consumers of wine (vv. 5–10), farmers (vv. 11–12), and priests (vv. 13–18). Then he cries out to God himself (vv. 19–20). **6:** *A nation has invaded my land* begins an extended metaphor,* by which Joel compares the incoming locust swarms to an invading army (compare 2.2, 4–11, 25). **7:** *Their branches have turned white:* In this and other vivid details of decimated vegetation, Joel's description matches that of eyewitnesses of Jerusalem's last great locust plague in 1915. **15:** *The day of the LORD* is a prophetic theme that reappears throughout Joel (2.1, 11, 31; 3.14). **19:** Joel uses the metaphor of *fire* together with the metaphor of an army for the devouring locust (compare 2.3).

2 Blow the trumpet in Zion;
 sound the alarm on my holy
  mountain!
Let all the inhabitants of the land
  tremble,
 for the day of the LORD is coming,
  it is near—
2 a day of darkness and gloom,
 a day of clouds and thick
  darkness!
Like blackness spread upon the
  mountains
 a great and powerful army comes;
their like has never been from of old,
 nor will be again after them
  in ages to come.

3 Fire devours in front of them,
 and behind them a flame burns.
Before them the land is like the garden
  of Eden,
 but after them a desolate wilderness,
 and nothing escapes them.

4 They have the appearance of horses,
 and like war-horses they charge.
5 As with the rumbling of chariots,
 they leap on the tops of the
  mountains,
like the crackling of a flame of fire
 devouring the stubble,
like a powerful army
 drawn up for battle.

6 Before them peoples are in anguish,
 all faces grow pale.^b
7 Like warriors they charge,
 like soldiers they scale the wall.
Each keeps to its own course,
 they do not swerve from^c their paths.
8 They do not jostle one another,
 each keeps to its own track;
they burst through the weapons
 and are not halted.
9 They leap upon the city,
 they run upon the walls;
they climb up into the houses,
 they enter through the windows like
  a thief.

10 The earth quakes before them,
 the heavens tremble.
The sun and the moon are darkened,
 and the stars withdraw their shining.
11 The LORD utters his voice
 at the head of his army;
how vast is his host!
 Numberless are those who obey his
  command.
Truly the day of the LORD is great;
 terrible indeed—who can endure it?

12 Yet even now, says the LORD,
 return to me with all your heart,

---

a Compare Gk Syr Vg: Meaning of Heb uncertain
b Meaning of Heb uncertain c Gk Syr Vg: Heb *they do not take a pledge along*

with fasting, with weeping, and with
      mourning;
13   rend your hearts and not
         your clothing.
   Return to the LORD, your God,
      for he is gracious and merciful,
   slow to anger, and abounding in
         steadfast love,
      and relents from punishing.
14 Who knows whether he will not turn
         and relent,
      and leave a blessing behind him,
   a grain offering and a drink offering
      for the LORD, your God?

15 Blow the trumpet in Zion;
      sanctify a fast;
   call a solemn assembly;
16   gather the people.
   Sanctify the congregation;
      assemble the aged;
   gather the children,
      even infants at the breast.
   Let the bridegroom leave his room,
      and the bride her canopy.

17 Between the vestibule and the altar
      let the priests, the ministers of the
         LORD, weep.
   Let them say, "Spare your people,
         O LORD,
      and do not make your heritage a
         mockery,
      a byword among the nations.
   Why should it be said among the
         peoples,
      'Where is their God?' "

2.1–17: The call to repentance. 1–3: Turning again
to the priests whom he had just addressed (1.13–18),
Joel directs them to *blow the trumpet in Zion** (a synonym for Jerusalem), assembling all the people to ask
for God's forgiveness (vv. 15–17). **2:** *Darkness* and
clouds are traditional images associated with the day
of the LORD, but they may also refer here to the dense
swarms of locusts that can obscure the sun. **4–11:** Joel
develops in detail his comparison of the locust swarms
with an invading army. **13:** *Rend your hearts and not
your clothing:* While not abandoning ritual—he directs the priests to lead the people in a liturgy* of repentance—Joel sees genuine religion as a matter of

inner renewal, as is common among the prophets. Like
other prophets, Joel regards disasters like this as acts
of divine judgment that require repentance, but unlike
them, he does not describe the particular sins that he
believes have brought on this punishment. *Gracious
and merciful . . . :* This is an adaptation of a traditional
description of God (Ex 34.6–7; Jon 4.2).

~~~~~~~~~~

18 Then the LORD became jealous for his
         land,
      and had pity on his people.
19 In response to his people the LORD said:
   I am sending you
      grain, wine, and oil,
      and you will be satisfied;
   and I will no more make you
      a mockery among the nations.

20 I will remove the northern army far
         from you,
      and drive it into a parched and
         desolate land,
   its front into the eastern sea,
      and its rear into the western sea;
   its stench and foul smell will rise up.
      Surely he has done great things!

21 Do not fear, O soil;
      be glad and rejoice,
      for the LORD has done great things!
22 Do not fear, you animals of the field,
      for the pastures of the wilderness are
         green;
   the tree bears its fruit,
      the fig tree and vine give their full
         yield.

23 O children of Zion, be glad
      and rejoice in the LORD your God;
   for he has given the early rain*a* for your
         vindication,
      he has poured down for you abundant
         rain,
      the early and the later rain, as before.
24 The threshing floors shall be full
         of grain,
      the vats shall overflow with wine
         and oil.

a Meaning of Heb uncertain

The Day of the LORD

Appearing five times in Joel (1.15; 2.1, 11, 31; 3.14), this expression is used in the Bible for a decisive divine act in human affairs. In its earliest occurrence, Amos uses it to describe an act of God's judgment on Israel (5.18–20). But since Amos implies that his audience believed this expression referred to an act of God's salvation, scholars think *the day of the* LORD originally had a positive meaning, describing God's victory on Israel's behalf. In some cases, in fact, this phrase is used for God's judgment on the nations and restoration of Judah (Ob 15–21; Zech 14.1–9). Scholars disagree whether *the day of the* LORD is used both ways in Joel—for judgment in 1.15; 2.1, 11 and for salvation in 2.31; 3.14—or whether all uses point toward the final salvation described in ch. 3.

25 I will repay you for the years
   that the swarming locust has eaten,
the hopper, the destroyer, and the
   cutter,
   my great army, which I sent against
   you.

26 You shall eat in plenty and be
   satisfied,
   and praise the name of the LORD
   your God,
who has dealt wondrously with you.
And my people shall never again be put
   to shame.
27 You shall know that I am in the midst
   of Israel,
   and that I, the LORD, am your God
   and there is no other.
And my people shall never again be put
   to shame.

2.18–27: God's renewal of the land. Joel anticipates new harvests to replace those the locusts have destroyed. Each crop ruined in 1.1–2.17 is to be restored. **20:** *The northern army* in Hebrew is simply "the northerner," used for the locust here because it is a traditional designation of the enemy, since enemies invaded from the north, or because the locusts themselves came in from the north, as did the first swarms in the 1915 plague in Jerusalem. The *eastern sea* is the Dead Sea and the *western sea* is the Mediterranean Sea.

28[a] Then afterward
   I will pour out my spirit on all flesh;

your sons and your daughters shall
   prophesy,
   your old men shall dream dreams,
   and your young men shall see visions.
29 Even on the male and female slaves,
   in those days, I will pour out
   my spirit.

30 I will show portents in the heavens and on the earth, blood and fire and columns of smoke. 31 The sun shall be turned to darkness, and the moon to blood, before the great and terrible day of the LORD comes. 32 Then everyone who calls on the name of the LORD shall be saved; for in Mount Zion and in Jerusalem there shall be those who escape, as the LORD has said, and among the survivors shall be those whom the LORD calls.

2.28–32: The outpouring of God's spirit. In the Hebrew Bible, these verses constitute a new chapter: 3.1–5. **28–29:** In the future, the prophetic gift will be spread among all people. **30–32:** *The day of the* LORD is pictured with traditional images of darkness as a day of judgment on Jerusalem, which only a few will survive. Whether these few are those who survived the locusts (which are not mentioned here) or the survivors of the destruction of Jerusalem in 586 BCE is not stated.

3 [b] For then, in those days and at that time, when I restore the fortunes of Judah and Jerusalem, 2 I will gather all the nations and

a Ch 3.1 in Heb   b Ch 4.1 in Heb

bring them down to the valley of Jehosha-phat, and I will enter into judgment with them there, on account of my people and my heritage Israel, because they have scattered them among the nations. They have divided my land, ³and cast lots for my people, and traded boys for prostitutes, and sold girls for wine, and drunk it down.

4 What are you to me, O Tyre and Sidon, and all the regions of Philistia? Are you pay-ing me back for something? If you are paying me back, I will turn your deeds back upon your own heads swiftly and speedily. ⁵For you have taken my silver and my gold, and have carried my rich treasures into your tem-ples.ᵃ ⁶You have sold the people of Judah and Jerusalem to the Greeks, removing them far from their own border. ⁷But now I will rouse them to leave the places to which you have sold them, and I will turn your deeds back upon your own heads. ⁸I will sell your sons and your daughters into the hand of the people of Judah, and they will sell them to the Sabeans, to a nation far away; for the LORD has spoken.

9 Proclaim this among the nations:
   Prepare war,ᵇ
      stir up the warriors.
   Let all the soldiers draw near,
      let them come up.
10 Beat your plowshares into swords,
      and your pruning hooks into spears;
      let the weakling say, "I am a warrior."

11 Come quickly,ᶜ
      all you nations all around,
      gather yourselves there.
   Bring down your warriors, O LORD.
12 Let the nations rouse themselves,
      and come up to the valley of
         Jehoshaphat;
   for there I will sit to judge
      all the neighboring nations.

13 Put in the sickle,
      for the harvest is ripe.
   Go in, tread,
      for the wine press is full.
   The vats overflow,
      for their wickedness is great.

14 Multitudes, multitudes,
      in the valley of decision!
   For the day of the LORD is near
      in the valley of decision.
15 The sun and the moon are darkened,
      and the stars withdraw their shining.

16 The LORD roars from Zion,
      and utters his voice from Jerusalem,
      and the heavens and the earth shake.
   But the LORD is a refuge for his
         people,
      a stronghold for the people of Israel.

17 So you shall know that I, the LORD
         your God,
      dwell in Zion, my holy mountain.
   And Jerusalem shall be holy,
      and strangers shall never again pass
         through it.

18 In that day
   the mountains shall drip sweet wine,
      the hills shall flow with milk,
   and all the stream beds of Judah
      shall flow with water;
   a fountain shall come forth from the
         house of the LORD
      and water the Wadi Shittim.

19 Egypt shall become a desolation
      and Edom a desolate wilderness,
   because of the violence done to the
         people of Judah,
      in whose land they have shed
         innocent blood.
20 But Judah shall be inhabited forever,
      and Jerusalem to all generations.
21 I will avenge their blood, and I will not
         clear the guilty,ᵈ
      for the LORD dwells in Zion.

3.1–21: Judgment on the nations and the restora-tion of Jerusalem. In the Hebrew Bible, these verses are 4.1–21. This poem does not mention the locusts, but takes as its backdrop the fall of Jerusalem in 586 BCE and the exile of its people (vv. 2, 5). It follows the

---

a Or palaces   b Heb sanctify war   c Meaning of Heb uncertain   d Gk Syr: Heb I will hold innocent their blood that I have not held innocent

traditional structure of hymns, such as Ex 15.1–18 and Zech 14.1–21, which celebrate the victory of God the warrior over Israel's enemies. The threat to divine rule (vv. 1–8) brings God into a battle (vv. 9–14) that shakes the cosmos (vv. 15–16). Victorious, God is enthroned on his holy mountain (v. 17), making the world fertile (v. 18) and saving his people (vv. 19–21). **2:** *Jehoshaphat* is a symbolic—rather than an actual, geographical—place, meaning "the LORD has judged." **4:** *Tyre* and *Sidon,* cities on the Mediterra-

nean coast north of Judah, and *Philistia* to the south are accused of participating in Judah's destruction and deporting its people. **8:** The *Sabeans* may be inhabitants of southern Arabia. **10:** This verse reverses the image of peace in Isa 2.4 and Mic 4.3. **19:** *Egypt,* sometimes ally and sometimes enemy, and *Edom,* elsewhere accused of participating in Jerusalem's destruction (Ob 8–14), are both counted here among the nations judged when Jerusalem is restored.

AMOS

Introduction

Amos is Israel's prophet* of social justice, proclaiming that true religion consists not just of ritual observances but in a moral life based on fair and equitable treatment of all members of society, powerful and powerless alike. This concern for justice lies at the heart of Israel's prophetic movement, but no other prophet expresses it with more passion and substance. Amos demands justice in all areas of society—political (6.10), judicial (5.10, 12), and economic (8.4–6)—and mercilessly attacks Israel's elite for their abuse of power (4.1, 6.1). He believes Israel's religious assemblies, sacred music, and elaborate sacrifices are pointless without principled and ethical behavior in daily affairs (5.21–24). And he regards the demise of Israelite society as the inevitable outcome of its internal corruption and injustices (5.6–7). The power of social justice in the imagination of Western society derives in large part from Israel's prophets and from Amos's passionate appeals in particular.

The book of Amos contains one brief narrative* about an event in his career (7.10–17) and several reports of his visions (7.1–9; 8.1–3; 9.1–4), but the book is primarily made up of short judgment speeches with a simple two-part structure: an indictment listing Israel's sins, and a sentence of judgment prescribing God's punishment for these sins. This structure is clearly visible, for example, in Amos's speech to the priest Amaziah at Bethel, in which Amos indicts Amaziah for restricting prophetic speech (7.16) and announces the divine sentence punishing Amaziah and his family (7.17). While judgment speeches against Israel predominate, the book of Amos actually begins with a series of judgment speeches, with this same two-part structure, directed against Israel's neighbors (1.3–2.5).

Although Amos reports his visions in the first person (8.1–3), the narrative about Amos's career (7.10–17) and the book's title (1.1) describe Amos in the third person, indicating that Amos's speeches were collected and passed down by his followers. Some contend that almost everything in Amos should be traced back to the prophet himself, while others think that Amos's followers have edited the collection of his speeches and added to them. Such additions are identified in particular with those texts that appear to update Amos's speeches against the northern kingdom of Israel with speeches that reflect the perspective of the southern kingdom of Judah, such as those that name Jerusalem and Judah (1.2; 2.4–5) and that predict the fall of the northern sanctuary of Bethel (3.13–14), which rivaled Judah's sanctuary in Jerusalem. Almost all scholars maintain that the oracle* of salvation for the royal family of David with which the book concludes (9.11–15) is a later addition, since it contrasts so strongly with the atmosphere of judgment that pervades the rest of the book.

Amos preached against the northern kingdom during the reign of Jeroboam II (1.1, 7.11) and is the first of Israel's prophets to have his speeches preserved in a collection bearing his name. Jeroboam's long 41-year reign (786–746 BCE) is presented in the accounts of Israel's history as a time of strength and expansion for Israel (2 Kings 14.23–29), a favorable portrait confirmed by Amos's repeated references to the prodigious wealth in its capital, Samaria (3.15; 5.11; 6.1, 4–6). Indeed, archaeologists have recovered from the ancient city of Samaria in this period examples of the fine ivory carvings of which Amos spoke (3.15; 6.4). During such an era of political and economic stability and growth, Amos's harsh criticism of Israelite society and his

expectation that its injustices would soon bring it down must have seemed exaggerated and outlandish to his audience (5.18; 6.6). A mere 25 years after Jeroboam's death, however, Amos's predictions came true when Samaria fell to Assyrian armies.

READING GUIDE

Amos must be read as an anthology of short, independent speeches rather than as a book with a single thesis developed from beginning to end. Since his editors did not mark the beginnings and ends of these speeches, the reader must make an effort to identify them, keeping in mind the typical two-part speech form: indictment of sins followed by announcement of punishment. The reader must also be aware that Amos (and other prophets) composed speeches in a poetic form based on verse units of two parallel lines: "But let justice roll down like waters,/ and righteousness like an ever-flowing stream" (5.24). Keeping these two features of Amos's work in mind can help make sense of a book that might otherwise appear disorganized and repetitious.

1 The words of Amos, who was among the shepherds of Tekoa, which he saw concerning Israel in the days of King Uzziah of Judah and in the days of King Jeroboam son of Joash of Israel, two years*a* before the earthquake.
2 And he said:
The LORD roars from Zion,
    and utters his voice from Jerusalem;
the pastures of the shepherds wither,
    and the top of Carmel dries up.

1.1–2: Introduction. Prophetic books customarily begin with data about their authors. **1:** Amos preached during the reigns of *King Uzziah of Judah* (783–742 BCE) and *King Jeroboam of Israel* (786–746), and he owned sheep and orchards (7.14). Though from *Tekoa*, a town in Judah, Amos preached primarily to Judah's northern neighbor, Israel (2.6). **2:** *Jerusalem* and *Zion** are both names of the capital city of Judah. *Carmel* is a mountain range near the Mediterranean coast in Israel.

〰〰〰〰〰〰〰〰〰〰〰〰〰〰〰

3 Thus says the LORD:
For three transgressions of Damascus,
    and for four, I will not revoke the
        punishment;*b*
because they have threshed Gilead
    with threshing sledges of iron.
4 So I will send a fire on the house
        of Hazael,
    and it shall devour the strongholds of
        Ben-hadad.

5 I will break the gate bars of Damascus,
    and cut off the inhabitants from the
        Valley of Aven,
and the one who holds the scepter from
        Beth-eden;
and the people of Aram shall go into
        exile to Kir,
                        says the LORD.

6 Thus says the LORD:
For three transgressions of Gaza,
    and for four, I will not revoke the
        punishment;*b*
because they carried into exile entire
        communities,
    to hand them over to Edom.
7 So I will send a fire on the wall
        of Gaza,
    fire that shall devour its strongholds.
8 I will cut off the inhabitants from
        Ashdod,
    and the one who holds the scepter
        from Ashkelon;
I will turn my hand against Ekron,
    and the remnant of the Philistines
        shall perish,
                        says the Lord GOD.

1.3–2.5: Judgments on Israel's neighbors. In typical two-part judgment speeches, containing indictments

a Or *during two years*   *b* Heb *cause it to return*

and sentences, Amos announces divine judgment on seven of Israel's closest neighbors (see map on page 1182). The indictments in each case involve acts of brutality against neighboring peoples. The repetition of *for three transgressions . . . and for four* in each indictment is a poetic convention meaning simply "several." The image of *fire* in each sentence predicts the violent destruction of the cities indicted. The phrase *says the* LORD, which begins and ends these speeches, identifies them as divine oracles★ and the prophet★ as a divine spokesperson. **3–5:** *Damascus* is the capital of the kingdom of Aram northeast of Israel, and *Hazael* and *Ben-hadad* are two of its kings. *Gilead* refers to Israelite territories east of the Jordan. The location of *Kir*, which Amos regarded as the original home of the Arameans (9.7), is uncertain. **6–8:** *Gaza, Ashdod, Ashkelon,* and *Ekron* are major Philistine cities southwest of Israel on the Mediterranean coast. *Edom*, to which both *Gaza* and *Tyre* (1.9–10) deported people, is Israel's neighbor southeast of the Dead Sea.

9 Thus says the LORD:
    For three transgressions of Tyre,
        and for four, I will not revoke the
            punishment;[a]
    because they delivered entire
            communities over to Edom,
        and did not remember the covenant
            of kinship.
10 So I will send a fire on the wall
        of Tyre,
    fire that shall devour its strongholds.

11 Thus says the LORD:
    For three transgressions of Edom,
        and for four, I will not revoke the
            punishment;[a]
    because he pursued his brother with the
            sword
        and cast off all pity;
    he maintained his anger perpetually,[b]
        and kept his wrath[c] forever.
12 So I will send a fire on Teman,
        and it shall devour the strongholds of
            Bozrah.

13 Thus says the LORD:
    For three transgressions of the
            Ammonites,
        and for four, I will not revoke the
            punishment;[a]

because they have ripped open pregnant
            women in Gilead
    in order to enlarge their territory.
14 So I will kindle a fire against the wall of
        Rabbah,
    fire that shall devour its strongholds,
        with shouting on the day of battle,
    with a storm on the day of the
            whirlwind;
15 then their king shall go into exile,
        he and his officials together,
                            says the LORD.

2 Thus says the LORD:
    For three transgressions of Moab,
        and for four, I will not revoke the
            punishment;[a]
    because he burned to lime
        the bones of the king of Edom.
2 So I will send a fire on Moab,
        and it shall devour the strongholds of
            Kerioth,
    and Moab shall die amid uproar,
        amid shouting and the sound of the
            trumpet;
3 I will cut off the ruler from its midst,
        and will kill all its officials with him,
                            says the LORD.

4 Thus says the LORD:
    For three transgressions of Judah,
        and for four, I will not revoke the
            punishment;[a]
    because they have rejected the law of
            the LORD,
        and have not kept his statutes,
    but they have been led astray by the
            same lies
        after which their ancestors walked.
5 So I will send a fire on Judah,
        and it shall devour the strongholds of
            Jerusalem.

1.9–2.5. 1.9–10: *Tyre* is a Phoenician city on the Mediterranean coast northwest of Israel. **11–12:** *Edom* is Israel's neighbor to the southeast, and *Teman* and *Bozrah* are two of its major cities. Edom's *brother* may refer to either Israel or Judah (Ob 8–12). **13–15:** The

a Heb *cause it to return*   *b* Syr Vg: Heb *and his anger tore perpetually*   *c* Gk Syr Vg: Heb *and his wrath kept*

``They sell the righteous for silver''

With this phrase, Amos strikes at the heart of Israel's guilt (2.6, 8.6). He criticizes not just an abuse here and an injustice there, but an economic system that condones the accumulation of great wealth in the hands of a few (6.1–6) and the growth in the gap between rich and poor (5.11). In Israel's traditional economy, families supported themselves by farming their ancestral lands, as Amos himself may have done (1.1; 7.14–15). But as the wealthy imposed heavy taxes (2.8; 5.11), took collateral for themselves (2.8), and cheated customers in the marketplace (8.5), the poor were eventually forced off of their lands and reduced to debt-slavery, where they were bought and sold by the rich. Such an economic system was intolerable, according to Amos, for a society that had itself been once freed from slavery (2.10; 3.1).

Ammonites, Israel's neighbors to the east, are accused, as is Damascus (1.3), of crimes against the Israelites in *Gilead*. **2.1–3:** *Moab*, located southeast of Israel, is accused of crimes against its southern neighbor *Edom*. **4–5:** *Judah*, like Israel to follow (2.6–16), is criticized not for crimes against its neighbors, but for crimes within its own society against God's *law*.

6 Thus says the LORD:
　For three transgressions of Israel,
　　and for four, I will not revoke the
　　　punishment;[a]
　because they sell the righteous
　　for silver,
　　and the needy for a pair of sandals—
7 they who trample the head of the poor
　　into the dust of the earth,
　　and push the afflicted out of the
　　　way;
　father and son go in to the same girl,
　　so that my holy name is profaned;
8 they lay themselves down beside every
　　altar
　　on garments taken in pledge;
　and in the house of their God
　　they drink
　　wine bought with fines they
　　　imposed.

2.6–16: Judgment on Israel. This judgment speech concludes the series of speeches directed against Israel's neighbors. By starting with judgments against Israel's neighbors, Amos may have intended to lure his

Israelite audience into agreement with him, only to shock them with a concluding speech listing their own sins, even more numerous than those of their neighbors. **6–8:** Amos's indictment begins with Israel's mistreatment of its poor (vv. 6b–7a), in particular, the sale of humans into slavery when they were unable to pay their debts (8.6). *Garments taken in pledge* (Ex 22.26–27; Deut 24.12–13) and *fines* refer to objects and money taken unfairly from the poor by the rich.

9 Yet I destroyed the Amorite
　　before them,
　　whose height was like the height of
　　　cedars,
　　and who was as strong as oaks;
　I destroyed his fruit above,
　　and his roots beneath.
10 Also I brought you up out of the land of
　　Egypt,
　　and led you forty years in
　　　the wilderness,
　　to possess the land of the Amorite.
11 And I raised up some of your children
　　to be prophets
　　and some of your youths to be
　　　nazirites.[b]
　　Is it not indeed so, O people
　　　of Israel?
　　　　　　　says the LORD.

a Heb *cause it to return*　　b That is, *those separated* or *those consecrated*

12 But you made the nazirites[a] drink wine,
  and commanded the prophets,
  saying, "You shall not prophesy."

13 So, I will press you down in your place,
  just as a cart presses down
  when it is full of sheaves.[b]
14 Flight shall perish from the swift,
  and the strong shall not retain their
    strength,
  nor shall the mighty save their lives;
15 those who handle the bow shall
    not stand,
  and those who are swift of foot shall
    not save themselves,
  nor shall those who ride horses save
    their lives;
16 and those who are stout of heart among
    the mighty
  shall flee away naked in that day,
      says the LORD.

2.9–16. 9–12: A brief historical summary stresses Israel's stubbornness by contrasting it with God's acts of salvation on Israel's behalf. **13–16:** The judgment imposed for Israel's crimes will bring an end to Israel's strongest defenses: its fastest runners, its strongest warriors, its most skilled archers, and its best horsemen.

3 Hear this word that the LORD has spoken against you, O people of Israel, against the whole family that I brought up out of the land of Egypt:
2 You only have I known
  of all the families of the earth;
  therefore I will punish you
  for all your iniquities.

3 Do two walk together
  unless they have made an appointment?
4 Does a lion roar in the forest,
  when it has no prey?
  Does a young lion cry out from its den,
  if it has caught nothing?
5 Does a bird fall into a snare on
    the earth,
  when there is no trap for it?
  Does a snare spring up from
    the ground,
  when it has taken nothing?

6 Is a trumpet blown in a city,
  and the people are not afraid?
  Does disaster befall a city,
  unless the LORD has done it?
7 Surely the Lord GOD does nothing,
  without revealing his secret
  to his servants the prophets.
8 The lion has roared;
  who will not fear?
  The Lord GOD has spoken;
  who can but prophesy?

3.1–8: The power of prophets. After a brief description of Israel's past salvation and future punishment (vv. 1–2), Amos begins a speech composed entirely of rhetorical* questions (vv. 3–8). With the first questions, Amos gains the audience's agreement on obvious issues in order to convince them of his real claim: When prophets speak, their words are the words of God (vv. 7–8).

9 Proclaim to the strongholds in Ashdod,
  and to the strongholds in the land of
    Egypt,
  and say, "Assemble yourselves on
    Mount[c] Samaria,
  and see what great tumults are
    within it,
  and what oppressions are in
    its midst."
10 They do not know how to do right, says
    the LORD,
  those who store up violence and
    robbery in their strongholds.
11 Therefore thus says the Lord GOD:
  An adversary shall surround the land,
  and strip you of your defense;
  and your strongholds shall be
    plundered.

12 Thus says the LORD: As the shepherd rescues from the mouth of the lion two legs, or a piece of an ear, so shall the people of Israel who live in Samaria be rescued, with the corner of a couch and part[b] of a bed.

3.9–12: Judgment on Samaria. Amos invites representatives from *Ashdod,* a Philistine city (1.8), and

a That is, *those separated* or *those consecrated*
b Meaning of Heb uncertain   c Gk Syr: Heb *the mountains of*

from *Egypt* to observe the *oppressions* of the poor on *Mount Samaria*, the capital of Israel. This indictment (vv. 9–10) is followed by God's sentence: Samaria's *strongholds shall be plundered* by an invading army (v. 11). The metaphor⋆ of the plundering *lion* in v. 12 emphasizes how little will remain in Samaria after the enemy strikes.

13 Hear, and testify against the house of
            Jacob,
       says the Lord GOD, the God of hosts:
14 On the day I punish Israel for its
            transgressions,
       I will punish the altars of Bethel,
   and the horns of the altar shall
            be cut off
       and fall to the ground.
15 I will tear down the winter house as
            well as the summer house;
   and the houses of ivory shall perish,
   and the great houses*a* shall come
            to an end,
                   says the LORD.

3.13–15: Judgment on Bethel. Located in the southern part of Israel, *Bethel,* together with Dan in the north, was one of Israel's major religious centers. The judgment against Israel's houses (v. 15) that follows the judgment on Bethel contains an implicit criticism of the rich. Israel's wealthiest citizens built *winter houses* in the Jordan valley to escape the cold winter climate in the mountains of Samaria, and they made furniture inlaid with ivory for their homes (6.4).

4 Hear this word, you cows of Bashan
       who are on Mount Samaria,
   who oppress the poor, who crush the
            needy,
       who say to their husbands, "Bring
            something to drink!"
2 The Lord GOD has sworn by his holiness:
       The time is surely coming upon you,
   when they shall take you away with
            hooks,
       even the last of you with fishhooks.
3 Through breaches in the wall you shall
            leave,
       each one straight ahead;
   and you shall be flung out into
            Harmon,*b*
                   says the LORD.

4 Come to Bethel—and transgress;
       to Gilgal—and multiply transgression;
   bring your sacrifices every morning,
       your tithes every three days;
5 bring a thank offering of leavened
            bread,
       and proclaim freewill offerings,
            publish them;
   for so you love to do, O people
            of Israel!
                   says the Lord GOD.

6 I gave you cleanness of teeth in all your
            cities,
       and lack of bread in all your places,
   yet you did not return to me,
                   says the LORD.

7 And I also withheld the rain from you
       when there were still three months to
            the harvest;
   I would send rain on one city,
       and send no rain on another city;
   one field would be rained upon,
       and the field on which it did not rain
            withered;
8 so two or three towns wandered to one
            town
       to drink water, and were not satisfied;
   yet you did not return to me,
                   says the LORD.

9 I struck you with blight and mildew;
       I laid waste*c* your gardens and your
            vineyards;
   the locust devoured your fig trees and
            your olive trees;
   yet you did not return to me,
                   says the LORD.

10 I sent among you a pestilence after the
            manner of Egypt;
       I killed your young men with the sword;
   I carried away your horses;*d*
       and I made the stench of your camp
            go up into your nostrils;
   yet you did not return to me,
                   says the LORD.

a Or *many houses*   b Meaning of Heb uncertain
c Cn: Heb *the multitude of*   d Heb *with the captivity of your horses*

11 I overthrew some of you,
    as when God overthrew Sodom and
        Gomorrah,
    and you were like a brand snatched
        from the fire;
  yet you did not return to me,
                    says the LORD.

12 Therefore thus I will do to you,
    O Israel;
  because I will do this to you,
    prepare to meet your God, O Israel!

13 For lo, the one who forms the
        mountains, creates the wind,
    reveals his thoughts to mortals,
  makes the morning darkness,
    and treads on the heights of
        the earth—
  the LORD, the God of hosts, is
        his name!

4.1–13. 1–3: Judgment on Samaria's elite women. In his indictment of their oppression of the poor (v. 1), Amos compares Israel's leading women to cattle grazing in Israel's prime pasture land, *Bashan*. The sentence for these women (vv. 2–3) is deportation, though the location of *Harmon* is uncertain. **4–13: Israel's stubbornness.** After criticizing the rituals practiced at two of Israel's religious centers, *Bethel* and *Gilgal* (vv. 4–5), perhaps because he judged them hypocritical, Amos lists a series of divine judgments that have failed to convince Israel of its injustices: famine (v. 6), drought (vv. 7–8), plant diseases and predators (v. 9), disease and death for Israel's army (v. 10), and defeat (v. 11). With the term *therefore*, which characteristically links indictments to sentences, Amos introduces God's judgment (vv. 12–13) for Israel's repeated refusal to reform.

〜〜〜〜〜〜〜〜〜〜〜〜〜

5 Hear this word that I take up over you
  in lamentation, O house of Israel:
2 Fallen, no more to rise,
    is maiden Israel;
  forsaken on her land,
    with no one to raise her up.

3 For thus says the Lord GOD:
  The city that marched out a thousand
    shall have a hundred left,

and that which marched out a hundred
    shall have ten left.*a*

4 For thus says the LORD to the house of
    Israel:
Seek me and live;
5   but do not seek Bethel,
  and do not enter into Gilgal
    or cross over to Beer-sheba;
  for Gilgal shall surely go into exile,
    and Bethel shall come to nothing.

6 Seek the LORD and live,
    or he will break out against the house
        of Joseph like fire,
    and it will devour Bethel, with no one
        to quench it.
7 Ah, you that turn justice to
        wormwood,
    and bring righteousness to
        the ground!

5.1–27: A lament over Israel. Within a lament* anticipating Israel's fall (vv. 1–3, 16–20), Amos indicts Israel for its injustices (vv. 10–13, 21–27) and pleads with Israel to seek God in order to avoid disaster (vv. 4–7, 14–15). **1–3:** Amos begins his lament by describing the conquest of Israel as if it had already happened. **4–7:** In his opening appeal to seek God, Amos criticizes the worship (v. 5) of those who are not just (v. 7). **5:** *Beer-sheba*, a southern religious center with old associations with the northern kingdom of Israel (1 Sam 8.2; 1 Kings 19.3), is mentioned here alongside two northern centers, *Bethel* and *Gilgal*, which Amos criticizes elsewhere (4.4). **6:** *Joseph*, father of the ancestors of the two most powerful northern tribes (Ephraim and Manasseh), is employed by Amos as a synonym for Israel.

〜〜〜〜〜〜〜〜〜〜〜〜〜

8 The one who made the Pleiades
        and Orion,
    and turns deep darkness into
        the morning,
    and darkens the day into night,
  who calls for the waters of the sea,
    and pours them out on the surface of
        the earth,
  the LORD is his name,

---

a Heb adds *to the house of Israel*

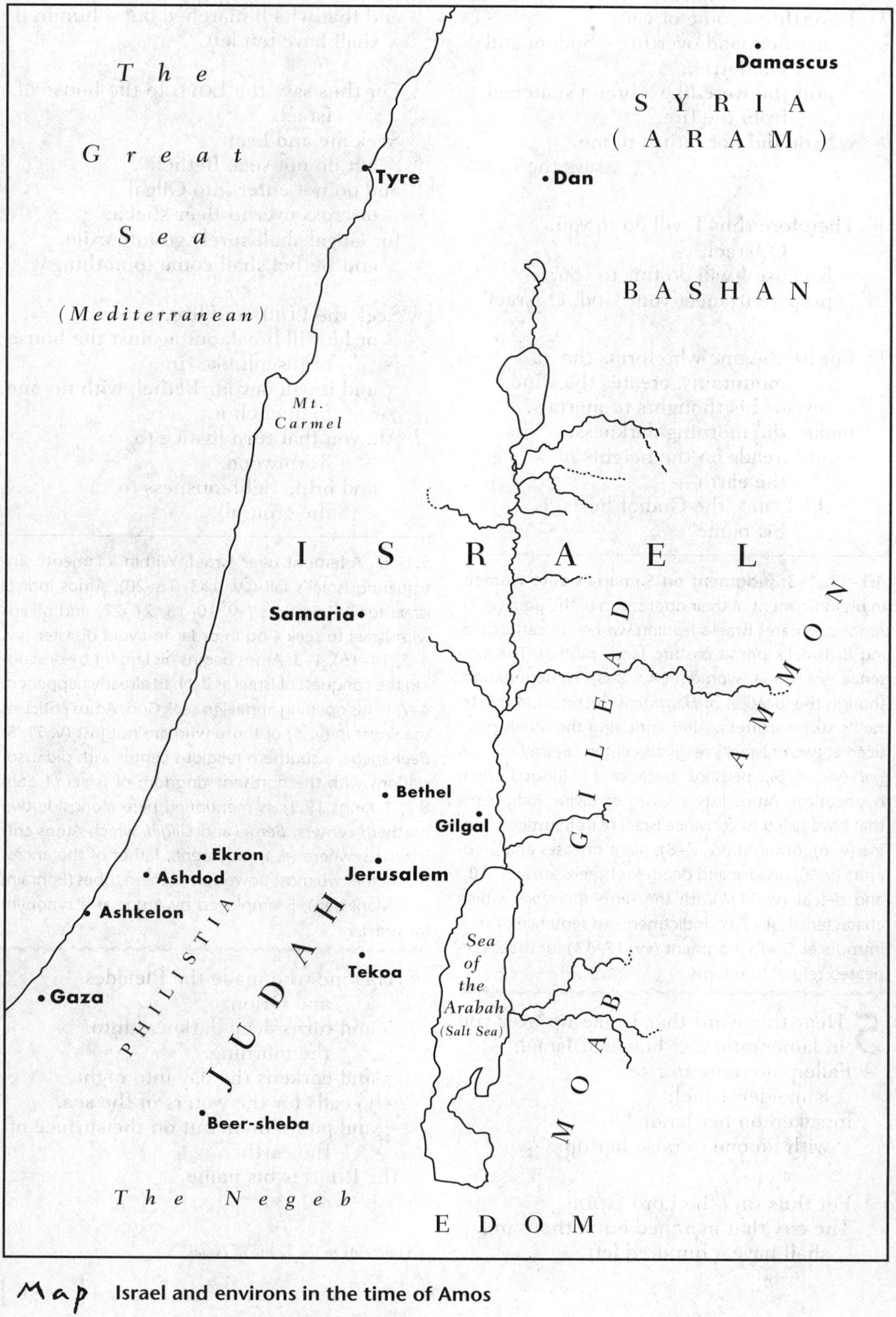
The Great Sea
(Mediterranean)
Damascus
SYRIA
(ARAM)
Tyre
Dan
BASHAN
Mt. Carmel
ISRAEL
Samaria
GILEAD
AMMON
Bethel
Gilgal
Ekron
Ashdod
Jerusalem
Ashkelon
PHILISTIA
JUDAH
Tekoa
Gaza
Sea of the Arabah
(Salt Sea)
MOAB
Beer-sheba
The Negeb
EDOM

Map Israel and environs in the time of Amos

9 who makes destruction flash out against
     the strong,
  so that destruction comes upon the
     fortress.

10 They hate the one who reproves in the
      gate,
   and they abhor the one who speaks
      the truth.
11 Therefore because you trample on the
      poor
   and take from them levies of grain,
   you have built houses of hewn stone,
      but you shall not live in them;
   you have planted pleasant vineyards,
      but you shall not drink their wine.
12 For I know how many are your
      transgressions,
   and how great are your sins—
   you who afflict the righteous, who take
      a bribe,
   and push aside the needy in the gate.
13 Therefore the prudent will keep silent in
      such a time;
   for it is an evil time.

5.8–13. 8–9: Hymns such as this one praising God's
power occur at several points in Amos (4.13; 9.5–6).
10–13: Amos indicts Israel for judicial and economic
abuses. Israel's judges heard and settled disputes at *the
gate* of the city (vv. 10, 12). *Levies of grain* are taxes
imposed by creditors or landlords on poor farmers.

---

14 Seek good and not evil,
     that you may live;
   and so the LORD, the God of hosts, will
     be with you,
     just as you have said.
15 Hate evil and love good,
     and establish justice in the gate;
   it may be that the LORD, the God
     of hosts,
     will be gracious to the remnant of
     Joseph.

16 Therefore thus says the LORD, the God
     of hosts, the Lord:
   In all the squares there shall be
     wailing;
   and in all the streets they shall say,
     "Alas! alas!"

They shall call the farmers to
     mourning,
   and those skilled in lamentation, to
     wailing;
17 in all the vineyards there shall
     be wailing,
   for I will pass through the midst of
     you,
                    says the LORD.

18 Alas for you who desire the day of
     the LORD!
   Why do you want the day of
     the LORD?
   It is darkness, not light;
19   as if someone fled from a lion,
     and was met by a bear;
   or went into the house and rested a
     hand against the wall,
     and was bitten by a snake.
20 Is not the day of the LORD darkness,
     not light,
   and gloom with no brightness in it?

21 I hate, I despise your festivals,
     and I take no delight in your solemn
     assemblies.
22 Even though you offer me your burnt
     offerings and grain offerings,
   I will not accept them;
   and the offerings of well-being of your
     fatted animals
   I will not look upon.
23 Take away from me the noise of your
     songs;
   I will not listen to the melody of your
     harps.
24 But let justice roll down like waters,
     and righteousness like an ever-flowing
     stream.

5.14–24. 14–15: Amos's appeal to seek God by living
justly (vv. 4–7) is resumed. **16–20**: Amos continues his
lament begun in vv. 1–3. The *day of the LORD* (vv. 18,
20) is a decisive act of God in human affairs. Although
Amos's audience believed it would be a day of salvation, Amos saw it as a day of judgment. **21–24**: This is
Amos's classic statement about the meaninglessness of
worship (vv. 21–23) if it is practiced by those who do
not do justice in their daily affairs (v. 24).

---

25 Did you bring to me sacrifices and offerings the forty years in the wilderness, O house of Israel? 26You shall take up Sakkuth your king, and Kaiwan your star-god, your images,*a* which you made for yourselves; 27therefore I will take you into exile beyond Damascus, says the LORD, whose name is the God of hosts.

5.25–27: In what may be an editorial addition, Israel is blamed for idolatry.* *Sakkuth* and *Kaiwan* are titles for Saturn, an astral deity in Mesopotamia. *Damascus* is the capital of the kingdom of Aram, northeast of Israel (1.3).

6 Alas for those who are at ease in Zion,
and for those who feel secure on
Mount Samaria,
the notables of the first of the nations,
to whom the house of Israel
resorts!
2 Cross over to Calneh, and see;
from there go to Hamath the great;
then go down to Gath of the
Philistines.
Are you better*b* than these kingdoms?
Or is your*c* territory greater than
their*d* territory,
3 O you that put far away the evil day,
and bring near a reign of violence?

4 Alas for those who lie on beds of ivory,
and lounge on their couches,
and eat lambs from the flock,
and calves from the stall;
5 who sing idle songs to the sound
of the harp,
and like David improvise on
instruments of music;
6 who drink wine from bowls,
and anoint themselves with the finest
oils,
but are not grieved over the ruin of
Joseph!
7 Therefore they shall now be the first to
go into exile,
and the revelry of the loungers shall
pass away.

8 The Lord GOD has sworn by himself
(says the LORD, the God of hosts):

I abhor the pride of Jacob
and hate his strongholds;
and I will deliver up the city and all
that is in it.

9 If ten people remain in one house, they shall die. 10And if a relative, one who burns the dead,*e* shall take up the body to bring it out of the house, and shall say to someone in the innermost parts of the house, "Is anyone else with you?" the answer will come, "No." Then the relative*f* shall say, "Hush! We must not mention the name of the LORD."

11 See, the LORD commands,
and the great house shall be shattered
to bits,
and the little house to pieces.
12 Do horses run on rocks?
Does one plow the sea with oxen?*g*
But you have turned justice
into poison
and the fruit of righteousness into
wormwood—
13 you who rejoice in Lo-debar,*h*
who say, "Have we not by our own
strength
taken Karnaim*i* for ourselves?"
14 Indeed, I am raising up against you a
nation,
O house of Israel, says the LORD, the
God of hosts,
and they shall oppress you from
Lebo-hamath
to the Wadi Arabah.

6.1–14: Judgment on Samaria's elite men. In this judgment speech, Amos indicts Israel's leaders for excessive wealth and complacency (vv. 1–6) and announces a sentence that includes the conquest of Samaria and deportation of its leaders (vv. 7–14). **2:** *Calneh* and *Hamath* are capital cities of important Syrian city-states. **6:** *Joseph* is a synonym for Israel (5.6). **13:** *Lo-debar* and *Karnaim* are cities east of the Jordan that may have been brought under Israelite control

a Heb *your images, your star-god*　　*b* Or *Are they better*
c Heb *their*　　*d* Heb *your*　　*e* Or *who makes a burning for him*　　*f* Heb *he*　　*g* Or *Does one plow them with oxen*　　*h* Or *in a thing of nothingness*　　*i* Or *horns*

DANIEL

Introduction

Daniel, the only example of an apocalyptic* book in the Hebrew Bible, appears among the Kethubim* ("Writings") of the Tanakh,* the Jewish version of the Bible, and among the Prophetic Books of the Christian First or Old Testament. Apocalyptic books are generally pseudonymous* or anonymous compositions, such as 1 Enoch,* 2 Baruch, or Revelation, in which a heavenly mediator reveals the future to a human being by means of an other-worldly journey or a review of world history. Apocalyptic literature is generally narrative* in form and employs various other-worldly images or motifs,* such as cosmic war, astronomical calculation, angels, mythological beings, and representations of God or other divine figures. Through a series of visions and dreams that provide a sweeping overview of world history from the Babylonian exile to the Hellenistic* period, Daniel is shown the impending downfall of the Seleucid* Syrian tyrant Antiochus IV Epiphanes* (175–163 BCE) and the emergence of God's kingdom, an independent Jewish state centered around the Jerusalem Temple.*

Although Daniel is initially portrayed as a Jewish exile in the court of the Babylonian King Nebuchadnezzar, the book clearly was not written during the sixth century BCE. Daniel is not a historical figure in Judah from this period, but his image is drawn from that of the legendary* sage and ruler of Canaanite mythology, Dan-El, who saves his son Aqhat from death in the fourteenth-century BCE Ugaritic tablets. Apocalyptic literature frequently employs well-known figures from the past, such as Enoch, Moses, or Ezra. Dan-El was known in Judah as early as the sixth century BCE (Ezek 14.14; 28.3). The literary history of the book is complicated and not well understood. It is written in two languages, Hebrew (1.1–2.4a; 8.1–12.13) and Aramaic* (2.4b–7.28), although these two portions do not correspond to its present literary structure. The tales in chs. 1–6 appear to have been composed in wisdom circles during the fourth or third centuries BCE to address the difficulties that Jews faced when living in the Diaspora.* As indicated by the precise historical knowledge conveyed in Daniel's final vision (chs. 10–12), the full form of the book was composed between 167 BCE, when Antiochus IV desecrated the Temple in Jerusalem, and 164 BCE, when Judah the Maccabee and his warriors rededicated the Temple, thereby inaugurating the festival of Hanukkah. The book supports the Maccabean revolt by positing a succession of four world empires, including Babylonia, Media, Persia, and Greece-Macedonia (see Nebuchadnezzar's dream, ch. 2; and the vision of the four beasts, ch. 7). The succession culminates in the emergence of the Seleucid Syrian empire and the rule of Antiochus IV, who is represented by the "little [horn]" with "human eyes . . . and a mouth speaking arrogantly" in 7.8 and "a contemptible person on whom royal majesty had not been conferred" in 11.21. Following his demise in battle, the anticipated Maccabean victory is symbolized by the deliverance of Daniel's people and the bringing of the dead to life (11.40–12.4). In later periods, Daniel has been read as an apocalyptic vision of the end of time. The Greek versions of Daniel in the Septuagint* and Theodotion contain additional chapters within the body of the work or added at the beginning or end of the book. These additional chapters, which appear separately in the Apocrypha* of Protestant Bibles, include the Prayer of Azariah and the Song of the Three Young Jews; Susanna; and Bel and the Dragon.

READING GUIDE

The book of Daniel is made up of two major sections. Chs. 1–6 presents six tales of Daniel and his companions in the Diaspora. Daniel appears as the epitome of a wise man, completely faithful to God and observant of Jewish tradition even in Babylonian exile. His wisdom and piety enable him to understand the will of God, to interpret it correctly to those around him, and to deliver himself and his companions from various threats. The tales employ these motifs to demonstrate that God will support those who adhere to Jewish identity and practice even when living outside of the land of Israel. They thereby establish both God's and Daniel's credibility as the basis for the visions that follow. The four visions of chs. 7–12 convey the major thrust of the book, insofar as the surveys of world history and the chronological calculations are designed to demonstrate the coming downfall of Antiochus IV and the emergence of the kingdom of God as a preordained divine act revealed to Daniel centuries before.

TALES CONCERNING DANIEL IN EXILE

Chs. 1–6: The tales establish Daniel's credibility as a righteous Jew whose God-given wisdom enables him to overcome the challenges of exile and to point to God's redemption of Jews from foreign domination.

1 In the third year of the reign of King Jehoiakim of Judah, King Nebuchadnezzar of Babylon came to Jerusalem and besieged it. ²The Lord let King Jehoiakim of Judah fall into his power, as well as some of the vessels of the house of God. These he brought to the land of Shinar,ᵃ and placed the vessels in the treasury of his gods.

1.1–21: Four young Jews in the Babylonian court. This tale establishes the theme of adherence to Jewish identity and practice by pointing to the success, wisdom, and good health of four young Jewish men who decline the delicacies and wine of the Babylonian king in order to observe Jewish dietary laws. **1–2:** *The third year of the reign of King Jehoiakim* was 606 BCE. Nebuchadnezzar assumed the throne of Babylon in 605 BCE, after he defeated Egypt and brought Judah under his rule. He besieged Jerusalem in 597 BCE during the reign of Jehoiachin (2 Kings 24.1–16) and again in 587 BCE during the regency of Zedekiah (2 Kings 25.1–7). *Shinar:* the location of Babylon (Gen 10.10; 11.2; Zech 5.11).

3 Then the king commanded his palace master Ashpenaz to bring some of the Israelites of the royal family and of the nobility,

⁴young men without physical defect and handsome, versed in every branch of wisdom, endowed with knowledge and insight, and competent to serve in the king's palace; they were to be taught the literature and language of the Chaldeans. ⁵The king assigned them a daily portion of the royal rations of food and wine. They were to be educated for three years, so that at the end of that time they could be stationed in the king's court. ⁶Among them were Daniel, Hananiah, Mishael, and Azariah, from the tribe of Judah. ⁷The palace master gave them other names: Daniel he called Belteshazzar, Hananiah he called Shadrach, Mishael he called Meshach, and Azariah he called Abednego.

1.3–7: The Babylonians trained persons from subject nations to serve in their courts. *Palace master:* Literally, "chief eunuch." *Chaldeans:* Aramaic-speaking Neo-Babylonians, used in Daniel for wise men. Daniel and his companions were given Babylonian names.

8 But Daniel resolved that he would not defile himself with the royal rations of food and wine; so he asked the palace master to allow him not to defile himself. ⁹Now God allowed Daniel to receive favor and compassion from the palace master. ¹⁰The palace master said to Daniel, "I am afraid of my lord the king; he has appointed your food and your drink. If he should see you in poorer condition than the other young men of your

ᵃ Gk Theodotion: Heb adds *to the house of his own gods*

own age, you would endanger my head with the king." 11Then Daniel asked the guard whom the palace master had appointed over Daniel, Hananiah, Mishael, and Azariah: 12"Please test your servants for ten days. Let us be given vegetables to eat and water to drink. 13You can then compare our appearance with the appearance of the young men who eat the royal rations, and deal with your servants according to what you observe." 14So he agreed to this proposal and tested them for ten days. 15At the end of ten days it was observed that they appeared better and fatter than all the young men who had been eating the royal rations. 16So the guard continued to withdraw their royal rations and the wine they were to drink, and gave them vegetables. 17To these four young men God gave knowledge and skill in every aspect of literature and wisdom; Daniel also had insight into all visions and dreams.

18 At the end of the time that the king had set for them to be brought in, the palace master brought them into the presence of Nebuchadnezzar, 19and the king spoke with them. And among them all, no one was found to compare with Daniel, Hananiah, Mishael, and Azariah; therefore they were stationed in the king's court. 20In every matter of wisdom and understanding concerning which the king inquired of them, he found them ten times better than all the magicians and enchanters in his whole kingdom. 21And Daniel continued there until the first year of King Cyrus.

1.8–21. 8–17: The *royal rations of food and wine* are not kosher* and therefore are unsuitable for Jews (Lev 11; Deut 14). Dream interpretation* is a mark of wisdom (Gen 40–41). **18–21:** God grants *wisdom and understanding* to those who adhere to divine requirements. *The first year of King Cyrus* was 539 BCE.

2 In the second year of Nebuchadnezzar's reign, Nebuchadnezzar dreamed such dreams that his spirit was troubled and his sleep left him. 2So the king commanded that the magicians, the enchanters, the sorcerers, and the Chaldeans be summoned to tell the king his dreams. When they came in and stood before the king, 3he said to them, "I have had such a dream that my spirit is troubled by the desire to understand it." 4The Chaldeans said to the king (in Aramaic),*ᵃ* "O king, live forever! Tell your servants the dream, and we will reveal the interpretation." 5The king answered the Chaldeans, "This is a public decree: if you do not tell me both the dream and its interpretation, you shall be torn limb from limb, and your houses shall be laid in ruins. 6But if you do tell me the dream and its interpretation, you shall receive from me gifts and rewards and great honor. Therefore tell me the dream and its interpretation." 7They answered a second time, "Let the king first tell his servants the dream, then we can give its interpretation." 8The king answered, "I know with certainty that you are trying to gain time, because you see I have firmly decreed: 9if you do not tell me the dream, there is but one verdict for you. You have agreed to speak lying and misleading words to me until things take a turn. Therefore, tell me the dream, and I shall know that you can give me its interpretation." 10The Chaldeans answered the king, "There is no one on earth who can reveal what the king demands! In fact no king, however great and powerful, has ever asked such a thing of any magician or enchanter or Chaldean. 11The thing that the king is asking is too difficult, and no one can reveal it to the king except the gods, whose dwelling is not with mortals."

12 Because of this the king flew into a violent rage and commanded that all the wise men of Babylon be destroyed. 13The decree was issued, and the wise men were about to be executed; and they looked for Daniel and his companions, to execute them. 14Then Daniel responded with prudence and discretion to Arioch, the king's chief executioner, who had gone out to execute the wise men of Babylon; 15he asked Arioch, the royal official, "Why is the decree of the king so urgent?" Arioch then explained the matter to Daniel. 16So Daniel went in and requested that the king give him

---

a The text from this point to the end of chapter 7 is in Aramaic

time and he would tell the king the interpretation.

2.1–49: Nebuchadnezzar's dream. This tale demonstrates God's superiority and Daniel's incomparable wisdom. **1–16:** Nebuchadnezzar's impossible demand prepares the reader for Daniel's role as a supremely competent interpreter in chs. 7–12. Dream and omen interpretation were widely practiced in Babylonia. **1:** *The second year of Nebuchadnezzar's reign* was 603 BCE. Daniel appears before his training is complete (1.1, 5). **4:** From 2.4b through 7.28 the text is written in Aramaic.* While Hebrew is a west Semitic language, Aramaic is an east Semitic language, originating in northern Aram (Syria), that was employed extensively throughout the Near East from the seventh or eighth century BCE until the emergence of Islam in the seventh century CE.

17 Then Daniel went to his home and informed his companions, Hananiah, Mishael, and Azariah, 18and told them to seek mercy from the God of heaven concerning this mystery, so that Daniel and his companions with the rest of the wise men of Babylon might not perish. 19Then the mystery was revealed to Daniel in a vision of the night, and Daniel blessed the God of heaven.

20 Daniel said:

"Blessed be the name of God from age
to age,
for wisdom and power are his.
21 He changes times and seasons,
deposes kings and sets up kings;
he gives wisdom to the wise
and knowledge to those who have
understanding.
22 He reveals deep and hidden things;
he knows what is in the darkness,
and light dwells with him.
23 To you, O God of my ancestors,
I give thanks and praise,
for you have given me wisdom
and power,
and have now revealed to me what we
asked of you,
for you have revealed to us what the
king ordered."

2.17–23: *A vision of the night:* Compare 1 Sam 3; 2 Sam 7.4. **18:** *The God of heaven:* A Persian title for

the Jewish deity (Ezra 1.2; 5.11; Neh 1.4; 2.4). **20–23:** A song of praise thanking God for the dream (compare Neh 9.5; Hab 3.4).

24 Therefore Daniel went to Arioch, whom the king had appointed to destroy the wise men of Babylon, and said to him, "Do not destroy the wise men of Babylon; bring me in before the king, and I will give the king the interpretation."

25 Then Arioch quickly brought Daniel before the king and said to him: "I have found among the exiles from Judah a man who can tell the king the interpretation." 26The king said to Daniel, whose name was Belteshazzar, "Are you able to tell me the dream that I have seen and its interpretation?" 27Daniel answered the king, "No wise men, enchanters, magicians, or diviners can show to the king the mystery that the king is asking, 28but there is a God in heaven who reveals mysteries, and he has disclosed to King Nebuchadnezzar what will happen at the end of days. Your dream and the visions of your head as you lay in bed were these: 29To you, O king, as you lay in bed, came thoughts of what would be hereafter, and the revealer of mysteries disclosed to you what is to be. 30But as for me, this mystery has not been revealed to me because of any wisdom that I have more than any other living being, but in order that the interpretation may be known to the king and that you may understand the thoughts of your mind.

31 "You were looking, O king, and lo! there was a great statue. This statue was huge, its brilliance extraordinary; it was standing before you, and its appearance was frightening. 32The head of that statue was of fine gold, its chest and arms of silver, its middle and thighs of bronze, 33its legs of iron, its feet partly of iron and partly of clay. 34As you looked on, a stone was cut out, not by human hands, and it struck the statue on its feet of iron and clay and broke them in pieces. 35Then the iron, the clay, the bronze, the silver, and the gold, were all broken in pieces and became like the chaff of the summer threshing floors; and the wind carried them away, so that not a trace of them could be found. But the stone that struck the

statue became a great mountain and filled the whole earth.

2.24–35. 31–33: Colossi, giant statues of gods or rulers, were erected throughout the Hellenistic* world to demonstrate Greek power. The five parts of the statue symbolize the succession of empires that would rule Judea prior to the kingdom of God: Babylon, Media, Persia, Greece, and the Hellenistic Ptolemaic* and Seleucid* dynasties.* The decreasing value of the materials symbolizes historical decline. The mixture of iron and clay in the feet represents the mixed Greek and indigenous ancestry of the Ptolemaic and Seleucid dynasties, as well as the weakness of their rule. **34:** *A stone was cut out, not by human hands:* An act of God.

36 "This was the dream; now we will tell the king its interpretation. ³⁷You, O king, the king of kings—to whom the God of heaven has given the kingdom, the power, the might, and the glory, ³⁸into whose hand he has given human beings, wherever they live, the wild animals of the field, and the birds of the air, and whom he has established as ruler over them all—you are the head of gold. ³⁹After you shall arise another kingdom inferior to yours, and yet a third kingdom of bronze, which shall rule over the whole earth. ⁴⁰And there shall be a fourth kingdom, strong as iron; just as iron crushes and smashes everything,ᵃ it shall crush and shatter all these. ⁴¹As you saw the feet and toes partly of potter's clay and partly of iron, it shall be a divided kingdom; but some of the strength of iron shall be in it, as you saw the iron mixed with the clay. ⁴²As the toes of the feet were part iron and part clay, so the kingdom shall be partly strong and partly brittle. ⁴³As you saw the iron mixed with clay, so will they mix with one another in marriage,ᵇ but they will not hold together, just as iron does not mix with clay. ⁴⁴And in the days of those kings the God of heaven will set up a kingdom that shall never be destroyed, nor shall this kingdom be left to another people. It shall crush all these kingdoms and bring them to an end, and it shall stand forever; ⁴⁵just as you saw that a stone was cut from the mountain not by hands, and that it crushed the iron, the bronze, the

clay, the silver, and the gold. The great God has informed the king what shall be hereafter. The dream is certain, and its interpretation trustworthy."

46 Then King Nebuchadnezzar fell on his face, worshiped Daniel, and commanded that a grain offering and incense be offered to him. ⁴⁷The king said to Daniel, "Truly, your God is God of gods and Lord of kings and a revealer of mysteries, for you have been able to reveal this mystery!" ⁴⁸Then the king promoted Daniel, gave him many great gifts, and made him ruler over the whole province of Babylon and chief prefect over all the wise men of Babylon. ⁴⁹Daniel made a request of the king, and he appointed Shadrach, Meshach, and Abednego over the affairs of the province of Babylon. But Daniel remained at the king's court.

2.36–49. 44: *The God of heaven will set up a kingdom:* An independent Jewish state under God, understood by later interpreters as an eschatological* kingdom of God. **46–49:** The pagan king acknowledges God (see Ex 15.14–16; Isa 45.14–17).

3 King Nebuchadnezzar made a golden statue whose height was sixty cubits and whose width was six cubits; he set it up on the plain of Dura in the province of Babylon. ²Then King Nebuchadnezzar sent for the satraps, the prefects, and the governors, the counselors, the treasurers, the justices, the magistrates, and all the officials of the provinces, to assemble and come to the dedication of the statue that King Nebuchadnezzar had set up. ³So the satraps, the prefects, and the governors, the counselors, the treasurers, the justices, the magistrates, and all the officials of the provinces, assembled for the dedication of the statue that King Nebuchadnezzar had set up. When they were standing before the statue that Nebuchadnezzar had set up, ⁴the herald proclaimed aloud, "You are commanded, O peoples, nations, and languages, ⁵that when you hear the sound of the horn, pipe, lyre, trigon,

a Gk Theodotion Syr Vg: Aram adds *and like iron that crushes*　　*b* Aram *by human seed*

harp, drum, and entire musical ensemble, you are to fall down and worship the golden statue that King Nebuchadnezzar has set up. 6Whoever does not fall down and worship shall immediately be thrown into a furnace of blazing fire." 7Therefore, as soon as all the peoples heard the sound of the horn, pipe, lyre, trigon, harp, drum, and entire musical ensemble, all the peoples, nations, and languages fell down and worshiped the golden statue that King Nebuchadnezzar had set up.

8 Accordingly, at this time certain Chaldeans came forward and denounced the Jews. 9They said to King Nebuchadnezzar, "O king, live forever! 10You, O king, have made a decree, that everyone who hears the sound of the horn, pipe, lyre, trigon, harp, drum, and entire musical ensemble, shall fall down and worship the golden statue, 11and whoever does not fall down and worship shall be thrown into a furnace of blazing fire. 12There are certain Jews whom you have appointed over the affairs of the province of Babylon: Shadrach, Meshach, and Abednego. These pay no heed to you, O king. They do not serve your gods and they do not worship the golden statue that you have set up."

13 Then Nebuchadnezzar in furious rage commanded that Shadrach, Meshach, and Abednego be brought in; so they brought those men before the king. 14Nebuchadnezzar said to them, "Is it true, O Shadrach, Meshach, and Abednego, that you do not serve my gods and you do not worship the golden statue that I have set up? 15Now if you are ready when you hear the sound of the horn, pipe, lyre, trigon, harp, drum, and entire musical ensemble to fall down and worship the statue that I have made, well and good.a But if you do not worship, you shall immediately be thrown into a furnace of blazing fire, and who is the god that will deliver you out of my hands?"

16 Shadrach, Meshach, and Abednego answered the king, "O Nebuchadnezzar, we have no need to present a defense to you in this matter. 17If our God whom we serve is able to deliver us from the furnace of blazing fire and out of your hand, O king, let him deliver us.b 18But if not, be it known to you,

O king, that we will not serve your gods and we will not worship the golden statue that you have set up."

3.1–30: The fiery furnace: The narrative* promotes adherence to Jewish identity and religion by demonstrating that God protects the righteous. **1–18:** Antiochus IV (175–163 BCE) erected a statue of Zeus in the Jerusalem Temple* and demanded that Jews worship Greek gods or be put to death (1 Macc 1.41–64; 2 Macc 6.1–11). His nickname, Epiphanes,* "manifest god," indicates that he expected worship as a god. Worship of national gods was generally understood as a sign of loyalty, but Jews are monotheistic and do not worship pagan gods. Charges of disloyalty prompted many anti-Jewish actions in the Greco-Roman and medieval periods and continue to underlie modern anti-Semitism.

19 Then Nebuchadnezzar was so filled with rage against Shadrach, Meshach, and Abednego that his face was distorted. He ordered the furnace heated up seven times more than was customary, 20and ordered some of the strongest guards in his army to bind Shadrach, Meshach, and Abednego and to throw them into the furnace of blazing fire. 21So the men were bound, still wearing their tunics,c their trousers,c their hats, and their other garments, and they were thrown into the furnace of blazing fire. 22Because the king's command was urgent and the furnace was so overheated, the raging flames killed the men who lifted Shadrach, Meshach, and Abednego. 23But the three men, Shadrach, Meshach, and Abednego, fell down, bound, into the furnace of blazing fire.

24 Then King Nebuchadnezzar was astonished and rose up quickly. He said to his counselors, "Was it not three men that we threw bound into the fire?" They answered the king, "True, O king." 25He replied, "But I see four men unbound, walking in the middle of the fire, and they are not hurt; and the fourth has the appearance of a

---

a Aram lacks *well and good*   b Or *If our God whom we serve is able to deliver us, he will deliver us from the furnace of blazing fire and out of your hand, O king.*
c Meaning of Aram word uncertain

god."[a] 26Nebuchadnezzar then approached the door of the furnace of blazing fire and said, "Shadrach, Meshach, and Abednego, servants of the Most High God, come out! Come here!" So Shadrach, Meshach, and Abednego came out from the fire. 27And the satraps, the prefects, the governors, and the king's counselors gathered together and saw that the fire had not had any power over the bodies of those men; the hair of their heads was not singed, their tunics[b] were not harmed, and not even the smell of fire came from them. 28Nebuchadnezzar said, "Blessed be the God of Shadrach, Meshach, and Abednego, who has sent his angel and delivered his servants who trusted in him. They disobeyed the king's command and yielded up their bodies rather than serve and worship any god except their own God. 29Therefore I make a decree: Any people, nation, or language that utters blasphemy against the God of Shadrach, Meshach, and Abednego shall be torn limb from limb, and their houses laid in ruins; for there is no other god who is able to deliver in this way." 30Then the king promoted Shadrach, Meshach, and Abednego in the province of Babylon.

3.19–30: The description of the fiery furnace is full of exaggeration, preparing the reader for the great miracle. **25:** The presence of a fourth man who *has the appearance of a god* (literally, *a son of the gods*) signifies divine intervention to save the young men (see v. 28). The pagan king acknowledges God's power and decrees destruction for nations that challenge God.

4[c]King Nebuchadnezzar to all peoples, nations, and languages that live throughout the earth: May you have abundant prosperity! 2The signs and wonders that the Most High God has worked for me I am pleased to recount.
3 How great are his signs,
　　how mighty his wonders!
His kingdom is an everlasting kingdom,
　　and his sovereignty is from generation
　　　　to generation.

4.1–37: Nebuchadnezzar's madness. Using the form of an epistle or public proclamation, this chapter dem-

onstrates God's power over pagan rulers. **1–2:** A typical epistolary introduction. *All peoples, nations, and languages that live throughout the earth:* Mesopotamian rulers generally claimed rule over the entire world. The motif* prepares the reader to recognize God's universal sovereignty. **3:** Again, Nebuchadnezzar acknowledges God.

4[d] I, Nebuchadnezzar, was living at ease in my home and prospering in my palace. 5I saw a dream that frightened me; my fantasies in bed and the visions of my head terrified me. 6So I made a decree that all the wise men of Babylon should be brought before me, in order that they might tell me the interpretation of the dream. 7Then the magicians, the enchanters, the Chaldeans, and the diviners came in, and I told them the dream, but they could not tell me its interpretation. 8At last Daniel came in before me—he who was named Belteshazzar after the name of my god, and who is endowed with a spirit of the holy gods[e]—and I told him the dream: 9"O Belteshazzar, chief of the magicians, I know that you are endowed with a spirit of the holy gods[e] and that no mystery is too difficult for you. Hear[f] the dream that I saw; tell me its interpretation. 10[g] Upon my bed this is what I saw;
　　there was a tree at the center of the
　　　　earth,
　　and its height was great.
11 The tree grew great and strong,
　　its top reached to heaven,
　　and it was visible to the ends of the
　　　　whole earth.
12 Its foliage was beautiful,
　　its fruit abundant,
　　and it provided food for all.
The animals of the field found shade
　　under it,
　　the birds of the air nested in
　　　　its branches,
　　and from it all living beings
　　　　were fed.

a Aram *a son of the gods*　b Meaning of Aram word uncertain　c Ch 3.31 in Aram　d Ch 4.1 in Aram　e Or *a holy, divine spirit*　f Theodotion: Aram *The visions of*　g Theodotion Syr Compare Gk: Aram adds *The visions of my head*

13 "I continued looking, in the visions of my head as I lay in bed, and there was a holy watcher, coming down from heaven. 14He cried aloud and said:

'Cut down the tree and chop off
        its branches,
    strip off its foliage and scatter its fruit.
Let the animals flee from beneath it
    and the birds from its branches.
15 But leave its stump and roots in the
        ground,
    with a band of iron and bronze,
    in the tender grass of the field.
Let him be bathed with the dew
        of heaven,
    and let his lot be with the animals of
        the field
    in the grass of the earth.
16 Let his mind be changed from that of a
        human,
    and let the mind of an animal be
        given to him.
    And let seven times pass over him.
17 The sentence is rendered by decree of
        the watchers,
    the decision is given by order of the
        holy ones,
in order that all who live may know
    that the Most High is sovereign over
        the kingdom of mortals;
he gives it to whom he will
    and sets over it the lowliest of human
        beings.'

18 "This is the dream that I, King Nebuchadnezzar, saw. Now you, Belteshazzar, declare the interpretation, since all the wise men of my kingdom are unable to tell me the interpretation. You are able, however, for you are endowed with a spirit of the holy gods."*a*

4.4–18: There are no extra-biblical accounts of Nebuchadnezzar's madness. The Babylonian king Nabonidus (556–539 BCE) lived in the Arabian desert while his son Belshazzar ruled in his stead. 8: *Named Belteshazzar after the name of my god:* Belteshazzar means "protect his life" and is styled to resemble the name Bel, a title for the Babylonian city god, Marduk. 10–17: The *tree at the center of the earth:* Ancient Near Eastern mythology frequently employs the image of a

cosmic tree (see Gen 2–3). See also Isa 10.5–34; Ezek 31, which portray Assyrian and Egyptian rulers as trees that will be cut down and sent to the netherworld. 13: *Holy watcher:* A celestial being (1 Enoch★ 1.5; 20.1; Jubilees 4.15). 15: *Stump and roots in the ground:* See Isa 6.13; 11.1. 16: *Let his mind be changed:* The motif is derived from Nabonidus, but also presupposes Babylonian traditions of Enkidu, the primal man of the Gilgamesh★ epic, who lived among the animals before he was civilized by a woman.

19 Then Daniel, who was called Belteshazzar, was severely distressed for a while. His thoughts terrified him. The king said, "Belteshazzar, do not let the dream or the interpretation terrify you." Belteshazzar answered, "My lord, may the dream be for those who hate you, and its interpretation for your enemies! 20The tree that you saw, which grew great and strong, so that its top reached to heaven and was visible to the end of the whole earth, 21whose foliage was beautiful and its fruit abundant, and which provided food for all, under which animals of the field lived, and in whose branches the birds of the air had nests— 22it is you, O king! You have grown great and strong. Your greatness has increased and reaches to heaven, and your sovereignty to the ends of the earth. 23And whereas the king saw a holy watcher coming down from heaven and saying, 'Cut down the tree and destroy it, but leave its stump and roots in the ground, with a band of iron and bronze, in the grass of the field; and let him be bathed with the dew of heaven, and let his lot be with the animals of the field, until seven times pass over him'— 24this is the interpretation, O king, and it is a decree of the Most High that has come upon my lord the king: 25You shall be driven away from human society, and your dwelling shall be with the wild animals. You shall be made to eat grass like oxen, you shall be bathed with the dew of heaven, and seven times shall pass over you, until you have learned that the Most High has sovereignty over the kingdom of mortals, and gives it to whom he will. 26As it was commanded to leave the stump and roots of the tree, your

a Or *a holy, divine spirit*

kingdom shall be re-established for you from the time that you learn that Heaven is sovereign. 27Therefore, O king, may my counsel be acceptable to you: atone for*a* your sins with righteousness, and your iniquities with mercy to the oppressed, so that your prosperity may be prolonged."

4.19–27: Nebuchadnezzar's greatness, symbolized by his monumental building programs, was well-known throughout the ancient world.

28 All this came upon King Nebuchadnezzar. 29At the end of twelve months he was walking on the roof of the royal palace of Babylon, 30and the king said, "Is this not magnificent Babylon, which I have built as a royal capital by my mighty power and for my glorious majesty?" 31While the words were still in the king's mouth, a voice came from heaven: "O King Nebuchadnezzar, to you it is declared: The kingdom has departed from you! 32You shall be driven away from human society, and your dwelling shall be with the animals of the field. You shall be made to eat grass like oxen, and seven times shall pass over you, until you have learned that the Most High has sovereignty over the kingdom of mortals and gives it to whom he will." 33Immediately the sentence was fulfilled against Nebuchadnezzar. He was driven away from human society, ate grass like oxen, and his body was bathed with the dew of heaven, until his hair grew as long as eagles' feathers and his nails became like birds' claws.

34 When that period was over, I, Nebuchadnezzar, lifted my eyes to heaven, and my reason returned to me.

I blessed the Most High,
  and praised and honored the one who
    lives forever.
For his sovereignty is an everlasting
    sovereignty,
  and his kingdom endures from
    generation to generation.
35 All the inhabitants of the earth are
    accounted as nothing,
  and he does what he wills with the
    host of heaven
  and the inhabitants of the earth.

There is no one who can stay his hand
  or say to him, "What are you doing?"
36At that time my reason returned to me; and my majesty and splendor were restored to me for the glory of my kingdom. My counselors and my lords sought me out, I was re-established over my kingdom, and still more greatness was added to me. 37Now I, Nebuchadnezzar, praise and extol and honor the King of heaven,
  for all his works are truth,
    and his ways are justice;
  and he is able to bring low
    those who walk in pride.

4.28–37. 28–33: The prediction of the dream is fulfilled. **34–37:** Nebuchadnezzar is restored when he acknowledges God's universal sovereignty.

5 King Belshazzar made a great festival for a thousand of his lords, and he was drinking wine in the presence of the thousand.

2 Under the influence of the wine, Belshazzar commanded that they bring in the vessels of gold and silver that his father Nebuchadnezzar had taken out of the temple in Jerusalem, so that the king and his lords, his wives, and his concubines might drink from them. 3So they brought in the vessels of gold and silver*b* that had been taken out of the temple, the house of God in Jerusalem, and the king and his lords, his wives, and his concubines drank from them. 4They drank the wine and praised the gods of gold and silver, bronze, iron, wood, and stone.

5 Immediately the fingers of a human hand appeared and began writing on the plaster of the wall of the royal palace, next to the lampstand. The king was watching the hand as it wrote. 6Then the king's face turned pale, and his thoughts terrified him. His limbs gave way, and his knees knocked together. 7The king cried aloud to bring in the enchanters, the Chaldeans, and the diviners; and the king said to the wise men of Babylon, "Whoever can read this writing and tell me its interpretation shall be clothed in

a Aram *break off*   *b* Theodotion Vg: Aram lacks *and silver*

purple, have a chain of gold around his neck, and rank third in the kingdom." ⁸Then all the king's wise men came in, but they could not read the writing or tell the king the interpretation. ⁹Then King Belshazzar became greatly terrified and his face turned pale, and his lords were perplexed.

10 The queen, when she heard the discussion of the king and his lords, came into the banqueting hall. The queen said, "O king, live forever! Do not let your thoughts terrify you or your face grow pale. ¹¹There is a man in your kingdom who is endowed with a spirit of the holy gods.ᵃ In the days of your father he was found to have enlightenment, understanding, and wisdom like the wisdom of the gods. Your father, King Nebuchadnezzar, made him chief of the magicians, enchanters, Chaldeans, and diviners,ᵇ ¹²because an excellent spirit, knowledge, and understanding to interpret dreams, explain riddles, and solve problems were found in this Daniel, whom the king named Belteshazzar. Now let Daniel be called, and he will give the interpretation."

5.1–31: Belshazzar's feast. This narrative* demonstrates the punishment of arrogant and sacrilegious rulers. 1: Belshazzar was not king of Babylon, but served as regent in place of his father Nabonidus. 2–4: Nebuchadnezzar was not Belshazzar's father (see comment on v. 1). Nebuchadnezzar's son Amel-Marduk (Evil-merodach, 2 Kings 25.27–30; Jer 52.31–34) ruled in 562–560 BCE and was assassinated by his brother-in-law. The use of holy Temple* vessels (see 2 Kings 24.13; 2 Chr 36.10) for drinking praise to the gods constitutes sacrilege like that of Antiochus IV (1 Macc 1.41–50; 2 Macc 5.15–6.11). 5–12: The fingers of a human hand: A supernatural response to Belshazzar's sacrilege. Both the servants and the king demonstrate their incompetence until the queen reminds them of Daniel.

13 Then Daniel was brought in before the king. The king said to Daniel, "So you are Daniel, one of the exiles of Judah, whom my father the king brought from Judah? ¹⁴I have heard of you that a spirit of the godsᶜ is in you, and that enlightenment, understanding, and excellent wisdom are found in you. ¹⁵Now the wise men, the enchanters, have been brought in before me to read this writing and tell me its interpretation, but they were not able to give the interpretation of the matter. ¹⁶But I have heard that you can give interpretations and solve problems. Now if you are able to read the writing and tell me its interpretation, you shall be clothed in purple, have a chain of gold around your neck, and rank third in the kingdom."

17 Then Daniel answered in the presence of the king, "Let your gifts be for yourself, or give your rewards to someone else! Nevertheless I will read the writing to the king and let him know the interpretation. ¹⁸O king, the Most High God gave your father Nebuchadnezzar kingship, greatness, glory, and majesty. ¹⁹And because of the greatness that he gave him, all peoples, nations, and languages trembled and feared before him. He killed those he wanted to kill, kept alive those he wanted to keep alive, honored those he wanted to honor, and degraded those he wanted to degrade. ²⁰But when his heart was lifted up and his spirit was hardened so that he acted proudly, he was deposed from his kingly throne, and his glory was stripped from him. ²¹He was driven from human society, and his mind was made like that of an animal. His dwelling was with the wild asses, he was fed grass like oxen, and his body was bathed with the dew of heaven, until he learned that the Most High God has sovereignty over the kingdom of mortals, and sets over it whomever he will. ²²And you, Belshazzar his son, have not humbled your heart, even though you knew all this! ²³You have exalted yourself against the Lord of heaven! The vessels of his temple have been brought in before you, and you and your lords, your wives and your concubines have been drinking wine from them. You have praised the gods of silver and gold, of bronze, iron, wood, and stone, which do not see or hear or know; but the God in whose power is your very breath, and to whom belong all your ways, you have not honored.

24 "So from his presence the hand was sent and this writing was inscribed. ²⁵And

a Or a holy, divine spirit   b Aram adds the king your father   c Or a divine spirit

this is the writing that was inscribed: MENE, MENE, TEKEL, and PARSIN. 26This is the interpretation of the matter: MENE, God has numbered the days of[a] your kingdom and brought it to an end; 27TEKEL, you have been weighed on the scales and found wanting; 28PERES,[b] your kingdom is divided and given to the Medes and Persians."

29 Then Belshazzar gave the command, and Daniel was clothed in purple, a chain of gold was put around his neck, and a proclamation was made concerning him that he should rank third in the kingdom.

30 That very night Belshazzar, the Chaldean king, was killed. 31c And Darius the Mede received the kingdom, being about sixty-two years old.

5.13–31. 13–29: Daniel chides Belshazzar for his arrogance, unlike "his father" Nebuchadnezzar, prior to interpreting the writing. The words are Aramaic* nouns for units of weight: "mené," a mina; "tequel," a shekel;* "parsin," a half mina. Daniel reads them as verbs: "menah," *to number;* "teqal," *to weigh;* and "peras," *to divide.* The root "prs" also serves as the base for the name Persia. 30: Nabonidus fled Babylon at the approach of the Persian army. There is no evidence that Belshazzar was killed. 31: *Darius the Mede* is not historical. Babylon submitted to Cyrus of Persia in 539. A Persian military commander and relative of the royal family, Darius, took the throne when Cyrus's son Cambyses was assassinated in 522 BCE. The Medes were part of the Persian empire, and various prophecies asserted that Babylon would fall to them (Isa 13.17–22; 21.1–10; Jer 51.11, 28).

6 It pleased Darius to set over the kingdom one hundred twenty satraps, stationed throughout the whole kingdom, 2and over them three presidents, including Daniel; to these the satraps gave account, so that the king might suffer no loss. 3Soon Daniel distinguished himself above all the other presidents and satraps because an excellent spirit was in him, and the king planned to appoint him over the whole kingdom. 4So the presidents and the satraps tried to find grounds for complaint against Daniel in connection with the kingdom. But they could find no grounds for complaint or any corruption, because he was faithful, and no negligence or corruption could be found in him. 5The men said, "We shall not find any ground for complaint against this Daniel unless we find it in connection with the law of his God."

6 So the presidents and satraps conspired and came to the king and said to him, "O King Darius, live forever! 7All the presidents of the kingdom, the prefects and the satraps, the counselors and the governors are agreed that the king should establish an ordinance and enforce an interdict, that whoever prays to anyone, divine or human, for thirty days, except to you, O king, shall be thrown into a den of lions. 8Now, O king, establish the interdict and sign the document, so that it cannot be changed, according to the law of the Medes and the Persians, which cannot be revoked." 9Therefore King Darius signed the document and interdict.

10 Although Daniel knew that the document had been signed, he continued to go to his house, which had windows in its upper room open toward Jerusalem, and to get down on his knees three times a day to pray to his God and praise him, just as he had done previously. 11The conspirators came and found Daniel praying and seeking mercy before his God. 12Then they approached the king and said concerning the interdict, "O king! Did you not sign an interdict, that anyone who prays to anyone, divine or human, within thirty days except to you, O king, shall be thrown into a den of lions?" The king answered, "The thing stands fast, according to the law of the Medes and Persians, which cannot be revoked." 13Then they responded to the king, "Daniel, one of the exiles from Judah, pays no attention to you, O king, or to the interdict you have signed, but he is saying his prayers three times a day."

14 When the king heard the charge, he was very much distressed. He was determined to save Daniel, and until the sun went down he made every effort to rescue him. 15Then the conspirators came to the king and said to him, "Know, O king, that it is a

---

a Aram lacks *the days of*   b The singular of *Parsin*
c Ch 6.1 in Aram

law of the Medes and Persians that no interdict or ordinance that the king establishes can be changed."

16 Then the king gave the command, and Daniel was brought and thrown into the den of lions. The king said to Daniel, "May your God, whom you faithfully serve, deliver you!" 17A stone was brought and laid on the mouth of the den, and the king sealed it with his own signet and with the signet of his lords, so that nothing might be changed concerning Daniel. 18Then the king went to his palace and spent the night fasting; no food was brought to him, and sleep fled from him.

19 Then, at break of day, the king got up and hurried to the den of lions. 20When he came near the den where Daniel was, he cried out anxiously to Daniel, "O Daniel, servant of the living God, has your God whom you faithfully serve been able to deliver you from the lions?" 21Daniel then said to the king, "O king, live forever! 22My God sent his angel and shut the lions' mouths so that they would not hurt me, because I was found blameless before him; and also before you, O king, I have done no wrong." 23Then the king was exceedingly glad and commanded that Daniel be taken up out of the den. So Daniel was taken up out of the den, and no kind of harm was found on him, because he had trusted in his God. 24The king gave a command, and those who had accused Daniel were brought and thrown into the den of lions—they, their children, and their wives. Before they reached the bottom of the den the lions overpowered them and broke all their bones in pieces.

25 Then King Darius wrote to all peoples and nations of every language throughout the whole world: "May you have abundant prosperity! 26I make a decree, that in all my royal dominion people should tremble and fear before the God of Daniel:

For he is the living God,
    enduring forever.
His kingdom shall never be destroyed,
    and his dominion has no end.
27 He delivers and rescues,
    he works signs and wonders in heaven
        and on earth;

for he has saved Daniel
    from the power of the lions."
28So this Daniel prospered during the reign of Darius and the reign of Cyrus the Persian.

6.1–28: Daniel in the lions' den. This narrative demonstrates God's protection of righteous Jews from foreign monarchs who demand worship of pagan gods and themselves. **1–9:** Darius I (522–486 BCE) organized the Persian empire into twenty "satrapies," administered by officials called *satraps*. See Esth 1.1; 8.9. Daniel's success as *president*, an otherwise unknown position, prompts a plot to bring him down by playing upon his religious piety. Darius is persuaded to demand worship of himself as a god, much like Antiochus IV Epiphanes, "manifest god." *So that it cannot be revoked:* Once signed with the royal signet, Persian laws could not be revoked, even by the king. **10–18:** Judaism requires three set times for prayer: morning, afternoon, and evening (see Ps 55.17; Jdt 9.1). The narrative portrays Darius as a victim of the plot since he intended no harm to Daniel. Cyrus authorized the building of the Second Temple* (2 Chr 36.22–23; Ezra 1.1–4), which was completed during the reign of Darius (Ezra 6). Darius calls upon God to save Daniel, and attempts to do so himself. **22:** God sends an *angel* to protect the righteous Daniel from the lions (compare 3.19–30). **24:** The families of criminals are punished as well to deter crime (Num 16.23–33; Josh 7.24; 2 Sam 21.6, 9; Esth 9–13). **25–27:** Darius's announcement of the kingdom of God serves the fundamental purpose of the book: to point to the establishment of an independent Jewish kingdom identified as the kingdom of God. **28:** Cyrus (539–530 BCE) preceded his son Cambyses (530–522 BCE) and Darius I (522–486 BCE) as ruler of Babylon.

DANIEL'S VISIONS CONCERNING THE COMING KINGDOM OF GOD

Chs. 7–12: The visions point to the establishment of the kingdom of God as the primary theme of the book. Scholars generally agree that these chapters were written in the mid second century BCE to support the Maccabean revolt against Seleucid* Syria. With the fall of Seleucid Syria, the kingdom of God would be realized as an independent Jewish state centered around the Jerusalem Temple.*

---

7 In the first year of King Belshazzar of Babylon, Daniel had a dream and visions

of his head as he lay in bed. Then he wrote down the dream:*a* 2I,*b* Daniel, saw in my vision by night the four winds of heaven stirring up the great sea, 3and four great beasts came up out of the sea, different from one another. 4The first was like a lion and had eagles' wings. Then, as I watched, its wings were plucked off, and it was lifted up from the ground and made to stand on two feet like a human being; and a human mind was given to it. 5Another beast appeared, a second one, that looked like a bear. It was raised up on one side, had three tusks*c* in its mouth among its teeth and was told, "Arise, devour many bodies!" 6After this, as I watched, another appeared, like a leopard. The beast had four wings of a bird on its back and four heads; and dominion was given to it. 7After this I saw in the visions by night a fourth beast, terrifying and dreadful and exceedingly strong. It had great iron teeth and was devouring, breaking in pieces, and stamping what was left with its feet. It was different from all the beasts that preceded it, and it had ten horns. 8I was considering the horns, when another horn appeared, a little one coming up among them; to make room for it, three of the earlier horns were plucked up by the roots. There were eyes like human eyes in this horn, and a mouth speaking arrogantly.

7.1–28: The vision of the four beasts. This narrative* points to God's overthrow of Antiochus IV. **1–8:** *First year of Belshazzar:* Belshazzar's regency began in 554 BCE. Daniel's vision draws upon creation traditions, which portray God's defeat of the sea or a sea dragon as the basis for the created world order (Ps 74.13–17; 89.9–10; Isa 27.1; 51.9–10; compare Gen 1; Ex 15). Here, the chaos monsters emerge from the sea to overturn creation. *The four winds* refer to the four cardinal directions, the universal context of *the four beasts,* which represent a succession of empires (ch. 2). The *lion* with *eagles' wings* is Babylon, which employed such figures extensively in art. The *bear* with *three tusks* (literally, "ribs") in its mouth is Media. The *leopard* with *four wings* and *four heads* is Persia, which ruled most of the Near Eastern world. The *beast* with *iron teeth* is the Greek-Macedonian empire of Alexander the Great. *The ten horns* represent the ten rulers of the Seleucid empire, who used horns as symbols of

their power. *The little horn* with *eyes . . . and a mouth speaking arrogantly* is Antiochus IV, who claimed to be a god and usurped the throne following the assassination of his brother, Seleucus IV.

〜〜〜〜〜〜〜〜〜〜〜〜〜〜〜

9 As I watched,
　　thrones were set in place,
　　　and an Ancient One*d* took his
　　　　throne,
　　his clothing was white as snow,
　　　and the hair of his head like
　　　　pure wool;
　　his throne was fiery flames,
　　　and its wheels were burning fire.
10 A stream of fire issued
　　and flowed out from his presence.
　　A thousand thousands served him,
　　　and ten thousand times ten thousand
　　　　stood attending him.
　　The court sat in judgment,
　　　and the books were opened.
11I watched then because of the noise of the arrogant words that the horn was speaking. And as I watched, the beast was put to death, and its body destroyed and given over to be burned with fire. 12As for the rest of the beasts, their dominion was taken away, but their lives were prolonged for a season and a time. 13As I watched in the night visions,
　　I saw one like a human being*e*
　　　coming with the clouds of heaven.
　　And he came to the Ancient One*f*
　　　and was presented before him.
14 To him was given dominion
　　　and glory and kingship,
　　that all peoples, nations, and languages
　　　should serve him.
　　His dominion is an everlasting dominion
　　　that shall not pass away,
　　and his kingship is one
　　　that shall never be destroyed.

7.9–14. 9: *An Ancient One* (literally, "One Ancient of Days"): God. The portrayal of the divine court builds upon traditions in 1 Kings 22; Isa 6; Ezek 1; Ps 82;

a Q Ms Theodotion: MT adds *the beginning of the words; he said*　*b* Theodotion: Aram *Daniel answered and said, "I*　*c* Or *ribs*　*d* Aram *an Ancient of Days*　*e* Aram *one like a son of man*　*f* Aram *the Ancient of Days*

Job 1. **13:** *One like a human being:* Literally, "one like a son of man" (compare "mortal," literally, "son of man/adam," in Ezek 2.1), a designation for a human being, in this case a messiah⋆ figure who will rule the world as king.

15 As for me, Daniel, my spirit was troubled within me,[a] and the visions of my head terrified me. [16]I approached one of the attendants to ask him the truth concerning all this. So he said that he would disclose to me the interpretation of the matter: [17]"As for these four great beasts, four kings shall arise out of the earth. [18]But the holy ones of the Most High shall receive the kingdom and possess the kingdom forever—forever and ever."

19 Then I desired to know the truth concerning the fourth beast, which was different from all the rest, exceedingly terrifying, with its teeth of iron and claws of bronze, and which devoured and broke in pieces, and stamped what was left with its feet; [20]and concerning the ten horns that were on its head, and concerning the other horn, which came up and to make room for which three of them fell out—the horn that had eyes and a mouth that spoke arrogantly, and that seemed greater than the others. [21]As I looked, this horn made war with the holy ones and was prevailing over them, [22]until the Ancient One[b] came; then judgment was given for the holy ones of the Most High, and the time arrived when the holy ones gained possession of the kingdom.

23 This is what he said: "As for the fourth beast,

there shall be a fourth kingdom
  on earth
 that shall be different from all the
    other kingdoms;
 it shall devour the whole earth,
  and trample it down, and break it to
    pieces.
24 As for the ten horns,
 out of this kingdom ten kings
    shall arise,
  and another shall arise after them.
This one shall be different from the
    former ones,
 and shall put down three kings.

25 He shall speak words against the Most
    High,
 shall wear out the holy ones of the
    Most High,
  and shall attempt to change the
    sacred seasons and the law;
and they shall be given into his power
 for a time, two times,[c] and half a
    time.
26 Then the court shall sit in judgment,
 and his dominion shall be taken away,
  to be consumed and totally destroyed.
27 The kingship and dominion
 and the greatness of the kingdoms
    under the whole heaven
shall be given to the people of the
    holy ones of the Most High;
 their kingdom shall be an everlasting
    kingdom,
  and all dominions shall serve and
    obey them."

28 Here the account ends. As for me, Daniel, my thoughts greatly terrified me, and my face turned pale; but I kept the matter in my mind.

7.15–28. 16: *One of the attendants:* An angel. **18:** *The holy ones of the Most High* are either angels or human beings, both of whom were believed to be fighting Antiochus. The Judean revolt was led by the Hasmonean⋆ priestly family, and the service of priests in the Temple⋆ was believed to reflect that of the angels in heaven. **25:** *Shall attempt to change the sacred seasons and the law:* Antiochus banned the observance of sabbath and Torah⋆ (1 Macc 1.41–50; 2 Macc 6.1–11), thus challenging the Jewish concept of creation, which is grounded in the sabbath as part of the created world order (Gen 2.1–3; Ex 31.12–17; compare Prov 8.22–36). *A time, two times, and half a time:* Three and a half years. Antiochus's persecution is of limited duration.

8 In the third year of the reign of King Belshazzar a vision appeared to me, Daniel, after the one that had appeared to me at first. [2]In the vision I was looking and saw myself in Susa the capital, in the province of Elam,[d]

a Aram *troubled in its sheath* b Aram *the Ancient of Days* c Aram *a time, times* d Gk Theodotion: MT Q Ms repeat *in the vision I was looking*

and I was by the river Ulai.[a] [3]I looked up and saw a ram standing beside the river.[b] It had two horns. Both horns were long, but one was longer than the other, and the longer one came up second. [4]I saw the ram charging westward and northward and southward. All beasts were powerless to withstand it, and no one could rescue from its power; it did as it pleased and became strong.

5 As I was watching, a male goat appeared from the west, coming across the face of the whole earth without touching the ground. The goat had a horn[c] between its eyes. [6]It came toward the ram with the two horns that I had seen standing beside the river,[b] and it ran at it with savage force. [7]I saw it approaching the ram. It was enraged against it and struck the ram, breaking its two horns. The ram did not have power to withstand it; it threw the ram down to the ground and trampled upon it, and there was no one who could rescue the ram from its power. [8]Then the male goat grew exceedingly great; but at the height of its power, the great horn was broken, and in its place there came up four prominent horns toward the four winds of heaven.

9 Out of one of them came another[d] horn, a little one, which grew exceedingly great toward the south, toward the east, and toward the beautiful land. [10]It grew as high as the host of heaven. It threw down to the earth some of the host and some of the stars, and trampled on them. [11]Even against the prince of the host it acted arrogantly; it took the regular burnt offering away from him and overthrew the place of his sanctuary. [12]Because of wickedness, the host was given over to it together with the regular burnt offering;[e] it cast truth to the ground, and kept prospering in what it did. [13]Then I heard a holy one speaking, and another holy one said to the one that spoke, "For how long is this vision concerning the regular burnt offering, the transgression that makes desolate, and the giving over of the sanctuary and host to be trampled?"[e] [14]And he answered him,[f] "For two thousand three hundred evenings and mornings; then the sanctuary shall be restored to its rightful state."

8.1–27: The vision of the ram and the goat. A second vision surveys Greece's defeat of Persia and points to the downfall of Antiochus IV. The language of the book reverts to Hebrew (see 2.4b). **1–4:** *Third year of Belshazzar:* 552 BCE. *Susa,* located in the province of *Elam* by the River *Ulai* in modern Iran, was the winter capital of the Persian empire. The *ram* with *two horns* is the combined Persian-Median empire. **5:** The *male goat* with a *horn* is the empire of Alexander, who swept through Persia in 333–330 BCE. Alexander died in 323 BCE, and his empire split into separate kingdoms. **9–14:** *Another horn, a little one:* Antiochus IV, who attempted to extend his power to the south and east, including *the beautiful land* of Israel. Alexander defiled the Temple* by turning it into a sanctuary for Zeus. *Two thousand three hundred evenings and mornings:* or 1,150 days, approximately three years and two months (see 7.25; 12.7), the time of Antiochus's persecution (1 Macc 1.54–4.52).

15 When I, Daniel, had seen the vision, I tried to understand it. Then someone appeared standing before me, having the appearance of a man, [16]and I heard a human voice by the Ulai, calling, "Gabriel, help this man understand the vision." [17]So he came near where I stood; and when he came, I became frightened and fell prostrate. But he said to me, "Understand, O mortal,[g] that the vision is for the time of the end."

18 As he was speaking to me, I fell into a trance, face to the ground; then he touched me and set me on my feet. [19]He said, "Listen, and I will tell you what will take place later in the period of wrath; for it refers to the appointed time of the end. [20]As for the ram that you saw with the two horns, these are the kings of Media and Persia. [21]The male goat[h] is the king of Greece, and the great horn between its eyes is the first king. [22]As for the horn that was broken, in place of which four others arose, four kingdoms shall arise from his[i] nation, but not with his power.

a Or *the Ulai Gate*   b Or *gate*   c Theodotion: Gk *one horn;* Heb *a horn of vision*   d Cn Compare 7.8: Heb *one*   e Meaning of Heb uncertain   f Gk Theodotion Syr Vg: Heb *me*   g Heb *son of man*   h Or *shaggy male goat*   i Gk Theodotion Vg: Heb *the*

23 At the end of their rule,
   when the transgressions have reached
      their full measure,
a king of bold countenance shall arise,
   skilled in intrigue.
24 He shall grow strong in power,[a]
   shall cause fearful destruction,
   and shall succeed in what he does.
He shall destroy the powerful
   and the people of the holy ones.
25 By his cunning
   he shall make deceit prosper under
      his hand,
   and in his own mind he shall
      be great.
Without warning he shall destroy many
   and shall even rise up against the
      Prince of princes.
But he shall be broken, and not by
   human hands.

26 The vision of the evenings and the mornings that has been told is true. As for you, seal up the vision, for it refers to many days from now."

27 So I, Daniel, was overcome and lay sick for some days; then I arose and went about the king's business. But I was dismayed by the vision and did not understand it.

8.15–27: The archangel Gabriel serves as the messenger to humanity in 8.15–26; 9.21–27; Lk 1.11–20. In 1 Enoch* 9 he intercedes on behalf of God's people and destroys the wicked. In Islam, he reveals the Quran to Muhammed. **17–18:** *The* (appointed) *time of the end:* The end of Antiochus's persecution. **25:** *Not by human hands:* God will act. **26:** *Seal up the vision:* Although given to Daniel in the sixth century, it will be realized in the second century (compare Isa 8.16; 29.11–12; 30.8; 34.16–17).

~~~~~~~~~~~~~~~~

9 In the first year of Darius son of Ahasuerus, by birth a Mede, who became king over the realm of the Chaldeans— 2 in the first year of his reign, I, Daniel, perceived in the books the number of years that, according to the word of the LORD to the prophet Jeremiah, must be fulfilled for the devastation of Jerusalem, namely, seventy years.

3 Then I turned to the Lord God, to seek an answer by prayer and supplication with fasting and sackcloth and ashes. 4 I prayed to the LORD my God and made confession, saying,

"Ah, Lord, great and awesome God, keeping covenant and steadfast love with those who love you and keep your commandments, 5 we have sinned and done wrong, acted wickedly and rebelled, turning aside from your commandments and ordinances. 6 We have not listened to your servants the prophets, who spoke in your name to our kings, our princes, and our ancestors, and to all the people of the land.

7 "Righteousness is on your side, O Lord, but open shame, as at this day, falls on us, the people of Judah, the inhabitants of Jerusalem, and all Israel, those who are near and those who are far away, in all the lands to which you have driven them, because of the treachery that they have committed against you. 8 Open shame, O LORD, falls on us, our kings, our officials, and our ancestors, because we have sinned against you. 9 To the Lord our God belong mercy and forgiveness, for we have rebelled against him, 10 and have not obeyed the voice of the LORD our God by following his laws, which he set before us by his servants the prophets.

11 "All Israel has transgressed your law and turned aside, refusing to obey your voice. So the curse and the oath written in the law of Moses, the servant of God, have been poured out upon us, because we have sinned against you. 12 He has confirmed his words, which he spoke against us and against our rulers, by bringing upon us a calamity so great that what has been done against Jerusalem has never before been done under the whole heaven. 13 Just as it is written in the law of Moses, all this calamity has come upon us. We did not entreat the favor of the LORD our God, turning from our iniquities and reflecting on his[b] fidelity. 14 So the LORD kept watch over this calamity until he brought it upon us. Indeed, the LORD our God is right in all that he has done; for we have disobeyed his voice.

a Theodotion and one Gk Ms: Heb repeats (from 8.22) *but not with his power* *b* Heb *your*

15 "And now, O Lord our God, who brought your people out of the land of Egypt with a mighty hand and made your name renowned even to this day—we have sinned, we have done wickedly. 16 O Lord, in view of all your righteous acts, let your anger and wrath, we pray, turn away from your city Jerusalem, your holy mountain; because of our sins and the iniquities of our ancestors, Jerusalem and your people have become a disgrace among all our neighbors. 17 Now therefore, O our God, listen to the prayer of your servant and to his supplication, and for your own sake, Lord,*a* let your face shine upon your desolated sanctuary. 18 Incline your ear, O my God, and hear. Open your eyes and look at our desolation and the city that bears your name. We do not present our supplication before you on the ground of our righteousness, but on the ground of your great mercies. 19 O Lord, hear; O Lord, forgive; O Lord, listen and act and do not delay! For your own sake, O my God, because your city and your people bear your name!"

9.1–27: The seventy weeks. This chapter applies Jeremiah's prophecy of a 70-year exile (Jer 25.11, 12; 29.10) together with the calculation of the jubilee year (Lev 25.8–17; "seven weeks of years") to predict the end of Antiochus's persecution. **1:** *Ahasuerus:* The Hebrew name for the Persian ruler Xerxes (see Esth 1.1; Ezra 4.6). Xerxes I (486–465 BCE) was the son of Darius I, and Xerxes II (425 BCE) was the son of Artaxerxes I (465–425 BCE). Darius II (423–405 BCE) was the son of Xerxes II, and Darius III (336–330 BCE), the son of Arses (338–336 BCE), was the last ruler of Persia; he was assassinated shortly after Alexander's final defeat of the Persian army. **2–19:** *Prayer and supplication:* Daniel employs a form of communal confession and petition (compare Ezra 9.6–15; Neh 1.5–11; 9.6–37). **11:** *The curse and the oath written in the law of Moses:* See Lev 26.14–45; Deut 28.15–68; 29.10–29.

20 While I was speaking, and was praying and confessing my sin and the sin of my people Israel, and presenting my supplication before the LORD my God on behalf of the holy mountain of my God— 21 while I was speaking in prayer, the man Gabriel, whom I had seen before in a vision, came to me in swift flight at the time of the evening sacri-

fice. 22 He came*b* and said to me, "Daniel, I have now come out to give you wisdom and understanding. 23 At the beginning of your supplications a word went out, and I have come to declare it, for you are greatly beloved. So consider the word and understand the vision:

24 "Seventy weeks are decreed for your people and your holy city: to finish the transgression, to put an end to sin, and to atone for iniquity, to bring in everlasting righteousness, to seal both vision and prophet, and to anoint a most holy place.*c* 25 Know therefore and understand: from the time that the word went out to restore and rebuild Jerusalem until the time of an anointed prince, there shall be seven weeks; and for sixty-two weeks it shall be built again with streets and moat, but in a troubled time. 26 After the sixty-two weeks, an anointed one shall be cut off and shall have nothing, and the troops of the prince who is to come shall destroy the city and the sanctuary. Its*d* end shall come with a flood, and to the end there shall be war. Desolations are decreed. 27 He shall make a strong covenant with many for one week, and for half of the week he shall make sacrifice and offering cease; and in their place*e* shall be an abomination that desolates, until the decreed end is poured out upon the desolator."

9.20–27. 24: *Seventy weeks:* Gabriel interprets Jeremiah's 70 years as "70 weeks of years" by applying the calculation of the jubilee year at "seven weeks of years" (Lev 25.8; see also 2 Chr 36.21). From 167 BCE, the total of 490 years would place the beginning of the calculation in 657 BCE during the reign of Manasseh, whose evil deeds prompted God to destroy Jerusalem and the Temple* (2 Kings 21.10–15). Gabriel's interpretation* points to the Maccabean revolt as the time when the punishment of Jerusalem would end. **25–26:** *Seven weeks:* Many claim that this is the 49 years that passed from the destruction of the Temple in 587 BCE to 538 BCE when Sheshbazzar laid the foundation for the Second Temple (Ezra 1.1–11; 5.13–16). The remaining *sixty-two weeks* or 434 years points to

a Theodotion Vg Compare Syr: Heb *for the Lord's sake*
b Gk Syr: Heb *He made to understand*   *c* Or *thing or one*   *d* Or *His*   *e* Cn: Meaning of Heb uncertain

104 BCE as the time of fulfillment, which goes beyond the period of the Maccabean revolt. *An anointed* one shall be cut off:* Antiochus removed the high priest Onias III, who was subsequently murdered (2 Macc 4.3–34). *The troops of the prince who is to come:* Antiochus sacked Jerusalem in 167 BCE following his humiliating withdrawal from Egypt. **27:** *He shall make a strong covenant* with many for one week:* Antiochus appointed Jason and then Menelaus as high priests in the Temple (2 Macc 4).

Daniel's vision of Antiochus's fall

Chs. 10–12: The culmination of the book describes the onset of the vision in 10.1–11.1; an overview of history from the fall of Persia to the projected fall of Antiochus IV in 11.2–12.4; and a conclusion that attempts to calculate the realization of the vision in 12.5–13. The author's description of historical events is accurate through 11.39, but the portrayal of Antiochus's demise in 11.40–12.4 is fictitious. The author wrote between December, 167 BCE, when the Temple* was desecrated, and December, 164 BCE, when it was rededicated by Judah the Maccabee.

10 In the third year of King Cyrus of Persia a word was revealed to Daniel, who was named Belteshazzar. The word was true, and it concerned a great conflict. He understood the word, having received understanding in the vision.

2 At that time I, Daniel, had been mourning for three weeks. ³I had eaten no rich food, no meat or wine had entered my mouth, and I had not anointed myself at all, for the full three weeks. ⁴On the twenty-fourth day of the first month, as I was standing on the bank of the great river (that is, the Tigris), ⁵I looked up and saw a man clothed in linen, with a belt of gold from Uphaz around his waist. ⁶His body was like beryl, his face like lightning, his eyes like flaming torches, his arms and legs like the gleam of burnished bronze, and the sound of his words like the roar of a multitude. ⁷I, Daniel, alone saw the vision; the people who were with me did not see the vision, though a great trembling fell upon them, and they fled and hid themselves. ⁸So I was left alone to see this great vision. My strength left me, and my complexion grew deathly pale, and I retained no strength. ⁹Then I heard the sound of his words; and when I heard the sound of his words, I fell into a trance, face to the ground.

10.1–11.1: The onset of Daniel's vision. Compare Ezekiel's vision (Ezek 1). **10.1:** *The third year of King Cyrus of Persia:* 536 BCE, 70 years after the date in 1.1 (see 9.24). **2–4:** Acts of self-denial are typical preparations for trances and other forms of mystical experience. **5:** *Twenty-fourth day of the month:* The 24th of Nissan, one day following the conclusion of Passover.* **5–6:** *A man clothed in linen:* An angel dressed as a priest and gleaming like the cherubim* of Ezekiel's vision (see Ezek 9.2; 40.3). *Uphaz:* See Jer 10.9. **7–9:** *Trance:* See Gen 2.21; 15.2.

10 But then a hand touched me and roused me to my hands and knees. ¹¹He said to me, "Daniel, greatly beloved, pay attention to the words that I am going to speak to you. Stand on your feet, for I have now been sent to you." So while he was speaking this word to me, I stood up trembling. ¹²He said to me, "Do not fear, Daniel, for from the first day that you set your mind to gain understanding and to humble yourself before your God, your words have been heard, and I have come because of your words. ¹³But the prince of the kingdom of Persia opposed me twenty-one days. So Michael, one of the chief princes, came to help me, and I left him there with the prince of the kingdom of Persia,ᵃ ¹⁴and have come to help you understand what is to happen to your people at the end of days. For there is a further vision for those days."

15 While he was speaking these words to me, I turned my face toward the ground and was speechless. ¹⁶Then one in human form touched my lips, and I opened my mouth to speak, and said to the one who stood before me, "My lord, because of the vision such pains have come upon me that I retain no strength. ¹⁷How can my lord's servant talk with my lord? For I am shaking,ᵇ no strength remains in me, and no breath is left in me."

18 Again one in human form touched me and strengthened me. ¹⁹He said, "Do not

---

a Gk Theodotion: Heb *I was left there with the kings of Persia*   *b* Gk: Heb *from now*

fear, greatly beloved, you are safe. Be strong and courageous!" When he spoke to me, I was strengthened and said, "Let my lord speak, for you have strengthened me." [20]Then he said, "Do you know why I have come to you? Now I must return to fight against the prince of Persia, and when I am through with him, the prince of Greece will come. [21]But I am to tell you what is inscribed in the book of truth. There is no one with me who contends against these princes

11 except Michael, your prince. [1]As for me, in the first year of Darius the Mede, I stood up to support and strengthen him.

10.10–11.1. 10–14: In ancient Near Eastern mythology, conflict among the nations often involves conflict among their gods. *The prince of Persia:* The angel or god of Persia. *Twenty-one days:* The duration of Daniel's fasting in v. 3. *Michael:* The archangel who protects the Jewish people (10.21; 12.1; see also Jude 9; Rev 12.7). **15–17:** Daniel speaks after his lips are touched (Isa 6.5–7; Ex 4.10–17; Ezek 3.26–27). *One in human form:* An angel. **10.18–11.1:** The angel, perhaps Michael, points to conflicts with Persia and Greece which are described in detail.

2 "Now I will announce the truth to you. Three more kings shall arise in Persia. The fourth shall be far richer than all of them, and when he has become strong through his riches, he shall stir up all against the kingdom of Greece. [3]Then a warrior king shall arise, who shall rule with great dominion and take action as he pleases. [4]And while still rising in power, his kingdom shall be broken and divided toward the four winds of heaven, but not to his posterity, nor according to the dominion with which he ruled; for his kingdom shall be uprooted and go to others besides these.

5 "Then the king of the south shall grow strong, but one of his officers shall grow stronger than he and shall rule a realm greater than his own realm. [6]After some years they shall make an alliance, and the daughter of the king of the south shall come to the king of the north to ratify the agreement. But she shall not retain her power, and his offspring shall not endure. She shall

be given up, she and her attendants and her child and the one who supported her.

"In those times [7]a branch from her roots shall rise up in his place. He shall come against the army and enter the fortress of the king of the north, and he shall take action against them and prevail. [8]Even their gods, with their idols and with their precious vessels of silver and gold, he shall carry off to Egypt as spoils of war. For some years he shall refrain from attacking the king of the north; [9]then the latter shall invade the realm of the king of the south, but will return to his own land.

11.2–12.4: Daniel's vision of history. Egypt did not attack Antiochus after 167 BCE. He died of tuberculosis in 164 or 163 BCE following campaigns in Armenia and Elymais (Elam). **2:** The three Persian kings are uncertain. **3–4:** Alexander, whose empire was divided after his death in 323 BCE. **5–6:** *The king of the south:* Ptolemy I (305–282 BCE), founder of the Ptolemaic★ dynasty★ of Egypt. *One of his officers:* Seleucus I (305–281 BCE), founder of the Syrian Seleucid★ dynasty. Ptolemy II's (282–246 BCE) daughter Berenice married Antiochus II (261–247 BCE), but the alliance failed after Berenice, her child, and Antiochus II were murdered. **7–9:** Berenice's brother, Ptolemy III (246–222 BCE), invaded Syria to avenge her death, but he was repulsed by Seleucus II (246–225 BCE). **10:** *His sons:* Seleucus III (225–223 BCE) and Antiochus III (223–187 BCE).

10 "His sons shall wage war and assemble a multitude of great forces, which shall advance like a flood and pass through, and again shall carry the war as far as his fortress. [11]Moved with rage, the king of the south shall go out and do battle against the king of the north, who shall muster a great multitude, which shall, however, be defeated by his enemy. [12]When the multitude has been carried off, his heart shall be exalted, and he shall overthrow tens of thousands, but he shall not prevail. [13]For the king of the north shall again raise a multitude, larger than the former, and after some years[a] he shall advance with a great army and abundant supplies.

a Heb *and at the end of the times years*

14 "In those times many shall rise against the king of the south. The lawless among your own people shall lift themselves up in order to fulfill the vision, but they shall fail. 15 Then the king of the north shall come and throw up siegeworks, and take a well-fortified city. And the forces of the south shall not stand, not even his picked troops, for there shall be no strength to resist. 16 But he who comes against him shall take the actions he pleases, and no one shall withstand him. He shall take a position in the beautiful land, and all of it shall be in his power. 17 He shall set his mind to come with the strength of his whole kingdom, and he shall bring terms of peace*a* and perform them. In order to destroy the kingdom,*b* he shall give him a woman in marriage; but it shall not succeed or be to his advantage. 18 Afterward he shall turn to the coastlands, and shall capture many. But a commander shall put an end to his insolence; indeed,*c* he shall turn his insolence back upon him. 19 Then he shall turn back toward the fortresses of his own land, but he shall stumble and fall, and shall not be found.

11.10–19. 11–12: Ptolemy IV (222–204 BCE) defeated Antiochus III at Raphia but failed to capitalize on his victory. 13–19: Antiochus III defeated Ptolemy V (204–180 BCE) in 200 BCE, taking control of the Sinai (and Judea). He later gave his daughter Cleopatra I to Ptolemy V in marriage.

20 "Then shall arise in his place one who shall send an official for the glory of the kingdom; but within a few days he shall be broken, though not in anger or in battle. 21 In his place shall arise a contemptible person on whom royal majesty had not been conferred; he shall come in without warning and obtain the kingdom through intrigue. 22 Armies shall be utterly swept away and broken before him, and the prince of the covenant as well. 23 And after an alliance is made with him, he shall act deceitfully and become strong with a small party. 24 Without warning he shall come into the richest parts*d* of the province and do what none of his predecessors had ever done, lavishing plunder, spoil, and wealth on them. He shall devise plans against strongholds, but only for a time. 25 He shall stir up his power and determination against the king of the south with a great army, and the king of the south shall wage war with a much greater and stronger army. But he shall not succeed, for plots shall be devised against him 26 by those who eat of the royal rations. They shall break him, his army shall be swept away, and many shall fall slain. 27 The two kings, their minds bent on evil, shall sit at one table and exchange lies. But it shall not succeed, for there remains an end at the time appointed. 28 He shall return to his land with great wealth, but his heart shall be set against the holy covenant. He shall work his will, and return to his own land.

11.20–28: The initial reign of Antiochus IV, who usurped the throne following the assassination of his brother Seleucus IV (187–175 BCE). His initial campaigns against Ptolemy VI (180–145 BCE) were successful.

29 "At the time appointed he shall return and come into the south, but this time it shall not be as it was before. 30 For ships of Kittim shall come against him, and he shall lose heart and withdraw. He shall be enraged and take action against the holy covenant. He shall turn back and pay heed to those who forsake the holy covenant. 31 Forces sent by him shall occupy and profane the temple and fortress. They shall abolish the regular burnt offering and set up the abomination that makes desolate. 32 He shall seduce with intrigue those who violate the covenant; but the people who are loyal to their God shall stand firm and take action. 33 The wise among the people shall give understanding to many; for some days, however, they shall fall by sword and flame, and suffer captivity and plunder. 34 When they fall victim, they shall receive a little help, and many shall join them insincerely. 35 Some of the wise shall fall, so that they may be refined, purified, and cleansed,*e* until the time of the

a Gk: Heb *kingdom, and upright ones with him*
b Heb *it* *c* Meaning of Heb uncertain *d* Or *among the richest men* *e* Heb *made them white*

end, for there is still an interval until the time appointed.

36 "The king shall act as he pleases. He shall exalt himself and consider himself greater than any god, and shall speak horrendous things against the God of gods. He shall prosper until the period of wrath is completed, for what is determined shall be done. [37] He shall pay no respect to the gods of his ancestors, or to the one beloved by women; he shall pay no respect to any other god, for he shall consider himself greater than all. [38] He shall honor the god of fortresses instead of these; a god whom his ancestors did not know he shall honor with gold and silver, with precious stones and costly gifts. [39] He shall deal with the strongest fortresses by the help of a foreign god. Those who acknowledge him he shall make more wealthy, and shall appoint them as rulers over many, and shall distribute the land for a price.

11.29–39: Following his forced withdrawal from Egypt, Antiochus sacked and occupied Jerusalem in 167 BCE, profaned the Temple,* and proscribed the practice of Judaism. **30:** *Kittim:* Originally Greeks or Cypriots (Gen 10.4; Ezek 27.6), later Romans. **34:** *A little help:* The Maccabean revolt. **36:** Antiochus called himself Epiphanes,* "manifest god." **37–39:** Antiochus set aside the worship of Tammuz-Adonis in favor of Zeus Olympus, whose statue he placed in the Temple (1 Macc 1.54–59).

40 "At the time of the end the king of the south shall attack him. But the king of the north shall rush upon him like a whirlwind, with chariots and horsemen, and with many ships. He shall advance against countries and pass through like a flood. [41] He shall come into the beautiful land, and tens of thousands shall fall victim, but Edom and Moab and the main part of the Ammonites shall escape from his power. [42] He shall stretch out his hand against the countries, and the land of Egypt shall not escape. [43] He shall become ruler of the treasures of gold and of silver, and all the riches of Egypt; and the Libyans and the Ethiopians[a] shall follow in his train. [44] But reports from the east and the north shall alarm him, and he shall go out with great fury to bring ruin and complete destruction to many. [45] He shall pitch his palatial tents between the sea and the beautiful holy mountain. Yet he shall come to his end, with no one to help him.

11.40–45: The scenario presented here did not take place. *The beautiful land:* Israel.

12 "At that time Michael, the great prince, the protector of your people, shall arise. There shall be a time of anguish, such as has never occurred since nations first came into existence. But at that time your people shall be delivered, everyone who is found written in the book. [2] Many of those who sleep in the dust of the earth[b] shall awake, some to everlasting life, and some to shame and everlasting contempt. [3] Those who are wise shall shine like the brightness of the sky,[c] and those who lead many to righteousness, like the stars forever and ever. [4] But you, Daniel, keep the words secret and the book sealed until the time of the end. Many shall be running back and forth, and evil[d] shall increase."

12.1–4: Michael calls upon Daniel to remain silent about the vision until its fulfillment. **2:** Resurrection of the righteous (Isa 26.19; Ezek 37). **3:** *Like the brightness of the sky:* The Hebrew word "zohar" ("brightness") from this verse serves as the title of the Zohar, the primary mystical work of Judaism.

5 Then I, Daniel, looked, and two others appeared, one standing on this bank of the stream and one on the other. [6] One of them said to the man clothed in linen, who was upstream, "How long shall it be until the end of these wonders?" [7] The man clothed in linen, who was upstream, raised his right hand and his left hand toward heaven. And I heard him swear by the one who lives forever that it would be for a time, two times, and half a time,[e] and that when the shattering of the power of the holy people comes to an end, all these things would be accom-

a Or *Nubians;* Heb *Cushites*   b Or *the land of dust*
c Or *dome*   d Cn Compare Gk: Heb *knowledge*
e Heb *a time, times, and a half*

plished. [8]I heard but could not understand; so I said, "My lord, what shall be the outcome of these things?" [9]He said, "Go your way, Daniel, for the words are to remain secret and sealed until the time of the end. [10]Many shall be purified, cleansed, and refined, but the wicked shall continue to act wickedly. None of the wicked shall understand, but those who are wise shall understand. [11]From the time that the regular burnt offering is taken away and the abomination that desolates is set up, there shall be one thousand two hundred ninety days. [12]Happy are those who persevere and attain the thousand three hundred thirty-five days. [13]But you, go your way,[a] and rest; you shall rise for your reward at the end of the days."

12.5–13: The realization of the vision. This section attempts to calculate the time when the vision will be realized. **5–6:** *Two others:* Angels. **7:** *A time, two times, and half a time:* Three and a half years, the approximate time from the desecration of the Temple* in 167 BCE to its rededication in 164 BCE (see 7.25). **11:** *One thousand two hundred ninety days:* An attempt to specify the figure in v. 7. **12:** *Thousand three hundred thirty-five days:* A second attempt to specify this figure. **13:** *The end of days:* The end of the period outlined in the vision (see 8.17; 9.26; 11.6, 13, 35, 40; 12.4, 9).

a Gk Theodotion: Heb adds *to the end*

HOSEA

Introduction

Hosea's central concern is Israel's loyalty to its God. He denounces Israel for worshipping other gods, in particular the Canaanite god Baal,☆ and pleads with Israel to return to the faithful worship of its God alone. To gain his audience's attention and to make his message vivid, Hosea used the metaphor☆ of marriage to describe Israel's relationship to God. God is pictured as a husband and Israel as his faithless and promiscuous wife. Israel, the disloyal wife, is urged to repent and return to her husband. The marriage metaphor is enacted by Hosea himself in chs. 1–3, when Hosea marries Gomer, described as a prostitute (2.2) and an adulteress (3.1). And Hosea uses the marriage metaphor repeatedly in the speeches in chs. 4–14, which make up the bulk of the book. A prophet☆ fond of metaphors, Hosea also compares Israel's disloyalty to a barren tree (9.13–17), a stubborn heifer (4.16; 10.11–15), and a rebellious son (11.1–7).

Hosea's prophecy can be divided into two parts, the first a collection of narratives☆ in chs. 1–3 that describes Israel's disloyalty in terms of Hosea's faithless wife. Narratives about prophets, such as these, typically take up less space in a prophetic book than the prophet's speeches themselves, and they frequently describe prophets acting out the message they wish to deliver. The second and larger part of Hosea is a collection of prophetic speeches (chs. 4–14) that condemn Israel's deceit, predict God's punishment, and express hope for Israel's renewal. It is difficult to know where one speech ends and the next begins, but a dominant pattern can be detected in which indictments of sin are followed by sentences of judgment. In the brief speech that begins this collection, for example, an indictment listing Israel's crimes (4.1–2) is followed by a sentence describing God's punishment (4.3). Much less common are speeches predicting Israel's restoration (11.8–11). Hosea's own speeches may have been supplemented at points by later editors who wished to relate Hosea's message to the southern kingdom of Judah or to the Judeans in exile (11.10–11).

Hosea lived and prophesied in the northern kingdom of Israel, also called Ephraim, at the time of the divided monarchy when Israel and Judah were separate kingdoms. Hosea was the only native northerner among the prophets, the rest of whom all lived in or came from Judah. His career covered the last 30 years of the kingdom of Israel (750–721 BCE), when Israel was under the constant threat of Assyrian imperialism and was wracked by a series of violent coups in its own capital, Samaria. Hosea deplores the internal political violence of this period (7.5–7) and Israel's attempt to protect itself by international alliances (7.11), and he believes Israel's impending doom in the face of Assyrian expansion to be God's punishment for its social and religious corruption.

Hosea is especially critical of the religious scene in Israelite society during this period. His frequent references to Baal (2.8, 13, 16) indicate that many Israelites had turned from their own God to worship this Canaanite deity. This attraction to Baal-worship among the Israelites was an old and continual problem, as the contest between Elijah and the prophets of Baal a century earlier shows (2 Kings 17–19). The Israelites believed that Baal, like Israel's own God, could deliver the rains and agricultural productivity on which their economy and survival depended. The calves that Hosea criticizes (8.5–6), though possibly pedestals or throne images for Israel's God, are also associated with Baal in this period, and Hosea regards them as idols of Baal.

Hosea begins a collection of twelve short prophetic books, often called the Minor Prophets because of their brief length when compared to the longer books of Isaiah, Jeremiah, and Ezekiel. These twelve books are arranged roughly in chronological order, starting with eighth-century prophets, as Hosea, Amos, and Micah are explicitly identified. The collection then moves to prophets of the seventh century and concludes with those of the sixth.

READING GUIDE

One key to understanding Hosea involves recognizing the variety of ways in which the image of marital infidelity is employed to picture Israel's religious disloyalty. Catching the basic point of the comparison and its shock value is more important than reconstructing the actual details of Hosea's marriage, which still elude scholars. It is also important to notice how much of Hosea's message of faithlessness is directed against abuses in Israelite religion: its priesthood, its rituals, its sacred sites and altars, and its basic integrity.

1 The word of the LORD that came to Hosea son of Beeri, in the days of Kings Uzziah, Jotham, Ahaz, and Hezekiah of Judah, and in the days of King Jeroboam son of Joash of Israel.

1.1: Title. The reigns of these Judean kings span almost a hundred years (783–687 BCE), while the reign of the single Israelite king mentioned, Jeroboam, lasts for only 41 of these years (786–746). Since Hosea's speeches are directed to Israel in particular and reflect events leading up to its fall to Assyria in 721 BCE, it is peculiar that the six kings who followed Jeroboam to the throne of Israel during this time are not mentioned here.

2 When the LORD first spoke through Hosea, the LORD said to Hosea, "Go, take for yourself a wife of whoredom and have children of whoredom, for the land commits great whoredom by forsaking the LORD." ³So he went and took Gomer daughter of Diblaim, and she conceived and bore him a son.

4 And the LORD said to him, "Name him Jezreel;ᵃ for in a little while I will punish the house of Jehu for the blood of Jezreel, and I will put an end to the kingdom of the house of Israel. ⁵On that day I will break the bow of Israel in the valley of Jezreel."

6 She conceived again and bore a daughter. Then the LORD said to him, "Name her Lo-ruhamah,ᵇ for I will no longer have pity on the house of Israel or forgive them. ⁷But I will have pity on the house of Judah, and I will save them by the LORD their God; I will not save them by bow, or by sword, or by war, or by horses, or by horsemen."

8 When she had weaned Lo-ruhamah, she conceived and bore a son. ⁹Then the LORD said, "Name him Lo-ammi,ᶜ for you are not my people and I am not your God."ᵈ

10ᵉ Yet the number of the people of Israel shall be like the sand of the sea, which can be neither measured nor numbered; and in the place where it was said to them, "You are not my people," it shall be said to them, "Children of the living God." ¹¹The people of Judah and the people of Israel shall be gathered together, and they shall appoint for themselves one head; and they shall take possession ofᶠ the land, for great shall be the day of Jezreel.

2 ᵍSay to your brother,ʰ Ammi,ⁱ and to your sister,ʲ Ruhamah.ᵏ

1.2–2.1: Hosea marries the prostitute Gomer. In chs. 1 and 3 Hosea acts out the message he wishes to convey to Israel: Just as the wife he marries has been promiscuous, seeking out other lovers, so Israel has been unfaithful to its LORD, seeking out other gods to worship. **1.2:** *Whoredom* translates the common Hebrew term for prostitution. **4:** Hosea's first son *Jezreel* is named after the broad valley in northern Israel where

a That is *God sows*   b That is *Not pitied*   c That is *Not my people*   d Heb *I am not yours*   e Ch 2.1 in Heb   f Heb *rise up from*   g Ch 2.3 in Heb   h Gk: Heb *brothers*   i That is *My people*   j Gk Vg: Heb *sisters*   k That is *Pitied*

Jehu led a bloody coup (2 Kings 9.14–10.11), establishing a dynasty* in which Jeroboam, Hosea's contemporary, was the fourth king. The name symbolizes the imminent end of that dynasty, which occurred during Hosea's career when Jeroboam's son Zechariah was assassinated in 745 BCE. **6–9:** The names of Hosea's daughter, *Lo-ruhamah* ("Not pitied"), and second son, *Lo-ammi* ("Not my people"), symbolize

Map   Kingdom of Israel in Hosea's time

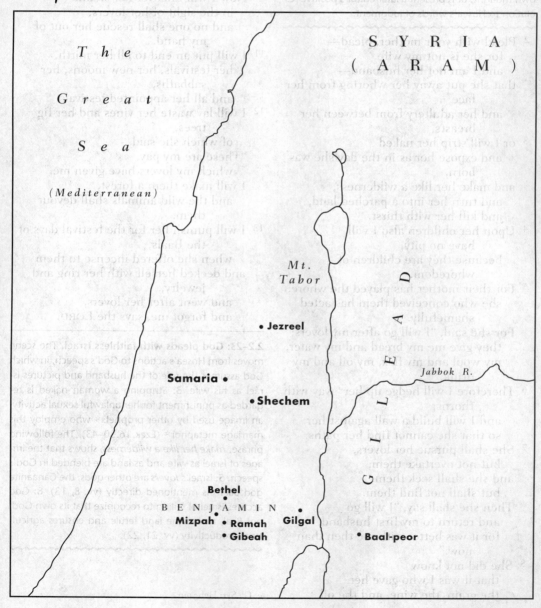

God's rejection of Israel for its faithlessness. **7:** Scholars disagree whether references to the southern kingdom of *Judah* here and elsewhere in Hosea are from Hosea himself or from later Judean editors who wished to relate Hosea's message to their own time and place. **1.10–2.1:** The marked shift to future salvation here, in which the meanings of Hosea's children's names are reversed to their positive counterparts, may either reflect the tension between despair and hope in Hosea's own thought, or represent a later editor's positive resolution to Hosea's words of judgment.

2 Plead with your mother, plead—
  for she is not my wife,
  and I am not her husband—
  that she put away her whoring from her
    face,
  and her adultery from between her
    breasts,
3 or I will strip her naked
  and expose her as in the day she was
    born,
  and make her like a wilderness,
  and turn her into a parched land,
  and kill her with thirst.
4 Upon her children also I will
    have no pity,
  because they are children of
    whoredom.
5 For their mother has played the whore;
  she who conceived them has acted
    shamefully.
  For she said, "I will go after my lovers;
  they give me my bread and my water,
  my wool and my flax, my oil and my
    drink."
6 Therefore I will hedge up her*a* way with
    thorns;
  and I will build a wall against her,
  so that she cannot find her paths.
7 She shall pursue her lovers,
  but not overtake them;
  and she shall seek them,
  but shall not find them.
  Then she shall say, "I will go
  and return to my first husband,
  for it was better with me then than
    now."
8 She did not know
  that it was I who gave her
  the grain, the wine, and the oil,
and who lavished upon her silver
  and gold that they used for Baal.
9 Therefore I will take back
  my grain in its time,
  and my wine in its season;
and I will take away my wool and my
    flax,
  which were to cover her
    nakedness.
10 Now I will uncover her shame
  in the sight of her lovers,
  and no one shall rescue her out of
    my hand.
11 I will put an end to all her mirth,
  her festivals, her new moons, her
    sabbaths,
  and all her appointed festivals.
12 I will lay waste her vines and her fig
    trees,
  of which she said,
"These are my pay,
  which my lovers have given me."
I will make them a forest,
  and the wild animals shall devour
    them.
13 I will punish her for the festival days of
    the Baals,
  when she offered incense to them
and decked herself with her ring and
    jewelry,
  and went after her lovers,
  and forgot me, says the LORD.

2.2–23: God pleads with faithless Israel. The scene moves from Hosea's actions to God's speech, in which God assumes the role of the husband and pictures Israel as his wife. **3:** Stripping a woman naked is regarded as punishment for her unlawful sexual activity, an image used by other prophets* who employ this marriage metaphor* (Ezek 16.30–43). The following phrase, *make her like a wilderness*, shows that the images of Israel as wife and as land are blended in God's speech. **5:** Israel's *lovers* are other gods; the Canaanite god Baal* is mentioned directly (vv. 8, 13). **8:** God accuses Israel of failing to recognize that its own God, not Baal, makes the land fertile and ensures agricultural productivity (vv. 21, 22).

a Gk Syr: Heb *your*

14 Therefore, I will now allure her,
  and bring her into the wilderness,
  and speak tenderly to her.
15 From there I will give her her
      vineyards,
  and make the Valley of Achor a door
      of hope.
There she shall respond as in the days
      of her youth,
  as at the time when she came out of
      the land of Egypt.
16 On that day, says the LORD, you will call
me, "My husband," and no longer will you
call me, "My Baal."*a* 17 For I will remove the
names of the Baals from her mouth, and they
shall be mentioned by name no more. 18 I
will make for you*b* a covenant on that day
with the wild animals, the birds of the air,
and the creeping things of the ground; and I
will abolish*c* the bow, the sword, and war
from the land; and I will make you lie down
in safety. 19 And I will take you for my wife
forever; I will take you for my wife in righteousness and in justice, in steadfast love,
and in mercy. 20 I will take you for my wife
in faithfulness; and you shall know the
LORD.
21 On that day I will answer, says the
      LORD,
  I will answer the heavens
      and they shall answer the earth;
22 and the earth shall answer the grain,
      the wine, and the oil,
  and they shall answer Jezreel;*d*
23 and I will sow him*e* for myself in the
      land.
  And I will have pity on Lo-ruhamah,*f*
  and I will say to Lo-ammi,*g* "You are
      my people";
  and he shall say, "You are my God."

3 The LORD said to me again, "Go, love a
woman who has a lover and is an adulteress, just as the LORD loves the people of
Israel, though they turn to other gods and
love raisin cakes." 2 So I bought her for fifteen shekels of silver and a homer of barley
and a measure of wine.*h* 3 And I said to her,
"You must remain as mine for many days;
you shall not play the whore, you shall not
have intercourse with a man, nor I with you."
4 For the Israelites shall remain many days
without king or prince, without sacrifice or
pillar, without ephod or teraphim. 5 Afterward the Israelites shall return and seek the
LORD their God, and David their king; they
shall come in awe to the LORD and to his
goodness in the latter days.

3.1–5: Hosea marries an adulteress. The details of
this account are so sketchy that it is difficult to decide
whether it describes (1) Hosea's first marriage to
Gomer in ch. 1, but from the first- rather than third-
person perspective; (2) Hosea's marriage to a second
woman; or (3) Hosea's remarriage to Gomer. In any
case, the point of his symbolic act is clear: Israel has
been an unfaithful wife but God desires her return. **1:**
While Hosea connects *raisin cakes* with worship of
other gods (as does Isa 16.7), they are also associated
with legitimate Israelite worship (2 Sam 6.19). **2:** The
nature of Hosea's transaction is unclear. Payment was
made in ancient Israel for women slaves (Ex 21.7–11)
and for wives (Ex 22.16–17), but this amount is not
mentioned elsewhere, and the narrative* does not
identify the recipient of the payment. **4:** Hosea predicts
a coming judgment in which Israel will lose both political and religious leadership. The *ephod** (Ex 28.4)
and the *teraphim* (Judg 17.5; Zech 10.2) are both associated with priestly activity. **5:** The reference to *David their king* may indicate that Hosea looked forward
to the reunification of Israel and Judah under a single
king (1.11), since David had once ruled over a united
kingdom (2 Sam 5; alternatively, it may represent the
perspective of a later editor from the southern kingdom of Judah, over which David's descendants ruled
for its entire history.

2.14–23. 14–15: References to *the wilderness, the Valley of Achor,* and *the land of Egypt* recall Israel's deliverance from slavery in Egypt (Ex 1–15), its journey
through the wilderness (Ex 16—Num 36), and its entrance into Canaan (Josh 7.24–26). **16:** Hosea plays on
the multiple meanings of the Hebrew word "ba'al": It
can be used as a common noun meaning "husband"
or "master" or as the name of the Canaanite god
Baal.

a That is, *"My master"*   *b* Heb *them*   *c* Heb *break*
d That is *God sows*   *e* Cn: Heb *her*   *f* That is *Not
pitied*   *g* That is *Not my people*   *h* Gk: Heb *a homer
of barley and a lethech of barley*

Prophets and Gender

Hosea's primary image for Israel's disloyalty to God is the wife who is unfaithful to her husband and has become a prostitute. One reason Hosea chose this image is the fact that his audience was primarily male—the men held the power and wealth in ancient patriarchal societies such as biblical Israel. For these men, faithless wives were a stinging shame. And by comparing the men's behavior to faithless wives, Hosea wanted to shock them so they would see the seriousness of their crimes. The image of the faithless wife gave Hosea a forceful means of criticizing the abuses of Israel's male elite. The problem of the image is that it connects disloyalty and sin with women in particular, a connection that must be clearly rejected in order to keep such an image from being used to disparage and mistreat women.

4 Hear the word of the LORD, O people
of Israel;
for the LORD has an indictment
against the inhabitants
of the land.
There is no faithfulness or loyalty,
and no knowledge of God in the land.
2 Swearing, lying, and murder,
and stealing and adultery break out;
bloodshed follows bloodshed.
3 Therefore the land mourns,
and all who live in it languish;
together with the wild animals
and the birds of the air,
even the fish of the sea are perishing.

4 Yet let no one contend,
and let none accuse,
for with you is my contention,
O priest.[a]
5 You shall stumble by day;
the prophet also shall stumble with
you by night,
and I will destroy your mother.
6 My people are destroyed for lack of
knowledge;
because you have rejected knowledge,
I reject you from being a priest to me.
And since you have forgotten the law of
your God,
I also will forget your children.

7 The more they increased,
the more they sinned against me;
they changed[b] their glory into shame.

8 They feed on the sin of my people;
they are greedy for their iniquity.
9 And it shall be like people, like priest;
I will punish them for their ways,
and repay them for their deeds.
10 They shall eat, but not be satisfied;
they shall play the whore, but not
multiply;
because they have forsaken the LORD
to devote themselves to
11 whoredom.

4.1–19: God puts Israel on trial. The language of this section puts God's accusations against Israel into the context of a legal proceeding initiated by an *indictment* (v. 1) describing the allegations against Israel. The judicial sentence that will follow (5.1–6.3) is already anticipated here (vv. 3, 6, 9–10). **2:** This list of crimes is similar to those outlawed in the ten commandments (Ex 20.7, 13–16). **4–10:** God prosecutes Israel's priests. **6:** The *law* (Heb., "torah") is the basis for Israel's life and worship.

Wine and new wine
take away the understanding.
12 My people consult a piece of wood,
and their divining rod gives
them oracles.
For a spirit of whoredom has led them
astray,
and they have played the whore,
forsaking their God.

a Cn: Meaning of Heb uncertain   *b* Ancient Heb
tradition: MT *I will change*

13 They sacrifice on the tops of the
    mountains,
     and make offerings upon the hills,
  under oak, poplar, and terebinth,
    because their shade is good.

    Therefore your daughters play
     the whore,
    and your daughters-in-law commit
    adultery.
14 I will not punish your daughters when
    they play the whore,
  nor your daughters-in-law when they
    commit adultery;
for the men themselves go aside with
    whores,
  and sacrifice with temple prostitutes;
thus a people without understanding
    comes to ruin.

15 Though you play the whore, O Israel,
    do not let Judah become guilty.
Do not enter into Gilgal,
    or go up to Beth-aven,
  and do not swear, "As the
    LORD lives."
16 Like a stubborn heifer,
    Israel is stubborn;
can the LORD now feed them
    like a lamb in a broad pasture?

17 Ephraim is joined to idols—
    let him alone.
18 When their drinking is ended, they
    indulge in sexual orgies;
  they love lewdness more than their
    glory.[a]
19 A wind has wrapped them[b] in its wings,
  and they shall be ashamed because of
    their altars.[c]

4.11–19: God prosecutes Israel for heretical worship, employing the image of prostitution introduced in chs. 1–3. **13:** Since mountains (Mt. Sinai and Mt. Zion*) and trees (Josh 24.26) are associated with authentic Israelite worship, Hosea appears to be criticizing the worship of other gods at these sites (as in Deut 12.2) rather than these natural features themselves. **14:** The term *temple prostitutes* translates the Hebrew word "qedeshot," literally "holy women." Partly because of the images of prostitution in the context, scholars have

suggested that these women may have been practicing ritual sex in sacred fertility rites. But the Hebrew term does not suggest this in itself, and there is very little concrete evidence of such practices in the biblical world. **15:** *Gilgal* likely refers to a religious sanctuary marking the site near Jericho where Israel entered Canaan (Josh 4.19–20). *Beth-aven,* literally "house of worthlessness," appears to be a scornful name for Bethel ("house of God"), one of the key northern religious shrines (1 Kings 12.26–30).

〰〰〰〰〰〰〰〰〰〰〰

5 Hear this, O priests!
   Give heed, O house of Israel!
Listen, O house of the king!
    For the judgment pertains to you;
for you have been a snare at Mizpah,
  and a net spread upon Tabor,
2 and a pit dug deep in Shittim;[d]
  but I will punish all of them.

3 I know Ephraim,
    and Israel is not hidden from me;
for now, O Ephraim, you have played
    the whore;
  Israel is defiled.
4 Their deeds do not permit them
    to return to their God.
For the spirit of whoredom is within
    them,
  and they do not know the LORD.

5 Israel's pride testifies against him;
    Ephraim[e] stumbles in his guilt;
  Judah also stumbles with them.
6 With their flocks and herds they shall
    go
    to seek the LORD,
but they will not find him;
  he has withdrawn from them.
7 They have dealt faithlessly with the
    LORD;
  for they have borne illegitimate
    children.
  Now the new moon shall devour them
    along with their fields.

5.1–6.3: **God sentences Israel.** An extended judgment speech describing God's punishment of Israel

a Cn Compare Gk: Meaning of Heb uncertain
b Heb *her*   *c* Gk Syr: Heb *sacrifices*   *d* Cn: Meaning of Heb uncertain
e Heb *Israel and Ephraim*

follows the indictment of ch. 4. **5.1–7: God reviews Israel's sins. 1:** Hosea does not explain the crimes of *Mizpah*, a town in southern Israel, or of *Tabor*, a mountain in the Jezreel Valley in northern Israel. **7:** The *new moon** marked the beginning of the month and of religious observances in Israel (Isa 1.13, Am 8.5).

8 Blow the horn in Gibeah,
   the trumpet in Ramah.
Sound the alarm at Beth-aven;
   look behind you, Benjamin!
9 Ephraim shall become a desolation
   in the day of punishment;
among the tribes of Israel
   I declare what is sure.
10 The princes of Judah have become
   like those who remove the landmark;
on them I will pour out
   my wrath like water.
11 Ephraim is oppressed, crushed in
      judgment,
   because he was determined to go
      after vanity.*ᵃ*
12 Therefore I am like maggots to
      Ephraim,
   and like rottenness to the house of
      Judah.
13 When Ephraim saw his sickness,
   and Judah his wound,
then Ephraim went to Assyria,
   and sent to the great king.*ᵇ*
But he is not able to cure you
   or heal your wound.
14 For I will be like a lion to Ephraim,
   and like a young lion to the house of
      Judah.
I myself will tear and go away;
   I will carry off, and no one shall rescue.
15 I will return again to my place
   until they acknowledge their guilt and
      seek my face.
   In their distress they will beg
      my favor:

6 "Come, let us return to the LORD;
   for it is he who has torn, and he will
      heal us;
   he has struck down, and he will bind
      us up.
2 After two days he will revive us;
   on the third day he will raise us up,
   that we may live before him.

3 Let us know, let us press on to know
      the LORD;
   his appearing is as sure as the dawn;
he will come to us like the showers,
   like the spring rains that water the
      earth."
4 What shall I do with you, O Ephraim?
   What shall I do with you, O Judah?
Your love is like a morning cloud,
   like the dew that goes away early.
5 Therefore I have hewn them by the
      prophets,
   I have killed them by the words of my
      mouth,
   and my*ᶜ* judgment goes forth as the
      light.
6 For I desire steadfast love and not
      sacrifice,
   the knowledge of God rather than
      burnt offerings.

5.8–6.3. 5.8–15: God summons the guilty to announce the sentence. **8:** Why Hosea sounds the alarm in *Gibeah, Ramah,* and *Beth-aven,* all cities in the southern part of Israel occupied by the tribe of *Benjamin,* is not entirely clear. **13:** Hosea criticizes Israel for trying to save itself by an alliance with *Assyria,* the imperial power threatening Israel in Hosea's time. Two of Israel's kings, Menahem (2 Kings 15.19–20) and Hoshea (2 Kings 17.3), paid tribute to Assyria to remain in power. **6.1–3:** Hosea anticipates Israel's response to judgment: Only after it is punished will it try to change its ways.

---

7 But at*ᵈ* Adam they transgressed the
      covenant;
   there they dealt faithlessly with me.
8 Gilead is a city of evildoers,
   tracked with blood.
9 As robbers lie in wait*ᵉ* for someone,
   so the priests are banded together;*ᶠ*
they murder on the road to Shechem,
   they commit a monstrous crime.
10 In the house of Israel I have seen a
      horrible thing;

a Gk: Meaning of Heb uncertain
b Cn: Heb *to a king who will contend*
c Gk Syr: Heb *your*   *d* Cn: Heb *like*
e Cn: Meaning of Heb uncertain
f Syr: Heb *are a company*

Ephraim's whoredom is there, Israel
    is defiled.

11 For you also, O Judah, a harvest
    is appointed.

6.4–11: Israel's disloyalty. God emphasizes Israel's lack of covenant* loyalty (v. 7), concluding with the image of prostitution (v. 10) that runs through the book. **6:** *Steadfast love* translates the Hebrew word "hesed," which describes loyalty to a relationship. Hosea's emphasis on right behavior rather than empty ritual is characteristic of prophetic thought (Am 5.21–24). **7–10:** The violent crime described here cannot be identified. *Adam* may refer to a city near the Jordan River (Josh 3.16). *Gilead*, located east of the Jordan, was the home of a band of men who assassinated Israel's king, Pekahiah (2 Kings 15.25). *Shechem*, Israel's first capital, was one of its most important cities.

When I would restore the fortunes of
    my people,
7 ¹when I would heal Israel,
    the corruption of Ephraim is revealed,
    and the wicked deeds of Samaria;
for they deal falsely,
    the thief breaks in,
    and the bandits raid outside.
2 But they do not consider
    that I remember all their wickedness.
Now their deeds surround them,
    they are before my face.
3 By their wickedness they make the king
    glad,
    and the officials by their treachery.
4 They are all adulterers;
    they are like a heated oven,
whose baker does not need to stir the
    fire,
    from the kneading of the dough until
    it is leavened.
5 On the day of our king the officials
    became sick with the heat of wine;
    he stretched out his hand with
    mockers.
6 For they are kindled*a* like an oven, their
    heart burns within them;
    all night their anger smolders;
    in the morning it blazes like a flaming
    fire.

7 All of them are hot as an oven,
    and they devour their rulers.
All their kings have fallen;
    none of them calls upon me.

7.1–16: Israel's political crimes. This speech focuses on the corruption of Israel's ruling elite by criticizing political intrigue at home (vv. 1–7) and alliances abroad (vv. 8–16). **1:** *Samaria* was Israel's capital through most of its history. **4–7:** Employing the image of a blazing oven, Hosea denounces the court officials responsible for numerous assassinations in Samaria. Four of the last six kings of Israel were killed in office.

8 Ephraim mixes himself with
    the peoples;
    Ephraim is a cake not turned.
9 Foreigners devour his strength,
    but he does not know it;
gray hairs are sprinkled upon him,
    but he does not know it.
10 Israel's pride testifies against*b* him;
    yet they do not return to the LORD
    their God,
    or seek him, for all this.

11 Ephraim has become like a dove,
    silly and without sense;
    they call upon Egypt, they go
    to Assyria.
12 As they go, I will cast my net over them;
    I will bring them down like birds of
    the air;
    I will discipline them according to the
    report made to their assembly.*c*
13 Woe to them, for they have strayed
    from me!
    Destruction to them, for they have
    rebelled against me!
I would redeem them,
    but they speak lies against me.

14 They do not cry to me from the heart,
    but they wail upon their beds;
they gash themselves for grain
    and wine;
    they rebel against me.

a Gk Syr: Heb *brought near*   *b* Or *humbles*
c Meaning of Heb uncertain

Chart The politics behind the prophet

King of Israel	Dates (BCE)	Path to Power	Historical Records
Jeroboam II	786–746	Son of Joash	2 Kings 14.23–29
Zechariah	746–745	Son of Jeroboam II	2 Kings 15.8–12
Shallum	745	Killed Zechariah	2 Kings 15.13–16
Menahem	745–738	Killed Shallum	2 Kings 15.17–22
Pekahiah	738–737	Son of Menahem	2 Kings 15.23–26
Pekah	737–732	Killed Pekahiah	2 Kings 15.25–27

15 It was I who trained and strengthened
  their arms,
  yet they plot evil against me.
16 They turn to that which does not profit;[a]
  they have become like a
    defective bow;
  their officials shall fall by the sword
  because of the rage of their tongue.
  So much for their babbling in the land
    of Egypt.

7.8–16. 11: Israel's foreign policy appears to have vacillated between alliances with *Egypt* and *Assyria*, the two great superpowers in whose sphere of influence Israel found itself. The history of Israel in 2 Kings mentions Israel's cooperation with Assyria (as explained in the comment on 5.13) and with Egypt (2 Kings 17.4) during Hosea's career. **14:** Gashing the body appears to be associated with earnest appeals to a deity, whether to Israel's God (Jer 41.5) or to Baal★ (1 Kings 18.28).

8 Set the trumpet to your lips!
  One like a vulture[b] is over the house
    of the LORD,
  because they have broken my covenant,
    and transgressed my law.
2 Israel cries to me,
  "My God, we—Israel—know you!"
3 Israel has spurned the good;
  the enemy shall pursue him.

4 They made kings, but not through me;
  they set up princes, but without my
    knowledge.

With their silver and gold they made
    idols
  for their own destruction.
5 Your calf is rejected, O Samaria.
  My anger burns against them.
  How long will they be incapable of
    innocence?
6   For it is from Israel,
  an artisan made it;
    it is not God.
  The calf of Samaria
  shall be broken to pieces.[c]

8.1–9.9: Israel's religious crimes. Hosea criticizes Israel's religious practices, blaming Israel for worshipping images (8.4–6), participating in empty rituals (8.13), following other gods (9.1), and persecuting the prophets★ (9.7–8). **8.4:** By accusing Israel of making kings without God's knowledge, Hosea may refer to the installation of kings through violent palace uprisings rather than through proper religious and prophetic legitimation (7.1–7). **5–6:** The calf was a prominent religious image in Israel from its beginnings when its first king, Jeroboam I, set up calves in the religious sanctuaries at Bethel and Dan (1 Kings 12.28–30). They may have been considered pedestals or throne images for God, as were the cherubim★ in the Jerusalem Temple★ (1 Kings 6.23–28, 8.10–11), rather than images of God or idols. But both Hosea and Israel's historian (1 Kings 12.28) regard these calves as idols.

a Cn: Meaning of Heb uncertain   *b* Meaning of Heb uncertain   *c* Or *shall go up in flames*

■▴▴■

The Canaanite God Baal

The god Baal,* whom Hosea sees as the main rival of Israel's God, was a prominent Canaanite deity. He is known not only from the Bible, where he is presented in a negative light, but also from ancient texts found at Ugarit, a Canaanite city north of Israel where Baal was worshipped. In these texts, Baal is pictured with many of the same attributes as Israel's God. Baal is associated with the storm and with its accompanying phenomena—thunder, lightning, and rain—and is considered the source of the land's fertility, just as Israel's God is (Hosea 2.8–9, 21–23). Baal is described as riding the clouds, just as Israel's God does (Ps 68.4; Deut 33.26). And both deities appear to be associated with calf iconography. Thus, it is not hard to understand why Baal would have had particular appeal to the people of Israel and why Hosea is so insistent that Israel not replace its allegiance to its own God with devotion to Baal.

■▴▴■

7 For they sow the wind,
   and they shall reap the whirlwind.
The standing grain has no heads,
   it shall yield no meal;
if it were to yield,
   foreigners would devour it.
8 Israel is swallowed up;
   now they are among the nations
   as a useless vessel.
9 For they have gone up to Assyria,
   a wild ass wandering alone;
   Ephraim has bargained for lovers.
10 Though they bargain with the
      nations,
   I will now gather them up.
They shall soon writhe
   under the burden of kings
   and princes.

11 When Ephraim multiplied altars to
      expiate sin,
   they became to him altars for
      sinning.
12 Though I write for him the multitude of
      my instructions,
   they are regarded as a strange thing.
13 Though they offer choice sacrifices,*a*
   though they eat flesh,
   the LORD does not accept them.
Now he will remember their iniquity,
   and punish their sins;
   they shall return to Egypt.

14 Israel has forgotten his Maker,
   and built palaces;
and Judah has multiplied fortified
      cities;
   but I will send a fire upon his cities,
   and it shall devour his strongholds.

9 Do not rejoice, O Israel!
   Do not exult*b* as other nations do;
for you have played the whore,
      departing from your God.
   You have loved a prostitute's pay
   on all threshing floors.
2 Threshing floor and wine vat shall not
      feed them,
   and the new wine shall fail them.
3 They shall not remain in the land of the
      LORD;
   but Ephraim shall return to Egypt,
   and in Assyria they shall eat unclean
      food.

4 They shall not pour drink offerings of
      wine to the LORD,
   and their sacrifices shall not please
      him.
Such sacrifices shall be like mourners'
      bread;
   all who eat of it shall be defiled;

a Cn: Meaning of Heb uncertain   *b* Gk: Heb To exultation

for their bread shall be for their hunger
 only;
  it shall not come to the house of the
   LORD.

8.7–9.4. 8.13: When Hosea describes Israel's punishment as a *return to Egypt*, he reverses the Exodus
(2.15; 9.3; Ex 1–15), in which God delivered Israel
from slavery. **9.1:** Since *threshing★ floors* are sites for
worship (2 Sam 24.24–25), Hosea denounces Israel's
worship of Baal★ there. The *prostitute's pay* to which
he refers is likely the grain harvest Israel attributed to
Baal rather than to God (2.8). **4:** *Mourners' bread* may
be translated literally in two ways: either "bread of sorrow," referring to bread eaten in exile (9.3), or "bread
of idolatry,★" referring to Israel's sacrifices that God
has rejected.

~~~~~~~~~~~~~~~~~~~~~~~~~~~~~~~~~

5   What will you do on the day of
   appointed festival,
  and on the day of the festival of the
   LORD?
6   For even if they escape destruction,
  Egypt shall gather them,
  Memphis shall bury them.
 Nettles shall possess their precious
   things of silver;*a*
 thorns shall be in their tents.

7   The days of punishment have come,
  the days of recompense have come;
  Israel cries,*b*
 "The prophet is a fool,
  the man of the spirit is mad!"
 Because of your great iniquity,
  your hostility is great.
8   The prophet is a sentinel for my God
   over Ephraim,
 yet a fowler's snare is on all his ways,
  and hostility in the house of his God.
9   They have deeply corrupted themselves
  as in the days of Gibeah;
 he will remember their iniquity,
  he will punish their sins.

9.5–9. 6: *Memphis* is a prominent Egyptian city
known for its pyramids, tombs, and burial grounds. **9:**
Hosea's reference here and in 10.9 to the corruption
in *Gibeah* may refer to the intertribal conflict and the
crimes that led to it (Judg 19–21).

~~~~~~~~~~~~~~~~~~~~~~~~~~~~~~~~~

10   Like grapes in the wilderness,
  I found Israel.
 Like the first fruit on the fig tree,
  in its first season,
  I saw your ancestors.
 But they came to Baal-peor,
  and consecrated themselves to a thing
   of shame,
  and became detestable like the thing
   they loved.
11   Ephraim's glory shall fly away like a
  bird—
  no birth, no pregnancy, no
   conception!
12   Even if they bring up children,
  I will bereave them until no one is
   left.
 Woe to them indeed
  when I depart from them!
13   Once I saw Ephraim as a young palm
  planted in a lovely meadow,*a*
 but now Ephraim must lead out his
  children for slaughter.
14   Give them, O LORD—
  what will you give?
 Give them a miscarrying womb
  and dry breasts.

15   Every evil of theirs began at Gilgal;
  there I came to hate them.
 Because of the wickedness of
   their deeds
 I will drive them out of my house.
 I will love them no more;
  all their officials are rebels.

16   Ephraim is stricken,
  their root is dried up,
  they shall bear no fruit.
 Even though they give birth,
  I will kill the cherished offspring of
   their womb.
17   Because they have not listened to him,
  my God will reject them;
 they shall become wanderers among
  the nations.

9.10–11.7: Images of a rebellious people. With a series of images taken from Israel's agricultural and fam-

a Meaning of Heb uncertain   *b* Cn Compare Gk: Heb
shall know

ily context—grapes and figs, a young palm tree, a vine, a female calf, a son—Hosea highlights Israel's past potential and present waywardness. **9.10–12:** The comparison of Israel to *grapes* and *figs* begins with images of fertility and a new harvest and concludes with images of infertility and barrenness. **10:** *Baal-peor* is a site east of the Jordan where the Israelites once worshipped Baal (Num 25.1–5). **13–17:** Israel is compared to a *young palm* with great potential (v. 13) whose roots dry up and whose fruit fails (v. 16). **15:** *Gilgal*, the site where Israel entered Canaan (Josh 4.19–20), is criticized by Hosea for its false worship (4.15). **17:** Hosea refers here and elsewhere (5.13–14; 10.14) to Israelites deported by conquering countries, a practice of the Assyrians described also by Israel's historian (2 Kings 15.29; 17.6).

10 Israel is a luxuriant vine
   that yields its fruit.
The more his fruit increased
   the more altars he built;
as his country improved,
   he improved his pillars.
2 Their heart is false;
   now they must bear their guilt.
The LORD [a] will break down
      their altars,
   and destroy their pillars.

3 For now they will say:
   "We have no king,
for we do not fear the LORD,
   and a king—what could he do for us?"
4 They utter mere words;
   with empty oaths they make
      covenants;
so litigation springs up like poisonous
      weeds
   in the furrows of the field.
5 The inhabitants of Samaria tremble
   for the calf [b] of Beth-aven.
Its people shall mourn for it,
   and its idolatrous priests shall wail [c]
      over it,
   over its glory that has departed from it.
6 The thing itself shall be carried to
      Assyria
   as tribute to the great king. [d]
Ephraim shall be put to shame,
   and Israel shall be ashamed of his
      idol. [e]

7 Samaria's king shall perish
   like a chip on the face of the waters.
8 The high places of Aven, the sin
      of Israel,
   shall be destroyed.
Thorn and thistle shall grow up
   on their altars.
They shall say to the mountains, Cover
      us,
   and to the hills, Fall on us.

10.1–8: The comparison of Israel to a vine begins with images of bountiful fruit (v. 1) and concludes with images of thorns and thistles (v. 8). **1–2:** *Pillars* were common installations in Israelite sanctuaries (Gen 28.18–22). **3:** The people's words, *"We have no king,"* could anticipate the end of Israel and its kingship; or they could mean that Israel has rejected the rule of God, its divine king (1 Sam 8.4–8), as the following line seems to indicate. **5:** For Hosea's view of Israel's calves, compare 13.2 and 8.5–6 (see comment at 8.5–6). **8:** *The high places* of Aven* (literally, "worthlessness") are the sites of Israel's false worship (4.13).

9 Since the days of Gibeah you have
      sinned, O Israel;
   there they have continued.
   Shall not war overtake them in
      Gibeah?
10 I will come [f] against the wayward
      people to punish them;
   and nations shall be gathered against
      them
   when they are punished [g] for their
      double iniquity.

11 Ephraim was a trained heifer
   that loved to thresh,
   and I spared her fair neck;
but I will make Ephraim break the
      ground;
   Judah must plow;
   Jacob must harrow for himself.
12 Sow for yourselves righteousness;
   reap steadfast love;
   break up your fallow ground;

a Heb *he*   *b* Gk Syr: Heb *calves*   *c* Cn: Heb *exult*
d Cn: Heb *to a king who will contend*   *e* Cn: Heb
counsel   *f* Cn Compare Gk: Heb *In my desire*
g Gk: Heb *bound*

for it is time to seek the LORD,
  that he may come and rain
    righteousness upon you.

13 You have plowed wickedness,
  you have reaped injustice,
    you have eaten the fruit of lies.
  Because you have trusted in
      your power
    and in the multitude of your
      warriors,
14 therefore the tumult of war shall rise
    against your people,
  and all your fortresses shall
      be destroyed,
  as Shalman destroyed Beth-arbel on the
      day of battle
    when mothers were dashed in pieces
      with their children.
15 Thus it shall be done to you, O Bethel,
    because of your great wickedness.
  At dawn the king of Israel
    shall be utterly cut off.

11 When Israel was a child, I loved him,
    and out of Egypt I called my son.
2 The more I[a] called them,
    the more they went from me;[b]
  they kept sacrificing to the Baals,
    and offering incense to idols.

3 Yet it was I who taught Ephraim to
      walk,
    I took them up in my[c] arms;
  but they did not know that I healed
      them.
4 I led them with cords of human
      kindness,
    with bands of love.
  I was to them like those
    who lift infants to their cheeks.[d]
  I bent down to them and fed them.

5 They shall return to the land of Egypt,
    and Assyria shall be their king,
  because they have refused to return
      to me.
6 The sword rages in their cities,
    it consumes their oracle-priests,
  and devours because of their
      schemes.

7 My people are bent on turning away
    from me.
  To the Most High they call,
    but he does not raise them up at all.[e]

10.9–11.7. 10.9–15: Israel is compared to a female calf (v. 11), once obedient but now plowing wickedness. **9:** For Hosea's criticism of *Gibeah,* see 9.9. **14:** Neither *Shalman* nor *Beth-arbel* can be positively identified, though some have suggested that *Shalman* is a shortened form of Shalmaneser V, who imprisoned Israel's last king, Hoshea, and laid siege to Samaria (2 Kings 17.3–5). **15:** *Bethel* was one of Israel's major religious sanctuaries. **11.1–7:** Israel is compared to a son who, though loved and raised with kindness, is stubborn and rebellious.

---

8 How can I give you up, Ephraim?
    How can I hand you over, O Israel?
  How can I make you like Admah?
    How can I treat you like Zeboiim?
  My heart recoils within me;
    my compassion grows warm
      and tender.
9 I will not execute my fierce anger;
    I will not again destroy Ephraim;
  for I am God and no mortal,
    the Holy One in your midst,
    and I will not come in wrath.[e]

10 They shall go after the LORD,
    who roars like a lion;
  when he roars,
    his children shall come trembling
      from the west.
11 They shall come trembling like birds
      from Egypt,
    and like doves from the land of
      Assyria;
  and I will return them to their homes,
    says the LORD.

11.8–11: A promise of restoration. The tone shifts from judgment to salvation: God shows compassion for Israel and promises to return its people to their homes. **8:** *Admah* and *Zeboiim* are cities which, like Sodom and Gomorrah, symbolize wickedness (Deut

---

a Gk: Heb *they*   b Gk: Heb *them*   c Gk Syr Vg: Heb *his*   d Or *who ease the yoke on their jaws*
e Meaning of Heb uncertain

29.23). **10:** This image of Israel returning *trembling from the west* assumes an exilic context and suggests that vv. 10–11 may have been added by a later Judean editor.

~~~~~~~~~~~~~~~~~~~~

12 [a] Ephraim has surrounded me with lies,
and the house of Israel with deceit;
but Judah still walks[b] with God,
and is faithful to the Holy One.

12 Ephraim herds the wind,
and pursues the east wind all day
long;
they multiply falsehood and violence;
they make a treaty with Assyria,
and oil is carried to Egypt.

2 The LORD has an indictment against
Judah,
and will punish Jacob according to his
ways,
and repay him according to his deeds.
3 In the womb he tried to supplant his
brother,
and in his manhood he strove with
God.
4 He strove with the angel and prevailed,
he wept and sought his favor;
he met him at Bethel,
and there he spoke with him.[c]
5 The LORD the God of hosts,
the LORD is his name!
6 But as for you, return to your God,
hold fast to love and justice,
and wait continually for your God.

7 A trader, in whose hands are false
balances,
he loves to oppress.
8 Ephraim has said, "Ah, I am rich,
I have gained wealth for myself;
in all of my gain
no offense has been found in me
that would be sin."[d]
9 I am the LORD your God
from the land of Egypt;
I will make you live in tents again,
as in the days of the appointed
festival.

_____

11.12–13.16: The history of a rebellious people. Hosea recalls major events in Israel's past to illustrate

God's acts of salvation and Israel's acts of rebellion. **12.3a:** Hosea describes the birth of Israel's ancestor Jacob (later renamed Israel) who struggled with *his brother* Esau in their mother's womb (Gen 25.21–26). **3b–4a:** Israel's ancestor Jacob *strove with God* at the Jabbok River when he returned home to meet Esau (Gen 32.22–32). **4b:** God appeared to Israel's ancestor Jacob at *Bethel* in a dream (Gen 28.10–22). **9:** Hosea recalls Israel's deliverance from slavery in *Egypt* and its journey through the wilderness.

~~~~~~~~~~~~~~~~~~~~

10 I spoke to the prophets;
it was I who multiplied visions,
and through the prophets I will bring
destruction.
11 In Gilead[e] there is iniquity,
they shall surely come to nothing.
In Gilgal they sacrifice bulls,
so their altars shall be like
stone heaps
on the furrows of the field.
12 Jacob fled to the land of Aram,
there Israel served for a wife,
and for a wife he guarded sheep.[f]
13 By a prophet the LORD brought Israel
up from Egypt,
and by a prophet he was guarded.
14 Ephraim has given bitter offense,
so his Lord will bring his crimes down
on him
and pay him back for his insults.

13 When Ephraim spoke, there was
trembling;
he was exalted in Israel;
but he incurred guilt through Baal
and died.
2 And now they keep on sinning
and make a cast image for
themselves,
idols of silver made according to their
understanding,
all of them the work of artisans.
"Sacrifice to these," they say.[g]
People are kissing calves!
3 Therefore they shall be like the morning
mist
or like the dew that goes away early,

_____

a Ch 12.1 in Heb   *b* Heb *roams* or *rules*   *c* Gk Syr: Heb *us*   *d* Meaning of Heb uncertain   *e* Compare Syr: Heb *Gilead*   *f* Heb lacks *sheep*   *g* Cn Compare Gk: Heb *To these they say sacrifices of people*

like chaff that swirls from the threshing
 floor
 or like smoke from a window.

4 Yet I have been the LORD your God
 ever since the land of Egypt;
you know no God but me,
 and besides me there is no savior.
5 It was I who fed[a] you in the
  wilderness,
 in the land of drought.
6 When I fed[b] them, they were satisfied;
 they were satisfied, and their heart
  was proud;
 therefore they forgot me.
7 So I will become like a lion to them,
 like a leopard I will lurk beside the
  way.
8 I will fall upon them like a bear robbed
  of her cubs,
 and will tear open the covering
  of their heart;
there I will devour them like a lion,
 as a wild animal would mangle them.

9 I will destroy you, O Israel;
 who can help you?[c]
10 Where now is[d] your king, that he may
  save you?
 Where in all your cities are your rulers,
of whom you said,
 "Give me a king and rulers"?
11 I gave you a king in my anger,
 and I took him away in my wrath.

12 Ephraim's iniquity is bound up;
 his sin is kept in store.
13 The pangs of childbirth come for him,
 but he is an unwise son;
for at the proper time he does not
  present himself
 at the mouth of the womb.

14 Shall I ransom them from the power of
  Sheol?
 Shall I redeem them from Death?
O Death, where are[e] your plagues?
 O Sheol, where is[e] your destruction?
 Compassion is hidden from my eyes.

15 Although he may flourish among
  rushes,[f]
 the east wind shall come, a blast from
  the LORD,
 rising from the wilderness;
and his fountain shall dry up,
 his spring shall be parched.
It shall strip his treasury
 of every precious thing.
16[g] Samaria shall bear her guilt,
 because she has rebelled against her
  God;
 they shall fall by the sword,
  their little ones shall be dashed in
   pieces,
 and their pregnant women
  ripped open.

12.10–13.16. 12.11: For Hosea's view of *Gilead* and *Gilgal*, compare 4.15, 6.8. **12:** *The land of Aram* was the territory to which Israel's ancestor Jacob fled from his brother Esau's anger (Gen 27.41–45; 29.1–30). **13:** The prophet to whom Hosea refers is Moses, who led Israel out of Egypt (Deut 34.10–12). **13.4:** Hosea's idea that Israel learned to know its God in Egypt appears to be based on the tradition that the name of God was revealed to Israel there (Ex 3.13–15). **5–6:** After delivering Israel from Egypt, God fed them manna in the wilderness (Num 11.7–9). **11:** Hosea may share the viewpoint of the author of 1 Sam 8.6–8, who saw Israel's request for a king as a rejection of God's rule. **14:** *Sheol** was a shadowy realm inhabited by the dead (Ps 6.5). **16:** Hosea anticipates Israel's end with a vivid image of the fall of its capital, *Samaria*.

---

14 Return, O Israel, to the LORD your
  God,
 for you have stumbled because of
  your iniquity.
2 Take words with you
 and return to the LORD;
say to him,
 "Take away all guilt;
accept that which is good,
 and we will offer
 the fruit[h] of our lips.

a Gk Syr: Heb *knew* b Cn: Heb *according to their pasture* c Gk Syr: Heb *for in me is your help* d Gk Syr Vg: Heb *I will be* e Gk Syr: Heb *I will be* f Or *among brothers* g Ch 14.1 in Heb h Gk Syr: Heb *bulls*

3 Assyria shall not save us;
  we will not ride upon horses;
  we will say no more, 'Our God,'
    to the work of our hands.
  In you the orphan finds mercy."

14.1–3: A call for repentance. Hosea urges Israel to turn from reliance on other nations to reliance on its God. **3:** To *ride upon horses* is to trust military strength more than God's protection.

4 I will heal their disloyalty;
  I will love them freely,
    for my anger has turned from them.
5 I will be like the dew to Israel;
  he shall blossom like the lily,
  he shall strike root like the forests of
    Lebanon.*a*
6 His shoots shall spread out;
  his beauty shall be like the olive tree,
  and his fragrance like that of
    Lebanon.
7 They shall again live beneath
    my*b* shadow,
  they shall flourish as a garden;*c*
  they shall blossom like the vine,

their fragrance shall be like the wine
  of Lebanon.

8 O Ephraim, what have I*d* to do with
    idols?
  It is I who answer and look after you.*e*
I am like an evergreen cypress;
  your faithfulness*f* comes from me.
9 Those who are wise understand these
    things;
  those who are discerning know them.
For the ways of the LORD are right,
  and the upright walk in them,
  but transgressors stumble in them.

14.4–9: A second promise of restoration. In the spirit of 11.8–11, God promises to restore Israel to faithfulness and well-being. **5:** The *forests of Lebanon* were legendary* for their magnificence (Ps 104.16). **9:** The concluding verse in Hosea shares the vocabulary and perspective of the book of Proverbs (10.29) and is likely a conclusion added by Israel's sages.

a Cn: Heb *like Lebanon*   *b* Heb *his*   *c* Cn: Heb *they shall grow grain*   *d* Or *What more has Ephraim*   *e* Heb *him*   *f* Heb *your fruit*

JOEL

Introduction

Joel is unique among the prophets* in his focus on a natural catastrophe, a widespread and destructive locust plague. Interpreting the plague as divine judgment on Jerusalem, the prophet calls on the people to mourn their predicament (1.5–20) and tells the priests to declare a solemn assembly to repent and ask for God's forgiveness (2.1–17). Then he predicts that God will restore the land to its former prosperity (2.18–27). Two concluding sections that do not mention the locusts, a prediction of the outpouring of God's spirit (2.28–32) and of the political renewal of Jerusalem (3.1–21), are either Joel's visions of the future set in motion by the plague or additions to Joel by a later editor.

No clear historical references in chs. 1–2 connect this plague to a precise period in Jerusalem's history. Such plagues were not uncommon (Am 7.1–3), and understanding the seriousness of these ancient plagues is more important for reading Joel than knowing the exact date of this particular plague. Because the vision of Jerusalem's political renewal in ch. 3 was composed after Jerusalem was destroyed and its citizens exiled, many believe all of Joel was written at this time, perhaps as late as the fourth or fifth centuries BCE. Editors placed Joel between Hosea and Amos, two eighth-century prophets, either because a tradition held that the plague happened in this period or because parts of Joel are so much like Amos (see Joel 3.16a; Amos 1.2a).

READING GUIDE

To appreciate the danger of the crisis Joel faced, the modern reader must recover a sense of the terrible destructiveness of a locust infestation for a pre-industrial agricultural society that lives year to year by its harvests. The key issue for reading the book as a whole is deciding whether the locust plague in 1.1–2.27 is the prelude to the religious and political renewal predicted in 2.28–3.21 or whether these two parts of Joel arise from different experiences in Jerusalem's history.

1 The word of the LORD that came to Joel son of Pethuel:

2 Hear this, O elders,
    give ear, all inhabitants of the land!
Has such a thing happened in
        your days,
    or in the days of your ancestors?
3 Tell your children of it,
    and let your children tell their
        children,
    and their children another generation.

4 What the cutting locust left,
    the swarming locust has eaten.

What the swarming locust left,
    the hopping locust has eaten,
and what the hopping locust left,
    the destroying locust has eaten.

1.1–4: The locust plague. Joel introduces the locust plague as one unparalleled in the living memory of his people (compare 2.2). **4:** The four terms for locust here and in 2.25 may refer to stages in the growth of the locust. The meanings of the Hebrew terms are unclear, and the translations, *cutting locust,* etc., are only suggestions.

---

5 Wake up, you drunkards, and weep;
    and wail, all you wine-drinkers,

The Desert Locust

The desert locust, known to scientists as "Schistocerca americana, subspecies gregaria," is a distant cousin of the American grasshopper. It lives and breeds in the great desert stretching from the Sahara in Africa to the Arabian Peninsula, including the Sinai and Judean deserts. In the right conditions, it multiplies rapidly, crowds into dense swarms, and sweeps into neighboring fertile areas, where it eats its own weight in green food each day. A swarm of desert locusts in Somaliland in 1957 was estimated to include 16 billion locusts and to weigh 50,000 tons. The desert locust's threat to Middle Eastern societies is recorded in the earliest human records and continues into the present, where it is monitored and combated by the United Nations Food and Agriculture Organization's Emergency Center for Locust Operations.

over the sweet wine,
    for it is cut off from your mouth.
6 For a nation has invaded my land,
    powerful and innumerable;
its teeth are lions' teeth,
    and it has the fangs of a lioness.

7 It has laid waste my vines,
    and splintered my fig trees;
it has stripped off their bark and thrown
      it down;
    their branches have turned white.

8 Lament like a virgin dressed in
      sackcloth
    for the husband of her youth.
9 The grain offering and the drink
      offering are cut off
    from the house of the LORD.
The priests mourn,
    the ministers of the LORD.
10 The fields are devastated,
    the ground mourns;
for the grain is destroyed,
    the wine dries up,
    the oil fails.

11 Be dismayed, you farmers,
    wail, you vinedressers,
over the wheat and the barley;
    for the crops of the field are ruined.
12 The vine withers,
    the fig tree droops.
Pomegranate, palm, and apple—
    all the trees of the field are dried up;

surely, joy withers away
    among the people.

13 Put on sackcloth and lament,
    you priests;
    wail, you ministers of the altar.
Come, pass the night in sackcloth,
    you ministers of my God!
Grain offering and drink offering
    are withheld from the house of
      your God.

14 Sanctify a fast,
    call a solemn assembly.
Gather the elders
    and all the inhabitants of the land
to the house of the LORD your God,
    and cry out to the LORD.

15 Alas for the day!
For the day of the LORD is near,
    and as destruction from the Almighty[a]
      it comes.
16 Is not the food cut off
    before our eyes,
joy and gladness
    from the house of our God?

17 The seed shrivels under the clods,[b]
    the storehouses are desolate;

a Traditional rendering of Heb *Shaddai*   b Meaning of Heb uncertain

the granaries are ruined
    because the grain has failed.
18 How the animals groan!
    The herds of cattle wander about
because there is no pasture for them;
    even the flocks of sheep are
        dazed.*a*

19 To you, O LORD, I cry.
    For fire has devoured
        the pastures of the wilderness,
    and flames have burned
        all the trees of the field.
20 Even the wild animals cry to you
    because the watercourses are
        dried up,
    and fire has devoured
        the pastures of the wilderness.

1.5–20: The call to mourning. Joel summons three groups into mourning: consumers of wine (vv. 5–10), farmers (vv. 11–12), and priests (vv. 13–18). Then he cries out to God himself (vv. 19–20). **6:** *A nation has invaded my land* begins an extended metaphor,* by which Joel compares the incoming locust swarms to an invading army (compare 2.2, 4–11, 25). **7:** *Their branches have turned white:* In this and other vivid details of decimated vegetation, Joel's description matches that of eyewitnesses of Jerusalem's last great locust plague in 1915. **15:** *The day of the LORD* is a prophetic theme that reappears throughout Joel (2.1, 11, 31; 3.14). **19:** Joel uses the metaphor of *fire* together with the metaphor of an army for the devouring locust (compare 2.3).

2 Blow the trumpet in Zion;
    sound the alarm on my holy
        mountain!
Let all the inhabitants of the land
    tremble,
    for the day of the LORD is coming,
        it is near—
2 a day of darkness and gloom,
    a day of clouds and thick
        darkness!
Like blackness spread upon the
    mountains
    a great and powerful army comes;
their like has never been from of old,
    nor will be again after them
        in ages to come.

3 Fire devours in front of them,
    and behind them a flame burns.
Before them the land is like the garden
        of Eden,
    but after them a desolate wilderness,
    and nothing escapes them.

4 They have the appearance of horses,
    and like war-horses they charge.
5 As with the rumbling of chariots,
    they leap on the tops of the
        mountains,
like the crackling of a flame of fire
    devouring the stubble,
like a powerful army
    drawn up for battle.

6 Before them peoples are in anguish,
    all faces grow pale.*b*
7 Like warriors they charge,
    like soldiers they scale the wall.
Each keeps to its own course,
    they do not swerve from*c* their paths.
8 They do not jostle one another,
    each keeps to its own track;
they burst through the weapons
    and are not halted.
9 They leap upon the city,
    they run upon the walls;
they climb up into the houses,
    they enter through the windows like
        a thief.

10 The earth quakes before them,
    the heavens tremble.
The sun and the moon are darkened,
    and the stars withdraw their shining.
11 The LORD utters his voice
    at the head of his army;
how vast is his host!
    Numberless are those who obey his
        command.
Truly the day of the LORD is great;
    terrible indeed—who can endure it?

12 Yet even now, says the LORD,
    return to me with all your heart,

---

a Compare Gk Syr Vg: Meaning of Heb uncertain
b Meaning of Heb uncertain   *c* Gk Syr Vg: Heb *they do not take a pledge along*

with fasting, with weeping, and with
    mourning;
13   rend your hearts and not
    your clothing.
Return to the LORD, your God,
    for he is gracious and merciful,
slow to anger, and abounding in
    steadfast love,
    and relents from punishing.
14 Who knows whether he will not turn
    and relent,
    and leave a blessing behind him,
a grain offering and a drink offering
    for the LORD, your God?

15 Blow the trumpet in Zion;
    sanctify a fast;
call a solemn assembly;
16   gather the people.
Sanctify the congregation;
    assemble the aged;
gather the children,
    even infants at the breast.
Let the bridegroom leave his room,
    and the bride her canopy.

17 Between the vestibule and the altar
    let the priests, the ministers of the
      LORD, weep.
Let them say, "Spare your people,
    O LORD,
    and do not make your heritage a
      mockery,
    a byword among the nations.
Why should it be said among the
    peoples,
    'Where is their God?' "

2.1–17: The call to repentance. 1–3: Turning again
to the priests whom he had just addressed (1.13–18),
Joel directs them to *blow the trumpet in Zion** (a synonym for Jerusalem), assembling all the people to ask
for God's forgiveness (vv. 15–17). 2: *Darkness* and
clouds are traditional images associated with the day
of the LORD, but they may also refer here to the dense
swarms of locusts that can obscure the sun. 4–11: Joel
develops in detail his comparison of the locust swarms
with an invading army. 13: *Rend your hearts and not
your clothing:* While not abandoning ritual—he directs the priests to lead the people in a liturgy* of repentance—Joel sees genuine religion as a matter of

inner renewal, as is common among the prophets. Like
other prophets, Joel regards disasters like this as acts
of divine judgment that require repentance, but unlike
them, he does not describe the particular sins that he
believes have brought on this punishment. *Gracious
and merciful . . . :* This is an adaptation of a traditional
description of God (Ex 34.6–7; Jon 4.2).

18 Then the LORD became jealous for his
    land,
    and had pity on his people.
19 In response to his people the LORD said:
I am sending you
    grain, wine, and oil,
    and you will be satisfied;
and I will no more make you
    a mockery among the nations.

20 I will remove the northern army far
    from you,
    and drive it into a parched and
      desolate land,
its front into the eastern sea,
    and its rear into the western sea;
its stench and foul smell will rise up.
    Surely he has done great things!

21 Do not fear, O soil;
    be glad and rejoice,
    for the LORD has done great things!
22 Do not fear, you animals of the field,
    for the pastures of the wilderness are
      green;
the tree bears its fruit,
    the fig tree and vine give their full
      yield.

23 O children of Zion, be glad
    and rejoice in the LORD your God;
for he has given the early rain*a* for your
    vindication,
    he has poured down for you abundant
      rain,
    the early and the later rain, as before.
24 The threshing floors shall be full
    of grain,
    the vats shall overflow with wine
      and oil.

a Meaning of Heb uncertain

The Day of the LORD

Appearing five times in Joel (1.15; 2.1, 11, 31; 3.14), this expression is used in the Bible for a decisive divine act in human affairs. In its earliest occurrence, Amos uses it to describe an act of God's judgment on Israel (5.18–20). But since Amos implies that his audience believed this expression referred to an act of God's salvation, scholars think *the day of the* LORD originally had a positive meaning, describing God's victory on Israel's behalf. In some cases, in fact, this phrase is used for God's judgment on the nations and restoration of Judah (Ob 15–21; Zech 14.1–9). Scholars disagree whether *the day of the* LORD is used both ways in Joel—for judgment in 1.15; 2.1, 11 and for salvation in 2.31; 3.14—or whether all uses point toward the final salvation described in ch. 3.

25 I will repay you for the years
    that the swarming locust has eaten,
the hopper, the destroyer, and the
    cutter,
    my great army, which I sent against
    you.

26 You shall eat in plenty and be
    satisfied,
    and praise the name of the LORD
    your God,
who has dealt wondrously with you.
And my people shall never again be put
    to shame.
27 You shall know that I am in the midst
    of Israel,
    and that I, the LORD, am your God
    and there is no other.
And my people shall never again be put
    to shame.

2.18–27: God's renewal of the land. Joel anticipates new harvests to replace those the locusts have destroyed. Each crop ruined in 1.1–2.17 is to be restored. **20:** *The northern army* in Hebrew is simply "the northerner," used for the locust here because it is a traditional designation of the enemy, since enemies invaded from the north, or because the locusts themselves came in from the north, as did the first swarms in the 1915 plague in Jerusalem. The *eastern sea* is the Dead Sea and the *western sea* is the Mediterranean Sea.

28*a*Then afterward
    I will pour out my spirit on all flesh;

your sons and your daughters shall
    prophesy,
your old men shall dream dreams,
and your young men shall see visions.
29 Even on the male and female slaves,
    in those days, I will pour out
    my spirit.

30 I will show portents in the heavens and on the earth, blood and fire and columns of smoke. 31The sun shall be turned to darkness, and the moon to blood, before the great and terrible day of the LORD comes. 32Then everyone who calls on the name of the LORD shall be saved; for in Mount Zion and in Jerusalem there shall be those who escape, as the LORD has said, and among the survivors shall be those whom the LORD calls.

2.28–32: The outpouring of God's spirit. In the Hebrew Bible, these verses constitute a new chapter: 3.1–5. **28–29:** In the future, the prophetic gift will be spread among all people. **30–32:** *The day of the* LORD is pictured with traditional images of darkness as a day of judgment on Jerusalem, which only a few will survive. Whether these few are those who survived the locusts (which are not mentioned here) or the survivors of the destruction of Jerusalem in 586 BCE is not stated.

3*b*For then, in those days and at that time, when I restore the fortunes of Judah and Jerusalem, 2I will gather all the nations and

a Ch 3.1 in Heb   *b* Ch 4.1 in Heb

bring them down to the valley of Jehosha-phat, and I will enter into judgment with them there, on account of my people and my heritage Israel, because they have scattered them among the nations. They have divided my land, ³and cast lots for my people, and traded boys for prostitutes, and sold girls for wine, and drunk it down.

4 What are you to me, O Tyre and Sidon, and all the regions of Philistia? Are you paying me back for something? If you are paying me back, I will turn your deeds back upon your own heads swiftly and speedily. ⁵For you have taken my silver and my gold, and have carried my rich treasures into your temples.*a* ⁶You have sold the people of Judah and Jerusalem to the Greeks, removing them far from their own border. ⁷But now I will rouse them to leave the places to which you have sold them, and I will turn your deeds back upon your own heads. ⁸I will sell your sons and your daughters into the hand of the people of Judah, and they will sell them to the Sabeans, to a nation far away; for the LORD has spoken.

9 Proclaim this among the nations:
    Prepare war,*b*
        stir up the warriors.
    Let all the soldiers draw near,
        let them come up.
10 Beat your plowshares into swords,
        and your pruning hooks into spears;
        let the weakling say, "I am a warrior."

11 Come quickly,*c*
        all you nations all around,
        gather yourselves there.
    Bring down your warriors, O LORD.
12 Let the nations rouse themselves,
        and come up to the valley of
            Jehoshaphat;
    for there I will sit to judge
        all the neighboring nations.

13 Put in the sickle,
        for the harvest is ripe.
    Go in, tread,
        for the wine press is full.
    The vats overflow,
        for their wickedness is great.

14 Multitudes, multitudes,
        in the valley of decision!
    For the day of the LORD is near
        in the valley of decision.
15 The sun and the moon are darkened,
        and the stars withdraw their shining.

16 The LORD roars from Zion,
        and utters his voice from Jerusalem,
        and the heavens and the earth shake.
    But the LORD is a refuge for his
            people,
        a stronghold for the people of Israel.

17 So you shall know that I, the LORD
            your God,
        dwell in Zion, my holy mountain.
    And Jerusalem shall be holy,
        and strangers shall never again pass
            through it.

18 In that day
    the mountains shall drip sweet wine,
        the hills shall flow with milk,
    and all the stream beds of Judah
        shall flow with water;
    a fountain shall come forth from the
            house of the LORD
        and water the Wadi Shittim.

19 Egypt shall become a desolation
        and Edom a desolate wilderness,
    because of the violence done to the
            people of Judah,
        in whose land they have shed
            innocent blood.
20 But Judah shall be inhabited forever,
        and Jerusalem to all generations.
21 I will avenge their blood, and I will not
            clear the guilty,*d*
        for the LORD dwells in Zion.

3.1–21: Judgment on the nations and the restoration of Jerusalem. In the Hebrew Bible, these verses are 4.1–21. This poem does not mention the locusts, but takes as its backdrop the fall of Jerusalem in 586 BCE and the exile of its people (vv. 2, 5). It follows the

---

a Or palaces   *b* Heb *sanctify war*   *c* Meaning of Heb uncertain   *d* Gk Syr: Heb *I will hold innocent their blood that I have not held innocent*

traditional structure of hymns, such as Ex 15.1–18 and Zech 14.1–21, which celebrate the victory of God the warrior over Israel's enemies. The threat to divine rule (vv. 1–8) brings God into a battle (vv. 9–14) that shakes the cosmos (vv. 15–16). Victorious, God is enthroned on his holy mountain (v. 17), making the world fertile (v. 18) and saving his people (vv. 19–21). **2:** *Jehoshaphat* is a symbolic—rather than an actual, geographical—place, meaning "the LORD has judged." **4:** *Tyre* and *Sidon,* cities on the Mediterra-nean coast north of Judah, and *Philistia* to the south are accused of participating in Judah's destruction and deporting its people. **8:** The *Sabeans* may be inhabitants of southern Arabia. **10:** This verse reverses the image of peace in Isa 2.4 and Mic 4.3. **19:** *Egypt,* sometimes ally and sometimes enemy, and *Edom,* elsewhere accused of participating in Jerusalem's destruction (Ob 8–14), are both counted here among the nations judged when Jerusalem is restored.

AMOS

Introduction

Amos is Israel's prophet* of social justice, proclaiming that true religion consists not just of ritual observances but in a moral life based on fair and equitable treatment of all members of society, powerful and powerless alike. This concern for justice lies at the heart of Israel's prophetic movement, but no other prophet expresses it with more passion and substance. Amos demands justice in all areas of society—political (6.10), judicial (5.10, 12), and economic (8.4–6)—and mercilessly attacks Israel's elite for their abuse of power (4.1, 6.1). He believes Israel's religious assemblies, sacred music, and elaborate sacrifices are pointless without principled and ethical behavior in daily affairs (5.21–24). And he regards the demise of Israelite society as the inevitable outcome of its internal corruption and injustices (5.6–7). The power of social justice in the imagination of Western society derives in large part from Israel's prophets and from Amos's passionate appeals in particular.

The book of Amos contains one brief narrative* about an event in his career (7.10–17) and several reports of his visions (7.1–9; 8.1–3; 9.1–4), but the book is primarily made up of short judgment speeches with a simple two-part structure: an indictment listing Israel's sins, and a sentence of judgment prescribing God's punishment for these sins. This structure is clearly visible, for example, in Amos's speech to the priest Amaziah at Bethel, in which Amos indicts Amaziah for restricting prophetic speech (7.16) and announces the divine sentence punishing Amaziah and his family (7.17). While judgment speeches against Israel predominate, the book of Amos actually begins with a series of judgment speeches, with this same two-part structure, directed against Israel's neighbors (1.3–2.5).

Although Amos reports his visions in the first person (8.1–3), the narrative about Amos's career (7.10–17) and the book's title (1.1) describe Amos in the third person, indicating that Amos's speeches were collected and passed down by his followers. Some contend that almost everything in Amos should be traced back to the prophet himself, while others think that Amos's followers have edited the collection of his speeches and added to them. Such additions are identified in particular with those texts that appear to update Amos's speeches against the northern kingdom of Israel with speeches that reflect the perspective of the southern kingdom of Judah, such as those that name Jerusalem and Judah (1.2; 2.4–5) and that predict the fall of the northern sanctuary of Bethel (3.13–14), which rivaled Judah's sanctuary in Jerusalem. Almost all scholars maintain that the oracle* of salvation for the royal family of David with which the book concludes (9.11–15) is a later addition, since it contrasts so strongly with the atmosphere of judgment that pervades the rest of the book.

Amos preached against the northern kingdom during the reign of Jeroboam II (1.1, 7.11) and is the first of Israel's prophets to have his speeches preserved in a collection bearing his name. Jeroboam's long 41-year reign (786–746 BCE) is presented in the accounts of Israel's history as a time of strength and expansion for Israel (2 Kings 14.23–29), a favorable portrait confirmed by Amos's repeated references to the prodigious wealth in its capital, Samaria (3.15; 5.11; 6.1, 4–6). Indeed, archaeologists have recovered from the ancient city of Samaria in this period examples of the fine ivory carvings of which Amos spoke (3.15; 6.4). During such an era of political and economic stability and growth, Amos's harsh criticism of Israelite society and his

expectation that its injustices would soon bring it down must have seemed exaggerated and outlandish to his audience (5.18; 6.6). A mere 25 years after Jeroboam's death, however, Amos's predictions came true when Samaria fell to Assyrian armies.

READING GUIDE

Amos must be read as an anthology of short, independent speeches rather than as a book with a single thesis developed from beginning to end. Since his editors did not mark the beginnings and ends of these speeches, the reader must make an effort to identify them, keeping in mind the typical two-part speech form: indictment of sins followed by announcement of punishment. The reader must also be aware that Amos (and other prophets) composed speeches in a poetic form based on verse units of two parallel lines: "But let justice roll down like waters,/ and righteousness like an ever-flowing stream" (5.24). Keeping these two features of Amos's work in mind can help make sense of a book that might otherwise appear disorganized and repetitious.

1 The words of Amos, who was among the shepherds of Tekoa, which he saw concerning Israel in the days of King Uzziah of Judah and in the days of King Jeroboam son of Joash of Israel, two years*a* before the earthquake.
2 And he said:
The LORD roars from Zion,
　and utters his voice from Jerusalem;
the pastures of the shepherds wither,
　and the top of Carmel dries up.

1.1–2: Introduction. Prophetic books customarily begin with data about their authors. **1:** Amos preached during the reigns of *King Uzziah of Judah* (783–742 BCE) and *King Jeroboam of Israel* (786–746), and he owned sheep and orchards (7.14). Though from *Tekoa*, a town in Judah, Amos preached primarily to Judah's northern neighbor, Israel (2.6). **2:** *Jerusalem* and *Zion** are both names of the capital city of Judah. *Carmel* is a mountain range near the Mediterranean coast in Israel.

3 Thus says the LORD:
For three transgressions of Damascus,
　and for four, I will not revoke the
　　punishment;*b*
because they have threshed Gilead
　with threshing sledges of iron.
4 So I will send a fire on the house
　of Hazael,
　and it shall devour the strongholds of
　　Ben-hadad.

5 I will break the gate bars of Damascus,
　and cut off the inhabitants from the
　　Valley of Aven,
　and the one who holds the scepter from
　　Beth-eden;
　and the people of Aram shall go into
　　exile to Kir,
　　　　　　　　　　says the LORD.

6 Thus says the LORD:
For three transgressions of Gaza,
　and for four, I will not revoke the
　　punishment;*b*
because they carried into exile entire
　communities,
　to hand them over to Edom.
7 So I will send a fire on the wall
　of Gaza,
　fire that shall devour its strongholds.
8 I will cut off the inhabitants from
　Ashdod,
　and the one who holds the scepter
　　from Ashkelon;
I will turn my hand against Ekron,
　and the remnant of the Philistines
　　shall perish,
　　　　　　　　　　says the Lord GOD.

1.3–2.5: Judgments on Israel's neighbors. In typical two-part judgment speeches, containing indictments

a Or *during two years*　*b* Heb *cause it to return*

and sentences, Amos announces divine judgment on seven of Israel's closest neighbors (see map on page 1182). The indictments in each case involve acts of brutality against neighboring peoples. The repetition of *for three transgressions . . . and for four* in each indictment is a poetic convention meaning simply "several." The image of *fire* in each sentence predicts the violent destruction of the cities indicted. The phrase *says the LORD*, which begins and ends these speeches, identifies them as divine oracles* and the prophet* as a divine spokesperson. **3–5:** *Damascus* is the capital of the kingdom of Aram northeast of Israel, and *Hazael* and *Ben-hadad* are two of its kings. *Gilead* refers to Israelite territories east of the Jordan. The location of *Kir*, which Amos regarded as the original home of the Arameans (9.7), is uncertain. **6–8:** *Gaza, Ashdod, Ashkelon,* and *Ekron* are major Philistine cities southwest of Israel on the Mediterranean coast. *Edom*, to which both *Gaza* and *Tyre* (1.9–10) deported people, is Israel's neighbor southeast of the Dead Sea.

9 Thus says the LORD:
For three transgressions of Tyre,
and for four, I will not revoke the punishment;*a*
because they delivered entire communities over to Edom,
and did not remember the covenant of kinship.
10 So I will send a fire on the wall of Tyre,
fire that shall devour its strongholds.

11 Thus says the LORD:
For three transgressions of Edom,
and for four, I will not revoke the punishment;*a*
because he pursued his brother with the sword
and cast off all pity;
he maintained his anger perpetually,*b*
and kept his wrath*c* forever.
12 So I will send a fire on Teman,
and it shall devour the strongholds of Bozrah.

13 Thus says the LORD:
For three transgressions of the Ammonites,
and for four, I will not revoke the punishment;*a*

because they have ripped open pregnant women in Gilead
in order to enlarge their territory.
14 So I will kindle a fire against the wall of Rabbah,
fire that shall devour its strongholds,
with shouting on the day of battle,
with a storm on the day of the whirlwind;
15 then their king shall go into exile,
he and his officials together,
says the LORD.

2 Thus says the LORD:
For three transgressions of Moab,
and for four, I will not revoke the punishment;*a*
because he burned to lime the bones of the king of Edom.
2 So I will send a fire on Moab,
and it shall devour the strongholds of Kerioth,
and Moab shall die amid uproar,
amid shouting and the sound of the trumpet;
3 I will cut off the ruler from its midst,
and will kill all its officials with him,
says the LORD.

4 Thus says the LORD:
For three transgressions of Judah,
and for four, I will not revoke the punishment;*a*
because they have rejected the law of the LORD,
and have not kept his statutes,
but they have been led astray by the same lies
after which their ancestors walked.
5 So I will send a fire on Judah,
and it shall devour the strongholds of Jerusalem.

1.9–2.5. 1.9–10: *Tyre* is a Phoenician city on the Mediterranean coast northwest of Israel. **11–12:** *Edom* is Israel's neighbor to the southeast, and *Teman* and *Bozrah* are two of its major cities. Edom's *brother* may refer to either Israel or Judah (Ob 8–12). **13–15:** The

a Heb *cause it to return*   b Syr Vg: Heb *and his anger tore perpetually*   c Gk Syr Vg: Heb *and his wrath kept*

"They sell the righteous for silver"

With this phrase, Amos strikes at the heart of Israel's guilt (2.6, 8.6). He criticizes not just an abuse here and an injustice there, but an economic system that condones the accumulation of great wealth in the hands of a few (6.1–6) and the growth in the gap between rich and poor (5.11). In Israel's traditional economy, families supported themselves by farming their ancestral lands, as Amos himself may have done (1.1; 7.14–15). But as the wealthy imposed heavy taxes (2.8; 5.11), took collateral for themselves (2.8), and cheated customers in the marketplace (8.5), the poor were eventually forced off of their lands and reduced to debt-slavery, where they were bought and sold by the rich. Such an economic system was intolerable, according to Amos, for a society that had itself been once freed from slavery (2.10; 3.1).

Ammonites, Israel's neighbors to the east, are accused, as is Damascus (1.3), of crimes against the Israelites in *Gilead*. **2.1–3:** *Moab*, located southeast of Israel, is accused of crimes against its southern neighbor *Edom*. **4–5:** *Judah*, like Israel to follow (2.6–16), is criticized not for crimes against its neighbors, but for crimes within its own society against God's *law*.

6 Thus says the LORD:
For three transgressions of Israel,
    and for four, I will not revoke the
        punishment;[a]
because they sell the righteous
        for silver,
    and the needy for a pair of sandals—
7 they who trample the head of the poor
        into the dust of the earth,
    and push the afflicted out of the
        way;
father and son go in to the same girl,
    so that my holy name is profaned;
8 they lay themselves down beside every
        altar
    on garments taken in pledge;
and in the house of their God
        they drink
    wine bought with fines they
        imposed.

2.6–16: Judgment on Israel. This judgment speech concludes the series of speeches directed against Israel's neighbors. By starting with judgments against Israel's neighbors, Amos may have intended to lure his

Israelite audience into agreement with him, only to shock them with a concluding speech listing their own sins, even more numerous than those of their neighbors. **6–8:** Amos's indictment begins with Israel's mistreatment of its poor (vv. 6b–7a), in particular, the sale of humans into slavery when they were unable to pay their debts (8.6). *Garments taken in pledge* (Ex 22.26–27; Deut 24.12–13) and *fines* refer to objects and money taken unfairly from the poor by the rich.

9 Yet I destroyed the Amorite
        before them,
    whose height was like the height of
        cedars,
    and who was as strong as oaks;
I destroyed his fruit above,
    and his roots beneath.
10 Also I brought you up out of the land of
        Egypt,
    and led you forty years in
        the wilderness,
    to possess the land of the Amorite.
11 And I raised up some of your children
        to be prophets
    and some of your youths to be
        nazirites.[b]
    Is it not indeed so, O people
        of Israel?
                        says the LORD.

a Heb *cause it to return*   b That is, *those separated* or *those consecrated*

12 But you made the nazirites*a* drink wine,
   and commanded the prophets,
   saying, "You shall not prophesy."

13 So, I will press you down in your place,
   just as a cart presses down
   when it is full of sheaves.*b*

14 Flight shall perish from the swift,
   and the strong shall not retain their
      strength,
   nor shall the mighty save their lives;

15 those who handle the bow shall
      not stand,
   and those who are swift of foot shall
      not save themselves,
   nor shall those who ride horses save
      their lives;

16 and those who are stout of heart among
      the mighty
   shall flee away naked in that day,
                              says the LORD.

2.9–16. 9–12: A brief historical summary stresses Israel's stubbornness by contrasting it with God's acts
of salvation on Israel's behalf. 13–16: The judgment
imposed for Israel's crimes will bring an end to Israel's
strongest defenses: its fastest runners, its strongest
warriors, its most skilled archers, and its best
horsemen.

3 Hear this word that the LORD has spoken against you, O people of Israel,
against the whole family that I brought up
out of the land of Egypt:

2 You only have I known
   of all the families of the earth;
   therefore I will punish you
   for all your iniquities.

3 Do two walk together
   unless they have made an appointment?

4 Does a lion roar in the forest,
   when it has no prey?
   Does a young lion cry out from its den,
   if it has caught nothing?

5 Does a bird fall into a snare on
      the earth,
   when there is no trap for it?
   Does a snare spring up from
      the ground,
   when it has taken nothing?

6 Is a trumpet blown in a city,
   and the people are not afraid?
   Does disaster befall a city,
   unless the LORD has done it?

7 Surely the Lord GOD does nothing,
   without revealing his secret
   to his servants the prophets.

8 The lion has roared;
   who will not fear?
   The Lord GOD has spoken;
   who can but prophesy?

3.1–8: The power of prophets. After a brief description of Israel's past salvation and future punishment
(vv. 1–2), Amos begins a speech composed entirely of
rhetorical* questions (vv. 3–8). With the first questions, Amos gains the audience's agreement on obvious issues in order to convince them of his real claim:
When prophets speak, their words are the words of
God (vv. 7–8).

9 Proclaim to the strongholds in Ashdod,
   and to the strongholds in the land of
      Egypt,
   and say, "Assemble yourselves on
      Mount*c* Samaria,
   and see what great tumults are
      within it,
   and what oppressions are in
      its midst."

10 They do not know how to do right, says
      the LORD,
   those who store up violence and
      robbery in their strongholds.

11 Therefore thus says the Lord GOD:
   An adversary shall surround the land,
   and strip you of your defense;
   and your strongholds shall be
      plundered.

12 Thus says the LORD: As the shepherd
rescues from the mouth of the lion two legs,
or a piece of an ear, so shall the people of
Israel who live in Samaria be rescued, with
the corner of a couch and part*b* of a bed.

3.9–12: Judgment on Samaria. Amos invites representatives from *Ashdod*, a Philistine city (1.8), and

a That is, *those separated* or *those consecrated*
b Meaning of Heb uncertain   c Gk Syr: Heb *the
mountains of*

from *Egypt* to observe the *oppressions* of the poor on *Mount Samaria*, the capital of Israel. This indictment (vv. 9–10) is followed by God's sentence: Samaria's *strongholds shall be plundered* by an invading army (v. 11). The metaphor* of the plundering *lion* in v. 12 emphasizes how little will remain in Samaria after the enemy strikes.

13 Hear, and testify against the house of
    Jacob,
    says the Lord GOD, the God of hosts:
14 On the day I punish Israel for its
    transgressions,
    I will punish the altars of Bethel,
    and the horns of the altar shall
        be cut off
    and fall to the ground.
15 I will tear down the winter house as
        well as the summer house;
    and the houses of ivory shall perish,
    and the great houses*a* shall come
        to an end,
    says the LORD.

3.13–15: Judgment on Bethel. Located in the southern part of Israel, *Bethel,* together with Dan in the north, was one of Israel's major religious centers. The judgment against Israel's houses (v. 15) that follows the judgment on Bethel contains an implicit criticism of the rich. Israel's wealthiest citizens built *winter houses* in the Jordan valley to escape the cold winter climate in the mountains of Samaria, and they made furniture inlaid with ivory for their homes (6.4).

4 Hear this word, you cows of Bashan
    who are on Mount Samaria,
    who oppress the poor, who crush the
        needy,
    who say to their husbands, "Bring
        something to drink!"
2 The Lord GOD has sworn by his holiness:
    The time is surely coming upon you,
    when they shall take you away with
        hooks,
    even the last of you with fishhooks.
3 Through breaches in the wall you shall
        leave,
    each one straight ahead;
    and you shall be flung out into
        Harmon,*b*
    says the LORD.

4 Come to Bethel—and transgress;
    to Gilgal—and multiply transgression;
    bring your sacrifices every morning,
    your tithes every three days;
5 bring a thank offering of leavened
        bread,
    and proclaim freewill offerings,
        publish them;
    for so you love to do, O people
        of Israel!
    says the Lord GOD.

6 I gave you cleanness of teeth in all your
        cities,
    and lack of bread in all your places,
    yet you did not return to me,
    says the LORD.

7 And I also withheld the rain from you
    when there were still three months to
        the harvest;
    I would send rain on one city,
    and send no rain on another city;
    one field would be rained upon,
    and the field on which it did not rain
        withered;
8 so two or three towns wandered to one
        town
    to drink water, and were not satisfied;
    yet you did not return to me,
    says the LORD.

9 I struck you with blight and mildew;
    I laid waste*c* your gardens and your
        vineyards;
    the locust devoured your fig trees and
        your olive trees;
    yet you did not return to me,
    says the LORD.

10 I sent among you a pestilence after the
        manner of Egypt;
    I killed your young men with the sword;
    I carried away your horses;*d*
    and I made the stench of your camp
        go up into your nostrils;
    yet you did not return to me,
    says the LORD.

a Or *many houses*   b Meaning of Heb uncertain
c Cn: Heb *the multitude of*   d Heb *with the captivity of your horses*

11 I overthrew some of you,
    as when God overthrew Sodom and
        Gomorrah,
    and you were like a brand snatched
        from the fire;
yet you did not return to me,
                        says the LORD.

12 Therefore thus I will do to you,
        O Israel;
    because I will do this to you,
    prepare to meet your God, O Israel!

13 For lo, the one who forms the
        mountains, creates the wind,
    reveals his thoughts to mortals,
makes the morning darkness,
    and treads on the heights of
        the earth—
    the LORD, the God of hosts, is
        his name!

4.1–13. 1–3: Judgment on Samaria's elite women.
In his indictment of their oppression of the poor (v. 1),
Amos compares Israel's leading women to cattle grazing in Israel's prime pasture land, *Bashan*. The sentence for these women (vv. 2–3) is deportation,
though the location of *Harmon* is uncertain. **4–13: Israel's stubbornness.** After criticizing the rituals practiced at two of Israel's religious centers, *Bethel* and *Gilgal* (vv. 4–5), perhaps because he judged them
hypocritical, Amos lists a series of divine judgments
that have failed to convince Israel of its injustices: famine (v. 6), drought (vv. 7–8), plant diseases and predators (v. 9), disease and death for Israel's army (v. 10),
and defeat (v. 11). With the term *therefore*, which
characteristically links indictments to sentences, Amos
introduces God's judgment (vv. 12–13) for Israel's repeated refusal to reform.

5 Hear this word that I take up over you
    in lamentation, O house of Israel:
2 Fallen, no more to rise,
    is maiden Israel;
forsaken on her land,
    with no one to raise her up.

3 For thus says the Lord GOD:
The city that marched out a thousand
    shall have a hundred left,

and that which marched out a hundred
    shall have ten left. *a*

4 For thus says the LORD to the house of
        Israel:
Seek me and live;
5   but do not seek Bethel,
    and do not enter into Gilgal
        or cross over to Beer-sheba;
    for Gilgal shall surely go into exile,
        and Bethel shall come to nothing.

6 Seek the LORD and live,
    or he will break out against the house
        of Joseph like fire,
    and it will devour Bethel, with no one
        to quench it.
7 Ah, you that turn justice to
        wormwood,
    and bring righteousness to
        the ground!

5.1–27: A lament over Israel. Within a lament* anticipating Israel's fall (vv. 1–3, 16–20), Amos indicts
Israel for its injustices (vv. 10–13, 21–27) and pleads
with Israel to seek God in order to avoid disaster (vv.
4–7, 14–15). **1–3:** Amos begins his lament by describing the conquest of Israel as if it had already happened.
4–7: In his opening appeal to seek God, Amos criticizes
the worship (v. 5) of those who are not just (v. 7). **5:**
Beer-sheba, a southern religious center with old associations with the northern kingdom of Israel (1 Sam
8.2; 1 Kings 19.3), is mentioned here alongside two
northern centers, *Bethel* and *Gilgal*, which Amos criticizes elsewhere (4.4). **6:** *Joseph*, father of the ancestors of the two most powerful northern tribes (Ephraim
and Manasseh), is employed by Amos as a synonym
for Israel.

8 The one who made the Pleiades
        and Orion,
    and turns deep darkness into
        the morning,
    and darkens the day into night,
who calls for the waters of the sea,
    and pours them out on the surface of
        the earth,
the LORD is his name,

a Heb adds *to the house of Israel*

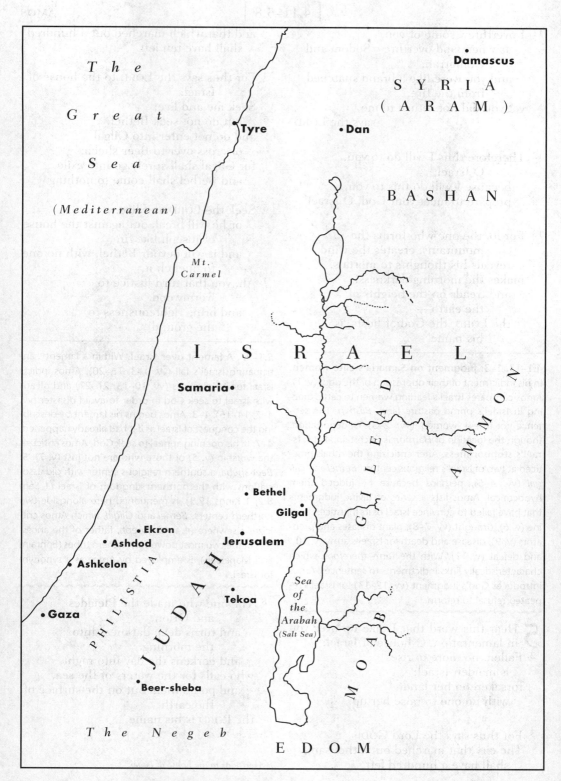

Map Israel and environs in the time of Amos

9 who makes destruction flash out against
      the strong,
   so that destruction comes upon the
      fortress.

10 They hate the one who reproves in the
      gate,
   and they abhor the one who speaks
      the truth.
11 Therefore because you trample on the
      poor
   and take from them levies of grain,
 you have built houses of hewn stone,
   but you shall not live in them;
 you have planted pleasant vineyards,
   but you shall not drink their wine.
12 For I know how many are your
      transgressions,
   and how great are your sins—
 you who afflict the righteous, who take
      a bribe,
   and push aside the needy in the gate.
13 Therefore the prudent will keep silent in
      such a time;
   for it is an evil time.

5.8–13. 8–9: Hymns such as this one praising God's power occur at several points in Amos (4.13; 9.5–6). 10–13: Amos indicts Israel for judicial and economic abuses. Israel's judges heard and settled disputes at *the gate* of the city (vv. 10, 12). *Levies of grain* are taxes imposed by creditors or landlords on poor farmers.

14 Seek good and not evil,
   that you may live;
 and so the LORD, the God of hosts, will
      be with you,
   just as you have said.
15 Hate evil and love good,
   and establish justice in the gate;
 it may be that the LORD, the God
      of hosts,
   will be gracious to the remnant of
      Joseph.

16 Therefore thus says the LORD, the God
      of hosts, the Lord:
 In all the squares there shall be
      wailing;
   and in all the streets they shall say,
      "Alas! alas!"

 They shall call the farmers to
   mourning,
 and those skilled in lamentation, to
   wailing;
17 in all the vineyards there shall
   be wailing
 for I will pass through the midst of
   you,
         says the LORD.

18 Alas for you who desire the day of
   the LORD!
 Why do you want the day of
   the LORD?
 It is darkness, not light;
19 as if someone fled from a lion,
   and was met by a bear;
 or went into the house and rested his
   hand against the wall,
   and was bitten by a snake.
20 Is not the day of the LORD darkness,
   not light,
   and gloom with no brightness in it?

21 I hate, I despise your festivals,
   and I take no delight in your solemn
      assemblies.
22 Even though you offer me your burnt
      offerings and grain offerings,
   I will not accept them;
 and the offerings of well-being of your
      fatted animals
   I will not look upon.
23 Take away from me the noise of your
      songs;
   I will not listen to the melody of your
      harps.
24 But let justice roll down like waters,
   and righteousness like an ever-flowing
      stream.

5.14–24. 14–15: Amos's appeal to seek God by living justly (vv. 4–7) is resumed. 16–20: Amos continues his lament begun in vv. 1–3. The *day of the LORD* (vv. 18, 20) is a decisive act of God in human affairs. Although Amos's audience believed it would be a day of salvation, Amos saw it as a day of judgment. 21–24: This is Amos's classic statement about the meaninglessness of worship (vv. 21–23) if it is practiced by those who do not do justice in their daily affairs (v. 24).

AMOS

25 Did you bring to me sacrifices and offerings the forty years in the wilderness, O house of Israel? 26 You shall take up Sakkuth your king, and Kawan your star-god, your images,ᵃ which you made for yourselves; 27 therefore I will take you into exile beyond Damascus, says the LORD, whose name is the God of hosts.

---

editorial addition, Israel

5.25–27: In what may buth and Kaiwan are titles is blamed for idolatry. Mesopotamia. *Damascus* for Saturn, an astral dom of Aram, northeast of is the capital of Israel (1.3).

who are at ease in Zion,
se who feel secure on

6 Alas nt Samaria,
aᵗs of the first of the nations,
n the house of Israel
sorts!
ver to Calneh, and see;
n there go to Hamath the great;
en go down to Gath of the
Philistines.
e you betterᵇ than these kingdoms?
Or is yourᶜ territory greater than
theirᵈ territory,
3 O you that put far away the evil day,
and bring near a reign of violence?

4 Alas for those who lie on beds of ivory,
and lounge on their couches,
and eat lambs from the flock,
and calves from the stall;
5 who sing idle songs to the sound
of the harp,
and like David improvise on
instruments of music;
6 who drink wine from bowls,
and anoint themselves with the finest
oils,
but are not grieved over the ruin of
Joseph!
7 Therefore they shall now be the first to
go into exile,
and the revelry of the loungers shall
pass away.

8 The Lord GOD has sworn by himself
(says the LORD, the God of hosts):

I abhor the pride of Jacob
and hate his strongholds;
and I will deliver up the city and all
that is in it.

9 If ten people remain in one house, they shall die. 10 And if a relative, one who burns the dead,ᵉ shall take up the body to bring it out of the house, and shall say to someone in the innermost parts of the house, "Is anyone else with you?" the answer will come, "No." Then the relativeᶠ shall say, "Hush! We must not mention the name of the LORD."

11 See, the LORD commands,
and the great house shall be shattered
to bits,
and the little house to pieces.
12 Do horses run on rocks?
Does one plow the sea with oxen?ᵍ
But you have turned justice
into poison
and the fruit of righteousness into
wormwood—
13 you who rejoice in Lo-debar,ʰ
who say, "Have we not by our own
strength
taken Karnaimⁱ for ourselves?"
14 Indeed, I am raising up against you a
nation,
O house of Israel, says the LORD, the
God of hosts,
and they shall oppress you from
Lebo-hamath
to the Wadi Arabah.

6.1–14: Judgment on Samaria's elite men. In this judgment speech, Amos indicts Israel's leaders for excessive wealth and complacency (vv. 1–6) and announces a sentence that includes the conquest of Samaria and deportation of its leaders (vv. 7–14). **2:** *Calneh* and *Hamath* are capital cities of important Syrian city-states. **6:** *Joseph* is a synonym for Israel (5.6). **13:** *Lo-debar* and *Karnaim* are cities east of the Jordan that may have been brought under Israelite control

---

a Heb *your images, your star-god*   b Or *Are they better*
c Heb *their*   d Heb *your*   e Or *who makes a burning for him*   f Heb *he*   g Or *Does one plow them with oxen*   h Or *in a thing of nothingness*   i Or *horns*

during Amos's career by the conquests of Jeroboam II (2 Kings 14.25). **14:** *Lebo-hamath* and the *Wadi★ Arabah* are the northern and southern boundaries established for the kingdom of Israel by Jeroboam II (2 Kings 14.25); they are used here by Amos to depict Israel in its entirety.

7 This is what the Lord GOD showed me: he was forming locusts at the time the latter growth began to sprout (it was the latter growth after the king's mowings). ²When they had finished eating the grass of the land, I said,

"O Lord GOD, forgive, I beg you!
How can Jacob stand?
He is so small!"

3 The LORD relented concerning this;
"It shall not be," said the LORD.

4 This is what the Lord GOD showed me: the Lord GOD was calling for a shower of fire,ª and it devoured the great deep and was eating up the land. ⁵Then I said,

"O Lord GOD, cease, I beg you!
How can Jacob stand?
He is so small!"

6 The LORD relented concerning this;
"This also shall not be," said the Lord GOD.

7 This is what he showed me: the Lord was standing beside a wall built with a plumb line, with a plumb line in his hand. ⁸And the LORD said to me, "Amos, what do you see?" And I said, "A plumb line." Then the Lord said,

"See, I am setting a plumb line
in the midst of my people Israel;
I will never again pass them by;
9 the high places of Isaac shall be made
desolate,
and the sanctuaries of Israel shall be
laid waste,
and I will rise against the house of
Jeroboam with the sword."

7.1–9: Amos's visions. In three separate visions—a locust plague (vv. 1–3); a fire storm (vv. 4–6); and a wall and plumb line (vv. 7–9)—God shows Amos judgments that will befall Israel. After the first two visions, Amos asks God to reconsider, and the punishment is

withheld. *Jacob* is used as a synonym for Israel in these two visions.

10 Then Amaziah, the priest of Bethel, sent to King Jeroboam of Israel, saying, "Amos has conspired against you in the very center of the house of Israel; the land is not able to bear all his words. ¹¹For thus Amos has said,

'Jeroboam shall die by the sword,
and Israel must go into exile
away from his land.'"

¹²And Amaziah said to Amos, "O seer, go, flee away to the land of Judah, earn your bread there, and prophesy there; ¹³but never again prophesy at Bethel, for it is the king's sanctuary, and it is a temple of the kingdom."

14 Then Amos answered Amaziah, "I amᵇ no prophet, nor a prophet's son; but I amᵇ a herdsman, and a dresser of sycamore trees, ¹⁵and the LORD took me from following the flock, and the LORD said to me, 'Go, prophesy to my people Israel.'

16 "Now therefore hear the word of the
LORD.
You say, 'Do not prophesy against Israel,
and do not preach against the house
of Isaac.'
17 Therefore thus says the LORD:
'Your wife shall become a prostitute in
the city,
and your sons and your daughters
shall fall by the sword,
and your land shall be parceled out by
line;
you yourself shall die in an
unclean land,
and Israel shall surely go into exile
away from its land.'"

7.10–17: Amos preaches at Bethel. This is the only narrative★ in Amos describing an event in Amos's career and a specific setting in which he preached. Upon hearing Amos's unfavorable prediction about *Jeroboam*, king of Israel, *Amaziah*, priest of Bethel, responds in two ways: He sends word to Jeroboam in Samaria (vv. 10–11), and he banishes Amos from Bethel, one of Israel's major religious centers (vv. 12–13). Amaziah appears to claim that Amos, from the

a Or *for a judgment by fire*   *b* Or *was*

Judean town of Tekoa (1.1), should earn his living as a prophet* in his own country of Judah ("*earn your bread there,*" v. 12), and stay out of Israel's affairs. When Amos responds that he is not a prophet but a shepherd and a farmer (v. 14), he may mean that he is not earning his living as a (professional) prophet at all, but rather communicating an unexpected but genuine divine revelation.

8 This is what the Lord GOD showed me—a basket of summer fruit.*ᵃ* ²He said, "Amos, what do you see?" And I said, "A basket of summer fruit."*ᵃ* Then the LORD said to me,

"The end*ᵇ* has come upon my people Israel;
I will never again pass them by.
³ The songs of the temple*ᶜ* shall become wailings in that day,"
says the Lord GOD;
"the dead bodies shall be many, cast out in every place. Be silent!"

8.1–3: Amos's visions continued. Like the visions described in 7.1–9, this vision reveals a coming judgment on Israel. **2:** The meaning of this vision is based on the similarity in Hebrew between the words for *summer fruit* ("qayits") and *end* ("qets").

---

⁴ Hear this, you that trample on the needy,
and bring to ruin the poor of the land,
⁵ saying, "When will the new moon be over
so that we may sell grain;
and the sabbath,
so that we may offer wheat for sale?
We will make the ephah small and the shekel great,
and practice deceit with false balances,
⁶ buying the poor for silver
and the needy for a pair of sandals,
and selling the sweepings of the wheat."

⁷ The LORD has sworn by the pride of Jacob:
Surely I will never forget any of their deeds.

⁸ Shall not the land tremble on this account,
and everyone mourn who lives in it,
and all of it rise like the Nile,
and be tossed about and sink again,
like the Nile of Egypt?

⁹ On that day, says the Lord GOD,
I will make the sun go down at noon,
and darken the earth in broad daylight.
¹⁰ I will turn your feasts into mourning,
and all your songs into lamentation;
I will bring sackcloth on all loins,
and baldness on every head;
I will make it like the mourning for an only son,
and the end of it like a bitter day.

¹¹ The time is surely coming, says the Lord GOD,
when I will send a famine on the land;
not a famine of bread, or a thirst for water,
but of hearing the words of the LORD.
¹² They shall wander from sea to sea,
and from north to east;
they shall run to and fro, seeking the word of the LORD,
but they shall not find it.
¹³ In that day the beautiful young women
and the young men
shall faint for thirst.
¹⁴ Those who swear by Ashimah of Samaria,
and say, "As your god lives, O Dan,"
and, "As the way of Beer-sheba lives"—
they shall fall, and never rise again.

8.4–14: Judgment on Israel's businessmen. In this judgment speech, Amos indicts Israel's merchants for economic abuses (vv. 4–6), and announces a sentence of widespread devastation (vv. 7–14). **5:** The *new moon** and the *sabbath* are religious holidays (Isa 1.13; Hos 2.11) considered an annoyance by merchants who cannot make a profit during their obser-

---

a Heb *qayits*   *b* Heb *qets*   *c* Or *palace*

vance. The *ephah* is used to measure an amount of grain by capacity, and the *shekel** is used to measure an amount of grain by weight. Reducing the *ephah* and enlarging the *shekel* are thus two ways merchants can cheat their customers. **14:** The Hebrew text rendered *Ashimah* here means literally "guilt," thus, "the guilt of Samaria." However, scholars have altered the Hebrew slightly to read either "Ashimah," a Syrian deity (2 Kings 17.30), or Asherah,* a Canaanite deity (1 Kings 16.33). Amos's mention of Israel's capital, *Samaria*, together with one of its major religious centers, *Dan*, and a southern center visited by northerners, *Beer-sheba* (5.5), includes within God's judgment the political and religious leaders of Israel.

9 I saw the LORD standing beside*ᵃ* the altar, and he said:
Strike the capitals until the thresholds shake,
and shatter them on the heads of all the people;*ᵇ*
and those who are left I will kill with the sword;
not one of them shall flee away,
not one of them shall escape.

2 Though they dig into Sheol,
from there shall my hand take them;
though they climb up to heaven,
from there I will bring them down.
3 Though they hide themselves on the top of Carmel,
from there I will search out and take them;
and though they hide from my sight at the bottom of the sea,
there I will command the sea-serpent, and it shall bite them.
4 And though they go into captivity in front of their enemies,
there I will command the sword, and it shall kill them;
and I will fix my eyes on them for harm and not for good.

9.1–4: Amos's visions concluded. Like Amos's other visions (7.1–9; 8.1–3), this vision shows Amos God's coming judgment, but the judgment predicted here is the harshest and most complete of them all. **2:** *Sheol** is the abode of the dead.

5 The Lord, GOD of hosts,
he who touches the earth and it melts,
and all who live in it mourn,
and all of it rises like the Nile,
and sinks again, like the Nile of Egypt;
6 who builds his upper chambers in the heavens,
and founds his vault upon the earth;
who calls for the waters of the sea,
and pours them out upon the surface of the earth—
the LORD is his name.

7 Are you not like the Ethiopians*ᶜ* to me,
O people of Israel? says the LORD.
Did I not bring Israel up from the land of Egypt,
and the Philistines from Caphtor and the Arameans from Kir?
8 The eyes of the Lord GOD are upon the sinful kingdom,
and I will destroy it from the face of the earth
—except that I will not utterly destroy the house of Jacob,
says the LORD.

9 For lo, I will command,
and shake the house of Israel among all the nations
as one shakes with a sieve,
but no pebble shall fall to the ground.
10 All the sinners of my people shall die by the sword,
who say, "Evil shall not overtake or meet us."

9.5–10: Master of the universe. Amos describes God's power over creation (vv. 5–6) and world history (vv. 7–10). **7:** *Caphtor* is likely Crete, while the location of *Kir* is uncertain. Just as God directed Israel's migration from Egypt (3.1), so God has directed the affairs of other nations.

11 On that day I will raise up
the booth of David that is fallen,
and repair its*ᵈ* breaches,

a Or *on* *b* Heb *all of them* *c* Or *Nubians*; Heb *Cushites* *d* Gk: Heb *their*

and raise up its[a] ruins,
  and rebuild it as in the days of old;
12 in order that they may possess the
      remnant of Edom
  and all the nations who are called by
      my name,
  says the LORD who does this.

13 The time is surely coming, says
      the LORD,
  when the one who plows shall
      overtake the one who reaps,
  and the treader of grapes the one who
      sows the seed;
the mountains shall drip sweet wine,
  and all the hills shall flow with it.
14 I will restore the fortunes of my people
      Israel,
  and they shall rebuild the ruined
      cities and inhabit them;
they shall plant vineyards and drink
      their wine,
  and they shall make gardens and eat
      their fruit.

15 I will plant them upon their land,
  and they shall never again be
      plucked up
    out of the land that I have
      given them,
        says the LORD your God.

9.11–15: Vision of renewal. These images of restoration, because they are unparalleled in the rest of
Amos and contrast so sharply with his expectation of
judgment, are widely regarded as a later addition to
Amos's prophecies. **11:** The ruined state of the *booth
of David*, a reference to the Davidic monarchy that
ruled Judah, appears to place this speech after the fall
of Jerusalem in 587 BCE. This image also suggests that
this text was written from the perspective of Judah, the
southern kingdom, rather than from the perspective
of the northern kingdom which Amos addressed. It
anticipates the return of the Babylonian exiles to rebuild their ruined country.

a Gk: Heb *his*

OBADIAH

Introduction

The book of Obadiah is unique among the prophetic* books because it contains only a single speech, and that speech is directed not against Israel or Judah but against a neighboring nation, Edom. Central to Obadiah's speech is a sense of betrayal, expressed most directly in vv. 8–14, which describe the Edomites entering Jerusalem, looting it, and mistreating its people, all the while gloating over Jersualem's misfortunes. God's judgment of Edom, predicted in the verses that precede and follow, is viewed as fair punishment for the Edomites' disloyalty to their Israelite neighbors. Though relations between the Israelites and Edomites were often marked by conflict over the years (2 Kings 8.20–22; 14.7), Israel believed the two peoples were closely related as descendants of the two brothers, Jacob and Esau (Gen 25–33). While rivalry is already present in these stories of their ancestors, it is resolved by reconciliation rather than revenge and betrayal (Gen 33).

Though this speech is not dated by reference to particular kings or events, it appears to have been composed sometime after the Babylonians destroyed Jerusalem in 587 BCE. Following Jerusalem's fall, the Edomites moved in and took advantage of Judah's weakness, taking booty and betraying its survivors (vv. 11, 14; Ps 137.7). The parallel themes of Edom's fall and Judah's rise with which the book ends (vv. 15–21) anticipate the return of the Judean exiles from Babylon and their resettlement of Judah and the surrounding areas.

READING GUIDE

Readers should attend to the structure of this book. Obadiah's judgment speech against Edom begins with the sentence imposed for Edom's crimes (vv. 1–7), then provides the indictment listing the crimes for which this sentence is imposed (vv. 8–14), and concludes by returning to the sentence itself (vv. 15–21). This final sentence for Edom is woven together with expectations for Judah's renewal.

1 The vision of Obadiah.

Thus says the Lord GOD concerning Edom:
We have heard a report from the LORD,
   and a messenger has been sent
      among the nations:
"Rise up! Let us rise against it
   for battle!"
2 I will surely make you least among the
   nations;
   you shall be utterly despised.
3 Your proud heart has deceived you,
   you that live in the clefts of
      the rock,*a*
   whose dwelling is in the heights.

You say in your heart,
   "Who will bring me down to
      the ground?"
4 Though you soar aloft like the eagle,
   though your nest is set among the
      stars,
   from there I will bring you down,
       says the LORD.
5 If thieves came to you,
   if plunderers by night
   —how you have been destroyed!—
   would they not steal only what they
      wanted?

a Or *clefts of Sela*

If grape-gatherers came to you,
would they not leave gleanings?
6 How Esau has been pillaged,
his treasures searched out!
7 All your allies have deceived you,
they have driven you to the border;
your confederates have prevailed
against you;
those who ate*a* your bread have set a
trap for you—
there is no understanding of it.
8 On that day, says the LORD,
I will destroy the wise out of Edom,
and understanding out of
Mount Esau.
9 Your warriors shall be shattered,
O Teman,
so that everyone from Mount Esau
will be cut off.
10 For the slaughter and violence done to
your brother Jacob,
shame shall cover you,
and you shall be cut off forever.
11 On the day that you stood aside,
on the day that strangers carried off
his wealth,
and foreigners entered his gates
and cast lots for Jerusalem,
you too were like one of them.
12 But you should not have gloated*b* over*c*
your brother
on the day of his misfortune;
you should not have rejoiced over the
people of Judah
on the day of their ruin;
you should not have boasted
on the day of distress.
13 You should not have entered the gate of
my people
on the day of their calamity;
you should not have joined in the
gloating over Judah's*d* disaster
on the day of his calamity;
you should not have looted his goods
on the day of his calamity.
14 You should not have stood at
the crossings
to cut off his fugitives;
you should not have handed over his
survivors
on the day of distress.

1–7: The fall of Edom. Obadiah announces the sentence for Edom's crimes. **1:** This *messenger* is a member of the heavenly council sent to announce God's plans. **3:** *The clefts of the rock* refer to the mountain range, rising sharply to the east of the Jordan rift valley, on which Edom was located. **6:** *Esau,* the ancestor of the Edomites (Gen 25.30), is used by Obadiah as a synonym for Edom. **7:** *Those who ate your bread* are the allies mentioned earlier in the verse. Alliances were sealed by covenant* meals (Gen 31.44–46). **8–14: Edom's betrayal of Judah.** Obadiah lists the details of Edom's exploitation of Judah following Babylon's destruction of Jerusalem (587 BCE). **9:** *Teman* is either a synonym for Edom or the name of a section or city in Edom. *Mount Esau* may be a particular Edomite mountain or the mountain range on which Edom was located. **10:** *Jacob,* the *brother* of Edom's ancestor Esau (Gen 25.24–26), is used by Obadiah to represent the citizens of Jerusalem and Judah. **11:** *Jerusalem* is the capital of Judah.

15 For the day of the LORD is near against
all the nations.
As you have done, it shall be done
to you;
your deeds shall return on your own
head.
16 For as you have drunk on my
holy mountain,
all the nations around you shall drink;
they shall drink and gulp down,*e*
and shall be as though they had never
been.
17 But on Mount Zion there shall be those
that escape,
and it shall be holy;
and the house of Jacob shall take
possession of those who
dispossessed them.
18 The house of Jacob shall be a fire,
the house of Joseph a flame,
and the house of Esau stubble;
they shall burn them and
consume them,
and there shall be no survivor of the
house of Esau;
for the LORD has spoken.

a Cn: Heb lacks *those who ate*   b Heb *But do not gloat*
(and similarly through verse 14)   c Heb *on the day of*
d Heb *his*   e Meaning of Heb uncertain

19 Those of the Negeb shall possess Mount
      Esau,
    and those of the Shephelah the land
      of the Philistines;
  they shall possess the land of Ephraim
      and the land of Samaria,
    and Benjamin shall possess Gilead.
20 The exiles of the Israelites who are in
      Halah*a*
    shall possess*b* Phoenicia as far
      as Zarephath;
  and the exiles of Jerusalem who are in
      Sepharad
    shall possess the towns of the Negeb.
21 Those who have been saved*c* shall go
      up to Mount Zion
    to rule Mount Esau;
  and the kingdom shall be the LORD's.

15–21: Edom's end and Judah's renewal. Obadiah
weaves together the themes of Edom's judgment and
Judah's salvation. **18:** *The house of Jacob* and *the
house of Joseph* refer to the southern kingdom of Judah or the Israelite people as a whole, while *the house
of Esau* refers to Edom. **19–20:** Listed here are the territories Obadiah expects to be resettled when Judah is
restored: *the Negeb*, south of Judah; *Mount Esau*, the
territory of Edom southeast of Judah; *the Shephelah*,
the foothills west of Judah; *the land of the Philistines*
on the Mediterranean coast west of Judah; *Ephraim*
and its capital *Samaria;* the old northern kingdom of
Israel; and *Phoenicia* and its city *Zarephath*, on the
Mediterranean coast northwest of Judah.

a Cn: Heb *in this army*   *b* Cn: Meaning of Heb
uncertain   *c* Or *Saviors*

JONAH

Introduction

The book of Jonah is unlike other prophetic books in that it contains a short story about a prophet* rather than a collection of prophetic speeches. Furthermore, Jonah is active not in his own country but in Nineveh, a great Assyrian city feared and hated by the Israelites, who more than once suffered at the hands of its conquering soldiers (2 Kings 18.9–16; Nah 3.1–4). Because the wicked Ninevites repent and are saved, though Jonah is displeased, the story has traditionally been understood to teach God's universal salvation, criticizing at the same time those who think salvation is limited to Israel alone. The story also emphasizes related themes: the importance of human repentance and the depth of divine compassion. In addition, the narrative also contrasts the frailty of the prophet with the power of the prophet's message (Jer 1.4–10).

Jonah has been unusually difficult to place into a particular historical setting. A Jonah son of Amittai (1.1) is mentioned by Israel's historian as an eighth-century prophet (2 Kings 14.25), which accounts for the book of Jonah's position together with other eighth-century prophets, such as Amos and Micah, among the twelve Minor Prophets. But these two prophets have nothing in common, and most scholars have preferred a post-exilic date (sixth to fourth centuries) for the book of Jonah, on the basis of its language and major themes. Nineveh was an important Assyrian city until its fall near the end of the seventh century (612 BCE), but it may well have remained a powerful symbol of the enemy among Israel's later prophets and storytellers.

READING GUIDE

The book of Jonah is full of humor and irony.* The author repeatedly undercuts the reader's expectations. Jonah is commanded to go in one direction and instead goes in the opposite direction; the sailors are more devout than the prophet; Jonah is disappointed when his mission succeeds; and he is more concerned about a plant than about a populous city. To appreciate the artistry of the story and its major themes most fully, the reader should watch for these and other ironies and humorous reversals.

1 Now the word of the LORD came to Jonah son of Amittai, saying, 2"Go at once to Nineveh, that great city, and cry out against it; for their wickedness has come up before me." 3But Jonah set out to flee to Tarshish from the presence of the LORD. He went down to Joppa and found a ship going to Tarshish; so he paid his fare and went on board, to go with them to Tarshish, away from the presence of the LORD.

4 But the LORD hurled a great wind upon the sea, and such a mighty storm came upon the sea that the ship threatened to break up. 5Then the mariners were afraid, and each cried to his god. They threw the cargo that was in the ship into the sea, to lighten it for them. Jonah, meanwhile, had gone down into the hold of the ship and had lain down, and was fast asleep. 6The captain came and said to him, "What are you doing sound asleep? Get up, call on your god! Perhaps the god will spare us a thought so that we do not perish."

7 The sailors*a* said to one another, "Come, let us cast lots, so that we may know on whose account this calamity has come

a Heb *They*

upon us." So they cast lots, and the lot fell on Jonah. ⁸Then they said to him, "Tell us why this calamity has come upon us. What is your occupation? Where do you come from? What is your country? And of what people are you?" ⁹"I am a Hebrew," he replied. "I worship the LORD, the God of heaven, who made the sea and the dry land." ¹⁰Then the men were even more afraid, and said to him, "What is this that you have done!" For the men knew that he was fleeing from the presence of the LORD, because he had told them so.

11 Then they said to him, "What shall we do to you, that the sea may quiet down for us?" For the sea was growing more and more tempestuous. ¹²He said to them, "Pick me up and throw me into the sea; then the sea will quiet down for you; for I know it is because of me that this great storm has come upon you." ¹³Nevertheless the men rowed hard to bring the ship back to land, but they could not, for the sea grew more and more stormy against them. ¹⁴Then they cried out to the LORD, "Please, O LORD, we pray, do not let us perish on account of this man's life. Do not make us guilty of innocent blood; for you, O LORD, have done as it pleased you." ¹⁵So they picked Jonah up and threw him into the sea; and the sea ceased from its raging. ¹⁶Then the men feared the LORD even more, and they offered a sacrifice to the LORD and made vows.

17ᵃ But the LORD provided a large fish to swallow up Jonah; and Jonah was in the belly of the fish three days and three nights.

2 Then Jonah prayed to the LORD his God from the belly of the fish, ²saying,

"I called to the LORD out of my distress,
    and he answered me;
out of the belly of Sheol I cried,
    and you heard my voice.
³ You cast me into the deep,
    into the heart of the seas,
    and the flood surrounded me;
all your waves and your billows
    passed over me.
⁴ Then I said, 'I am driven away
    from your sight;
how ᵇ shall I look again
    upon your holy temple?'
⁵ The waters closed in over me;
    the deep surrounded me;
weeds were wrapped around my head
⁶   at the roots of the mountains.
I went down to the land
    whose bars closed upon me forever;
yet you brought up my life from
        the Pit,
    O LORD my God.
⁷ As my life was ebbing away,
    I remembered the LORD;
and my prayer came to you,
    into your holy temple.
⁸ Those who worship vain idols
    forsake their true loyalty.
⁹ But I with the voice of thanksgiving
    will sacrifice to you;
what I have vowed I will pay.
    Deliverance belongs to the LORD!"
¹⁰Then the LORD spoke to the fish, and it spewed Jonah out upon the dry land.

1.1–17: Jonah flees from God. The book of Jonah begins, as do other prophetic books, with the phrase *the word of the LORD came to . . .* (1.1; Hos 1.1), but unlike other prophets, Jonah embarks on an elaborate plan to escape his calling. The motif* of descent runs through the narrative* of Jonah's attempt to escape (vv. 3, 5, 15). **3:** *Tarshish* is a site of uncertain location on the Mediterranean coast west of Israel (Isa 23.1), in the opposite direction from Nineveh to the east. *Joppa* is an ancient Mediterranean port city, just south of modern Tel Aviv. **4:** Israel's God is frequently associated with the thunderstorm (Ex 19.16–17; Ps 18.7–15).

2.1–10: Jonah's prayer. Jonah's prayer, an appeal to God in poetic form, may be a traditional text taken over by the narrator to represent Jonah's petition. It is composed in the form of a lament,* a common psalm type in which the worshipper pleads for God's help in a time of great distress (Ps 3, 5, 7). **2:** The lament opens with an address, in which the worshipper calls out to God. *Sheol* is the land of the dead. **3–6:** The description of distress follows the opening address. The image of deep waters swallowing the worshipper is common in such descriptions of distress (Ps 69.1–2, 14–15).

a Ch 2.1 in Heb   *b* Theodotion: Heb *surely*

The *holy temple* refers to the Temple* in Jerusalem. **7:** A petition to God follows the description of distress. **8–9:** Laments customarily end, as does this one, with the worshipper anticipating God's aid and promising to thank God by presenting a sacrifice at the Temple.

3 The word of the LORD came to Jonah a second time, saying, [2]"Get up, go to Nineveh, that great city, and proclaim to it the message that I tell you." [3]So Jonah set out and went to Nineveh, according to the word of the LORD. Now Nineveh was an exceedingly large city, a three days' walk across. [4]Jonah began to go into the city, going a day's walk. And he cried out, "Forty days more, and Nineveh shall be overthrown!" [5]And the people of Nineveh believed God; they proclaimed a fast, and everyone, great and small, put on sackcloth.

6 When the news reached the king of Nineveh, he rose from his throne, removed his robe, covered himself with sackcloth, and sat in ashes. [7]Then he had a proclamation made in Nineveh: "By the decree of the king and his nobles: No human being or animal, no herd or flock, shall taste anything. They shall not feed, nor shall they drink water. [8]Human beings and animals shall be covered with sackcloth, and they shall cry mightily to God. All shall turn from their evil ways and from the violence that is in their hands. [9]Who knows? God may relent and change his mind; he may turn from his fierce anger, so that we do not perish."

10 When God saw what they did, how they turned from their evil ways, God changed his mind about the calamity that he had said he would bring upon them; and he did not do it.

3.1–10: The Ninevites repent and are saved. An irony* that underlies the response of the people of Nineveh to Jonah's preaching is that, while the people of Israel and Judah seldom respond to their own prophets by repenting (Hos 9.7; Am 4.6–12), these wicked enemies repent immediately. **6:** *Sackcloth** and *ashes* are traditional signs of mourning and repentance (Joel 1.13; Isa 58.5). **7–8:** By including Nineveh's *animals* in the rituals of fasting, wearing sackcloth, and praying to God, the narrator emphasizes

through humor and irony Nineveh's total response to Jonah's preaching.

4 But this was very displeasing to Jonah, and he became angry. [2]He prayed to the LORD and said, "O LORD! Is not this what I said while I was still in my own country? That is why I fled to Tarshish at the beginning; for I knew that you are a gracious God and merciful, slow to anger, and abounding in steadfast love, and ready to relent from punishing. [3]And now, O LORD, please take my life from me, for it is better for me to die than to live." [4]And the LORD said, "Is it right for you to be angry?" [5]Then Jonah went out of the city and sat down east of the city, and made a booth for himself there. He sat under it in the shade, waiting to see what would become of the city.

6 The LORD God appointed a bush,[a] and made it come up over Jonah, to give shade over his head, to save him from his discomfort; so Jonah was very happy about the bush. [7]But when dawn came up the next day, God appointed a worm that attacked the bush, so that it withered. [8]When the sun rose, God prepared a sultry east wind, and the sun beat down on the head of Jonah so that he was faint and asked that he might die. He said, "It is better for me to die than to live."

9 But God said to Jonah, "Is it right for you to be angry about the bush?" And he said, "Yes, angry enough to die." [10]Then the LORD said, "You are concerned about the bush, for which you did not labor and which you did not grow; it came into being in a night and perished in a night. [11]And should I not be concerned about Nineveh, that great city, in which there are more than a hundred and twenty thousand persons who do not know their right hand from their left, and also many animals?"

4.1–11: God's lesson to Jonah. In the final episode of Jonah's story, the prophet's self-interest is contrasted with God's compassion for others, even for those people considered enemies of Israel and Judah. **2:** When Jonah says "*You are a gracious God and merciful,*" he

a Heb *qiqayon,* possibly *the castor bean plant*

is quoting an ancient Israelite creedal statement affirming God's compassion for the repentant and judgment on the unrepentant (Ex 34.6–7; Joel 2.13). **6:** The castor bean, the best suggestion for the Hebrew "qiqayon" (rendered here *bush*), is a perennial herb whose oil was used in antiquity for medicine and as fuel for oil lamps. Its large leaves could provide a modest amount of shade. **11:** The final phrase of the story, *many animals*, recalls the repentance of the animals in 3.7–8 and, not without a bit of humor and irony, emphasizes again the extent of God's compassion.

MICAH

Introduction

The book of Micah is a collection of two distinct kinds of prophetic speeches. One kind of speech is the judgment speech that indicts its listeners for the crimes they have committed and sentences them to an appropriate punishment. Such judgment speeches, found in chs. 1–3, 6, and 7.17, focus on Samaria, the capital of the northern kingdom of Israel; on Jerusalem, the capital of the southern kingdom of Judah; and on their ruling elite. Rulers, judges, priests, and prophets* are accused of corruption and of mistreating and misleading their people (3.1, 5, 11). The other kind of address is the salvation speech. Such speeches, found in chs. 4–5, and 7.8–20, describe the misfortune their listeners have experienced and predict a period of renewal and restoration for them. The misfortune described in these speeches is most often the exile of Israelites that followed the fall of Samaria and Jerusalem (4.6, 10; 5.8). And the prediction of renewal anticipates the restoration of Jerusalem as a religious and political center (4.2, 7, 13; 7.11). Both kinds of speeches may have been delivered by a single prophet who predicted both judgment and the salvation that would follow it. The character of these speeches, however, suggests that they arose in two different historical contexts.

The judgment speeches in the book of Micah (chs. 1–3, 6; 7.1–7) come from a period in which both Samaria and Jerusalem were threatened by the imperial expansion of the Assyrian empire (1.6–9). Such was the case during the period assigned in the book's title (1.1) to Micah's prophetic career, the latter part of the eighth century BCE marked by the reigns of the Judean kings Jotham (742–735), Ahaz (735–715), and Hezekiah (715–687). Therefore these speeches are widely regarded as those of the prophet Micah, after whom the book was named. They were delivered to a ruling elite that was both corrupt and complacent, unaware of the grave danger in which they and their people lived (3.11–12). The salvation speeches (chs. 4–5; 7.8–20), by contrast, are addressed to people in exile and express many of the themes—the shame of defeat (4.11), life among the nations (5.7), divine forgiveness (7.18), return to Judah (4.6), the restoration of Jerusalem (4.8; 7.11), and judgment on the nations (4.13; 7.10)—of other exilic literature (Isa 40–55). Therefore it may be best to understand these parts of Micah as supplements added in the sixth century by those who preserved Micah's prophecy, in order to link Micah's message to a new era.

READING GUIDE

Like many other prophetic books, Micah must be read as an anthology of short speeches rather than as a unified narrative* or as a single, continuous argument. In Micah's case, it is especially important to distinguish the judgment speeches from the salvation speeches and to keep their distinct historical contexts in mind.

1

The word of the LORD that came to Micah of Moresheth in the days of Kings Jotham, Ahaz, and Hezekiah of Judah, which he saw concerning Samaria and Jerusalem.

1.1: Title. Micah's home is the small village of *Moresheth*, southwest of Jerusalem in the southern kingdom of Judah, but his speeches are directed to *Samaria* and *Jerusalem*, capital cities of the north and the south.

2 Hear, you peoples, all of you;
  listen, O earth, and all that is in it;
and let the Lord GOD be a witness
    against you,
  the Lord from his holy temple.
3 For lo, the LORD is coming out of his
    place,
  and will come down and tread upon
    the high places of the earth.
4 Then the mountains will melt under
    him
  and the valleys will burst open,
like wax near the fire,
  like waters poured down a
    steep place.
5 All this is for the transgression of Jacob
  and for the sins of the house of Israel.
What is the transgression of Jacob?
  Is it not Samaria?
And what is the high place*a* of Judah?
  Is it not Jerusalem?
6 Therefore I will make Samaria a heap in
    the open country,
  a place for planting vineyards.
I will pour down her stones into
    the valley,
  and uncover her foundations.
7 All her images shall be beaten to pieces,
  all her wages shall be burned with
    fire,
  and all her idols I will lay waste;
for as the wages of a prostitute she
    gathered them,
  and as the wages of a prostitute they
    shall again be used.

8 For this I will lament and wail;
  I will go barefoot and naked;
I will make lamentation like the jackals,
  and mourning like the ostriches.

9 For her wound*b* is incurable.
  It has come to Judah;
it has reached to the gate of my people,
  to Jerusalem.

1.2–9: Judgment on Samaria and Jerusalem. Micah's opening speech focuses on his primary audience: the ruling elite in the capitals of Israel and Judah. **3–4:** Divine appearances so powerful that they throw nature into disarray are common at the beginning of prophetic books (Am 1.2; Nah 1.3–5). **5:** *Samaria* and *Jerusalem* are viewed as the centers of corruption in their respective kingdoms. **6–7:** The end of *Samaria*, forecast here, occurred during Micah's career in 721 BCE when the Assyrians conquered Israel. **9:** A threat to *Jerusalem*, but not its end, is described.

10 Tell it not in Gath,
  weep not at all;
in Beth-leaphrah
  roll yourselves in the dust.
11 Pass on your way,
  inhabitants of Shaphir,
  in nakedness and shame;
the inhabitants of Zaanan
  do not come forth;
Beth-ezel is wailing
  and shall remove its support from you.
12 For the inhabitants of Maroth
  wait anxiously for good,
yet disaster has come down from
    the LORD
  to the gate of Jerusalem.
13 Harness the steeds to the chariots,
  inhabitants of Lachish;
it was the beginning of sin
  to daughter Zion,
for in you were found
  the transgressions of Israel.
14 Therefore you shall give parting gifts
  to Moresheth-gath;
the houses of Achzib shall be
    a deception
  to the kings of Israel.
15 I will again bring a conqueror upon you,
  inhabitants of Mareshah;
the glory of Israel
  shall come to Adullam.

a Heb *what are the high places*   *b* Gk Syr Vg: Heb *wounds*

The Assyrian Invasion

The invasion of Judah by Sennacherib of Assyria, described in 1.10–16, is also documented in other ancient sources. Additional perspective is supplied by the following accounts, one from Israel's historians (2 Kings 18.13–16) and another from an Assyrian source.

As to Hezekiah, the Jew, he did not submit to my yoke, I laid siege to 46 of his strong cities, walled forts and to the countless small villages in their vicinity, and conquered (them) by means of well-stamped (earth-)ramps, and battering-rams brought (thus) near (to the walls) (combined with) the attack by foot soldiers, (using) mines, breeches as well as sapper work. I drove out (of them) 200,150 people, young and old, male and female, horses, mules, donkeys, camels, big and small cattle beyond counting, and considered (them) booty. Himself I made a prisoner in Jerusalem, his royal residence, like a bird in a cage. I surrounded him with earthwork in order to molest those who were leaving his city's gate. His towns which I had plundered, I took away from his country and gave them (over) to Mitini, king of Ashdod, Padi, king of Ekron, and Sillibel, king of Gaza. Thus I reduced his country, but I still increased the tribute and the *katrû*-presents (due) to me (as his) overlord which I imposed (later) upon him beyond the former tribute, to be delivered annually.—From the Annals of Sennacherib

In the fourteenth year of King Hezekiah, King Sennacherib of Assyria came up against all the fortified cities of Judah and captured them. King Hezekiah of Judah sent to the king of Assyria at Lachish, saying, "I have done wrong; withdraw from me; whatever you impose on me I will bear." The king of Assyria demanded of King Hezekiah of Judah three hundred talents of silver and thirty talents of gold. Hezekiah gave him all the silver that was found in the house of the LORD and in the treasuries of the king's house. At that time Hezekiah stripped the gold from the doors of the temple of the LORD, and from the doorposts that King Hezekiah of Judah had overlaid and gave it of the king of Assyria.—2 Kings 18.13–16 (NRSV)

16 Make yourselves bald and cut off your
        hair
    for your pampered children;
    make yourselves as bald as the eagle,
        for they have gone from you
            into exile.

1.10–16: A lament* over the invasion of Judah. This speech may have been composed in response to the invasion in 701 BCE of the Assyrian King Sennacherib, who conquered *Lachish* (v. 13) together with other cities and towns in the Judean foothills in the vicinity of Micah's own village *Moresheth-gath* (v. 14; see sidebar above). Among the towns Micah lists as bearing the brunt of the Assyrian attack, *Beth-ezel* (v. 11), *Lachish* (v. 13), *Moresheth-gath* and *Achzib* (v. 14), and *Mareshah* and *Adullam* (v. 15) have all been identified with sites in the Judean foothills (see map on p.

1200), and the other places mentioned were likely situated in this vicinity as well.

2 Alas for those who devise wickedness
    and evil deeds*a* on their beds!
When the morning dawns, they
        perform it,
    because it is in their power.
2 They covet fields, and seize them;
        houses, and take them away;
    they oppress householder and house,
        people and their inheritance.
3 Therefore thus says the LORD:
    Now, I am devising against this family
        an evil

a Cn: Heb *work evil*

from which you cannot remove your
    necks;
and you shall not walk haughtily,
    for it will be an evil time.
4 On that day they shall take up a taunt
        song against you,
    and wail with bitter lamentation,
and say, "We are utterly ruined;
    the LORD *a* alters the inheritance of
        my people;
    how he removes it from me!
        Among our captors *b* he parcels out
            our fields."
5 Therefore you will have no one to cast
        the line by lot
    in the assembly of the LORD.

2.1–5: Judgment for economic crimes. The theme of
this speech is the exploitation of the poor by the rich.
1–2: The indictment blames the wealthy for seizing
fields unfairly, including the ancestral *inheritance*
which was not to leave a family's possession. **3–5:** The
sentence imposes a punishment that suits the crime:
The wealthy will lose their own *fields* and others will
divide them among themselves.

6 "Do not preach"—thus they preach—
    "one should not preach of such things;
        disgrace will not overtake us."
7 Should this be said, O house of Jacob?
    Is the LORD's patience exhausted?
    Are these his doings?
Do not my words do good
    to one who walks uprightly?
8 But you rise up against my people *c* as
        an enemy;
    you strip the robe from the peaceful, *d*
from those who pass by trustingly
    with no thought of war.
9 The women of my people you drive out
    from their pleasant houses;
from their young children you take away
    my glory forever.
10 Arise and go;
    for this is no place to rest,
because of uncleanness that destroys
    with a grievous destruction. *e*
11 If someone were to go about uttering
        empty falsehoods,
    saying, "I will preach to you of wine
        and strong drink,"

such a one would be the preacher for
    this people!

2.6–11: The true prophets' message rejected. Opposition to prophets* such as Micah who pronounce
judgment arises from the belief that a disaster is un-
thinkable: *"Disgrace will not overtake us"* (v. 6; 3.5,
11). **9:** Micah tells the male elite (*you* is a masculine
plural form in Hebrew) that *women* and *children* will
bear the punishment for their sins. **11:** False prophets
dull the senses like liquor.

12 I will surely gather all of you, O Jacob,
    I will gather the survivors of Israel;
I will set them together
    like sheep in a fold,
like a flock in its pasture;
    it will resound with people.
13 The one who breaks out will go up
        before them;
    they will break through and pass the
        gate,
    going out by it.
Their king will pass on before them,
    the LORD at their head.

2.12–13: Salvation for the survivors. This brief
speech, describing returning exiles as a flock of sheep
led by the LORD, is characteristic of the later, exilic parts
of Micah (4.6–8) and of other exilic literature (Isa
40.10–11). It is likely a supplement added to Micah's
own speeches.

3 And I said:
  Listen, you heads of Jacob
    and rulers of the house of Israel!
  Should you not know justice?—
2   you who hate the good and love the
            evil,
    who tear the skin off my people, *f*
        and the flesh off their bones;
3 who eat the flesh of my people,
    flay their skin off them,
break their bones in pieces,
    and chop them up like meat *g* in a
        kettle,
    like flesh in a caldron.

a Heb *he*   *b* Cn: Heb *the rebellious*   *c* Cn: Heb *But
yesterday my people rose*   *d* Cn: Heb *from before a
garment*   *e* Meaning of Heb uncertain   *f* Heb *from
them*   *g* Gk: Heb *as*

⁴ Then they will cry to the LORD,
  but he will not answer them;
he will hide his face from them at that
    time,
  because they have acted wickedly.

⁵ Thus says the LORD concerning
    the prophets
  who lead my people astray,
who cry "Peace"
  when they have something to eat,

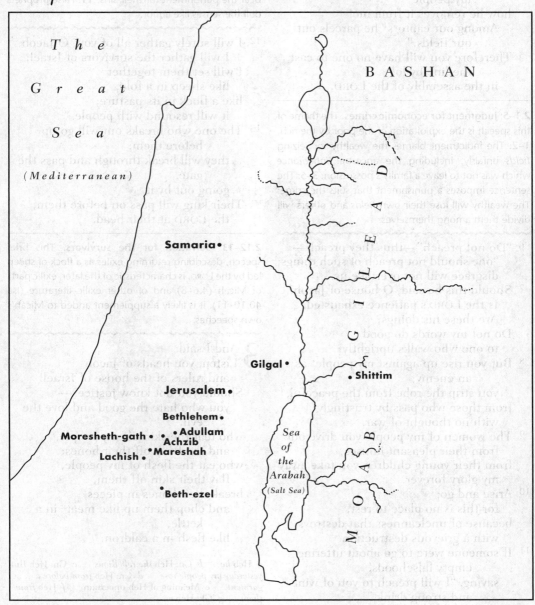

Map The Assyrian conquest of southwestern Judah

*The
Great
Sea*

(Mediterranean)

BASHAN

G I L E A D

Samaria•

Gilgal •

Jerusalem •

•Shittim

Bethlehem •

Moresheth-gath • •Adullam
        •Achzib
Lachish • •Mareshah

*Sea
of
the
Arabah
(Salt Sea)*

M O A B

•Beth-ezel

but declare war against those
    who put nothing into their mouths.
6 Therefore it shall be night to you,
    without vision,
   and darkness to you, without
    revelation.
The sun shall go down upon
    the prophets,
   and the day shall be black over
    them;
7 the seers shall be disgraced,
   and the diviners put to shame;
they shall all cover their lips,
   for there is no answer from God.
8 But as for me, I am filled with power,
   with the spirit of the LORD,
   and with justice and might,
to declare to Jacob his transgression
   and to Israel his sin.

9 Hear this, you rulers of the house of
    Jacob
   and chiefs of the house of Israel,
who abhor justice
   and pervert all equity,
10 who build Zion with blood
   and Jerusalem with wrong!
11 Its rulers give judgment for a bribe,
   its priests teach for a price,
   its prophets give oracles for money;
yet they lean upon the LORD and say,
   "Surely the LORD is with us!
   No harm shall come upon us."
12 Therefore because of you
   Zion shall be plowed as a field;
Jerusalem shall become a heap of ruins,
   and the mountain of the house a
    wooded height.

3.1–12: Judgment on the ruling elite. Chapter 3 is composed of three typical judgment speeches, each with an indictment of crimes and a sentence of punishment for them, directed at political and religious leaders. The theme introduced in Micah's opening speech, that the corruption of Israel and Judah stems from the highest levels of power in its capital cities, continues here. **1–4:** The first judgment speech, directed to political officials, includes an indictment (vv.1–3), accusing them of devouring their people by their injustices, and a sentence (v. 4), according to which they are abandoned by God. **5–8:** The second

judgment speech, directed to false *prophets*, indicts them for accepting bribes to give favorable prophecies (v. 5). The sentence by which they are blocked from receiving further revelations (vv. 6–7) is contrasted with Micah's own power to preach (v. 8). **9–12:** The third judgment speech indicts Jerusalem's political and religious leaders alike: its political *rulers,* its *priests,* and its *prophets* (vv. 9–11). The sentence Micah announces, the fall of *Jerusalem* (v. 12), sets him off from his contemporary Isaiah, who thought Jerusalem would be threatened but not conquered (Isa 29.1–8). Jerusalem in fact survived the Assyrian invasion and did not fall during Micah's career. Nearly a hundred years later, when the prophet Jeremiah also predicted the fall of Jerusalem and was about to be sentenced to death for his prediction, Micah's prophecy was recalled in Jeremiah's defense (Jer 26.16–19).

4 In days to come
   the mountain of the LORD's house
shall be established as the highest of the
    mountains,
   and shall be raised up above
    the hills.
Peoples shall stream to it,
2   and many nations shall come
    and say:
"Come, let us go up to the mountain of
    the LORD,
   to the house of the God of Jacob;
that he may teach us his ways
   and that we may walk in his paths."
For out of Zion shall go forth
    instruction,
   and the word of the LORD
    from Jerusalem.
3 He shall judge between many peoples,
   and shall arbitrate between strong
    nations far away;
they shall beat their swords into
    plowshares,
   and their spears into pruning
    hooks;
nation shall not lift up sword against
    nation,
   neither shall they learn war
    any more;
4 but they shall all sit under their own
    vines and under their own fig
    trees,
   and no one shall make them afraid;

for the mouth of the LORD of hosts
    has spoken.

5 For all the peoples walk,
    each in the name of its god,
but we will walk in the name of the
    LORD our God
    forever and ever.

4.1–5: God rules from Jerusalem. This begins a new collection of speeches (chs. 4–5) that announce salvation rather than judgment. They stress the return of the Israelite exiles and the restoration of Jerusalem to its former power and prestige. This same speech, celebrating God's rule over the nations in an era of universal disarmament, is preserved also among the speeches of Micah's contemporary Isaiah (2.1–5). **1:** The *mountain* on which the Temple★ in Jerusalem is located is in reality overshadowed by higher peaks in the vicinity.

~~~~~~~~~~~~~~~~~~~~~~~~~~~~~~~~~

6 In that day, says the LORD,
    I will assemble the lame
and gather those who have been driven
        away,
    and those whom I have afflicted.
7 The lame I will make the remnant,
    and those who were cast off, a strong
        nation;
and the LORD will reign over them in
        Mount Zion
    now and forevermore.

8 And you, O tower of the flock,
    hill of daughter Zion,
to you it shall come,
    the former dominion shall come,
    the sovereignty of daughter
        Jerusalem.

9 Now why do you cry aloud?
    Is there no king in you?
Has your counselor perished,
    that pangs have seized you like a
        woman in labor?
10 Writhe and groan,*a* O daughter Zion,
    like a woman in labor;
for now you shall go forth from
        the city
    and camp in the open country;
    you shall go to Babylon.

There you shall be rescued,
    there the LORD will redeem you
    from the hands of your enemies.

11 Now many nations
    are assembled against you,
saying, "Let her be profaned,
    and let our eyes gaze upon Zion."
12 But they do not know
    the thoughts of the LORD;
they do not understand his plan,
    that he has gathered them as sheaves
        to the threshing floor.
13 Arise and thresh,
    O daughter Zion,
for I will make your horn iron
    and your hoofs bronze;
you shall beat in pieces many peoples,
    and shall*b* devote their gain to the
        LORD,
    their wealth to the Lord of the whole
        earth.

5 *c*Now you are walled around with
    a wall;*d*
    siege is laid against us;
with a rod they strike the ruler of Israel
    upon the cheek.

4.6–5.1: God gathers the exiles to Jerusalem. 6: This characterization of the returning exiles as *lame* recalls other exilic descriptions of them as similarly disabled (Zeph 3.19–20; Isa 35.5–10). **8:** The phrase *former dominion* looks back to the time of the prophet Micah when Jerusalem was capital of an independent kingdom. **9–10:** The image of *a woman in labor*, commonly used to describe excruciating pain, is also employed by Jeremiah to describe the suffering of the exiles (30.1–7). **10:** *Babylon* is the Mesopotamian city to which Jerusalem's leaders were deported when the city fell to the Babylonians in 587 BCE. **13:** The image of an ox threshing★ grain is used to describe God's judgment of the nations that have oppressed and exiled the Israelites (Isa 41.14–16).

~~~~~~~~~~~~~~~~~~~~~~~~~~~~~~~~~

2 *e*But you, O Bethlehem of Ephrathah,
    who are one of the little clans
        of Judah,

a Meaning of Heb uncertain   *b* Gk Syr Tg: Heb *and I will*   *c* Ch 4.14 in Heb   *d* Cn Compare Gk: Meaning of Heb uncertain   *e* Ch 5.1 in Heb

from you shall come forth for me
  one who is to rule in Israel,
whose origin is from of old,
  from ancient days.
3 Therefore he shall give them up until
    the time
  when she who is in labor has brought
    forth;
then the rest of his kindred shall
    return
  to the people of Israel.
4 And he shall stand and feed his flock in
    the strength of the LORD,
  in the majesty of the name of the
    LORD his God.
And they shall live secure, for now he
    shall be great
  to the ends of the earth;
5 and he shall be the one of peace.

5.2–5a: A new ruler. 2: By associating the new ruler over a restored Israel with *Bethlehem*, David's home town, and with *Ephrathah*, David's clan* (1 Sam 17.12), the author announces that the coming ruler will revive the dynasty* of David, which ruled in Jerusalem before it fell to the Babylonians in 587 BCE.

If the Assyrians come into our land
  and tread upon our soil,[a]
we will raise against them seven
    shepherds
  and eight installed as rulers.
6 They shall rule the land of Assyria with
    the sword,
  and the land of Nimrod with the
    drawn sword;[b]
they[c] shall rescue us from the Assyrians
  if they come into our land
  or tread within our border.

7 Then the remnant of Jacob,
  surrounded by many peoples,
shall be like dew from the LORD,
  like showers on the grass,
which do not depend upon people
  or wait for any mortal.
8 And among the nations the remnant of
    Jacob,
  surrounded by many peoples,
shall be like a lion among the animals of
    the forest,

like a young lion among the flocks of
    sheep,
which, when it goes through,
    treads down
  and tears in pieces, with no one to
    deliver.
9 Your hand shall be lifted up over your
    adversaries,
  and all your enemies shall be cut off.

10 In that day, says the LORD,
  I will cut off your horses from among
    you
  and will destroy your chariots;
11 and I will cut off the cities of your
    land
  and throw down all your strongholds;
12 and I will cut off sorceries from your
    hand,
  and you shall have no more
    soothsayers;
13 and I will cut off your images
  and your pillars from among you,
and you shall bow down no more
  to the work of your hands;
14 and I will uproot your sacred poles[d]
    from among you
  and destroy your towns.
15 And in anger and wrath I will execute
    vengeance
  on the nations that did not obey.

5.5b–15: Israel will be restored and its oppressors punished. 5–6: The *Assyrians* conquered the northern kingdom of Israel with its capital Samaria in 721 BCE. *Nimrod* was a legendary Assyrian ruler (Gen 10.8–12). **10–15:** It is unclear whether this judgment is intended for Israel or its enemies: The pronoun *you* appears to refer to Israel as it does in v. 9 and the content is typical of judgments on Israel, but the context of Israel's restoration and the reference to Israel's enemies in vv. 9 and 15 imply that this judgment is directed to them.

6 Hear what the LORD says:
  Rise, plead your case before
    the mountains,
  and let the hills hear your voice.

---

a Gk: Heb *in our palaces*   b Cn: Heb *in its entrances*
c Heb *he*   d Heb *Asherim*

2 Hear, you mountains, the controversy of
the LORD,
    and you enduring foundations of the
    earth;
for the LORD has a controversy with his
people,
    and he will contend with Israel.

3 "O my people, what have I done
to you?
    In what have I wearied you? Answer
    me!
4 For I brought you up from the land of
Egypt,
    and redeemed you from the house of
    slavery;
and I sent before you Moses,
    Aaron, and Miriam.
5 O my people, remember now what King
Balak of Moab devised,
    what Balaam son of Beor answered
    him,
and what happened from Shittim
    to Gilgal,
    that you may know the saving acts of
    the LORD."

6 "With what shall I come before
the LORD,
    and bow myself before God on
    high?
Shall I come before him with
    burnt offerings,
    with calves a year old?
7 Will the LORD be pleased with
    thousands of rams,
    with ten thousands of rivers of oil?
Shall I give my firstborn for my
    transgression,
    the fruit of my body for the sin of my
    soul?"
8 He has told you, O mortal, what
    is good;
and what does the LORD require
    of you
but to do justice, and to love kindness,
    and to walk humbly with your God?

message to Israel as a lawsuit brought against the people. **1:** Elements of nature, like the *mountains* here,
are often called to witness solemn announcements
(1.2; Deut 32.1). **4:** *Moses, Aaron,* and *Miriam* were
Israel's leaders at the time of the exodus from *Egypt*
(Ex 4.10–17; 15.20–21). **5:** *King Balak of Moab* paid
Balaam son of Beor to curse the Israelites before they
entered Canaan, but God intervened (Num 22). The
Israelites passed *from Shittim to Gilgal* when they
crossed the Jordan River to enter the land of Canaan
(Josh 3–4). **6–8:** Like other prophets* (Am 5.21–24),
Micah asserts that religious rituals are meaningless
without the pursuit of justice in all areas of life (see
sidebar on p. 1205).

9 The voice of the LORD cries to the city
    (it is sound wisdom to fear
    your name):
Hear, O tribe and assembly of the
    city!ᵃ
10   Can I forgetᵇ the treasures of
    wickedness in the house of the
    wicked,
    and the scant measure that is
    accursed?
11 Can I tolerate wicked scales
    and a bag of dishonest weights?
12 Yourᶜ wealthy are full of violence;
    yourᵈ inhabitants speak lies,
    with tongues of deceit in
    their mouths.
13 Therefore I have begunᵉ to strike you
    down,
    making you desolate because of your
    sins.
14 You shall eat, but not be satisfied,
    and there shall be a gnawing hunger
    within you;
you shall put away, but not save,
    and what you save, I will hand over to
    the sword.
15 You shall sow, but not reap;
    you shall tread olives, but not anoint
    yourselves with oil;
    you shall tread grapes, but not drink
    wine.

6.1–8: God demands justice above all. This speech,
beginning the second collection from the eighth-
century prophet Micah (6.1–7.7), describes God's

a Cn Compare Gk: Heb *tribe, and who has appointed it
yet?*   *b* Cn: Meaning of Heb uncertain
c Heb *Whose*   *d* Heb *whose*   *e* Gk Syr Vg: Heb *have
made sick*

"What does the LORD require of you?"

Micah 6.8 is a concise summary of prophetic thought, based on three important Hebrew terms. The first, "mishpat," *justice*, is the basic word used by Israel's prophets to describe the fairness and equality they believed should govern all social relationships (Isa 1.27; Am 5.24). The second, "hesed," usually translated *kindness* (as here) or "mercy," is better translated "loyalty" or "integrity," since the word describes fulfilling one's social obligations responsibly. The third, "hatsnea' lekhet," *to walk humbly*, describes a way of life directly opposed to the exploitation of power that Micah sees as the root of the corruption and injustice in his society (1.5; 3.11; 7.3).

16 For you have kept the statutes of Omri[a]
    and all the works of the house
        of Ahab,
    and you have followed their counsels.
Therefore I will make you a desolation,
    and your[b] inhabitants an object
        of hissing;
    so you shall bear the scorn of
        my people.

6.9–16: Judgment on Israel's businessmen. Micah resumes his attack on Israel's leadership, indicting its wealthy citizens for cheating the poor (vv. 9–12) and imposing a sentence by which they will be unable to enjoy the profits they have earned unfairly (vv. 13–16). **11:** Merchants use false *weights* to shortchange customers (Am 8.5). **16:** *Omri* and *Ahab* were the first two kings of a dynasty that ruled Samaria for 131 years (876–745 BCE).

7 Woe is me! For I have become like
    one who,
    after the summer fruit has
        been gathered,
    after the vintage has been gleaned,
finds no cluster to eat;
    there is no first-ripe fig for which I
        hunger.
2 The faithful have disappeared from the
        land,
    and there is no one left who
        is upright;
they all lie in wait for blood,
    and they hunt each other with nets.
3 Their hands are skilled to do evil;

the official and the judge ask for a
        bribe,
and the powerful dictate what
        they desire;
    thus they pervert justice.[c]
4 The best of them is like a brier,
    the most upright of them a
        thorn hedge.
The day of their[d] sentinels, of their[d]
        punishment, has come;
    now their confusion is at hand.
5 Put no trust in a friend,
    have no confidence in a loved one;
guard the doors of your mouth
    from her who lies in your embrace;
6 for the son treats the father with
        contempt,
    the daughter rises up against
        her mother,
the daughter-in-law against her
        mother-in-law;
    your enemies are members of your
        own household.
7 But as for me, I will look to the LORD,
    I will wait for the God of my
        salvation;
    my God will hear me.

7.1–7: "The powerful dictate what they desire" **(v. 3).** From the opening speech, in which Micah singles out for criticism the capitals of Israel and Judah, to this concluding speech (7.8–20 is an exilic supple-

a Gk Syr Vg Tg: Heb *the statutes of Omri are kept*
b Heb *its*   c Cn: Heb *they weave it*   d Heb *your*

ment), the abuse of power is a central concern in Micah's message. In this speech, Micah laments the spread of corruption from the powerful (vv. 1–4) to friend and family (vv. 5–6).

8 Do not rejoice over me, O my enemy;
    when I fall, I shall rise;
when I sit in darkness,
    the LORD will be a light to me.
9 I must bear the indignation of
        the LORD,
    because I have sinned against him,
until he takes my side
    and executes judgment for me.
He will bring me out to the light;
    I shall see his vindication.
10 Then my enemy will see,
    and shame will cover her who said
        to me,
    "Where is the LORD your God?"
My eyes will see her downfall;*a*
    now she will be trodden down
    like the mire of the streets.

11 A day for the building of your walls!
    In that day the boundary shall be far
        extended.
12 In that day they will come to you
    from Assyria to*b* Egypt,
and from Egypt to the River,
    from sea to sea and from mountain to
        mountain.
13 But the earth will be desolate
    because of its inhabitants,
    for the fruit of their doings.

14 Shepherd your people with your staff,
    the flock that belongs to you,
which lives alone in a forest
    in the midst of a garden land;
let them feed in Bashan and Gilead
    as in the days of old.
15 As in the days when you came out of
        the land of Egypt,
    show us*c* marvelous things.

16 The nations shall see and be ashamed
    of all their might;
they shall lay their hands on
    their mouths;
    their ears shall be deaf;
17 they shall lick dust like a snake,
    like the crawling things of the earth;
they shall come trembling out of their
        fortresses;
    they shall turn in dread to the LORD
        our God,
    and they shall stand in fear of you.

18 Who is a God like you, pardoning
        iniquity
    and passing over the transgression
    of the remnant of your*d* possession?
He does not retain his anger forever,
    because he delights in showing
        clemency.
19 He will again have compassion upon us;
    he will tread our iniquities under foot.
You will cast all our*e* sins
    into the depths of the sea.
20 You will show faithfulness to Jacob
    and unswerving loyalty to Abraham,
as you have sworn to our ancestors
    from the days of old.

7.8–20: Israel is pardoned and restored. Like the speeches in chs. 4–5, this speech addresses the plight of the exiles after the fall of Jerusalem in 587 BCE. **11:** *The building of your walls* anticipates the reconstruction of Jerusalem. **12:** The surrounding nations will recognize Jerusalem's new stature (4.1–5). **14:** *Bashan* and *Gilead*, east of the Jordan, were prime pasture land. **15:** The return from Babylonian captivity is viewed as a second Exodus, an event as significant as the first deliverance from slavery (Isa 51.9–11).

---

a Heb lacks *downfall*   b One Ms: MT *Assyria and cities of*   c Cn: Heb *I will show him*   d Heb *his*
e Gk Syr Vg Tg: Heb *their*

NAHUM

Introduction

Like the speeches of the prophet* Obadiah, Nahum's speeches are directed entirely to one of Israel's neighbors rather than to Israel itself. The object of Nahum's speeches is Nineveh, the capital city of the Assyrian empire for almost a hundred years, and the subject of his speeches is God's judgment on this city for its cruel treatment of its neighbors. Feelings of anger and vengeance run through the book (1.2, 6) together with a delight in the complete devastation of the city (3.19). Yet behind these emotions lies a belief in God's just government of world affairs. Assyria was an ancient superpower that had dominated its smaller, weaker neighbors through policies of colonial expansion and heavy taxation. Thus its demise was viewed by citizens of its satellite countries, such as Israel and Judah, as just punishment for its oppressive exploitation (2.10–13) and as a time of new freedom (1.12–13) and economic and religious revival (1.15; 2.2).

Nineveh, an ancient and powerful Assyrian city, became capital of the Assyrian empire during the reign of Sennacherib (704–681 BCE). It was, thereafter, the chief Assyrian city and a symbol of the empire itself, until it fell to the armies of the Medes and the Babylonians in 612 BCE. It was not long before Nineveh's fall that these speeches predicting its end were likely composed by the prophet Nahum. This distinguishes Nahum from the eighth-century prophets, Hosea, Amos, and Micah, who precede him in the collection of Minor Prophets, and it makes him a contemporary of Habakkuk and Zephaniah, who follow.

READING GUIDE

The strong emotions and extended descriptions of destruction in Nahum are best understood if the reader keeps in mind that Nahum was a citizen of a country that had been cruelly oppressed as a result of Nineveh's colonial ambitions.

1 An oracle concerning Nineveh. The book of the vision of Nahum of Elkosh.

2 A jealous and avenging God is
the LORD,
the LORD is avenging and wrathful;
the LORD takes vengeance on his
adversaries
and rages against his enemies.
3 The LORD is slow to anger but great in
power,
and the LORD will by no means clear
the guilty.

His way is in whirlwind and storm,
and the clouds are the dust of
his feet.

4 He rebukes the sea and makes it dry,
and he dries up all the rivers;
Bashan and Carmel wither,
and the bloom of Lebanon fades.
5 The mountains quake before him,
and the hills melt;
the earth heaves before him,
the world and all who live in it.

1.1–5. 1: **Title.** The location of the Judean town *Elkosh* is unknown. **2–8: God's terrifying power.** These verses make up an incomplete acrostic* poem, in which each two-line verse unit begins with the succeeding letter of the Hebrew alphabet.* **2:** The emphasis on the *vengeance* and *wrath* of God at the beginning of Nahum is related to the book's central theme: God's judgment of Nineveh for its cruelties.

3: God often appears in the form of a thunderstorm (Ex 19.16–17; Ps 77.17–18). **4:** The traditional enemy of the storm god in ancient Near Eastern mythology is the *sea* (alias river), a tradition reflected at points in biblical thought (Ps 89.9–10; Hab 3.8, 15). **4–5:** God's appearance shakes the world of nature (Am 1.2; Mic 1.3–4). *Bashan,* the highlands east of the Jordan, *Carmel,* the mountain range touching the Mediterranean Sea in northern Israel, and *Lebanon,* the coastal range north of Israel, were famous for their elevation and natural vegetation.

6 Who can stand before his indignation?
    Who can endure the heat of
        his anger?
    His wrath is poured out like fire,
        and by him the rocks are broken in
            pieces.
7 The LORD is good,
    a stronghold in a day of trouble;
    he protects those who take refuge
        in him,
8   even in a rushing flood.
    He will make a full end of his
        adversaries,[a]
    and will pursue his enemies into
        darkness.
9 Why do you plot against the LORD?
    He will make an end;
    no adversary will rise up twice.
10 Like thorns they are entangled,
    like drunkards they are drunk;
    they are consumed like dry straw.
11 From you one has gone out
    who plots evil against the LORD,
    one who counsels wickedness.

12 Thus says the LORD,
    "Though they are at full strength
        and many,[b]
    they will be cut off and pass away.
    Though I have afflicted you,
    I will afflict you no more.
13 And now I will break off his yoke
        from you
    and snap the bonds that bind you."

14 The LORD has commanded
        concerning you:
    "Your name shall be perpetuated no
        longer;

from the house of your gods I will
    cut off
    the carved image and the cast image.
I will make your grave, for you
    are worthless."

15c Look! On the mountains the feet of one
    who brings good tidings,
    who proclaims peace!
Celebrate your festivals, O Judah,
    fulfill your vows,
for never again shall the wicked
    invade you;
    they are utterly cut off.

2 A shatterer[d] has come up against you.
    Guard the ramparts;
    watch the road;
    gird your loins;
    collect all your strength.

1.9–15: Nineveh will be judged and Judah restored. The audience shifts repeatedly in this brief speech from Nineveh to Judah and back again. **9:** Nahum addresses the Ninevites (*you* is masculine plural in Hebrew). **10:** *Thorns* (Isa 34.13), *drunkards* (Lam 4.21), and stubble (Ob 18) are all images used for enemies whom God punishes. **11:** Nahum addresses the city of Nineveh (*you* is now feminine singular) and describes its king as *one who has gone out.* **12–13:** While *you* is still feminine singular in form, Nahum is now addressing Judah, describing its new freedom from Assyrian control as a release from imprisonment. **14:** Nahum turns to address the Assyrian king (*you* is now masculine singular). **15:** The poem concludes with words of hope to *Judah,* delivered by a member of the heavenly court.

2 (For the LORD is restoring the majesty
        of Jacob,
    as well as the majesty of Israel,
    though ravagers have ravaged them
        and ruined their branches.)

3 The shields of his warriors are red;
    his soldiers are clothed in crimson.
The metal on the chariots flashes
    on the day when he musters them;
    the chargers[e] prance.

a Gk: Heb *of her place*   b Meaning of Heb uncertain
c Ch 2.1 in Heb   d Cn: Heb *scatterer*
e Cn Compare Gk Syr: Heb *cypresses*

4 The chariots race madly through the
        streets,
    they rush to and fro through
            the squares;
their appearance is like torches,
    they dart like lightning.
5 He calls his officers;
    they stumble as they come forward;
they hasten to the wall,
    and the mantelet*a* is set up.
6 The river gates are opened,
    the palace trembles.
7 It is decreed*a* that the city*b* be exiled,
    its slave women led away,
moaning like doves
    and beating their breasts.
8 Nineveh is like a pool
    whose waters*c* run away.
    "Halt! Halt!"—
    but no one turns back.
9 "Plunder the silver,
    plunder the gold!
There is no end of treasure!
    An abundance of every precious
            thing!"

2.1–3.7: Nineveh is attacked. The detailed descriptions of a military assault on Nineveh and of battles in
its streets anticipate the imminent end of the city. **2.1:**
The *shatterer* (or "scatterer"; see note *d*) is the enemy
army attacking Nineveh. **2:** This verse appears to be
out of place, as the parentheses added by the translators indicate. It describes the restoration of Judah,
interrupting the narrative* of the attack on Nineveh.
It probably once followed 1.15 or is a later scribal addition. **3–5:** The description of the army attacking Nineveh continues from v. 1. **5:** The Hebrew term translated by *mantelet* is a noun from the root, "weave,"
and may be a woven shield to protect soldiers in battle.
6: These *river gates* controlled a network of canals that
brought water into Nineveh from the Tigris and Khoser
rivers nearby. They appear to have been opened by
the enemy to flood the city (v. 8).

---

10 Devastation, desolation, and
        destruction!
    Hearts faint and knees tremble,
all loins quake,
    all faces grow pale!
11 What became of the lions' den,
    the cave*d* of the young lions,

where the lion goes,
    and the lion's cubs, with no one to
            disturb them?
12 The lion has torn enough for
        his whelps
    and strangled prey for his lionesses;
he has filled his caves with prey
    and his dens with torn flesh.

13 See, I am against you, says the LORD
of hosts, and I will burn your*e* chariots in
smoke, and the sword shall devour your
young lions; I will cut off your prey from the
earth, and the voice of your messengers shall
be heard no more.

3 Ah! City of bloodshed,
    utterly deceitful, full of booty—
    no end to the plunder!
2 The crack of whip and rumble of wheel,
    galloping horse and bounding
            chariot!
3 Horsemen charging,
    flashing sword and glittering spear,
piles of dead,
    heaps of corpses,
dead bodies without end—
    they stumble over the bodies!
4 Because of the countless debaucheries
        of the prostitute,
    gracefully alluring, mistress
        of sorcery,
who enslaves*f* nations through her
        debaucheries,
    and peoples through her sorcery,
5 I am against you,
    says the LORD of hosts,
    and will lift up your skirts over your
            face;
and I will let nations look on your
        nakedness
    and kingdoms on your shame.
6 I will throw filth at you
    and treat you with contempt,
    and make you a spectacle.
7 Then all who see you will shrink from
        you and say,

---

a Meaning of Heb uncertain   *b* Heb *it*
c Cn Compare Gk: Heb *a pool, from the days that she has
become, and they*   *d* Cn: Heb *pasture*   *e* Heb *her*
f Heb *sells*

"Nineveh is devastated; who will
    bemoan her?"
Where shall I seek comforters
    for you?

2.10–3.7. 2.11–13: The *lion* is frequently used in the Bible as an image for a king and a royal family (Ezek 19.2–7), in this case for the king of Nineveh filling his caves with plundered prey. **3.1:** The *City of bloodshed* is Nineveh. **4–7:** Nahum now takes up the image of a *prostitute* to describe Nineveh. *Nakedness* and the accompanying *shame* are traditional punishments for promiscuous behavior (Isa 47.3; Jer 13.26).

~~~~~~~~~~

8 Are you better than Thebes[a]
        that sat by the Nile,
    with water around her,
        her rampart a sea,
        water her wall?
9 Ethiopia[b] was her strength,
        Egypt too, and that without limit;
    Put and the Libyans were her[c]
        helpers.

10 Yet she became an exile,
        she went into captivity;
    even her infants were dashed
            in pieces
        at the head of every street;
    lots were cast for her nobles,
        all her dignitaries were bound
            in fetters.
11 You also will be drunken,
        you will go into hiding;[d]
    you will seek
        a refuge from the enemy.
12 All your fortresses are like fig trees
        with first-ripe figs—
    if shaken they fall
        into the mouth of the eater.
13 Look at your troops:
        they are women in your midst.
    The gates of your land
        are wide open to your foes;
    fire has devoured the bars of
        your gates.

14 Draw water for the siege,
        strengthen your forts;
    trample the clay,
        tread the mortar,
        take hold of the brick mold!
15 There the fire will devour you,
        the sword will cut you off.
    It will devour you like the locust.

    Multiply yourselves like the locust,
        multiply like the grasshopper!
16 You increased your merchants
        more than the stars of the heavens.
    The locust sheds its skin and
            flies away.
17 Your guards are like grasshoppers,
        your scribes like swarms[d] of locusts
    settling on the fences
        on a cold day—
    when the sun rises, they fly away;
        no one knows where they have gone.

18 Your shepherds are asleep,
        O king of Assyria;
        your nobles slumber.
    Your people are scattered on the
            mountains
        with no one to gather them.
19 There is no assuaging your hurt,
        your wound is mortal.
    All who hear the news about you
        clap their hands over you.
    For who has ever escaped
        your endless cruelty?

3.8–19: Nineveh's fate is sealed. 8: *Thebes* was the capital of Upper Egypt which, though heavily defended, was destroyed by the Assyrians in 663 BCE. **9:** *Put* is a North African people associated with *Egypt* and *Ethiopia* (Jer 46.8–9). **19:** Nahum's final verse summarizes the image of Nineveh held by all who had suffered as a result of its imperial ambitions.

~~~~~~~~~~

a Heb *No-amon*   *b* Or Nubia; Heb *Cush*
c Gk: Heb *your*   *d* Meaning of Heb uncertain

HABAKKUK

Introduction

The prophet* Habakkuk is primarily concerned about believing in God's just rule over a world that appears to be overwhelmingly unjust. In this regard, he is more like Job and the psalmists who lament undeserved suffering than he is like Israel's other prophets. The book of Habakkuk is organized as a dialogue between the prophet and God, in which Habakkuk twice challenges God's power and plan. To Habakkuk's first complaint about injustices in Judean society (1.2–4), God promises that the guilty will be punished by invading Chaldeans (1.5–11). To Habakkuk's second complaint that the Chaldeans themselves are corrupt (1.12–2.1), God assures Habakkuk that his rule is reliable, and God calls for the righteous to be steadfast (2.2–4). Following this dialogue, a series of sayings describes the suicidal nature of tyranny (2.5–20), confirming the inevitable and just end of oppressive power. The book's concluding hymn (ch. 3) has been interpreted variously as the full description of Habakkuk's vision (2.2), as Habakkuk's prayer that this vision be fulfilled, and as a hymn that later editors added to Habakkuk's speeches to further resolve the dilemma they raise. In any case, the theophany* in this hymn (3.3–15) draws heavily on ancient traditions in which God establishes order in the cosmos by conquering chaos, symbolized by raging seas.

Habakkuk's initial proclamation about injustices in Judean society (1.2–4) and God's announcement of the Chaldean invasion (1.5–11) probably occurred during the violent reign of Jehoiakim (609–598 BCE; 2 Kings 23.36–24.7) before the first Babylonian (Chaldean) invasion of Judah in 597 BCE. Habakkuk's second complaint, and perhaps the arrangement of the dialogues as a whole, logically arises from his firsthand experience of the Babylonians between their first invasion (597) and their final conquest of Judah and destruction of Jerusalem (587). The hymn in ch. 3 may be a very old victory hymn added by Habakkuk's editors after the fall of Jerusalem to reemphasize God's universal rule.

READING GUIDE

The dialogue between Habakkuk and God around which the book is organized can best be followed if the reader keeps in mind the major concern that drives it: believing in God's just rule in an unjust world.

1 The oracle that the prophet Habakkuk saw.

2 O LORD, how long shall I cry for help,
    and you will not listen?
Or cry to you "Violence!"
    and you will not save?
3 Why do you make me see wrongdoing
    and look at trouble?
Destruction and violence are before me;
    strife and contention arise.

4 So the law becomes slack
    and justice never prevails.
The wicked surround the righteous—
    therefore judgment comes forth
        perverted.

1.1–4. 1: Title. The customary information about family, home, and date are not provided for Habakkuk. **2–4: Habakkuk's opening complaint: Judean corruption.** Habakkuk draws attention to crimes in his society, not by an indictment as is customary for Israel's

prophets* (Mic 3.9–12), but by a lament.* His lament begins, as do laments in the Psalms (3, 13), with an address to God (v. 2) followed by a description of distress (vv. 3–4). **3:** *Destruction* (or "plunder") and *violence* are used by other prophets (Am 3.10; Ezek 45.9) to describe the ruthless accumulation of wealth. *Strife* and *contention* describe a breakdown in Judah's legal and judicial systems.

5 Look at the nations, and see!
    Be astonished! Be astounded!
  For a work is being done in your days
    that you would not believe if you were
      told.
6 For I am rousing the Chaldeans,
    that fierce and impetuous nation,
  who march through the breadth of the
      earth
    to seize dwellings not their own.
7 Dread and fearsome are they;
    their justice and dignity proceed from
      themselves.
8 Their horses are swifter than leopards,
    more menacing than wolves at dusk;
    their horses charge.
  Their horsemen come from far away;
    they fly like an eagle swift to devour.
9 They all come for violence,
    with faces pressing*a* forward;
    they gather captives like sand.
10 At kings they scoff,
    and of rulers they make sport.
  They laugh at every fortress,
    and heap up earth to take it.
11 Then they sweep by like the wind;
    they transgress and become guilty;
    their own might is their god!

1.5–11: God's response: a Chaldean invasion. God announces to Habakkuk that Judah's injustices will be punished by means of a foreign nation that will depose its current leadership. **6:** The *Chaldeans* are the Neo-Babylonians, who rose to prominence in the ancient Near East during the reign of Nebuchadnezzar II (605–562 BCE). **8:** The typical ancient Near Eastern military machine was built around horse-drawn chariots and cavalry.

12 Are you not from of old,
    O LORD my God, my Holy One?
  You*b* shall not die.

O LORD, you have marked them for
      judgment;
  and you, O Rock, have established
    them for punishment.
13 Your eyes are too pure to behold evil,
    and you cannot look on wrongdoing;
  why do you look on the treacherous,
    and are silent when the wicked
      swallow
  those more righteous than they?
14 You have made people like the fish of
      the sea,
    like crawling things that have
      no ruler.
15 The enemy*c* brings all of them up with
      a hook;
  he drags them out with his net,
    he gathers them in his seine;
    so he rejoices and exults.
16 Therefore he sacrifices to his net
    and makes offerings to his seine;
  for by them his portion is lavish,
    and his food is rich.
17 Is he then to keep on emptying his net,
    and destroying nations without
      mercy?

1.12–2.1: Habakkuk's second complaint: Chaldean corruption. In his second complaint—probably composed after the Babylonians invaded Judah in 597, replaced its king, deported its leading citizens, and collected tribute (2 Kings 24)—Habakkuk claims that the very instruments of God's *judgment* (v. 12), the Babylonians, are themselves *wicked* (v. 13). **16:** When the Babylonian enemy *sacrifices to his net*, he is worshipping his own military armaments. **1.17–2.1:** Habakkuk wonders whether the Babylonians' injustices will go unpunished (1.17) or whether God will respond (2.1).

2 I will stand at my watchpost,
    and station myself on the rampart;
  I will keep watch to see what he will say
      to me,
    and what he*d* will answer concerning
      my complaint.

a Meaning of Heb uncertain   *b* Ancient Heb tradition: MT *We*   *c* Heb *He*   *d* Syr: Heb *I*

2 Then the LORD answered me and said:
Write the vision;
    make it plain on tablets,
    so that a runner may read it.
3 For there is still a vision for the
        appointed time;
    it speaks of the end, and does not lie.
If it seems to tarry, wait for it;
    it will surely come, it will not delay.
4 Look at the proud!
    Their spirit is not right in them,
    but the righteous live by their faith.^a
5 Moreover, wealth^b is treacherous;
    the arrogant do not endure.
They open their throats wide as Sheol;
    like Death they never have enough.
They gather all nations for themselves,
    and collect all peoples as their own.

2.2–4: God's response: God's rule is reliable. 2: God tells Habakkuk to record his revelation so that the prophet as God's messenger can carry and announce it to the people. **3:** God emphasizes the reliability of Habakkuk's revelation. **4:** This verse may contain the content of Habakkuk's revelation or instructions about waiting for it. The main point is that *the righteous live by their faith.* ''Faithfulness'' (see note *a*) is a better translation, since the Hebrew ''emunah'' means ''firmness, steadfastness,'' or ''fidelity.''

6 Shall not everyone taunt such people
and, with mocking riddles, say about them,
    "Alas for you who heap up what is not
            your own!"
    How long will you load yourselves
        with goods taken in pledge?
7 Will not your own creditors suddenly
        rise,
    and those who make you tremble
        wake up?
    Then you will be booty for them.
8 Because you have plundered many
        nations,
    all that survive of the peoples shall
        plunder you—
because of human bloodshed, and
        violence to the earth,
    to cities and all who live in them.

9 "Alas for you who get evil gain for your
        houses,

setting your nest on high
    to be safe from the reach of harm!"
10 You have devised shame for your house
    by cutting off many peoples;
    you have forfeited your life.
11 The very stones will cry out from the
        wall,
    and the plaster^c will respond from
        the woodwork.

12 "Alas for you who build a town by
        bloodshed,
    and found a city on iniquity!"
13 Is it not from the LORD of hosts
    that peoples labor only to feed the
        flames,
    and nations weary themselves for
        nothing?
14 But the earth will be filled
    with the knowledge of the glory of
        the LORD,
    as the waters cover the sea.

15 "Alas for you who make your neighbors
        drink,
    pouring out your wrath^d until they
        are drunk,
    in order to gaze on their
        nakedness!"
16 You will be sated with contempt instead
        of glory.
    Drink, you yourself, and stagger!^e
The cup in the LORD's right hand
    will come around to you,
    and shame will come upon
        your glory!
17 For the violence done to Lebanon will
        overwhelm you;
    the destruction of the animals will
        terrify you—^f
because of human bloodshed and
        violence to the earth,
    to cities and all who live in them.

18 What use is an idol
    once its maker has shaped it—
    a cast image, a teacher of lies?

---

a Or *faithfulness*   *b* Other Heb Mss read *wine*
c Or *beam*   *d* Or *poison*   *e* Q Ms Gk: MT *be*
uncircumcised   *f* Gk Syr: Meaning of Heb uncertain

For its maker trusts in what has been
made,
though the product is only an idol
that cannot speak!
19 Alas for you who say to the wood,
"Wake up!"
to silent stone, "Rouse yourself!"
Can it teach?
See, it is gold and silver plated,
and there is no breath in it at all.

20 But the LORD is in his holy temple;
let all the earth keep silence before
him!

2.5–20: Five proverbial sayings about the fall of tyrants. These sayings all claim that oppressors, like the Babylonians, will be suitably judged (1.17). In each saying, all of which except the last begin with "Alas," the tyrant experiences a reversal of fortune, as if imperial power has within it the seeds of its own destruction. **5:** The introduction to these sayings describes the insatiable greed of the tyrant. *Sheol*⋆ is the realm of the dead. **6–8:** Stolen wealth will itself be stolen. The Hebrew term translated *creditors* may also mean "debtors," a double meaning intended here. **9–11:** Security will be lost in the very strongholds built to ensure it. **12–14:** The greatest efforts of tyrants are only fuel for the fire. **15–17:** Honor gained by shaming others will itself turn to shame. **18–20:** False gods will fall silent.

〰〰〰〰〰〰〰〰〰〰〰

3 A prayer of the prophet Habakkuk according to Shigionoth.

2 O LORD, I have heard of your renown,
and I stand in awe, O LORD, of your
work.
In our own time revive it;
in our own time make it known;
in wrath may you remember mercy.
3 God came from Teman,
the Holy One from Mount Paran.
Selah
His glory covered the heavens,
and the earth was full of his praise.
4 The brightness was like the sun;
rays came forth from his hand,
where his power lay hidden.
5 Before him went pestilence,
and plague followed close behind.

6 He stopped and shook the earth;
he looked and made the
nations tremble.
The eternal mountains were shattered;
along his ancient pathways
the everlasting hills sank low.
7 I saw the tents of Cushan under
affliction;
the tent-curtains of the land of
Midian trembled.
8 Was your wrath against the rivers,ᵃ
O LORD?
Or your anger against the rivers,ᵃ
or your rage against the sea,ᵇ
when you drove your horses,
your chariots to victory?
9 You brandished your naked bow,
satedᶜ were the arrows at your
command.ᵈ   Selah
You split the earth with rivers.
10 The mountains saw you, and writhed;
a torrent of water swept by;
the deep gave forth its voice.
The sunᵉ raised high its hands;
11 the moonᶠ stood still in its exalted
place,
at the light of your arrows
speeding by,
at the gleam of your flashing spear.
12 In fury you trod the earth,
in anger you trampled nations.
13 You came forth to save your people,
to save your anointed.
You crushed the head of the
wicked house,
laying it bare from foundation
to roof.ᵈ   Selah
14 You pierced with theirᵍ own arrows the
headʰ of his warriors,ⁱ
who came like a whirlwind to
scatter us,ʲ
gloating as if ready to devour the poor
who were in hiding.
15 You trampled the sea with your horses,
churning the mighty waters.

---

a Or *against River*   b Or *against Sea*   c Cn: Heb
oaths   d Meaning of Heb uncertain   e Heb *It*
f Heb *sun, moon*   g Heb *his*   h Or *leader*
i Vg Compare Gk Syr: Meaning of Heb uncertain
j Heb *me*

16 I hear, and I tremble within;
    my lips quiver at the sound.
Rottenness enters into my bones,
    and my steps tremble^a beneath me.
I wait quietly for the day of calamity
    to come upon the people who
        attack us.

17 Though the fig tree does not blossom,
    and no fruit is on the vines;
though the produce of the olive fails,
    and the fields yield no food;
though the flock is cut off from the fold,
    and there is no herd in the stalls,
18 yet I will rejoice in the LORD;
    I will exult in the God of my
        salvation.
19 GOD, the Lord, is my strength;
    he makes my feet like the feet of a
        deer,
    and makes me tread upon the
        heights.^b

To the leader: with stringed^c
    instruments.

3.1–19: A hymn praising God's rule. This hymn describes a theophany,* a direct appearance of God (vv. 3–15), placed in a framework describing the poet's response to it (vv. 2, 16–19). **1:** Though attributing the hymn to Habakkuk, the title contains a musical notation, *according to Shigionoth* (a Hebrew word no longer understood), which is found elsewhere only in Ps 7. Other features of ch. 3 found elsewhere only in the Psalms—the term *Selah* (vv. 3, 9, 13; a Hebrew word no longer understood) and the musical notations in v. 19—suggest that this hymn may once have existed as a psalm, independent of the prophetic book

that it now concludes. **2:** The hymn's introduction and conclusion (vv. 16–19) are composed in the first-person perspective of the poet. **3–15:** The theophany describes God's march into battle (vv. 3–7) and conquest of his enemies (vv. 8–15). **3:** *Teman* and *Mount Paran* refer to a sacred mountain in the southern desert, perhaps to be identified with Mount Sinai (Horeb) and where God appeared to Moses and Israel (Ex 19; Deut 33.2–3). **5:** *Pestilence* and *plague* are divine figures in antiquity; they may be part of the heavenly armies God leads into battle. **7:** *Cushan* and *Midian* are inhabitants of the southern desert where God's march begins. They are shaken together with nature (v. 6) when God appears. **8:** The forces of chaos that challenge God's rule of the world are personified* in ancient mythology as Sea and River, as they may be here (see the alternative translations in notes *a* and *b*). By describing God's enemies here and in v. 15 as *sea* and *river*, the poet claims that God conquers chaotic forces in both cosmic and historical realms. **10–11:** The *sun* and *moon* are heavenly figures who are members of God's armies, like pestilence and plague (v. 5), or are simply startled by God's appearance together with the rest of nature. **13:** The *anointed** is Israel's military or political leader. As note *d* indicates, the Hebrew text of the second half of this verse is difficult. It may also be understood as *laying bare* the body of the *wicked* (Sea/River) from buttocks to neck, thus describing God's defeat of the powers of cosmic chaos as well as Israel's historical enemies. **16–19:** The conclusion resumes the first-person perspective of the introduction (v.2), describing the poet's own awe at God's appearance (v. 16) and joy because of God's victory and rule (vv. 18–19).

---

a Cn Compare Gk: Meaning of Heb uncertain
b Heb *my heights*   *c* Heb *my stringed*

ZEPHANIAH

Introduction

Most distinctive about Zephaniah is the absolute devastation that characterizes his images of God's punishment of the people of Judah and Jerusalem. Like most other prophets,✶ Zephaniah calls attention to the crimes of Judah's leaders, their corruption and idolatry✶ (1.4–9; 3.1–7). And like other prophets, he anticipates and announces an impending disaster brought on Judah by God to punish it for its crimes (1.2–2.3). But Zephaniah's description of this disaster, called by him "the day of the LORD," is unmatched in its intensity. The disaster is so sweeping and unbounded that nothing can survive it (1.2–3, 18). Two other kinds of material found in Zephaniah are typical of prophetic books. One is a collection of judgment speeches against Judah's neighbors (2.4–15; Am 1.3–2.3); the other is a speech announcing the restoration of Judah and the return of its exiles (3.8–20; Mic 4.6–13).

The title of Zephaniah's prophecy places his ministry during the reign of Josiah, who governed the southern kingdom of Judah during 640–609 BCE, not long before its fall in 587 BCE. Zephaniah's protest against the worship of other gods and his condemnation of foreign practices (1.4–9) may indicate that he preached during the height of Assyrian influence in the early years of Josiah's reign, before Josiah initiated the reforms recorded by Israel's historians (1 Kings 22.1–23.30). Such a date would make Zephaniah a contemporary of Jeremiah, who also predicted the fall of Judah and Jerusalem (Jer 7). The conclusion of the book of Zephaniah (3.8–20), if not from Zephaniah himself, was added by editors after Judah's fall to announce hope for its survivors and exiles.

READING GUIDE

Zephaniah's criticism of Jerusalem (3.1–7) is directly related to his announcement of judgment on Judah and Jerusalem (1.2–2.3). Supplementing this core of the book are judgments on the nations (2.4–15) and an announcement of Judah's renewal (3.8–20).

1 The word of the LORD that came to Zephaniah son of Cushi son of Gedaliah son of Amariah son of Hezekiah, in the days of King Josiah son of Amon of Judah.

1.1: Title. *Josiah* governed the southern kingdom of Judah during 640–609 BCE (2 Kings 22.1–23.30). *Hezekiah*, Zephaniah's great-great-grandfather, may be the earlier Judean king who governed from 715–687 (2 Kings 18–20).

〰〰〰〰〰〰〰〰

2 I will utterly sweep away everything
    from the face of the earth, says
        the LORD.
3 I will sweep away humans and animals;
    I will sweep away the birds of the air

and the fish of the sea.
    I will make the wicked stumble.*a*
    I will cut off humanity
        from the face of the earth, says
            the LORD.
4 I will stretch out my hand against
        Judah,
    and against all the inhabitants of
        Jerusalem;
    and I will cut off from this place every
            remnant of Baal
    and the name of the idolatrous
        priests;*b*

a Cn: Heb *sea, and those who cause the wicked to stumble*   *b* Compare Gk: Heb *the idolatrous priests with the priests*

5 those who bow down on the roofs
      to the host of the heavens;
   those who bow down and swear to
         the LORD,
      but also swear by Milcom;[a]
6 those who have turned back from
         following the LORD,
      who have not sought the LORD or
         inquired of him.

7 Be silent before the Lord GOD!
      For the day of the LORD is at hand;
   the LORD has prepared a sacrifice,
      he has consecrated his guests.
8 And on the day of the LORD's sacrifice
   I will punish the officials and the king's
         sons
      and all who dress themselves in
         foreign attire.
9 On that day I will punish
      all who leap over the threshold,
   who fill their master's house
      with violence and fraud.

10 On that day, says the LORD,
      a cry will be heard from the Fish Gate,
   a wail from the Second Quarter,
      a loud crash from the hills.
11 The inhabitants of the Mortar wail,
      for all the traders have perished;
   all who weigh out silver are cut off.
12 At that time I will search Jerusalem
         with lamps,
      and I will punish the people
   who rest complacently[b] on their dregs,
      those who say in their hearts,
   "The LORD will not do good,
      nor will he do harm."
13 Their wealth shall be plundered,
      and their houses laid waste.
   Though they build houses,
      they shall not inhabit them;
   though they plant vineyards,
      they shall not drink wine from them.

14 The great day of the LORD is near,
      near and hastening fast;
   the sound of the day of the LORD
         is bitter,
      the warrior cries aloud there.

15 That day will be a day of wrath,
      a day of distress and anguish,
   a day of ruin and devastation,
      a day of darkness and gloom,
   a day of clouds and thick darkness,
16   a day of trumpet blast and battle
         cry
      against the fortified cities
      and against the lofty battlements.

17 I will bring such distress upon people
      that they shall walk like the blind;
   because they have sinned against
         the LORD,
   their blood shall be poured out
         like dust,
      and their flesh like dung.
18 Neither their silver nor their gold
      will be able to save them
      on the day of the LORD's wrath;
   in the fire of his passion
      the whole earth shall be consumed;
   for a full, a terrible end
      he will make of all the inhabitants of
         the earth.

2 Gather together, gather,
      O shameless nation,
2 before you are driven away
      like the drifting chaff,[c]
   before there comes upon you
      the fierce anger of the LORD,
   before there comes upon you
      the day of the LORD's wrath.
3 Seek the LORD, all you humble of the
         land,
      who do his commands;
   seek righteousness, seek humility;
      perhaps you may be hidden
      on the day of the LORD's wrath.
4 For Gaza shall be deserted,
      and Ashkelon shall become a
         desolation;
   Ashdod's people shall be driven out at
         noon,
      and Ekron shall be uprooted.

---

a Gk Mss Syr Vg: Heb *Malcam* (or, *their king*)
b Heb *who thicken*   c Cn Compare Gk Syr: Heb *before
a decree is born; like chaff a day has passed away*

1.2–2.3: The day of the Lord: Judah is judged.
Though Zephaniah does include in this speech an indictment of Judah's sins (1.4–9), as is customary in prophetic judgment speeches, he emphasizes the sentence, God's punishment on Judah and its people. **1.2–3:** This is one of the most desolate images of judgment in prophetic literature (Jer 4.23–26). **4:** *Jerusalem*, the capital city of *Judah*, is singled out for further criticism in 3.1–7. With this mention of *Baal,*⋆ the Canaanite god who is the major rival of Judah's God (Hos 2), Zephaniah begins the indictment of Judah's crimes, focusing on its rejection of Yahweh and its worship of other gods (vv. 4–9). **5:** *The host of the heavens* are the sun, moon, planets, and stars, the worship of which became widespread in Judah under Assyrian influence (2 Kings 21.3–5). *Milcom* is the god of the Ammonites (2.8; 2 Kings 23.13). **7:** Zephaniah introduces the theme of *the day of the Lord* for God's judgment on Judah, a theme that carries this judgment speech forward to its conclusion in 2.3. God's *sacrifice* is not the customary animal sacrifice but God's enemies (Jer 46.10), in this case the people of Judah themselves. **9:** Those *who leap over the threshhold* may be priests practicing a ritual associated with the Philistine god Dagon (1 Sam 5.5). **10:** *The Fish Gate* is located in the north wall of Jerusalem (Neh 12.39). *The Second Quarter* is a district in Jerusalem near the Temple⋆ complex (2 Kings 22.14). **11:** *The Mortar* is Jerusalem's business district. **12:** The phrase "who thicken (note *b;* or *rest complacently) on their dregs*" may be translated: "Who are as undisturbed as the sediment of wine." **18:** While the picture of destruction in this verse appears to include the entire world, Zephaniah's concern is Judah in particular, as the preceding and following verses show. **2.1–3:** Zephaniah's judgment speech concludes with an appeal to Judah (*shameless nation*, v. 1) to *seek the Lord* and reform in order to avert disaster (Am 5.6, 14–15).

5 Ah, inhabitants of the seacoast,
　　you nation of the Cherethites!
　The word of the Lord is against you,
　　O Canaan, land of the Philistines;
　　and I will destroy you until no
　　　　inhabitant is left.
6 And you, O seacoast, shall be pastures,
　　meadows for shepherds
　　and folds for flocks.
7 The seacoast shall become the
　　possession

of the remnant of the house of Judah,
　on which they shall pasture,
and in the houses of Ashkelon
　they shall lie down at evening.
For the Lord their God will be mindful
　　of them
　and restore their fortunes.

8 I have heard the taunts of Moab
　　and the revilings of the Ammonites,
how they have taunted my people
　　and made boasts against
　　　their territory.
9 Therefore, as I live, says the Lord of
　　hosts,
　　the God of Israel,
Moab shall become like Sodom
　　and the Ammonites like Gomorrah,
a land possessed by nettles and salt pits,
　　and a waste forever.
The remnant of my people shall plunder
　　them,
　　and the survivors of my nation shall
　　　possess them.
10 This shall be their lot in return for their
　　　pride,
　　because they scoffed and boasted
　　against the people of the Lord
　　　of hosts.
11 The Lord will be terrible against them;
　　he will shrivel all the gods of
　　　the earth,
and to him shall bow down,
　　each in its place,
　　all the coasts and islands of
　　　the nations.

12 You also, O Ethiopians,ᵃ
　　shall be killed by my sword.

13 And he will stretch out his hand against
　　　the north,
　　and destroy Assyria;
and he will make Nineveh a desolation,
　　a dry waste like the desert.
14 Herds shall lie down in it,
　　every wild animal;ᵇ

___
a Or *Nubians;* Heb *Cushites*　　*b* Tg Compare Gk:
Heb *nation*

the desert owl[a] and the screech owl[a]
    shall lodge on its capitals;
the owl[b] shall hoot at the window,
    the raven[c] croak on the threshold;
    for its cedar work will be laid bare.
15 Is this the exultant city
    that lived secure,
that said to itself,
    "I am, and there is no one else"?
What a desolation it has become,
    a lair for wild animals!
Everyone who passes by it
    hisses and shakes the fist.

2.4–15: The nations are judged. The lengthy speech describing Judah's judgment is followed by a collection of shorter speeches describing judgment on four of Judah's neighbors: Philistia (vv. 4–7), Moab and Ammon (vv. 8–11), Ethiopia (v. 12), and Assyria (vv. 13–15). **4:** *Gaza, Ashkelon, Ashdod,* and *Ekron* are major cities of Philistia, Judah's neighbor on the Mediterranean coast. **5:** *Cherethites* is a synonym for, or a subgroup of, the Philistines, who are associated with Crete, part of the larger Aegean area from which the Philistines came. **8:** *Moab* and *Ammon* are Judah's neighbors east of the Jordan River. **9:** *Sodom* and *Gomorrah* were destroyed by God in a fierce firestorm (Gen 19.12–29) and therefore represent divine judgment. **13:** *Assyria,* with its capital in *Nineveh,* is an ancient Near Eastern superpower that destroyed the northern kingdom of Israel in 721 BCE and dominated the southern kingdom of Judah for a century before Zephaniah's career. **15:** *The exultant city* is Nineveh. The images of its fall here mirror those in the speeches of Nahum.

3 Ah, soiled, defiled,
    oppressing city!
2 It has listened to no voice;
    it has accepted no correction.
It has not trusted in the LORD;
    it has not drawn near to its God.

3 The officials within it
    are roaring lions;
its judges are evening wolves
    that leave nothing until the morning.
4 Its prophets are reckless,
    faithless persons;
its priests have profaned what is sacred,
    they have done violence to the law.

5 The LORD within it is righteous;
    he does no wrong.
Every morning he renders his
        judgment,
    each dawn without fail;
but the unjust knows no shame.

6 I have cut off nations;
    their battlements are in ruins;
I have laid waste their streets
    so that no one walks in them;
their cities have been made desolate,
    without people, without inhabitants.
7 I said, "Surely the city[d] will fear me,
    it will accept correction;
it will not lose sight[e]
    of all that I have brought upon it."
But they were the more eager
    to make all their deeds corrupt.

3.1–7: Jerusalem is indicted. The sins listed here, together with those in 1.4–9, are the basis for the devastating judgment described in 1.2–2.3. **1:** The *oppressing city* is Jerusalem, Judah's capital. **3–4:** While Zephaniah's first indictment of Judah's sins focuses on the worship of other gods (1.4–9), this indictment focuses, as do those of Micah (4.6–8), on Judah's political and religious leadership. **7:** *The city* is Jerusalem.

8 Therefore wait for me, says the LORD,
    for the day when I arise as a witness.
For my decision is to gather nations,
    to assemble kingdoms,
to pour out upon them my indignation,
    all the heat of my anger;
for in the fire of my passion
    all the earth shall be consumed.

9 At that time I will change the speech of
        the peoples
    to a pure speech,
that all of them may call on the name of
        the LORD
    and serve him with one accord.
10 From beyond the rivers of Ethiopia[f]
    my suppliants, my scattered ones,
    shall bring my offering.

---

a Meaning of Heb uncertain   *b* Cn: Heb *a voice*
c Gk Vg: Heb *desolation*   *d* Heb *it*   *e* Gk Syr: Heb
its dwelling will not be cut off   *f* Or *Nubia;* Heb *Cush*

11 On that day you shall not be put
    to shame
      because of all the deeds by which you
      have rebelled against me;
  for then I will remove from your midst
    your proudly exultant ones,
  and you shall no longer be haughty
    in my holy mountain.
12 For I will leave in the midst of you
    a people humble and lowly.
  They shall seek refuge in the name of
    the LORD—
13   the remnant of Israel;
  they shall do no wrong
    and utter no lies,
  nor shall a deceitful tongue
    be found in their mouths.
  Then they will pasture and lie down,
    and no one shall make them afraid.

14 Sing aloud, O daughter Zion;
    shout, O Israel!
  Rejoice and exult with all your heart,
    O daughter Jerusalem!
15 The LORD has taken away the
      judgments against you,
    he has turned away your enemies.
  The king of Israel, the LORD, is in your
      midst;
    you shall fear disaster no more.
16 On that day it shall be said to
    Jerusalem:
  Do not fear, O Zion;
    do not let your hands grow weak.
17 The LORD, your God, is in your midst,
    a warrior who gives victory;
  he will rejoice over you with gladness,
    he will renew you[a] in his love;
  he will exult over you with
    loud singing

18   as on a day of festival.[b]
  I will remove disaster from you,[c]
    so that you will not bear reproach
      for it.
19 I will deal with all your oppressors
    at that time.
  And I will save the lame
    and gather the outcast,
  and I will change their shame
    into praise
    and renown in all the earth.
20 At that time I will bring you home,
    at the time when I gather you;
  for I will make you renowned
    and praised
    among all the peoples of the earth,
  when I restore your fortunes
    before your eyes, says the LORD.

3.8–20: Judah is restored. A major shift occurs here in the book of Zephaniah from the criticism of Judah and announcement of its destruction (1.2–2.3; 3.1–7) to the anticipation of its renewal. Either Zephaniah himself looked forward to a new era after Judah's fall, or this speech was added by Zephaniah's editors after Judah's fall to provide hope to its exiles. The speech shares numerous images with literature composed during and after the Exile* (after 587 BCE). **9:** The expectation of the conversion of the nations is characteristic of exilic literature (Isa 55.4–5; Mic 4.1–2). **11:** *My holy mountain* is the Temple* mount in Jerusalem. **19–20:** The return of Judah's exiles, often pictured as *lame* and *outcast*, was a widespread hope during the Exile and afterwards (Isa 35.5–10; Mic 4.6–8).

---

a Gk Syr: Heb *he will be silent*   b Gk Syr: Meaning of Heb uncertain   c Cn: Heb *I will remove from you; they were*

[1220]   OLD TESTAMENT

HAGGAI

Introduction

Haggai's main concern is the reconstruction of the Temple* in Jerusalem, which was reduced to ruins when Nebuchadnezzar conquered and destroyed Jerusalem in 587 BCE (2 Kings 25). His messages, all delivered in the fall of 520 BCE, make a single point: Judah's poor harvests and depressed economy stem from the people's disregard for their religious life, at the center of which is the Temple. By reconstructing the Temple and its ritual practices the people will again experience the divine blessing of agricultural bounty. The belief that God, preeminently present in the Temple, blessed the righteous with plenty was deeply imbedded in Israelite thought (Ps 36.5–9; Joel 2.18–27).

Haggai, together with Zechariah and Malachi whose prophecies conclude the Minor Prophets, lived in the post-exilic era, the period following the fall of Jerusalem (587 BCE) and the Babylonian exile (587–538), when the entire Near East was under Persian rule.* The policies of the first Persian monarch, Cyrus, allowed exiles to return to their homelands and govern their affairs with some autonomy (see the texts of Cyrus's decree). Many of the events of this era are recorded in the books of Ezra and Nehemiah. It appears from Haggai's speeches, dating to the second year of the reign of Persia's third king Darius (520 BCE), that exiles returning to Judah had rebuilt their own homes (1.4) but—nearly 20 years after Cyrus had allowed their return—had not yet begun the reconstruction of the Temple. This effort, begun as a result of Haggai's preaching (1.12–15), was completed five years later in 515 BCE (Ezra 5.1–2; 6.1–22).

READING GUIDE

The context and mood of Haggai's audience is entirely different from the audience of the pre-exilic prophets* who preceded him, a fact that must be kept in mind when reading his speeches. Whereas earlier prophets spoke to a powerful Israelite and Judean elite who were smug and complacent, Haggai addresses a people who have returned to a ruined land, are no longer in control of their own affairs, and often question whether the renewal of their homeland is a realistic possibility.

1 In the second year of King Darius, in the sixth month, on the first day of the month, the word of the LORD came by the prophet Haggai to Zerubbabel son of Shealtiel, governor of Judah, and to Joshua son of Jehozadak, the high priest: ²Thus says the LORD of hosts: These people say the time has not yet come to rebuild the LORD's house. ³Then the word of the LORD came by the prophet Haggai, saying: ⁴Is it a time for you yourselves to live in your paneled houses, while this house lies in ruins? ⁵Now therefore thus says the LORD of hosts: Consider how you have fared. ⁶You have sown much, and harvested little; you eat, but you never have enough; you drink, but you never have your fill; you clothe yourselves, but no one is warm; and you that earn wages earn wages to put them into a bag with holes.

7 Thus says the LORD of hosts: Consider how you have fared. ⁸Go up to the hills and bring wood and build the house, so that I may take pleasure in it and be honored, says the LORD. ⁹You have looked for much, and, lo, it came to little; and when you brought it home, I blew it away. Why? says the LORD

The Decree of Cyrus

After Cyrus, ruler of the Persian empire, conquered Babylon, he issued a decree that allowed exiles to return to their homelands. Two descriptions of that decree, one Cyrus's own text from the Cyrus Cylinder, and one the biblical text from Ezra 1.2–4, are reprinted here.

(As to the region) from . . . as far as Ashur and Susa, Agade, Eshnunna, the towns Zamban, Me-Turnu, Der as well as the region of the Gutians, I returned to (these) sacred cities on the other side of the Tigris, the sanctuaries of which have been ruins for a long time, the images which (used) to live therein and established for them permanent sanctuaries. I (also) gathered all their (former) inhabitants and returned (to them) their habitations.—From the Cyrus Cylinder

"Thus says King Cyrus of Persia: The LORD, the God of heaven, has given me all the kingdoms of the earth, and he has charged me to build him a house at Jerusalem in Judah. Any of those among you who are of his people—may their God be with them!—are now permitted to go up to Jerusalem in Judah, and rebuild the house of the LORD, the God of Israel—he is the God who is in Jerusalem; and let all survivors, in whatever place they reside, be assisted by the people of their place with silver and gold, with goods and with animals, besides freewill offerings for the house of God in Jerusalem."—Ezra 1.2–4 (NRSV)

of hosts. Because my house lies in ruins, while all of you hurry off to your own houses. ¹⁰Therefore the heavens above you have withheld the dew, and the earth has withheld its produce. ¹¹And I have called for a drought on the land and the hills, on the grain, the new wine, the oil, on what the soil produces, on human beings and animals, and on all their labors.

12 Then Zerubbabel son of Shealtiel, and Joshua son of Jehozadak, the high priest, with all the remnant of the people, obeyed the voice of the LORD their God, and the words of the prophet Haggai, as the LORD their God had sent him; and the people feared the LORD. ¹³Then Haggai, the messenger of the LORD, spoke to the people with the LORD's message, saying, I am with you, says the LORD. ¹⁴And the LORD stirred up the spirit of Zerubbabel son of Shealtiel, governor of Judah, and the spirit of Joshua son of Jehozadak, the high priest, and the spirit of all the remnant of the people; and they came and worked on the house of the LORD of hosts, their God, ¹⁵on the twenty-fourth day of the month, in the sixth month.

1.1–15a: The charge to rebuild the Temple.* Haggai's first speech directs those who have returned to Jerusalem from exile to begin reconstruction of the Temple. **1:** *King Darius* (522–486) is the third monarch of the Persian empire, of which Judah became a province when the Persian king Cyrus conquered Babylon in 538 BCE. The *second year* of Darius's reign is 520 BCE. *Zerubbabel*, grandson of Jehoiachin ("Jeconiah"; 1 Chr 3.16–19), the king of Judah exiled to Babylon in 597 BCE (2 Kings 24.8–17; 25.27–30), had returned to Judah with other exiles (Ezra 2.1–2; see sidebar above). *Joshua's* grandfather Seraiah, chief priest of Jerusalem, was killed when Jerusalem was conquered by the Babylonians (2 Kings 25.18–21), and Joshua's father, *Jehozadak*, was deported to Babylon (1 Chr 6.14–15). **12:** *The remnant of the people* refers to those who had returned to Judah from Babylonian exile (Jer 43.5; see sidebar above).

2 In the second year of King Darius, ¹in the seventh month, on the twenty-first day of the month, the word of the LORD came by the prophet Haggai, saying: ²Speak now to Zerubbabel son of Shealtiel, governor of Judah, and to Joshua son of Jehozadak,

the high priest, and to the remnant of the people, and say, ³Who is left among you that saw this house in its former glory? How does it look to you now? Is it not in your sight as nothing? ⁴Yet now take courage, O Zerubbabel, says the LORD; take courage, O Joshua, son of Jehozadak, the high priest; take courage, all you people of the land, says the LORD; work, for I am with you, says the LORD of hosts, ⁵according to the promise that I made you when you came out of Egypt. My spirit abides among you; do not fear. ⁶For thus says the LORD of hosts: Once again, in a little while, I will shake the heavens and the earth and the sea and the dry land; ⁷and I will shake all the nations, so that the treasure of all nations shall come, and I will fill this house with splendor, says the LORD of hosts. ⁸The silver is mine, and the gold is mine, says the LORD of hosts. ⁹The latter splendor of this house shall be greater than the former, says the LORD of hosts; and in this place I will give prosperity, says the LORD of hosts.

1.15b–2.9: The vision of the new Temple's glory. Haggai encourages those whose first efforts at reconstruction of the Temple* seem insignificant. **2.3:** *Its former glory* recalls the splendor of Solomon's Temple (1 Kings 6), which was destroyed when Jerusalem fell to the Babylonians in 587 BCE (2 Kings 25.9, 13–17). **4:** The *people of the land* may refer to those who had remained in Judah after its conquest by Babylon. **5:** Haggai reminds the people that God delivered them from slavery in *Egypt* (Ex 1–15). **6–7:** Descriptions of Judah's restoration are often accompanied by images of the cosmos in disarray (Isa 51.6) and of the nations bringing tribute to Jerusalem (Isa 45.14).

10 On the twenty-fourth day of the ninth month, in the second year of Darius, the word of the LORD came by the prophet Haggai, saying: ¹¹Thus says the LORD of hosts: Ask the priests for a ruling: ¹²If one carries consecrated meat in the fold of one's garment, and with the fold touches bread, or stew, or wine, or oil, or any kind of food, does it become holy? The priests answered, "No." ¹³Then Haggai said, "If one who is unclean by contact with a dead body touches any of these, does it become unclean?" The priests

answered, "Yes, it becomes unclean." ¹⁴Haggai then said, So is it with this people, and with this nation before me, says the LORD; and so with every work of their hands; and what they offer there is unclean. ¹⁵But now, consider what will come to pass from this day on. Before a stone was placed upon a stone in the LORD's temple, ¹⁶how did you fare?ᵃ When one came to a heap of twenty measures, there were but ten; when one came to the wine vat to draw fifty measures, there were but twenty. ¹⁷I struck you and all the products of your toil with blight and mildew and hail; yet you did not return to me, says the LORD. ¹⁸Consider from this day on, from the twenty-fourth day of the ninth month. Since the day that the foundation of the LORD's temple was laid, consider: ¹⁹Is there any seed left in the barn? Do the vine, the fig tree, the pomegranate, and the olive tree still yield nothing? From this day on I will bless you.

2.10–19: The promise of agricultural bounty. Haggai announces that God will bless the people's work on the Temple by granting them good harvests. **12:** The point of this priestly decision is that holiness cannot be transferred (from *consecrated meat* carried home to eat; Lev 6.26–27; 7.16–17). **13:** The point of this priestly decision is that uncleanness can be transferred (from a "corpse" through a person to other objects; Num 5.1–4). **14:** Both of these previous questions (vv. 12–13) simply set up Haggai's point in this verse: Without a proper worship space, uncleanness has tainted all that the people have done.

20 The word of the LORD came a second time to Haggai on the twenty-fourth day of the month: ²¹Speak to Zerubbabel, governor of Judah, saying, I am about to shake the heavens and the earth, ²²and to overthrow the throne of kingdoms; I am about to destroy the strength of the kingdoms of the nations, and overthrow the chariots and their riders; and the horses and their riders shall fall, every one by the sword of a comrade. ²³On that day, says the LORD of hosts, I will take you, O Zerubbabel my servant, son of Shealtiel, says the LORD, and make you

a Gk: Heb *since they were*

like a signet ring; for I have chosen you, says the LORD of hosts.

2.20–23: The promise to Zerubbabel. The focus shifts from the reconstruction of the Temple to the installation of Zerubbabel as Judah's leader. **21–22:** Descriptions of Judah's restoration are often accompanied by references to the conquest of other nations

(Joel 3). **23:** While *Zerubbabel* is only a governor of Judah (1.1; 2.21) under Persian authority, he is a member of the Davidic family that had ruled Jerusalem (see comment on 1.1), and Haggai may be announcing a greater role for him. Both *my servant* (2 Sam 7.5) and *signet ring* (Jer 22.24) may be royal images anticipating a revival of the Davidic dynasty.*

ZECHARIAH

Introduction

Zechariah, together with his contemporary Haggai, lived in a time of great crisis, the period following the destruction of Jerusalem (587 BCE) and the exile of its leading citizens to Babylon (587–538). Twenty years after the new Persian monarch Cyrus allowed exiles to return to their homelands, Zechariah spoke to those who had returned to the ruins of Judah and Jerusalem, encouraging them not to lose hope. His words of hope emphasize God's control of history and God's plans to restore the fortunes of Judah. In a series of eight visions, which make up the core of Zechariah's prophecy, these themes are elaborated in detail (see sidebar on p. 1230). The first and last visions describe God's universal rule along with the heavenly emissaries who carry out God's plans in the world (1.7–17; 6.1–8). The intervening visions announce the restoration and purification of Judah (1.18–2.5; 5.1–11) and the establishment of a new government in which leadership will be shared by priestly and political officials (chs. 3–4). The aim of these visions is to give the people of Judah confidence in the future and a new religious and political structure within which to build their future. Framing these visions are two speeches (1.1–6; 7.1–8.23) in which Zechariah urges his listeners to build a society more principled and just than their ancestors'.

Appended to the visions and speeches of Zechariah are two prophetic collections (chs. 9–11 and 12–14) that differ in style and content and are believed to have been composed by another prophetic figure or group. These collections lack the specific references to dates and people present in chs. 1–8, are composed in different literary forms and styles, and reflect a crisis in leadership and internal Judean conflicts absent in Zechariah's messages. Two themes dominate chs. 9–14, one unique to this section of the book, the other shared with chs. 1–8. Unique to chs. 9–14 is a criticism of Judah's political leaders, described as shepherds, and of Judah's proph-ets.* Judah's leaders are blamed for exploiting their people (11.4–17) and its prophets for preach-ing lies (13.1–6). Shared with chs. 1–8 is a vision of Judah's restoration, detailed in several lengthy speeches (chs. 9, 10, 12, 14).

The historical period in which Zechariah spoke can be determined precisely by the dates prefixed to the book's major sections (1.1, 7; 7.1). These speeches were all delivered between the years 520 and 518 BCE, the second to the fourth years of rule by the Persian monarch Darius. This was about 20 years after the Persian king Cyrus had conquered Babylon (538 BCE) and issued a decree repatriating exiles and supporting their return to their homelands (see sidebar on p. 1222). Urged by the great exilic prophet Second Isaiah (Isa 40–55), many Judean exiles took this opportunity to return home from Babylon and to begin the reconstruction of Jerusalem and its environs (Ezra 1–5). But the land lay in ruins (2.1–4), and the future did not look bright for those who returned (8.6). In such difficult circumstances Zechariah and his contemporary Haggai spoke, both to instill hope and to urge the people to begin the concrete process of re-building their cities and institutions.

The context of the supplements to Zechariah, chs. 9–14, cannot be determined as precisely as the prophecies of Zechariah themselves, since they contain no specific dates or references to identifiable people or events. They certainly reflect the same general environment in Judah during the post-exilic period. The crisis in leadership they address (11.4–17; 13.1–6), however, may

place these supplements later than chs. 1–8, in a time when the sanctified leadership expected by Zechariah (chs. 3–4) had become corrupt and exploitive.

READING GUIDE

Zechariah should be read as a book in two parts: the visions and speeches of the prophet after whom the book is named (chs. 1–8), and the speeches of an anonymous prophetic figure or group added at a later time (chs. 9–12). Zechariah's own prophecies are best understood when the careful design of his visions, which progressively narrows the reader's focus from the world to Jerusalem, is kept in mind (see sidebar, p. 1230).

1 In the eighth month, in the second year of Darius, the word of the LORD came to the prophet Zechariah son of Berechiah son of Iddo, saying: 2 The LORD was very angry with your ancestors. 3 Therefore say to them, Thus says the LORD of hosts: Return to me, says the LORD of hosts, and I will return to you, says the LORD of hosts. 4 Do not be like your ancestors, to whom the former prophets proclaimed, "Thus says the LORD of hosts, Return from your evil ways and from your evil deeds." But they did not hear or heed me, says the LORD. 5 Your ancestors, where are they? And the prophets, do they live forever? 6 But my words and my statutes, which I commanded my servants the prophets, did they not overtake your ancestors? So they repented and said, "The LORD of hosts has dealt with us according to our ways and deeds, just as he planned to do."

1.1–6: Zechariah's opening speech. Zechariah's visions (1.7–6.8) are introduced and concluded (chs. 7–8) by speeches in which Zechariah urges his listeners to embrace the social responsibilities and just behavior preached by the prophets✶ before him. **1:** Zechariah's opening and closing speeches (1.1; 7.1), together with his visions (1.7), are dated. The *second year of Darius* (522–486 BCE) is 520 BCE, the same year in which Haggai preached (Hag 1.1; 2.1, 10). **4:** The *former prophets* are Zechariah's predecessors who preached before the fall of Jerusalem. Zechariah quotes words similar to Jeremiah's (Jer 25.5).

~~~~~~~~~~~~

7 On the twenty-fourth day of the eleventh month, the month of Shebat, in the second year of Darius, the word of the LORD came to the prophet Zechariah son of Bere-

chiah son of Iddo; and Zechariah[a] said, 8 In the night I saw a man riding on a red horse! He was standing among the myrtle trees in the glen; and behind him were red, sorrel, and white horses. 9 Then I said, "What are these, my lord?" The angel who talked with me said to me, "I will show you what they are." 10 So the man who was standing among the myrtle trees answered, "They are those whom the LORD has sent to patrol the earth." 11 Then they spoke to the angel of the LORD who was standing among the myrtle trees, "We have patrolled the earth, and lo, the whole earth remains at peace." 12 Then the angel of the LORD said, "O LORD of hosts, how long will you withhold mercy from Jerusalem and the cities of Judah, with which you have been angry these seventy years?" 13 Then the LORD replied with gracious and comforting words to the angel who talked with me. 14 So the angel who talked with me said to me, Proclaim this message: Thus says the LORD of hosts; I am very jealous for Jerusalem and for Zion. 15 And I am extremely angry with the nations that are at ease; for while I was only a little angry, they made the disaster worse. 16 Therefore, thus says the LORD, I have returned to Jerusalem with compassion; my house shall be built in it, says the LORD of hosts, and the measuring line shall be stretched out over Jerusalem. 17 Proclaim further: Thus says the LORD of hosts: My cities shall again overflow with prosperity; the LORD will again comfort Zion and again choose Jerusalem.

a Heb *and he*

1.7–17: The first vision: The heavenly horsemen and God's plans for Jerusalem. This is the first of eight visions that make up the core of Zechariah's prophecy. **7:** The chronological notice dates the entire vision complex three months later than Zechariah's opening speech, or early in 519 BCE. **8:** These horsemen are God's heavenly patrol, keeping watch over the world's affairs (v. 10). The significance of the horses' colors is uncertain, but the number four represents totality. **11:** *Peace* in this case is undesirable, since the plight of Jerusalem remains unchanged. **12:** The Babylonian exile lasted only 50 years (587–538 BCE), not *seventy,* but Jeremiah mentions a 70-year period of servitude to Babylon (Jer 25.11–12), to which Zechariah may be referring. **16:** The rebuilding of the Temple* is the central concern of Zechariah's contemporary Haggai.

18ᵃ And I looked up and saw four horns. 19I asked the angel who talked with me, "What are these?" And he answered me, "These are the horns that have scattered Judah, Israel, and Jerusalem." 20Then the LORD showed me four blacksmiths. 21And I asked, "What are they coming to do?" He answered, "These are the horns that scattered Judah, so that no head could be raised; but these have come to terrify them, to strike down the horns of the nations that lifted up their horns against the land of Judah to scatter its people."ᵇ

1.18–21: The second vision: The four horns and Judah's security. 18: The *horn,* a symbol of power (Ps 18.2), represents the strength of the nations that have conquered and exiled the Israelite people. The number four probably represents totality rather than specific countries. **20–21:** The *four blacksmiths* strike off the horns, thus putting an end to the power of the nations to dominate Judah.

2ᶜI looked up and saw a man with a measuring line in his hand. 2Then I asked, "Where are you going?" He answered me, "To measure Jerusalem, to see what is its width and what is its length." 3Then the angel who talked with me came forward, and another angel came forward to meet him, 4and said to him, "Run, say to that young man: Jerusalem shall be inhabited like villages without walls, because of the multitude of people and animals in it. 5For I will be a wall of fire all around it, says the LORD, and I will be the glory within it."

2.1–5: The third vision: The measuring line and Jerusalem's resettlement. 1: The *man with a measuring line* is a surveyor making preparations for rebuilding Jerusalem. **5:** God, not its walls (v. 4), will protect Jerusalem.

6 Up, up! Flee from the land of the north, says the LORD; for I have spread you abroad like the four winds of heaven, says the LORD. 7Up! Escape to Zion, you that live with daughter Babylon. 8For thus said the LORD of hosts (after his gloryᵈ sent me) regarding the nations that plundered you: Truly, one who touches you touches the apple of my eye.ᵉ 9See now, I am going to raiseᶠ my hand against them, and they shall become plunder for their own slaves. Then you will know that the LORD of hosts has sent me. 10Sing and rejoice, O daughter Zion! For lo, I will come and dwell in your midst, says the LORD. 11Many nations shall join themselves to the LORD on that day, and shall be my people; and I will dwell in your midst. And you shall know that the LORD of hosts has sent me to you. 12The LORD will inherit Judah as his portion in the holy land, and will again choose Jerusalem.

13 Be silent, all people, before the LORD; for he has roused himself from his holy dwelling.

2.6–13: A charge to the exiles. A brief speech, urging Judah's exiles to return from exile in Babylon, interrupts the sequence of visions. **7:** Babylon is the city to which the majority of Judah's exiles were deported (2 Kings 24.14–15; 25.11–12). **10:** *Daughter Zion** is Jerusalem.

3 Then he showed me the high priest Joshua standing before the angel of the LORD, and Satanᵍ standing at his right hand to accuse him. 2And the LORD said to Satan,ᵍ "The LORD rebuke you, O Satan!ᵍ The

---

a Ch 2.1 in Heb   b Heb *it*   c Ch 2.5 in Heb
d Cn: Heb *after glory he*   e Heb *his eye*   f Or *wave*
g Or *the Accuser;* Heb *the Adversary*

LORD who has chosen Jerusalem rebuke you! Is not this man a brand plucked from the fire?" 3 Now Joshua was dressed with filthy clothes as he stood before the angel. 4 The angel said to those who were standing before him, "Take off his filthy clothes." And to him he said, "See, I have taken your guilt away from you, and I will clothe you with festal apparel." 5 And I said, "Let them put a clean turban on his head." So they put a clean turban on his head and clothed him with the apparel; and the angel of the LORD was standing by.

6 Then the angel of the LORD assured Joshua, saying 7 "Thus says the LORD of hosts: If you will walk in my ways and keep my requirements, then you shall rule my house and have charge of my courts, and I will give you the right of access among those who are standing here. 8 Now listen, Joshua, high priest, you and your colleagues who sit before you! For they are an omen of things to come: I am going to bring my servant the Branch. 9 For on the stone that I have set before Joshua, on a single stone with seven facets, I will engrave its inscription, says the LORD of hosts, and I will remove the guilt of this land in a single day. 10 On that day, says the LORD of hosts, you shall invite each other to come under your vine and fig tree."

3.1–10: The fourth vision: Joshua's installation as high priest. This vision may have been a later addition to the vision sequence; it does not open with the question and answer exchange between Zechariah and the interpreting angel that begins the other visions. **1:** The term *Satan* does not refer to the prince of evil familiar from early Christian writings. It is a common noun, not a name, in Hebrew and means "adversary" or "accuser" (see note *g*), that member of God's heavenly court designated to bring cases against individuals (Job 1.6). **2:** *A brand plucked from the fire* refers to someone who has survived God's judgment of Israel and Judah (Am 4.11). **3–5:** The reclothing of Joshua symbolizes his sanctification for priestly office (Lev 8.6–9). **7:** *My house* is the Temple* in Jerusalem. **8:** *My servant* and *the Branch* are royal titles used of the Davidic dynasty* (2 Sam 7.5; Jer 23.5) and may be used here of Zerubbabel (4.6–10a; Hag 2.23), governor of Judah and a member of the Davidic family. **9:**

The seven-faceted *stone* and its *inscription* are images of royalty (2 Sam 12.30; 2 Kings 11.12).

4 The angel who talked with me came again, and wakened me, as one is wakened from sleep. 2 He said to me, "What do you see?" And I said, "I see a lampstand all of gold, with a bowl on the top of it; there are seven lamps on it, with seven lips on each of the lamps that are on the top of it. 3 And by it there are two olive trees, one on the right of the bowl and the other on its left." 4 I said to the angel who talked with me, "What are these, my lord?" 5 Then the angel who talked with me answered me, "Do you not know what these are?" I said, "No, my lord." 6 He said to me, "This is the word of the LORD to Zerubbabel: Not by might, nor by power, but by my spirit, says the LORD of hosts. 7 What are you, O great mountain? Before Zerubbabel you shall become a plain; and he shall bring out the top stone amid shouts of 'Grace, grace to it!' "

8 Moreover the word of the LORD came to me, saying, 9 "The hands of Zerubbabel have laid the foundation of this house; his hands shall also complete it. Then you will know that the LORD of hosts has sent me to you. 10 For whoever has despised the day of small things shall rejoice, and shall see the plummet in the hand of Zerubbabel.

"These seven are the eyes of the LORD, which range through the whole earth." 11 Then I said to him, "What are these two olive trees on the right and the left of the lampstand?" 12 And a second time I said to him, "What are these two branches of the olive trees, which pour out the oil*a* through the two golden pipes?" 13 He said to me, "Do you not know what these are?" I said, "No, my lord." 14 Then he said, "These are the two anointed ones who stand by the Lord of the whole earth."

4.1–14: The fifth vision: The golden lampstand and Judah's leadership. This vision may originally have been the central vision in a seven-vision sequence. **2:** The *lampstand* (Heb., "menorah") in the Temple* is unusually elaborate and difficult to describe, though it

a Cn: Heb *gold*

is related to the lampstand in the tabernacle* (Ex 25.31–37). The *bowl* may have contained the oil for the lamps, and the *lips* held the lamps' wicks. **3:** Images of *trees* adorned the walls of Solomon's Temple (1 Kings 6.29). **6–10a:** This speech to *Zerubbabel,* encouraging him in the rebuilding of the Temple (Hag 2.1–4; Ezra 5.1–2), interrupts the vision narrative* and may be a later addition. **10b:** The vision narrative resumes with the explanation that the seven lamps represent God's *eyes,* watching the entire *earth.* **14:** The *anointed* ones,* symbolized in the vision by the two olive trees (vv. 3, 11), represent Judah's leadership, shared by a religious figure (the high priest Joshua; 3.1–10) and by a political figure (Zerubbabel; 4.6–10a).

5 Again I looked up and saw a flying scroll. ²And he said to me, "What do you see?" I answered, "I see a flying scroll; its length is twenty cubits, and its width ten cubits." ³Then he said to me, "This is the curse that goes out over the face of the whole land; for everyone who steals shall be cut off according to the writing on one side, and everyone who swears falsely*ᵃ* shall be cut off according to the writing on the other side. ⁴I have sent it out, says the LORD of hosts, and it shall enter the house of the thief, and the house of anyone who swears falsely by my name; and it shall abide in that house and consume it, both timber and stones."

5.1–4: The sixth vision: The flying scroll and social justice. The scroll's flight indicates that the power of its message covers the whole land. **3–4:** The two crimes mentioned in the scroll's text are theft and deceit in official transactions (*swearing falsely*), two of the ten commandments (Ex 20.7, 15). Why these two are singled out is not stated, but they represent the elimination of corruption from Judean society, the theme of the next vision as well.

5 Then the angel who talked with me came forward and said to me, "Look up and see what this is that is coming out." ⁶I said, "What is it?" He said, "This is a basket*ᵇ* coming out." And he said, "This is their iniquity*ᶜ* in all the land." ⁷Then a leaden cover was lifted, and there was a woman sitting in the basket! *ᵇ* ⁸And he said, "This is Wickedness." So he thrust her back into the basket,*ᵇ* and

pressed the leaden weight down on its mouth. ⁹Then I looked up and saw two women coming forward. The wind was in their wings; they had wings like the wings of a stork, and they lifted up the basket*ᵇ* between earth and sky. ¹⁰Then I said to the angel who talked with me, "Where are they taking the basket?"*ᵇ* ¹¹He said to me, "To the land of Shinar, to build a house for it; and when this is prepared, they will set the basket*ᵇ* down there on its base."

5.5–11: The seventh vision: The basket and Judah's purification. 6: *Basket* translates the Hebrew term "ephah," a unit of measure. **8:** *Wickedness* is a general term referring to corruption and unrighteousness in general. **11:** The removal of the basket containing wickedness to *Shinar,* a name for the plain in which Babylon was located (Gen 11.1–9), symbolizes the elimination of wickedness from Judean society.

6 And again I looked up and saw four chariots coming out from between two mountains—mountains of bronze. ²The first chariot had red horses, the second chariot black horses, ³the third chariot white horses, and the fourth chariot dappled gray*ᵈ* horses. ⁴Then I said to the angel who talked with me, "What are these, my lord?" ⁵The angel answered me, "These are the four winds*ᵉ* of heaven going out, after presenting themselves before the Lord of all the earth. ⁶The chariot with the black horses goes toward the north country, the white ones go toward the west country,*ᶠ* and the dappled ones go toward the south country." ⁷When the steeds came out, they were impatient to get off and patrol the earth. And he said, "Go, patrol the earth." So they patrolled the earth. ⁸Then he cried out to me, "Lo, those who go toward the north country have set my spirit at rest in the north country."

6.1–8: The eighth vision: The heavenly chariots and international peace. In this, Zechariah's final vision, as in his first vision (1.7–17), the world is at peace, but

---

a The word *falsely* added from verse 4　　*b* Heb *ephah*
c Gk Compare Syr: Heb *their eye*　　*d* Compare Gk:
Meaning of Heb uncertain　　*e* Or *spirits*　　*f* Cn: Heb
go after them

The Design of Zechariah's Visions

Zechariah's visions are organized by a concentric structure to draw the reader's attention from the universal to the particular, from the perspective of God to the realities of life in Judah. The first and last visions describe the world from the perspective of God and God's heavenly emissaries (1.7–17; 6.1–8). The second and third visions (1.18–2.5), together with the sixth and seventh visions (5.1–11), narrow the reader's focus to the restoration of Judah and Jerusalem. And the two visions at the center of the design describe the officials who will preside over a renewed Jerusalem (chs. 3–4). If ch. 3 is a later addition as some claim, the concentric pattern is even more balanced and focused on the two anointed✶ leaders of the people.

- 1.1–17 The first vision: The heavenly horsemen and God's plans for Jerusalem
  - 1.18–21 The second vision: The four horns and Judah's security
    - 2.1–5 The third vision: The measuring line and Jerusalem's resettlement
      - [3.1–10 The fourth vision: Joshua's installation as high priest]
      - 4.1–14 The fifth vision: The golden lampstand and Judah's leadership
    - 5.1–4 The sixth vision: The flying scroll and social justice
  - 5.5–11 The seventh vision: The basket and Judah's purification
- 6.1–8 The eighth vision: The heavenly chariots and international peace

now that peace includes the restoration of Judah and Jerusalem among the nations. **1–3:** These four chariots parallel the four horsemen in Zechariah's first vision (1.8–10) and represent God's heavenly patrol (v. 7) assigned to watch over the world's affairs. *Mountains* signify the abode of the gods in antiquity (Ps 48.1). **8:** The chariot patrol that sets God's *spirit at rest in the north country* thereby establishes the security of Judah on the international scene. It was from the north that Judah's enemies attacked (Jer 6.22), and it was from the north that Judah's exiles returned from captivity in Babylon (Jer 3.18).

9 The word of the LORD came to me: [10]Collect silver and gold[a] from the exiles—from Heldai, Tobijah, and Jedaiah—who have arrived from Babylon; and go the same day to the house of Josiah son of Zephaniah. [11]Take the silver and gold and make a crown,[b] and set it on the head of the high priest Joshua son of Jehozadak; [12]say to him: Thus says the LORD of hosts: Here is a man whose name is Branch: for he shall branch out in his place, and he shall build the temple of the LORD. [13]It is he that shall build

the temple of the LORD; he shall bear royal honor, and shall sit upon his throne and rule. There shall be a priest by his throne, with peaceful understanding between the two of them. [14]And the crown[c] shall be in the care of Heldai,[d] Tobijah, Jedaiah, and Josiah[e] son of Zephaniah, as a memorial in the temple of the LORD.

15 Those who are far off shall come and help to build the temple of the LORD; and you shall know that the LORD of hosts has sent me to you. This will happen if you diligently obey the voice of the LORD your God.

6.9–15: A charge to the high priest Joshua. This speech, placed between Zechariah's last vision and his concluding speech (chs. 7–8) may be an editorial addition. **10:** *Josiah* is a priestly figure, whose father *Zephaniah* was killed alongside Joshua's grandfather

a Cn Compare verse 11: Heb lacks *silver and gold*
b Gk Mss Syr Tg: Heb *crowns*   c Gk Syr: Heb *crowns*
d Syr Compare verse 10: Heb *Helem*   e Syr Compare verse 10: Heb *Hen*

Seraiah when Jerusalem was conquered (2 Kings 25.18–21). **11–13:** While this speech is directed to *Joshua*, its content seems more suitable for Zerubbabel. In 3.8 the *Branch* is not Joshua but an individual presented to him. In 4.6–10 Zerubbabel, not Joshua, is commissioned as the Temple✶ builder. Moreover, the Hebrew text does not say that *a crown* but that (two?) crowns were made (see note *b*), perhaps for both the royal figure and the priest mentioned in v. 13. It appears almost as if a speech once directed to Judah's political leader has been redirected to its religious leader. In any case, the concept of a leadership shared between religious and political figures found elsewhere in Zechariah (4.14) is present here too.

7 In the fourth year of King Darius, the word of the LORD came to Zechariah on the fourth day of the ninth month, which is Chislev. ²Now the people of Bethel had sent Sharezer and Regem-melech and their men, to entreat the favor of the LORD, ³and to ask the priests of the house of the LORD of hosts and the prophets, "Should I mourn and practice abstinence in the fifth month, as I have done for so many years?" ⁴Then the word of the LORD of hosts came to me: ⁵Say to all the people of the land and the priests: When you fasted and lamented in the fifth month and in the seventh, for these seventy years, was it for me that you fasted? ⁶And when you eat and when you drink, do you not eat and drink only for yourselves? ⁷Were not these the words that the LORD proclaimed by the former prophets, when Jerusalem was inhabited and in prosperity, along with the towns around it, and when the Negeb and the Shephelah were inhabited?

7.1–14: A charge to live justly. Zechariah's concluding speech is divided into two parts: an appeal—with an eye on the past—to create a just society (ch. 7), and a promise—with an eye on the future—of renewal and celebration (ch. 8). **1:** This speech is dated two years later (518 BCE) than Zechariah's opening speech (1.1). **2:** *Bethel* is 10 miles north of Jerusalem. **3:** *Prophets*✶ were often asked for divine instructions (Ezek 8.1; 14.1). The period of mourning in the *fifth month*, about which the envoys ask Zechariah, may have commemorated the destruction of the Temple in the fifth month (2 Kings 25.8–9). **5:** *Seventy years* appears to refer to the Exile,✶ though the Exile was

shorter (see comment on 1.12). **7:** Zechariah refers to the period before Jerusalem's fall in 587 BCE.

8 The word of the LORD came to Zechariah, saying: ⁹Thus says the LORD of hosts: Render true judgments, show kindness and mercy to one another; ¹⁰do not oppress the widow, the orphan, the alien, or the poor; and do not devise evil in your hearts against one another. ¹¹But they refused to listen, and turned a stubborn shoulder, and stopped their ears in order not to hear. ¹²They made their hearts adamant in order not to hear the law and the words that the LORD of hosts had sent by his spirit through the former prophets. Therefore great wrath came from the LORD of hosts. ¹³Just as, when I*ᵃ* called, they would not hear, so, when they called, I would not hear, says the LORD of hosts, ¹⁴and I scattered them with a whirlwind among all the nations that they had not known. Thus the land they left was desolate, so that no one went to and fro, and a pleasant land was made desolate.

7.8–11: By responding to a question about mourning rituals (v. 3) with a charge to create a just society, Zechariah appears to side with his predecessors, the former prophets (v. 7), who claimed that religious rituals were meaningless apart from the practice of justice in all areas of life (Am 5.21–24). This same concern is also present in Zechariah's sixth and seventh visions (5.1–11). Throughout this speech Zechariah uses his ancestors who disobeyed as a lesson for his own audience.

8 The word of the LORD of hosts came to me, saying: ²Thus says the LORD of hosts: I am jealous for Zion with great jealousy, and I am jealous for her with great wrath. ³Thus says the LORD: I will return to Zion, and will dwell in the midst of Jerusalem; Jerusalem shall be called the faithful city, and the mountain of the LORD of hosts shall be called the holy mountain. ⁴Thus says the LORD of hosts: Old men and old women shall again sit in the streets of Jerusalem, each with staff in hand because of

a Heb *he*

their great age. ⁵And the streets of the city shall be full of boys and girls playing in its streets. ⁶Thus says the LORD of hosts: Even though it seems impossible to the remnant of this people in these days, should it also seem impossible to me, says the LORD of hosts? ⁷Thus says the LORD of hosts: I will save my people from the east country and from the west country; ⁸and I will bring them to live in Jerusalem. They shall be my people and I will be their God, in faithfulness and in righteousness.

9 Thus says the LORD of hosts: Let your hands be strong—you that have recently been hearing these words from the mouths of the prophets who were present when the foundation was laid for the rebuilding of the temple, the house of the LORD of hosts. ¹⁰For before those days there were no wages for people or for animals, nor was there any safety from the foe for those who went out or came in, and I set them all against one another. ¹¹But now I will not deal with the remnant of this people as in the former days, says the LORD of hosts. ¹²For there shall be a sowing of peace; the vine shall yield its fruit, the ground shall give its produce, and the skies shall give their dew; and I will cause the remnant of this people to possess all these things. ¹³Just as you have been a cursing among the nations, O house of Judah and house of Israel, so I will save you and you shall be a blessing. Do not be afraid, but let your hands be strong.

14 For thus says the LORD of hosts: Just as I purposed to bring disaster upon you, when your ancestors provoked me to wrath, and I did not relent, says the LORD of hosts, ¹⁵so again I have purposed in these days to do good to Jerusalem and to the house of Judah; do not be afraid. ¹⁶These are the things that you shall do: Speak the truth to one another, render in your gates judgments that are true and make for peace, ¹⁷do not devise evil in your hearts against one another, and love no false oath; for all these are things that I hate, says the LORD.

18 The word of the LORD of hosts came to me, saying: ¹⁹Thus says the LORD of hosts: The fast of the fourth month, and the fast of the fifth, and the fast of the seventh, and the fast of the tenth, shall be seasons of joy and gladness, and cheerful festivals for the house of Judah: therefore love truth and peace.

20 Thus says the LORD of hosts: Peoples shall yet come, the inhabitants of many cities; ²¹the inhabitants of one city shall go to another, saying, "Come, let us go to entreat the favor of the LORD, and to seek the LORD of hosts; I myself am going." ²²Many peoples and strong nations shall come to seek the LORD of hosts in Jerusalem, and to entreat the favor of the LORD. ²³Thus says the LORD of hosts: In those days ten men from nations of every language shall take hold of a Jew, grasping his garment and saying, "Let us go with you, for we have heard that God is with you."

8.1–23: A promise of restoration. In this second part of his final speech, Zechariah includes many of the typical themes of post-exilic prophecy: the renewal of Jerusalem (vv. 2–5), the return of the exiles (vv. 6–8), the rebuilding of the Temple (vv. 9–13), and the respect of the nations (vv. 20–23). **6:** The *remnant* refers to the exiles who are returning to Judah (vv. 7–8; Hag 1.12). To these returnees the process of reconstruction *seems impossible* (4.10; Hag 2.3). **9:** Laying the Temple's foundation is described in Hag 1.12–14 and Ezra 5.1–2. **10:** The difficult times described here appear to reflect those mentioned by Haggai (1.2–11). **17:** *False oaths* are a major concern in Zechariah's sixth vision (5.1–4). **19:** Though not addressed directly to those who had asked Zechariah about mourning rituals (7.3), this speech instructs the people to substitute festivals of celebration for fasting. **22–23:** The conversion of the nations is a common theme in the post-exilic period (Isa 60.1–7; Mic 4.1–4).

~~~~~~~~~~~~~~~~~~~~~~~~~~~~~~~~~~~~~~~

9 An Oracle.

The word of the LORD is against the
   land of Hadrach
   and will rest upon Damascus.
For to the LORD belongs the capital*ᵃ* of
   Aram,*ᵇ*
   as do all the tribes of Israel;

a Heb *eye*   *b* Cn: Heb *of Adam* (or *of humankind*)

2 Hamath also, which borders on it,
  Tyre and Sidon, though they are very
    wise.
3 Tyre has built itself a rampart,
  and heaped up silver like dust,
  and gold like the dirt of the streets.
4 But now, the Lord will strip it of its
    possessions
  and hurl its wealth into the sea,
  and it shall be devoured by fire.

5 Ashkelon shall see it and be afraid;
  Gaza too, and shall writhe in anguish;
  Ekron also, because its hopes
    are withered.
  The king shall perish from Gaza;
  Ashkelon shall be uninhabited;
6 a mongrel people shall settle in Ashdod,
  and I will make an end of the pride of
    Philistia.
7 I will take away its blood from
    its mouth,
  and its abominations from between
    its teeth;
  it too shall be a remnant for our God;
  it shall be like a clan in Judah,
  and Ekron shall be like the Jebusites.
8 Then I will encamp at my house as a
    guard,
  so that no one shall march to and fro;
  no oppressor shall again overrun them,
  for now I have seen with my
    own eyes.

9.1–17: The divine warrior★ defends Judah. This
chapter begins the second part of Zechariah, which,
because of its differences in style and content, appears
to have been composed later than chs. 1–8 and to
have been added to the prophecies of Zechariah. The
title *An Oracle*★ (9.1; 12.1) divides these supplementary speeches into two collections, chs. 9–11 and
12–14. 1–8: God marches from north to south, defeating Judah's traditional enemies and taking up
residence in Jerusalem. 1–2a: *Hadrach, Damascus,* and
Hamath are important Aramean cities north of Israel
and Judah. 2b–4: *Tyre* and *Sidon* are important Phoenician cities on the Mediterranean coast northwest of
Judah. Tyre's legendary★ wisdom and wealth are described in Ezek 28. 5–7: *Ashkelon, Gaza, Ekron,* and
Ashdod are important Philistine cities on the Mediterranean coast west of Judah. The *Jebusites* (v. 7) were

defeated by David when he conquered Jerusalem
(2 Sam 5.6–10). 8: Following victory, the divine warrior is enthroned in his temple (Ps 29.9–11).

~~~~~~~~~~~~~~~~~~~~~~~~~~~~~~

9 Rejoice greatly, O daughter Zion!
  Shout aloud, O daughter Jerusalem!
  Lo, your king comes to you;
  triumphant and victorious is he,
  humble and riding on a donkey,
  on a colt, the foal of a donkey.
10 He[a] will cut off the chariot
    from Ephraim
  and the war-horse from Jerusalem;
  and the battle bow shall be cut off,
  and he shall command peace to the
    nations;
  his dominion shall be from sea to sea,
  and from the River to the ends of the
    earth.

11 As for you also, because of the blood of
    my covenant with you,
  I will set your prisoners free from the
    waterless pit.
12 Return to your stronghold, O prisoners
    of hope;
  today I declare that I will restore to
    you double.
13 For I have bent Judah as my bow;
  I have made Ephraim its arrow.
  I will arouse your sons, O Zion,
  against your sons, O Greece,
  and wield you like a warrior's sword.

14 Then the LORD will appear over them,
  and his arrow go forth like lightning;
  the Lord GOD will sound the trumpet
  and march forth in the whirlwinds of
    the south.
15 The LORD of hosts will protect them,
  and they shall devour and tread down
    the slingers;[b]
  they shall drink their blood[c] like wine,
  and be full like a bowl,
  drenched like the corners of the altar.

16 On that day the LORD their God will
    save them

a Gk: Heb I   b Cn: Heb *the slingstones*
c Gk: Heb *shall drink*

for they are the flock of his people;
 for like the jewels of a crown
  they shall shine on his land.
17 For what goodness and beauty are his!
 Grain shall make the young
  men flourish,
  and new wine the young women.

9.9–17. 9: While God may be referred to as *king* in late prophetic literature (Zeph 3.14–15), a human *king* reviving the Davidic dynasty* may be intended here (Jer 23.5–6; Hag 2.20–23). The Davidic king from the tribe of Judah referred to in Gen 49.10–11 is pictured with a *donkey*, the traditional transportation for gods and kings in antiquity. **10:** *Ephraim* is a name for the northern kingdom of Israel (Hos 5.5). International *peace* is a typical element in visions of the future (Mic 4.3–4). **11:** The exilic prophet* Second Isaiah also combines God's remembrance of the covenant* with God's liberation of the exiles (Isa 42.6–7). **13:** *Greece* (Heb., "Javan") is one of the lands to which Judeans were exiled (Isa 66.18–20; Joel 3.6).

〜〜〜〜〜〜〜

10 Ask rain from the LORD
 in the season of the spring rain,
 from the LORD who makes the storm
  clouds,
  who gives showers of rain to you,*a*
  the vegetation in the field
  to everyone.
2 For the teraphim*b* utter nonsense,
 and the diviners see lies;
 the dreamers tell false dreams,
  and give empty consolation.
 Therefore the people wander like
  sheep;
  they suffer for lack of a shepherd.

3 My anger is hot against the shepherds,
 and I will punish the leaders;*c*
 for the LORD of hosts cares for his
  flock, the house of Judah,
  and will make them like his proud
  war-horse.
4 Out of them shall come the
  cornerstone,
  out of them the tent peg,
 out of them the battle bow,
  out of them every commander.
5 Together they shall be like warriors in
  battle,

trampling the foe in the mud of the
  streets;
 they shall fight, for the LORD is with
  them,
  and they shall put to shame the riders
  on horses.

10.1–12: God gathers the exiles. This speech continues the theme of restoration in the previous oracle* by focusing on God's work of returning the exiles of Israel and Judah. **2:** *Teraphim* are objects or images used in worship (Judg 17.5) and were condemned by some writers (2 Kings 23.24). Here the main concern seems to be that all media of revelation have become silent. **3:** It is uncertain whether these *shepherds*, the people's *leaders*, are rulers of foreign countries oppressing Judah (Jer 12.10) or Judah's own rulers who have become corrupt (Isa 56.11), like those denigrated in 11.4–6. In either case, they will be punished so God can restore *the house of Judah.*

〜〜〜〜〜〜〜

6 I will strengthen the house of Judah,
 and I will save the house of Joseph.
 I will bring them back because I have
  compassion on them,
  and they shall be as though I had not
  rejected them;
 for I am the LORD their God and I
  will answer them.
7 Then the people of Ephraim shall
  become like warriors,
  and their hearts shall be glad as with
  wine.
 Their children shall see it and rejoice,
  their hearts shall exult in the LORD.

8 I will signal for them and gather them in,
 for I have redeemed them,
  and they shall be as numerous as they
  were before.
9 Though I scattered them among
  the nations,
  yet in far countries they shall
  remember me,
 and they shall rear their children and
  return.
10 I will bring them home from the land of
  Egypt,
  and gather them from Assyria;

a Heb *them*   *b* Or *household gods*   *c* Or *male goats*

I will bring them to the land of Gilead
　　　and to Lebanon,
　　until there is no room for them.
11 They[a] shall pass through the sea of
　　　　distress,
　　　and the waves of the sea shall be
　　　　struck down,
　　　and all the depths of the Nile
　　　　dried up.
The pride of Assyria shall be laid low,
　　　and the scepter of Egypt shall depart.
12 I will make them strong in the LORD,
　　　and they shall walk in his name,
　　　　　　　　　　　　　says the LORD.

10.6–12. 6–7: The *house of Joseph* and *Ephraim* are references to the northern kingdom of Israel. **10:** *Egypt* and *Assyria* are two of the countries to which Israelites were exiled (2 Kings 17.5–6; 25.26). *Gilead* and *Lebanon* are territories to the north of Israel.

11 Open your doors, O Lebanon,
　　　so that fire may devour your cedars!
2 Wail, O cypress, for the cedar
　　　　has fallen,
　　　for the glorious trees are ruined!
　　Wail, oaks of Bashan,
　　　for the thick forest has been felled!
3 Listen, the wail of the shepherds,
　　　for their glory is despoiled!
　　Listen, the roar of the lions,
　　　for the thickets of the Jordan
　　　　are destroyed!

11.1–3: God brings down wicked rulers. As in 10.3, the details are too few to indicate whether these *shepherds* (v. 3) are leaders of foreign nations, such as those God defeats in the previous verses (10.11–12), or leaders of Judah, such as those criticized in the following verses (11.4–6). The *cedars* and *cypress* of Lebanon and *the oaks of Bashan*, legendary* forests, are symbolic of the great and powerful.

4 Thus said the LORD my God: Be a shepherd of the flock doomed to slaughter. 5 Those who buy them kill them and go unpunished; and those who sell them say, "Blessed be the LORD, for I have become rich"; and their own shepherds have no pity on them. 6 For I will no longer have pity on the inhabitants of the earth, says the LORD.

I will cause them, every one, to fall each into the hand of a neighbor, and each into the hand of the king; and they shall devastate the earth, and I will deliver no one from their hand.

7 So, on behalf of the sheep merchants, I became the shepherd of the flock doomed to slaughter. I took two staffs; one I named Favor, the other I named Unity, and I tended the sheep. 8 In one month I disposed of the three shepherds, for I had become impatient with them, and they also detested me. 9 So I said, "I will not be your shepherd. What is to die, let it die; what is to be destroyed, let it be destroyed; and let those that are left devour the flesh of one another!" 10 I took my staff Favor and broke it, annulling the covenant that I had made with all the peoples. 11 So it was annulled on that day, and the sheep merchants, who were watching me, knew that it was the word of the LORD. 12 I then said to them, "If it seems right to you, give me my wages; but if not, keep them." So they weighed out as my wages thirty shekels of silver. 13 Then the LORD said to me, "Throw it into the treasury"[b]—this lordly price at which I was valued by them. So I took the thirty shekels of silver and threw them into the treasury[b] in the house of the LORD. 14 Then I broke my second staff Unity, annulling the family ties between Judah and Israel.

15 Then the LORD said to me: Take once more the implements of a worthless shepherd. 16 For I am now raising up in the land a shepherd who does not care for the perishing, or seek the wandering,[c] or heal the maimed, or nourish the healthy,[d] but devours the flesh of the fat ones, tearing off even their hoofs.
17 Oh, my worthless shepherd,
　　　who deserts the flock!
　　May the sword strike his arm
　　　and his right eye!
　　Let his arm be completely withered,
　　　his right eye utterly blinded!

---

a Gk: Heb *He*　　b Syr: Heb *it to the potter*
c Syr Compare Gk Vg: Heb *the youth*　　d Meaning of Heb uncertain

11.4–17: The prophet satirizes Judah's corrupt leaders. In this first-person narrative,* an anonymous prophet acts out the corrupt practices of Judah's leaders in order to expose and denounce them. **5:** *Their own shepherds* are Judah's leaders, who *buy* and *kill them*, that is, their own people symbolized as sheep. **7:** The *sheep merchants* are Judah's leaders, buying and selling their people (v. 5). The names of the *two staffs*, *Favor* (or "pleasantness") and *Unity*, reflect the goals of the good shepherd for the sheep. **8:** The identity of the *three shepherds* is unknown. **9:** Having disposed of the three shepherds (v. 8), the prophet apparently becomes impatient with the people themselves. **10:** Breaking the staffs of *Favor* and *Unity* (v. 14) consigns the flock, the people of Judah, to a time of trouble and conflict. **12–13:** The reason for the amount of the wages and their deposit in the Temple* is uncertain. Donations of about this amount were made to the Temple to "redeem" people devoted to Temple service from their obligation (Lev 27.1–8). On the other hand, the prophet may, by placing tainted money in the Temple's treasuries, want to indict the Temple and its leaders as corrupt. **14:** The prophet abandons hope for the reunion of the old northern kingdom of *Israel* and southern kingdom of *Judah*, which traced their origins back to a single ancestor, Jacob (Gen 49). **15–17:** The prophet anticipates, by dressing up a second time as a shepherd (v. 4), the arrival of another corrupt leader.

12

An Oracle.

The word of the LORD concerning Israel: Thus says the LORD, who stretched out the heavens and founded the earth and formed the human spirit within: 2See, I am about to make Jerusalem a cup of reeling for all the surrounding peoples; it will be against Judah also in the siege against Jerusalem. 3On that day I will make Jerusalem a heavy stone for all the peoples; all who lift it shall grievously hurt themselves. And all the nations of the earth shall come together against it. 4On that day, says the LORD, I will strike every horse with panic, and its rider with madness. But on the house of Judah I will keep a watchful eye, when I strike every horse of the peoples with blindness. 5Then the clans of Judah shall say to themselves, "The inhabi-

tants of Jerusalem have strength through the LORD of hosts, their God."

6 On that day I will make the clans of Judah like a blazing pot on a pile of wood, like a flaming torch among sheaves; and they shall devour to the right and to the left all the surrounding peoples, while Jerusalem shall again be inhabited in its place, in Jerusalem.

7 And the LORD will give victory to the tents of Judah first, that the glory of the house of David and the glory of the inhabitants of Jerusalem may not be exalted over that of Judah. 8On that day the LORD will shield the inhabitants of Jerusalem so that the feeblest among them on that day shall be like David, and the house of David shall be like God, like the angel of the LORD, at their head. 9And on that day I will seek to destroy all the nations that come against Jerusalem.

12.1–9: Judah defeats the nations. This text, like ch. 9, describes Judah's defense against its neighboring nations. **1:** The title *An Oracle* marks the beginning of the second collection of speeches in chs. 9–14. **2:** The *cup of reeling*, a traditional image of judgment, renders the enemy drunk and senseless (Isa 51.17–22). **6:** The *flaming torch*, another traditional image of judgment, consumes the enemy, pictured as sheaves or stubble (Ob 18). **7:** *The house of David* refers to a revival of the Davidic dynasty* which ruled from Jerusalem before its fall in 587 BCE.

10 And I will pour out a spirit of compassion and supplication on the house of David and the inhabitants of Jerusalem, so that, when they look on the one*a* whom they have pierced, they shall mourn for him, as one mourns for an only child, and weep bitterly over him, as one weeps over a firstborn. 11On that day the mourning in Jerusalem will be as great as the mourning for Hadadrimmon in the plain of Megiddo. 12The land shall mourn, each family by itself; the family of the house of David by itself, and their wives by themselves; the family of the house of Nathan by itself, and their wives by themselves; 13the family of the house of Levi by

a Heb *on me*

itself, and their wives by themselves; the family of the Shimeites by itself, and their wives by themselves; 14and all the families that are left, each by itself, and their wives by themselves.

12.10–14: Mourning in Jerusalem. 10: The identification of the object of mourning, *the one whom they have pierced*, is uncertain; but due to the wide extent of the mourning and the leading role of the house of David in it (vv. 10, 12), the person mourned may have been a member of the royal family. **11:** *Hadad-rimmon* is the name of the Syrian storm god, a figure like Baal, ✻ the Canaanite storm god. If taken as the name of a place named after his deity *in the plain of Megiddo*, however, this may be a reference to the mourning for the Judean king, Josiah, who was killed by the Egyptians in the plain of Megiddo and mourned by all of Judah and Jerusalem (2 Chr 35.20–25). **13:** *Levi* and *Shimei* are priestly families.

13 On that day a fountain shall be opened for the house of David and the inhabitants of Jerusalem, to cleanse them from sin and impurity.

2 On that day, says the LORD of hosts, I will cut off the names of the idols from the land, so that they shall be remembered no more; and also I will remove from the land the prophets and the unclean spirit. 3And if any prophets appear again, their fathers and mothers who bore them will say to them, "You shall not live, for you speak lies in the name of the LORD"; and their fathers and their mothers who bore them shall pierce them through when they prophesy. 4On that day the prophets will be ashamed, every one, of their visions when they prophesy; they will not put on a hairy mantle in order to deceive, 5but each of them will say, "I am no prophet, I am a tiller of the soil; for the land has been my possession*a* since my youth." 6And if anyone asks them, "What are these wounds on your chest?"*b* the answer will be "The wounds I received in the house of my friends."

7 "Awake, O sword, against my shepherd,
    against the man who is my associate,"
        says the LORD of hosts.

Strike the shepherd, that the sheep may
    be scattered;
I will turn my hand against
    the little ones.
8 In the whole land, says the LORD,
    two-thirds shall be cut off
        and perish,
    and one-third shall be left alive.
9 And I will put this third into the fire,
    refine them as one refines silver,
    and test them as gold is tested.
They will call on my name,
    and I will answer them.
I will say, "They are my people";
    and they will say, "The LORD is
        our God."

13.1–9: God removes false prophets and leaders. This text, like 11.4–17, focuses on corruption within Judah itself, especially among its leaders. **2–3:** The prophets whose writings have been preserved in the Bible often find themselves in conflict with other prophets preaching opposite messages (Jer 14.14; Ezek 13.1–7). Here the prophet accuses his opponents of preaching *lies in the name of the LORD* and announces God's judgment on them. *The unclean spirit* (or "breath") is the source of the prophets' false inspiration or revelation (1 Kings 22.19–23). **7:** The judgment on Judah's *shepherd* resumes the criticism of Judah's leadership in 11.4–17. **8–9:** The division of Judah into thirds for punishment is reminiscent of Ezekiel's prophecy (5.1–12). But here the prophet concentrates on a third that, though punished, will survive and renew their relationship to God.

14 See, a day is coming for the LORD, when the plunder taken from you will be divided in your midst. 2For I will gather all the nations against Jerusalem to battle, and the city shall be taken and the houses looted and the women raped; half the city shall go into exile, but the rest of the people shall not be cut off from the city. 3Then the LORD will go forth and fight against those nations as when he fights on a day of battle. 4On that day his feet shall

---

a Cn: Heb *for humankind has caused me to possess*
b Heb *wounds between your hands*

stand on the Mount of Olives, which lies before Jerusalem on the east; and the Mount of Olives shall be split in two from east to west by a very wide valley; so that one half of the Mount shall withdraw northward, and the other half southward. 5And you shall flee by the valley of the LORD's mountain,[a] for the valley between the mountains shall reach to Azal;[b] and you shall flee as you fled from the earthquake in the days of King Uzziah of Judah. Then the LORD my God will come, and all the holy ones with him.

14.1–21: God defeats the nations and restores Jerusalem. Speeches such as this one describing the defense and restoration of Jerusalem in the context of God's intervention against the neighboring nations that have oppressed it are common in the period after the Exile,* as chs. 9, 10, and 12 illustrate (Isa 59.15–20; Joel 3). **1:** The *plunder* once taken from Jerusalem will be returned. **2:** This is the only verse in the chapter that describes judgment, rather than restoration, for Jerusalem. The prophet either anticipates a coming judgment on Jerusalem's corrupt leadership (11.4–17; 13.2–9) or recalls the fall of Jerusalem in 587 BCE. **4–5:** The citizens of Jerusalem will escape God's attack on the nations by fleeing east through a great rift in the Mount of Olives, which in reality towers over the city of Jerusalem.

6 On that day there shall not be[c] either cold or frost.[d] 7And there shall be continuous day (it is known to the LORD), not day and not night, for at evening time there shall be light.

8 On that day living waters shall flow out from Jerusalem, half of them to the eastern sea and half of them to the western sea; it shall continue in summer as in winter.

14.8: The upwelling of Jerusalem's Gihon spring with abundant water is a common theme in visions of the future (Ezek 47.1–12; Joel 3.18).

9 And the LORD will become king over all the earth; on that day the LORD will be one and his name one.

10 The whole land shall be turned into a plain from Geba to Rimmon south of Jerusalem. But Jerusalem shall remain aloft on its site from the Gate of Benjamin to the place of the former gate, to the Corner Gate, and from the Tower of Hananel to the king's wine presses. 11And it shall be inhabited, for never again shall it be doomed to destruction; Jerusalem shall abide in security.

12 This shall be the plague with which the LORD will strike all the peoples that wage war against Jerusalem: their flesh shall rot while they are still on their feet; their eyes shall rot in their sockets, and their tongues shall rot in their mouths. 13On that day a great panic from the LORD shall fall on them, so that each will seize the hand of a neighbor, and the hand of the one will be raised against the hand of the other; 14even Judah will fight at Jerusalem. And the wealth of all the surrounding nations shall be collected—gold, silver, and garments in great abundance. 15And a plague like this plague shall fall on the horses, the mules, the camels, the donkeys, and whatever animals may be in those camps.

16 Then all who survive of the nations that have come against Jerusalem shall go up year after year to worship the King, the LORD of hosts, and to keep the festival of booths.[e] 17If any of the families of the earth do not go up to Jerusalem to worship the King, the LORD of hosts, there will be no rain upon them. 18And if the family of Egypt do not go up and present themselves, then on them shall[f] come the plague that the LORD inflicts on the nations that do not go up to keep the festival of booths.[e] 19Such shall be the punishment of Egypt and the punishment of all the nations that do not go up to keep the festival of booths.[e]

14.16: The surrounding nations will make an annual pilgrimage to worship Israel's God in Jerusalem (8.22–23) in the fall for *the festival of booths*, a festival commemorating the autumn harvest (Deut 16.13–15).

a Heb *my mountains*   *b* Meaning of Heb uncertain   *c* Cn: Heb *there shall not be light*   *d* Compare Gk Syr Vg Tg: Meaning of Heb uncertain   *e* Or *tabernacles;* Heb *succoth*   *f* Gk Syr: Heb *shall not*

20 On that day there shall be inscribed on the bells of the horses, "Holy to the LORD." And the cooking pots in the house of the LORD shall be as holy as*a* the bowls in front of the altar; 21 and every cooking pot in Jerusalem and Judah shall be sacred to the LORD of hosts, so that all who sacrifice may come and use them to boil the flesh of the sacrifice. And there shall no longer be trad-ers*b* in the house of the LORD of hosts on that day.

14.20–21: The holiness of the Temple's most sacred precincts will spread to all of Jerusalem.

a Heb *shall be like*   *b* Or *Canaanites*

MALACHI

Introduction

Malachi is primarily concerned about a lack of devotion and seriousness in Judah's Temple* worship and about a lack of fidelity in Judah's social relationships. The prophet* addresses these issues in a series of disputations, in which he often quotes his audience. He blames the Temple priesthood for its impure offerings (1.6–2.3) and improper teachings (2.4–9) and Judah's people for their meager contributions (3.6–12). Furthermore, he blames the people for a lack of faithfulness in family relations, in particular marriage (2.10–16), and in obligations to the poor and powerless (3.5). In his concern for social fidelity and justice, Malachi stands in the tradition of the pre-exilic prophets, such as Amos and Micah, who preached against injustice and the abuse of power. In his concern for proper worship in a sanctified temple, Malachi shares the concerns of other post-exilic prophets, such as Haggai and Zechariah. Malachi also expresses the post-exilic expectation of a great day of salvation when the righteous are restored and the wicked punished (4.1–3).

Since the book of Malachi contains no references to dates or to identifiable contemporary people or events, it is difficult to identify its precise social and historical setting. The mention of a governor (1.8; Hag 1.1) places it in the post-exilic period, together with Haggai and Zechariah which precede it, following the return to Judah of the Babylonian exiles. Because of a sense of disillusionment in Malachi's audience (1.2, 17) and a failure of leadership in the Temple and society (1.6–2.9), Malachi may have preached at a time later than Haggai and Zechariah (1–8), who initiated the reconstruction of the Temple and who had a positive view of Judah's new leadership.

READING GUIDE

If Malachi preached to a people disillusioned with early hopes of the restoration of their homeland (1.2, 17; 3.14–15), he faced a daunting challenge that must be kept in mind while reading his speeches. How does a people remain faithful when its efforts seem fruitless?

---

1 An oracle. The word of the LORD to Israel by Malachi.*

2 I have loved you, says the LORD. But you say, "How have you loved us?" Is not Esau Jacob's brother? says the LORD. Yet I have loved Jacob ³but I have hated Esau; I have made his hill country a desolation and his heritage a desert for jackals. ⁴If Edom says, "We are shattered but we will rebuild the ruins," the LORD of hosts says: They may build, but I will tear down, until they are called the wicked country, the people with whom the LORD is angry forever. ⁵Your own eyes shall see this, and you shall say, "Great is the LORD beyond the borders of Israel!"

1.1–5. 1: Title. Malachi, meaning "my messenger" (see note a), is either the name of an individual or a title selected for the author of this prophetic collection on the basis of 3.1. **2–5: Edom's ruins.** For those who think their modest efforts at the reconstruction of Judah do not reflect God's presence or love, the uninhabited ruins of their neighbor Edom are a stark reminder of God's real absence and anger. **2:** *Esau,* Edom's ancestor, was the *brother* of *Jacob,* Israel's an-

a Or *by my messenger*

cestor (Gen 25.21–34). **3–4:** God's destruction of Edom is viewed elsewhere as punishment for Edom's participation in the sacking of Jerusalem when it was conquered by the Babylonians (Obadiah; Ps 137.7–8).

6 A son honors his father, and servants their master. If then I am a father, where is the honor due me? And if I am a master, where is the respect due me? says the LORD of hosts to you, O priests, who despise my name. You say, "How have we despised your name?" 7 By offering polluted food on my altar. And you say, "How have we polluted it?"*a* By thinking that the LORD's table may be despised. 8 When you offer blind animals in sacrifice, is that not wrong? And when you offer those that are lame or sick, is that not wrong? Try presenting that to your governor; will he be pleased with you or show you favor? says the LORD of hosts. 9 And now implore the favor of God, that he may be gracious to us. The fault is yours. Will he show favor to any of you? says the LORD of hosts. 10 Oh, that someone among you would shut the temple*b* doors, so that you would not kindle fire on my altar in vain! I have no pleasure in you, says the LORD of hosts, and I will not accept an offering from your hands. 11 For from the rising of the sun to its setting my name is great among the nations, and in every place incense is offered to my name, and a pure offering; for my name is great among the nations, says the LORD of hosts. 12 But you profane it when you say that the Lord's table is polluted, and the food for it*c* may be despised. 13 "What a weariness this is," you say, and you sniff at me,*d* says the LORD of hosts. You bring what has been taken by violence or is lame or sick, and this you bring as your offering! Shall I accept that from your hand? says the LORD. 14 Cursed be the cheat who has a male in the flock and vows to give it, and yet sacrifices to the Lord what is blemished; for I am a great King, says the LORD of hosts, and my name is reverenced among the nations.

2 And now, O priests, this command is for you. 2 If you will not listen, if you will not lay it to heart to give glory to my name, says the LORD of hosts, then I will send the curse on you and I will curse your blessings; indeed I have already cursed them,*e* because you do not lay it to heart. 3 I will rebuke your offspring, and spread dung on your faces, the dung of your offerings, and I will put you out of my presence.*f*

4 Know, then, that I have sent this command to you, that my covenant with Levi may hold, says the LORD of hosts. 5 My covenant with him was a covenant of life and well-being, which I gave him; this called for reverence, and he revered me and stood in awe of my name. 6 True instruction was in his mouth, and no wrong was found on his lips. He walked with me in integrity and uprightness, and he turned many from iniquity. 7 For the lips of a priest should guard knowledge, and people should seek instruction from his mouth, for he is the messenger of the LORD of hosts. 8 But you have turned aside from the way; you have caused many to stumble by your instruction; you have corrupted the covenant of Levi, says the LORD of hosts, 9 and so I make you despised and abased before all the people, inasmuch as you have not kept my ways but have shown partiality in your instruction.

1.6–2.9: The priests' sins. Making up a third of the entire book, this accusation singles out two priestly sins: making improper offerings (1.6–2.3) and giving improper instruction (2.4–9). **1.8:** Priestly (Lev 1.3; 22.17–25) and deuteronomic (Deut 15.19–23) laws prohibit the sacrifice of blemished animals, Deuteronomy specifically forbidding the *lame* and *blind*. **2.4:** *Levi* is the ancestor of Israel's priestly families (1 Chr 6.1–48). **8:** Priests were responsible for teaching and *instruction*. Micah also blames priests for abusing their teaching office (3.11).

10 Have we not all one father? Has not one God created us? Why then are we faithless to one another, profaning the covenant of our ancestors? 11 Judah has been faithless, and abomination has been committed in Israel and in Jerusalem; for Judah has profaned the sanctuary of the LORD, which he loves, and has married the daughter of a for-

a Gk: Heb *you*   *b* Heb lacks *temple*   *c* Compare Syr Tg: Heb *its fruit, its food*   *d* Another reading is *at it* *e* Heb *it*   *f* Cn Compare Gk Syr: Heb *and he shall bear you to it*

eign god. 12 May the LORD cut off from the tents of Jacob anyone who does this—any to witness[a] or answer, or to bring an offering to the LORD of hosts.

13 And this you do as well: You cover the LORD's altar with tears, with weeping and groaning because he no longer regards the offering or accepts it with favor at your hand. 14 You ask, "Why does he not?" Because the LORD was a witness between you and the wife of your youth, to whom you have been faithless, though she is your companion and your wife by covenant. 15 Did not one God make her?[b] Both flesh and spirit are his.[c] And what does the one God[d] desire? Godly offspring. So look to yourselves, and do not let anyone be faithless to the wife of his youth. 16 For I hate[e] divorce, says the LORD, the God of Israel, and covering one's garment with violence, says the LORD of hosts. So take heed to yourselves and do not be faithless.

2.10–16: Judah's unfaithfulness. This speech is either a criticism of idolatry,* by means of the metaphor* of unfaithfulness in marriage, or, more likely, a criticism of unfaithful marriage relationships themselves. **10–12:** Judean men have been *faithless* by marrying foreign women, *the daughter of a foreign god* (v. 11). The prohibition against marrying foreign women appears to stem from the concern that the husband will abandon worship of Israel's God (Ex 34.16; 1 Kings 11.1–2). **13–16:** Judean men have also been *faithless* by divorcing their wives. While deuteronomic law provides stipulations for divorce (Deut 24.1–4), this speech appears to be more critical of it.

---

17 You have wearied the LORD with your words. Yet you say, "How have we wearied him?" By saying, "All who do evil are good in the sight of the LORD, and he delights in them." Or by asking, "Where is the God of justice?"

3 See, I am sending my messenger to prepare the way before me, and the Lord whom you seek will suddenly come to his temple. The messenger of the covenant in whom you delight—indeed, he is coming, says the LORD of hosts. 2 But who can endure the day of his coming, and who can stand when he appears?

For he is like a refiner's fire and like fullers' soap; 3 he will sit as a refiner and purifier of silver, and he will purify the descendants of Levi and refine them like gold and silver, until they present offerings to the LORD in righteousness.[f] 4 Then the offering of Judah and Jerusalem will be pleasing to the LORD as in the days of old and as in former years.

5 Then I will draw near to you for judgment; I will be swift to bear witness against the sorcerers, against the adulterers, against those who swear falsely, against those who oppress the hired workers in their wages, the widow and the orphan, against those who thrust aside the alien, and do not fear me, says the LORD of hosts.

2.17–3.5: God's judgment. Malachi announces a divine judgment as a response to those who weary God by complaining that the wicked prosper (v. 17). **3.1:** The identity of the *messenger* is not stated, though the conclusion to Malachi connects him with the prophet* Elijah (4.5). **3:** The first group singled out for judgment is the *descendants of Levi*, the priests who have been making improper *offerings* (see 1.6–2.9). **5:** *The adulterers* judged here may be the faithless Judeans (2.10–16). By describing God's judgment against those who *oppress* the poor and powerless, including *the widow and the orphan*, Malachi takes up the theme of social justice preached by Israel's pre-exilic prophets (Isa 1.17).

---

6 For I the LORD do not change; therefore you, O children of Jacob, have not perished. 7 Ever since the days of your ancestors you have turned aside from my statutes and have not kept them. Return to me, and I will return to you, says the LORD of hosts. But you say, "How shall we return?"

8 Will anyone rob God? Yet you are robbing me! But you say, "How are we robbing you?" In your tithes and offerings! 9 You are cursed with a curse, for you are robbing me—the whole nation of you! 10 Bring the full tithe into the storehouse, so that there

---

a Cn Compare Gk: Heb *arouse*   *b* Or *Has he not made one?*   *c* Cn: Heb *and a remnant of spirit was his*   *d* Heb *he*   *e* Cn: Heb *he hates*   *f* Or *right offerings to the LORD*

may be food in my house, and thus put me to the test, says the LORD of hosts; see if I will not open the windows of heaven for you and pour down for you an overflowing blessing. ¹¹I will rebuke the locust[a] for you, so that it will not destroy the produce of your soil; and your vine in the field shall not be barren, says the LORD of hosts. ¹²Then all nations will count you happy, for you will be a land of delight, says the LORD of hosts.

3.6–12: Judah's miserliness. Just as Judah's priests are not fulfilling their obligations for proper worship at the Temple* (1.6–2.3), so Judah's people are not fulfilling theirs. They are not bringing to the Temple the *full tithes* (v. 10) of their produce required by Israelite law (Lev 27.30–33; Deut 14.22–29). **10:** The connection between proper worship and divine blessing in Malachi's message mirrors Haggai's thought (Hag 1.9–10).

---

13 You have spoken harsh words against me, says the LORD. Yet you say, "How have we spoken against you?" ¹⁴You have said, "It is vain to serve God. What do we profit by keeping his command or by going about as mourners before the LORD of hosts? ¹⁵Now we count the arrogant happy; evildoers not only prosper, but when they put God to the test they escape."

16 Then those who revered the LORD spoke with one another. The LORD took note and listened, and a book of remembrance was written before him of those who revered the LORD and thought on his name. ¹⁷They shall be mine, says the LORD of hosts, my special possession on the day when I act, and I will spare them as parents spare their children who serve them. ¹⁸Then once more you shall see the difference between the righteous and the wicked, between one who serves God and one who does not serve him.

4 ᵇSee, the day is coming, burning like an oven, when all the arrogant and all evildoers will be stubble; the day that comes shall burn them up, says the LORD of hosts, so that it will leave them neither root nor branch. ²But for you who revere my name the sun of righteousness shall rise, with healing in its wings. You shall go out leaping like calves from the stall. ³And you shall tread down the wicked, for they will be ashes under the soles of your feet, on the day when I act, says the LORD of hosts.

4 Remember the teaching of my servant Moses, the statutes and ordinances that I commanded him at Horeb for all Israel.

5 Lo, I will send you the prophet Elijah before the great and terrible day of the LORD comes. ⁶He will turn the hearts of parents to their children and the hearts of children to their parents, so that I will not come and strike the land with a curse.[c]

3.13–4.6: God's judgment of the wicked and salvation of the righteous. The announcement of God's judgment, like the announcement in 2.17–3.5, is made in response to those who believe that there is no justice, that the wicked prosper while the righteous do not (vv. 13–15). Such a concern was not unique to Malachi's audience, as the books of Job (21.28–31) and Ecclesiastes (7.15) illustrate. **3.16:** The *book of remembrance* is unique to Malachi, though it is based on older traditions (Ex 32.32; Ps 69.28). **4.2:** *The sun of righteousness* is a title for God, who is elsewhere described with solar imagery (Ps 4.6; 84.11). **4:** This event is summarized in Deut 5–6. **5:** The expectation of the return of *Elijah* may be related to the tradition that he did not die but was taken up into heaven (2 Kings 2.11–12). The phrase *"I will send . . . "* associates him with God's messenger, mentioned in 3.1.

---

a Heb *devourer*   *b* Ch 4.1–6 are Ch 3.19–24 in Heb
c Or *a ban of utter destruction*

THE APOCRYPHAL/DEUTEROCANONICAL
BOOKS OF THE OLD TESTAMENT

*New Revised
Standard Version*

(a) The books and parts of books from Tobit through 2 Maccabees are recognized as Deuterocanonical Scripture by the Roman Catholic, Greek, and Russian Orthodox Churches.

TOBIT

Introduction

The books of Tobit, Judith, the Greek version of Esther, the expanded form of Daniel, and *Joseph and Aseneth*★ are the only ancient Jewish novels★ known to have survived. Tobit is an entertaining work that recounts the intertwined stories of Tobit and his future daughter-in-law, Sarah. Their respective problems—Tobit has become blind and each of Sarah's seven successive husbands has died on his wedding night before the marriage can be consummated—are solved by the intervention of the angel Raphael, who comes to them in the guise of one of their kinsmen. Tobit, although set at the time of the fall of the northern kingdom of Israel (late eighth century BCE), was likely written much later, about third to second century BCE, in Hebrew or Aramaic. It contains many references to Persian lands, and though it may not have been written in the east, it has an eastern orientation. Many extended Jewish families, including the Tobiad family, engaged in commerce across the boundaries from west to east, and some may be reflected in this work's central characters.

The book can be divided into three parts: (1) Tobit's piety is demonstrated by his courage in burying the corpses of dead Jews in violation of a royal decree (ch. 1); (2) Tobit's and Sarah's problems are resolved through the intervention of the angel Raphael (chs. 2–12); and (3) Tobit pronounces his deathbed prayers and testament (chs. 13–14). The three parts may not have been written by the same hand, but they fit together as a satisfying three-part novel for the Jewish audience in the Greco-Roman period.

The book communicates a charming piety, in that family and religious values are paramount. Very little tension is created as to whether their problems will be solved (3.16), but the reader is thoroughly entertained by discovering precisely how the plot will proceed. In addition, the author utilizes humor and irony★ to create a comic tone throughout, making the happy ending seem inevitable.

1 This book tells the story of Tobit son of Tobiel son of Hananiel son of Aduel son of Gabael son of Raphael son of Raguel of the descendants*a* of Asiel, of the tribe of Naphtali, ²who in the days of King Shalmaneser*b* of the Assyrians was taken into captivity from Thisbe, which is to the south of Kedesh Naphtali in Upper Galilee, above Asher toward the west, and north of Phogor.

1.1–2: Introduction. Tobit is identified by genealogy,★ and the story is dated to the period of the fall of the ten northern tribes of Israel in 722 BCE, when many Israelites were deported to Assyria (2 Kings

17.1–6). The meanings of most of the names in this book are significant for the story. *Tobit* is probably from the Hebrew Tobiah ("God is my good"), from which is also derived the name of Tobit's son Tobias. **2:** *Thisbe* may be Thebez (Judg 9.50–57); *Asher* is probably Hazor.

〰〰〰〰〰〰〰〰〰〰〰〰〰〰

3 I, Tobit, walked in the ways of truth and righteousness all the days of my life. I performed many acts of charity for my kindred and my people who had gone with me in exile to Nineveh in the land of the Assyri-

a Other ancient authorities lack *of Raphael son of Raguel of the descendants*   *b* Gk *Enemessaros*

ans. ⁴When I was in my own country, in the land of Israel, while I was still a young man, the whole tribe of my ancestor Naphtali deserted the house of David and Jerusalem. This city had been chosen from among all the tribes of Israel, where all the tribes of Israel should offer sacrifice and where the temple, the dwelling of God, had been consecrated and established for all generations forever.

5 All my kindred and our ancestral house of Naphtali sacrificed to the calf[a] that King Jeroboam of Israel had erected in Dan and on all the mountains of Galilee. ⁶But I alone went often to Jerusalem for the festivals, as it is prescribed for all Israel by an everlasting decree. I would hurry off to Jerusalem with the first fruits of the crops and the firstlings of the flock, the tithes of the cattle, and the first shearings of the sheep. ⁷I would give these to the priests, the sons of Aaron, at the altar; likewise the tenth of the grain, wine, olive oil, pomegranates, figs, and the rest of the fruits to the sons of Levi who ministered at Jerusalem. Also for six years I would save up a second tenth in money and go and distribute it in Jerusalem. ⁸A third tenth[b] I would give to the orphans and widows and to the converts who had attached themselves to Israel. I would bring it and give it to them in the third year, and we would eat it according to the ordinance decreed concerning it in the law of Moses and according to the instructions of Deborah, the mother of my father Tobiel,[c] for my father had died and left me an orphan. ⁹When I became a man I married a woman,[d] a member of our own family, and by her I became the father of a son whom I named Tobias.

10 After I was carried away captive to Assyria and came as a captive to Nineveh, everyone of my kindred and my people ate the food of the Gentiles, ¹¹but I kept myself from eating the food of the Gentiles. ¹²Because I was mindful of God with all my heart, ¹³the Most High gave me favor and good standing with Shalmaneser,[e] and I used to buy everything he needed. ¹⁴Until his death I used to go into Media, and buy for him there. While in the country of Media I left bags of silver worth ten talents in trust with Gabael, the brother of Gabri. ¹⁵But when Shalmaneser[e] died, and his son Sennacherib reigned in his place, the highways into Media became unsafe and I could no longer go there.

1.3–15: Tobit is deported to Assyria and rises in the court of Shalmaneser. Beginning at 1.3 the text is narrated in the first person, but at 3.7 it shifts to the third person without explanation. **6–15:** Even after deportation, Tobit makes the required offerings in Jerusalem and keeps kosher* (that is, observes the traditional Jewish food laws). God rewards him by causing him to rise in the court of Shalmaneser. **9:** Tobit marries his kinswoman, according to the preferred practice of endogamy, or marrying within the extended family (4.12–13). **14:** *Ten talents* of silver, about 750 pounds, or a huge sum of money. **15:** Here and elsewhere, the account of the Assyrian kings contains some inaccuracies; Shalmaneser had died earlier, succeeded by Sargon and Sennacherib.

---

16 In the days of Shalmaneser[e] I performed many acts of charity to my kindred, those of my tribe. ¹⁷I would give my food to the hungry and my clothing to the naked; and if I saw the dead body of any of my people thrown out behind the wall of Nineveh, I would bury it. ¹⁸I also buried any whom King Sennacherib put to death when he came fleeing from Judea in those days of judgment that the king of heaven executed upon him because of his blasphemies. For in his anger he put to death many Israelites; but I would secretly remove the bodies and bury them. So when Sennacherib looked for them he could not find them. ¹⁹Then one of the Ninevites went and informed the king about me, that I was burying them; so I hid myself. But when I realized that the king knew about me and that I was being searched for to be put to death, I was afraid and ran away. ²⁰Then all my property was confiscated; nothing was left to me that was not taken into the royal treasury except my wife Anna and my son Tobias.

a Other ancient authorities read *heifer*   b *A third tenth* added from other ancient authorities   c Lat: Gk *Hananiel*   d Other ancient authorities add *Anna*   e Gk *Enemessaros*

21 But not forty[a] days passed before two of Sennacherib's[b] sons killed him, and they fled to the mountains of Ararat, and his son Esar-haddon[c] reigned after him. He appointed Ahikar, the son of my brother Hanael[d] over all the accounts of his kingdom, and he had authority over the entire administration. 22 Ahikar interceded for me, and I returned to Nineveh. Now Ahikar was chief cupbearer, keeper of the signet, and in charge of administration of the accounts under King Sennacherib of Assyria; so Esar-haddon[c] reappointed him. He was my nephew and so a close relative.

1.16–22: Tobit's charitable acts land him in trouble. The Jewish practice of burying the dead was different from many other ancient near eastern cultures, but this prohibition by Sennacherib is meant to dishonor the bodies of enemies. 19–22: The character of *Ahikar*★ is borrowed from the popular ancient "Story of Ahikar." In this story Ahikar, prime minister to the king of Assyria, adopts his orphaned nephew, Nadab, as his own son in order to instruct him. Betrayed by his ungrateful nephew, Ahikar is condemned to death. The nephew, however, is found out and punished, and Ahikar is returned to his former position. The motifs★ of Tobit's disgrace, fall, and vindication at court are mirrored in this ancient near eastern tale, and also in Gen 37–50, Esther, Dan 3 and 6, and Bel and the Dragon. 20: *Anna* in Hebrew means "grace."

2 Then during the reign of Esar-haddon[c] I returned home, and my wife Anna and my son Tobias were restored to me. At our festival of Pentecost, which is the sacred festival of weeks, a good dinner was prepared for me and I reclined to eat. 2 When the table was set for me and an abundance of food placed before me, I said to my son Tobias, "Go, my child, and bring whatever poor person you may find of our people among the exiles in Nineveh, who is wholeheartedly mindful of God,[e] and he shall eat together with me. I will wait for you, until you come back." 3 So Tobias went to look for some poor person of our people. When he had returned he said, "Father!" And I replied, "Here I am, my child." Then he went on to say, "Look, father, one of our own people has been murdered and thrown into the market place, and now he lies there strangled." 4 Then I sprang up, left the dinner before even tasting it, and removed the body[f] from the square[g] and laid it[f] in one of the rooms until sunset when I might bury it.[f] 5 When I returned, I washed myself and ate my food in sorrow. 6 Then I remembered the prophecy of Amos, how he said against Bethel,[h]

"Your festivals shall be turned into
         mourning,
     and all your songs into lamentation."
And I wept.

7 When the sun had set, I went and dug a grave and buried him. 8 And my neighbors laughed and said, "Is he still not afraid? He has already been hunted down to be put to death for doing this, and he ran away; yet here he is again burying the dead!" 9 That same night I washed myself and went into my courtyard and slept by the wall of the courtyard; and my face was uncovered because of the heat. 10 I did not know that there were sparrows on the wall; their fresh droppings fell into my eyes and produced white films. I went to physicians to be healed, but the more they treated me with ointments the more my vision was obscured by the white films, until I became completely blind. For four years I remained unable to see. All my kindred were sorry for me, and Ahikar took care of me for two years before he went to Elymais.

2.1–10: Tobit is restored but becomes blind. Tobit's righteousness and charity are constant and may even seem excessive. 1: *Pentecost*★ is Shavuot or Festival of Weeks (Lev 23.15–21; Acts 2.1). 4: Tobit cannot bury the corpse on a religious holiday and also cannot sleep in the house (v. 9) because contact with a corpse would render him ritually unclean. 6: Amos 8.10. 7: Burial, like charity, kinfolk, and blessing, is a recurring motif★ in this work. The constant repetition, even overuse, of some of these terms is probably intended to create a lighthearted tone. 9–10: It is not clear whether Tobit's blindness is caused by the supposedly

a Other ancient authorities read either *forty-five* or *fifty*
b Gk *his*   c Gk *Sacherdonos*   d Other authorities read *Hananael*   e Lat: Gk *wholeheartedly mindful*
f Gk *him*   g Other ancient authorities lack *from the square*   h Other ancient authorities read *against Bethlehem*

■◣▲▲■

Chart   **The parallel problems of Tobit and Sarah**

Tobit's piety (2.1–7)	Sarah's innocence (3.14)
Tobit's problem: blindness (2.9–10)	Sarah's problem: demon (3.8a)
Tobit reproached (2.14b)	Sarah reproached (3.7, 8b–9)
Tobit's prayer (3.1–6)	Sarah's prayer (3.10–15)

■◣▲▲■

natural effects of the bird droppings, by the demon Asmodeus (3.8), or by God to put a divine plan into motion.

11 At that time, also, my wife Anna earned money at women's work. 12She used to send what she made to the owners and they would pay wages to her. One day, the seventh of Dystrus, when she cut off a piece she had woven and sent it to the owners, they paid her full wages and also gave her a young goat for a meal. 13When she returned to me, the goat began to bleat. So I called her and said, "Where did you get this goat? It is surely not stolen, is it? Return it to the owners; for we have no right to eat anything stolen." 14But she said to me, "It was given to me as a gift in addition to my wages." But I did not believe her, and told her to return it to the owners. I became flushed with anger against her over this. Then she replied to me, "Where are your acts of charity? Where are your righteous deeds? These things are known about you!"*a*

2.11–14: Tobit reproves Anna and is reproved by her. A seemingly unrelated plot development actually serves to demonstrate the limits of Tobit's charity and also to dramatize his personal suffering (see chart).

3 Then with much grief and anguish of heart I wept, and with groaning began to pray:
2 "You are righteous, O Lord,
  and all your deeds are just;
all your ways are mercy and truth;
  you judge the world.*b*
3 And now, O Lord, remember me
  and look favorably upon me.

Do not punish me for my sins
  and for my unwitting offenses
  and those that my ancestors
    committed before you.
They sinned against you,
4   and disobeyed your commandments.
So you gave us over to plunder, exile,
    and death,
  to become the talk, the byword, and
    an object of reproach
  among all the nations among whom
    you have dispersed us.
5 And now your many judgments are true
  in exacting penalty from me for my
    sins.
For we have not kept your
    commandments
  and have not walked in accordance
    with truth before you.
6 So now deal with me as you will;
  command my spirit to be taken from
    me,
  so that I may be released from the
    face of the earth and become
    dust.
For it is better for me to die than to
    live,
  because I have had to listen to
    undeserved insults,
  and great is the sorrow within me.
Command, O Lord, that I be released
    from this distress;
  release me to go to the eternal home,
  and do not, O Lord, turn your face
    away from me.

a Or *to you*; Gk *with you*   *b* Other ancient authorities read *you render true and righteous judgment forever*

For it is better for me to die
than to see so much distress in my
life
and to listen to insults."

3.1–6: Tobit prays for death. Tobit's prayer is typical of the penitential prayers of late biblical texts (Neh 9; Dan 9.4–19; Bar 1.15–3.8), even where there is no apparent sin (Prayer of Azariah). Tobit concludes it, however, by asking for death. Is he overreacting to his affliction (as 5.10 implies), or is he broken in spirit because he feels God has forsaken him?

7 On the same day, at Ecbatana in Media, it also happened that Sarah, the daughter of Raguel, was reproached by one of her father's maids. 8For she had been married to seven husbands, and the wicked demon Asmodeus had killed each of them before they had been with her as is customary for wives. So the maid said to her, "You are the one who kills[a] your husbands! See, you have already been married to seven husbands and have not borne the name of[b] a single one of them. 9Why do you beat us? Because your husbands are dead? Go with them! May we never see a son or daughter of yours!"

10 On that day she was grieved in spirit and wept. When she had gone up to her father's upper room, she intended to hang herself. But she thought it over and said, "Never shall they reproach my father, saying to him, 'You had only one beloved daughter but she hanged herself because of her distress.' And I shall bring my father in his old age down in sorrow to Hades. It is better for me not to hang myself, but to pray the Lord that I may die and not listen to these reproaches anymore." 11At that same time, with hands outstretched toward the window, she prayed and said,

"Blessed are you, merciful God!
Blessed is your name forever;
let all your works praise you forever.
12 And now, Lord,[c] I turn my face to
you,
and raise my eyes toward you.
13 Command that I be released from the
earth
and not listen to such reproaches any
more.

14 You know, O Master, that I am
innocent
of any defilement with a man,
15 and that I have not disgraced my name
or the name of my father in the land
of my exile.
I am my father's only child;
he has no other child to be his heir;
and he has no close relative or other
kindred
for whom I should keep myself as
wife.
Already seven husbands of mine have
died.
Why should I still live?
But if it is not pleasing to you, O Lord,
to take my life,
hear me in my disgrace."

3.7–15: Far away, Sarah suffers a similar fate. Sarah's suffering has been at the hands of the *demon Asmodeus,* but like Tobit, she is also reproved by a member of her household. While protesting her innocence, she also prays for death. 8: *Asmodeus,* probably to be identified with "Aeshma Daeva," an archdemon in Persian lore.

16 At that very moment, the prayers of both of them were heard in the glorious presence of God. 17So Raphael was sent to heal both of them: Tobit, by removing the white films from his eyes, so that he might see God's light with his eyes; and Sarah, daughter of Raguel, by giving her in marriage to Tobias son of Tobit, and by setting her free from the wicked demon Asmodeus. For Tobias was entitled to have her before all others who had desired to marry her. At the same time that Tobit returned from the courtyard into his house, Sarah daughter of Raguel came down from her upper room.

3.16–17: Tobit's and Sarah's prayers are heard in heaven. The solutions to both their problems are announced, seemingly undercutting any suspense in the story. However, the interest now revolves around how the angel *Raphael* ("God has healed") will resolve the

a Other ancient authorities read *strangles*   b Other ancient authorities read *have had no benefit from*
c Other ancient authorities lack *Lord*

problems, and how the two unrelated plotlines will become intertwined. In addition, here and elsewhere the author creates irony* by providing the reader important information about the incidents of the story that the protagonists do not have; the reader in effect has an omniscient perspective.

4 That same day Tobit remembered the money that he had left in trust with Gabael at Rages in Media, ²and he said to himself, "Now I have asked for death. Why do I not call my son Tobias and explain to him about the money before I die?" ³Then he called his son Tobias, and when he came to him he said, "My son, when I die,ᵃ give me a proper burial. Honor your mother and do not abandon her all the days of her life. Do whatever pleases her, and do not grieve her in anything. ⁴Remember her, my son, because she faced many dangers for you while you were in her womb. And when she dies, bury her beside me in the same grave.

5 "Revere the Lord all your days, my son, and refuse to sin or to transgress his commandments. Live uprightly all the days of your life, and do not walk in the ways of wrongdoing; ⁶for those who act in accordance with truth will prosper in all their activities. To all those who practice righteousnessᵇ ⁷give alms from your possessions, and do not let your eye begrudge the gift when you make it. Do not turn your face away from anyone who is poor, and the face of God will not be turned away from you. ⁸If you have many possessions, make your gift from them in proportion; if few, do not be afraid to give according to the little you have. ⁹So you will be laying up a good treasure for yourself against the day of necessity. ¹⁰For almsgiving delivers from death and keeps you from going into the Darkness. ¹¹Indeed, almsgiving, for all who practice it, is an excellent offering in the presence of the Most High.

12 "Beware, my son, of every kind of fornication. First of all, marry a woman from among the descendants of your ancestors; do not marry a foreign woman, who is not of your father's tribe; for we are the descendants of the prophets. Remember, my son, that Noah, Abraham, Isaac, and Jacob, our ancestors of old, all took wives from among their kindred. They were blessed in their children, and their posterity will inherit the land. ¹³So now, my son, love your kindred, and in your heart do not disdain your kindred, the sons and daughters of your people, by refusing to take a wife for yourself from among them. For in pride there is ruin and great confusion. And in idleness there is loss and dire poverty, because idleness is the mother of famine.

14 "Do not keep over until the next day the wages of those who work for you, but pay them at once. If you serve God you will receive payment. Watch yourself, my son, in everything you do, and discipline yourself in all your conduct. ¹⁵And what you hate, do not do to anyone. Do not drink wine to excess or let drunkenness go with you on your way. ¹⁶Give some of your food to the hungry, and some of your clothing to the naked. Give all your surplus as alms, and do not let your eye begrudge your giving of alms. ¹⁷Place your bread on the grave of the righteous, but give none to sinners. ¹⁸Seek advice from every wise person and do not despise any useful counsel. ¹⁹At all times bless the Lord God, and ask him that your ways may be made straight and that all your paths and plans may prosper. For none of the nations has understanding, but the Lord himself will give them good counsel; but if he chooses otherwise, he casts down to deepest Hades. So now, my child, remember these commandments, and do not let them be erased from your heart.

4.1–19: Tobit, thinking he is about to die, delivers his testament to his son. **1:** *Money* deposited earlier (1.14) must be recovered so that Tobit can face death. *Gabael* means "God is exalted." **3–19:** Tobit's testament is a combination of general wisdom precepts (e.g., v. 5) and motifs* specific to the story: burial, marriage to a kinswoman, and charity. Interestingly, Tobit's situation appears to contradict his own advice

ᵃ Lat ᵇ The text of codex Sinaiticus goes directly from verse 6 to verse 19, reading *To those who practice righteousness* ¹⁹*the Lord will give good counsel.* In order to fill the lacuna verses 7 to 18 are derived from other ancient authorities

(vv. 6–7). **15:** The Golden Rule is found in many cultures in this negative form, but the positive form (Mt 7.12; Lk 6.31) is rarer.

～～～～～～～～～

20 "And now, my son, let me explain to you that I left ten talents of silver in trust with Gabael son of Gabrias, at Rages in Media. ²¹Do not be afraid, my son, because we have become poor. You have great wealth if you fear God and flee from every sin and do what is good in the sight of the Lord your God."

5 Then Tobias answered his father Tobit, "I will do everything that you have commanded me, father; ²but how can I obtain the money*a* from him, since he does not know me and I do not know him? What evidence*b* am I to give him so that he will recognize and trust me, and give me the money? Also, I do not know the roads to Media, or how to get there." ³Then Tobit answered his son Tobias, "He gave me his bond and I gave him my bond. I*c* divided his in two; we each took one part, and I put one with the money. And now twenty years have passed since I left this money in trust. So now, my son, find yourself a trustworthy man to go with you, and we will pay him wages until you return. But get back the money from Gabael."*d*

4.20–5.3: Tobit tells Tobias how to recover the money. The trip to retrieve the silver will set in motion the main events of the story. The next few chapters will include travel, adventure, demons, angels, magic, and love, the staples of exciting storytelling.

～～～～～～～～～

4 So Tobias went out to look for a man to go with him to Media, someone who was acquainted with the way. He went out and found the angel Raphael standing in front of him; but he did not perceive that he was an angel of God. ⁵Tobias*e* said to him, "Where do you come from, young man?" "From your kindred, the Israelites," he replied, "and I have come here to work." Then Tobias*f* said to him, "Do you know the way to go to Media?" ⁶"Yes," he replied, "I have been there many times; I am acquainted with it and know all the roads. I have often traveled to Media, and would stay with our kinsman Gabael who lives in Rages of Media. It is a journey of two days from Ecbatana to Rages; for it lies in a mountainous area, while Ecbatana is in the middle of the plain." ⁷Then Tobias said to him, "Wait for me, young man, until I go in and tell my father; for I do need you to travel with me, and I will pay you your wages." ⁸He replied, "All right, I will wait; but do not take too long."

9 So Tobias*f* went in to tell his father Tobit and said to him, "I have just found a man who is one of our own Israelite kindred!" He replied, "Call the man in, my son, so that I may learn about his family and to what tribe he belongs, and whether he is trustworthy enough to go with you."

10 Then Tobias went out and called him, and said, "Young man, my father is calling for you." So he went in to him, and Tobit greeted him first. He replied, "Joyous greetings to you!" But Tobit retorted, "What joy is left for me any more? I am a man without eyesight; I cannot see the light of heaven, but I lie in darkness like the dead who no longer see the light. Although still alive, I am among the dead. I hear people but I cannot see them." But the young man*f* said, "Take courage; the time is near for God to heal you; take courage." Then Tobit said to him, "My son Tobias wishes to go to Media. Can you accompany him and guide him? I will pay your wages, brother." He answered, "I can go with him and I know all the roads, for I have often gone to Media and have crossed all its plains, and I am familiar with its mountains and all of its roads."

11 Then Tobit*f* said to him, "Brother, of what family are you and from what tribe? Tell me, brother." ¹²He replied, "Why do you need to know my tribe?" But Tobit*f* said, "I want to be sure, brother, whose son you are and what your name is." ¹³He replied, "I am Azariah, the son of the great Hananiah, one of your relatives." ¹⁴Then Tobit said to him, "Welcome! God save you, brother. Do not feel bitter toward me, brother, because I wanted to be sure about your ancestry. It turns out that you are a kinsman, and

a Gk *it*   *b* Gk *sign*   *c* Other authorities read *He*
d Gk *from him*   *e* Gk *He*   *f* Gk *he*

Novel

The terms novel* and romance* are often used by scholars to describe the fanciful and entertaining prose narratives* from the ancient world. A novel is a fictional story in prose. The increase in education in the ancient world during the third and second centuries BCE (see Sirach 51.23–26) created a literate class, and novels arose in various cultures as a new form of diversion and entertainment. Ancient Greek novels, often called romances as well, feature stereotyped plots that involve the separation and reunion of lovers: A handsome hero and beautiful heroine, engaged or newly married, are separated and tested during a series of adventures, but remain faithful to each other and are eventually reunited to live happily ever after. The storylines are often complicated and involve various marvelous occurrences, including the intervention of gods and goddesses to protect the protagonists. Jewish novels generally portray extended families rather than the nuclear family of husband and wife, and in many cases (Judith, Esther, Susanna, *Joseph and Aseneth,** and to some extent, Tobit) the heroine is at the center of the action. Her challenge is not to be reunited with her husband but to overcome the obstacles to Jews or to her religious life.

of good and noble lineage. For I knew Hananiah and Nathan,*a* the two sons of Shemeliah,*b* and they used to go with me to Jerusalem and worshiped with me there, and were not led astray. Your kindred are good people; you come of good stock. Hearty welcome!"

15 Then he added, "I will pay you a drachma a day as wages, as well as expenses for yourself and my son, 16 and*c* I will add something to your wages." Raphael*d* answered, "I will go with him; so do not fear. We shall leave in good health and return to you in good health, because the way is safe." 17 So Tobit*e* said to him, "Blessings be upon you, brother."

Then he called his son and said to him, "Son, prepare supplies for the journey and set out with your brother. May God in heaven bring you safely there and return you in good health to me; and may his angel, my son, accompany you both for your safety."

Before he went out to start his journey, he kissed his father and mother. Tobit then said to him, "Have a safe journey."

18 But his mother*f* began to weep, and said to Tobit, "Why is it that you have sent my child away? Is he not the staff of our hand as he goes in and out before us? 19 Do not

heap money upon money, but let it be a ransom for our child. 20 For the life that is given to us by the Lord is enough for us." 21 Tobit*d* said to her, "Do not worry; our child will leave in good health and return to us in good health. Your eyes will see him on the day when he returns to you in good health. Say no more! Do not fear for them, my sister. 22 For a good angel will accompany him; his journey will be successful, and he will come back in good health." 1 So she stopped weeping.

5.4–6.1a: The angel Raphael is hired to guide Tobias. There is irony* and humor in the interviews with Raphael. Tobit and Tobias are brusque with Raphael, pressing to learn his identity, while the audience knows he is an angel. It is also significant that, with the exception of the Assyrian kings, every character in the book is related to Tobit, even Raphael in his human guise. **17a:** The irony continues when Tobit prays for an angel to accompany them. **17b–21:** Although Anna wisely counsels caution, Tobit now expresses a more

a Other ancient authorities read *Jathan* or *Nathaniah*
b Other ancient authorities read *Shemaiah*
c Other ancient authorities add *when you return safely*
d Gk *He*　　*e* Gk *he*　　*f* Other ancient authorities add *Anna*

optimistic outlook. The section of the story set in Nineveh thus concludes on a reassuring, rather than suspenseful, note.

The young man went out and the angel went with him; [2]and the dog came out with him and went along with them. So they both journeyed along, and when the first night overtook them they camped by the Tigris river. [3]Then the young man went down to wash his feet in the Tigris river. Suddenly a large fish leaped up from the water and tried to swallow the young man's foot, and he cried out. [4]But the angel said to the young man, "Catch hold of the fish and hang on to it!" So the young man grasped the fish and drew it up on the land. [5]Then the angel said to him, "Cut open the fish and take out its gall, heart, and liver. Keep them with you, but throw away the intestines. For its gall, heart, and liver are useful as medicine." [6]So after cutting open the fish the young man gathered together the gall, heart, and liver; then he roasted and ate some of the fish, and kept some to be salted.

The two continued on their way together until they were near Media.[a] [7]Then the young man questioned the angel and said to him, "Brother Azariah, what medicinal value is there in the fish's heart and liver, and in the gall?" [8]He replied, "As for the fish's heart and liver, you must burn them to make a smoke in the presence of a man or woman afflicted by a demon or evil spirit, and every affliction will flee away and never remain with that person any longer. [9]And as for the gall, anoint a person's eyes where white films have appeared on them; blow upon them, upon the white films, and the eyes[b] will be healed."

6.1b–9: On their way Raphael instructs Tobias in the exorcising of demons. Tobias is very quickly plunged into the world of magic and danger, and in the process, the reader learns how the *fish* will provide the means to solve the protagonists' problems. The information given the reader once again removes some of the suspense as to the role of the fish organs, yet at the same time, it gives the reader insights into how the lives of Tobit and Sarah will become intertwined. **2:** The *dog* that accompanies them, although serving little narrative purpose, is a common folktale motif✳ and may suggest a faithful traveling companion for an important quest.

10 When he entered Media and already was approaching Ecbatana,[c] [11]Raphael said to the young man, "Brother Tobias." "Here I am," he answered. Then Raphael[d] said to him, "We must stay this night in the home of Raguel. He is your relative, and he has a daughter named Sarah. [12]He has no male heir and no daughter except Sarah only, and you, as next of kin to her, have before all other men a hereditary claim on her. Also it is right for you to inherit her father's possessions. Moreover, the girl is sensible, brave, and very beautiful, and her father is a good man." [13]He continued, "You have every right to take her in marriage. So listen to me, brother; tonight I will speak to her father about the girl, so that we may take her to be your bride. When we return from Rages we will celebrate her marriage. For I know that Raguel can by no means keep her from you or promise her to another man without incurring the penalty of death according to the decree of the book of Moses. Indeed he knows that you, rather than any other man, are entitled to marry his daughter. So now listen to me, brother, and tonight we shall speak concerning the girl and arrange her engagement to you. And when we return from Rages we will take her and bring her back with us to your house."

14 Then Tobias said in answer to Raphael, "Brother Azariah, I have heard that she already has been married to seven husbands and that they died in the bridal chamber. On the night when they went in to her, they would die. I have heard people saying that it was a demon that killed them. [15]It does not harm her, but it kills anyone who desires to approach her. So now, since I am the only son my father has, I am afraid that I may die and bring my father's and mother's life down to their grave, grieving for me—and they have no other son to bury them."

a Other ancient authorities read *Ecbatana*   b Gk *they*
c Other ancient authorities read *Rages*   d Gk *he*

16 But Raphael[a] said to him, "Do you not remember your father's orders when he commanded you to take a wife from your father's house? Now listen to me, brother, and say no more about this demon. Take her. I know that this very night she will be given to you in marriage. [17]When you enter the bridal chamber, take some of the fish's liver and heart, and put them on the embers of the incense. An odor will be given off; [18]the demon will smell it and flee, and will never be seen near her any more. Now when you are about to go to bed with her, both of you must first stand up and pray, imploring the Lord of heaven that mercy and safety may be granted to you. Do not be afraid, for she was set apart for you before the world was made. You will save her, and she will go with you. I presume that you will have children by her, and they will be as brothers to you. Now say no more!" When Tobias heard the words of Raphael and learned that she was his kinswoman,[b] related through his father's lineage, he loved her very much, and his heart was drawn to her.

6.10–18: Raphael plays matchmaker for Tobias and Sarah. 12: Under the Jewish law of levirate marriage* (Deut 25.5–10; compare Gen 38), if a husband died and left no heirs, the nearest male relative was to marry the widow in order to produce heirs for the deceased. More distant relatives could marry the widow if there were no closer relatives, or if the closer relatives waived their right to marry her (compare Ruth 3–4). **13–15:** Tobias has heard of the demon who kills Sarah's husbands, but he points out the need to bury his parents as an overriding concern. The constant references to death and burial are probably intended as comic exaggeration; they begin in ch. 1 and reach a climax* in 8.9b–21. **16–18:** Raphael assures Tobias that choosing a kinswoman is also his father's wish, and that it will result in a happy marriage.

7 Now when they[c] entered Ecbatana, Tobias[a] said to him, "Brother Azariah, take me straight to our brother Raguel." So he took him to Raguel's house, where they found him sitting beside the courtyard door. They greeted him first, and he replied, "Joyous greetings, brothers; welcome and good health!" Then he brought them into his house. [2]He said to his wife Edna, "How much the young man resembles my kinsman Tobit!" [3]Then Edna questioned them, saying, "Where are you from, brothers?" They answered, "We belong to the descendants of Naphtali who are exiles in Nineveh." [4]She said to them, "Do you know our kinsman Tobit?" And they replied, "Yes, we know him." Then she asked them, "Is he[d] in good health?" [5]They replied, "He is alive and in good health." And Tobias added, "He is my father!" [6]At that Raguel jumped up and kissed him and wept. [7]He also spoke to him as follows, "Blessings on you, my child, son of a good and noble father![e] O most miserable of calamities that such an upright and beneficent man has become blind!" He then embraced his kinsman Tobias and wept. [8]His wife Edna also wept for him, and their daughter Sarah likewise wept. [9]Then Raguel[a] slaughtered a ram from the flock and received them very warmly.

7.1–9a: Tobias and Raphael proceed to the home of Raguel, Edna, and Sarah. 1: *Brothers,* in both Aramaic and Greek, can mean kinsmen. It is often used in Tobit, as family relations are emphasized. Note also *sister* for wife at vv. 11, 15, and 8.4.

When they had bathed and washed themselves and had reclined to dine, Tobias said to Raphael, "Brother Azariah, ask Raguel to give me my kinswoman[b] Sarah." [10]But Raguel overheard it and said to the lad, "Eat and drink, and be merry tonight. For no one except you, brother, has the right to marry my daughter Sarah. Likewise I am not at liberty to give her to any other man than yourself, because you are my nearest relative. But let me explain to you the true situation more fully, my child. [11]I have given her to seven men of our kinsmen, and all died on the night when they went in to her. But now, my child, eat and drink, and the Lord will act on behalf of you both." But Tobias said, "I will neither eat nor drink anything until you set-

a Gk *he* *b* Gk *sister* *c* Other ancient authorities read *he* *d* Other ancient authorities add *alive and* *e* Other ancient authorities add *When he heard that Tobit had lost his sight, he was stricken with grief and wept. Then he said,*

tle the things that pertain to me." So Raguel said, "I will do so. She is given to you in accordance with the decree in the book of Moses, and it has been decreed from heaven that she be given to you. Take your kinswoman;[a] from now on you are her brother and she is your sister. She is given to you from today and forever. May the Lord of heaven, my child, guide and prosper you both this night and grant you mercy and peace." [12]Then Raguel summoned his daughter Sarah. When she came to him he took her by the hand and gave her to Tobias,[b] saying, "Take her to be your wife in accordance with the law and decree written in the book of Moses. Take her and bring her safely to your father. And may the God of heaven prosper your journey with his peace." [13]Then he called her mother and told her to bring writing material; and he wrote out a copy of a marriage contract, to the effect that he gave her to him as wife according to the decree of the law of Moses. [14]Then they began to eat and drink.

15 Raguel called his wife Edna and said to her, "Sister, get the other room ready, and take her there." [16]So she went and made the bed in the room as he had told her, and brought Sarah[c] there. She wept for her daughter.[c] Then, wiping away the tears,[d] she said to her, "Take courage, my daughter; the Lord of heaven grant you joy[e] in place of your sorrow. Take courage, my daughter." Then she went out.

7.9b–16: A marriage is arranged between Tobias and Sarah. 10: Raguel is bound by the levirate* law to have his daughter marry Tobias (see comment on 6.12). **11:** The marriage of Tobias and Sarah is arranged contractually between Tobias and Raguel according to Jewish law, but Raguel also warns Tobias that his predecessors have died.

~~~

8 When they had finished eating and drinking they wanted to retire; so they took the young man and brought him into the bedroom. [2]Then Tobias remembered the words of Raphael, and he took the fish's liver and heart out of the bag where he had them and put them on the embers of the incense. [3]The odor of the fish so repelled the demon

that he fled to the remotest parts[f] of Egypt. But Raphael followed him, and at once bound him there hand and foot.

4 When the parents[g] had gone out and shut the door of the room, Tobias got out of bed and said to Sarah,[c] "Sister, get up, and let us pray and implore our Lord that he grant us mercy and safety." [5]So she got up, and they began to pray and implore that they might be kept safe. Tobias[h] began by saying,

"Blessed are you, O God of our
     ancestors,
   and blessed is your name in all
     generations forever.
Let the heavens and the whole creation
   bless you forever.
[6] You made Adam, and for him you made
     his wife Eve
   as a helper and support.
From the two of them the human
     race has sprung.
You said, 'It is not good that the man
     should be alone;
   let us make a helper for him like
     himself.'
[7] I now am taking this kinswoman of
     mine,
   not because of lust,
   but with sincerity.
Grant that she and I may find mercy
   and that we may grow old
     together."

[8]And they both said, "Amen, Amen." [9]Then they went to sleep for the night.

8.1–9a: Tobias and Sarah consummate their marriage. 1–3: Because Tobias is appropriately prepared, the *demon* is easily exorcised. The struggle between Raphael and the demon, and the subsequent binding, are typical ways of describing the conflict of supernatural figures, but the description of the procedure is also humorous here. **5–7:** Tobias and Sarah sanctify their marriage with a blessing that recalls the first marriage, that of Adam and Eve. In this scene, the dramatic center of the story, the importance of marriage and the

---

a Gk *sister*   *b* Gk *him*   *c* Gk *her*   *d* Other ancient authorities read *the tears of her daughter*   *e* Other ancient authorities read *favor*   *f* Or *fled through the air to the parts*   *g* Gk *they*   *h* Gk *He*

solidifying of the extended family is affirmed. From this point on, the problems of the story begin to be resolved.

〜〜〜〜〜〜〜〜〜〜

But Raguel arose and called his servants to him, and they went and dug a grave, 10for he said, "It is possible that he will die and we will become an object of ridicule and derision." 11When they had finished digging the grave, Raguel went into his house and called his wife, 12saying, "Send one of the maids and have her go in to see if he is alive. But if he is dead, let us bury him without anyone knowing it." 13So they sent the maid, lit a lamp, and opened the door; and she went in and found them sound asleep together. 14Then the maid came out and informed them that he was alive and that nothing was wrong. 15So they blessed the God of heaven, and Raguel*a* said,

"Blessed are you, O God, with every
pure blessing;
let all your chosen ones bless you.*b*
Let them bless you forever.

16 Blessed are you because you have made
me glad.
It has not turned out as I expected,
but you have dealt with us according
to your great mercy.

17 Blessed are you because you had
compassion
on two only children.
Be merciful to them, O Master, and
keep them safe;
bring their lives to fulfillment
in happiness and mercy."

18Then he ordered his servants to fill in the grave before daybreak.

19 After this he asked his wife to bake many loaves of bread; and he went out to the herd and brought two steers and four rams and ordered them to be slaughtered. So they began to make preparations. 20Then he called for Tobias and swore on oath to him in these words:*c* "You shall not leave here for fourteen days, but shall stay here eating and drinking with me; and you shall cheer up my daughter, who has been depressed. 21Take at once half of what I own and return in safety to your father; the other half will be yours when my wife and I die. Take courage, my child. I am your father and Edna is your mother, and we belong to you as well as to your wife*d* now and forever. Take courage, my child."

8.9b–21: Raguel and Edna expect to bury another son-in-law but are surprised. In this humorous scene, Raguel wants Tobias buried quickly before anyone finds out that he has died. **15–17:** Raguel greets the good news with a heartfelt *blessing.* **18–21:** The filling in of the grave represents the end of the ordeal for Sarah's family, and Raguel can now celebrate a truly joyful wedding feast. His benevolence is indicated by his generous overtures to Tobias.

〜〜〜〜〜〜〜〜〜〜

9 Then Tobias called Raphael and said to him, 2"Brother Azariah, take four servants and two camels with you and travel to Rages. Go to the home of Gabael, give him the bond, get the money, and then bring him with you to the wedding celebration. 4For you know that my father must be counting the days, and if I delay even one day I will upset him very much. 3You are witness to the oath Raguel has sworn, and I cannot violate his oath."*e* 5So Raphael with the four servants and two camels went to Rages in Media and stayed with Gabael. Raphael*f* gave him the bond and informed him that Tobit's son Tobias had married and was inviting him to the wedding celebration. So Gabael*g* got up and counted out to him the money bags, with their seals intact; then they loaded them on the camels.*h* 6In the morning they both got up early and went to the wedding celebration. When they came into Raguel's house they found Tobias reclining at table. He sprang up and greeted Gabael,*i* who wept and blessed him with the words, "Good and noble son of a father good and noble, upright and generous! May the Lord grant the blessing of heaven to you and your wife, and to your wife's father and mother. Blessed be God, for I see in Tobias the very image of my cousin Tobit."

a Gk *they*   *b* Other ancient authorities lack this line
c Other ancient authorities read *Tobias and said to him*
d Gk *sister*   *e* In other ancient authorities verse 3
precedes verse 4   *f* Gk *He*   *g* Gk *he*   *h* Other
ancient authorities lack *on the camels*   *i* Gk *him*

9.1–6: Tobias sends Raphael on ahead to retrieve the deposited money. 2: It is part of the fairytale-like tone of the text that Tobias trusts Raphael to retrieve the fortune on deposit with Gabael. **6:** Gabael greets Tobias enthusiastically. All of the characters are part of one extended family and they act accordingly.

10 Now, day by day, Tobit kept counting how many days Tobias[a] would need for going and for returning. And when the days had passed and his son did not appear, [2]he said, "Is it possible that he has been detained? Or that Gabael has died, and there is no one to give him the money?" [3]And he began to worry. [4]His wife Anna said, "My child has perished and is no longer among the living." And she began to weep and mourn for her son, saying, [5]"Woe to me, my child, the light of my eyes, that I let you make the journey." [6]But Tobit kept saying to her, "Be quiet and stop worrying, my dear;[b] he is all right. Probably something unexpected has happened there. The man who went with him is trustworthy and is one of our own kin. Do not grieve for him, my dear;[b] he will soon be here." [7]She answered him, "Be quiet yourself! Stop trying to deceive me! My child has perished." She would rush out every day and watch the road her son had taken, and would heed no one.[c] When the sun had set she would go in and mourn and weep all night long, getting no sleep at all.

10.1–7a: Tobit and Anna wait anxiously for Tobias and Raphael to return. Because the reader knows that Tobias is happily married, the suffering of Tobit and Anna has an ironic poignance. The opposite situation occurs in Judg 5.28–30, where a mother celebrates her son's victories, unaware that he has been killed. The disagreement here between Tobit and Anna mirrors the disagreement in ch. 2, although in this case the reader knows that they are about to be made exceedingly happy.

Now when the fourteen days of the wedding celebration had ended that Raguel had sworn to observe for his daughter, Tobias came to him and said, "Send me back, for I know that my father and mother do not be-lieve that they will see me again. So I beg of you, father, to let me go so that I may return to my own father. I have already explained to you how I left him." [8]But Raguel said to Tobias, "Stay, my child, stay with me; I will send messengers to your father Tobit and they will inform him about you." [9]But he said, "No! I beg you to send me back to my father." [10]So Raguel promptly gave Tobias his wife Sarah, as well as half of all his property: male and female slaves, oxen and sheep, donkeys and camels, clothing, money, and household goods. [11]Then he saw them safely off; he embraced Tobias[d] and said, "Farewell, my child; have a safe journey. The Lord of heaven prosper you and your wife Sarah, and may I see children of yours before I die." [12]Then he kissed his daughter Sarah and said to her, "My daughter, honor your father-in-law and your mother-in-law,[e] since from now on they are as much your parents as those who gave you birth. Go in peace, daughter, and may I hear a good report about you as long as I live." Then he bade them farewell and let them go. Then Edna said to Tobias, "My child and dear brother, the Lord of heaven bring you back safely, and may I live long enough to see children of you and of my daughter Sarah before I die. In the sight of the Lord I entrust my daughter to you; do nothing to grieve her all the days of your life. Go in peace, my child. From now on I am your mother and Sarah is your be-loved wife.[b] May we all prosper together all the days of our lives." Then she kissed them both and saw them safely off. [13]Tobias parted from Raguel with happiness and joy, praising the Lord of heaven and earth, King over all, because he had made his journey a success. Finally, he blessed Raguel and his wife Edna, and said, "I have been commanded by the Lord to honor you all the days of my life."[f]

10.7b–13: Tobias asks leave to return home. Raguel generously provides the dowry for his daughter and

a Gk *he*   *b* Gk *sister*   *c* Other ancient authorities read *and she would eat nothing*   *d* Gk *him*   *e* Other ancient authorities lack parts of *Then . . . mother-in-law*   *f* Lat: Meaning of Gk uncertain

Joseph and Aseneth

Joseph and Aseneth,★ a story about Joseph in Egypt, takes as its point of departure the account of Joseph and his brothers in Egypt in Gen 37–50. Aseneth, the beautiful but haughty daughter of an Egyptian priest, falls in love with Joseph, is converted by a heavenly messenger to belief in Joseph's God, and is married to him. As in the Greek romances, the protagonists here are both extravagantly beautiful, pious, and modest. Aseneth's conversion is accompanied by a meal consisting of the honey of heaven, which gives her eternal life. Despite an evil plot between Pharaoh's jealous son and two of Joseph's brothers, Joseph and Aseneth overcome all obstacles and Joseph, with Aseneth as his wife, becomes the ruler of Egypt when Pharaoh dies.

cements the bonds between the two branches of the extended family.

11 When they came near to Kaserin, which is opposite Nineveh, Raphael said, 2"You are aware of how we left your father. 3Let us run ahead of your wife and prepare the house while they are still on the way." 4As they went on together Raphael*a* said to him, "Have the gall ready." And the dog*b* went along behind them.

5 Meanwhile Anna sat looking intently down the road by which her son would come. 6When she caught sight of him coming, she said to his father, "Look, your son is coming, and the man who went with him!"

7 Raphael said to Tobias, before he had approached his father, "I know that his eyes will be opened. 8Smear the gall of the fish on his eyes; the medicine will make the white films shrink and peel off from his eyes, and your father will regain his sight and see the light."

9 Then Anna ran up to her son and threw her arms around him, saying, "Now that I have seen you, my child, I am ready to die." And she wept. 10Then Tobit got up and came stumbling out through the courtyard door. Tobias went up to him, 11with the gall of the fish in his hand, and holding him firmly, he blew into his eyes, saying, "Take courage, father." With this he applied the medicine on his eyes, 12and it made them smart.*c* 13Next, with both his hands he peeled off the white films from the corners of his eyes. Then Tobit*a* saw his son and*d* threw his arms around him, 14and he wept and said to him, "I see you, my son, the light of my eyes!" Then he said,

"Blessed be God,
 and blessed be his great name,
 and blessed be all his holy angels.
May his holy name be blessed*e*
 throughout all the ages.
15 Though he afflicted me,
 he has had mercy upon me.*f*
 Now I see my son Tobias!"

So Tobit went in rejoicing and praising God at the top of his voice. Tobias reported to his father that his journey had been successful, that he had brought the money, that he had married Raguel's daughter Sarah, and that she was, indeed, on her way there, very near to the gate of Nineveh.

11.1–15: Tobias and Raphael return and cure Tobit's blindness. In a romance★ such as this, the distinction between magic and religion becomes less relevant. It was God who made the fish available in 6.1b–9, and Raphael who explained its usefulness to Tobias (8.1–9a). Working in tandem, God and Raphael have manipulated events toward a happy ending. **14–15:** Tobit begins a series of blessings, which becomes a common motif★ at this point in the narrative.

a Gk *he*   b Codex Sinaiticus reads *And the Lord*
c Lat: Meaning of Gk uncertain   d Other ancient authorities lack *saw his son and*   e Codex Sinaiticus reads *May his great name be upon us and blessed be all the angels*   f Lat: Gk lacks this line

16 Then Tobit, rejoicing and praising God, went out to meet his daughter-in-law at the gate of Nineveh. When the people of Nineveh saw him coming, walking along in full vigor and with no one leading him, they were amazed. ¹⁷Before them all, Tobit acknowledged that God had been merciful to him and had restored his sight. When Tobit met Sarah the wife of his son Tobias, he blessed her saying, "Come in, my daughter, and welcome. Blessed be your God who has brought you to us, my daughter. Blessed be your father and your mother, blessed be my son Tobias, and blessed be you, my daughter. Come in now to your home, and welcome, with blessing and joy. Come in, my daughter." So on that day there was rejoicing among all the Jews who were in Nineveh. ¹⁸Ahikar and his nephew Nadab were also present to share Tobit's joy. With merriment they celebrated Tobias's wedding feast for seven days, and many gifts were given to him.ᵃ

11.16–18: Tobit meets his daughter-in-law, Sarah. The general celebration is extended further, encompassing the *Jews* who reside in *Nineveh*. The term "Jews" is normally applied to the residents of Judah from the time of the exile on, but here this term is inappropriately used of an earlier period.

12 When the wedding celebration was ended, Tobit called his son Tobias and said to him, "My child, see to paying the wages of the man who went with you, and give him a bonus as well." ²He replied, "Father, how much shall I pay him? It would do no harm to give him half of the possessions brought back with me. ³For he has led me back to you safely, he cured my wife, he brought the money back with me, and he healed you. How much extra shall I give him as a bonus?" ⁴Tobit said, "He deserves, my child, to receive half of all that he brought back." ⁵So Tobiasᵇ called him and said, "Take for your wages half of all that you brought back, and farewell."

12.1–5: Tobit and Tobias decide to pay Raphael. Since the amount of money on deposit in Rages was so large, the payment of half to Raphael would be very generous. It is part of the mood of celebration for all the blessings the family has received.

6 Then Raphaelᵇ called the two of them privately and said to them, "Bless God and acknowledge him in the presence of all the living for the good things he has done for you. Bless and sing praise to his name. With fitting honor declare to all people the deedsᶜ of God. Do not be slow to acknowledge him. ⁷It is good to conceal the secret of a king, but to acknowledge and reveal the works of God, and with fitting honor to acknowledge him. Do good and evil will not overtake you. ⁸Prayer with fastingᵈ is good, but better than both is almsgiving with righteousness. A little with righteousness is better than wealth with wrongdoing.ᵉ It is better to give alms than to lay up gold. ⁹For almsgiving saves from death and purges away every sin. Those who give alms will enjoy a full life, ¹⁰but those who commit sin and do wrong are their own worst enemies.

11 "I will now declare the whole truth to you and will conceal nothing from you. Already I have declared it to you when I said, 'It is good to conceal the secret of a king, but to reveal with due honor the works of God.' ¹²So now when you and Sarah prayed, it was I who brought and readᶠ the record of your prayer before the glory of the Lord, and likewise whenever you would bury the dead. ¹³And that time when you did not hesitate to get up and leave your dinner to go and bury the dead, ¹⁴I was sent to you to test you. And at the same time God sent me to heal you and Sarah your daughter-in-law. ¹⁵I am Raphael, one of the seven angels who stand ready and enter before the glory of the Lord."

16 The two of them were shaken; they fell face down, for they were afraid. ¹⁷But he said to them, "Do not be afraid; peace be with you. Bless God forevermore. ¹⁸As for me, when I was with you, I was not acting on my own will, but by the will of God. Bless

---

a Other ancient authorities lack parts of this sentence
b Gk *he*   *c* Gk *words*; other ancient authorities read *words of the deeds*   *d* Codex Sinaiticus *with sincerity*
e Lat   *f* Lat: Gk lacks *and read*

him each and every day; sing his praises. [19]Although you were watching me, I really did not eat or drink anything—but what you saw was a vision. [20]So now get up from the ground,[a] and acknowledge God. See, I am ascending to him who sent me. Write down all these things that have happened to you." And he ascended. [21]Then they stood up, and could see him no more. [22]They kept blessing God and singing his praises, and they acknowledged God for these marvelous deeds of his, when an angel of God had appeared to them.

12.6–22: Raphael gives parting instructions and reveals his identity. 7–10: Raphael's instructions emphasize *almsgiving*, as did Tobit's at 4.6–11. The implication of this is that God has rewarded Tobit for his earlier acts of charity. **20:** *Write down all these things that have happened to you:* The present text of Tobit, which begins in the first person, is presumed to be the result of this command.

13

Then Tobit[b] said:
"Blessed be God who lives forever,
because his kingdom[c] lasts throughout all ages.
[2] For he afflicts, and he shows mercy;
he leads down to Hades in the lowest regions of the earth,
and he brings up from the great abyss,[d]
and there is nothing that can escape his hand.
[3] Acknowledge him before the nations, O children of Israel;
for he has scattered you among them.
[4] He has shown you his greatness even there.
Exalt him in the presence of every living being,
because he is our Lord and he is our God;
he is our Father and he is God forever.
[5] He will afflict[e] you for your iniquities,
but he will again show mercy on all of you.
He will gather you from all the nations
among whom you have been scattered.
[6] If you turn to him with all your heart
and with all your soul,
to do what is true before him,
then he will turn to you
and will no longer hide his face from you.
So now see what he has done for you;
acknowledge him at the top of your voice.
Bless the Lord of righteousness,
and exalt the King of the ages.[f]
In the land of my exile I acknowledge him,
and show his power and majesty to a nation of sinners:
'Turn back, you sinners, and do what is right before him;
perhaps he may look with favor upon you and show you mercy.'
[7] As for me, I exalt my God,
and my soul rejoices in the King of heaven.
[8] Let all people speak of his majesty,
and acknowledge him in Jerusalem.
[9] O Jerusalem, the holy city,
he afflicted[g] you for the deeds of your hands,[h]
but will again have mercy on the children of the righteous.
[10] Acknowledge the Lord, for he is good,[i]
and bless the King of the ages,
so that his tent[j] may be rebuilt in you in joy.
May he cheer all those within you who are captives,
and love all those within you who are distressed,
to all generations forever.
[11] A bright light will shine to all the ends of the earth;

a Other ancient authorities read *now bless the Lord on earth*   b Gk *he*   c Other ancient authorities read *forever, and his kingdom*   d Gk *from destruction*   e Other ancient authorities read *He afflicted*   f The lacuna in codex Sinaiticus, verses 6b to 10a, is filled in from other ancient authorities   g Other ancient authorities read *will afflict*   h Other ancient authorities read *your children*   i Other ancient authorities read *Lord worthily*   j Or *tabernacle*

many nations will come to you from
 far away,
the inhabitants of the remotest parts of
 the earth to your holy name,
 bearing gifts in their hands for the
  King of heaven.
Generation after generation will give
 joyful praise in you;
 the name of the chosen city will
  endure forever.

12 Cursed are all who speak a harsh word
  against you;
 cursed are all who conquer you
  and pull down your walls,
all who overthrow your towers
 and set your homes on fire.
 But blessed forever will be all who
  revere you.ᵃ

13 Go, then, and rejoice over the children
  of the righteous,
 for they will be gathered together
 and will praise the Lord of the ages.

14 Happy are those who love you,
 and happy are those who rejoice in
  your prosperity.
 Happy also are all people who grieve
  with you
 because of your afflictions;
 for they will rejoice with you
 and witness all your glory forever.

15 My soul blessesᵇ the Lord, the great
  King!

16 For Jerusalem will be builtᶜ as his
  house for all ages.
How happy I will be if a remnant of my
 descendants should survive
 to see your glory and acknowledge the
  King of heaven.
The gates of Jerusalem will be built with
 sapphire and emerald,
 and all your walls with precious
  stones.
The towers of Jerusalem will be built
 with gold,
 and their battlements with pure gold.
The streets of Jerusalem will be paved
 with ruby and with stones of Ophir.

17 The gates of Jerusalem will sing hymns
  of joy,
 and all her houses will cry,
  'Hallelujah!

Blessed be the God of Israel!'
 and the blessed will bless the holy
  name forever and ever."

13.1–17: Tobit's hymn of praise. It is possible that chs. 13–14 (except for 14.1–2) were not originally part of the story of Tobit but were added at different times. Although the hymn provides a fitting celebration to the happy ending of the story and emphasizes the motif* of "blessing," it does not refer to any of the incidents of the story.

〜〜〜〜〜〜〜〜〜〜〜〜〜

14 So ended Tobit's words of praise.
2 Tobitᵈ died in peace when he was one hundred twelve years old, and was buried with great honor in Nineveh. He was sixty-twoᵉ years old when he lost his eyesight, and after regaining it he lived in prosperity, giving alms and continually blessing God and acknowledging God's majesty.

3 When he was about to die, he called his son Tobias and the seven sons of Tobiasᶠ and gave this command: "My son, take your children ⁴and hurry off to Media, for I believe the word of God that Nahum spoke about Nineveh, that all these things will take place and overtake Assyria and Nineveh. Indeed, everything that was spoken by the prophets of Israel, whom God sent, will occur. None of all their words will fail, but all will come true at their appointed times. So it will be safer in Media than in Assyria and Babylon. For I know and believe that whatever God has said will be fulfilled and will come true; not a single word of the prophecies will fail. All of our kindred, inhabitants of the land of Israel, will be scattered and taken as captives from the good land; and the whole land of Israel will be desolate, even Samaria and Jerusalem will be desolate. And the temple of God in it will be burned to the ground, and it will be desolate for a while.ᵍ

5 "But God will again have mercy on them, and God will bring them back into the

---

ᵃ Other ancient authorities read *who build you up*
ᵇ Or *O my soul, bless* ᶜ Other ancient authorities add *for a city* ᵈ Gk *He* ᵉ Other ancient authorities read *fifty-eight* ᶠ Lat: Gk lacks *and the seven sons of Tobias* ᵍ Lat: Other ancient authorities read *of God will be in distress and will be burned for a while*

land of Israel; and they will rebuild the temple of God, but not like the first one until the period when the times of fulfillment shall come. After this they all will return from their exile and will rebuild Jerusalem in splendor; and in it the temple of God will be rebuilt, just as the prophets of Israel have said concerning it. [6]Then the nations in the whole world will all be converted and worship God in truth. They will all abandon their idols, which deceitfully have led them into their error; [7]and in righteousness they will praise the eternal God. All the Israelites who are saved in those days and are truly mindful of God will be gathered together; they will go to Jerusalem and live in safety forever in the land of Abraham, and it will be given over to them. Those who sincerely love God will rejoice, but those who commit sin and injustice will vanish from all the earth. [8,9]So now, my children, I command you, serve God faithfully and do what is pleasing in his sight. Your children are also to be commanded to do what is right and to give alms, and to be mindful of God and to bless his name at all times with sincerity and with all their strength. So now, my son, leave Nineveh; do not remain here. [10]On whatever day you bury your mother beside me, do not stay overnight within the confines of the city. For I see that there is much wickedness within it, and that much deceit is practiced within it, while the people are without shame. See, my son, what Nadab did to Ahikar who had reared him. Was he not, while still alive, brought down into the earth? For God repaid him to his face for this shameful treatment. Ahikar came out into the light, but Nadab went into the eternal darkness, because he tried to kill Ahikar. Because he gave alms, Ahikar[a] escaped the fatal trap that Nadab had set for him, but Nadab fell into it himself, and was destroyed. [11]So now, my children, see what almsgiving accomplishes, and what injustice does—it brings death! But now my breath fails me."

Then they laid him on his bed, and he died; and he received an honorable funeral. [12]When Tobias's mother died, he buried her beside his father. Then he and his wife and children[b] returned to Media and settled in Ecbatana with Raguel his father-in-law. [13]He treated his parents-in-law[c] with great respect in their old age, and buried them in Ecbatana of Media. He inherited both the property of Raguel and that of his father Tobit. [14]He died highly respected at the age of one hundred seventeen[d] years. [15]Before he died he heard[e] of the destruction of Nineveh, and he saw its prisoners being led into Media, those whom King Cyaxares[f] of Media had taken captive. Tobias[g] praised God for all he had done to the people of Nineveh and Assyria; before he died he rejoiced over Nineveh, and he blessed the Lord God forever and ever. Amen.[h]

14.1–15: The testament of Tobit. Unlike the first testament of Tobit (ch. 4), this one does not relate to the story directly but predicts future events and has parallels to Zech 8.20–23 and Isa 40–55. It does not emphasize coexistence in the Diaspora* as the rest of the book does but instead envisions a renewal of Jewish life in Jerusalem. **10:** *What Nadab did to Ahikar:* See comments on 1.19–22.

---

a Gk *he*; other ancient authorities read *Manasses*
b Codex Sinaiticus lacks *and children*　　c Gk *them*
d Other authorities read other numbers　　e Codex Sinaiticus reads *saw and heard*　　f Cn: Codex Sinaiticus *Ahikar*; other ancient authorities read *Nebuchadnezzar and Ahasuerus*　　g Gk *He*　　h Other ancient authorities lack *Amen*

JUDITH

Introduction

Judith is one of the most developed examples of the Jewish novelistic* literature of antiquity (see introduction to Tobit). It is the rousing story of the young Jewish woman Judith, who through her bravery saves her village and, ultimately, Jerusalem. Though the style is typical of other Jewish novels of the period (Daniel and Esther with their Apocryphal* additions, Tobit, and *Joseph and Aseneth**), the central theme is also similar to biblical stories that depict a warrior killed by a woman, such as Judg 4–5, 9, and 2 Sam 20.14–22.

The story, probably written in Hebrew in about the middle of the second century BCE, is set in a much earlier period. The historical setting, however, seems to be intentionally blurred, since Assyria, the imperial power that threatens Israel, is here headed by Nebuchadnezzar, who was actually king of the Neo-Babylonian empire. The two worst empires in Jewish history—Assyria had conquered the northern part of Israel and the Neo-Babylonians the southern, or Judah— have been merged to create a fictitious "evil empire."

Judith is very carefully structured. It is divisible into two acts of about equal length: the growing threat of the Assyrian army, commanded by Holofernes (chs. 1–7), and the response to that threat, which is focused on one woman in one Jewish village, Bethulia (chs. 8–12; see chart on page 22). The overarching symbolic opposition that governs the entire drama, however, is that between the "lord" Nebuchadnezzar, whose servant is his general Holofernes, and the Lord God, whose servant is Judith. This theme in Judith may be derived from the depiction of Nicanor and his claim to be "sovereign on earth" in 2 Macc 15.1–5. There are also other parallels to the defeat of Nicanor (see comments).

Although the Book of Judith requires twelve chapters of preparation before reaching the climactic* decapitation scene, the author uses many effective narrative* techniques to create excitement and a sense of the impending threat along the way. The geographical references, for example, often strung together, communicate the idea of a world at war and the immensity of Nebuchadnezzar's threat. The descriptions of the mustering of the troops and their movements likewise make for a very vivid, almost cinematic drama, and the path of destruction of the invading armies can be seen as descending inexorably upon Israel and, even more dramatically, on the small mountain town of Bethulia, which means "virgin."

No fragment of the Book of Judith was found at Qumran, and it is not quoted or alluded to in Philo, Josephus, or the New Testament, but Judith is mentioned in First Clement 55.3–4, an early Christian text. The story, retaining its appeal over the centuries, has been retold in various versions and has inspired many works of art.

1 It was the twelfth year of the reign of Nebuchadnezzar, who ruled over the Assyrians in the great city of Nineveh. In those days Arphaxad ruled over the Medes in Ecbatana. ²He built walls around Ecbatana with hewn stones three cubits thick and six cubits long; he made the walls seventy cubits high and fifty cubits wide. ³At its gates he raised towers one hundred cubits high and sixty cubits wide at the foundations. ⁴He made its gates seventy cubits high and forty cubits wide to allow his armies to march out in force and his infantry to form their ranks. ⁵Then King Nebuchadnezzar made war

against King Arphaxad in the great plain that is on the borders of Ragau. ⁶There rallied to him all the people of the hill country and all those who lived along the Euphrates, the Tigris, and the Hydaspes, and, on the plain, Arioch, king of the Elymeans. Thus, many nations joined the forces of the Chaldeans.^a

1.1–6: Nebuchadnezzar declares war against Arphaxad of Media. *Nebuchadnezzar* reigned over the Neo-Babylonian empire, not the *Assyrians*, from 605–562 BCE; his father, Nabopolassar, had destroyed the Assyrian capital in 612 BCE. The Assyrians may have been seen as equivalent to Syrians, or the Greek/Seleucid rulers from whom the Maccabees won their independence. *Arphaxad* is a fictional king. **6:** *Chaldeans* is another name for the Neo-Babylonians. The import of this reference is unclear, since Nebuchadnezzar is here associated with the Assyrians.

7 Then Nebuchadnezzar, king of the Assyrians, sent messengers to all who lived in Persia and to all who lived in the west, those who lived in Cilicia and Damascus, Lebanon and Antilebanon, and all who lived along the seacoast, ⁸and those among the nations of Carmel and Gilead, and Upper Galilee and the great plain of Esdraelon, ⁹and all who were in Samaria and its towns, and beyond the Jordan as far as Jerusalem and Bethany and Chelous and Kadesh and the river of Egypt, and Tahpanhes and Raamses and the whole land of Goshen, ¹⁰even beyond Tanis and Memphis, and all who lived in Egypt as far as the borders of Ethiopia. ¹¹But all who lived in the whole region disregarded the summons of Nebuchadnezzar, king of the Assyrians, and refused to join him in the war; for they were not afraid of him, but regarded him as only one man.^b So they sent back his messengers empty-handed and in disgrace.

12 Then Nebuchadnezzar became very angry with this whole region, and swore by his throne and kingdom that he would take revenge on the whole territory of Cilicia and Damascus and Syria, that he would kill with his sword also all the inhabitants of the land of Moab, and the people of Ammon, and all Judea, and every one in Egypt, as far as the coasts of the two seas.

13 In the seventeenth year he led his forces against King Arphaxad and defeated him in battle, overthrowing the whole army of Arphaxad and all his cavalry and all his chariots. ¹⁴Thus he took possession of his towns and came to Ecbatana, captured its towers, plundered its markets, and turned its glory into disgrace. ¹⁵He captured Arphaxad in the mountains of Ragau and struck him down with his spears, thus destroying him once and for all. ¹⁶Then he returned to Nineveh, he and all his combined forces, a vast body of troops; and there he and his forces rested and feasted for one hundred twenty days.

1.7–16: The rising threat of Nebuchadnezzar and his response to the nations who spurn him. The geographical expanse of the area threatened by Nebuchadnezzar is emphasized. The area is larger than either the Assyrian or Babylonian empires, but corresponds to lands ruled by the later Persian and Greek empires. **13–16:** The easy victory of Nebuchadnezzar over the great *Arphaxad* of *Ecbatana* demonstrates the threat that looms over smaller nations. This episode concludes with Nebuchadnezzar's celebration and a temporary pause in the action. A number of these pauses will occur throughout the novel,* framing the scenes of dramatic action and allowing for a more deliberate pacing of the story.

2 In the eighteenth year, on the twenty-second day of the first month, there was talk in the palace of Nebuchadnezzar, king of the Assyrians, about carrying out his revenge on the whole region, just as he had said. ²He summoned all his ministers and all his nobles and set before them his secret plan and recounted fully, with his own lips, all the wickedness of the region.^c ³They decided that every one who had not obeyed his command should be destroyed.

4 When he had completed his plan, Nebuchadnezzar, king of the Assyrians, called Holofernes, the chief general of his army, second only to himself, and said to him, ⁵"Thus says the Great King, the lord of the whole earth: Leave my presence and take with you men confident in their strength,

a Syr: Gk *Cheleoudites*   *b* Or *a man*   *c* Meaning of Gk uncertain

...ered them, "Truly I ...th and do not doubt, ...hat has been done to ... you say to this moun- ...thrown into the sea,' ...hatever you ask for in ...tell ...u will receive."

...1.17, 15–19; Lk 19.45–48; Jn ... **protest. 12–13:** The activity ...the Gentiles.* Selling animals ...(many with pagan symbols) for ... ...eis* were necessary in order for pilgrims to participate in Temple worship. Matthew does not condemn Temple worship per se (5.23; 12.5–6; 17.24; 23.16–20), but Jesus becomes the new site of divine presence. **13:** *Den of robbers* indicates not dishonesty in the Temple system (see Jer 7.1–11) but a haven for those who sin elsewhere. **14:** Jesus casts out insiders and welcomes the sick. **15:** The leaders are more concerned with the children's acclamation than with Jesus' actions. **16:** Ps 8.2. **18–22** (Mk 11.12–14; 20.25): **The fig tree.** Matthew condenses Mark's two-stage account into an instantaneous miracle. The tree may symbolize Jerusalem and the Temple. **19:** *Fruit* connotes proper action. **21–22:** See 17.20.

23 When he entered the temple, the chief priests and the elders of the people came to him as he was teaching, and said, "By what authority are you doing these things, and who gave you this authority?" [24]Jesus said to them, "I will also ask you one question; if you tell me the answer, then I will also tell you by what authority I do these things. [25]Did the baptism of John come from heaven, or was it of human origin?" And they argued with one another, "If we say, 'From heaven,' he will say to us, 'Why then did you not believe him?' [26]But if we say, 'Of human origin,' we are afraid of the crowd; for all regard John as a prophet." [27]So they answered Jesus, "We do not know." And he said to them, "Neither will I tell you by what authority I am doing these things.

28 "What do you think? A man had two sons; he went to the first and said, 'Son, go and work in the vineyard today.' [29]He answered, 'I will not'; but later he changed his mind and went. [30]The father[a] went to the second and said the same; and he answered,

'I go, sir'; but he did not go. [31]Which of the two did the will of his father?" They said, "The first." Jesus said to them, "Truly I tell you, the tax collectors and the prostitutes are going into the kingdom of God ahead of you. [32]For John came to you in the way of righteousness and you did not believe him, but the tax collectors and the prostitutes believed him; and even after you saw it, you did not change your minds and believe him.

21.23–32 (Mk 11.27–33; Lk 20.1–8; Jn 2.18–22): **Temple* teaching.** While Jesus teaches in the Temple, the chief priests and elders will later plot his death (26.3). **23–24:** Jesus' opponents seek to trap him with a question, and Jesus responds in kind. *Authority* is a Matthean theme (7.29; 8.9; 9.8; 10.1; 28.17). **28–32:** The parable* of the two sons is unique to Matthew. Consistent with the Gospel's themes, the parable emphasizes the importance of deeds (see 7.21–23) and denigrates empty promises. The Sadducees* and Pharisees* heard John the Baptist (3.5–7) but rejected his teaching. **32:** Tax collectors and prostitutes place themselves deliberately outside the communal standards of righteousness.

33 "Listen to another parable. There was a landowner who planted a vineyard, put a fence around it, dug a wine press in it, and built a watchtower. Then he leased it to tenants and went to another country. [34]When the harvest time had come, he sent his slaves to the tenants to collect his produce. [35]But the tenants seized his slaves and beat one, killed another, and stoned another. [36]Again he sent other slaves, more than the first; and they treated them in the same way. [37]Finally he sent his son to them, saying, 'They will respect my son.' [38]But when the tenants saw the son, they said to themselves, 'This is the heir; come, let us kill him and get his inheritance.' [39]So they seized him, threw him out of the vineyard, and killed him. [40]Now when the owner of the vineyard comes, what will he do to those tenants?" [41]They said to him, "He will put those wretches to a miserable death, and lease the vineyard to other tenants who will give him the produce at the harvest time."

a Gk He

42 Jesus said to them, "Have you never read in the scriptures:

'The stone that the builders rejected
　　has become the cornerstone;[a]
this was the Lord's doing,
　　and it is amazing in our eyes'?
43Therefore I tell you, the kingdom of God will be taken away from you and given to a people that produces the fruits of the kingdom.[b] 44The one who falls on this stone will be broken to pieces; and it will crush anyone on whom it falls."[c]

45 When the chief priests and the Pharisees heard his parables, they realized that he was speaking about them. 46They wanted to arrest him, but they feared the crowds, because they regarded him as a prophet.

21.33–46 (Mk 12.1–12; Lk 20.9–19): **The parable★ of the vineyard**. The vineyard symbolizes Israel (Isa 5.1–7). **34:** *Produce* is "fruits," Matthew's term for good works. *Slaves* likely represent the prophets.★ **39:** The son's death corresponds to that of Jesus (27.32); the parable makes sense with this allegorical★ meaning, while on a literal level, the father's action in sending the son is foolishness at best. **40–41:** The *tenants* are, allegorically, the chief priests and elders; the *other tenants* are the Jews and gentiles★ of Matthew's church. **42:** See Ps 118.22–23 (Septuagint★).

22 Once more Jesus spoke to them in parables, saying: 2"The kingdom of heaven may be compared to a king who gave a wedding banquet for his son. 3He sent his slaves to call those who had been invited to the wedding banquet, but they would not come. 4Again he sent other slaves, saying, 'Tell those who have been invited: Look, I have prepared my dinner, my oxen and my fat calves have been slaughtered, and everything is ready; come to the wedding banquet.' 5But they made light of it and went away, one to his farm, another to his business, 6while the rest seized his slaves, mistreated them, and killed them. 7The king was enraged. He sent his troops, destroyed those murderers, and burned their city. 8Then he said to his slaves, 'The wedding is ready, but those invited were not worthy. 9Go therefore into the main streets, and invite everyone you find to the wedding banquet.' 10Those

slaves went out ￼nto the ￼ all whom they fou￼d, bot￼ the wedding h￼ll was filled ￼

11 "But whe￼ the king can￼ guests, he notic￼d a man there ￼ wearing a weddi￼g robe, 12and ￼ him, 'Friend, how ￼id you get in her￼ a wedding robe?' ￼nd he was spee￼ 13Then the king said to the attendants, ￼ him hand and foot, a￼d throw him into t￼ outer darkness, where ￼here will be weeping and gnashing of teeth.' 14For many are called, but few are chosen."

22.1–14 (see Lk 14.15–24; see Gospel of Thomas★ 64): **The parable of the marriage feast**. Refusing a royal invitation constitutes rebellion (2 Sam 10.4). **11–13:** New clothing represents a new identity (see Rom 13.12–14; Rev 3.4). **14:** *Chosen* (Gk., "elektos") means accepted at final judgment.

15 Then the Pharisees went and plotted to entrap him in what he said. 16So they sent their disciples to him, along with the Herodians, saying, "Teacher, we know that you are sincere, and teach the way of God in accordance with truth, and show deference to no one; for you do not regard people with partiality. 17Tell us, then, what you think. Is it lawful to pay taxes to the emperor, or not?" 18But Jesus, aware of their malice, said, "Why are you putting me to the test, you hypocrites? 19Show me the coin used for the tax." And they brought him a denarius. 20Then he said to them, "Whose head is this, and whose title?" 21They answered, "The emperor's." Then he said to them, "Give therefore to the emperor the things that are the emperor's, and to God the things that are God's." 22When they heard this, they were amazed; and they left him and went away.

23 The same day some Sadducees came to him, saying there is no resurrection;[d] and they asked him a question, saying, 24"Teacher, Moses said, 'If a man dies childless, his brother shall marry the widow, and raise up children for his brother.' 25Now

a Or *keystone*　　*b* Gk *the fruits of it*　　*c* Other ancient authorities lack verse 44　　*d* Other ancient authorities read *who say that there is no resurrection*

...rs among us; the first ...ildless, leaving the ...²⁶The second did the ..., down to the seventh. ...man herself died. ²⁸In ...en, whose wife of the ...or all of them had mar-

...d them, "You are wrong, ...neither the scriptures nor ...³⁰For in the resurrection ...nor are given in marriage, ...ᵃ in heaven. ³¹And as for ...ion of the dead, have you not ...at was said to you by God, ³²'I am ...e God of Abraham, the God of Isaac, and the God of Jacob'? He is God not of the dead, but of the living." ³³And when the crowd heard it, they were astounded at his teaching.

22.15–33 (Mk 12.13–17; Lk 20.20–26): **Paying taxes. 16**: *Herodians* are supporters of Rome (see Mk 3.6). The Roman head-tax was instituted in 6 CE to indicate Judea's status as a Roman province. Roman coinage usually contained Caesar's portrait and an inscription proclaiming his divinity; Jesus apparently does not carry money (see 6.24). Jesus' enigmatic answer satisfies both pro- and anti-Roman factions: For pro-Roman factions, the line appears to support payment of taxes; for those who believe everything belongs to God, the line supports their protest against Roman presence. **23–33** (Mk 12.18–27; Lk 20.27–40): **Angelic bodies**. On levirate marriage* (Latin, "levir," brother-in-law) see Deut 25.5–6, Gen 38, Ruth 3 (Tamar and Ruth also appear in Matthew's genealogy*). The rationale of the practice is to continue the family name. **32**: See Ex 3.6. Jesus envisages the resurrected body to be without sexual desire or the desire for procreation (see also 1 Cor 15).

34 When the Pharisees heard that he had silenced the Sadducees, they gathered together, ³⁵and one of them, a lawyer, asked him a question to test him. ³⁶"Teacher, which commandment in the law is the greatest?" ³⁷He said to him, " 'You shall love the Lord your God with all your heart, and with all your soul, and with all your mind.' ³⁸This is the greatest and first commandment. ³⁹And a second is like it: 'You shall love your

neighbor as yourself.' ⁴⁰On these two commandments hang all the law and the prophets."

41 Now while the Pharisees were gathered together, Jesus asked them this question: ⁴²"What do you think of the Messiah?ᵇ Whose son is he?" They said to him, "The son of David." ⁴³He said to them, "How is it then that David by the Spiritᶜ calls him Lord, saying,

44 'The Lord said to my Lord,
    "Sit at my right hand,
        until I put your enemies under your
            feet" '?

⁴⁵If David thus calls him Lord, how can he be his son?" ⁴⁶No one was able to give him an answer, nor from that day did anyone dare to ask him any more questions.

22.34–46. 34–40 (Mk 28.34; Lk 10.25–28): **The great commandment**. Rabbinic authorities in antiquity also discussed which commandments summarized the others (see comment on 7.12). **37**: The first commandment (Deut 6.4–9), Deut 11.18–20, and Ex 13.9 are contained in the "tefillin" (phylacteries) worn by Jewish men (and, today, some women). *Love* is a verbal form of the Greek noun "agape." **41–46: Son of David**. See comment on Mk 12.35–37 (Lk 20.41–44).

23 Then Jesus said to the crowds and to his disciples, ²"The scribes and the Pharisees sit on Moses' seat; ³therefore, do whatever they teach you and follow it; but do not do as they do, for they do not practice what they teach. ⁴They tie up heavy burdens, hard to bear,ᵈ and lay them on the shoulders of others; but they themselves are unwilling to lift a finger to move them. ⁵They do all their deeds to be seen by others; for they make their phylacteries broad and their fringes long. ⁶They love to have the place of honor at banquets and the best seats in the synagogues, ⁷and to be greeted with respect in the marketplaces, and to have people call them rabbi. ⁸But you are not to be called rabbi, for you have one teacher, and you are all students.ᵉ ⁹And call no one your father

---

a Other ancient authorities add *of God*   b Or *Christ*
c Gk in *spirit*   d Other ancient authorities lack *hard to bear*   e Gk *brothers*

on earth, for you have one Father—the one in heaven. [10]Nor are you to be called instructors, for you have one instructor, the Messiah.[a] [11]The greatest among you will be your servant. [12]All who exalt themselves will be humbled, and all who humble themselves will be exalted.

13 "But woe to you, scribes and Pharisees, hypocrites! For you lock people out of the kingdom of heaven. For you do not go in yourselves, and when others are going in, you stop them.[b] [15]Woe to you, scribes and Pharisees, hypocrites! For you cross sea and land to make a single convert, and you make the new convert twice as much a child of hell[c] as yourselves.

16 "Woe to you, blind guides, who say, 'Whoever swears by the sanctuary is bound by nothing, but whoever swears by the gold of the sanctuary is bound by the oath.' [17]You blind fools! For which is greater, the gold or the sanctuary that has made the gold sacred? [18]And you say, 'Whoever swears by the altar is bound by nothing, but whoever swears by the gift that is on the altar is bound by the oath.' [19]How blind you are! For which is greater, the gift or the altar that makes the gift sacred? [20]So whoever swears by the altar, swears by it and by everything on it; [21]and whoever swears by the sanctuary, swears by it and by the one who dwells in it; [22]and whoever swears by heaven, swears by the throne of God and by the one who is seated upon it.

23 "Woe to you, scribes and Pharisees, hypocrites! For you tithe mint, dill, and cummin, and have neglected the weightier matters of the law: justice and mercy and faith. It is these you ought to have practiced without neglecting the others. [24]You blind guides! You strain out a gnat but swallow a camel!

25 "Woe to you, scribes and Pharisees, hypocrites! For you clean the outside of the cup and of the plate, but inside they are full of greed and self-indulgence. [26]You blind Pharisee! First clean the inside of the cup,[d] so that the outside also may become clean.

27 "Woe to you, scribes and Pharisees, hypocrites! For you are like whitewashed tombs, which on the outside look beautiful, but inside they are ... dead and of all kinds... on the outside look righteo... inside you are full of ... lawlessness.

29 "Woe to you, scribes and hypocrites! For you build the to... prophets and decorate the graves of ... teous, [30]and you say, 'If we had live... days of our ancestors, we would no... taken part with them in shedding the b... of the prophets.' [31]Thus you testify agai... yourselves that you are descendants of thos... who murdered the prophets. [32]Fill up, then, the measure of your ancestors. [33]You snakes, you brood of vipers! How can you escape being sentenced to hell?[c] [34]Therefore I send you prophets, sages, and scribes, some of whom you will kill and crucify, and some you will flog in your synagogues and pursue from town to town, [35]so that upon you may come all the righteous blood shed on earth, from the blood of righteous Abel to the blood of Zechariah son of Barachiah, whom you murdered between the sanctuary and the altar. [36]Truly I tell you, all this will come upon this generation.

23.1–36: Woes against Pharisees* and scribes.* Matthew defines the church and its members in contrast to synagogues* and its leaders. 2: *Moses' seat* represents synagogue teaching and administrative authority. 5: On *phylacteries*, see comment on 22.37; *fringes*, see comment on 9.20. 13–36: The seven "woe oracles*" all concern self-definition and self-regulation; Jesus' pronouncements against the Pharisees also function as Matthew's warnings to church members. 15: Refers either to a gentile* mission or to Pharisaic attempts to convince other Jews of their teachings. 16–22: Suggests 5.33–37. 23–24 (Lk 11.42): *Camel* and *gnat* sound similar in Aramaic.* 25–26: See Lk 11.39–41. 27–28 (Lk 11.44): Tombs were *whitewashed* to prevent accidental contact and so impurity (Num 19.11–22); contact with a corpse prevented immediate entry into the Temple.* 29–32 (Lk 11.47–

a Or *the Christ* *b* Other authorities add here (or after verse 12) verse 14, *Woe to you, scribes and Pharisees, hypocrites! For you devour widows' houses and for the sake of appearance you make long prayers; therefore you will receive the greater condemnation* *c* Gk *Gehenna* *d* Other ancient authorities add *and of the plate*